Small Business Sourcebook

ISSN 0883-3397

Small Business Sourcebook

The Entrepreneur's Resource

THIRTIETH EDITION

Volume 4

General Small Business Topics

(Entries 30408-43315)

Sonya D. Hill
Project Editor

GALE
CENGAGE Learning

Detroit • New York • San Francisco • New Haven, Conn • Waterville, Maine • London

GALE
CENGAGE Learning

Small Business Sourcebook, 30th edition

Project Editor: Sonya D. Hill

Editorial Support Services: Charles Beaumont

Composition and Electronic Prepress: Gary Leach

Manufacturing: Rita Wimberley

Gale
27500 Drake Rd.
Farmington Hills, MI, 48331-3535

ISBN-13: 978-1-4144-7957-6 (set)
ISBN-10: 1-4144-7957-3 (set)
ISBN-13: 978-1-4144-7958-3 (vol. 1)
ISBN-10: 1-4144-7958-1 (vol. 1)
ISBN-13: 978-1-4144-7959-0 (vol. 2)
ISBN-10: 1-4144-7959-X (vol. 2)
ISBN-13: 978-1-4144-7960-6 (vol. 3)
ISBN-10: 1-4144-7960-3 (vol. 3)
ISBN-13: 978-1-4144-7961-3 (vol. 4)
ISBN-10: 1-4144-7961-1 (vol. 4)
ISBN-13: 978-1-4144-7962-0 (vol. 5)
ISBN-10: 1-4144-7962-X (vol. 5)
ISBN-13: 978-1-4144-7963-7 (vol. 6)
ISBN-10: 1-4144-7963-8 (vol. 6)

ISSN 0883-3397

Printed in the United States of America
1 2 3 4 5 17 16 15 14 13

Contents

Introduction

The appeal of small business ownership remains perpetually entrenched in American culture as one of the most viable avenues for achieving the American Dream. To many entrepreneurs going into business for themselves represents financial independence, an increased sense of identity and self-worth, and the fulfillment of personal goals. Small business owners strive to make their mark in today's competitive marketplace by establishing healthy businesses that can, over time, become legacies handed down from one generation to the next. Entrepreneurs from each generation tackle the obstacles and adversities of the current business and economic climate to test their business savvy and generate opportunities. Today's entrepreneurs face many of the problems of their predecessors, as well as some distinctly new challenges.

With the rightsizing, downsizing, and reorganization of-corporate America, many individuals have decided to confront the risks of developing and operating their own businesses. Small business ownership is rapidly becoming a viable alternative to what is perceived as an equally unstable corporate environment. These entrepreneurs, many of whom have firsthand experience with the problems and inefficiencies inherent in today's large corporations, seek to improve upon an archaic business model and to capitalize on their own ingenuity and strengths. Led by their zeal, many would-be entrepreneurs let their desire, drive, and determination overshadow the need for business knowledge and skill. Ironically, aids in obtaining these components of entrepreneurial success are widely available, easily accessible, and often free of charge.

Small Business Sourcebook (*SBS*) is a six-volume annotated guide to more than 21,310 listings of live and print sources of information designed to facilitate the start-up, development, and growth of specific small businesses, as well as over 26,280 similar listings on general small business topics. An additional 12,367 state-specific listings and over 2,220 U.S. federal government agencies and offices specializing in small business issues, programs, and assistance are also included. *SBS* covers 340 specific small business profiles and 99 general small business topics.

Features of This Edition

This edition of *Small Business Sourcebook* has been revised and updated, incorporating thousand of changes to names, addresses, contacts, and descriptions of listings from the previous edition.

Contents and Arrangement

The geographical scope of *SBS* encompasses the United States and Canada, with expanded coverage for resources pertaining to international trade and for resources that have a U.S. or Canadian distributor or contact. Internet sites that are maintained outside of the U.S. and Canada are also included if they contain relevant information for North American small businesses. Resources that do not relate specifically to small businesses are generally not included.

The information presented in *SBS* is grouped within four sections: Specific Small Business Profiles, General Small Business Topics, State Listings, and Federal Government Assistance. Detailed outlines of these sections may be found in the Users' Guide following this Introduction. Also included is a Master Index to Volumes 1 through 6.

Specific Small Business Profiles This section includes the following types of resources: start-up information, associations and other organizations, educational programs, directories of educational programs, reference works, sources of supply, statistical sources, trade periodicals, videocassettes/audiocassettes, trade shows and conventions, consultants, franchises and business opportunities, computerized databases, computer systems/software, Internet databases, libraries, and research centers-all arranged by business type. Entries range from Accounting Service to Word Processing Service, and include such businesses as Airbag Replacement Service Centers, Computer Consulting, Damage Restoration Service, and Web Site Design.

General Small Business Topics This section offers such resources as associations, books, periodicals, articles, pamphlets, educational programs, directories of educational programs,videocassettes/audiocassettes, trade shows and conventions, consultants, computerized databases, Internet databases, software, libraries, and research centers, arranged alphabetically by business topic.

State Listings Entries include government, academic, and commercial agencies and organizations, as well as select coverage of relevant state-specific publications; listings are arranged alphabetically by state, territory, and Canadian province. Some examples include small business development consultants, educational programs, financing and loan programs, better business bureaus, and chambers of commerce.

Federal Government Assistance Listings specializing in small business issues, programs, assistance, and policyare arranged alphabetically by U.S. government agency or office; regional or branch offices are listed alphabetically by state.

Master Index All entries in Volumes 1 through 6 are arranged in one alphabetic index for convenience.

Entries in *SBS* include (as appropriate andavailable):

- Organization, institution, or product name
- Contact information, including contact name, address and phone, toll-free, and fax numbers
- Author/editor, date(s), and frequency
- Availability, including price
- Brief description of purpose, services, or content
- Company and/or personal E-mail addresses
- Web site addresses

SBS also features the following:

Guide to Publishers—An alphabetic listing of 2,470 companies, associations, institutions, and individuals that publish the periodicals, directories, guidebooks, and other publications noted in the Small Business Profiles and General Topics sections. Users are provided with full contact information, including address, phone, fax,and e-mail and URL when available. The Guide to Publishers facilitates contact with publishers and provides a one- stop resource for valuable information.

Method of Compilation

SBS was compiled by consulting small business experts and entrepreneurs, as well as a variety of resources, including direct contact with the associations, organizations, and agencies through telephone surveys, Internet research, or through materials provided by those listees; government resources; and data obtained from other relevant Gale directories. *SBS* was reviewed by a team of small business advisors, all of whom have numerous years of expertise in small business counseling and identification of small business information resources. The last and perhaps most important resource we utilize is direct contact with our readers, who provide valuable comments and suggestions to improve our publication. *SBS* relies on these comprehensive market contacts to provide today's entrepreneurs with relevant, current, and accurate informationon all aspects of small business.

Available in Electronic Formats

Licensing. *Small Business Sourcebook* is available for licensing. The complete database is provided in a fielded format and is deliverable on such media as disk or CD-ROM. For more information, contact Gale's Business Development Group at1-800-877-GALE, or visit our website at www.gale.com/bizdev.

Comments and Suggestions Welcome

Associations, agencies, business firms, publishers, and other organizations that provide assistance and information to the small business community are encouraged to submit material about their programs, activities, services, or products. Comments and suggestions from users of this directory are also welcomed and appreciated. Please contact:

Project Editor
Small Business Sourcebook
Gale, Cengage Learning
27500 Drake Rd.
Farmington Hills, MI 48331-3535
Phone: (248) 699-4253
Fax: (248) 699-8070
E-mail: BusinessProductsgale.com
URL: www.gale.com

Small Business Sourcebook (*SBS*) provides information in a variety of forms and presentations for comprehensive coverage and ease of use. The directory contains four parts within two volumes:

- Specific Small Business Profiles
- General Small Business Topics
- State Listings
- Federal Government Assistance

Information on specific businesses is arranged by type of business; the many general topics that are of interest to the owners, operators, or managers of all small businesses are grouped in a separate section for added convenience. Users should consult the various sections to benefit fully from the information *SBS* offers. For example, an entrepreneur with a talent or interest in the culinary arts could peruse a number of specific small business profiles, such as Restaurant, Catering, Cooking School, Specialty Food/Wine Shop, Bakery/Doughnut Shop, Healthy Restaurant, or Candy/Chocolate Store. Secondly, the General Small Business Topics section could be consulted for any applicable subjects, such as Service Industry, Retailing, Franchising, and other relevant topics. Then, the appropriate state within the State Listings section would offer area programs and offices providing information and support to small businesses, including venture capital firms and small business development consultants. Finally, the Federal Government Assistance section could supply relevant government offices, such as procurement contacts.

Features Included in Volumes 1 through 3

List of Small Business Profiles. This list provides an alphabetic outline of the small businesses profiled, with cross-references for related profiles and for alternate names by which businesses may be identified. The page number for each profile is indicated.

Standard Industrial Classification (SIC) Codes for-Profiled Small Businesses. This section lists four-digit SIC codes and corresponding classification descriptions for the small businesses profiled in this edition. The SIC system, which organizes businesses by type, is a product of the Statistical Policy Division of the U.S. Office of Management and Budget. Statistical data produced by government, public, and private organizations is usually categorized according to SIC codes, thereby facilitating the collection, comparison, and analysis of data as well as providing a uniform method for presenting statistical information. Hence, knowing the SIC code for a particular small business increases access and the use of a variety of statistical data from many sources.

Guide to Publishers. This resource lists alphabetically the companies, associations, institutions, and individuals that publish the periodicals, directories, guidebooks, and other publications noted in the "Small Business Profiles" and "General Topics" sections. Users are provided with full contact information, including address, phone, fax, and e-mail and URL when available. The "Guide" facilitates contact with publishers and provides a one-stop resource for valuable information.

Glossary of Small Business Terms. This glossary defines nearly 400 small business terms, including financial, governmental, insurance, procurement, technical, and general business definitions. Cross-references and acronyms are also provided.

Small Business Profiles A-Z. A total of 340 small businesses is represented in volumes 1 through 3. Profiles are listed alphabetically by business name. Entries within each profile are arranged alphabetically by resource type, within up to 17 subheadings.These subheadings are detailed below:

- ***Start-up Information***—Includes periodical articles, books, manuals, book excerpts, kits, and other sources of information. Entries offer title; publisher; address; phone, fax, toll-free numbers; company e-mail and URL addresses; and a description. Bibliographic data is provided for cited periodical articles whenever possible.
- ***Associations and Other Oganizations***—Includes trade and professional associations whose members gather and disseminate information of interest to small business owners. Entries offer the association's

name; address; phone, toll-free and fax numbers; company e-mail address; contact name; purpose and objective; a description of membership; telecommunication services; and a listing of its publications, including publishing frequency.

- ***Educational Programs***—Includes university and college programs, schools, training opportunities, association seminars, correspondence courses, and other educational programs.Entries offer name of program or institution, sponsor name, address, phone, toll-free and fax numbers, e-mail and URL addresses; and description of program.
- ***Directories of Educational Programs***—Includes directories and other publications that list educational programs. Entries offer name of publication; publisher name, address, and phone, toll-free and fax numbers; editor; frequency or date of publication; price; and description of contents, including directory arrangement and indexes.
- ***Reference Works***—Includes handbooks, manuals, textbooks, guides, directories, dictionaries, encyclopedias, and other published reference materials. Entries offer name of publication; publisher name, address, and phone, toll-free and fax numbers; e-mail and URL addresses; and, when available, name of author or editor, publication year or frequency, and price. A brief description is often featured.
- ***Sources of Supply***—Includes buyer's guides,directories, special issues of periodicals, and other publications that list sources of equipment, supplies, and services related to the operation of the profiled small business. Entries offer publication name; publisher name, address, and phone, toll-free and fax numbers; e-mail and URL addresses; and, when available, editor's name, frequency or publication year, and price. A brief description of the publication, including directory arrangement and indexes, is often provided.
- ***Statistical Sources***—Includes books, reports, pamphlets, and other sources of statistical data of interest to an owner, operator or manager of the profiled small business, such as wage, salary, and compensation data; financial and operating ratios; prices and costs; demographics; and other statistical information. Entries offer publication/data source name; publisher (if applicable); address; phone, toll-free and fax numbers of data source; publication date or frequency; and price. A brief description of the publication/data source is often provided.
- ***Trade Periodicals***—Includes trade journals, newsletters, magazines, and other serials that offer information about the management and operation of the profiled small business. Such periodicals often contain industry news; trends and developments; reviews; articles about new equipment and supplies; and other information related to business operations. Entries offer publication name; publisher name, address, phone, toll-free and fax numbers, and e-mail and URL addresses; editor name; publication frequency; andprice. A brief description of the publication's content is also included, when known.
- ***Videocassettes/Audiocassettes***—Includes videocassettes, audiocassettes, and other audiovisual media offering information on the profiled small business. Entries offer program title; distributor name, address, phone, toll-free and fax numbers, and e-mail and URL addresses; description of program; release date; price; and format(s).
- ***Trade Shows and Conventions***—Includes tradeshows, exhibitions, expositions, conventions, and other industry meetings that provide prospective and existing business owners with the opportunity to meet and exchange information with their peers, review commercial exhibits, establish business or sales contacts, and attend educational programs. Entries offer event name; sponsor or management company name, address, phone, toll-free and fax numbers, and e-mail and URL addresses; a description of the event, including audience, frequency, principal exhibits, and dates and locations of event for as many years ahead as provided by the event's sponsor.
- ***Consultants***—Includes consultants and consulting organizations that provide services specifically related to the profiled small business. Entries offer individual consultant or consulting organization name, address, and phone, toll-free and fax numbers; company and individual e-mail addresses; and a brief description of consulting services. (For e-mail and URL addresses, see the Small Business Development Consultants subheadings in the State Listings section in Volume 2.)
- ***Franchises and Business Opportunities***—Includes companies granting franchise licenses for enterprises falling within the scope of the profiled small business, as well as other non-franchised business opportunities that operate within a given network or system. Entries offer franchise name, address, phone, toll-free and fax numbers, and e-mail and URL addresses, as well as a description of the franchise or business opportunity, which has been expanded whenever possible to include the number of existing franchises, the founding date of the franchise, franchise fees, equity capital requirements, royalty fees, any managerial assistance offered, and available training.
- ***Computerized Databases***—Includes diskettes, magnetic tapes, CD-ROMs, online systems, and other computer-readable databases. Entries offer database name; producer name, address, phone, toll-free and fax numbers, e-mail and URL addresses; description; and available format(s), including vendor name.

(Many university and public libraries offer online information retrieval services that provide searches of databases, including those listed in this category.)

- ***Computer Systems/Software***—Includes softwar-eand computerized business systems designed to assist in the operation of the profiled small business. Entries offer name of the software or system; publisher name, address, phone, toll-free and fax-numbers; price; and description.
- ***Libraries***—Includes libraries and special collections that contain material especially applicable to the profiled small business. Entries offer library or collection name; parent organization (where applicable); address; phone, toll-free and fax numbers; e-mail and URL addresses; contact name and title; scope of collection; and description of holdings, subscriptions, and services.
- ***Research Centers***—Includes university-related and independently operated research institutes and information centers that generate, through their research programs, data related to the operation of the profiled small business. Also listed are associations and other business-related organizations that conduct research programs. Entries offer name of organization; address; phone, toll-free and fax numbers; company web site address; contact name and personale-mail; a description of principal fields of research or services; publications, including title and frequency; and related conferences.

Features Included in Volumes 2 through 6

General Small Business Topics. This section offers chapters on different topics in the operation of any small business, for example, venture capital and other funding, or compensation. Chapters are listed alphabetically by small business topic; entries within each chapter are arranged alphabetically, within up to 14 subheadings, by resource type:

- ***Associations and Other Organizations***—Includes trade and professional associations that gather and disseminate information of interest to small business owners. Entries offer the association's name; address; phone, toll-free and fax numbers; organization e-mail and URL addresses; contact name;purpose and objectives; a description of membership; telecommunication services; and a listing of its publications, including publishing frequency.
- ***Educational Programs***—Includes university and college programs, schools, training opportunities, association seminars, correspondence courses, and other educational programs. Entries offer name of program or institution, sponsor name, address, phone, toll-free and fax numbers, e-mail and URL addresses, and description of program.
- ***Directories of Educational Programs***—Includes directories and other publications that list educational programs. Entries offer name of publication; publisher name, address, phone, toll-free and fax numbers, and e-mail and URL addresses; editor; frequency or date of publication; price; and description of contents, including arrangement and indexes.
- ***Reference Works***—Includes articles, handbooks, manuals, textbooks, guides, directories, dictionaries, encyclopedias, and other published reference materi-als. Entries offertitle of article, including bibliographic information; name of publication; publisher name, address, phone, toll-free and fax numbers, and e-mail and URL addresses; and, when available, name of author oreditor, publication year or frequency, and price. A brief descriptionis often featured.
- ***Sources of Supply***—Includes buyer's guides,directories, special issues of periodicals, and other publications that list sources of equipment, supplies, and services. Entries offer publication name; publisher name, address, phone, toll-free and fax numbers, and e-mail and URL addresses; editor's name, frequency or publication year, price, and a brief description of the publication, when available.
- ***Statistical Sources***—Includes books, reports, pamphlets, and other sources of statistical data of interest to an owner, operator, or manager of a small business, such as wage, salary, and compensation data; financial and operating ratios; prices and costs; demographics; and other statistical information. Entries offer publication/data source name; publisher (if applicable); address; phone, toll-free and fax numbers of data source; publication date or frequency; and price. A brief description is often provided.
- ***Trade Periodicals***—Includes journals, newsletters, magazines, and other serials. Entries offer name of publication; publisher name, address, phone, toll-free and fax numbers, and e-mail and URL addresses; and name of editor, frequency, and price.A brief description of the periodical's content is included when known.
- ***Videocassettes/Audiocassettes***—Includes videocassettes, audiocassettes, and other audiovisual media. Entries offer program title; distributor name, address, phone, toll-free and fax numbers, and e-mail and URL addresses; price; description of program; release date; and format(s).
- ***Trade Shows and Conventions***—Includes tradeshows, exhibitions, expositions, seminars, and conventions. Entries offer event name; sponsor or management company name, address, phone, toll-free and fax numbers, and e-mail and URL ad-

dresses; frequency of event; and dates and locations of the event for as many years ahead as known.

- ***Consultants***—Includes consultants and consulting organizations. Entries offer individual consultant or-consulting organization name, address, and phone, toll-free and fax numbers; company and individual e-mail addresses; and a brief description of consulting services. (See also Consultants in the State Listings section.)
- ***Computerized Databases***—Includes diskettes, CD-ROMs, magnetic tape, online systems and other computer-readable databases. Entries offer database name; producer, address, phone, toll-free and fax numbers, and e-mail and URL addresses; description; and available format(s), including vendor name. (Many university and public libraries offer online information retrieval services that provide searches of databases, including those listed in this category.)
- ***Computer Systems/Software***—Includes software and computerized business systems. Entries offer name of the software or system; publisher name, address, phone, toll-free and fax numbers, and e-mail and URL addresses; price; and description.
- ***Libraries***—Includes libraries and special collections that contain material applicable to the small business topic. Entries offer library or collection name, parent organization (where applicable), address, phone and fax numbers, e-mail and URL addresses, scope of collection, and description of holdings and services.
- ***Research Centers***— Includes university-related and independently operated research institutes and information centers that generate, through their research programs, data related to specific small business topics. Entries offer name of organization, address, phone, toll-free and fax numbers, e-mail and URL addresses, a description of principal fields of research or services, and related conferences.

State Listings. This section lists various sources of information and assistance available within given states, territories, and Canadian provinces; entries include governmental, academic, and commercial agencies, and are arranged alphabetically within up to 15 subheadings by resource type:

- ***Small Business Development Center Lead Office***— Includes the lead small business development center (SBDC) for each state.
- ***Small Business Development Centers***—Includes any additional small business development centers (SBDC) in the state, territory, or province. SBDCs provide support services to small businesses, including individual counseling, seminars, conferences, and learning center activities.
- ***Small Business Assistance Programs***—Includes state small business development offices and other programs offering assistance to small businesses.
- ***SCORE Offices***—Includes SCORE office(s) for each state. The Service Corps of Retired Executives Association (SCORE), a volunteer program sponsored by the Small Business Administration, offers counseling, workshops, and seminars across the U.S. for small business entrepreneurs.
- ***Better Business Bureaus***—Includes various better business bureaus within each state. By becoming a member of the local Better Business Bureau, a small business owner can increase the prestige and credibility of his or her business within the community, as well as make valuable business contacts.
- ***Chambers of Commerce***—Includes various chambers of commerce within each state. Chambers of Commerce are valuable sources of small business advice and information; often, local chambers sponsor SCORE counseling several times per month for a small fee, seminars, conferences, and other workshops to its members. Also, by becoming a member of the local Chamber of Commerce, a small business owner can increase the prestige and credibility of his or herbusiness within the community, as well as make valuable business contacts.
- ***Minority Business Assistance Programs***—Includes minority business development centers and other sources of assistance for minority-owned business.
- ***Financing and Loan Programs***—Includes venture capital firms, small business investment companies (SBIC), minority enterprise small business investment companies (MESBIC), and other programs that provide funding to qualified small businesses.
- ***Procurement Assistance Programs***—Includes state services such as counseling, set-asides, and sheltered-market bidding, which are designed to aid small businesses in bidding on government contracts.
- ***Incubators/Research and Technology Parks***—Includes small business incubators, which provide newly established small business owners with work sites, business services, training, and consultation; also includes research and technology parks, which sponsor research and facilitate commercialization of new technologies.
- ***Educational Programs***—Includes university and college programs, as well as those sponsored by other organizations that offer degree, nondegree, certificate, and correspondence programs in entrepreneurship and in small business development.
- ***Legislative Assistance***—Includes committees, subcommittees, and joint committees of each state's

senate and house of representatives that are concerned with small business issues and regulations.

- ***Consultants***—Includes consultants and consulting firms offering expertise in small business development.
- ***Publications***—Includes publications related to small business operations within the profiled state.
- ***Publishers***—Includes publishers operating in or for the small business arena within the profiled state.

Federal Government Assistance. This section lists federal government agencies and offices, many with additional listings for specific offices, as well as regional or district branches. Main agencies or offices are listed alphabetically; regional, branch, ordistrict offices are listed after each main office or agency.

Master Index. This index provides an alphabetic listing of all entries contained in Volumes 1 throgh 6. Citations are referenced by their entry numbers. Publication titles are rendered in italics.

Acknowledgements

The editors would like to extend sincere thanks to the following members of the Small Business Sourcebook advisory board for their expert guidance, recommendations, and suggestions for the ongoing development of this title:

Susan C. Awe
Assistant Director,
William J. Parish Memorial Business Library

Jill Clever
Business Technology Specialist,
Toledo-Lucas County Public Library

Jules Matsoff
District Manager,
Service Corps of Retired Executives (SCORE) Milwaukee Chapter

Ken MacKenzie
President,
Southeast Business Appraisal

The editors would also like to thank the individuals from associations and other organizations who provided information for the compilation of this directory.

List of General Small Business Topics

This section covers sources of assistance applicable to a variety of small businesses. Resources are arranged by topic and include associations, educational programs, directories of educational programs, reference works, sources of supply, statistical sources, periodicals, videocassettes/audiocassettes, trade shows and conventions, consultants, computerized databases, computer systems/software, Internet databases, libraries, and research centers.

Environmentally Responsible Business Practices

START-UP INFORMATION

30408 ■ *75 Green Businesses You Can Start to Make Money and Make a Difference*
Pub: Entrepreneur Press
Ed: Glenn Croston. **Released:** August 1, 2008. **Price:** $19.95 paper. **Description:** Descriptions of seventy-five environmentally-friendly business startups are presented.

30409 ■ *"EDCO Doling Out Capital Along Border" in Austin Business JournalInc. (Vol. 28, August 1, 2008, No. 20, pp. 1)*
Pub: American City Business Journals
Ed: Sandra Zaragoza. **Description:** Non-profit business incubator Economic Development Catalyst Organization Ventures is searching for promising startup companies. The company is targeting startups in green energy, technology and consumer markets. EDCO has partnered with consumer electronics repair company CherryFusion and technology firm MiniDonations.

30410 ■ *"Green Acre$ Tope 10 Green Biz To Start Right Now" in Small Business Opportunities (September 2010)*
Pub: Harris Publications Inc.
Description: A list of the top ten green businesses to start in 2010 is provided.

30411 ■ *"Green Clean Machine" in Small Business Opportunities (Winter 2010)*
Pub: Harris Publications Inc.
Description: Eco-friendly maid franchise plans to grow its $62 million sales base. Profile of Maid Brigade, a green-cleaning franchise is planning to expand across the country.

30412 ■ *Starting Green: An Ecopreneur's Guide to Starting a Green Business from Business Plans to Profits*
Pub: Entrepreneur Press
Contact: Perlman Neil, President
Ed: Glenn E. Croston. **Released:** September 9, 2010. **Price:** $21.95. **Description:** Entrepreneur and scientist outlines green business essentials and helps uncover eco-friendly business opportunities, build a sustainable business plan, and gain the competitive advantage.

ASSOCIATIONS AND OTHER ORGANIZATIONS

30413 ■ *Between the Issues*
2705 Fern Ln.
Halifax, NS, Canada B3K 4L7
Ph: (902)429-2202
Fax: (902)405-3716
Co. E-mail: info@ecologyaction.ca
URL: http://www.ecologyaction.ca
Contact: Karen Hollett, Co-Chairperson
Released: Quarterly **Price:** included in membership dues.

30414 ■ Canadian Association on Water Quality (CAWQ)—Association canadienne sur la qualite de l'eau (ACQE)
PO Box 5050
Burlington, ON, Canada L7R 4A6
Ph: (289)780-0378
Fax: (905)336-6444
Co. E-mail: members@cawq.ca
URL: http://www.cawq.ca
Contact: Dr. C. Tiedemann, President
Description: Corporations, learned societies, universities, organizations, and individuals. Promotes research on water quality and water pollution. Furthers the exchange of information and practical application of such research for public benefit. **Founded:** 1967. **Publications:** *Water Quality Research Journal of Canada* (Quarterly). **Awards:** Philip H. Jones Award (3/year). **Telecommunication Services:** ctiedema@epcor.ca.

30415 ■ Canadian Environmental Network (CEN)—Reseau canadien de l'environment (RCEN)
39 McArthur Ave., Level 1-1
Ottawa, ON, Canada K1L 8L7
Ph: (613)728-9810
Fax: (613)728-2963
Co. E-mail: info@cen-rce.org
URL: http://www.cen-rce.org
Contact: Maggie Paquet, Chairman
Description: Environmental organizations. Seeks to advance the projects and activities of members. Promotes ecologically sustainable development. Serves as a clearinghouse on environmental issues; provides support and assistance to members. **Founded:** 1988. **Publications:** *Canadian Environmental Network News* (Annual). **Awards:** Caucus Achievement Award.

30416 ■ *Canadian Environmental Network News*
39 McArthur Ave., Level 1-1
Ottawa, ON, Canada K1L 8L7
Ph: (613)728-9810
Fax: (613)728-2963
Co. E-mail: info@cen-rce.org
URL: http://www.cen-rce.org
Contact: Maggie Paquet, Chairman
Released: Annual

30417 ■ Canadian Water Resources Association (CWRA)—Association Canadienne des Resources Hydriques (ACRH)
c/o Rick Ross, Exec. Dir.
1401 14th St. N
Lethbridge, AB, Canada T1H 2W6
Ph: (403)317-0017
Co. E-mail: executivedirector@cwra.org
URL: http://www.cwra.org
Contact: Rick Ross, Executive Director
Description: Corporations, government agencies, public libraries, and individuals with an interest in water resources. Seeks to increase public awareness and understanding of water resources; serves as a forum for the exchange of information relating to their management and use. Encourages governments at all levels to recognize the importance of water as a resource and supports formulation of appropriate water use policies. Conducts educational programs. **Founded:** 1947. **Publications:** *Canadian Water Resources Journal* (Quarterly); *Water News* (Quarterly). **Awards:** Hoskin Scientific Award; CWRA Scholarships in Water Resources (Annual); Ken Thompson Scholarship (Annual).

30418 ■ *Canadian Water Resources Journal*
c/o Rick Ross, Exec. Dir.
1401 14th St. N
Lethbridge, AB, Canada T1H 2W6
Ph: (403)317-0017
Co. E-mail: executivedirector@cwra.org
URL: http://www.cwra.org
Contact: Rick Ross, Executive Director
Released: Quarterly **Price:** C$25, /copy.

30419 ■ Compost Council of Canada—Conseil Canadien du Compost
16, rue Northumberland St.
Toronto, ON, Canada M6H 1P7
Ph: (416)535-0240
Free: 877-571-4769
Fax: (416)536-9892
Co. E-mail: info@compost.org
URL: http://www.compost.org
Contact: Susan Antler, Executive Director
Description: Serves to advocate and advance composting and compost usage across Canada. Serves as the central resource and network for the composting industry in Canada. Contributes to the environmental sustainability of communities. Sponsors International Composting Awareness Week; "Plant a Row Grow a Row". Conducts seminars and educational programs. Compiles statistics, maintains speakers' bureau. **Founded:** 1991. **Publications:** *Compost Council of Canada Communique.*

30420 ■ *Compost Council of Canada Communique*
16, rue Northumberland St.
Toronto, ON, Canada M6H 1P7
Ph: (416)535-0240
Free: 877-571-4769
Fax: (416)536-9892
Co. E-mail: info@compost.org
URL: http://www.compost.org
Contact: Susan Antler, Executive Director

30421 ■ *Connector*
PO Box 23
Bluffton, AB, Canada T0C 0M0
Ph: (403)843-6563
Fax: (403)843-4156
Co. E-mail: info@recycle.ab.ca
URL: http://www.recycle.ab.ca
Contact: Jason London, Director
Released: Quarterly **Price:** free.

30422 ■ Ecology Action Centre (EAC)
2705 Fern Ln.
Halifax, NS, Canada B3K 4L7

Ph: (902)429-2202
Fax: (902)405-3716
Co. E-mail: info@ecologyaction.ca
URL: http://www.ecologyaction.ca
Contact: Karen Hollett, Co-Chairperson
Description: Works to develop solutions to ecological problems. Fosters communication between members. **Founded:** 1971. **Publications:** *Between the Issues* (Quarterly).

30423 ■ *Enviro Business Guide*
PO Box 23
Bluffton, AB, Canada T0C 0M0
Ph: (403)843-6563
Fax: (403)843-4156
Co. E-mail: info@recycle.ab.ca
URL: http://www.recycle.ab.ca
Contact: Jason London, Director

30424 ■ *For R Information*
127 Wyndham St. N, Ste. 100
Guelph, ON, Canada N1H 4E9
Ph: (519)823-1990
Fax: (519)823-0084
Co. E-mail: mwa@municipalwaste.ca
URL: http://www.municipalwaste.ca
Contact: Sue McCrae, Chairman
Released: Quarterly

30425 ■ Green Hotels Association
PO Box 420212
Houston, TX 77242-0212
Ph: (713)789-8889
Fax: (713)789-9786
Co. E-mail: green@greenhotels.com
URL: http://greenhotels.com
Contact: Patricia Griffin, President
Description: Hotels, motels, inns, bed and breakfasts, and all other lodging establishments with an interest in protecting the environment. Encourages, promotes and supports ecological consciousness in the hospitality industry. **Founded:** 1993. **Publications:** *Greening Newsletter* (Bimonthly); *Membership Conservation Guidelines and Ideas* (Quadrennial).

30426 ■ Municipal Waste Association (MWA)
127 Wyndham St. N, Ste. 100
Guelph, ON, Canada N1H 4E9
Ph: (519)823-1990
Fax: (519)823-0084
Co. E-mail: mwa@municipalwaste.ca
URL: http://www.municipalwaste.ca
Contact: Sue McCrae, Chairman
Description: Municipal waste management professionals. Promotes more effective and environmentally sustainable removal of solid wastes. Facilitates sharing of municipal waste management, reduction, recycling, and reuse information and facilities. Conducts continuing professional education courses for members; operates job hotline; represents members' interests before government agencies and the public. Sponsors research; compiles statistics. **Founded:** 1987. **Publications:** *For R Information* (Quarterly). **Awards:** Promotion and Education Awards.

30427 ■ Pellet Fuels Institute (PFI)
1901 N Moore St., Ste. 600
Arlington, VA 22209-1708
Ph: (703)522-6778
Fax: (703)522-0548
Co. E-mail: pfimail@pelletheat.org
URL: http://www.pelletheat.org
Contact: Scott Jacobs, President
Description: Pellet and briquette manufacturers; processors of wood, and agricultural fuels; pellet burner manufacturers and distributors; combustion and handling equipment manufacturers and distributors; industry suppliers; and companies and organizations that use wood, agricultural residues, and paper as fuel. Promotes the increased use of pellets, briquettes, chips, and other renewable fiber fuels. Supports lobbying efforts promoting fiber fuels. Acts as an information clearinghouse among members. **Founded:** 1982. **Publications:** *PFI Newsletter* (Quarterly).

30428 ■ Pembina Institute for Appropriate Development (PIAD)
219 19 St. NW
Calgary, AB, Canada T2N 2H9
Ph: (403)269-3344
Fax: (403)269-3377
Co. E-mail: info@pembina.org
URL: http://www.pembina.org
Contact: Ed Whittingham, Executive Director
Description: Organizations and individuals with an interest in environmental protection and global development. Promotes increased public awareness of environmental and development issues. Conducts environmental research and educational programs; provides corporate environmental strategic management services, sponsors charitable activities. **Founded:** 1985.

30429 ■ Planetary Association for Clean Energy (PACE)—Societe Planetaire pour l'Assainissement de l'Energie
100 Bronson Ave., No. 1001
Ottawa, (ON), Canada K1R 6G8
Ph: (613)236-6265
Fax: (613)235-5876
Co. E-mail: paceincnet@gmail.com
URL: http://pacenet.homestead.com
Description: Researchers, individuals, corporations, and institutions worldwide seeking to facilitate research, development, demonstration, and evaluation of clean energy systems. Defines clean energy systems as those that utilize natural sources, and are inexpensive, non-polluting, and universally applicable. Concerns include the bioeffects of low-level electromagnetics, bioenergetics, new energy technology, decontamination of nuclear and toxic wastes, production of clean water from ambient air, and pesticide and fertilizer-free ultra-productive agricultural practices. Tests and recommends products that facilitate the implementation of clean energy systems. Serves as a consultant to governments and other agencies. Maintains speaker's bureau. **Scope:** new energy technologies, bioeffects of electromagnetic fields. **Founded:** 1975. **Subscriptions:** 5000 articles books periodicals.

30430 ■ Pollution Probe Foundation
12 Madison Ave.
Toronto, ON, Canada M5R 2S1
Ph: (416)926-1907
Fax: (416)926-1601
Co. E-mail: pprobe@pollutionprobe.org
URL: http://www.pollutionprobe.org
Contact: Bob Oliver, Chief Executive Officer
Description: Works to define environmental problems through research; seeks to raise public awareness of environmental issues through education; lobbies for environmental protection and remediation before government agencies and industrial associations. Focuses on smog and climate change, reduction and elimination of mercury in water, child health and the environment, indoor air quality, and water quality. **Founded:** 1969. **Publications:** *ProbeAbilities* (Quarterly); *Probe Post: Canada's Environmental Magazine* (Quarterly).

30431 ■ *ProbeAbilities*
12 Madison Ave.
Toronto, ON, Canada M5R 2S1
Ph: (416)926-1907
Fax: (416)926-1601
Co. E-mail: pprobe@pollutionprobe.org
URL: http://www.pollutionprobe.org
Contact: Bob Oliver, Chief Executive Officer
Released: Quarterly **Price:** available to members only.

30432 ■ Recycling Council of Alberta (RCA)
PO Box 23
Bluffton, AB, Canada T0C 0M0
Ph: (403)843-6563
Fax: (403)843-4156
Co. E-mail: info@recycle.ab.ca
URL: http://www.recycle.ab.ca
Contact: Jason London, Director
Description: Promotes and facilitates waste reduction, recycling and resource conservation in the province of Alberta. **Founded:** 1987. **Publications:** *Connector* (Quarterly); *Enviro Business Guide*. **Awards:** Rs of Excellence Awards; R's of Excellence (Annual).

30433 ■ Resource Efficient Agricultural Production - Canada (REAPC)
21, 111 Lakeshore Rd.
Centennial Centre CCB13
Ste.-Anne-de-Bellevue, QC, Canada H9X 3V9
Ph: (514)398-7743
Fax: (514)398-7972
Co. E-mail: info@reap-canada.com
URL: http://www.reap-canada.com
Contact: Roger Samson, Executive Director
Description: Agricultural researchers and educators. Promotes development and implementation of environmentally sustainable and economically viable agricultural techniques in Canada and internationally. Conducts research and disseminates results in areas including ecology, energy, agri-fibre, and food production. Maintains on-farm research programs. **Founded:** 1986. **Educational Activities:** International Agriculture Program.

30434 ■ Saskatchewan Environmental Society (SES)
Box 1372
Saskatoon, SK, Canada S7K 3N9
Ph: (306)665-1915
Fax: (306)665-2128
Co. E-mail: info@environmentalsociety.ca
URL: http://www.environmentalsociety.ca
Contact: Allyson Brady, Executive Director
Description: Seeks to support and encourage the creation of a global community in which all needs are met in sustainable ways. **Founded:** 1970. **Publications:** *SES Newsletter* (Bimonthly).

30435 ■ *SES Newsletter*
Box 1372
Saskatoon, SK, Canada S7K 3N9
Ph: (306)665-1915
Fax: (306)665-2128
Co. E-mail: info@environmentalsociety.ca
URL: http://www.environmentalsociety.ca
Contact: Allyson Brady, Executive Director
Released: Bimonthly **Price:** C$40, /subscription.

30436 ■ Society Promoting Environmental Conservation (SPEC)
2060-B Pine St.
Vancouver, BC, Canada V6J 4P8
Ph: (604)736-7732
Fax: (604)736-7115
Co. E-mail: admin@spec.bc.ca
URL: http://www.spec.bc.ca
Contact: Tara Moreau, President
Description: Promotes environmental research, advocacy, and education. **Founded:** 1969. **Publications:** *SPECTRUM* (Quarterly).

30437 ■ *SPECTRUM*
2060-B Pine St.
Vancouver, BC, Canada V6J 4P8
Ph: (604)736-7732
Fax: (604)736-7115
Co. E-mail: admin@spec.bc.ca
URL: http://www.spec.bc.ca
Contact: Tara Moreau, President
Released: Quarterly **Price:** free.

30438 ■ *Walk Softly*
302 Hawkins St.
Whitehorse, YT, Canada Y1A 1X6
Ph: (867)668-5678
Fax: (867)668-6637
Co. E-mail: ycs@ycs.yk.ca
URL: http://www.yukonconservation.org
Contact: Mary Whitley, President
Released: Quarterly **Price:** included in membership dues.

30439 ■ *Water News*
c/o Rick Ross, Exec. Dir.
1401 14th St. N
Lethbridge, AB, Canada T1H 2W6

Ph: (403)317-0017
Co. E-mail: executivedirector@cwra.org
URL: http://www.cwra.org
Contact: Rick Ross, Executive Director
Released: Quarterly **Price:** C$25, /copy.

30440 ■ *Water Quality Research Journal of Canada*
PO Box 5050
Burlington, ON, Canada L7R 4A6
Ph: (289)780-0378
Fax: (905)336-6444
Co. E-mail: members@cawq.ca
URL: http://www.cawq.ca
Contact: Dr. C. Tiedemann, President
Released: Quarterly **Price:** C$250, in U.S. and Canada; C$295, overseas.

30441 ■ *Women and Environments*
215 Spadina Ave., Ste. 400
Toronto, ON, Canada M5T 2C7
Ph: (416)928-0880
Fax: (416)644-0116
Co. E-mail: office@womenshealthyenvironments.ca
URL: http://www.womenshealthyenvironments.ca
Contact: Marie Lorenzo, Chairperson
Released: Quarterly **Price:** C$8, /issue; C$21.97, /year.

30442 ■ Women's Healthy Environments Network (WHEN)
215 Spadina Ave., Ste. 400
Toronto, ON, Canada M5T 2C7
Ph: (416)928-0880
Fax: (416)644-0116
Co. E-mail: office@womenshealthyenvironments.ca
URL: http://www.womenshealthyenvironments.ca
Contact: Marie Lorenzo, Chairperson
Description: Women experts in environmental studies and issues. Works to implement community development projects to improve the environment. Provides a forum for discussion, information exchange, and the conducting of research related to women in the fields of planning, health, workplace, design, economy, urban and rural sociology, and community development. Initiates and organizes community projects. Advocates environmental protection, anti-discriminatory zoning practices, and the development of affordable housing. **Founded:** 1994. **Publications:** *Women and Environments* (Quarterly); *Whitewash*.

30443 ■ Yukon Conservation Society (YCS)
302 Hawkins St.
Whitehorse, YT, Canada Y1A 1X6
Ph: (867)668-5678
Fax: (867)668-6637
Co. E-mail: ycs@ycs.yk.ca
URL: http://www.yukonconservation.org
Contact: Mary Whitley, President
Description: Seeks to protect Canada's natural environment; particularly that of the Yukon region. Encourages the conservation of Yukon wilderness, wildlife and natural resources. **Founded:** 1968. **Publications:** *Walk Softly* (Quarterly). **Awards:** Ted Parnell Scholarship (Annual).

EDUCATIONAL PROGRAMS

30444 ■ Advanced Hazardous Waste Management (Onsite)
Seminar Information Service, Inc.
20 Executive Park, Ste. 120
Irvine, CA 92614
Ph: (949)261-9104
Free: 877-SEM-INFO
Fax: (949)261-1963
Co. E-mail: info@seminarinformation.com
URL: http://www.seminarinformation.com
Price: $499.00. **Description:** Learn to minimize your hazardous waste generation and make sure you are complying fully with all hazardous regulations. **Dates and Locations:** Atlanta, GA.

30445 ■ ASTM Phase I & Phase II Environmental Site Assessment Processes (Onsite)
Seminar Information Service, Inc.
20 Executive Park, Ste. 120
Irvine, CA 92614
Ph: (949)261-9104
Free: 877-SEM-INFO
Fax: (949)261-1963
Co. E-mail: info@seminarinformation.com
URL: http://www.seminarinformation.com
Price: $1,095.00. **Description:** Gain an understanding how to use the standards and how the standards affect the way you do business. The 'Innocent Landowner Defense' under the Comprehensive Environmental Response, Compensation and Liability Act (CERCLA) and why due diligence is necessary will be covered. **Dates and Locations:** Boston, MA; Columbus, OH; West Conshohocken, PA; New Orleans, LA; and Las Vegas, NV.

30446 ■ Climatic Test Techniques (Onsite)
Seminar Information Service, Inc.
20 Executive Park, Ste. 120
Irvine, CA 92614
Ph: (949)261-9104
Free: 877-SEM-INFO
Fax: (949)261-1963
Co. E-mail: info@seminarinformation.com
URL: http://www.seminarinformation.com
Price: $1,595.00. **Description:** An introduction to climatic testing with an overview of field test measurement and analysis, with primary emphasis on understanding the physics of each environment, and available measurement and control techniques.

30447 ■ Comprehensive 5-Day Training Program for Business Energy Professionals (Onsite)
Seminar Information Service, Inc.
20 Executive Park, Ste. 120
Irvine, CA 92614
Ph: (949)261-9104
Free: 877-SEM-INFO
Fax: (949)261-1963
Co. E-mail: info@seminarinformation.com
URL: http://www.seminarinformation.com
Price: $1,895.00; $1,695.00 for members government/non-profits. **Description:** Gain an understanding of how energy efficiency opportunities impact the bottom line for their customers. **Dates and Locations:** Atlanta, GA.

30448 ■ Comprehensive 5-Day Training Program For Energy Managers (Onsite)
Seminar Information Service, Inc.
20 Executive Park, Ste. 120
Irvine, CA 92614
Ph: (949)261-9104
Free: 877-SEM-INFO
Fax: (949)261-1963
Co. E-mail: info@seminarinformation.com
URL: http://www.seminarinformation.com
Price: $1,895.00. **Description:** Provides detailed coverage of all of the six training areas specified for energy managers in the Energy Policy Act, and offers a comprehensive learning and problem-solving forum for those who want a broader understanding of the latest energy cost reduction techniques and strategies. **Dates and Locations:** San Antonio, TX; Nashville, TN; San Juan, PR; Washington, DC; and Las Vegas, NV.

30449 ■ Crude Oil: Sampling, Testing, and Evaluation (Onsite)
Seminar Information Service, Inc.
20 Executive Park, Ste. 120
Irvine, CA 92614
Ph: (949)261-9104
Free: 877-SEM-INFO
Fax: (949)261-1963
Co. E-mail: info@seminarinformation.com
URL: http://www.seminarinformation.com
Price: $1,095.00. **Description:** Learn how to obtain representative samples of crude oil using automatic and manual methods. Learn the test methods available for obtaining the basic data necessary to determine quantity for custody transfer purposes and conformance to expected quality. **Dates and Locations:** Houston, TX.

30450 ■ DOT Hazardous Materials Training (Onsite)
Seminar Information Service, Inc.
20 Executive Park, Ste. 120
Irvine, CA 92614
Ph: (949)261-9104
Free: 877-SEM-INFO
Fax: (949)261-1963
Co. E-mail: info@seminarinformation.com
URL: http://www.seminarinformation.com
Price: $449.00. **Description:** DOT is changing virtually all of the rules for hazardous materials containers, labeling, shipping papers, placards, and shipping names. Learn how to comply with the regulations. **Dates and Locations:** Cities throughout the United States.

30451 ■ Energy Auditing 101: Identifying Cost Saving Opportunities in Plants & Buildings (Onsite)
Seminar Information Service, Inc.
20 Executive Park, Ste. 120
Irvine, CA 92614
Ph: (949)261-9104
Free: 877-SEM-INFO
Fax: (949)261-1963
Co. E-mail: info@seminarinformation.com
URL: http://www.seminarinformation.com
Price: $1,150.00. **Description:** Seminar designed to provide you with the knowledge you need to identify where energy consumption can be reduced, and utilize the latest methods and technologies to accomplish real savings, with emphasis on providing useful calculation methods and practical examples.

30452 ■ Fundamentals of Carbon Reduction (Onsite)
Seminar Information Service, Inc.
20 Executive Park, Ste. 120
Irvine, CA 92614
Ph: (949)261-9104
Free: 877-SEM-INFO
Fax: (949)261-1963
Co. E-mail: info@seminarinformation.com
URL: http://www.seminarinformation.com
Price: $1,450.00. **Description:** First step for organizations that want to become more environmentally-friendly, including how to conduct a 'carbon audit' and how to begin a carbon reduction program. **Dates and Locations:** Atlanta,GA.

30453 ■ Fundamentals of Energy Auditing (Onsite)
Seminar Information Service, Inc.
20 Executive Park, Ste. 120
Irvine, CA 92614
Ph: (949)261-9104
Free: 877-SEM-INFO
Fax: (949)261-1963
Co. E-mail: info@seminarinformation.com
URL: http://www.seminarinformation.com
Price: $1,450.00. **Description:** Learn to evaluate how energy is being used in a facility, and to identify where consumption can be reduced, covering useful calculation methods and practical examples. **Dates and Locations:** Atlanta, GA; Chicago, IL; and Las Vegas, NV.

30454 ■ Gasoline: Specifications, Testing, and Technology (Onsite)
Seminar Information Service, Inc.
20 Executive Park, Ste. 120
Irvine, CA 92614
Ph: (949)261-9104
Free: 877-SEM-INFO
Fax: (949)261-1963
Co. E-mail: info@seminarinformation.com
URL: http://www.seminarinformation.com
Price: $1,195.00. **Description:** Covers the properties and specifications of gasoline and how they affect its performance in a spark ignition engine, including a tour of a gasoline testing laboratory. **Dates and Locations:** San Antonio, TX; and Savannah, GA.

30455 ■ Hazardous Waste Management: The Complete Course
Seminar Information Service, Inc.
20 Executive Park, Ste. 120
Irvine, CA 92614
Ph: (949)261-9104
Free: 877-SEM-INFO
Fax: (949)261-1963
Co. E-mail: info@seminarinformation.com
URL: http://www.seminarinformation.com
Price: $795.00. **Description:** Covers how to meet your annual training requirement and learn a systematic approach to understanding and complying with the latest state and federal regulations. **Dates and Locations:** Cities throughout the United States.

30456 ■ Marine Fuels: Specifications, Testing, Purchase & Use
Seminar Information Service, Inc.
20 Executive Park, Ste. 120
Irvine, CA 92614
Ph: (949)261-9104
Free: 877-SEM-INFO
Fax: (949)261-1963
Co. E-mail: info@seminarinformation.com
URL: http://www.seminarinformation.com
Price: $1,095.00. **Description:** Learn how the properties of marine fuels affect fuel handling, combustion, and cost, including a detailed understanding of fuel quality requirements, and why they are necessary for good handling and combustion performance. **Dates and Locations:** Houston, TX; San Francisco, CA.

30457 ■ Risk-Based Corrective Action RBCA Applied at Petroleum Release Sites (Onsite)
Seminar Information Service, Inc.
20 Executive Park, Ste. 120
Irvine, CA 92614
Ph: (949)261-9104
Free: 877-SEM-INFO
Fax: (949)261-1963
Co. E-mail: info@seminarinformation.com
URL: http://www.seminarinformation.com
Price: $895.00. **Description:** Receive the same RBCA training your state regulators are receiving from the organization that developed the RBCA standard from RBCA process overview and risk assessment to fate and transport and policy decisions. **Dates and Locations:** Lansing, MI.

DIRECTORIES OF EDUCATIONAL PROGRAMS

30458 ■ *Recycling in America: A Reference Handbook*
Pub: ABC-Clio Inc.
Contact: Ron Boehm, President
E-mail: rboehm@abc-clio.com
URL(s): www.abc-clio.com. **Released:** Latest edition 2nd, November 1997. **Publication includes:** Lists of private, state, and federal agencies and organizations, and online sources. Principal content of publication is a history of recycling; brief biographical section; facts on recycled materials; and laws and regulations.

REFERENCE WORKS

30459 ■ *"21st Century Filling Station" in Austin Business JournalInc. (Vol. 29, December 11, 2009, No. 40, pp. 1)*
Pub: American City Business Journals
Ed: Jacob Dirr. **Description:** Clean Energy Fuels Corporation announced plans for the construction of a $1 million, 17,000 square foot compressed natural gas fueling station at or near the Austin-Bergstrom International Airport (ABIA). Clean Energy Fuels hopes to encourage cab and shuttle companies in the ABIA to switch from gasoline to natural gas.

30460 ■ *"$40M Fund Created for Big Energy Project" in Austin Business JournalInc. (Vol. 29, November 27, 2009, No. 38, pp. 1)*
Pub: American City Business Journals
Ed: Christopher Calnan. **Description:** A group of Texas businessmen, called Republic Power Partners LP, is planning to raise $40 million in order to launch an alternative energy project. The 6,000-megawatt initiative would generate solar, biomass and wind power in West Texas and could cost as much as $10 billion.

30461 ■ *"2008 Woman of the Year Gala" in Hispanic Business (Vol. 30, July-August 2008, No. 7-8, pp. 58)*
Pub: Hispanic Business, Inc.
Ed: Brynne Chappell. **Description:** Brief report on the sixth annual Women of the Year Awards gala which was held at JW Marriott Desert Ridge Resort and Spa is given; 20 women were honored with these awards for their professional contribution, commitment to the advancement of the Hispanic community and involvement with charitable organizations.

30462 ■ *"2010: Important Year Ahead for Waterfront" in Bellingham Business Journal (Vol. March 2010, pp. 2)*
Pub: Sound Publishing Inc.
Ed: Isaac Bonnell. **Description:** A tentative timeline has been established for the environmental impact statement (EIS) slated for completion in May 2010. The plan for the Waterfront District includes detailed economic and architectural analysis of the feasibility of reusing remaining structures and retaining some industrial icons.

30463 ■ *"2011 FinOvation Awards" in Farm Industry News (January 19, 2011)*
Pub: Penton Business Media Inc.
Ed: Jodie Wehrspann. **Description:** The 2011 FinOvation Award winners are announced, covering new products that growers need for corn and soybean crops. Winners range from small turbines and a fuel-efficient pickup to a Class 10 combine and drought-tolerant hybrids.

30464 ■ *"2011 a Record Year for New Wind Energy Installations in Canada" in CNW Group (September 26, 2011)*
Pub: CNW Group
Contact: Carolyn McGill-Davidson, President
Description: Canada reports a record for new wind energy projects in 2011 with about 1,338 MW of newly installed wind energy capacity expected to come on line, compared to 690 MW installed in 2010. Statistical data included.

30465 ■ *"2011 U.S. Smart Grid - Saving Energy/Saving Money" in Ecology,Environment & Conservation Business (October 8, 2011, pp. 3)*
Pub: HighBeam Research
Description: Highlights of the '2011 U.S. Smart Grid —Saving Energy/Saving Money Customers' Prospective Demand-Response assesses residential energy consumers' willingness to decrease their power consumption in order to mitigate power issues. Statistical details included.

30466 ■ *"A123-Fisker Deal May Mean 540 Jobs" in Crain's Detroit Business (Vol. 26, January 18, 2010, No. 3, pp. 4)*
Pub: Crain Communications Inc.
Ed: Dustin Walsh. **Description:** Manufacturing plants in Livonia and Romulous may be hiring up to 540 skilled workers due to a contract that was won by A123 Systems Inc. that will result in the company supplying lithium-ion batteries to Fisker Automotive Inc. to be used in their Karma plug-in hybrid electric vehicle.

30467 ■ *"The ABCs of a Good Show" in Playthings (Vol. 106, October 1, 2008, No. 9, pp. 18)*
Pub: Reed Business Information
Contact: Jeff Greisch, President
Ed: Karyn M. Peterson. **Description:** ABC Kids Expo 2008 made a strong showing with products for babies, kids and new/expecting parents. The new Naturally Kids section promoting eco-friendly products was the highlight of the show.

30468 ■ *"Acing the Test" in Contractor (Vol. 57, January 2010, No. 1, pp. 32)*
Pub: Penton Media, Inc.
Ed: Robert P. Mader. **Description:** A ward winning mechanical system retrofitting of a middle school in Ohio is discussed. The school now operates at 37,800 Btu/sq. ft and reduced a significant amount of pollutants from being emitted into the environment.

30469 ■ *"Actiontec and Verizon Team Up for a Smarter Home" in Ecology,Environment & Conservation Business (November 5, 2011, pp. 3)*
Pub: HighBeam Research
Description: Verizon is implementing Actiontec Electronics' SG200 Service Gateway as a basic component of its Home Monitoring and Control service. This new smart home service allows customers to remotely check their homes, control locks and appliances, view home-energy use and more using a smartphone, PC, or FiOS TV.

30470 ■ *"Adventures at Hydronicahh" in Contractor (Vol. 56, September 2009, No. 9, pp. 52)*
Pub: Penton Media, Inc.
Ed: Mark Eatherton. **Description:** Installation of the heating system of a lakeview room are described. The room's radiant windows are powered by electricity from a solar PV array and a propane-powered hydrogen fuel cell. The system will be programmed to use the most energy available.

30471 ■ *"Adventures at Hydronicahh" in Contractor (Vol. 56, November 2009, No. 11, pp. 36)*
Pub: Penton Media, Inc.
Ed: Mark Eatherton. **Description:** Part 6 of the installation of a five stage ground-source heat pump for a hydronic heating system is discussed. The heat exchanger will be bidirectional in the plan described.

30472 ■ *"Adventures at Hydronicahh" in Contractor (Vol. 56, October 2009, No. 10, pp. 42)*
Pub: Penton Media, Inc.
Ed: Mark Eatherton. **Description:** Design and installation of a solar thermal system for a hydronic heating project is described. This portion has two 32-square feet of flat plate glazed solar collectors that are tied to a 120-gallon reverse indirect DHW heater.

30473 ■ *"AF Expands in New Green Building in Gothenburg" in Ecology,Environment & Conservation Business (September 24, 2011, pp. 2)*
Pub: HighBeam Research
Description: AF signed a ten-year tenancy contract with Skanska for the premises of its new green building in Gothenburg, Sweden. AF offers qualified services and solutions for industrial processes, infrastructure projects and the development of products and IT systems.

30474 ■ *"Agricultural Community Implements Green Technologies, Building Team" in Contractor (Vol. 56, September 2009, No. 9, pp. 5)*
Pub: Penton Media, Inc.
Ed: Candace Ruolo. **Description:** John DeWald and Associates has initiated a residential development project which uses green technologies in Illinois. The community features a community center, organic farm and recreational trails. Comments from executives are also provided.

30475 ■ *"Ahead of the Pack" in Small Business Opportunities (Fall 2010)*
Pub: Harris Publications Inc.
Description: Profile of an organic fast-food business that is carving out a niche that is gaining favor. Elevation Burger is a unique concept offering healthier burgers in sustainable buildings.

30476 ■ *"Allowing Ethanol Tax Incentive to Expire Would Risk Jobs, RFAas Dinneen Says" in Farm Industry News (November 3, 2010)*
Pub: Penton Business Media Inc.
Description: Jobs would be at risk if the ethanol tax incentive expires.

30477 ■ *"Alstom Launches te ECO 122 - 2.7MW Wind Turbine for Low Wind Sites" in CNW Group (September 28, 2011)*
Pub: CNW Group
Contact: Carolyn McGill-Davidson, President
Description: Alstom is launching its new ECO 122, a 2.7MW onshore wind turbine that combines high power and high capacity factor (1) to boost energy yield in low wind regions around the world. The ECO 122 will produce about 25 percent increased wind farm yield that current turbines and fewer turbines would be installed in areas.

30478 ■ *"Alternative Energy Calls for Alternative Marketing" in Indoor Comfort Marketing (Vol. 70, June 2011, No. 6, pp. 8)*
Pub: Industry Publications Inc.
Ed: Richard Rutigliano. **Description:** Advice for marketing solar energy products and services is given.

30479 ■ *"Alternative Energy is a Major Topic at Agritechnica 2011" in Farm Industry News (November 16, 2011)*
Pub: Penton Business Media Inc.
Ed: Mark Moore. **Description:** Sustainable agricultural systems were a hot topic at this year's Agritechnia 2011, held in Germany. Germany is a leader in the development of on-farm biogas systems.

30480 ■ *"American Chemistry Council Launches Flagship Blog" in Ecology,Environment & Conservation Business (October 29, 2011, pp. 5)*
Pub: HighBeam Research
Description: American Chemistry Council (ACC) launched its blog, American Chemistry Matters, where interactive space allows bloggers to respond to news coverage and to discuss policy issues and their impact on innovation, competitiveness, job creation and safety.

30481 ■ *"ANATURALCONCEPT" in Crain's Cleveland Business (Vol. 30, June 22, 2009, No. 24, pp. 1)*
Pub: Crain Communications, Inc.
Ed: Dan Shingler. **Description:** Cleveland-based Biomimicry Institute, led by Cleveland's Entrepreneurs for Sustainability and the Cuyahoga County Planning Commission, are using biomimicry to incorporate eco-friendliness with industry. Biomimicry studies nature's best ideas then imitates these designs and processes to solve human problems.

30482 ■ *"Ann Alexander; Senior Attorney, Natural Resources Defense Council" in Crain's Chicago Business (Vol. 31, May 5, 2008, No. 18)*
Pub: Crain Communications, Inc.
Ed: Emily Stone. **Description:** Profile of Ann Alexander who is the senior attorney at the Natural Resources Defense Council and is known for her dedication to the environment and a career spent battling oil companies, steelmakers and the government to change federal regulations. One recent project aims to improve the Bush administration's fuel economy standards for SUVs. Past battles include her work to prevent permits from slipping through the cracks such as the proposal by London-based BP PLC to dump 54 percent more ammonia and 35 percent more suspended solids from its Whiting, Indiana refinery into Lake Michigan-the source of drinking water for Chicago and its surrounding communities.

30483 ■ *"Answers About Commercial Wind Farms Could Come from Downstate" in Erie Times-News (September 27, 2011)*
Pub: Erie Times-News
Ed: Valerie Myers. **Description:** Texas-based Pioneer Green Energy is measuring wind and leasing land in North East Township, Pennsylvania. The firm plans to build a 7,000-acre wind farm along wine-country ridges. About 70 turbines would harness wind in order to generate electricity that would be sold into the eastern power grid.

30484 ■ *"Aquarium's Solar Demonstration Project Exceeds Expectations" in Contractor (Vol. 57, February 2010, No. 2, pp. 1)*
Pub: Penton Media, Inc.
Ed: Candace Roulo. **Description:** Seattle Aquarium cafe installed flat-plate solar collectors to preheat water and data has shown that the system has allowed them to off-set almost double their expected consumption of natural gas. It is estimated that rthe solar panels will shrink the aquarium's carbon footprint by 2.5 tons of carbon dioxide each year.

30485 ■ *"Are You Looking for an Environmentally Friendly Dry Cleaner?" in Inc. (Vol. 30, December 2008, No. 12, pp. 34)*
Pub: Mansueto Ventures LLC
Ed: Shivani Vora. **Description:** Greenopia rates the greenness of 52 various kinds of businesses, including restaurants, nail salons, dry cleaners, and clothing stores. The guidebooks are sold through various retailers including Barnes & Noble and Amazon.com.

30486 ■ *"Areva Diversifies Further Into Wind" in Wall Street Journal Eastern Edition (November 29, 2011, pp. B7)*
Pub: Dow Jones & Company Inc. Enterprise Media Group
Contact: Clare Hart, President
Ed: Max Colchester, Noemie Bisserbe. **Description:** French engineering company Areva SA is diversifying and moving away from nuclear energy projects. One sign of that is its recent discussion to construct 120 wind turbines to be located at two German wind farms. Such a deal, if signed, would be worth about US$1.59 billion.

30487 ■ *"Art Institute of Chicago Goes Green" in Contractor (Vol. 56, July 2009, No. 7, pp. 1)*
Pub: Penton Media, Inc.
Ed: Candace Roulo. **Description:** Art Institute of Chicago's Modern Wing museum addition will receive a certification that makes them one of the most environmentally sound museum expansions in the U.S. A modified variable-air-volume system is being used to meet temperature and humidity requirements in the building and it also has a double curtain wall to capture summer heat.

30488 ■ *"Attorney Covers Climate in Copenhagen" in Houston Business Journal (Vol. 40, December 25, 2009, No. 33, pp. 1)*
Pub: American City Business Journals
Ed: Ford Gunter. **Description:** Houston environmental attorney Richard Faulk talks to the United Nations Climate Change Conference in Copenhagen, Denmark. Faulk believes the conference failed due to political differences between countries like US and China. Faulk believed the discussion of developed and developing countries on verification and limits on carbon emissions is something good that came from the conference.

30489 ■ *"Austin to Buy $1.1B of Wind Power from Two" in Austin Business Journal (Vol. 31, August 19, 2011, No. 24, pp. A1)*
Pub: American City Business Journals Inc.
Ed: Vicky Garza. **Description:** Austin City Council is set to approve contracts to purchase wind energy from Duke Energy Corporation and MAP Royalty Inc. The city will get 200MW from Duke and 91MW from MAP and the total contract is estimated to be worth $1.1 million.

30490 ■ *"Austin Energy May Build $2.3B Biomass Plant" in Austin Business JournalInc. (Vol. 28, July 25, 2008, No. 19, pp. A1)*
Pub: American City Business Journals
Ed: Kate Harrington. **Description:** An approval from the Austin City Council is being sought by Austin Energy for a 20-year supply contract with Nacogdoches Power LLC to build a $2.3 billion biomass plant in East Texas. The 100-megawatt biomass plant, which is to run on waste wood, will have Austin Energy as its sole buyer.

30491 ■ *"Auto Show Aims to Electrify" in Crain's Detroit Business (Vol. 26, January 11, 2010, No. 2, pp. 1)*
Pub: Crain Communications, Inc.
Ed: Ryan Beene. **Description:** Overview of the North American International Auto show include sixteen production and concept vehicles including eight from the Detroit 3. High-tech battery suppliers as well as hybrid and electric vehicles will highlight the show.

30492 ■ *"Automaker Foundations Run Leaner" in Crain's Detroit Business (Vol. 26, January 11, 2010, No. 2, pp. 1)*
Pub: Crain Communications Inc.
Ed: Sherri Welch. **Description:** Overview of the Detroit automobile industry includes restoring profitability, smarter marketing strategies and philanthropy. Each company comprising the Big 3 is examined, as is their vision for the future.

30493 ■ *"AV Concept Expands Into Green Energy Storage" in Wireless News (January 25, 2010)*
Pub: Close-Up Media
Description: Electronics distributor and manufacturer AV Concept Holdings Limited announced a marketing partnership with Boston-Power, a provider of lithium-ion batteries, with a focus in the Chinese and Korean markets.

30494 ■ *"Award Win Highlights Slingsby's Green Credentials" in Ecology,Environment & Conservation Business (August 20, 2011, pp. 3)*
Pub: HighBeam Research
Description: Slingsby, an industrial and commercial equipment supplier, was joint winner with Hallmark Cards of the Baildon Business in the Community's Yorkshire and Humber Long Term Environmental Improvement Award. The firm cites its commitment to reducing environmental impact.

30495 ■ *"Babynut.com to Shut Down" in Bellingham Business Journal (Vol. February 2010, pp. 3)*
Pub: Sound Publishing Inc.
Description: Saralee Sky and Jerry Kilgore, owners of Babynut.com will close their online store. The site offered a free online and email newsletter to help mothers through pregnancy and the first three years of their child's life. Products being sold at clearance prices include organic and natural maternity and nursing clothing, baby and toddler clothes, books on pregnancy, and more.

30496 ■ *"Back to Business for Bishop Museum" in Hawaii Business (Vol. 54, August 2008, No. 2, pp. 53)*
Pub: Hawaii Business Publishing
Ed: Shara Enay. **Description:** Bishop Museum, ranked 224 in Hawaii Business' top 250 companies for 2008, had $29.5 million in gross sales for 2007, up 52.8 percent from the $19.3 million gross sales in 2006. The company has cut 24 positions in a restructuring effort for the museum's sustainability. Grants, artifacts and plans for sustainable operations are discussed.

30497 ■ *"Bank on It" in Hawaii Business (Vol. 53, November 2007, No. 5, pp. 60)*
Pub: Hawaii Business Publishing
Ed: Kathleen Bryan. **Description:** Many Baby Boomers that are preparing to retire would like to give back and make a difference. One way is to make gifts of Individual Retirement Assets (IRA). During 2007 people over 70 years can make withdrawals from an IRA and donate it without realizing the income as taxable.

30498 ■ *"Be Wary of Dual-Flush Conversion Kits" in Contractor (Vol. 56, September 2009, No. 9, pp. 66)*
Pub: Penton Media, Inc.
Ed: John Koeller; Bill Gauley. **Description:** Recommendation of untested dual-flush conversion devices for tank-type toilets in the United States have been questioned. The products are being advertised as

having the ability to convert single-flush to a dual-flush toilet. No evidence of water conservation from using such devices has been recorded.

30499 ■ *"BETC Backers Plot Future" in Business Journal Portland (Vol. 27, December 10, 2010, No. 41, pp. 1)*
Pub: Portland Business Journal

Ed: Erik Siemers. **Description:** A coalition of clean energy groups and industrial manufacturers have spearheaded a campaign aimed at persuading Oregon legislators that the state's Business Energy Tax Credit (BETC) is vital in job creation. Oregon's BETC grants tax credits for 50 percent of an eligible renewable or clean energy project's cost. However, some legislators propose BETC's abolition.

30500 ■ *"Beware of E15" in Rental Product News (Vol. 33, October 2011)*
Pub: Cygnus Business Media

Ed: Curt Bennink. **Description:** Environmental Protection Agency (EPA) set a new regulation that grants partial waivers to allow gasoline containing up to 15 percent ethanol (E15) to be introduced into commerce for use in model year 2001 and newer light-duty motor vehicles, subject to certain conditions.

30501 ■ *Big-Box Swindle: The True Cost of Mega-Retailers and the Fight for America's Independent Businesses*
Pub: Beacon Press

Ed: Stacy Mitchell. **Released:** October 2007. **Price:** $15.00. **Description:** Examination of the economic, environmental, and social damage done by big-box retailers like Wal-Mart, Costco, and Home Depot. Labor policies of these retailers, particularly those enforced by Wal-Mart, are discussed at length.

30502 ■ *"Big Energy Deals Power OptiSolar's Local Growth" in Sacramento Business Journal (Vol. 25, August 22, 2008, No. 25, pp. 1)*
Pub: American City Business Journals, Inc.

Ed: Celia Lamb. **Description:** Solar energy projects are driving Sacramento, California-based OptiSolar's growth. The company is set to begin construction of its first photovoltaic project in Ontario. It also plans to build the world largest photovoltaic project in San Luis Obispo County.

30503 ■ *"Big Energy Ideas for Our Times" in Canadian Business (Vol. 83, August 17, 2010, No. 13-14, pp. 49)*
Pub: Rogers Media Ltd.

Description: Five ideas Canada must consider in the production of energy are explored. These ideas are run-off-river hydroelectric projects, the tapping of natural gas inside shale formation, the water's role in creating energy, the development of a smart grid, and the reduction of energy consumption.

30504 ■ *"Bigger is Definitely Not Better When It Comes to Cooling" in Indoor Comfort Marketing (Vol. 70, May 2011, No. 5, pp. 49)*
Pub: Industry Publications Inc.

Ed: Eugene Silberstein. **Description:** Efficiency is more important when installing air conditioning equipment over size of the unit. Details are provided.

30505 ■ *"Biodiesel Poised to Regain Growth" in Farm Industry News (January 21, 2011)*
Pub: Penton Business Media Inc.

Description: According to Gary Haer, vice president of sales and marketing for Renewable Energy Group, the biodiesel industry is positioned to regain growth in 2011 with the reinstatement of the biodiesel blendersa tax credt of $1 per gallon.

30506 ■ *"Bioheat - Alternative for Fueling Equipment" in Indoor Comfort Marketing (Vol. 70, May 2011, No. 5, pp. 14)*
Pub: Industry Publications Inc.

Ed: Gary Hess. **Description:** Profile of Worley and Obetz, supplier of biofuels used as an alternative for fueling industry equipment.

30507 ■ *"Blackwater is LEED Golden for Port of Portland Building" in Contractor (Vol. 56, October 2009, No. 10, pp. 3)*
Pub: Penton Media, Inc.

Ed: Robert P. Mader. **Description:** Worrel Water Technologies' Tidal Wetlands Living Machine recycles blackwater from the toilets and sends it right back to flush the toilets. The Technology is being installed in the new headquarters of the Port of Portland which aims to get awarded a gold certificate from the Leadership in Energy and Environmental Design.

30508 ■ *"Board This Powertrain" in Barron's (Vol. 89, July 27, 2009, No. 30, pp. 30)*
Pub: Dow Jones & Co., Inc.

Ed: Naureen S. Malik. **Description:** Siemens' American Depositary Receipts have risen 60 percent from their March 2009 low and they should continue heading higher. The company has solid earnings and revenue growth since they lead in growing markets such as alternative energy and health-care infrastructure. Their shares also look cheap at 1.9 times book value.

30509 ■ *"Bold Goals Will Require Time" in Contractor (Vol. 56, October 2009, No. 10, pp. S2)*
Pub: Penton Media, Inc.

Ed: Ted Lower. **Description:** Offering a broad range of courses is the Radiant Panel Association (RPA), an organization that holds education as its top priority. The RPA must lead the industry by raising the educational bar for future installers.

30510 ■ *"Brown At Center of Local CleanTech Lobbying Efforts" in Boston Business Journal (Vol. 30, October 15, 2010, No. 36, pp. 1)*
Pub: Boston Business Journal

Ed: Kyle Alspach. **Description:** U.S. Senator Scott Brown has been active in lobbying for energy reform in Massachusetts. Brown has been meeting with business groups seeking the reforms.

30511 ■ *"Burner Handles Everything From #2 to B100" in Indoor Comfort Marketing (Vol. 70, May 2011, No. 5, pp. 24)*
Pub: Industry Publications Inc.

Description: A new oil burner being offered by AMERIgreen Energy is profiled.

30512 ■ *"Burning Issues: Four of Today's Hottest Energy Topics" in Canadian Business (Vol. 83, August 17, 2010, No. 13-14, pp. 45)*
Pub: Rogers Media Ltd.

Description: A look at four issues dominating Canada's energy industry is presented. These issues are lack of transmission capacity and difficulty in transferring power across provincial boundaries, the management of intermittency of renewable generation, techniques that would clean up the Alberta's oil sands, and the impending massive use of electric cars in North America.

30513 ■ *"The Business of Activism" in Entrepreneur (Vol. 37, September 2009, No. 9, pp. 43)*
Pub: Entrepreneur Media, Inc.

Ed: Mary Catherine O'Connor. **Description:** San Francisco, California-based business incubator Virgance has been promoting sustainable projects by partnering with businesses. The company has launched campaigns which include organizing homeowners in negotiating with solar installers. The company is also planning to expand its workforce.

30514 ■ *"Buy the Pants, Save the Planet?" in Globe & Mail (February 5, 2007, pp. B1)*
Pub: CTVglobemedia Publishing Inc.

Ed: Keith McArthur. **Description:** The marketing campaign of the clothing company Diesel S.p.A. is discussed. The company has based its latest collection of T-shirt designs on the problem of global warming.

30515 ■ *"Caber Engineering Helps to Reduce Canada's Carbon Footprint" in Ecology,Environment & Conservation Business (July 16, 2011, pp. 7)*
Pub: HighBeam Research

Description: Calgary-based Caber Engineering Inc. will assist in the engineering design of the Alberta Carbon Trunk Line (ACTL). The ACTL is Alberta's first sizable commercial carbon capture and storage project focusing on the reduction of environmental impacts while being economically beneficial.

30516 ■ *"Calendar" in Crain's Detroit Business (Vol. 24, April 14, 2008, No. 15, pp. 25)*
Pub: Crain Communications Inc.

Description: Listing of events in the Detroit area include conferences addressing entrepreneurialism, economic development, and ways in which to develop environmentally friendly buildings.

30517 ■ *"Campaign Not Stirred by Wind Issue in Roanoke County" in Roanoke Times (September 18, 2011)*
Pub: Roanoke Times

Ed: Katelyn Polantz. **Description:** Wind energy has brought citizens of the Roanoke area into activism this year. Comments from citizen on both sides of the issue are provided.

30518 ■ *"Canada's Clean Energy Advantages Offer a Bright Future" in Canadian Business (Vol. 83, August 17, 2010, No. 13-14, pp. 38)*
Pub: Rogers Media Ltd.

Ed: Don McKinnon. **Description:** Canada has clean energy advantages in the greenhouse gas emission-free CANada Deuterium Uranium reactor technology and carbon neutral biomass fuels that were continuously ignored by policy makers. Both are proven to significantly reduce emissions while providing reliable, affordable and secure electricity.

30519 ■ *"Canada's Largest Bakery Officially Opened Today" in Ecology,Environment & Conservation Business (October 15, 2011, pp. 7)*
Pub: HighBeam Research

Description: Maple Leaf Foods opened Canada's largest commercial bakery in Hamilton, Ontario. The firm's 385,000 square foot Trillium bakery benefits from efficient design flow and best-in-class technologies.

30520 ■ *"Canadian Hydronics Businesses Promote 'Beautiful Heat"' in Indoor Comfort Marketing (Vol. 70, September 2011, No. 9, pp. 20)*
Pub: Industry Publications Inc.

Description: Canadian hydronics companies are promoting their systems as beautiful heat. Hydronics is the use of water as the heat-transfer medium in heating and cooling system.

30521 ■ *"Canadian Wind Farm Sued Due to Negative Health Effects" in PC Magazine Online (September 22, 2011)*
Pub: PC Magazine

Description: Suncor Energy is being sued by a family in Ontario, Canada. The family claims that Suncor's wind turbines have created health problems for them, ranging from vertigo and sleep disturbance to depression and suicidal thoughts. The family's home is over 1,000 meters from the eight wind turbines, and according to Ontario officials, wind turbines must be a minimum of 550 meters from existing homes.

30522 ■ *"Candidates Differ On State's Green Streak" in Business Journal Portland (Vol. 27, October 22, 2010, No. 34, pp. 1)*
Pub: Portland Business Journal

Ed: Andy Giegerich. **Description:** The views of Oregon gubernatorial candidates Chris Dudley and John Kitzhaber on the state's economy and on environmental policies are presented. Both Dudley, who is a Republican, and his Democratic challenger believe that biomass could help drive the state's economy. Both candidates also pledged changes in Oregon's business energy tax credit (BETC) program.

30523 ■ *"C&W Gets Green Star" in Crain's New York Business (Vol. 24, January 7, 2008, No. 1, pp. 25)*
Pub: Crain Communications, Inc.
Ed: Theresa Agovino. **Description:** Cushman & Wakefield Inc. has hired Eleni Reed as director of sustainability strategies; the real estate firm wants to ensure that the 500 million square feet of office space it manages around the globe meets environmental standards.

30524 ■ *"CanWEA Unveils WindVision for BC: 5,250 MW of Wind Energy by 2025" in CNW Group (October 4, 2011)*
Pub: CNW Group
Contact: Carolyn McGill-Davidson, President
Description: Wind industry leaders are asking British Columbia, Canada policy makers to created conditions to further develop and integrate wind energy in accordance with greenhouse gas emission targets and projected economic growth. Statistical data included.

30525 ■ *"The Carbon Equation" in Canadian Business (Vol. 81, October 27, 2008, No. 18, pp. 109)*
Pub: Rogers Media Ltd.
Ed: Jack M. Mintz. **Description:** Economic and environmental impacts of the likely rejection of a carbon tax for the cap-and-trade system in Canada are discussed. The Conservative Party is expected tow in the 2008 elections and would likely pursue the cap-and-trade system.

30526 ■ *"Carbon Trading: Current Schemes and Future Developments" in Energy Policy (Vol. 39, October 2011, No. 10, pp. 6040-6054)*
Pub: Reed Elsevier Reference Publishing
Ed: Slobodan Perdan, Adisa Azapagic. **Description:** Current and future developments regarding carbon trading is highlighted.

30527 ■ *"Case IH Announces Strategy to Meet 2014 Clean Air Standards" in Farm Industry News (September 15, 2011)*
Pub: Penton Business Media Inc.
Ed: Jodie Wehrspann. **Description:** Case IH will meet EPA's stringent engine emissions limits imposed in 2014, called Tier 4. The limits call for a 90 percent reduction in particulate matter and nitrogen oxides (NOx) over the Tier 3 requirements from a few years ago.

30528 ■ *"Cash for Appliances Targets HVAC Products, Water Heaters" in Contractor (Vol. 56, October 2009, No. 10, pp. 1)*
Pub: Penton Media, Inc.
Ed: Candace Roulo. **Description:** States and territories would need to submit a full application that specifies their implementation plans if they are interested in joining the Cash for Appliances program funded by the American Recovery and Reinvestment Act. The Department of Energy urges states to focus on heating and cooling equipment, appliances and water heaters since these offer the greatest energy savings potential.

30529 ■ *"Catch the Wind Announces Filing of Injunction Against Air Data Systems LLC and Philip Rogers" in CNW Group (September 30, 2011)*
Pub: CNW Group
Contact: Carolyn McGill-Davidson, President
Description: Catch the Wind, providers of laser-based wind sensor products and technology, filed an injunction against Optical Air Data Systems (OADS) LLC and its former President and CEO Philip L. Rogers. The complaint seeks to have OADS and Rogers return tangible and intangible property owned by Catch the Wind, which the firm believes to be critical to the operations of their business.

30530 ■ *"Catch the Wind to Hold Investor Update Conference Call on October 18, 2011" in CNW Group (October 4, 2011)*
Pub: CNW Group
Contact: Carolyn McGill-Davidson, President
Description: Catch the Wind Ltd., providers of laser-based wind sensor products and technology, held a conference call for analysts and institutional investors. The high-growth technology firm is headquartered in Manassas, Virginia.

30531 ■ *"CE2 Carbon Capital and Dogwood Carbon Solutions Partner With Missouri Landowners" in Nanotechnolgy Business Journal (Jan. 25, 2010)*
Pub: Investment Weekly News
Description: Dogwood Carbon Solutions, a developer of agriculture and forestry based conservation projects, has partnered with CE2 Carbon Capital, one of the largest investors and owners of U.S. carbon commodities and carbon emissions reduction projects, to develop high-quality carbon offsets from over 30,000 acres of privately-owned non-industrial forest in the Ozark mountain region of Arkansas and Missouri.

30532 ■ *"CEO Forecast" in Hispanic Business (January-February 2009, pp. 34, 36)*
Pub: Hispanic Business
Ed: Jessica Haro, Richard Kaplan. **Description:** As economic uncertainty fogs the future, executives turn to government contracts in order to boost business. Revenue sources, health care challenges, environmental consulting and remediation services, as well as technological strides are discussed.

30533 ■ *"Certification Experts Germanischer Lloyd Wind Energy Assist NaiKun's Offshore Wind Project" in Canadian Corporate News (May 14, 2007)*
Pub: Comtex News Network Inc.
Description: Germanischer Lloyd Wind Energy (GL Wind) will examine, inspect, and provide quality management services for the engineering, design, and construction of the offshore wind project planned by NaiKun Wind Development Inc. in northwest British Columbia.

30534 ■ *"Changing Fuel Compositions: What It Means To You and Your Business" in Indoor Comfort Marketing (Vol. 70, June 2011, No. 6, pp. 30)*
Pub: Industry Publications Inc.
Ed: Paul Nazzaro. **Description:** Biofuels are outlined and the way it is changing the HVAC/R industry are discussed.

30535 ■ *"Charged Up for Sales" in Charlotte Business Journal (Vol. 25, October 15, 2010, No. 30, pp. 1)*
Pub: Charlotte Business Journal
Ed: Susan Stabley. **Description:** Li-Ion Motors Corporation is set to expand its production lines of electric cars in Sacramento, California. The plan is seen to create up to 600 jobs. The company's total investment is seen to reach $500 million.

30536 ■ *"Chicago Botanic Garden Builds Green Research Facility" in Contractor (Vol. 56, December 2009, No. 12, pp. 5)*
Pub: Penton Media, Inc.
Ed: Candace Roulo. **Description:** Chicago Botanic Garden has built a laboratory and research facility in Illinois. The facility is set to receive a United States Green Building Council LEED Gold certification. The building features a solar photovoltaic array, radiant flooring and water-conserving plumbing products.

30537 ■ *"Chicago Public School District Builds Green" in Contractor (Vol. 56, October 2009, No. 10, pp. 5)*
Pub: Penton Media, Inc.
Ed: Candace Roulo. **Description:** Chicago Public Schools district has already built six U.S. Green Building Council LEED certified schools and one addition in five years and will continue to build new green buildings. The district has an Environmental Action Plan that strives to reduce energy usage, improve indoor air quality, and reduce contribution to climate change.

30538 ■ *"China Wind Power Generates Stronger First Quarter Results" in Marketwire Canada (September 28, 2011)*
Pub: MarketWire Canada
Description: China Wind Power International Corporation, an independent wind power producer in China reported strong growth for the first quarter 2011. Details of the company and its future developments are highlighted.

30539 ■ *"China's Transition to Green Energy Systems" in Energy Policy (Vol. 39, October 2011, No. 10, pp. 5909-5919)*
Pub: Reed Elsevier Reference Publishing
Ed: Wei Li, Guojun Song, Melanie Beresford, Ben Ma. **Description:** The economics of home solar water heaters and their growing popularity in Dezhous City, China is discussed.

30540 ■ *"Chinese Solar Panel Manufacturer Scopes Out Austin" in Austin Business Journallnc. (Vol. 29, October 30, 2009, No. 34, pp. 1)*
Pub: American City Business Journals
Ed: Jacob Dirr. **Description:** China's Yingli Green Energy Holding Company Ltd. is looking for a site in order to construct a $20 million photovoltaic panel plant. Both Austin and San Antonio are vying to house the manufacturing hub. The project could create about 300 jobs and give Austin a chance to become a player in the solar energy market. Other solar companies are also considering Central Texas as an option to set up shop.

30541 ■ *"City's New Energy Audits to Spawn 'Fantastic' Market" in Austin Business Journallnc. (Vol. 28, November 14, 2008, No. 35, pp. 1)*
Pub: American City Business Journals
Ed: Jean Kwon. **Description:** A new law requiring older homes to undergo energy use audits is seen to provide new business for some companies in the Austin, Texas area. The new law is seen to create a new industry of performance testers. Details of the new ordinance are also given.

30542 ■ *"Clean-Tech Focus Sparks Growth" in Philadelphia Business Journal (Vol. 28, January 15, 2010, No. 48, pp. 1)*
Pub: American City Business Journals
Ed: Peter Key. **Description:** Keystone Redevelopment Group and economic development organization Ben Franklin Technology Partners of Southeastern Pennsylvania have partnered in supporting the growth of new alternative energy and clean technology companies. Keystone has also been developing the Bridge Business Center.

30543 ■ *"Clean Wind Energy Tower Transitions from R&D Stage Company" in Professional Services Close-Up (September 30, 2011)*
Pub: Close-Up Media
Description: Clean Wind Energy designed and is developing large downdraft towers that use benevolent, non-toxic natural elements to generate electricity and clean water. The firm is closing its internally staffed engineering office in Warrenton, Virginia and transitioning a development team to oversee and coordinate industry consultants and advisors to construct their first dual renewable energy tower.

30544 ■ *"Cleaner and Greener" in Canadian Business (Vol. 80, February 12, 2007, No. 4, pp. 45)*
Pub: Rogers Media
Ed: Zena Olijnyk. **Description:** Canadian research and government investments in clean coal technology is discussed.

30545 ■ *"Climate Law Could Dig into our Coal-Dusted Pockets" in Business Courier (Vol. 26, November 20, 2009, No. 30, pp. 1)*
Pub: American City Business Journals, Inc.
Ed: Lucy May. **Description:** Passage of federal climate legislation into law is set to increase household cost for Greater Cincinnati, according to the calculation by the Brookings Institute. The increase for residents of the area will amount to $244 in 2020 and the city was ranked the sixth-highest rate in the nation, behind Indianapolis.

30546 ■ *"Cloudy Skies" in Canadian Business (Vol. 81, October 27, 2008, No. 18, pp. 101)*
Pub: Rogers Media Ltd.
Ed: Andrew Wahl. **Description:** Canada's federal government is expected to implement its regulations on greenhouse-gas emissions by January 1, 2010, but companies are worried because the plan took so long and some details are yet to be revealed. Corporate Canada wants a firm, long-range plan similar to the European Union Emissions Trading Scheme in dealing with greenhouse-gas emissions.

30547 ■ *"CO2 Emissions Embodied in China-US Trade" in Energy Policy (Vol. 39, October 2011, No. 10, pp. 5980-5987)*
Pub: Reed Elsevier Reference Publishing
Ed: Huibin Du, Guozhu Mao, Alexander M. Smith, Xuxu Wang, Yuan Wang, Jianghong Guo. **Description:** Input and output analysis based on the energy per dollar ratio for carbon dioxide emissions involved in China-United States trade is outlined.

30548 ■ *"Combo Dorm-Field House Built to Attain LEED Gold" in Contractor (Vol. 56, September 2009, No. 9, pp. 1)*
Pub: Penton Media, Inc.
Ed: Candace Roulo; Robert P. Mader. **Description:** North Central College in Illinois has built a new dormitory that is expected to attain Leadership in Energy and Environmental Design Gold certification from the United States Green Building Council. The structure features a geo-exchange heat pump system and radiant floor heat. A description of the facility is also provided.

30549 ■ *"Coming Soon: Electric Tractors" in Farm Industry News (November 21, 2011)*
Pub: Penton Business Media Inc.
Ed: Jodie Wehrspann. **Description:** The agricultural industry is taking another look at electric farm vehicles. John Deere Product Engineering Center said that farmers can expect to see more diesel-electric systems in farm tractors, sprayers, and implements.

30550 ■ *"Commercial Water Efficiency Initiatives Announced" in Contractor (Vol. 56, November 2009, No. 11, pp. 5)*
Pub: Penton Media, Inc.
Ed: Robert P. Mader. **Description:** Plumbing engineers John Koeller and Bill Gauley are developing a testing protocol for commercial toilets. The team said commercial toilets should have a higher level of flush performance than residential toilets for certification. The Environmental Protection Agency's WaterSense program wants to expand the program into the commercial/institutional sector.

30551 ■ *"Community Food Co-op Creates Revolving Loan Program for Local Farmers" in Bellingham Business Journal (Vol. February 2010, pp. 3)*
Pub: Sound Publishing Inc.
Description: Community Food Co-op's Farm Fund received a $12,000 matching grant from the Sustainable Whatcom Fund of the Whatcom Community Foundation. The Farm Fund will create a new revolving loan program for local farmers committed to using sustainable practices.

30552 ■ *The Company We Keep: Reinventing Small Business for People, Community, and Place*
Pub: Chelsea Green Publishing
Ed: John Abrams, William Grieder. **Released:** June 2006. **Price:** $18.00. **Description:** The new business trend in social entrepreneurship as a business plan enables small business owners to meet the triple bottom line of profits for people (employees and owners), community, and the environment.

30553 ■ *"Consumers Like Green, But Not Mandates" in Business Journal-Milwaukee (Vol. 28, December 10, 2010, No. 10, pp. A1)*
Pub: Milwaukee Business Journal
Ed: Sean Ryan. **Description:** Milwaukee, Wisconsin consumers are willing to spend more on green energy, a survey has revealed. Respondents also said they will pay more for efficient cars and appliances. Support for public incentives for homeowners and businesses that reduce energy use has also increased.

30554 ■ *"Contractors Debate Maximizing Green Opportunities, Education" in Contractor (Vol. 56, November 2009, No. 11, pp. 3)*
Pub: Penton Media, Inc.
Ed: Robert P. Mader. **Description:** Attendees at the Mechanical Service Co ntractors Association convention were urged to get involved with their local U.S. Green Building Council chapter by one presenter. Another presenter says that one green opportunity for contractors is the commissioning of new buildings.

30555 ■ *"Convert New Customers to Long Term Accounts" in Indoor Comfort Marketing (Vol. 70, February 2011, No. 2, pp. 22)*
Pub: Industry Publications Inc.
Description: Marketing to new customers and suggestions for retaining them is covered.

30556 ■ *"Corporate Park Retrofits for Water Savings" in Contractor (Vol. 56, October 2009, No. 10, pp. 5)*
Pub: Penton Media, Inc.
Description: Merrit Corporate Park in Norwalk, Connecticut has been interested in improving building efficiency and one of their buildings has been retrofitted with water-efficient plumbing systems which will allow them to save as much as two million gallons of water. ADP Service Corp. helped the park upgrade their plumbing system.

30557 ■ *Corporate Radar: Tracking the Forces That Are Shaping Your Business*
Pub: Amacom
Ed: Karl Albrecht. **Released:** December 2008. **Price:** $24.95. **Description:** Ways for a business to assess the forces operating in the external environment that can affect the business and solutions to protect from outside threats.

30558 ■ *"Corporate Responsibility" in Professional Services Close-Up (July 2, 2010)*
Pub: Close-Up Media
Description: List of firms awarded the inaugural Best Corporate Citizens in Government Contracting by the Corporate Responsibility Magazine is presented. The list is based on the methodology of the Magazine's Best Corporate Citizen's List, with 324 data points of publicly-available information in seven categories which include: environment, climate change, human rights, philanthropy, employee relations, financial performance, and governance.

30559 ■ *"The Cost of Energy" in Canadian Business (Vol. 83, August 17, 2010, No. 13-14, pp. 39)*
Pub: Rogers Media Ltd.
Description: Canada's cheap energy has bred complacency among Canadian companies and most have not strived to conserve or develop other forms of energy. However, even costs of traditional energy such as oil are set to rise, fueled by recent events in Saudi Arabia and the Gulf of Mexico.

30560 ■ *"Cost Remains Top Factor In Considering Green Technology" in Canadian Sailings (June 30, 2008)*
Pub: UBM Global Trade
Contact: Leonard J. Corallo, President
Ed: Julie Gedeon. **Description:** Improving its environmental performance remains a priority in the shipping industry; however, testing new technologies can prove difficult due to the harsh conditions that ships endure as well as installation which usually requires a dry dock.

30561 ■ *"Could This Be Your Next Office Building?" in Austin Business Journal (Vol. 31, May 13, 2011, No. 10, pp. A1)*
Pub: American City Business Journals Inc.
Ed: Cody Lyon. **Description:** Falcon Containers moved to a 51-acre site in Far East Austin, Texas and started construction of a 2,500-square-foot headquarters made from eight 40-foot shipping containers. Falcon's CEO Stephen Shang plans to use his headquarters building as a showroom to attract upscale, urban hipsters. Insights on the construction's environmental and social impact are shared.

30562 ■ *"Council Power Shift Could Benefit Business" in Business Courier (Vol. 26, November 6, 2009, No. 28, pp. 1)*
Pub: American City Business Journals, Inc.
Ed: Lucy May. **Description:** A majority in the Cincinnati City Council, which is comprised of reelected members, might be created by Charlie Winburn's impending return to the council. It would be empowered to decide on public safety, stock options taxes, and environmental justice. How the presumed majority would affect the city's economic progress is discussed.

30563 ■ *"Crude Awakening" in Canadian Business (Vol. 81, October 27, 2008, No. 18, pp. 14)*
Pub: Rogers Media Ltd.
Ed: Jeff Sanford. **Description:** Jim Grays believes that a global liquid fuels crisis is coming and hopes the expected transition from oil dependence will be smooth. Charles Maxwell, on the other hand, predicts that a new world economy will arrive in three waves. Views of both experts are examined.

30564 ■ *"Customized Before Custom Was Cool" in Green Industry Pro (July 2011)*
Pub: Cygnus Business Media
Ed: Gregg Wartgow. **Description:** Profile of Turf Care Enterprises and owner Kevin Vogeler, who discusses his desire to use more natural programs using little or no chemicals in 1986. At that time, that sector represented 20 percent of his business, today it shares 80 percent.

30565 ■ *"Cut Energy Waste" in Inc. (Vol. 31, January-February 2009, No. 1, pp. 42)*
Pub: Mansueto Ventures LLC
Description: Carbon Control, Edison, and Saver software programs help companies cut carbon emissions by reducing the amount of energy consumed by computers while they are idle.

30566 ■ *"David Robinson Column" in Buffalo News (October 2, 2011)*
Pub: Buffalo News
Ed: David Robinson. **Description:** New York Power Authority ceased development of an offshore wind farm project. Wind farming in the waters of Lake Erie or Lake Ontario would be too costly. Details of the project are discussed.

30567 ■ *"A Day Late and a Dollar Short" in Indoor Comfort Marketing (Vol. 70, March 2011, No. 3, pp. 30)*
Pub: Industry Publications Inc.
Ed: Philip J. Baratz. **Description:** A discussion involving futures options and fuel oil prices is presented.

30568 ■ *"Design Programs for HVAC Sizing Solutions" in Contractor (Vol. 57, January 2010, No. 1, pp. 44)*
Pub: Penton Media, Inc.
Ed: William Feldman; Patti Feldman. **Description:** Rhvac 8 is an HVAC design program that lets users calculate peak heating and cooling load requirements for rooms, zones, systems, and entire buildings. The HVAC Pipe Sizer software for the iPhone enables quick sizing of a simple piping system.

30569 ■ *"Despite Economic Upheaval Generation Y is Still Feeling Green: RSA Canada Survey" in CNW Group (October 28, 2010)*
Pub: CNW Group
Contact: Carolyn McGill-Davidson, President
Description: Canadian Generation Y individuals believe it is important for their company to be environmentally-friendly and one-third of those surveyed would quit their job if they found their employer was environmentally irresponsible, despite the economy.

30570 ■ *"Detroit Hosts Conferences on Green Building, IT, Finance" in Crain's Detroit Business (Vol. 25, June 1, 2009, No. 22, pp. 9)*
Pub: Crain Communications Inc. - Detroit
Ed: Tom Henderson. **Description:** Detroit will host three conferences in June 2009, one features green technology, one information technology and the third will gather black bankers and financial experts from across the nation.

30571 ■ *"DeWind Delivering Turbines to Texas Wind Farm" in Professional Services Close-Up (September 25, 2011)*
Pub: Close-Up Media
Description: DeWind Company has begun shipment of turbines to the 20 MW Frisco Wind Farm located in Hansford County, Texas. DeWind is a subsidiary of Daewoo Shipbuilding and Marine Engineering Company. Details of the project are discussed.

30572 ■ *"DOE Proposes New Water Heater Efficiency Standards" in Contractor (Vol. 57, January 2010, No. 1, pp. 3)*
Pub: Penton Media, Inc.
Ed: Robert P. Mader. **Description:** U.S. Department of Energy is proposing higher efficiency standards for gas and electric water heaters which will not take effect until 2015. The proposal calls for gas-fired storage water heaters less than 60 gallons to have an Energy Factor of 0.675 and those larger than 60 gallons to have an Energy Factor of 0.717.

30573 ■ *"Doing Good: Fair Fashion" in Entrepreneur (Vol. 35, October 2007, No. 10, pp. 36)*
Pub: Entrepreneur Media Inc.
Ed: J.J. Ramberg. **Description:** Indigenous Designs was launched in 1993, when organic clothing was not yet popular. However, the company has become successful in the industry, with $4 million dollars in revenue, owing to the growing environment awareness of consumers. A history of how the company was formed and an overview of their production process are provided.

30574 ■ *"Doing the Right Thing" in Black Enterprise (Vol. 38, July 2008, No. 12, pp. 50)*
Pub: Earl G. Graves Publishing Co. Inc.
Ed: Tamara E. Holmes. **Description:** More business owners are trying to become more environmentally friendly, either due to their belief in social responsibility or for financial incentives or for both reasons. Tips for making one's business more environmentally responsible are included as well as a listing of resources that may be available to help owners in their efforts.

30575 ■ *"Dow Champions Innovative Energy Solutions for Auto Industry at NAIAS" in Business of Global Warming (January 25, 2010, pp. 7)*
Pub: Investment Weekly News
Description: This year's North American International Auto Show in Detroit will host the 'Electric Avenue' exhibit sponsored by the Dow Chemical Company. The display will showcase the latest in innovative energy solutions from Dow as well as electric vehicles and the technology supporting them. This marks the first time a non-automotive manufacturer is part of the main floor of the show.

30576 ■ *"Drop in the Bucket Makes a lot of Waves" in Globe & Mail (March 22, 2007, pp. B1)*
Pub: CTVglobemedia Publishing Inc.
Ed: Greg Keenan. **Description:** The concern of several auto makers in Canada over the impact of providing heavy rebates to customers buying energy-efficient cars is discussed.

30577 ■ *"Dry Idea" in Entrepreneur (Vol. 36, April 2008, No. 4, pp. 20)*
Pub: Entrepreneur Media, Inc.
Ed: Tiffany Meyers. **Description:** Lucky Earth LLC is an Inglewood, California-based company that markets 'Waterless' Carwash, an organic product that is sprayed on to the car and wiped down without using water. Businesses related to water conservation are being created, as water shortage is anticipated in 36 states in the U.S. by 2013.

30578 ■ *"Earth Angels" in Playthings (Vol. 106, September 1, 2008, No. 8, pp. 10)*
Pub: Reed Business Information
Contact: Jeff Greisch, President
Ed: Karyn M. Peterson. **Description:** ImagiPlay toy company has partnered with Whole Foods Market to distribute the company's wooden playthings across the country. The company's Earth-friendly business model is outlined.

30579 ■ *Earth: The Sequel*
Pub: W. W. Norton & Company, Inc.
Ed: Fred Krupp; Miriam Horn. **Released:** March 16, 2009. **Price:** $15.95. **Description:** President of the Environmental Defense Fund offers suggestions for small businesses to help solve global warming. Investigation into the new industries, jobs, and opportunities is provided.

30580 ■ *"East Coast Solar" in Contractor (Vol. 57, February 2010, No. 2, pp. 17)*
Pub: Penton Media, Inc.
Ed: Dave Yates. **Description:** U.S. Department of Energy's Solar Decathlon lets 20 college student-led teams from around the world compete to design and build a solar-powered home. A mechanical contractor discusses his work as an advisor during the competition.

30581 ■ *Eco Barons: The New Heroes of Environmental Activism*
Pub: Ecco/HarperCollins
Ed: Edward Humes. **Released:** January 19, 2010. **Price:** $14.99. **Description:** Profiles of business leaders who have dedicated their lives to saving the planet from ecological devastation.

30582 ■ *"Eco-Preneuring" in Small Business Opportunities (July 2008)*
Pub: Entrepreneur Media Inc.
Ed: Mary C. Pearl. **Description:** Profile of Wildlife Trust, a rapidly growing global organization dedicated to innovative conservation science linking health and ecology. With partners in nearly twenty countries, Wildlife Trust draws on global strengths in order to respond to well-defined local needs. In the Dominican Republic, they are working with the community and local biologists in order to restore fishing and create jobs in the field of ecotourism.

30583 ■ *Ecopreneuring: Putting Purpose and the Planet Before Profits*
Pub: New Society Publishers
Ed: John Ivanko; Lisa Kivirist. **Released:** July 1, 2008. **Price:** $17.95 paperback. **Description:** Ecopreneurs in America are shifting profits and market share towards green living. The book provides a guideline for ecopreneurs in the areas of eco-business basics, purposeful management, marketing in the green economy, and running a lifestyle business.

30584 ■ *"Editor's Note" in Canadian Business (Vol. 81, March 17, 2008, No. 4, pp. 7)*
Pub: Rogers Media
Ed: Joe Chidley. **Description:** Canadian Consolidated government expenditures increased by an average of 4.5 percent annually from 2003 to 2007. Health care, housing, and the environment were some of the areas which experienced higher spending. However, government spending in labor, employment, and immigration dropped 6.6 percent.

30585 ■ *"Election Could Undo Renewable Energy Quotas" in The Business Journal - Serving Phoenix and the Valley of the Sun (Vol. 28, July 11, 2008, No. 45, pp. 1)*
Pub: American City Business Journals, Inc.
Ed: Patrick O'Grady. **Description:** Competition for the three open seats in the Arizona Corporation Commission is intense, with 12 candidates contesting for the three slots. The commission's mandates for renewable energy and infrastructure investment will also be at stake.

30586 ■ *"Electronic Design and a Greener Environment" in Canadian Electronics (Vol. 23, June-July 2008, No. 4, pp. 6)*
Pub: Action Communication Inc.
Ed: Nicholas Deeble. **Description:** Companies seeking to minimize their environmental impact are using Design methodologies of Cadence Design Systems Ltd. The company's Low Power Format and Low Power Design Flow help reduce carbon dioxide emissions.

30587 ■ *"EMC Greens Its Machines" in Boston Business Journal (Vol. 31, July 15, 2011, No. 25, pp. 3)*
Pub: Boston Business Journal
Ed: Kyle Alspach. **Description:** Hopkinton, Massachusetts-based EMC Corporation has been pursuing a sustainability strategy even though it would not directly pay back money to the company or customers who use the products. EMC has been increasingly requiring sustainable practices from its suppliers and evaluating the full lifecycle impacts of its products.

30588 ■ *"Energy Consulting Company to Expand" in Austin Business JournalInc. (Vol. 28, November 7, 2008, No. 34, pp. A1)*
Pub: American City Business Journals
Ed: Kate Harrington. **Description:** CLEAResult Consulting Inc. is planning to increase its workforce and move its headquarters to a larger office. The company has posted 1,000 percent increase in revenues. The company's adoption of best practices and setting of benchmark goals are seen as the reason for its growth.

30589 ■ *"Energy Efficiency Ordinance Softened" in Austin Business JournalInc. (Vol. 28, October 3, 2008, No. 29)*
Pub: American City Business Journals
Ed: Jean Kwon. **Description:** City of Austin has eliminated mandatory energy efficiency upgrades to single-family housing as a condition for selling or renting homes or buildings. The new law proposes that an energy performance audit be conducted on single-family homes before being sold and the results of the audit disclosed to perspectives buyers.

30590 ■ *"Energy Is Put to Good Use in Antarctica" in Contractor (Vol. 56, July 2009, No. 7, pp. 32)*
Pub: Penton Media, Inc.
Ed: Carol Fey. **Description:** Recapturing waste heat is an important part of the heating system at the McMurdo Station in Antarctica. The radiators of generators are the heat source and this is supplemented by modular boilers when seasonal demands for heat increase. Waste heat is also used to make 55,000 gallons of fresh water a day.

30591 ■ *Environmental Guide to the Internet*
Pub: Government Institutes
Contact: Judith Rothman, Director
URL(s): www.govinstpress.com. **Ed:** Carol Briggs-Erickson, Toni Murphy. **Released:** Latest edition 4th. **Price:** $83, Individuals Paperback; £51.95, Individuals Paperback. **Covers:** 1,200 resources covering the environment on the Internet, including organizations, products, and resources, including discussion groups, electronic journals, newsgroups, and discussion groups. **Entries include:** Name, online address, description, e-mail address. **Arrangement:** Categories.

30592 ■ *"EPA 'Finalizes' WaterSense for Homes" in Contractor (Vol. 57, January 2010, No. 1, pp. 70)*
Pub: Penton Media, Inc.
Ed: Bob Mader. **Description:** U.S. Environmental Protection Agency released its 'final' version of the WaterSense for Homes standard. The standard's provisions that affect plumbing contractors includes the specification that everything has to be leak tested and final service pressure cannot exceed 60 psi.

30593 ■ *"EPA Grants E15 Waiver for 2001-2006 Vehicles" in Farm Industry News*

(January 21, 2011)
Pub: Penton Business Media Inc.
Description: U.S. Environmental Protection Agency waived a limitation on selling gasoline that contains more than 10 percent ethanol for model year 2001-2006 cars and light trucks, allowing fuel to contain up to 15 percent ethanol (E15) for these vehicles.

30594 ■ *"EPA to Tighten Energy Star Standards for 2011" in Contractor (Vol. 56, September 2009, No. 9, pp. 6)*
Pub: Penton Media, Inc.
Description: United States Environmental Protection Agency will tighten standards for its Energy Star for Homes program in 2011. The green trend in the construction industry has been cited as reason for the plan. The agency is adding requirements for energy-efficient equipment and building techniques.

30595 ■ *"ESolar Partners With Penglai on Landmark Solar Thermal Agreement for China" in Business of Global Warming (January 25, 2010, pp. 8)*
Pub: Investment Weekly News
Description: Penglai Electric, a privately-owned Chinese electrical power equipment manufacturer, and eSolar, a global provider of cost-effective and reliable solar power plants, announced a master licensing agreement in which eSolar will build at least 2 gigawatts of solar thermal power plants in China over the next 10 years.

30596 ■ *"Everett Dowling" in Hawaii Business (Vol. 54, August 2008, No. 2, pp. 32)*
Pub: Hawaii Business Publishing
Ed: Jason Ubay. **Description:** Real estate developer Everett Dowling, president of Dowling Company Inc., talks about the company's sustainable management and services. The company's office has been retrofitted to earn a Leadership in Energy and Environmental Design (LEED) certification. Dowling believes that real estate development can be part of the sustainable solution.

30597 ■ *"Expansions Signal Growing Interest in Waste-to-Energy Plants" in Crain's Cleveland Business (Vol. 28, November 5, 2007, No. 44)*
Pub: Crain Communications, Inc.
Ed: Bruce Geiselman. **Description:** According to industry insiders, concerns about greenhouse gas emissions as well as escalating energy and waste disposal prices are fueling increased interest in waste-to-energy plants. Many plants are expanding and considering building new trash-burning plants; this marks the first growth in capacity in more than a decade.

30598 ■ *"Family Takes Wind Turbine Companies to Court Over Gag Clauses on Health Effects of Turbines" in CNW Group (September 12, 2011)*
Pub: CNW Group
Contact: Carolyn McGill-Davidson, President
Description: Shawn and Trisha Drennan are concerned about the negative experiences other have had with wind turbines close to their homes, including adverse health effects. The couple's home will be approximately 650 meters from the Kingsbridge II wind farm project in Ontario, Canada.

30599 ■ *Fast-Track Business Start-Up Kit: California*
Pub: DP Group, Incorporated
Ed: Carolyn Usinger. **Released:** September 2006. **Price:** $29.00. **Description:** Step-by-step guide for starting and running a business in California, including information on sole proprietors, partnerships, limited liability companies, S and C corporations, as well as details concerning business entities, sales taxes, environmental issues, human resources, and more.

30600 ■ *"Fed May Ban Amphibian Trade" in Pet Product News (Vol. 64, November 2010, No. 11, pp. 13)*
Pub: BowTie Inc.
Description: U.S. Fish and Wildlife Service is seeking public input on a petition submitted by the conservation activist group Defenders of Wildlife. The petition involves possible classification of chytrid fungus-infected amphibians and amphibian eggs as 'injurious wildlife' under the Lacey Act. Interstate trading or importation of injurious wildlife into the U.S. is not allowed.

30601 ■ *"Federal Buildings to Achieve Zero-Net Energy by 2030" in Contractor (Vol. 56, December 2009, No. 12, pp. 5)*
Pub: Penton Media, Inc.
Ed: Candace Roulo. **Description:** United States president Barack Obama has issued sustainable goals for federal buildings. Federal agencies are also required to increase energy efficiency, conserve water and support sustainable communities. Obama has also announced a $3.4 billion investment in a smart energy creed.

30602 ■ *"The Final Frontier" in Canadian Business (Vol. 80, October 8, 2007, No. 20, pp. 127)*
Pub: Rogers Media
Ed: Andy Holloway. **Description:** Effects of economic development in Northern Canada's natural environment are discussed. The caribou, which are still a primary source of food and clothing in the region, are dying. It is assumed that mining and petroleum projects are affecting the migration patterns of the animals inhabiting the region. The need to maintain a balance between the needs of resource companies and traditional businesses is also discussed.

30603 ■ *"Find Private Money for FutureGen Plant" in Crain's Chicago Business (Vol. 34, September 12, 2011, No. 37, pp. 18)*
Pub: Crain Communications Inc.
Description: FutureGen is a clean-coal power plant being developed in Southern Illinois. The need for further funding is discussed.

30604 ■ *"First Suzlon S97 Turbines Arrive in North America for Installation" in PR Newswire (September 28, 2011)*
Pub: United Business Media
Description: Suzlon Energy Ltd., the world's fifth largest manufacturer of wind turbines, will install its first S97 turbine at the Amherst Wind Farm Project. These turbines will be installed on 90-meter hub height towers and at full capacity, will generate enough electricity to power over 10,000 Canadian homes.

30605 ■ *"First Venture Reports Proprietary Yeasts Further Reduce Ethyl Carbamate in Sake" in Canadian Corporate News (May 16, 2007)*
Pub: Comtex News Network Inc.
Description: First Ventures Technologies Corp., a biotechnology company that develops and commercializes advanced yeast products, confirmed that two of their proprietary yeasts used in the making of sake have yielded reductions in ethyl carbamate compared to previous sake brewing trials.

30606 ■ *"Five-Ring Circus" in Entrepreneur (Vol. 35, November 2007, No. 11, pp. 76)*
Pub: Entrepreneur Media Inc.
Ed: Scott Bernard Nelson. **Description:** China's economy is growing and is expected to do well even after the 2008 Olympics, but growth could slow from eleven percent to eight or nine percent. Chinese portfolio concerns with regard to health and environmental records and bureaucratic fraud are discussed.

30607 ■ *The Flaw of Averages: Why We Underestimate Risk in the Face of Uncertainty*
Pub: John Wiley & Sons, Inc.
Ed: Sam L. Savage. **Released:** June 3, 2009. **Price:** $22.95. **Description:** Personal and business plans are based on uncertainties on a daily basis. The common avoidable mistake individuals make in assessing risk in the face of uncertainty is defined. The explains why plans based on average assumptions are wrong, on average, in areas as diverse as finance, healthcare, accounting, the war on terror, and climate change.

30608 ■ *"Florida's Bright Upside" in Tampa Bay Business Journal (Vol. 29, November 6, 2009, No. 46, pp. 1)*
Pub: American City Business Journals
Ed: Michael Hinman. **Description:** Florida's Public Service Commission (PSC) decision on a power purchase agreement that could add 25 megawatts of solar energy on Tampa Electric Company's offerings is presented. The decision could support the growing market for suppliers and marketers of renewable energy such as Jabil Circuit Inc., which manufactures photovoltaic modules. Details of the agreement are discussed.

30609 ■ *"Floyd County Considers Wind Farms" in Roanoke Times (September 19, 2011)*
Pub: Roanoke Times
Ed: Jeff Sturgeon. **Description:** German firm, Nordex USA Inc. is proposing a $100 million, 30-50 megawatt wind farm atop Wills Ridge, Virginia within the next four years. This project is one of several large wind project considered in the Roanoke and New River valleys of Virginia.

30610 ■ *"Flue Vaccines are Going Green" in Canadian Business (Vol. 83, September 14, 2010, No. 15, pp. 24)*
Pub: Rogers Media Ltd.
Ed: Angelia Chapman. **Description:** Quebec-based Medicago has found a solution to the bottleneck in the production of influenza vaccines by using plant-based processes instead of egg-based systems. Medicago's US Department of Defense funded research has produced the technology that speeds up the production time for vaccines by almost two-thirds. Insights into Medicago's patented process are also given.

30611 ■ *"For Giving Us a Way To Say Yes To Solar: Lynn Jurich and Edward Fenster" in Inc. (Volume 32, December 2010, No. 10, pp. 110)*
Pub: Inc. Magazine
Description: Profile of entrepreneurs Lynn Jurich and Edward Fenster, cofounders of SunRun. The firm installs solar panels at little or no cost and homeowners sign 20-year contracts to buy power at a fixed price.

30612 ■ *"For Putting Down Roots in Business: Amy Norquist: Greensulate, New York City" in Inc. (Volume 32, December 2010, No. 10, pp. 106)*
Pub: Inc. Magazine
Ed: Christine Lagorio. **Description:** Profile of Amy Norquist who left her position at an environmental nonprofit organization to found Greensulate. Her firm insulates rooftops with lavender, native grasses and succulents called sedum in order to eliminate carbon from the atmosphere.

30613 ■ *"Forum at UNCW to Explore Offshore Wind Farming" in Star-News (October 4, 2011)*
Pub: Star-News
Ed: Kate Elizabeth Queram. **Description:** North Carolina is poised to profit from offshore wind farming, according to regional environmental experts. The Sierra Club, in conjunction with the University of North Carolina Wilmington and Oceana are hosting an offshore wind forum featuring five panelists, focusing on potential impacts on birds and sea life, tourism and cost, as well as other pertinent issues.

30614 ■ *"Fossil Fuel, Renewable Fuel Shares Expected to Flip Flop" in Farm Industry News (April 29, 2011)*
Pub: Penton Business Media Inc.
Description: Total energy use of fossil fuels is predicted to fall 5 percent by the year 2035, with renewable fuel picking it up.

30615 ■ *"Franchising's Green Scene" in Entrepreneur (Vol. 37, August 2009, No. 8, pp. 85)*
Pub: Entrepreneur Media, Inc.
Ed: Gwen Moran. **Description:** Trends in favor of environmentally friendly franchises have been growing for about 25 years but have now become main-

stream. The challenges for a prospective green franchisee is that these companies may be tricky to evaluate and they need to ask franchisors a lot of questions to weed out ones that falsely claim to be green.

30616 ■ *"FSU's OGZEB Is Test Bed for Sustainable Technology" in Contractor (Vol. 56, October 2009, No. 10, pp. 1)*
Pub: Penton Media, Inc.
Ed: Candace Roulo. **Description:** Florida State University has one of 14 off-grid zero emissions buildings (OGZEB) in the U.S.; it was built to research sustainable and alternative energy systems. The building produces electricity from 30 photovoltaic panels and it also has three AET water heating solar panels on the roof.

30617 ■ *"Fuel King: The Most Fuel-Efficient Tractor of the Decade is the John Deere 8295R" in Farm Industry News (November 10, 2011)*
Pub: Penton Business Media Inc.
Description: Farm Industry News compiled a list of the most fuel-efficient tractors with help from the Nebraska Tractor Test Lab, with the John Deere 8295R PTO winner of the most fuel-efficient tractor of the decade.

30618 ■ *"Fuel for Thought; Canadian Business Leaders on Energy Policy" in Canadian Business (Vol. 81, September 15, 2008, No. 14-15, pp. 12)*
Pub: Rogers Media Ltd.
Ed: Joe Castaldo. **Description:** Most Canadian business leaders worry about the unreliability of the oil supply but feel that Canada is in a better position to benefit from the energy supply crisis than other countries. Many respondents also highlighted the need to invest in renewable energy sources.

30619 ■ *"Funeral Directors Get Creative As Boomers Near Great Beyond" in Advertising Age (Vol. 79, October 13, 2008, No. 38, pp. 30)*
Pub: Crain Communications, Inc.
Ed: Lenore Skenazy. **Description:** Despite the downturn in the economy, the funeral business is thriving due to the number of baby boomers who realize the importance of making preparations for their death. Marketers are getting creative in their approach and many companies have taken into consideration the need for a more environmental friendly way to dispose of bodies and thus have created innovative businesses that reflect this need.

30620 ■ *"Game On: The Hunt Is On for Nation's Top Keeper" in Farmer's Weekly (March 28, 2008, No. 320)*
Pub: Reed Business Information
Contact: Jeff Greisch, President
Description: Gamekeepers must strike the natural balance that encourages wildlife and protects game. CLA Game Fair and Farmer's Weekly are holding a competition for Gamekeeper of the Year 2008.

30621 ■ *"GE Milestone: 1,000th Wind Turbine Installed in Canada" in CNW Group (October 4, 2011)*
Pub: CNW Group
Contact: Carolyn McGill-Davidson, President
Description: GE installed its 1,000th wind turbine in Canada at Cartier Wind Energy's Gros Morne project in the Gaspesie Region of Quebec, Canada. As Canada continues to expand its use of wind energy, GE plans to have over 1,100 wind turbines installed in the nation by the end of 2011.

30622 ■ *"Germans Win Solar Decathlon - Again" in Contractor (Vol. 56, November 2009, No. 11, pp. 1)*
Pub: Penton Media, Inc.
Ed: Robert P. Mader. **Description:** Students from Technische Universtat Darmstadt won the U.S. Department of Energy's Solar Decathlon by designing and building the most attractive and efficient solar-powered home. The winner's design produced a surplus of power even during three days of rain and photovoltaic panels covered nearly every exterior surface.

30623 ■ *"Getting the Bioheat Word Out" in Indoor Comfort Marketing (Vol. 70, September 2011, No. 9, pp. 32)*
Pub: Industry Publications Inc.
Description: Ways to market advanced liquid fuels to the public are outlined.

30624 ■ *"Getting Going on Going Green" in HRMagazine (Vol. 53, August 2008, No. 8, pp. 8)*
Pub: Society for Human Resource Management
Contact: Henry G. Jackson, President
E-mail: hjackson@shrm.org
Ed: Rita Zeidner. **Description:** Being eco-friendly can help recruit and retain workers. Resources to help firms create green initiatives are presented.

30625 ■ *"Getting NORA reauthorized is high priority" in Indoor Comfort Marketing (Vol. 70, February 2011, No. 2, pp. 14)*
Pub: Industry Publications Inc.
Description: The importance of reauthorizing the National Oilheat Research Alliance is stressed.

30626 ■ *"The GHG Quandary: Whose Problem Is It Anyway?" in Canadian Business (Vol. 81, September 15, 2008, No. 14-15, pp. 72)*
Pub: Rogers Media Ltd.
Ed: Matthew McClearn. **Description:** Nongovernmental organizations were able to revoke the permit for Imperial Oil Ltd's Kearl oilsands project on the grounds of its expected greenhouse gas emission but the court's ruling was rendered irrelevant by bureaucratic paper-shuffling shortly after. The idea of an environmental impact assessment as a guide to identify the consequences of a project is also discussed.

30627 ■ *"The Global Environment Movement is Bjorn Again" in Canadian Business (Vol. 83, September 14, 2010, No. 15, pp. 11)*
Pub: Rogers Media Ltd.
Ed: Steve Maich. **Description:** Danish academic Bjorn Lomborg is in favor of decisive action to combat climate change in his new book and was given front page treatment by a London newspaper. Environmentalist groups see this as a victory since Lomborg had not previously considered climate change an immediate issue.

30628 ■ *"GM's Volt Woes Cast Shadow on E-Cars" in Wall Street Journal Eastern Edition (November 28, 2011, pp. B1)*
Pub: Dow Jones & Company Inc. Enterprise Media Group
Contact: Clare Hart, President
Ed: Sharon Terlep. **Description:** The future of electric cars is darkened with the government investigation by the National Highway Traffic Safety Administration into General Motor Company's Chevy Volt after two instances of the car's battery packs catching fire during crash tests conducted by the Agency.

30629 ■ *"Go Green Or Go Home" in Black Enterprise (Vol. 41, August 2010, No. 1, pp. 53)*
Pub: Earl G. Graves Publishing Co. Inc.
Ed: Tennille M. Robinson. **Description:** The green economy has become an essential part of every business, however, small business owners need to learn how to participate, including minority owned entrepreneurs.

30630 ■ *"Going Green, Going Slowly" in Playthings (Vol. 106, September 1, 2008, No. 8, pp. 17)*
Pub: Reed Business Information
Contact: Jeff Greisch, President
Ed: Nancy Zwiers. **Description:** Sustainability and greener materials for both product and packaging in the toy industry has become important for protecting our environment. However, in a recent survey nearly 60 percent of responders stated environmental issues did not play a part in purchasing a toy or game for their children.

30631 ■ *"Golden Valley, Fling Hills Plan LNG Plant" in Alaska Business Monthly (Vol. 27, October 2011, No. 10, pp. 9)*
Pub: Alaska Business Publishing Company
Ed: Nancy Pounds. **Description:** Golden Valley Electric Association and Flint Hills Resources have partnered on a natural gas liquefaction facility on the North Slope. The deal will deliver gas at cost to GVEA and Flint Hills and Flint Hills will become more competitive and efficient by burning LNG instead of refined crude oil at the refinery.

30632 ■ *Good Green Guide for Small Businesses: How to Change the Way Your Business Works for the Better*
Pub: A. & C. Black
Ed: Impetus Consulting Ltd. Staff. **Released:** September 1, 2009. **Price:** $19.95. **Description:** Guide for small businesses to take an environmental audit of their company and shows how to minimize the impact of office essentials such as utilities, insulation, recycling and waste, electrical equipment, water systems, lighting options, food and drink, and office cleaning arrangements and products.

30633 ■ *"Got to be Smarter than the Average Bear" in Contractor (Vol. 56, September 2009, No. 9, pp. 82)*
Pub: Penton Media, Inc.
Ed: Bob Mader. **Description:** International Association of Plumbing and Mechanical Officials Green Technical Committee has debated the need for contractors to have certifications in installing green plumbing. Some have argued that qualifications would discourage homeowners from improving their properties. Comments from executives are also included.

30634 ■ *"Gov. Kasich to Put DOD On Short Leash" in Business Courier (Vol. 27, November 26, 2010, No. 30, pp. 1)*
Pub: Business Courier
Ed: Dan Monk. **Description:** Ohio Governor-elect John Kasich proposed the privatization of the Ohio Department of Development in favor of a nonprofit corporation called JobsOhio. Kasich believes that the department has lost its focus by adding to its mission issues such as energy efficiency and tourism.

30635 ■ *"Grainger Show Highlights Building Green, Economy" in Contractor (Vol. 57, February 2010, No. 2, pp. 3)*
Pub: Penton Media, Inc.
Ed: Candace Roulo. **Description:** chief U.S. economist told attendees of the Grainger's 2010 Total MRO Solutions National Customer Show that the economic recovery would be subdued. Mechanical contractors who attended the event also learned about building sustainable, green products, and technologies, and economic and business challenges.

30636 ■ *"Grave Concerns" in Canadian Business (Vol. 81, July 21 2008, No. 11, pp. 25)*
Pub: Rogers Media Ltd.
Ed: Andrew Nikiforuk. **Description:** Air pollution control regulations to reduce greenhouse gasses have been implemented by the Canadian government. The federal government is planning to construct a carbon funeral industry that will store the global warming gases, however the expenditure for the project will be shifted to the taxpayers. Details of the Bruce Peachy's initiative on how to reduce GHGs are presented.

30637 ■ *"Green Acres" in Hawaii Business (Vol. 54, September 2008, No. 3, pp. 48)*
Pub: Hawaii Business Publishing
Ed: Jan Tenbruggencate. **Description:** Bill Cowern's Hawaiian Mahogany is a forestry business that processes low-value trees to be sold as wood chips, which can be burned to create biodiesel. Cowern is planning to obtain certification to market carbon credits and is also working with Green Energy Hawaii for the permit of a biomass-fueled power plant. Other details about Cowern's business are discussed.

30638 ■ *"Green Assets Powering Boralex Shares" in Globe & Mail (March 30, 2007, pp. B10)*
Pub: CTVglobemedia Publishing Inc.
Ed: Richard Blackwell. **Description:** The impact of econ-friendly power plant portfolio on the stock performance of Kingsey Falls-based Boralex Inc. is analyzed.

30639 ■ *Green Business: A Five-Part Model for Creating an Environmentally Responsible Company*
Pub: Schiffer Publishing Ltd.
Contact: Peter B. Schiffer, President
E-mail: petes@schifferbooks.com
Ed: Amy K. Townsend. **Released:** 2006. **Price:** $29.95 paperback. **Description:** Five-part model for small companies to become a green business; the book discusses the advantages to following the current trend using environmentally-friendly practices.

30640 ■ *Green Business Practices for Dummies*
Pub: John Wiley and Sons, Inc.
Ed: Lisa Swallow. **Released:** January 2009. **Price:** $21.99. **Description:** The book provides information for any small business to help reduce environmental impact without reducing their company's bottom line.

30641 ■ *"Green Business Push Blooms" in Charlotte Observer (February 7, 2007)*
Pub: Knight-Ridder/Tribune Business News
Ed: Christopher D. Kirkpatrick. **Description:** Many energy companies are capitalizing on corporate guild about global warming. Companies offering environmental peace of mind are discussed.

30642 ■ *"Green and Clean" in Retail Merchandiser (Vol. 51, July-August 2011, No. 4, pp. 56)*
Pub: Phoenix Media Corporation
Description: Green Valley Grocery partnered with Paragon Solutions consulting firm to make their stores environmentally green.

30643 ■ *"'Green' Cleaner Buys Local Firm" in Puget Sound Business Journal (Vol. 29, December 19, 2008, No. 35, pp. 3)*
Pub: American City Business Journals
Ed: Greg Lamm. **Description:** Washington-based Blue Sky Cleaners has purchased Four Seasons Cleaners. The green company also purchased Queen Anne store and Four Seasons' routes fro Snohomish County through Seattle.

30644 ■ *The Green Collar Economy: How One Solution Can Fix Our Two Biggest Problems*
Pub: HarperCollins Publishers
Ed: Van Jones. **Released:** November 1, 2009. **Price:** $14.99. **Description:** This book offers insight into rebuilding the nation's infrastructure and creating alternative energy sources that could boost the economy through increased employment and higher wages while decreasing our dependence on fossil fuels.

30645 ■ *"The Green Conversation" in Harvard Business Review (Vol. 86, September 2008, No. 9, pp. 58)*
Pub: Harvard Business School Press
Description: Six guidelines are presented for addressing and benefiting from environmentally conscious corporate decision making and practices. Topics covered include marketing, supply chain, and leadership.

30646 ■ *"Green Counting" in Canadian Business (Vol. 81, October 13, 2008, No. 17, pp. 27)*
Pub: Rogers Media Ltd.
Ed: Joe Castaldo. **Description:** Procter and Gamble research revealed that only 10 percent of North American consumers are willing to accept trade-offs for a greener product. Three out of four North American consumers will not accept a higher price or a decrease in a product's performance for an environmental benefit. Details on green marketing are also discussed.

30647 ■ *"Green Energy Exec Hits State Policy" in Boston Business Journal (Vol. 30, December 3, 2010, No. 45, pp. 1)*
Pub: Boston Business Journal
Ed: Kyle Alspach. **Description:** American Superconductor Corporation President Dan McGahn believes that the state government of Massachusetts is not proactive enough to develop the state into a manufacturing hub for wind power technology. McGahn believes that while Governor Deval Patrick campaigned for wind turbines in the state, his administration does not have the focus required to build the turbines in the state.

30648 ■ *"Green Firm Scouts Sites in Tri-State" in Business Courier (Vol. 27, July 23, 2010, No. 12, pp. 1)*
Pub: Business Courier
Ed: Dan Monk. **Description:** CresaPartners is searching for a manufacturing facility in Cincinnati, Ohio. The company is set to tour about ten sites in the area.

30649 ■ *Green to Gold*
Pub: Yale University Press
Contact: John Donatich, Director
Ed: Daniel C. Esty; Andrew S. Winston. **Released:** January 2009. **Price:** $19.95. **Description:** Examples are given for small businesses to beat competition while tackling sustainability, engage stakeholders, develop NGO partnerships, and work environmental stewardship into corporate culture.

30650 ■ *The Green Guide for Business: The Ultimate Environment for Businesses of All Sizes*
Pub: Profile Books Limited
Ed: Roger East, Hannah Bullock, Chris Goodall. **Released:** May 10, 2010. **Description:** Everyone wants to go green these days, but for small businesses that's easier said than done. How do you measure a company's carbon footprint? Are dryers or hand towels more eco-friendly? Recycled paper or FSC-certified? All these questions and more are explored.

30651 ■ *"Green Housing for the Rest of Us" in Inc. (November 2007, pp. 128-129)*
Pub: Gruner & Jahr USA Publishing
Ed: Nitasha Tiku. **Description:** Profile of Full Spectrum NY, real estate developer firm, offering residences at the Kalahari, a green high-rise with state-of-the-art features at a reasonable price.

30652 ■ *"Green It Like You Mean It" in Special Events Magazine (Vol. 28, February 1, 2009, No. 2)*
Pub: Special Events Magazine
Ed: Christine Landry. **Description:** Eco-friendly party planners offer advice for planning and hosting green parties or events. Tips include information for using recycled paper products, organic food and drinks. The Eco Nouveau Fashion Show held by Serene Star Productions reused old garments to create new fashions as well as art pieces from discarded doors and window frames for the show; eco-friendly treats and gift bags were highlighted at the event.

30653 ■ *"Green Light" in The Business Journal-Portland (Vol. 25, July 11, 2008, No. 18, pp. 1)*
Pub: American City Business Journals, Inc.
Ed: Erik Siemers. **Description:** Ecos Consulting, a sustainability consulting company based in Portland, Oregon, is seeing a boost in revenue as more businesses turn to sustainable practices. The company's revenue rose by 50 percent in 2007 and employees increased from 57 to 150. Other details about Ecos' growth are discussed.

30654 ■ *"Green Pipe Helps Miners Remove the Black" in Contractor (Vol. 57, January 2010, No. 1, pp. 1)*
Pub: Penton Media, Inc.
Description: Lyons Co. Mechanical Contractors and Engineers installed a piping system for the River View Coal Mine facility's shower rooms. Lyons used Aquatherm's polypropylene piping system which creates seamless connections in the piping.

30655 ■ *"Green Shift Sees Red" in Canadian Business (Vol. 81, September 29, 2008, No. 16)*
Pub: Rogers Media Ltd.
Ed: Jeff Sanford. **Description:** Green Shift Inc. is suing the Liberal Party of Canada in an $8.5 million lawsuit for using the phrase 'green shift' when they rolled out their carbon tax and climate change policy. The company has come to be recognized as a consultant and provider of green products such as non-toxic, biodegradable cups, plates, and utensils for events.

30656 ■ *"The Green Trap" in Canadian Business (Vol. 80, April 9, 2007, No. 8, pp. 19)*
Pub: Rogers Media
Ed: Al Rosen. **Description:** Expert advice to companies on investing in environmental-friendly measures is presented.

30657 ■ *Green Your Small Business: Profitable Ways to Become an Ecopreneur*
Pub: McGraw-Hill
Ed: Scott Cooney. **Released:** November 7, 2008. **Price:** $19.95 paperback. **Description:** Advice and guidance is given to help any entrepreneur start, build or grow a green business, focusing on green business basics, market research and financing, as well as handling legal and insurance issues.

30658 ■ *"Greenhouse Announces Merger With Custom Q, Inc." in Investment Weekly (January 30, 2010, pp. 338)*
Pub: Investment Weekly News
Description: In accordance with an Agreement and Plan of Share Exchange, GreenHouse Holdings, Inc., an innovative green solutions provider, has gone public via a reverse merger with Custom Q, Inc.

30659 ■ *"Greening the Auto Industry" in Business Journal-Serving Phoenix & the Valley of the Sun (Vol. 30, July 23, 2010, No. 46, pp. 1)*
Pub: Phoenix Business Journal
Ed: Patrick O'Grady. **Description:** Thermo Fluids Inc. has been recycling used oil products since 1993 and could become Arizona's first home for oil filter recycling after retrofitting its Phoenix facility to include a compaction machine. The new service could help establish Thermo Fluids as a recycling hub for nearby states.

30660 ■ *"The Greening of Lunch" in Entrepreneur (Vol. 37, October 2009, No. 10, pp. 44)*
Pub: Entrepreneur Media, Inc.
Ed: Deborah Song. **Description:** Kids Konserve is a self-funded online business selling reusable and recycled lunch kits for kids. The company also aims to increase awareness about waste reduction.

30661 ■ *"Greening the Manscape" in Canadian Business (Vol. 81, October 13, 2008, No. 17, pp. S19)*
Pub: Rogers Media Ltd.
Ed: David Lackie. **Description:** Buyer's guide of environmentally friendly grooming products for men is provided. Improved formulations have solved the problems of having synthetic ingredients in grooming products. Details about a face scrub, after shave conditioner, and a nourishing cream made of 91 percent organic ingredients are given, including prices.

30662 ■ *Greening Your Small Business: How to Improve Your Bottom Line, Grow Your Brand, Satisfy Your Customers and Save the Planet*
Pub: Prentice Hall Press
Contact: Dame Marjorie M. Scardino, Chief Executive Officer
Ed: Jennifer Kaplan. **Released:** November 3, 2009. **Price:** $19.95. **Description:** A definitive resource for anyone who wants their small business to be cutting-edge, competitive, profitable, and eco-conscious. Stories from small business owners address every aspect of going green, from basics such as recycling waste, energy efficiency, and reducing information

technology footprint, to more in-depth concerns such as green marketing and communications, green business travel, and green employee benefits.

30663 ■ *"A Growing Concern" in Canadian Business (Vol. 79, October 9, 2006, No. 20, pp. 90)*
Pub: Rogers Media
Ed: Jeff Sanford. **Description:** With rich dividends being harvested by companies producing ethanol, after ethanol became a petrol additive, is discussed.

30664 ■ *Guerrilla Marketing Goes Green: Winning Strategies to Improve Your Profits and Your Planet*
Pub: John Wiley & Sons, Inc.
Ed: Jay Conrad Levinson, Shel Horowitz. **Released:** January 10, 2010. **Price:** $21.95. **Description:** The latest tips on green marketing and sustainable business strategies are shared.

30665 ■ *"Guide to Carbon Footprinting" in American Printer (Vol. 128, June 1, 2011, No. 6)*
Pub: Penton Media Inc.
Description: PrintCity Alliance published its new report, 'Carbon Footprint & Energy Reduction for Graphic Industry Value Chain.' The report aims to help improve the environmental performance of printers, converters, publishers, brand owners and their suppliers.

30666 ■ *"Habitat, Home Depot Expand Building Programs" in Contractor (Vol. 56, September 2009, No. 9, pp. 16)*
Pub: Penton Media, Inc.
Description: Habitat for Humanity International and The Home Depot Foundation are planning to expand their Partners in Sustainable Building program. The program will provide funds to help Habitat affiliates build 5,000 homes. Comments from executives are also included.

30667 ■ *"Hard Rock on Pike" in Puget Sound Business Journal (Vol. 29, September 5, 2008, No. 20, pp. 1)*
Pub: American City Business Journals
Ed: Jeanne Lang Jones. **Description:** A branch of the Hard Rock Cafe is opening in 2009 in the Liberty Building on Pike Street in downtown Seattle, Washington. The location is being renovated as a green building; the restaurant and concert venue will seat 300 patrons and has a rooftop deck and memorabilia shop.

30668 ■ *"Helping Customers Fight Pet Waste" in Pet Product News (Vol. 64, November 2010, No. 11, pp. 52)*
Pub: BowTie Inc.
Ed: Sandy Robins. **Description:** Pet cleaning products manufacturers have been enjoying high sales figures by paying attention to changing pet ownership trends and environmental awareness. Meanwhile, the inclusion of user-friendly features in these products has also been boosted by the social role of pets and the media attention to pet waste. How manufacturers have been responding to this demand is explored.

30669 ■ *"Hey, You Can't Do That" in Green Industry Pro (Vol. 23, September 2011)*
Pub: Cygnus Business Media
Ed: Rod Dickens. **Description:** Manufacturers of landscape equipment are making better use of energy resources, such as the use of fuel-injection systems instead of carburetors, lightweight materials, better lubricants, advanced battery technology, and innovative engine designs.

30670 ■ *"High Energy: Gaurdie Banister Joins Aera As President and CEO" in Black Enterprise (Vol. 38, July 2008, No. 12, pp. 30)*
Pub: Earl G. Graves Publishing Co. Inc.
Ed: Brenda Porter. **Description:** Gaurdie Banister Jr. has been appointed president and CEO of Aera Energy L.L.C., becoming one of the first African Americans in the nation to run a major energy corporation. His plans for the firm include utilizing new, sophisticated technologies in order to unlock the 3-1/2 billion barrels of resources the company has on their books in a safe and environmentally friendly way. He also hopes to increase production and maintain cost leadership.

30671 ■ *"Homing In On the Future" in Black Enterprise (Vol. 38, October 2007, No. 3, pp. 61)*
Pub: Earl G. Graves Publishing Co. Inc.
Ed: Sean Drakes. **Description:** More and more people are wanting new homes wired automated systems that integrate multiple home devices such as computers, audio/visual entertainment, security, communications, utilities, and lighting and environmental controls.

30672 ■ *"Hot Air" in Canadian Business (Vol. 81, July 22, 2008, No. 12-13, pp. 16)*
Pub: Rogers Media Ltd.
Ed: Joe Castaldo. **Description:** Over half of 101 business leaders who were recently surveyed oppose Liberal leader Stephane Dion's carbon-tax proposal, saying that manufacturers in Canada are likely to suffer from the plan. Additional key results of the survey are presented.

30673 ■ *"Hot Air: On Global Warming and Carbon Tax" in Canadian Business (Vol. 81, October 13, 2008, No. 17, pp. 12)*
Pub: Rogers Media Ltd.
Ed: Joe Castaldo. **Description:** Survey of Canadian business leaders revealed that the environment is a key issue in Canada's federal elections. Respondents believe that Prime Minister Stephen Harper's views on global warming and climate change are closer to their own views. Other key information on the survey is presented.

30674 ■ *Hot, Flat and Crowded: Why We Need a Green Revolution - and How It Can Renew America*
Pub: Farrar, Straus and Giroux
Ed: Thomas L. Friedman. **Released:** September 8, 2008. **Price:** $27.95. **Description:** Author explains how global warming, rapidly growing populations, and the expansion of the world's middle class through globalization have impacted the environment.

30675 ■ *Housecleaning Business: Organize Your Business - Get Clients and Referrals - Set Rates and Services*
Pub: Globe Pequot Press
Ed: Laura Jorstad, Melinda Morse. **Released:** June 1, 2009. **Price:** $18.95. **Description:** This book shares insight into starting a housecleaning businesses. It shows how to develop a service manual, screen clients, serve customers, select cleaning products, competition, how to up a home office, using the Internet to grow the business and offering green cleaning options to clients.

30676 ■ *"How Bad Is It?" in Hawaii Business (Vol. 54, July 2008, No. 1, pp. 35)*
Pub: Hawaii Business Publishing
Ed: Jolyn Okimoto Rosa. **Description:** Donald G. Horner, chief executive officer of First Hawaiian Bank, says that the current Hawaiian economic situation is a cyclical slowdown. Maurice Kaya, an energy consultant, says the slowdown is due to overdependence on imported fuels. Other local leaders, such as Constance H. Lau, also discuss their view on the current economic situation in Hawaii.

30677 ■ *"How Green Is The Valley?" in Barron's (Vol. 88, July 4, 2008, No. 28, pp. 13)*
Pub: Dow Jones & Co., Inc.
Description: San Jose, California has made a good start towards becoming a leader in alternative energy technology through the establishment of United Laboratories' own lab in the city. The certification process for photovoltaic cells will be dramatically shortened with this endeavor.

30678 ■ *"Hybrid Popularity Pushes Automakers to Add to Offerings" in Crain's Cleveland Business (Vol. 28, November 12, 2007, No. 45, pp. 30)*
Pub: Crain Communications, Inc.
Ed: David Sedgwick. **Description:** Due in part to Toyota's innovative marketing, automotive hybrids have caught on with consumers thus forcing other automakers to add hybrids to their product plans.

30679 ■ *"Hydronicahh - Everything in Modulation" in Contractor (Vol. 56, December 2009, No. 12, pp. 24)*
Pub: Penton Media, Inc.
Ed: Mark Eatherton. **Description:** Management and the environmental impact of a home hydronic system are discussed. Radiant windows have the potential to reduce energy consumption. A variable speed delta T pump is required for the construction of a hydronic wood pit.

30680 ■ *"IAPMO GTC Debates Supplement" in Contractor (Vol. 56, September 2009, No. 9, pp. 3)*
Pub: Penton Media, Inc.
Ed: Robert P. Mader. **Description:** Green Technical Committee of the International Association of Plumbing and Mechanical Officials is developing a Green Plumbing and Mechanical Supplement. The supplement provides for installation of systems by licensed contractors and installers. Comments from officials are also presented.

30681 ■ *"IAPMO GTC Finalizes Green Supplement" in Contractor (Vol. 57, January 2010, No. 1, pp. 1)*
Pub: Penton Media, Inc.
Description: International Association of Plumbing and Mechanical Officials' Green Technical Committee finalized the Green Plumbing & Mechanical Code Supplement. The supplement was created to provide a set of provisions that encourage sustainable practices and work towards the design and construction of plumbing and mechanical systems.

30682 ■ *"IAPMO GTC Votes to Limit Showers to 2.0-GPM" in Contractor (Vol. 56, September 2009, No. 9, pp. 1)*
Pub: Penton Media, Inc.
Ed: Robert P. Mader. **Description:** Green Technical Committee of the International Association of Plumbing and Mechanical Officials has voted to limit showers to 2.0 GPM. It is also developing a Green Plumbing and Mechanical Supplement. Comments from executives are also supplied.

30683 ■ *"ICC Works on Prescriptive Green Construction Code" in Contractor (Vol. 56, October 2009, No. 10, pp. 1)*
Pub: Penton Media, Inc.
Ed: Robert P. Mader. **Description:** International Code Council launched an initiative to create a green construction code that focuses on existing commercial buildings. The initiative's timeline will include public meetings leading up to a final draft that will be available in 2010.

30684 ■ *"Illinois Bets On Recycling Program" in Chicago Tribune (November 29, 2008)*
Pub: McClatchy-Tribune Information Services
Ed: Joel Hood. **Description:** Traditionally the holiday gift-giving season is one of the most wasteful times of year and the state of Illinois is granting $760,000 to small businesses and cities in an attempt to expand curbside recycling programs and hire additional workers to address electronic waste.

30685 ■ *"Illinois Residential Building Legislation Includes New HVAC Requirements" in Contractor (Vol. 56, July 2009, No. 7, pp. 3)*
Pub: Penton Media, Inc.
Ed: Candace Roulo. **Description:** Illinois' Energy Efficient Building Act will require all new buildings and houses to conform to the International Energy Conservation Code. The code includes a duct leakage requirement followed by a post-construction test to verify leakage rates and requires programmable thermostats on all houses.

30686 ■ *"Independence Station Utilizes Sustainable Technologies" in Contractor (Vol. 56, September 2009, No. 9, pp. 3)*
Pub: Penton Media, Inc.
Ed: Candace Ruolo. **Description:** Independence Station building in Oregon is seen to receive the most LEED points ever awarded by the United States Green Building Council. The building will use an ice-

based cooling storage system, biofuel cogeneration system and phovoltaic system. Other building features and dimensions are also supplied.

30687 ■ *"Indoor Air Quality - a Tribute to Efficiency" in Indoor Comfort Marketing (Vol. 70, August 2011, No. 8, pp. 8)*
Pub: Industry Publications Inc.
Ed: Matthew Maleske. **Description:** Efficiency of new HVAC/R equipment has helped improve indoor air quality.

30688 ■ *"Industry Escalates Lobbying Efforts For Loan Program" in Crain's Detroit Business (Vol. 24, September 22, 2008, No. 38, pp. 22)*
Pub: Crain Communications Inc.
Ed: Jay Greene; Ryan Beene; Harry Stoffer. **Description:** Auto suppliers such as Lear Corp., which is best known for vehicle seating, also supplies high-voltage wiring for Ford hybrids and is developing other hybrid components. These suppliers are joining automakers in lobbying for the loan program which would promote the accelerated development of fuel-efficient vehicles.

30689 ■ *"Info Junkie" in Crain's Chicago Business (Vol. 34, October 24, 2011, No. 42, pp. 35)*
Pub: Crain Communications Inc.
Ed: Christina Le Beau. **Description:** Greg Colando, president of Flor Inc., an eco-friendly carpet company located I Chicago discusses his marketing program to increase sales.

30690 ■ *"Insider" in Canadian Business (Vol. 81, Summer 2008, No. 9, pp. 170)*
Pub: Rogers Media Ltd.
Ed: Thomas Watson; Jeff Sanford. **Description:** Oil peak theory posits that the world has consumed half of the non-renewable resources is indicated by the surging oil prices. However, critics argued that the high oil prices are effects of market speculation and not the depletion of the supply. Ten reasons on why to buy and not buy peak oil are presented.

30691 ■ *"Integral USA Magazine Sponsors Eco-Fashion in the Park" in Entertainment Close-Up (September 2, 2011)*
Pub: Close-Up Media
Description: Integral Magazine sponsored Eco-Fashion in the Park, a fashion show for the fashion conscious. Eleven independent designers will show their eco-friendly fashions at the event.

30692 ■ *"Interested in 12 Billion Dollars?" in Indoor Comfort Marketing (Vol. 70, March 2011, No. 3, pp. 18)*
Pub: Industry Publications Inc.
Ed: Matthew Maleske. **Description:** Trends in the indoor quality industry are cited, with insight into expanding an existing indoor heating and cooling business.

30693 ■ *"Iogen in Talks to Build Ethanol Plant in Canada" in Globe & Mail (March 21, 2007, pp. B7)*
Pub: CTVglobemedia Publishing Inc.
Ed: Shawn McCarthy. **Description:** Ottawa based Iogen Corp. is planning to construct a cellulosic ethanol plant in Saskatchewan region. The company will be investing an estimated $500 million for this purpose.

30694 ■ *"Iogen, VW Look to Build Ethanol Plant" in Globe & Mail (January 9, 2006, pp. B3)*
Pub: CTVglobemedia Publishing Inc.
Ed: Simon Tuck. **Description:** Iogen Corp. and Volkswagen AG plan cellulose ethanol plant in Germany. The details of the project are presented.

30695 ■ *"Iron Man Forges New Path" in Canadian Business (Vol. 80, February 12, 2007, No. 4, pp. 41)*
Pub: Rogers Media
Ed: Rachel Pulfer. **Description:** The research of Donald Sadoway of Massachusetts Institute of Technology in making iron in an environmentally friendly method using electrolysis is discussed.

30696 ■ *"It's Always 55 Degrees F" in Contractor (Vol. 56, September 2009, No. 9, pp. 38)*
Pub: Penton Media, Inc.
Ed: Carol Fey. **Description:** Geothermal-exchange heating and cooling systems can save businesses up to 60 percent on energy costs for heating and cooling. Geothermal systems get heat from the earth during winter. Design, features and installation of geothermal systems are also discussed.

30697 ■ *"It's Not Easy Investing Green" in Entrepreneur (Vol. 37, August 2009, No. 8, pp. 64)*
Pub: Entrepreneur Media, Inc.
Ed: Rosalind Resnick. **Description:** Some venture capitalists remain bullish on green investing despite signs of stagnation. One way for an investor to cash in on green investing is to invest in large public companies that are investing big in green initiatives. Being an angel investor to a local clean-tech company is another avenue.

30698 ■ *"Jennifer Hernandez Helps Developers Transform Contaminated Properties" in Hispanic Business (Vol. 30, April 2008, No. 4, pp. 32)*
Pub: Hispanic Business
Ed: Hildy Medina. **Description:** Jennifer Hernandez is a partner and head of the law firm of Holland & Knight's environmental practice which specializes in the restoration of polluted land where former industrial and commercial buildings once stood, known as brownfields. Brownfield redevelopment can be lucrative but costly due to the cleaning up of contaminated land and challenging because of federal and state environmental laws.

30699 ■ *"KC Sewer Solutions May Overflow With Green Ideas" in The Business Journal-Serving Metropolitan Kansas City (August 22, 2008)*
Pub: American City Business Journals, Inc.
Ed: Suzanna Stagemeyer. **Description:** Adding green solutions such as small, dispersed basins to catch runoffs and the use of deep rooted natural plants to fix the sewer system of Kansas could probably justify the $2.3 billion worth of funds needed for the project. The city has been ordered by the EPA and the Missouri Department of Natural Resources to fix their sewer systems that are overwhelmed by significant rains.

30700 ■ *"Keeping the Faith in Fuel-Tech" in Barron's (Vol. 88, March 24, 2008, No. 12, pp. 20)*
Pub: Dow Jones & Company, Inc.
Ed: Christopher C. Williams. **Description:** Shares of air pollution control company Fuel-Tech remain on track to reach $40 each from their $19 level due to a continued influx of contracts. The stock has suffered from lower-than-expected quarterly earnings and tougher competition but stand to benefit from increased orders.

30701 ■ *"Kelvin Taketa" in Hawaii Business (Vol. 53, October 2007, No. 4, pp. 30)*
Pub: Hawaii Business Publishing
Ed: Scott Radway. **Description:** Hawaii Community Foundation chief executive officer Kelvin Taketa believes that the leadership shortage for nonprofit sector in Hawaii is a result of leaders retiring or switching to part-time work. Taketa adds that the duties of a nonprofit organization leader are very challenging, with the organizations being usually thinly staffed. His opinion on the prospects of young leadership in Hawaii is also given.

30702 ■ *"Know the Facts About Natural Gas!" in Indoor Comfort Marketing (Vol. 70, August 2011, No. 8, pp. 26)*
Pub: Industry Publications Inc.
Description: AEC Activity Update is presented on the American Energy Coalition's Website.

30703 ■ *"Kohler Building Earns LEED Silver Certification" in Contractor (Vol. 56, September 2009, No. 9, pp. 12)*
Pub: Penton Media, Inc.
Description: United States Green Building Council has awarded Kohler Co. with the Silver Leadership in Energy and Environmental Design Status. The award has highlighted the company's work to transform its building into a more environmentally efficient structure. A description of the facility is also provided.

30704 ■ *"The Lap of Eco-Luxury" in Entrepreneur (Vol. 37, August 2009, No. 8, pp. 38)*
Pub: Entrepreneur Media, Inc.
Ed: Dina Mishev. **Description:** Founder Rob DesLauriers of the Terra Resort Group says that the natural world has taken very good care of him and that he wants to do his part to take care of it. The mattresses that their hotel uses are made from recycled steel springs and their TVs are Energy Star-approved. Their linens are made from organically grown cottons and their walls use by-products from coal burning.

30705 ■ *"Large Homes can be Energy Efficient Too" in Contractor (Vol. 56, October 2009, No. 10, pp. 5)*
Pub: Penton Media, Inc.
Ed: Candace Roulo. **Description:** Eco Estate at Briggs Chaney subdivision in Silver Spring, Maryland has model houses that use sustainable technologies and products and the homes that will be built on the subdivision will feature some of the technologies featured on the model home. The energy efficient HVAC system of the model homes are discussed.

30706 ■ *"Legislation Introduced" in Indoor Comfort Marketing (Vol. 70, July 2011, No. 7, pp. 6)*
Pub: Industry Publications Inc.
Description: New industry legislation is examined by the National Oilheat Research Alliance.

30707 ■ *"Let's Put On a Show" in Inc. (November 2007, pp. 127)*
Pub: Gruner & Jahr USA Publishing
Ed: Elaine Appleton Grant. **Description:** Profile of Jeff Baker, CEO of Image 4, designer of trade show exhibits. Baker shares details of the firm's commitment to being green.

30708 ■ *"Letting the Sunshine In" in Barron's (Vol. 89, July 6, 2009, No. 27, pp. 11)*
Pub: Dow Jones & Co., Inc.
Ed: Katherine Cheng. **Description:** Solar energy industry leaders believe the industry needs aid from the US government regarding the funding of its research efforts and lowering solar energy costs. The climate change bill passed by the US House of Representatives signifies the US government's desire to significantly reduce carbon dioxide emissions.

30709 ■ *"A Light Bulb Came On, and It Was Energy Efficient" in Globe & Mail (January 27, 2007, pp. B3)*
Pub: CTVglobemedia Publishing Inc.
Ed: Shawn McCarthy. **Description:** A brief profile of Edward Weinstein, chief executive officer of the Montreal-based family-run lighting firm Globe Electric Co., is presented The firm's management strategies are described.

30710 ■ *"Lincoln Electric Installs Large Wind Tower" in Modern Machine Shop (Vol. 84, October 2011, No. 5, pp. 42)*
Pub: Gardner Business Media, Inc.
Contact: Richard G. Kline, President
E-mail: rkline@gardnerweb.com
Description: Lincoln Electric, a welding product manufacturer, constructed a 443-foot-tall wind tower at its plant in Euclid, Ohio. The tower is expected to generate as much as 10 percent of the facility's energy and save as much as $500,000 annually in energy costs.

30711 ■ *"Lining Up at the Ethanol Trough (Ethanol Production in Canada)" in Globe & Mail (January 25, 2007, pp. B2)*
Pub: CTVglobemedia Publishing Inc.
Ed: Eric Reguly. **Description:** The future of ethanol production in Canada is discussed, alternate fuel market is expected to reach 35 billion gallons by 2017.

30712 ■ *"The Lithium Deficit" in Canadian Business (Vol. 82, April 27, 2009, No. 7, pp. 17)*
Pub: Rogers Media
Ed: Joe Castaldo. **Description:** Experts are concerned that there may not be enough lithium available to support the expected rise in demand for the natural resource. Lithium is used in lithium ion batteries, the standard power source for electric and hybrid vehicles. Experts believe that the demand for lithium can only be measured once the technology is out in the market.

30713 ■ *"A Little Less Hot Air" in Canadian Business (Vol. 81, March 17, 2008, No. 4, pp. 9)*
Pub: Rogers Media
Description: British Columbia will levy an extra tax on all carbon-emitting fuels starting July 1, 2008. The tax will raise $1.8 billion in three years and in effect, the province will reduce general corporate income tax from 12 percent to 11 percent. The tax on small businesses and personal income will also be reduced.

30714 ■ *"Loan Dollars Sit Idle for Energy Plan" in Baltimore Business Journal (Vol. 28, September 10, 2010, No. 18, pp. 1)*
Pub: Baltimore Business Journal
Ed: Scott Dance. **Description:** The Maryland Energy Administration has millions of dollars in Federal stimulus and state energy efficiency cash sitting idle and might be lost once the window for stimulus spending is gone. However, businesses have no interest in betting on renewable energy because some cannot afford to take out more loans. Other challenges faced by these businesses are presented.

30715 ■ *"Local Green Technology on Display" in Crain's Detroit Business (Vol. 26, January 18, 2010, No. 3, pp. 1)*
Pub: Crain Communications Inc.
Ed: Ryan Beene. **Description:** Detroit's 2010 North American International Auto Show put the newest, most innovative green technologies on display showing that the Southeast Michigan automobile industry is gaining traction with its burgeoning e-vehicle infrastructure. Think, a Norwegian electric city-car manufacturer is eyeing sites in Southeast Michigan in which to locate its corporate headquarters and technical center for its North American branch.

30716 ■ *"Long Live Rock" in Inc. (November 2007, pp. 130)*
Pub: Gruner & Jahr USA Publishing
Ed: Nitasha Tiku. **Description:** Profile of a family business using chemistry to recycle concrete products.

30717 ■ *"The Long View: Roberta Bondar on Science and the Need for Education" in Canadian Business (Vol. 81, October 27, 2008, No. 18)*
Pub: Rogers Media Ltd.
Ed: Alex Mlynek. **Description:** Roberta Bondar believes that energy and renewable energy is a critical environmental issue faced by Canada today. Bondar is the first Canadian woman and neurologist in space.

30718 ■ *"A Look At Three Gas-Less Cars" in Hispanic Business (Vol. 30, September 2008, No. 9, pp. 90)*
Pub: Hispanic Business, Inc.
Ed: Daniel Soussa. **Description:** Three major car manufacturers, Chevrolet, BMW, and Honda, are giving market leader Toyota competition for the next generation of eco-friendly car. The latest and most advanced of the gasoline-less cars designed by the three firms, namely, the Chevrolet Volt, BMW's Hydrogen 7, and the Honda FCX Clarity, are reviewed.

30719 ■ *"Lunch Box Maker Gives Back" in Marketing to Women (Vol. 23, November 2010, No. 11, pp. 5)*
Pub: EPM Communications Inc.
Contact: Ira Mayer, President
E-mail: imayer@epmcom.com
Description: Female entrepreneurs launched a new program called, 'Share Your Lunch Project' that encourages mothers to give back and replace their child's lunchbox with their eco-friendly lunch boxes, which are available at select retailers. All proceeds from the project will benefit the World Food Program USA, which feeds children in developing countries.

30720 ■ *"Magpower May Build Solar Panels Here" in Austin Business Journal (Vol. 31, May 13, 2011, No. 10, pp. A1)*
Pub: American City Business Journals Inc.
Ed: Christopher Calnan. **Description:** RRE Austin Solar LLC CEO Doven Mehta has revealed plans to partner with Portugal-based Magpower SA, only if Austin energy buys electricity from planned solar energy farm in Pflugerville. Austin Energy has received 100 bids from 35 companies to supply 200 megawatts of solar- and wind-generated electricity.

30721 ■ *"Making Waves" in Business Journal Portland (Vol. 27, November 26, 2010, No. 39, pp. 1)*
Pub: Portland Business Journal
Ed: Erik Siemers. **Description:** Corvallis, Oregon-based Columbia Power Technologies LLC is about to close a $2 million Series A round of investment initiated by $750,000 from Oregon Angel Fund. The wave energy startup company was formed to commercialize the wave buoy technology developed by Oregon State University researchers.

30722 ■ *"Manufacturers Become Part of Coalition" in Contractor (Vol. 56, July 2009, No. 7, pp. 40)*
Pub: Penton Media, Inc.
Description: Bradford White Water Heaters, Rheem Water Heating, Rinnai America Corp., and A.O. Smith Water Heaters have joined the Consortium for Energy Efficiency in the Coalition for Energy Star Water Heaters. The coalition seeks to increase the awareness of Energy Star water heaters.

30723 ■ *"Marine Act Amendments Gain Parliamentary Approval" in Canadian Sailings (July 7, 2008)*
Pub: UBM Global Trade
Contact: Leonard J. Corallo, President
Ed: Alex Binkley. **Description:** Changes to the Canada Marine Act provides better borrowing deals as well as an ability to tap into federal infrastructure funding for environmental protection measures, security improvements and other site enhancements.

30724 ■ *"Market Takes Shape for Emissions Credits" in Globe & Mail (April 16, 2007, pp. B3)*
Pub: CTVglobemedia Publishing Inc.
Ed: Shawn McCarthy. **Description:** The effort of Canadian companies to prepare for emissions trading after the government imposes climate change regulations is discussed.

30725 ■ *"Meet the Jetsons" in Entrepreneur (Vol. 35, November 2007, No. 11, pp. 21)*
Pub: Entrepreneur Media Inc.
Ed: Amanda C. Kooser. **Description:** An overview of modern home devices is presented, including an organic light-emitting diode (OLED) wall display with changeable artwork, networked appliances like refrigerators, biometric door locks, and a television that can serve as a computer monitor.

30726 ■ *"Mexican Companies to Rent Space in TechTown, Chinese Negotiating" in Crain's Detroit Business (Vol. 24, September 29, 2008, No. 39)*
Pub: Crain Communications Inc.
Ed: Tom Henderson. **Description:** Wayne State University's TechTown, the business incubator and research park, has signed an agreement with the Mexican government that will provide temporary office space to 25 Mexican companies looking to find customers or establish partnerships in Michigan. TechTown's executive director is negotiating with economic development officials from China. To accommodate foreign visitors the incubator is equipping offices with additional equipment and resources.

30727 ■ *"Minnesota State Park Building Exemplifies Sustainability" in Contractor (Vol. 56, November 2009, No. 11, pp. 5)*
Pub: Penton Media, Inc.
Ed: Candace Roulo. **Description:** Camden State Park's newly remodeled information/office building in Lynd, Minnesota features a 10 kw wind turbine which is capable of offsetting most of the facility's electricity and a geothermal heat pump system. The heat pump is a 4-ton vertical closed-loop ground source heat pump by ClimateMaster.

30728 ■ *"Missouri Public Service Commission Chooses APX" in Wireless News (January 22, 2010)*
Pub: Investment Weekly News
Description: Missouri Public Service Commission, with the help of APX Inc., an infrastructure provider for environmental and energy markets, has selected the North American Registry as the renewable energy certificate management system for Missouri Renewable Energy Standard compliance. APX will continue to support the state's renewable energy programs and manage their environmental assets.

30729 ■ *"Mixing Business and Pleasure On the Green" in Black Enterprise (Vol. 41, October 2010, No. 3, pp. 65)*
Pub: Earl G. Graves Publishing Co. Inc.
Ed: Annya M. Lott. **Description:** Glow Golf, sponsored by Glow Sports, will offer instruction to 150 female corporate executives and entrepreneurs to learn the fundamentals of the game of golf.

30730 ■ *"Molycorp Funds Wind Energy Technology Company" in Manufacturing Close-Up (September 19, 2011)*
Pub: Close-Up Media
Description: Molycorp Inc., producer of rare earth oxides (REO) and a REO producer outside of China, announced it will invest in Boulder Wind Power, which has designed a rare earth magnet powered wind turbine generator. This new generator can produce electricity as low as $0.04 per Kilowatt Hour. Boulder Wind Power's patented wind turbine technology allows for use of rare earth permanent magnets that do not require dysprosium, which is relatively scarce.

30731 ■ *"Motorola's New Cell Phone Lineup Includes Green Effort" in Chicago Tribune (January 14, 2009)*
Pub: McClatchy-Tribune Information Services
Ed: Eric Benderoff. **Description:** Motorola Inc. introduced a new line of mobile phones at the Consumer Electronics Show in Las Vegas; the phones are made using recycled water bottles for the plastic housing.

30732 ■ *"Mr. Clean" in Canadian Business (Vol. 81, October 27, 2008, No. 18, pp. 74)*
Pub: Rogers Media Ltd.
Ed: Rachel Pulfer. **Description:** Profile of Nicholas Parker, co-founder of Cleantech Group LLC, a pioneer in clean technology investing. Cleantech, now a global industry, accounts for 10 percent of all venture capital investments made by U.S. companies in 2007.

30733 ■ *The Necessary Revolution: Working Together to Create a Sustainable World*
Pub: Broadway Books
Contact: David Drake, Manager
E-mail: ddrake@randomhouse.com
Ed: Peter M. Senge, Bryan Smith, Nina Kruschwitz, Joe Laur, Sara Schley. **Released:** April 6, 2010. **Price:** $18.00. **Description:** The book outlines various examples for companies to implement sustainable change and go green in the process.

30734 ■ *"N.E.'s Largest Solar Site Set for Scituate Landfill" in Boston Business Journal (Vol. 30, December 17, 2010, No. 47, pp. 1)*
Pub: Boston Business Journal
Ed: Kyle Alspach. **Description:** A closed 12-acre landfill in Scituate, Massachusetts is the proposed site for a 2.4-megawatt solar power plant. The town government will buy the power at a discounted rate, saving it $200,000 annually.

30735 ■ *"The New Alchemists" in Canadian Business (Vol. 81, October 27, 2008, No. 18, pp. 22)*
Pub: Rogers Media Ltd.
Ed: Joe Castaldo. **Description:** Ethanol industry expects second-generation ethanol or cellulosic biofuels to provide ecologically friendly technologies than the ethanol made from food crops. Government and industries are investing on producing cellulosic biofuels.

30736 ■ *"A New Alliance For Global Change" in Harvard Business Review (Vol. 88, September 2010, No. 9, pp. 56)*
Pub: Harvard Business School Publishing
Ed: Bill Drayton, Valeria Budinich. **Description:** Collaboration between social organizations and for-profit firms through the development of hybrid value chains to target complex global issues is promoted. While social organizations offer links to communities and consumers, firms provide financing and scale expertise.

30737 ■ *"New Book Takes Alternate View on Ontario's Wind Industry" in CNW Group (September 19, 2011)*
Pub: CNW Group
Contact: Carolyn McGill-Davidson, President
Description: Dirty Business: The Reality Behind Ontario's Rush to Wind Power, was written by editor and health care writer Jane Wilson of Ottawa, Ontario, Canada along with contributing editor Parker Gallant. The book contains articles and papers on the wind business, including information on illnesses caused from the environmental noise.

30738 ■ *"A New Day is Dawning" in Indoor Comfort Marketing (Vol. 70, August 2011, No. 8, pp. 18)*
Pub: Industry Publications Inc.
Ed: Paul Nazzaro. **Description:** New trends in the HVAC/R industry regarding biofuels and bioheat are explored.

30739 ■ *"New Hydronic Heating Technologies Work" in Contractor (Vol. 57, January 2010, No. 1, pp. 58)*
Pub: Penton Media, Inc.
Ed: Carol Fey. **Description:** Technology behind hydronic heating systems is reviewed. These technologies include radiant and geothermal hydronic heating. System requirements for installing these greener forms of heating are discussed.

30740 ■ *"A New World" in Canadian Business (Vol. 80, October 8, 2007, No. 20, pp. 136)*
Pub: Rogers Media
Ed: Deborah Harford. **Description:** Effects of climate change in Canada's economy are presented. A report published by Natural Resources Canada's Climate Change Impacts and Adaptation Program shows severe weather events such as droughts and storms will cause severe economic problems. Canada's infrastructure could also be affected by the rise in sea level over the next century.

30741 ■ *"The Next Great Canadian Idea?" in Canadian Business (Vol. 81, July 21, 2008, No. 11, pp. 45)*
Pub: Rogers Media Ltd.
Ed: Sharda Prashad. **Description:** Thane Heins has invented a generator that produces energy in an isolated system which contradicts the law of conservation of energy. Perepiteia generator is referred to as a 'perpetual motion machine.' Other inventions slated for the Canadian invention competition include Rob Matthies' batteries and Frank Naumann's Smart Trap.

30742 ■ *"Next Stage of Green Building will be Water Efficiency" in Contractor (Vol. 56, July 2009, No. 7, pp. 41)*
Pub: Penton Media, Inc.
Description: One market report says that water efficiency and conservation will become critical factors in green design, construction, and product selection in the next five years from 2009. The report outlines how critical it will be for the construction industry to address responsible water practices in the future.

30743 ■ *"N.H. Near the LEED in Green Space" in New Hampshire Business Review (Vol. 33, March 25, 2011, No. 6, pp. 30)*
Pub: Business Publications Inc.
Description: New Hamphire's architects, contractors and suppliers are among the leaders with LEED-certified space per capita.

30744 ■ *"Niche Markets, Green Will Be Okay in 2010" in Contractor (Vol. 57, January 2010, No. 1, pp. 1)*
Pub: Penton Media, Inc.
Ed: Robert P. Mader . **Description:** Mechanical contractors will see most of their work stemming from niche markets, such as green work, as well as service work in 2010. It is said that things will turn around for the industry in 2012 and 2013 and one forecast believes that anything outside of the institutional or more public sector work could be down 15 to 30 percent.

30745 ■ *"Nothing But Green Skies" in Inc. (November 2007, pp. 115-120)*
Pub: Gruner & Jahr USA Publishing
Ed: Alison Stein Wellner. **Description:** Profile of Enterprise Rent-A-Car, one of the largest family-owned businesses in the U.S. Andy Taylor, CEO, discusses the company's talks about the idea of offering carbon off-sets for a few years.

30746 ■ *"NStar Feels the Heat" in Cape Cod Times (September 30, 2011)*
Pub: Cape Cod Media Group
Ed: Patrick Cassidy. **Description:** Massachusetts energy officials wish to delay a merger between NStar and Northeast Utilities until it is clear how the partnership would meet the state's green energy goals. Governor Deval Patrick supports the proposed Nantucket Sound wind farm.

30747 ■ *"Nuclear Renaissance" in Canadian Business (Vol. 83, August 17, 2010, No. 13-14, pp. 46)*
Pub: Rogers Media Ltd.
Description: Nuclear energy has come back into the public's favor in Canada because it has virtually no emissions and is always available anytime of the day. Canada's nuclear industry has also achieved an incomparable record of safe, economic and reliable power generation in three provinces for 48 years.

30748 ■ *"On Growth Path of Rising Star" in Boston Business Journal (Vol. 31, June 24, 2011, No. 22, pp. 3)*
Pub: Boston Business Journal
Ed: Kyle Alspach. **Description:** 1366 Technologies Inc. of Lexington, Massachusetts is considered a rising solar power technology company. The firm secured $150 million loan guarantee from the US Department of Energy that could go to the construction of a 1,000 megawatt solar power plant.

30749 ■ *"One on One With SEIA's President, CEO" in Contractor (Vol. 57, January 2010, No. 1, pp. 40)*
Pub: Penton Media, Inc.
Ed: Dave Yates. **Description:** Solar Energy Industries Association President and CEO Rhone Resch says that the deployment of solar systems in the U.S. has exploded since 2005 and that there is a need to make inroads for shaping the U.S. energy policy. Resch says one of the hurdles they face is that there are no universal standards.

30750 ■ *"OPEC Exposed" in Hawaii Business (Vol. 54, September 2008, No. 3, pp. 2)*
Pub: Hawaii Business Publishing
Ed: Serena Lim. **Description:** Organization of the Petroleum Exporting Countries (OPEC) has said that their effort in developing an alternative energy source has driven prices up. The biofuel sector is criticizing the statement, saying that a research study found that biofuels push petroleum prices down by 15 percent. Details on the effect of rising petroleum prices are discussed.

30751 ■ *"Ottawa Advised to Underwrite Carbon Technology" in Globe & Mail (March 10, 2007, pp. B3)*
Pub: CTVglobemedia Publishing Inc.
Ed: Shawn McCarthy. **Description:** A federal panel's suggestion that carbon tax in Canada was not adequate to encourage oil companies and utilities to take up costly technologies to reduce carbon emissions is discussed.

30752 ■ *"Our Company is Dedicated to the Environment, But We Work With Vendors that Aren't" in Inc. (March 2008, pp. 78)*
Pub: Gruner & Jahr USA Publishing
Ed: Myra Goodman. **Description:** Insight into working with vendors, such as construction and janitorial contractors, to comploy with your company's environmental policies is given.

30753 ■ *"Out of Juice?" in Canadian Business (Vol. 81, October 27, 2008, No. 18, pp. 32)*
Pub: Rogers Media Ltd.
Ed: Joe Castaldo. **Description:** Alternative energy experts suggest Canada should be more aggressive and should make major policy changes on energy alternatives despite an Ernst & Young research that rated the country high on renewable energy.

30754 ■ *"Overheating Taking Place? Pay Attention to Details.." in Indoor Comfort Marketing (Vol. 70, March 2011, No. 3, pp.)*
Pub: Industry Publications Inc.
Ed: George R. Carey. **Description:** Boiler facts are outlined to help the small HVAC company when servicing customers.

30755 ■ *"An Overview of Energy Consumption of the Globalized World Economy" in Energy Policy (Vol. 39, October 2011, No. 10, pp. 5920-2928)*
Pub: Reed Elsevier Reference Publishing
Ed: Z.M. Chen, G.Q. Chen. **Description:** Energy consumption and its impact on the global world economy is examined.

30756 ■ *"Phoenix Conference Reveals Opportunities are Coming" in Indoor Comfort Marketing (Vol. 70, March 2011, No. 3, pp. 24)*
Pub: Industry Publications Inc.
Ed: Paul J. Nazzaro. **Description:** Advanced liquid fuels were spotlighted at the Phoenix conference revealing the opportunities for using liquid fuels.

30757 ■ *"Plans for Coal-Fired Electricity Could Go Up in Smoke" in Globe & Mail (March 5, 2007, pp. B7)*
Pub: CTVglobemedia Publishing Inc.
Ed: Steve James. **Description:** The coal-fired power project initiated by Texas-based utility company TXU Corp. is receiving legal challenges from green groups. The possible disasters caused by the coal-fired plant are presented.

30758 ■ *"Positive Transformational Change" in Indoor Comfort Marketing (Vol. 70, April 2011, No. 4, pp. 30)*
Pub: Industry Publications Inc.
Ed: Blaine Fox. **Description:** Management changes taking place at Shark Bites HVAC firm are discussed.

30759 ■ *"Power Ranger" in Inc. (November 2007, pp. 131)*
Pub: Gruner & Jahr USA Publishing
Ed: Nitasha Tiku. **Description:** Surveyor software is designed to power down computers when not in use, in order to save energy.

30760 ■ *"PPC's Major Commitment to Biofuel Infrastructure" in Indoor Comfort Marketing (Vol. 70, April 2011, No. 4, pp. 6)*
Pub: Industry Publications Inc.
Description: Petroleum Products Corporation's commitment to the biofuel infrastructure is outlined.

30761 ■ *"Pre-Certified LEED Hotel Prototype Reduces Energy Use, Conserves Water" in Contractor (Vol. 57, January 2010, No. 1, pp. 3)*
Pub: Penton Media, Inc.
Ed: Candace Roulo. **Description:** Marriott International Inc.'s LEED pre-certified prototype hotel will reduce a hotel's energy and water consumption by 25 percent and save owners approximately $100,000. Their Courtyard Settler's Ridge in Pittsburgh will be the first hotel built based on the prototype.

30762 ■ *"Preparing for Weed Control" in Farmer's Weekly (March 28, 2008, No. 320)*
Pub: Reed Business Information
Contact: Jeff Greisch, President
Description: Profile of Richard Beachell who farms in a joint venture with his neighbor. Beachell discusses nitrogen applications, fungicides and the reduction of pesticides.

30763 ■ *"Provinces Tackle E-Waste Problem" in Canadian Electronics (Vol. 23, June-July 2008, No. 4, pp. 1)*
Pub: Action Communication Inc.
Ed: Ken Manchen. **Description:** Canadian provinces are implementing measures concerning the safe and environmentally friendly disposal of electronic waste. Alberta, British Columbia, Nova Scotia, and Saskatchewan impose an e-waste recycling fee on electronic equipment purchases.

30764 ■ *"PSC Approves $130M TECO Solar Project" in Tampa Bay Business Journal (Vol. 30, December 18, 2009, No. 52, pp. 1)*
Pub: American City Business Journals
Ed: Michael Hinman. **Description:** Florida's Public Service Commission has endorsed Tampa Electric Company's plan to add 25 megawatts of solar energy to its portfolio. TECO's plan needed the approval by PSC to defray additional costs for the project through ratepayers.

30765 ■ *"A Quick Guide to NATE" in Indoor Comfort Marketing (Vol. 70, February 2011, No. 2, pp. 12)*
Pub: Industry Publications Inc.
Description: Guide for training and certification in the North American Technician Excellence award.

30766 ■ *"Radiant - the Hottest Topic in .. Cooling" in Indoor Comfort Marketing (Vol. 70, February 2011, No. 2, pp. 8)*
Pub: Industry Publications Inc.
Description: Examination of radiant cooling systems, a new trend in cooling homes and buildings.

30767 ■ *"Radiant Commences In-Lab Testing for US Air Mobility Command" in Canadian Corporate News (May 16, 2007)*
Pub: Comtex News Network Inc.
Description: The Boeing Company will be conducting in-lab infrared material testing for the Radiant Energy Corporation, developer and marketer of InfraTek, the environmentally friendly, patented infrared pre-flight aircraft deicing system.

30768 ■ *"Recycling 202: How to Take Your Recycling Practices to the Next Level" in Black Enterprise (Vol. 41, September 2010, No. 2, pp. 38)*
Pub: Earl G. Graves Publishing Co. Inc.
Ed: Tamara E. Holmes. **Description:** Consumer Electronics Association and other organizations, manufacturers and retailers list ways to recycle all household items.

30769 ■ *Recycling and Waste Management Guide to the Internet*
Pub: Government Institutes
Contact: Judith Rothman, Director
URL(s): www.govinstpress.com. **Price:** $72, Individuals. **Covers:** More than 350 web sites, discussion lists, and news groups on the internet covering waste management and recycling issues. **Entries include:** Site name, address, subject, site summary, contact name and e-mail. **Arrangement:** Alphabetical. **Indexes:** Subject.

30770 ■ *"Red Diesel Cost Sparks a Move to Home-Grown Fuel" in Farmer's Weekly (March 28, 2008, No. 320)*
Pub: Reed Business Information
Contact: Jeff Greisch, President
Description: Due to the rising cost of red diesel, the idea of growing one's own tractor fuel has an undeniable attraction for many farmers. A growing pressure is weighing on engine manufacturers to produce designs that can run on both SVO as well as biodiesel.

30771 ■ *"Red, Pink and More: Cause Marketing Surges as a Prime Tactic to Reach Female Customers" in Marketing to Women (April 2008)*
Pub: EPM Communications Inc.
Contact: Ira Mayer, President
E-mail: imayer@epmcom.com
Description: According to the American Marketing Association, forty percent of women say they are more likely to purchase a product or service if they know a certain amount of the price is being donated directly to a cause or campaign that they believe in supporting.

30772 ■ *"Reduce or Repay" in Canadian Business (Vol. 80, November 5, 2007, No. 22, pp. 35)*
Pub: Rogers Media
Ed: Regan Ray. **Description:** The new greenhouse gas (GHG) policy of Alberta, Canada requires about 100 industrial facilities that emit over 100,000 tons of GHG per year to reduce emissions by 12 percent by the end of 2007. Facilities that fail to comply will pay $15 per ton of GHG emission beyond target. The economic impacts of the regulation are evaluated.

30773 ■ *"Reducing the Book's Carbon Footpring" in American Printer (Vol. 128, July 1, 2011, No. 7)*
Pub: Penton Media Inc.
Description: Green Press Initiative's Book Industry Environmental Council is working to achieve a 20 percent reduction in the book industry's carbon footprint by 2020. The Council is made up of publishers, printers, paper suppliers, and non-governmental organizations.

30774 ■ *"Reinventing the Cheeseburger" in Inc. (November 2007, pp. 124-125)*
Pub: Gruner & Jahr USA Publishing
Ed: Chris Lydgate. **Description:** Profile of Burgerville's Tom Mears, who turned his drive-through burger restaurant green.

30775 ■ *"Reinventing Marketing to Manage the Environmental Imperative" in Journal of Marketing (Vol. 75, July 2011, No. 4, pp. 132)*
Pub: American Marketing Association
Ed: Philip Kotler. **Description:** Marketers must now examine their theory and practices due to the growing recognition of finite resources and high environmental costs. Companies also need to balance more carefully their growth goals with the need to purse sustainability. Insights on the rise of demarketing and social marketing are also given.

30776 ■ *"Renewable Energy Adoption in an Aging Population" in Energy Policy (Vol. 39, October 2011, No. 10, pp. 6021-6029)*
Pub: Reed Elsevier Reference Publishing
Ed: Ken Willis, Riccardo Scarpa, Rose Gilroy, Neveen Hamza. **Description:** Attitudes and impacts of renewable energy adoption on an aging population is examined.

30777 ■ *"Renewable Energy Market Opportunities: Wind Testing" in PR Newswire (September 22, 2011)*
Pub: United Business Media
Description: Global wind energy test systems markets are discussed. Research conducted covers both non-destructive test equipment and condition monitoring equipment product segments.

30778 ■ *Resource and Environmental Management in Canada*
Pub: Oxford University Press
Ed: Bruce Mitchell. **Released:** April 1, 2004. **Price:** $45.00. **Description:** Discusses resource management in Canada, focusing on business and industry, environmental groups, First Nations, the public, local communities with resource-based economies.

30779 ■ *"ReVenture Plan Appears Close to Landing Key Legislative Deal" in Charlotte Business Journal (Vol. 25, July 9, 2010, No. 16, pp. 1)*
Pub: Charlotte Business Journal
Ed: John Downey. **Description:** North Carolina lawmakers acted on special legislation that would boost development of Forsite Development 667-acre ReVenture Energy Park. The legislation could also improve chances that Duke Energy Carolinas will contract to purchase the power from the planned 50-megawatt biomass power plant located at the park. How utilities would benefit from the legislation is also discussed.

30780 ■ *"Rivals Blow In" in Crain's Cleveland Business (Vol. 30, June 1, 2009, No. 21, pp. 1)*
Pub: Crain Communications, Inc.
Ed: Chuck Soder. **Description:** U.S. and Canadian competitors are hoping to start construction of offshore wind farm project proposed by Cuyahoga County's Great Lakes Energy Development Task Force. Details of the project are included.

30781 ■ *"Rosewood Site Faces Big Cleanup" in Baltimore Business Journal (Vol. 27, February 6, 2010, No. 40, pp. 1)*
Pub: American City Business Journals
Ed: Daniel J. Sernovitz. **Description:** Environmental assessment report states that Maryland's Rosewood Center for the Developmentally Disabled has significant amounts of toxic chemicals, which could impact Stevenson University's decision to purchase the property. Senator Robert A. Zirkin believes that the state should pay for the cleanup, which is expected to cost millions.

30782 ■ *"Rough Headwinds" in Boston Business Journal (Vol. 30, November 12, 2010, No. 42, pp. 1)*
Pub: Boston Business Journal
Ed: Kyle Alspach. **Description:** Views of residents, as well as key information on First Wind's plan to install wind power turbines in Brimfield, Massachusetts are presented. Residents believe that First Wind's project will devalue properties, compromise quality of life, and ruin the rural quality of Brimfield. First Wind expects to produce 2,000 megawatts of power from wind by 2020.

30783 ■ *"San Diego Museum Receives LEED Certification" in Contractor (Vol. 57, January 2010, No. 1, pp. 14)*
Pub: Penton Media, Inc.
Description: San Diego Natural History Museum received an LEED certification for existing buildings. The certification process began when they committed to displaying the Dead Sea Scrolls in 2007 and they had to upgrade their buildings' air quality and to control for air moisture, temperature, and volume. They reduced their energy consumption by upwards of 20 percent.

30784 ■ *"Sandvik Expands Energy-Saving Program" in Modern Machine Shop (Vol. 84, September 2011, No. 4, pp. 48)*
Pub: Gardner Business Media, Inc.
Contact: Richard G. Kline, President
E-mail: rkline@gardnerweb.com
Description: Sandvik Coromant, based in Fair Lawn, New Jersey, expanded its Sustainable Manufacturing Program that originally was developed to help Japanese-based firms reduce electricity consumption by 15 percent after the recent earthquake that cause loss of electrical power. The program now provides energy reduction through the Sandvick cutting tool technology, application techniques and productivity increases.

30785 ■ *"Saudi Overtures" in The Business Journal-Portland (Vol. 25, August 15, 2008, No. 23, pp. 1)*
Pub: American City Business Journals, Inc.
Ed: Aliza Earnshaw. **Description:** Saudi Arabia's huge revenue from oil is creating opportunities for Oregon companies as the country develops new cities, industrial zones, and tourism centers. Oregon exported only $46.8 million worth of goods to Saudi Arabia in 2007 but the kingdom is interested in green building materials and methods, renewable energy and water quality control, and nanotechnology all of which Oregon has expertise in.

30786 ■ *"Scorched Earth: Will Environmental Risks in China Overwhelm Its Opportunities?" in Harvard Business Review (Vol. 85, June 2007, No. 6)*
Pub: Harvard Business School Publishing
Ed: Elizabeth Economy, Kenneth Lieberthal. **Description:** Environmental risks for business in China include water supply access, energy needs, pollution, and soil erosion. However, the nation's government is investing money to develop green technology and alternative energy sources.

30787 ■ *"The Second Most Fuel-Efficient Tractor of the Decade: John Deere 8320R" in Farm Industry News (November 10, 2011)*
Pub: Penton Business Media Inc.
Description: John Deere's 8320R Tractor was ranked second in the Farm Industry News listing of the top 40 most fuel-efficient tractors of the decade, following the winner, John Deere's 8295R PTO tractor.

30788 ■ *"Seeing Green in Going Green" in The Business Journal-Serving Greater Tampa Bay (Vol. 28, July 4, 2008, No. 28, pp. 1)*
Pub: American City Business Journals, Inc.
Ed: Janet Leiser. **Description:** Atlanta, Georgia-based developer IDI Corp. is pushing for Leadership in Energy and Environmental Design certification for the warehouse that is currently under construction at Madison Business Center along Port Sutton and U.S. 41. The industrial building is the first in Tampa Bay to seek certification for LEED as set by the U.S. Green Building Council.

30789 ■ *"Shaw Joins Green Institute Launch" in Home Textiles Today (Vol. 31, May 24, 2011, No. 13, pp. 4)*
Pub: Reed Business Information
Contact: Jeff Greisch, President
Description: Shaw Industries Group joined the Green Products Innovation Institute, the first nonprofit institute of its kind in America. The institute promotes the concepts of reverse engineering, elimination of waste, safe chemistries, and closed loop technical nutrients.

30790 ■ *"Shifting Gears" in Business Journal-Serving Phoenix & the Valley of the Sun (Vol. 31, November 12, 2010, No. 10, pp. 1)*
Pub: Phoenix Business Journal
Ed: Patrick O'Grady. **Description:** Automotive parts recyclers in Arizona are benefiting from the challenging national economic conditions as well as from the green movement. Recyclers revealed that customers prefer recycled parts more because they are cheaper and are more environmentally friendly. Other information about the automotive parts recycling industry is presented.

30791 ■ *"Should I or Shouldn't I?" in Indoor Comfort Marketing (Vol. 70, February 2011, No. 2, pp. 30)*
Pub: Industry Publications Inc.
Ed: Philip J. Baratz. **Description:** Investment tips are shared for investing in futures options.

30792 ■ *"Slick Science" in Canadian Business (Vol. 81, September 15, 2008, No. 14-15, pp. 55)*
Pub: Rogers Media Ltd.
Ed: Andrew Nikiforuk. **Description:** N-Solv Corp's John Nenniger has discovered a better alternative to steam-assisted gravity drainage methods for extracting bitumen. Nenniger's technique also relies on gravity but replaces steam with propane, which leaves behind impurities like asphaltenes and heavy metals that are too dirty to burn.

30793 ■ *"Small Changes Can Mean Big Energy Savings" in Crain's Cleveland Business (Vol. 28, November 5, 2007, No. 44, pp. 21)*
Pub: Crain Communications, Inc.
Ed: Harriet Tramer. **Description:** Many Northeast Ohio businesses are taking their cues from the residential real estate market to draw and capitalize on interest in energy efficiency and is regularly taken into account by local architects.

30794 ■ *"Small Wind Power Market to Double by 2015 at $634 Million" in Western Farm Press (September 30, 2011)*
Pub: Penton Media, Inc.
Description: Small wind power provides cost-effective electricity on a highly localized level, in both remote settings as well as in conjunction with power from the utility grid. Government incentives are spurring new growth in the industry.

30795 ■ *"Smart Car Sales Take Big Hit in Recession" in Business Journal-Milwaukee (Vol. 28, December 10, 2010, No. 10, pp. A1)*
Pub: Milwaukee Business Journal
Ed: Stacey Vogel Davis. **Description:** Sales of smart cars in Milwaukee declined in 2010. Smart Center Milwaukee sold only 52 new cars through October 2010. Increased competition is seen as a reason for the decline in sales.

30796 ■ *"Snow Melt Systems Offer Practical Solutions" in Contractor (Vol. 56, October 2009, No. 10, pp. S6)*
Pub: Penton Media, Inc.
Ed: Lisa Murton Beets. **Description:** Cases are discussed in which the installation of a snow melt system becomes a necessity. One example describes how limited space means there would be no place to put plowed snow; snow melt systems can also resolve problems that arise due to an excess of melting snow.

30797 ■ *"Software Solutions from Trane and Carrier" in Contractor (Vol. 56, July 2009, No. 7, pp. 38)*
Pub: Penton Media, Inc.
Ed: William Feldman; Patti Feldman. **Description:** Trane Trace 700 software helps HVAC contractors optimize the design of a building's HVAC system and aids in the evaluation of various key energy-saving concepts, including daylighting, high-performance glazing, and other optimization strategies. Carrier's E20-II family of software programs lets contractors increase the accuracy of an HVAC system estimate.

30798 ■ *"Solar Credit Lapse Spur Late Demand" in The Business Journal - Serving Phoenix and the Valley of the Sun (Vol. 28, July 18, 2008)*
Pub: American City Business Journals, Inc.
Ed: Patrick O'Grady. **Description:** Businesses looking to engage in the solar energy industry are facing the problems of taxation and limited solar panel supply. Solar panels manufacturers are focusing more on the European market. Political issues surrounding the federal tax credit policy on solar energy users are also discussed.

30799 ■ *"Something Different in the Air? The Collapse of the Schwarzenegger Health Plan in California" in WorkingUSA (June 2008)*
Pub: Blackwell Publishers Ltd.
Ed: Daniel J.B. Mitchell. **Description:** In January 2007, California Governor Arnold Schwarzenegger proposed a state universal health care plan modeled after the Massachusetts individual mandate program. A year later, the plan was dead. Although some key interest groups eventually backed the plan, it was overwhelmed by a looming state budget crisis and a lack of gubernatorial focus. Although much acclaimed for his stance on greenhouse gases, stem cells, hydrogen highways, and other Big Ideas, diffused gubernatorial priorities and a failure to resolve California's chronic fiscal difficulties let the clock run out on universal health care.

30800 ■ *"Star Power Versus (Somewhat) Green Power" in Globe & Mail (January 18, 2007, pp. B2)*
Pub: CTVglobemedia Publishing Inc.
Ed: Konrad Yakabuski. **Description:** The views of the Canadian actor Roy Dupuis on the trends of energy consumption by Quebeckers are presented, along with statistics of energy consumption in the Quebec region.

30801 ■ *"Start Connecting Today" in Indoor Comfort Marketing (Vol. 70, May 2011, No. 5, pp. 34)*
Pub: Industry Publications Inc.
Ed: Paul Nazzaro. **Description:** An in-depth discussion regarding the use of biofuels on bioheat use and dealership.

30802 ■ *"Start Moving Toward Advanced Fuels" in Indoor Comfort Marketing (Vol. 70, March 2011, No. 3, pp. 4)*
Pub: Industry Publications Inc.
Ed: Michael L. SanGiovanni. **Description:** Commentary on advanced fuels is presented.

30803 ■ *"Start Thinking About Carbon Assets - Now" in Harvard Business Review (Vol. 86, September 2008, No. 9, pp. 28)*
Pub: Harvard Business School Press
Ed: Alex Rau; Robert Toker. **Description:** Economic and strategic benefits of adopting a corporate carbon assets policy are discussed. Topics include renewable energy and capturing waste energy.

30804 ■ *"State Investment Goes Sour" in Business Journal Portland (Vol. 26, December 4, 2009, No. 39, pp. 1)*
Pub: American City Business Journals Inc.
Ed: Erik Siemers. **Description:** Oregon might recoup only $500,000 of a $20 million loan to Vancouver-based Cascade Grain Products LLC. Cascade Grain's ethanol plant in Clatskanie, OR will be put into auction under the supervision of a bankruptcy court.

30805 ■ *"Stimulus 'Loser' Won't Build Plant in Mass." in Boston Business Journal (Vol. 30, November 5, 2010, No. 41, pp. 1)*
Pub: Boston Business Journal
Ed: Kyle Alspach. **Description:** Boston-Power Inc. no longer plans to build an electric vehicle battery plant in Massachusetts after it failed to obtain stimulus funds from the federal government. The company is instead looking to build a lithium-ion battery plant in China and possibly Europe.

30806 ■ *"Stock Car Racing" in Canadian Business (Vol. 81, September 15, 2008, No. 14-15, pp. 29)*
Pub: Rogers Media Ltd.
Ed: Thomas Watson. **Description:** Some analysts predict a Chapter 11-style tune-up making GM and Ford a speculative turnaround stock. However, the price of oil could make or break the shares of the Big Three U.S. automobile manufacturers and if oil goes up too high then a speculative stock to watch is an electric car company called Zenn Motor Co.

30807 ■ *"The Superpower Dilemma" in Canadian Business (Vol. 83, August 17, 2010, No. 13-14, pp. 42)*
Pub: Rogers Media Ltd.
Description: Canada has been an energy superpower partly because it controls the energy source and the production means, particularly of fossil fuels. However, Canada's status as superpower could diminish if it replaces petroleum exports with renewable technology for using sources of energy available globally.

30808 ■ *"Survey Finds State Execs Cool On Climate Change" in The Business Journal-Milwaukee (Vol. 25, August 8, 2008,*

No. 46, pp. A1)
Pub: American City Business Journals, Inc.

Ed: David Doege. **Description:** According to a survey of business executives in Wisconsin, business leaders do not see climate change as a pressing concern, but businesses are moving toward more energy-efficient operations. The survey also revealed that executives believe that financial incentives can promote energy conservation. Other survey results are provided.

30809 ■ *"Sustainability Is Top Priority for GreenTown Chicago" in Contractor (Vol. 56, November 2009, No. 11, pp. 1)*
Pub: Penton Media, Inc.

Ed: Candace Roulo. **Description:** GreenTown Chicago 2009 conference tackled energy-efficient practices and technologies, green design and building, and sustainable policies. Water conservation was also a topic at the conference and one mayor who made a presentation said that reducing the water loss in the system is a priority in the city's endeavor.

30810 ■ *"Sustaining Supply" in Crain's Cleveland Business (Vol. 28, November 19, 2007, No. 46, pp. 3)*
Pub: Crain Communications, Inc.

Ed: David Bennett. **Description:** Local firms are playing key roles in preparing Wal-Mart suppliers to develop sustainable, or ecologically conscious, packaging. New products such as the innovative 'eco-bottle' - a collapsed container made of recyclable plastic that will expand to its traditional size and shape once water is added and would transform to such items as window cleaner when the water mixes with the container's dry contents - are being designed by firms such as Nottingham Spirk.

30811 ■ *"Suzlon S88-Powered Wind Farm in Minnesota Secures Long-Term Financing" in PR Newswire (September 21, 2011)*
Pub: United Business Media

Description: Suzlon Energy Limited is the world's fifth largest manufacturer of wind turbines. Owners of the Grant County Wind Farm in Minnesota have secured a long-term financing deal for the ten Suzlon S88 2.1 MW wind turbines that generate enough electricity to power 7,000 homes.

30812 ■ *"Taiwan Technology Initiatives Foster Growth" in Canadian Electronics (Vol. 23, February 2008, No. 1, pp. 28)*
Pub: CLB Media Inc.

Description: A study conducted by the Market Intelligence Center shows that currently, Taiwan is the world's larges producer of information technology products such as motherboards, servers, and LCD monitors. In 2006, Taiwan's LED industry reached a production value of NTD 21 billion. This push into the LED sector shows the Ministry of Economic Affairs' plan to target industries that are environmentally friendly.

30813 ■ *"The Tapestry of Life" in Women In Business (Vol. 61, December 2009, No. 6, pp. 8)*
Pub: American Business Women's Association

Ed: Kathleen Leighton. **Description:** Suzanne Fanch, co-owner of the Devil's Thumb Ranch, discusses the family and career-related influences that helped her to achieve success as a small business proprietor. She advises that opportunities should be treated as building blocks towards success. Fanch's involvement in advocacies that take care of the welfare of community, children, and environment is also discussed.

30814 ■ *"Taxis Are Set to Go Hybrid" in Philadelphia Business Journal (Vol. 30, September 16, 2011, No. 31, pp. 1)*
Pub: American City Business Journals Inc.

Ed: Natalie Kostelni. **Description:** Taxis are going hybrid in several major states such as New York, California and Maryland where it is mandated, but it is yet to happen in Philadelphia, Pennsylvania with the exception of one taxi company. Freedom Taxi is awaiting Philadelphia Parking Authority's sign off.

30815 ■ *"Taylor Tests Land Grant Program" in Austin Business Journal (Vol. 31, June 3, 2011, No. 13, pp. 1)*
Pub: American City Business Journals Inc.

Ed: Vicky Garza. **Description:** Taylor Economic Development Corporation implemented a land grant program called Build On Our Lot to lure businesses to Taylor City, Austin, Texas. They are targeting small businesses, especially those in the renewable energy, advanced manufacturing, technical services and food products. Program details are included.

30816 ■ *"Think the Oilsands Are an Environmental Disaster?" in Canadian Business (Vol. 83, October 12, 2010, No. 17, pp. 52)*
Pub: Rogers Media Ltd.

Ed: Michael McCullough. **Description:** Studies which were commissioned by the Alberta Energy Research Institute in 2008 found that the life-cycle carbon emissions of oil derived from oilsands was 10 percent greater than the average from all sources. Synthetic crude from the oilsands is 38 percent less carbon-intensive than it was 20 years ago due to productivity improvements.

30817 ■ *"Thirsty? Now There's a Water Cooler to Suit Every Taste" in Inc. (Vol. 33, October 2011, No. 8, pp. 43)*
Pub: Inc. Magazine

Ed: John Brandon. **Description:** Brita's Hydration Station is a wall-mounted unit with a touch-free sensor for dispensing water. This water cooler cuts down on landfill waste and offers special features.

30818 ■ *"Thomas Morley; President, The Lube Stop Inc., 37" in Crain's Cleveland Business (Vol. 28, November 19, 2007, No. 46, pp. F-12)*
Pub: Crain Communications, Inc.

Ed: David Bennett. **Description:** Profile of Thomas Morley, president of The Lube Stop Inc., who is dedicated to promoting the company's strong environmental record as an effective way to differentiate Lube Stop from its competition. Since Mr. Morley came to the company in 2004, Lube Stop has increased sales by 10 percent and has boosted its operating profits by 30 percent.

30819 ■ *The Three Secrets of Green Business: Unlocking Competitive Advantage in a Low Carbon Economy*
Pub: Earthscan

Ed: Gareth Kane. **Released:** February 10, 2010. **Price:** $96.00. **Description:** Small business is coming under increasing pressure from government, customers and campaigning groups to improve environmental performance. Soaring utility and compliance costs are critical financial burdens on small companies.

30820 ■ *"Timberland's CEO On Standing Up to 65,000 Angry Activists" in Harvard Business Review (Vol. 88, September 2010, No. 9, pp. 39)*
Pub: Harvard Business School Publishing

Ed: Jeff Swartz. **Description:** Timberland Company avoided a potential boycott by taking a two-way approach. It addressed a supplier issue that posed a threat to the environment, and launched an email campaign to keep Greenpeace activists informed of the development of a new supplier agreement.

30821 ■ *"Time to Green Your Business" in Gallup Management Journal (April 22, 2011)*
Pub: Gallup

Ed: Bryant Ott. **Description:** It's Earth Day, so expect to hear companies touting their commitment to the environment. However, according to Gallup, more companies are finding it more interested to talk about being green than actually taking the steps to become a green business.

30822 ■ *"Too Much Precaution About Biotech Corn" in Barron's (Vol. 88, March 17, 2008, No. 11, pp. 54)*
Pub: Dow Jones & Company, Inc.

Ed: Mark I. Schwartz. **Description:** In the U.S., 90 percent of cultivated soybeans are biotech varietals as well as 60 percent of the corn. Farmers have significantly reduced their reliance on pesticides in the growing of biotech corn. Biotech cotton cultivation has brought hundreds of millions of dollars in net financial gains to farmers. The European Union has precluded the cultivation or sale of biotech crops within its border.

30823 ■ *"Toolmakers' New Tack" in Crain's Detroit Business (Vol. 25, June 8, 2009,)*
Pub: Crain Communications Inc. - Detroit

Ed: Ryan Beene, Amy Lane. **Description:** MAG Industrial Automation Systems LLC and Dowding Machining Inc. have partnered to advance wind-turbine technology. The goal is to cut costs of wind energy to the same level as carbon-based fuel.

30824 ■ *"Top 50 Exporters" in Hispanic Business (Vol. 30, July-August 2008, No. 7-8, pp. 42)*
Pub: Hispanic Business, Inc.

Ed: Hildy Medina. **Description:** Increases in exports revenues reported by food exporters and green companies in a time of economic slowdown in the U.S are described. Food exporters have benefited from the growth of high-volume grocery stores in underdeveloped countries and the German governments' promotion of solar energy has benefited the U.S. solar heating equipment and solar panel manufactures.

30825 ■ *"Tory Green?" in Canadian Business (Vol. 80, January 15, 2007, No. 2, pp. 72)*
Pub: Rogers Media

Ed: Joe Chidley. **Description:** The need for the government to participate actively in protecting the environment through proper enforcement of the Tories Clean Air Act, is discussed.

30826 ■ *"Toward a Better Future" in Canadian Business (Vol. 83, August 17, 2010, No. 13-14, pp. 51)*
Pub: Rogers Media Ltd.

Description: A look at certain realities in order to build a better future for Canada's energy industry is presented. Canada must focus on making the oil cleaner, instead of replacing it with another source since dependency on oil will remain in this lifetime. Canada must also develop solutions toward clean technology power sources.

30827 ■ *"Traer Turning to Wind Power to Meet Long-Term Energy Needs" in Waterloo Courier (September 20, 2011)*
Pub: Lee Enterprises

Ed: Josh Nelson. **Description:** Traer Municipal Utilities is working with Clark Thompson, a Story City wind turbine developer, to erect a wind turbine to supply electrical energy to the city. Details are included.

30828 ■ *"Transportation Enterprise" in Advertising Age (Vol. 79, June 9, 2008, No. 23, pp. S10)*
Pub: Crain Communications, Inc.

Ed: Jean Halliday. **Description:** Overview of Enterprise rent-a-car's plan to become a more environmentally-friendly company. The family-owned business has spent $1 million a year to plant trees since 2006 and has added more fuel-efficient cars, hybrids and flex-fuel models.

30829 ■ *"Tritium: A Hot Topic in Canada" in Canadian Business (Vol. 80, January 29, 2007, No. 3, pp. 8)*
Pub: Rogers Media

Ed: Marlene Rego. **Description:** The views of Canadian environmental activists, on the effects of the release of tritium into the Ottwa river, are presented.

30830 ■ *True Green at Work: 100 Ways You Can Make the Environment Your Business*
Pub: National Geographic

Ed: Kim McKay; Jenny Bonnin; Tim Wallace. **Released:** February 19, 2008. **Price:** $19.95 paperback. **Description:** Manual to help any small business minimize its carbon footprint by reducing waste.

30831 ■ *"Tucson Tech Column" in AZ Daily Star (September 27, 2011)*
Pub: Arizona Daily Star
Ed: David Wichner. **Description:** Western Wind Energy, based in Vancouver, British Columbia, Canada is able to harness energy from the sun when the wind is not blowing at the Kingman I Project wind farm. Details of this technology are outlined.

30832 ■ *"Turning Green Ink to Black" in The Business Journal-Serving Metropolitan Kansas City (Vol. 26, August 8, 2008, No. 48, pp. 1)*
Pub: American City Business Journals, Inc.
Ed: James Dornbrook. **Description:** InkCycle has introduced grenk, a line of environmentally-friendly printer toner and ink cartridges. The cartridges are collected and recycled after use by the company, which separates them into their metal, cardboard, and plastic components.

30833 ■ *"Tweaking On-Board Activities, Equipment Saves Fuel, Reduces CO2" in Canadian Sailings (June 30, 2008)*
Pub: UBM Global Trade
Contact: Leonard J. Corallo, President
Description: Optimizing ship activities and equipment uses less fuel and therefore reduces greenhouse gas emissions. Ways in which companies are implementing research and development techniques in order to monitor ship performance and analyze data in an attempt to become more efficient are examined.

30834 ■ *"UA Turns Ann Arbor Green" in Contractor (Vol. 56, September 2009, No. 9, pp. 5)*
Pub: Penton Media, Inc.
Ed: Robert P. Mader. **Description:** Instructors at the United Association of Plumbers and Steamfitters have studied the latest in green and sustainable construction and service at the Washtenaw Community College in Michigan. Classes included building information modeling, hydronic heating and cooling and advanced HVACR troubleshooting. The UA is currently focusing on green training.

30835 ■ *"The Ultimate Comfort System" in Contractor (Vol. 56, July 2009, No. 7, pp. 30)*
Pub: Penton Media, Inc.
Ed: Mark Eatherton. **Description:** Retrofitting of a hydronic heating system to an existing home is presented. The project approaches near net-zero energy production.

30836 ■ *"Ultra Green Energy Services Opens NJ Biodiesel Transload Facility" in Indoor Comfort Marketing (Vol. 70, June 2011, No. 6, pp. 35)*
Pub: Industry Publications Inc.
Description: Profile of Ultra Green Energy Services and the opening of their new biodiesel facility in New Jersey is discussed.

30837 ■ *"Ultra Low Sulfur Diesel: The Promise and the Reality" in Indoor Comfort Marketing (Vol. 70, July 2011, No. 7, pp. 22)*
Pub: Industry Publications Inc.
Ed: Ed Kitchen. **Description:** Impacts of ultra low sulfur diesel are examined.

30838 ■ *"Unilever to Sustainably Source All Paper and Board Packaging" in Ice Cream Reporter (Vol. 23, July 20, 2010, No. 8, pp. 1)*
Pub: Ice Cream Reporter
Description: Unilever, a leader in the frozen dessert market, has developed a new sustainable paper and board packaging sourcing policy that will reduce environmental impact by working with suppliers to source 75 percent of paper and board packaging from sustainably managed forests or from recycled material. Unilever is parent company to Breyers, Haagen-Dazs, Klondike, Popsicle and other ice cream brands.

30839 ■ *"University Data Center Goes Off-Grid, Is Test Bed" in Contractor (Vol. 57, February 2010, No. 2, pp. 1)*
Pub: Penton Media, Inc.
Ed: Candace Roulo. **Description:** Syracuse University's Green Data Center has gone off-grid through the use of natural gas fired turbines. It is expected to use 50 percent less energy than a typical computer center. The center's heating and cooling system setup is also discussed.

30840 ■ *"Uranium Energy Corp Provides an Update on Its Goliad Operations" in Canadian Corporate News (May 16, 2007)*
Pub: Comtex News Network Inc.
Description: Complaints against Uranium Energy Corp. and its Goliad Project in South Texas have been dismissed. The Railroad Commission of Texas (RRC), the regulatory authority which oversees mineral exploration in Texas, concluded that Uranium Energy Corp.'s drilling activities on the Goliad Project have not contaminated certain water wells or the related aquifier.

30841 ■ *"Valener Announces that Gaz Metro has Achieved a Key Step in Acquiring CVPS" in CNW Group (September 30, 2011)*
Pub: CNW Group
Contact: Carolyn McGill-Davidson, President
Description: Valener Inc., which owns about 29 percent of Gaz Metro Ltd. Partnership, announced that Gaz Metro welcomes the sale of Central Vermont Public Service Corporation (CVPS). Valener owns an indirect interest of 24.5 percent in the wind power projects jointly developed by Beaupre Eole General Partnership and Boralex Inc. on private lands in Quebec. Details of the deal are included.

30842 ■ *Values-Centered Entrepreneurship*
Pub: Routledge
Ed: David Y. Choi, Edmund Gray. **Released:** August 10, 2010. **Price:** $39.95. **Description:** A new brand of entrepreneurs has arrived on the business scene, carrying with them a new set of values. They possess a sense of social responsibility, the need to protect the planet, and to do the right thing for all stakeholders.

30843 ■ *"Volunteers Needed" in Canadian Business (Vol. 81, October 27, 2008, No. 18, pp. 60)*
Pub: Rogers Media Ltd.
Ed: Megan Harman. **Description:** Emissions-targeting regulations focus on the biggest polluters, missing out on other companies that leave carbon footprints in things such as shipping and travel. Some companies in Canada have initiated programs to offset their carbon emissions. Critics claim that offsetting does not reduce emissions and the programs merely justify pollution.

30844 ■ *"Warm Floors Make Warm Homes" in Contractor (Vol. 56, October 2009, No. 10, pp. S18)*
Pub: Penton Media, Inc.
Ed: Lisa Murton Beets. **Description:** Three award winning radiant floor-heating installations are presented. The design and the equipment used for these systems are discussed.

30845 ■ *"Was Mandating Solar Power Water Heaters For New Homes Good Policy?" in Hawaii Business (Vol. 54, August 2008, No. 2, pp. 28)*
Pub: Hawaii Business Publishing
Description: Senator Gary L. Kooser of District 7 Kauai-Niihau believes that the mandating of energy-efficient water heaters for new single-family homes starting in 2010 will help cut Hawaii's oil consumption. Ron Richmond of the Hawaii Solar Energy Association says that the content of SB 644 has negative consequences as it allows for choice of energy and not just solar, and it also eliminates tax credits for new homebuyers.

30846 ■ *"Waste Not" in Entrepreneur (Vol. 36, April 2008, No. 4, pp. 21)*
Pub: Entrepreneur Media, Inc.
Ed: JJ Ramberg. **Description:** RecycleBank is a company that provides homes with carts in which recyclables are thrown. An identification chip measures the amount of recyclables and converts them into points, which can be redeemed in stores, such as Starbucks and Whole Foods. RecycleBank earns revenue from cities that save landfill waste spending with the use of the program.

30847 ■ *"Water Conservation Helps GC's Building Attain LEED Gold Status" in Contractor (Vol. 56, September 2009, No. 9, pp. 5)*
Pub: Penton Media, Inc.
Description: Green contractor Marshall Erdman has built a new office building using green design. The facility is seen to become a prime Leadership in Energy and Environmental Design (LEED) building model. Details of the building's design and features are also provided.

30848 ■ *"Water Distiller" in Canadian Business (Vol. 81, September 29, 2008, No. 16, pp. 52)*
Pub: Rogers Media Ltd.
Ed: Matthew McClearn. **Description:** Les Fairn's invention of a water distiller called a Solarsphere was recognized in the Great Canadian Invention Competition. Fairn's invention resembles a buoy that uses the sun's energy to vaporize dirty water then leaves the impurities behind in a sump. The invention has an application for producing potable water in impoverished countries.

30849 ■ *"Water Efficiency Bill Move Through Congress" in Contractor (Vol. 56, July 2009, No. 7, pp. 20)*
Pub: Penton Media, Inc.
Ed: Kevin Schwalb. **Description:** National Association, a plumbing-heating-cooling contractor, was instrumental in drafting the Water Advanced Technologies for Efficient Resource Use Act of 2009 and they are also backing the Water Accountability Tax Efficiency Reinvestment Act. The first bill promotes WaterSense-labeled products while the other promotes water conservation through tax credits.

30850 ■ *"Watershed Solution" in Business Courier (Vol. 24, December 14, 2008, No. 35, pp. 1)*
Pub: American City Business Journals, Inc.
Ed: Dan Monk. **Description:** Discusses the Metropolitan Sewer District of Greater Cincinnati which is planning to spend around $128 million for its 20-year green-infrastructure improvement projects. Part of the project involves construction of green roofs, rain gardens and restored wetlands to manage water overflows.

30851 ■ *"Western Wind Energy Corporation" in CNW Group (October 4, 2011)*
Pub: CNW Group
Contact: Carolyn McGill-Davidson, President
Description: Profile of Western Wind Energy Corporation will complete the installation of 60 wind turbines by the end of 2011. The first 106MW are ready for pre-commissioning with the ability to sell power in November when the site is interconnected.

30852 ■ *"What Are Canada's Industrial Polluters Doing to Reduce Emissions?" in Canadian Business (Vol. , pp.)*
Pub: Rogers Media Ltd.
Ed: Matthew McClearn. **Description:** Efforts by Canada's industrial polluters to reduce emissions are examined. Syncrude Canada plans to reduce sulphur emissions by 60 percent in 2011, while TransAlta invests in emission reduction programs. Environmental groups, however, claim that companies are not doing enough to protect the environment.

30853 ■ *"What Is a Geothermal Heat Pump" in Indoor Comfort Marketing (Vol. 70, August 2011, No. 8, pp. 14)*
Pub: Industry Publications Inc.
Ed: George Carey. **Description:** Examination of geothermal heat pumps is provided, citing new trends in the industry.

30854 ■ *"What's In That Diaper?" in Inc. (November 2007, pp. 126)*
Pub: Gruner & Jahr USA Publishing
Ed: Nitasha Tiku. **Description:** Profile of Jason and Kimberly Graham-Nye, inventors of the gDiaper, consisting of a washable cotton elastine outer pant and an insert made of fluffed wood pulp and viscose rayon, both harvested from trees certified by the Sustainable Forestry Initiative.

30855 ■ *"Where the Future is Made" in Indoor Comfort Marketing (Vol. 70, May 2011, No. 5, pp. 48)*
Pub: Industry Publications Inc.
Description: Research being performed at Brookhaven National Laboratory, located in Upton, New York, is discussed, focusing on new energy sources for our nation.

30856 ■ *"Where Rubber Meets Road" in Canadian Business (Vol. 80, March 12, 2007, No. 6, pp. 15)*
Pub: Rogers Media
Ed: Michelle Magnan. **Description:** The partnership between Engineered Drilling Solutions Inc. and EnCana Corp. to build road from rubber wastes and follow environment-friendly methods in work is discussed.

30857 ■ *"A Whiff of TV Reality" in Houston Business Journal (Vol. 40, January 22, 2010, No. 37, pp. A1)*
Pub: American City Business Journals
Ed: Christine Hall. **Description:** Houston, Texas-based Waste Management Inc.'s president and chief operation officer, Larry O'Donnell shares some of his experience as CBS Television Network reality show 'Undercover Boss' participant. O'Donnell believes the show was a great way to show the customers how tough their jobs are and reveals that the most difficult job was being a sorter at the recycling center.

30858 ■ *"The Whole Package" in Entrepreneur (Vol. 36, February 2008, No. 2, pp. 24)*
Pub: Entrepreneur Media Inc.
Description: Holy Bohn, owner of The Honest Statute, developed an environmentally-friendly packaging for her pet food products. The company hired a packaging consultant and spent $175,000. Big corporations also spend money and plunge into the latest trends in packaging ranging from lighter and flexible to temperature-sensitive labels.

30859 ■ *"Why the Ethanol King Loves Driving his SUV" in Globe & Mail (January 29, 2007, pp. B17)*
Pub: CTVglobemedia Publishing Inc.
Ed: Gordon Pitts. **Description:** Ken Field, chairman of Canada's leading ethanol manufacturer Green-Field Ethanol, talks about the cars he drives, the commercial use of cellulose, ethanol's performance as an alternative to gasoline and about the plans of his firm to go public.

30860 ■ *"Will Home Buyers Pay for Green Features?" in Contractor (Vol. 56, October 2009, No. 10, pp. 70)*
Pub: Penton Media, Inc.
Ed: Bob Mader. **Description:** National Association of Home Builders commissioned a survey which shows that homeowners are interested in green as long as they do no have to pay much for it. The association did not allow a board member to read the survey which raises questions about how the questions were phrased and how the sample was selected.

30861 ■ *"Wind Gets Knocked Out of Energy Farm Plan" in Buffalo News (September 28, 2011)*
Pub: Buffalo News
Ed: David Robinson. **Description:** New York Power Authority formally killed the proposal for a wind energy farm off the shores of Lake Erie and Lake Ontario. The Authority cited high subsidy costs would be required to make the wind farm economically feasible. Details of the proposal are outlined.

30862 ■ *"Winning Gold" in The Business Journal-Milwaukee (Vol. 25, August 8, 2008, No. 46, pp. A1)*
Pub: American City Business Journals, Inc.
Ed: Rich Rovito. **Description:** Johnson Controls Inc. of Milwaukee, Wisconsin is taking part in the 2008 Beijing Olympics with the installation of its sustainable control equipment and technology that monitor over 58,000 points in 18 Olympic venues. Details of Johnson Controls' green products and sustainable operations in China are discussed.

30863 ■ *"WQA's Leadership Conference Tackles Industry Issues" in Contractor (Vol. 56, October 2009, No. 10, pp. 3)*
Pub: Penton Media, Inc.
Ed: Candace Roulo. **Description:** Water Quality Association's Mid-Year Leadership Conference held in Bloomingdale, Illinois in September 2009 tackled lead regulation, water softeners, and product efficiency. The possibility of a WQA green seal was discussed by the Water Sciences Committee and the Government Relations Committee meeting.

30864 ■ *"Xerox Diverts Waste from Landfills" in Canadian Electronics (Vol. 23, February 2008, No. 1, pp. 1)*
Pub: CLB Media Inc.
Description: Xerox Corporation revealed that it was able to divert more than two billion pounds of electronic waste from landfills through waste-free initiatives. The company's program, which was launched in 1991, covers waste avoidance in imaging supplies and parts reuse. Environmental priorities are also integrated into manufacturing operations.

30865 ■ *"Yates Helps Turn Log Home Green" in Contractor (Vol. 56, December 2009, No. 12, pp. 40)*
Pub: Penton Media, Inc.
Description: Upgrading and greening of a log home's HVAC system in Pennsylvania is discussed. F. W. Behler Inc. president Dave Yates was chosen to manage the project. A large coil of R-flex was used to connect the buffer tank to the garage's radiant heat system.

30866 ■ *"Yates Helps Turn Log Home Green" in Contractor (Vol. 56, November 2009, No. 11, pp. 1)*
Pub: Penton Media, Inc.
Description: Dave Yates of F.W. Behler Inc. helped homeowners from James Creek, Pennsylvania achieve energy efficiency on the heating system of their log cabin. The mechanical system installed on the cabin had high-temp 'THW' water-to-water geothermal system by ClimateMaster, two twin-coil indirect water heaters, and several pre-assembled, pre-engineered Hydronex panels by Watts Radiant.

30867 ■ *"Yates Turns Log Home Green - Part Three" in Contractor (Vol. 57, January 2010, No. 1, pp. 5)*
Pub: Penton Media, Inc.
Description: Dave Yates of F.W. Behler Inc. discusses remodeling a log home's HVAC system with geo-to-radiant heat and thermal-solar systems. The solar heater's installation is discussed.

30868 ■ *"You're a What? Wind Turbine Service Technician" in Occupational Outlook Quarterly (Vol. 54, Fall 2010, No. 3, pp. 34)*
Pub: U.S. Bureau of Labor Statistics
Ed: Drew Liming. **Description:** Profile of Brandon Johnson, former member of the Air Force, found a career as a wind turbine service technician.

30869 ■ *"Yudelson Challenges San Antonio Groups" in Contractor (Vol. 56, October 2009, No. 10, pp. 6)*
Pub: Penton Media, Inc.
Description: Green building consultant and author Jerry Yudelson made a presentation for the Central Texas Green Building Council and Leadership San Antonio where he discussed the European approach to sustainability and how it can be used for designing green buildings. Yudelson also discussed how to use sustainable practices for planning 25 years into the future.

TRADE PERIODICALS

30870 ■ *Composting News*
Pub: McEntee Media Corp.
Ed: Ken McEntee, Editor, ken@recycle.cc. **Released:** Monthly. **Price:** $83, individuals; $93, Canada and Mexico; $105, other countries. **Description:** Covers news and trends in the composting industry. Also reports on compost product prices. Recurring features include letters to the editor, interviews, news of research, a calendar of events, reports of meetings, and notices of publications available.

30871 ■ *The Davlin Report*
Pub: The Davlin Report Inc.
Ed: Andrew Davlin, Jr., Editor, aquaandy@aol.com. **Released:** Periodic. **Price:** $39.95, U.S. 4 issues; $59.95, U.S. 8 issues. **Description:** Reports on the aquaculture industry & companies, oil & gas companies & attractive common stocks.

30872 ■ *The Green Business Letter*
Pub: Tilden Press Inc.
Ed: Joel Makower, Editor. **Released:** Monthly. **Price:** $95 electronic edition; $45 for students and academics. **Description:** Helps companies integrate environmental considerations into their operations in a way that creates business value and environmental improvement. Recurring features include interviews, news of research, reports of meetings, book reviews, and notices of publications available.

30873 ■ *The GreenMoney Journal & Online Guide*
Pub: The Greenmoney Journal
Contact: Cliff Feigenbaum, Editor
E-mail: cliff@greenmoney.com
Released: Bimonthly. **Price:** $50, individuals; $50, Canada plus $10 postage; $50, elsewhere plus $20. **Description:** Encourages and promotes the awareness of socially and environmentally responsible business, investing and consumer resources in publications and online. Our goal is to educate and empower individuals and businesses to make informed financial decisions through aligning their personal, corporate and financial principles. Recurring features include a calendar.

30874 ■ *Inside Cal/EPA*
Pub: Inside Washington Publishers
Contact: Korila Malecha, Manager
Released: Weekly (Fri.). **Price:** $585, U.S. and Canada; $635, elsewhere. **Description:** Reports on environmental legislation, regulation, and litigation.

30875 ■ *Water Policy Report*
Pub: Inside Washington Publishers
Contact: Korila Malecha, Manager
Released: Biweekly, every other Monday. **Price:** $650, U.S. and Canada; $700, elsewhere. **Description:** Reports on federal water quality programs and policies. Covers topics such as drinking water, toxics, enforcement, monitoring, and state/EPA relations.

30876 ■ *Wind Energy Weekly*
Pub: American Wind Energy Association
Ed: Thomas O. Gray, Editor, tom_gray@igc.org. **Released:** Weekly. **Price:** Included in membership; $595, nonmembers. **Description:** Provides wind energy trade news, plus covers energy and environmental policy. Recurring features include news of research, reports of meetings, job listings, and notices of publications available. Remarks: Available only via E-mail account.

VIDEOCASSETTES/ AUDIOCASSETTES

30877 ■ *Cleaning Up Toxics*
The Video Project
PO Box 411376
San Francisco, CA 94141-1376
Free: 800-4-PLANET
Fax: (888)562-9012
Co. E-mail: support@videoproject.com
URL: http://www.videoproject.com
Released: 1990. **Price:** $59.95. **Description:** A series containing practical suggestions on reducing the amount of hazardous substances introduced into the environment from homes and businesses. **Availability:** VHS; 3/4 U; Special order formats.

30878 ■ *Free Energy: The Race to Zero Point*
Lightworks Audio & Video
PO Box 661593
Los Angeles, CA 90066
Ph: (310)398-4949
Free: 800-795-8273

Fax: (310)397-4401
Co. E-mail: sales1@lightworksav.com
URL: http://www.lightworksav.com

Released: 1998. **Price:** $29.95. **Description:** Documentary takes a look at the quest to find safe non-polluting energy sources that are available to everyone. Features segments on Nikola Tesla's method of "broadcasting" free energy, electric cars, zero-point "space" energy and cold fusion. **Availability:** DVD.

30879 ■ *Greenbucks: The Challenge of Sustainable Development*
The Video Project
PO Box 411376
San Francisco, CA 94141-1376
Free: 800-4-PLANET
Fax: (888)562-9012
Co. E-mail: support@videoproject.com
URL: http://www.videoproject.com

Released: 1992. **Price:** $195.00. **Description:** Major corporations change their attitudes and look for environmental solutions. Designed to inspire other businesses to higher ecological awareness. **Availability:** VHS.

30880 ■ *Grime Goes Green: Your Business & the Environment*
Video Arts, Inc.
c/o Aim Learning Group
8238-40 Lehigh
Morton Grove, IL 60053-2615
Free: 877-444-2230
Fax: (416)252-2155
Co. E-mail: service@aimlearninggroup.com
URL: http://www.aimlearninggroup.com

Released: 1991. **Price:** $435.00. **Description:** How to implement effective organizational enviromental policies. Shows how to avoid waste, use resources more efficiently, and institute re-cycling systems. **Availability:** VHS; 8 mm; 3/4 U; Special order formats.

30881 ■ *The Impact of Environmental Regulations on Business Transactions*
Practising Law Institute (PLI)
810 7th Ave., 21st Fl.
New York, NY 10019-5818
Ph: (212)824-5700
Free: 800-260-4754
Co. E-mail: info@pli.edu
URL: http://www.pli.edu
Contact: Victor J. Rubino, President
E-mail: vrubino@pli.edu

Released: 1988. **Price:** $245.00. **Description:** A look at how environmental standards affect business dealings. **Availability:** VHS.

30882 ■ *Nuclear Power: The Hot Debate*
Filmakers Library, Inc.
124 E. 40th St.
New York, NY 10016
Ph: (212)808-4980
Free: 800-555-9815
Fax: (212)808-4983
URL: http://www.filmakers.com

Released: 19??. **Price:** $395. **Description:** Looks at the pros and cons of nuclear power and at possible energy alternatives. **Availability:** VHS.

CONSULTANTS

30883 ■ GE Energy
888 N Industrial Dr.
Elmhurst, IL 60126-1121
Ph: (630)530-6656
Free: 866-758-9042
Fax: (630)530-6630
Co. E-mail: daniel.grabowski@ge.com
URL: http://www.gepower.com
Contact: John Krenicki, Jr., President
Scope: Provides environmental compliance, permitting and site assessment services including compliance management systems, environmental outsourcing, remediation design and management, asbestos project management, wetlands investigations, risk management planning, OSHA Compliance, and indoor air quality. **Founded:** 1976. **Publications:** "Energy consulting".

30884 ■ Occusafe Inc.
608 S Washington St., Ste. 9
Naperville, IL 60540
Ph: (630)851-3255
Free: 800-323-7597
Fax: (630)851-9339
Co. E-mail: info@occusafe-inc.com
Contact: Robert K. McKinley, President
E-mail: rkm@occusafe-inc.com
Scope: Assist clients in resolving employee safety, health or environmental problems or concerns by providing practical and economical solutions. **Founded:** 1972.

30885 ■ Prindle Hinds Environmental Inc.
7208 Jefferson St. NE
Albuquerque, NM 87109
Ph: (505)345-8732
Fax: (505)345-0393
Contact: William V. Hinds, Vice President
Scope: Provides environmental engineering/consulting services needed by clients to prevent/solve regulatory compliance problems and/or reduce their potential liabilities. Services include: geology, hydrology, and engineering; hazardous waste management; non-hazardous waste management; permit preparation/delisting; site/risk assessments; and site characterization/remedial action planning and training. Additional specialized expertise includes underground storage tanks, regulatory negotiations and expert witness testimony. **Founded:** 1981. **Seminars:** Firm has presented over a hundred specialized seminars/workshops, most pertaining to hazardous waste management.

30886 ■ SENES Consultants Ltd.
121 Granton Dr., Ste. 12
Richmond Hill, ON, Canada L4B 3N4
Ph: (905)764-9380
Fax: (905)764-9386
Co. E-mail: info@senes.ca
URL: http://www.senes.ca
Contact: Donald Gorber, President
Scope: Provider of environmental and solid waste management solutions. It offers site investigations, air quality assessment, preparation of solid waste management master plans, and data management services. **Founded:** 1980. **Seminars:** Risk assessments; Environmental audits and other environmental matters.

30887 ■ Smyth Fivenson Co.
8513 Irvington Ave.
Bethesda, MD 20817-3815
Ph: (301)493-6600
Fax: (301)530-7557
URL: http://www.smythfivenson.com
Contact: A. Jack Smyth, President
E-mail: jsmyth@smythfivenson.com
Scope: A Human Resources consulting firm providing services to two business areas, both nationally. First, provides temporary human resource professionals to all industries. Second, Smyth Fivenson Co. performs recruiting and placement services for the environmental industry. **Founded:** 1982.

30888 ■ Versar Inc.—Versar
6850 Versar Ctr.
Springfield, VA 22151-4175
Ph: (703)750-3000
Free: 800-283-7727
Fax: (703)642-6807
Co. E-mail: info@versar.com
URL: http://www.versar.com
Contact: Jeffrey A. Wagonhurst, President
Scope: Consultants offering environmental services; complete regulatory assistance to industry; applied research services to industry and government, emergency planning services; nuclear power plant emergency plan development; engineering services; atmospheric and meteorological modeling; and recent experience in evaluation of off site consequences of chemical accidents. Serves private industries as well as government agencies. **Founded:** 1969.

LIBRARIES

30889 ■ Environmental Bankers Association Library
510 King St., Ste. 410
Alexandria, VA 22314
Ph: (703)549-0977
Fax: (703)548-5945
Co. E-mail: nsingh@envirobank.org
URL: http://www.envirobank.org
Contact: Rick Ferguson, President
Scope: Environmental lender liability, insurance, EPA and FDIC regulations, environment risk management, sustaibale development, green baking. **Services:** Library not open to the public. **Founded:** 1994. **Holdings:** 50 books, periodicals, and clippings. **Subscriptions:** 125 journals and other serials. **Telecommunication Services:** eba@envirobank.org.

RESEARCH CENTERS

30890 ■ Colorado State University - Industrial Assessment Center (IAC)
Department of Mechanical Engineering
Fort Collins, CO 80523-1374
Ph: (970)491-8617
Fax: (970)491-3827
Co. E-mail: hittle@engr.colostate.edu
URL: http://www.engr.colostate.edu/IAC/
Contact: Prof. Douglas C. Hittle, Director
Services: Pollution prevention, energy conservation & productivity improvement: to industry. **Founded:** 1984.

30891 ■ Tarleton State University - Texas Institute for Applied Environmental Research (TIAER)
Box T-0410
Stephenville, TX 76402
Ph: (254)968-9569
Fax: (254)968-9336
Co. E-mail: dhunter@tiaer.tarleton.edu
URL: http://tiaer.tarleton.edu
Contact: Dan Hunter, Executive Director

30892 ■ University of California, Davis - Information Center for the Environment (ICE)
1 Shields Ave.
Davis, CA 95616
Ph: (530)752-8027
Fax: (530)752-8027
Co. E-mail: jfquinn@ucdavis.edu
URL: http://ice.ucdavis.edu
Contact: Prof. James F. Quinn, Director
Founded: 1991.

30893 ■ University of Florida - Powell Center for Construction and Environment
342 Rinker Hall
Gainesville, FL 32611-5703
Ph: (352)273-1172
Fax: (352)273-9606
Co. E-mail: ckibert@ufl.edu
URL: http://www.cce.ufl.edu
Contact: Dr. Charles J. Kibert, Director
Founded: 1991. **Publications:** *Powell Center for Construction and Environment Conference proceedings*; *Powell Center for Construction and Environment Research reports*. **Educational Activities:** Powell Center for Construction and Environment Conferences; Continuing education courses; Powell Center for Construction and Environment Workshops. **Awards:** Research/Teaching assistantships, for graduate students. **Telecommunication Services:** dlisaacs@ufl.edu.

ASSOCIATIONS AND OTHER ORGANIZATIONS

30894 ■ *Communique*
240 rue Catherine St., Ste. 208
Ottawa, ON, Canada K2P 2G8
Ph: (613)233-5445
Fax: (613)233-0658
Co. E-mail: office@ncehr-cnerh.org
URL: http://www.ncehr-cnerh.org
Contact: Deborah Poff, President
Released: Annual **Price:** free.

30895 ■ Council for Ethical Leadership (CEE)
1 College and Main
Columbus, OH 43209
Ph: (614)236-7222
Fax: (614)221-8707
URL: http://www.businessethics.org
Contact: James D. Abrams, Chairman of the Board
Description: Leaders in business, education, and the professions. Seeks to "strengthen the ethical fabric of business and economic life". Facilitates the development of international networks of business-people interested in economic ethics; sponsors educational programs and develops and distributes educational materials; advises and supports communities wishing to implement character educational programs; makes available consulting services. **Founded:** 1982. **Publications:** *Ethical Leadership* (3/year).

30896 ■ National Council on Ethics in Human Research (NCEHR)—Le Conseil national d'ethique en recherche chez l'humain - Conseil national d'Ethique en recherche chez l'Humain
240 rue Catherine St., Ste. 208
Ottawa, ON, Canada K2P 2G8
Ph: (613)233-5445
Fax: (613)233-0658
Co. E-mail: office@ncehr-cnerh.org
URL: http://www.ncehr-cnerh.org
Contact: Deborah Poff, President
Description: Encourages high ethical standards research involving human subjects. Consults with universities, government agencies and businesses engaged in human research; recommends standards for research projects using human subjects. Conducts educational programs. **Founded:** 1989. **Subscriptions:** books periodicals. **Publications:** *Communique* (Annual).

30897 ■ Society for Business Ethics (SBE)
c/o Jeff Frooman, Exec. Dir.
University of New Brunswick
PO Box 4400
Fredericton, NB, Canada E3B 5A3
Co. E-mail: frooman@unb.ca
URL: http://www.societyforbusinessethics.org
Contact: Jeff Frooman, Executive Director
Description: Philosophy and theology professors, business school professors, and business executives. Facilitates information exchange regarding research and activities in business ethics. **Founded:** 1980. **Publications:** *Society For Business Ethics Newsletter* (Quarterly). **Educational Activities:** Society for Business Ethics Annual Conference (Annual).

REFERENCE WORKS

30898 ■ *"The Accountability Lens: A New Way to View Management Issues" in Business Horizons (September-October 2007, pp. 405)*
Pub: Elsevier Technology Publications
Ed: Angela T. Hall, Michael G. Bowen, Gerald R. Ferris, M. Todd Royle, Dale E. Fitzgibbons. **Description:** Organizations are viewed through an accountability lens in terms of source, focus, salience, and intensity to explain issues on corporate governance and ethics. Accountability environment, the individual's immediate work environment that directly affects the subjective experience of felt accountability, and its four main aspects are discussed.

30899 ■ *"Accountants Get the Hook" in Canadian Business (Vol. 80, October 22, 2007, No. 21, pp. 19)*
Pub: Rogers Media
Ed: John Gray. **Description:** Chartered Accountants of Ontario handed down the decision on Douglas Barrington, Anthony Power and Claudio Russo's professional misconduct case. The three accountants of Deloitte & Touche LLP must pay C$100,000 in fines and C$417,000 in costs. Details of the disciplinary case are presented.

30900 ■ *"Battling Back from Betrayal" in Harvard Business Review (Vol. 88, December 2010, No. 12, pp. 130)*
Pub: Harvard Business School Publishing
Ed: Daniel McGinn. **Description:** Stephen Greer's scrap metal firm, Hartwell Pacific, lost several million dollars due to a lack of efficient and appropriate inventory audits, accounting procedures, and new-hire reference checks for his foreign operations. Greer believes that balancing growth with control is a key component of success.

30901 ■ *"Biovail Hits SAC With $4.6 Billion Suit" in Globe & Mail (February 23, 2006, pp. B1)*
Pub: CTVglobemedia Publishing Inc.
Ed: Shawn McCarthy. **Description:** The details of Biovail Corp.'s securities fraud case against SAC Management LLC are presented.

30902 ■ *"Blood Diamonds are Forever" in Canadian Business (Vol. 83, August 17, 2010, No. 13-14, pp. 59)*
Pub: Rogers Media Ltd.
Ed: Matthew McClearn. **Description:** The failed case against Donald McKay who was found in possession of rough diamonds in a raid by Royal Canadian Mounted Police has raised doubts about Kimberley Process (KP) attempts to stop the illicit global trade in diamonds. KP has managed to reduce total global trade of blood diamonds by 1 percent in mid-2000.

30903 ■ *The Board Book: An Insider's Guide for Directors and Trustees*
Pub: W.W. Norton & Company
Ed: William G. Bowen. **Released:** 2009. **Price:** $26.95. **Description:** A primer for all directors and trustees that provides suggestions for getting back to good-governance basics in business.

30904 ■ *"Bridging the Gap: Contextualing Professional Ethics in Collaborative Writing Projects" in Business Communication Quarterly (Dec.2007)*
Pub: SAGE Publications USA
Contact: Blaise R. Simqu, President
Ed: J.A. Rice. **Description:** A classroom activity for business management students integrates ethical concepts with business writing strategies, while increasing understanding of writing ethics by emphasizing its rhetorical, contingent, and public nature.

30905 ■ *"Business Ethics, Strategic Decision Making, and Firm Performance" in Business Horizons (September-October 2007, pp. 353)*
Pub: Elsevier Technology Publications
Ed: Michael A. Hitt, Jaime D. Collins. **Description:** Strategic management and decision-making process are linked to business ethics. The Strengths, Weakness, Opportunities, and Threats (SWOT) analysis model is employed to design an effective strategy for companies.

30906 ■ *Business Fairy Tales*
Pub: Thomson South-Western
Ed: Cecil W. Jackson. **Released:** July 2006. **Price:** $39.95. **Description:** The seven most-common business schemes are uncovered.

30907 ■ *"Business Through Hollywood's Lens" in Harvard Business Review (Vol. 88, October 2010, No. 10, pp. 146)*
Pub: Harvard Business School Publishing
Ed: Batia Wiesnefeld, Gino Cattani. **Description:** The authors contend that businesses are likely to be portrayed as villains in movies because corruption has higher entertainment draw. However, movies also depict popular opinion, which encourages businesses to be accountable and to help build communities.

30908 ■ *"The Case for Treating the Sex Trade as an Industry" in Canadian Business (Vol. 83, October 12, 2010, No. 17, pp. 9)*
Pub: Rogers Media Ltd.
Ed: Steve Maich. **Description:** It is believed that the worst aspects of prostitution in Canada are exacerbated by the fact that it must take place in secret. The laws that deal with the market for sex have led to an unsafe working environment. Prostitutes believe their industry needs to be sanctioned and regulated rather than ignored and reviled.

30909 ■ *"Chesley Fighting Ky. Disbarment" in Business Courier (Vol. 27, September 10, 2010, No. 19, pp. 1)*
Pub: Business Courier
Ed: Jon Newberry. **Description:** Stan Chesley, a Cincinnati attorney, has been accused of making false statements to the courts and bar officials, self-

dealing in violation of the bar's conflict of interest rules, and failing to adequately inform clients. Kentucky Bar Association officials will seek to have Chesley permanently disbarred.

30910 ■ *"Chino Valley Ranches: a Family of Farmers" in Retail Merchandiser (Vol. 51, September-October 2011, No. 5, pp. 79)*
Pub: Phoenix Media Corporation
Ed: Angela Forsyth. **Description:** Charles B. Nichols and his wife Isabella purchased their ranch in Beaumont, California in the early 1950s. The family has been raising their chickens, producing eggs with quality, integrity and honesty the foundation of their business.

30911 ■ *"Citi Ruling Could Chill SEC, Street Legal Pacts" in Wall Street Journal Eastern Edition (November 29, 2011, pp. C1)*
Pub: Dow Jones & Company Inc. Enterprise Media Group
Contact: Clare Hart, President
Ed: Jean Eaglesham, Chad Bray. **Description:** A $285 million settlement was reached between the Securities and Exchange Commission and Citigroup Inc. over allegations the bank misled investors over a mortgage-bond deal. Now, Judge Jed S. Rakoff has ruled against the settlement, a decision that will affect the future of such attempts to prosecute Wall Street fraud. Rakoff said that the settlement was 'neither fair, nor reasonable, nor adequate, nor in the public interest.'.

30912 ■ *"The Classless Workplace: The Digerati and the New Spirit of Technocapitalism" in WorkingUSA (Vol. 11, June 2008, No. 2, pp. 181)*
Pub: Blackwell Publishers Ltd.
Ed: Eran Fisher. **Description:** Article argues the formation of a new type of economic actor at the intersection of a new capitalism and a new technology: The Dierati. The discourse in based on the analysis of the popular magazine Wired, which registers the culture of contemporary technocapitalism. The suggestion that the new persona of the digerati is constructed as a rejection of the ethics, which dominated the Fordist workplace and Fordist society: Hierarchy and differentiation between workers, on the one hand and capitalists and managers, on the other hand. The transformation of these two categories, workers and capitalists into the digerati worker and the digerati entrepreneur, is described. Set within the context of the structural transformations of capitalism from Fordism to post-Fordism, the article shows the ideological fit of the new ethics of the digerati to the new working arrangements of post-Fordist capitalism, characterized by more privatizes, flexible, and precarious working arrangements.

30913 ■ *"Corporate Responsibility" in Professional Services Close-Up (July 2, 2010)*
Pub: Close-Up Media
Description: List of firms awarded the inaugural Best Corporate Citizens in Government Contracting by the Corporate Responsibility Magazine is presented. The list is based on the methodology of the Magazine's Best Corporate Citizen's List, with 324 data points of publicly-available information in seven categories which include: environment, climate change, human rights, philanthropy, employee relations, financial performance, and governance.

30914 ■ *"CR Magazine Taps ITT As a 'Best Corporate Citizen' in Government Contracting" in Profesisonal Services Close-Up (July 30, 2010)*
Pub: Close-Up Media
Description: ITT Corporation was named by Corporate Responsibility Magazine as a Best Corporate Citizen in Government Contracting. The list recognizes publicly-traded companies that exemplify transparency and accountability while serving the U.S. government.

30915 ■ *"Crime and Punishment" in Canadian Business (Vol. 81, December 24, 2007, No. 1, pp. 21)*
Pub: Rogers Media
Ed: Joe Castaldo. **Description:** Cmpass Inc.'s survey of 137 Canadian chief executive officers showed that they want tougher imposition of sentences on white-collar criminals, as they believe that the weak enforcement of securities laws gives an impression that Canada is a country where it is easy to get away with fraud.

30916 ■ *"Critics Target Bribery Law" in Wall Street Journal Eastern Edition (November 28, 2011, pp. B1)*
Pub: Dow Jones & Company Inc. Enterprise Media Group
Contact: Clare Hart, President
Ed: Joe Palazzuolo. **Description:** Concern about how the Foreign Corrupt Practices Act, the United States' anti-bribery law, is enforced has drawn the focus of corporate lobbyists. Corporations have paid some $4 billion in penalties in cases involving the law, which prohibits companies from paying foreign officials bribes. The US Chamber of Commerce believes amending the act should be a priority.

30917 ■ *Data Driven Investing: Professional Edition*
Pub: Data Driven Publishing, LLC
Ed: Mitchell R. Hardy; Bill Matson. **Released:** 2004. **Description:** Investment concepts and trading techniques are explored in a simple and practical way. The book covers the unreliability of financial markets due to malpractices, appalling analysis, insider training and more. Information is based on data and common sense and easy to use for beginner as well as professional.

30918 ■ *"Dating Games" in Canadian Business (Vol. 79, September 25, 2006, No. 19, pp. 23)*
Pub: Rogers Media
Ed: John Gray. **Description:** Increasing stock option scandals in Canada and American companies is discussed.

30919 ■ *"Diary of a Short-Seller" in Conde Nast Portfolio (Vol. 2, June 2008, No. 6, pp. 44)*
Pub: Conde Nast Publications
Contact: David Carey, President
Ed: Jesse Eisinger. **Description:** Profile of David Einhorn who is a fund manager that spoke out against finance company Allied Capital whose stock fell nearly 20 percent the day after Einhorn's critique; Einhorn subsequently had to contend with attacks against his credibility as well as investigations by the S.E.C.; Einhorn's experience illuminates our current economic crisis.

30920 ■ *"Do the Math" in Canadian Business (Vol. 79, October 9, 2006, No. 20, pp. 17)*
Pub: Rogers Media
Ed: Al Rosen. **Description:** Faulty practices followed by regulators in Canadian stock market are discussed. The need for authorities to protect investors against these frauds are emphasized.

30921 ■ *Doing Business Anywhere: The Essential Guide to Going Global*
Pub: John Wiley and Sons, Inc.
Ed: Tom Travis. **Released:** 2007. **Price:** $24.95. **Description:** Plans are given for new or existing businesses to organize, plan, operate and execute a business on a global basis. Trade agreements, brand protection and patents, ethics, security as well as cultural issues are among the issues addressed.

30922 ■ *"Don't Lie To Me: Dishonesty Can Ruin Professional and Personal Relationships" in Black Enterprise (Vol. 38, January 2008)*
Pub: Earl G. Graves Publishing Co. Inc.
Ed: Marcia A. Reed-Woodard. **Description:** Consequences of lying can be devastating in any business environment. When a person lies he loses integrity, credibility, confidence and self-esteem.

30923 ■ *"easyhome Ltd. Discovers Employee Fraud at an Easyfinancial Kiosk Company" in Internet Wire (October 14, 2010)*
Pub: Comtex
Description: Canada's leading merchandise leasing company and provider of financial services, easyhome Ltd., reported employee fraud totaling $3.4 million that was perpetrated against the firm's easyfinancial services business.

30924 ■ *The Economics of Integrity*
Pub: HarperStudio/HarperCollins
Ed: Anna Bernasek. **Released:** February 23, 2010. **Price:** $19.99. **Description:** Integrity is built over time and the importance of trust in starting and building business relationships is stressed.

30925 ■ *The Ethical Executive: Becoming Aware of the Root Causes of Unethical Behavior*
Pub: Stanford University Press
Ed: Robert Hoyk, Paul Hersey. **Released:** February 28, 2010. **Price:** $17.95. **Description:** Forty-five lessons to help avoid becoming a victim to day-to-day ethical traps are outlined using moral lapses at Enron, Tyco International, Adelphia, World Com and other businesses as examples.

30926 ■ *"Ethics Commission May Hire Collection Agency" in Tulsa World (August 21, 2010)*
Pub: World Publishing
Ed: Barbara Hoberock. **Description:** Oklahoma Ethics Commission is considering a more to hire a collection agency or law firm in order to collect fees from candidates owing money for filing late financial reports.

30927 ■ *"Ethics and the End of Life" in Crain's Chicago Business (Vol. 34, October 24, 2011, No. 42, pp. 31)*
Pub: Crain Communications Inc.
Ed: Lisa Bertagnoli. **Description:** Technology has enabled doctors to provide more and better methods for helping patients, however end of life issues faced by medical ethicists are discussed.

30928 ■ *"The Ethics of Price Discrimination" in Business Ethics Quarterly (Vol. 21, October 2011, No. 4, pp. 633)*
Pub: Society for Business Ethics
Ed: Juan M. Elegido. **Description:** Price discrimination is the practice of charging different customers different prices for the same product. Many people consider price discrimination unfair, but economists argue that in many cases price discrimination is more likely to lead to greater welfare than is the uniform pricing alternative, sometimes even for every party in the transaction.

30929 ■ *"The Evolution of Corporate Social Responsibility" in Business Horizons (November-December 2007, pp. 449)*
Pub: Elsevier Technology Publications
Ed: Philip L. Cochran. **Description:** Corporate social responsibility is now perceived as vital in enhancing the profitability of businesses while improving their reputation. It has changed business practices such as philanthropy, investment, and entrepreneurship.

30930 ■ *Extraordinary Circumstances: The Journey of a Corporate Whistleblower*
Pub: John Wiley & Sons, Inc.
Ed: Cynthia Cooper. **Released:** 2009. **Price:** $27.95. **Description:** Cynthia Cooper offers details of the events that led to the implosion of telecom giant WorldCom.

30931 ■ *"FBI Initiates Fraud Inquiry Into Mortgage Lenders" in Miami Daily Business Review (March 26, 2008)*
Pub: ALM Media Inc.
Description: FBI has launched investigations into Countrywide Financial, the nation's largest mortgage lender, along with sixteen other firms, tied to the subprime mortgage crisis.

30932 ■ *"Final Player In Big Mortgage Fraud Operation Gets Jail Time" in Boston Business Journal (Vol. 31, May 27, 2011, No. 18, pp. 3)*
Pub: Boston Business Journal
Ed: Galen Moore. **Description:** Real estate broker Ralp Appolon has been sentenced to 70 months in prison for wire fraud. Appolon was part of a group that falsified information about property purchase prices. A total of ten mortgage lenders have become victims of the group.

30933 ■ *"Finally, Justice" in Canadian Business (Vol. 82, April 27, 2009, No. 7, pp. 12)*
Pub: Rogers Media
Ed: John Gray. **Description:** Former investment adviser Alex Winch feels that he was vindicated with the Canadian Court's ruling that Livent Inc. founders Garth Drabinsky and Myron Gottlieb were guilty of fraud. Drabinsky filed a libel case on Winch over Winch's letter that complained over Livent's accounting procedures. Winch also criticized the inconsistent accounting during Drabinsky's term as chief executive of another firm.

30934 ■ *"Five-Ring Circus" in Entrepreneur (Vol. 35, November 2007, No. 11, pp. 76)*
Pub: Entrepreneur Media Inc.
Ed: Scott Bernard Nelson. **Description:** China's economy is growing and is expected to do well even after the 2008 Olympics, but growth could slow from eleven percent to eight or nine percent. Chinese portfolio concerns with regard to health and environmental records and bureaucratic fraud are discussed.

30935 ■ *"A Hacker in India Hijacked His Website Design and Was Making Good Money Selling It" in Inc. (December 2007, pp. 77-78, 80)*
Pub: Gruner & Jahr USA Publishing
Ed: Darren Dahl. **Description:** John Anton, owner of an online custom T-shirt business and how a company in India was selling software Website templates identical to his firm's Website.

30936 ■ *High Performance with High Integrity*
Pub: Harvard Business School Press
Ed: Ben W. Heineman Jr. **Released:** May 28, 2008. **Price:** $18.00. **Description:** The dark side of today's free-market capitalist system is examined. Under intense pressure to make the numbers, executives and employees are tempted to cut corners, falsify accounts, or worse. In today's unforgiving environment that can lead to catastrophe for a small company.

30937 ■ *"Home Builder, Four Others, Face Sentencing" in Business Courier (Vol. 27, November 26, 2010, No. 30, pp. 1)*
Pub: Business Courier
Ed: Jon Newberry. **Description:** Home builder Bernie Kurlemann was convicted on November 10, 2010 on six felony counts and faces up to 65 years in prison due to his part in a 2006 Warren County mortgage fraud scheme. Four other business people have pleaded guilty to related charges, and all are awaiting sentencing in early 2011.

30938 ■ *House of Cards: A Tale of Hubris and Wretched Excess on Wall Street*
Pub: Anchor Press
Ed: William D. Cohan. **Released:** February 9, 2010. **Price:** $16.95. **Description:** A historical account of the events leading up to the Bear Stearns implosion.

30939 ■ *How to Salvage More Millions from Your Small Business*
Pub: Mike French Publishing
Ed: Ron Sturgeon. **Released:** April 1, 2009. **Price:** $14.95. **Description:** Entrepreneurs in any industry will learn how strong work ethics and sound business principles will make any small business successful.

30940 ■ *How to Start a Home-Based Senior Care Business: Develop a Winning Business Plan*
Pub: Globe Pequot Press
Ed: James L. Ferry. **Released:** January 10, 2010. **Price:** $18.95. **Description:** Everything needed to know in order to start and run a profitable, ethical, and satisfying senior care business from your home. Information covers writing a good business plan, marketing services to families, creating a fee structure, and developing a network of trusted caregivers and service providers.

30941 ■ *"Identity Thieves Hit a New Low" in Information Today (Vol. 26, February 2009, No. 2, pp. 1)*
Pub: Information Today, Inc.
Ed: Phillip Britt. **Description:** Identity thieves are opening credit lines after reading obituaries. Actual identity theft cases are examined.

30942 ■ *"Institutional Logics in the Study of Organizations" in Business Ethics Quarterly (Vol. 21, July 2011, No. 3, pp. 409)*
Pub: Society for Business Ethics
Ed: Marc Orlitzky. **Description:** Examination into whether the empirical evidence on the relationship between corporate social performance (CSP) and corporate financial performance (CFP) differs depending on the publication outlet in which that evidence appears.

30943 ■ *"Internal Auditor Wants Ethics Review of City's Casper Golf Contract" in Business Courier (Vol. 27, September 10, 2010, No. 19, pp. 1)*
Pub: Business Courier
Ed: Dan Monk. **Description:** Mark Ashworth, an internal auditor for Cincinnati, Ohio is pushing for an ethics review of management contract for seven city-owned golf courses. Ashworth wants the Ohio Ethics Commission to investigate family ties between a superintendent for the Cincinnati Recreation Commission and Billy Casper Golf.

30944 ■ *"Investment Manager Disciplined" in Sacramento Business Journal (Vol. 25, July 4, 2008, No. 18, pp. 1)*
Pub: American City Business Journals, Inc.
Ed: Mark Anderson. **Description:** Community Capital Management's David A. Zwick is permanently barred by the Securities and Exchange Commission (SEC) from associating with any broker or dealer, after investigations revealed that he took part in paying kickbacks to a bond trader. Other views and information on Community Capital, and on the SEC investigation on Zwick, are presented.

30945 ■ *"Is Business Ethics Getting Better? A Historical Perspective" in Business Ethics Quarterly (Vol. 21, April 2011, No. 2, pp. 335)*
Pub: Society for Business Ethics
Ed: Joanne B. Ciulla. **Description:** The question 'Is Business Ethics Getting Better?' as a heuristic for discussing the importance of history in understanding business and ethics is answered. The article uses a number of examples to illustrate how the same ethical problems in business have been around for a long time. It describes early attempts at the Harvard School of Business to use business history as a means of teaching students about moral and social values. In the end, the author suggests that history may be another way to teach ethics, enrich business ethics courses, and develop the perspective and vision in future business leaders.

30946 ■ *"It's Time to Take Full Responsibility" in Harvard Business Review (Vol. 88, October 2010, No. 10, pp. 42)*
Pub: Harvard Business School Publishing
Ed: Rosabeth Moss Kanter. **Description:** A case for corporate responsibility is cited, focusing on long-term impact and the effects of public accountability.

30947 ■ *"It's Time to Wise Up: Income Trusts" in Canadian Business (Vol. 79, November 6, 2006, No. 22, pp. 24)*
Pub: Rogers Media
Ed: Mark Rosen. **Description:** The effects bogus financial reporting of income trusts on investors are analyzed.

30948 ■ *"Kraft Not Alone" in Crain's Chicago Business (Vol. 30, February 2007, No. 6, pp. 8)*
Pub: Crain Communications, Inc.
Description: Consumer watchdog group, The Center for Science in the Public Interest, has been putting pressure on food companies to be more truthful on their product labels. Listing of companies who have had misleading claims on their products is included.

30949 ■ *Liespotting: Proven Techniques to Detect Deception*
Pub: St. Martins Press/Macmillan
Ed: Pamela Meyer. **Released:** July 20, 2010. **Price:** $24.99. **Description:** Liespotting links three disciplines: facial recognition training, interrogation training, and a comprehensive survey of research in the field - into a specialized body of information developed specifically to help business leaders detect deception and get the information they need to successfully conduct their most important interactions and transactions.

30950 ■ *"Life's Work: Ben Bradlee" in Harvard Business Review (Vol. 88, September 2010, No. 9, pp. 128)*
Pub: Harvard Business School Publishing
Ed: Alison Beard. **Description:** Newspaper publisher Ben Bradlee discusses factors that lead to success, including visible supervisors, enthusiasm, appropriate expansion, and the importance in truth in reporting.

30951 ■ *"Making the Tough Call: Great Leaders Recognize When Their Values Are On the Line" in Inc. (November 2007, pp. 36, 38)*
Pub: Gruner & Jahr USA Publishing
Ed: Noel M. Tichy, Warren G. Bennis. **Description:** Good judgment by company leaders is a process involving preparation, making the call, and executing the process. Character provides a moral compass for these decision makers.

30952 ■ *MBA In a Day*
Pub: John Wiley and Sons, Inc.
Ed: Steven Stralser, PhD. **Released:** 2004. **Price:** $34.95. **Description:** Management professor presents important concepts, business topics and strategies that can be used by anyone to manage a small business or professional practice. Topics covered include: human resources and personal interaction, ethics and leadership skills, fair negotiation tactics, basic business accounting practices, project management, and the fundamentals of economics and marketing.

30953 ■ *"Millions of Senior Citizens Swindled by Financial Fraud" in Black Enterprise (Vol. 41, September 2010, No. 2, pp. 24)*
Pub: Earl G. Graves Publishing Co. Inc.
Description: One of every five citizens over the age of 65 have been victims of financial fraud. Statistical data included.

30954 ■ *"Missing MF Global Funds Could Top $1.2 Billion" in Wall Street Journal Eastern Edition (November 22 , 2011, pp. A1)*
Pub: Dow Jones & Company Inc.
Ed: Aaron Lucchetti, Dan Strumpf. **Description:** As the investigation into the collapse of securities brokerage MF Global Holdings Ltd. continues, the question of what happened to customers' funds has to be answered. Now, it is believed that the actual amount of missing funds is much more than the $600 million originally thought, and could be well over $1.2 billion.

30955 ■ *"Model Citizen" in Entrepreneur (Vol. 36, February 2008, No. 2, pp. 42)*
Pub: Entrepreneur Media Inc.
Ed: Guy Kawasaki. **Description:** A mensch is a person of noble character, as defined by Leo Rosten. Tips on how to be a mensch and a better person, in relation to being an entrepreneur, are given. These include: helping others without expecting something in return, giving back to society, and knowing the line between right and wrong.

30956 ■ *"The Moral Legitimacy of NGOs as Partners of Corporations" in Business Ethics Quarterly (Vol. 21, October 2011, No. 4, pp. 579)*
Pub: Society for Business Ethics
Contact: Jeff Frooman, Executive Director
Ed: Dorothea Baur, Guido Palazzo. **Description:** Partnerships between companies and NGOs have received considerable attention in CSR in the past years. However, the role of NGO legitimacy in such partnerships has thus far been neglected. The article argues that NGOs assume a status as special stakeholders of corporations which act on behalf of the common good. This role requires a particular focus on their moral legitimacy. An introduction to the conceptual framework analyzing the moral legitimacy of NGOs along three dimensions, building on the theory of deliberative democracy.

30957 ■ *"The Murky Tale of a Failed Fund" in Globe & Mail (January 3, 2006, pp. B1)*
Pub: CTVglobemedia Publishing Inc.
Ed: Bertrand Marotte. **Description:** The opinions of chief executive officer John Xanthoudakis of Norshield Financial Group, on controversy surrounding the company's handling of investors' money, are presented.

30958 ■ *"'No Snitch' Culture in American Business" in Business Owner (Vol. 35, September-October 2011, No. 5, pp. 7)*
Pub: DL Perkins Company
Description: It is important to make known the fact that a businessman is performing unethical or illegal activities in his firm.

30959 ■ *"Now That's Rich" in Canadian Business (Vol. 80, February 12, 2007, No. 4, pp. 92)*
Pub: Rogers Media
Ed: Thomas Watson. **Description:** The effort of chief executive officer of Stelco Inc. Rodney Mott in resolving the issue of financial loss of the company by taking up backdating options for share price is discussed.

30960 ■ *"One-Time Area Trust Executive Finds Trouble in N.H." in The Business Journal-Serving Metropolitan Kansas City (September 12, 2008)*
Pub: American City Business Journals, Inc.
Ed: Steve Vockrodt. **Description:** About 200 investors, some from Missouri's Kansas City area, claim that they had conducted business with Noble Trust Co. The trust company was placed under New Hampshire Banking Department's conservatorship after $15 million was discovered to be missing from its account. It is alleged that the money was lost in a Colorado Ponzi scheme.

30961 ■ *"Only in Canada, Eh?" in Canadian Business (Vol. 79, November 6, 2006, No. 22, pp. 17)*
Pub: Rogers Media
Ed: Al Rosen. **Description:** The ethics of corporate spying with relation to competitive information leakage are analyzed.

30962 ■ *"Organizational Virtue Orientation and Family Firms" in Business Ethics Quarterly (Vol. 21, April 2011, No. 2, pp. 257)*
Pub: Society for Business Ethics
Ed: G. Tyge Payne, Keith H. Brigham, J. Christian Broberg, Todd W. Moss, Jeremy C. Short. **Description:** The concept of organizational virtue orientation (OVO) and the differences between family and nonfamily firms on six organizational virtue dimensions of Integrity, Empathy, Warmth, Courage, Conscientiousness, and Zeal are examined.

30963 ■ *"Paging Dr. Phil" in Canadian Business (Vol. 79, September 25, 2006, No. 19, pp. 21)*
Pub: Rogers Media
Ed: John Gray. **Description:** Increasing corporate crimes in software industry is discussed by focusing on recent case of Hewlett and Packard.

30964 ■ *"People Often Trust Eloquence More Than Honesty" in Harvard Business Review (Vol. 88, November 2010, No. 11, pp. 36)*
Pub: Harvard Business School Publishing
Ed: Todd Rogers, Michael I. Norton. **Description:** The article shows how deftly side-stepping a question in an eloquent manner generates a more positive response in an audience than does a direct answer that is ineffectively delivered. Implications for both politics and business are discussed.

30965 ■ *"Pet Food Insider Sold Shares Before Recall" in Globe & Mail (April 10, 2007, pp. B1)*
Pub: CTVglobemedia Publishing Inc.
Ed: Keith McArthur. **Description:** The issue related the selling of share units by Mark Weins, chief financial officer of pet food firm Menu Foods Income Fund, just before the recall of contaminated pet food is discussed.

30966 ■ *The Power of Many: Values for Success in Business and in Life*
Pub: Crown Business
Ed: Meg Whitman, Joan O'C Hamilton. **Released:** January 26, 2010. **Price:** $26.00. **Description:** Meg Whitman discusses the important values for success in business and in life: integrity, accountability, authenticity and courage.

30967 ■ *Principled Profit: Marketing that Puts People First*
Pub: Accurate Writing & More
Ed: Shel Horowitz. **Price:** $17.50. **Description:** The importance for companies to market ethically and honestly is stressed. Quality marketing will build customer loyalty and that will translate into new customers and repeat business. A customer-retention strategy is outlined along with ideas to increase profits of any small business.

30968 ■ *"A Property Rights Analysis of Newly Private Firms" in Business Ethics Quarterly (Vol. 21, July 2011, No. 3, pp. 445)*
Pub: Society for Business Ethics
Ed: Marguerite Schneider, Alix Valenti. **Description:** A key factor in the decision to convert a publicly owned company to private status is the expectation that value will be create, providing the firm with rent. These rents have implications regarding the property rights of the firm's capital-contributing constituencies. The article identifies and analyzes the types of rent associated with the newly private firm. Compared to public firms, going private allows owners the potential to partition part of the residual risk to bond holders and employees, rendering them to be co-residual risk bearers with owners.

30969 ■ *"Q&A: David Labistour" in Canadian Business (Vol. 81, March 17, 2008, No. 4, pp. 10)*
Pub: Rogers Media
Ed: Lauren McKeon. **Description:** David Labistour says that the difference between being a co-op retailer and a corporate-owned retailer in the case of Mountain Equipment Co-op (MEC) is that the company is owned by their customers and not by shareholders. Labistour also says that MEC works with their factories to ensure that these maintain ethical standards in the manufacturing process.

30970 ■ *"A Research Firm With More Than One Foe" in Globe & Mail (February 24, 2006, pp. B1)*
Pub: CTVglobemedia Publishing Inc.
Ed: Shawn McCarthy. **Description:** The details of Biovail Corp.'s securities fraud case against Gradient Analytics Inc. are presented.

30971 ■ *"Risk Management Starts at the Top" in Business Strategy Review (Vol. 21, Spring 2010, No. 1, pp. 18)*
Pub: Wiley-Blackwell
Ed: Paul Strebel, Hongze Lu. **Description:** Authors question why, at the end of 2008, Citigroup, Merrill Lynch and UBS had well over $40 billion in sub-prime write-downs and credit losses, while some of their competitors were much less exposed. Their research into the situation revealed correlations of great import to today's firms.

30972 ■ *"Rogue's Gallery" in Canadian Business (Vol. 81, November 10, 2008, No. 19, pp. 44)*
Pub: Rogers Media Ltd.
Ed: Rachel Pulfer. **Description:** Laissez-faire capitalism or poor oversight of Fannie Mae and Freddie Mac are causes for the financial crisis in the U.S., depending or Democrat or Republican viewpoint. Events leading up to the 2008 financial crisis are covered.

30973 ■ *Rogues' Gallery: The Secret Story of the Lust, Lies, Greed, and Betrayals That Made the Metropolitan Museum of Art*
Pub: Crown Business Books
Ed: Michael Gross. **Released:** May 11, 2010. **Price:** $16.99. **Description:** Michael Gross, leading chronicler of the American rich, looks at the saga of the nation's largest museum, the Metropolitan Museum of Art.

30974 ■ *"Save the Date" in Barron's (Vol. 90, September 13, 2010, No. 37, pp. 35)*
Pub: Barron's Editorial & Corporate Headquarters
Ed: Mark Veverka. **Description:** Mark Hurd is the new Co-President of Oracle after being forced out at Hewlett-Packard where he faced a harassment complaint. HP fired Hurd due to expense account malfeasance. Hurd is also set to speak at an Oracle trade show in San Francisco on September 20, 2010.

30975 ■ *The SEO Manifesto: A Practical and Ethical Guide to Internet Marketing and Search Engine Optimization*
Pub: Cape Project Management Inc.
Ed: Dan Tousignant, Pamela Gobiel. **Released:** December 5, 2011. **Price:** $14.99. **Description:** Comprehensive guide for each phase of launching an online business; chapters include checklists, process descriptions, and examples.

30976 ■ *Small Business Desk Reference*
Pub: Penguin Books USA Inc.
Ed: Gene Marks. **Released:** December 2004. **Description:** Comprehensive guide for starting or running a successful small business, focusing on buying a business or franchise, writing a business plan, financial management, accounting, legal issues, human resources management, operations, marketing, sales, customer service, taxes, insurance, and ethics. Information for launching a restaurant, property management firm, retail outlet, consulting firm, and service business is included.

30977 ■ *Small Business Management*
Pub: John Wiley & Sons, Incorporated
Ed: Margaret Burlingame. **Released:** March 2007. **Price:** $44.95. **Description:** Advice for starting and running a small business as well as information on the value and appeal of small businesses, is given. Topics include budgets, taxes, inventory, ethics, e-commerce, and current laws.

30978 ■ *"Soldiering On to Remake the SBA" in Inc. (February 2008, pp. 21)*
Pub: Gruner & Jahr USA Publishing
Description: Steven Preston discusses efforts to improve the Small Business Administration's processes to improve services to small businesses. Topics covered include customer service issues, loans, and fraud.

30979 ■ *The SPEED of Trust: The One Thing That Changes Everything*
Pub: Free Press/Simon & Schuster Inc.
Ed: Stephen M.R. Covey. **Released:** February 5, 2008. **Price:** $15.95. **Description:** Because of recent business scandals, trust and a desire for accountability is addressed by the author.

30980 ■ *"Stent Cases at Md. Hospitals Falling" in Baltimore Business Journal (Vol. 28, November 12, 2010, No. 27, pp. 1)*
Pub: Baltimore Business Journal
Ed: Emily Mullin. **Description:** Cardiologists believe that the recent drop in cardiac stent procedures in Maryland can be associated with the ongoing investigation of Dr. Mark G. Midei and St. Joseph Medical Center. Midei is accused of performing unnecessary stent procedures on patients and was let go from the clinical practice in St. Joseph in 2009.

30981 ■ *"Talent Scout: How This Exec Finds and Develops Leaders Internally" in Black Enterprise (Vol. 38, November 2007, No. 4, pp. 63)*
Pub: Earl G. Graves Publishing Co. Inc.
Ed: Faith Chukwudi. **Description:** Profile of Bernard Bedon, director at Public Group Media. Bedon helps attract, develop, retain, and reward talent in his media group of 10,000 employees worldwide.

30982 ■ *"The Ten Commandments of Legal Risk Management" in Business Horizons (Vol. 51, January-February 2008, No. 1, pp. 13)*
Pub: Elsevier Advanced Technology Publications
Ed: Michael B. Metzger. **Description:** Effective legal risk management is tightly linked with ethical and good management, and managers' behaviors have to be professional and based on ethically defensible

principles of action. Basic human tendencies cannot be used in justifying questionable decisions in court. Guidelines for legal risk management are presented.

30983 ■ *"Toward a Theory of Stakeholder Salience in Family Firms" in Business Ethics Quarterly (Vol. 21, April 2011, No. 2, pp. 235)*
Pub: Society for Business Ethics
Ed: Ronald K. Mitchell, Bradley R. Agle, James J. Chrisman, Laura J. Spence. **Description:** The notion of stakeholder salience based on attributes (e.g. power, legitimacy, urgency) is applied in the family business setting.

30984 ■ *Trade-Off: The Ever-Present Tension Between Quality and Conscience*
Pub: Crown Business Books
Ed: Kevin Maney. **Released:** August 17, 2010. **Price:** $15.00. **Description:** The tension between fidelity (the quality of a consumer's experience) and convenience (the ease of getting and paying for a product) are shown to be the forces that determine the success or failure of new products and services in the marketplace.

30985 ■ *"Trial of Enron Ex-Bosses to Begin Today" in Globe & Mail (January 30, 2006, pp. B1)*
Pub: CTVglobemedia Publishing Inc.
Ed: Shawn McCarthy. **Description:** The details of the case against former executives Kenneth L. Lay and Jeffrey Skilling of Enron Corp. are presented.

30986 ■ *"Union Ethics Training: Building the Legitimacy and Effectiveness of Organized Labor" in WorkingUSA (Vol. 11, September 2008, No. 3)*
Pub: Blackwell Publishers Ltd.
Ed: Maggie Cohen. **Description:** Arguments are presented for the implementation of serious ethics training at all levels of labor unions and their contribution to union effectiveness by enhancing union legitimacy-understood as an amalgam of legal, pragmatic, and moral legitimacy and by paving the way to stable recognition of the labor movement as an integral part of American society, necessary to economic prosperity and the realization of fundamental American moral and social values.

30987 ■ *Values-Centered Entrepreneurship*
Pub: Routledge
Ed: David Y. Choi, Edmund Gray. **Released:** August 10, 2010. **Price:** $39.95. **Description:** A new brand of entrepreneurs has arrived on the business scene, carrying with them a new set of values. They possess a sense of social responsibility, the need to protect the planet, and to do the right thing for all stakeholders.

30988 ■ *"Voice: Rebuilding Trust" in Business Strategy Review (Vol. 21, Summer 2010, No. 2, pp. 79)*
Pub: Blackwell Publishers Ltd.
Ed: David De Cremer. **Description:** An examination of the financial sector's attempt to rebuild trust is given. Three steps to jump start the process are explored.

30989 ■ *"Voices: Breaking the Corruption Habit" in Business Strategy Review (Vol. 21, Autumn 2010, No. 3, pp. 67)*
Pub: Wiley-Blackwell
Ed: David De Cremer. **Description:** In times of crisis, it seems natural that people will work together for the common good. David De Cremer cautions that, on the contrary, both economic and social research prove otherwise. He proposes steps for organizations to take to prevent corrupt behaviors.

30990 ■ *"Voices: Climategate Leads Nowhere" in Business Strategy Review (Vol. 21, Summer 2010, No. 2, pp. 76)*
Pub: Blackwell Publishers Ltd.
Ed: Mick Blowfield. **Description:** An examination of the recent Climategate scandal that explores the damage caused by managers who are too easily mystified or misled.

30991 ■ *"When You Need Strong Millennials in Your Workplace" in Agency Sales Magazine (Vol. 39, November 2009, No. 10, pp. 22)*
Pub: MANA
Ed: Joanne G. Sujansky. **Description:** Millennials are bringing a new set of skills and a different kind of work ethics to the workplace. This generation is used to receiving a great deal of positive feedback and they expect to continue receiving this on the job. Expectations should be made clear to this generation and long-term career plans and goals should also be discussed with them.

30992 ■ *Work at Home Now*
Pub: Career Press, Inc.
Ed: Christine Durst, Michael Haaren. **Released:** October 9, 2010. **Price:** $14.99. **Description:** There are legitimate home-based jobs and projects that can be found on the Internet, but trustworthy guidance is scarce. There is a 58 to 1 scam ratio in work at-home advertising filled with fraud.

TRADE PERIODICALS

30993 ■ *Business Ethics: The Magazine of Corporate Responsibility*
Pub: Business Ethics
URL(s): business-ethics.com/. **Ed:** Michael Connor. **Released:** Quarterly

30994 ■ *Ethics & Policy*
Pub: Center for Ethics and Social Policy
Ed: Chris Adams, Editor. **Released:** Quarterly. **Price:** Included in membership. **Description:** Voices the concerns of the Center, which was founded to develop new modes of ethical analysis applicable to the major institutions of our society. Acts as a forum for various points of view on contemporary social problems. Recurring features include editorials from staff members; news of research in areas covering business ethics, economic policy, environmental ethics, religion and society, medical ethics, and book reviews.

30995 ■ *Ethics Today*
Pub: Ethics Resource Center Inc.
Contact: Dr. Patricia J. Harned, President
E-mail: pat@ethics.org
Ed: Lauren Larsen, Editor, lauren@ethics.org. **Released:** Monthly. **Price:** Free. **Description:** Presents discussions on issues in the field of organizational ethics and character education.

30996 ■ *The GreenMoney Journal & Online Guide*
Pub: The Greenmoney Journal
Contact: Cliff Feigenbaum, Editor
E-mail: cliff@greenmoney.com
Released: Bimonthly. **Price:** $50, individuals; $50, Canada plus $10 postage; $50, elsewhere plus $20. **Description:** Encourages and promotes the awareness of socially and environmentally responsible business, investing and consumer resources in publications and online. Our goal is to educate and empower individuals and businesses to make informed financial decisions through aligning their personal, corporate and financial principles. Recurring features include a calendar.

30997 ■ *Issues in Ethics*
Pub: Markkula Center for Applied Ethics
Contact: Amy Gomersall, Designer
Ed: Miriam Schulman, Editor. **Released:** Semiannual. **Price:** $30. **Description:** Covers ethics in fields of education, business, biotech, healthcare, and technology. Recurring features include letters to the editor, interviews, news of research, and book reviews.

30998 ■ *Poynter Center Newsletter*
Pub: Poynter Center for the Study of Ethics and American Institutions
Contact: Glinda Murray, Author
Ed: Glenda MurrayJudith A. Granbois, Editor, glmurrayindianaiana.edu. **Released:** Semiannual. **Price:** Free. **Description:** Focuses on Center programs in American ethics and institutions, such as political institutions, research ethics and biomedical ethics.

VIDEOCASSETTES/ AUDIOCASSETTES

30999 ■ *Concerns Quarterly with Footage from CBS News: General Business*
Harcourt Brace College Publishers
301 Commerce, Ste. 3700
Fort Worth, TX 76102
Ph: (817)334-7500
Free: 800-237-2665
Fax: (817)334-0947
Co. E-mail: info@harcourt.com
URL: http://www.hmhco.com
Released: 1995. **Price:** $80.00. **Description:** Video newsletter containing footage from such CBS programs as CBS Evening News, 48 Hours, Street Stories, and CBS This Morning. Provides information on such topics as ethical responsibilities in business, people in business, competition, manufacturing, and marketing. Comes with instructor's guide. Available at an annual subscription rate of $300.00. **Availability:** VHS.

31000 ■ *Ethics in American Business*
Phoenix Learning Group
2349 Chaffee Dr.
Saint Louis, MO 63146-3306
Ph: (314)569-0211
Free: 800-221-1274
Fax: (314)569-2834
URL: http://www.phoenixlearninggroup.com
Released: 1988. **Price:** $475.00. **Description:** This video provides suggestions for formulating a legal code of business ethics. **Availability:** VHS; 3/4 U.

CONSULTANTS

31001 ■ Frederick A. Bornhofen & Associates—Bornhofen & Associates
220 Isabella Rd.
Elverson, PA 19520-9141
Ph: (610)942-9140
Fax: (610)942-9576
Contact: Frederick A. Bornhofen, President
E-mail: fborn@comcast.net
Scope: Offers commercial and industrial security services, specializes in areas of robbery and violence prevention, business ethics, cargo security, commercial loss prevention techniques, and security management. Industries served: retail, convenience store, transportation, manufacturing, and energy. **Founded:** 1989. **Publications:** "Everything Changes Sometime". **Seminars:** Business Ethics; Fraud in the Business World.

31002 ■ Siebrand-Wilton Associates Inc.
PO Box 369
Marlboro, NJ 07746-0369
Ph: (732)917-0239
Fax: (732)972-0214
Co. E-mail: clientsvcs@s-wa.com
URL: http://www.s-wa.com
Contact: John S. Sturges, President
E-mail: bencomp@s-wa.com
Scope: Assesses, plans and implements human resources aspects of mergers and acquisitions. Offers human resources consulting in compensation and benefit plan design, mergers and acquisitions (HR aspects), business ethics assessment and development, editing, writing and association management services, and contract professionals and interim executives. **Founded:** 1986. **Publications:** "Should Government or Business Try to Save Medicare," HR News; "Executive Temping," HR Horizons; "When is an Employee Truly an Employee," HR Magazine; "Examining Your Insurance Carrier," HR Magazine.

LIBRARIES

31003 ■ Ethics Centre CA Library
One Yonge St., Ste. 1801
Toronto, ON, Canada M5E 1W7
Ph: (416)368-7525

Fax: (416)348-8689
Co. E-mail: info@ethicscentre.ca
URL: http://www.ethicscentre.ca
Contact: Helene Yaremko-Jarvis, Executive Director
Scope: Ethics, business, corporate policy. **Services:** Library open to the public for reference use only. **Holdings:** Books; periodicals; videocassettes.

31004 ■ University of South Florida, Saint Petersburg - Nelson Poynter Memorial Library and Special Collections
140 7th Ave. S., POY 321
St. Petersburg, FL 33701-5016
Ph: (727)873-4094
Fax: (727)873-4768
Co. E-mail: schnur@nelson.usf.edu
URL: http://www.nelson.usf.edu/spccoll
Contact: Jim Schnur, Librarian, Special Collections
Scope: Marine science and ichthyology, local and regional history, oral history, journalism and media studies, campus archives, ethics. **Services:** Interlibrary loan; copying; library open to the public by appointment. **Founded:** 1968. **Holdings:** 4750 books; 200 bound periodical volumes; 100 reports; 500 lin.ft. of archival material; 1700 audio/visual materials.

RESEARCH CENTERS

31005 ■ Josephson Institute of Ethics
9841 Airport Blvd., No. 300
Los Angeles, CA 90045
Ph: (310)846-4800
Free: 800-711-2670
Fax: (310)846-4858
URL: http://josephsoninstitute.org
Contact: Michael S. Josephson, President
Services: Radio commentaries. **Founded:** 1987. **Publications:** *Ethics in Action*; *Good Ideas Books—The Power of Character*. **Educational Activities:** Aspen Summit Conference; Character Counts!, youth education project; Character Development Seminars; Ethics in the Workplace training; Pursuing Victory with Honor, sportsmanship campaign; Character Counts! Coalition Meeting (Annual).

31006 ■ Loyola University Chicago - Center for Ethics and Social Justice
6525 N Sheridan Rd.
Chicago, IL 60626
Ph: (773)508-8349
Fax: (773)508-8879
Co. E-mail: ethics@luc.edu
URL: http://www.luc.edu/ethics
Contact: William French, Director
Services: Consulting. **Founded:** 1991. **Educational Activities:** Ethics Breakfast Series; Integration Courses; Moral Reasoning Workshop; Nursing Ethics Workshops; Center for Ethics and Social Justice Short courses, about health care ethics for ethics committees. **Awards:** Fellowships for internal faculty. **Telecommunication Services:** wfrench@luc.edu.

31007 ■ San Jose State University - Institute for Social Responsibility, Ethics, and Education (ISREE)
1 Washington Sq.
San Jose, CA 95192-0096
Ph: (408)924-5563
Fax: (408)924-4527
Co. E-mail: lawrence.quill@sjsu.edu
URL: http://www.sjsu.edu/isree
Contact: Prof. Lawrence Quill, Director
Founded: 1987. **Educational Activities:** Lecture series, corporate roundtables, seminars, training session, and workshops.

31008 ■ Western Michigan University - Center for the Study of Ethics in Society
3024 Moore Hall
Kalamazoo, MI 49008-5328
Ph: (269)387-4397
Fax: (269)387-4390
Co. E-mail: michael.pritchard@wmich.edu
URL: http://www.wmich.edu/ethics
Contact: Prof. Michael S. Pritchard, Director
Services: Consulting. **Founded:** 1985. **Publications:** *Occasional papers* (Quarterly). **Educational Activities:** Colloquia; Public presentations, 20 per academic year. **Telecommunication Services:** ethicscenter@wmich.edu.

START-UP INFORMATION

31009 ■ *"Family Dynamics and Family Business Financial Performance: Spousal Commitment" in Family Business Review (Vol. 19, March 2006)*
Pub: Family Firm Institute
Contact: Judy L. Green, President
Ed: Howard Van Auken. **Description:** Study examining the effect of spousal commitment on launch and survival of family-owned businesses is presented.

31010 ■ *"Hand-Held Heaven: Smallcakes Cupcakery" in Tulsa World (February 15, 2011)*
Pub: McClatchy Company
Description: Franchisee Carolyn Archer displays her products at Smallcakes Cupcakery, a Jenks shop that's the first to be co-branded with FreshBerry under the Beautiful Brands International banner. The shop's launch is part of a franchise deal between BBI and Jeff and Brandy Martin, co-owners of Smallcakes; twelve concepts have been developed and marketed already by Tulsa-based BBI.

31011 ■ *"Securing a Fortune" in Small Business Opportunities (Fall 2010)*
Pub: Harris Publications Inc.
Description: Profile of Whelan Security based in Saint Louis and is a private security company operating in 17 states. The family owned business started as a safety patrol unit.

31012 ■ *"Should You Go Into Business With Your Spouse?" in Women Entrepreneur (September 1, 2008)*
Pub: Entrepreneur Media Inc.
Ed: Tamara Monosoff. **Description:** Things to consider before starting a business with one's spouse are discussed. Compatible work ethics, clear expectations of one another, long-term goals for the company and the status of the relationship are among the things to consider before starting a business endeavor with a spouse.

ASSOCIATIONS AND OTHER ORGANIZATIONS

31013 ■ Canadian Association of Family Enterprise (CAFE)—Association Canadienne des Entreprises Familiales
465 Morden Rd., Ste. 112
Oakville, ON, Canada L6K 3W6
Ph: (905)337-8375
Free: 866-849-0099
Fax: (905)337-0572
Co. E-mail: office@cafenational.org
URL: http://www.cafecanada.ca
Contact: Peter G. White, Director
Description: Family-owned businesses. Seeks to "encourage, educate, and inform members in disciplines unique to the family business." Fosters increased understanding of the importance of family-owned enterprises in the national economy among government agencies and the public. Gathers and disseminates information of interest to members. Conducts educational and lobbying activities. Provides technical support and advisory services to small businesses in areas including succession planning, taxation, family law, and arbitration and mediation. Maintains network of Family Councils, which serve as a forum for discussion of family and business matters. **Scope:** business, personal wellness, family business. **Founded:** 1983. **Subscriptions:** books. **Publications:** *Family Business Magazine* (Quarterly); *Family Enterpriser* (Quarterly); *International Magazine for Family Businesses* (Bimonthly); *Canadian Association of Family Enterprise--Annual Membership Directory*. **Educational Activities:** National Symposium for Families in Business (Semiannual). **Awards:** Family Enterprise of the Year Award.

31014 ■ *Family Business Magazine*
465 Morden Rd., Ste. 112
Oakville, ON, Canada L6K 3W6
Ph: (905)337-8375
Free: 866-849-0099
Fax: (905)337-0572
Co. E-mail: office@cafenational.org
URL: http://www.cafecanada.ca
Contact: Peter G. White, Director
Released: Quarterly

31015 ■ *Family Enterpriser*
465 Morden Rd., Ste. 112
Oakville, ON, Canada L6K 3W6
Ph: (905)337-8375
Free: 866-849-0099
Fax: (905)337-0572
Co. E-mail: office@cafenational.org
URL: http://www.cafecanada.ca
Contact: Peter G. White, Director
Released: Quarterly

31016 ■ Focus on the Family (FOTF)
8605 Explorer Dr.
Colorado Springs, CO 80920
Ph: (719)531-3400
Free: 800-232-6459
Fax: (719)531-3424
Co. E-mail: help@focusonthefamily.com
URL: http://www.family.org
Contact: Dr. James D. Daly, President
Description: Promotes traditional Judeo-Christian values and strong family ties. Gathers and disseminates practical resource information on marriage, parenting, and other subjects related to family life. Produces fourteen different radio programs, aired in 96 countries. Conducts research and educational programs; sponsors charitable activities; makes available children's services; maintains speakers' bureau. Broadcasts and resources are also available in Hebrew, Hungarian, Indonesian, Italian, Japanese, Korean, Lithuanian, Norwegian, Polish, Portuguese, Romanian, Russian, Slovakian, Spanish, Swedish, Thai, Ukrainian and Zulu. **Founded:** 1977. **Publications:** *Citizen*; *Clubhouse Jr.* (Monthly); *Plugged In* (Monthly); *Brio Magazine* (Monthly); *Breakaway Magazine* (Monthly); *Focus on the Family Magazine* (Monthly); *Boundless* (Weekly); *Breakaway* (Monthly); *Brio* (Monthly); *Clubhouse* (Monthly); *Clubhouse, Jr.* (Monthly); *Focus on the Family Citizen* (Monthly); *Focus on the Family Physician* (Bimonthly); *LifeWise* (Bimonthly); *Plugged In* (Monthly); *Physician Magazine: A Publication of Focus on the Family* (Bimonthly); *Plugged In* (Monthly); *Focus on the Family Clubhouse* (Monthly); *Teachers in Focus Magazine*. **Educational Activities:** Pillars (Annual); Counseling Enrichment Program (Periodic); Crisis Pregnancy Center Directors Conference (Periodic). **Telecommunication Services:** news@fotf.org.

31017 ■ *International Magazine for Family Businesses*
465 Morden Rd., Ste. 112
Oakville, ON, Canada L6K 3W6
Ph: (905)337-8375
Free: 866-849-0099
Fax: (905)337-0572
Co. E-mail: office@cafenational.org
URL: http://www.cafecanada.ca
Contact: Peter G. White, Director
Released: Bimonthly

EDUCATIONAL PROGRAMS

31018 ■ Kennesaw State University - Cox Family Enterprise Center
1000 Chastain Rd.
Kennesaw, GA 30144-5591
Ph: (770)423-6000
Fax: (770)423-6721
Co. E-mail: cfec@kennesaw.edu
URL: http://www.kennesaw.edu
Description: Four-day course covering family business. Topics include: strategic and family business planning, leadership and management, conlict resolutions, total quality management (TQM), working with boards and other advisors, family and business values, and succession.

REFERENCE WORKS

31019 ■ *"Achieving Sustained Competitive Advantage: A Family Capital Theory" in Family Business Review (Vol. 19, June 2006, No. 2, pp. 135)*
Pub: Family Firm Institute
Contact: Judy L. Green, President
Ed: James Hoffman, Mark Hoelscher, Ritch Sorenson. **Description:** Impact of capital assets on performance of family businesses is discussed.

31020 ■ *"Advantage Tutoring Center" in Bellingham Business Journal (Vol. February 2010, pp. 16)*
Pub: Sound Publishing Inc.
Ed: Ashley Mitchell. **Description:** Profile of the newly opened Advantage Tutoring, owned by Mary and Peter Morrison. The center offers programs ranging from basic homework help to subject-specific enrichment.

31021 ■ *"After the Storm: Following a Tragic Loss, the Chambers Family Is Starting To See the Light" in Black Enterprise (November 2007)*
Pub: Earl G. Graves Publishing Co. Inc.
Ed: Sheryl Nance Nash. **Description:** A family law firm filed bankruptcy after the death of a daughter.

31022 ■ *"All In The Family" in Canadian Business (Vol. 79, September 25, 2006, No. 19, pp. 75)*
Pub: Rogers Media
Ed: Zena Olijnyk. **Description:** Continuing ownership of Weston dynasty on Canada's largest chain Loblaw Co. is discussed.

31023 ■ *"Always Striving" in Women In Business (Vol. 61, December 2009, No. 6, pp. 28)*
Pub: American Business Women's Association
Ed: Kathleen Leighton. **Description:** Jennifer Mull discusses her responsibilities and how she attained success as CEO of Backwoods, a gear and clothing store founded by her father in 1973. She places importance on being true to one's words and beliefs, while emphasizing the capacity to tolerate risks in business. Mull defines success as an evolving concept and believes there must always be something to strive for.

31024 ■ *"Auction Company Grows with Much Smaller Sites" in Automotive News (Vol. 86, October 31, 2011, No. 6488, pp. 23)*
Pub: Crain Communications Inc.
Ed: Arlena Sawyers. **Description:** Auction Broadcasting Company has launched auction sites and is expanding into new areas. The family-owned business will provide auctions half the size traditionally used. The firm reports that 40 percent of the General Motors factory-owned vehicles sold on consignment were purchased by online buyers, up 30 percent over 2010.

31025 ■ *"B. Jannetta" in Ice Cream Reporter (Vol. 21, August 20, 2008, No. 9, pp. 8)*
Pub: Ice Cream Reporter
Description: B. Jannetta ice cream parlor, run by Owen and Nicola Hazel, is celebrating its 100th Anniversary. The ice cream parlor is believed to be the oldest business still operating in its original shop in Saint Andrews. Owen and Nicola are the fourth generation to run the shop since Hazel's grandfather founded the business in 1908.

31026 ■ *"Baxter Baker Wins in Hot Finale of 'Cupcake Wars" in Fort Mill Times (September 13, 2011)*
Pub: McClatchy Company
Ed: Jenny Overmann. **Description:** Heather McDonnell, owner of Cupcrazed Cakery, and her assistant Debbie McDonnell, vied for a chance to win $10,000 on the cable network show called 'Cupcake Wars', and to serve cupcakes at the album release party for country singer Jennette McCurdy. At the end of the show, the sisters-in-law won the top prize.

31027 ■ *"Bellingham Boatbuilder Norstar Yachts Maintains Family Tradition" in Bellingham Business Journal (Vol. February 2010, pp. 12)*
Pub: Sound Publishing Inc.
Ed: Isaac Bonnell. **Description:** Profile of Norstar Yachts and brothers Gary and Steve Nordtvedt who started the company in 1994. The company recently moved its operations to a 12,000 square foot space in the Fairhaven Marine Industrial Park.

31028 ■ *"Better Than New" in Bellingham Business Journal (Vol. February 2010, pp. 16)*
Pub: Sound Publishing Inc.
Ed: Ashley Mitchell. **Description:** Profile of family owned Better Than New clothing store that sells overstock items from department stores and clothing manufacturers. The stores location makes it easy to miss and its only advertising is a large sign posted outside. This is the sixth store owned by the couple, Keijeo and Sirba Halmekanqas.

31029 ■ *"Boston Printer Celebrates 60th Anniversary" in American Printer (Vol. 128, August 1, 2011, No. 8)*
Pub: Penton Media Inc.
Description: Shawmut printing is celebrating its 60th anniversary. The family business plans to increase efficiency through automation, monitoring job progress online from start to finish.

31030 ■ *"Brewing a Love-Haiti Relationship" in The Business Journal - Serving Phoenix and the Valley of the Sun (Vol. 28, July 4, 2008, No. 44)*
Pub: American City Business Journals, Inc.
Ed: Yvonne Zusel. **Description:** Jean and Alicia Marseille have ventured into a coffee distribution company called Ka Bel LLC which markets Marabou brand of coffee imported from Haiti. Part of the proceeds of the business is donated to entrepreneurs from Jean's country, Haiti. Details of the Marseille's startup business and personal mission to help are discussed.

31031 ■ *"Builders Land Rutenberg Deal" in Charlotte Observer (February 2, 2007)*
Pub: Knight-Ridder/Tribune Business News
Ed: Bob Fliss. **Description:** Jim and Larry Sanders purchased a franchise from builder, Arthur Rutenberg Homes. The brothers will build custom homes in the area.

31032 ■ *"Business Succession Planning" in New Jersey Law Review (December 7, 2007)*
Pub: New Jersey Law Journal
Ed: Robert W. Cockren, Elga A. Goodman. **Description:** Ninety percent of American businesses are family-owned. The importance of estate planning for family-owned or controlled firms is covered.

31033 ■ *"Businessman Legend Passes: Charles H. James II Credited With Transforming Family Business" in Black Enterprise (December 2007)*
Pub: Earl G. Graves Publishing Co. Inc.
Ed: Tara C. Walker. **Description:** Profile of Charles H. James II, president and chairman of The James Corporation, a family-owned multigenerational food distribution company that started as a produce firm.

31034 ■ *"Carving Passion, Talent Help Couple Craft Business on Wood-Rich Land" in Crain's Cleveland Business (October 8, 2007)*
Pub: Crain Communications, Inc.
Ed: Sharon Schnall. **Description:** Profile of Woodcarved Art Gallery & Studio, a family-owned business which includes several ventures of the husband-and-wife team, Jim Stadtlander and Diane Harto.

31035 ■ *"Changing Prescriptions" in Business North Carolina (Vol. 28, March 2008, No. 3, pp. 52)*
Pub: Business North Carolina
Description: Profile of Moose Drug Company, founded by Archibald Walter Moose in 1882. Family owners share how they focus on pharmacoeconomics (cost-benefit analyses of drugs or drug therapy) and customer service.

31036 ■ *"Chino Valley Ranches: a Family of Farmers" in Retail Merchandiser (Vol. 51, September-October 2011, No. 5, pp. 79)*
Pub: Phoenix Media Corporation
Ed: Angela Forsyth. **Description:** Charles B. Nichols and his wife Isabella purchased their ranch in Beaumont, California in the early 1950s. The family has been raising their chickens, producing eggs with quality, integrity and honesty the foundation of their business.

31037 ■ *"Cleaning Up" in Small Business Opportunities (Get Rich At Home 2010)*
Pub: Harris Publications Inc.
Description: Break into the $23 billion pro car wash business with no experience needed. Profile of Team Blue, founded by father and son team, Jeff and Jason Haas along with franchise opportunities is included.

31038 ■ *"Connie Ozan; Founder, Design Director, Twist Creative, 37" in Crain's Cleveland Business (Vol. 28, November 19, 2007, No. 46)*
Pub: Crain Communications, Inc.
Ed: John Booth. **Description:** Profile of Connie Ozan, design director and founder of Twist Creative, an advertising agency that she runs with her husband, Michael; Ms. Ozan credits her husband's business sense in bringing a more strategic side to the company in which to complement her art direction.

31039 ■ *"Cupcake Craze" in Mail Tribune (March 2, 2011)*
Pub: Southern Oregon Media Group
Ed: Sarah Lemon. **Description:** Gourmet cupcake shops are sprouting up in large cities in Oregon. The Cupcake Company, a family business, is profiled.

31040 ■ *"Cupcake Maker Grabs Outpost" in Crain's New York Business (Vol. 27, August 15, 2011, No. 33, pp. 16)*
Pub: Crain Communications, Inc.
Ed: Jermaine Taylor. **Description:** Family-owned miniature cupcake maker, Baked by Melissa, singed a ten-year lease, expanding their stores to five. The business was started three years ago by advertising executive Melissa Bushell.

31041 ■ *"Dancing With Giants: Acquisition and Survival of the Family Firm" in Family Business Review (Vol. 19, December 2006, No. 4, pp. 289)*
Pub: Family Firm Institute
Contact: Judy L. Green, President
Ed: Adam Steen, Lawrence S. Welch. **Description:** Responses of family firms to mergers and acquisitions are analyzed taking the example of the takeover of an Australian wine producer and family firm.

31042 ■ *"Detroit Pawn Shop to be Reality TV Venue" in UPI NewsTrack (July 10, 2010)*
Pub: United Press International-USA
Description: TruTV will present a new series called 'Hardcore Pawn' to compete with the History Channel's successful show 'Pawn Stars'. The show will feature American Jewelry and Loan in Detroit, Michigan and its owner Les Gold, who runs the store with his wife and children.

31043 ■ *"The Duty of Wealth: Canadian Business Leaders on Nepotism and Philanthropy" in Canadian Business (Vol. 80, Winter 2007, No. 24)*
Pub: Rogers Media
Ed: Joe Castaldo. **Description:** Fifty-one percent of the respondents in a survey of business leaders say that the decision to allow adult children to join a family firm should be based on the circumstances at the time. He CEOs that were surveyed also believed that billionaires should donate an average of forty percent of their estates and keep the rest for their family.

31044 ■ *"The Effect of Cunfucian Values On Succession In Family Business" in Family Business Review (Vol. 19, September 2006, No. 3)*
Pub: Family Firm Institute
Contact: Judy L. Green, President
Ed: Jun Yan, Ritch Sorenson. **Description:** Position of family business in a social context using Confucian values is examined.

31045 ■ *Entrepreneurship and Small Business*
Pub: Palgrave Macmillan
Ed: Paul Burns. **Released:** January 2007. **Price:** $74.95. **Description:** Entrepreneurial skills, focusing on good management practices are discussed. Topics include family businesses, corporate, international and social entrepreneurship.

31046 ■ *Ethnic Solidarity for Economic Survival: Korean Greengrocers in New York City*
Pub: Russell Sage Foundation Publications
Ed: Pyong Gap Min. **Released:** August 2008. **Price:** $32.50. **Description:** Investigations into the entrepreneurial traditions of Korean immigrant families in New

York City running ethnic businesses, particularly small grocery stores and produce markets. Social, cultural and economic issues facing these retailers are discussed.

31047 ■ *"Fairfax Announces Acquisition of William Ashley" in Benzinga.com (August 16, 2011)*
Pub: Benzinga.com
Ed: Benzinga Staff. **Description:** Fairfax Financial Holdings Limited acquired the family-owned William Ashley China company, leader within the dinnerware and wedding registry industries and was the first company in North America to introduce a computerized wedding registry system.

31048 ■ *Family Business*
Pub: Cengage South-Western
Ed: Ernesto J. Poza. **Released:** January 1, 2009. **Price:** $96.95. **Description:** Family-owned businesses face unique challenges in today's economy. This book provides the next generation of knowledge and skills required for profitable management and leadership in a family enterprise.

31049 ■ *Family Business Models*
Pub: Palgrave Macmillan
Ed: Alberto Gimeno. **Released:** June 10, 2010. **Price:** $45.00. **Description:** A unique new model for understanding family businesses gives readers the potential to build better managed and more stable family firms and to plan for a success future.

31050 ■ *"Family Business Research" in International Journal of Entrepreneurship and Small Business (Vol. 12, December 3, 2010, No. 1)*
Pub: Publishers Communication Group
Ed: A. Bakr Ibrahim, Jean B. McGuire. **Description:** Assessment of the growing field of family business and suggestions for an integrated framework. The paper addresses a number of key issues facing family business research.

31051 ■ *"Family Feud: Pawn Shop Empire Stalls with Transition to Second Generation" in Billings Gazette (December 19, 2010)*
Pub: Billings Gazette
Ed: Jan Falstad. **Description:** Profile of Ben L. Brown Sr. and his pawn shop located in Billings, Montana is presented. Brown discusses his plan to transition his business to his children.

31052 ■ *"Family Firm Performance: Further Evidence" in Family Business Review (Vol. 19, June 2006, No. 2, pp. 103)*
Pub: Family Firm Institute
Contact: Judy L. Green, President
Ed: Jim Lee. **Description:** Empirical results of regression analysis, which is used to examine the competitiveness of family owned businesses and non-family firms are presented.

31053 ■ *"Family Governance and Firm Performance: Agency, Stewardship, and Capabilities" in Family Business Review (Vol. 19, March 2006)*
Pub: Family Firm Institute
Contact: Judy L. Green, President
Ed: Danny Miller, Isabelle Le Breton-Miller. **Description:** Study examining the effect of governance, agency perspective, and stewardship perspective on performances of major publicly-traded family-controlled businesses in the U.S. is presented.

31054 ■ *Family Limited Partnership Deskbook*
Pub: American Bar Association
Contact: Carolyn Lamm, President
Ed: David T. Lewis; Andrea C. Chomakos. **Released:** March 25, 2008. **Price:** $169.95. **Description:** Forming and funding a family limited partnership or limited liability company is complicated. In-depth analysis of all facets of this business entity are examined using detailed guidance on the basic principles of drafting, forming, funding, and valuing an FLP or LLC and also covers tax concerns. Examples and extensive sample forms are included on a CD-ROM included with the book.

31055 ■ *Family Limited Partnerships Deskbook: Forming and Funding FLPs and Other Closely Held Business Entities*
Pub: American Bar Association
Contact: Carolyn Lamm, President
Ed: David T. Lewis. **Released:** March 2008. **Price:** $169.95. **Description:** Forming and funding a family limited partnership (FLP) or limited liability company (LLC) is common and complicated. This handbook offers in-depth analysis of issues facing these types of businesses. Guidance is given on the principles of drafting, forming, funding, and valuing an FLP or LLC as well as tax matters. Examples and sample forms are included on a CD-ROM.

31056 ■ *"Family Matters: Founding Family Firms and Corporate Political Activity" in Business and Society (December 2007, pp. 395-428)*
Pub: SAGE Publications USA
Contact: Blaise R. Simqu, President
Ed: Michael Hadani. **Description:** The impact of publicly traded family founding firms and their inclination for corporate political activity is examined. Publicly traded family founding firms are more predisposed to engage in corporate political activity when the founder is in an executive position. Details of these findings are reported.

31057 ■ *"Family Matters: Founding Family Firms and Corporate Political Activity" in Business and Society (Vol. 46, December 2007, No. 4)*
Pub: SAGE Publications USA
Contact: Blaise R. Simqu, President
Ed: Michael Hadani. **Description:** The impact of publicly traded family founding firms and their inclination for corporate political activity is examined. Publicly traded family founding firms are more predisposed to engage in corporate political activity when the founder is in an executive position.

31058 ■ *"The Family-Run Business" in Small Business Opportunities (Get Rich At Home 2010)*
Pub: Harris Publications Inc.
Ed: Gene Siciliano. **Description:** The good, the bad and the ugly of succession planning for any small business is spotlighted.

31059 ■ *"Family Throne" in Hawaii Business (Vol. 53, March 2008, No. 9, pp. 51)*
Pub: Hawaii Business Publishing
Ed: Cathy S. Cruz-George. **Description:** Jeanette and George Grace inherited Paradise Lua Inc., a portable toilet company founded by George's father. The toilets are rented by Aloha Stadium during football season and St. Patrick's Day block party among others. The company has 2,500 toilets and 20 pumping trucks and had earnings of $1.3 million in 2007.

31060 ■ *"The Family Tools" in Canadian Business (Vol. 80, March 26, 2007, No. 7, pp. 14)*
Pub: Rogers Media
Description: A few strategies for running family businesses successfully are presented.

31061 ■ *Family Wars*
Pub: Kogan Page, Ltd.
Ed: Grant Gordon. **Released:** April 1, 2008. **Price:** $37.50. **Description:** Family feuding, sibling rivalries, and petty jealousies are among the greatest issues faced by family owned companies. Family Wars explores behind the scenes issues of some of the largest family-run firms in the world, and shows how family in-fighting has threatened their downfall. Ford, Gucci, McCain, Guinness, Fallo, and Restone are among the families discussed. Advice is given to anyone involved in a family business and offers suggestions to avoid problems.

31062 ■ *"A Family's Fortune" in Canadian Business (Vol. 80, Winter 2007, No. 24, pp. 103)*
Pub: Rogers Media
Ed: Graham F. Scott. **Description:** James Richardson started as a tailor before moving into the grain business because his clients paid him in sacks of wheat and barley. The James Richardson and Sons Ltd. entered the radio business in 1927 but later sold it off in 1951.

31063 ■ *"Finalist: Private Company, Less Than $100M" in Crain's Detroit Business (Vol. 25, June 22, 2009, No. 25)*
Pub: Crain Communications Inc. - Detroit
Ed: Sherri Begin Welch. **Description:** Profile of family-owned Guardian Alarm Company is presented. The firm has expanded to include medical monitoring and video equipment of doors and windows.

31064 ■ *"Firm Stays In the 'Family'; After Owner's Death, Employees Buy Company" in Crain's Detroit Business (Vol. 24, January 28, 2008)*
Pub: Crain Communications Inc. - Detroit
Ed: Chad Halcom. **Description:** Sterling Office Systems Inc., distributor of photocopiers and other office machines was purchased from the owner's family after his demise. The new owners would like to hit $1.75 million in sales their first year.

31065 ■ *"For the Seasoned Buyer" in Inc. (Vol. 30, November 2008, No. 11, pp. 32)*
Pub: Mansueto Ventures LLC
Ed: Darren Dahl. **Description:** Dominick Fimiano shares his plans to sell his ten-year-old business that manufactures and sells frozen pizza dough and crusts as well as a variety of topped pizzas. Products are purchased by schools, hospitals, bowling alleys and amusement parks. The business sale includes the buyer's taking on Fimiano's son the firm's most senior employee.

31066 ■ *"Former NFL Player Tackles a New Restaurant Concept" in Inc. (Vol. 33, September 2011, No. 7, pp. 32)*
Pub: Inc. Magazine
Ed: Nadine Heintz. **Description:** Matt Chatham, former NFL player, launched SkyCrepers, a chain of fast-serve crepe shops with his wife Erin. Chatham entered Babson College's MBA program after retiring from football.

31067 ■ *"Freeman Beauty Labs" in Retail Merchandiser (Vol. 51, September-October 2011, No. 5, pp. 74)*
Pub: Phoenix Media Corporation
Description: Profile of Freeman Beauty Labs, the family owned beauty product developer supplying retailers and salons with quality products. The firm promotes its bath, foot care, hair care, and skincare brands as a whole, not as individual products.

31068 ■ *"Fromm Family Foods Converts Old Feed Mill Into Factory for Gourmet Pet Food" in Wisconsin State Journal (August 3, 2011)*
Pub: Capital Newspapers
Ed: Barry Adams. **Description:** Fromm Family Foods, a gourmet cat and dog food company spent $10 million to convert an old feed mill into a pet food manufacturing facility. The owner forecasts doubling or tripling its production of 600 tons of feed per week in about five years.

31069 ■ *"Generational Savvy" in Hawaii Business (Vol. 54, August 2008, No. 2, pp. 135)*
Pub: Hawaii Business Publishing
Ed: Jolyn Okimoto Rosa. **Description:** Lawrence Takeo Kagawa founded Security Insurance Agency, later renamed Occidental Underwriters of Hawaii Ltd., in 1933 to provide insurance to Asian-Americans in Hawaii at lower premiums. Details on the company's history, growth investment products and Transamerica Life products and 75 years of family-run business are discussed.

31070 ■ *"Gillette Creamery" in Ice Cream Reporter (Vol. 23, September 20, 2010, No. 10, pp. 8)*
Pub: Ice Cream Reporter
Description: Gillette family of Gillette Creamery in Ellenville have been Entrepreneurs of the Year in Ulster County, New York. Gillette is the largest supplier of ice cream products in Eastern New York.

31071 ■ *"Good Price, Best Brands" in Retail Merchandiser (Vol. 51, July-August 2011, No. 4, pp. 58)*
Pub: Phoenix Media Corporation
Description: Flemington Department Store has been a family-owned and operated retailer for over 50 years. Customer service is key to the store's success.

31072 ■ *"Grape Expectations" in Canadian Business (Vol. 80, Winter 2007, No. 24, pp. 57)*
Pub: Rogers Media
Ed: Joe Castaldo. **Description:** Laura McCain-Jensen bought a 15-acre vineyard in the Niagara wine country after a trip to Ontario for her husband's hair transplant. The vineyard has since been renamed Creekside Estate Winery and now produces two celebrity-branded wines under the name of golfer Mike Weir and hockey player Wayne Gretsky.

31073 ■ *"'Groundhog Day' B & B Likely Will Be Converted Into One In Real Life" in Chicago Tribune (October 21, 2008)*
Pub: McClatchy-Tribune Information Services
Ed: Carolyn Starks. **Description:** Everton Martin and Karla Stewart Martin have purchased the Victorian house that was featured as a bed-and-breakfast in the 1993 hit move 'Groundhog Day'; the couple was initially unaware of the structure's celebrity status when they purchased it with the hope of fulfilling their dream of owning a bed-and-breakfast.

31074 ■ *"Growing Pains" in Canadian Business (Vol. 81, July 22, 2008, No. 12-13, pp. 35)*
Pub: Rogers Media Ltd.
Ed: Alex Mylnek. **Description:** Laughing Stock Vineyards' Cynthia Enns and David Enns plan to target young buyers by using social media. The Enns however, are concerned that targeting younger buyers may affect Laughing Stock's image as a premium brand. Additional information regarding the company's future plans is presented.

31075 ■ *"Guidelines For Family Business Boards of Directors" in Family Business Review (Vol. 19, June 2006, No. 2, pp. 147)*
Pub: Family Firm Institute
Contact: Judy L. Green, President
Ed: Suzanne Lane. **Description:** Effective corporate governance standards for boards of directors of family businesses are examined.

31076 ■ *"Halls Give Hospital Drive $11 Million Infusion" in The Business Journal-Serving Metropolitan Kansas City (Vol. 26, July 18, 2008)*
Pub: American City Business Journals, Inc.
Ed: Rob Roberts. **Description:** Don Hall, chairman of Hallmark Cards Inc., and eight family members have announced that they will give $11 million to Children's Mercy Hospitals and Clinics for its $800 million expansion plan. Hall Family Foundation president Bill Hall that contributions such as that for Children's Mercy reflect the charitable interests of the foundation's board and founders. The possible impacts of the Hall's donation are analyzed.

31077 ■ *"Hometown Value" in Retail Merchandiser (Vol. 51, July-August 2011, No. 4, pp. 50)*
Pub: Phoenix Media Corporation
Ed: Todd Vowell. **Description:** Profile of family-owned Vowell's Marketplace located in Noxapater, Mississippi. The 10-store chain caters to its Southern roots and is run by the third generation of the Vowell family.

31078 ■ *"How-To Workshops Teach Sewing, Styles" in St. Louis Post-Dispatch (September 14, 2010)*
Pub: St. Louis Post-Dispatch
Ed: Kalen Ponche. **Description:** Profile of DIY Style Workshop in St. Charles, Missouri, where sewing, designing and teaching is offered. The shop is home base for DIY Style, a Website created by mother and daughter to teach younger people how to sew.

31079 ■ *"Impact of Family Relationships On Attitudes of the Second Generation In Family Business" in Family Business Review (September 2006)*
Pub: Family Firm Institute
Contact: Judy L. Green, President
Ed: Jean Lee. **Description:** Relationship of family functioning with organizational variables, with particular attention given to family cohesion and family adaptability is examined.

31080 ■ *In-N-Out Burger: A Behind-the-Counter Look at the Fast-Food Chain That Breaks All the Rules*
Pub: HarperCollins Publishers
Ed: Stacy Perman. **Released:** April 2009. **Price:** $24.99. **Description:** Business analysis of the factors that helped In-N-Out Burgers, a family owned burger chain in California, along with a history of its founding family, the Synders.

31081 ■ *"Internationalization of Australian Family Businesses" in Family Business Review (Vol. 19, September 2006)*
Pub: Family Firm Institute
Contact: Judy L. Green, President
Ed: Chris Graves, Jill Thomas. **Description:** Concept that managerial capabilities of family firms lag behind those of non-family counterparts as they expand is discussed.

31082 ■ *"It All Comes Back to Trust" in Canadian Business (Vol. 80, March 26, 2007, No. 7, pp. S11)*
Pub: Rogers Media
Description: Eileen Fischer, family business expert at York University, shares her views on the challenges involved in running family businesses.

31083 ■ *"Juicy Feud; Deal Caps Years of Rancor in Wrigley Gum Dynasty" in Crain's Chicago Business (Vol. 31, May 5, 2008, No. 18, pp. 1)*
Pub: Crain Communications, Inc.
Ed: David Sterrett. **Description:** Discusses the sale of Wm. Wrigley Jr. Co. to Mars Inc. and Warren Buffett for $23 billion as well as the intra-family feuding which has existed for nearly a decade since William Wrigley Jr. took over as CEO of the company following his father's death.

31084 ■ *"A Life of Spice" in Entrepreneur (Vol. 37, September 2009, No. 9, pp. 46)*
Pub: Entrepreneur Media, Inc.
Ed: Jason Daley. **Description:** Matt and Bryan Walls have successfully grown their Atlanta, Georgia-based Snorg Tees T-shirt company. The company has expanded its product offering and redesigned its Website to be more user-friendly. The company has registered between $5 and 10 million in 2008.

31085 ■ *"Life's Work: Manolo Blahnik" in Harvard Business Review (Vol. 88, December 2010, No. 12, pp. 144)*
Pub: Harvard Business School Publishing
Ed: Alison Beard. **Description:** Shoe designer Manolo Blahnik recounts his beginnings in the shoe industry and the influence art has had on his work, as well as balancing art and commerce. He also discusses the importance of quality materials and craftsmanship and the benefits of managing an independent, family-owned business.

31086 ■ *"Long Live Rock" in Inc. (November 2007, pp. 130)*
Pub: Gruner & Jahr USA Publishing
Ed: Nitasha Tiku. **Description:** Profile of a family business using chemistry to recycle concrete products.

31087 ■ *"Lots More Mr. Nice Guy" in Canadian Business (Vol. 80, October 22, 2007, No. 21, pp. 58)*
Pub: Rogers Media
Ed: Zena Olijnyk. **Description:** Galen Weston Jr., executive chairman of Loblaw and heir to the Weston family business, has his hands full running the company. Details of his turnaround strategies and ambitious plans to increase profitability of the business are discussed.

31088 ■ *"Mars Advertising's Orbit Grows as Other Ad Segments Fall" in Crain's Detroit Business (Vol. 25, June 1, 2009, No. 22, pp. 10)*
Pub: Crain Communications Inc. - Detroit
Ed: Bill Shea. **Description:** An electrical fire burned at Mars Advertising's headquarters in Southfield, Michigan. The company talks about its plans for regrouping and rebuilding. The family firm specializes in in-store marketing that targets consumers already in the buying mode.

31089 ■ *"McIntosh Family Sells Car Dealership" in Black Enterprise (Vol. 38, December 2007, No. 5)*
Pub: Earl G. Graves Publishing Co. Inc.
Ed: Brenda Porter. **Description:** Seattle's McIntosh family sold its Kirkland Chrysler Jeep dealership to private equity firm Cerberus Capital Management. Details of the deal are given.

31090 ■ *"Measuring Success In Family Businesses: The Concept of Configurational Fit" in Family Business Review (Vol. 19, June 2006, No. 2)*
Pub: Family Firm Institute
Contact: Judy L. Green, President
Ed: Christoph Hienerth, Alexander Kessler. **Description:** Strategic benchmarking, which are used to examine business success of family-owned enterprises are investigated.

31091 ■ *"The Molson Way" in Canadian Business (Vol. 80, April 9, 2007, No. 8, pp. 36)*
Pub: Rogers Media
Ed: Andy Holloway. **Description:** The success of the seventh generation of Molson family in running the Molson Coors Brewing Co. since it was established 221 years ago by John Molson is discussed.

31092 ■ *The Mom and Pop Store: How the Unsung Heroes of the American Economy Are Surviving and Thriving*
Pub: Walker & Company
Ed: Robert Spector. **Released:** September 1, 2009. **Price:** $26.00. **Description:** The history of small independent retail enterprises and how mom and pop stores in the U.S. continue to thrive through customer service and renewed community support for local businesses.

31093 ■ *"MPI Expansion Goes Back to Family Roots" in Crain's Detroit Business (Vol. 25, June 1, 2009, No. 22, pp. M007)*
Pub: Crain Communications Inc. - Detroit
Ed: Sherri Begin Welch. **Description:** William Parfet, grandson of Upjohn Company founder, is expanding MPI Research's clinical and early clinical research operations into two buildings in Kalamazoo, land which was once part of his grandfather's farm.

31094 ■ *"Muirhead Farmhouse B & B Owners Get Hospitality Right" in Chicago Tribune (July 31, 2008)*
Pub: McClatchy-Tribune Information Services
Ed: Glenn Jeffers. **Description:** Profile of the Muirhead Farmhouse, a bed-and-breakfast owned by Mike Petersdorf and Sarah Muirhead Petersdorf; Frank Lloyd Wright designed the historic farmhouse which blends farm life and history into a unique experience that is enhanced by the couple's hospitality.

31095 ■ *"The Natural Environment, Innovation, and Firm Performance" in Family Business Review (Vol. 19, December 2006, No. 4)*
Pub: Family Firm Institute
Contact: Judy L. Green, President
Ed: Justin Craig, Clay Dibrell. **Description:** Comparative study of the impact of firm-level natural environment-related policies on innovation and performance of family and non-family firms is presented.

31096 ■ *"A New Perspective On the Development Model for Family Business" in Family Business Review (Vol. 19, December 2006, No. 4, pp. 317)*
Pub: Family Firm Institute
Contact: Judy L. Green, President
Ed: Matthew W. Rutherford, Lori A. Muse, Sharon L. Oswald. **Description:** Empirical test model of the developmental model for family business is proposed and owner, firm and family characteristics which have an impact on the development model are examined.

31097 ■ *Nirvana in a Cup: The Founding of Oregon Chai*
Pub: Moby Press
Ed: Tedde McMillen; Heather Hale. **Released:** July 2006. **Price:** $12.99. **Description:** Profile of a mother-daughter team who founded Oregon Chai, a tea company.

31098 ■ *"Nothing But Green Skies" in Inc. (November 2007, pp. 115-120)*
Pub: Gruner & Jahr USA Publishing
Ed: Alison Stein Wellner. **Description:** Profile of Enterprise Rent-A-Car, one of the largest family-owned businesses in the U.S. Andy Taylor, CEO, discusses the company's talks about the idea of offering carbon off-sets for a few years.

31099 ■ *"Oberweis Tests Home Ice Cream Delivery" in Ice Cream Reporter (Vol. 21, November 20, 2008, No. 12, pp. 1)*
Pub: Ice Cream Reporter
Description: Oberwies Dairy launched its Treat Delivery Program in the Saint Louis area. The program allows customers to order milkshakes, ice cream cones, sundaes and scoops of ice cream and they are delivered to their home or office. Oberweis is a fourth generation family run business.

31100 ■ *"Organizational Virtue Orientation and Family Firms" in Business Ethics Quarterly (Vol. 21, April 2011, No. 2, pp. 257)*
Pub: Society for Business Ethics
Ed: G. Tyge Payne, Keith H. Brigham, J. Christian Broberg, Todd W. Moss, Jeremy C. Short. **Description:** The concept of organizational virtue orientation (OVO) and the differences between family and non-family firms on six organizational virtue dimensions of Integrity, Empathy, Warmth, Courage, Conscientiousness, and Zeal are examined.

31101 ■ *"Ownership Preferences, Competitive Heterogeneity, and Family-Controlled Businesses" in Family Business Review (June 2006)*
Pub: Family Firm Institute
Contact: Judy L. Green, President
Ed: David G. Hoopes, Danny Miller. **Description:** Impact of ownership structure and corporate governance choices on competition among family-owned businesses is explored.

31102 ■ *"A Panel Study of Copreneurs In Business" in Family Business Review (Vol. 19, September 2006, No. 3, pp. 193)*
Pub: Family Firm Institute
Contact: Judy L. Green, President
Ed: Glenn Muske, Margaret A. Fitzgerald. **Description:** Analysis of three groups of copreneurs of family businesses, and their entrepreneurial impact on business success is presented.

31103 ■ *"Perry's Goes Organic" in Ice Cream Reporter (Vol. 22, December 20, 2008, No. 1, pp. 1)*
Pub: Ice Cream Reporter
Description: Family-owned Perry's Ice Cream is starting a new line of organic ice cream in both vanilla and chocolate flavors. All Perry's products are made with milk and cream from local dairy farmers.

31104 ■ *"A Pioneer of Paying With Plastic" in Crain's Chicago Business (Vol. 31, April 28, 2008, No. 17, pp. 39)*
Pub: Crain Communications, Inc.
Ed: Phuong Ly. **Description:** Profile of Perfect Plastic Printing Corp., a family-owned company which manufactures credit cards, bank cards and gift cards and whose sales hit $50.1 million last year, a 16 percent jump from 2006.

31105 ■ *"Please Pass the Mayo" in Crain's Chicago Business (Vol. 31, April 28, 2008, No. 17, pp. 32)*
Pub: Crain Communications, Inc.
Ed: Samantha Stainburn. **Description:** Fort Dearborn Co. has come a long way since it started as on one-press print shop; the family-owned company was struggling to keep up with the technology of making consumer product labels for curvy bottles of products like V8 V-Fusion juice and in 2006 sold off to Genstar Capital LLC which has pushed for acquisitions; last year, Fort Derborn bought its biggest competitor, Renaissance Mark Inc., doubling its size and adding spirit and wine makers to its client roster.

31106 ■ *"Printing Company Edwards Brothers Grapples With a Shrinking Market" in Crain's Detroit Business (Vol. 26, Jan. 4, 2010)*
Pub: Crain Communications Inc.
Ed: Bill Shea. **Description:** Overview of the publishing industry, which has seen a huge decline in revenue; Edwards Brothers, Inc., a family printing business that was founded 117 years ago is struggling due to a variety of factors, many of which are explored.

31107 ■ *Race and Entrepreneurial Success: Black-, Asian-, and White-Owned Businesses in the United States*
Pub: The MIT Press
Contact: Ellen W. Faran, Director
E-mail: ewfaran@mit.edu
Ed: Robert W. Fairlie. **Released:** September 30, 2008. **Price:** $35.00. **Description:** Trends in minority small business ownership are explored, focusing on the importance of human capital, financial capital, and family business background in successful business ownership.

31108 ■ *"The Relationship Between Boards and Planning In Family Businesses" in Family Business Review (Vol. 19, March 2006, No. 1, pp. 65)*
Pub: Family Firm Institute
Contact: Judy L. Green, President
Ed: Timothy Blumentritt. **Description:** Study determining the extent of control exercised by board of directors and advisory boards on business planning within family-owned businesses is covered.

31109 ■ *"The Romance of Good Deeds: a Business With a Cause Can Do Good in the World" in Inc. (Volume 32, December 2010, No. 10, pp. 47)*
Pub: Inc. Magazine
Ed: Meg Cadoux Hirshberg. **Description:** Entrepreneurship and family relationships are discussed. When a small business has a passion for philanthropy it can help any marriage by creating even greater passion for each other.

31110 ■ *"Root, Root, Root for the P.A. Hutchison Co." in American Printer (Vol. 128, August 1, 2011, No. 8)*
Pub: Penton Media Inc.
Description: The P.A. Hutchison Company celebrate 100 years in the printing business. President and CEO Chris Hutchison presented awards to employees, however employees also presented awards to Chris and his father as Employer of the Century.

31111 ■ *"Savvy Solutions" in Black Enterprise (Vol. 41, October 2010, No. 3, pp. 52)*
Pub: Earl G. Graves Publishing Co. Inc.
Ed: Tennille M. Robinson. **Description:** Husband and wife team seek advice for expanding their catering business. They are also seeking funding resources.

31112 ■ *Small Business Survival Guide*
Pub: Adams Media Corporation
Contact: Gary Krebs, Director
E-mail: swatrous@adamsmedia.com
Ed: Cliff Ennico. **Price:** $12.95. **Description:** Small business expert provides strategies to start a company and survive in the 21st Century. He shows small business owners how to succeed despite challenges that can defeat any firm. His advice covers suppliers; customers and contractors; competitors and creditors; spouses, family and friends; as well as the ways lawyers, accountants and other can steal an entrepreneur's success. Ennico also describes how startups can comply with local regulations.

31113 ■ *Sneaker Wars: The Enemy Brothers Who Founded Adidas and Puma and the Family Feud that Forever Changed the Business of Sport*
Pub: Ecco
Ed: Barbara Smit. **Released:** 2009. **Price:** $26.95. **Description:** A history of Puma and Adidas shoes and the two German brothers who built the empires.

31114 ■ *"Solutions to Family Business Problems" in Contractor (Vol. 56, October 2009, No. 10, pp. 51)*
Pub: Penton Media, Inc.
Ed: Irv Blackman. **Description:** Several common business problems that family owned firms face are presented together with their solutions. These problems include giving the children stock bonus options while another discusses the tax burden when a father wants to transfer the business to his son.

31115 ■ *"Son of Sandman: Can Tom Gaglardi Really Outdo His Old Man?" in Canadian Business (Vol. 80, Winter 2007, No. 24, pp. 106)*
Pub: Rogers Media
Ed: Calvin Leung. **Description:** Bob Gagliardi of Northland Properties started to learn about his family's business by working at a construction site at one of the high-rise buildings in downtown Vancouver. Gagliardi wants to expand their Moxie's restaurant chain and increase the market share of their Sandman hotel by 2018.

31116 ■ *"Soured Relationship Plays Out in Courts" in The Business Journal-Serving Greater Tampa Bay (Vol. 28, September 19, 2008, No. 39)*
Pub: American City Business Journals, Inc.
Ed: Janet Leiser. **Description:** Heirs of developer Julian Hawthorne Lifset won a court battle to end a 50-year lease with Specialty Restaurants Corp. in Rocky Point. The decision opens the Tampa Bay prime waterfront property for new development.

31117 ■ *"Stockerts Open Repair Business" in Dickinson Press (July 13, 2010)*
Pub: Dickinson Press
Ed: Ashley Martin. **Description:** Ed Stockert is opening his new appliance repair firm in Dickinson, North Dakota with his wife Anna.

31118 ■ *A Successful Family Business*
Pub: Penguin Group USA Inc.
Ed: Neil Pahel, Janis Raye. **Released:** August 1, 2009. **Price:** $18.95. **Description:** Guide to running a family business includes information for expanding beyond the original family firm and family versus hired management.

31119 ■ *"Swedes Swoop In To Save Time4" in Advertising Age (Vol. 78, January 29, 2007, No. 5, pp. 4)*
Pub: Crain Communications, Inc.
Ed: Nat Ives. **Description:** Overview of Stockholm's Bonnier Group, a family-owned publisher that is looking to expand its U.S. presence; Bonnier recently acquired a number of Time Inc. magazines.

31120 ■ *"A Tale of Two Brothers" in Canadian Business (Vol. 80, March 26, 2007, No. 7, pp. 18)*
Pub: Rogers Media
Description: The successful business strategies followed by Tyler Gompf and Kirby Gompf, owners of Tell Us About Us Inc., are presented.

31121 ■ *"Ted Stahl: Executive Chairman" in Inside Business (Vol. 13, September-October 2011, No. 5, pp. NC6)*
Pub: Great Lakes Publishing Co.
Ed: Miranda S. Miller. **Description:** Profile of Ted Stahl, who started working in his family's business when he was ten years old is presented. The firm makes dies for numbers and letters used on team

uniforms. Another of the family firms manufactures stock and custom heat-printing products, equipment and supplies. It also educates customers on ways to decorate garments with heat printing products and offers graphics and software for customers to create their own artwork.

31122 ■ *"Teeling and Gallagher: A Textbook for Success" in Agency Sales Magazine (Vol. 39, September-October 2009, No. 9, pp. 20)*
Pub: MANA

Ed: Jack Foster. **Description:** Profile of Teeling & Gallagher, a manufacturing firm that was founded in 1946 as the D.G. Teeling Company and continued as a one-person agency until 1960 when Tom Gallagher joined the company. Tom Gallagher talks about how things have changed and his work with his son Bob in the agency.

31123 ■ *"Termite Trouble" in Arkansas Business (Vol. 28, March 28, 2011, No. 13, pp. 5)*
Pub: Arkansas Business Publishing Group

Description: Thomas Pest Control of Little Rock, Arkansas has had liens placed against it by the Internal Revenue Service. The owner's daughter took over the business after her father passed away and is trying to rectify the situation.

31124 ■ *"To Sell or Not To Sell" in Inc. (December 2007, pp. 80)*
Pub: Gruner & Jahr USA Publishing

Ed: Patrick J. Sauer. **Description:** Owner of a private equity discusses the challenges he faces when deciding to sell his family's business.

31125 ■ *"Toward a Theory of Stakeholder Salience in Family Firms" in Business Ethics Quarterly (Vol. 21, April 2011, No. 2, pp. 235)*
Pub: Society for Business Ethics

Ed: Ronald K. Mitchell, Bradley R. Agle, James J. Chrisman, Laura J. Spence. **Description:** The notion of stakeholder salience based on attributes (e.g. power, legitimacy, urgency) is applied in the family business setting.

31126 ■ *"Transportation Enterprise" in Advertising Age (Vol. 79, June 9, 2008, No. 23, pp. S10)*
Pub: Crain Communications, Inc.

Ed: Jean Halliday. **Description:** Overview of Enterprise rent-a-car's plan to become a more environmentally-friendly company. The family-owned business has spent $1 million a year to plant trees since 2006 and has added more fuel-efficient cars, hybrids and flex-fuel models.

31127 ■ *"Trouble With Transport" in Farmer's Weekly (March 28, 2008, No. 320)*
Pub: Reed Business Information
Contact: Jeff Greisch, President

Description: Profile of Richard Crewe and his wife Jane who farm alongside a main trans-Canadian railway line but keep getting pushed back on their delivery of malt barley.

31128 ■ *"UC's Goering Center to Get New Director" in Business Courier (Vol. 24, February 15, 2008, No. 45, pp. 3)*
Pub: American City Business Journals, Inc.

Ed: Dan Monk. **Description:** Kent Lutz, director of University of Cincinnati Goering (UC) Center for Family & Private Business is to leave the resource center in June 2008 after nine years of service. Changes in the UC-affiliated institute include the expansion of the board from three to seven members and developing new programs related to family businesses.

31129 ■ *"Ultimate Business of the Week: McDougals Sewing Center" in Houston Chronicle (December 2, 2010)*
Pub: Houston Chronicle

Description: Profile of family owned, McDouglas Sewing Center located in Houston, Texas. The shop offers computerized sewing machines, supplies, classes and repairs.

31130 ■ *"Up, Up and Away" in Small Business Opportunities (November 2007)*
Pub: Harris Publications Inc.

Ed: Stan Roberts. **Description:** Profile of Miniature Aircraft USA, a mail order business providing kits to build flying machines priced from $500 to $2,500.

31131 ■ *"We All Scream for Ice Cream" in Crain's Chicago Business (Vol. 31, April 28, 2008, No. 17, pp. 48)*
Pub: Crain Communications, Inc.

Ed: Phuong Ly. **Description:** Profile of Oberweis' ice cream shops which has expanded its business by delivering dairy products to grocery stores.

31132 ■ *"We Do: Copreneurs Simultaneously Build Happy Marriages and Thriving Enterprises" in Black Enterprise (Vol. 38, February 2008)*
Pub: Earl G. Graves Publishing Co. Inc.

Ed: Krissah Williams. **Description:** Of the 2.7 million businesses in the U.S. that are equally owned by male-female partnerships, about 79,000 are black-owned. One couple shares their experiences of working and growing their business together.

31133 ■ *When Family Businesses are Best*
Pub: Palgrave Macmillan

Ed: Randel S. Carlock, John L. Ward. **Released:** March 1, 2010. **Price:** $45.00. **Description:** An exploration into effective planning and communication to help small businesses grow into multi-generation family enterprises.

31134 ■ *"Wowing Her Customers" in Women In Business (Vol. 61, August-September 2009, No. 4, pp. 34)*
Pub: American Business Women's Association

Ed: Kathleen Leighton. **Description:** Gail Worth, together with her brother, bought her parents' Harley-Davidson motorcycle dealership in Grandview, Missouri. She eventually had the dealership to herself when her brother broke out of the partnership. Gail says she is comfortable in a man's world kind of business and has expanded the business with a 10-acre site.

31135 ■ *"Your Lawyer: An Owner's Manual, a Business Owner's Guide to Managing Your Lawyer" in Family Business Review (June 2006)*
Pub: Family Firm Institute
Contact: Judy L. Green, President

Ed: Jane Hilburt-Davis. **Description:** Profile of the guide for managing a lawyer for a family-owned small business.

31136 ■ *"Your Turn in the Spotlight" in Inc. (Volume 32, December 2010, No. 10, pp. 57)*
Pub: Inc. Magazine

Ed: John Brandon. **Description:** Examples of three video blogs created by entrepreneurs to promote their businesses and products are used to show successful strategies. Wine Library TV promotes a family's wine business; SHAMA.TV offers marketing tips and company news; and Will It Blend? promotes sales of a household blender.

TRADE PERIODICALS

31137 ■ *Estate Planners Alert*
Pub: Research Institute of America
Contact: Peter Warwick, President

Released: Monthly. **Price:** $210. **Description:** Spotlights critical developments in estate and financial planning.

31138 ■ *Family Business Advisor*
Pub: Family Enterprise Publishers

Ed: Craig E. Aronoff, Ph.D., Editor. **Released:** Monthly, 12/year. **Price:** $195, U.S.; $210, Canada; $225, elsewhere. **Description:** Covers business management, family relations, and asset protection. Addresses succession planning, estate planning, conflict management, compensation, family meetings, strategic planning, and board composition. Recurring features include news of research.

VIDEOCASSETTES/ AUDIOCASSETTES

31139 ■ *The Agony and the Ecstasy—The Special Problems of Running a Closely-Held or Family Business*
RMI Media
1365 N. Winchester St.
Olathe, KS 66061-5880
Ph: (913)768-1696
Free: 800-745-5480
Fax: (800)755-6910
Co. E-mail: actmedia@act.org
URL: http://www.actmedia.com
Released: 1989. **Price:** $149.00. **Description:** About 90% of American businesses are family-owned. Find out their disadvantages and advantages and what makes them so special. **Availability:** VHS; 3/4 U.

CONSULTANTS

31140 ■ Calmas Associates
62 Fairway Rd.
Chestnut Hill, MA 02467
Ph: (617)277-9244
Fax: (617)277-2021
Co. E-mail: wcalmas@calmasassociates.com
URL: http://www.calmasassociates.com
Contact: Paul Mazonson, President
Scope: Offers sales productivity services, specializing in intra-corporate communications, employee relations, and motivation. Offers unique coaching program for increasing sales force productivity. Also serves in resolving family conflicts. Industries served: all, but primarily insurance and stock brokerage in New England. Executive coach. **Founded:** 1984. **Publications:** "Overcoming People Problems"; "How to Combat High Sales Force Turnover," Boston Business Journal. **Seminars:** How to Communicate with Difficult People, Jan, 2009; Succession Issues for Family Owned Businesses; Role of Psychoanalysis in the Succession Process; The Sports Approach for Success in Sales.

31141 ■ Dean Fowler Associates Inc.
200 S Executive Dr., Ste. 101
Brookfield, WI 53005
Ph: (262)271-5979
Co. E-mail: dean@deanfowler.com
URL: http://www.deanfowler.com
Contact: Dr. Dean R. Fowler, President
E-mail: dean@deanfowler.com
Scope: Offers management services in family dynamics in family owned businesses. Services include: management development and peer interaction, maintaining family harmony and business success, and resolving personal and interpersonal issues. Industries served: Family businesses, all industries. **Founded:** 1983. **Publications:** "Forums for Family Business," 2006; "The Family Forum," 2005; "The Bermuda Triangle," 2003; "Love, Power and Money: Family Business Between Generations," Glengrove Publishing, May, 2002.

31142 ■ Family Business Institute Inc.—Family Business Experts
904 Steffi Ct.
Lawrenceville, GA 30044-6933
Ph: (770)952-4085
Fax: (770)432-6660
Co. E-mail: asktheexpert@family-business-experts.com
URL: http://www.family-business-experts.com
Contact: Wayne Rivers, President
Scope: Assists families in business to achieve personal, family, and organizational goals by meeting challenges that are unique to family-owned businesses. Provides coordinated and integrated assessments and solutions for family issues and needs; for company finance and for human resource and operational requirements. **Founded:** 1985. **Publications:** "Professional Intervention in the Family Owned Business"; "Building Consensus in a Family Business"; "Professionalizing Family Business Management"; "Recognizing generations - know them by their weekends"; "Succession planning tactics"; "Succession Planning Obstacles in Family Business"; "Suc-

cession: three ways to ease the transition"; "Pruning the family business tree"; "Responsibility diffusion - the most critical impediment to successfully growing any kind of business"; "Breaking Up is Hard to Do: Divorce in the Family Business".

31143 ■ Frankel and Topche P.C.
1700 Galloping Hill Rd.
Kenilworth, NJ 07033
Ph: (908)298-7700
Fax: (908)298-7701
Co. E-mail: info@frankelandtopche.com
URL: http://www.frankelandtopche.com
Contact: Mark J. Tikkanen, Director
E-mail: mtikkanen@frankelandtopche.com
Scope: Offers financial consulting for closely held businesses. Assists in mergers and acquisitions, tax planning, strategic business planning, family succession planning, accounting, auditing, and obtaining financing. The firm serves small businesses in the service, retail, wholesale, and manufacturing industries. Specializes in real estate, lumber and building materials, and service businesses. **Founded:** 1990. **Seminars:** Annual Tax Seminar.

31144 ■ Management Growth Institute (MGI)
27 Chelmsford Rd.
Rochester, NY 14618
Ph: (585)461-1353
Fax: (585)461-5266
Co. E-mail: kbalbertini@managementgrowth.com
URL: http://www.managementgrowth.com
Contact: Kathleen B. Albertini, Chief Executive Officer
E-mail: kbalbertini@managementgrowth.com
Scope: Offers assistance in the specification, design, and implementation of management development programs. Clients include individuals, small businesses, national trade associations, and government agencies. **Founded:** 1961. **Publications:** "Cost Reduction Is Your Company the Target," InFocus Magazine, Apr, 2010; "Fall-I hired this great person," The Canadian Mover, Dec, 2009; "Profit Strategies," Direction Magazine, Jul, 2009; "Customer Loyalty," InFocus Magazine, Jul, 2009; "Cash Management," The Portal Magazine, Jul, 2009; "What is Customer Loyalty," In FOCUS Magazine, Dec, 2008; "Strategies to Improve Profits," Aug, 2008; "A Question of Management," Moving World. **Seminars:** Profit Enhancement; Family-Owned Businesses; Strategic Planning; Survival and Growth in a Down Economy.

31145 ■ Profit Planning Consultants
617 Fields Dr.
Lafayette Hill, PA 19444-1511
Ph: (610)828-1999
Contact: Martin Feinberg, Owner
Scope: Strengthening the Family Firm; Increasing the value of the business and preserving the heritage; Provides a full range of management services to independently-owned companies; Services cover such areas as operations analysis, planning and budgeting, marketing and sales, organizational development, succession planning, debt and equity financing, employee training and motivation as well as acquisitions, mergers and sales of business. Client's sales range from over $1 million to $50 million; Client base covers a broad range of family-owned businesses in all industries; Teaches the entrepreneur survival and growth techniques that become his own and develop with him/her the company's succession plan. **Founded:** 1982. **Seminars:** How to Enter International Markets; Time Management; Leadership, Professional Selling Skills; Managing a Family Owned Business; Profit Opportunities for Your Business; Family vs. Business; Doubling Your Net Profit; Transferring Management in a Family Owned Business.

31146 ■ ReGENERATION Partners
3811 Turtle Creek, Blvd., Ste. 300
Dallas, TX 75219
Ph: (214)559-3999
Free: 800-406-1112
Fax: (214)559-4299
Co. E-mail: info@regeneration-partners.com
URL: http://www.regeneration-partners.com
Contact: James Olan Hutcheson, President
E-mail: jim@regeneration-partners.com
Scope: Specializes in business expertise growth strategies, competitive planning, crisis intervention, dispute resolution, interim management, bridge management, strategic planning, team selection, transitional management, employee assessment, business planning, management skills training, profit enhancement, family perspective, conflict management, communication barriers, family meetings, wealth preservation, succession planning, management mentoring, family values, family retreats. **Founded:** 1995. **Publications:** "When Siblings Share Leadership," May, 2007; "The End of a 1400-Year-Old Business," Apr, 2007; "Building a Family Business to Last," Mar, 2007; "Dealing with Death in a Family Business," Feb, 2007; "Best Practices for Family Business," Dec, 2006; "Resolving Family Business Conflicts," Nov, 2006; "Coping with Family-Business Ills," Oct, 2006; "Should You Join the Family Business," Sep, 2006; "A Transfer Tsunami for Family Biz," Jun, 2006; "When Kids Play the Guilt Card," Apr, 2006.

31147 ■ Schneider Consulting Group Inc.
50 S Steele St., Ste. 390
Denver, CO 80209-2834
Ph: (303)320-4413
Fax: (303)320-5795
Contact: Kim Schneider Malek, Vice President
E-mail: kim@scgfambus.com
Scope: Assists family-owned and privately-held business transition to the next generation and/or to a more professionally managed company, turn around consulting for small and medium size companies. **Founded:** 1987.

31148 ■ Stier Associates
4 Dunellen
Cromwell, CT 06416-2702
Ph: (860)635-1590
Fax: (860)635-1591
Co. E-mail: sstier7@comcast.net
Contact: Dr. Suzanne Stier, President
Scope: Offers personal development consulting. Services include: succession planning, executive coaching, strategic management, team building, and board development. Consulting services for public companies include: process consulting, team building, executive coaching, diversity management, strategic management and religious institutions. **Founded:** 1981.

31149 ■ The Titens Consulting Group
12612 Cedar St.
Leawood, KS 66209-3148
Ph: (913)469-5279
Fax: (913)469-5192
Co. E-mail: sherman@redzeus.com
URL: http://www.redzeus.com
Contact: Sherman Titens, Owner
E-mail: sherman.titens@gmail.com
Scope: Provider of market positioning, strategic planning and continuing education design, standards, certification for trade associations, professional societies and professional service providers and family businesses. Industries served include banking, financial services, automotive, jewellery, health care, law, materials, joining, retail, environmental programs and distribution. **Founded:** 1993. **Publications:** "NFP"; "Applied Research at the Graduate Level," Parkway Press; "123 Secrets for Success in Your Family Business". **Seminars:** Making Family Business Work; Getting Started With Strategic Planning; Using the Internet as an Educational Tool.

31150 ■ Turnaround Inc.
3415 A St. NW
Gig Harbor, WA 98335
Ph: (253)857-6730
Fax: (253)857-6344
Co. E-mail: info@turnround-inc.com
URL: http://www.turnaround-inc.com
Contact: Miles Stover, President
E-mail: mstover@turnaround-inc.com
Scope: Provider of interim executive management assistance and management advisory to small, medium and family-owned businesses that are not meeting their goals. Services include acting as an interim executive or on-site manager. Extensive practices in arena of bankruptcy management. **Founded:** 1997. **Publications:** "How to Identify Problem and Promising Management"; "How to Tell if Your Company is a Bankruptcy Candidate"; "Signs that Your Company is in Trouble"; "The Turnaround Specialist: How to File a Petition Under 11 USC 11". **Seminars:** Competitive Intelligence Gathering.

START-UP INFORMATION

31151 ■ ***Entrepreneurship and the Financial Community Starting Up and Growing New Businesses***
Pub: Edward Elgar Publishing, Incorporated
Ed: Clarysse. **Released:** November 2006. **Price:** $75.00. **Description:** Understanding the role of private equity providers in the development and growth processes of small business.

31152 ■ ***How to Get the Financing for Your New Small Business: Innovative Solutions from the Experts Who Do It Every Day***
Pub: Atlantic Publishing Company
Ed: Sharon L. Fullen. **Released:** May 2006. **Price:** $39.95, includes companion CD-Rom. **Description:** Ready capital is essential for starting and expanding a small business. Topics include traditional financing methods, financial statements, and a good business plan.

31153 ■ ***How to Start a Bankruptcy Forms Processing Service***
Pub: Graphico Publishing Company
Ed: Victoria Ring. **Released:** September 2004. **Price:** $39.00. **Description:** Due to the increase in bankruptcy filings, attorneys are outsourcing related jobs in order to reduce overhead.

31154 ■ ***Working for Yourself: An Entrepreneur's Guide to the Basics***
Pub: Kogan Page, Limited
Contact: Ben Glover, Director of Marketing
Ed: Jonathan Reuvid. **Released:** September 2006. **Description:** Guide for starting a new business venture, focusing on raising financing, legal and tax issues, marketing, information technology, and site location.

EDUCATIONAL PROGRAMS

31155 ■ Advanced Auditing for In-Charge Auditors (Onsite)
Seminar Information Service, Inc.
20 Executive Park, Ste. 120
Irvine, CA 92614
Ph: (949)261-9104
Free: 877-SEM-INFO
Fax: (949)261-1963
Co. E-mail: info@seminarinformation.com
URL: http://www.seminarinformation.com
Price: $2,050.00. **Description:** Learn all of the elements involved in traditional and operational auditing from the unique perspective of the in-charge position, while reviewing concepts such as audit program flexibility, risk assessment, priority setting during fieldwork, and effective oral and written communications of audit findings. **Dates and Locations:** Chicago, IL; Las Vegas, NV; Atlanta, GA; and New York, NY.

31156 ■ Advanced Collection Strategies (Onsite)
Seminar Information Service, Inc.
20 Executive Park, Ste. 120
Irvine, CA 92614
Ph: (949)261-9104
Free: 877-SEM-INFO
Fax: (949)261-1963
Co. E-mail: info@seminarinformation.com
URL: http://www.seminarinformation.com
Price: $369.00. **Description:** Learn the secrets to getting what's owed while complying with strict debtor protection laws, including strategies for defending against collection harassment claims should they arise.

31157 ■ Advanced Cost Accounting (Onsite)
Seminar Information Service, Inc.
20 Executive Park, Ste. 120
Irvine, CA 92614
Ph: (949)261-9104
Free: 877-SEM-INFO
Fax: (949)261-1963
Co. E-mail: info@seminarinformation.com
URL: http://www.seminarinformation.com
Price: $2,195.00 for non-members; $1,995.00 for AMA members. **Description:** Learn to incorporate Activity-Based Costing with advanced traditional costing methodologies determining true product cost information.

31158 ■ AMA's Finance Workshop for Nonfinancial Executives (Onsite)
American Management Association
600 AMA Way
Saranac Lake, NY 12983-5534
Ph: (212)586-8100
Free: 877-566-9441
Fax: (518)891-0368
Co. E-mail: customerservice@amanet.org
URL: http://www.amaseminars.org
Price: $2,645.00 for non-members; $2,395.00 for AMA members; and $2,051.00 for General Services Administration (GSA) members. **Description:** Comprehensive four-day seminar covering all aspects of corporate finance. **Dates and Locations:** New York, NY; Chicago, IL; San Francisco, CA; Washington, DC; and Arlington, VA.

31159 ■ Collections Law (Onsite)
Fred Pryor Seminars & CareerTrack
5700 Broadmoor St., Ste. 300
Mission, KS 66202
Free: 800-780-8476
Fax: (913)967-8849
Co. E-mail: customerservice@pryor.com
URL: http://www.pryor.com
Price: $149.00; $139.00 for groups of 5 or more. **Description:** Ensure your organization is legally compliant, including strategies and techniques to gain quicker results in collecting money. **Dates and Locations:** Cities throughout the United States.

31160 ■ Corporate Cash Management (onsite)
Seminar Information Service, Inc.
20 Executive Park, Ste. 120
Irvine, CA 92614
Ph: (949)261-9104
Free: 877-SEM-INFO
Fax: (949)261-1963
Co. E-mail: info@seminarinformation.com
URL: http://www.seminarinformation.com
Price: $1,995.00. **Description:** Introductory course that covers how money moves, how to accelerate cash receipts, how to select the right cash management bank, and how to make better use of excess funds through short-term investments.

31161 ■ Creative Ways to Cut and Control Costs (Onsite)
Fred Pryor Seminars & CareerTrack
5700 Broadmoor St., Ste. 300
Mission, KS 66202
Free: 800-780-8476
Fax: (913)967-8849
Co. E-mail: customerservice@pryor.com
URL: http://www.pryor.com
Price: $149.00; $139.00 for groups of 5 or more. **Description:** Learn how to control business expenses to create an organization that is competitive, profitable, and growth focused. **Dates and Locations:** Cities throughout the United States.

31162 ■ The Essentials of Cash Flow Forecasting (Onsite)
Fred Pryor Seminars & CareerTrack
5700 Broadmoor St., Ste. 300
Mission, KS 66202
Free: 800-780-8476
Fax: (913)967-8849
Co. E-mail: customerservice@pryor.com
URL: http://www.pryor.com
Price: $249.00; $229.00 for groups of 3 or more. **Description:** Learn to make better budget decisions through proven strategies and techniques. **Dates and Locations:** Cities throughout the United States.

31163 ■ Export/Import Procedures and Documentation (Onsite)
American Management Association
600 AMA Way
Saranac Lake, NY 12983-5534
Ph: (212)586-8100
Free: 877-566-9441
Fax: (518)891-0368
Co. E-mail: customerservice@amanet.org
URL: http://www.amaseminars.org
Price: $2,195.00 for non-members; $1,995.00 for AMA members; and $1,708.00 for General Services Administration (GSA) members. **Description:** Covers export and import guidelines and regulations, business documentation practices, using foreign trade zones, and financial aspects of importing and exporting. **Dates and Locations:** Chicago, IL; and New York, NY.

31164 ■ Financial & Accounting Concepts, Statements & Terminology: 2 Day (Onsite)
Seminar Information Service, Inc.
20 Executive Park, Ste. 120
Irvine, CA 92614
Ph: (949)261-9104
Free: 877-SEM-INFO

Fax: (949)261-1963
Co. E-mail: info@seminarinformation.com
URL: http://www.seminarinformation.com
Price: $399.00. **Description:** Financial and accounting training in plain English. **Dates and Locations:** Cities throughout the United States.

31165 ■ Financial Modeling and Forecasting
Canadian Management Centre (CMC)
150 York St., 5th Fl.
Toronto, ON, Canada M5H 3S5
Ph: (416)214-5678
Free: 877-262-2519
Fax: (416)313-4985
Co. E-mail: cmcinfo@cmctraining.org
URL: http://www.cmctraining.org
Contact: John Wright, President
Price: $2,195.00 for members; $2,395.00 for non-members. **Description:** This highly interactive course helps you build more powerful and accurate forecasting models that fast-track decision making and improve end results. **Dates and Locations:** Toronto, ON.

31166 ■ Financial Statement Analysis (Onsite)
Seminar Information Service, Inc.
20 Executive Park, Ste. 120
Irvine, CA 92614
Ph: (949)261-9104
Free: 877-SEM-INFO
Fax: (949)261-1963
Co. E-mail: info@seminarinformation.com
URL: http://www.seminarinformation.com
Price: $199.00. **Description:** Enhance your ability to read, analyze and use financial statements to manage, drive and stay on top of your company's growth, including how to understand the specialized language of finance and quickly scan a financial report and pick out the numbers that matter and detect variance while there's time to take corrective action. **Dates and Locations:** Cities throughout the United States.

31167 ■ How to Implement Effective Internal Controls (Onsite)
Fred Pryor Seminars & CareerTrack
5700 Broadmoor St., Ste. 300
Mission, KS 66202
Free: 800-780-8476
Fax: (913)967-8849
Co. E-mail: customerservice@pryor.com
URL: http://www.pryor.com
Price: $199.00; $189.00 for groups of 5 or more. **Description:** Learn to protect, maintain, and control your financial structure while streamlining your business. **Dates and Locations:** Cities throughout the United States.

31168 ■ How to Manage & Organize Accounts Payable (Onsite)
Fred Pryor Seminars & CareerTrack
5700 Broadmoor St., Ste. 300
Mission, KS 66202
Free: 800-780-8476
Fax: (913)967-8849
Co. E-mail: customerservice@pryor.com
URL: http://www.pryor.com
Price: $195.00; $185.00 for groups of 5 or more. **Description:** Learn how to organize your files, records, and workspace for maximum organization and flow. **Dates and Locations:** Cities throughout the United States.

31169 ■ How to Read and Understand Financial Statements (Onsite)
Fred Pryor Seminars & CareerTrack
5700 Broadmoor St., Ste. 300
Mission, KS 66202
Free: 800-780-8476
Fax: (913)967-8849
Co. E-mail: customerservice@pryor.com
URL: http://www.pryor.com
Price: $249.00; $229.00 for groups of 3 or more. **Description:** Learn how to read financial statements, interpret their data, and put that information to positive use. **Dates and Locations:** Cities throughout the United States.

31170 ■ Know Your Basic Finance (Onsite)
Seminar Information Service, Inc.
20 Executive Park, Ste. 120
Irvine, CA 92614
Ph: (949)261-9104
Free: 877-SEM-INFO
Fax: (949)261-1963
Co. E-mail: info@seminarinformation.com
URL: http://www.seminarinformation.com
Price: $370.00. **Description:** Learn and understand the principles of accounting and interpret statements to determine the financial health of the organization, including how to create and monitor budgets.

31171 ■ The Nonfinancial Manager's Guide to Understanding Financial Statements (Onsite)
Padgett-Thompson Seminars
Rockhurst University CEC
14502 W. 105th St.
Lenexa, KS 66215
Free: 800-349-1935
URL: http://www.findaseminar.com/tpd/Padgett-Thompson-Seminars.asp
Price: $299.00. **Description:** Comprehensive, fast-paced, one-day seminars that covers all the essentials of understanding financial statements. **Dates and Locations:** Baltimore, MD; San Antonio, TX; Houston, TX; Oklahoma City, OK.

31172 ■ Principles of Cost and Finance for Engineers (Onsite)
Seminar Information Service, Inc.
20 Executive Park, Ste. 120
Irvine, CA 92614
Ph: (949)261-9104
Free: 877-SEM-INFO
Fax: (949)261-1963
Co. E-mail: info@seminarinformation.com
URL: http://www.seminarinformation.com
Price: $1,545.00. **Description:** Learn to make and justify financial decisions using sound economic principles, including how to use current economic strategies to reduce costs and improve productivity, estimate capital and manufacturing or service costs, identify the relationship between direct and marginal costs in the decision making process, and execute strategies for resource allocation and cost-control measures. **Dates and Locations:** Norwalk, CA.

31173 ■ Successful Inventory Management (Onsite)
Fred Pryor Seminars & CareerTrack
5700 Broadmoor St., Ste. 300
Mission, KS 66202
Free: 800-780-8476
Fax: (913)967-8849
Co. E-mail: customerservice@pryor.com
URL: http://www.pryor.com
Price: $199.00; $189.00 for groups of 5 or more. **Description:** Learn proven cost saving methods that improve inventory and cycle count accuracy. **Dates and Locations:** Cities throughout the United States.

31174 ■ Valuation Strategies for Both Sides of the Deal (Onsite)
American Management Association
600 AMA Way
Saranac Lake, NY 12983-5534
Ph: (212)586-8100
Free: 877-566-9441
Fax: (518)891-0368
Co. E-mail: customerservice@amanet.org
URL: http://www.amaseminars.org
Price: $2,345.00 for non-members; $2,095.00 for AMA members; and $1,794.00 for General Services Administration (GSA) members. **Description:** Learn how to establish the real value of any company. **Dates and Locations:** Atlanta, GA.

REFERENCE WORKS

31175 ■ *"13D Filings" in Barron's (Vol. 88, March 24, 2008, No. 12, pp. M13)*
Pub: Dow Jones & Company, Inc.
Description: HealthCor Management called as problematic the plan of Magellan Health Services to use its high cash balances for acquisitions. Carlson Capital discussed with Energy Partners possible changes in the latter's board. Investor Carl Icahn suggested that Enzon Pharmaceuticals consider selling itself or divest some of its assets.

31176 ■ *"13D Filings" in Barron's (Vol. 88, March 10, 2008, No. 10, pp. M11)*
Pub: Dow Jones & Company, Inc.
Description: Barington Capital and Clinton Group sent a letter to Dillard's demanding a list of the company's stockholders. Elliott Associates announced that it is prepared to take over Packeteer for $5.50 a share. Strongbow capital suggested a change in leadership in Duckwall-ALCO Stores.

31177 ■ *"13D Filings: Investors Report to the SEC" in Barron's (Vol. 88, March 31, 2008, No. 13, pp. M10)*
Pub: Dow Jones & Company, Inc.
Description: Obrem Capital Management wants Micrel to rescind Micrel's shareholder-rights plan and to boost its board to six members from five. Patricia L. Childress plans to nominate herself to the board of Sierra Bancorp, and Luther King Capital Management may consider a competing acquisition proposal for Industrial Distribution Group.

31178 ■ *"13D Filings: Investors Report to the SEC" in Barron's (Vol. 88, March 17, 2008, No. 11, pp. M11)*
Pub: Dow Jones & Company, Inc.
Description: Nanes Delorme wants Vaalco Energy to keep an investment bank to start an open-bid process to sell the company. West Creek Capital plans to nominate two directors at the 2008 annual meeting of the Capital Senior Living just as ValueVest Management wants to nominate the same number of people at Ampex's annual meeting.

31179 ■ *"13D Filings: Investors Report to the SEC" in Barron's (Vol. 89, July 13, 2009, No. 28, pp. M9)*
Pub: Dow Jones & Co., Inc.
Description: Bulldog Investors wants Hicks Acquisition Co. to liquidate and return money to shareholders and they believe that the acquisition of Graham Packaging by Hicks will not be completed in a timely manner. Discovery Group raised their holdings to 5.2 percent of Nobel Learning Communities.

31180 ■ *"13D Filings: Investors Report to the SEC" in Barron's (Vol. 89, July 27, 2009, No. 30, pp. M14)*
Pub: Dow Jones & Co., Inc.
Description: Duquesne Capital Management is opposed to Alpha Natural Resources' proposed merger with Foundation Coal Holdings since it is against the long-term interest of shareholders. Lime Rock Partners increased their holdings of Tesco to 5,234,516 shares while Nova A/S increased their holdings of BioMimetic Therapeutics to 3,729,065 shares.

31181 ■ *"A 16-Year Housing Slump? It Could Happen" in Barron's (Vol. 88, March 17, 2008, No. 11, pp. 27)*
Pub: Dow Jones & Company, Inc.
Ed: Gene Epstein. **Description:** Housing remains a good protection against inflation but over very long periods. Inflation-adjusted stock prices did even better but have greater volatility. Commodities, on the other hand, underperformed both housing and stocks as inflation hedges. House prices tend to rise faster than the consumer price index is because land is inherently limited.

31182 ■ *"The 100 Most Bullish Stocks" in Canadian Business (Vol. 81, Summer 2008, No. 9, pp. 81)*
Pub: Rogers Media Ltd.
Ed: Megan Harman; Lauren McKeon. **Description:** 100 of the most bullish stocks are taken from the list of the 500 best-performing stocks. The idea is to narrow the list help investors in their investment decisions since it is difficult to choose from a large list. Analysts rate the companies with 5 being the most bullish and 1 the least. Other details of the roster are presented.

31183 ■ *"401(k) Keys to Stable Value" in Barron's (Vol. 88, March 10, 2008, No. 10, pp. 40)*
Pub: Dow Jones & Company, Inc.
Ed: Tom Sullivan. **Description:** Stable-value funds offer investors stability in a period of volatility in financial markets, attracting $888 million in funds. The Securities and Exchange Commission approved the launch of actively managed exchange-traded funds.

31184 ■ *"529.com Wins Outstanding Achievement in Web Development" in Investment Weekly (November 14, 2009, pp. 152)*
Pub: Investment Weekly News
Description: Web Marketing Association's 2009 WebAward for Financial Services Standard of Excellence and Investment Standard of Excellence was won by 529.com, the website from Upromise Investments, Inc., the leading administrator of 529 college savings plans.

31185 ■ *"2010 Book of Lists" in Tampa Bay Business Journal (Vol. 30, December 22, 2009, No. 53, pp. 1)*
Pub: American City Business Journals
Description: Rankings of companies and organizations within the human resources, banking and finance, business services, healthcare, real estate, technology, hospitality and travel, and education industries in the Greater Tampa Bay area are presented. Rankings are based on sales, business size, and more.

31186 ■ *Access to Finance*
Pub: Brookings Institution Press
Ed: Barr. **Released:** December 2006. **Price:** $39.95. **Description:** Challenges to help make financial systems more inclusive to promote successful venture in new markets while utilizing new technologies and government policies to expand financial access to smaller companies.

31187 ■ *The Accidental Entrepreneur: The 50 Things I Wish Someone Had Told Me About Starting a Business*
Pub: AMACOM
Ed: Susan Urquhart-Brown. **Released:** March 2008. **Price:** $17.95. **Description:** Advice is offered to any would-be entrepreneur, including eight questions to ask before launching a new business, ten traits of a successful entrepreneur, how to obtain licenses and selling permits, best way to create a business plan, ten ways to get referrals, six secrets of marketing, investment and financial information, ways to avoid burnout, and the seven biggest pitfalls to avoid.

31188 ■ *Accounting and Finance for Your Small Business*
Pub: John Wiley & Sons, Incorporated
Ed: Steven M. Bragg; E. James Burton. **Released:** April 2006. **Price:** $49.00. **Description:** Financial procedures and techniques for establishing and maintaining a profitable small company are outlined.

31189 ■ *"Accrual vs. Cash Accounting, Explained" in Business Owner (Vol. 35, July-August 2011, No. 4, pp. 13)*
Pub: DL Perkins Company
Description: Cash method versus accrual accounting methods are examined, using hypothetical situations.

31190 ■ *"After Price Cuts, Competition GPS Makers Lose Direction" in Brandweek (Vol. 49, April 21, 2008, No. 16, pp. 16)*
Pub: VNU Business Media, Inc.
Ed: Steve Miller. **Description:** Garmin and TomTom, two of the leaders in portable navigation devices, have seen lowering revenues due to dramatic price cuts and unexpected competition from the broadening availability of personal navigation on mobile phones. TomTom has trimmed its sales outlook for its first quarter while Garmin's stock dropped 40 percent since February.

31191 ■ *"Ag Firms Harvest Revenue Growth" in The Business Journal-Serving Metropolitan Kansas City (Vol. 26, July 18, 2008, No. 45, pp. 1)*
Pub: American City Business Journals, Inc.
Ed: Steve Vockrodt. **Description:** Five of the biggest agricultural companies in the Kansas City area, except one, reported multibillion-dollar revenue increases in 2007. The companies, which include Lansing Trade Group, posted a combined $9.5 billion revenue growth. The factors that affected the revenue increase in the area's agricultural companies, such as prices and high demand, are also examined.

31192 ■ *"AIG Fixed; Is Michigan Next?" in Crain's Detroit Business (Vol. 24, September 22, 2008, No. 38, pp. 1)*
Pub: Crain Communications Inc.
Ed: Jay Greene. **Description:** Michigan's economic future is examined as is the mortgage buyout plan and American International Group Inc.'s takeover by the U.S. government.

31193 ■ *"All Eyes On Iris" in Canadian Business (Vol. 81, July 22, 2008, No. 12-13, pp. 20)*
Pub: Rogers Media Ltd.
Ed: Jack Mintz. **Description:** Provincial governments in Canada are believed to be awaiting Alberta Finance Minister Iris Evans' financial and investment policies as well as Evans' development of a new saving strategy. Alberta is the only Canadian province that is in position to invest in sovereign wealth funds after it eliminated its debt in 2005.

31194 ■ *All the Money in the World: How the Forbes 400 Make - and Spend - Their Fortunes*
Pub: AMACOM
Ed: Peter W. Bernstein; Annalyn Swan. **Released:** September 2007. **Description:** A fascinating and historical breakdown of the 400 richest Americans according to Forbes magazine. The book examines how the list's members actually make and spend their money. Illustrating the text with charts and informational sidebars, readers are given the opportunity to look at both production and consumption and insights in social and historical context.

31195 ■ *American Bar Association Legal Guide for Small Business: Everything You Need to Know About Small Business*
Pub: Random House Information Group
Contact: Markus Dohle, Accountant
Ed: American Bar Association. **Released:** June 10, 2010. **Description:** The American Bar Association provides insight into financial, health and family issues affecting small business, including start up issues, employment laws, financing a business, and selling a business.

31196 ■ *"The Annual Entitlement Lecture: Trustees of Medicare and Social Security Issue Another Dismal Report" in Barron's (March 31, 2008)*
Pub: Dow Jones & Company, Inc.
Ed: Thomas G. Donlan. **Description:** Expenditures on Medicare hospital insurance and the revenues available to pay for it have led to a gap of capital valued at $38.6 trillion. Slashing the benefits or raising taxes will not solve the gap which exists unless the government saves the money and invests it in private markets.

31197 ■ *"Antwerpen Takes on Chrysler Financial Over Foreclosure Sales" in Baltimore Business Journal (Vol. 28, July 30, 2010, No. 12, pp. 1)*
Pub: Baltimore Business Journal
Ed: Gary Haber. **Description:** Antwerpen Motorcars Ltd. aims to fight the scheduled foreclosure sale of real estate it leases in Baltimore County, including the showroom for its Hyundai dealership on Baltimore National Pike in Catonsville, Maryland. The company is planning to file papers in court to stop the scheduled August 11, 2010 auction sought by Chrysler Financial Services Americas LLC.

31198 ■ *Are the Rich Necessary? Great Economic Arguments and How They Reflect Our Personal Values*
Pub: Axios Press
Contact: Stephanie Bosserman, President
Ed: Hunter Lewis. **Released:** 2007. **Price:** $20.00. **Description:** Investment advisor argues whether today's economic system promotes greed. Each chapter of the book poses a question and then he answers.

31199 ■ *"Are You Ready for Dow 20,000?" in Barron's (Vol. 88, March 24, 2008, No. 12, pp. 26)*
Pub: Dow Jones & Company, Inc.
Ed: Jonathan R. Laing. **Description:** Stock strategist James Finucane forecasts that the Dow Jones Industrial Average will rise from its 12,361 level to as high as 20,000 from 2008 to 2009. He believes that stock liquidation and a buildup of cash provide the perfect conditions for a huge rally.

31200 ■ *"Are You Ready To Do It Yourself? Discipline and Self-Study Can Help You Profit From Online Trading" in Black Enterprise (Feb. 2008)*
Pub: Earl G. Graves Publishing Co. Inc.
Ed: Steve Garmhausen. **Description:** Steps to help individuals invest in stocks online is given by an expert broker. Discount brokerage houses can save money for online investors.

31201 ■ *The Ascent of Money: A Financial History of the World*
Pub: Penguin Group USA Inc.
Ed: Niall Ferguson. **Released:** 2009. **Price:** $29.95. **Description:** How financial considerations prompted the Crusades and other surprising explanations of famous events are uncovered.

31202 ■ *"Asia Breathes a Sigh of Relief" in Business Week (September 22, 2008, No. 4100, pp. 32)*
Pub: McGraw-Hill Companies, Inc.
Ed: Bruce Einhorn; Theo Francis; Chi-Chu Tschang; Moon Ihlwan; Hiroko Tashiro. **Description:** Foreign bankers, such as those in Asia, that had been investing heavily in the United States began to worry as the housing crisis deepened and the impact on Freddie Mac and Fannie Mae became increasingly clear. Due to the government bailout, however, central banks will most likely continue to buy American debt.

31203 ■ *"ATS Secures Investment From Goldman Sachs" in The Business Journal - Serving Phoenix and the Valley of the Sun (Vol. 29, September 26, 2008, No. 4, pp. 1)*
Pub: American City Business Journals, Inc.
Ed: Patrick O'Grady. **Description:** Goldman Sachs made an investment to American Traffic Solutions Inc. (ATS) which will allow it to gain two seats on the board of the red-light and speed cameras maker. The investment will help ATS maintain its rapid growth which is at 83 percent over the past 18 months leading up to September 2008.

31204 ■ *"Attend To Your Corporate Housekeeping" in Women Entrepreneur (December 4, 2008)*
Pub: Entrepreneur Media Inc.
Ed: Nina Kaufman. **Description:** Business owners can lose all the benefits and privileges of the corporate form if they do not follow proper corporate formalities such as holding an annual meeting, electing officers and directors and adopting or passing corporate resolutions. Creditors are able to take from one's personal assets if such formalities have not been followed.

31205 ■ *"Au Revoir Or Goodbye?" in Barron's (Vol. 88, July 14, 2008, No. 28, pp. 5)*
Pub: Dow Jones & Co., Inc.
Ed: Alan Abelson. **Description:** Former Senator Phil Gramm's opinion that the U.S. is a 'nation of whiners' as they moan about recession is another example of the disconnection between Washington and Wall Street on one hand and the real world on the

other. It would be a catastrophe for most of the world if Fannie Mae and Freddie Mac were to go under and take their trillions of mortgage debt with them.

31206 ■ *"Auction-Rate Cash Frees Up" in The Business Journal-Portland (Vol. 25, August 15, 2008, No. 23, pp. 1)*
Pub: American City Business Journals, Inc.
Ed: Aliza Earnshaw. **Description:** FEI Co. and RadiSys Corp. have received notices that UBS AG will buy back the auction-rate securities that were sold to them in around two years from 2008. FEI had $110.1 million invested in auction-rate securities while RadiSys holds $62.8 million of these securities.

31207 ■ *"Auto Supplier Stock Battered In Wake Of Wall Street Woes" in Crain's Detroit Business (Vol. 24, September 29, 2008, No. 39, pp. 4)*
Pub: Crain Communications Inc.
Ed: Ryan Beene. **Description:** Due to the volatility of the stock market and public perception of the $700 billion banking bailout, auto suppliers are now facing a dramatic drop in their shares. Statistical data included.

31208 ■ *"BABs in Bond Land" in Barron's (Vol. 89, July 6, 2009, No. 27, pp. 14)*
Pub: Dow Jones & Co., Inc.
Ed: Jim McTague. **Description:** American Recovery and Reinvestment Act has created taxable Build America Bonds (BAB) to finance new construction projects. The issuance of the two varieties of taxable BABs is expected to benefit the municipal bond market.

31209 ■ *"Baby's Room Franchisee Files Bankruptcy" in Crain's Detroit Business (Vol. 25, June 22, 2009, No. 25, pp. 15)*
Pub: Crain Communications Inc. - Detroit
Ed: Gabe Nelson. **Description:** Emery L, a franchisee of USA Baby Inc. and ran the franchised Baby's Room Nursery Furniture stores in the area has filed for bankruptcy. Details of the bankruptcy are included.

31210 ■ *"Back in the Race" in Barron's (Vol. 88, March 17, 2008, No. 11, pp. 43)*
Pub: Dow Jones & Company, Inc.
Ed: Leslie P. Norton. **Description:** Katherine Schapiro was able to get Sentinel International Equity's Morningstar classification to blended fund from a value fund rating after joining Sentinel from her former jobs at Strong Overseas Fund. Schapiro aims to benefit from the global rebalancing as the U.S.'s share of the world economy shrinks.

31211 ■ *"Back Talk with Chris Gardner" in Black Enterprise (Vol. 37, January 2007, No. 6, pp. 112)*
Pub: Earl G. Graves Publishing Co. Inc.
Ed: Kenneth Meeks. **Description:** Profile of with Chris Gardner and his Chicago company, Gardner Rich L.L.C., a multimillion-dollar investment firm. During an interview, Gardner discusses his rise from homelessness. His story became a book, The Pursuit of Happyness and was recently released as a film starring Will Smith.

31212 ■ *"Back on Track-Or Off the Rails?" in Business Week (September 22, 2008, No. 4100, pp. 22)*
Pub: McGraw-Hill Companies, Inc.
Ed: Peter Coy; Tara Kalwarski. **Description:** Discusses the possible scenarios the American economy may undergo due to the takeover of Fannie Mae and Freddie Mac. Statistical data included.

31213 ■ *"Bad-Loan Bug Bites Mid-Tier Banks; More Pain, Tighter Lending Standards Ahead, CEOs Say" in Crain's Chicago Business (May 5, 2008)*
Pub: Crain Communications, Inc.
Ed: Steve Daniels. **Description:** Mid-sized commercial banks form the bedrock of Chicago's financial-services industry and they are now feeling the results of the credit crisis that has engulfed the nation's largest banks and brokerages. Commercial borrowers are seeing tighter terms on loans and higher interest rates while bank investors are unable to forecast lenders' earnings performance from quarter to quarter. Statistical data included.

31214 ■ *"Bad Loans Start Piling Up" in Crain's New York Business (Vol. 24, January 7, 2008, No. 1, pp. 2)*
Pub: Crain Communications, Inc.
Ed: Tom Fredrickson. **Description:** Problems in the subprime mortgage industry have extended to other lending activities as evidenced by bank charge-offs on bad commercial and industrial loans which have more than doubled in the third quarter.

31215 ■ *Bad Money*
Pub: Viking Press/Penguin Group
Ed: Kevin Phillips. **Released:** April 15, 2008. **Description:** How the financial sector has hijacked the American economy, aided by Washington's ruinous faith in the efficiency of markets.

31216 ■ *"Bailout Forgets the 'Little Guys'" in The Business Journal-Milwaukee (Vol. 25, September 26, 2008, No. 53, pp. A1)*
Pub: American City Business Journals, Inc.
Ed: Rich Kirchen. **Description:** Community Bankers of Wisconsin and the Wisconsin Bankers Association are urging members to approach congressional representatives and remind them to include local banks in building the $700 billion bailout plan. WBA president and CEO Kurt Bauer thinks that it is only fair to include smaller institutions in the bailout. The initial bailout plan and its benefit for the smaller banks are examined.

31217 ■ *"Bailout May Force Cutbacks, Job Losses" in The Business Journal - Serving Phoenix and the Valley of the Sun (Vol. 29, September 26, 2008, No. 4, pp. 1)*
Pub: American City Business Journals, Inc.
Ed: Mike Sunnucks. **Description:** Economists say the proposed $700 billion bank bailout could affect Arizona businesses as banks could be forced to reduce the amount and number of loans it has thereby forcing businesses to shrink capital expenditures and then jobs. However, the plan could also stimulate the economy by taking bad loans off banks balance sheets according to another economist.

31218 ■ *"Balancing Risk and Return in a Customer Portfolio" in Journal of Marketing (Vol. 75, May 2011, No. 3, pp. 1)*
Pub: American Marketing Association
Ed: Crina O. Tarasi, Ruth N. Bolton, Michael D. Hutt, Beth A. Walker. **Description:** A framework for reducing the vulnerability and volatility of cash flows in customer portfolios is presented. The efficient portfolios of firms are identified and tested against their current portfolios and hypothetical profit maximization portfolios.

31219 ■ *"BancVue to Expand" in Austin Business JournalInc. (Vol. 29, November 27, 2009, No. 38, pp. 1)*
Pub: American City Business Journals
Ed: Kate Harrington. **Description:** Significant growth of BancVue in the past six years has prompted the company to look for a site that could increase its office space from 25,000 square feet to 65,000 square feet. BancVue offers bank and credit union software solutions and is planning to lease or buy a property in Austin, Texas.

31220 ■ *"Bank Bullish on Austin" in Austin Business JournalInc. (Vol. 29, November 13, 2009, No. 36, pp. A1)*
Pub: American City Business Journals
Ed: Kate Harrington. **Description:** American Bank's presence in Austin, Texas has been boosted by new management and a new 20,000 square foot building. This community bank intends to focus on building relationship with commercial banking customers. American Bank also plans to extend investment banking, treasury management, and commercial lending services.

31221 ■ *The Bank Directory*
Pub: Accuity Inc.
Contact: Hugh M. Jones, IV, President
URL(s): store.accuitysolutions.com/order.html. **Released:** Semiannual; June and December. **Price:** $1195, Individuals. **Covers:** In five volumes, about 11,000 banks and 50,000 branches of United States banks, and 60,000 foreign banks and branches engaged in foreign banking; Federal Reserve system and other United States government and state government banking agencies; 500 largest North American and International commercial banks; paper and automated clearinghouses. Volumes 1 and 2 contain North American listings; volumes 3 and 4, international listings (also cited as 'Thomson International Bank Directory; volume 5, Worldwide Correspondents Guide containing key correspondent data to facilitate funds transfer. **Entries include:** For domestic banks--Bank name, address, phone, telex, cable, date established, routing number, charter type, bank holding company affiliation, memberships in Federal Reserve System and other banking organizations, principal officers by function performed, principal correspondent banks, and key financial data (deposits, etc.). For international banks--Bank name, address, phone, fax, telex, cable, SWIFT address, transit or sort codes within home country, ownership, financial data, names and titles of key personnel, branch locations. For branches--Bank name, address, phone, charter type, ownership and other details comparable to domestic bank listings. **Database includes:** Bank operations information, asset ranking in state and country, bank routing numbers in numeric sequence, discontinued or changed bank names in geographical sequence. **Arrangement:** Geographical. **Indexes:** Alphabetical, geographical.

31222 ■ *"Bank Forces Brooke Founder To Sell His Holdings" in The Business Journal-Serving Metropolitan Kansas City (October 10, 2008)*
Pub: American City Business Journals, Inc.
Ed: James Dornbrook. **Description:** Robert Orr who is the founder of Brooke Corp., a franchise of insurance agencies, says that he was forced to sell virtually all of his stocks in the company by creditors. First United Bank held the founder's stock as collateral for two loans worth $5 million and $7.9 million, which were declared in default in September 2008. Details of the selling of the company's stocks are provided.

31223 ■ *"Bank on It" in Hawaii Business (Vol. 53, November 2007, No. 5, pp. 60)*
Pub: Hawaii Business Publishing
Ed: Kathleen Bryan. **Description:** Many Baby Boomers that are preparing to retire would like to give back and make a difference. One way is to make gifts of Individual Retirement Assets (IRA). During 2007 people over 70 years can make withdrawals from an IRA and donate it without realizing the income as taxable.

31224 ■ *"Banking Bailout: Boost or Bust?" in Crain's Detroit Business (Vol. 24, September 29, 2008, No. 39, pp. 1)*
Pub: Crain Communications Inc.
Ed: Amy Lane. **Description:** Economic insiders discuss the banking bailout and how it might impact the state of Michigan.

31225 ■ *"A Banking Play Without Banking Plagues" in Barron's (Vol. 88, March 31, 2008, No. 13, pp. 26)*
Pub: Dow Jones & Company, Inc.
Ed: Jack Willoughby. **Description:** Fiserv's shares have been dragged down by about 20 percent which presents an appealing entry point since the shares could rise by 30 percent or more by 2009. The company enables banks to post and open new checks and keeps track of loans which are not discretionary processes of banks.

31226 ■ *"Banking on Twitter" in Baltimore Business Journal (Vol. 27, February 6, 2010, No. 40, pp. 1)*
Pub: American City Business Journals
Ed: Gary Haber. **Description:** Ways that banks are using Twitter, Facebook and other social networking sites to provide customer services is discussed. First Mariner Bank is one of those banks that are finding the social media platform as a great way to reach customers. Privacy issues regarding this marketing trend are examined.

31227 ■ *"The Bankrate Double Pay" in Barron's (Vol. 88, March 24, 2008, No. 12, pp. 27)*
Pub: Dow Jones & Company, Inc.
Ed: Neil A. Martin. **Description:** Shares of Bankrate may rise as much as 25 percent from their level of $45.08 a share due to a strong cash flow and balance sheet. The company's Internet business remains strong despite weakness in the online advertising industry and is a potential takeover target.

31228 ■ *"Bankruptcies Shoot Up 68 Percent" in Sacramento Business Journal (Vol. 25, July 18, 2008, No. 20, pp. 1)*
Pub: American City Business Journals, Inc.
Ed: Kathy Robertson. **Description:** Personal bankruptcy in the Sacramento area rose by 88 percent for the first half of 2008 while business bankruptcies rose by 50 percent for the same period. The numbers of consumer bankruptcy reflects the effect of high debt, rising mortgage costs, and declining home values on U.S. households.

31229 ■ *"Bankruptcy Blowback" in Business Week (September 22, 2008, No. 4100, pp. 36)*
Pub: McGraw-Hill Companies, Inc.
Ed: Jessica Silver-Greenberg. **Description:** Changes to bankruptcy laws which were enacted in 2005 after banks and other financial institutions lobbied hard for them are now suffering the consequences of the laws which force more troubled borrowers to let their homes go into foreclosure; lenders suffer financially every time they have to take on a foreclosure and the laws in which they lobbied so hard to see enacted are now becoming a problem for these lending institutions. Details of the changes in the laws are outlined as are the affects on the consumer, the economy and the lenders.

31230 ■ *Bankruptcy for Small Business*
Pub: Sphinx Publishing
Ed: Wendell Schollander. **Released:** July 1, 2008. **Price:** $22.95 paperback. **Description:** Bankruptcy laws can be used to save a small business, homes or other property. The book provides general information for small business owners regarding the reasons for money problems, types of bankruptcy available and their alternatives, myths about bankruptcy, and the do's and don'ts for filing for bankruptcy.

31231 ■ *Bankruptcy for Small Business, 2E: Know Your Legal Rights and Recover from Mistakes and Start Over Successfully*
Pub: Sourcebooks, Inc.
Contact: Len Vlahos, President
E-mail: dominique@sourcebooks.com
Ed: Wendell Schollander; Wes Schollander. **Released:** July 2008. **Price:** $22.95. **Description:** Bankruptcy laws can actually help small business owners save their companies, homes and other property. This book offers general information regarding reasons for money problems, types of bankruptcy available to small business owners as well as alternatives to bankruptcy and more.

31232 ■ *"Banks Beef Up Deposits, But Lending Lags" in Baltimore Business Journal (Vol. 28, October 29, 2010, No. 25, pp. 1)*
Pub: Baltimore Business Journal
Ed: Gary Haber. **Description:** Bank deposits in the Greater Baltimore area have increased but commercial loans have not. Small business owners complain that banks do not help them expand their businesses, but banks argue that they want to lend but the borrowers have to meet standard qualifications.

31233 ■ *"Banks Deposit Reassurance, Calm Customers" in The Business Journal-Serving Greater Tampa Bay (Vol. 28, August 22, 2008)*
Pub: American City Business Journals, Inc.
Ed: Margie Manning. **Description:** Community banks in the Tampa Bay Area are training tellers and other customer care workers to help reassure customers that their deposits are safe. Other measures to reassure depositors include joining a network that allows banks to share deposits. Additional information on moves community banks are making to reassure consumers is presented.

31234 ■ *"Banks Fall Short in Online Services for Savvy Traders" in Barron's (Vol. 88, March 17, 2008, No. 11, pp. 35)*
Pub: Dow Jones & Company, Inc.
Ed: Theresa W. Carey. **Description:** Banc of America Investment Services, WellsTrade, and ShareBuilder are at the bottom of the list of online brokerages because they offer less trading technologies and product range. Financial shoppers miss out on a lot of customized tools and analytics when using these services.

31235 ■ *"Banks Find Borrowers Off the Beaten Path" in Boston Business Journal (Vol. 30, December 3, 2010, No. 45, pp. 1)*
Pub: Boston Business Journal
Ed: Tim McLaughlin. **Description:** Banks in Boston have found unlikely applicants for bank loans in organizations such as the Dorchester Collegiate Academy. Dorchester is a charter school in its second year of operation, but qualified for $1.08 million to finance its own building. Other information, as well as views on the unexpected borrowers in Boston, is presented.

31236 ■ *"Banks Fret About Gist Of Bailout" in The Business Journal-Serving Metropolitan Kansas City (Vol. 27, September 26, 2008, No. 2)*
Pub: American City Business Journals, Inc.
Ed: James Dornbrook. **Description:** Banks from the Kansas City area hope that the proposed $700 billion bailout will not send the wrong message. UMB Financial Corp. chairman says that he hopes that the bailout would benefit companies that were more risk restrained and punish those that took outsized risk. Other bank executives' perceptions on the planned bailout are given.

31237 ■ *"Banks Lower Rates on CDs, Deposits" in Baltimore Business Journal (Vol. 27, January 1, 2010, No. 35, pp. 1)*
Pub: American City Business Journals
Ed: Gary Haber. **Description:** Greater Baltimore area banks in Maryland have lowered their rates on certificates of deposits (CDs) and money market accounts, which could indicate the incoming trend for the first half of 2010. A banking industry forecast shows that lower Federal Funds rate, low inflation, and a new Federal Deposit Insurance Corporation (FDIC) rule might cause the rates to drop even further. Details on the FDIC rule are given.

31238 ■ *"Banks, Retailers Squabble Over Fees" in Baltimore Business Journal (Vol. 28, June 18, 2010, No. 6, pp. 1)*
Pub: Baltimore Business Journal
Ed: Gary Haber. **Description:** How an amendment to the financial regulatory reform bill would affect the bankers' and retailers' conflict over interchange fees is discussed. Interchange fees are paid for by retailers every time consumers make purchases through debit cards. Industry estimates indicate that approximately $50 million in such fees are paid by retailers.

31239 ■ *"Banks Seeing Demand for Home Equity Loans Slowing" in Crain's Cleveland Business (Vol. 28, December 3, 2007, No. 48, pp. 1)*
Pub: Crain Communications, Inc.
Ed: Shawn A. Turner. **Description:** Discusses the reasons for the decline in demand for home equity loans and lines of credit. Statistical data included.

31240 ■ *"Bargain Hunting In Vietnam" in Barron's (Vol. 88, July 14, 2008, No. 28, pp. M6)*
Pub: Dow Jones & Co., Inc.
Ed: Elliot Wilson. **Description:** Vietnam's economy grew by just 6.5 percent for the first half of 2008 and its balance of payments ballooned to $14.4 billion. The falling stock prices in the country is a boon for bargain hunters and investing in the numerous domestic funds is one way of investing in the country. Some shares that investors are taking an interest in are also discussed.

31241 ■ *"Barron's Lipper Fund Listings" in Barron's (Vol. 89, July 13, 2009, No. 28, pp. 19)*
Pub: Dow Jones & Co., Inc.
Description: Statistical tables are presented which show the assets and return of mutual funds up to a ten year period. The listing covers funds with at least $200 million in assets.

31242 ■ *"Basel3 Quick Fix Actually Neither" in Canadian Business (Vol. 83, October 12, 2010, No. 17, pp. 19)*
Pub: Rogers Media Ltd.
Ed: Thomas Watson. **Description:** Information about the so-called Basel 3 standards, which will require banks to hold top-quality capital totaling at least 7 percent of their risk-bearing assets is provided. The rules' supporters believe that a good balance has been reached between improving the Basel 2 framework and maintaining enough lending capital to stimulate an economic growth.

31243 ■ *"Battle of the Titans" in Canadian Business (Vol. 81, March 17, 2008, No. 4, pp. 15)*
Pub: Rogers Media
Ed: Rachel Pulfer. **Description:** Regulatory authorities in Canada gave Thomson Corp and Reuters Group PLC the permission to go ahead with their merger. The merged companies could eclipse Bloomberg LP's market share of 33 percent. Authorities also required Thomson and Reuters to sell some of their databases to competitors.

31244 ■ *Battling Big Box: How Nimble Niche Companies Can Outmaneuver Giant Companies*
Pub: Career Press, Inc.
Ed: Henry Dubroff, Susan J. Marks. **Released:** January 1, 2009. **Price:** $15.99. **Description:** Small companies can compete with larger firms through agility, adaptability, customer service, and credibility. Topics include information to help empower employees, build a powerful brand, manage cash flow, and maintaining a business vision.

31245 ■ *"BDC Launches New Online Business Advice Centre" in Internet Wire (July 13, 2010)*
Pub: Comtex
Description: The Business Development Bank of Canada (BDC) offers entrepreneurs the chance to use their new online BDC Advice Centre in order to seek advice regarding the challenges of entrepreneurship. Free online business tools and information to help both startups and established firms are also provided.

31246 ■ *"The Bear Arrives - With Bargain Hunters" in Barron's (Vol. 88, July 7, 2008, No. 27, pp. M3)*
Pub: Dow Jones & Co., Inc.
Ed: Kopin Tan. **Description:** US stock markets have dropped 20 percent below their highs, entering the bear market at the end of June 2008. It was also the worst performance of the stock markets during June. Wine maker Constellation Brands, however, reported a 50 percent rise in net income for the first quarter of 2008.

31247 ■ *"Bear Market Tough On Investors" in The Business Journal-Milwaukee (Vol. 25, July 4, 2008, No. 41, pp. A1)*
Pub: American City Business Journals, Inc.
Ed: Rich Kirchen. **Description:** Public companies and their investors in the Milwaukee area suffered as the bear market took hold of the Wisconsin stock market. There were 18 stocks out of the 36 publicly traded stocks that have fallen into the bear market, meaning a 20 percent decline from the market peak in the fall of 2007. The impacts of the bear market on investors are evaluated.

31248 ■ *"The Bear's Back" in Barron's (Vol. 88, July 7, 2008, No. 27, pp. 17)*
Pub: Dow Jones & Co., Inc.
Ed: Randall W. Forsyth; Vito Racanelli. **Description:** US stock markets have formally entered the bear market after the Dow Jones Industrial Average

dropped 20 percent from its high as of June 2008. Investors remain uncertain as to how long the bear market will persist, especially with the US economy on the edge of recession.

31249 ■ *"Beat the Buck: Bartering Tips from In-The-Know Authors" in (June 23, 2010)*
Pub: The Telegraph

Ed: Jill Moon. **Description:** The Art of Barter is a new book to help small businesses learn this art form in order to expand customer base and reserve cash flow.

31250 ■ *"Beaumont Outsources Purchasing as Route to Supply Cost Savings" in Crain's Detroit Business (Vol. 25, June 1, 2009, No. 22)*
Pub: Crain Communications Inc. - Detroit

Ed: Jay Greene. **Description:** William Beaumont Hospitals in Royal Oak have begun outsourcing the purchasing of supplies in order to cut costs. So far, Beaumont is the only hospital in southeast Michigan to outsource its purchasing department. Other hospitals employ their own purchasing supply workers.

31251 ■ *"The Beauty of Banking's Big Ugly" in Barron's (Vol. 89, July 27, 2009, No. 30, pp. 31)*
Pub: Dow Jones & Co., Inc.

Ed: Andrew Bary. **Description:** Appeal of the shares of Citigroup comes from its sharp discount to its tangible book value and the company's positive attributes include a strong capital position, high loan-loss reserves, and their appealing global-consumer. The shares have the potential to generate nice profits and decent stock gains as the economy turns.

31252 ■ *"Behind the Numbers: When It Comes to Earnings, Look for Quality, Not Just Quantity" in Black Enterprise (July 2008, pp. 35)*
Pub: Earl G. Graves Publishing Co. Inc.

Ed: Chris Keenan. **Description:** It is important for investors to examine the quality of a company's earnings rather than fixate on the quantity of those earnings. Advice is given regarding issues investors can look at when trying to determine the potential growth of a firm.

31253 ■ *"Bertha's Birth Stirs Juice" in Barron's (Vol. 88, July 14, 2008, No. 28, pp. M11)*
Pub: Dow Jones & Co., Inc.

Ed: Tom Sellen. **Description:** Price of frozen concentrated orange juice, which has risen to four-month highs of $1.3620 in July 2008 is due, in part, to the hurricane season that has come earlier than normal in the far eastern Atlantic thereby possibly harming the 2008-2009 Florida orange crop. Future tropical-storm development will affect the prices of this commodity.

31254 ■ *"Best Cash Flow Generators" in Canadian Business (Vol. 81, Summer 2008, No. 9, pp. 73)*
Pub: Rogers Media Ltd.

Ed: Calvin Leung. **Description:** Table showing the five-year annualized growth rate and one-year stock performance of companies that have grown their cash flow per share at an annualized rate of 15 percent or more over the past five years. Analysts project that the cash flow trend will continue. Other details of the stock performance index are presented.

31255 ■ *"Best Cash Flow Generators" in Canadian Business (Vol. 82, Summer 2009, No. 8, pp. 40)*
Pub: Rogers Media

Ed: Calvin Leung. **Description:** Agrium Inc. and FirstService Corporation are in the list of firms that are found to have the potential to be the best cash flow generators in Canada. The list also includes WestJet Airlines Ltd., which accounts for 385 flights each day. More than 80 percent of analysts rate the airline stocks a Buy.

31256 ■ *"Best Defensive Stocks" in Canadian Business (Vol. 81, Summer 2008, No. 9, pp. 67)*
Pub: Rogers Media Ltd.

Ed: Calvin Leung. **Description:** Stocks of the companies presented have market capitalization of greater than $1 billion and dividend gains of at least 2 percent. A table showing the average one-year total return of the stocks is provided.

31257 ■ *"The Best Five-Month Run Since 1938" in Barron's (Vol. 89, August 3, 2009, No. 31, pp. M3)*
Pub: Dow Jones & Co., Inc.

Ed: Kopin Tan. **Description:** US stock markets ended July 2009 registering the highest five-month rise since 1938. The shares of Cablevision could rise as the company simplifies its structure and spins off its Madison Square Garden unit. The shares of Potash Corp. could fall as the company faces lower earnings due to falling potash purchases.

31258 ■ *"Best Growth Stocks" in Canadian Business (Vol. 81, Summer 2008, No. 9, pp. 61)*
Pub: Rogers Media Ltd.

Ed: Calvin Leung. **Description:** Table showing the one-year performance of growth stocks is presented. Edmonton-based Stantec Inc. expects to advance its sales and profits by 15 percent to 20 percent per year through tapping international markets and acquisitions. Analysts forecast a 17.1 percent growth rate annually over the next 3 to 5 years.

31259 ■ *"Best Growth Stocks" in Canadian Business (Vol. 82, Summer 2009, No. 8, pp. 28)*
Pub: Rogers Media

Ed: Calvin Leung. **Description:** Canadian stocks that are considered as the best growth stocks, and whose price-earnings ratio is less than their earnings growth rate, are suggested. Suggestions include pharmaceutical firm Paladin Labs, which was found to have 13 consecutive years of revenue growth. Paladin Labs acquires or licenses niche drugs and markets them in Canada.

31260 ■ *"Best Income Trust" in Canadian Business (Vol. 81, Summer 2008, No. 9, pp. 69)*
Pub: Rogers Media Ltd.

Ed: Calvin Leung. **Description:** Table showing five-year annualized growth rate and one-year stock performance of real estate investment trusts firms in Canada is presented. Calgary-based Boardwalk REIT is projected to grow the fastest among North American REITs over the next two years. Other details on the stock performance analysis are presented.

31261 ■ *"Best Managed Companies" in Canadian Business (Vol. 81, Summer 2008, No. 9, pp. 71)*
Pub: Rogers Media Ltd.

Ed: Calvin Leung. **Description:** Table showing the five-year annualized growth rate and one-year stock performance of companies that have grown their cash flow per share at an annualized rate of 15 percent or more over the past five years. Analysts project that the cash flow trend will continue. Other details of the stock performance index are presented.

31262 ■ *"Best Turnaround Stocks" in Canadian Business (Vol. 81, Summer 2008, No. 9, pp. 65)*
Pub: Rogers Media Ltd.

Ed: Calvin Leung. **Description:** Share prices of Sierra Wireless Inc. and EXFO Electro Optical Engineering Inc. have fallen over the past year but have good chance at a rebound considering that the companies have free cash flow and no long-term debt. One-year stock performance analysis of the two companies is presented.

31263 ■ *"Best Value Stocks" in Canadian Business (Vol. 81, Summer 2008, No. 9, pp. 63)*
Pub: Rogers Media Ltd.

Ed: Calvin Leung. **Description:** Table showing the one-year performance of bargain or best-value stocks is presented. These stocks are undervalued compared to their North American peers, but it is projected that their five-year average return on equity is greater.

31264 ■ *"Best Value Stocks" in Canadian Business (Vol. 82, Summer 2009, No. 8, pp. 30)*
Pub: Rogers Media

Ed: Calvin Leung. **Description:** Canadian companies that are believed to have the best value stocks are suggested. Suggestions include publishing firm Glacier Media, which has reported a four-fold growth in sales in the last three years. While publishers like Glacier Media face challenges such as declining circulation, the firm's industry diversification is expected to help it weather the economic downturn.

31265 ■ *"Bet on the Subcontinent" in Canadian Business (Vol. 81, April 14, 2008, No. 6, pp. 27)*
Pub: Rogers Media

Ed: Calvin Leung. **Description:** Morgan Stanley Capital International India Index is down 28 percent for the first half of 2008 but this index rebounded 6 percent in 2002 then skyrocketed 65 percent in 2003. The economic reforms in the 1990's have created a growing middle class and households that can afford discretionary items will grow from eight million to 94 million by 2025. India's equity market could outperform developed markets if its economy grows at its current rate.

31266 ■ *"Betting Big, Winning Big" in Barron's (Vol. 88, March 17, 2008, No. 11, pp. 49)*
Pub: Dow Jones & Company, Inc.

Ed: Lawrence C. Strauss. **Description:** Bruce Berkowitz explains that the reason that his portfolio is concentrated is because getting more positions makes the portfolio more average compared to putting the money into your 10th or 20th-best idea. Berkowitz' picks include Berkshire Hathaway, Well-Care Health Plus, Sears Holdings, and Mohawk Industries.

31267 ■ *"Betting on a Happy Ending" in Barron's (Vol. 88, July 7, 2008, No. 27, pp. 14)*
Pub: Dow Jones & Co., Inc.

Ed: Dimitra DeFotis. **Description:** Shares of Time Warner, priced at $14.69 each, appear under-priced as financial analysts discount the value of the company. The company should be worth more than $20 a share as the company is spinning off Time Warner Cable.

31268 ■ *"Betting On Volatile Materials" in Barron's (Vol. 88, July 14, 2008, No. 28, pp. M11)*
Pub: Dow Jones & Co., Inc.

Ed: John Marshall. **Description:** Economic slowdowns in the U.S., Europe and China could cause sharp short-term declines in the materials sector. The S&P Materials sector is vulnerable to shifts in the flow of funds. Statistical data included.

31269 ■ *"Beware the Ides of March" in Canadian Business (Vol. 81, April 14, 2008, No. 6, pp. 13)*
Pub: Rogers Media

Ed: Jeff Sanford. **Description:** Financial troubles of Bear Stearns in March, 2008 was part of the credit crunch that started in the summer of 2007 in the U.S. when subprime mortgages that were written for people who could barely afford the payments started defaulting. The bankruptcy protection given to 20 asset backed commercial paper trusts is being fought by the investors in these securities who could stand to lose 40 percent of their money under the agreement.

31270 ■ *"Beware of Rotting Money" in Barron's (Vol. 89, July 13, 2009, No. 28, pp. 31)*
Pub: Dow Jones & Co., Inc.

Ed: Thomas G. Donlan. **Description:** Inflation can take hold of a country and do it great harm; it is caused by people, most particularly central bankers in charge of the world's reserve currency. Arrogant economists pushed the belief that the government can engineer the economy and it is argued that there is trouble ahead when the government tries to control the economy.

31271 ■ *"Beyond Microsoft and Yahoo!: Some M&A Prospects" in Barron's (Vol. 88, March 17, 2008, No. 11, pp. 39)*
Pub: Dow Jones & Company, Inc.
Ed: Eric J. Savitz. **Description:** Weak quarterly earnings report for Yahoo! could pressure the company's board to cut a deal with Microsoft. Electronic Arts is expected to win its hostile $26-a-share bid for Take-Two Interactive Software. Potential targets and buyers for mergers and acquisitions are mentioned.

31272 ■ *"The Big 50" in Canadian Business (Vol. 81, Summer 2008, No. 9, pp. 125)*
Pub: Rogers Media Ltd.
Description: Large publicly held corporations are ranked based on market capitalization and stock performance. Potash Corp. of Saskatchewan topped the roster with 169.3 percent of return and even surpassing its 2007 result of 107 percent. A table showing the 2008 rankings of the companies is presented.

31273 ■ *"Big Losses Mount for Hospitals" in Baltimore Business Journal (Vol. 27, October 23, 2009, No. 24, pp. 1)*
Pub: American City Business Journals
Ed: Scott Graham. **Description:** Reported losses by nine of the 22 hospitals in the Greater Baltimore area during fiscal 2009 have proven that the health care industry is not immune to the recession. The rising costs of doing business and losses in the stock market have strongly affected the financial status of hospitals.

31274 ■ *The Big Squeeze: Tough Times for the American Workers*
Pub: Pantheon Books
Ed: Steven Greenhouse. **Released:** 2009. **Price:** $25.95. **Description:** Labor correspondent for the New York Times reports on the bleak condition of the current workplace environment, citing violations of child labor laws and forced slave labor conditions in third world countries and robber baron era occurring often here in America that are expanding the number of working poor.

31275 ■ *"Big Trouble at Sony Ericsson" in Barron's (Vol. 88, March 24, 2008, No. 12, pp. M9)*
Pub: Dow Jones & Company, Inc.
Ed: Angelo Franchini. **Description:** Sony Ericsson is facing trouble as it warned that its sales and net income before taxes will fall by nearly half for the first quarter of 2008. The joint venture of Sony and Ericsson has a global mobile phone market share of nine percent as of 2007, fourth largest in the world.

31276 ■ *"Blackstone's Outlook Still Tough" in Barron's (Vol. 88, March 17, 2008, No. 11, pp. 19)*
Pub: Dow Jones & Company, Inc.
Ed: Andrew Bary. **Description:** Earnings for the Blackstone Group may not recover soon since the company's specialty in big leveraged buyouts is floundering and may not recover until 2009. The company earns lucrative incentive fees on its funds but those fees went negative in the fourth quarter of 2007 and there could be more fee reversals in the future.

31277 ■ *"A Bleak Earnings View" in Barron's (Vol. 88, March 10, 2008, No. 10, pp. 15)*
Pub: Dow Jones & Company, Inc.
Description: Analysts expect consumer discretionary profits in the S&P 500 to drop 8.4 percent in the first quarter of 2008. A less confident consumer is expected to pull profits down, putting forecasts of earnings growth in the S&P 500 at risk. Statistical data included.

31278 ■ *"Bloody Monday for Bear?" in Barron's (Vol. 88, March 17, 2008, No. 11, pp. M14)*
Pub: Dow Jones & Company, Inc.
Ed: Steven M. Sears. **Description:** Shares of Bear Stearns could slip further at the start of the trading week unless the company is bought out or bolstered by some other development over the weekend. Prices of the company's shares in the options market suggests about a 30 percent chance that the stock falls below $20 before March expirations expire.

31279 ■ *"BMW Revs Up for a Rebound" in Barron's (Vol. 89, July 13, 2009, No. 28, pp. M7)*
Pub: Dow Jones & Co., Inc.
Ed: Jonathan Buck. **Description:** Investors may like BMW's stocks because the company has maintained its balance sheet strength and has an impressive production line of new models that should boost sales in the next few years. The company's sales are also gaining traction, although their vehicle delivery was down 1.7 percent year on year on June 2009, this was still the best monthly sales figure for 2009.

31280 ■ *"Boar Market: Penny-Wise Consumers Favoring Pork" in Crain's Chicago Business (Vol. 31, April 14, 2008, No. 15, pp. 4)*
Pub: Crain Communications, Inc.
Ed: Bruce Blythe. **Description:** Interview with Alan Cole who is the president of Cedar Hill Associates Inc. and who discusses ways in which his company is taking advantage of the record highs of oil and natural gas as well as his overall outlook on the market.

31281 ■ *"Board This Powertrain" in Barron's (Vol. 89, July 27, 2009, No. 30, pp. 30)*
Pub: Dow Jones & Co., Inc.
Ed: Naureen S. Malik. **Description:** Siemens' American Depositary Receipts have risen 60 percent from their March 2009 low and they should continue heading higher. The company has solid earnings and revenue growth since they lead in growing markets such as alternative energy and health-care infrastructure. Their shares also look cheap at 1.9 times book value.

31282 ■ *"Boeing Earns Its Wings With Strong Quarter" in Crain's Chicago Business (Vol. 31, April 28, 2008, No. 17, pp. 4)*
Pub: Crain Communications, Inc.
Ed: Daniel Rome Levine. **Description:** Interview with Michael A. Crowe, the senior managing director at Mesirow Financial Investment Management, who discusses highlights from the earnings season so far, his outlook for the economy and the stock market as well as what his company is purchasing. Mr. Crowe also recommends shares of five companies.

31283 ■ *"BofA Goes for Small Business" in Austin Business Journal (Vol. 31, July 22, 2011, No. 20, pp. A1)*
Pub: American City Business Journals Inc.
Ed: Christopher Calnan. **Description:** Bank of America is planning to target small businesses as new customers. The bank lost its number one market share in Austin, Texas in 2010.

31284 ■ *"BofA May Part With U.S. Trust" in Boston Business Journal (Vol. 31, May 20, 2011, No. 17, pp. 1)*
Pub: Boston Business Journal
Ed: Tim McLaughlin. **Description:** Bank of America Corporation is willing to sell its U.S. Trust private banking division to improve its capital ratio. The unit remains to be the corporation's core asset and posted $696 million revenue in the first quarter 2010 in contract with Merrill Lynch Global Wealth Management's $3.5 billion. Analysts say that U.S. Trust would fetch more than $3 billion.

31285 ■ *Bonds - the Other Market*
Pub: AuthorHouse
Ed: George L. Fulton. **Released:** March 16, 2005. **Price:** $15.50. **Description:** Professional bond broker provides fundamental information to help investors choose the bond market an alternative to the stock market. The book describes the various types of bonds available, including treasury bonds, issued by the U.S. Government; municipal bonds, issued by a municipal authority of a local or state government; and corporate bonds, issued by corporations. Risk vs. reward in bond investing is also covered.

31286 ■ *"Bonds v. Stocks: Who's Right About Recession?" in Barron's (Vol. 90, August 23, 2010, No. 34, pp. M3)*
Pub: Barron's Editorial & Corporate Headquarters
Ed: Kopin Tan. **Description:** The future of treasury securities and stocks should the U.S. enter or avoid a recession are discussed. The back to school business climate and BHP Billiton's bid for Potash Corporation of Saskatchewan are also discussed.

31287 ■ *"Book of Lists 2010" in Philadelphia Business Journal (Vol. 28, December 25, 2009, No. 45, pp. 1)*
Pub: American City Business Journals
Description: Rankings of companies and organizations within the banking, biotechnology, economic development, healthcare, hospitality, law and accounting, marketing and media, real estate, and technology industries in the Philadelphia, Pennsylvania area are presented. Rankings are based on sales, business size, and more.

31288 ■ *"The Book On Indigo" in Canadian Business (Vol. 81, July 22, 2008, No. 12-13, pp. 29)*
Pub: Rogers Media Ltd.
Ed: Thomas Watson. **Description:** Indigo Books & Music Inc. reported record sales of $922 million resulting in a record net profit of $52.8 million for the 2008 fiscal year ended March 29, 2008. Earnings per share were $2.13, greater than Standard & Poor's expected $1.70 per share. Additional information concerning Indigo Books is presented.

31289 ■ *"Boston Hedge Fund Pours Money Into Real Estate Projects" in Charlotte Business Journal (Vol. 25, December 3, 2010, No. 37, pp. 1)*
Pub: Charlotte Business Journal
Ed: Will Boye. **Description:** Boston-based hedge fund Baupost Group has been financing real estate project in Charlotte, North Carolina including more than 80 acres just north of uptown. Aside from purchasing the $23.8 million note for the Rosewood Condominiums from Regions Financial Corporation, the Baupost Group is also negotiating with Regions to buy the $93.9 million debt of the EipCentre real estate project.

31290 ■ *"Bottler Will Regain Its Pop" in Barron's (Vol. 88, March 17, 2008, No. 11, pp. 56)*
Pub: Dow Jones & Company, Inc.
Ed: Alexander Eule. **Description:** Discusses he 30 percent drop in the share price of PepsiAmericas Inc. from their 2007 high which presents an opportunity to buy into the company's dependable U.S. market and fast growing Eastern European business. The bottler's Eastern European operating profits in 2007 grew to $101 million from $21 million in 2006.

31291 ■ *"Bottom-Fishing and Speed-Dating in India" in Barron's (Vol. 88, March 24, 2008, No. 12, pp. M12)*
Pub: Dow Jones & Company, Inc.
Ed: Elliot Wilson. **Description:** Indian stocks have fallen hard in 2008, with Mumbai's Sensex 30 down 30 percent from its January 2008 peak of 21,000 to 14,995 in March. The India Private Equity Fair 2008 attracted 140 of the world's largest private equity firms and about 24 of India's fastest-growing corporations. Statistical data included.

31292 ■ *"Bountiful Barrels: Where to Find $140 Trillion" in Barron's (Vol. 88, July 14, 2008, No. 28, pp. 40)*
Pub: Dow Jones & Co., Inc.
Ed: Andrew Bary. **Description:** Surge in oil prices has caused a large transfer of wealth to oil-producing countries thereby reshaping the global economy. Oil reserves of oil exporting countries are now valued at $140 trillion. Economist Stephen Jen believes that this wealth will be transformed into paper assets as these countries invest in global stocks and bonds.

31293 ■ *"Bracing for a Bear of a Week" in Barron's (Vol. 88, March 17, 2008, No. 11, pp. 24)*
Pub: Dow Jones & Company, Inc.
Ed: Jacqueline Doherty. **Description:** JPMorgan Chase and the Federal Reserve Bank of New York's opening of a line of credit to Bear Stearns cut the

stock price of Bear Stearns by 47 percent to 30 followed by speculation of an imminent sale. JP Morgan may be the only potential buyer for the firm and some investors say Bears could be sold at $20 to $30. Bears prime assets include its enormous asset base worth $395 billion.

31294 ■ *Bridging the Equity Gap for Innovative SMEs*
Pub: Palgrave Macmillan
Ed: Elisabetta Gualandri. **Released:** December 1, 2009. **Price:** $85.00. **Description:** This book addresses the evaluation of financial constraints faced by innovative and startup companies and explores ways for bridging the financing and equity gap faced by small to medium business enterprises.

31295 ■ *"Brooke Agents Claim Mistreatment" in The Business Journal-Serving Metropolitan Kansas City (Vol. 27, October 24, 2008, No. 7, pp. 1)*
Pub: American City Business Journals, Inc.
Ed: James Dornbrook. **Description:** Franchisees of Brooke Corp., an insurance franchise, face uncertainty as their bills remain unpaid and banks threaten to destroy their credit. The company bundled and sold franchisee loans to different banks, but the credit crunch left the company with massive debts and legal disputes.

31296 ■ *"Building Portfolios for a World of 2.5 Percent Gains" in Barron's (Vol. 88, July 7, 2008, No. 27, pp. L9)*
Pub: Dow Jones & Co., Inc.
Ed: Karen Hube. **Description:** Interview with Harold Evenski whom is a financial planner running a fee-only planning practice; he continues to caution investors against pursuing short-term gains and focusing on long-term trends. He advises investors against investing in commodity and real estate stocks and is concerned about the possible effects of high inflation.

31297 ■ *Business Black Belt: Develop the Strength, Flexibility and Agility to Run Your Company*
Pub: Career Press, Inc.
Ed: Burke Franklin. **Released:** November 1, 2010. **Price:** $15.99. **Description:** Manual offering insights that will enable anyone to become successful in small business. Seventy short chapters included topics such as attitude, management, marketing, selling, employees, money, MBAs, lawyers, consultants, and investors.

31298 ■ *"Business Execs Await Walker's Tax Cut Plan" in Business Journal-Milwaukee (Vol. 28, December 17, 2010, No. 11, pp. A1)*
Pub: Milwaukee Business Journal
Ed: Rich Kirchen. **Description:** Wisconsin governor-elect Scott Walker has to tackle the state's projected $3.3 billion budget deficit, which became the subject of speculation among business groups and state politic watchers. Walker has pledged to reduce the state taxes without driving costs down to the local government and school district level.

31299 ■ *Business Management for Tropical Dairy Farmers*
Pub: CSIRO Publishing
Ed: John Moran. **Released:** August 1, 2009. **Price:** $33.95. **Description:** Business management skills required for dairy farmers are addressed, focusing on financial management and ways to improve cattle housing and feeding systems.

31300 ■ *"But Who's Counting.." in Canadian Business (Vol. 79, Winter 2006, No. 24, pp. 27)*
Pub: Rogers Media
Ed: David Wolf. **Description:** The analysis of the debt management policies of the Canadian government is presented. The plans of the Canadian government to repay all of its debts by the year 2020 are discussed.

31301 ■ *"Buyers' Market" in Baltimore Business Journal (Vol. 27, November 20, 2009, No. 28, pp. 1)*
Pub: American City Business Journals
Ed: Daniel J. Sernovitz. **Description:** Some business owners in Maryland are removing their leases and purchasing buildings due to the lower costs of real estate. This trend has enabled small business owners to avoid rent hikes, while setting equity into their companies. The pros and cons of owning buildings and how business owners assess their return on investment are examined.

31302 ■ *"C.A. Bancorp Inc. (TSX:BKP) Announces First Quarter 2007 Financial Results" in Canadian Corporate News (May 16, 2007)*
Pub: Comtex News Network Inc.
Description: Financial report for the first quarter of 2007 for C.A. Bancorp Inc., a publicly traded Canadian merchant bank and asset manager providing investors access to a range of private equity and alternative asset class investment opportunities. Statistical data and highlights included.

31303 ■ *"Calming Customers" in The Business Journal-Portland (Vol. 25, August 29, 2008, No. 25, pp. 1)*
Pub: American City Business Journals, Inc.
Ed: Kirsten Grind; Rob Smith. **Description:** Credit unions and banks in the Portland area are reaching out to clients in an effort to reassure them on the security of their money and the firms' financial stability. Roy Whitehead of Washington Federal Savings, for instance, wrote 41,000 customers of the bank to reassure them. The strategies of different banks and credit unions to answer their client's worries are discussed.

31304 ■ *"Cambodia Calls" in Barron's (Vol. 89, July 27, 2009, No. 30, pp. M7)*
Pub: Dow Jones & Co., Inc.
Ed: Leslie P. Norton. **Description:** Interest in frontier markets could jump if enthusiasm about growth in the developed world gathers steam. Cambodia is the latest market to get attention where a handful of investors are trying to set up funds. One investor believes that Cambodia is back open for business but others are still cautious about investing in the country.

31305 ■ *Canadian Multinationals and International Finance*
Pub: International Specialized Books Services
Ed: Greg Marchildon. **Released:** October 1, 1992. **Price:** $190.00. **Description:** Seven stories that explore the role of Canadian multinational enterprise in world finance, trade and direct investment.

31306 ■ *"Candidates Won't Bash Fed; Rate Cuts Bash Savers" in Barron's (Vol. 88, March 24, 2008, No. 12, pp. 31)*
Pub: Dow Jones & Company, Inc.
Ed: Jim McTague. **Description:** Candidates in the 2008 US presidential election, like the current administration, do not and will not bash the Federal Reserve. The Federal Reserve's aggressive interest rate cuts hurt the incomes of people depending on their savings accounts.

31307 ■ *"Capturing Generation Y: Ready, Set, Transform" in Credit Union Times (Vol. 21, July 14, 2010, No. 27, pp. 20)*
Pub: Summit Business Media
Ed: Senthil Kumar. **Description:** The financial services sector recognizes that Generation Y will have a definite impact on the way business is conducted in the future. The mindset of Generation Y is social and companies need to use networking tools such as Facebook in order to reach this demographic.

31308 ■ *Cash In a Flash*
Pub: Crown Business Books
Ed: Robert G. Allen, Mark Victor Hansen. **Released:** December 28, 2010. **Price:** $15.00. **Description:** Proven, practical advice and techniques are given to help entrepreneurs make money quickly using skills and resources known to generate permanent and recurring income.

31309 ■ *"Cautions On Loans With Your Business" in Business Owner (Vol. 35, July-August 2011, No. 4, pp. 5)*
Pub: DL Perkins Company
Description: Caution must be used when borrowing from or lending to any small business. Tax guidelines for the borrowing and lending practice are also included.

31310 ■ *"Cemex Paves a Global Road to Solid Growth" in Barron's (Vol. 88, March 10, 2008, No. 10, pp. 24)*
Pub: Dow Jones & Company, Inc.
Ed: Sandra Ward. **Description:** Shares of Cemex are expected to perform well with the company's expected strong performance despite fears of a US recession. The company has a diverse geographical reach and benefits from a strong worldwide demand for cement.

31311 ■ *"Centrue Sets Down New Roots in St. Louis; Bank Looks to Expand in Exurbs of Chicago" in Crain's Chicago Business (May 5, 2008)*
Pub: Crain Communications, Inc.
Ed: H. Lee Murphy. **Description:** Centrue Financial Corp. has moved its headquarters from Ottawa to suburban St. Louis in search of higher-growth markets. The banks acquisitions and expansion plans are also discussed.

31312 ■ *"Change of Plans" in Entrepreneur (Vol. 35, November 2007, No. 11, pp. 74)*
Pub: Entrepreneur Media Inc.
Ed: C.J. Prince. **Description:** Companies should provide 401K plans that meet employee needs and demographics, with new technology allowing providers to lower their own costs. Details on finding a plans that appeal to employees are examined.

31313 ■ *The Changing Geography of Banking and Finance*
Pub: Springer Publishing Company
Ed: Pietro Alessandrini, Michele Fratianni, Alberto Zazzaro. **Released:** May 1, 2009. **Price:** $139.00. **Description:** The two contrasting trends that have emerged from the integration and consolidation processes of the banking industry in both Europe and the United States in the 1990s is examined.

31314 ■ *"Chasing Credit" in Canadian Business (Vol. 81, November 10, 2008, No. 19, pp. 59)*
Pub: Rogers Media Ltd.
Ed: Joe Castaldo. **Description:** Small and medium sized companies are dealing with tightening credit because they appear riskier than usual. Some of these businesses are turning to private investors, but this is not easy since many have invested everything in the stock market. The sector is expected to weaken with the broader Canadian market in the next six months from October 2008.

31315 ■ *"Cheap Deposits Fuel Bank Profits" in Boston Business Journal (Vol. 31, July 29, 2011, No. 27, pp. 1)*
Pub: Boston Business Journal
Ed: Tim MacLaughlin. **Description:** Massachusetts-are banks increased profits primarily due to inexpensive deposits. The cheaper deposits have provided profit stability and fuel loan growth in an environment of historically low interest rates and uncertain economic recovery. Details of the banks' move to shed the more expensive certificates of deposit in favor of money market accounts are discussed.

31316 ■ *"Chuck's Big Chance" in Barron's (Vol. 89, July 13, 2009, No. 28, pp. L3)*
Pub: Dow Jones & Co., Inc.
Ed: Leslie P. Norton. **Description:** Charles Schwab is cutting prices and rolling out new products to lure customers and the company is well positioned to benefit from Wall Street's misery. Their shares are trading at just 17 times earnings, which should be at least at a multiple of 20.

31317 ■ *"Citadel Hires Three Lehman Execs" in Chicago Tribune (October 2, 2008)*
Pub: McClatchy-Tribune Information Services
Ed: James P. Miller. **Description:** Citadel Investment Group LLC, Chicago hedge-fund operator, has hired three former senior executives of bankrupt investment banker Lehman Brothers Holding Inc. Citadel believes that the company's hiring spree will help them to further expand the firm's capabilities in the global fixed income business.

31318 ■ *"Citi Ruling Could Chill SEC, Street Legal Pacts" in Wall Street Journal Eastern Edition (November 29, 2011, pp. C1)*
Pub: Dow Jones & Company Inc. Enterprise Media Group
Contact: Clare Hart, President
Ed: Jean Eaglesham, Chad Bray. **Description:** A $285 million settlement was reached between the Securities and Exchange Commission and Citigroup Inc. over allegations the bank misled investors over a mortgage-bond deal. Now, Judge Jed S. Rakoff has ruled against the settlement, a decision that will affect the future of such attempts to prosecute Wall Street fraud. Rakoff said that the settlement was 'neither fair, nor reasonable, nor adequate, nor in the public interest.'.

31319 ■ *"Citizens Unveils Mobile App for Business Customers" in New Hampshire Business Review (Vol. 33, March 25, 2011, No. 6, pp. 27)*
Pub: Business Publications Inc.
Description: Citizens Financial Group offers a new mobile banking application that allows business customers to manage cash and payments from a mobile device.

31320 ■ *"A Click In the Right Direction: Website Teaches Youth Financial Literacy" in Black Enterprise (Vol. 38, December 2007, No. 5)*
Pub: Earl G. Graves Publishing Co. Inc.
Ed: Nicole Norfleet. **Description:** Profile of Donald Lee Robinson who launched SkillsThatClick, a Website that teaches young individuals ages 12 to 15 about money management. Robinson shares how he used his Navy career as a model for designing the site.

31321 ■ *"Climbing the Wall of Worry, Two Steps at a Time" in Barron's (Vol. 89, July 13, 2009, No. 28, pp. L16)*
Pub: Dow Jones & Co., Inc.
Ed: Brian Blackstone. **Description:** Statistical table that shows the performance of different mutual funds for the second quarter of 2009 is presented. The data shows that on average, the 8,272 diversified equity funds gained 17 percent for this quarter.

31322 ■ *"Clock Ticks On Columbia Sussex Debt" in Business Courier (Vol. 27, July 30, 2010, No. 13, pp. 1)*
Pub: Business Courier
Ed: Dan Monk. **Description:** Cincinnati, Ohio-based Columbia Sussex Corporation has made plans to restructure a $1 billion loan bundle that was scheduled to mature in October 2010. The privately held hotel has strived in a weak hotel market to keep pace with its $3 billion debt load.

31323 ■ *"CN 'Extremely Optimistic' After Record Profit" in Globe & Mail (January 24, 2007, pp. B3)*
Pub: CTVglobemedia Publishing Inc.
Ed: Brent Jang. **Description:** The increase in Canadian National Railway Co.'s profits to $2.1 billion despite a harsh winter is discussed.

31324 ■ *"Coca-Cola Looks Ready to Pause" in Barron's (Vol. 88, March 10, 2008, No. 10, pp. 18)*
Pub: Dow Jones & Company, Inc.
Ed: Michael Santoli. **Description:** Shares of Coca-Cola are expected to turn sideways or experience a slight drop from $59.50 each to the mid-50 level. The company has seen its shares jump 40 percent since 2006, when it was in a series of measures to improve profitability.

31325 ■ *Code of Federal Regulations: Title 13: Business Credit and Assistance*
Pub: U.S. Government Printing Office
Ed: Department of Commerce Staff. **Released:** May 2007. **Price:** $55.00. **Description:** Title 13 covers regulations governing the activities of the Small Business Administration and the Department of Commerce. Book covers information on business credit, finance, and economic development.

31326 ■ *"Coming: Cheaper Oil and a Stronger Buck" in Barron's (Vol. 88, March 24, 2008, No. 12, pp. 53)*
Pub: Dow Jones & Company, Inc.
Ed: Lawrence C. Strauss. **Description:** Carl C. Weinberg, the chief economist of High Frequency Economics, forecasts that Chinese economic growth will slow down and that oil prices will drop to $80 a barrel in 2008. He also believes that the US dollar will start rising the moment the Federal Reserve stops cutting interest rates.

31327 ■ *"Coming Soon: Bailouts of Fannie and Freddie" in Barron's (Vol. 88, July 14, 2008, No. 28, pp. 14)*
Pub: Dow Jones & Co., Inc.
Ed: Jonathan R. Laing. **Description:** Assurances from the government that Fannie Mae and Freddie Mac are adequately capitalized and able to carry on their duties as guarantors or owners of over $5 trillion of U.S. home mortgages are designed to keep both entities afloat until they attempt to raise $10 billion in new equity. The government would assume any losses in a bailout and owners of the banks' papers would profit as yields drop.

31328 ■ *"A Comment on 'Balancing Risk and Return in a Customer Portfolio"' in Journal of Marketing (Vol. 75, May 2011, No. 3, pp. 18)*
Pub: American Marketing Association
Ed: Fred Selnes. **Description:** Issues regarding the use of approaches to managing customer portfolios are described. These are related to assumptions in modern financial portfolio theory and return and risk.

31329 ■ *"Commentary. On Federal Reserve's Cut of Interest Rates" in Small Business Economic Trends (January 2008, pp. 3)*
Pub: National Federation of Independent Business
Description: Federal Reserve cut interest rates and announced its economic outlook on September 18, 2007 to stimulate spending. The cut in interest rates, however, may not help in supporting consumer spending because savers may lose interest income. The expected economic impact of the interest rate cuts and the U.S. economic outlook are also discussed.

31330 ■ *"Commentary. Small Business Economic Trends" in Small Business Economic Trends (March 2008, pp. 3)*
Pub: National Federation of Independent Business
Ed: William C. Dunkelberg, Holly Wade. **Description:** Commentary on the economic trends for small businesses in the U.S. is presented. Analysis of the labor market and low interest rates is given. The effect of the Federal Reserve's policy announcement on small business owner optimism is also discussed.

31331 ■ *"Commentary. Small Business Economic Trends" in Small Business Economic Trends (February 2008, pp. 3)*
Pub: National Federation of Independent Business
Ed: William C. Dunkelberg, Holly Wade. **Description:** Commentary on the economic trends for small businesses in the U.S. is presented. Analysis of the U.S. Federal Reserve Board's efforts to prevent a recession is given. Reduction in business inventories is also discussed.

31332 ■ *"Commodities: Who's Behind the Boom?" in Barron's (Vol. 88, March 31, 2008, No. 13, pp. 3)*
Pub: Dow Jones & Company, Inc.
Ed: Gene Epstein. **Description:** Proliferation of mutual funds and exchange traded funds tied to commodities indexes has helped speculative buying reach unusual levels. Index funds are estimated to account for 40 percent of all bullish bets on commodities. Commodities could drop by 30 percent as speculators retreat. Statistical data included.

31333 ■ *"Commodity Speculation: Over the Top?" in Barron's (Vol. 89, July 13, 2009, No. 28, pp. 22)*
Pub: Dow Jones & Co., Inc.
Ed: Gene Epstein. **Description:** Commodity Futures Trading Commission is planning to impose position limits on speculators of oil and other commodities as energy costs rebound from their lows. These regulations make much sense and these position limits would greatly diminish the cash commitment of the commodity index traders if these were imposed on speculators and swaps dealers properly.

31334 ■ *"Compelling Opportunities" in Barron's (Vol. 88, March 10, 2008, No. 10, pp. 39)*
Pub: Dow Jones & Company, Inc.
Ed: Neil A. Martin. **Description:** Michael L. Reynal, portfolio manager of Principal International Emerging Markets Fund, is bullish on the growth prospects of stocks in emerging markets. He is investing big on energy, steel, and transportation companies.

31335 ■ *"Competitors Line Up to Save Failing Banks" in The Business Journal - Serving Phoenix and the Valley of the Sun (Vol. 28, July 25, 2008, No. 47, pp. 1)*
Pub: American City Business Journals, Inc.
Ed: Chris Casacchia. **Description:** Financial institutions in Arizona are positioning themselves as possible buyers in the event of failure of one of their competitors. These banks have already approached the Federal Deposit Insurance Corp. about their ability to take over their more troubled competitors.

31336 ■ *The Complete Idiot's Guide to Finance for Small Business*
Pub: Penguin Group Incorporated
Ed: Kenneth E. Little. **Released:** April 2006. **Price:** $19.95. **Description:** Financial experts helps small business owners through strategies for long-term financial success.

31337 ■ *"Comtech's Winning Streak" in Crain's New York Business (Vol. 24, January 7, 2008, No. 1, pp. 3)*
Pub: Crain Communications, Inc.
Description: Comtech Telecommunications Corp., a designer and manufacturer of equipment that helps military track troops and vehicles on the field, has been one of the stock market's biggest winners over the past decade. Statistical data included.

31338 ■ *"Conquering Your Fear of Fees" in Entrepreneur (Vol. 37, October 2009, No. 10, pp. 86)*
Pub: Entrepreneur Media, Inc.
Ed: Rosalind Resnick. **Description:** Entrepreneurs should study money management charges carefully before investing. They should understand how different forms of investments work and how much money managers and mutual funds charge for their services.

31339 ■ *"Consumers Finding It Harder to Get and Keep Credit" in Chicago Tribune (January 10, 2009)*
Pub: McClatchy-Tribune Information Services
Ed: Susan Chandler. **Description:** Five tips to maintain a good credit rating in these economic times are outlined and discussed.

31340 ■ *"Consumers Seek to Redo Rate Structure: Smaller Biz Paid Big Rates" in Crain's Detroit Business (Vol. 25, June 22, 2009)*
Pub: Crain Communications Inc. - Detroit
Ed: Amy Lane. **Description:** Consumers Energy Company charged small business customers disproportionately higher rates on June 2009 electric bills than other consumers.

31341 ■ *"Controlling Costs: Update Your Information Technology Program" in Franchising World (Vol. 42, August 2010, No. 8, pp. 18)*
Pub: International Franchise Association
Ed: Jeff Dumont. **Description:** It is imperative for any franchise to understand its technology needs in order to control costs. Needs analysis; creating a Request for Proposal; and information regarding the choices between renting, buying or building technology are covered. Relationship contingency in franchised organizations is also covered.

31342 ■ *"Conversation Starters for the Holiday" in Barron's (Vol. 89, July 6, 2009, No. 27, pp. 7)*
Pub: Dow Jones & Co., Inc.
Ed: Michael Santoli. **Description:** Investors are concerned that the US will experience high inflation due to low interest rates and improved money supply. US consumer spending has increased to 70 percent of gross domestic product, brought by health-care spending increases, while savings rates have risen to 6.9 percent.

31343 ■ *"A Conversation With Money Manager William Vellon" in Crain's Chicago Business (Vol. 31, November 17, 2008, No. 46, pp. 4)*
Pub: Crain Communications, Inc.
Ed: Mike Colias. **Description:** Interview with William Vellon, the executive vice-president of Kingsbury Capital Investment Advisors; Vellon discusses ways in which the government can help the financial sector, his client base and bargains that investors should consider.

31344 ■ *"A Conversation With; Ron Gatner, Jones Lang LaSalle" in Crain's Detroit Business (Vol. 24, October 6, 2008, No. 40, pp. 9)*
Pub: Crain Communications, Inc.
Description: Interview with Ron Gatner who is a corporate real estate adviser with the real estate company Jones Lang LaSalle as well as the company's executive vice president and part of the tenant advisory team; Gatner speaks about the impact that the Wall Street crisis is having on the commercial real estate market in Detroit.

31345 ■ *"Copy Karachi?" in Barron's (Vol. 88, June 30, 2008, No. 26, pp. 5)*
Pub: Dow Jones & Co., Inc.
Ed: Randall W. Forsyth. **Description:** Karachi bourse had a historic 8.6 percent one-day gain because the bourse banned short-selling for a month and announced a 30 billion rupee fund to stabilize the market. The shares of General Motors are trading within the same values that it had in 1974. The reasons for this decline are discussed.

31346 ■ *"Corn May Get Shucked By Soy" in Barron's (Vol. 88, March 31, 2008, No. 13, pp. M12)*
Pub: Dow Jones & Company, Inc.
Ed: Angie Pointer. **Description:** Acreage allotted to soybeans could jump by 12 percent from 2007's 63.6 million as the price for soybeans reaches record highs. Corn acreage could drop by 6.7 percent as other crops expand and higher fertilizer prices shift farmers away from corn.

31347 ■ *"Corporate Elite Show Resilience" in The Business Journal-Serving Greater Tampa Bay (Vol. 28, August 1, 2008, No. 32, pp. 1)*
Pub: American City Business Journals, Inc.
Ed: Margie Manning; Alexis Muellner. **Description:** Stocks of the largest public companies in Tampa Bay, Florida, outperformed the S&P 500 index by 28 percent in the first half of 2008. The escalation is attributed to the growth orientation of the companies in the area and the lack of exposure to the real estate and financial services sectors.

31348 ■ *"Corporate Responsibility" in Professional Services Close-Up (July 2, 2010)*
Pub: Close-Up Media
Description: List of firms awarded the inaugural Best Corporate Citizens in Government Contracting by the Corporate Responsibility Magazine is presented. The list is based on the methodology of the Magazine's Best Corporate Citizen's List, with 324 data points of publicly-available information in seven categories which include: environment, climate change, human rights, philanthropy, employee relations, financial performance, and governance.

31349 ■ *"Corus Eases Off Ailing Condo Market; Office Developers Get Majority of 1Q Loans" in Crain's Chicago Business (April 28, 2008)*
Pub: Crain Communications, Inc.
Ed: H. Lee Murphy. **Description:** Corus Bankshares Inc., a specialist in lending for the condominium high-rise construction market, is diversifying its portfolio by making loans to office developers and expects to be investing in hotels through the rest of the year. Corus' $7.57 billion loan portfolio is also discussed in detail as well as the company's earnings and share price. Statistical data included.

31350 ■ *"COSE Turns On To Electricity Market" in Crain's Cleveland Business (Vol. 30, June 22, 2009, No. 24, pp. 4)*
Pub: Crain Communications, Inc.
Ed: Jay Miller. **Description:** Council of Smaller Enterprises is working to offer small businesses and their employees electricity at discount prices set at auction by the Public Utilities Commission of Ohio and even lower prices from the Northern Ohio Public Energy Council. Details of the program are offered.

31351 ■ *"Cost of Business Banking May Soon Go Up" in Baltimore Business Journal (Vol. 28, October 29, 2010, No. 25, pp. 1)*
Pub: Baltimore Business Journal
Ed: Gary Haber. **Description:** Experts in the financial industry expect banks to charge credit card transactions, especially to small business owners and consumers to recover about $11 million in lost revenue annually. Banks are expected to charge old fees and new ones, including $5 to $10 a month for a checking account.

31352 ■ *"Cost of Md. Health Plan Not Known" in Baltimore Business Journal (Vol. 28, September 3, 2010, No. 17, pp. 1)*
Pub: Baltimore Business Journal
Ed: Emily Mullin. **Description:** United States health reform is seen to result in increased health insurance prices in Maryland. However, health care reform advocates claim a new marketplace and increased competition will help keep costs down.

31353 ■ *"Countdown" in Canadian Business (Vol. 81, March 3, 2008, No. 3, pp. 27)*
Pub: Rogers Media
Ed: Al Rosen. **Description:** According to a recent poll only 42 percent of portfolio managers in Canada are aware that the country is planning to adopt the International Financial Reporting Standards beginning 2011. The shift to the new standards will have significant impacts on investment values and will be the biggest revolution in Canadian financial reporting. The effects of the transition on portfolio managers and investors are analyzed.

31354 ■ *"Crain's Picks Top '08 Stocks" in Crain's New York Business (Vol. 24, January 7, 2008, No. 1, pp. 3)*
Pub: Crain Communications, Inc.
Ed: Aaron Elstein. **Description:** Listing of five stocks that Crain's believes can deliver solid gains for shareholders.

31355 ■ *Crash Proof 2.0: How to Profit From the Economic Collapse*
Pub: John Wiley & Sons, Inc.
Ed: Peter D. Schiff. **Released:** September 22, 2009. **Price:** $27.95. **Description:** Factors that will affect financial stability in the coming years are explained. A three step plan to battle the current economic downturn is also included.

31356 ■ *Creating a World without Poverty: Social Business and the Future of Capitalism*
Pub: Basic Books
Released: April 26, 2009. **Price:** $26.00. **Description:** Explanation of how microcredit lending practices and more collaborative business strategies can be used to alleviate poverty worldwide.

31357 ■ *"Creative In-Sourcing Boosts Franchisee Performance" in Franchising World (Vol. 42, September 2010, No. 9, pp. 16)*
Pub: International Franchise Association
Ed: Daniel M. Murphy. **Description:** Operational training and support is usually provided by franchisors. To be successful in this process it is important to balance the reality of limited financial and human resources.

31358 ■ *"The Credit Crisis Continues" in Barron's (Vol. 88, March 10, 2008, No. 10, pp. M12)*
Pub: Dow Jones & Company, Inc.
Ed: Randall W. Forsyth. **Description:** Short-term Treasury yields dropped to new cyclical lows in early March 2008, with the yield for the two-year Treasury note falling to 1.532 percent. Spreads of the mortgage-backed securities of Fannie Mae and Freddie Mac rose on suspicion of collapses in financing.

31359 ■ *"Credit Crisis Puts Market in Unprecedented Territory" in Crain's New York Business (Vol. 24, January 7, 2008, No. 1, pp. 14)*
Pub: Crain Communications, Inc.
Ed: Aaron Elstein. **Description:** Banks are being forced to take enormous losses due to investors who are refusing to buy anything linked to subprime mortgages and associated securities.

31360 ■ *"Credit Crunch Takes Bite Out Of McDonald's" in Advertising Age (Vol. 79, September 29, 2008, No. 36, pp. 1)*
Pub: Crain Communications, Inc.
Ed: Emily Bryson York. **Description:** McDonald's will delay its launch of coffee bars inside its restaurants due to the banking crisis which has prompted Bank of America to halt loans to the franchise chains.

31361 ■ *"Credit Reporting Myths and Reality" in Black Enterprise (Vol. 41, December 2010, No. 5, pp. 34)*
Pub: Earl G. Graves Publishing Co. Inc.
Ed: Denise Campbell. **Description:** It is critical to understand all the factors affecting credit scores before making any major purchase.

31362 ■ *"Credit Unions Cast Wary Eye at Paulson Plan, But Not Panicking Yet" in The Business Review Albany (Vol. 35, April 11, 2008, No. 1)*
Pub: The Business Review
Ed: Barbara Pinckney. **Description:** Credit unions are suspicious of US Treasury Secretary Henry Paulson's plan to establish a single federally insured depository institution charter for all institutions covered by federal deposit insurance. The charter would replace national banks, federal savings associations, and federal credit union charters.

31363 ■ *"CreFirst To Reward Doctors for Reducing Costs, Improving Care" in Baltimore Business Journal (Vol. 28, June 4, 2010, No. 4, pp. 1)*
Pub: Baltimore Business Journal
Ed: Scott Graham. **Description:** CareFirst Blue Cross Blue Shield plans to introduce a program that dangles big financial rewards to physicians who change the way they deliver primary care by improving the health of their sickest patients while reducing costs. The company will soon begin recruiting primary care physicians in Maryland, Washington DC, and Northern Virginia.

31364 ■ *"Currency: I'm Otta Here" in Entrepreneur (Vol. 35, October 2007, No. 10, pp. 72)*
Pub: Entrepreneur Media Inc.
Ed: C.J. Prince. **Description:** Liberum Research revealed that 193 chief financial officers (CFOs) at small companies have either resigned or retired during the first half of 2007. A survey conducted by Tatum found that unreasonable expectations from the management and compliance to regulations are the main reasons why CFOs are leaving small firms. The chief executive officer's role in making CFOs stay is also discussed.

31365 ■ *Currency Internationalization: Global Experiences and Implications for the Renminbi*
Pub: Palgrave Macmillan
Ed: Wensheng Peng, Chang Shu. **Released:** January 5, 2010. **Price:** $100.00. **Description:** A collection of academic studies relating to the potential internationalization of China's remninbi. It also discusses the increasing use of China's remninbi currency in international trade and finance.

31366 ■ *"Customers Turned Off? Not at Best Buy" in Barron's (Vol. 88, March 24, 2008, No. 12, pp. 29)*
Pub: Dow Jones & Company, Inc.
Ed: Sandra Ward. **Description:** Shares of Best Buy, trading at $42.41 each, are expected to rise to an average of $52 a share due to the company's solid fundamentals. The company's shares have fallen 20 percent from their 52-week high and are attractive given the company's bright prospects in the video game sector and high-definition video.

31367 ■ *"Cyclicals, Your Day Is Coming" in Barron's (Vol. 89, July 27, 2009, No. 30, pp. 24)*
Pub: Dow Jones & Co., Inc.
Ed: Dimitra DeFotis. **Description:** Cyclical stocks are likely to be big winners when the economy improves and 13 stocks that have improving earnings, decent balance sheets, and dividends are presented. These candidates include U.S. Steel, Alcoa, Allegheny Tech, Dow Chemical, and Nucor.

31368 ■ *"Darkness Falling.." in Barron's (Vol. 89, July 20, 2009, No. 29, pp. 13)*
Pub: Dow Jones & Co., Inc.
Description: Newsletter writer Arch Crawford believes that market indicators signal a possible downturn in US stock markets. High risk areas also include China and Japan .

31369 ■ *"Data Dispel Some Notions About Value of Stock Buybacks" in Crain's Cleveland Business (Vol. 28, November 19, 2007, No. 46, pp. 9)*
Pub: Crain Communications, Inc.
Ed: Megan Johnston. **Description:** According to new research on buybacks and their benefits, companies engaged in stock buybacks frequently do not enjoy a nice boost in their share prices despite the conventional wisdom that states that investors like stock buybacks.

31370 ■ *Data Driven Investing: Professional Edition*
Pub: Data Driven Publishing, LLC
Ed: Mitchell R. Hardy; Bill Matson. **Released:** 2004. **Description:** Investment concepts and trading techniques are explored in a simple and practical way. The book covers the unreliability of financial markets due to malpractices, appalling analysis, insider training and more. Information is based on data and common sense and easy to use for beginner as well as professional.

31371 ■ *"Deal Braces Cramer for Growth Run" in The Business Journal-Serving Metropolitan Kansas City (Vol. 26, July 4, 2008, No. 43, pp. 1)*
Pub: American City Business Journals, Inc.
Ed: James Dornbook. **Description:** Gardner, Kansas-based Cramer Products Inc. bought 100 percent of the stocks of Louisville, Kentucky-based Active Ankle Inc. from 26 private investors increasing its revenue by 20 percent. The latter is the second largest vendor of Cramer. Other details of the merger are presented.

31372 ■ *"The Deal - Rhymes With Steal - Of A Lifetime" in Barron's (Vol. 88, March 24, 2008, No. 12, pp. 24)*
Pub: Dow Jones & Company, Inc.
Ed: Andrew Bary. **Description:** JPMorgan Chase's impending acquisition of Bear Stearns for $2.50 a share is a huge steal for the former. JPMorgan is set to acquire a company with a potential annual earnings of $1 billion while the Federal Reserve funds Bear's illiquid assets by providing $30 billion in nonrecourse loans.

31373 ■ *"Decline in Assets Is Costly for Advisers" in The Business Journal-Serving Metropolitan Kansas City (Vol. 27, October 24, 2008)*
Pub: American City Business Journals, Inc.
Ed: James Dornbrook. **Description:** Financial advisers in the Kansas City, Missouri area are forced to cut costs as their assets have decreased sharply due to the huge drop in stock prices. American Century Investments was forced to diversify into foreign assets and cut 90 jobs as its assets dropped to $84 billion. Diversification has softened the impact of the steep decline in stock prices for Waddell & Reed Financial Inc.

31374 ■ *"Deutsche Bank Joins the Club" in Barron's (Vol. 88, March 31, 2008, No. 13, pp. M6)*
Pub: Dow Jones & Company, Inc.
Ed: Arindam Nag. **Description:** Deutsche Bank's tangible leverage has worsened sharply in the past year from 2.1 percent to 2.3 percent during 2002-2006 to only 1.6 percent. The bank has also been accumulating a lot of illiquid assets and its Level-3 assets are three times its tangible equity.

31375 ■ *"Developers Compete for APG Project" in Baltimore Business Journal (Vol. 27, October 16, 2009, No. 23, pp. 1)*
Pub: American City Business Journals
Ed: Daniel J. Sernovitz. **Description:** Corporate Office Properties Trust has lost the case in Delaware bankruptcy court to prevent rival St. John Properties Inc. from going ahead with its plans to develop the 400 acres at Aberdeen Proving Ground (APG) in Maryland. Both developers have competed for the right to develop the two million square foot business park in APG.

31376 ■ *The Dhandho Investor: The Low Risk Value Method to High Returns*
Pub: John Wiley and Sons Inc.
Ed: Mohnish Pabrai. **Released:** April 2007. **Price:** $27.95. **Description:** Value investing is described using the Dhandho capital allocation framework for successfully investing in the stock market.

31377 ■ *"Diary of a Short-Seller" in Conde Nast Portfolio (Vol. 2, June 2008, No. 6, pp. 44)*
Pub: Conde Nast Publications
Contact: David Carey, President
Ed: Jesse Eisinger. **Description:** Profile of David Einhorn who is a fund manager that spoke out against finance company Allied Capital whose stock fell nearly 20 percent the day after Einhorn's critique; Einhorn subsequently had to contend with attacks against his credibility as well as investigations by the S.E.C.; Einhorn's experience illuminates our current economic crisis.

31378 ■ *"Dick Haskayne" in Canadian Business (Vol. 81, March 31, 2008, No. 5, pp. 72)*
Pub: Rogers Media
Ed: Andy Holloway. **Description:** Dick Haskayne says that he learned a lot about business from his dad who ran a butcher shop where they had to make a decision on buying cattle and getting credit. Haskayne says that family, friends, finances, career, health, and infrastructure are benchmarks that have to be balanced.

31379 ■ *Dictionary of Finance, Investment and Banking*
Pub: Palgrave Macmillan
Ed: Erik Banks. **Released:** 2010. **Price:** $42.95. **Description:** Comprehensive dictionary covering terms used in finance, investment and banking sectors.

31380 ■ *"Different This Time?" in Canadian Business (Vol. 81, April 14, 2008, No. 6, pp. 38)*
Pub: Rogers Media
Ed: Matthew McClearn. **Description:** Irving Fisher believed that the low interest rates of the 1920's spurred investors to borrow and use the money to speculate with the proceeds thereby increasing the debt to unmanageable levels prior to the stock market crash in Oct. 29, 1929. The U.S. economic conditions in 1929 and U.S. economic conditions in 2008 are discussed.

31381 ■ *"Digging Deep for Gold" in Barron's (Vol. 88, March 24, 2008, No. 12, pp. 49)*
Pub: Dow Jones & Company, Inc.
Ed: Suzanne McGee. **Description:** David Iben, manager of the Nuveen Tradewinds Value Opportunities Fund, looks for value in companies and industries where the consensus of analysts is negative. He started investing in gold stocks well before gold prices started to rise.

31382 ■ *"Dividing to Conquer" in Barron's (Vol. 88, March 31, 2008, No. 13, pp. 22)*
Pub: Dow Jones & Company, Inc.
Ed: Andrew Bary. **Description:** Altria's spin off of Philip Morris International could unlock substantial value for both domestic and international cigarette concerns. The strong brands and ample payouts from both companies will most likely impress investors.

31383 ■ *"Do-It-Yourself Portfolio Management" in Barron's (Vol. 89, July 13, 2009, No. 28, pp. 25)*
Pub: Dow Jones & Co., Inc.
Ed: Mike Hogan. **Description:** Services of several portfolio management web sites are presented. These web sites include MarketRiders E.Adviser, TD Ameritrade and E.

31384 ■ *"DoEs and DonEts" in Canadian Business (Vol. 79, July 17, 2006, No. 14-15, pp. 29)*
Pub: Rogers Media
Ed: Andy Holloway; Erin Pooley; Thomas Watson. **Description:** Strategic tips for planning systematic investments, in order to make life more enjoyable after retirement, are elucidated.

31385 ■ *"The Dogs of TSX" in Canadian Business (Vol. 81, Summer 2008, No. 9, pp. 77)*
Pub: Rogers Media Ltd.
Ed: Calvin Leung. **Description:** Table showing the one-year stock performance of the ten highest dividend-yielding stocks on the S&P/TSX 60 Composite Index is presented. This technique is similar to the 'Dogs of the Dow' approach. The idea in this investment strategy is to buy equal amounts of stocks from these companies and selling them a year later, and then repeat the process.

31386 ■ *"The Dominance of Doubt" in Barron's (Vol. 89, July 13, 2009, No. 28, pp. M3)*
Pub: Dow Jones & Co., Inc.
Description: Five straight down days leading up to July 10, 2009 in the U.S. stock market reminds one strategist of 1982 when there was a feeling that things could never be the same again. One analyst is bullish on the stocks of Apple Inc. and sees the stocks rising to at least 180 in 12 months. The prospects of the shares of GM and Ford are also discussed.

31387 ■ *"Don't Bet Against The House" in Barron's (Vol. 88, July 14, 2008, No. 28, pp. 20)*
Pub: Dow Jones & Co., Inc.
Ed: Sandra Ward. **Description:** Shares of Nasdaq OMX have lost more than 50 percent of their value from November 2007 to July 2008 but the value of these shares could climb 50 percent on the strength of world security exchanges. Only 15 percent of the company's revenues come from the U.S. and the shares are trading at 12.5 times the amount expected for 2008.

31388 ■ *"Don't Expect Quick Fix" in The Business Journal-Serving Metropolitan Kansas City (Vol. 27, October 3, 2008, No. 3, pp. 1)*
Pub: American City Business Journals, Inc.
Ed: James Dornbrook. **Description:** United States governmental entities cannot provide a quick fix solution to the current financial crisis. The economy requires a systemic change in the way people think about credit. The financial services industry should also focus on core lending principles.

31389 ■ *"Don't Get Lulled by the Calm" in Barron's (Vol. 89, July 27, 2009, No. 30, pp. M13)*
Pub: Dow Jones & Co., Inc.
Ed: Steven M. Sears. **Description:** Options traders expect volatility to return in the fall of 2009 and to bring correlation with it. September and October are typically the most volatile months and the trick is to survive earnings season.

31390 ■ *"Don't' Hang Up On FairPoint" in Barron's (Vol. 88, July 7, 2008, No. 27, pp. M5)*
Pub: Dow Jones & Co., Inc.
Ed: Fleming Meeks. **Description:** Shares of FairPoint Communications, priced at $6.63 each, are undervalued and should be worth over $12 each. The company increased its size by more than five times by acquiring Verizon's local telephone operations in Vermont, New Hampshire, and Maine, but must switch customers in those areas into their system by the end of September 2007.

31391 ■ *"Downtown Bank Got High Marks for Irwin Purchase, Is Looking For More" in Business Courier (Vol. 27, September 3, 2010, No. 18, pp. 1)*
Pub: Business Courier
Ed: Steve Watkins. **Description:** First Financial Bancorp is looking to acquire more troubled banks following its purchase of Irwin Union Bank. The bank has reported a $383 million bargain purchase gain during the third quarter of 2009.

31392 ■ *"Drilling Deep and Flying High" in Barron's (Vol. 88, June 30, 2008, No. 26, pp. 34)*
Pub: Dow Jones & Co., Inc.
Ed: Kenneth Rapoza. **Description:** Shares of Petrobras could rise another 25 percent if the three deepwater wells that the company has found proves as lucrative as some expect. Petrobras will become an oil giant if the reserves are proven.

31393 ■ *"Drug-Maker Plans IPO" in Business Courier (Vol. 24, November 23, 2008, No. 32, pp. 1)*
Pub: American City Business Journals, Inc.
Ed: James Ritchie; Steve Watkins. **Description:** Xanodyne Pharmaceuticals Inc. filed plans with the Securities and Exchange Commission on November 9, 2007 for an initial public offering. The company, with annual sales of $75 million, had lost $222 million since it was founded in 2001.

31394 ■ *"Drug, Seed Firms Offer Antidote For Inflation" in Crain's Chicago Business (Vol. 31, April 21, 2008, No. 16, pp. 4)*
Pub: Crain Communications, Inc.
Ed: Daniel Rome Levine. **Description:** Interview with Jerrold Senser, the CEO of Institutional Capital LLC in Chicago, in which he discusses the ways that the company is adjusting to the economic slowdown and rising inflation, his favorite firms for investment and his prediction of an economic turnaround; he also recommends five companies he feels are worth investing in.

31395 ■ *"Dueling Visions" in Barron's (Vol. 89, July 27, 2009, No. 30, pp. 13)*
Pub: Dow Jones & Co., Inc.
Ed: Michael Santoli. **Description:** Goldman Sachs' market strategists believe the stock market has entered a 'sustained-rally' mode while Morgan Stanley's strategist believes this is a 'rally to sell into'. What is not known in the stock market is how much of a 'V'-shaped recovery in earning the market rebound has already priced in.

31396 ■ *"Dynamic Duo" in Barron's (Vol. 88, March 10, 2008, No. 10, pp. 45)*
Pub: Dow Jones & Company, Inc.
Ed: Shirley A. Lazo. **Description:** General Dynamics, the world's sixth-largest military contractor, raised its dividend payout by 20.7 percent from 29 cents to 35 cents a share. Steel Dynamics, producer of structural steel and steel bar products, declared a 2-for-1 stock split and raised its quarterly dividend by 33 percent to a split-adjusted 10 cents a share.

31397 ■ *"Economic Prognosis" in Barron's (Vol. 89, July 13, 2009, No. 28, pp. 11)*
Pub: Dow Jones & Co., Inc.
Ed: Karen Hube. **Description:** Loomis Sayles Bond Fund manager Dan Fuss believes that the economy is bottoming and that recovery will be long and drawn out. Fuss guesses that the next peak in 10-year Treasury yields will be about 6.25% in around 4 and a half or five years ahead of 2009.

31398 ■ *"An Educated Play on China" in Barron's (Vol. 88, June 30, 2008, No. 26, pp. M6)*
Pub: Dow Jones & Co., Inc.
Ed: Mohammed Hadi. **Description:** New Oriental Education & Technology Group sells English-language courses to an increasingly competitive Chinese workforce that values education. The shares in this company have been weighed down by worries on the impact of the Beijing Olympics on enrollment and the Sichuan earthquake. These shares could be a great way to get exposure to the long-term growth in China.

31399 ■ *"Effect of Oil Prices on the Economy" in Canadian Business (Vol. 81, September 15, 2008, No. 14-15, pp. 5)*
Pub: Rogers Media Ltd.
Ed: Joe Chidley. **Description:** Rise of oil prices above $100 in February 2008 and $140 in July signals the birth of a 'new economy' according to commentators; this shift is causing uneasiness from oil industry professionals who are unsure of how this trend could be sustained. Oil dropped below $120 in August, which could slow down global economic growth followed by oil demand, then oil prices.

31400 ■ *"Egg Fight: The Yolk's on the Short" in Barron's (Vol. 88, July 7, 2008, No. 27, pp. 20)*
Pub: Dow Jones & Co., Inc.
Ed: Christopher C. Williams. **Description:** Shares of Cal-Maine Foods, the largest egg producer and distributor in the US, are due for a huge rise because of the increase in egg prices. Short sellers, however, continue betting that the stock, priced at $31.84 each, will eventually go down.

31401 ■ *"Elder Care Costs Surge" in National Underwriter Life & Health (Vol. 114, November 8, 2020, No. 21, pp. 25)*
Pub: Summit Business Media
Ed: Trevor Thomas. **Description:** Nursing home and assisted living rates rose from 2009 to 2010, according to MetLife Mature Market Institute. Statistical data included.

31402 ■ *"End of an Era" in Barron's (Vol. 88, July 7, 2008, No. 27, pp. 3)*
Pub: Dow Jones & Co., Inc.
Ed: Alan Abelson. **Description:** June 2008 was a very bad month for US stocks, with investors losing as much as 41.9 percent in the first half of 2008 signaling an end to the financial environment that prevailed around the world since the 1980's. The US job market lost 62,000 jobs in June 2008.

31403 ■ *"The End of the Line for Line Extensions?" in Advertising Age (Vol. 79, July 7, 2008, No. 26, pp. 3)*
Pub: Crain Communications, Inc.
Description: After years of double-digit growth, some of the most heavily extended personal-care products have slowed substantially or even declined in the U.S. Unilever's Dove and P&G's Pantene and Olay are two such brands that have been affected. Statistical data included.

31404 ■ *"Energy, MLPs: Pipeline to Profits" in Barron's (Vol. 89, July 27, 2009, No. 30, pp. 9)*
Pub: Dow Jones & Co., Inc.
Ed: Dimitra DeFotis. **Description:** Energy master limited partnership stocks are range-bound in the next few months from July 2009 but there are there are some opportunities that remain. These include Energy Transfer Equity, Enterprise GP holdings, NuStar GP Holdings, and Plains All American Pipeline.

31405 ■ *"Engine of Growth: U.S. Industry Funk hasn't Hurt Cummins or Its Investors" in Barron's (Vol. 88, July 14, 2008, No. 28, pp. 43)*
Pub: Dow Jones & Co., Inc.
Ed: Shirley A. Lazo. **Description:** Engine maker Cummins increased its quarterly common dividend by 40 percent to 17.5 cents per share from 12.5 cents. CVS Caremark's dividend saw a hike of 18.4 percent from 9.5 cents to 11.25 cents per share while its competitor Walgreen is continuing its 75th straight year of dividend distribution and its 33rd straight year of dividend hikes.

31406 ■ *Entrepreneurial Finance*
Pub: Pearson Education, Limited
Contact: Steven A. Dowling, President
Ed: Philip J. Adelman; Alan M. Marks. **Released:** July 2006. **Price:** $87.35. **Description:** Financial aspects of running a small business are covered; topics include sole proprietorships, partnerships, limited liability companies, and private corporations.

31407 ■ *Entrepreneurial Finance: A Casebook*
Pub: John Wiley and Sons Inc.
Ed: Paul A. Gompers; William Sahlman. **Released:** September 2006. **Price:** $63.00. **Description:** Investment analysis, entrepreneurial financing, harvesting, and renewal in the entrepreneurial firm are among the topics discussed.

31408 ■ *Entrepreneurial Small Business*
Pub: McGraw-Hill Higher Education
Ed: Richard P. Green; Jerome A. Katz. **Released:** January 2008. **Price:** $139.43. **Description:** Students are able to get a clear vision of small enterprise in today's business climate. The textbook helps focus on the goal of having personal independence with financial security as an entrepreneur.

31409 ■ *The Entrepreneur's Edge: Finding Money, Making Money, Keeping Money*
Pub: Silver Lake Publishing
Ed: Daniel Hogan. **Released:** October 2006. **Price:** $24.95. **Description:** Advice for starting, running and growing a new business is given.

31410 ■ *"An Equity Fund of Their Own" in Entrepreneur (Vol. 35, October 2007, No. 10, pp. 68)*
Pub: Entrepreneur Media Inc.
Ed: Lee Gimpel. **Description:** About 100 new private equity funds have formed since 2002, proof that private equity investing is becoming popular among companies. There is also an increase in competition to close deals owing to the large number of investors that companies can choose; advantages of smaller funds over the larger one is explained.

31411 ■ *"Essential Releases Record First Quarter Results" in Canadian Corporate News (May 14, 2007)*
Pub: Comtex News Network Inc.
Description: The first quarter of 2007 saw record financial performance despite numerous challenges for Essential Energy Services Trust. Statistical data included.

31412 ■ *Essentials of Entrepreneurship and Small Business Management*
Pub: Prentice Hall PTR
Ed: Thomas W. Zimmerer; Norman M. Scarborough; Doug Wilson. **Released:** February 2007. **Price:** $106.67. **Description:** New venture creation and the knowledge required to start a new business are shared. The challenges of entrepreneurship, business plans, marketing, e-commerce, and financial considerations are explored.

31413 ■ *"ETF Score Card" in Barron's (Vol. 89, July 13, 2009, No. 28, pp. 51)*
Pub: Dow Jones & Co., Inc.
Description: Statistical table is presented which shows the net assets of various exchange-traded funds is presented. The table also shows the total return of these funds up to a three-year time period.

31414 ■ *"Ethics Commission May Hire Collection Agency" in Tulsa World (August 21, 2010)*
Pub: World Publishing
Ed: Barbara Hoberock. **Description:** Oklahoma Ethics Commission is considering a more to hire a collection agency or law firm in order to collect fees from candidates owing money for filing late financial reports.

31415 ■ *"European Stocks on Deck" in Barron's (Vol. 89, July 27, 2009, No. 30, pp. M7)*
Pub: Dow Jones & Co., Inc.
Ed: Vito J. Racanelli. **Description:** European stocks are cheap and these trade at a discount to U.S. equities rarely seen in the past 40 years. This represents an opportunity for Americans and trends show that Europe's stocks outperform when there is a discrepancy between the price to earnings ratio in European stocks versus U.S. stocks and when sentiment on European equities are downbeat.

31416 ■ *"Even Gold Gets Tarnished When Everyone Wants Cash" in Globe & Mail (February 28, 2007, pp. B1)*
Pub: CTVglobemedia Publishing Inc.
Ed: John Partridge. **Description:** The impact of fall in Chinese equities on the United States stock market and metal prices, including gold, is discussed.

31417 ■ *"Everyone Out of the Pool" in Barron's (Vol. 89, July 20, 2009, No. 29, pp. 18)*
Pub: Dow Jones & Co., Inc.
Ed: Sandra Ward. **Description:** Shares of Pool Corp. could drop as continued weakness in the housing market weakens the market for swimming pool equipment. The company's shares are trading at $18.29, about 20 times projected 2009 earnings of $0.91 a share.

31418 ■ *"Expect a Rally as Waders Dive In" in Barron's (Vol. 89, July 20, 2009, No. 29, pp. 11)*
Pub: Dow Jones & Co., Inc.
Ed: Vito J. Racanelli. **Description:** US stock markets may experience a rally in the autumn of 2009 as skeptical investors start to return to the market. The Standard & Poor's Index may jump to the 1025-1050 point levels during this rally.

31419 ■ *"Experts: Market Shaky But Resilient" in The Business Journal-Serving Metropolitan Kansas City (Vol. 27, September 19, 2008, No. 1)*
Pub: American City Business Journals, Inc.
Ed: Steve Vockrodt. **Description:** Investment advisers believe that the local investors in Kansas City who have a long-term approach towards their portfolios may come out even or even experience gains despite the Wall Street financial crisis. The impacts of the crisis are expected to take time to reach the area of Kansas City. The potential impacts of the Wall Street meltdown are examined further.

31420 ■ *"Export Initiative Launched" in Philadelphia Business Journal (Vol. 28, December 11, 2009, No. 43, pp. 1)*
Pub: American City Business Journals
Ed: Athena D. Merritt. **Description:** The first initiative that came out of the partnership between the Export-Import Bank of the US, the city of Philadelphia, and the World Trade Center of Greater Philadelphia is presented. A series of export finance workshops have featured Ex-Im Bank resources that can provide Philadelphia businesses with working capital, insurance protection and buyer financing.

31421 ■ *"Extra Rehab Time Boosts M-B's Off-Lease Profits" in Automotive News (Vol. 86, October 31, 2011, No. 6488, pp. 22)*
Pub: Crain Communications Inc.
Ed: Arlena Sawyers. **Description:** Mercedes-Benz Financial Services USA is holding on to off-lease vehicles in order to recondition them and the move is boosting profits for the company.

31422 ■ *Facing Financial Dysfunction*
Pub: Infinity Publishing
Ed: Bert Whitehead. **Released:** April 2004. **Description:** Handbook to help individuals manage their finances, investments, taxes and retirement.

31423 ■ *"Fair Exchange" in Food and Drink (Winter 2010, pp. 84)*
Pub: Schofield Media Group
Ed: Don Mardak. **Description:** Bartering can assist firms in the food and beverage industry to attract new customers, maximize resources, and reduce cash expenses.

31424 ■ *"Falling Local Executive Pay Could Suggest a Trend" in Tampa Bay Business Journal (Vol. 30, January 15, 2010, No. 4, pp. 1)*
Pub: American City Business Journals
Ed: Margie Manning. **Description:** Tampa Bay, Florida-based Raymond James Financial Inc. and MarineMax Inc.'s proxy statements have shown the decreasing compensation of the companies' highest paid executives. The falling trend in executive compensation was a result of intensified shareholder scrutiny and the economy.

31425 ■ *"Falling Markets' Nastiest Habits" in Barron's (Vol. 88, July 7, 2008, No. 27, pp. 7)*
Pub: Dow Jones & Co., Inc.
Ed: Michael Santoli. **Description:** US market conditions reflect a bear market, with the S&P 500 index falling 20 percent below its recent high as of June 2008. The bear market is expected to persist in the immediate future, although bear market rallies are likely to occur.

31426 ■ *A Family Matter: A Guide to Operating Your Personal Estate*
Pub: Brown Books Publishing Group
Ed: William A. Verkest. **Released:** May 2003. **Price:** $22.95. **Description:** Guidebook to financial management of personal assets is presented. Important documents must be maintained in a safe, secure place for family members or attorneys to access when necessary. The author suggests that a personal diary be kept with important information regarding records of investment accounts and financial summaries for every year in order to calculate taxes and manage financial matters more efficiently.

31427 ■ *"Fannie and Freddie: How They'll Change" in Business Week (September 22, 2008, No. 4100, pp. 30)*
Pub: McGraw-Hill Companies, Inc.
Ed: Jane Sasseen. **Description:** Three possible outcomes of the fate of struggling mortgage giants Freddie Mac and Fannie Mae after the government bailout are outlined.

31428 ■ *"Fast Revival Unlikely For Indian 'Net Stocks" in Barron's (Vol. 88, July 7, 2008, No. 27, pp. 12)*
Pub: Dow Jones & Co., Inc.
Ed: Leslie P. Norton. **Description:** Shares of Indian Internet companies Rediff.com and Sify are not likely to stage a rebound due to weak financial results. Rediff.com shares have declined 39.2 percent in 2008, while Sify shares are down 35.8 percent.

31429 ■ *"February Hot for Mutual Fund Sales" in Globe & Mail (March 3, 2006, pp. B10)*
Pub: CTVglobemedia Publishing Inc.
Ed: Keith Damsell. **Description:** The details on Canadian mutual fund sector, which posted $4.7 billion for February 2005, are presented.

31430 ■ *"Fed Tackles Bear of a Crisis" in Barron's (Vol. 88, March 17, 2008, No. 11, pp. M10)*
Pub: Dow Jones & Company, Inc.
Ed: Randall W. Forsyth. **Description:** Emergency funding package for Bear Stearns from the Federal Reserve Bank of New York through JPMorgan Chase is one of the steps taken by the central bank shore up bank liquidity. Prior to the emergency funding, the central bank announced the Term Securities Lending Facility to allow dealers to borrow easily saleable Treasuries in exchange for less-liquid issues.

31431 ■ *"Fees Come Down; Markets Come Down More" in Barron's (Vol. 89, July 13, 2009, No. 28, pp. L8)*
Pub: Dow Jones & Co., Inc.
Ed: J.R. Brandstrader. **Description:** Investors spent less on mutual fund fees in 2009 than they did in the last 25 years. These fees include administration, accounting, and legal expense. Despite the popularity of money market funds which has contributed to this decline, the short-term yields of these funds fell in the last year.

31432 ■ *"A Few Points of Contention" in Barron's (Vol. 88, July 14, 2008, No. 28, pp. 3)*
Pub: Dow Jones & Co., Inc.
Ed: Michael Santoli. **Description:** Headline inflation tends to revert to the lower core inflation, which excludes food and energy in its calculation over long periods. Prominent private equity figures believe that regulators should allow more than the de facto 10 percent to 25 percent limit of commercial banks to hasten the refunding of the financial sector.

31433 ■ *"Fewer Banks Offer Big Gifts to Lure Clients" in Globe & Mail (March 14, 2006, pp. D1)*
Pub: CTVglobemedia Publishing Inc.
Ed: Chris Reidy. **Description:** Fewer banks are offering gifts to lure the customers in this year in the wake of less favorable interest rates in the spring season. The market climate is analyzed.

31434 ■ *"Fifth Third CEO Kabat: A World of Difference" in Business Courier (Vol. 26, January 1, 2010, No. 37, pp. 1)*
Pub: American City Business Journals, Inc.
Ed: Steve Watkins. **Description:** CEO Kevin Kabat of Cincinnati-based Fifth Third Bancorp believes that the bank's assets of $111 billion and stock value of more than $10 indicate the recovery from the low stock prices posted in February 2009. He attributes the recovery from the federal government's stress test finding in May 2009 that Fifth Third needs to generate $1.1 billion.

31435 ■ *"Fifth Third Grapples With Account Snafu" in Business Courier (Vol. 24, December 7, 2008, No. 34, pp. 1)*
Pub: American City Business Journals, Inc.
Ed: Jon Newberry. **Description:** Fifth Third Bank's vendor committed an error which led to a badly damaged credit score for Brett and Karen Reloka. The couple reported the incident to the bank and are still waiting for action to be taken. A major outourced services vendor caused paid-off mortgages to be reported delinquent.

31436 ■ *"Fifth Third Spinoff" in Business Courier (Vol. 27, July 16, 2010, No. 11, pp. 1)*
Pub: Business Courier
Ed: Dan Monk, Steve Watkins. **Description:** Electronic-funds transfer company Fifth Third Solutions (FTPS), a spinoff of Fifth Third Bancorp, is seeking as much as 200,000 square feet of new office space in Ohio. The bank's sale of 51 percent ownership stake to Boston-based Advent International Corporation has paved the way for the growth of FTPS. How real estate brokers' plans have responded to FTPS' growth mode is discussed.

31437 ■ *"Fighting Detroit" in Baltimore Business Journal (Vol. 27, January 22, 2010, No. 38, pp. 1)*
Pub: American City Business Journals
Ed: Daniel J. Sernovitz. **Description:** Baltimore, Maryland-based car dealers could retrieve their franchises from car manufacturers, Chrysler LLC and General Motors Corporation, through a forced arbitration. A provision in a federal budget mandates the arbitration. The revoking of franchises has been attributed to the car manufacturers' filing of bankruptcy protection.

31438 ■ *"The File On..Skoda Minotti" in Crain's Cleveland Business (Vol. 28, October 8, 2007, No. 40, pp. 26)*
Pub: Crain Communications, Inc.
Ed: Kimberly Bonvissuto. **Description:** Overview of Skoda Minotti, the accounting and financial services firm located in Mayfield Village; the company has 140 employees and an expanded slate of services.

31439 ■ *"Finalist: BlackEagle Partners L.L.C." in Crain's Detroit Business (Vol. 24, March 24, 2008, No. 12, pp. 12)*
Pub: Crain Communications, Inc.
Ed: Brent Snavely. **Description:** Overview of private-equity firm, BlackEagle Partners L.L.C., an upstart that acquired Rockford Products Corp. in order to improve the performance of the company who does business with several major tier-one automotive sup-

pliers; Rockford manufactures highly engineered chassis and suspension components for automakers and the automotive aftermarket.

31440 ■ *Finance & Accounting: How to Keep Your Books and Manage Your Finances with an MBA, a CPA, or a Ph.D*
Pub: Adams Media Corporation
Ed: Suzanne Caplan. **Price:** $19.95.

31441 ■ *"The Finance Function In A Global Corporation" in Harvard Business Review (Vol. 86, July-August 2008, No. 8, pp. 108)*
Pub: Harvard Business School Press
Ed: Mihir A. Desai. **Description:** Designing and implementing a successful finance function in a global setting is discussed. Additional topics include the internal capital market, managing risk and budgeting capital internationally.

31442 ■ *"Financial Education: Boomer's Spending Hurts Retirement" in Employee Benefit News (Vol. 25, November 1, 2011, No. 14, pp. 18)*
Pub: SourceMedia Inc.
Ed: Ann Marsh. **Description:** Financial planners and employers need to educate clients and employees about retirement planning. Boomers are spending money that should be saved for their retirement.

31443 ■ *Financial Management 101: Get a Grip on Your Business Numbers*
Pub: Self-Counsel Press, Incorporated
Ed: Angie Mohr. **Released:** November 2007. **Price:** $16.95. **Description:** An overview of business planning, financial statements, budgeting and advertising for small businesses. s.

31444 ■ *Financial Management for the Small Business*
Pub: Kogan Page, Limited
Contact: Ben Glover, Director of Marketing
Ed: Colin Barrow. **Released:** April 2006. **Description:** Keys to successful financial management are presented to help small business owners to address the principles and problems associated with financial planning.

31445 ■ *Financing Growth: Strategies, Capital Structure, and M and A Transactions*
Pub: John Wiley and Sons, Inc.
Ed: Kenneth H. Marks, Larry E. Robbins, Gonzalo Fernandez, John P. Funkhouser, D.L. Williams. **Released:** September 1, 2009. **Price:** $95.00. **Description:** Guide for emerging growth and middle market companies includes information to help understand and apply the basics of corporate finance using empirical data and actual company cases to illustrate capital structures and financing approaches.

31446 ■ *"Finding Good Bets Down on the Farm" in Crain's Chicago Business (Vol. 31, March 24, 2008, No. 12, pp. 4)*
Pub: Crain Communications, Inc.
Ed: Daniel Rome Levine. **Description:** Interview with money manager Jeff James, the portfolio manager for Driehaus Capital Management LLC, who discusses the Federal Reserve and recommends several companies in which to make investments.

31447 ■ *"Finger-Pointing Time" in Barron's (Vol. 88, March 10, 2008, No. 10, pp. 9)*
Pub: Dow Jones & Company, Inc.
Ed: Michael Santoli. **Description:** Discusses who is to blame for the financial crisis brought about by the credit crunch in the United States; the country's financial markets will eventually digest this crisis but will bottom out first before the situation improves.

31448 ■ *"First Financial Aiming for Banking Big Leagues" in Business Courier (Vol. 26, December 4, 2009, No. 32, pp. 1)*
Pub: American City Business Journals, Inc.
Ed: Steve Watkins. **Description:** First Financial Bancorp could dominate the community banking market of Greater Cincinnati after buying failed banks with the supervision of the FDIC. Details of the transactions are presented.

31449 ■ *"First Mariner's New Ads No Passing Fancy" in Boston Business Journal (Vol. 29, September 16, 2011, No. 19, pp. 1)*
Pub: American City Business Journals Inc.
Ed: Gary Haber. **Description:** Baltimore, Maryland-based First Mariner Bank replaced Ed Hale, the bank's CEO and founder, as the pitchman for its television ads with Ravens quarterback Joe Flacco. Hales' exit from the advertisements is the result of First Mariner's struggle to raise money for recapitalization.

31450 ■ *"FirstMerit's Top Executive Turns Around Credit Quality" in Crain's Cleveland Business (Vol. 28, October 15, 2007, No. 41, pp. 3)*
Pub: Crain Communications, Inc.
Ed: Shawn A. Turner. **Description:** Discusses the ways in which chairman and CEO Paul Greig has been able to improve FirstMerit Corp.'s credit quality and profit margin. Strategies included selling more than $70 million in bad loans, hiring a new chief credit officer and redirecting its focus on cross-selling its wealth and investment services to its commercial customers. Statistical data included.

31451 ■ *The Flaw of Averages: Why We Underestimate Risk in the Face of Uncertainty*
Pub: John Wiley & Sons, Inc.
Ed: Sam L. Savage. **Released:** June 3, 2009. **Price:** $22.95. **Description:** Personal and business plans are based on uncertainties on a daily basis. The common avoidable mistake individuals make in assessing risk in the face of uncertainty is defined. The explains why plans based on average assumptions are wrong, on average, in areas as diverse as finance, healthcare, accounting, the war on terror, and climate change.

31452 ■ *"A Flawed Yardstick for Banks" in Barron's (Vol. 88, July 14, 2008, No. 28, pp. M6)*
Pub: Dow Jones & Co., Inc.
Ed: Arindam Nag. **Description:** Return on equity is no longer the best measure for investors to judge banks by in a post-subprime-crises world. Investors should consider the proportion of a bank's total assets that are considered risky and look out for any write-downs of goodwill when judging a bank's financial health.

31453 ■ *"Florida's Housing Gloom May Add To Woes of National City" in Crain's Cleveland Business (Vol. 28, October 29, 2007, No. 43, pp. 1)*
Pub: Crain Communications, Inc.
Ed: Shawn A. Turner. **Description:** Already suffering by bad loans in the troubled mortgage market, National City Corp. is attempting to diversify its geographic presence beyond the slow-growth industrial Midwest by acquiring two Florida firms. Analysts worry that the acquisitions may end up making National City vulnerable to a takeover if the housing slump continues and credit quality becomes more of an issue for the bank.

31454 ■ *Fooling Some of the People All of the Time*
Pub: John Wiley & Sons, Inc.
Ed: David Einhorn. **Released:** March 10, 2010. **Price:** $29.95. **Description:** A chronicle of the ongoing saga between author, David Einhorn's hedge fund, Greenlight Capital, and Allied Capital, a leader in the private finance industry.

31455 ■ *"For Baxter, A Lingering PR Problem; Ongoing Focus On Heparin Deaths Ups Heat On CEO" in Crain's Chicago Business (April 21, 2008)*
Pub: Crain Communications, Inc.
Ed: Mike Colias. **Description:** Baxter International Inc.'s recall of the blood-thinning medication heparin has exposed the company to costly litigation and put the perils of overseas drug manufacturing in the spotlight. Wall Street investors predict that an indefinite halt in production of the drug should not hurt the company's bottom line since heparin represents a tiny sliver of the business. Since Baxter began recalling the drug in January its shares have continued to outpace most other medical stocks.

31456 ■ *"For Buffet Fans, the Price Is Right" in Barron's (Vol. 89, July 13, 2009, No. 28, pp. 17)*
Pub: Dow Jones & Co., Inc.
Ed: Andrew Bary. **Description:** Shares of Warren Buffett's Berkshire Hathaway have fallen to $85,000 and these are cheap since they are trading at just 1.2 times estimated book value and are well below its peak of $149,000. One fan of the stock expects it to top $110,000 in the next year from June 2009.

31457 ■ *"For Gilead, Growth Beyond AIDS" in Barron's (Vol. 88, June 30, 2008, No. 26, pp. 18)*
Pub: Dow Jones & Co., Inc.
Ed: Jay Palmer. **Description:** First-quarter 2008 revenue for Gilead Sciences grew by 22 percent and an earnings gain of 19 percent thanks to their HIV-treatment drugs that comprised over two-thirds of the company's sales in 2007. An analyst has a 12-month target from June, 2008 of 65 per share. The factors behind the company's prospects are also discussed.

31458 ■ *"Foreclosures Crisis Expected to Significantly Drain Wealth" in Black Enterprise (Vol. 41, September 2010, No. 2, pp. 24)*
Pub: Earl G. Graves Publishing Co. Inc.
Description: African American communities will lose billions in wealth because of the current foreclosure crisis. Statistical data included.

31459 ■ *"Foreign (In)Direct Investment and Corporate Taxation" in Canadian Journal of Economics (Vol. 44, November 2011, No. 4, pp. 1497)*
Pub: Blackwell Publishers Ltd.
Ed: Georg Wamser. **Description:** Foreign investments of multinational firms are often complex in that they involve conduit entities. In particular, a multinational can pursue either a direct or an indirect investment strategy, where the latter involves an intermediate corporate entity and is associated with enhanced opportunities for international tax planning. As a consequence, in the case of indirect investments, the role of corporate taxation in destination countries may change. An investigation into the effects of corporation taxation on foreign investment decisions of German multinationals, taking explicitly into account that firms choose in a first stage the investment regime, (direct vs. indirect) is provided.

31460 ■ *"Former Mayor Driving $500 Million Real Estate Equity Fund" in The Business Journal - Serving Phoenix and the Valley of the Sun (Vol. 28, August 15, 2008, No. 50, pp. 1)*
Pub: American City Business Journals, Inc.
Ed: Jan Buchholz. **Description:** Paul John, the former mayor of Phoenix, is establishing a $500 million real estate asset management fund. The fund is dubbed Southwest Next Capital Management and has attracted three local partners, namely Joseph Meyer, Jay Michalowski, and James Mullany, who all have background in finance and construction.

31461 ■ *"Forward Motion" in Green Industry Pro (July 2011)*
Pub: Cygnus Business Media
Ed: Gregg Wartgow. **Description:** Several landscape contractors have joined this publication's Working Smarter Training Challenge over the last year. This process is helping them develop ways to improve work processes, boost morale, drive out waste, reduce costs, improve customer service, and be more competitive.

31462 ■ *"The Four Cheapest Plays in Emerging Markets" in Barron's (Vol. 89, July 27, 2009, No. 30, pp. 34)*
Pub: Dow Jones & Co., Inc.
Ed: Lawrence C. Strauss. **Description:** Portfolio manager Arjun Divecha of the GMO Emerging Markets III Fund says that the main thing in investing in emerging markets is getting the country right since

getting it wrong makes it harder to add value. Divecha says that the four countries that they are positive on are Turkey, Russia, South Korea, and Thailand.

31463 ■ *"Friends With Money" in Canadian Business (Vol. 81, Summer 2008, No. 9, pp. 22)*
Pub: Rogers Media Ltd.
Description: Two of the most well connected managers in Canadian capital markets Rob Farquharson and Brian Gibson will launch Panoply Capital Asset Management in June. The investment management company aims to raise a billion dollars from institutions and high-net worth individuals.

31464 ■ *"From Buyout to Busted" in Business Week (September 22, 2008, No. 4100, pp. 18)*
Pub: McGraw-Hill Companies, Inc.
Ed: Emily Thornton; Deborah Stead. **Description:** Bankruptcy filings by private equity-backed companies are at a record high with 134 American firms taken private (or invested in) by buyout firms that have filed for protection this year under Chapter 11; this is 91 percent higher than the previous year, which had set a record when 70 of such companies filed for protection under Chapter 11.

31465 ■ *"From Fastenal, a Boost" in Barron's (Vol. 89, July 20, 2009, No. 29, pp. M13)*
Pub: Dow Jones & Co., Inc.
Ed: Shirley A. Lazo. **Description:** Fastenal increased its semi-annual common payout from $0.35 to $0.37 a share. Core Laboratories declared a special dividend of $0.75 a share along with its quarterly payout of $0.10. Ryder System and Landstar System raised their payouts to $0.23 and $0.045 a share respectively.

31466 ■ *"Full-Court Press for Apple" in Barron's (Vol. 88, March 24, 2008, No. 12, pp. 47)*
Pub: Dow Jones & Company, Inc.
Ed: Mark Veverka. **Description:** Apple Inc. is facing more intellectual property lawsuits in 2008, with 30 patent lawsuits filed compared to 15 in 2007 and nine in 2006. The lawsuits, which involve products such as the iPod and the iPhone, present some concern for Apple's shareholders.

31467 ■ *"Function Over Forms?" in Barron's (Vol. 88, June 30, 2008, No. 26, pp. 17)*
Pub: Dow Jones & Co., Inc.
Ed: Eric Savitz. **Description:** Securities and Exchange Commission (SEC) chairman Christopher Cox wants the SEC to consider an overhaul of the forms used to meet the agency's disclosure requirements. Cox also said that the U.S. Generally Accepted Accounting Standards has too many rules with exceptions and alternative interpretations.

31468 ■ *"Funds "Friend" Facebook" in Barron's (Vol. 89, July 27, 2009, No. 30, pp. 30)*
Pub: Dow Jones & Co., Inc.
Ed: Leslie P. Norton. **Description:** Mutual-fund companies are the latest entrants to the 'social media' space and several companies have already set up Facebook and Twitter pages. The use of this technology pose special challenges for compliance and regulators especially since the Financial Industry Regulatory Authority reminds companies that advertising, sales and literature are governed by regulations.

31469 ■ *"Future's Brighter for Financial Stocks" in Barron's (Vol. 89, July 20, 2009, No. 29, pp. 14)*
Pub: Dow Jones & Co., Inc.
Ed: Jacqueline Doherty. **Description:** Shares of US financial companies are projected to rise as their earnings start to normalize. Earnings of these companies have been hurt by credit losses but have been bolstered by one-time gains.

31470 ■ *"Futures Shock for the CME" in Crain's Chicago Business (Vol. 31, November 10, 2008, No. 45, pp. 8)*
Pub: Crain Communications, Inc.
Ed: Ann Saphir. **Description:** Chicago-based CME Group Inc., the largest futures exchange operator in the U.S., is facing a potentially radically altered regulatory landscape as Congress weighs sweeping reform of financial oversight. The possible merger of the CFTC and the Securities and Exchange Commission are among CME's concerns. Other details of possible regulatory measures are provided.

31471 ■ *"Futures of the Street" in Barron's (Vol. 88, June 30, 2008, No. 26, pp. 27)*
Pub: Dow Jones & Co., Inc.
Ed: Michael Santoli. **Description:** Prospects of the securities industry in terms of jobs and profit sources are discussed. Suggestions on what the industry needs with regards to its use of capital are also discussed.

31472 ■ *"Gas Glut Pummels Prices" in Barron's (Vol. 89, July 27, 2009, No. 30, pp. M8)*
Pub: Dow Jones & Co., Inc.
Ed: Christine Buurma. **Description:** Natural gas-futures prices have fallen 73 percent and the glut of output from onshore gas fields and the weak demand signals that a rebound is not near. An analyst expects U.S. production to show increasingly steep declines but the oversupply situation is not good for prices.

31473 ■ *"Gateway Delays Start" in The Business Journal-Serving Metropolitan Kansas City (Vol. 27, October 31, 2008, No. 8, pp. 1)*
Pub: American City Business Journals, Inc.
Ed: Rob Roberts. **Description:** Economic problems caused, in part, by the Wall Street crisis has resulted in the setback of a proposed mixed-use redevelopment project, The Gateway. The $307 million project, which includes the Kansas Aquarium, will be delayed due to financing problems. Details of the project are given.

31474 ■ *"GE Looking to Extend Hot Streak" in Business Courier (Vol. 24, January 25, 2008, No. 42, pp. 1)*
Pub: American City Business Journals, Inc.
Ed: John Newberry. **Description:** GE Aviation has enjoyed strong revenues and sales due to increase aircraft engine orders. It has an engine backlog order of $19 million as of the end of 2007. Data on the aviation company's revenues, operating profit and total engine orders for the year 2004 to 2007 are presented.

31475 ■ *"General Motors Can't Kick Incentives-But They Work" in Advertising Age (Vol. 79, July 7, 2008, No. 26, pp. 3)*
Pub: Crain Communications, Inc.
Ed: Jean Halliday. **Description:** General Motors Corp. was able to maintain their market share just as Toyota Motor Corp. was beginning to pass the manufacturer; GM lured in customers with a sales incentive that they heavily advertised and subsequently helped build demand; investors, however, were not impressed and GM shares were hammered to their lowest point in 50 years after analysts speculated the company might go bankrupt.

31476 ■ *"Generation Y - An Opportunity for a Fresh Financial Start" in (September 11, 2010, pp. 241)*
Pub: VerticalNews
Description: Eleanor Blayney, the consumer advocate for the Certified Financial Planner Board of Standards, offers a financial strategy for Generation Y individuals starting their financial planning. The first segment of the non-profit's Lifelong Financial Strategies initiative is called 'Starting Out', and focuses on ways Generation Y people can avoid pitfalls of earlier generations by making smart financial decisions.

31477 ■ *"Genzyme: Underrated Oversold" in Barron's (Vol. 88, March 24, 2008, No. 12, pp. 58)*
Pub: Dow Jones & Company, Inc.
Ed: Johanna Bennett. **Description:** Shares of biotechnology company Genzyme appear oversold and underrated at their $71.86 level. The company's finances are on a solid foundation, with revenues over $3.8 billion in 2007 and forecasts of $4.5-4.7 billion in revenue for 2008.

31478 ■ *"Get Off The Rollercoaster" in Michigan Vue (Vol. 13, July-August 2008, No. 4, pp. 19)*
Pub: Entrepreneur Media Inc.
Ed: Donald N. Hobley Jr. **Description:** Benefits of creating and implementing a solid financial plan during these rocky economic times are examined. Things to keep in mind before meeting with a financial planner include risk assessment, investment goals, the length of time required to meet those goals and the amount of money one has available to invest.

31479 ■ *Get Your Credit Straight: A Sister's Guide to Ditching Your Debt, Mending Your Credit, and Building a Strong Financial Future*
Pub: Broadway Books
Contact: David Drake, Manager
E-mail: ddrake@randomhouse.com
Ed: Glinda Bridgforth. **Price:** $19.95. **Description:** Third book in the series is aimed primarily at African American women and offers helpful and understandable information for a larger audience. The sidebars on how women in particular tend to get into credit trouble and ways they can increase their financial knowledge and reign in their spending habits are especially notable.

31480 ■ *"Getting In on the Ground Floor" in Barron's (Vol. 89, July 27, 2009, No. 30, pp. 32)*
Pub: Dow Jones & Co., Inc.
Ed: Jacqueline Doherty. **Description:** Shares of AvalonBay Communities have fallen 61 percent in the past two and a half years to July 2009 but at $56, the stock is trading near the asset value. The shares could rise as the economy improves and if the recovery takes longer, investors will be rewarded with a yield of 3.5 percent.

31481 ■ *"Getting More Out of Retirement" in Agency Sales Magazine (Vol. 39, November 2009, No. 10, pp. 48)*
Pub: MANA
Ed: Joshua D. Mosshart. **Description:** Overview of the Tax Increase Prevention and Reconciliation Act, which lets employees convert to a Roth IRA in 2010. The benefits of conversion depend on age and wealth and it is best to consult a tax advisor to determine the best strategy for retirement planners.

31482 ■ *"Getting Out of an IRS Mess" in Black Enterprise (Vol. 37, December 2006, No. 5, pp. 53)*
Pub: Earl G. Graves Publishing Co. Inc.
Ed: Carolyn M. Brown. **Description:** Owing back taxes to the IRS can lead to huge penalties and interest. Here are some tips on how to handle paying the IRS what you owe them.

31483 ■ *Getting Rich In Your Underwear: How To Start and Run a Profitable Home-Based Business*
Pub: HCM Publishing
Ed: Peter I. Hupalo. **Released:** April 1, 2005. **Price:** $17.95. **Description:** Book offers insight into starting a home-based business. Entrepreneurs will learn about business models and the home business; distribution and fulfillment of product or service; marketing and sales; how to overcome the fear of starting a business; personal success characteristics; naming a business; zoning and insurance; intellectual capital; copyrights, trademarks, and patents; limited liability companies and S-corporations; business expenses and accounting; taxes; fifteen basic steps for starting a home-based business, state resources for starting a home company; and seven home-based business ideas.

31484 ■ *"Giants Now Admit They Roam Planet Earth; Time To Buy?" in Barron's (Vol. 88, March 31, 2008, No. 13, pp. 39)*
Pub: Dow Jones & Company, Inc.
Ed: Eric J. Savitz. **Description:** Oracle's third-quarter results showed that top-line growth fell short of expectations but the company is expected to fare

better than most applications companies in the downturn. Google had a flat growth in the number of people who click their online ads. The time for investors in the tech sector with a long-term horizon has arrived.

31485 ■ *"Give Me Liberty With DirecTV" in Barron's (Vol. 89, July 13, 2009, No. 28, pp. M5)*
Pub: Dow Jones & Co., Inc.
Ed: Fleming Meeks. **Description:** Shares of Liberty Entertainment look cheap at $25.14 and the same goes for DirecTV at $23.19. A merger between the two companies was announced and the deal will likely close by September 2009. Barclays Capital has a target of $30 for Liberty Media and $32 for DirecTV.

31486 ■ *"Gold Still Has That Glitter" in Barron's (Vol. 89, July 20, 2009, No. 29, pp. M8)*
Pub: Dow Jones & Co., Inc.
Ed: Allen Sykora. **Description:** Gold prices appear to be ready for an increase starting in the fall of 2009 due to an increase in demand. The price of the August 2009 gold contract fell to as low as $904.08 an ounce before recovering to $937.50.

31487 ■ *"A Good Book Is Worth a Thousand Blogs" in Barron's (Vol. 88, July 14, 2008, No. 28, pp. 42)*
Pub: Dow Jones & Co., Inc.
Ed: Gene Epstein. **Description:** Nine summer book suggestions on economics are presented. The list includes 'The Revolution' by Ron Paul, 'The Forgotten Man' by Amity Shales, 'The Commitments of Traders Bible' by Stephen Briese, and 'Economic Facts and Fallacies' by Thomas Sowell.

31488 ■ *"Good Going, Partners: Energy-Asset Firms Do Their Parents Proud" in Barron's (Vol. 89, July 27, 2009, No. 30, pp. M8)*
Pub: Dow Jones & Co., Inc.
Ed: Shirley A. Lazo. **Description:** Four master limited partnerships boosted their dividends. Sunoco Logistics raised theirs by 11.2 percent, El Paso Pipeline by 12 percent, Holly Energy upped their dividends by a penny, and Western Gas hiked their dividend to 31 cents per unit.

31489 ■ *"A Good Step, But There's a Long Way to Go" in Business Week (September 22, 2008, No. 4100, pp. 10)*
Pub: McGraw-Hill Companies, Inc.
Ed: James C. Cooper. **Description:** Despite the historic action by the U.S. government to nationalize the mortgage giants Freddie Mac and Fannie Mae, rising unemployment rates may prove to be an even bigger roadblock to bringing back the economy from its downward spiral. The takeover is meant to restore confidence in the credit markets and help with the mortgage crisis but the rising rate in unemployment may make many households unable to take advantage of any benefits which arise from the bailout. Statistical data included.

31490 ■ *"Good Things Happen When We Buy Local" in Crain's Detroit Business (Vol. 24, October 6, 2008, No. 40, pp. 7)*
Pub: Crain Communications, Inc.
Description: Michigan is facing incredibly difficult economic times. One way in which each one of us can help the state and the businesses located here is by purchasing our goods and services from local vendors. The state Agriculture Department projected that if Michigan households earmarked $10 per week in their grocery purchases to made-in-Michigan products, this would generate $30 million a week in economic impact.

31491 ■ *"Google's Next Stop: Below 350?" in Barron's (Vol. 88, March 10, 2008, No. 10, pp. 17)*
Pub: Dow Jones & Company, Inc.
Ed: Jacqueline Doherty. **Description:** Share prices of Google Inc. are expected to drop from their level of $433 each to below $350 per share. The company is expected to miss its earnings forecast for the first quarter of 2008, and its continued aggressive spending on non-core areas will eventually bring down earnings.

31492 ■ *"Graduates to the TSX in 2008" in Canadian Business (Vol. 81, Summer 2008, No. 9, pp. 79)*
Pub: Rogers Media Ltd.
Ed: Calvin Leung. **Description:** Table showing the market capitalization and stock performance of the companies that jumped to the TSX Venture Exchange is presented. The 17 companies that made the leap to the list will have an easier time raising capital, although leeway must be made in investing since they are still new businesses.

31493 ■ *"The Great Fall" in Barron's (Vol. 88, March 10, 2008, No. 10, pp. 5)*
Pub: Dow Jones & Company, Inc.
Ed: Alan Abelson. **Description:** Discusses the US economy is considered to be in a recession, with the effects of the credit crisis expected to intensify as a result. Inflation is estimated at 4.3 percent in January 2008, while 63,000 jobs were lost in February 2008.

31494 ■ *The Great Inflation and Its Aftermath: The Past and Future of American Affluence*
Pub: Random House Inc.
Contact: Richard Sarnoff, President
Ed: Robert J. Samuelson. **Released:** 2009. **Price:** $26.00. **Description:** How inflation has shaped the economics in today's United States is examined.

31495 ■ *"A Greenish Light for Financial-Sector Funds" in Barron's (Vol. 88, March 24, 2008, No. 12, pp. 52)*
Pub: Dow Jones & Company, Inc.
Ed: Tom Sullivan. **Description:** Financial sector funds have lost value in 2008 through 17 March, and investors are advised to reduce investments in the financial sector. Exchange-traded funds present a good way to own financial stocks.

31496 ■ *"Greg Stringham" in Canadian Business (Vol. 81, March 3, 2008, No. 3, pp. 8)*
Pub: Rogers Media
Ed: Michelle Magnan. **Description:** Canadian Association of Petroleum Producers' Greg Stringham thinks that the new royalty plan will result in companies pulling out their investments for Alberta's conventional oil and gas sector. Stringham adds that Alberta is losing its competitive advantage and companies must study their cost profiles to retrieve that advantage. The effects of the royalty system on Alberta's economy are examined further.

31497 ■ *"A Gripping Read: Bargains & Noble" in Barron's (Vol. 88, March 17, 2008, No. 11, pp. 20)*
Pub: Dow Jones & Company, Inc.
Ed: Jonathan R. Laing. **Description:** Barnes & Noble's earnings forecast for the fiscal year ending in January, 2008 to be $1.70 to $1.90 per share which is way lower than the $2.12 analyst consensus. The company also said that sales at stores one-year old or older dropped 0.5 percent in the fourth quarter. However, the shares are now cheap at 4.9 times enterprise value with some analysts putting a price target of 41 per share.

31498 ■ *Grow Your Money: 101 Easy Tips to Plan, Save and Invest*
Pub: HarperBusiness
Ed: Jonathan D. Pond. **Released:** December 2007. **Price:** $26.95. **Description:** In what should be required reading for anyone entering the work world, the author offers helpful investment and financial definitions, debt-management strategies, retirement and home ownerships considerations and more.

31499 ■ *"Growth Back on CIBC's Agenda" in Globe & Mail (March 3, 2006, pp. B1)*
Pub: CTVglobemedia Publishing Inc.
Ed: Sinclair Stewart. **Description:** The details on business growth of Canadian Imperial Bank of Commerce, which posted $547 million profit for first quarter 2006, are presented.

31500 ■ *The Handbook of Financing Growth: Strategies and Capital Structure*
Pub: John Wiley & Sons, Incorporated
Ed: Kenneth H. Marks, John P. Funkhouser, Larry E. Robbins. **Released:** March 2005. **Price:** $85.00 (US), $123.95 (Canadian). **Description:** Using empirical data and actual case studies, strategies are presented to illustrate capital structures and fund raising techniques for emerging growth and middle-market companies.

31501 ■ *"Handleman Liquidation Leaves Questions For Shareholders" in Crain's Detroit Business (Vol. 24, October 6, 2008, No. 40, pp. 4)*
Pub: Crain Communications, Inc.
Ed: Nancy Kaffer. **Description:** Discusses Handleman Co., a Troy-based music distribution company, and their plan of liquidation and dissolution as well as how shareholders will be affected by the company's plan. Handleman filed its plan to liquidate and dissolve assets with the Securities and Exchange Commission in mid-August, following several quarters of dismal earnings.

31502 ■ *"Hank and Ben: Hedgies' BFFs" in Barron's (Vol. 88, March 31, 2008, No. 13, pp. 50)*
Pub: Dow Jones & Company, Inc.
Ed: Tom Sullivan. **Description:** David Ballin of Alternative Investment Solutions says that everything in the financial markets is tainted and beaten-up which presents an extraordinary opportunity for hedge funds as long as they back up their decisions with sharp and intensive research. He adds that money managers should short suspect stocks and go long on undeservedly battered stocks in the same sector.

31503 ■ *"Hank Paulson On the Housing Bailout and What's Ahead" in Business Week (September 22, 2008, No. 4100, pp. 19)*
Pub: McGraw-Hill Companies, Inc.
Ed: Maria Bartiromo. **Description:** Interview with Treasury Secretary Henry Paulson in which he discusses the bailout of Fannie Mae and Freddie Mac as well as the potential impact on the American economy and foreign interests and investments in the country. Paulson has faith that the government's actions will help to stabilize the housing market.

31504 ■ *"A Harbinger?" in The Business Journal-Milwaukee (Vol. 25, August 29, 2008, No. 49, pp. A1)*
Pub: American City Business Journals, Inc.
Ed: Rich Kirchen. **Description:** Stock prices of Marshall & Ilsley Corp. (M&I) and MGIC Investment Corp. are expected to rebound after insiders were reported to have bought stocks of the companies. M&I director David Lubar bought $4.3 million, while MGIC CEO and chairman Curt Culver bought 20,000 stocks of MGIC. Other views and information on the insiders' purchase of stocks are presented.

31505 ■ *"Hartco Income Fund Announces the Completion of the CompuSmart Strategic Review" in Canadian Corporate News (May 14, 2007)*
Pub: Comtex News Network Inc.
Description: Hartco Income Fund announced that it has completed the process of exploring strategic options for CompuSmart and found that it should implement a plan to sell select stores and assets while consolidating remaining CompuSmart locations over the next sixty days.

31506 ■ *"Has Microsoft Found a Way to Get at Yahoo?" in Advertising Age (Vol. 79, July 7, 2008, No. 26, pp. 4)*
Pub: Crain Communications, Inc.
Ed: Abbey Klaassen. **Description:** Microsoft's attempt to acquire Yahoo's search business is discussed as is Yahoo's plans for the future at a time when the company's shares have fallen dangerously low.

31507 ■ *"Hastily Enacted Regulation Will Not Cure Economic Crisis" in Crain's Chicago*

Business (Vol. 31, May 5, 2008, No. 18, pp. 18)
Pub: Crain Communications, Inc.

Ed: Stephen P. D'Arcy. **Description:** Policymakers are looking for ways to respond to what is possibly the greatest financial crisis of a generation due to the collapse of the housing market, the credit crisis and the volatility of Wall Street.

31508 ■ *"Hawaii's Identity Crisis" in Hawaii Business (Vol. 53, November 2007, No. 5, pp. 10)*
Pub: Hawaii Business Publishing

Ed: Kelli Abe Trifonovitch. **Description:** Some Hawaiians have shown that the Superferry controversy makes it seem to the rest of the world as if they do not know what they are doing, and intensifies several issues regarding the stability of investing in Hawaii. With or without the Superferry, there is still no evidence that investors are afraid to put their money in Hawaii.

31509 ■ *"Hawaii's Top Twenty Financial Advisors" in Hawaii Business (Vol. 53, February 2008, No. 8, pp. 32)*
Pub: Hawaii Business Publishing

Description: Listing of Hawaii's top 20 financial advisors is presented. Details on the methodology used to create the rankings are discussed.

31510 ■ *"HBDiversityStockIndex" in Hispanic Business (October 2009, pp. 1)*
Pub: Hispanic Business

Description: Data covering the Hispanic Business Diversity Stock Index is highlighted. The HBDSI was up 0.12 percent through September 3, 2009. Statistical data included.

31511 ■ *"Headwinds From the New Sod Slow Aer Lingus" in Barron's (Vol. 88, March 10, 2008, No. 10, pp. M6)*
Pub: Dow Jones & Company, Inc.

Ed: Sean Walters; Arindam Nag. **Description:** Aer Lingus faces a drop in its share prices with a falling US market, higher jet fuel prices, and lower long-haul passenger load factors. British media companies Johnston Press and Yell Group are suffering from weaker ad revenue and heavier debt payments due to the credit crunch.

31512 ■ *"The Heat Is On" in Crain's Chicago Business (Vol. 31, April 28, 2008, No. 17, pp. 4)*
Pub: Crain Communications, Inc.

Ed: Steve Daniels. **Description:** Discusses Nicor Inc., a natural-gas utility serving 2 million customers in Chicago's suburbs, and its potential acquirers; shares of the company have dropped 17 percent this year making Nicor the second-worst among 31 utilities in an index tracked by Standrd & Poor's. Statistical data included.

31513 ■ *"A Heavy Burden" in Crain's Cleveland Business (Vol. 30, June 8, 2009, No. 22, pp. 13)*
Pub: Crain Communications, Inc.

Ed: Chuck Soder. **Description:** Small business owners are making sacrifices in the tight economy. In a recent survey conducted by American Express, 30 percent of the 727 small business owners questioned said they no longer take salaries from their firms.

31514 ■ *"Hello, 9000! The Dow's Run Is Far From Over" in Barron's (Vol. 89, July 27, 2009, No. 30, pp. 20)*
Pub: Dow Jones & Co., Inc.

Ed: Andrew Bary. **Description:** Another 10 percent gain is possible for the rest of 2009 as the Dow Jones Industrial Average moved above 9000 level for the week ending July 24, 2009. Blue chip stocks could do well in the next 10 years.

31515 ■ *Here Come the Regulars: How to Run a Record Label on a Shoestring Budget*
Pub: Faber & Faber, Inc.

Ed: Ian Anderson. **Released:** October 1, 2009. **Price:** $15.00. **Description:** Author, Ian Anderson launched his own successful record label, Afternoon Records when he was 18 years old. Anderson shares insight into starting a record label, focusing on label image, budget, blogging, potential artists, as well as legal aspects.

31516 ■ *"Here are the Stocks of the Decade" in Business Courier (Vol. 26, December 18, 2009, No. 34, pp. 1)*
Pub: American City Business Journals, Inc.

Ed: Steve Watkins. **Description:** Listing of companies with stocks that made big gains since December 1999 to November 30, 2009 is presented.

31517 ■ *"Here's How Buffett Spent 2007" in Barron's (Vol. 88, March 10, 2008, No. 10, pp. 48)*
Pub: Dow Jones & Company, Inc.

Ed: Andrew Bary. **Description:** Earnings of Berkshire Hathaway may decline in 2008 due to a tighter insurance market, but its portfolio is expected to continue growing. Warren Buffett purchased $19.1 billion worth of stocks in 2007.

31518 ■ *"The Hidden Tax" in Canadian Business (Vol. 81, April 14, 2008, No. 6, pp. 28)*
Pub: Rogers Media

Ed: Al Rosen. **Description:** Accounting fraud could take out a sizable sum from one's retirement fund when computed over a long period of time. The much bigger tax on savings is the collective impact of the smaller losses that do not attract the attention they deserve. Ensuring that investors are not unnecessarily taxed 2 percent of their total investments every year outweighs the benefit of a 2 percent reduction in personal tax rates.

31519 ■ *"High-End Jeweler Loses Street Sparkle" in Houston Business Journal (Vol. 40, November 27, 2009, No. 29, pp. 1)*
Pub: American City Business Journals

Ed: Allison Wollam. **Description:** High-end jeweler Bailey Banks & Biddle's 7,000 square foot prototype store in Houston, Texas' CityCentre will be ceasing operations despite its parent company's filing for Chapter 11 protection from creditors. According to the bankruptcy filing, parent company Finlay Enterprises Inc. of New York intends to auction off its business and assets. Finlay has 67 Bailey Banks locations throughout the US.

31520 ■ *"High Hopes: Ralph Mitchell's Picks Have Growth Potential" in Black Enterprise (Vol. 37, February 2007, No. 7, pp. 42)*
Pub: Earl G. Graves Publishing Co. Inc.

Ed: Carolyn M. Brown. **Description:** Ralph Mitchell, president and senior financial advisor of Braintree-Carthage Financial Group, offers three recommendations: Toll Brothers, Home Depot, and Lowe's.

31521 ■ *High Wire: The Precarious Financial Lives of American Families*
Pub: Basic Books

Ed: Peter Gosselin. **Released:** 2009. **Price:** $26.95. **Description:** Despite the general prosperity in America, household finances are growing more precarious making people more anxious about their economic prospects in the future.

31522 ■ *"High-Yield Turns Into Road Kill" in Barron's (Vol. 88, July 7, 2008, No. 27, pp. M7)*
Pub: Dow Jones & Co., Inc.

Ed: Emily Barrett. **Description:** High-yield bonds have returned to the brink of collapse after profits have recovered from the shock brought about by the collapse of Bear Stearns. The high-yield bond market could decline again due to weakness in the automotive sector, particularly in Ford and General Motors.

31523 ■ *"Hispantelligence Report" in Hispanic Business (July-August 2009, pp. 8)*
Pub: Hispanic Business

Description: After forty years, Hispanic-owned businesses have grown to more than three million, according to a U.S. Census report. The Hispanic business stock index is also presented. Statistical data included.

31524 ■ *"Hit the Books" in Black Enterprise (Vol. 38, July 2008, No. 12, pp. 42)*
Pub: Earl G. Graves Publishing Co. Inc.

Ed: Mellody Hobson. **Description:** Four books that deal with investing are discussed as is the idea that reading even 15 minutes a day from one of these books will give you tools that far exceed what you can learn from magazines and the business section of your daily newspaper.

31525 ■ *"Hitting Bottom?" in Barron's (Vol. 88, March 24, 2008, No. 12, pp. 21)*
Pub: Dow Jones & Company, Inc.

Ed: Jacqueline Doherty. **Description:** Brokerage houses and banks may stabilize in 2008 as a result of regulatory responses brought about by the near-collapse of Bear Stearns. Some of their shares may rise by as much as 20 percent from 2008 to 2009.

31526 ■ *"Hollinger Shares Plummet on Reports" in Globe & Mail (March 10, 2007, pp. B5)*
Pub: CTVglobemedia Publishing Inc.

Ed: Richard Blackwell. **Description:** The fall in the share prices of Hollinger Inc. to 49 percent soon after the company filed its annual statements is discussed.

31527 ■ *Home-Based Business for Dummies*
Pub: John Wiley and Sons, Inc.

Ed: Paul Edwards, Sarah Edwards, Peter Economy. **Released:** February 25, 2005. **Price:** $19.99. **Description:** Provides all the information needed to start and run a home-based business. Topics include: selecting the right business; setting up a home office; managing money, credit, and financing; marketing; and ways to avoid distractions while working at home.

31528 ■ *"A Home of Her Own" in Hawaii Business (Vol. 53, October 2007, No. 4, pp. 51)*
Pub: Hawaii Business Publishing

Ed: Maria Torres-Kitamura. **Description:** It was observed that the number of single women in Hawaii purchasing their own home has increased, as that in the whole United States where the percentage has increased from 14 percent in 1995 to 22 percent in 2006. However, First Hawaiian Bank's Wendy Lum thinks that the trend will not continue in Hawaii due to lending restrictions. The factors that women consider in buying a home of their own are presented.

31529 ■ *"Homebuilders Continue to be Our Nemesis" in Contractor (Vol. 56, July 2009, No. 7, pp. 50)*
Pub: Penton Media, Inc.

Ed: Bob Mader. **Description:** Homebuilders rank high on the greed scale along with Wall Street brokers. There is this one instance when a builder gave copies of another contractor's quotes that have just been blackened out and another instance when one builder let other bidders visit a site while the current mechanical contractor is working.

31530 ■ *"Hong Kong's Boom in IPO" in Barron's (Vol. 89, July 13, 2009, No. 28, pp. M7)*
Pub: Dow Jones & Co., Inc.

Ed: Nick Lord. **Description:** Hong Kong's IPO (initial public offering) market is booming with 13 Chinese IPOs already on the market for the year as July 2009. One of them is Bawang International which raised $214 million after generating $9 billion in order which makes it 42 times oversubscribed.

31531 ■ *"Hospital Revenue Healthier in 2009" in Orlando Business Journal (Vol. 26, February 5, 2010, No. 36, pp. 1)*
Pub: American City Business Journals

Ed: Melanie Stawicki Azam. **Description:** Orlando Health, Health Central and Adventist Health System are Florida-based hospital systems that generated the most profits in 2009. Orlando Health had the highest profit in 2009 at $73.3 million, contrary to about $31 million in losses in 2008. The increased profits are attributed to stock market recovery, cost-cutting initiatives, and rising patient volumes.

31532 ■ *"Hospitals Feel Pain from Slow Economy" in Business Courier (Vol. 27, September 3, 2010, No. 18, pp. 1)*
Pub: Business Courier
Ed: James Ritchie. **Description:** Hospitals in Cincinnati, Ohio have suffered from decreased revenues owing to the economic crises. Declining patient volumes and bad debt have also adversely impacted hospitals.

31533 ■ *"Hospitals Try to Buy Smarter" in Crain's Detroit Business (Vol. 25, June 1, 2009, No. 22, pp. M025)*
Pub: Crain Communications Inc. - Detroit
Ed: Jay Greene. **Description:** Hospitals in southeast Michigan are using bulk discount purchasing of medical and non-medical supplies through group purchasing organizations in order to cut costs.

31534 ■ *House of Cards: A Tale of Hubris and Wretched Excess on Wall Street*
Pub: Anchor Press
Ed: William D. Cohan. **Released:** February 9, 2010. **Price:** $16.95. **Description:** A historical account of the events leading up to the Bear Stearns implosion.

31535 ■ *"Housing Hedge" in Canadian Business (Vol. 79, July 17, 2006, No. 14-15, pp. 66)*
Pub: Rogers Media
Ed: Jeff Sanford. **Description:** The idea of starting a hedge scheme for housing is presented using the advent of pension schemes as an example to follow.

31536 ■ *"How to Avoid the Three Big Mistakes" in Barron's (Vol. 88, March 10, 2008, No. 10, pp. 30)*
Pub: Dow Jones & Company, Inc.
Ed: Karen Hube. **Description:** Investors, particularly those having retirement investments, are advised to diversify their investments, refrain from market timing, and minimize payments to maximize investment gains. An investor committing these mistakes could lose as much as $375,000 dollars over ten years.

31537 ■ *"How to Beat the Pros" in Canadian Business (Vol. 81, Summer 2008, No. 9, pp. 59)*
Pub: Rogers Media Ltd.
Ed: Calvin Leung. **Description:** Table showing the results of the Investor 500 beat the S&P/TSX composite index is presented. The average total return, best performing stocks and total return of the 2007 stock screen are provided.

31538 ■ *How Come That Idiot's Rich and I'm Not?*
Pub: Crown Publishing/Random House
Ed: Robert Shemin. **Released:** April 2009. **Price:** $13.95. **Description:** The book shows the average person not only how to get rich, but to create, connect and contribute greatly.

31539 ■ *"How to Handle a Bank Error: Act Quickly When You See a Mistake on Your Statement" in Black Enterprise (Vol. 41, December 2010, No. 5)*
Pub: Earl G. Graves Publishing Co. Inc.
Ed: Sheiresa Ngo. **Description:** Contact your bank or financial institution immediately after discovering an error in your account.

31540 ■ *"How High Can Soybeans Fly?" in Barron's (Vol. 88, March 10, 2008, No. 10, pp. M14)*
Pub: Dow Jones & Company, Inc.
Ed: Kenneth Rapoza. **Description:** Prices of soybeans have risen to $14.0875 a bushel, up 8.3 percent for the week. Increased demand, such as in China and in other developing economies, and the investment-driven commodities boom are boosting prices.

31541 ■ *"How Interest Rate Changes Affect You" in Agency Sales Magazine (Vol. 39, September-October 2009, No. 9, pp. 50)*
Pub: MANA
Ed: Lee Eisinberg. **Description:** Falling interest rates make the prices of previously issued bonds rise and new issues are offered at lower rates. For stock investors, rising interest rates can have a positive or negative effect. Terminologies related to investing are explained.

31542 ■ *How to Make Big Money*
Pub: Hyperion Books
Ed: Jeffrey J. Fox. **Released:** May 19, 2004. **Price:** $16.95. **Description:** Entrepreneur and consultant offers advice to help others create successful startups and prosper. Fox directs new business owners with a counterintuitive style and describes essential methods that beat the competition. Tips include: setting priorities, getting a personal driver, creating a contingency plan for employees, pricing to value, saving money, and getting an office outside of the home.

31543 ■ *How to Make Money in Stocks: A Winning System in Good Times and Bad*
Pub: The McGraw-Hill Companies
Ed: William J. O'Neil. **Released:** June 12. 2009. **Price:** $16.95. **Description:** The bestselling guide to buying stocks, from the founder of Investor's Business Daily. The technique is based on a study of the greatest stock market winners dating back to 1953 and includes a seven-step process for minimizing risk, maximizing return, and finding stocks that are ready to perform.

31544 ■ *"How Not to Raise Bank Capital" in Barron's (Vol. 88, June 30, 2008, No. 26, pp. M6)*
Pub: Dow Jones & Co., Inc.
Ed: Sean Walters. **Description:** French bank Natixis wants to raise 1 billion euros from cash provided by their two major owners. Natixis will reimburse Banque Populaire and Caisses d'Epargne with hybrid securities so this move will not benefit Natixis' core Tier 1 ratio. This has also given the impression that the company is afraid of a full rights issue which could shake investors' faith in the bank.

31545 ■ *"How Our Picks Beat The Bear" in Barron's (Vol. 88, July 14, 2008, No. 28, pp. 18)*
Pub: Dow Jones & Co., Inc.
Ed: Andrew Bary. **Description:** Performance of the stocks that Barron's covered in the first half of 2008 is discussed; some of the worst picks and most rewarding pans have been in the financial sector while the best plays were in the energy, materials, and the transportation sectors.

31546 ■ *How to Protect and Manage Your 401K: Shield, Save, and Grow Your Money, Guard Against Corporate Corruption, Do What It Takes to Protect Your Future*
Pub: Career Press, Incorporated
Ed: Elizabeth Opalka. **Released:** May 2003. **Description:** Ways to protect and manage 401(K) investments.

31547 ■ *How to Start a Small Business in Canada: Your Road Map to Financial Freedom*
Pub: Self-Help Publishers
Ed: Tariq Nadeem. **Released:** September 30, 2004. **Price:** $17.95. **Description:** Provides information for starting and managing a small business in Canada.

31548 ■ *"How Sweet It Will Be" in Barron's (Vol. 89, July 13, 2009, No. 28, pp. M13)*
Pub: Dow Jones & Co., Inc.
Ed: Debbie Carlson. **Description:** Raw sugar experienced a rally in the first half of 2009 and the long term outlook for sugar prices is still good. However, there is a likely near-term correction due to the onset of Brazilian harvest that could be 20.7 percent higher for 2009 as compared to the previous year and October contracts could fall to 15.61 cents per pound.

31549 ■ *"How To: Manage Your Cash Better" in Inc. (Volume 32, December 2010, No. 10, pp. 69)*
Pub: Inc. Magazine
Description: A monthly guide to policies, procedures and practices for managing cash for a small business.

31550 ■ *How to Use the Internet to Advertise, Promote, and Market Your Business or Web Site: With Little or No Money*
Pub: Atlantic Publishing Company
Released: December 1, 2010. **Price:** $24.95. **Description:** Information is given to help build, promote, and make money from your Website or brick and mortar store using the Internet, with minimal costs.

31551 ■ *How to Write a Great Business Plan for Your Small Business in 60 Minutes or Less*
Pub: Atlantic Publishing
Ed: Sharon L. Fullen. **Released:** January 2006. **Price:** $39.95 includes CD-Rom. **Description:** A good business plan outlines goals and works as a company's resume to obtain funding, credit from suppliers, management of the operations and finances, promotion and marketing, and more.

31552 ■ *Hug Your Customers*
Pub: Hyperion Books
Ed: Jack Mitchell. **Price:** $19.95. **Description:** The CEO of Mitchells/Roberts, two very successful clothing stores, professes his belief in showering customers with attention. His secrets for long-term business success include advice about attracting a good staff, lowering marketing costs, and maintaining higher gross margins and revenues.

31553 ■ *"Huntington's Future At a Crossroads" in Crain's Cleveland Business (Vol. 30, June 22, 2009, No. 24, pp. 1)*
Pub: Crain Communications, Inc.
Ed: Arielle Kass. **Description:** Despite Huntington Bancshares plans to expand in the Cleveland, Ohio area, experts wonder if the bank will be able to take advantage of the area's growth in the long run. Statistical data included.

31554 ■ *"Ian Gordon" in Canadian Business (Vol. 81, Summer 2008, No. 9, pp. 10)*
Pub: Rogers Media Ltd.
Ed: Matthew McClearn. **Description:** Bolder Investment Partners' Ian Gordon discussed the economic theory promulgated by Russian economist Nikolai Kondratieff. The cycle begins with a rising economy then followed by deflationary depression. Details of his views on the Kondratieff cycle and its application to the current economy are presented.

31555 ■ *"Ideas at Work: The Reality of Costs" in Business Strategy Review (Vol. 21, Summer 2010, No. 2, pp. 40)*
Pub: Wiley-Blackwell
Ed: Jules Goddard. **Description:** If you think that cost cutting is the surest way to business success, the author wants to challenge every assumption you hold. Costs are an outcome of sound strategy, never the goal of strategy. He offers a new perspective on what counts when it comes to costs.

31556 ■ *"Identity Crisis: The Battle For Your Data" in Canadian Business (Vol. 81, March 17, 2008, No. 4, pp. 12)*
Pub: Rogers Media
Description: Nigel Brown explains that businesses must protect their data through encryption and tightening up access to data. Brown also points out that banks and merchants bear most of the costs for identity fraud and leaves individuals with a lot of pain and heartache in clearing their name.

31557 ■ *"If You Go Into the Market Today.." in Canadian Business (Vol. 82, Summer 2009, No. 8, pp. 18)*
Pub: Rogers Media
Ed: Jeff Sanford. **Description:** Opinions of experts and personalities who are known to have bear attitudes towards the economy were presented in the event 'A Night with the Bears' in Toronto in April 2009. Known bears that served as resource persons in the event were Nouriel Roubini, Eric Sprott, Ian Gordon, and Meredith Whitney. The bears were observed to have differences regarding consumer debt.

31558 ■ *"Immigration Issues Frustrate Owners From Overseas" in The Business Journal-Serving Greater Tampa Bay (Vol. 28, August 15, 2008)*
Pub: American City Business Journals, Inc.
Ed: Margie Manning. **Description:** Investors who availed the E-2 visa program believe that the tightened restrictions on the visa program has trapped them in the United States. The E-2 investor visa program was designed to attract investors into the

U.S., but restrictions were tightened after the September 11, 2001 attacks. Other views and information on E-2 and its impact on investors are presented.

31559 ■ *"In the Bag?" in Canadian Business (Vol. 81, March 3, 2008, No. 3, pp. 57)*
Pub: Rogers Media
Ed: Calvin Leung. **Description:** American stocks are beginning to appear cheap amidst the threat of a worldwide economic slowdown, United States economic crisis and declining stock portfolios. Investors looking for bargain stocks should study the shares of Apple and Oshkosh Corp. Evaluation of other cheap-looking stocks such as the shares of Coach and 3M is also given.

31560 ■ *"In China, Railways to Riches" in Barron's (Vol. 88, July 7, 2008, No. 27, pp. M9)*
Pub: Dow Jones & Co., Inc.
Ed: Assif Shameen. **Description:** Shares of Chinese railway companies look to benefit from multimillion-dollar investments aimed at upgrading the Chinese railway network. Investment in the sector is expected to reach $210 billion for the 2006-2010 period.

31561 ■ *"In India, A Gold-Price Threat?" in Barron's (Vol. 88, June 30, 2008, No. 26, pp. M12)*
Pub: Dow Jones & Co., Inc.
Ed: Melanie Burton. **Description:** Gold purchases in India are falling as record prices take its toll on demand. Gold imports to India fell by 52 percent in May 2008 from the previous year and local prices are higher by one-third from the previous year to 12,540 rupees for 10 grams.

31562 ■ *"In Praise of How Not to Invest" in Barron's (Vol. 89, July 13, 2009, No. 28, pp. 11)*
Pub: Dow Jones & Co., Inc.
Ed: Vito J. Racanelli. **Description:** One research study found that the shares of companies that have growing market shares and expanding asset bases underperform. This is contrary to the widely held premise that stock prices for these companies rise. It is argued that this result is caused by these companies' tendency to sacrifice profitability to grab market share and this is reflected in their stock prices.

31563 ■ *"In the Public Eye" in Entrepreneur (Vol. 35, November 2007, No. 11, pp. 75)*
Pub: Entrepreneur Media Inc.
Ed: David Worrell. **Description:** The market for initial public offerings (IPOs) was booming in 2007 and strong fundamentals for companies that would like to go public are needed. The basics that companies should review before planning an IPO are outlined.

31564 ■ *"In Sickness and In Wealth Management" in Hispanic Business (Vol. 30, March 2008, No. 3, pp. 28)*
Pub: Hispanic Business
Ed: Rick Munarriz. **Description:** Discusses the investment and wealth management firms owned and operated by Hispanics. There are only a handful of these firms owned by Hispanics, as most of them prefer capital preservation by investing in hard assets like cash and real estate than in capital appreciation.

31565 ■ *"In Sickness and in Wealth Management" in Hispanic Business (March 2008, pp. 28, 30)*
Pub: Hispanic Business
Ed: Rick Munarriz. **Description:** Financial advice is offered by experts, Myrna Rivera and Samuel Ramirez Jr., with an overview of Hispanic-owned investment firms.

31566 ■ *"In Surging Oil Industry, Good Fortune Comes In Stages" in Barron's (Vol. 88, July 7, 2008, No. 27, pp. 12)*
Pub: Dow Jones & Co., Inc.
Ed: Sandra Ward. **Description:** Shares of US land oil and gas driller Helmerich and Payne, priced at $69 each, are estimated to be at peak levels. The shares are trading at 17 times 2008 earnings and could be in for some profit taking.

31567 ■ *"Inch by Inch, Employees Lose Ground" in Business Courier (Vol. 26, November 13, 2009, No. 29, pp. 1)*
Pub: American City Business Journals, Inc.
Ed: James Ritchie. **Description:** Employees in Ohio who retained their jobs have suffered losses in salary and other benefits, as companies exert efforts to save money. Thirty-four percent of employees experienced pay cuts. Statistical data included.

31568 ■ *"Inflation Woes: Secure Your Portfolio Against Rising Prices" in Black Enterprise (Vol. 37, January 2007, No. 6, pp. 40)*
Pub: Earl G. Graves Publishing Co. Inc.
Ed: Donald Jay Korn. **Description:** Inflation has a huge impact on investing and it is important to take the steady increase on cost into account when looking at your financial goals and investing in your future. Statistical data included.

31569 ■ *"Inland Snaps Up Rival REITs" in Crain's Chicago Business (Vol. 31, November 17, 2008, No. 46, pp. 3)*
Pub: Crain Communications, Inc.
Ed: Alby Gallun. **Description:** Discusses Inland American Real Estate Trust Inc., a real estate investment trust that is napping up depressed shares of publicly traded competitors, a possible first step toward taking over these companies; however, with hotel and retail properties accounting for approximately 70 percent of its portfolio, the company could soon face its own difficulties.

31570 ■ *"Insider" in Canadian Business (Vol. 81, March 31, 2008, No. 5, pp. 76)*
Pub: Rogers Media
Ed: John Gray. **Description:** Discusses a comparison of an average Canadian family's finances in 1990 with the data from 2007. The average family in 2007 has over $80,000 in debt compared to just under $52,000 in 1990. However, Canadians have also been accumulating solid assets such as homes and stocks. This means that Canadian debt load has fallen from 22 percent in 1990 to 20 percent in 2007 when taken as a percentage of total net worth.

31571 ■ *"Insider" in Canadian Business (Vol. 81, March 3, 2008, No. 3, pp. 96)*
Pub: Rogers Media
Description: History of gold usage and gold trading is presented in a timeline. Gold was a symbol of power and wealth in 2500 B.C., and in 1500 B.C., it became the first currency to be recognized internationally. Other remarkable events in the gold industry and laws that covered gold are discussed.

31572 ■ *Instant Cashflow: Hundreds of Proven Strategies to Win Customers, Boost Margins and Take More Money Home*
Pub: McGraw-Hill Companies Inc.
Contact: Deven Sharma, President
Ed: Bradley J. Sugars. **Released:** December 2005. **Price:** $17.95 (US), $22.95 (Canadian). **Description:** Nearly 300 proven marketing and sales strategies are shared by the author, a self-made millionaire. Advice on creating the proper mindset, generating new leads, boosting the conversion rate of leads to sales, maximizing the value of the average sale, and measuring results is included.

31573 ■ *Instant Profit: Successful Strategies to Boost Your Margin and Increase the Profitability of Your Business*
Pub: McGraw-Hill Companies Inc.
Contact: Deven Sharma, President
Ed: Bradley J. Sugars. **Released:** December 2005. **Price:** $16.95 (US), $22.95 (Canadian). **Description:** Advice on management, money, marketing, and merchandising a successful small business is offered.

31574 ■ *"An Insurance Roll-Up In Danger of Unraveling" in Barron's (Vol. 88, March 17, 2008, No. 11, pp. 51)*
Pub: Dow Jones & Company, Inc.
Ed: Bill Alpert. **Description:** Shares of National Financial Partners have fallen below their initial offering price as sputtering sales and management turnover leave many investors wondering. One of the company's star brokers is being sued for their 'life settlement' contracts while another broker is being pursued by the IRS for unpaid taxes.

31575 ■ *"International ETFs: Your Passport to the World" in Barron's (Vol. 89, July 13, 2009, No. 28, pp. L10)*
Pub: Dow Jones & Co., Inc.
Ed: John Hintze. **Description:** International exchange traded funds give investors more choices in terms of investment plays and there are 174 U.S. ETF listings worth $141 billion as of July 2009. Suggestions on how to invest in these funds based on one's conviction on how the global economy will unfold are presented.

31576 ■ *"Investment Manager Disciplined" in Sacramento Business Journal (Vol. 25, July 4, 2008, No. 18, pp. 1)*
Pub: American City Business Journals, Inc.
Ed: Mark Anderson. **Description:** Community Capital Management's David A. Zwick is permanently barred by the Securities and Exchange Commission (SEC) from associating with any broker or dealer, after investigations revealed that he took part in paying kickbacks to a bond trader. Other views and information on Community Capital, and on the SEC investigation on Zwick, are presented.

31577 ■ *"Investors Shrug Off the Turmoil" in Globe & Mail (March 1, 2007, pp. B1)*
Pub: CTVglobemedia Publishing Inc.
Ed: Geoffrey York. **Description:** The decision of Chinese investors to continue to buy stocks despite the decade's biggest market crash is discussed. The rise in the stock price indexes of China is described.

31578 ■ *"Iowa Tax Case Could Cost Nation's Franchises" in Franchising World (Vol. 42, September 2010, No. 9, pp. 38)*
Pub: International Franchise Association
Ed: Bruce A. Ackerman, Adam B. Thimmesch. **Description:** Ruling by the Iowa Supreme Court could have a financial impact on franchisors across the U.S. Iowa asserted that Kentucky Fried Chicken is subject to Iowa corporate income tax based solely on the fact that it received royalties from franchises in the state.

31579 ■ *"Is Raising CPP Premiums a Good Idea?" in Canadian Business (Vol. 83, July 20, 2010, No. 11-12, pp. 37)*
Pub: Rogers Media Ltd.
Description: Big labor is pushing for an increase in Canada Pension Plan premiums but pension consultants believe this system is not broken and that the government needs to focus on addressing the low rate of personal retirement savings. If the premiums go up, even those with high savings will be forced to pay more and it could block other plans that really address the real issue.

31580 ■ *"Is There a Doctor In the House?" in Black Enterprise (Vol. 41, December 2010, No. 5, pp. 42)*
Pub: Earl G. Graves Publishing Co. Inc.
Ed: Renita Burns. **Description:** Health insurance premiums have increased between 15 percent and 20 percent for small business owners, making it one of the most expensive costs. Ways to evaluate a health plan's costs and effectiveness are examined.

31581 ■ *"Is the VIX in Denial?" in Barron's (Vol. 88, July 7, 2008, No. 27, pp. M12)*
Pub: Dow Jones & Co., Inc.
Ed: Lawrence McMillan. **Description:** Volatility Index (VIX) of the Chicago Board Options Exchange did not rise significantly despite the drop in the US stock markets, rising to near 25. This market decline, however, will eventually result in investor panic and the rise of the VIX.

31582 ■ *"Islamic Banks Get a 'Libor' of Their Own" in Wall Street Journal Eastern Edition (November 25 , 2011, pp. C4)*
Pub: Dow Jones & Company Inc. Enterprise Media Group
Contact: Clare Hart, President
Ed: Katy Burne. **Description:** The London interbank offered rate, or Libor, has been used by banks internationally for years. It is the rate at which banks

lend money to each other. The rate has not been used by Islamic banks, but now sixteen banks have come up with the Islamic Interbank Benchmark Rate.

31583 ■ *"It Could Be Worse" in Barron's (Vol. 89, July 27, 2009, No. 30, pp. 5)*
Pub: Dow Jones & Co., Inc.
Ed: Alan Abelson. **Description:** Media sources are being fooled by corporate America who is peddling an economic recovery rather than reality as shown by the report of a rise in existing home sales which boosted the stock market even if it was a seasonal phenomenon. The phrase 'things could be worse' sums up the reigning investment philosophy in the U.S. and this has been stirring up the market.

31584 ■ *"It May Be Cheaper to Manufacture At Home" in Harvard Business Review (Vol. 88, October 2010, No. 10, pp. 84)*
Pub: Harvard Business School Publishing
Ed: Suzanne de Treville, Lenos Trigeorgis. **Description:** Using a real options framework rather than a discounted cash flow model to assess and value supply chain processes is examined. This enables companies to assess costs for a variety of situations, not just ideal or normal circumstances, which can make the difference between domestic and foreign manufacturing decisions.

31585 ■ *"It Takes More Than One" in Black Enterprise (Vol. 38, July 2008, No. 12, pp. 38)*
Pub: Earl G. Graves Publishing Co. Inc.
Ed: James A. Anderson. **Description:** Interview with Eric Small, the CEO of SBK-Brooks Investment Corp., whom discusses the importance of versatility when trying to find the best investment choices; the primary factors investors should be mindful of; his current stock picks; and recommendations for investing in an uncertain and volatile market.

31586 ■ *"It's Good to be Goldman" in Barron's (Vol. 89, July 20, 2009, No. 29, pp. 5)*
Pub: Dow Jones & Co., Inc.
Ed: Randall W. Forsyth. **Description:** Profits of Goldman Sachs rose to $3.44 billion in the second quarter of 2009, aided by federal financial stimulus programs. CIT Group is facing bankruptcy and may need up to $6 billion to survive. The federal economic stimulus programs are benefiting Wall Street more than the US economy itself.

31587 ■ *It's Your Ship*
Pub: Warner Books Inc.
Ed: Michael Abrashoff. **Released:** May 1, 2002. **Price:** $24.95. **Description:** Naval Captain D. Michael Abrashoff shares management principles he used to shape his ship, the U.S.S. Benfold, into a model of progressive leadership. Abrashoff revolutionized ways to face the challenges of excessive costs, low morale, sexual harassment, and constant turnover.

31588 ■ *"J.C. Evans Seeks Bankruptcy Protection" in Austin Business Journal (Vol. 31, August 12, 2011, No. 23, pp. A1)*
Pub: American City Business Journals Inc.
Ed: Vicky Garza. **Description:** J.C. Evans Construction Holdings Inc., as well as its affiliated companies, has filed for Chapter 11 bankruptcy following its continued financial breakdown which it blames on the tough economy. Details are included.

31589 ■ *"The Judgment Deficit" in Harvard Business Review (Vol. 88, September 2010, No. 9, pp. 44)*
Pub: Harvard Business School Publishing
Ed: Amar Bhide. **Description:** The importance of individual, decentralized initiative and judgment in the capitalist system is outlined. While financial models have their use, they cannot always account appropriately for the inherent uncertainty in economic decision making.

31590 ■ *"Juiced on Energy" in Barron's (Vol. 88, July 14, 2008, No. 28, pp. 33)*
Pub: Dow Jones & Co., Inc.
Ed: Leslie P. Norton. **Description:** Brad Evans and his team at Heartland Value Plus were able to outperform their peers by significantly undercommitting to financials and overexposing themselves with energy stocks. Brad Evans believes that there is a lot of value left in energy stocks such as natural gas.

31591 ■ *"Julie Holzrichter; Managing Director of Operations, CME Group Inc." in Crain's Chicago Business (Vol. 31, May 5, 2008, No. 18)*
Pub: Crain Communications, Inc.
Ed: Ann Saphir. **Description:** Profile of Julie Holzrichter who works as the managing director of operations for CME Group Inc. and is known as a decisive leader able to intercept and solve problems.

31592 ■ *"Just Hang Up" in Barron's (Vol. 88, March 10, 2008, No. 10, pp. 45)*
Pub: Dow Jones & Company, Inc.
Ed: Tiernan Ray. **Description:** Sprint's shares are expected to continue falling while the company attempts to attract subscribers by cutting prices, cutting earnings in the process. The company faces tougher competition from better-financed AT&T and Verizon Communications.

31593 ■ *"Keeping the Faith in Fuel-Tech" in Barron's (Vol. 88, March 24, 2008, No. 12, pp. 20)*
Pub: Dow Jones & Company, Inc.
Ed: Christopher C. Williams. **Description:** Shares of air pollution control company Fuel-Tech remain on track to reach $40 each from their $19 level due to a continued influx of contracts. The stock has suffered from lower-than-expected quarterly earnings and tougher competition but stand to benefit from increased orders.

31594 ■ *"Kenyans Embrace Moving Money By Text Message" in Chicago Tribune (October 7, 2008)*
Pub: McClatchy-Tribune Information Services
Ed: Laurie Goering. **Description:** Cell phone banking services are becoming more common, especially for foreign residents; customers are able to establish a virtual cell phone bank account through companies such as M-Pesa which allows their customers to pay bills, withdraw cash, pay merchants or text money to relatives.

31595 ■ *"Kid Rock" in Canadian Business (Vol. 81, Summer 2008, No. 9, pp. 54)*
Pub: Rogers Media Ltd.
Ed: John Gray. **Description:** Damien Reynolds is the founder, chairman and chief executive officer of Vancouver-based Longview Capital Partners. The investment bank, founded in 2005, is one of the fastest-growing companies in British Columbia. The recent economic downturn has battered the stocks of the company and its portfolio of junior miners.

31596 ■ *"Know Your Numbers" in Inc. (Volume 32, December 2010, No. 10, pp. 39)*
Pub: Inc. Magazine
Ed: Norm Brodsky. **Description:** Ways to maximize profit and minimize tax burden are presented.

31597 ■ *"The Latin Beat Goes On" in Barron's (Vol. 88, July 7, 2008, No. 27, pp. L5)*
Pub: Dow Jones & Co., Inc.
Ed: Tom Sullivan. **Description:** Latin American stocks have outperformed other regional markets due to rising commodities prices and favorable economic climate. Countries such as Brazil, Mexico, Chile, and Peru provide investment opportunities, while Argentina and Venezuela are tougher places to invest.

31598 ■ *"Laugh or Cry?" in Barron's (Vol. 88, March 24, 2008, No. 12, pp. 7)*
Pub: Dow Jones & Company, Inc.
Ed: Alan Abelson. **Description:** Discusses the American economy which is just starting to feel the effect of the credit and housing crises. JPMorgan Chase purchased Bear Stearns for $2 a share, much lower than its share price of $60, while quasi-government entities Fannie Mae and Freddie Mac are starting to run into trouble.

31599 ■ *Law for the Small and Growing Business*
Pub: Jordans Publishing Limited
Ed: P. Bohm. **Released:** February 2007. **Price:** $59.98. **Description:** Legal and regulatory issues facing small businesses, including employment law, health and safety, commercial property, company law and finance are covered.

31600 ■ *"Leaders and Lagards" in Barron's (Vol. 89, July 13, 2009, No. 28, pp. 14)*
Pub: Dow Jones & Co., Inc.
Ed: J.R. Brandstrader. **Description:** Statistical table that shows the returns of different mutual funds in different categories that include U.S. stock funds, sector funds, world equity funds, and mixed equity funds is presented. The data presented is for the second quarter of 2009.

31601 ■ *"Leaders and Lagards" in Barron's (Vol. 89, July 13, 2009, No. 28, pp. 14)*
Pub: Dow Jones & Co., Inc.
Ed: J.R. Brandstrader. **Description:** Statistical table that shows the returns of different mutual funds in different categories that include U.S. stock funds, sector funds, world equity funds, and mixed equity funds is presented. The data presented is for the second quarter of 2009.

31602 ■ *"Leaders Weigh In On Fannie Mae, Freddie Mac Failure, Fed Bailout" in The Business Journal - Serving Phoenix and the Valley of the Sun (Vol. 28, September 12, 2008, No. 53, pp. 1)*
Pub: American City Business Journals, Inc.
Ed: Chris Casacchia; Mike Sunnucks; Jan Buchholz. **Description:** Fannie Mae and Freddie Mac's federal takeover was a move to help stabilize the financial market and it helped bring down interest rates in the past week. Local executives from Arizona's Phoenix area share their thoughts on the immediate effect of the takeover and its upside and downside.

31603 ■ *"Legg's Compensation Committee Chair Defends CEO Fetting's Pay" in Boston Business Journal (Vol. 29, July 22, 2011, No. 11, pp. 1)*
Pub: American City Business Journals Inc.
Ed: Gary Haber. **Description:** Legg Mason Inc. CEO Mark R. Fetting has been awarded $5.9 million pay package and he expects to receive questions regarding it in the coming shareholders meeting. However, Baltimore, Maryland-based RKTL Associates chairman emeritus Harold R. Adams believes Fetting has done a tremendous job in bringing Legg's through a tough market.

31604 ■ *"Lehman's Hail Mary Pass" in Business Week (September 22, 2008, No. 4100, pp. 28)*
Pub: McGraw-Hill Companies, Inc.
Ed: Matthew Goldstein; David Henry; Ben Levison. **Description:** Overview of Lehman Brothers' CEO Richard Fuld's plan to keep the firm afloat and end the stock's plunge downward; Fuld's strategy calls for selling off a piece of the firm's investment management business.

31605 ■ *"Lenders" in The Business Journal - Serving Phoenix and the Valley of the Sun (Vol. 28, July 25, 2008, No. 47, pp. 1)*
Pub: American City Business Journals, Inc.
Ed: Jan Buchholz. **Description:** Private equity lender Investor Mortgage Holdings Inc. has continued growing despite the crisis surrounding the real estate and financial industries and has accumulated a $700 million loan portfolio. Private lending has become increasingly important in financing real estate deals as commercial credit has dried up.

31606 ■ *"Lenders Capitalize on a Thinning Bulge Bracket" in Mergers & Acquisitions: The Dealmaker's Journal (March 1, 2008)*
Pub: SourceMedia, Inc.
Description: Regardless of what the economic markets look like, private equity firms will continue to invest capital and mid-market finance firms are becoming very attractive acquisition opportunities since not as much capital is needed to buy them.

31607 ■ *"Lending Stays Down at Local Banks" in Business Courier (Vol. 27, October 1, 2010, No. 22, pp. 1)*
Pub: Business Courier
Ed: Steve Watkins. **Description:** Greater Cincinnati's largest banks have experienced decreases in loans in the past year due to weak economy and sagging loan demands. Analysis of mid-year data has shown that loans drop by a total of $3.6 billion or 4 percent at the ten largest banks as of June 30, 2010 compared to same period in 2009.

31608 ■ *"Less Malaise in Malaysia" in Barron's (Vol. 88, March 17, 2008, No. 11, pp. M12)*
Pub: Dow Jones & Company, Inc.
Ed: Assif Shameen. **Description:** Shares of Malaysia's Bursa have been in freefall while the Malaysia government prolongs its pitch to sell a 10 percent stake of the exchange to NYSE Euronext. Asian bourses had produced very good returns for five years and charge some of the highest fees for exchanges. A key growth driver for Asian bourses could be the derivatives markets and exchange-traded funds.

31609 ■ *"Let Us Count the Ways" in Barron's (Vol. 88, July 7, 2008, No. 27, pp. M10)*
Pub: Dow Jones & Co., Inc.
Ed: Bennet Sedacca. **Description:** Investors are advised to remain cautious after the drop in stock prices in June 2008. The stock markets remain in the downtrend after reaching a peak in October 2007 and are on the verge of a collapse.

31610 ■ *"Lifesavers" in Black Enterprise (Vol. 41, December 2010, No. 5, pp. 38)*
Pub: Earl G. Graves Publishing Co. Inc.
Ed: Tamara E. Holmes. **Description:** Profile of Interventional Nephrology Specialists Access Center and founders Dr. Omar Davis and Dr. Natarsha Grant; the center generated $5.5 million in revenue for 2009. Details on how they run their successful center are included.

31611 ■ *"A Lifetime of Making Deals" in Crain's Detroit Business (Vol. 24, March 24, 2008, No. 12, pp. 11)*
Pub: Crain Communications, Inc.
Ed: Tom Henderson. **Description:** Profile of Walter 'Bud' Aspatore who received Crain's Lifetime Achievement Award for mergers and acquisitions; Aspatore is chairman and co-founder of Amherst Partners L.L.C., an investment banking firm that does evaluations and financings, specializes in turnarounds and advises private and public companies on mergers and acquisitions.

31612 ■ *"Lifetime Planning with a Twist" in Contractor (Vol. 56, July 2009, No. 7, pp. 40)*
Pub: Penton Media, Inc.
Ed: Irv Blackman. **Description:** Private Placement Life Insurance lets wealthy investors make their investment gains tax-free and can be set up so investors can make tax-free loans from the policy. This can be used on a younger member of the family as a wealth-building strategy if the investor is uninsurable.

31613 ■ *"Like Mom and Apple Pie" in Canadian Business (Vol. 79, October 9, 2006, No. 20, pp. 19)*
Pub: Rogers Media
Ed: Peter Shawn Taylor. **Description:** Impact of paying huge tax bills on the social benefits of family income is discussed. Income splitting as an effective way to lower household's overall tax bill is presented.

31614 ■ *"Listen Up: There's a Revolution in the Cubicle" in Barron's (Vol. 89, July 27, 2009, No. 30, pp. 18)*
Pub: Dow Jones & Co., Inc.
Ed: Jay Palmer. **Description:** Plantronics will be among the first beneficiaries when the unified communications revolution arrives in the office. Plantronics' shares could rise to around 30 in 2009 from the 20s as of July 2009. Unified communications could create a huge new multimillion-dollar market for Plantronics.

31615 ■ *"The Little Biotech that Could" in Barron's (Vol. 89, July 27, 2009, No. 30, pp. 19)*
Pub: Dow Jones & Co., Inc.
Ed: Christopher C. Williams. **Description:** OSI Pharmaceuticals' shares is a compelling investment bet among small biotech firms due to its Tarceva anticancer drug which has a 23 percent market share as well as their strong balance sheet. OSI is planning to expand the use of Tarceva which could re-ignite sales and one analyst expects the shares to trade in the 40s one year from July 2009.

31616 ■ *"A Load of Bull?" in Canadian Business (Vol. 82, Summer 2009, No. 8, pp. 12)*
Pub: Rogers Media
Ed: Joe Castaldo. **Description:** Some experts and analysts believe that the improvement of some economic indicators in Canada suggest an economic recovery. A survey of Russell Investment in March 2009 found that 60 percent of investment managers are bullish on Canadian stocks. Some experts like Mike Zyblock, however, remain cautious on the economy.

31617 ■ *"Local Firms Will Feel Impact Of Wall St. Woes" in The Business Journal-Milwaukee (Vol. 25, September 19, 2008, No. 52, pp. A1)*
Pub: American City Business Journals, Inc.
Ed: Rich Kirchen. **Description:** Wall Street's crisis is expected to affect businesses in Wisconsin, in terms of decreased demand for services and products and increased financing costs. Businesses in Milwaukee area may face higher interest rates and tougher loan standards. The potential impacts of the Wall Street crisis on local businesses are examined further.

31618 ■ *"Locally Based Stocks Escape Worst of Market's Turmoil" in Crain's Detroit Business (Vol. 24, September 22, 2008, No. 38, pp. 4)*
Pub: Crain Communications Inc.
Ed: Daniel Duggan. **Description:** Locally-based companies did not take as big a hit as might be expected with the shock to the financial markets last week; this is due mainly to the fact that the region does not have heavy exposure to energy or capital markets.

31619 ■ *"Long - And Leery" in Barron's (Vol. 88, March 31, 2008, No. 13, pp. 47)*
Pub: Dow Jones & Company, Inc.
Ed: Jack Willoughby. **Description:** Tom Claugus' Bay Resource Partners hedge fund has returned 20 percent annually since it started in 1993. Claugus says that he is as aggressively long as he has ever been despite the dangers of the U.S. market. Claugus' stock picks include Canadian Natural Resources, NII Holdings, and Discover Financial.

31620 ■ *"Loonie Tunes: When Will the Dollar Rise Again?" in Canadian Business (Vol. 81, November 10, 2008, No. 19, pp. 62)*
Pub: Rogers Media Ltd.
Ed: Joe Castaldo. **Description:** The Canadian dollar has weakened against the U.S. Dollar as the U.S. financial crisis rocked global markets. A currency strategist says that the strength of the U.S. dollar is not based on people's optimism on the U.S. economy but on a structural demand where U.S. non-financial corporations have been repatriating greenbacks from foreign subsidiaries.

31621 ■ *"Lotus Starts Slowly, Dodges Subprime Woes" in Crain's Detroit Business (Vol. 24, April 14, 2008, No. 15, pp. 3)*
Pub: Crain Communications, Inc.
Ed: Tom Henderson. **Description:** Discusses Lotus Bancorp Inc. and their business plan, which although is not right on target due to the subprime mortgage meltdown, is in a much better position than its competitors due to the quality of their loans.

31622 ■ *"Loyalty Cards Score Points" in Crain's Cleveland Business (Vol. 30, June 8, 2009, No. 22, pp. 1)*
Pub: Crain Communications, Inc.
Ed: Chuck Soder. **Description:** Northeast Ohio retailers are promoting loyalty and rewards programs in order to attract and maintain loyal customers.

31623 ■ *"Loyalty Pays" in Entrepreneur (Vol. 36, February 2008, No. 2, pp. 63)*
Pub: Entrepreneur Media Inc.
Ed: David Worrell. **Description:** Michael Vadini, chief executive officer of Titan Technology Partners looks after his stockholders and investors by making sure that they are protected from risk. Having been affected by the downturn in the technology industry between 2001 and 2004, Vadini granted his investors a liquidity preference. Details regarding his actions to retain investor loyalty are discussed.

31624 ■ *"Make Money in 2011" in Small Business Opportunities (January 2011)*
Pub: Harris Publications Inc.
Description: Top twenty ways to pick up extra cash, boost your income and generate new revenue. There has never been a better time to start a small business.

31625 ■ *"Making Automated Royalty Payments Work for Your Franchise" in Franchising World (Vol. 42, October 2010, No. 10, pp. 30)*
Pub: International Franchise Association
Ed: J.P. O'Brien. **Description:** In the past, royalty payments were sent by franchisees through regular postal mail and accompanied by a single slip of paper with handwritten notes indicating the month's revenue numbers and royalty amounts.

31626 ■ *"Making It Click" in Barron's (Vol. 88, March 17, 2008, No. 11, pp. 31)*
Pub: Dow Jones & Company, Inc.
Ed: Theresa W. Carey. **Description:** Listing of 23 online brokers that are evaluated based on their trade experience, usability, range of offerings, research amenities, customer service and access, and costs. TradeStation Securities takes the top spot followed by thinkorswim by just a fraction.

31627 ■ *"The Man Behind Brascan" in Canadian Business (Vol. 79, Winter 2006, No. 24, pp. 64)*
Pub: Rogers Media
Ed: Andy Holloway. **Description:** The role of Jack Cockwell in the growth of Brookfield Asset Management Inc., is described.

31628 ■ *Managing Business Growth: Get a Grip on the Numbers That Count*
Pub: Self-Counsel Press, Incorporated
Ed: Angie Mohr. **Released:** October 2004. **Price:** $14.95. **Description:** Fourth book in the Numbers 101 for Small Business Series, teaches how small company owners can expand their businesses using sound financial planning.

31629 ■ *Managing a Small Business Made Easy*
Pub: Entrepreneur Press
Ed: Martin E. Davis. **Released:** September 2005. **Price:** $19.95 (US), $26.95 (Canadian). **Description:** Examination of the essential elements for an entrepreneur running a business, including advice on leadership, customer service, financials, and more.

31630 ■ *"M&T On the March?" in Baltimore Business Journal (Vol. 28, November 12, 2010, No. 27, pp. 1)*
Pub: Baltimore Business Journal
Ed: Gary Haber. **Description:** Information on the growth of M&T Bank, as well as its expansion plans are presented. M&T recently acquired Wilmington Trust and took over $500 million in deposits from the failed K Bank. Analysts believe that M&T would continue its expansion through Washington DC and Richmond, Virginia, especially after a bank executive acknowledged that the markets in those areas are attractive.

31631 ■ *"Many Roads Lead to Value" in Barron's (Vol. 88, March 10, 2008, No. 10, pp. 46)*
Pub: Dow Jones & Company, Inc.
Ed: Lawrence C. Strauss. **Description:** David J. Williams, lead manager of Excelsior Value & Restructuring Fund, invests in struggling companies and those companies whose turnarounds show promise. Morgan Stanley, Lehman Brothers, and Petroleo

Brasileiro are some of the companies he holds shares in, while he has unloaded shares of Citigroup, Freddie Mac, and Sallie Mae.

31632 ■ *"Market Recoups Its Losses - And Its Optimism" in Barron's (Vol. 89, July 20, 2009, No. 29, pp. M3)*
Pub: Dow Jones & Co., Inc.
Ed: Kopin Tan. **Description:** US stock markets gained heavily in the third week of July 2009, rising by about 7 percent during the week. The shares of human resource management companies could be overpriced as they are trading at very high price-earnings multiples. Baxter International faces a class-action suit due to its alleged conspiracy with CSL to fix blood-plasma product prices.

31633 ■ *"Market Swings Intensify Yearning for Bonds" in Globe & Mail (March 9, 2007, pp. B9)*
Pub: CTVglobemedia Publishing Inc.
Ed: Keith Damsell. **Description:** The rise in demand for proper fixed-income bonds in Canada as a result of uncertainties in the equity market is discussed. Some big Canadian fixed-income funds are presented.

31634 ■ *"Market Volatility and Your Retirement" in Agency Sales Magazine (Vol. 39, August 2009, No. 8, pp. 48)*
Pub: MANA
Ed: Joshua D. Mosshart. **Description:** Strategies for retirees in managing investments amid market volatility are presented. Retirees should keep their withdrawal assumptions conservative, maintain sensible asset allocation, review and rebalance their portfolio and allow a financial professional to guide them. Insights on market volatility are also given.

31635 ■ *"Market Watch" in Barron's (Vol. 88, March 24, 2008, No. 12, pp. M18)*
Pub: Dow Jones & Company, Inc.
Ed: Ashraf Laidi; Marc Pado; David Kotok. **Description:** Latest measures implemented by the Federal Reserve to address the credit crisis did not benefit the US dollar, with the Japanese yen and the euro recouping earlier losses against the dollar. Goldman Sachs reported earnings of $3.23 per share, claiming a stronger liquidity position. The US markets bottomed early on 22 January 2007, according to evidence.

31636 ■ *"Market Watch" in Barron's (Vol. 89, July 20, 2009, No. 29, pp. M10)*
Pub: Dow Jones & Co., Inc.
Ed: Peter Greene; Michael Darda; Ian Wyatt; Stephanie Pomboy. **Description:** Concerns about a possible increase in US inflation rates are overblown as the country remains in a deflationary environment. Goldman Sachs's second quarter 2009 earnings have already been priced in as its shares rose. Germany's plans of a possible dollar bond sale are in anticipation of a rise in the euro's value.

31637 ■ *"Market Watch: A Sampling of Advisory Opinion" in Barron's (Vol. 88, March 17, 2008, No. 11, pp. M10)*
Pub: Dow Jones & Company, Inc.
Ed: Paul Schatz; William Gibson; Michael Darda. **Description:** S&P 500 bank stocks were down 46 percent from their 2007 peak while the peak to through fall in 1989-1990 was just over 50 percent. This suggests that the bottom on the bank stocks could be near. The Federal Reserve Board announced they will lend up to $200 billion to primary lenders in exchange other securities.

31638 ■ *Marketing in a Web 2.0 World - Using Social Media, Webinars, Blogs, and More to Boost Your Small Business on a Budget*
Pub: Atlantic Publishing Company
Ed: Peter VanRysdam. **Released:** June 1, 2010. **Price:** $24.95. **Description:** Web 2.0 technologies have leveled the playing field for small companies trying to boost their presence by giving them an equal voice against larger competitors. Advice is given to help target your audience using social networking hubs.

31639 ■ *"Markets Defy the Doomsayers" in Barron's (Vol. 88, March 24, 2008, No. 12, pp. M5)*
Pub: Dow Jones & Company, Inc.
Ed: Leslie P. Norton. **Description:** US stock markets registered strong gains, with the Dow Jones Industrial Average rising 3.43 percent on the week to close at 12,361.32, in a rally that may be seen as short-covering. Shares of Hansen Natural are poised for further drops with a slowdown in the energy drink market.

31640 ■ *"The Market's (Very) Tender Spring Shoots" in Barron's (Vol. 88, March 31, 2008, No. 13, pp. M3)*
Pub: Dow Jones & Company, Inc.
Ed: Kopin Tan. **Description:** Expansion in price-earnings multiples and a lower credit-default risk index has encouraged fans of the spring-awakening theory. Shares of industrial truckers have gone up 32 percent in 2008 and some shares are pushing five-year highs brought on by higher efficiency and earnings from more load carried. The prospects of the shares of Foot Locker are also discussed.

31641 ■ *"A Matter of Interest" in Canadian Business (Vol. 79, July 17, 2006, No. 14-15, pp. 21)*
Pub: Rogers Media
Ed: Jeff Sanford. **Description:** With the steady decrease in savings, the need for growth in Canada's payloan industry is discussed. Also emphasized are the challenges faced by payloan operators.

31642 ■ *"The Medium 150" in Canadian Business (Vol. 81, Summer 2008, No. 9, pp. 129)*
Pub: Rogers Media Ltd.
Description: Medium-sized companies are ranked based on market capitalization and stock performance. Timminico Ltd. topped the roster with 1,294.2 percent returns, while Petrominerales Ltd. ranked second with 325.4 percent. A table showing the 2008 rankings of the companies is presented.

31643 ■ *"Merrill Lynch in Talks to Buy BlackRock Stake" in Globe & Mail (February 13, 2006, pp. B4)*
Pub: CTVglobemedia Publishing Inc.
Ed: Dennis K. Breman; Randall Smith. **Description:** Financial services firm Merrill Lynch and Co. Inc. is planning to acquire money managing company BlackRock Inc. for 8 million dollars. Sources report that this deal would create 1-trillion dollar huge fund management venture.

31644 ■ *"Mettle Detector" in Canadian Business (Vol. 79, July 17, 2006, No. 14-15, pp. 63)*
Pub: Rogers Media
Ed: Calvin Leung. **Description:** The difficulties faced in completing the Certified Financial Analyst course, and the rewards one can expect after its completion, are discussed.

31645 ■ *"MF Global Moved Clients' Funds to BNY Mellon" in Wall Street Journal Eastern Edition (November 19 , 2011, pp. B2)*
Pub: Dow Jones & Company Inc.
Ed: Aaron Lucchetti. **Description:** Since the collapse of securities brokerage MF Global Holdings Ltd., one question has remained: where did the hundreds of millions of dollars in customers' accounts go? It has been revealed that MF Global moved those millions from its own brokerage unit to Bank of New York Mellon Corporation in August of this year, just two months before filing for bankruptcy protection.

31646 ■ *"MFS Survey: Generation X/Y Perplexed and Conservative about Future Investing" in Wireless News (November 16, 2010)*
Pub: Close-Up Media Inc.
Description: Generation X and Y tend to have a conservative approach to investing according to a survey conducted by MFS Investment Management. Statistical data included.

31647 ■ *"Micro-Cap Companies" in Canadian Business (Vol. 81, Summer 2008, No. 9, pp. 157)*
Pub: Rogers Media Ltd.
Description: Micro-cap companies have lower than $221 million in terms of market capitalization. Burnaby, British Columbia-based Fancamp Exploration Ltd. topped the roster with 1,116.7 percent in return. A table showing the 2008 rankings of the companies is presented.

31648 ■ *"Micro-Finance Agencies and SMEs" in International Journal of Entrepreneurship and Small Business (Vol. 11, August 3, 2010)*
Pub: Publishers Communication Group
Ed: Patricia A. Rowe, Michael J. Christie, Frank Hoy. **Description:** Institutional preparedness of economic development agencies for developing small and medium-sized enterprises (SMEs) is discussed. The cases presented illustrate variations in the micro-finance lender agency-enterprise development of processes for sharing vision and interdependence.

31649 ■ *Microfinance*
Pub: Palgrave Macmillan
Ed: Mario La Torre; Gianfranco A. Vento; Philip Molyneux. **Released:** October 2006. **Price:** $80.00. **Description:** Microfinance involves the analysis of operational, managerial and financial aspects of a small business.

31650 ■ *"Microsoft's Big Gamble" in Canadian Business (Vol. 81, March 3, 2008, No. 3, pp. 13)*
Pub: Rogers Media
Ed: Andrew Wahl. **Description:** Microsoft Corp. is taking a big risk in buying Yahoo, as it is expected to pay more than $31 a share to finalize the acquisition. The deal would be seven and a half times bigger than any other that Microsoft has entered before, an execution of such deal is also anticipated to become a challenge for Microsoft. Recommendations on how Microsoft should handle the integration of the two businesses are given.

31651 ■ *The Middle Class Millionaire: The Rise of the New Rich and How They Are Changing America*
Pub: Currency/Doubleday Broadway Publishing Group
Ed: Russ Alan Prince; Lewis Schiff. **Released:** February 26, 2008. **Price:** $23.95. **Description:** Examination of the far-reaching impact of the middle class millionaires with net worth ranging from one million to ten million dollars and have earned rather than inherited their wealth.

31652 ■ *Millionaire Republican*
Pub: Penguin Group Incorporated
Ed: Wayne Allyn Root. **Released:** September 2006. **Price:** $12.95. **Description:** Eighteen steps to create personal wealth in a Republican-dominated era.

31653 ■ *"Millions of Senior Citizens Swindled by Financial Fraud" in Black Enterprise (Vol. 41, September 2010, No. 2, pp. 24)*
Pub: Earl G. Graves Publishing Co. Inc.
Description: One of every five citizens over the age of 65 have been victims of financial fraud. Statistical data included.

31654 ■ *Minding Her Own Business, 4th Ed.*
Pub: Sphinx Publishing
Ed: Jan Zobel. **Released:** January 1, 2005. **Price:** $16.95. **Description:** A guide to taxes and financial records for women entrepreneurs is presented.

31655 ■ *"Mine Woes Could Rouse Zinc" in Barron's (Vol. 88, July 7, 2008, No. 27, pp. M12)*
Pub: Dow Jones & Co., Inc.
Ed: Andrea Hotter. **Description:** Prices of zinc could increase due to supply problems in producing countries such as Australia and China. London Metal Exchange prices for the metal have dropped about 36 percent in 2008.

31656 ■ *"Mining Goldman for Insight" in Barron's (Vol. 89, July 20, 2009, No. 29, pp. M8)*
Pub: Dow Jones & Co., Inc.
Ed: Steven M. Sears. **Description:** Methods of investing in options for companies with earnings estimates from Goldman Sachs are discussed. These methods take advantage of increased volatility generated by earnings revisions.

31657 ■ *"Misguided" in Canadian Business (Vol. 81, July 22, 2008, No. 12-13, pp. 30)*
Pub: Rogers Media Ltd.
Ed: Al Rosen. **Description:** Canada's securities regulations are discussed; differing views on using principles-based and rules-based securities regulations are also presented.

31658 ■ *"A Mixed-Bag Quarter" in Barron's (Vol. 88, July 7, 2008, No. 27, pp. 19)*
Pub: Dow Jones & Co., Inc.
Ed: Shirley A. Lazo. **Description:** Seven component companies of the Dow Jones Industrial Average increased their dividend payouts in the second quarter of 2008 despite the weak performance of the index. Five companies in the Dow Jones Transportation index and three in the Dow Jones Utilities also increased their dividends.

31659 ■ *The Mommy Manifesto: How to Use Our Power to Think Big, Break Limitations and Achieve Success*
Pub: John Wiley & Sons, Inc.
Ed: Kim Lavine. **Released:** September 1, 2009. **Price:** $24.95. **Description:** A new women's revolution will help women take control of their careers, their lives, and their economic future. The book shows how mom's control the economy and have the power to become successful entrepreneurs.

31660 ■ *"Moms Mull Money" in Marketing to Women (Vol. 21, February 2008, No. 2, pp. 6)*
Pub: EPM Communications Inc.
Contact: Ira Mayer, President
E-mail: imayer@epmcom.com
Description: According to a survey by Countrywide Bank, women, especially mothers, are more concerned about their financial fitness than men.

31661 ■ *"Moody and Paranoid" in Barron's (Vol. 88, March 10, 2008, No. 10, pp. M14)*
Pub: Dow Jones & Company, Inc.
Ed: Steven M. Sears. **Description:** Discusses the options market which remains liquid but is cautious of possible failures, especially for financial companies. Investors are in absolute fear when trading with options involving the financial sector.

31662 ■ *"More Gains in the Pipeline" in Barron's (Vol. 89, August 3, 2009, No. 31, pp. M5)*
Pub: Dow Jones & Co., Inc.
Ed: Fleming Meeks. **Description:** Shares of El Paso Corp. could recover as the company concludes a deal with a private-equity group to fund pipeline construction. The company's shares are trading at $10.06 and could move up to $12 as bad news has already been priced into the stock.

31663 ■ *"More Jobs Moving Out of City" in Business Courier (Vol. 24, March 14, 2008, No. 49, pp. 1)*
Pub: American City Business Journals, Inc.
Ed: Steve Watkins; Laura Baverman. **Description:** UBS Financial Services Inc. is moving Gradison to Kenwood Town Place in Sycamore Township a year after UBS acquired Gradison. The township does not have a tax on earnings so the move will save Gradison's employees the 2.1 percent Cincinnati tax.

31664 ■ *"More Pain" in Canadian Business (Vol. 81, December 24, 2007, No. 1, pp. 12)*
Pub: Rogers Media
Ed: Lauren McKeon. **Description:** Manufacturing sector in Canada is sinking with a forecast by as much as 23 percent for 2008, which can be offset as manufacturers say they plan to increase productivity by 25 percent. Details on the sector's competitiveness, workforce, importing of machinery from the U.S. and financial needs for research and development are examined.

31665 ■ *"Mortgage Securities Drop Hits Home" in The Business Journal-Serving Metropolitan Kansas City (Vol. 27, October 17, 2008, No. 5)*
Pub: American City Business Journals, Inc.
Ed: Rob Roberts. **Description:** Sale of commercial mortgage-backed securities (CMBS) in Kansas City, Missouri have declined. The area may avoid layoffs if the United States government succeeds in stabilizing the economy. Major CMBS players in the area include Midland Loan Services Inc. and KeyBank Real Estate Capital.

31666 ■ *"Mortgages Going Under" in Black Enterprise (Vol. 41, December 2010, No. 5, pp. 20)*
Pub: Earl G. Graves Publishing Co. Inc.
Description: Nearly one-fifth of the country's homeowners are underwater in their mortgages, which means they owe more on their home than the home's worth. Statistical data included.

31667 ■ *"Mover and Sheika" in Conde Nast Portfolio (Vol. 2, June 2008, No. 6, pp. 104)*
Pub: Conde Nast Publications
Contact: David Carey, President
Ed: John Arlidge. **Description:** Profile of Princess Sheika Lubna who is the first female foreign trade minister in the Middle East, the United Arab Emirates biggest business envoy, paving the way for billions in new investment, and also a manufacturer of her own perfume line.

31668 ■ *"Mr. Deeds" in Canadian Business (Vol. 81, March 31, 2008, No. 5, pp. 24)*
Pub: Rogers Media
Ed: Thomas Watson. **Description:** Ron Sandler has the right experience to save Northern Rock PLC get through its liquidity problems. Sandler is known for saving Lloyd's of London in the mid-90's and he is not afraid to make enemies. Ron Sandler's assignment to help Northern Rock comes at a time when the health of the U.K. housing is not great.

31669 ■ *"MTI Faces Touch Choices" in The Business Review Albany (Vol. 35, April 4, 2008, No. 53, pp. 1)*
Pub: The Business Review
Ed: Richard A. D'Errico. **Description:** Mechanical Technology Inc.'s auditor, PricewaterhouseCoopers LLP is concerned about the company's limited current cash and its $105 million accumulated deficit. MTI has already sold 1.45 million of its PlugPower Inc. shares, but still considers to sell more of the Plug stock. The problems at MTI and the difficult decisions it has to face to solve them are examined.

31670 ■ *"Muddy Portfolio Raises a Question: Just What Is National City Worth?" in Crain's Detroit Business (Vol. 24, April 7, 2008, No. 14)*
Pub: Crain Communications, Inc.
Ed: Jay Miller. **Description:** National City Bank is looking at strategies to help it deal with its credit and loan problems which are reflected in its falling stock price. One possible solution is a merger with another bank, however most national banks are facing their own home-loan portfolio issues and may be unable to tackle another company's unresolved problems. Statistical data included.

31671 ■ *"My Favorite Tool for Managing Expenses" in Inc. (Volume 32, December 2010, No. 10, pp. 60)*
Pub: Inc. Magazine
Ed: J.J. McCorvey. **Description:** Web-based service called Expensify is outlined. The service allows companies to log expenses while away from the office using the service's iPhone application.

31672 ■ *"Nanoready?" in Entrepreneur (Vol. 36, May 2008, No. 5, pp. 20)*
Pub: Entrepreneur Media, Inc.
Ed: Andrea Cooper. **Description:** Experts predict that the medicine and energy sectors are among those that will see nanotechnology innovations in the coming years, and that nanotechnology will produce significant commercial value in new products. Some entrepreneurs are investing in nanotech and are partnering with universities. Details on nanotech funding concerns are discussed.

31673 ■ *"Need Grub? Start Texting at Kroger" in Business Courier (Vol. 24, December 21, 2008, No. 36, pp. 1)*
Pub: American City Business Journals, Inc.
Ed: Laura Baverman. **Description:** Discusses the University of Cincinnati which is teaming up to release a technology platform called Macopay that would link a cell phone to a bank account and allow a person to make payments at participating retailers by sending a text message. Details with regard to the new service and its growth potential are discussed.

31674 ■ *"Needed: A Strategy; Banking In China" in The Economist (Vol. 390, January 3, 2009, No. 8612, pp. 54)*
Pub: The Economist Newspaper Inc.
Description: International banks are competing for a role in China but are finding obstacles in their paths such as a reduction in the credit their operations may receive from Chinese banks and the role they can play in the public capital markets which remain limited.

31675 ■ *"Netflix Gets No Respect" in Barron's (Vol. 89, July 27, 2009, No. 30, pp. 26)*
Pub: Dow Jones & Co., Inc.
Ed: Tiernan Ray. **Description:** Netflix met expectations when they announced their second quarter sales but their shares still fell by almost 10 percent. Analysts say their entry into the 'streaming video' business is a mixed bag since customers are increasingly buying the cheaper monthly plan and this is dragging the economics of the business.

31676 ■ *Never Bet the Farm*
Pub: Jossey-Bass Publishers
Ed: Anthony L. Iaquinto; Stephen Spinelli, Jr. **Price:** R19.95 paperback.

31677 ■ *"The New Arsenal of Risk Management" in Harvard Business Review (Vol. 86, September 2008, No. 9, pp. 92)*
Pub: Harvard Business School Press
Ed: Kevin Bueler; Andrew Freeman; Ron Hulme. **Description:** Goldman Sachs Group Inc. is used to illustrate methods for successful risk management. The investment bank's business principles, partnerships, and oversight practices are discussed.

31678 ■ *"New Century's Fall Has a New Culprit" in Barron's (Vol. 88, March 31, 2008, No. 13, pp. 20)*
Pub: Dow Jones & Company, Inc.
Ed: Jonathan R. Laing. **Description:** Court examiner Michael Missal reports that New Century Financial's auditor contributed to New Century's demise by its negligence in permitting improper and imprudent practices related to New Century's accounting processes. New Century's bankruptcy filing is considered the start of the subprime-mortgage crisis.

31679 ■ *"New Drug Could Revitalize Amgen" in Barron's (Vol. 88, July 7, 2008, No. 27, pp. 23)*
Pub: Dow Jones & Co., Inc.
Ed: Johanna Bennett. **Description:** Shares of the biotechnology company Amgen could receive a boost from the release of the anti-osteoporosis drug denosumab. The shares, priced at $48.84 each, are trading at 11 times expected earnings for 2008 and could also be boosted by cost cutting measures.

31680 ■ *"A New Kid on the Block" in Barron's (Vol. 88, March 17, 2008, No. 11, pp. 58)*
Pub: Dow Jones & Company, Inc.
Ed: Thomas G. Donlan. **Description:** Discusses the Federal Reserve which has offered to lend $100 billion in cash to banks and $200 billion in Treasuries to Wall Street investment banks that have problems with liquidity. The reluctance of the banks to lend money to meet a margin call on securities that could still depreciate is the reason why the agency is going into the direct loan business.

31681 ■ *"New Money" in Entrepreneur (Vol. 36, February 2008, No. 2, pp. 62)*
Pub: Entrepreneur Media Inc.

Ed: C.J. Prince. **Description:** Tips on how to handle business finance, with regard to the tightened credit standards imposed by leading institutions, are provided. These include: selling receivables, margining blue chips, and selling purchase orders.

31682 ■ *"The New Risk Tolerance" in Entrepreneur (Vol. 37, September 2009, No. 9, pp. 66)*
Pub: Entrepreneur Media, Inc.

Ed: Rosalind Resnick. **Description:** Offers advice on where to invest personal money in the United States. One could lose money from investing in gold and treasuries. High-quality corporate bonds and Treasury Inflation-Protected Securities are seen as ideal investments.

31683 ■ *"New Rule Rankles In Jersey" in Philadelphia Business Journal (Vol. 30, September 16, 2011, No. 31, pp. 1)*
Pub: American City Business Journals Inc.

Ed: Jeff Blumenthal. **Description:** A new rule in New Jersey which taxes out-of-state companies that conduct business in the state earned the ire of several banks, mortgage lenders and credit card companies and prompted opponents to threaten to file lawsuits. The new rule is an amendment to New Jersey Division of Taxation's corporate business tax regulation and is retroactive to 2002. Details are given.

31684 ■ *"New Thinking for a New Financial Order" in Harvard Business Review (Vol. 86, September 2008, No. 9, pp. 26)*
Pub: Harvard Business School Press

Ed: Diana Farell. **Description:** Factors driving the current global economy are analyzed with a focus on the influence of new public and private sectors and the impact of unregulated markets.

31685 ■ *"A New Way to Tell When to Fold" in Barron's (Vol. 88, July 7, 2008, No. 27, pp. 27)*
Pub: Dow Jones & Co., Inc.

Ed: Theresa W. Carey. **Description:** Overview of the Online trading company SmartStops, a firm that aims to tell investors when to sell the shares of a particular company. The company's Web site categorizes stocks as moving up, down, or sideways, and calculates exit points for individual stocks based on an overall market trend.

31686 ■ *"New Ways to Catch a Thief" in Barron's (Vol. 88, March 10, 2008, No. 10, pp. 37)*
Pub: Dow Jones & Company, Inc.

Ed: Theresa W. Carey. **Description:** Online brokerage firms employ different methods to protect the accounts of their customers from theft. These methods include secure Internet connections, momentary passwords, and proprietary algorithms.

31687 ■ *"New Year, New Estate Plan" in Hawaii Business (Vol. 53, February 2008, No. 8, pp. 54)*
Pub: Hawaii Business Publishing

Ed: Antony M. Orme. **Description:** Discusses the start of the new year which can be a time to revise wills and estate plans as failure to do so may create problems of unequal inheritance and increase in estate tax exemption, which could disinherit beneficiaries. Other circumstances that can prompt changes in wills and estate plans are presented.

31688 ■ *"The Next Government Bailout?" in Barron's (Vol. 88, March 10, 2008, No. 10, pp. 21)*
Pub: Dow Jones & Company, Inc.

Ed: Jonathan Laing. **Description:** Fannie Mae may need a government bailout as it faces huge hits brought about by the effects of the housing crisis. The shares of the government-sponsored enterprise have dropped 65 percent since the housing crisis began.

31689 ■ *"Nightmare on Wall Street" in Canadian Business (Vol. 81, October 13, 2008, No. 17, pp. 9)*
Pub: Rogers Media Ltd.

Ed: Rachel Pulfer. **Description:** Information on events that happened on Wall Street on the week that started September 15, 2008, as well on its effect on financial markets around the world, are presented. Lehman Brothers filed for bankruptcy on September 15, 2008 after negotiations with Barclays Group and Bank of America failed. Details on AIG and Morgan Stanley are also presented.

31690 ■ *"No Fast Cash Class" in Black Enterprise (Vol. 37, December 2006, No. 5, pp. 72)*
Pub: Earl G. Graves Publishing Co. Inc.

Description: There are no shortcuts to a obtaining a career as a financial planner. Certified Financial Planner Board of Standards has specific requirements for certification which include having a bachelor's degree from an accredited U.S. school before candidates are even eligible for taking the certification exam. Other criteria and requirements are discussed.

31691 ■ *"No More Debt" in Black Enterprise (Vol. 37, November 2006, No. 4, pp. 159)*
Pub: Earl G. Graves Publishing Co. Inc.

Ed: Tanisha A. Sykes. **Description:** Eliminating debt is not necessarily easy and can be overwhelming. Here are some tips for reducing and eventually getting out of debt.

31692 ■ *"Nonprofits Pressured to Rein in Fundraising Events" in Crain's Detroit Business (Vol. 25, June 15, 2009, No. 24, pp. 1)*
Pub: Crain Communications Inc. - Detroit

Ed: Sherri Begin Welch. **Description:** Local corporations have asked nonprofit= s to limit fundraising events in order to cut costs during the recession.

31693 ■ *North American Financial Institutions Directory*
Pub: Accuity Inc.
Contact: Hugh M. Jones, IV, President

URL(s): store.accuitysolutions.com/order.html. **Released:** Semiannual; January and July. **Price:** $955, Individuals. **Covers:** 15,000 banks and their branches; over 2,000 head offices, and 15,500 branches of savings and loan associations; over 5,500 credit unions with assets over $5 million; Federal Reserve System and other U.S. government and state government banking agencies; bank holding, commercial finance, and leasing companies; coverage includes the United States, Canada, Mexico, and Central America. **Entries include:** Bank name, address, phone, fax, telex, principal officers and directors, date established, financial data, association memberships, attorney or counsel, correspondent banks, out-of-town branch, holding company affiliation, ABA transit number and routing symbol, MICR number with check digit, credit card(s) issued, trust powers, current par value and dividend of common stock, kind of charter. **Database includes:** Bank routing numbers in numeric sequence; maps; discontinued banks. **Arrangement:** Geographical. **Indexes:** Alphabetical.

31694 ■ *"Not In My Backyard" in Entrepreneur (Vol. 36, May 2008, No. 5, pp. 42)*
Pub: Entrepreneur Media, Inc.

Ed: Farnoosh Torabi. **Description:** More investors are turning to overseas real estate investments as the U.S. market sees a slowdown. Analysts say that risk-averse investors opt for funds with record of strong returns and U.S. real estate investment trusts that partner with foreign businesses for transparency purposes. Other details about foreign real estate investments are discussed.

31695 ■ *"A Novel Fix for the Credit Mess" in Barron's (Vol. 88, March 31, 2008, No. 13, pp. 10)*
Pub: Dow Jones & Company, Inc.

Ed: Michael Santoli. **Description:** Due to the common bank-leverage factor of 10, the $250 billion of lost bank capital would have supported $2.5 trillion in lending capacity. Jeffrey Lewis suggests onerous regulations on bank-holding companies that own 10 to 25 percent, as they are partly to blame. Statistical data included.

31696 ■ *"Now You See It.." in Canadian Business (Vol. 81, November 10, 2008, No. 19, pp. 20)*
Pub: Rogers Media Ltd.

Ed: Sharda Prashad. **Description:** Total return swaps were offered by Deutsche Bank AG and UBS AG to foreign investors for them to avoid paying taxes on the proceeds of their shares of Fording Canadian Coal Trust when Teck Cominco offered to buy the company. This means that the Canadian government is losing tax revenue from foreigners and it is argued that a simpler tax system would avoid this practice.

31697 ■ *"Number of Mechanic's Liens Triple Since 2005" in The Business Journal - Serving Phoenix and the Valley of the Sun (Vol. 28, August 22, 2008, No. 51, pp. 1)*
Pub: American City Business Journals, Inc.

Ed: Jan Buchholtz. **Description:** Experts are blaming the mortgage and banking industries for the tripling of mechanic's liens that were filed in Arizona from 2005 through August 6, 2008. The rise in mechanic's liens is believed to indicate stress in the real estate community. Other views and information on the rise of mechanic's liens filed in Arizona are presented.

31698 ■ *"The Numbers Speak For Themselves" in Barron's (Vol. 88, July 14, 2008, No. 28, pp. 16)*
Pub: Dow Jones & Co., Inc.

Ed: Bill Alpert. **Description:** Discusses quant fund managers versus traditional long-short equity funds after quants outperformed traditional funds in the year 2000. Causes for the underperformance are outlined and statistical data is included.

31699 ■ *"Nvidia Shares Clobbered After Gloomy Warning" in Barron's (Vol. 88, July 7, 2008, No. 27, pp. 25)*
Pub: Dow Jones & Co., Inc.

Ed: Eric J. Savitz. **Description:** Shares of graphics chip manufacturer Nvidia suffered a 30 percent drop in its share price after the company warned that revenue and gross margin forecasts for the quarter ending July 27, 2008 will be below expectations. Stan Glasgow, chief operating officer of Sony Electronics, believes the US economic slowdown will not affect demand for the company's products. Statistical data included.

31700 ■ *"Nvidia's Picture Brighter Than Stock Price Indicates" in Barron's (Vol. 88, March 24, 2008, No. 12, pp. 46)*
Pub: Dow Jones & Company, Inc.

Ed: Eric J. Savitz. **Description:** Shares of graphics chip maker Nvidia, priced at $18.52 each, do not indicate the company's strong position in the graphics chip market. The company's shares have dropped due to fears of slower demand for PCs, but the company is not as exposed to broader economic forces.

31701 ■ *"Nymex Dissidents Rattle Sabers" in Crain's Chicago Business (Vol. 31, April 21, 2008, No. 16, pp. 2)*
Pub: Crain Communications, Inc.

Ed: Ann Saphir. **Description:** Two groups of New York Mercantile Exchange members say they have more than enough votes to stop CME Group Inc.'s $10 billion deal to acquire the oil and metals exchange and they are threatening a proxy fight if the Chicago exchange doesn't raise its offer.

31702 ■ *"October 2009: Recovery Plods Along" in Hispanic Business (October 2009, pp. 10-11)*
Pub: Hispanic Business

Ed: Dr. Juan Solana. **Description:** Economist reports on a possible economic recovery which will not be allowed to rely on a strong domestic demand in order to sustain it. Consumers, looking to counterbalance years of leverage financing based on unrealistic, ever-increasing home and portfolio valuations, are saving rather than spending money.

31703 ■ *"Office Market May Turn Down" in Crain's New York Business (Vol. 24, January 14, 2008, No. 2, pp. 26)*
Pub: Crain Communications, Inc.
Description: Although still dominated by Wall Street, the downturn in the economy is raising fears that the continuing fallout from the subprime mortgage crisis could result in layoffs that will derail the office market.

31704 ■ *"Ohio Commerce Draws Closer to Profitability" in Crain's Cleveland Business (Vol. 28, October 29, 2007, No. 43, pp. 14)*
Pub: Crain Communications, Inc.
Ed: Shawn A. Turner. **Description:** Overview of the business plan of Ohio Commerce Bank, a de novo, or startup bank that is close to turning the corner to profitability. The bank opened in November 2006 and focuses on dealing with small businesses totaling $5 million or less in annual revenues.

31705 ■ *"Ok, So Now What?" in Canadian Business (Vol. 79, November 6, 2006, No. 22, pp. 113)*
Pub: Rogers Media
Ed: Calvin Leung. **Description:** Details of healthy income-generating corporations, such as Cedar Fair L.P., are presented.

31706 ■ *"On the Trail of the Bear" in Canadian Business (Vol. 81, March 17, 2008, No. 4, pp. 28)*
Pub: Rogers Media
Ed: Thomas Watson. **Description:** Discusses the conservative rule of thumb which is to invest in equity markets when a five to ten percent market rally is sustained for more than a few months. Bear markets on the S&P 500 bear markets in the 20th century only lasts over a year based on average. It is also good to remember that bear markets are followed by bulls that exceed the previous market highs.

31707 ■ *The One Minute Entrepreneur*
Pub: Doubleday
Ed: Ken Blanchard; assisted by Don Hutson and Ethan Willis. **Released:** 2008. **Price:** $19.95. **Description:** Four traditional business ideas are covered including: revenue needs to exceed expenses, bill collection, customer service, and employee motivation in order to be successful.

31708 ■ *"One-Time Area Trust Executive Finds Trouble in N.H." in The Business Journal-Serving Metropolitan Kansas City (September 12, 2008)*
Pub: American City Business Journals, Inc.
Ed: Steve Vockrodt. **Description:** About 200 investors, some from Missouri's Kansas City area, claim that they had conducted business with Noble Trust Co. The trust company was placed under New Hampshire Banking Department's conservatorship after $15 million was discovered to be missing from its account. It is alleged that the money was lost in a Colorado Ponzi scheme.

31709 ■ *"Opportunity Now Lies at Short End of the Market" in Barron's (Vol. 88, June 30, 2008, No. 26, pp. M9)*
Pub: Dow Jones & Co., Inc.
Ed: Michael S. Derby. **Description:** Renewed credit concerns and the lesser chance of a Federal Reserve interest rate hike boosted the bond market. Some portfolio managers are more bullish on short-dated securities as they expect the market to adjust to a more appropriate outlook.

31710 ■ *"An Opportunity for Patience" in Barron's (Vol. 88, June 30, 2008, No. 26, pp. M5)*
Pub: Dow Jones & Co., Inc.
Ed: Fleming Meeks. **Description:** Shares of Louisiana-Pacific are near their 52-week low at $8.95 per share making them look like a better buy than they were at $11.51 in May, 2008. The company is a to player in a cyclical business and its balance sheet is sound compared to its peers with net debt at just $84 million or 20 percent of total capital.

31711 ■ *"Optimism Index" in Black Enterprise (Vol. 41, September 2010, No. 2, pp. 24)*
Pub: Earl G. Graves Publishing Co. Inc.
Description: According to a Pew Research Center report, 81 percent of African Americans expect to improve their finances in 2011. Blacks have carried a disproportionate share of job losses and housing foreclosures in the recession that began in 2007.

31712 ■ *"Optimize.ca Supplies Free Online Financial Advice" in Entertainment Close-Up (October 9, 2010)*
Pub: Close-Up Media Inc.
Description: Optimize.ca provides free online financial advice, focusing on instant savings for their mutual funds and other banking products while improving rates of return and overall financial health.

31713 ■ *"Oracle: No Profit of Doom" in Barron's (Vol. 88, March 31, 2008, No. 13, pp. 40)*
Pub: Dow Jones & Company, Inc.
Ed: Mark Veverka. **Description:** Oracle's revenues grew by 21 percent but fell short of expectation and their profits came in at the low-end of expectations. The company's shares dropped 8 percent but investors are advised to pay more attention to the company's earnings expansion rather than revenue growth in a slow economy. Nokia's Rick Simonson points out that their markets in Asia and particularly India is growing so they are not as affected by the U.S. economic conditions.

31714 ■ *"Our Rich Past: a Guide to Some of Canada's Historic Fortunes" in Canadian Business (Vol. 80, Winter 2007, No. 24, pp. 131)*
Pub: Rogers Media
Ed: Graham F. Scott. **Description:** Donald Alexander Smith rose through the ranks at Hudson's Bay Company to become the company's principal shareholder. John Wilson McConnell started his career at the Standard Chemical Company but later shifted to selling stocks and receiving equity stocks in return for his endorsement. Bud McDougald is well known for his deal making skills before he died in 1978.

31715 ■ *"Out of Fashion" in Barron's (Vol. 88, March 17, 2008, No. 11, pp. 48)*
Pub: Dow Jones & Company, Inc.
Ed: Robin Goldwyn Blumenthal. **Description:** Shares of Perry Ellis International and G-III Apparel Group have taken some beating in the market despite good growth earnings prospects. Perry Ellis sees earnings growth of 8 to 11 percent for fiscal 2009, while G-III Apparel expects earnings growth of 25 percent.

31716 ■ *"Over A Barrel" in Canadian Business (Vol. 81, July 21, 2008, No. 11, pp. 13)*
Pub: Rogers Media Ltd.
Ed: Thomas Watson. **Description:** Analysts predict that the skyrocketing price of fuel will cause a crackdown in the market as purported in the peak oil theory. It is forecasted that the price of oil will reach $200 per barrel. Details of the effect of the increasing oil prices on the market are presented.

31717 ■ *Own Your Own Corporation: Why the Rich Own Their Own Companies and Everyone Else Works for Them*
Pub: Business Plus
Ed: Garrett Sutton; Robert T. Kiyosaki; Ann Blackman. **Released:** June 2008. **Price:** $17.99 paperback. **Description:** Part of the Rich Dad Advisor's Series, this edition shows how individuals can incorporate themselves and their businesses to save thousands of dollars in taxes and protect against financial disaster.

31718 ■ *"Owning the Right Risks" in Harvard Business Review (Vol. 86, September 2008, No. 9, pp. 102)*
Pub: Harvard Business School Press
Ed: Kevin Bueler; Andrew Freeman; Ron Hulme. **Description:** TXU Corp. is used to illustrate methods for successful risk management. The electric utility's practices include determining which risks are natural, embedding risk in all processes and decisions, and organizing corporate governance around risk.

31719 ■ *"Packaging Firm Wraps Up Remake; Overseas Plants Help Firm Fatten Margins" in Crain's New York Business (January 7, 2008)*
Pub: Crain Communications, Inc.
Description: Sealed Air Corp., a packaging manufacturer, has seen its share price fall nearly 20 percent over the past two years, making it one of the worst performers in the packaging sector.

31720 ■ *"Pain Ahead as Profit Pressure Increases" in Crain's Chicago Business (Vol. 31, May 5, 2008, No. 18, pp. 4)*
Pub: Crain Communications, Inc.
Ed: Daniel Rome Levine. **Description:** Interview with David Klaskin, the chairman and chief investment officer at Oak Ridge Investments LLC, who discusses the outlook for the economy and corporate earnings, particularly in the housing and auto industries, the impact of economic stimulus checks, the weakness of the dollar and recommendations of stocks that individual investors may find helpful.

31721 ■ *Panic! The Story of Modern Financial Insanity*
Pub: W.W. Norton & Company
Ed: Michael Lewis. **Released:** 2009. **Price:** $27.95. **Description:** Two decades of stock market crashes are outlined.

31722 ■ *Paper Fortunes: Modern Wall Street: Where It's Been and Where It's Going*
Pub: St. Martin's Press LLC
Ed: Roy C. Smith. **Released:** 2010. **Price:** $35.00. **Description:** Comprehensive history of Wall Street and lessons learned with insight into ways Wall Street will reinvent itself in this new economy.

31723 ■ *"Passing It On: Using Life Insurance as an Estate Planning Tool" in Inc. (October 2007, pp. 47-49)*
Pub: Gruner & Jahr USA Publishing
Ed: Elaine Appleton Grant. **Description:** Permanent life insurance policies can be used to cover estate taxes for heirs inheriting large estates, while allowing them time to sell any small business. Six tips are included to assist in choosing the right policy.

31724 ■ *"Paying for the Recession: Rebalancing Economic Growth" in Montana Business Quarterly (Vol. 49, Spring 2011, No. 1, pp. 2)*
Pub: Bureau of Business & Economic Research
Ed: Patrick M. Barkey. **Description:** Four key issues required to address in order to rebalance economic growth in America are examined. They include: savings rates, global trade imbalances, government budgets and most importantly, housing price correction.

31725 ■ *"Peak Performer" in Canadian Business (Vol. 81, October 13, 2008, No. 17, pp. 30)*
Pub: Rogers Media Ltd.
Ed: Andrea Jezovit. **Description:** Jerry Del Missier's promotion as president of Barclays Capital (BarCap) has made him the likely successor to BarCap chief executive Bob Diamond. Diamond believes the technology Jerry Del Missier built on BarCap is producing record performance for the company. Public opinion on Jerry Del Missier, as well as his views, is discussed.

31726 ■ *"Penny Chief Shops For Shares" in Barron's (Vol. 88, July 7, 2008, No. 27, pp. 29)*
Pub: Dow Jones & Co., Inc.
Ed: Teresa Rivas. **Description:** Myron Ullman III, chairman and chief executive officer of J.C. Penney, purchased $1 million worth of shares of the company. He now owns 393,140 shares of the company and an additional 1,282 on his 401(k) plan.

31727 ■ *Personal Success and the Bottom Line*
Pub: Successful Publishing
Ed: Mark C. Middleton. **Released:** March 2006. **Price:** $24.95. **Description:** Retired certified public accountant provides a primer for those wishing to achieve a balance between career and their personal life.

31728 ■ ***"Peter Bynoe Trades Up" in Black Enterprise (Vol. 38, July 2008, No. 12, pp. 30)***
Pub: Earl G. Graves Publishing Co. Inc.

Ed: Alexis McCombs. **Description:** Chicago-based Loop Capital Markets L.L.C. has named Peter Bynoe managing director of corporate finance. Bynoe was previously a senior partner at the law firm DLA Piper U.S. L.L.P., where he worked on stadium deals.

31729 ■ ***"Pioneering Strategies for Entrepreneurial Success" in Business Horizons (Vol. 51, January-February 2008, No. 1, pp. 21)***
Pub: Elsevier Advanced Technology Publications

Ed: Candida G. Brush. **Description:** Entrepreneurs are known for new products, services, processes, markets and industries. In order to achieve success, they have to develop a clear vision, creatively manage finances, and use social skills to persuade others to commit to the venture. Pioneering strategies and their implementation are examined.

31730 ■ ***"Place Restrictions on Your Stock Shares" in Business Owner (Vol. 35, July-August 2011, No. 4, pp. 14)***
Pub: DL Perkins Company

Description: It is critical for any small business owner to be certain that the buyer or recipient of any part of the company represents that the stock is being acquired or given for investment purposes only.

31731 ■ ***"A Place in the Sun" in Canadian Business (Vol. 81, July 22, 2008, No. 12-13, pp. 56)***
Pub: Rogers Media Ltd.

Description: Experts believe that it is the best time for Canadians to own a retirement home in the U.S., where real estate prices are up to 50 percent below their peak. Other views concerning the economic conditions occurring in the United States, as well as on the implications for Canadians planning to invest in the country are presented.

31732 ■ ***"Plan Targets Small Banks" in Business Journal Portland (Vol. 26, December 11, 2009, No. 40, pp. 1)***
Pub: American City Business Journals Inc.

Ed: Courtney Sherwood. **Description:** Senator Jeff Merkley of Oregon has proposed an expansion of the Troubled Assets Relief Program to accommodate banks with capital levels of less than 10 percent. In his proposal, affected banks would be mandated on a stress test to evaluate capital requirements.

31733 ■ ***"Planning Ahead: Steven Taylor Mulls a Second Career After Retirement" in Black Enterprise (Vol. 37, November 2006, No. 4, pp. 82)***
Pub: Earl G. Graves Publishing Co. Inc.

Ed: Sheryl Nance Nash. **Description:** Many workers are unprepared for retirement. Profile of Steven Taylor, a soon to retire dietary correctional officer who looked to Walt Clark, president of Clark Capital Financial in Maryland, to assess his retirement goals. Detailed advice and statistical data included.

31734 ■ ***"Playing Citigroup's Woes" in Barron's (Vol. 88, March 31, 2008, No. 13, pp. M7)***
Pub: Dow Jones & Company, Inc.

Ed: Steven M. Sears. **Description:** Citigroup's first-quarter earnings estimate was slashed to a $1.15-per-share-loss from 28 cents. A strategist recommends buying the company's shares at Sept. 20, 2008 put and selling a Sept. 17.50 put with a maximum profit of $166 if the shares is at or below $17.50 at expiration.

31735 ■ ***"Playing Defense" in Crain's Chicago Business (Vol. 31, November 10, 2008, No. 45, pp. 4)***
Pub: Crain Communications, Inc.

Ed: Monee Fields-White. **Description:** Chicago's money managers are increasingly investing in local companies such as Caterpillar Inc., a maker of construction and mining equipment, Kraft Foods Inc. and Baxter International Inc., a manufacturer of medical products, in an attempt to bolster their portfolios. These companies have a history of surviving tough economic times.

31736 ■ ***"PNC Begins Search for New Local HQ" in Baltimore Business Journal (Vol. 28, June 4, 2010, No. 4, pp. 1)***
Pub: Baltimore Business Journal

Ed: Daniel J. Sernovitz. **Description:** PNC Financial Services Group Inc. is searching for a new headquarters building in Greater Baltimore, Maryland. The company is seeking about 150,000 square feet for its regional operations. However, PNC could also end up moving out of Baltimore for space in the surrounding suburbs.

31737 ■ ***"Point, Click, Buy" in Barron's (Vol. 90, September 6, 2010, No. 36, pp. 11)***
Pub: Barron's Editorial & Corporate Headquarters

Ed: Vito J. Racanelli. **Description:** Non-travel online retail sales from January to July 2010 increased nine percent which indicates that online shopping for the coming holidays will be good. Online sales are outpacing traditional shopping, but pricing is still critical.

31738 ■ ***"Portfolio: Written in the Polls" in Entrepreneur (Vol. 35, October 2007, No. 10, pp. 74)***
Pub: Entrepreneur Media Inc.

Ed: Scott Bernard Nelson. **Description:** Ibbotsen Associates looked at trends in the U.S. presidential elections to see if the election has something to do with stock market behavior. It was found that election years beat non-election years in the stock market by nearly three percentage points each year. Details of the presidential elections' impact on the stock market are given.

31739 ■ ***"Powder River Reports First Quarter Revenues Over 5 Million" in Canadian Corporate News (May 16, 2007)***
Pub: Comtex News Network Inc.

Description: Financial report for Powder River Basin Gas Corp., a revenue generating producer, marketer, and acquirer of crude oil and natural gas properties. Statistical data included.

31740 ■ ***Prepare to Be a Teen Millionaire***
Pub: Health Communications, Inc.
Contact: Peter Vegso, President

Ed: Robyn Collins; Kimberly Spinks Burleson. **Released:** April 1, 2008. **Price:** $16.95. **Description:** Business reference for any teenager wishing to become a successful entrepreneur; advice is given from successful teenage millionaires. Topics covered include: choosing a business name, type, and location; use of the Internet; legal issues; branding, sales, and marketing; funding and financial management; return on investment; retirement; development of a sound business plan; and certification for minority or women-owned companies.

31741 ■ ***"Private Equity Firms Shopping Valley For Deals" in The Business Journal - Serving Phoenix and the Valley of the Sun (Vol. 29, September 19, 2008, No. 3, pp. 1)***
Pub: American City Business Journals, Inc.

Ed: Mike Sunnucks. **Description:** Private equity firms from California, Boston, New York, and overseas are expected to invest in growth-oriented real estate markets that include Phoenix. Real estate experts revealed that privately held investment and acquisition firms are looking to invest in real estate markets hit by the housing crisis. Views and information on private equity firms' real estate investments are presented.

31742 ■ ***"Profit Predictions Look Too Plump" in Barron's (Vol. 88, March 31, 2008, No. 13, pp. 37)***
Pub: Dow Jones & Company, Inc.

Ed: Johanna Bennett. **Description:** Full-year forecast points to a 14 percent gain for 2008 but the second-half profit increases would have to grow at a fast rate and peak at 61 percent in the fourth quarter to achieve this. Trends in the U.S. economic conditions are also discussed.

31743 ■ ***Profits Aren't Everything. They're the Only Thing: No-Nonsense Rules from the Ultimate Contrarian and Small Business Guru***
Pub: HarperCollins Publishers

Ed: George Cloutier. **Released:** September 9, 2010. **Price:** $24.99. **Description:** In difficult economic times, the only way for small businesses to survive is to maximize profits. Thirteen steps to maximize profits in a slow economy are outlined.

31744 ■ ***Progress-Driven Entrepreneurs, Private Equity Finance and Regulatory Issues***
Pub: Palgrave Macmillan

Ed: Zuhayr Mikdashi. **Released:** October 1, 2009. **Price:** $90.00. **Description:** Durable business performance is critically dependent on a stakeholders strategy along with accessible entrepreneurial financing availability within macro-economic and economic regulatory environments.

31745 ■ ***"Proof That Good Entrepreneurs Can Make Bad Investors" in Inc. (October 2007, pp. 77-78)***
Pub: Gruner & Jahr USA Publishing

Ed: Norm Brodsky. **Description:** Information for small business owners is offered to help decide which investments are right for them.

31746 ■ ***"Public Opinion" in Entrepreneur (Vol. 36, April 2008, No. 4, pp. 28)***
Pub: Entrepreneur Media, Inc.

Ed: Aliza Sherman. **Description:** According to a 2007 report from Group and Organization Management, women in top positions can lead publicly traded companies to stock price and earnings growth. Some women business owners say that going public has provided them with the capital to grow. Details on the potential of women-managed publicly traded companies are discussed.

31747 ■ ***"Put It on MasterCard" in Barron's (Vol. 89, July 27, 2009, No. 30, pp. 16)***
Pub: Dow Jones & Co., Inc.

Ed: Bill Alpert. **Description:** Shares of MasterCard trade at a discount at just 15 times its anticipated earnings and some believe that these shares may be a better play in an economic recovery. The prospects of these shares are compared with those of Visa.

31748 ■ ***"Putting SogoTrade Through Its Paces" in Barron's (Vol. 89, July 27, 2009, No. 30, pp. 27)***
Pub: Dow Jones & Co., Inc.

Ed: Theresa W. Carey. **Description:** SogoTrade options platform streams options quotes in real time and lets users place a trade in several ways. The site also features notable security tactics and is a reasonable choice for bargain-seekers. OptionsXpress' Xtend platform lets users place trades and get real time quotes.

31749 ■ ***"Putting the World at Your Fingertips" in Barron's (Vol. 88, July 7, 2008, No. 27, pp. L13)***
Pub: Dow Jones & Co., Inc.

Ed: Neil A. Martin. **Description:** Currency-traded exchange funds allow investors to diversify their assets and take advantage of investment opportunities such as speculation and hedging. Investors can use these funds to build positions in favor of or against the US dollar.

31750 ■ ***"Q&A: David Labistour" in Canadian Business (Vol. 81, March 17, 2008, No. 4, pp. 10)***
Pub: Rogers Media

Ed: Lauren McKeon. **Description:** David Labistour says that the difference between being a co-op retailer and a corporate-owned retailer in the case of Mountain Equipment Co-op (MEC) is that the company is owned by their customers and not by shareholders. Labistour also says that MEC works with their factories to ensure that these maintain ethical standards in the manufacturing process.

31751 ■ ***"Q&A Patrick Pichette" in Canadian Business (Vol. 81, October 13, 2008, No. 17, pp. 6)***
Pub: Rogers Media Ltd.

Ed: Andrew Wahl. **Description:** Patrick Pichette finds challenge in taking over the finances of an Internet company that has a market cap of about $140 billion.

He feels, however, that serving as Google's chief financial officer is nothing compared to running Bell Canada Enterprises (BCE). Pichette's other views on Google and BCE are presented.

31752 ■ *"Qualcomm Could Win Big as the IPhone 3G Calls" in Barron's (Vol. 88, July 4, 2008, No. 28, pp. 30)*
Pub: Dow Jones & Co., Inc.
Ed: Eric J. Savitz. **Description:** Apple iPhone 3G's introduction could widen the smartphone market thereby benefiting handset chipmaker Qualcomm in the process. Qualcomm Senior V.P., Bill Davidson sees huge potential for his company's future beyond phones with their Snapdragon processor. The prospects of Sun Microsystems' shares are also discussed.

31753 ■ *The Quants*
Pub: Crown Business Books
Ed: Scott Patterson. **Released:** January 25, 2011. **Price:** $16.00. **Description:** The story of four rich and powerful men, along with Jim Simons, the founder of the most successful hedge fund in history and how they felt and what they thought in the days and weeks during the crash of Wall Street.

31754 ■ *"Quarreling Parties Keep Schenectady Redevelopment Plan In Limbo" in The Business Review Albany (Vol. 35, April 4, 2008, No. 53)*
Pub: The Business Review
Ed: Michael DeMasi. **Description:** First National Bank of Scotia chairman Louis H. Buhrmaster opposes the Erie Boulevard design project. as it could negatively affect access to the bank. Buhrmaster, aslo a vice president for Schenectady Industrial Corp, prohibits environmental assessment at the former American Locomotive property. The issues affecting the progress of the planned redevelopment at Schenectady are analyzed.

31755 ■ *"A Questionable Chemical Romance" in Barron's (Vol. 88, July 14, 2008, No. 28, pp. 28)*
Pub: Dow Jones & Co., Inc.
Ed: Andrew Bary. **Description:** Dow Chemical paid $78-a-share for the surprise takeover of Rohm & Haas. The acquisition is reducing Dow Chemical's financial flexibility at a time when chemical companies are being affected by high costs and a weak U.S. economy.

31756 ■ *"Quick Earnings Revival Unlikely" in Barron's (Vol. 88, June 30, 2008, No. 26, pp. 31)*
Pub: Dow Jones & Co., Inc.
Ed: Johanna Bennett. **Description:** Analysts are pushing back their prediction of a U.S. economy turnaround to 2009. A recession in the first half of 2008 may not have happened but unemployment is rising and house prices continue to fall.

31757 ■ *"Quicken Starter Edition 2008" in Black Enterprise (Vol. 38, March 2008, No. 8, pp. 54)*
Pub: Earl G. Graves Publishing Co. Inc.
Ed: Sonya A. Donaldson. **Description:** Profile of Quicken Starter Edition 2008 offering programs that track spending; it will also categorize tax deductible expenses.

31758 ■ *"The RBC Dynasty Continues" in Globe & Mail (January 30, 2006, pp. B1)*
Pub: CTVglobemedia Publishing Inc.
Ed: Gordon Pitts. **Description:** The details on business growth of Royal Bank of Canada, under chief executive officer Gordon Nixon, are presented.

31759 ■ *Reading Financial Reports for Dummies*
Pub: John Wiley and Sons, Inc.
Ed: Lita Epstein. **Released:** January 2009. **Price:** $21.99. **Description:** This second edition contains more new and updated information, including new information on the separate accounting and financial reporting standards for private/small businesses versus public/large businesses; updated information reflecting 2007 laws on international financial reporting standards; new content to match SEC and other governmental regulatory changes over the last three years; new information about how the analyst-corporate connection has changed the playing field; the impact of corporate communications and new technologies; new examples that reflect the current trends; and updated Websites and resources.

31760 ■ *"Ready for the Back Burner" in Barron's (Vol. 88, March 17, 2008, No. 11, pp. 47)*
Pub: Dow Jones & Company, Inc.
Ed: Vito J. Racanelli. **Description:** McDonald's has promised to return $15 billion to $17 billion to shareholders in 2007-2009 but headwinds are rising for the company. December, 2007 same-store sales were flat and the company's traffic growth in the U.S. is slowing. Its shares are likely to trade in tandem with the market until recession fears recede.

31761 ■ *"Ready for a Rally?" in The Economist (Vol. 390, January 3, 2009, No. 8612, pp. 54)*
Pub: The Economist Newspaper Inc.
Description: Analysts predict that the recession could end by 2010. The current economic crisis is presented in detail.

31762 ■ *"Real Estate Defaults Top $300M" in Business Courier (Vol. 26, January 15, 2010, No. 39, pp. 1)*
Pub: American City Business Journals, Inc.
Ed: Dan Monk. **Description:** Cincinnati commercial real estate owners defaulting in securitized loans reached $306 million at the end of 2009. The trend has lifted the region's default rate to nearly 9 percent. National average for commercial real estate default is examined.

31763 ■ *"Real Opportunities: Don't Let Mortgage Mayhem Steer You Away From Sound Investments" in Black Enterprise (December 2007)*
Pub: Earl G. Graves Publishing Co. Inc.
Ed: James A. Anderson. **Description:** Real estate investment trusts (REITs) that operate office buildings, industrial parks, shopping malls, hotels, hospitals, or other commercial properties may be a sound investment, despite the mortgage crisis facing the U.S. financial sector.

31764 ■ *"Recession Fears Power Gold" in Barron's (Vol. 88, March 17, 2008, No. 11, pp. M14)*
Pub: Dow Jones & Company, Inc.
Ed: Melanie Burton. **Description:** Gold prices have been more attractive as the U.S. dollar weakens and the Dow Jones Industrial Average has slipped almost 10 percent in 2008. The rate cuts from the Federal Reserve Board has also spurred inflation fears adding upward pressure to the price of the metal.

31765 ■ *"Recession Management" in Canadian Business (Vol. 81, March 3, 2008, No. 3, pp. 62)*
Pub: Rogers Media
Ed: Joe Castaldo. **Description:** Some companies such as Capital One Financial Corp. are managing their finances as if a recession has already taken place to prepare themselves for the looming economic downturn. Intel Corp., meanwhile shows how increasing its investments during a recession could be advantageous. Tips on how companies can survive a recession are provided.

31766 ■ *"Reduce the Risk of Failed Financial Judgments" in Harvard Business Review (Vol. 86, July-August 2008, No. 8, pp. 24)*
Pub: Harvard Business School Press
Ed: Robert G. Eccles; Edward J. Fiedl. **Description:** Utilization of business consultants, evaluators, appraisers, and actuaries to decrease financial management risks is discussed.

31767 ■ *"Reform Law Spares Community Banks from FDIC Fee Hike" in Baltimore Business Journal (Vol. 28, July 23, 2010, No. 11, pp. 1)*
Pub: Baltimore Business Journal
Ed: Gary Haber. **Description:** A new financial regulator bill has exempted community banks from increased Federal Insurance Deposit Corporation fees. Large banks with assets of $10 billion and above will be required to pay the higher fee in 2010. Small banks are seen to hold bank fees at bay owing to the exemption.

31768 ■ *"Regulation Papered Over" in Charlotte Business Journal (Vol. 25, November 5, 2010, No. 33, pp.)*
Pub: Charlotte Business Journal
Ed: Adam O'Daniel. **Description:** County courts in North Carolina are having challenges coping with its oversight and regulation duties as it becomes too busy with foreclosure cases. Clerks in some county courts have presided over foreclosure hearings because of the flooding of foreclosure cases.

31769 ■ *"Reports of Banks' Revival were Greatly Exaggerated" in Barron's (Vol. 88, July 7, 2008, No. 27, pp. L14)*
Pub: Dow Jones & Co., Inc.
Ed: Jack Willoughby. **Description:** Performance of mutual funds improved for the second quarter of 2008 compared to the previous quarter, registering an average gain of 0.13 percent; funds focusing on natural resources rose the highest, their value rising by an average of 24.50 percent.

31770 ■ *"Research Reports" in Barron's (Vol. 88, March 24, 2008, No. 12, pp. M10)*
Pub: Dow Jones & Company, Inc.
Description: Investors are recommending purchasing shares of Ampco Pittsburgh due to an expected surge in earnings. Deteriorating credit quality presents problems for the shares of BankAtlantic Bancorp, whose price targets have been lowered from $7 to $5 each. Shares of Helicos Biosciences are expected to move sideways from their $6 level. Statistical data included.

31771 ■ *"Research Reports" in Barron's (Vol. 88, March 10, 2008, No. 10, pp. M13)*
Pub: Dow Jones & Company, Inc.
Description: Research reports on different company stocks by investment analysts are given. Shares of Cal Dive are rated Outperform by analysts, citing the shares' continued attractiveness and the company's acquisition of Horizon. Analysts recommend buying the shares of California Water Service Group.

31772 ■ *"Research Reports" in Barron's (Vol. 89, July 20, 2009, No. 29, pp. M12)*
Pub: Dow Jones & Co., Inc.
Description: Shares of Bank of the Ozarks, Broadpoint Gleacher Securities Group, Halozyme Therapeutics, and Take Two Interactive are rated as Buy. The shares of Fluor and PetMed Express are rated as Outperform, while those of Humana and Janus Capital Group are rated as Hold and Underweight respectively.

31773 ■ *"Research Reports: How Analysts Size Up Companies" in Barron's (Vol. 88, March 31, 2008, No. 13, pp. M13)*
Pub: Dow Jones & Company, Inc.
Ed: Anita Peltonen. **Description:** Sirius Satellite's shares are ranked Outperform as it awaits approval from the Federal Communications Commission in its merger with XM. TiVo's shares are ranked Avoid as the company is in a sector that's being commoditized. Verizon Communications' rising dividend yield earns it a Focus List ranking. The shares of Bear Stearns, Churchill Downs, Corning, and Deerfield Triarc Capital are also reviewed. Statistical data included.

31774 ■ *"Research Reports: How Analysts Size Up Companies" in Barron's (Vol. 88, March 17, 2008, No. 11, pp. M13)*
Pub: Dow Jones & Company, Inc.
Ed: Anita Peltonen. **Description:** Shares of Applied Industrial Technologies are ranked Market Perform while the shares of Google get a buy rating. Salix Pharmaceuticals gets a Sell/Above-Average risk rating. The shares of Dune Energy, Franklin Resources, Internet Brands, Piper Jaffray, and Texas Instruments are also rated.

31775 ■ *"Research Reports: How Analysts Size Up Companies" in Barron's (Vol. 88,*

June 30, 2008, No. 26, pp. M11)
Pub: Dow Jones & Co., Inc.
Ed: Anita Peltonen. **Description:** Shares of Developers Diversified Realty Corp. get a 'Long-Term Buy' rating while the shares of HealthSouth Corp. and Onyx Pharmaceutical get a rating of 'Underperform' and a 'Buy' rating respectively. The shares of American Capital Agency, American Public Education, Bankrate, and Werner Enterprises are also ranked.

31776 ■ *"Research Reports: How Analysts Size Up Companies" in Barron's (Vol. 88, July 14, 2008, No. 28, pp. M13)*
Pub: Dow Jones & Co., Inc.
Ed: Anita Peltonen. **Description:** Shares of Bankrate and AutoZone both get a 'Buy' rating from analysts while Zions Bancorporation's shares are downgraded from 'Outperform' to 'Neutral'. The shares of Jet Blue Airline and Deckers Outdoor, a manufacturer of innovative footwear, are also rated and discussed. Statistical data included.

31777 ■ *"Research Reports: How Analysts Size Up Companies" in Barron's (Vol. 89, July 13, 2009, No. 28, pp. M11)*
Pub: Dow Jones & Co., Inc.
Description: Shares of Alaska Air Group get a 'Hold' rating while the shares of Art Technology Group and Cathay General Bancorp both get a 'Buy' rating. The shares of HCC Insurance Holdings, HMS Holdings, H&R Block, Intel, McDonald's, People's United Financial, Pride International, Sino Forest, and Virgin Media are also given ratings.

31778 ■ *"Research Reports: How Analysts Size Up Companies" in Barron's (Vol. 89, July 27, 2009, No. 30, pp. M12)*
Pub: Dow Jones & Co., Inc.
Ed: Anita Peltonen. **Description:** Shares of Allscripts-Misys gets an 'Outperform' rating while the shares of M&T Bank and Precision Castparts get a 'Sell' and 'Hold' rating respectively. The shares of Supervalu, Syniverse Holdings, Valley National Bancorp, Volterra, and Wesco are also rated.

31779 ■ *"Retail Woes: The Shoe Doesn't Fit for Gerald Loftin's Stock Picks" in Black Enterprise (Vol. 38, July 2008, No. 12, pp. 40)*
Pub: Earl G. Graves Publishing Co. Inc.
Ed: Steve Garmhausen. **Description:** Each of the three stocks that Gerald Loftin picked in May 2007 have lost money; DSW, the designer shoe retailer, fell by 63.7 percent; paint and coatings retailer Sherwin-Williams Co. fell by 7.2 percent; and Verizon Communications Inc. fell by 1.4 percent. Statistical data included.

31780 ■ *Retire Dollar Smart*
Pub: Trafford Publishing
Ed: Jim Miller. **Released:** July 2006. **Price:** $25.99. **Description:** The difference between savings and investments and their importance is examined, along with four rules for converting good investments into even greater ones. Contingency plans for healthcare costs as well as ways to manage taxes on investments are discussed. Five methods to control the costs of investing and saving include the use of smart strategies; getting independent, accurate, complete information; investing passively; asking for a discount; and taking off your blinders. Ten steps for designing a foolproof retirement investment portfolio are also provided.

31781 ■ *The Return of Depression Economics and the Crisis of 2008*
Pub: W.W. Norton & Company, Inc.
Ed: Paul Krugman. **Price:** $16.95. **Description:** The recipient of the 2008 Nobel Memorial Prize in Economics revises his earlier work from 1999 to reflect the current economic crisis of 2008.

31782 ■ *"Return to Wealth; Bank Strategy" in The Economist (Vol. 390, January 3, 2009, No. 8612, pp. 56)*
Pub: The Economist Newspaper Inc.
Description: UBS' strategy to survive these trying economic times is presented. Statistical data included. UBS has a stronger balance-sheet than most of its investment-banking peers and has reduced its portfolio.

31783 ■ *Rich Dad, Poor Dad*
Pub: Warner Books Inc.
Ed: Robert Kiyosaki with Sharon Lechter. **Price:** $16. 95. **Description:** What the wealthy teach their children about money that others do not.

31784 ■ *Rich Dad, Poor Dad: What the Rich Teach Their Kids About Money-That the Poor and Middle Class Do Not!*
Pub: Time Warner Paperbacks
Ed: Robert T. Kiyosaki; Sharon L. Lechter. **Released:** December 5, 2002. **Price:** $16.95. **Description:** Personal finance expert shares his economic perspective through exposure to a pair of disparate influences: his own highly education but fiscally unstable father and the multimillionaire eighth-grade dropout father of his closest friend.

31785 ■ *Rich Dad's Increase Your Financial IQ: Get Smarter with Your Money*
Pub: Business Plus
Ed: Robert T. Kiyosaki. **Released:** $16.99. **Price:** March 26, 2008. **Description:** Author describes his five key principles of financial knowledge to help readers build wealth.

31786 ■ *"The Right Time for REITs" in Barron's (Vol. 88, July 14, 2008, No. 28, pp. 32)*
Pub: Dow Jones & Co., Inc.
Ed: Mike Hogan. **Description:** Discusses the downturn in U.S. real estate investment trusts so these are worth considering for investment. Several Websites that are useful for learning about real estate investment trusts for investment purposes are presented.

31787 ■ *"Risk and Reward" in Canadian Business (Vol. 81, October 13, 2008, No. 17, pp. 21)*
Pub: Rogers Media Ltd.
Ed: Calvin Leung. **Description:** Macro-economist and currency analyst Mark Venezia believes that stable financial institutions, free-market reforms, and the role of central banks in keeping inflation and exchange rates stable could make emerging-market bonds strong performers for better future returns. Venezia's other views on emerging-market bonds are discussed.

31788 ■ *"Risky Business" in Canadian Business (Vol. 79, October 23, 2006, No. 21, pp. 153)*
Pub: Rogers Media
Ed: C.J. Burton. **Description:** Tips for Canadian managers on how to handle business risks are presented.

31789 ■ *"Rock Festival: High Spirited Conventioneers Celebrate Their Good Fortune" in Canadian Business (Vol. 81, March 31, 2008, No. 5)*
Pub: Rogers Media
Ed: Jeff Sanford. **Description:** Soaring prices of commodities in the mining industry have been very good for the attendees of the 76th annual conference of the Prospectors & Developers Association of Canada. A speaker at the conference expects commodity prices to come off a bit but not fall dramatically as it did in the 1980's.

31790 ■ *"Ryder's Shock Absorbers Are In Place" in Barron's (Vol. 88, March 24, 2008, No. 12, pp. 19)*
Pub: Dow Jones & Company, Inc.
Ed: Christopher C. Williams. **Description:** Shares of Ryder System Inc. are expected to continue rising on the back of rising earnings, forecast at $5.20 a share for 2009. The shares of the truck freight company hit a 52-week high of $62.27 each and may reach $70 a share.

31791 ■ *Safety Net*
Pub: Crown Business Books
Ed: James Glassman. **Released:** February 22, 2011. **Price:** $23.00. **Description:** Ways to build a financial investment strategy that protects you, while ensuring growth in a strong financial future are presented.

31792 ■ *"Sales Gave W&S Record '07" in Business Courier (Vol. 24, March 14, 2008, No. 49, pp. 1)*
Pub: American City Business Journals, Inc.
Ed: Jon Newberry. **Description:** Western & Southern Financial Group was able to achieve a record $365 million in net income thanks in large part to the double-digit increases in profits by its W&S Agency Group field offices and non-insurance businesses. The sale of their Integrated Investment Services Subsidiary and shares in several Marriot hotels also added to the record profit.

31793 ■ *"Samll Fortunes" in Business Courier (Vol. 27, July 23, 2010, No. 12, pp. 1)*
Pub: Business Courier
Ed: Steve Watkins. **Description:** Small banks in Cincinnati, Ohio have been faring well despite the economic crisis, a survey has revealed. Sixty percent of local small banks have capital levels above 15.8 percent median. But regulators are seen to close more banks in 2010 than since the financial crises began.

31794 ■ *Sarbanes-Oxley for Dummies, 2nd Ed.*
Pub: John Wiley and Sons, Inc.
Ed: Jill Gilbert Welytok. **Released:** February 2008. **Price:** $21.99. **Description:** Provides the latest Sarbanes-Oxley (SOX) legislation with procedures to safely and effectively reduce compliance costs. Topics include way to: establish SOX standards for IT professionals, minimize compliances costs for every aspect of a business, survive a Section 404 audit, avoid litigation under SOX, anticipate future rules and trends, create a post-SOX paper trail, increase a company's standing and reputation, work with SOX in a small business, meet new SOX standards, build a board that can't be bought, and to comply with all SOX management mandates.

31795 ■ *"Satellite Down, Stock Up: Raytheon Is On Target With Ten Percent Dividend Increase" in Barron's (Vol. 88, March 31, 2008, No. 13)*
Pub: Dow Jones & Company, Inc.
Ed: Shirley A. Lazo. **Description:** Raytheon hiked their quarterly dividend to 28 cents per share from 25.5 cents. Aircastle slashed their quarterly common dividend by 64 percent for them to retain additional capital that can be used to increase their liquidity position.

31796 ■ *Save Your Small Business: 10 Crucial Strategies to Survive Hard Times or Close Down and Move On*
Pub: NOLO
Contact: Ralph Warner, Chief Executive Officer
Ed: Ralph Warner, Bethany Laurence. **Released:** August 1, 2009. **Price:** $29.99. **Description:** According to a study among 500 businesses, 44 percent used credit cards in order to meet their firm's needs in the previous six months. Written by a business owner, this book provides twelve strategies to protect personal assets from creditors and survive the current recession.

31797 ■ *"A Say on Pay" in Canadian Business (Vol. 82, April 27, 2009, No. 7, pp. 14)*
Pub: Rogers Media
Ed: Joe Castaldo. **Description:** A COMPAS Inc. survey of 134 Canadian chief executive officers found that 44 percent agree that CEO compensation should be subject to a non-binding vote. The respondents were also divided on whether to allow shareholders to exercise retroactive clawbacks on executive compensation if firm performance turns out to be worse than projected.

31798 ■ *"SBA Can Improve Your Cash Flow" in Business Owner (Vol. 35, September-October 2011, No. 5, pp. 3)*
Pub: DL Perkins Company
Description: Federal assistance available to small business is examined. The Small Business Administration loan guarantee program is designed to improve availability and attractiveness of small business loans.

31799 ■ *Schaum's Outline Financial Management, Third Edition*
Pub: McGraw-Hill

Ed: Jae K. Shim; Joel G. Siegel. **Released:** May 2007. **Price:** $22.95 (CND). **Description:** Rules and regulations governing corporate finance, including the Sarbanes-Oxley Act are discussed.

31800 ■ *"Schwab: Lower Returns Ahead" in Barron's (Vol. 89, July 13, 2009, No. 28, pp. L4)*
Pub: Dow Jones & Co., Inc.

Ed: Leslie P. Norton. **Description:** Charles Schwab says that 8 percent to 10 percent equity-market returns are not realistic these days and that 4 percent to 5 percent are more realistic in the next four to five years from 2009. Schwab expects inflation to be close to 10 percent per annum in a couple of years.

31801 ■ *"Score One for 'Barron's'" in Barron's (Vol. 89, July 13, 2009, No. 28, pp. 14)*
Pub: Dow Jones & Co., Inc.

Ed: Andrew Bary. **Description:** 57 companies that were bullishly covered on 'Barron's' for the first half of 2009 were up an average of 20.4 percent compared to the 10.2 percent gain in the relevant market indexes. The bearish stock picks by 'Barron's' were down 3.4 percent compared to a 6.4 percent for the benchmarks.

31802 ■ *"Scottsdale Bank Plans 4Q Opening" in The Business Journal - Serving Phoenix and the Valley of the Sun (Vol. 28, August 15, 2008, No. 50)*
Pub: American City Business Journals, Inc.

Ed: Chris Casacchia. **Description:** Arizona's Department of Financial Institutions has approved Scottsdale Business Bank, a community bank which plans to open in the fourth quarter of 2008. The bank, which is to be located near McCormick Ranch in Scottsdale, Arizona, will cater to small business owners in the professional sector, such as accountants and doctors.

31803 ■ *"Screening for the Best Stock Screens" in Barron's (Vol. 90, September 13, 2010, No. 37, pp. 36)*
Pub: Barron's Editorial & Corporate Headquarters

Ed: Mike Hogan. **Description:** Pros and cons of the new and revised stock screening tools from Zack, Finviz.com, and GuruFocus are discussed. FinVix.com is more capable for screening through stocks and the service is free.

31804 ■ *"SEC Doesn't Buy Biovail's Claims" in Barron's (Vol. 88, March 31, 2008, No. 13, pp. 20)*
Pub: Dow Jones & Company, Inc.

Ed: Bill Alpert. **Description:** Overstatement of earnings and chronic fraudulent conduct has led the SEC to file a stock fraud suit against Biovail, Eugene Melnyk and three others present or former employees of Biovail. Melnyk had the firm file suit in 2006 that blames short-sellers and stock researchers for the company's drop in share price.

31805 ■ *"SEC Report On Rating Agencies Falls Short" in Barron's (Vol. 88, July 14, 2008, No. 28, pp. 35)*
Pub: Dow Jones & Co., Inc.

Ed: Jack Willoughby. **Description:** The Securities and Exchange Commissions report on credit-rating firms should have drawn attention to the slipshod practices in the offerings of collateralized debt obligations. The report fell short of prescribing correctives for the flawed system of these agencies' relationship with their clients.

31806 ■ *"A Security Risk?" in Canadian Business (Vol. 80, October 22, 2007, No. 21, pp. 36)*
Pub: Rogers Media

Ed: Joe Castaldo. **Description:** Garda World Security Corporation declared a C$1.5 million loss in the second quarter of 2007. The company's securities have been falling since June and hit a 52-week low of $15.90 in September. Details of the physical and cash-handling firm's strategy to integrate its acquisitions are discussed.

31807 ■ *"Selling Pressures Rise in China" in Barron's (Vol. 88, March 10, 2008, No. 10, pp. M9)*
Pub: Dow Jones & Company, Inc.
Ed: Mohammed Hadi. **Description:** There are about 1.6 trillion yuan worth of shares up for sale in Chinese stock markets in 2008, adding to the selling pressures in these markets. The Chinese government has imposed restrictions to prevent a rapid rise in selling stocks.

31808 ■ *"Sense and Consensus" in Canadian Business (Vol. 81, October 13, 2008, No. 17, pp. 22)*
Pub: Rogers Media Ltd.
Ed: David Wolf. **Description:** Stock analysts' agree that earning estimates are seen to be optimistic in relation to their global economic outlook. Analysts are expected to cut earnings projections by fall because it may negatively affect the Canadian stock market. Other view on market analysis are presented.

31809 ■ *"Sentiment Split on Financials" in Barron's (Vol. 88, March 24, 2008, No. 12, pp. M14)*
Pub: Dow Jones & Company, Inc.
Ed: Steven M. Sears. **Description:** Experts in the financial sector are split as to whether or not the worst of the financial crisis brought on by the credit crunch is over. Some options traders are trading on are defensive puts, expecting the worst, while investors buying calls are considered as bullish.

31810 ■ *"Serious Signal Flashing?" in Barron's (Vol. 88, July 7, 2008, No. 27, pp. 11)*
Pub: Dow Jones & Co., Inc.
Description: Discusses the Hindenburg Omen, named after the airship disaster of May 1937, which is considered a predictor of market crashes and has appeared twice in June 2008. There is a 25 percent probability that the US stock market will suffer a crash in the July-October 2008 period.

31811 ■ *"A Shallow Pool" in Canadian Business (Vol. 81, Summer 2008, No. 9, pp. 44)*
Pub: Rogers Media Ltd.
Ed: Joe Castaldo. **Description:** Bank of Canada projected in its 'Monetary Policy Report' a growth rate of 1.4 percent in 2008 and does not expect the economy to fully recover until mid-2010. The Canadian stock market has been recovering although slowly with just a 1.6 percent gain by April 30. Other details on the Canadian equity market are presented.

31812 ■ *"Shopped Out; Retailing Gloom" in The Economist (Vol. 390, January 3, 2009, No. 8612, pp. 26)*
Pub: The Economist Newspaper Inc.
Description: Economic volatility in the retail sector is having an impact on a number of countries around the globe. Europe is experiencing hard economic times as well and unless businesses have a strong business plan banks feel unable to lend the money necessary to tide the retailers over. The falling pound has increased the cost of imported goods and small to midsize retail chains may not be able to weather such an unforgiving economic climate.

31813 ■ *"Shoppes of Kenwood Files Chap. 11" in Business Courier (Vol. 26, December 18, 2009, No. 34, pp. 1)*
Pub: American City Business Journals, Inc.
Ed: Jon Newberry. **Description:** Shoppes of Kenwood filed for Chapter 11 reorganization in US Bankruptcy Court just as the property was scheduled to be offered at a sheriff's auction. Details of the filing are included.

31814 ■ *"Shorts Story" in Barron's (Vol. 89, July 6, 2009, No. 27, pp. 16)*
Pub: Dow Jones & Co., Inc.
Ed: Gene Epstein. **Description:** Shares of Compass Minerals, J2 Global Communications, K12, Middleby, and Pactiv should be shorted by investors. These companies suffer from weaknesses in their business models, making them vulnerable to a share price decline.

31815 ■ *"Shorts Story" in Barron's (Vol. 89, July 6, 2009, No. 27, pp. 16)*
Pub: Dow Jones & Co., Inc.

Ed: Gene Epstein. **Description:** Shares of Compass Minerals, J2 Global Communications, K12, Middleby, and Pactiv should be shorted by investors. These companies suffer from weaknesses in their business models, making them vulnerable to a share price decline.

31816 ■ *"Should the Fed Regulate Wall Street?" in Barron's (Vol. 88, March 24, 2008, No. 12, pp. M15)*
Pub: Dow Jones & Company, Inc.

Ed: Randall W. Forsyth. **Description:** Greater regulation of the financial sector by the Federal Reserve is essential for it to survive the crisis it is experiencing. The resulting regulation could be in complete contrast with the deregulation the sector previously experienced.

31817 ■ *"Should I or Shouldn't I?" in Indoor Comfort Marketing (Vol. 70, February 2011, No. 2, pp. 30)*
Pub: Industry Publications Inc.

Ed: Philip J. Baratz. **Description:** Investment tips are shared for investing in futures options.

31818 ■ *"Silver Standard Reports First Quarter 2007 Results" in Canadian Corporate News (May 14, 2007)*
Pub: Comtex News Network Inc.

Description: Silver Standard Resources Inc. reports a first quarter loss of $1.6 million compared with the first quarter of 2006 in which the loss was $1.1 million. Statistical data included.

31819 ■ *"Singapore Airlines' Balancing Act" in Harvard Business Review (Vol. 88, July-August 2010, No. 7-8, pp. 145)*
Pub: Harvard Business School Publishing

Ed: Loizos Heracleous, Jochen Wirtz. **Description:** Singapore Airlines is used as an illustration of organizational effectiveness. The article includes the firm's 4-3-3 rule of spending, its promotion of centralized as well as decentralized innovation, use of technology, and strategic planning.

31820 ■ *"Six Great Stock Funds for the Long Haul" in Barron's (Vol. 89, July 13, 2009, No. 28, pp. L5)*
Pub: Dow Jones & Co., Inc.

Ed: Lawrence C. Strauss; Tom Sullivan. **Description:** Six mutual funds that have solid long-term performance, transparency, savvy stock picking, and discipline are presented. The managers of these funds are also evaluated. These funds include the T. Rowe Price Emerging Market Stock Fund, Fairholme, and Dodge & Cox Stock.

31821 ■ *Six SIGMA for Small Business*
Pub: Entrepreneur Press

Ed: Greg Brue. **Released:** October 2005. **Price:** $19.95 (US), $26.95 (Canadian). **Description:** Jack Welch's Six SIGMA approach to business covers accounting, finance, sales and marketing, buying a business, human resource development, and new product development.

31822 ■ *"Six Things You Can Do To Ride Out A Turbulent Market" in Hispanic Business (Vol. 30, March 2008, No. 3, pp. 20)*
Pub: Hispanic Business

Ed: Hildy Medina; Michael Bowker. **Description:** Top financial experts' views on managing investment portfolios during turbulent periods in the stock market are reported. Experts prefer investing in health care, short term investments, international bonds and preferred stocks or just maintain cash until such times as the market settles.

31823 ■ *"A Slice of Danish; Fixing Finance" in The Economist (Vol. 390, January 3, 2009, No. 8612, pp. 55)*
Pub: The Economist Newspaper Inc.

Description: Denmark's mortgage-holders and the county's lending system is presented.

31824 ■ *"The Small 300" in Canadian Business (Vol. 81, Summer 2008, No. 9, pp. 137)*
Pub: Rogers Media Ltd.
Description: Small cap-companies are ranked based on market capitalization and stock performance. Calgary-based Grande Cache Coal Corp. topped the roster with 1,000 percent of return resulting from strong sales. A table showing the 2008 rankings of the companies is presented.

31825 ■ *The Small Business Bible: Everything You Need to Know to Succeed in Your Small Business*
Pub: John Wiley and Sons, Inc.
Ed: Steven D. Strauss. **Released:** September 2008. **Price:** $19.95 (US), $28.99 (Canadian). **Description:** Comprehensive guide to starting and running a successful small business. Topics include bookkeeping and financial management, marketing, publicity, and advertising.

31826 ■ *"Small Business Capital Outlays" in Small Business Economic Trends (April 2008, pp. 16)*
Pub: National Federation of Independent Business
Ed: William C. Dunkelberg, Holly Wade. **Description:** Graphs and tables that present the capital outlays of small businesses in the U.S. are provided. The tables include figures on planned and actual capital expenditures, and type and amount of capital expenditures.

31827 ■ *"Small Business Capital Outlays" in Small Business Economic Trends (March 2008, pp. 16)*
Pub: National Federation of Independent Business
Ed: William C. Dunkelberg, Holly Wade. **Description:** Graphs and tables that present the capital outlays of small businesses in the U.S. are provided. The tables include figures on planned and actual capital expenditures, and type and amount of capital expenditures.

31828 ■ *"Small Business Capital Outlays" in Small Business Economic Trends (February 2008, pp. 16)*
Pub: National Federation of Independent Business
Ed: William C. Dunkelberg, Holly Wade. **Description:** Graphs and tables that present the capital outlays of small businesses in the U.S. are provided. The tables include figures on planned and actual capital expenditures, and type and amount of capital expenditures.

31829 ■ *"Small Business Capital Outlays" in Small Business Economic Trends (January 2008, pp. 16)*
Pub: National Federation of Independent Business
Description: Graph representing actual and planned capital expenditures among small businesses surveyed in the U.S. from January 1986 to December 2007 is given. Tables showing actual capital expenditures, type of capital expenditures made, amount of capital expenditures made, and capital expenditure plans are also presented.

31830 ■ *"Small Business Capital Outlays" in Small Business Economic Trends (September 2010, pp. 16)*
Pub: National Federation of Independent Business
Ed: William C. Dunkelberg, Holly Wade. **Description:** A graph representing actual and planned expenditures among small businesses surveyed in the U.S. from January 1986 to August 2010 is given. Tables showing actual capital expenditures, type of capital expenditures made, amount of capital expenditures made, and capital expenditure plans are also presented.

31831 ■ *"Small Business Capital Outlays" in Small Business Economic Trends (July 2010, pp. 16)*
Pub: National Federation of Independent Business
Description: A graph representing actual and planned capital expenditures among small businesses surveyed in the U.S. from January 1986 to June 2010 is given. Tables showing actual capital expenditures, type of capital expenditures made, amount of capital expenditures made, and capital expenditure plans are also presented.

31832 ■ *Small Business Cash Flow: Strategies for Making Your Business a Financial Success*
Pub: John Wiley & Sons, Incorporated
Ed: Denise O'Berry. **Released:** October 2006. **Price:** $19.95. **Description:** Tips to help small businesses manage money are given.

31833 ■ *Small Business Clustering Technology: Applications in Marketing, Management, Finance, and IT*
Pub: Idea Group Publishing
Ed: Robert C. MacGregor; Ann Hodgkinson. **Released:** June 2006. **Description:** An overview of the development and role of small business clusters in disciplines that include economics, marketing, management and information systems.

31834 ■ *Small Business Desk Reference*
Pub: Penguin Books USA Inc.
Ed: Gene Marks. **Released:** December 2004. **Description:** Comprehensive guide for starting or running a successful small business, focusing on buying a business or franchise, writing a business plan, financial management, accounting, legal issues, human resources management, operations, marketing, sales, customer service, taxes, insurance, and ethics. Information for launching a restaurant, property management firm, retail outlet, consulting firm, and service business is included.

31835 ■ *Small Business for Dummies, 3rd Ed.*
Pub: John Wiley and Sons, Inc.
Ed: Eric Tyson; Jim Schell. **Released:** March 2008. **Price:** $21.99. **Description:** Guidebook for anyone wanting to start or grow a small business; topics include information financing, budgeting, marketing, management and more.

31836 ■ *"Small Business Earnings" in Small Business Economic Trends (March 2008, pp. 6)*
Pub: National Federation of Independent Business
Ed: William C. Dunkelberg, Holly Wade. **Description:** Two tables and a graph representing the earnings of small businesses in the U.S. are presented. Statistics for actual earnings changes are provided. The figures in the graph include data from 1986 to 2008.

31837 ■ *"Small Business Earnings" in Small Business Economic Trends (February 2008, pp. 6)*
Pub: National Federation of Independent Business
Ed: William C. Dunkelberg, Holly Wade. **Description:** Two tables and a graph representing the earnings of small businesses in the U.S. are presented. Statistics for actual earnings changes are provided. The figures in the graph include data from 1974 to 2008.

31838 ■ *"Small Business Earnings" in Small Business Economic Trends (January 2008, pp. 6)*
Pub: National Federation of Independent Business
Description: Graph from a survey of small businesses in the U.S. is given, representing actual small business earnings from January 1986 to December 2007. Tables showing actual earnings changes and most important reason for lower earnings are also presented.

31839 ■ *"Small Business Earnings" in Small Business Economic Trends (September 2010, pp. 6)*
Pub: National Federation of Independent Business
Ed: William C. Dunkelberg, Holly Wade. **Description:** A graph from a survey of small businesses in the U.S. is given, representing actual small business earnings from January 1986 to August 2010. Tables showing actual earnings changes and most important reason for lower earnings are also presented.

31840 ■ *The Small Business Savings Plan: 101 Tactics for Controlling Costs and Boosting the Bottom Line*
Pub: Kaplan Books
Ed: Timothy R. Gase. **Released:** May 2007. **Price:** $28.00. **Description:** Strategies for small business owners to develop a savings plan and increase profits are outlined.

31841 ■ *"Smart Investor's Shopping List: Coke, Walgreen, Drill Bits; A Conversation with Money Manager Paula Dorion-Gray" in Crain's Chicago Business*
Pub: Crain Communications, Inc.
Ed: Bruce Blythe. **Description:** Interview with Paula Dorion-Gray, president of Dorion-Gray Retirement Planning Inc., discusses the state of the investing environment, favored industries, industries to avoid, and her approach towards investing.

31842 ■ *"The Smell of Fear: Is a Bottom Near?" in Barron's (Vol. 88, March 17, 2008, No. 11, pp. M3)*
Pub: Dow Jones & Company, Inc.
Ed: Kopin Tan. **Description:** Liquidity problems at Bear Stearns frightened investors in markets around the world due to the fear of the prospects of a big bank's failure. Shares of health maintenance organizations got battered led by WellPoint, and Humana but longer-term investors who could weather short-term volatility may find value here. The value of J. Crew shares is also discussed.

31843 ■ *"A Socko Payout Menu: Rural Phone Carrier Plots to Supercharge Its Shares" in Barron's (Vol. 88, June 30, 2008, No. 26, pp. M5)*
Pub: Dow Jones & Co., Inc.
Ed: Shirley A. Lazo. **Description:** CenturyTel boosted its quarterly common payout to 70 cents from 6.75 cents per share die to its strong cash flows and solid balance sheet. Eastman Kodak's plan for a buyback will be partially funded by its $581 million tax refund. CME Group will buyback stocks through 2009 worth $1.1 billion.

31844 ■ *"Solace for the Freshly Flaherty'd" in Canadian Business (Vol. 79, November 6, 2006, No. 22, pp. 114)*
Pub: Rogers Media
Ed: Ian McGugan. **Description:** Tips to manage investments with relation to cash distribution tax on income trusts are presented.

31845 ■ *"Some Big Biotechs Buying Own Stock" in Boston Business Journal (Vol. 30, November 5, 2010, No. 41, pp. 1)*
Pub: Boston Business Journal
Ed: Julie M. Donnelly. **Description:** Biotechnology companies such as Biogen Idec and Genzyme Corporation are conducting stock buybacks as they look to invest their cash holdings. Other analysts see the buybacks as reluctance in committing to longer-term investments.

31846 ■ *"Some Relief Possible Following Painful Week" in Barron's (Vol. 88, July 14, 2008, No. 28, pp. M3)*
Pub: Dow Jones & Co., Inc.
Ed: Kopin Tan. **Description:** Dow Chemical is offering a 74 percent premium to acquire Rohm & Haas' coatings and electronics materials operations. Frontline amassed a 5.6 percent stake in rival Overseas Shipholding Group and a merger between the two would create a giant global fleet with pricing power. Highlights of the U.S. stock market during the week that ended in July 11, 2008 are discussed. Statistical data included.

31847 ■ *"Something to Like" in Canadian Business (Vol. 81, April 14, 2008, No. 6, pp. 22)*
Pub: Rogers Media
Ed: Jack Mintz. **Description:** Jim Flaherty's policy on tax-free savings account (TFSA) will allow Canadians to accumulate wealth at a much faster rate and these accounts could be especially good for people who are subject to high effective taxes on savings. Investors should put their money into a Registered

Retirement Savings Plan (RRSP) when it comes to risky investments but the TFSA is better than an RRSP if investors expect very high taxes on withdrawals from their RRSP.

31848 ■ *"Spotlight on Pensions" in Business Horizons (Vol. 51, March-April 2008, No. 2, pp. 105)*
Pub: Elsevier Advanced Technology Publications
Ed: Laureen A. Maines. **Description:** Perceptions of pension burden and risk among financial statement users is likely to increase with changes in pension accounting. These perceptions might affect decisions on pension commitments and investments.

31849 ■ *"Spread Your Wings" in Canadian Business (Vol. 81, March 17, 2008, No. 4, pp. 31)*
Pub: Rogers Media
Ed: Megan Harman. **Description:** Financing from angel investors is one avenue that should be explored by startups. Angel investors are typically affluent individuals who invest their own money. Angel investors usually want at least 10 times their initial investment within eight years but they benefit the businesses through their help in decision-making and the industry expertise they provide.

31850 ■ *"Sprint Tries to Wring Out Positives" in The Business Journal-Serving Metropolitan Kansas City (Vol. 26, August 8, 2008, No. 48)*
Pub: American City Business Journals, Inc.
Ed: Suzanna Stagemeyer. **Description:** Sprint Nextel Corp. reported that 901,000 subscribers left the company in the quarter ending June 30, 2008; fewer than the nearly 1.1 million it lost in the previous quarter. Customer turnover also dropped to just less than 2 percent, compared to 2.45 percent in the first quarter of 2008.

31851 ■ *"Staffing Firm Grows by Following Own Advice-Hire a Headhunter" in Crain's Detroit Business (Vol. 24, October 6, 2008, No. 40, pp. 1)*
Pub: Crain Communications, Inc.
Ed: Sherri Begin. **Description:** Profile of Venator Holdings L.L.C., a staffing firm that provides searches for companies in need of financial-accounting and technical employees; the firm's revenue has increased from $1.1 million in 2003 to a projected $11.5 million this year due to a climate in which more people are exiting the workforce than are coming in with those particular specialized skills and the need for a temporary, flexible workforce for contract placements at companies that do not want to take on the legacy costs associated with permanent employees. The hiring of an external headhunter to find the right out-of-state manager for Venator is also discussed.

31852 ■ *"Stand-Up Guy" in Barron's (Vol. 88, July 7, 2008, No. 27, pp. L11)*
Pub: Dow Jones & Co., Inc.
Ed: Suzanne McGee. **Description:** James O'Shaughnessy, a mutual fund manager with O'Shaughnessy Asset Management, is bullish on both financial and energy stocks. He was formerly involved with Bear Stearns until he left the firm in March 2008.

31853 ■ *"State Shock Prices Take Large Tumble" in The Business Journal-Milwaukee (Vol. 25, September 12, 2008, No. 51, pp. A1)*
Pub: American City Business Journals, Inc.
Ed: Rich Rovito. **Description:** Weak economic times have caused the stocks of most publicly traded companies in Wisconsin to dip in 2008. Companies that appeared on the worst performing stocks list also experienced drops in share price to as much as 70 percent. Information about the companies that experienced increases in stock prices is also presented. Statistical data included.

31854 ■ *"Stay Calm, Bernanke Urges Markets" in Globe & Mail (March 1, 2007, pp. B1)*
Pub: CTVglobemedia Publishing Inc.
Ed: Brian McKenna. **Description:** The views of Ben Bernanke, the chief of the United States Federal Reserve Board, on the future trends of the United States' economy are presented. The effect of the global stock market trends on the American stock markets is discussed.

31855 ■ *"Stock Analysts' Pans" in Canadian Business (Vol. 81, Summer 2008, No. 9, pp. 75)*
Pub: Rogers Media Ltd.
Ed: Calvin Leung. **Description:** Table showing the one-year stock performance of companies that are least loved by analysts and are rated either to be a Hold or Sell. These companies should not be included in the investment portfolio, at least in the short term.

31856 ■ *"Stock Car Racing" in Canadian Business (Vol. 81, September 15, 2008, No. 14-15, pp. 29)*
Pub: Rogers Media Ltd.
Ed: Thomas Watson. **Description:** Some analysts predict a Chapter 11-style tune-up making GM and Ford a speculative turnaround stock. However, the price of oil could make or break the shares of the Big Three U.S. automobile manufacturers and if oil goes up too high then a speculative stock to watch is an electric car company called Zenn Motor Co.

31857 ■ *"Stock Delisting Could Hamper First Mariner" in Boston Business Journal (Vol. 29, July 29, 2011, No. 12, pp. 1)*
Pub: American City Business Journals Inc.
Ed: Gary Haber. **Description:** Possible delisting of First Mariner Bancorp from the Nasdaq stock exchange could adversely impact the bank's ability to attract institutional investors. Some institutions limit their investments to companies trading on the Nasdaq.

31858 ■ *Streetwise Finance and Accounting for Entrepreneurs: Set Budgets, Manage Costs, Keep Your Business Profitable*
Pub: Adams Media Corporation
Ed: Suzanne Caplan. **Released:** November 2006. **Price:** $25.95. **Description:** Book offers a basic understanding of accounting and finance for small businesses, including financial statements, credits and debits, as well as establishing a budget. Strategies for small companies in financial distress are included.

31859 ■ *"Stressed Out: 7 Banks Rated 'At Riks" in Saint Louis Business Journal (Vol. 32, September 16, 2011, No. 3, pp. 1)*
Pub: Saint Louis Business Journal
Ed: Greg Edwards. **Description:** St. Louis, Missouri has seven banks that are well above the 100 percent level that is considered 'at risk' based on a risk measurement called the Texas ratio. The banks are the Sun Security bank, 1st Advantage Bank, Superior Bank, Truman Bank, Reliance Bank, St. Louis Bank and Meramec Valley Bank.

31860 ■ *"Stretch Your Last Dollar Or Invest It?" in Business Owner (Vol. 35, November-December 2011, No. 6, pp. 4)*
Pub: DL Perkins Company
Description: Should small business owners cut expenses or invest in a downturned economy? Difficult times can be an opportunity to build a business brad.

31861 ■ *Structuring Your Business*
Pub: Adams Media Corporation
Contact: Gary Krebs, Director
E-mail: swatrous@adamsmedia.com
Ed: Michele Cagan. **Released:** 2004. **Price:** $19.95. **Description:** Accountant and author shares insight into starting a new company. The guide assists entrepreneurs through the process, whether it is a corporation, an LLC, a sole proprietorship, or a partnership. Tax codes, accounting practices and legislation affecting every business as well as tips on managing finances are among the topics covered.

31862 ■ *"Struggling Community Banks Find Little Help In Wall Street Bailout" in Crain's Detroit Business (Vol. 24, September 29, 2008)*
Pub: Crain Communications Inc.
Ed: Tom Henderson. **Description:** Both public and private Michigan bands have been hit hard by poorly performing loan portfolios and although their problems were not caused by high-risk securities but by a longtime statewide recession and a housing slump, these community banks have little hope of seeing any of the bailout money that has been allotted for the larger institutions.

31863 ■ *"Sudden Shift Leaves Wells Vendor Scrambling" in Charlotte Business Journal (Vol. 25, July 9, 2010, No. 16, pp. 1)*
Pub: Charlotte Business Journal
Ed: Adam O'Daniel. **Description:** Rubber stamps vendor Carolina Marking Devices is facing a 30 percent drop in business after banking firm Wells Fargo & Company decided to buy its rubber stamps from another vendor. Carolina Marking Devices had provided rubber to First Union Corporation and its successor Wachovia Corporation, which was eventually acquired by Wells Fargo. Other reactions from Carolina Marking Device owners are given.

31864 ■ *"The Suits Look Better Than the Shares" in Barron's (Vol. 88, March 31, 2008, No. 13, pp. 25)*
Pub: Dow Jones & Company, Inc.
Ed: Bill Alpert. **Description:** Jos. A. Bank's inventory has increased sharply raising questions about the company's growth prospects. The company's shares have already dropped significantly from 46 to 23 and could still continue its slide. The company is also battling a class action suit where plaintiffs allege that the Bank inventories were bloated.

31865 ■ *"Surprise Package" in Business Courier (Vol. 27, June 25, 2010, No. 8, pp. 1)*
Pub: Business Courier
Ed: Dan Monk, Jon Newberry, Steve Watkins. **Description:** More than 60 percent of the chief executive officers (CEOs) in Greater Cincinnati's 35 public companies took a salary cut in 2009, but stock grants resulted in large paper gains for the CEOs. The salary cuts show efforts of boards of directors to observe austerity. Statistics on increased values of stock awards for CEOs, median pay for CEOs, and median shareholder return are also presented.

31866 ■ *"Survey Distorts Cost of Capitals" in Canadian Business (Vol. 83, October 12, 2010, No. 17, pp. 22)*
Pub: Rogers Media Ltd.
Ed: Matthew McClearn. **Description:** Swiss bank UBS publishes a study comparing the costs of goods and services in megalopolises every three years. The study ranked Toronto and Montreal outside the Top 30 in 2009, but the two cities jumped to eighth and ninth in a recent update. This change can be contributed to the conversion of prices into Euros before making comparisons.

31867 ■ *"A Survival Guide for Crazy Times" in Canadian Business (Vol. 81, March 3, 2008, No. 3, pp. 61)*
Pub: Rogers Media
Ed: David Wolf. **Description:** Investors should ensure that their portfolios are positioned defensively more than the average as the U.S. and Canadian markets face turbulent times. They should not assume that U.S. residential property is a good place to invest only because prices have dropped and the Canadian dollar is showing strength. Other tips that investors can use during unstable periods are supplied.

31868 ■ *"Surviving the Storm" in Canadian Business (Vol. 81, July 22, 2008, No. 12-13, pp. 50)*
Pub: Rogers Media Ltd.
Ed: Jeff Sanford. **Description:** Investment adviser Harry Dent and finance professor Paul Marsh discuss their views and forecasts on the United States' economic condition. Dent believes advisors should concentrate on wealth preservation rather than on returns. Other views regarding U.S. economic conditions are also presented.

31869 ■ *"A Swifter, Better Marketplace" in Barron's (Vol. 89, July 13, 2009, No. 28, pp. M13)*
Pub: Dow Jones & Co., Inc.
Ed: Eric W. Noll. **Description:** Listed-derivatives market is moving towards greater trading through computerized systems with an emphasis on speed

and innovation. The market for listed options is also being changed by new techniques from other markets such as algorithmic trading, dark pools, and new-order priority systems.

31870 ■ *"Sykes Group Targets GunnAllen" in The Business Journal-Serving Greater Tampa Bay (Vol. 28, September 5, 2008, No. 37, pp. 1)*
Pub: American City Business Journals, Inc.
Ed: Margie Manning. **Description:** GAH Holdings LLC. a newly formed investment company by John H. Sykes of Sykes Enterprises Inc., will add capital to Tampa Bay Area investment banking firm GunnAllen Holdings Inc. The capital infusion is to aid GunnAllen Holdings in expanding and diversifying as GAH becomes its largest shareholder.

31871 ■ *"Take Control of Your Company's Finances" in Green Industry Pro (Vol. 23, March 2011, No. 3, pp. 24)*
Pub: Cygnus Business Media
Ed: Gregg Wartgow. **Description:** Understanding that when certain leading indicators that affect the outcome of certain lagging indicators are aligned, companies will be able to take control of their firm's finances. Ways to improve the processes that drive financial performance for landscape firms are outlined.

31872 ■ *"Take It to the Bank" in Barron's (Vol. 89, July 13, 2009, No. 28, pp. 20)*
Pub: Dow Jones & Co., Inc.
Ed: Jim McTague. **Description:** Banks are one of the safest place to put one's principal due to the temporary increase in the Federal Deposit Insurance Corp.'s insurance of bank accounts up to $250,000 and also because of the Cdars (Certificates of Deposit Registry Service) program which spreads the deposit to several banks thereby making the account covered as if it the money was deposited at multiple banks.

31873 ■ *"Take the Wheel: the Pension Protection Act Doesn't Mean You Can Sit Back and Relax" in Black Enterprise (October 2007)*
Pub: Earl G. Graves Publishing Co. Inc.
Ed: Mellody Hobson. **Description:** Pension Protection Act provides multiple benefits and tax advantages for retirement, however the investment options and contribution rates are very conservative.

31874 ■ *"Taking the Over-the-Counter Route to US" in Barron's (Vol. 88, July 7, 2008, No. 27, pp. 24)*
Pub: Dow Jones & Co., Inc.
Ed: Eric Uhlfelder. **Description:** Many multinational companies have left the New York Stock Exchange and allowed their shares to trade over-the-counter. The companies have taken advantage of a 2007 SEC rule allowing publicly listed foreign companies to change trading venues if less than 5 percent of global trading volume in the past 12 months occurred in the US.

31875 ■ *"Tanganyika Announces First Quarter 2007 Results" in Canadian Corporate News (May 14, 2007)*
Pub: Comtex News Network Inc.
Description: Tanganyika Oil Company Ltd., announced the interim operating and financial results for the first quarter ending March 31, 2007. Statistical data included.

31876 ■ *"Tao of Downfall" in International Journal of Entrepreneurship and Small Business (Vol. 11, August 31, 2010, No. 2, pp. 121)*
Pub: Publishers Communication Group
Ed: Wenxian Zhang, Ilan Alon. **Description:** Through historical reviews and case studies, this research seeks to understand why some initially successful entrepreneurs failed in the economic boom of past decades. Among various factors contributing to their downfall are a unique political and business environment, fragile financial systems, traditional cultural influences and personal characteristics.

31877 ■ *"Tax Reform Analysis: Reforms Equal Smaller 401(k)s" in Employee Benefit News (Vol. 25, December 1, 2011, No. 15, pp. 19)*
Pub: SourceMedia Inc.
Ed: Lisa V. Gillespie. **Description:** According to a new analysis by the Employee Benefit Research Institute, two recent proposals to change existing tax treatment of 401(k) retirement plans could cost workers because they would lower their account balances towards retirement.

31878 ■ *"TD Pares in U.S., Still Aims for Growth" in Globe & Mail (March 24, 2007, pp. B6)*
Pub: CTVglobemedia Publishing Inc.
Ed: Tara Perkins. **Description:** The decision of TD Banknorth Inc. to close some of its branches and remove 400 jobs, with a view to cutting down operational expenses, is discussed.

31879 ■ *"TerraVest Income Fund Releases 2007 First Quarter Financial Results" in Canadian Corporate News (May 14, 2007)*
Pub: Comtex News Network Inc.
Description: Overview of TerraVest Income Fund's financial results for the quarter ended March 31, 2007 in which the net earnings increased 36.7 percent to $3.7 million from the 2006 first quarter. Statistical data included.

31880 ■ *"That's About It for Quantitative Easing" in Barron's (Vol. 89, July 20, 2009, No. 29, pp. M11)*
Pub: Dow Jones & Co., Inc.
Ed: Brian Blackstone. **Description:** US Federal Reserve appears to have decided to halt quantitative easing, causing bond prices to drop and yields to rise. The yield for the 1-year Treasury bond rose more than 0.3 percentage point to about 3.65 percent.

31881 ■ *"TheStree.com: Study Abroad" in Entrepreneur (Vol. 35, October 2007, No. 10, pp. 44)*
Pub: Entrepreneur Media Inc.
Ed: Farnoosh Torabi. **Description:** Businessmen who wish to pursue foreign investments should study the country in which they will operate. Some investors do their research by completely exposing themselves to their prospective country, while others prefer studying the market home-based. Details of how investors pick their country and the different ways of investing in foreign land are presented.

31882 ■ *"They've Fallen, But They Can Get Up" in Barron's (Vol. 88, March 10, 2008, No. 10, pp. 43)*
Pub: Dow Jones & Company, Inc.
Ed: Kopin Tan. **Description:** Shares of senior housing companies present buying opportunities to investors because of their low prices. Companies such as Brookdale Senior Living are not as dependent on housing prices but have suffered declines in share prices.

31883 ■ *"THL Credit Is Hunting In Middle Market" in Boston Business Journal (Vol. 30, October 22, 2010, No. 39, pp. 1)*
Pub: Boston Business Journal
Ed: Tim McLaughlin. **Description:** THL Credit has been supplying capital to middle market companies in Massachusetts. The company has reported investment income of $2.44 million at the end of June 2010.

31884 ■ *The Three Secrets of Green Business: Unlocking Competitive Advantage in a Low Carbon Economy*
Pub: Earthscan
Ed: Gareth Kane. **Released:** February 10, 2010. **Price:** $96.00. **Description:** Small business is coming under increasing pressure from government, customers and campaigning groups to improve environmental performance. Soaring utility and compliance costs are critical financial burdens on small companies.

31885 ■ *"Time to Leave the Party?" in Barron's (Vol. 88, March 24, 2008, No. 12, pp. M16)*
Pub: Dow Jones & Company, Inc.
Ed: Andrea Hotter. **Description:** Prices of commodities such as gold, copper, crude oil, sugar, cocoa, and wheat have fallen from their all-time highs set in the middle of March 2008. Analysts, however, caution that this decline in prices may be temporary, and that a banking crisis may trigger new price rises in commodities.

31886 ■ *"Time for a Little Pruning" in Barron's (Vol. 89, July 6, 2009, No. 27, pp. 13)*
Pub: Dow Jones & Co., Inc.
Ed: Dimitra DeFotis. **Description:** Investors are advised to avoid the shares of Whole Foods, American Tower, T. Rowe Price, Iron Mountain, Intuitive Surgical, Salesforce.com, and Juniper Networks due to their high price to earnings ratios. The shares of Amazon.com, Broadcom, and Expeditors International of Washington remain attractive to investors despite their high price to earnings ratios due to their strong growth.

31887 ■ *"Time Value of Money Rate of Return" in Business Owner (Vol. 35, September-October 2011, No. 5, pp. 8)*
Pub: DL Perkins Company
Description: Estimating value of an income-generating asset or group of assets requires the small business owner to consider concepts such as the time value of money, risk and required rate of return. A brief summary explaining this theory is presented.

31888 ■ *"A Timely Boon for Small Investors" in Barron's (Vol. 88, March 24, 2008, No. 12, pp. 48)*
Pub: Dow Jones & Company, Inc.
Ed: Theresa W. Carey. **Description:** Nasdaq Data Store's new program called Market Replay allows investors to accurately track stock price movements. The replay can be as long as a day of market time and allows investors to determine whether they executed stock trades at the best possible price.

31889 ■ *"Tiptoeing Beyond Treasuries" in Barron's (Vol. 88, March 31, 2008, No. 13, pp. M6)*
Pub: Dow Jones & Company, Inc.
Ed: Michael S. Derby. **Description:** Risk-free assets like treasuries are still a good place for cash even if market conditions have calmed down and Treasury yields are low. Investors looking for yield and safety might want to consider Treasury inflation-indexed securities that are attractive given new inflation pressures.

31890 ■ *"To Give and Receive: How to Pass On 401k Assets and Manage an Inheritance" in Black Enterprise (Vol. 38, October 2007, No. 3)*
Pub: Earl G. Graves Publishing Co. Inc.
Ed: Steven Garmhausen. **Description:** Without proper planning, heirs could pay large tax bills to the government unless assets are managed properly. A common error is to avoid updating account records to reflect the names of designated beneficiaries.

31891 ■ *"To Thine Own Self" in Entrepreneur (Vol. 35, November 2007, No. 11, pp. 50)*
Pub: Entrepreneur Media Inc.
Ed: Torabi Farnoosh. **Description:** Self-directed individual retirement account (IRA) provides more investment options as payoff from this can be higher than an average mutual fund. Details on how to manage self-directed IRAs are discussed.

31892 ■ *"A Tonic for Irrationality" in Barron's (Vol. 89, July 13, 2009, No. 28, pp. 12)*
Pub: Dow Jones & Co., Inc.
Description: Financial-personality assessment being introduced by Barclays Wealth, measures six personality aspects related to financial behavior through a profile that measures such traits including risk tolerance, composure and perceived financial expertise. The profile helps the company create a portfolio that are structured to meet their client's personality needs.

31893 ■ *"Too Much Information?" in Black Enterprise (Vol. 37, December 2006, No. 5, pp. 59)*
Pub: Earl G. Graves Publishing Co. Inc.
Ed: James C. Johnson. **Description:** African American business owners often face the dilemma of whether or not to divulge their minority status when soliciting new customers and financial institutions. The quality of the products or services is always the key factor and race should never define one's business; however, it is appropriate to market oneself as a minority or women-owned business, especially if the company is in an industry where those clients are offered top-tier contracts.

31894 ■ *"Too Much Precaution About Biotech Corn" in Barron's (Vol. 88, March 17, 2008, No. 11, pp. 54)*
Pub: Dow Jones & Company, Inc.
Ed: Mark I. Schwartz. **Description:** In the U.S., 90 percent of cultivated soybeans are biotech varietals as well as 60 percent of the corn. Farmers have significantly reduced their reliance on pesticides in the growing of biotech corn. Biotech cotton cultivation has brought hundreds of millions of dollars in net financial gains to farmers. The European Union has precluded the cultivation or sale of biotech crops within its border.

31895 ■ *"Too Much too Soon" in Barron's (Vol. 89, July 27, 2009, No. 30, pp. 33)*
Pub: Dow Jones & Co., Inc.
Ed: Leslie P. Norton. **Description:** Shares of hhgregg have risen 85 percent in the year leading up to July 2009 and analysts believe the stock could hit 25. However, their 113 outlets are concentrated in states where unemployment is above 10 percent and expanding into areas already overstored. Competition is also rife and credit availability is still tight.

31896 ■ *"Top 10 Retirement Mistakes and How to Avoid Them" in Canadian Business (Vol. 83, July 20, 2010, No. 11-12, pp. 39)*
Pub: Rogers Media Ltd.
Ed: Jacqueline Nelson, Angelina Chapin. **Description:** Some of the top retirement mistakes is relying on selling one's house to find a retirement. Other mistakes are paying too much for investments and planning to work in retirement since no one can be sure that they will be healthy enough to accomplish this. Suggestions to avoid these pitfalls are discussed.

31897 ■ *"Top 50 By 1-Year Return" in Canadian Business (Vol. 81, Summer 2008, No. 9, pp. 121)*
Pub: Rogers Media Ltd.
Description: Table showing the top 50 Canadian companies ranked in terms of one-year return is presented. Toronto, Canada-based Timminco Ltd. topped the roster with a 1,294.2 percent in one-year return. However, the share prices of the company were affected by the recent controversy in its silicon purification process.

31898 ■ *"Top 50 By 5-Year Return" in Canadian Business (Vol. 81, Summer 2008, No. 9, pp. 123)*
Pub: Rogers Media Ltd.
Description: Table showing the rankings of the top 50 Canadian companies in terms of five-year return is presented. Silver Wheaton Corp. topped the roster with a 178.5 percent in five-year return. The company's share prices have skyrocketed despite increasing silver prices.

31899 ■ *"Top 50 in the Capital Market" in Canadian Business (Vol. 81, Summer 2008, No. 9, pp. 117)*
Pub: Rogers Media Ltd.
Description: Research in Motion Ltd. topped the list of companies in Canada in terms of market capitalization. The company's share prices surge to 119.8 percent in the year ended April 4. A table showing the top 50 Canadian companies in terms of market capitalization is presented.

31900 ■ *"Top 50 In Profits" in Canadian Business (Vol. 81, Summer 2008, No. 9, pp. 116)*
Pub: Rogers Media Ltd.
Description: Royal Bank of Canada topped the Investor 500 by profits list despite the slower economic growth in Canada and the U.S. The bank was in the runner-up position in the 2007. RBC's growth strategy is through hefty acquisitions in the U.S. A table ranking the top 50 companies in Canada in terms of profits is presented.

31901 ■ *"Top 50 In Total Revenue" in Canadian Business (Vol. 81, Summer 2008, No. 9, pp. 119)*
Pub: Rogers Media Ltd.
Description: Table showing the top 50 Canadian companies in terms of total revenue is presented. Manulife Financial Corp. topped the list with revenue of 34.5 billion. The financial services firm is the 6th largest provider of life insurance in the world and the second largest in North America.

31902 ■ *"Top Law Firms Join Forces" in Business Journal Portland (Vol. 27, December 3, 2010, No. 40, pp. 1)*
Pub: Portland Business Journal
Ed: Andy Giegerich. **Description:** Law Firms Powell PC and Roberts Kaplan LLP will forge a collaboration, whereby 17 Roberts Kaplan attorneys will join the Portland, Oregon-based office of Lane Powell. The partnership is expected to strengthen the law firms' grip on Portland's banking clients.

31903 ■ *The Total Money Makeover*
Pub: Nelson Thomson Learning
Ed: Dave Ramsey. **Released:** February 6, 2007. **Price:** $24.99. **Description:** How to get rid of debt and build up your rainy-day reserves.

31904 ■ *"The Trader's Edge" in Barron's (Vol. 88, March 31, 2008, No. 13, pp. 56)*
Pub: Dow Jones & Company, Inc.
Ed: Dan McGuire. **Description:** There is a $3,000 a year annual limit to deducting investor's losses and normal investment expenses are purportedly deductible as miscellaneous expenses on Schedule A only to the extent that they exceed two percent of adjusted gross income. Professional gamblers who can use Schedule C are unable deduct a net gaming loss against income from any other sources.

31905 ■ *"Traditional VS. Roth IRA" in Black Enterprise (Vol. 37, October 2006, No. 3, pp. 58)*
Pub: Earl G. Graves Publishing Co. Inc.
Ed: K. Parker; Carolyn M. Brown. **Description:** Government taxes the traditional IRAs different than it taxes Roth IRAs.

31906 ■ *"Treasuries Buffeted by Stocks" in Barron's (Vol. 89, July 27, 2009, No. 30, pp. M9)*
Pub: Dow Jones & Co., Inc.
Ed: Randall W. Forsyth. **Description:** Warren Buffett favors equities over long-term government bonds or stocks even with the Dow index at an eight-month high. The 10-year Treasury was up two basis points to 3.67 percent as of July 24, 2009. Corporate bond issuance hit a record $1.79 trillion for the first half of 2009.

31907 ■ *"Treasuries Rally Despite Huge Supply" in Barron's (Vol. 89, July 13, 2009, No. 28, pp. M10)*
Pub: Dow Jones & Co., Inc.
Ed: Randall W. Forsyth. **Description:** Prices of U.S. Treasuries were sent higher and their yields lower despite four auctions of coupon securities because of the strong appetite for government securities around the world. The reopening of the 10-year note in the week ending July 10, 2009 drew the strongest bidding since 1995.

31908 ■ *"A Trend Is His Friend" in Barron's (Vol. 89, July 27, 2009, No. 30, pp. 28)*
Pub: Dow Jones & Co., Inc.
Ed: Eric Uhlfelder. **Description:** Global Diversified Program fund under Quality Capital Management is managed through a trading system called the Advanced Resource Allocator which rebalances short-term tactical moves to gather quick profits. CEO Aref Karim's allocations are based on risk and he says their sentiments toward the market conditions are agnostic.

31909 ■ *"The Trials of Brian Hunter" in Canadian Business (Vol. 81, March 3, 2008, No. 3, pp. 64)*
Pub: Rogers Media
Ed: Thomas Watson. **Description:** Brian Hunter was a considered a brilliant trader in Wall Street before he was blamed for the fall of the Amaranth hedge fund. Some people blame Hunter for placing bets based on unpredictable weather when he was a trader for Amaranth Advisors LLC. The accusation against Hunter that he conspired to manipulate natural gas prices is also discussed.

31910 ■ *"Trilogy Metals Inc.: Private Placement" in Canadian Corporate News (May 16, 2007)*
Pub: Comtex News Network Inc.
Description: Trilogy Metals Inc. announces a private placement of 10,000,000 units at $0.08 per unit in an effort to raise total gross proceeds of $800,000 which will be allocated to working capital, new acquisitions, and to service existing debt.

31911 ■ *"Try, Try Again" in Baltimore Business Journal (Vol. 28, August 20, 2010, No. 15, pp. 1)*
Pub: Baltimore Business Journal
Ed: Gary Haber. **Description:** Customers' refinancing of mortgages has boosted Baltimore, Maryland mortgage banking business. The housing decline has resulted in a decrease in the number of people looking for new mortgages.

31912 ■ *"TUSK Announces 2007 First Quarter Results" in Canadian Corporate News (May 14, 2007)*
Pub: Comtex News Network Inc.
Description: TUSK Energy Corp. announced its financial and operating results for the first quarter ending March 31, 2007.

31913 ■ *"Uncashed Checks: Retirement Plans in a Quandry" in Employee Benefit News (Vol. 25, December 1, 2011, No. 15, pp. 18)*
Pub: SourceMedia Inc.
Ed: Terry Dunne. **Description:** Complex issues arise when employees don't cash their 401(k) balance checks. The US Department of Labor permits plans to cash out accounts of former employees with less than $1,000 to reduce the cost and time required to manage them.

31914 ■ *"Understanding the Fed" in Black Enterprise (Vol. 38, December 2007, No. 5, pp. 66)*
Pub: Earl G. Graves Publishing Co. Inc.
Ed: Steve Garmhausen. **Description:** The Federal Reserve System along with twelve regional banks regulates the value of money through the law of supply and demand. The Feds increase or decrease the supply of dollars in circulation which makes them cheap or expensive.

31915 ■ *"Unemployment Tax Surge Could Hit Businesses Hard" in Orlando Business Journal (Vol. 26, January 1, 2010, No. 31, pp. 1)*
Pub: American City Business Journals
Ed: Christopher Boyd. **Description:** Consequences of the almost 1,100 percent increase in Florida's minimum unemployment compensation insurance tax to businesses in the state are discussed. Employers pay for the said tax, which is used to fund the state's unemployment claims.

31916 ■ *"An Unfair Knock on Nokia" in Barron's (Vol. 88, March 10, 2008, No. 10, pp. 36)*
Pub: Dow Jones & Company, Inc.
Ed: Mark Veverka. **Description:** Discusses the decision by the brokerage house Exane to recommend a Sell on Nokia shares, presumably due to higher inventories, which is unfounded. The news that the company's inventories are rising is not an indicator of falling demand for its products. The company is also benefiting from solid management and rising market share.

31917 ■ *"Unify Corp. Back in the Black, Poised to Grow" in Sacramento Business Journal (Vol. 25, August 29, 2008, No. 26, pp. 1)*
Pub: American City Business Journals, Inc.
Ed: Melanie Turner. **Description:** It was reported that Unify Corp. returned to profitability in the fiscal year ended April 30, 2008 with a net income of $1.6 million, under the guidance of Todd Wille. Wille, who took over as the company's chief executive officer in October 2000, was named as Turnaround CEO of the Year in June 2008 for his efforts.

31918 ■ *"Universal Energy Group Releases March 31, 2007 Financial Statements" in Canadian Corporate News (May 14, 2007)*
Pub: Comtex News Network Inc.
Description: Universal Energy Group Ltd., a company that sells electricity and natural gas to small to mid-size commercial and small industrial customers as well as residential customers, announced the release of its March 31, 2007 financial statements. Management's analysis and discussion of the company's financial condition and results of operations are listed. Statistical data included.

31919 ■ *"Univest Charter Switch Signals Banking Trend" in Philadelphia Business Journal (Vol. 30, September 2, 2011, No. 29, pp. 1)*
Pub: American City Business Journals Inc.
Ed: Jeff Blumenthal. **Description:** Univest Corporation of Pennsylvania changed from a federal to state charter because of cost savings and state agency has greater understanding of the intricacies of the local economy. The Pennsylvania Department of Banking has also received inquiries from seven other banks about doing the same this year.

31920 ■ *"Unpleasant Surprise" in Barron's (Vol. 88, March 24, 2008, No. 12, pp. 60)*
Pub: Dow Jones & Company, Inc.
Ed: Shirley A. Lazo. **Description:** Discusses the $175 million that footwear company Genesco received in a settlement with Finish Line and UBS is considered as a stock distribution and is taxable as dividend income. Railroad company CSX raised its quarterly common payout from 15 cents to 18 cents.

31921 ■ *"The Upside of Fear and Loathing" in Barron's (Vol. 88, March 24, 2008, No. 12, pp. 11)*
Pub: Dow Jones & Company, Inc.
Ed: Michael Santoli. **Description:** Fear and risk aversion prevalent among investors may actually serve to cushion the decline and spark a rally in US stock prices. Surveys of investors indicate rising levels of anxiety and bearishness, indicating a possible positive turnaround.

31922 ■ *"USAmeriBank Deals for Growth" in The Business Journal-Serving Greater Tampa Bay (Vol. 28, September 26, 2008, No. 40, pp. 1)*
Pub: American City Business Journals, Inc.
Ed: Margie Manning. **Description:** It is believed that the pending $14.9 million purchase of Liberty Bank by USAmeriBank could be at the forefront of a trend. Executives of both companies expect the deal to close by the end of 2008. USAmeriBank will have $430 million in assets and five offices in Pinellas, Florida once the deal is completed.

31923 ■ *Using Other People's Money To Get Rich: Secrets, Techniques, and Strategies Investors Use Every Day Using OPM*
Pub: Atlantic Publishing Company
Ed: Eric J. Leech. **Released:** December 2009. **Price:** $24.95 paperback. **Description:** Discussion showing individuals how to invest using other people's money.

31924 ■ *"Valenti: Roots of Financial Crisis Go Back to 1998" in Crain's Detroit Business (Vol. 24, October 6, 2008, No. 40, pp. 25)*
Pub: Crain Communications, Inc.
Ed: Tom Henderson; Nathan Skid. **Description:** Interview with Sam Valenti III who is the chairman and CEO of Valenti Capital L.L.C., a wealth-management firm; Valenti discusses in detail the history that led up to the current economic crisis as well as his prediction for the future of the country.

31925 ■ *Valuing the Closely Held Firm*
Pub: Oxford University Press
Ed: Michael S. Long; Thomas A. Bryant. **Released:** March 2007. **Price:** $65.00. **Description:** The differences between a large and small firm and their ability to generate future cash flow are discussed.

31926 ■ *"Virtus.com Wins 'Best of Industry' WebAward for Excellence in Financial Services" in Investment Weekly News (October 24, 2009)*
Pub: Investment Weekly News
Description: Web Marketing Association honored Virtus.com, the Website of Virtus Investment Partners, Inc., for Outstanding Achievement in Web Development and Acsys Interactive was awarded the Financial Services Standard of Excellence Award for developing the site. The site was part of a rebranding effort and is a one-stop portal for both financial advisors and their investors.

31927 ■ *"Virtus.com Wins 'Best of Industry' WebAward for Excellence in Financial Services" in Investment Weekly News (Oct. 24, 2009, pp. 227)*
Pub: Investment Weekly News
Description: Web Marketing Association honored Virtus.com, the Website of Virtus Investment Partners, Inc., for Outstanding Achievement in Web Development and Acsys Interactive was awarded the Financial Services Standard of Excellence Award for developing the site. The site was part of a rebranding effort and is a one-stop portal for both financial advisors and their investors.

31928 ■ *"Vital Signs: The Big Picture" in Canadian Business (Vol. 81, Summer 2008, No. 9, pp. 153)*
Pub: Rogers Media Ltd.
Description: Results of the Investor 500 showing percentage of companies with positive returns, most actively traded companies over the past six months and market capitalization by industry are presented. Stock performance and revenues of publicly held corporations in Canada are also provided.

31929 ■ *"W&S to Trim Rich Retirement Plan" in Business Courier (Vol. 27, October 15, 2010, No. 24, pp. 1)*
Pub: Business Courier
Ed: Dan Monk. **Description:** Insurance firm Western & Southern Financial Group announced that it will reduce the pension benefits of its 4,000 associates by more than 30 percent starting January 1, 2011. The move is expected to reduce annual retirement payments by several thousand dollars per associate. Western is a Fortune 500 company and has $34 billion in total assets.

31930 ■ *"Want People to Save? Force Them" in Harvard Business Review (Vol. 88, September 2010, No. 9, pp. 36)*
Pub: Harvard Business School Publishing
Ed: Dan Ariely. **Description:** Contrasts in U.S. attitudes towards savings and government regulation with those of Chile, where all employees are required to save 11 percent of their salary in a retirement account, are highlighted.

31931 ■ *"Watchful Eye: Entrepreneur Protects Clients and His Bottom Line" in Black Enterprise (Vol. 38, March 2008, No. 8, pp. 46)*
Pub: Earl G. Graves Publishing Co. Inc.
Ed: Tennille M. Robinson. **Description:** Profile of Elijah Shaw, founder of Icon Services Corporation, a full service security and investigative service; Shaw shares his plans to protect clients while growing his business.

31932 ■ *The Way We'll Be: The Zogby Report on the Transformation of the American Dream*
Pub: Crown Business
Ed: John Zogby. **Released:** 2009. **Price:** $26.00. **Description:** According to a recent poll, the next generation of Americans are not as concerned about making money as they are about making a difference in the world.

31933 ■ *We Are Smarter Than Me: How to Unleash the Power of Crowds in Your Business*
Pub: Wharton School Publishing
Ed: Barry Libert; Jon Spector; Don Tapscott. **Released:** October 5, 2007. **Price:** $21.99. **Description:** Ways to use social networking and community in order to make decisions and plan your business, with a focus on product development, manufacturing, marketing, customer service, finance, management, and more.

31934 ■ *"Website for Women 50 Launches" in Marketing to Women (Vol. 21, April 2008, No. 4, pp. 5)*
Pub: EPM Communications Inc.
Contact: Ira Mayer, President
E-mail: imayer@epmcom.com
Description: Vibrantnation.com is an online community targeting women over age 50; members can share recommendations on a variety of topics such as vacation spots, retailers and financial issues.

31935 ■ *"A Week of the Worst Kind of Selling" in Barron's (Vol. 88, June 30, 2008, No. 26, pp. M3)*
Pub: Dow Jones & Co., Inc.
Ed: Kopin Tan. **Description:** In the week that ended in June 27, 2008 the selloff in the U.S. stock market was brought on by mounting bank losses and the spread of economic slowdown on top of high oil prices. The 31 percent decrease in the share price of Ingersoll-Rand since October 2007 may have factored in most of its risks. The company has completed its acquisition of Trane to morph into a refrigeration-equipment company.

31936 ■ *A Weekend with Warren Buffett: And Other Shareholder Meeting Adventures*
Pub: Basic Books/Perseus Books Group
Ed: Randy Cepuch. **Released:** February 23, 2007. **Price:** $23.95. **Description:** Financial writer and personal investor relates his experiences attending various shareholder meetings, reviewing each meeting and grading its educational value. The book is essential for those hoping to learn more about the way companies invest and do business.

31937 ■ *"Welcome Back" in Canadian Business (Vol. 82, April 27, 2009, No. 7, pp. 25)*
Pub: Rogers Media
Ed: Sarka Halas. **Description:** Some Canadian companies such as Gennum Corporation have taken advantage of corporate sale-leasebacks to raise money at a time when credit is hard to acquire. Corporate sale-leasebacks allow companies to sell their property assets while remaining as tenants of the building. Sale-leasebacks allow firms to increase capital while avoiding the disruptions that may result with moving.

31938 ■ *"Welcome to the Neighborhood" in Hawaii Business (Vol. 53, October 2007, No. 4, pp. 48)*
Pub: Hawaii Business Publishing
Ed: Jolyn Okimoto Rosa. **Description:** Finance Factors is planning to build branches in Manoa, and Liliha, as part of its strategy to position itself in high-yield areas. The company chose Manoa and Liliha due to thee sites' rich deposits. Its strategy with regards to the branches' location and to the building design is discussed.

31939 ■ *"Wenzel Downhole Tools Ltd. Announces First Quarter Results for 2007" in Canadian Corporate News (May 14, 2007)*
Pub: Comtex News Network Inc.
Description: Wenzel Downhole Tools Ltd., a manufacturer, renter, and seller of drilling tools used in gas and oil exploration, announced its financial results for the first quarter ended March 31, 2007 which includes achieved revenues of $14.5 million. Statistical data included.

31940 ■ *"Weyerhaeuser's REIT Decision Shouldn't Scare Investors Away" in Barron's (Vol. 88, June 30, 2008, No. 26, pp. 18)*
Pub: Dow Jones & Co., Inc.
Ed: Christopher Williams. **Description:** Weyerhaeuser Co.'s management said that a conversion to a real estate investment trust was not likely in 2009 since the move is not tax-efficient as of the moment and would overload its non-timber assets with debt. The company's shares have fallen by 19.5 percent. However, the company remains an asset-rich outfit and its activist shareholder is pushing for change.

31941 ■ *"What Ever Happened to TGIF?" in Barron's (Vol. 88, March 10, 2008, No. 10, pp. M3)*
Pub: Dow Jones & Company, Inc.
Ed: Kopin Tan. **Description:** US stock markets fell in early March 2008 to their lowest level in 18 months, venturing close to entering a bear market phase. The S&P 500 has dropped an average of 0.78 percent on Fridays for 2008.

31942 ■ *"What Has Sergey Wrought?" in Barron's (Vol. 89, July 13, 2009, No. 28, pp. 8)*
Pub: Dow Jones & Co., Inc.
Ed: Alan Abelson. **Description:** Sergey Aleynikov is a computer expert that once worked for Goldman Sachs but he was arrested after he left the company and charged with theft for bringing with him the code for the company's proprietary software for high-frequency trading. The stock market has been down for four straight weeks as of July 13, 2009 which reflects the reality of how the economy is still struggling.

31943 ■ *"What Most Banks Fail to See; New and Complex Financial Regulations Can be Daunting" in Gallup Management Journal (March 10, 2011)*
Pub: Gallup
Ed: Sean Williams, Daniel Porcelli. **Description:** New financial regulations are complicated and politically charged. But banks that move beyond the fear of those regulations will find a new opportunity to engage customers.

31944 ■ *"What You Should Know If Your Bank Fails" in Black Enterprise (Vol. 41, December 2010, No. 5, pp. 29)*
Pub: Earl G. Graves Publishing Co. Inc.
Ed: John Simons. **Description:** The Federal Deposit Insurance Corporation announced that the number of banks in trouble has reached the highest level since March 1993. Advice from the FDIC is cited. Statistical data included.

31945 ■ *"What'll You Have Tonight?" in Barron's (Vol. 88, July 4, 2008, No. 28, pp. 22)*
Pub: Dow Jones & Co., Inc.
Ed: Neil A. Martin. **Description:** Shares of Diageo could rise by 30 percent a year from June 2008 after it slipped due to U.S. sales worries. The company also benefits from the trend toward more premium alcoholic beverage brands worldwide especially in emerging markets.

31946 ■ *"What's In a Name?" in Barron's (Vol. 88, March 17, 2008, No. 11, pp. 7)*
Pub: Dow Jones & Company, Inc.
Ed: Alan Abelson. **Description:** Eliot Spitzer's resignation incidentally caused the stock market to go up by 400 points. The Federal Reserve Board's new Term Securities Lending Facility provides liquidity to the big lenders by funneling $200 billion in the form of 28-day loans of Treasuries. The analysis of Paul Brodsky and Lee Quaintance of QB Partners on the demand for commodities is also discussed.

31947 ■ *"What's More Important: Stag or Inflation?" in Barron's (Vol. 88, July 14, 2008, No. 28, pp. M8)*
Pub: Dow Jones & Co., Inc.
Ed: Randall W. Forsyth. **Description:** Economists are divided on which part of stagflation, an economic situation in which inflation and economic stagnation occur simultaneously and remain unchecked for a period of time, is more important. Some economists say that the Federal government is focusing on controlling inflation while others see the central bank as extending its liquidity facilities to the financial sector.

31948 ■ *"When Dov Cries" in Canadian Business (Vol. 83, June 15, 2010, No. 10, pp. 71)*
Pub: Rogers Media Ltd.
Ed: Joe Castaldo. **Description:** American Apparel disclosed that they will have problems meeting one of its debt covenants which could trigger a chain reaction that could lead to bankruptcy. The prospects look bleak, but eccentric company founder Dov Charney, has always defied expectations.

31949 ■ *"When R&D Spending Is Not Enough" in Human Resource Management (Vol. 49, July-August 2010, No. 4, pp. 767-792)*
Pub: John Wiley
Ed: Sheng Wang, Rebecca M. Guidice, Judith W. Tansky, Zhong-Ming Wang. **Description:** A study was conducted to examine the effect of contextual contingencies on innovation. Findings indicate that Chinese manufacturers with cultures emphasizing innovation and teamwork more effectively utilize financial resources in the innovation process. Results also show that a culture emphasizing outcomes and stability leads to lower levels innovation irrespective of investments.

31950 ■ *"When to Roll Over" in Black Enterprise (Vol. 37, November 2006, No. 4, pp. 50)*
Pub: Earl G. Graves Publishing Co. Inc.
Ed: Carolyn M. Brown. **Description:** Being proactive and rolling over your funds if you own stock of your former employee will give you more control over your money, especially if the company merges or is sold.

31951 ■ *"Where the Money Is" in Conde Nast Portfolio (Vol. 2, June 2008, No. 6, pp. 113)*
Pub: Conde Nast Publications
Contact: David Carey, President
Description: Revenue generated from treatments for common brain disorders that are currently on the market are listed.

31952 ■ *"Where Oil-Rich Nations Are Placing Their Bets" in Harvard Business Review (Vol. 86, September 2008, No. 9, pp. 119)*
Pub: Harvard Business School Press
Ed: Rawi Abdelal; Ayesha Khan; Tarun Khanna. **Description:** Investment strategies of the Gulf Cooperation Council nations are examined in addition to how these have impacted the global economy and capitalism.

31953 ■ *"Where to Stash Your Cash" in Barron's (Vol. 88, March 17, 2008, No. 11, pp. 41)*
Pub: Dow Jones & Company, Inc.
Ed: Mike Hogan. **Description:** Investors are putting their money in money-market mutual funds seeking fractionally better yields and a safe haven from the uncertainties that was brought about by subprime lending. These funds, however, are hovering near 3.20 percent which is less than the 4 percent inflation rate.

31954 ■ *"Where To Look for Income" in Women In Business (Vol. 63, Summer 2011, No. 2, pp. 50)*
Pub: American Business Women's Association
Ed: William J. Lynott. **Description:** Advice on ways to invest in the US market are presented, with information on Certificates of Deposit and Money Markets included.

31955 ■ *"Whiplashed? That's a Bullish Sign" in Barron's (Vol. 88, March 31, 2008, No. 13, pp. 34)*
Pub: Dow Jones & Company, Inc.
Ed: Richard W. Arms. **Description:** Huge volatility often occurs just ahead of a substantial rally, according to an analysis of the volatility in the Dow Jones Index since 2000. The Average Percentage Change based on a 10-day moving average of volatility is a way to measure the level of fear in the market and reveals when buying or selling have been overdone.

31956 ■ *"Whistling Past the Graveyard?" in Barron's (Vol. 88, March 17, 2008, No. 11, pp. 15)*
Pub: Dow Jones & Company, Inc.
Ed: Michael Santoli. **Description:** Discusses the Federal Reserve's move to provide $200 billion to the system which can be seen as an effort to avoid the liquidity problems that Bear Stearns suffered. The Federal Reserve's move seems to frighten investors rather than reassure them.

31957 ■ *"Who Gets the Last Laugh?" in Barron's (Vol. 88, March 31, 2008, No. 13, pp. 17)*
Pub: Dow Jones & Company, Inc.
Ed: Leslie P. Norton. **Description:** Nord/LB will take a charge of 82.5 million euros to cover potential losses apparently related to Vatas' refusal to take the shares of Remote MDx Inc. after buying the shares. Remote MDx's main product is an ankle bracelet to monitor criminals; the firm has lost over half of its market cap due to the Nord/LB troubles and questions about its revenues.

31958 ■ *"Why Intel Should Dump Its Flash-Memory Business" in Barron's (Vol. 88, March 10, 2008, No. 10, pp. 35)*
Pub: Dow Jones & Company, Inc.
Ed: Eric J. Savitz. **Description:** Intel Corp. must sell its NAND flash-memory business as soon as it possibly can to the highest bidder to focus on its PC processor business and take advantage of other business opportunities. Apple should consider a buyback of 10 percent of the company's shares to lift its stock.

31959 ■ *"Why the Rally Should Keep Rolling..for Now" in Barron's (Vol. 89, July 27, 2009, No. 30, pp. M3)*
Pub: Dow Jones & Co., Inc.
Ed: Kopin Tan. **Description:** Stocks rallied for the second straight week as of July 24, 2009 and more companies reported better than expected earnings but the caveat is that companies are beating estimates chiefly by slashing expenses and firing workers. The regulatory risks faced by CME Group and the IntercontinentalExchange are discussed as well as the shares of KKR Private Equity Investors LP.

31960 ■ *"Why the Rout in Financials Isn't Over" in Barron's (Vol. 88, June 30, 2008, No. 26, pp. 23)*
Pub: Dow Jones & Co., Inc.
Ed: Robin Goldwyn Blumenthal. **Description:** Top market technician Louise Yamada warns that the retreat in the shares of financial services is not yet over based on her analysis of stock charts. Yamada's analysis of the charts of Citigroup, Fifth Third Bancorp and Merrill Lynch are discussed together with the graphs for these shares. Statistical data included.

31961 ■ *Why We Want You to be Rich: Two Men - One Message*
Pub: Rich Publishing LLC
Ed: Donald J. Trump; Robert T. Kiyosaki; Meredith McIver; Sharon Lechter. **Released:** October 9, 2006. **Price:** $24.95. **Description:** Authors explain why some people get rich while others don't.

31962 ■ *"Wielding a Big Ax" in Barron's (Vol. 89, July 13, 2009, No. 28, pp. 26)*
Pub: Dow Jones & Co., Inc.
Ed: Shirley A. Lazo. **Description:** Weyerhaeuser cut their quarterly common payout by 80 percent from 25 cents to a nickel a share which they say will help them preserve their long-term value and improve their performance. Paccar also cut their quarterly dividend by half to nine cents a share. Walgreen however, boosted their quarterly dividend by 22.2 percent to 13.75 cents a share.

31963 ■ *"Will the Force Be With Salesforce?" in Barron's (Vol. 88, March 24, 2008, No. 12, pp. 20)*
Pub: Dow Jones & Company, Inc.
Ed: Mark Veverka. **Description:** Shares of Salesforce.com are likely to drop from the $44.83-a-share level in the face of a deteriorating economy and financial sector and thus lower demand for business

software. The company is unlikely to deliver on its ambitious earnings forecasts for 2008 especially with strengthening competition from Oracle.

31964 ■ *"Wind Point Partners Closes Southfield HQ" in Crain's Detroit Business (Vol. 26, January 18, 2010, No. 3, pp. 18)*
Pub: Crain Communications Inc.
Ed: Tom Henderson. **Description:** Wind Point Partners, a private-equity firm that expanded its headquarters to Southfield in 1997, has closed down its Michigan operations opting to move its headquarters back to Illinois.

31965 ■ *Wine Investment for Portfolio Diversification: How Investing in Wine Can Yield Greater Returns than Stocks and Bonds*
Pub: Wine Appreciation Guild
Contact: Donna Bottrell, President
E-mail: donna@wineappreciation.com
Ed: Mahesh Kumar. **Released:** October 2005. **Price:** $45.00. **Description:** Analysis of the performance of investments in fine wines, particularly Bordeaux, is presented. History verifies that wine has traditionally been a sound investment offering a higher expected return over the market relative to its overall contribution of risk. Wine can be used as an effective means of diversifying one's portfolio.

31966 ■ *"WNY Casing In On Loonie's Climb" in Business First Buffalo (November 23, 2007, pp. 1)*
Pub: American City Business Journals, Inc.
Ed: Scott Thomas. **Description:** Economy of Western New York has rebounded since the 9/11 recession and the rise of the Canadian dollar, which has contributed to the areas economic growth. Canadian shoppers are frequenting markets in the area due to the parity of the U.S. and Canadian dollar. Details of the cross-border shopping and its impact in WNY are discussed.

31967 ■ *"Wobbling Economy" in The Business Journal-Serving Metropolitan Kansas City (Vol. 27, September 26, 2008, No. 2, pp. 1)*
Pub: American City Business Journals, Inc.
Ed: Rob Roberts. **Description:** Real estate developers in Kansas City Metropolitan Area are worried of the possible impacts of the crisis at Wall Street. They expect tightening of the credit market, which will result in difficulty of financing their projects. The potential effects of the Wall Street crisis are examined further.

31968 ■ *"Woes Portend Consumer Shift" in The Business Journal-Serving Metropolitan Kansas City (Vol. 27, September 26, 2008, No. 2, pp. 1)*
Pub: American City Business Journals, Inc.
Ed: Suzanna Stagemeyer. **Description:** Black Bamboo owner Tim Butt believes that prolonged tightening of the credit market will result in consumer spending becoming more cash-driven that credit card driven. The financial crisis has already constricted spending among consumers. Forecasts for the US economy are provided.

31969 ■ *The Working Man and Woman's Guide to Becoming a Millionaire*
Pub: Prentiss Publishing
Ed: Al Herron. **Released:** November 2006. **Description:** President and CEO of a Century 21 office in Dallas, Texas shares insight into financial security and commitment to community.

31970 ■ *Working Papers, Chapters 1-14 for Needles/Powers/Crosson's Financial and Managerial Accounting*
Pub: Cengage South-Western
Ed: Belverd E. Needles, Marian Powers, Susan V. Crosson. **Released:** May 10, 2010. **Price:** $62.95. **Description:** Appropriate accounting forms for completing all exercises, problems and cases in the text are provided for financial management of a small company.

31971 ■ *"A World of Opportunity: Foreign Markets Offer Diversity to Keen Investors" in Canadian Business (Vol. 81, Summer 2008, No. 9)*
Pub: Rogers Media Ltd.
Ed: Andrew Wahl. **Description:** International Monetary Fund projected in its 'World Economy Outlook' that there is a 25 percent chance that a global recession will occur in 2008 and 2009. Global growth rate is forecasted at 3.7 percent in 2008. Inflation in Asia emerging markets and forecasts on stock price indexes are presented.

31972 ■ *"World's Best CEOs" in Barron's (Vol. 88, March 24, 2008, No. 12, pp. 33)*
Pub: Dow Jones & Company, Inc.
Ed: Andrew Bary. **Description:** Listing of the 30 best chief executive officers worldwide which was compiled through interviews with investors and analysts, analysis of financial and stock market performance, and leadership and industry stature.

31973 ■ *The Worst-Case Scenario Business Survival Guide*
Pub: John Wiley & Sons, Inc.
Released: September 28, 2009. **Price:** $17.95. **Description:** Since 1999, the Worst-Case Scenario survival handbooks have provided readers with real answers for the most extreme situations. Now, in a time of economic crisis, the series returns with a new, real-world guide to avoiding the worst business cataclysms.

31974 ■ *"The Worst Lies Ahead for Wall Street; More Losses Certain" in Crain's New York Business (Vol. 24, January 21, 2008, No. 3, pp. 1)*
Pub: Crain Communications, Inc.
Ed: Aaron Elstein. **Description:** Due to the weakening economy, many financial institutions will face further massive losses forcing them to borrow more at higher interest rates and dragging down their earnings for years to come. The effects on commercial real estate and credit card loans are also discussed as well as the trend to investing in Asia and the Middle East.

31975 ■ *"Yahoo! - Microsoft Pact: Alive Again?" in Barron's (Vol. 89, July 27, 2009, No. 30, pp. 8)*
Pub: Dow Jones & Co., Inc.
Ed: Mark Veverka. **Description:** Yahoo! reported higher than expected earnings in the second quarter of 2009 under CEO Carol Bartz who has yet to articulate her long-term vision and strategy for turning around the company. The media reported that Yahoo! and Microsoft are discussing an advertising-search partnership which should benefit both companies.

31976 ■ *"YoCream" in Ice Cream Reporter (Vol. 23, September 20, 2010, No. 10, pp. 6)*
Pub: Ice Cream Reporter
Description: YoCream reported a sales increase for third quarter 2010 at 15.6 percent and net income increasing 25 percent to $2,141,000 for that quarter.

31977 ■ *"You Won't Go Broke Filling Up On These Stocks" in Barron's (Vol. 88, July 14, 2008, No. 28, pp. 38)*
Pub: Dow Jones & Co., Inc.
Ed: Assif Shameen. **Description:** Due to high economic growth, pro-business policies and a consumption boom, the Middle East is a good place to look for equities. The best ways in which to gain exposure to this market include investing in the real estate industry and telecommunications markets as well as large banks that serve corporations and consumers.

31978 ■ *Young Bucks: How to Raise a Future Millionaire*
Pub: Thomas Nelson Inc.
Ed: Troy Dunn. **Released:** November 2007. **Price:** $17.99. **Description:** Advice is given to parents to teach their children how to save money, invest wisely and even start their own business.

31979 ■ *"Young People Speak Out On Credit Union Board Involvement" in Credit Union Times (Vol. 21, July 14, 2010, No. 27, pp. 20)*
Pub: Summit Business Media
Ed: Myriam Di Giovanni. **Description:** Results of a Credit Union Times survey of Generation Y individuals about serving on Credit Union boards across the country are examined.

31980 ■ *"Your 2010 Windfall" in Small Business Opportunities (July 2010)*
Pub: Harris Publications Inc.
Description: Make this a year of fiscal health and wealth. A survey says most will strive to save this year.

31981 ■ *"Your Exposure to Bear Stearns" in Barron's (Vol. 88, March 17, 2008, No. 11, pp. 45)*
Pub: Dow Jones & Company, Inc.
Ed: Tom Sullivan; Jack Willoughby. **Description:** Bear Stearns makes up 5.5 percent of Pioneer Independence's portfolio, 1.4 percent of Vanguard Windsor II's portfolio, 1.2 percent of Legg Mason Value Trust, about 1 percent of Van Kampen Equity & Income, and 0.79 percent of Putnam Fund for Growth & Income. Ginnie Mae securities are now trading at 1.78 percentage points over treasuries due to the mortgage crises.

31982 ■ *Your Guide to Arranging Bank and Debt Financing for Your Own Business in Canada*
Pub: Productive Publications
Ed: Iain Williamson. **Released:** December 31, 2000. **Description:** Bank financing for small businesses in Canada is discussed.

31983 ■ *Your Guide to Canadian Export Financing: Successful Techniques for Financing Your Exports from Canada*
Pub: Productive Publications
Ed: Iain Williamson. **Released:** December 31, 2000. **Description:** Canadian export financing is covered.

31984 ■ *Your Guide to Preparing a Plan to Raise Money for Your Own Business*
Pub: Productive Publications
Ed: Iain Williamson. **Released:** June 1991. **Description:** A good business plan is essential for raising money for any small business.

TRADE PERIODICALS

31985 ■ *CFO & Controller Alert*
Pub: Progressive Business Publications
Ed: John Hiatt, Editor, hiatt@pbp.com. **Released:** Semimonthly. **Price:** $299, individuals. **Description:** Assists busy financial executives to boost cash flow, control expenses, manage resources, and comply with changing regulations. Recurring features include case studies, success stories, financial and tax developments, cost-saving ideas and columns titled Management and Sharpen Your Judgment.

31986 ■ *The COINfidential Report*
Pub: Bale Publications
Ed: Don Bale, Jr., Editor. **Released:** Bimonthly, except July and August. **Price:** $19.95, individuals; $99 lifetime subscription. **Description:** Features coin, stock and bullion market forecasts and analyses, plus inside information and best coin and stock bets. Recurring features include interviews, book reviews, and notices of publications available.

31987 ■ *Deposit Growth Strategies*
Pub: Siefer Consultants Inc.
Ed: Joe Sheller, Editor. **Released:** Monthly. **Price:** $329, U.S.; $259 charter rate. **Description:** Cover methods to increase deposits at financial institutions, as well as marketing strategies for deposit growth. Both personal accounts and commercial accounts are covered.

31988 ■ *Financial Services Review: The Journal of Individual Financial Management*
Pub: Cadmus Journal Services
URL(s): www.drsm.org/FSR_journal/Financial_Services_Review_home.htm. **Ed:** Stuart Michelson. **Released:** Quarterly

31989 ■ *Financial Studies of the Small Business*
Pub: Financial Research Association Inc.
Contact: Karen E. Klein, Manager
URL(s): aern.cba.ua.edu. **Released:** Annual

31990 ■ *NACOMEX Insider*
Pub: NACOMEX USA Inc.
Ed: Robert Zises, Editor, zises@nacomex.com. **Released:** Quarterly. **Price:** $199, U.S.. **Description:** Provides information on historical values, current tactics, and residual value forecasting for ad valorem tax, bankruptcy, loss compensation, and related purposes. Recurring features include news of research and a column titled Industry Round-up.

31991 ■ *Quarterly Journal of Finance and Accounting*
Pub: University of Nebraska
URL(s): www.qjbe.unl.edu. **Ed:** Gordon V. Karels. **Released:** Quarterly **Price:** $35, Individuals; $55, Institutions; $47, Other countries; $65, Institutions, other countries.

VIDEOCASSETTES/ AUDIOCASSETTES

31992 ■ *Accounting and Finance for Non-Financial Managers*
SmartPros Ltd.
12 Skyline Dr.
Hawthorne, NY 10532-2133
Ph: (914)345-2620
Co. E-mail: admin@smartpros.com
URL: http://www.smartpros.com
Contact: Jack Fingerhut, President
Released: 1986. **Description:** This tape shows non-financial executives how to handle and process business finances. **Availability:** VHS; 3/4 U.

31993 ■ *American Institute of Small Business: Your Personal Financial Guide to Success, Power & Security*
American Institute of Small Business
23075 Highway 7, Ste. 200
Shorewood, MN 55331
Ph: (952)545-7001
Free: 800-328-2906
Fax: (952)545-7020
Co. E-mail: judy@aisb.biz
URL: http://www.pfa.com/AISB.htm
Released: 199?. **Price:** $69.95. **Description:** Covers money management, financial planning, budgeting, record keeping, and spending and savings plans. **Availability:** VHS.

31994 ■ *Corporate Financial Management: Emerging Trends and Recent Developments*
Bisk Education
9417 Princess Palm Ave.
Tampa, FL 33619
Free: 800-874-7877
Co. E-mail: info@bisk.com
URL: http://www.bisk.com
Released: 19??. **Price:** $179.00. **Description:** Discusses financial management techniques and recent developments in corporate finance. Furnishes information on Activity-Based Cost Management (ABC), Total Quality Management (TQM), and Internal Controls and Management Accounting. Includes workbook and quizzer. **Availability:** VHS.

31995 ■ *Financial Success Strategies for the 1990s*
Cambridge Educational
c/o Films Media Group
132 West 31st Street, 17th Floor
Ste. 124
New York, NY 10001
Free: 800-257-5126
Fax: (609)671-0266
Co. E-mail: custserve@films.com
URL: http://www.cambridgeol.com
Released: 1992. **Price:** $99.00. **Description:** Best-selling financial author Charles J. Givens gives advice that could save or earn viewers thousands of dollars. **Availability:** VHS.

31996 ■ *Money in America*
Ambrose Video Publishing, Inc.
145 W. 45th St., Ste. 1115
New York, NY 10036
Ph: (212)768-7373
Free: 800-526-4663
Fax: (212)768-9282
Co. E-mail: customerservice@ambrosevideo.com
URL: http://www.ambrosevideo.com
Released: 1989. **Price:** $795.00. **Description:** A video series which explains everything about banks and banking. **Availability:** VHS.

31997 ■ *Reading Financial Reports: The Income Statement*
Phoenix Learning Group
2349 Chaffee Dr.
Saint Louis, MO 63146-3306
Ph: (314)569-0211
Free: 800-221-1274
Fax: (314)569-2834
URL: http://www.phoenixlearninggroup.com
Released: 1985. **Description:** An explanation of the income statement-how to read it and use it. **Availability:** VHS; 3/4 U; Special order formats.

31998 ■ *Return on Investment*
Video Arts, Inc.
c/o Aim Learning Group
8238-40 Lehigh
Morton Grove, IL 60053-2615
Free: 877-444-2230
Fax: (416)252-2155
Co. E-mail: service@aimlearninggroup.com
URL: http://www.aimlearninggroup.com
Released: 1986. **Price:** $790.00. **Description:** For the business owner, a look at assessing and justifying capital expenditures. **Availability:** VHS; 8 mm; 3/4 U; Special order formats.

TRADE SHOWS AND CONVENTIONS

31999 ■ ABA/BMA National Conference for Community Bankers
American Bankers Association (ABA)
1120 Connecticut Ave. NW
Washington, DC 20036
Ph: (202)663-5564
Free: 800-226-5377
Fax: (202)663-7543
Co. E-mail: custserv@aba.com
URL: http://www.aba.com
Contact: Edward L. Yingling, President
Frequency: Annual. **Audience:** Chairmen and presidents, mainly of banks with less than $500 million in assets, community bank CEOs, bank directors, and other community bank executives. **Principal Exhibits:** Products and services related to investment management, customer service improvements, advertising, asset/liability management, bank management, electronic data interchange, employee recruitment/training, insurance, strategic planning models, including preparation for the 21st century, new revenue sources, cost control techniques, mainframe computers, market research, MCIF technology, minicomputers in community banking applications, software: platform, optical disk, and loan pricing, sweep accounts, and relationship banking for community bankers.

32000 ■ BMA Annual Marketing Forum
American Bankers Association (ABA)
1120 Connecticut Ave. NW
Washington, DC 20036
Ph: (202)663-5564
Free: 800-226-5377
Fax: (202)663-7543
Co. E-mail: custserv@aba.com
URL: http://www.aba.com
Contact: Edward L. Yingling, President
Frequency: Annual. **Audience:** Bankers including community bank CEOs, marketing directors, sales managers, advertising directors, public relations managers. **Principal Exhibits:** Financial services marketing offering banking solutions in advertising services, bank equipment/systems, computer software, database marketing, direct marketing/sales, incentive/premium programs, insurance services, investment services, marketing consulting, merchandising, publishing, research, retail delivery, sales training, service quality, signage, and telemarketing.

32001 ■ BMA Private Wealth Sales Management Workshop, an ABA Program
American Bankers Association (ABA)
1120 Connecticut Ave. NW
Washington, DC 20036
Ph: (202)663-5564
Free: 800-226-5377
Fax: (202)663-7543
Co. E-mail: custserv@aba.com
URL: http://www.aba.com
Contact: Edward L. Yingling, President
Frequency: Annual. **Audience:** Trust, private banking and asset management officers, bank brokerage managers, sales managers, business development managers, and regional department managers. **Principal Exhibits:** Provides marketing education and information, professional growth and networking resources to marketing professionals in the financial services industry.

32002 ■ Financial Managers Society Annual Conference
Financial Managers Society (FMS)
100 W Monroe St., Ste. 1700
Chicago, IL 60603-1907
Ph: (312)578-1300
Free: 800-275-4367
Fax: (312)578-1308
Co. E-mail: info@fmsinc.org
URL: http://www.fmsinc.org
Contact: Dick Yingst, President
E-mail: dyingst@fmsinc.org
URL(s): www.fmsinc.org. **Price:** $849, Pre-registered, members; $1049, Pre-registered, non-members. **Frequency:** Annual. **Audience:** CEOs, CFOs, treasurers, controllers, investment officers, internal auditors of banks, thrift and credit unions. **Principal Exhibits:** Companies offering products/services to CEOs, CFOs, treasurers, controllers, investment officers, and internal auditors of banks, thrifts, and credit unions. **Telecommunication Services:** info@fmsinc.org.

32003 ■ National Agricultural Bankers Conference
American Bankers Association (ABA)
1120 Connecticut Ave. NW
Washington, DC 20036
Ph: (202)663-5564
Free: 800-226-5377
Fax: (202)663-7543
Co. E-mail: custserv@aba.com
URL: http://www.aba.com
Contact: Edward L. Yingling, President
URL(s): www.aba.com. **Price:** $830, Pre-registered, members; $900, Pre-registered, members; $830, Pre-registered, members; $900, Pre-registered, members. **Frequency:** Annual. **Audience:** Bank CEOs, mainly from community banks in rural areas, executive vice presidents, senior vice presidents, economists, analysts. **Principal Exhibits:** The latest developments in the agricultural lending business, as well as strategies for better market share, profitability and customer service. **Telecommunication Services:** jblanchf@aba.com.

CONSULTANTS

32004 ■ 2010 Fund 5
24351 Spartan St.
Mission Viejo, CA 92691-3920
Ph: (949)583-1992
Fax: (949)583-0474
Contact: Wally Eater, Principal
Scope: Funds in formation that will invest in technologies licensed from 30 universities. **Founded:** 1982.

32005 ■ ADG Group
4261 Northside Dr., Ste. 200
Atlanta, GA 30327
Ph: (404)264-9301

Fax: (404)261-3439
Contact: Cameron Adair, Chairman of the Board
E-mail: camadair@aol.com
Scope: Corporate finance advisory firm specializing in arranging venture capital financing for emerging companies. Assists with mergers, acquisitions, and divestitures. Offers balance sheet restructuring services for bankrupt and financially troubled companies. Also offers independent due diligence investigations. **Founded:** 1986.

32006 ■ Aurora Management Partners Inc.
4485 Tench Rd., Ste. 340
Suwanee, GA 30024
Ph: (770)904-5209
Fax: (770)904-5226
Co. E-mail: rturcotte@auroramp.com
URL: http://www.auroramp.com
Contact: William A. Barbee, Director
E-mail: abarbee@auroramp.com
Scope: Specializes in turnaround management and reorganization consulting. Firm develop strategic initiatives, organize and analyze solutions, deal with creditor issues, review organizational structure and develop time frames for decision making. Turnaround services offered include Recovery plans and their implementation, Viability analysis, Crisis management, Financial restructuring, Corporate and organizational restructuring, Facilities rationalization, Liquidation management, Loan workout, Litigation support and Expert testimony, Contract renegotiation, Sourcing loan refinancing and Sourcing equity investment. **Founded:** 2005. **Publications:** "TMA Turnaround of the Year Award, Small Company, Honorable Mention," Nov, 2005; "Back From The Brink - Bland Farms," Progressive Farmer, Oct, 2004; "New Breed of Turnaround Managers," Catalyst Magazine, Aug, 2004; "Key Performance Drivers - Bland Farms," The Produce News, Apr, 2004; "Corporate Governance: Averting Crisis's Before They Happen," ABJ journal, Feb, 2004.

32007 ■ Beacon Management - Management Consultants
1000 W McNab Rd.
Pompano Beach, FL 33069
Ph: (954)782-1119
Free: 800-771-8721
Fax: (954)969-2566
Co. E-mail: md@beaconmgmt.com
URL: http://www.beaconmgmt.com
Contact: Joyce Slencak, Manager
Scope: Specializes in change management, organized workplaces, multicultural negotiations and dispute resolutions and internet based decision making. **Founded:** 1985. **Publications:** "Sun-Sentinel Article," Oct, 2012.

32008 ■ Benchmark Consulting Group Inc.—Benchmark Advisors
283 Franklin St., Ste. 400
Boston, MA 02110-3100
Ph: (617)482-7661
Fax: (617)423-2158
Contact: Walter E. Robb, III, President
E-mail: werobb35@aol.com
Scope: Provides financial and management services to companies. Helps companies grow through debt, equity sourcing and restructuring, business valuation, acquisition and divestiture, computer information systems and improved operation profitability. **Founded:** 1978.

32009 ■ Samuel E. Bodily Associates
Office:172, 100 Darden Blvd.
Charlottesville, VA 22903
Ph: (434)924-4813
Fax: (434)243-7677
Contact: Samuel E. Bodily, Principal
E-mail: bodilys@virginia.edu
Scope: Consultant specializes in financial analysis, capital investment, business/product/market planners, financial risk analysis and decision sciences. **Founded:** 1977. **Publications:** "I Can't Get No Satisfaction: How Bundling and Multi-Part Pricing Can Satisfy Consumers and Suppliers," Feb, 2006; "Organizational Use of Decision Analysis," Oct, 2004; "Real Options," Oct, 2004.

32010 ■ The Business Guide Inc.
Torbay Rd.
Saint John, NL, Canada A1A 5B8
Ph: (709)754-8433
Free: 877-754-8433
Fax: (709)754-8434
Co. E-mail: info@businessguide.net
URL: http://www.businessguide.net
Contact: Sharon Monahan, President
E-mail: sharon@businessguide.net
Scope: Assists private sector firms in acquiring financial assistance to start or expand a business. **Founded:** 1998. **Publications:** "Accessing Government Funding".

32011 ■ CBIZ Inc.
6050 Oak Tree Blvd. S, Ste. 500
Cleveland, OH 44131-6951
Ph: (216)447-9000
Fax: (216)447-9007
URL: http://www.cbizinc.com
Contact: Jerome P. Grisko, President
URL(s): www.cbiz.com. **Scope:** A business consulting and tax services firm providing financial, consulting, tax and business services through seven groups: Financial management, tax advisory, construction and real estate, health-care, litigation support, capital resource and CEO outsource. **Founded:** 1996. **Publications:** "FAS 154: Changes in the Way We Report Changes," 2006; "Equity-Based Compensation: How Much Does it Really Cost Your Business," 2006; "Preventing Fraud - Tips for Nonprofit Organizations"; "Today's Workforce and Nonprofit Organizations: Meeting a Critical Need"; "IRS Highlights Top Seven Form 990 Errors". **Seminars:** Health Care - What the Future Holds; Consumer Driven Health Plans; Executive Plans; Health Savings Accounts; Healthy Wealthy and Wise; Legislative Update; Medicare Part D; Retirement Plans.

32012 ■ C.C. Comfort Consulting
3370 N Hayden Rd., Ste. 123-127
Scottsdale, AZ 85251
Ph: (480)483-8364
Contact: Clifton C. Comfort, Jr., Principal
Scope: Evaluates, develops and implements financial, operational and compliance management systems strategies, programs and practices. Has professional recognition as certified public accountant, internal auditor, cost analyst and fraud examiner plus investigatory, law enforcement, and court experience ensure confidential handling of sensitive and legal matters. Works with management, audit, legal, security and outside personnel to evaluate and improve compliance, efficiency and effectiveness. **Founded:** 1983.

32013 ■ Chartered Management Co.
10 S Riverside Plz., Ste. 1800
Chicago, IL 60606
Ph: (312)214-2575
Contact: William B. Avellone, President
Scope: Operations improvement consultants. Specializes in strategic planning; feasibility studies; management audits and reports; profit enhancement; start-up businesses; mergers and acquisitions; joint ventures; divestitures; interim management; crisis management; turnarounds; business process re-engineering; venture capital; and due diligence. **Founded:** 1985.

32014 ■ Clayton/Curtis/Cottrell
1722 Madison Ct.
Louisville, CO 80027-1121
Ph: (303)665-2005
Contact: Robert Cottrell, President
Scope: Market research firm specializes in providing consultations for packaged goods, telecommunications, direct marketing and printing, and packaging industries. Services include strategic planning; profit enhancement; startup businesses; mergers and acquisitions; joint ventures; divestitures; interim management; crisis management; turnarounds; market size, segmentation and rates of growth; competitor intelligence; image and reputation, and competitive analysis. **Founded:** 1981. **Publications:** "Turn an attitude into a purchase," Jul, 1995; "Mixed results for private label; price assaults by the national brands are getting heavy, but there's still a place for private label," Jun, 1995; "In-store promotion goes high-tech: is the conventional coupon destined for obsolescence?," Jun, 1995.

32015 ■ John Alan Cohan
433 N Camden Dr., Ste. 600
Beverly Hills, CA 90210
Ph: (310)278-0203
Free: 800-255-1529
Fax: (310)859-8656
Co. E-mail: johnalancohan@aol.com
URL: http://www.johnalancohan.com
Contact: Cohan John Alan, Principal
Scope: Consultant assists in the development of business plans for startups in the fields of livestock, horses, farming, or aviation. Also provides tax consultations and tax opinion letters to support deductions. **Founded:** 1981.

32016 ■ Colmen Menard Company Inc. (CMCI)
The Woods, 994 Old Eagle School Rd., Ste. 1000
Wayne, PA 19087
Ph: (484)367-0300
Fax: (484)367-0305
Co. E-mail: cmci@colmenmenard.com
URL: http://www.colmenmenard.com
Contact: David W. Menard, President
E-mail: dmenard@colmenmenard.com
Scope: Merger and acquisition corporate finance and business advisory services for public and private companies located in North America. **Founded:** 1982. **Publications:** "Success in Selling a Troubled Company," Nov, 2002; "Savvy Dealmakers," May, 2001; "Success in Selling a Troubled Company feature article from The Technology Times bimonthly newspaper," Apr, 2002; "Truisms," M&A Today, Nov, 2000.

32017 ■ Community Development Consulting
73 Michelle Ave.
Cotuit, MA 02635-2429
Ph: (508)420-9661
Fax: (508)420-4444
Co. E-mail: bobibanez@comcast.net
Contact: Robert Ibanez, Principal
Scope: A consulting practice offering business planning, financial management, organizational assessments and capital formation to non-profit, community development organizations. **Founded:** 2001.

32018 ■ Comprehensive Business Services
3201 Lucas Cir.
Lafayette, CA 94549
Ph: (925)283-8272
Fax: (925)283-8272
Contact: Walter H. Diebold, President
Scope: Business/financial consultants with related experience in marketing, finance, organization, business planning, and profit development. Industries served include construction, manufacturing, and wholesale. **Founded:** 1985.

32019 ■ Comprehensive Professional Management Inc.
222 E Dundee Rd.
Wheeling, IL 60090-3009
Ph: (847)520-1301
Fax: (847)520-0372
Co. E-mail: bob@cpmincfs.com
Contact: Kathy Rathunde, Principal
Scope: Services include accounting, financial planning, litigation support, pension profit sharing administration, practice surveys, professional corporation issues, retirement and estate planning and tax advice.

32020 ■ Controlled Resources
1021 E 1st Ave., Apt. 822
Broomfield, CO 80020
Ph: (708)798-2978
Fax: (727)532-3955
Co. E-mail: lwightman@mindspring.com
Scope: Firm offers business and management consultancy services.

32021 ■ Corporate Consulting Inc.
3333 Belcaro Dr.
Denver, CO 80209-4912

Ph: (303)698-9292
Fax: (303)698-9292
Co. E-mail: corpcons@compuserve.com
Contact: Devereux C. Josephs, President
Scope: Specializes in feasibility studies, organizational development, small business management, mergers and acquisitions, joint ventures, divestitures, interim management, crisis management, turnarounds, financing, appraisals valuations and due diligence studies. **Founded:** 1983.

32022 ■ Crystal Clear Communications Inc.
1633 W Winslow Dr., Ste. 210
Mequon, WI 53092
Ph: (262)240-0072
Fax: (262)240-0073
Co. E-mail: contact@crystalclear1.com
URL: http://www.crystalclear1.com
Contact: Barry J. Moze, Partner
E-mail: barrymoze@crystalclearl.com
Scope: Specialize in helping executives identify impediments to success, and then develop strategies to surmount them. Serves to identify core problems, suggest appropriate business changes, work with the organization to support these changes, and help executives articulate the behavior that will uphold these changes. Specializes in strategic planning; organizational development; small business management; executive coaching. **Founded:** 1986. **Publications:** "Weakest Link"; "Aware Leadership"; "Integrity"; "When Your Plate is Full"; "Problem Solving"; "Strategic Thinking".

32023 ■ Dubuc Lucke & Company Inc.—Adventa Global Intermediaries
120 W 5th St.
Cincinnati, OH 45202-2713
Ph: (513)579-8330
Fax: (513)241-6669
Contact: Kenneth E. Dubuc, President
Scope: Provides consulting services in the areas of profit enhancement; small business management; mergers and acquisitions; joint ventures; divestitures; interim management; crisis management; turnarounds; appraisals; valuations; due diligence; and international trade. **Founded:** 1999.

32024 ■ Effective Compensation Inc. (ECI)
30792 Southview Dr., Ste. 101
Evergreen, CO 80439
Ph: (303)854-1000
Free: 877-746-4324
Fax: (303)854-1030
Co. E-mail: eci@effectivecompensation.com
URL: http://www.effectivecompensation.com
Contact: Terry L. Isselhardt, Chief Executive Officer
E-mail: tisselhardt@effectivecompensation.com
Scope: Independent compensation consulting firm specializing in working with clients on a collaborative basis to improve their organization's efficiency through competitive, focused total compensation processes. Helps organizations determine how to competitively pay their employees. Provides quality, culture sensitive, compensation consulting assistance to all types of employers. Specializes in surveys like drilling industry compensation surveys, environmental industry compensation surveys, liquid pipeline round table compensation surveys; and oil and gas E and P industry compensation surveys. **Founded:** 1991. **Publications:** "Alternative Job Evaluation Approaches"; "Broad Banding: A Management Overview"; "Job Evaluation: Understanding the Issues"; "Industry Compensation Surveys"; "Skill Based Pay"; "Four Levels of Team Membership"; "Factors in Designing an Incentive Plan"; "Key Stock Allocation Issues"; "Stock Plans Primer". **Seminars:** Alternative Job Evaluation Approaches; Broad Banding: A Management Overview; Skill Based Pay; Job Evaluation: Understanding the Issues; Designing Compensation Programs that Motivate Employees; Master the Compensation Maze; Base Salary Administration Manual.

32025 ■ Everett & Co.
3126 S Franklin St.
Englewood, CO 80113
Ph: (303)761-7999
Fax: (303)781-8296
Contact: Robert W. Everett, Manager
Scope: Provides strategic real estate solutions and project management. **Founded:** 1993.

32026 ■ Steven S. Feinbert
412 Beacon St.
Boston, MA 02115
Ph: (617)247-2881
Fax: (617)247-2881
Scope: Offers small business consulting with emphasis on budgeting and financial management needs of small manufacturing firms. Also offers plant layout and work simplification services. Serves private industries. **Founded:** 1980.

32027 ■ Financial Management Solutions Inc.
1720 Windward Condourse Rm. 200
Alpharetta, GA 30005-1727
Ph: (770)619-3443
Free: 877-887-3022
Fax: (770)619-3095
Co. E-mail: JanP@fmsi.com
URL: http://www.fmsi.com
Contact: Walter M. Scott, President
Scope: Provider of staff models, industry comparative and benchmark data, measurement and monitoring systems. Also offers data processing evaluations, process improvements, and operational reviews. They have also developed resource management and sales management systems. Industries served: communications, banking, insurance, retail. **Founded:** 1988. **Publications:** "Teller Management System and Empowered Process Improvement". **Seminars:** Staff Productivity: Effective Use of Databases to Improve Performance and Statistical Models - the New Wave of Management; Micro-Analysis process to Profitability in the Financial Services Industry. **Telecommunication Services:** mikes@fmsi.com; gordonw@fmsi.com. **Special Services:** The Teller Management System™; The Resource ManagementSystem™; The Sales Management System™.

32028 ■ The Foster Group Inc.
180 N Stetson, Ste. 3470
Chicago, IL 60601
Ph: (312)609-1009
Fax: (312)609-1109
Co. E-mail: info@thefostergroup.com
URL: http://www.thefostergroup.com
Contact: John L. Foster, Jr., Managing Partner
E-mail: rpike@thefostergroup.com
Scope: Offers information systems and data security, financial accounting services, and management consulting. **Founded:** 1986.

32029 ■ Frankel and Topche P.C.
1700 Galloping Hill Rd.
Kenilworth, NJ 07033
Ph: (908)298-7700
Fax: (908)298-7701
Co. E-mail: info@frankelandtopche.com
URL: http://www.frankelandtopche.com
Contact: Mark J. Tikkanen, Director
E-mail: mtikkanen@frankelandtopche.com
Scope: Offers financial consulting for closely held businesses. Assists in mergers and acquisitions, tax planning, strategic business planning, family succession planning, accounting, auditing, and obtaining financing. The firm serves small businesses in the service, retail, wholesale, and manufacturing industries. Specializes in real estate, lumber and building materials, and service businesses. **Founded:** 1990. **Seminars:** Annual Tax Seminar.

32030 ■ Global Technology Transfer L.L.C.
1500 Dixie Hwy.
Park Hills, KY 41011-2819
Ph: (859)431-1262
Fax: (859)431-5148
Contact: Anthony Zembrodt, President
Scope: Firm specializes in product development; quality assurance; new product development; and total quality management focusing on household chemical specialties, especially air fresheners. Utilizes latest technology from global resources. Specializes in enhancement products for home and automobile. **Founded:** 1992.

32031 ■ Joseph Goldsten & Associates Inc.
401 Jackson Ave.
Lexington, VA 24450-1905
Ph: (540)463-4593
Contact: Joseph Goldsten, President
Scope: Offers counsel to financial institutions, corporations and individuals on planning, financial management, new ventures, small business development, investment counseling, real estate and banking. Active in mergers, acquisitions and valuations. Primarily clients: Financial institutions and manufacturers. **Founded:** 1996.

32032 ■ Gordian Concepts & Solutions
16 Blueberry Ln.
Lincoln, MA 01773
Ph: (617)259-8341
Contact: Stephen R. Low, President
Scope: Engineering and management consultancy offering general, financial, and valuation services, civil and tax litigation support. Assists clients in entering new businesses, planning new products and services, and evaluating feasibility. Targets industrial concerns engaged in manufacturing, assembly, warehousing, energy production, process systems and biotechnology, steel, paper, and electronics. Serves businesses such as retailing, financial services, health care, satellite broadcasting and cable television, outdoor advertising and professional practices. **Founded:** 1990. **Publications:** "Establishing Rural Cellular Company Values," Cellular Business.

32033 ■ Herpers Gowling L.L.P.—310 DEBT Herpers Chagani Gowling Inc.
4 Hughson St. S, Ste. 300
Hamilton, ON, Canada L8N 3Z1
Ph: (905)529-3328
Free: 888-735-9909
Fax: (905)529-3980
Contact: Alex Herpers, President
Scope: Provides services to small and medium size businesses in the areas of financial management, strategic planning, mergers and acquisitions and re-engineering/restructuring. **Founded:** 1996. **Special Services:** 310 DEBT®.

32034 ■ Hewitt Development Enterprises (HDE)
1717 N Bayshore Dr., Ste. 2154
Miami, FL 33132
Ph: (305)372-0941
Fax: (305)372-0941
Co. E-mail: info@hewittdevelopment.com
URL: http://www.hewittdevelopment.com
Contact: Robert G. Hewitt, Principal
E-mail: bob@hewittdevelopment.com
Scope: Specializes in strategic planning; profit enhancement; start-up businesses; interim management; crisis management; turnarounds; production planning; just-in-time inventory management; and project management. Serves senior management (CEOs, CFOs, division presidents, etc.) and acquirers of distressed businesses. **Founded:** 1985.

32035 ■ Hickey & Hill Inc.
1009 Oak Hill Rd., Ste. 201
Lafayette, CA 94549-3812
Ph: (925)906-5331
Contact: Edwin L. Hill, Chief Executive Officer
Scope: Firm provides management consulting services to companies in financial distress. Expertise area: Corporate restructuring and turnaround. **Founded:** 1984.

32036 ■ C. W. Hines and Associates Inc.—C&W Associates Inc.
344 Churchill Cir., Sanctuary Bay
White Stone, VA 22578
Ph: (804)435-8844
Fax: (804)435-8855
Co. E-mail: turtlecwh@aol.com
URL: http://www.cwhinesassociates.org
Contact: Dr. Carolyn C.W. Hines, President
Scope: Management consultants with expertise in the following categories: advertising and public relations; health and human resources; management sciences; organizational development; computer sciences; financial management; behavioral sciences;

environmental design; technology transfer; project management; facility management; program evaluation; and business therapy. Also included are complementary areas such as sampling procedures; job training; managerial effectiveness; corporate seminars; gender harassment; training for trainers and leadership and management skills development. **Founded:** 1979. **Publications:** "Money Muscle, 120 Exercises To Build Spiritual And Financial Strength," 2004; "Inside Track: Executives Coaching Executives"; "Money Muscle: 122 Exercises to Build Financial Strength"; "Nuts and Bolts of Work Force Diversity"; "Legal Issues, published in the Controllers Business Advisor"; "Identifying Racism: Specific Examples"; "BOSS Spelled Backwards is double SSOB! Or is it?"; "A No-Nonsense Guide to Being Stressed". **Seminars:** Career Development; Coaching and Counseling for Work Success; Communicating More Effectively in a Diverse Work Environment; Communications 600: Advanced Skills for Relationship Building; Customer Service: Building a Caring Culture.

32037 ■ Hollingsworth & Associates
395 Wellington Rd. S, Ste. 101
London, ON, Canada N6C 4P9
Ph: (519)649-2001
Fax: (519)649-7880
Co. E-mail: jack@hollingsworth.net
Contact: Jack Hollingsworth, President
E-mail: jack@hollingsworth.net
Scope: Acts as management accountants, tax and management consultants, and offsite controllers. Consulting services include software selection, and financial information systems. Accounting and tax preparation. **Founded:** 1993.

32038 ■ Holt Capital
1916 Pike Pl., Ste. 12-344
Seattle, WA 98101
Ph: (206)484-0403
Fax: (206)789-8034
Co. E-mail: info@holtcapital.com
URL: http://www.holtcapital.com
Contact: Marilyn J. Holt, Chief Executive Officer
E-mail: mjholt@holtcapital.com
Scope: Registered investment advisory firm. Services include: Debt planning, private equity, mergers, divestitures and acquisitions, transaction support services. Connects companies with capital. **Founded:** 1980. **Publications:** "Early Sales Key to Early-Stage Funding"; "Financial Transactions: Who Should Be At Your Table"; "Get the Deal Done: The Four Keys to Successful Mergers and Acquisitions"; "Is Your First Paragraph a Turn-off"; "Bubble Rubble: Bridging the Price Gap for an Early-Stage Business"; "Are You Ready For The new Economy"; "Could I Get Money or Jail Time With That The Sarbanes-Oxley Act Of 2002 gives early-stage companies More Risks". **Seminars:** Attracting Private Investors; Five Proven Ways to Finance Your Company; How to Get VC Financing; Venture Packaging; How to Finance Company Expansion.

32039 ■ Human Capital Research Corp. (HCRC)
1560 Sherman Ave., Ste. 1010
Evanston, IL 60201
Ph: (847)475-7580
Fax: (847)475-7584
Co. E-mail: fraya@humancapital.com
URL: http://www.humancapital.com
Contact: Brian Zucker, President
E-mail: brian@humancapital.com
Scope: provides colleges and universities with a wide range of services, including enrollment management, market development, long-term strategic planning, program evaluation, institutional research and learning outcomes assessment. **Founded:** 1991.

32040 ■ InfoSource Management Services Inc.
PO Box 590
Sicamous, BC, Canada V0E 2V0
Ph: (250)804-6113
Fax: (250)836-3667
Contact: Sherry Leggett, President
Scope: Firm provides customized financial reports that highlight the areas where change will improve the bottom line. **Founded:** 1995.

32041 ■ Integrated Financial Consultants
3625 Dufferin St., Ste. 340
Toronto, ON, Canada M3K 1Z2
Ph: (416)630-4000
Free: 800-263-4570
Fax: (416)630-4022
Co. E-mail: qfs@qfscanada.com
URL: http://www.qfscanada.com
Contact: Kevin Cott, President
E-mail: kevin.cott@qfscanada.com
Scope: Designs and implements a financial plan for the shareholders partners of small businesses. Services include investment management, tax planning risk management in the form of structuring and funding shareholders agreements estate planning and creditor protection. **Founded:** 1999.

32042 ■ Interminds & Federer Resources Inc.
106 E 6th St., Ste. 310
Austin, TX 78701-3659
Ph: (512)476-8800
Fax: (512)476-8811
Co. E-mail: yesyoucan@interminds.com
URL: http://www.interminds.com
Contact: Frank Federer, President
E-mail: ffederer@integra100.com
Scope: Specializes in feasibility studies; startup businesses; small business management; mergers and acquisitions; joint ventures; divestitures; interim management; crisis management; turnarounds; production planning; team building; appraisals and valuations. **Founded:** 1985. **Publications:** "Yes You Can: How To Be A Success No Matter Who You Are Or Where You're From".

32043 ■ Johnston Co.
78 Bedford St.
Lexington, MA 02420
Ph: (781)862-7595
Fax: (781)862-9066
Co. E-mail: info@johnstoncompany.com
URL: http://www.johnstoncompany.com
Contact: Claire Sehringer, Manager
Scope: Specializes in management audits and reports; start-up businesses; small business management; mergers and acquisitions; joint ventures; divestitures; interim management; crisis management; turnarounds; cost controls; financing; venture capital; controller services; financial management, strategic and advisory services. **Founded:** 1987. **Publications:** "Why are board meetings such a waste of time," Boston Business Journal, Apr, 2004.

32044 ■ Keiei Senryaku Corp.
19191 S Vermont Ave., Ste. 530
Torrance, CA 90502-1049
Ph: (310)366-3331
Free: 800-951-8780
Fax: (310)366-3330
Co. E-mail: takenakaes@earthlink.net
Contact: Kurt Miyamoto, President
Scope: Offers consulting services in the areas of strategic planning; feasibility studies; profit enhancement; organizational development; start-up businesses; mergers and acquisitions; joint ventures; divestitures; executive searches; sales management; and competitive analysis. **Founded:** 1989.

32045 ■ Charles A. Krueger—Scheree L. Krueger
1908 Innsbrooke Dr.
Sun Prairie, WI 53590
Ph: (608)837-5247
Fax: (608)825-7538
Co. E-mail: ckrueger@bus.wisc.edu
Contact: Charles Krueger, Owner
Scope: Financial management consultant specializing in professional education programs for managers and executives. Programs include: Finance and accounting for nonfinancial executives, financial management for executives, and developing and using financial information for decision making. Major industries served include manufacturing, service, healthcare and insurance. **Founded:** 1982. **Publications:** "Monitoring Financial Results, chapter in Corporate Controllers Manual," Warren Gorham and Lamont. **Seminars:** Finance and Accounting for Nonfinancial Executives; Financial Management for Health Care Executives; Financial Management for Insurance Executives; Direct Costing; Flexible Budgeting; Contribution Reporting; Building Value and Driving Profits - A Business Simulation.

32046 ■ William E. Kuhn & Associates
234 Cook St.
Denver, CO 80206-5305
Ph: (303)322-8233
Fax: (303)331-9032
Co. E-mail: billkuhn1@cs.com
Contact: William E. Kuhn, Owner
E-mail: billkuhn1@cs.com
Scope: Firm specializes in strategic planning; profit enhancement; small business management; mergers and acquisitions; joint ventures; divestitures; human resources management; performance appraisals; team building; sales management; appraisals and valuations. **Founded:** 1980. **Publications:** "Creating a High-Performance Dealership," Office SOLUTIONS & Office DEALER, Jul-Aug, 2006.

32047 ■ LaCloche Manitoulin Business Assistance Corp.
30 Meredith St.
Gore Bay, ON, Canada P0P 1H0
Ph: (705)282-3215
Free: 800-461-5131
Fax: (705)282-2989
Co. E-mail: info@lambac.org
URL: http://www.lambac.org
Contact: Amanda Morrison, Manager
E-mail: amanda@lambac.org
Scope: Encourages a strong, vibrant, sustainable, environmentally-friendly, business community through financial investment and support services. **Founded:** 1986. **Publications:** "Packed Panniers on Manitoulin," Sep, 2005; "One Wind Farm Gains License, Another Proposes 60 Windmills," Jul, 2005; "The Great Spirit Circle Trail," Jan, 2005.

32048 ■ Management Resource Partners
181 2nd Ave., Ste. 542
San Mateo, CA 94401
Ph: (650)401-5850
Fax: (650)401-5850
Contact: John C. Roberts, Owner
Scope: Firm specializes in strategic planning; small business management; mergers and acquisitions; joint ventures; divestitures; interim management; crisis management; turn around; venture capital; appraisals and valuations. **Founded:** 1981.

32049 ■ McShane Group Inc.
2345 York Rd., Ste. 102
Timonium, MD 21093
Ph: (410)560-0077
Fax: (410)560-2718
Co. E-mail: tmcshane@mcshanegroup.com
URL: http://www.mcshanegroup.com
Contact: Thomas P. McShane, President
E-mail: tmcshane@mcshanegroup.com
Scope: Turnaround consulting and crisis management firm. Specializes in due diligence services, interim management, strategic business realignments, business sale and asset depositions and debt restructuring. Industries served: technology, financial, retail, distribution, medical, educational, manufacturing, contracting, environmental and health care. **Founded:** 1987.

32050 ■ Mefford, Knutson & Associates Inc. (MK)
6437 Lyndale Ave. S, Ste. 103
Richfield, MN 55423-1465
Ph: (612)869-8011
Free: 800-831-0228
Fax: (612)869-8004
Co. E-mail: info@mkaonline.net
URL: http://www.mkaonline.net
Contact: Jeanette Mefford, Director
E-mail: jmefford@mkaonline.com
Scope: A consulting and licensed business brokerage firm specializing in start-up businesses; strategic planning; mergers and acquisitions; joint ventures;

divestitures; business process re-engineering; personnel policies and procedures; market research; new product development and cost controls. **Founded:** 1990.

32051 ■ Merrimac Associates Inc.
190 N Evergreen Ave., Ste. 100
Woodbury, NJ 08096-1862
Ph: (856)428-4350
Free: 888-777-5215
Fax: (856)848-7770
Co. E-mail: mo@merrimac.com
URL: http://www.merrimac.com
Contact: David B. Shaffer, President
E-mail: dbs@merrimac.com
Scope: Offers financial management consulting to help with financial problems of small or medium sized businesses of any type on a long or short term basis. Assists with a wide variety of management problems. **Founded:** 1992. **Special Services:** XtremePM™.

32052 ■ Metro Accounting Services Inc.
167 Oxmoor Blvd.
Homewood, AL 35209
Ph: (205)916-0900
Fax: (205)945-1784
Co. E-mail: info@metroaccountingservice.com
URL: http://www.metroaccountingservice.com
Contact: James Waligora, President
E-mail: jim@metroaccountingservice.com
Scope: Consults on tax planning, retirement planning, investment analysis and personal financial planning on a fee basis for individuals and small businesses and on real estate partnerships. Also specializes in employee benefit analysis, pension investment analysis and investment management for small businesses. **Founded:** 1982. **Seminars:** How to Win the Money Game; Using Mutual Funds for Financial Independence; IRA's, Keogh and Other Retirement Plans; How to Quit Paying Income Taxes. **Special Services:** IRS problem solving, Quick Books® installation and training.

32053 ■ Miller/Cook & Associates Inc.
20 Marco Lake Dr., Ste. 12
Marco Island, FL 34145-3644
Ph: (239)394-5040
Free: 800-591-1141
Fax: (239)394-2652
Co. E-mail: info@millercook.com
URL: http://www.millercook.com
Contact: William B. Miller, President
Scope: Specializes in all areas of enrollment management, admissions and financial aid. Involves in institutional and enrollment analysis, strategic positioning/institutional image, enrollment integration/operation, re-recruitment, financial aid and planning, integrated communications, training and workshops, and on-site management. **Founded:** 1988. **Publications:** "Capital gains: Surviving in an increasingly for profit world"; "Making steps to a brighter future". **Seminars:** Admissions: An overview of a changing profession; Admission practices: Managing the admissions office; Admission practices: Internal operations often make the difference; Effective communication and the enrollment process; Telemarketing or Tele counseling: How to use the telephone to effectively enroll and re-enroll students; Graduate and professional program recruitment: An overview Re-Recruitment: What is it? Is it necessary?; The effective use of electronic mediums in the recruitment process; The use of alumni to support and sustain your recruiting efforts.

32054 ■ Mitchell and Titus L.L.P.—Mitchell/Titus
1 Battery Park Plz., 27th Fl.
New York, NY 10004-1405
Ph: (212)709-4500
Fax: (212)709-4680
URL: http://www.mitchelltitus.com
Contact: Bert N. Mitchell, Chief Executive Officer
Scope: Firm provides assurance, advisory business services, transaction support and tax services. Specializes in auditing and accounting services, tax planning and preparation services management and business advisory services. **Founded:** 1974. **Publications:** "ITEM Club Budget preview report," 2010; "Year end personal planning," 2010; "Steering towards the future using the Pre Budget Report to help the UK rebound," 2009; "Be careful what you wish for," 2009; "Year end personal planning," 2009. **Seminars:** Budget Seminar 2010, Mar, 2010.

32055 ■ Partners for Market Leadership L.L.C.
400 Galleria Pky., Ste. 1500
Atlanta, GA 30339
Ph: (770)850-1409
Free: 800-984-1110
Co. E-mail: dcarpenter@market-leadership.com
URL: http://www.market-leadership.com
Contact: Nancy Surdyka, Manager
E-mail: nsurdyka@market-leadership.com
Scope: Boutique consulting firm focused on assisting clients to develop sustainable market leadership in geographic, practice area and/or industry markets. Provides consulting on market leadership, revenue enhancement, strategic development and change facilitation. Additional services are offered to legal, accounting, valuation and financial firms. **Founded:** 1995.

32056 ■ Penny & Associates Inc.
2748 Bur Oak Ave., Unit 2
Markham, ON, Canada L6B 1K4
Ph: (905)985-0712
Free: 800-699-6190
Fax: (905)985-9461
Co. E-mail: mail@pennyinc.com
URL: http://www.pennyinc.com
Contact: Betty Penny, President
E-mail: betty@pennyinc.com
Scope: Accounting and management firm that offers accounting and business solutions. Assistance in preparation of financial reports, reconciliation of inter company accounts, foreign currency transactions, investment trades and auditor working paper files and assistance in developing accounting policies and procedures. Provides part-time controllers to prepare financial statements, cash flow management, credit negotiations and give financial management advice or oversee accounting staff. **Founded:** 1994. **Seminars:** Quick Books, Aug, 2001; How to Stand Up to People Without Being a Jerk; How to Build Influence and Rapport With Almost Anyone; Dealing With Dissatisfied, Different and Difficult People; Effective Public Speaking; How to Incorporate Yourself; Company Perks: Attracting & Retaining Good People; FIRST AID. **Telecommunication Services:** info@pennyinc.com. **Special Services:** Quickbooks®.

32057 ■ Queens Business Consulting (QBC)
Queens School of Business, Goodes Hall, 143 Union St.
Kingston, ON, Canada K7L 3N6
Ph: (613)533-2309
Fax: (613)533-2370
Co. E-mail: qbc@business.queensu.ca
URL: http://www.qsbc.com
Contact: Michelle Miatello, Director
E-mail: mmiatello@business.queensu.ca
Scope: Provides business plans, feasibility studies, financial planning, competitor analysis, market research, marketing strategies, production planning and systems implementation. **Founded:** 1973. **Publications:** "Information technology, network structure and competitive action. Information Systems Research," 2010; "The role of dominance in the appeal of violent media depictions. Journal of Advertising," 2010; "Great expectations and broken promises: Misleading claims, product failure, expectancy disconfirmation and consumer distrust. Journal of the Academy of Marketing Science," 2010; "Development and psychometric properties of the Transformational Teaching Questionnaire. Journal of Health Psychology," 2010; ". Predicting workplace aggression: myths, realities, and remaining questions," 2009; "The Inconvenient Truth about Improving Vehicle Fuel Efficiency: An MultiAttribute Analysis of the Efficient Frontier of the U.S. Automobile Industry, Transportation Research-Part," 2009; "Fraud in Canadian Nonprofit Organizations as Seen through the Eyes of Canadian Newspapers," 2009; "Disentangling the Indirect Links between SES and Health: The Dynamic Roles of Work Stressors and Personal Contro," 2009; "The strong situation hypothesis. Personality and Social Psychology Review," 2009; " Planning Your Next Crisis Decisively and Effectively. Ivey Business Journal," 2009. **Seminars:** Enabling Innovation Discussion Highlights, 2011; Intellectual Capital, 2010; On the diffusion of knowledge inside the organization, 2010; A model of the tacit knowledge lifecycle for decision-making: From creation to utilization, 2010; Individual, group, and organizational learning; A knowledge management perspective, 2009; Political economies of knowledge, with an example, 2009; The alignment of business and knowledge strategies and structures, 2009; Using IT To Support the Discovery of Novel Knowledge in Organizations, 2008; Leadership: Knowledge Management by a New Name?, 2007; Every User Tells a Story, 2007.

32058 ■ Rainwater Gish & Associates
317 3rd St., Ste. 3
Eureka, CA 95501
Ph: (707)443-0030
Fax: (707)443-5683
Contact: Joan Rainwater Gish, President
Scope: Offers financial management for small business: includes asset management (controlling cash, inventory, A/R), cash flow control, credit policies, and securing/structuring financing for growth. Also offers assistance in business planning, preparing proforma statements and other loan documents to secure financing. Majority of financial loan packages have been SBA loans. Firm provides SBA marketing and portfolio management services to banks. **Founded:** 1986.

32059 ■ Scannell & Kurz Inc.
71-B Munroe Ave.
Pittsford, NY 14534
Ph: (585)381-1120
Free: 877-266-0847
Fax: (585)381-2383
Co. E-mail: info@scannellkurz.com
URL: http://www.scannellkurz.com
Contact: James Scannell, President
E-mail: scannell@scannellkurz.com
Scope: Provides pricing and financial aid strategies, admissions market analysis, enrollment management, and retention strategies. **Founded:** 1996. **Publications:** "Financial Aid Strategies in Tough Economic Times," Jan, 2010; "Financial Aid Trends in the Current Economy: Lessons for the Future," Dec, 2009; "Data-Driven Retention Strategies," Feb, 2009; "Enrollment Management 101," Mar, 2008; "Don't Get Distracted: Top Audit Issues in Financial Aid," Sep, 2007; "Financial Aid and the Business Office," Jul, 2007; "Understanding the Value of Transfers," May, 2007; "Financial Aid Appeal Pitfalls," Mar, 2007; "Is Affordability Really the Issue," Nov, 2006; "Building a Financial Fundraising Case," Jul, 2006; "Enrollment Management Grows Up," May, 2006; "Just One Stop, But Many Potential Pitfalls," Mar, 2006; "Bond Rating: Beyond the Balance," Jan, 2006; "Strategy and Operations in Financial Aid," Nov, 2005; "The Evolution of a Successful Admissions Director"; "Profile of an Effective Enrollment Manager". **Seminars:** 2009 Enrollment and Financial Aid Results: Lessons for the Future, Presidents Institute, Jan, 2010; The Bottom Line on Student Retention: Data-Driven Approaches that Work, Nov, 2009; Thriving Without Deep Pockets--Achieving Enrollment Success on an Uneven Playing Field, Feb, 2009.

32060 ■ Harvey C. Skoog
7151 E Addis Ave.
Prescott Valley, AZ 86314
Ph: (928)772-1448
Scope: Firm has expertise in taxes, payroll, financial planning, budgeting, buy/sell planning, business startup, fraud detection, troubled business consulting, acquisition, and marketing. Serves the manufacturing, construction, and retailing industries in Arizona. **Founded:** 1977.

32061 ■ The Stillwater Group—Stillwater Consulting Group Inc.
920 E Shore Dr.
Stillwater, NJ 07875
Ph: (973)579-7080
Fax: (973)579-7970
Co. E-mail: education@stillwater.com
URL: http://www.stillwater.com
Contact: David Woodward, Chief Operating Officer
Scope: Provides strategic planning, budget and financial management, process improvement, organi-

zational design and assessment, and college student services operations. **Founded:** 1993. **Publications:** "Integrated Resource Planning (Irp)," Business Officer Magazine, 2005; "The Economic Risk Conundrum," University Business Magazine; "Revenue Analysis and Tuition Strategy"; "Managing Advancement Services: Processes and Paper".

32062 ■ Swigert & Associates Inc.
505 Chicago Ave.
Evanston, IL 60202-2916
Ph: (847)864-4690
Fax: (847)864-0802
Co. E-mail: ryan@swigert.biz
URL: http://www.swigert.biz
Contact: Thomas C. Swigert, President
Scope: Offers assistance to businesses and individuals on matters related to finance, investment decisions, taxes and general management concerns. **Founded:** 1970.

32063 ■ Value Creation Group Inc.
7820 Scotia Dr., Ste. 2000
Dallas, TX 75248-3115
Ph: (972)980-7407
Fax: (972)980-4619
Co. E-mail: john.antos@valuecreationgroup.com
URL: http://www.valuecreationgroup.com
Contact: John Antos, Chief Executive Officer
E-mail: john.antos@valuecreationgroup.com
Scope: General business experts offering predictive strategic planning, Activity Based Costing ABC, Activity Based Management ABM, mergers and acquisitions, outsourcing, re engineering, process management, web enabling technology, bench marking, installation of financial systems, executive search, training, teams, activity based budgeting, operational auditing, feature costing. Industries served financial services, food, health care, insurance, manufacturing, electronics, real estate, consumer products, nonprofit, telecommunication, oil, service, data processing, hotel and resort and government agencies. **Founded:** 1984. **Publications:** "Handbook of Process Management Based Predictive Accounting," Alcpa 2002; "Cost Management for Today's Manufacturing Environment and Activity Based Management for Service Environments, Government Entities and Nonprofit Organizations"; "Risks and Opportunities in International Finance and Treasury"; "Driving Value Using Activity Based Budgeting"; "Process Based Accounting Leveraging Processes to Predict Results"; "Handbook of Supply Chain Management"; "Economic Value Management Applications and Techniques"; "The Change Handbook": "Group Methods for Creating the Future"; "Why Value Management and Performance Measurement Through U.S. Binoculars," Journal of Strategic Performance Measurement; "Real Options, Intangibles Measurement and the Benefits of Human Capital Investment to Power the Organization," Journal of Strategic Performance Measurement. **Seminars:** Activity Based Management; Predictive Accounting; Performance measures; ABM for Manufacturing; ABM for Service Organizations; Finance and Accounting for Non-Financial Executives; Return on Investment/Capital Expenditure Evaluation; Planning and Cost Control; The Next Step Intermediate Finance and Accounting for Non-financial Managers; Activity-Based Budgeting; Friendly Finance for Fund Raisers; Strategic Outsourcing. **Telecommunication Services:** assistu@valuecreationgroup.com; consultu@valuecreationgroup.com.

32064 ■ ValueNomics Value Specialists
50 W San Fernando St., Ste. 600
San Jose, CA 95113
Fax: (408)200-6401
Co. E-mail: info@amllp.com
Contact: Gary E. Jones, Chief Executive Officer
Scope: Consulting is offered in the areas of financial management, process re-engineering, growth business services; governance, risk/compliance, SOX readiness and compliance, SAS 70, enterprise risk management, system security, operational and internal audit; business advisory services; valuation services; CORE assessment; contract assurance; transaction advisory services, IT solutions and litigation support services. **Founded:** 1993. **Publications:** "Dueling Appraisers: How Differences in Input and Assumptions May Control the Value," Apr, 2005; "The Business of Business Valuation and the CPA as an expert witness"; "The Business of Business Valuation," McGraw-Hill Professional Publishers Inc.

32065 ■ Mark Vanderstelt
9831 Gulfstream Ct.
Fishers, IN 46037
Ph: (317)576-9328
Fax: (317)576-9328
Contact: Mark Vanderstelt, Owner
Scope: Consulting services include financial planning and analysis, inventory control, cash management, return on investment, budgeting, pricing, system design and analysis, mergers and acquisitions, feasibility studies, data processing, cost systems and controls, and performance measurement. Also performs operational and financial reviews. **Founded:** 1985.

32066 ■ VelociTel Inc.
200 N Glebe Rd., Ste. 1000
Arlington, VA 22203-3728
Ph: (703)558-2200
Fax: (703)276-1169
Contact: John Powers, President
Scope: Provides expertise in developing wireless networks. Services include: project management; site acquisition; land use planning; architecture and engineering; construction and construction management. **Founded:** 1987. **Special Services:** VelociTel®.

32067 ■ VenturEdge Corp.
4711 Yonge St., Ste. 1105
Toronto, ON, Canada M2N 6K8
Ph: (416)224-2000
Fax: (416)224-2376
Co. E-mail: info@venturedge.com
URL: http://www.venturedge.com
Contact: Morris Langer, President
E-mail: langer@venturedge.com
Scope: Provides services including strategy formulation; business planning; financial management; business coaching; performance improvement; information management; merger, acquisitions and divestitures; family succession planning; competitive intelligence. **Founded:** 1972. **Publications:** "Reputation," Harvard Business School Press, 1996; "Competing for the Future," Harvard Business School Press, 1994; "The Fifth Discipline," 1990.

32068 ■ Verbit & Co.
19 Bala Ave.
Bala Cynwyd, PA 19004-3202
Ph: (610)668-9840
Co. E-mail: verbitcompany@earthlink.net
Contact: Alan C. Verbit, President
Scope: Management consulting firm to assist executives and managers fulfill their mission and to assure that adequate planning of day-to-day operations occurs; that controls sufficient to safeguard valuable resources; and that results of decisions reviewed in sufficient time to effect continuing action. Financial planning and control-to develop accounting, budgeting, forecasting and other information systems for the management of resources and evaluation of strategies. Services also include: Evaluation of desk-top computer systems for small firms; CAD/CAM implementation plan and orderly introduction of CAD/CAM. Industries served: manufacturing, distribution, metals casting, equipment and components, professional services, health care, retail, nonprofit and government. **Founded:** 1981. **Seminars:** Integrating Manufacturing Management Systems with Business Systems; Negotiating Information Systems Agreements with Suppliers.

32069 ■ Vision Management
149 Meadows Rd.
Lafayette, NJ 07848-3120
Ph: (973)702-1116
Fax: (973)702-8311
Contact: Norman L. Naidish, President
Scope: Firm specializes in profit enhancement; strategic planning; business process reengineering; industrial engineering; facilities planning; team building; inventory management; and total quality management (TQM). **Founded:** 1984. **Publications:** "To increase profits, improve quality," Manufacturing Engineering, May, 2000.

32070 ■ WestCap Partners Inc.
750 Lexington Ave., 24th Fl.
New York, NY 10022
Ph: (212)949-1825
Fax: (212)223-7363
Contact: Charles J. Cernansky, Owner
Scope: Business and financial consultants provide corporate finance (debt, equity, private placements) and advisory services to emerging and medium-sized companies; investment and merchant banking; trade assistance, planning, strategy and financing and financial consulting. Also temporarily assist growing companies in operational roles. Offer troubled company assistance through work-outs and turnarounds. Industries served: All including environmental, manufacturing, information technology (hardware, software, systems integration and implementation) direct marketing, sales service/wholesaling/distribution, construction materials and services, advertising, financial services and emerging technologies. **Founded:** 1992. **Seminars:** Financial Negotiations for Mergers, Acquisitions and Projects.

32071 ■ Western Capital Holdings Inc.
10050 E Applewood Dr.
Parker, CO 80138
Ph: (303)841-1022
Contact: Patrick T. Frasco, President
Scope: Specialists in all phases of financial and management consulting. Provide strong emphasis in strategic planning and corporate development, financial analysis, acquisitions, investment banking and corporate finance. Projects range in size and duration to fit clients needs. Services can be applied to many diverse financial projects that may include the following: Business plan development, budgeting and forecasting, strategic planning, cash flow analysis, cash flow management, corporate development, banking relations, asset management, and financial analysis. Industries served: Food industry, manufacturing, distribution, retailing, computer services, agribusiness, financial services, insurance, and government agencies. **Founded:** 1986. **Seminars:** Buy Low, Sell High, Collect Early and Pay Late; Preparing Your Company for Sale; Venture Capital - Finding an Angel.

32072 ■ Westlife Consultants & Counsellors
95 October Ln.
Aurora, ON, Canada L4G 7A1
Ph: (905)867-0686
Fax: (416)799-5242
Co. E-mail: westlifeconsultant@hotmail.com
URL: http://www.westlifeconsultants.com
Contact: Dr. Syed N. Hussain, President
E-mail: westlifeconsultant@hotmail.com
Scope: Provider of entrepreneurs and businesses with a highly commercial and global perspectives on the international business development ideas under consideration. **Founded:** 1990. **Publications:** "Innovative Management"; "Team Building and Leadership"; "Financial Planning"; "Estate Planning"; "Risk Management"; "Export/Import Trade Finance Mechanics"; "Marketing and Sales Management"; "What Your Banker Needs to Know"; "Building A Successful Financial Plan".

32073 ■ Donald C. Wright CPA
3906 Lawndale Ln. N
Plymouth, MN 55446-2940
Ph: (763)478-6999
Co. E-mail: donaldwright@compuserve.com
URL: http://www.donaldwrightcpa.com
Contact: Donald C. Wright, President
E-mail: donaldwright@compuserve.com
Scope: Offers accounting, tax, and small business consulting services. Services include cash flow and budgeting analysis; financial forecast and projections; financial statements; reviews and compilations; tax planning, tax preparation; IRS and state/local representation; international taxation; estate, gift and trust tax return preparation; benefit plan services; business succession planning; estate planning; financial planning; management advisory services, pension and profit sharing plans, retirement planning, expert

witness services and employee benefits plans. Serves individuals, corporations, partnerships, and non-profit organizations. **Founded:** 1968. **Seminars:** Qualified pension plans and employee welfare benefit plans.

COMPUTERIZED DATABASES

32074 ■ *e-JEP*
2014 Broadway, Ste. 305
Nashville, TN 37203
Ph: (615)322-2595
Fax: (615)343-7590
Co. E-mail: aeainfo@vanderbilt.edu
URL: http://www.vanderbilt.edu/AEA
Contact: Angus Deaton, President
Availability: Online: American Economic Association; Thomson Reuters - Westlaw. CD-ROM: American Economic Association. **Type:** Full-text.

32075 ■ *InvestmentNews*
711 3rd Ave.
New York, NY 10017
Ph: (212)210-0111
Free: 888-909-9111
Fax: (212)210-0200
Co. E-mail: rcrain@adage.com
URL: http://www.crain.com
URL(s): www.investmentnews.com/. **Availability:** Online: Crain Communications Inc. **Type:** Full-text; Numeric.

32076 ■ *Offshore Money Fund Report™*
1 Research Dr., Ste. 400A
Westborough, MA 01581
Ph: (508)616-6600
Fax: (508)616-5511
Co. E-mail: info@imoneynet.com
URL: http://www.imoneynet.com
Contact: Kenneth B. Bohlin, President
Availability: Online: Informa Financial Information Inc.-Informa Financial Information-iMoneyNet. **Type:** Full-text; Numeric.

32077 ■ *Vickers Weekly Insider Report*
61 Broadway St., Ste. 1700
New York, NY 10006
Ph: (212)425-7500
Free: 800-645-5043
Fax: (212)809-2975
Co. E-mail: info@vickers-stock.com
URL: http://www.vickers-stock.com
Availability: Online: Vickers Stock Research Corp. **Type:** Full-text; Numeric.

LIBRARIES

32078 ■ Business Development Bank of Canada Research & Information Centre
5 Place Ville Marie, Ste. 300
Montreal, QC, Canada H3B 5E7
Ph: (514)283-7632
Free: 877-232-2269
Fax: (514)283-2304
URL: http://www.bdc.ca
Contact: Odette Lavoie, Specialist
Scope: Small business, management, Canadian business and industry, banking and finance, development banking. **Services:** Interlibrary loan; Library not open to the public. **Founded:** 1977. **Holdings:** 5000 books. **Subscriptions:** 100 journals and other serials; 7 newspapers.

32079 ■ Carnegie Library of Pittsburgh - Downtown & Business
612 Smithfield St.
Pittsburgh, PA 15222-2506
Ph: (412)281-7141
Fax: (412)471-1724
Co. E-mail: downtown@carnegielibrary.org
URL: http://www.carnegielibrary.org/locations/downtown
Contact: Karen Rossi, Department Head
Scope: Investments, small business, entrepreneurship, management, marketing, insurance, advertising, personal finance, accounting, real estate, job and career, International business. **Services:** Library open to the public. **Founded:** 1924. **Holdings:** 13,000 business volumes; VF materials; microfilm; looseleaf services; AV materials.

32080 ■ Nichols College - Conant Library
124 Center Rd.
Dudley, MA 01571
Ph: (508)213-2333
Free: 800-470-3379
Co. E-mail: reference@nichols.edu
URL: http://www.nichols.edu/academics/academics/Library
Contact: Jim Douglas, Director, Library Services
Scope: Management, advertising, finance and accounting, small business, marketing, taxation, economics, International trade, humanities. **Services:** Interlibrary loan; copying; information service to groups; document delivery; library open to Dudley and Webster residents. **Founded:** 1962. **Holdings:** 48,000 volumes; 1677 audio/visual titles; 3804 reels of microfilm. **Subscriptions:** 278 journals and electronic subscriptions. **Telecommunication Services:** jim.douglas@nichols.edu.

32081 ■ Strategic Account Management Association - Resource Search Library
33 N. LaSalle St., Ste. 3700
Chicago, IL 60602
Ph: (312)251-3131
Fax: (312)251-3132
URL: http://www.strategicaccounts.org/search/resourcesearch.asp
Contact: Elisabeth Cornell, Director, Education
Scope: National and global account management programs, account managers, strategic account management, strategic partnering and alliances, cross-functional teams, channel conflict, supply chain management, internal selling, customer viewpoint, value-added selling, account planning, account segmentation, compensation. **Services:** Library not open to the public (numerous sample documents available to non-members, and most can be purchased). **Founded:** 1964. **Holdings:** 1500 documents, periodicals, audiocassettes, case studies, white papers, research studies, books, reports, archives, PDFs, and presentation materials. **Subscriptions:** 1 journal; 3 newsletters.

32082 ■ University of Kentucky - Business & Economics Information Center
B&E Info. Ctr., Rm. 116
335-BA Gatton College of Business & Economics
Lexington, KY 40506-0034
Ph: (859)257-8936
Fax: (859)257-1333
Co. E-mail: mrazeeq@pop.uk.edu
URL: http://www.uky.edu//Provost/academicprograms.html
Contact: Michael A. Razeeq, Librarian, Business
URL(s): gatton.uky.edu/. **Scope:** Business, economics, business management, marketing, finance, accounting. **Services:** Library open to the public for reference use only. **Founded:** 1993. **Telecommunication Services:** cber@uky.edu; klimar@pop.uky.edu; provost@email.uky.edu.

RESEARCH CENTERS

32083 ■ University of Oklahoma - Center for Financial Studies (CFS)
Price College of Business
307 W Brooks, Ste. 205A
Norman, OK 73019
Ph: (405)325-5591
Fax: (405)325-5491
Co. E-mail: pyadav@ou.edu
URL: http://www.ou.edu/price/finance/cfs.html
Contact: Prof. Pradeep Yadav, Director
Founded: 1990. **Publications:** *Center for Financial Studies working paper series.* **Educational Activities:** CFS Seminar (Weekly). **Awards:** Research Scholarships, Fellowships and Grants (Annual).

START-UP INFORMATION

32084 ■ ***"Biz Pays Tribute: Franchise Helps Owners Grieve and Honor Their Beloved Pets" in Small Business Opportunities (November 2007)***
Pub: Harris Publications Inc.
Description: Paws and Remember is a franchise company that provides pet cremation and memorial products while assisting veterinary clinics and other pet specialists to help clients when they lose a pet.

32085 ■ ***"Building a Business: Directbuild Helps Clients Build Their Own Home" in Small Business Opportunities (Winter 2007)***
Pub: Harris Publications Inc.
Description: Mike New, founder of Directbuild, a franchise company that helps individuals with no construction knowledge build their own home.

32086 ■ ***Building a Dream: A Canadian Guide to Starting Your Own Business***
Pub: McGraw-Hill Ryerson Ltd.
Ed: Walter S. Good. **Released:** 2005. **Description:** Topics covered include evaluating business potential, new business ideas, starting or buying a business, franchise opportunities, business organization, protecting an idea, arranging financing, and developing a business plan.

32087 ■ ***The Canadian Small Business Survival Guide: How to Start and Operate Your Own Successful Business***
Pub: Dundurn Group
Ed: Benj Gallander. FRQ June 2002. **Price:** $26.99. **Description:** Ideas for starting and running a successful small business. Topics include selecting a business, financing, government assistance, locations, franchises, and marketing ideas.

32088 ■ ***"Cheap Ticket" in Entrepreneur (Vol. 35, November 2007, No. 11, pp. 126)***
Pub: Entrepreneur Media Inc.
Description: List of 69 franchises that can be started for less than $25,000 is spotlighted.

32089 ■ ***"Cleaning Up" in Small Business Opportunities (Get Rich At Home 2010)***
Pub: Harris Publications Inc.
Description: Break into the $23 billion pro car wash business with no experience needed. Profile of Team Blue, founded by father and son team, Jeff and Jason Haas along with franchise opportunities is included.

32090 ■ ***"Courier Service Delivers Big Profits and Top-Notch Customer Service" in Small Business Opportunities (November 2007)***
Pub: Harris Publications Inc.
Description: Profile of Relay Express, a courier franchising business started by three friends in 1986. The company focuses on customer service and calls them every 19 minutes to report on progress of a parcel until it is delivered.

32091 ■ ***"Driving Home Success: Stamped Asphalt for Driveways and Paths is Hottest New Trend" in Small Business Opportunities (Winter 2007)***
Pub: Harris Publications Inc.
Description: Profile of technology that turns asphalt into three-dimensional replicas of hand-laid brick, slate, cobblestone and other design effects. Profiles of franchise opportunities in this industry are included.

32092 ■ ***Franchise: Freedom or Fantasy***
Pub: iUniverse
Ed: Mitchell York. **Released:** June 22, 2009. **Price:** $13.95. **Description:** Successful franchisee and professional certified coach guides individuals through the many steps involved in deciding whether or not to buy a franchise and how to do it correctly.

32093 ■ ***Franchising for Dummies***
Pub: John Wiley & Sons, Incorporated
Ed: Dave Thomas, Michael Seid. **Released:** October 2006. **Price:** $24.99. **Description:** Advice to help entrepreneurs choose the right franchise, as well as financing, managing and expanding the business.

32094 ■ ***"Geo-Marketing: Site Selection by the Numbers" in Franchising World (Vol. 42, September 2010, No. 9, pp.)***
Pub: International Franchise Association
Ed: Kellen Vaughan. **Description:** Site location is critical when starting a new franchise. Information to help franchisees choose the right location is included.

32095 ■ ***"Hand-Held Heaven: Smallcakes Cupcakery" in Tulsa World (February 15, 2011)***
Pub: McClatchy Company
Description: Franchisee Carolyn Archer displays her products at Smallcakes Cupcakery, a Jenks shop that's the first to be co-branded with FreshBerry under the Beautiful Brands International banner. The shop's launch is part of a franchise deal between BBI and Jeff and Brandy Martin, co-owners of Smallcakes; twelve concepts have been developed and marketed already by Tulsa-based BBI.

32096 ■ ***"Home: Where the Money Is!" in Small Business Opportunities (May 2008)***
Pub: Harris Publications Inc.
Description: Profile of ComForcare, a franchise company that serves the senior population in America; a franchise can be started with one owner and add and build a team as it grows.

32097 ■ ***"Hot Market Opportunity" in Small Business Opportunities (January 2011)***
Pub: Harris Publications Inc.
Description: Mobility products for seniors give this small business a $3 million lift. Profile of 101 Mobility, the nation's first full-service sales, service and installation provider of mobility and accessibility products and equipment including stair lifts, auto lifts, ramps, porch lifts, power wheelchairs and scooters as well as other medical equipment such as walkers, hospital beds and more.

32098 ■ ***"It's Tea-Riffic! Natural Bottled Tea Satisfies Void In Beverage Market" in Small Business Opportunities (November 2007)***
Pub: Harris Publications Inc.
Description: Profile of Skae Beverage International LLC, offering franchise opportunities for its New Leaf all-natural tea beverage, available in eight flavors of green, white and blue tea.

32099 ■ ***"Making Money? Child's Play!" in Small Business Opportunities (March 2008)***
Pub: Harris Publications Inc.
Description: Proven system helps launch a successful child care business.

32100 ■ ***Microfranchising: Creating Wealth at the Bottom of the Pyramid***
Pub: Edward Elgar Publishing, Incorporated
Ed: W. Gibb Dyer; Jason Fairbourne; Stephen W. Gibson. **Released:** July 2008. **Price:** $35.00. **Description:** Ideas from researchers and social entrepreneurs discusses the movement that moves microfranchising into a mechanism for sustainable poverty reduction on a scale to match microfinance.

32101 ■ ***"New Wave" in Entrepreneur (Vol. 36, March 2008, No. 3, pp. 100)***
Pub: Entrepreneur Media Inc.
Description: List of top new franchise opportunities is presented. The list ranks the franchises according to their order in Entrepreneur Magazine's 2008 Franchise 500 issue.

32102 ■ ***"Proven Success Pays Off" in Small Business Opportunities (January 2011)***
Pub: Harris Publications Inc.
Description: Industry pioneers of the fast-casual restaurant launch new venture with sales of $43 million. Profile of Newk's Express Cafe and its founders is included.

32103 ■ ***"Pump Up the Profits" in Small Business Opportunities (Summer 2010)***
Pub: Harris Publications Inc.
Description: New fitness franchise offers customized personal training at bargain rates. Profile of Alan Katz, president of EduFit, a concept that allows small groups of people to workout with customized training is provided.

32104 ■ ***"Pump Up the Profits: Teaching Small Biz How to Handle Fuel and Reduce Costs!" in Small Business Opportunities (March 2008)***
Pub: Harris Publications Inc.
Description: Profile of 4Refuel, a company that delivers diesel and biodiesel fuel to customers individual fuelings.

32105 ■ ***"Rev Up Your Engine" in Small Business Opportunities (Fall 2010)***
Pub: Harris Publications Inc.
Description: Industry giant Meineke is adding franchisees whose average sales top $500,000 annually. Profile of Meineke is also included.

32106 ■ *"Revel in Riches!" in Small Business Opportunities (May 2008)*
Pub: Harris Publications Inc.
Description: Profile of Proforma, a business-to-business franchise firm providing print and promotional products.

32107 ■ *"Riches In Recreation" in Small Business Opportunities (March 2011)*
Pub: Harris Publications Inc.
Description: Making money is child's play thanks to new gym concept that makes parents and franchisors happy. Profile of Great Play, the franchised children's gym is provided.

32108 ■ *"Savvy Solutions" in Black Enterprise (Vol. 40, July 2010, No. 12, pp. 44)*
Pub: Earl G. Graves Publishing Co. Inc.
Ed: Tennille M. Robinson. **Description:** Advice is offered to an African American interested in starting a franchise operation.

32109 ■ *"Secure Fortune: New Twist In Security: The Marketplace Is Going Digital" in Small Business Opportunities (November 2007)*
Pub: Harris Publications Inc.
Description: Profile of EYESthere, providing digital video security franchise opportunities.

32110 ■ *Start Small, Finish Big*
Pub: Business Plus/Warner Business Books
Ed: Fred DeLuca with John P. Hayes. **Released:** April 2009. **Price:** $16.95. **Description:** Fred DeLuca is profiled; after founding the multi-billion dollar chain of Subway sandwich restaurants, DeLuca is committed to helping microentrepreneurs, people who start successful small businesses with less than $1,000.

32111 ■ *"Stepping Out" in Small Business Opportunities (Get Rich At Home 2010)*
Pub: Harris Publications Inc.
Description: Earn $1 million a year selling flip flops? A Flip Flop Shop franchise will help individuals start their own business.

32112 ■ *"Victoria Colligan; Co-Founder, Ladies Who Launch Inc., 38" in Crain's Cleveland Business (Vol. 28, November 19, 2007, No. 46)*
Pub: Crain Communications, Inc.
Ed: Jay Miller. **Description:** Profile of Victoria Colligan who is the co-founder of Ladies Who Launch Inc., an organization with franchises in nearly 50 cities; the company offers women entrepreneurs workshops and a newsletter to help women balance their businesses with other aspects of their lives. Ms. Colligan found that women were learning about being business owners differently than men and she felt that there was a need to create opportunities for networking for women launching businesses that had more of a lifestyle purpose.

ASSOCIATIONS AND OTHER ORGANIZATIONS

32113 ■ American Association of Franchisees & Dealers (AAFD)
3500 5th Ave.
San Diego, CA 92103
Ph: (619)209-3775
Free: 800-733-9858
Fax: (619)209-3777
Co. E-mail: benefits@aafd.org
URL: http://www.aafd.org
Contact: Peter Hanson, President
Description: Franchisees and business services. **Scope:** A nonprofit organization providing referrals and other member benefits and services for franchisees. **Founded:** 1992. **Publications:** "Nsights the Art of Positive Emotions," Sep-Oct, 2003; "Nsights Understanding Basic Human Behaviors at Work," Aug, 2003; "Nsights Pinkerton," Aug, 2002. **Educational Activities:** Total Quality Franchising (Annual). **Awards:** Fair Franchising Seal (Periodic). **Seminars:** Driving Your Association to the Next Level; Keeping your Association on the Fairway: Re-Model and Re-Imaging in Today's Economy; Avoid being an Association duffer: Recruiting and Retaining Membership Dos and Don'ts!; Clubhouse Chatter: The Most Cost Effective Ways to Communicate.

32114 ■ American Franchisee Association (AFA)
53 W Jackson Blvd., Ste. 1256
Chicago, IL 60604
Ph: (312)431-0545
Fax: (312)431-1469
Co. E-mail: webmasterafa@franchisee.org
URL: http://www.franchisee.org
Contact: Susan P. Kezios, President
Description: Works to promote and enhance the economic interests of small business franchisees; promote the growth and development of members' enterprises; assist in the formation of independent franchisee associations; offer support, assistance, and legal referral services to members. **Scope:** Offers expertise to potential franchise business opportunity buyers. **Founded:** 1993. **Publications:** *E-news* (Monthly); *How to Form an Association.* **Telecommunication Services:** spkezios@franchisee.org.

32115 ■ Canadian Franchise Association (CFA)—Association Canadienne de la Franchise
5399 Eglinton Ave. W, Ste. 116
Toronto, ON, Canada M9C 5K6
Ph: (416)695-2896
Free: 800-665-4232
Fax: (416)695-1950
Co. E-mail: info@cfa.ca
URL: http://www.cfa.ca
Contact: Lorraine Mclachlan, President
Description: Franchise businesses. Represents the shared interests of businesses and professionals active in the Canadian franchise sector. Provides information and guidance to aspiring franchisees. **Scope:** franchising. **Founded:** 1968. **Subscriptions:** 30. **Publications:** *FranchiseCanada* (Bimonthly). **Awards:** Award of Excellence (Annual).

32116 ■ *FranchiseCanada*
5399 Eglinton Ave. W, Ste. 116
Toronto, ON, Canada M9C 5K6
Ph: (416)695-2896
Free: 800-665-4232
Fax: (416)695-1950
Co. E-mail: info@cfa.ca
URL: http://www.cfa.ca
Contact: Lorraine Mclachlan, President
Released: Bimonthly **Price:** C$4.99, /issue; C$17.35, /year.

32117 ■ International Franchise Association (IFA)
1501 K St. NW, Ste. 350
Washington, DC 20005
Ph: (202)628-8000
Fax: (202)628-0812
Co. E-mail: ifa@franchise.org
URL: http://www.franchise.org
Contact: Jon Luther, Chairman
Description: Firms in 100 countries utilizing the franchise method of distribution for goods and services in all industries. **Founded:** 1960. **Publications:** *Franchising World Magazine* (Bimonthly). **Educational Activities:** Legal Symposium (Annual). **Awards:** Entrepreneur of the Year; Bonny LeVine Award; Hall of Fame Award; Don Debolt Franchising Scholarship Program; Franchise Law Diversity Scholarship Awards.

32118 ■ Women in Franchising (WIF)
53 W Jackson Blvd., Ste. 1157
Chicago, IL 60604
Ph: (312)431-1467
Fax: (312)431-1469
Co. E-mail: spkezios@womeninfranchising.com
URL: http://www.womeninfranchising.com
Contact: Susan P. Kezios, President
Description: Assists women interested in all aspects of franchise business development including those buying a franchised business and those expanding their businesses via franchising. Provides franchise technical assistance in both of these areas. Surveys the industry on the status of women. **Scope:** The firm offers franchise consulting services for women and minorities interested in becoming franchisees or franchisors. Also Offers a number of consulting services including presenting workshops and seminars that teach prospective franchisees the skills and knowledge needed to evaluate, finance and purchase a franchise, providing one-on-one assistance to persons considering buying a franchise by conducting a UFOC (Uniform Franchise Offering Circular) Review and feasibility studies. Provides a variety of tools and one-on-one assistance to prospective franchisees and franchisors including audio seminars, a detailed Operations Manual and sales guidance and national public relations contracts for recruiting franchisees. **Founded:** 1987. **Seminars:** Buying a Franchise: How To Make The Right Choice; Growing Your Business: The Franchise Option.

DIRECTORIES OF EDUCATIONAL PROGRAMS

32119 ■ *Bond's Franchise Guide 2007*
Pub: Source Book Publications
Ed: Robert E. Bond. **Released:** December 2006. **Price:** $34.95. **Description:** Directory of 1,000 franchise opportunities, includes supplemental profiles on franchise attorneys and consultants. The companies are divided into 45 business categories with comparisons.

32120 ■ *Bond's Franchise Guide 2009*
Pub: Source Book Publications
Contact: Stephanie Woo, Editor
Ed: Robert E. Bond, Michelle Yang. **Released:** April 7, 2009. **Description:** Comprehensive directory offering prospective franchise owners a current and detailed profile of 1,000 franchises, as well as supplemental profiles of franchise attorneys and consultants; companies are divided into 45 categories for easy comparison.

REFERENCE WORKS

32121 ■ *"Affordable Financing for Acquisitions" in Franchising World (Vol. 42, September 2010, No. 9, pp. 47)*
Pub: International Franchise Association
Ed: Gene Cerrotti. **Description:** Acquisition pricing is reasonable and interest rates are low and quality franchised resale opportunities are priced 4.5 times EBITDA. Information about Small Business Administration loans is also included.

32122 ■ *"All Fired Up!" in Small Business Opportunities (November 2008)*
Pub: Entrepreneur Media Inc.
Ed: Stan Roberts. **Description:** Profile of Brixx Wood Fired Pizza, which has launched a franchising program due to the amount of interest the company's founders received over the years; franchisees do not need experience in the food industry or pizza restaurant service business in order to open a franchise of their own because all franchisees receive comprehensive training in which they are educated on all of the necessary tools to effectively run the business.

32123 ■ *"All Those Applications, and Phone Users Just Want to Talk" in Advertising Age (Vol. 79, August 11, 2008, No. 31, pp. 18)*
Pub: Crain Communications, Inc.
Ed: Mike Vorhaus. **Description:** Although consumers are slowly coming to text messaging and other data applications, a majority of those Americans surveyed stated that they simply want to use their cell phones to talk and do not care about other activities. Statistical data included.

32124 ■ *"Allied Brands Loses Baskin-Robbins Franchise Down Under" in Ice Cream Reporter (Vol. 23, November 20, 2010, No. 12, pp. 2)*
Pub: Ice Cream Reporter
Description: Dunkin Brands, worldwide franchisor of Baskin-Robbins, terminated the master franchise agreement for Australia held by the food marketer Allied Brands Services.

32125 ■ *"Ampm Focus Has BP Working Overtime; New Convenience-Store Brand Comes to Chicago" in Crain's Chicago Business (April 28, 2008)*
Pub: Crain Communications, Inc.
Ed: John T. Slania. **Description:** Britian's oil giant BP PLC is opening its ampm convenience stores in the Chicago market and has already begun converting most of its 78 Chicago-area gas stations to ampms. The company has also started to franchise the stores to independent operators. BP is promoting the brand with both traditional and unconventional marketing techniques such s real or simulated 3D snacks embedded in bus shelter ads and an in-store Guitar Hero contest featuring finalists from a recent contest at the House of Blues.

32126 ■ *"Area Small Businesses Enjoy Benefits of Bartering Group" in News-Herald (August 22, 2010)*
Pub: The News-Herald
Ed: Brandon C. Baker. **Description:** ITEX is a publicly traded firm that spurs cashless, business-to-business transactions within its own marketplace. Details of the bartering of goods and services within the company are outlined.

32127 ■ *"Attracting Veteran-Franchisees To Your System" in Franchising World (Vol. 42, November 2010, No. 11, pp. 53)*
Pub: International Franchise Association
Ed: Mary Kennedy Thompson. **Description:** As military servicemen and women return home, the franchising industry expects an increase in veterans as franchise owners. The Veterans Transition Franchise Initiative, also known as VetFran, is described.

32128 ■ *"Baby's Room Franchisee Files Bankruptcy" in Crain's Detroit Business (Vol. 25, June 22, 2009, No. 25, pp. 15)*
Pub: Crain Communications Inc. - Detroit
Ed: Gabe Nelson. **Description:** Emery L, a franchisee of USA Baby Inc. and ran the franchised Baby's Room Nursery Furniture stores in the area has filed for bankruptcy. Details of the bankruptcy are included.

32129 ■ *"Bank Forces Brooke Founder To Sell His Holdings" in The Business Journal-Serving Metropolitan Kansas City (October 10, 2008)*
Pub: American City Business Journals, Inc.
Ed: James Dornbrook. **Description:** Robert Orr who is the founder of Brooke Corp., a franchise of insurance agencies, says that he was forced to sell virtually all of his stocks in the company by creditors. First United Bank held the founder's stock as collateral for two loans worth $5 million and $7.9 million, which were declared in default in September 2008. Details of the selling of the company's stocks are provided.

32130 ■ *"Bankruptcy Claims Brooke, Gives Franchisees Hope" in The Business Journal-Serving Metropolitan Kansas City (October 31, 2008)*
Pub: American City Business Journals, Inc.
Ed: James Dornbrook; Steve Vockrodt. **Description:** Insurer Brooke Corp. was required to file for Chapter 11 bankruptcy for a deal to sell all of its assets to businessmen Terry Nelson and Lysle Davidson. The new Brooke plans to share contingency fees with franchisees. The impacts of the bankruptcy case on Brooke franchisees are discussed.

32131 ■ *"Bark Up The Right Tree" in Small Business Opportunities (Winter 2009)*
Pub: Entrepreneur Press
Contact: Perlman Neil, President
Description: Profile of Central Bark, a daycare company catering to pets that offers franchise opportunities and is expanding rapidly despite the economic downturn; the company's growth strategy is also discussed.

32132 ■ *"Baskin-Robbins Expanding to South Texas" in Ice Cream Reporter (Vol. 23, July 20, 2010, No. 8, pp. 4)*
Pub: Ice Cream Reporter
Description: Baskin-Robbins will develop six new shops in south Texas after signing agreements with two franchisees.

32133 ■ *"Baskin-Robbins: New in U.S., Old in Japan" in Ice Cream Reporter (Vol. 23, August 20, 2010, No. 9, pp. 2)*
Pub: Ice Cream Reporter
Description: Baskin-Robbins is celebrating its first franchise in Japan.

32134 ■ *"Best Practices: Developing a Rewards Program" in Franchising World (Vol. 42, September 2010, No. 9, pp. 13)*
Pub: International Franchise Association
Ed: Leah Templeton. **Description:** Rewards for a job well done are examined in order to recognize franchisees for outstanding performance. Ways to customize a rewards program are outlined.

32135 ■ *"BK Franchisees Lose Sleep Over Late-Night Rule" in Advertising Age (Vol. 79, August 11, 2008, No. 31, pp. 1)*
Pub: Crain Communications, Inc.
Ed: Emily Bryson York. **Description:** Burger King's corporate headquarters mandates that franchisees remain open until at least 2 a.m. Three Miami operators have filed a lawsuit that alleges the extended hours can be dangerous, do not make money and overtax the workforce.

32136 ■ *"BK Menu Gives Casual Dining Reason to Worry" in Advertising Age (Vol. 79, November 17, 2008, No. 43, pp. 12)*
Pub: Crain Communications, Inc.
Ed: Emily Bryson York. **Description:** Burger King is beginning to compete with such casual dining restaurants as Applebees and the Cheesecake Factory with new premium menu items, including thicker burgers and ribs; statistical data regarding the casual dining segment which continues to fall and Burger King, whose sales continue to rise is included.

32137 ■ *"Blog Buzz Heralds Arrival of IPhone 2.0" in Advertising Age (Vol. 79, June 9, 2008, No. 40, pp. 8)*
Pub: Crain Communications, Inc.
Ed: Abbey Klaasen. **Description:** Predictions concerning the next version of the iPhone include a global-positioning-system technology as well as a configuration to run on a faster, 3G network.

32138 ■ *"Blueprint for Profit: Family-Run Lumberyard Sets Sites On Sales of $100 Million a Year" in Small Business Opportunities (Jan. 2008)*
Pub: Harris Publications Inc.
Ed: Stan Roberts. **Description:** Profile of family-run lumberyard whose owner shares insight into the challenges of competing with big box operations like Home Depot and Lowe's.

32139 ■ *Bond's Franchise Guide 2007*
Pub: Source Book Publications
Contact: Stephanie Woo, Editor
Ed: Robert E. Bond. **Released:** December 2006. **Price:** $34.95. **Description:** Comprehensive directory of franchise opportunities, divided into 45 categories.

32140 ■ *"Bookkeeping Service Opens First Sacramento Franchise" in Sacramento Bee (April 13, 2011)*
Pub: Sacramento Bee
Ed: Mark Glover. **Description:** Franchise bookkeeping service called BookKeeping Express opened its new office in Roseville, California; its first shop in the area.

32141 ■ *"Boosting Your Merchant Management Services With Wireless Technology" in Franchising World (Vol. 42, August 2010, No. 8, pp. 27)*
Pub: International Franchise Association
Ed: Michael S. Slominski. **Description:** Franchises should have the capability to accept credit cards away from their businesses. This technology will increase sales.

32142 ■ *"Breadwinner Tries on Designer Jeans" in Houston Business Journal (Vol. 40, December 18, 2009, No. 32, pp. 1)*
Pub: American City Business Journals
Ed: Allison Wollam. **Description:** Chuck Cain, the franchisee who introduced Panera Bread to Houston, Texas has partnered with tax accountant Jim Jacobsen to introduce custom-make Tattu Jeans. As more Tattu Jeans outlets are being planned, Cain is using entrepreneurial lessons learned from Panera Bread in the new venture. Both Panera Bread and Tattu Jeans were opened by Cain during economic downturns.

32143 ■ *"Breaking the Mold" in Entrepreneur (Vol. 37, September 2009, No. 9, pp. 87)*
Pub: Entrepreneur Media, Inc.
Ed: Tracy Stapp. **Description:** Profiles of top franchise businesses in the United States are presented. Hey Buddy! Pet Supply Vending Co. offers pet supply vending machines. Home Health Mates, on the other hand, provides professional medical care at home.

32144 ■ *"Brooke Agents Claim Mistreatment" in The Business Journal-Serving Metropolitan Kansas City (Vol. 27, October 24, 2008, No. 7, pp. 1)*
Pub: American City Business Journals, Inc.
Ed: James Dornbrook. **Description:** Franchisees of Brooke Corp., an insurance franchise, face uncertainty as their bills remain unpaid and banks threaten to destroy their credit. The company bundled and sold franchisee loans to different banks, but the credit crunch left the company with massive debts and legal disputes.

32145 ■ *"Builders Land Rutenberg Deal" in Charlotte Observer (February 2, 2007)*
Pub: Knight-Ridder/Tribune Business News
Ed: Bob Fliss. **Description:** Jim and Larry Sanders purchased a franchise from builder, Arthur Rutenberg Homes. The brothers will build custom homes in the area.

32146 ■ *"Burritos New Bag for Shopping Developer" in Houston Business Journal (Vol. 40, December 4, 2009, No. 30, pp. 4A)*
Pub: American City Business Journals
Ed: Allison Wollam. **Description:** Houston, Texas-based Rob Johnson is the newest franchisee for Bullritos and plans to open eight area locations to market the quick-casual burrito concept. The former shopping center developer was looking for a new business sector after selling off his shopping center holdings.

32147 ■ *"Carvel Offers Franchisee Discount" in Ice Cream Reporter (Vol. 21, August 20, 2008, No. 9, pp. 2)*
Pub: Ice Cream Reporter
Description: Carvel Ice Cream is offering new franchise opportunities in Florida, New Jersey, and New York. The company will offer incentive for new franchise owners.

32148 ■ *"Cold Stone Creamery" in Ice Cream Reporter (Vol. 22, January 20, 2009, No. 2, pp. 8)*
Pub: Ice Cream Reporter
Description: Franchise News reports that Cold Stone Creamery is looking for master franchisees to support its expansion into the North German market. The report notes that following its successful launch in Denmark, the firm is also preparing for expansion into France.

32149 ■ *The Commonsense Way to Build Wealth: One Entrepreneur Shares His Secrets*
Pub: Griffin Publishing Group
Ed: Jack Chou. **Released:** September 2004. **Price:** $19.95. **Description:** Entrepreneurial tips to accumulate wealth, select the proper business or franchise, choose and manage rental property, and how to negotiate a good lease.

32150 ■ *"Community Commitment Safeguards Franchising Industry" in Franchising World (Vol. 42, November 2010,*

No. 11, pp. 38)
Pub: International Franchise Association
Description: Individuals who are dedicated to committing time and resources to bring to the attention of legislators those laws and proposals affecting franchise small businesses are highlighted in a monthly format.

32151 ■ *"Controlling Costs: Update Your Information Technology Program" in Franchising World (Vol. 42, August 2010, No. 8, pp. 18)*
Pub: International Franchise Association
Ed: Jeff Dumont. **Description:** It is imperative for any franchise to understand its technology needs in order to control costs. Needs analysis; creating a Request for Proposal; and information regarding the choices between renting, buying or building technology are covered. Relationship contingency in franchised organizations is also covered.

32152 ■ *"Convention Budgeting Best Practice" in Franchising World (Vol. 42, November 2010, No. 11, pp. 11)*
Pub: International Franchise Association
Contact: Stephen J. Caldeira, Chief Executive Officer
E-mail: scaldeira@franchise.org
Ed: Steve Friedman. **Description:** Franchise conventions can offer benefits to both franchisor and franchisee in terms of culture-building, professional education and networking. However, these conventions can be costly. Tips for planning a successful franchising convention on a budget are outlined.

32153 ■ *"Creative In-Sourcing Boosts Franchisee Performance" in Franchising World (Vol. 42, September 2010, No. 9, pp. 16)*
Pub: International Franchise Association
Ed: Daniel M. Murphy. **Description:** Operational training and support is usually provided by franchisors. To be successful in this process it is important to balance the reality of limited financial and human resources.

32154 ■ *"Credit Crunch Takes Bite Out Of McDonald's" in Advertising Age (Vol. 79, September 29, 2008, No. 36, pp. 1)*
Pub: Crain Communications, Inc.
Ed: Emily Bryson York. **Description:** McDonald's will delay its launch of coffee bars inside its restaurants due to the banking crisis which has prompted Bank of America to halt loans to the franchise chains.

32155 ■ *"Culture, Community and Chicken Fingers" in Entrepreneur (Vol. 37, July 2009, No. 7, pp. 96)*
Pub: Entrepreneur Media, Inc.
Ed: Jason Daley. **Description:** Raising Cane's Chicken Fingers founder Todd Graves shares his experiences in running the company - from getting funding to plans for company. Graves believes that the company wants franchisees to live and breathe the brand, and that the key to its success is doing one thing and doing it right. Cane's Pillar Program, a financial support program for franchisees, is also discussed.

32156 ■ *"Customer Loyalty: Making Your Program Excel" in Franchising World (Vol. 42, August 2010, No. 8, pp. 47)*
Pub: International Franchise Association
Ed: Steve Baxter. **Description:** Customer loyalty is key to any franchise operation's growth. Tips for identifying preferred customers are outlined.

32157 ■ *"Day Care for Affluent Drawing a Crowd" in Business First Columbus (Vol. 24, August 15, 2008, No. 52, pp. 1)*
Pub: American City Business Journals
Ed: Carrie Ghose. **Description:** Day care centers for affluent families have grown in popularity in Columbus, Ohio. Primrose Schools Franchising Company has opened three such schools in the area. Statistical data included.

32158 ■ *"Daycare Dollars" in Small Business Opportunities (Winter 2009)*
Pub: Entrepreneur Media Inc.
Description: Profile of Maui Playcare, a franchise that provides parents drop-in daycare for their children without having to purchase a membership, make reservations or pay costly dues; the company is expanding beyond its Hawaiian roots onto the mainland and is expected to have between 40 and 50 locations signed by the end of 2010.

32159 ■ *"Dunkin' Donuts Franchise Looking Possible for 2011" in Messenger-Inquirer (January 2, 2010)*
Pub: Messenger-Inquirer
Ed: Joy Campbell. **Description:** Dunkin' Donuts has approved expansion of their franchises in the Owensboro, Kentucky region.

32160 ■ *The E Myth Revisited: Why Most Small Businesses Don't Work and What to Do*
Pub: HarperCollins Publishers
Ed: Michael E. Gerber. **Released:** January 18, 2010. **Price:** $11.10. **Description:** The book dispels the myths surrounding starting a business and shows how traditional assumptions can get in the way of running a small company. Topics cover entrepreneurship from infancy to growth and covers franchising.

32161 ■ *"Eat Up!" in Entrepreneur (Vol. 36, April 2008, No. 4, pp. 104)*
Pub: Entrepreneur Media, Inc.
Ed: Tracy Stapp. **Description:** Provides a list of the top restaurant franchises. The restaurant franchises presented are picked out from the 2008 Franchise 500 ranking and are listed according to category.

32162 ■ *"The Economic Loss Rule and Franchise Attorneys" in Franchise Law Journal (Vol. 27, Winter 2008, No. 3, pp. 192)*
Pub: American Bar Association
Contact: Carolyn Lamm, President
Ed: Christian C. Burden, Sean Trende. **Description:** Economic loss rule prohibits recovery of damages in tort when the subject injury is unaccompanied by either property damage or personal injury.

32163 ■ *Entrepreneur Magazine--Franchise 500 Survey Issue*
Pub: Entrepreneur Press
Contact: Perlman Neil, President
URL(s): www.entrepreneur.com. **Ed:** Rieva Lesonsky. **Released:** Annual; Latest edition 2012. **Publication includes:** Listing and ranking of top 500 franchises in the United States and Canada. **Entries include:** Company name, address, and, in tabular form, key statistics. **Arrangement:** Classified by industry and ranking.

32164 ■ *"Explosive Growth: Wings Over To Triple In Size By 2010" in Small Business Opportunities (Fall 2007)*
Pub: Harris Publications Inc.
Ed: Michael L. Corne. **Description:** Profile of Wings Over, a franchised chain of restaurants offering chicken wings in 22 flavors; all items are cooked to order.

32165 ■ *"Fashion Forward - Frugally" in Entrepreneur (Vol. 37, July 2009, No. 7, pp. 18)*
Pub: Entrepreneur Media, Inc.
Ed: Jason Daley. **Description:** Staci Deal, a Fayetteville-based franchisee of fashion brand Plato's Closet, shares her experiences on the company's growth. Deal believes that the economy, and the fact that Fayetteville is a college town, played a vital role in boosting the used clothing store's popularity. Her thoughts on being a young business owner, and the advantages of running a franchise are also given.

32166 ■ *"Fighting Detroit" in Baltimore Business Journal (Vol. 27, January 22, 2010, No. 38, pp. 1)*
Pub: American City Business Journals
Ed: Daniel J. Sernovitz. **Description:** Baltimore, Maryland-based car dealers could retrieve their franchises from car manufacturers, Chrysler LLC and General Motors Corporation, through a forced arbitration. A provision in a federal budget mandates the arbitration. The revoking of franchises has been attributed to the car manufacturers' filing of bankruptcy protection.

32167 ■ *"First Franchising Census Report Highlights Industry's Economic Role" in Franchising World (Vol. 42, November 2010, No. 11, pp. 41)*
Pub: International Franchise Association
Ed: John Reynolds. **Description:** Franchise businesses accounted for 10.5 percent of businesses with paid employees in the year 2007.

32168 ■ *"Fiscally Fit" in Entrepreneur (Vol. 37, October 2009, No. 10, pp. 130)*
Pub: Entrepreneur Media, Inc.
Ed: Jason Daley. **Description:** Landrie Peterman, owner of an Anytime Fitness franchise in Oregon, describes how she turned her business around. The franchise, located in an industrial park, saw growth after six months with the help of corporate clients.

32169 ■ *"Former Chrysler Dealers Build New Business Model" in Crain's Detroit Business (Vol. 25, June 22, 2009, No. 25, pp. 3)*
Pub: Crain Communications Inc. - Detroit
Ed: Daniel Duggan. **Description:** Joe Ricci is one of 14 Detroit area dealerships whose franchises have been terminated. Ricci and other Chrysler dealers in the area are starting new businesses or switching to new franchises.= Ricci's All American Buyer's Service will be located in Dearborn and will sell only used cars.

32170 ■ *Franchise Handbook*
Pub: Enterprise Magazines Inc.
Contact: Maria A. Lahm, Chief Executive Officer
E-mail: maria@franchisehandbook.com
URL(s): www.franchisehandbook.com. **Ed:** Michael J. McDermott. **Released:** Quarterly; Latest edition 2012. **Price:** $6.99, Single issue; $22.95, Individuals 1 year subscription (4 issues); $42.95, Individuals 2 years (4 issues); $60.95, Individuals 3 years (4 issues). **Covers:** Firms offering franchises. **Entries include:** Franchisor name, headquarters address, phone, president or other contact, description of operation, number of franchises, year founded, and equity capital needed, financial assistance available, training provided, managerial assistance available. **Arrangement:** Classified by line of business, alphabetical. **Indexes:** Franchising company name.

32171 ■ *"Franchise Law in China: Law, Regulations, and Guidelines" in Franchise Law Journal (Vol. 27, Summer 2007, No. 1, pp. 57)*
Pub: American Bar Association
Contact: Carolyn Lamm, President
Ed: Paul Jones, Erik Wulff. **Description:** Issues faced by foreign franchising are discussed, with a focus on China.

32172 ■ *"Franchisees Lose Battle Against BK" in Advertising Age (Vol. 79, June 2, 2008, No. 22, pp. 46)*
Pub: Crain Communications, Inc.
Ed: Emily Bryson York. **Description:** Burger King has had continuing litigation with former franchisees from New York, Luan and Elizabeth Sadik, who claim that Burger King's double cheeseburger, along with additional problems, created the environment for their eventual insolvency. Burger King has since terminated its test of selling the double cheeseburger for $1, although the company declined to comment on the reason for this decision.

32173 ■ *"Franchises with an Eye on Chicago" in Crain's Chicago Business (Vol. 34, March 14, 2011, No. 11, pp. 20)*
Pub: Crain Communications Inc.
Description: Profiles of franchise companies seeking franchisees for the Chicago area include: Extreme Pita, a sandwich shop; Hand and Stone, offering massage, facial and waxing services; Molly Maid, homecleaning service; Primrose Schools, private accredited schools for children 6 months to 6 hears and after-school programs; Protect Painters, residential

and light-commercial painting contractor; and Wingstop, a restaurant offering chicken wings in nine flavors, fries and side dishes.

32174 ■ *"Franchising Lures Boomers" in Business Journal-Portland (Vol. 24, November 9, 2007, No. 36, pp. 1)*
Pub: American City Business Journals, Inc.
Ed: Wendy Culverwell. **Description:** Popularity of franchising has increased, and investors belonging to the baby boom generation contribute largely to this growth. The number of aging baby boomers is also increasing, particularly in Oregon, which means further growth of franchises can be expected. Reasons why franchising is a good investment for aging baby boomers are given.

32175 ■ *"Franchising's Green Scene" in Entrepreneur (Vol. 37, August 2009, No. 8, pp. 85)*
Pub: Entrepreneur Media, Inc.
Ed: Gwen Moran. **Description:** Trends in favor of environmentally friendly franchises have been growing for about 25 years but have now become mainstream. The challenges for a prospective green franchisee is that these companies may be tricky to evaluate and they need to ask franchisors a lot of questions to weed out ones that falsely claim to be green.

32176 ■ *"Fries With That?" in Canadian Business (Vol. 81, September 29, 2008, No. 16, pp. 33)*
Pub: Rogers Media Ltd.
Ed: Calvin Leung. **Description:** Profile of Toronto-based New York Fries, which has four stores in South Korea, is planning to expand further as well as into Hong Kong and Macau; the company also has a licensee in the United Arab Emirates whom is also planning to expand.

32177 ■ *"From War Zone to Franchise Zone" in Entrepreneur (Vol. 37, August 2009, No. 8, pp. 104)*
Pub: Entrepreneur Media, Inc.
Ed: Jason Daley. **Description:** Ross Paterson says that he realized that the material he used in the Growth Coach franchise could give the people of Afghanistan the systematic model they need. Paterson says that the Afghans are very business-oriented people but that they work in a different system than Americans.

32178 ■ *"George Cohon" in Canadian Business (Vol. 79, November 20, 2006, No. 23, pp. 70)*
Pub: Rogers Media
Ed: Zena Olijnyk. **Description:** George Cohon, the founder of McDonald's in Canada and Russia, speaks about the Canadian market and the experience of starting McDonald's in Canada.

32179 ■ *"Getting In On the Ground Floor" in Entrepreneur (Vol. 37, September 2009, No. 9, pp. 90)*
Pub: Entrepreneur Media, Inc.
Description: Franchise businesses in the United States are listed. Franchise services are mentioned. Statistical data and contact information included.

32180 ■ *"The Global Economy, the Labor Force and Franchising's Future" in Franchising World (Vol. 42, September 2010, No. 9, pp. 35)*
Pub: International Franchise Association
Ed: Jeffrey A. Rosensweig. **Description:** Point forecasting and the methodology called scenario analysis are presented looking at the global economy and future of franchising in the U.S. and abroad.

32181 ■ *"GM's Decision to Boot Dealer Prompts Sale" in Baltimore Business Journal (Vol. 27, November 6, 2009, No. 26, pp. 1)*
Pub: American City Business Journals
Ed: Daniel J. Sernovitz. **Description:** General Motors Corporation's (GM) decision to strip Baltimore's Anderson Automotive Group Inc. of its GM franchise has prompted the owner, Bruce Mortimer, to close the automotive dealership and sell the land to a developer. The new project could make way for new homes, a shopping center and supermarket.

32182 ■ *"Golden Spoon Accelerates Expansion Here and Abroad" in Ice Cream Reporter (Vol. 22, December 20, 2008, No. 1, pp. 2)*
Pub: Ice Cream Reporter
Description: Golden Spoon frozen yogurt franchise chain is developing 35 more locations in the Phoenix, Arizona area along with plans to open a store in Japan.

32183 ■ *"Ground Floor Opportunity" in Small Business Opportunities (July 2008)*
Pub: Entrepreneur Press
Contact: Perlman Neil, President
Description: Profile of Doug Disney, the founder of the booming franchise Tile Outlet Always in Stock, which sells ceramic and porcelain tile and stone products at wholesale prices; Disney found inspiration in a book he read in two days and that motivated him to expand his venture into a huge franchise opportunity.

32184 ■ *"Haagen-Dazs Recruits Shop Owners through Facebook" in Ice Cream Reporter (Vol. 23, November 20, 2010, No. 12, pp. 1)*
Pub: Ice Cream Reporter
Description: Haagen-Dazs Shoppe Company is using Facebook, the leading social media, to recruit new franchises.

32185 ■ *"Happy Trails: RV Franchiser Gives Road Traveling Enthusiasts a Lift" in Black Enterprise (Vol. 38, July 2008, No. 12, pp. 47)*
Pub: Earl G. Graves Publishing Co. Inc.
Ed: Tamara E. Holmes. **Description:** Overview of Bates International Motor Home Rental Systems Inc., a growing franchise that gives RV owners the chance to rent out their big-ticket purchases to others when they are not using them; Sandra Williams Bate launched the company as a franchise in July 1997 and now has a fleet of 30 franchises across the country. She expects the company to reach 2.2 million for 2008 due to a marketing initiative that will expand the company's presence.

32186 ■ *"Hospitals Face Big Whammy From State Fees" in Business Courier (Vol. 26, October 2, 2009, No. 23, pp. 1)*
Pub: American City Business Journals, Inc.
Ed: James Ritchie. **Description:** Ohio hospitals are facing losses of nearly $145 million in franchise fees which are set to be levied by the state. Ohio hospitals will be responsible for a total of $718 million franchise fees as required by 2010-2011 state budget but will recover only 80 percent of the amount in increased Medicaid fees. Possible effects of anticipated losses to Ohio hospitals are examined.

32187 ■ *"Hyannis Mercedes Franchise Sold" in Cape Cod Times (December 2, 2010)*
Pub: Cape Cod Times
Ed: Sarah Shemkus. **Description:** Trans-Atlantic Motors franchise has been sold to Mercedes-Benz of Westwood.

32188 ■ *"IFA-AAG Professional Athlete Franchise Summit Scores" in Franchising World (Vol. 42, August 2010, No. 8, pp. 56)*
Pub: International Franchise Association
Ed: Miriam L. Brewer. **Description:** The first International Franchise Association-Allied Athlete Group Franchise summit spotlighted athletes turned business owners addressing peers on franchising. The summit is expected to become an annual event.

32189 ■ *"Integrating Your Compliance Program" in Franchising World (Vol. 42, November 2010, No. 11, pp. 49)*
Pub: International Franchise Association
Ed: Melanie Bergeron. **Description:** Compliance is integral to every part of any business operation and it is necessary for a company to make standards and compliance to those standards a priority.

32190 ■ *International Franchise Association--Franchise Opportunities Guide*
Pub: International Franchise Association
Contact: Anne Poodiack, Director
E-mail: apoodiack@franchise.org
URL(s): www.franchise.org. **Released:** Semiannual; October and April; Latest edition 2009. **Price:** $20, Nonmembers plus $10.00 shipping; $12, Members plus $10.00 shipping. **Covers:** Over 5,000 companies offering franchises. **Entries include:** Company name, address, phone, type of business, contact, number of franchised and company-owned outlets, years in business, qualifications expected of prospective franchisees, investment required, training & support provided. **Arrangement:** Classified.

32191 ■ *"Iowa Tax Case Could Cost Nation's Franchises" in Franchising World (Vol. 42, September 2010, No. 9, pp. 38)*
Pub: International Franchise Association
Ed: Bruce A. Ackerman, Adam B. Thimmesch. **Description:** Ruling by the Iowa Supreme Court could have a financial impact on franchisors across the U.S. Iowa asserted that Kentucky Fried Chicken is subject to Iowa corporate income tax based solely on the fact that it received royalties from franchises in the state.

32192 ■ *"IPhone 3G" in Advertising Age (Vol. 79, November 17, 2008, No. 43, pp. 15)*
Pub: Crain Communications, Inc.
Ed: Beth Snyder Bulik. **Description:** Review of Apple's new iPhone 3G which includes the addition of smart-phone applications as well as a price drop; the new functionalities as well as the lower price seems to be paying off for Apple who reported sales of 6.9 million iPhones in its most recent quarter, in which the 3G hit store shelves.

32193 ■ *"Learn New Ideas from Experienced Menu Makers" in Nation's Restaurant News (Vol. 45, June 27, 2011, No. 13, pp. 82)*
Pub: Penton Media Inc.
Contact: John French, President
Ed: Nancy Kruse. **Description:** National Restaurant Association Restaurant, Hotel-Motel Show featured the Food Truck Spot, a firm committed to all aspects of mobile catering, foodtruck manufacturers, leasers of fully equipped truck and a food-truck franchising group.

32194 ■ *"Local Firm Snaps up 91 Area Pizza Huts" in Orlando Business Journal (Vol. 26, January 8, 2010, No. 32, pp. 1)*
Pub: American City Business Journals
Ed: Alexis Muellner, Anjali Fluker. **Description:** Orlando, Florida-based CFL Pizza LLC bought the 91 Orlando-area Pizza Hut restaurants for $35 million from parent company Yum! Brands Inc. CFL Pizza plans to distribute parts of the business to Central Florida vendors and the first business up for grabs is the advertising budget.

32195 ■ *"Making Automated Royalty Payments Work for Your Franchise" in Franchising World (Vol. 42, October 2010, No. 10, pp. 30)*
Pub: International Franchise Association
Ed: J.P. O'Brien. **Description:** In the past, royalty payments were sent by franchisees through regular postal mail and accompanied by a single slip of paper with handwritten notes indicating the month's revenue numbers and royalty amounts.

32196 ■ *"Marketers Push for Mobile Tuesday as the New Black Friday" in Advertising Age (Vol. 79, December 1, 2008, No. 44, pp. 21)*
Pub: Crain Communications, Inc.
Ed: Natalie Zmuda. **Description:** Marketers are using an innovative approach in an attempt to stimulate business on the Tuesday following Thanksgiving by utilizing consumer's cell phones to alert them of sales or present them with coupons for this typically slow retail business day; with this campaign both advertisers and retailers are hoping to start Mobile Tuesday, another profitable shopping day in line with Black Friday and Cyber Monday.

32197 ■ *"Mattel's Got a Monster Holiday Hit, But Will Franchise Have Staying Power?" in Advertising Age (Vol. 81, December 6, 2010, No. 43)*
Pub: Crain Communications, Inc.
Ed: Beth Snyder Bulik. **Description:** Monster High transmedia play expands beyond dolls to merchandise, apparel and entertainment.

32198 ■ *"Maximize Your Marketing Results In a Down Economy" in Franchising World (Vol. 42, November 2010, No. 11, pp. 45)*
Pub: International Franchise Association
Ed: Loren Rakich. **Description:** Strategies to help any franchisee to maximize their marketing efforts in a slow economy are outlined.

32199 ■ *"MBA Project Turns on Tastebuds" in The Business Journal - Serving Phoenix and the Valley of the Sun (Vol. 28, August 15, 2008, No. 50)*
Pub: American City Business Journals, Inc.
Ed: Angela Gonzales. **Description:** Amol Khade, Venkat Nallapati and Govind Arora, master of businesss administration graduates from Thunderbird School of Global Management, have opened an Indian restaurant, called The Daba, in Tempe, Arizona. The Indian name of the restaurant means 'a place for travelers to stop for rest and food'. Franchise plans for the restaurant are discussed.

32200 ■ *"McD's Dollar-Menu Fixation Sparks Revolt" in Advertising Age (Vol. 79, June 2, 2008, No. 22, pp. 1)*
Pub: Crain Communications, Inc.
Ed: Emily Bryson York. **Description:** McDonald's franchisees say that low-cost dollar-menu offerings are impacting their bottom line and many have discontinued the dollar-menu altogether due to rising commodity costs, an increase in minimum wage and consumers trading down to the lower-price items.

32201 ■ *"McD's Picks a Soda Fight; Takes on 7-Eleven With $1 Pop as Economy Softens" in Crain's Chicago Business (April 14, 2008)*
Pub: Crain Communications, Inc.
Ed: David Sterrett. **Description:** McDonald's Corp. is urging franchise owners to slash prices on large soft drinks to one dollar this summer to win customers from convenience store chains like 7-Eleven.

32202 ■ *"McD's Tries to Slake Consumer Thirst for Wider Choice of Drinks" in Advertising Age (Vol. 79, June 9, 2008, No. 23, pp. 1)*
Pub: Crain Communications, Inc.
Ed: Natalie Zmuda; Emily Bryson York. **Description:** McDonald's is testing the sale of canned and bottled drinks in about 150 locations in an attempt to offer more options to consumers who are going elsewhere for their beverage choices.

32203 ■ *"McD's Warms Up For Olympics Performance" in Advertising Age (Vol. 79, July 7, 2008, No. 26, pp. 8)*
Pub: Crain Communications, Inc.
Description: Overview of McDonald's marketing plans for the company's sponsorship of the Olympics which includes a website, an alternate-reality game, names featured on U.S. athletes and on-the-ground activities.

32204 ■ *"Menchie's Tops Restaurant Business' Future 50 List" in Ice Cream Reporter (Vol. 23, August 20, 2010, No. 9, pp. 4)*
Pub: Ice Cream Reporter
Description: Menchie's, frozen yogurt shop, announced it placed first in the Restaurant Business Magazine's Future 50, ranking the franchise the fastest-growing in the food industry.

32205 ■ *"Mount Laurel Woman Launches Venture Into Children's Used Clothing" in Philadelphia Inquirer (September 17, 2010)*
Pub: Philadelphia Media Network
Ed: Maria Panaritis. **Description:** Profile of Jennifer Frisch, stay-at-home mom turned entrepreneur. Frisch started a used-clothing store Once Upon a Child after opening her franchised Plato's Closet, selling unwanted and used baby clothing and accessories at her new shop, while offering used merchandise to teens at Plato's Closet.

32206 ■ *"A New Way to Arrive in Style" in Inc. (Vol. 33, September 2011, No. 7, pp. 54)*
Pub: Inc. Magazine
Ed: Matthew Rist. **Description:** EagleRider is a franchise offering various two-wheeled rentals, including BMWs and Harley-Davidsons at more than 100 locations worldwide.

32207 ■ *"New Ways To Think About Data Loss: Data Loss Is Costly and Painful" in Franchising World (Vol. 42, August 2010, No. 8, pp. 21)*
Pub: International Franchise Association
Ed: Ken Colburn. **Description:** Information for maintaining data securely for franchised organizations, including smart phones, tablets, copiers, computers and more is given.

32208 ■ *"NexCen Brands Sells Chains and Will Liquidate" in Ice Cream Reporter (Vol. 23, August 20, 2010, No. 9, pp. 1)*
Pub: Ice Cream Reporter
Description: NexCen Brands is closing the sale of its franchise businesses, which include the frozen dessert chains MaggieMoo's and Marbel Slab Creamery, to Global Franchise Group.

32209 ■ *"NFL Labor, Legal Issues Hang Over Detroit Lions' Rebuilding Efforts" in Crain's Detroit Business (Vol. 26, January 11, 2010, No. 2)*
Pub: Crain Communications Inc.
Ed: Bill Shea. **Description:** Overview of the possible outcomes regarding labor talks with Detroit Lion's players as well as the outcome of a U.S. Supreme Court decision that could boost franchise values but at the expense of fans and corporate sponsors.

32210 ■ *"Ohio Franchise Buys 21 Jacksonville Area Papa John's" in Florida Times-Union (December 20, 2010)*
Pub: Florida Times-Union
Ed: Mark Basch. **Description:** Ohio-based Papa John's pizza franchise acquired 21 of the restaurants in Duval, Clay and St. Johns counties in Jacksonville, Florida.

32211 ■ *"Open Price Agreements: Good Faith Pricing in the Franchise Relationship" in Franchise Law Journal (Vol. 27, Summer 2007, No. 1)*
Pub: American Bar Association
Contact: Carolyn Lamm, President
Ed: Douglas C. Berry, David M. Byers, Daniel J. Oates. **Description:** Open price term contracts are important to franchise businesses. Details of open price contracts are examined.

32212 ■ *"Opportunity Knocks" in Small Business Opportunities (September 2008)*
Pub: Entrepreneur Media Inc.
Description: Profile of YourOffice USA, a franchise that provides home-based and small businesses cost-effective and efficient support through 'virtual' offices that are available as much or as little as the client needs it; they also supply necessary tools such as a professional business address, private mailbox service, personalized telephone answering and more that supports clients who want to look, act and operate with an advanced business image.

32213 ■ *"Ordering Pizza Hut From Your Facebook Page?" in Advertising Age (Vol. 79, November 10, 2008, No. 42, pp. 50)*
Pub: Crain Communications, Inc.
Ed: Emily Bryson York. **Description:** Fast-food chains are experimenting with delivery/takeout services via social networks such as Facebook and iPhone applications. This also allows the chains to build valuable databases of their customers.

32214 ■ *"Ownership Form, Managerial Incentives, and the Intensity of Rivalry" in Academy of Management Journal (Vol. 50, No. 4, August 2007)*
Pub: Academy of Management
Contact: Ming-Jer Chen, President
Ed: Govert Vroom, Javier Gimeno. **Description:** Ways in which differences in ownership form between franchised and company-owned units alter managerial incentives and competitive pricing in different oligopolistic contexts, or following competitors into foreign markets, is presented.

32215 ■ *"Personal Pizza Goes Franchise Route" in Atlanta Journal-Constitution (December 22, 2010)*
Pub: Atlanta Journal-Constitution
Ed: Bob Townsend. **Description:** Your Pie, developer of the personal-size pizza franchise concept is profiled.

32216 ■ *"A Practical Approach to Addressing Holdover Ex-Franchisee Trademark Issues" in Franchise Law Journal (Vol. 27, Summer 2007, No. 1)*
Pub: American Bar Association
Contact: Carolyn Lamm, President
Ed: Christopher P. Bussert, William M. Bryner. **Description:** Franchisor-franchisee relationships can become legally complicated when they are terminated. Laws governing trademarks and other proprietary materials are examined.

32217 ■ *"Prepaid Cards and State Unclaimed Property Laws" in Franchise Law Journal (Vol. 27, Summer 2007, No. 1, pp. 23)*
Pub: American Bar Association
Contact: Carolyn Lamm, President
Ed: Phillip W. Bohl, Kathryn J. Bergstrom, Kevin J. Moran. **Description:** Unredeemed value of electronic prepaid stored-value credit cards for retail purchases is known as breakage. Laws governing unclaimed property as it relates to these gift cards is covered.

32218 ■ *"The Profitability of Mobility" in Entrepreneur (Vol. 37, September 2009, No. 9, pp. 98)*
Pub: Entrepreneur Media, Inc.
Ed: John Daley. **Description:** Wireless Zone franchisee Jonah Engler says he manages the business by hiring managers that could do the job. He has given his employees small equity ownership in the company. He also says great service and referrals have contributed to his business' growth.

32219 ■ *"Prominent Hispanic Businessman Signs With Choice Hotels" in Hispanic Business (Vol. 30, March 2008, No. 3, pp. 36)*
Pub: Hispanic Business
Ed: Melinda Burns. **Description:** Chairman of the board of Lopez Food Inc., John C. Lopez signs the agreement with Choice Hotels International to build five new Cambria suites in the USA. This is his first hotel venture and also the first Hispanic franchisee to enter into business with Choice Hotels.

32220 ■ *"Q&A With Devin Ringling: Franchise's Services Go Beyond Elder Care" in Gazette (October 2, 2010)*
Pub: The Gazette
Ed: Bill Radford. **Description:** Profile of franchise, Interim HealthCare, in Colorado Springs, Colorado; the company offers home care services that include wound care and specialized feedings to shopping and light housekeeping. It also runs a medical staffing company that provides nurses, therapists and other health care workers to hospitals, prisons, schools and other facilities.

32221 ■ *"Quiznos Franchisees Walloped by Recession" in Advertising Age (Vol. 79, October 20, 2008, No. 39, pp. 3)*
Pub: Crain Communications, Inc.
Ed: Emily Bryson York. **Description:** While the recession has taken a toll on the entire restaurant industry, a number of Quiznos franchisees claim to have been disproportionately affected due to lackluster marketing, higher-than-average commodity costs, competition with Subway and a premium-pricing structure that is incompatible with a tight economy.

32222 ■ *"Ready for the Back Burner" in Barron's (Vol. 88, March 17, 2008, No. 11, pp. 47)*
Pub: Dow Jones & Company, Inc.
Ed: Vito J. Racanelli. **Description:** McDonald's has promised to return $15 billion to $17 billion to shareholders in 2007-2009 but headwinds are rising for the company. December, 2007 same-store sales were flat and the company's traffic growth in the U.S. is slowing. Its shares are likely to trade in tandem with the market until recession fears recede.

32223 ■ *"Report: McD's Pepsi Score Best With Young Hispanics" in Brandweek (Vol. 49, April 21, 2008, No. 16, pp. 8)*
Pub: VNU Business Media, Inc.
Ed: Della de Lafuente. **Description:** According to a new report, in order to reach Hispanic Gen Yers, marketing strategists need to understand this demographic's 'bi-dentity,' something which has proved an elusive task to many marketers. Another trend is the emergence of Latinas who have careers, as opposed to just jobs. There is an opportunity to tap this new, young and empowered female market with innovative messaging. Statistical data included.

32224 ■ *"Retail Franchises to Start Now" in Entrepreneur (Vol. 37, August 2009, No. 8, pp. 88)*
Pub: Entrepreneur Media, Inc.
Ed: Tracy Stapp. **Description:** Listing of retail franchises is presented and is categorized based on their products sold. The total cost of the franchise and the website are also included as well as additional statistical data.

32225 ■ *"A Road Map to the New FTC Franchise Rule" in Franchise Law Journal (Vol. 27, Fall 2007, No. 2, pp. 105)*
Pub: American Bar Association
Contact: Carolyn Lamm, President
Ed: Gerald C. Wells, Dennis E. Wieczorek. **Description:** Information about the Federal Trade Commission's revised Franchise Rule (16 C.F.R. Part 436 Disclosure Requirements and Prohibitions Concerning Franchising) (the New Rule) which replaces the original 1978 Franchise Rule (the Old Rule) is given; a comprehensive overview of the New Rule and its implications for the franchise industry is included.

32226 ■ *"Rooting for Hispanic Dollars" in Hispanic Business (October 2007, pp. 76, 80)*
Pub: Hispanic Business
Description: Sports franchises are working to gain and retain the Hispanic market.

32227 ■ *"Running the Numbers" in Entrepreneur (Vol. 37, July 2009, No. 7, pp. 87)*
Pub: Entrepreneur Media, Inc.
Ed: Carol Tice. **Description:** Ways in which entrepreneurs can assess if they are ready to be a multi-unit franchisee are presented. Choosing the right locations, knowing how much assistance they can get from the franchisor, and financing are the key considerations when planning additional franchise units. Examples of success in multi-unit operations and multi-unit terms are also presented.

32228 ■ *"Salad Creations To Open 2nd Location" in Crain's Detroit Business (Vol. 24, March 3, 2008, No. 9, pp. 26)*
Pub: Crain Communications Inc. - Detroit
Ed: Brent Snavely. **Description:** Salad Creations, a franchise restaurant that allows customers to create their own salads and also offers soups and sandwiches; Salad Creations plans to open a total of five locations by the end of 2008.

32229 ■ *"SBA Lauds Anchorage DQ Franchise" in Alaska Business Monthly (Vol. 27, October 2011, No. 10, pp. 9)*
Pub: Alaska Business Publishing Company
Ed: Nancy Pounds. **Description:** US Small Business Administration (SBA) honored Greg Todd, operator of four DQ Grill and Chill eateries in Anchorage, Alaska. The firm has created 100 jobs since receiving SBA assistance.

32230 ■ *"Seasonal Franchises" in Franchising World (Vol. 42, August 2010, No. 8, pp. 50)*
Pub: International Franchise Association
Ed: Jennifer Lemcke. **Description:** Seasonal franchises, such as tax businesses can be slow during the summer months. Restaurants are slow during the months of January and February. The various challenges faced by seasonal franchises are examined.

32231 ■ *"Sellers Shift Gears" in Crain's Detroit Business (Vol. 25, June 22, 2009, No. 25, pp. 3)*
Pub: Crain Communications Inc. - Detroit
Description: Of the 14 new car Chrysler dealerships in the Detroit area who had franchises terminated, Joe Ricci of Dearborn will sell used cars at his new business called All American Buyer's Service; Lochmoor Automotive Group in Detroit will focus on Mahindra & Mahindra trucks; Mt. Clemens Dodge, Clinton Township is also selling Mahindra & Mahindra trucks; and Monicatti Chrysler Jeep, Sterling Heights, will offer service along with selling used cars.

32232 ■ *"Setting Out on Your Own? Think Franchises" in Crain's Cleveland Business (Vol. 28, October 8, 2007, No. 40, pp. 20)*
Pub: Crain Communications, Inc.
Description: Franchisers are targeting baby boomers due to their willingness to put up some of their own money to open their own business. According to local franchising expert, Joel Libava, entrepreneurs should expect to pay about 15 to 30 percent of the total cost of starting the franchise out of their own pocket.

32233 ■ *"Shout and Devour" in Tulsa World (November 7, 2009)*
Pub: Tulsa World
Ed: Kyle Arnold. **Description:** Profile of convenience store Shout and Sack whose owners have distanced themselves from the corporate fray of the chain stores by offering homemade lunches served at a counter; the store recently gained national exposure that highlighted the popularity despite a market share heavily dominated by franchises and chains.

32234 ■ *"Silver Dollars" in Small Business Opportunities (September 2008)*
Pub: Entrepreneur Media Inc.
Description: Profile of Always Best Care Senior Services, a franchise created by Michael Newman, which offers non-medical In-Home Care, Personal Emergency Response Systems, and Assisted Living Placement Services to seniors; the company offers franchisees the opportunity to fill what is oftentimes a void for the seniors and their families in the community.

32235 ■ *"Simplifying Social Media for Optimum Results" in Franchising World (Vol. 42, August 2010, No. 8, pp. 12)*
Pub: International Franchise Association
Ed: Paul Segreto. **Description:** Keys to effective technology usage requires the development of an integrated plan, choosing the most complementary tools and implementing well-planned strategies.

32236 ■ *"Skinner's No Drive-Thru CEO" in Crain's Chicago Business (Vol. 31, April 28, 2008, No. 17, pp. 1)*
Pub: Crain Communications, Inc.
Ed: David Sterrett. **Description:** Profile of James Skinner who was named CEO for McDonald's Corp. in November 2004 and has proved to be a successful leader despite the number of investors who doubted him when he came to the position. Mr. Skinner has overseen three years of unprecedented sales growth and launched the biggest menu expansion in 30 years.

32237 ■ *Small Business Desk Reference*
Pub: Penguin Books USA Inc.
Ed: Gene Marks. **Released:** December 2004. **Description:** Comprehensive guide for starting or running a successful small business, focusing on buying a business or franchise, writing a business plan, financial management, accounting, legal issues, human resources management, operations, marketing, sales, customer service, taxes, insurance, and ethics. Information for launching a restaurant, property management firm, retail outlet, consulting firm, and service business is included.

32238 ■ *"Steering Toward Profitability" in Black Enterprise (Vol. 41, December 2010, No. 5, pp. 72)*
Pub: Earl G. Graves Publishing Co. Inc.
Ed: Alan Hughes. **Description:** Systems Electro Coating LLC had to make quick adjustments when auto manufacturers were in a slump. The minority father-daughter team discuss their strategies during the auto industry collapse.

32239 ■ *"Sun Capital Partners Affiliate Acquires Timothy's Coffees" in Miami Daily Business Review (March 26, 2008)*
Pub: ALM Media Inc.
Description: An affiliate of Sun Capital Partners acquired Timothy's Coffees of the World. Timothy's operates and franchises 166 stores offering coffees, muffins, and Michel's Baguette products.

32240 ■ *"Sweet Tea; Neil Golden" in Advertising Age (Vol. 79, November 17, 2008, No. 43, pp. 4)*
Pub: Crain Communications, Inc.
Ed: Emily Bryson York. **Description:** McDonald's launch of iced coffee and sweat tea, which were promoted via price cuts over the summer, helped to boost sales at the fast-food chain.

32241 ■ *"Taco Bell; David Ovens" in Advertising Age (Vol. 79, November 17, 2008, No. 43, pp. S2)*
Pub: Crain Communications, Inc.
Ed: Emily Bryson York. **Description:** Due to the addition of new products such as a low-calorie, low-fat Fresco menu; a fruity iced beverage; and a value initiative, Taco Bell now accounts for half of Yum Brands' profits. The chain has also benefited from a new chief marketing officer, David Ovens, who oversees ad support.

32242 ■ *"Taking the Right Road" in Entrepreneur (Vol. 37, October 2009, No. 10, pp. 104)*
Pub: Entrepreneur Media, Inc.
Ed: Jason Daley. **Description:** Joe Grubb's franchise of BrightStar Healthcare, a home health care provider, in Knoxville, Tennessee has grown into a $1 million business. Grubb, a former sales agent, experienced slow growth for his franchise and had to deal with cash flow issues during its first few months.

32243 ■ *"Tap the iPad and Mobile Internet Device Market" in Franchising World (Vol. 42, September 2010, No. 9, pp. 43)*
Pub: International Franchise Association
Ed: John Thomson. **Description:** The iPad and other mobile Internet devices will help franchise owners interact with customers. It will be a good marketing tool for these businesses.

32244 ■ *"Tasti D-Lite Has Franchise Agreement for Australia" in Ice Cream Reporter (Vol. 23, November 20, 2010, No. 12, pp. 3)*
Pub: Ice Cream Reporter
Description: Tasti D-Lite signed an international master franchise agreement with Friezer Australia Pty. Ltd. and will open 30 units throughout Australia over the next five years.

32245 ■ *"A Team Sport" in Business Courier (Vol. 26, October 2, 2009, No. 23, pp. 1)*
Pub: American City Business Journals, Inc.
Ed: Lisa Biank Fasig. **Description:** Procter & Gamble (P&G) revised the way it works with marketing, design and public relations firms. Creative discussions will be managed by only two representatives, the franchise leader and the brand agency leader in order for P&G to simplify operations as it grows larger and more global.

32246 ■ *"Technology Drivers to Boost Your Bottom Line" in Franchising World (Vol. 42,*

August 2010, No. 8, pp. 15)
Pub: International Franchise Association
Ed: Dan Dugal. **Description:** Technological capabilities are expanding quickly and smart franchises should stay updated on all the new developments, including smart phones, global positioning systems, and social media networks.

32247 ■ *"Thinking Strategically About Technology" in Franchising World (Vol. 42, August 2010, No. 8, pp. 9)*
Pub: International Franchise Association
Ed: Bruce Franson. **Description:** Nearly 25 percent of companies waste money from their technology budget. Most of the budget is spent on non-strategic software. Ways to spend money on technology for any franchise are examined.

32248 ■ *"Tim Hortons Aims for Breakfast Breakout" in Globe & Mail (February 13, 2006, pp. B3)*
Pub: CTVglobemedia Publishing Inc.
Ed: Andy Hoffman. **Description:** Fast food chain Tim Hortons will be launching its new breakfast menu with more combinations that include bacons, eggs and coffee. Tim Horton is subsidiary of Wendy's International Inc and has 290 outlets in America.

32249 ■ *"Top IPhone Apps" in Advertising Age (Vol. 79, December 15, 2008, No. 46, pp. 17)*
Pub: Crain Communications, Inc.
Ed: Marissa Miley. **Description:** Free and low cost applications for the iPhone are described including Evernote, an application that allows users to outsource their memory to keep track of events, notes, ides and more; Handshake, a way for users to exchange business cards and pictures across Wi-Fi and 3G; CityTransit, an interactive map of the New York subway system that uses GPS technology to find nearby stations and also tells the user if a train is out of commission that day; and Stage Hand which allows users to deliver a presentation, control timing and slide order on the spot.

32250 ■ *"Training: an Investment in Performance Improvement" in Franchising World (Vol. 42, September 2010, No. 9, pp. 22)*
Pub: International Franchise Association
Ed: Catherine Monson. **Description:** Advantages of training provided by franchisors that are available to franchisees and their employees is discussed.

32251 ■ *"Tulsa-Based Dollar Thrifty Adds Franchises" in Journal Record (December 7, 2010)*
Pub: Dolan Media Newswires
Ed: D. Ray Tuttle. **Description:** Dollar Thrifty Automotive Group Inc. opened 31 franchise locations in 2010 as part of its expansion plan in the U.S.

32252 ■ *"U-Swirl Added to SBA's Franchise Registry" in Ice Cream Reporter (Vol. 23, September 20, 2010, No. 10, pp. 1)*
Pub: Ice Cream Reporter
Description: Healthy Fast Food Inc., parent to the U-SWIRL Frozen Yogurt cafe chain announced that the U.S. Small Business Administration listed U-SWIRL Frozen Yogurt on its official franchise registry. This move will allow U-SWIRL the benefits of a streamlined review process for SBA financing.

32253 ■ *"U-Swirl To Open in Salt Lake City Metro Market" in Ice Cream Reporter (Vol. 23, November 20, 2010, No. 12, pp. 4)*
Pub: Ice Cream Reporter
Description: Healthy Fast Food Inc., parent company to U-SWIRL International Inc., the owner and franchisor of U-SWIRL Frozen Yogurt cafes signed a franchising area development agreement for the Salt Lake City metropolitan area with Regents Management and will open 5 cafes over a five year period.

32254 ■ *Ultimate Guide to Buying or Selling Your Business*
Pub: Entrepreneur Press
Ed: Ira N. Nottonson. **Released:** September 2004. **Price:** $24.95 (US), $35.95 (Canadian). **Description:** Proven strategies to evaluate, negotiate, and buy or sell a small business. Franchise and family business succession planning is included.

32255 ■ *"Valuation of Intangible Assets in Franchise Companies and Multinational Groups" in Franchise Law Journal (Winter 2008)*
Pub: American Bar Association
Contact: Carolyn Lamm, President
Ed: Bruce S. Schaeffer, Susan J. Robins. **Description:** Intangible assets, also known as intellectual properties are the most valuable assets for companies today. Legal intellectual property issues faced by franchises firms are discussed.

32256 ■ *"V&J Scores Partnership with Shaq" in Business Journal-Milwaukee (Vol. 25, October 12, 2007, No. 2, pp. A1)*
Pub: American City Business Journals, Inc.
Ed: Rich Kirchen. **Description:** O'Neal Franchise Group has agreed to a partnership with V&J Foods of Milwaukee to handle Auntie Anne's shops in New York, South Africa, Michigan, and the Caribbean. V&J O'Neal Enterprises will open six Auntie Anne's soft pretzel shops in Detroit towards the end of 2007. Planned international ventures of the partnership are presented.

32257 ■ *"Visionary Riches" in Small Business Opportunities (Winter 2009)*
Pub: Entrepreneur Press
Contact: Perlman Neil, President
Description: Profile of Sterling Optical, which was included in a recent listing of 25 franchise high performers in The Wall Street Journal and is poised for mega-growth due to its offerings of professional eye exams, impeccable customer service, convenient locations and a great selection of eyewear.

32258 ■ *"V's Barbershop Opening in Bakerview Square in May" in Bellingham Business Journal (Vol. March 2010, pp. 2)*
Pub: Sound Publishing Inc.
Description: Upscale barbershop franchise catering to men, V's Barbershop, will open a new location in Bakerview Square (its first in Washington) in 2010. The new location will include six chairs and will appear like an old-time barbershop with a contemporary flavor featuring real barber chairs, flat-screen TVs, and hot lather shaves using a straight-edge razor.

32259 ■ *"Want Leverage? Multi-Unit Franchisees Deliver Substantial Savings" in Franchising World (Vol. 42, October 2010, No. 10, pp. 39)*
Pub: International Franchise Association
Ed: Aziz Hashim. **Description:** Many retail franchises selling the same product are able to buy in bulk. Volume-buying can save money for any franchise.

32260 ■ *"Wendy's Mulls Total Hortons Selloff" in Globe & Mail (January 7, 2006, pp. B5)*
Pub: CTVglobemedia Publishing Inc.
Ed: Sinclair Stewart; Omar El Akkad. **Description:** The plans of Wendy's International Inc. to spin off Tim Hortons are presented.

32261 ■ *"Wendy's Speeds Up Tim's Spinout" in Globe & Mail (January 11, 2006, pp. B1)*
Pub: CTVglobemedia Publishing Inc.
Ed: Andrew Willis. **Description:** The reasons behind the decision of Wendy's International Inc. to bid Tim Hortons are presented.

32262 ■ *"What Dead Zone?" in Entrepreneur (Vol. 37, October 2009, No. 10, pp. 128)*
Pub: Entrepreneur Media, Inc.
Ed: Jason Daley. **Description:** Joe Purifico, Halloween Adventure franchises co-owner and chief executive officer, discusses the Halloween superstore phenomenon. Malls allow seasonal leasing for Halloween stores due to the high number of customers these stores attract.

32263 ■ *"When Are Sales Representatives Also Franchisees?" in Franchise Law Journal (Vol. 27, Winter 2008, No. 3, pp. 151)*
Pub: American Bar Association
Contact: Carolyn Lamm, President
Ed: John R.F. Baer, David A. Beyer, Scott P. Weber. **Description:** Review of the traditional definitions of sales representatives along with information on how these distribution models could fit into various legal tests for a franchise.

32264 ■ *"When Worlds Collide: The Enforceability of Arbitration Agreements in Bankruptcy" in Franchise Law Journal (Summer 2007)*
Pub: American Bar Association
Contact: Carolyn Lamm, President
Ed: Mark A. Salzberg, Gary M. Zinkgraf. **Description:** Most franchise agreements carry broad arbitration clauses requiring arbitration of nearly all disputes between franchisor and franchisee; how these clauses govern issues of bankruptcy are explored.

32265 ■ *"While Competitors Shut Doors, Subway Is Still Growing" in Advertising Age (Vol. 79, July 21, 2008, No. 28, pp. 4)*
Pub: Crain Communications, Inc.
Ed: Emily Bryson York. **Description:** Subway, the largest fast-food chain, with 22,000 U.S. locations, is adding 800 this year, despite the economic downturn that has caused competitors such as Starbucks to close stores and McDonald's to focus its expansion abroad.

32266 ■ *"Whopper; Russ Klein" in Advertising Age (Vol. 79, November 17, 2008, No. 43, pp. S10)*
Pub: Crain Communications, Inc.
Ed: Emily Bryson York. **Description:** Burger King has seen a double digit increase in the sales of its Whopper hamburger despite the economic recession that has hit many in the restaurant industry particularly hard. For most of the spring, U.S. same-store-sales gains beat McDonald's.

32267 ■ *"Wild-Goose Chaser" in Entrepreneur (Vol. 37, September 2009, No. 9, pp. 96)*
Pub: Entrepreneur Media, Inc.
Ed: Jason Daley. **Description:** Geese Police owner David Marcks says he discovered that trained collies could chase geese off golf courses, which started his business. He gives new franchises two dogs to start their business. The company has fared well even during the economic crisis.

32268 ■ *"Worth His Salt" in Hawaii Business (Vol. 53, January 2008, No. 7, pp. 45)*
Pub: Hawaii Business Publishing
Ed: Jolyn Okimoto Rosa. **Description:** Bryan Zada owns three PretzelMaker franchises, whose total loss amounted to $40,000 in 2003. Zada believes that listening to employees was one of the key steps in turning the business around. The efforts made to improve the franchises' products are also given.

32269 ■ *"Yogun Fruz Adds First Location in Southern New York State" in Ice Cream Reporter (Vol. 23, September 20, 2010, No. 10, pp. 2)*
Pub: Ice Cream Reporter
Description: Yogen Fruz signed a master franchise agreement to expand into the southern counties of New York State. The firm offers a healthy and beneficial option to fast food and typical dessert choices.

TRADE PERIODICALS

32270 ■ *Business Opportunities Journal*
Pub: Business Service Corp.
URL(s): www.boj.com. **Ed:** Mark Adkins. **Released:** Monthly

32271 ■ *Canadian Pizza Magazine*
Pub: Annex Publishing & Printing Inc.
URL(s): www.canadianpizzamag.comwww.annexweb.com/. **Ed:** Laura Aiken. **Released:** 8/yr. **Price:** $18, Canada.

32272 ■ *Franchise News*
Pub: Franchise News
Ed: C. Richey, Editor. **Released:** Quarterly. **Price:** Included in membership. **Description:** Provides information about franchising. Recurring features include letters to the editor, interviews, news of research, a calendar of events, news of educational opportunities, reports of meetings, notices of publications available, and legal and global franchising news.

32273 ■ *Franchising World*
Pub: International Franchise Association
Contact: Stephen J. Caldeira, Chief Executive Officer
E-mail: scaldeira@franchise.org
URL(s): www.franchise.org/. **Released:** Monthly **Price:** $50, Individuals.

VIDEOCASSETTES/ AUDIOCASSETTES

32274 ■ *The Franchising Explosion*
GPN Educational Media
1550 Executive Drive
Elgin, IL 60123
Ph: (402)472-2007
Free: 800-228-4630
Fax: (800)306-2330
Co. E-mail: askgpn@smarterville.com
URL: http://www.shopgpn.com
Released: 1989. **Price:** $29.95. **Description:** The business phenomenon of franchising is explained by the experts at the University of Nebraska-Lincoln. **Availability:** VHS; 3/4 U.

32275 ■ *How to Buy a Franchise*
Chesney Communications
2302 Martin St., Ste. 125
Irvine, CA 92612
Ph: (949)263-5500
Free: 800-223-8878
Fax: (949)263-5506
Co. E-mail: videocc@aol.com
URL: http://www.videocc.com
Released: 1987. **Price:** $39.95. **Description:** Find out how to become a francisee. **Availability:** VHS; 3/4 U.

TRADE SHOWS AND CONVENTIONS

32276 ■ Franchising Conference & Expo
E.J. Krause & Associates, Inc.
6550 Rock Spring Dr., Ste. 500
Bethesda, MD 20817
Ph: (301)493-5500
Fax: (301)493-5705
Co. E-mail: info@ejkrause.com
URL: http://www.ejkrause.com
Contact: Sharon Deutch, Director
E-mail: deutch@ejkrause.com
URL(s): www.franquiciaweb.com. **Frequency:** Annual. **Principal Exhibits:** Franchise systems and conference about purchasing a franchise. **Telecommunication Services:** centro@franquiciaweb.com.

CONSULTANTS

32277 ■ Damas & Associates
6810 S Cedar St., Ste. 2B
Lansing, MI 48911-6961
Ph: (517)694-0910
Fax: (517)694-1377
Contact: Raymond J. Damas, Owner
Scope: Franchise developers and consultants for franchisers in such areas as structuring the franchise, drafting agreements and disclosures statements, registering the franchise offerings where necessary, advising on matters pertaining to anti-trust trade name and trademark protection and rights, and corporate matters, developing marketing materials and operating manuals, and marketing franchises. **Founded:** 1979.

32278 ■ Follow-Up News
185 Pine St., Ste. 818
Manchester, CT 06040-5882
Ph: (860)647-7542
Free: 800-708-0696
Fax: (860)646-6544
Co. E-mail: followupnews@aol.com
URL: http://www.follow-upnewsadvertising.com
Contact: Mark Merrill, Owner
Scope: Offers low cost, low volume, target marketing solutions, to small and medium size businesses that never thought before, they had the time or money to advertise, and implement loyalty, referral, frequency, retention, reference, name recognition, and new customer prospecting programs. **Founded:** 1986. **Special Services:** Database management.

32279 ■ Franchise Architects
250 Parkway Dr., Ste. 150
Lincolnshire, IL 60069
Ph: (847)465-3400
Free: 888-237-2624
Fax: (847)325-5566
Co. E-mail: info@franchisearchitects.com
URL: http://www.franchisearchitects.com
Contact: Craig S. Slavin, President
E-mail: craig@franchisearchitects.com
Scope: Creates and manages indirect channels of distribution, which include franchising, licensing, dealerships and distributorships. Development and consulting services include strategic planning, positioning, naming, creation or refinement of training programs, operational manuals, marketing strategies and collateral brochures; organizational surveys and development; and human resource assessment. Industries served: retail, transportation, food service, technology, service and communications. **Founded:** 1980. **Seminars:** Making the Transition from Entrepreneurial to a Professionally Managed Company; Franchising - Is It for You?; The Franchise Success System.

32280 ■ Franchise Brokers Network
3617 Silverside Rd., Ste. A
Wilmington, DE 19810-5117
Ph: (302)478-0200
Contact: N. Norman Schutzman, President
Scope: Serves companies that interested in expanding their business by way of franchising. Provides all services including feasibility studies, contracts, disclosure statement, brochure, marketing plan, advertising program and a sales organization to bring the franchise to market. Active with manufacturing, sales, service, retail and food and beverage companies. Services individuals who: interested into going into their own business. **Founded:** 1976.

32281 ■ Franchise Developments Inc. (FDI)
5001 Baum Blvd., Ste. 660
Pittsburgh, PA 15213
Ph: (412)687-8484
Free: 800-576-5115
Fax: (412)687-0541
Co. E-mail: franchise-dev@earthlink.net
URL: http://www.franchise-dev.com
Contact: Kenneth Franklin, President
Description: Develop, implement and launch franchise programs. **Scope:** Offers clients full development services for the purpose of designing and implementing a total franchise program. **Founded:** 1970. **Publications:** "Franchising Your Business," May/Jun, 2003; "Female Entrepreneur," May/Jun, 2003; "Franchising World," May/Jun, 2003; "Canadian Business Franchise," Jul/Aug, 2000. **Seminars:** Has presented franchising seminars under auspices of American Management Association, Management Center Europe and International Franchise Association. Recent programs include Expanding Your Business by Franchising; Writing Effective Franchise Operations Manuals. Also has franchise seminar on Prodigy.

32282 ■ Franchise Masters Inc. (FMI)
8301 Golden Valley Rd.
Golden Valley, MN 55427-4435
Ph: (763)541-1385
Free: 800-328-4158
Fax: (763)542-2246
Co. E-mail: johncampbell@franchisemasters.com
URL: http://www.franchisemasters.com
Contact: David Mitchell, President
Scope: Provider of franchise development and consulting services that include franchise legal services, advertising brochures and media advertising, manual preparation, video presentation, training programs, franchiser franchisee relations, franchise sales and marketing, venture capital funding, business planning and human resource evaluation and planning. **Founded:** 1981. **Seminars:** How to Choose a Business or a Franchise. **Telecommunication Services:** johnca@franchisemasters.com.

32283 ■ Francorp Inc.
20200 Governors Dr.
Olympia Fields, IL 60461
Ph: (708)481-2900
Free: 800-372-6244
Fax: (708)481-5885
Co. E-mail: info@francorp.com
URL: http://www.francorp.com
Contact: Ramon Vinay, President
Description: Offers consultancy on franchising business. Consultants have provided full development programs, including feasibility studies, business plans, legal documents, operations manuals, and marketing materials for clients since 1976. **Scope:** A management consulting firm specializing in franchise development. Provides full development programs, including feasibility studies, business plans, legal documents, operations manuals and marketing materials. Also provides post-development services for established franchisers including lead generation programs, franchise brochures, videotapes, international brokerage, public relations and expert witness services. **Founded:** 1976. **Training:** Provides post-development services for establishing franchisors, including lead generation programs, brochures, videotapes, international brokerage, PR, and expert witness service. **Seminars:** Franchise Your Business, Sep, 2006; A review of both Federal and State laws which govern franchising; An overview of different franchise strategies available for expansion, as well as guidance in choosing the right one for your business; A comparison of the cost of various growth strategies; An overview of revenue streams through franchising; The estimated costs of franchising your business; Calculating returns on franchise development and support costs.

32284 ■ General Business Services Corp.
1020 N University Parks Dr.
Waco, TX 76707
Ph: (817)745-2525
Free: 800-583-6181
Fax: (817)745-2544
Contact: Gary Mattson, Principal
Scope: Provider of financial management, business counseling, and tax-related products and services to business owners and professionals. Additional services include proper record-keeping systems, accurate tax return preparation, computer software services, and financial planning services. Initial and continuous training is available to franchisees in all areas: Business and tax counseling, client acquisition and business operations. **Founded:** 1962. **Publications:** "Tax Tips for the Small Business Owner and Professional," 1993.

32285 ■ David Goodwin, PhD
23 Barnsley Cres.
Mount Sinai, NY 11766
Ph: (631)474-3290
Fax: (631)234-2649
Contact: David Goodwin, President
Scope: Specializes in franchise and organizational development, sales and operation support, and business and marketing plans.

32286 ■ ISO Healthcare Consulting—Intelligence Strategy Organization
650 Madison Ave., 9th Fl.
New York, NY 10022
Ph: (212)940-6000
Fax: (212)940-6100
Co. E-mail: info@isohc.com
Contact: David Amar, President
E-mail: damar@isohc.com
Scope: Provides strategic management consulting services to major pharmaceutical, medical device and biotech companies worldwide. ISO helps its clients create and implement strategies that drive top-line growth, performance and competitiveness.

The company provides customized services that enhance commercial and R and D performance and alignment. The firm's areas of focus include corporate, functional and brand strategy; marketing and sales effectiveness; R and D portfolio management; R and D productivity; life cycle management; franchise planning; and organizational effectiveness design. **Founded:** 1975. **Seminars:** Strategy workshops are customized to specific client needs.

32287 ■ JC Ventures Inc.
4 Arnold St.
Old Greenwich, CT 06870
Ph: (203)698-1990
Free: 800-698-1997
Fax: (203)698-2638
Contact: James O. Campbell, President
Scope: Specialize in business strategy consulting services to the middle market and provide venture management services. Venture management services include development of business plans, franchise advisory services, and assistance in attaining financing. Industries served: Financial services and high-technology. **Founded:** 1988. **Publications:** "The Commandants of Franchising". **Seminars:** Provide seminars for individuals looking for franchise opportunities.

32288 ■ Harold L. Kestenbaum P.C.—Harold L. Kestenbaum and Kick Solutions
1425 Rexcorp Plz., E Twr., 15th Fl.
Uniondale, NY 11556
Ph: (516)745-0099
Fax: (516)745-0293
Co. E-mail: hkestenbaum@farrellfritz.com
URL: http://www.franchiseatty.com
Contact: Harold L. Kestenbaum, Principal
E-mail: hkesten@worldnet.att.net
Scope: Provider of consulting services for startup and existing franchisors. Services include feasibility studies, determination of franchise format, business plan development, capital resources, manual preparation and legal services. Practices franchise law and provides marketing services as well. Serves all industries. **Founded:** 1977. **Publications:** "Four tips to starting a successful franchise".

32289 ■ Koach Enterprises
5529 N 18th St.
Arlington, VA 22205
Ph: (703)241-8361
Fax: (703)241-8623
Co. E-mail: info@koach.com
Contact: Joseph L. Koach, President
Scope: Business consultants specializing in franchise development, distribution and small business start-ups. Services include business development plans, preparation of operations manuals, marketing programs and training programs. Serves private industries as well as government agencies. **Founded:** 1981. **Publications:** "How to Franchise Your Business and How to Buy a Franchise". **Seminars:** Taking the Mystique Out of Franchising; Franchising in the 1990's; Franchising Internationally; How to Avoid Bankruptcy; International Franchising.

32290 ■ Lupfer & Associates (L&A)
92 Glen St.
Natick, MA 01760-5646
Ph: (508)655-3950
Fax: (508)655-7826
Co. E-mail: donlupfer@aol.com
Contact: Donald Lupfer, Owner
E-mail: don.lupfer@lupferassociates.com
Scope: Assists off shore hi-tech companies in entering United States markets and specializes in channel development for all sorts of products. Perform MARCOM support for hi-tech United States clients. **Founded:** 1988. **Publications:** "What's Next For Distribution-Feast or Famine"; "The Changing Global Marketplace"; "Making Global Distribution Work". **Seminars:** How to do Business in the United States.

32291 ■ Management Action Programs Inc.
14140 Ventura Blvd., Ste. 208
Sherman Oaks, CA 91423
Ph: (818)380-1177
Free: 888-834-3040
Fax: (818)981-2717
Co. E-mail: rkwacker@mapconsulting.com
URL: http://www.mapconsulting.com
Contact: Lee Froschheiser, President
E-mail: lfroschheiser@mapconsulting.com
Scope: Counsels distributors of products and services in improving productivity and profitability through the MAP management system. Also specializes in dealer and distributor systems, franchised companies, strategic planning and business planning to use investment capital. **Founded:** 1961. **Publications:** "Vital Factors," Oct, 2006. **Seminars:** How to Finance a Growing Business; Venture Capital for Growing Business; Franchise Relations for the Large Accounting Firm; Should You Franchise Your Business; The Pitfalls of TQM; Productivity in the Manufacturing Sector and Re-engineering to Get Results; Management Development Workshop. **Special Services:** Vital Factor®.

32292 ■ Marketing Resources Group Franchise Consulting
7158 Austin St.
Forest Hills, NY 11375
Ph: (718)261-8882
Contact: Bill Alexander, President
Scope: Provider of franchise sales, development and consulting solutions. It offers sales prospecting, competitive analysis, customer evaluation, and strategic planning services.

32293 ■ National Cooperative Bank, Corporate Banking Div. (NCB)
2011 Crystal Dr., Ste. 800
Arlington, VA 22202
Ph: (703)302-8000
Free: 800-955-9622
Fax: (703)647-3460
Co. E-mail: marcom@ncb.coop
URL: http://www.ncb.coop
Contact: Charles E. Snyder, President
Scope: In addition to offering various banking services to franchise cooperatives, this Division consults on the establishment of employee stock ownership plans within the franchising system.

32294 ■ National Franchise Associates Inc.
240 Lake View Ct.
Lavonia, GA 30553
Ph: (770)945-0660
Fax: (770)356-5180
Co. E-mail: nfa@nationalfranchise.com
URL: http://www.nationalfranchise.com
Contact: Stephen S. Raines, President
Description: Full service consulting and developmental firm with expertise in feasibility studies, Franchise agreements and UFOC's, advertising and public relations campaigns, operations and training manuals, franchise sales programs, and ongoing franchise consulting. **Scope:** An international franchise consulting firm providing full-service program to franchise companies. Services include: Feasibility studies, franchise plans, venture capital, franchise agreement, FTC disclosure document, state registration applications, operations manuals, training materials, advertising and public relations, computer software programs and sales and marketing of franchises. **Founded:** 1981. **Publications:** "Keys To Successful Franchising: Franchise Marketing Reflections Of A Franchise Consultant"; "Keys To A Successful Franchise Training"; "Keys To Successful Franchise Development: Will The Franchise Generate Sufficient Money? Reflections Of A Franchise Consultant"; "Focus on Operations Manuals & Marketing"; "Keys To Successful Franchising: Will Your Franchise Program Make Enough Money?"; "Keys To Successful Franchise Planning: Selecting The Right Franchisees"; "DePalma's expanding into Asia"; "Spirit Of Ingenuity"; "Why a Franchise Consultant Can Be Helpful". **Seminars:** Franchise Training Program.

32295 ■ National Franchise Sales (NFS)
1601 Dove St., Ste. 150
Newport Beach, CA 92660
Ph: (949)428-0480
Free: 888-982-4446
Fax: (949)428-0490
Co. E-mail: pp@nationalfranchisesales.com
URL: http://www.nationalfranchisesales.com
Contact: Mike Deegan, President
E-mail: md@nationalfranchisesales.com
Scope: A business brokerage firm specializing in the resale of franchise businesses and small chains. Assists in the asset recovery of non-performing franchise businesses in bankruptcy, foreclosure, or default, by re-franchising the businesses. **Founded:** 1978. **Seminars:** Franchising - How to Start a Franchise; Franchising - How to Market Your Franchise.

32296 ■ Nationwide Franchise Marketing Services
18715 Gibbons Dr.
Dallas, TX 75287-4045
Ph: (972)733-9942
Free: 866-740-5815
Fax: (972)733-9942
Co. E-mail: fmmigdol@tx.rr.com
Contact: Marvin J. Migdol, President
E-mail: marvmigdol@aol.com
Description: Full service franchise development evaluations. **Scope:** Helps franchisors in areas such as food services, automotive products and services, apparel, education, personnel, health and beauty aids, maintenance, entertainment and service businesses. **Founded:** 1971. **Publications:** "Starting a Business"; "Winning in the 90S"; "How to Get Organized in 30Days"; "25 Tips for Producing an Effective Direct Mail Brochure"; "How to Land That Job"; "How to Keep a Job"; "How to Buy the Right Franchise"; "Fund-Raising for Business"; "Fund-Raising for Non-Profit Organizations, Public Relations: A Growing Management Function for Today"; "How to Prevent Legal Problems in Hiring"; "Comics As a Public Relations Tool in Communications and Greater Virility".

32297 ■ Sommers Consultants Inc.—Sommers Financial Group Inc.
301 N Main St., Ste. 5
New City, NY 10956
Ph: (845)639-0195
Fax: (845)639-0198
Contact: Leslie Sommers, President
Scope: Provider of the full scope of services necessary for planning, designing and implementing franchise programs. Industries presently served include: juvenile furniture, uniforms and maternity, fashion and footwear, instant shoe repair, and specialty baking and foods. Other services provided include: Business forms and systems, marketing programs and services, real estate site selection and lease negotiations, and small business development. **Founded:** 1982. **Publications:** "Estate Planning"; "Living Trusts"; "Avoiding Probate"; "Charitable Gifts"; "Controlling the Distribution"; "Paying Estate Taxes"; "Benefits of A-B Trusts"; "Gifting Strategies"; "Charitable Lead Trusts"; "Charitable Remainder Trusts"; "Wealth Replacement Trusts"; "Family Limited Partnerships"; "Property Ownership"; "Eliminating the Estate Tax".

32298 ■ Tarbutton Associates Inc.
1072 Laskin Rd.
Virginia Beach, VA 23451-6364
Ph: (757)422-2020
Contact: Kenton L. Tarbutton, President
Scope: A consulting firm specializing in franchise consulting worldwide for expert witness court and legislative testimony as well as the sale or acquisition of franchising parent companies. **Founded:** 1962. **Publications:** "Franchising: The How-To Book," Prentice-Hall Inc. **Seminars:** 21st Century Management Techniques; Developing Your Business for Franchising; Developing People into Producers; The Franchising Possibilities.

32299 ■ Venture Marketing Associates L.L.C.
800 Palisade Ave., Ste. 907
Fort Lee, NJ 07024
Ph: (201)924-7435

Fax: (201)224-8757
Co. E-mail: venturemkt@aol.com
URL: http://www.venturemarketingassociates.com
Contact: Brian Furber, Market Analyst Director, Marketing
Scope: Provider of consulting services in business development and franchising. Provides hands-on assistance in planning and implementing strategic marketing/management plans. Clients include franchisers, small business owners and individuals. Cost-effective fees for those in transition, facing unemployment, researching a franchise or starting a business. Industries served: service, retail and distribution. **Seminars:** Franchise Your Business; How to Research a Franchise Services.

FRANCHISES AND BUSINESS OPPORTUNITIES

32300 ■ Aloha Hotels and Resorts
PO Box 3347
Princeville, HI 96722
Ph: (808)826-6244
URL: http://www.franchisedirectory.ca
Description: Provides independent Inn, Hotel and Resort owners with the ability to obtain new sources of revenue. Membership in the Aloha Hotels and Resort chain brings a wide variety of benefits to the property owner. Aloha Hotel and Resort president has over 25 years of enhancing financial performance for 3 major hotel and resort chains. **Equity Capital Needed:** $1,000-$200,000 total investment; $1,000-$200,000 required cash liquidity. **Training:** Provides training an support programs. There is one assigned management team member to your property that is available to answer any questions and take you through the steps to become an Aloha Hotel and Resort member. There are many training and support areas that are included in your membership.

32301 ■ Dorsey & Whitney, LLP
701 5th Ave., Ste. 6100
Seattle, WA 98104
Ph: (206)903-8700
Fax: (206)903-8820
Description: Franchise Lawyers.

32302 ■ FD & MG Franchise Company Inc.
949 E Pioneer Rd., Ste. B-2
Draper, UT 84020
Ph: (801)352-1400
Fax: (801)619-4038
Description: Franchise consulting. **No. of Franchise Units:** 2. **No. of Company-Owned Units:** 1. **Founded:** 2003.. **Franchised:** 2007. **Equity Capital Needed:** $120,500-$152,100. **Franchise Fee:** $75,000. **Royalty Fee:** 6%. **Financial Assistance:** Third party financing and limited in-house financing available. **Training:** Includes 2 weeks training at headquarters and ongoing support.

32303 ■ Franchise Development International, LLC
370 SE 15 Ave.
Pompano Beach, FL 33060
Ph: (954)942-9424
Fax: (954)783-5177
Description: Franchise development and marketing. **Founded:** 1991..

32304 ■ Franchise Development & Marketing Group
Franchise Development & Marketing Group, Inc.
949 E Pioneer Rd., Ste. 2B
Draper, UT 84020
Ph: (801)352-1400
Fax: (801)619-4038
Description: Assist businesses in all franchise phase. **Founded:** 2003..

32305 ■ Franchise Developments Inc. (FDI)
5001 Baum Blvd., Ste. 660
Pittsburgh, PA 15213
Ph: (412)687-8484
Free: 800-576-5115
Fax: (412)687-0541
Co. E-mail: franchise-dev@earthlink.net
URL: http://www.franchise-dev.com
Contact: Kenneth Franklin, President
Description: Develop, implement and launch franchise programs. **Scope:** Offers clients full development services for the purpose of designing and implementing a total franchise program. **Founded:** 1970. **Publications:** "Franchising Your Business," May/Jun, 2003; "Female Entrepreneur," May/Jun, 2003; "Franchising World," May/Jun, 2003; "Canadian Business Franchise," Jul/Aug, 2000. **Seminars:** Has presented franchising seminars under auspices of American Management Association, Management Center Europe and International Franchise Association. Recent programs include Expanding Your Business by Franchising; Writing Effective Franchise Operations Manuals. Also has franchise seminar on Prodigy.

32306 ■ Franchise Foundations
4157 23rd St.
San Francisco, CA 94114
Free: 800-942-4402
Description: Franchise consulting. **Founded:** 1980..

32307 ■ Franchise Recruiters Ltd.
Saddlebrooke Country Club
63284 E Flower Ridge Dr.
Tucson, AZ 85739
Ph: (520)825-9588
Description: Placement of franchise management professionals. **Founded:** 1977..

32308 ■ Franchise Sales
1315 S Villa Ave.
Villa Park, IL 60181
Ph: (630)819-2418
Description: Self franchisees in business now. **Founded:** 1991..

32309 ■ Franchise Search, Inc.
Kushell Associates Inc.
48 Burd St., Ste. 101
Nyack, NY 10960
Ph: (845)727-4103
Description: International executive search firm for franchisors. **Founded:** 1982..

32310 ■ Franchise Specialists, Inc.
1234 Maple St. Ext.
Moon Twp., PA 15108
Ph: (412)262-5055
Description: Professional franchise development and sales. **Founded:** 1978..

32311 ■ FranchiseInc!
2148 Pelham Pky., Bldg. 300
Pelham, AL 35124
Free: 800-961-0420
Fax: (205)682-2939
Description: Franchise consulting service. **No. of Franchise Units:** 24. **No. of Company-Owned Units:** 1. **Founded:** 1995.. **Franchised:** 2006. **Equity Capital Needed:** $36,600-$48,500. **Franchise Fee:** $29,500. **Training:** Includes 5 days training at headquarters, 52 weeks mentoring via teleconference and ongoing support.

32312 ■ FranchiseMart / Biz1Brokers
2121 Vista Pky.
West Palm Beach, FL 33411
Ph: (877)757-6550
Fax: (561)478-4340
Co. E-mail: franchise@franchisemart.com
URL: http://www.franchisemart.com
Description: Franchise consulting services. **No. of Franchise Units:** 5. **Founded:** 2006.. **Franchised:** 2007. **Equity Capital Needed:** $30,000-$35,000 initial, total investment $110,000-$115,000. **Franchise Fee:** $29,500. **Financial Assistance:** Yes. **Training:** Yes.

32313 ■ Franchises Unlimited Network LLC
36601 Samoa Dr.
Sterling Heights, MI 48312
Free: 866-583-5311
Description: Franchise consulting service.

32314 ■ Franchoice, Inc.
7500 Flying Cloud Dr., Ste. 600
Eden Prairie, MN 55344
Ph: (952)345-8400
Free: 877-396-4238
Fax: (952)942-5793
Co. E-mail: info@franchoice.com
URL: http://www.franchoice.com
Description: Provides consumers with free guidance and advice to help them select a franchise that matches their individual interests and financial qualifications. **Founded:** 2000..

32315 ■ Francorp Inc.
20200 Governors Dr.
Olympia Fields, IL 60461
Ph: (708)481-2900
Free: 800-372-6244
Fax: (708)481-5885
Co. E-mail: info@francorp.com
URL: http://www.francorp.com
Contact: Ramon Vinay, President
Description: Offers consultancy on franchising business. Consultants have provided full development programs, including feasibility studies, business plans, legal documents, operations manuals, and marketing materials for clients since 1976. **Scope:** A management consulting firm specializing in franchise development. Provides full development programs, including feasibility studies, business plans, legal documents, operations manuals and marketing materials. Also provides post-development services for established franchisers including lead generation programs, franchise brochures, videotapes, international brokerage, public relations and expert witness services. **Founded:** 1976. **Training:** Provides post-development services for establishing franchisors, including lead generation programs, brochures, videotapes, international brokerage, PR, and expert witness service. **Seminars:** Franchise Your Business, Sep, 2006; A review of both Federal and State laws which govern franchising; An overview of different franchise strategies available for expansion, as well as guidance in choosing the right one for your business; A comparison of the cost of various growth strategies; An overview of revenue streams through franchising; The estimated costs of franchising your business; Calculating returns on franchise development and support costs.

32316 ■ iFranchise Group
905 W 175th St., 2nd Fl.
Homewood, IL 60430
Ph: (708)957-2300
Fax: (708)957-2395
Co. E-mail: info@ifranchise.net
URL: http://www.ifranchise.com
Description: Offers services on strategic planning, franchise law, operations documentation, marketing and sales, and executive recruiting for franchisors.

32317 ■ Jones & Co.
365 Bay St., 2nd Fl.
Toronto, ON, Canada M5H 2V1
Ph: (416)703-5716
Fax: (416)703-6180
Description: Law firm experienced in franchising and distribution. **Founded:** 2004..

32318 ■ Kanouse & Walker, P.A.
2255 Glades Rd., Ste. 324
Boca Raton, FL 33431
Ph: (561)451-8090
Fax: (561)451-8089
Description: Represents franchisees in buying a franchise. **Founded:** 1974..

32319 ■ Kaufman & Canoles, P.C.
150 W Main St., Ste. 2100
Norfolk, VA 23510
Ph: (757)624-3257
Fax: (757)624-3169
Description: Franchise attorneys. **Founded:** 1974..

32320 ■ L. Michael Schwartz, P.A.
10561 Barkley Pl., Ste. 510
Overland Park, KS 66212-1860
Ph: (913)341-1919

Fax: (913)341-0007
Description: Franchise consulting and full legal services.

32321 ■ Leon Gottlieb USA/Int'l Franchise/ Restaurant Consultants
Leon Gottlieb & Associates
4601 Sendero Pl.
Tarzana, CA 91356-4821
Ph: (818)757-1131
Fax: (818)757-1816
Description: Consultant, expert witness, arbitrator. **Founded:** 1960..

32322 ■ Marketing Resources Group
83-26 Lefferts Blvd.
Kew Gardens, NY 11415
Ph: (718)261-8882
Description: Franchise development, marketing, and sales.

32323 ■ National Franchise Associates Inc.
240 Lake View Ct.
Lavonia, GA 30553
Ph: (770)945-0660
Fax: (770)356-5180
Co. E-mail: nfa@nationalfranchise.com
URL: http://www.nationalfranchise.com
Contact: Stephen S. Raines, President
Description: Full service consulting and developmental firm with expertise in feasibility studies, Franchise agreements and UFOC's, advertising and public relations campaigns, operations and training manuals, franchise sales programs, and ongoing franchise consulting. **Scope:** An international franchise consulting firm providing full-service program to franchise companies. Services include: Feasibility studies, franchise plans, venture capital, franchise agreement, FTC disclosure document, state registration applications, operations manuals, training materials, advertising and public relations, computer software programs and sales and marketing of franchises. **Founded:** 1981. **Publications:** "Keys To Successful Franchising: Franchise Marketing Reflections Of A Franchise Consultant"; "Keys To A Successful Franchise Training"; "Keys To Successful Franchise Development: Will The Franchise Generate Sufficient Money? Reflections Of A Franchise Consultant"; "Focus on Operations Manuals & Marketing"; "Keys To Successful Franchising: Will Your Franchise Program Make Enough Money?"; "Keys To Successful Franchise Planning: Selecting The Right Franchisees"; "DePalma's expanding into Asia"; "Spirit Of Ingenuity"; "Why a Franchise Consultant Can Be Helpful". **Seminars:** Franchise Training Program.

32324 ■ Oxford Business Consulting Group, LLC
19 Beech Pl.
Huntington, NY 11743
Ph: (631)423-8570
Fax: (631)423-8580
Description: Outsourced franchise sales & development. **Founded:** 2000..

32325 ■ Webber Consulting Group, Inc.
3506 SW Sawgrass Pky.
Ankeny, IA 50023
Ph: (515)419-6122
Fax: (253)679-4351
Description: Franchise development and accounting service.

LIBRARIES

32326 ■ Alberta Securities Commission Library
250-5th St. SW, Ste. 600
Calgary, AB, Canada T2P 0R4
Ph: (403)297-6454
Free: 877-355-0585
Fax: (403)297-6156
Co. E-mail: inquiries@asc.ca
URL: http://www.albertasecurities.com
Contact: Yanming Fei, Librarian
Scope: Securities legislation, corporate law. **Services:** Library not open to the public. **Holdings:** Figures not available.

32327 ■ Franchise Consultants International Association Library
5147 S. Angela Rd.
Memphis, TN 38117
Ph: (901)368-3361
Fax: (901)368-1144
Co. E-mail: franmark@msn.com
URL: http://www.FranchiseStores.com
Contact: R. Richey
URL(s): www.FranchiseStores.Net, consultantsamerica.net. **Scope:** Franchise law, demographics, statistics, logistics, suppliers, technology, advertising, management, legal consulting. **Services:** Members only participants for reference use. **Founded:** 1976. **Holdings:** 2800 books, periodicals, clippings, audio/visuals, and audio recordings; reports; manuscripts; archives; patents. **Subscriptions:** 143 magazines.

RESEARCH CENTERS

32328 ■ The Nature Conservancy - New Jersey Chapter Office
200 Pottersville Rd.
Chester, NJ 07930
Ph: (908)879-7262
Fax: (908)879-2172
Co. E-mail: newjersey@tnc.org
URL: http://www.nature.org/ourinitiatives/regions/northamerica/unitedstates/newjersey
Contact: Barbara Brummer, Director
Founded: 1988. **Publications:** *Brochures and fact sheets*; *Nature Conservancy Magazine*; *The Oak Leaf*. **Educational Activities:** Field trips and special events throughout the state; Annual Members Meeting, each fall.

START-UP INFORMATION

32329 ■ *75 Green Businesses You Can Start to Make Money and Make a Difference*
Pub: Entrepreneur Press

Ed: Glenn Croston. **Released:** August 1, 2008. **Price:** $19.95 paper. **Description:** Descriptions of seventy-five environmentally-friendly business startups are presented.

32330 ■ *The 100 Best Businesses to Start When You Don't Want To Work Hard Anymore*
Pub: Career Press Inc.

Ed: Lisa Rogak. **Price:** $16.99. **Description:** Author helps burned-out workers envision a new future as a small business owner. Systems analysis, adventure travel outfitting, bookkeeping, food delivery, furniture making, and software development are among the industries examined.

32331 ■ *The 100 Best Businesses to Start When You Don't Want to Work Hard Anymore*
Pub: Career Press

Ed: Lisa Rogak. **Price:** $14.99.

32332 ■ *101 Businesses You Can Satrt at with Less Thank One Thousand Dollars: For Retirees*
Pub: Atlantic Publishing Company

Ed: Christina Bultinck. **Released:** December 2006. **Price:** $21.95. **Description:** Business ideas to help retirees start a home-based business on a low budget.

32333 ■ *101 Businesses You Can Start at with Less Than One Thousand Dollars: For Stay-At-Home Moms and Dads*
Pub: Atlantic Publishing Company

Ed: Christina Bultinck. **Released:** December 2006. **Price:** $21.95. **Description:** Business ideas to help stay-at-home moms and dads start a home-based business on a low budget.

32334 ■ *101 Businesses You Can Start with Less Than One Thousand Dollars: for Retirees*
Pub: Atlantic Publishing Company

Ed: Heather Lee Shepherd. **Released:** October 2007. **Price:** $21.95. **Description:** According to a study by the U.S. Department of Health and Human Resources, people starting their work careers will face the following situation when they retire at the age of 65: they will have annual incomes between $4,000 and $26,000. According to the Social Security Administration, today's retirees can count on corporate pensions and Social Security for 61 percent of their retirement income. The remainder must come from other sources. Therefore, if this holds true for the future, today's workers need to accumulate enough in personal savings to make up the 39 percent shortfall in retirement income. The solution for many will be to start a small part-time business.

32335 ■ *101 Businesses You Can Start with Less Than One Thousand Dollars: for Stay-at-Home Moms and Dads*
Pub: Atlantic Publishing Company
Ed: Heather Lee Shepherd. **Released:** October 2007. **Price:** $21.95. **Description:** Over 100 business ideas are detailed to help stay-at-home parents earn extra money to add to the family income. These businesses can be started with minimum training and investment and most can be easily operated by one person and eventually be sold for an additional profit; many are started with less than one hundred dollars and can be run from home.

32336 ■ *101 Businesses You Can Start with Less Than One Thousand Dollars: for Students*
Pub: Atlantic Publishing Company
Ed: Heather Lee Shepherd. **Released:** September 2007. **Price:** $21.95. **Description:** More than 100 business ideas for busy students; these ideas can be started for very little money yet provide striving students with more money than they would make working a job paying an hourly wage. Web links for additional information are provides along with detailed instruction and examples for starting a successful business.

32337 ■ *101 Small Business Ideas for Under $5000*
Pub: John Wiley & Sons, Incorporated
Ed: Corey Sandler, Janice Keefe. **Released:** April 2005. **Price:** $21.95. **Description:** Entrepreneurial ideas for starting companies that can be run part-time or full-time, and some as an absentee owner.

32338 ■ *202 Things You Can Buy and Sell for Big Profits*
Pub: Entrepreneur Press
Ed: James Stephenson; Jason R. Rich. **Released:** July 2008. **Price:** $19.95. **Description:** Become an entrepreneur at selling new and used products. This handbook will help individuals cash in on the boom in reselling new and used products online. A new section defines ways to set realistic goals while distinguishing between 'get-rich schemes' and long term, viable businesses. A discussion about targeting and reaching the right customer base is included, along with finding and obtaining the service support needed for starting a new business.

32339 ■ *"218 More Programs" in Entrepreneur (Vol. 35, November 2007, No. 11, pp. 96)*
Pub: Entrepreneur Media Inc.
Description: List of 218 colleges and universities in the U.S. offering entrepreneurship programs is presented.

32340 ■ *250 Questions Every Self-Employed Person Should Ask*
Pub: Adams Media Corporation
Contact: Gary Krebs, Director
E-mail: swatrous@adamsmedia.com
Ed: Mary Mihaly. **Released:** January 1, 2010. **Price:** $10.95. **Description:** Comprehensive information is given for anyone wishing to start their own business.

32341 ■ *The Accidental Entrepreneur: Practical Wisdom for People Who Never Expected to Work for Themselves*
Pub: Career Steps
Ed: Susan Urquhart-Brown. **Released:** October 20, 2005. **Description:** Steps for launching, growing and running a successful small company.

32342 ■ *The Accidental Entrepreneur: The 50 Things I Wish Someone Had Told Me About Starting a Business*
Pub: AMACOM
Ed: Susan Urquhart-Brown. **Released:** March 2008. **Price:** $17.95. **Description:** Advice is offered to any would-be entrepreneur, including eight questions to ask before launching a new business, ten traits of a successful entrepreneur, how to obtain licenses and selling permits, best way to create a business plan, ten ways to get referrals, six secrets of marketing, investment and financial information, ways to avoid burnout, and the seven biggest pitfalls to avoid.

32343 ■ *The Accidental Startup: How to Realize Your True Potential by Becoming Your Own Boss*
Pub: Penguin Group USA Inc.
Ed: Danielle Babb. **Released:** May 1, 2009. **Price:** $18.95. **Description:** Advice is given to help would-be entrepreneurs realize their goals for starting and running a successful small business.

32344 ■ *"Ailing Economy Nibbling at Tech-Sector Jobs" in Puget Sound Business Journal (Vol. 29, November 7, 2008, No. 29, pp. 1)*
Pub: American City Business Journals
Ed: Eric Engleman, John Cook. **Description:** Seattle-area tech start-up companies including Redfin, Zillow, WildTangent, Daptiv, Avelle, and Intrepid Learning Solutions have cut staff as the nation's economy staggers. The layoffs are reminiscent of the tech bubble era, but most startups these days have been more prudent about spending and hiring as compared to that period.

32345 ■ *American Bar Association Legal Guide for Small Business: Everything You Need to Know About Small Business*
Pub: Random House Information Group
Contact: Markus Dohle, Accountant
Ed: American Bar Association. **Released:** June 10, 2010. **Description:** The American Bar Association provides insight into financial, health and family issues affecting small business, including start up issues, employment laws, financing a business, and selling a business.

32346 ■ *"Angel Investors Across State Collaborate" in Austin Business Journal (Vol. 31, May 20, 2011, No. 11, pp. 1)*
Pub: American City Business Journals Inc.
Ed: Christopher Calnan. **Description:** Texas' twelve angel investing groups are going to launch the umbrella organization Alliance of Texas Angel Net-

works (ATAN) to support more syndicated deals and boost investments in Texas. In 2010, these investing groups infused more than $24 million to startups in 61 deals.

32347 ■ *The Art of the Start*
Pub: Portfolio Publishing
Ed: Guy Kawasaki. **Price:** $26.95. **Description:** Apple's Guy Kawasaki offers information to help would-be entrepreneurs create new enterprises. As founder and CEO of Garage Technology Ventures, he has field-tested his ideas with newly hatched companies and he takes readers through every phase of creating a business, from the very basics of raising money and designing a business model through the many stages that eventually lead to success and thus giving back to society.

32348 ■ *The Art of the Start: The Time-Tested, Battle-Hardened Guide for Anyone Starting Anything*
Pub: Penguin Books USA Inc.
Ed: Guy Kawasaki. **Released:** September 2004. **Price:** $26.95. **Description:** Advice for someone starting a new business covering topics such as hiring employees, building a brand, business competition, and management.

32349 ■ *Awakening the Entrepreneur Within: How Ordinary People Can Create Extraordinary Companies*
Pub: HarperCollins Publishers
Ed: Michael E. Gerber. **Released:** December 1, 2009. **Price:** $15.99. **Description:** Four dimensions of the entrepreneurial personality are explored: dreamer, thinker, performer and leader.

32350 ■ *"Barriers to Small Business Creations in Canada" in International Journal of Entrepreneurship and Small Business (Vol. , pp.)*
Pub: Publishers Communication Group
Ed: Amarjit Gill, Nahum Biger, Vivek Nagpal. **Description:** Studies of Hatala (2005) and Choo and Wong (2006) related to the barriers to new venture creations in Canada are examined.

32351 ■ *"BDC Launches New Online Business Advice Centre" in Internet Wire (July 13, 2010)*
Pub: Comtex
Description: The Business Development Bank of Canada (BDC) offers entrepreneurs the chance to use their new online BDC Advice Centre in order to seek advice regarding the challenges of entrepreneurship. Free online business tools and information to help both startups and established firms are also provided.

32352 ■ *Be the Elephant: Build a Bigger, Better Business*
Pub: Workman Publishing Company
Ed: Steve Kaplan. **Price:** $19.95. **Description:** Entrepreneur and author sets out an accessible, no-frills plan for business owners, managers, and other industrialists to grow their businesses into elephants: big and strong but also smart. Advice is given on fostering a growth mind-set, assessing risk, and creating unique selling propositions.

32353 ■ *Be Your Own Boss*
Pub: Wet Feet, Incorporated
Ed: Marcia Passos. **Released:** November 2006. **Price:** $24.95. **Description:** Tips for starting a freelance business in any career or industry are covered.

32354 ■ *Become Your Own Boss in 12 Months: A Month-by-Month Guide to a Business that Works*
Pub: Adams Media Corporation
Contact: Gary Krebs, Director
E-mail: swatrous@adamsmedia.com
Ed: Melinda F. Emerson. **Released:** March 10, 2010. **Price:** $14.95. **Description:** Realistic planning guide to help would-be entrepreneurs transition from working for someone else to working for themselves is given. The key to successfully starting a new company lies in thoughtful preparation at least a year and a half before quitting a job.

32355 ■ *The Beermat Entrepreneur: Turn Your Good Idea Into a Great Business*
Pub: Pearson Education Ltd.
Contact: Rod Bristow, President
Ed: Mike Southon, Andrew Leigh, Chris West. **Released:** March 1, 2009. **Price:** $39.50. **Description:** Information to help start, maintain and grow a small business is given, along with suggestions for working with a bank.

32356 ■ *Boss of You: Everything a Woman Needs to Know to Start, Run, and Maintain Her Own Business*
Pub: Seal Press
Contact: Charlie Winton, Manager
Ed: Lauren Bacon; Emira Mears. **Released:** June 2008. **Price:** $15.95. **Description:** Women entrepreneurs start businesses at twice the rate of male counterparts. Information is shared to help a woman start, run and maintain a successful company.

32357 ■ *Breaking Free: How to Quit Your Job and Start Your Own Business*
Pub: Greenwood Publishing Group, Inc.
Ed: Chris Lauer. **Released:** March 1, 2009. **Price:** $34.95. **Description:** This books helps individuals transition from working for others to starting their own business.

32358 ■ *Brewing Up a Business: Adventures in Entrepreneurship from the Founder of Dogfish Head Craft*
Pub: John Wiley and Sons, Inc.
Ed: Sam Calagione. **Released:** October 2006. **Price:** $16.95. **Description:** Author shares nontraditional success secrets. Calgione began his business with a home brewing kit and grew it into Dogfish Head Craft Beer, the leading craft brewery in the U.S.

32359 ■ *Building a Dream: A Canadian Guide to Starting Your Own Business*
Pub: McGraw-Hill Ryerson Ltd.
Ed: Walter S. Good. **Released:** 2005. **Description:** Topics covered include evaluating business potential, new business ideas, starting or buying a business, franchise opportunities, business organization, protecting an idea, arranging financing, and developing a business plan.

32360 ■ *Business for Beginners, Canadian Edition: A Simple Step-By-Step Guide to Starting a Small Business*
Pub: Sourcebooks Mediafusion
Ed: Frances McGuckin. **Released:** March 15, 2005. **Price:** $16.95. **Description:** Small business advice is shared by seven successful entrepreneurs.

32361 ■ *A Business of My Own? 21 Steps to Successfully Starting and Running a Small Business*
Pub: Enfield Publishing
Ed: Marjorie Cleveland Fisher. **Released:** January 2005. **Description:** New ideas to start or grow a small business, including ideas for writing business plans with examples, adopting a business structure, and setting goals and objectives.

32362 ■ *Canadian Small Business Kit for Dummies*
Pub: CDG Books Canada, Incorporated
Ed: Margaret Kerr, JoAnn Kurtz. **Released:** March 2007. **Price:** $37.99 (Canadian). **Description:** Entrepreneurial guide to starting and running a small business in Canada.

32363 ■ *The Canadian Small Business Survival Guide: How to Start and Operate Your Own Successful Business*
Pub: Dundurn Group
Ed: Benj Gallander. FRQ June 2002. **Price:** $26.99. **Description:** Ideas for starting and running a successful small business. Topics include selecting a business, financing, government assistance, locations, franchises, and marketing ideas.

32364 ■ *Careers for Self-Starters and Other Entrepreneurial Types*
Pub: McGraw-Hill Companies Inc.
Contact: Deven Sharma, President
Ed: Blythe Camenson. **Released:** September 2004. **Price:** $9.99 (US). **Description:** Advice to entrepreneurs wishing to start their own small company. Tips for turning hobbies into job skills are included.

32365 ■ *Cash In On Cash Flow*
Pub: Simon and Schuster Inc.
Contact: Carolyn Reidy, President
E-mail: carolyn.reidy@simonandschuster.com
Ed: Lawrence J. Pino. **Released:** July 2005. **Price:** $19.95. **Description:** Guide to assist entrepreneurs with starting a new business as a cash flow specialist.

32366 ■ *Coin Laundries - Road to Financial Independence: A Complete Guide to Starting and Operating Profitable Self-Service Laundries*
Pub: Mountain Publishing Company
Ed: Emerson G. Higdon. **Released:** June 2001. **Description:** Guide to starting and operating a self-service laundry.

32367 ■ *Common Sense Business: Starting, Operating, and Growing Your Small Business-In Any Economy!*
Pub: HarperInformation
Ed: Steve Gottry. **Released:** July 2005. **Price:** $19.95 (US), $26.95 (Canadian). **Description:** Strategies for starting, operating and growing a small business in any economy. .

32368 ■ *Complete Idiot's Guide to Starting an Ebay Business*
Pub: Penguin Books USA Inc.
Ed: Barbara Weltman, Malcolm Katt. **Released:** February 2008. **Price:** $19.95 (US), $29.00 (Canadian). **Description:** Guide for starting an eBay business includes information on products to sell, how to price merchandise, and details for working with services like PayPal, and how to organize fulfillment services.

32369 ■ *The Complete Startup Guide for the Black Entrepreneur*
Pub: Career Press
Ed: Bill Bourdreaux. **Price:** $15.99.

32370 ■ *Corporation: Small Business Start-Up Kit*
Pub: Nova Publishing Company
Ed: Daniel Sitarz. **Released:** February 2005. **Price:** $29.95. **Description:** Guidebook to help entrepreneurs start up and run a small business corporation. Book includes state and federal forms with instructions.

32371 ■ *Crush It!*
Pub: HarperStudio/HarperCollins
Ed: Gary Vaynerchuk. **Released:** 2009. **Price:** $19.99. **Description:** Ways the Internet can help entrepreneurs turn their passions into successful companies.

32372 ■ *E-Myth Enterprise: How to Turn a Great Idea into a Thriving Business*
Pub: HarperCollins Publishers
Ed: Michael E. Gerber. **Released:** July 1, 2009. **Price:** $21.99. **Description:** This book explores the requirement needed to start and run a successful small business.

32373 ■ *Effective Small Business Management: An Entrepreneurial Approach*
Pub: Prentice Hall Higher Education
Ed: Norman M. Scarborough; Thomas W. Zimmerer; Douglas L. Wilson. **Released:** March 2006. **Price:** $178.33. **Description:** Provides undergraduate and graduate entrepreneurship and/or small business management courses with information to successfully launch a new company. The books offers entrepreneurs the tools required to develop staying power to succeed and grow their new business.

32374 ■ *The Elements of Small Business*
Pub: Silver Lake Publishing
Ed: John Thaler. **Released:** October 2004. **Price:** $12.95. **Description:** Concepts, markets, worksheets, letters, business plans, and sample legal forms for starting and running a small business are included.

32375 ■ *Enterprise Planning and Development: Small Business and Enterprise Start-Up Survival and Growth*
Pub: Elsevier Science and Technology Books
Ed: David Butler. **Released:** August 2006. **Price:** $42.95. **Description:** Innovation, intellectual property, and exit strategies are among the issues discussed in this book involving current entrepreneurship.

32376 ■ *Entrepreneurial Itch: What No One Tells You About Starting Your Own Business*
Pub: Self-Counsel Press Inc.
Ed: David Trahair. **Released:** December 2006. **Price:** $13.95. **Description:** Small business accountant shares a plan for starting a business.

32377 ■ *Entrepreneurial Management*
Pub: McGraw-Hill
Ed: Robert J. Calvin. **Description:** Starting a new business takes careful consideration, determined preparation and a well-developed plan president of an international company that helps startups offers strategies, tools, techniques, models and methodologies for starting a new business. This guidebook covers all aspects of launching a new company as well as hands-on business skills and the motivation to keep new business owners moving towards success while conquering the entrepreneurial challenges along with way.

32378 ■ *The Entrepreneur's Edge: Finding Money, Making Money, Keeping Money*
Pub: Silver Lake Publishing
Ed: Daniel Hogan. **Released:** October 2006. **Price:** $24.95. **Description:** Advice for starting, running and growing a new business is given.

32379 ■ *"Entrepreneurs: Search Party" in Business Strategy Review (Vol. 21, Autumn 2010, No. 3, pp. 30)*
Pub: Wiley-Blackwell
Ed: Georgina Peters. **Description:** Entrepreneurs tend to be fixated on coming up with a foolproof idea for a new business and then raising money to start it. Raising startup funds is difficult, but it doesn't have to be that way. Search funds offers an innovative alternative, and the results are often impressive.

32380 ■ *Entrepreneurship: A Small Business Approach*
Pub: McGraw-Hill Higher Education
Ed: Charles E. Bamford, Garry D. Bruton. **Released:** January 10, 2010. **Price:** $83.44. **Description:** This text takes a hands-on, problem-based learning approach that works through real problems faced by entrepreneurs and small business owners.

32381 ■ *Entrepreneurship and the Creation of Small Firms Empirical Studies of New Ventures*
Pub: Edward Elgar Publishing, Inc.
Ed: C. Holmquist Wiklund. **Released:** February 10, 2010. **Price:** $110.00. **Description:** Study focuses on the important issue of new venture creation. Using a variety of data sources, methods and theories, the authors demonstrate the factors that aid or hinder new venture creation in a number of settings.

32382 ■ *Entrepreneurship: Successfully Launching New Ventures*
Pub: Pearson Education Canada
Ed: Bruce Barringer; Duane Ireland. **Released:** January 2007. **Price:** $139.95 (CND). **Description:** Guide to help any entrepreneur successfully launch a new venture.

32383 ■ *Escape from Corporate America: A Practical Guide to Creating the Career of Your Dreams*
Pub: Ballantine/Random House
Ed: Pamela Skillings. **Released:** 2008. **Price:** $15.00. **Description:** How to quit your job and start your own business.

32384 ■ *Escape from Cubicle Nation: From Corporate Prisoner to Thriving Entrepreneur*
Pub: Penguin Group USA Inc.
Ed: Pamela Slim. **Released:** April 1, 2009. **Price:** $25.95. **Description:** Insight if offered to help anyone wishing to leave their corporate position and start their own small business is offered.

32385 ■ *Extraordinary Entrepreneurship: The Professional's Guide to Starting an Exceptional Enterprise*
Pub: John Wiley and Sons, Inc.
Ed: Stephen C. Harper. **Released:** October 2006. **Price:** $45.00. **Description:** New rules to assist entrepreneurs in the 21st Century. The book focuses on thinking outside the box.

32386 ■ *Fast-Track Business Start-Up Kit: California*
Pub: DP Group, Incorporated
Ed: Carolyn Usinger. **Released:** September 2006. **Price:** $29.00. **Description:** Step-by-step guide for starting and running a business in California, including information on sole proprietors, partnerships, limited liability companies, S and C corporations, as well as details concerning business entities, sales taxes, environmental issues, human resources, and more.

32387 ■ *Financial Times Guide to Business Start Up 2007*
Pub: Pearson Education, Limited
Contact: Steven A. Dowling, President
Ed: Sara Williams; Jonquil Lowe. **Released:** November 2006. **Price:** $52.50. **Description:** Guide for starting and running a new business is presented. Sections include ways to get started, direct marketing, customer relations, management and accounting.

32388 ■ *Foreclosure Cleanout Business: High Profits — Low Start Up Cost*
Pub: James R. Tolliver
Ed: James Tolliver. **Released:** October 11, 2011. **Price:** $17.99. **Description:** Foreclosure cleanout business is booming. This manual teaches how to start a foreclosure firm, who to contact, what to charge, services provided and more.

32389 ■ *Franchising for Dummies*
Pub: John Wiley & Sons, Incorporated
Ed: Dave Thomas, Michael Seid. **Released:** October 2006. **Price:** $24.99. **Description:** Advice to help entrepreneurs choose the right franchise, as well as financing, managing and expanding the business.

32390 ■ *The Girl's Guide to Starting Your Own Business: Candid Advice, Frank Talk, and True Stories*
Pub: Collins Publications
Contact: Rachel Anderson, Director
Ed: Caitlin Friedman; Kimberly Yorio. **Released:** January 1, 2005. **Price:** $14.95. **Description:** Advice is given to help any woman start her own company. Every chapter includes interviews, charts, quizzes and witty directives about self-employment. Topics include, choosing a name and logo, business law, communication and information about business associations.

32391 ■ *"Gordon Stollery" in Canadian Business (Vol. 81, December 24, 2007, No. 1, pp. 76)*
Pub: Rogers Media
Ed: Michelle Magnan. **Description:** Gordon Stollery of Highpine Oil and Gas Ltd. talks about being a hard-rock geologist and his move to start his oil and gas business. Other aspects of his business career are discussed.

32392 ■ *Harmonic Wealth*
Pub: Hyperion Books
Ed: Linda Sivertsen; James Arthur Ray. **Released:** May 6, 2008. **Price:** $24.95. **Description:** Secrets for attracting the life you want through entrepreneurship; tips for timing a startup are included.

32393 ■ *Home-Based Business for Dummies*
Pub: John Wiley and Sons, Inc.
Ed: Paul Edwards, Sarah Edwards, Peter Economy. **Released:** February 25, 2005. **Price:** $19.99. **Description:** Provides all the information needed to start and run a home-based business. Topics include: selecting the right business; setting up a home office; managing money, credit, and financing; marketing; and ways to avoid distractions while working at home.

32394 ■ *How to Form Your Own California Corporation*
Pub: NOLO
Ed: Anthony Mancuso. **Released:** March 2009. **Price:** $39.99. **Description:** Instructions and forms required to incorporate any business in the State of California.

32395 ■ *How to Get the Financing for Your New Small Business: Innovative Solutions from the Experts Who Do It Every Day*
Pub: Atlantic Publishing Company
Ed: Sharon L. Fullen. **Released:** May 2006. **Price:** $39.95, includes companion CD-Rom. **Description:** Ready capital is essential for starting and expanding a small business. Topics include traditional financing methods, financial statements, and a good business plan.

32396 ■ *How I Made It: 40 Successful Entrepreneurs Reveal How They Made Millions*
Pub: Kogan Page, Limited
Contact: Ben Glover, Director of Marketing
Ed: Rachel Bridge. **Released:** May 10, 2010. **Price:** $19.95. **Description:** Inspiration is given to anyone wishing to become a successful entrepreneur.

32397 ■ *How to Make Big Money*
Pub: Hyperion Books
Ed: Jeffrey J. Fox. **Released:** May 19, 2004. **Price:** $16.95. **Description:** Entrepreneur and consultant offers advice to help others create successful startups and prosper. Fox directs new business owners with a counterintuitive style and describes essential methods that beat the competition. Tips include: setting priorities, getting a personal driver, creating a contingency plan for employees, pricing to value, saving money, and getting an office outside of the home.

32398 ■ *How to Start a Home-Based Mail Order Business*
Pub: Globe Pequot Press
Ed: Georganne Fiumara. **Released:** January 2005. **Price:** $17.95. **Description:** Step-by-step guide for starting and growing a home-based mail order business. Information about equipment, pricing, online marketing, are included along with worksheets and checklists for planning.

32399 ■ *How to Start an Internet Sales Business*
Pub: Lulu.com
Ed: Dan Davis. **Released:** August 2005. **Price:** $19.95. **Description:** Small business guide for launching an Internet sales company. Topics include business structure, licenses, and taxes.

32400 ■ *How to Start, Operate and Market a Freelance Notary Signing Agent Business*
Pub: Gom Publishing, LLC
Ed: Victoria Ring. **Released:** September 2004. **Price:** $8.18. **Description:** Due to the changes in the 2001 Uniform Commercial Code allowing notary public agents to serve as a witness to mortgage loan closings (eliminating the 2-witness requirement under the old code), notaries are working directly for mortgage, title and signing companies as mobile notaries.

32401 ■ *How to Start and Run a Small Book Publishing Company: A Small Business Guide to Self-Publishing and Independent Publishing*
Pub: HCM Publishing
Ed: Peter I. Hupalo. **Released:** August 30, 2002. **Price:** $18.95. **Description:** The book teaches all aspects of starting and running a small book publishing company. Topics covered include: inventory accounting in the book trade, just-in-time inventory management, turnkey fulfillment solutions, tax deduct-

ible costs, basics of sales and use tax, book pricing, standards in terms of the book industry, working with distributors and wholesalers, cover design and book layout, book promotion and marketing, how to select profitable authors to publish, printing process, printing on demand, the power of a strong backlist, and how to value copyright.

32402 ■ *How to Start and Run Your Own Corporation: S-Corporations For Small Business Owners*
Pub: HCM Publishing

Ed: Peter I. Hupalo. **Released:** March 6, 2003. **Price:** $22.95. **Description:** Basics of corporate business structure are explained. Topics include discovering the best business structure for your company; how to decided between an S-Corporation and LLC; choosing the state in which to incorporate, how to form a corporation, angel investing, special issues for one-person corporations, the role of bylaws and corporate minutes, board of directors, taxes, workers' compensation issues, retirement plans, and more.

32403 ■ *How to Start a Small Business in Canada: Your Road Map to Financial Freedom*
Pub: Self-Help Publishers

Ed: Tariq Nadeem. **Released:** September 30, 2004. **Price:** $17.95. **Description:** Provides information for starting and managing a small business in Canada.

32404 ■ *How to Start Your Own Business for Entrepreneurs*
Pub: FT Press

Ed: Robert Ashton. **Released:** December 9, 2010. **Price:** $24.99. **Description:** More than 300,000 individuals start a business every year. That number will rise over the next year or two if the current economic downturn leads to widespread job losses.

32405 ■ *How to Succeed As a Lifestyle Entrepreneur*
Pub: Dearborn Trade Publishing Inc.
Contact: Roy Lipner, President

Ed: Gary Schine. **Released:** May 12, 2003. **Description:** Consultant helps entrepreneurs start a new business on their own terms and create flexibility in their lifestyles. Shine offers various ways to create a business around your passions while utilizing the same business tools used by more traditional businesses.

32406 ■ *"Hype: If You Build It.." in Entrepreneur (Vol. 35, October 2007, No. 10, pp. 138)*
Pub: Entrepreneur Media Inc.

Ed: John Jantsch. **Description:** Marketing strategy can be achieved by determining what a company's target market is, and how that company is unique in its industry. Narrowing the market will make promoting the company's products or services easier, and identifying the company's unique qualities will help in sending out a uniform message to the clients. Details of how to develop a marketing strategy are provided.

32407 ■ *"It's Not Perfect; But Illinois a Good Home for Business" in Crain's Chicago Business (Vol. 34, October 24, 2011, No. 42, pp. 18)*
Pub: Crain Communications Inc.

Description: Focusing on all factors that encompass Illinois' business environment, findings show that Illinois is a good place to start and grow a business. The study focused on corporate income tax rates and the fact that talent, access to capital and customers along with transportation connections are among the important factors the state has for small businesses.

32408 ■ *Kick Start Your Dream Business: Getting it Started and Keeping You Going*
Pub: Celestial Arts Publishing Co.
Contact: Patricia Kelly, Manager

Ed: Romanus Wolter. **Released:** March 2004. **Description:** Comprehensive guide covering the start-up process for any new company.

32409 ■ *Legal Guide for Starting and Running a Small Business*
Pub: NOLO

Ed: Fred S. Steingold. **Released:** August 2006. **Price:** $34.99. **Description:** Legal issues any small business owner needs to know for starting and running a successful business are outlined.

32410 ■ *Life Entrepreneurs*
Pub: Jossey Bass

Ed: Christopher Gergen; Gregg Vanourek. **Released:** 2008. **Price:** $24.95. **Description:** Consultants Christopher Gergen and Gregg Vanourek present the basic principles for becoming a successful entrepreneur: recognizing opportunity, taking risks, and innovation.

32411 ■ *"Looking To Leap?" in Black Enterprise (Vol. 38, January 2008, No. 6, pp. 64)*
Pub: Earl G. Graves Publishing Co. Inc.

Ed: Tennille M. Robinson. **Description:** Websites and organizations providing resources for any young entrepreneur wishing to start a new business are outlined.

32412 ■ *Low Risk, High Reward*
Pub: R & R Publishing

Ed: Bob Reiss with Jeffrey L. Cruikshank. **Released:** 2000. **Price:** $19.95. **Description:** Successful entrepreneur teaches others about creating, growing and maintaining a successful business venture. The book offers a step-by-step approach to helping entrepreneurs minimize the risk involved in a new business while examining the skills and resources needed to succeed.

32413 ■ *"Make Money in 2011" in Small Business Opportunities (January 2011)*
Pub: Harris Publications Inc.

Description: Top twenty ways to pick up extra cash, boost your income and generate new revenue. There has never been a better time to start a small business.

32414 ■ *Making a Living Without a Job: Winning Ways for Creating Work That You Love*
Pub: Random House Publishing Group

Ed: Barbara Winter. **Released:** August 9, 2010. **Price:** $16.00. **Description:** For all Americans who are out of work, soon to be out of work, or wishing to be freed from unrewarding work: here is the must-have book that shows how to make a living by working when, where, and how you want to work.

32415 ■ *Making a Living Without a Job: Winning Ways For Creating Work That You Love, Revised Ed.*
Pub: Bantam Books

Ed: Barbara Winter. **Released:** August 25, 2009. **Price:** $16.00 paperback. **Description:** Winter gives advice to help anyone turn an interest or hobby into a lucrative business.

32416 ■ *"Making Social Ventures Work" in Harvard Business Review (Vol. 88, September 2010, No. 9, pp. 66)*
Pub: Harvard Business School Publishing

Ed: James D. Thompson, Ian C. MacMillan. **Description:** Five steps are to define, examine the political aspects, focus on discovery-driven planning, develop an appropriate exit strategy, and anticipate unexpected consequences when starting a new social venture.

32417 ■ *MBA In a Day*
Pub: John Wiley and Sons, Inc.

Ed: Steven Stralser, PhD. **Released:** 2004. **Price:** $34.95. **Description:** Management professor presents important concepts, business topics and strategies that can be used by anyone to manage a small business or professional practice. Topics covered include: human resources and personal interaction, ethics and leadership skills, fair negotiation tactics, basic business accounting practices, project management, and the fundamentals of economics and marketing.

32418 ■ *Mobile Office: The Essential Small Business Guide to Office Technology*
Pub: Double Storey Books

Ed: Arthur Goldstruck, Steven Ambrose. **Released:** September 1, 2009. **Price:** $6.95. **Description:** Essential pocket guide for startup businesses and entrepreneurs which provides information to create a mobile office in order to maximize business potential while using current technologies.

32419 ■ *"The New Face of Detroit" in Inc. (Vol. 33, October 2011, No. 8, pp. 6)*
Pub: Inc. Magazine

Ed: Elizabeth Sile. **Description:** Basketball legend Magic Johnson has joined Detroit Venture Partners and Detroit will be one of the firm's three inaugural cities to host fellows from Venture for America, a new organization that places recent college graduates in start-up companies.

32420 ■ *"New Program for Entrepreneurs" in Austin Business JournalInc. (Vol. 29, February 12, 2010, No. 29, pp. 1)*
Pub: American City Business Journals

Ed: Christopher Calnan. **Description:** Nonprofit group Economic Development Catalyst Organization (ECDO) is formalizing its BizLaunch mentoring program, which was stated in 2009. The program aims to offer support networks to entrepreneurs and assistance regarding early-stage venture capital.

32421 ■ *New Venture Creation: Entrepreneurship for the 21st Century with Online Learning Center Access Card*
Pub: McGraw-Hill

Ed: Jeffrey A. Timmons; Stephen Spinelli. **Released:** November 1, 2008. **Price:** $71.97. **Description:** A handbook for students that explores all the concepts necessary for successfully launching a new enterprise.

32422 ■ *Niche and Grow Rich*
Pub: Entrepreneur Press

Ed: Jennifer Basye Sander; Peter Sander. **Released:** 2003. **Description:** Consultants share insight to entrepreneurs wishing to find a profitable niche market. Authors write that good niche businesses are easy to start and easy to defend from competitors. They also report that finding a successful niche can attract and maintain good customers who are willing to pay more for unique goods and services.

32423 ■ *"Oh, Grow Up!" in Entrepreneur (Vol. 35, October 2007, No. 10, pp. 120)*
Pub: Entrepreneur Media Inc.

Ed: Mark Henricks. **Description:** Most entrepreneurs are overwhelmed with the idea of expanding their business, forgetting to strategically plan the process of business growth. However, there are certain steps entrepreneurs must take in turning a startup business into a bigger venture. Eight steps to growing a business, such as asking for advice and deciding on a focus are presented.

32424 ■ *The Owners Manual for Small Business*
Pub: Planning Shop

Ed: Rhonda Abrams. **Released:** December 2005. **Price:** $19.95. **Description:** Reference book offering tips for starting a small business, low-cost marketing, and communicating effectively.

32425 ■ *Partnership: Small Business Start-Up Kit*
Pub: Nova Publishing Company

Ed: Daniel Sitarz. **Released:** November 2005. **Price:** $29.95. **Description:** Guidebook detailing partnership law by state covering the formation and use of partnerships as a business form. Information on filing requirements, property laws, legal liability, standards, and the new Revised Uniform Partnership Act is covered.

32426 ■ *Running Your Small Business on a MAC*
Pub: Peachpit Press

Ed: Doug Hanley. **Released:** November 2007. **Price:** $29.99. **Description:** Information to effectively start and run a small business using a MAC, including setting up a network and accounting.

32427 ■ *"Slow-Down Startups Hot" in Austin Business JournalInc. (Vol. 28, September 12, 2008, No. 26, pp. 1)*
Pub: American City Business Journals
Ed: Sandra Zaragoza. **Description:** A number of entrepreneurs from Austin, Texas are starting their own small business despite the economic slowdown. The Small Business Development Program in Austin has seen a 50 percent increase in the demand for its services in 2008 as compared to demand in 2007. Other details about the entrepreneurship trend are discussed.

32428 ■ *Small Business, Big Life: Five Steps to Creating a Great Life with Your Own Small Business*
Pub: Thomas Nelson Inc.
Ed: Louis Barajas. **Price:** $22.99. **Description:** Barajas describes his and his father's independent entrepreneurial paths and suggests an inspirational approach to business that relies on four personal greatness cornerstones: truth, responsibility, awareness, and courage, and on keeping in mind your vision and your team's needs. The book provides a new look at achieving a work/life balance.

32429 ■ *Small Business for Dummies*
Pub: John Wiley & Sons, Incorporated
Ed: Eric Tyson, Jim Schell. **Released:** March 2008. **Price:** $21.99. **Description:** Advice for launching and growing a small business; insights into using the Internet as business tool are included.

32430 ■ *Small Business for Dummies, 3rd Ed.*
Pub: John Wiley and Sons, Inc.
Ed: Eric Tyson; Jim Schell. **Released:** March 2008. **Price:** $21.99. **Description:** Guidebook for anyone wanting to start or grow a small business; topics include information financing, budgeting, marketing, management and more.

32431 ■ *Small Business Entrepreneur: Launching a New Venture and Managing a Business on a Day-to-Day Basis*
Pub: Austin & Company, Incorporated
Ed: Rory Burke. **Released:** February 2006. **Price:** $19.95. **Description:** Comprehensive guide examining the management skills required to launch and run a small business.

32432 ■ *Small Business Legal Tool Kit*
Pub: Entrepreneur Press
Ed: Ira Nottonson; Theresa A. Pickner. **Released:** May 2007. **Price:** $36.95. **Description:** Legal expertise is provided by two leading entrepreneurial attorneys. Issues covered include forming and operating a business: taxes, contracts, leases, bylaws, trademarks, small claims court, etc.

32433 ■ *Small Business Management: Launching and Managing New Ventures*
Pub: Nelson Thomson Learning
Ed: Justin G. Longenecker. **Released:** March 2006. **Price:** $78.95. **Description:** Tips for starting and running a successful new company are provided.

32434 ■ *The Small Business Owner's Manual: Everything You Need to Know to Start Up and Run Your Business*
Pub: Career Press, Incorporated
Ed: Joe Kennedy. **Released:** June 2005. **Price:** $19.99 (US), $26.95 (Canadian). **Description:** Comprehensive guide for starting a small business, focusing on twelve ways to obtain financing, business plans, selling and advertising products and services, hiring and firing employees, setting up a Web site, business law, accounting issues, insurance, equipment, computers, banks, financing, customer credit and collection, leasing, and more.

32435 ■ *The Small Business Start-Up Kit*
Pub: NOLO
Ed: Peri Pakroo. **Released:** January 2008. **Price:** $29.99. **Description:** Entrepreneurial advice for launching a new business. Topics include compliance with state regulations, sole proprietorships, partnerships, corporations, limited liability companies, as well as accounting and tax information.

32436 ■ *The Small Business Start-Up Kit for California*
Pub: NOLO
Ed: Peri Pakroo. **Released:** March 2008. **Price:** $29.99. **Description:** Handbook covering all aspects of starting a business in California, including information about necessary fees, forms, and taxes.

32437 ■ *Small Business Start-Up Workbook: A Step-by-Step Guide to Starting the Business You've Dreamed Of*
Pub: How To Books
Ed: Cheryl D. Rickman. **Released:** February 2006. **Price:** $24.75. **Description:** Book provides practical exercises for starting a small business, including marketing and management strategies.

32438 ■ *Small Business Survival Guide*
Pub: Adams Media Corporation
Contact: Gary Krebs, Director
E-mail: swatrous@adamsmedia.com
Ed: Cliff Ennico. **Price:** $12.95. **Description:** Small business expert provides strategies to start a company and survive in the 21st Century. He shows small business owners how to succeed despite challenges that can defeat any firm. His advice covers suppliers; customers and contractors; competitors and creditors; spouses, family and friends; as well as the ways lawyers, accountants and other can steal an entrepreneur's success. Ennico also describes how startups can comply with local regulations.

32439 ■ *Small Time Operator: How to Start Your Own Business, Keep Your Books, Pay Your Taxes, and Stay Out of Trouble*
Pub: Bell Springs Publishing
Ed: Bernard B. Kamoroff. **Released:** January 2008. **Price:** $18.95. **Description:** Comprehensive guide for starting any kind of business.

32440 ■ *So You Want to Start a Business?*
Pub: Pearson Education, Limited
Contact: Steven A. Dowling, President
Ed: Edward D. Hess; Charles Goetz. **Released:** August 30, 2008. **Price:** $18.99. **Description:** Over sixty percent of Americans say they would like to own their own business and more than five million business startups are launched annually. However, fifty to seventy percent of new businesses fail. This book identifies the eight mistakes that cause these business failures and offers entrepreneurs the knowledge, tools, templates, strategies, and hands-on how-to advice needed to avoid these errors and succeed.

32441 ■ *Soul Proprietor: 101 Lessons from a Lifestyle Entrepreneur*
Pub: Crossing Press, Incorporated
Ed: Jane Pollak. **Released:** September 2004. **Description:** More than 100 tips and stores to inspire and guide any would-be entrepreneur to earn a living from a favorite hobby or passion.

32442 ■ *The Spirit of Entrepreneurship: Exploring the Essence of Entrepreneurship Through Personal Stories*
Pub: Springer
Ed: Sharda S. Nandram; Karel J. Samson. **Released:** October 2006. **Price:** $79.95. **Description:** Case studies involving 60 entrepreneurs and executives explores the fundamentals in starting a new business, techniques and mindsets.

32443 ■ *The Spiritual Entrepreneur*
Pub: New Paradigm Media
Ed: Robert Morgen. **Released:** January 1, 2010. **Price:** $16.95. **Description:** Step-by-step guide to start a small business and then use that business to create various streams of passive income to support yourself and charities is presented.

32444 ■ *Start Business in California, 3E*
Pub: Sourcebooks, Inc.
Contact: Len Vlahos, President
E-mail: dominique@sourcebooks.com
Ed: John J. Talamo. **Released:** July 2006. **Price:** $24.95. **Description:** Information required for starting any business in California.

32445 ■ *Start and Run a Bookkeeping Business*
Pub: Self-Counsel, Incorporated
Ed: Angie Mohr. **Released:** October 2005. **Price:** $17.95 (US), $22.95 (Canadian). **Description:** Advice for starting and running a bookkeeping service business. Includes MS Word and PDF formats for use in Windows-based PC.

32446 ■ *Start, Run, and Grow a Successful Small Business, 2nd Edition*
Pub: CCH Inc.
Contact: Mike Sabbatis, President
Ed: Susan M. Jacksack. **Price:** $24.95.

32447 ■ *"Start-Up Pointers" in Inside Business (Vol. 13, September-October 2011, No. 5, pp. Y3)*
Pub: Great Lakes Publishing Co.
Description: Four tips to help entrepreneurs with startup firms are provided by Youngstown Business Incubator.

32448 ■ *Start-ups That Work: Surprise Research on What Makes or Breaks a New Company*
Pub: Penguin Group
Ed: Joel Kurtzman; Glenn Rifkin. **Released:** October 2005. **Price:** $25.95.

32449 ■ *Start Your Own Business, Fifth Edition*
Pub: Entrepreneur Press
Contact: Perlman Neil, President
Ed: Rieva Lesonsky. **Released:** October 1, 2010. **Price:** $24.95. **Description:** Author and the staff of Entrepreneur Magazine provide business resources and information for starting a successful business. The book guides you through the first three years of ownership and provides work sheets and checklists.

32450 ■ *Start Your Own Lawn Care Business: Your Step-by-Step Guide to Success*
Pub: Entrepreneur Press
Ed: Eileen Figure Sandlin. **Released:** March 2007. **Price:** $17.95. **Description:** Steps for starting and running a lawn care service.

32451 ■ *Start Your Own Wedding Consultant Business*
Pub: Entrepreneur Press
Ed: Eileen Figure Sandlin. **Released:** December 2003. **Description:** Advice for starting and running a wedding consulting business.

32452 ■ *Starting Green: An Ecopreneur's Guide to Starting a Green Business from Business Plans to Profits*
Pub: Entrepreneur Press
Contact: Perlman Neil, President
Ed: Glenn E. Croston. **Released:** September 9, 2010. **Price:** $21.95. **Description:** Entrepreneur and scientist outlines green business essentials and helps uncover eco-friendly business opportunities, build a sustainable business plan, and gain the competitive advantage.

32453 ■ *Starting and Running a Coaching Business*
Pub: How To Books
Ed: Aryanne Oade. **Released:** August 9, 2010. **Price:** $26.00. **Description:** Guide for the comprehensive, practical and personalized process of starting and running a coaching business is presented.

32454 ■ *Starting a Successful Business in Canada*
Pub: Self-Counsel Press Inc.
Ed: Jack D. James. **Released:** 2000. **Description:** Provides a framework for entrepreneurs launching a new business in Canada.

32455 ■ *StartingUp Now Facilitator Guide*
Pub: StartingUp Now
Ed: L. Jenkins. **Released:** September 11, 2011. **Price:** $29.95. **Description:** Guide for those teaching entrepreneurship using StartingUp Now; the guide provides 24 lesson plans for each of the 24 steps/chapters in the book.

32456 ■ *Steps to Small Business Start-Up*
Pub: Kaplan Books
Ed: Linda Pinson; Jerry Jinnett. **Released:** July 2006. **Price:** $29.00. **Description:** Tips for starting and running a new company are presented.

32457 ■ *Stop Working: Start a Business, Globalize It, and Generate Enough Cash Flow to Get Out of the Rat Race*
Pub: Eye Contact Media
Ed: Rohan Hall. **Released:** November 2004. **Price:** $15.99. **Description:** Advice is given to small companies to compete in the global marketplace by entrepreneur using the same strategy for his own business.

32458 ■ *Straight Talk About Small Business Success in New Jersey: How to Maximize the Growth, Cash Flow and Profitability of Your Small Business*
Pub: Business Success Systems, Incorporated
Ed: Salim Omar. **Released:** April 2004. **Description:** Small business information geared to new and existing small businesses in New Jersey.

32459 ■ *"Survival of the Fittest" in Black Enterprise (November 2007)*
Pub: Earl G. Graves Publishing Co. Inc.
Ed: Tennille M. Robinson. **Description:** Black Enterprise has developed the Small Business Success Guide for prospective and current entrepreneurs.

32460 ■ *Swimming Against the Stream: Launching Your Business and Making Your Life*
Pub: Macmillan Publishers Limited
Ed: Tim Waterstone. **Released:** March 2007. **Price:** $17.99. **Description:** Ten rules for launching a new business are outlined using real-life experiences.

32461 ■ *The Toilet Paper Entrepreneur: The Tell-It-Like-It-Is Guide to Cleaning Up In Business, Even If You Are At the End of Your Roll*
Pub: Obsidian Launch LLC
Ed: Mike Michalowicz. **Price:** $24.95. **Description:** The founder of three multimillion-dollar companies, including Obsidian Launch, a company that partners with first-time entrepreneurs to grow their concepts into industry leaders.

32462 ■ *"Top 25 Graduate Programs" in Entrepreneur (Vol. 35, November 2007, No. 11, pp. 92)*
Pub: Entrepreneur Media Inc.
Description: List of the top twenty-five graduate entrepreneurship programs of different colleges and universities in the U.S. for 2007, as ranked by Entrepreneur Magazine and the Princeton Review, is presented.

32463 ■ *"Top 25 Undergrad Programs" in Entrepreneur (Vol. 35, November 2007, No. 11, pp. 88)*
Pub: Entrepreneur Media Inc.
Description: List of the top twenty-five undergraduate entrepreneurship programs of different colleges and universities in the U.S. for 2007, as ranked by Entrepreneur Magazine and the Princeton Review, is highlighted.

32464 ■ *"Top of the Class" in Entrepreneur (Vol. 35, November 2007, No. 11, pp. 82)*
Pub: Entrepreneur Media Inc.
Ed: Nichole L. Torres. **Description:** Education in entrepreneurship is being pursued by many students and it is important to understand what entrepreneurship program fits you. Aspiring entrepreneurs should also ask about the program's focus. Considerations searched for by students regarding the particular school they chose to study entrepreneurship are discussed.

32465 ■ *"Troy Patent Law Firm Launches Rent-Free Tech Incubator" in Crain's Detroit Business (Vol. 25, June 8, 2009, No. 23, pp. 4)*
Pub: Crain Communications Inc. - Detroit
Ed: Tom Henderson. **Description:** Young Basile Hanlon MacFarlane & Helmholdt PC, a patent law firm located in Troy, Michigan has created a small, rent-free technology incubator on site. The incubator will be called North Woodward Tech Incubator and has room for four or five startups. The incubator is for the earliest or pre-seed stage for entrepreneurs who have not yet gotten significant investment capital.

32466 ■ *Trump University Entrepreneurship 101: How to Turn Your Idea Into a Money Machine*
Pub: John Wiley & Sons, Inc.
Ed: Michael E. Gordon. **Released:** September 1, 2009. **Price:** $24.95. **Description:** Current and expanded edition to the Trump guide to starting a business where Trump teams with Professor Michael Gordon to show how to take a dream and turn it into a successful enterprise.

32467 ■ *"Turning Bright Ideas Into Profitable Businesses" in Inside Business (Vol. 13, September-October 2011, No. 5, pp. SS6)*
Pub: Great Lakes Publishing Co.
Ed: Susan Keen Flynn. **Description:** Startup Lakewood was launched by Mickie Rinehart. She provides free resources to entrepreneurs in the city in order to help them turn their small business vision into reality.

32468 ■ *Ultimate Startup Directory: Expert Advice and 1,500 Great Startup Ideas*
Pub: Entrepreneur Press
Ed: James Stephenson. **Released:** February 2007. **Price:** $30.95 (CND). **Description:** Startup opportunities in over 30 industries are given, along with information on investment, earning potential, skills, legal requirements and more.

32469 ■ *The Unofficial Guide to Starting a Small Business*
Pub: John Wiley & Sons, Incorporated
Ed: Marcia Layton Turner. **Released:** October 2004. **Price:** $16.99. **Description:** Information and tools for starting a small business, covering the start-up process, from market research, to business plans, to marketing programs.

32470 ■ *Up and Running: Opening a Chiropractic Office*
Pub: PageFree Publishing, Incorporated
Ed: John L. Reizer. **Released:** March 2002. **Price:** $30.00. **Description:** Tips for starting a chiropractic business.

32471 ■ *"USM Focuses on Turning Science Into New Companies, Cash" in Boston Business Journal (Vol. 29, July 1, 2011, No. 8, pp. 1)*
Pub: American City Business Journals Inc.
Ed: Alexander Jackson. **Description:** University System of Maryland gears up to push for its plan for commercializing its scientific discoveries which by 2020 could create 325 companies and double the $1.4 billion the system's eleven schools garner in yearly research grants. It is talking with University of Utah and University Maryland, Baltimore to explore ways to make this plan a reality.

32472 ■ *"UT Deans Serious about Biz" in Austin Business Journal (Vol. 31, May 20, 2011, No. 11, pp. 1)*
Pub: American City Business Journals Inc.
Ed: Sandra Zaragoza. **Description:** Dean Thomas Gilligan of the University of Texas, McCombs School of Business and engineering school Dean Gregory Fenves have partnered to develop a joint engineering and business degree. Their partnership has resulted in an undergraduate course on initiating startups.

32473 ■ *Valuing Early Stage and Venture Backed Companies*
Pub: John Wiley & Sons, Inc.
Ed: Neil J. Beaton. **Released:** December 1, 2009. **Price:** $110.00. **Description:** Valuation techniques that can be used to value early stage companies with complex capital structures are examined.

32474 ■ *"Virtual Playground" in Entrepreneur (Vol. 36, March 2008, No. 3, pp. 112)*
Pub: Entrepreneur Media Inc.
Ed: Amanda C. Kooser. **Description:** The growing number of children visiting virtual worlds provides opportunity for entrepreneurs to start online businesses catering to this market. Entrepreneurs need to be aware of the Children's Online Privacy Protection Act with regard to collecting children's information. Details of other things to know about with reference to these businesses are examined.

32475 ■ *Weekend Small Business Start*
Pub: Sourcebooks, Inc.
Contact: Len Vlahos, President
E-mail: dominique@sourcebooks.com
Ed: Mark Warda. **Released:** June 2007. **Price:** $19.95. **Description:** Information for starting a new business is presented.

32476 ■ *What No One Ever Tells You About Starting Your Own Business: Real-Life Start-Up Advice from 101 Successful Entrepreneurs*
Pub: Kaplan Publishing
Ed: Jan Norman. **Released:** July 2004. **Price:** $18.95 (US), $28.95 (Canadian). **Description:** From planning to marketing, advice is given to entrepreneurs starting new companies. s.

32477 ■ *Working for Yourself: An Entrepreneur's Guide to the Basics*
Pub: Kogan Page, Limited
Contact: Ben Glover, Director of Marketing
Ed: Jonathan Reuvid. **Released:** September 2006. **Description:** Guide for starting a new business venture, focusing on raising financing, legal and tax issues, marketing, information technology, and site location.

32478 ■ *"The Y Factor" in Entrepreneur (Vol. 35, November 2007, No. 11, pp. 58)*
Pub: Entrepreneur Media Inc.
Ed: Sara Wilson. **Description:** Venture capital company Y Cominbator hosts a three-month program wherein the firm's founders select technology entrepreneurs from across the U.S. to help and to mentor them on starting a business.

32479 ■ *You Can Do It Too: The 20 Essential Things Every Budding Entrepreneur Should Know*
Pub: Kogan Page, Limited
Contact: Ben Glover, Director of Marketing
Ed: Rachel Bridge. **Released:** May 10, 2010. **Price:** $29.95. **Description:** Collective wisdom of successful entrepreneurs in the form of twenty essential elements to focus on when starting a new company is illustrated by real-life entrepreneurial stories.

32480 ■ *You Need to be a Little Bit Crazy: The Truth about Starting and Growing Your Business*
Pub: Dearborn Trade Publishing Inc.
Contact: Roy Lipner, President
Ed: Barry J. Moltz. **Description:** Offers entrepreneurs and small business owners insight into the ups and downs of running a business.

32481 ■ *You Need To Be a Little Crazy*
Pub: Dearborn Trade Publishing Inc.
Contact: Roy Lipner, President
Ed: Barry J. Moltz. **Released:** December 2008. **Price:** $14.95. **Description:** Entrepreneur and investor who has founded several successful startups provides a guide using personal experience to help anyone start a new business.

32482 ■ *Your First Business Plan: A Simple Question-and-Answer Format Designed to Help You Write Your Own Plan*
Pub: Sourcebooks, Inc.
Contact: Len Vlahos, President
E-mail: dominique@sourcebooks.com
Ed: Joseph A. Covello. **Released:** May 2005. **Price:** $14.95. **Description:** Writing a good first business plan outlines successful business growth.

32483 ■ *Your Million-Dollar Idea: From Concept to Marketplace*
Pub: Adams Media Corporation
Ed: Sandy Abrams. **Released:** March 1, 2010. **Price:** $14.95. **Description:** Self-taught entrepreneur provides a 12-step plan to make a new product or service a profitable reality.

ASSOCIATIONS AND OTHER ORGANIZATIONS

32484 ■ Association for Enterprise Information (AFEI)
2111 Wilson Blvd., Ste. 400
Arlington, VA 22201
Ph: (703)247-9474
Fax: (703)522-3192
Co. E-mail: dchesebrough@afei.org
URL: http://www.afei.org
Contact: Margaret E. Myers, Chairperson
Description: Strives to advance enterprise integration and electronic business practices for industries and governments. **Founded:** 1998.

32485 ■ BC Innovation Council
1188 W Georgia St., 9th Fl.
Vancouver, BC, Canada V6E 4A2
Ph: (604)683-2724
Free: 800-665-7222
Fax: (604)683-6567
Co. E-mail: info@bcic.ca
URL: http://www.bcic.ca
Contact: Jill Leversage, Chairperson
Description: Provides support and access to companies and institutions by using research results, development projects and programs to further enhance in creating innovations. **Awards:** BCIC Awards; BC Science and Technology Champion (Annual); Cecil Green Award for Technology Entrepreneurship (Annual).

32486 ■ Canadian Federation of Independent Business (CFIB)—Federation Canadienne de l'Entreprise Independandante
401-4141 Yonge St., Ste. 401
Toronto, ON, Canada M2P 2A6
Ph: (416)222-8022
Free: 888-234-2232
Fax: (416)222-6103
Co. E-mail: cfib@cfib.ca
URL: http://www.cfib-fcei.ca/english/index.html
Contact: Danny Kelly, President
Description: Independent businesses. Promotes economic well-being of members and seeks to maintain a healthy domestic business climate. Represents members' interests before government agencies, labor and industrial organizations, and the public. **Scope:** entrepreneurship, economic policy, small business, public policy. **Founded:** 1971. **Subscriptions:** 4000 books periodicals reports. **Publications:** *Mandate* (Quarterly); *Quarterly Business Barometer* (3/year). **Awards:** Canada Awards for Excellence.

32487 ■ International Council for Small Business (ICSB)
GWU School of Business
Washington, DC 20052
Ph: (202)994-0704
Fax: (202)994-4930
Co. E-mail: icsb@gwu.edu
URL: http://www.icsb.org
Contact: Sylvio Rosa, Jr., President
E-mail: srosa@parqtec.com.br
Description: Management educators, researchers, government officials and professionals in 80 countries. Fosters discussion of topics pertaining to the development and improvement of small business management. **Founded:** 1955. **Publications:** *Journal of Small Business Management* (Quarterly). **Telecommunication Services:** aymanelt@icsb.org.

32488 ■ *Mandate*
401-4141 Yonge St., Ste. 401
Toronto, ON, Canada M2P 2A6
Ph: (416)222-8022
Free: 888-234-2232
Fax: (416)222-6103
Co. E-mail: cfib@cfib.ca
URL: http://www.cfib-fcei.ca/english/index.html
Contact: Danny Kelly, President
Released: Quarterly

32489 ■ National Association for Business Organizations (NAFBO)
5432 Price Ave.
Baltimore, MD 21215
Ph: (410)367-5309
Co. E-mail: nahbb@msn.com
URL: http://www.ameribizs.com/global
Contact: Rudolph Lewis, President
Description: Business organizations that develop and support small businesses that have the capability to provide their products or services on a national level. Promotes small business in a free market system; represents the interests of small businesses to government and community organizations on small business affairs; monitors and reviews laws that affect small businesses; promotes a business code of ethics. Supplies members with marketing and management assistance; encourages joint marketing services between members. Operates a Home Based Business Television Network that provides an affordable audio/visual media for small and home based businesses. **Founded:** 1986. **Awards:** Entrepreneur Certificate.

32490 ■ National Association of Small Business Investment Companies (NASBIC)
1100 H St. NW, Ste. 610
Washington, DC 20005
Ph: (202)628-5055
Fax: (202)628-5080
Co. E-mail: bpalmer@nasbic.org
URL: http://www.nasbic.org
Contact: Brett Palmer, President
E-mail: bpalmer@nasbic.org
URL(s): www.nasbic.com/. **Description:** Firms licensed as Small Business Investment Companies (SBICs) under the Small Business Investment Act of 1958. **Founded:** 1958. **Publications:** *NASBIC News* (Quarterly); *NASBIC Membership Directory* (Annual); *NASBIC Membership Directory* (Annual); *Today's SBICs: Investing in America's Future*; *Venture Capital: Where to Find It* (Annual). **Educational Activities:** Venture Capital Institute for Entrepreneurs (Annual); Venture Capital Institute for Entrepreneurs (Annual); National Association of Small Business Investment Companies Annual Convention (Annual). **Awards:** Portfolio Company of the Year Award (Annual). **Telecommunication Services:** info@sbia.org; nasbic@nasbic.org.

32491 ■ National Small Business Association (NSBA)
1156 15th St. NW, Ste. 1100
Washington, DC 20005
Ph: (202)293-8830
Free: 800-345-6728
Fax: (202)872-8543
Co. E-mail: membership@nsba.biz
URL: http://www.nsba.biz
Contact: Chris Holman, Chairman
Description: Small businesses including manufacturing, wholesale, retail, service, and other firms. Works to advocate at the federal level on behalf of smaller businesses. **Founded:** 1937. **Publications:** *Advocate* (Bimonthly). **Educational Activities:** Small Business Meetup Day (Monthly). **Awards:** Lewis I. Shattuck Advocate of the Year Award (Annual).

32492 ■ *Quarterly Business Barometer*
401-4141 Yonge St., Ste. 401
Toronto, ON, Canada M2P 2A6
Ph: (416)222-8022
Free: 888-234-2232
Fax: (416)222-6103
Co. E-mail: cfib@cfib.ca
URL: http://www.cfib-fcei.ca/english/index.html
Contact: Danny Kelly, President
Released: 3/year

32493 ■ SCORE
1175 Herndon Pkwy., Ste. 900
Herndon, VA 20170
Free: 800-634-0245
Co. E-mail: help@score.org
URL: http://www.score.org
Contact: Kenneth W. Yancey, Jr., Chief Executive Officer
Description: Serves as volunteer program sponsored by U.S. Small Business Administration in which working and retired business management professionals provide free business counseling to men and women who are considering starting a small business, encountering problems with their business, or expanding their business. Offers free one-on-one counseling, online counseling and low cost workshops on a variety of business topics. **Scope:** business. **Founded:** 1964. **Subscriptions:** books clippings periodicals. **Publications:** *SCORE eNews* (Monthly); *SCORE Today* (Monthly). **Awards:** Outstanding Woman-owned Business Award (Annual); SCORE Chapter of the Year Award (Annual).

REFERENCE WORKS

32494 ■ *The 4-Hour Workweek*
Pub: Crown Publishing/Random House
Ed: Timothy Ferris. **Released:** April 24, 2007. **Price:** $19.95. **Description:** Examination of ways to cut the hours you work and find more enjoyment in your life.

32495 ■ *The 4 Routes to Entrepreneurial Success*
Pub: Berrett-Koehler Publishers
Ed: John B. Miner. **Price:** $18.95. **Description:** After researching one hundred successful entrepreneurs, the author discovered there are basically four personality types of entrepreneurs: the personal achiever, the super salesperson, the real manager, and the expert idea generator.

32496 ■ *The 5 Big Lies About American Business: Combating Smears Against the Free-Market Economy*
Pub: Crown Business Books
Ed: Michael Medved. **Released:** November 2, 2010. **Price:** $15.00. **Description:** Michael Medved, talk-radio personality and bestselling author, argues for capitalism. He presents popular myths about the free market system and discusses why each myth is instead good for Americans and our economy.

32497 ■ *The 7 Irrefutable Rules of Small Business Growth*
Pub: John Wiley & Sons, Incorporated
Ed: Steven S. Little. **Released:** February 2005. **Price:** $18.95. **Description:** Proven strategies to maintain small business growth are outlined, covering topics such as technology, business plans, hiring, and more.

32498 ■ *The 29 Percent Solution*
Pub: Greenleaf Book Group Press
Ed: Ivan Misner, Michele Donovan. **Released:** 2008. **Price:** $21.95. **Description:** It is true that some people are better connected than others. That means that connecting is a skill that can be acquired. Networking skills used to increase business connections are highlighted.

32499 ■ *32 Ways to Be a Champion in Business*
Pub: Three Rivers Press
Ed: Earvin Magic Johnson. **Released:** December 29, 2009. **Price:** $18.94. **Description:** Earvin Johnson discusses his transition from athlete to entrepreneur and discusses the importance of hard work in order to pursue your dreams of starting and running a successful business.

32500 ■ *"The 40-Year-Old Intern" in Entrepreneur (Vol. 37, October 2009, No. 10, pp. 90)*
Pub: Entrepreneur Media, Inc.
Ed: Kristin Ladd. **Description:** Brian Kurth's VocationVacation is an internship program aimed at helping people experience their dream job. The website, launched in January 2004, matches people with businesses that allow them to experience their fantasy jobs.

32501 ■ *"The 100 Fastest-Growing Companies" in Hispanic Business (Vol. 30, July-August 2008, No. 7-8, pp. 22)*
Pub: Hispanic Business, Inc.
Ed: Michael Bowker. **Description:** CEO's of the five fastest growing Hispanic-owned companies discuss the success of their companies; most of them at-

tribute their success to proper investment and diversification, effective innovations and seeing growth opportunities where others see roadblocks.

32502 ■ *101 Secrets to Building a Winning Business*
Pub: Allen & Unwin
Ed: Andrew Griffiths. **Released:** September 1, 2009. **Price:** $14.95. **Description:** Provides expert information for running and growing a small business.

32503 ■ *201 Great Tips for Your Small Business: Increase Your Profit and Joy in Your Work*
Pub: Dundren Press Limited
Ed: Julie V. Watson. **Released:** April 2006. **Price:** $24.99. **Description:** Tips and hints for home-based, micro, and small businesses are presented.

32504 ■ *401 Questions Every Entrepreneur Should Ask*
Pub: Career Press, Incorporated
Ed: James L. Silvester. **Released:** October 2006. **Price:** $17.99. **Description:** Review of 25 functional areas of running a small business are covered along with questions entrepreneurs should ask in order to correct and avoid unwanted issues.

32505 ■ *"2007 Fittest CEOs" in Hawaii Business (Vol. 53, October 2007, No. 4, pp. 40)*
Pub: Hawaii Business Publishing
Description: Discusses the outcome of the fittest chief executive officers in Hawaii competition for 2007. Hawaii Capital Management's David Low leads the list while Group Pacific (Hawaii) Inc.'s Chip Doyle and Greater Good Inc.'s Kari Leong placed second and third, respectively. The CEO's routines, eating habits, and inspirations for staying fit are provided.

32506 ■ *"2009: A Call For Vision" in Women Entrepreneur (January 28, 2009)*
Pub: Entrepreneur Media Inc.
Ed: Elinor Robin. **Description:** Providing exemplary customer service, reducing expenses and creating an out-of-the-box niche are three key factors that will help business survive during this economic crisis. Business owners must see potential where others see failure in order to create new opportunities that may not only allow their business to survive during these times but may actually cause some businesses to thrive despite this economic downturn.

32507 ■ *"2010 Book of Lists" in Business Courier (Vol. 26, December 26, 2009, No. 36, pp. 1)*
Pub: American City Business Journals, Inc.
Description: Rankings of companies and organizations within the business services, education, finance, health care, hospitality and tourism, real estate, and technology industries in the Cincinnati, Ohio-Northern Kentucky area are presented. Rankings are based on sales, business size, or other statistics.

32508 ■ *"Abaddon Acquires Pukaskwa Uranium Properties in NW Ontario" in Canadian Corporate News (May 16, 2007)*
Pub: Comtex News Network Inc.
Description: Rubicon Minerals Corp. has entered into an Option Agreement with Consolidated Abaddon Resources Inc. for the acquisition of Pukaskwa uranium properties and plans to conduct an extensive exploration program to prove out the resource and geological potential of the area. Statistical data included.

32509 ■ *"Ace Every Introduction" in Women Entrepreneur (September 10, 2008)*
Pub: Entrepreneur Media Inc.
Ed: Cynthia McKay. **Description:** Making a powerful first impression is one of the most important marketing tools a business owner can possess. Advice about meeting new business contacts is given.

32510 ■ *The Age Curve: How to Profit from the Demographic Storm*
Pub: AMACOM
Ed: Kenneth W. Gronbach. **Released:** July 3, 2008. **Price:** $24.95. **Description:** Reveals how America's largest generations are redefining consumer behavior and how businesses can anticipate their growing needs more effectively.

32511 ■ *"Aging Boomers to Slow Growth, Study Says" in Globe & Mail (March 15, 2006, pp. B5)*
Pub: CTVglobemedia Publishing Inc.
Ed: Heather Scoffield. **Description:** Acording to a research study by economic forecasters at Global Insight (Canada) Inc., an issue about Canada controlling its economy, as the country's population is aging, is discussed.

32512 ■ *Ahead of the Curve: Two Years at Harvard Business School*
Pub: Penguin Group USA Inc.
Ed: Philip Delves Broughton. **Released:** 2009. **Price:** $25.95. **Description:** A behind-the-scenes glimpse at Harvard Business School is given. The author believes Harvard succeeds in transforming students into business leaders but feels they are failing them in every other way.

32513 ■ *"Alberta: Help Wanted, Badly" in Globe & Mail (March 11, 2006, pp. B5)*
Pub: CTVglobemedia Publishing Inc.
Ed: Patrick Brethour; Dawn Walton. **Description:** The issue of unemployment rate, which fell by 3.1 percent in Alberta, is discussed.

32514 ■ *"Alberta Slashes Tax Rate to Ten Percent" in Globe & Mail (March 23, 2006, pp. B1)*
Pub: CTVglobemedia Publishing Inc.
Ed: Patrick Brethour. **Description:** Alberta province has slashed its corporate taxes from 11.5 to 10 percent to draw more business to the state. Details of the tax cut and its impact is analyzed.

32515 ■ *"Alcan Statement on Water Rights Could Encourgage Bid" in Globe & Mail (April 25, 2007, pp. B5)*
Pub: CTVglobemedia Publishing Inc.
Ed: Andy Hoffman. **Description:** The possibility for a foreign firm to bid for Alcan Inc. in the light of its agreement with Canadian government over water rights is discussed.

32516 ■ *"All In The Family" in Canadian Business (Vol. 79, September 25, 2006, No. 19, pp. 75)*
Pub: Rogers Media
Ed: Zena Olijnyk. **Description:** Continuing ownership of Weston dynasty on Canada's largest chain Loblaw Co. is discussed.

32517 ■ *Alpha Dogs: How Your Small Business Can Become a Leader of the Pack*
Pub: HarperInformation
Ed: Donna Fenn. **Released:** May 2007. **Price:** $14.95. **Description:** Ways for an entrepreneur to outsmart competitors in the marketplace, to generate higher sales, and earn lasting customer and employee loyalty.

32518 ■ *Alpha Dogs: How Your Small Business Can Become a Leader of the Pack*
Pub: HarperCollins Publishers, Inc.
Ed: Donna Fenn. **Released:** May 2007. **Price:** $14.95. **Description:** Profiles of eight successful entrepreneurs along with information for developing customer service, technology and competition.

32519 ■ *America's Corporate Families*
Pub: Dun and Bradstreet Corp.
Contact: David J. Emery, President
URL(s): www.dnb.com. **Released:** Annual **Covers:** Approximately 12,700 U.S. corporations. Ultimate companies must meet all of the following criteria for inclusion: two or more business locations, 250 or more employees at that location or in excess of $25 million in sales volume or a tangible net worth greater than $500,000, and controlling interest in one or more subsidiary company. **Entries include:** D&B D-U-N-S number, company name, address, phone, state of incorporation, line of business, primary/secondary SIC codes, sales volume, net worth, number of employees, current ownership date, year started, number of sites, key executives' names/titles, directors and officers, primary bank and accounting firm, import/export designation, stock exchange symbol and indicator for publicly owned companies, parent company and location. **Arrangement:** Alphabetical, geographical, industry classification. **Indexes:** Geographical, SIC code (both with address and SIC code).

32520 ■ *"Angels for the Jobless; Church Volunteer Groups Give Career Guidance" in Crain's Detroit Business (Vol. 24, March 31, 2008, No. 13)*
Pub: Crain Communications, Inc.
Ed: Sherri Begin. **Description:** St. Andrew Catholic Church, located in Rochester, offers the St. Andrew Career Mentoring Ministry, a program that brings in professionals who volunteer to aid those seeking jobs or, in numerous cases, new careers.

32521 ■ *"Arcelor Bid Wins Dofasco Board's Blessing" in Globe & Mail (January 17, 2006, pp. B1)*
Pub: CTVglobemedia Publishing Inc.
Ed: Greg Keenan. **Description:** The details surrounding Arcelor SA's proposed acquisition of Dofasco Inc., for $5.5 billion, are presented.

32522 ■ *Are Government Purchasing Policies Failing Small Business?: Congressional Hearing*
Pub: DIANE Publishing Company
Ed: John F. Kerry. **Released:** September 2002. **Price:** Paperback $35.00. **Description:** Covers Congressional hearing: Steven App, Treasury Department; Fred Armendariz and Major Clark, Small Business Administration; Susan Allen, Pan Asian American Chamber of Commerce; Stephen Denlinger, Latin American Management Association; Charles Henry, National Veteran's Business Development Corporation; Morris Hudson, MO Procurement Technology Assistance Centers; Bar Kasoff, Women Impact, Public Policy; Pam Mazza, Piliero, Massa and Pargament; Ron Newlan, HubZone Contract National Council; Pat Parker, Native American Management Service; Joann Payne, Women First National Legislative Commission; Mike Robinson, MA Small Business Development Centers; Ramon Rodriguez, Hispanic Chamber of Commerce; Angela Styles, Office of Management and Budget; Ralph Thomas, NASA; John Turner, MN Business Enterprise Legal Defense Fund; James Turpin, American Subcontractor's Association, Inc.; and Henry Wilfong, National Association of Small Disadvantaged Business.

32523 ■ *"Are There Material Benefits To Social Diversity?" in Hispanic Business (Vol. 30, September 2008, No. 9, pp. 10)*
Pub: Hispanic Business, Inc.
Ed: Brigida Benitez. **Description:** Diversity in American colleges and universities, where students view and appreciate their peers as individuals and do not judge them on the basis of race, gender, or ethnicity is discussed. The benefits of diversity in higher education are also acknowledged by the U.S. Supreme Court and by leading American corporations.

32524 ■ *"Are You Rich?" in Barron's (Vol. 88, March 10, 2008, No. 10, pp. 27)*
Pub: Dow Jones & Company, Inc.
Ed: Tom Sullivan. **Description:** Discusses the minimum net worth of people considered as rich in America is now at $25 million. There are about 125,000 households in America that meet this threshold, while 49,000 households have a net worth between $25 million and $ 500 million, and about 1,400 US households have a net worth over $500 million.

32525 ■ *"The Art of War for Women" in Hawaii Business (Vol. 54, July 2008, No. 1, pp. 23)*
Pub: Hawaii Business Publishing
Description: Business consultant Chi-Ning Chu talks about her new book 'The Art of War for Women: Sun Tzu's Ancient Strategies and Wisdom for Winning at Work', which discusses how women can more effectively win in business. She also shares her thoughts about the advantages that women have, which they can use in businesses decisions.

32526 ■ *"At Your Career Crossroads" in Women In Business (Vol. 61, December 2009, No. 6, pp. 26)*
Pub: American Business Women's Association
Ed: Diane Stafford. **Description:** Guidelines for employees who are considering a job or career change are presented. Among the reasons for lead employees to make these changes are downsizing, job loss, environments that are not conducive to work or unfavorable work relationships with bosses.

32527 ■ *"Attend To Your Corporate Housekeeping" in Women Entrepreneur (December 4, 2008)*
Pub: Entrepreneur Media Inc.
Ed: Nina Kaufman. **Description:** Business owners can lose all the benefits and privileges of the corporate form if they do not follow proper corporate formalities such as holding an annual meeting, electing officers and directors and adopting or passing corporate resolutions. Creditors are able to take from one's personal assets if such formalities have not been followed.

32528 ■ *"Austin's GMP Growth Top in Nation" in Austin Business JournalInc. (Vol. 29, January 8, 2010, No. 44, pp. 1)*
Pub: American City Business Journals
Ed: Jacob Dirr. **Description:** Austin's gross metropolitan product (GMP) has grown by 2 percent, putting it in the top 5 for GMP growth among the largest 100 American metropolitan areas. Insights into the area's business and technology services are examined.

32529 ■ *"The Bad Dresser" in Canadian Business (Vol. 80, April 23, 2007, No. 9, pp. 66)*
Pub: Rogers Media
Ed: Calvin Leung. **Description:** The need of maintaining formal dressing to fit into corporate culture is emphasized.

32530 ■ *Balls!: 6 Rules for Winning Today's Business Game*
Pub: John Wiley & Sons, Incorporated
Ed: Alexi Venneri. **Released:** January 2005. **Price:** $29.95. **Description:** In order to be successful business leaders must be brave, authentic, loud, lovable, and spunky and they need to lead their competition.

32531 ■ *"Bankruptcies" in Crain's Detroit Business (Vol. 24, March 24, 2008, No. 12, pp. 6)*
Pub: Crain Communications, Inc.
Description: Current list of business that filed for Chapter 7 or 11 protection in U.S. Bankruptcy Court in Detroit include a construction company, a medical care company, a physical therapy firm and a communications firm.

32532 ■ *Bankruptcy for Small Business*
Pub: Sphinx Publishing
Ed: Wendell Schollander. **Released:** July 1, 2008. **Price:** $22.95 paperback. **Description:** Bankruptcy laws can be used to save a small business, homes or other property. The book provides general information for small business owners regarding the reasons for money problems, types of bankruptcy available and their alternatives, myths about bankruptcy, and the do's and don'ts for filing for bankruptcy.

32533 ■ *Beans: Four Principles for Running a Business in Good Times or Bad*
Pub: John Wiley & Sons, Incorporated
Ed: Leslie Yerkes, Charles Decker, Bob Nelson. **Released:** June 2003. **Price:** $19.95. **Description:** Profile of Monorail Espresso, the popular Seattle coffee company that has become prosperous by intentionally staying small and building a strong customer service program.

32534 ■ *Being Self-Employed: How to Run a Business Out of Your Home, Claim Travel and Depreciation and Earn a Good Income Well into Your 70s or 80s*
Pub: Allyear Tax Guides
Ed: Holmes F. Crouch, Irma Jean Crouch, Barbara J. MacRae. **Released:** September 2004. **Price:** $24.95 (US), $37.95 (Canadian). **Description:** Guide for small business to keep accurate tax records.

32535 ■ *Ben Franklin: America's Original Entrepreneur, Franklin's Autobiography Adapted for Modern Times*
Pub: McGraw-Hill
Ed: Blaine McCormick; Benjamin Franklin. **Released:** September 2005.

32536 ■ *"Best Companies for Diversity" in Black Enterprise (Vol. 38, July 2008, No. 12, pp. 12)*
Pub: Earl G. Graves Publishing Co. Inc.
Description: Maintaining excellence in a company's diversity efforts requires critical challenges such as recruiting, retaining and developing talent in the executive pipeline. Top young and diverse emerging executives in corporate America are featured.

32537 ■ *"The Best Execs in Canada" in Canadian Business (Vol. 79, October 9, 2006, No. 20, pp. 68)*
Pub: Rogers Media
Description: The annual list of the most outstanding and innovative business executives of Canada is presented.

32538 ■ *The Big Book of Small Business: You Don't Have to Run Your Business by the Seat of Your Pants*
Pub: HarperCollins Publishers, Inc.
Ed: Tom Gegax; Phil Bolsta. **Released:** February 2007. **Price:** $29.95. **Description:** Entrepreneur shares his experiences starting and running his small business.

32539 ■ *Big Vision, Small Business*
Pub: Ivy Sea, Inc.
Ed: Jamie S. Walters. **Released:** October 10, 2002. **Price:** $17.95. **Description:** The power of the small enterprise is examined. The author shares her expertise as an entrepreneur and founder of a business consulting firm to help small business owners successfully run their companies. Interviews with more than seventy small business owners provide insight into visioning, planning, and establishing a small company, as well as strategies for good employee and customer relationships.

32540 ■ *Bigger Isn't Always Better*
Pub: AMACOM
Ed: Robert M. Tomasko. **Price:** $24.95.

32541 ■ *"Billion-Dollar Impact" in Business First Buffalo (November 9, 2007, pp. 1)*
Pub: American City Business Journals, Inc.
Ed: Tracey Dury. **Description:** Western New York has thousands of nonprofit organizations, 240 of which have collective revenue of $1.74 billion based on federal tax returns for the 2005 and 2006 fiscal years. The nonprofit sector has a large impact on WNY's economy, but it is not highly recognized. The financial performance of notable nonprofit organizations is given.

32542 ■ *The Black Swan*
Pub: Random House
Description: A black swan is a highly improbably event with three principle characteristics: it is unpredictable, it carries a massive impact, and after the fact, we concoct an explanation that makes it appear less random and more predictable than it really was. The success of Google was a black swan; so was 9/11. According to the author, black swans underlie almost everything about the world, from the rise of religions to events in personal lives.

32543 ■ *The Board Book: An Insider's Guide for Directors and Trustees*
Pub: W.W. Norton & Company
Ed: William G. Bowen. **Released:** 2009. **Price:** $26.95. **Description:** A primer for all directors and trustees that provides suggestions for getting back to good-governance basics in business.

32544 ■ *"Bombardier Wins Chinese Rail Deal" in Globe & Mail (March 20, 2006, pp. B1)*
Pub: CTVglobemedia Publishing Inc.
Ed: Geoffrey York. **Description:** Bombardier Inc. has won a $68 million (U.S) contract to provide railway cars for rapid transit-link between Beijing and its international airport for 2008 Olympics in China. Details of the contract are presented.

32545 ■ *The Book of Entrepreneurs' Wisdom*
Pub: John Wiley and Sons Inc.
Ed: Peter Krass. **Price:** $26.95.

32546 ■ *"Book of Lists 2010" in Philadelphia Business Journal (Vol. 28, December 25, 2009, No. 45, pp. 1)*
Pub: American City Business Journals
Description: Rankings of companies and organizations within the banking, biotechnology, economic development, healthcare, hospitality, law and accounting, marketing and media, real estate, and technology industries in the Philadelphia, Pennsylvania area are presented. Rankings are based on sales, business size, and more.

32547 ■ *"The Bottom Line: Did CN Push Too Hard?" in Globe & Mail (February 23, 2007, pp. B1)*
Pub: CTVglobemedia Publishing Inc.
Ed: Brett Jang. **Description:** The effect of the efficiency drive started by Hunter Harrison at Canadian National Railway Company on the company's labor relations is discussed.

32548 ■ *Brag!: The Art of Tooting Your Own Horn Without Blowing It*
Pub: Warner Books, Incorporated
Ed: Peggy Klaus. **Released:** May 2004. **Price:** $13.95. **Description:** A plan to promote a small business by effectively selling one's self.

32549 ■ *The Breakthrough Company*
Pub: Crown Publishing/Random House
Ed: Keith McFarland. **Released:** September 1, 2009. **Price:** $16.00 paperback. **Description:** Traits of high-growth players that actually make it in business.

32550 ■ *"Brett Wilson" in Canadian Business (Vol. 81, July 22, 2008, No. 12-13, pp. 80)*
Pub: Rogers Media Ltd.
Ed: Michelle Magnan. **Description:** Interview with Brett Wilson who believes he became a 'capitalist with a heart' because he had a father who sold cars and a mother who was a social worker. He feels that being accelerated a grade was one of the biggest opportunities and challenges in his life. Brett Wilson's other views on business and on his family are presented.

32551 ■ *"Bridging the Ingenuity Gap" in Canadian Business (Vol. 79, November 6, 2006, No. 22, pp. 12)*
Pub: Rogers Media
Ed: Rachel Pulfer. **Description:** The views of Patrick Whitney, director of Illinois Institute of Technology's Institute of design, on globalization and business design methods are presented.

32552 ■ *"Bryan Berg" in Hawaii Business (Vol. 53, March 2008, No. 9, pp. 28)*
Pub: Hawaii Business Publishing
Ed: David K. Choo. **Description:** Bryan Berg, senior vice president at Target Corp.'s Region 1, shares his thoughts about entering the Hawaiian market and Target representatives bringing malasadas when visiting a business in the state. Berg finds the state's aloha spirit interesting and feels that it is important to be respectful of the Hawaiian culture and traditions in doing their business there.

32553 ■ *Building a Business the Buddhist Way*
Pub: Celestial Arts Publishing Company
Ed: Geri Larkin. **Released:** September 2004. **Price:** $11.67 (Canadian). **Description:** Principles of entrepreneurship for starting and growing a business while maintaining a balance between business goals and spiritual goals.

32554 ■ *Built to Last: Successful Habits of Visionary Companies*
Pub: HarperCollins Publishers Inc.
Ed: James C. Collins; Jerry I. Porras. **Released:** January 2002. **Price:** $17.95 paperback.

32555 ■ *Business Diagnostics: The Canadian Edition 2nd Ed.*
Pub: Trafford Publishing
Ed: Michael Thompson; Richard Mimick. **Released:** July 6, 2006. **Price:** $70.00. **Description:** Business management skills are outlined.

32556 ■ *"Business Diary" in Crain's Detroit Business (Vol. 24, October 6, 2008, No. 40, pp. 23)*
Pub: Crain Communications, Inc.
Description: Detailed listing of acquisitions, expansions, new products, new services, business contracts and startups from the Detroit area is provided.

32557 ■ *Business Fairy Tales*
Pub: Thomson South-Western
Ed: Cecil W. Jackson. **Released:** July 2006. **Price:** $39.95. **Description:** The seven most-common business schemes are uncovered.

32558 ■ *Business Know-How: An Operational Guide for Home-Based and Micro-Sized Businesses with Limited Budgets*
Pub: Adams Media Corporation
Ed: Janet Attard. **Price:** $17.95.

32559 ■ *"Business Looks for Results in Congress" in Baltimore Business Journal (Vol. 28, November 5, 2010, No. 26, pp. 1)*
Pub: Baltimore Business Journal
Ed: Kent Hoover. **Description:** Republican candidates in the 2010 Congressional elections were overwhelmingly supported by the business community. Republican John Boehner, who will be the next Speaker of the House, says that the party's victory would end economic uncertainty and would assist small businesses to rehire workers.

32560 ■ *"Business Must Stand Up And Be Counted" in Crain's Detroit Business (Vol. 24, October 6, 2008, No. 40, pp. 6)*
Pub: Crain Communications, Inc.
Description: Discusses the challenges that the new mayor of Detroit faces concerning business, the state of the economy and the exceptionally tight budget the city is running on, which includes a lot of red ink. It is very likely that the city is going to see tax revenues fall substantially in the next few months and business leaders may find it in their favor to lend their support to the new mayor as well as provide him with the executive talent necessary to overcome some of these crucial issues.

32561 ■ *Business, Occupations, Professions and Vocations in the Bible*
Pub: ABC Book Publishing
Ed: Rich Brott. **Released:** 2008. **Price:** $19.99. **Description:** The important role small business has played in all societies and cultures throughout history is examined. The ingenuity of individuals and their ability to design, craft, manufacture and harvest has kept countries and kingdoms prosperous.

32562 ■ *"The Business Owner's Flight Plan" in Entrepreneur (Vol. 37, July 2009, No. 7, pp. 22)*
Pub: Entrepreneur Media, Inc.
Description: Greg Rosner, author of 'The Road Warrior Survival Guide: Practical Tips for the Business Traveler,' shares insights on the stages of a typical business trip. Delegating a trusted colleague who can assume certain tasks that you cannot deal with remotely, expecting that the trip is not a vacation, and taking a Thursday night flight are some of the tips given to business travelers.

32563 ■ *Business Plans Kit for Dummies, 2nd Edition*
Pub: John Wiley and Sons Inc.
Released: September 2005.

32564 ■ *Business Plans That Work: A Guide for Small Business*
Pub: McGraw-Hill Companies Inc.
Contact: Deven Sharma, President
Ed: Jeffry A. Timmons, Stephen Spinelli, Andrew Zacharakis. **Released:** April 2004. **Price:** $12.89 (US), $24.95 (Canadian). **Description:** Guide for preparing a small business plan along with an analysis of potential business opportunities.

32565 ■ *The Business of Small Business: Succeeding and Prospering in Business for Reasonably Intelligent Entrepreneurs*
Pub: Allen-Reed Publishing Company
Released: August 2006. **Price:** $27.95. **Description:** Tips for running a successful company are presented to entrepreneurs.

32566 ■ *"Business Still Expected to Take Hit in 2008" in Business Journal-Serving Phoenix and the Valley of the Sun (December 28, 2007)*
Pub: American City Business Journals, Inc.
Ed: Chris Casacchia. **Description:** Community banks in 2008 are still projected to suffer from the repercussions of the subprime mortgage and credit crises. Meanwhile, the asset devaluation of big banks and global investment companies are higher than that of smaller banks. The third quarter and fourth quarter losses of banks such as Bear Stearns are discussed as well.

32567 ■ *"Business Travel Can be a Trip if Structured Right" in Globe & Mail (February 3, 2007, pp. B11)*
Pub: CTVglobemedia Publishing Inc.
Ed: Roma Luciw. **Description:** The importance of arranging a proper business trip for executives by employers, in order to achieve good benefits for the company, is discussed.

32568 ■ *Business Unusual*
Pub: Thorsons
Ed: Anita Roddick. **Price:** $24.95.

32569 ■ *Business Warrior: Strategy for Entrepreneurs*
Pub: Clearbridge Publishing
Ed: Sun Tzu. **Released:** September 2006. **Price:** $19.95. **Description:** Advice to help entrepreneurs understand competitive strategies in order to succeed, focusing on sales, marketing, and personnel management.

32570 ■ *Business Week--1,000 Issue*
Pub: McGraw-Hill Inc.
Contact: Henry Hirschberg, President
URL(s): www.ccife.org/usa/new_york/. **Released:** Annual; March. **Publication includes:** List of 1,000 U.S. Corporations by market value in all business, industrial, and financial categories, with financial results from preceding year and extensive analytical text. **Entries include:** Company name, several types of sales and earnings data in dollars, line of business. **Arrangement:** Ranked by market value.

32571 ■ *Business Week--Corporate Scoreboard Issue*
Pub: McGraw-Hill Inc.
Contact: Henry Hirschberg, President
URL(s): search.businessweek.com. **Released:** Quarterly; March, May, August, November. **Publication includes:** List of sales and profits for 900 major U.S. Companies in all business, industrial, and financial categories, with extensive analytical text. **Entries include:** Company name, several types of sales and earnings data. **Arrangement:** Alphabetical within line of business categories.

32572 ■ *BUZZ: How to Create It and Win With It*
Pub: AMACOM
Ed: Edward I. Koch; Christy Heady. **Released:** June 2007. **Price:** $21.95. **Description:** Former New York City Mayor, Edward Koch demonstrates buss to define a small business image, how to create buzz with honesty, engage the media, withstand public scrutiny, turn mistakes into opportunities, and create loyal followers.

32573 ■ *"Calgary East" in Canadian Business (Vol. 80, January 15, 2007, No. 2, pp. 13)*
Pub: Rogers Media
Ed: Charles Mandel. **Description:** The positive impact on the economy of Saint John city of New Brunswick province of Canada, due to the establishment of oil refineries by Irving Oil Ltd. in the area, is discussed.

32574 ■ *"A Call to Make SOX More Elastic" in Canadian Business (Vol. 80, February 12, 2007, No. 4, pp. 14)*
Pub: Rogers Media
Ed: Rachel Pulfer. **Description:** The suggestion of New York City Governor Eliot Spitzer to relax the Sarbanes-Oxley Act of 2002 due to its 'excessive' regulation is discussed.

32575 ■ *"Can America Invent Its Way Back?" in Business Week (September 22, 2008, No. 4100, pp. 52)*
Pub: McGraw-Hill Companies, Inc.
Description: Business leaders as well as economists agree that innovative new products, services and ways of doing business may be the only way in which America can survive the downward spiral of the economy; innovation economics may be the answer and may even provide enough growth to enable Americans to prosper in the years to come.

32576 ■ *"Can the State Afford a Big Time College Football Program?" in Hawaii Business (Vol. 53, March 2008, No. 9, pp. 26)*
Pub: Hawaii Business Publishing
Description: Jill Nunokawa, civil rights at University of Hawaii, believes that athletics are extra-curricular and that the state needs to focus on priorities. State representative K. Mark Takai says that a football program brings pride and inspiration and can generate revenue and provide economic opportunities.

32577 ■ *"Can We Talk?" in Canadian Business (Vol. 79, September 11, 2006, No. 18, pp. 131)*
Pub: Rogers Media
Ed: Sarah B. Hood. **Description:** The importance of informal communications and steps to build strong social networks within the organizations are discussed.

32578 ■ *"Can You Hear Me Now?" in Harvard Business Review (Vol. 86, July-August 2008, No. 8, pp. 23)*
Pub: Harvard Business School Press
Ed: Katharina Pick. **Description:** Tips for improving communication among boardroom members are presented. These include encouraging frankness via in-meeting leaders, and the ability of directors to meet without managers.

32579 ■ *"Canada Tops Again in G7: Study" in Globe & Mail (March 22, 2006, pp. B8)*
Pub: CTVglobemedia Publishing Inc.
Ed: Roma Luciw. **Description:** Canada is still the cheapest place to do business among G7 countries, even though the rising dollar has eroded some of its advantages over the United States. The survey is detailed.

32580 ■ *Canadian Small Business Kit for Dummies*
Pub: John Wiley & Sons, Incorporated
Ed: Margaret Kerr; JoAnn Kurtz. **Released:** May 2006. **Price:** $28.99. **Description:** Resources include information on changes to laws and taxes for small businesses in Canada.

32581 ■ *"Capital Ideas: Regions to Lansing: Focus on Taxes, Reform, Keeping Talent" in Crain's Detroit Business (Vol. 24, October 6, 2008)*
Pub: Crain Communications, Inc.
Ed: Amy Lane. **Description:** Michigan must make bold and dramatic changes in public policy regarding business legislation. The tax structure, unemployment issues and attracting and retaining talent are among the issues the state must confront, especially in this tough economic climate.

32582 ■ *"A Capitol Opportunity" in Hispanic Business (Vol. 30, September 2008, No. 9, pp. 82)*
Pub: Hispanic Business, Inc.
Ed: John Schumacher. **Description:** Launched in 2003, the Polanco fellows program is named after former state Senator Richard Polanco, a founder and chairman of the California Latino Caucus Institute. The program offers young Hispanics a chance to

experience public policy and the functioning of the California Capitol through a 12-month, on-the-job Capitol training.

32583 ■ *"The Case for Professional Boards" in Harvard Business Review (Vol. 88, December 2010, No. 12, pp. 50)*
Pub: Harvard Business School Publishing
Ed: Robert C. Pozen. **Description:** A professional directorship model can be applied to corporate governance. Suggestions for this include the reduction of board size to seven members in order to improve the effectiveness of decision making, along with the requirement that directors have industry expertise.

32584 ■ *"Cashing in Before You Join: Negotiating a Signing Bonus" in Black Enterprise (Vol. 37, October 2006, No. 3, pp. 90)*
Pub: Earl G. Graves Publishing Co. Inc.
Ed: Chauntelle Folds. **Description:** Information on how to research and negotiate a signing deal, including how to avoid a tax hit.

32585 ■ *"Cashing In: Gleaning an Education from Our Economic State" in Agency Sales Magazine (Vol. 39, August 2009, No. 8, pp. 22)*
Pub: MANA
Ed: John Graham. **Description:** Businesses have learned that cutting price can kill business and being tough is normal. The recession has also taught that getting the right vision and gaining the confidence and trust of consumers are important.

32586 ■ *The Catalyst Code: The Strategies Behind the World's Most Dynamic Companies*
Pub: Harvard Business School Press
Ed: David S. Evans; Richard Schmalensee. **Released:** May 9, 2007. **Price:** $29.95. **Description:** Economic catalysts businesses can bring consumers and merchants together in order to survive in an economy where markets, consumers and technology are always changing.

32587 ■ *CCH Toolkit Tax Guide 2007*
Pub: CCH Inc.
Contact: Mike Sabbatis, President
Ed: Paul Gada. **Released:** January 2007. **Price:** $17. 95. **Description:** Guide for filing 2007 tax forms for both personal and small businesses with expert line-by-line explanations.

32588 ■ *"Centerra Caught in Kyrgyzstan Dispute" in Globe & Mail (April 19, 2007, pp. B5)*
Pub: CTVglobemedia Publishing Inc.
Ed: Andy Hoffman. **Description:** The details of the demonstrations carried against government proposal to nationalize Centerra Gold Inc.'s assets are presented.

32589 ■ *"C'est Bon" in Canadian Business (Vol. 79, September 25, 2006, No. 19, pp. 39)*
Pub: Rogers Media
Ed: Benoit Aubin. **Description:** Economic development of Quebec City are evaluated on the eve of its formation anniversary.

32590 ■ *Change in SMEs: The New European Capitalism*
Pub: Palgrave Macmillan
Ed: Katharina Bluhm; Rudi Schmidt. **Released:** October 2008. **Price:** $95.00. **Description:** Effects of global change on corporate governance, management, competitive strategies and labor relations in small-to-medium sized enterprises in various European countries are discussed.

32591 ■ *"The China Syndrome" in Canadian Business (Vol. 79, July 17, 2006, No. 14-15, pp. 25)*
Pub: Rogers Media
Ed: Peter Diekmeyer. **Description:** Contrasting pace of growth in China and India are presented. Reasons for the slow pace of growth of Canadian companies like CAE Inc. and Magna in India are also discussed.

32592 ■ *China's Rational Entrepreneurs: The Development of the New Private Business Sector*
Pub: Routledge
Ed: Barbara Krug. **Released:** March 2004. **Price:** $195.00 (US). **Description:** Difficulties faced by entrepreneurs in China are discussed, including analysis for understanding their behavior and relations with local governments in order to secure long-term business success.

32593 ■ *"Choosing Strategies For Change" in Harvard Business Review (Vol. 86, July-August 2008, No. 8, pp. 130)*
Pub: Harvard Business School Press
Ed: John P. Kotter; Leonard A. Schlesinger. **Description:** Methods for implementing organizational change include identifying potential areas of resistance, providing the necessary skills and information to counteract resistance, and assessing situational factors that may influence results.

32594 ■ *Cities from the Arabian Desert: The Building of Jubail and Yanbu in Saudi Arabia*
Pub: Turnaround Associates
Ed: Andrea H. Pampanini. **Released:** May 2005. **Price:** $35.00. **Description:** An overview of Saudi Arabia's government to take control of the nation's natural resources and change the government, educational system, and its culture by evolving into a modern industrial society.

32595 ■ *"City Struggles to Iron Out Tangled Transportation" in Crain's New York Business (Vol. 24, January 14, 2008, No. 2, pp. 33)*
Pub: Crain Communications, Inc.
Ed: Judith Messina. **Description:** Discusses the possible solutions to improve lower Manhattan's transportation infrastructure including the construction of three new transit centers, an expansion in ferry service and the plan to get parked buses off the street.

32596 ■ *"The Classless Workplace: The Digerati and the New Spirit of Technocapitalism" in WorkingUSA (Vol. 11, June 2008, No. 2, pp. 181)*
Pub: Blackwell Publishers Ltd.
Ed: Eran Fisher. **Description:** Article argues the formation of a new type of economic actor at the intersection of a new capitalism and a new technology: The Dierati. The discourse in based on the analysis of the popular magazine Wired, which registers the culture of contemporary technocapitalism. The suggestion that the new persona of the digerati is constructed as a rejection of the ethics, which dominated the Fordist workplace and Fordist society: Hierarchy and differentiation between workers, on the one hand and capitalists and managers, on the other hand. The transformation of these two categories, workers and capitalists into the digerati worker and the digerati entrepreneur, is described. Set within the context of the structural transformations of capitalism from Fordism to post-Fordism, the article shows the ideological fit of the new ethics of the digerati to the new working arrangements of post-Fordist capitalism, characterized by more privatizes, flexible, and precarious working arrangements.

32597 ■ *"CN Rail Strike Ends With Fragile Truce" in Globe & Mail (February 26, 2007, pp. B1)*
Pub: CTVglobemedia Publishing Inc.
Ed: Brent Jang. **Description:** The agreement between Canadian National Railway Co. and the United Transportation Union on wage increase that ended employee strike is discussed.

32598 ■ *Code of Federal Regulations: Title 13: Business Credit and Assistance*
Pub: U.S. Government Printing Office
Ed: Department of Commerce Staff. **Released:** May 2007. **Price:** $55.00. **Description:** Title 13 covers regulations governing the activities of the Small Business Administration and the Department of Commerce. Book covers information on business credit, finance, and economic development.

32599 ■ *"College Opens On St. Luke's Site" in The Business Journal - Serving Phoenix and the Valley of the Sun (Vol. 28, September 5, 2008)*
Pub: American City Business Journals, Inc.
Ed: Angela Gonzales. **Description:** Fortis College is planning to offer classes in Phoenix, Arizona. It has made its home at the St. Luke's Medical Center. Courses to be offered by the college are also provided.

32600 ■ *"Commentary. Economic Trends for Small Business" in Small Business Economic Trends (April 2008, pp. 3)*
Pub: National Federation of Independent Business
Ed: William C. Dunkelberg, Holly Wade. **Description:** Commentary on the economic trends for small businesses in the U.S. is presented. Analysis of recession possibilities is given. Reports indicate that the number of business owners citing inflation as their number one problem is at its highest point since 1982.

32601 ■ *Common Problems; Common Sense Solutions: Practical Advice for Small Business Owners*
Pub: iUniverse, Incorporated
Ed: Greg Hadley. **Released:** September 2004. **Price:** $14.95. **Description:** Common sense advice for entrepreneurs running a small business.

32602 ■ *The Commonsense Way to Build Wealth: One Entrepreneur Shares His Secrets*
Pub: Griffin Publishing Group
Ed: Jack Chou. **Released:** September 2004. **Price:** $19.95. **Description:** Entrepreneurial tips to accumulate wealth, select the proper business or franchise, choose and manage rental property, and how to negotiate a good lease.

32603 ■ *"Companies Must Set Goals for Diversity" in Crain's Detroit Business (Vol. 24, April 14, 2008, No. 15, pp. 16)*
Pub: Crain Communications Inc.
Ed: Laura Weiner. **Description:** Diversity programs should start with a plan that takes into account exactly what the company wants to accomplish; this may include wanting to increase the bottom line with new contracts or wanting a staff that is more innovative in their ideas due to their varied backgrounds.

32604 ■ *"Companies Urged to Take Steps to Replenish Work Force" in Crain's Cleveland Business (Vol. 28, October 29, 2007, No. 43, pp. 9)*
Pub: Crain Communications, Inc.
Ed: Mike Verespej. **Description:** If America wants to stay competitive in the global marketplace, experts say that the education system will need serious improvements. According to Thomas J. Donahue, president and CEO of the U.S. Chamber of Commerce, one-third of the K-through-12 students in the United States don't graduate from high school.

32605 ■ *The Company We Keep: Reinventing Small Business for People, Community, and Place*
Pub: Chelsea Green Publishing
Ed: John Abrams, William Grieder. **Released:** June 2006. **Price:** $18.00. **Description:** The new business trend in social entrepreneurship as a business plan enables small business owners to meet the triple bottom line of profits for people (employees and owners), community, and the environment.

32606 ■ *"Competing On Resources" in Harvard Business Review (Vol. 86, July-August 2008, No. 8, pp. 140)*
Pub: Harvard Business School Press
Ed: David J. Collis; Cynthia A. Montgomery. **Description:** Guidelines regarding assessing the value of resources, such as slow depreciation and superiority to competitors' similar resources are discussed.

32607 ■ *"The Competitive Imperative Of Learning" in Harvard Business Review (Vol.*

86, July-August 2008, No. 8, pp. 60)
Pub: Harvard Business School Press
Ed: Amy C. Edmondson. **Description:** Experimentation and reflection are important components for maintaining success in the business world and are the kind of character traits that can help one keep his or her competitive edge.

32608 ■ *The Complete Idiot's Guide to Finance for Small Business*
Pub: Penguin Group Incorporated
Ed: Kenneth E. Little. **Released:** April 2006. **Price:** $19.95. **Description:** Financial experts helps small business owners through strategies for long-term financial success.

32609 ■ *The Complete Small Business Guide: A Sourcebook for New and Small Businesses*
Pub: John Wiley & Sons, Incorporated
Ed: Colin Barrow. **Released:** March 2006. **Price:** $27.95. **Description:** Sourcebook for creating new small companies and running established small businesses.

32610 ■ *"Confessions Of Serial Entrepreneurs" in Entrepreneur (January 8, 2009)*
Pub: Entrepreneur Media Inc.
Ed: Jennifer Wang. **Description:** Serial entrepreneurs are those individuals that are able to start business after business. These individuals enjoy the process of starting a company then handing off the finished product and starting over with a new endeavor. Several serial entrepreneurs are profiled.

32611 ■ *"Congratulations to the 2010 Top Ten Business Women of ABWA" in Women In Business (Vol. 61, August-September 2009, No. 4, pp. 12)*
Pub: American Business Women's Association
Description: Listing of the top 10 members of the American Business Women's Association (ABWA) for 2010 is presented. The lists of the top ten 2010 members selected by each of the six ABWA chapters are also provided.

32612 ■ *"Convention Calendar" in Black Enterprise (Vol. 37, February 2007, No. 7, pp. 68)*
Pub: Earl G. Graves Publishing Co. Inc.
Description: Listing of conventions and trade show of interest to minority and women business leaders.

32613 ■ *Coolhunting*
Pub: AMACOM
Ed: Peter A. Gloor; Scott W. Cooper. **Released:** June 1, 2007. **Price:** $24.95. **Description:** Lessons for unlocking and applying swarm creativity in organizations to increase creativity, productivity, and efficiency.

32614 ■ *Corporate Affiliations Library: Who Owns Whom*
Pub: LexisNexis
Contact: Michael Walsh, President
URL(s): www.corporateaffiliations.com. **Released:** Annual; Latest edition 2008. **Description:** A 8-volume set listing public and private companies worldwide. Comprises the following: Master Index (volumes 1 and 2); U.S. Public Companies (volume 3 and 4), listing 6,200 parent companies and 52,000 subsidiaries, affiliates, and divisions worldwide; U.S. Private Companies (volume 5), listing 15,000 privately held companies and 70,000 U.S. and international subsidiaries; and International Public and Private Companies (volume 7 and 8), listing 4,800 parent companies and 69,000 subsidiaries worldwide. **Entries include:** Parent company name, address, phone, fax, telex, e-mail addresses, names and titles of key personnel, financial data, fiscal period, type and line of business, SIC codes; names and locations of subsidiaries, divisions, and affiliates, outside service firms (accountants, legal counsel, etc.). **Arrangement:** Alphabetical within each volume. **Indexes:** Each volume includes company name index; separate Master Index volumes list all company names in the set in one alphabetic sequence in five indexes including private, public, international, alphabetical, geographical, brand name, SIC, and corporate responsibilities.

32615 ■ *"Corporate Canada Eyes Retiree Benefit Cuts" in Globe & Mail (March 8, 2006, pp. B3)*
Pub: CTVglobemedia Publishing Inc.
Ed: Virginia Galt. **Description:** A survey on Canadian companies reveals that due to rising health care costs and increasing number of baby boomer retirements, these companies are to cut down on health benefits they are providing to these retired employees.

32616 ■ *Corporate Crisis and Risk Management: Modeling, Strategies and SME Application*
Pub: Elsevier Science and Technology Books
Ed: M. Aba-Bulgu; S.M.N. Islam. **Released:** December 2006. **Price:** $115.00. **Description:** Methods and tools for handling corporate risk and crisis management are profiled for small to medium-sized businesses.

32617 ■ *"Corporate Diversity Driving Profits" in Hispanic Business (Vol. 30, September 2008, No. 9, pp. 12)*
Pub: Hispanic Business, Inc.
Ed: Michael Bowker. **Description:** U.S. businesses are beginning to appreciate the importance of diversity and are developing strategies to introduce a diverse workforce that reflects the cultural composition of their customers. The realization that diversity increases profits and the use of professional networks to recruit and retain skilled minority employees are two other new trends impacting corporate diversity in the U.S.

32618 ■ *Corporate Entrepreneurship & Innovation*
Pub: Thomson South-Western
Ed: Michael H. Morris; Donald F. Kuratko. **Released:** January 2007. **Price:** $104.95. **Description:** Innovation is the key to running a successful small business. The book helps entrepreneurs to develop the skills and business savvy to sustain a competitive edge.

32619 ■ *"Corporate Etiquette: The Art of Apology" in Canadian Business (Vol. 80, January 29, 2007, No. 3, pp. 62)*
Pub: Rogers Media
Ed: John Gray. **Description:** The methods of nurturing professional relationships, by apologizing for the mistakes committed by individuals and institutions, are described.

32620 ■ *Corporate Radar: Tracking the Forces That Are Shaping Your Business*
Pub: Amacom
Ed: Karl Albrecht. **Released:** December 2008. **Price:** $24.95. **Description:** Ways for a business to assess the forces operating in the external environment that can affect the business and solutions to protect from outside threats.

32621 ■ *"Crafting Kinship at Home and Work: Women Miners in Wyoming" in WorkingUSA (Vol. 11, December 2008, No. 4, pp. 439)*
Pub: Blackwell Publishers Ltd.
Ed: Jessica M. Smith. **Description:** Institutional policies and social dynamics shaping women working in the northeastern Wyoming mining industry are examined. Ethnographic research suggests that the women's successful integration into this nontraditional workplace is predicated on their ability to craft and maintain kin-like social relationships in two spheres. First, women miners have addressed the challenges of managing their home and work responsibilities by cultivating networks of friends and family to care for their children while they are at work. Second, women miners craft close relationships with coworkers in what are called 'crew families'. These relationships make their work more enjoyable and the ways in which they create camaraderie prompt a reconsideration of conventional accounts of sexual harassment in the mining industry.

32622 ■ *"Credit Crunch Gives, Takes Away" in The Business Journal-Serving Metropolitan Kansas City (Vol. 27, October 17, 2008, No. 5, pp. 1)*
Pub: American City Business Journals, Inc.
Ed: Suzanna Stagemeyer. **Description:** Although many Kansas City business enterprises have been adversely affected by the U.S. credit crunch, others have remained relatively unscathed. Examples of how local businesses are being impacted by the crisis are provided including: American Trailer & Storage Inc., which declared bankruptcy after failing to pay a long-term loan; and NetStandard, a technology firm who, on the other hand, is being pursued by prospective lenders.

32623 ■ *Crunch Point: The Secret to Succeeding When it Matters Most*
Pub: American Management Association
Contact: Charles R. Craig, Chairman
Ed: Brian Tracy. **Released:** 2006. **Price:** $17.95.

32624 ■ *"Culture Club" in Canadian Business (Vol. 79, October 9, 2006, No. 20, pp. 115)*
Pub: Rogers Media
Ed: Calvin Leung. **Description:** Positive impacts of an effective corporate culture on the employees' productivity and the performance of the business are discussed.

32625 ■ *"Cutting Credit Card Processing Costs" in Hawaii Business (Vol. 53, March 2008, No. 9, pp. 56)*
Pub: Hawaii Business Publishing
Ed: Robert K.O. Lum. **Description:** Accepting credit card payments offers businesses with profits from the discount rate. The discount rate includes processing fee, VISA & MasterCard assessment and interchange. Details regarding merchant service cost and discount rate portions are discussed. Statistical data included.

32626 ■ *"Danger, Will Robinson!" in Business Owner (Vol. 35, July-August 2011, No. 4, pp. 3)*
Pub: DL Perkins Company
Description: Critical measures each small business owner must take to ensure the success of their company are outlined.

32627 ■ *Dare to Prepare - How to Win Before You Begin*
Pub: Crown Publishing/Random House
Ed: Ronald M. Shapiro; Gregory Jordan. **Released:** February 24, 2009. **Price:** $14.95 paperback. **Description:** Shapiro uses his experience as one of America's top negotiators and lawyers to show how meticulous planning can raise the odds of success in business as well as in life.

32628 ■ *"Dark Horse Murphy Means Business In Gubernatorial Race" in Baltimore Business Journal (Vol. 28, June 25, 2010, No. 7, pp. 1)*
Pub: Baltimore Business Journal
Ed: Scott Dance. **Description:** Maryland gubernatorial candidate Brian Murphy has claimed better knowledge in helping small business owners than the other candidates, Governor Martin O'Malley and former Governor Robert Ehrlich. Murphy, who faces off against Ehrlich in the Republican primary, is banking on the benefit of his business background.

32629 ■ *"David Saunders Q&A" in Canadian Business (Vol. 80, October 22, 2007, No. 21, pp. 11)*
Pub: Rogers Media
Ed: Erin Pooley. **Description:** David Saunders, chairman of the Federation of Business School Deans, talks about the changes in business education in Canada. He stresses that a master's degree in business administration is vital and a good investment that would reap rewards in a business career.

32630 ■ *Dead on Arrival: How the Anti-Business Backlash is Destroying Entrepreneurship in America and What We Can Still Do About It!*
Pub: HarperCollins Publishers, Inc.
Ed: Bernie Marcus; Steve Gottry. **Released:** November 2006. **Price:** $23.95. **Description:** Bernie Marcus, Home Depot leader, addresses regulations hurting small businesses in America.

32631 ■ ***Dealing with the Tough Stuff: Practical Wisdom for Running a Values-Driven Business***
Pub: Berrett-Koehler Publishers, Inc.
Ed: Margot Fraser, Lisa Lorimer. **Released:** November 1, 2009. **Price:** $16.95. **Description:** Advice is given to help small firms run a value-driven business.

32632 ■ ***"Deals Still Get Done at Drake's Coq d'Or" in Crain's Chicago Business (Vol. 31, November 17, 2008, No. 46, pp. 35)***
Pub: Crain Communications, Inc.
Ed: Shia Kapos. **Description:** Chicago's infamous Coq d'Or, a restaurant and lounge located at the Drake Hotel, is still a favorite establishment for noted executives but the eatery is now trying to cater to younger professionals through marketing and offering new beverages that appeal to that demographic. Many find it the perfect environment in which to close deals, relax or network.

32633 ■ ***"The Dean of Design" in Canadian Business (Vol. 79, November 6, 2006, No. 22, pp. 42)***
Pub: Rogers Media
Ed: Erin Pooley. **Description:** The need of a good business design to increase the business in saturated markets with relation to customer satisfaction is emphasized.

32634 ■ ***"Dedge Rejects Inflation Concerns" in Globe & Mail (January 26, 2007, pp. B3)***
Pub: CTVglobemedia Publishing Inc.
Ed: Heather Scoffield. **Description:** The rejection of concern over inflation by Governor of the Bank of Canada David Dodge and his views on checking inflation in Alberta are discussed.

32635 ■ ***Delivering Knock Your Socks Off Service, 4th Edition***
Pub: American Management Association
Contact: Charles R. Craig, Chairman
Ed: Performance Research Associates. **Released:** 2006.

32636 ■ ***"Dick Evans" in Canadian Business (Vol. 82, April 27, 2009, No. 7, pp. 78)***
Pub: Rogers Media
Ed: Sean Silcoff. **Description:** Former Rio Tinto Alcan chief executive officer Dick Evans believes that the 1982 downturn was worse than the current recession, at least for the mining sector. He also believes that while people are anxious, there is confidence that the economy will recover in two to three years. Key information on Evans, as well as his other views on being a CEO is presented.

32637 ■ ***"Did I Do That?" in Entrepreneur (Vol. 35, November 2007, No. 11, pp. 144)***
Pub: Entrepreneur Media Inc.
Ed: Romanus Wolter. **Description:** Entrepreneurs need to watch habits as some bad habits can affect business operations. Tips on ways to identify bad habits and how to address them are presented.

32638 ■ ***"Director Elections Campaign Pays Off" in Globe & Mail (March 9, 2006, pp. B1)***
Pub: CTVglobemedia Publishing Inc.
Ed: Janet McFarland. **Description:** The details pertaining to the introduction of new voting standards by electing company directors by 20 major Canadian companies, after the Canadian Coalition for Good Governance campaigned for it, are presented.

32639 ■ ***"Dirty Work Required" in Workforce Management (Vol. 88, November 16, 2009, No. 12, pp. 34)***
Pub: Crain Communications Inc.
Ed: John Hollon. **Description:** Due to salary freezes, pay cuts, layoffs, buyouts and a number of other stress factors brought about by the recession, employee engagement has been difficult to maintain by managers.

32640 ■ ***Divine Wisdom at Work: 10 Universal Principles for Enlightened Entrepreneurs***
Pub: Aha! House
Ed: Tricia Molloy. **Released:** July 2006. **Price:** $20.00. **Description:** Entrepreneurial advice for managing a small enterprise is given using inspiration, anecdotes and exercises.

32641 ■ ***Do You! 12 Laws to Access the Power in You to Achieve Happiness and Success***
Pub: Gotham/Penguin Group Incorporated
Ed: Russell Simmons; Chris Morrow. **Released:** April 2008. **Price:** $15.00. **Description:** Hip-Hop mogul describes his successful visions and ventures.

32642 ■ ***"Dodge Frets Over Flood of Fast Money" in Globe & Mail (May 2, 2007, pp. B1)***
Pub: CTVglobemedia Publishing Inc.
Ed: Heather Scoffield. **Description:** The concern of governor of Bank of Canada, David Dodge, over the increase in global liquidity due to growth in the business of private equity, is discussed.

32643 ■ ***Doing Business Anywhere: The Essential Guide to Going Global***
Pub: John Wiley and Sons, Inc.
Ed: Tom Travis. **Released:** 2007. **Price:** $24.95. **Description:** Plans are given for new or existing businesses to organize, plan, operate and execute a business on a global basis. Trade agreements, brand protection and patents, ethics, security as well as cultural issues are among the issues addressed.

32644 ■ ***"Donald Tarlton" in Canadian Business (Vol. 80, March 26, 2007, No. 7, pp. 70)***
Pub: Rogers Media
Ed: Andy Holloway. **Description:** Donald Tarlton, owner of Donald K Donald Entertainment Group, shares few things about his childhood and career.

32645 ■ ***"Don't Expect Quick Fix" in The Business Journal-Serving Metropolitan Kansas City (Vol. 27, October 3, 2008, No. 3, pp. 1)***
Pub: American City Business Journals, Inc.
Ed: James Dornbrook. **Description:** United States governmental entities cannot provide a quick fix solution to the current financial crisis. The economy requires a systemic change in the way people think about credit. The financial services industry should also focus on core lending principles.

32646 ■ ***"Don't Quit When The Road Gets Bumpy" in Women Entrepreneur (November 25, 2008)***
Pub: Entrepreneur Media Inc.
Ed: Bonnie Price. **Description:** Discusses techniques four women entrepreneurs are utilizing to keep their businesses successful despite the credit crunch and the economic downturn.

32647 ■ ***"Don't Touch My Laptop, If You Please Mr. Customs Man" in Canadian Electronics (Vol. 23, June-July 2008, No. 4, pp. 6)***
Pub: Action Communication Inc.
Ed: Mark Borkowski. **Description:** Canadian businessmen bringing electronic devices to the US can protect the contents of their laptops by hiding their data from US border agents. They can also choose to clean up the contents of their laptop using file erasure programs.

32648 ■ ***"Down a 'Peg' in Canadian Business (Vol. 79, September 25, 2006, No. 19, pp. 41)***
Pub: Rogers Media
Ed: Bryan Borzykowski. **Description:** Economic development in Canada's Winnipeg city is evaluated.

32649 ■ ***The Dynamic Small Business Manager***
Pub: Lulu.com
Ed: Frank Vickers. **Released:** March 2006. **Price:** $39.99. **Description:** Practical advice is given to help small business owners successfully manage their company.

32650 ■ ***e-Business, e-Government and Small and Medium-Size Enterprises: Opportunities and Challenges***
Pub: Idea Group Publishing
Ed: Brian J. Corbitt, Nabeel A.Y. Al-Qirim. **Released:** February 2004. **Price:** $64.95. **Description:** Electronic commerce and information technology research in small and medium-sized enterprises (SMEs). Policymakers, legislators, researchers and professionals address significant issues of importance to the small business sector.

32651 ■ ***The E Myth Revisited: Why Most Small Businesses Don't Work and What to Do***
Pub: HarperCollins Publishers
Ed: Michael E. Gerber. **Released:** January 18, 2010. **Price:** $11.10. **Description:** The book dispels the myths surrounding starting a business and shows how traditional assumptions can get in the way of running a small company. Topics cover entrepreneurship from infancy to growth and covers franchising.

32652 ■ ***The E-Myth Revisited: Why Most Small Businesses Don't Work and What to Do About It***
Pub: HarperInformation
Ed: Michael E. Gerber. **Released:** November 2005. **Price:** $39.00. **Description:** Keys for developing a prosperous small business is presented in an updated version of the author's best-seller published in the nineties.

32653 ■ ***Earth: The Sequel***
Pub: W. W. Norton & Company, Inc.
Ed: Fred Krupp; Miriam Horn. **Released:** March 16, 2009. **Price:** $15.95. **Description:** President of the Environmental Defense Fund offers suggestions for small businesses to help solve global warming. Investigation into the new industries, jobs, and opportunities is provided.

32654 ■ ***The Economics of Integrity***
Pub: HarperStudio/HarperCollins
Ed: Anna Bernasek. **Released:** February 23, 2010. **Price:** $19.99. **Description:** Integrity is built over time and the importance of trust in starting and building business relationships is stressed.

32655 ■ ***"Economics at Play When Allocating Seats to Series" in Boston Business Journal (Vol. 27, October 26, 2007, No. 39, pp. 1)***
Pub: American City Business Journals Inc.
Ed: Jesse Noyes, Naomi R. Kooker. **Description:** Business executives are trying to obtain as many baseball tickets to the World Series as possible. Allocating corporate seats to the Series is about maintaining tight relationships and influence clients. It is a key to business relationships.

32656 ■ ***The Economics of Small Firms***
Pub: Routledge Inc.
Ed: Johnson. **Released:** December 2006. **Price:** $41.95. **Description:** Introduction to the economics of small business, covering both theoretical and empirical issues.

32657 ■ ***Edgewalkers: People and Organizations That Take Risks, Build Bridges, and Break New Ground***
Pub: Greenwood Publishing Group Inc.
Contact: Janann Sherman, Manager
Ed: Judi Neal. **Released:** October 2006. **Price:** $39.95. **Description:** Profiles of entrepreneurs who thrive on change and challenge in order to create successful companies in today's complex business climate.

32658 ■ ***"The Effect of Cunfucian Values On Succession In Family Business" in Family Business Review (Vol. 19, September 2006, No. 3)***
Pub: Family Firm Institute
Contact: Judy L. Green, President
Ed: Jun Yan, Ritch Sorenson. **Description:** Position of family business in a social context using Confucian values is examined.

32659 ■ ***"Effect of Oil Prices on the Economy" in Canadian Business (Vol. 81, September 15, 2008, No. 14-15, pp. 5)***
Pub: Rogers Media Ltd.
Ed: Joe Chidley. **Description:** Rise of oil prices above $100 in February 2008 and $140 in July signals the birth of a 'new economy' according to commentators; this shift is causing uneasiness from oil industry professionals who are unsure of how this

trend could be sustained. Oil dropped below $120 in August, which could slow down global economic growth followed by oil demand, then oil prices.

32660 ■ *Effective Operations and Controls for the Small Privately Held Business*
Pub: John Wiley and Sons, Inc.
Ed: Rob Reider. **Released:** January 2008. **Price:** $75.00. **Description:** Guide for implementing effective operations and controls for non-regulated small businesses with the least cost possible is presented.

32661 ■ *Effectuation*
Pub: Edward Elgar Publishing, Incorporated
Ed: Sarasvathy. **Released:** October 2006. **Price:** $85.00. **Description:** Effectuation is the idea that the future is unpredictable while being controllable. A study of 27 entrepreneurs shows effective effectuators.

32662 ■ *The Emerging Markets Century: How a New Breed of World-Class Companies is Overtaking the World*
Pub: Free Press/Simon & Schuster Inc.
Ed: Antoine van Agtmael. **Released:** 2007. **Price:** $29.00. **Description:** An exploration of how companies like Lenovo and Haier who are presently in emerging economies are already competing with household name brands like Ford and Sony, thus proving globalization is here to stay.

32663 ■ *"Employee Motivation: A Powerful New Model" in Harvard Business Review (Vol. 86, July-August 2008, No. 8, pp. 78)*
Pub: Harvard Business School Press
Ed: Nitin Nohria; Boris Groysbert; Linda Eling Lee. **Description:** Four drives underlying employee motivation are discussed as well as processes for leveraging these drives through corporate culture, job design, reward systems, and resource-allocation priorities.

32664 ■ *Encyclopedia of Small Business*
Pub: Cengage Gale
Ed: Arsen Darnay; Monique D. Magee; Kevin Hillstrom. **Released:** November 2010. **Description:** Concise encyclopedia of small business information.

32665 ■ *"Energy Slide Slows Fourth Quarter Profits" in Globe & Mail (April 13, 2007, pp. B9)*
Pub: CTVglobemedia Publishing Inc.
Ed: Angela Barnes. **Description:** The decrease in the fourth quarter profits of several companies across various industries in Canada, including mining and manufacturing, due to global decrease in oil prices, is discussed.

32666 ■ *Enterprise, Entrepreneurship and Innovation: Concepts, Context and Commercialization*
Pub: Elsevier Science and Technology Books
Ed: Robin Lowe, Sue Marriott. **Released:** June 2006. **Price:** $39.95. **Description:** Application of enterprise, innovation and entrepreneurship are discussed to help companies grow.

32667 ■ *Enterprise and Small Business: Principles, Practice and Policy*
Pub: Pearson Education, Limited
Contact: Steven A. Dowling, President
Ed: Sara Carter; Dylan Jones-Evans. **Released:** September 2006. **Price:** $79.50. **Description:** Introduction to small business, challenges of a changing environment, and the nature of entrepreneurship are among the issues covered.

32668 ■ *The Entrepreneur Next Door: Discover the Secrets to Financial Independence*
Pub: Entrepreneur Press
Ed: William F. Wagner. **Released:** May 2006. **Price:** $19.95. **Description:** Traits required to become a successful entrepreneur are highlighted.

32669 ■ *The Entrepreneur and Small Business Problem Solver*
Pub: John Wiley & Sons, Incorporated
Ed: William A. Cohen. **Released:** December 2005. **Price:** $24.95 (US), $31.99 (Canadian). **Description:** Revised edition of the resource for entrepreneurs and small business owners that covers everything from start-up financing and loans to new product promotion and more.

32670 ■ *Entrepreneurial Small Business*
Pub: McGraw-Hill Higher Education
Ed: Richard P. Green; Jerome A. Katz. **Released:** January 2008. **Price:** $139.43. **Description:** Students are able to get a clear vision of small enterprise in today's business climate. The textbook helps focus on the goal of having personal independence with financial security as an entrepreneur.

32671 ■ *"Entrepreneurs Save the World" in Women In Business (Vol. 61, December 2009, No. 6, pp. 12)*
Pub: American Business Women's Association
Ed: Leigh Elmore. **Description:** American economic growth is attributed to small businesses but more than one-third of these businesses have had to cut jobs in 2009, while only five percent have increased workforces. This trend motivated organizations, such as the Ewing Marion Kauffman Foundation, to bring together entrepreneurs and assist them in having greater participation in public dialogues about America's economy.

32672 ■ *Entrepreneurs in the Southern Upcountry: Commercial Culture in Spartanburg, South Carolina, 1845-1880*
Pub: University of Georgia Press
Contact: Stacey Hayes, Manager
E-mail: shayes@ugapress.uga.edu
Ed: Bruce W. Eelman. **Released:** February 2008. **Price:** $42.95. **Description:** Historical account of the entrepreneurial culture in a nineteenth-century southern community outside the plantation belt is given.

32673 ■ *The Entrepreneur's Strategy Guide: Ten Keys for Achieving Marketplace Leadership and Operational Excellence*
Pub: Greenwood Publishing Group Inc.
Contact: Janann Sherman, Manager
Ed: Tom Cannon. **Released:** June 2006. **Price:** $38. 45. **Description:** Business plan for entrepreneurs is offered from a fifty-year business veteran. The book is divided into tow parts: the marketplace and the internal environment.

32674 ■ *Entrepreneurship*
Pub: Blackwell Publishing Inc.
Contact: Gordon Tibbitts, President
Ed: R. Duane Ireland; Michael A. Hitt. **Released:** June 2006. **Price:** $99.95. **Description:** Overview of entrepreneurship through the use of dictionary definitions as well as entries of 2,500 words explaining advanced issues and debates.

32675 ■ *Entrepreneurship*
Pub: Thomson South-Western
Ed: Donald F. Kuratko; Richard M. Hodgetts. **Released:** April 2006. **Price:** $125.95. **Description:** Understanding the process of entrepreneurship.

32676 ■ *Entrepreneurship*
Pub: Greenwood Publishing Group Inc.
Contact: Janann Sherman, Manager
Ed: Alan L. Carsrud; Malin E. Brannback. **Released:** March 2007. **Price:** $55.00. **Description:** Entrepreneurial process is profiles, examining how these individuals identify opportunity and ways they address the personal, social, and financial risks involved in starting a new business venture.

32677 ■ *Entrepreneurship*
Pub: John Wiley and Sons Inc.
Ed: William D. Bygrave; Andrew Zacharakis. **Released:** March 2007. **Price:** $109.95. **Description:** Process for starting a new business is shared, focusing on marketing and financing a product or service.

32678 ■ *Entrepreneurship: A Process Perspective*
Pub: Thomson South-Western
Ed: Robert A. Baron; Scott A. Shane. **Released:** February 2007. **Price:** $137.95. **Description:** Entrepreneurial process covering team building, finances, business plan, legal issues, marketing, growth and exit strategies.

32679 ■ *Entrepreneurship: From Opportunity to Action*
Pub: Palgrave Macmillan
Ed: David Rae. **Released:** March 2007. **Price:** $63.95 (CND). **Description:** Learning enterprise theory is discussed, focusing on the individual as an entrepreneur and ways to create and take advantage of opportunities.

32680 ■ *Entrepreneurship and How to Establish Your Own Business*
Pub: Double Storey Books
Ed: Johan Strydon. **Released:** March 1, 2009. **Price:** $37.95. **Description:** Guidelines are given to help develop a small business idea and to establish a successful enterprise. .

32681 ■ *Entrepreneurship and Small Business*
Pub: Palgrave Macmillan
Ed: Paul Burns. **Released:** January 2007. **Price:** $74.95. **Description:** Entrepreneurial skills, focusing on good management practices are discussed. Topics include family businesses, corporate, international and social entrepreneurship.

32682 ■ *Entrepreneurship and Small Business Development in the Former Soviet Bloc*
Pub: Routledge
Ed: David Smallbone, Friederike Welter. **Released:** January 10, 2010. **Price:** $140.00. **Description:** Examination of entrepreneurship and small business in Russia and other key countries of Eastern Europe, showing how far small businesses have developed in the region.

32683 ■ *The Ethical Executive: Becoming Aware of the Root Causes of Unethical Behavior*
Pub: Stanford University Press
Ed: Robert Hoyk, Paul Hersey. **Released:** February 28, 2010. **Price:** $17.95. **Description:** Forty-five lessons to help avoid becoming a victim to day-to-day ethical traps are outlined using moral lapses at Enron, Tyco International, Adelphia, World Com and other businesses as examples.

32684 ■ *"Even Money on Recession" in Barron's (Vol. 88, March 10, 2008, No. 10, pp. M9)*
Pub: Dow Jones & Company, Inc.
Ed: Gene Epstein. **Description:** Discusses the US unemployment rate which was steady in February 2008 at 4.8 percent, while nonfarm payroll employment decreased by 63,000 in the same month, with the private sector losing 101,000 jobs. The economic indicators showed mixed signals on whether or not the US economy is in a recession.

32685 ■ *Everything I Know About Business I Learned from My Mama: A Down-Home Approach to Business and Personal Success*
Pub: John Wiley & Sons, Incorporated
Ed: Tim Knox. **Released:** June 22, 2007. **Price:** $22. 95. **Description:** Part memoir, part self-help, and part business how-to manual designed to help any small business owner/entrepreneur.

32686 ■ *"The Evolution of the Mobile Entrepreneur" in Entrepreneur (Vol. 37, August 2009, No. 8, pp. 31)*
Pub: Entrepreneur Media, Inc.
Ed: Dan O'Shea. **Description:** Covers the timeline of important events that led to the mobile businessperson today; includes the first cell phone call made by Martin Cooper in 1973 and the invention of Apple and the Newton in 1989. The first BlackBerry appeared in 1999 and the iPod was launched in 2001.

32687 ■ *Falling Behind: How Rising Inequality Harms the Middle Class*
Pub: University of California Press
Contact: Alison Mudditt, Director
Ed: Robert H. Frank. **Released:** July 2007. **Price:** $21.95 paperback. **Description:** Economist argues that though middle-class American families aren't earning much more than they were a few decades

ago, they are spending considerably more, a pattern attributed primarily to the context of seeing and emulating the spending habits of the rich.

32688 ■ *"Family Matters: Founding Family Firms and Corporate Political Activity" in Business and Society (Vol. 46, December 2007, No. 4)*
Pub: SAGE Publications USA
Contact: Blaise R. Simqu, President
Ed: Michael Hadani. **Description:** The impact of publicly traded family founding firms and their inclination for corporate political activity is examined. Publicly traded family founding firms are more predisposed to engage in corporate political activity when the founder is in an executive position.

32689 ■ *Fast Company's Greatest Hits: Ten Years of the Most Innovative Ideas in Business*
Pub: Penguin Group Incorporated
Ed: John Byrne; David Lidsky; Mark N. Vamos. **Released:** July 2006. **Price:** $24.95. **Description:** Offering of Fast Company's best articles covering business ideas and profiles of successful firms and their leaders.

32690 ■ *Fast-Track Employer's Kit: California*
Pub: Kaplan Books
Ed: Carolyn Usinger. **Released:** May 2006. **Price:** $29.95. **Description:** Requirements for running a small business in California re outlined.

32691 ■ *"Festivals Press on Despite Loss of Sponsors" in Crain's Detroit Business (Vol. 25, June 22, 2009, No. 25, pp. 3)*
Pub: Crain Communications Inc. - Detroit
Ed: Sherri Began Welch. **Description:** Organizers of local festivals are experiencing a decrease in sponsorship this summer due to the slow economy. These events help keep areas vibrant and stress the importance of community and cultural events.

32692 ■ *Financial Management 101: Get a Grip on Your Business Numbers*
Pub: Self-Counsel Press, Incorporated
Ed: Angie Mohr. **Released:** November 2007. **Price:** $16.95. **Description:** An overview of business planning, financial statements, budgeting and advertising for small businesses. s.

32693 ■ *Financing Your Business: Get a Grip on Finding the Money*
Pub: Self-Counsel Press, Incorporated
Ed: Angie Mohr. **Released:** October 2004. **Price:** $14.95 (US), $19.95 (Canadian). **Description:** Recommendations to help raise capital for a new or expanding small company.

32694 ■ *"Finishing Touches: the Fashion Statement is in the Detail" in Black Enterprise (Vol. 37, January 2007, No. 6, pp. 106)*
Pub: Earl G. Graves Publishing Co. Inc.
Ed: Sonia Alleyne. **Description:** Men are discovering the importance of dressing for success. Paying attention to the details such as shoes, socks, cuffs, and collars are just as important as finding the right suit.

32695 ■ *First, Break All the Rules: What the World's Greatest Managers Do Differently*
Pub: Simon and Schuster Inc.
Contact: Carolyn Reidy, President
E-mail: carolyn.reidy@simonandschuster.com
Ed: Marcus Buckingham, Curt Coffman. **Released:** May 1999. **Price:** $19.80. **Description:** Great managers break virtually every rule revered by conventional wisdom.

32696 ■ *"Five More Great Books on Entrepreneurship" in Entrepreneur (Vol. 37, July 2009, No. 7, pp. 19)*
Pub: Entrepreneur Media, Inc.
Description: 800-CEO-Read founder, Jack Covert, and president, Todd Stattersten, share five books that would have been included in the book, 'The 100 Business Books of All Time' if space was not an issue. 'You Need to Be a Little Crazy,' 'Oh, the Places You'll Go!,' 'Founders at Work,' 'The Innovator's Dilemma,' and 'Purple Cow' are highly recommended for entrepreneurs.

32697 ■ *"Five Steps to an Effective Meeting" in Hawaii Business (Vol. 53, March 2008, No. 9, pp. 55)*
Pub: Hawaii Business Publishing
Ed: Jason Ubay. **Description:** Identifying goals and writing them down can help in knowing what needs get done. Engaging everyone is a way to get cooperation in reaching the goals set. Other tips on how to have an effective meeting are discussed.

32698 ■ *"Five Steps for Handling Independent Contractors" in Hawaii Business (Vol. 53, January 2008, No. 7, pp. 49)*
Pub: Hawaii Business Publishing
Ed: Jason Ubay. **Description:** Small companies should be cautious in dealing with independent contractors. They must understand that they cannot dictate specific operational procedures, job duties, standards of conduct and performance standards to the contractors, and they cannot interfere with the evaluation and training of the contractors' employees. Tips on negotiating with independent contractors are given.

32699 ■ *"Five Steps to Killer Business Ideas" in Hawaii Business (Vol. 53, December 2007, No. 6, pp. 135)*
Pub: Hawaii Business Publishing
Ed: Jason Ubay. **Description:** Five ways to formulating good business concepts are presented. The importance of keeping an open mind and analyzing the market is discussed.

32700 ■ *"Five Things" in Hawaii Business (Vol. 53, November 2007, No. 5, pp. 20)*
Pub: Hawaii Business Publishing
Ed: Jason Ubay. **Description:** Discusses products that are allowed to be carried on board airplane flights by business travelers.

32701 ■ *"Five Tips for New Managers" in Hawaii Business (Vol. 53, November 2007, No. 5, pp. 59)*
Pub: Hawaii Business Publishing
Ed: Jason Ubay. **Description:** New managers should remember to know what their roles are, learn from others, build an infrastructure according to the customer's needs, communicate professionally and have consideration.

32702 ■ *"Follow the ABCs of Buying a Business" in Women Entrepreneur (September 10, 2008)*
Pub: Entrepreneur Media Inc.
Ed: Nina Kaufman. **Description:** Buying a business will likely result in the largest single asset one will ever own. A list of steps one can take in order to educate and protect themselves is provided.

32703 ■ *Forbes--Platinum 400-America's Best Big Companies*
Pub: Forbes Magazine
URL(s): www.forbes.com. **Ed:** William Baldwin. **Released:** Annual; Latest edition 2009. **Publication includes:** List of 400 leading publicly owned corporations. **Entries include:** Company name, sales and net income growth rates, return on capital, debt/capital, net profit margin, and operating margin. **Arrangement:** Classified alphabetically by industry. **Indexes:** Alphabetical.

32704 ■ *Forbes--Up-and-Comers 200: Best Small Companies in America Issue*
Pub: Forbes Magazine
URL(s): www.forbes.com. **Ed:** Steve Kichen. **Released:** Weekly; Latest edition October, 2007. **Publication includes:** List of 200 small companies judged to be high quality and fast-growing on the basis of 5-year return on equity and other qualitative measurements. Also includes a list of the 100 best small companies outside the U.S. Note: Issue does not carry address or CEO information for the foreign companies. **Entries include:** Company name, shareholdings data on chief executive officer; financial data. **Arrangement:** Alphabetical. **Indexes:** Ranking.

32705 ■ *Foundations of Small Business Enterprise*
Pub: Routledge Inc.
Ed: G. Reid. **Released:** December 2006. **Price:** $120.00. **Description:** Insight is given into the life cycle of entrepreneurial ventures; 150 new firms are tracked through early years.

32706 ■ *"Four Big Fat Business Plan Lies" in Entrepreneur (December 11, 2008)*
Pub: Entrepreneur Media Inc.
Ed: Tim Berry. **Description:** Business plans are essential for every business and do not necessarily have to be a complex document containing a full list of components. Other misconceptions concerning business plans are also discussed.

32707 ■ *Free Lunch: How the Wealthiest Americans Enrich Themselves at Government Expense*
Pub: Portfolio
Description: Johnston uses the case of the Texas Rangers as an example to support his belief that the nation's monied elite bend the rules of capitalism for their own benefit.

32708 ■ *The Future Arrived Yesterday: The Rise of the Protean Corporation and What It Means for You*
Pub: Crown Business
Ed: Michael S. Malone. **Released:** 2009. **Price:** $27.50. **Description:** Reasons why dominant companies of the next decade will behave like perpetual entrepreneurial startups are investigated.

32709 ■ *"The Future of Work" in Black Enterprise (Vol. 41, August 2010, No. 1, pp. 65)*
Pub: Earl G. Graves Publishing Co. Inc.
Ed: Annya M. Lott. **Description:** Technology, globalization, and outsourcing will continue to shape the future of work. Social media is a means for small companies to market goods and services.

32710 ■ *"The Future of Work" in Business Strategy Review (Vol. 21, Autumn 2010, No. 3, pp. 16)*
Pub: Blackwell Publishers Ltd.
Ed: Lynda Gratton. **Description:** Work is universal. But how, why, where and when we work has never been so open to individual interpretation. The certainties of the past have been replaced by ambiguity, questions and the steady hum of technology. Now, in a groundbreaking research project covering 21 global companies and more than 200 executives, the author is making sense of the future of work.

32711 ■ *Gen X*
Pub: Entrepreneur Press
Ed: Brian O'Connell. **Price:** $17.95.

32712 ■ *Gendered Processes: Korean Immigrant Small Business Ownership*
Pub: LFB Scholarly Publishing LLC
Ed: Eunju Lee. **Released:** November 2005. **Price:** $60.00. **Description:** Examination of the gender processes among Korean immigrants becoming small business owners in the New York City metropolitan area.

32713 ■ *"Generation Y Goes To Work; Management" in The Economist (Vol. 390, January 3, 2009, No. 8612, pp. 48)*
Pub: The Economist Newspaper Inc.
Description: Unemployment rates among people in their 20s has increased significantly and there is a lower turnover in crisis-hit firms, which has made it more difficult to simply find another job if one is unsatisfied with the management style of his or her company. Managers are adopting a more command-and-control approach which is the antithesis of the open, collaborative style that younger employees prefer.

32714 ■ *The Geography of Small Firm Innovation*
Pub: Springer
Ed: Grant Black. **Released:** January 2005. **Price:** $49.95. **Description:** Concentration of high-tech innovation across metropolitan areas in the U.S. during the 1990s and the role geography plays in innovation.

32715 ■ *Get in the Game: 8 Elements of Perseverance that Make the Difference*
Pub: Gotham/Penguin Group Incorporated
Ed: Cal Ripken, Jr.; Donald T. Phillips. **Released:** April 10, 2008. **Price:** $15.00. **Description:** Guidebook written by superstar athlete Cal Ripkin to help managers and entrepreneurs achieve success.

32716 ■ *"Get in Line" in Canadian Business (Vol. 79, September 25, 2006, No. 19, pp. 43)*
Pub: Rogers Media
Ed: Andy Holloway. **Description:** The needs of economically developing Canada's urban regions are discussed.

32717 ■ *"Get More Time Off" in Canadian Business (Vol. 80, March 12, 2007, No. 6, pp. 32)*
Pub: Rogers Media
Ed: June Morrow. **Description:** Expert advice to employees to make use of leaves of absence to improve their career instead of working continuously for a long period is presented.

32718 ■ *Get Your Business to Work!: 7 Steps to Earning More, Working Less and Living the Life You Want*
Pub: BenBella Books
Contact: Glen Yeffeth, President
Ed: George Hedley. **Released:** June 9, 2010. **Price:** $24.95. **Description:** Complete step-by-step guide for the small business owner to realize profits, wealth and freedom.

32719 ■ *"Getting in the Swing" in Canadian Business (Vol. 80, February 26, 2007, No. 5, pp. 67)*
Pub: Rogers Media
Ed: Andrew Wahl. **Description:** The economic issues associated with the acquisition of Adams, Harkness and Hill Inc. by Canaccord Capital are presented. A large number of Canadian companies are entering into the United States.

32720 ■ *Getting Things Done: The Art of Stress-Free Productivity*
Pub: Penguin Books USA Inc.
Ed: David Allen. **Released:** December 2002. **Price:** $16.00. **Description:** Coach and management consultant recommends methods for stress-free performance under the premise that productivity is directly related to our ability to relax.

32721 ■ *"Glamis Reserves Get Boost With Western Silver Deal" in Globe & Mail (February 25, 2006, pp. B3)*
Pub: CTVglobemedia Publishing Inc.
Ed: Wendy Stueck. **Description:** The details on Glamis Gold Ltd.'s proposed acquisition of Western Silver Corp., for $1.2 billion, are presented.

32722 ■ *Global Economic Crisis: Impact on Small Business*
Pub: Cengage South-Western
Ed: Global Economics Crisis Resource Center. **Released:** March 1, 2009. **Price:** $17.95. **Description:** A discussion of the historical context of the global economic crisis is presented, along with a discussion on the impact of this crisis on small businesses. It also provides learning goals, questions, key terms, and digital access to the Global Economic Crisis Resource Center.

32723 ■ *The Go-Giver: A Little Story About a Powerful Business Idea*
Pub: Penguin Group
Ed: Bob Burg; John David Mann. **Released:** December 27, 2007. **Price:** $19.95. **Description:** Story of an ambitious young man named Joe who years for success. The book is a heartwarming tale that brings new relevance to the old proverb, 'Give and you shall receive'.

32724 ■ *Going to Extremes: How Like Minds Unite and Divide*
Pub: Oxford University Press
Ed: Cass R. Sunstein. **Released:** 2009. **Price:** $21.95. **Description:** Solutions to marketplace problems are examined.

32725 ■ *Good to Great*
Pub: Harper Business
Ed: Jim Collins. **Price:** $27.50.

32726 ■ *Good to Great: Why Some Companies Make the Leap..and Others Don't*
Pub: HarperInformation
Ed: Jim Collins. **Released:** October 2001. **Price:** $29.99. **Description:** Management styles for growing a modern business.

32727 ■ *"Good Things Happen When We Buy Local" in Crain's Detroit Business (Vol. 24, October 6, 2008, No. 40, pp. 7)*
Pub: Crain Communications, Inc.
Description: Michigan is facing incredibly difficult economic times. One way in which each one of us can help the state and the businesses located here is by purchasing our goods and services from local vendors. The state Agriculture Department projected that if Michigan households earmarked $10 per week in their grocery purchases to made-in-Michigan products, this would generate $30 million a week in economic impact.

32728 ■ *"Got Skills? (Entrepreneurs' Adeptness In Other Fields)" in Entrepreneur (Vol. 35, October 2007, No. 10, pp. 31)*
Pub: Entrepreneur Media Inc.
Ed: Laura Tifanny. **Description:** Entrepreneurs such as Jim Mousner, Hugh Briathwaite, and Joi Ito, has been known to apply their skills and interests in other fields on their business operations. Knowing something outside the realm of their industry helps entrepreneurs think of fresh ideas that are beneficial not only to them but also to their clients. Details of how having a different kind of interest helped Mousner, Braithwaite and Ito are presented.

32729 ■ *Goventure: Live the Life of an Entrepreneur*
Pub: Houghton Mifflin College Division
Ed: Hatten. **Released:** May 2006. **Price:** $28.47. **Description:** Challenges of operating a small business are presented with more than 6,000 graphics, audio, and interactive video.

32730 ■ *"Grand Action Makes Grand Changes in Grand Rapids" in Crain's Detroit Business (Vol. 25, June 1, 2009, No. 22, pp. M012)*
Pub: Crain Communications Inc. - Detroit
Ed: Amy Lane. **Description:** Businessman Dick DeVos believes that governments are not always the best to lead certain initiatives. That's why, in 1991, he gathered 50 west Michigan community leaders and volunteers to look consider the construction of an arena and expanding or renovating local convention operations. Grand Action has undertaken four major projects in the city.

32731 ■ *"The Grass is Greener" in Canadian Business (Vol. 79, August 14, 2006, No. 16-17, pp. 43)*
Pub: Rogers Media
Ed: Thomas Watson. **Description:** Owner of New Image Plans LLC, Joe White, shares his views on the Canadian market for the marijuana drug.

32732 ■ *Great Big Book of Business Lists: All the Info You Need to Run a Small Business*
Pub: Entrepreneur Press
Ed: Courtney Thurman; Ashlee Gardner. **Released:** April 2006. **Price:** $45.95. **Description:** Reference guide for small business that includes information for starting and running a small business; lists are organized for easy access and cover every aspect of small business.

32733 ■ *Green Business Practices for Dummies*
Pub: John Wiley and Sons, Inc.
Ed: Lisa Swallow. **Released:** January 2009. **Price:** $21.99. **Description:** The book provides information for any small business to help reduce environmental impact without reducing their company's bottom line.

32734 ■ *The Gridlock Economy: How Too Much Ownership Wrecks Markets, Stops Innovation, and Costs Lives*
Pub: Basic Books
Ed: Michael Heller. **Released:** 2009. **Price:** $26.00. **Description:** While private ownership generally creates wealth, the author believes that economic gridlock results when too many people own pieces of one thing, which results in too many people being able to block each other from creating or using a scarce source.

32735 ■ *"A Growing Concern" in Canadian Business (Vol. 79, October 9, 2006, No. 20, pp. 90)*
Pub: Rogers Media
Ed: Jeff Sanford. **Description:** With rich dividends being harvested by companies producing ethanol, after ethanol became a petrol additive, is discussed.

32736 ■ *Growing Local Value: How to Build Business Partnerships That Strengthen Your Community*
Pub: Berrett-Koehler Publishers, Incorporated
Ed: Laury Hammel; Gun Denhart. **Released:** December 2006. **Price:** $15.00. **Description:** Advice and examples are provided for building socially responsible entrepreneurship.

32737 ■ *Growing and Managing a Small Business: An Entrepreneurial Perspective*
Pub: Houghton Mifflin College Division
Ed: Kathleen R. Allen. **Released:** July 2006. **Price:** $105.27. **Description:** Introduction to business ownership and management from startup through growth.

32738 ■ *"Growth Seen Climbing Out of a Trough" in Globe & Mail (March 3, 2007, pp. B5)*
Pub: CTVglobemedia Publishing Inc.
Ed: Tavia Grant. **Description:** The economic condition of Canada in the fourth quarter 2006 is analyzed. The gross domestic product rose 1.4 percent in the fourth quarter.

32739 ■ *A Guide to the Project Management Body of Knowledge*
Pub: Project Management Institute
Contact: Peter Monkhouse, Chairman
Ed: Project Management Institute. **Released:** July 31, 2009. **Price:** $65.95. **Description:** A guide for project management using standard language, with new data flow diagrams; the Identify Stakeholders and Collect Requirements processes defined; and with greater attention placed on how knowledge areas integrate in the context of initiating, planning, executing, monitoring and controlling, and closing process groups.

32740 ■ *Happy About Joint Venturing: The 8 Critical Factors of Success*
Pub: Happy About
Ed: Valerie Orsoni-Vauthey. **Released:** June 2006. **Price:** $23.95. **Description:** An overview of joint venturing is presented.

32741 ■ *"Hawaii Business 2008 SB Success Awards" in Hawaii Business (Vol. 53, February 2008, No. 8, pp. 43)*
Pub: Hawaii Business Publishing
Description: Winners in the Hawaii Business 2008 SB Success Awards are presented; the awards give recognition for Hawaii small businesses with less than 100 employees and are based on four criteria, namely: unique service or product; rapid expansion or sales growth; longevity; and competency in overcoming challenges.

32742 ■ *"Heavy Duty: The Case Against Packing Lightly" in Crain's Chicago Business (Vol. 31, April 21, 2008, No. 16, pp. 29)*
Pub: Crain Communications, Inc.
Ed: Sarah A. Klein. **Description:** Penelope Biggs, a Northern Trust executive who manages sales teams in North America, Europe and Asia gives advice on traveling abroad for business including time management skills, handling time-zone hops and avoiding jet-lag.

32743 ■ *"Help for Job Seekers" in Crain's Detroit Business (Vol. 26, January 18, 2010, No. 3, pp. 14)*
Pub: Crain Communications Inc.
Description: CareerWorks is aimed at helping those who are in career transition or are looking for new jobs; this weekly collection of news, advertising and information includes weekly stories, events and the highlighting of a person who has successfully made the transition from one profession to another. On the Website, readers are welcome to post an anonymous resume in order to attract employers.

32744 ■ *"Higher Education" in Canadian Business (Vol. 79, October 23, 2006, No. 21, pp. 129)*
Pub: Rogers Media
Ed: Erin Pooley; Laura Bogomolny; Joe Castaldo; Michelle Magnan. **Description:** Details of some Canadian business schools, where students can simultaneously pursue a master of business administration degree and also be employed on a part time basis, are presented.

32745 ■ *"Hire Education" in Canadian Business (Vol. 79, September 11, 2006, No. 18, pp. 114)*
Pub: Rogers Media
Ed: Erin Pooley. **Description:** Study results showing the perceptions of students while considering full-time employment and the attributes they look for in their future employers are presented.

32746 ■ *"Hispanic Representation in Boardrooms Remains Static" in Hispanic Business (January-February 2008, pp. 36, 38, 40)*
Pub: Hispanic Business
Description: Estimated 3 percent of Hispanic representation in corporate boardroom in America has remained the same, despite the growth in the Hispanic population. Statistical data and board member names are included.

32747 ■ *History of Canadian Business 1867-1914*
Pub: University of Toronto Press
Ed: R.T. Naylor. **Released:** 1975. **Description:** Covers the growth of business in Canada.

32748 ■ *A History of Small Business in America*
Pub: University of North Carolina Press
Contact: Kate Douglas Torrey, Director
E-mail: kate_torrey@unc.edu
Ed: Mansel G. Blackford. **Released:** May 2003. **Price:** $22.95. **Description:** History of American small business from the colonial era to present, showing how it has played a role in the nation's economic, political, and cultural development across manufacturing, sales, services and farming.

32749 ■ *"Holidays Should Foster Mutual Respect" in Women In Business (Vol. 61, October-November 2009, No. 5, pp. 33)*
Pub: American Business Women's Association
Ed: Diane Stafford. **Description:** Workplaces have modified the way year-end holiday celebrations are held in an effort to promote mutual respect. The workers' varying religious beliefs, political affiliations, and other differences have brought about the modifications. The importance of developing mutual understanding is emphasized as a mechanism to stimulate successful business ties.

32750 ■ *Hoover's Vision*
Pub: Cengage Learning Inc.
Contact: Michael Hansen, Chief Executive Officer
Ed: Gary Hoover. **Description:** Founder of Bookstop Inc. and Hoover's Inc. provides a plan to turn an enterprise into a success by showing entrepreneurs how to address inputs with an open mind in order to see more than what other's envision. Hoover pushes business owners to create and feed a clear and consistent vision by recognizing the importance of history and trends, then helps them find the essential qualities of entrepreneurial leadership.

32751 ■ *"How Innovative Is Michigan? Index Aims To Keep Track" in Crain's Detroit Business (Vol. 24, February 4, 2008, No. 5, pp. 1)*
Pub: Crain Communications Inc. - Detroit
Ed: Chad Halcom. **Description:** Profile of the newly created 'Innovation Index', released by the University of Michigan-Dearborn. The report showed a combination of indicators that gauged innovation activity in the state slightly lower for second quarter 2007, but ahead of most levels for most of 2006. Statistical data included.

32752 ■ *How to Make Big Money in Your Own Small Business: Unexpected Rules Every Small Business Owner Needs to Know*
Pub: Hyperion Press
Ed: Jeffrey J. Fox. **Released:** May 2004. **Price:** $16. 95. **Description:** Former sales and marketing pro offers advice on growing a small business.

32753 ■ *How the Mighty Fall: And Why Some Companies Never Give In*
Pub: HarperCollins Publishers
Ed: Jim Collins. **Released:** May 19, 2008. **Price:** $23.99. **Description:** Companies fail in stages and their decline can be detected and reversed.

32754 ■ *"How to Pick an All-Star" in Canadian Business (Vol. 79, October 9, 2006, No. 20, pp. 15)*
Pub: Rogers Media
Ed: Andy Holloway. **Description:** Factors that determine the competency levels o f individuals are discussed. The need for firms to take into consideration the right selection factors while hiring an employee is presented.

32755 ■ *How to Raise Capital: Techniques and Strategies for Financing and Valuing Your Small Business*
Pub: McGraw-Hill Companies Inc.
Contact: Deven Sharma, President
Ed: Jeffrey A. Timmons, Stephen Spinelli, Andrew Zacharakis. **Released:** May 2004. **Price:** $16.95 (US), $24.95 (Canadian). **Description:** Small business financing process is examined. Tips for identifying the financial life cycle of new ventures, developing a framework for financial strategies, and understanding an investor's prospective.

32756 ■ *How to Run Your Business Like a Girl: Successful Strategies from Entrepreneurial Women Who Made It Happen*
Pub: Adams Media Corporation
Contact: Gary Krebs, Director
E-mail: swatrous@adamsmedia.com
Ed: Elizabeth Cogswell Baskin. **Released:** September 2005. **Description:** Tour of three women entrepreneurs and their successful companies.

32757 ■ *How to Succeed As a Lifestyle Entrepreneur*
Pub: Dearborn Trade Publishing Inc.
Contact: Roy Lipner, President
Ed: Gary Schine. **Price:** $18.95.

32758 ■ *"How To Live To Be 100; John E. Green Co. Grows Through Diversification" in Crain's Detroit Business (February 18, 2008)*
Pub: Crain Communications Inc. - Detroit
Ed: Chad Halcom. **Description:** Continuity, name recognition, and inventiveness are keys to continuing growth for Highland Park, Michigan's John E. Green Company, designer of pipe systems and mechanical contractor.

32759 ■ *How Walmart is Destroying America (And the World): And What You Can Do About It*
Pub: Celestial Arts Publishing Co.
Contact: Patricia Kelly, Manager
Ed: Bill Quinn. **Released:** April 2005. **Price:** $10.95. **Description:** Wal-Mart employs 1.5 million employees and operates more than 3,500 stores, making it the largest private employer globally. Wal-Mart's impact on mom-and-pop business is discussed.

32760 ■ *How: Why How We Do Anything Means Everything..in Business*
Pub: John Wiley and Sons, Inc.
Ed: Dov L. Seidman. **Released:** June 4, 2007. **Price:** $27.95. **Description:** Author shares his unique approach to building successful companies using case studies, anecdotes, research, and interviews to help entrepreneurs succeed in the 21st Century.

32761 ■ *How to Write a Business Plan*
Pub: NOLO
Ed: Mike McKeever. **Released:** January 2007. **Price:** $34.99. **Description:** Author, teacher and financial manager shows how to write an effective business plan. Examples and worksheets are included.

32762 ■ *How to Write a Great Business Plan for Your Small Business in 60 Minutes or Less*
Pub: Atlantic Publishing
Ed: Sharon L. Fullen. **Released:** January 2006. **Price:** $39.95 includes CD-Rom. **Description:** A good business plan outlines goals and works as a company's resume to obtain funding, credit from suppliers, management of the operations and finances, promotion and marketing, and more.

32763 ■ *"How to Write a Report" in Canadian Business (Vol. 80, November 5, 2007, No. 22, pp. 41)*
Pub: Rogers Media
Ed: Gabriel Fuchs. **Description:** Basic rule in writing a report is the so-called USNA, which stands for Use Synonyms, No Acronyms. Synonyms make the report seem more interesting while acronyms increase the chance of being misunderstood. Details of how to write an impressive business report are given.

32764 ■ *HRD in Small Organizations: Research and Practice*
Pub: Routledge
Ed: Jim Steward, Graham Beaver. **Released:** February 2004. **Price:** $190.00. **Description:** Approaches to human resource development in small organizations are evaluated.

32765 ■ *"The Human Factor" in Canadian Business (Vol. 80, October 8, 2007, No. 20, pp. 22)*
Pub: Rogers Media
Ed: Alex Mynek. **Description:** David Foot, a demographer and an economics professor at the University of Toronto, talks about Canada's future, including economic and demographic trends. He discusses activities that should be done by businessmen in order to prepare for the future. He also addresses the role of the Canadian government in economic development.

32766 ■ *Human Resources for Small Business Made Easy*
Pub: Skilled Learning Incorporated
Ed: Ruth Zimmerman. **Released:** November 2006. **Description:** Guide for human resource development for small businesses.

32767 ■ *"Ian Delaney" in Canadian Business (Vol. 81, Summer 2008, No. 9, pp. 168)*
Pub: Rogers Media Ltd.
Ed: Joe Castaldo. **Description:** Interview with Ian Delaney who is the executive chairman of chemical company Sherritt International Corp.; Delaney previously worked as chief executive for a holding company owned by Peter Munk. Details of his beliefs, profession and family life are discussed.

32768 ■ *ICTs and SMEs Antecedents and Consequences of Technology Adoption*
Pub: Edward Elgar Publishing, Incorporated
Ed: Ordanini. **Released:** November 2006. **Price:** $85.00. **Description:** Issues involving information communication technology adoption among small and medium-sized firms are discussed.

32769 ■ *"The 'In-Crowd' Online: Professionals Take Networking To New Levels" in Black Enterprise (Vol. 38, January*

2008, No. 6, pp. 47)
Pub: Earl G. Graves Publishing Co. Inc.
Ed: Alwin A.D. Jones. **Description:** The Internet is providing new ways for professionals to network with others. New sites like LinkedIn.com provide entrepreneurs with access to others with a business life similar to theirs.

32770 ■ *"In Everyone's Interests" in Canadian Business (Vol. 80, April 23, 2007, No. 9, pp. 62)*
Pub: Rogers Media
Ed: Rachel Pulfer. **Description:** The need of strategic negotiations during a labor contract to prevent disputes with employer is emphasized.

32771 ■ *Inc.--The Inc. 500 Issue*
Pub: Gruner & Jahr USA Publishing
URL(s): www.inc.comwww.inc.com/inc5000/2009/index.html. **Released:** Annual; Latest edition 2010. **Publication includes:** List of 500 fastest-growing privately held companies based on percentage increase in sales over the five year period prior to compilation of current year's list. **Entries include:** Company name, headquarters city, description of business, year founded, number of employees, sales five years earlier and currently, profitability range, and growth statistics. **Arrangement:** Ranked by sales growth.

32772 ■ *Innovation Methodologies in Enterprise Research*
Pub: Edward Elgar Publishing, Incorporated
Ed: Hine. **Released:** December 2006. **Price:** $75.00. **Description:** The importance of qualitative, interpretist research in the field of enterprise research is discussed. The book stresses how enterprise research is a new method and permits a wide scope for new and innovative research studies.

32773 ■ *Innovative Approaches to Global Sustainability*
Pub: Palgrave Macmillan
Ed: Charles Wankel, James A.F. Stoner. **Released:** April 13, 2010. **Price:** $30.00. **Description:** Examples are given to help businesses become sustainable as we move towards a sustainable world.

32774 ■ *"The Inside and Outside Scoop on CEO Succession" in Globe & Mail (January 2, 2006, pp. B8)*
Pub: CTVglobemedia Publishing Inc.
Ed: Shirley Won. **Description:** The career profile of Randy Eresman as the chief executive officer of Encana Corp. is presented.

32775 ■ *"Interview Advisory; Warning! Do YOU Have VD?" in Canadian Corporate News (May 18, 2007)*
Pub: Comtex News Network Inc.
Description: Interview with Beverly Beuermann-King, a stress and wellness specialist, who provides insights on the problems associated with Vacation Deprivation.

32776 ■ *Introduction to Business*
Pub: The McGraw-Hill Companies
Ed: Laura Portolese Dias, Amit J. Shah. **Released:** January 1, 2009. **Price:** $70.94. **Description:** Introduction to business course discusses the changing educational environment for teaching business courses in colleges and universities.

32777 ■ *"Is Globalization Threatening U.S. Hispanic Progress?" in Hispanic Business (Vol. 30, September 2008, No. 9, pp. 16)*
Pub: Hispanic Business, Inc.
Ed: Jessica Haro. **Description:** Talented Hispanic employees are making progress within the increasingly diverse American corporate scenario. However, while some experts believe the induction of foreign professionals through globalization will not impact this progress, others feel it could hamper opportunities for American Hispanics.

32778 ■ *"Is It Time to Move to a Real Office?" in Women Entrepreneur (December 30, 2008)*
Pub: Entrepreneur Media Inc.
Ed: Aliza Sherman. **Description:** Before moving a company from a home-office to a real office it is important to make sure that the additional overhead that will be incurred by the move is comfortably covered and that the move is being done for the right reasons. Several women entrepreneurs who have moved their businesses from their homes to an actual rental space are profiled.

32779 ■ *"Is the Sun Setting on Oil Sector's Heydey?" in Globe & Mail (January 25, 2007, pp. B3)*
Pub: CTVglobemedia Publishing Inc.
Ed: Shawn McCarthy. **Description:** The effects of fuel efficiency management policies of the United States on Canadian petroleum industry are discussed. Canada is the largest exporter of crude oil to America after the Middle East.

32780 ■ *"Is That the Best You Can Do?" in Entrepreneur (Vol. 37, October 2009, No. 10, pp. 85)*
Pub: Entrepreneur Media, Inc.
Ed: Jennifer Wang. **Description:** Small business owners can deal with hagglers better by setting parameters in advance. They should convince hagglers by offering the best value and separating this from price.

32781 ■ *"Is Your Company Ready to Succeed?" in Business Strategy Review (Vol. 21, Spring 2010, No. 1, pp. 68)*
Pub: Wiley-Blackwell
Ed: Srikumar Rao. **Description:** The author asked thousands of students about the ideal company of the future, the kind of place where they would want to spend their lives.

32782 ■ *"Is Your Supply Chain Sustainable?" in Harvard Business Review (Vol. 88, October 2010, No. 10, pp. 74)*
Pub: Harvard Business School Publishing
Description: Charts and models are presented to help a firm assess its sustainability.

32783 ■ *"It All Comes Back to Trust" in Canadian Business (Vol. 80, March 26, 2007, No. 7, pp. S11)*
Pub: Rogers Media
Description: Eileen Fischer, family business expert at York University, shares her views on the challenges involved in running family businesses.

32784 ■ *It's Not Just Who You Know: Transform Your Life (and Your Organization) by Turning Colleagues and Contacts into Lasting Relationships*
Pub: Crown Business Books
Ed: Tommy Spaulding. **Released:** August 10, 2010. **Price:** $23.00. **Description:** Tommy Spaulding teaches the reader how to reach out to others in order to create lasting relationships that go beyond superficial contacts.

32785 ■ *"Jobless Rate Climbs Unexpectedly in December" in Globe & Mail (January 7, 2006, pp. B5)*
Pub: CTVglobemedia Publishing Inc.
Description: The reasons behind increase in unemployment rate by 6.5 percent, in Canada, are presented.

32786 ■ *"Jobs Boom Ramps Up in March" in Globe & Mail (April 7, 2007, pp. B1)*
Pub: CTVglobemedia Publishing Inc.
Ed: Tara Perkins. **Description:** The increase in the number of jobs by 54,900 in Canada and 180,000 in the United States in March 2007 is discussed.

32787 ■ *"Jobs, Export Surge Confirm Recovery" in Globe & Mail (March 10, 2007, pp. B5)*
Pub: CTVglobemedia Publishing Inc.
Ed: Heather Scoffield. **Description:** The increase in the number of jobs and exports that is forecast to reverse the slowdown in the Canadian economy is discussed.

32788 ■ *"Key Budgeting Tips: For Your Management Team" in Agency Sales Magazine (Vol. 39, December 2009, No. 11, pp. 49)*
Pub: MANA
Ed: Gene Siciliano. **Description:** Constructing a budget must be the result of coordinated input and effort. Practice is also important in creating a budget and accurately predicting actual results is not the objective but giving the company a direction for course correction.

32789 ■ *"Kirnross Holds Firm on Offer for Bema" in Globe & Mail (January 20, 2007, pp. B5)*
Pub: CTVglobemedia Publishing Inc.
Ed: Andy Hoffman. **Description:** The acquisition of Bema Gold Corp. by Kinross Gold Corp. is discussed.

32790 ■ *Kiss Theory Good Bye: Five Proven Ways to Get Extraordinary Results in Any Company*
Pub: Gold Pen Publishing
Ed: Bob Prosen. **Released:** August 2006. **Price:** $21.95. **Description:** Author provides wisdom from his career as a high-level executive at AT&T Global Information Solutions, Sabre, and Hitachi, as well as his consulting firm. The book focuses on business execution rather than processes or theory of business management and provides step-by-step instructions allowing organizations to maximize profitability and results.

32791 ■ *Knockout Entrepreneur: My Ten Count Strategy for Winning at Business*
Pub: Thomas Nelson Inc.
Ed: George Foreman. **Released:** September 1, 2009. **Price:** $22.99. **Description:** George Foreman offers ten key strategies for running a successful small business.

32792 ■ *"Knowledge Workers" in Canadian Business (Vol. 79, October 9, 2006, No. 20, pp. 59)*
Pub: Rogers Media
Ed: Doug Cooper. **Description:** Knowledge workers as an integral part of organizations and the need for business leaders to effectively manage and recognize the talent of knowledge workers is discussed.

32793 ■ *"The Labor Crunch is Coming" in Canadian Business (Vol. 80, December 25, 2006, No. 1, pp. 74)*
Pub: Rogers Media
Description: The need for skilled and educated workforce to meet labor shortage in future in Canada is discussed.

32794 ■ *"Laurent Beaudoin" in Canadian Business (Vol. 80, April 9, 2007, No. 8, pp. 68)*
Pub: Rogers Media
Ed: Thomas Watson. **Description:** Chief executive officer of Bombardier Inc., Laurent Beaudoin, talks about his personal life and career.

32795 ■ *Law (in Plain English) for Small Business*
Pub: Sourcebooks, Inc.
Contact: Len Vlahos, President
E-mail: dominique@sourcebooks.com
Ed: Leonard D. DuBoff. **Released:** November 2006. **Description:** Small business law is described in easy to read format.

32796 ■ *"Leaders in Denial" in Harvard Business Review (Vol. 86, July-August 2008, No. 8, pp. 18)*
Pub: Harvard Business School Press
Ed: Richard S. Tedlow. **Description:** Identifying denial in the corporate arena is discussed, along with its impact on business and how to prevent it from occurring.

32797 ■ *Lean Six Sigmas That Works: A Powerful Action Plan for Dramatically Improving Quality, Increasing Speed, and Reducing Waste*
Pub: American Management Association
Contact: Charles R. Craig, Chairman
Ed: Bill Carreira; Bill Trudell. **Released:** 2006. **Price:** $21.95.

32798 ■ *"Leave It Behind; Novel Packing Strategy" in Crain's Chicago Business (Vol. 31, April 21, 2008, No. 16, pp. 32)*
Pub: Crain Communications, Inc.
Ed: Sarah A. Klein. **Description:** Patrick Brady who investigates possible violations of the Foreign Corrupt Practices Act has a novel approach when travel-

ing to frequent destinations which allows him to travel with only a carry-on piece of luggage: he leaves suits at dry cleaners in the places he visits most often and since he mainly stays at the same hotels, he also leaves sets of workout clothes and running shoes with hotel staff.

32799 ■ *"Legal Aid: Sample Legal Documents can Lower Your Attorney Fees" in Black Enterprise (Vol. 37, October 2006, No. 3, pp. 210)*
Pub: Earl G. Graves Publishing Co. Inc.
Ed: Tamara E. Holmes. **Description:** FreeLegalForms.net provides thousands of free legal forms. These forms are not a substitute for consultation with an attorney but the sample documents can help save you time and money.

32800 ■ *Lessons in Service From Charlie Trotter*
Pub: Celestial Arts Publishing Co.
Contact: Patricia Kelly, Manager
Ed: Edmund Lawler. **Released:** March 2004. **Price:** $24.95. **Description:** Chef Charlie Trotter, owner of a restaurant, shares insight into managing any business successfully.

32801 ■ *The Life Cycle of Entrepreneurial Ventures*
Pub: Springer
Ed: Simon Parker. **Released:** October 2006. **Price:** $199.00. **Description:** Issues involved in creating a new business are explored, including venture creation, development and performance.

32802 ■ *"Lines of Communication" in Entrepreneur (Vol. 37, October 2009, No. 10, pp. 80)*
Pub: Entrepreneur Media, Inc.
Ed: Brad Feld. **Description:** Entrepreneurial companies should establish a clear and open communication culture between their management teams and their venture capital backers. Chief executive officers should trust their leadership teams when it comes to communicating with venture capitalists.

32803 ■ *"Live and Learn" in Canadian Business (Vol. 79, October 23, 2006, No. 21, pp. 160)*
Pub: Rogers Media
Ed: Joe Castaldo. **Description:** Philip Kives, founder and chief executive officer of K-Tel International Inc. discusses his professional achievements.

32804 ■ *"Local Knowledge" in Hawaii Business (Vol. 53, December 2007, No. 6, pp. 40)*
Pub: Hawaii Business Publishing
Ed: David K. Choo. **Description:** Rules and facts business professionals need to know about the local life in Hawaii are presented. The important components in island life include knowledge Hawaiian high schools' histories and image, the local sports scene, special events, potluck ethics, and locals' favorite destination, which is Las Vegas.

32805 ■ *"Local M&A Activity Sputters in 1Q" in Crain's Chicago Business (Vol. 31, April 21, 2008, No. 16, pp. 20)*
Pub: Crain Communications, Inc.
Ed: H. Lee Murphy. **Description:** Local mergers-and-acquisitions activity is down by 34 percent in the first quarter compared to the fourth quarter of last year due to the credit crisis making financing harder to obtain.

32806 ■ *The Logic of Life: The Rational Economics of an Irrational World*
Pub: Random House
Ed: Tim Harford. **Released:** February 2009. **Price:** $15.00 paperback. **Description:** Harford excels at making economists' studies palatable for discerning but non-expert readers. The uses hard data to show why promiscuous teens are actually health-conscious, divorce hasn't gotten a fair shake, corporate bosses will always be overpaid and job prospects for minorities continue to be grim.

32807 ■ *"Look Before You Lease" in Women Entrepreneur (February 3, 2009)*
Pub: Entrepreneur Media Inc.
Ed: Nina L. Kaufman. **Description:** Top issues to consider before leasing an office space are discussed including: additional charges that may be expected on top of the basic rental price; determining both short- and long-term goals; the cost of improvements to the space; the cost of upkeep; and the conditions of the lease.

32808 ■ *"Looking For Financing?" in Hispanic Business (Vol. 30, July-August 2008, No. 7-8, pp. 16)*
Pub: Hispanic Business, Inc.
Ed: Frank Nelson. **Description:** Investment firms want to know about businesses that need funding for either expansion or acquisition; companies fitting this profile are interviewed and their perceptions are discussed. Investment firms need businesses to be realistic in their expectations and business plans which show spending of funds and expected benefits, long term goals, track record and strong management teams.

32809 ■ *"Lost in America" in Canadian Business (Vol. 79, October 23, 2006, No. 21, pp. 23)*
Pub: Rogers Media
Ed: David Wolf. **Description:** The impact of a decline in the economy of the United States on global economy is analyzed.

32810 ■ *"Lots of Qualified Women, But Few Sit on Boards" in Globe & Mail (March 2, 2006, pp. B1)*
Pub: CTVglobemedia Publishing Inc.
Ed: Virginia Galt. **Description:** The findings of Catalyst Canada survey on the rise in women executives on boards of directors are presented.

32811 ■ *"Magna Banks on Big Cash Hoard" in Globe & Mail (March 1, 2006, pp. B3)*
Pub: CTVglobemedia Publishing Inc.
Ed: Greg Keenan. **Description:** The details on Magna International Inc., which posted decline in profits at $639 million for 2005, are presented.

32812 ■ *Make It Big With Yuvi: How to Achieve Poolside Living by Growing Your Small Business*
Pub: AuthorHouse
Ed: Ron Peltier. **Released:** March 2006. **Price:** $17. 00. **Description:** Successful entrepreneurship is profiled.

32813 ■ *Make Your Business Survive and Thrive! 100+ Proven Marketing Methods to Help You Beat the Odds*
Pub: John Wiley & Sons, Incorporated
Ed: Priscilla Y. Huff. **Released:** December 2006. **Price:** $19.95. **Description:** Small business and entrepreneurial expert gives information to help small and home-based businesses grow.

32814 ■ *"Making Diverse Teams Click" in Harvard Business Review (Vol. 86, July-August 2008, No. 8, pp. 20)*
Pub: Harvard Business School Press
Ed: Jeffrey T. Polzer. **Description:** 360-degree feedback to increase the efficacy of diverse-member workplace teams, which involves each member providing feedback to the others on the team is discussed.

32815 ■ *"Making Your Mark: Five Steps To Brand Your Success" in Black Enterprise (Vol. 38, November 2007, No. 4, pp. 106)*
Pub: Earl G. Graves Publishing Co. Inc.
Ed: Erinn R. Johnson. **Description:** Founder of Velvet Suite Marketing Consulting Group, Melissa D. Johnson, assists clients in building brands. Johnson offers tips to develop and build a sold brand in her new book, 'Brand Me! Make Your Mark: Turn Passion Into Profit'.

32816 ■ *"Managing Corporate Social Networks" in Harvard Business Review (Vol. 86, July-August 2008, No. 8, pp. 26)*
Pub: Harvard Business School Press
Ed: Adam M. Kleinbaum; Michael L. Tushman. **Description:** Tips on how to promote business creativity and foster knowledge building through business social networks are given.

32817 ■ *Managing Labour in Small Firms*
Pub: Routledge
Ed: Susan Marlow. **Released:** December 2004. **Price:** $170.00. **Description:** Essays addressing conditions of workers in small business.

32818 ■ *Managing a Small Business Made Easy*
Pub: Entrepreneur Press
Ed: Martin E. Davis. **Released:** September 2005. **Price:** $19.95 (US), $26.95 (Canadian). **Description:** Examination of the essential elements for an entrepreneur running a business, including advice on leadership, customer service, financials, and more.

32819 ■ *"Many Sectors Lost Jobs In Detroit Area" in Crain's Detroit Business (Vol. 24, February 11, 2008, No. 6, pp. 3)*
Pub: Crain Communications Inc. - Detroit
Ed: Amy Lane. **Description:** Southeast Michigan reported its highest jobless rate since 1992 in fourth quarter 2007. Statistical data included.

32820 ■ *"Market Forces" in Canadian Business (Vol. 79, October 23, 2006, No. 21, pp. 93)*
Pub: Rogers Media
Ed: Erin Pooley. **Description:** The tremendous rise in the number of business schools offering Master of business administration degree in Canada and the depletion in the quality of education provided in these business schools is discussed.

32821 ■ *The Martha Rules: 10 Essentials for Achieving Success as You Start, Build, or Manage a Business*
Pub: Rodale Inc.
Contact: Maria Rodale, Chief Executive Officer
Ed: Martha Stewart. **Released:** October 2006. **Price:** $15.95. **Description:** Martha Stewart offers insight into starting, building and managing a successful business.

32822 ■ *The Martha Rules: 10 Essentials for Achieving Success as You Start, Grow, or Manage a Business*
Pub: Rodale Press, Inc.
Ed: Martha Stewart. **Released:** October 2005.

32823 ■ *Mastering Business Growth and Change Made Easy*
Pub: Entrepreneur Press
Ed: Jeffrey A. Hansen. **Released:** October 2005. **Price:** $19.95 (US), $26.95 (Canadian). **Description:** Tips for growing a small business, regardless of state or environment.

32824 ■ *"Maurice Strong" in Canadian Business (Vol. 81, December 8, 2008, No. 21, pp. 70)*
Pub: Rogers Media Ltd.
Ed: Andrew Wahl. **Description:** Peking University honorary professor Maurice Strong believes that a lot of Westerners, including Canadians, do not take time to understand the business culture in China.

32825 ■ *"MBA Essentials: Real-Life Instruction" in Women In Business (Vol. 61, October-November 2009, No. 5, pp. 28)*
Pub: American Business Women's Association
Ed: Leigh Elmore. **Description:** University of Kansas School of Business allied itself with the American Business Women's Association (ABWA) which led to the formation of the ABWA-KU MBA essentials program. With this program, ABWA members are exposed to graduate-level coursework that delves on business topics, such as strategy and operations.

32826 ■ *"MBT Add On: Gone by 2012?" in Crain's Detroit Business (Vol. 24, October 6, 2008, No. 40, pp. 1)*
Pub: Crain Communications, Inc.
Ed: Amy Lane. **Description:** Discusses the Michigan Business Tax (MBT), which has angered many businesses in the state due to the addition of a 21.99 percent surcharge. Although the tax policy will cut taxes on 63 percent of businesses in the state and represent no tax liability change for another nine percent of firms, other businesses will see increases of 100 percent or more. This increase means that many business owners will be forced to relocate or close their establishment and others will have to eliminate jobs. Lawmakers are attempting to find a solution to this problem.

32827 ■ *"MBT 'Sticker Shock' Surprises Business; Reaction? 'You Can't Print It,' Owner Says" in Crain's Detroit Business (March 17, 2008)*
Pub: Crain Communications, Inc.
Ed: Amy Lane. **Description:** Overview of the new Michigan Business Tax which is raising many middle-sized businesses' taxes by up to 400 percent.

32828 ■ *"McClatchy Believed Front-Runner in Knight Ridder Sale" in Globe & Mail (March 13, 2006, pp. B6)*
Pub: CTVglobemedia Publishing Inc.
Ed: Joseph T. Hallinan; Dennis K. Berman. **Description:** The details on proposed acquisition of Knight Ridder Inc. by McClatchy Co. are presented.

32829 ■ *"Measure Your Business Plan Results" in Entrepreneur (January 6, 2009)*
Pub: Entrepreneur Media Inc.
Ed: Tim Berry. **Description:** Although no business plan is ever right on target, it is still essential for every business owner to create one; the way in which to analyze the actual results compared to the plan are discussed.

32830 ■ *"Measuring Success In Family Businesses: The Concept of Configurational Fit" in Family Business Review (Vol. 19, June 2006, No. 2)*
Pub: Family Firm Institute
Contact: Judy L. Green, President
Ed: Christoph Hienerth, Alexander Kessler. **Description:** Strategic benchmarking, which are used to examine business success of family-owned enterprises are investigated.

32831 ■ *Medium Sized Firms and Economics Growth*
Pub: Nova Science Publishers, Incorporated
Ed: Janez Prasniker. **Released:** April 2005. **Price:** $130.00. **Description:** Medium sized companies should have a more definitive presence in modern microeconomic theory, the theory of entrepreneurship, and the theory of financial markets.

32832 ■ *Memos to the Prime Minister: What Canada Could Be in the 21st Century*
Pub: John Wiley & Sons, Incorporated
Ed: Harvey Schacter. **Released:** April 11, 2003. **Price:** $16.95. **Description:** A look into the business future of Canada. Topics include business, healthcare, think tanks, policy groups, education, the arts, economy, and social issues.

32833 ■ *Microtrends*
Pub: Twelve Books/Hachette Book Group USA
Ed: Mark J. Pen with E. Kinney Zalesne. **Released:** September 2007. **Price:** $25.99. **Description:** Detecting small patterns the great impact they can have on business.

32834 ■ *"The Middle Ages" in Hawaii Business (Vol. 53, October 2007, No. 4, pp. 42)*
Pub: Hawaii Business Publishing
Ed: Cathy S. Cruz-George. **Description:** Starcom Builders Inc.'s Theodore 'Ted' Taketa, School Kine Cookies' Steven Gold And Sharon Serene of Sharon Serene Creative are among the participants in Hawaii's Fittest CEO competition for executives over 50 years old. Taketa takes yoga classes, and also goes to the gym while Serne has Mike Hann as her professional trainer. Eating habits of the aforementioned executives are also described.

32835 ■ *"Mind the Gap" in Canadian Business (Vol. 80, November 5, 2007, No. 22, pp. 21)*
Pub: Rogers Media
Ed: Matthew McCleam. **Description:** The average difference in median wages between men and women who have full-time jobs, according to the Organization Co-operation and Development is over 15 percent and that number is above 20 percent in Canada. The difference in earnings has become smaller since the 1960s, as more women have joined the labor market. The reasons for the wage gap are examined.

32836 ■ *"Mitch D'Olier" in Hawaii Business (Vol. 53, November 2007, No. 5, pp. 27)*
Pub: Hawaii Business Publishing
Ed: Cathy S. Cruz-George. **Description:** Mitch D'Olier chief executive officer of Kaneohe Ranch/ Harold K.L. Castle Foundation thinks that achievement gaps are a nationwide problem and that the Knowledge is Power Program is one of the programs that focuses on achievement gaps in some communities across the US. He also provides his insights on education in Hawaii and the current shortage of teachers.

32837 ■ *"Molson Coors Ends Ill-Fated Foray Into Brazil" in Globe & Mail (January 17, 2006, pp. B1)*
Pub: CTVglobemedia Publishing Inc.
Ed: Andy Hoffman. **Description:** The details of loss incurred by Molson Coors Brewing Co., from the sale of Cervejarias Kaiser SA to Fomento Economico Mexicano S.A. de C.V., are presented.

32838 ■ *"More Than a Feeling" in Entrepreneur (Vol. 36, April 2008, No. 4, pp. 10)*
Pub: Entrepreneur Media, Inc.
Ed: Rieva Lesonsky. **Description:** It is said that emotion has no place when it comes to business matters, but it may not be the case as entrepreneurs and other people in business feel passionate about what they do. Emotions can help bring out a positive outlook in them. Other details on the topic are discussed.

32839 ■ *"Most See Gloomy Year For Michigan Business" in Crain's Detroit Business (Vol. 24, October 6, 2008, No. 40, pp. 4)*
Pub: Crain Communications, Inc.
Ed: Amy Lane. **Description:** Michigan residents are extremely concerned about the economic climate and business conditions in the state. According to the latest quarterly State of the State Survey, conducted by Michigan State University's Institute for Public Policy and Social Research, 63.9 percent of those surveyed anticipate bad times for Michigan businesses over the next year. Additional findings from the survey are also included.

32840 ■ *Never Bet the Farm*
Pub: Jossey-Bass Publishers
Ed: Anthony L. Iaquinto; Stephen Spinelli, Jr. **Price:** R19.95 paperback.

32841 ■ *"New BMO Boss Set to Cut 1,000 Jobs" in Globe & Mail (February 1, 2007, pp. B3)*
Pub: CTVglobemedia Publishing Inc.
Ed: Andrew Willis. **Description:** The decision of the new chief executive officer of the Bank of Montreal, Bill Downe, to cut down 1,000 jobs, to boost the company's performance is discussed.

32842 ■ *"A New Era for Raiders" in Harvard Business Review (Vol. 88, November 2010, No. 11, pp. 34)*
Pub: Harvard Business School Publishing
Ed: Guhan Subramanian. **Description:** The article presents evidence that Section 203 is vulnerable, and a new wave of corporate takeovers may develop. The authors suggest that since no bidders have able to use the 85 percent stipulation over the last 19 years, it does not present a meaningful opportunity for success.

32843 ■ *"New Year, New Estate Plan" in Hawaii Business (Vol. 53, February 2008, No. 8, pp. 54)*
Pub: Hawaii Business Publishing
Ed: Antony M. Orme. **Description:** Discusses the start of the new year which can be a time to revise wills and estate plans as failure to do so may create problems of unequal inheritance and increase in estate tax exemption, which could disinherit beneficiaries. Other circumstances that can prompt changes in wills and estate plans are presented.

32844 ■ *"No, Management Is Not a Profession" in Harvard Business Review (Vol. 88, July-August 2010, No. 7-8, pp. 52)*
Pub: Harvard Business School Publishing
Ed: Richard Barker. **Description:** An argument is presented that management is not a profession, as it is less focused on mastering a given body of knowledge than it is on obtaining integration and collaboration skills. Implications for teaching this new approach are also examined.

32845 ■ *No Man's Land: What to Do When Your Company Is Too Big to Be Small but Too Small to Be Big*
Pub: Penguin Group Incorporated
Ed: Doug Tatum. **Released:** September 2007. **Price:** $24.95. **Description:** Tips for managing a small business.

32846 ■ *No Man's Land: What to Do When Your Company Is Too Big to Be Small but Too Small to Be Big*
Pub: Portfolio Publishing
Ed: Doug Tatum. **Released:** September 13, 2007. **Price:** $24.95. **Description:** Insight to help fast-growing companies navigate the fatal trap of no-man's land, a perilous zone where they have outgrown the habits and practices that fueled their early growth but have not yet adopted new practices and resources in order to cope with new situations and challenges.

32847 ■ *"Northern Overexposure" in Canadian Business (Vol. 79, August 14, 2006, No. 16-17, pp. 36)*
Pub: Rogers Media
Description: Fall in revenue from foreign film productions in Canada due to its overexposure, and incentives offered by other nations to foreign film productions, are discussed.

32848 ■ *"Not Your Dad's Business Card" in Small Business Opportunities (July 2008)*
Pub: Entrepreneur Press
Contact: Perlman Neil, President
Ed: Rob Schlacter. **Description:** Provides tips on how to effectively design and use business cards.

32849 ■ *"Note to Leonard: Swim Fast" in Canadian Business (Vol. 80, January 15, 2007, No. 2, pp. 29)*
Pub: Rogers Media
Ed: Zena Olijnyk. **Description:** The decision of Can-West Entertainment Inc and Goldman Sachs Capital Partners to collectively acquire Toronto-based Alliance Atlantis Communications Inc. is discussed.

32850 ■ *"Nothing But Net: Fran Harris Offers Advice On Winning the Game of Business" in Black Enterprise (Vol. 38, March 2008, No. 8, pp. 50)*
Pub: Earl G. Graves Publishing Co. Inc.
Ed: Chana Garcia. **Description:** Fran Harris, certified life coach, business consultant, and CEO of her business, a multimedia development company, reveals five tips to ensure entrepreneurial success.

32851 ■ *"Ocean Choice in Running to Acquire Assets of FPI" in Globe & Mail (March 15, 2007, pp. B9)*
Pub: CTVglobemedia Publishing Inc.
Description: Ocean Choice International is bidding vigorously for acquiring assets St. Johns based of FPI Ltd. Complete details of these bids are discussed.

32852 ■ *Off-Ramps and On-Ramps: Keeping Talented Women on the Road to Success*
Pub: Harvard Business School Press
Ed: Sylvia Ann Hewlett. **Price:** $29.95. **Description:** Hewlett (founding president for the Center for Work-Life Policy) examines why many women exit their careers, taking 'off-ramps' (leaving altogether) or 'scenic routes' (opting to work part-time), often during critical, competitive times. She also provides valuable suggestions for companies hoping to retain talented employees of any gender.

32853 ■ *"Office Party Attire" in Women In Business (Vol. 61, October-November 2009, No. 5, pp. 27)*
Pub: American Business Women's Association
Ed: Leigh Elmore. **Description:** Office holiday party attire should conform to factors such as time, location, scheduled events, and other company-furnished details. Observing this guideline can help in upholding the business nature of the party. Party attendees are also encouraged to network with other attendees, while tips on how to behave during the party are also presented.

32854 ■ *"Office Pests" in Canadian Business (Vol. 79, October 9, 2006, No. 20, pp. 122)*
Pub: Rogers Media
Ed: Calvin Leung. **Description:** Personality traits of employees and strategies for managers to effectively handle them are discussed.

32855 ■ *"O'Malley, Ehrlich, Court Business Vote" in Baltimore Business Journal (Vol. 28, October 1, 2010, No. 21, pp. 1)*
Pub: Baltimore Business Journal
Ed: Scott Dance. **Description:** Maryland Governor Martin O'Malley and former Governor Robert Ehrlich reveal their business plans and platforms as they court business-minded votes in the state. Ehrlich, a Republican and O'Malley, a Democrat have both initiated programs that helped small businesses, but both have also introduced programs that made it more expensive and difficult to do business in the state.

32856 ■ *"Omniplex on the Case" in Black Enterprise (Vol. 37, December 2006, No. 5, pp. 38)*
Pub: Earl G. Graves Publishing Co. Inc.
Ed: Glenn Townes. **Description:** Office of Personnel Management in Washington D.C. recently awarded a service contract to Omniplex World Services Corp. Virginia-based, The Chantilly, will perform security investigations and background checks on current and prospective federal employees and military personnel and contractors.

32857 ■ *"On Track" in Canadian Business (Vol. 79, July 17, 2006, No. 14-15, pp. 51)*
Pub: Rogers Media
Ed: John Gray. **Description:** Results of the annual survey conducted by CanadaEs boards, to measure the levels of corporate governance of firms in Canada, which are presented.

32858 ■ *"One Hundred Years of Excellence in Business Education: What Have We Learned?" in Business Horizons (January-February 2008)*
Pub: Elsevier Advanced Technology Publications
Ed: Frank Acito, Patricia M. McDougall, Daniel C. Smith. **Description:** Business schools have to be more innovative, efficient and nimble, so that the quality of the next generation of business leaders is improved. The Kelley School of Business, Indiana University ahs long been a leader in business education. The trends that influence the future of business education and useful success principles are discussed.

32859 ■ *Organizations Alive!: Six Things That Challenge - Seven That Bring Success*
Pub: Yuill & Associates
Ed: Jan Yuill. **Released:** January 2005. **Price:** $35.12 for book and guide. **Description:** New insight into understanding how organizations function as individuals is presented by an international consultant. Customer service, resource management, outsourcing, and management are among the issues covered.

32860 ■ *"Our Gadget of the Week: Business Buddy" in Barron's (Vol. 88, July 7, 2008, No. 27, pp. 26)*
Pub: Dow Jones & Co., Inc.
Ed: Jay Palmer. **Description:** Review and evaluation of the Lenovo X300 laptop computer which offers executives a variety of features despite its smaller size and weight. The laptop is about 0.73 inch thick, comes with a 64-gigabyte solid-state drive from Samsung, and weighs less than three pounds.

32861 ■ *Outfoxing the Small Business Owner*
Pub: Adams Media Corporation
Ed: Gene Marks. **Released:** January 2005. **Description:** Special skill sets are required to sell, service or deal with small business customers.

32862 ■ *Outliers*
Pub: Little, Brown and Company
Ed: Malcolm Gladwell. **Released:** 2008. **Description:** The book explores reasons for individual success.

32863 ■ *"Overview - Small Business Optimism" in Small Business Economic Trends (April 2008, pp. 4)*
Pub: National Federation of Independent Business
Ed: William C. Dunkelberg, Holly Wade. **Description:** Graph and table representing the optimism index for small businesses in the U.S., based on ten survey indicators, are presented. The index values include data from 1986 to 2008.

32864 ■ *"Overview - Small Business Optimism" in Small Business Economic Trends (July 2009, pp. 4)*
Pub: National Federation of Independent Business
Description: Small businesses surveyed in the United States regarding their optimism index from 1986 to 2009 shows a marked difference as is presented in a graph. A small business optimism index from January 2004 to June 2009 is also given in tabular form. The index value was seasonally adjusted at 1986=100.

32865 ■ *Own Your Own Corporation: Why the Rich Own Their Own Companies and Everyone Else Works for Them*
Pub: Business Plus
Ed: Garrett Sutton; Robert T. Kiyosaki; Ann Blackman. **Released:** June 2008. **Price:** $17.99 paperback. **Description:** Part of the Rich Dad Advisor's Series, this edition shows how individuals can incorporate themselves and their businesses to save thousands of dollars in taxes and protect against financial disaster.

32866 ■ *"Owning the Right Risks" in Harvard Business Review (Vol. 86, September 2008, No. 9, pp. 102)*
Pub: Harvard Business School Press
Ed: Kevin Bueler; Andrew Freeman; Ron Hulme. **Description:** TXU Corp. is used to illustrate methods for successful risk management. The electric utility's practices include determining which risks are natural, embedding risk in all processes and decisions, and organizing corporate governance around risk.

32867 ■ *The Oxford Handbook of Entrepreneurship*
Pub: Oxford University Press, Incorporated
Ed: Mark Casson; Bernard Young; Anuradha Basu. **Released:** October 2006. **Price:** $155.00. **Description:** Research covering entrepreneurship is presented by an international team of leading scholars.

32868 ■ *"Pau Hana" in Hawaii Business (Vol. 53, December 2007, No. 6, pp. 118)*
Pub: Hawaii Business Publishing
Ed: Cathy Cruz-George. **Description:** Presented are the hobbies of four Hawaii executives as well as the reason these hobbies are an important part of their lives and add to their ability to manage effectively. Mike Wilkins, for example, is not only Turtle Bay Resort's director of sales and marketing, but is also a glider pilot, while Aubrey Hawk Public Relations president Aubrey Hawk loves baking. The interests of Queen Liliuokalani Trust's Thomas K. Kaulukukui Jr., Reyn Spooner's Tim McCullough, and Heide and Cook Ltd.'s Dexter S. Kekua, are discussed.

32869 ■ *"People and Places" in Entrepreneur (Vol. 36, February 2008, No. 2, pp. 12)*
Pub: Entrepreneur Media Inc.
Ed: Rieva Lesonsky. **Description:** Websites of different organizations that can provide entrepreneurs with business help are presented. Business-related events such as the Women in Charge conference and Xerox Smart Business Symposium are mentioned.

32870 ■ *"Personal File: Dean Williams" in Canadian Business (Vol. 80, April 23, 2007, No. 9, pp. 55)*
Pub: Rogers Media
Description: A brief profile of Dean Williams, architect at Softchoice Corp., including his services to the company, is presented.

32871 ■ *Petty Capitalists and Globalization: Flexibility, Entrepreneurship, and Economic Development*
Pub: State University of New York Press
Ed: Alan Smart, Josephine Smart. **Released:** January 2006. **Price:** $26.95. **Description:** Investigation into ways small businesses in Europe, Asia, and Latin America are required to operate and compete in the fast-growing transnational economy.

32872 ■ *"Pick A Trademark You Can Protect" in Women Entrepreneur (November 3, 2008)*
Pub: Entrepreneur Media Inc.
Ed: Nina L. Kaufman. **Description:** Provides information regarding trademarks, how to choose a name that will win approval from the U.S. Patent and Trademark Office, and how to choose a trademark that one can protect.

32873 ■ *A Piece of the Pie*
Pub: Outskirts Press, Incorporated
Ed: Shelton P. Rhodes, Peter Fretty. **Released:** July 2005. **Description:** Examination of the U.S. Small Business Administration's program 8(a), designed to help disadvantaged individuals grow their small businesses.

32874 ■ *"Pioneers Get All The Perks" in Canadian Business (Vol. 81, March 3, 2008, No. 3, pp. 18)*
Pub: Rogers Media
Description: Suncor Energy Inc. will face royalty payments from 25% to 30% of net profits as it signs a new deal with Alberta. Biovail Corp., meanwhile, is under a U.S. grand jury investigation for supposed improprieties in Cardizem LA heart drug launch. The Conference Board of Canada's proposal to impose taxes on greenhouse gas emissions and other developments in the business community are discussed.

32875 ■ *"Plan: Put Health Centers in ERs" in Crain's Detroit Business (Vol. 25, June 22, 2009, No. 25, pp. 1)*
Pub: Crain Communications Inc. - Detroit
Ed: Jay Greene. **Description:** It has been suggested by top CEOs in the Detroit, Michigan area to put satellites of federally qualified health centers within emergency room departments. The plan would have the health centers pay a monthly fee for each patient treated.

32876 ■ *The Platinum Rule for Small Business Success*
Pub: Morgan James Publishing, LLC
Ed: Scott Zimmerman; Tony Allesandra; Ron Finklestein. **Released:** August 2006. **Description:** Rules for running a successful and profitable small business are shared.

32877 ■ *"Playing to Win" in Entrepreneur (Vol. 36, May 2008, No. 5, pp. 40)*
Pub: Entrepreneur Media, Inc.
Ed: Robert Kiyosaki. **Description:** Four personality types needed by entrepreneurs to drive their leadership in business are given. 'I must be liked' are social directors and go-betweens; 'I must be comfortable'

are those who seek job security and are not at ease with deadlines; I must be right are those strong in opinion; and 'I must win' are people in charge.

32878 ■ *Poker Winners are Different*
Pub: Kensington Publishing Corporation
Ed: Alan N. Schoonmaker. **Released:** 2009. **Description:** Poker success requires reading the context and reading people, two skills every entrepreneur needs to possess.

32879 ■ *PPC's Guide to Compensation Planning for Small Business*
Pub: Practitioners Publishing Company
Released: September 2004. **Price:** $119.00. **Description:** Technical guide for developing a compensation system for small business. Forms and letters included.

32880 ■ *"The Preparation Gap" in Hawaii Business (Vol. 53, February 2008, No. 8, pp. 37)*
Pub: Hawaii Business Publishing
Ed: Ashley Hamershock. **Description:** Discussion of the educational gap in Hawaii's workforce is being addressed by educational workshops that aim to improve students' knowledge in science, technology, math, and engineering, and prepare them for their entry into the workforce. Education beyond high school is required for jobs to be filled in the coming years.

32881 ■ *Prepare for the Worst, Plan for the Best: Disaster Preparedness and Recovery for Small Businesses*
Pub: John Wiley & Sons, Incorporated
Ed: Donna R. Childs. **Released:** July 2009. **Price:** $24.95. **Description:** Guide to help small businesses protect themselves from disasters. New information is presented on Redundant Arrays of Independent Disk (RAID) hardware backups, calling trees and the Internet, power outages and suppliers, as well as wireless networks.

32882 ■ *Prescriptive Entrepreneurship*
Pub: Edward Elgar Publishing, Inc.
Ed: James O. Fiet. **Released:** March 10, 2010. **Price:** $130.00. **Description:** In the only known program of prescriptive entrepreneurship, the author provides a marked contract to the standard descriptive focus of entrepreneurship studies.

32883 ■ *Principles of Private Firm Valuation*
Pub: John Wiley & Sons, Incorporated
Ed: Stanley J. Feldman. **Released:** April 2005. **Price:** $85.00. **Description:** Tools and techniques to correctly perform private firm valuation, including value and how to measure it, valuing control, determining the size of the marketability discount, creating transparency and the implications for value, the value of tax pass-through entities versus a C corporation, etc.

32884 ■ *Print Solutions--Buyers' Guide Issue*
Pub: Print Services and Distribution Association
Contact: Robert O'Connell, President
URL(s): www.psda.org/?page=nmk_annbuygu. **Released:** Annual; October; Latest edition 2011. **Price:** $49, Individuals. **Publication includes:** List of about 600 suppliers of business forms and other business printing, such as ad specialties, bar-coded forms & labels, commercial printing calendars, tags, cards, labels, and printed stationery. **Entries include:** name, address, phone, fax, capabilities, product/service. **Arrangement:** Alphabetical. **Indexes:** Product/service.

32885 ■ *"Priority: In Memoriam" in Inc. (December 2007, pp. 25-26, 28, 30)*
Pub: Gruner & Jahr USA Publishing
Ed: Ryan McCarthy. **Description:** Profiles of entrepreneurs who died in 2007; these individuals helped to create some major business trends in the last fifty years, from the advent of socially responsible business to development of quality manufacturing.

32886 ■ *"Private Equity Party Fuelled by Cheap Debt" in Globe & Mail (February 27, 2007, pp. B1)*
Pub: CTVglobemedia Publishing Inc.
Ed: Sinclair Stewart. **Description:** The funding of private equity fund Kohlberg Kravis through cheap debt, during the buyout of the TXU Corp. is discussed.

32887 ■ *"Profit Predictions Look Too Plump" in Barron's (Vol. 88, March 31, 2008, No. 13, pp. 37)*
Pub: Dow Jones & Company, Inc.
Ed: Johanna Bennett. **Description:** Full-year forecast points to a 14 percent gain for 2008 but the second-half profit increases would have to grow at a fast rate and peak at 61 percent in the fourth quarter to achieve this. Trends in the U.S. economic conditions are also discussed.

32888 ■ *Project Management for Small Business Made Easy*
Pub: Entrepreneur Press
Ed: Sid Kemp. **Released:** April 2006. **Price:** $26.95. **Description:** Strategies for implementing project management for small business are offered.

32889 ■ *Purple Cow*
Pub: Penguin Group USA Inc.
Ed: Seth Godin. **Description:** Being a purple cow means you are exciting, phenomenal and unforgettable, the traits required to be a successful entrepreneur.

32890 ■ *The Pursuit of Happyness*
Pub: HarperCollins Publishers Inc.
Ed: Chris Gardner. **Released:** May 2006. **Price:** $25. 95. **Description:** Rags-to-riches saga of a homeless father who raised and cared for his son on the streets of San Francisco and worked to become a powerful leader on Wall Street.

32891 ■ *Put Your Business on Autopilot: The 7-Step System to Create a Business That Works So Well That You Don't Have To*
Pub: Morgan James Publishing LLC
Ed: Greg Roworth. **Released:** April 1, 2009. **Price:** $16.95. **Description:** Failure rates still remain as high as 80 percent within five years of starting a small business despite the hard work by their owners. The author suggests that working harder doesn't necessarily equate to a successful enterprise.

32892 ■ *"Randy Perreira" in Hawaii Business (Vol. 53, February 2008, No. 8, pp. 28)*
Pub: Hawaii Business Publishing
Ed: David K. Choo. **Description:** Randy Perreira is recently named executive director of Hawaii Government Employees Association. He talks about how he was shaped growing up with a father who was a labor leader and how the challenges in 2008 compare with those in the time of his father. He also shares his thoughts about the importance of employees fighting for their rights.

32893 ■ *Re-Imagine! Business Excellence in a Disruptive Age*
Pub: DK Publishing/Penguin Group
Ed: Tom Peters. **Released:** 2006. **Price:** $20.00. **Description:** Examination of today's business order. Peters urges business owners to re-imagine business.

32894 ■ *"Reaching Your Potential" in Harvard Business Review (Vol. 86, July-August 2008, No. 8, pp. 45)*
Pub: Harvard Business School Press
Ed: Robert S. Kaplan. **Description:** Being proactive in developing one's career is an important part of entrepreneurship. Keys to successful development include knowing oneself and one's goals, and taking calculated risks.

32895 ■ *"The Real Job of Boards" in Business Strategy Review (Vol. 21, Autumn 2010, No. 3, pp. 36)*
Pub: Wiley-Blackwell
Ed: Harry Korine, Macrus Alexander, Pierre-Yves Gomez. **Description:** Widely seen as the key for ensuring quality in corporate governance, the board of directors has been a particular focal point for reform. The authors believe that more leadership at board level could avert many corporate crises in the future.

32896 ■ *Reality Check: The Irreverent Guide to Outsmarting, Outmanaging, and Outmarketing Your Competition*
Pub: Penguin Group USA Inc.
Ed: Guy Kawasaki. **Price:** $29.95. **Description:** Marketing guru and entrepreneur, Guy Kawasaki, provides a compilation of his blog posts on all aspects of starting and operating a business.

32897 ■ *"Recession Drags Down CEO Pay; Full Impact May Not Have Played Out" in Crain's Detroit Business (Vol. 25, June 22, 2009, No. 25)*
Pub: Crain Communications Inc. - Detroit
Ed: Ryan Beene. **Description:** Median overall compensation package for Detroit's top-compensated 50 CEOs was down 10.67 percent from $2.3 million in 2007 to $2.06 million in 2008. Statistical data included.

32898 ■ *"The Recession: Problem or Opportunity" in Women In Business (Vol. 61, October-November 2009, No. 5, pp. 34)*
Pub: American Business Women's Association
Ed: J. Douglas Bate. **Description:** Business organizations' success during a recession is based on how management views the economic situation. The recession may be deemed as a setback or may be visualized as an opportunity that has to be grabbed for the organization. Suggestions on what management should do in the opportunity-creating or proactive approach are also highlighted.

32899 ■ *"Redefining Failure" in Harvard Business Review (Vol. 88, September 2010, No. 9, pp. 34)*
Pub: Harvard Business School Publishing
Ed: Seth Godin. **Description:** Specific forms of failure, including design failure, failure of priorities, failure of opportunity, and failure to quit are examined. The negative implications of maintaining the status quo are discussed.

32900 ■ *"Reduce the Risk of Failed Financial Judgments" in Harvard Business Review (Vol. 86, July-August 2008, No. 8, pp. 24)*
Pub: Harvard Business School Press
Ed: Robert G. Eccles; Edward J. Fiedl. **Description:** Utilization of business consultants, evaluators, appraisers, and actuaries to decrease financial management risks is discussed.

32901 ■ *"Region and City Need Influx of Youth" in Crain's Detroit Business (Vol. 24, April 14, 2008, No. 15, pp. 8)*
Pub: Crain Communications Inc.
Description: Discusses an upcoming report from Michigan Future Inc. which finds that young professionals, including those with children, are interested in living in an active urban environment. It also states that because many of those young professionals are entrepreneurial in nature, oftentimes businesses follow.

32902 ■ *"Relocation, Relocation, Relocation" in Conde Nast Portfolio (Vol. 2, June 2008, No. 6, pp. 36)*
Pub: Conde Nast Publications
Contact: David Carey, President
Ed: Michelle Leder. **Description:** Perks regarding executive relocation are discussed.

32903 ■ *"A Research Firm With More Than One Foe" in Globe & Mail (February 24, 2006, pp. B1)*
Pub: CTVglobemedia Publishing Inc.
Ed: Shawn McCarthy. **Description:** The details of Biovail Corp.'s securities fraud case against Gradient Analytics Inc. are presented.

32904 ■ *Resource and Environmental Management in Canada*
Pub: Oxford University Press
Ed: Bruce Mitchell. **Released:** April 1, 2004. **Price:** $45.00. **Description:** Discusses resource management in Canada, focusing on business and industry, environmental groups, First Nations, the public, local communities with resource-based economies.

32905 ■ *The RFA at 25: Needed Improvements for Small Business Regulatory Relief*
Pub: U.S. Government Printing Office
Released: February 2006. **Price:** $62.00. **Description:** Information regarding the hearing on needed improvements for small business regulatory relief

before the Committee on Small Business, House of Representatives, One Hundred Ninth Congress, First Session, Washington, DC, March 16, 2005 is provided.

32906 ■ *"The Rich 100" in Canadian Business (Vol. 79, Winter 2006, No. 24, pp. 78)*
Pub: Rogers Media
Description: The rankings of the 100 richest billionaires in Canada are presented, along with the description of their achievements and their net worth.

32907 ■ *"The Right Stuff" in Canadian Business (Vol. 79, October 23, 2006, No. 21, pp. 151)*
Pub: Rogers Media
Ed: Laura Bogomolny. **Description:** The profile of Linda Duxbury, the winner of the Sprott MBA Students Society 2003-04 Best teacher award as well as Carleton University Students' Association 2002-03 award, is presented.

32908 ■ *Risk Takers and Innovators, Great Canadian Business Ventures Since 1950*
Pub: Altitude Publishing
Ed: Sandra Phinney. **Released:** June 15, 2004. **Price:** $7.95. **Description:** Successful business leaders share their creativity, technology skills, and entrepreneurship.

32909 ■ *The Road from Ruin: How to Revive Capitalism and Put American Back on Top*
Pub: Crown Business
Ed: Matthew Bishop, Michael Green. **Released:** January 26, 2010. **Price:** $27.00. **Description:** Authors show why American companies must respond to the economic crisis with long term vision and a renewed emphasis on values.

32910 ■ *"Rob Ritchie" in Canadian Business (Vol. 80, January 15, 2007, No. 2, pp. 70)*
Pub: Rogers Media
Ed: Michelle Magnan. **Description:** The former president of the Canadian Pacific Railway, Rob Ritchie, reveals facts about his personal and professional life.

32911 ■ *"Sage Advice" in Canadian Business (Vol. 80, October 22, 2007, No. 21, pp. 70)*
Pub: Rogers Media
Ed: John Gray. **Description:** Seymour Schulich, one of Canada's richest men and generous philanthropist, wrote the book, 'Get Smarter: Life and Business Lessons'. The business book sold more than 50,000 copies and now sits on Canada's bestseller's list. Its popularity is attributed to the marketing efforts of the entrepreneur and author.

32912 ■ *Save Your Small Business: 10 Crucial Strategies to Survive Hard Times or Close Down and Move On*
Pub: NOLO
Contact: Ralph Warner, Chief Executive Officer
Ed: Ralph Warner, Bethany Laurence. **Released:** August 1, 2009. **Price:** $29.99. **Description:** According to a study among 500 businesses, 44 percent used credit cards in order to meet their firm's needs in the previous six months. Written by a business owner, this book provides twelve strategies to protect personal assets from creditors and survive the current recession.

32913 ■ *"Say Goodbye to Shy" in Canadian Business (Vol. 79, September 11, 2006, No. 18, pp. 125)*
Pub: Rogers Media
Ed: Alex Mlynek. **Description:** Tips and practices for effective communications at workplaces are presented.

32914 ■ *"Say No to Slackers" in Canadian Business (Vol. 79, November 6, 2006, No. 22, pp. 105)*
Pub: Rogers Media
Ed: Erin Pooley. **Description:** The effects of underperformers on performance of other colleagues with relation to company productivity are analyzed.

32915 ■ *"Scotiabank Tapped as Likely Buyer in Puerto Rico" in Globe & Mail (January 30, 2007, pp. B3)*
Pub: CTVglobemedia Publishing Inc.
Ed: Andrew Willis. **Description:** Speculation over Bank of Nova Scotia's proposed acquisition of First BanCorp is discussed.

32916 ■ *"The Search for Big Oil" in Canadian Business (Vol. 80, April 9, 2007, No. 8, pp. 10)*
Pub: Rogers Media
Ed: Joe Castaldo. **Description:** The continuing effort of Canmex Minerals Corp. to explore for oil in Somalia despite the failure of several other companies is discussed.

32917 ■ *The Secret of Exiting Your Business Under Your Terms!*
Pub: Outskirts Press, Incorporated
Ed: Gene H. Irwin. **Released:** August 2005. **Price:** $29.95. **Description:** Topics include how to sell a business for the highest value, tax laws governing the sale of a business, finding the right buyer, mergers and acquisitions, negotiating the sale, and using a limited auction to increase future value of a business.

32918 ■ *"The Secret's Out About Kansas City" in Women In Business (Vol. 61, August-September 2009, No. 4, pp. 26)*
Pub: American Business Women's Association
Ed: Leigh Elmore. **Description:** Missouri's Kansas City offers various attractions, such as public fountains, the 18th and Vine Historic Districts for jazz enthusiasts, and the Crossroads Arts District with a variety of art galleries. Details on other cultural attractions and neighborhoods in the city are presented.

32919 ■ *"Secrets To Trade Show Success" in Women Entrepreneur (September 12, 2008)*
Pub: Entrepreneur Media Inc.
Ed: Lesley Spencer Pyle. **Description:** Trade shows require an enormous amount of work, but they are an investment that can pay off handsomely because they allow a business to get their product or service in front of their target market. Advice regarding trade shows is given including selecting the correct venue, researching the affair and following up on leads obtained at the event.

32920 ■ *Serves You Right!*
Pub: Serves You Right!, Incorporated
Ed: Susan Brooks. **Released:** May 2004. **Price:** $15. 95. **Description:** Profile of excellence in customer service.

32921 ■ *Services in Canada*
Pub: Routledge Inc.
Ed: W.R. Frisbee. **Released:** March 29, 1990. **Price:** $215.00. **Description:** Profiles of the services industry in Canada.

32922 ■ *Setting the Table: The Transforming Power of Hospitality in Business*
Pub: HarperCollins Publishers Inc.
Released: October 2006.

32923 ■ *"Seven Ways to Fail Big" in Harvard Business Review (Vol. 86, September 2008, No. 9, pp. 82)*
Pub: Harvard Business School Press
Ed: Paul B. Carroll; Chunka Mui. **Description:** Seven factors involved in business failures are identified, and ways to avoid them are described. These factors include flawed financial engineering, hurrying into consolidation, and investing in technology that is not a good fit.

32924 ■ *Shop Class as Soulcraft*
Pub: Penguin Group USA Inc.
Ed: Matthew B. Crawford. **Released:** May 28, 2009. **Price:** $25.95. **Description:** A philosopher and mechanic argues for the satisfaction and challenges of manual work.

32925 ■ *"Shopping Around for New Ideas" in Canadian Business (Vol. 79, July 17, 2006, No. 14-15, pp. 76)*
Pub: Rogers Media
Description: Pensions should be a win-win situation for both the employer and the employee. The perspective of both parties concerning pension plans is explored as well as the need to amend laws in order to make sure that one class of merchant does not suffer at the cost of another.

32926 ■ *Simplified Incorporation Kit*
Pub: Nova Publishing Company
Ed: Daniel Sitarz. **Released:** March 2007. **Price:** $19.95. **Description:** Kit includes all the forms, instructions, and information necessary for incorporating any small business in any state (CD-ROM included).

32927 ■ *"Simply Therapeutic" in Women In Business (Vol. 61, December 2009, No. 6, pp. 34)*
Pub: American Business Women's Association
Ed: Maureen Sullivan. **Description:** Steps on minimizing office clutter are presented in an effort to also eliminate clutter from the office worker's mind. Allotting time for clutter reduction, setting realistic goals, file organization, labeling, and sticking to a clutter reduction system are suggested. Clutter reduction is expected to contribute to increased productivity in the workplace.

32928 ■ *"Single Most Important Problem" in Small Business Economic Trends (April 2008, pp. 18)*
Pub: National Federation of Independent Business
Ed: William C. Dunkelberg, Holly Wade. **Description:** Two graphs and a table presenting the economic problems encountered by small businesses in the U.S. are provided. The figures presented in the graphs include data from 1986 to 2008.

32929 ■ *"Single Most Important Problem" in Small Business Economic Trends (March 2008, pp. 18)*
Pub: National Federation of Independent Business
Ed: William C. Dunkelberg, Holly Wade. **Description:** Two graphs and a table representing the economic problems encountered by small businesses in the U.S. are presented. The figures presented in the graphs include data from 1986 to 2008.

32930 ■ *"Single Most Important Problem" in Small Business Economic Trends (February 2008, pp. 18)*
Pub: National Federation of Independent Business
Ed: William C. Dunkelberg, Holly Wade. **Description:** Two graphs and a table representing the economic problems encountered by small businesses in the U.S. are presented. The figures presented in the graphs include data from 1974 to 2008.

32931 ■ *"Single Most Important Problem" in Small Business Economic Trends (January 2008, pp. 18)*
Pub: National Federation of Independent Business
Description: Table of the single most important problem among small businesses surveyed in the U.S. in December 2007 is presented. Taxes were selected by 21 percent of firms as the single most important problem, followed by cost and availability of insurance at 16 percent. Graphs comparing selected single most important problem from January 1986 to December 2007 are also given.

32932 ■ *"Single Most Important Problem" in Small Business Economic Trends (September 2010, pp. 18)*
Pub: National Federation of Independent Business
Ed: William C. Dunkelberg, Holly Wade. **Description:** A table of the single most important problem among small businesses surveyed in the U.S. in August 2010 is presented. 'Poor sales' was selected by 31 percent of firms as the single most important problem, followed by taxes at 21 percent. Graphs comparing selected single most important problem from January 1986 to August 2010 are also provided.

32933 ■ *Six SIGMA for Small Business*
Pub: Entrepreneur Press
Ed: Greg Brue. **Released:** October 2005. **Price:** $19.95 (US), $26.95 (Canadian). **Description:** Jack Welch's Six SIGMA approach to business covers accounting, finance, sales and marketing, buying a business, human resource development, and new product development.

32934 ■ *The Six Sigma for Small and Medium Businesses: What You Need to Know Explained Simply*
Pub: Atlantic Publishing Company
Ed: Marsha R. Ford. **Released:** January 1, 2009. **Price:** $24.95. **Description:** The Six Sigma set of practices used to systematically improve business practices by eliminating defects. To be Six Sigma compliant, a company must produce no more than 3.4 defects per one million products, and if achieved will save the firm millions of dollars. The two main methodologies of Six Sigma are outlined.

32935 ■ *"A Skimmer's Guide to the Latest Business Books" in Inc. (Volume 32, December 2010, No. 10, pp. 34)*
Pub: Inc. Magazine
Ed: Leigh Buchanan. **Description:** A list of new books published covering all aspects of small business is offered.

32936 ■ *Small Business: An Entrepreneur's Business Plan*
Pub: South-Western
Ed: J.D Ryan, Gail P. Hiduke. **Released:** October 2008. **Price:** $119.95. **Description:** Assistance in preparing a business plan that identifies opportunities and ways to target a customer market.

32937 ■ *Small Business: An Entrepreneur's Plan*
Pub: Nelson Thomson Learning
Ed: Ronald A. Knowles. **Released:** December 2006. **Description:** Entrepreneur's guide to planning a small business.

32938 ■ *The Small Business Bible: Everything You Need to Know to Succeed in Your Small Business*
Pub: John Wiley and Sons, Inc.
Ed: Steven D. Strauss. **Released:** September 2008. **Price:** $19.95 (US), $28.99 (Canadian). **Description:** Comprehensive guide to starting and running a successful small business. Topics include bookkeeping and financial management, marketing, publicity, and advertising.

32939 ■ *Small Business, Big Life: Five Steps to Creating a Great Life with Your Own Small Business*
Pub: Rutledge Books Inc.
Ed: Louis Barajas. **Released:** May 2007. **Price:** $22.99. **Description:** Five steps for planning, starting and running a small business, while maintaining a good life, are presented.

32940 ■ *"Small Business Compensation" in Small Business Economic Trends (April 2008, pp. 10)*
Pub: National Federation of Independent Business
Ed: William C. Dunkelberg, Holly Wade. **Description:** Graphs and tables that present compensation plans and compensation changes of small businesses in the U.S. are provided. The figures include data from 1986 to 2008.

32941 ■ *"Small Business Compensation" in Small Business Economic Trends (March 2008, pp. 10)*
Pub: National Federation of Independent Business
Ed: William C. Dunkelberg, Holly Wade. **Description:** Graphs and tables that present compensation plans and compensation changes of small businesses in the U.S. are provided. The figures include data from 1968 to 2008.

32942 ■ *"Small Business Compensation" in Small Business Economic Trends (February 2008, pp. 10)*
Pub: National Federation of Independent Business
Ed: William C. Dunkelberg, Holly Wade. **Description:** Graphs and tables that present compensation plans and compensation changes of small businesses in the U.S. are provided. The figures include data from 1974 to 2008.

32943 ■ *"Small Business Compensation" in Small Business Economic Trends (January 2008, pp. 10)*
Pub: National Federation of Independent Business
Description: Graph from a survey of small businesses in the U.S. is given, representing small business compensation from January 1986 to December 2007. Tables showing actual compensation changes and compensation plans are also presented. A graph comparing small business prices and labor compensation is supplied.

32944 ■ *Small Business Desk Reference*
Pub: Penguin Books USA Inc.
Ed: Gene Marks. **Released:** December 2004. **Description:** Comprehensive guide for starting or running a successful small business, focusing on buying a business or franchise, writing a business plan, financial management, accounting, legal issues, human resources management, operations, marketing, sales, customer service, taxes, insurance, and ethics. Information for launching a restaurant, property management firm, retail outlet, consulting firm, and service business is included.

32945 ■ *Small Business and Entrepreneurship*
Pub: SAGE Publications USA
Contact: Blaise R. Simqu, President
Ed: Robert Blackburn. **Released:** January 2008. **Price:** $1,275.00. **Description:** Research covering small business and entrepreneurship.

32946 ■ *Small Business: Innovation, Problems and Strategies*
Pub: Nova Science Publishers, Inc.
Ed: John E. Michaels, Leonardo F. Piraro. **Released:** April 1, 2009. **Price:** $89.00. **Description:** Innovation is a fundamental determinant of value creation in businesses and can also be a key to successful economic growth. The innovative process and innovative effort of small companies are examined and evaluated, along with alternative strategies.

32947 ■ *Small Business Legal Strategies*
Pub: Aspatore Books, Incorporated
Released: July 2004. **Price:** $37.95. **Description:** Corporate Chairs and Partners from top firms in the U.S. offering insight into selecting, engaging, employing, and benefiting from external corporate counsel for the small business owner or executive.

32948 ■ *"Small Business Outlook" in Small Business Economic Trends (July 2009, pp. 4)*
Pub: National Federation of Independent Business
Description: Outlook among small businesses surveyed in the United States from January 1986 to June 2009 is presented. Tables showing small business outlook for expansion and outlook for general business conditions from January 2004 to June 2009 and the most important reasons for expansion outlook are also given.

32949 ■ *Small Business Sourcebook*
Pub: Cengage Gale
Released: July 2009. **Price:** $578.00. **Description:** Two-volume guide to more than 27,300 listings of live and print sources for small business startups as well as small business growth and development. Over 30,500 topics are included.

32950 ■ *Small Business Survival Guide*
Pub: Adams Media Corporation
Ed: Cliff Ennico. **Price:** $12.95.

32951 ■ *Small Business Survival Guide: Starting, Protecting, and Securing Your Business for Long-Term Success*
Pub: Adams Media Corporation
Ed: Cliff Ennico. **Released:** September 2005. **Price:** $12.95 (US), $17.95 (Canadian). **Description:** Entrepreneurship in the new millennium. Topics include creditors, taxes, competition, business law, and accounting.

32952 ■ *Small Business Taxes 2006: Your Complete Guide to a Better Bottom Line*
Pub: John Wiley & Sons, Incorporated
Ed: Barbara Weltman. **Released:** November 2008. **Price:** $18.95. **Description:** Detailed information on new tax laws and IRS rules for small businesses.

32953 ■ *Small Business Taxes Made Easy: How to Increase Your Deductions, Reduce What You Owe, and Boost Your Profits*
Pub: McGraw-Hill Companies Inc.
Contact: Deven Sharma, President
Ed: Eva Rosenberg. **Released:** December 2004. **Price:** $16.95. **Description:** Tax expert gives advice to small business owners regarding tax issues. TaxMamma.com, run by Eva Rosenberg, is one of the top seven tax advice Websites on the Internet.

32954 ■ *Small Business Turnaround*
Pub: Adams Media Corporation
Ed: Marc Kramer. **Price:** $17.95 paperback.

32955 ■ *Small Businesses and Workplace Fatality Risk: An Exploratory Analysis*
Pub: RAND Corp.
Contact: Michael D. Rich, President
E-mail: michael_rich@rand.org
Ed: John F. Mendelhoff; Christopher Nelson; Kilkon Ko. **Released:** June 2006. **Price:** $20.00. **Description:** According to previous research, small business worksites report higher rates of deaths or serious injuries than larger corporations. Statistical data included.

32956 ■ *Small Giants: Companies that Choose to Be Great Instead of Big*
Pub: Penguin Group
Ed: Bo Burllingham. **Price:** $19.96.

32957 ■ *Small Giants: Companies That Choose to Be Great Instead of Big*
Pub: Penguin Group
Ed: Bo Burlingame. **Released:** March 27, 2007. **Price:** $16.00. **Description:** Profiles of privately held companies that have become huge in their field without becoming large corporations.

32958 ■ *Small and Medium-Sized Enterprises in Countries in Transition*
Pub: United Nations Publications
Contact: Christopher Woodthrope, Director (Acting)
Released: January 2005. **Price:** $18.00. **Description:** Characteristics of small and medium enterprise (SME) sector in transition countries and emerging market economies.

32959 ■ *"Smart Businesses See Value, and Profit, in Promoting Women" in Crain's Chicago Business (Vol. 30, February 2007, No. 6, pp. 30)*
Pub: Crain Communications, Inc.
Ed: Marc J. Lane. **Description:** Despite U.S. corporations making little progress in advancing women to leadership positions over the past ten years, enlightened corporate decision makers understand that gender diversity is good business as the highest percentages of women officers yielded, on average, a 34 percent higher total return to shareholders and a 35.1 percent higher return on equity than those firms with the lowest percentages of women officers, according to a 2004 Catalyst study of Fortune 500 companies.

32960 ■ *SME Cluster Development: A Dynamic View on Survival Clusters in Developing Countries*
Pub: Palgrave Macmillan
Ed: Mario Davide Parrilli. **Released:** April 2007. **Price:** $90.00. **Description:** Survival clustering in developing countries is discussed in order to increase effectiveness of policy-making and development operations in local contexts.

32961 ■ *"Social Intelligence and the Biology of Leadership" in Harvard Business Review (Vol. 86, September 2008, No. 9, pp. 74)*
Pub: Harvard Business School Press
Ed: Daniel Goleman; Richard Boyatzis. **Description:** Social intelligence within the framework of corporate leadership is defined and described. Guidelines for assessing one's own capabilities as a socially intelligent leader include empathy, teamwork, inspiration, and influence.

32962 ■ *"Sound Advice From Dr. Sleep" in Crain's Chicago Business (Vol. 31, April 21, 2008, No. 16, pp. 30)*
Pub: Crain Communications, Inc.
Ed: Sarah A. Klein. **Description:** James K. Wyatt, the director of the Sleep Disorders Centers at Rush University Medical Center in Chicago, gives advice to business executives concerning what to eat, how to nap and which drugs to take or avoid in order to ease the strain of air travel, particularly on overseas flights.

32963 ■ *"Speak Better: Five Tips for Polished Presentations" in Women Entrepreneur (September 19, 2008)*
Pub: Entrepreneur Media Inc.
Ed: Suzannah Baum. **Description:** Successful entrepreneurs agree that exemplary public speaking skills are among the core techniques needed to propel their business forward. A well-delivered presentation can result in securing a new distribution channel, gaining new customers, locking into a new referral stream or receiving extra funding.

32964 ■ *The SPEED of Trust: The One Thing That Changes Everything*
Pub: Free Press/Simon & Schuster Inc.
Ed: Stephen M.R. Covey. **Released:** February 5, 2008. **Price:** $15.95. **Description:** Because of recent business scandals, trust and a desire for accountability is addressed by the author.

32965 ■ *"Stains Still Set After SBA Scrub" in Black Enterprise (March 2008)*
Pub: Earl G. Graves Publishing Co. Inc.
Ed: Marcia A. Wade. **Description:** Small Business Administration's attempt to ensure that federal contracts were legitimately rewarded to small businesses, however the report filed showed that $4.6 billion in incorrectly coded contracts were removed from the SBA database. Critics contend the report is filled with inaccuracies. Statistical data included.

32966 ■ *"Standard-of-Living Gap With U.S. Closing" in Globe & Mail (March 27, 2007, pp. B3)*
Pub: CTVglobemedia Publishing Inc.
Ed: Heather Scoffield. **Description:** According to latest report released by Statistics Canada, standard-of-living in Canada has increased considerably in last decade to match-up with American economy. Complete analysis in this context is presented.

32967 ■ *"Star Power" in Small Business Opportunities (September 2008)*
Pub: Entrepreneur Press
Contact: Perlman Neil, President
Description: Employee retention is an important factor for corporate executives to consider because the impact of excessive turnovers can be devastating to a company causing poor morale, unemployment claims, hiring costs, lost production and customer loss. Although there is no specific formula for retaining employees, there are several things every organization can do to keep their workers happy and increase the chances that they will stay loyal and keep working for the company for years to come; tips aimed at management regarding good employee relationships are included.

32968 ■ *"Star Power Versus (Somewhat) Green Power" in Globe & Mail (January 18, 2007, pp. B2)*
Pub: CTVglobemedia Publishing Inc.
Ed: Konrad Yakabuski. **Description:** The views of the Canadian actor Roy Dupuis on the trends of energy consumption by Quebeckers are presented, along with statistics of energy consumption in the Quebec region.

32969 ■ *The Starfish and the Spider*
Pub: Portfolio
Ed: Ori Brafman; Rod A. Beckstrom. **Released:** 2007. **Price:** $24.95.

32970 ■ *The Starfish and the Spider: The Unstoppable Power of Leaderless Organizations*
Pub: Portfolio Publishing
Ed: Ori Brafman; Rod A. Beckstrom. **Released:** 2008. **Price:** $15.00 paperback. **Description:** Through their experiences promoting peace and economic development through decentralizing networking, the authors offer insight into ways that decentralizing can change organizations. Three techniques for combating a decentralized competitor are examined.

32971 ■ *Start Small, Finish Big*
Pub: Warner Business Books
Ed: Fred DeLuca. **Price:** $14.95.

32972 ■ *"Stay Calm, Bernanke Urges Markets" in Globe & Mail (March 1, 2007, pp. B1)*
Pub: CTVglobemedia Publishing Inc.
Ed: Brian McKenna. **Description:** The views of Ben Bernanke, the chief of the United States Federal Reserve Board, on the future trends of the United States' economy are presented. The effect of the global stock market trends on the American stock markets is discussed.

32973 ■ *"Step Up to Help Regionalism Step Forward" in Crain's Cleveland Business (Vol. 28, November 12, 2007, No. 45, pp. 10)*
Pub: Crain Communications, Inc.
Ed: Rob Briggs; William Currin. **Description:** Discusses the importance of regionalism for Northeast Ohio as being a broad, collaborative approach to spur economic development.

32974 ■ *Strategic Entrepreneurship*
Pub: Prentice Hall PTR
Ed: Philip A. Wickham. **Released:** September 2006. **Price:** $90.00. **Description:** Conceptual and practical ideas for managing a small business are explored.

32975 ■ *Strategizing, Disequilibrium, and Profit*
Pub: Stanford University Press
Ed: John A. Mathews. **Released:** June 2006. **Price:** $24.95. **Description:** Author proposes the use of a conceptual framework that is consistent with real economies instead of equilibrium-based foundations when creating a business strategy.

32976 ■ *"Streaming Hot Currie" in Canadian Business (Vol. 80, April 23, 2007, No. 9, pp. 10)*
Pub: Rogers Media
Ed: Paul Brent. **Description:** The views of Richard Currie, former president of Loblow Cos. Ltd., on the human resource policy of the company are presented.

32977 ■ *Streetwise Small Business Book of Lists: Hundreds of Lists to Help You Reduce Costs, Increase Revenues, and Boost Your Profits!*
Pub: Adams Media Corporation
Contact: Gary Krebs, Director
E-mail: swatrous@adamsmedia.com
Ed: Gene Marks. **Released:** September 2006. **Price:** $25.95. **Description:** Strategies to help small business owners locate services, increase sales, and lower expenses.

32978 ■ *Strengthsfinder 2.0*
Pub: Gallup Press
Ed: Tom Rath. **Released:** 2007. **Price:** $22.95. **Description:** Author helps people uncover their talents in order to achieve their best each day.

32979 ■ *"Stronach Confirms Magna Eyeing Chrysler" in Globe & Mail (March 9, 2007, pp. B1)*
Pub: CTVglobemedia Publishing Inc.
Ed: Greg Keenan. **Description:** The decision of auto parts manufacturing firm Magna International Inc. to participate in the take-over bid for Chrysler Group, as announced by its founder Frank Stronach, is discussed.

32980 ■ *"Succeed at a New Job" in Canadian Business (Vol. 79, November 20, 2006, No. 23, pp. 65)*
Pub: Rogers Media
Ed: Claire Gagne. **Description:** Collections of questions that job-seekers can ask the interviewer during employment interviews are presented.

32981 ■ *"Success Fees" in Canadian Business (Vol. 80, March 12, 2007, No. 6, pp.)*
Pub: Rogers Media
Ed: David Baines. **Description:** Legal issues regarding payment of lawyer fees termed 'fair fee' in Canada are discussed with an instance of Inmet Mining Corp.'s dealing with lawyer Irwin Nathanson.

32982 ■ *Success Secrets to Maximize Business in Canada*
Pub: Graphic Arts Center Publishing Company
Ed: Ken Coates. **Released:** October 5, 2000. **Description:** Part of the Culture Shock! Series that helps companies maximize business opportunities in Canada.

32983 ■ *The Successful Entrepreneur's Guidebook: Where You Are Now, Where You Want to Be and How to Get There*
Pub: Kogan Page, Limited
Contact: Ben Glover, Director of Marketing
Ed: Colin Barrow; Robert Brown. **Released:** January 2007. **Price:** $35.00. **Description:** Characteristics of successful entrepreneurship are examined. The book helps new business owners to develop and grow a business.

32984 ■ *Successful Proposal Strategies for Small Business: Using Knowledge Management to Win Government, Private-Sector, and International Contracts, Fourth E*
Pub: Artech House, Incorporated
Ed: Robert S. Frey. **Released:** February 2008. **Price:** $129.00. **Description:** Front-end proposal planning and storyboarding, focusing on the customer mission in proposals, along with the development of grant proposals.

32985 ■ *"Surprise Offer for Dofasco Puts Heat on Arcelor" in Globe & Mail (January 16, 2006, pp. B1)*
Pub: CTVglobemedia Publishing Inc.
Ed: Greg Keenan. **Description:** The details of competition between ThyssenKrupp AG and Arcelor SA to bid Dofasco Inc. are presented.

32986 ■ *"Survey Finds State Execs Cool On Climate Change" in The Business Journal-Milwaukee (Vol. 25, August 8, 2008, No. 46, pp. A1)*
Pub: American City Business Journals, Inc.
Ed: David Doege. **Description:** According to a survey of business executives in Wisconsin, business leaders do not see climate change as a pressing concern, but businesses are moving toward more energy-efficient operations. The survey also revealed that executives believe that financial incentives can promote energy conservation. Other survey results are provided.

32987 ■ *"Survey Profile" in Small Business Economic Trends (April 2008, pp. 19)*
Pub: National Federation of Independent Business
Ed: William C. Dunkelberg, Holly Wade. **Description:** Two graphs and a table presenting the profile of small businesses that participated in the National Federation of Independent Business (NFIB) survey are provided. The actual number of firms, their industry types, and the number of full and part-time employees are also given.

32988 ■ *"Survey Profile" in Small Business Economic Trends (March 2008, pp. 19)*
Pub: National Federation of Independent Business
Ed: William C. Dunkelberg, Holly Wade. **Description:** Two graphs and a table that present the profile of small businesses that participated in the National Federation of Independent Business (NFIB) survey are provided. The actual number of firms, their industry types, and the number of full and part-time employees are also given.

32989 ■ *"Survey Profile" in Small Business Economic Trends (February 2008, pp. 19)*
Pub: National Federation of Independent Business
Ed: William C. Dunkelberg, Holly Wade. **Description:** Two graphs and a table that present the profile of small businesses that participated in the National

Federation of Independent Business (NFIB) survey are provided. The actual number of firms, their industry types, and the number of full and part-time employees are also given.

32990 ■ *"Survey Profile" in Small Business Economic Trends (September 2010, pp. 19)*
Pub: National Federation of Independent Business

Ed: William C. Dunkelberg, Holly Wade. **Description:** Two graphs and a table presenting the profile of small businesses that participated in the National Federation of Independent Business (NFIB) survey are provided. The actual number of firms, their industry types, and the number of full and part-time employees are presented.

32991 ■ *"Survive the Small-to-Big Transition" in Entrepreneur (November 4, 2008)*
Pub: Entrepreneur Media Inc.

Ed: Elizabeth Wilson. **Description:** Transitioning a small company to a large company can be a challenge, especially during the time when it is too big to be considered small and too small to be considered big. Common pitfalls during this time are discussed as well as techniques business owners should implement when dealing with this transitional period.

32992 ■ *"Surviving the Storm" in Canadian Business (Vol. 81, July 22, 2008, No. 12-13, pp. 50)*
Pub: Rogers Media Ltd.

Ed: Jeff Sanford. **Description:** Investment adviser Harry Dent and finance professor Paul Marsh discuss their views and forecasts on the United States' economic condition. Dent believes advisors should concentrate on wealth preservation rather than on returns. Other views regarding U.S. economic conditions are also presented.

32993 ■ *Swimming Against the Tide*
Pub: Macmillan Publishers Limited

Ed: Tim Waterstone. **Released:** October 2006. **Price:** $29.95. **Description:** Tim Waterstone shares ten rules for creating successful small businesses.

32994 ■ *The Ten Faces of Innovation*
Pub: Doubleday Broadway Publishing Group

Ed: Tom Kelley. **Price:** $29.95.

32995 ■ *"Ten Ways to Save on Business Travel" in Women Entrepreneur (November 21, 2008)*
Pub: Entrepreneur Media Inc.

Ed: Julie Moline. **Description:** Advice regarding ways in which to save money when traveling for business is given.

32996 ■ *"The Ten Worst Leadership Habits" in Canadian Business (Vol. 81, March 31, 2008, No. 5, pp. 63)*
Pub: Rogers Media

Ed: Michael Stern. **Description:** Ten leadership behaviors that aspiring leaders need to avoid are presented. These include expecting colleagues and subordinates to be like themselves, attending too many meetings, being miserly when it comes to recognition and praise, and giving an opinion often.

32997 ■ *They Made America*
Pub: Little Brown Company/Time Warner Book Group

Ed: Harold Evans, Gail Buckland, David Lefer. **Released:** 2006. **Price:** $18.95. **Description:** Coffee table book highlighting entrepreneurship; this book is filled with interesting illustrated portraits of entrepreneurs and innovators like Thomas Edison, George Doriot (a venture capital pioneer), and Ida Rosenthal (inventor of the Maidenform bra).

32998 ■ *Think Big and Kick Ass in Business and Life*
Pub: HarperBusiness

Ed: Donald J. Trump; Bill Zanker. **Price:** $26.95. **Description:** The philosophy of thinking big and acting aggressively on the path to prosperity is examined.

32999 ■ *"The Thinker" in Canadian Business (Vol. 81, March 31, 2008, No. 5, pp. 52)*
Pub: Rogers Media

Ed: Andrew Wahl. **Description:** Mihnea Moldoveanu provides much of the academic rigor that underpins Roger Martin's theories on how to improve the way business leaders think. Moldoveanu is also a classically trained pianist and founder of Redline Communications and has a mechanical engineering degree from MIT on top of his astounding knowledge on many academic fields.

33000 ■ *This Is Not Your Parents' Retirement: A Revolutionary Guide for a Revolutionary Generation*
Pub: Entrepreneur Press

Ed: Patrick P. Astre. **Released:** July 2005. **Price:** $19.95 (US), $26.95 (Canadian). **Description:** Mutual funds, stocks, bonds, insurance products, and tax strategies for retirement planning.

33001 ■ *"Three Funds Look to Join CPP, Bypassing Teachers in BCE Hunt" in Globe & Mail (April 23, 2007, pp. B1)*
Pub: CTVglobemedia Publishing Inc.

Ed: Sinclair Stewart. **Description:** The plans of the Ontario Municipal Employees Retirement Board, British Columbia Investment Management Corp. and the Alberta Investment Corp. to join the bidding consortium led by Canadian Pension Plan Investment Board, for the buyout of BCE Inc. are discussed. The efforts of the Ontario Teachers Pension Plan Board to form a bidding consortium for the same purpose are discussed.

33002 ■ *Three Moves Ahead*
Pub: John Wiley and Sons, Inc.

Ed: Bob Rice. **Released:** March 30, 2008. **Price:** $24.95. **Description:** Things the game of chess can teach about business are explored.

33003 ■ *"To Win, Create What's Scarce" in Harvard Business Review (Vol. 88, November 2010, No. 11, pp. 46)*
Pub: Harvard Business School Publishing

Ed: Seth Godin. **Description:** It is recommended to identify what is scarce yet valuable and applying this principle to business in order to be successful.

33004 ■ *"Top 49ers Alphabetical Listing with Five Years Rank and Revenue" in Alaska Business Monthly (Vol. 27, October 2011, No. 10, pp. 100)*
Pub: Alaska Business Publishing Company

Description: A listing of Alaska's top 49 performing companies ranked by revenue for years 2010 and 2011.

33005 ■ *"Top Marks" in Canadian Business (Vol. 79, October 23, 2006, No. 21, pp. 143)*
Pub: Rogers Media

Ed: Erin Pooley; Laura Bogomolny. **Description:** Profiles of some top grade master of business administration students like Hogan Mullally and Will mercer, belonging to reputed business schools, are presented.

33006 ■ *"Tough Sell" in Black Enterprise (Vol. 37, October 2006, No. 3, pp. 92)*
Pub: Earl G. Graves Publishing Co. Inc.

Ed: Sonia Alleyne. **Description:** Career coaches can evaluate your talents and skills. In an era where more companies are downsizing a coach can help you decide if you are suited for your industry or should try switching careers.

33007 ■ *Trading Places: SMEs in the Global Economy, A Critical Research Handbook*
Pub: Edward Elgar Publishing, Incorporated

Ed: Lloyd-Reason. **Released:** September 2006. **Price:** $110.00. **Description:** An overview of international research for small and medium-sized companies wishing to expand in the global economy.

33008 ■ *"TransCanada Builds on Proud Olympic History by Joining Vancouver 2010" in Canadian Corporate News (May 14, 2007)*
Pub: Comtex News Network Inc.

Description: TransCanada is the official supplier in the Natural Gas Pipeline Operator category for the Vancouver 2010 Olympic and Paralympic Winter Games.

33009 ■ *"Trimming Costs, But Not Looking It" in Crain's Chicago Business (Vol. 31, November 17, 2008, No. 46, pp. 35)*
Pub: Crain Communications, Inc.

Ed: Shia Kapos. **Description:** Advice is given concerning ways in which to keep up appearances of success during these troubled financial times.

33010 ■ *"The Trouble With $150,000 Wine" in Barron's (Vol. 88, July 7, 2008, No. 27, pp. 33)*
Pub: Dow Jones & Co., Inc.

Ed: Orley Ashenfelter. **Description:** Review of the book, 'The Billionaire's Vinegar: The Mystery of the World's Most Expensive Bottle of Wine,' which discusses vintners along with the marketing and distribution of wine as well as the winemaking industry as a whole.

33011 ■ *"The Trusty Sidekick" in Canadian Business (Vol. 81, March 31, 2008, No. 5, pp. 33)*
Pub: Rogers Media

Ed: John Gray. **Description:** Being second-in-command is a good opportunity to be mentored by the boss and puts the executive in the position to see the whole organization and have influence to make changes. However, the chief operating officer has the unenviable task of trying to achieve unattainable goals. Executives who want to become the right hand man must go beyond their job description.

33012 ■ *The Truth About Middle Managers: Who They Are, How They Work, Why They Matter*
Pub: Harvard Business School Publishing

Ed: Paul Osterman. **Released:** 2009. **Price:** $35.00. **Description:** The alienation of middle managers is bad for a company.

33013 ■ *"TSX Linkup Sets Stage for Battle" in Globe & Mail (March 6, 2007, pp. B1)*
Pub: CTVglobemedia Publishing Inc.

Ed: Boyd Erman; Sinclair Stewart. **Description:** The strategic alliance between TSX Group Inc. and International Securities Exchange Holdings Inc. for the establishment of a derivatives exchange in Canada is discussed. The prospects of competition between the new exchange and the Montreal Exchange are discussed.

33014 ■ *"A Turn in the South" in The Economist (Vol. 390, January 3, 2009, No. 8612, pp. 34)*
Pub: The Economist Newspaper Inc.

Description: Overview of Charleston, South Carolina, a region that lost its navy base in 1996, which had provided work for more than 22,000 people; the city developed a plan called Noisette in order to redevelop the area and today the economy is healthier and more diversified than it was a decade ago. Charleston was described as among the best cities for doing business by Inc. Magazine and seems to be handling the downturn of the economy fairly well. Statistical data regarding growth, business and population is included.

33015 ■ *"Twenty Years of Advocacy and Education" in Women Entrepreneur (January 18, 2009)*
Pub: Entrepreneur Media Inc.

Ed: Eve Gumpel. **Description:** Profile of Sharon Hadary who served as executive director of the Center for Women's Business Research for two decades; Hadary discusses what she has learned about women business owners, their impact on the economy and what successful business owners share in common.

33016 ■ *"Two of a Kind" in Entrepreneur (Vol. 35, November 2007, No. 11, pp. 103)*
Pub: Entrepreneur Media Inc.

Ed: Chris Penttila. **Description:** Entrepreneurs need support and advice once in a while as pressure from work gets to them. It is good to have people from the same industry to give advice on particular topics when needed.

33017 ■ *The Ugly Truth About Small Business: 50 Things That Can Go Wrong..and What You Can Do About It*
Pub: Sourcebooks, Inc.
Contact: Len Vlahos, President
E-mail: dominique@sourcebooks.com
Ed: Ruth King. **Released:** November 2005. **Price:** $14.95. **Description:** More than 50 percent of small businesses fail within their first year and 95 percent fail within the first five years.

33018 ■ *"The Ultimate Business Tune-Up: For Times Like These" in Inc. (Vol. 31, January-February 2009, No. 1, pp. 70)*
Pub: Mansueto Ventures LLC
Description: Twenty-three things do energize a small business in tough economic times are outlined with insight from successful entrepreneurs.

33019 ■ *Ultimate Guide to Project Management*
Pub: Entrepreneurial Press
Ed: Sid Kemp. **Released:** October 2005. **Price:** $29.95 (US), $39.95 (Canadian). **Description:** Project management strategies including writing a business plan and developing a good advertising campaign.

33020 ■ *Ultimate Small Business Advisor*
Pub: Entrepreneur Press
Ed: Andi Axman. **Released:** May 2007. **Price:** $30. 95. **Description:** Tip for starting and running a small business, including new tax rulings and laws affecting small business, are shared.

33021 ■ *"The Uncompromising Leader" in Harvard Business Review (Vol. 86, July-August 2008, No. 8, pp. 50)*
Pub: Harvard Business School Press
Ed: Russell A. Eisenstat; Michael Beer; Nathaniel Foote; Tobias Fredburg; Flemming Norrgren. **Description:** Advice regarding how to drive performance without sacrificing commitment to people is given. Topics include development of shared purpose, organizational engagement, the fostering of collective leadership capability, and maintaining perspective.

33022 ■ *"Under Pressure" in Canadian Business (Vol. 81, July 21, 2008, No. 11, pp. 18)*
Pub: Rogers Media Ltd.
Ed: Joe Castaldo. **Description:** According to a survey conducted by COMPASS Inc., meeting revenue targets is the main cause of job stress for chief executive officers. Staffing and keeping expenditures lower also contribute to the workplace stress experienced by business executives. Other results of the survey are presented.

33023 ■ *"Unemployment Rates" in The Economist (Vol. 390, January 3, 2009, No. 8612, pp. 75)*
Pub: The Economist Newspaper Inc.
Description: Countries that are being impacted the worst by rising unemployment rates are those that have also been suffering from the housing market crisis. Spain has been the hardest hit followed by Ireland. America and Britain are also seeing levels of unemployment that indicate too much slack in the economy.

33024 ■ *"Unmasking Manly Men" in Harvard Business Review (Vol. 86, July-August 2008, No. 8, pp. 20)*
Pub: Harvard Business School Press
Ed: Robin J. Ely; Debra Meyerson. **Description:** Oil rig work is used to explore how focusing on job requirements and performance successfully challenged stereotypical views of masculinity and competence.

33025 ■ *"The Upside of Fear and Loathing" in Barron's (Vol. 88, March 24, 2008, No. 12, pp. 11)*
Pub: Dow Jones & Company, Inc.
Ed: Michael Santoli. **Description:** Fear and risk aversion prevalent among investors may actually serve to cushion the decline and spark a rally in US stock prices. Surveys of investors indicate rising levels of anxiety and bearishness, indicating a possible positive turnaround.

33026 ■ *"Use Common Sense in Office Gift-Giving" in Women In Business (Vol. 61, October-November 2009, No. 5, pp. 32)*
Pub: American Business Women's Association
Ed: Maureen Sullivan. **Description:** Tips on office gift-giving during the Christmas season are discussed. Aside from ensuring appropriateness of the gift with respect to the recipient, a fixed giving budget must be adhered to. Gifts that can be used by anyone may be selected and those with religious overtones must be avoided.

33027 ■ *"Valenti: Roots of Financial Crisis Go Back to 1998" in Crain's Detroit Business (Vol. 24, October 6, 2008, No. 40, pp. 25)*
Pub: Crain Communications, Inc.
Ed: Tom Henderson; Nathan Skid. **Description:** Interview with Sam Valenti III who is the chairman and CEO of Valenti Capital L.L.C., a wealth-management firm; Valenti discusses in detail the history that led up to the current economic crisis as well as his prediction for the future of the country.

33028 ■ *"Valuation: Confusing and Misunderstood" in Business Owner (Vol. 35, July-August 2011, No. 4, pp. 10)*
Pub: DL Perkins Company
Description: Business valuation is explained to help small business owners realize the value of their company.

33029 ■ *"The Valuation of Players" in Canadian Business (Vol. 80, October 22, 2007, No. 21, pp. 39)*
Pub: Rogers Media
Ed: Jeff Sanford. **Description:** Business professionals are supplementing their Masters in Business Administration degrees with CBV or chartered business valuator. CBVs are trained, not only in business tangibles, but also in business intangibles such as market position, reputation, intellectual property, and patent. Details of employment opportunities for chartered business valuators are discussed.

33030 ■ *Wake Up and Smell the Zeitgeist*
Pub: Basic Books
Ed: Grand McCracken. **Released:** 2010. **Price:** $26. 95. **Description:** Insight is given into an element of corporate success that's often overlooked and valuable suggestions are offered for any small business to pursue.

33031 ■ *"Walker Seeks More Business Participation" in Business Journal-Milwaukee (Vol. 28, December 10, 2010, No. 10, pp. A1)*
Pub: Milwaukee Business Journal
Ed: Rich Kirchen. **Description:** Wisconsin governor Scott Walker is seeking the aid of Milwaukee business leaders to participate in resolving the challenges posed by the economic crisis. Walker is aiming to create 250,000 jobs. He is also planning to call a special session of the legislature to enact strategies to jumpstart the economy.

33032 ■ *The Wall Street Journal. Complete Small Business Guidebook*
Pub: Three Rivers Press
Ed: Colleen DeBaise. **Released:** December 29, 2009. **Price:** $15.00. **Description:** The mechanics of building, running and growing a profitable business are outlined, teaching how to write a business plan, ways to finding money during lean years, how to keep stress in check, time management, investment in technology, hiring, marketing, management basics, angel investing and venture capital, as well as an exit strategy.

33033 ■ *Ward's Business Directory of U.S. Private and Public Companies*
Pub: Cengage Learning Inc.
Contact: Ronald Dunn, President
URL(s): www.gale.cengage.com. **Released:** Annual; Latest edition 54th; June, 2011. **Price:** Edition 48 (2002): 8-vol. set, $3,075.00 (includes inter-edition supplement). Some individual volumes also sold separately.; $3627, Individuals five-volume set; $3205, Individuals four-volume set; $1697, Individuals volumes 5, 6, or 7; $1149, Individuals volume 8. **Covers:** Approximately 112,000 companies, 90% of which are privately owned, representing all industries. **Entries include:** Company name, address, phone, fax, toll-free, e-mail, URL, names and titles of up to five officers, up to four Standard Industrial Classification (SIC) codes, NAICS code, revenue figure, number of employees, year founded, ticker symbol, stock exchange, immediate parent, fiscal year end, import/export, type of company (public, private, subsidiary, etc.). In Vol. 4, lists of top 1,000 privately held companies ranked by sales vol., top 1,000 publicly held companies ranked by sales volume, and top 1,000 employers ranked by number of employees; analyses of public and private companies by state, revenue per employee for top 1,000 companies, public and private companies by SIC code and NAICS code. In volume 5, national Standard Industrial Classification (SIC) code rankings are listed, while volumes 6 and 7 lists Standard Industrial Classification (SIC) code rankings by state. In all volumes, guide to abbreviations, codes, and symbols; explanation of classification system; numerical and alphabetical listings of SIC and NAICS codes. In volume 8, NAICS rankings. In the supplement, 10,000 new listings not contained in the main edition are included. **Arrangement:** Volumes 1, 2, and 3, alphabetical; volume 4 is geographical by state, then ascending zip; volume 5 is classified by 4-digit SIC code, then ranked by sales; volumes 6 and 7 are classified by Standard Industrial Classification (SIC) code within state; volume 8 classified by NAICS, then ranked; supplement arranged alphabetical and Standard Industrial Classification (SIC) code. **Indexes:** Company name index in volumes 5, 7, and 8. **Availability:** Online: Cengage Learning Inc. CD-ROM: Cengage Learning Inc. **Type:** Directory; Numeric.

33034 ■ *"We Move Forward as a Team" in Women In Business (Vol. 61, December 2009, No. 6, pp. 6)*
Pub: American Business Women's Association
Ed: Rene Street. **Description:** Based on her experiences in ABWA's National Board of Directors retreat, an executive director of the American Business Women's Association, shares her belief that interaction is necessary for a successful business enterprise. She believes that the problems presented in the retreat's team-building exercises are similar to challenges which are faced in ABWA, in the workplace, and in the marketplace.

33035 ■ *"WestJet Hires a New CFO After Lengthy Search" in Globe & Mail (January 23, 2007, pp. B8)*
Pub: CTVglobemedia Publishing Inc.
Ed: Brent Jang. **Description:** Vito Culmone, formerly vice of Malson Canada, is appointed as chief financial officer.

33036 ■ *"What Are Your Party's Legislative Priorities for 2008?" in Hawaii Business (Vol. 53, January 2008, No. 7, pp. 22)*
Pub: Hawaii Business Publishing
Description: Discusses the Democratic Party of Hawaii which will prioritize giving more opportunities to earn a living a wage in 2008, according to the party chairwoman Jeani Withington. The Republican Party chairman Willes K. Lee, meanwhile, states that his party will seek to enhance the local business climate. The political parties' plans for Hawaii for the year 2008 are presented in detail.

33037 ■ *What Losing Taught Me about Winning: The Ultimate Guide for Success in Small and Home-Based Business*
Pub: Fireside Publishing
Ed: Fran Tarkenton; Wes Smith. **Released:** April 7, 1999. **Price:** $17.95. **Description:** Provides insight into running a successful small business.

33038 ■ *What Men Don't Tell Woman about Business: Opening Up the Heavily Guarded Alpha Male Playbook*
Pub: John Wiley and Sons, Inc.
Ed: Christopher V. Fleet. **Released:** October 26, 2007. **Description:** Valuable guide for any woman in business, this book helps reveal everything a woman needs to know in order to understand, communicate, and compete with men in business.

33039 ■ *"What School Did You Attend?" in Hawaii Business (Vol. 53, December 2007, No. 6, pp. 14)*
Pub: Hawaii Business Publishing
Ed: Kelli Abe Trifonovitch. **Description:** Discusses the question 'what school did you attend?' which is observed to be the most important inquiry in Hawaiian business discourse. The principle behind the question is based on establishing connections. The relation between the aforementioned inquiry and Hawaiian culture is explained.

33040 ■ *What Works: Success in Stressful Times*
Pub: Harper Press
Ed: Hamish McRae. **Released:** January 21, 2010. **Price:** $30.12. **Description:** Exploration of success stories from across the glove, and what Michelle Obama referred to as 'the flimsy difference between success and failure.' Why do some initiatives take off while others flounder? How have communities managed to achieve so much while others struggle? What distinguishes the good companies from the bad? What lessons can be learned from the well-ordered Mumbai community made famous by 'Slumdog Millionaire'? Why have Canadian manners helped Whistler become the most popular ski resort in North America?.

33041 ■ *"When Good Deals Go Bad: How to Renegotiate a Contract" in Inc. (November 2007, pp. 33-34)*
Pub: Gruner & Jahr USA Publishing
Ed: Dee Gill. **Description:** Ways to renegotiate contracts are discussed. Robb Corwin of Gorilla Fuel discusses how he was able to renegotiate contracts in order to save his business.

33042 ■ *"When Profit Is Not the Incentive" in Business North Carolina (Vol. 28, February 2008, No. 2, pp. 42)*
Pub: Business North Carolina
Ed: Amanda Parry. **Description:** Novant Health is North Carolina's fifth-largest private-sector employer and one of the largest nonprofit companies. Nonprofits grew 35 percent in North Carolina from 1995 to 2003.

33043 ■ *"When Virtue Is A Vice" in Harvard Business Review (Vol. 86, July-August 2008, No. 8, pp. 22)*
Pub: Harvard Business School Press
Ed: Anat Keinan; Ran Kivetz. **Description:** Negative consequences of habitually denying self-indulgence, from work and life balance to consumer shopping behaviors are discussed.

33044 ■ *"Where Are They Now?" in Canadian Business (Vol. 79, October 9, 2006, No. 20, pp. 71)*
Pub: Rogers Media
Description: The profile of the top chief executive officers of Canada for the year 2005 is discussed.

33045 ■ *"Where to Buy the Right MBA" in Canadian Business (Vol. 79, October 23, 2006, No. 21, pp. 99)*
Pub: Rogers Media
Ed: Erin Pooley; Laura Bogomolny; Joe Castaldo; Michelle Magnan; Claire Gagne. **Description:** Details of Canadian graduate business schools offering Master of business administration degree are presented.

33046 ■ *Who's Got Your Back*
Pub: Broadway Books, a Division of Random House
Ed: Keith Ferrazzi. **Price:** $25.00. **Description:** Achieving goals by building close relationships with a small circle of trusted individuals.

33047 ■ *"Why Did We Ever Go Into HR?" in Harvard Business Review (Vol. 86, July-August 2008, No. 8, pp. 39)*
Pub: Harvard Business School Press
Ed: Matthew D. Breitfelder; Daisy Wademan Dowling. **Description:** Examines the role of human resource directors and how their jobs foster new ideas and generate optimism.

33048 ■ *"Why LinkedIn is the Social Network that Will Never Die" in Advertising Age (Vol. 81, December 6, 2010, No. 43, pp. 2)*
Pub: Crain Communications, Inc.
Ed: Irina Slutsky. **Description:** Despite the popularity of Facebook, LinkIn in will always be a source for professionals who wish to network.

33049 ■ *"Why Oil Fell, and How It May Rise" in Globe & Mail (January 18, 2007, pp. B2)*
Pub: CTVglobemedia Publishing Inc.
Ed: Eric Reguly. **Description:** The causes of the decline in oil prices in Canada are discussed, along with prospects of an increase in the same.

33050 ■ *Wikinomics: How Mass Collaboration Changes Everything*
Pub: Penguin Group
Ed: Don Tapscott. **Released:** November 2006. **Price:** $25.95. **Description:** Guide to collaborate plans change beliefs about business hierarchies.

33051 ■ *"Will Focus on Business Continue?" in Baltimore Business Journal (Vol. 28, November 5, 2010, No. 26, pp. 1)*
Pub: Baltimore Business Journal
Ed: Scott Dance. **Description:** The 2010 election may call for new efforts to teach new lawmakers to assure that the viewpoints of businesses are considered and accurately delivered. The Greater Baltimore Committee and similar groups have gathered reports on the competitiveness of Maryland and are planning to use them to make a case of keeping business a top priority.

33052 ■ *"Will Small Business be Stimulated" in Entrepreneur (Vol. 37, July 2009, No. 7, pp. 18)*
Pub: Entrepreneur Media, Inc.
Ed: Jennifer Wang. **Description:** Steven Strauss, Alberto G. Alvarado, Jeff Rosenweig, Al Gordon, and Theresa Alfaro Daytner share their views on how the American Recovery and Reinvestment Act of 2009, also known as the economic stimulus, will affect small businesses. Their backgrounds are also provided.

33053 ■ *Winner Take All: How Competitiveness Shapes the Fate of Nations*
Pub: Basic Books
Ed: Richard J. Elkus Jr. **Released:** 2009. **Price:** $27.00. **Description:** American government and misguided business practices has allowed the U.S. to fall behind other countries in various market sectors such as cameras and televisions, as well as information technologies. It will take a national strategy to for America to regain its lead in crucial industries.

33054 ■ *Winning!*
Pub: HarperCollins Publishers Inc.
Ed: Jack and Suzy Welch. **Price:** $27.95.

33055 ■ *The Wisdom of Crowds: Why the Many Are Smarter Than the Few and How Collective Wisdom Shapes Business, Economies, Societies and Nations*
Pub: Doubleday Canada, Limited
Ed: James Surrowiecki. **Released:** May 2004. **Description:** The premise that the many are smarter than the few and its impact on business, economics, societies and nations is discussed.

33056 ■ *"Women Draw Less Pension Income" in Marketing to Women (Vol. 21, March 2008, No. 3, pp. 6)*
Pub: EPM Communications Inc.
Contact: Ira Mayer, President
E-mail: imayer@epmcom.com
Description: According to a study by the Employee Benefit Research Institute, women over the age of 50 are much less likely to receive annuity and/or pension income. Statistical data included.

33057 ■ *"Work Buds" in Canadian Business (Vol. 80, April 23, 2007, No. 9, pp. 56)*
Pub: Rogers Media
Ed: Andrew Wahl. **Description:** The role of team work and cooperation in improving workplace environment is presented.

33058 ■ *"Work Is An Action Word" in Black Enterprise (Vol. 38, December 2007, No. 5, pp. 86)*
Pub: Earl G. Graves Publishing Co. Inc.
Ed: Marcia Reed-Woodard. **Description:** Understanding your company's culture, knowing the importance of networking, and connecting with the right mentors to guide you are the ingredients required for any entrepreneur.

33059 ■ *"Work Less, Earn More" in Canadian Business (Vol. 80, March 12, 2007, No. 6, pp. 30)*
Pub: Rogers Media
Ed: Erin Pooley. **Description:** Expert advice on ways to work efficiently to complete the job instead of extending work hours is presented.

33060 ■ *"Work Naked" in Canadian Business (Vol. 80, March 12, 2007, No. 6, pp. 33)*
Pub: Rogers Media
Ed: Andrew Wahl. **Description:** The disadvantages of teleworking for both employees and the company, in view of lack of an office environment and self-discipline on the part of workers, are discussed.

33061 ■ *"Working His Magic at Home" in Business Courier (Vol. 24, February 22, 2008, No. 46, pp. 1)*
Pub: American City Business Journals, Inc.
Ed: Lucy May. **Description:** Rob Portman has left his position at the White House as budget director and decided to practice law at Squire, Sanders & Dempsey in Cincinnati. However, analysts believe that Portman's political career is not finished yet, as some expect him to become a gubernatorial or senatorial candidate in 2010. Portman's impacts on Cincinnati's business community are also evaluated.

33062 ■ *"Working It Out! How a Young Executive Overcomes Obstacles on the Job" in Black Enterprise (Vol. 37, January 2007, No. 6, pp. 55)*
Pub: Earl G. Graves Publishing Co. Inc.
Ed: Laura Egodigwe. **Description:** Interview with Susan Chapman, Global Head of Operations for Citigroup Realty Services, in which she discusses issues such as the important skills necessary for overcoming obstacles in the workplace.

33063 ■ *Working Together: Why Great Partnerships Succeed*
Pub: HarperBusiness
Ed: Michael D. Eisner with Aaron Cohen. **Price:** $25.99. **Description:** Michael D. Eisner, former CEO of the Walt Disney Company interviews corporate partners from various industries, including Bill and Melinda Gates and Warren Buffet and Charlie Munger. Why certain business partnerships succeed in the corporate world is discussed.

33064 ■ *The World Is Flat: A Brief History of the Twenty-First Century*
Pub: Picador USA
Ed: Thomas L. Friedman. **Released:** July 2007. **Price:** $16.00. **Description:** Globalization's impact on business.

33065 ■ *Ya Gotta Wanna*
Pub: Creative Book Publishers
Ed: Malcolm Paice. **Released:** July 2005. **Price:** $12.95. **Description:** Three phases of teamwork are outlined: identifying the people and creating the team, analyzing the components of the team, and implementing the project. The author compares a soccer team to a management team and that a successful soccer team has three main area attributes: a solid defense, a creative midfield, and a potent strike force.

33066 ■ *"Year-End Tax Tips" in Hawaii Business (Vol. 53, December 2007, No. 6, pp. 136)*
Pub: Hawaii Business Publishing
Ed: Kathleen Bryan. **Description:** Tax planning tips for the end of 2007, in relation to the tax breaks that are scheduled to expire, are presented. Among the tax breaks that will be expiring at the 2007 year-end are sales tax deduction in the state and local level, premiums on mortgage insurance, and deduction on tuition. The impacts of these changes are discussed.

33067 ■ *"Your Guide to Local Style Business" in Hawaii Business (Vol. 53, December 2007, No. 6, pp. 36)*
Pub: Hawaii Business Publishing
Ed: David K. Choo. **Description:** Discusses the importance of studying the Hawaiian culture when doing business locally. It was observed that geographical aspects increase emphasis on culture and lifestyle more than the need to rectify false imaging do. Details of how locals adhere to their culture are supplied.

33068 ■ *Your Lawyer: An Owner's Manual*
Pub: Agate Publishing, Incorporated
Ed: Henry C. Krasnow. **Released:** November 2005. **Price:** $14.00. **Description:** Small business guide that assists owners and managers to find, work with, and inspire attorneys. Includes an overview of the legal processes involved in running a small company.

TRADE PERIODICALS

33069 ■ *Business Asia*
Pub: Economist Intelligence Unit
Released: Biweekly. **Price:** $985. **Description:** Provides news on political, economic, and legal developments throughout the region, including business and e-business news; regulatory changes; distribution, human resources, market-entry strategies and regulatory development issues; economic and political risk analysis; company case studies; business intelligence.

33070 ■ *Business China*
Pub: Economist Intelligence Unit
Released: Biweekly. **Price:** $985. **Description:** Provides news on political, economic, and legal developments throughout the region, including business and e-business news; regulatory changes; distribution, human resources, market-entry strategies and regulatory development issues; company case studies; business intelligence.

33071 ■ *Business Eastern Europe*
Pub: Economist Intelligence Unit
Released: Weekly. **Price:** $1455, individuals for print version; $1530, individuals for online. **Description:** Provides news on political, economic, and legal developments throughout the region, including business and e-business news; regulatory changes; distribution, human resources, market-entry strategies and regulatory development issues; economic and political risk analysis; company case studies; business intelligence.

33072 ■ *Business India Intelligence*
Pub: Economist Intelligence Unit
Released: Monthly. **Price:** $845, individuals for print version; $895 for online version per year;. **Description:** Provides news on political, economic, and legal developments throughout the region, including business and e-business news; regulatory changes; distribution, human resources, market-entry strategies and regulatory development issues; economic and political risk analysis; company case studies; business intelligence.

33073 ■ *Business Middle East*
Pub: Economist Intelligence Unit
Released: Biweekly. **Price:** $1055, individuals for print version; $1095 for online version per year;. **Description:** Provides news on political, economic, and legal developments throughout the region, including business and e-business news; regulatory changes; distribution, human resources, market-entry strategies and regulatory development issues; economic and political risk analysis; company case studies; business intelligence.

33074 ■ *Business Periodicals Index (BPI)*
Pub: The H.W. Wilson Co.
URL(s): www.hwwilson.com/dd/bus_i.htm. **Ed:** Hiyol Yang. **Released:** Monthly; with annual cumulation. **Price:** An annual subscription is $1,495.00. **Covers:** Index of articles in business periodicals. **Entries include:** Publisher name, address, subscription rate, and frequency. Principal content of publication is annotated index of articles from 400 business periodicals, including book reviews.

33075 ■ *Business Russia*
Pub: Economist Intelligence Unit
Released: Monthly. **Price:** $955 for online version per year; $90 for most recent online issue. **Description:** Provides news on political, economic, and legal developments throughout the region, including business and e-business news; regulatory changes; distribution, human resources, market-entry strategies and regulatory development issues; political and economic risk analysis; company case studies; business intelligence.

33076 ■ *Business Week*
Pub: McGraw-Hill Inc.
Contact: Henry Hirschberg, President
URL(s): www.businessweek.com. **Released:** Weekly **Price:** $40, Canada; $40, Individuals.

33077 ■ *Cincy Business Magazine: The Magazine for Business Professionals*
Pub: Great Lakes Publishing Co.
URL(s): www.cincybusinessmag.com. **Ed:** Dianne Gebhardt-French.

33078 ■ *Forbes*
Pub: Forbes Inc.
URL(s): www.forbes.com. **Ed:** John Chamberlain, Scott DeCarlo. **Released:** Biweekly **Price:** $19.99, Individuals; $22.25, Canada. **Availability:** Online: LexisNexis Group; Forbes Inc. **Type:** Full-text.

33079 ■ *Fortune*
Pub: Time Inc.
Contact: Wayne Powers, President
URL(s): money.cnn.com/magazines/fortunewww.timeinc.com/brands/international.php. **Released:** 25/yr. **Price:** $19.99, Individuals; $39.98, Two years; $59.97, Individuals 3 years.

33080 ■ *Inc. Magazine: The Magazine for Growing Companies*
Pub: Gruner & Jahr USA
URL(s): www.inc.com. **Released:** Monthly **Price:** $22, Canada; $46, Other countries surface mail; $9.97, Individuals APO/FPO.

33081 ■ *Independent Operations*
Pub: American Financial Services Association
Contact: Chris Stinebert, President
Ed: Thomas L. Thomas, Editor. **Released:** Quarterly. **Price:** Included in membership; $15, nonmembers. **Description:** Furnishes members with news of the financial services industry, small business, and other areas of concern to the members of the Association's Section on Independent Operations. Provides news of current legislation, regulations, and individual/company profiles. Recurring features include letters to the editor, interviews, reports of meetings, news of Association events and conferences, and notices of publications available. Also contains columns titled Chairman's Report, Profile, Marketplace, Want Ads, For Your Information, and Question and Answer.

33082 ■ *The Journal of Business Valuation*
Pub: Carswell
Contact: Gregory Azeff, President
URL(s): www.carswell.com/description.asp?docid=7393. **Released:** Annual **Price:** C$85, Individuals; $52.52, Individuals.

33083 ■ *Marple's Pacific Northwest Letter*
Pub: Newsletter Publishing Corp.
Ed: Michael J. Parks, Editor. **Released:** Biweekly. **Price:** $125; $225 2 years. **Description:** Reports business and economic conditions in the Pacific Northwest (Washington, Oregon, Idaho, Montana), with some coverage of Alaska. Includes coverage of publicly-held companies of the region, with emphasis on basic industry such as forest products. Includes an analysis of long-term regional economic trends.

33084 ■ *Print Solutions: Award-Winning Coverage of the Printing Industry*
Pub: Print Services and Distribution Association
Contact: Robert O'Connell, President
URL(s): www.printsolutionsmag.com. **Ed:** John Delavan. **Released:** Monthly **Price:** Free to members; $29, Nonmembers.

33085 ■ *Review of Business Information Systems*
Pub: The Clute Institute for Academic Research
URL(s): journals.cluteonline.com/index.php/RBIS. **Released:** Quarterly **Price:** $300, Institutions.

VIDEOCASSETTES/ AUDIOCASSETTES

33086 ■ *The Business File*
PBS Home Video
Catalog Fulfillment Center
Charlotte, NC 28275-1089
Ph: (800)531-4727
Free: 800-645-4PBS
Co. E-mail: info@pbs.org
URL: http://www.pbs.org
Released: 1985. **Price:** $130.00. **Description:** An extensive course for college students, introducing them to the basic concepts of business. **Availability:** VHS; 3/4 U.

33087 ■ *Career Insights*
RMI Media
1365 N. Winchester St.
Olathe, KS 66061-5880
Ph: (913)768-1696
Free: 800-745-5480
Fax: (800)755-6910
Co. E-mail: actmedia@act.org
URL: http://www.actmedia.com
Released: 1987. **Description:** Describes 50 occupations, including skill requirements and interviews with people employed in these fields. **Availability:** VHS; 3/4 U.

33088 ■ *Managing the Emerging Company*
Leslie T. McClure
PO Box 1223
Pebble Beach, CA 93953
Ph: (831)656-0553
Fax: (831)656-0555
Co. E-mail: leslie@411videoinfo.com
URL: http://www.411videoinfo.com
Released: 1997. **Price:** $990.00. **Description:** Ten-volume set deals with the functions of developing and running a business. **Availability:** VHS.

33089 ■ *Take It from the Top: The Business of Business Success*
Video Arts, Inc.
c/o Aim Learning Group
8238-40 Lehigh
Morton Grove, IL 60053-2615
Free: 877-444-2230
Fax: (416)252-2155
Co. E-mail: service@aimlearninggroup.com
URL: http://www.aimlearninggroup.com
Released: 1991. **Price:** $295.00. **Description:** David Frost interviews three of England's most successful businessmen, who share their secrets of success. In the first tape, Lord Hanson talks about organization and change. In the second, Sir John Harvey-Jones tells the difference between leadership and management. In the third, Sir James Goldsmith shares his business philosophy. **Availability:** VHS; 8 mm; 3/4 U; Special order formats.

TRADE SHOWS AND CONVENTIONS

33090 ■ Age Small Business Show
Business Connect
PO Box 576
Crows Nest, NSW 1585, Australia
Ph: 61 2 9437 9333
URL(s): www.businessconnect.com.au. **Principal Exhibits:** Small Business equipment, supplies, and services.

33091 ■ Sydney Morning Herald Small Business Show
Business Connect
PO Box 576
Crows Nest, NSW 1585, Australia

Ph: 61 2 9437 9333
URL(s): www.businessconnect.com.au. **Frequency:** Annual. **Principal Exhibits:** Small Business equipment, supplies, and services.

CONSULTANTS

33092 ■ Shriner-Midland Co.
7347 Stuart Cir.
Warrenton, VA 20187
Ph: (540)349-8193
Fax: (540)349-8799
Contact: Robert D. Shriner, Manager
E-mail: rshriner@aol.com
Scope: Business and economic analysis for corporations, investors, associations and law firms. Services include development of management strategies, financial management and analysis, financial due diligence, turnaround and work-out support. Also provides analysis and expert testimony for legislative, regulatory, and trial proceedings. Specializes in high-tech, services, and nonprofit organizations. **Founded:** 1976. **Publications:** "Economic Impact Estimates of the Clinton Health Plan"; "Modeling Product Liability Costs in Large Class Action Cases"; "Minimum Wage Research Review"; "Cost Analysis for Nonprofit Organizations".

33093 ■ Value Creation Group Inc.
7820 Scotia Dr., Ste. 2000
Dallas, TX 75248-3115
Ph: (972)980-7407
Fax: (972)980-4619
Co. E-mail: john.antos@valuecreationgroup.com
URL: http://www.valuecreationgroup.com
Contact: John Antos, Chief Executive Officer
E-mail: john.antos@valuecreationgroup.com
Scope: General business experts offering predictive strategic planning, Activity Based Costing ABC, Activity Based Management ABM, mergers and acquisitions, outsourcing, re engineering, process management, web enabling technology, bench marking, installation of financial systems, executive search, training, teams, activity based budgeting, operational auditing, feature costing. Industries served financial services, food, health care, insurance, manufacturing, electronics, real estate, consumer products, nonprofit, telecommunication, oil, service, data processing, hotel and resort and government agencies. **Founded:** 1984. **Publications:** "Handbook of Process Management Based Predictive Accounting," Alcpa 2002; "Cost Management for Today's Manufacturing Environment and Activity Based Management for Service Environments, Government Entities and Nonprofit Organizations"; "Risks and Opportunities in International Finance and Treasury"; "Driving Value Using Activity Based Budgeting"; "Process Based Accounting Leveraging Processes to Predict Results"; "Handbook of Supply Chain Management"; "Economic Value Management Applications and Techniques"; "The Change Handbook": "Group Methods for Creating the Future"; "Why Value Management and Performance Measurement Through U.S. Binoculars," Journal of Strategic Performance Measurement; "Real Options, Intangibles Measurement and the Benefits of Human Capital Investment to Power the Organization," Journal of Strategic Performance Measurement. **Seminars:** Activity Based Management; Predictive Accounting; Performance measures; ABM for Manufacturing; ABM for Service Organizations; Finance and Accounting for Non-Financial Executives; Return on Investment/Capital Expenditure Evaluation; Planning and Cost Control; The Next Step Intermediate Finance and Accounting for Non-financial Managers; Activity-Based Budgeting; Friendly Finance for Fund Raisers; Strategic Outsourcing. **Telecommunication Services:** assistu@valuecreationgroup.com; consultu@valuecreationgroup.com.

COMPUTERIZED DATABASES

33094 ■ *Academic OneFile*
10650 Toebben Dr.
Independence, KY 41051
Free: 800-354-9706
Fax: (800)487-8488
Co. E-mail: investors@cengage.com
URL: http://www.gale.cengage.com
Contact: Ronald Dunn, President
Availability: Online: Cengage Learning Inc. **Type:** Full-text.

33095 ■ *Bloomberg BusinessWeek*
731 Lexington Ave.
New York, NY 10022-1331
Ph: (212)318-2000
URL: http://www.bloomberg.com
Contact: Daniel Doctoroff, President
Availability: Online: ProQuest LLC - Dialog; Bloomberg L.P. **Type:** Full-text.

33096 ■ *BtoB*
1155 Gratiot Ave.
Detroit, MI 48207
Ph: (313)446-6000
Free: 800-678-2427
Fax: (313)446-1616
Co. E-mail: info@crain.com
URL: http://www.crain.com
Availability: Online: Crain Communications Inc. **Type:** Full-text.

33097 ■ *Business Periodicals Index Retrospective™: 1913-1982*
10 Estes St.
Ipswich, MA 01938-2106
Ph: (978)356-6500
Free: 800-653-2726
Fax: (978)356-6565
Co. E-mail: information@ebscohost.com
URL: http://www.ebscohost.com
Contact: Tim Collins, President
E-mail: tcollins@ebscohost.com
Availability: Online: EBSCO Publishing. **Type:** Bibliographic.

33098 ■ *Business Source® Alumni Edition*
10 Estes St.
Ipswich, MA 01938-2106
Ph: (978)356-6500
Free: 800-653-2726
Fax: (978)356-6565
Co. E-mail: information@ebscohost.com
URL: http://www.ebscohost.com
Contact: Tim Collins, President
E-mail: tcollins@ebscohost.com
Availability: Online: EBSCO Publishing. **Type:** Full-text.

33099 ■ *The CorpTech Directory of Technology Companies*
1020 E 1st St.
Papillin, NE 68046
Free: 866-313-6367
Co. E-mail: corptech@corptech.com
URL: http://www.corptech.com
Availability: Online: infoUSA Inc. - Corporate Technology Information Services Inc. CD-ROM: infoUSA Inc. - Corporate Technology Information Services Inc. **Type:** Full-text; Directory.

33100 ■ *NewsEdge™*
3 Becker Farm Rd., Ste. 401
Roseland, NJ 07068
Ph: (973)422-0800
Co. E-mail: info@acquiremedia.com
URL: http://www.acquiremedia.com
Availability: Online: Acquire Media. **Type:** Full-text; Numeric; Statistical.

33101 ■ *Small Business Resource Center*
10650 Toebben Dr.
Independence, KY 41051
Free: 800-354-9706
Fax: (800)487-8488
Co. E-mail: investors@cengage.com
URL: http://www.gale.cengage.com
Contact: Ronald Dunn, President
Availability: Online: Cengage Learning Inc. **Type:** Full-text.

33102 ■ *Vente et Gestion*
10 Estes St.
Ipswich, MA 01938-2106
Ph: (978)356-6500
Free: 800-653-2726
Fax: (978)356-6565
Co. E-mail: information@ebscohost.com
URL: http://www.ebscohost.com
Contact: Tim Collins, President
E-mail: tcollins@ebscohost.com
Availability: Online: EBSCO Publishing. **Type:** Full-text.

LIBRARIES

33103 ■ Broome County Public Library - J. Donald Ahearn Business Resource Center
185 Court St., Rm. 138
Binghamton, NY 13901
Ph: (607)778-6451
Co. E-mail: reference@bclibrary.info
URL: http://www.bclibrary.info/ahearn.html
Contact: Sherry Kowalski, Director, Information Services
Scope: Business. **Services:** Center open to the public. **Holdings:** Audio and video tapes; CD-ROMs. **Telecommunication Services:** skowalski@co.broome.ny.us.

33104 ■ College of William and Mary - Mason School of Business - McLeod Business Library
Alan B. Miller Hall, Rm. 2034
101 Ukrop Way
Williamsburg, VA 23187-8795
Ph: (757)221-2916
Fax: (757)221-7482
Co. E-mail: charlotte.brown@mason.wm.edu
URL: http://mason.wm.edu/about/library
Contact: Charlotte Davis Brown, Director
URL(s): mason.wm.edu/about/library/index.php. **Scope:** Business. **Founded:** 1985. **Holdings:** Reference materials; corporation records; videocassettes; periodicals and serials; reserve materials.

33105 ■ Community Futures Development Corporation of Greater Trail - Kootenay Regional Business Library
825 Spokane St
Trail, BC, Canada V1R 3W4
Ph: (250)364-2595
Fax: (250)364-2728
Co. E-mail: kristi@communityfutures.com
URL: http://www.communityfutures.com/cms/Business_Library.181.0.html
Contact: Kristi Loughlin, Coordinator
Scope: Business. **Services:** Library open to the public. **Founded:** 1994. **Holdings:** Books; publications. **Subscriptions:** 4 journals and other serials.

33106 ■ Charles Darwin University - Palmerston Campus Library
University Ave.
Palmerston, NT 0830, Australia
Ph: 61 8 89467870
Fax: 61 8 89467880
Co. E-mail: referencedesk@cdu.edu.au
URL: http://www.cdu.edu.au/library/about/campuses.html
Contact: Heather Moorcroft
Scope: Business, cookery, computing, ESL (English as a Second Language), hospitality, tourism. **Holdings:** Books; park guides; magazines; restaurant menus; travel brochures; videos. **Telecommunication Services:** library-liaison@cdu.edu.au.

33107 ■ East Baton Rouge Parish Library - Main Library - Special Collections
7711 Goodwood Blvd.
Baton Rouge, LA 70806
Ph: (225)231-3700
Co. E-mail: dfarrar@brgov.com
URL: http://www.ebr.lib.la.us/libcollections.htm
Contact: David Farrar, Director, Library Services
Scope: Louisiana history and genealogy, business, automobile repair. **Services:** Library open to the public. **Holdings:** Books; government publications; microfilm; vertical files. **Telecommunication Services:** mstein@ebr.lib.la.us.

33108 ■ Florida State University - Panama Branch Library
PO Box 0819-05390
Panama City 6A, Panama
Ph: (507)314-0374
Fax: (507)314-0366
Co. E-mail: ablackie@mailer.fsu.edu
URL: http://www.lib.fsu.edu/panama/index.html
Contact: Anthony Blackie, Librarian
Scope: Business, computer science, engineering, environmental studies, information science, International affairs, Latin America and Caribbean studies, mathematics. **Services:** Interlibrary loan; copying. **Holdings:** Figures not available.

33109 ■ The New Library at New Hampshire Technical Institute, Concord
31 College Dr.
Concord, NH 03301-7412
Ph: (603)230-4028
Fax: (603)230-9310
Co. E-mail: nhtilibrary@ccsnh.edu
URL: http://www.nhti.edu/student-resources/library
Contact: Stephen Ambra, Director, Library Services
URL(s): www.nhti.edu. **Scope:** Full-range community college Library including: business, computers, education, engineering, health, justice/legal studies, architecture, autism, nursing, dental assisting, anthropology, film studies, gaming, sports management. **Services:** Interlibrary loan; library open to the public with restrictions. **Founded:** 1968. **Holdings:** 62,000 titles, including over 140,000 e-books; 50,000 microfilms, DVDs and videocassettes, recordings, CDs, and other media. **Subscriptions:** 191 journals and other serials. **Telecommunication Services:** sambra@ccsnh.edu.

33110 ■ Oxford Brookes University - Wheatley Library
Wheatley
Oxford OX33 1HX, United Kingdom
Ph: 44 1865 485869
Co. E-mail: cmjeffery@brookes.ac.uk
URL: http://www.brookes.ac.uk/library
Contact: Claire Jeffery, Director, Education
Scope: Business, computing, engineering, mathematics. **Holdings:** Books; company reports; dissertations and theses; exam papers; journals; statistics. **Telecommunication Services:** libraryenquiries@brookes.ac.uk.

33111 ■ Southern Methodist University - Cox School of Business - Business Information Center
6214 Bishop Blvd.
Dallas, TX 75275-0333
Ph: (214)768-4496
Fax: (214)768-1884
Co. E-mail: bicstaff@smu.edu
URL: http://bic.cox.smu.edu
Contact: Sandy Miller, Director
Scope: Business. **Services:** Instructional workshops; classroom instruction; group presentation room; multimedia studio; Investing and Trading Center; copying and printing; center not open to public. **Founded:** 1987. **Holdings:** Reference materials; faculty papers. **Subscriptions:** 36 journals and other serials; 480 e-journals.

33112 ■ Texas Southern University - Robert James Terry Library - Business Library
3100 Cleburne St.
Houston, TX 77004
Ph: (713)313-4379
Co. E-mail: west_lg@tsu.edu
URL: http://www.tsu.edu/academics/Robert_J_Terry_Library
Contact: Louis G. West, Librarian
Scope: Business, economics. **Holdings:** 50,000 bound periodical volumes, periodicals, and microforms, CD-ROM. **Subscriptions:** 500 journals and other serials. **Telecommunication Services:** harris_dl@tsu.edu.

33113 ■ Touro College - Bensonhurst Library
1870 Stillwell Ave., No. 86
Brooklyn, NY 11223
Ph: (718)265-6534, x1006
Fax: (718)265-0616
Co. E-mail: miriam.magill@touro.edu
URL: http://www.tourolib.org/about/libraries/bensonhurst
Contact: Miriam Magill
Scope: Business, computer science, human services, ESL. **Services:** Computer access; library open to college affiliates. **Holdings:** Books; diskettes; audio and video tapes; CD-ROMs; DVDs; microfiche.

33114 ■ Touro College - Boro Park Library (53rd Street)
1273 53rd St.
Brooklyn, NY 11219
Ph: (718)871-6187, x-17
Fax: (718)686-7071
Co. E-mail: leibk@touro.edu
URL: http://www.tourolib.org/about/libraries
Contact: Leib Klein, Librarian
Scope: Business, computer science, human services, ESL. **Holdings:** Books; diskettes; audio and video tapes; CD-ROMs; DVDs; microfiche.

33115 ■ Touro College - Brighton Beach Library
532 Neptune Ave.
Brooklyn, NY 11224
Ph: (718)449-6160, x-118
Fax: (718)265-6341
Co. E-mail: bella.reytblat@touro.edu
URL: http://www.tourolib.org/about/libraries
Contact: Bella Reytblat
Scope: Business, computer science, human services, ESL. **Services:** Research and reference; copying; computer access; library open to college students, staff and affiliates. **Holdings:** Books; diskettes; audio and video tapes; CD-ROMs; DVDs; microfiche.

33116 ■ Touro College - Flushing Library
133-35 Roosevelt Ave.
Flushing, NY 11354
Ph: (718)353-6400, x112
Fax: (718)495-3809
Co. E-mail: xuanwen.huang@touro.edu
URL: http://www.tourolib.org/about/libraries/flushing
Contact: Xuan Wen Huang
Scope: Business, computer science, human services, ESL. **Services:** Interlibrary loan; copying. **Holdings:** Books; diskettes; audio and video tapes; CD-ROMs; DVDs; microfiche.

33117 ■ Touro College - Forest Hills Library
71-02 113th St.
Forest Hills, NY 11375
Ph: (718)520-5107
Fax: (718)793-3610
Co. E-mail: dorai@touro.edu
URL: http://www.tourolib.org/about/libraries/forest-hills
Contact: Dora Isakova
Scope: Business, computer science, human services, ESL. **Services:** Copying; computer access for research purposes; Ilibrary open to college student, staff and alumni only. **Holdings:** Books; diskettes; audio and video tapes; CD-ROMs; DVDs; microfiche.

33118 ■ Touro College - Lander College for Men Library
75-31 150th St.
Kew Gardens Hills, NY 11367
Ph: (718)820-4894
Fax: (718)495-3824
Co. E-mail: joan.wagner2@touro.edu
URL: http://www.tourolib.org/about/libraries/kew-gardens-hills
Contact: Debora Duerksen, Librarian
Scope: Biology, business, computer science, management information science, political science, psychology, social sciences, Judaica. **Services:** Interlibrary loan; copying; library open to college staff and students. **Holdings:** Books; diskettes; audio and video tapes; CD-ROMs; DVDs; microfiche. **Telecommunication Services:** irene.cherry@touro.edu.

33119 ■ Touro College - Midtown Library
43 W. 23rd St.
New York, NY 10010
Ph: (212)463-0400
Fax: (212)627-3696
Co. E-mail: marina.zilberman@touro.edu
URL: http://www.tourolib.org/about/libraries/midtown
Contact: Marina Zilberman, Librarian
Scope: Business, education, ethnic studies, psychology, pre-clinical and clinical medicine, occupational and physical therapy, physician assistant, Oriental medicine. **Services:** Copying; computer access; research and reference; library open to college staff and students only. **Holdings:** Books; diskettes; audio and video tapes; CD-ROMs; DVDs; microfiche. **Telecommunication Services:** carol.schapiro@touro.edu.

33120 ■ Touro College - Midwood Library (Flatbush)
1602 Ave. J
Brooklyn, NY 11230
Ph: (718)252-7800
Fax: (718)338-7732
Co. E-mail: edlira.agalliu@touro.edu
URL: http://www.tourolib.org/about/libraries/midwood
Contact: Bashe Simon, Director, Library Services
Scope: Business, computer science, education, human services, neuroscience, political science, psychology, speech pathology, Judaica. **Services:** Copying; research services; library open to student and staff only. **Holdings:** Books; CD-ROMs; DVDs; microfiche; audio and video tapes. **Telecommunication Services:** caitlin.bernstein@touro.edu.

33121 ■ Touro College - Starrett City Library
1390 Pennsylvania Ave.
Brooklyn, NY 11239
Ph: (718)642-6562, x-104
Fax: (718)642-6807
Co. E-mail: rita.hilu@touro.edu
URL: http://www.tourolib.org/about/libraries/starett-city
Contact: Rita Hilu
Scope: Business, computer science, human services, ESL. **Services:** Interlibrary loan; computer access for research use; library open to college staff and students only. **Holdings:** Books; diskettes; audio and video tapes; CD-ROMs; DVDs; microfiche.

33122 ■ Touro College - Sunset Park Library
475 53rd St.
Brooklyn, NY 11220
Ph: (718)748-2776, x-4
Fax: (718)492-9031
Co. E-mail: faina.katsnelson@touro.edu
URL: http://www.tourolib.org/about/libraries/sunset-park
Contact: Faina G. Katsnelson
Scope: Business, computer science, human services, ESL. **Services:** Interlibrary loan; library open to college students and staff. **Holdings:** Books; diskettes; audio and video tapes; CD-ROMs; DVDs; microfiche.

33123 ■ University of Nevada, Reno - Mathewson-IGT Knowledge Center
1664 N. Virginia St.
Mail Stop 322
Reno, NV 89557-0001
Ph: (775)682-4636
Fax: (775)784-4398
Co. E-mail: ragains@unr.edu
URL: http://knowledgecenter.unr.edu/
Contact: Patrick Ragains, Librarian, Business Librarian, Government Documents
Scope: Business, government. **Holdings:** Regional Federal Depository Library Collection; Presidential Papers; Indian Agency Correspondence; Census Materials, Patent & Trademark Depository Library Materials; Nevada State and Local Publications.

33124 ■ University of Northampton - Park Campus Library
Boughton Green Rd.
Northampton NN2 7AL, United Kingdom
Ph: 44 1604 892222
Co. E-mail: jenny.townend@northampton.ac.uk
URL: http://www.northampton.ac.uk/info/200208/library/
Contact: Jenny Townend
Scope: Business, education, health, humanities, law, local history, natural sciences, waste management. **Services:** Interlibrary loan. **Holdings:** 375,000

books. **Subscriptions:** 15,000 journals and other serials. **Telecommunication Services:** libraryhelp@northampton.ac.uk.

33125 ■ University of Nottingham - Business Library
Business School, Top Fl.
Jubilee Campus
Wollaton Rd.
Nottingham NG8 1BB, United Kingdom
Ph: 44 115 8468069
URL: http://www.nottingham.ac.uk/is/libraries/locations/businesslibrary.aspx
Scope: Business. **Services:** Copying; scanning; laptop loan. **Holdings:** Figures not available.

33126 ■ University of Paisley - Ayr Campus Library
Beech Grove
Ayr KA8 0SR, United Kingdom
Ph: 44 1292 886000
Fax: 44 1292 886288
Co. E-mail: libraryayr@uws.ac.uk
URL: http://library.paisley.ac.uk
Contact: Neal Buchanan, Librarian
Scope: Business, primary and secondary education, media, commercial music, nursing. **Founded:** 1965. **Holdings:** Books; journals; audio/visual item. **Telecommunication Services:** info@uws.ac.uk.

33127 ■ University of Queensland - Graduate Economics and Business Library
St. Lucia Campus
Bldg. 39
St. Lucia, QLD 4072, Australia
Ph: 61 7 33654860
Fax: 61 7 33654855
Co. E-mail: ecob@library.uq.edu.au
URL: http://www.library.uq.edu.au/ecob
Contact: Dale Drysdale, Librarian
Scope: Business, economics. **Founded:** 1996. **Holdings:** 9500 books; 12,000 bound periodical volumes; theses. **Subscriptions:** 80 journals and other serials; 16,000 e-journals. **Telecommunication Services:** d.drysdale@library.uq.edu.au.

33128 ■ Winthrop University - Small Business Development Center Library
118 Thurmond Bldg.
Rock Hill, SC 29733
Ph: (803)323-2283
Fax: (803)323-4281
Co. E-mail: stevensl@winthrop.edu
URL: http://cba.winthrop.edu/sbdc/help2.htm
Contact: Larry Stevens, Director
Scope: Business. **Services:** Performs searches on fee basis. **Holdings:** Books; audio/visual items.

START-UP INFORMATION

33129 ■ *The Canadian Small Business Survival Guide: How to Start and Operate Your Own Successful Business*
Pub: Dundurn Group
Ed: Benj Gallander. FRQ June 2002. **Price:** $26.99. **Description:** Ideas for starting and running a successful small business. Topics include selecting a business, financing, government assistance, locations, franchises, and marketing ideas.

33130 ■ *Getting Rich In Your Underwear: How To Start and Run a Profitable Home-Based Business*
Pub: HCM Publishing
Ed: Peter I. Hupalo. **Released:** April 1, 2005. **Price:** $17.95. **Description:** Book offers insight into starting a home-based business. Entrepreneurs will learn about business models and the home business; distribution and fulfillment of product or service; marketing and sales; how to overcome the fear of starting a business; personal success characteristics; naming a business; zoning and insurance; intellectual capital; copyrights, trademarks, and patents; limited liability companies and S-corporations; business expenses and accounting; taxes; fifteen basic steps for starting a home-based business, state resources for starting a home company; and seven home-based business ideas.

33131 ■ *"New Program for Entrepreneurs" in Austin Business JournalInc. (Vol. 29, February 12, 2010, No. 29, pp. 1)*
Pub: American City Business Journals
Ed: Christopher Calnan. **Description:** Nonprofit group Economic Development Catalyst Organization (ECDO) is formalizing its BizLaunch mentoring program, which was stated in 2009. The program aims to offer support networks to entrepreneurs and assistance regarding early-stage venture capital.

33132 ■ *"SBA Streamlines Loans and Ramps Up Web Presence" in Hispanic Business (January-February 2008, pp. 64)*
Pub: Hispanic Business
Description: Federal government's Small Business Administration offers informational resources and tools to individuals wishing to start a new company as well as those managing existing firms. The site consists of over 20,000 pages with information, advice and tips on starting, financing and managing any small business. Free online courses are also provided.

33133 ■ *"Slow-Down Startups Hot" in Austin Business JournalInc. (Vol. 28, September 12, 2008, No. 26, pp. 1)*
Pub: American City Business Journals
Ed: Sandra Zaragoza. **Description:** A number of entrepreneurs from Austin, Texas are starting their own small business despite the economic slowdown. The Small Business Development Program in Austin has seen a 50 percent increase in the demand for its services in 2008 as compared to demand in 2007. Other details about the entrepreneurship trend are discussed.

ASSOCIATIONS AND OTHER ORGANIZATIONS

33134 ■ National Association of Government Guaranteed Lenders (NAGGL)
215 E 9th Ave.
Stillwater, OK 74074
Ph: (405)377-4022
Fax: (405)377-3931
Co. E-mail: info@naggl.com
URL: http://www.naggl.org
Contact: Anthony R. Wilkinson, President
Description: Aims to serve the needs and represents the interests of the small business lending community who utilize the Small Business Administrations and other government guaranteed loan programs. **Founded:** 1984. **Educational Activities:** National Association of Government Guaranteed Lenders Conference (Annual).

REFERENCE WORKS

33135 ■ *"3CDC's Biggest Year" in Business Courier (Vol. 26, December 18, 2009, No. 34, pp. 1)*
Pub: American City Business Journals, Inc.
Ed: Lucy May. **Description:** Cincinnati Center City Development Corporation (3CDC) will make 2010 its biggest year with nearly $164 million projects in the works. Historic tax credits and continued help from the city have allowed the private nonprofit organization to finance mega projects such as the $43 million renovation and expansion of Washington Park. Other projects that 3CDC will start or complete in 2010 are presented.

33136 ■ *"$49M Defense Contracts Hits Austin" in Austin Business JournalInc. (Vol. 28, August 8, 2008, No. 21, pp. A1)*
Pub: American City Business Journals
Ed: Laura Hipp. **Description:** BAE Systems PLC has landed a $49 million contract to build thermal cameras, which are expected to be installed on tanks in 2009 and 2010. BAE is expected to land other defense contracts and is likely to add employees in order to meet production demands.

33137 ■ *"$100 Million in Projects Jeopardized" in Business Courier (Vol. 24, March 28, 2008, No. 51, pp. 1)*
Pub: American City Business Journals, Inc.
Ed: Dan Monk. **Description:** Ohio's historic preservation tax credit program may be reinstated after some companies planned to sue over its stoppage. The Ohio Department of Development said the program was halted because it exceeded the allocated budget for the credit. $34 million in credits are at stake for more than two dozen local projects if the program is reinstated.

33138 ■ *"Abroad, Not Overboard" in Entrepreneur (Vol. 36, April 2008, No. 4, pp. 68)*
Pub: Entrepreneur Media, Inc.
Ed: Crystal Detamore-Rodman. **Description:** Export-Import Bank is an agency created by the U.S. government to help exporters get credit insurance and capital loans by providing them with loan guarantees. The bank, being criticized as supporting more the bigger exporters, has allotted to smaller businesses a bigger portion of the annual credit being approved.

33139 ■ *"Affordable Financing for Acquisitions" in Franchising World (Vol. 42, September 2010, No. 9, pp. 47)*
Pub: International Franchise Association
Ed: Gene Cerrotti. **Description:** Acquisition pricing is reasonable and interest rates are low and quality franchised resale opportunities are priced 4.5 times EBITDA. Information about Small Business Administration loans is also included.

33140 ■ *"Affordable Housing on the Rise" in Philadelphia Business Journal (Vol. 28, October 23, 2009, No. 36, pp. 1)*
Pub: American City Business Journals
Ed: Natalie Kostelni. **Description:** Philadelphia, Pennsylvania led an affordable housing boom with more than 800 new affordable housing units in the works in spite of the recession. The converging of developers and federal stimulus money has driven the sudden increase with the launching of several projects across the city.

33141 ■ *"AIG Fixed; Is Michigan Next?" in Crain's Detroit Business (Vol. 24, September 22, 2008, No. 38, pp. 1)*
Pub: Crain Communications Inc.
Ed: Jay Greene. **Description:** Michigan's economic future is examined as is the mortgage buyout plan and American International Group Inc.'s takeover by the U.S. government.

33142 ■ *"Airlines Mount PR Push to Win Public Support Against Big Oil" in Advertising Age (Vol. 79, July 14, 2008, No. 7, pp. 1)*
Pub: Crain Communications, Inc.
Ed: Michael Bush. **Description:** Top airline executives from competing companies have banded together in a public relations plan in which they are sending e-mails to their frequent fliers asking for aid in lobbying legislators to put a restriction on oil speculation.

33143 ■ *"All Indicators in Michigan Innovation Index Drop in 4Q" in Crain's Detroit Business (Vol. 25, June 22, 2009, No. 25, pp. 9)*
Pub: Crain Communications Inc. - Detroit
Ed: Ryan Beene. **Description:** Economic indicators that rate Michigan's innovation fell in the fourth quarter of 2008. The index of trademark applications, SBA loans, venture capital funding, new incorporations and other indicators traced dropped 12.6 points.

33144 ■ *"Amount Md. Pays to Unemployed Dips to Lowest Level Since '08" in Baltimore Business Journal (Vol. 28, November 12, 2010, No. 27)*
Pub: Baltimore Business Journal
Ed: Scott Dance. **Description:** Maryland paid out $50 million for unemployment benefits in September 2010 for its lowest payout since 2008. The drop in unemployment payout could mean lower taxes for employers who pay for the benefits. The unemployment rate in Maryland, however, increased to 7.5 percent.

33145 ■ *"The Annual Entitlement Lecture: Trustees of Medicare and Social Security Issue Another Dismal Report" in Barron's (March 31, 2008)*
Pub: Dow Jones & Company, Inc.
Ed: Thomas G. Donlan. **Description:** Expenditures on Medicare hospital insurance and the revenues available to pay for it have led to a gap of capital valued at $38.6 trillion. Slashing the benefits or raising taxes will not solve the gap which exists unless the government saves the money and invests it in private markets.

33146 ■ *"Are There Material Benefits To Social Diversity?" in Hispanic Business (Vol. 30, September 2008, No. 9, pp. 10)*
Pub: Hispanic Business, Inc.
Ed: Brigida Benitez. **Description:** Diversity in American colleges and universities, where students view and appreciate their peers as individuals and do not judge them on the basis of race, gender, or ethnicity is discussed. The benefits of diversity in higher education are also acknowledged by the U.S. Supreme Court and by leading American corporations.

33147 ■ *"ATI Now Ready to Pounce on Biotech" in Austin Business JournalInc. (Vol. 28, August 22, 2008, No. 23, pp. 1)*
Pub: American City Business Journals
Ed: Laura Hipp. **Description:** Austin Technology Incubator has entered the biotechnology sector through a program of the University of Texas incubator. The company's bioscience program was set off by a grant from the City of Austin worth $125,000. The growth of Austin's biotechnology sector is examined.

33148 ■ *"Auto Supplier Stock Battered In Wake Of Wall Street Woes" in Crain's Detroit Business (Vol. 24, September 29, 2008, No. 39, pp. 4)*
Pub: Crain Communications Inc.
Ed: Ryan Beene. **Description:** Due to the volatility of the stock market and public perception of the $700 billion banking bailout, auto suppliers are now facing a dramatic drop in their shares. Statistical data included.

33149 ■ *"Automotive Trouble" in Canadian Business (Vol. 82, April 27, 2009, No. 7, pp. 11)*
Pub: Rogers Media
Ed: Thomas Watson. **Description:** The likely effects of a possible bailout of the U.S. automotive industry are examined. Some experts believe that a bailout will be good for the automotive industry and on the U.S. economy. Others argue however, that the nationalization may have a negative impact on the industry and on the economy.

33150 ■ *"Auxis Introduces Services for Government Contracting" in Entertainment Close-Up (December 22, 2010)*
Pub: Close-Up Media
Description: Profile of Auxis Inc., a management consulting and outsourcing company has launched a new service for companies involved in or bidding for government contracts. Details of the program are provided.

33151 ■ *"BABs in Bond Land" in Barron's (Vol. 89, July 6, 2009, No. 27, pp. 14)*
Pub: Dow Jones & Co., Inc.
Ed: Jim McTague. **Description:** American Recovery and Reinvestment Act has created taxable Build America Bonds (BAB) to finance new construction projects. The issuance of the two varieties of taxable BABs is expected to benefit the municipal bond market.

33152 ■ *"Back on Track-Or Off the Rails?" in Business Week (September 22, 2008, No. 4100, pp. 22)*
Pub: McGraw-Hill Companies, Inc.
Ed: Peter Coy; Tara Kalwarski. **Description:** Discusses the possible scenarios the American economy may undergo due to the takeover of Fannie Mae and Freddie Mac. Statistical data included.

33153 ■ *"Bailout Forgets the 'Little Guys" in The Business Journal-Milwaukee (Vol. 25, September 26, 2008, No. 53, pp. A1)*
Pub: American City Business Journals, Inc.
Ed: Rich Kirchen. **Description:** Community Bankers of Wisconsin and the Wisconsin Bankers Association are urging members to approach congressional representatives and remind them to include local banks in building the $700 billion bailout plan. WBA president and CEO Kurt Bauer thinks that it is only fair to include smaller institutions in the bailout. The initial bailout plan and its benefit for the smaller banks are examined.

33154 ■ *"Bailout May Force Cutbacks, Job Losses" in The Business Journal - Serving Phoenix and the Valley of the Sun (Vol. 29, September 26, 2008, No. 4, pp. 1)*
Pub: American City Business Journals, Inc.
Ed: Mike Sunnucks. **Description:** Economists say the proposed $700 billion bank bailout could affect Arizona businesses as banks could be forced to reduce the amount and number of loans it has thereby forcing businesses to shrink capital expenditures and then jobs. However, the plan could also stimulate the economy by taking bad loans off banks balance sheets according to another economist.

33155 ■ *"Banking Bailout: Boost or Bust?" in Crain's Detroit Business (Vol. 24, September 29, 2008, No. 39, pp. 1)*
Pub: Crain Communications Inc.
Ed: Amy Lane. **Description:** Economic insiders discuss the banking bailout and how it might impact the state of Michigan.

33156 ■ *"Bankruptcies Shoot Up 68 Percent" in Sacramento Business Journal (Vol. 25, July 18, 2008, No. 20, pp. 1)*
Pub: American City Business Journals, Inc.
Ed: Kathy Robertson. **Description:** Personal bankruptcy in the Sacramento area rose by 88 percent for the first half of 2008 while business bankruptcies rose by 50 percent for the same period. The numbers of consumer bankruptcy reflects the effect of high debt, rising mortgage costs, and declining home values on U.S. households.

33157 ■ *"Bankruptcy Blowback" in Business Week (September 22, 2008, No. 4100, pp. 36)*
Pub: McGraw-Hill Companies, Inc.
Ed: Jessica Silver-Greenberg. **Description:** Changes to bankruptcy laws which were enacted in 2005 after banks and other financial institutions lobbied hard for them are now suffering the consequences of the laws which force more troubled borrowers to let their homes go into foreclosure; lenders suffer financially every time they have to take on a foreclosure and the laws in which they lobbied so hard to see enacted are now becoming a problem for these lending institutions. Details of the changes in the laws are outlined as are the affects on the consumer, the economy and the lenders.

33158 ■ *"Banks Fret About Gist Of Bailout" in The Business Journal-Serving Metropolitan Kansas City (Vol. 27, September 26, 2008, No. 2)*
Pub: American City Business Journals, Inc.
Ed: James Dornbrook. **Description:** Banks from the Kansas City area hope that the proposed $700 billion bailout will not send the wrong message. UMB Financial Corp. chairman says that he hopes that the bailout would benefit companies that were more risk restrained and punish those that took outsized risk. Other bank executives' perceptions on the planned bailout are given.

33159 ■ *"BETC Backers Plot Future" in Business Journal Portland (Vol. 27, December 10, 2010, No. 41, pp. 1)*
Pub: Portland Business Journal
Ed: Erik Siemers. **Description:** A coalition of clean energy groups and industrial manufacturers have spearheaded a campaign aimed at persuading Oregon legislators that the state's Business Energy Tax Credit (BETC) is vital in job creation. Oregon's BETC grants tax credits for 50 percent of an eligible renewable or clean energy project's cost. However, some legislators propose BETC's abolition.

33160 ■ *"Bigger TIF Makes Development Inroads" in The Business Journal-Serving Metropolitan Kansas City (Vol. 26, July 11, 2008, No. 44)*
Pub: American City Business Journals, Inc.
Ed: Rob Roberts. **Description:** On July 9, 2008 the Tax Increment Financing Commission voted to expand a TIF district to Tiffany Springs Road. The plan for the TIF district close to Kansas City International Airport is to include a-half mile of the road. The impacts of the expansion on construction projects and on the road network are analyzed.

33161 ■ *"Boeing Scores $21.7 Billion Order in Indonesia" in Wall Street Journal Eastern Edition (November 18 , 2011, pp. B6)*
Pub: Dow Jones & Company Inc.
Ed: David Kesmodel, Laura Meckler. **Description:** Boeing has garnered a large contract to deliver Boeing 737 jets to Indonesia's Lion Air. There are those who are lobbying against the US government's practice of subsidizing foreign companies that make contracts with American aerospace companies.

33162 ■ *Bold Endeavors: How Our Government Built America, and Why It Must Rebuild Now*
Pub: Simon and Schuster Inc.
Contact: Carolyn Reidy, President
E-mail: carolyn.reidy@simonandschuster.com
Ed: Felix Rohatyn. **Released:** 2009. **Price:** $26.00. **Description:** The federal government built the nation by investing in initiatives like the Erie Canal and the G.I. Bill and why it should do the same at this point in history is examined.

33163 ■ *"Brad Wall" in Canadian Business (Vol. 82, April 27, 2009, No. 7, pp. 9)*
Pub: Rogers Media
Ed: Joe Castaldo. **Description:** Saskatchewan Premier Brad Wall believes that the mood in the province is positive, as its economy is one of the few that is expected to post growth in 2009. Wall actively promotes the province in job fairs, offering $20,000 in tuition for recent college and university graduates that relocate in the province for seven years. Wall's views on the province's economy and challenges are presented.

33164 ■ *"Budget Woes Endanger E-Prep Progress" in Crain's Cleveland Business (Vol. 30, June 22, 2009, No. 24, pp. 6)*
Pub: Crain Communications, Inc.
Ed: Brian Tucker. **Description:** The future of the Entrepreneurship Preparatory School located in Cleveland is being threatened by State budget concerns. The charter school requires all students to wear uniforms, respect discipline, and attend for longer hours and more weeks.

33165 ■ *"Business Looks for Results in Congress" in Baltimore Business Journal (Vol. 28, November 5, 2010, No. 26, pp. 1)*
Pub: Baltimore Business Journal
Ed: Kent Hoover. **Description:** Republican candidates in the 2010 Congressional elections were overwhelmingly supported by the business community. Republican John Boehner, who will be the next Speaker of the House, says that the party's victory would end economic uncertainty and would assist small businesses to rehire workers.

33166 ■ *"Cabela's Repays Incentives as Sales Lag" in Business Journal-Milwaukee (Vol. 28, November 19, 2010, No. 7, pp. A1)*
Pub: Milwaukee Business Journal
Ed: Stacy Vogel Davis. **Description:** Cabela's has given back $266,000 to the government of Wisconsin owing to its failure to meet projected revenue goals for its Richfield, Wisconsin store. It has also failed to meet sales tax and hiring projection. The company received $4 million in incentives from Washington County.

33167 ■ *"Cal-ISO Plans $125 Million Facility" in Sacramento Business Journal (Vol. 25, August 1, 2008, No. 22, pp. 1)*
Pub: American City Business Journals, Inc.
Ed: Celia Lamb; Michael Shaw. **Description:** Sacramento, California-based nonprofit organization California Independent System Operator (ISO) is planning to build a new headquarters in Folsom. The new building would double its current leased space to 227,000 square feet. The ISO will seek tax-exempt bond financing for the project.

33168 ■ *"Can Avenue be Fashionable Again? Livernois Merchants, City Want Revival" in Crain's Detroit Business (March 10, 2008)*
Pub: Crain Communications, Inc.
Ed: Nancy Kaffer. **Description:** Once a busy retail district, the Avenue of Fashion, a Livernois Avenue strip between Six Mile and Eight Mile roads, is facing a community business effort being backed by city support whose aim is to restore the area to its former glory.

33169 ■ *"A Capitol Opportunity" in Hispanic Business (Vol. 30, September 2008, No. 9, pp. 82)*
Pub: Hispanic Business, Inc.
Ed: John Schumacher. **Description:** Launched in 2003, the Polanco fellows program is named after former state Senator Richard Polanco, a founder and chairman of the California Latino Caucus Institute. The program offers young Hispanics a chance to experience public policy and the functioning of the California Capitol through a 12-month, on-the-job Capitol training.

33170 ■ *"Cash for Appliances Targets HVAC Products, Water Heaters" in Contractor (Vol. 56, October 2009, No. 10, pp. 1)*
Pub: Penton Media, Inc.
Ed: Candace Roulo. **Description:** States and territories would need to submit a full application that specifies their implementation plans if they are interested in joining the Cash for Appliances program funded by the American Recovery and Reinvestment Act. The Department of Energy urges states to focus on heating and cooling equipment, appliances and water heaters since these offer the greatest energy savings potential.

33171 ■ *"City Council Committee Votes Against Establishing Small and Minority Business Fund" in Commercial Appeal (November 10, 2010)*
Pub: Commercial Appeal
Ed: Amos Maki. **Description:** Memphis, Tennessee City Council decided against the establishment of a $1 million small and minority business fund until criteria can be set in place for disbursing the money.

33172 ■ *"City Eyeing Tax Breaks for Arena" in Boston Business Journal (Vol. 29, June 3, 2011, No. 4, pp. 1)*
Pub: American City Business Journals Inc.
Ed: Daniel J. Sernovitz. **Description:** Baltimore City is opting to give millions of dollars in tax breaks and construction loans to a group of private investors led by William Hackerman who is proposing to build a new arena and hotel at the Baltimore Convention Center. The project will cost $500 million with the state putting up another $400 million for the center's expansion.

33173 ■ *"City Plans Downtown Congestion Fees" in Crain's Chicago Business (Vol. 31, May 5, 2008, No. 18, pp. 12)*
Pub: Crain Communications, Inc.
Description: By penalizing downtown drivers and rewarding public-transit users, Chicago officials plan to unclog Loop streets. The $153 million federal grant would establish a pilot network of express bus routes and set up a peak-period pricing system for city, street and private garage parking and for building loading zones.

33174 ■ *"City Sets Yamhill Makeover" in The Business Journal-Portland (Vol. 25, July 4, 2008, No. 17, pp. 1)*
Pub: American City Business Journals, Inc.
Ed: Andy Giegerich. **Description:** City government is scheduled to redevelop Peterson's property on Yamhill Street in Portland. The redevelopment is seen as a way to better developing commercial properties in the area. Problems associated with the project, which include cost and developer selection, are also discussed.

33175 ■ *"City's Streetcar Utility Estimate Way Off Mark" in Business Courier (Vol27, November 19, 2010, No. 29. , pp. 1)*
Pub: Business Courier
Ed: Dan Monk, Lucy May. **Description:** Duke Energy Corporation has released new estimates that show moving electric and gas lines alone for Cincinnati, Ohio's proposed streetcar project could cost more than $20 million. However, the city has only estimated the relocation to cost $5 million in federal grant applications.

33176 ■ *"Cleaner and Greener" in Canadian Business (Vol. 80, February 12, 2007, No. 4, pp. 45)*
Pub: Rogers Media
Ed: Zena Olijnyk. **Description:** Canadian research and government investments in clean coal technology is discussed.

33177 ■ *"Cleanup to Polish Plating Company's Bottom Line" in Crain's Cleveland Business (Vol. 28, October 29, 2007, No. 43, pp. 4)*
Pub: Crain Communications, Inc.
Ed: Jay Miller. **Description:** Barker Products Co, a manufacturer of nuts and bolts, is upgrading its aging facility which will allow them to operate at capacity and will save the company several hundred thousand dollars a year in operating costs. The new owners secured a construction loan from the county's new Commercial Redevelopment Fund which will allow them to upgrade the building which was hampered by years of neglect.

33178 ■ *"Clock Ticking for Hotel Berry" in Sacramento Business Journal (Vol. 25, July 25, 2008, No. 21, pp. 1)*
Pub: American City Business Journals, Inc.
Ed: Michael Shaw. **Description:** Federal tax credits worth $13.6 million have been awarded to boost the renovation project for the aging Hotel Berry in downtown Sacramento, California. The owners of the hotel have five months before the expiration of the tax credits to raise the remaining funding for the $20 million renovation.

33179 ■ *Code of Federal Regulations: Title 13: Business Credit and Assistance*
Pub: U.S. Government Printing Office
Ed: Department of Commerce Staff. **Released:** May 2007. **Price:** $55.00. **Description:** Title 13 covers regulations governing the activities of the Small Business Administration and the Department of Commerce. Book covers information on business credit, finance, and economic development.

33180 ■ *"Coming Soon: Bailouts of Fannie and Freddie" in Barron's (Vol. 88, July 14, 2008, No. 28, pp. 14)*
Pub: Dow Jones & Co., Inc.
Ed: Jonathan R. Laing. **Description:** Assurances from the government that Fannie Mae and Freddie Mac are adequately capitalized and able to carry on their duties as guarantors or owners of over $5 trillion of U.S. home mortgages are designed to keep both entities afloat until they attempt to raise $10 billion in new equity. The government would assume any losses in a bailout and owners of the banks' papers would profit as yields drop.

33181 ■ *"Companies Press Ottawa to End CN Labor Dispute" in Globe & Mail (April 16, 2007, pp. B1)*
Pub: CTVglobemedia Publishing Inc.
Ed: Brent Jang. **Description:** The plea of several industries to the Canadian parliament to end the labor dispute at the Canadian National Railway Co. is discussed.

33182 ■ *"Congress Ponders Annuity Trusts" in National Underwriter Life & Health (Vol. 114, June 21, 2010, No. 12, pp. 10)*
Pub: Summit Business Media
Ed: Arthur D. Postal. **Description:** Congress is looking over several bills, including the Small Business Jobs Tax Relief Act that would significantly narrow the advantages of using grantor-retained annuity trusts (GRATs) to avoid estate and gift taxes.

33183 ■ *"Corporate Responsibility" in Professional Services Close-Up (July 2, 2010)*
Pub: Close-Up Media
Description: List of firms awarded the inaugural Best Corporate Citizens in Government Contracting by the Corporate Responsibility Magazine is presented. The list is based on the methodology of the Magazine's Best Corporate Citizen's List, with 324 data points of publicly-available information in seven categories which include: environment, climate change, human rights, philanthropy, employee relations, financial performance, and governance.

33184 ■ *"Countywide Tax Could Fund Metro" in Business Courier (Vol. 26, January 15, 2010, No. 39, pp. 1)*
Pub: American City Business Journals, Inc.
Ed: Lucy May, Dan Monk. **Description:** Cincinnati officials are considering a new countywide tax to fund the Metro bus system and extend healthcare to the poor.

33185 ■ *"CR Magazine Taps ITT As a 'Best Corporate Citizen' in Government Contracting" in Profesisonal Services Close-Up (July 30, 2010)*
Pub: Close-Up Media
Description: ITT Corporation was named by Corporate Responsibility Magazine as a Best Corporate Citizen in Government Contracting. The list recognizes publicly-traded companies that exemplify transparency and accountability while serving the U.S. government.

33186 ■ *"Crowdsourcing Solutions to Prepare Our Communities" in The America's Intelligence Wire (November 2, 2010)*
Pub: HighBeam Research
Description: The 2010 TEDMED conference in San Diego, California, held in October 2010, challenged leaders from government and the public sector to offer ideas to help communities prepare for disasters.

33187 ■ *"The Cudgel of Samson" in Barron's (Vol. 88, March 24, 2008, No. 12, pp. 62)*
Pub: Dow Jones & Company, Inc.
Ed: Thomas G. Donlan. **Description:** Discusses the Federal Reserve is jawboning businesses against inflation while inflation is starting to rise because of the abundance of cheap money. The practice of jawboning has been used by the administrations of past US presidents with limited effect.

33188 ■ *"Daley's Efforts to Ease Traffic Woes Fall Short" in Crain's Chicago Business (Vol. 31, May 5, 2008, No. 18, pp. 18)*
Pub: Crain Communications, Inc.
Description: Discusses some of the inherent problems of Mayor Daley's plan to reduce traffic congestion by creating a tax on drivers who park their cars downtown during peak traffic periods and putting articulated buses on new bus-only lanes on major arterial streets leading into the Loop.

33189 ■ *"Defense Budge Ax May Not Come Down So Hard On the Region" in Baltimore Business Journal (Vol. 28, August 20, 2010,*

No. 15, pp. 1)
Pub: Baltimore Business Journal
Ed: Daniel J. Sernovitz. **Description:** U.S. Defense Secretary Robert M. Gates' planned budget cuts are having little effect on Maryland's defense industry. Gates will reduce spending on intelligence service contracts by 10 percent.

33190 ■ *"Delaware Diaper Maker Wanting To Expand Less Than a Year After Move" in Business First-Columbus (December 7, 2007, pp. A6)*
Pub: American City Business Journals, Inc.
Ed: Dan Eaton. **Description:** Duluth, Georgia-based Associated Hygienic Products LLC is planning to expand its production operations by 20 percent and hire new workers. The diaper maker was awarded state incentives to facilitate its transfer from Marion to Delaware. Details are included.

33191 ■ *"Detroit Residential Market Slows; Bright Spots Emerge" in Crain's Detroit Business (Vol. 24, October 6, 2008, No. 40, pp. 11)*
Pub: Crain Communications, Inc.
Ed: Daniel Duggan. **Description:** Discusses the state of the residential real estate market in Detroit; although condominium projects receive the most attention, deals for single-family homes are taking place in greater numbers due to financing issues. Buyers can purchase a single family home with a 3.5 percent down payment compared to 20 percent for some condo deals because of the number of first-time homebuyer programs under the Federal Housing Administration.

33192 ■ *"The Display Group Is Super-Sized" in Michigan Vue (Vol. 13, July-August 2008, No. 4, pp. 34)*
Pub: Entrepreneur Media Inc.
Description: Profile of the Display Group, located in downtown Detroit, this company provides custom designed mobile marketing displays as well as special event production services for trade show displays. The rental house and design service is also beginning to see more business due to the film initiative, which provides incentives for films that are shooting in Michigan.

33193 ■ *"Doctors Warn of Problems" in Austin Business JournalInc. (Vol. 29, December 4, 2009, No. 39, pp. 1)*
Pub: American City Business Journals
Ed: Sandra Zaragoza. **Description:** Texas physicians have voiced their concern regarding the potential cuts in Medicare reimbursement rates due to the 21 percent cut imposed by Centers for Medicare and Medicaid at the start of 2010. Experts believe the large cuts would result in the closure of some physician practices. Details of the Texas Medical Association's stand on the health reform bill are examined.

33194 ■ *"Dodge Pushes Reform Agenda" in Globe & Mail (February 6, 2006, pp. B1)*
Pub: CTVglobemedia Publishing Inc.
Ed: Heather Scoffield. **Description:** The impact of variations in global economy, on Canadian economy, is discussed. The recommendations of Governor David Dodge of Bank of Canada to resolve the issue are presented.

33195 ■ *"Doing the Right Thing" in Black Enterprise (Vol. 38, July 2008, No. 12, pp. 50)*
Pub: Earl G. Graves Publishing Co. Inc.
Ed: Tamara E. Holmes. **Description:** More business owners are trying to become more environmentally friendly, either due to their belief in social responsibility or for financial incentives or for both reasons. Tips for making one's business more environmentally responsible are included as well as a listing of resources that may be available to help owners in their efforts.

33196 ■ *"Don't Expect Quick Fix" in The Business Journal-Serving Metropolitan Kansas City (Vol. 27, October 3, 2008, No. 3, pp. 1)*
Pub: American City Business Journals, Inc.
Ed: James Dornbrook. **Description:** United States governmental entities cannot provide a quick fix solution to the current financial crisis. The economy requires a systemic change in the way people think about credit. The financial services industry should also focus on core lending principles.

33197 ■ *"Down the Tracks, a Whistle Is a Blowin" in Barron's (Vol. 89, July 27, 2009, No. 30, pp. 36)*
Pub: Dow Jones & Co., Inc.
Ed: Jim McTague. **Description:** Higher numbers of freight-rail carloads are a sign that the economy is improving and it is no stretch to imagine that this is aided by the American Recovery and Reinvestment Act. It is also predicted that 2009 municipal bond issuance will be above $373 billion with at least $55 billion of it made up of Buy America Bonds that are subsidized by the federal government.

33198 ■ *"Dream On: California's Budget Fix may not Last for Long." in Barron's (Vol. 89, July 27, 2009, No. 30, pp. 21)*
Pub: Dow Jones & Co., Inc.
Ed: Jonathan R. Laing. **Description:** California's budget agreement which purports to eliminate a $26 billion deficit is discussed. The frequent budgetary dustups in the state calls for several reforms including a rainy day fund of 15 percent of any budget and a constitutional convention. Other reform suggestions are discussed.

33199 ■ *"Editor's Note" in Canadian Business (Vol. 81, March 17, 2008, No. 4, pp. 7)*
Pub: Rogers Media
Ed: Joe Chidley. **Description:** Canadian Consolidated government expenditures increased by an average of 4.5 percent annually from 2003 to 2007. Health care, housing, and the environment were some of the areas which experienced higher spending. However, government spending in labor, employment, and immigration dropped 6.6 percent.

33200 ■ *"Emerging Tech Fund Strong in 2009" in Austin Business JournalInc. (Vol. 29, December 25, 2009, No. 42, pp. 1)*
Pub: American City Business Journals
Ed: Christopher Calnan. **Description:** Texas' Emerging Technology Fund (ETF) has seen an increase in applications from the state's technology companies in 2009. ETF received 87 applications in 2009 from Central Texas companies versus 50 during 2008 while $10.5 million was given to seven Texas companies compared with $10.6 million to ten companies in 2008.

33201 ■ *"Employer Jobless Tax Could Rise" in Sacramento Business Journal (Vol. 28, May 27, 2011, No. 13, pp. 1)*
Pub: Sacramento Business Journal
Ed: Kathy Robertson. **Description:** The government of California is facing an estimated $16 billion deficit in its unemployment insurance fund. Unemployment insurance spending has exceeded employer contributions to the fund. Statistics on unemployment insurance is included.

33202 ■ *"Encouraging Study in Critical Languages" in Occupational Outlook Quarterly (Vol. 55, Summer 2011, No. 2, pp. 23)*
Pub: U.S. Bureau of Labor Statistics
Description: Proficiency in particular foreign languages is vital to the defense, diplomacy, and security of the United States. Several federal programs provide scholarships and other funding to encourage high school and college students to learn languages of the Middle East, China, and Russia.

33203 ■ *"ETF Process May be Tweaked" in Austin Business JournalInc. (Vol. 28, December 26, 2008, No. 41, pp. 3)*
Pub: American City Business Journals
Ed: Christopher Calnan. **Description:** Some government officials are proposing for an adjustment of the Texas Emerging Technology Fund's (ETF) policies. The ETF was created to get startup companies capital to get off the ground. Reports show that the global recession had made it more difficult for startup companies to garner investment.

33204 ■ *"Exit Strategy" in Barron's (Vol. 89, July 6, 2009, No. 27, pp. 3)*
Pub: Dow Jones & Co., Inc.
Ed: Alan Abelson. **Description:** US Federal Reserve is not likely to change its easy-money strategy in the short term. States such as California are suffering from spiraling costs and declining revenues and are struggling to balance their budgets. The US unemployment rate climbed to 9.5 percent in June 2009.

33205 ■ *"Exiting Stage Left" in Baltimore Business Journal (Vol. 28, June 18, 2010, No. 6, pp. 1)*
Pub: Baltimore Business Journal
Ed: Scott Dance. **Description:** Film professionals including crew members and actors have been leaving Maryland to find work in other states such as Michigan, Louisiana, and Georgia where bigger budgets and film production incentives are given. Other consequences of this trend in local TV and film production are discussed.

33206 ■ *"Experts Take the Temp of Obama Plan" in The Business Journal-Serving Metropolitan Kansas City (Vol. 27, November 14, 2008, No. 10)*
Pub: American City Business Journals, Inc.
Ed: Rob Roberts. **Description:** Kansas City, Missouri-based employee benefits experts say president-elect Barack Obama's health care reform plan is on track. Insurance for children and capitalization for health information technology are seen as priority areas. The plan is aimed at reducing the number of uninsured people in the United States.

33207 ■ *"Fannie and Freddie: How They'll Change" in Business Week (September 22, 2008, No. 4100, pp. 30)*
Pub: McGraw-Hill Companies, Inc.
Ed: Jane Sasseen. **Description:** Three possible outcomes of the fate of struggling mortgage giants Freddie Mac and Fannie Mae after the government bailout are outlined.

33208 ■ *"Farm Aid" in Canadian Business (Vol. 80, November 5, 2007, No. 22, pp. 123)*
Pub: Rogers Media
Ed: Calvin Leung. **Description:** Canadian farmers experiencing difficulties with increasing their earning as the price of production is greater than the amount they earn from produce. Government assistance programs, including the Canadian Agricultural Income Stabilization, are aimed at helping farmers mitigate the impacts of the high prices of production. The effectiveness of Canadian farm policies are evaluated.

33209 ■ *"Fast-Release Calcium Could Help Control Club Root" in Farmer's Weekly (March 28, 2008, No. 320)*
Pub: Reed Business Information
Contact: Jeff Greisch, President
Description: According to initial observations from a new HGCA club root research study, applications of fertilizers that rapidly release calcium may help improve performance of both susceptible and resistant oilseed rape varieties.

33210 ■ *"The Fed Still Has Ammunition" in Barron's (Vol. 90, August 30, 2010, No. 35, pp. M9)*
Pub: Barron's Editorial & Corporate Headquarters
Ed: Randall W. Forsyth. **Description:** Federal Reserve chairman Ben Bernanke said the agency still has tools to combat deflation and a second downturn but these strategies are not needed at this time. The prospects of the Federal Open Market Committee's purchasing of treasuries are also discussed.

33211 ■ *"Fed Tackles Bear of a Crisis" in Barron's (Vol. 88, March 17, 2008, No. 11, pp. M10)*
Pub: Dow Jones & Company, Inc.
Ed: Randall W. Forsyth. **Description:** Emergency funding package for Bear Stearns from the Federal Reserve Bank of New York through JPMorgan Chase is one of the steps taken by the central bank shore up bank liquidity. Prior to the emergency funding, the

central bank announced the Term Securities Lending Facility to allow dealers to borrow easily saleable Treasuries in exchange for less-liquid issues.

33212 ■ *"Federal Bailout, Three Years Later" in Business Owner (Vol. 35, September-October 2011, No. 5, pp. 6)*
Pub: DL Perkins Company
Description: State of the economy and small business sector three years after the government stimulus and bailout programs were instituted.

33213 ■ *"Federal Fund Valuable Tool For Small-Biz Innovators" in Crain's Detroit Business (Vol. 24, September 29, 2008, No. 39, pp. 42)*
Pub: Crain Communications Inc.
Ed: Nancy Kaffer. **Description:** Grants from the Small Business Innovation Research Program, or SBIR grants, are federal funds that are set aside for 11 federal agencies to allocate to tech-oriented small-business owners. Firms such as Biotechnology Business Consultants help these companies apply for SBIR grants.

33214 ■ *"Feds to Pay University $20M" in Business Courier (Vol. 27, July 23, 2010, No. 12, pp. 3)*
Pub: Business Courier
Ed: James Ritchie. **Description:** The U.S. government is set to pay University Hospital and medical residents who trained there $20 million as part of a tax dispute settlement. Around 1,000 former residents are to receive tax refunds. But the hospital must provide the U.S. Internal Revenue Service with extensive documentation.

33215 ■ *"A Few Points of Contention" in Barron's (Vol. 88, July 14, 2008, No. 28, pp. 3)*
Pub: Dow Jones & Co., Inc.
Ed: Michael Santoli. **Description:** Headline inflation tends to revert to the lower core inflation, which excludes food and energy in its calculation over long periods. Prominent private equity figures believe that regulators should allow more than the de facto 10 percent to 25 percent limit of commercial banks to hasten the refunding of the financial sector.

33216 ■ *"Fifth Third CEO Kabat: A World of Difference" in Business Courier (Vol. 26, January 1, 2010, No. 37, pp. 1)*
Pub: American City Business Journals, Inc.
Ed: Steve Watkins. **Description:** CEO Kevin Kabat of Cincinnati-based Fifth Third Bancorp believes that the bank's assets of $111 billion and stock value of more than $10 indicate the recovery from the low stock prices posted in February 2009. He attributes the recovery from the federal government's stress test finding in May 2009 that Fifth Third needs to generate $1.1 billion.

33217 ■ *"Fight Against Fake" in The Business Journal-Portland (Vol. 25, July 18, 2008, No. 19, pp. 1)*
Pub: American City Business Journals, Inc.
Ed: Erik Siemers. **Description:** Companies, such as Columbia Sportswear Co. and Nike Inc., are fighting the counterfeiting of their sportswear and footwear products through the legal process of coordinating with law enforcement agencies to raid factories. Most of the counterfeiting factories are in China and India. Other details on the issue are discussed.

33218 ■ *"Film Incentives: A Hit or a Flop?" in Michigan Vue (Vol. 13, July-August 2008, No. 4, pp. 10)*
Pub: Entrepreneur Media Inc.
Description: Michigan's new film incentive legislation is fulfilling its core purpose, according to Lisa Dancsok of the Michigan Economic Development Corp. (MEDC), by kickstarting the state's entry into the multi-billion dollar industry; the initiative is considered to be very competitive with other states and countries and is thought to be a way in which to help revitalize Michigan's struggling economy.

33219 ■ *"Final State Budget Is a Mixed Bag of Key Industries" in The Business Journal - Serving Phoenix and the Valley of the Sun (Vol. 28, July 4, 2008, No. 44, pp. 3)*
Pub: American City Business Journals, Inc.
Ed: Mike Sunnucks; Patrick O'Grady. **Description:** Approved by Governor Janet Napolitano and passed by the Arizona Legislature, the $9.9 billion state budget is beneficial to some industries in the business community. The tax cap for on Arizona Lottery has been removed which is beneficial to the industry, while the solar energy industry and real estate developers stand to lose from the spending bill. Other details of the finance budget are presented.

33220 ■ *"Finding Room for Financing" in The Business Journal-Serving Metropolitan Kansas City (Vol. 26, August 1, 2008, No. 47, pp. 1)*
Pub: American City Business Journals, Inc.
Ed: Rob Roberts. **Description:** Kansas City officials are expecting to receive financing recommendations for a new 1,000-room convention headquarters hotel. The $300-million project could be financed either through private ownership with public subsidies, or through public ownership with tax-exempt bond financing. Other views and information on the project and its expected economic impact, are presented.

33221 ■ *"First-Time Homebuyer Credit May Add Some Momentum to Market" in Crain's Cleveland Business (Vol. 30, May 18, 2009, No. 20)*
Pub: Crain Communications, Inc.
Ed: Stan Bullard. **Description:** Federal tax credits for first-time homebuyers have increased the number of homes being sold. Details of the tax credit are defined.

33222 ■ *"Five Area Businesses Win State Tax Breaks" in Crain's Detroit Business (Vol. 25, June 22, 2009, No. 25, pp. 9)*
Pub: Crain Communications Inc. - Detroit
Ed: Amy Lane. **Description:** Michigan Economic Growth Authority approved tax breaks for five area businesses among 15 across the state. Details of the tax credits are provided.

33223 ■ *"Five New Scientists Bring Danforth Center $16 Million" in Saint Louis Business Journal (Vol. 32, October 7, 2011, No. 6, pp. 1)*
Pub: Saint Louis Business Journal
Ed: E.B. Solomont. **Description:** Donald Danforth Plant Science Center's appointment of five new lead scientists has increased its federal funding by $16 million. Cornell University scientist Tom Brutnell is one of the five new appointees.

33224 ■ *"Freedom Center May have New Path" in Business Courier (Vol. 26, October 30, 2009, No. 27, pp. 1)*
Pub: American City Business Journals, Inc.
Ed: Dan Monk, Lucy May. **Description:** National Underground Railroad Freedom Center in Price Hill, Cincinnati is in negotiations with US Rep. John Conyers for its possible classification as an independent establishment within the US federal government. If this happens, funding for the museum might be possibly augmented and the rights to use national archives might be furnished.

33225 ■ *"Freshman Lawmaker Graves Keeping Busy" in Atlanta Journal-Constitution (June 20, 2010, pp. A6)*
Pub: Atlanta Journal Constitution
Ed: Bob Keefe. **Description:** Newly elected Republican Representative Tom Graves of Ranger supports the Small Business Jobs Tax Relief Act.

33226 ■ *"From Buyout to Busted" in Business Week (September 22, 2008, No. 4100, pp. 18)*
Pub: McGraw-Hill Companies, Inc.
Ed: Emily Thornton; Deborah Stead. **Description:** Bankruptcy filings by private equity-backed companies are at a record high with 134 American firms taken private (or invested in) by buyout firms that have filed for protection this year under Chapter 11; this is 91 percent higher than the previous year, which had set a record when 70 of such companies filed for protection under Chapter 11.

33227 ■ *"Glendale Pumping $29 Million Into Redevelopment" in The Business Journal - Serving Phoenix and the Valley of the Sun (Vol. 28, August 1, 2008, No. 48, pp. 1)*
Pub: American City Business Journals, Inc.
Ed: Mike Sunnucks. **Description:** Glendale City is planning to invest $29 million to improve city infrastructure like roadways and water and sewer lines over the next five years. Glendale's city council is also planning to hold a workshop on the redevelopment projects in September 2008. Other views and information on the redevelopment project, are presented.

33228 ■ *"A Good Step, But There's a Long Way to Go" in Business Week (September 22, 2008, No. 4100, pp. 10)*
Pub: McGraw-Hill Companies, Inc.
Ed: James C. Cooper. **Description:** Despite the historic action by the U.S. government to nationalize the mortgage giants Freddie Mac and Fannie Mae, rising unemployment rates may prove to be an even bigger roadblock to bringing back the economy from its downward spiral. The takeover is meant to restore confidence in the credit markets and help with the mortgage crisis but the rising rate in unemployment may make many households unable to take advantage of any benefits which arise from the bailout. Statistical data included.

33229 ■ *"Growing Field" in Crain's Detroit Business (Vol. 26, January 11, 2010, No. 2, pp. 3)*
Pub: Crain Communications Inc.
Description: Detroit's TechTown was awarded a combination loan and grant of $4.1 million from the U.S. Department of Housing and Urban Development to build a 15,000-square-foot stem cell center, a collection of laboratories that will be available to both for-profit companies and university researchers.

33230 ■ *"Half a World Away" in Tampa Bay Business Journal (Vol. 30, December 4, 2009, No. 50, pp. 1)*
Pub: American City Business Journals
Ed: Jane Meinhardt. **Description:** Enterprise Florida has offered four trade grants for Florida's marine industry businesses to give them a chance to tap into the Middle East market at the Dubai International Boat Show on March 9 to 13, 2010. The grants pay for 50 percent of the exhibition costs for the qualifying business.

33231 ■ *"Hank Paulson On the Housing Bailout and What's Ahead" in Business Week (September 22, 2008, No. 4100, pp. 19)*
Pub: McGraw-Hill Companies, Inc.
Ed: Maria Bartiromo. **Description:** Interview with Treasury Secretary Henry Paulson in which he discusses the bailout of Fannie Mae and Freddie Mac as well as the potential impact on the American economy and foreign interests and investments in the country. Paulson has faith that the government's actions will help to stabilize the housing market.

33232 ■ *"Hastily Enacted Regulation Will Not Cure Economic Crisis" in Crain's Chicago Business (Vol. 31, May 5, 2008, No. 18, pp. 18)*
Pub: Crain Communications, Inc.
Ed: Stephen P. D'Arcy. **Description:** Policymakers are looking for ways to respond to what is possibly the greatest financial crisis of a generation due to the collapse of the housing market, the credit crisis and the volatility of Wall Street.

33233 ■ *"Have High-Tech Tax Credits Helped or Hurt Hawaii?" in Hawaii Business (Vol. 53, December 2007, No. 6, pp. 28)*
Pub: Hawaii Business Publishing
Description: Presents the opinons of Channel Capital LLC's Walter R. Roth and Hawaii Venture Capital Association's Bill Spencer concerning the impacts of tax credits. Roth thinks that Act 221 appeals to investors who can earn despite business failure while Spencer thinks that the legislation promotes investments in innovative technology firms. The need to support tax credits is also discussed.

33234 ■ *"Health Care Braces for Federal Cuts" in Boston Business Journal (Vol. 29, August 19, 2011, No. 15, pp. 1)*
Pub: American City Business Journals Inc.

Ed: Scott Dance. **Description:** The healthcare industry in Baltimore is expecting negative effects from the federal debt ceiling on Medicare and Medicaid spending. Medicare funds are expected to be slashed and could impact hospitals and doctors.

33235 ■ *"Health Care of the Future" in Business Journal Serving Greater Tampa Bay (Vol. 30, November 19, 2010, No. 48, pp. 1)*
Pub: Tampa Bay Business Journal

Ed: Margie Manning. **Description:** Information about accountable care organizations (ACO), which are integrated care systems with doctors and hospitals working closely together to handle patient care, is provided. The Patient Protection and Affordable Care Act paved the way for ACOs as Medicare demonstration projects.

33236 ■ *"Health Centers Plan Expansion" in Crain's Detroit Business (Vol. 25, June 15, 2009, No. 24, pp. 3)*
Pub: Crain Communications Inc. - Detroit

Ed: Jay Greene. **Description:** Detroit has five federally qualified health centers that plan to receive over $3 million in federal stimulus money that will be used to expand projects that will care for uninsured patients.

33237 ■ *"Heart Hospitals Analyzed" in Philadelphia Business Journal (Vol. 30, September 2, 2011, No. 29, pp. 1)*
Pub: American City Business Journals Inc.

Ed: John George. **Description:** Centers for Medicare and Medicaid Services (CMS) released updated data on mortality rates for heart attack patients as hospitals in Pennsylvania. Doylestown Hospital posted the lowest mortality rates with 10.9 percent, tying the fourth best in the entire nation. Other details on the CMS data are presented.

33238 ■ *"Help, For Some" in Canadian Business (Vol. 81, December 8, 2008, No. 21, pp. 10)*
Pub: Rogers Media Ltd.

Ed: Joe Castaldo. **Description:** Over 80 percent of Canadian chief executives believe that government bailouts merely reward mediocre management and encourages companies to take risks because they know the government will help prevent their bankruptcy. Respondents to a COMPAS online survey believe bailouts are unfair for properly managed companies.

33239 ■ *"Help Wanted: 100 Hospitals IT Workers" in Business Courier (Vol. 27, October 8, 2010, No. 23, pp. 1)*
Pub: Business Courier

Ed: James Ritchie. **Description:** Hospitals in the Greater Cincinnati area are expected to hire more than 100 information technology (IT) workers to help digitize medical records. Financial incentives from the health care reform bill encouraged investments in electronic medical record systems, increasing the demand for IT workers that would help make information exchange across the healthcare system easier.

33240 ■ *"Help in Wings for Aviation, Defense" in Globe & Mail (March 12, 2007, pp. B1)*
Pub: CTVglobemedia Publishing Inc.

Ed: Simon Tuck. **Description:** The creation of a corporate subsidy fund by the Canadian government, to facilitate the growth of the aerospace and defense industries, is described.

33241 ■ *"Helping Small Businesses Create Jobs" in America's Intelligence Wire (August 27, 2010)*
Pub: HighBeam Research

Ed: Ross Raihala. **Description:** Ways the Small Business Jobs Tax Relief Act will help small businesses create jobs are investigated.

33242 ■ *"His Record, Not Polls, Is What Matters" in Bangor Daily News (October 13, 2010)*
Pub: Bangor Daily News

Ed: Nick Sambides Jr. **Description:** The Small Business Jobs Tax Relief Act could spur investment in small businesses by increasing capital gains tax cuts for investors in small business in 2010 and increase to $20,000 from $5,000 the deduction for start-up businesses.

33243 ■ *"Historic Tax Credit Plan Gains Support" in Baltimore Business Journal (Vol. 27, January 8, 2010, No. 36, pp. 1)*
Pub: American City Business Journals

Ed: Heather Harlan Warnack. **Description:** Maryland Governor Martin O'Malley plans to push legislation in the General Assembly to extend for three more years the tax credit program for rehabilitation of obsolete buildings. The Maryland Heritage Structure Rehabilitation Tax Credit Program has declined from almost $75 million in expenses in 2001 to roughly $5 million in 2010 fiscal year. Details on the projects that benefited from the program are explored.

33244 ■ *"Hopkins, UMd Worry Reduced NIH Budget Will Impact Research" in Boston Business Journal (Vol. 29, August 19, 2011, No. 15, pp. 1)*
Pub: American City Business Journals Inc.

Ed: Scott Dance. **Description:** The budget for the National Institutes of Health (NIH) is slated to be cut by at least 7.9 percent to $2.5 billion in 2013. This will have a big negative effect on medical and biotech research in Maryland, especially Johns Hopkins University and University of Maryland, Baltimore which could face stiffer completion for grants from the NIH.

33245 ■ *"Hospital Fighting for Its Life; Board of St. Anthony Scrambles to Stem Losses" in Crain's Chicago Business (April 28, 2008)*
Pub: Crain Communications, Inc.

Ed: Mike Colias. **Description:** Chicago's Catholic health chain was looking to sell the money-losing hospital St. Anthony Hospital on the West Side but with the financial picture improving and no merger offers in the works the investment bank hired to shop the hospital is hoping to operate the 111-year-old facility as an independent entity. St. Anthony serves as a 'safety net' for the region since an increasing number of its patients are uninsured or on public aid, which pays far less than commercial insurers.

33246 ■ *"Hot-Button Ordinances May Go Up for Review" in Crain's Detroit Business (Vol. 26, January 18, 2010, No. 3, pp. 1)*
Pub: Crain Communications Inc.

Ed: Nancy Kaffer. **Description:** Detroit's economic fate may be tied to the city's anti-privatization ordinance and its policy of giving contract preference to Detroit-based businesses. The new administration feels that it is time to put everything on the table in an attempt to look for ways in which to save the city money.

33247 ■ *"House Committee on Small Business Calls for Sweeping Changes to SBIR Program" in Hispanic Business (March 2008, pp. 44)*
Pub: Hispanic Business

Description: Changes in the Small Business Innovation and Research Program would allow greater flexibility for firms participating in the program to leverage venture capital funds.

33248 ■ *"How Green Is The Valley?" in Barron's (Vol. 88, July 4, 2008, No. 28, pp. 13)*
Pub: Dow Jones & Co., Inc.

Description: San Jose, California has made a good start towards becoming a leader in alternative energy technology through the establishment of United Laboratories' own lab in the city. The certification process for photovoltaic cells will be dramatically shortened with this endeavor.

33249 ■ *"Illinois Bets On Recycling Program" in Chicago Tribune (November 29, 2008)*
Pub: McClatchy-Tribune Information Services

Ed: Joel Hood. **Description:** Traditionally the holiday gift-giving season is one of the most wasteful times of year and the state of Illinois is granting $760,000 to small businesses and cities in an attempt to expand curbside recycling programs and hire additional workers to address electronic waste.

33250 ■ *In Fed We Trust: Ben Bernanke's Ware on the Great Panic*
Pub: Crown Business

Ed: David Wessel. **Released:** 2009. **Price:** $27.99. **Description:** A look at the central bank's reaction to the crisis and Ben Bernanke has been forced to play the crisis by ear in order to keep the economy from imploding.

33251 ■ *"In the SBA's Face" in Hispanic Business (December 2010)*
Pub: Hispanic Business

Ed: Richard Larsen. **Description:** Lloyd Chapman uses the American Small Business League to champion small business. Statistical data included.

33252 ■ *"Incentives Debate Rages On Unabated" in The Business Journal-Serving Metropolitan Kansas City (Vol. 26, September 5, 2008, No. 52)*
Pub: American City Business Journals, Inc.

Ed: Rob Roberts. **Description:** Debate on the new economic development and incentives policy adopted by the Kansas City Council is still on. The city's Planned Industrial Expansion Authority has rejected a standard property tax abatement proposal. The real estate development community has opposed the rejection of proposed the tax incentives policy.

33253 ■ *"Incentives In Play for Astronautics" in Business Journal-Milwaukee (Vol. 28, November 5, 2010, No. 5, pp. A1)*
Pub: Milwaukee Business Journal

Ed: Sean Ryan. **Description:** Astronautics Corporation was offered incentives by local government officials in Milwaukee, Wisconsin and by Brewery Project LLC to move into a building in The Brewery in the city. The company's officials remain indecisive over the offers and incentives.

33254 ■ *"Intel: Tax Breaks Key" in Business Journal Portland (Vol. 27, October 22, 2010, No. 34, pp. 1)*
Pub: Portland Business Journal

Ed: Erik Siemers. **Description:** Intel Corporation believes that state tax incentives will be critical, especially in the purchase of manufacturing equipment, as they build a new chip factory in Hillsboro, Oregon. The tax breaks would help Intel avoid paying 10 times more in property taxes compared to average Washington County firms. Critics argue that Intel has about $15 billion in cash assets, and can afford the factory without the tax breaks.

33255 ■ *"It's Good to be Goldman" in Barron's (Vol. 89, July 20, 2009, No. 29, pp. 5)*
Pub: Dow Jones & Co., Inc.

Ed: Randall W. Forsyth. **Description:** Profits of Goldman Sachs rose to $3.44 billion in the second quarter of 2009, aided by federal financial stimulus programs. CIT Group is facing bankruptcy and may need up to $6 billion to survive. The federal economic stimulus programs are benefiting Wall Street more than the US economy itself.

33256 ■ *"It's Not Easy Being Small" in Baltimore Business Journal (Vol. 27, October 9, 2009, No. 22, pp. 1)*
Pub: American City Business Journals

Ed: Scott Dance. **Description:** A look at how small businesses were left out of the stimulus-funded federal contracts in Maryland. Small contractors were not listed in the federal contracts database USAspending.gov and none were hired for work in the state.

33257 ■ *"It's Time To Swim" in Canadian Business (Vol. 81, March 3, 2008, No. 3, pp. 37)*
Pub: Rogers Media

Ed: Megan Harman. **Description:** Canadian manufacturers should consider Asian markets such as India and the United Arab Emirates as the U.S. economic downturn continues. Canada's shortage in skilled labor is also expected to negatively affect manufacturing industries. Ontario's plans to assist manufacturers are also presented.

33258 ■ *"KC Sewer Solutions May Overflow With Green Ideas" in The Business Journal-Serving Metropolitan Kansas City (August 22, 2008)*
Pub: American City Business Journals, Inc.
Ed: Suzanna Stagemeyer. **Description:** Adding green solutions such as small, dispersed basins to catch runoffs and the use of deep rooted natural plants to fix the sewer system of Kansas could probably justify the $2.3 billion worth of funds needed for the project. The city has been ordered by the EPA and the Missouri Department of Natural Resources to fix their sewer systems that are overwhelmed by significant rains.

33259 ■ *"Leaders Weigh In On Fannie Mae, Freddie Mac Failure, Fed Bailout" in The Business Journal - Serving Phoenix and the Valley of the Sun (Vol. 28, September 12, 2008, No. 53, pp. 1)*
Pub: American City Business Journals, Inc.
Ed: Chris Casacchia; Mike Sunnucks; Jan Buchholz. **Description:** Fannie Mae and Freddie Mac's federal takeover was a move to help stabilize the financial market and it helped bring down interest rates in the past week. Local executives from Arizona's Phoenix area share their thoughts on the immediate effect of the takeover and its upside and downside.

33260 ■ *"Legislature to Tackle Crisis in Jobless Fund" in Baltimore Business Journal (Vol. 27, December 18, 2009, No. 32, pp. 1)*
Pub: American City Business Journals
Ed: Scott Dance. **Description:** Maryland's General Assembly is set to finalize changes to the state's unemployment insurance system as soon as it convenes for the 2010 session. The move was aimed to draw $127 million in stimulus money that can support the nearly depleted fund of unemployment benefits within 45 days.

33261 ■ *"Lending Act Touted by Michaud" in Morning Sentinel (June 21, 2010)*
Pub: Morning Sentinel
Ed: Doug Harlow. **Description:** If passed, the Small Business Jobs Tax Relief Act will leverage up to $300 billion in loans for small businesses through a $30 billion lending fund for small and medium-sized community banks, which focus on lending to small firms.

33262 ■ *"Lending Idea Gets Mixed Review" in Tampa Bay Business Journal (Vol. 29, October 30, 2009, No. 45, pp. 1)*
Pub: American City Business Journals
Ed: Kent Hoover, Margie Manning. **Description:** Tampa Bay area, Florida's community banks have expressed disapproval to the proposal of President Obama to increase lending to small business, wherein the government will provide cheap capital through US Treasury Troubled Asset Relief Program (TARP). The banks were hesitant on the plan because of the strings attached to TARP.

33263 ■ *"Letting the Sunshine In" in Barron's (Vol. 89, July 6, 2009, No. 27, pp. 11)*
Pub: Dow Jones & Co., Inc.
Ed: Katherine Cheng. **Description:** Solar energy industry leaders believe the industry needs aid from the US government regarding the funding of its research efforts and lowering solar energy costs. The climate change bill passed by the US House of Representatives signifies the US government's desire to significantly reduce carbon dioxide emissions.

33264 ■ *"A Limited Sphere of Influence" in Mergers & Acquisitions: The Dealmaker's Journal (March 1, 2008)*
Pub: SourceMedia, Inc.
Ed: Ken MacFadyen. **Description:** Changes to the interest rate has had little impact on the mergers and acquisitions market since the federal funds rate does not link directly to the liquidity available to the M&A market; lenders are looking at cash flows and are likely to remain cautious due to other factors impacting the market.

33265 ■ *"Loan Dollars Sit Idle for Energy Plan" in Baltimore Business Journal (Vol. 28, September 10, 2010, No. 18, pp. 1)*
Pub: Baltimore Business Journal
Ed: Scott Dance. **Description:** The Maryland Energy Administration has millions of dollars in Federal stimulus and state energy efficiency cash sitting idle and might be lost once the window for stimulus spending is gone. However, businesses have no interest in betting on renewable energy because some cannot afford to take out more loans. Other challenges faced by these businesses are presented.

33266 ■ *"Local Hospitals Wage Wars on 'Bounce-Backs" in Business Courier (Vol. 27, July 30, 2010, No. 13, pp. 1)*
Pub: Business Courier
Ed: James Ritchie. **Description:** Health care organizations in Greater Cincinnati area have tried a number of care and follow up programs, primarily focused on congestive heart failure to prevent readmissions to hospitals. Hospital administrators have made the averting of bounce-backs a priority due to new federal government plans on reimbursement.

33267 ■ *"Local Researchers Get Cash Infusion" in Business Courier (Vol. 26, October 9, 2009, No. 24, pp. 1)*
Pub: American City Business Journals, Inc.
Ed: James Ritchie. **Description:** Cincinnati's Children's Hospital Medical Center and the University of Cincinnati researchers are set to receive at least $56 million from the stimulus bill. The cash infusion has reenergized research scientists and enhances Cincinnati's national clout as a major research center.

33268 ■ *"Lords Should Get Real About Food" in Farmer's Weekly (March 28, 2008, No. 320)*
Pub: Reed Business Information
Contact: Jeff Greisch, President
Description: Discusses the reasons why farming needs subsidies and suggests that the House of Lords should look at the way that grocery stores are operating.

33269 ■ *"Major Renovation Planned for Southridge" in Business Journal-Milwaukee (Vol. 28, November 12, 2010, No. 6, pp. A1)*
Pub: Milwaukee Business Journal
Ed: Stacy Vogel Davis. **Description:** Simon Property Group plans to invest more than $20 million in upgrading and renovating Southridge Mall in Milwaukee County, Wisconsin. The project, which is partially financed by a $10 million grant from the Village of Greendale, could boost the property's value by $52.5 million.

33270 ■ *"Making It Stick" in Business Courier (Vol. 24, November 9, 2008, No. 30, pp. 1)*
Pub: American City Business Journals, Inc.
Ed: Lucy May. **Description:** Discusses a report by the Brookings Institution which shows the need for the U.S. government to offer greater support to the country's metro areas in order to excel globally. Ohio, which has seven of the country's 100 largest metropolitan areas, does not receive enough funds, due to the need to finance less populated areas. Because of this, Ohio politicians have to spread less funding in order to cover more constituents.

33271 ■ *"M&I Execs May Get Golden Parachutes" in Business Journal-Milwaukee (Vol. 28, December 31, 2010, No. 14, pp. A3)*
Pub: Milwaukee Business Journal
Ed: Rich Kirchen. **Description:** Marshall and Isley Corporation's top executives have a chance to receive golden-parachute payments it its buyer, BMO Financial Group, repays the Troubled Asset Relief Program (TARP) loan on behalf of the company. One TARP rule prevents golden-parachute payments to them and the next five most highly paid employees of TARP recipients.

33272 ■ *"Manufacturers Urged to Adapt to Defense" in Crain's Cleveland Business (Vol. 30, June 22, 2009, No. 24, pp. 3)*
Pub: Crain Communications, Inc.
Ed: Dan Shingler. **Description:** Manufacturers in Northeast Ohio are making products for the military from steel, polymers or composite materials. The U.S. Department of Defense is teaching companies to work with titanium and other advanced metals in order to further manufacture for the military.

33273 ■ *"Market Watch" in Barron's (Vol. 88, March 24, 2008, No. 12, pp. M18)*
Pub: Dow Jones & Company, Inc.
Ed: Ashraf Laidi; Marc Pado; David Kotok. **Description:** Latest measures implemented by the Federal Reserve to address the credit crisis did not benefit the US dollar, with the Japanese yen and the euro recouping earlier losses against the dollar. Goldman Sachs reported earnings of $3.23 per share, claiming a stronger liquidity position. The US markets bottomed early on 22 January 2007, according to evidence.

33274 ■ *"Mayor Unveils Business Plan" in Boston Business Journal (Vol. 29, September 16, 2011, No. 19, pp. 1)*
Pub: American City Business Journals Inc.
Ed: Gary Haber. **Description:** Mayor Stephanie Rawlings-Blake of Baltimore, Maryland unveiled her plan to push the economy forward. Her key objectives include giving more support for the city's technology companies and refocusing the Baltimore Development Corporation on job creation and retention.

33275 ■ *"Md. Bankers Say 'Devil Is In the Details' of New $30B Loan Fund" in Baltimore Business Journal (Vol. 28, October 8, 2010, No. 22)*
Pub: Baltimore Business Journal
Ed: Gary Haber. **Description:** Maryland community bankers have expressed doubts over a new federal loan program for small business. The new law will also earmark $80 billion for community banks. Comments from executives also given.

33276 ■ *"MEDC: Put Venture Funds to Work" in Crain's Detroit Business (Vol. 25, June 22, 2009, No. 25, pp. 1)*
Pub: Crain Communications Inc. - Detroit
Ed: Tom Henderson. **Description:** Michigan Strategic Fund board will finalize approval for ESP Holdings II LLC, Peninsula Capital Partners LLC, Triathlon Medical Ventures LLC and Arsenal Venture Partners Inc. are expected to share $35.5 million from the fund.

33277 ■ *"Medicaid Expansion Could Prompt New Taxes, Program Cuts" in Baltimore Business Journal (Vol. 27, October 23, 2009, No. 24, pp. 1)*
Pub: American City Business Journals
Ed: Julekha Dash. **Description:** Effects of the expected federal expansion of Medicaid under federal health care reform on Maryland tax policy are presented. Health care executives believe new taxes are necessary for the state to pay for an expansion that could cost over $400 million to $600 million.

33278 ■ *"Mercy Parent Nets Almost $1B in 2011" in Sacramento Business Journal (Vol. 28, September 30, 2011, No. 31, pp. 1)*
Pub: Sacramento Business Journal
Ed: Kathy Robertson. **Description:** Catholic Healthcare West has reported almost $1 billion in profits for 2010. The company has reported a profit margin of 8.7 percent. It also absorbed more than $1 billion in costs from charity care and government programs.

33279 ■ *"Michaud Touts Small-Business Credentials" in Bangor Daily News (September 10, 2010)*
Pub: Bangor Daily News
Ed: Nick Sambides Jr. **Description:** Mike Michaud, Democrat, is running against a Republican challenger in the 2nd District and states he will support the Small Business Jobs Tax Relief Act if reelected.

33280 ■ *"Microlending Seen as Having a Major Impact" in Business Journal Serving Greater Tampa Bay (Vol. 30, November 26, 2010, No. 49, pp. 1)*
Pub: Tampa Bay Business Journal
Ed: Margie Manning. **Description:** There are several organizations that are planning to offer microlending services in Tampa Bay, Florida. These include the

Children's Board of Hillsborough County, and OUR Microlending Florida LLC. Organizations that are already offering these services in the area include the Small Business Administration and the Tampa Bay Black Business Investment Corp.

33281 ■ *"Minnesota ABC Event Looks at Government Contracting" in Finance and Commerce Daily Newspaper (November 23, 2010)*
Pub: Dolan Media Newswires
Ed: Brian Johnson. **Description:** Minnesota Associated Builders and Contractors hosted an event focusing on doing business with government agencies. Topics included bidding work, awarding jobs, paperwork, guidelines, certifications and upcoming projects.

33282 ■ *"Minority Auto Suppliers Get Help Diversifying" in Crain's Detroit Business (Vol. 26, January 11, 2010, No. 2, pp. 3)*
Pub: Crain Communications, Inc.
Ed: Sherri Welch. **Description:** Displaced minority auto suppliers are being given assistance by the Kauffman's Foundation Urban Entrepreneur Partnership Detroit program, a three-year effort to assist 150 of the region's suppliers into more diversified businesses.

33283 ■ *"Mission: Recruitment" in HRMagazine (Vol. 54, January 2009, No. 1, pp. 42)*
Pub: Society for Human Resource Management
Contact: Henry G. Jackson, President
E-mail: hjackson@shrm.org
Ed: Theresa Minton-Eversole. **Description:** Due to the hiring challenges faced by Army recruiters, they are partnering with employers in order to establish connections to high quality, Army-trained individuals when they separate from active duty.

33284 ■ *"More Corporate Welfare?" in Canadian Business (Vol. 80, February 12, 2007, No. 4, pp. 96)*
Pub: Rogers Media
Description: The burden on Canadian taxpayers by governmental efforts to finance loss-making companies in the name of corporate welfare is discussed.

33285 ■ *"More Jobs Heading to Suburb" in Austin Business JournalInc. (Vol. 29, November 20, 2009, No. 37, pp. 1)*
Pub: American City Business Journals
Ed: Kate Harrington. **Description:** Site of Advanced Integration Technologies (AIT) in Pflugerville, Texas might increase its workforce to 80 employees in the next six months due to the creation of an incentive package. Funds from the Pflugerville Community Development Corporation have been helping AIT's initiative to hire more workers. The firm receives $2,000 from the plan for every new employee it hires.

33286 ■ *"Nampa Police Department: Electronic Systems Just One Tool in Business Security Toolbox" in Idaho Business Review (October 29, 2010)*
Pub: Dolan Media Newswires
Ed: Brad Carlson. **Description:** Police departments and private security firms can help small businesses with hard security and business consultants can assist with internal audit security and fraud prevention.

33287 ■ *Navigating Your Way to Business Success: An Entrepreneur's Journey*
Pub: FreeBridge Publishing, Inc.
Ed: Kathryn B. Freeland. **Released:** January 10, 2010. **Price:** $24.95. **Description:** Learn first-hand from a successful entrepreneur about assessing skills and talent, envisioning your company, planning a path to success, and then tapping into available government agencies to make your business become a reality.

33288 ■ *"NAWBO Takes the Stage at Press Conference for Small Business Jobs, Credit and Tax Relief Acts" in Internet Wire (June 17, 2010)*
Pub: Comtex
Description: A survey of the National Association of Women Business Owners reported optimism returning and women business owners are ready to invest in job creation. The Small Business Jobs Tax Relief Act will aid in their progress.

33289 ■ *"Neighborhood Watch" in Baltimore Business Journal (Vol. 28, July 23, 2010, No. 11, pp. 1)*
Pub: Baltimore Business Journal
Ed: Daniel J. Sernovitz. **Description:** Maryland government and housing leaders are set to spend $100 million in federal funding to stem the increase in foreclosures in the area. The federal funding is seen as inadequate to resolve the problem of foreclosures.

33290 ■ *"A New Kid on the Block" in Barron's (Vol. 88, March 17, 2008, No. 11, pp. 58)*
Pub: Dow Jones & Company, Inc.
Ed: Thomas G. Donlan. **Description:** Discusses the Federal Reserve which has offered to lend $100 billion in cash to banks and $200 billion in Treasuries to Wall Street investment banks that have problems with liquidity. The reluctance of the banks to lend money to meet a margin call on securities that could still depreciate is the reason why the agency is going into the direct loan business.

33291 ■ *"The Next Government Bailout?" in Barron's (Vol. 88, March 10, 2008, No. 10, pp. 21)*
Pub: Dow Jones & Company, Inc.
Ed: Jonathan Laing. **Description:** Fannie Mae may need a government bailout as it faces huge hits brought about by the effects of the housing crisis. The shares of the government-sponsored enterprise have dropped 65 percent since the housing crisis began.

33292 ■ *"Nine Sectors to Watch: Biotech" in Canadian Business (Vol. 81, December 24, 2007, No. 1, pp. 48)*
Pub: Rogers Media
Ed: Calvin Leung. **Description:** Forecasts on the Canadian biotechnology sector for 2008 are presented. Details on the increase in the number of biotechnology companies and prediction on the government's plan for business incentives are discussed.

33293 ■ *"NJ Tries to Push Stimulus Funds to Minorities" in Philadelphia Business Journal (Vol. 28, September 25, 2009, No. 32, pp. 1)*
Pub: American City Business Journals
Ed: Athena D. Merritt. **Description:** New Jersey Governor Jon S. Corzine signed an executive order that seeks to ease the way for minority and women-owned business to take on federal stimulus-funded work. New Jersey has also forged new relations with different organizations to reduce the time and cost of certifications for businesses.

33294 ■ *"No End to the Nightmare; America's Car Industry" in The Economist (Vol. 390, January 3, 2009, No. 8612, pp. 46)*
Pub: The Economist Newspaper Inc.
Description: Detroit's struggling auto industry and the government loan package is discussed as well as the United Auto Worker union, which is loathed by Senate Republicans.

33295 ■ *"Nonprofit to Grow" in Austin Business JournalInc. (Vol. 29, January 22, 2010, No. 46, pp. 1)*
Pub: American City Business Journals
Ed: Sandra Zaragoza. **Description:** Southwest Key Programs Inc. received a $2.1 million grant from the U.S. Economic Development Administration to help finance the building of a $3.6 million 'Social Enterprise Complex'. The complex is expected to create at least 100 jobs in East Austin, Texas. Details of the plan for the complex are presented.

33296 ■ *"Not Enough To Go Around" in The Business Journal-Milwaukee (Vol. 25, August 15, 2008, No. 47, pp. A1)*
Pub: American City Business Journals, Inc.
Ed: David Doege. **Description:** Most of the creditors of bankrupt real estate developer Scott Fergus are likely to remain unpaid as he only has an estimated $30,000 available for paying debts. Creditors, as of the 13 August 2008 deadline for filing claims, have filed a total of $79.1 million in claims.

33297 ■ *"Now Entering A Secure Area" in Women Entrepreneur (January 14, 2009)*
Pub: Entrepreneur Media Inc.
Ed: Aliza Sherman. **Description:** Despite the fact that the field of government intelligence and security is dominated by males, many women entrepreneurs are finding opportunities for their products and services in homeland security. Profiles of several women who have found such opportunities are included.

33298 ■ *"Numbers Game" in Baltimore Business Journal (Vol. 27, February 6, 2010, No. 40, pp. 1)*
Pub: American City Business Journals
Ed: Scott Dance. **Description:** Doubts are being raised regarding the impact of the federal stimulus spending in addressing unemployment in Maryland, which has experienced 1,800 jobs created so far. Details on the view of companies and the insufficient amount of contracts that lead to the fewer number of workers being hired are discussed.

33299 ■ *"On Growth Path of Rising Star" in Boston Business Journal (Vol. 31, June 24, 2011, No. 22, pp. 3)*
Pub: Boston Business Journal
Ed: Kyle Alspach. **Description:** 1366 Technologies Inc. of Lexington, Massachusetts is considered a rising solar power technology company. The firm secured $150 million loan guarantee from the US Department of Energy that could go to the construction of a 1,000 megawatt solar power plant.

33300 ■ *"OPSEU: Developmental Service Workers Picketing Across Ontario to Raise Community Awareness" in Canadian Corporate News (May 16, 2007)*
Pub: Comtex News Network Inc.
Description: Across Ontario staff who support people with developmental disabilities are picketing local MPP offices and other community hubs to highlight the Ontario government's inadequate response to the crisis in developmental services.

33301 ■ *"Pain Ahead as Profit Pressure Increases" in Crain's Chicago Business (Vol. 31, May 5, 2008, No. 18, pp. 4)*
Pub: Crain Communications, Inc.
Ed: Daniel Rome Levine. **Description:** Interview with David Klaskin, the chairman and chief investment officer at Oak Ridge Investments LLC, who discusses the outlook for the economy and corporate earnings, particularly in the housing and auto industries, the impact of economic stimulus checks, the weakness of the dollar and recommendations of stocks that individual investors may find helpful.

33302 ■ *"Past Promises Haunt Project" in The Business Journal-Portland (Vol. 25, August 1, 2008, No. 21, pp. 1)*
Pub: American City Business Journals, Inc.
Ed: Aliza Earnshaw. **Description:** Oregon University System and Oregon Health and Science University will face the state Legislature to defend their request for a $250 million in state bonds to fund a life-sciences collaborative research building. The project is meant to help grow the Oregon bioscience industry. Comments from industry observers and legislators are also presented.

33303 ■ *"The People Puzzle; Re-Training America's Workers" in The Economist (Vol. 390, January 3, 2009, No. 8612, pp. 32)*
Pub: The Economist Newspaper Inc.
Description: With thousands of workers losing their jobs, America is now facing the task of getting them back to work. With an overall unemployment rate of 6.7 percent, the federal government has three main ways for leading workers back to employment: training them for new jobs, providing unemployment insurance in order to replace lost wages during the period of job-hunting; and matching employers who desire a skill with workers who have that skill. Specialized staffing agencies provide employers and potential employees with the help necessary to find a job in some of the more niche markets.

33304 ■ ***A Piece of the Pie***
Pub: Outskirts Press, Incorporated
Ed: Shelton P. Rhodes, Peter Fretty. **Released:** July 2005. **Description:** Examination of the U.S. Small Business Administration's program 8(a), designed to help disadvantaged individuals grow their small businesses.

33305 ■ ***"Pitch for SPX Expansion was Full of Energy" in Charlotte Business Journal (Vol. 25, November 19, 2010, No. 35, pp. 1)***
Pub: Charlotte Business Journal
Ed: John Downey. **Description:** SPX Corporation announced that it will expand their headquarters in Ballantyne after Charlotte and North Carolina leaders made an aggressive push to retain the company. SPX Corporation is expected to invest $70 million for the expansion, which would mean 180 new jobs in Charlotte.

33306 ■ ***"Plan Targets Small Banks" in Business Journal Portland (Vol. 26, December 11, 2009, No. 40, pp. 1)***
Pub: American City Business Journals Inc.
Ed: Courtney Sherwood. **Description:** Senator Jeff Merkley of Oregon has proposed an expansion of the Troubled Assets Relief Program to accommodate banks with capital levels of less than 10 percent. In his proposal, affected banks would be mandated on a stress test to evaluate capital requirements.

33307 ■ ***"Political Environments and Business Strategy: Implications for Managers" in Business Horizons (Vol. 51, January-February 2008)***
Pub: Elsevier Advanced Technology Publications
Ed: Gerald D. Keim, Amy J. Hillman. **Description:** Various government bodies and business organizations work together in shaping new business opportunities and policies that arise from globalization. Presented is framework of public policy considerations for business managers. The framework is based on Nobel laureate Douglas North's work.

33308 ■ ***"Possible Green Light On Transit" in The Business Journal-Milwaukee (Vol. 25, July 25, 2008, No. 44, pp. A1)***
Pub: American City Business Journals, Inc.
Ed: David Doege. **Description:** $50 million in federal funding is being sought by Wisconsin's Milwaukee County Executive Scott Walker for the creation of two bus rapid transit lines, and is to be added to the unspent Milwaukee area federal funds worth $91.5 million. The new transit line will have new higher-speed buses and fewer stops than the traditional line.

33309 ■ ***"The Power of Innovation" in Canadian Business (Vol. 81, March 17, 2008, No. 4, pp. 57)***
Pub: Rogers Media
Ed: Andrew Wahl. **Description:** Canada ranks badly in terms innovation yardsticks that directly translate to economic growth such as business R&D as a percentage of GDP and R&D per capita. Canada's reliance on natural resources does not provide incentives to innovate unlike smaller countries with little natural resources. Canada could spur innovation through regulations that encourage industrial research.

33310 ■ ***"The Price of Citizenship" in Canadian Business (Vol. 79, August 14, 2006, No. 16-17, pp. 13)***
Pub: Rogers Media
Ed: Jack Mintz. **Description:** Safety and insurance benefits provided by the Canadian government to Canadian passport holders returning from Lebanon, is discussed.

33311 ■ ***"Providers Ride First Wave of eHealth Dollars" in Boston Business Journal (Vol. 31, June 10, 2011, No. 20, pp. 1)***
Pub: Boston Business Journal
Ed: Julie M. Donnelly. **Description:** Health care providers in Massachusetts implementing electronic medical records technology started receiving federal stimulus funds. Beth Israel Deaconess Medical Center was the first hospital to qualify for the funds.

33312 ■ ***"Public Health Care Funding and the Montana Economy" in Montana Business Quarterly (Vol. 49, Spring 2011, No. 1, pp. 23)***
Pub: Bureau of Business & Economic Research
Ed: Gregg Davis. **Description:** Montana has more baby boomers and veterans per capita than any other state in the nation. The role of public health in the state is a crucial part of the state's economy.

33313 ■ ***"The Quest for the Smart Prosthetic" in Canadian Business (Vol. 83, October 12, 2010, No. 17, pp. 26)***
Pub: Rogers Media Ltd.
Ed: Jacqueline Nelson. **Description:** Information about a two-year research project led by Southern Methodist University (SMU) and funded by the Defense Advance Research Projects Agency (DARPA) is provided. The agency aims to create a 'smart prosthetic' which will improve the lives of military amputees. The planned prosthetic will use a sensor that can carry nerve signals through synthetic channels.

33314 ■ ***"Real Estate Vets Take Times In Stride" in The Business Journal-Serving Metropolitan Kansas City (Vol. 26, July 25, 2008, No. 46)***
Pub: American City Business Journals, Inc.
Ed: Rob Roberts. **Description:** Kansas City, Missouri's real estate industry veterans like Allen Block believe that the challenges faced by the industry in the 1980s, when the Federal Reserve Board controlled the money supply to slow down inflation, were worse than the challenges faced today. Other views, trends and information on the real estate industry of the city, are presented.

33315 ■ ***"Recession Fears Power Gold" in Barron's (Vol. 88, March 17, 2008, No. 11, pp. M14)***
Pub: Dow Jones & Company, Inc.
Ed: Melanie Burton. **Description:** Gold prices have been more attractive as the U.S. dollar weakens and the Dow Jones Industrial Average has slipped almost 10 percent in 2008. The rate cuts from the Federal Reserve Board has also spurred inflation fears adding upward pressure to the price of the metal.

33316 ■ ***"Red Tape Ties Detroit Housing Rehab Plan" in Crain's Detroit Business (Vol. 24, September 22, 2008, No. 38, pp. 1)***
Pub: Crain Communications Inc.
Ed: Ryan Beene. **Description:** Venture-capital firm Wilherst Oxford LLC is a Florida-based company that has purchased 300 inner-city homes which were in foreclosure in Detroit. Wilherst Oxford is asking the city to forgive the existing tax and utility liens so the firm can utilize the money for home improvements. The city, however, is reluctant but has stated that they are willing to negotiate.

33317 ■ ***"Region to Be Named Innovation Hub" in Business Courier (Vol. 27, July 2, 2010, No. 9, pp. 1)***
Pub: Business Courier
Ed: Dan Monk. **Description:** The selection of Cincinnati's consumer-marketing cluster as a 'Hub of Innovation' by the Ohio Department of Development could boost Cincinnati's chances of receiving $100 million in grants from Ohio's Third Frontier program and other funding sources. Implications of the University of Cincinnati's designation as a Center of Excellence in Advanced Transportation and Aerospace are also discussed.

33318 ■ ***"Region Ready to Dig Deeper into Tech Fund" in Business Courier (Vol. 26, October 30, 2009, No. 27, pp. 1)***
Pub: American City Business Journals, Inc.
Ed: James Ritchie. **Description:** Southwest Ohio region aims for a bigger share in the planned renewal of Ohio's Third Frontier technology funding program. Meanwhile, University of Cincinnati vice president Sarah Degen will be appointed to the program's advisory board if the renewal proceeds.

33319 ■ ***"Rich or Poor, Hospitals Must Work Together" in Crain's Chicago Business (Vol. 31, April 28, 2008, No. 17, pp. 22)***
Pub: Crain Communications, Inc.
Description: Chicago=area safety-net hospitals that serve the poor, uninsured and underinsured are struggling to stay open while wealthier areas compete to build advanced facilities for the expensive surgical procedures their privately insured patients can afford. If these safety-net hospitals close, their patients, many of them in ambulances, will show up at the remaining hospitals resulting in a strain that will test the ability of hospitals across the region to care for all of their patients. Hospitals need to address the threats to the local health care system before it slips into crisis since the current every-hospital-for-itself approach that pays off big for some will eventually will make losers of everyone.

33320 ■ ***"RIM Reinforces Claim as Top Dog by Expanding BlackBerry" in Globe & Mail (March 11, 2006, pp. B3)***
Pub: CTVglobemedia Publishing Inc.
Ed: Simon Avery. **Description:** The plans of Research In Motion Ltd. to enhance the features of BlackBerry, through acquisition of Ascendent Systems, are presented.

33321 ■ ***"Rosewood Site Faces Big Cleanup" in Baltimore Business Journal (Vol. 27, February 6, 2010, No. 40, pp. 1)***
Pub: American City Business Journals
Ed: Daniel J. Sernovitz. **Description:** Environmental assessment report states that Maryland's Rosewood Center for the Developmentally Disabled has significant amounts of toxic chemicals, which could impact Stevenson University's decision to purchase the property. Senator Robert A. Zirkin believes that the state should pay for the cleanup, which is expected to cost millions.

33322 ■ ***"RT Seeking Ways to Finance Expansion" in Sacramento Business Journal (Vol. 28, July 29, 2011, No. 22, pp. 1)***
Pub: Sacramento Business Journal
Ed: Melanie Turner. **Description:** Sacramento Regional Transit District is considering ways to finance all its capital projects outlined in a 30-year transit master plan which would cost more than $7 billion to complete. Current funding sources include developer fees and state and federal assistance and fares. Part of the master plan is a light-rail line to Sacramento International Airport.

33323 ■ ***"S3 Entertainment Group Partners with WFW International for Film Services in Michigan" in Michigan Vue (July-August 2008)***
Pub: Entrepreneur Media Inc.
Description: William F. White (WFW), one of North America's largest production equipment providers has partnered with S3 Entertainment Group (S3EG), a Michigan-based full-service film production services company due to the new incentives package which currently offers the highest incentives in the United States, up to 42 percent. S3EG will actively store, lease, manage, distribute and sell WFW's equipment to the growing number of production teams that are filming in the state.

33324 ■ ***"A Safety Net in Need of Repair" in The Economist (Vol. 390, January 3, 2009, No. 8612, pp. 33)***
Pub: The Economist Newspaper Inc.
Description: America's unemployment-insurance scheme is outdated and skimpy compared to other industrialized countries despite the fact that Americans tend to work harder at returning to the job market; the benefits are lower and available for a smaller amount of time and less unemployed workers are even able to collect these benefits. Statistical data included.

33325 ■ ***"Samsung 'Holding Breath" in Austin Business JournalInc. (Vol. 29, January 29, 2010, No. 47, pp. 1)***
Pub: American City Business Journals
Ed: Jacob Dirr. **Description:** Samsung Austin Semiconductor LLC entered into an incentives agreement with the State of Texas in 2005, which involved $230 million in tax breaks and public financing. Terms of

the agreement have been met, but some are questioning whether the company will be able to meet its goals for the Austin operations in 2010.

33326 ■ *"SBA Can Improve Your Cash Flow" in Business Owner (Vol. 35, September-October 2011, No. 5, pp. 3)*
Pub: DL Perkins Company
Description: Federal assistance available to small business is examined. The Small Business Administration loan guarantee program is designed to improve availability and attractiveness of small business loans.

33327 ■ *"SBA Intervenes to Keep Cash Flowing" in Business First Columbus (Vol. 25, November 21, 2008, No. 14, pp. A1)*
Pub: American City Business Journals
Ed: Adrian Burns. **Description:** U.S. Small Business Administration's loan volumes fell as it tried to cushion the impact of the economic crisis on small businesses. Large investors have pulled back buying SBA loans due to declining profits, but demand for SBA loans are seen to resurge due to low risk.

33328 ■ *"SBA Lauds Anchorage DQ Franchise" in Alaska Business Monthly (Vol. 27, October 2011, No. 10, pp. 9)*
Pub: Alaska Business Publishing Company
Ed: Nancy Pounds. **Description:** US Small Business Administration (SBA) honored Greg Todd, operator of four DQ Grill and Chill eateries in Anchorage, Alaska. The firm has created 100 jobs since receiving SBA assistance.

33329 ■ *"SBA Lending Hits Record" in Saint Louis Business Journal (Vol. 32, September 30, 2011, No. 5, pp. 1)*
Pub: Saint Louis Business Journal
Ed: Rick Desloge. **Description:** US Small Business Administration loans have reached a record high of $200 million in 2011. The agency decreased the usual loan fees.

33330 ■ *"SBA Lending Jumps in May; Loan Guarantee Raised, Fee Axed" in Crain's Detroit Business (Vol. 25, June 8, 2009, No. 23, pp. 1)*
Pub: Crain Communications Inc. - Detroit
Ed: Nancy Kaffer. **Description:** U.S. Small Business Administration backed 102 loans through its 7(a) program in May. Statistical data included.

33331 ■ *"SBA Reinvigorates Loan Program" in Crain's Cleveland Business (Vol. 30, June 29, 2009, No. 25, pp. 1)*
Pub: Crain Communications, Inc.
Ed: Arielle Kass. **Description:** U.S. Small Business Administration has changed its loan programs that encourage banks to lend and businesses to borrow. Details of the program are discussed.

33332 ■ *"A Second Chance at Road Dollars" in Orlando Business Journal (Vol. 26, February 5, 2010, No. 36, pp. 1)*
Pub: American City Business Journals
Ed: Bill Orben. **Description:** Nearly $10 million worth of construction projects in Central Florida would give construction companies that missed the initial round of federal stimulus-funded local road building projects another opportunity. Cost savings in the initial round of road projects enabled Orange, Osceola, and Seminole Counties to secure additional projects.

33333 ■ *"Second to None" in Crain's Detroit Business (Vol. 26, January 18, 2010, No. 3, pp. 9)*
Pub: Crain Communications Inc.
Ed: Nancy Kaffer. **Description:** Second-stage companies are beginning to attract more attention from government entities and the business community alike, due in part to their ability to create jobs more rapidly than their counterparts both smaller and larger. Second-stage companies have between 10-99 employees and consistently have supplied the most jobs, despite overall job declines in recent years.

33334 ■ *"Seeking Local SBA Loan?" in Business Courier (Vol. 26, October 16, 2009, No. 25, pp. 1)*
Pub: American City Business Journals, Inc.
Ed: Steve Watkins. **Description:** The largest banks in Greater Cincinnati reduced Small Business Administration (SBA) lending by 41 percent for the fiscal year ended September 2009. For the year, local SBA loans from all banks in the area declined 25 percent. The importance of SBA loans for growth of small business is examined.

33335 ■ *"Sen. Mark Warner Holds a Hearing on Government Contracting Modernization" in Political/Congressional Transcript Wire (July 20, 2010)*
Pub: Roll Call CQ
Description: Senate Committee on the Budget, Task Force on Government Performance held a hearing on modernizing the business of government. Details of that hearing are included.

33336 ■ *"Should the Fed Regulate Wall Street?" in Barron's (Vol. 88, March 24, 2008, No. 12, pp. M15)*
Pub: Dow Jones & Company, Inc.
Ed: Randall W. Forsyth. **Description:** Greater regulation of the financial sector by the Federal Reserve is essential for it to survive the crisis it is experiencing. The resulting regulation could be in complete contrast with the deregulation the sector previously experienced.

33337 ■ *"Small-Business Agenda: Increase Capital, Education, Tax Breaks" in Crain's Detroit Business (Vol. 24, March 17, 2008)*
Pub: Crain Communications, Inc.
Ed: Nancy Kaffer. **Description:** Discusses the policy suggestions detailed in the Small Business Association of Michigan's entrepreneurial agenda which include five main categories of focus: making entrepreneurial education a higher state priority; increasing capital available to entrepreneurs; using the state's tax structure as an incentive for entrepreneurial growth; getting university research from the lab to the market; and limiting government regulation that's burdensome to small businesses and getting legislative support of entrepreneurial assistance efforts.

33338 ■ *The Small Business Guide to HSAs*
Pub: Brick Tower Press
Ed: JoAnn Mills Laing. **Released:** September 2004. **Price:** $14.95. **Description:** Government-assisted Health Savings Accounts (HSAs) offer employees a tax-free way to accumulate savings to be used for qualified medical expenses, they can be rolled over without penalty for future spending, or invested to accumulate savings to pay for health needs after retirement. Employers offering HSAs can save up to two-thirds of business expenses on health insurance costs.

33339 ■ *Small Business Loan Program Kit*
Pub: International Wealth Success, Inc.
Ed: Tyler G. Hicks. **Released:** 2006. **Price:** $100.00. **Description:** Guide to the Small Business Loan Program that offers loans to small and minority-owned companies doing work for government agencies, large corporations, hospitals, universities, and similar organizations.

33340 ■ *"Small Wind Power Market to Double by 2015 at $634 Million" in Western Farm Press (September 30, 2011)*
Pub: Penton Media, Inc.
Description: Small wind power provides cost-effective electricity on a highly localized level, in both remote settings as well as in conjunction with power from the utility grid. Government incentives are spurring new growth in the industry.

33341 ■ *"Soldiering On to Remake the SBA" in Inc. (February 2008, pp. 21)*
Pub: Gruner & Jahr USA Publishing
Description: Steven Preston discusses efforts to improve the Small Business Administration's processes to improve services to small businesses. Topics covered include customer service issues, loans, and fraud.

33342 ■ *"South Lake Hospital Starting $47M Patient Tower" in Orlando Business Journal (Vol. 26, December 4, 2009, No. 26, pp. 1)*
Pub: American City Business Journals
Ed: Melanie Stawicki Azam. **Description:** Clermont, Florida's South Lake Hospital has divulged intentions to issue $50.9 million in bonds in order to fund construction of the $47 million patient tower. The three-story, 124,000 square foot tower would add eighteen inpatient rooms, a new lobby and expanded pharmacy, diagnostic and lab services, and treatment areas.

33343 ■ *"Spending the Stimulus" in Crain's Cleveland Business (Vol. 30, June 29, 2009, No. 25, pp. 3)*
Pub: Crain Communications, Inc.
Ed: Dan Shingler. **Description:** Three of northeast Ohio's industrial firms will receive funding from the President's economic stimulus package. Eaton Corporation, Cleveland, Ohio; Parker Hannifin Corporation and Timken Company are expected to see higher revenues from the government spending plans.

33344 ■ *"Stains Still Set After SBA Scrub" in Black Enterprise (March 2008)*
Pub: Earl G. Graves Publishing Co. Inc.
Ed: Marcia A. Wade. **Description:** Small Business Administration's attempt to ensure that federal contracts were legitimately rewarded to small businesses, however the report filed showed that $4.6 billion in incorrectly coded contracts were removed from the SBA database. Critics contend the report is filled with inaccuracies. Statistical data included.

33345 ■ *"State Budget Woes Hurt Many Vendors, Senior Services" in Sacramento Business Journal (Vol. 25, August 15, 2008, No. 24, pp. 1)*
Pub: American City Business Journals, Inc.
Ed: Melanie Turner. **Description:** Delays in the passage of the California state budget have adversely affected the health care industry. The Robertson Adult Day Health Care had taken out loans to keep the business afloat. The state Legislature has reduced Medi-Cal reimbursement to health care providers by 10 percent.

33346 ■ *"State Expects Increase of $50 Million from Film Bills; Come Back, Al Roker" in Crain's Detroit Business (March 24, 2008)*
Pub: Crain Communications, Inc.
Ed: Bill Shea. **Description:** Overview of the new film initiative and its incentives designed to entice more film work to Michigan; the measures could bring $50 million to $100 million in movie production work for the rest of this year compared to the $4 million total the state saw last year. Also discusses the show 'DEA' which was filmed in Detroit and stars Al Roker.

33347 ■ *"State Investment Goes Sour" in Business Journal Portland (Vol. 26, December 4, 2009, No. 39, pp. 1)*
Pub: American City Business Journals Inc.
Ed: Erik Siemers. **Description:** Oregon might recoup only $500,000 of a $20 million loan to Vancouver-based Cascade Grain Products LLC. Cascade Grain's ethanol plant in Clatskanie, OR will be put into auction under the supervision of a bankruptcy court.

33348 ■ *"Stimulus Effect Slow" in Baltimore Business Journal (Vol. 27, October 23, 2009, No. 24, pp. 1)*
Pub: American City Business Journals
Ed: Scott Dance. **Description:** Companies in Maryland have reported only 154 new jobs being created or saved in Greater Baltimore and 965 jobs overall in the state because of stimulus cash. The federal stimulus program was expected to create thousands of new jobs but statistics show its failure to reduce unemployment in the state.

33349 ■ *"Stimulus 'Loser' Won't Build Plant in Mass." in Boston Business Journal (Vol. 30, November 5, 2010, No. 41, pp. 1)*
Pub: Boston Business Journal
Ed: Kyle Alspach. **Description:** Boston-Power Inc. no longer plans to build an electric vehicle battery plant in Massachusetts after it failed to obtain

stimulus funds from the federal government. The company is instead looking to build a lithium-ion battery plant in China and possibly Europe.

33350 ■ *"Struggling Community Banks Find Little Help In Wall Street Bailout" in Crain's Detroit Business (Vol. 24, September 29, 2008)*
Pub: Crain Communications Inc.
Ed: Tom Henderson. **Description:** Both public and private Michigan bands have been hit hard by poorly performing loan portfolios and although their problems were not caused by high-risk securities but by a longtime statewide recession and a housing slump, these community banks have little hope of seeing any of the bailout money that has been allotted for the larger institutions.

33351 ■ *"Struggling States Slashing Health Care For Poor" in Chicago Tribune (January 15, 2009)*
Pub: McClatchy-Tribune Information Services
Ed: Noam N. Levey. **Description:** Health officials warn that even the huge federal rescue plan may not be enough to restore health services being eliminated due to the economic crisis.

33352 ■ *"Sunwest Vies To Stave Off Bankruptcy" in The Business Journal-Portland (Vol. 25, August 15, 2008, No. 23, pp. 1)*
Pub: American City Business Journals, Inc.
Ed: Robin J. Moody. **Description:** Sunwest Management Inc. is teetering on the edge of bankruptcy as creditors start foreclosure on nine of their properties. This could potentially displace residents of the assisted living operator. Sunwest is trying to sell smaller packages of properties to get a $100 million bridge loan to maintain operations.

33353 ■ *"The Surplus Shell Game" in Canadian Business (Vol. 80, March 12, 2007, No. 6, pp. 72)*
Pub: Rogers Media
Description: The effort of successive federal governments in Canada to ensure budget surpluses and its impact on the economy are discussed.

33354 ■ *"Survey: Don't Expect Big Results From Stimulus" in Crain's Detroit Business (Vol. 25, June 1, 2009, No. 22)*
Pub: Crain Communications Inc. - Detroit
Ed: Nancy Kaffer, Chad Halcom. **Description:** In a recent survey, Michigan business owners, operators or managers showed that 48 percent of respondents oppose the President's stimulus package and believe it will have little or no effect on the economy.

33355 ■ *"Suspense Hangs Over Fledging Film Industry" in Crain's Detroit Business (Vol. 26, January 18, 2010, No. 3, pp. 3)*
Pub: Crain Communications Inc.
Ed: Bill Shea. **Description:** Overview of the film incentive package which has fostered a growth in the industry with 52 productions completed in 2009, bringing in $223.6 million in gross in-state production expenditures of which the state will refund $87.2 million. Opposition to the incentives has been growing among legislatures who believe that the initiatives cost more than they ultimately bring into the state. Experts believe that the initiatives will remain since they have already fostered economic growth and are good for the state's image.

33356 ■ *"Tax Credit Crunch" in Miami Daily Business Review (March 26, 2008)*
Pub: ALM Media Inc.
Ed: Paula Iuspa-Abbott. **Description:** Uncertainty is growing over the future of the low-income housing project in South Florida and the tax credit program that helps fuel the projects.

33357 ■ *"Taxpayers' Banks Share Even Higher" in Business Courier (Vol. 24, October 26, 2008, No. 28, pp. 1)*
Pub: American City Business Journals, Inc.
Ed: Dan Monk; Lucy May. **Description:** Banks Working Group originally announced that it needs $106 million in public funds to build the Banks riverfront development but then declared it needs $45 million more from Cincinnati and Hamilton County after it approved a deal for the project. It would not be easy for the city and the county to come up with the money but many decision-makers think it's worth it.

33358 ■ *"Taylor Tests Land Grant Program" in Austin Business Journal (Vol. 31, June 3, 2011, No. 13, pp. 1)*
Pub: American City Business Journals Inc.
Ed: Vicky Garza. **Description:** Taylor Economic Development Corporation implemented a land grant program called Build On Our Lot to lure businesses to Taylor City, Austin, Texas. They are targeting small businesses, especially those in the renewable energy, advanced manufacturing, technical services and food products. Program details are included.

33359 ■ *"Tempel Steel To Expand Its Chicago Plant" in Chicago Tribune (August 22, 2008)*
Pub: McClatchy-Tribune Information Services
Ed: James P. Miller. **Description:** Tempel Steel Co. is no longer considering transferring a Libertyville factory's production to Mexico; the company has responded to government incentives and will instead shift that work to its plant on Chicago's North Side.

33360 ■ *"Testing Firm to Add Jobs" in Business Courier (Vol. 26, December 11, 2009, No. 33, pp. 1)*
Pub: American City Business Journals, Inc.
Ed: Dan Monk. **Description:** Cincinnati-based Q Laboratories announced plans to add dozens of jobs with the $1.6 million stimulus assisted expansion. The company hired Michael Lichtenberg & Sons Construction Co. to build a new 9,000 square foot laboratory building.

33361 ■ *"This Just In" in Crain's Detroit Business (Vol. 25, June 1, 2009, No. 22, pp. 1)*
Pub: Crain Communications Inc. - Detroit
Description: Three veterans of the auto industry have partnered to create, Revitalizing Michigan, a nonprofit dedicated to help manufacturers improve their processes. The firm is seeking federal, state and private grants to fund the mission.

33362 ■ *"This Just In. State House Introduces Film-Industry Stimulus Bills" in Crain's Detroit Business (Vol. 24, March 3, 2008, No. 9)*
Pub: Crain Communications Inc. - Detroit
Description: House Bills 5841-5856 would give Michigan the most competitive incentives in the U.S. to encourage projects by film industry. Provisions of the bill are outlined.

33363 ■ *"Tied to Home: Female Owned Businesses Export Less, And It's Not Just Because They're Smaller" in Canadian Business (April 14, 2008)*
Pub: Rogers Media
Ed: Lauren McKeon. **Description:** Only 12 percent of small and midsized enterprises that are run by women export their products and services. Government agencies can be more proactive in promoting the benefits of exporting by including women in case studies and recruiting women as mentors. Exporting provides great growth potential especially for the service sector where women have an advantage.

33364 ■ *"TMC Development Closes $1.1 Million Real Estate Purchase" in Internet Wire (September 17, 2009)*
Pub: Comtex News Network, Inc.
Description: TMC Development announced the closing of a $1.1 million real estate purchase for Mansa, LLC dba Kwikee Mart, a Napa-based convenience store; TMC helped the company secure a Small Business Administration 504 loan in order to purchase the acquisition of a 3,464 square foot building. SBA created the 504 loan program to provide financing for growing small and medium-sized businesses.

33365 ■ *"Today's Business Sale Climate" in Business Owner (Vol. 35, September-October 2011, No. 5, pp. 10)*
Pub: DL Perkins Company
Description: Despite the weak economy, there is a surplus of individuals wanting to purchase a small business. The Small Business Administration loan guarantees program helps with its loans for purchase/ sale of business assistance.

33366 ■ *"Top Private Companies" in Baltimore Business Journal (Vol. 28, August 27, 2010, No. 16, pp. 1)*
Pub: Baltimore Business Journal
Ed: Gary Haber. **Description:** The combined revenue of the 100 largest private firms in Maryland's Baltimore region dropped from about $22.7 billion in 2008 to $21 billion in 2009, an annual decrease of more than 7 percent. To survive the recession's impact, these firms resorted to strategies such as government contracting and overseas expansion. How these strategies affected the revenue of some firms is described.

33367 ■ *"Triad, Fortune Dump TARP Cut Costs, Boost Lending" in Saint Louis Business Journal (Vol. 32, October 7, 2011, No. 6, pp. 1)*
Pub: Saint Louis Business Journal
Ed: Greg Edwards. **Description:** St. Louis, Missouri-based Triad Bank and Fortune Bank have been using an alternative federal loan program to pay back financing from the Troubled Asset Relief Program. Triad got a $5 million loan at one percent interest rate from the US Small Business Lending Fund.

33368 ■ *"Turbulent Skies" in The Business Journal-Portland (Vol. 25, August 29, 2008, No. 25, pp. 1)*
Pub: American City Business Journals, Inc.
Ed: Erik Siemers. **Description:** Small airlines are struggling to keep their commercial services amid the troubled commercial airline sector. Small communities, for example, were expected to pony up about $650,000 in revenue guarantees each in order to convince SkyWest Airlines to offer two direct flights to Portland daily beginning October 12, 2008. The trends in the commercial airline industry are analyzed.

33369 ■ *"U-Swirl Added to SBA's Franchise Registry" in Ice Cream Reporter (Vol. 23, September 20, 2010, No. 10, pp. 1)*
Pub: Ice Cream Reporter
Description: Healthy Fast Food Inc., parent to the U-SWIRL Frozen Yogurt cafe chain announced that the U.S. Small Business Administration listed U-SWIRL Frozen Yogurt on its official franchise registry. This move will allow U-SWIRL the benefits of a streamlined review process for SBA financing.

33370 ■ *"UC Lobbies for Big Chunk of New Funds" in Business Courier (Vol. 24, February 22, 2008, No. 46, pp. 1)*
Pub: American City Business Journals, Inc.
Ed: Laura Baverman. **Description:** Discusses the University of Cincinnati (UC) which has requested $192 million funding from the Ohio Innovation Partnership. The program was launched by governor Stickland in an attempt to drive research and innovation in the studies of biotechnology, aeronautics, and other fields that reflects Ohio's strengths. Details of UC's grant proposals are supplied.

33371 ■ *"Union, Heal Thyself" in Canadian Business (Vol. 81, July 21, 2008, No. 11, pp. 9)*
Pub: Rogers Media Ltd.
Description: General Motors Corp. was offered by the federal government a $250 million fund after the company declared plans to close its facility in Ontario. The government move is geared towards supporting the workers who have refused to support the automotive company. Details of the labor contract between General Motors and the Canadian Auto Workers are presented.

33372 ■ *"Unions Pony Up $1 Million for McBride Stimulus" in Saint Louis Business Journal (Vol. 31, July 29, 2011, No. 49, pp. 1)*
Pub: Saint Louis Business Journal
Ed: Evan Binns. **Description:** Carpenters District Council of Greater St. Louis and International Brotherhood of Electrical Workers Local 1 were among the nine unions that agreed to split the cost of

nearly $1 million in incentives for homebuyers who purchase homes in McBride communities. McBride & Son has spent over $100,000 to promote the incentive program.

33373 ■ *"U.S. Attorney Post the Latest Twist" in The Business Journal-Serving Greater Tampa Bay (Vol. 28, July 25, 2008, No. 31, pp. 1)*
Pub: American City Business Journals, Inc.
Ed: Jane Meinhardt. **Description:** Tampa, Florida-based lawyer A. Brian Albritton has been nominated to be the U.S. Attorney for the Middle District of Florida. He is an expert in cases involving white-collar crime, secret theft, noncompete agreements, and other agreements.

33374 ■ *"US Cavalry Store" in Retail Merchandiser (Vol. 51, September-October 2011, No. 5, pp. 70)*
Pub: Phoenix Media Corporation
Description: US Cavalry Store serves enlisted military members. The store has launched a newly upgraded Website and has expanded its distribution center.

33375 ■ *"Valenti: Roots of Financial Crisis Go Back to 1998" in Crain's Detroit Business (Vol. 24, October 6, 2008, No. 40, pp. 25)*
Pub: Crain Communications, Inc.
Ed: Tom Henderson; Nathan Skid. **Description:** Interview with Sam Valenti III who is the chairman and CEO of Valenti Capital L.L.C., a wealth-management firm; Valenti discusses in detail the history that led up to the current economic crisis as well as his prediction for the future of the country.

33376 ■ *"Vanity Plates" in Canadian Business (Vol. 82, April 27, 2009, No. 7, pp. 26)*
Pub: Rogers Media
Ed: Andy Holloway. **Description:** Politicians in the U.S. called for the review of firms that availed of the bailout money but are under deals for naming rights of sports stadiums. Angus Reid's Corporate Reputation and Sponsorship Index found for example, that there is little correlation between sponsoring arenas on having a better brand image. It is suggested that firms who enter these deals build closer to people's homes.

33377 ■ *"Venture Capital's Capital Infusion: Federal Incentives Mean More Money for VC Firms" in Entrepreneur (August 2009)*
Pub: Entrepreneur Media, Inc.
Ed: Carol Tice. **Description:** American Recovery and Reinvestment Act of 2009 changed the rules for the Small Business Investment Corporations (SBIC) program under the Small Business Authority. The rule changes are meant to put more money from the program into circulation and it increases funding to existing SBICs.

33378 ■ *"Venture Capital's Capital Infusion: Federal Incentives Mean More Money for VC Firms" in Entrepreneur (Vol. 37, August 2009)*
Pub: Entrepreneur Media, Inc.
Ed: Carol Tice. **Description:** American Recovery and Reinvestment Act of 2009 changed the rules for the Small Business Investment Corporations (SBIC) program under the Small Business Authority. The rule changes are meant to put more money from the program into circulation and it increases funding to existing SBICs.

33379 ■ *"VPA to Pay $9.5 Million to Settle Whistle-Blower Lawsuits" in Crain's Detroit Business (Vol. 26, January 11, 2010, No. 2, pp. 13)*
Pub: Crain Communications Inc.
Ed: Jay Greene. **Description:** According to Terrence Berg, first assistant with the U.S. Attorney's Office in Detroit, Voluntary Physicians Association, a local home health care company, has agreed to pay $9.5 million to settle four whistle-blower lawsuits; the agreement settles allegations that VPA submitted claims to TriCare, the Michigan Medicaid program and Medicare for unnecessary home visits, tests and procedures.

33380 ■ *"Walker Seeks More Business Participation" in Business Journal-Milwaukee (Vol. 28, December 10, 2010, No. 10, pp. A1)*
Pub: Milwaukee Business Journal
Ed: Rich Kirchen. **Description:** Wisconsin governor Scott Walker is seeking the aid of Milwaukee business leaders to participate in resolving the challenges posed by the economic crisis. Walker is aiming to create 250,000 jobs. He is also planning to call a special session of the legislature to enact strategies to jumpstart the economy.

33381 ■ *"Weighing the Write-Off" in Baltimore Business Journal (Vol. 28, September 10, 2010, No. 18, pp. 1)*
Pub: Baltimore Business Journal
Ed: Daniel J. Sernovitz. **Description:** President Barrack Obama has proposed to let business write off their investments in plant and equipment upgrades under a plan aimed at getting the economy going. The plan would allow a company to write off 100 percent of the depreciation for their new investments at one time instead of over several years.

33382 ■ *"What Are Your Party's Legislative Priorities for 2008?" in Hawaii Business (Vol. 53, January 2008, No. 7, pp. 22)*
Pub: Hawaii Business Publishing
Description: Discusses the Democratic Party of Hawaii which will prioritize giving more opportunities to earn a living a wage in 2008, according to the party chairwoman Jeani Withington. The Republican Party chairman Willes K. Lee, meanwhile, states that his party will seek to enhance the local business climate. The political parties' plans for Hawaii for the year 2008 are presented in detail.

33383 ■ *"What's Ahead for Fannie and Fred?" in Barron's (Vol. 90, August 30, 2010, No. 35, pp. 26)*
Pub: Barron's Editorial & Corporate Headquarters
Ed: Jonathan R. Laing. **Description:** A meeting presided by Treasury Secretary Timothy Geithner discussed the future of Fannie Mae and Freddie Mac. The two government sponsored enterprises were mismanaged and reforming these two agencies is critical.

33384 ■ *"Whistling in the Dark" in Canadian Business (Vol. 79, September 25, 2006, No. 19, pp. 17)*
Pub: Rogers Media
Ed: Jack Mintz. **Description:** Increasing subsidies for research projects in Canada is discussed.

33385 ■ *"Whistling Past the Graveyard?" in Barron's (Vol. 88, March 17, 2008, No. 11, pp. 15)*
Pub: Dow Jones & Company, Inc.
Ed: Michael Santoli. **Description:** Discusses the Federal Reserve's move to provide $200 billion to the system which can be seen as an effort to avoid the liquidity problems that Bear Stearns suffered. The Federal Reserve's move seems to frighten investors rather than reassure them.

33386 ■ *"Will Focus on Business Continue?" in Baltimore Business Journal (Vol. 28, November 5, 2010, No. 26, pp. 1)*
Pub: Baltimore Business Journal
Ed: Scott Dance. **Description:** The 2010 election may call for new efforts to teach new lawmakers to assure that the viewpoints of businesses are considered and accurately delivered. The Greater Baltimore Committee and similar groups have gathered reports on the competitiveness of Maryland and are planning to use them to make a case of keeping business a top priority.

33387 ■ *"Will Small Business be Stimulated" in Entrepreneur (Vol. 37, July 2009, No. 7, pp. 18)*
Pub: Entrepreneur Media, Inc.
Ed: Jennifer Wang. **Description:** Steven Strauss, Alberto G. Alvarado, Jeff Rosenweig, Al Gordon, and Theresa Alfaro Daytner share their views on how the American Recovery and Reinvestment Act of 2009, also known as the economic stimulus, will affect small businesses. Their backgrounds are also provided.

33388 ■ *"Winburn's Big Idea" in Business Courier (Vol. 27, October 8, 2010, No. 23, pp. 1)*
Pub: Business Courier
Ed: Dan Monk, Lucy May. **Description:** Cincinnati Councilman Charlie Winburn proposed the creation of Cincinnati Competitive Edge Division and to remake a small-business division of the city in order to start a job-creation program. The new division will monitor compliance to the city's small business inclusion regulations, as well as to help small business owners grow.

33389 ■ *"Young-Kee Kim; Deputy Director, Fermi National Accelerator Laboratory" in Crain's Chicago Business (Vol. 31, May 5, 2008, No. 18)*
Pub: Crain Communications, Inc.
Ed: Phuong Ly. **Description:** Profile of Young-Kee Kim who is the deputy director of Fermilab, a physics lab where scientists study the smallest particles in the universe; Ms. Kim was a researcher at Fermilab before becoming deputy director two years ago; Fermilab is currently home to the most powerful particle accelerator in the world and is struggling to compete with other countries despite cuts in federal funding.

RESEARCH CENTERS

33390 ■ Center for International Private Enterprise (CIPE)—Centre International pour l'Entreprise Privée
1155 15th St. NW, Ste. 700
Washington, DC 20005
Ph: (202)721-9200
Fax: (202)721-9250
Co. E-mail: cipe@cipe.org
URL: http://www.cipe.org
Contact: John D. Sullivan, Executive Director
Founded: 1983. **Publications:** *Economic Reform Feature Service.* **Educational Activities:** Training program for Business Association Management.

ASSOCIATIONS AND OTHER ORGANIZATIONS

33391 ■ Coalition for Government Procurement (CGP)
1990 M St. NW, Ste. 450
Washington, DC 20036-3466
Ph: (202)331-0975
Fax: (202)822-9788
Co. E-mail: rwaldron@thecgp.org
URL: http://netforum.avectra.com
Contact: Roger Waldron, President
E-mail: rwaldron@thecgp.org
URL(s): thecgp.org/, www.netforumondemand.com. **Description:** Represents large and small businesses interested in commercial product procurement issues. Works to help protect the interests of federal government commercial product suppliers; to monitor commercial product legislation, policies, regulations and procurement trends of federal agencies. Provides members with current information, changes and developments in procurement policies and their impact. Conducts phone consultations. **Founded:** 1979. **Publications:** *Off the Shelf* (Monthly). **Awards:** Excellence in Partnership Award (Annual). **Telecommunication Services:** info@netforumondemand.com; info@thecgp.org.

33392 ■ National Contract Management Association
21740 Beaumeade Cir., Ste. 125
Ashburn, VA 20147
Ph: (571)382-0082
Free: 800-344-8096
Fax: (703)448-0939
Co. E-mail: wearelistening@ncmahq.org
URL: http://www.ncmahq.org
Contact: Charles D. Chadwick, President
Description: Professional individuals concerned with administration, procurement, acquisition, negotiation and management of contracts and subcontracts. Works for the education, improvement and professional development of members and nonmembers through national and chapter programs, symposia and educational materials. Offers certification in Contract Management (CPCM, CFCM, and CCCM) designations as well as a credential program. Operates speakers' bureau. **Publications:** *National Contract Management Journal* (Annual); *Contract Management* (Monthly); *Journal of Contract Management* (Annual); *Contract Management*; *Journal of Contract Management* (Annual). **Awards:** James E. Cravens Membership Award (Annual); National Achievement Award (Annual); Outstanding Fellow Award (Annual); James E. Cravens Membership Award; Outstanding Fellow Award; Staff Achievement Award.

EDUCATIONAL PROGRAMS

33393 ■ Advanced Writing and Editing for Government Proposals
EEI Communications
8945 Guilford Rd., Ste. 145
Columbia, MD 21046
Ph: (410)309-8200
Free: 888-253-2762
Fax: (410)630-3980
Co. E-mail: train@eeicom.com
URL: http://www.eeicom.com/eei-training-services
Price: $745.00. **Description:** Developed for anyone who regularly writes, edits, or manages government proposals to explore proposal-specific writing and editing challenges, including how to ensure consistent voice no matter how many writers are involved. **Dates and Locations:** Alexandria, VA.

33394 ■ Basics of Government Contract Administration (Onsite)
Seminar Information Service, Inc.
20 Executive Park, Ste. 120
Irvine, CA 92614
Ph: (949)261-9104
Free: 877-SEM-INFO
Fax: (949)261-1963
Co. E-mail: info@seminarinformation.com
URL: http://www.seminarinformation.com
Price: $1,025.00. **Description:** Designed to show you how to fill out the most common standard forms, where the forms are found, and how proper forms preparation avoids administration pitfalls. **Dates and Locations:** Arlington, VA; and Norfolk, VA.

33395 ■ Fundamentals of Buying and Selling Energy (Onsite)
Seminar Information Service, Inc.
20 Executive Park, Ste. 120
Irvine, CA 92614
Ph: (949)261-9104
Free: 877-SEM-INFO
Fax: (949)261-1963
Co. E-mail: info@seminarinformation.com
URL: http://www.seminarinformation.com
Price: $1,350.00; $1,250.00 member/government/non-profit.. **Description:** Covers the full spectrum of topics essential to the energy procurement process, covering both electricity and natural gas from both a purchasing/procurement and a selling/marketing perspective. **Dates and Locations:** Atlanta, GA.

33396 ■ Government Contract Accounting (Onsite)
Seminar Information Service, Inc.
20 Executive Park, Ste. 120
Irvine, CA 92614
Ph: (949)261-9104
Free: 877-SEM-INFO
Fax: (949)261-1963
Co. E-mail: info@seminarinformation.com
URL: http://www.seminarinformation.com
Price: $1,025.00. **Description:** Accounting principles as they relate to procurement activities with the Federal Government, with focus on Government forms and formats, direct and indirect cost rate submissions, cost principles, dealing with Government auditors, changes and delay claims and terminations. **Dates and Locations:** Las Vegas, NV.

33397 ■ Government Proposal Writing Basics
EEI Communications
8945 Guilford Rd., Ste. 145
Columbia, MD 21046
Ph: (410)309-8200
Free: 888-253-2762
Fax: (410)630-3980
Co. E-mail: train@eeicom.com
URL: http://www.eeicom.com/eei-training-services
Price: $745.00. **Description:** Designed for proposal novices at any level of writing ability, this course explains the unique features of government proposals and the government procurement process. **Dates and Locations:** Alexandria, VA.

REFERENCE WORKS

33398 ■ *"$161.9M 'Pit Stop' Fix-Up Will Create About 1,600 Jobs" in Orlando Business Journal (Vol. 26, January 22, 2010, No. 34, pp. 1)*
Pub: American City Business Journals
Ed: Anjali Fluker. **Description:** State of Florida will be providing $161.9 million to renovate eight service plazas starting November 2010. The project is expected to create 1,600 jobs across the state and is expected to be completed by 2012. Details on bid advertisements and facilities slated for improvement are discussed.

33399 ■ *"AG Warns Slots MBE Plan Risky" in Boston Business Journal (Vol. 29, May 27, 2011, No. 3, pp. 1)*
Pub: American City Business Journals Inc.
Ed: Scott Dance. **Description:** Attorney General Doug Gansler states that the law extending the minority business program on slots parlors contracting through 2018 could be open to lawsuits. He recommended that the state should conduct a study proving that minority- and women-owned businesses do not get a fair share in the gaming industry before it signs the bill to avoid lawsuits from majority-owned firms.

33400 ■ *"Airmall Mulls I-95 Travel Plazas Bid" in Boston Business Journal (Vol. 29, September 2, 2011, No. 17, pp. 3)*
Pub: American City Business Journals Inc.
Ed: Alexander Jackson. **Description:** Airmall USA is planning to move its food courts from the Baltimore/Washington International Thurgood Marshall Airport to the new travel plazas on Interstate 95. The plazas are up for bid.

33401 ■ *"Annapolis Seeks City Market Vendors" in Boston Business Journal (Vol. 29, June 10, 2011, No. 5, pp. 3)*
Pub: American City Business Journals Inc.
Ed: Daniel J. Sernovitz. **Description:** The city of Annapolis, Maryland is planning to revive the historical landmark Market House and it is now accepting bids from vendors until June 10, 2011. The city hopes to reopen the facility by July 2011 for a six-month period after which it will undergo renovations.

33402 ■ *"Apples, Decoded: WSU Scientist Unraveling the Fruit's Genetics" in Puget Sound Business Journal (Vol. 29, September 5, 2008, No. 20)*
Pub: American City Business Journals
Ed: Clay Holtzman. **Description:** Washington State University researcher is working to map the apple's genome in order to gain information about how the fruit grows, looks and tastes. His work, funded by a research grant from the US Department of Agriculture and the Washington Apple Commission is crucial to improving the state's position as an apple-producing region.

33403 ■ *Are Government Purchasing Policies Failing Small Business?: Congressional Hearing*
Pub: DIANE Publishing Company
Ed: John F. Kerry. **Released:** September 2002. **Price:** Paperback $35.00. **Description:** Covers Congressional hearing: Steven App, Treasury Department; Fred Armendariz and Major Clark, Small Business Administration; Susan Allen, Pan Asian American Chamber of Commerce; Stephen Denlinger, Latin American Management Association; Charles Henry, National Veteran's Business Development Corporation; Morris Hudson, MO Procurement Technology Assistance Centers; Bar Kasoff, Women Impact, Public Policy; Pam Mazza, Piliero, Massa and Pargament; Ron Newlan, HubZone Contract National Council; Pat Parker, Native American Management Service; Joann Payne, Women First National Legislative Commission; Mike Robinson, MA Small Business Development Centers; Ramon Rodriguez, Hispanic Chamber of Commerce; Angela Styles, Office of Management and Budget; Ralph Thomas, NASA; John Turner, MN Business Enterprise Legal Defense Fund; James Turpin, American Subcontractor's Association, Inc.; and Henry Wilfong, National Association of Small Disadvantaged Business.

33404 ■ *"Auto Bankruptcies Could Weaken Defense" in Crain's Detroit Business (Vol. 25, June 8, 2009, No. 23, pp. 1)*
Pub: Crain Communications Inc. - Detroit
Ed: Chad Halcom. **Description:** Bankruptcy and supplier consolidation of General Motors Corporation and Chrysler LLC could interfere with the supply chains of some defense contractors, particularly makers of trucks and smaller vehicles.

33405 ■ *"Behind the Scenes: Companies at the Heart of Everyday Life" in Inc. (March 2008, pp. 34-35)*
Pub: Gruner & Jahr USA Publishing
Ed: Athena Schindelheim. **Description:** Profiles of companies used to improve road conditions at the Bedford, New Hampshire Toll Plaza are presented. General Traffic Equipment provides LED traffic lights; TRMI, provided 8-foot strips treadles that count the number of axles that drive over them; E-Z Pass system is an antenna from Mark IV Industries that uses radio-frequency identification (RFID) technology to scan a small device attached to a car's windshield; and Transport Data Systems installed cameras that snap photos of passengers and license plates in order to catch individuals who try to dodge fees.

33406 ■ *"Capital Metro May Soon Seek Contractor to Replace Star Tran" in Austin Business Journal (Vol. 31, June 10, 2011, No. 14, pp. 1)*
Pub: American City Business Journals Inc.
Ed: Vicky Garza. **Description:** Capital Metropolitan Transportation Authority may be forced to contract out its bus services provided by StarTran Inc. as early as September 2012 following legislation approved by the Texas legislature. The bill originates in a report by the Sunset Advisory Commission. Details are included.

33407 ■ *"Centerra Caught in Kyrgyzstan Dispute" in Globe & Mail (April 19, 2007, pp. B5)*
Pub: CTVglobemedia Publishing Inc.
Ed: Andy Hoffman. **Description:** The details of the demonstrations carried against government proposal to nationalize Centerra Gold Inc.'s assets are presented.

33408 ■ *"CEO Forecast" in Hispanic Business (January-February 2009, pp. 34, 36)*
Pub: Hispanic Business
Ed: Jessica Haro, Richard Kaplan. **Description:** As economic uncertainty fogs the future, executives turn to government contracts in order to boost business. Revenue sources, health care challenges, environmental consulting and remediation services, as well as technological strides are discussed.

33409 ■ *"City Seeks More Minorities" in Austin Business JournalInc. (Vol. 28, November 7, 2008, No. 34, pp. A1)*
Pub: American City Business Journals
Ed: Jean Kwon. **Description:** Austin, Texas is planning to increase the participation of minority- and women-owned businesses in government contracts. Contractors are required to show 'good faith' to comply with the specified goals. The city is planning to effect the changes in the construction and professional services sector.

33410 ■ *"Combat Mission: Rebuffed, BAE Systems Fights Army Contract Decision" in Business Courier (Vol. 26, September 25, 2009)*
Pub: American City Business Journals, Inc.
Ed: Jon Newberry. **Description:** BAE Systems filed a complaint with the US Government Accountability Office after the US Army issued an order to BAE's competitor for armoured trucks which is potentially worth over $3 billion. Hundreds of jobs in Butler County, Ohio hinge on the success of the contract protest.

33411 ■ *"Complete Discovery Source, Inc. (CDS) Receives Minority Owned Business Certification" in Internet Wire (December 14, 2010)*
Pub: Comtex
Description: Complete Discovery Source Inc. (CDS) was granted Minority-Owned Business Enterprise status by the New York State Department of Economic Development. The certification provides CDS, an end-to-end eDiscovery services provider, with access to contracting opportunities with 130 government agencies throughout New York state.

33412 ■ *"Construction Firms Support NAACP Plan" in Business Courier (Vol. 27, September 24, 2010, No. 21, pp. 1)*
Pub: Business Courier
Ed: Lucy May. **Description:** Executives of Turner Construction Company and Messer Construction Company expressed their support for the Cincinnati National Association for the Advancement of Colored People Construction Partnership Agreement. The agreement involves the setting of rules for the involvement of firms owned by African Americans in major projects in Cincinnati.

33413 ■ *Contractor's Directory*
Pub: Government Data Publications Inc.
Contact: Siegfried Lobel, President
URL(s): www.govdata.com. **Released:** Annual; February. **Price:** $49.50, Diskette edition; $15; $49.50, CD-ROM. **Covers:** Contractors who have received government contract under Public Law 95-507, which requires preferential treatment of small business for subcontracts. **Entries include:** Contractor name and address. Supplementary to 'Small Business Preferential Subcontracts Opportunities Monthly,' which lists companies with government contracts over $500,000 ($1,000,000 for construction) (see separate entry). **Arrangement:** Same information given alphabetically and by ZIP code.

33414 ■ *"Contractors Scramble for Jobs" in Business Journal Portland (Vol. 26, December 18, 2009, No. 41, pp. 1)*
Pub: American City Business Journals Inc.
Ed: Andy Giegerich. **Description:** Contractors in Portland area are expected to bid for capital construction projects that will be funded by municipalities in the said area. Contracts for companies that work on materials handling, road improvement, and public safety structure projects will be issued.

33415 ■ *"Corner Office" in Hispanic Business (December 2010)*
Pub: Hispanic Business
Ed: Jesus Chavarria. **Description:** The gap opens up between government contracts and small businesses. The state of minority enterprise development in federal markets as well as other levels of government throughout the U.S. is examined.

33416 ■ *"County Limited in Awarding Contracts" in Crain's Cleveland Business (Vol. 30, June 15, 2009, No. 23, pp. 8)*
Pub: Crain Communications, Inc.
Description: Cuyahoga County government has been accused of not offering fair levels of county-issued contracts to minority-owned companies.

33417 ■ *"DCAA-Compliant Accounting Solution Provider Intros Redesign of Website at sympaq.com" in Entertainment Close-Up (April 18, 2011)*
Pub: Close-Up Media
Description: Aldebaron Inc., developer of DCAA-compliant accounting solution SYMPAQ SQL, launched a new Website that will assist government contractors access information about their products and services.

33418 ■ *"Decorated Marine Sues Contractor" in Wall Street Journal Eastern Edition (November 29, 2011, pp. A4)*
Pub: Dow Jones & Company Inc. Enterprise Media Group
Contact: Clare Hart, President
Ed: Julian E. Barnes. **Description:** Marine Devon Maylie, who was awarded the Congressional Medal of Honor for bravery, has filed a lawsuit against defense contractor BAE Systems PLC claiming that the company prevented his hiring by another firm by saying he has a mental condition and a drinking problem. Maylie says that this was in retaliation for his objections to the company's plan to sell the Pakistani military high-tech sniper scopes.

33419 ■ *e-Business, e-Government and Small and Medium-Size Enterprises: Opportunities and Challenges*
Pub: Idea Group Publishing
Ed: Brian J. Corbitt, Nabeel A.Y. Al-Qirim. **Released:** February 2004. **Price:** $64.95. **Description:** Electronic commerce and information technology research in small and medium-sized enterprises (SMEs). Policymakers, legislators, researchers and professionals address significant issues of importance to the small business sector.

33420 ■ *"El Paso Firm Rides Boom to the Top" in Hispanic Business (Vol. 30, July-August 2008, No. 7-8, pp. 28)*
Pub: Hispanic Business, Inc.
Ed: Jeremy Nisen. **Description:** VEMAC, a commercial construction management and general contracting firm that is experiencing success despite the plummeting construction market is discussed. VEMAC's success is attributed to the Pentagons' $5 billion investment in construction for the benefit of new personnel and their families to be transferred to Fort Bliss, a U.S. army base adjacent to El Paso.

33421 ■ *Electronic Commerce: Technical, Business, and Legal Issues*
Pub: Prentice Hall PTR
Ed: Oktay Dogramaci; Aryya Gangopadhyay; Yelena Yesha; Nabil R. Adam. **Released:** August 1998. **Description:** Provides insight into the goals of using the Internet to grow a business in the areas of networking and telecommunication, security, and storage and retrieval; business areas such as marketing, procurement and purchasing, billing and payment, and supply chain management; and legal aspects such as privacy, intellectual property, taxation, contractual and legal settlements.

33422 ■ *"Eminent Domain Fight Looks Imminent" in The Business Journal-Serving Metropolitan Kansas City (Vol. 26, August 1,*

2008, No. 47)
Pub: American City Business Journals, Inc.
Ed: Rob Roberts. **Description:** Views and information on the proposed constitutional amendments that will limit the use of eminent domain in Missouri, are presented. The proposals are expected to largely ban the taking of private property for private development. It may be included in a November 4,2008 statewide vote for approval.

33423 ■ *"EOTech Product Improves Holographic Gun Sights" in Crain's Detroit Business (Vol. 24, February 4, 2008, No. 5, pp. 9)*
Pub: Crain Communications Inc. - Detroit
Description: L-3 Communications EOTech Inc. procured new business contracts to fulfill military and law enforcement's demand for improved holographic sites used on handheld weapons.

33424 ■ *"Flu is a Booster for Firms Here" in Philadelphia Business Journal (Vol. 28, September 25, 2009, No. 32, pp. 1)*
Pub: American City Business Journals
Ed: John George. **Description:** GlaxoSmithKline, AstraZeneca, CSL Biotherapies, and Sanofi Aventis were awarded contract by the US Government to supply swine flu vaccines. It is estimated that global sales of the vaccine could reach billions of dollars.

33425 ■ *"For Bombardier, a Case of Deja Vu" in Canadian Business (Vol. 83, August 17, 2010, No. 13-14, pp. 28)*
Pub: Rogers Media Ltd.
Ed: Laura Cameron. **Description:** Foreign competitors have accused the Quebec government and the Societe de transport de Montreal of giving Bombardier preferential treatment when it bids for contract to replace Montreal metro's rail cars. Bombardier was in a similar situation in 1974 when it won the contract to build the metro's second generation rail cars.

33426 ■ *"Getting Out of an IRS Mess" in Black Enterprise (Vol. 37, December 2006, No. 5, pp. 53)*
Pub: Earl G. Graves Publishing Co. Inc.
Ed: Carolyn M. Brown. **Description:** Owing back taxes to the IRS can lead to huge penalties and interest. Here are some tips on how to handle paying the IRS what you owe them.

33427 ■ *Getting Started in Federal Contracting: A Guide through the Federal Procurement Maze*
Pub: Panoptic Enterprises
Contact: Vivina H. McVay, President
URL(s): www.fedgovcontracts.com. **Released:** Irregular; Latest edition 5th, 2009. **Price:** $49.95, Individuals. **Publication includes:** Lists of 26 offices of small and disadvantaged business utilization; 10 Department of Labor regional offices, 11 General Services Administration business service centers, and 11 Small Business Administration regional offices, plus 14 Government resource offices; 35 commercial resources; training; books; newsletters; and associations. These agencies are of use to those privately-owned businesses wishing to sell their products and services to the federal government. Plus 26 Federal Acquisition Computer Network (FACNET) Certified Value Added Networks (VANS). **Entries include:** Agency name, address, phone, geographical territory covered. Principal content is discussion of current procurement regulations and information on how to submit proposals. **Arrangement:** Classified by agency represented; type of resource. **Indexes:** Organization name.

33428 ■ *"Goldbelt Inc.: Targeting Shareholder Development" in Alaska Business Monthly (Vol. 27, October 2011, No. 10, pp. 108)*
Pub: Alaska Business Publishing Company
Ed: Tracy Kalytiak. **Description:** Profile of Goldbelt Inc., the company that has changed its original focus of timber to real estate to tourism and then to government contracting opportunities.

33429 ■ *Government Contracts & Subcontract Leads Directory*
Pub: Government Data Publications Inc.
Contact: Siegfried Lobel, President
URL(s): www.govdata.com. **Released:** Annual; March. **Price:** $89.50, Individuals print, CD-ROM, disk. **Covers:** Firms which received prime contracts for production of goods or services from federal government agencies during the preceding twelve months. **Entries include:** Name and address of recipient, awarding agency, product, quantity, contact number, and dollar amount. Cumulates listings in 'Government Primecontracts Monthly.'. **Arrangement:** Classified by product.

33430 ■ *Government Prime Contractors Directory*
Pub: Government Data Publications Inc.
Contact: Siegfried Lobel, President
URL(s): www.govdata.com. **Released:** Annual; July. **Price:** $15, Individuals; $49.95, Individuals diskettes; $49.95, Individuals CD-ROM. **Covers:** Organizations that received government prime contracts during the previous two years. **Entries include:** Contractor name and address, product/service; contractors with contracts of more than $500,000 are marked. **Arrangement:** In two parts; Part 1 is alphabetical by company name and Part 2 is classified by zip code.

33431 ■ *"Green Shift Sees Red" in Canadian Business (Vol. 81, September 29, 2008, No. 16)*
Pub: Rogers Media Ltd.
Ed: Jeff Sanford. **Description:** Green Shift Inc. is suing the Liberal Party of Canada in an $8.5 million lawsuit for using the phrase 'green shift' when they rolled out their carbon tax and climate change policy. The company has come to be recognized as a consultant and provider of green products such as non-toxic, biodegradable cups, plates, and utensils for events.

33432 ■ *"Half a World Away" in Tampa Bay Business Journal (Vol. 30, December 4, 2009, No. 50, pp. 1)*
Pub: American City Business Journals
Ed: Jane Meinhardt. **Description:** Enterprise Florida has offered four trade grants for Florida's marine industry businesses to give them a chance to tap into the Middle East market at the Dubai International Boat Show on March 9 to 13, 2010. The grants pay for 50 percent of the exhibition costs for the qualifying business.

33433 ■ *"HBMG Targets Federal Contracts from Under Raytheon's Wing" in Austin Business Journallnc. (Vol. 29, January 15, 2010, No. 45, pp. 1)*
Pub: American City Business Journals
Ed: Christopher Calnan. **Description:** Information Technology firm HBMG Inc. of Austin Texas has been chosen by Massachusetts-based subcontractor Raytheon Company and the US Department of Defense (DoD) to join DoD's Mentor-Protege program. HBMG will be allowed to vie for government contracts through the said program, potentially increasing business with the DoD by at least 700 percent.

33434 ■ *"High-Tech Job-Apalooza!" in Orlando Business Journal (Vol. 26, January 15, 2010, No. 33, pp. 1)*
Pub: American City Business Journals
Ed: Christopher Boyd. **Description:** Science Applications International Corporation, Saab Training USA LLC, CAE USA, and Pelliconi &C.SPA attempt to obtain $939,000 in tax incentives to generate 222 technology and defense-related jobs in Orange County, Florida. Each job will provide an average salary of $67,000. Future plans of each technology and defense firm are also presented.

33435 ■ *"Hilliard Scans Horizon, Finds Defense Contractor" in Business First Columbus (Vol. 25, October 17, 2008, No. 8, pp. A1)*
Pub: American City Business Journals
Ed: Brian R. Ball. **Description:** An incentive package being offered by Hilliard may prompt a Powell defense contractor to relocate in 2009. The package offered to Star Dynamics Corporation incorporates incentives that return a sizeable amount of income taxes to the company.

33436 ■ *"Hospitals Face Big Whammy From State Fees" in Business Courier (Vol. 26, October 2, 2009, No. 23, pp. 1)*
Pub: American City Business Journals, Inc.
Ed: James Ritchie. **Description:** Ohio hospitals are facing losses of nearly $145 million in franchise fees which are set to be levied by the state. Ohio hospitals will be responsible for a total of $718 million franchise fees as required by 2010-2011 state budget but will recover only 80 percent of the amount in increased Medicaid fees. Possible effects of anticipated losses to Ohio hospitals are examined.

33437 ■ *"How to Keep a US Naval Destroyer Warm" in Indoor Comfort Marketing (Vol. 70, April 2011, No. 4, pp. 34)*
Pub: Industry Publications Inc.
Ed: George R. Carey. **Description:** Boiler facts regarding US Naval destroyers are discussed.

33438 ■ *"It's Not Easy Being Small" in Baltimore Business Journal (Vol. 27, October 9, 2009, No. 22, pp. 1)*
Pub: American City Business Journals
Ed: Scott Dance. **Description:** A look at how small businesses were left out of the stimulus-funded federal contracts in Maryland. Small contractors were not listed in the federal contracts database USAspending.gov and none were hired for work in the state.

33439 ■ *"Job Corps Center Remains Vacant After Operator is Booted" in Tampa Bay Business Journal (Vol. 30, January 15, 2010, No. 4, pp. 1)*
Pub: American City Business Journals
Ed: Jane Meinhardt. **Description:** Pinellas County, Florida Job Corps Center has remained vacant due to a conflict over the $16 million contract awarded to Res-Care Inc. by the US Department of Labor (DOL) The DOL has ordered Res-Care to stop operation at the center and it is uncertain when it will open or what company will operate it.

33440 ■ *"Local Company Seeks Patent For Armored Trucks" in Crain's Detroit Business (Vol. 24, February 4, 2008, No. 5, pp. 10)*
Pub: Crain Communications Inc. - Detroit
Description: Profile of James LeBlanc Sr., mechanical engineer and defense contractor, discusses his eleven utility patents pending for a set of vehicles and subsystems that would work as countermeasures to explosively formed projectiles.

33441 ■ *"Maryland Ready to Defend Slots Minority Policy" in Boston Business Journal (Vol. 29, July 8, 2011, No. 9, pp. 3)*
Pub: American City Business Journals Inc.
Ed: Scott Dance. **Description:** The legality of Maryland's minority inclusion policy may be put under scrutiny once the lawsuit filed by rejected slots developer Baltimore City Entertainment Group on July 5, 2011 is heard in court. The lawsuit aims to stop the bidding process on a proposed casino in Baltimore because the minority policy amounts to reverse discrimination.

33442 ■ *"Military Center a Go" in Austin Business Journallnc. (Vol. 29, December 11, 2009, No. 40, pp. 1)*
Pub: American City Business Journals
Ed: Kate Harrington. **Description:** The $40 million Armed Forces Guard and Reserve Center project at Austin-Bergstrom International Airport has resumed work after a delay of several years. The project is in both the House and Senate versions of the fiscal 2010 Military Construction and Veterans Appropriations Bill that would earmark $16.5 million for the center and $5.7 million for the maintenance facility. Details of construction plans are covered.

33443 ■ *"Montgomery & Barnes: a Service-Disabled, Veteran-Owned Small Business" in Underground Construction (Vol. 65, October 2010, No. 10)*
Pub: Oildom Publishing Company of Texas Inc.
Description: Gary Montgomery, chairman of Montgomery and Barnes announced that President Wendell (Buddy) Barnes is now majority owner, thus mak-

ing the Houston-based civil engineering and consulting services firm, eligible to quality as a Service-Disabled Veteran-Owned Small Business (SDVOSB).

33444 ■ *"N.E.'s Largest Solar Site Set for Scituate Landfill" in Boston Business Journal (Vol. 30, December 17, 2010, No. 47, pp. 1)*
Pub: Boston Business Journal
Ed: Kyle Alspach. **Description:** A closed 12-acre landfill in Scituate, Massachusetts is the proposed site for a 2.4-megawatt solar power plant. The town government will buy the power at a discounted rate, saving it $200,000 annually.

33445 ■ *"NJ Tries to Push Stimulus Funds to Minorities" in Philadelphia Business Journal (Vol. 28, September 25, 2009, No. 32, pp. 1)*
Pub: American City Business Journals
Ed: Athena D. Merritt. **Description:** New Jersey Governor Jon S. Corzine signed an executive order that seeks to ease the way for minority and women-owned business to take on federal stimulus-funded work. New Jersey has also forged new relations with different organizations to reduce the time and cost of certifications for businesses.

33446 ■ *"Nonprofits May Lose MBE Status in MD" in Boston Business Journal (Vol. 29, September 2, 2011, No. 17, pp. 1)*
Pub: American City Business Journals Inc.
Ed: Scott Dance. **Description:** A business group has been pushing to bar nonprofits from Maryland's Minority Business program. Nonprofits have been found to take a large portion of state contracts intended for women- and minority-owned businesses. The group is also crafting proposed legislation to remove nonprofits from the program.

33447 ■ *"Not in Your Backyard?" in Canadian Business (Vol. 80, March 12, 2007, No. 6, pp. 44)*
Pub: Rogers Media
Ed: John Gray. **Description:** The threat of losing residential property rights of persons whose land has rightful stakes from miners due to availability of minerals at the place is discussed.

33448 ■ *"Numbers Game" in Baltimore Business Journal (Vol. 27, February 6, 2010, No. 40, pp. 1)*
Pub: American City Business Journals
Ed: Scott Dance. **Description:** Doubts are being raised regarding the impact of the federal stimulus spending in addressing unemployment in Maryland, which has experienced 1,800 jobs created so far. Details on the view of companies and the insufficient amount of contracts that lead to the fewer number of workers being hired are discussed.

33449 ■ *"Post-Prison Center Idea Rankles OTR" in Business Courier (Vol. 26, November 27, 2009, No. 31, pp. 1)*
Pub: American City Business Journals, Inc.
Ed: Lucy May. **Description:** Cincinnati officials and community leaders oppose Firetree Ltd.'s plan to launch a residential program for federal offenders near the School for the Creative and Performing Arts in Over-the-Rhine. Firetree, a Pennsylvania-based reentry center services firm, proposed a five-year contract with the Federal Bureau of Prisons based on a letter to Cincinnati Police Chief Thomas Streicher.

33450 ■ *"Procurement Benefits" in Black Enterprise (Vol. 38, February 2008, No. 7, pp. 72)*
Pub: Earl G. Graves Publishing Co. Inc.
Ed: Aisha Sylvester. **Description:** Nearly 18 percent of all U.S. firms are minority-owned according to the recent report called Minorities in Business: A Demographic Review of Minority Business Ownership produced by the Small Business Administration. Issues for working with diversity suppliers are addressed.

33451 ■ *"Proposed Law Would Stop REIS Bid for Annexation by Livonia" in Crain's Detroit Business (Vol. 24, March 10, 2008, No. 10, pp. 2)*
Pub: Crain Communications, Inc.
Ed: Chad Halcom. **Description:** REIS Northville L.L.C., a joint venture made up of Real Estate Interests Group Inc. and Schostak Bros. & Co., has proposed an $800 million project called Highwood at the former Northville Psychiatric Hospital site but has been stalled due to a disagreement with Northville Township on several terms including: the amount of retail at the site and the paying for cleanup of environmental and medical waste.

33452 ■ *"The Quest for the Smart Prosthetic" in Canadian Business (Vol. 83, October 12, 2010, No. 17, pp. 26)*
Pub: Rogers Media Ltd.
Ed: Jacqueline Nelson. **Description:** Information about a two-year research project led by Southern Methodist University (SMU) and funded by the Defense Advance Research Projects Agency (DARPA) is provided. The agency aims to create a 'smart prosthetic' which will improve the lives of military amputees. The planned prosthetic will use a sensor that can carry nerve signals through synthetic channels.

33453 ■ *"A Safe Bet" in Entrepreneur (Vol. 35, October 2007, No. 10, pp. 26)*
Pub: Entrepreneur Media Inc.
Ed: Carol Tice. **Description:** U.S. Department of Defense has developed a program, called the Defense Venture Catalyst Initiative or DeVenCI, that will match defense officials to the products that they need. DeVenCI uses conferences to showcase the defense contractors and their technologies to defense managers. Details of how this program helps both contractors and defense officials are overviewed.

33454 ■ *"SBA Makes Reforms To Federal Government Contracting" in Black Enterprise (Vol. 38, January 2008, No. 6, pp. 26)*
Pub: Earl G. Graves Publishing Co. Inc.
Ed: Alexis McCombs. **Description:** U.S. Small Business Administration's new requirement that small businesses recertify size status in order to remain eligible for federal contracts lasting more than five years. Prior regulations allowed companies declared small in earlier contracts may have grown through acquisitions, making them ineligible. This move may impact black businesses.

33455 ■ *"A Second Chance at Road Dollars" in Orlando Business Journal (Vol. 26, February 5, 2010, No. 36, pp. 1)*
Pub: American City Business Journals
Ed: Bill Orben. **Description:** Nearly $10 million worth of construction projects in Central Florida would give construction companies that missed the initial round of federal stimulus-funded local road building projects another opportunity. Cost savings in the initial round of road projects enabled Orange, Osceola, and Seminole Counties to secure additional projects.

33456 ■ *"State Efforts to Boost Contract Efficiency Hurt Smaller Firms" in Boston Business Journal (Vol. 27, November 9, 2007, No. 41, pp. 1)*
Pub: American City Business Journals Inc.
Ed: Lisa van der Pool. **Description:** Massachusetts Operational Services Division, which provides statewide telecommunications and data infrastructure contracts, announced that it is cutting the list of companies on the new contract from twelve to six. The cost-cutting efforts began in 2005, after a review by an independent consultant advised the state to adopt strategies that would save millions of dollars.

33457 ■ *"Stimulus Effect Slow" in Baltimore Business Journal (Vol. 27, October 23, 2009, No. 24, pp. 1)*
Pub: American City Business Journals
Ed: Scott Dance. **Description:** Companies in Maryland have reported only 154 new jobs being created or saved in Greater Baltimore and 965 jobs overall in the state because of stimulus cash. The federal stimulus program was expected to create thousands of new jobs but statistics show its failure to reduce unemployment in the state.

33458 ■ *"TIA Wrestles with Procurement Issues" in Business Journal Serving Greater Tampa Bay (Vol. 30, November 12, 2010, No. 47, pp. 1)*
Pub: Tampa Bay Business Journal
Ed: Mark Holan. **Description:** Tampa International Airport (TIA) has been caught in conflict of interest and procurement policy issues after the Hillsborough County Aviation Authority learned of the spousal relationship of an employee with his wife's firm, Gresham Smith and Partners. Gresham already won contracts with TIA and was ahead of other firms in a new contract.

33459 ■ *"Training the Troops: Battlefield Simulations Bring Growth to UNITECH" in Black Enterprise (Vol. 38, February 2008, No. 7, pp. 30)*
Pub: Earl G. Graves Publishing Co. Inc.
Ed: Cliff Hocker. **Description:** Universal Systems and Technology (UNITECH) received a total of over $45 million U.S. Department of Defense orders during September and October 2007. UNITECH designs and manufactures battlefield simulation devices used to train troops in the Army and Marine Corps.

33460 ■ *"U-Swirl Added to SBA's Franchise Registry" in Ice Cream Reporter (Vol. 23, September 20, 2010, No. 10, pp. 1)*
Pub: Ice Cream Reporter
Description: Healthy Fast Food Inc., parent to the U-SWIRL Frozen Yogurt cafe chain announced that the U.S. Small Business Administration listed U-SWIRL Frozen Yogurt on its official franchise registry. This move will allow U-SWIRL the benefits of a streamlined review process for SBA financing.

33461 ■ *"U.S. Widens Rocket Field" in Wall Street Journal Eastern Edition (October 17, 2011, pp. B4)*
Pub: Dow Jones & Company Inc. Enterprise Media Group
Contact: Clare Hart, President
Ed: Andy Pasztor. **Description:** An agreement has been reached between National Aeronautics and Space Administration, the Department of Defense and the Air Force that will assist small commercial space ventures in bidding for profitable contracts for government launching. The program will give those companies a chance to compete against larger corporations.

33462 ■ *"Water Works Spinoff Could Make Big Splash" in Business Courier (Vol. 24, October 19, 2008, No. 27, pp. 1)*
Pub: American City Business Journals, Inc.
Ed: Dan Monk. **Description:** Cincinnati, Ohio city manager Milton Dohoney proposed to spin off the city-owned Greater Cincinnati Water Works into a regionally focused water district that could allow the city to receive millions of dollars in annual dividends. A feasibility study is to be conducted by a team of outside consultants and city staffers and is expected to be finished by summer of 2008.

33463 ■ *"Wi-Fi Finds Its Way Despite Nixed Plan for Free System" in Crain's Cleveland Business (Vol. 28, November 12, 2007, No. 45, pp. 3)*
Pub: Crain Communications, Inc.
Ed: Jay Miller. **Description:** Discusses the issues facing Cleveland and Northeast Ohio concerning their proposal to offer citizens wireless Internet services for free or a small fee.

33464 ■ *Win Government Contracts for Your Small Business*
Pub: CCH Inc.
Contact: Mike Sabbatis, President
Ed: John DiGiacomo. **Released:** June 2007. **Price:** $24.95. **Description:** Techniques to help small companies negotiate and win government contracts.

33465 ■ *"Your Next Big Customer" in Business Owner (Vol. 35, November-December 2011, No. 6, pp. 7)*
Pub: DL Perkins Company
Description: Learn how to sell goods and services to the Federal Government. The Office of Government Contracting is the agency responsible for coordinating government purchases.

TRADE PERIODICALS

33466 ■ *Inside Missile Defense*
Pub: Inside Washington Publishers
Ed: Thomas Duffy, Editor. **Released:** Biweekly, every other Wednesday. **Price:** $795, U.S. and Canada;

$845, elsewhere. **Description:** Reports on U.S. missile defense programs, procurement, and policymaking.

33467 ■ *The Nash & Cibinic Report*
Pub: West Group
Ed: Ralph Nash, Editor. **Released:** Monthly. **Price:** $1,706.88. **Description:** Discusses government contracts analysis and reporting. Topics include procurement management, contractor claims, and competition and awards.

TRADE SHOWS AND CONVENTIONS

33468 ■ Alliance Texas
Showorks Inc.
1205 N. Napa St.
Spokane, WA 99202
Ph: (509)838-8755
Fax: (509)838-2838
Co. E-mail: showorks@showorksinc.com
URL: http://www.showorksinc.com
URL(s): www.allianceforbiz.com. **Price:** $140, registered before early bird date; $165, registered through early bird date; $195, Onsite. **Audience:** Buyers and contracting officers from military bases. **Principal Exhibits:** Small business procurement opportunities.

CONSULTANTS

33469 ■ Margiloff & Associates
621 Royalview St.
Duarte, CA 91010-1346
Ph: (626)303-1266
Fax: (626)303-0127
Contact: Dorine Margiloff, Manager
Scope: Energy and water conservation studies, analysis of research and development, licensing, economics and project management. Projects involve development, training, utility review, cost analysis, manufacturing system improvement, process modeling and expert witness services. Clients include in the field of food, chemical, fermentation, energy, financial and legal services, government and general manufacturing fields. **Founded:** 1983.

COMPUTERIZED DATABASES

33470 ■ *Commerce Business Daily Online (CBD)*
2 Washingtonian Ctr.
9737 Washingtonian Blvd., Ste. 100
Gaithersburg, MD 20878-7364
Ph: (301)287-2700
Free: 800-824-1195
Fax: (301)287-2039
Co. E-mail: webmaster@ucg.com
URL: http://www.ucg.com
Availability: Online: U.S. Government Printing Office-Federal Digital System. **Type:** Full-text; Directory.

33471 ■ *Federal Contracts Report™*
1801 S Bell St.
Arlington, VA 22202
Free: 800-372-1033
Co. E-mail: customercare@bna.com
URL: http://www.bna.com
Availability: Online: Bloomberg LP-Bloomberg BNA; Thomson Reuters - Westlaw. **Type:** Full-text.

LIBRARIES

33472 ■ Georgia State University - Small Business Development Center
10 Park Place South SE, Ste. 450
Atlanta, GA 30302
Ph: (404)413-7830
Co. E-mail: sbpmbp@langate.gsu.edu
URL: http://www2.gsu.edu/~wwwsbp/
Contact: Bernard J. Meineke, Regional Director
Scope: Small business, marketing, finance, International business, government procurement. **Services:** Counseling; Center open to the public for reference use only. **Founded:** 1979. **Holdings:** Business directories; government publications and journals, periodicals, training manuals and videotapes. **Subscriptions:** 11 journals and other serials.

33473 ■ National Institute of Governmental Purchasing, Inc. - Specifications/Searchable Forms/Documents
151 Spring St., Ste. 200
Herndon, VA 20170
Ph: (703)736-8900
Free: 800-367-6447
Fax: (703)736-9639
Co. E-mail: rgrimm@nigp.org
URL: http://www.nigp.org
Contact: Rick Grimm, Chief Executive Officer
Scope: Governmental purchasing. **Services:** Library open to NIGP members. **Founded:** 1946. **Holdings:** Files of specifications, government procurement (13,000), searchable forms and documents (350).

Government Regulations

START-UP INFORMATION

33474 ■ *The Small Business Start-Up Kit*
Pub: NOLO
Ed: Peri Pakroo. **Released:** January 2008. **Price:** $29.99. **Description:** Entrepreneurial advice for launching a new business. Topics include compliance with state regulations, sole proprietorships, partnerships, corporations, limited liability companies, as well as accounting and tax information.

33475 ■ *Small Business Survival Guide*
Pub: Adams Media Corporation
Contact: Gary Krebs, Director
E-mail: swatrous@adamsmedia.com
Ed: Cliff Ennico. **Price:** $12.95. **Description:** Small business expert provides strategies to start a company and survive in the 21st Century. He shows small business owners how to succeed despite challenges that can defeat any firm. His advice covers suppliers; customers and contractors; competitors and creditors; spouses, family and friends; as well as the ways lawyers, accountants and other can steal an entrepreneur's success. Ennico also describes how startups can comply with local regulations.

ASSOCIATIONS AND OTHER ORGANIZATIONS

33476 ■ American Senior Benefits Association (ASBA)
PO Box 300777
Chicago, IL 60630-0777
Ph: (773)714-7990
Free: 877-906-2722
Co. E-mail: info@asbaonline.org
URL: http://www.asbaonline.org
Contact: Eileen Philbin, Executive Director
Description: Represents small business owners. Supports legislation favorable to the small business enterprise; organizes members to collectively oppose unfavorable legislation. Informs members of proposed legislation affecting small businesses; conducts business education programs. Operates scholarship program. **Founded:** 1975. **Publications:** *ASBA Benefits Guide* (Annual); *ASBA Quarterly* (Quarterly). **Awards:** College Scholarship Program (Annual); ASBA College Scholarship Program.

33477 ■ Small Business Council of America (SBCA)
1523 Concord Pike, Ste. 300
Brandywine E
Wilmington, DE 19803
Ph: (302)691-7222
Free: 877-404-1329
Co. E-mail: calimafde@sbca.net
URL: http://www.sbca.net
Contact: Leanne H. Redstone, Executive Director
Description: Small business and professional organizations. Goals are to keep federal tax and employee benefit legislation from becoming burdensome, and to support legislation creating economic incentives for small businesses. Lobbies Congress on behalf of members; alerts members to proposed legislation so that opposition or support can be mustered before a bill becomes law; operates ad hoc committees on specific legislation. Maintains speakers' bureau; compiles statistics. **Founded:** 1979. **Publications:** *News Flashes*; *Tax Report* (Monthly); *SBCA Member and Congressional Directory* (Annual). **Educational Activities:** Congressional Awards Ceremony (Annual). **Awards:** Connie Murdoch Award; Small Business Person of the Year; Humanitarian of the Year.

33478 ■ Small Business Legislative Council (SBLC)
1100 H St. NW, Ste. 540
Washington, DC 20005
Ph: (202)639-8500
Co. E-mail: email@sblc.org
URL: http://www.sblc.org
Contact: John Satagaj, President
Description: Serves as an independent coalition of trade and professional associations that share a common commitment to the future of small business. Represents the interests of small businesses in such diverse economic sectors as manufacturing, retailing, distribution, professional and technical services, construction, transportation, and agriculture. **Founded:** 1976.

EDUCATIONAL PROGRAMS

33479 ■ 2011 National Electrical Code (Onsite) (NEC)
American Trainco
9785 S Maroon Cir., Ste. 300
Englewood, CO 80112
Ph: (303)531-4560
Free: 877-978-7246
Fax: (303)531-4565
Co. E-mail: Sales@AmericanTrainco.com
URL: http://www.americantrainco.com
Price: $990.00. **Description:** Provides anyone working with electricity the most up-to-date, best practices for safe installation and maintenance of electrical systems and equipment, including the new 2011 Code changes. **Dates and Locations:** Cities throughout the United States.

33480 ■ Adobe Acrobat Section 508 Accessibility (Onsite)
EEI Communications
8945 Guilford Rd., Ste. 145
Columbia, MD 21046
Ph: (410)309-8200
Free: 888-253-2762
Fax: (410)630-3980
Co. E-mail: train@eeicom.com
URL: http://www.eeicom.com/eei-training-services
Price: $425.00. **Description:** Covers the regulations by the Federal Government's Section 508 accessibility and the features of Adobe Acrobat software designed to meet the regulations, including definition of accessibility, authoring for accessibility, working with existing PDF files, forms, and scanned documents, using the accessibility checker, and tags palette, and testing your PDF files for accessibility. **Dates and Locations:** Alexandria, VA.

33481 ■ Advanced Hazardous Waste Management (Onsite)
Seminar Information Service, Inc.
20 Executive Park, Ste. 120
Irvine, CA 92614
Ph: (949)261-9104
Free: 877-SEM-INFO
Fax: (949)261-1963
Co. E-mail: info@seminarinformation.com
URL: http://www.seminarinformation.com
Price: $499.00. **Description:** Learn to minimize your hazardous waste generation and make sure you are complying fully with all hazardous regulations. **Dates and Locations:** Atlanta, GA.

33482 ■ ASTM Phase I & Phase II Environmental Site Assessment Processes (Onsite)
Seminar Information Service, Inc.
20 Executive Park, Ste. 120
Irvine, CA 92614
Ph: (949)261-9104
Free: 877-SEM-INFO
Fax: (949)261-1963
Co. E-mail: info@seminarinformation.com
URL: http://www.seminarinformation.com
Price: $1,095.00. **Description:** Gain an understanding how to use the standards and how the standards affect the way you do business. The 'Innocent Landowner Defense' under the Comprehensive Environmental Response, Compensation and Liability Act (CERCLA) and why due diligence is necessary will be covered. **Dates and Locations:** Boston, MA; Columbus, OH; West Conshohocken, PA; New Orleans, LA; and Las Vegas, NV.

33483 ■ Automotive Glazing Materials (Onsite)
Seminar Information Service, Inc.
20 Executive Park, Ste. 120
Irvine, CA 92614
Ph: (949)261-9104
Free: 877-SEM-INFO
Fax: (949)261-1963
Co. E-mail: info@seminarinformation.com
URL: http://www.seminarinformation.com
Price: $1,225.00; $1,130.00 for Society of Automotive Engineers members. **Description:** An overview of the different automotive glazing materials, past, present and future, including the laws that govern their use, and manufacture, installation, usage, testing, safety aspects and how they affect automotive performance. Topics include the chemical, physical and design issues of annealed, laminated, tempered, glass-plastic and plastic glazing materials. **Dates and Locations:** Troy, MI.

33484 ■ Automotive Lighting (Onsite)
Seminar Information Service, Inc.
20 Executive Park, Ste. 120
Irvine, CA 92614
Ph: (949)261-9104

Free: 877-SEM-INFO
Fax: (949)261-1963
Co. E-mail: info@seminarinformation.com
URL: http://www.seminarinformation.com

Price: $1,155.00; $1,035.00 for Society of Automotive Engineers members. **Description:** Provides broad information about automotive lighting systems with emphasis on lighting functions, effectiveness, and technologies, including the legal aspects and implications related to automotive lighting and examine safety measurements used with lighting functions and human factors costs. **Dates and Locations:** Detroit, MI.

33485 ■ Collections Law (Onsite)
Fred Pryor Seminars & CareerTrack
5700 Broadmoor St., Ste. 300
Mission, KS 66202
Free: 800-780-8476
Fax: (913)967-8849
Co. E-mail: customerservice@pryor.com
URL: http://www.pryor.com

Price: $149.00; $139.00 for groups of 5 or more. **Description:** Ensure your organization is legally compliant, including strategies and techniques to gain quicker results in collecting money. **Dates and Locations:** Cities throughout the United States.

33486 ■ DOT Hazardous Materials Training (Onsite)
Seminar Information Service, Inc.
20 Executive Park, Ste. 120
Irvine, CA 92614
Ph: (949)261-9104
Free: 877-SEM-INFO
Fax: (949)261-1963
Co. E-mail: info@seminarinformation.com
URL: http://www.seminarinformation.com

Price: $449.00. **Description:** DOT is changing virtually all of the rules for hazardous materials containers, labeling, shipping papers, placards, and shipping names. Learn how to comply with the regulations. **Dates and Locations:** Cities throughout the United States.

33487 ■ Environmental, Health, and Safety Laws and Regulations
Seminar Information Service, Inc.
20 Executive Park, Ste. 120
Irvine, CA 92614
Ph: (949)261-9104
Free: 877-SEM-INFO
Fax: (949)261-1963
Co. E-mail: info@seminarinformation.com
URL: http://www.seminarinformation.com

Price: $699.00; $349.00 for four or more. **Description:** Common sense approach to compliance with environmental, health, and safety laws and regulations. **Dates and Locations:** Cary, NC; and Indianapolis, IN.

33488 ■ Environmental Regulations Seminars
Seminar Information Service, Inc.
20 Executive Park, Ste. 120
Irvine, CA 92614
Ph: (949)261-9104
Free: 877-SEM-INFO
Fax: (949)261-1963
Co. E-mail: info@seminarinformation.com
URL: http://www.seminarinformation.com

Price: $895.00. **Description:** 2-day seminar on how to comply with federal environmental regulations. **Dates and Locations:** Atlanta, GA; Virginia Beach, VA; and Newark, NJ.

33489 ■ Hazardous Waste Management: The Complete Course
Seminar Information Service, Inc.
20 Executive Park, Ste. 120
Irvine, CA 92614
Ph: (949)261-9104
Free: 877-SEM-INFO
Fax: (949)261-1963
Co. E-mail: info@seminarinformation.com
URL: http://www.seminarinformation.com

Price: $795.00. **Description:** Covers how to meet your annual training requirement and learn a systematic approach to understanding and complying with the latest state and federal regulations. **Dates and Locations:** Cities throughout the United States.

33490 ■ Hazardous Waste Management: The Complete Course (Onsite)
Seminar Information Service, Inc.
20 Executive Park, Ste. 120
Irvine, CA 92614
Ph: (949)261-9104
Free: 877-SEM-INFO
Fax: (949)261-1963
Co. E-mail: info@seminarinformation.com
URL: http://www.seminarinformation.com

Price: $795.00. **Description:** Learn a systematic approach to understanding and complying with the latest state and federal regulations. **Dates and Locations:** Cities throughout the United States.

33491 ■ Records Retention and Destruction (Onsite)
Fred Pryor Seminars & CareerTrack
5700 Broadmoor St., Ste. 300
Mission, KS 66202
Free: 800-780-8476
Fax: (913)967-8849
Co. E-mail: customerservice@pryor.com
URL: http://www.pryor.com

Price: $149.00; $139.00 for groups of 5 or more. **Description:** Gain valuable information for successfully organizing, storing, archiving and destroying your organization's critical business documents while eliminating risk and ensuring compliance with the latest legal requirements. **Dates and Locations:** Cities throughout the United States.

33492 ■ SARA Title III Workshop (Onsite)
Seminar Information Service, Inc.
20 Executive Park, Ste. 120
Irvine, CA 92614
Ph: (949)261-9104
Free: 877-SEM-INFO
Fax: (949)261-1963
Co. E-mail: info@seminarinformation.com
URL: http://www.seminarinformation.com

Price: $399.00. **Description:** Step-by-step procedures for compliance with Title III of the Superfund Amendments. **Dates and Locations:** Charlotte, NC.

33493 ■ Storm Water Management: How to Comply with Federal and State Regulations (Onsite)
Seminar Information Service, Inc.
20 Executive Park, Ste. 120
Irvine, CA 92614
Ph: (949)261-9104
Free: 877-SEM-INFO
Fax: (949)261-1963
Co. E-mail: info@seminarinformation.com
URL: http://www.seminarinformation.com

Price: $499.00. **Description:** Learn what discharges must be permitted, how to apply for a permit, and requirements for maintaining permit compliance. **Dates and Locations:** Charlotte, NC.

33494 ■ Workers' Compensation (Onsite)
Fred Pryor Seminars & CareerTrack
5700 Broadmoor St., Ste. 300
Mission, KS 66202
Free: 800-780-8476
Fax: (913)967-8849
Co. E-mail: customerservice@pryor.com
URL: http://www.pryor.com

Price: $199.00; $189.00 for groups of 5 or more. **Description:** Learn strategies, insider tips, tools, and more to help manage entire workers' compensation plan more effectively, including how workers' compensation, FMLA, and ADA regulations can overlap. **Dates and Locations:** Cities throughout the United States.

DIRECTORIES OF EDUCATIONAL PROGRAMS

33495 ■ *Neal-Schuman Guide to Finding Legal and Regulatory Information on the Internet*
Pub: Neal-Schuman Publishers Inc.
Contact: Patricia Glass Schuman, President
E-mail: pgs@neal-schuman.com

URL(s): www.neal-schuman.com. **Ed:** Yvonne J. Chandler. **Released:** new edition expected 2005. **Price:** $135, Individuals. **Covers:** 900 Internet sites offering local, state, and federal legal and government information. **Entries include:** Title, publishing agency, URL, brief description of the site.

REFERENCE WORKS

33496 ■ *"11th Circuit: Don't Break the Law to Comply with It" in Miami Daily Business Review (October 21, 2009)*
Pub: Incisive Media
Contact: Lee Feldman, Manager
E-mail: lee.feldman@incisivemedia.com

Ed: Janet L. Conley. **Description:** Niagara Credit Solutions argued with a three-judge panel that the company broke the rule saying debt collectors must identify themselves so that they could comply with a rule barring debt collectors from communicating about a debt with third parties.

33497 ■ *"$100 Million in Projects Jeopardized" in Business Courier (Vol. 24, March 28, 2008, No. 51, pp. 1)*
Pub: American City Business Journals, Inc.

Ed: Dan Monk. **Description:** Ohio's historic preservation tax credit program may be reinstated after some companies planned to sue over its stoppage. The Ohio Department of Development said the program was halted because it exceeded the allocated budget for the credit. $34 million in credits are at stake for more than two dozen local projects if the program is reinstated.

33498 ■ *"401(k) Keys to Stable Value" in Barron's (Vol. 88, March 10, 2008, No. 10, pp. 40)*
Pub: Dow Jones & Company, Inc.

Ed: Tom Sullivan. **Description:** Stable-value funds offer investors stability in a period of volatility in financial markets, attracting $888 million in funds. The Securities and Exchange Commission approved the launch of actively managed exchange-traded funds.

33499 ■ *"AAAFCO Unveils Pet Food Resource" in Feedstuffs (Vol. 83, August 29, 2011, No. 35, pp. 15)*
Pub: Miller Publishing Company

Description: The Association of American Feed Control Officials has launched a Website called The Business of Pet Food, which will address frequently asked questions about U.S. regulatory requirements for pet food. The site serves as an initial reference for anyone wishing to start a pet food business because it provides information and guidance.

33500 ■ *Access to Finance*
Pub: Brookings Institution Press

Ed: Barr. **Released:** December 2006. **Price:** $39.95. **Description:** Challenges to help make financial systems more inclusive to promote successful venture in new markets while utilizing new technologies and government policies to expand financial access to smaller companies.

33501 ■ *"AG Warns Slots MBE Plan Risky" in Boston Business Journal (Vol. 29, May 27, 2011, No. 3, pp. 1)*
Pub: American City Business Journals Inc.

Ed: Scott Dance. **Description:** Attorney General Doug Gansler states that the law extending the minority business program on slots parlors contracting through 2018 could be open to lawsuits. He recommended that the state should conduct a study proving that minority- and women-owned businesses do not get a fair share in the gaming industry before it signs the bill to avoid lawsuits from majority-owned firms.

33502 ■ *"Airlines Mount PR Push to Win Public Support Against Big Oil" in Advertising Age (Vol. 79, July 14, 2008, No. 7, pp. 1)*
Pub: Crain Communications, Inc.
Ed: Michael Bush. **Description:** Top airline executives from competing companies have banded together in a public relations plan in which they are sending e-mails to their frequent fliers asking for aid in lobbying legislators to put a restriction on oil speculation.

33503 ■ *"Alberta Star Begins Phase 2 Drilling On Its Eldorado & Contact Lake IOCG & Uranium Projects" in Canadian Corporate News (May 16, 2007)*
Pub: Comtex News Network Inc.
Description: Profile of Alberta Star Development Corp., a Canadian mineral exploration company that identifies, acquires, and finances advanced stage exploration projects in Canada, and its current undertaking of its 2007 drill program in which the company intends to begin accelerating its uranium and poly-metallic exploration and drilling activities on all of its drill targets for 2007 now that it has been granted its permits.

33504 ■ *"Alcan Statement on Water Rights Could Encourgage Bid" in Globe & Mail (April 25, 2007, pp. B5)*
Pub: CTVglobemedia Publishing Inc.
Ed: Andy Hoffman. **Description:** The possibility for a foreign firm to bid for Alcan Inc. in the light of its agreement with Canadian government over water rights is discussed.

33505 ■ *"All Bubbles Must Burst" in Canadian Business (Vol. 83, August 17, 2010, No. 13-14, pp. 12)*
Pub: Rogers Media Ltd.
Ed: Matthew McClearn. **Description:** Canada's housing markets is showing signs of cooling down as home and condo sales both fell for the first time in 16 years. The Canadian government has fueled the market over an extended period through Canada Mortgage and Housing Corporation's role in insuring mortgage lenders against risk of defaults.

33506 ■ *"All Eyes On Iris" in Canadian Business (Vol. 81, July 22, 2008, No. 12-13, pp. 20)*
Pub: Rogers Media Ltd.
Ed: Jack Mintz. **Description:** Provincial governments in Canada are believed to be awaiting Alberta Finance Minister Iris Evans' financial and investment policies as well as Evans' development of a new saving strategy. Alberta is the only Canadian province that is in position to invest in sovereign wealth funds after it eliminated its debt in 2005.

33507 ■ *"All For One, None for All?" in Canadian Business (Vol. 83, October 12, 2010, No. 17, pp. 60)*
Pub: Rogers Media Ltd.
Ed: Michael McCullogh. **Description:** The effect of the growth of Canada's overseas provincial trade offices on Canadian trade is discussed. Economic development commissions in the country have devised a single 'Consider Canada' campaign to pitch foreign investors. It is hoped that large cities will gain from banding together rather than competing against one another.

33508 ■ *"An Amazing Race" in Canadian Business (Vol. 81, March 3, 2008, No. 3, pp. 25)*
Pub: Rogers Media
Ed: Rachel Pulfer. **Description:** U.S. presidential candidates Barack Obama and Hilary Clinton lead the Democratic Part primaries while John McCain is a frontrunner at the Republican Party. These leading candidates have different plans for the U.S. economy which will affect Canada's own economy particularly concerning trade policies. The presidential candidates' proposals and the impacts of U.S. economic downturn on Canada are examined.

33509 ■ *"American Chemistry Council Launches Flagship Blog" in Ecology,Environment & Conservation Business (October 29, 2011, pp. 5)*
Pub: HighBeam Research
Description: American Chemistry Council (ACC) launched its blog, American Chemistry Matters, where interactive space allows bloggers to respond to news coverage and to discuss policy issues and their impact on innovation, competitiveness, job creation and safety.

33510 ■ *"Analysts: More Mergers for the Region's Hospitals" in Boston Business Journal (Vol. 30, October 15, 2010, No. 36, pp. 1)*
Pub: Boston Business Journal
Ed: Julie M. Donnelly. **Description:** A number of hospitals in Boston, Massachusetts are engaging in mergers and acquisitions. Caritas Christi Health Care is set to be purchased by Cerberus Capital Management. The U.S. healthcare reform law is seen to drive the development.

33511 ■ *"And The Winner Is.." in Canadian Business (Vol. 81, March 3, 2008, No. 3, pp. 21)*
Pub: Rogers Media
Ed: Joe Castaldo. **Description:** Thirty out of 141 Canadian chief executive officers think that Hilary Clinton would be best for U.S.-Canada relations if elected as U.S. president. Findings also revealed that 60 respondents believe that presidential candidate John McCain would be best on handling issues of international military-security. Views on the candidates' performance and their ability to deal with the declining U.S. economy as well as international trade issues are also given.

33512 ■ *"Ann Alexander; Senior Attorney, Natural Resources Defense Council" in Crain's Chicago Business (Vol. 31, May 5, 2008, No. 18)*
Pub: Crain Communications, Inc.
Ed: Emily Stone. **Description:** Profile of Ann Alexander who is the senior attorney at the Natural Resources Defense Council and is known for her dedication to the environment and a career spent battling oil companies, steelmakers and the government to change federal regulations. One recent project aims to improve the Bush administration's fuel economy standards for SUVs. Past battles include her work to prevent permits from slipping through the cracks such as the proposal by London-based BP PLC to dump 54 percent more ammonia and 35 percent more suspended solids from its Whiting, Indiana refinery into Lake Michigan-the source of drinking water for Chicago and its surrounding communities.

33513 ■ *"Another Baby Step" in Canadian Business (Vol. 81, March 31, 2008, No. 5, pp. 32)*
Pub: Rogers Media
Ed: Andrew Wahl. **Description:** Discusses the Canadian government's federal budget which makes it easier to tap into tax credits for corporate research and development. However, these steps do not really go far enough to boost industrial research levels in Canada. Making these incentives at least partially refundable could help during tough economic times.

33514 ■ *"Are EO Programs Right for Your Business?" in Contractor (Vol. 56, October 2009, No. 10, pp. 49)*
Pub: Penton Media, Inc.
Ed: Susan Linden McGreevy. **Description:** Some of the laws regarding equal opportunity programs are discussed. Suggestions for mechanical contractors who are considering certification to qualify for these programs are presented.

33515 ■ *Are Government Purchasing Policies Failing Small Business?: Congressional Hearing*
Pub: DIANE Publishing Company
Ed: John F. Kerry. **Released:** September 2002. **Price:** Paperback $35.00. **Description:** Covers Congressional hearing: Steven App, Treasury Department; Fred Armendariz and Major Clark, Small Business Administration; Susan Allen, Pan Asian American Chamber of Commerce; Stephen Denlinger, Latin American Management Association; Charles Henry, National Veteran's Business Development Corporation; Morris Hudson, MO Procurement Technology Assistance Centers; Bar Kasoff, Women Impact, Public Policy; Pam Mazza, Piliero, Massa and Pargament; Ron Newlan, HubZone Contract National Council; Pat Parker, Native American Management Service; Joann Payne, Women First National Legislative Commission; Mike Robinson, MA Small Business Development Centers; Ramon Rodriguez, Hispanic Chamber of Commerce; Angela Styles, Office of Management and Budget; Ralph Thomas, NASA; John Turner, MN Business Enterprise Legal Defense Fund; James Turpin, American Subcontractor's Association, Inc.; and Henry Wilfong, National Association of Small Disadvantaged Business.

33516 ■ *"Attend To Your Corporate Housekeeping" in Women Entrepreneur (December 4, 2008)*
Pub: Entrepreneur Media Inc.
Ed: Nina Kaufman. **Description:** Business owners can lose all the benefits and privileges of the corporate form if they do not follow proper corporate formalities such as holding an annual meeting, electing officers and directors and adopting or passing corporate resolutions. Creditors are able to take from one's personal assets if such formalities have not been followed.

33517 ■ *"Au Revoir Or Goodbye?" in Barron's (Vol. 88, July 14, 2008, No. 28, pp. 5)*
Pub: Dow Jones & Co., Inc.
Ed: Alan Abelson. **Description:** Former Senator Phil Gramm's opinion that the U.S. is a 'nation of whiners' as they moan about recession is another example of the disconnection between Washington and Wall Street on one hand and the real world on the other. It would be a catastrophe for most of the world if Fannie Mae and Freddie Mac were to go under and take their trillions of mortgage debt with them.

33518 ■ *"Austin to Make it Easier for Stores to Just Pop In" in Austin Business Journal (Vol. 31, August 19, 2011, No. 24, pp. A1)*
Pub: American City Business Journals Inc.
Ed: Vicky Garza. **Description:** Temporary retail stores may soon become common in Austin as City Council has urged the city manager to look into the possibility of amending the city codes to permit businesses to temporarily fill the vacant spaces downtown.

33519 ■ *"Austin Ponders Annexing F1 Racetrack" in Austin Business Journal (Vol. 31, July 8, 2011, No. 18, pp. 1)*
Pub: American City Business Journals Inc.
Ed: Vicky Garza. **Description:** City planners in Austin, Texas are studying the feasibility of annexing the land under and around the Circuit of the Americas Formula One Racetrack being constructed east of the city. The annexation could generate at least $13 million in financial gain over 25 years from property taxes alone.

33520 ■ *"Austin Ventures: Is It a VC Firm?" in Austin Business Journal (Vol. 31, June 17, 2011, No. 15, pp. 1)*
Pub: American City Business Journals Inc.
Ed: Christopher Calnan. **Description:** Investment firm Austin Ventures could lose its classification as a venture capital firm under a new definition of venture capital by the Securities and Exchange Commission. The reclassification could result in additional expenses for Austin Ventures, which has two-thirds of its investments in growth equity transactions.

33521 ■ *"Austin on Verge of Losing 7,500 Jobs" in Austin Business Journal (Vol. 31, May 6, 2011, No. 9, pp. 1)*
Pub: American City Business Journals Inc.
Ed: Jacob Dirr. **Description:** Proposed state budget cuts are seen to result in the loss of as many as 7,500 public and private sector jobs in Austin, Texas, with the private sector losing the majority of workers. Comments from analysts are included.

33522 ■ *"Auto Supplier Stock Battered In Wake Of Wall Street Woes" in Crain's Detroit Business (Vol. 24, September 29, 2008, No. 39, pp. 4)*
Pub: Crain Communications Inc.
Ed: Ryan Beene. **Description:** Due to the volatility of the stock market and public perception of the $700 billion banking bailout, auto suppliers are now facing a dramatic drop in their shares. Statistical data included.

33523 ■ *"Automotive Trouble" in Canadian Business (Vol. 82, April 27, 2009, No. 7, pp. 11)*
Pub: Rogers Media
Ed: Thomas Watson. **Description:** The likely effects of a possible bailout of the U.S. automotive industry are examined. Some experts believe that a bailout will be good for the automotive industry and on the U.S. economy. Others argue however, that the nationalization may have a negative impact on the industry and on the economy.

33524 ■ *"A Baby Step to the South" in Canadian Business (Vol. 81, July 22, 2008, No. 12-13, pp. 21)*
Pub: Rogers Media Ltd.
Ed: Jane Bao. **Description:** Canada's free trade agreement (FTA) with Colombia is seen as Canada's re-engagement with Latin America. Some politicians believe that the FTA is more of a political agreement than a trade agreement with Colombia. Key information on Canada's trade agreements, as well as trade with Colombia and Latin American countries, is presented.

33525 ■ *"Back to Business for Bishop Museum" in Hawaii Business (Vol. 54, August 2008, No. 2, pp. 53)*
Pub: Hawaii Business Publishing
Ed: Shara Enay. **Description:** Bishop Museum, ranked 224 in Hawaii Business' top 250 companies for 2008, had $29.5 million in gross sales for 2007, up 52.8 percent from the $19.3 million gross sales in 2006. The company has cut 24 positions in a restructuring effort for the museum's sustainability. Grants, artifacts and plans for sustainable operations are discussed.

33526 ■ *"Back Off on ABM Legislation, Banks Warn MPs" in Globe & Mail (April 20, 2007, pp. B1)*
Pub: CTVglobemedia Publishing Inc.
Ed: Steven Chase. **Description:** The efforts of banks to prevent legislation by the Canadian government on the automated banking machine levies charged from customers of other institutions are described.

33527 ■ *"Back on Track-Or Off the Rails?" in Business Week (September 22, 2008, No. 4100, pp. 22)*
Pub: McGraw-Hill Companies, Inc.
Ed: Peter Coy; Tara Kalwarski. **Description:** Discusses the possible scenarios the American economy may undergo due to the takeover of Fannie Mae and Freddie Mac. Statistical data included.

33528 ■ *Bad Money*
Pub: Viking Press/Penguin Group
Ed: Kevin Phillips. **Released:** April 15, 2008. **Description:** How the financial sector has hijacked the American economy, aided by Washington's ruinous faith in the efficiency of markets.

33529 ■ *"Bad Paper" in Canadian Business (Vol. 80, November 19, 2007, No. 23, pp. 34)*
Pub: Rogers Media
Ed: Al Rosen. **Description:** The Canadian government froze the market for non-bank asset-backed commercial paper (ABCP) August 2007, which means holders will be unable to withdraw investments. The crisis and value of ABCP are discussed.

33530 ■ *Bad Samaritans: The Myth of Free Trade and the Secret History of Capitalism*
Pub: Bloomsbury USA
Ed: Ha-Joon Chang. **Released:** 2009. **Price:** $26.95. **Description:** Economist challenges open-market proponents and believes that free trade would do more harm than good.

33531 ■ *"Bailout Forgets the 'Little Guys" in The Business Journal-Milwaukee (Vol. 25, September 26, 2008, No. 53, pp. A1)*
Pub: American City Business Journals, Inc.
Ed: Rich Kirchen. **Description:** Community Bankers of Wisconsin and the Wisconsin Bankers Association are urging members to approach congressional representatives and remind them to include local banks in building the $700 billion bailout plan. WBA president and CEO Kurt Bauer thinks that it is only fair to include smaller institutions in the bailout. The initial bailout plan and its benefit for the smaller banks are examined.

33532 ■ *"Banking Bailout: Boost or Bust?" in Crain's Detroit Business (Vol. 24, September 29, 2008, No. 39, pp. 1)*
Pub: Crain Communications Inc.
Ed: Amy Lane. **Description:** Economic insiders discuss the banking bailout and how it might impact the state of Michigan.

33533 ■ *"Bankruptcy Blowback" in Business Week (September 22, 2008, No. 4100, pp. 36)*
Pub: McGraw-Hill Companies, Inc.
Ed: Jessica Silver-Greenberg. **Description:** Changes to bankruptcy laws which were enacted in 2005 after banks and other financial institutions lobbied hard for them are now suffering the consequences of the laws which force more troubled borrowers to let their homes go into foreclosure; lenders suffer financially every time they have to take on a foreclosure and the laws in which they lobbied so hard to see enacted are now becoming a problem for these lending institutions. Details of the changes in the laws are outlined as are the affects on the consumer, the economy and the lenders.

33534 ■ *"Banks Lower Rates on CDs, Deposits" in Baltimore Business Journal (Vol. 27, January 1, 2010, No. 35, pp. 1)*
Pub: American City Business Journals
Ed: Gary Haber. **Description:** Greater Baltimore area banks in Maryland have lowered their rates on certificates of deposits (CDs) and money market accounts, which could indicate the incoming trend for the first half of 2010. A banking industry forecast shows that lower Federal Funds rate, low inflation, and a new Federal Deposit Insurance Corporation (FDIC) rule might cause the rates to drop even further. Details on the FDIC rule are given.

33535 ■ *"Banks, Retailers Squabble Over Fees" in Baltimore Business Journal (Vol. 28, June 18, 2010, No. 6, pp. 1)*
Pub: Baltimore Business Journal
Ed: Gary Haber. **Description:** How an amendment to the financial regulatory reform bill would affect the bankers' and retailers' conflict over interchange fees is discussed. Interchange fees are paid for by retailers every time consumers make purchases through debit cards. Industry estimates indicate that approximately $50 million in such fees are paid by retailers.

33536 ■ *"Bark and Bite" in Canadian Business (Vol. 81, March 31, 2008, No. 5, pp. 20)*
Pub: Rogers Media
Ed: Rachel Pulfer. **Description:** Hillary Clinton and Barack Obama both want to renegotiate NAFTA but the most job losses in the American manufacturing industry is caused by technological change and Asian competition than with NAFTA. The risk of protectionist trade policies has increased given the political atmosphere.

33537 ■ *"Barred Collection Agency Sued by Colorado AG" in Collections & Credit Risk (Vol. 15, August 1, 2010, No. 7, pp. 7)*
Pub: SourceMedia Inc.
Description: Collection agency run by Chad Lee received notice that it is barred from collecting in the State of Colorado by Attorney General John Suther's office. A ruling cited that the firm engages in harassment or abuse and/or threats of violence, made false representations as to its legal status of debts, made false and misleading representations of nonpayment of debts that would result in arrest, and that Lee failed to disclose his previous felony conviction.

33538 ■ *"Basel3 Quick Fix Actually Neither" in Canadian Business (Vol. 83, October 12, 2010, No. 17, pp. 19)*
Pub: Rogers Media Ltd.
Ed: Thomas Watson. **Description:** Information about the so-called Basel 3 standards, which will require banks to hold top-quality capital totaling at least 7 percent of their risk-bearing assets is provided. The rules' supporters believe that a good balance has been reached between improving the Basel 2 framework and maintaining enough lending capital to stimulate an economic growth.

33539 ■ *"Battle of the Titans" in Canadian Business (Vol. 81, March 17, 2008, No. 4, pp. 15)*
Pub: Rogers Media
Ed: Rachel Pulfer. **Description:** Regulatory authorities in Canada gave Thomson Corp and Reuters Group PLC the permission to go ahead with their merger. The merged companies could eclipse Bloomberg LP's market share of 33 percent. Authorities also required Thomson and Reuters to sell some of their databases to competitors.

33540 ■ *"Belmont Annexation Approved" in Charlotte Observer (February 7, 2007)*
Pub: Knight-Ridder/Tribune Business News
Ed: Jefferson George. **Description:** Belmont, North Carolina City Council approved annexation of nearly 64 acres. The land will be used to develop a residential community.

33541 ■ *"Beltway Monitor" in Mergers & Acquisitions: The Dealmaker's Journal (March 1, 2008)*
Pub: SourceMedia, Inc.
Description: Discusses in detail The Foreign Investment and National Security Act of 2007 which was put into legislation due to the initially approved acquisition of certain U.S. ports by Dubai Ports World which set off a firestorm of controversy.

33542 ■ *"Bernier Open to Telecom Changes" in Globe & Mail (March 22, 2006, pp. B1)*
Pub: CTVglobemedia Publishing Inc.
Ed: Simon Tuck. **Description:** Federal Industry Minister Maxime Bernier of Canada says that he is open to scrapping restrictions on foreign ownership in telecommunications. His views on telecom industry are detailed.

33543 ■ *"BETC Backers Plot Future" in Business Journal Portland (Vol. 27, December 10, 2010, No. 41, pp. 1)*
Pub: Portland Business Journal
Ed: Erik Siemers. **Description:** A coalition of clean energy groups and industrial manufacturers have spearheaded a campaign aimed at persuading Oregon legislators that the state's Business Energy Tax Credit (BETC) is vital in job creation. Oregon's BETC grants tax credits for 50 percent of an eligible renewable or clean energy project's cost. However, some legislators propose BETC's abolition.

33544 ■ *"Bethesda Stepping Out" in Business Courier (Vol. 27, October 15, 2010, No. 24, pp. 1)*
Pub: Business Courier
Ed: James Ritchie. **Description:** Nonprofit organization Bethesda Inc. is planning to donate $5 million a year for the next three years to Greater Cincinnati health care reforms. Bethesda revealed that it announced its donations to pressure other organizations to help.

33545 ■ *"Beware of E15" in Rental Product News (Vol. 33, October 2011)*
Pub: Cygnus Business Media
Ed: Curt Bennink. **Description:** Environmental Protection Agency (EPA) set a new regulation that grants partial waivers to allow gasoline containing up to 15 percent ethanol (E15) to be introduced into commerce for use in model year 2001 and newer light-duty motor vehicles, subject to certain conditions.

33546 ■ *"Beware of Rotting Money" in Barron's (Vol. 89, July 13, 2009, No. 28, pp. 31)*
Pub: Dow Jones & Co., Inc.
Ed: Thomas G. Donlan. **Description:** Inflation can take hold of a country and do it great harm; it is caused by people, most particularly central bankers in charge of the world's reserve currency. Arrogant economists pushed the belief that the government can engineer the economy and it is argued that there is trouble ahead when the government tries to control the economy.

33547 ■ *"Bigger TIF Makes Development Inroads" in The Business Journal-Serving Metropolitan Kansas City (Vol. 26, July 11, 2008, No. 44)*
Pub: American City Business Journals, Inc.
Ed: Rob Roberts. **Description:** On July 9, 2008 the Tax Increment Financing Commission voted to expand a TIF district to Tiffany Springs Road. The plan for the TIF district close to Kansas City International Airport is to include a-half mile of the road. The impacts of the expansion on construction projects and on the road network are analyzed.

33548 ■ *"Bill Kaneko" in Hawaii Business (Vol. 53, December 2007, No. 6, pp. 32)*
Pub: Hawaii Business Publishing
Ed: David K. Choo. **Description:** Hawaii Institute for Public Affairs chief executive officer and president Bill Kaneko believes that the Hawaiian economy is booming, however, he also asserts that the economy is too focused on tourism and real estate. Kaneko has also realized the that the will of the people is strong while he was helping with the Hawaiian 2050 Sustainability Plan. The difficulties of making a sustainable Hawaii are discussed.

33549 ■ *"Bills Raise Blues Debate; An Unfair Edge or Level Playing Field?" in Crain's Detroit Business (Vol. 24, January 21, 2008, No. 3)*
Pub: Crain Communications Inc. - Detroit
Ed: Sherri Begin. **Description:** Changes in Michigan state law would change the way health insurance can be sold to individuals. Michigan Blue Cross Blue Shield is working to keep its tax-exempt status while staying competitive against for-profit insurers and nonprofit HMOs.

33550 ■ *"Bills Would Regulate Mortgage Loan Officers" in Crain's Detroit Business (Vol. 24, February 25, 2008, No. 8, pp. 9)*
Pub: Crain Communications Inc. - Detroit
Ed: Amy Lane. **Description:** New legislation in Michigan, if passed, would create a registration process for mortgage loan officers in the state in order to address the mortgage loan crisis.

33551 ■ *"Blues at the Toy Fair: Industry Reeling From Recalls, Lower Sales Volumes" in Crain's New York Business (February 18, 2008)*
Pub: Crain Communications Inc.
Ed: Elisabeth Cordova. **Description:** Over 1,500 toy developers and vendors will attend the American International Toy Fair, expected to be low-key due to recent recalls of toys not meeting American safety standards. Toy retailers and manufacturers, as well as the Chinese government, are promoting product testing to prevent toxic metals in toys.

33552 ■ *Bold Endeavors: How Our Government Built America, and Why It Must Rebuild Now*
Pub: Simon and Schuster Inc.
Contact: Carolyn Reidy, President
E-mail: carolyn.reidy@simonandschuster.com
Ed: Felix Rohatyn. **Released:** 2009. **Price:** $26.00. **Description:** The federal government built the nation by investing in initiatives like the Erie Canal and the G.I. Bill and why it should do the same at this point in history is examined.

33553 ■ *"Borrow For Tomorrow" in Canadian Business (Vol. 80, October 8, 2007, No. 20, pp. 193)*
Pub: Rogers Media
Ed: David Wolf. **Description:** The possibility of running deficits in order to finance infrastructures in Canada is discussed. Statistics show that the country's net government debt is below 25 percent of GDP as of 2007, and that the government is spending less on public infrastructure. Based on these figures, it is expected that an increase in government debt could help in making infrastructure investments.

33554 ■ *"Boston Globe" in Ice Cream Reporter (Vol. 21, August 20, 2008, No. 9, pp. 7)*
Pub: Ice Cream Reporter
Description: Boston City Council approved an ordinance that will limit when ice cream vendors can announce their presence with music over loud speakers. The rules are simple: when the wheels stop moving, the jingles stop playing.

33555 ■ *"Both Eyes on the Prize" in Canadian Business (Vol. 83, September 14, 2010, No. 15, pp. 42)*
Pub: Rogers Media Ltd.
Ed: Jacqueline Nelson. **Description:** North American executive compensation has fundamentally shifted partly due to pressure from the US government and recent adjustments in the way CEO pay packages are structured. The changes have also become common practice in Canada and helped in scrutinizing the executive pay.

33556 ■ *"Brace for the Bill" in Boston Business Journal (Vol. 27, December 28, 2007, No. 48, pp. 1)*
Pub: American City Business Journals Inc.
Ed: Mark Hollmer. **Description:** Historic 2006 Massachusetts Health Care Reform Law seems successful because many people have signed up for health insurance within one year of its implementation. However, rising premiums and other factors are threatening the health industry.

33557 ■ *"Bringing Manufacturing Concerns to Springfield" in Crain's Chicago Business (Vol. 31, March 31, 2008, No. 13, pp. 6)*
Pub: Crain Communications, Inc.
Ed: Paul Merrion. **Description:** Profile of the new executive vice-president of Tooling & Manufacturing Assn., Paul Merrion, a man who plans to grow TMA's membership with an aggressive legislative agenda in Springfield.

33558 ■ *"Broadway Casino Climbing Hills to Get to Gambling" in Business Courier (Vol. 26, January 1, 2010, No. 37, pp. 1)*
Pub: American City Business Journals, Inc.
Ed: Dan Monk. **Description:** Rock Ventures LLC, operators of the Broadway Commons Casino, needs approval from the Ohio General Assembly and the to-be-created Ohio Casino Control Commission to commence operations.

33559 ■ *"Brown At Center of Local CleanTech Lobbying Efforts" in Boston Business Journal (Vol. 30, October 15, 2010, No. 36, pp. 1)*
Pub: Boston Business Journal
Ed: Kyle Alspach. **Description:** U.S. Senator Scott Brown has been active in lobbying for energy reform in Massachusetts. Brown has been meeting with business groups seeking the reforms.

33560 ■ *"Builders, Unions Aim to Cut Costs; Pushing Changes to Regain Share of Residential Market; Seek Council's Help" in Crain's New York Business*
Pub: Crain Communications, Inc.
Ed: Erik Engquist. **Description:** Union contractors and workers are worried about a decline in their market share for housing so they intend to ask the City Council to impose new safety and benefit standards on all contractors to avoid being undercut by nonunion competitors.

33561 ■ *"Building Targeted for Marriott in Violation" in Business Journal-Milwaukee (Vol. 28, December 24, 2010, No. 12, pp. A1)*
Pub: Milwaukee Business Journal
Ed: Sean Ryan. **Description:** Milwaukee, Wisconsin's Department of Neighborhood Services has ordered structural improvements and safeguards for the Pioneer Building after three violations from structural failures were found. Pioneer was among the five buildings wanted by Jackson Street Management LLC to demolish for the new Marriott Hotel.

33562 ■ *"Business Looks for Results in Congress" in Baltimore Business Journal (Vol. 28, November 5, 2010, No. 26, pp. 1)*
Pub: Baltimore Business Journal
Ed: Kent Hoover. **Description:** Republican candidates in the 2010 Congressional elections were overwhelmingly supported by the business community. Republican John Boehner, who will be the next Speaker of the House, says that the party's victory would end economic uncertainty and would assist small businesses to rehire workers.

33563 ■ *"The Business of Medicine: Maintaining a Healthy Bottom Line" in Black Enterprise (Vol. 41, October 2010, No. 3, pp. 60)*
Pub: Earl G. Graves Publishing Co. Inc.
Ed: Marcia A. Reed-Woodard. **Description:** Sustainable government reform requires reconstruction in the areas of financing and delivery of services in the field of medicine.

33564 ■ *"Business Must Stand Up And Be Counted" in Crain's Detroit Business (Vol. 24, October 6, 2008, No. 40, pp. 6)*
Pub: Crain Communications, Inc.
Description: Discusses the challenges that the new mayor of Detroit faces concerning business, the state of the economy and the exceptionally tight budget the city is running on, which includes a lot of red ink. It is very likely that the city is going to see tax revenues fall substantially in the next few months and business leaders may find it in their favor to lend their support to the new mayor as well as provide him with the executive talent necessary to overcome some of these crucial issues.

33565 ■ *"Business Put Cash Behind Bernstein" in Baltimore Business Journal (Vol. 28, August 20, 2010, No. 15, pp. 1)*
Pub: Baltimore Business Journal
Ed: Scott Dance. **Description:** Baltimore, Maryland-based businesses have invested $40,000 to support lawyer Gregg L. Bernstein in the 2010 State Attorney election. The election campaign is being fueled by fear of a crime surge. Many businesses have been dealing with crimes such as muggings, shootings, and car break-ins.

33566 ■ *"Business Tax Complaints Prompt Action" in Sacramento Business Journal (Vol. 28, July 29, 2011, No. 22, pp. 1)*
Pub: Sacramento Business Journal
Ed: Michael Shaw. **Description:** California's Board of Equalization has amended a program to collect taxes from businesses for out-of-state purchases due to a flood of complaints from owners who find the paperwork costly and time consuming. The program was created in 2009 and fell short of expectations as it only brought in $56 million in the first two years against the projected $264 million.

33567 ■ *"Businesses Balk at 1099 Provision in Health Reform Law" in Baltimore Business Journal (Vol. 28, August 13, 2010, No. 14, pp. 1)*
Pub: Baltimore Business Journal
Ed: Scott Dance. **Description:** Small business advocates and accountants have criticized the Internal Revenue Service Form 1099 provision in the health care reform law as not worth the cost of time and money. Critics believe the policy would create a deluge of the documents that is too much for the companies or the IRS to handle. Details of the provision are also discussed.

33568 ■ *"Businesses Keep a Watchful Eye on Worker's Comp" in The Business Journal-Serving Greater Tampa Bay (September 5, 2008)*
Pub: American City Business Journals, Inc.
Ed: Jane Meinhardt. **Description:** Pending a ruling from the Florida Supreme Court that could uphold the 2003 changes on workers' compensation law, the

outcome would include restrictions on claimant attorneys' fees and allow the competitive workers' compensation insurance rates to remain low. However, insurance rates are expected to go up if the court overturns the changes.

33569 ■ *"By Land, Air, and Sea: New Passport Rules in Effect" in Black Enterprise (Vol. 37, January 2007, No. 6., pp. 101)*
Pub: Earl G. Graves Publishing Co. Inc.
Ed: Stephanie Young. **Description:** As part of a new security measure by the Western Hemisphere Travel Initiative, a passport will now be required for U.S. citizens traveling by air between Mexico, Canada, South and Central America, and the Caribbean. This initiative, designed to easily identify travelers and enforce border security, will most likely extend to land or sea travel no later than January 1, 2008.

33570 ■ *"A Call to Make SOX More Elastic" in Canadian Business (Vol. 80, February 12, 2007, No. 4, pp. 14)*
Pub: Rogers Media
Ed: Rachel Pulfer. **Description:** The suggestion of New York City Governor Eliot Spitzer to relax the Sarbanes-Oxley Act of 2002 due to its 'excessive' regulation is discussed.

33571 ■ *"Can Turfway Park Stay in the Race?" in Business Courier (Vol. 26, January 8, 2010, No. 38, pp. 1)*
Pub: American City Business Journals, Inc.
Ed: Jon Newberry. **Description:** Legalization of slot machine gambling in Kentucky could affect raceway Turfway Park and the state's thoroughbred industry. Thousands of farms and jobs in the industry could be lost if slot machine gambling is approved.

33572 ■ *"Canada Nears European Trade Treaty" in Globe & Mail (February 5, 2007, pp. B1)*
Pub: CTVglobemedia Publishing Inc.
Ed: Steven Chase. **Description:** The probable establishment of a treaty by Canada with Norway, Switzerland and Iceland for free-trade is discussed. The treaty will allow an annual business of $11 billion to take place in Canada.

33573 ■ *"Canada Wins Second NAFTA Decision on Softwood Tariffs" in Globe & Mail (March 18, 2006, pp. B2)*
Pub: CTVglobemedia Publishing Inc.
Ed: Steven Chase; Peter Kennedy. **Description:** Canada has won a second major North American Free Trade Agreement (NAFTA) victory in five years of legal battles over U.S. tariffs on softwood. Details of the controversy and ruling are presented.

33574 ■ *"Canada's Clean Energy Advantages Offer a Bright Future" in Canadian Business (Vol. 83, August 17, 2010, No. 13-14, pp. 38)*
Pub: Rogers Media Ltd.
Ed: Don McKinnon. **Description:** Canada has clean energy advantages in the greenhouse gas emission-free CANada Deuterium Uranium reactor technology and carbon neutral biomass fuels that were continuously ignored by policy makers. Both are proven to significantly reduce emissions while providing reliable, affordable and secure electricity.

33575 ■ *"Canada's New Government Introduces Amendments to Deny Work Permits to Foreign Strippers" in Canadian Corporate News (May 16, 2007)*
Pub: Comtex News Network Inc.
Description: Honourable Diane Finley, Minister of Citizenship and Immigration, introduced amendments to the Immigration and Refugee Protection Act (IRPA) to help prevent the exploitation and abuse of vulnerable foreign workers, such as strippers.

33576 ■ *"Candidates Differ On State's Green Streak" in Business Journal Portland (Vol. 27, October 22, 2010, No. 34, pp. 1)*
Pub: Portland Business Journal
Ed: Andy Giegerich. **Description:** The views of Oregon gubernatorial candidates Chris Dudley and John Kitzhaber on the state's economy and on environmental policies are presented. Both Dudley, who is a Republican, and his Democratic challenger believe that biomass could help drive the state's economy. Both candidates also pledged changes in Oregon's business energy tax credit (BETC) program.

33577 ■ *"Candidates Won't Bash Fed; Rate Cuts Bash Savers" in Barron's (Vol. 88, March 24, 2008, No. 12, pp. 31)*
Pub: Dow Jones & Company, Inc.
Ed: Jim McTague. **Description:** Candidates in the 2008 US presidential election, like the current administration, do not and will not bash the Federal Reserve. The Federal Reserve's aggressive interest rate cuts hurt the incomes of people depending on their savings accounts.

33578 ■ *"CanWEA Unveils WindVision for BC: 5,250 MW of Wind Energy by 2025" in CNW Group (October 4, 2011)*
Pub: CNW Group
Contact: Carolyn McGill-Davidson, President
Description: Wind industry leaders are asking British Columbia, Canada policy makers to created conditions to further develop and integrate wind energy in accordance with greenhouse gas emission targets and projected economic growth. Statistical data included.

33579 ■ *"Capital Ideas: Regions to Lansing: Focus on Taxes, Reform, Keeping Talent" in Crain's Detroit Business (Vol. 24, October 6, 2008)*
Pub: Crain Communications, Inc.
Ed: Amy Lane. **Description:** Michigan must make bold and dramatic changes in public policy regarding business legislation. The tax structure, unemployment issues and attracting and retaining talent are among the issues the state must confront, especially in this tough economic climate.

33580 ■ *"Capital Metro May Soon Seek Contractor to Replace Star Tran" in Austin Business Journal (Vol. 31, June 10, 2011, No. 14, pp. 1)*
Pub: American City Business Journals Inc.
Ed: Vicky Garza. **Description:** Capital Metropolitan Transportation Authority may be forced to contract out its bus services provided by StarTran Inc. as early as September 2012 following legislation approved by the Texas legislature. The bill originates in a report by the Sunset Advisory Commission. Details are included.

33581 ■ *"A Capitol Opportunity" in Hispanic Business (Vol. 30, September 2008, No. 9, pp. 82)*
Pub: Hispanic Business, Inc.
Ed: John Schumacher. **Description:** Launched in 2003, the Polanco fellows program is named after former state Senator Richard Polanco, a founder and chairman of the California Latino Caucus Institute. The program offers young Hispanics a chance to experience public policy and the functioning of the California Capitol through a 12-month, on-the-job Capitol training.

33582 ■ *"Carbon Trading: Current Schemes and Future Developments" in Energy Policy (Vol. 39, October 2011, No. 10, pp. 6040-6054)*
Pub: Reed Elsevier Reference Publishing
Ed: Slobodan Perdan, Adisa Azapagic. **Description:** Current and future developments regarding carbon trading is highlighted.

33583 ■ *"Case IH Announces Strategy to Meet 2014 Clean Air Standards" in Farm Industry News (September 15, 2011)*
Pub: Penton Business Media Inc.
Ed: Jodie Wehrspann. **Description:** Case IH will meet EPA's stringent engine emissions limits imposed in 2014, called Tier 4. The limits call for a 90 percent reduction in particulate matter and nitrogen oxides (NOx) over the Tier 3 requirements from a few years ago.

33584 ■ *"The Case for Treating the Sex Trade as an Industry" in Canadian Business (Vol. 83, October 12, 2010, No. 17, pp. 9)*
Pub: Rogers Media Ltd.
Ed: Steve Maich. **Description:** It is believed that the worst aspects of prostitution in Canada are exacerbated by the fact that it must take place in secret. The laws that deal with the market for sex have led to an unsafe working environment. Prostitutes believe their industry needs to be sanctioned and regulated rather than ignored and reviled.

33585 ■ *"CBC Chief: Future is Now" in Business Courier (Vol. 27, August 13, 2010, No. 15, pp. 1)*
Pub: Business Courier
Ed: Lucy May. **Description:** Tom Williams, chairman of the Cincinnati Business Committee (CBC), maintains that politicians and business leaders must cooperate to ensure the competitiveness of the city for the 21st Century. Under Williams' leadership, the CBC has put emphasis on initiatives related to government efficiency, economic development, and public education. Williams' views on a proposed inland port are given.

33586 ■ *"Cell Tower Potential" in Black Enterprise (Vol. 37, October 2006, No. 3, pp. 86)*
Pub: Earl G. Graves Publishing Co. Inc.
Ed: James C. Johnson. **Description:** Due to local zoning that does not allow new cell towers to be too close to existing ones along with other issues only certain properties are eligible as leasing cites to wireless carriers.

33587 ■ *"CEOs Divided About Census" in Canadian Business (Vol. 83, August 17, 2010, No. 13-14, pp. 20)*
Pub: Rogers Media Ltd.
Ed: Jacqueline Nelson. **Description:** A Compass poll of Canadian CEOs on what the government should do with controversial long-form census is presented. The poll results show that 30 percent believe the government should remove any threat of punishment for failure to complete the survey. The CEOs also believe the law must be enforced by the government to encourage participation.

33588 ■ *"The CEO's New Armor" in Conde Nast Portfolio (Vol. 2, June 2008, No. 6, pp. 56)*
Pub: Conde Nast Publications
Contact: David Carey, President
Ed: John Cassidy. **Description:** Due to a new breed in C.E.O.'s contracts it is nearly impossible to fire them regardless of their performance. Despite the Sarbanes-Oxley Act in which attempted to codify C.E.O. responsibilities, corporate bosses responded by quietly demanding individual contracts, which, in many cases, were drawn up by their own lawyers and accepted by company boards with no outside oversight or review.

33589 ■ *"CEOs Split on Migrant Workers" in Canadian Business (Vol. 83, September 14, 2010, No. 15, pp. 23)*
Pub: Rogers Media Ltd.
Ed: Jacqueline Nelson. **Description:** A survey of Canadian CEOs shows that 49 percent of the respondents believe it was wrong to suspend the immigration programs and companies should be allowed to hire the most skilled workers regardless of citizenship. However, 42 percent believe the suspension was right because employment of Canadians must take precedence.

33590 ■ *"Changes Sought to Health Law" in Baltimore Business Journal (Vol. 28, July 30, 2010, No. 12, pp. 1)*
Pub: Baltimore Business Journal
Ed: Kent Hoover. **Description:** Business groups that opposed health care reform are working to undo parts of the new laws even before they go into effect. Business groups are gaining support for one legislative fix, which is repealing the law's provision that requires all businesses to file 1099 forms with the IRS any time they pay more than $600 a year to another business.

33591 ■ *"Changing the Rules of the Accounting Game" in Canadian Business (Vol. 81, December 8, 2008, No. 21, pp. 19)*
Pub: Rogers Media Ltd.
Ed: Al Rosen. **Description:** Interference from world politicians in developing accounting standards is believed to have resulted in untested rules that are

inferior to current standards. European lawmakers have recently asked to change International Financial Reporting Standards.

33592 ■ *"Chesley Fighting Ky. Disbarment" in Business Courier (Vol. 27, September 10, 2010, No. 19, pp. 1)*
Pub: Business Courier
Ed: Jon Newberry. **Description:** Stan Chesley, a Cincinnati attorney, has been accused of making false statements to the courts and bar officials, self-dealing in violation of the bar's conflict of interest rules, and failing to adequately inform clients. Kentucky Bar Association officials will seek to have Chesley permanently disbarred.

33593 ■ *"China Vs. the World: Whose Technology Is It?" in Harvard Business Review (Vol. 88, December 2010, No. 12, pp. 94)*
Pub: Harvard Business School Publishing
Ed: Thomas M Hout, Pankaj Ghemawat. **Description:** Examination of the regulation the Chinese government is implementing that require foreign corporations wishing to do business in the country to give up their new technologies. These regulations avoid World Trade Organization technology transfer provisions and complicate the convergence of socialism and capitalism.

33594 ■ *"China's Transition to Green Energy Systems" in Energy Policy (Vol. 39, October 2011, No. 10, pp. 5909-5919)*
Pub: Reed Elsevier Reference Publishing
Ed: Wei Li, Guojun Song, Melanie Beresford, Ben Ma. **Description:** The economics of home solar water heaters and their growing popularity in Dezhous City, China is discussed.

33595 ■ *Chinese Ethnic Business: Global and Local Perspectives*
Pub: Routledge
Ed: Eric Fong; Chiu Luk. **Released:** May 2009. **Price:** $39.95 paperback. **Description:** Globalization impacts on the development of Chinese businesses are analyzed, focusing on economic globalization of the United States, Australia, and Canada. Information is focused on economic globalization and Chinese community development, transnational linkages, local urban structures, homogenization and place attachment, as well as methodology such as ethnographic studies, historical analysis, geographic studies and statistical analysis.

33596 ■ *Cities from the Arabian Desert: The Building of Jubail and Yanbu in Saudi Arabia*
Pub: Turnaround Associates
Ed: Andrea H. Pampanini. **Released:** May 2005. **Price:** $35.00. **Description:** An overview of Saudi Arabia's government to take control of the nation's natural resources and change the government, educational system, and its culture by evolving into a modern industrial society.

33597 ■ *"City Board Tweaks Internet Cafe Ordinance" in Ocala Star-Banner (July 19, 2011)*
Pub: Ocala Star-Banner
Ed: Susan Latham Carr. **Description:** Ocala Planning and Zoning Commission revised the proposed draft of the Internet Cafe ordinance by eliminating the cap on the number of locations allowed, but keeping fees and number of devices the same.

33598 ■ *"City Consults Executives on Police Hire" in Business Courier (Vol. 27, August 27, 2010, No. 17, pp. 1)*
Pub: Business Courier
Ed: Lucy May, Dan Monk. **Description:** The City of Cincinnati, Ohio has begun a selection process for the new police chief by consulting the city's business executives. The city charter amendment known as Issue 5 has removed civil service protection from the chief's post and enables City Manager Milton Dohoney to hire a chief from outside the department.

33599 ■ *"CityLink Project On Hold" in Business Courier (Vol. 24, November 9, 2008, No. 30, pp. 3)*
Pub: American City Business Journals, Inc.
Ed: Dan Monk. **Description:** Developers of the CityLink project have indicated that it will be at least a year before they start the planned social services mall at 800 Bank West End. According to Tim Senff, Citylink CEO, the company wants to build bridges before constructing the buildings. The project's critics are still considering whether to appeal a court ruling regarding the facility's compliance with the city's zoning code.

33600 ■ *"City's New Energy Audits to Spawn 'Fantastic' Market" in Austin Business JournalInc. (Vol. 28, November 14, 2008, No. 35, pp. 1)*
Pub: American City Business Journals
Ed: Jean Kwon. **Description:** A new law requiring older homes to undergo energy use audits is seen to provide new business for some companies in the Austin, Texas area. The new law is seen to create a new industry of performance testers. Details of the new ordinance are also given.

33601 ■ *"Climate Law Could Dig into our Coal-Dusted Pockets" in Business Courier (Vol. 26, November 20, 2009, No. 30, pp. 1)*
Pub: American City Business Journals, Inc.
Ed: Lucy May. **Description:** Passage of federal climate legislation into law is set to increase household cost for Greater Cincinnati, according to the calculation by the Brookings Institute. The increase for residents of the area will amount to $244 in 2020 and the city was ranked the sixth-highest rate in the nation, behind Indianapolis.

33602 ■ *"Cloudy Skies" in Canadian Business (Vol. 81, October 27, 2008, No. 18, pp. 101)*
Pub: Rogers Media Ltd.
Ed: Andrew Wahl. **Description:** Canada's federal government is expected to implement its regulations on greenhouse-gas emissions by January 1, 2010, but companies are worried because the plan took so long and some details are yet to be revealed. Corporate Canada wants a firm, long-range plan similar to the European Union Emissions Trading Scheme in dealing with greenhouse-gas emissions.

33603 ■ *"Clusters Last Stand?" in Canadian Electronics (Vol. 23, February 2008, No. 1, pp. 6)*
Pub: CLB Media Inc.
Description: Survival of technology clusters was the focus of Strategic Microelectronics Council's conference entitled, 'The Power of Community: Building Technology Clusters in Canada'. Clusters can help foster growth in the microelectronics sector, and it was recognized that government intervention is needed to maintain these clusters.

33604 ■ *"CO2 Emissions Embodied in China-US Trade" in Energy Policy (Vol. 39, October 2011, No. 10, pp. 5980-5987)*
Pub: Reed Elsevier Reference Publishing
Ed: Huibin Du, Guozhu Mao, Alexander M. Smith, Xuxu Wang, Yuan Wang, Jianghong Guo. **Description:** Input and output analysis based on the energy per dollar ratio for carbon dioxide emissions involved in China-United States trade is outlined.

33605 ■ *Code of Federal Regulations: Title 13: Business Credit and Assistance*
Pub: U.S. Government Printing Office
Ed: Department of Commerce Staff. **Released:** May 2007. **Price:** $55.00. **Description:** Title 13 covers regulations governing the activities of the Small Business Administration and the Department of Commerce. Book covers information on business credit, finance, and economic development.

33606 ■ *"Collateral Damage" in Business Courier (Vol. 26, October 16, 2009, No. 25, pp. 1)*
Pub: American City Business Journals, Inc.
Ed: Jon Newberry. **Description:** Non-union construction firms representing Ohio Valley Associated Builders and Contractors Inc. have filed cases against unionized shops claiming violations of wage law in Ohio. Defendants say the violations are minor, however, they believe they are caught in the middle of the group's campaign to change the state's wage law.

33607 ■ *"Collection Agency Issues Whitepaper on Legal and Ethical Methods of Collecting on Overdue Accounts" in Internet Wire (July 20, 2009)*
Pub: Comtex News Network, Inc.
Description: American Profit Recovery, a collection agency based in Massachusetts and Michigan, has updated and reissued a whitepaper on what businesses can and cannot do regarding conversing with their customers in an attempt to collect on overdue accounts and payments. A detailed summary on the federal laws associated with collecting on overdue accounts is outlined in such a way that any business owner, manager, or responsible party can easily understand.

33608 ■ *"Combat Mission: Rebuffed, BAE Systems Fights Army Contract Decision" in Business Courier (Vol. 26, September 25, 2009)*
Pub: American City Business Journals, Inc.
Ed: Jon Newberry. **Description:** BAE Systems filed a complaint with the US Government Accountability Office after the US Army issued an order to BAE's competitor for armoured trucks which is potentially worth over $3 billion. Hundreds of jobs in Butler County, Ohio hinge on the success of the contract protest.

33609 ■ *"Coming Soon: Bailouts of Fannie and Freddie" in Barron's (Vol. 88, July 14, 2008, No. 28, pp. 14)*
Pub: Dow Jones & Co., Inc.
Ed: Jonathan R. Laing. **Description:** Assurances from the government that Fannie Mae and Freddie Mac are adequately capitalized and able to carry on their duties as guarantors or owners of over $5 trillion of U.S. home mortgages are designed to keep both entities afloat until they attempt to raise $10 billion in new equity. The government would assume any losses in a bailout and owners of the banks' papers would profit as yields drop.

33610 ■ *"Commentary" in Small Business Economic Trends (September 2010, pp. 3)*
Pub: National Federation of Independent Business
Ed: William C. Dunkelberg, Holly Wade. **Description:** A commentary on the economic trends for small businesses in the U.S. is presented. An analysis of the unemployment rate and inflation is given. Economic growth is also expected to remain sub-par for some time, unless new policies are introduced.

33611 ■ *"Commentary. On Federal Reserve's Cut of Interest Rates" in Small Business Economic Trends (January 2008, pp. 3)*
Pub: National Federation of Independent Business
Description: Federal Reserve cut interest rates and announced its economic outlook on September 18, 2007 to stimulate spending. The cut in interest rates, however, may not help in supporting consumer spending because savers may lose interest income. The expected economic impact of the interest rate cuts and the U.S. economic outlook are also discussed.

33612 ■ *"Commentary. Small Business Economic Trends" in Small Business Economic Trends (March 2008, pp. 3)*
Pub: National Federation of Independent Business
Ed: William C. Dunkelberg, Holly Wade. **Description:** Commentary on the economic trends for small businesses in the U.S. is presented. Analysis of the labor market and low interest rates is given. The effect of the Federal Reserve's policy announcement on small business owner optimism is also discussed.

33613 ■ *"Commentary. Small Business Economic Trends" in Small Business Economic Trends (February 2008, pp. 3)*
Pub: National Federation of Independent Business
Ed: William C. Dunkelberg, Holly Wade. **Description:** Commentary on the economic trends for small businesses in the U.S. is presented. Analysis of the

U.S. Federal Reserve Board's efforts to prevent a recession is given. Reduction in business inventories is also discussed.

33614 ■ *"Commentary: US Economic Recovery and Policy" in Small Business Economic Trends (July 2010, pp. 3)*
Pub: National Federation of Independent Business
Description: U.S. Government is making economic recovery difficult, with one of the largest tax increases in history arriving in six months. Meanwhile, Congress is looking into taxing successful businesses, which will potentially hamper growth and real investment. Other insights on the government's role in the country's economic growth are presented.

33615 ■ *"Commodity Speculation: Over the Top?" in Barron's (Vol. 89, July 13, 2009, No. 28, pp. 22)*
Pub: Dow Jones & Co., Inc.
Ed: Gene Epstein. **Description:** Commodity Futures Trading Commission is planning to impose position limits on speculators of oil and other commodities as energy costs rebound from their lows. These regulations make much sense and these position limits would greatly diminish the cash commitment of the commodity index traders if these were imposed on speculators and swaps dealers properly.

33616 ■ *"Commotion Pictures; Bill C-10: Is It Censorship or Merely Inept?" in Canadian Business (Vol. 81, March 31, 2008, No. 5, pp. 10)*
Pub: Rogers Media
Ed: Denis Seguin. **Description:** Filmmakers are claiming that Bill C-10 amounts to censorship as it could retract a production's eligibility for a tax credit if it is deemed offensive. However, the bill's backers say that the bill protects against tax dollars being directed at productions that run contrary to public policy.

33617 ■ *"Company Goes High-Tech To Attack Some Sore Spots" in Boston Business Journal (Vol. 27, December 7, 2007, No. 45, pp. 10)*
Pub: American City Business Journals Inc.
Ed: Mark Hollmer. **Description:** Transport Pharmaceuticals Inc. hopes to raise $35 million to fund a drug and a treatment device for treating cold sores, and seek federal regulatory approval. Dennis Goldberg, the company's CEO, believes that existing treatments that use acyclovir cream are relatively weak. Transport's drug uses a soluble gel cartridge with a higher concentration of acyclovir.

33618 ■ *"Competition At Last?" in Canadian Business (Vol. 81, July 22, 2008, No. 12-13, pp. 7)*
Pub: Rogers Media Ltd.
Description: Competition Policy Review Panel's 'Compete to Win' report revealed that Canada is being 'hollowed-out' by foreign acquisitions. The panel investigated competition and foreign investment policies in Canada. Key information on the report, as well as views on the Investment Canada Act and the Competition Act, is presented.

33619 ■ *"Complete Discovery Source, Inc. (CDS) Receives Minority Owned Business Certification" in Internet Wire (December 14, 2010)*
Pub: Comtex
Description: Complete Discovery Source Inc. (CDS) was granted Minority-Owned Business Enterprise status by the New York State Department of Economic Development. The certification provides CDS, an end-to-end eDiscovery services provider, with access to contracting opportunities with 130 government agencies throughout New York state.

33620 ■ *"Computer Forensics Firms Get Boost From New Evidence Rules" in Crain's Detroit Business (Vol. 24, March 24, 2008, No. 12, pp. 28)*
Pub: Crain Communications, Inc.
Ed: Chad Halcom. **Description:** Computer forensics is a growing niche for firms such as the Center for Computer Forensics in Southfield; driving some of the growth are new amendments to the Federal Rules of Civil Procedure, which took effect about a year ago and address standards of evidence for electronic records, or 'e-discovery,' that are admissible for civil cases in federal courts.

33621 ■ *"Congress Targets Ad Tracking" in Inc. (Vol. 33, November 2011, No. 9, pp. 30)*
Pub: Inc. Magazine
Ed: Issie Lapowsky. **Description:** Congressional bills dealing with behavioral tracking whereby advertising networks monitor people's online behavior and use the date to tailor ads to people's interest propose Do Not Track measures which would allow consumers to turn off online behavior tracking by clicking a button.

33622 ■ *"Contractors Must be Lead Certified by April 2010" in Contractor (Vol. 57, February 2010, No. 2, pp. 3)*
Pub: Penton Media, Inc.
Description: Contractors should be trained and certified to comply with the U.S. Environmental Protection Agency's Lead Renovation, Repair, and Painting regulation if they work on housing built before 1978 by April 2010. Contractors with previous lead abatement training must be trained and certified under this new program.

33623 ■ *"Contractors Should Expand Their Services" in Contractor (Vol. 56, July 2009, No. 7, pp. 34)*
Pub: Penton Media, Inc.
Ed: Steven Scandaliato. **Description:** All single family homes will be required to have fire sprinkler systems installed when the 2009 International Residential Code arrives. This presents an opportunity for plumbing contractors and they can be competitively priced against a fire protection contractor if they train their workforce to install sprinklers.

33624 ■ *"Controversial Bill Could Raise Rates for Homeowners" in Orlando Business Journal (Vol. 26, January 22, 2010, No. 34, pp. 1)*
Pub: American City Business Journals
Ed: Oscar Pedro Musibay; Christopher Boyd. **Description:** Florida Senate Bill 876 and its companion House Bill 447 are pushing for the deregulation of rates in the state's home insurance market. The bill is being opposed by consumer advocates as it could mean higher rates for homeowner insurance policies.

33625 ■ *"Convergence Collaboration: Revising Revenue Recognition" in Management Accounting Quarterly (Vol. 12, Spring 2011, No. 3, pp. 18)*
Pub: Management Accounting Quarterly
Ed: Jack T. Ciesielski, Thomas R. Weirich. **Description:** While revenue recognition is critical, regulations have been developed on an ad hoc basis until now. The joint FASB/IASB proposed accounting standard on revenue recognition is a meaningful convergence of standards that will require a major adjustment for financial statement preparers. The proposal is a radical departure from the way revenue has been recognized by the U.S. GAAP. For industries such as consulting, engineering, construction, and technology, it could dramatically change revenue recognition, impacting the top line. The new proposed standard, its potential impact, and the critical role that contracts play is examined thoroughly.

33626 ■ *"A Conversation With Money Manager William Vellon" in Crain's Chicago Business (Vol. 31, November 17, 2008, No. 46, pp. 4)*
Pub: Crain Communications, Inc.
Ed: Mike Colias. **Description:** Interview with William Vellon, the executive vice-president of Kingsbury Capital Investment Advisors; Vellon discusses ways in which the government can help the financial sector, his client base and bargains that investors should consider.

33627 ■ *"Convictions Under the Fisheries Act" in Canadian Corporate News (May 16, 2007)*
Pub: Comtex News Network Inc.
Description: Fisheries and Oceans Canada is mandated to protect and conserve marine resources and thus released a list of fishers fined for various offences under the Fisheries Act in March and April.

33628 ■ *"Council Power Shift Could Benefit Business" in Business Courier (Vol. 26, November 6, 2009, No. 28, pp. 1)*
Pub: American City Business Journals, Inc.
Ed: Lucy May. **Description:** A majority in the Cincinnati City Council, which is comprised of reelected members, might be created by Charlie Winburn's impending return to the council. It would be empowered to decide on public safety, stock options taxes, and environmental justice. How the presumed majority would affect the city's economic progress is discussed.

33629 ■ *"Councilman May Revive Labor Bill" in Baltimore Business Journal (Vol. 28, August 13, 2010, No. 14, pp. 1)*
Pub: Baltimore Business Journal
Ed: Daniel J. Sernovitz. **Description:** Baltimore, Maryland Councilman Bill Henry has started reviving controversial legislation that would force developers and contractors to give preference to union labor. The legislation requires contractors to give preference to city workers in order to lower Baltimore's unemployment rate.

33630 ■ *"Countdown" in Canadian Business (Vol. 81, March 3, 2008, No. 3, pp. 27)*
Pub: Rogers Media
Ed: Al Rosen. **Description:** According to a recent poll only 42 percent of portfolio managers in Canada are aware that the country is planning to adopt the International Financial Reporting Standards beginning 2011. The shift to the new standards will have significant impacts on investment values and will be the biggest revolution in Canadian financial reporting. The effects of the transition on portfolio managers and investors are analyzed.

33631 ■ *"Credit Card Crackdown" in Business Journal-Portland (Vol. 24, November 23, 2007, No. 38, pp. 1)*
Pub: American City Business Journals, Inc.
Ed: Andy Giegerich. **Description:** Oregon's U.S. Senator Ron Wyden is sponsoring Credit Card Safety Act of 2007, a bill that requires credit card companies to reduce the jargon of credit card agreements and require the Federal Reserve Board to launch a public education campaign among credit card users. The legislation will also impose a rating system for credit card contracts with five being the safest for consumers to use.

33632 ■ *"Credit Unions Cast Wary Eye at Paulson Plan, But Not Panicking Yet" in The Business Review Albany (Vol. 35, April 11, 2008, No. 1)*
Pub: The Business Review
Ed: Barbara Pinckney. **Description:** Credit unions are suspicious of US Treasury Secretary Henry Paulson's plan to establish a single federally insured depository institution charter for all institutions covered by federal deposit insurance. The charter would replace national banks, federal savings associations, and federal credit union charters.

33633 ■ *"CTV's CHUM Proposal Gets Chilly Reception" in Globe & Mail (May 1, 2007, pp. B1)*
Pub: CTVglobemedia Publishing Inc.
Ed: Grant Robertson. **Description:** The possible violation of broadcast regulations in case of acquisition of CHUM Ltd. by CTV Inc. for $1.4 billion is discussed.

33634 ■ *"The Cudgel of Samson" in Barron's (Vol. 88, March 24, 2008, No. 12, pp. 62)*
Pub: Dow Jones & Company, Inc.
Ed: Thomas G. Donlan. **Description:** Discusses the Federal Reserve is jawboning businesses against inflation while inflation is starting to rise because of the abundance of cheap money. The practice of jawboning has been used by the administrations of past US presidents with limited effect.

33635 ■ *"Curbing the Debt Collector" in Business Journal-Portland (Vol. 24, October 5, 2007, No. 32, pp. 1)*
Pub: American City Business Journals, Inc.
Ed: Andy Giegerich. **Description:** Republican representative Sal Esquivel, who had a bad personal experience with a Houston collector, is developing

legislation that would give the state attorney general's office enforcement powers over debt collecting agencies. The existing Oregon legislation concerning the debt collection industry is also discussed.

33636 ■ *"Currency: I'm Otta Here" in Entrepreneur (Vol. 35, October 2007, No. 10, pp. 72)*
Pub: Entrepreneur Media Inc.
Ed: C.J. Prince. **Description:** Liberum Research revealed that 193 chief financial officers (CFOs) at small companies have either resigned or retired during the first half of 2007. A survey conducted by Tatum found that unreasonable expectations from the management and compliance to regulations are the main reasons why CFOs are leaving small firms. The chief executive officer's role in making CFOs stay is also discussed.

33637 ■ *"Daley's Efforts to Ease Traffic Woes Fall Short" in Crain's Chicago Business (Vol. 31, May 5, 2008, No. 18, pp. 18)*
Pub: Crain Communications, Inc.
Description: Discusses some of the inherent problems of Mayor Daley's plan to reduce traffic congestion by creating a tax on drivers who park their cars downtown during peak traffic periods and putting articulated buses on new bus-only lanes on major arterial streets leading into the Loop.

33638 ■ *"The Data Drivers" in Canadian Business (Vol. 81, September 15, 2008, No. 14-15, pp. 1)*
Pub: Rogers Media Ltd.
Ed: Andrew Wahl. **Description:** Canadian regulators hope that an auction of telecommunications companies will inject more competition into the industry; however, newcomers may not be able to rely on lower prices in order to gain market share from the three major telecommunications companies that already have a stronghold on the market. Analysts feel that providing additional data service is the key to surviving market disruptions.

33639 ■ *Dead on Arrival: How the Anti-Business Backlash is Destroying Entrepreneurship in America and What We Can Still Do About It!*
Pub: HarperCollins Publishers, Inc.
Ed: Bernie Marcus; Steve Gottry. **Released:** November 2006. **Price:** $23.95. **Description:** Bernie Marcus, Home Depot leader, addresses regulations hurting small businesses in America.

33640 ■ *"Deal With Tribes Revives Revenue Stream" in Crain's Detroit Business (Vol. 24, March 24, 2008, No. 12, pp. 6)*
Pub: Crain Communications, Inc.
Ed: Amy Lane. **Description:** Michigan Bureau of State Lottery's 2003 launch of its Club Keno game caused the Little River Band of Ottawa Indians and the Little Traverse Bay Bands of Odawa Indians to halt payments of shared casino revenue with the state. The federal lawsuit that resulted has now been settled and tribal revenue-sharing will resume as well as $26 million in previous payments to the state of Michigan that the tribes had put into escrow.

33641 ■ *"Dealing With Dangers Abroad" in Financial Executive (Vol. 23, December 2007, No. 10, pp. 32)*
Pub: Financial Executives International
Ed: Jeffrey Marshall. **Description:** Clear processes and responsibilities for risk management for all companies going global are essential. U.S. toy manufacturer, Matel was put into crisis mode after its Chinese-made toys were recalled due to the use of lead-based paint or tiny magnets in its products.

33642 ■ *"Death Spiral" in Business Journal Serving Greater Tampa Bay (Vol. 30, October 29, 2010, No. 45, pp. 1)*
Pub: Tampa Bay Business Journal
Ed: Margie Manning. **Description:** Bay Cities Bank has started working on the loan portfolio of its acquisition, Progress Bank of Florida. Regulators closed Progress Bank in October 2010 after capital collapsed due to charge-offs and increases in the provision for future loan losses.

33643 ■ *"Defense Budge Ax May Not Come Down So Hard On the Region" in Baltimore Business Journal (Vol. 28, August 20, 2010, No. 15, pp. 1)*
Pub: Baltimore Business Journal
Ed: Daniel J. Sernovitz. **Description:** U.S. Defense Secretary Robert M. Gates' planned budget cuts are having little effect on Maryland's defense industry. Gates will reduce spending on intelligence service contracts by 10 percent.

33644 ■ *Democratization Without Representation: The Politics of Small Industry in Mexico*
Pub: Pennsylvania State University Press
Ed: Kenneth C. Shalden. **Released:** March 2006. **Price:** $31.95. **Description:** Opportunities for individuals to participate in Mexico's democracy and how it is affecting the way industries do business.

33645 ■ *A Demon of Our Own Design: Markets, Hedge Funds, and the Perils of Financial Innovation*
Pub: John Wiley and Sons, Inc.
Ed: Richard Bookstaber. **Released:** December 2008. **Price:** $16.95 paperback. **Description:** Longtime hedge-fund manager offers his take on a market and investment system that he believes is needlessly complex owing to investment banks, hedge funds, innovation, regulation, and safeguards and further compounded by investor and market instabilities. These complexities could create a large-scale disaster.

33646 ■ *"Department of Agriculture" in Ice Cream Reporter (Vol. 23, November 20, 2010, No. 12, pp. 8)*
Pub: Ice Cream Reporter
Description: Department of Agriculture notes that food price inflation for 2010 will be at its lowest since 1992.

33647 ■ *The Department of Labor's Overtime Regulations Effect on Small Business: Congressional Hearing*
Pub: DIANE Publishing Company
Ed: W. Todd Akin. **Released:** April 2006. **Price:** $20. 00. **Description:** An overview of the Congressional hearing regarding the Department of Labor's regulations governing overtime and how they impact small business.

33648 ■ *"Despite Hot Toys, Holiday Sales Predicted To Be Ho-Ho-Hum" in Drug Store News (Vol. 29, November 12, 2007, No. 14, pp. 78)*
Pub: Drug Store News
Ed: Doug Desjardins. **Description:** Summer toy recalls have retailers worried about holiday sales in 2007. Mattel was heavily impacted from the recall of millions of toys manufactured in China.

33649 ■ *"DHS Finalizes Rules Allowing Electronic I-9s" in HR Specialist (Vol. 8, September 2010, No. 9, pp. 5)*
Pub: Capitol Information Group Inc.
Description: U.S. Department of Homeland Security issued regulations that give employers more flexibility to electronically sing and store I-9 employee verification forms.

33650 ■ *"Diary of a Short-Seller" in Conde Nast Portfolio (Vol. 2, June 2008, No. 6, pp. 44)*
Pub: Conde Nast Publications
Contact: David Carey, President
Ed: Jesse Eisinger. **Description:** Profile of David Einhorn who is a fund manager that spoke out against finance company Allied Capital whose stock fell nearly 20 percent the day after Einhorn's critique; Einhorn subsequently had to contend with attacks against his credibility as well as investigations by the S.E.C.; Einhorn's experience illuminates our current economic crisis.

33651 ■ *"A Different Kind of Waiting List" in Canadian Business (Vol. 80, April 9, 2007, No. 8, pp. 17)*
Pub: Rogers Media
Ed: Erin Pooley. **Description:** The adverse impact on drug companies' profitability due to regulatory delays in approving drugs is discussed.

33652 ■ *"Director Elections Campaign Pays Off" in Globe & Mail (March 9, 2006, pp. B1)*
Pub: CTVglobemedia Publishing Inc.
Ed: Janet McFarland. **Description:** The details pertaining to the introduction of new voting standards by electing company directors by 20 major Canadian companies, after the Canadian Coalition for Good Governance campaigned for it, are presented.

33653 ■ *"The Display Group Is Super-Sized" in Michigan Vue (Vol. 13, July-August 2008, No. 4, pp. 34)*
Pub: Entrepreneur Media Inc.
Description: Profile of the Display Group, located in downtown Detroit, this company provides custom designed mobile marketing displays as well as special event production services for trade show displays. The rental house and design service is also beginning to see more business due to the film initiative, which provides incentives for films that are shooting in Michigan.

33654 ■ *The Diversity Code: Unlocking the Secrets to Making Differences Work in the Real World*
Pub: AMACOM
Ed: Michelle T. Johnson. **Released:** September 8, 2010. **Price:** $19.95. **Description:** The most diligent compliance with laws and regulations can't foster true work place diversity. The best organizations have become genuine cross-cultural communities that believe equality in reconciling difference and valuing them. The book promotes understanding by answering many of the toughest questions that professionals and their employers are afraid to ask.

33655 ■ *"Do the Math" in Canadian Business (Vol. 79, October 9, 2006, No. 20, pp. 17)*
Pub: Rogers Media
Ed: Al Rosen. **Description:** Faulty practices followed by regulators in Canadian stock market are discussed. The need for authorities to protect investors against these frauds are emphasized.

33656 ■ *"Doctors, Health Insurers Squabble Over Who Sends Patients the Bill" in Baltimore Business Journal (Vol. 27, February 6, 2010)*
Pub: American City Business Journals
Ed: Scott Graham. **Description:** Issue of allowing patients to send reimbursement checks to physicians who are not part of their health insurer's provider network is being debated in Maryland. Details on the proposed Maryland bill and the arguments presented by doctors and insurers are outlined.

33657 ■ *"Does it Add Up?" in Canadian Business (Vol. 81, October 13, 2008, No. 17, pp. 18)*
Pub: Rogers Media Ltd.
Ed: Jack Mintz. **Description:** Views on Canada's tax policy, as well as on tax reforms planned by major parties and their expected economic impact are discussed. The Tories' proposal to cut federal diesel fuel tax is seen as politically smart, but reforms on other taxes could help generate economic growth. High income tax rates are believed to discourage talented individuals from working in Canada.

33658 ■ *Doing Business Anywhere: The Essential Guide to Going Global*
Pub: John Wiley and Sons, Inc.
Ed: Tom Travis. **Released:** 2007. **Price:** $24.95. **Description:** Plans are given for new or existing businesses to organize, plan, operate and execute a business on a global basis. Trade agreements, brand protection and patents, ethics, security as well as cultural issues are among the issues addressed.

33659 ■ *"DOL Sets Stiff New Child Labor Penalties" in HR Specialist (Vol. 8, September 2010, No. 9, pp. 2)*
Pub: Capitol Information Group Inc.
Description: U.S. Department of Labor (DOL) will impose new penalties for employers that violate U.S. child labor laws. Details of the new law are included.

33660 ■ *"Domestic Workers Organize!" in WorkingUSA (Vol. 11, December 2008, No. 4, pp. 413)*
Pub: Blackwell Publishers Ltd.
Ed: Eileen Boris, Premilla Nadasen. **Description:** History of domestic workers in the U.S. is examined. The article challenges the long-standing assumption that these, primarily women of color cleaners, nannies, and elder care providers are unable to organize and assesses the possibilities and limitations of recent organizing efforts. The nature of the occupation, its location in the home, the isolated character of the work, informal arrangements with employers, and exclusions from labor law protection, has fostered community-based, social movement organizing to build coalitions, reform legislation and draw public attention to the plight of domestic workers.

33661 ■ *"Don't Expect Quick Fix" in The Business Journal-Serving Metropolitan Kansas City (Vol. 27, October 3, 2008, No. 3, pp. 1)*
Pub: American City Business Journals, Inc.
Ed: James Dornbrook. **Description:** United States governmental entities cannot provide a quick fix solution to the current financial crisis. The economy requires a systemic change in the way people think about credit. The financial services industry should also focus on core lending principles.

33662 ■ *"Don't Fall Foul of Farming's Workplace Killer" in Farmer's Weekly (March 28, 2008, No. 320)*
Pub: Reed Business Information
Contact: Jeff Greisch, President
Description: Discusses the Work at Height Regulations that were introduced to reduce the risk of injury and death caused by accidental falls in the workplace.

33663 ■ *"Down the Tracks, a Whistle Is a Blowin'" in Barron's (Vol. 89, July 27, 2009, No. 30, pp. 36)*
Pub: Dow Jones & Co., Inc.
Ed: Jim McTague. **Description:** Higher numbers of freight-rail carloads are a sign that the economy is improving and it is no stretch to imagine that this is aided by the American Recovery and Reinvestment Act. It is also predicted that 2009 municipal bond issuance will be above $373 billion with at least $55 billion of it made up of Buy America Bonds that are subsidized by the federal government.

33664 ■ *"Duro Bag to Expand, Add 130 Jobs" in Business Courier (Vol. 27, August 6, 2010, No. 14, pp. 1)*
Pub: Business Courier
Ed: Jon Newberry. **Description:** Duro Bag Manufacturing Company will expand capacity at its Florence, Kentucky plant and will add around 130 jobs over the next few years. The state of Kentucky has given preliminary approval for up to $1 million in tax incentives over 10 years, tied to the creation of new jobs. The company's investment will include new production and packaging equipment and building improvements.

33665 ■ *E-Commerce in Regional Small to Medium Enterprises*
Pub: Idea Group Publishing
Ed: Robert MacGregor. **Released:** July 2007. **Price:** $99.95. **Description:** Strategies small to medium enterprises (SMEs) need to implement in order to compete with larger, global businesses and the role electronic commerce plays in this process are outlined. Studies of e-commerce in multiple regional areas, focusing on the role of business size, business sector, market focus, gender of CEO, and education level of the CEO are discussed.

33666 ■ *Effect of the Overvalued Dollar on Small Exporters: Congressional Hearing*
Pub: DIANE Publishing Company
Ed: Donald Manzullo. **Released:** September 2002. **Price:** $30.00. **Description:** Congressional hearing: Witnesses: Dr. Lawrence Chimerine, Economist; Tony Raimondo, President and CEO, Behlen Manufacturing Company; Robert J. Weskamp, President, Wes-Tech, Inc.; Wayne Dollar, President, Georgia Farm Bureau; and Vargese George, President and CEO, Westex International, Inc. Appendix includes correspondence sent to committee on the overvalued dollar.

33667 ■ *"Elanco Challenges Bayer's Advantage, K9 Advantix Ad Claims" in Pet Product News (Vol. 64, November 2010, No. 11, pp. 11)*
Pub: BowTie Inc.
Description: Elanco Animal Health has disputed Bayer Animal Health's print and Web advertising claims involving its flea, tick, and mosquito control products Advantage and K9 Advantix. The National Advertising Division of the Council of Better Business Bureaus recommended the discontinuation of ads, while Bayer Animal Health reiterated its commitment to self-regulation.

33668 ■ *"Elder Care, Rx Drugs Reforms Top Zoeller's Agenda" in Times (December 21, 2010)*
Pub: The Times
Ed: Sarah Tompkins. **Description:** Indiana Attorney General Greg Zoeller is hoping to develop a program in the state that will help regulate care for the elderly; freeze medical licenses for doctors involved in criminal investigations; address illegal drug use; and to establish a program to help individuals dispose of old prescription medications easily at pharmacies.

33669 ■ *"Election Could Undo Renewable Energy Quotas" in The Business Journal - Serving Phoenix and the Valley of the Sun (Vol. 28, July 11, 2008, No. 45, pp. 1)*
Pub: American City Business Journals, Inc.
Ed: Patrick O'Grady. **Description:** Competition for the three open seats in the Arizona Corporation Commission is intense, with 12 candidates contesting for the three slots. The commission's mandates for renewable energy and infrastructure investment will also be at stake.

33670 ■ *Electronic Commerce: Technical, Business, and Legal Issues*
Pub: Prentice Hall PTR
Ed: Oktay Dogramaci; Aryya Gangopadhyay; Yelena Yesha; Nabil R. Adam. **Released:** August 1998. **Description:** Provides insight into the goals of using the Internet to grow a business in the areas of networking and telecommunication, security, and storage and retrieval; business areas such as marketing, procurement and purchasing, billing and payment, and supply chain management; and legal aspects such as privacy, intellectual property, taxation, contractual and legal settlements.

33671 ■ *"Eminent Domain Fight Looks Imminent" in The Business Journal-Serving Metropolitan Kansas City (Vol. 26, August 1, 2008, No. 47)*
Pub: American City Business Journals, Inc.
Ed: Rob Roberts. **Description:** Views and information on the proposed constitutional amendments that will limit the use of eminent domain in Missouri, are presented. The proposals are expected to largely ban the taking of private property for private development. It may be included in a November 4,2008 statewide vote for approval.

33672 ■ *The Employer's Legal Advisor*
Pub: AMACOM
Ed: Thomas M. Hanna. **Released:** April 30, 2007. **Price:** $24.00. **Description:** Attorney provides tips for reducing the possibility of a lawsuit and winning a case if one does go to court.

33673 ■ *"Employers Plan to Fill Jobs" in Philadelphia Business Journal (Vol. 28, February 5, 2010, No. 51, pp. 1)*
Pub: American City Business Journals
Ed: Peter van Allen. **Description:** Philadelphia, Pennsylvania's largest employers have openings for at least 6,000 jobs. But businesses remain cautious and are selective in hiring or waiting to see what happens to federal policy changes.

33674 ■ *"Employers Tied in Knots" in Sacramento Business Journal (Vol. 25, August 15, 2008, No. 24, pp. 1)*
Pub: American City Business Journals, Inc.
Ed: Kathy Robertson. **Description:** Conflicting laws on same sex marriage have been posing problems for companies, and insurers in California. The court ruling that allowed gay marriages has created differences between state and federal laws. Federal laws on same-sex spouse taxation are also seen to complicate the issue.

33675 ■ *Enabling Environments for Jobs and Entrepreneurship: The Role of Policy and Law in Small Enterprise Employment*
Pub: International Labour Office
Ed: Gerhard Reinecke. **Released:** February 2004. **Price:** $83.25. **Description:** National policies, laws and regulations governing workplace safety.

33676 ■ *"End of the Beginning" in Canadian Business (Vol. 81, November 10, 2008, No. 19, pp. 17)*
Pub: Rogers Media Ltd.
Ed: David Wolf. **Description:** The freeze in the money markets and historic decline in equity markets around the world finally forced governments into aggressive coordinated action. The asset price inflation brought on by cheap credit will now work in reverse and the tightening of credit will be difficult economically. Canada is exposed to the fallout everywhere, given that the U.S, the U.K. and Japan buy 30 percent of Canada's output.

33677 ■ *"The End of Clock-Punching" in Canadian Business (Vol. 83, September 14, 2010, No. 15, pp. 96)*
Pub: Rogers Media Ltd.
Ed: Lyndsie Bourgon. **Description:** Workplace consultant Peter Hadwen is pushing for the transformation of Canada's government departments into results-only work environments (ROWE). ROWE does not require employees to show up to work at a certain time as long as they are meeting goals and achieving results in their jobs. Details of studies regarding ROWE in US companies are examined.

33678 ■ *"Ending the Ebola Death Sentence" in Canadian Business (Vol. 83, August 17, 2010, No. 13-14, pp. 22)*
Pub: Rogers Media Ltd.
Ed: Michael McCullough. **Description:** US Army Medical Research Institute of Infectious Diseases made a $140 million agreement with Tekmira Pharmaceuticals Corporation to develop both a drug delivery system and delivery technology for curing the Ebola virus. Tekmira's delivery technology, which has been shown to halt Ebola in laboratory animals, might be the key to finding a cure.

33679 ■ *"Energy Efficiency Ordinance Softened" in Austin Business JournalInc. (Vol. 28, October 3, 2008, No. 29)*
Pub: American City Business Journals
Ed: Jean Kwon. **Description:** City of Austin has eliminated mandatory energy efficiency upgrades to single-family housing as a condition for selling or renting homes or buildings. The new law proposes that an energy performance audit be conducted on single-family homes before being sold and the results of the audit disclosed to perspectives buyers.

33680 ■ *"Energy Firms Face Stricter Definitions" in Globe & Mail (March 26, 2007, pp. B3)*
Pub: CTVglobemedia Publishing Inc.
Ed: David Ebner. **Description:** The Alberta Securities Commission has imposed strict securities regulations on oil and gas industries. Energy industries will have to submit revenue details to stake holders.

33681 ■ *"Enforcer In Fantasyland" in Crain's New York Business (Vol. 24, February 25, 2008, No. 8, pp. 10)*
Pub: Crain Communications Inc.
Ed: Hilary Potkewitz. **Description:** Patent law, particularly in the toy and game industry, is recession-proof according to Barry Negrin, partner at Pryor Cashman. Negrin co-founded his patent practice

group. Despite massive recalls of toys and the concern over toxic toys, legal measures are in place in this industry.

33682 ■ *Entrepreneurship and Technology Policy*
Pub: Edward Elgar Publishing, Incorporated
Ed: Link. **Released:** August 2006. **Price:** $190.00. **Description:** Journal articles focusing how and the ways small businesses' technical contributions are affecting business. The book is divided into four parts: Government's Direct Support of R&D, Government's Leveraging of R&D, Government's Infrastructure Policies; and Knowledge Flows from Universities and Laboratories.

33683 ■ *"EPA Grants E15 Waiver for 2001-2006 Vehicles" in Farm Industry News (January 21, 2011)*
Pub: Penton Business Media Inc.
Description: U.S. Environmental Protection Agency waived a limitation on selling gasoline that contains more than 10 percent ethanol for model year 2001-2006 cars and light trucks, allowing fuel to contain up to 15 percent ethanol (E15) for these vehicles.

33684 ■ *"Evaluating the 1996-2006 Employment Projections" in Montly Labor Review (Vol. 133, September 2010, No. 9, pp. 33)*
Pub: Bureau of Labor Statistics
Description: Bureau of Labor Statistics employment projections outperformed alternative naive models, but not projecting the housing bubble or the rise in oil prices caused some inaccuracies in the projects. These projections are used by policymakers, economists, and students.

33685 ■ *"Executives Exit at Wal-Mart in China" in Wall Street Journal Eastern Edition (October 17 , 2011, pp. B3)*
Pub: Dow Jones & Company Inc.
Ed: Laurie Burkitt. **Description:** Woes for Wal-Mart Inc.'s subsidiary in China are adding up as Wal-Mart China president and chief executive Ed Chan stepped down, as well as the company's senior vice president for human resources, Clara Wong. The company has been charged by regulators with mislabeling pork products, the result which has forced stores to close. Sales in China have been slow at the retail stores.

33686 ■ *"Expect Action on Health Care and the Economy" in Contractor (Vol. 57, January 2010, No. 1, pp. 30)*
Pub: Penton Media, Inc.
Ed: Kevin Schwalb. **Description:** The Plumbing-Heating-Cooling Contractors National Association is working to solidify its standing in the public policy arena as the legislative agenda will focus on health care reform, estate tax and immigration reform, all of which will impact the industries.

33687 ■ *"Expert Sees No Radical Reform of 401(K) System" in Workforce Management (Vol. 88, November 16, 2009, No. 12, pp. 12)*
Pub: Crain Communications Inc.
Ed: Ed Frauenheim. **Description:** Although many would like to see an overhaul of the 401(k) retirement system, it is unlikely to occur anytime soon; however, the drastic stock market drop of 2008 has raised pointed questions about the 401(k) system and if it enables a secure retirement for American workers.

33688 ■ *"Experts Take the Temp of Obama Plan" in The Business Journal-Serving Metropolitan Kansas City (Vol. 27, November 14, 2008, No. 10)*
Pub: American City Business Journals, Inc.
Ed: Rob Roberts. **Description:** Kansas City, Missouri-based employee benefits experts say president-elect Barack Obama's health care reform plan is on track. Insurance for children and capitalization for health information technology are seen as priority areas. The plan is aimed at reducing the number of uninsured people in the United States.

33689 ■ *"Fair Play? China Cheats, Carney Talks and Rankin Walks; Here's the Latest" in Canadian Business (Vol. 81, March 17, 2008, No. 4)*
Pub: Rogers Media
Description: Discusses the World Trade Organization which says that China is breaking trade rules by taxing imports of auto parts at the same rate as foreign-made finished cars. Mark Carney first speech as the governor of the Bank of Canada made economists suspect a rate cut on overnight loans. Andre Rankin was ordered by the Ontario Securities Commission to pay $250,000 in investigation costs.

33690 ■ *"Fair Tax Backers Hope MBT Anger Will Bring Votes" in Crain's Detroit Business (Vol. 24, March 31, 2008, No. 13, pp. 32)*
Pub: Crain Communications, Inc.
Description: Discusses the Michigan Fair Tax Proposal which would eliminate Michigan's business taxes and income tax, raise the state sales tax to 9.75 percent and expand it to services.

33691 ■ *"Familiar Fun" in Crain's Cleveland Business (Vol. 28, October 22, 2007, No. 42, pp. 3)*
Pub: Crain Communications Inc.
Ed: John Booth. **Description:** Marketing for the 2007 holiday season has toy retailers focusing on American-made products because of recent recalls of toys produced in China that do not meet U.S. safety standards.

33692 ■ *"Fannie and Freddie: How They'll Change" in Business Week (September 22, 2008, No. 4100, pp. 30)*
Pub: McGraw-Hill Companies, Inc.
Ed: Jane Sasseen. **Description:** Three possible outcomes of the fate of struggling mortgage giants Freddie Mac and Fannie Mae after the government bailout are outlined.

33693 ■ *Fast-Track Business Start-Up Kit: California*
Pub: DP Group, Incorporated
Ed: Carolyn Usinger. **Released:** September 2006. **Price:** $29.00. **Description:** Step-by-step guide for starting and running a business in California, including information on sole proprietors, partnerships, limited liability companies, S and C corporations, as well as details concerning business entities, sales taxes, environmental issues, human resources, and more.

33694 ■ *"FCC Adopts New Media Ownership Rules" in Black Enterprise (Vol. 38, March 2008, No. 8, pp. 26)*
Pub: Earl G. Graves Publishing Co. Inc.
Ed: Joyce Jones. **Description:** Federal Communications Commission approved a ruling that lifts a ban on newspaper and/or broadcast cross ownership. Because of declining sales in newspaper advertising and readership the ban will allow companies to share local news gathering costs across multiple media platforms.

33695 ■ *"Fed May Ban Amphibian Trade" in Pet Product News (Vol. 64, November 2010, No. 11, pp. 13)*
Pub: BowTie Inc.
Description: U.S. Fish and Wildlife Service is seeking public input on a petition submitted by the conservation activist group Defenders of Wildlife. The petition involves possible classification of chytrid fungus-infected amphibians and amphibian eggs as 'injurious wildlife' under the Lacey Act. Interstate trading or importation of injurious wildlife into the U.S. is not allowed.

33696 ■ *"Feds, Not City, Will Pick GSA Office Site" in Business Journal-Serving Metropolitan Kansas City (Vol. 26, November 30, 2007, No. 12)*
Pub: American City Business Journals, Inc.
Ed: Jim Davis. **Description:** Mark Funkhouser wants the federal government to decide the location of the General Services Administration building site. The act of the Mayor enraged the executive director of Kansas City Port Authority, Vincent Gauthier. Details of the GSAs building location plans are discussed.

33697 ■ *"A Few Points of Contention" in Barron's (Vol. 88, July 14, 2008, No. 28, pp. 3)*
Pub: Dow Jones & Co., Inc.
Ed: Michael Santoli. **Description:** Headline inflation tends to revert to the lower core inflation, which excludes food and energy in its calculation over long periods. Prominent private equity figures believe that regulators should allow more than the de facto 10 percent to 25 percent limit of commercial banks to hasten the refunding of the financial sector.

33698 ■ *"Fighting Detroit" in Baltimore Business Journal (Vol. 27, January 22, 2010, No. 38, pp. 1)*
Pub: American City Business Journals
Ed: Daniel J. Sernovitz. **Description:** Baltimore, Maryland-based car dealers could retrieve their franchises from car manufacturers, Chrysler LLC and General Motors Corporation, through a forced arbitration. A provision in a federal budget mandates the arbitration. The revoking of franchises has been attributed to the car manufacturers' filing of bankruptcy protection.

33699 ■ *"Film Incentives: A Hit or a Flop?" in Michigan Vue (Vol. 13, July-August 2008, No. 4, pp. 10)*
Pub: Entrepreneur Media Inc.
Description: Michigan's new film incentive legislation is fulfilling its core purpose, according to Lisa Dancsok of the Michigan Economic Development Corp. (MEDC), by kickstarting the state's entry into the multi-billion dollar industry; the initiative is considered to be very competitive with other states and countries and is thought to be a way in which to help revitalize Michigan's struggling economy.

33700 ■ *"Final State Budget Is a Mixed Bag of Key Industries" in The Business Journal - Serving Phoenix and the Valley of the Sun (Vol. 28, July 4, 2008, No. 44, pp. 3)*
Pub: American City Business Journals, Inc.
Ed: Mike Sunnucks; Patrick O'Grady. **Description:** Approved by Governor Janet Napolitano and passed by the Arizona Legislature, the $9.9 billion state budget is beneficial to some industries in the business community. The tax cap for on Arizona Lottery has been removed which is beneficial to the industry, while the solar energy industry and real estate developers stand to lose from the spending bill. Other details of the finance budget are presented.

33701 ■ *"Financing for NNSA Plant Is a Work in Progress" in The Business Journal-Serving Metropolitan Kansas City (October 24, 2008)*
Pub: American City Business Journals, Inc.
Ed: Rob Roberts. **Description:** The Kansas City Council approved a development plan for a $500 million nuclear weapons parts plant in south Kansas City. The US Congress approved a $59 million annual lease payment to the plant's developer. Financing for the construction of the plant remains in question as the plant's developers have to shoulder construction costs.

33702 ■ *"Firm Restricts Cellphone Use While Driving" in Globe & Mail (January 30, 2006, pp. B3)*
Pub: CTVglobemedia Publishing Inc.
Ed: Catherine McLean. **Description:** The details on AMEC Plc, which adopted cellphone-free driving policy, are presented.

33703 ■ *The Flaw of Averages: Why We Underestimate Risk in the Face of Uncertainty*
Pub: John Wiley & Sons, Inc.
Ed: Sam L. Savage. **Released:** June 3, 2009. **Price:** $22.95. **Description:** Personal and business plans are based on uncertainties on a daily basis. The common avoidable mistake individuals make in assessing risk in the face of uncertainty is defined. The explains why plans based on average assumptions are wrong, on average, in areas as diverse as finance, healthcare, accounting, the war on terror, and climate change.

33704 ■ *"For All It's Worth" in Entrepreneur (Vol. 36, April 2008, No. 4, pp. 46)*
Pub: Entrepreneur Media, Inc.
Ed: Farnoosh Torabi. **Description:** Discusses the federal estate tax system requires that 45 percent of the money beyond $2 million be given to the government. Ways on how to minimize the effects of estate tax on assets include: creating bypass trusts for married couples; setting up an irrevocable life insurance trust to avoid taxation of estate for insurance benefactors; and having annual gift tax exclusion.

33705 ■ *"For Yung, Lady Luck a Fickle Mistress" in Business Courier (Vol. 24, November 30, 2008, No. 33, pp. 1)*
Pub: American City Business Journals, Inc.
Ed: Dan Monk. **Description:** Bill Yung's Columbia Sussex Corp. won the bid for the parent company of Tropicana casinos in November 2006, and a year after, the company is facing regulatory and labor issues.

33706 ■ *"Former Synthes Officers Receive Prison Sentences" in Wall Street Journal Eastern Edition (November 22 , 2011, pp. B4)*
Pub: Dow Jones & Company Inc.
Ed: Peter Loftus. **Description:** Michael D. Huggins, formerly chief operating officer of medical-device maker Synthes Ltd., and Thomas B. Higgins, formerly the president of Synthes spine unit, were given prison sentences of nine months while a third executive, John J. Walsh, formerly director of regulatory and clinical affairs in the spine division, was given a five-month sentence for their involvement in the promotion of the unauthorized use of a bone cement produced by the company.

33707 ■ *"Forsys Metals Corporation Goes "Live" With Q4's On-Demand Disclosure Management Software" in Canadian Corporate News (May 16, 2007)*
Pub: Comtex News Network Inc.
Description: Forsys Metals Corp. selected Q4 Web Systems to automate its corporate website disclosure with Q4's software platform which also automates and simplifies many of the administrative tasks that Forsys was doing manually, allowing them to focus their internal resources on the business.

33708 ■ *"Free Speech Vs. Privacy in Data Mining" in Information Today (Vol. 28, September 2011, No. 8, pp. 22)*
Pub: Information Today, Inc.
Ed: George H. Pike. **Description:** The U.S. Constitution does not explicitly guarantee the right of privacy. Organizations and businesses that require obtaining and disseminating information can be caught in the middle of privacy rights. The long-term impact on data mining, Internet marketing, and Internet privacy issues are examined.

33709 ■ *"Freedom Center May have New Path" in Business Courier (Vol. 26, October 30, 2009, No. 27, pp. 1)*
Pub: American City Business Journals, Inc.
Ed: Dan Monk, Lucy May. **Description:** National Underground Railroad Freedom Center in Price Hill, Cincinnati is in negotiations with US Rep. John Conyers for its possible classification as an independent establishment within the US federal government. If this happens, funding for the museum might be possibly augmented and the rights to use national archives might be furnished.

33710 ■ *"Freeing the Wheels of Commerce" in Hispanic Business (July-August 2007, pp. 50, 52, 54)*
Pub: Hispanic Business
Ed: Keith Rosenblum. **Description:** SecureOrigins, a border-based partnership with high-tech innovators is working to move goods faster, more efficiently, and securely.

33711 ■ *"Fresh Direct's Crisis" in Crain's New York Business (Vol. 24, January 14, 2008, No. 2, pp. 3)*
Pub: Crain Communications, Inc.
Ed: Lisa Fickenscher. **Description:** Freshdirect, an Internet grocery delivery service, finds itself under siege from federal immigration authorities, customers and labor organizations due to its employment practice of hiring illegals. At stake is the grocer's reputation as well as its ambitious growth plans, including an initial public offering of its stock.

33712 ■ *"FTC Takes Aim At Foreclosure 'Rescue' Firm" in The Business Journal-Serving Greater Tampa Bay (Vol. 28, September 19, 2008, No. 39)*
Pub: American City Business Journals, Inc.
Ed: Michael Hinman. **Description:** United Home Savers LLP has been ordered to halt its mortgage foreclosure rescue services after the Federal Trade Commission accused it of deceptive advertising. The company is alleged to have charged customers $1,200 in exchange for unfulfilled promises to keep them in their homes.

33713 ■ *"Fuel for Thought; Canadian Business Leaders on Energy Policy" in Canadian Business (Vol. 81, September 15, 2008, No. 14-15, pp. 12)*
Pub: Rogers Media Ltd.
Ed: Joe Castaldo. **Description:** Most Canadian business leaders worry about the unreliability of the oil supply but feel that Canada is in a better position to benefit from the energy supply crisis than other countries. Many respondents also highlighted the need to invest in renewable energy sources.

33714 ■ *Fugitive Denim: A Moving Story of People and Pants in the Borderless World of Global Trade*
Pub: W.W. Norton & Company
Ed: Rachel Snyder. **Released:** April 2009. **Price:** $16.95. **Description:** In-depth study of the global production and processes of how jeans are designed, sewn, and transported as well as how the cotton for denim is grown, regulated, purchased and processed.

33715 ■ *"Function Over Forms?" in Barron's (Vol. 88, June 30, 2008, No. 26, pp. 17)*
Pub: Dow Jones & Co., Inc.
Ed: Eric Savitz. **Description:** Securities and Exchange Commission (SEC) chairman Christopher Cox wants the SEC to consider an overhaul of the forms used to meet the agency's disclosure requirements. Cox also said that the U.S. Generally Accepted Accounting Standards has too many rules with exceptions and alternative interpretations.

33716 ■ *"Funds "Friend" Facebook" in Barron's (Vol. 89, July 27, 2009, No. 30, pp. 30)*
Pub: Dow Jones & Co., Inc.
Ed: Leslie P. Norton. **Description:** Mutual-fund companies are the latest entrants to the 'social media' space and several companies have already set up Facebook and Twitter pages. The use of this technology pose special challenges for compliance and regulators especially since the Financial Industry Regulatory Authority reminds companies that advertising, sales and literature are governed by regulations.

33717 ■ *"Futures Shock for the CME" in Crain's Chicago Business (Vol. 31, November 10, 2008, No. 45, pp. 8)*
Pub: Crain Communications, Inc.
Ed: Ann Saphir. **Description:** Chicago-based CME Group Inc., the largest futures exchange operator in the U.S., is facing a potentially radically altered regulatory landscape as Congress weighs sweeping reform of financial oversight. The possible merger of the CFTC and the Securities and Exchange Commission are among CME's concerns. Other details of possible regulatory measures are provided.

33718 ■ *"German Win Through Sharing" in Canadian Business (Vol. 83, September 14, 2010, No. 15, pp. 16)*
Pub: Rogers Media Ltd.
Ed: Jordan Timm. **Description:** German economic historian Eckhard Hoffner has a two-volume work showing how German's relaxed attitude toward copyright and intellectual property helped it catch up to industrialized United Kingdom. Hoffner's research was in response to his interest in the usefulness of software patents. Information on the debate regarding Canada's copyright laws is given.

33719 ■ *"Get Prepared for New Employee Free Choice Act" in HRMagazine (Vol. 53, December 2008, No. 12, pp. 22)*
Pub: Society for Human Resource Management
Contact: Henry G. Jackson, President
E-mail: hjackson@shrm.org
Ed: Allen Smith. **Description:** According to the director of global labor and employee relations with Ingersoll Rand Company, unions may have started having employees signing authorization cards in anticipation of the Employee Free Choice Act. Once signed, the cards are good for one year and employers would have only ten days in which to prepare for bargaining with unions over the first labor contract. The Act also requires these negotiations be subject to mandatory arbitration if a contract is not reached within 120 days of negotiations with unions, resulting in employers' wage rates, health insurance, retirement benefits and key language about flexibility would be determined by an arbitrator with no vested interest in the success of the company.

33720 ■ *"Getting NORA reauthorized is high priority" in Indoor Comfort Marketing (Vol. 70, February 2011, No. 2, pp. 14)*
Pub: Industry Publications Inc.
Description: The importance of reauthorizing the National Oilheat Research Alliance is stressed.

33721 ■ *"Getting Out of an IRS Mess" in Black Enterprise (Vol. 37, December 2006, No. 5, pp. 53)*
Pub: Earl G. Graves Publishing Co. Inc.
Ed: Carolyn M. Brown. **Description:** Owing back taxes to the IRS can lead to huge penalties and interest. Here are some tips on how to handle paying the IRS what you owe them.

33722 ■ *"Getting Rid of Global Glitches: Choosing Software For Trade Compliance" in Black Enterprise (Vol. 41, September 2010, No. 2, pp. 48)*
Pub: Earl G. Graves Publishing Co. Inc.
Ed: Marcia Wade Talbert. **Description:** Compliance software for trading with foreign companies must be compatible with the U.S. Census Bureau's Automated Export System (www.aesdirect.gov). It has to be current with regulatory requirements for any country in the world. Whether owners handle their own compliance or hire a logistics company, they need to be familiar with this software in order to access reports and improve transparency and efficiency of theft supply chain.

33723 ■ *"The GHG Quandary: Whose Problem Is It Anyway?" in Canadian Business (Vol. 81, September 15, 2008, No. 14-15, pp. 72)*
Pub: Rogers Media Ltd.
Ed: Matthew McClearn. **Description:** Nongovernmental organizations were able to revoke the permit for Imperial Oil Ltd's Kearl oilsands project on the grounds of its expected greenhouse gas emission but the court's ruling was rendered irrelevant by bureaucratic paper-shuffling shortly after. The idea of an environmental impact assessment as a guide to identify the consequences of a project is also discussed.

33724 ■ *"Give Us Your Skilled" in Canadian Business (Vol. 80, October 8, 2007, No. 20, pp. 78)*
Pub: Rogers Media
Ed: Zena Olijnyk. **Description:** Demand for skilled workers in Canada is discussed. Despite a strong demand, as evidenced by shortages in both skilled and unskilled labor, the country's immigration policy is affecting the recruitment process. Peter Veress, founder and president of Vermax Group, believes the country is wasting opportunities to take advantage of its attractiveness as a destination for foreign workers.

33725 ■ *"GM's Volt Woes Cast Shadow on E-Cars" in Wall Street Journal Eastern Edition*

(November 28, 2011, pp. B1)
Pub: Dow Jones & Company Inc. Enterprise Media Group
Contact: Clare Hart, President
Ed: Sharon Terlep. **Description:** The future of electric cars is darkened with the government investigation by the National Highway Traffic Safety Administration into General Motor Company's Chevy Volt after two instances of the car's battery packs catching fire during crash tests conducted by the Agency.

33726 ■ *"The Good Guys of ABWA" in Women In Business (Vol. 63, Fall 2011, No. 3, pp. 9)*
Pub: American Business Women's Association
Ed: Rene Street. **Description:** The American Business Women's Association (ABWA) was an all-woman group since its founding in 1949. However, a Supreme Court ruling in 1987 opened all-male and all-female organizations of the opposite sex. Some of the male members of the ABWA are Bill Hense, James Drager, and John Lester.

33727 ■ *"A Good Step, But There's a Long Way to Go" in Business Week (September 22, 2008, No. 4100, pp. 10)*
Pub: McGraw-Hill Companies, Inc.
Ed: James C. Cooper. **Description:** Despite the historic action by the U.S. government to nationalize the mortgage giants Freddie Mac and Fannie Mae, rising unemployment rates may prove to be an even bigger roadblock to bringing back the economy from its downward spiral. The takeover is meant to restore confidence in the credit markets and help with the mortgage crisis but the rising rate in unemployment may make many households unable to take advantage of any benefits which arise from the bailout. Statistical data included.

33728 ■ *"Gordon Nixon" in Canadian Business (Vol. 80, November 5, 2007, No. 22, pp. 9)*
Pub: Rogers Media
Ed: Rachel Pulfer. **Description:** Royal Bank of Canada (RBC) CEO, Gordon Nixon, believes the Canadian financial services segment is heavily regulated. Nixon also feels that it has become difficult for local banks to enter the market since foreign banks can easily come in and compete with them. His views on RBC's success are provided.

33729 ■ *"Gordon Nixon Q&A" in Canadian Business (Vol. 80, November 5, 2007, No. 22, pp. 9)*
Pub: Rogers Media
Ed: Rachel Pulfer. **Description:** Royal Bank of Canada (RBC) chief executive officer Gordon Nixon believes that the Canadian financial services segment is heavily regulated. Nixon also feels that it has become difficult for local banks to enter the market since foreign banks can easily come in and compete with Canadian banks. His views on RBC's success are provided.

33730 ■ *"Government Says Self-Regulation of Online Privacy is Coming Up Short" in Advertising Age (Vol. 81, December 6, 2010, No. 43, pp. 1)*
Pub: Crain Communications, Inc.
Ed: Edmund Lee. **Description:** U.S. Federal Trade Commission and the Department of Commerce are concerned about the current state of digital privacy and stated that self-regulation has not been sufficient to date.

33731 ■ *"Grave Concerns" in Canadian Business (Vol. 81, July 21 2008, No. 11, pp. 25)*
Pub: Rogers Media Ltd.
Ed: Andrew Nikiforuk. **Description:** Air pollution control regulations to reduce greenhouse gasses have been implemented by the Canadian government. The federal government is planning to construct a carbon funeral industry that will store the global warming gases, however the expenditure for the project will be shifted to the taxpayers. Details of the Bruce Peachy's initiative on how to reduce GHGs are presented.

33732 ■ *"The Great Cleanup" in Canadian Business (Vol. 81, April 14, 2008, No. 6, pp. 50)*
Pub: Rogers Media
Ed: Graham Silnicki. **Description:** China's rectification program includes the licensing of 100 percent of food producers and monitoring of 100 percent of raw materials for exports between August and December, 2007. There is a lot of money to be made for those who are willing to help China win its quality battle. PharmEng International Inc. is one of the companies that helps Chinese companies meet international quality standards.

33733 ■ *"Green Acres" in Hawaii Business (Vol. 54, September 2008, No. 3, pp. 48)*
Pub: Hawaii Business Publishing
Ed: Jan Tenbruggencate. **Description:** Bill Cowern's Hawaiian Mahogany is a forestry business that processes low-value trees to be sold as wood chips, which can be burned to create biodiesel. Cowern is planning to obtain certification to market carbon credits and is also working with Green Energy Hawaii for the permit of a biomass-fueled power plant. Other details about Cowern's business are discussed.

33734 ■ *"Green Energy Exec Hits State Policy" in Boston Business Journal (Vol. 30, December 3, 2010, No. 45, pp. 1)*
Pub: Boston Business Journal
Ed: Kyle Alspach. **Description:** American Superconductor Corporation President Dan McGahn believes that the state government of Massachusetts is not proactive enough to develop the state into a manufacturing hub for wind power technology. McGahn believes that while Governor Deval Patrick campaigned for wind turbines in the state, his administration does not have the focus required to build the turbines in the state.

33735 ■ *"Green Shift Sees Red" in Canadian Business (Vol. 81, September 29, 2008, No. 16)*
Pub: Rogers Media Ltd.
Ed: Jeff Sanford. **Description:** Green Shift Inc. is suing the Liberal Party of Canada in an $8.5 million lawsuit for using the phrase 'green shift' when they rolled out their carbon tax and climate change policy. The company has come to be recognized as a consultant and provider of green products such as non-toxic, biodegradable cups, plates, and utensils for events.

33736 ■ *"Greenberg Sues U.S. Over AIG Rescue" in Wall Street Journal Eastern Edition (November 22 , 2011, pp. C3)*
Pub: Dow Jones & Company Inc.
Ed: Liam Pleven, Serena Ng. **Description:** Former Chief Executive Officer of American International Group Inc., Maurice R. 'Hank' Greenberg, has filed a lawsuit against the United States and the Federal Reserve Bank of New York on behalf of shareholders and his company, Starr International Company Inc., claiming that the government was wrong in taking control of the insurance giant and used it to move tens of millions of dollars to the trading partners of AIG.

33737 ■ *"Greg Stringham" in Canadian Business (Vol. 81, March 3, 2008, No. 3, pp. 8)*
Pub: Rogers Media
Ed: Michelle Magnan. **Description:** Canadian Association of Petroleum Producers' Greg Stringham thinks that the new royalty plan will result in companies pulling out their investments for Alberta's conventional oil and gas sector. Stringham adds that Alberta is losing its competitive advantage and companies must study their cost profiles to retrieve that advantage. The effects of the royalty system on Alberta's economy are examined further.

33738 ■ *"Hank Paulson On the Housing Bailout and What's Ahead" in Business Week (September 22, 2008, No. 4100, pp. 19)*
Pub: McGraw-Hill Companies, Inc.
Ed: Maria Bartiromo. **Description:** Interview with Treasury Secretary Henry Paulson in which he discusses the bailout of Fannie Mae and Freddie Mac as well as the potential impact on the American economy and foreign interests and investments in the country. Paulson has faith that the government's actions will help to stabilize the housing market.

33739 ■ *"Has Daylight Savings Time Fuelled Gasoline Consumption" in Globe & Mail (April 14, 2007, pp. B1)*
Pub: CTVglobemedia Publishing Inc.
Ed: Shawn McCarthy. **Description:** The prospects of the acquisition of BCE Inc, by Canadian pension funds are discussed. The effect of the growth of these pension funds on the Canadian economy is described.

33740 ■ *"Hastily Enacted Regulation Will Not Cure Economic Crisis" in Crain's Chicago Business (Vol. 31, May 5, 2008, No. 18, pp. 18)*
Pub: Crain Communications, Inc.
Ed: Stephen P. D'Arcy. **Description:** Policymakers are looking for ways to respond to what is possibly the greatest financial crisis of a generation due to the collapse of the housing market, the credit crisis and the volatility of Wall Street.

33741 ■ *"Have High-Tech Tax Credits Helped or Hurt Hawaii?" in Hawaii Business (Vol. 53, December 2007, No. 6, pp. 28)*
Pub: Hawaii Business Publishing
Description: Presents the opinons of Channel Capital LLC's Walter R. Roth and Hawaii Venture Capital Association's Bill Spencer concerning the impacts of tax credits. Roth thinks that Act 221 appeals to investors who can earn despite business failure while Spencer thinks that the legislation promotes investments in innovative technology firms. The need to support tax credits is also discussed.

33742 ■ *"Health Care of the Future" in Business Journal Serving Greater Tampa Bay (Vol. 30, November 19, 2010, No. 48, pp. 1)*
Pub: Tampa Bay Business Journal
Ed: Margie Manning. **Description:** Information about accountable care organizations (ACO), which are integrated care systems with doctors and hospitals working closely together to handle patient care, is provided. The Patient Protection and Affordable Care Act paved the way for ACOs as Medicare demonstration projects.

33743 ■ *"Health IT Regulations Generate Static Among Providers" in Philadelphia Business Journal (Vol. 28, January 29, 2010, No. 50, pp. 1)*
Pub: American City Business Journals
Ed: John George. **Description:** US Centers for Medicaid and Medicare Services and the Office of the National Coordinator for Health Information Technology have proposed rules regarding the meaningful use of electronic health records. The rules must be complied with by hospitals and physicians to qualify for federal stimulus funds.

33744 ■ *"Health Job Shift Looms" in Boston Business Journal (Vol. 31, June 3, 2011, No. 19, pp. 3)*
Pub: Boston Business Journal
Ed: Julie M. Donnelly. **Description:** Pending health care payment reform in Massachusetts is seen to adversely impact hospital staff. Hospitals are also seen to serve more patients once the bill is approved.

33745 ■ *"Health Reform Could Expand HSA-Based Plans" in Workforce Management (Vol. 88, December 14, 2009, No. 13, pp. 6)*
Pub: Crain Communications Inc.
Ed: Jeremy Smerd. **Description:** HSA-qualified plans are the cheapest insurance plans on the market as they have a higher deductible but cost less upfront. If health care reform passes, HSA-qualified plans should benefit greatly.

33746 ■ *"Health Reform How-To" in Business Courier (Vol. 26, December 11, 2009, No. 33, pp. 1)*
Pub: American City Business Journals, Inc.
Ed: James Ritchie. **Description:** Greater Cincinnati health care leaders shared views about the health care reform bill. Respondents included the Cincinnati

Visiting Nurse's Wallen Falberg, healthcare consultant Hirsch Cohen, Greater Cincinnati Health Council's Coleen O'Toole, Employer Health Care Alliance's Sharron DiMario, Legal Aid Society of Greater Cincinnati's Col Owens, Christ Hospital's Susan Croushore, and Humana of Ohio's Tim Cappel.

33747 ■ *"Hike in Md.'s Alcohol Tax May Be Hard For Lawmakers to Swallow" in Baltimore Business Journal (Vol. 28, November 19, 2010, No. 28)*
Pub: Baltimore Business Journal
Ed: Emily Mullin. **Description:** Maryland's General Assembly has been reluctant to support a dime-per-drink increase in alcohol tax that was drafted in the 2009 bill if the tax revenue goes into a separate fund. The alcohol tax increase is considered unnecessary by some lawmakers and business leaders due to impending federal spending boosts.

33748 ■ *"His Way" in Inc. (February 2008, pp. 90-97)*
Pub: Gruner & Jahr USA Publishing
Ed: Stephanie Clifford. **Description:** Profile of Chris Reed, founder of a natural soda company, who undertook an initial public offering (IPO). Reed discusses the challenges he faced mediating with the Securities Exchange Commission regarding his firm's IPO.

33749 ■ *"Hispanic Business 100 Influentials" in Hispanic Business (October 2009, pp. 22)*
Pub: Hispanic Business
Description: Profiles of the top one hundred influential Hispanics in business and government are presented.

33750 ■ *"Hispanic Business 100 Influentials: Profiles of the Top 100 Influentials" in Hispanic Business (October 2009, pp. 22)*
Pub: Hispanic Business
Description: Profiles of the top one hundred influential Hispanics in business and government are presented.

33751 ■ *"Historic Tax Credit Plan Gains Support" in Baltimore Business Journal (Vol. 27, January 8, 2010, No. 36, pp. 1)*
Pub: American City Business Journals
Ed: Heather Harlan Warnack. **Description:** Maryland Governor Martin O'Malley plans to push legislation in the General Assembly to extend for three more years the tax credit program for rehabilitation of obsolete buildings. The Maryland Heritage Structure Rehabilitation Tax Credit Program has declined from almost $75 million in expenses in 2001 to roughly $5 million in 2010 fiscal year. Details on the projects that benefited from the program are explored.

33752 ■ *"A History of Neglect" in Canadian Business (Vol. 79, September 11, 2006, No. 18, pp. 21)*
Pub: Rogers Media
Ed: Al Rosen. **Description:** Faulty practices being followed by auditors and regulators of Canada are discussed. The need for appropriate steps to protect investors against these frauds are emphasized.

33753 ■ *"Hitting Bottom?" in Barron's (Vol. 88, March 24, 2008, No. 12, pp. 21)*
Pub: Dow Jones & Company, Inc.
Ed: Jacqueline Doherty. **Description:** Brokerage houses and banks may stabilize in 2008 as a result of regulatory responses brought about by the near-collapse of Bear Stearns. Some of their shares may rise by as much as 20 percent from 2008 to 2009.

33754 ■ *"The Hollow Debate" in Canadian Business (Vol. 81, March 3, 2008, No. 3, pp. 26)*
Pub: Rogers Media
Ed: Thomas Watson. **Description:** According to a report conducted by the Conference Board of Canada, the Canadian business community is not being hollowed out by acquisitions made by foreign companies. Findings further showed that local businesses are protected by dual shares and that the economy can benefit more from foreign acquisitions than local mergers. The need to relax foreign ownership restrictions and other recommendations are presented.

33755 ■ *"Home Sprinklers Blocked in Texas, Long Beach, California" in Contractor (Vol. 56, July 2009, No. 7, pp. 1)*
Pub: Penton Media, Inc.
Ed: Robert P. Mader. **Description:** Long Beach, California has exempted older residential high rises and large apartment complexes from a rule to install fire sprinkler systems. Texas has also prohibited municipalities from enacting residential sprinkler ordinances.

33756 ■ *"Hot Air" in Canadian Business (Vol. 81, July 22, 2008, No. 12-13, pp. 16)*
Pub: Rogers Media Ltd.
Ed: Joe Castaldo. **Description:** Over half of 101 business leaders who were recently surveyed oppose Liberal leader Stephane Dion's carbon-tax proposal, saying that manufacturers in Canada are likely to suffer from the plan. Additional key results of the survey are presented.

33757 ■ *"Hot Air: On Global Warming and Carbon Tax" in Canadian Business (Vol. 81, October 13, 2008, No. 17, pp. 12)*
Pub: Rogers Media Ltd.
Ed: Joe Castaldo. **Description:** Survey of Canadian business leaders revealed that the environment is a key issue in Canada's federal elections. Respondents believe that Prime Minister Stephen Harper's views on global warming and climate change are closer to their own views. Other key information on the survey is presented.

33758 ■ *"House Committee on Small Business Calls for Sweeping Changes to SBIR Program" in Hispanic Business (Vol. 30, March 2008, No. 3)*
Pub: Hispanic Business
Description: Proposals suggested by the House Committee on small business to revamp the Small Business Innovation and Research Program (SBIR) are reported. These include allowing participating firms greater flexibility to use venture capital funds, increasing SBIR grants and faster processing of applications.

33759 ■ *"How To: Manage Your Cash Better" in Inc. (Volume 32, December 2010, No. 10, pp. 69)*
Pub: Inc. Magazine
Description: A monthly guide to policies, procedures and practices for managing cash for a small business.

33760 ■ *"The HST Hornet's Nest" in Canadian Business (Vol. 83, September 14, 2010, No. 15, pp. 17)*
Pub: Rogers Media Ltd.
Ed: Michael McCullough. **Description:** Canadian Premier Gordon Campbell's Harmonized Sales Tax (HST) initiative has left British Columbia's economic and political future stuck in uncertainty. The petition of a coalition group forced a bill to abolish the HST through legislation or referendum. How the HST's abolition will affect British Columbia's revenues is also discussed.

33761 ■ *"The Human Factor" in Canadian Business (Vol. 80, October 8, 2007, No. 20, pp. 22)*
Pub: Rogers Media
Ed: Alex Mynek. **Description:** David Foot, a demographer and an economics professor at the University of Toronto, talks about Canada's future, including economic and demographic trends. He discusses activities that should be done by businessmen in order to prepare for the future. He also addresses the role of the Canadian government in economic development.

33762 ■ *"I-5 Bridge Funding Unclear" in The Business Journal-Portland (Vol. 25, July 11, 2008, No. 18, pp. 1)*
Pub: American City Business Journals, Inc.
Ed: Andy Giegerich. **Description:** Financing for a new Interstate 5 bridge is unclear as Washington lawmakers identify two priority projects other than the planned bridge, which is shared with Oregon. An estimate says that the two states could pay between $487.6 million and $1.5 billion for the new bridge. Other details on the financing of the project are discussed.

33763 ■ *"If Just One Person Applies, Are You Required to Hire Him?" in HR Specialist (Vol. 8, September 2010, No. 9, pp. 7)*
Pub: Capitol Information Group Inc.
Description: It is legal to decline hiring an applicant, or even promoting a current employee, if they are the only applicant for a particular position. It may be good choice to wait for more applicants or to change recruiting strategy.

33764 ■ *"IFRS Monopoly: the Pied Piper of Financial Reporting" in Accounting and Business Research (Vol. 41, Summer 2011, No. 3, pp. 291)*
Pub: American Institute of Certified Public Accountants
Contact: Barry C. Melancon, President
E-mail: bmelancon@aicpa.org
Ed: Shyam Sunder. **Description:** The disadvantages of granting monopoly to the international financial reporting standards (IFRS) are examined. Results indicate that an IFRS monopoly removes the chances for comparing alternative practices and learning from them. An IFRS monopoly also eliminates customization of financial reporting to fit local differences in governance, business, economic, and legal conditions.

33765 ■ *"Illinois Regulators Revoke Collection Agency's License" in Collections & Credit Risk (Vol. 15, August 1, 2010, No. 7, pp. 13)*
Pub: SourceMedia Inc.
Description: Creditors Service Bureau of Springfield, Illinois had its license revoked by a state regulatory agency and was fined $55,000 because the owner and president, Craig W. Lewis, did not turn over portions of collected funds to clients.

33766 ■ *"Illinois Residential Building Legislation Includes New HVAC Requirements" in Contractor (Vol. 56, July 2009, No. 7, pp. 3)*
Pub: Penton Media, Inc.
Ed: Candace Roulo. **Description:** Illinois' Energy Efficient Building Act will require all new buildings and houses to conform to the International Energy Conservation Code. The code includes a duct leakage requirement followed by a post-construction test to verify leakage rates and requires programmable thermostats on all houses.

33767 ■ *"Immigration Issues Frustrate Owners From Overseas" in The Business Journal-Serving Greater Tampa Bay (Vol. 28, August 15, 2008)*
Pub: American City Business Journals, Inc.
Ed: Margie Manning. **Description:** Investors who availed the E-2 visa program believe that the tightened restrictions on the visa program has trapped them in the United States. The E-2 investor visa program was designed to attract investors into the U.S., but restrictions were tightened after the September 11, 2001 attacks. Other views and information on E-2 and its impact on investors are presented.

33768 ■ *"Importers Share Safety Liability" in Feedstuffs (Vol. 80, January 21, 2008, No. 3, pp. 19)*
Pub: Miller Publishing Company, Inc.
Description: Pet food and toys containing lead paint are among products from China being recalled due to safety concerns. American Society for Quality's list of measures that outsourcing companies can take to help ensure safer products being imported to the U.S.

33769 ■ *In Fed We Trust: Ben Bernanke's Ware on the Great Panic*
Pub: Crown Business
Ed: David Wessel. **Released:** 2009. **Price:** $27.99. **Description:** A look at the central bank's reaction to the crisis and Ben Bernanke has been forced to play the crisis by ear in order to keep the economy from imploding.

33770 ■ *"In the SBA's Face" in Hispanic Business (December 2010)*
Pub: Hispanic Business
Ed: Richard Larsen. **Description:** Lloyd Chapman uses the American Small Business League to champion small business. Statistical data included.

33771 ■ *"In With the Good" in Canadian Business (Vol. 80, November 5, 2007, No. 22, pp. 22)*
Pub: Rogers Media
Ed: Jack Mintz. **Description:** Restriction on foreign direct investment in Canada is unlikely to materialize despite Minister of Industry Jim Prentice's opinion that new rules be set in Ottawa regarding foreign state-owned businesses. Reasons why governments would not unreasonably regulate foreign investments are investigated.

33772 ■ *"Incentives Debate Rages On Unabated" in The Business Journal-Serving Metropolitan Kansas City (Vol. 26, September 5, 2008, No. 52)*
Pub: American City Business Journals, Inc.
Ed: Rob Roberts. **Description:** Debate on the new economic development and incentives policy adopted by the Kansas City Council is still on. The city's Planned Industrial Expansion Authority has rejected a standard property tax abatement proposal. The real estate development community has opposed the rejection of proposed the tax incentives policy.

33773 ■ *"Inco Takeover Faces Foreign Hurdles" in Globe & Mail (February 14, 2006, pp. B1)*
Pub: CTVglobemedia Publishing Inc.
Ed: Paul Waldie. **Description:** The issues that impact Inco Ltd.'s acquisition of Falconbridge Ltd., for $12.5 billion, are presented. Inco Ltd. is awaiting foreign regulatory approval in the United States and Europe.

33774 ■ *Incorporate Your Business: A 50 State Legal Guide to Forming a Corporation*
Pub: Nolo
Ed: Anthony Mancuso. **Released:** January 2004. **Description:** Legal guide to incorporating a business in the U.S., covering all 50 states.

33775 ■ *"Inco's Takeover Offer Extended Four Months" in Globe & Mail (February 22, 2006, pp. B1)*
Pub: CTVglobemedia Publishing Inc.
Ed: Wendy Stueck. **Description:** United States and Europe competition authorities wanted more time to investigate Inco Ltd.'s takeover of Falconbridge Ltd. and compelling Inco to extend its $12.5 billion offer for the third time.

33776 ■ *"Industry Escalates Lobbying Efforts For Loan Program" in Crain's Detroit Business (Vol. 24, September 22, 2008, No. 38, pp. 22)*
Pub: Crain Communications Inc.
Ed: Jay Greene; Ryan Beene; Harry Stoffer. **Description:** Auto suppliers such as Lear Corp., which is best known for vehicle seating, also supplies high-voltage wiring for Ford hybrids and is developing other hybrid components. These suppliers are joining automakers in lobbying for the loan program which would promote the accelerated development of fuel-efficient vehicles.

33777 ■ *"Injured Workers Caught in the Middle" in Sacramento Business Journal (Vol. 28, June 10, 2011, No. 15, pp. 1)*
Pub: Sacramento Business Journal
Ed: Kelly Johnson. **Description:** A bill that would extend the cap on disability payments to nearly five years is in the works, but employers and insurance companies fear it would increase their costs. Proponents of the bill say, however, that it would correct unfairness suffered by the employees. Features of the bill are discussed as well as its effects on both parties and the State of California.

33778 ■ *"Internet Cafe Logging in to Chardon Plaza?" in News-Herald (July 16, 2011)*
Pub: Journal Register Ohio
Ed: Betsy Scott. **Description:** Pearl's High Rollers Inc. applied for an Internet sweepstakes cafe license that would reside in a vacant space in Chardon Plaza. City officials have created regulations for such businesses and Pearl's applied for a license and is awaiting approval.

33779 ■ *"Internet Cafe Regulations Head to City Council Vote" in Vindicator (April 13, 2011)*
Pub: Vindicator
Ed: David Skolnick. **Description:** Youngstown City Council's safety committee agrees with proposed changes to the policy regulating Internet gaming cafes and sweepstakes businesses. The new amendments allow Internet cafe customers to buy Internet time and go to Websites and play sweepstakes games of change.

33780 ■ *"Investigation Hints at Workers' Comp Trouble" in Sacramento Business Journal (Vol. 25, July 4, 2008, No. 18, pp. 1)*
Pub: American City Business Journals, Inc.
Ed: Kelly Johnson. **Description:** In 500 California firms, a survey of worker compensation revealed that 38 percent of the companies had problems with required coverage. Government investigators are bothered that 107 companies did not respond to the official inquiry. Other views and information on the survey and on the expected economic implications of the findings are presented.

33781 ■ *"IRS Announces New Standards for Tax Preparers" in Bellingham Business Journal (Vol. February 2010, pp. 9)*
Pub: Sound Publishing Inc.
Ed: Isaac Bonnell. **Description:** A new oversight plan was announced by the Internal Revenue Services (IRS) that will require tax professionals to pass a competency test and register with the government in order to ensure greater accountability in the industry.

33782 ■ *"Is Hawaii Ready for Universal Health Care?" in Hawaii Business (Vol. 53, February 2008, No. 8, pp. 26)*
Pub: Hawaii Business Publishing
Description: Representative Lyn Finnegan does not believe that a universal health is good for Hawaii as health insurance for everyone will be difficult to achieve. Representative John M. Mizuno says that House Bill 1008 introduced in the state was a landmark for Hawaii as it will provide the people with health care insurance. Other details about their opinion on the topic are presented.

33783 ■ *"It's All in the Details" in Canadian Business (Vol. 80, December 25, 2006, No. 1, pp. 11)*
Pub: Rogers Media
Description: The failure of several Canadian clothing retailers to disclose their labor practices is discussed.

33784 ■ *"Ivernia Mine Closing Could Boost Lead" in Globe & Mail (April 4, 2007, pp. B5)*
Pub: CTVglobemedia Publishing Inc.
Ed: Andy Hoffman. **Description:** The closing of Ivernia Inc.'s mine in view of government investigation into alleged lead contamination at the port of Esperance is discussed. The likely increase in the price of lead is also discussed.

33785 ■ *"Jennifer Hernandez Helps Developers Transform Contaminated Properties" in Hispanic Business (Vol. 30, April 2008, No. 4, pp. 32)*
Pub: Hispanic Business
Ed: Hildy Medina. **Description:** Jennifer Hernandez is a partner and head of the law firm of Holland & Knight's environmental practice which specializes in the restoration of polluted land where former industrial and commercial buildings once stood, known as brownfields. Brownfield redevelopment can be lucrative but costly due to the cleaning up of contaminated land and challenging because of federal and state environmental laws.

33786 ■ *"Job Losses and Budget Shortfall Adding to Economic Woes" in Sacramento Business Journal (Vol. 25, July 11, 2008, No. 19, pp. 1)*
Pub: American City Business Journals, Inc.
Ed: Kathy Robertson. **Description:** Budget cuts in California have been approved amid rising unemployment in a slowing economy. Statistics show that total industry employment in the Sacramento region decreased by 3,700 jobs from May 2007 to May 2008. Governor Arnold Schwarzenegger has ordered a 10 percent budget cut for state departments, but this cut will likely mean few layoffs.

33787 ■ *"Jump Ship On Your Wireless Contract" in Black Enterprise (Vol. 38, January 2008, No. 6, pp. 87)*
Pub: Earl G. Graves Publishing Co. Inc.
Ed: Nicole Norfleet. **Description:** Better Business Bureau reported it received more than 28,000 complaints in 2007. Four situations that allow consumers to be released from a long-term service contract with a carrier without paying penalty fees are addressed.

33788 ■ *"Kaboom!" in Canadian Business (Vol. 81, November 10, 2008, No. 19, pp. 18)*
Pub: Rogers Media Ltd.
Ed: Al Rosen, Mark Rosen. **Description:** International Financial Reporting Standards (IFRS) is a good idea in theory but was implemented in a hurry and had poor quality standards from the beginning.

33789 ■ *"KC Sewer Solutions May Overflow With Green Ideas" in The Business Journal-Serving Metropolitan Kansas City (August 22, 2008)*
Pub: American City Business Journals, Inc.
Ed: Suzanna Stagemeyer. **Description:** Adding green solutions such as small, dispersed basins to catch runoffs and the use of deep rooted natural plants to fix the sewer system of Kansas could probably justify the $2.3 billion worth of funds needed for the project. The city has been ordered by the EPA and the Missouri Department of Natural Resources to fix their sewer systems that are overwhelmed by significant rains.

33790 ■ *"Keltic Gets Nod to Build N.S. Petrochemical Plant" in Globe & Mail (March 15, 2007, pp. B9)*
Pub: CTVglobemedia Publishing Inc.
Ed: Shawn McCarthy. **Description:** The government of Nova Scotia has awarded clearance to Keltic Inc. for the construction of new petrochemical plant in Goldboro region. Complete details in this context are discussed.

33791 ■ *"Key FDA Approval Yanked for Avastin" in Wall Street Journal Eastern Edition (November 19 , 2011, pp. B1)*
Pub: Dow Jones & Company Inc.
Ed: Thomas M. Burton, Jennifer Corbett Dooren. **Description:** Avastin, a drug manufactured by Genetech Inc. and used in the treatment of metastatic breast cancer in women, has had its approval by the US Food and Drug Administration withdrawn by the agency, which says there is no evidence the widely-used drug is successful in increasing the longevity of breast cancer patients.

33792 ■ *"LA Passes HET Ordinance, California Greens Code" in Contractor (Vol. 56, September 2009, No. 9, pp. 1)*
Pub: Penton Media, Inc.
Ed: Candace Ruolo. **Description:** Los Angeles City Council has passed a Water Efficiency Requirements ordinance. The law mandates lower low-flow plumbing requirements for plumbing fixtures installed in new buildings and retrofits. Under the ordinance, a toilet's maximum flush volume may not exceed 1.28-gpf.

33793 ■ *"Land Swap Key to Ending Royal Oak Project Impasse" in Crain's Detroit Business (Vol. 25, June 8, 2009, No. 23, pp. 20)*
Pub: Crain Communications Inc. - Detroit
Ed: Chad Halcom. **Description:** Details of the new construction of the LA Fitness health club near Woodward and Washington Avenues in Royal Oak, Michigan are discussed.

33794 ■ *"The Latest on E-Verify" in Contractor (Vol. 56, September 2009, No. 9, pp. 58)*
Pub: Penton Media, Inc.
Ed: Susan McGreevy. **Description:** United States government has required federal contractors to use its E-Verify program to verify the eligibility of incoming and existent employees. The use of the program is seen to eliminate Social Security mismatches.

33795 ■ *"Latest Volley Tries to Press Port Group" in Business Courier (Vol. 26, November 20, 2009, No. 30, pp. 1)*
Pub: American City Business Journals, Inc.
Ed: Dan Monk. **Description:** Subcontractors filed a new legal argument to force the Port of Greater Cincinnati Development Authority to pursue default claim against Bank of America. The bank issued letters of credit to guarantee bond payments in addition to holding the mortgage of the Kenwood Towne Place. Details of the claim are discussed.

33796 ■ *"Law Allows Captive Insurance Companies to Form in State" in Crain's Detroit Business (Vol. 24, March 31, 2008, No. 13, pp. 29)*
Pub: Crain Communications, Inc.
Description: Discusses new legislation allowing the formation of captive insurance companies in the state of Michigan; these companies are subsidiaries of non-insurers that are formed primarily to insure some or all of the risks of its parent company.

33797 ■ *"Law Reform, Collective Bargaining, and the Balance of Power: Results of an Empirical Study" in WorkingUSA (June 2008)*
Pub: Blackwell Publishers Ltd.
Ed: Ellen Dannin, Michelle Dean, Gangaram Singh. **Description:** Despite Congress' having made clear policy statements in the National Labor Relations Act that the law was intended to promote equality of bargaining power between employers and employees, to promote the practice and procedure of collective bargaining as the method of setting workplace terms and conditions of employment, and forbidding construing the law 'so as to either interfere with or impede or diminish in any way the right to strike,' by early 1940, the courts had given employers the right to permanently replace strikers and implement their final offer at impasse. Judges have often justified these doctrines as promoting balance in bargaining. Critics contend that the doctrines have the capacity to destroy the right to strike, unbalance bargaining power, and divert parties from the process of bargaining collectively. Some have proposed allowing temporary but not permanent striker replacement. The article uses a bargaining simulation followed by a survey and debriefing comments to test these opposing claims.

33798 ■ *"Lawyers Cash In On Alcohol" in Business Journal Portland (Vol. 27, November 19, 2010, No. 38, pp. 1)*
Pub: Portland Business Journal
Ed: Andy Giegerich. **Description:** Oregon-based law firms have continued to corner big business on the state's growing alcohol industry as demand for their services increased. Lawyers, who represent wine, beer and liquor distillery interests, have seen their workload increased by 20 to 30 percent in 2009.

33799 ■ *"LCB Puts a Cork in Kiosk Wine Sales" in Times Leader (December 22, 2010)*
Pub: Wilkes-Barre Publishing Company
Ed: Andrew M. Seder. **Description:** The Pennsylvania Liquor Control Board closed down thirty Pronto Wine Kiosks located in supermarkets throughout the state. The Board cited mechanical and technological issues such as products not dispensing.

33800 ■ *"Lead-Free Products must Meet Requirements" in Contractor (Vol. 56, September 2009, No. 9, pp. 30)*
Pub: Penton Media, Inc.
Ed: Robert Gottermeier. **Description:** United States Environmental Protection Agency's adoption of the Safe Drinking Water Act is aimed at lowering lead extraction levels from plumbing products. Manufacturers have since deleaded brass and bronze potable water products. Meanwhile, California and Vermont have passed a law limiting lead content for potable water conveying plumbing products.

33801 ■ *"Legislating the Cloud" in Information Today (Vol. 28, October 2011, No. 9, pp. 1)*
Pub: Information Today, Inc.
Description: Internet and telecommunications industry leaders are asking for legislation to address the emerging market in cloud computing. Existing communications laws do not adequately govern the modern Internet.

33802 ■ *"Legislation Introduced" in Indoor Comfort Marketing (Vol. 70, July 2011, No. 7, pp. 6)*
Pub: Industry Publications Inc.
Description: New industry legislation is examined by the National Oilheat Research Alliance.

33803 ■ *"Legislators Must Cut Cost of Government" in Crain's Detroit Business (Vol. 24, October 6, 2008, No. 40, pp. 6)*
Pub: Crain Communications, Inc.
Description: Southeast and West Michigan business leaders are setting aside their differences and have proposed clear agendas, ranging from eliminating the Michigan Business Tax to overhauling public employee and retiree benefits and pensions. Lawmakers must also come together to find solutions for the state's economy and discover an entirely new vision for the future of Michigan business.

33804 ■ *"Legislature Passes Increased Tax Credit for Urban Brownfield Projects" in Crain's Detroit Business (Vol. 24, March 31, 2008, No. 13)*
Pub: Crain Communications, Inc.
Ed: Amy Lane. **Description:** Discusses the bill passed by the Legislature that creates a tax credit of up to 20 percent for projects in urban development areas.

33805 ■ *"Legislature to Tackle Crisis in Jobless Fund" in Baltimore Business Journal (Vol. 27, December 18, 2009, No. 32, pp. 1)*
Pub: American City Business Journals
Ed: Scott Dance. **Description:** Maryland's General Assembly is set to finalize changes to the state's unemployment insurance system as soon as it convenes for the 2010 session. The move was aimed to draw $127 million in stimulus money that can support the nearly depleted fund of unemployment benefits within 45 days.

33806 ■ *"Legoland Plans Could Tumble After State's Modesa Denial" in Business Journal-Serving Metropolitan Kansas City (November 16, 2007)*
Pub: American City Business Journals, Inc.
Ed: Jim Davis. **Description:** RED Development LLC's officials are not giving up after the Missouri Department of Economic Development said RED could not exploit the Missouri Downtown and Rural Economic Stimulus Act (Modesa) for the Legoland theme park development in Lee's Summit. Legoland's proposed site southeast of Interstate 470 and U.S. Highway 50 does not fit the Modesa because it is outside Lee's Summit.

33807 ■ *"Lending Idea Gets Mixed Review" in Tampa Bay Business Journal (Vol. 29, October 30, 2009, No. 45, pp. 1)*
Pub: American City Business Journals
Ed: Kent Hoover, Margie Manning. **Description:** Tampa Bay area, Florida's community banks have expressed disapproval to the proposal of President Obama to increase lending to small business, wherein the government will provide cheap capital through US Treasury Troubled Asset Relief Program (TARP). The banks were hesitant on the plan because of the strings attached to TARP.

33808 ■ *"Less Malaise in Malaysia" in Barron's (Vol. 88, March 17, 2008, No. 11, pp. M12)*
Pub: Dow Jones & Company, Inc.
Ed: Assif Shameen. **Description:** Shares of Malaysia's Bursa have been in freefall while the Malaysia government prolongs its pitch to sell a 10 percent stake of the exchange to NYSE Euronext. Asian bourses had produced very good returns for five years and charge some of the highest fees for exchanges. A key growth driver for Asian bourses could be the derivatives markets and exchange-traded funds.

33809 ■ *"Less Than Zero" in Canadian Business (Vol. 80, November 5, 2007, No. 22, pp. 36)*
Pub: Rogers Media
Ed: Andy Holloway. **Description:** Zero-tolerance policy with regards to discrimination and harassment at the workplace has been adopted by many companies. However, employers must exercise caution in terminating employees based on zero-tolerance policies since there are laws governing illegal dismissals. Important considerations employers should make in dismissing workers, such as proof of willful misconduct, are discussed.

33810 ■ *"Let Markets Decide?" in Canadian Business (Vol. 80, October 8, 2007, No. 20, pp. 67)*
Pub: Rogers Media
Ed: James Gillies. **Description:** Need to protect Canadian companies that could help boost the country's economy is discussed. It is expected that free markets alone will solve economic problems. Suggested policies that will discourage the takeover of major companies in the country, such as the organization of capitalization with multiple voting shares, are also presented.

33811 ■ *"The Letter of the Law" in Collections and Credit Risk (Vol. 14, November 1, 2009, No. 9, pp. 40)*
Pub: SourceMedia, Inc.
Ed: Michelle Dunn. **Description:** Analyzes the regulatory landscape regarding debt collection and the ways in which those in the field are dealing with a tough economy, unclear laws and the newest regulations.

33812 ■ *"Letting the Sunshine In" in Barron's (Vol. 89, July 6, 2009, No. 27, pp. 11)*
Pub: Dow Jones & Co., Inc.
Ed: Katherine Cheng. **Description:** Solar energy industry leaders believe the industry needs aid from the US government regarding the funding of its research efforts and lowering solar energy costs. The climate change bill passed by the US House of Representatives signifies the US government's desire to significantly reduce carbon dioxide emissions.

33813 ■ *"Levy Boards: From Unity Comes Farming's Strength" in Farmer's Weekly (March 28, 2008, No. 320)*
Pub: Reed Business Information
Contact: Jeff Greisch, President
Description: Discusses the amalgamation of five farming levy boards to create the Agriculture and Horticulture Development Board.

33814 ■ *"A Little Less Hot Air" in Canadian Business (Vol. 81, March 17, 2008, No. 4, pp. 9)*
Pub: Rogers Media
Description: British Columbia will levy an extra tax on all carbon-emitting fuels starting July 1, 2008. The tax will raise $1.8 billion in three years and in effect, the province will reduce general corporate income tax from 12 percent to 11 percent. The tax on small businesses and personal income will also be reduced.

33815 ■ *"Living in a 'Goldfish Bowl'" in WorkingUSA (Vol. 11, June 2008, No. 2, pp. 277)*
Pub: Blackwell Publishers Ltd.
Ed: John Lund. **Description:** Recent changes in laws, regulations and even the reporting format of labor organization annual financial reports in both the U.S. and Australia have received surprisingly little attention, yet they have significantly increased the amount of information available both to union members and the public in general, as reports in both countries are available via government Websites. While such financial reporting laws are extremely rare in European countries, with the exception of the

UK and Ireland, the U.S. and Australian reporting systems have become among the most detailed in the world. After reviewing these changes in financial reporting and the availability of these reports, as well as comparing and contrasting the specific reporting requirements of each country, this paper then examines the cost-benefit impact of more detailed financial reporting.

33816 ■ *"Local Hospitals Wage Wars on 'Bounce-Backs" in Business Courier (Vol. 27, July 30, 2010, No. 13, pp. 1)*
Pub: Business Courier
Ed: James Ritchie. **Description:** Health care organizations in Greater Cincinnati area have tried a number of care and follow up programs, primarily focused on congestive heart failure to prevent readmissions to hospitals. Hospital administrators have made the averting of bounce-backs a priority due to new federal government plans on reimbursement.

33817 ■ *"Local Manufacturers See Tax Proposal Hurting Global Operations" in Crain's Cleveland Business (Vol. 30, May 18, 2009, No. 20)*
Pub: Crain Communications, Inc.
Ed: Dan Shingler. **Description:** New tax laws proposed by the Obama Administration could hinder the efforts of some Northeast Ohio industrial companies from expanding their overseas markets. The law is designed to prevent companies from moving jobs overseas.

33818 ■ *"Lofty Ambitions" in Canadian Business (Vol. 80, October 22, 2007, No. 21, pp. 26)*
Pub: Rogers Media
Ed: Thomas Watson. **Description:** Canada has made its first trade deal in six years through the European Free Trade Agreement. This is a boost to the Canadian economy, but focus must be made on taking out internal barriers to inter-provincial trade and from third-party trade liberalization.

33819 ■ *"A Long Road to Recovery" in Barron's (Vol. 89, July 27, 2009, No. 30, pp. 37)*
Pub: Dow Jones & Co., Inc.
Ed: Henry Kaufman. **Description:** United States' economy remains hobbled by some underlying constraint and real recovery remains ephemeral. Much of the financial problems could have been avoided if t he Federal Reserve was effectively guarding the financial system.

33820 ■ *"Looking for a Sales Tax Extension" in Milwaukee Business Journal (Vol. 27, January 29, 2010, No. 18, pp. A1)*
Pub: American City Business Journals
Ed: Mark Kass. **Description:** Milwaukee, Wisconsin-area business executives believe the extension of the Miller Park 0.1 percent sales tax could help fund a new basketball arena to replace the 21-year-old Bradley Center in downtown Milwaukee. However, any sales tax expansion that includes the new basketball arena would need approval by Wisconsin's legislature.

33821 ■ *"Looking To Hire Young? Be Careful" in Boston Business Journal (Vol. 30, November 19, 2010, No. 43, pp. 1)*
Pub: Boston Business Journal
Ed: Lisa van der Pool. **Description:** The Massachusetts Commission Against Discrimination (MCAD) has been using undercover job applicants to expose discrimination. Cabot's Ice Cream and Restaurant has been accused of denying older workers equal employment opportunities. MCAD has discovered unfair hiring practices such as hiring high school and college students.

33822 ■ *"Lower Prices No Shoo-In as Telcos Near Deregulation" in Globe & Mail (March 28, 2007, pp. B1)*
Pub: CTVglobemedia Publishing Inc.
Ed: Catherine McLean. **Description:** The fall in market share and low quality of service among other issues that may disallow telecommunication industries in Canada from setting their phone rates is discussed.

33823 ■ *"Make a Resolution: ADA Training" in HRMagazine (Vol. 54, January 2009, No. 1, pp. 81)*
Pub: Society for Human Resource Management
Contact: Henry G. Jackson, President
E-mail: hjackson@shrm.org
Ed: Victoria Zellers. **Description:** Americans with Disabilities Act (ADA) Amendments Act took effect January 1, 2009. The ADA Amendments Act means that more applicants and employees are eligible for reasonable accommodations and that employers need to develop a new ADA compliance strategy.

33824 ■ *"M&I Execs May Get Golden Parachutes" in Business Journal-Milwaukee (Vol. 28, December 31, 2010, No. 14, pp. A3)*
Pub: Milwaukee Business Journal
Ed: Rich Kirchen. **Description:** Marshall and Isley Corporation's top executives have a chance to receive golden-parachute payments it its buyer, BMO Financial Group, repays the Troubled Asset Relief Program (TARP) loan on behalf of the company. One TARP rule prevents golden-parachute payments to them and the next five most highly paid employees of TARP recipients.

33825 ■ *"The Many Hats and Faces of NAOHSM" in Indoor Comfort Marketing (Vol. 70, May 2011, No. 5, pp. 8)*
Pub: Industry Publications Inc.
Description: Profile of the National Association of Oil Heating Service Managers, and its role in the industry, is presented.

33826 ■ *"Marine Act Amendments Gain Parliamentary Approval" in Canadian Sailings (July 7, 2008)*
Pub: UBM Global Trade
Contact: Leonard J. Corallo, President
Ed: Alex Binkley. **Description:** Changes to the Canada Marine Act provides better borrowing deals as well as an ability to tap into federal infrastructure funding for environmental protection measures, security improvements and other site enhancements.

33827 ■ *"Market Takes Shape for Emissions Credits" in Globe & Mail (April 16, 2007, pp. B3)*
Pub: CTVglobemedia Publishing Inc.
Ed: Shawn McCarthy. **Description:** The effort of Canadian companies to prepare for emissions trading after the government imposes climate change regulations is discussed.

33828 ■ *"Market Watch" in Barron's (Vol. 88, March 24, 2008, No. 12, pp. M18)*
Pub: Dow Jones & Company, Inc.
Ed: Ashraf Laidi; Marc Pado; David Kotok. **Description:** Latest measures implemented by the Federal Reserve to address the credit crisis did not benefit the US dollar, with the Japanese yen and the euro recouping earlier losses against the dollar. Goldman Sachs reported earnings of $3.23 per share, claiming a stronger liquidity position. The US markets bottomed early on 22 January 2007, according to evidence.

33829 ■ *"Martin Marietta Expands Rock Solid Port Manatee Presence" in Tampa Bay Business Journal (Vol. 30, January 8, 2010, No. 3, pp. 1)*
Pub: American City Business Journals
Ed: Jane Meinhardt. **Description:** Raleigh, North Carolina-based Martin Marietta Materials Inc. has been granted by Florida's Manatee County Port Authority with a 30-year, $42 million contract. Through the contract, an aggregate terminal will be built by Martin Marietta at the port. Construction work is anticipated to start in earl 2010 with terminal operations commencing by late summer 2010.

33830 ■ *"Maryland Ready to Defend Slots Minority Policy" in Boston Business Journal (Vol. 29, July 8, 2011, No. 9, pp. 3)*
Pub: American City Business Journals Inc.
Ed: Scott Dance. **Description:** The legality of Maryland's minority inclusion policy may be put under scrutiny once the lawsuit filed by rejected slots developer Baltimore City Entertainment Group on July 5, 2011 is heard in court. The lawsuit aims to stop the bidding process on a proposed casino in Baltimore because the minority policy amounts to reverse discrimination.

33831 ■ *"Mass-Transit Backers: Change in State Funding Needed" in Crain's Detroit Business (Vol. 24, October 6, 2008, No. 40, pp. 19)*
Pub: Crain Communications, Inc.
Ed: Bill Shea. **Description:** Options to reform transportation and infrastructure funding in the state of Michigan are examined. Transit revitalization investment zones are also discussed.

33832 ■ *"A Matter of Perspective" in Business Journal-Portland (Vol. 24, November 2, 2007, No. 35, pp. 1)*
Pub: American City Business Journals, Inc.
Ed: Andy Giegerich. **Description:** Oregon Governor Ted Kulongoski assembled the Mortgage Lending Work Group, made up of members of the mortgage industry and consumer groups, to recommend possible bills for the Oregon Senate and House to consider. How its members try to balance philosophical differences in mortgage lending rules is discussed.

33833 ■ *"MBT Add On: Gone by 2012?" in Crain's Detroit Business (Vol. 24, October 6, 2008, No. 40, pp. 1)*
Pub: Crain Communications, Inc.
Ed: Amy Lane. **Description:** Discusses the Michigan Business Tax (MBT), which has angered many businesses in the state due to the addition of a 21.99 percent surcharge. Although the tax policy will cut taxes on 63 percent of businesses in the state and represent no tax liability change for another nine percent of firms, other businesses will see increases of 100 percent or more. This increase means that many business owners will be forced to relocate or close their establishment and others will have to eliminate jobs. Lawmakers are attempting to find a solution to this problem.

33834 ■ *"Medicaid Expansion Could Prompt New Taxes, Program Cuts" in Baltimore Business Journal (Vol. 27, October 23, 2009, No. 24, pp. 1)*
Pub: American City Business Journals
Ed: Julekha Dash. **Description:** Effects of the expected federal expansion of Medicaid under federal health care reform on Maryland tax policy are presented. Health care executives believe new taxes are necessary for the state to pay for an expansion that could cost over $400 million to $600 million.

33835 ■ *"Medical Pot Backers Say Industry Will Survive" in Sacramento Business Journal (Vol. 28, October 14, 2011, No. 33, pp. 1)*
Pub: Sacramento Business Journal
Ed: Melanie Turner. **Description:** Medical marijuana supporters have expected the industry to decline but will survive the federal restriction on growers and dispensaries across California. California Cannabis Association and National Cannabis Industry Association believe that some of the dispensaries will remain and the shakeout will lead to stronger state regulations.

33836 ■ *Memos to the Prime Minister: What Canada Could Be in the 21st Century*
Pub: John Wiley & Sons, Incorporated
Ed: Harvey Schacter. **Released:** April 11, 2003. **Price:** $16.95. **Description:** A look into the business future of Canada. Topics include business, healthcare, think tanks, policy groups, education, the arts, economy, and social issues.

33837 ■ *"Minimizing Import Risks" in Canadian Sailings (July 7, 2008)*
Pub: UBM Global Trade
Contact: Leonard J. Corallo, President
Ed: Jack Kohane. **Description:** New food and product safety laws may be enacted by Canada's Parliament; importers, retailers and manufacturers could face huge fines if the new laws are passed.

33838 ■ *"Misguided" in Canadian Business (Vol. 81, July 22, 2008, No. 12-13, pp. 30)*
Pub: Rogers Media Ltd.
Ed: Al Rosen. **Description:** Canada's securities regulations are discussed; differing views on using principles-based and rules-based securities regulations are also presented.

33839 ■ *"Missouri Public Service Commission Chooses APX" in Wireless News (January 22, 2010)*
Pub: Investment Weekly News
Description: Missouri Public Service Commission, with the help of APX Inc., an infrastructure provider for environmental and energy markets, has selected the North American Registry as the renewable energy certificate management system for Missouri Renewable Energy Standard compliance. APX will continue to support the state's renewable energy programs and manage their environmental assets.

33840 ■ *"Modular Home Center Opens in Arcadia" in Charlotte Observer (February 1, 2007)*
Pub: Knight-Ridder/Tribune Business News
Ed: John Lawhorne. **Description:** Arcadia Home Center features modular homes constructed on a steel frame; regulations regarding the manufacture and moving of these homes are included.

33841 ■ *"Monopoly Money Madness" in Canadian Business (Vol. 81, March 17, 2008, No. 4, pp. 9)*
Pub: Rogers Media
Description: Enbridge was given permission by the Ontario Energy Board to collect $22 million it spent on an out-of-court settlement for charging unfair fees from 1994 to 2002. Customers are essentially being gouged twice in this scenario. The monopoly of Enbridge should end and the consumers should not have to pay for the system's faults.

33842 ■ *"Monsanto's Next Single-Bag Refuge Product Approved" in Farm Industry News (December 5, 2011)*
Pub: Penton Business Media Inc.
Description: Monsanto's refuge-in-a-bag (RIB) product was approved for commercialization in 2012. The Genuity VT Double Pro RIB Complete is a blend of 95 percent Genuity VT Double Pro and 5 percent refuge (non-Bt) seed and provides above-ground pest control and not corn rootworm protection.

33843 ■ *"More SouthPark Shopping" in Charlotte Business Journal (Vol. 25, July 16, 2010, No. 17, pp. 1)*
Pub: Charlotte Business Journal
Ed: Will Boye. **Description:** Charlotte, North Carolina-based Bissel Companies has announced plans to expand its retail presence at the Siskey and Sharon properties in SouthPark. Bissel Companies has requested a rezoning to a mixed-use development classification so that it can utilize the entire ground floor of the Siskey building for restaurant and retail uses.

33844 ■ *"Mortgage Mess Continues To Trigger Bids To Ease Crisis" in Business First-Columbus (December 14, 2007, pp. A1)*
Pub: American City Business Journals, Inc.
Ed: Adrian Burns. **Description:** Measures to prevent foreclosures in Ohio are presented. On December 6, 2007, the Bush Administration started a national incentive that will establish a streamlined process for modifying loans. Some have questioned the proposal, since it is expected the plan will only help about 90,000 of the 1.8 million borrowers. According to Ohio Treasurer, Richard Cordray, one of the state's objectives is to calm the markets on Wall Street.

33845 ■ *"Mulroney on the Record" in Canadian Business (Vol. 79, September 11, 2006, No. 18, pp. 43)*
Pub: Rogers Media
Description: Canada's former prime minister and senior partner at the law firm Ogilvy Renault, Brain Mulroney speaks about the major policies and initiatives of the current government and its impact on the country's economy.

33846 ■ *"New Chief Walking the Talk" in Business Courier (Vol. 27, August 27, 2010, No. 17, pp. 1)*
Pub: Business Courier
Ed: Lucy May. **Description:** National Brand & Tag Company president, Eric Haas, has vowed to put his various work experiences when he assumes the presidency of North Kentucky Chamber of Commerce. Haas wants to help the Chamber influence government policies that could help various businesses through the economic depression.

33847 ■ *"A New Era for Raiders" in Harvard Business Review (Vol. 88, November 2010, No. 11, pp. 34)*
Pub: Harvard Business School Publishing
Ed: Guhan Subramanian. **Description:** The article presents evidence that Section 203 is vulnerable, and a new wave of corporate takeovers may develop. The authors suggest that since no bidders have able to use the 85 percent stipulation over the last 19 years, it does not present a meaningful opportunity for success.

33848 ■ *"New Health Law, Lack of Docs Collide on Cape Cod" in Boston Business Journal (Vol. 27, October 12, 2007, No. 37, pp. 1)*
Pub: American City Business Journals Inc.
Ed: Mark Hollmer. **Description:** There is a shortage of primary care providers at Outer Cape Health Services in Massachusetts, with the isolation of the area and as physicians look for higher paying careers in specialty positions. The Commonwealth Health Insurance Connector Authority is pushing for a new health insurance law and is working with Cape Cod Chamber of Commerce to conduct outreach programs.

33849 ■ *"New Law Lets Shareholders Play Hardball With Firms" in Globe & Mail (January 2, 2006, pp. B1)*
Pub: CTVglobemedia Publishing Inc.
Ed: Janet McFarland. **Description:** Business lawyer Wes Voorheis discusses about the launching of Bill 198 by plaintiffs' lawyers on behalf of ordinary retail investors.

33850 ■ *"New Rule Rankles In Jersey" in Philadelphia Business Journal (Vol. 30, September 16, 2011, No. 31, pp. 1)*
Pub: American City Business Journals Inc.
Ed: Jeff Blumenthal. **Description:** A new rule in New Jersey which taxes out-of-state companies that conduct business in the state earned the ire of several banks, mortgage lenders and credit card companies and prompted opponents to threaten to file lawsuits. The new rule is an amendment to New Jersey Division of Taxation's corporate business tax regulation and is retroactive to 2002. Details are given.

33851 ■ *"New State Rules Require Cranes and Operators to be Certified" in Bellingham Business Journal (Vol. February 2010, pp. 11)*
Pub: Sound Publishing Inc.
Ed: Isaac Bonnell. **Description:** All construction cranes in Washington state must be inspected annually to be certified for use. The move is part of a larger L&I crane safety program that also requires crane operators to pass a written exam and a skill test.

33852 ■ *New Technology-Based Firms in the New Millennium, Volume 6*
Pub: Elsevier Science & Technology Books
Ed: Ray Oakey, R. Oakey. **Released:** May 2008. **Price:** $149.00. **Description:** Collection of papers from the Annual International High Technology Firms (HTSFs) Conference cover issues of importance to governments as they develop technological program. Papers are grouped into three sections: theory, strategy and clustering, and spin-off firms.

33853 ■ *"New York Collection Agency's Bribery Case Resolved" in Collections & Credit Risk (Vol. 15, August 1, 2010, No. 7, pp. 19)*
Pub: SourceMedia Inc.
Description: Criminal conviction and civil settlement in a bribery case and Medicaid scam involving H.I.S. Holdings Inc. and owner Deborah Kantor is examined.

33854 ■ *"The Next Step in Patent Reform" in Information Today (Vol. 28, November 2011, No. 10, pp. 1)*
Pub: Information Today, Inc.
Ed: George H. Pike. **Description:** The Leahy-Smith America Invents Act was signed into law in September 2011. The new act reformed the previous US patent system. Information involving the new patent law process is discussed.

33855 ■ *"The Next Waive" in Hawaii Business (Vol. 53, January 2008, No. 7, pp. 27)*
Pub: Hawaii Business Publishing
Ed: Cathy S. Cruz-George. **Description:** Only 40,000 Koreans took a visit to Hawaii in 2007, a decline from the pre-September averages of 123,000 visits. The number of Korean visitors in Hawaii could increase if the visa waiver proposal is passed. Efforts to improve Hawaiian tourism are presented.

33856 ■ *"Nixon Assails Insurance Rules" in Globe & Mail (March 4, 2006, pp. B5)*
Pub: CTVglobemedia Publishing Inc.
Ed: Sinclair Stewart. **Description:** The opinions of chief executive officer Gordon Nixon of Royal Bank of Canada on the need to amend banking regulations, in order to provide insurance services, are presented.

33857 ■ *"No End to the Nightmare; America's Car Industry" in The Economist (Vol. 390, January 3, 2009, No. 8612, pp. 46)*
Pub: The Economist Newspaper Inc.
Description: Detroit's struggling auto industry and the government loan package is discussed as well as the United Auto Worker union, which is loathed by Senate Republicans.

33858 ■ *"No Shortage of Challenges for Cross-Border Trade" in Canadian Sailings (June 30, 2008)*
Pub: UBM Global Trade
Contact: Leonard J. Corallo, President
Ed: Kathlyn Horibe. **Description:** Pros and cons of the North American Free Trade Agreement are examined. The agreement between the U.S. and Canada concerning trade was an essential step toward securing economic growth for Canadian citizens. Two-way trade between the counties has tripled since the agreement and accounts for 7.1 million American and 3 million Canadian jobs.

33859 ■ *Non-Standard Employment under Globalization*
Pub: Palgrave Macmillan
Ed: Koichi Usami. **Released:** January 19, 2010. **Price:** $100.00. **Description:** Expansion of non-standard employment under globalization is being recognized in all of the newly industrialized countries. The book examines deregulation of labor markets, social protection for nonstandard workers, and social security reforms in accordance with the transformation of employment.

33860 ■ *"Nonprofits May Lose MBE Status in MD" in Boston Business Journal (Vol. 29, September 2, 2011, No. 17, pp. 1)*
Pub: American City Business Journals Inc.
Ed: Scott Dance. **Description:** A business group has been pushing to bar nonprofits from Maryland's Minority Business program. Nonprofits have been found to take a large portion of state contracts intended for women- and minority-owned businesses. The group is also crafting proposed legislation to remove nonprofits from the program.

33861 ■ *"Not In Our Backyard" in Canadian Business (Vol. 80, October 22, 2007, No. 21, pp. 76)*
Pub: Rogers Media
Ed: Anrew Nikiforuk. **Description:** Alberta Energy and Utilities Board's proposed construction of electric transmission line has let to protests by landowners. The electric utility was also accused of spying on ordinary citizens and violating impartiality rules. Details of the case between Lavesta Area Group and the Board are discussed.

33862 ■ *"A Novel Fix for the Credit Mess" in Barron's (Vol. 88, March 31, 2008, No. 13, pp. 10)*
Pub: Dow Jones & Company, Inc.
Ed: Michael Santoli. **Description:** Due to the common bank-leverage factor of 10, the $250 billion of lost bank capital would have supported $2.5 trillion in lending capacity. Jeffrey Lewis suggests onerous regulations on bank-holding companies that own 10 to 25 percent, as they are partly to blame. Statistical data included.

33863 ■ *"Now the Real Work Begins" in Baltimore Business Journal (Vol. 28, October 15, 2010, No. 23, pp. 1)*
Pub: Baltimore Business Journal
Ed: Emily Mullin. **Description:** The Henry J. Kaiser Family Foundation's survey shows nearly 53 percent of Americans remain confused about health care reform and it was up to the states to educate the people. However, Maryland is still trying to figure out how to conduct the campaign without guidance or funding from the Federal government.

33864 ■ *"Numbers Game" in Baltimore Business Journal (Vol. 27, February 6, 2010, No. 40, pp. 1)*
Pub: American City Business Journals
Ed: Scott Dance. **Description:** Doubts are being raised regarding the impact of the federal stimulus spending in addressing unemployment in Maryland, which has experienced 1,800 jobs created so far. Details on the view of companies and the insufficient amount of contracts that lead to the fewer number of workers being hired are discussed.

33865 ■ *"Obama Plan May Boost Maryland Cyber Security" in Boston Business Journal (Vol. 29, May 20, 2011, No. 2, pp. 1)*
Pub: American City Business Journals Inc.
Ed: Scott Dance. **Description:** May 12, 2011 outline of the cyber security policies of President Obama may improve the cyber security industry in Maryland as the state is home to large defense and intelligence activities. Details of the proposed policies are discusses as well as their advantages to companies that deal in developing cyber security plans for other companies.

33866 ■ *"Ohio Collection Agency Settles Second Lawsuit" in Collections & Credit Risk (Vol. 15, July 1, 2010, No. 6, pp. 9)*
Pub: SourceMedia Inc.
Description: National Enterprise Systems, will pay $75,000 for illegal and abusive collection charged in a lawsuit filed by West Virginia's Attorney General's office. Money will be used to reimburse students and consumers who paid the illegal fees to the company.

33867 ■ *"O'Malley, Ehrlich, Court Business Vote" in Baltimore Business Journal (Vol. 28, October 1, 2010, No. 21, pp. 1)*
Pub: Baltimore Business Journal
Ed: Scott Dance. **Description:** Maryland Governor Martin O'Malley and former Governor Robert Ehrlich reveal their business plans and platforms as they court business-minded votes in the state. Ehrlich, a Republican and O'Malley, a Democrat have both initiated programs that helped small businesses, but both have also introduced programs that made it more expensive and difficult to do business in the state.

33868 ■ *"Omniplex on the Case" in Black Enterprise (Vol. 37, December 2006, No. 5, pp. 38)*
Pub: Earl G. Graves Publishing Co. Inc.
Ed: Glenn Townes. **Description:** Office of Personnel Management in Washington D.C. recently awarded a service contract to Omniplex World Services Corp. Virginia-based, The Chantilly, will perform security investigations and background checks on current and prospective federal employees and military personnel and contractors.

33869 ■ *"On Policy: Where Talk is Cheap" in Canadian Business (Vol. 80, January 29, 2007, No. 3, pp. 19)*
Pub: Rogers Media
Ed: Jack Mintz. **Description:** The comparative analysis of the telecommunications policy of Canada and the United States of America is presented. The methods of improving Canada's telecommunications policy are discussed.

33870 ■ *"On tap: More Could Get MEGA Credits; Need to Look Outside State May Be Cut" in Crain's Detroit Business (April 7, 2008)*
Pub: Crain Communications, Inc.
Ed: Amy Lane. **Description:** In order to qualify for Michigan Economic Growth Authority tax credits Michigan businesses may no longer have to shop outside the state due to a new bill which has already passed the state Senate and will move on to the House; the bill, along with further changes to the MEGA program, is designed to provide incentives for investments that would add relevance and make Michigan more competitive.

33871 ■ *"Open the Telecom Market" in Canadian Business (Vol. 80, April 23, 2007, No. 9, pp. 80)*
Pub: Rogers Media
Description: The effects of federal telecommunication law on foreign investments in telecommunication industry are presented.

33872 ■ *"Oracle and Tauri Group Honored by Homeland Security and Defense Business Council" in Wireless News (December 15, 2009)*
Pub: Close-Up Media
Description: Selected as members of the year by the Homeland Security and Defense Business Council were Oracle, a software company that has provided thought leadership and strategic insights as well as The Tauri Group, an analytical consultancy, that has demonstrated a unique understanding of the role of small business and its vital contribution to the success of the country's security.

33873 ■ *"OSC Eyes New Tack on Litigation" in Globe & Mail (April 9, 2007, pp. B1)*
Pub: CTVglobemedia Publishing Inc.
Ed: Janet McFarland. **Description:** The efforts of the Ontario Securities Commission to set up a tribunal for the investigation and control of securities fraud are described. The rate of the conviction of corporate officials in cases heard by the courts is discussed.

33874 ■ *"OSHA Proposes Historic Safety Penalty on BP" in Workforce Management (Vol. 88, November 16, 2009, No. 12, pp. 8)*
Pub: Crain Communications Inc.
Ed: Mark Schoeff Jr. **Description:** Labor Secretary Hilda Solis has warned that she aims to toughen the enforcement of workplace laws; OSHA, the Occupational Safety and Health Administration, an agency within the Department of Labor, is penalizing BP Products North America Inc. for their failure to improve workplace safety.

33875 ■ *"Ottawa Advised to Underwrite Carbon Technology" in Globe & Mail (March 10, 2007, pp. B3)*
Pub: CTVglobemedia Publishing Inc.
Ed: Shawn McCarthy. **Description:** A federal panel's suggestion that carbon tax in Canada was not adequate to encourage oil companies and utilities to take up costly technologies to reduce carbon emissions is discussed.

33876 ■ *"Ottawa Attacks!" in Canadian Business (Vol. 79, November 6, 2006, No. 22, pp. 21)*
Pub: Rogers Media
Ed: Jeff Sanford. **Description:** The effects of new tax policy developed by Jim Flaherty, Finance Minister of Canada, on income trusts are presented.

33877 ■ *Overcoming Barriers to Entrepreneurship in the United States*
Pub: Lexington Books
Ed: Diana Furchtgott-Roth. **Released:** March 28, 2008. **Price:** $24.95. **Description:** Real and perceived barriers to the founding and running of small businesses in America are discussed. Each chapter outlines how policy and economic environments can hinder business owners and offers tips to overcome these obstacles. Starting with venture capital access in Silicon Valley during the Internet bubble, the book goes on to question the link between personal wealth and entrepreneurship, examines how federal tax rates affect small business creation and destruction, explains the low rate of self-employment among Mexican immigrants, and suggests ways pension coverage can be increased in small businesses.

33878 ■ *"An Overview of Energy Consumption of the Globalized World Economy" in Energy Policy (Vol. 39, October 2011, No. 10, pp. 5920-2928)*
Pub: Reed Elsevier Reference Publishing
Ed: Z.M. Chen, G.Q. Chen. **Description:** Energy consumption and its impact on the global world economy is examined.

33879 ■ *"PA Tax Reforms See Some Progress" in Philadelphia Business Journal (Vol. 28, October 16, 2009, No. 35, pp. 1)*
Pub: American City Business Journals
Ed: Athena D. Merritt. **Description:** It was reported that Pennsylvania's $27.8 billion budget arrived 101 days late, but business groups are encouraged that progress continues to be made on long-called-for tax reforms. The Research and Development Tax Credit, currently at $40 million, will drop to $20 million in 2009-2010.

33880 ■ *"Panel to Call for Reduced Restraints on Telecom Sector" in Globe & Mail (March 17, 2006, pp. B1)*
Pub: CTVglobemedia Publishing Inc.
Ed: Simon Tuck. **Description:** A federal panel called to adopt a more market-friendly approach to the lucrative telecommunications sector in Canada. Details of the report are presented.

33881 ■ *"Panel Calls for 'Fundamental' Change to Telecom Regulation" in Globe & Mail (March 23, 2006, pp. B1)*
Pub: CTVglobemedia Publishing Inc.
Ed: Catherine McLean. **Description:** A federal panel review at Ottawa called for a shakeup of regulations and policies that govern telecommunications companies to contend with sweeping technological changes. Details of the panel review are presented.

33882 ■ *"Papal Permit Trumps the Plumbing Codes" in Contractor (Vol. 57, February 2010, No. 2, pp. 20)*
Pub: Penton Media, Inc.
Ed: Dave Yates. **Description:** Despite the plumbing code, a plumbing contractor was able to convince the inspector to approve his application to install a sacristy sink which drains into the ground instead of the sewer system. Details of the church's system are presented.

33883 ■ *"The Paper Shredder" in Business Courier (Vol. 26, September 11, 2009, No. 20, pp. 1)*
Pub: American City Business Journals, Inc.
Ed: Dan Monk. **Description:** DotLoop Company, owned by entrepreneur Austin Allison, is developing the DotLoop software, which eliminates paperwork in the processing of real estate contracts. The software allows realtors to take control of the negotiation process and is adaptable to the rules of different US states.

33884 ■ *"Paralysis Foundation has Big Plans" in Austin Business JournalInc. (Vol. 29, December 11, 2009, No. 40, pp. 1)*
Pub: American City Business Journals
Ed: Sandra Zaragoza. **Description:** Lone Star Paralysis Foundation revealed plans to launch a fundraising effort for the advancement of cures for spinal cord injuries via adult stem cells and also fund a new spinal injury rehabilitation center. Efforts to raise about $3 million will begin as soon as the adult stem cell research study by Dr. Wise Young receives Food and Drug Administration approval.

33885 ■ *"Past Promises Haunt Project" in The Business Journal-Portland (Vol. 25, August 1, 2008, No. 21, pp. 1)*
Pub: American City Business Journals, Inc.
Ed: Aliza Earnshaw. **Description:** Oregon University System and Oregon Health and Science University will face the state Legislature to defend their request for a $250 million in state bonds to fund a life-sciences collaborative research building. The project is meant to help grow the Oregon bioscience industry. Comments from industry observers and legislators are also presented.

33886 ■ *"Paying for the Recession: Rebalancing Economic Growth" in Montana Business Quarterly (Vol. 49, Spring 2011, No. 1, pp. 2)*
Pub: Bureau of Business & Economic Research
Ed: Patrick M. Barkey. **Description:** Four key issues required to address in order to rebalance economic growth in America are examined. They include: savings rates, global trade imbalances, government budgets and most importantly, housing price correction.

33887 ■ *"PCH Gets Trauma Center Status" in The Business Journal - Serving Phoenix and the Valley of the Sun (Vol. 28, July 11, 2008, No. 45)*
Pub: American City Business Journals, Inc.
Ed: Angela Gonzales. **Description:** Phoenix Children's Hospital has been allowed by the Arizona Department of Health Services to launch the state's first trauma center for children. The trauma center is expected to cost the hospital $7 million a year.

33888 ■ *"People Often Trust Eloquence More Than Honesty" in Harvard Business Review (Vol. 88, November 2010, No. 11, pp. 36)*
Pub: Harvard Business School Publishing
Ed: Todd Rogers, Michael I. Norton. **Description:** The article shows how deftly side-stepping a question in an eloquent manner generates a more positive response in an audience than does a direct answer that is ineffectively delivered. Implications for both politics and business are discussed.

33889 ■ *"Perspective: Borderline Issues" in Entrepreneur (Vol. 35, October 2007, No. 10, pp. 48)*
Pub: Entrepreneur Media Inc.
Ed: Joshua Kurlantzick. **Description:** Failure of the immigration reform bill is expected to result in increased difficulty in finding workers that would take on the dirty and perilous jobs, which are usually taken by immigrants. Regularizing immigration on the other hand will cost business owners money by making them spend for the legality of their employees' stay in the U.S. Other effects of immigration laws on entrepreneurs are discussed.

33890 ■ *"Peter Gilgan" in Canadian Business (Vol. 82, April 27, 2009, No. 7, pp. 58)*
Pub: Rogers Media
Ed: Calvin Leung. **Description:** Mattamy Homes Ltd. president and chief executive officer Peter Gilgan believes that their business model of building communities in an organized way brings advantages to the firm and for their customers. He also believes in adopting their product prices to new market realities. Gilgan considers the approvals regime in Ontario his biggest challenge in the last 20 years.

33891 ■ *"Piece of Health Law 'A Goner'" in Baltimore Business Journal (Vol. 28, November 19, 2010, No. 28, pp. 1)*
Pub: Baltimore Business Journal
Ed: Kent Hoover. **Description:** Montana Senator Max Baucus, a Democrat who heads the Senate Finance Committee, has revealed his plan to push legislation that would repeal the 1099 IRS provision that was created by the health care reform law and will result in more paperwork for small businesses when it goes into effect in 2012.

33892 ■ *"Pipe Show Finds a Way for Smokers to Light Up" in Crain's Chicago Business (Vol. 31, April 28, 2008, No. 17, pp. 57)*
Pub: Crain Communications, Inc.
Ed: H. Lee Murphy. **Description:** With the help of attorneys within its local membership of 150 pipe collectors, the Chicagoland Pipe Collectors Club will be allowed to smoke at its 13th International Pipe & Tobacciana Show at Pheasant Run Resort. The event is expected to draw 4,000 pipe enthusiasts from as far as China and Russia.

33893 ■ *"Pipeline Dreams" in Canadian Business (Vol. 80, October 22, 2007, No. 21, pp. 19)*
Pub: Rogers Media
Ed: Rachel Pulfer. **Description:** Northwest Mackenzie Valley Pipeline has been under review by the National Energy Board since 2004. Hearings on the construction of the gas pipeline will wrap up in 2008. Pius Rolheiser, the spokesman of Imperial Oil Company Inc. believes the change of government in the area will not affect the negotiations on the pipeline construction.

33894 ■ *"Play It Safe" in Entrepreneur (Vol. 35, November 2007, No. 11, pp. 26)*
Pub: Entrepreneur Media Inc.
Ed: Gwen Moran. **Description:** U.S.-based toy manufacturers find opportunity from concerns regarding the recent recalls of toys that are made in China. The situation can provide better probability of parents buying toys made in the U.S. or Europe, where manufacturing standards are stricter.

33895 ■ *"Playfair Receives Drill Permit for Risby, Yukon Tungsten Deposit" in Canadian Corporate News (May 16, 2007)*
Pub: Comtex News Network Inc.
Description: Playfair Mining announced that it has received a 5 year Class III land use permit from the Mineral Resources Branch, Yukon which will allow the company to carry out a drill program during the upcoming drill season on the company-owned Risby, Yukon tungsten deposit. Statistical data included.

33896 ■ *"Political Environments and Business Strategy: Implications for Managers" in Business Horizons (Vol. 51, January-February 2008)*
Pub: Elsevier Advanced Technology Publications
Ed: Gerald D. Keim, Amy J. Hillman. **Description:** Various government bodies and business organizations work together in shaping new business opportunities and policies that arise from globalization. Presented is framework of public policy considerations for business managers. The framework is based on Nobel laureate Douglas North's work.

33897 ■ *"Port Authority Taking Heat in Kenwood Mess" in Business Courier (Vol. 26, September 18, 2009, No. 21, pp. 1)*
Pub: American City Business Journals, Inc.
Ed: Dan Monk. **Description:** Port of Greater Cincinnati Development Authority is being criticized for not requiring payment and performance bonds to ensure that contractors would be paid. The criticism occurred after the general contractor for the project to build a parking garage at Kenwood Towne Plaza stopped paying its subcontractors.

33898 ■ *"Potash Sale Must Be Blocked" in Canadian Business (Vol. 83, October 12, 2010, No. 17, pp. 24)*
Pub: Rogers Media Ltd.
Ed: Kasey Coholan. **Description:** Chief executive officers (CEOs) and corporate leaders in Canada are concerned about the possible sale of Potash Corporation to foreign buyers. A Compas Inc. poll recently asked CEOs whether the Canadian Government should step in to block the sale of the country's largest fertilizer firm.

33899 ■ *"The Power Brokers" in Crain's Chicago Business (Vol. 31, April 28, 2008, No. 17, pp. 41)*
Pub: Crain Communications, Inc.
Ed: Samantha Stainburn. **Description:** Profile of BlueStar Energy Services Inc., one of the first suppliers to cash in on the deregulation f the electricity market by the Illinois Legislature; last year BlueStar's revenue was $171.1 million, up from $600,000 in 2002, the year the company was founded.

33900 ■ *"The Power of Innovation" in Canadian Business (Vol. 81, March 17, 2008, No. 4, pp. 57)*
Pub: Rogers Media
Ed: Andrew Wahl. **Description:** Canada ranks badly in terms innovation yardsticks that directly translate to economic growth such as business R&D as a percentage of GDP and R&D per capita. Canada's reliance on natural resources does not provide incentives to innovate unlike smaller countries with little natural resources. Canada could spur innovation through regulations that encourage industrial research.

33901 ■ *"President Obama Appoints Record Number of Hispanics to High Office" in Hispanic Business (October 2009, pp. 12-13)*
Pub: Hispanic Business
Ed: Rob Kuznia. **Description:** Fourteen percent, or 43 of the Senate-approved appointees by President Obama are Hispanic; President George W. Bush appointed 34 Hispanics, Bill Clinton, 30 Hispanics.

33902 ■ *"Prime Site Lands Retirement Center" in Business Courier (Vol. 24, November 2, 2008, No. 29, pp. 1)*
Pub: American City Business Journals, Inc.
Ed: Laura Baverman. **Description:** Erickson Retirement Communities plans to build a $220 milllion campus on 65 acres of land between Evendale and Glendale. The project will depend on votes casted by village councils in Evendale and Glendale, expected to take place in December 2007. Both areas must sign on and alter zoning rules before the development can proceed.

33903 ■ *"Prison Farms are Closing, but the Manure Remains" in Canadian Business (Vol. 83, August 17, 2010, No. 13-14, pp. 9)*
Pub: Rogers Media Ltd.
Ed: Steve Maich. **Description:** The explanation given by Canada's government ministers on planned closure of the prison farms and scrapping of the long form census are designed by mixing of spin, argument and transparent justification. The defense should have been plausible but the ministers could not handle the simple questions about statistics and prison job training with pretense.

33904 ■ *"Privacy Concern: Are 'Group' Time Sheets Legal?" in HR Specialist (Vol. 8, September 2010, No. 9, pp. 4)*
Pub: Capitol Information Group Inc.
Description: Under the Fair Labor Standards Act (FLSA) employers are required to maintain and preserve payroll or other records, including the number of hours worked, but it does not prescribe a particular order or form in which these records must be kept.

33905 ■ *"Proposal Ruffles Builders" in Austin Business JournalInc. (Vol. 29, November 20, 2009, No. 37, pp. 1)*
Pub: American City Business Journals
Ed: Jacob Dirr. **Description:** A proposal that requires heating, ventilation and cooling equipment checking for a new commercial building having an area of at least 10,000 square feet might cost 25 cents to 50 cents per square foot for the owners. This may lead to higher housing costs. Both the Building and Fire Code Board of Appeals and the Mechanical Plumbing and Solar Board have recommended the plan.

33906 ■ *"Proposed Law Would Stop REIS Bid for Annexation by Livonia" in Crain's Detroit Business (Vol. 24, March 10, 2008, No. 10, pp. 2)*
Pub: Crain Communications, Inc.
Ed: Chad Halcom. **Description:** REIS Northville L.L.C., a joint venture made up of Real Estate Interests Group Inc. and Schostak Bros. & Co., has proposed an $800 million project called Highwood at the former Northville Psychiatric Hospital site but has been stalled due to a disagreement with Northville Town-

ship on several terms including: the amount of retail at the site and the paying for cleanup of environmental and medical waste.

33907 ■ *"Proposed Transit Legislation" in Crain's Detroit Business (Vol. 24, October 6, 2008, No. 40, pp. 19)*
Pub: Crain Communications, Inc.
Description: Breakdown of state Representative Marie Donigan's proposed transit legislation includes tax increment financing. Other pieces of the proposed legislation are examined.

33908 ■ *"Protection, Flexibility Make Single-Member LLCs Attractive" in Crain's Cleveland Business (Vol. 28, November 12, 2007, No. 45)*
Pub: Crain Communications, Inc.
Ed: Peter DeMarco. **Description:** Discusses the reasons why single-member limited liability companies are gaining popularity; LLC structure allows a great deal of flexibility and protects the owner from liability.

33909 ■ *"Provinces Tackle E-Waste Problem" in Canadian Electronics (Vol. 23, June-July 2008, No. 4, pp. 1)*
Pub: Action Communication Inc.
Ed: Ken Manchen. **Description:** Canadian provinces are implementing measures concerning the safe and environmentally friendly disposal of electronic waste. Alberta, British Columbia, Nova Scotia, and Saskatchewan impose an e-waste recycling fee on electronic equipment purchases.

33910 ■ *"PSC Approves $130M TECO Solar Project" in Tampa Bay Business Journal (Vol. 30, December 18, 2009, No. 52, pp. 1)*
Pub: American City Business Journals
Ed: Michael Hinman. **Description:** Florida's Public Service Commission has endorsed Tampa Electric Company's plan to add 25 megawatts of solar energy to its portfolio. TECO's plan needed the approval by PSC to defray additional costs for the project through ratepayers.

33911 ■ *"Que Pasa? A Canadian-Cuban Credit Card Crisis" in Canadian Business (Vol. 81, March 31, 2008, No. 5, pp. 10)*
Pub: Rogers Media
Ed: Geoff Kirbyson. **Description:** Discusses the acquisition of CUETS Financial Ltd. by the Bank of America which means that CUETS-issued credit cards in Cuba are worthless since U.S. laws prohibit transactions from Cuba and other sanctioned countries. CUETS members are advised to take multiple payment methods to Cuba.

33912 ■ *"Quicksilver Resources Receives Favorable Judgement" in Canadian Corporate News (May 16, 2007)*
Pub: Comtex News Network Inc.
Description: The 236th Judicial District Court of Texas ruled in favor of Quicksilver Resources Inc., a crude oil and natural gas exploration and production company, in the litigation between Quicksilver and CMS Marketing Services and Trading Company regarding the sale and purchase of 10,000 million British thermal units of natural gas per day at a minimum price of $2.47 per MMbtu, with the condition that the parties share any upside equally. The Court has rescinded the contract, rendering it void.

33913 ■ *"The Rabbi Trust" in Barron's (Vol. 88, March 24, 2008, No. 12, pp. 55)*
Pub: Dow Jones & Company, Inc.
Ed: Joseph F. Gelband. **Description:** Discusses a rabbi trust which is a method of deferring taxes on compensation allowed by the Internal Revenue Service. Funding of the trust is not considered taxable. Other regulations concerning tax deferment are also discussed.

33914 ■ *"Raising Money: the Bond that Lasts" in Entrepreneur (Vol. 35, October 2007, No. 10, pp. 73)*
Pub: Entrepreneur Media Inc.
Ed: Crystal Detamore-Rodman. **Description:** Tax-exempt bonds can be the solution to long-term financing needs of entrepreneurs. However, high initial costs may discourage some entrepreneurs to apply for these bonds, with transactions usually costing $3 mor more. How tax-exempt bonds work, and how rules vary with different states are discussed.

33915 ■ *Reading Financial Reports for Dummies*
Pub: John Wiley and Sons, Inc.
Ed: Lita Epstein. **Released:** January 2009. **Price:** $21.99. **Description:** This second edition contains more new and updated information, including new information on the separate accounting and financial reporting standards for private/small businesses versus public/large businesses; updated information reflecting 2007 laws on international financial reporting standards; new content to match SEC and other governmental regulatory changes over the last three years; new information about how the analyst-corporate connection has changed the playing field; the impact of corporate communications and new technologies; new examples that reflect the current trends; and updated Websites and resources.

33916 ■ *"Realtors Signing Out" in The Business Journal-Serving Metropolitan Kansas City (Vol. 27, November 21, 2008, No. 11, pp. 1)*
Pub: American City Business Journals, Inc.
Ed: Rob Roberts. **Description:** The Kansas City Regional Association of Realtors has lost 1,000 of its members due to the downturn in the housing market. Applications for realtor licenses have dropped by 159 percent. Changes in Missouri's licensing requirements are seen as additional reasons for the declines.

33917 ■ *"Recession Fears Power Gold" in Barron's (Vol. 88, March 17, 2008, No. 11, pp. M14)*
Pub: Dow Jones & Company, Inc.
Ed: Melanie Burton. **Description:** Gold prices have been more attractive as the U.S. dollar weakens and the Dow Jones Industrial Average has slipped almost 10 percent in 2008. The rate cuts from the Federal Reserve Board has also spurred inflation fears adding upward pressure to the price of the metal.

33918 ■ *"Reduce or Repay" in Canadian Business (Vol. 80, November 5, 2007, No. 22, pp. 35)*
Pub: Rogers Media
Ed: Regan Ray. **Description:** The new greenhouse gas (GHG) policy of Alberta, Canada requires about 100 industrial facilities that emit over 100,000 tons of GHG per year to reduce emissions by 12 percent by the end of 2007. Facilities that fail to comply will pay $15 per ton of GHG emission beyond target. The economic impacts of the regulation are evaluated.

33919 ■ *"Reform Law Spares Community Banks from FDIC Fee Hike" in Baltimore Business Journal (Vol. 28, July 23, 2010, No. 11, pp. 1)*
Pub: Baltimore Business Journal
Ed: Gary Haber. **Description:** A new financial regulator bill has exempted community banks from increased Federal Insurance Deposit Corporation fees. Large banks with assets of $10 billion and above will be required to pay the higher fee in 2010. Small banks are seen to hold bank fees at bay owing to the exemption.

33920 ■ *"Reform or Perish" in Canadian Business (Vol. 82, April 27, 2009, No. 7, pp. 20)*
Pub: Rogers Media
Ed: Al Rosen. **Description:** It is believed that Canada needs to fix its financial regulatory framework in order to provide more oversight on accounting procedures that is often left up to auditors. While the U.S. has constantly rebuilt its regulatory framework, Canada has not instituted reforms on its regulations. Canada entered the recession with a strong system but needs to build more substance into it.

33921 ■ *"Regulation Papered Over" in Charlotte Business Journal (Vol. 25, November 5, 2010, No. 33, pp.)*
Pub: Charlotte Business Journal
Ed: Adam O'Daniel. **Description:** County courts in North Carolina are having challenges coping with its oversight and regulation duties as it becomes too busy with foreclosure cases. Clerks in some county courts have presided over foreclosure hearings because of the flooding of foreclosure cases.

33922 ■ *"Regulators Revoke Mann Bracken's Collection Agency Licenses" in Collections & Credit Risk (Vol. 15, September 1, 2010, No. 8, pp. 19)*
Pub: SourceMedia Inc.
Description: Maryland regulators have revoked the collections licenses of defunct law firm Mann Bracken LLP.

33923 ■ *"REIT's Decry Foreign Limits on Investment" in Globe & Mail (March 29, 2007, pp. B4)*
Pub: CTVglobemedia Publishing Inc.
Ed: Elizabeth Church. **Description:** The planned legislation by Canadian government for regulation foreign investments by real estate investment trusts is discussed.

33924 ■ *"Renewable Energy Adoption in an Aging Population" in Energy Policy (Vol. 39, October 2011, No. 10, pp. 6021-6029)*
Pub: Reed Elsevier Reference Publishing
Ed: Ken Willis, Riccardo Scarpa, Rose Gilroy, Neveen Hamza. **Description:** Attitudes and impacts of renewable energy adoption on an aging population is examined.

33925 ■ *"Rep. Loretta Sanchez Holds a Hearing on Small Business Cyber Security" in Political/Congressional Transcript Wire (July 29, 2010)*
Pub: CQ Roll Call
Description: U.S. House Committee on Armed Services, Subcommittee on Terrorism, Unconventional Threats and Capabilities held a hearing on small business cyber security innovation.

33926 ■ *"Research Reports: How Analysts Size Up Companies" in Barron's (Vol. 88, March 31, 2008, No. 13, pp. M13)*
Pub: Dow Jones & Company, Inc.
Ed: Anita Peltonen. **Description:** Sirius Satellite's shares are ranked Outperform as it awaits approval from the Federal Communications Commission in its merger with XM. TiVo's shares are ranked Avoid as the company is in a sector that's being commoditized. Verizon Communications' rising dividend yield earns it a Focus List ranking. The shares of Bear Stearns, Churchill Downs, Corning, and Deerfield Triarc Capital are also reviewed. Statistical data included.

33927 ■ *"Retailers, City Clash Over Wages" in Baltimore Business Journal (Vol. 28, July 9, 2010, No. 9, pp. 1)*
Pub: Baltimore Business Journal
Ed: Daniel J. Sernovitz. **Description:** A bill pending before the City Council of Baltimore, Maryland would mandate the city's major retailers to pay their employees at least $10.57 per hour, $3 higher than was state law requires. Major retailers, as defined in the said bill by Councilwoman Mary Pat Clarke, have gross sales of at least $10 million. Reactions of the retailers affected are presented.

33928 ■ *"Retirement Plan Disclosures: Prepare Now for Fiduciary Rules" in Employee Benefit News (Vol. 25, November 1, 2011, No. 14, pp. 24)*
Pub: SourceMedia Inc.
Ed: Brian M. Pinheiro, Kurt R. Anderson. **Description:** Department of Labor has delayed the deadlines on new affirmative obligations for fiduciaries of retirement plans subject to the Employee Retirement Income Security Act. Details included.

33929 ■ *"ReVenture Plan Appears Close to Landing Key Legislative Deal" in Charlotte Business Journal (Vol. 25, July 9, 2010, No. 16, pp. 1)*
Pub: Charlotte Business Journal
Ed: John Downey. **Description:** North Carolina lawmakers acted on special legislation that would boost development of Forsite Development 667-acre ReVenture Energy Park. The legislation could also improve chances that Duke Energy Carolinas will

contract to purchase the power from the planned 50-megawatt biomass power plant located at the park. How utilities would benefit from the legislation is also discussed.

33930 ■ *The RFA at 25: Needed Improvements for Small Business Regulatory Relief*
Pub: U.S. Government Printing Office
Released: February 2006. **Price:** $62.00. **Description:** Information regarding the hearing on needed improvements for small business regulatory relief before the Committee on Small Business, House of Representatives, One Hundred Ninth Congress, First Session, Washington, DC, March 16, 2005 is provided.

33931 ■ *"Riding the Export Wave: How To Find a Good Distributor Overseas" in Inc. (January 2008, pp. 49)*
Pub: Gruner & Jahr USA Publishing
Ed: Sarah Goldstein. **Description:** Small companies should contact the U.S. embassy in foreign companies in order to connect with the U.S. Commercial Service's Gold Key program that is designed to work with small and midsize exporters.

33932 ■ *"River Plan in Disarray" in Business Journal Portland (Vol. 26, December 4, 2009, No. 39, pp. 1)*
Pub: American City Business Journals Inc.
Ed: Andy Giegerich. **Description:** Portland's proposed rules on a waterfront development plan for the Willamette River calls for fees intended for river bank preservation, a move that could drive industrial manufacturers away. The manufacturers, under the Working Waterfront Coalition, claim that the proposals could increase riverfront building costs by 15 percent.

33933 ■ *"Rogue's Gallery" in Canadian Business (Vol. 81, November 10, 2008, No. 19, pp. 44)*
Pub: Rogers Media Ltd.
Ed: Rachel Pulfer. **Description:** Laissez-faire capitalism or poor oversight of Fannie Mae and Freddie Mac are causes for the financial crisis in the U.S., depending or Democrat or Republican viewpoint. Events leading up to the 2008 financial crisis are covered.

33934 ■ *"S3 Entertainment Group Partners with WFW International for Film Services in Michigan" in Michigan Vue (July-August 2008)*
Pub: Entrepreneur Media Inc.
Description: William F. White (WFW), one of North America's largest production equipment providers has partnered with S3 Entertainment Group (S3EG), a Michigan-based full-service film production services company due to the new incentives package which currently offers the highest incentives in the United States, up to 42 percent. S3EG will actively store, lease, manage, distribute and sell WFW's equipment to the growing number of production teams that are filming in the state.

33935 ■ *"Sales of Pension Income Targeted by Senator" in Wall Street Journal Eastern Edition (November 21 , 2011, pp. C7)*
Pub: Dow Jones & Company Inc.
Ed: Leslie Scism. **Description:** Senator Tom Harkin is concerned about a widening business in which retirees and veterans sell pension income to investors in the secondary market. The business provides major profits for middlemen. Harkin wants those who are considering such a sale to have adequate information provided and knowledge in order to avoid unscrupulous dealings.

33936 ■ *"Samll Fortunes" in Business Courier (Vol. 27, July 23, 2010, No. 12, pp. 1)*
Pub: Business Courier
Ed: Steve Watkins. **Description:** Small banks in Cincinnati, Ohio have been faring well despite the economic crisis, a survey has revealed. Sixty percent of local small banks have capital levels above 15.8 percent median. But regulators are seen to close more banks in 2010 than since the financial crises began.

33937 ■ *"San Marcos May Ban Smoking" in Austin Business Journal (Vol. 31, June 17, 2011, No. 15, pp. 1)*
Pub: American City Business Journals Inc.
Ed: Vicky Garza. **Description:** The City Council of San Marcos, Texas will hold a public hearing regarding a proposed citywide smoking ban. The city is moving towards the smoking ban because it appears a statewide ban may be enacted.

33938 ■ *"Sandi Jackson; Alderman, 7th Ward, City of Chicago" in Crain's Chicago Business (Vol. 31, May 5, 2008, No. 18, pp. 31)*
Pub: Crain Communications, Inc.
Ed: Sarah A. Klein. **Description:** Profile of Sandi Jackson who is an alderman of the 7th ward of the city of Chicago and is addressing issues such as poverty and crime as well as counting on a plan to develop the former USX Corp. steel mill to revitalize the area's economic climate.

33939 ■ *Sarbanes-Oxley for Dummies, 2nd Ed.*
Pub: John Wiley and Sons, Inc.
Ed: Jill Gilbert Welytok. **Released:** February 2008. **Price:** $21.99. **Description:** Provides the latest Sarbanes-Oxley (SOX) legislation with procedures to safely and effectively reduce compliance costs. Topics include way to: establish SOX standards for IT professionals, minimize compliances costs for every aspect of a business, survive a Section 404 audit, avoid litigation under SOX, anticipate future rules and trends, create a post-SOX paper trail, increase a company's standing and reputation, work with SOX in a small business, meet new SOX standards, build a board that can't be bought, and to comply with all SOX management mandates.

33940 ■ *"SBA Makes Reforms To Federal Government Contracting" in Black Enterprise (Vol. 38, January 2008, No. 6, pp. 26)*
Pub: Earl G. Graves Publishing Co. Inc.
Ed: Alexis McCombs. **Description:** U.S. Small Business Administration's new requirement that small businesses recertify size status in order to remain eligible for federal contracts lasting more than five years. Prior regulations allowed companies declared small in earlier contracts may have grown through acquisitions, making them ineligible. This move may impact black businesses.

33941 ■ *"SCPA Members Seek Senate Support for H.R. 872" in Farm Industry News (May 26, 2011)*
Pub: Penton Business Media Inc.
Ed: Forrest Laws. **Description:** U.S. House of Representatives passed legislation, H.R. 872 the Reducing Regulatory Burdens Act that frees pesticide applicators from having to obtain NPDES permits for applications over or near water.

33942 ■ *"SEC Extends Small Business Deadline for SOX Audit Requirement" in HRMagazine (Vol. 53, August 2008, No. 8, pp. 20)*
Pub: Society for Human Resource Management
Contact: Henry G. Jackson, President
E-mail: hjackson@shrm.org
Description: Securities and Exchange Commission has approved a one-year extension of the compliance date for smaller public companies to meet the Section 404(b) auditor attestation requirement of the Sarbanes-Oxley Act.

33943 ■ *"SEC Report On Rating Agencies Falls Short" in Barron's (Vol. 88, July 14, 2008, No. 28, pp. 35)*
Pub: Dow Jones & Co., Inc.
Ed: Jack Willoughby. **Description:** The Securities and Exchange Commissions report on credit-rating firms should have drawn attention to the slipshod practices in the offerings of collateralized debt obligations. The report fell short of prescribing correctives for the flawed system of these agencies' relationship with their clients.

33944 ■ *"Seed-Count Labeling" in Farm Industry News (October 20, 2010)*
Pub: Penton Business Media Inc.
Ed: Mark Moore. **Description:** National Conference on Weights and Measures voted to standardize testing methods and procedures that will verify seed-count labeling.

33945 ■ *"Selling Pressures Rise in China" in Barron's (Vol. 88, March 10, 2008, No. 10, pp. M9)*
Pub: Dow Jones & Company, Inc.
Ed: Mohammed Hadi. **Description:** There are about 1.6 trillion yuan worth of shares up for sale in Chinese stock markets in 2008, adding to the selling pressures in these markets. The Chinese government has imposed restrictions to prevent a rapid rise in selling stocks.

33946 ■ *"Sen. Mark Warner Holds a Hearing on Government Contracting Modernization" in Political/Congressional Transcript Wire (July 20, 2010)*
Pub: Roll Call CQ
Description: Senate Committee on the Budget, Task Force on Government Performance held a hearing on modernizing the business of government. Details of that hearing are included.

33947 ■ *"Senate Bill Would Eliminate MBT Surcharge in 2011" in Crain's Detroit Business (Vol. 24, April 7, 2008, No. 14, pp. 33)*
Pub: Crain Communications, Inc.
Ed: Amy Lane. **Description:** Discusses possible changes to the new Michigan Business Tax, including a proposed bill which would phase out a 21.99 percent surcharge on the tax.

33948 ■ *"Senate OKs Funds for Promoting Tourism" in Crain's Detroit Business (Vol. 24, March 31, 2008, No. 13, pp. 6)*
Pub: Crain Communications, Inc.
Ed: Amy Lane. **Description:** Discusses the Senate proposal which allocates funds for Michigan tourism and business promotion as well as Michigan's No Worker Left Behind initiative, a program that provides free tuition at community colleges and other venues to train displaced workers for high-demand occupations.

33949 ■ *"Senate's Effort to Reform Immigration Policies Fizzles Out" in Hispanic Business (July-August 2007, pp. 62)*
Pub: Hispanic Business
Description: Legislators predict no further work towards comprehensive immigration reform is likely to occur until a new administration is in place in Washington, DC.

33950 ■ *"Senators Predict Online School Changes" in Puget Sound Business Journal (Vol. 29, September 19, 2008, No. 22, pp. 1)*
Pub: American City Business Journals
Ed: Clay Holtzman. **Description:** State senators promise to create new legislation that would tighten the monitoring and oversight of online public schools. The officials are concerned about the lack of oversight of the programs as well as lack of knowledge about content of the lessons.

33951 ■ *"Servicers Back National Effort" in Business First-Columbus (October 19, 2007, pp. A1)*
Pub: American City Business Journals, Inc.
Ed: Adrian Burns. **Description:** Ohio is having difficulty convincing mortgage companies to sign a compact containing guidelines when working with troubled borrowers. Many of Ohio's mortgage companies are supporting a national initiative to respond to the mortgage crisis instead.

33952 ■ *"Setting Up Shop in a Political Hot Spot" in Harvard Business Review (Vol. 88, October 2010, No. 10, pp. 141)*
Pub: Harvard Business School Publishing
Ed: Patrick Chun, John Coleman, Nabil el-Hage. **Description:** A fictitious foreign operations scenario is presented, with contributors providing comments

and advice. The scenario involves a politically charged North Korean-South Korean business venture; suggestions range from ensuring financial flexibility in case of adverse events to avoiding any business venture until political stability is achieved.

33953 ■ *"Shaky on Free Trade" in Canadian Business (Vol. 81, December 24, 2007, No. 1, pp. 29)*
Pub: Rogers Media
Ed: Rachel Pulfer. **Description:** Rhetoric at the U.S. presidential elections seems to be pointing toward a weaker free trade consensus, with Democratic candidates being against the renewal of free trade deals, while Republican candidates seem to be for free trade.

33954 ■ *"Shopping Around for New Ideas" in Canadian Business (Vol. 79, July 17, 2006, No. 14-15, pp. 76)*
Pub: Rogers Media
Description: Pensions should be a win-win situation for both the employer and the employee. The perspective of both parties concerning pension plans is explored as well as the need to amend laws in order to make sure that one class of merchant does not suffer at the cost of another.

33955 ■ *"Should the Fed Regulate Wall Street?" in Barron's (Vol. 88, March 24, 2008, No. 12, pp. M15)*
Pub: Dow Jones & Company, Inc.
Ed: Randall W. Forsyth. **Description:** Greater regulation of the financial sector by the Federal Reserve is essential for it to survive the crisis it is experiencing. The resulting regulation could be in complete contrast with the deregulation the sector previously experienced.

33956 ■ *"A Simple Old Reg that Needs Dusting Off" in Barron's (Vol. 88, June 30, 2008, No. 26, pp. 35)*
Pub: Dow Jones & Co., Inc.
Ed: Gene Epstein. **Description:** Senator Joe Lieberman has a point when he accused speculators of inflating the prices of food and fuel futures but introducing legislation to address speculation has an alternative. The senator's committee should instead demand that the Commodity Futures Trading Commission enforce position limits on the maximum number of contracts in a given market per speculative entity.

33957 ■ *"Single Most Important Problem" in Small Business Economic Trends (July 2010, pp. 18)*
Pub: National Federation of Independent Business
Description: A table showing the single most important problem among small businesses surveyed in the U.S. for June 2010 is presented. Poor sales was selected by 30 percent of firms as the single most important problem, followed by taxes and government requirements and red tape. Graphs comparing selected single most important problem from January 1986 to June 2010 are also given.

33958 ■ *Small Business Access to Health Care: Congressional Hearing*
Pub: DIANE Publishing Company
Ed: Donald A. Manzullo. **Released:** 2001. **Price:** $20.00. **Description:** Congressional hearing held at Crystal Lake, Illinois. Witnesses: Mary Blankenbaker, Co-Owner, Benjamin's Restaurant; Ryan Brauns, Senior Vice President, Rockford Consulting and Brokerage; Scott Shalek, RHU, Shalek Financial Services; Brad Close, National Federation of Independent Businesses; Ken Koehler, Flowerwood, Inc.; Brad Buxton, Vice President of Networks and Medical Management, Blue Cross and Blue Shield of Illinois; Isabella Wilson, Chief Financial Office, Illinois Blower, Inc.; and James Milam, Illinois State Medical Society.

33959 ■ *"Small, But Mighty" in Employee Benefit News (Vol. 25, November 1, 2011, No. 14, pp. 32)*
Pub: SourceMedia Inc.
Ed: Andrea Davis. **Description:** Three consulting firms are facing the challenge of helping clients understand the new health care reform in a tight economy.

33960 ■ *"Small Firms Punch Ticket for Growth" in Houston Business Journal (Vol. 40, January 29, 2010, No. 38, pp. 1)*
Pub: American City Business Journals
Ed: Allison Wollam. **Description:** Independent ticket agencies anticipate growth as American and Canadian authorities approved a merger between Ticketmaster and concert promoter Live Nation. Expansion of service offerings and acquisition of venues have also been done by independent ticket agencies in light of the merger. Details of the merger are included.

33961 ■ *"A Smarter Kind of Taxes" in Canadian Business (Vol. 80, October 8, 2007, No. 20, pp. 203)*
Pub: Rogers Media
Ed: Jack Mintz. **Description:** Forecasts on Canada's tax system by 2020 are analyzed. It is expected that the country's aging society will place great demands on elderly-related spending such as pensions and healthcare. And, since the elderly pay fewer taxes, the revenue available to the government will be reduced. Other trends also show that several factors will cause significant change to the country's tax system.

33962 ■ *"Some Atlantic Beach Leaders Leery About Convenience Store Safety Measure" in Florida Times-Union (November 3, 2010)*
Pub: Florida Times-Union
Ed: Drew Dixon. **Description:** Jacksonville, Florida authorities are proposing a new ordinance that would require convenience stores to upgrade safety measures to protect store workers and customers from robbery and other crimes.

33963 ■ *"Some More Equal Than Others" in Canadian Business (Vol. 80, April 23, 2007, No. 9, pp. 23)*
Pub: Rogers Media
Ed: Jack Mintz. **Description:** The details of the equalization program to be started by United States to improve economic conditions of Canada are presented.

33964 ■ *"Something Different in the Air? The Collapse of the Schwarzenegger Health Plan in Calfornia" in WorkingUSA (June 2008)*
Pub: Blackwell Publishers Ltd.
Ed: Daniel J.B. Mitchell. **Description:** In January 2007, California Governor Arnold Schwarzenegger proposed a state universal health care plan modeled after the Massachusetts individual mandate program. A year later, the plan was dead. Although some key interest groups eventually backed the plan, it was overwhelmed by a looming state budget crisis and a lack of gubernatorial focus. Although much acclaimed for his stance on greenhouse gases, stem cells, hydrogen highways, and other Big Ideas, diffused gubernatorial priorities and a failure to resolve California's chronic fiscal difficulties let the clock run out on universal health care.

33965 ■ *"Sour Grapes" in Canadian Business (Vol. 79, November 20, 2006, No. 23, pp. 28)*
Pub: Rogers Media
Ed: Michael Mainville. **Description:** The impact of the sanctions imposed by Russia on the Georgian wine exports to Russia is discussed.

33966 ■ *"Soured Relationship Plays Out in Courts" in The Business Journal-Serving Greater Tampa Bay (Vol. 28, September 19, 2008, No. 39)*
Pub: American City Business Journals, Inc.
Ed: Janet Leiser. **Description:** Heirs of developer Julian Hawthorne Lifset won a court battle to end a 50-year lease with Specialty Restaurants Corp. in Rocky Point. The decision opens the Tampa Bay prime waterfront property for new development.

33967 ■ *"Squeeze Play" in Baltimore Business Journal (Vol. 28, September 3, 2010, No. 17, pp. 1)*
Pub: Baltimore Business Journal
Ed: Daniel J. Sernovitz. **Description:** The Baltimore Grand Prix is seen to benefit businesses in Baltimore, Maryland's Inner Harbor. It is also seen to create a rift between the city government and some office workers.

33968 ■ *"Stains Still Set After SBA Scrub" in Black Enterprise (March 2008)*
Pub: Earl G. Graves Publishing Co. Inc.
Ed: Marcia A. Wade. **Description:** Small Business Administration's attempt to ensure that federal contracts were legitimately rewarded to small businesses, however the report filed showed that $4.6 billion in incorrectly coded contracts were removed from the SBA database. Critics contend the report is filled with inaccuracies. Statistical data included.

33969 ■ *"State Barks At Servicers Over Reluctance To Back Compact" in Business First-Columbus (2007, pp.)*
Pub: American City Business Journals, Inc.
Ed: Adrian Burns. **Description:** State of Ohio asked members of the mortgage industry to back a compact as a way to prevent foreclosures. Mortgage services denied the state's request. Other measures to help borrowers avoid foreclosure are investigated.

33970 ■ *"State Democrats Push for Changes to Plant Security Law" in Chemical Week (Vol. 172, July 19, 2010, No. 17, pp. 8)*
Pub: Access Intelligence L.L.C.
Contact: Donald Pazour, President
Ed: Kara Sissell. **Description:** Legislation has been introduced to revise the existing U.S. Chemical Facility Anti-Terrorism Standards (CFATS) that would include a requirement for facilities to use inherently safer technology (IST). The bill would eliminate the current law's exemption of water treatment plants and certain port facilities and preserve the states' authority to establish stronger security standards.

33971 ■ *"State Film Business Tops $1.3 Billion" in The Business Journal-Portland (Vol. 25, August 22, 2008, No. 24, pp. 1)*
Pub: American City Business Journals, Inc.
Ed: Andy Giegerich. **Description:** Oregon's film industry has generated $1.39 billion in direct and indirect economic impact in 2007, a 55 percent rise from 2005 levels. The growth of the industry is attributed to tax incentives issued in 2007, which attracted film production companies from other states.

33972 ■ *"State Lawmakers Should Try Raising Jobs, Not Taxes" in Crain's Chicago Business (Vol. 31, March 24, 2008, No. 12, pp. 20)*
Pub: Crain Communications, Inc.
Ed: Diug Whitley. **Description:** According to U.S. Department of Labor figures through December 2007, Illinois has ranked 45th in the nation in job growth for seven straight months. Many feel that the state would not need to raise taxes if they spent more time working to keep and attract employers that create jobs.

33973 ■ *"State Printing Plant on the Move" in Sacramento Business Journal (Vol. 25, August 29, 2008, No. 26, pp. 1)*
Pub: American City Business Journals, Inc.
Ed: Michael Shaw; Celia Lamb. **Description:** California is planning to replace its printing plant on Richards Boulevard and 7th Street with a newly built or leased facility in the Sacramento area. It was revealed that the project will meet the state's standards for new buildings. It is believed that the new site will require 15 acres or more depending on requirements.

33974 ■ *"State Targets Credit Fixers" in Business Journal-Portland (Vol. 24, October 12, 2007, No. 33, pp. 1)*
Pub: American City Business Journals, Inc.
Ed: Andy Giegerich, Justin Matlick. **Description:** Number of companies that offer quick fix to consumers is growing; the State of Oregon is considering rules to target them. A group working on a study in the state's mortgage lending regulations could craft bills to be examined for legislative session in February 2008.

33975 ■ *"State VC Fund To Get At Least $7.5 Million" in Crain's Detroit Business (Vol. 24, February 25, 2008, No. 8, pp. 14)*
Pub: Crain Communications Inc. - Detroit
Description: Michigan's 21st Century Investment Fund is expected to receive $7.5 million, financed by tobacco-settlement money. The Michigan Strategic

Fund Board will determine which firms will receive venture capital, which is mandated by legislation to invest the fund within three years.

33976 ■ *"State Wants to Add Escape Clause to Leases" in Sacramento Business Journal (Vol. 28, October 14, 2011, No. 33, pp. 1)*
Pub: Sacramento Business Journal
Ed: Michael Shaw. **Description:** California Governor Jerry Brown's administration has decided to add escape clauses to new lease agreements, which created new worry for building owners and brokers in Sacramento, California. Real estate brokers believe the appropriation of funds clauses have been making the lenders nervous and would result in less competition.

33977 ■ *Stay Out of Court: The Small Business Owners Guide to Prevent or Resolve Disputes and Avoid Lawsuit Hell*
Pub: Entrepreneur Press
Ed: Andrew A. Caffey. **Released:** January 24, 2005. **Price:** $17.95. **Description:** Business law attorney offers tools to help small company owners to solve disputes without going to court.

33978 ■ *"Stelco Investors Told Their Stock Now Worthless" in Globe & Mail (January 23, 2006, pp. B4)*
Pub: CTVglobemedia Publishing Inc.
Ed: Greg Keenan. **Description:** The reasons behind Ontario Superior Court's approval of Stelco Inc.'s restructuring proposal are presented.

33979 ■ *"Strathmore Receives Permit to Drill oca Honda Project in New Mexico" in Canadian Corporate News (May 14, 2007)*
Pub: Comtex News Network Inc.
Description: New Mexico's Mining and Minerals Division approved a permit to allow Strathmore Minerals Corp. to conduct drilling at its Roca Honda Project located in McKinley County, New Mexico.

33980 ■ *Structuring Your Business*
Pub: Adams Media Corporation
Contact: Gary Krebs, Director
E-mail: swatrous@adamsmedia.com
Ed: Michele Cagan. **Released:** 2004. **Price:** $19.95. **Description:** Accountant and author shares insight into starting a new company. The guide assists entrepreneurs through the process, whether it is a corporation, an LLC, a sole proprietorship, or a partnership. Tax codes, accounting practices and legislation affecting every business as well as tips on managing finances are among the topics covered.

33981 ■ *Studies of Entrepreneurship, Business and Government in Hong Kong: The Economic Development of a Small Open Economy*
Pub: Edwin Mellen Press
Ed: Fu-Lai Tony Yu. **Released:** November 2006. **Price:** $109.95. **Description:** Institutional and Austrian theories are used to analyze the transformation taking place in Hong Kong's economy.

33982 ■ *"Taiwan Technology Initiatives Foster Growth" in Canadian Electronics (Vol. 23, February 2008, No. 1, pp. 28)*
Pub: CLB Media Inc.
Description: A study conducted by the Market Intelligence Center shows that currently, Taiwan is the world's larges producer of information technology products such as motherboards, servers, and LCD monitors. In 2006, Taiwan's LED industry reached a production value of NTD 21 billion. This push into the LED sector shows the Ministry of Economic Affairs' plan to target industries that are environmentally friendly.

33983 ■ *"Take the Wheel: the Pension Protection Act Doesn't Mean You Can Sit Back and Relax" in Black Enterprise (October 2007)*
Pub: Earl G. Graves Publishing Co. Inc.
Ed: Mellody Hobson. **Description:** Pension Protection Act provides multiple benefits and tax advantages for retirement, however the investment options and contribution rates are very conservative.

33984 ■ *"Taking the 'Comprehensive' Out of Immigration Reform" in Hispanic Business (September 2007, pp. 8)*
Pub: Hispanic Business
Ed: Patricia Guadalupe. **Description:** Information about the AgJOBS bill, legislation that would grant legal residency to migrant agricultural workers is discussed.

33985 ■ *"Tao of Downfall" in International Journal of Entrepreneurship and Small Business (Vol. 11, August 31, 2010, No. 2, pp. 121)*
Pub: Publishers Communication Group
Ed: Wenxian Zhang, Ilan Alon. **Description:** Through historical reviews and case studies, this research seeks to understand why some initially successful entrepreneurs failed in the economic boom of past decades. Among various factors contributing to their downfall are a unique political and business environment, fragile financial systems, traditional cultural influences and personal characteristics.

33986 ■ *"Tauri Group Partner Joining Homeland Security and Defense" in Wireless News (December 15, 2009)*
Pub: Close-Up Media
Description: Managing partner Cosmo DiMaggio III of the Tauri Group, a provider of analytic consulting for homeland security, defense and space clients, has been elected to the Board of Directors at Homeland Security and Defense Business Council.

33987 ■ *"Tax Reform Analysis: Reforms Equal Smaller 401(k)s" in Employee Benefit News (Vol. 25, December 1, 2011, No. 15, pp. 19)*
Pub: SourceMedia Inc.
Ed: Lisa V. Gillespie. **Description:** According to a new analysis by the Employee Benefit Research Institute, two recent proposals to change existing tax treatment of 401(k) retirement plans could cost workers because they would lower their account balances towards retirement.

33988 ■ *"Tax Talk; Usual Election-Year Obstacles to Income Tax May Not Apply This Time" in Crain's Chicago Business (March 24, 2008)*
Pub: Crain Communications, Inc.
Ed: Greg Hinz. **Description:** Discusses the possible raising of the state's income tax; The latest version of the income tax hike bill, sponsored by Senator James Meeks, D-Chicago, would boost individual rates to 5 percent from 3 percent, with the corporate rate rising to a total of 8 percent from 4.8 percent; about $3 billion of the projected $8 billion that would be brought in would be used to cut local property taxes and experts believe the business community overall would benefit.

33989 ■ *"Tax Thriller in D.C." in Barron's (Vol. 90, August 30, 2010, No. 35, pp. 17)*
Pub: Barron's Editorial & Corporate Headquarters
Ed: Jim McTague. **Description:** There are speculations on how Senator Harry Reid can push his bill to raise taxes on the wealthy while retaining the George W. Bush tax rates for the rest. Reid's challenge is to get the 60 votes needed to pass the bill.

33990 ■ *"Taxes, Right-To-Work Top West Michigan Concerns" in Crain's Detroit Business (Vol. 24, September 22, 2008, No. 38, pp. 6)*
Pub: Crain Communications Inc.
Ed: Amy Lane. **Description:** Two of the top priorities of business leaders in Western Michigan are the new business tax which they want to end as well as making the state a 'right-to-work' one through laws to prohibit unions from requiring workers to pay dues and membership as a condition of their employment.

33991 ■ *"Technology and Returnable Asset Management" in Canadian Electronics (Vol. 23, February 2008, No. 1, pp. 6)*
Pub: CLB Media Inc.
Ed: Mark Borkowski. **Description:** Peter Kastner, president of Vestigo Corporation, believes that public companies without an asset track, trace, and control system in place could face Sarbanes-Oakley liability if error-prone processes result to misstatements of asset inventory positions. He also thinks that the system can improve return on assets by increasing the utilization of returnables.

33992 ■ *"Tenacious Trailblazer" in Hispanic Business (Vol. 30, April 2008, No. 4, pp. 26)*
Pub: Hispanic Business
Ed: Melinda Burns. **Description:** Dr. Sandra Hernandez has been named as Hispanic Business Woman of the Year for her pioneering work in health care reform. Dr. Hernandez is the first Hispanic and the first woman to serve as public health director for the city and county of San Francisco.

33993 ■ *"Texas Fold 'Em" in Canadian Business (Vol. 79, October 9, 2006, No. 20, pp. 44)*
Pub: Rogers Media
Ed: John Gray. **Description:** New policies of the United States law makers for the online casino industries that could force many of them out of business are discussed.

33994 ■ *"They're Hopping Mad" in Canadian Business (Vol. 80, October 22, 2007, No. 21, pp. 20)*
Pub: Rogers Media
Description: Alberta Review Panel is calling for a 20 percent increase in oil and gas development taxes. SABMiller and Molson Coors Brewing Company combined its U.S. and Puerto Rican operations, though the deal is still subject to regulatory approvals. Montreal Exchange Inc. filed for approval of the trade of Montreal Climate Exchange futures contracts.

33995 ■ *"Things Fall Apart" in Canadian Business (Vol. 80, October 8, 2007, No. 20, pp. 187)*
Pub: Rogers Media
Ed: Jeff Sanford. **Description:** Infrastructure crisis in Canada and in other countries in North America is examined. Incidents that demonstrate this crisis, such as the collapse of a bridge in Minneapolis and the collapse of an overpass in Quebec, Canada are presented. It is estimated that the reconstruction in the country will cost between C$44 billion and C$200 billion.

33996 ■ *"Thomas D'Aquino" in Canadian Business (Vol. 80, November 19, 2007, No. 23, pp. 92)*
Pub: Rogers Media
Ed: Calvin Leung. **Description:** Thomas D'Aquino is the CEO and president of the Canadian Council of Chief Executives since 1981. D'Aquino thinks he has the best job in Canada because he can change the way policies are made and the way people think. Details of his career as a lawyer and CEO and his views on Canada's economy are provided.

33997 ■ *"Thomas and His Washington Friends" in CFO (Vol. 23, October 2007, No. 10, pp. 18)*
Pub: CFO Publishing Corporation
Ed: Alix Stuart. **Description:** Reliance on Chinese suppliers to America's toymakers may become quite costly as Congress considers legislation that would increase fines to as high as $50 million for companies selling tainted products. The legislation would also require independent mandatory testing for makers of products for children.

33998 ■ *"Thousands Balk at Health Law Sign-Up Mandate" in Boston Business Journal (Vol. 27, November 9, 2007, No. 41, pp. 1)*
Pub: American City Business Journals Inc.
Ed: Mark Hollmer. **Description:** About 100,000 Massachusetts residents have not signed up for insurance plans created as part of the state's health care reform law. Insurers have underestimated the number of new customers signing up for insurance and come close to risking penalties if they do not get insurance by the end of 2007. The Commonwealth Health Insurance Connector Authority's deadline to buy insurance before penalties kick in is November 15, 2007.

33999 ■ *The Three Secrets of Green Business: Unlocking Competitive Advantage in a Low Carbon Economy*
Pub: Earthscan
Ed: Gareth Kane. **Released:** February 10, 2010. **Price:** $96.00. **Description:** Small business is coming under increasing pressure from government, customers and campaigning groups to improve environmental performance. Soaring utility and compliance costs are critical financial burdens on small companies.

34000 ■ *"Three Trails Blazes Tax Credit Deal" in The Business Journal-Serving Metropolitan Kansas City (Vol. 27, November 7, 2008, No. 9)*
Pub: American City Business Journals, Inc.
Ed: Rob Roberts. **Description:** Three Trails Redevelopment LLC plans to redevelop the Bannister Mall area. The Missouri Development Finance Board is expected to approve $30 million in tax credits for the project. A verbal agreement on the terms and conditions has already been reached according to the agency's executive director.

34001 ■ *"TIA Wrestles with Procurement Issues" in Business Journal Serving Greater Tampa Bay (Vol. 30, November 12, 2010, No. 47, pp. 1)*
Pub: Tampa Bay Business Journal
Ed: Mark Holan. **Description:** Tampa International Airport (TIA) has been caught in conflict of interest and procurement policy issues after the Hillsborough County Aviation Authority learned of the spousal relationship of an employee with his wife's firm, Gresham Smith and Partners. Gresham already won contracts with TIA and was ahead of other firms in a new contract.

34002 ■ *"Time to Fight Back" in Green Industry Pro (Vol. 23, March 2011, No. 3, pp. 8)*
Pub: Cygnus Business Media
Ed: Rod Dickens. **Description:** Lawn care operators in the United States must learn from Canada that a shift to socialism will impact their industry in a negative way. Government regulation over the application of control products regarding environmental health in Canada has been a death sentence for small lawn care businesses.

34003 ■ *"Time is Right for Fiscal Authority" in Canadian Business (Vol. 83, July 20, 2010, No. 11-12, pp. 24)*
Pub: Rogers Media Ltd.
Ed: Jacqueline Nelson. **Description:** A survey of Canadian CEOs show that only 5 percent of them believe that the world is in a severe recession. Almost 80 percent of them believe that economic recessions and depressions are caused by failures of the free market and the government.

34004 ■ *"Time for State Tax Restructure?" in Crain's Detroit Business (Vol. 26, January 18, 2010, No. 3, pp. 3)*
Pub: Crain Communications Inc.
Ed: Amy Lane. **Description:** Business Leaders for Michigan, a statewide CEO group, launched a proposal to cut the Michigan Business Tax by about $1.1 billion and replace the revenue by taxing services. Statistical data included.

34005 ■ *"Tory Green?" in Canadian Business (Vol. 80, January 15, 2007, No. 2, pp. 72)*
Pub: Rogers Media
Ed: Joe Chidley. **Description:** The need for the government to participate actively in protecting the environment through proper enforcement of the Tories Clean Air Act, is discussed.

34006 ■ *"Tougher Securities Rules on the Way" in Globe & Mail (February 21, 2007, pp. B1)*
Pub: CTVglobemedia Publishing Inc.
Ed: Janet McFarland. **Description:** The Canadian Securities Administration will implement new regulation for the securities industry by early next year. Securities companies will now have to register its employee details and earnings according to this new rule.

34007 ■ *"Tourism Bureau Seeks Hotel Tax Hike" in Baltimore Business Journal (Vol. 27, December 18, 2009, No. 32, pp. 1)*
Pub: American City Business Journals
Ed: Rachel Bernstein. **Description:** Baltimore, Maryland's tourism agency, Visit Baltimore, has proposed a new hotel tax that could produce $2 million annually for its marketing budget, fund improvements to the city's 30-year-old convention center and help it compete for World Cup soccer games. Baltimore hotel leaders discuss the new tax.

34008 ■ *"Toy Scares Drive Business" in Boston Business Journal (Vol. 27, November 23, 2007, No. 43, pp. 1)*
Pub: American City Business Journals, Inc.
Ed: Joan Goodchild. **Description:** Several Boston businesses have tapped into the lead content scare in toys and other products manufactured in China. ConRoy Corporation LLC launched Toy Recall Alert!, an online tool to alert consumers about new recalls while Hybrivet Systems introduced screening test kit, LeadCheck. Other new products pertaining to toy safety are discussed.

34009 ■ *"Toy Story" in Forbes (Vol. 180, October 15, 2007, No. 8, pp. 102)*
Pub: Forbes Inc.
Description: Three voluntary recalls of Chinese-made toys were announced by American toymakers, sending Mattel stocks plummeting.

34010 ■ *"Toy Story: U.S.-Made a Hot Seller" in Crain's Detroit Business (Vol. 23, December 17, 2007, No. 51, pp. 3)*
Pub: Crain Communications Inc. - Detroit
Ed: Chad Halcom. **Description:** American Plastic Toys, located in Walled Lake, Michigan reports all its toys are made in the U.S. and have passed all U.S. safety standards. Revenue for American Plastic Toys reached nearly $33 million in 2005, and the company expects to exceed that because of recent toy safety recalls of products produced in China.

34011 ■ *"Training Center Wants to be College" in Austin Business JournalInc. (Vol. 29, November 13, 2009, No. 36, pp. A1)*
Pub: American City Business Journals
Ed: Sandra Zaragoza. **Description:** Texas-based CyberTex Institute, a job training center, has established technical careers in an effort to obtain federal accreditation as a college. A college status would allow CyperTex to extend financial assistance to students. Aside from potentially having an enlarged student body and expanded campus, CyberTex would be allowed to engage in various training programs.

34012 ■ *"Transborder Short-Sea Shipping: Hurdles Remain" in Canadian Sailings (June 30, 2008)*
Pub: UBM Global Trade
Contact: Leonard J. Corallo, President
Ed: Kathlyn Horibe. **Description:** Legislation that would exempt non-bulk commercial cargo by water in the Great Lakes region from U.S. taxation is discussed.

34013 ■ *"Trillium Turmoil" in Canadian Business (Vol. 81, December 8, 2008, No. 21, pp. 16)*
Pub: Rogers Media Ltd.
Ed: Jeff Sanford. **Description:** Ontario's manufacturing success in the past was believed to have been built by the 1965 Canada-U.S. automotive pact and by advantages such as low-cost energy. The loss of these advantages along with the challenging economic times has hurt Ontario's manufacturing industry.

34014 ■ *"Trust But Verify: FMLA Software Isn't Foolproof, So Apply a Human Touch" in HR Specialist (Vol. 8, September 2010, No. 9, pp. 3)*
Pub: Capitol Information Group Inc.
Description: Employers are using software to track FMLA information, however, it is important for employers to review reasons for eligibility requirements, particularly when an employee is reportedly overstepping the bounds within leave regulations due to software error.

34015 ■ *"Turfway Slowing its Gait" in Business Courier (Vol. 26, November 6, 2009, No. 28, pp. 1)*
Pub: American City Business Journals, Inc.
Ed: Jon Newberry. **Description:** Kentucky's Turfway Park will be decreasing its weekly race schedule from five days to three days in the first two months of 2010, and to four days in March 2010. The decision to make reductions in the schedule is attributed to the relocation of thoroughbred racing to states that allow casino gambling. As a result, Turfway Park's resources and purse money would be focused on less days.

34016 ■ *"Uncashed Checks: Retirement Plans in a Quandry" in Employee Benefit News (Vol. 25, December 1, 2011, No. 15, pp. 18)*
Pub: SourceMedia Inc.
Ed: Terry Dunne. **Description:** Complex issues arise when employees don't cash their 401(k) balance checks. The US Department of Labor permits plans to cash out accounts of former employees with less than $1,000 to reduce the cost and time required to manage them.

34017 ■ *"Uncle Volodya's Flagging Christmas Spirit; Russia" in The Economist (Vol. 390, January 3, 2009, No. 8612, pp. 22)*
Pub: The Economist Newspaper Inc.
Description: Overview of Russia's struggling economy as well as unpopular government decisions such as raising import duties on used foreign vehicles so as to protect Russian carmakers.

34018 ■ *"Understanding the Fed" in Black Enterprise (Vol. 38, December 2007, No. 5, pp. 66)*
Pub: Earl G. Graves Publishing Co. Inc.
Ed: Steve Garmhausen. **Description:** The Federal Reserve System along with twelve regional banks regulates the value of money through the law of supply and demand. The Feds increase or decrease the supply of dollars in circulation which makes them cheap or expensive.

34019 ■ *"Union, Heal Thyself" in Canadian Business (Vol. 81, July 21, 2008, No. 11, pp. 9)*
Pub: Rogers Media Ltd.
Description: General Motors Corp. was offered by the federal government a $250 million fund after the company declared plans to close its facility in Ontario. The government move is geared towards supporting the workers who have refused to support the automotive company. Details of the labor contract between General Motors and the Canadian Auto Workers are presented.

34020 ■ *"Union Questions Patrick Cudahy Layoffs" in Business Journal-Milwaukee (Vol. 28, December 3, 2010, No. 9, pp. A1)*
Pub: Milwaukee Business Journal
Ed: Rich Ravito. **Description:** United Food and Commercial Workers Local 1473 is investigating Patrick Cudahy Inc.'s termination of 340 jobs. The union said the company has violated the law for failing to issue proper notice of a mass layoff.

34021 ■ *"U.S. Enters BlackBerry Dispute Compromise Sought Over Security Issues" in Houston Chronicle (August 6, 2010)*
Pub: Houston Chronicle
Ed: Matthew Lee. **Description:** U.S. State Department is working for a compromise with Research in Motion, manufacturer of the BlackBerry, over security issues. The Canadian company makes the smartphones and foreign governments believe they pose a security risk.

34022 ■ *United States Taxes and Tax Policy*
Pub: Cambridge University Press
Contact: Richard Ziemacki, President
E-mail: rziemacki@cambridge.org
Ed: David G. Davies. **Released:** January 22, 2010. **Price:** $34.99. **Description:** This book expands the information on taxes found in public finance texts by

using a combination of institutional, factual, theoretical and empirical information. It also stresses the economic effects of taxes and tax policy.

34023 ■ *"United's Next Hurdle: Costly Repairs" in Crain's Chicago Business (Vol. 31, April 14, 2008, No. 15, pp. 1)*
Pub: Crain Communications, Inc.

Ed: John Pletz. **Description:** Discusses the recent crackdown by aviation regulators concerning airline safety at United Airlines as well as other carriers. Maintenance costs at United for the upkeep on the company's older planes is severely affecting its bottom line which is already sagging under heavy fuel costs.

34024 ■ *"Univest Charter Switch Signals Banking Trend" in Philadelphia Business Journal (Vol. 30, September 2, 2011, No. 29, pp. 1)*
Pub: American City Business Journals Inc.

Ed: Jeff Blumenthal. **Description:** Univest Corporation of Pennsylvania changed from a federal to state charter because of cost savings and state agency has greater understanding of the intricacies of the local economy. The Pennsylvania Department of Banking has also received inquiries from seven other banks about doing the same this year.

34025 ■ *"Unlicensed Utah Collection Agency Settles with Idaho Department of Finance" in Idaho Business Review, Boise (July 15, 2010)*
Pub: Idaho Business Review

Description: Federal Recovery Acceptance Inc., doing business as Paramount Acceptance in Utah, agreed to pay penalties and expenses after the firm was investigated by the state for improprieties. The firm was charged with conducting unlicensed collection activity.

34026 ■ *"Up on the Farm" in Canadian Business (Vol. 81, October 27, 2008, No. 18, pp. 119)*
Pub: Rogers Media Ltd.

Ed: Sean Silcoff. **Description:** Investing in Saskatchewan's agricultural land is explored. Calvert government's lifting of restrictions on ownership of land have enabled Doug Emsley and Brad Farquhar to invest in farmlands in the area. Emsley and Farquhar lease the farmlands they own, enabling farmers to buy equipment and improve crop yields.

34027 ■ *"Up To Code? Website Eases Compliance Burden for Entrepreneurs" in Black Enterprise (Vol. 38, March 2008, No. 8, pp. 48)*
Pub: Earl G. Graves Publishing Co. Inc.

Ed: Robin White-Goode. **Description:** Business.gov is a presidential E-government project created to help small businesses easily find, understand, and comply with laws and regulations pertaining to a particular industry.

34028 ■ *"Valenti: Roots of Financial Crisis Go Back to 1998" in Crain's Detroit Business (Vol. 24, October 6, 2008, No. 40, pp. 25)*
Pub: Crain Communications, Inc.

Ed: Tom Henderson; Nathan Skid. **Description:** Interview with Sam Valenti III who is the chairman and CEO of Valenti Capital L.L.C., a wealth-management firm; Valenti discusses in detail the history that led up to the current economic crisis as well as his prediction for the future of the country.

34029 ■ *"Vanity Plates" in Canadian Business (Vol. 82, April 27, 2009, No. 7, pp. 26)*
Pub: Rogers Media

Ed: Andy Holloway. **Description:** Politicians in the U.S. called for the review of firms that availed of the bailout money but are under deals for naming rights of sports stadiums. Angus Reid's Corporate Reputation and Sponsorship Index found for example, that there is little correlation between sponsoring arenas on having a better brand image. It is suggested that firms who enter these deals build closer to people's homes.

34030 ■ *"VC Boosts WorkForce; Livonia Software Company to Add Sales, Marketing Staff" in Crain's Detroit Business (March 24, 2008)*
Pub: Crain Communications, Inc.

Ed: Tom Henderson. **Description:** WorkForce Software Inc., a company that provides software to manage payroll processes and oversee compliance with state and federal regulations and with union rules, plans to use an investment of $5.5 million in venture capital to hire more sales and marketing staff.

34031 ■ *"Volunteers Needed" in Canadian Business (Vol. 81, October 27, 2008, No. 18, pp. 60)*
Pub: Rogers Media Ltd.

Ed: Megan Harman. **Description:** Emissions-targeting regulations focus on the biggest polluters, missing out on other companies that leave carbon footprints in things such as shipping and travel. Some companies in Canada have initiated programs to offset their carbon emissions. Critics claim that offsetting does not reduce emissions and the programs merely justify pollution.

34032 ■ *"Walker Seeks More Business Participation" in Business Journal-Milwaukee (Vol. 28, December 10, 2010, No. 10, pp. A1)*
Pub: Milwaukee Business Journal

Ed: Rich Kirchen. **Description:** Wisconsin governor Scott Walker is seeking the aid of Milwaukee business leaders to participate in resolving the challenges posed by the economic crisis. Walker is aiming to create 250,000 jobs. He is also planning to call a special session of the legislature to enact strategies to jumpstart the economy.

34033 ■ *"Want People to Save? Force Them" in Harvard Business Review (Vol. 88, September 2010, No. 9, pp. 36)*
Pub: Harvard Business School Publishing

Ed: Dan Ariely. **Description:** Contrasts in U.S. attitudes towards savings and government regulation with those of Chile, where all employees are required to save 11 percent of their salary in a retirement account, are highlighted.

34034 ■ *"Was Mandating Solar Power Water Heaters For New Homes Good Policy?" in Hawaii Business (Vol. 54, August 2008, No. 2, pp. 28)*
Pub: Hawaii Business Publishing

Description: Senator Gary L. Kooser of District 7 Kauai-Niihau believes that the mandating of energy-efficient water heaters for new single-family homes starting in 2010 will help cut Hawaii's oil consumption. Ron Richmond of the Hawaii Solar Energy Association says that the content of SB 644 has negative consequences as it allows for choice of energy and not just solar, and it also eliminates tax credits for new homebuyers.

34035 ■ *"Water Efficiency Bill Move Through Congress" in Contractor (Vol. 56, July 2009, No. 7, pp. 20)*
Pub: Penton Media, Inc.

Ed: Kevin Schwalb. **Description:** National Association, a plumbing-heating-cooling contractor, was instrumental in drafting the Water Advanced Technologies for Efficient Resource Use Act of 2009 and they are also backing the Water Accountability Tax Efficiency Reinvestment Act. The first bill promotes WaterSense-labeled products while the other promotes water conservation through tax credits.

34036 ■ *"Wealth and Jobs: the Broken Link" in Harvard Business Review (Vol. 88, November 2010, No. 11, pp. 44)*
Pub: Harvard Business School Publishing

Ed: Nitin Nohria. **Description:** Rebuilding the link between business and job creation to shore up the middle class is advocated. A blend of government policies and business strategies that foster entrepreneurship and innovation are essential.

34037 ■ *"Weaving a Stronger Fabric: Organizing a Global Sweat-Free Apparel Production Agreement" in WorkingUSA (Vol. 11, June 2008, No. 2)*
Pub: Blackwell Publishers Ltd.

Ed: Eric Dirnbach. **Description:** Tens of millions of workers working under terrible sweatshop conditions in the global apparel industry. Workers are employed at apparel contractors and have been largely unsuccessful in organizing and improving their working conditions. The major apparel manufacturers and retailers have the most power in this industry, and they have adopted corporate social responsibility programs as a false solution to the sweatshop problem. The major North American apparel unions dealt with similar sweatshop conditions a century ago by organizing the contractors and brands into joint association contracts that significantly raised standards. Taking inspiration from their example, workers and their anti-sweatshop allies need to work together to coordinate a global organizing effort that builds worker power and establishes a global production agreement that negotiates with both contractors and the brands for improved wages, benefits, and working conditions.

34038 ■ *"What Are Your Party's Legislative Priorities for 2008?" in Hawaii Business (Vol. 53, January 2008, No. 7, pp. 22)*
Pub: Hawaii Business Publishing

Description: Discusses the Democratic Party of Hawaii which will prioritize giving more opportunities to earn a living a wage in 2008, according to the party chairwoman Jeani Withington. The Republican Party chairman Willes K. Lee, meanwhile, states that his party will seek to enhance the local business climate. The political parties' plans for Hawaii for the year 2008 are presented in detail.

34039 ■ *"What Do Your ISO Procedures Say?" in Modern Machine Shop (Vol. 84, September 2011, No. 4, pp. 34)*
Pub: Gardner Business Media, Inc.
Contact: Richard G. Kline, President
E-mail: rkline@gardnerweb.com

Ed: Wayne S. Chaneski. **Description:** ISO 9000 certification can be time-consuming and costly, but it is a necessary step in developing a quality management system that meets both current and potential customer needs.

34040 ■ *"What Enforcement?" in Canadian Business (Vol. 81, December 24, 2007, No. 1, pp. 26)*
Pub: Rogers Media

Ed: Al Rosen. **Description:** Securities enforcement in Canada needs to be improved in order to tackle white collar crimes that influence investors' opinion of the country. There have been high-profile cases where investigations have not been initiated. Details on the responsibilities of the securities commissions and the need for enforcement mandate in a separate agency are discussed.

34041 ■ *"What the Future Holds for Consumers" in Black Enterprise (Vol. 41, August 2010, No. 1, pp. 47)*
Pub: Earl G. Graves Publishing Co. Inc.

Ed: Sheiresa Ngo. **Description:** The way people purchase goods and service has changed with technology. With an increased focus on security (as well as privacy and fairness) the U.S. Congress began regulating the credit card industry with the Fair Credit Reporting Act of 1970 and the Credit Card Accountability, Responsibility, and Disclosure (CARD) Act of 2009.

34042 ■ *"What Happens in Vegas Could Happen in Baltimore, Too" in Boston Business Journal (Vol. 29, June 17, 2011, No. 6, pp. 1)*
Pub: American City Business Journals Inc.

Ed: Daniel J. Sernovitz. **Description:** At least 36 companies expressed their interest in developing a casino in South Baltimore following the state commission's announcement for bids. Developers have until July 28, 2011 to submit their proposals. Baltimore's strong economy is the major factor for the interest, yet the fact that blackjack and poker are outlawed in Maryland could be a drawback.

34043 ■ *"What Most Banks Fail to See; New and Complex Financial Regulations Can be Daunting" in Gallup Management Journal (March 10, 2011)*
Pub: Gallup
Ed: Sean Williams, Daniel Porcelli. **Description:** New financial regulations are complicated and politically charged. But banks that move beyond the fear of those regulations will find a new opportunity to engage customers.

34044 ■ *"What Will Green Power Cost? Surcharge, Spending Cap Considered" in Crain's Detroit Business (Vol. 24, March 10, 2008, No. 10, pp. 1)*
Pub: Crain Communications, Inc.
Ed: Amy Lane. **Description:** Due to a proposed mandate, which states that 10 percent of power will have to come from renewable sources by 2015 in the state of Michigan, concern is being raised about the higher electricity prices this legislation will undoubtedly cause to business and residential customers.

34045 ■ *"What You Should Know If Your Bank Fails" in Black Enterprise (Vol. 41, December 2010, No. 5, pp. 29)*
Pub: Earl G. Graves Publishing Co. Inc.
Ed: John Simons. **Description:** The Federal Deposit Insurance Corporation announced that the number of banks in trouble has reached the highest level since March 1993. Advice from the FDIC is cited. Statistical data included.

34046 ■ *"What's Ahead for Fannie and Fred?" in Barron's (Vol. 90, August 30, 2010, No. 35, pp. 26)*
Pub: Barron's Editorial & Corporate Headquarters
Ed: Jonathan R. Laing. **Description:** A meeting presided by Treasury Secretary Timothy Geithner discussed the future of Fannie Mae and Freddie Mac. The two government sponsored enterprises were mismanaged and reforming these two agencies is critical.

34047 ■ *"What's In a Name?" in Barron's (Vol. 88, March 17, 2008, No. 11, pp. 7)*
Pub: Dow Jones & Company, Inc.
Ed: Alan Abelson. **Description:** Eliot Spitzer's resignation incidentally caused the stock market to go up by 400 points. The Federal Reserve Board's new Term Securities Lending Facility provides liquidity to the big lenders by funneling $200 billion in the form of 28-day loans of Treasuries. The analysis of Paul Brodsky and Lee Quaintance of QB Partners on the demand for commodities is also discussed.

34048 ■ *"What's More Important: Stag or Inflation?" in Barron's (Vol. 88, July 14, 2008, No. 28, pp. M8)*
Pub: Dow Jones & Co., Inc.
Ed: Randall W. Forsyth. **Description:** Economists are divided on which part of stagflation, an economic situation in which inflation and economic stagnation occur simultaneously and remain unchecked for a period of time, is more important. Some economists say that the Federal government is focusing on controlling inflation while others see the central bank as extending its liquidity facilities to the financial sector.

34049 ■ *"Where Canada Meets the World" in Canadian Business (Vol. 80, October 8, 2007, No. 20, pp. 86)*
Pub: Rogers Media
Ed: Zena Olijnyk. **Description:** An overview of facilities within Canada's borders that contributes to the country's economy is presented. The facilities include fishing vessels and seaports. Agencies that regulate the borders such as the Canada Border Services Agency and the Department of Fisheries and Oceans are also presented.

34050 ■ *"Whistling Past the Graveyard?" in Barron's (Vol. 88, March 17, 2008, No. 11, pp. 15)*
Pub: Dow Jones & Company, Inc.
Ed: Michael Santoli. **Description:** Discusses the Federal Reserve's move to provide $200 billion to the system which can be seen as an effort to avoid the liquidity problems that Bear Stearns suffered. The Federal Reserve's move seems to frighten investors rather than reassure them.

34051 ■ *"Why Change?" in Canadian Business (Vol. 80, October 8, 2007, No. 20, pp. 9)*
Pub: Rogers Media
Ed: Joe Chidley. **Description:** The need for economic change in Canada is discussed. Despite the country's economic growth and low unemployment rate, economic reform is needed in order to maximize its economic potential in the future. Other reasons for the need to further develop its economy, such as the rise of manufacturing and service industries in Asia and the emergence of regional trade pacts in South America are also tackled.

34052 ■ *"Why the Rally Should Keep Rolling..for Now" in Barron's (Vol. 89, July 27, 2009, No. 30, pp. M3)*
Pub: Dow Jones & Co., Inc.
Ed: Kopin Tan. **Description:** Stocks rallied for the second straight week as of July 24, 2009 and more companies reported better than expected earnings but the caveat is that companies are beating estimates chiefly by slashing expenses and firing workers. The regulatory risks faced by CME Group and the IntercontinentalExchange are discussed as well as the shares of KKR Private Equity Investors LP.

34053 ■ *"The Wild West" in Canadian Business (Vol. 80, January 15, 2007, No. 2, pp. 57)*
Pub: Rogers Media
Ed: David Baines. **Description:** The impact of the introduction of regulations by the British Columbia Securities Commission on trading of securities by investors is discussed.

34054 ■ *"Will Focus on Business Continue?" in Baltimore Business Journal (Vol. 28, November 5, 2010, No. 26, pp. 1)*
Pub: Baltimore Business Journal
Ed: Scott Dance. **Description:** The 2010 election may call for new efforts to teach new lawmakers to assure that the viewpoints of businesses are considered and accurately delivered. The Greater Baltimore Committee and similar groups have gathered reports on the competitiveness of Maryland and are planning to use them to make a case of keeping business a top priority.

34055 ■ *"Winburn's Big Idea" in Business Courier (Vol. 27, October 8, 2010, No. 23, pp. 1)*
Pub: Business Courier
Ed: Dan Monk, Lucy May. **Description:** Cincinnati Councilman Charlie Winburn proposed the creation of Cincinnati Competitive Edge Division and to remake a small-business division of the city in order to start a job-creation program. The new division will monitor compliance to the city's small business inclusion regulations, as well as to help small business owners grow.

34056 ■ *Winner Take All: How Competitiveness Shapes the Fate of Nations*
Pub: Basic Books
Ed: Richard J. Elkus Jr. **Released:** 2009. **Price:** $27. 00. **Description:** American government and misguided business practices has allowed the U.S. to fall behind other countries in various market sectors such as cameras and televisions, as well as information technologies. It will take a national strategy to for America to regain its lead in crucial industries.

34057 ■ *"With Mine Approval, Crystallex's Value as Target Seen on Rise" in Globe & Mail (March 28, 2006, pp. B3)*
Pub: CTVglobemedia Publishing Inc.
Ed: Wendy Stueck. **Description:** Crystallex International Corp. obtains Venezuelan Ministry of Basic Industry and Mining's authorization on Las Cristinas mining project. The impact of the approval, which posted rise in shares by 21 percent for the company, is discussed.

34058 ■ *"Workers' Comp System Cuts Through Paper" in Sacramento Business Journal (Vol. 25, July 11, 2008, No. 19, pp. 1)*
Pub: American City Business Journals, Inc.
Ed: Kelly Johnson. **Description:** California has started testing a new paperless system for handling disputed workers' compensation claims. It is believed that the shift will affect people both inside and outside of the state Division of Workers' Compensation and the state Workers' Compensation Appeals Board. The other details of the planned system are also presented.

34059 ■ *"WQA Develops Certification Program" in Contractor (Vol. 57, January 2010, No. 1, pp. 56)*
Pub: Penton Media, Inc.
Description: Water Quality Association is now offering a new certification program for companies that may be affected by California's law that prohibits any products intended to convey or dispense water for human consumption that is not lead-free. All pipe or plumbing fixtures must be certified by a third party certification body.

34060 ■ *"WQA's Leadership Conference Tackles Industry Issues" in Contractor (Vol. 56, October 2009, No. 10, pp. 3)*
Pub: Penton Media, Inc.
Ed: Candace Roulo. **Description:** Water Quality Association's Mid-Year Leadership Conference held in Bloomingdale, Illinois in September 2009 tackled lead regulation, water softeners, and product efficiency. The possibility of a WQA green seal was discussed by the Water Sciences Committee and the Government Relations Committee meeting.

34061 ■ *"You Won't Go Broke Filling Up On These Stocks" in Barron's (Vol. 88, July 14, 2008, No. 28, pp. 38)*
Pub: Dow Jones & Co., Inc.
Ed: Assif Shameen. **Description:** Due to high economic growth, pro-business policies and a consumption boom, the Middle East is a good place to look for equities. The best ways in which to gain exposure to this market include investing in the real estate industry and telecommunications markets as well as large banks that serve corporations and consumers.

STATISTICAL SOURCES

34062 ■ *Regulatory Spending Soars: An Analysis of the US Budget for 2003*
Weidenbum Center
Price: Free. **Description:** Provides information on government regulation, covering 2004 overall cost, barriers to economic growth, and benefits of deregulation, Includes graphs, charts, and statistics.

TRADE PERIODICALS

34063 ■ *Compliance Action*
Pub: Compliance Action
Contact: George B. Milner, Jr., Publisher
Ed: Lucy Griffin, Editor. **Released:** 16/year. **Price:** $299. **Description:** Covers issues pertaining to regulatory compliance in financial institutions.

34064 ■ *Dickinson's FDA Review*
Pub: Ferdic Inc.
Ed: James G. Dickinson, Editor. **Released:** Monthly. **Price:** $735, U.S. and Canada. **Description:** Recurring features include interviews, news of research, a calendar of events, reports of meetings, and notices of publications available.

34065 ■ *Document Center--Update*
Pub: Document Center Inc.
Contact: Claudia Bach, President
Description: Informs of the Center's specifications and standards services available to customers.

34066 ■ *FDA Week*
Pub: Inside Washington Publishers
Contact: Korila Malecha, Manager
Ed: Donna Haseley, Editor. **Released:** Weekly (Fri.). **Price:** $595, U.S. and Canada; $645, elsewhere. **Description:** Reports on Food and Drug Administration policy, regulation, and enforcement.

34067 ■ *Legislative Watch*
Pub: American Tort Reform Association
Contact: Sherman Joyce, President
Released: Weekly. **Price:** Included in membership. **Description:** Membership newsletter of the American Tort Reform Association.

34068 ■ *The Nash & Cibinic Report*
Pub: West Group
Ed: Ralph Nash, Editor. **Released:** Monthly. **Price:** $1,706.88. **Description:** Discusses government contracts analysis and reporting. Topics include procurement management, contractor claims, and competition and awards.

34069 ■ *Ottawa Letter*
Pub: CCH Canadian Ltd.
Contact: Ian Rhind, President
Released: Biweekly. **Price:** $920. **Description:** Reports on current events and topics of Canada, such as free trade, human rights, employment, and defense. Also provides statistics, lending, and foreign exchange rates.

34070 ■ *PCS Direct Marketing Newsletter*
Pub: PCS Mailing List Company
Contact: Ed Nasser, Associate Editor
E-mail: ednasser@pcslist.com
Ed: Ann Guyer, Editor, aguyer@pcslist.com. **Released:** Bimonthly. **Price:** Free. **Description:** Offers research tools, publications, and other advice on legal, medical, financial & consumer, direct marketing. Also covers mailing lists, databases, and software to assist with direct mailings. Reports on news and conferences in this field as well. Recurring features include notices of publications available and book reviews.

34071 ■ *Russian Telecom Newsletter*
Pub: Information Gatekeepers Inc.
Contact: Jeremy Awori, Publisher
Ed: Prof. Sergei L. Galkin, Editor. **Released:** Monthly. **Price:** $695, U.S. and Canada; $745, elsewhere; $695 PDF email version. **Description:** Covers the telecommunications industry in Russia, including competition, government regulations, international business and ventures, cellular, satellites, and market intelligence. Also features new products and conference reports.

34072 ■ *The Small Business Advocate*
Pub: Office of Advocacy
Contact: Kathryn Tobias, Senior Editor
Ed: Rebecca Kraft, Editor. **Released:** Bimonthly, Monthly or Bi-monthly. **Price:** Free. **Description:** Provides updates on activities and issues of the Office of Advocacy, which examines the impact of legislative proposals and other public policy issues on small businesses.

34073 ■ *The Tan Sheet*
Pub: F-D-C Reports Inc.
Contact: Jaimie Kelley, Managing Editor
Ed: Christopher Walker, Editor. **Released:** Weekly, 50/year. **Price:** $2,020, U.S. print and web. **Description:** Provides 'in-depth coverage of nonprescription pharmaceuticals and dietary supplement/nutritionals.' Topics include congressional hearings and legislation, business and marketing news, FDA recalls and seizures, regular listing of product trademarks, and activities of FTC, CPSC, and FDA.

34074 ■ *Utilities Telecommunications News*
Pub: Information Gatekeepers Inc.
Contact: Paul Polishuk, Managing Editor
Released: Monthly. **Price:** $695, U.S. and Canada; $745, elsewhere; $695 PDF email version. **Description:** Focuses on the role of utilities in telecommunications. Topics include government and regulations, business, and the Internet. Also features new products and conferences.

34075 ■ *Water Policy Report*
Pub: Inside Washington Publishers
Contact: Korila Malecha, Manager
Released: Biweekly, every other Monday. **Price:** $650, U.S. and Canada; $700, elsewhere. **Description:** Reports on federal water quality programs and policies. Covers topics such as drinking water, toxics, enforcement, monitoring, and state/EPA relations.

34076 ■ *Windstar Wildlife Garden Weekly*
Pub: WindStar Wildlife Institute
Contact: Thomas D. Patrick, Editor
Released: Weekly. **Price:** Included in membership; $25, nonmembers. **Description:** Communicates how to attract wildlife to one's property and improve wildlife habitat at the same time, including personal experiences. Includes profiles of wildlife and plants, and what to plant and feed. Recurring features include interviews, news of research, reports of meetings, news of educational opportunities, book reviews, and notices of publications available. Also includes a column titled From the President.

CONSULTANTS

34077 ■ ARDITO Information & Research Inc.
1019 Sedwick Dr., Ste. G
Wilmington, DE 19803
Ph: (302)479-5373
Free: 800-836-9068
Fax: (302)479-5375
Co. E-mail: sardito@ardito.com
Contact: Stephanie C. Ardito, President
E-mail: sardito@ardito.com
Scope: A full-service information and research firm. Provides information in areas of financial data, published research, demographic data, industry-specific publications, competitor data, marketing and sales trends, new product developments, government relations, bibliographies. Industries served are pharmaceutical, health, publishing, and environment, and business. **Founded:** 1990. **Publications:** "The Swine flu pandemic: Authoritative information versus community gossip," Searcher, Oct, 2009; "The Medical blogosphere: How social networking platforms are changing medical searching," Searcher, May, 2009; "Social Networking and Video Web Sites: MySpace and YouTube Meet the Copyright Cops," Searcher, May, 2007; "Copyright Clearance Center raises transactional fees," Information Today, Jul, 2004.

34078 ■ Daniel Bloom and Associates Inc. (DBAI)
11517 128th Ave. N
Largo, FL 33778
Ph: (727)581-6216
Fax: (727)216-8532
Co. E-mail: dan@dbaiconsulting.com
URL: http://www.dbaiconsulting.com
Contact: Sharon Megiel, Consultant
Scope: Human resources management consultant with a specialization in corporate relocation. Offers clients a turn key service aimed at meeting the unique relocation needs of their employees. Develops and implements training programs within the relocation industry. **Founded:** 1980. **Publications:** "Where Have All the Elders Gone," Aug, 2002; "Recoup Your Hiring Investment," Brainbuzz.com, Aug, 2000; "Managing Your Lump Sum Program," Brainbuzz.com, Jun, 2000; "Buyer Value Options," Brainbuzz.com, Apr, 2000; "Just Get Me There". **Seminars:** Chaos in the Workplace: Multiple Generational Interactions; Training Effectiveness: Is the Cost Justified?; Human Capital Resource Management: A Six-Sigma Based Approach to Paving Your Way to the Table; Welcome to My World.

34079 ■ Compliance Consultants—C2
1151 Hope St.
Stamford, CT 06907
Ph: (203)329-2700
Fax: (203)329-2345
Co. E-mail: rkeen@fda-complianceconsultants.com
URL: http://www.fda-complianceconsultants.com
Contact: Lou Kale, Principal
Scope: A consultancy with expertise in regulatory engineering, product development, and medical devices. Firm advises manufacturers of regulatory requirements and submits detailed engineering facts and marketing reports to obtain market approval from Federal Drug Administration. Serves domestic and foreign clients who wish to market products in the United States. **Founded:** 1988.

34080 ■ Envar Services Inc.
505 Milltown Rd.
North Brunswick, NJ 08902-3326
Ph: (732)296-9601
Fax: (732)296-9602
Co. E-mail: mail@envarservices.com
URL: http://www.envarservices.com
Contact: John F. Shultis, President
Scope: Provider of consultation services in the following areas: Engineering design and construction; environmental compliance; plant and process appraisals and upgrades; environmental audits and impact statements; air/oil pollution control and test analyses; feasibility studies; spill prevention; underground storage tank upgrades, removals, and remediation; waste-water treatment studies; and groundwater remediation. Industries served include chemical, petrochemical, pharmaceutical, and manufacturing. Serves eastern United States and Texas. **Founded:** 1960. **Publications:** "Method of Detoxification and Stabilization of Soils Contaminated with Chromium Ore Waste".

34081 ■ Environmental Affairs Management Inc.
455 Dan St.
Akron, OH 44310-3906
Ph: (330)384-9150
Free: 888-878-3664
Fax: (330)384-9169
Contact: John W. Brasnell, President
E-mail: envafsmgt@aol.com
Scope: Company provides facilities support services and Phase I and Phase II site assessment, regulatory compliance management and training programs, including OSHA HAZ-COM training, remedial operations, and maintenance of underground storage tanks throughout the United States, Eastern sea board and southern states. Also facility decontamination and demolition services. **Founded:** 1988. **Seminars:** Hazard communication.

34082 ■ Environmental Assessment Services Inc.
124 S Main St.
Middletown, OH 45044-4002
Ph: (513)424-3400
Fax: (513)424-2020
Contact: David W. Armentrout, Owner
Scope: Offers environmental and health and safety services in compliance auditing, program management and implementation, field services (monitoring/testing) and real estate assessment. **Founded:** 1988.

34083 ■ Environmental Management Consultants Inc. (EMC)
427 Main St.
Evansville, IN 47708
Ph: (812)424-7768
Free: 800-280-7768
Fax: (812)424-7797
URL: http://www.emcevv.com
Contact: Mark E. Phillips, Manager
E-mail: mphillips@emcevv.com
Scope: Offers environmental consulting in the following areas: Asbestos related services; air and water quality monitoring; environmental site assessments; training; underground and above-ground storage tanks; industrial regulatory compliance; and hazardous materials cleanups. Serves private sector and government environmental organizations, industry, financial, educational, hospitals, judicial, school systems, developers, petro-chemical, and insurance agents and adjusters in Indiana, Kentucky, and Illinois areas. **Founded:** 1988.

34084 ■ Environmental Monitoring Inc. (EMI)
5730 Industrial Park Rd.
Norton, VA 24273-4047
Ph: (276)679-6544
Free: 888-236-4522
Fax: (276)679-6549
Co. E-mail: rjporter@emilab.com
URL: http://www.emilab.com
Contact: Randall J. Porter, President
E-mail: rjporter@emilab.com
Scope: Designer of environmental inspection solutions. It offers groundwater monitoring, industrial waste characterization, visible emissions evaluations,

municipal and industrial waste sampling, and analysis services. Provide sampling and analytical services as well as interpretative consultation services. **Founded:** 1983.

34085 ■ Environmental Solutions Inc.
1129 Woodmere Ave., Ste. I
Traverse City, MI 49686-4282
Ph: (231)941-2025
Free: 800-968-0400
Fax: (231)941-8752
Contact: Rebecca Cooper, President
Scope: Full service environmental consulting firm providing environmental management systems, auditing, hydro geological, regulatory, waste minimization, site redevelopment and remediation services. It serves all industries. **Founded:** 1989.

34086 ■ Environmental Support Network Inc.
5376 Fulton Dr. NW
Canton, OH 44718-1808
Ph: (330)494-0905
Fax: (330)494-1650
Co. E-mail: esn@sssnet.com
URL: http://www.environmental-support.com
Contact: William P. Racine, President
Scope: Provides environmental, health, and safety consulting and project management services. These include compliance auditing and remediation specifications concerning air, groundwater, and soil quality. Also offers health and safety reviews, asbestos and lead-based paint handling, noise sampling, industrial permitting, and UST management. Industries served: education, finance, industry and government. **Founded:** 1989. **Seminars:** Environmental Health and Safety Management in Ohio; Managing Compliance in Ohio; Environmental Site Remediation in Ohio and Surrounding States; Conducting ESAs by ASTM Standards; Health and Safety Management in the Medical Setting; Exposure Monitoring in Schools and Public Buildings.

34087 ■ G. Ferrell & Associates
251 Mulholland St.
Ann Arbor, MI 48103
Ph: (734)663-1230
Fax: (734)663-1230
Co. E-mail: gferrell@umich.edu
Contact: George D. Ferrell, President
Scope: Firm provides a full range of services to assist businesses with meeting their regulatory and compliance obligations under Affirmative Action and Equal Employment Opportunity (EEO) requirements. These services include: Affirmative Action Plan (AAP) development for government contractors, preparation and management of government compliance audits; personnel and EEO data tracking systems; statistical discrimination analysis; technical compliance assessment for affirmative action and non-discrimination requirements; risk management strategies; EEO census data research; public policy and economic research; Americans with Disabilities Act (ADA) compliance assistance; I-9 audit preparation and management. Serves all industries except construction. Firm also provides training and instructional services in computer software applications. **Founded:** 1994. **Publications:** Affirmative Action Planning for Individuals with Disabilities; Excel Exercises: Spreadsheet Applications Workbook; EEO Checklist for Employers. **Seminars:** How to Prepare an Affirmative Action Plan; Affirmative Action Planning for Individuals with Disabilities; I-9 Compliance Training; ADA Compliance Training; Sexual Orientation in the Workplace.

34088 ■ Floyd Browne Group (FBG)
450 Grant St., Ste. 201
Akron, OH 44311
Ph: (330)375-1390
Free: 800-835-1390
Fax: (330)375-1590
Co. E-mail: info@floydbrowne.com
URL: http://www.floydbrowne.com
Contact: Jay W. Shutt, Chief Executive Officer
E-mail: jshutt@floydbrowne.com
Scope: Manages environmental affairs such as assessments, compliance reviews, audits, remedial investigations and feasibility studies, asbestos inspection and abatement management, pollution prevention and spill plans, hazardous and solid waste management, modeling, environmental risk assessments, remediation, and underground storage tank management. Firm does building inventory analysis, facade design and street scape planning.

34089 ■ Safety Management Services
4012 Santa Nella Pl.
San Diego, CA 92130-2291
Ph: (858)259-0591
Fax: (858)792-2350
Contact: Bob Harrell, President
Scope: Offers safety consulting services: Evaluates safety policies and procedures to determine degree of effectiveness; advises on compliance with OSHA standards; and provides safety programs for managers, supervisors, and workers. Industries served: general contractors in new construction, renovation, and demolition; and tenant improvement companies which hire general contractors to perform construction activities on their premises. Also assists litigation as construction safety expert witness. Safety training programs customized to meet clients needs. **Founded:** 1978. **Publications:** "What Can Go Wrong?," International Cranes magazine, Apr, 1994. **Seminars:** Federal OSHA Construction Safety and Health Course for Trainers, University of California, San Diego; OSHA 10-Hour Construction Safety Course; 90-Hour Construction Safety Management Certificate Course - 1991 to 1993; Fall Protection; Confined Space Standards; Cranes and Rigging; Scaffold or Trenching and Excavation; and Safe Construction Work Practices.

COMPUTERIZED DATABASES

34090 ■ *CCH Tax Protos™*
90 Sheppard Ave. E, Ste. 300
Toronto, ON, Canada M2N 6X1
Ph: (416)224-2224
Free: 800-268-4522
Fax: (416)224-2243
Co. E-mail: cservice@cch.ca
URL: http://www.cch.ca
Availability: Online: Wolters Kluwer - CCH Canadian Ltd. **Type:** Bulletin board.

34091 ■ *KeyCite®*
610 Opperman Dr.
Eagan, MN 55123
Ph: (651)687-7000
Free: 800-344-5008
Fax: (651)687-5827
Co. E-mail: west.customer.service@thomsonreuters.com
URL: http://www.westlaw.com
Availability: Online: Thomson Reuters - Westlaw. **Type:** Bibliographic; Full-text.

34092 ■ *Product Safety & Liability Reporter™*
1801 S Bell St.
Arlington, VA 22202
Free: 800-372-1033
Co. E-mail: customercare@bna.com
URL: http://www.bna.com
Availability: Online: Bloomberg LP-Bloomberg BNA. **Type:** Full-text.

34093 ■ *The Tax Directory®*
400 S Maple Ave., Ste. 400
Falls Church, VA 22046
Ph: (703)533-4400
Free: 800-955-2444
Co. E-mail: cservice@tax.org
URL: http://www.taxanalysts.com
Availability: Online: LexisNexis Group. CD-ROM: Tax Analysts. **Type:** Directory.

34094 ■ *TOMES Plus® System*
777 E Eisenhower Pky.
Ann Arbor, MI 48108
Co. E-mail: info@truvenhealth.com
URL: http://www.truvenhealth.com
Availability: Online: Truven Health Analytics Inc. **Type:** Bibliographic; Full-text; Numeric.

LIBRARIES

34095 ■ Bryan Cave LLP Law Library
1155 F St., NW
Washington, DC 20004
Ph: (202)508-6000
Fax: (202)508-6200
Co. E-mail: john.peirce@bryancave.com
URL: http://www.bryancave.com
Contact: John Peirce
Scope: Government and politics; law - commercial, corporate, environmental, intellectual property, taxation. **Services:** Interlibrary loan; copying; faxing; library open to the public with restrictions. **Founded:** 1978. **Holdings:** 11,000 volumes. **Subscriptions:** 200 journals and other serials.

RESEARCH CENTERS

34096 ■ American Enterprise Institute (AEI)
1150 17th St. NW
Washington, DC 20036
Ph: (202)862-5800
Fax: (202)862-7177
Co. E-mail: arthur.brooks@aei.org
URL: http://www.aei.org
Contact: Arthur C. Brooks, President
Founded: 1943. **Publications:** *AEI Newsletter* (Monthly); *The American Enterprise* (Bimonthly). **Educational Activities:** Debates and meetings, featuring discussions among experts on major public policy issues.

START-UP INFORMATION

34097 ■ *"Former Gov. Fletcher Starts Blue Ash Firm" in Business Courier (Vol. 26, October 9, 2009, No. 24, pp. 1)*
Pub: American City Business Journals, Inc.
Ed: Lucy May. **Description:** Former Kentucky Governor Ernie Fletcher partnered with Belcan Corporation founder Ralph Anderson to purchase Blue Ash, Ohio-based Virtual Medical Network and form Alton Healthcare LLC. The company's goal is to increase practice revenues by adapting technology to reinvent clinical practices and deliver best possible care to more patients.

34098 ■ *Up and Running: Opening a Chiropractic Office*
Pub: PageFree Publishing, Incorporated
Ed: John L. Reizer. **Released:** March 2002. **Price:** $30.00. **Description:** Tips for starting a chiropractic business.

ASSOCIATIONS AND OTHER ORGANIZATIONS

34099 ■ AcademyHealth
1150 17th St. NW, Ste. 600
Washington, DC 20036
Ph: (202)292-6700
Fax: (202)292-6800
URL: http://www.academyhealth.org
Contact: Katherine Baicker, Chairperson
Description: Promotes interaction across the health research and policy arenas by bringing together a broad spectrum of players to share their perspectives, learn from each other and strengthen their working relationships. Convenes national scientific and health policy conferences; helps public and private policymakers transform research and policy into workable programs; educates policymakers, researchers, government officials, and business leaders; disseminates vital information through research syntheses, special report findings, newsletters and website; and conducts major programs that serve the research community, health policy leaders, and business and government decision-makers. **Founded:** 1981. **Publications:** *AcademyHealth Reports* (Quarterly); *AcademyHealth Health Services Research*. **Educational Activities:** National Health Policy Conference. **Awards:** Alice S. Hersh New Investigator Award (Annual); Article of the Year (Annual); Distinguished Investigator (Annual).

34100 ■ American Health Care Association (AHCA)
1201 L St. NW
Washington, DC 20005
Ph: (202)842-4444
Free: 800-321-0343
Fax: (202)842-3860
Co. E-mail: hr@ahca.org
URL: http://www.ahcancal.org/Pages/Default.aspx
Contact: Mark Parkinson, President
Description: Federation of state associations of long-term health care facilities. Promotes standards for professionals in long-term health care delivery and quality care for patients and residents in a safe environment. Focuses on issues of availability, quality, affordability, and fair payment. Operates as liaison with governmental agencies, Congress, and professional associations. Compiles statistics. **Scope:** long-term care, nursing facilities, assisted living, subacute care. **Services:** Interlibrary loan; copying; Library open to the public with restrictions by appointment. **Founded:** 1949. **Holdings:** 5000 volumes. **Subscriptions:** audiovisuals books clippings monographs periodicals; 100 journals and other serials. **Publications:** *Caring for Someone with Alzheimer's*; *Tips on Visiting Friends and Relatives*; *Family Questions: The First Thirty Days*; *Making the Transition to Nursing Facility Life*; *Paying for Long Term Care*; *Glossary of Terms*; *Advice for Families*; *Coping with the Transition*; *Capitol Connection*; *NCAL Focus*; *AHCA Notes* (Monthly); *American Health Care Association: Provider*; *Choosing a Nursing Home*; *Having Your Say: Advance Directives*; *Understanding Long Term Care Insurance*; *NCAL Connections*; *Assessing Your Needs: Consumer Guides to Nursing and Assisted Living Facilities*; *Living in a Nursing Home: Myths and Realities*; *Moving Into an Assisted Living Residence: Making a Successful Transition*; *Advance Preparation: Having the Conversation About Long Term Care*; *Talking To Your Loved Ones About Their Care*; *Provider: For Long Term Care Professionals* (Monthly); *Provider--LTC Buyers' Guide Issue* (Annual); *Choosing An Assisted Living Residence: A Consumer's Guide*; *Assisted Living State Regulatory Review*; *Resident Assistant Newsletter*. **Educational Activities:** American Health Care Association Annual Convention and Exposition (Annual). **Awards:** Adult Volunteer of the Year; Group Volunteer of the Year; AHCA/NCAL Quality Award (Annual); James Durante Nurse Scholarship (Annual); Young Adult Volunteer of the Year Award. **Telecommunication Services:** webmaster@ahca.org.

34101 ■ Associated Medical Services (AMS)
162 Cumberland St., Ste. 228
Toronto, ON, Canada M5R 3N5
Ph: (416)924-3368
Fax: (416)323-3338
Co. E-mail: info@ams-inc.on.ca
URL: http://php.ams-inc.on.ca
Contact: Dorothy Pringle, President
Description: Health services. Promotes increased availability of quality health care. Facilitates communication and cooperation among members; represents members' interests before government agencies, professional medical organizations, and the public. **Founded:** 1937. **Publications:** *Corporate Report* (Biennial). **Awards:** Hannah Independent Scholar Grant (Annual); Hannah Junior General Scholarship (Annual); Hannah Post Doctoral Fellowship (Annual); Jason A. Hannah Medal (Annual); Hannah Junior General Scholarships; Hannah Senior General Scholarships; Canadian Region Member Recognition Award; John B. Neilson Award; William B. Spaulding Award.

34102 ■ Association for Behavioral Health and Wellness (ABHW)
1325 G St. NW, Ste. 500
Washington, DC 20005
Ph: (202)449-7660
Fax: (202)449-7659
Co. E-mail: info@abhw.org
URL: http://www.abhw.org
Contact: Pamela Greenberg, President
Description: Managed behavioral healthcare organizations. Works to advance the value of managed behavioral healthcare and promotes the inclusion of mental illnesses and addiction disorders in benefit coverage. **Founded:** 1994. **Publications:** *Catalog of Special Reports*.

34103 ■ *CAG Newsletter*
263 McCaul St., Ste. 328
Toronto, ON, Canada M5T 1W7
Ph: (416)978-7977
Free: 855-224-2240
Co. E-mail: contact@cagacg.ca
URL: http://www.cagacg.ca
Contact: Neena L. Chappell, President
Released: Quarterly **Price:** free for members; C$32. 10, for nonmembers.

34104 ■ Canadian Academy of Periodontology (CAP)—Academie Canadienne de Parodontologie
1815 Alta Vista Dr., No. 201
Ottawa, ON, Canada K1G 3Y6
Ph: (613)523-9800
Fax: (613)523-1968
Co. E-mail: info@cap-acp.ca
URL: http://www.cap-acp.ca
Description: Periodontologists, educators, and students. Promotes advancement in the practice and teaching of periodontology. Conducts continuing professional education courses for members. Maintains speakers' bureau. **Founded:** 1955. **Publications:** *CAPsule* (3/year). **Awards:** Book Award (Annual); Book Award.

34105 ■ Canadian Association of Gerontology (CAG)—Association canadienne de gerontologie
263 McCaul St., Ste. 328
Toronto, ON, Canada M5T 1W7
Ph: (416)978-7977
Free: 855-224-2240
Co. E-mail: contact@cagacg.ca
URL: http://www.cagacg.ca
Contact: Neena L. Chappell, President
Description: Focuses on the problems and process of aging. **Founded:** 1971. **Publications:** *CAG Newsletter* (Quarterly); *Canadian Journal on Aging* (Quarterly). **Educational Activities:** Canadian Association of Gerontology Conference (Annual). **Awards:** Award For Contribution to Gerontology; Distinguished Member Award; Donald Menzies Bursary Award; Honorary Member; Margery Boyce Bursary Awards; CAG Award for Contribution to Gerontology (Annual); CAG Distinguished Member Award (Annual); CAG Donald Menzies Bursary (Annual); CAG Honorary Member (Annual); Margery Boyce Bursary (Annual); Evelyn Shapiro Mentoring Award (Biennial); Betty Havens Award (Biennial).

34106 ■ Canadian Association for School Health (CASH)
1669 62A Ave.
Surrey, BC, Canada V3S 9L5
Ph: (604)575-3199
Co. E-mail: info@cash-aces.ca
URL: http://www.cash-aces.ca
Description: School health services. Promotes increased availability and quality of school health programs. Serves as a clearinghouse on school health services; facilitates communication and cooperation among members.

34107 ■ Canadian Cancer Society (CCS)—Societe Canadienne du Cancer
55 St. Clair Ave. W, Ste. 300
Toronto, ON, Canada M4V 2Y7
Ph: (416)961-7223
Fax: (416)961-4189
Co. E-mail: ccs@cancer.ca
URL: http://www.cancer.ca
Contact: Marc Genereux, Chairman
Description: Community-based volunteers. Promotes research into the causes, detection, and cure of cancer; seeks to improve the quality of life of people with cancer. Conducts fundraising activities benefiting cancer research; sponsors volunteer training programs; makes available educational courses. **Scope:** cancer. **Founded:** 1938. **Subscriptions:** archival material books clippings periodicals.

34108 ■ Canadian Cardiovascular Society (CCS)—Societe Canadienne de Cardiologie
222 Queen St., Ste. 1403
Ottawa, ON, Canada K1P 5V9
Ph: (613)569-3407
Free: 877-569-3407
Fax: (613)569-6574
Co. E-mail: info@ccs.ca
URL: http://www.ccs.ca/home/index_e.aspx
Contact: Dr. Mario Talajic, President
Description: Physicians, surgeons, and scientists practicing or conducting research in cardiology and related fields. Works to advance the cardiovascular health and care of Canadians through leadership on professional development, advocacy, and the promotion, dissemination of research. **Founded:** 1946. **Publications:** *The Canadian Journal of Cardiology*; *CCS News* (Biweekly). **Awards:** Achievement Award (Annual); Distinguished Teacher Award (Annual); Dr. Robert E. Beamish Award (Annual); Research Achievement (Annual); Student Presentation Award (Annual); Trainee Excellence in Education Award (Annual); Young Investigator Award (Annual); Research Achievement Award; Achievement Award; Distinguished Teacher Award; Student Presentation Award; Trainee Excellence in Education Award; Young Investigator Award; Dr. Harold N. Segall Award of Merit (Annual); Harold N. Segall Award of Merit.

34109 ■ Canadian College of Health Leaders—College Canadien des Leaders en Sante
292 Somerset St. W
Ottawa, ON, Canada K2P 0J6
Ph: (613)235-7218
Free: 800-363-9056
Fax: (613)235-5451
Co. E-mail: info@cchl-ccls.ca
URL: http://www.cchl-ccls.ca/default1.asp
Contact: Ray J. Racette, President
Description: Serves health service executives in Canada. Offers a forum for the exchange of ideas and information, a career network, and professional development opportunities. **Scope:** healthcare management forum. **Founded:** 1970. **Publications:** *Healthcare Management FORUM* (Quarterly). **Educational Activities:** Canadian College of Health Leaders Convention (Annual); Scientific Basis of Health Services (Annual). **Awards:** Quality of Life Award (Annual); Robert Wood Johnson Award (Annual); Outstanding Young Health Executive of the Year (Annual); 3M Health Care Quality Team Awards (Annual). **Telecommunication Services:** rracette@cchl-ccls.ca.

34110 ■ Canadian Dermatology Association (CDA)—Association Canadienne de Dermatologie (ACD)
1385 Bank St., Ste. 425
Ottawa, ON, Canada K1H 8N4
Ph: (613)738-1748
Free: 800-267-3376
Fax: (613)738-4695
Co. E-mail: info@dermatology.ca
URL: http://www.dermatology.ca
Contact: Denise Wexler, President
Description: Certified dermatologists and related professionals interested in the professional advancement of dermatology. Promotes continuing education programs in dermatology. Provides public education program on skin cancer prevention. Holds an annual National Sun Awareness Week. Recognizes sun protection products. **Scope:** dermatology. **Founded:** 1925. **Subscriptions:** 80 archival material books. **Publications:** *Journal of Cutaneous Medicine and Surgery* (Bimonthly); *Membership and Corporate Directory* (Annual). **Educational Activities:** Canadian Dermatology Association Annual Conference (Annual). **Awards:** Award of Merit; Barney Usher Research Award in Dermatology; President's Cup; Young Dermatologists' Volunteer Award; Award of Honour; Public Education Awards; Young Dermatologists' Volunteer Award (Annual); Award of Honour (Annual); Barney Usher Award (Annual); CDA Public Education Award (Annual); President's Cup (Annual).

34111 ■ *Canadian Family Physician*
340 Richmond St. W
Toronto, ON, Canada M5V 1X2
Ph: (416)867-9646
Free: 800-670-6237
Fax: (416)867-9990
Co. E-mail: jk_ocfp@cfpc.ca
URL: http://www.cfpc.ca/Chapter_Offices
Contact: Dr. David Tannenbaum, President
Released: Monthly **Price:** C$8.56, /issue.

34112 ■ Canadian Health Coalition (CHC)—Coalition Canadienne de la Sante
2841 Riverside Dr.
Ottawa, ON, Canada K1V 8X7
Ph: (613)521-3400
Fax: (613)521-9638
Co. E-mail: info@healthcoalition.ca
URL: http://healthcoalition.ca
Contact: Kathleen Connors, Chairperson
Description: Individuals and organizations with an interest in health care. Promotes increased availability and quality of health services. Monitors the performance of health care facilities and services and makes recommendations for their improvement. **Founded:** 1979.

34113 ■ Canadian Healthcare Association (CHA)—Association canadienne des soins de sante
17 York St., Ste. 100, 3rd Fl.
Ottawa, ON, Canada K1N 9J6
Ph: (613)241-8005
Free: 855-236-0213
Fax: (613)241-5055
Co. E-mail: info@cha.ca
URL: http://www.cha.ca
Contact: Pamela C. Fralick, President
Description: Promotes a humane, effective, and efficient health system of the highest quality. **Founded:** 1931. **Publications:** *Guide to Canadian Healthcare Facilities* (Annual); *CHA Guide to Canadian Healthcare Facilities* (Annual); *Leadership in Health Services* (Bimonthly); *Canada's Health Care System: Its Funding and Organization.* **Educational Activities:** Navigating the Health System Data, Dollars and Decision (Annual). **Awards:** Award for Distinguished Service (Annual); Marion Stephenson Award (Annual).

34114 ■ *Canadian Journal on Aging*
263 McCaul St., Ste. 328
Toronto, ON, Canada M5T 1W7
Ph: (416)978-7977
Free: 855-224-2240
Co. E-mail: contact@cagacg.ca
URL: http://www.cagacg.ca
Contact: Neena L. Chappell, President
Released: Quarterly **Price:** free for members; C$52.50, individual, plus GST; C$80.25, institution, plus GST.

34115 ■ *The Canadian Journal of Cardiology*
222 Queen St., Ste. 1403
Ottawa, ON, Canada K1P 5V9
Ph: (613)569-3407
Free: 877-569-3407
Fax: (613)569-6574
Co. E-mail: info@ccs.ca
URL: http://www.ccs.ca/home/index_e.aspx
Contact: Dr. Mario Talajic, President
Released: 14/year.

34116 ■ *Canadian Journal of Infection Control*
PO Box 46125
Winnipeg, MB, Canada R3R 3S3
Ph: (204)897-5990
Free: 866-999-7111
Fax: (204)895-9595
Co. E-mail: chicacanada@mts.net
URL: http://www.chica.org
Contact: Jim Gauthier, President
Released: Quarterly **Price:** C$36.

34117 ■ *Canadian Journal of Psychiatry*
141 Laurier Ave. W., Ste. 701
Ottawa, ON, Canada K1P 5J3
Ph: (613)234-2815
Fax: (613)234-9857
Co. E-mail: cpa@cpa-apc.org
URL: http://www.cpa-apc.org
Contact: Donald Addington, Chairman of the Board
Released: Monthly **Price:** C$160, /year in Canada; C$250, /year outside Canada.

34118 ■ Canadian Medical Association (CMA)
1867 Alta Vista Dr.
Ottawa, ON, Canada K1G 5W8
Ph: (613)520-7685
Free: 866-913-3427
Fax: (613)236-8864
Co. E-mail: cmamsc@cma.ca
URL: http://www.cma.ca
Contact: Dr. Anna Reid, President
Description: Seeks to improve medical care for persons living in Canada. Works to maintain high standards of hospital care and health related services. Encourages constant improvement in the medical profession. **Founded:** 1867. **Publications:** *Canadian Medical Association Journal (CMAJ)*; *CMA News* (Biweekly); *Canadian Association of Radiologists Journal*; *Strategy: The Financial Digest for Physicians* (Monthly); *Canadian Association of Radiologists Journal*; *Mediscan*; *Clinical and Investigative Medicine* (Bimonthly); *Canadian Medical Association Journal* (Biweekly); *Journal of Psychiatry and Neuroscience* (Bimonthly); *Humane Medicine* (Quarterly).

34119 ■ Canadian Medical Protective Association (CMPA)—Association Canadienne de Protection Medicale
Sta. T
Ottawa, ON, Canada K1G 3H7
Ph: (613)725-2000
Free: 800-267-6522
Fax: (613)725-1300
Co. E-mail: feedback@cmpa.org
URL: http://www.cmpa-acpm.ca
Contact: John E. Gray, Chief Executive Officer
Description: Defense organization for physicians practicing in Canada. **Founded:** 1901.

34120 ■ Canadian Mental Health Association (CMHA)—Association Canadienne pour la Sante Mentale
Phenix Professional Bldg.
595 Montreal Rd., Ste. 303
Ottawa, ON, Canada K1K 4L2
Ph: (613)745-7750
Free: 800-875-6213

Fax: (613)745-5522
Co. E-mail: info@cmha.ca
URL: http://www.cmha.ca
Contact: Peter Coleridge, Chief Executive Officer
URL(s): www.ontario.cmha.ca. **Description:** Mental health professionals and other individuals with an interest in community mental health. Works to enable individuals, groups and communities to increase control over and enhance their mental health. Serves as a social advocate to encourage public action to strengthen community mental health services; conducts lobbying activities. Promotes mental health research; organizes and operates grass roots programs to help people whose mental health is at risk make use of the services available to them. Sponsors educational programs. **Founded:** 1918. **Publications:** *Mental Health Promotion-Train the Trainer.* **Awards:** C.M. Hincks Award (Annual); Consumer Involvement Award (Periodic); Media Award (Periodic); Outstanding Volunteer Service Award (Periodic); Marjorie Hiscott Keyes Award; Consumer Involvement Award; National Distinguished Service Award; Mental Health in the Workplace Award; Media Award; C. M. Hincks Award. **Telecommunication Services:** info@ontario.cmha.ca.

34121 ■ Canadian Paediatric Society (CPS)—Societe canadienne de pediatrie
2305 St. Laurent Blvd.
Ottawa, ON, Canada K1G 4J8
Ph: (613)526-9397
Fax: (613)526-3332
Co. E-mail: info@cps.ca
URL: http://www.cps.ca
Contact: Pascale Gervais, Director
URL(s): www.caringforkids.cps.ca. **Description:** Professional organization of pediatricians serving on committees and sections focusing on adolescent medicine, bioethics, drug therapy, hazardous substances, fetus and newborns, Indian and Inuit health, infectious disease and immunization, injury prevention, pediatric practice, nutrition, and psychological pediatrics. Provides services to Canadian children and to its membership. Serves as an advocate on issues relating to child health and welfare. Provides continuing education for the maintenance of competence of its members. Establishes Canadian standards/guidelines for pediatric care and practice, and promotes the interest of pediatricians. **Founded:** 1922. **Publications:** *Clinical Practice Guidelines* (Periodic); *CPS News* (5/year); *Pediatrics & Child Health* (10/year). **Awards:** Aventis Pasteur Research Award (Annual); Geoffrey C. Robinson Award (Annual); Noni MacDonald Award (Annual); Ross Award (Annual); Canadian Pediatric Society Research Award; Alan Ross Award.

34122 ■ Canadian Pain Society (CPS)—La Societe Canadienne De La Douleur
1143 Wentworth St. W, Ste. 202
Oshawa, ON, Canada L1J 8P7
Ph: (905)404-9545
Fax: (905)404-3727
Co. E-mail: catherine.bushnell@mcgill.ca
URL: http://www.canadianpainsociety.ca
Contact: Judy Watt-Watson, President
Description: Health care professionals and medical and pharmaceutical researchers with an interest in pain and its alleviation. Fosters research on the causes of pain; seeks improved methods of pain management. Facilitates communication and cooperation among pain researchers and clinicians; sponsors educational and research programs. **Founded:** 1982. **Publications:** *CPS Newsletter* (Quarterly); *Pain Research and Management* (Quarterly). **Awards:** Canadian Pain Society Post-Doctoral Fellowship Awards; Clinical Pain Management Fellowship Awards; CPS Excellence in Interprofessional Pain Education Awards; CPS Interprofessional Nursing Project Awards; CPS Knowledge Translation Research Awards; CPS Nursing Excellence in Pain Management Awards; CPS Nursing Research and Education Awards; CPS Outstanding Pain Mentorship Awards; CPS Trainee Research Awards; CPS Toronto Poly Clinic - ROD Inter-Disciplinary Pain Education Grants. **Telecommunication Services:** office@canadianpainsociety.ca.

34123 ■ Canadian Psychiatric Association (CPA)—Association des Psychiatres du Canada
141 Laurier Ave. W., Ste. 701
Ottawa, ON, Canada K1P 5J3
Ph: (613)234-2815
Fax: (613)234-9857
Co. E-mail: cpa@cpa-apc.org
URL: http://www.cpa-apc.org
Contact: Donald Addington, Chairman of the Board
Description: Works to improve mental health and psychiatric care delivery systems in Canada. Fosters high standards among Canadian psychiatrists; promotes continuing education of members; encourages and participates in educational programs for patient care providers; promotes research into psychiatric disorders; advocates for mental health system reforms and on related issues affecting the practice of psychiatry. **Founded:** 1951. **Publications:** *The Canadian Journal of Psychiatry*; *Canadian Journal of Psychiatry* (Monthly); *Canadian Psychology* (Quarterly). **Educational Activities:** Canadian Psychiatric Association Annual Conference (Annual); Canadian Psychiatric Association Conference (Annual). **Awards:** President's Commendation; Special Recognition Award; Honorary Members; Fellow of the CPA; Alex Leighton Award in Psychiatric Epidemiology; Awards for Best Posters; C.A. Roberts Award for Clinical Leadership (Annual); Paul Patterson Education Leadership Award (Annual); C.A. Roberts Award for Clinical Leadership; J.M. Cleghorn Award for Excellence and Leadership in Clinical Research; Paul Patterson Innovation in Education Leadership Award; Award for the Most Outstanding Continuing Education Activity in Psychiatry in Canada; R.O. Jones Awards for Best Papers; J.M. Cleghorn Award for Excellence and Leadership in Clinical Research (Annual).

34124 ■ Canadian Public Health Association (CPHA)—Association Canadienne De Sante Publique
404-1525 Carling Ave.
Ottawa, ON, Canada K1Z 8R9
Ph: (613)725-3769
Fax: (613)725-9826
Co. E-mail: info@cpha.ca
URL: http://www.cpha.ca/en/default.aspx
Contact: Debra Lynkowski, Chief Executive Officer
Description: Works to mobilize national charitable and volunteer resources to address public health concerns worldwide. Conducts immunization, maternal and child health, and HIV/AIDS programs in at-risk areas. **Founded:** 1910. **Educational Activities:** Canadian Public Health Association Conference (Annual). **Awards:** R. D. Defries Award; Honorary Life Member; Certificate of Merit; Ron Draper Health Promotion Award; International Award; CPHA International Award (Annual); Dr. John Hastings Student Award (Annual); Population and Public Health Student Awards (Annual); R.D. Defries Award (Annual); Ron Draper Health Promotion Award (Annual); Dr. John Hastings Student Award; Public Health Agency of Canada/Canadian Public Health Association Health Human Resources Awards (Annual).

34125 ■ Canadian Society for Clinical Investigation (CSCI)—Societe canadienne de recherches cliniques
114 Cheyenne Way
Ottawa, ON, Canada K2J 0E9
Ph: (613)730-6240
Free: 877-968-9449
Fax: (613)491-0073
Co. E-mail: csci@rcpsc.edu
URL: http://www.csci-scrc.ca
Contact: Dr. Bing Siang Gan, President
Description: Canadian clinical investigators working in the field of human health. Represents members' interests. **Founded:** 1951. **Publications:** *Clinical and Investigative Medicine* (Periodic). **Awards:** Distinguished Scientist Lecture and Award (Annual); Henry Friesen Awards and Lectures; Dr. Mel Silverman Distinguished Service Award (Annual); CSCI Distinguished Scientist Lectures and Awards.

34126 ■ Canadian Society for International Health (CSIH)—La Societe Canadienne de Sante Internationale (SCSI)
1 Nicholas St., Ste. 1105
Ottawa, ON, Canada K1N 7B7
Ph: (613)241-5785
Co. E-mail: csih@csih.org
URL: http://www.csih.org
Contact: Ms. Janet Hatcher Roberts, Executive Director
Description: Health care services and individuals and organizations with an interest in global public health. Promotes increased availability and quality of health services in previously underserved areas worldwide. Advocates for health policy and programming that contributes to global objectives of health for all; equity, and social justice through partnership building with Canadian and other institutions and organizations. **Founded:** 1977. **Publications:** *Online Synergy* (Weekly); *PAHO News* (Weekly). **Awards:** Lifetime Achievement Award; CSIH Lifetime Achievement Award for International Health (Annual).

34127 ■ *CAPsule*
1815 Alta Vista Dr., No. 201
Ottawa, ON, Canada K1G 3Y6
Ph: (613)523-9800
Fax: (613)523-1968
Co. E-mail: info@cap-acp.ca
URL: http://www.cap-acp.ca
Released: 3/year

34128 ■ Catholic Health Association of Canada (CHAC)
1247 Kilborn Pl.
Ottawa, ON, Canada K1H 6K9
Ph: (613)731-7148
Fax: (613)731-7797
Co. E-mail: info@chac.ca
URL: http://www.chac.ca
Contact: James Roche, Executive Director
Description: Represents the interests of Catholic Hospitals and nursing homes in Canada. Works to administer Christian principles within the Canadian healthcare system. Fosters competent and efficient health care services. **Scope:** healthcare, ethics, medicine, pastoral care. **Subscriptions:** 6000 articles books periodicals. **Publications:** *Catholic Health Association of Canada--Membership Directory*; *CHAC Info*.

34129 ■ *CCS News*
222 Queen St., Ste. 1403
Ottawa, ON, Canada K1P 5V9
Ph: (613)569-3407
Free: 877-569-3407
Fax: (613)569-6574
Co. E-mail: info@ccs.ca
URL: http://www.ccs.ca/home/index_e.aspx
Contact: Dr. Mario Talajic, President
Released: Biweekly

34130 ■ *CFPC-Liaison Newsletter*
340 Richmond St. W
Toronto, ON, Canada M5V 1X2
Ph: (416)867-9646
Free: 800-670-6237
Fax: (416)867-9990
Co. E-mail: jk_ocfp@cfpc.ca
URL: http://www.cfpc.ca/Chapter_Offices
Contact: Dr. David Tannenbaum, President
Released: Quarterly

34131 ■ *CHA Guide to Canadian Healthcare Facilities*
17 York St., Ste. 100, 3rd Fl.
Ottawa, ON, Canada K1N 9J6
Ph: (613)241-8005
Free: 855-236-0213
Fax: (613)241-5055
Co. E-mail: info@cha.ca
URL: http://www.cha.ca
Contact: Pamela C. Fralick, President
Released: Annual **Price:** C$159.95, /year for individuals.

34132 ■ *Clinical and Investigative Medicine*
114 Cheyenne Way
Ottawa, ON, Canada K2J 0E9

Ph: (613)730-6240
Free: 877-968-9449
Fax: (613)491-0073
Co. E-mail: csci@rcpsc.edu
URL: http://www.csci-scrc.ca
Contact: Dr. Bing Siang Gan, President
Released: Periodic

34133 ■ *Clinical Practice Guidelines*
2305 St. Laurent Blvd.
Ottawa, ON, Canada K1G 4J8
Ph: (613)526-9397
Fax: (613)526-3332
Co. E-mail: info@cps.ca
URL: http://www.cps.ca
Contact: Pascale Gervais, Director
Released: Periodic

34134 ■ College of Family Physicians of Canada - Ontario Chapter (CFPC)—College des Medecins de Famille du Canada
340 Richmond St. W
Toronto, ON, Canada M5V 1X2
Ph: (416)867-9646
Free: 800-670-6237
Fax: (416)867-9990
Co. E-mail: jk_ocfp@cfpc.ca
URL: http://www.cfpc.ca/Chapter_Offices
Contact: Dr. David Tannenbaum, President
URL(s): www.ocfp.on.ca. **Description:** National medical association of family physicians and general practitioners. Members must maintain a minimum of 50 hours of continuing medical education credits annually. Works to maintain standards of family medicine training in the 16 Canadian medical schools through support of the Departments of Family Medicine and the accreditation of family practice residency programs. Administers certification examinations in emergency medicine and family medicine. Runs practice assessment program. Offers public education programs on family medicine topics. **Scope:** Canadian library of family medicine. **Founded:** 1954. **Publications:** *Canadian Family Physician* (Monthly); *CFPC-Liaison Newsletter* (Quarterly); *Self-Evaluation*. **Awards:** Member Awards Program (Annual); Ontario's Family Physicians of the Year.

34135 ■ Community Health Nurses Association of Canada (CHNC)—Association canadienne des infirmieres et infirmiers en sante communantaire
182 Clendenan Ave.
Toronto, ON, Canada M6P 2X2
Ph: (416)604-8692
Co. E-mail: info@chnc.ca
URL: http://www.chnc.ca
Contact: Ruth Schofield, President
Description: Community health nurses and provincial organizations. Seeks to advance the practice of community health nursing and enhance members' professional status. Represents members' interests before government agencies and medical associations; provides support, services, and assistance to members. **Scope:** community health nursing. **Founded:** 1989. **Subscriptions:** archival material business records. **Publications:** *Electronic Newsletters* (3/year).

34136 ■ Community and Hospital Infection Control Association - Canada (CHICA)—Association Pour La Prevention Des Infections A l'hopital et dans La Communaute
PO Box 46125
Winnipeg, MB, Canada R3R 3S3
Ph: (204)897-5990
Free: 866-999-7111
Fax: (204)895-9595
Co. E-mail: chicacanada@mts.net
URL: http://www.chica.org
Contact: Jim Gauthier, President
Description: Health care professionals engaged in the prevention and control of infections. Seeks to improve the health of Canadians by promoting excellence in the practice of infection prevention and control. Serves as a clearinghouse on infection control standards and practices; facilitates communication and exchange of information among members; conducts continuing professional education programs for members. Collaborates with government agencies responsible for public health in the formulation and enforcement of certification standards and in the development of public policies. Provides advice and assistance to organizations and agencies concerned with specific diseases, including AIDS. Maintains speakers' bureau. **Founded:** 1971. **Publications:** *Canadian Journal of Infection Control* (Quarterly). **Educational Activities:** National Education Conference (Annual).

34137 ■ *Corporate Report*
162 Cumberland St., Ste. 228
Toronto, ON, Canada M5R 3N5
Ph: (416)924-3368
Fax: (416)323-3338
Co. E-mail: info@ams-inc.on.ca
URL: http://php.ams-inc.on.ca
Contact: Dorothy Pringle, President
Released: Biennial

34138 ■ *CPS News*
2305 St. Laurent Blvd.
Ottawa, ON, Canada K1G 4J8
Ph: (613)526-9397
Fax: (613)526-3332
Co. E-mail: info@cps.ca
URL: http://www.cps.ca
Contact: Pascale Gervais, Director
Released: 5/year

34139 ■ *CPS Newsletter*
1143 Wentworth St. W, Ste. 202
Oshawa, ON, Canada L1J 8P7
Ph: (905)404-9545
Fax: (905)404-3727
Co. E-mail: catherine.bushnell@mcgill.ca
URL: http://www.canadianpainsociety.ca
Contact: Judy Watt-Watson, President
Released: Quarterly **Price:** free for members.

34140 ■ *Electronic Newsletters*
182 Clendenan Ave.
Toronto, ON, Canada M6P 2X2
Ph: (416)604-8692
Co. E-mail: info@chnc.ca
URL: http://www.chnc.ca
Contact: Ruth Schofield, President
Released: 3/year

34141 ■ Epilepsy Canada (EC)—Epilepsie Canada
2255B Queen St. E, Ste. 336
Toronto, ON, Canada M4E 1G3
Free: 877-734-0873
Fax: (905)764-1231
Co. E-mail: epilepsy@epilepsy.ca
URL: http://www.epilepsy.ca
Contact: Denise Crepin, Executive Director
Description: People with epilepsy and their families; health care professionals with an interest in epilepsy and related disorders. Seeks to improve the quality of life of people affected by epilepsy through promotion and support of research. Offers education and awareness initiatives that build understanding and acceptance of epilepsy. **Scope:** epilepsy. **Founded:** 1966. **Subscriptions:** archival material. **Publications:** *Lumina* (Semiannual). **Awards:** Research Awards (Annual).

34142 ■ *Heads Up*
36 Eglinton W, Ste. 704
Toronto, ON, Canada M4R 1A1
Ph: (416)596-2700
Fax: (416)596-2721
Co. E-mail: info@smartrisk.ca
URL: http://www.smartrisk.ca
Contact: Philip Groff, President
Released: Monthly

34143 ■ Health Information Resource Center (HIRC)
1850 W Winchester Rd., Ste. 213
Libertyville, IL 60048
Ph: (847)816-8660
Free: 800-828-8225
Fax: (847)816-8662
Co. E-mail: info@healthprograms.com
URL: http://www.healthawards.com
Contact: Patricia Henze, Executive Director
URL(s): www.health.gov, www.fitnessday.com. **Description:** Clearinghouse for consumer health information. Provides information and referral services to many organizations that use or produce consumer health information materials. Conducts market research. **Scope:** consumer health. **Founded:** 1993. **Subscriptions:** articles audiovisuals books clippings monographs periodicals. **Publications:** *Health and Medical Media: The Comprehensive Sourcebook of Media Contacts for Healthcare Professionals* (Biennial); *Health and Medical Media* (Annual); *The Health Events Calendar* (Annual). **Awards:** National Health Information Awards (Annual); WWW Health Awards (Semiannual). **Telecommunication Services:** maturemkt@aol.com.

34144 ■ *Healthcare Management FORUM*
292 Somerset St. W
Ottawa, ON, Canada K2P 0J6
Ph: (613)235-7218
Free: 800-363-9056
Fax: (613)235-5451
Co. E-mail: info@cchl-ccls.ca
URL: http://www.cchl-ccls.ca/default1.asp
Contact: Ray J. Racette, President
Released: Quarterly; always March, June, September, and December. **Price:** C$85, individual in Canada; C$170, institution in Canada; C$115, international.

34145 ■ International Institute of Concern for Public Health (IICPH)
PO Box 40017
Toronto, ON, Canada M5R 0A2
Ph: (905)906-6128
Co. E-mail: info@iicph.org
URL: http://www.iicph.org
Contact: Dr. Marion Odell, President
Description: Promotes dissemination of information on public health and related topics including environmental and occupational health and human rights. Serves as a clearinghouse on international public health and related issues; assists in the development of model health-related human rights legislation. Conducts research and educational programs; compiles statistics; maintains speakers' bureau. Provides support and assistance to communities wishing to maintain their own public health databases. **Scope:** environmental health. **Founded:** 1984. **Subscriptions:** 4000 articles audio recordings audiovisuals books business records periodicals. **Publications:** *International Perspectives in Public Health* (Annual).

34146 ■ *International Perspectives in Public Health*
PO Box 40017
Toronto, ON, Canada M5R 0A2
Ph: (905)906-6128
Co. E-mail: info@iicph.org
URL: http://www.iicph.org
Contact: Dr. Marion Odell, President
Released: Annual

34147 ■ *Journal of Cutaneous Medicine and Surgery*
1385 Bank St., Ste. 425
Ottawa, ON, Canada K1H 8N4
Ph: (613)738-1748
Free: 800-267-3376
Fax: (613)738-4695
Co. E-mail: info@dermatology.ca
URL: http://www.dermatology.ca
Contact: Denise Wexler, President
Released: Bimonthly **Price:** $230.35, /year for individuals in U.S.; C$242.55, /year for individuals in Canada.

34148 ■ Let's Face It USA
University of Michigan
School of Dentistry
Dentistry Library
1011 N University Ave.
Ann Arbor, MI 48109-1078
Co. E-mail: faceit@umich.edu
URL: http://www.dent.umich.edu/faceit
Contact: Betsy Wilson, Director
Description: Provides information and support for people who have or who care for those with facial

disfigurement. Website and annual publication with over 150 resources for professionals and families. Links to all related networks for specific conditions i.e. Genetic Disorders, Burns, Cancer, etc. **Founded:** 1987. **Publications:** *Resources for People with Facial Difference* (Semiannual).

34149 ■ *Liaison*
1101 Upper Middle Rd. E, Ste. 1430
Oakville, ON, Canada L6H 5Z9
Ph: (905)849-9925
Fax: (905)338-8523
Co. E-mail: oemac@oemac.org
URL: http://www.oemac.org
Contact: Oscar Howell, President
Released: Quarterly **Price:** included in membership dues.

34150 ■ *Lumina*
2255B Queen St. E, Ste. 336
Toronto, ON, Canada M4E 1G3
Free: 877-734-0873
Fax: (905)764-1231
Co. E-mail: epilepsy@epilepsy.ca
URL: http://www.epilepsy.ca
Contact: Denise Crepin, Executive Director
Released: Semiannual

34151 ■ *Membership and Corporate Directory*
1385 Bank St., Ste. 425
Ottawa, ON, Canada K1H 8N4
Ph: (613)738-1748
Free: 800-267-3376
Fax: (613)738-4695
Co. E-mail: info@dermatology.ca
URL: http://www.dermatology.ca
Contact: Denise Wexler, President
Released: Annual

34152 ■ *Mental Health Promotion-Train the Trainer*
Phenix Professional Bldg.
595 Montreal Rd., Ste. 303
Ottawa, ON, Canada K1K 4L2
Ph: (613)745-7750
Free: 800-875-6213
Fax: (613)745-5522
Co. E-mail: info@cmha.ca
URL: http://www.cmha.ca
Contact: Peter Coleridge, Chief Executive Officer
Price: C$15.

34153 ■ National Council Against Health Fraud (NCAHF)—Quackwatch
11312 US 15 501 N, Ste. 107/108
Chapel Hill, NC 27517-6377
Ph: (919)533-6009
Co. E-mail: sbinfo@quackwatch.org
URL: http://www.ncahf.org
Contact: Stephen Barrett, Board Member Editor
Description: Health professionals, researchers, legal professionals, and other interested individuals. Seeks to educate the public on fraud and quackery in health care. Offers advice to consumers. Provides witnesses for health fraud trials. Assists law enforcement officials with health fraud cases. Sponsors speaker's bureau and research programs. Offers aid to victims in the form of free legal screening. **Founded:** 1977. **Awards:** Consumer Service Awards (Annual).

34154 ■ National Health Policy Forum (NHPF)
2131 K St. NW, Ste. 500
Washington, DC 20037-1882
Ph: (202)872-1390
Fax: (202)862-9837
Co. E-mail: nhpf@gwu.edu
URL: http://www.nhpf.org
Contact: Judith Miller Jones, Director
Description: Nonpartisan education program serving primarily senior federal legislative and executive branch health staff but also addressing the interests of state officials and their Washington representatives. Seeks to foster more informed government decision-making. Helps decision makers forge the personal acquaintances and understanding necessary for cooperation among government agencies and between government and the private sector. **Founded:** 1971. **Publications:** *Site Visit Reports* (Periodic).

34155 ■ Occupational and Environmental Medical Association of Canada (OEMAC)—Association canadienne de la medecine du travail et de l'environnement
1101 Upper Middle Rd. E, Ste. 1430
Oakville, ON, Canada L6H 5Z9
Ph: (905)849-9925
Fax: (905)338-8523
Co. E-mail: oemac@oemac.org
URL: http://www.oemac.org
Contact: Oscar Howell, President
Description: Health care professionals with an active interest in occupational and environmental medicine. Promotes improved standards of education and practice in the field. Serves as a unified voice for Canadian occupational and environmental medicine; acts as a forum for exchange of scientific and professional information. Conducts continuing professional education programs. **Scope:** occupational medicine, environmental medicine. **Founded:** 1985. **Subscriptions:** periodicals. **Publications:** *Liaison* (Quarterly); *Occupational Medicine*. **Awards:** Meritorious Service Award (Annual); Meritorious Service Award.

34156 ■ *Occupational Medicine*
1101 Upper Middle Rd. E, Ste. 1430
Oakville, ON, Canada L6H 5Z9
Ph: (905)849-9925
Fax: (905)338-8523
Co. E-mail: oemac@oemac.org
URL: http://www.oemac.org
Contact: Oscar Howell, President
Price: C$75, hard copy; C$250, /year.

34157 ■ *Online Synergy*
1 Nicholas St., Ste. 1105
Ottawa, ON, Canada K1N 7B7
Ph: (613)241-5785
Co. E-mail: csih@csih.org
URL: http://www.csih.org
Contact: Ms. Janet Hatcher Roberts, Executive Director
Released: Weekly **Price:** included in membership dues.

34158 ■ Operation Eyesight Universal (OEU)
4 Parkdale Crescent NW
Calgary, AB, Canada T2N 3T8
Ph: (403)283-6323
Free: 800-585-8265
Fax: (403)270-1899
Co. E-mail: info@operationeyesight.com
URL: http://www.operationeyesight.ca/netcommunity
Contact: Brian Foster, Chief Executive Officer
Description: Individuals, firms, churches, schools, service clubs, and other organizations united to promote sight restoration and blindness prevention through programs in developing countries. Provides medical and educational assistance to needy individuals. Assists in the establishment of: special programs to combat blindness due to malnutrition; eye care hospitals; eye care departments in health care institutions; rural mobile eye programs. Works with local blindness prevention societies. Operates training programs. **Founded:** 1963. **Publications:** *Sightlines* (Triennial).

34159 ■ *Osteoblast*
1090 Don Mills Rd., Ste. 301
Toronto, ON, Canada M3C 3R6
Ph: (416)696-2663
Free: 800-463-6842
Fax: (416)696-2673
Co. E-mail: fjiwa@osteoporosis.ca
URL: http://www.osteoporosis.ca
Contact: Dr. Famida Jiwa, President
Released: Quarterly

34160 ■ Osteoporosis Canada—Osteoporose Canada
1090 Don Mills Rd., Ste. 301
Toronto, ON, Canada M3C 3R6
Ph: (416)696-2663
Free: 800-463-6842
Fax: (416)696-2673
Co. E-mail: fjiwa@osteoporosis.ca
URL: http://www.osteoporosis.ca
Contact: Dr. Famida Jiwa, President
Description: Individuals and organizations interested in the prevention, diagnosis, and treatment of osteoporosis. Supports research programs that seek to improve the quality of life for women with osteoporosis. Promotes education about osteoporosis among professional health practitioners. Disseminates informational materials to individuals with osteoporosis, physicians, and the public. Offers audio visual programs; participates in public forums. **Founded:** 1982. **Publications:** *Osteoblast*; *Osteoblast* (Quarterly); *Osteoporosis Update* (Quarterly). **Telecommunication Services:** info@osteoporosis.ca.

34161 ■ *Osteoporosis Update*
1090 Don Mills Rd., Ste. 301
Toronto, ON, Canada M3C 3R6
Ph: (416)696-2663
Free: 800-463-6842
Fax: (416)696-2673
Co. E-mail: fjiwa@osteoporosis.ca
URL: http://www.osteoporosis.ca
Contact: Dr. Famida Jiwa, President
Released: Quarterly **Price:** free to physicians.

34162 ■ *PAHO News*
1 Nicholas St., Ste. 1105
Ottawa, ON, Canada K1N 7B7
Ph: (613)241-5785
Co. E-mail: csih@csih.org
URL: http://www.csih.org
Contact: Ms. Janet Hatcher Roberts, Executive Director
Released: Weekly **Price:** included in membership dues.

34163 ■ *Pain Research and Management*
1143 Wentworth St. W, Ste. 202
Oshawa, ON, Canada L1J 8P7
Ph: (905)404-9545
Fax: (905)404-3727
Co. E-mail: catherine.bushnell@mcgill.ca
URL: http://www.canadianpainsociety.ca
Contact: Judy Watt-Watson, President
Released: Quarterly **Price:** free for members.

34164 ■ *Pediatrics & Child Health*
2305 St. Laurent Blvd.
Ottawa, ON, Canada K1G 4J8
Ph: (613)526-9397
Fax: (613)526-3332
Co. E-mail: info@cps.ca
URL: http://www.cps.ca
Contact: Pascale Gervais, Director
Released: 10/year

34165 ■ People's Medical Society (PMS)
462 Walnut St.
Allentown, PA 18102
Ph: (610)770-1670
Fax: (610)285-2694
Co. E-mail: cbi@peoplesmed.org
URL: http://www.peoplesmed.org
Description: Promotes citizen involvement in the cost, quality, and management of the American health care system. Seeks to: train and encourage individuals to study local health care systems, practitioners, and institutions and promote preventive health care and medical cost control by these groups; address major policy issues and control health costs; encourage more preventive practice and research; promote self-care and alternative health care procedures; launch an information campaign to assist individuals in maintaining personal health and to prepare them for appointments with medical professionals. Convention/Meeting: none. **Founded:** 1983. **Publications:** *Dial 800 for Health* (Irregular); *People's Medical Society Newsletter* (Bimonthly); *Allergies: Questions You Have...Answers You Need*; *Alzheimer's and Dementia: Questions You Have...Answers You Need*; *Take This Book to the Gynecologist With You*; *Take This Book to the Hospital With You.*

34166 ■ Physicians Committee for Responsible Medicine (PCRM)
5100 Wisconsin Ave. NW, Ste. 400
Washington, DC 20016
Ph: (202)686-2210
Fax: (202)686-2216
Co. E-mail: pcrm@pcrm.org
URL: http://www.pcrm.org
Contact: Neal D. Barnard, President
Description: Physicians, scientists, healthcare professionals, and interested others. Increases public awareness about the importance of preventive medicine and nutrition, and raises scientific and ethical questions pertaining to the use of humans and animals in medical research. Supports research into U.S. agricultural and public health policies. Promotes the New Four Food Groups, a no-cholesterol, low-fat alternative to U.S.D.A. dietary recommendations. Maintains the Gold Plan program, which includes information on low-fat, cholesterol-free entrees and nutrition for institutional food services. Offers fact sheets on nutrition, preventive medicine, and non-animal research topics. Maintains speakers' bureau. **Publications:** *Good Medicine Magazine* (Quarterly); *Good Medicine* (Quarterly).

34167 ■ *Self-Evaluation*
340 Richmond St. W
Toronto, ON, Canada M5V 1X2
Ph: (416)867-9646
Free: 800-670-6237
Fax: (416)867-9990
Co. E-mail: jk_ocfp@cfpc.ca
URL: http://www.cfpc.ca/Chapter_Offices
Contact: Dr. David Tannenbaum, President

34168 ■ *Sightlines*
4 Parkdale Crescent NW
Calgary, AB, Canada T2N 3T8
Ph: (403)283-6323
Free: 800-585-8265
Fax: (403)270-1899
Co. E-mail: info@operationeyesight.com
URL: http://www.operationeyesight.ca/netcommunity
Contact: Brian Foster, Chief Executive Officer
Released: Triennial **Price:** free.

34169 ■ SMARTRISK
36 Eglinton W, Ste. 704
Toronto, ON, Canada M4R 1A1
Ph: (416)596-2700
Fax: (416)596-2721
Co. E-mail: info@smartrisk.ca
URL: http://www.smartrisk.ca
Contact: Philip Groff, President
Description: Works to reduce the number of injuries in Canada. Sponsors campaigns to raise public awareness of preventable causes of injury in all aspects of daily life. **Subscriptions:** 1000. **Publications:** *Heads Up* (Monthly); *Will It Float.*

34170 ■ Society for the Psychological Study of Social Issues (SPSSI)
208 I St. NE
Washington, DC 20002-4340
Ph: (202)675-6956
Free: 877-310-7778
Fax: (202)675-6902
Co. E-mail: spssi@spssi.org
URL: http://www.spssi.org
Contact: Susan Dudley, Executive Director
Description: Psychologists, sociologists, anthropologists, psychiatrists, political scientists, and social workers. Works to: obtain and disseminate to the public scientific knowledge about social change and other social processes; promote psychological research on significant theoretical and practical questions of social issues; encourage application of findings to problems of society. **Scope:** social issues. **Founded:** 1936. **Subscriptions:** 100 books. **Publications:** *Journal of Social Issues* (Quarterly); *Journal of Social Issues* (Quarterly); *Forward* (3/year); *Journal of Social Issues* (Quarterly); *SPSSI Newsletter* (3/year); *Analyses of Social Issues and Public Policy* (Annual); *Research Methods in Social Relations*; *SPSSI Newsletter, Forward* (3/year); *Analysis of Social Issues and Public Policy (ASAP)*; *Analysis of Social Issues and Public Policy* (Annual); *Social Issues and Policy Review* (Annual); *The Complete Academic: A Career Guide, 2nd Edition 2003.* **Educational Activities:** International conferences; Social Justice: Research, Action & Policy (Biennial). **Awards:** SAGES Grant Program (Annual); Social Issues Dissertation Award (Annual); Social Issues Dissertation Award (Annual); Social Issues Dissertation Award; Applied Social Issues Internship; Clara Mayo Grants; Grants-in-aid; Applied Social Issues Internship Program (Annual); Clara Mayo Grants Program (Annual); Dalmas A. Taylor Summer Minority Fellow (Annual); Gordon Allport Intergroup Relations Prize (Annual); Grants-In-Aid Program (Annual); Kurt Lewin Memorial Award (Annual); Louise Kidder Early Career Award (Annual); Michele Alexander Early Career Award (Annual); Otto Klineberg Intercultural and International Relations Award (Annual); Outstanding Teaching and Mentoring Awards (Annual); Gordon Allport Prize; Social Issues Dissertation Award; Applied Social Issues Internship; Grants-in-Aid Program; Otto Klineberg Award; Louise Kidder Early Career Award; Michele Alexander Early Career Award; Awards for Outstanding Teaching and Mentoring; Kurt Lewin Memorial Award; Applied Social Issues Internship Program (Annual); Clara Mayo Grants Program (Semiannual); Dalmas A. Taylor Summer Minority Policy Fellowship (Annual); Gordon Allport Intergroup Relations Prize (Annual); Grants-in-Aid Program (Semiannual); James Marshall Public Policy Scholar (Biennial); Louise Kidder Early Career Award (Annual); Michele Alexander Junior Scholars Award (Annual); Otto Klineberg Intercultural and International Relations Award (Annual); SPSSI Action Grants for Experienced Scholars (Annual); Gordon Allport Intergroup Relations Prize; Louise Kidder Early Career Award; Michele Alexander Early Career Award, for scholarships and services; Otto Klineberg Intercultural and International Relations Award; SPSSI Action Grants for Experienced Scholars. **Telecommunication Services:** sdudley@spssi.org.

34171 ■ Society for the Study of Social Problems (SSSP)
901 McClung Tower
University of Tennessee
Knoxville, TN 37996-0490
Ph: (865)689-1531
Fax: (865)689-1534
Co. E-mail: sssp@utk.edu
URL: http://www.sssp1.org
Contact: Wendy Simonds, President
Description: An interdisciplinary community of scholars, activists, practitioners, and students endeavoring to create greater social justice through social research. Members are often social scientists working in colleges and universities, in non-profit organizations and in other applied and policy settings. **Founded:** 1951. **Publications:** *SSSP Social Problems* (Quarterly). **Awards:** C. Wright Mills Award (Annual); Joseph B. Gittler (Annual); Lee-Founders Award; Social Action Award (Annual); Lee Founders Award; Racial/Ethnic Minority Graduate Scholarship (Annual); C. Wright Mills Award; Thomas C. Hood Social Action Award; Racial/Ethnic Minority Graduate Scholarship.

34172 ■ Society for Women's Health Research (SWHR)
1025 Connecticut Ave. NW, Ste. 701
Washington, DC 20036
Ph: (202)223-8224
Fax: (202)833-3472
Co. E-mail: info@swhr.org
URL: http://www.womenshealthresearch.org
Contact: Phyllis Greenberger, President
Description: Seeks to improve the health of women by promoting equity in research. Advocates policies which promotes the inclusion of women in clinical trials; informs government agencies and private industry of issues affecting women's health and sex-based biology; educates women consumers on conditions that affect women; promotes funding for women's health research. **Founded:** 1990. **Publications:** *SWHR Journal of Women's Health* (10/year); *Sexx Matters* (Quarterly). **Educational Activities:** Scientific Advisory Meeting (Annual); Scientific Advisory Meeting: Update on Women's Health (Annual). **Awards:** Excellence in Media (Annual).

34173 ■ United Methodist Association of Health and Welfare Ministries (UMA)
407 B Corporate Center Dr.
Vandalia, OH 45377-1165
Ph: (937)415-3624
Free: 800-411-9901
Fax: (937)222-7364
Co. E-mail: uma@umassociation.org
URL: http://www.umassociation.org
Contact: Steve L. Rumford, President
Description: Offers communications and church relations guidance. Provides leadership development training for health and human service professionals in United Methodist-related organizations and agencies. Develops ethical and theological statements on institutional care. Operates Educational Assessment Guidelines Leading Toward Excellence(EAGLE), a self-assessment and peer review accreditation program. Operates a Field Consultation Program; members may access skilled professionals to assist with governance questions. Offers audiovisual services to members. Administers the Order of Good Shepherds program designed to recognize ministry in the workplace by employees at member organizations. Maintains speakers' bureau; compiles statistics. **Founded:** 1940. **Publications:** *National Directory of Healthcare and Human Service Ministries* (Annual); *National Directory of all United Methodist Related Health and Welfare Ministries* (Annual). **Awards:** Chaplain of the Year; Hall of Fame in Philanthropy.

34174 ■ *Will It Float*
36 Eglinton W, Ste. 704
Toronto, ON, Canada M4R 1A1
Ph: (416)596-2700
Fax: (416)596-2721
Co. E-mail: info@smartrisk.ca
URL: http://www.smartrisk.ca
Contact: Philip Groff, President

REFERENCE WORKS

34175 ■ *"13D Filings" in Barron's (Vol. 88, March 24, 2008, No. 12, pp. M13)*
Pub: Dow Jones & Company, Inc.
Description: HealthCor Management called as problematic the plan of Magellan Health Services to use its high cash balances for acquisitions. Carlson Capital discussed with Energy Partners possible changes in the latter's board. Investor Carl Icahn suggested that Enzon Pharmaceuticals consider selling itself or divest some of its assets.

34176 ■ *"2007 Fittest CEOs" in Hawaii Business (Vol. 53, October 2007, No. 4, pp. 40)*
Pub: Hawaii Business Publishing
Description: Discusses the outcome of the fittest chief executive officers in Hawaii competition for 2007. Hawaii Capital Management's David Low leads the list while Group Pacific (Hawaii) Inc.'s Chip Doyle and Greater Good Inc.'s Kari Leong placed second and third, respectively. The CEO's routines, eating habits, and inspirations for staying fit are provided.

34177 ■ *"2010 Book of Lists" in Austin Business JournalInc. (Vol. 29, December 25, 2009, No. 42, pp. 1)*
Pub: American City Business Journals
Description: Rankings of companies and organizations within the business services, finance, healthcare, hospitality and travel, insurance, marketing and media, professional services, real estate, education and technology industries in Austin, Texas are presented. Rankings are based on sales, business size, and other statistics.

34178 ■ *"2010 Book of Lists" in Business Courier (Vol. 26, December 26, 2009, No. 36, pp. 1)*
Pub: American City Business Journals, Inc.
Description: Rankings of companies and organizations within the business services, education, finance, health care, hospitality and tourism, real estate, and technology industries in the Cincinnati, Ohio-Northern Kentucky area are presented. Rankings are based on sales, business size, or other statistics.

34179 ■ *"2010 Book of Lists" in Tampa Bay Business Journal (Vol. 30, December 22, 2009, No. 53, pp. 1)*
Pub: American City Business Journals
Description: Rankings of companies and organizations within the human resources, banking and finance, business services, healthcare, real estate, technology, hospitality and travel, and education industries in the Greater Tampa Bay area are presented. Rankings are based on sales, business size, and more.

34180 ■ *"Abraxis Bets On Biotech Hub" in Business Journal-Serving Phoenix and the Valley of the Sun (Vol. 10, November 9, 2007, No. 28)*
Pub: American City Business Journals, Inc.
Ed: Angela Gonzales. **Description:** Abraxis BioScience Inc. purchased a 200,000 square foot manufacturing facility in Phoenix, Arizona from Watson Pharmaceuticals Inc. The company has the technology to allow chemotherapy drugs to be injected directly into tumor cell membranes. A human protein, albumin is used to deliver the chemotherapy.

34181 ■ *"Achieve Tampa Bay Thrown a Lifeline in Proposed Merger" in Tampa Bay Business Journal (Vol. 30, January 22, 2010, No. 5, pp. 1)*
Pub: American City Business Journals
Ed: Margie Manning. **Description:** Mental Health Care Inc. proposed a merger with Achieve Tampa Bay Inc. The former proposes to administer the latter's operations and take over its assets while paying its debts.

34182 ■ *Achieving Planned Innovation: A Proven System for Creating Successful New Products and Services*
Pub: Simon and Schuster
Ed: Frank R. Bacon. **Released:** August 2007. **Price:** $16.95. **Description:** Planned innovation is a disciplined and practical step-by-step sequence of procedures for reaching the intended destination point: successful products. This easy-to-read book explains the system along with an action-oriented program for continuous success in new-product innovations. Five steps outlined include: a disciplined reasoning process; lasting market orientation; proper selection criteria that reflect both strategic and tactical business objectives and goals along with dynamic matching of resources to present and future opportunities, and positive and negative requirements before making major expenditures; and proper organizational staffing. The author explains what to do and evaluating the potential of any new product or service, ranging from ventures in retail distribution to the manufacture of goods as diverse as bicycles, motorcycles, aerospace communication and navigation equipment, small business computers, food packaging, and medical products.

34183 ■ *"Acsys Interactive Announces Crowdsourcing Comes to the Hospital Industry" in Internet Wire (August 23, 2010)*
Pub: Comtex
Description: Hospital marketers are obtaining data through crowdsourcing as strategy to gain ideas and feedback. The Hospital Industry Crowdsourced Survey of Digital, Integrated and Emerging Marketing is the first initiative among hospitals.

34184 ■ *"Active Duty" in Crain's Cleveland Business (Vol. 28, November 26, 2007, No. 47, pp. 3)*
Pub: Crain Communications, Inc.
Ed: David Bennett. **Description:** Discusses the Veteran Workforce Training Program, sponsored by the Volunteers of America - Greater Ohio; the program is meant to provide employment training for military veterans and to assist them in transitioning back into the work force.

34185 ■ *Adoption Resource Book*
Pub: HarperCollins
URL(s): www.harpercollins.com/Book/Browse.aspx. **Released:** Irregular; Latest edition 4th. **Price:** $16.95, Individuals paperback. **Publication includes:** List of public and private adoption agencies, support groups, and services. **Entries include:** Agency name, address, phone, special requirements. Principal content of the publication is a discussion of adoption procedures and requirements, including adoption of foreign children and open adoption. **Arrangement:** Geographical.

34186 ■ *"Aggenix Completes Merger with German Giant" in Houston Business Journal (Vol. 40, December 25, 2009, No. 33, pp. 2)*
Pub: American City Business Journals
Ed: Mary Ann Azevedo. **Description:** Agennix Inc. has completed its transformation into a German company after Germany-based GPC Biotech merged into the former publicly traded Agennix AG. One quarter of Agennix's 60 employees will remain in Houston. Details on Agennix's drug trials are examined.

34187 ■ *"Albany Molecular on Hiring Spree as Big Pharma Slashes Work Force" in Business Review, Albany New York (December 28, 2007)*
Pub: American City Business Journals, Inc.
Ed: Barbara Pinckney. **Description:** Albany Molecular Research Inc. (AMRI) is an outsourcing company that provides work forces for pharmaceutical companies due to large numbers of downsizings in the year 2007. In 2008, AMRI plans to hire several workers.

34188 ■ *"Analysts: More Mergers for the Region's Hospitals" in Boston Business Journal (Vol. 30, October 15, 2010, No. 36, pp. 1)*
Pub: Boston Business Journal
Ed: Julie M. Donnelly. **Description:** A number of hospitals in Boston, Massachusetts are engaging in mergers and acquisitions. Caritas Christi Health Care is set to be purchased by Cerberus Capital Management. The U.S. healthcare reform law is seen to drive the development.

34189 ■ *"The Annual Entitlement Lecture: Trustees of Medicare and Social Security Issue Another Dismal Report" in Barron's (March 31, 2008)*
Pub: Dow Jones & Company, Inc.
Ed: Thomas G. Donlan. **Description:** Expenditures on Medicare hospital insurance and the revenues available to pay for it have led to a gap of capital valued at $38.6 trillion. Slashing the benefits or raising taxes will not solve the gap which exists unless the government saves the money and invests it in private markets.

34190 ■ *"An Apple a Day" in Entrepreneur (Vol. 36, February 2008, No. 2, pp. 19)*
Pub: Entrepreneur Media Inc.
Ed: Mark Henricks. **Description:** Businesses are handling rising health coverage costs by providing employees with wellness programs, which include smoking-cessation programs, consumer-directed plans for savings on premiums, and limited medical care plans. Details on the growing trend regarding employee health coverage are discussed.

34191 ■ *"Area Hurt By Doctor Deficiency" in The Business Journal-Serving Metropolitan Kansas City (Vol. 27, October 17, 2008, No. 5, pp. 1)*
Pub: American City Business Journals, Inc.
Ed: Rob Roberts. **Description:** Kansas City, Missouri may face a shortage of doctors, according to the Metropolitan Medical Society of Greater Kansas City. Over the next ten years the city needs to recruit more doctors in order to address the problem. Practicing physicians are having difficulties recruiting.

34192 ■ *"Attorney Guides Biotech Company in $6 Million Initial Public Offering" in Miami Daily Business Review (March 26, 2008)*
Pub: ALM Media Inc.
Description: In order to raise capital to engage in a full-scale trial of MyoCell to receive clinical approval, Bioheart Inc., launched an initial public offering. Bioheart researches and develops cell therapies to treat heart damage.

34193 ■ *"Back Talk With Terrie M. Williams" in Black Enterprise (Vol. 38, December 2007, No. 5, pp. 204)*
Pub: Earl G. Graves Publishing Co. Inc.
Ed: Tennille M. Robinson. **Description:** Profile of Terrie M. Williams, president of a public relations agency as well as founder of a youth empowerment organization called Stay Strong Foundation. Williams reflects on her bouts with depression and how the disease impacts sufferers and talks about her book that will inspire others dealing with depression.

34194 ■ *"Banking on Cord Blood" in Business Journal-Serving Phoenix & the Valley of the Sun (Vol. 31, September 10, 2010, No. 1, pp. 1)*
Pub: Phoenix Business Journal
Ed: Angela Gonzales. **Description:** Celebration Stem Cell Centre obtained contracts from Mercy Gilbert Medical Center and its two sister hospitals, St. Joseph Hospital and Medical Center in Phoenix, Arizona and Chandler Regional Medical Center. The contract will facilitate the donation of unused umbilical cord blood for research.

34195 ■ *"Bankruptcies" in Crain's Detroit Business (Vol. 24, March 24, 2008, No. 12, pp. 6)*
Pub: Crain Communications, Inc.
Description: Current list of business that filed for Chapter 7 or 11 protection in U.S. Bankruptcy Court in Detroit include a construction company, a medical care company, a physical therapy firm and a communications firm.

34196 ■ *"Barbara West" in Crain's Cleveland Business (Vol. 30, June 29, 2009, No. 25, pp. 14)*
Pub: Crain Communications, Inc.
Ed: Shannon Mortland. **Description:** Profile of Barbara West, administrative director of emergency medicine at MetroHealth Medical Center in Ohio. Ms. West manages Metro Life Flight that uses helicopters to transport patients to MetroHealth. She discusses the challenges of taking care of patients when big emergencies occur.

34197 ■ *"Bethesda Stepping Out" in Business Courier (Vol. 27, October 15, 2010, No. 24, pp. 1)*
Pub: Business Courier
Ed: James Ritchie. **Description:** Nonprofit organization Bethesda Inc. is planning to donate $5 million a year for the next three years to Greater Cincinnati health care reforms. Bethesda revealed that it announced its donations to pressure other organizations to help.

34198 ■ *"Big Losses Mount for Hospitals" in Baltimore Business Journal (Vol. 27, October 23, 2009, No. 24, pp. 1)*
Pub: American City Business Journals
Ed: Scott Graham. **Description:** Reported losses by nine of the 22 hospitals in the Greater Baltimore area during fiscal 2009 have proven that the health care industry is not immune to the recession. The rising costs of doing business and losses in the stock market have strongly affected the financial status of hospitals.

34199 ■ *"Big Paychecks for Hospital CEOs" in Sacramento Business Journal (Vol. 28, April 8, 2011, No. 6, pp. 1)*
Pub: Sacramento Business Journal
Ed: Kathy Robertson. **Description:** Hospital chief executives in Sacramento, California have been receiving large salaries, tax records show. The huge salaries reflect the high demand for successful hospital chief executives. Statistical data included.

34200 ■ *"Biotechnology Wants a Lead Role" in Business North Carolina (Vol. 28, March 2008, No. 3, pp. 14)*
Pub: Business North Carolina
Description: According to experts, North Carolina is poised as a leader in the biotechnology sector. Highlights of a recent roundtable discussion sponsored by the North Carolina Biotechnology Center in Research Triangle Park are presented.

34201 ■ *"Blue Cross Confronts Baby Blues" in Marketing to Women (Vol. 21, March 2008, No. 3, pp. 3)*
Pub: EPM Communications Inc.
Contact: Ira Mayer, President
E-mail: imayer@epmcom.com
Description: Blue Cross of California has launched a Maternity Depression Program aimed at educating mothers suffering from postpartum depression.

34202 ■ *"Blue Cross to Put Kiosk in Mall" in News & Observer (November 9, 2010)*
Pub: News & Observer
Ed: Alan M. Wolf. **Description:** Blue Cross and Blue Shield of North Carolina has placed a kiosk in Durham's Streets of Southpoint in order to market its health insurance.

34203 ■ *"Board This Powertrain" in Barron's (Vol. 89, July 27, 2009, No. 30, pp. 30)*
Pub: Dow Jones & Co., Inc.
Ed: Naureen S. Malik. **Description:** Siemens' American Depositary Receipts have risen 60 percent from their March 2009 low and they should continue heading higher. The company has solid earnings and revenue growth since they lead in growing markets such as alternative energy and health-care infrastructure. Their shares also look cheap at 1.9 times book value.

34204 ■ *"Book of Lists 2010" in Philadelphia Business Journal (Vol. 28, December 25, 2009, No. 45, pp. 1)*
Pub: American City Business Journals
Description: Rankings of companies and organizations within the banking, biotechnology, economic development, healthcare, hospitality, law and accounting, marketing and media, real estate, and technology industries in the Philadelphia, Pennsylvania area are presented. Rankings are based on sales, business size, and more.

34205 ■ *"Brace for the Bill" in Boston Business Journal (Vol. 27, December 28, 2007, No. 48, pp. 1)*
Pub: American City Business Journals Inc.
Ed: Mark Hollmer. **Description:** Historic 2006 Massachusetts Health Care Reform Law seems successful because many people have signed up for health insurance within one year of its implementation. However, rising premiums and other factors are threatening the health industry.

34206 ■ *"Budget Cuts Afflict Health Department" in Business Courier (Vol. 24, November 23, 2008, No. 32, pp. 1)*
Pub: American City Business Journals, Inc.
Ed: Lucy May; James Ritchie. **Description:** Cincinnati must cut $25 million to balance its budget for 2008. As a result, the city will be cutting $704,000 from its Health Department's budget of $42 million, and will eliminate 31.6 positions by the end of 2007.

34207 ■ *"Building Alexian Brothers' Clinical Reputation" in Crain's Chicago Business (Vol. 31, May 5, 2008, No. 18, pp. 6)*
Pub: Crain Communications, Inc.
Ed: Mike Colias. **Description:** Profile of the CEO of Alexian Brothers Medical Center in Elk Grove Village who plans to stabilize Alexian Brothers' financial performance in part by eliminating $20 million in annual costs.

34208 ■ *"The Business of Medicine: Maintaining a Healthy Bottom Line" in Black Enterprise (Vol. 41, October 2010, No. 3, pp. 60)*
Pub: Earl G. Graves Publishing Co. Inc.
Ed: Marcia A. Reed-Woodard. **Description:** Sustainable government reform requires reconstruction in the areas of financing and delivery of services in the field of medicine.

34209 ■ *"Businesses Balk at 1099 Provision in Health Reform Law" in Baltimore Business Journal (Vol. 28, August 13, 2010, No. 14, pp. 1)*
Pub: Baltimore Business Journal
Ed: Scott Dance. **Description:** Small business advocates and accountants have criticized the Internal Revenue Service Form 1099 provision in the health care reform law as not worth the cost of time and money. Critics believe the policy would create a deluge of the documents that is too much for the companies or the IRS to handle. Details of the provision are also discussed.

34210 ■ *"California Company Suing City's Lupin Over its Generic Diabetes Drug" in Baltimore Business Journal (Vol. 27, January 1, 2010)*
Pub: American City Business Journals
Ed: Gary Haber. **Description:** California-based Depomed Inc. is suing Baltimore, Maryland-based Lupin Pharmaceuticals Inc. and its parent company in India over the patents to a diabetes drug. Lupin allegedly infringed on Depomed's four patents for Glumetza when it filed for permission to sell its own version of the drug with the US Food and Drug Administration. Details on generic pharmaceutical manufacturer tactics are discussed.

34211 ■ *"Canadian Patients Give Detroit Hospitals a Boost" in Crain's Detroit Business (Vol. 24, April 14, 2008, No. 15, pp. 10)*
Pub: Crain Communications Inc.
Ed: Jay Greene. **Description:** Each year thousands of Canadians travel to Detroit area hospitals seeking quicker solutions to medical problems or access to services that are limited or unavailable in Canada.

34212 ■ *"Canadian Wind Farm Sued Due to Negative Health Effects" in PC Magazine Online (September 22, 2011)*
Pub: PC Magazine
Description: Suncor Energy is being sued by a family in Ontario, Canada. The family claims that Suncor's wind turbines have created health problems for them, ranging from vertigo and sleep disturbance to depression and suicidal thoughts. The family's home is over 1,000 meters from the eight wind turbines, and according to Ontario officials, wind turbines must be a minimum of 550 meters from existing homes.

34213 ■ *"Cancer Care's Quantum Leap" in Hawaii Business (Vol. 53, October 2007, No. 4, pp. 17)*
Pub: Hawaii Business Publishing
Ed: Cathy S. Cruz-George. **Description:** TomoTherapy is an innovative device for cancer treatment that gives high-intensity radiation to more accurate parts of the body compared to conventional treatments. Hawaii has one of the 70 TomoTherapy machines in the nation, and it is expected to help advance cancer care in the area. Details on how the machine works are provided.

34214 ■ *"Cancer Therapy Raises Debate Over Shared Technology" in Crain's Detroit Business (Vol. 24, March 10, 2008, No. 10, pp. 1)*
Pub: Crain Communications, Inc.
Ed: Jay Greene. **Description:** Overview of a proposed collaborative approach among select hospitals that would allow the consortium to utilize proton-beam accelerators in order to treat cancer patients; this expensive new technology is possibly a better way to destroy cancers by using the proton beams to direct high dosages of radiation to destroy small tumors.

34215 ■ *"Cannabis Science Signs Exclusive and Non-Exclusive Agreement with Prescription Vending Machines" in Benzinga.com (October 29, 2011)*
Pub: Benzinga.com
Ed: Benzinga Staff. **Description:** Cannabis Science Inc., a biotech company developing pharmaceutical cannabis products has partnered with Prescription Vending Machines Inc. and its principal Vincent Meddizadeh to provide industry specific consulting and advisory services to Cannabis Science.

34216 ■ *CARES Directory: Social and Health Services in the Greater New York Area*
URL(s): www.unitedwaynyc.org/?id=65. **Released:** Biennial **Covers:** Over 2,469 nonprofit social service agencies in the greater New York area. **Entries include:** Name, address, phone, names and titles of key personnel, agency mission, programs offered, eligibility requirements, fees, application procedure, geographic area served, other locations, site director name and title, accessibility to the handicapped, hours open, languages spoken, transportation facilities. **Arrangement:** Alphabetical by agency name. **Indexes:** Program, Keyword/Target Group.

34217 ■ *"Centerpoint Nurses Unionize Despite Change In Hospital CEO" in Business Journal-Serving Metropolitan Kansas City (November 16, 2007)*
Pub: American City Business Journals, Inc.
Ed: Rob Roberts. **Description:** The change in Centerpoint Medical Center's CEO did not stop the hospital's 336 registered nurses from joining Nurses United for Improved Patient Care. Carolyn Caldwell was named CEO of Centerpoint on October 8, 2007, one week after Dan Jones announced his resignation. Poor communications are pointed out as the reason why the nurses joined the union.

34218 ■ *"CEO Forecast" in Hispanic Business (January-February 2009, pp. 34, 36)*
Pub: Hispanic Business
Ed: Jessica Haro, Richard Kaplan. **Description:** As economic uncertainty fogs the future, executives turn to government contracts in order to boost business. Revenue sources, health care challenges, environmental consulting and remediation services, as well as technological strides are discussed.

34219 ■ *"Cerner Works the Business Circuit" in Business Journal-Serving Metropolitan Kansas City (Vol. 26, October 5, 2007, No. 4, pp. 1)*
Pub: American City Business Journals, Inc.
Ed: Rob Roberts. **Description:** Cerner Corporation is embracing the coming of the electronic medical record exchange by creating a regional health information organization (RHIO) called the CareEntrust. The RHIO convinced health insurers to share claims data with patients and clinicians. At the Center Health Conference, held October 7 to 10, Cerner will demonstrate the software it developed for CareEntrust to the 40,000 healthcare and information technology professionals.

34220 ■ *"Changes Sought to Health Law" in Baltimore Business Journal (Vol. 28, July 30, 2010, No. 12, pp. 1)*
Pub: Baltimore Business Journal
Ed: Kent Hoover. **Description:** Business groups that opposed health care reform are working to undo parts of the new laws even before they go into effect. Business groups are gaining support for one legislative fix, which is repealing the law's provision that requires all businesses to file 1099 forms with the IRS any time they pay more than $600 a year to another business.

34221 ■ *"Chelsea Community Hospital to Merge with St. Joseph Mercy Health" in Crain's Detroit Business (Vol. 24, March 24, 2008, No. 12)*
Pub: Crain Communications, Inc.
Ed: Jay Greene. **Description:** Chelsea Community Hospital has signed a letter of intent to merge with St. Joseph Mercy Health System and will negotiate merger terms, including a plan to fund an unspecified amount of facility improvements and equipment purchases at Chelsea.

34222 ■ *"Chemed's Vitas Aims to Acquire" in Business Courier (Vol. 27, July 9, 2010, No. 10, pp. 1)*
Pub: Business Courier
Ed: James Ritchie. **Description:** Chemed Corporation's Vitas Healthcare Corporation is looking for smaller nonprofit hospices as it looks to become more streamlined in a tougher reimbursement environment. CFO David Williams syas they want to acquire these hospices as fast as they can integrate them.

34223 ■ *"Chief Boo Boo Officer" in Marketing to Women (Vol. 21, February 2008, No. 2, pp. 1)*
Pub: EPM Communications Inc.
Contact: Ira Mayer, President
E-mail: imayer@epmcom.com
Ed: Ellen Neuborne. **Description:** Pharmaceutical companies are reaching out to women through innovative marketing techniques.

34224 ■ *"Children's Hospital to Grow" in Austin Business Journal (Vol. 31, July 22, 2011, No. 20, pp. A1)*
Pub: American City Business Journals Inc.
Ed: Sandra Zaragoza. **Description:** Austin, Texas-based Dell Children's Medical Center is set to embark on a tower expansion. The plan will accommodate more patients and make room for the hospital's growing specialty program.

34225 ■ *"Christ Hospital to Expand" in Business Courier (Vol. 27, June 25, 2010, No. 8, pp. 3)*
Pub: Business Courier
Ed: Dan Monk, James Ritchie. **Description:** Christ Hospital intends to invest more than $300 million and generate 200 jobs in an expansion of its Mount Auburn campus in Cincinnati, Ohio. About $22 million in retail activity can be created by the hospital expansion, which will also include a replacement garage and new surgery facilities.

34226 ■ *"Clinic to Use Medical Summit to Pump Up Cardiology Center" in Crain's Cleveland Business (Vol. 28, October 1, 2007, No. 39, pp. 6)*
Pub: Crain Communications, Inc.
Ed: Chuck Soder. **Description:** Overview of the Medical Innovation Summit, sponsored by the Cleveland Clinic and regional business recruitment group Team NEO, whose theme was cardiology. The goal for this year's summit went beyond finding companies for the cardiovascular center, it also looked to market the region to other industries with growth potential.

34227 ■ *"College Opens On St. Luke's Site" in The Business Journal - Serving Phoenix and the Valley of the Sun (Vol. 28, September 5, 2008)*
Pub: American City Business Journals, Inc.
Ed: Angela Gonzales. **Description:** Fortis College is planning to offer classes in Phoenix, Arizona. It has made its home at the St. Luke's Medical Center. Courses to be offered by the college are also provided.

34228 ■ *"Columbia Sale Narrowed To Two Developers" in The Business Journal-Milwaukee (Vol. 25, July 18, 2008, No. 43, pp. A1)*
Pub: American City Business Journals, Inc.
Ed: Corrinne Hess. **Description:** Officials of Columbia St. Mary's Inc plan to pick one of two real-estate developers who will buy the 8-acre property of the Columbia Hospital which the company will move away from when their new hospital has been constructed. The hospital on Newport Ave. has been on the market since 2001.

34229 ■ *"Commercial Builders Take It on the Chin" in Crain's Chicago Business (Vol. 31, April 28, 2008, No. 17, pp. 16)*
Pub: Crain Communications, Inc.
Ed: Alby Gallun. **Description:** Although the health care development sector has seen growth, the rest of Chicago's local commercial building industry has seen steep declines in the first quarter of this year. According to McGraw-Hill Construction, Chicago-area non-residential construction starts totaled $731 million in the quarter, a 60 percent drop from the year-earlier period. Volume in the retail, office and hotel markets fell by nearly 70 percent.

34230 ■ *"Company Goes High-Tech To Attack Some Sore Spots" in Boston Business Journal (Vol. 27, December 7, 2007, No. 45, pp. 10)*
Pub: American City Business Journals Inc.
Ed: Mark Hollmer. **Description:** Transport Pharmaceuticals Inc. hopes to raise $35 million to fund a drug and a treatment device for treating cold sores, and seek federal regulatory approval. Dennis Goldberg, the company's CEO, believes that existing treatments that use acyclovir cream are relatively weak. Transport's drug uses a soluble gel cartridge with a higher concentration of acyclovir.

34231 ■ *"Connecting the Dots Between Wellness and Elder Care" in Benefits and Compensation Digest (Vol. 47, August 2010, No. 8, pp. 18)*
Pub: International Foundation of Employee Benefit Plans
Contact: Richard Lyall, President
Ed: Sandra Timmermann. **Description:** Employees caring for aged and infirm parents deal with time and financial issues and other stresses. The connection between health status of caregivers and employers' health care costs could be aided by linking programs and benefits with wellness and caregiving.

34232 ■ *"Consulting Firm Goes Shopping" in Crain's Chicago Business (Vol. 31, April 28, 2008, No. 17, pp. 45)*
Pub: Crain Communications, Inc.
Ed: Phuong Ly. **Description:** Clark & Wamberg LLC was created last year after the merger of Clark Inc. to a Dutch insurance conglomerate. Clark Inc. was a life insurance and benefits consultancy which had been on a downslide, returning just 5.6 percent a year to shareholders. In contrast Clark & Wamberg posted first-year revenue of $106.8 million, fueled by business from its executive compensation and health care clients.

34233 ■ *"Contracting Firm Sees Timing Right for Expansion" in Tampa Bay Business Journal (Vol. 29, November 13, 2009, No. 47, pp. 1)*
Pub: American City Business Journals
Ed: Janet Leiser. **Description:** Construction management company Moss & Associates LLC of Fort Lauderdale, Florida has launched its expansion to Tampa Bay. Moss & Associates has started the construction of the Marlins stadium in Miami, Florida's Little Havana section. It also plans to diversify by embarking on other government development, such as health care facilities and airports.

34234 ■ *"Conversation Starters for the Holiday" in Barron's (Vol. 89, July 6, 2009, No. 27, pp. 7)*
Pub: Dow Jones & Co., Inc.
Ed: Michael Santoli. **Description:** Investors are concerned that the US will experience high inflation due to low interest rates and improved money supply. US consumer spending has increased to 70 percent of gross domestic product, brought by health-care spending increases, while savings rates have risen to 6.9 percent.

34235 ■ *"Corporate Canada Eyes Retiree Benefit Cuts" in Globe & Mail (March 8, 2006, pp. B3)*
Pub: CTVglobemedia Publishing Inc.
Ed: Virginia Galt. **Description:** A survey on Canadian companies reveals that due to rising health care costs and increasing number of baby boomer retirements, these companies are to cut down on health benefits they are providing to these retired employees.

34236 ■ *"COSE: More Small Companies Offering Wellness Plans" in Crain's Cleveland Business (Vol. 28, December 3, 2007, No. 48, pp. 22)*
Pub: Crain Communications, Inc.
Ed: Shannon Mortland. **Description:** Discusses the Council of Smaller Enterprises (COSE) which is offering incentives to companies who implement wellness programs and can show that their employees are living healthier lives.

34237 ■ *"Cost of Md. Health Plan Not Known" in Baltimore Business Journal (Vol. 28, September 3, 2010, No. 17, pp. 1)*
Pub: Baltimore Business Journal
Ed: Emily Mullin. **Description:** United States health reform is seen to result in increased health insurance prices in Maryland. However, health care reform advocates claim a new marketplace and increased competition will help keep costs down.

34238 ■ *"Could UNCC Be Home to Future Med School Here?" in Charlotte Business Journal (Vol. 25, July 23, 2010, No. 18, pp. 1)*
Pub: Charlotte Business Journal
Ed: Jennifer Thomas. **Description:** University of North Carolina, Charlotte chancellor Phil Dubois is proposing that a medical school be established at the campus. The idea began in 2007 and Dubois' plan is for students to spend all four years in Charlotte and train at the Carolinas Medical Center.

34239 ■ *"Countywide Tax Could Fund Metro" in Business Courier (Vol. 26, January 15, 2010, No. 39, pp. 1)*
Pub: American City Business Journals, Inc.
Ed: Lucy May, Dan Monk. **Description:** Cincinnati officials are considering a new countywide tax to fund the Metro bus system and extend healthcare to the poor.

34240 ■ *"CreFirst To Reward Doctors for Reducing Costs, Improving Care" in Baltimore Business Journal (Vol. 28, June 4, 2010, No. 4, pp. 1)*
Pub: Baltimore Business Journal
Ed: Scott Graham. **Description:** CareFirst Blue Cross Blue Shield plans to introduce a program that dangles big financial rewards to physicians who change the way they deliver primary care by improving the health of their sickest patients while reducing costs. The company will soon begin recruiting primary care physicians in Maryland, Washington DC, and Northern Virginia.

34241 ■ *"Criticare Sees Rapid Expansion" in Business Journal-Milwaukee (Vol. 28, December 31, 2010, No. 14, pp. A1)*
Pub: Milwaukee Business Journal
Ed: Rich Rovito. **Description:** Criticare Systems Inc. expanded its distribution network, added customers, launched two new products and transferred into a new building in Pewaukee, Wisconsin at the start of their fiscal year. Criticare expanded its workforce and now has nearly 140 full time employees.

34242 ■ *Dakotas-Montana Medical Directory*
Pub: Jola Publications
URL(s): www.orderpoint.comwww.jolapub.com. **Released:** Biennial; Latest edition March, 2010. **Price:** $25, Individuals. **Covers:** Approximately 5,000 doctors, hospitals, clinics, nursing homes, and other selected health care providers in North Dakota, South Dakota, and Montana. **Entries include:** Doctor or facility name, address, phone. **Arrangement:** Classified by type of facility or care provided. **Indexes:** Name, product/service, subject.

34243 ■ *"David Low" in Hawaii Business (Vol. 53, October 2007, No. 4, pp. 38)*
Pub: Hawaii Business Publishing
Ed: Cathy S. Cruz-George. **Description:** Hawaii Capital Management managing director David Low ranked first in the 2007 competition for fittest male executives in Hawaii. This 5-foot-9 executive, who weighed 225 lbs. in 2003, weighs 150 lbs. in 2007. The activities that improved Low's fitness, such as weight training, swimming, biking, and running, are discussed.

34244 ■ *"Diana Bonta: Keeping People Healthy and Thriving" in Hispanic Business (Vol. 30, April 2008, No. 4, pp. 30)*
Pub: Hispanic Business
Ed: Leanndra Martinez. **Description:** Diana Bonta serves as vice president of public affairs for Kaiser Permanente and is a strong advocate for health reform and improving access to health care. In order to better serve the underinsured and uninsured, she directs Kaiser's Community Benefit division that devoted $369 million last year to this cause.

34245 ■ *Directory of Catholic Charities USA Directories*
Pub: Catholic Charities USA
Contact: Bill Jones, Director
URL(s): www.catholiccharitiesusa.org. **Ed:** Mary Reed. **Released:** Annual **Price:** $25, Individuals. **Covers:** Nearly 1,200 Catholic community and social service agencies. Listings include diocesan agencies, state Catholic conferences. **Entries include:** Organi-

zation name, address, name and title of director, phone, fax. **Arrangement:** Geographical by state, then classified by diocese.

34246 ■ *Directory of Human Services and Self Help Support Groups--Maricopa County*
Pub: Community Information & Referral Inc.
Contact: Roberto Armijo, President
URL(s): www.cir.org/publications-dhs.html. **Released:** Annual; Latest edition 2009. **Price:** $35, plus 5 for shipping; $35, CD-ROM. **Covers:** More than 2,300 governmental and private non-profit human service organizations in Maricopa County, Arizona. **Entries include:** Organization name, address, phone, fax, e-mail, URL, Name and title of contact, affiliations, location, geographical area served, eligibility requirements, description of services, days and hours of operation, complete program and service descriptions. **Arrangement:** Alphabetical. **Indexes:** Subject, alphabetical.

34247 ■ *"Discovery Communications" in Workforce Management (Vol. 88, December 14, 2009, No. 13, pp. 17)*
Pub: Crain Communications Inc.
Ed: Jeremy Smerd. **Description:** Discovery Communications provides its employees a wealth of free health services via a comprehensive work-site medical clinic that is available to its employees and their dependents. Overview of the company's innovative approach to healthcare is presented.??.

34248 ■ *"Docs Might Hold Cure for Real Estate, Banks" in Baltimore Business Journal (Vol. 28, November 5, 2010, No. 26, pp. 1)*
Pub: Baltimore Business Journal
Ed: Gary Haber. **Description:** Health care providers, including physicians are purchasing their office space instead of renting it as banks lower interest rates to 6 percent on mortgages for medical offices. The rise in demand offers relief to the commercial real estate market. It has also resulted in a boom in building new medical offices.

34249 ■ *"Docs Prop Up Health Insurer" in Business First-Columbus (December 14, 2007, pp. A1)*
Pub: American City Business Journals, Inc.
Ed: Carrie Ghose. **Description:** Doctors and executives supporting Physicians Assurance Corporation, a startup health insurer in Central Ohio, were required to raise $2.5 million before they could apply for a license from the state Department of Insurance. The company, which hopes to acquire its license by January 2007, will focus on doctor's offices and businesses with two to ninety-nine employees.

34250 ■ *"Doctor On the Go: Concessions International Founder Opens Airport Clinic" in Black Enterprise (Vol. 38, October 2007, No. 3, pp. 34)*
Pub: Earl G. Graves Publishing Co. Inc.
Ed: Tara C. Walker. **Description:** Aero Clinic is an onsite healthcare facility designed to care for travelers. Located at Atlanta's Hartsfield-Jackson International Airport, the clinic is the first of its kind.

34251 ■ *"Doctors Buy In to Medical Timeshares" in Houston Business Journal (Vol. 40, December 11, 2009, No. 31, pp. 1)*
Pub: American City Business Journals
Ed: Mary Ann Azevedo. **Description:** Memorial Hermann Hospital System has leased to doctors three examination rooms and medical office space in the Memorial Hermann Medical Plaza in line with its new timeshare concept. The concept was designed to bring primary care physicians to its Texas Medical Center campus.

34252 ■ *"Doctors Eye Rating Plan With Caution" in The Business Journal-Portland (Vol. 25, July 4, 2008, No. 17, pp. 1)*
Pub: American City Business Journals, Inc.
Ed: Robin J. Moody. **Description:** Doctors in Portland, Oregon are wary of a new Providence Health Plan system that rates their performance on patients with certain medical conditions. The system is expected to discourage wasteful procedures, thereby, saving employers' money. Other mechanics of the rating system are also discussed.

34253 ■ *"Doctor's Orders" in Canadian Business (Vol. 79, November 20, 2006, No. 23, pp. 73)*
Pub: Rogers Media
Ed: Jeff Sanford. **Description:** George Cohon, the founder of McDonald's in Canada and Russia, speaks about the Canadian market and the experience of starting McDonald's in Canada.

34254 ■ *"Doctors Warn of Problems" in Austin Business Journallnc. (Vol. 29, December 4, 2009, No. 39, pp. 1)*
Pub: American City Business Journals
Ed: Sandra Zaragoza. **Description:** Texas physicians have voiced their concern regarding the potential cuts in Medicare reimbursement rates due to the 21 percent cut imposed by Centers for Medicare and Medicaid at the start of 2010. Experts believe the large cuts would result in the closure of some physician practices. Details of the Texas Medical Association's stand on the health reform bill are examined.

34255 ■ *Dorland's Medical Directory*
Pub: Phillips Business Information Inc. Access Intelligence L.L.C.
Contact: Heather Farley, President
E-mail: hfarley@accessintel.com
URL(s): www.dorlandhealth.com. **Released:** Annual; latest edition 2004. **Price:** $69.95, Individuals plus $3.95 shipping. **Covers:** Nearly 15,000 physicians in Eastern Pennsylvania and Southern New Jersey, Northern Delaware. Also includes group practices, hospitals, healthcare facilities, and medical organizations. **Entries include:** For physicians--Name, office and home addresses and phone, fax numbers, email addresses, medical school attended and year graduated, medical specialties, certifications, hospital affiliations. For hospitals--Name, address, names and specialties of staff members. **Arrangement:** Geographical, subject. **Indexes:** Speciality.

34256 ■ *"E-Medical Records Save Money, Time in Ann Arbor" in Crain's Detroit Business (Vol. 24, January 21, 2008, No. 3, pp. 6)*
Pub: Crain Communications Inc. - Detroit
Ed: Jay Greene. **Description:** Ann Arbor Area Health Information Exchange is improving patient outcomes by sharing clinical and administrative data in electronic medical record systems.

34257 ■ *"Editor's Note" in Canadian Business (Vol. 81, March 17, 2008, No. 4, pp. 7)*
Pub: Rogers Media
Ed: Joe Chidley. **Description:** Canadian Consolidated government expenditures increased by an average of 4.5 percent annually from 2003 to 2007. Health care, housing, and the environment were some of the areas which experienced higher spending. However, government spending in labor, employment, and immigration dropped 6.6 percent.

34258 ■ *"Elder Care At Work" in HRMagazine (Vol. 53, September 2008, No. 9, pp. 111)*
Pub: Society for Human Resource Management
Contact: Henry G. Jackson, President
E-mail: hjackson@shrm.org
Ed: Pamela Babcock. **Description:** Many employers are helping workers who face sudden, short-term elder care needs.

34259 ■ *"Elements For Success" in Small Business Opportunities (November 2008)*
Pub: Entrepreneur Press
Contact: Perlman Neil, President
Description: Profile of Elements, a physical fitness club that approach a healthy lifestyle for women, which includes the components of body, beauty and mind; the network of upscale, boutique style health clubs differ from other providers in its 'balanced lifestyle' approach to a healthy lifestyle. This unique niche is gaining in popularity despite the faltering economy.

34260 ■ *"Elevated Status" in Business Courier (Vol. 24, March 21, 2008, No. 50, pp. 1)*
Pub: American City Business Journals, Inc.
Ed: James Ritchie. **Description:** Overview of Tri-Health Inc.'s growth is presented. Currently, the company's revenue is estimated to be around $1 billion. Since 2004, the company was able to build patient towers, an outpatient facility in Lebanon, and was able to acquire the Group Health Associates physician practice. TriHealth recently hired 500 nurses in order to meet its needs.

34261 ■ *"Employers See Workers' Comp Rates Rising" in Sacramento Business Journal (Vol. 28, April 8, 2011, No. 6, pp. 1)*
Pub: Sacramento Business Journal
Ed: Kelly Johnson. **Description:** Employers in California are facing higher workers compensation costs. Increased medical costs and litigation are seen to drive the trend.

34262 ■ *"Employers Waking Up to Effects of Workers' Sleep Problems" in Crain's Cleveland Business (Vol. 28, December 3, 2007, No. 48, pp. 18)*
Pub: Crain Communications, Inc.
Ed: Jennifer Keirn. **Description:** Employers are beginning to realize that poor sleep quality can impact their bottom lines with higher health care costs and more lost-time accidents. The National Institutes of Health estimates that sleep deprivation, sleep disorders and excessive daytime sleepiness add about $15 billion to our national health care bill and cost employers $50 billion in lost productivity.

34263 ■ *"Ending the Ebola Death Sentence" in Canadian Business (Vol. 83, August 17, 2010, No. 13-14, pp. 22)*
Pub: Rogers Media Ltd.
Ed: Michael McCullough. **Description:** US Army Medical Research Institute of Infectious Diseases made a $140 million agreement with Tekmira Pharmaceuticals Corporation to develop both a drug delivery system and delivery technology for curing the Ebola virus. Tekmira's delivery technology, which has been shown to halt Ebola in laboratory animals, might be the key to finding a cure.

34264 ■ *Episcopal Church Annual*
Pub: Morehouse Publishing
Contact: Jeanne Smith, Manager
E-mail: jsmith@morehousegroup.com
URL(s): www.morehousepublishing.org/epchan.htm. **Released:** Annual; February. **Price:** $45, Individuals list price. **Covers:** The churches and clergy of the Episcopal Church; seminaries, training schools, retreat centers, and social service agencies; dioceses, and provinces of Anglican Communion. **Entries include:** Name, address, phone of churches; name and address of clergy members; staff size, membership; the organizations, officers, and other information for the Episcopal Church in the United States of America with contacts, addresses, and phone numbers. **Database includes:** Information and statistics on dioceses, the structure of the church, and its institutions; biographies, with photographs, of recently consecrated bishops. **Arrangement:** Clergy list is alphabetical; diocesan list is alphabetical. **Indexes:** Alphabetical by categories; Classified Buyers' Guide classified by subject; alphabetical by advertisers.

34265 ■ *"Ethics and the End of Life" in Crain's Chicago Business (Vol. 34, October 24, 2011, No. 42, pp. 31)*
Pub: Crain Communications Inc.
Ed: Lisa Bertagnoli. **Description:** Technology has enabled doctors to provide more and better methods for helping patients, however end of life issues faced by medical ethicists are discussed.

34266 ■ *"Everett Hospice Planned" in Puget Sound Business Journal (Vol. 29, September 26, 2008, No. 23, pp. 1)*
Pub: American City Business Journals
Ed: Peter Neurath. **Description:** Providence Senior and Community Services is pursuing a purchase-and-sales agreement for land in Everett to build a $9.7 million 20-bed hospice facility. The organization plans to break ground on the new facility in 2009.

34267 ■ *"Expect Action on Health Care and the Economy" in Contractor (Vol. 57, January 2010, No. 1, pp. 30)*
Pub: Penton Media, Inc.

Ed: Kevin Schwalb. **Description:** The Plumbing-Heating-Cooling Contractors National Association is working to solidify its standing in the public policy arena as the legislative agenda will focus on health care reform, estate tax and immigration reform, all of which will impact the industries.

34268 ■ *"Experts Take the Temp of Obama Plan" in The Business Journal-Serving Metropolitan Kansas City (Vol. 27, November 14, 2008, No. 10)*
Pub: American City Business Journals, Inc.

Ed: Rob Roberts. **Description:** Kansas City, Missouri-based employee benefits experts say president-elect Barack Obama's health care reform plan is on track. Insurance for children and capitalization for health information technology are seen as priority areas. The plan is aimed at reducing the number of uninsured people in the United States.

34269 ■ *"Family Takes Wind Turbine Companies to Court Over Gag Clauses on Health Effects of Turbines" in CNW Group (September 12, 2011)*
Pub: CNW Group
Contact: Carolyn McGill-Davidson, President

Description: Shawn and Trisha Drennan are concerned about the negative experiences other have had with wind turbines close to their homes, including adverse health effects. The couple's home will be approximately 650 meters from the Kingsbridge II wind farm project in Ontario, Canada.

34270 ■ *"Feds to Pay University $20M" in Business Courier (Vol. 27, July 23, 2010, No. 12, pp. 3)*
Pub: Business Courier

Ed: James Ritchie. **Description:** The U.S. government is set to pay University Hospital and medical residents who trained there $20 million as part of a tax dispute settlement. Around 1,000 former residents are to receive tax refunds. But the hospital must provide the U.S. Internal Revenue Service with extensive documentation.

34271 ■ *"Fitness: Dispelling Rocky Mountain Myths Key to Wellness" in Employee Benefit News (Vol. 25, November 1, 2011, No. 14, pp. 12)*
Pub: SourceMedia Inc.

Ed: Andrea Davis. **Description:** Andrew Sykes, chairman of Health at Work Wellness Actuaries, states that it is a myth that Colorado is ranked as the healthiest state in America. Sykes helped implement a wellness programs at Brighton School District in the Denver area.

34272 ■ *"Five-Ring Circus" in Entrepreneur (Vol. 35, November 2007, No. 11, pp. 76)*
Pub: Entrepreneur Media Inc.

Ed: Scott Bernard Nelson. **Description:** China's economy is growing and is expected to do well even after the 2008 Olympics, but growth could slow from eleven percent to eight or nine percent. Chinese portfolio concerns with regard to health and environmental records and bureaucratic fraud are discussed.

34273 ■ *The Flaw of Averages: Why We Underestimate Risk in the Face of Uncertainty*
Pub: John Wiley & Sons, Inc.

Ed: Sam L. Savage. **Released:** June 3, 2009. **Price:** $22.95. **Description:** Personal and business plans are based on uncertainties on a daily basis. The common avoidable mistake individuals make in assessing risk in the face of uncertainty is defined. The explains why plans based on average assumptions are wrong, on average, in areas as diverse as finance, healthcare, accounting, the war on terror, and climate change.

34274 ■ *"Flue Vaccines are Going Green" in Canadian Business (Vol. 83, September 14, 2010, No. 15, pp. 24)*
Pub: Rogers Media Ltd.

Ed: Angelia Chapman. **Description:** Quebec-based Medicago has found a solution to the bottleneck in the production of influenza vaccines by using plant-based processes instead of egg-based systems. Medicago's US Department of Defense funded research has produced the technology that speeds up the production time for vaccines by almost two-thirds. Insights into Medicago's patented process are also given.

34275 ■ *"For Gilead, Growth Beyond AIDS" in Barron's (Vol. 88, June 30, 2008, No. 26, pp. 18)*
Pub: Dow Jones & Co., Inc.

Ed: Jay Palmer. **Description:** First-quarter 2008 revenue for Gilead Sciences grew by 22 percent and an earnings gain of 19 percent thanks to their HIV-treatment drugs that comprised over two-thirds of the company's sales in 2007. An analyst has a 12-month target from June, 2008 of 65 per share. The factors behind the company's prospects are also discussed.

34276 ■ *"For Hospitals, a Dating Game" in Business Courier (Vol. 26, December 4, 2009, No. 32, pp. 1)*
Pub: American City Business Journals, Inc.

Ed: James Ritchie. **Description:** Drake Center, Fort Hamilton Hospital, and West Chester Medical Center are among the members of Cincinnati's Health Alliance looking for potential buyers or partners. Meanwhile, Jewish Hospital, another member of the Alliance, will be bought by Mercy Health Partners by January 7, 2010.

34277 ■ *"Former Synthes Officers Receive Prison Sentences" in Wall Street Journal Eastern Edition (November 22 , 2011, pp. B4)*
Pub: Dow Jones & Company Inc.

Ed: Peter Loftus. **Description:** Michael D. Huggins, formerly chief operating officer of medical-device maker Synthes Ltd., and Thomas B. Higgins, formerly the president of Synthes spine unit, were given prison sentences of nine months while a third executive, John J. Walsh, formerly director of regulatory and clinical affairs in the spine division, was given a five-month sentence for their involvement in the promotion of the unauthorized use of a bone cement produced by the company.

34278 ■ *"From OTC Sellers to Surgeons, Healthcare Marketers Target Women to Achieve Growth" in Marketing to Women (February 2008)*
Pub: EPM Communications Inc.
Contact: Ira Mayer, President
E-mail: imayer@epmcom.com

Description: Healthcare companies are targeting women with ad campaigns, new product development and new technology in order to reach and develop brand loyalty.

34279 ■ *"Generation Y: Engaging the Invincibles" in Employee Benefit News (Vol. 25, November 1, 2011, No. 14, pp. 22)*
Pub: SourceMedia Inc.

Ed: Bremma Shebel, Dannel Dan. **Description:** Employers will need to engage younger workers about healthcare decisions and lifestyle improvement as they become the majority worker as boomers retire.

34280 ■ *"Genetic Counselor" in Occupational Outlook Quarterly (Vol. 55, Summer 2011, No. 2, pp. 34)*
Pub: U.S. Bureau of Labor Statistics

Ed: John Mullins. **Description:** Genetic counseling involves the practice of informing clients about genetic disorders and to help them understand and manage a disorder. There are approximately 2,400 certified genetic counselors in the U.S. and earn a median annual salary of about $63,000, according to the American Board of Genetic Counseling. The US Bureau of Labor Statistics does not have data on employment or wages for genetic counselors.

34281 ■ *"Giving Biotech Startups a Hand" in Philadelphia Business Journal (Vol. 28, January 8, 2010, No. 47, pp. 1)*
Pub: American City Business Journals

Ed: John George. **Description:** Elkins Park, Pennsylvania-based BioStrategy Partners is a virtual life sciences incubator that is seeking to improve the dull ranking of Philadelphia in the small business vitality index of life sciences. BioStrategy provides technology and business development services to startup life sciences companies and university-based research projects.

34282 ■ *Global Health Directory*
Pub: Global Health Council
Contact: William Foege, Director

URL(s): www.globalhealth.org. **Ed:** Annmarie Christensen. **Released:** Irregular; latest edition 2003-2004. **Covers:** Over 500 private voluntary organizations, universities, civic groups, professional associations, and other groups involved with global health. **Entries include:** Organization name, address, e-mail, website, contact name, number of employees, mission, services, regions served, publications, internships available, and volunteer information. **Arrangement:** Classified by title of organization.

34283 ■ *"Glossary of Health Benefit Terms" in HRMagazine (Vol. 53, August 2008, No. 8, pp. 78)*
Pub: Society for Human Resource Management
Contact: Henry G. Jackson, President
E-mail: hjackson@shrm.org

Description: Glossary of health benefit terms is presented to help when choosing a health benefits package.

34284 ■ *"Good for Business: Houston is a Hot Spot for Economic Growth" in Black Enterprise (Vol. 37, October 2006, No. 3, pp. 216)*
Pub: Earl G. Graves Publishing Co. Inc.

Ed: Jeanette Valentine. **Description:** Fast-growing sectors in the biotechnology and healthcare industries are among the driving forces of Houston's economic growth. More than 76,000 small businesses in the area employ about one in four area workers, according to the Small Business Administration. Housing and business costs are 26 and 11 percent below the national average, respectively, garnering the attention of corporate giants.

34285 ■ *"Halls Give Hospital Drive $11 Million Infusion" in The Business Journal-Serving Metropolitan Kansas City (Vol. 26, July 18, 2008)*
Pub: American City Business Journals, Inc.

Ed: Rob Roberts. **Description:** Don Hall, chairman of Hallmark Cards Inc., and eight family members have announced that they will give $11 million to Children's Mercy Hospitals and Clinics for its $800 million expansion plan. Hall Family Foundation president Bill Hall that contributions such as that for Children's Mercy reflect the charitable interests of the foundation's board and founders. The possible impacts of the Hall's donation are analyzed.

34286 ■ *"Health Alliance Could Sell Group" in Business Courier (Vol. 27, June 18, 2010, No. 7, pp. 1)*
Pub: Business Courier

Ed: James Ritchie. **Description:** Health Alliance could sell the 31-doctor Greater Cincinnati Associated Physicians Group. The group has seen several members withdraw ever since the group filed a complaint asking to be released from services to Health Alliance.

34287 ■ *"Health Care Braces for Federal Cuts" in Boston Business Journal (Vol. 29, August 19, 2011, No. 15, pp. 1)*
Pub: American City Business Journals Inc.

Ed: Scott Dance. **Description:** The healthcare industry in Baltimore is expecting negative effects from the federal debt ceiling on Medicare and Medicaid spending. Medicare funds are expected to be slashed and could impact hospitals and doctors.

34288 ■ *"Health Care Checkup" in Business Courier (Vol. 24, November 16, 2008, No. 31, pp. 1)*
Pub: American City Business Journals, Inc.
Ed: James Ritchie. **Description:** Discusses a survey of 300 Greater Cincinnati residents about the quality of local health care and access to doctors indicates that there were improvements from five years ago. About 65 percent of those surveyed said the quality of their health care is good or excellent, a 12 percent improvement from a similar survey conducted five years ago. The other findings of the survey are also presented.

34289 ■ *"Health Care of the Future" in Business Journal Serving Greater Tampa Bay (Vol. 30, November 19, 2010, No. 48, pp. 1)*
Pub: Tampa Bay Business Journal
Ed: Margie Manning. **Description:** Information about accountable care organizations (ACO), which are integrated care systems with doctors and hospitals working closely together to handle patient care, is provided. The Patient Protection and Affordable Care Act paved the way for ACOs as Medicare demonstration projects.

34290 ■ *"Health-Care Highway" in Saint Louis Business Journal (Vol. 32, October 14, 2011, No. 7, pp. 1)*
Pub: Saint Louis Business Journal
Ed: Angela Mueller. **Description:** Around $2.6 billion will be invested in health care facilities along the Highway 64/40 corridor in St. Louis, Missouri. Mercy Hospital is planning to invest $19 million in a virtual care center. St. Elizabeth's Hospital on the other hand, will purchase 105 acres in the corridor.

34291 ■ *"Health Care Leads Sectors Attracting Capital" in Hispanic Business (March 2008, pp. 14-16, 18)*
Pub: Hispanic Business
Ed: Scott Williams. **Description:** U. S. Hispanic healthcare, media, and food were the key industries in the U.S. gaining investors in 2007.

34292 ■ *"Health Care Leads Sectors Attracting Capital" in Hispanic Business (Vol. 30, March 2008, No. 3, pp. 14)*
Pub: Hispanic Business
Ed: Scott Williams. **Description:** Discusses the capital gains of Hispanic-owned companies and other Hispanic leaders in the investment and retail fields in the year 2007. Sectors like health care, media, food and technology saw a healthy flow of capital due to successful mergers, acquisitions and increased private equity investments.

34293 ■ *"Health Centers Plan Expansion" in Crain's Detroit Business (Vol. 25, June 15, 2009, No. 24, pp. 3)*
Pub: Crain Communications Inc. - Detroit
Ed: Jay Greene. **Description:** Detroit has five federally qualified health centers that plan to receive over $3 million in federal stimulus money that will be used to expand projects that will care for uninsured patients.

34294 ■ *Health Groups in Washington: A Directory*
Pub: National Health Council
Contact: Myrl Weinberg, President
URL(s): www.nationalhealthcouncil.org/pages/publications.php. **Released:** Biennial; August of odd years; Latest edition 2009. **Price:** $40, Members; $60, Nonmembers. **Covers:** Over 900 professional, voluntary, consumer, insurance, union, business, and academic organizations with some impact on the development of federal health policies. **Entries include:** Name of organization, address, phone, e-mail address, website address, names of Washington representatives. **Arrangement:** Alphabetical. **Indexes:** Subject index; personnel index.

34295 ■ *"Health IT Regulations Generate Static Among Providers" in Philadelphia Business Journal (Vol. 28, January 29, 2010, No. 50, pp. 1)*
Pub: American City Business Journals
Ed: John George. **Description:** US Centers for Medicaid and Medicare Services and the Office of the National Coordinator for Health Information Technology have proposed rules regarding the meaningful use of electronic health records. The rules must be complied with by hospitals and physicians to qualify for federal stimulus funds.

34296 ■ *"Health Job Shift Looms" in Boston Business Journal (Vol. 31, June 3, 2011, No. 19, pp. 3)*
Pub: Boston Business Journal
Ed: Julie M. Donnelly. **Description:** Pending health care payment reform in Massachusetts is seen to adversely impact hospital staff. Hospitals are also seen to serve more patients once the bill is approved.

34297 ■ *"Health Nuts and Bolts" in Entrepreneur (Vol. 36, April 2008, No. 4, pp. 24)*
Pub: Entrepreneur Media, Inc.
Ed: Jacquelyn Lynn. **Description:** Encouraging employees to develop good eating habits can promote productivity at work. Ways on how to improve employee eating habits include employers setting a good example themselves and offering employees healthy options. Other details about the topic are discussed.

34298 ■ *"Health Providers Throw Lifeline to Clinics" in Sacramento Business Journal (Vol. 25, July 25, 2008, No. 21, pp. 1)*
Pub: American City Business Journals, Inc.
Ed: Kathy Robertson. **Description:** Health Net of California Inc., Catholic Healthcare West and Sutter Health are each providing up to $5 million in no-interest and low-interest loans to clinics in California, while the Sisters of Mercy of the Americas Burlingame Regional Community is offering $300,000. Other details on the short term loans are discussed.

34299 ■ *"Health Reform Could Expand HSA-Based Plans" in Workforce Management (Vol. 88, December 14, 2009, No. 13, pp. 6)*
Pub: Crain Communications Inc.
Ed: Jeremy Smerd. **Description:** HSA-qualified plans are the cheapest insurance plans on the market as they have a higher deductible but cost less upfront. If health care reform passes, HSA-qualified plans should benefit greatly.

34300 ■ *"Health Reform How-To" in Business Courier (Vol. 26, December 11, 2009, No. 33, pp. 1)*
Pub: American City Business Journals, Inc.
Ed: James Ritchie. **Description:** Greater Cincinnati health care leaders shared views about the health care reform bill. Respondents included the Cincinnati Visiting Nurse's Wallen Falberg, healthcare consultant Hirsch Cohen, Greater Cincinnati Health Council's Coleen O'Toole, Employer Health Care Alliance's Sharron DiMario, Legal Aid Society of Greater Cincinnati's Col Owens, Christ Hospital's Susan Croushore, and Humana of Ohio's Tim Cappel.

34301 ■ *"Healthcare: How To Get a Better Deal" in Inc. (November 2007, pp. 34)*
Pub: Gruner & Jahr USA Publishing
Ed: Sarah Goldstein. **Description:** Things to consider when choosing an insurance carrier for your employees are explored.

34302 ■ *"HealthTronics Eager to Buy" in Austin Business Journallnc. (Vol. 28, September 12, 2008, No. 26, pp. 1)*
Pub: American City Business Journals
Ed: Laura Hipp. **Description:** HealthTronics Inc., an Austin, Texas urology equipment company has repeated its offer to buy Endocare Inc., an Irvine, California tumor technology firm for $26.9 million. The proposal has been revised to allow Endocare shareholders to choose between HealthTronics cash or shares. Endocare has not commented on the offer.

34303 ■ *"Healthy Dose of Vitality" in Business Courier (Vol. 24, February 29, 2008, No. 47, pp. 1)*
Pub: American City Business Journals, Inc.
Ed: Dan Monk. **Description:** Healthy Advice plans to become a leading consumer brand and expand to pharmacies and hospitals. The growth opportunities for healthy Advice are discussed.

34304 ■ *"Hearing Damage Leads to Settlement" in Register-Guard (August 13, 2011)*
Pub: The Register-Guard
Ed: Karen McCowan. **Description:** Cynergy Pest Control lost a court battle when a rural Cottage Grove man was granted a $37,000 settlement after his hearing was damaged by the pest control companies method to eradicate gophers, using blasts in his neighbor's yard.

34305 ■ *"Heart Hospitals Analyzed" in Philadelphia Business Journal (Vol. 30, September 2, 2011, No. 29, pp. 1)*
Pub: American City Business Journals Inc.
Ed: John George. **Description:** Centers for Medicare and Medicaid Services (CMS) released updated data on mortality rates for heart attack patients as hospitals in Pennsylvania. Doylestown Hospital posted the lowest mortality rates with 10.9 percent, tying the fourth best in the entire nation. Other details on the CMS data are presented.

34306 ■ *"Heart Test No Boom for BG Medical" in Boston Business Journal (Vol. 31, June 17, 2011, No. 21, pp. 1)*
Pub: Boston Business Journal
Ed: Julie M. Donnelly. **Description:** The Galectin-3 test failed to boost stock prices of its manufacturer, BG Medicine, which has fallen to $6.06/share. The company hopes that its revenue will be boosted by widespread adoption of an automated and faster version of the test, which diagnoses for heart failure.

34307 ■ *"Help Wanted: 100 Hospitals IT Workers" in Business Courier (Vol. 27, October 8, 2010, No. 23, pp. 1)*
Pub: Business Courier
Ed: James Ritchie. **Description:** Hospitals in the Greater Cincinnati area are expected to hire more than 100 information technology (IT) workers to help digitize medical records. Financial incentives from the health care reform bill encouraged investments in electronic medical record systems, increasing the demand for IT workers that would help make information exchange across the healthcare system easier.

34308 ■ *"Henry Ford Health Leases Lab Space at TechTown" in Crain's Detroit Business (Vol. 24, March 31, 2008, No. 13, pp. 5)*
Pub: Crain Communications, Inc.
Ed: Tom Henderson. **Description:** Henry Ford Health System has signed a seven-year lease at TechTown, the high-tech incubator and research park affiliated with Wayne State University, to take over 14,000 square feet of space for four research groups and laboratories. Construction has already begun and Henry Ford officials hope to take occupancy as early as June 1.

34309 ■ *"HER's: the Future is Free" in Benzinga.com (October 29, 2011)*
Pub: Benzinga.com
Ed: Benzinga Staff. **Description:** In order to create and maintain electronic health records that connects every physician and hospital it is essential to create a reliable, easy-to-use, certified Web-based ambulatory ERH using an ad-supported model. eBay seems to be the company showing the most potential for improving services to physicians and consumers, but requires sellers to pay fees based upon sales price.

34310 ■ *"His Banking Industry Software Never Caught On, so Bill Randle is Now Targeting the Health Care Market" in Inc. (March 2008)*
Pub: Gruner & Jahr USA Publishing
Ed: Alex Salkever. **Description:** Profile of Bill Randle, bank executive turned entrepreneur; Randle tells how he changed his focus for his company from banking

software to healthcare software. The firm employs ten people who secure online billing and recordkeeping systems for hospitals and insurers. Randle discusses critical decisions that will impact his firm in the coming year. Three experts offer advice.

34311 ■ *"Hopkins, UMd Worry Reduced NIH Budget Will Impact Research" in Boston Business Journal (Vol. 29, August 19, 2011, No. 15, pp. 1)*
Pub: American City Business Journals Inc.
Ed: Scott Dance. **Description:** The budget for the National Institutes of Health (NIH) is slated to be cut by at least 7.9 percent to $2.5 billion in 2013. This will have a big negative effect on medical and biotech research in Maryland, especially Johns Hopkins University and University of Maryland, Baltimore which could face stiffer completion for grants from the NIH.

34312 ■ *"Hospital Errors Made Public" in Sacramento Business Journal (Vol. 25, August 8, 2008, No. 23, pp. 1)*
Pub: American City Business Journals, Inc.
Ed: Kathy Robertson. **Description:** California hospitals reported 1,224 serious and preventable errors for the fiscal year ended June 30, 2008. Consumer groups have expressed concerns at the number and level of violations. Views and information on the errors, as well as a table detailing the number of hospital errors classified by error type, are presented.

34313 ■ *"Hospital Fighting for Its Life; Board of St. Anthony Scrambles to Stem Losses" in Crain's Chicago Business (April 28, 2008)*
Pub: Crain Communications, Inc.
Ed: Mike Colias. **Description:** Chicago's Catholic health chain was looking to sell the money-losing hospital St. Anthony Hospital on the West Side but with the financial picture improving and no merger offers in the works the investment bank hired to shop the hospital is hoping to operate the 111-year-old facility as an independent entity. St. Anthony serves as a 'safety net' for the region since an increasing number of its patients are uninsured or on public aid, which pays far less than commercial insurers.

34314 ■ *"Hospital to Get $72M Makeover" in Austin Business JournalInc. (Vol. 29, January 15, 2010, No. 45, pp. 1)*
Pub: American City Business Journals
Ed: Sandra Zaragoza. **Description:** St. David's South Austin Medical Center, formerly St. David's South Austin Hospital, is undertaking an expansion and renovation project worth $72 million. Meanwhile, CEO Erol Akdamar has resigned to serve as CEO of Medical City Hospital in Dallas, Texas. A new CEO and a general contractor for the project are yet to be chosen by the hospital.

34315 ■ *"Hospital Jobs" in Baltimore Business Journal (Vol. 28, June 25, 2010, No. 7, pp. 1)*
Pub: Baltimore Business Journal
Ed: Scott Graham. **Description:** Greater Baltimore, Maryland has four hospitals that are in the middle of transforming their campuses with new facilities for treating various patients. Construction at Mercy Medical Center, Johns Hopkins Hospital, Franklin Square Hospital and Anne Rundle Hospital has helped bring the construction industry back to life. Insights into the hiring plans of these hospitals are also included.

34316 ■ *"Hospital Moves Toward Self-Rule" in Business Courier (Vol. 24, December 7, 2008, No. 34, pp. 1)*
Pub: American City Business Journals, Inc.
Ed: James Ritchie. **Description:** Christ Hospital is planning on hiring 100 employees that will work on its newly leased facility located in Eden Park Drive.

34317 ■ *"Hospital Pegged for Lakeway" in Austin Business JournalInc. (Vol. 28, August 8, 2008, No. 21, pp. A1)*
Pub: American City Business Journals
Ed: Kate Harrington. **Description:** Views and information on the development of the Lakeway Regional Medical Center in Texas, are presented. The hospital, which is expected to cost more than $250 million, will include 244,000 square feet of medical space. Shops, offices, hike-and-bike trails are also planned around hospital.

34318 ■ *"Hospital Revenue Healthier in 2009" in Orlando Business Journal (Vol. 26, February 5, 2010, No. 36, pp. 1)*
Pub: American City Business Journals
Ed: Melanie Stawicki Azam. **Description:** Orlando Health, Health Central and Adventist Health System are Florida-based hospital systems that generated the most profits in 2009. Orlando Health had the highest profit in 2009 at $73.3 million, contrary to about $31 million in losses in 2008. The increased profits are attributed to stock market recovery, cost-cutting initiatives, and rising patient volumes.

34319 ■ *"Hospital Tax Could Be a Separate Bill" in Business Journal-Milwaukee (Vol. 25, October 26, 2007, No. 4, pp. A1)*
Pub: American City Business Journals, Inc.
Ed: Elizabeth Sanders. **Description:** Hospital officials are working on reintroducing a hospital tax proposal that would increase Medicaid reimbursement, thereby generating millions of dollars of revenue for the Milwaukee-area hospitals. The bill sponsored by Governor Jim Doyle was supported by the Wisconsin Hospital Association. Details of the proposed hospital tax are presented.

34320 ■ *"Hospitals Face Big Whammy From State Fees" in Business Courier (Vol. 26, October 2, 2009, No. 23, pp. 1)*
Pub: American City Business Journals, Inc.
Ed: James Ritchie. **Description:** Ohio hospitals are facing losses of nearly $145 million in franchise fees which are set to be levied by the state. Ohio hospitals will be responsible for a total of $718 million franchise fees as required by 2010-2011 state budget but will recover only 80 percent of the amount in increased Medicaid fees. Possible effects of anticipated losses to Ohio hospitals are examined.

34321 ■ *"Hospitals Feel Pain from Slow Economy" in Business Courier (Vol. 27, September 3, 2010, No. 18, pp. 1)*
Pub: Business Courier
Ed: James Ritchie. **Description:** Hospitals in Cincinnati, Ohio have suffered from decreased revenues owing to the economic crises. Declining patient volumes and bad debt have also adversely impacted hospitals.

34322 ■ *"Hospitals Mandate Shots" in Business Courier (Vol. 27, November 19, 2010, No. 29, pp. 1)*
Pub: Business Courier
Ed: James Ritchie. **Description:** TriHealth has mandated that employees who refuse to get the vaccination shot for 2010 could be penalized with unpaid administrative leave. Other hospital employers, such as University Hospital and Cincinnati Children's Hospital and Medical Center have fired employees for forgoing flu shots. Vaccination rates among hospital employees are given.

34323 ■ *"Hospitals See Major Shift To Outpatient Care" in The Business Journal-Milwaukee (Vol. 25, September 12, 2008, No. 51, pp. A1)*
Pub: American City Business Journals, Inc.
Ed: Corrinne Hess. **Description:** Statistics show that the revenue of Wisconsin hospitals from outpatient medical care is about to surpass revenue from hospital patients who stay overnight. This revenue increase is attributed to new technology and less-invasive surgery. Trends show that the shift toward outpatient care actually started in the late 1980s and early 1990s.

34324 ■ *"Hospitals Try to Buy Smarter" in Crain's Detroit Business (Vol. 25, June 1, 2009, No. 22, pp. M025)*
Pub: Crain Communications Inc. - Detroit
Ed: Jay Greene. **Description:** Hospitals in southeast Michigan are using bulk discount purchasing of medical and non-medical supplies through group purchasing organizations in order to cut costs.

34325 ■ *How to Start a Home-Based Senior Care Business: Check-in-Care, Transportation Services, Shopping and Cooking*
Pub: Globe Pequot Press
Ed: James L. Ferry. **Released:** January 1, 2010. **Price:** $18.95. **Description:** Information is provided to start a home-based senior care business.

34326 ■ *"Human Bone Breakthrough" in Houston Business Journal (Vol. 40, January 8, 2010, No. 35, pp. 1)*
Pub: American City Business Journals
Ed: Casey Wooten. **Description:** Biotech startup company Osteosphere in Houston, Texas aims to market a technology in which laboratory-grown bone tissues can be processed to appear like a real human bone tissue. The technology was developed by a co-founder of the startup and it can be applied to bone disease and injury treatment. Osteophere's future plans, such as the search for possible investors, is also outlined.

34327 ■ *"Humana: Take Pay Cut or Get Out" in Business Courier (Vol. 24, February 1, 2008, No. 43, pp. 1)*
Pub: American City Business Journals, Inc.
Ed: James Ritchie. **Description:** Insurer Humana Inc. is removing some surgery centers from its network for refusing to welcome the new payment system. Evendale Surgery Center and the Surgery Center of Cincinnati will be removed from the network because they resist the newly imposed lower rates. Speculations over Humana's decision are discussed.

34328 ■ *"IBC Reverses Member Slide" in Philadelphia Business Journal (Vol. 30, September 23, 2011, No. 32, pp. 1)*
Pub: American City Business Journals Inc.
Ed: John George. **Description:** Health insurer Independence Blue Cross (IBC) added more than 40,000 members across all product lines since the start of 2011. It has 2.2 million members in Pennsylvania's Philadelphia region and 3.1 million members across the U.S. Services and other growth-related plans of IBC are covered.

34329 ■ *"Impressive Numbers: Companies Experience Substantial Increases in Dollars, Employment" in Hispanic Business (July-August 2007)*
Pub: Hispanic Business
Ed: Derek Reveron. **Description:** Profiles of five fastest growing Hispanic companies reporting increases in revenue and employment include Brightstar, distributor of wireless products; Greenway Ford Inc., a car dealership; Fred Loya Insurance, auto insurance carrier; and Group O, packaging company; and Diverse Staffing, Inc., an employment and staffing firm.

34330 ■ *"IMRA's Ultrafast Lasers Bring Precision, profits; Ann Arbor Company Eyes Expansion" in Crain's Detroit Business (March 10, 2008)*
Pub: Crain Communications, Inc.
Ed: Tom Henderson. **Description:** IMRA America Inc. plans to expand its headquarters and has applied for permits to build a fourth building that will house research and development facilities and allow the company more room for manufacturing; the company plans to add about 20 more employees that would include research scientists, manufacturing and assembly workers, engineers and salespeople. The growth is due mainly to a new technology of ultrafast fiber lasers that reduce side effects for those getting eye surgeries and help manufacturers of computer chips to reduce their size and cost.

34331 ■ *"In It For the Long Run" in Business Journal-Serving Phoenix & the Valley of the Sun (Vol. 30, August 20, 2010, No. 50, pp. 1)*
Pub: Phoenix Business Journal
Ed: Angela Gonzales. **Description:** Cancer survivor Helene Neville has finished a record-breaking 2,520-mile run in 93 days and then celebrated her 50th birthday despite being diagnosed with Hodgkins' lymphoma in 1991. Neveille, who is also a Phoenix area

registered nurse, made stops along the way to promote her book, 'Nurses in Shape'. Neville also discusses how she fought her cancer through running.

34332 ■ *"In the Raw: Karyn Calabrese Brings Healthy Dining to a New Sophisticated Level" in Black Enterprise (Vol. 41, September 2010)*
Pub: Earl G. Graves Publishing Co. Inc.

Ed: Sonia Alleyne. **Description:** Profile of Karyn Calabrese whose businesses are based in Chicago, Illinois. Calabrese has launched a complete line of products (vitamins and beauty items), services (spa, chiropractic, and acupuncture treatments), and restaurants to bring health dining and lifestyles to a better level.

34333 ■ *"Injury and Illness Data" in Montly Labor Review (Vol. 133, September 2010, No. 9, pp. 147)*
Pub: Bureau of Labor Statistics

Description: Occupational injury and illness rates by industry in the U.S. are presented.

34334 ■ *"Insurers Warn Brokers" in Sacramento Business Journal (Vol. 25, August 22, 2008, No. 25, pp. 1)*
Pub: American City Business Journals, Inc.

Ed: Kathy Robertson. **Description:** Sacramento, California-based health plans have warned insurance brokers not to combine two different kinds of insurance products or they will be stricken from the sales network. The health plans also asked employers to promise not to combine plans with self-insurance. Such schemes are seen to destroy lower-premium health products.

34335 ■ *"Internet Translation Service Helps Burmese" in News-Sentinel (May 10, 2011)*
Pub: New-Sentinel

Ed: Ellie Bogue. **Description:** Catherine Kasper Place, Parkview Health Community Outreach, Allen County-Fort Wayne Department of Health and Advantage Health have partnered to help the Burmese Community in the area by providing an online service that links doctors' offices with translators in order to provide better healthcare.

34336 ■ *"Inventive Doctor New Venture Partner" in Houston Business Journal (Vol. 40, January 29, 2010, No. 38, pp. A2)*
Pub: American City Business Journals

Ed: Ford Gunter. **Description:** Dr. Billy Cohn, a surgeon from Houston, Texas has been named as venture partner for venture firm Sante Ventures LLC of Austin, Texas. Cohn will be responsible for seeing marketable developing technologies in the medical industry. The motivation for Cohn's naming as venture partner is his development of a minimally invasive therapy for end-stage renal disease.

34337 ■ *"Investigation Hints at Workers' Comp Trouble" in Sacramento Business Journal (Vol. 25, July 4, 2008, No. 18, pp. 1)*
Pub: American City Business Journals, Inc.

Ed: Kelly Johnson. **Description:** In 500 California firms, a survey of worker compensation revealed that 38 percent of the companies had problems with required coverage. Government investigators are bothered that 107 companies did not respond to the official inquiry. Other views and information on the survey and on the expected economic implications of the findings are presented.

34338 ■ *"Is Hawaii Ready for Universal Health Care?" in Hawaii Business (Vol. 53, February 2008, No. 8, pp. 26)*
Pub: Hawaii Business Publishing

Description: Representative Lyn Finnegan does not believe that a universal health is good for Hawaii as health insurance for everyone will be difficult to achieve. Representative John M. Mizuno says that House Bill 1008 introduced in the state was a landmark for Hawaii as it will provide the people with health care insurance. Other details about their opinion on the topic are presented.

34339 ■ *"Is Your Employees' BMI Your Business?" in Canadian Business (Vol. 83, September 14, 2010, No. 15, pp. 98)*
Pub: Rogers Media Ltd.

Ed: Jacqueline Nelson. **Description:** Canada's Public Health Agency's research shows that there is a solid business case for companies to promote active living to their employees. However, employers must toe the line between being helpful and being invasive. Insights into the issues faces by companies when introducing health programs are discussed.

34340 ■ *It's Your Life!: A Gynecologist's Guide for Taking Control of It*
Pub: Blue Dolphin Publishing Inc.
Contact: Paul M. Clemens, President
URL(s): www.bluedolphinpublishing.com. **Price:** $16.95, Individuals Paperback; $24.95, Individuals Cloth. **Publication includes:** Resources covering health care for women. **Entries include:** Publication name, address. Principal content of publication is articles and suggestions on health care and social and emotional issues for women. **Indexes:** Yes.

34341 ■ *"Kaiser Permanente's Innovation on the Front Lines" in Harvard Business Review (Vol. 88, September 2010, No. 9, pp. 92)*
Pub: Harvard Business School Publishing
Ed: Lew McCreary. **Description:** Kaiser Permanente's human-centered model for organizational effectiveness emphasizes the roles of patients and providers as collaborators driving quality improvement and innovation.

34342 ■ *"Kari Leong" in Hawaii Business (Vol. 53, October 2007, No. 4, pp. 39)*
Pub: Hawaii Business Publishing
Ed: Cathy S. Cruz-George. **Description:** Greater Good Inc. president Kari Leong is the number 1 fittest female executive in Hawaii for 2007. Leong exercises at the gym and at her home, and carries her two children for strength training. The physical activities she had undergone during her college life at the Gonzaga University are discussed.

34343 ■ *"The Keeper of Records" in Black Enterprise (Vol. 41, December 2010, No. 5, pp. 54)*
Pub: Earl G. Graves Publishing Co. Inc.
Ed: Denise Campbell. **Description:** Medical billing and coding, submission of claims to health insurance companies and Medicare or Medicaid for payment is one of the fastest growing disciplines in healthcare.

34344 ■ *"Kids in Crisis" in Employee Benefit News (Vol. 25, November 1, 2011, No. 14, pp. 26)*
Pub: SourceMedia Inc.
Ed: Lisa V. Gillespie. **Description:** Employers and vendor are taking more aggressive steps to help battle childhood obesity.

34345 ■ *"King of the Crib: How Good Samaritan Became Ohio's Baby HQ" in Business Courier (Vol. 27, June 18, 2010, No. 7, pp. 1)*
Pub: Business Courier
Ed: James Ritchie. **Description:** Cincinnati's Good Samaritan hospital had 6,875 live births in 2009, which is more than any other hospital in Ohio. They specialize in the highest-risk pregnancies and deliveries and other hospitals are trying to grab Good Samaritan's share in this niche.

34346 ■ *"Know Your Bones: Take Your Bone Health Seriously" in Women In Business (Vol. 62, June 2010, No. 2, pp. 40)*
Pub: American Business Women's Association
Description: Bone health for women with postmenopausal osteoporosis is encouraged to help create an appropriate health plan that includes exercise, diet and medication. Questions to consider when discussing possible plans with health care providers are presented.

34347 ■ *"Kubicki Juggles Lineup at Vianda" in Business Courier (Vol. 26, December 11, 2009, No. 33, pp. 1)*
Pub: American City Business Journals, Inc.
Ed: Dan Monk. **Description:** Cincinnati real estate developer Chuck Kubicki replaced the management team of Vianda LLC and cancelled contracts with two vendors that caused a surge of customer complaints. Vianda is a direct-response marketing firm that sells and distributes dietary supplements for wellness and sexual performance.

34348 ■ *"A Late Night Run: After-Hours Pediatric Practice Fills Void for Affordable Urgent Care" in Black Enterprise (February 2008)*
Pub: Earl G. Graves Publishing Co. Inc.
Ed: Erinn R. Johnson. **Description:** Practicing pediatricians in Texas founded the Night Light After Hours Pediatrics facility in order to provide urgent care to children without the trauma witnessed in emergency rooms at hospitals.

34349 ■ *"Lawrence: Larger than Life Sciences" in Business Journal-Serving Metropolitan Kansas City (Vol. 26, November 2, 2007, No. 8, pp. 1)*
Pub: American City Business Journals, Inc.
Ed: Rob Roberts. **Description:** Greater Kansas City Community Foundation has more than $1 billion to spend on life sciences initiatives and chairwoman Sandra Lawrence will unveil a multimillion-dollar master plan for Children's Mercy Hospitals and Clinics. Details regarding Lawrence's dedication to the foundation are discussed.

34350 ■ *"Lean Machine" in Crain's Detroit Business (Vol. 26, Jan. 11, 2010)*
Pub: Crain Communications Inc.
Ed: Jay Greene. **Description:** Reducing waste and becoming more efficient is a goal of many businesses involved in the health care industry. These firms are looking to the local manufacturing sector, comparing themselves in specifically to the auto industry, for ways in which to become more efficient.

34351 ■ *"Lean Machine; Health Care Follows Auto's Lead, Gears Up for Efficiency" in Crain's Detroit Business (Vol. 26, January 11, 2010)*
Pub: Crain Communications, Inc.
Ed: Jay Greene. **Description:** Reducing waste and becoming more efficient is a goal of many businesses involved in the health care industry. These firms are looking to the local manufacturing sector, comparing themselves in specifically to the auto industry, for ways in which to become more efficient.

34352 ■ *"Life's Work: Oliver Sacks" in Harvard Business Review (Vol. 88, November 2010, No. 11, pp. 152)*
Pub: Harvard Business School Publishing
Ed: Lisa Burrell. **Description:** Neurologist and author Oliver Sacks discusses whether different types of minds tend toward certain skills, physician-patient communication, and his own perspectives from being a patient himself.

34353 ■ *"Lifesavers" in Black Enterprise (Vol. 41, December 2010, No. 5, pp. 38)*
Pub: Earl G. Graves Publishing Co. Inc.
Ed: Tamara E. Holmes. **Description:** Profile of Interventional Nephrology Specialists Access Center and founders Dr. Omar Davis and Dr. Natarsha Grant; the center generated $5.5 million in revenue for 2009. Details on how they run their successful center are included.

34354 ■ *"The Little Biotech that Could" in Barron's (Vol. 89, July 27, 2009, No. 30, pp. 19)*
Pub: Dow Jones & Co., Inc.
Ed: Christopher C. Williams. **Description:** OSI Pharmaceuticals' shares is a compelling investment bet among small biotech firms due to its Tarceva anticancer drug which has a 23 percent market share as well as their strong balance sheet. OSI is planning to expand the use of Tarceva which could re-ignite sales and one analyst expects the shares to trade in the 40s one year from July 2009.

34355 ■ *"Local Hospitals Wage Wars on 'Bounce-Backs"' in Business Courier (Vol. 27, July 30, 2010, No. 13, pp. 1)*
Pub: Business Courier
Ed: James Ritchie. **Description:** Health care organizations in Greater Cincinnati area have tried a number of care and follow up programs, primarily

focused on congestive heart failure to prevent readmissions to hospitals. Hospital administrators have made the averting of bounce-backs a priority due to new federal government plans on reimbursement.

34356 ■ *"Local Researchers Get Cash Infusion" in Business Courier (Vol. 26, October 9, 2009, No. 24, pp. 1)*
Pub: American City Business Journals, Inc.
Ed: James Ritchie. **Description:** Cincinnati's Children's Hospital Medical Center and the University of Cincinnati researchers are set to receive at least $56 million from the stimulus bill. The cash infusion has reenergized research scientists and enhances Cincinnati's national clout as a major research center.

34357 ■ *"Losses Threaten Comp Care's Future Viability" in The Business Journal-Serving Greater Tampa Bay (Vol. 28, August 15, 2008, No. 34)*
Pub: American City Business Journals, Inc.
Ed: Margie Manning. **Description:** Comprehensive Care Corp. expressed that it may have to cease or drastically curtail its operations if it won't be able to raise additional funding in the next two or three months. The firm, which provides managed behavioral health care services, is also believed to be exploring a sale. Other views and information on Comprehensive Care's finances and plans are presented.

34358 ■ *Management Lessons from Mayo Clinic*
Pub: McGraw-Hill
Ed: Leonard L. Berry; Kent D. Seltman. **Released:** June 6, 2008. **Price:** $27.95. **Description:** Management practices employed by the Mayo Clinic are examined to show why it is one of the world's most successful health care facilities.

34359 ■ *Managing Health Benefits in Small and Mid-Sized Organizations*
Pub: Amacom
Ed: Patricia Halo. **Released:** July 1999. **Description:** Comprehensive guide for developing health care plans for companies employing between 50 and 5,000 employees in order to provide employees with better health care at lower prices.

34360 ■ *"Maryland Hospitals Cope with Rare Drop in Patient Admissions" in Boston Business Journal (Vol. 29, September 23, 2011, No. 20, pp. 1)*
Pub: American City Business Journals Inc.
Ed: Scott Dance. **Description:** Admissions to Maryland hospitals have dropped to less than 700,000 in fiscal year 2010 and initial figures for fiscal 2011 show in-patient admissions are now nearing 660,000. The decline can be partly attributed to new ways health insurers are paying hospitals for care and to the financial reward hospitals get for cutting back on admissions.

34361 ■ *"The Massachusetts Mess: Good Health Care Is Expensive" in Barron's (Vol. 89, July 27, 2009, No. 30, pp. 39)*
Pub: Dow Jones & Co., Inc.
Ed: Thomas G. Donlan. **Description:** Massachusetts' mandatory health insurance has produced the highest rate of insurance coverage among the states but the state is now unable to afford its dream of universal coverage just three years after they enacted it. This supposed model for federal health-care reform is turning out to be a joke.

34362 ■ *"mChip: Claros Diagnostics" in Inc. (Vol. 33, November 2011, No. 9, pp. 42)*
Pub: Inc. Magazine
Ed: Christine Lagorio. **Description:** Harvard University researchers have developed a device called the mChip that produces accurate blood tests in about 10 minutes. Plans to apply for FDA approval for the mChip in the US should happen in 2012.

34363 ■ *"Medicaid Expansion Could Prompt New Taxes, Program Cuts" in Baltimore Business Journal (Vol. 27, October 23, 2009, No. 24, pp. 1)*
Pub: American City Business Journals
Ed: Julekha Dash. **Description:** Effects of the expected federal expansion of Medicaid under federal health care reform on Maryland tax policy are presented. Health care executives believe new taxes are necessary for the state to pay for an expansion that could cost over $400 million to $600 million.

34364 ■ *"Medical Connectors: Meeting the Demands of Reliability, Portability, Size and Cost" in Canadian Electronics (February 2008)*
Pub: CLB Media Inc.
Ed: Murtaza Fidaali, Ted Worroll. **Description:** Component manufacturers who serve the medical industry need to ensure component reliability in order to maintain patient safety. Because of this, connectors in medical equipment are becoming more versatile. It is concluded that these manufacturers are facing challenges meeting the medical industry standards or reliability, miniaturization, portability, and cost.

34365 ■ *"Medical Pot Backers Say Industry Will Survive" in Sacramento Business Journal (Vol. 28, October 14, 2011, No. 33, pp. 1)*
Pub: Sacramento Business Journal
Ed: Melanie Turner. **Description:** Medical marijuana supporters have expected the industry to decline but will survive the federal restriction on growers and dispensaries across California. California Cannabis Association and National Cannabis Industry Association believe that some of the dispensaries will remain and the shakeout will lead to stronger state regulations.

34366 ■ *"Medicare Inc." in Canadian Business (Vol. 80, October 8, 2007, No. 20, pp. 160)*
Pub: Rogers Media
Ed: Erin Pooley. **Description:** State of Canada's health care system is discussed. A report by the Fraser Institute in Vancouver predicts that public health spending in six of ten provinces in the country will use more than half the revenues from all sources by 2020. Experts believe competition in the health care industry will help solve the current problems in the sector.

34367 ■ *"Medicare Plans Step Up Battle for Subscribers" in Sacramento Business Journal (Vol. 28, October 21, 2011, No. 34, pp. 1)*
Pub: Sacramento Business Journal
Ed: Kathy Robertson. **Description:** California's market for health plans have become increasingly competitive as more than 313,000 seniors try to figure out the best plans to meet their needs for 2012. Health plans are rated on Medicare materials to help consumers distinguish among the Medicare health maintenance organizations (HMOs).

34368 ■ *Medicare & You Handbook*
Pub: Health Care Financing Administration U.S. Department of Health & Human Service
URL(s): www.os.dhhs.gov/about/opdivs/hcfa.html. **Released:** Irregular; Latest edition 2010. **Price:** Free. **Publication includes:** Lists of Medicare carriers in individual states. Principal content includes discussion of what Medicare is, what its various options are, and what new benefits have been added recently.

34369 ■ *Memos to the Prime Minister: What Canada Could Be in the 21st Century*
Pub: John Wiley & Sons, Incorporated
Ed: Harvey Schacter. **Released:** April 11, 2003. **Price:** $16.95. **Description:** A look into the business future of Canada. Topics include business, healthcare, think tanks, policy groups, education, the arts, economy, and social issues.

34370 ■ *"Mercy Parent Nets Almost $1B in 2011" in Sacramento Business Journal (Vol. 28, September 30, 2011, No. 31, pp. 1)*
Pub: Sacramento Business Journal
Ed: Kathy Robertson. **Description:** Catholic Healthcare West has reported almost $1 billion in profits for 2010. The company has reported a profit margin of 8.7 percent. It also absorbed more than $1 billion in costs from charity care and government programs.

34371 ■ *"Michigan Institute of Urology Grows in Expertise, Services" in Crain's Detroit Business (Vol. 24, April 7, 2008, No. 14, pp. 13)*
Pub: Crain Communications, Inc.
Ed: Jay Greene. **Description:** One of the nation's largest urology groups, the Michigan Institute of Urology, plans to continue its growth by adding doctors and offering new treatment options. The growth is financially beneficial to the group, but it also cuts down on health care costs since the group can perform procedures for a lesser rate than at a hospital.

34372 ■ *Microtrends: The Small Forces Behind Tomorrow's Big Changes*
Pub: Business Plus
Ed: Mark J. Penn. **Released:** 2007. **Price:** $25.99. **Description:** Political pollster and lead presidential campaign strategist for Hillary Clinton, identifies seventy-five microtrends he believes are changing the social and cultural landscape in the U.S. and globally. The book covers the areas of health and wellness, technology, education and more.

34373 ■ *"The Moody Blues" in Entrepreneur (Vol. 36, April 2008, No. 4, pp. 87)*
Pub: Entrepreneur Media, Inc.
Ed: Mark Henricks. **Description:** Depression among employees can affect their productivity and cost the company. Businesses with a workforce that is likely to have depression should inform their employees about the health benefits covered by insurance. Other details on how to address depression concerns among employees are discussed.

34374 ■ *"More Businesses Will Shift Health Costs to Workers" in Business Review, Albany New York (Vol. 34, November 16, 2007, No. 33, pp. 1)*
Pub: American City Business Journals, Inc.
Ed: Barbara Pinckney. **Description:** Survey conducted by consulting firm Benetech Inc. showed that sixty percent of employers are planning to increase payroll deductions to pay for health insurance premiums. More than ninety percent of the employers prefer HMO plans, followed by Preferred Provider Organizations. Other details of the survey are discussed.

34375 ■ *"More Small Businesses Willing to Fund Employees' Benefits" in Baltimore Business Journal (Vol. 28, June 18, 2010, No. 6, pp. 1)*
Pub: Baltimore Business Journal
Ed: Scott Graham. **Description:** An increasing number of small businesses in Maryland are tapping into potentially cheaper self-funded health plans instead of providing fully insured benefits to employees through traditional health plans. Self-funded health plans charge employers for health care up to a specified level. Economic implications of self-funded plans to small businesses are discussed.

34376 ■ *"Most States Have High-Risk Health Insurance Pools" in Crain's Detroit Business (Vol. 24, March 24, 2008, No. 12, pp. 31)*
Pub: Crain Communications, Inc.
Ed: Jay Greene. **Description:** High-risk health insurance pools, designed to cover individuals with medical conditions that essentially make them otherwise uninsurable, are being debated by the Senate Health Policy Committee; the pool concept is supported by Blue Cross Blue Shield of Michigan and contested by a number of consumer groups and competing health insurers.

34377 ■ *National Wellness Institute--Member Directory*
Pub: National Wellness Institute
Contact: Judd Allen, Director
E-mail: judda@healthyculture.com
URL(s): www.nationalwellness.org. **Released:** updated daily. **Covers:** more than 1,600 health and wellness promotion professionals in corporations, hospitals, colleges, government agencies, universities, community organizations, schools (K-12), and consulting firms, and managed care. **Entries include:**

Member name, address, and phone, fax, email. **Arrangement:** Same information given in alphabetical, and geographical and work setting arrangements.

34378 ■ *"Neurosciences, Orthopedics Push Mease Dunedin Plan" in Tampa Bay Business Journal (Vol. 29, October 30, 2009, No. 45, pp. 1)*
Pub: American City Business Journals
Ed: Margie Manning. **Description:** Mease Dunedin Hospital has pushed with a $19 million renovation and expansion plan that would triple the space in its operating suites, in line with its effort to become a center of excellence focused on neurosciences, orthopedics and the spine. The hospital expects these kinds of specialties will help offset the cost of less profitable services.

34379 ■ *"New Book Takes Alternate View on Ontario's Wind Industry" in CNW Group (September 19, 2011)*
Pub: CNW Group
Contact: Carolyn McGill-Davidson, President
Description: Dirty Business: The Reality Behind Ontario's Rush to Wind Power, was written by editor and health care writer Jane Wilson of Ottawa, Ontario, Canada along with contributing editor Parker Gallant. The book contains articles and papers on the wind business, including information on illnesses caused from the environmental noise.

34380 ■ *"New Database Brings Doctors Out of the Dark" in Business Courier (Vol. 26, October 23, 2009, No. 26, pp. 1)*
Pub: American City Business Journals, Inc.
Ed: James Ritchie. **Description:** A database created by managed care consulting firm Praesentia allows doctors in Cincinnati to compare average reimbursements from health insurance companies to doctors in different areas. Specialist doctors in the city are paid an average of $172.25 for every office consultation.

34381 ■ *"New Drug Could Revitalize Amgen" in Barron's (Vol. 88, July 7, 2008, No. 27, pp. 23)*
Pub: Dow Jones & Co., Inc.
Ed: Johanna Bennett. **Description:** Shares of the biotechnology company Amgen could receive a boost from the release of the anti-osteoporosis drug denosumab. The shares, priced at $48.84 each, are trading at 11 times expected earnings for 2008 and could also be boosted by cost cutting measures.

34382 ■ *"New Health Care Sector" in Hispanic Business (July-August 2009, pp. 10-12)*
Pub: Hispanic Business
Ed: Rob Kuznia. **Description:** Despite the recession and reform, the health care sector continues to grow at a fast rate. The top ten health care organizations are outlined.

34383 ■ *"New Health Law, Lack of Docs Collide on Cape Cod" in Boston Business Journal (Vol. 27, October 12, 2007, No. 37, pp. 1)*
Pub: American City Business Journals Inc.
Ed: Mark Hollmer. **Description:** There is a shortage of primary care providers at Outer Cape Health Services in Massachusetts, with the isolation of the area and as physicians look for higher paying careers in specialty positions. The Commonwealth Health Insurance Connector Authority is pushing for a new health insurance law and is working with Cape Cod Chamber of Commerce to conduct outreach programs.

34384 ■ *The New Wellness Revolution: Make a Fortune in the Next Trillion Dollar Industry*
Pub: John Wiley & Sons, Incorporated
Ed: Paul Zane Pilzer. **Released:** February 16, 2007. **Price:** $24.95. **Description:** Tips for starting and running a healthcare business.

34385 ■ *The No Asshole Rule*
Pub: Warner Books Inc.
Ed: Robert I. Sutton PhD. **Released:** February 22, 2007. **Price:** $22.99. **Description:** Problem employees are more than just a nuisance they are a serious and costly threat to corporate success and employee health.

34386 ■ *"Not Just for Kids: ADHD can be Debilitating for an Employee, and Frustrating for Bosses" in Canadian Business (April 14, 2008)*
Pub: Rogers Media
Ed: Andy Holloway. **Description:** Up to four percent of North American adults continue to feel the effects of Attention Deficit Hyperactivity Disorder or Attention Deficit Disorder. Explaining the value of the task at hand to people who are afflicted with these conditions is one way to keep them engaged in the workplace. Giving them opportunities to create their own working structure is another strategy to manage these people.

34387 ■ *"Notes on Current Labor Statistics" in Montly Labor Review (Vol. 133, September 2010, No. 9, pp. 75)*
Pub: Bureau of Labor Statistics
Description: Principal statistics and calculated by the Bureau of Labor Statistics are presented. The series includes statistics on labor force; employment; unemployment; labor compensation; consumer, producer, and international prices; productivity; international comparisons; and injury and illness statistics.

34388 ■ *"Novi Eyed for $11 Million, 100-Bed Medilodge" in Crain's Detroit Business (Vol. 25, June 1, 2009, No. 22, pp. M032)*
Pub: Crain Communications Inc. - Detroit
Description: Novi, Michigan is one of the cities being considered for construction of a new 110-bed skilled nursing facility. Details of the project are included.

34389 ■ *"Now the Real Work Begins" in Baltimore Business Journal (Vol. 28, October 15, 2010, No. 23, pp. 1)*
Pub: Baltimore Business Journal
Ed: Emily Mullin. **Description:** The Henry J. Kaiser Family Foundation's survey shows nearly 53 percent of Americans remain confused about health care reform and it was up to the states to educate the people. However, Maryland is still trying to figure out how to conduct the campaign without guidance or funding from the Federal government.

34390 ■ *"Oakland County Hopes Auto Suppliers Can Drive Medical Industry Growth" in Crain's Detroit Business (March 10, 2008)*
Pub: Crain Communications, Inc.
Ed: Chad Halcom. **Description:** Oakland County officials are hoping to create further economic development for the region by pairing health care companies and medical device makers with automotive suppliers in an attempt to discover additional crossover technology.

34391 ■ *"On Their Own" in Crain's Cleveland Business (Vol. 28, November 12, 2007, No. 45, pp. 19)*
Pub: Crain Communications, Inc.
Ed: Eileen Beal. **Description:** Discusses the reasons more physicians with entrepreneurial spirit are opening their own practices as well the added challenges and responsibilities that comes with owning one's own practice.

34392 ■ *"The One Thing That's Holding Back Your Wellness Program" in Employee Benefit News (Vol. 25, December 1, 2011, No. 15, pp. 8)*
Pub: SourceMedia Inc.
Ed: Kelley M. Butler. **Description:** A 13-year study shows that women who sat for more than six hours a day were 94 percent more likely to die during the study period. Most women sit at their desks an average of 7.7 hours while at work.

34393 ■ *"Open Enrollment: Staying Healthy During Enrollment Season" in Employee Benefit News (Vol. 25, November 1, 2011, No. 14, pp. 41)*
Pub: SourceMedia Inc.
Ed: Shana Sweeney. **Description:** Tips for staying healthy during your benefit open enrollment period are outlined.

34394 ■ *"Orlando Health to Build $24M Proton Therapy Facility" in Orlando Business Journal (Vol. 26, January 22, 2010, No. 34, pp. 1)*
Pub: American City Business Journals
Ed: Melanie Stawicki Azam. **Description:** Orlando Health is planning to construct a $24 million proton therapy facility at its MD Anderson Cancer Center Orlando in Florida. The facility, which aims for a 2011 opening, will be using radiation for more accurate targeting of tumors and avoiding the damage to surrounding tissues and organs.

34395 ■ *"Over and Out" in Entrepreneur (Vol. 36, February 2008, No. 2, pp. 25)*
Pub: Entrepreneur Media Inc.
Ed: Julie Moline. **Description:** Ben Wolin, owner of Waterfront Media that operates wellness and health Websites, had employed the services of human resource consulting firm to advise him in regard to overtime pay. Guidelines on how to avoid overtime pay violations are presented.

34396 ■ *"Paralysis Foundation has Big Plans" in Austin Business JournalInc. (Vol. 29, December 11, 2009, No. 40, pp. 1)*
Pub: American City Business Journals
Ed: Sandra Zaragoza. **Description:** Lone Star Paralysis Foundation revealed plans to launch a fund-raising effort for the advancement of cures for spinal cord injuries via adult stem cells and also fund a new spinal injury rehabilitation center. Efforts to raise about $3 million will begin as soon as the adult stem cell research study by Dr. Wise Young receives Food and Drug Administration approval.

34397 ■ *"Patients to Elect to Cut Care" in The Business Journal-Serving Metropolitan Kansas City (Vol. 27, November 21, 2008, No. 11, pp. 1)*
Pub: American City Business Journals, Inc.
Ed: Rob Roberts. **Description:** Patients in Kansas City, Missouri are cutting down on health care services due to the economic crisis. A decline in diagnostic procedures has been observed at Northland Cardiology. Elective reconstructive procedures have also been reduced by 25 percent. Additional information and statistics regarding the healthcare sector is included.

34398 ■ *"Patients: Make Mine a Single" in Business Courier (Vol. 24, March 28, 2008, No. 51, pp. 1)*
Pub: American City Business Journals, Inc.
Ed: James Ritchie. **Description:** Hospitals in the Tri-State area are switching from double to private rooms since patients heal better in private rooms and also they provide peace and quiet to patients. Private rooms also contribute to the reduction of medical errors and hospital acquired infection rates.

34399 ■ *"Patricia Hemingway Hall; President, Chief Operating Officer, Health Care Service Corp." in Crain's Chicago Business (May 5, 2008)*
Pub: Crain Communications, Inc.
Ed: Mike Colias. **Description:** Profile of Patricia Hemingway Hall who is the president and chief operating officer of Health Care Service Corp., a new strategy launched by Blue Cross & Blue Shield of Illinois; the new endeavor will emphasize wellness rather than just treatment across its four health plans.

34400 ■ *"PCH Gets Trauma Center Status" in The Business Journal - Serving Phoenix and the Valley of the Sun (Vol. 28, July 11, 2008, No. 45)*
Pub: American City Business Journals, Inc.
Ed: Angela Gonzales. **Description:** Phoenix Children's Hospital has been allowed by the Arizona Department of Health Services to launch the state's first trauma center for children. The trauma center is expected to cost the hospital $7 million a year.

34401 ■ *"Physics for Females" in Occupational Outlook Quarterly (Vol. 55, Summer 2011, No. 2, pp. 22)*
Pub: U.S. Bureau of Labor Statistics
Description: Free resources to help females investigate careers in medical physics and health physics are available from the American Physical Society.

The booklet is designed for girls in middle and high school and describes the work of 15 women who use physics to solve medical mysteries, discover planets, research new materials, and more.

34402 ■ *"Piece of Health Law 'A Goner" in Baltimore Business Journal (Vol. 28, November 19, 2010, No. 28, pp. 1)*
Pub: Baltimore Business Journal
Ed: Kent Hoover. **Description:** Montana Senator Max Baucus, a Democrat who heads the Senate Finance Committee, has revealed his plan to push legislation that would repeal the 1099 IRS provision that was created by the health care reform law and will result in more paperwork for small businesses when it goes into effect in 2012.

34403 ■ *"Pioneers Get All The Perks" in Canadian Business (Vol. 81, March 3, 2008, No. 3, pp. 18)*
Pub: Rogers Media
Description: Suncor Energy Inc. will face royalty payments from 25% to 30% of net profits as it signs a new deal with Alberta. Biovail Corp., meanwhile, is under a U.S. grand jury investigation for supposed improprieties in Cardizem LA heart drug launch. The Conference Board of Canada's proposal to impose taxes on greenhouse gas emissions and other developments in the business community are discussed.

34404 ■ *"Plan: Put Health Centers in ERs" in Crain's Detroit Business (Vol. 25, June 22, 2009, No. 25, pp. 1)*
Pub: Crain Communications Inc. - Detroit
Ed: Jay Greene. **Description:** It has been suggested by top CEOs in the Detroit, Michigan area to put satellites of federally qualified health centers within emergency room departments. The plan would have the health centers pay a monthly fee for each patient treated.

34405 ■ *"Positive Social Interactions and the Human Body at Work" in Academy of Management Review (January 2008, pp. 137)*
Pub: ScholarOne, Inc.
Ed: Emily D. Heaphy, Jane E. Dutton. **Description:** Research is recommended for the manner in which positive social interactions in organizational contexts can influence employees' health and physiological resourcefulness.

34406 ■ *"Prescription for Health: Choosing the Best Healthcare Plan" in Black Enterprise (Vol. 38, July 2008, No. 12, pp. 48)*
Pub: Earl G. Graves Publishing Co. Inc.
Ed: Tamara E. Holmes. **Description:** According to a survey of small-business owners conducted by SurePayroll Inc., 20 percent of respondents have had a prospective employee refuse a job offer because healthcare benefits did not come with it. Cost is not the only reason many small-business owners do not offer these benefits. Guidelines to help take some of the confusion out of the guesswork that comes with trying to find the proper fit concerning healthcare benefits are outlined.

34407 ■ *"Presidential Address: Innovation in Retrospect and Prospect" in Canadian Journal of Electronics (Vol. 43, November 2010, No. 4)*
Pub: Journal of the Canadian Economics Association
Ed: James A. Brander. **Description:** Has innovation slowed in recent decades? While there has been progress in information and communications technology, the recent record of innovation in agriculture, energy, transportation and healthcare sectors is cause for concern.

34408 ■ *"Priority: Business For Sale" in Inc. (January 2008, pp. 28)*
Pub: Gruner & Jahr USA Publishing
Ed: Elaine Appleton Grant. **Description:** Profile of an employment agency providing registered nurses to hospitals and nursing homes. The company began as an temporary placement agency for IT professionals and is now for sale at the asking price of $4.2 million.

34409 ■ *"Providers Ride First Wave of eHealth Dollars" in Boston Business Journal (Vol. 31, June 10, 2011, No. 20, pp. 1)*
Pub: Boston Business Journal
Ed: Julie M. Donnelly. **Description:** Health care providers in Massachusetts implementing electronic medical records technology started receiving federal stimulus funds. Beth Israel Deaconess Medical Center was the first hospital to qualify for the funds.

34410 ■ *"Public Health Care Funding and the Montana Economy" in Montana Business Quarterly (Vol. 49, Spring 2011, No. 1, pp. 23)*
Pub: Bureau of Business & Economic Research
Ed: Gregg Davis. **Description:** Montana has more baby boomers and veterans per capita than any other state in the nation. The role of public health in the state is a crucial part of the state's economy.

34411 ■ *Public Human Services Directory*
Pub: American Public Human Services Association
Contact: Kevin McGuire, President
URL(s): www.aphsa.org. **Ed:** Sybil Walker Barnes. **Released:** Annual; Latest edition 2009. **Price:** $225, Individuals; $200, Members; $350, Institutions. **Covers:** Federal, state, territorial, county, and major municipal public human service agencies. **Entries include:** Agency name, address, phone, fax, e-mail address, web site address, names of key personnel, program area. **Database includes:** Information on all major human service programs, such as child welfare, child support enforcement. Medicaid eligibility and claims, interstate compacts, and other programs. **Arrangement:** Geographical.

34412 ■ *"Q&A With Devin Ringling: Franchise's Services Go Beyond Elder Care" in Gazette (October 2, 2010)*
Pub: The Gazette
Ed: Bill Radford. **Description:** Profile of franchise, Interim HealthCare, in Colorado Springs, Colorado; the company offers home care services that include wound care and specialized feedings to shopping and light housekeeping. It also runs a medical staffing company that provides nurses, therapists and other health care workers to hospitals, prisons, schools and other facilities.

34413 ■ *"The Quest for the Smart Prosthetic" in Canadian Business (Vol. 83, October 12, 2010, No. 17, pp. 26)*
Pub: Rogers Media Ltd.
Ed: Jacqueline Nelson. **Description:** Information about a two-year research project led by Southern Methodist University (SMU) and funded by the Defense Advance Research Projects Agency (DARPA) is provided. The agency aims to create a 'smart prosthetic' which will improve the lives of military amputees. The planned prosthetic will use a sensor that can carry nerve signals through synthetic channels.

34414 ■ *"Rebels' Cause: Adult Stem Cell" in Austin Business Journal (Vol. 31, June 3, 2011, No. 13, pp. 1)*
Pub: American City Business Journals Inc.
Ed: Sandra Zaragoza. **Description:** MedRebels Foundation was launched in February 2011 with the goal of providing millions of dollars for research funding, education and advocacy for adult stem cell-focused medicine. The foundation, whose major contributor is SpineSmith LP, is a collaboration of other adult stem cell-related companies and nonprofit partners. It hopes to raise $200,000 by the end of 2011.

34415 ■ *"Recovery on Tap for 2010?" in Orlando Business Journal (Vol. 26, January 1, 2010, No. 31, pp. 1)*
Pub: American City Business Journals
Ed: Melanie Stawicki Azam, Richard Bilbao, Christopher Boyd, Anjali Fluker. **Description:** Economic forecasts for Central Florida's leading business sectors in 2010 are presented. These sectors include housing, film and TV, sports business, law, restaurants, aviation, tourism and hospitality, banking and finance, commercial real estate, retail, health care, insurance, higher education, and manufacturing. According to some local executives, Central Florida's economy will slowly recover in 2010.

34416 ■ *"Renewed Vision" in Hawaii Business (Vol. 54, August 2008, No. 2, pp. 49)*
Pub: Hawaii Business Publishing
Ed: Jason Ubay. **Description:** Saint Francis Healthcare System of Hawaii, ranked 81 in Hawaii's top 250 companies for 2008, has been rebranding to focus on senior community healthcare and sold some of its operations, which explains the decline in gross sales from $219.5M in 2006 to $122.7M in 2007. The system's senior services and home hospice service expansion are provided.

34417 ■ *"Research Reports: How Analysts Size Up Companies" in Barron's (Vol. 88, June 30, 2008, No. 26, pp. M11)*
Pub: Dow Jones & Co., Inc.
Ed: Anita Peltonen. **Description:** Shares of Developers Diversified Realty Corp. get a 'Long-Term Buy' rating while the shares of HealthSouth Corp. and Onyx Pharmaceutical get a rating of 'Underperform' and a 'Buy' rating respectively. The shares of American Capital Agency, American Public Education, Bankrate, and Werner Enterprises are also ranked.

34418 ■ *"Retail Health Clinics Sprout in Area; Doctors Feel Threat, Have Concerns" in Crain's Detroit Business (April 7, 2008)*
Pub: Crain Communications, Inc.
Ed: Mike Scott. **Description:** Competing with doctors' offices for routine patient visits are the retail health clinics which have made their way into the metro Detroit area. Physicians are concerned about the limited doctor supervision on site.

34419 ■ *"Retailers, Your Will, and More" in Agency Sales Magazine (Vol. 39, July 2009, No. 7, pp. 46)*
Pub: MANA
Ed: Melvin H. Daskal. **Description:** IRS audit guide for small retail businesses is presented. Tips on how to make a will with multiple beneficiaries are discussed together with medical expenses that can not be deducted.

34420 ■ *Rhode Island Directory of Human Service Agencies & Government Agencies*
Pub: Travelers Aid Society of Rhode Island
URL(s): riroads.com/links/listdetail.cgi?Lookup=378039. **Released:** Biennial **Covers:** about 1,200 public and private nonprofit human service agencies and organizations in Rhode Island. **Entries include:** Agency name, address, phone, name of contact or director; description of services; hours open; eligibility requirements; ages and geographic area served; fee for service; funding. **Arrangement:** Alphabetical. **Indexes:** Service, alphabetical, government agency name.

34421 ■ *"Rich or Poor, Hospitals Must Work Together" in Crain's Chicago Business (Vol. 31, April 28, 2008, No. 17, pp. 22)*
Pub: Crain Communications, Inc.
Description: Chicago=area safety-net hospitals that serve the poor, uninsured and underinsured are struggling to stay open while wealthier areas compete to build advanced facilities for the expensive surgical procedures their privately insured patients can afford. If these safety-net hospitals close, their patients, many of them in ambulances, will show up at the remaining hospitals resulting in a strain that will test the ability of hospitals across the region to care for all of their patients. Hospitals need to address the threats to the local health care system before it slips into crisis since the current every-hospital-for-itself approach that pays off big for some will eventually will make losers of everyone.

34422 ■ *"The Right Remedy: Entrepreneur's Success Is a Matter of Life and Death" in Black Enterprise (Vol. 38, February 2008, No. 7, pp. 46)*
Pub: Earl G. Graves Publishing Co. Inc.
Ed: Tamara E. Holmes. **Description:** Profile of Leah Brown, whose company conducts clinical trials to determine if specific drugs will relieve particular

symptoms. Her company will also visit physician's offices to make certain doctors are following proper protocol for a clinical trial or will collect data from patients.

34423 ■ *"Roseville Ob-Gyn Group Grows With Patient Focus, Diverse Services" in Crain's Detroit Business (Vol. 24, April 7, 2008, No. 14)*
Pub: Crain Communications, Inc.
Ed: Christine Snyder. **Description:** According to the American Medical Association, the number of medical groups of 10 or more physicians has been growing. Eastside Gynecology Obstetrics is one such group which has seen its yearly revenue grow due to a good business plan and a diversity of services and doctors.

34424 ■ *"St. Elizabeth Fights for Share at St. Lukes" in Business Courier (Vol. 27, November 12, 2010, No. 28, pp. 1)*
Pub: Business Courier
Ed: James Ritchie. **Description:** Key information on how St. Elizabeth Healthcare helps partner St. Luke's Hospitals increase market share in the healthcare industry are presented. Some of St. Luke's hospitals, such as the St. Elizabeth Fort Thomas in Kentucky, are struggling with low occupancy rates, prompting St. Elizabeth to invest about $24 million to help St. Luke's increase its market share.

34425 ■ *"St. Luke's Gets Shot in the Arm From Outpatient Services" in Saint Louis Business Journal (Vol. 31, August 19, 2011, No. 52, pp. 1)*
Pub: Saint Louis Business Journal
Ed: Angela Mueller, E.B. Solomont. **Description:** St. Louis, Missouri-based St. Luke's Hospital benefited from investing in outpatient services as contained in its latest bond offering. Fitch Ratings gave the bond issuance an A rating.

34426 ■ *"Scottsdale Bank Plans 4Q Opening" in The Business Journal - Serving Phoenix and the Valley of the Sun (Vol. 28, August 15, 2008, No. 50)*
Pub: American City Business Journals, Inc.
Ed: Chris Casacchia. **Description:** Arizona's Department of Financial Institutions has approved Scottsdale Business Bank, a community bank which plans to open in the fourth quarter of 2008. The bank, which is to be located near McCormick Ranch in Scottsdale, Arizona, will cater to small business owners in the professional sector, such as accountants and doctors.

34427 ■ *Selling the Invisible: A Field Guide to Modern Marketing*
Pub: Business Plus
Ed: Harry Beckwith. **Price:** $22.95. **Description:** Tips for marketing and selling intangibles such as health care, entertainment, tourism, legal services, and more are provided.

34428 ■ *"Seton Grows Heart Institute" in Austin Business Journal (Vol. 31, July 15, 2011, No. 19, pp. A1)*
Pub: American City Business Journals Inc.
Ed: Sandra Zaragoza. **Description:** Seton Heart Institute experienced significant growth in the last six months. The organization added physicians, specialists and outreach offices across Central Texas.

34429 ■ *"Shape Up! Jamal Williams Develops KIDFIT App to Combat Childhood Obesity" in Black Enterprise (Vol. 41, August 2010, No. 1, pp. 62)*
Pub: Earl G. Graves Publishing Co. Inc.
Ed: Sonya A. Donaldson. **Description:** Profile of Jamal Williams who developed KIDFIT, an app that helps to combat childhood obesity by offering 150 various exercises for children, with an emphasis on training, conditioning, coordination, and flexibility.

34430 ■ *"Sinai Doctor Seeks FDA OK for Drug" in Baltimore Business Journal (Vol. 28, July 16, 2010, No. 10, pp. 1)*
Pub: Baltimore Business Journal
Ed: Emily Mullin. **Description:** Paul Gurbel, Sinai Hospital Center for Thrombosis Research director, is seeking an FDA approval of Brilinta, a drug which he helped create and test. Gurbel says that the approval could bring the drug to market as early as December 2010. The drug is expected to rival Bristol-Myers' Plavix, which generated almost $6.2 billion in 2009.

34431 ■ *"Six Things You Can Do To Ride Out A Turbulent Market" in Hispanic Business (Vol. 30, March 2008, No. 3, pp. 20)*
Pub: Hispanic Business
Ed: Hildy Medina; Michael Bowker. **Description:** Top financial experts' views on managing investment portfolios during turbulent periods in the stock market are reported. Experts prefer investing in health care, short term investments, international bonds and preferred stocks or just maintain cash until such times as the market settles.

34432 ■ *"Sixty-Acre Vision for North Suburbs" in Business Courier (Vol. 24, April 4, 2008, No. 52, pp. 1)*
Pub: American City Business Journals, Inc.
Ed: Laura Baverman. **Description:** Al Neyer Inc. plans for a mixed-use development at the 60-acre site it has recently purchased. The mixed-use project could cost up to $100 million, and will include medical offices, residential buildings, and corporate offices. Details of Al Neyer's plans for the site are given.

34433 ■ *"Sluggish Market Gives Hospitals the Financial Chills" in The Business Journal-Serving Greater Tampa Bay (Vol. 28, August 1, 2008)*
Pub: American City Business Journals, Inc.
Ed: Margie Manning. **Description:** Operating margins for hospitals in the Tampa Bay, Florida area have been reduced from 2 percent in 2006 to 0.8 percent in 2007 due to a weaker US economy. Total margins, on the other hand, rose from 2.9 percent to 3.3 percent in the same period.

34434 ■ *"Small Biz Owners Are Tapping Into Health Savings Plans" in Small Business Opportunities (Fall 2007)*
Pub: Harris Publications Inc.
Ed: Michael L. Corne. **Description:** Health savings accounts were developed by Golden Rule, a United Healthcare company. Today, more than 40 percent of the company's customers are covered by health savings account plans.

34435 ■ *Small Business Access and Alternatives to Health Care: Congressional Hearing*
Pub: DIANE Publishing Company
Ed: Donald A. Manzullo. **Released:** July 2006. **Price:** $35.00. **Description:** Congressional hearings regarding the health care crisis facing America's small businesses is discussed.

34436 ■ *Small Business Access to Health Care: Congressional Hearing*
Pub: DIANE Publishing Company
Ed: Donald A. Manzullo. **Released:** 2001. **Price:** $20.00. **Description:** Congressional hearing held at Crystal Lake, Illinois. Witnesses: Mary Blankenbaker, Co-Owner, Benjamin's Restaurant; Ryan Brauns, Senior Vice President, Rockford Consulting and Brokerage; Scott Shalek, RHU, Shalek Financial Services; Brad Close, National Federation of Independent Businesses; Ken Koehler, Flowerwood, Inc.; Brad Buxton, Vice President of Networks and Medical Management, Blue Cross and Blue Shield of Illinois; Isabella Wilson, Chief Financial Office, Illinois Blower, Inc.; and James Milam, Illinois State Medical Society.

34437 ■ *The Small Business Guide to HSAs*
Pub: Brick Tower Press
Ed: JoAnn Mills Laing. **Released:** September 2004. **Price:** $14.95. **Description:** Government-assisted Health Savings Accounts (HSAs) offer employees a tax-free way to accumulate savings to be used for qualified medical expenses, they can be rolled over without penalty for future spending, or invested to accumulate savings to pay for health needs after retirement. Employers offering HSAs can save up to two-thirds of business expenses on health insurance costs.

34438 ■ *"Small Businesses Changing Their Health Plan Preferences" in Boston Business Journal (Vol. 29, June 24, 2011, No. 7, pp. 1)*
Pub: American City Business Journals Inc.
Ed: Scott Dance. **Description:** Small businesses in Maryland are shifting from traditional health plans to the consumer-oriented health savings accounts or HSAs. Health insurance industry experts say the change is indicative of the insurance buyers' desire to be more thrifty and discerning in their health care purchases.

34439 ■ *"Small, But Mighty" in Employee Benefit News (Vol. 25, November 1, 2011, No. 14, pp. 32)*
Pub: SourceMedia Inc.
Ed: Andrea Davis. **Description:** Three consulting firms are facing the challenge of helping clients understand the new health care reform in a tight economy.

34440 ■ *"A Smarter Kind of Taxes" in Canadian Business (Vol. 80, October 8, 2007, No. 20, pp. 203)*
Pub: Rogers Media
Ed: Jack Mintz. **Description:** Forecasts on Canada's tax system by 2020 are analyzed. It is expected that the country's aging society will place great demands on elderly-related spending such as pensions and healthcare. And, since the elderly pay fewer taxes, the revenue available to the government will be reduced. Other trends also show that several factors will cause significant change to the country's tax system.

34441 ■ *"The Smell of Fear: Is a Bottom Near?" in Barron's (Vol. 88, March 17, 2008, No. 11, pp. M3)*
Pub: Dow Jones & Company, Inc.
Ed: Kopin Tan. **Description:** Liquidity problems at Bear Stearns frightened investors in markets around the world due to the fear of the prospects of a big bank's failure. Shares of health maintenance organizations got battered led by WellPoint, and Humana but longer-term investors who could weather short-term volatility may find value here. The value of J. Crew shares is also discussed.

34442 ■ *"Something Different in the Air? The Collapse of the Schwarzenegger Health Plan in Calfornia" in WorkingUSA (June 2008)*
Pub: Blackwell Publishers Ltd.
Ed: Daniel J.B. Mitchell. **Description:** In January 2007, California Governor Arnold Schwarzenegger proposed a state universal health care plan modeled after the Massachusetts individual mandate program. A year later, the plan was dead. Although some key interest groups eventually backed the plan, it was overwhelmed by a looming state budget crisis and a lack of gubernatorial focus. Although much acclaimed for his stance on greenhouse gases, stem cells, hydrogen highways, and other Big Ideas, diffused gubernatorial priorities and a failure to resolve California's chronic fiscal difficulties let the clock run out on universal health care.

34443 ■ *"Sorry: Good Defense for Mal Offense" in The Business Journal-Serving Metropolitan Kansas City (Vol. 26, July 4, 2008, No. 43, pp. 1)*
Pub: American City Business Journals, Inc.
Ed: Rob Roberts. **Description:** According to a survey conducted by the Kansas City Business Journal, ten hospitals in Kansas City showed that they have adopted disclosure policies that include prompt apologies and settlement offers. The policy is effective in minimizing medical malpractice lawsuits. Other details of the survey are presented.

34444 ■ *"South Lake Hospital Starting $47M Patient Tower" in Orlando Business Journal (Vol. 26, December 4, 2009, No. 26, pp. 1)*
Pub: American City Business Journals
Ed: Melanie Stawicki Azam. **Description:** Clermont, Florida's South Lake Hospital has divulged intentions to issue $50.9 million in bonds in order to fund construction of the $47 million patient tower. The

three-story, 124,000 square foot tower would add eighteen inpatient rooms, a new lobby and expanded pharmacy, diagnostic and lab services, and treatment areas.

34445 ■ *"State Budget Woes Hurt Many Vendors, Senior Services" in Sacramento Business Journal (Vol. 25, August 15, 2008, No. 24, pp. 1)*
Pub: American City Business Journals, Inc.
Ed: Melanie Turner. **Description:** Delays in the passage of the California state budget have adversely affected the health care industry. The Robertson Adult Day Health Care had taken out loans to keep the business afloat. The state Legislature has reduced Medi-Cal reimbursement to health care providers by 10 percent.

34446 ■ *"The Stem Cell Revolution" in Canadian Business (Vol. 79, November 20, 2006, No. 23, pp. 31)*
Pub: Rogers Media
Ed: Erin Pooley. **Description:** The commercial prospects and the future of stem cell therapeutics are presented. The use of stem cell therapy to heal the chronic conditions of patients is also discussed.

34447 ■ *"Stent Cases at Md. Hospitals Falling" in Baltimore Business Journal (Vol. 28, November 12, 2010, No. 27, pp. 1)*
Pub: Baltimore Business Journal
Ed: Emily Mullin. **Description:** Cardiologists believe that the recent drop in cardiac stent procedures in Maryland can be associated with the ongoing investigation of Dr. Mark G. Midei and St. Joseph Medical Center. Midei is accused of performing unnecessary stent procedures on patients and was let go from the clinical practice in St. Joseph in 2009.

34448 ■ *"Strategic Issue Management as Change Catalyst" in Strategy and Leadership (Vol. 39, September-October 2011, No. 5, pp. 20-29)*
Pub: Emerald Group Publishing Inc.
Ed: Bruce E. Perrott. **Description:** A study analyzes the case of a well-known Australian healthcare organization to examine how a company's periodic planning cycle is supplemented with a dynamic, real-time, strategic-issue-management system under high turbulence conditions. Findings highlight the eight steps that a company's management can use in its strategic issue management (SIM) process to track, monitor and manage strategic issues so as to ensure that the corporate, strategy, and capability are aligned with one another in turbulent times.

34449 ■ *"Struggling States Slashing Health Care For Poor" in Chicago Tribune (January 15, 2009)*
Pub: McClatchy-Tribune Information Services
Ed: Noam N. Levey. **Description:** Health officials warn that even the huge federal rescue plan may not be enough to restore health services being eliminated due to the economic crisis.

34450 ■ *"Survey: Most Approve of Donating Used Pacemakers to Medically Underserved" in Crain's Detroit Business (Vol. 25, June 1, 2009)*
Pub: Crain Communications Inc. - Detroit
Description: According to a survey conducted by University of Michigan Cardiovascular Center, 87 percent of those with pacemakers and 71 percent of the general population would donate the device to patients in underserved nations.

34451 ■ *"Sutter, CHW Reject Blue Cross Deal" in Sacramento Business Journal (Vol. 25, August 15, 2008, No. 24, pp. 1)*
Pub: American City Business Journals, Inc.
Ed: Kathy Robertson. **Description:** California-based Sutter Health and Catholic Healthcare West have rejected the $11.8 million class action settlement in connection with contract rescissions between California hospitals and Anthem Blue Cross. Blue Cross can halt the settlement if not enough hospitals accept it. The deal covers all hospitals that owe money due to rescinded Blue Cross coverage.

34452 ■ *"Swift Shift" in Crain's Cleveland Business (Vol. 28, November 12, 2007, No. 45, pp. 1)*
Pub: Crain Communications, Inc.
Ed: Shannon Mortland. **Description:** Discusses the ways in which Southwest General Health Center is working to stay competitive in a region that is highly saturated with health care providers.

34453 ■ *"Taking the Right Road" in Entrepreneur (Vol. 37, October 2009, No. 10, pp. 104)*
Pub: Entrepreneur Media, Inc.
Ed: Jason Daley. **Description:** Joe Grubb's franchise of BrightStar Healthcare, a home health care provider, in Knoxville, Tennessee has grown into a $1 million business. Grubb, a former sales agent, experienced slow growth for his franchise and had to deal with cash flow issues during its first few months.

34454 ■ *"Tenacious Trailblazer" in Hispanic Business (Vol. 30, April 2008, No. 4, pp. 26)*
Pub: Hispanic Business
Ed: Melinda Burns. **Description:** Dr. Sandra Hernandez has been named as Hispanic Business Woman of the Year for her pioneering work in health care reform. Dr. Hernandez is the first Hispanic and the first woman to serve as public health director for the city and county of San Francisco.

34455 ■ *"Thousands Balk at Health Law Sign-Up Mandate" in Boston Business Journal (Vol. 27, November 9, 2007, No. 41, pp. 1)*
Pub: American City Business Journals Inc.
Ed: Mark Hollmer. **Description:** About 100,000 Massachusetts residents have not signed up for insurance plans created as part of the state's health care reform law. Insurers have underestimated the number of new customers signing up for insurance and come close to risking penalties if they do not get insurance by the end of 2007. The Commonwealth Health Insurance Connector Authority's deadline to buy insurance before penalties kick in is November 15, 2007.

34456 ■ *"To Help Maintain an Adequate Blood Supply During the Summer Months" in Ice Cream Reporter (Vol. 21, August 20, 2008, No. 9, pp. 8)*
Pub: Ice Cream Reporter
Description: Friendly's and the American Red Cross have partnered to offer blood donors a coupon for one free carton of Friendly's ice cream in order to maintain an adequate supply during summer months.

34457 ■ *"Top 10 Retirement Mistakes and How to Avoid Them" in Canadian Business (Vol. 83, July 20, 2010, No. 11-12, pp. 39)*
Pub: Rogers Media Ltd.
Ed: Jacqueline Nelson, Angelina Chapin. **Description:** Some of the top retirement mistakes is relying on selling one's house to find a retirement. Other mistakes are paying too much for investments and planning to work in retirement since no one can be sure that they will be healthy enough to accomplish this. Suggestions to avoid these pitfalls are discussed.

34458 ■ *"Top 100 Consolidate Gains" in Hispanic Business (Vol. 30, July-August 2008, No. 7-8, pp. 30)*
Pub: Hispanic Business, Inc.
Ed: Richard Kaplan. **Description:** Data developed by HispanTelligence on the increase in revenue posted by the top 100 fastest-growing U.S. Hispanic firms over the last five years is reported. Despite the economic downturn, the service sector, IT and health suppliers showed an increase in revenue whereas construction companies showed a marginal slump in revenue growth.

34459 ■ *"Trisun Healthcare Eager to Add Centers" in Austin Business Journallnc. (Vol. 28, August 22, 2008, No. 23, pp. 1)*
Pub: American City Business Journals
Ed: Kate Harrington. **Description:** Austin-based nursing and rehabilitation centers operator Trisun Healthcare plans to build more facilities as part of a growth strategy that can expand beyond Texas. Trisun has 16 facilities along the corridor from San Antonio to Temple, and projects to have three more in Texas in 2008.

34460 ■ *"Types of Health Plans" in HRMagazine (Vol. 53, August 2008, No. 8, pp. 72)*
Pub: Society for Human Resource Management
Contact: Henry G. Jackson, President
E-mail: hjackson@shrm.org
Description: Definitions are given for various types of health care coverage available. Fee-for-service (FFS), health maintenance organization (HMO), preferred provider organization (PPO), point of service (POS) and consumer-directed health plan (CDHP) are outlined.

34461 ■ *"The Ultimate Cure" in Conde Nast Portfolio (Vol. 2, June 2008, No. 6, pp. 110)*
Pub: Conde Nast Publications
Contact: David Carey, President
Ed: David Ewing Duncan. **Description:** Small upstarts as well as pharmaceutical giants are developing drugs for the neurotechnology industry; these firms are attempting to adapt groundbreaking research into the basic workings of the brain to new drugs for ailments ranging from multiple sclerosis to dementia to insomnia.

34462 ■ *"UnitedHealthcare Resists Prognosis" in The Business Journal-Serving Metropolitan Kansas City (Vol. 26, August 29, 2008, No. 51)*
Pub: American City Business Journals, Inc.
Ed: Rob Roberts. **Description:** Saint Luke's Hospital Systems terminated UnitedHealthcare from its insurance provider network on July 25, 2008. Negotiators with both parties have stopped speaking, and employees under UnitedHealthcare plans will have to pay higher bills unless Saint Luke's reconsiders its decision. The parties' previous negotiations are discussed.

34463 ■ *"Unwanted News for Hospitals" in Business Courier (Vol. 24, October 26, 2008, No. 28, pp. 1)*
Pub: American City Business Journals, Inc.
Description: Christ and St. Luke Hospital might be sharing responsibility costs on the $207 million hospital being built by Health Alliance, the group they are parting with. Christ and St. Lu ke hospitals will be paying $60 million and $25 miilion for partial liability res pectively because the plans for the said project were already underway before they decided to withdraw. Christ Hospital is involved in a whistleblower case that might cause $424 million in liability across the group.

34464 ■ *"VA Seeking Bidders for Ft. Howard" in Baltimore Business Journal (Vol. 28, June 25, 2010, No. 7, pp. 1)*
Pub: Baltimore Business Journal
Ed: Daniel J. Sernovitz. **Description:** The Veterans Affairs Maryland Health Care Systems has requested proposals from developers to build a retirement community at Fort Howard in Baltimore County. The historic site, which has about 36 mostly vacant buildings, could become the home to hundreds of war veterans. Details of the proposed development are discussed.

34465 ■ *"Vernon Revamp" in Business Courier (Vol. 26, October 9, 2009, No. 24, pp. 1)*
Pub: American City Business Journals, Inc.
Ed: Dan Monk. **Description:** Al Neyer Inc. will redevelop the Vernon Manor Hotel as an office building for the Cincinnati Children's Hospital Medical Center. The project will cost $35 million and would generate a new investment vehicle for black investors who plan to raise $2.7 million in private offerings to claim majority ownership of the property after its renovations.

34466 ■ *"VPA to Pay $9.5 Million to Settle Whistle-Blower Lawsuits" in Crain's Detroit Business (Vol. 26, January 11, 2010, No. 2, pp. 13)*
Pub: Crain Communications Inc.
Ed: Jay Greene. **Description:** According to Terrence Berg, first assistant with the U.S. Attorney's Office in Detroit, Voluntary Physicians Association, a local

home health care company, has agreed to pay $9.5 million to settle four whistle-blower lawsuits; the agreement settles allegations that VPA submitted claims to TriCare, the Michigan Medicaid program and Medicare for unnecessary home visits, tests and procedures.

34467 ■ *"Walgreen Takes Up Doctoring" in Crain's Chicago Business (Vol. 31, March 31, 2008, No. 13, pp. 18)*
Pub: Crain Communications, Inc.
Ed: Mark Bruno. **Description:** Walgreen Co. has agreed to acquire two firms that provide on-site medical and pharmaceutical services to large companies. Walgreen feels that these facilities mark the future of health care for a number of large corporations.

34468 ■ *"Wayne, Oakland Counties Create Own 'Medical Corridor" in Crain's Detroit Business (Vol. 24, October 6, 2008, No. 40, pp. 8)*
Pub: Crain Communications, Inc.
Ed: Jay Greene. **Description:** Woodward Medical Corridor that runs along Woodward Avenue and currently encompasses twelve hospitals and is rapidly growing with additional physician offices, advanced oncology centers and new hospitals. Beaumont Hospital is building a $160 million proton-beam therapy cancer center on its Royal Oak campus in a joint venture with Procure Treatment Centers of Bloomington Ind. That is expected to open in 2010 and will employ approximately 145 new workers.

34469 ■ *"'We Are Not a Marketing Company" in Boston Business Journal (Vol. 31, June 10, 2011, No. 20, pp. 1)*
Pub: Boston Business Journal
Ed: Julie M. Donnelly. **Description:** Vertex Pharmaceuticals Inc. is marketing its new Hepatitis C treatment, Incivek. The company hired people to connect patients to the drug. Vertex is also set to move to a new facility in Boston, Massachusetts.

34470 ■ *"Week on the Web" in Crain's Detroit Business (Vol. 25, June 22, 2009, No. 25, pp. 19)*
Pub: Crain Communications Inc. - Detroit
Description: Blue Cross Blue Shield of Michigan, in a class-action lawsuit, will pay about 100 families whose children were either denied coverage for autism treatment or paid for treatment out of pocket. The settlement is worth about $ million.

34471 ■ *"What Choice Did I Have?" in Entrepreneur (Vol. 37, October 2009, No. 10, pp. 88)*
Pub: Entrepreneur Media, Inc.
Ed: Craig Matsuda. **Description:** Profile of a worker at a financial services company who acquired first hand knowledge concerning the relationship between health insurance costs and coverage. The worker's son got severely ill, forcing the worker to spend above what is covered by health insurance.

34472 ■ *"Where the Money Is" in Conde Nast Portfolio (Vol. 2, June 2008, No. 6, pp. 113)*
Pub: Conde Nast Publications
Contact: David Carey, President
Description: Revenue generated from treatments for common brain disorders that are currently on the market are listed.

34473 ■ *"Winner Nonprofit, Hospitals" in Crain's Detroit Business (Vol. 25, June 22, 2009, No. 25, pp. E002)*
Pub: Crain Communications Inc. - Detroit
Ed: Jay Greene. **Description:** James Connelly, CFO for Henry Ford Health System, discusses the financial status of the system. Statistical data included.

34474 ■ *Wisconsin Medical Directory*
Pub: Jola Publications
URL(s): www.orderpoint.comwww.jolapub.com. **Released:** Annual; Latest edition June, 2011-2012. **Price:** $25, Individuals Orderpoint tentative price. **Covers:** Approximately 15,000 doctors, hospitals, clinics, nursing homes, and other selected health care providers in Wisconsin. **Entries include:** Doctor or facility name, address, phone, fax, doctors' UPINS. **Arrangement:** Classified by type of facility or care provided. **Indexes:** Name, product/service, subject.

34475 ■ *Women's Health Concerns Sourcebook*
Pub: Omnigraphics Inc.
Contact: Frederick G. Ruffner,, Jr., President
URL(s): www.omnigraphics.com. **Ed:** Sandra J. Judd. **Released:** Irregular; latest edition 3rd; May 2009. **Price:** $85, Individuals Hardcover; $95, Individuals List price. **Publication includes:** Resources on women's health issues. **Entries include:** Publication name, address. Principal content of publication is articles on specific health issues, definitions, symptoms, risks, treatment, and answers to frequently asked questions. **Arrangement:** Topic. **Indexes:** subject index/alpha.

34476 ■ *"Work At It!" in Hawaii Business (Vol. 53, October 2007, No. 4, pp. 44)*
Pub: Hawaii Business Publishing
Ed: Cathy S. Cruz-George. **Description:** Employers in Hawaii are mitigating the effects of rising healthcare costs by giving their employees health insurance and offering wellness programs. Employer-based health insurance has increases by 87 percent in the United States over the 2000-2006 period. Wellness programs that address different aspects of employees' health, such as food consumption, drug compliance and smoking habits, are discussed.

34477 ■ *"Workers' Comp System Cuts Through Paper" in Sacramento Business Journal (Vol. 25, July 11, 2008, No. 19, pp. 1)*
Pub: American City Business Journals, Inc.
Ed: Kelly Johnson. **Description:** California has started testing a new paperless system for handling disputed workers' compensation claims. It is believed that the shift will affect people both inside and outside of the state Division of Workers' Compensation and the state Workers' Compensation Appeals Board. The other details of the planned system are also presented.

34478 ■ *"The World Is Your Hospital" in Canadian Business (Vol. 81, July 22, 2008, No. 12-13, pp. 62)*
Pub: Rogers Media Ltd.
Ed: Sharda Prashad. **Description:** Medical tourism is seen as a booming industry around the world and is expected to grow to around $40 billion in 2010. Key information regarding medical tourism and services are presented. Views on the possible impact of medical tourism on Canada's health care industry, as well as medical tourism opportunities in Canada, are also given.

34479 ■ *"The Worst-Run Industry in Canada: Health Care" in Canadian Business (Vol. 83, October 12, 2010, No. 17, pp. 39)*
Pub: Rogers Media Ltd.
Ed: Rachel Mendleson. **Description:** Most Canadians believe that the problem of the country's health care system is rooted in insufficient funding, demographic overload, or corporate profiteering. However, health economists and policy analysts think the real issues is mismanagement, as the pervasive inefficiency is affecting the system's structure.

TRADE PERIODICALS

34480 ■ *The AARP Pharmacy Service Enjoying Good Health Newsletter*
Pub: Retired Persons Services Inc.
Ed: Joan M. Zimmermann, Editor, jzimmermann@rpsrx.com. **Released:** Bimonthly. **Description:** Offers health information and medical tips on topics relevant for the elderly. Recurring features include notices of publications available.

34481 ■ *Abbeyfield Houses Society of Canada Newsletter*
Pub: Abbeyfield Houses Society of Canada
Ed: Robert McMullan, Editor. **Released:** Quarterly. **Description:** Reports on news of Abbeyfield Houses Society of Canada, a provider of care and companionship for the elderly. Also features articles related to aging, housing, and lifestyle in Canada and internationally. Recurring features include letters to the editor, and columns titled News of Local Societies and Bits 'n Bites.

34482 ■ *Academic Emergency Medicine: Official Journal of the Society for Academic Emergency Medicine*
Pub: Blackwell Publishing Inc.
Contact: Gordon Tibbitts, President
URL(s): as.wiley.com/WileyCDA/WileyTitle/productCd-ACEM.html. **Ed:** Carey D. Chisholm, James G. Adams. **Released:** Monthly **Price:** $178, Individuals print + online; €134, Individuals print + online; £89, Other countries print + online; $331, Institutions print + online; £174, Institutions print + online; $289, Institutions online; £153, Institutions online; $97, Members; €72, Members; £49, Members.

34483 ■ *Advances*
Pub: The Robert Wood Johnson Foundation
Ed: Larry Blumenthal, Editor, lblumen@rwjf.org. **Released:** Quarterly. **Price:** Included in membership. **Description:** The National Newsletter of The Robert Wood Johnson Foundation. Reports on issues related to the Foundations grantmaking. Recurring features include interviews, news of research, and columns titled Profile, Abridge, Grants, and People.

34484 ■ *AHA News: American Hospital Association News*
Pub: Health Forum L.L.C.
Contact: Neil Jesuele, President
E-mail: njesuel1@aha.org
URL(s): www.ahanews.com/. **Released:** Biweekly **Price:** $75, Members 2 years; 2nd class mail; $125, Members 2 years; 1st class mail; $195, Members 2 years; other countries (prepaid); $375, Members 2 years; international air (prepaid); $160, Nonmembers 2 years; 2nd class mail; $210, Nonmembers 2 years; 1st class mail; $280, Nonmembers 2 years; other countries (prepaid); $460, Nonmembers international air (prepaid).

34485 ■ *Air Medical Journal*
Pub: Mosby Inc.
URL(s): journals.elsevierhealth.com/periodicals/ymam. **Ed:** Jacqueline C. Stocking, Eric R. Swanson. **Released:** Bimonthly **Price:** $125, Individuals online and print; $177, Canada and Mexico online and print; $177, Other countries online and print.

34486 ■ *Alcohol Research and Health*
Pub: U.S. Government Printing Office
URL(s): www.niaaa.nih.gov/Publications/AlcoholResearch/Pages/default.aspx. **Released:** Quarterly **Price:** $33, Individuals; $46.20, Other countries; $13.75, Single issue; $19.25, Single issue in other countries.

34487 ■ *Alive*
Pub: Alive Publishing Group Inc.
Contact: Siegfried Gursche, Owner
URL(s): www.alive.com/. **Released:** Monthly **Price:** $37, Individuals.

34488 ■ *American Journal of Electroneurodiagnostic Technology: Journal of the American Society of Electroneurodiagnostic Technologists, Inc*
Pub: American Society of Electroneurodiagnostic Technologists
Contact: Arlen Reimnitz, Executive Director
E-mail: arlen@aset.org
URL(s): www.aset.org/i4a/pages/index.cfm?pageid=3314. **Released:** Quarterly **Price:** $110, Individuals; $130, Other countries individual; $150, Institutions; $180, Institutions, other countries.

34489 ■ *American Journal of Infection Control (AJIC)*
Pub: Mosby Inc.
URL(s): journals.elsevierhealth.com/periodicals/ymic. **Ed:** Elaine L. Larson. **Released:** 10/yr. **Price:** $196, Individuals; $252, Canada and Mexico; $252, Other countries.

34490 ■ *The Arc News*
Pub: The Arc of Carroll County Inc.
Price: Included in membership. **Description:** Spotlights issues concerning the mentally and physically disabled. Discusses rehabilitation, safety, housing, and centers.

34491 ■ *Archives of Environmental & Occupational Health: An International Journal*
Pub: Taylor & Francis Group Journals
Contact: Kevin J. Bradley, President
URL(s): www.tandfonline.com/toc/vaeh20/current. **Released:** 4/yr. **Price:** $486, Institutions print & online; $338, Individuals print & online; $437, Institutions online only.

34492 ■ *Bulletin of Experimental Treatments for AIDS: Bulletin of Experimental Treatments for AIDS (BETA)*
Pub: San Francisco AIDS Foundation
URL(s): www.sfaf.org/hiv-info/hot-topics/beta/. **Ed:** Reilly O'Neal, Liz Highleyman. **Released:** Biennial **Price:** Free.

34493 ■ *Business & Health Institute: Keys to Workforce Productivity*
Pub: Advanstar Communications
Contact: Robert Krakoff, President
URL(s): managedhealthcareexecutive.modernmedicine.com/mhe/Business-and-Healt h-Institute/static/detail/134801. **Released:** 10/yr.

34494 ■ *Business Insurance*
Pub: Crain Communications Inc.
URL(s): www.businessinsurance.com. **Released:** Weekly **Price:** $399, Individuals print; $149, Individuals print & digital; $69, Individuals digital edition.

34495 ■ *Cambridge Quarterly of Healthcare Ethics*
Pub: Cambridge University Press
Contact: Richard Ziemacki, President
E-mail: rziemacki@cambridge.org
URL(s): journals.cambridge.org/action/displayJournal?jid=CQH. **Ed:** Steve Heilig, Dr. Thomasine Kushner. **Released:** Quarterly **Price:** $360, Institutions online & print; $300, Institutions online; $45, Single issue article; £225, Institutions online & print; £188, Institutions online.

34496 ■ *Canadian Journal of Dietetic Practice and Research*
Pub: Dietitians of Canada
Contact: Marsha Sharp, Chief Executive Officer
URL(s): www.dietitians.ca/public/content/research/journal.asp. **Released:** Quarterly **Price:** $110, Canada online and print; $85, Canada print only; $110, Other countries print only; $95, Individuals print only; $125, Individuals online and print; $135, Other countries online and print.

34497 ■ *Canadian Journal of Public Health*
Pub: Canadian Public Health Association
Contact: Jerry Dafoe, Chief Executive Officer
URL(s): www.cpha.ca/en/cjph.aspx. **Ed:** Dr. Gilles Paradis. **Released:** Bimonthly **Price:** $117, Canada regular; C$151, U.S. regular; $193, Other countries regular; $26, Canada single issue; $31, U.S. single issue; $36, Other countries single issue.

34498 ■ *Canadian Journal of Respiratory Therapy: Leadership through Advocacy, Service and Unity for Respiratory Therapists in Canada*
Pub: Canadian Society of Respiratory Therapists
Contact: Christiane Menard, Executive Director
URL(s): www.csrt.com/en/publications/journal.asp. **Released:** 5/yr. **Price:** $50, Canada; $60, Other countries; $15, Single issue; Free members.

34499 ■ *Canadian Respiratory Journal: The Official Journal of the Canadian Thorasic Society*
Pub: Pulsus Group Inc.
URL(s): www.pulsus.com/journals/journalHome.jsp?jnlKy=4&/home2.htm. **Released:** 8/yr. **Price:** C$215, Canada; $195, Individuals print; $250, Other countries; C$240, Canada print and online; $295, Individuals print and online; $330, Other countries print and online.

34500 ■ *Care Management Journals: "Journal of Case Management" and "The Journal of Long Term Home Health Care"*
Pub: Springer Publishing Co.
Contact: Ursula Springer, President
URL(s): www.springerpub.com/product/15210987#.UB8RbPbiZIR. **Ed:** F. Russell Kellogg, Joan Quinn. **Released:** Quarterly **Price:** $110, Individuals print or online; $165, Individuals print & online; $289, Individuals print or online; $240, Institutions print & online.

34501 ■ *Caring People*
Pub: National Association for Home Care
URL(s): www.nahc.org/CARINGMAGAZINE/. **Ed:** Val Halamandaris. **Released:** Monthly

34502 ■ *The Case Manager: The Official Publication of the Case Management Society of America*
Pub: Mosby Inc.
Contact: Brian Nairin, President
URL(s): www.elsevier.com/wps/find/journaldescription.cws_home/623112/descri p tion#description. **Ed:** Catherine M. Mullahy. **Released:** Bimonthly; 6 /yr. **Price:** $131, Institutions, other countries; $91, Other countries; $100, Institutions; $91, Single issue; $67, Individuals.

34503 ■ *Child and Youth Services*
Pub: Routledge Journals Taylor & Francis Group
URL(s): www.tandfonline.com/toc/wcys20/current. **Ed:** Doug Magnuson, Jerome Beker. **Released:** Quarterly **Price:** $114, Individuals online only; $123, Individuals print + online; $684, Institutions online only; $616, Institutions online only.

34504 ■ *Children's Voice*
Pub: Child Welfare League of America Inc.
Contact: Chris James-Brown, President
E-mail: cjamesbrown@cwla.org
URL(s): www.cwla.org/pubs/welcome.htm. **Released:** Bimonthly **Price:** $140, Nonmembers; $255, Nonmembers 2 years.

34505 ■ *Clinical Laboratory News*
Pub: American Association of Clinical Chemistry
Contact: Mozella Place, Manager
E-mail: mplace@aacc.org
URL(s): www.aacc.org/publications/cln/Pages/default.aspx. **Ed:** Nancy Sasavage. **Released:** Monthly

34506 ■ *Clinical Leadership and Management Review: CLMR*
Pub: Clinical Laboratory Management Association
Contact: Rodney W. Forsman, President
URL(s): www.clma.org/?page=Publications_Overvie. **Ed:** Tony Kurec. **Released:** Bimonthly

34507 ■ *The CMA Today: Professional Medical Assistant*
Pub: American Association of Medical Assistants
Contact: Boni Bruntz, President
URL(s): www.aama-ntl.org/cmatoday/about.aspx. **Released:** Bimonthly **Price:** $30, free to members; $60, Nonmembers.

34508 ■ *Contemporary Long Term Care*
Pub: Leisure Publications Inc.
Contact: Nancy Field, President
URL(s): www.cltcmag.com. **Released:** Monthly; 11/yr. **Price:** $80, Individuals; $95, Canada and Mexico; $130, Two years; $129, Other countries.

34509 ■ *The Counselor*
Pub: The Counselor
Ed: Steve Erickson, Editor. **Released:** 6/year. **Description:** Reports on membership news and other public relations topics.

34510 ■ *Dentaletter*
Pub: MPL Communications Inc.
Contact: Barrie Martland, President
E-mail: bmartland@mplcomm.com
Ed: Dr. Brian Waters, Editor. **Released:** 11/year. **Price:** $119. **Description:** Publishes news of dental research. Also covers related web sites.

34511 ■ *Dietary Manager Magazine*
Pub: Dietary Managers Association
Contact: Ricky Clark, Chairman of the Board
URL(s): www.dmaonline.org/Publications/Dietary_Manager.shtml. **Ed:** Diane Everett. **Released:** Monthly; 10/yr. **Price:** $40, Individuals.

34512 ■ *EHS Today: The Magazine of Safety, Health and Loss Prevention*
Pub: Penton Media Inc.
URL(s): ehstoday.com/. **Ed:** Sandy Smith. **Released:** Monthly

34513 ■ *Encounters*
Pub: Venice Family Clinic
Contact: Carmen Ibara, Chief Operating Officer
Released: Biennial. **Price:** Free. **Description:** Reports on news, events, programs, and activities of the Venice Family Clinic in Los Angeles, California whose mission is 'to provide comprehensive primary health care that is affordable, accessible and compassionable for people with no other access to such care.'.

34514 ■ *Equilibrium*
Pub: The Mood Disorders Association of Ontario
Ed: Eric Jonasson, Editor. **Released:** Quarterly. **Price:** $25. **Description:** Reports on news, events, and updates of The Mood Disorders Association of Metropolitan Toronto, as well as related topics.

34515 ■ *European Clinical Laboratory*
Pub: International Scientific Communications Inc.
Contact: William N. Wham, Publisher
E-mail: iscpubs@iscpubs.com
URL(s): www.iscpubs.comwww.iscpubs.com/publications/#eu. **Released:** Bimonthly; 6 times.

34516 ■ *Evaluation & the Health Professions*
Pub: SAGE Publications USA
Contact: Blaise R. Simqu, President
URL(s): www.sagepub.com/journalsProdDesc.nav?prodId=Journal200787&. **Ed:** R. Barker Bausell, Carolyn F. Waltz. **Released:** Quarterly **Price:** $720, Institutions combined (print & e-access); $792, Institutions current volume (print & all online content); $648, Institutions e-access; $720, Institutions backfile lease, e-access plus backfile; $1157, Institutions backfile purchase, e-access (content through 1998); $706, Institutions print only; $147, Individuals print only; $194, Institutions single print; $48, Individuals single print.

34517 ■ *FDA Week*
Pub: Inside Washington Publishers
Contact: Korila Malecha, Manager
Ed: Donna Haseley, Editor. **Released:** Weekly (Fri.). **Price:** $595, U.S. and Canada; $645, elsewhere. **Description:** Reports on Food and Drug Administration policy, regulation, and enforcement.

34518 ■ *Fertility Weekly*
Pub: Keith Key
Contact: Keith Key, Publisher
E-mail: keithkey@mindspring.com
Released: Weekly. **Price:** $799, U.S. and Canada; $899, elsewhere; $1,299, U.S. and Canada two years;. **Description:** Discusses information pertaining to fertility. Recurring features include news of research, a calendar of events, reports of meetings, and a column titled Periodical Review.

34519 ■ *Focus on Autism and Other Developmental Disabilities*
Pub: SAGE Publications USA
Contact: Blaise R. Simqu, President
URL(s): www.sagepub.com/journalsProdEditBoards.nav?prodId=Journal201875. **Ed:** Paul Alberto, Juane Helfin, Richard Simpson, Joel Arick, Diane Adreon, Paul E. Bates. **Released:** Quarterly **Price:** $63, Individuals print & e-access; $187, Institutions print & e-access; $172, Institutions e-access; $187, Institutions print only.

34520 ■ *Forensic Drug Abuse Advisor*
Pub: Forensic Drug Abuse Advisor Inc.
Ed: Steven B. Karch, M.D., Editor. **Released:** 10/year. **Price:** $197, individuals. **Description:** Acts as a drug information source. Emphasizes the latest scientific discoveries in drug abuse, workplace drug

testing, federal drug law, and forensic pathology. An absolute necessity in drug related litigation. Recurring features include letters to the editor, news of research, a calendar of events, reports of meetings, news of educational opportunities, book reviews, and notices of publications available. Continuing medical education available.

34521 ■ *Frontiers of Health Services Management*
Pub: Health Administration Press
Contact: Thomas C. Dolan, President
E-mail: tdolan@ache.org
URL(s): www.ache.org/pubs/frontiers.cfm. **Ed:** Margaret F. Schulte. **Released:** Quarterly **Price:** $110, Individuals; $32, Single issue.

34522 ■ *Georgia Tech Sports and Performance Newsletter*
Pub: Georgia Tech University
Ed: H.G. Knuttgen, Ph.D., Editor. **Released:** Monthly. **Price:** $34, U.S.; $42, Canada; $48, elsewhere. **Description:** Discusses sports training, nutrition, injury prevention, and sports medicine research and news. Recurring features include letters to the editor, interviews, and news of research.

34523 ■ *Good Health Bulletin*
Pub: Harvey W. Watt & Company Inc.
Released: Monthly. **Price:** $19.95, U.S. and Canada. **Description:** Contains up-to-date helpful medical and related information concerning health, fitness, and longevity. Recurring features include news of research.

34524 ■ *Government Recreation and Fitness*
Pub: Executive Business Media Inc.
URL(s): www.ebmpubs.com/GFS/index.asp. **Released:** 10/yr. **Price:** $35, Individuals; $60, Two years; $40, Other countries; $5, Single issue; $87, Other countries airmail.

34525 ■ *Health Affairs: The Policy Journal of the Health Sphere*
Pub: Project HOPE
Contact: Dr. John Howe, III, President
URL(s): www.healthaffairs.org. **Ed:** John K. Iglehart, Meredith S. Zimmerman. **Released:** Bimonthly **Price:** $138, Individuals print & online; $188, Other countries print & online; $235, Two years print & online; $285, Other countries print & online, 2 years; $84, Students print & online; $134, Students print & online, international; $37, Single issue print & online; $355, Institutions print online, tier 1; $405, Institutions, other countries print & online, tier 1; $335, Institutions online only.

34526 ■ *Health Care for Women International: Official Journal of the International Council on Women's Health Issues*
Pub: Routledge, Taylor & Francis Group
Contact: David Smith, Chief Executive Officer
URL(s): www.tandf.co.uk/journals/titles/07399332.asp. **Ed:** Carole Anne McKenzie. **Released:** 12/yr. **Price:** $260, Individuals print only; $1001, Institutions online only; $1112, Institutions print and online.

34527 ■ *Health Progress: Official Journal of the Catholic Health Association of the United States*
Pub: Healing Ministry of Catholic Health Care
Contact: Sr. Carol Keehan, President
E-mail: ckeehan@chausa.org
URL(s): www.chausa.org/pages/publications/health_progress/current_issue. **Ed:** Pamela Schaeffer. **Released:** Bimonthly **Price:** $55, Members CHA; $65, Other countries; $65, Nonmembers; $10, Nonmembers single copy; Free to members, single copy; $55, Members; $65, Nonmembers.

34528 ■ *Health and Safety Science Abstracts*
Pub: Cambridge Scientific Abstracts L.P.
Contact: Chris Jahn, Manager
URL(s): www.csa.com/factsheets/health-safety-set-c.php. **Released:** Monthly

34529 ■ *Health Science: Living Well Into the Future*
Pub: National Health Association
Contact: Jerry Deutsch, President
URL(s): www.healthscience.org/index.php?option=com_content&view=article&id= 37&Itemid=265. **Released:** Quarterly **Price:** $35, U.S. and Canada; $55, Other countries; $65, Two years; $95, Other countries 2 years.

34530 ■ *Healthcare Advertising Review: Creative Forum for the People who Plan and Create Healthcare Advertising Programs*
Pub: The Business Word
Contact: Susan J. Alt, President
URL(s): www.businessword.com/pubs/har.html. **Ed:** Tom Rees. **Released:** Bimonthly **Price:** $294, Individuals print; $294, Individuals online.

34531 ■ *Healthcare Corporate Finance News*
Pub: Irving Levin Associates Inc.
Contact: Stephen M. Monroe, Managing Editor
Ed: Gretchen S. Swanson, Editor. **Released:** Monthly. **Price:** $495. **Description:** Reports on the growth strategies of managed care providers, hospitals, drug companies, medical device manufacturers, and other healthcare organizations. Also reports on the latest deals in the healthcare sector, and how healthcare companies are doing on Wall Street.

34532 ■ *Healthcare Executive*
Pub: American College of Healthcare Executives
Contact: Thomas C. Dolan, President
URL(s): www.ache.org/PUBS/hcexecsub.cfm. **Released:** Bimonthly **Price:** $100, Individuals in the U.S.

34533 ■ *Healthcare Purchasing News: Business News and Analysis for Purchasing Decision-Makers*
Pub: Nelson Publishing Inc.
URL(s): www.hpnonline.com. **Ed:** Susan Cantrell. **Released:** Monthly **Price:** $72, Individuals; $110, Canada; $130, Other countries.

34534 ■ *Heart and Lung: The Journal of Acute and Critical Care*
Pub: Mosby An Imprint of Elsevier Science Inc. Elsevier Inc. Health Sciences
URL(s): www.elsevier.com/wps/find/journaldescription.cws_home/623089/descrip tion#description. **Ed:** Nancy S. Redeker. **Released:** Bimonthly; Jan, Mar, May, July, Sept, Nov. **Price:** $103, Individuals; $445, Institutions; $524, Institutions, other countries; $153, Other countries.

34535 ■ *Hemophilia Ontario News*
Pub: Hemophilia Ontario
Released: Quarterly, 3-4/yr. **Price:** $15, individuals in Canada; $20, institutions in Canada. **Description:** Hemophilia Ontario is commited to improve the quality of life of people affected by hemophilia and related blood conditions, and to work towards a cure. Publishes on current events, new treatments, volunteer update, and advocacy news. Recurring features include news of research, a calendar of events, and job listings.

34536 ■ *Home Health Care Management and Practice*
Pub: SAGE Publications USA
Contact: Blaise R. Simqu, President
URL(s): www.sagepub.com/journalsProdDesc.nav?prodId=Journal201504. **Ed:** Barbara Stover Gingerich. **Released:** Bimonthly **Price:** $555, Institutions print & e-access; $611, Institutions current volume print & all online content; $500, Institutions e-access; $556, Institutions all online content; $500, Institutions content through 1998; $544, Institutions print only; $170, Individuals print only; $100, Institutions single print; $37, Individuals single print.

34537 ■ *Home Health Care Services Quarterly*
Pub: Routledge Journals Taylor & Francis Group
URL(s): www.tandf.co.uk/journals/WHHC. **Ed:** Maria Aranda. **Released:** Quarterly **Price:** $125, Individuals online; $134, Individuals print & online.

34538 ■ *Homecare Administrative HORIZONS*
Pub: Beacon Health Corp.
Contact: Diane J. Omdahl, Editor-in-Chief
Released: Monthly. **Price:** $347, individuals. **Description:** Provides homecare agency management information on all kinds of business and personnel topics. Incorporates comprehensive how-to information, current regulatory requirements, and documentation strategies. Runs a series of articles, including how to move into managed care, how to manage and measure outcomes, how to survive scrutiny by medicare's fraud squad, strengthening agency/physician relationships, and personnel issues. Recurring features include columns titled Peaks & Valleys, Fine-tuning the Fundamentals, Clearing the Fog, and Higher Ground.

34539 ■ *Hospital News Canada*
Pub: Trader Media Corp.
URL(s): www.hospitalnews.com. **Released:** Monthly **Price:** $29.40, Canada; $77, Individuals bulk subscriptions; 25 copies per month; $104.50, Individuals bulk subscriptions; 50 copies per month; $187, Individuals bulk subscriptions; 100 copies per month; $330, Individuals bulk subscriptions; 150 copies per month; $374, Individuals bulk subscriptions; 200 copies per month; $42.90, Two years; $55, Other countries; $33, Individuals in U.S.

34540 ■ *Hospital Topics*
Pub: Routledge, Taylor & Francis Group
Contact: David Smith, Chief Executive Officer
URL(s): www.tandf.co.uk/journals/titles/00185868.asp. **Released:** Quarterly **Price:** $62, Individuals print & online; $177, Institutions print & online.

34541 ■ *Industrial Hygiene News*
Pub: Rimbach Publishing Inc.
URL(s): www.rimbach.com. **Released:** Bimonthly

34542 ■ *The Informer*
Pub: Simon Foundation for Continence
Contact: Ms. Cheryle Gartley, President
Released: Quarterly. **Price:** $15, U.S.. **Description:** Discusses topics concerned with bladder or bowel incontinence.

34543 ■ *International Journal of Health Planning and Management*
Pub: John Wiley & Sons Inc.
Contact: Stephen M. Smith, President
URL(s): onlinelibrary.wiley.com/journal/10.1002/(ISSN)1099-1751. **Ed:** Prof. Kenneth Lee, Dr. Ruby Barrow. **Released:** Quarterly **Price:** $1742, Other countries print only; $2494, Institutions, other countries print only; $2868, Institutions, other countries print with online; €1609, Institutions print only; £1272, Institutions print only; €1850, Institutions print with online; £1463, Institutions print with online.

34544 ■ *International Journal of Health Services*
Pub: Baywood Publishing Company Inc.
Contact: Stuart Cohen, President
URL(s): www.baywood.com/journals/PreviewJournals.asp?Id=0020-7314. **Ed:** Linda Strange. **Released:** Quarterly **Price:** $402, Institutions; $381, Institutions online.

34545 ■ *International Journal of Technology Assessment in Health Care*
Pub: Cambridge University Press
Contact: Richard Ziemacki, President
E-mail: rziemacki@cambridge.org
URL(s): journals.cambridge.org/action/displayJournal?jid=THC. **Ed:** Prof. Egon Jonsson. **Released:** 4/yr. **Price:** £327, Institutions online & print; £278, Institutions online; £164, Individuals online & print; $580, Institutions online & print; $485, Institutions online; $281, Individuals online & print; $45, Individuals article.

34546 ■ *The Joint Commission Journal on Quality Improvement*
Pub: The Joint Commission Journal on Quality Improvement
URL(s): www.jcrinc.com/26813/newsletters/32/. **Released:** Monthly **Price:** $319, Individuals.

34547 ■ *Journal of Agromedicine*
Pub: Taylor & Francis Group Ltd.
Contact: William Germanno, Manager
E-mail: williamgermano@gmail.com
URL(s): www.tandfonline.com/toc/wagr20/current. **Ed:** Matthew C. Keifer. **Released:** 4/yr. **Price:** $132, Individuals online; $145, Individuals print & online; $293, Institutions online; $326, Institutions print & online.

34548 ■ *Journal of the American Board of Family Medicine*
Pub: American Board of Family Medicine
Contact: Samuel Jones, Chairman
URL(s): www.jabfm.org. **Ed:** Anne Victoria Neale, Marjorie Bowman. **Released:** Bimonthly **Price:** $140, Institutions print; $70, Individuals print; $35, Single issue print; $175, Institutions, other countries print; $105, Other countries print; $45, Other countries single issue.

34549 ■ *Journal of American College Health*
Pub: Routledge, Taylor & Francis Group
Contact: David Smith, Chief Executive Officer
URL(s): www.tandf.co.uk/journals/titles/07448481.asp. **Released:** Bimonthly **Price:** $124, Individuals print & online; $327, Institutions print & online.

34550 ■ *Journal of the Association of Nurses in AIDS Care*
Pub: Elsevier
URL(s): www.elsevier.com/wps/find/journaldescription.cws_home/704632/descrip tion#description. **Ed:** Lucy Bradley-Springer. **Released:** Bimonthly **Price:** $552, Institutions, other countries; $116, Individuals; $500, Institutions; $162, Other countries.

34551 ■ *Journal of Behavioral Health Services & Research*
Pub: Springer-Verlag New York Inc.
Contact: Ruediger Gebauer, President
URL(s): jbhsr.fmhi.usf.eduwww.springer.com/public+health/journal/11414. **Released:** Quarterly **Price:** €337, Institutions print or online; €404, Institutions print & enchanced access.

34552 ■ *Journal of Ethnic & Cultural Diversity in Social Work: Innovations in Theory, Research & Practice*
Pub: Routledge Journals Taylor & Francis Group
URL(s): www.tandfonline.com/toc/wecd20/current. **Released:** Quarterly **Price:** $125, Individuals online only; $134, Individuals print + online; $505, Institutions online only; $562, Institutions print + online.

34553 ■ *Journal of Health Care Chaplaincy*
Pub: Routledge Journals Taylor & Francis Group
URL(s): www.tandfonline.com/toc/whcc20/current. **Released:** Semiannual **Price:** $52, Individuals online only; $58, Individuals print + online; $291, Institutions online only; $323, Institutions print + online.

34554 ■ *Journal of Health Care Finance*
Pub: Aspen Publishers Inc.
Contact: Mark Dorman, President
URL(s): www.aspenpublishers.com/Product.asp?catalog_name=Aspen&product_id=S S 10786767. **Released:** Quarterly **Price:** $369, Individuals.

34555 ■ *Journal of Health Care for the Poor and Underserved (JHCPU)*
Pub: Association of Clinicians for the Underserved
Contact: Kathie Westpheling, Executive Director
URL(s): www.press.jhu.edu/journals/journal_of_health_care_for_the_poor_and_u nderserved/. **Ed:** Virginia Brennan. **Released:** Quarterly; February, May, August, and November. **Price:** $705, Individuals print; $370, Institutions print; $740, Institutions print, 2 years; $35, Students print; $140, Two years individual.

34556 ■ *Journal of Health & Social Behavior*
Pub: American Sociological Association
Contact: Sally T. Hillsman, Executive Director
E-mail: hillsman@asanet.org
URL(s): www.asanet.org/journals/jhsb/index.cfm. **Ed:** Debra Umberson, Ronald J. Angel, Chloe E. Bird. **Released:** Quarterly **Price:** $40, Members; $30, Students members; $255, Institutions print/online; $229, Institutions online only; $20, Individuals postage outside the U.S./Canada.

34557 ■ *Journal for Healthcare Quality: The Official Journal of the National Association for Healthcare Quality*
Pub: National Association for Healthcare Quality
Contact: Stacy Sochacki, Executive Director
E-mail: ssochacki@nahq.org
URL(s): www.wiley.com/bw/journal.asp?ref=1062-2551. **Released:** Bimonthly **Price:** $193, Individuals print and online; $252, Institutions print and online.

34558 ■ *Journal of Intensive Care Medicine*
Pub: SAGE Publications USA
Contact: Blaise R. Simqu, President
URL(s): www.sagepub.com/journalsProdDesc.nav?prodId=Journal201630. **Ed:** Nicholas Smyrnios, James M. Rippe. **Released:** Bimonthly **Price:** $845, Institutions print & e-access; $930, Institutions (current volume print & all online content); $761, Institutions e-access; $846, Institutions e-access; $841, Institutions back file purchase, e-access content through 1998; $828, Institutions print; $306, Individuals print; $152, Institutions single print; $66, Individuals single print.

34559 ■ *Journal of Nuclear Cardiology: Official Journal of the American Society of Nuclear Cardiology*
Pub: Springer-Verlag New York Inc.
Contact: Ruediger Gebauer, President
URL(s): www.springer.com/medicine/cardiology/journal/12350. **Ed:** Barry L. Zaret. **Released:** Bimonthly **Price:** €405, Institutions print + online; €486, Institutions print + enhanced access.

34560 ■ *Journal of School Health*
Pub: American School Health Association
Contact: Susan F. Wooley, Director
E-mail: swooley@ashaweb.org
URL(s): www.ashaweb.org/i4a/pages/index.cfm?pageid=3341. **Released:** Monthly; (not published in June and July).

34561 ■ *Journal of Social Service Research*
Pub: Routledge Journals Taylor & Francis Group
URL(s): www.tandfonline.com/toc/wssr20/current. **Released:** Quarterly **Price:** $110, Individuals online only; $122, Individuals print + online; $832, Institutions online only; $925, Institutions print + online.

34562 ■ *The League Letter*
Pub: Center for Hearing and Communication
Contact: Laurie Hanin, Executive Director
Price: Included in membership. **Description:** Reports on news and events of the The League for the Hard of Hearing. Recurring features include a calendar of events. Remarks: TTY available at (917)305-7999.

34563 ■ *Leaven*
Pub: La Leche League International
Contact: Viola Lennon, Director
URL(s): www.llli.org/llleaderweb/lv/index.html. **Released:** Quarterly **Price:** $30, Members box of back issues; $35, Individuals box of back issues; online; $35, Individuals box of back issues.

34564 ■ *Managed Healthcare Executive: The News Magazine for Health Care Costs and Quality*
Pub: Advanstar Communications Inc.
Contact: Mr. Joseph Loggia, Chief Executive Officer
E-mail: jloggia@advanstar.com
URL(s): managedhealthcareexecutive.modernmedicine.com. **Released:** Monthly **Price:** $89.25, Individuals; $131.25, Two years; $7.35, Single issue prepaid; $173.25, Canada and Mexico; $267.25, Canada and Mexico two years; $19.95, Single issue Canada & Mexico.

34565 ■ *Marketing Health Services*
Pub: American Marketing Association
Contact: Lucille Pointer, President
URL(s): www.marketingpower.com. **Ed:** Rhoda Weiss. **Released:** Quarterly **Price:** $100, Individuals print only; $135, Institutions print only; $105, Canada print only; $141.75, Institutions, Canada print only; $165, Institutions, other countries print only; $135, Other countries print only.

34566 ■ *Massage Therapy Journal*
Pub: American Massage Therapy Association
Contact: Shelly Johnson, Executive Director
URL(s): www.amtamassage.org/. **Ed:** Michael Schwanz. **Released:** Annual **Price:** $25, U.S. and Canada; $45, U.S. and Canada 2 years; $70, Other countries; $120, Other countries 2 years.

34567 ■ *Materials Management in Health Care*
Pub: Health Forum L.L.C.
Contact: Neil Jesuele, President
E-mail: njesuel1@aha.org
URL(s): www.matmanmag.com/matmanmag_app/index.jsp. **Ed:** Bob Kehoe. **Released:** Monthly

34568 ■ *Medicine on the Net*
Pub: COR Healthcare Resources
Ed: Bridget Meaney, Editor. **Released:** Monthly. **Price:** $147, U.S. and Canada; $159, elsewhere. **Description:** Spotlights developing issues in the use of the Internet by medical professionals. Recurring features include letters to the editor, interviews, news of research, and book reviews.

34569 ■ *Modern Healthcare: The Weekly Healthcare Business News Magazine*
Pub: Crain Communications Inc.
URL(s): www.modernhealthcare.com. **Ed:** David Burda. **Released:** Weekly **Price:** $164, Individuals; $255, Canada; $218, Other countries.

34570 ■ *Morbidity and Mortality Weekly Report: Morbidity and Mortality Weekly Report*
Pub: Centers for Disease Control and Prevention Office of Scientific and Health Communications
Contact: Karen White, Director
E-mail: kew1@cdc.gov
URL(s): www.cdc.gov/. **Released:** Weekly (Fri.) **Price:** Free electronic copy; $4.25, Single issue domestic; $5.95, Single issue foreign.

34571 ■ *The Nation's Health*
Pub: American Public Health Association
Contact: Melvin D. Shipp, President
E-mail: mshipp@optometry.osu.edu
URL(s): thenationshealth.aphapublications.org. **Released:** 10/yr. **Price:** $75, U.S. and Canada; $90, Other countries; $8, Single issue; $9, Other countries single issue.

34572 ■ *NCPD National Update*
Pub: National Catholic Partnership on Disability
Contact: Janice Benton, Executive Director
Released: Quarterly. **Price:** Free. **Description:** Focuses on disabled persons with a Catholic slant.

34573 ■ *New Beginnings*
Pub: La Leche League International
Contact: Viola Lennon, Director
URL(s): www.llli.org/nbdate.html. **Released:** Bimonthly

34574 ■ *New Horizons*
Pub: San Fernando Valley Association for the Retarded
Ed: Nancy Banks, Editor. **Released:** 3/year. **Price:** Included in membership. **Description:** Reports on membership news of the San Fernando Valley Association for the Retarded. Spotlights volunteers, activities, and events. Recurring features include columns titled Legislative Corner and President's Corner.

34575 ■ *Nursing Education Perspectives*
Pub: National League for Nursing
Contact: Judith A. Halstead, President
URL(s): www.nln.org/nlnjournal/index.htm. **Ed:** Joyce Fitzpatrick. **Released:** Bimonthly; January, March, May, July, September, and November. **Price:** $40, Individuals; $90, Nonmembers; $110, Canada nonmembers; $120, Other countries non-member; $152, Institutions; C$172, Libraries; $182, Other countries libraries.

34576 ■ *Nutrition & Mental Health*
Pub: International Schizophrenia Foundation
Contact: Dr. Abram Hoffer, President
Released: Quarterly. **Price:** $30, U.S. and Canada. **Description:** Acquaints readers with the effects of nutrition on mental health, with on emphasis on schizophrenia.

34577 ■ *Nutrition Today*
Pub: Lippincott Williams & Wilkins
Contact: Rich Wohl, Executive Vice President
URL(s): journals.lww.com/nutritiontodayonline/pages/default.aspx. **Ed:** Johanna Dwyer. **Released:** Bimonthly **Price:** $94, Individuals; $325, Institutions; $56, Individuals in-training; $189, Other countries; $445, Institutions, other countries.

34578 ■ *Occupational Therapy in Health Care: A Journal of Contemporary Practice*
Pub: Informa Healthcare
URL(s): informahealthcare.com/loi/ohc. **Ed:** Anne Elizabeth Dickerson. **Released:** Quarterly **Price:** $645, Institutions; €480, Institutions; £360, Institutions.

34579 ■ *Osteoporosis International*
Pub: Springer-Verlag New York Inc.
Contact: Ruediger Gebauer, President
URL(s): www.springer.com/medicine/orthopedics/journal/198. **Released:** Monthly **Price:** €2275, Institutions print + online; €2730, Institutions print + enhanced access.

34580 ■ *Peritoneal Dialysis International*
Pub: Multimed Inc.
URL(s): www.pdiconnect.comwww.multi-med.com/peritoneal-dialysis-international. **Ed:** D.G. Oreopoulos, Nicholas Topley. **Released:** Bimonthly **Price:** $475, U.S. and Canada libraries & institutions; print; $625, Other countries libraries & institutions; print; $630, Other countries libraries & institutions; online; $700, U.S. and Canada libraries & institutions; print & online; $1595, Other countries 2 years; libraries/institutions-print & online; $315, Individuals Medical Doctor/PhD; print; $370, Individuals Medical Doctor/PhD; print & online.

34581 ■ *Physical and Occupational Therapy in Pediatrics: A Quarterly Journal of Developmental Therapy*
Pub: Informa Healthcare
URL(s): informahealthcare.com/loi/pop. **Ed:** Robert J. Palisano, Doreen Bartlett. **Released:** Quarterly **Price:** $1020, Institutions; €755, Institutions; £570, Institutions.

34582 ■ *Physician Executive*
Pub: American College of Physician Executives
Contact: Martin E. Hickey, President
E-mail: mhickey@acpe.org
URL(s): www.acpe.org/publications/pej.aspx. **Ed:** Bill Steiger. **Released:** Bimonthly **Price:** $80, Individuals; $96, Other countries.

34583 ■ *The Prevention Researcher*
Pub: Integrated Research Services Inc.
Ed: Steven Ungerleider, Ph.D., Editor, suinteg@attglobal.net. **Released:** Quarterly, 4/year. **Price:** $36, individuals; $48 libraries. **Description:** Specializes in prevention topics for at-risk youth.

34584 ■ *Provider: For Long Term Care Professionals*
Pub: American Health Care Association
Contact: Mark Parkinson, President
URL(s): www.providermagazine.com. **Released:** Monthly **Price:** free to long-term health care professionals; $48, /year for nonmembers and libraries; $61, Canada and Mexico; $85, Other countries.

34585 ■ *Psychoanalytic Social Work*
Pub: Routledge Journals Taylor & Francis Group
URL(s): www.tandfonline.com/toc/wpsw20/current. **Ed:** Morton Chethik, Max Bruck, William Borden, Shoshana Ringel, Linda A. Chernus, Naomi Abramowitz, Eda Goldstein. **Released:** Semiannual **Price:** $107, Individuals online only; $115, Individuals print + online; $516, Institutions online only; $573, Institutions print + online.

34586 ■ *PT in Motion*
Pub: American Physical Therapy Association
Contact: R. Scott Ward, President
E-mail: scottward@apta.org
URL(s): www.apta.org/PTinMotion. **Ed:** Eric Ries, Donald Tepper. **Released:** Monthly **Price:** $119, Institutions non-members; $139, Institutions, other countries non-members.

34587 ■ *Qualitative Health Research*
Pub: SAGE Publications USA
Contact: Blaise R. Simqu, President
URL(s): www.sagepub.com/journalsProdDesc.nav?prodId=Journal200926. **Ed:** Janice M. Morse. **Released:** 10/yr. **Price:** $1320, Institutions combined (print & e-access); $1452, Institutions backfile lease, combined plus backfile; $1188, Institutions e-access; $1320, Institutions backfile lease, e-access plus backfile; $1188, Institutions backfile, e-access (content through 1998); $1294, Institutions print only; $229, Individuals print only; $119, Institutions single print; $25, Individuals single print.

34588 ■ *Revista Panamericana de Salud Publica*
Pub: Pan American Health Organization
Contact: Dr. Carissa Etienne, Director
URL(s): journal.paho.org/www.scielosp.org/scielo.php?script=sci_serial&pid=1020-4989&lng=en&nrm=iso. **Ed:** Carlos Campbell, Susana Belmartino, Celia Maria de Almeida. **Released:** Monthly **Price:** $44, Individuals electronic; Free print; $81, Individuals electronic; $133, Institutions electronic; $72, Institutions two years, electronic.

34589 ■ *Roswellness*
Pub: Roswell Park Cancer Institute
Contact: Dr. Donald L. Trump, President
Released: 3/year. **Price:** Free. **Description:** Focuses on health and wellness with a special emphasis on cancer prevention, research, and patient care. Features include patient testimonials and special events.

34590 ■ *Seizure: European Journal of Epilepsy*
Pub: Elsevier
URL(s): www.elsevier.com/wps/find/journaldescription.cws_home/623071/descrip tion#description. **Ed:** T. Betts. **Released:** 10/yr. **Price:** €406, Individuals online or print; $521, Individuals online or print; $58400, Individuals online or print; €1253, Institutions print only; $1111, Institutions print only; $135000, Institutions print only.

34591 ■ *Share*
Pub: SHARE
Contact: Alice Yaker, Executive Director
Released: Semiannual. **Description:** Acts as a forum for information, meetings, resources, and support groups for women with breast or ovarian cancer.

34592 ■ *SIECUS Report*
Pub: Sexuality Information and Education Council of the U.S.
Contact: Monica Rodriguez, President
URL(s): www.siecus.org. **Released:** Quarterly **Price:** $49, Individuals; $9.20, Single issue.

34593 ■ *Sleep*
Pub: American Academy of Sleep Medicine
Contact: Sam Fleishman, President
URL(s): www.journalsleep.org/. **Released:** Monthly **Price:** $225, Individuals online only; $425, Institutions print only; $375, Other countries print & online.

34594 ■ *Social Work with Groups: A Journal of Community and Clinical Practice*
Pub: Routledge Journals Taylor & Francis Group
URL(s): www.tandfonline.com/toc/wswg20/current. **Ed:** Andrew Malekoff. **Released:** Quarterly **Price:** $125, Individuals online only; $134, Individuals print + online; $729, Institutions online only; $810, Institutions print + online.

34595 ■ *Social Work in Health Care: A Quarterly Journal Adopted by the Society for Social Work Leadership in Health Care*
Pub: Routledge Journals Taylor & Francis Group
URL(s): www.tandf.co.uk/journals/WSHC. **Ed:** Toba Schwaber Kerson, Gary Rosenberg. **Released:** Quarterly; (4 issues per vol./2 vols. per year). **Price:** $303, Individuals online only; $337, Individuals print + online; $1248, Institutions online only; $1386, Institutions print + online.

34596 ■ *Social Work in Public Health*
Pub: Routledge Journals Taylor & Francis Group
URL(s): www.tandfonline.com/toc/whsp20/current. **Ed:** Marvin D. Feit, Stanley F. Battle. **Released:** 6/yr. **Price:** $130, Individuals online only; $145, Individuals print + online; $835, Institutions online only; $928, Institutions print + online.

34597 ■ *Therapeutic Recreation Journal*
Pub: National Recreation and Park Association
Contact: Barbara Tulipane, Chief Executive Officer
URL(s): www.nrpa.org/trj/. **Released:** Quarterly **Price:** $52, Members; $66, Nonmembers; $299, Libraries.

34598 ■ *Topics in Clinical Nutrition (TICN)*
Pub: Lippincott Williams & Wilkins
URL(s): www.lww.com/webapp/wcs/stores/servlet/product__11851_-1_9012052_Prod -08835691. **Ed:** Judith A. Gilbride. **Released:** Quarterly **Price:** $98.99, Individuals; $354.49, Institutions; $197.73, Other countries; $453.73, Institutions, other countries; $60.99, Individuals in-training.

34599 ■ *Trustee: The Magazine for Hospital Governing Boards*
Pub: Health Forum L.L.C.
Contact: Neil Jesuele, President
E-mail: njesuel1@aha.org
URL(s): www.trusteemag.com. **Ed:** Jane Jeffries. **Released:** Monthly **Price:** $52, Individuals; $120, Canada; $200, Other countries; $10, Single issue domestic; $16, Single issue other countries.

34600 ■ *Women and Health: A Multi Disciplinary Journal of Women's Health Issues*
Pub: Routledge Journals Taylor & Francis Group
URL(s): www.tandfonline.com/toc/wwah20/current. **Released:** 8/yr. **Price:** $251, Individuals online only; $279, Individuals print + online; $1527, Institutions online only; $1696, Institutions print + online.

34601 ■ *Worksight*
Pub: Rehabilitation Research and Training Center on Blindness and Low Vision
Released: Annual. **Price:** Free. **Description:** Discusses news, activities, research, and training programs of the Rehabilitation Research and Training Center on Blindness and Low Vision. Remarks: TDD available at (662)325-8693.

VIDEOCASSETTES/ AUDIOCASSETTES

34602 ■ *Confidentiality: Ethical and Legal Considerations*
Channing Bete Company
One Community Pl.
South Deerfield, MA 01373-7328
Ph: (413)665-7611
Free: 800-477-4776
Fax: (800)499-6464
Co. E-mail: custsvcs@channing-bete.com
URL: http://www.channing-bete.com
Released: 1994. **Price:** $295.00. **Description:** Discusses privacy issues, defamation, instances when information must be shared, patient and family access to information, and the impact of computers on confidentiality. Program approved for 1 hour of CEU credits. **Availability:** VHS.

34603 ■ *Continuous Quality Improvement in Health Care*
Channing Bete Company
One Community Pl.
South Deerfield, MA 01373-7328

Ph: (413)665-7611
Free: 800-477-4776
Fax: (800)499-6464
Co. E-mail: custsvcs@channing-bete.com
URL: http://www.channing-bete.com
Released: 1993. **Price:** $199.00. **Description:** Discusses leadership, training, empowerment, data collection, and tools for interpreting data. Program approved for 3 hours of CEU credits. **Availability:** VHS.

34604 ■ *Continuous Quality Improvement in Long-Term Care*
Channing Bete Company
One Community Pl.
South Deerfield, MA 01373-7328
Ph: (413)665-7611
Free: 800-477-4776
Fax: (800)499-6464
Co. E-mail: custsvcs@channing-bete.com
URL: http://www.channing-bete.com
Released: 1993. **Price:** $99.00. **Description:** Discusses leadership, training, empowerment, data collection, and tools for interpreting data. Program approved for 2 hours of CEU credits. **Availability:** VHS.

34605 ■ *Controlling Violence in Health Care*
Channing Bete Company
One Community Pl.
South Deerfield, MA 01373-7328
Ph: (413)665-7611
Free: 800-477-4776
Fax: (800)499-6464
Co. E-mail: custsvcs@channing-bete.com
URL: http://www.channing-bete.com
Released: 1994. **Price:** $199.00. **Description:** Covers verbal de-escalation, limit setting, pharmacological intervention, and physical containment. Program approved for 1 hour of CEU credit. **Availability:** VHS.

34606 ■ *Coronary Artery Disease*
Concept Media
PO Box 6904
Florence, KY 41022-6904
Free: 800-354-9706
Fax: (800)487-8488
Co. E-mail: cpgcs@cengage.com
URL: http://www.conceptmedia.com
Released: 1997. **Description:** Four-volume series discusses nursing assessment, diagnosis, intervention and evaluation of patients with this condition. **Availability:** VHS.

34607 ■ *Health Care for the Homeless*
National Film Board of Canada
1123 Broadway, Ste. 307
New York, NY 10010
Ph: (212)629-8890
Free: 800-542-2164
Fax: (212)629-8502
URL: http://www.nfb.ca
Released: 1989. **Price:** $295.00. **Description:** This program examines the nexus of poverty and ill health in its extremes, and asks questions about the responsibility of physicians to treat any and all ill people that come to them. **Availability:** VHS; 3/4 U.

34608 ■ *Issues in Homecare Nursing*
Concept Media
PO Box 6904
Florence, KY 41022-6904
Free: 800-354-9706
Fax: (800)487-8488
Co. E-mail: cpgcs@cengage.com
URL: http://www.conceptmedia.com
Released: 1997. **Description:** Four-volume series that helps healthcare professionals, experienced practitioners and students address aspects of care in the home. **Availability:** VHS.

34609 ■ *Patient Rights: The Art of Caring*
Channing Bete Company
One Community Pl.
South Deerfield, MA 01373-7328
Ph: (413)665-7611
Free: 800-477-4776
Fax: (800)499-6464
Co. E-mail: custsvcs@channing-bete.com
URL: http://www.channing-bete.com
Released: 1990. **Price:** $199.00. **Description:** Explains patients rights to information, self-determination, communication, privacy, personal property, and freedom from abuse and restraint. Program approved for 2 hours of CEU credits. **Availability:** VHS.

34610 ■ *S.O.S. Kids: Infant/Child Emergency Life Saving Video*
Tapeworm Video Distributors
25876 The Old Road #141
Stevenson Ranch, CA 91381
Ph: (661)257-4904
Fax: (661)257-4820
Co. E-mail: sales@tapeworm.com
URL: http://www.tapeworm.com
Released: 1997. **Price:** $19.95. **Description:** EMT Paramedic Richard Hardman describes and demonstrates what to do in various medical emergencies. **Availability:** VHS.

34611 ■ *What Tadoo*
Tapeworm Video Distributors
25876 The Old Road #141
Stevenson Ranch, CA 91381
Ph: (661)257-4904
Fax: (661)257-4820
Co. E-mail: sales@tapeworm.com
URL: http://www.tapeworm.com
Released: 1997. **Price:** $14.95. **Description:** Puppet frogs, What and Tadoo help children deal with issues of child abuse and prevention. **Availability:** VHS.

TRADE SHOWS AND CONVENTIONS

34612 ■ American Public Health Association Public Health Expo
American Public Health Association (APHA)
800 I St. NW
Washington, DC 20001-3710
Ph: (202)777-2742
Fax: (202)777-2534
Co. E-mail: comments@apha.org
URL: http://www.apha.org
Contact: Melvin D. Shipp, President
E-mail: mshipp@optometry.osu.edu
URL(s): www.apha.org. **Frequency:** Annual. **Audience:** Public health professionals, physicians, nurses, and health administrators. **Principal Exhibits:** Medical, products-related and pharmaceutical, health services, publishers, computer/software, educational, government, schools of public health. **Telecommunication Services:** comments@apha.org.

34613 ■ American School Health Association National School Health Conference
American School Health Association (ASHA)
4340 East West Hwy., Ste. 403
Bethesda, MD 20814
Ph: (301)652-8072
Free: 800-445-2742
Fax: (301)652-8077
Co. E-mail: info@ashaweb.org
URL: http://www.ashaweb.org
Contact: Stephen Conley, Executive Director
URL(s): www.ashaweb.org. **Price:** $195, Members; $290, Non-members; $215, Onsite registered, members; $310, Onsite registered, non-members. **Frequency:** Annual. **Audience:** School nurses, health educators, physicians, teachers, school administrators, dentists, school counselors, physical educators, and school health coordinators. **Principal Exhibits:** Publications, pharmaceuticals, clinical and medical equipment and supplies, information on health organizations, and health education methods and materials. **Telecommunication Services:** mbramsier@ashaweb.org.

34614 ■ Association for Research on Nonprofit Organizations and Voluntary Action Conference (ACNOVA)
Association for Research on Nonprofit Organizations and Voluntary Action
550 W. North St., Ste. 301
Indianapolis, IN 46202
Ph: (317)684-2120
Fax: (317)684-2128
URL: http://www.arnova.org
Contact: Roseanne Mirabella, President
E-mail: roseanne.mirabella@shu.edu
URL(s): www.arnova.org. **Frequency:** Annual. **Audience:** Scholars and non-profit organization professionals. **Principal Exhibits:** Exhibits for citizen participation and voluntary action, including social movements, interest groups, consumer groups, political participation, community development, and religious organizations. **Telecommunication Services:** conference@arnova.org.

34615 ■ Virginia Health Care Association Annual Convention and Trade Show
Virginia Health Care Association
2112 W. Laburnum Ave., Ste. 206
Richmond, VA 23227
Ph: (804)353-9101
Fax: (804)353-3098
Co. E-mail: kathy.robertson@vhca.org
URL: http://www.vhca.org
Contact: Stephen Morrisette, President
E-mail: steve.morrisette@vhca.org
URL(s): www.vhca.org. **Price:** $495, Members. **Frequency:** Annual. **Audience:** Nursing homeowners, administrators, purchasing agents, and nurses; dietary, housekeeping, social services, and activities departments' heads. **Principal Exhibits:** Equipment, supplies, and services for nursing home operations, including food, medical supplies, furniture, computer systems, linen, medical equipment, insurance, pharmaceuticals, optometrists, psychologists, and transportation.

CONSULTANTS

34616 ■ Alternative Services Inc.
32625 7 Mile Rd., Ste. 10
Livonia, MI 48152
Ph: (248)471-4880
Fax: (248)471-5230
URL: http://www.asi-mi.org
Contact: Arthur Mack, President
Scope: Provider of social services management support to group homes for the mentally disabled. Also offers marketing, training, and financial services to businesses and nonprofit organizations. **Founded:** 1978.

34617 ■ BioSciCon Inc.
14905 Forest Landing Cir.
Rockville, MD 20850
Ph: (301)610-9130
Fax: (301)610-7662
Co. E-mail: info@bioscicon.com
URL: http://www.bioscicon.com
Contact: Nenad Markovic, President
Scope: Sponsoring development of the technology of the Pap test accuracy via introduction of a new bio-marker that enhances visibility of abnormal cells on Pap smears or mono-layers of cervical cells obtained in solution. Conducts clinical trials for assessment of the test efficacy and safety, manufactures research tools for conduct of trials, and markets IP to license manufacturing, marketing, sales and distribution rights of the new technology line of products. **Founded:** 1996. **Publications:** "Cervical Acid Phosphates: A Biomarker of Cervical Dysplasia and Potential Surrogate Endpoint for Colposcopy," 2004; "Enhancing Pap test with a new biological marker of cervical dysplasia," 2004; "A cytoplasmic biomarker for liquid-based Pap," The FACEB Journal Experimental Biology, 2004; "Pap test and new biomarker-based technology for enhancing visibility of abnormal cells," 2004. **Special Services:** MarkPap®; PreservCyt®.

34618 ■ Center for Lifestyle Enhancement - Columbia Medical Center of Plano
3901 W 15th St.
Plano, TX 75075
Ph: (972)596-6800
Fax: (972)519-1299
Co. E-mail: mcp.cle@hcahealthcare.com
URL: http://www.medicalcenterofplano.com
Contact: Harvey Fishero, President
Scope: Provides professional health counseling in the areas of general nutrition for weight management, eating disorders, diabetic education, cholesterol reduction and adolescent weight management. Offers work site health promotion and preventive services. Also coordinates speaker's bureau, cooking classes and physician referrals. Industries served: education, insurance, healthcare, retail or wholesale, data processing and manufacturing throughout Texas. **Founded:** 1975. **Seminars:** Rx Diet and Exercise; Smoking Cessation; Stress Management; Health Fairs; Fitness Screenings; Body Composition; Nutrition Analysis; Exercise Classes; Prenatal Nutrition; SHAPEDOWN; Successfully Managing Diabetes; Gourmet Foods for Your Heart; The Aging Heart; Heart Smart Saturday featuring Day of Dance; Weight-Loss Management Seminars; The Right Stroke for Men; Peripheral Artery Disease Screening; Menstruation: The Cycle Begins; Boot Camp for New Dads; Grand parenting 101: Caring for Kids Today; Teddy Bear Camp; New Baby Day Camp; Safe Sitter Baby-Sitting Class.

34619 ■ The Children's Psychological Trauma Center
2105 Divisadero St.
San Francisco, CA 94115
Ph: (415)292-7119
Fax: (415)749-2802
Co. E-mail: gil.kliman@cphc-sf.org
URL: http://www.cphc-sf.org
Contact: Gilbert Kliman, Director
Scope: Treats those with psychological trauma claimed from stressors including institutional negligence, vehicular and aviation accidents, wrongful death in the family, rape, molestation, fire, explosion, flood, earthquake, loss of parents, terrorism, kidnapping, disfiguring events, emotional damage from social work, medical malpractice or defective products. Provides evaluation and reports to referring professionals. Experienced in forensic consultation and testimony. **Founded:** 1992. **Publications:** "My Personal Story About Tropical Storm Stan," Feb, 2006; "My Personal Story About Hurricanes Katrina and Rita: A guided activity workbook to help coping, learning and Healthy expression," Sep, 2005; "Helping Patients and their Families Cope in a National Disaster," Jan, 2002; "The practice of behavioral treatment in the acute rehabilitation setting".

34620 ■ Diversified Health Resources Inc.
875 N Michigan Ave., Ste. 3250
Chicago, IL 60611-1901
Ph: (312)266-0466
Fax: (312)266-0715
Contact: Andrea R. Rozran, President
Scope: Offers health care consulting for hospitals, nursing homes including homes for the aged, and other health related facilities and companies. Specializes in planning and marketing. Also conducts executive searches for top level health care administrative positions. Serves private industries as well as government agencies. **Founded:** 1979. **Publications:** "City Finance".

34621 ■ Environmental Health Science Inc.
418 Wall St.
Princeton, NJ 08540
Ph: (609)924-7616
Free: 800-841-8923
Fax: (609)924-0793
Co. E-mail: healthscience@comcast.net
URL: http://www.speechgeneratingdevices.com
Contact: David Goldberg, President
E-mail: davidg@patmedia.net
Scope: Specialists in rehabilitation technology for speech disorder and physically disabled persons. Offers demonstrations, evaluations and sales of the following types of equipment: augmentative speech communication systems, adaptive switches and specialty controls, and computer access devices. Industries served: hospitals and rehabilitation centers, schools, and special service organizations such as United Cerebral Palsy Association, Department of Human Services, etc. **Founded:** 1984. **Publications:** "Play & Learn"; "Bookworm Literacy Tool"; "Meville to Weville". **Seminars:** Augmentative Communication and Assistive Devices. **Special Services:** Boardmaker®; Dynamically Pro®.

34622 ■ Family Resource Center on Disabilities (FRCD)
20 E Jackson Blvd., Ste. 300
Chicago, IL 60604-2265
Ph: (312)939-3519
Free: 800-952-4199
Fax: (312)939-7297
Co. E-mail: contact@frcd.org
URL: http://www.frcd.org
Contact: Michelle Phillips, Executive Director
Description: Parents, professionals, and volunteers seeking to improve services for all children with disabilities. Originally organized as a result of the 1969 Illinois law mandating the education of all children with disabilities and operates as a coalition to inform and activate parents. Provides information and referral services, individualized support services for low-income Chicago families, transition services, and special education rights training. **Scope:** Provider of consulting services to advocacy groups and individuals seeking support for children with disabilities. **Founded:** 1969. **Publications:** "How to Get Services By Being Assertive"; "How to Organize an Effective Parent/Advocacy Group and Move Bureaucracies"; "Main roads Travel to Tomorrow - a Road Map for the Future"; "Does Your Child Have Special Education Needs"; "How to Prepare for a Successful Due Process Hearing"; "How to Participate Effectively in Your Child's IEP Meeting"; "Tax Guide for Parents". **Seminars:** How to Support Parents as Effective Advocates; How to Get Services by Being Assertive; How to Develop an Awareness Program for Nondisabled Children; How to Organize a Parent Support Group; How to Move Bureaucratic Mountains; How to Raise Money Painlessly through Publishing; How to Use Humor in Public Presentations. **Telecommunication Services:** frcdptiil@ameritech.net; info@frcd.org.

34623 ■ Grief Counseling & Support Services
8600 W Chester Pke., Ste. 304
Upper Darby, PA 19082
Ph: (610)789-7707
Fax: (610)469-9499
Contact: Jeffrey Kauffman, President
E-mail: jkharry@voicenet.com
Scope: Specializing in consulting and training services for organizations dealing with loss, trauma and grief issues. These services may include management consultations, crisis intervention, educational programming, policy development, program design, group process work, individual counseling or other support services. Training and support services also provided for loss issues for mental retardation service providers. Serves private industries as well as government agencies. **Founded:** 1984.

34624 ■ Jest for the Health of It Services
PO Box 8484
Santa Cruz, CA 95061-8484
Ph: (831)425-8436
Fax: (831)425-8437
Co. E-mail: pwooten@jesthealth.com
URL: http://www.jesthealth.com
Contact: Shirley Trout, Manager
E-mail: strout@nurseswhostay.com
Scope: Develops and presents seminars, keynotes and skill shops about the power of humor. Provides consulting services for development of humor rooms and comedy carts in hospitals. Conducts training for clowns to make visits in hospitals and nursing homes. Industries served: health professionals and businesses wishing to educate staff about healthy lifestyle choices. **Founded:** 1982. **Publications:** "Heart Humor and Healing"; "Compassionate Laughter: Jest for Your Health"; "The Hospital Clown: A Closer Look"; "Humor: An Antidote for Stress"; "Humor, Laughter and Play: Maintaining Balance in a Serious World"; "You've Got to Be Kidding: Humor Skills for Surviving Managed Care"; "Laughter as Therapy for Patient and Caregiver"; "Patty Wooten: Nurse Healer"; "Humor: An antidote for stress".

34625 ■ Kanata Intercultural Consulting Inc.
82 Douglas Woods Close SE
Calgary, AB, Canada T2Z 1Z5
Ph: (403)807-9200
Fax: (403)207-9405
Co. E-mail: info@kanataint.ca
Contact: Jim Potts, Manager
Scope: Firm helps organizations reach their diversity objectives by creating and implementing custom solutions that address inter cultural issues. Consulting services include diversity assessments; diversity initiative creation and execution; an on-site diversity consultant in house to eliminate the need to hire additional staff to address issues of diversity; and diversity training workshops tailored to address specific issues facing a business. **Seminars:** Diverse Staff Hiring/Retention; Building A Culture of Diversity In Your Business; Problem solving and conflict resolution; How to effectively reach intercultural communities.

34626 ■ Occupational & Environmental Health Consulting Services Inc.
635 Harding Rd.
Hinsdale, IL 60521-4814
Ph: (630)325-2083
Fax: (630)325-2098
Co. E-mail: bobb@safety-epa.com
URL: http://www.oehcs.com
Contact: Robert C. Brandys, President
E-mail: bobb@safety-epa.com
Scope: Provider of consulting to industry on safety program development and implementation, industrial hygiene monitoring programs, occupational health nursing, wellness programs, medical monitoring, accident trending and statistics, emergency response planning, multilingual training, right-to-know compliance and training, hazardous waste management, random monitoring and mitigation, asbestos school inspection, and project management. Also offers indoor air quality, expert witnessing service. **Founded:** 1984. **Publications:** "Worldwide Exposure Standards for Mold and Bacteria"; "Global Occupational Exposure Limits for Over 5000 Specific Chemicals"; "Post-Remediation Verification and Clearance Testing for Mold and Bacteria Risk Based Levels of Cleanliness". **Seminars:** Right-To-Know Compliance; Setting Internal Exposure Standards; Hospital Right-to-Know and Contingency Response; Ethylene Oxide Control; Industrial Hygiene Training; Asbestos Worker Training; Biosafety; Asbestos Operations and Maintenance. **Special Services:** Safety Software Program, Audiogram Analysis, First Report of Injury Form, Human Resources Database; Material Safety Data Sheet (MSDS); NPDES Monthly Reports; Lockout/Tagout (LOTO) Procedure Software; VOC Usage Tracking and Reporting Software, Medical Department Patient Records Database, Pictorial Labels for Chemical Containers, TIER II Hazardous Material Inventory Form & Database.

34627 ■ Pathways To Wellness
617 Everhart Rd.
Corpus Christi, TX 78411
Ph: (361)985-9642
Fax: (361)949-4627
Co. E-mail: path2wellness@earthlink.net
URL: http://www.path2wellness.com
Contact: Evy Coppola, Owner
Scope: Offer natural holistic health counseling, yoga and hatha yoga classes, teachers training and cookery classes for individuals and companies. Health counseling includes nutritional guidance, kinesiology, iridology, reflexology, energy healing, massage therapy, herbal and vitamin therapy, creative visualization and meditation. Provides supplements which bring about the same effects as that of natural sunshine. **Founded:** 1988. **Seminars:** Is It You Holding You Back?; The Balancing Act. . .Career. . . Family. . .and Self; Learning the Art of Friendly Persuasion; Stop Accepting What You Are Getting and Start Asking for What You Want!; Introduction to Natural Health and Healthy Living; Learn Why One Size Ap-

proaches to the Answers on Health Do Not Work; Introduction to Yoga. What is it? Who can do it? What can it do for you.

34628 ■ Professional Counseling Centers Inc.
543 Coventry Way
Noblesville, IN 46062-9024
Ph: (317)877-3111
Contact: Jack W. Schinderle, President
Scope: Business counselors offering services in the following areas: employee assistance, managed care, alcohol and drug treatment, labor and union consultation, and industrial mental health.

FRANCHISES AND BUSINESS OPPORTUNITIES

34629 ■ Boston Bartenders School of America
Boston Bartenders School Associates, Inc.
64 Enterprise Rd.
Hyannis, MA 02601
Free: 800-357-3210
Fax: (508)771-1165
Description: Program in mixology and alcohol awareness. **No. of Franchise Units:** 10. **No. of Company-Owned Units:** 3. **Founded:** 1968.. **Franchised:** 1994. **Equity Capital Needed:** $50,000. **Franchise Fee:** $10,000. **Financial Assistance:** Yes. **Training:** Yes.

34630 ■ ComForcare Senior Services
ComForcare Healthcare Holdings Inc.
2510 Telegraph Rd., Ste. 100
Bloomfield Hills, MI 48302
Ph: (248)745-9700
Free: 800-886-4044
Fax: (248)745-9763
URL: http://www.ComForcare.com
Description: Franchise provides home health care for seniors. **No. of Franchise Units:** 150. **No. of Company-Owned Units:** 1. **Founded:** 1996.. **Franchised:** 2001. **Equity Capital Needed:** $105,000-$155,000 includes franchise fee. **Franchise Fee:** $39,500. **Training:** Yes.

34631 ■ CPR Services
CPR Services, Inc.
158 Pond St., Ste. A
Ashland, MA 01721
Ph: (508)881-5107
Free: 800-547-5107
Fax: (508)881-4718
Description: CPR and First Aid Training. **No. of Franchise Units:** 1. **No. of Company-Owned Units:** 1. **Founded:** 1985.. **Franchised:** 1998. **Equity Capital Needed:** $13,500-$16,500. **Franchise Fee:** $7,500. **Training:** Yes.

34632 ■ The Dentist Choice, Inc.
Choice Corporation, Inc.
33971 Selva Rd., Ste. 200
Dana Point, CA 92629
Free: 888-757-1333
Fax: (949)443-2074
Description: Dental health services. **No. of Franchise Units:** 120. **No. of Company-Owned Units:** 1. **Founded:** 1994.. **Franchised:** 1994. **Equity Capital Needed:** $60,000. **Franchise Fee:** $45,000. **Financial Assistance:** Yes. **Training:** Provides 1 week at headquarters and ongoing support.

34633 ■ Interim Health Care
1601 Sawgrass Corporate Pkwy.
Sunrise, FL 33323
Ph: (800)338-7786
Fax: (954)858-4832
Description: Franchises nursing and home health care personnel services. **No. of Franchise Units:** 267. **No. of Company-Owned Units:** 20. **Founded:** 1966.. **Franchised:** 1966. **Equity Capital Needed:** Medical staffing $100,000-$125,000; home health care $250,000-$400,000. **Franchise Fee:** $5,000; $20,000-$30,000. **Training:** Yes.

34634 ■ Superior Senior Care
Superior Senior Care Franchises, L.L.C.
PO Box 505
Hot Springs, AR 71902
Ph: (479)783-1206
Fax: (479)783-1232
Co. E-mail: Franchise@SuperiorSeniorCare.com
URL: http://www.SuperiorSeniorCare.com
Description: Provider of light housekeeping and home management, meal preparation, shopping, transportation and companionship. **No. of Franchise Units:** 7. **No. of Company-Owned Units:** 7. **Founded:** 1985.. **Franchised:** 2000. **Equity Capital Needed:** $18,771. **Franchise Fee:** $15,000. **Training:** Yes.

COMPUTERIZED DATABASES

34635 ■ *GrantSelect™*
Kurz Purdue Technology Ctr.
1281 Win Hintschel Blvd.
West Lafayette, IN 47906
Ph: (765)237-3390
Fax: (765)463-3501
Co. E-mail: webmaster@schoolhousepartners.net
URL: http://www.schoolhousepartners.net
Availability: Online: Schoolhouse Partners L.L.C. **Type:** Directory; Numeric.

34636 ■ *Health Care Daily Report™*
1801 S Bell St.
Arlington, VA 22202
Free: 800-372-1033
Co. E-mail: customercare@bna.com
URL: http://www.bna.com
Availability: Online: Bloomberg LP-Bloomberg BNA; Thomson Reuters - Westlaw. **Type:** Full-text.

34637 ■ *Health Care Policy Report*
1801 S Bell St.
Arlington, VA 22202
Free: 800-372-1033
Co. E-mail: customercare@bna.com
URL: http://www.bna.com
Availability: Online: Bloomberg LP-Bloomberg BNA; Thomson Reuters - Westlaw. **Type:** Full-text.

34638 ■ *Health Reference Center*
10650 Toebben Dr.
Independence, KY 41051
Free: 800-354-9706
Fax: (800)487-8488
Co. E-mail: investors@cengage.com
URL: http://www.gale.cengage.com
Contact: Ronald Dunn, President
Availability: CD-ROM: Cengage Learning Inc. **Type:** Full-text; Directory.

34639 ■ *Health & Wellness InSite<svs>*
610 Opperman Dr.
Eagen, MN 55122
Free: 800-477-4300
Co. E-mail: gale.contentlicensing@cengage.com
URL: http://www.insite2.gale.com
Availability: Online: Cengage Learning Inc. - Gale - InSite2. **Type:** Full-text.

LIBRARIES

34640 ■ Association of Gospel Rescue Missions Library
7222 Commerce Center Dr., Ste. 120
Colorado Springs, CO 80919
Ph: (719)266-8300
Free: 800-4RE-SCUE
Fax: (719)266-8600
Co. E-mail: info@agrm.org
URL: http://www.agrm.org
Contact: John Ashmen, President
Scope: Homelessness, urban ministry, alcohol and drug assistance, history of Christian efforts to inner city poor. **Services:** Library open to the public for reference use only. **Founded:** 1913. **Holdings:** 2118 periodicals, books, clippings, audio/visuals, and archival material.

34641 ■ National Families in Action Library
2957 Clairmont Rd. NE, Ste. 150
Atlanta, GA 30329
Ph: (404)248-9676
Fax: (404)248-9676
Co. E-mail: nfia@nationalfamilies.org
URL: http://www.nationalfamilies.org
Scope: Drug use, drug legalization, drug usage prevention. **Services:** Library open to the public for reference use only. **Founded:** 1977. **Holdings:** 1 million books, periodicals, clippings, audio/visuals, monographs, and archival material.

34642 ■ Wisconsin HIV/STD/Hepatitis Information & Referral Center
PO Box 510498
Milwaukee, WI 53203
Free: 800-334-2437
Co. E-mail: irc-wisconsin@arcw.org
URL: http://www.irc-wisconsin.org/
Contact: Angie Clark, Manager
Scope: AIDS, HIV, STDs, hepatitis. **Services:** Library open to the public. **Founded:** 1985.

RESEARCH CENTERS

34643 ■ African Medical and Research Foundation, U.S.A. (AMREF USA)
4 W 43rd St., 2nd Fl.
New York, NY 10036
Ph: (212)768-2440
Fax: (212)768-4230
Co. E-mail: info@amrefusa.org
URL: http://www.amrefusa.org
Contact: Lisa K. Meadowcraft, Executive Director
Founded: 1957. **Educational Activities:** Health education courses.

34644 ■ American College of Apothecaries - Research and Education Resource Center
2830 Summer Oaks Dr.
Memphis, TN 38184-3811
Ph: (901)383-8119
Free: 800-828-5933
Fax: (901)383-8882
Co. E-mail: aca@acainfo.org
URL: http://www.americancollegeofapothecaries.com/AboutACA/ACAResearchEducationFoundation/REFResourceCenter.aspx
Contact: Edward J. Hesterlee, Executive Vice President
Founded: 1978. **Educational Activities:** Community pharmacy residency program; Community education program; Research and Education Resource Center Conferences; Speakers bureau.

34645 ■ Baylor College of Medicine - Center for Medical Ethics and Health Policy
1 Baylor Plz., MS BCM420
Houston, TX 77030
Ph: (713)798-3503
Fax: (713)798-5678
Co. E-mail: bbrody@bcm.edu
URL: http://www.bcm.edu/ethics
Contact: Prof. Baruch A. Brody, Director
Services: Consultation Services. **Founded:** 1982. **Publications:** *News Bulletin* (Semimonthly). **Educational Activities:** Clinical Instruction; Continuing Education Programs; Education Courses, in medical ethics; Center for Medical Ethics and Health Policy Lectures, visiting scholars.

34646 ■ Benaroya Research Institute at Virginia Mason (BRI)
1201 9th Ave.
Seattle, WA 98101-2795
Ph: (206)583-6525
Fax: (206)223-7543
Co. E-mail: info@benaroyaresearch.org
URL: http://www.benaroyaresearch.org
Contact: Jack Nagan, Executive Director
Founded: 1956. **Publications:** *Bulletin of the Virginia Mason Clinic.* **Educational Activities:** Educational opportunities through high school programs and post-doctoral training. **Awards:** Fellowships for foreign students. **Telecommunication Services:** jnepom@benaroyaresearch.org.

34647 ■ Blanton-Peale Institute
3 W 29th St.
New York, NY 10001
Ph: (212)725-7850
Fax: (212)689-3212
Co. E-mail: pbradley@blantonpeale.org
URL: http://www.blantonpeale.org
Contact: Rev. Paul W. Bradley, President
Founded: 1937. **Publications:** *Journal of Religion and Health* (Quarterly); *Labyrinth Newsletter* (Semiannual). **Educational Activities:** Blanton-Peale Institute Lectures; Marriage and Family Therapy Residency; Pastoral Care Studies Program; Psychoanalytic Residency. **Telecommunication Services:** info@blantonpeale.org.

34648 ■ Brandeis University - Schneider Institutes for Health Policy (SIHP)
Heller School for Social Policy & Management, MS 035
415 S St.
Waltham, MA 02454-9110
Ph: (781)736-3900
Fax: (781)736-3905
Co. E-mail: wallack@brandeis.edu
URL: http://sihp.brandeis.edu
Contact: Stanley S. Wallack, Executive Director
Founded: 1978. **Publications:** *Background Reports*; *Heller Highlights* (Quarterly); *Program Analyses*; *Publication Catalogue*; *Major Issue Papers*. **Educational Activities:** AHRQ Training Program (3/year); NIAAA Training Program (3/year). **Telecommunication Services:** colnon@brandeis.edu.

34649 ■ Brown University - Watson Institute for International Studies
111 Thayer St., Box 1970
Providence, RI 02912-1970
Ph: (401)863-2809
Fax: (401)863-1270
Co. E-mail: watson_institute@brown.edu
URL: http://www.watsoninstitute.org
Contact: Prof. Michael D. Kennedy, Director
Services: Extensive outreach activities: for community and policy makers. **Founded:** 1986. **Publications:** *Blogs*; *Conference Reports*; *Documentaries*; *Watson Institute for International Studies Newsletters*; *Streaming video*; *Watson Institute for International Studies Annual Report*; *Studies in Comparative International Development*. **Educational Activities:** Development studies undergraduate major; International relations undergraduate major; Watson Institute for International Studies Lectures; Watson Institute for International Studies Seminars; Watson Institute for International Studies Conferences; Choices for the 21st Century Education program; Faculty and student foreign exchange programs. **Telecommunication Services:** michael_kennedy@brown.edu.

34650 ■ California State University, Los Angeles - Edmund G. "Pat" Brown Institute of Public Affairs
5151 State University Dr.
Los Angeles, CA 90032-8261
Ph: (323)343-3770
Fax: (323)343-3774
Co. E-mail: jregalado@cslanet.calstatela.edu
URL: http://www.patbrowninstitute.org/
Contact: Prof. Jaime A. Regalado, Executive Director
Services: Technical assistance and consulting: on policy issues. **Founded:** 1980. **Educational Activities:** Conferences and forums. **Awards:** Edmund G. "Pat" Brown Institute of Public Affairs Internships, in public service. **Telecommunication Services:** pbi@cslanet.calstatela.edu.

34651 ■ Center for the Study of Social Policy (CSSP)
1575 Eye St. NW, Ste. 500
Washington, DC 20005
Ph: (202)371-1565
Fax: (202)371-1472
Co. E-mail: info@cssp.org
URL: http://www.cssp.org
Contact: Frank Farrow, Director
Founded: 1979.

34652 ■ Dalhousie University - Population Health Research Unit (PHRU)
Department of Community Health & Epidemiology
Faculty of Medicine
5790 University Ave.
Halifax, NS, Canada B3H 1V7
Ph: (902)494-1785
Fax: (902)494-1597
Co. E-mail: pfnestma@dal.ca
URL: http://www.phru.dal.ca
Contact: Upal Nath, Director
Founded: 1993. **Telecommunication Services:** upal@dal.ca.

34653 ■ Dartmouth College - Dartmouth Institute for Health Policy and Clinical Practice
35 Centerra Pky., Ste. 300
Lebanon, NH 03766
Ph: (603)653-3268
Fax: (603)653-0820
Co. E-mail: the.dartmouth.institute@dartmouth.edu
URL: http://tdi.dartmouth.edu
Contact: Dr. Wiley Souba, Director (Acting)
Founded: 1989. **Publications:** *The Dartmouth Atlas of Health Care*. **Educational Activities:** Fellowships to physicians, administrators, and health policy makers; Graduate programs in evaluative clinical science.

34654 ■ Evergreen Freedom Foundation (EFF)
PO Box 552
Olympia, WA 98507
Ph: (360)956-3482
Fax: (360)352-1874
Co. E-mail: info@myfreedomfoundation.org
URL: http://www.myfreedomfoundation.com
Contact: Jonathan Bechtle, Chief Executive Officer
Services: Briefings,: during legislative session when requested. **Founded:** 1991. **Publications:** *In-Briefs*; *EFF Newsletter* (Monthly); *Policy Highlighters*. **Educational Activities:** Speaking engagements, at service clubs and community organizations.

34655 ■ Forum for State Health Policy Leadership
National Conference of State Legislatures
444 N Capitol St. NW, Ste. 515
Washington, DC 20001
Ph: (202)624-5400
Fax: (202)737-1069
Co. E-mail: donna.folkemer@ncsl.org
URL: http://www.ncsl.org/Default.aspx?tabid=160#NCSL_programs
Contact: Donna Folkemer, Director
Services: Assistance: on particular issues and research projects; Legislative and state clearinghouses; Maintains a network of health policy correspondents: in each of the 50 states who keep the project abreast of significant developments in the states; State legislative tracking service. **Founded:** 1977. **Publications:** *Primary Care News*; *State Health Notes* (Semimonthly); *Reports on long-term care, primary care, and children's health*. **Educational Activities:** Health Policy Conference (Annual).

34656 ■ Georgia State University - Center for Risk Management and Insurance Research
PO Box 4036
Atlanta, GA 30302-4036
Ph: (404)413-7515
Fax: (404)413-7516
Co. E-mail: rwklein@gsu.edu
URL: http://rmictr.gsu.edu
Contact: Robert W. Klein, Director
Services: Consultation; Develops technical and professional materials; Issues working papers; Responds to proposal requests. **Founded:** 1969. **Publications:** *Reprint series*; *Research report series*; *Working paper series*. **Educational Activities:** Research and analysis (Daily); Center for Risk Management and Insurance Research Seminars and workshops, on risk management and insurance industry financial, actuarial and regulatory topics.

34657 ■ Health Research and Educational Trust (HRET)
155 N Wacker, Ste. 400
Chicago, IL 60606
Ph: (312)422-2600
Fax: (312)422-4568
URL: http://www.hret.org
Contact: Maulik S. Joshi, President
Description: Advances ideas and practices beneficial to health care practitioners, institutions, consumers and society at large. Principal activities focus on identifying, exploring, demonstrating and evaluating key strategic health care issues affecting innovative health care delivery systems, educating the field about the implications of changing health policies and developing strategies for community health improvement. **Founded:** 1944. **Publications:** *Health Services Research* (Bimonthly); *HSR: Impacting Health Practice and policy through state-of-the-art Research and Thinking* (Bimonthly). **Educational Activities:** HRET Conference (Annual). **Awards:** Trust Award (Annual); Crosby Fellowship; Walter J. Mcnerney Fellowship.

34658 ■ Health Research and Educational Trust of New Jersey
760 Alexander Rd.
Princeton, NJ 08543-0001
Ph: (609)275-4000
Fax: (609)275-4271
Co. E-mail: eryan@njha.com
URL: http://www.njha.com/hret/
Contact: Elizabeth A. Ryan, President
Founded: 1964. **Publications:** *Shaping Healthier Tomorrows*. **Educational Activities:** Continuing education courses; HRET Annual Meeting; Specialized training workshops. **Awards:** Community outreach awards; Health careers scholarships.

34659 ■ Heartland Institute (HI)
19 S LaSalle St., Ste. 903
Chicago, IL 60603
Ph: (312)377-4000
Fax: (312)377-5000
Co. E-mail: jbast@heartland.org
URL: http://www.heartland.org
Contact: Joseph L. Bast, President
Founded: 1984. **Publications:** *Budget & Tax News* (Monthly); *Environment and Climate News* (Monthly); *FIRE Policy News* (Monthly); *Health Care News* (Monthly); *IT&T News* (Monthly); *Policy Studies*; *School Reform News* (Monthly). **Educational Activities:** Book tours (Occasionally); Mealtime conferences and seminars (Periodic), open to the public. **Awards:** Heartland Liberty Prize. **Telecommunication Services:** think@heartland.org.

34660 ■ Indiana University-Purdue University at Indianapolis - Hall Center for Law and Health
Lawrence W Inlow Hall
School of Law
530 W New York St.
Indianapolis, IN 46202-3225
Ph: (317)274-1912
Fax: (317)274-0455
Co. E-mail: dorentli@iupui.edu
URL: http://indylaw.indiana.edu/centers/clh/
Contact: Prof. David Orentlicher, Director
Founded: 1987. **Publications:** *Hall Centre Newsletter* (Semiannual). **Educational Activities:** Information resource, on law issues. **Awards:** Research, scholarships, health law policy and law school courses (Annual).

34661 ■ Institute for SocioEconomic Studies (ISES)
10 New King St.
White Plains, NY 10604
Ph: (914)686-7112
Fax: (914)686-0581
Co. E-mail: mail@socioeconomic.org
URL: http://www.socioeconomic.org
Contact: Allan Ostergren, Director
Founded: 1974. **Publications:** *Socioeconomic Bulletin* (Bimonthly).

34662 ■ Institute for Women's Policy Research (IWPR)
1200 18th St. NW, Ste. 301
Washington, DC 20036
Ph: (202)785-5100
Fax: (202)833-4362
Co. E-mail: iwpr@iwpr.org
URL: http://www.iwpr.org
Contact: Dr. Heidi Hartmann, President
E-mail: hartmann@iwpr.org
Description: Individuals and organizations concerned with economic and social justice for women and families. Designs, executes, and disseminates research findings that illuminate policy issues affecting women and families. Works to addressing complex issues engendered by race, ethnicity, and class. Focuses on survival issues such as welfare reform, family and medical leave, childcare, pay equity and the wage gap, the glass ceiling, labor law reform, and equal opportunity for women of all race and ethnic backgrounds. Builds a network of individuals and organizations that conduct and use women-oriented policy research. **Services:** First Friday Forums: a discussion series. **Founded:** 1987. **Educational Activities:** IWPR Conferences; IWPR Workshops. **Awards:** 2 fellowships, for the academic year (9 months); Research action minigrants; IWPR Summer internships; Mariam K. Chamberlain Fellowships in Women and Public Policy; IWPR/GW Fellowships in Women's Public Policy Research. **Telecommunication Services:** hhartmann@iwpr.org.

34663 ■ International Development Research Centre (IDRC)—Centre de Recherches pour le Développement International (CRDI)
PO Box 8500
Ottawa, ON, Canada K1G 3H9
Ph: (613)236-6163
Fax: (613)238-7230
Co. E-mail: info@idrc.ca
URL: http://publicwebsite.idrc.ca
Contact: David M. Malone, President
Founded: 1970. **Publications:** *IDRC Annual Report*; *IDRC Reports* (Quarterly); *Searching Series*. **Awards:** Young Canadian Researchers Award; Gemini and Periscoop internships, in journalism; John Bene Fellowship in Social Forestry; Pearson Fellowship, for outstanding public servants; Training fellowships, for junior and senior scientists, managers, and planners from developing countries; Bentley Fellowship in Forage Crops in Sustainably Managed Agro-ecosystems.

34664 ■ Jacobs Institute of Women's Health (JIWH)
School of Public Health & Health Services
George Washington University
2021 K St. NW, Ste. 800
Washington, DC 20006
Ph: (202)994-4184
Fax: (202)994-4040
Co. E-mail: whieditor@gwu.edu
URL: http://www.jiwh.org
Contact: Susan Wood, Executive Director
Founded: 1990. **Publications:** *Women's Health Issues* (Bimonthly). **Educational Activities:** JIWH Seminars; JIWH Symposia. **Awards:** Charles E. Gibbs MD Leadership Prize.

34665 ■ Johns Hopkins University - Center for Hospital Finance and Management
624 N Broadway, Rm. 493
Baltimore, MD 21205
Ph: (410)955-3241
Fax: (410)955-2301
Co. E-mail: ganderso@jhsph.edu
URL: http://www.jhsph.edu/dept/hpm/research/centers.html
Contact: Prof. Gerard Anderson, Director
Services: Offers Congressional testimony. **Founded:** 1979. **Educational Activities:** Training to pre- and postdoctoral fellows.

34666 ■ Johns Hopkins University - Health Services Research and Development Center
Hampton House, 6th Fl.
Department of Health Policy & Management
624 N Broadway
Baltimore, MD 21205-1901
Ph: (410)955-6562
Fax: (410)955-0470
Co. E-mail: dsteinwa@jhsph.edu
URL: http://www.jhsph.edu/HSR/index.html
Contact: Prof. Donald M. Steinwachs, Director
Services: Technical assistance: for local and national groups. **Founded:** 1969. **Educational Activities:** Presentations, at national meetings.

34667 ■ Kaiser Permanente Center for Health Research (CHR)
3800 N Interstate Ave.
Portland, OR 97227-1098
Ph: (503)335-2400
Fax: (503)335-2424
Co. E-mail: information@kpchr.org
URL: http://www.kpchr.org/research/public/default.aspx
Contact: Mary L. Durham, Director
Founded: 1964. **Educational Activities:** Residence program, in public health; Saward Lecture (Annual). **Telecommunication Services:** mary.durham@kpchr.org.

34668 ■ Kaiser Permanente Medical Care Program - Division of Research (DOR)
3505 Broadway
Oakland, CA 94611
Ph: (510)891-3400
Fax: (510)450-2073
Co. E-mail: alan.s.go@kp.org
URL: http://www.dor.kaiser.org
Contact: Dr. Alan S. Go, Director (Acting)
Services: Staff teaches at local universities and performs editorial and review services for scientific and medical journals. **Founded:** 1961. **Educational Activities:** In-house seminars and conferences.

34669 ■ La Rabida Children's Hospital and Research Center
E 65th St. at Lake Michigan
Chicago, IL 60649
Ph: (773)363-6700
Fax: (773)363-7160
Co. E-mail: info@larabida.org
URL: http://www.larabida.org
Contact: Dr. Brenda J. Wolf, President
Services: Technical assistance and consulting for the community. **Founded:** 1989. **Educational Activities:** Informal mentoring program; Professional symposium, at pediatricians, therapists, social workers, psychologists and other health care professionals; La Rabida Children's Hospital and Research Center Seminars and workshops (Periodic).

34670 ■ Marshall University Research Corp. (MURC)
Coal Exchange Bldg., Ste. 1400
401 11th St.
Huntington, WV 25701
Ph: (304)696-6598
Fax: (304)697-2770
Co. E-mail: maherj@marshall.edu
URL: http://www.marshall.edu/murc/
Contact: John Maher, Executive Director
Services: Counseling and referral services; Technical and research assistance. **Founded:** 1984. **Educational Activities:** Educational seminars, workshops, and lectures; Graduate cooperative education programs.

34671 ■ Medical Technology and Practice Patterns Institute, Inc. (MTPPI)
4733 Bethesda Ave., Ste. 510
Bethesda, MD 20814
Ph: (301)652-4005
Fax: (301)652-8335
Co. E-mail: info@mtppi.org
URL: http://www.mtppi.org
Contact: Dennis J. Cotter, President
Services: Consulting for public and private organizations. **Founded:** 1986. **Publications:** *Diagnostic Imaging and Child Abuse*; *Direct and Indirect Costs of Diabetes*; *Implications of NAFTA for Trade in Health Care Technology*; *Rational Use of Health Technologies*; *Reports on various health technologies*. **Educational Activities:** Senior Resident Scholar Program. **Telecommunication Services:** dcott@mtppi.org.

34672 ■ Methodist Research Institute (MRI)
1812 N Capitol Ave.
Indianapolis, IN 46202
Ph: (317)962-3749
Fax: (317)962-5954
Co. E-mail: rmcnamee@clarian.org
URL: http://www.clarian.org/portal/patients/education-?clarianContentID=/education/mri/m ri_welcome.xml
Services: Statistical analysis, abstract and manuscript preparation, and grant proposal writing. **Founded:** 1956. **Educational Activities:** Educational seminars on research topics; MRI Seminars; Staff physician training in surgical techniques; Summer Student Research Program.

34673 ■ Michigan Family Forum (MFF)
PO Box 15216
Lansing, MI 48901-5216
Ph: (517)374-1171
Free: 800-644-9111
Fax: (517)374-6112
Co. E-mail: info@michiganfamily.org
URL: http://www.michiganfamily.org
Contact: Brad Snavely, Executive Director
Founded: 1990. **Publications:** *The Forum* (Quarterly); *Forum Online* (Weekly); *Voter Guides*. **Educational Activities:** Choose Freedom Peer Abstinence Network; Special events (Periodic). **Telecommunication Services:** brad@michiganfamily.org.

34674 ■ Mount Sinai School of Medicine of City University of New York - International Longevity Center-USA (ILC)
60 E 86th St.
New York, NY 10028
Ph: (212)288-1468
Fax: (212)288-3132
Co. E-mail: info@ilcusa.org
URL: http://www.ilcusa.org
Contact: Dr. Robert N. Butler, President
Services: Consulting services: for policymakers, the general public, and the media. **Founded:** 1990. **Publications:** *ILC Annual report*; *ILC Newsletter*. **Educational Activities:** Exchange program, for scholars and students.

34675 ■ New Mexico Clinical Research and Osteoporosis Center
300 Oak St. NE
Albuquerque, NM 87106
Ph: (505)855-5525
Fax: (505)884-4006
URL: http://www.nmbonecare.com
Contact: Dr. Lance A. Rudolph, Director, Research
Founded: 1987. **Publications:** *New Mexico Clinical Research and Osteoporosis Center Newsletter* (Quarterly).

34676 ■ New School University - Center for New York City Affairs
72 5th Ave., 6th Fl.
New York, NY 10011
Ph: (212)229-5418
Fax: (212)229-5335
Co. E-mail: centernyc@newschool.edu
URL: http://www.newschool.edu/milano/nycaffairs/
Contact: Andrew White, Director
Founded: 1964. **Publications:** *Child Welfare Watch* (Semiannual); *Developmental Disabilities Watch* (Annual); *Center for New York City Affairs Working papers* (Occasionally). **Educational Activities:** Conferences, lectures, short courses, and seminars. **Telecommunication Services:** whitea@newschool.edu.

34677 ■ Oklahoma Family Policy Council (OFPC)
Bethany Bank Twr., Ste. 100
3908 N Peniel Ave.
Bethany, OK 73008-3458
Ph: (405)787-7744
Free: 888-381-0044

Fax: (405)787-3900
Co. E-mail: mljestes@okfamilypc.org
URL: http://www.okfamilypc.org
Contact: Michael L. Jestes, Executive Director
Founded: 1990. **Publications:** *Community Impact Bulletin*; *OFPC Fact Sheet*; *Oklahoma Citizen* (Quarterly); *Viewpoint on Public Issues*. **Educational Activities:** Title V abstinence-only education program, in Oklahoma City; OFPC Training courses, on citizenship and policy issues. **Telecommunication Services:** info@okfamilypc.org.

34678 ■ Pacific Health Research Institute (PHRI)
700 Bishop St., Ste. 900
Honolulu, HI 96813
Ph: (808)524-4411
Fax: (808)524-5559
Co. E-mail: info@phrihawaii.org
URL: http://www.phrihawaii.org
Contact: Bruce R. Stevenson, Chief Executive Officer
Founded: 1960. **Telecommunication Services:** ceo@phrihawaii.org.

34679 ■ Pacific Research Institute (PRI)
1 Embarcadero Ctr., Ste. 350
San Francisco, CA 94111
Ph: (415)989-0833
Free: 800-276-7600
Fax: (415)989-2411
Co. E-mail: info@pacificresearch.org
URL: http://www.pacificresearch.org
Contact: Sally C. Pipes, President
E-mail: spipes@pacificresearch.org
Description: Aims to inform the public about issues that affect the free enterprise system and the rights of individuals. Studies public policy issues, including education, environment, technology, economics, health and welfare. Maintains speakers' bureau. Conducts educational programs. **Founded:** 1979. **Publications:** *Capital Ideas*; *The Contrarian*; *PRI Newsletter* (Quarterly); *Policy Briefings*; *Studies*. **Educational Activities:** Issues Luncheons (Periodic); Privatization Competition (Annual). **Telecommunication Services:** spipes@pacificresearch.org.

34680 ■ Portland VA Research Foundation, Inc. (PVARF)
PO Box 69539
Portland, OR 97239
Ph: (503)220-8262
Fax: (503)402-2866
Co. E-mail: david.hickam@va.gov
URL: http://www.visn20.med.va.gov/portland/Research/pvarf/index.htm
Contact: David Hickam, President
Founded: 1989.

34681 ■ Public Citizen - Health Research Group
1600 20th St. NW
Washington, DC 20009
Ph: (202)588-1000
Fax: (202)588-7796
Co. E-mail: hrg1@citizen.org
URL: http://www.citizen.org/hrg
Contact: Sidney M. Wolfe, Director
Founded: 1971. **Publications:** *Health Letter* (Monthly); *Health Research Group List of Publications* (Annual); *Worst Pills, Best Bills*; *Worst Pills Best Pills News* (Monthly).

34682 ■ Regenstrief Institute, Inc.
410 W 10th St., Ste. 2000
Indianapolis, IN 46202-3012
Ph: (317)630-6083
Co. E-mail: wtierney@iupui.edu
URL: http://www.regenstrief.org
Contact: William M. Tierney, President
Founded: 1969.

34683 ■ RTI International
3040 Cornwallis Rd.
Research Triangle Park, NC 27709-2194
Ph: (919)485-2666
Fax: (919)541-5985
Co. E-mail: listen@rti.org
URL: http://www.rti.org
Contact: Victoria F. Haynes, President
Founded: 1958. **Publications:** *RTI International Annual report*; *Hypotenuse* (8/year).

34684 ■ Rush University - Center for Health Management Studies
1700 W Van Burren St., Rm. 126-B
Chicago, IL 60612
Ph: (312)942-5402
Fax: (312)942-4957
Co. E-mail: rush_hsm@rush.edu
URL: http://www.rushu.rush.edu/hsm/
Contact: Andy Garman, Associate
Services: Methodological and statistical assistance to health care clinicians, managers, and students for developing research projects. **Founded:** 1978. **Publications:** *Center for Health Management Studies Annual report*; *Center for Health Management Studies Working papers* (Semiannual). **Educational Activities:** Journal Club; Annual Symposium of Health Affairs, on current topics in healthcare management research and policy; Faculty Development Program; Symposia, seminars, continuing education/executive development programs, and other special programs. **Telecommunication Services:** andy_n_garman@rush.edu.

34685 ■ Rutgers University - Institute for Health, Health Care Policy, and Aging Research
30 College Ave.
New Brunswick, NJ 08901-1283
Ph: (732)932-8415
Fax: (732)932-6872
Co. E-mail: mechanic@rci.rutgers.edu
URL: http://www-ihhcpar.rutgers.edu/
Contact: David Mechanic, Director
Founded: 1986. **Publications:** *Peer-reviewed articles*. **Educational Activities:** Brown Bag luncheon seminars (Weekly), on health, mental health and health policy; Research training, for undergraduates from minority backgrounds; Institute for Health, Health Care Policy, and Aging Research Seminars (Occasionally), open to the public. **Telecommunication Services:** ihhcpar_webmaster@ifh.rutgers.edu.

34686 ■ Rutgers University - Institute for Health, Health Care Policy, and Aging Research - Division on Aging - AIDS Policy Research Group (ARG)
112 Paterson St.
New Brunswick, NJ 08901
Ph: (732)932-8413
Fax: (732)932-1253
Co. E-mail: caboyer@rci.rutgers.edu
URL: http://www.ihhcpar.rutgers.edu/org_units/default.asp?v=2&o=6
Contact: Dr. Carol A. Boyer, Associate Director
Founded: 1987. **Publications:** *ARG Annual report*; *State health policy reports*; *White papers*. **Educational Activities:** Major talks and presentations (Weekly); ARG Seminars; Training programs for undergraduate, graduate and postdoctoral students (Weekly); Group meetings.

34687 ■ Seton Hall University - Center for Public Service
Jubilee Hall
400 S Orange Ave.
South Orange, NJ 07079
Ph: (973)761-9501
Fax: (973)275-2463
Co. E-mail: wishnaom@shu.edu
URL: http://www.shu.edu/academics/artsci/public-service
Contact: Naomi B. Wish, Director
Services: Technical assistance and training. **Founded:** 1986. **Educational Activities:** Graduate certificates, in Health Care Administration and Nonprofit Organization Management; Master's program, in public and healthcare administration; Distinguished Lecture Series in Philanthropy. **Awards:** Center for Public Service Scholarships, on a competitive basis to managers of community-based organizations.

34688 ■ Southern Illinois University at Carbondale - Center for Rural Health and Social Service Development (CRHSSD)
MC 6892
Carbondale, IL 62901-6892
Ph: (618)453-1262
Fax: (618)453-5040
Co. E-mail: ksanders@rural.siu.edu
URL: http://crhssd.siuc.edu
Contact: Dr. Kimberly J. (Kim) Sanders, Director
Services: Community needs assessments; Project development and management. **Founded:** 1989. **Publications:** *Center Briefs* (Quarterly). **Educational Activities:** Research projects, program evaluations; Training, curriculum development.

34689 ■ Texas A&M University - Institute for Science, Technology and Public Policy (ISTPP)
1112 Allen Bldg.
Bush School of Government & Public Service
4350 TAMU
College Station, TX 77843-4350
Ph: (979)862-8855
Fax: (979)862-8856
Co. E-mail: avedlitz@bushschool.tamu.edu
URL: http://bush.tamu.edu/istpp
Contact: Arnold Vedlitz, Director
Founded: 1993. **Publications:** *Articles in scholarly, peer-reviewed journals*; *ISTPP Reports* (Occasionally). **Educational Activities:** ISTPP Conferences, workshops (Occasionally); ISTPP Scholarship.

34690 ■ Texas Tech University - Center for Healthcare Innovation, Education and Research (CHIER)
College of Business Administration
Lubbock, TX 79409-2102
Ph: (806)742-1236
Fax: (806)742-3434
Co. E-mail: tim.huerta@ttu.edu
URL: http://chier.ba.ttu.edu/index.asp
Contact: Timothy R. Huerta, Director
Founded: 1997. **Publications:** *Advances in Health Care Management* (Annual). **Educational Activities:** Graduate programs, on health organization management; John A. Buesseler Lecture Series; Management education and development series; Professional development programming, related to healthcare organizations. **Telecommunication Services:** hom@ttu.edu.

34691 ■ Texas Tech University - Institute for Leadership Research (ILR)
Rawls College of Business Administration
Lubbock, TX 79409-2101
Ph: (806)742-3175
Fax: (806)742-3848
Co. E-mail: ilr@ttu.edu
URL: http://www.ilr.ba.ttu.edu
Contact: Prof. Michael Ryan, Executive Director
Founded: 1988. **Publications:** *ILR Monographs*; *Journal of Management Inquiry* (Quarterly). **Educational Activities:** Forums for chief executive officers; Leadership Development Series (5/year), series of workshop offered to the regional business community to enhance leadership development in the business and community sectors; Distinguished lecturer and panel discussions.

34692 ■ Thomas Jefferson University - Center for Research in Medical Education and Health Care
Jefferson Medical College
1020 Walnut St.
Philadelphia, PA 19107-5587
Ph: (215)955-5492
Fax: (215)923-6939
Co. E-mail: joseph.gonnella@jefferson.edu
URL: http://www.tju.edu/jmc/crmehc
Contact: Joseph S. Gonnella, Director
Services: Consultation and technical services. **Founded:** 1983. **Publications:** *ABSTRACTS: Longitudinal Study of Medical Students and Graduates*; *Center for Research in Medical Education and Health Care Annual report*. **Educational Activities:** Provides

abstracts of graduating students' performance to graduate program coordinators; Center for Research in Medical Education and Health Care Seminars.

34693 ■ University of Alabama at Birmingham - Lister Hill Center for Health Policy
Ryals Public Health Bldg.
1665 University Blvd.
Birmingham, AL 35294-0022
Ph: (205)975-9007
Fax: (205)934-3347
Co. E-mail: morrisey@uab.edu
URL: http://www.soph.uab.edu/index.php?q=listerhill
Contact: Michael A. Morrisey, Director
Founded: 1987. **Publications:** *Health Policy Abstract* (Monthly). **Educational Activities:** Methods workshops (Semiannual); Lister Hill Center for Health Policy Research seminars (Monthly). **Awards:** Intramural Grant Program (Annual); Health Policy Fellowship (Annual).

34694 ■ University of Arizona - Native American Research and Training Center (NARTC)
1642 E Helen
Tucson, AZ 85719
Ph: (520)621-5075
Fax: (520)621-9802
Co. E-mail: jrjoe@email.arizona.edu
URL: http://nartc.fcm.arizona.edu
Contact: Jennie R. Joe, Director
Founded: 1983. **Publications:** *NARTC Books*; *Dual track videotapes*; *NARTC Reports*. **Educational Activities:** NARTC Conferences and workshops; Training programs for indigenous trainers and direct-service providers.

34695 ■ University of California, Berkeley - Center for Labor Research and Education
2521 Channing Way, No. 5555
Berkeley, CA 94720-5555
Ph: (510)642-0323
Fax: (510)642-6432
Co. E-mail: kjacobs9@berkeley.edu
URL: http://laborcenter.berkeley.edu
Contact: Ken Jacobs, Chairperson
Founded: 1964. **Publications:** *California Workers Rights, and various pamphlets*; *Eyes on the Fries*; *Falling Apart: Declining Job-Based Health Coverage for Working Families in California and the United States*; *Hidden Costs of Wal-Mart Jobs*; *Hidden Public Costs of Low Wage Work*; *Kids at Risk: Declining Employer-Based Health Coverage in California and the U.S.*; *Organize to Improve the Quality of Jobs in the Black Community*; *The State of Labor Education in the U.S.*; *Trade Secrets*; *The Weingarten Decision and the Right to Representation on the Job*; *Winning at Work*. **Educational Activities:** California Lead Organizers Institute; California Union Leadership School; China labor rights curriculum; C.L. Dellums African American Leadership School; Export processing zone workers organizing curriculum; Financial Skills Workshop; Labor summer internships, in unions and community organizations; Latino American Leadership School; Media Skills Workshop; Strategic Campaigns Workshop; Strategic Research Workshop. **Telecommunication Services:** laborcenter@berkeley.edu.

34696 ■ University of California, San Francisco - Institute for Health Policy Studies
3333 California St., Ste. 265, Box 0936
San Francisco, CA 94118
Ph: (415)476-5255
Fax: (415)476-0705
Co. E-mail: hal.luft@ucsf.edu
URL: http://ihps.medschool.ucsf.edu
Contact: Claire Brindis, Director
Founded: 1972. **Awards:** Institute for Health Policy Studies Postdoctoral Fellowships. **Telecommunication Services:** claire.brindis@ucsf.edu.

34697 ■ University of Colorado at Denver - Center for Health Services Research
Division of Health Care Policy & Research
13611 E Colfax Ave., Ste. 100
Aurora, CO 80045-5701
Ph: (303)724-2400
Fax: (303)724-2530
Contact: Dr. Andrew Kramer, Director
Founded: 1977.

34698 ■ University of Connecticut - Center for International Community Health Studies (CICHS)
Department of Community Medicine & Health Care
School of Medicine, MC 6325
263 Farmington Ave.
Farmington, CT 06030-6325
Ph: (860)679-1570
Fax: (860)679-5464
Co. E-mail: schensul@nso2.uchc.edu
URL: http://www.commed.uchc.edu/cichs/default.htm
Contact: Stephen L. Schensul, Director
Founded: 1981. **Publications:** *Annual Training Program Catalogue*; *CICHS Connections Newsletter*. **Educational Activities:** Develops curricula in the medical, dental, and other health professional schools; Language training programs, short-term research, evaluation, curriculum design, and management training programs, for health professionals from Africa, Asia, the Middle East, Latin America, and The New Independent States (NIS); Conference on International Community Health (Annual).

34699 ■ University of Illinois at Chicago - Institute for Health Research and Policy - Center for Health Services Research (CHSR)
Westside Research Office Bldg., Rm. 560 CU3
1747 W Roosevelt Rd., MC 275
Chicago, IL 60608
Ph: (312)996-1062
Fax: (312)996-5356
Co. E-mail: jzwanzig@uic.edu
URL: http://ihrp.uic.edu/center/center-health-services-research
Contact: Jack Zwanziger, Director
Founded: 1972. **Educational Activities:** Internships and independent studies. **Awards:** CHSR Fellowships; CHSR Research assistantships, for graduate students.

34700 ■ University of Illinois - Health Systems Research (HSR)
College of Medicine
1601 Parkview Ave.
Rockford, IL 61107
Ph: (815)395-5639
Fax: (815)395-5602
Co. E-mail: joelc@uic.edu
URL: http://www.rockford.medicine.uic.edu
Founded: 1972. **Publications:** *Information Service Letter* (Quarterly).

34701 ■ University of Manitoba - Manitoba Centre for Nursing and Health Research (MCNHR)—University of Manitoba - Manitoba Nursing Research Institute (MNRI)
Helen Glass Ctr. for Nursing
Ft. Garry Campus
89 Curry Pl.
Winnipeg, MB, Canada R3T 2N2
Ph: (204)474-9080
Fax: (204)474-7683
Co. E-mail: mcnhr@cc.umanitoba.ca
URL: http://umanitoba.ca/nursing/mcnhr/index.html
Contact: Lesley Degner, Director
Services: Consultation: for faculty, graduate students and community nurses; Research support: for research grant applications and knowledge translation activities. **Founded:** 1985. **Publications:** *MCNHR Annual reports*; *Research activity reports* (Semiannual). **Educational Activities:** Dr. Helen P. Glass Researcher in Residence Program (Annual); Research seminars, workshops and training. **Awards:** Fort Garry Branch Royal Canadian Legion Poppy Trust Fund (Annual); Kathleen & Winnifred Ruane Graduate Student Research Grant for Nurses (Annual); Nursing research grants (Annual), for outcomes research. **Telecommunication Services:** lesley_degner@umanitoba.ca.

34702 ■ University of Maryland at College Park - Center on Aging
2367 SPH Bldg.
College Park, MD 20742-2611
Ph: (301)405-2469
Fax: (301)405-2542
Co. E-mail: lwilson@umd.edu
URL: http://www.sph.umd.edu/hlsa/aging/index.cfm
Contact: Dr. Laura B. Wilson, Director
Services: Curriculum development. **Founded:** 1974. **Publications:** *Community Gerontology*. **Educational Activities:** Legacy College, for age 50 and over; Graduate Gerontology Certificate Program; Legacy Leadership Institutes.

34703 ■ University of Michigan - Health Management Research Center (UM-HMRC)
1015 E Huron St.
Ann Arbor, MI 48104-1688
Ph: (734)763-2462
Co. E-mail: dwe@umich.edu
URL: http://www.hmrc.umich.edu
Contact: Dr. D.W. Edington, Director
Services: Consultation on wellness programs. **Founded:** 1977. **Publications:** *Cost Benefit Analysis* (Annual). **Educational Activities:** Wellness in the Workplace Seminar. **Awards:** Internships and research assistantships in the study of worksite health promotion programs. **Telecommunication Services:** hmrc-contact@umich.edu.

34704 ■ University of Minnesota - Division of Health Policy and Management (HPM)
School of Public Health, MMC 729
420 Delaware St. SE
Minneapolis, MN 55455-0392
Ph: (612)624-6151
Fax: (612)624-2196
Co. E-mail: mosco001@umn.edu
URL: http://www.sph.umn.edu/hpm
Contact: Ira Moscovice, Director
Founded: 1978. **Publications:** *Institute News* (3/year); *Research brief* (Monthly). **Educational Activities:** Minnesota Health Services Research Conference (Annual); Postdoctoral training program. **Awards:** Fellowships, scholarships, traineeships.

34705 ■ University of Pennsylvania - Leonard Davis Institute of Health Economics (LDI)
Colonial Penn Ctr.
3641 Locust Walk
Philadelphia, PA 19104-6218
Ph: (215)898-5611
Fax: (215)898-0229
Co. E-mail: asch@wharton.upenn.edu
URL: http://ldi.upenn.edu
Contact: David A. Asch, Executive Director
Founded: 1967. **Publications:** *LDI Brochures*; *Issue briefs* (Occasionally). **Educational Activities:** Advanced management education programs, to senior health care executives and other health care professionals; Health Policy Seminar Series; Research conference (Semimonthly); Research Seminar Series; Summer Undergraduate Minority Research Program.

34706 ■ University of South Florida - Center for HIV Education and Research
13301 Bruce B. Downs Blvd.
Tampa, FL 33612
Ph: (813)974-4430
Free: 866-352-2382
Fax: (813)974-8451
Co. E-mail: knox@usf.edu
URL: http://www.usfcenter.org
Contact: Dr. Michael D. Knox, Director
Services: Consulting: to hospitals, clinics, public health centers, community health centers, and substance abuse centers. **Founded:** 1988. **Publications:** *HIV/AIDS Primary Care Guide*; *HIV Carelink Newsletter*, *Pocket Transmission Treatment Cards*. **Educational Activities:** Educational events, on HIV and AIDS for physicians and other primary care clinicians; Florida/Caribbean AIDS Education and Training Center; HIV Conference (Annual), designed to increase the knowledge and skills of HIV healthcare providers; Perinatal Transmission Prevention Program; Center for HIV Education and Research Workshops, on topics related to and on clinical management for public health and correctional medical personnel specifically addressing HIV/AIDS. **Telecommunication Services:** contact@fcaetc.org.

34707 ■ University of Tennessee at Knoxville - Society for the Study of Social Problems, Inc. (SSSP)
901 McClung Twr.
Knoxville, TN 37996-0490
Ph: (865)689-1531
Fax: (865)689-1534
Co. E-mail: hector.delgado49@gmail.com
URL: http://www.sssp1.org
Contact: Dr. Hector L. Delgado, Executive Officer
Founded: 1951. **Publications:** *SSSP Newsletters* (3/year); *Social Problems* (Quarterly). **Educational Activities:** Panels; SSSP Symposia; Training workshops. **Awards:** Lee Student Support Fund (Annual); Thomas C. Hood Social Action Award (Annual); Racial/Ethnic Minority Graduate Scholarship; C. Wright Mills Award (Annual); Erwin O. Smigel Award (Annual); Lee Founders Award (Annual); Lee Scholar Support Fund (Annual). **Telecommunication Services:** mkoontz3@utk.edu.

34708 ■ University of Wisconsin—Madison - Center for Health System Research and Analysis (CHSRA)
WARF Bldg., 11th Fl.
610 Walnut St.
Madison, WI 53726-2397
Ph: (608)263-5722
Fax: (608)263-4523
Co. E-mail: robinson@chsra.wisc.edu
URL: http://www.chsra.wisc.edu
Contact: James M. Robinson, Director
Founded: 1973. **Telecommunication Services:** chsra_help@chsra.wisc.edu.

34709 ■ Vanderbilt University - Center for Health Policy
1207 18th Ave. S
Nashville, TN 37212
Ph: (615)322-0045
Fax: (615)322-8081
URL: http://www.vanderbilt.edu/VIPPS/HPC/HPChome.html
Contact: James F. Blumstein, Director

34710 ■ Vanderbilt University - Vanderbilt Institute for Public Policy Studies (VIPPS)
Department of Sociology
Nashville, TN 37235-1811
Ph: (615)322-7536
Fax: (615)322-7505
Co. E-mail: daniel.b.cornfield@vanderbilt.edu
URL: http://www.vanderbilt.edu/VIPPS/
Contact: Dr. Daniel B. Cornfield, Director (Acting)
Founded: 1975. **Publications:** *VIPPS Annual Report*; *Semiannual Newsletter*. **Educational Activities:** VIPPS Conferences; Faculty discussion groups; Freshman Tennessee Legislator Issue Workshop (Biennial); Orientation and budget workshops; Technical and general interest seminars.

34711 ■ Walther Cancer Institute, Inc. - Mary Margaret Walther Program for Cancer Care Research
Indiana University School of Nursing
1033 E 3rd St., NU 340 G
Bloomington, IN 47405-7005
Ph: (317)274-7563
Fax: (317)278-2021
Co. E-mail: vchampio@iupui.edu
URL: http://www.research.indiana.edu/centers/mmw-pccr.html
Contact: Dr. Victoria L. Champion, Director, Science
Founded: 1985. **Publications:** *Mary Margaret Walther Program for Cancer Care Research Brochures* (Annual). **Awards:** Postdoctoral and predoctoral fellowships.

34712 ■ Welfare Research, Inc. (WRI)
112 State St., Ste. 1340
Albany, NY 12207
Ph: (518)432-2563
Fax: (518)432-2564
Co. E-mail: vhswri@yahoo.com
URL: http://www.welfareresearch.org
Contact: Virginia Hayes Sibbison, Executive Director
Services: Management assistance; Program evaluation projects: health and human services and public administration. **Founded:** 1967. **Publications:** *WRI Annual Report*. **Educational Activities:** Communication and public information programs.

START-UP INFORMATION

34713 ■ *"Ailing Economy Nibbling at Tech-Sector Jobs" in Puget Sound Business Journal (Vol. 29, November 7, 2008, No. 29, pp. 1)*
Pub: American City Business Journals
Ed: Eric Engleman, John Cook. **Description:** Seattle-area tech start-up companies including Redfin, Zillow, WildTangent, Daptiv, Avelle, and Intrepid Learning Solutions have cut staff as the nation's economy staggers. The layoffs are reminiscent of the tech bubble era, but most startups these days have been more prudent about spending and hiring as compared to that period.

34714 ■ *"ATI Now Ready to Pounce on Biotech" in Austin Business JournalInc. (Vol. 28, August 22, 2008, No. 23, pp. 1)*
Pub: American City Business Journals
Ed: Laura Hipp. **Description:** Austin Technology Incubator has entered the biotechnology sector through a program of the University of Texas incubator. The company's bioscience program was set off by a grant from the City of Austin worth $125,000. The growth of Austin's biotechnology sector is examined.

34715 ■ *"EDCO Doling Out Capital Along Border" in Austin Business JournalInc. (Vol. 28, August 1, 2008, No. 20, pp. 1)*
Pub: American City Business Journals
Ed: Sandra Zaragoza. **Description:** Non-profit business incubator Economic Development Catalyst Organization Ventures is searching for promising startup companies. The company is targeting startups in green energy, technology and consumer markets. EDCO has partnered with consumer electronics repair company CherryFusion and technology firm MiniDonations.

34716 ■ *"ETF Process May be Tweaked" in Austin Business JournalInc. (Vol. 28, December 26, 2008, No. 41, pp. 3)*
Pub: American City Business Journals
Ed: Christopher Calnan. **Description:** Some government officials are proposing for an adjustment of the Texas Emerging Technology Fund's (ETF) policies. The ETF was created to get startup companies capital to get off the ground. Reports show that the global recession had made it more difficult for startup companies to garner investment.

34717 ■ *"Former Gov. Fletcher Starts Blue Ash Firm" in Business Courier (Vol. 26, October 9, 2009, No. 24, pp. 1)*
Pub: American City Business Journals, Inc.
Ed: Lucy May. **Description:** Former Kentucky Governor Ernie Fletcher partnered with Belcan Corporation founder Ralph Anderson to purchase Blue Ash, Ohio-based Virtual Medical Network and form Alton Healthcare LLC. The company's goal is to increase practice revenues by adapting technology to reinvent clinical practices and deliver best possible care to more patients.

34718 ■ *"Giving Biotech Startups a Hand" in Philadelphia Business Journal (Vol. 28, January 8, 2010, No. 47, pp. 1)*
Pub: American City Business Journals
Ed: John George. **Description:** Elkins Park, Pennsylvania-based BioStrategy Partners is a virtual life sciences incubator that is seeking to improve the dull ranking of Philadelphia in the small business vitality index of life sciences. BioStrategy provides technology and business development services to startup life sciences companies and university-based research projects.

34719 ■ *"Head West, Young Startup?" in Boston Business Journal (Vol. 30, October 22, 2010, No. 39, pp. 1)*
Pub: Boston Business Journal
Ed: Galen Moore. **Description:** Startup companies Lark Technologies, Baydin and E la Cart Inc. are planning to leave Boston, Massachusetts for Silicon Valley. Lark has developed a vibrating wrist strap that syncs with a mobile phone's alarm clock.

34720 ■ *High Tech Start Up*
Pub: Free Press
Ed: John L. Nesheim. **Price:** $50.00.

34721 ■ *The Mousedriver Chronicles*
Pub: Perseus Books Group
Ed: John Lusk; Kyle Harrison. **Released:** 2003. **Price:** $16.95. **Description:** Entrepreneurial voyage through the startup business of two ivy-league business school graduates and the lessons they learned while developing their idea of a computer mouse that looks like a golf driver into the marketplace. The book is an inspiration for those looking to turn an idea into a company.

34722 ■ *"Online Fortunes" in Small Business Opportunities (Fall 2008)*
Pub: Entrepreneur Media Inc.
Description: Fifty hot, e-commerce enterprises for the aspiring entrepreneur to consider are featured; virtual assistants, marketing services, party planning, travel services, researching, web design and development, importing as well as creating an online store are among the businesses featured.

34723 ■ *Seed-Stage Venture Investing: The Ins and Outs for Entrepreneurs, Start-Ups, and Investors on Successfully Starting a New Business*
Pub: Aspatore Books, Incorporated
Ed: William J. Robbins. **Released:** July 2006. **Price:** $199.95. **Description:** Ideas for starting, funding, and managing technology-based firms, also known as, venture capitalists, are featured.

34724 ■ *"Startup Aims to Cut Out Coupon Clipping" in The Business Journal-Serving Metropolitan Kansas City (Vol. 26, August 15, 2008, No. 49)*
Pub: American City Business Journals, Inc.
Ed: Suzanna Stagemeyer. **Description:** TDP Inc., who started operations 18 months ago, aims to transform stale coupon promotions using technology by digitizing the entire coupon process. The process is expected to enable consumers to hunt coupons online where they will be automatically linked to loyalty cards. Other views and information on TDP and its services are presented.

34725 ■ *"Startup to Serve Bar Scene" in Austin Business JournalInc. (Vol. 29, December 18, 2009, No. 41, pp. 1)*
Pub: American City Business Journals
Ed: Christopher Calnan. **Description:** Startup ATX Innovation Inc. of Austin, Texas has developed a test version of TabbedOut, a Web-based tool that would facilitate mobile phone-based restaurant and bar bill payment. TabbedOut has been tested by six businesses in Austin and will be available to restaurant and bar owners for free. Income would be generated by ATX through a 99-cent convenience charge per transaction.

34726 ■ *Technology Ventures: From Idea to Enterprise*
Pub: McGraw-Hill Higher Education
Ed: Thomas Byers, Richard Dorf, Andrew Nelson. **Released:** January 10, 2010. **Description:** An action-approached through the use of examples, exercises, cases, sample business plans, and recommended sources helps entrepreneurs start and run a technology-base small business.

34727 ■ *Technology Ventures: From Idea to Enterprise with Student DVD*
Pub: McGraw-Hill Higher Education
Ed: Richard C. Dorf; Thomas H. Byers. **Released:** October 2006. **Price:** $100.68. **Description:** Textbook examining technology entrepreneurship on a global basis; technology management theories are explored.

34728 ■ *"Troy Patent Law Firm Launches Rent-Free Tech Incubator" in Crain's Detroit Business (Vol. 25, June 8, 2009, No. 23, pp. 4)*
Pub: Crain Communications Inc. - Detroit
Ed: Tom Henderson. **Description:** Young Basile Hanlon MacFarlane & Helmholdt PC, a patent law firm located in Troy, Michigan has created a small, rent-free technology incubator on site. The incubator will be called North Woodward Tech Incubator and has room for four or five startups. The incubator is for the earliest or pre-seed stage for entrepreneurs who have not yet gotten significant investment capital.

34729 ■ *"Wanted: Angels in the Country" in Austin Business JournalInc. (Vol. 28, July 18, 2008, No. 18, pp. 1)*
Pub: American City Business Journals
Ed: Laura Hipp. **Description:** A proposal is being pushed forward by managers of Texas' Emerging Technology Fund to create an angel investors' network. The proposal is asking that tax credits for those who invest in research and development projects be granted in order to boost the number of technology companies in the state.

34730 ■ *"The Y Factor" in Entrepreneur (Vol. 35, November 2007, No. 11, pp. 58)*
Pub: Entrepreneur Media Inc.
Ed: Sara Wilson. **Description:** Venture capital company Y Cominbator hosts a three-month program

wherein the firm's founders select technology entrepreneurs from across the U.S. to help and to mentor them on starting a business.

EDUCATIONAL PROGRAMS

34731 ■ Application Systems Development Audit and Security
Seminar Information Service, Inc.
20 Executive Park, Ste. 120
Irvine, CA 92614
Ph: (949)261-9104
Free: 877-SEM-INFO
Fax: (949)261-1963
Co. E-mail: info@seminarinformation.com
URL: http://www.seminarinformation.com
Price: $1,950.00. **Description:** Learn an end-to-end approach for ensuring the design, security, integrity, and performance of your application system. **Dates and Locations:** San Francisco, CA; New York, NY; and Atlanta, GA.

34732 ■ Auditing Business Application Systems (Onsite)
Seminar Information Service, Inc.
20 Executive Park, Ste. 120
Irvine, CA 92614
Ph: (949)261-9104
Free: 877-SEM-INFO
Fax: (949)261-1963
Co. E-mail: info@seminarinformation.com
URL: http://www.seminarinformation.com
Price: $2,150.00. **Description:** Three-day seminar attendees will learn how to audit and how to develop controls for complex automated applications which use online/real-time, distributed processing, and/or database technologies, including an opportunity to actually prepare an audit plan for a complex application system. **Dates and Locations:** Chicago, IL.

34733 ■ Auditing Networked Computers (Onsite)
Seminar Information Service, Inc.
20 Executive Park, Ste. 120
Irvine, CA 92614
Ph: (949)261-9104
Free: 877-SEM-INFO
Fax: (949)261-1963
Co. E-mail: info@seminarinformation.com
URL: http://www.seminarinformation.com
Price: $1,950.00. **Description:** Seminar designed as a first look at LANs, WANs, workstations, and servers where you will focus on understanding the technology, evaluating the risks, and establishing n audit approach.

34734 ■ Auditing and Securing Oracle Databases (Onsite)
Seminar Information Service, Inc.
20 Executive Park, Ste. 120
Irvine, CA 92614
Ph: (949)261-9104
Free: 877-SEM-INFO
Fax: (949)261-1963
Co. E-mail: info@seminarinformation.com
URL: http://www.seminarinformation.com
Price: $2,695.00. **Description:** Learn Oracle's database facilities and terminology along with the commands you need to know to provide security, audit and query controls for Oracle and Oracle-controlled data. **Dates and Locations:** Washington, DC.

34735 ■ BGP - Configuring BGP on Cisco Routers (Onsite)
Seminar Information Service, Inc.
20 Executive Park, Ste. 120
Irvine, CA 92614
Ph: (949)261-9104
Free: 877-SEM-INFO
Fax: (949)261-1963
Co. E-mail: info@seminarinformation.com
URL: http://www.seminarinformation.com
Price: $3,295.00. **Description:** Comprehensive five-day course explores the theory of BGP, configuration of BGP on Cisco IOS routers, and detailed troubleshooting information. **Dates and Locations:** Dallas, TX; and New York, NY.

34736 ■ Comprehensive 5-Day Training Program for Business Energy Professionals (Onsite)
Seminar Information Service, Inc.
20 Executive Park, Ste. 120
Irvine, CA 92614
Ph: (949)261-9104
Free: 877-SEM-INFO
Fax: (949)261-1963
Co. E-mail: info@seminarinformation.com
URL: http://www.seminarinformation.com
Price: $1,895.00; $1,695.00 for members government/non-profits. **Description:** Gain an understanding of how energy efficiency opportunities impact the bottom line for their customers. **Dates and Locations:** Atlanta, GA.

34737 ■ Computer Forensics and Incident Response: Hands-On - Analyzing Windows-Based Systems (Onsite)
Seminar Information Service, Inc.
20 Executive Park, Ste. 120
Irvine, CA 92614
Ph: (949)261-9104
Free: 877-SEM-INFO
Fax: (949)261-1963
Co. E-mail: info@seminarinformation.com
URL: http://www.seminarinformation.com
Price: $2,890.00. **Description:** Learn how to: Implement a computer forensics incident-response strategy; Lead a successful investigation from the initial response to completion; Conduct disk-based analysis and recover deleted files; Identify information-hiding techniques; Reconstruct user activity from e-mail, temporary Internet files and cached data; Assess the integrity of system memory and process architecture to reveal malicious code. **Dates and Locations:** New York, NY.

34738 ■ Deploying Intrusion Detection Systems: Hands-On (Onsite)
Seminar Information Service, Inc.
20 Executive Park, Ste. 120
Irvine, CA 92614
Ph: (949)261-9104
Free: 877-SEM-INFO
Fax: (949)261-1963
Co. E-mail: info@seminarinformation.com
URL: http://www.seminarinformation.com
Price: $2,890.00. **Description:** Learn how to: Detect and respond to network- and host-based intruder attacks; Integrate intrusion detection systems (IDS) into your current network topology; Analyze IDS alerts using the latest tools and techniques; Identify methods hackers use to attack systems; Recognize detection avoidance schemes; Stop attackers with Intrusion Prevention Systems (IPSs). **Dates and Locations:** Rockville, MD.

34739 ■ Deterring Social Engineering Attacks: Resisting Human Deception (Onsite)
Seminar Information Service, Inc.
20 Executive Park, Ste. 120
Irvine, CA 92614
Ph: (949)261-9104
Free: 877-SEM-INFO
Fax: (949)261-1963
Co. E-mail: info@seminarinformation.com
URL: http://www.seminarinformation.com
Price: $1,890.00. **Description:** Learn how to: Help prevent social engineering exploits by heightening your security awareness; Decode the art of human deception; Identify the social engineering attack cycle; Define and help protect corporate and personal assets; Assess and quantify the impact of social engineering attacks; Integrate your corporate security policy into your professional responsibilities; Apply an employee social engineering defense checklist. **Dates and Locations:** Alexandria, VA.

34740 ■ Developing High-Performance SQL Server Databases: Hands-On (Onsite)
Seminar Information Service, Inc.
20 Executive Park, Ste. 120
Irvine, CA 92614
Ph: (949)261-9104
Free: 877-SEM-INFO
Fax: (949)261-1963
Co. E-mail: info@seminarinformation.com
URL: http://www.seminarinformation.com
Price: $3,190.00. **Description:** Learn how to design and implement high-performance databases for SQL Server 2005 and 2000; Create indexes that optimize different types of queries; Design transactions that maximize concurrency and minimize contention; Interpret the data access plans produced by the query optimizer; Minimize I/O by designing efficient physical data structures; Improve response time by introducing controlled redundancy; and analyze and cure performance problems using SQL Server's tools. **Dates and Locations:** Rockville, MD; Toronto, CN; New York, NY; and Reston, VA.

34741 ■ Disaster Recovery Planning: Ensuring Business Continuity (Onsite)
Seminar Information Service, Inc.
20 Executive Park, Ste. 120
Irvine, CA 92614
Ph: (949)261-9104
Free: 877-SEM-INFO
Fax: (949)261-1963
Co. E-mail: info@seminarinformation.com
URL: http://www.seminarinformation.com
Price: $2,890.00. **Description:** Learn how to: Create, document and test continuity arrangements for your organization; Perform a risk assessment and Business Impact Assessment (BIA) to identify vulnerabilities; Select and deploy an alternate site for continuity of mission-critical activities; Identify appropriate strategies to recover the infrastructure and processes; Organize and manage recovery teams; Test and maintain an effective recovery plan in a rapidly changing technology environment. **Dates and Locations:** Rockvile, MD; New York, NY; and Reston, VA.

34742 ■ DSP: Digital Signal Processing (Onsite)
Seminar Information Service, Inc.
20 Executive Park, Ste. 120
Irvine, CA 92614
Ph: (949)261-9104
Free: 877-SEM-INFO
Fax: (949)261-1963
Co. E-mail: info@seminarinformation.com
URL: http://www.seminarinformation.com
Price: $1,895.00. **Description:** Introduction to DSP concepts and implementation, including a complete model of a DSP system from the input transducer through all the stages.

34743 ■ Ethical Hacking and Countermeasures: Hands-On - Preventing Network and System Breaches (Onsite)
Seminar Information Service, Inc.
20 Executive Park, Ste. 120
Irvine, CA 92614
Ph: (949)261-9104
Free: 877-SEM-INFO
Fax: (949)261-1963
Co. E-mail: info@seminarinformation.com
URL: http://www.seminarinformation.com
Price: $2,890.00. **Description:** Learn how to deploy ethical hacking to expose weaknesses in your organization and select countermeasures; Gather intelligence by employing social engineering, published data and scanning tools; Probe and compromise your network using hacking tools to improve your security; Discover how malicious hackers exploit weaknesses to 'own' the network; Protect against privilege escalation to prevent intrusions; Defend against evasions of antivirus, firewalls and IDS. **Dates and Locations:** Reston, VA; Rockville, MD; and New York, NY.

34744 ■ Fundamentals of Information Security (Onsite)
Seminar Information Service, Inc.
20 Executive Park, Ste. 120
Irvine, CA 92614
Ph: (949)261-9104
Free: 877-SEM-INFO

Fax: (949)261-1963
Co. E-mail: info@seminarinformation.com
URL: http://www.seminarinformation.com
Price: $2,050.00. **Description:** Three-day seminar will guide you through the basics of information security in today's high-tech, business environment, including external threats, establishing effective security policies, contingency planning, and employee privacy rights.

34745 ■ Introduction to Soundtrack Pro
EEI Communications
8945 Guilford Rd.., Ste. 145
Columbia, MD 21046
Ph: (410)309-8200
Free: 888-253-2762
Fax: (410)630-3980
Co. E-mail: train@eeicom.com
URL: http://www.eeicom.com/eei-training-services
Price: $745.00. **Description:** Course includes an introduction to Soundtrack Pro Interface, basic audio editing, importing audio, post-production techniques with audio and video, producing podcasts with Soundtrack Pro, and exporting your audio projects. **Dates and Locations:** Alexandria, VA.

34746 ■ IT Auditing and Controls (Onsite)
Seminar Information Service, Inc.
20 Executive Park, Ste. 120
Irvine, CA 92614
Ph: (949)261-9104
Free: 877-SEM-INFO
Fax: (949)261-1963
Co. E-mail: info@seminarinformation.com
URL: http://www.seminarinformation.com
Price: $2,150.00. **Description:** Three-day seminar outlines the concepts of information systems you need to know in order to understand the audit concerns in the IS environment. You will learn the necessary controls for application systems- the session pinpoints specific controls to evaluate when auditing currently installed system, new systems under development, and the various activities within the information systems department, as well as techniques for auditing automated systems. **Dates and Locations:** Cities throughout the United States.

34747 ■ A Practical Guide to Controls for IT Professionals (Onsite)
Seminar Information Service, Inc.
20 Executive Park, Ste. 120
Irvine, CA 92614
Ph: (949)261-9104
Free: 877-SEM-INFO
Fax: (949)261-1963
Co. E-mail: info@seminarinformation.com
URL: http://www.seminarinformation.com
Price: Contact for fees. **Description:** Designed to provide all levels of IT personnel with an understanding of what controls are and why they are critical to safeguarding information assets. Discover why it is important to have a business-process view of IT controls and review the critical role they play in providing for a smooth running, efficiently manager IT environment.

REFERENCE WORKS

34748 ■ *The 7 Irrefutable Rules of Small Business Growth*
Pub: John Wiley & Sons, Incorporated
Ed: Steven S. Little. **Released:** February 2005. **Price:** $18.95. **Description:** Proven strategies to maintain small business growth are outlined, covering topics such as technology, business plans, hiring, and more.

34749 ■ *"2010 Book of Lists" in Austin Business JournalInc. (Vol. 29, December 25, 2009, No. 42, pp. 1)*
Pub: American City Business Journals
Description: Rankings of companies and organizations within the business services, finance, healthcare, hospitality and travel, insurance, marketing and media, professional services, real estate, education and technology industries in Austin, Texas are presented. Rankings are based on sales, business size, and other statistics.

34750 ■ *"2010 Book of Lists" in Business Courier (Vol. 26, December 26, 2009, No. 36, pp. 1)*
Pub: American City Business Journals, Inc.
Description: Rankings of companies and organizations within the business services, education, finance, health care, hospitality and tourism, real estate, and technology industries in the Cincinnati, Ohio-Northern Kentucky area are presented. Rankings are based on sales, business size, or other statistics.

34751 ■ *"2010 Book of Lists" in Tampa Bay Business Journal (Vol. 30, December 22, 2009, No. 53, pp. 1)*
Pub: American City Business Journals
Description: Rankings of companies and organizations within the human resources, banking and finance, business services, healthcare, real estate, technology, hospitality and travel, and education industries in the Greater Tampa Bay area are presented. Rankings are based on sales, business size, and more.

34752 ■ *"Abraxis Bets On Biotech Hub" in Business Journal-Serving Phoenix and the Valley of the Sun (Vol. 10, November 9, 2007, No. 28)*
Pub: American City Business Journals, Inc.
Ed: Angela Gonzales. **Description:** Abraxis BioScience Inc. purchased a 200,000 square foot manufacturing facility in Phoenix, Arizona from Watson Pharmaceuticals Inc. The company has the technology to allow chemotherapy drugs to be injected directly into tumor cell membranes. A human protein, albumin is used to deliver the chemotherapy.

34753 ■ *"Achieving Greatness" in Black Enterprise (Vol. 38, January 2008, No. 6, pp. 50)*
Pub: Earl G. Graves Publishing Co. Inc.
Description: Randall Pinkett, winner of a reality show on television and chairman of BCT Partners, insists that a business cannot survive by doing just enough or more of the same. Pinkett's New Jersey company provides management, technology and consulting to other firms.

34754 ■ *Achieving Planned Innovation: A Proven System for Creating Successful New Products and Services*
Pub: Simon and Schuster
Ed: Frank R. Bacon. **Released:** August 2007. **Price:** $16.95. **Description:** Planned innovation is a disciplined and practical step-by-step sequence of procedures for reaching the intended destination point: successful products. This easy-to-read book explains the system along with an action-oriented program for continuous success in new-product innovations. Five steps outlined include: a disciplined reasoning process; lasting market orientation; proper selection criteria that reflect both strategic and tactical business objectives and goals along with dynamic matching of resources to present and future opportunities, and positive and negative requirements before making major expenditures; and proper organizational staffing. The author explains what to do and evaluating the potential of any new product or service, ranging from ventures in retail distribution to the manufacture of goods as diverse as bicycles, motorcycles, aerospace communication and navigation equipment, small business computers, food packaging, and medical products.

34755 ■ *Advanced Manufacturing Technology*
Pub: Wiley-Blackwell
Contact: William J. Pesce, President
E-mail: wpesce@wiley.com
URL(s): www.apnf.org/frostbody.htm. **Ed:** Leo O'Connor. **Released:** Monthly **Publication includes:** List of companies involved in developing advanced manufacturing technologies such as robotics, artificial intelligence in computers, ultrasonics, lasers, and waterjet cutters; also lists sources of information and education on high-technology. **Entries include:** Company or organization name, address, phone, name of contact; description of process, product, or service. Principal content is articles and analysis of advanced manufacturing technology. **Arrangement:** Classified by subject.

34756 ■ *"After Price Cuts, Competition GPS Makers Lose Direction" in Brandweek (Vol. 49, April 21, 2008, No. 16, pp. 16)*
Pub: VNU Business Media, Inc.
Ed: Steve Miller. **Description:** Garmin and TomTom, two of the leaders in portable navigation devices, have seen lowering revenues due to dramatic price cuts and unexpected competition from the broadening availability of personal navigation on mobile phones. TomTom has trimmed its sales outlook for its first quarter while Garmin's stock dropped 40 percent since February.

34757 ■ *Aging and Working in the New Economy: Changing Career Structures in Small IT Firms*
Pub: Edward Elgar Publishing, Inc.
Ed: Julie McMullin, Victor W. Marshall. **Released:** March 1, 2010. **Price:** $110.00. **Description:** Case studies and analyses provide insight into the structural features of small- and medium-sized firms in the information technology sector, and the implications of these features for the careers of people employed by them.

34758 ■ *"Agricharts Launches New Mobile App for Ag Market" in Farm Industry News (December 1, 2011)*
Pub: Penton Business Media Inc.
Description: AgriCharts provides market data, agribusiness Website hosting and technology solutions for the agricultural industry. AgriCharts is a division of Barchart.com Inc. and announced the release of a new mobile applications that offers real-time or delayed platform for viewing quotes, charts and analysis of grains, livestock and other commodity markets.

34759 ■ *"Airlines Mount PR Push to Win Public Support Against Big Oil" in Advertising Age (Vol. 79, July 14, 2008, No. 7, pp. 1)*
Pub: Crain Communications, Inc.
Ed: Michael Bush. **Description:** Top airline executives from competing companies have banded together in a public relations plan in which they are sending e-mails to their frequent fliers asking for aid in lobbying legislators to put a restriction on oil speculation.

34760 ■ *"All About The Benjamins" in Canadian Business (Vol. 81, September 29, 2008, No. 16, pp. 92)*
Pub: Rogers Media Ltd.
Ed: David Baines. **Description:** Discusses real estate developer Royal Indian Raj International Corp., a company that planned to build a $3 billion 'smart city' near the Bangalore airport; to this day nothing has ever been built. The company was incorporated in 1999 by Manoj C. Benjamin one investor, Bill Zack, has been sued by the developer for libel due to his website that calls the company a scam. Benjamin has had a previous case of fraud issued against him as well as a string of liabilities and lawsuits.

34761 ■ *"All Those Applications, and Phone Users Just Want to Talk" in Advertising Age (Vol. 79, August 11, 2008, No. 31, pp. 18)*
Pub: Crain Communications, Inc.
Ed: Mike Vorhaus. **Description:** Although consumers are slowly coming to text messaging and other data applications, a majority of those Americans surveyed stated that they simply want to use their cell phones to talk and do not care about other activities. Statistical data included.

34762 ■ *Alpha Dogs: How Your Small Business Can Become a Leader of the Pack*
Pub: HarperCollins Publishers, Inc.
Ed: Donna Fenn. **Released:** May 2007. **Price:** $14. 95. **Description:** Profiles of eight successful entrepreneurs along with information for developing customer service, technology and competition.

34763 ■ *"Analysts: Intel Site May Be Last Major U.S.-Built Fab" in Business Journal-Serving Phoenix and the Valley of the Sun (Oct. 19, 2007)*
Pub: American City Business Journals, Inc.

Ed: Ty Young. **Description:** Intel's million-square-foot manufacturing facility, called Fab 32, is expected to open in 2007. The plant will mass-produce the 45-nanometer microchip. Industry analysts believe Fab 32 may be the last of its kind to be built in the U.S., as construction costs are higher in America than in other countries. Intel's future in Chandler is examined.

34764 ■ *"Ann Arbor Google's Growth Dips" in Crain's Detroit Business (Vol. 25, June 8, 2009, No. 23, pp. 3)*
Pub: Crain Communications Inc. - Detroit

Ed: Bill Shea. **Description:** Global recession has slowed the growth of Google Inc. Three years ago, when Google moved to Ann Arbor, Michigan it estimated it would provide 1,000 new jobs within five years, so far the firm employs 250.

34765 ■ *"Anybody Out There?" in Canadian Business (Vol. 81, July 21 2008, No. 11, pp. 31)*
Pub: Rogers Media Ltd.

Ed: Andrew Wahl. **Description:** Virtual offices or shared office services provide solutions to companies that can no longer accommodate additional workspaces. The alternative working arrangement allows the company to have a kind of distributed work system. The disadvantages of employing virtual offices are presented.

34766 ■ *"Anything Could Happen" in Inc. (March 2008, pp. 116-123)*
Pub: Gruner & Jahr USA Publishing

Ed: Max Chafkin. **Description:** Profile of Evan Williams, founder of Blogger and Twitter, a new type of technology idea; Williams answers ten questions and share insight into growing both of his companies.

34767 ■ *"Anytime Access" in Crain's Cleveland Business (Vol. 28, October 22, 2007, No. 42, pp. 17)*
Pub: Crain Communications, Inc.

Ed: Brad Dicken. **Description:** Technology continues to evolve in the competitive world of mobile communications in which the phone has become a sleek multitool that can take a call, send and e-mail, calculate the tip after dinner and snap a photograph.

34768 ■ *"App Time: Smartphone Applications Aren't Just for Fun and Games Anymore" in Inc. (Volume 32, December 2010, No. 10, pp. 116)*
Pub: Inc. Magazine

Ed: Jason Del Rey. **Description:** Smart phone technology can help any small business market their products and services.

34769 ■ *"Apps For Anybody With an Idea" in Advertising Age (Vol. 79, October 20, 2008, No. 39, pp. 29)*
Pub: Crain Communications, Inc.

Ed: Beth Snyder Bulik. **Description:** Apple's new online App Store is open to anyone with an idea and the ability to write code and many of these developers are not only finding a sense of community through this venue but are also making money since the sales are split with Apple, 30/70 in the developer's favor.

34770 ■ *"ART Announces New Distribution Arrangement with GE Healthcare for eXplore Optix" in Canadian Corporate News (May 14, 2007)*
Pub: Comtex News Network Inc.

Description: ART Advanced Research Technologies Inc., a medical device company and a leader in optical molecular imaging products for the pharmaceutical and healthcare industries, announced that it signed an agreement with GE Healthcare regarding worldwide distribution of its eXplore Optix preclinical optical molecular imaging system.

34771 ■ *"As Technology Changes, So Must African American Business" in Black Enterprise (Vol. 41, August 2010, No. 1, pp. 61)*
Pub: Earl G. Graves Publishing Co. Inc.

Ed: Sonya A. Donaldson. **Description:** Social media is essential to compete in today's business environment, especially for African American firms.

34772 ■ *"Asterand Eyes Jump to Ann Arbor; TechTown Tenant" in Crain's Detroit Business (Vol. 25, June 22, 2009)*
Pub: Crain Communications Inc. - Detroit

Ed: Tom Henderson. **Description:** Asterand PLC is considering a move to Ann Arbor from its current location as anchor tenant at TechTown, an incubator and technology park associated with Wayne State University. The university believes the Ann Arbor location's rent is too expensive for the tissue bank company.

34773 ■ *"Astral Fine-Tunes Details of Standard Purchase" in Globe & Mail (February 26, 2007, pp. B1)*
Pub: CTVglobemedia Publishing Inc.

Ed: Grant Robertson. **Description:** The proposed acquisition of Standard Radio Inc. by Astral Media Inc. for $1.2 billion is discussed.

34774 ■ *"Attention, Please" in Entrepreneur (Vol. 36, April 2008, No. 4, pp. 52)*
Pub: Entrepreneur Media, Inc.

Ed: Andrea Cooper. **Description:** Gurbaksh Chahal created his own company ClickAgents at the age of 16, and sold it two years later for $40 million to ValueClick. He then founded BlueLithium, an online advertising network on behavioral targeting, which Yahoo! Inc. bought in 2007 for $300 million. Chahal, now 25, talks about his next plans and describes how BlueLithium caught Yahoo's attention.

34775 ■ *"Attivio Brings Order to Data" in Information Today (Vol. 26, February 2009, No. 2, pp. 14)*
Pub: Information Today, Inc.

Ed: Marji McClure. **Description:** Profile of Attivio, the high tech firm offering next-generation software that helps businesses to consolidate data and eliminate enterprise silos.

34776 ■ *"Auction-Rate Cash Frees Up" in The Business Journal-Portland (Vol. 25, August 15, 2008, No. 23, pp. 1)*
Pub: American City Business Journals, Inc.

Ed: Aliza Earnshaw. **Description:** FEI Co. and RadiSys Corp. have received notices that UBS AG will buy back the auction-rate securities that were sold to them in around two years from 2008. FEI had $110.1 million invested in auction-rate securities while RadiSys holds $62.8 million of these securities.

34777 ■ *"Back Off on ABM Legislation, Banks Warn MPs" in Globe & Mail (April 20, 2007, pp. B1)*
Pub: CTVglobemedia Publishing Inc.

Ed: Steven Chase. **Description:** The efforts of banks to prevent legislation by the Canadian government on the automated banking machine levies charged from customers of other institutions are described.

34778 ■ *"Baker Building A Snapshot Of Corridor's Future; Long-Empty Euclid Avenue Site Already Houses Two Tech Tenants" in Crain's Cleveland Business*
Pub: Crain Communications, Inc.

Ed: Stan Bullard. **Description:** Due to a new transit line and the redevelopment of the old Baker Electric Building, the Euclid Ave. area of Cleveland is transforming from a known drug activity area to a new area for high-tech ventures.

34779 ■ *"Banks Fall Short in Online Services for Savvy Traders" in Barron's (Vol. 88, March 17, 2008, No. 11, pp. 35)*
Pub: Dow Jones & Company, Inc.

Ed: Theresa W. Carey. **Description:** Banc of America Investment Services, WellsTrade, and ShareBuilder are at the bottom of the list of online brokerages because they offer less trading technologies and product range. Financial shoppers miss out on a lot of customized tools and analytics when using these services.

34780 ■ *"Bark and Bite" in Canadian Business (Vol. 81, March 31, 2008, No. 5, pp. 20)*
Pub: Rogers Media

Ed: Rachel Pulfer. **Description:** Hillary Clinton and Barack Obama both want to renegotiate NAFTA but the most job losses in the American manufacturing industry is caused by technological change and Asian competition than with NAFTA. The risk of protectionist trade policies has increased given the political atmosphere.

34781 ■ *"BCE Wireless Growth Flags in Fourth Quarter" in Globe & Mail (February 8, 2007, pp. B5)*
Pub: CTVglobemedia Publishing Inc.

Ed: Catherine McLean. **Description:** BCE Inc., the largest telecommunications provider in Canada, reported $699 million profit in the final quarter of 2006. The company signed up 169,000 wireless customers in the important holiday season.

34782 ■ *Behind the Cloud*
Pub: Jossey-Bass

Ed: Marc Benioff, Carlye Adler. **Released:** 2010. **Price:** $27.95. **Description:** Salesforce.com is the world's most successful business-to-business cloud-computing company that sells an online service that helps businesses manage sales, customer service, and marketing functions.

34783 ■ *"Being Big By Design" in Canadian Business (Vol. 82, April 27, 2009, No. 7, pp. 39)*
Pub: Rogers Media

Ed: Andrew Wahl. **Description:** Gennum expects that its planned acquisition of Tundra Semiconductor will expand its market presence and leverage its research and development better than working alone. The proposed friendly acquisition could challenge Zarlink Semiconductor as the largest Canadian semiconductor firm in terms of revenue. The merger could expand Gennum's addressable market to about $2 billion.

34784 ■ *"The Bell Tolls for Thee" in Canadian Business (Vol. 81, March 3, 2008, No. 3, pp. 36)*
Pub: Rogers Media

Ed: Andrew Wahl. **Description:** Bell Canada has formed the Canadian Coalition for Tomorrow's IT Skills to solve the shortage of technology talent in the country. Canada's total workforce has only around 4%, or 600,000 people employed in information technology-related fields. The aims of the Bell-led coalition, which is supported by different industry associations and 30 corporations, are investigated.

34785 ■ *"Bernier Open to Telecom Changes" in Globe & Mail (March 22, 2006, pp. B1)*
Pub: CTVglobemedia Publishing Inc.

Ed: Simon Tuck. **Description:** Federal Industry Minister Maxime Bernier of Canada says that he is open to scrapping restrictions on foreign ownership in telecommunications. His views on telecom industry are detailed.

34786 ■ *"Beyond Microsoft and Yahoo!: Some M&A Prospects" in Barron's (Vol. 88, March 17, 2008, No. 11, pp. 39)*
Pub: Dow Jones & Company, Inc.

Ed: Eric J. Savitz. **Description:** Weak quarterly earnings report for Yahoo! could pressure the company's board to cut a deal with Microsoft. Electronic Arts is expected to win its hostile $26-a-share bid for Take-Two Interactive Software. Potential targets and buyers for mergers and acquisitions are mentioned.

34787 ■ *"Beyond the RAZR's Edge" in Canadian Business (Vol. 79, November 6, 2006, No. 22, pp. 15)*
Pub: Rogers Media

Ed: Andrew Wahl. **Description:** Features of Motorola RAZR, such as low weight and camera accessibility, are presented.

34788 ■ *"The Big Picture" in Canadian Business (Vol. 79, Winter 2006, No. 24, pp. 142)*
Pub: Rogers Media
Ed: Andy Holloway. **Description:** The features of the new range of high-definition television sets released by Matushita Electric Corporation of America are described. The pricing of the television sets is discussed.

34789 ■ *The Big Switch*
Pub: W. W. Norton & Company, Inc.
Ed: Nicholas Carr. **Released:** January 19, 2009. **Price:** $16.95 paperback. **Description:** Today companies are dismantling private computer systems and tapping into services provided via the Internet. This shift is remaking the computer industry, bringing competitors such as Google to the forefront ant threatening traditional companies like Microsoft and Dell. The book weaves together history, economics, and technology to explain why computing is changing and what it means for the future.

34790 ■ *The Big Switch: Rewiring the World, From Edison to Google*
Pub: W.W. Norton & Company
Ed: Nicholas Carr. **Released:** 2009. **Price:** $25.95. **Description:** Companies such as Google, Microsoft, and Amazon.com are building huge centers in order to create massive data centers. Together these centers form a giant computing grid that will deliver the digital universe to scientific labs, companies and homes in the future. This trend could bring about a new, darker phase for the Internet, one where these networks could operate as a fearsome entity that will dominate the lives of individuals worldwide.

34791 ■ *"Biotechnology Wants a Lead Role" in Business North Carolina (Vol. 28, March 2008, No. 3, pp. 14)*
Pub: Business North Carolina
Description: According to experts, North Carolina is poised as a leader in the biotechnology sector. Highlights of a recent roundtable discussion sponsored by the North Carolina Biotechnology Center in Research Triangle Park are presented.

34792 ■ *"Biotechs Are Using Back Door to Go Public" in Boston Business Journal (Vol. 31, May 27, 2011, No. 18, pp. 1)*
Pub: Boston Business Journal
Ed: Julie M. Donnelly. **Description:** Members of Massachusetts' biotechnology sector have been engaging in reverse mergers as an alternative to initial public offerings. Reverse mergers provide access to institutional investors and hedge funds.

34793 ■ *"Biz Assesses 'Textgate' Fallout; Conventions, Smaller Deals Affected" in Crain's Detroit Business (Vol. 24, March 31, 2008)*
Pub: Crain Communications, Inc.
Ed: Tom Henderson. **Description:** Businesspeople who were trying to measure the amount of economic damage is likely to be caused due to Mayor Kwame Kilpatrick's indictment on eight charges and found that: automotive and other large global deals are less likely to be affected than location decisions by smaller companies and convention site decisions. Also being affected are negotiations in which Mexican startup companies were planning a partnership with the TechTown incubator to pursue opportunities in the auto sector; those plans are being put on hold while they look at other sites.

34794 ■ *"Biz U: Cool for School" in Entrepreneur (Vol. 35, October 2007, No. 10, pp. 144)*
Pub: Entrepreneur Media Inc.
Ed: Nichole L. Torres. **Description:** Forming a high technology business while still in college has its advantages such as having information resources nearby and having students from various fields to ask for help and advice. School business competitions are also helpful in building networks with investors. Ways that the college environment can be useful to aspiring entrepreneurs, particularly to those who are into high technology business, are discussed.

34795 ■ *"Blacks Go Broadband: High Speed Internet Adoption Grows Among African Americans" in Black Enterprise (Vol. 38, February 2008)*
Pub: Earl G. Graves Publishing Co. Inc.
Ed: Cliff Hocker. **Description:** Number of black households using broadband Internet services tripled since 2005 according to a survey conducted by Pew Internet and American Life Project.

34796 ■ *"Blockbuster Launches Internet Movie Downloads to Compete Against Netflix, Others" in Chicago Tribune (December 3, 2008)*
Pub: McClatchy-Tribune Information Services
Ed: Eric Benderoff. **Description:** Blockbuster Inc., the DVD rental giant, has launched a new service that delivers movies to their customer's homes via the Internet in an attempt to compete against Netflix and other competitors.

34797 ■ *"Blog Buzz Heralds Arrival of IPhone 2.0" in Advertising Age (Vol. 79, June 9, 2008, No. 40, pp. 8)*
Pub: Crain Communications, Inc.
Ed: Abbey Klaasen. **Description:** Predictions concerning the next version of the iPhone include a global-positioning-system technology as well as a configuration to run on a faster, 3G network.

34798 ■ *"BofA Cutting 70 Charlotte Tech Jobs" in Charlotte Observer (January 31, 2007)*
Pub: Knight-Ridder/Tribune Business News
Ed: Rick Rothacker. **Description:** Bank of America announced the elimination of 70 technology positions at their Charlotte, North Carolina facility. The move is part of the company's effort to increase efficiency.

34799 ■ *"Bon Voyager" in Entrepreneur (Vol. 36, April 2008, No. 4, pp. 58)*
Pub: Entrepreneur Media, Inc.
Ed: Heather Clancy. **Description:** LG Voyager, especially made for Verizon Wireless, is a smart phone that is being compared to Apple iPhone. The Voyager has a 2.8-inch external touchscreen and has a clamshell design, which features an internal keyboard. It does not have Wi-Fi support like iPhone, but it has 3G support. Other differences between the two phones are discussed.

34800 ■ *"Book of Lists 2010" in Philadelphia Business Journal (Vol. 28, December 25, 2009, No. 45, pp. 1)*
Pub: American City Business Journals
Description: Rankings of companies and organizations within the banking, biotechnology, economic development, healthcare, hospitality, law and accounting, marketing and media, real estate, and technology industries in the Philadelphia, Pennsylvania area are presented. Rankings are based on sales, business size, and more.

34801 ■ *"Boom has Tech Grads Mulling Their Options" in Globe & Mail (March 14, 2006, pp. B1)*
Pub: CTVglobemedia Publishing Inc.
Ed: Grant Robertson. **Description:** Internet giant Google Inc. has stepped up its efforts to hire the talented people, in Canada, at Waterloo University in southern Ontario, to expand its operations. The details of the job market and increasing salaries are analyzed.

34802 ■ *"Boosting Your Merchant Management Services With Wireless Technology" in Franchising World (Vol. 42, August 2010, No. 8, pp. 27)*
Pub: International Franchise Association
Ed: Michael S. Slominski. **Description:** Franchises should have the capability to accept credit cards away from their businesses. This technology will increase sales.

34803 ■ *"Boots Treat Street Rolls Out Trolley Dash App on Androis and iPhone OS" in Entertainment Close-Up (October 24, 2011)*
Pub: Close-Up Media
Description: Shoppers using Boots Treat Street can now download the Trolley Dash app game, available from the Apple Store and the Android Market, and enjoy the pastel colored street featuring favorite retailers such as eBay, New Look and Play.com collecting prizes while avoiding hazards.

34804 ■ *"Border Boletin: UA to Take Lie-Detector Kiosk to Poland" in Arizona Daily Star (September 14, 2010)*
Pub: Arizona Daily Star
Ed: Brady McCombs. **Description:** University of Arizona's National Center for Border Security and Immigration Research will send a team to Warsaw, Poland to show border guards from 27 European Union countries the center's Avatar Kiosk. The Avatar technology is designed for use at border ports and airports to assist Customs officers detect individuals who are lying.

34805 ■ *"Boxing, Tech Giants Team to Help Teens" in Hispanic Business (January-February 2009, pp. 44)*
Pub: Hispanic Business
Ed: Daniel Soussa. **Description:** Microsoft and Oscar de la Hoya are providing teens a head start for careers in the sciences by offering a competition in the categories of photography, short films or Web-based games.

34806 ■ *"Branding Your Way" in Canadian Business (Vol. 80, February 12, 2007, No. 4, pp. 31)*
Pub: Rogers Media
Ed: Erin Pooley. **Description:** The trend in involving consumers in brand marketing by seeking their views through contests or inviting them to produce and submit commercials through Internet is discussed.

34807 ■ *"Broadband Reaches Access Limits in Europe" in Information Today (Vol. 26, February 2009, No. 2, pp. 22)*
Pub: Information Today, Inc.
Ed: Jim Ashling. **Description:** Eurostat (the Statistical Office of the European communities) reports results from is survey regarding Internet use by businesses throughout its 27-member states. Iceland, Finland and the Netherlands provide the most access at broadband speeds, followed by Belgium, Spain and France.

34808 ■ *"Brown At Center of Local CleanTech Lobbying Efforts" in Boston Business Journal (Vol. 30, October 15, 2010, No. 36, pp. 1)*
Pub: Boston Business Journal
Ed: Kyle Alspach. **Description:** U.S. Senator Scott Brown has been active in lobbying for energy reform in Massachusetts. Brown has been meeting with business groups seeking the reforms.

34809 ■ *"Building His Dream" in Business Courier (Vol. 24, January 25, 2008, No. 42, pp. 1)*
Pub: American City Business Journals, Inc.
Ed: Laura Baverman. **Description:** Technology entrepreneur Mahendra Vora plans to build a more than $100 million local IT headquarters for VTech Holdings Ltd by 2010. Acquisition of four $5 million companies within 2008 are part of the owner's plan to expand the office equipment company. Other plans for the IT company are discussed.

34810 ■ *"The Business Case for Mobile Content Acceleration" in Streaming Media (November 2011, pp. 78)*
Pub: Information Today Inc.
Ed: Dan Rayburn. **Description:** Last holiday season, eBay became a mobile commerce (m-commerce) giant when sales rose by 134 percent, as most online retailers offered customers the ability to purchase items using their mobile devices.

34811 ■ *"Business Still Expected to Take Hit in 2008" in Business Journal-Serving Phoenix and the Valley of the Sun (December 28, 2007)*
Pub: American City Business Journals, Inc.
Ed: Ty Young. **Description:** Semiconductor industry is forecasting a slow first quarter for 2008 and industry analysts believe there will be decreased growth for the rest of the year. The impending reces-

sion in the U.S. will lead to a fall in consumer spending, which will in turn drive down the demand for electronics. The semiconductor revenue forecast for 2010 is also discussed.

34812 ■ *"Buyer's Guide: Room for Improvement" in Entrepreneur (Vol. 35, October 2007, No. 10, pp. 62)*
Pub: Entrepreneur Media Inc.

Ed: Amanda C. Kooser. **Description:** Buyers guide for wireless routers is presented. Price, features and availability of the Belkin N1 Vision, Buffalo Wireless-N Nfinit Router, D-Link Xtreme Gigabit Router DIR 655, Linksys Wireless-N Gigabit Security Router, Netgear RangeMax Next Wireless-N Router and Zyxel NBG-460N are provided.

34813 ■ *"The Buzz About HD Radio" in Black Enterprise (Vol. 37, February 2007, No. 7, pp. 58)*
Pub: Earl G. Graves Publishing Co. Inc.

Ed: James C. Johnson. **Description:** HD radio broadcasting will send CD quality sound and extra information to more radio stations using the same amount of bandwidth.

34814 ■ *"Call Them Gorgeous" in Entrepreneur (Vol. 35, October 2007, No. 10, pp. 54)*
Pub: Entrepreneur Media Inc.

Ed: Amanda C. Kooser. **Description:** Smart phones are known for their high technology features, unique names and extraordinary design. Features of the Apple iPhone, Helio Ocean, Blackberry Curve, T-Mobile Wing and Motorola Razr2 V9 are described.

34815 ■ *"Can America Invent Its Way Back?" in Business Week (September 22, 2008, No. 4100, pp. 52)*
Pub: McGraw-Hill Companies, Inc.

Description: Business leaders as well as economists agree that innovative new products, services and ways of doing business may be the only way in which America can survive the downward spiral of the economy; innovation economics may be the answer and may even provide enough growth to enable Americans to prosper in the years to come.

34816 ■ *"Can You Hear Them Now?" in Hawaii Business (Vol. 54, August 2008, No. 2, pp. 48)*
Pub: Hawaii Business Publishing

Ed: Jason Ubay. **Description:** Coral Wireless LLC (dba Mobi PCS) is ranked 237 in Hawaii Business' list of the state's top 250 companies for 2008. The company is a local wireless phone provider, which has expanded its market to Oahu, Maui and the Big Island since opening in 2006, offering 13 phones and unlimited texts and calls. Details on the company's sales are provided.

34817 ■ *"Canada Tomorrow" in Canadian Business (Vol. 80, October 8, 2007, No. 20, pp. 14)*
Pub: Rogers Media

Ed: Donald J. Johnston. **Description:** An assessment of Canada's future in terms of its educational, social, and economic environment is presented. Concerns regarding the country's educational system such as the declining interest in science and technology and the possible lack of teachers in the future are discussed. In terms of its social and economic aspects, the need to support entrepreneurs and other qualified people is explained.

34818 ■ *"Canada's Clean Energy Advantages Offer a Bright Future" in Canadian Business (Vol. 83, August 17, 2010, No. 13-14, pp. 38)*
Pub: Rogers Media Ltd.

Ed: Don McKinnon. **Description:** Canada has clean energy advantages in the greenhouse gas emission-free CANada Deuterium Uranium reactor technology and carbon neutral biomass fuels that were continuously ignored by policy makers. Both are proven to significantly reduce emissions while providing reliable, affordable and secure electricity.

34819 ■ *"Canadians Keep Memories in 'Inboxes' Instead of Shoe Boxes; MSN Canada" in Canadian Corporate News (May 14, 2007)*
Pub: Comtex News Network Inc.

Description: According to an MSN Canada online poll, 76 percent of Canadians are creating 'virtual shoeboxes' with their email inboxes and archiving important messages, photos, and documents.

34820 ■ *"Cancer Care's Quantum Leap" in Hawaii Business (Vol. 53, October 2007, No. 4, pp. 17)*
Pub: Hawaii Business Publishing

Ed: Cathy S. Cruz-George. **Description:** TomoTherapy is an innovative device for cancer treatment that gives high-intensity radiation to more accurate parts of the body compared to conventional treatments. Hawaii has one of the 70 TomoTherapy machines in the nation, and it is expected to help advance cancer care in the area. Details on how the machine works are provided.

34821 ■ *"The Case for a Bright Future" in Canadian Business (Vol. 83, July 20, 2010, No. 11-12, pp. 58)*
Pub: Rogers Media Ltd.

Ed: Andrew Potter. **Description:** Writer Matt Ridley argues that trade is the determinant of development and that it is the reason why humans got rich. Ridley believes that the important innovations are often low-tech and is often processes rather than products.

34822 ■ *"Catch the Wind Announces Filing of Injunction Against Air Data Systems LLC and Philip Rogers" in CNW Group (September 30, 2011)*
Pub: CNW Group
Contact: Carolyn McGill-Davidson, President

Description: Catch the Wind, providers of laser-based wind sensor products and technology, filed an injunction against Optical Air Data Systems (OADS) LLC and its former President and CEO Philip L. Rogers. The complaint seeks to have OADS and Rogers return tangible and intangible property owned by Catch the Wind, which the firm believes to be critical to the operations of their business.

34823 ■ *"Catch the Wind to Hold Investor Update Conference Call on October 18, 2011" in CNW Group (October 4, 2011)*
Pub: CNW Group
Contact: Carolyn McGill-Davidson, President

Description: Catch the Wind Ltd., providers of laser-based wind sensor products and technology, held a conference call for analysts and institutional investors. The high-growth technology firm is headquartered in Manassas, Virginia.

34824 ■ *"CBC Eyes Partners for TV Downloads" in Globe & Mail (February 9, 2006, pp. B1)*
Pub: CTVglobemedia Publishing Inc.

Ed: Grant Robertson. **Description:** The details on Canadian Broadcasting Corp.'s distribution agreement with Google Inc. and Apple Computer Inc. are presented.

34825 ■ *"Cell Phone the Ticket on American Airlines" in Chicago Tribune (November 14, 2008)*
Pub: McClatchy-Tribune Information Services

Ed: Julie Johnsson. **Description:** American Airlines is testing a new mobile boarding pass at O'Hare International Airport. Travelers on American can board flights and get through security checkpoints by flashing a bar code on their phones. Passengers must have an Internet-enabled mobile device and an active e-mail address in order to utilize this service.

34826 ■ *"Cell Tower Potential" in Black Enterprise (Vol. 37, October 2006, No. 3, pp. 86)*
Pub: Earl G. Graves Publishing Co. Inc.

Ed: James C. Johnson. **Description:** Due to local zoning that does not allow new cell towers to be too close to existing ones along with other issues only certain properties are eligible as leasing cites to wireless carriers.

34827 ■ *"CEO Forecast" in Hispanic Business (January-February 2009, pp. 34, 36)*
Pub: Hispanic Business

Ed: Jessica Haro, Richard Kaplan. **Description:** As economic uncertainty fogs the future, executives turn to government contracts in order to boost business. Revenue sources, health care challenges, environmental consulting and remediation services, as well as technological strides are discussed.

34828 ■ *"Certification Experts Germanischer Lloyd Wind Energy Assist NaiKun's Offshore Wind Project" in Canadian Corporate News (May 14, 2007)*
Pub: Comtex News Network Inc.

Description: Germanischer Lloyd Wind Energy (GL Wind) will examine, inspect, and provide quality management services for the engineering, design, and construction of the offshore wind project planned by NaiKun Wind Development Inc. in northwest British Columbia.

34829 ■ *"China Vs. the World: Whose Technology Is It?" in Harvard Business Review (Vol. 88, December 2010, No. 12, pp. 94)*
Pub: Harvard Business School Publishing

Ed: Thomas M Hout, Pankaj Ghemawat. **Description:** Examination of the regulation the Chinese government is implementing that require foreign corporations wishing to do business in the country to give up their new technologies. These regulations avoid World Trade Organization technology transfer provisions and complicate the convergence of socialism and capitalism.

34830 ■ *"The Chips Are In" in Business Journal-Portland (Vol. 24, November 2, 2007, No. 35, pp. 1)*
Pub: American City Business Journals, Inc.

Ed: Aliza Earnshaw. **Description:** The $30 million funding round of Ambric Inc., which brings a total investment of $51 million, is about to close, and its clients are releasing over half-dozen products containing Ambric chips in January 2008. The features of Ambric's semiconductors, its market sectors and market positioning, as well as its investor relations, are discussed.

34831 ■ *"Clash of the Titans" in Canadian Business (Vol. 80, March 12, 2007, No. 6, pp. 27)*
Pub: Rogers Media

Ed: Andrew Wahl. **Description:** The frequent allegations of Google Inc. and Microsoft Corp. against each other over copyright and other legal issues, with a view to taking away other's market share, is discussed.

34832 ■ *"Clusters Last Stand?" in Canadian Electronics (Vol. 23, February 2008, No. 1, pp. 6)*
Pub: CLB Media Inc.

Description: Survival of technology clusters was the focus of Strategic Microelectronics Council's conference entitled, 'The Power of Community: Building Technology Clusters in Canada'. Clusters can help foster growth in the microelectronics sector, and it was recognized that government intervention is needed to maintain these clusters.

34833 ■ *"CN to Webcast 2007 Analyst Meeting in Toronto May 23-24" in Canadian Corporate News (May 16, 2007)*
Pub: Comtex News Network Inc.

Description: Canadian National Railway Company (CN) broadcast its analyst meeting in Toronto with a webcast which focused on CN's opportunities, strategies, and financial outlook through the year 2010.

34834 ■ *"Combat Mission: Rebuffed, BAE Systems Fights Army Contract Decision" in Business Courier (Vol. 26, September 25, 2009)*
Pub: American City Business Journals, Inc.

Ed: Jon Newberry. **Description:** BAE Systems filed a complaint with the US Government Accountability Office after the US Army issued an order to BAE's competitor for armoured trucks which is potentially worth over $3 billion. Hundreds of jobs in Butler County, Ohio hinge on the success of the contract protest.

34835 ■ *"Company Goes High-Tech To Attack Some Sore Spots" in Boston Business Journal (Vol. 27, December 7, 2007, No. 45, pp. 10)*
Pub: American City Business Journals Inc.
Ed: Mark Hollmer. **Description:** Transport Pharmaceuticals Inc. hopes to raise $35 million to fund a drug and a treatment device for treating cold sores, and seek federal regulatory approval. Dennis Goldberg, the company's CEO, believes that existing treatments that use acyclovir cream are relatively weak. Transport's drug uses a soluble gel cartridge with a higher concentration of acyclovir.

34836 ■ *"Computer Forensics Firms Get Boost From New Evidence Rules" in Crain's Detroit Business (Vol. 24, March 24, 2008, No. 12, pp. 28)*
Pub: Crain Communications, Inc.
Ed: Chad Halcom. **Description:** Computer forensics is a growing niche for firms such as the Center for Computer Forensics in Southfield; driving some of the growth are new amendments to the Federal Rules of Civil Procedure, which took effect about a year ago and address standards of evidence for electronic records, or 'e-discovery,' that are admissible for civil cases in federal courts.

34837 ■ *"Conferencing Takes on High-Tech Futuristic Feel" in Crain's Cleveland Business (Vol. 28, October 29, 2007, No. 43, pp. 17)*
Pub: Crain Communications, Inc.
Ed: Chuck Soder. **Description:** Overview of the newest technologies which are making local company's meetings more effective including: tele-presence, a videoconferencing technology, as well as virtual flip charts.

34838 ■ *"Congestion Relief" in Canadian Business (Vol. 80, February 12, 2007, No. 4, pp. 31)*
Pub: Rogers Media
Ed: Andrea Jezovit. **Description:** The development of a satellite-based system for traffic management including paying for parking fees by Skymeter Corp. is discussed.

34839 ■ *"Connections: United We Gab" in Entrepreneur (Vol. 35, October 2007, No. 10, pp. 60)*
Pub: Entrepreneur Media Inc.
Ed: Mike Hogan. **Description:** T-Mobile and AT&T introduced dual-mode service to consumers, helping them to switch between cellular and Wi-Fi networks easily. These services, such as Hotspot@Home, reduces the cost of long distance calls by routing them over the Internet with the use of WiFi. Benefits of dual mode service, such as lower hardware price and better call coverage are given.

34840 ■ *"Connectors for Space, Mil/Aero and Medical Applications" in Canadian Electronics (Vol. 23, June-July 2008, No. 4, pp. 13)*
Pub: Action Communication Inc.
Ed: Gilles Parguey. **Description:** Product information on electrical connectors for use in space, military, aeronautics, and medical applications is provided. These connectors are built to withstand the extreme conditions offered by the harsh working environments in those applications.

34841 ■ *"Contec Innovations Inc.: MovieSet.com First to Mobilize Content Using BUZmob" in Canadian Corporate News (May 16, 2007)*
Pub: Comtex News Network Inc.
Description: Contec Innovations Inc., a provider of mobile infrastructure software, announced that MovieSet.com is the first Internet portal to mobilize their content using BUZmob, the company's new mobile publishing service that allows content publishers to enable mobile access to their feed-based content on any mobile device or network in real-time.

34842 ■ *"Controlling Costs: Update Your Information Technology Program" in Franchising World (Vol. 42, August 2010, No. 8, pp. 18)*
Pub: International Franchise Association
Ed: Jeff Dumont. **Description:** It is imperative for any franchise to understand its technology needs in order to control costs. Needs analysis; creating a Request for Proposal; and information regarding the choices between renting, buying or building technology are covered. Relationship contingency in franchised organizations is also covered.

34843 ■ *"Conversations Need to Yield Actions Measured in Dollars" in Advertising Age (Vol. 79, July 7, 2008, No. 26, pp. 18)*
Pub: Crain Communications, Inc.
Ed: Jonathan Salem Baskin. **Description:** New ways in which to market to consumers are discussed.

34844 ■ *"Credit Crunch Gives, Takes Away" in The Business Journal-Serving Metropolitan Kansas City (Vol. 27, October 17, 2008, No. 5, pp. 1)*
Pub: American City Business Journals, Inc.
Ed: Suzanna Stagemeyer. **Description:** Although many Kansas City business enterprises have been adversely affected by the U.S. credit crunch, others have remained relatively unscathed. Examples of how local businesses are being impacted by the crisis are provided including: American Trailer & Storage Inc., which declared bankruptcy after failing to pay a long-term loan; and NetStandard, a technology firm who, on the other hand, is being pursued by prospective lenders.

34845 ■ *Crossing the Chasm: Marketing and Selling Disruptive Products to Mainstream Customers*
Pub: HarperInformation
Ed: Geoffrey A. Moore. **Released:** September 2002. **Price:** $17.95. **Description:** A guide for marketing in high-technology industries, focusing on the Internet.

34846 ■ *"Customers Turned Off? Not at Best Buy" in Barron's (Vol. 88, March 24, 2008, No. 12, pp. 29)*
Pub: Dow Jones & Company, Inc.
Ed: Sandra Ward. **Description:** Shares of Best Buy, trading at $42.41 each, are expected to rise to an average of $52 a share due to the company's solid fundamentals. The company's shares have fallen 20 percent from their 52-week high and are attractive given the company's bright prospects in the video game sector and high-definition video.

34847 ■ *"Cyberwise" in Black Enterprise (Vol. 41, December 2010, No. 5, pp. 50)*
Pub: Earl G. Graves Publishing Co. Inc.
Ed: Marica Wade Talbert. **Description:** Information is given regarding single platforms that can be used to develop applications for iPhone, Android, Blackberry, and Nokia.

34848 ■ *"Danaher to Acquire Tectronix" in Canadian Electronics (Vol. 22, November-December 2007, No. 7, pp. 1)*
Pub: CLB Media Inc.
Description: Leading supplier of measurement, test and monitoring equipment Tektronix will be acquired by Danaher Corporation for $2.8 billion. Tektronix products are expected to complement Danaher's test equipment sector. The impacts of the deal on Tektronix shareholders and Danaher's operations are discussed.

34849 ■ *"The Data Drivers" in Canadian Business (Vol. 81, September 15, 2008, No. 14-15, pp. 1)*
Pub: Rogers Media Ltd.
Ed: Andrew Wahl. **Description:** Canadian regulators hope that an auction of telecommunications companies will inject more competition into the industry; however, newcomers may not be able to rely on lower prices in order to gain market share from the three major telecommunications companies that already have a stronghold on the market. Analysts feel that providing additional data service is the key to surviving market disruptions.

34850 ■ *"Dear Diary, Arbitron is Dumping You" in Business Courier (Vol. 26, September 25, 2009, No. 22, pp. 1)*
Pub: American City Business Journals, Inc.
Ed: Dan Monk. **Description:** Arbitron Inc. is replacing hand-written ratings diaries with Portable People Meters or electronic sensors that measure local radio audiences. The technology counts all exposure to radio and stations; those that penetrate the workplace will see success, while the more 'niche' oriented formats will have a more difficult time.

34851 ■ *"Design Programs for HVAC Sizing Solutions" in Contractor (Vol. 57, January 2010, No. 1, pp. 44)*
Pub: Penton Media, Inc.
Ed: William Feldman; Patti Feldman. **Description:** Rhvac 8 is an HVAC design program that lets users calculate peak heating and cooling load requirements for rooms, zones, systems, and entire buildings. The HVAC Pipe Sizer software for the iPhone enables quick sizing of a simple piping system.

34852 ■ *"Detroit Hosts Conferences on Green Building, IT, Finance" in Crain's Detroit Business (Vol. 25, June 1, 2009, No. 22, pp. 9)*
Pub: Crain Communications Inc. - Detroit
Ed: Tom Henderson. **Description:** Detroit will host three conferences in June 2009, one features green technology, one information technology and the third will gather black bankers and financial experts from across the nation.

34853 ■ *"Digital Duplication" in Crain's Cleveland Business (Vol. 28, October 1, 2007, No. 39, pp. 3)*
Pub: Crain Communications, Inc.
Ed: David Bennett. **Description:** Profile of the business plan of eBlueprint Holdings LLC, a reprographics company that found success by converting customers' paper blueprints to an electronic format; the company plans to expand into other geographic markets by acquiring solid reprographics companies and converting their computer systems so that customers' blueprints can be managed electronically.

34854 ■ *"Digital Edge: Stay Tuned" in Entrepreneur (Vol. 35, October 2007, No. 10, pp. 56)*
Pub: Entrepreneur Media Inc.
Ed: Mike Hogan. **Description:** Future of set-top boxes, particularly the digital video recorders is promising. TiVo HD, for example, already receives content from Websites, while companies such as Diego and Microsoft are soon to release similar devices. The potential applications of television and computer convergence are provided.

34855 ■ *"Digital Power Management and the PMBus" in Canadian Electronics (Vol. 23, June-July 2008, No. 4, pp. 8)*
Pub: Action Communication Inc.
Ed: Torbjorn Hohnberg. **Description:** PMBus is an interface that can be applied to a variety of devices including power management devices. Information on digital power management products using this interface are also provided.

34856 ■ *"The Digital Revolution is Over. Long Live the Digital Revolution!" in Business Strategy Review (Vol. 21, Spring 2010, No. 1, pp. 74)*
Pub: Wiley-Blackwell
Ed: Gianvito Lanzolla, Jamie Anderson. **Description:** Many businesses are now involved in the digital marketplace. The authors argue that the new reality of numerous companies offering overlapping products means that it is critical for managers to understand digital convergence and to observe the imperatives for remaining competitive.

34857 ■ *"The Dominance of Doubt" in Barron's (Vol. 89, July 13, 2009, No. 28, pp. M3)*
Pub: Dow Jones & Co., Inc.
Description: Five straight down days leading up to July 10, 2009 in the U.S. stock market reminds one strategist of 1982 when there was a feeling that things could never be the same again. One analyst is

bullish on the stocks of Apple Inc. and sees the stocks rising to at least 180 in 12 months. The prospects of the shares of GM and Ford are also discussed.

34858 ■ *"Don't Touch My Laptop, If You Please Mr. Customs Man" in Canadian Electronics (Vol. 23, June-July 2008, No. 4, pp. 6)*
Pub: Action Communication Inc.
Ed: Mark Borkowski. **Description:** Canadian businessmen bringing electronic devices to the US can protect the contents of their laptops by hiding their data from US border agents. They can also choose to clean up the contents of their laptop using file erasure programs.

34859 ■ *"Downturn Tests HCL's Pledge to Employees" in Workforce Management (Vol. 88, November 16, 2009, No. 12, pp. 23)*
Pub: Crain Communications Inc.
Ed: Ed Frauenheim. **Description:** HCL Technologies has kept its promise to keep from laying any employees off during the recession which served as a test for the tech firm's Employee First program, which seeks to give workers greater income security as well as a stronger voice in the firm.

34860 ■ *"Drive Traffic To Your Blog" in Women Entrepreneur (January 13, 2009)*
Pub: Entrepreneur Media Inc.
Ed: Lesley Spencer Pyle. **Description:** Internet social networking has become a vital component to marketing one's business. Tips are provided on how to establish a blog that will attract attention to one's business and keep one's customers coming back for more.

34861 ■ *"Dropped Calls" in Canadian Business (Vol. 80, November 5, 2007, No. 22, pp. 34)*
Pub: Rogers Media
Ed: Andrew Wahl. **Description:** Control over Canada's telecommunications market by Telus, Rogers and Bell Canada has resulted in a small number of innovations. The pricing regimes of these carriers have also stifled innovations in the telecommunications industry. The status of Canada's telecommunications industry is further analyzed.

34862 ■ *"DST Turns to Banks for Credit" in The Business Journal-Serving Metropolitan Kansas City (Vol. 27, October 3, 2008, No. 3, pp. 1)*
Pub: American City Business Journals, Inc.
Ed: Rob Roberts. **Description:** Kansas City, Missouri-based DST Systems Inc., a company that provides sophisticated information processing, computer software services and business solutions, has secured a new five-year, $120 million credit facility from Enterprise Bank and Bank of the West. The deal is seen to reflect that the region and community-banking model remain stable. Comments from executives are also provided.

34863 ■ *"The Easy Route" in Entrepreneur (Vol. 36, April 2008, No. 4, pp. 60)*
Pub: Entrepreneur Media, Inc.
Ed: Amanda C. Kooser. **Description:** Buyer's guide of wireless office routers is presented. All products included in the list use the latest draft-n technology. Price and availability of the products are provided.

34864 ■ *"eBay Introduces Open Commerce Ecosystem" in Entertainment Close-Up (October 24, 2011)*
Pub: Close-Up Media
Description: eBay's new X.commerce is an open commerce ecosystem that will arm developers and merchants with the technology tools required to keep pace with the ever-changing industry. X.commerce brings together the technology assets and developer communities of eBay, PayPal, Magento and partners to expand on eBays vision for enabling commerce.

34865 ■ *Electronic Commerce*
Pub: Course Technology
Ed: Gary Schneider, Bryant Chrzan, Charles McCormick. **Released:** May 1, 2010. **Price:** $117.95. **Description:** E-commerce can open the door to more opportunities than ever before for small business. Packed with real-world examples and cases, the book delivers comprehensive coverage of emerging online technologies and trends and their influence on the electronic marketplace. It details how the landscape of online commerce is evolving, reflecting changes in the economy and how business and society are responding to those changes. Balancing technological issues with the strategic business aspects of successful e-commerce, the new edition includes expanded coverage of international issues, social networking, mobile commerce, Web 2.0 technologies, and updates on spam, phishing, and identity theft.

34866 ■ *"Electronics Assembly" in Canadian Electronics (Vol. 23, February 2008, No. 1, pp. 12)*
Pub: CLB Media Inc.
Description: I&J Fisnar Inc. has launched a new system of bench top dispensing robots while Vitronics Soltec and KIC have introduced a new reflow soldering machine. Teknek, on the other hand, has announced a new product, called the CM10, which an be used in cleaning large format substrates. Other new products and their description are presented.

34867 ■ *"Elemental Nabs $5.5 Million" in The Business Journal-Portland (Vol. 25, July 18, 2008, No. 19, pp. 1)*
Pub: American City Business Journals, Inc.
Ed: Aliza Earnshaw. **Description:** Elemental Technologies Inc., a Portland, Oregon-based software company got $5.5 million in new funding, bringing its total invested capital to $7.1 million in nine months since October 2008. The company plans to launch Badaboom, software for converting video into various formats, later in 2008.

34868 ■ *Elsewhere, U.S.A.: How We Got From the Company Man, Family Dinners, and the Affluent Society to the Home Office, Blackberry Moms, and Economic Anxiety*
Pub: Pantheon Books
Ed: Dalton Conley. **Released:** 2009. **Price:** $24.00. **Description:** The alienation of the working middle class in America and the downturned economy is examined.

34869 ■ *"Emerging Tech Fund Strong in 2009" in Austin Business JournalInc. (Vol. 29, December 25, 2009, No. 42, pp. 1)*
Pub: American City Business Journals
Ed: Christopher Calnan. **Description:** Texas' Emerging Technology Fund (ETF) has seen an increase in applications from the state's technology companies in 2009. ETF received 87 applications in 2009 from Central Texas companies versus 50 during 2008 while $10.5 million was given to seven Texas companies compared with $10.6 million to ten companies in 2008.

34870 ■ *"Ending the Ebola Death Sentence" in Canadian Business (Vol. 83, August 17, 2010, No. 13-14, pp. 22)*
Pub: Rogers Media Ltd.
Ed: Michael McCullough. **Description:** US Army Medical Research Institute of Infectious Diseases made a $140 million agreement with Tekmira Pharmaceuticals Corporation to develop both a drug delivery system and delivery technology for curing the Ebola virus. Tekmira's delivery technology, which has been shown to halt Ebola in laboratory animals, might be the key to finding a cure.

34871 ■ *"Engineering Services Supplier Launches 'Robotic Renaissance" in Modern Machine Shop (Vol. 84, September 2011, No. 4, pp. 46)*
Pub: Gardner Business Media, Inc.
Contact: Richard G. Kline, President
E-mail: rkline@gardnerweb.com
Description: Profile of Applied Manufacturing Technologies (AMT) new hiring initiative that supports continuing growth in the robotics industry. AMT is located in Orion, Michigan and supplies factory automation design, engineering and process consulting services.

34872 ■ *Entrepreneurial Finance: A Casebook*
Pub: John Wiley and Sons Inc.
Ed: Paul A. Gompers; William Sahlman. **Released:** September 2006. **Price:** $63.00. **Description:** Investment analysis, entrepreneurial financing, harvesting, and renewal in the entrepreneurial firm are among the topics discussed.

34873 ■ *Entrepreneurial Strategies: New Technologies and Emerging Markets*
Pub: Blackwell Publishing Inc.
Contact: Gordon Tibbitts, President
Ed: Arnold Cooper; Sharon Alvarez; Alejandro Carrera; Luiz Mesquita; Robert Vassolo. **Released:** August 2006. **Price:** $69.95. **Description:** Ideas to help a small business expand into emerging market economies (EMEs) are discussed. Despite the high failure rate, this book helps a small firm develop a successful plan.

34874 ■ *Entrepreneurship and Technology Policy*
Pub: Edward Elgar Publishing, Incorporated
Ed: Link. **Released:** August 2006. **Price:** $190.00. **Description:** Journal articles focusing how and the ways small businesses' technical contributions are affecting business. The book is divided into four parts: Government's Direct Support of R&D, Government's Leveraging of R&D, Government's Infrastructure Policies; and Knowledge Flows from Universities and Laboratories.

34875 ■ *"EOTech Product Improves Holographic Gun Sights" in Crain's Detroit Business (Vol. 24, February 4, 2008, No. 5, pp. 9)*
Pub: Crain Communications Inc. - Detroit
Description: L-3 Communications EOTech Inc. procured new business contracts to fulfill military and law enforcement's demand for improved holographic sites used on handheld weapons.

34876 ■ *"Ethics and the End of Life" in Crain's Chicago Business (Vol. 34, October 24, 2011, No. 42, pp. 31)*
Pub: Crain Communications Inc.
Ed: Lisa Bertagnoli. **Description:** Technology has enabled doctors to provide more and better methods for helping patients, however end of life issues faced by medical ethicists are discussed.

34877 ■ *"Etiquette, Common Sense Often Lag Behind Smarter Devices" in Crain's Cleveland Business (Vol. 28, October 22, 2007, No. 42, pp. 21)*
Pub: Crain Communications, Inc.
Ed: Chrissy Kadleck. **Description:** Discusses the importance of good etiquette in regards to electronic communication both within as well as outside the business world.

34878 ■ *"The Evolution of the Mobile Entrepreneur" in Entrepreneur (Vol. 37, August 2009, No. 8, pp. 31)*
Pub: Entrepreneur Media, Inc.
Ed: Dan O'Shea. **Description:** Covers the timeline of important events that led to the mobile businessperson today; includes the first cell phone call made by Martin Cooper in 1973 and the invention of Apple and the Newton in 1989. The first BlackBerry appeared in 1999 and the iPod was launched in 2001.

34879 ■ *"Experts Take the Temp of Obama Plan" in The Business Journal-Serving Metropolitan Kansas City (Vol. 27, November 14, 2008, No. 10)*
Pub: American City Business Journals, Inc.
Ed: Rob Roberts. **Description:** Kansas City, Missouri-based employee benefits experts say president-elect Barack Obama's health care reform plan is on track. Insurance for children and capitalization for health information technology are seen as priority areas. The plan is aimed at reducing the number of uninsured people in the United States.

34880 ■ *"Facebook, Adobe, Kenshoo, Outright and Cignex Datamatics Sign On to X.commerce" in Entertainment Close-Up (October 24, 2011)*
Pub: Close-Up Media
Description: Facebook, Adobe, Kenshoo, Outright and Cignex Datamatics have all partnered with X.commerce's ecosystem, where developers build and merchants can come to shop for new technologies and services.

34881 ■ *"Far Out: Satellite Radio Finds New Way to Tally Listeners" in Globe & Mail (March 14, 2007, pp. B14)*
Pub: CTVglobemedia Publishing Inc.
Ed: Grant Robertson. **Description:** The marketing strategy adopted by satellite radio broadcasting firm XM Satellite Radio Inc. in Canada for increasing its subscriber based is discussed.

34882 ■ *"Fast Revival Unlikely For Indian 'Net Stocks" in Barron's (Vol. 88, July 7, 2008, No. 27, pp. 12)*
Pub: Dow Jones & Co., Inc.
Ed: Leslie P. Norton. **Description:** Shares of Indian Internet companies Rediff.com and Sify are not likely to stage a rebound due to weak financial results. Rediff.com shares have declined 39.2 percent in 2008, while Sify shares are down 35.8 percent.

34883 ■ *"Federal Fund Valuable Tool For Small-Biz Innovators" in Crain's Detroit Business (Vol. 24, September 29, 2008, No. 39, pp. 42)*
Pub: Crain Communications Inc.
Ed: Nancy Kaffer. **Description:** Grants from the Small Business Innovation Research Program, or SBIR grants, are federal funds that are set aside for 11 federal agencies to allocate to tech-oriented small-business owners. Firms such as Biotechnology Business Consultants help these companies apply for SBIR grants.

34884 ■ *"Finalist: Private Company, Less Than $100M" in Crain's Detroit Business (Vol. 25, June 22, 2009, No. 25)*
Pub: Crain Communications Inc. - Detroit
Ed: Nancy Kaffer. **Description:** Profile of W3R Consulting and CFO Patrick Tom= ina. The company offers information technology consulting. Tomina discusses the company's 505 strategy: to grow its annual revenue to $50 million in five years.

34885 ■ *"First Impression of Robotic Farming Systems" in Farm Industry News (September 30, 2011)*
Pub: Penton Business Media Inc.
Ed: Jodie Wehrspann. **Description:** Farm Science Review featured tillage tools and land rollers, including John Deere's GPS system where a cart tractor is automatically controlled as well as a new line of Kinze's carts and a video of their robotic system for a driver-less cart tractor.

34886 ■ *"FIS-Metavante Deal Paying Off for Many" in Business Journal-Milwaukee (Vol. 28, December 17, 2010, No. 11, pp. A1)*
Pub: Milwaukee Business Journal
Ed: Rich Kirchen. **Description:** Jacksonville, Florida-based Fidelity National Information Services Inc., also known as FIS, has remained committed to Milwaukee, Wisconsin more than a year after purchasing Metavante Technologies Inc. FIS has transferred several operations into Metropolitan Milwaukee and has continued its contribution to charitable organizations in the area.

34887 ■ *"Five Things..For Photo Fun" in Hawaii Business (Vol. 53, October 2007, No. 4, pp. 20)*
Pub: Hawaii Business Publishing
Ed: Cathy S. Cruz-George. **Description:** Featured is a buyers guide of products used for capturing or displaying digital photos; products featured include the Digital Photo Wallet and Light Affection.

34888 ■ *"For Apple, It's Showtime Again" in Barron's (Vol. 90, August 30, 2010, No. 35, pp. 29)*
Pub: Barron's Editorial & Corporate Headquarters
Ed: Eric J. Savitz. **Description:** Speculations on what Apple Inc. will unveil at its product launch event are presented. These products include a possible new iPhone Nano, a new update to its Apple TV, and possibly a deal with the Beatles to distribute their songs over iTunes.

34889 ■ *"Forsys Metals Corporation Goes "Live" With Q4's On-Demand Disclosure Management Software" in Canadian Corporate News (May 16, 2007)*
Pub: Comtex News Network Inc.
Description: Forsys Metals Corp. selected Q4 Web Systems to automate its corporate website disclosure with Q4's software platform which also automates and simplifies many of the administrative tasks that Forsys was doing manually, allowing them to focus their internal resources on the business.

34890 ■ *"The Fort" in Hawaii Business (Vol. 53, November 2007, No. 5, pp. 19)*
Pub: Hawaii Business Publishing
Ed: Jason Ubay. **Description:** DRFortress' flagship data center The Fort located at Honolulu's Airport Industrial Park provides companies a place to store their servers in an ultra-secure environment. Anything stored in here that requires power has a back up and in case of an outage generators can supply power up to 80 hrs. The Fort caters to major carriers and Internet service providers.

34891 ■ *Founders at Work*
Pub: Apress
Ed: Jessica Livingston. **Description:** Through interviews with founders of companies such as Apple, Flickr and PayPal, the book shows the qualities required to be a successful entrepreneur.

34892 ■ *"Free Your Mind" in Entrepreneur (Vol. 37, October 2009, No. 10, pp. 24)*
Pub: Entrepreneur Media Inc.
Ed: Joe Robinson. **Description:** Writer Chris Anderson believes that firms in the digital age should allow products and services to initially be sold for free. These companies could then charge for premium versions of these products and services after the free versions have gained attention.

34893 ■ *"Freeing the Wheels of Commerce" in Hispanic Business (July-August 2007, pp. 50, 52, 54)*
Pub: Hispanic Business
Ed: Keith Rosenblum. **Description:** SecureOrigins, a border-based partnership with high-tech innovators is working to move goods faster, more efficiently, and securely.

34894 ■ *"Full-Court Press for Apple" in Barron's (Vol. 88, March 24, 2008, No. 12, pp. 47)*
Pub: Dow Jones & Company, Inc.
Ed: Mark Veverka. **Description:** Apple Inc. is facing more intellectual property lawsuits in 2008, with 30 patent lawsuits filed compared to 15 in 2007 and nine in 2006. The lawsuits, which involve products such as the iPod and the iPhone, present some concern for Apple's shareholders.

34895 ■ *"Funbrain Launches Preschool Content" in Marketing to Women (Vol. 21, March 2008, No. 3, pp. 3)*
Pub: EPM Communications Inc.
Contact: Ira Mayer, President
E-mail: imayer@epmcom.com
Description: Funbrain.com launches The Moms and Kids Playground, a section of the website devoted to activities and games for moms and kids aged 2 to 6; content aims at building early computer skills and to teach basic concepts such as counting and colors.

34896 ■ *"Funds "Friend" Facebook" in Barron's (Vol. 89, July 27, 2009, No. 30, pp. 30)*
Pub: Dow Jones & Co., Inc.
Ed: Leslie P. Norton. **Description:** Mutual-fund companies are the latest entrants to the 'social media' space and several companies have already set up Facebook and Twitter pages. The use of this technology pose special challenges for compliance and regulators especially since the Financial Industry Regulatory Authority reminds companies that advertising, sales and literature are governed by regulations.

34897 ■ *"Funny Business" in Canadian Business (Vol. 82, April 27, 2009, No. 7, pp. 27)*
Pub: Rogers Media
Ed: Rachel Pulfer. **Description:** Companies are advised to use humor in marketing to drive more revenue. IBM Canada, for example, commissioned Second City Communications for a marketing campaign that involved humor. While IBM Canada declined to give sales or traffic figures, firm executives rank the marketing campaign as an overall success.

34898 ■ *"The Future of Work" in Black Enterprise (Vol. 41, August 2010, No. 1, pp. 65)*
Pub: Earl G. Graves Publishing Co. Inc.
Ed: Annya M. Lott. **Description:** Technology, globalization, and outsourcing will continue to shape the future of work. Social media is a means for small companies to market goods and services.

34899 ■ *"The Future of Work" in Business Strategy Review (Vol. 21, Autumn 2010, No. 3, pp. 16)*
Pub: Blackwell Publishers Ltd.
Ed: Lynda Gratton. **Description:** Work is universal. But how, why, where and when we work has never been so open to individual interpretation. The certainties of the past have been replaced by ambiguity, questions and the steady hum of technology. Now, in a groundbreaking research project covering 21 global companies and more than 200 executives, the author is making sense of the future of work.

34900 ■ *"The Future of Work" in Business Strategy Review (Vol. 21, Autumn 2010, No. 3, pp. 16)*
Pub: Wiley-Blackwell
Ed: Lynda Gratton. **Description:** Work is universal. Buy, how, why, where and when we work has never been so open to individual interpretation. The certainties of the past have been replaced by ambiguity, questions and the steady hum of technology. Research covering 21 global companies and more than 200 executives covers the future of work.

34901 ■ *"Gadget Makers Aim for New Chapter in Reading" in Crain's Cleveland Business (Vol. 28, October 22, 2007, No. 42, pp. 20)*
Pub: Crain Communications, Inc.
Ed: Jennifer McKevitt. **Description:** Although e-books and e-audiobooks are becoming more popular, e-readers, devices that display digital books, still haven't caught on with the public. Experts feel that consumers, many of whom have to look at a computer screen all day for work, still like the feel of a real book in their hands.

34902 ■ *"Galvanizing the Scientific Community" in Information Today (Vol. 26, February 2009, No. 2, pp. 20)*
Pub: Information Today, Inc.
Ed: Barbara Brynko. **Description:** Profile of John Haynes, newly appointed vice president of publishing for the American Institute of Physics; the Institute consists of ten organizations specializing in STM publishing as well as providing publishing services for over 170 science and engineering journals.

34903 ■ *"Game On" in Canadian Business (Vol. 80, February 12, 2007, No. 4, pp. 15)*
Pub: Rogers Media
Ed: Calvin Leung. **Description:** The plan of president of TransGaming Vikas Gupta to create innovative software programs for games that can be played in different operating systems is discussed.

34904 ■ *"Game On! African Americans Get a Shot at $17.9 Billion Video Game Industry" in*

Black Enterprise (Vol. 38, July 2008, No. 12, pp. 56)
Pub: Earl G. Graves Publishing Co. Inc.

Ed: Carolyn M. Brown. **Description:** Despite the economic crisis, consumers are still purchasing the hottest video games and hardware. Tips for African American developers who want to become a part of this industry that lacks content targeting this demographic are offered.

34905 ■ *"Game Plan" in Canadian Business (Vol. 79, September 11, 2006, No. 18, pp. 50)*
Pub: Rogers Media

Ed: Joe Castaldo. **Description:** Strategies adopted by gaming companies to revitalize their business and give a stimulus to their falling resources are presented.

34906 ■ *"gdgt: The New Online Home for Gadget Fans" in Hispanic Business (July-August 2009, pp. 15)*
Pub: Hispanic Business

Ed: Jeremy Nisen. **Description:** Profile of the new online Website for gadget lovers. The site combines a leek interface, gadget database, and social networking-type features which highlights devices for the consumer.

34907 ■ *"GeckoSystems Reduces Sensor Fusion Costs Due to Elder Care Robot Trials" in Internet Wire (December 14, 2010)*
Pub: Comtex

Description: GeckoSystems International Corporation has been able to reduce the cost of its sensor fusion system while maintaining reliability and performance. The firm's ongoing first in-home elder care robot trials have sparked interest regarding its business model, technologies available for licensing, and joint domestic and international ventures.

34908 ■ *"Genzyme: Underrated Oversold" in Barron's (Vol. 88, March 24, 2008, No. 12, pp. 58)*
Pub: Dow Jones & Company, Inc.

Ed: Johanna Bennett. **Description:** Shares of biotechnology company Genzyme appear oversold and underrated at their $71.86 level. The company's finances are on a solid foundation, with revenues over $3.8 billion in 2007 and forecasts of $4.5-4.7 billion in revenue for 2008.

34909 ■ *The Geography of Small Firm Innovation*
Pub: Springer

Ed: Grant Black. **Released:** January 2005. **Price:** $49.95. **Description:** Concentration of high-tech innovation across metropolitan areas in the U.S. during the 1990s and the role geography plays in innovation.

34910 ■ *"Get Online or Be Left Behind" in Women In Business (Vol. 61, August-September 2009, No. 4, pp. 33)*
Pub: American Business Women's Association

Ed: Diane Stafford. **Description:** Technology's significance for the connectivity purposes among business people is discussed. Details on the use of wireless tools and online social media to boost technology IQ are presented.

34911 ■ *"Get Paid and Get Moving" in Entrepreneur (Vol. 37, October 2009, No. 10, pp. 38)*
Pub: Entrepreneur Media, Inc.

Description: GoPayments application from Intuit allows mobile telephones to process payments like credit card terminals. The application costs $19.95 a month and can be used on the Internet browsers of mobile telephones.

34912 ■ *"Get Personal" in Entrepreneur (Vol. 36, April 2008, No. 4)*
Pub: Entrepreneur Media, Inc.

Ed: Romanus Wolter. **Description:** Customers appreciate personal contact, and communicating with them can help business owners' customer relations. Some ways on how to keep a personal touch with customers and improve business dealings include blending technology with personal interaction and knowing what the customers want. Other tips are provided.

34913 ■ *"Getting a Grip on the Saddle: Chasms or Cycles?" in Journal of Marketing (Vol. 75, July 2011, No. 4, pp. 21)*
Pub: American Marketing Association

Ed: Deepa Chandrasekaran, Gerald J. Tellis. **Description:** A study of the saddle's generality across products and countries is presented. The saddle is fairly pervasive based on empirical analysis of historical sales data from ten products across 19 countries. The results indicate chasms and technological cycles for information/entertainment products while business cycles and technological cycles affect kitchen/laundry products.

34914 ■ *"Giants Now Admit They Roam Planet Earth; Time To Buy?" in Barron's (Vol. 88, March 31, 2008, No. 13, pp. 39)*
Pub: Dow Jones & Company, Inc.

Ed: Eric J. Savitz. **Description:** Oracle's third-quarter results showed that top-line growth fell short of expectations but the company is expected to fare better than most applications companies in the downturn. Google had a flat growth in the number of people who click their online ads. The time for investors in the tech sector with a long-term horizon has arrived.

34915 ■ *"Go Beyond Local Search With Hyper-Local" in Women Entrepreneur (October 30, 2008)*
Pub: Entrepreneur Media Inc.

Ed: Lena West. **Description:** According to Forrester Research, as much as $500 billion in local spending in 2007 was influenced by the Internet and industry analysts report that consumers spend approximately 80 percent of their income within 50 miles of their home. Discussion of ways in which to capitalize on the hyper-local trend that is being driven by greater Internet connectivity and use of the web to find information is provided.

34916 ■ *"Google Edges into Wireless E-Mail" in Globe & Mail (February 19, 2007, pp. B5)*
Pub: CTVglobemedia Publishing Inc.

Ed: Simon Avery. **Description:** Google Inc. has introduced a free mobile e-mail service in Canada. The mobile users can read, send, and search messages using the new software.

34917 ■ *"Google, MySpace Deal Hits Snag" in Globe & Mail (February 7, 2007, pp. B11)*
Pub: CTVglobemedia Publishing Inc.

Ed: Julia Angwin; Kevin J. Delaney. **Description:** MySpace's intention to partner with eBay which is delaying the finalization of its $900 million online advertising deal signed with Google Inc. is discussed.

34918 ■ *"Google Places a Call to Bargain Hunters" in Advertising Age (Vol. 79, September 29, 2008, No. 36, pp. 13)*
Pub: Crain Communications, Inc.

Ed: Abbey Klaassen. **Description:** Google highlighted application developers who have created tools for its Android mobile phone in the device's unveiling; applications such as ShopSavvy and CompareEverywhere help shoppers to find bargains by allowing them to compare prices in their local areas and across the web.

34919 ■ *The Google Story: Inside the Hottest Business, Media, and Technology Success of Our Time*
Pub: Random Housing Publishing Group

Ed: David A. Vise; Mark Malseed. **Price:** $26.00.

34920 ■ *"Google's Next Stop: Below 350?" in Barron's (Vol. 88, March 10, 2008, No. 10, pp. 17)*
Pub: Dow Jones & Company, Inc.

Ed: Jacqueline Doherty. **Description:** Share prices of Google Inc. are expected to drop from their level of $433 each to below $350 per share. The company is expected to miss its earnings forecast for the first quarter of 2008, and its continued aggressive spending on non-core areas will eventually bring down earnings.

34921 ■ *"Green Energy Exec Hits State Policy" in Boston Business Journal (Vol. 30, December 3, 2010, No. 45, pp. 1)*
Pub: Boston Business Journal

Ed: Kyle Alspach. **Description:** American Superconductor Corporation President Dan McGahn believes that the state government of Massachusetts is not proactive enough to develop the state into a manufacturing hub for wind power technology. McGahn believes that while Governor Deval Patrick campaigned for wind turbines in the state, his administration does not have the focus required to build the turbines in the state.

34922 ■ *"Greg Lueck: Glass Blowing" in Inc. (Volume 32, December 2010, No. 10, pp. 36)*
Pub: Inc. Magazine

Ed: April Joyner. **Description:** Profile of Greg Lueck, partner and COO of Centerstance, a tech consulting firm in Portland, Oregon. Lueck opened Firehouse Glass, a studio that provides workspace and equipment for glass blowers. He says glass blowing serves as a welcome counterbalance to the cerebral work he does at the office.

34923 ■ *Groundswell: Winning in a World Transformed by Social Technologies*
Pub: Harvard Business School Press

Ed: Charlene Li; Josh Bernoff. **Released:** April 21, 2008. **Price:** $29.95. **Description:** Individuals are using online social technologies such as blogs, social networking sites, YouTube, and podcasts to discuss products and companies, write their own news, and find their own deals. When consumers you've never met are rating your company's products in public forums with which you have no experience or influence, your company is vulnerable. This book teaches the tools and data necessary to turn this treat into an opportunity.

34924 ■ *Grown Up Digital: How the Net Generation Is Changing Your World*
Pub: The McGraw-Hill Companies

Ed: Don Tapscott. **Released:** 2009. **Price:** $27.95. **Description:** As baby boomers retire, business needs to understand what makes the Internet work for business.

34925 ■ *"Happy New Year, Celestica?" in Canadian Business (Vol. 80, January 15, 2007, No. 2, pp. 25)*
Pub: Rogers Media

Ed: Andrew Wahl. **Description:** Speculations on the performance of the electronics manufacturing company Celestica Inc. in 2007, which has been labelled as a 'sick' company in recent times, are presented.

34926 ■ *"Harlequin Leads the Way" in Marketing to Women (Vol. 22, July 2009, No. 7, pp. 1)*
Pub: EPM Communications Inc.
Contact: Ira Mayer, President
E-mail: imayer@epmcom.com

Description: Although the publishing industry has been slow to embrace new media options, the Internet is now a primary source for reaching women readers. Harlequin has been eager to court their female consumers over the Internet and often uses women bloggers in their campaigns strategies.

34927 ■ *"Has Microsoft Found a Way to Get at Yahoo?" in Advertising Age (Vol. 79, July 7, 2008, No. 26, pp. 4)*
Pub: Crain Communications, Inc.

Ed: Abbey Klaassen. **Description:** Microsoft's attempt to acquire Yahoo's search business is discussed as is Yahoo's plans for the future at a time when the company's shares have fallen dangerously low.

34928 ■ *"Have High-Tech Tax Credits Helped or Hurt Hawaii?" in Hawaii Business (Vol. 53, December 2007, No. 6, pp. 28)*
Pub: Hawaii Business Publishing

Description: Presents the opinons of Channel Capital LLC's Walter R. Roth and Hawaii Venture Capital Association's Bill Spencer concerning the impacts of tax credits. Roth thinks that Act 221 appeals to investors who can earn despite business failure while Spencer thinks that the legislation promotes investments in innovative technology firms. The need to support tax credits is also discussed.

34929 ■ *"HBMG Targets Federal Contracts from Under Raytheon's Wing" in Austin Business JournalInc. (Vol. 29, January 15, 2010, No. 45, pp. 1)*
Pub: American City Business Journals
Ed: Christopher Calnan. **Description:** Information Technology firm HBMG Inc. of Austin Texas has been chosen by Massachusetts-based subcontractor Raytheon Company and the US Department of Defense (DoD) to join DoD's Mentor-Protege program. HBMG will be allowed to vie for government contracts through the said program, potentially increasing business with the DoD by at least 700 percent.

34930 ■ *"Health Care Leads Sectors Attracting Capital" in Hispanic Business (Vol. 30, March 2008, No. 3, pp. 14)*
Pub: Hispanic Business
Ed: Scott Williams. **Description:** Discusses the capital gains of Hispanic-owned companies and other Hispanic leaders in the investment and retail fields in the year 2007. Sectors like health care, media, food and technology saw a healthy flow of capital due to successful mergers, acquisitions and increased private equity investments.

34931 ■ *"HealthTronics Eager to Buy" in Austin Business JournalInc. (Vol. 28, September 12, 2008, No. 26, pp. 1)*
Pub: American City Business Journals
Ed: Laura Hipp. **Description:** HealthTronics Inc., an Austin, Texas urology equipment company has repeated its offer to buy Endocare Inc., an Irvine, California tumor technology firm for $26.9 million. The proposal has been revised to allow Endocare shareholders to choose between HealthTronics cash or shares. Endocare has not commented on the offer.

34932 ■ *High-Tech Entrepreneurship: Managing Innovation in a World of Uncertainty*
Pub: Routledge Inc.
Ed: Michel Bernasconi; Simon Harris. **Released:** September 2006. **Price:** $42.95. **Description:** Profiles of successful high tech companies is included; high tech companies are driving innovation globally.

34933 ■ *"High-Tech Job-Apalooza!" in Orlando Business Journal (Vol. 26, January 15, 2010, No. 33, pp. 1)*
Pub: American City Business Journals
Ed: Christopher Boyd. **Description:** Science Applications International Corporation, Saab Training USA LLC, CAE USA, and Pelliconi &C.SPA attempt to obtain $939,000 in tax incentives to generate 222 technology and defense-related jobs in Orange County, Florida. Each job will provide an average salary of $67,000. Future plans of each technology and defense firm are also presented.

34934 ■ *"High-Tech Machines Show a New Age of Vending" in Wisconsin State Journal (October 14, 2011)*
Pub: Wisconsin State Journal
Ed: Barry Adams. **Description:** Vending machines are looking more like an iPad than the machines of the past. These high tech machines are seeing sharp rises in use.

34935 ■ *"High-Tech, Niche Options Change Sports Marketing" in Crain's Detroit Business (Vol. 24, March 17, 2008, No. 11, pp. 14)*
Pub: Crain Communications, Inc.
Ed: Leah Boyd. **Description:** Sports advertisers have an ever-increasing menu of high-tech or niche marketing options such as interactive campaigns through cell phones and electronic banners which can span arenas.

34936 ■ *"His Banking Industry Software Never Caught On, so Bill Randle is Now Targeting the Health Care Market" in Inc. (March 2008)*
Pub: Gruner & Jahr USA Publishing
Ed: Alex Salkever. **Description:** Profile of Bill Randle, bank executive turned entrepreneur; Randle tells how he changed his focus for his company from banking software to healthcare software. The firm employs ten people who secure online billing and recordkeeping systems for hospitals and insurers. Randle discusses critical decisions that will impact his firm in the coming year. Three experts offer advice.

34937 ■ *"Homing In On the Future" in Black Enterprise (Vol. 38, October 2007, No. 3, pp. 61)*
Pub: Earl G. Graves Publishing Co. Inc.
Ed: Sean Drakes. **Description:** More and more people are wanting new homes wired automated systems that integrate multiple home devices such as computers, audio/visual entertainment, security, communications, utilities, and lighting and environmental controls.

34938 ■ *"How to Beat Jet Lag for $550,000" in Globe & Mail (January 3, 2006, pp. B1)*
Pub: CTVglobemedia Publishing Inc.
Ed: Simon Avery. **Description:** The details on DreamWorks Animation SKG Inc., which developed videoconferencing software 'Halo' in association with Hewlett-Packard Co., are presented.

34939 ■ *"How Dell Will Dial for Dollars" in Austin Business JournalInc. (Vol. 29, December 4, 2009, No. 39, pp. 1)*
Pub: American City Business Journals
Ed: Christopher Calnan. **Description:** Dell Inc. revealed plans to launch a Mini3i smartphone in China which could enable revenue sharing by bundling with wireless service subscription. Dell's smartphone plan is similar to the netbook business, which Dell sold with service provided by AT&T Inc.

34940 ■ *"How Not to Build a Website" in Women Entrepreneur (December 24, 2008)*
Pub: Entrepreneur Media Inc.
Ed: Erica Ruback; Joanie Reisen. **Description:** Tips for producing a unique and functional Website are given as well as a number of lessons a pair of entrepreneurs learned while trying to launch their networking website, MomSpace.com.

34941 ■ *"How to Play the Tech Mergers" in Barron's (Vol. 90, August 30, 2010, No. 35, pp. 18)*
Pub: Barron's Editorial & Corporate Headquarters
Ed: Tiernan Ray. **Description:** The intense bidding by Hewlett-Packard and Dell for 3Par was foreseen in a previous Barron's cover story and 3Par's stock has nearly tripled since reported. Other possible acquisition targets in the tech industry include Brocade Communication Systems, NetApp, Xyratex, and Isilon Systems.

34942 ■ *"How to Plug in to the Wireless Revolution" in Globe & Mail (March 11, 2006, pp. B3)*
Pub: CTVglobemedia Publishing Inc.
Ed: Catherine McLean. **Description:** The plans of president David Dobbin of Toronto Hydro Telecom Inc., to establish WiFi service, are presented.

34943 ■ *"HP Eats Into Rival Dell Sales as Profits Soar" in Globe & Mail (February 21, 2007, pp. B15)*
Pub: CTVglobemedia Publishing Inc.
Ed: Connie Guglielmo. **Description:** The world's largest personal computer maker Hewlett Packard Co. has reported increased profits by 26 percent to $1.55 billion during the first quarter. The company has outpaced its competitor Dell Inc. by offering low priced personal computers during this period.

34944 ■ *"HR Tech on the Go" in Workforce Management (Vol. 88, November 16, 2009, No. 12, pp. 1)*
Pub: Crain Communications Inc.
Ed: Ed Frauenheim. **Description:** Examination of the necessity of mobile access of human resources software applications that allow managers to recruit, schedule and train employees via their mobile devices; some industry leaders believe that mobile HR applications are vital while others see this new technology as hype.

34945 ■ *"Human Bone Breakthrough" in Houston Business Journal (Vol. 40, January 8, 2010, No. 35, pp. 1)*
Pub: American City Business Journals
Ed: Casey Wooten. **Description:** Biotech startup company Osteosphere in Houston, Texas aims to market a technology in which laboratory-grown bone tissues can be processed to appear like a real human bone tissue. The technology was developed by a co-founder of the startup and it can be applied to bone disease and injury treatment. Osteophere's future plans, such as the search for possible investors, is also outlined.

34946 ■ *IBM on Demand Technology for the Growing Business: How to Optimize Your Computing Environment for Today and Tomorrow*
Pub: Maximum Press
Ed: Jim Hoskins. **Released:** June 2005. **Price:** $29. 95. **Description:** IBM is offering computer solutions to small companies entering the On Demand trend in business.

34947 ■ *"IBM's Best-Kept Secret" in Canadian Business (Vol. 79, September 25, 2006, No. 19, pp. 19)*
Pub: Rogers Media
Ed: Andrew Wahl. **Description:** The contribution of IBM vice-president Steve Mills in company's development is discussed.

34948 ■ *ICTs and SMEs Antecedents and Consequences of Technology Adoption*
Pub: Edward Elgar Publishing, Incorporated
Ed: Ordanini. **Released:** November 2006. **Price:** $85.00. **Description:** Issues involving information communication technology adoption among small and medium-sized firms are discussed.

34949 ■ *"Image Conscious" in Canadian Business (Vol. 81, March 17, 2008, No. 4, pp. 36)*
Pub: Rogers Media
Ed: Andrew Wahl. **Description:** Idee Inc. is testing an Internet search engine for images that does not rely on tags but compares its visual data to a database of other images. The company was founded and managed by Leila Boujnane as an off-shoot of their risk-management software firm. Their software has already been used by image companies to track copyrighted images and to find images within their own archives.

34950 ■ *Imagining India: The Idea of a Renewed Nation*
Pub: Penguin Group USA Inc.
Ed: Nandan Nilekani. **Released:** 2009. **Price:** $29. 95. **Description:** National technology leader, Nandan Nilekan warns of pitfalls, obstacles and the danger of letting down the people of India.

34951 ■ *"The Impact of Acquisitions On the Productivity of Inventors at Semiconductor Firms" in Academy of Management Journal (October 2007)*
Pub: Academy of Management
Contact: Ming-Jer Chen, President
Ed: Rahul Kapoor, Kwanghui Lim. **Description:** Study examined the relation between knowledge-based and incentive-based outlook in explaining the impact of acquisitions on the productivity of inventors at acquired semiconductor firms. Results showed a definite relation between the two perspectives.

34952 ■ *"Impressive Numbers: Companies Experience Substantial Increases in Dollars, Employment" in Hispanic Business (July-August 2007)*
Pub: Hispanic Business
Ed: Derek Reveron. **Description:** Profiles of five fastest growing Hispanic companies reporting increases in revenue and employment include Brightstar, distributor of wireless products; Greenway Ford Inc.,

a car dealership; Fred Loya Insurance, auto insurance carrier; and Group O, packaging company; and Diverse Staffing, Inc., an employment and staffing firm.

34953 ■ *"In the Bag?" in Canadian Business (Vol. 81, March 3, 2008, No. 3, pp. 57)*
Pub: Rogers Media
Ed: Calvin Leung. **Description:** American stocks are beginning to appear cheap amidst the threat of a worldwide economic slowdown, United States economic crisis and declining stock portfolios. Investors looking for bargain stocks should study the shares of Apple and Oshkosh Corp. Evaluation of other cheap-looking stocks such as the shares of Coach and 3M is also given.

34954 ■ *"In the Fast Lane" in Chain Store Age (Vol. 85, November 2009, No. 11, pp. 44)*
Pub: Chain Store Age
Ed: Samantha Murphy. **Description:** Quick Chek, which operates some 120 convenience stores in New Jersey and southern New York, is testing a new self-checkout system in order to examine how speed affects its in-store experience.

34955 ■ *"In the Mobikey of Life" in Canadian Business (Vol. 81, July 21, 2008, No. 11, pp. 42)*
Pub: Rogers Media Ltd.
Ed: John Gray. **Description:** Toronto-based Route1 has created a data security software system that allows employees to access files and programs stored in the head office without permanently transferring data to the actual computer being used. Mobikey technology is useful in protecting laptops of chief executive officers, which contain confidential financial and customer data.

34956 ■ *"Incentives In Play for Astronautics" in Business Journal-Milwaukee (Vol. 28, November 5, 2010, No. 5, pp. A1)*
Pub: Milwaukee Business Journal
Ed: Sean Ryan. **Description:** Astronautics Corporation was offered incentives by local government officials in Milwaukee, Wisconsin and by Brewery Project LLC to move into a building in The Brewery in the city. The company's officials remain indecisive over the offers and incentives.

34957 ■ *Information Technology for the Small Business: How to Make IT Work For Your Company*
Pub: TAB Computer Systems, Incorporated
Ed: T.J. Benoit. **Released:** June 2006. **Price:** $17.95. **Description:** Basics of information technology to help small companies maximize benefits are covered. Topics include pitfalls to avoid, email and Internet use, data backup, recovery and overall IT organization.

34958 ■ *"Ingrian and Channel Management International Sign Distribution Agreement" in Canadian Corporate News (May 16, 2007)*
Pub: Comtex News Network Inc.
Description: Channel Management International (CMI), a Canadian channel management and distribution company, and Ingrian Networks, Inc., the leading provider of data privacy solutions, announced a Canadian distribution agreement to resell Ingrian encryption solutions to the Canadian market.

34959 ■ *Innov and Entrepren in Biotech*
Pub: Edward Elgar Publishing, Incorporated
Ed: Hine. **Released:** April 2006. **Price:** $100.00. **Description:** Innovation processes underlying successful entrepreneurship in the biotechnology sector are explored.

34960 ■ *"Innovation in 3D: NextFab" in Philadelphia Business Journal (Vol. 28, January 22, 2010, No. 49, pp. 1)*
Pub: American City Business Journals
Ed: Peter Key. **Description:** NextFab Studio LLC is set to offer product development services using 3D technology. The company has developed a three-dimensional printer which fabricates objects usually made of plastic.

34961 ■ *Innovation Nation: Canadian Leadership from Java to Jurassic Park*
Pub: John Wiley & Sons, Incorporated
Ed: Leonard Brody; Wendy Cukier; Ken Grant; Matt Holland; Catherine Middleton; Denise Shortt. **Released:** January 30, 2003. **Price:** $28.95. **Description:** Canadian's have risen to the top of the largest technology firms, from development of the Java and the Blackberry to defining specifications for XML.

34962 ■ *"Innovation Station" in Canadian Business (Vol. 80, October 8, 2007, No. 20, pp. 42)*
Pub: Rogers Media
Ed: Andrew Wahl. **Description:** Study and teaching of entrepreneurship at the University of Waterloo is discussed. Research projects in the university are expected to be influential in Canada's economic development. In spite of the success of these studies, financing is still a problem for the university, especially in technological innovations.

34963 ■ *"Innovators Critical in Technical Economy" in Crain's Cleveland Business (Vol. 28, November 5, 2007, No. 44, pp. 10)*
Pub: Crain Communications, Inc.
Ed: Peter Rea. **Description:** Discusses the importance to attract, develop and retain talented innovators on Ohio's economy. Also breaks down the four fronts on which the international battle for talent is being waged.

34964 ■ *"Inside the New Nortel" in Canadian Business (Vol. 79, November 6, 2006, No. 22, pp. 93)*
Pub: Rogers Media
Ed: Andrew Wahl. **Description:** The team plans of Nortel Networks to improve its technology market by appointing new team are analyzed.

34965 ■ *"Intel Forges New Strategy With Chinese Fabrication Plant" in Globe & Mail (March 26, 2007, pp. B6)*
Pub: CTVglobemedia Publishing Inc.
Ed: Don Clark. **Description:** World's largest semiconductor manufacturing giant Intel Corp. is planning to construct a new chip fabrication plant in China. It will be investing an estimated $2.5 billion for this purpose.

34966 ■ *"Interactive Stores a Big Part of Borders' Turnaround Plan" in Crain's Detroit Business (Vol. 24, February 18, 2008, No. 7, pp. 4)*
Pub: Crain Communications Inc. - Detroit
Description: Borders Group Inc. is using digital technology and interactive media as a part of the firm's turnaround plan. The digital store will allow shoppers to create CDs, download audio books, publish their own works, print photos and search family genealogy.

34967 ■ *"Into the Groove: Fine-Tune Your Biz By Getting Into the Good Habit Groove" in Small Business Opportunities (Spring 2008)*
Pub: Harris Publications Inc.
Description: Profile of Ty Freyvogel and his consulting firm Freyvogel Communications. Freyvogel serves the telecommunications need of Fortune 500 and mid-sized businesses.

34968 ■ *"Investing in the IT that Makes a Competitive Difference" in Harvard Business Review (Vol. 86, July-August 2008, No. 8, pp. 98)*
Pub: Harvard Business School Press
Ed: Andrew McAfee; Erik Brynjolfsson. **Description:** Components of a successful information technology management strategy are examined. These techniques are broad in spectrum, produce immediate results, are consistent and precise, facilitate monitoring, and promote enforceability.

34969 ■ *"IPhone 3G" in Advertising Age (Vol. 79, November 17, 2008, No. 43, pp. 15)*
Pub: Crain Communications, Inc.
Ed: Beth Snyder Bulik. **Description:** Review of Apple's new iPhone 3G which includes the addition of smart-phone applications as well as a price drop; the new functionalities as well as the lower price seems to be paying off for Apple who reported sales of 6.9 million iPhones in its most recent quarter, in which the 3G hit store shelves.

34970 ■ *"iPhone Apps Big Business" in Austin Business JournalInc. (Vol. 28, November 14, 2008, No. 35, pp. 1)*
Pub: American City Business Journals
Ed: Christopher Calnan. **Description:** Members of the computer software industry in Austin, Texas have benefited from developing applications for Apple Inc.'s iPhone. Pangea Software Inc.'s revenues have grown by developing iPhone applications. Lexcycle LLC, on the other hand, has created an application that enables users to read books on the iPhone.

34971 ■ *"IPod Killers?" in Canadian Business (Vol. 79, November 20, 2006, No. 23, pp. 68)*
Pub: Rogers Media
Ed: Gerry Blackwell. **Description:** The features of Apple iPod that distinguishes it from other MP3 players available in the market are discussed.

34972 ■ *"iSymmetry's Technological Makeover Or, How a Tech Company Finally Grew Up and Discovered the World Wide Web" in Inc. (October 2007)*
Pub: Gruner & Jahr USA Publishing
Description: Profile of iSymmetry, an Atlanta, Georgia-based IT recruiting firm, covering the issues the company faces keeping its technology equipment up-to-date. The firm has devised a program that will replace its old server-based software systems with on-demand software delivered via the Internet, known as software-as-a-service. Statistical information included.

34973 ■ *"The IT Department: Understanding Geeks: A Field Guide To Your Tech Staff" in Inc. (December 2007, pp. 62-63)*
Pub: Gruner & Jahr USA Publishing
Ed: Adam Bluestein. **Description:** Guide to demystify managing the information technology staff of any small business is presented, including a list of do's and don'ts and a glossary of technical terms.

34974 ■ *"It's Not About the G1; Google Just Wants You to Use the Mobile Web" in Advertising Age (Vol. 79, September 29, 2008, No. 36, pp. 32)*
Pub: Crain Communications, Inc.
Ed: Abbey Klaassen. **Description:** Google's Android is the first serious competitor to Apple's iPhone; the company says that its goal is to simplify the mobile market and get wireless subscribers to use the mobile Internet and purchase smartphones.

34975 ■ *"Jack Be Nimble" in Business Courier (Vol. 24, October 26, 2008, No. 28, pp. 1)*
Pub: American City Business Journals, Inc.
Ed: Laura Baverman. **Description:** Cincinnati Bell is losing around 47,000 phone lines a year due to the advent of wireless technology and increased competition from cable companies.

34976 ■ *"JumpTV to Hold Conference Call to Discuss Q1 Results and Annual General Meeting" in Canadian Corporate News (May 16, 2007)*
Pub: Comtex News Network Inc.
Description: Profile of JumpTv, the world's leading broadcaster of ethnic television over the Internet, and the results of a conference that discussed their first quarter 2007 financial report as well as the company's business goals. Statistical data included.

34977 ■ *"Just Following Directions" in Entrepreneur (Vol. 36, February 2008, No. 2, pp. 56)*
Pub: Entrepreneur Media Inc.
Ed: Amanda C. Kooser. **Description:** Buyer's guide for purchasing Global Positioning System units is presented.

34978 ■ *"Keeping Up With the Joneses: Outfitting Your Company With Up-To-Date Technology is Vital" in Black Enterprise*

(November 2007)
Pub: Earl G. Graves Publishing Co. Inc.
Ed: Sonya A. Donaldson. **Description:** Small businesses, whether home-based or not, need to keep up with new technological developments including hardware, software, and the Internet.

34979 ■ *"Kenyans Embrace Moving Money By Text Message" in Chicago Tribune (October 7, 2008)*
Pub: McClatchy-Tribune Information Services
Ed: Laurie Goering. **Description:** Cell phone banking services are becoming more common, especially for foreign residents; customers are able to establish a virtual cell phone bank account through companies such as M-Pesa which allows their customers to pay bills, withdraw cash, pay merchants or text money to relatives.

34980 ■ *"Kodak Cuts Deep in Effort to Change Focus" in Globe & Mail (February 9, 2007, pp. B8)*
Pub: CTVglobemedia Publishing Inc.
Ed: Gillian Wee. **Description:** Eastman Kodak Co., the world's largest photography company, is eliminating 5,000 more jobs than the originally planned 28,000 jobs. The job cuts are being driven by the sale of Kodak's health-imaging unit.

34981 ■ *"Kodiak Bucks Bear Market" in Austin Business JournalInc. (Vol. 29, December 18, 2009, No. 41, pp. 1)*
Pub: American City Business Journals
Ed: Kate Harrington. **Description:** Austin, Texas-based Kodiak Assembly Solutions LLC, a company that installs components into printed circuit boards for product or evaluation tool kit prototyping purposes, will expand despite the recession. It will relocate from a 28,000 square foot space to a 42,000 square foot space in North Austin. The firm will also increase its workforce by 20 employees.

34982 ■ *"LED Screen Technology Takes Centre Stage" in Canadian Electronics (Vol. 23, June-July 2008, No. 4, pp. 17)*
Pub: Action Communication Inc.
Ed: Ed Whitaker. **Description:** Display technologies based on light emitting diodes are becoming more popular due to their flexibility, versatility and reproducibility of displays. These are being increasingly used in different applications, such as advertising and concerts.

34983 ■ *"Legislators Must Cut Cost of Government" in Crain's Detroit Business (Vol. 24, October 6, 2008, No. 40, pp. 6)*
Pub: Crain Communications, Inc.
Description: Southeast and West Michigan business leaders are setting aside their differences and have proposed clear agendas, ranging from eliminating the Michigan Business Tax to overhauling public employee and retiree benefits and pensions. Lawmakers must also come together to find solutions for the state's economy and discover an entirely new vision for the future of Michigan business.

34984 ■ *"Let the Online Games Begin" in Canadian Business (Vol. 80, January 29, 2007, No. 3, pp. 23)*
Pub: Rogers Media
Ed: Andy Holloway. **Description:** The trends pertaining to the promotion of the products and services of different Canadian companies on the internet are discussed.

34985 ■ *"Like Being There" in Canadian Business (Vol. 79, August 14, 2006, No. 16-17, pp. 77)*
Pub: Rogers Media
Ed: Gerry Blackwell. **Description:** Latest video conferencing facilities at the Halo Collaboration Studio, are discussed.

34986 ■ *"The Lithium Deficit" in Canadian Business (Vol. 82, April 27, 2009, No. 7, pp. 17)*
Pub: Rogers Media
Ed: Joe Castaldo. **Description:** Experts are concerned that there may not be enough lithium available to support the expected rise in demand for the natural resource. Lithium is used in lithium ion batteries, the standard power source for electric and hybrid vehicles. Experts believe that the demand for lithium can only be measured once the technology is out in the market.

34987 ■ *"The Little Insect" in Canadian Electronics (Vol. 23, June-July 2008, No. 4, pp. 6)*
Pub: Action Communication Inc.
Ed: Tim Gouldson. **Description:** Electronics designers should not be underestimated because they can manufacture technologies vital to saving lives and bringing peace. They have designed robots and other electronic equipment that are as small as insects.

34988 ■ *"A Look Ahead Into 2007" in Canadian Business (Vol. 80, December 25, 2006, No. 1, pp. 40)*
Pub: Rogers Media
Description: The 2007 forecasts for various industrial sectors like telecom, information technology, manufacturing, retail, financial and energy among others is discussed.

34989 ■ *"Looking Out for the Little Guys" in Black Enterprise (Vol. 38, October 2007, No. 3, pp. 58)*
Pub: Earl G. Graves Publishing Co. Inc.
Ed: Kaylyn Kendall Dines. **Description:** Biz Tech-Connect is a Web portal that offers free online and social networking, along with four modules that help small businesses with marketing and advertising, communications and mobility, financial management, and customer relationship management.

34990 ■ *"Loyalty Pays" in Entrepreneur (Vol. 36, February 2008, No. 2, pp. 63)*
Pub: Entrepreneur Media Inc.
Ed: David Worrell. **Description:** Michael Vadini, chief executive officer of Titan Technology Partners looks after his stockholders and investors by making sure that they are protected from risk. Having been affected by the downturn in the technology industry between 2001 and 2004, Vadini granted his investors a liquidity preference. Details regarding his actions to retain investor loyalty are discussed.

34991 ■ *"Made In Canada" in Canadian Business (Vol. 80, March 12, 2007, No. 6, pp. 11)*
Pub: Rogers Media
Ed: Ian Harvey. **Description:** The devision of Christie Digital Systems Canada Inc. to increase production of its DLP projectors, in view of high demand from the United States, is discussed.

34992 ■ *"Major Tech Employers Pulling Out" in Sacramento Business Journal (Vol. 25, August 1, 2008, No. 22, pp. 1)*
Pub: American City Business Journals, Inc.
Ed: Celia Lamb. **Description:** Biotechnology company Affymetrix Inc. is planning to close its West Sacramento, California plant and lay off 110 employees. The company said it will expand a corporate restructuring plan. Affymetrix also plans to lease out or sell its building at Riverside Parkway.

34993 ■ *"Make It Easy" in Entrepreneur (Vol. 36, May 2008, No. 5, pp. 49)*
Pub: Entrepreneur Media, Inc.
Ed: Mike Hogan. **Description:** Zoho has a Planner that keep contacts, notes and reminders and a DB & Reports feature for reports, data analysis and pricing comparisons. WebEx WebOffice Workgroup supports document management and templates for contacts lists, time sheets and sales tracking. Other online data manages are presented.

34994 ■ *"Making Visitors Out Of Listeners" in Hawaii Business (Vol. 54, July 2008, No. 1, pp. 18)*
Pub: Hawaii Business Publishing
Ed: Casey Chin. **Description:** Japanese workers are subscribing to the Official Hawaii Podcast in iTunes, which offers a free 20-minute, Japanese-language audio content on different topics, such as dining reviews and music from local artists. The concept is a way to attract Japanese travelers to come to Hawaii.

34995 ■ *"Making Waves" in Business Journal Portland (Vol. 27, November 26, 2010, No. 39, pp. 1)*
Pub: Portland Business Journal
Ed: Erik Siemers. **Description:** Corvallis, Oregon-based Columbia Power Technologies LLC is about to close a $2 million Series A round of investment initiated by $750,000 from Oregon Angel Fund. The wave energy startup company was formed to commercialize the wave buoy technology developed by Oregon State University researchers.

34996 ■ *"Managing the Facebookers; Business" in The Economist (Vol. 390, January 3, 2009, No. 8612, pp. 10)*
Pub: Economist Newspaper Ltd.
Description: According to a report from PricewaterhouseCoopers, a business consultancy, workers from Generation Y, also known as the Net Generation, are more difficult to recruit and integrate into companies that practice traditional business acumen. 61 percent of chief executive managers say that they have trouble with younger employees who tend to be more narcissistic and more interested in personal fulfillment with a need for frequent feedback and an over-precise set of objectives on the path to promotion which can be hard for managers who are used to a different relationship with their subordinates. Older bosses should prepare to make some concessions to their younger talent since some of the issues that make them happy include cheaper online ways to communicate and additional coaching, both of which are good for business.

34997 ■ *"Marketers Push for Mobile Tuesday as the New Black Friday" in Advertising Age (Vol. 79, December 1, 2008, No. 44, pp. 21)*
Pub: Crain Communications, Inc.
Ed: Natalie Zmuda. **Description:** Marketers are using an innovative approach in an attempt to stimulate business on the Tuesday following Thanksgiving by utilizing consumer's cell phones to alert them of sales or present them with coupons for this typically slow retail business day; with this campaign both advertisers and retailers are hoping to start Mobile Tuesday, another profitable shopping day in line with Black Friday and Cyber Monday.

34998 ■ *"Matchmakers Anticipating Tech Valley Boom" in Business Review, Albany New York (Vol. 34, November 2, 2007, No. 31, pp. 1)*
Pub: American City Business Journals, Inc.
Ed: Adam Sichko. **Description:** Qualified candidates are coming to permanent placement companies after being downsized elsewhere. The top five projected fastest-growing and top five projected fasted-decreasing jobs in the Capital Region are presented.

34999 ■ *"Mayor Unveils Business Plan" in Boston Business Journal (Vol. 29, September 16, 2011, No. 19, pp. 1)*
Pub: American City Business Journals Inc.
Ed: Gary Haber. **Description:** Mayor Stephanie Rawlings-Blake of Baltimore, Maryland unveiled her plan to push the economy forward. Her key objectives include giving more support for the city's technology companies and refocusing the Baltimore Development Corporation on job creation and retention.

35000 ■ *"Me First!" in Black Enterprise (Vol. 38, December 2007, No. 5, pp. 107)*
Pub: Earl G. Graves Publishing Co. Inc.
Ed: Tamara E. Holmes. **Description:** Profile of Andrew J. Milisits Jr., entrepreneur and operating manager of an information technology firm; Milisits shares his experiences when taking on increasing responsibilities and his inability to balance the conflicting demands of career and family.

35001 ■ *"Medical Connectors: Meeting the Demands of Reliability, Portability, Size and Cost" in Canadian Electronics (February 2008)*
Pub: CLB Media Inc.
Ed: Murtaza Fidaali, Ted Worroll. **Description:** Component manufacturers who serve the medical industry need to ensure component reliability in order

to maintain patient safety. Because of this, connectors in medical equipment are becoming more versatile. It is concluded that these manufacturers are facing challenges meeting the medical industry standards or reliability, miniaturization, portability, and cost.

35002 ■ *"Meet the White-Label Cash Kings" in Globe & Mail (April 23, 2007, pp. B1)*
Pub: CTVglobemedia Publishing Inc.
Ed: Tara Perkins; Tavia Grant. **Description:** The services provided by the independent Canadian companies managing automated banking machines are described. The trends of ownership of automated banking machines in Canada are discussed.

35003 ■ *"Meetings Go Virtual" in HRMagazine (Vol. 54, January 2009, No. 1, pp. 74)*
Pub: Society for Human Resource Management
Contact: Henry G. Jackson, President
E-mail: hjackson@shrm.org
Ed: Elizabeth Agnvall. **Description:** Microsoft Office Live Meeting conferencing software allows companies to schedule meetings from various company locations, thus saving travel costs.

35004 ■ *"Merkle Lands $75M" in Baltimore Business Journal (Vol. 28, October 15, 2010, No. 23, pp. 1)*
Pub: Baltimore Business Journal
Ed: Gary Haber. **Description:** Baltimore, Maryland-based Merkle has received a $75 million investment from Silicon Valley-based Technology Crossover Ventures. The private equity firm's cash infusion was considered the biggest stake made in a company in the region and provides a healthy sign for Greater Baltimore's company.

35005 ■ *"Microsoft Clicks Into High Speed" in Hispanic Business (Vol. 30, July-August 2008, No. 7-8, pp. 54)*
Pub: Hispanic Business, Inc.
Ed: Derek Reveron. **Description:** Microsoft's diversity hiring and vendor diversity program to capture more Hispanic consumer and business-to-business market is described. One of the main goals of these programs is to hire more Hispanic executives and managers who will help the company develop and market products and services that will appeal and benefit Hispanic consumers.

35006 ■ *"Microsoft Goes Macrosoft" in Barron's (Vol. 89, July 27, 2009, No. 30, pp. 25)*
Pub: Dow Jones & Co., Inc.
Ed: Mark Veverka. **Description:** Microsoft reported a weak quarter on the heels of a tech rally which suggests the economy has not turned around. Marc Andreesen describes his new venture-capital fund as focused on 'classic tech' and that historical reference places him in the annals of the last millennium.

35007 ■ *"Microsoft's Big Gamble" in Canadian Business (Vol. 81, March 3, 2008, No. 3, pp. 13)*
Pub: Rogers Media
Ed: Andrew Wahl. **Description:** Microsoft Corp. is taking a big risk in buying Yahoo, as it is expected to pay more than $31 a share to finalize the acquisition. The deal would be seven and a half times bigger than any other that Microsoft has entered before, an execution of such deal is also anticipated to become a challenge for Microsoft. Recommendations on how Microsoft should handle the integration of the two businesses are given.

35008 ■ *"MicroTech: No. 1 Fastest-Growing Company" in Hispanic Business (July-August 2009, pp. 20, 22)*
Pub: Hispanic Business
Ed: Suzanne Heibel. **Description:** Profile of Tony Jimenez, former lieutenant colonel in the Army and CEO and founder of Virginia-based information technology firm, Micro Tech LLC. Jimenez was named Latinos in Information Science and Technology Association's CEO of the Year for 2008.

35009 ■ *Microtrends: The Small Forces Behind Tomorrow's Big Changes*
Pub: Business Plus
Ed: Mark J. Penn. **Released:** 2007. **Price:** $25.99. **Description:** Political pollster and lead presidential campaign strategist for Hillary Clinton, identifies seventy-five microtrends he believes are changing the social and cultural landscape in the U.S. and globally. The book covers the areas of health and wellness, technology, education and more.

35010 ■ *"Miller's Crossroad" in Canadian Business (Vol. 83, September 14, 2010, No. 15, pp. 58)*
Pub: Rogers Media Ltd.
Ed: Joe Castaldo. **Description:** Future Electronics founder and billionaire Robert Miller shares the secret of Future's unique operating model, which is based on inventory and market research. Miller attributes much of the company's success to its privately held status that enables quick movement against competitors.

35011 ■ *"Mobile: Juanes Fans Sing for Sprint" in Advertising Age (Vol. 79, November 3, 2008, No. 41, pp. 22)*
Pub: Crain Communications, Inc.
Ed: Laurel Wentz. **Description:** Marketers are appealing to the Hispanic market since they are more prone to use their cell phones to respond to contests, download videos, ringtones, or other data activity. Sprint recently sponsored a contest inviting people to sing like Colombian megastar Juanes; the participants filmed and sent their videos using their cell phones rather than laptops or camcorders illustrating the Hispanic overindex on mobile-phone technology. The contest generated hundreds of thousands of dollars in additional fee revenue, as monthly downloads increased 63 percent.

35012 ■ *"Mobile Marketing Grows With Size of Cell Phone Screens" in Crain's Detroit Business (Vol. 24, January 14, 2008, No. 2, pp. 13)*
Pub: Crain Communications Inc. - Detroit
Ed: Bill Shea. **Description:** Experts are predicting increased marketing for cell phones with the inception of larger screens and improved technology.

35013 ■ *Mobile Office: The Essential Small Business Guide to Office Technology*
Pub: Double Storey Books
Ed: Arthur Goldstruck, Steven Ambrose. **Released:** September 1, 2009. **Price:** $6.95. **Description:** Essential pocket guide for startup businesses and entrepreneurs which provides information to create a mobile office in order to maximize business potential while using current technologies.

35014 ■ *"Mobile Security for Business V5" in SC Magazine (Vol. 20, August 2009, No. 8, pp. 55)*
Pub: Haymarket Media, Inc.
Description: Review of F-Secure's Mobile Security for Business v5 which offers protection for business smartphones that can be centralized for protection monitoring by IT administrators.

35015 ■ *"Mobility: So Happy Together" in Entrepreneur (Vol. 35, October 2007, No. 10, pp. 64)*
Pub: Entrepreneur Media Inc.
Ed: Heather Clancy. **Description:** Joshua Burnett, CEO and founder of 9ci, uses index cards to keep track of what he needs to do despite the fact that he has a notebook computer, cell phone and PDA. Kim Hahn, a media entrepreneur, prefers jotting her ideas down in a spiral notebook, has a team that would organize her records for her, and a personal assistant that would keep track of changes to her schedule. Reasons why these entrepreneurs use old-fashioned methods along with new technology are given.

35016 ■ *"A Model Development" in Crain's Cleveland Business (Vol. 28, October 1, 2007, No. 39, pp. 12)*
Pub: Crain Communications, Inc.
Description: Profile a Forest City Enterprises Inc., a firm that is developing a project in New Mexico called Mesa del Sol. The Albuquerque development is being seen as the vanguard of master-planned communities with its high-tech economic development center which is expected to become the site of 60,000 jobs, 38,000 homes and a town center.

35017 ■ *"Molycorp Funds Wind Energy Technology Company" in Manufacturing Close-Up (September 19, 2011)*
Pub: Close-Up Media
Description: Molycorp Inc., producer of rare earth oxides (REO) and a REO producer outside of China, announced it will invest in Boulder Wind Power, which has designed a rare earth magnet powered wind turbine generator. This new generator can produce electricity as low as $0.04 per Kilowatt Hour. Boulder Wind Power's patented wind turbine technology allows for use of rare earth permanent magnets that do not require dysprosium, which is relatively scarce.

35018 ■ *"Moosylvania Releases Latest XL Marketing Trends Report" in Wireless News (October 6, 2009)*
Pub: Close-Up Media
Description: Moosylvania, a digital promotion and branding agency that also has an on-site research facility, has released its 2nd XL Marketing Trends Report which focuses on digital video; the study defines the top digital video trends marketers must focus on now and well into the future and notes that in 2010, Mobile Web Devices, such as smart phones will outnumber computers in this country. Statistical data included.

35019 ■ *"More Jobs Heading to Suburb" in Austin Business JournalInc. (Vol. 29, November 20, 2009, No. 37, pp. 1)*
Pub: American City Business Journals
Ed: Kate Harrington. **Description:** Site of Advanced Integration Technologies (AIT) in Pflugerville, Texas might increase its workforce to 80 employees in the next six months due to the creation of an incentive package. Funds from the Pflugerville Community Development Corporation have been helping AIT's initiative to hire more workers. The firm receives $2,000 from the plan for every new employee it hires.

35020 ■ *"Mosaid Grants First Wireless Parent License To Matsushita" in Canadian Electronics (Vol. 23, June-July 2008, No. 5, pp. 1)*
Pub: Action Communication Inc.
Description: Matsushita Electric Industrial Co. Ltd. has been granted a six-and-a-half-year license by Mosaid Technologies Inc. to manufacture the latter's products. The patent portfolio license agreement covers Mosaid's Wi-Fi, Wi-Max, CDMA-enabled notebook computers and other products.

35021 ■ *"A Motorola Spinoff Is No Panacea" in Barron's (Vol. 88, March 31, 2008, No. 13, pp. 19)*
Pub: Dow Jones & Company, Inc.
Ed: Mark Veverka. **Description:** Motorola's plan to try and spinoff their handset division is bereft of details as to how or specifically when in 2009 the spinoff would occur. There's no reason to buy the shares since there's a lot of execution risk to the plan. Motorola needs to hire a proven cellphone executive and develop a compelling new cellphone platform.

35022 ■ *"Motors and Motion Control" in Canadian Electronics (Vol. 23, February 2008, No. 1, pp. 23)*
Pub: CLB Media Inc.
Description: A new version of MicroMo Electronics Inc.'s Smoovy Series 0303..B has been added to MicroMo's DC motor product line. United Electronic Industries, on the other hand, has introduced the new UEIPAC series of programmable automation controllers that can offer solutions to various applications such as unmanned vehicle controllers. Features and functions of other new motors and motion control devices are given.

35023 ■ *My Start-Up Life: What a (Very) Young C.E.O. Learned on His Journey*

Through Silicon Valley
Pub: Jossey-Bass Publishers
Ed: Ben Casnocha. **Released:** May 25, 2007. **Price:** $24.95. **Description:** Profile of Ben Casnocha, a young entrepreneur who shares insight into starting a running a new business.

35024 ■ *"Naked Ambitions Put Telus on the Spot" in Globe & Mail (February 6, 2007, pp. B3)*
Pub: CTVglobemedia Publishing Inc.
Ed: Catherine McLean. **Description:** The offering of pornographic content on mobile phones by the telecommunications company Telus Corp., is discussed.

35025 ■ *"Nanoready?" in Entrepreneur (Vol. 36, May 2008, No. 5, pp. 20)*
Pub: Entrepreneur Media, Inc.
Ed: Andrea Cooper. **Description:** Experts predict that the medicine and energy sectors are among those that will see nanotechnology innovations in the coming years, and that nanotechnology will produce significant commercial value in new products. Some entrepreneurs are investing in nanotech and are partnering with universities. Details on nanotech funding concerns are discussed.

35026 ■ *"Nanotech Impact is Smaller Than Hoped For" in Boston Business Journal (Vol. 27, October 26, 2007, No. 39, pp. 1)*
Pub: American City Business Journals Inc.
Ed: Jackie Noblett. **Description:** Survey by the Massachusetts Technology Collaborative showed that nanotechnology firms are within the early stages of operations and need funding to make them profitable. Details on some nanotech companies and their operations and difficulties in developing or mass producing their products are discussed.

35027 ■ *"National Automatic Merchandising Association Takes Vending on the Road" in Food and Beverage Close-Up (September 6, 2011)*
Pub: Close-Up Media
Description: National Automatic Merchandising Association launched the new age of vending and is taking its machines, products and technology on the road to say thank you to loyal users of vending machines.

35028 ■ *"Nat'l Instruments Connects with Lego" in Austin Business JournalInc. (Vol. 28, August 22, 2008, No. 23, pp. 1)*
Pub: American City Business Journals
Ed: Laura Hipp. **Description:** Austin-based National Instruments Corporation has teamed with Lego Group from Denmark to create a robot that can be built by children and can be used to perform tasks. Lego WeDo, their latest product, uses computer connection to power its movements. The educational benefits of the new product are discussed.

35029 ■ *"Need Grub? Start Texting at Kroger" in Business Courier (Vol. 24, December 21, 2008, No. 36, pp. 1)*
Pub: American City Business Journals, Inc.
Ed: Laura Baverman. **Description:** Discusses the University of Cincinnati which is teaming up to release a technology platform called Macopay that would link a cell phone to a bank account and allow a person to make payments at participating retailers by sending a text message. Details with regard to the new service and its growth potential are discussed.

35030 ■ *Nerds on Wall Street: Math, Machines and Wired Markets*
Pub: John Wiley & Sons, Inc.
Ed: David J. Leinweber. **Released:** May 27, 2009. **Price:** $39.95. **Description:** The history of technology and how it will transform investing and trading on Wall Street is outlined.

35031 ■ *"Network TV" in Canadian Business (Vol. 79, September 11, 2006, No. 18, pp. 136)*
Pub: Rogers Media
Ed: Gerry Blackwell. **Description:** The functions and features of the new Mediasmart LCD TV offered by Hewlett-Packard are discussed.

35032 ■ *The New Innovators: How Canadians are Shaping the Knowledge-Based Economy*
Pub: James Lorimer & Company Ltd.
Ed: Roger Voyer; Patti Ryan. **Released:** January 1, 1994. **Price:** $29.95. **Description:** Details are examined showing how the innovation process works and how ideas are successfully translated into marketable products.

35033 ■ *"New IPhone Also Brings New Way of Mobile Marketing" in Advertising Age (Vol. 79, June 16, 2008, No. 24, pp. 23)*
Pub: Crain Communications, Inc.
Ed: Abbey Klaasen. **Description:** Currently there are two kinds of applications for the iPhone and other mobile devices: native applications that allow for richer experiences and take advantage of features that are built into a phone and web applications, those that allow access to the web through specific platforms. Marketers are interested in creating useful experiences for customers and opening up the platforms which will allow them to do this.

35034 ■ *"New Sony HD Ads Tout Digital" in Brandweek (Vol. 49, April 21, 2008, No. 16, pp. 5)*
Pub: VNU Business Media, Inc.
Description: Looking to promote Sony Electronics' digital imaging products, the company has launched another campaign effort known as HDNA, a play on the words high-definition and DNA; originally Sony focused the HDNA campaign on their televisions, the new ads will include still and video cameras as well and marketing efforts will consist of advertising in print, Online, television spots and publicity at various venues across the country.

35035 ■ *"New Sprint Phone Whets Appetite for Applications" in The Business Journal-Serving Metropolitan Kansas City (Vol. 26, July 25, 2008)*
Pub: American City Business Journals, Inc.
Ed: Suzanna Stagemeyer. **Description:** Firms supporting the applications of the new Samsung Instinct, which was introduced by Sprint Nextel Corp. in June 2008, have reported usage rates increase for their products. Handmark, whose mobile services Pocket Express comes loaded with Instinct, has redirected employees to meet the rising demand for the services. Other views and information on Instinct, are presented.

35036 ■ *New Technology-Based Firms in the New Millennium, Volume 5*
Pub: Elsevier Science and Technology Books
Ed: Ray Oakey; Saleema Kauser; Aard Groen; Peter van der Sijde. **Released:** November 2006. **Price:** $145.00. **Description:** Papers from the Annual High Technology Smal Firms conference are presented. Experts address strategic growth for these small firms.

35037 ■ *New Technology-Based Firms in the New Millennium, Volume 6*
Pub: Elsevier Science & Technology Books
Ed: Ray Oakey, R. Oakey. **Released:** May 2008. **Price:** $149.00. **Description:** Collection of papers from the Annual International High Technology Firms (HTSFs) Conference cover issues of importance to governments as they develop technological program. Papers are grouped into three sections: theory, strategy and clustering, and spin-off firms.

35038 ■ *"A New Way to Tell When to Fold" in Barron's (Vol. 88, July 7, 2008, No. 27, pp. 27)*
Pub: Dow Jones & Co., Inc.
Ed: Theresa W. Carey. **Description:** Overview of the Online trading company SmartStops, a firm that aims to tell investors when to sell the shares of a particular company. The company's Web site categorizes stocks as moving up, down, or sideways, and calculates exit points for individual stocks based on an overall market trend.

35039 ■ *"New Ways to Catch a Thief" in Barron's (Vol. 88, March 10, 2008, No. 10, pp. 37)*
Pub: Dow Jones & Company, Inc.
Ed: Theresa W. Carey. **Description:** Online brokerage firms employ different methods to protect the accounts of their customers from theft. These methods include secure Internet connections, momentary passwords, and proprietary algorithms.

35040 ■ *"New Work Order" in Black Enterprise (Vol. 38, March 2008, No. 8, pp. 60)*
Pub: Earl G. Graves Publishing Co. Inc.
Description: Today's management challenges includes issues of more competition, globalization, outsourcing and technological advances. Suggestions to help create progressive leadership in small business that sustains a competitive edge are listed.

35041 ■ *"The Next Big Thing" in Farm Industry News (Vol. 42, January 1, 2009, No. 1)*
Pub: Penton Media Inc.
Contact: John French, President
Ed: David Hest. **Description:** Communication technology that allows farmers to detect equipment location, travel speed and real-time fuel and sprayer/combine tank levels will pay off with better machine use efficiency, improved maintenance and reduced downtime. These telemetry systems will be widely available in the next few years.

35042 ■ *"The Next Dimension" in Entrepreneur (Vol. 35, November 2007, No. 11, pp. 62)*
Pub: Entrepreneur Media Inc.
Ed: Heather Clancy. **Description:** Entrepreneurs can make use of virtual worlds like Second Life to promote their products or services. Details and cautions on the use of virtual worlds are discussed.

35043 ■ *"The Next Generation of Bluetooth Headsets" in Inc. (Vol. 31, January-February 2009, No. 1, pp. 41)*
Pub: Mansueto Ventures LLC
Ed: Mark Spoonauer. **Description:** Information on the latest Bluetooth headsets that allow users to talk hands-free and the new technology that blocks ambient sounds is given. Aliph Jawbone, Plantronics Voyager Jabra BT530, and Motorola Motopure H15 are profiled.

35044 ■ *"Nine Sectors to Watch: Biotech" in Canadian Business (Vol. 81, December 24, 2007, No. 1, pp. 48)*
Pub: Rogers Media
Ed: Calvin Leung. **Description:** Forecasts on the Canadian biotechnology sector for 2008 are presented. Details on the increase in the number of biotechnology companies and prediction on the government's plan for business incentives are discussed.

35045 ■ *"Nine Sectors to Watch: Telecom" in Canadian Business (Vol. 81, December 24, 2007, No. 1, pp. 44)*
Pub: Rogers Media
Ed: Andrew Wahl. **Description:** Forecasts on the Canadian telecommunications industry for 2008 are presented. Details on consumer spending growth, the popularity of broadband, and activities in the wireless sector are also discussed.

35046 ■ *The Nokia Revolution: The Story of an Extraordinary Company That Transformed an Industry*
Pub: AMACOM
Ed: Dan Steinbock. **Released:** May 31, 2001. **Description:** Profile of Nokia, the world's largest wireless communications company. Nokia started in 1865 in rural Finland and merged its rubber company and a cabling firm to form the corporation around 1965. The firm's corporate strategy in the mobile communications industry is highlighted.

35047 ■ *"Nonprofit Ready to Get More Girls into 'STEM' Jobs" in Austin Business JournalInc. (Vol. 29, December 25, 2009, No. 42, pp. 1)*
Pub: American City Business Journals
Ed: Sandra Zaragoza. **Description:** Girlstart has completed its $1.5 million capital campaign to buy the building it will care the Girlstart Tech Center. Girlstart is a nonprofit organization that prepares girls for science, technology, engineering and mathematics or STEM careers. Details of the program are highlighted.

35048 ■ *"Nortel Makes Customers Stars in New Campaign" in Brandweek (Vol. 49, April 21, 2008, No. 16, pp. 8)*
Pub: VNU Business Media, Inc.

Ed: Mike Beirne. **Description:** Nortel has launched a new television advertising campaign in which the business-to-business communications technology provider cast senior executives in 30-second TV case studies that show how Nortel's technology helped their businesses innovate.

35049 ■ *"Nortel Romances Chinese Rival Huawei" in Globe & Mail (February 2, 2006, pp. B1)*
Pub: CTVglobemedia Publishing Inc.

Ed: Simon Avery. **Description:** The reasons behind Nortel Networks Corp.'s joint venture with Huawei Technologies Company Ltd. are presented.

35050 ■ *"Not Your Father's Whiteboard" in Inc. (Vol. 33, November 2011, No. 9, pp. 50)*
Pub: Inc. Magazine

Ed: Adam Baer. **Description:** Sharp's new interactive whiteboard is really a 70-inch touch screen monitor with software for importing presentations from any Windows 7 computer.

35051 ■ *"NovAtel Inc. Licensed to Sell Galileo Receivers" in Canadian Corporate News (May 14, 2007)*
Pub: Comtex News Network Inc.

Description: NovAtel Inc., a leading provider of precision Global Navigation Satellite System (GNSS) components and subsystems that afford its customers rapid integration of precise positioning technology, has received a license valid for ten years that allows NovAtel to sell receivers that track Galileo signals.

35052 ■ *"Now See This" in Entrepreneur (Vol. 36, April 2008, No. 4, pp. 53)*
Pub: Entrepreneur Media, Inc.

Ed: Mike Hogan. **Description:** New high definition (HD) products are to be introduced in 2008 at the Consumer Electronics Show and the Macworld Conference & Expo. HD lineup from companies such as Dell Inc. and Hewlett-Packard Co. are discussed.

35053 ■ *"Nvidia Shares Clobbered After Gloomy Warning" in Barron's (Vol. 88, July 7, 2008, No. 27, pp. 25)*
Pub: Dow Jones & Co., Inc.

Ed: Eric J. Savitz. **Description:** Shares of graphics chip manufacturer Nvidia suffered a 30 percent drop in its share price after the company warned that revenue and gross margin forecasts for the quarter ending July 27, 2008 will be below expectations. Stan Glasgow, chief operating officer of Sony Electronics, believes the US economic slowdown will not affect demand for the company's products. Statistical data included.

35054 ■ *"Nvidia's Picture Brighter Than Stock Price Indicates" in Barron's (Vol. 88, March 24, 2008, No. 12, pp. 46)*
Pub: Dow Jones & Company, Inc.

Ed: Eric J. Savitz. **Description:** Shares of graphics chip maker Nvidia, priced at $18.52 each, do not indicate the company's strong position in the graphics chip market. The company's shares have dropped due to fears of slower demand for PCs, but the company is not as exposed to broader economic forces.

35055 ■ *"NYC Tops Hub in Tech VC Dollars" in Boston Business Journal (Vol. 31, August 5, 2011, No. 28, pp. 1)*
Pub: Boston Business Journal

Ed: Kyle Alspach. **Description:** New York City has been outdoing Boston in terms of venture capital for technology firms since second quarter 2010. New York tech firms raised $865 million during the first two quarters of 2011 against Boston techs' $682 million. Boston has the edge, though, when it comes to hiring engineering talent as it is home to the Massachusetts Institute of Technology.

35056 ■ *"Obama Plan May Boost Maryland Cyber Security" in Boston Business Journal (Vol. 29, May 20, 2011, No. 2, pp. 1)*
Pub: American City Business Journals Inc.

Ed: Scott Dance. **Description:** May 12, 2011 outline of the cyber security policies of President Obama may improve the cyber security industry in Maryland as the state is home to large defense and intelligence activities. Details of the proposed policies are discusses as well as their advantages to companies that deal in developing cyber security plans for other companies.

35057 ■ *"Office Retooled" in Canadian Business (Vol. 80, March 26, 2007, No. 7, pp. 67)*
Pub: Rogers Media

Ed: Andrew Wahl. **Description:** The merits and demerits of using new Google Apps Premier Edition are presented.

35058 ■ *"Online Training Requires Tools, Accessories" in Contractor (Vol. 56, September 2009, No. 9, pp. 67)*
Pub: Penton Media, Inc.

Ed: Larry Drake. **Description:** Importance of the right equipment and tools to members of the United States plumbing industry undergoing online training is discussed. Portable devices such as Blackberrys and I-phones could be used for online training. The use of headphones makes listening easier for the trainee.

35059 ■ *"Optimal Awarded US $256 Thousand Contract to Conduct LiDAR Survey for a Major Electric Utility in the Southwest" in Canadian Corporate News*
Pub: Comtex News Network Inc.

Description: Optimal Geomatics, a company specializing in the science and technology of analyzing, gathering, interpreting, distributing, and using geographic information, was awarded a new contract from a long-standing electric utility customer in the Southwest to conduct a LiDAR survey for a part of the utility's overhead transmission line system.

35060 ■ *"Oracle: No Profit of Doom" in Barron's (Vol. 88, March 31, 2008, No. 13, pp. 40)*
Pub: Dow Jones & Company, Inc.

Ed: Mark Veverka. **Description:** Oracle's revenues grew by 21 percent but fell short of expectation and their profits came in at the low-end of expectations. The company's shares dropped 8 percent but investors are advised to pay more attention to the company's earnings expansion rather than revenue growth in a slow economy. Nokia's Rick Simonson points out that their markets in Asia and particularly India is growing so they are not as affected by the U.S. economic conditions.

35061 ■ *"Ordering Pizza Hut From Your Facebook Page?" in Advertising Age (Vol. 79, November 10, 2008, No. 42, pp. 50)*
Pub: Crain Communications, Inc.

Ed: Emily Bryson York. **Description:** Fast-food chains are experimenting with delivery/takeout services via social networks such as Facebook and iPhone applications. This also allows the chains to build valuable databases of their customers.

35062 ■ *"Our Gadget of the Week" in Barron's (Vol. 88, March 24, 2008, No. 12, pp. 47)*
Pub: Dow Jones & Company, Inc.

Ed: Tiernan Ray. **Description:** Review of the $299 Apple Time Capsule, which is a 500-megabyte hard disk drive and a Wi-Fi router, rolled into one device. The device allows users to create backup files without the need for sophisticated file management software.

35063 ■ *"Our Gadget of the Week" in Barron's (Vol. 88, March 10, 2008, No. 10, pp. 36)*
Pub: Dow Jones & Company, Inc.

Ed: Jay Palmer. **Description:** Review of the $1,599 Fujitsu Lifebook T2010 tablet notebook which is a lightweight notebook offering a comfortable keyboard and a 12-inch screen illuminated by light emitting diodes. The notebook, however, also offers limited capability with its low-end processor and the lack of a built-in optical drive and a touchpad.

35064 ■ *"Our Gadget of the Week" in Barron's (Vol. 89, July 27, 2009, No. 30, pp. 26)*
Pub: Dow Jones & Co., Inc.

Ed: Jay Palmer. **Description:** Zeo Sleep Coach has a lightweight headband with built-in sensors which measures the user's brain waves and records their sleep patterns. The device details the time the users spends in deep sleep, light sleep and the restorative REM (rapid eye movement) sleep mode. Users can get lifestyle change recommendations from a website to improve their sleep.

35065 ■ *"Our Gadget of the Week: Balancing Act" in Barron's (Vol. 88, March 31, 2008, No. 13, pp. 40)*
Pub: Dow Jones & Company, Inc.

Ed: Naureen S. Malik. **Description:** Wii Fit gives users the experience of a virtual personal trainer and workouts that become progressively harder. The device turns the typical fitness regimes into fun exercises and users can choose workouts in four categories including yoga, balance, strength-training and, low impact aerobics.

35066 ■ *"Our Gadget of the Week: Business Buddy" in Barron's (Vol. 88, July 7, 2008, No. 27, pp. 26)*
Pub: Dow Jones & Co., Inc.

Ed: Jay Palmer. **Description:** Review and evaluation of the Lenovo X300 laptop computer which offers executives a variety of features despite its smaller size and weight. The laptop is about 0.73 inch thick, comes with a 64-gigabyte solid-state drive from Samsung, and weighs less than three pounds.

35067 ■ *"Our Gadget of the Week: Mostly, I Liked It" in Barron's (Vol. 88, July 14, 2008, No. 28, pp. 31)*
Pub: Dow Jones & Co., Inc.

Ed: Jay Palmer. **Description:** Review of the Apple iPhone 3G, which costs $199, has better audio and is slightly thicker than its predecessor; using the 3G wireless connection makes going online faster but drains the battery faster too.

35068 ■ *Out of the Comfort Zone: Learning to Expect the Unexpected*
Pub: Morgan & Claypool Publishers

Ed: Lisbeth Borbye. **Released:** May 10, 2010. **Price:** $35.00. **Description:** A collection of lectures covering technology, management and entrepreneurship.

35069 ■ *Outsourcing: Information Technology, Original Equipment Manufacturer, Leo, Oursourcing, Offshoring Research Network, Crowdsourcing*
Pub: General Books LLC

Released: May 1, 2010. **Price:** $14.14. **Description:** Chapters include information for outsourcing firms and how to maintain an outsourcing business.

35070 ■ *Overcoming Barriers to Entrepreneurship in the United States*
Pub: Lexington Books

Ed: Diana Furchtgott-Roth. **Released:** March 28, 2008. **Price:** $24.95. **Description:** Real and perceived barriers to the founding and running of small businesses in America are discussed. Each chapter outlines how policy and economic environments can hinder business owners and offers tips to overcome these obstacles. Starting with venture capital access in Silicon Valley during the Internet bubble, the book goes on to question the link between personal wealth and entrepreneurship, examines how federal tax rates affect small business creation and destruction, explains the low rate of self-employment among Mexican immigrants, and suggests ways pension coverage can be increased in small businesses.

35071 ■ *"Paging Dr. Phil" in Canadian Business (Vol. 79, September 25, 2006, No. 19, pp. 21)*
Pub: Rogers Media

Ed: John Gray. **Description:** Increasing corporate crimes in software industry is discussed by focusing on recent case of Hewlett and Packard.

35072 ■ *"Panel to Call for Reduced Restraints on Telecom Sector" in Globe & Mail (March 17, 2006, pp. B1)*
Pub: CTVglobemedia Publishing Inc.
Ed: Simon Tuck. **Description:** A federal panel called to adopt a more market-friendly approach to the lucrative telecommunications sector in Canada. Details of the report are presented.

35073 ■ *"Panel Calls for 'Fundamental' Change to Telecom Regulation" in Globe & Mail (March 23, 2006, pp. B1)*
Pub: CTVglobemedia Publishing Inc.
Ed: Catherine McLean. **Description:** A federal panel review at Ottawa called for a shakeup of regulations and policies that govern telecommunications companies to contend with sweeping technological changes. Details of the panel review are presented.

35074 ■ *"Paterson Plots Comeback With Internet IPO" in Globe & Mail (February 20, 2006, pp. B1)*
Pub: CTVglobemedia Publishing Inc.
Ed: Grant Robertson. **Description:** The initial public offering plans of chief executive officer Scott Paterson of JumpTV.com are presented.

35075 ■ *"PC Connection Acquires Cloud Software Provider" in New Hampshire Business Review (Vol. 33, March 25, 2011, No. 6, pp. 8)*
Pub: Business Publications Inc.
Description: Merrimack-based PC Connection Inc. acquired ValCom Technology, a provider of cloud-based IT service management software. Details of the deal are included.

35076 ■ *"PDAs Are Great - As Long As You Can Find Them" in Crain's Chicago Business (Vol. 31, May 5, 2008, No. 18, pp. 41)*
Pub: Crain Communications, Inc.
Ed: Jennifer Olvera. **Description:** Discusses a new service from Global Lost & Found Inc. in which after paying a one-time fee, customers receive a label with an identification number and a toll free phone number so if they lose a gadget such as a cell phone, PDA or laptop the finder can return the device and are rewarded with a gift card.

35077 ■ *"Philanthropy Good For Business" in Crain's Detroit Business (Vol. 24, February 18, 2008, No. 7, pp. 14)*
Pub: Crain Communications Inc. - Detroit
Ed: Sheena Harrison. **Description:** Profile of Burce McCully, founder of Dynamic Edge Inc., and his views on philanthropy as a key to any small company's success. The Ann Arbor, Michigan information technology firm has volunteered and raised funds for many causes since 1999 when the company was founded.

35078 ■ *"Pioneers Get All The Perks" in Canadian Business (Vol. 81, March 3, 2008, No. 3, pp. 18)*
Pub: Rogers Media
Description: Suncor Energy Inc. will face royalty payments from 25% to 30% of net profits as it signs a new deal with Alberta. Biovail Corp., meanwhile, is under a U.S. grand jury investigation for supposed improprieties in Cardizem LA heart drug launch. The Conference Board of Canada's proposal to impose taxes on greenhouse gas emissions and other developments in the business community are discussed.

35079 ■ *Power Up Your Small-Medium Business: A Guide to Enabling Network Technologies*
Pub: Cisco Press
Ed: Robyn Aber. **Released:** March 2004. **Price:** $39.95 (US), $57.95 (Canadian). **Description:** Network technologies geared to small and medium-size business, focusing on access, IP telephony, wireless technologies, security, and computer network management.

35080 ■ *Practical Tech for Your Business*
Pub: Kiplinger Books and Tapes
Ed: Michael J. Martinez. **Released:** 2002. **Description:** Advice is offered to help small business owners choose the right technology for their company. The guide tells how to get started, network via the Internet, create an office network, use database software, and conduct business using mobile technology.

35081 ■ *"Prepaid Phones Surge in Bad Economy" in Advertising Age (Vol. 79, November 17, 2008, No. 43, pp. 6)*
Pub: Crain Communications, Inc.
Ed: Rita Chang. **Description:** Prepay cell phone offerings are becoming increasingly competitive amid a greater choice of plans and handsets. In an economic environment in which many consumers are unable to pass the credit checks required for traditional cell phone plans, the prepay market is surging.

35082 ■ *"Presidential Address: Innovation in Retrospect and Prospect" in Canadian Journal of Electronics (Vol. 43, November 2010, No. 4)*
Pub: Journal of the Canadian Economics Association
Ed: James A. Brander. **Description:** Has innovation slowed in recent decades? While there has been progress in information and communications technology, the recent record of innovation in agriculture, energy, transportation and healthcare sectors is cause for concern.

35083 ■ *"Pressed for Time" in Marketing to Women (Vol. 21, March 2008, No. 3, pp. 1)*
Pub: EPM Communications Inc.
Contact: Ira Mayer, President
E-mail: imayer@epmcom.com
Description: Statistical data concerning the tools women use for time management which include gadgets as well as traditional media such as calendars.

35084 ■ *"Products and Services" in Canadian Electronics (Vol. 23, August 2008, No. 5, pp. 46)*
Pub: Action Communication Inc.
Description: Directory of companies under the alphabetical listing of electronic equipment and allied components that they offer is presented.

35085 ■ *"Providing Expertise Required to Develop Microsystems" in Canadian Electronics (Vol. 23, February 2008, No. 1, pp. 6)*
Pub: CLB Media Inc.
Ed: Ian McWalter. **Description:** CMC Microsystems, formerly Canadian Microelectronics Corporation, is focused on empowering microelectronics and Microsystems research in Canada. Microsystems offers the basis for innovations in the fields of science, environment, technology, automotives, energy, aerospace and communications technology. CMC's strategy in developing Microsystems in Canada is described.

35086 ■ *"Punta Gorda Interested in Wi-Fi Internet" in Charlotte Observer (February 1, 2007)*
Pub: Knight-Ridder/Tribune Business News
Ed: Steve Reilly. **Description:** Punta Gorda officials are developing plans to provide free wireless Internet services to businesses and residents.

35087 ■ *"Put a Projector in Your Pocket" in Inc. (Vol. 31, January-February 2009, No. 1, pp. 42)*
Pub: Mansueto Ventures LLC
Description: PowerPoint presentations can be given using the Optoma Pico Pocket Projector. The device can be connected to laptops, cell phones, digital cameras, and iPods.

35088 ■ *"Put Your Data to Work in the Marketplace" in Harvard Business Review (Vol. 86, September 2008, No. 9, pp. 34)*
Pub: Harvard Business School Press
Ed: Thomas C. Redman. **Description:** Nine strategies are presented for data asset marketing including exploiting asymmetries, unbundling, repackaging, and offering new content.

35089 ■ *"Putting the App in Apple" in Inc. (Vol. 30, November 2008, No. 11, pp.)*
Pub: Mansueto Ventures LLC
Ed: Nitasha Tiku. **Description:** Aftermarket companies are scrambling to develop games and widgets for Apple's iPhone. Apple launched a kit for developers interested in creating iPhone-specific software along with the App Store, and an iTunes spinoff. Profiles of various software programs that may be used on the iPhone are given.

35090 ■ *"Qualcomm Could Win Big as the IPhone 3G Calls" in Barron's (Vol. 88, July 4, 2008, No. 28, pp. 30)*
Pub: Dow Jones & Co., Inc.
Ed: Eric J. Savitz. **Description:** Apple iPhone 3G's introduction could widen the smartphone market thereby benefiting handset chipmaker Qualcomm in the process. Qualcomm Senior V.P., Bill Davidson sees huge potential for his company's future beyond phones with their Snapdragon processor. The prospects of Sun Microsystems' shares are also discussed.

35091 ■ *"Quantivo Empowers Online Media Companies to Immediately Expand Audiences and Grow Online Profits" in Internet Wire (Nov. 18, 2009)*
Pub: Comtex News Network, Inc.
Description: Quantivo, the leader in on-demand Behavioral Analytics, has launched a new solution that includes 22 of the most critical Internet audience behavior insights as out-of-the-box reports; Internet marketers need to understand their audience, what they want and how often to offer it to them in order to gain successful branding and campaigns online.

35092 ■ *The Race for a New Game Machine: Creating the Chips Inside the Xbox 360 and the PlayStation 3*
Pub: Citadel Press
Contact: Steven Zacharius, President
E-mail: szacharius@kensingtonbooks.com
Ed: David Shippy, Mickie Phipps. **Released:** 2009. **Price:** $21.95. **Description:** The story of Microsoft and Sony's race to deliver the goods for the Xbox 360 and Playstation 3 is explored.

35093 ■ *"Radiant Commences In-Lab Testing for US Air Mobility Command" in Canadian Corporate News (May 16, 2007)*
Pub: Comtex News Network Inc.
Description: The Boeing Company will be conducting in-lab infrared material testing for the Radiant Energy Corporation, developer and marketer of InfraTek, the environmentally friendly, patented infrared pre-flight aircraft deicing system.

35094 ■ *"Radio Feels Heat from IPod Generation" in Globe & Mail (March 16, 2006, pp. B1)*
Pub: CTVglobemedia Publishing Inc.
Ed: Simon Tuck; Grant Robertson. **Description:** Conventional radio stations are losing the younger generation listeners to new technology such as MP3 players, satellite radio and music-playing cell phones. The report of Canadian Association of Broadcasters (CAB) is detailed.

35095 ■ *"Raptor Opens Consultancy" in Austin Business Journal (Vol. 31, July 8, 2011, No. 18, pp. 1)*
Pub: American City Business Journals Inc.
Ed: Christopher Calnan. **Description:** Boston hedge fund operator Raptor Group launched Raptor Accelerator, a consulting business providing sales and advisory services to early-stage companies in Central Texas. Aside from getting involved with the startups in which the Raptor Group invests, Raptor Accelerator will target firms operating in the sports, media, entertainment, and content technology sectors.

35096 ■ *Reading Financial Reports for Dummies*
Pub: John Wiley and Sons, Inc.
Ed: Lita Epstein. **Released:** January 2009. **Price:** $21.99. **Description:** This second edition contains more new and updated information, including new information on the separate accounting and financial

reporting standards for private/small businesses versus public/large businesses; updated information reflecting 2007 laws on international financial reporting standards; new content to match SEC and other governmental regulatory changes over the last three years; new information about how the analyst-corporate connection has changed the playing field; the impact of corporate communications and new technologies; new examples that reflect the current trends; and updated Websites and resources.

35097 ■ *"Recent Deals Signal an M&A Resurgence" in Austin Business JournalInc. (Vol. 29, January 22, 2010, No. 46, pp. 1)*
Pub: American City Business Journals

Ed: Jacob Dirr. **Description:** The acquisition of at least six Austin, Texas technology companies reflects the growing acquisition activity in the US. Corporations have bought 86 companies and spent $7.3 billion during the fourth quarter of 2009. Insights into the impact of the acquisition activity to Austin's entrepreneurial energy are also given.

35098 ■ *"Recession Management" in Canadian Business (Vol. 81, March 3, 2008, No. 3, pp. 62)*
Pub: Rogers Media

Ed: Joe Castaldo. **Description:** Some companies such as Capital One Financial Corp. are managing their finances as if a recession has already taken place to prepare themselves for the looming economic downturn. Intel Corp., meanwhile shows how increasing its investments during a recession could be advantageous. Tips on how companies can survive a recession are provided.

35099 ■ *"Red One and The Rain Chronicles" in Michigan Vue (Vol. 13, July-August 2008, No. 4, pp. 30)*
Pub: Entrepreneur Media Inc.

Ed: Evan Cornish. **Description:** Troy-based film school the Motion Picture Institute (MPI) implemented the latest technology by shooting the second of their trilogy, 'The Rain Chronicles', on the Red One camera. This is the first feature film in Michigan to utilize this exciting new camera, which includes proprietary software for rendering and color correction. Brian K. Johnson heads up the visual effects team as visual effects supervisor and lead CG artist. His company, Dream Conduit Studios, had to tackle the task of employing the new work flow through a post-production pipeline that would allow him to attack complex visual effects shots, many of which were shot with a moving camera, a technique rarely seen in films at this budgetary level where the camera is traditionally locked off.

35100 ■ *"Region to Be Named Innovation Hub" in Business Courier (Vol. 27, July 2, 2010, No. 9, pp. 1)*
Pub: Business Courier

Ed: Dan Monk. **Description:** The selection of Cincinnati's consumer-marketing cluster as a 'Hub of Innovation' by the Ohio Department of Development could boost Cincinnati's chances of receiving $100 million in grants from Ohio's Third Frontier program and other funding sources. Implications of the University of Cincinnati's designation as a Center of Excellence in Advanced Transportation and Aerospace are also discussed.

35101 ■ *"Region Ready to Dig Deeper into Tech Fund" in Business Courier (Vol. 26, October 30, 2009, No. 27, pp. 1)*
Pub: American City Business Journals, Inc.

Ed: James Ritchie. **Description:** Southwest Ohio region aims for a bigger share in the planned renewal of Ohio's Third Frontier technology funding program. Meanwhile, University of Cincinnati vice president Sarah Degen will be appointed to the program's advisory board if the renewal proceeds.

35102 ■ *Remix: Making Art and Commerce Thrive in the Hybrid Economy*
Pub: Penguin Group USA Inc.

Ed: Lawrence Lessig. **Released:** 2009. **Price:** $25. 95. **Description:** An examination of copyright laws in the digital age.

35103 ■ *"Remote Control: Working From Wherever" in Inc. (February 2008, pp. 46-47)*
Pub: Gruner & Jahr USA Publishing

Ed: Ryan Underwood. **Description:** New technology allows workers to perform tasks from anywhere via the Internet. Profiles of products to help connect to your office from afar include, LogMein Pro, a Web-based service that allowsaccess to a computer from anywhere; Xdrive, an online service that allows users to store and swap files; Basecamp, a Web-based tools that works like a secure version of MySpace; MojoPac Freedom, is software that allows users to copy their computer's desktop to a removable hard drive and plug into any PC; WatchGuard Firebox X Core e-Series UTM Bundle, hardware that blocks hackers and viruses while allowing employees to work remotely; TightVNC, a free open-source software that lets you control another computer via the Internet.

35104 ■ *"Reportlinker.com Adds Report: GeoWeb and Local Internet Markets: 2008 Edition" in Entertainment Close-Up (September 11, 2009)*
Pub: Close-Up Media

Description: Reportlinker.com is adding a new market research report that is available in its catalogue: GeoWeb and Local Internet Markets - 2008 Edition; highlights include the outlook for consumer mapping services and an examination of monetizing services and an analysis the development outlook for geospacial Internet market, also referred to as the Geoweb.

35105 ■ *"Research and Market Adds Report: Endpoint Security for Business" in Wireless News (October 26, 2009)*
Pub: Close-Up Media

Description: Summarizes Research and Markets Adds Report: Endpoint Security for Business: Desktops, Laptops & Mobile Devices 2009-2014; highlights include a detailed analysis of where the industry is at present and forecasts regarding how it will develop over the next five years.

35106 ■ *"Research and Markets Adds Report: The U.S. Mobile Web Market" in Entertainment Close-Up (December 10, 2009)*
Pub: Close-Up Media

Description: Highlights of the new Research and Markets report 'The U.S. Mobile Web Market: Taking Advantage of the iPhone Phenomenon' include: mobile Internet marketing strategies; the growth of mobile web usage; the growth of revenue in the mobile web market; and a look at Internet business communications, social media and networking.

35107 ■ *"Research Reports: How Analysts Size Up Companies" in Barron's (Vol. 88, March 31, 2008, No. 13, pp. M13)*
Pub: Dow Jones & Company, Inc.

Ed: Anita Peltonen. **Description:** Sirius Satellite's shares are ranked Outperform as it awaits approval from the Federal Communications Commission in its merger with XM. TiVo's shares are ranked Avoid as the company is in a sector that's being commoditized. Verizon Communications' rising dividend yield earns it a Focus List ranking. The shares of Bear Stearns, Churchill Downs, Corning, and Deerfield Triarc Capital are also reviewed. Statistical data included.

35108 ■ *"Research Reports: How Analysts Size Up Companies" in Barron's (Vol. 88, March 17, 2008, No. 11, pp. M13)*
Pub: Dow Jones & Company, Inc.

Ed: Anita Peltonen. **Description:** Shares of Applied Industrial Technologies are ranked Market Perform while the shares of Google get a buy rating. Salix Pharmaceuticals gets a Sell/Above-Average risk rating. The shares of Dune Energy, Franklin Resources, Internet Brands, Piper Jaffray, and Texas Instruments are also rated.

35109 ■ *"RIM Reinforces Claim as Top Dog by Expanding BlackBerry" in Globe & Mail (March 11, 2006, pp. B3)*
Pub: CTVglobemedia Publishing Inc.

Ed: Simon Avery. **Description:** The plans of Research In Motion Ltd. to enhance the features of BlackBerry, through acquisition of Ascendent Systems, are presented.

35110 ■ *"Ring Ka-Ching" in Canadian Business (Vol. 79, November 6, 2006, No. 22, pp. 106)*
Pub: Rogers Media

Description: A brief profile of Jajah including its web activated telephone services is presented.

35111 ■ *"Rising in the East; Research and Development" in The Economist (Vol. 390, January 3, 2009, No. 8612, pp. 47)*
Pub: The Economist Newspaper Inc.

Description: Impressive growth of the technological research and development in Asian countries is discussed. Statistical data included.

35112 ■ *Risk Takers and Innovators, Great Canadian Business Ventures Since 1950*
Pub: Altitude Publishing

Ed: Sandra Phinney. **Released:** June 15, 2004. **Price:** $7.95. **Description:** Successful business leaders share their creativity, technology skills, and entrepreneurship.

35113 ■ *"RS Information Systems Signs Buyout Deal" in Black Enterprise (February 2008)*
Pub: Earl G. Graves Publishing Co. Inc.

Ed: Alan Hughes. **Description:** Details of the RS Information Systems buyout by Wyle, a privately held provider of high-tech aerospace engineering, testing, and research services.

35114 ■ *"Rule of Thumb" in Entrepreneur (Vol. 36, May 2008, No. 5, pp. 44)*
Pub: Entrepreneur Media, Inc.

Ed: Guy Kawasaki. **Description:** Business presentations using PowerPoint are recommended to have no more than 10 slides, last no longer than 20 minutes and have font no smaller than 30 points. Topics covered should include problem, solution, business model, underlying technology, and projections among others.

35115 ■ *"The Rypple Effect; Performance Management" in The Economist (Vol. 390, January 3, 2009, No. 8612, pp. 48)*
Pub: The Economist Newspaper Inc.

Description: New companies such as Rypple, a new, web-based service, claim that they can satisfy the Net Generation's need for frequent assessments while easing the burden this creates for management.

35116 ■ *"Sales Communications in a Mobile World" in Business Communication Quarterly (December 2007, pp. 492)*
Pub: SAGE Publications USA
Contact: Blaise R. Simqu, President

Ed: Daniel T. Norris. **Description:** Salespeople can take advantage of the latest mobile technologies while maintaining a personal touch with clients and customers through innovation, formality in interactions, client interactions, and protection and security of mobile data.

35117 ■ *"Samsung 'Holding Breath" in Austin Business JournalInc. (Vol. 29, January 29, 2010, No. 47, pp. 1)*
Pub: American City Business Journals

Ed: Jacob Dirr. **Description:** Samsung Austin Semiconductor LLC entered into an incentives agreement with the State of Texas in 2005, which involved $230 million in tax breaks and public financing. Terms of the agreement have been met, but some are questioning whether the company will be able to meet its goals for the Austin operations in 2010.

35118 ■ *"Samsung's Metamorphosis" in Austin Business Journal (Vol. 31, May 20, 2011, No. 11, pp. 1)*
Pub: American City Business Journals Inc.

Ed: Christopher Calnan. **Description:** Samsung Austin Semiconductor LP, a developer of semiconductors for smartphones and tablet computers, plans to diversify its offerings to include niche products: flash memory devices and microprocessing devices. In light of this strategy, Samsung Austin will be hiring 300 engineers as part of a $3.6 billion expansion of its plant.

35119 ■ *"Satellite Down, Stock Up: Raytheon Is On Target With Ten Percent Dividend Increase" in Barron's (Vol. 88, March 31, 2008, No. 13)*
Pub: Dow Jones & Company, Inc.
Ed: Shirley A. Lazo. **Description:** Raytheon hiked their quarterly dividend to 28 cents per share from 25.5 cents. Aircastle slashed their quarterly common dividend by 64 percent for them to retain additional capital that can be used to increase their liquidity position.

35120 ■ *"Say Goodbye to Voicemail" in Agency Sales Magazine (Vol. 39, November 2009, No. 10, pp. 3)*
Pub: MANA
Description: Salespeople should think twice before leaving a voicemail. The emerging modern etiquette is to send a text message or to e-mail the customer or client. Communication suggestions for both salespeople and their principals are presented.

35121 ■ *"Scanning the Field" in Business Courier (Vol. 26, January 8, 2010, No. 38, pp. 1)*
Pub: American City Business Journals, Inc.
Ed: Jon Newberry. **Description:** Anti-terror detection systems developer Valley Force Composite Technologies Inc. of Kentucky plans to enter the market with its high-resolution ODIN and Thor-LVX screening systems. These systems are expected to meet the increasing demand for airport security equipment.

35122 ■ *Science Lessons: What the Business of Biotech Taught Me About Management*
Pub: Harvard Business School Press
Ed: Gordon Binder, Philip Bashe. **Released:** 2009. **Price:** $29.95. **Description:** Former CFO of biotechnology startup Amgen and veteran of Ford Motor Company provides a universal guide to management based on some of the same scientific principles used to create new drugs.

35123 ■ *"Scientific American Builds Novel Blog Network" in Information Today (Vol. 28, September 2011, No. 8, pp. 12)*
Pub: Information Today, Inc.
Ed: Kurt Schiller. **Description:** Scientific American launched a new blog network that joins a diverse lineup of bloggers cover various scientific topics under one banner. The blog network includes 60 bloggers providing insights into the ever-changing world of science and technology.

35124 ■ *"Second Cup?" in Canadian Business (Vol. 81, July 21, 2008, No. 11, pp. 50)*
Pub: Rogers Media Ltd.
Ed: Calvin Leung. **Description:** Profile of James Gosling who is credited as the inventor of the Java programming language; however, the 53-year-old software developer feels ambivalent for being credited as inventor since many people contributed to the language. Netscape and Sun Microsystems incorporation of the programming language into Java is presented.

35125 ■ *"Security Alert: Data Server" in Entrepreneur (Vol. 36, February 2008, No. 2, pp. 28)*
Pub: Entrepreneur Media Inc.
Ed: Amanda C. Kooser. **Description:** Michael Kogon is the founder of Definition 6, a technology consulting and interactive marking firm. He believes in the philosophy that the best way to keep sensitive data safe is not to store it. Details on the security policies of his firm are discussed.

35126 ■ *"Seven Ways to Fail Big" in Harvard Business Review (Vol. 86, September 2008, No. 9, pp. 82)*
Pub: Harvard Business School Press
Ed: Paul B. Carroll; Chunka Mui. **Description:** Seven factors involved in business failures are identified, and ways to avoid them are described. These factors include flawed financial engineering, hurrying into consolidation, and investing in technology that is not a good fit.

35127 ■ *"Sherwin-Williams Workers Forgo Travel for Virtual Trade Show" in Crain's Cleveland Business (Vol. 28, October 15, 2007, No. 41)*
Pub: Crain Communications, Inc.
Ed: John Booth. **Description:** Overview of CyberCoating 2007, a cutting-edge virtual three-dimensional trade show that exhibitors such as Sherwin-Williams Co.'s Chemical Coatings Division will take part in by chatting verbally or via text messages in order to exchange information and listen to pitches just like they would on an actual trade show floor.

35128 ■ *"Show and Tell" in Entrepreneur (Vol. 36, May 2008, No. 5, pp. 54)*
Pub: Entrepreneur Media, Inc.
Ed: Heather Clancy. **Description:** FreshStart Telephone uses recorded video testimonials of customers, by using Pure Digital Flip Video that downloads content directly to the computer, and uploads it in the company's website to promote their wireless phone service.

35129 ■ *"Silicon Valley's Economic Recovery Picking Up Pace" in Globe & Mail (January 29, 2007, pp. B13)*
Pub: CTVglobemedia Publishing Inc.
Ed: Pui-Wing Tam. **Description:** The addition of 30,000 new jobs, rise in average annual wages and household income, along with other factors that have contributed to Silicon Valley's economic recovery are discussed.

35130 ■ *"Singapore Airlines' Balancing Act" in Harvard Business Review (Vol. 88, July-August 2010, No. 7-8, pp. 145)*
Pub: Harvard Business School Publishing
Ed: Loizos Heracleous, Jochen Wirtz. **Description:** Singapore Airlines is used as an illustration of organizational effectiveness. The article includes the firm's 4-3-3 rule of spending, its promotion of centralized as well as decentralized innovation, use of technology, and strategic planning.

35131 ■ *"The Skype's the Limit" in Canadian Business (Vol. 80, February 12, 2007, No. 4, pp. 70)*
Pub: Rogers Media
Ed: Gerry Blackwell. **Description:** The increase in the market share of Skype Technologies S.A.'s Internet phone service to 171 million users is discussed.

35132 ■ *"Slow but Steady into the Future" in Barron's (Vol. 88, July 7, 2008, No. 27, pp. M)*
Pub: Dow Jones & Co., Inc.
Ed: Mark Veverka. **Description:** Investors are advised to maintain their watch on the shares of business software company NetSuite. The company's chief executive officer, Zach Nelson, claims that the company has a 10-year lead on its competitors with the development of software-as-a service.

35133 ■ *Small Business Clustering Technology: Applications in Marketing, Management, Finance, and IT*
Pub: Idea Group Publishing
Ed: Robert C. MacGregor; Ann Hodgkinson. **Released:** June 2006. **Description:** An overview of the development and role of small business clusters in disciplines that include economics, marketing, management and information systems.

35134 ■ *SMEs and New Technologies: Learning E-Business and Development*
Pub: Palgrave Macmillan
Ed: Banji Oyelaran-Oyeyinka; Kaushalesh Lal. **Released:** October 2006. **Price:** $85.00. **Description:** Adoption and learning of new information technologies in developing nations is covered. New technologies are opening opportunities for small companies in these countries.

35135 ■ *"Social Media Event Slated for March 25" in Bellingham Business Journal (Vol. February 2010, pp. 3)*
Pub: Sound Publishing Inc.
Description: Center for Economic Vitality (CEV) and the Technology Alliance Group (TAG) will host the 2010 Social Media Conference at the McIntyre Hall Performing Arts & Conference Center in Mt. Vernon, Washington. The event will provide networking opportunities for attendees.

35136 ■ *"Social Networking Site for Moms" in Marketing to Women (Vol. 21, March 2008, No. 3, pp. 3)*
Pub: EPM Communications Inc.
Contact: Ira Mayer, President
E-mail: imayer@epmcom.com
Description: The Cradle is a social networking site devoted to pregnancy and new parenthood.

35137 ■ *"The Solution" in Entrepreneur (Vol. 37, October 2009, No. 10, pp. 71)*
Pub: Entrepreneur Media, Inc.
Ed: Jennifer Wang. **Description:** Ford's 2010 Transit Connect is a compact commercial van developed specifically for small business owners. The compact van offers an integrated in-dash computer system providing a cellular broadband connection.

35138 ■ *"Some Big Biotechs Buying Own Stock" in Boston Business Journal (Vol. 30, November 5, 2010, No. 41, pp. 1)*
Pub: Boston Business Journal
Ed: Julie M. Donnelly. **Description:** Biotechnology companies such as Biogen Idec and Genzyme Corporation are conducting stock buybacks as they look to invest their cash holdings. Other analysts see the buybacks as reluctance in committing to longer-term investments.

35139 ■ *"Sources" in Canadian Electronics (Vol. 23, August 2008, No. 5, pp. 12)*
Pub: Action Communication Inc.
Description: Directory of electronic manufacturers, distributors and representatives in Canada is provided. The list presents distributors and representatives under each manufacturer.

35140 ■ *"The Spark's Back in Sanyo" in Barron's (Vol. 88, March 31, 2008, No. 13, pp. M9)*
Pub: Dow Jones & Company, Inc.
Ed: Jay Alabaster. **Description:** Things are looking up for Sanyo Electric after its string of calamities that range from major losses brought on by earthquake damage to its semiconductor operations and its near collapse and bailout. The company looks poised for a rebound as they are on track for their first net profit since 2003 and could beat its earnings forecast for 2008.

35141 ■ *"Spell It Out" in Entrepreneur (Vol. 36, April 2008, No. 4, pp. 123)*
Pub: Entrepreneur Media, Inc.
Ed: Emily Weisberg. **Description:** IM:It is an apparel and accessories company that markets products with instant messaging (IM) acronyms and emoticons. Examples of these are 'LOL' and 'GTG'. Other details on IM:It products are discussed.

35142 ■ *"A Sports Extravaganza - To Go" in Canadian Business (Vol. 79, June 19, 2006, No. 13, pp. 21)*
Pub: Rogers Media
Ed: Andy Holloway. **Description:** Television broadcasting industry in Canada utilizing advanced technologies like mobile television and internet protocol television in broadcasting major sports events. Large number of new technologies are being invented to support increasing demand.

35143 ■ *"Staffing Firm Grows by Following Own Advice-Hire a Headhunter" in Crain's Detroit Business (Vol. 24, October 6, 2008, No. 40, pp. 1)*
Pub: Crain Communications, Inc.
Ed: Sherri Begin. **Description:** Profile of Venator Holdings L.L.C., a staffing firm that provides searches for companies in need of financial-accounting and technical employees; the firm's revenue has increased from $1.1 million in 2003 to a projected $11.5 million this year due to a climate in which more people are exiting the workforce than are coming in with those particular specialized skills and the need for a temporary, flexible workforce for contract placements at companies that do not want to take on the

legacy costs associated with permanent employees. The hiring of an external headhunter to find the right out-of-state manager for Venator is also discussed.

35144 ■ *"STAR TEC Incubator's Latest Resident Shows Promise" in The Business Journal-Serving Greater Tampa Bay (August 8, 2008)*
Pub: American City Business Journals, Inc.
Ed: Jane Meinhardt. **Description:** Field Forensics Inc., a resident of the STAR Technology Enterprise Center, has grown after being admitted into the business accelerator. The producer of defense and security devices and equipment has doubled 2007 sales as of 2008.

35145 ■ *"State Efforts to Boost Contract Efficiency Hurt Smaller Firms" in Boston Business Journal (Vol. 27, November 9, 2007, No. 41, pp. 1)*
Pub: American City Business Journals Inc.
Ed: Lisa van der Pool. **Description:** Massachusetts Operational Services Division, which provides statewide telecommunications and data infrastructure contracts, announced that it is cutting the list of companies on the new contract from twelve to six. The cost-cutting efforts began in 2005, after a review by an independent consultant advised the state to adopt strategies that would save millions of dollars.

35146 ■ *"State of Play" in Canadian Business (Vol. 79, June 19, 2006, No. 13, pp. 25)*
Pub: Rogers Media
Ed: Andrew Wahl; Zena Olijnyk; Jeff Sanford. **Description:** Top 100 information technology companies in Canada are ranked by their market capitalization as of June 1. The statistics that show the revenues of these companies are also presented.

35147 ■ *"Sticking to Stories; Havey Ovshinksy Changes Method, Keeps the Mission" in Crain's Detroit Business (Vol. 24, March 31, 2008)*
Pub: Crain Communications, Inc.
Ed: Daniel Duggan. **Description:** Profile of Harvey Ovshinsky, an award-winning documentary filmmaker who has reinvented his work with corporations who want to market themselves with the transition to digital media. His company, HKO Media, takes Ovshinsky's art of storytelling and enhances it through multimedia operations on the Internet through a joint venture with a man he once mentored, Bob Kernen.

35148 ■ *"STMicroelectronics" in Canadian Electronics (Vol. 23, February 2008, No. 1, pp. 1)*
Pub: CLB Media Inc.
Description: STMicroelectronics, a semiconductor maker, revealed that it plans to acquire Genesis Microchip Inc. Genesis develops image and video processing systems. It was reported that the acquisition has been approved by Genesis' Board of Directors. It is expected that Genesis will enhance STMicroelectronics' technological capabilities.

35149 ■ *"The Story Of Diane Greene" in Barron's (Vol. 88, July 14, 2008, No. 28, pp. 31)*
Pub: Dow Jones & Co., Inc.
Ed: Mark Veverka. **Description:** Discusses the ousting of Diane Greene as a chief executive of VMWare, a developer of virtualization software, after the firm went public; in this case Greene, a brilliant engineer, should not be negatively impacted by the decision because it is common for companies to bring in new executive leadership that is more operations oriented after the company goes public.

35150 ■ *"Study Puts Hub On Top of the Tech Heap" in Boston Business Journal (Vol. 30, November 26, 2010, No. 44, pp. 1)*
Pub: Boston Business Journal
Ed: Galen Moore. **Description:** The Ewing Marion Kauffman Foundation ranked Massachusetts at the top in its evaluations of states' innovative industries, government leadership, and education. Meanwhile, research blog formDs.com also ranked Massachusetts number one in terms of venture-capital financings per capita.

35151 ■ *"Suited for Success" in Retail Merchandiser (Vol. 51, July-August 2011, No. 4, pp. 6)*
Pub: Phoenix Media Corporation
Description: MyBestFit is a size-matching body scanner that helps consumers find the perfect size clothing for themselves, giving brick and mortar retailers an edge on ecommerce competitors.

35152 ■ *"The Superfluous Position" in Entrepreneur (Vol. 37, July 2009, No. 7, pp. 62)*
Pub: Entrepreneur Media, Inc.
Description: Profile of an anonymous editor at a multimedia company that publishes tourism guides who shares his experiences in dealing with an officemate who was promoted as creative manager of content. Everyone was irritated by this person, who would constantly do something to justify his new title. The biggest problem was the fact that this person didn't have a clear job description.

35153 ■ *"The Superpower Dilemma" in Canadian Business (Vol. 83, August 17, 2010, No. 13-14, pp. 42)*
Pub: Rogers Media Ltd.
Description: Canada has been an energy superpower partly because it controls the energy source and the production means, particularly of fossil fuels. However, Canada's status as superpower could diminish if it replaces petroleum exports with renewable technology for using sources of energy available globally.

35154 ■ *"A Swifter, Better Marketplace" in Barron's (Vol. 89, July 13, 2009, No. 28, pp. M13)*
Pub: Dow Jones & Co., Inc.
Ed: Eric W. Noll. **Description:** Listed-derivatives market is moving towards greater trading through computerized systems with an emphasis on speed and innovation. The market for listed options is also being changed by new techniques from other markets such as algorithmic trading, dark pools, and new-order priority systems.

35155 ■ *"Symbility Solutions Joins Motion Computing Partner Program" in Canadian Corporate News (May 14, 2007)*
Pub: Comtex News Network Inc.
Description: Symbility Solutions Inc., a wholly owned subsidiary of Automated Benefits Corp., announced an agreement with Alliance Partner of Motion Computing, a leader in wireless communications and mobile computing, in which both companies will invest in a sales and marketing strategy that focuses specifically on the insurance market.

35156 ■ *"Tabular Dreams" in Canadian Business (Vol. 80, February 12, 2007, No. 4, pp. 36)*
Pub: Rogers Media
Ed: Christina Campbell. **Description:** The research of Raymor Industries in developing carbon nanotubes by bonding carbon atoms using high technology is discussed.

35157 ■ *"Taiwan Technology Initiatives Foster Growth" in Canadian Electronics (Vol. 23, February 2008, No. 1, pp. 28)*
Pub: CLB Media Inc.
Description: A study conducted by the Market Intelligence Center shows that currently, Taiwan is the world's larges producer of information technology products such as motherboards, servers, and LCD monitors. In 2006, Taiwan's LED industry reached a production value of NTD 21 billion. This push into the LED sector shows the Ministry of Economic Affairs' plan to target industries that are environmentally friendly.

35158 ■ *"Taking on Intel" in Canadian Business (Vol. 79, October 23, 2006, No. 21, pp. 27)*
Pub: Rogers Media
Ed: Andrew Wahl. **Description:** The decision of ATI Technologies Inc., a Canadian computer peripherals company to acquire cash and stocks worth US$5.4-billion from American microprocessor maker Advanced Micro Devices Inc., is discussed.

35159 ■ *"Taking the Steps Into the Clouds" in New Hampshire Business Review (Vol. 33, March 25, 2011, No. 6, pp. 19)*
Pub: Business Publications Inc.
Ed: Tim Wessels. **Description:** Cloud services include Internet and Web security, spam filtering, message archiving, work group collaboration, IT asset management, help desk and disaster recovery backup.

35160 ■ *"Tale of a Gun" in Canadian Business (Vol. 80, February 26, 2007, No. 5, pp. 37)*
Pub: Rogers Media
Ed: Matthew McClearn. **Description:** The technology behind automated ballistic identification systems, which can be used to analyze fired ammunition components and link them to crime guns and suspects, developed by Canadian companies is presented.

35161 ■ *"Tale of the Tape: IPhone Vs. G1" in Advertising Age (Vol. 79, October 27, 2008, No. 40, pp. 6)*
Pub: Crain Communications, Inc.
Ed: Rita Chang. **Description:** T-Mobile's G1 has been positioned as the first serious competitor to Apple's iPhone. G1 is the first mobile phone to run on the Google-backed, open-source platform Android.

35162 ■ *"Taylor Tests Land Grant Program" in Austin Business Journal (Vol. 31, June 3, 2011, No. 13, pp. 1)*
Pub: American City Business Journals Inc.
Ed: Vicky Garza. **Description:** Taylor Economic Development Corporation implemented a land grant program called Build On Our Lot to lure businesses to Taylor City, Austin, Texas. They are targeting small businesses, especially those in the renewable energy, advanced manufacturing, technical services and food products. Program details are included.

35163 ■ *"The Tech 100" in Canadian Business (Vol. 81, July 21, 2008, No. 11, pp. 48)*
Pub: Rogers Media Ltd.
Ed: Calvin Leung. **Description:** Absolute Software Corp. Day4 Energy Inc., Sandvine Corp., Norsat International Inc. and Call Genie Inc. are the five technology firms included in the annual ranking of top companies in Canada by market capitalization. The services and the one-year total return potential of the companies are presented.

35164 ■ *"Tech Coaltion Warns Takeover Spree is Nigh" in Globe & Mail (February 6, 2007, pp. B1)*
Pub: CTVglobemedia Publishing Inc.
Ed: Steven Chase. **Description:** The declaration by an alliance of technology-rich companies, that the huge credits that these companies have to endure due to research and development activities may lead to company takeovers, is discussed.

35165 ■ *"Tech Data Launches Unified Communications and Network Security Specialized Business Units" in Wireless News (October 22,2009)*
Pub: Close-Up Media
Description: Responding to the growing demand for unified communications and network security, Tech Data announced the formation of two new Specialized Business Units.

35166 ■ *"Tech Giving 2.0" in Boston Business Journal (Vol. 31, August 5, 2011, No. 28, pp. 1)*
Pub: Boston Business Journal
Ed: Mary Moore. **Description:** Entrepreneurs and venture capitalists in Boston have launched Technology Underwriting Greater Good, the tech industry's answer to the criticism that they are not charitable. The foundation finances nonprofits that aid young

people through entrepreneurship, education and life experience. Other tech firms in Boston doing charitable works are discussed.

35167 ■ *"Tech Godfather Steve Walker Winding Down Howard Venture Fund" in Baltimore Business Journal (Vol. 27, December 11, 2009, No. 31)*
Pub: American City Business Journals
Ed: Scott Dance. **Description:** Steve Walker, president of venture capital fund firm Walker Ventures, will be closing the Howard County, Maryland-based firm as the economic situation is finding it difficult to recover investor's money. According to Walker, the economy also constrained investors from financing venture funds. Despite the closure, Walker will continue his work in the local angel investing community.

35168 ■ *"Tech Investing: March's Long Road" in Canadian Business (Vol. 80, January 29, 2007, No. 3, pp. 67)*
Pub: Rogers Media
Ed: Calvin Leung. **Description:** The efforts of March Networks, a manufacturer of digital surveillance equipment, from the decline in the price of its shares at the beginning of the year 2007 are described.

35169 ■ *"Tech Tax Heroes Go from Political Neophytes to Savvy Fundraisers" in Baltimore Business Journal (Vol. 27, November 20, 2009, No. 28)*
Pub: American City Business Journals
Ed: Scott Dance. **Description:** A group of computer services and information technology executives in Maryland have arranged a private dinner that will function as a fundraiser for Governor Martin O'Malley and Lieutenant Governor Anthony Brown. The event is seen as an effort to ensure the industry's involvement in the state after fighting for the repeal of the tech tax in 2007.

35170 ■ *"TechLift Strives to Fill in Gaps in Entrepreneurial Support Efforts" in Crain's Cleveland Business (November 12, 2007)*
Pub: Crain Communications, Inc.
Ed: Marsha Powers. **Description:** Profile of the program, TechLift, a new business model launched by NorTech, that is aiming to provide assistance to technology-based companies that may not be a good fit for other entrepreneurial support venues.

35171 ■ *"Technically Speaking" in Black Enterprise (Vol. 38, February 2008, No. 7, pp. 64)*
Pub: Earl G. Graves Publishing Co. Inc.
Ed: Sonia Alleyne. **Description:** Marketing manager for Texas Instruments discusses the Strategic Marketing of Technology Products course offered at the California Institute of Technology. The course helps turn products into profits.

35172 ■ *Technological Entrepreneurship*
Pub: Edward Elgar Publishing, Incorporated
Ed: Donald Siegel. **Released:** October 2006. **Price:** $230.00. **Description:** Technological entrepreneurship at universities is discussed. The book covers four related topics: university licensing and patenting; science parks and incubators; university-based startups; and the role of academic science in entrepreneurship.

35173 ■ *"Technology Drivers to Boost Your Bottom Line" in Franchising World (Vol. 42, August 2010, No. 8, pp. 15)*
Pub: International Franchise Association
Ed: Dan Dugal. **Description:** Technological capabilities are expanding quickly and smart franchises should stay updated on all the new developments, including smart phones, global positioning systems, and social media networks.

35174 ■ *"Technology Protects Lottery" in Arkansas Business (Vol. 26, September 28, 2009, No. 39, pp. 1)*
Pub: Journal Publishing Inc.
Ed: George Waldon. **Description:** Arkansas Lottery Commission was initially criticized for what was seen as a major breach in security protocol by revealing the exact location of 26 million lottery tickets during a publicity stunt in which the media was invited to the main distribution center; however, due to the high-tech security that has been implemented the tickets are worthless until their status is changed after passing through multiple security scans.

35175 ■ *"Technology and Returnable Asset Management" in Canadian Electronics (Vol. 23, February 2008, No. 1, pp. 6)*
Pub: CLB Media Inc.
Ed: Mark Borkowski. **Description:** Peter Kastner, president of Vestigo Corporation, believes that public companies without an asset track, trace, and control system in place could face Sarbanes-Oakley liability if error-prone processes result to misstatements of asset inventory positions. He also thinks that the system can improve return on assets by increasing the utilization of returnables.

35176 ■ *"Tech's Payout Problem" in Barron's (Vol. 90, September 13, 2010, No. 37, pp. 19)*
Pub: Barron's Editorial & Corporate Headquarters
Ed: Andrew Bary. **Description:** Big tech companies have the potential to be good dividend payers, but instead just hoard their cash for acquisitions and share buybacks. If these companies offered more dividends, they could boost their shares and attract more income-oriented investors.

35177 ■ *"TELUS Drawing More Power From Its Wireless Operations" in Globe & Mail (February 17, 2007, pp. B3)*
Pub: CTVglobemedia Publishing Inc.
Ed: Catherine McLean. **Description:** TELUS Corp., the fast-growing wireless business company, posted tripled profits in the fourth quarter of 2006. The revenues of the company increased 8 percent in the same period.

35178 ■ *"Texas Fold 'Em" in Canadian Business (Vol. 79, October 9, 2006, No. 20, pp. 44)*
Pub: Rogers Media
Ed: John Gray. **Description:** New policies of the United States law makers for the online casino industries that could force many of them out of business are discussed.

35179 ■ *"They Like It Cold" in Business Journal Portland (Vol. 27, October 15, 2010, No. 33, pp. 1)*
Pub: Portland Business Journal
Ed: Erik Siemers. **Description:** Ajinomoto Frozen Foods USA Inc. has been investing in its Portland, Oregon facility. The company has completed a new rice production line. It has also spent $1.2 million on a new packaging technology.

35180 ■ *"Thinking Strategically About Technology" in Franchising World (Vol. 42, August 2010, No. 8, pp. 9)*
Pub: International Franchise Association
Ed: Bruce Franson. **Description:** Nearly 25 percent of companies waste money from their technology budget. Most of the budget is spent on non-strategic software. Ways to spend money on technology for any franchise are examined.

35181 ■ *"Thumbing Around" in Canadian Business (Vol. 79, October 9, 2006, No. 20, pp. 143)*
Pub: Rogers Media
Ed: Gerry Blackwell. **Description:** The features, functions of Cruzer Titanium, a serial bus standard to interface device developed by SanDisk Corporation are discussed.

35182 ■ *"Tim Armstrong" in Canadian Business (Vol. 81, July 21, 2008, No. 11, pp. 10)*
Pub: Rogers Media Ltd.
Ed: Calvin Leung. **Description:** Interview with Tim Armstrong who is the president of advertising and commerce department of Google Inc. for North America; the information technology company executive talked about the emerging trends and changes to YouTube made by the company since its acquisition in 2006.

35183 ■ *"A Timely Boon for Small Investors" in Barron's (Vol. 88, March 24, 2008, No. 12, pp. 48)*
Pub: Dow Jones & Company, Inc.
Ed: Theresa W. Carey. **Description:** Nasdaq Data Store's new program called Market Replay allows investors to accurately track stock price movements. The replay can be as long as a day of market time and allows investors to determine whether they executed stock trades at the best possible price.

35184 ■ *"TiVo, Domino's Team to Offer Pizza Ordering by DVR" in Advertising Age (Vol. 79, November 17, 2008, No. 43, pp. 48)*
Pub: Crain Communications, Inc.
Ed: Brian Steinberg. **Description:** Domino's Pizza and TiVo are teaming up to make it possible for customers to order from the restaurant straight from their DVR. The companies see that this kind of interactive television and consumer experience will only serve to generate more sales as the customer can be exposed to a fuller range of menu selections and will not have to interrupt their viewing, while workers can spend more time making the product.

35185 ■ *"To Build for the Future, Reach Beyond the Skies" in Canadian Business (Vol. 83, June 15, 2010, No. 10, pp. 11)*
Pub: Rogers Media Ltd.
Ed: Richard Branson. **Description:** Richard Branson says that tackling an engineering challenge or a scientific venture is a real adventure for an entrepreneur. Branson discusses Virgin's foray into the aviation business and states that at Virgin, they build for the future.

35186 ■ *"TomTom GO910: On the Road Again" in Black Enterprise (Vol. 37, January 2007, No. 6, pp. 52)*
Pub: Earl G. Graves Publishing Co. Inc.
Ed: Stephanie Young. **Description:** TomTom GO 910 is a GPS navigator that offers detailed maps of the U.S., Canada, and Europe. Consumers view their routes by a customizable LCD screen showing everything from the quickest to the shortest routes available or how to avoid toll roads. Business travelers may find this product invaluable as it also functions as a cell phone and connects to a variety of other multi-media devices.

35187 ■ *"Too Much Precaution About Biotech Corn" in Barron's (Vol. 88, March 17, 2008, No. 11, pp. 54)*
Pub: Dow Jones & Company, Inc.
Ed: Mark I. Schwartz. **Description:** In the U.S., 90 percent of cultivated soybeans are biotech varietals as well as 60 percent of the corn. Farmers have significantly reduced their reliance on pesticides in the growing of biotech corn. Biotech cotton cultivation has brought hundreds of millions of dollars in net financial gains to farmers. The European Union has precluded the cultivation or sale of biotech crops within its border.

35188 ■ *"Top 100 Consolidate Gains" in Hispanic Business (Vol. 30, July-August 2008, No. 7-8, pp. 30)*
Pub: Hispanic Business, Inc.
Ed: Richard Kaplan. **Description:** Data developed by HispanTelligence on the increase in revenue posted by the top 100 fastest-growing U.S. Hispanic firms over the last five years is reported. Despite the economic downturn, the service sector, IT and health suppliers showed an increase in revenue whereas construction companies showed a marginal slump in revenue growth.

35189 ■ *"Top IPhone Apps" in Advertising Age (Vol. 79, December 15, 2008, No. 46, pp. 17)*
Pub: Crain Communications, Inc.
Ed: Marissa Miley. **Description:** Free and low cost applications for the iPhone are described including Evernote, an application that allows users to outsource their memory to keep track of events, notes, ides and more; Handshake, a way for users to exchange business cards and pictures across Wi-Fi and 3G; CityTransit, an interactive map of the New York subway system that uses GPS technology to

find nearby stations and also tells the user if a train is out of commission that day; and Stage Hand which allows users to deliver a presentation, control timing and slide order on the spot.

35190 ■ *"A Torch in the Darkness" in Canadian Business (Vol. 83, August 17, 2010, No. 13-14, pp. 66)*
Pub: Rogers Media Ltd.
Ed: Joe Castaldo. **Description:** Research In Motion (RIM) unveiled the BlackBerry Touch, featuring a touch screen as well as a physical keyboard, in an attempt to repel competitors and expand share in the consumer smart phone market. RIM shares have fallen 43 percent from its peak in 2009.

35191 ■ *"The Total Cost of Ignorance: Avoiding Top Tech Mistakes" in Black Enterprise (Vol. 38, October 2007, No. 3, pp. 64)*
Pub: Earl G. Graves Publishing Co. Inc.
Ed: Alwin A.D. Jones. **Description:** Cost of data loss for any small business can be devastating; lack of security is another mistake companies make when it comes to technology.

35192 ■ *"Touching the Future" in Canadian Business (Vol. 81, July 21, 2008, No. 11, pp. 41)*
Pub: Rogers Media Ltd.
Ed: Matt McClearn. **Description:** Microsoft Corp. has launched a multi-touch product which is both a software and hardware technology called Microsoft Surface. The innovative product allows people to use it at the same time, however touch-based computers are reported to be around $100,000. Other features and benefits of the product are presented.

35193 ■ *"Toward a Better Future" in Canadian Business (Vol. 83, August 17, 2010, No. 13-14, pp. 51)*
Pub: Rogers Media Ltd.
Description: A look at certain realities in order to build a better future for Canada's energy industry is presented. Canada must focus on making the oil cleaner, instead of replacing it with another source since dependency on oil will remain in this lifetime. Canada must also develop solutions toward clean technology power sources.

35194 ■ *"Training Center Wants to be College" in Austin Business JournalInc. (Vol. 29, November 13, 2009, No. 36, pp. A1)*
Pub: American City Business Journals
Ed: Sandra Zaragoza. **Description:** Texas-based CyberTex Institute, a job training center, has established technical careers in an effort to obtain federal accreditation as a college. A college status would allow CyperTex to extend financial assistance to students. Aside from potentially having an enlarged student body and expanded campus, CyberTex would be allowed to engage in various training programs.

35195 ■ *"Training the Troops: Battlefield Simulations Bring Growth to UNITECH" in Black Enterprise (Vol. 38, February 2008, No. 7, pp. 30)*
Pub: Earl G. Graves Publishing Co. Inc.
Ed: Cliff Hocker. **Description:** Universal Systems and Technology (UNITECH) received a total of over $45 million U.S. Department of Defense orders during September and October 2007. UNITECH designs and manufactures battlefield simulation devices used to train troops in the Army and Marine Corps.

35196 ■ *"The Transparent Supply Chain" in Harvard Business Review (Vol. 88, October 2010, No. 10, pp. 76)*
Pub: Harvard Business School Publishing
Ed: Steve New. **Description:** Examination of the use of new technologies to create a transparent supply chain, such as next-generation 2D bar codes in clothing labels that can provide data on a garment's provenance.

35197 ■ *"The Traveler's Traveler" in Entrepreneur (Vol. 37, September 2009, No. 9, pp. 22)*
Pub: Entrepreneur Media, Inc.
Ed: Kim Orr. **Description:** Business travel columnist Joe Sharkey says technology may someday replace business travel. Airlines are realizing that a part of the business travel market has disappeared. Sharkey also says airlines can never get those customers back.

35198 ■ *"Turnaround Plays: The Return of Wi-LAN" in Canadian Business (Vol. 80, January 29, 2007, No. 3, pp. 68)*
Pub: Rogers Media
Ed: Joe Castaldo. **Description:** The recovery of the wireless equipment manufacturing firm Wi-LAN from near-bankruptcy, under the leadership of Jim Skippen, is described.

35199 ■ *"Twice the Innovation, Half the Tears" in Business Courier (Vol. 24, March 7, 2008, No. 48, pp. 1)*
Pub: American City Business Journals, Inc.
Ed: Lisa Biank Fasig. **Description:** Procter & Gamble was able to develop a pant-style diaper called Pampers First Pants by creating a virtual, three-dimensional baby. The company was able to reduce the number of real mock-ups that it had to make by putting the diapers on the virtual baby first. Specifics about product designs were not revealed by the company.

35200 ■ *"Two Local Firms Make Inc. List: Minority Business" in Indianapolis Business Journal (Vol. 31, August 30, 2010, No. 26, pp. 13A)*
Pub: Indianapolis Business Journal Corporation
Description: Smart IT staffing agency and Entap Inc., an IT outsourcing firm were among the top ten fastest growing black-owned businesses in the U.S. by Inc. magazine.

35201 ■ *"Unbreakable" in Canadian Business (Vol. 79, October 9, 2006, No. 20, pp. 111)*
Pub: Rogers Media
Ed: Robert Hercz. **Description:** The features and functions of Neutrino, an embedded operating system developed by QNX Software Systems are discussed.

35202 ■ *"Valenti: Roots of Financial Crisis Go Back to 1998" in Crain's Detroit Business (Vol. 24, October 6, 2008, No. 40, pp. 25)*
Pub: Crain Communications, Inc.
Ed: Tom Henderson; Nathan Skid. **Description:** Interview with Sam Valenti III who is the chairman and CEO of Valenti Capital L.L.C., a wealth-management firm; Valenti discusses in detail the history that led up to the current economic crisis as well as his prediction for the future of the country.

35203 ■ *"VC Boosts WorkForce; Livonia Software Company to Add Sales, Marketing Staff" in Crain's Detroit Business (March 24, 2008)*
Pub: Crain Communications, Inc.
Ed: Tom Henderson. **Description:** WorkForce Software Inc., a company that provides software to manage payroll processes and oversee compliance with state and federal regulations and with union rules, plans to use an investment of $5.5 million in venture capital to hire more sales and marketing staff.

35204 ■ *The Venture Cafe*
Pub: Business Plus
Ed: Teresa Esser. **Released:** 2002. **Description:** Research covering the types of entrepreneurs who build new, high-technology ventures from the ground up. Author interviewed over 150 high-tech professionals in order to gather information to help others start high-tech companies.

35205 ■ *"VeriFone Announces Global Security Solutions Business" in Marketing Weekly News (October 3, 2009)*
Pub: Investment Weekly News
Description: Focused on delivering innovative security solutions, VeriFone Holdings, Inc. announced the formation of its Global Security Solutions Business Unit, including VeriShield Protect, an end-to-end encryption to protect cardholder data throughout the merchant and processor systems. The business will focus on consulting, sales and implementation of these new products in order to help retailers and processors protect customer data.

35206 ■ *"Verizon Small Business Awards Give Companies a Technology Edge" in Hispanic Business (July-August 2009, pp. 32)*
Pub: Hispanic Business
Ed: Patricia Marroquin. **Description:** Verizon Wireless awards grants to twenty-four companies in California. The winning businesses ranged from barbershop to coffee shop, tattoo parlor to florist.

35207 ■ *"Verizon's Big Gamble Comes Down to the Wire" in Globe & Mail (February 3, 2007, pp. B1)*
Pub: CTVglobemedia Publishing Inc.
Ed: Catherine McLean. **Description:** The launch of a new broadband service by Verizon Communications Inc. based on fibre optic cable technology is discussed. The company has spent $23 billion for introducing the new service.

35208 ■ *"Video Surveillance Enters Digital Era, Makes Giant Strides" in Arkansas Business (Vol. 26, September 28, 2009, No. 39, pp. 1)*
Pub: Journal Publishing Inc.
Ed: Jamie Walden. **Description:** Arkansas business owners are finding that the newest technology in video surveillance is leading to swift apprehension of thieves due to the high-quality digital imagery now being captured on surveillance equipment. Motion detection software for these systems is enhancing the capabilities of these systems and providing opportunities for businesses that would normally have problems integrating these systems.

35209 ■ *"Virgin Mobile has Big Plans for Year Two" in Globe & Mail (March 6, 2006, pp. B5)*
Pub: CTVglobemedia Publishing Inc.
Ed: Catherine McLean. **Description:** The business growth plans of Virgin Mobile Canada are presented.

35210 ■ *"The Virtual Office" in Canadian Business (Vol. 80, April 9, 2007, No. 8, pp. 64)*
Pub: Rogers Media
Ed: Andrew Wahl. **Description:** The business operation of Eloqua which runs all its IT systems using its own online software is discussed.

35211 ■ *"Vonage V-Phone: Use Your Laptop to Make Calls Via the Internet" in Black Enterprise (Vol. 37, January 2007, No. 6, pp. 52)*
Pub: Earl G. Graves Publishing Co. Inc.
Ed: James C. Johnson. **Description:** Overview of the Vonage V-Phone, which is small flash drive device that lets you make phone calls through a high-speed Internet connection and plugs into any computer's USB port. Business travels may find this product to be a wonderful solution as it includes 250MB of memory and can store files, digital photos, MP3s, and more.

35212 ■ *"VTech Targets Tots With a Wee Wii" in Advertising Age (Vol. 79, September 8, 2008, No. 33, pp. 14)*
Pub: Crain Communications, Inc.
Ed: Beth Snyder Bulik. **Description:** V-Motion is a video-game console targeting 3-to-7-year-olds and is manufactured by educational toy company VTech. The company is marketing the product as a kind of Wii for preschoolers and hopes to build a formidable brand presence in the kids' electronics market.

35213 ■ *"Weathering the BlackBerry Storm" in Hispanic Business (January-February 2009, pp. 52)*
Pub: Hispanic Business
Ed: Jeremy Nisen. **Description:** Profile of BlackBerry Storm, the smartphone from Research in Motion.

35214 ■ *"Web Biz Brulant Surfing for Acquisition Candidates" in Crain's Cleveland Business (Vol. 28, December 3, 2007, No. 48, pp. 6)*
Pub: Crain Communications, Inc.
Ed: Chuck Soder. **Description:** Brulant Inc., a provider of web development and marketing services, is looking to acquire other companies after growing for five years straight. The company is one of the largest technology firms in Northeast Ohio.

35215 ■ *"The Web Gets Real" in Canadian Business (Vol. 79, July 17, 2006, No. 14-15, pp. 19)*
Pub: Rogers Media
Ed: Andrew Wahl. **Description:** Ron Lake's efforts of bringing the virtual and physical worlds more closely together by using Geographic Markup Language (GML) are presented.

35216 ■ *"What's Working Now: In Providing Jobs for North Carolinians" in Business North Carolina (Vol. 28, February 2008, No. 2, pp. 16)*
Pub: Business North Carolina
Ed: Edward Martin, Frank Maley. **Description:** Individuals previously employed in the furniture, tobacco, or textile manufacturing sectors have gone back to school to be trained in new sectors in the area such as life sciences, finances and other emerging sectors.

35217 ■ *"Who's Next?" in Boston Business Journal (Vol. 27, November 16, 2007, No. 42, pp. 1)*
Pub: American City Business Journals Inc.
Ed: Lisa van der Pool. **Description:** Boston, Massachusetts' burgeoning technology and biotech industries along with rising billing rates make it a unique legal market. Law firms cross the threshold either by merging with or acquiring a smaller law firm. Boston as a unique legal market is discussed.

35218 ■ *"Why Intel Should Dump Its Flash-Memory Business" in Barron's (Vol. 88, March 10, 2008, No. 10, pp. 35)*
Pub: Dow Jones & Company, Inc.
Ed: Eric J. Savitz. **Description:** Intel Corp. must sell its NAND flash-memory business as soon as it possibly can to the highest bidder to focus on its PC processor business and take advantage of other business opportunities. Apple should consider a buyback of 10 percent of the company's shares to lift its stock.

35219 ■ *"Why-Max?" in Canadian Business (Vol. 81, July 22, 2008, No. 12-13, pp. 19)*
Pub: Rogers Media Ltd.
Ed: Andrew Wahl. **Description:** Nascent technology known as LTE (Long Term Evolution) is expected to challenge Intel's WiMax wireless technology as the wireless broadband standard. LTE , which is believed to be at least two years behind WiMax in development, is likely to be supported by wireless and mobile-phone carriers. Views and information on WiMax and LTE are presented.

35220 ■ *"Why Some Get Shaften By Google Pricing" in Advertising Age (Vol. 79, July 14, 2008, No. 7, pp. 3)*
Pub: Crain Communications, Inc.
Ed: Abbey Klaassen. **Description:** Google's search advertising is discussed as well as the company's pricing structure for these ads.

35221 ■ *"Wi-Fi Finds Its Way Despite Nixed Plan for Free System" in Crain's Cleveland Business (Vol. 28, November 12, 2007, No. 45, pp. 3)*
Pub: Crain Communications, Inc.
Ed: Jay Miller. **Description:** Discusses the issues facing Cleveland and Northeast Ohio concerning their proposal to offer citizens wireless Internet services for free or a small fee.

35222 ■ *"Wi-Fi On Steroids: Will WiMAX Provide the Juice For Souped-Up Connections?" in Black Enterprise (November 2007)*
Pub: Earl G. Graves Publishing Co. Inc.
Ed: Fiona Haley. **Description:** WiMAX, Worldwide Interoperability for Microwave Access in the U.S. WiMax is technology that moves data and connects faster and at greater distances than before.

35223 ■ *"The Wiki-Powered Workplace" in Workforce Management (Vol. 88, November 16, 2009, No. 12, pp. 8)*
Pub: Crain Communications Inc.
Description: Many organizations are successfully using wikis inside the corporate structure for business communications and knowledge sharing. Wikis can be a very powerful tool due to the inherent transparency that comes with allowing everything to be edited with the accountability of seeing who is doing the editing. A brilliant employee may be noticed sooner because they are doing work in the wiki and the work is being judged on its own merit.

35224 ■ *"Will Work for Equity" in Inc. (March 2008, pp. 50, 52)*
Pub: Gruner & Jahr USA Publishing
Ed: Ryan McCarthy. **Description:** Profile of Dave Graham and his information technology company; Graham built his business by taking equity in client firms rather than charging fees. Four tips to consider before signing a work-for-equity business deal are outlined.

35225 ■ *Winner Take All: How Competitiveness Shapes the Fate of Nations*
Pub: Basic Books
Ed: Richard J. Elkus Jr. **Released:** 2009. **Price:** $27. 00. **Description:** American government and misguided business practices has allowed the U.S. to fall behind other countries in various market sectors such as cameras and televisions, as well as information technologies. It will take a national strategy to for America to regain its lead in crucial industries.

35226 ■ *"Wireless: Full Service" in Entrepreneur (Vol. 35, October 2007, No. 10, pp. 60)*
Pub: Entrepreneur Media Inc.
Ed: Amanda C. Kooser. **Description:** Palm Foleo, the $599 smart phone enables users to access and compose email, browse the Internet, view documents and play Powerpoint files. It weighs 2.5 pounds and has a 10-inch screen. Other features, such as built-in WiFi are described.

35227 ■ *"Wireless Provider's Star Grows $283 Million Brighter" in Hispanic Business (July-August 2007, pp. 60)*
Pub: Hispanic Business
Description: Profile of Brightstar Corporation, the world's largest wireless phone distribution and supply chain reported record growth in 2007.

35228 ■ *"Women Losing IT Ground" in Marketing to Women (Vol. 21, February 2008, No. 2, pp. 6)*
Pub: EPM Communications Inc.
Contact: Ira Mayer, President
E-mail: imayer@epmcom.com
Description: According to a study conducted by The National Center for Women & Information Technology, women in technology are losing ground. Statistical data included.

35229 ■ *"Work Naked" in Canadian Business (Vol. 80, March 12, 2007, No. 6, pp. 33)*
Pub: Rogers Media
Ed: Andrew Wahl. **Description:** The disadvantages of teleworking for both employees and the company, in view of lack of an office environment and self-discipline on the part of workers, are discussed.

35230 ■ *"Work Smarter" in Entrepreneur (Vol. 36, April 2008, No. 4, pp. 70)*
Pub: Entrepreneur Media, Inc.
Ed: Amanda C. Kooser. **Description:** Online applications that address a business' particular needs are presented. These web applications offer email services, collaboration services of sharing and editing documents and presentations, and tie-ups with online social networking sites. Details on various web applications are provided.

35231 ■ *"A World of Investors" in Entrepreneur (Vol. 35, November 2007, No. 11, pp. 72)*
Pub: Entrepreneur Media Inc.
Ed: Gail Dutton. **Description:** Information technology services company mPortal Inc. raised nearly $15 million in financing from venture capital company Friedli Corporate Finance. The biggest international investors are European companies, while the venture capital market is growing in Asia.

35232 ■ *"World Wide Technology Expands" in Black Enterprise (Vol. 37, December 2006, No. 5, pp. 34)*
Pub: Earl G. Graves Publishing Co. Inc.
Ed: Marcia A. Wade. **Description:** World Wide Technology Inc. opened a streamlined, higher capacity 12,000-square-foot Integration Technology Center near its corporate headquarters in St. Louis. The new venture will transfer lower costs to customers.

35233 ■ *"XM Burning Through Cash to Catch Sirius" in Globe & Mail (April 17, 2007, pp. B5)*
Pub: CTVglobemedia Publishing Inc.
Ed: Grant Robertson. **Description:** The effort of XM Satellite Radio Holdings Inc. to spend about $45 million to increase sale of its radio in Canada is discussed.

35234 ■ *"XM Mulls Betting the Bank in Competitive Game of Subscriber Growth" in Globe & Mail (March 18, 2006, pp. B3)*
Pub: CTVglobemedia Publishing Inc.
Ed: Grant Robertson. **Description:** Canadian Satellite Radio Inc., XM Canada, president and Chief Operating Officer Stephen Tapp feel that establishing a profile in satellite radio to attract subscribers is a very big challenge. His views on the Canadian radio market are detailed.

35235 ■ *"XM and Sirius Satellite Radio Face Up to Their Losses and Decide to Get Hitched" in Globe & Mail (February 20, 2007, pp. B17)*
Pub: CTVglobemedia Publishing Inc.
Ed: Grant Robertson. **Description:** XM Satellite Radio and Sirius Satellite Radio are planning to merge operations, after years of losses. The possible merger could create a $13 billion company.

35236 ■ *"The Yahoo Family Tree" in Conde Nast Portfolio (Vol. 2, June 2008, No. 6, pp. 34)*
Pub: Conde Nast Publications
Contact: David Carey, President
Ed: Blaise Zerega. **Description:** Yahoo, founded in 1994 by Stanford students Jerry Yang and David Filo, is still an Internet powerhouse. The company's history is also outlined as well as the reasons in which Microsoft desperately wants to acquire the firm.

35237 ■ *"Yahoo! - Microsoft Pact: Alive Again?" in Barron's (Vol. 89, July 27, 2009, No. 30, pp. 8)*
Pub: Dow Jones & Co., Inc.
Ed: Mark Veverka. **Description:** Yahoo! reported higher than expected earnings in the second quarter of 2009 under CEO Carol Bartz who has yet to articulate her long-term vision and strategy for turning around the company. The media reported that Yahoo! and Microsoft are discussing an advertising-search partnership which should benefit both companies.

35238 ■ *"Young-Kee Kim; Deputy Director, Fermi National Accelerator Laboratory" in Crain's Chicago Business (Vol. 31, May 5, 2008, No. 18)*
Pub: Crain Communications, Inc.
Ed: Phuong Ly. **Description:** Profile of Young-Kee Kim who is the deputy director of Fermilab, a physics lab where scientists study the smallest particles in the universe; Ms. Kim was a researcher at Fermilab before becoming deputy director two years ago; Fermilab is currently home to the most powerful particle accelerator in the world and is struggling to compete with other countries despite cuts in federal funding.

35239 ■ *"Zebra's Changing Stripes" in Crain's Chicago Business (Vol. 31, November 17, 2008, No. 46, pp. 4)*
Pub: Crain Communications, Inc.
Ed: John Pletz. **Description:** Zebra Technologies Corp., the world's largest manufacturer of bar-code printers is profiled; the company's stock has plunged with shares declining 40 percent in the past three months grinding the firm's growth to a halt. Zebra's plans to regain revenue growth are also discussed.

SOURCES OF SUPPLY

35240 ■ *High-Tech Materials Alert*
Wiley-Blackwell
Contact: William J. Pesce, President
E-mail: wpesce@wiley.com
URL(s): apnf.org/frostbody.htm. **Released:** Monthly **Publication includes:** List of manufacturers and suppliers of high performance alloys, metals, ceramics, plastics, graphite, and other materials. **Entries include:** Company name, address, phone. Principal content is articles and analyses of new materials for industrial processes.

TRADE PERIODICALS

35241 ■ *Optics & Photonics News*
Pub: Optical Society of America
Contact: Christopher Dainty, President
Released: Monthly. **Price:** Free. **Description:** Concerned with optical research, instruction, applications, manufacturing, and equipment. Supplies information on developments in all branches of optics, such as space optics, medical optics, fiber optics, lasers, color optics, and optical communications. Recurring features include reports on Society activities, news of members, and a calendar of events.

35242 ■ *Robotics Online E-Newsletter*
Pub: Robotic Industries Association
Ed: Mary Kay Morel, Editor. **Released:** Quarterly. **Price:** Included in membership; Free. **Description:** Promotes the use and acceptance of robotic technology through the exchange of technical and trade-related information. Provides news of the Association and its affiliate organization, the Automated Imaging Association.

35243 ■ *Sensor Technology*
Pub: Technical Insights
Ed: Leo O'Connor, Editor. **Released:** Monthly. **Price:** $650, U.S. and Canada year; $710, elsewhere year. **Description:** Informs readers of the latest scientific and technological developments in the field of sensors. Focuses on process and machine control, including robotics; also covers environmental and medical uses. Recurring features include a calendar of events, news of research, book reviews, and columns titled Key Patents and Keep an Eye On.

CONSULTANTS

35244 ■ I.H.R. Solutions
3333 E Bayaud Ave., Ste. 219
Denver, CO 80209
Ph: (303)588-4243
Fax: (303)978-0473
Co. E-mail: dhollands@ihrsolutions.com
Contact: Deborah Hollands, Owner
E-mail: dhollands@ihrsolutions.com
Scope: Provides joint-venture and start-up human resource consulting services as well as advice on organization development for international human capital. Industries served: high-tech and telecommunications. **Founded:** 1997.

35245 ■ ProActive English
4355 SE 29th Ave.
Portland, OR 97202
Ph: (503)231-2906
Co. E-mail: infopae@proactive-english.com
URL: http://www.proactive-english.com
Contact: Margaret Lyman, Manager
E-mail: mlyman@proactive-english.com
Scope: Offers on-site individual and small group language and communication training. Sets up learning plans tailored to the needs and schedules of managers and executives who are non-native English speakers. Serves all industries. **Founded:** 1997. **Seminars:** Communicating in Business Situations; Presentations and Pronunciation; Tailored Curriculum; One-on-One Programs.

RESEARCH CENTERS

35246 ■ Georgia Institute of Technology - Advanced Technology Development Center (ATDC)
75 5th St. NW, Ste. 202
Atlanta, GA 30308
Ph: (404)894-3575
URL: http://atdc.org
Contact: Stephen Fleming, Director (Acting)
Services: Business assistance: to start-up technology companies; General management consulting; Technical and business management services: to entrepreneurs. **Founded:** 1979. **Publications:** *Technology Partners* (Quarterly).

35247 ■ National Center for Technology Planning (NCTP)
PO Box 2393
Tupelo, MS 38803-2393
Ph: (662)844-9630
Fax: (662)844-9630
Co. E-mail: larry@nctp.com
URL: http://www.nctp.com
Contact: Dr. Larry S. Anderson, Director
Services: Consulting. **Founded:** 1992. **Educational Activities:** Speeches and presentations; NCTP Workshops.

35248 ■ Progress Corporate Park
13709 Progress Blvd., Box 10
Alachua, FL 32615
Ph: (386)462-4040
Free: 877-457-6489
Fax: (386)462-3932
Co. E-mail: sandy@progresscorporatepark.com
URL: http://www.progresscorporatepark.com
Services: Assistance: in entrepreneurial development, commercialization of scientific and technological innovations, and international marketing. **Founded:** 1984.

35249 ■ University of California, Berkeley - Berkeley Roundtable on International Economy (BRIE)
2234 Piedmont Ave., MC 2322
Berkeley, CA 94720-2322
Ph: (510)642-3067
Fax: (510)643-6617
Co. E-mail: brie@berkeley.edu
URL: http://brie.berkeley.edu
Contact: Prof. Stephen S. Cohen, Director
Founded: 1982. **Publications:** *BRIE Working Paper Series.*

35250 ■ University of Illinois at Urbana-Champaign - Technology Commercialization Laboratory (TCL)
2004 S Wright St.
Urbana, IL 61802
Ph: (217)244-7742
Fax: (217)333-4050
Co. E-mail: kybrown@uiuc.edu
URL: http://www.researchpark.uiuc.edu
Services: Assistance in identifying specialists in the areas of accounting, business start-up, planning and budgeting, and financial management; Provides specialists in industrial relations, manufacturing operations, organizational development, and strategic planning; Provides specialists in management of marketing and sales, human resources, and personnel areas.

35251 ■ Washington Technology Center (WTC)
300 Fluke Hall, Box 352140
Seattle, WA 98195-2140
Ph: (206)685-1920
Fax: (206)543-3059
Co. E-mail: info@watechcenter.org
URL: http://www.watechcenter.org
Contact: Steve Goll, Director, Communications
Services: Statewide Technology Assistance Program. **Founded:** 1983. **Publications:** *At-A-Glance Newsletter* (Quarterly); *Index of Innovation* (Annual); *WTC Annual Report.* **Educational Activities:** SBIR training; WTC Workshops and seminars, on future research projects. **Awards:** Focused Technology Initiatives; Research and Technology Development Grants. **Telecommunication Services:** sgoll@watechcenter.org.

START-UP INFORMATION

35252 ■ *The Art of the Start: The Time-Tested, Battle-Hardened Guide for Anyone Starting Anything*
Pub: Penguin Books USA Inc.
Ed: Guy Kawasaki. **Released:** September 2004. **Price:** $26.95. **Description:** Advice for someone starting a new business covering topics such as hiring employees, building a brand, business competition, and management.

35253 ■ *The Complete Idiot's Guide to Starting and Running a Thrift Store*
Pub: Alpha Publishing House
Ed: Ravel Buckley, Carol Costa. **Released:** January 5, 2010. **Price:** $18.95. **Description:** Thrift stores saw a 35 percent increase in sales during the falling economy in 2008. Despite the low startup costs, launching and running a thrift store is complicated. Two experts cover the entire process, including setting up a store on a nonprofit basis, choosing a location, funding, donations for saleable items, recruiting and managing staff, sorting items, pricing, and recycling donations.

ASSOCIATIONS AND OTHER ORGANIZATIONS

35254 ■ International Association of Corporate and Professional Recruitment (IACPR)
327 N Palm Dr., Ste. 201
Beverly Hills, CA 90210
Ph: (310)550-0304
Fax: (206)202-4838
Co. E-mail: office@iacpr.org
URL: http://www.iacpr.org
Contact: Kay Kennedy, Executive Director
Description: Human resources executives and executive search professionals who are leaders in executive recruitment and retention. Serves as a communications network for sharing information and solving problems within the corporate recruiting industry. **Founded:** 1978. **Publications:** *Quick Takes* (Bimonthly). **Awards:** Professional Recruiters Ovation Award (Annual).

35255 ■ National Association of Executive Recruiters (NAER)
1 E Wacker Dr., Ste. 2600
Chicago, IL 60601
Ph: (618)398-6027
Co. E-mail: lisom@hhisearch.com
URL: http://www.naer.org
Contact: Jim Schneider, President
Description: Executive recruitment and search specialist firms providing counsel and assistance in identifying and hiring candidates for middle- and senior-level management positions. Promotes and enhances the public image, awareness, and understanding of the executive search profession. Serves as a forum for exchange of ideas among members; conducts educational programs and owners' roundtable. Maintains code of ethics and professional practice guidelines. **Founded:** 1984. **Educational Activities:** National Association of Executive Recruiters Conference (Annual).

REFERENCE WORKS

35256 ■ *The 7 Irrefutable Rules of Small Business Growth*
Pub: John Wiley & Sons, Incorporated
Ed: Steven S. Little. **Released:** February 2005. **Price:** $18.95. **Description:** Proven strategies to maintain small business growth are outlined, covering topics such as technology, business plans, hiring, and more.

35257 ■ *"$49M Defense Contracts Hits Austin" in Austin Business JournalInc. (Vol. 28, August 8, 2008, No. 21, pp. A1)*
Pub: American City Business Journals
Ed: Laura Hipp. **Description:** BAE Systems PLC has landed a $49 million contract to build thermal cameras, which are expected to be installed on tanks in 2009 and 2010. BAE is expected to land other defense contracts and is likely to add employees in order to meet production demands.

35258 ■ *"$50 Million Project for West Chester" in Business Courier (Vol. 24, December 14, 2008, No. 35, pp. 1)*
Pub: American City Business Journals, Inc.
Ed: Laura Baverman. **Description:** Commercial developer Scott Street Partners is planning to invest $50 million for the development of a site south of the Streets of West Chester retail center. The 31-acre project will generate 1,200 jobs, and will bring in offices, restaurants and a hotel. The development plans and the features of the site are discussed as well.

35259 ■ *"$161.9M 'Pit Stop' Fix-Up Will Create About 1,600 Jobs" in Orlando Business Journal (Vol. 26, January 22, 2010, No. 34, pp. 1)*
Pub: American City Business Journals
Ed: Anjali Fluker. **Description:** State of Florida will be providing $161.9 million to renovate eight service plazas starting November 2010. The project is expected to create 1,600 jobs across the state and is expected to be completed by 2012. Details on bid advertisements and facilities slated for improvement are discussed.

35260 ■ *"A123-Fisker Deal May Mean 540 Jobs" in Crain's Detroit Business (Vol. 26, January 18, 2010, No. 3, pp. 4)*
Pub: Crain Communications Inc.
Ed: Dustin Walsh. **Description:** Manufacturing plants in Livonia and Romulous may be hiring up to 540 skilled workers due to a contract that was won by A123 Systems Inc. that will result in the company supplying lithium-ion batteries to Fisker Automotive Inc. to be used in their Karma plug-in hybrid electric vehicle.

35261 ■ *"Active Duty" in Crain's Cleveland Business (Vol. 28, November 26, 2007, No. 47, pp. 3)*
Pub: Crain Communications, Inc.
Ed: David Bennett. **Description:** Discusses the Veteran Workforce Training Program, sponsored by the Volunteers of America - Greater Ohio; the program is meant to provide employment training for military veterans and to assist them in transitioning back into the work force.

35262 ■ *"AdvacePierre Heats Up" in Business Courier (Vol. 27, October 29, 2010, No. 26, pp. 1)*
Pub: Business Courier
Ed: John Newberry. **Description:** Bill Toler, chief executive officer of AdvancePierre Foods, is aiming for more growth and more jobs. The company was formed after the merger of Pierre Foods with two Oklahoma-based food processing companies. Toler wants to expand production and is set to start adding employees in the next 6-12 months.

35263 ■ *"Advancing the Ball" in Inside Healthcare (Vol. 6, December 2010, No. 7, pp. 31)*
Pub: RedCoat Publishing Inc.
Ed: Michelle McNickle. **Description:** Profile of Medicalodges an elder-care specialty company that provides both patient care and technology development. President and CEO of the firm believes that hiring good employees is key to growth for any small business.

35264 ■ *"Akron Community Foundation Hires Help for CEO Search" in Crain's Cleveland Business (Vol. 28, October 29, 2007, No. 43, pp. 6)*
Pub: Crain Communications, Inc.
Ed: Shannon Mortland. **Description:** Waverly Partners LLC, an executive search firm, has been hired by the Akron Community Foundation to search for its next president and CEO as Jody Bacon, the company's current CEO, will retire on July 31, 2008.

35265 ■ *"Albany Molecular on Hiring Spree as Big Pharma Slashes Work Force" in Business Review, Albany New York (December 28, 2007)*
Pub: American City Business Journals, Inc.
Ed: Barbara Pinckney. **Description:** Albany Molecular Research Inc. (AMRI) is an outsourcing company that provides work forces for pharmaceutical companies due to large numbers of downsizings in the year 2007. In 2008, AMRI plans to hire several workers.

35266 ■ *"Apprenticeship: Earn While You Learn" in Occupational Outlook Quarterly (Vol. 54, Fall 2010, No. 3, pp. 24)*
Pub: U.S. Bureau of Labor Statistics
Description: Paid training, or apprenticeships, are examined. Registered apprenticeship programs conform to certain guidelines and industry-established training standards and may be run by businesses, trade or professional associations, or partnerships with business and unions.

35267 ■ *"Are There Material Benefits To Social Diversity?" in Hispanic Business (Vol. 30, September 2008, No. 9, pp. 10)*
Pub: Hispanic Business, Inc.
Ed: Brigida Benitez. **Description:** Diversity in American colleges and universities, where students view and appreciate their peers as individuals and do not judge them on the basis of race, gender, or ethnicity is discussed. The benefits of diversity in higher education are also acknowledged by the U.S. Supreme Court and by leading American corporations.

35268 ■ *"Area Hurt By Doctor Deficiency" in The Business Journal-Serving Metropolitan Kansas City (Vol. 27, October 17, 2008, No. 5, pp. 1)*
Pub: American City Business Journals, Inc.
Ed: Rob Roberts. **Description:** Kansas City, Missouri may face a shortage of doctors, according to the Metropolitan Medical Society of Greater Kansas City. Over the next ten years the city needs to recruit more doctors in order to address the problem. Practicing physicians are having difficulties recruiting.

35269 ■ *"The Art of Persuasion: How You Can Get the Edge You Need To Reach Every Goal" in Small Business Opportunities (November 2007)*
Pub: Harris Publications Inc.
Ed: Paul Endress. **Description:** Expert in the field of psychology to business in the areas of communication, hiring and retention discusses a unique approach to solving business problems.

35270 ■ *"Ask Inc." in Inc. (December 2007, pp. 83-84)*
Pub: Gruner & Jahr USA Publishing
Ed: Ari Weinzweig. **Description:** Questions regarding knowledge management in the case of a retiring CFO, issues involved in opening a satellite office for a New York realtor, and information for hiring a multicultural workforce are all discussed.

35271 ■ *"At the Drugstore, the Nurse Will See You Now" in Globe & Mail (April 13, 2007, pp. B1)*
Pub: CTVglobemedia Publishing Inc.
Ed: Marina Strauss. **Description:** The appointment of several health professionals including nurse, podiatrists, etc. by Rexall Co. at its drugstores to face competition from rivals, is discussed.

35272 ■ *"At This Bakery, Interns' Hope Rises Along With the Bread" in Chicago Tribune (October 31, 2008)*
Pub: McClatchy-Tribune Information Services
Ed: Mary Schmich. **Description:** Profile of Sweet Miss Givings Bakery and its diverse founder, interns and employees; the bakery was founded by Stan Sloan, an Episcopal priest who started the business to help fund his ministry; Sloan saw a need for jobs for those living with HIV and other disabilities and through the bakery the interns learn the skills needed to eventually find work elsewhere.

35273 ■ *"At Your Career Crossroads" in Women In Business (Vol. 61, December 2009, No. 6, pp. 26)*
Pub: American Business Women's Association
Ed: Diane Stafford. **Description:** Guidelines for employees who are considering a job or career change are presented. Among the reasons for lead employees to make these changes are downsizing, job loss, environments that are not conducive to work or unfavorable work relationships with bosses.

35274 ■ *"Battling Back from Betrayal" in Harvard Business Review (Vol. 88, December 2010, No. 12, pp. 130)*
Pub: Harvard Business School Publishing
Ed: Daniel McGinn. **Description:** Stephen Greer's scrap metal firm, Hartwell Pacific, lost several million dollars due to a lack of efficient and appropriate inventory audits, accounting procedures, and new-hire reference checks for his foreign operations. Greer believes that balancing growth with control is a key component of success.

35275 ■ *"The Bell Tolls for Thee" in Canadian Business (Vol. 81, March 3, 2008, No. 3, pp. 36)*
Pub: Rogers Media
Ed: Andrew Wahl. **Description:** Bell Canada has formed the Canadian Coalition for Tomorrow's IT Skills to solve the shortage of technology talent in the country. Canada's total workforce has only around 4%, or 600,000 people employed in information technology-related fields. The aims of the Bell-led coalition, which is supported by different industry associations and 30 corporations, are investigated.

35276 ■ *"Best Companies for Diversity" in Black Enterprise (Vol. 38, July 2008, No. 12, pp. 12)*
Pub: Earl G. Graves Publishing Co. Inc.
Description: Maintaining excellence in a company's diversity efforts requires critical challenges such as recruiting, retaining and developing talent in the executive pipeline. Top young and diverse emerging executives in corporate America are featured.

35277 ■ *"BETC Backers Plot Future" in Business Journal Portland (Vol. 27, December 10, 2010, No. 41, pp. 1)*
Pub: Portland Business Journal
Ed: Erik Siemers. **Description:** A coalition of clean energy groups and industrial manufacturers have spearheaded a campaign aimed at persuading Oregon legislators that the state's Business Energy Tax Credit (BETC) is vital in job creation. Oregon's BETC grants tax credits for 50 percent of an eligible renewable or clean energy project's cost. However, some legislators propose BETC's abolition.

35278 ■ *"Black Gold" in Canadian Business (Vol. 79, August 14, 2006, No. 16-17, pp. 57)*
Pub: Rogers Media
Ed: Erin Pooley. **Description:** A list of the top ten jobs in the petroleum industry in Canada along with pay and nature of jobs, is presented.

35279 ■ *"The Board Shorts Executive" in Hawaii Business (Vol. 53, January 2008, No. 7, pp. 33)*
Pub: Hawaii Business Publishing
Ed: Mike Markrich. **Description:** Vans Triple Crown of Surfing executive director Randy Rarick believes that the surfing business requires knowledge of the sport and integity to the game's lifestyle and spirit. His organization manages surfing events, and has generated jobs for the locals. Plans for Vans Triple Crown are supplied.

35280 ■ *"Boom has Tech Grads Mulling Their Options" in Globe & Mail (March 14, 2006, pp. B1)*
Pub: CTVglobemedia Publishing Inc.
Ed: Grant Robertson. **Description:** Internet giant Google Inc. has stepped up its efforts to hire the talented people, in Canada, at Waterloo University in southern Ontario, to expand its operations. The details of the job market and increasing salaries are analyzed.

35281 ■ *"Brad Wall" in Canadian Business (Vol. 82, April 27, 2009, No. 7, pp. 9)*
Pub: Rogers Media
Ed: Joe Castaldo. **Description:** Saskatchewan Premier Brad Wall believes that the mood in the province is positive, as its economy is one of the few that is expected to post growth in 2009. Wall actively promotes the province in job fairs, offering $20,000 in tuition for recent college and university graduates that relocate in the province for seven years. Wall's views on the province's economy and challenges are presented.

35282 ■ *"Business Looks for Results in Congress" in Baltimore Business Journal (Vol. 28, November 5, 2010, No. 26, pp. 1)*
Pub: Baltimore Business Journal
Ed: Kent Hoover. **Description:** Republican candidates in the 2010 Congressional elections were overwhelmingly supported by the business community. Republican John Boehner, who will be the next Speaker of the House, says that the party's victory would end economic uncertainty and would assist small businesses to rehire workers.

35283 ■ *"Businesses Need to Know State, Federal Laws for Employing Minors" in Crain's Detroit Business (Vol. 25, June 15, 2009, No. 24)*
Pub: Crain Communications Inc. - Detroit
Ed: Nancy Kaffer. **Description:** Small business owners must know the law before employing minors. According to Steven Fishman, partner with Bodman LLP, who practices workplace law, most small business owners are not aware of laws regarding employment of minors.

35284 ■ *"Cabela's Repays Incentives as Sales Lag" in Business Journal-Milwaukee (Vol. 28, November 19, 2010, No. 7, pp. A1)*
Pub: Milwaukee Business Journal
Ed: Stacy Vogel Davis. **Description:** Cabela's has given back $266,000 to the government of Wisconsin owing to its failure to meet projected revenue goals for its Richfield, Wisconsin store. It has also failed to meet sales tax and hiring projection. The company received $4 million in incentives from Washington County.

35285 ■ *"Cancer-Fighting Entrepreneurs" in Austin Business Journal (Vol. 31, August 5, 2011, No. 22, pp. 1)*
Pub: American City Business Journals Inc.
Ed: Sandra Zaragoza. **Description:** Cancer Prevention and Research Institute of Texas has invested $10 million in recruiting known faculty to the University of Texas. The move is seen to bolster Austin's position as a major cancer research market. The institute has awarded grants to researchers Jonghwan Kim, Guangbin Dong and Kyle Miller.

35286 ■ *"Capital Ideas: Regions to Lansing: Focus on Taxes, Reform, Keeping Talent" in Crain's Detroit Business (Vol. 24, October 6, 2008)*
Pub: Crain Communications, Inc.
Ed: Amy Lane. **Description:** Michigan must make bold and dramatic changes in public policy regarding business legislation. The tax structure, unemployment issues and attracting and retaining talent are among the issues the state must confront, especially in this tough economic climate.

35287 ■ *"Capital Position" in Business Journal-Milwaukee (Vol. 28, December 24, 2010, No. 12, pp. A1)*
Pub: Milwaukee Business Journal
Ed: Rich Kirchen. **Description:** Canada-based BMO Financial Group has purchased Marshall and Isley Corporation (M and I), which dominated lending among Wisconsin businesses for decades. The sale of M and I will enable other banks to recruit M and I's customers but BMO Financial remains a stronger competitor since it possesses a more potent capital position.

35288 ■ *"A Capitol Opportunity" in Hispanic Business (Vol. 30, September 2008, No. 9, pp. 82)*
Pub: Hispanic Business, Inc.
Ed: John Schumacher. **Description:** Launched in 2003, the Polanco fellows program is named after former state Senator Richard Polanco, a founder and chairman of the California Latino Caucus Institute. The program offers young Hispanics a chance to experience public policy and the functioning of the California Capitol through a 12-month, on-the-job Capitol training.

35289 ■ *"Cashing in Before You Join: Negotiating a Signing Bonus" in Black Enterprise (Vol. 37, October 2006, No. 3, pp. 90)*
Pub: Earl G. Graves Publishing Co. Inc.
Ed: Chauntelle Folds. **Description:** Information on how to research and negotiate a signing deal, including how to avoid a tax hit.

35290 ■ *"Casinos See College as Job Jackpot" in The Business Journal-Serving Metropolitan Kansas City (Vol. 26, August 1, 2008, No. 47)*
Pub: American City Business Journals, Inc.
Ed: Suzanna Stagemeyer. **Description:** Wyandotte County casino managers revealed plans to develop partnerships with Kansas City Kansas Community College. The planned partnership is expected to include curriculum development and degree programs that would help train employees for the planned casinos. Other views and information on the project are presented.

35291 ■ *"Catching Creatives; Detroit Group Gets Grant to Attract 1,000 Design Pros" in Crain's Detroit Business (March 24, 2008)*
Pub: Crain Communications, Inc.
Ed: Sherri Begin. **Description:** Design Detroit was given a $200,000 planning grant by the Knight Foundation, an organization that strives to back initiatives that leverage talent and resources in each of the 26 U.S. cities it funds, to inspire strategies to attract up to 1,000 creative professionals to live in Detroit.

35292 ■ *"Cautious Hiring in January Report" in Charlotte Observer (February 3, 2007)*
Pub: Knight-Ridder/Tribune Business News
Ed: Kerry Hall. **Description:** U.S. Labor Department released a report that shows 111,000 new positions in January 2007, compared to 206,000 in December 2006. Employers remain cautious about hiring.

35293 ■ *"CEOs Split on Migrant Workers" in Canadian Business (Vol. 83, September 14, 2010, No. 15, pp. 23)*
Pub: Rogers Media Ltd.
Ed: Jacqueline Nelson. **Description:** A survey of Canadian CEOs shows that 49 percent of the respondents believe it was wrong to suspend the immigration programs and companies should be allowed to hire the most skilled workers regardless of citizenship. However, 42 percent believe the suspension was right because employment of Canadians must take precedence.

35294 ■ *"Channeling for Growth" in The Business Journal-Serving Greater Tampa Bay (Vol. 28, July 11, 2008, No. 29, pp. 1)*
Pub: American City Business Journals, Inc.
Ed: Margie Manning. **Description:** HSN Inc., one of the largest employers in Tampa Bay, Florida, is expected to spend an additional $9.7 million annually as it plans to hire more accounting, internal audit, legal, treasury and tax personnel after its spin-off to a public company. Details on the company's sales growth are provided.

35295 ■ *"Charged Up for Sales" in Charlotte Business Journal (Vol. 25, October 15, 2010, No. 30, pp. 1)*
Pub: Charlotte Business Journal
Ed: Susan Stabley. **Description:** Li-Ion Motors Corporation is set to expand its production lines of electric cars in Sacramento, California. The plan is seen to create up to 600 jobs. The company's total investment is seen to reach $500 million.

35296 ■ *"Christ Hospital to Expand" in Business Courier (Vol. 27, June 25, 2010, No. 8, pp. 3)*
Pub: Business Courier
Ed: Dan Monk, James Ritchie. **Description:** Christ Hospital intends to invest more than $300 million and generate 200 jobs in an expansion of its Mount Auburn campus in Cincinnati, Ohio. About $22 million in retail activity can be created by the hospital expansion, which will also include a replacement garage and new surgery facilities.

35297 ■ *"Citadel Hires Three Lehman Execs" in Chicago Tribune (October 2, 2008)*
Pub: McClatchy-Tribune Information Services
Ed: James P. Miller. **Description:** Citadel Investment Group LLC, Chicago hedge-fund operator, has hired three former senior executives of bankrupt investment banker Lehman Brothers Holding Inc. Citadel believes that the company's hiring spree will help them to further expand the firm's capabilities in the global fixed income business.

35298 ■ *"City Consults Executives on Police Hire" in Business Courier (Vol. 27, August 27, 2010, No. 17, pp. 1)*
Pub: Business Courier
Ed: Lucy May, Dan Monk. **Description:** The City of Cincinnati, Ohio has begun a selection process for the new police chief by consulting the city's business executives. The city charter amendment known as Issue 5 has removed civil service protection from the chief's post and enables City Manager Milton Dohoney to hire a chief from outside the department.

35299 ■ *"ClearEdge Hums Along" in Business Journal Portland (Vol. 26, December 18, 2009, No. 41, pp. 1)*
Pub: American City Business Journals Inc.
Ed: Erik Siemers. **Description:** Hillsboro-based ClearEdge Power Inc. expanded its workforce and facilities with $15M capital from investors. Since May 2009, the number of employees increased from 40 to 150 and headquarters expanded from 5,000 to 80,000 square feet.

35300 ■ *"Commentary. On Federal Reserve's Cut of Interest Rates" in Small Business Economic Trends (January 2008, pp. 3)*
Pub: National Federation of Independent Business
Description: Federal Reserve cut interest rates and announced its economic outlook on September 18, 2007 to stimulate spending. The cut in interest rates, however, may not help in supporting consumer spending because savers may lose interest income. The expected economic impact of the interest rate cuts and the U.S. economic outlook are also discussed.

35301 ■ *"Commentary. Small Business Economic Trends" in Small Business Economic Trends (March 2008, pp. 3)*
Pub: National Federation of Independent Business
Ed: William C. Dunkelberg, Holly Wade. **Description:** Commentary on the economic trends for small businesses in the U.S. is presented. Analysis of the labor market and low interest rates is given. The effect of the Federal Reserve's policy announcement on small business owner optimism is also discussed.

35302 ■ *"Commentary. Small Business Economic Trends" in Small Business Economic Trends (February 2008, pp. 3)*
Pub: National Federation of Independent Business
Ed: William C. Dunkelberg, Holly Wade. **Description:** Commentary on the economic trends for small businesses in the U.S. is presented. Analysis of the U.S. Federal Reserve Board's efforts to prevent a recession is given. Reduction in business inventories is also discussed.

35303 ■ *"Comparative Indicators" in Montly Labor Review (Vol. 133, September 2010, No. 9, pp. 87)*
Pub: Bureau of Labor Statistics
Description: Labor market indicators for years 2008 and 2009 are given. Statistical data included.

35304 ■ *"Competing for Jobs" in Women In Business (Vol. 63, Summer 2011, No. 2, pp. 37)*
Pub: American Business Women's Association
Ed: Leigh Elmore. **Description:** Job hunting tips for women in the US in relation to generation demographic groups are presented. Effective communications and positive interactions are essential to career development. Generation groups' strengths and weaknesses as job seekers are also given.

35305 ■ *"Contractors Scramble for Jobs" in Business Journal Portland (Vol. 26, December 18, 2009, No. 41, pp. 1)*
Pub: American City Business Journals Inc.
Ed: Andy Giegerich. **Description:** Contractors in Portland area are expected to bid for capital construction projects that will be funded by municipalities in the said area. Contracts for companies that work on materials handling, road improvement, and public safety structure projects will be issued.

35306 ■ *"Conversation" in Harvard Business Review (Vol. 86, September 2008, No. 9, pp. 32)*
Pub: Harvard Business School Press
Ed: Susan Donovan. **Description:** Danish software entrepreneur Thorkil Sonne has helped improve employment for individuals with autism after discovering the perception of detail and remarkable memory skills in his own son, who has autism. His company, Specialisterne, was built via focusing on these strengths.

35307 ■ *"Cool Jobs in Hot Markets" in Canadian Business (Vol. 80, March 26, 2007, No. 7, pp. 66)*
Pub: Rogers Media
Ed: Marlene Rego. **Description:** The growth in employment opportunities in various parts of the Canada is analyzed.

35308 ■ *"Corporate Diversity Driving Profits" in Hispanic Business (Vol. 30, September 2008, No. 9, pp. 12)*
Pub: Hispanic Business, Inc.
Ed: Michael Bowker. **Description:** U.S. businesses are beginning to appreciate the importance of diversity and are developing strategies to introduce a diverse workforce that reflects the cultural composition of their customers. The realization that diversity increases profits and the use of professional networks to recruit and retain skilled minority employees are two other new trends impacting corporate diversity in the U.S.

35309 ■ *"Crain's Makes Ad Sales, Custom Marketing Appointments" in Crain's Chicago Business (Vol. 34, October 24, 2011, No. 42, pp. 13)*
Pub: Crain Communications Inc.
Description: Crain's Chicago Business announced key appointments in its sales department: David Denor has been named first director of custom marketing services and Kate Van Etten will succeed Denor as advertising director.

35310 ■ *"Criticare Sees Rapid Expansion" in Business Journal-Milwaukee (Vol. 28, December 31, 2010, No. 14, pp. A1)*
Pub: Milwaukee Business Journal
Ed: Rich Rovito. **Description:** Criticare Systems Inc. expanded its distribution network, added customers, launched two new products and transferred into a new building in Pewaukee, Wisconsin at the start of their fiscal year. Criticare expanded its workforce and now has nearly 140 full time employees.

35311 ■ *"CSX Transportation: Supplier Diversity on the Right Track" in Hispanic Business (July-August 2009, pp. 34)*
Pub: Hispanic Business
Description: CSX Transportation is a leader in delivering essential products, operating as many as 1,200 trains and a fleet of more than 100,000 freight cars. CSX attributes its success by valuing diversity in both hiring and supplier contracts.

35312 ■ *"Cultural Due Diligence" in Canadian Business (Vol. 80, April 23, 2007, No. 9, pp. 60)*
Pub: Rogers Media
Ed: Graham Lowe. **Description:** The factors to be considered by job seekers during judging good workplace with relation to corporate culture are presented.

35313 ■ *"Custom Fit" in Canadian Business (Vol. 80, November 19, 2007, No. 23, pp. 42)*
Pub: Rogers Media
Ed: Andy Holloway. **Description:** Proper employee selection will help ensure a company has the people with the skills it really needs. Employee development is integral in coping with changes in the company. The importance of hiring the right employee and developing his skills is examined.

35314 ■ *"Datebook" in Crain's Chicago Business (Vol. 31, March 24, 2008, No. 12, pp. 18)*
Pub: Crain Communications, Inc.
Description: Listing of events in the Detroit area include conferences addressing entrepreneurialism,

economic development, secrets of getting hired, and women business ownership.

35315 ■ *"Datebook" in Crain's Chicago Business (Vol. 31, March 31, 2008, No. 13, pp. 1)*

Pub: Crain Communications, Inc.

Description: Listing of events in the Detroit area include conferences addressing entrepreneurialism, economic development, secrets of getting hired, and women business ownership.

35316 ■ *"David Maus Debuting New Dealership" in Orlando Business Journal (Vol. 26, February 5, 2010, No. 36, pp. 1)*

Pub: American City Business Journals

Ed: Anjali Fluker. **Description:** Automotive dealers David Maus Automotive Group and Van Tuyl Automotive Investment Group will launch David Maus Chevrolet in Sanford, Florida in fall 2010. The 12-acre site of the Chevy dealership will be located adjacent to the David Maus Toyota dealership. The new store is expected to generate nearly 125 new jobs.

35317 ■ *"Dealer Gets a Lift with Acquisitions at Year's End" in Crain's Detroit Business (Vol. 26, January 11, 2010, No. 2, pp. 3)*

Pub: Crain Communications, Inc.

Ed: Ryan Beene. **Description:** Alta Equipment Co., a forklift dealer, closed 2009 with a string of acquisitions expecting to double the firm's employee headcount and triple its annual revenue. Alta Lift Truck Services, Inc., as the company was known before the acquisitions, was founded in 1984 as Michigan's dealer for forklift manufacturer Yale Materials Handling Corp.

35318 ■ *"Debt-Collection Agency to Lay Off 368 in Hampton Center" in Virginian-Pilot (December 4, 2010)*

Pub: Virginian-Pilot

Ed: Tom Shean. **Description:** NCO Financial Systems Inc., provider of debt-collection and outsourcing services will permanently lay off 368 workers at its Hampton call center in 2011.

35319 ■ *"Decorated Marine Sues Contractor" in Wall Street Journal Eastern Edition (November 29, 2011, pp. A4)*

Pub: Dow Jones & Company Inc. Enterprise Media Group

Contact: Clare Hart, President

Ed: Julian E. Barnes. **Description:** Marine Devon Maylie, who was awarded the Congressional Medal of Honor for bravery, has filed a lawsuit against defense contractor BAE Systems PLC claiming that the company prevented his hiring by another firm by saying he has a mental condition and a drinking problem. Maylie says that this was in retaliation for his objections to the company's plan to sell the Pakistani military high-tech sniper scopes.

35320 ■ *"Delaware Diaper Maker Wanting To Expand Less Than a Year After Move" in Business First-Columbus (December 7, 2007, pp. A6)*

Pub: American City Business Journals, Inc.

Ed: Dan Eaton. **Description:** Duluth, Georgia-based Associated Hygienic Products LLC is planning to expand its production operations by 20 percent and hire new workers. The diaper maker was awarded state incentives to facilitate its transfer from Marion to Delaware. Details are included.

35321 ■ *"Delta Looks at Downtown Departure" in Business Courier (Vol. 27, October 1, 2010, No. 22, pp. 1)*

Pub: Business Courier

Ed: Dan Monk. **Description:** Delta Air Lines Inc. has been looking for a smaller office for its reservations center in downtown Cincinnati, Ohio. Delta has informed the city of its plan to seek proposals on office space alternatives in advance of the 2011 lease expiration. Insights on the current employment status at the reservations center are also given.

35322 ■ *"Do You Have A Retirement Parachute?" in Barron's (Vol. 88, July 7, 2008, No. 27, pp. 32)*

Pub: Dow Jones & Co., Inc.

Ed: Jane White. **Description:** The idea that American companies should emulate the Australian retirement system which implements a forced contribution rate for all employers regarding an adequate retirement plan for their employees is discussed.

35323 ■ *"Downtowns Must Court Young, CEOs for Cities President Says" in Crain's Detroit Business (Vol. 24, October 6, 2008, No. 40, pp. 18)*

Pub: Crain Communications, Inc.

Ed: Amy Lane. **Description:** It is important to produce more college graduates, and keep them in Michigan, according to CEOs for Cities President Carol Coletta when she spoke to a session at the West Michigan Regional Policy Conference which was held in September in Grand Rapids. Ways in which city leaders can connect students to communities, resulting in employees who have vested interest in the region, are also discussed.

35324 ■ *"Dreyer's Grand Ice Cream" in Ice Cream Reporter (Vol. 23, September 20, 2010, No. 10, pp. 8)*

Pub: Ice Cream Reporter

Description: Dreyer's Grand Ice Cream will add one hundred new manufacturing jobs at its plant in Laurel, Maryland and another 65 new hires before the end of 2010 and another 35 in 2011.

35325 ■ *"Duro Bag to Expand, Add 130 Jobs" in Business Courier (Vol. 27, August 6, 2010, No. 14, pp. 1)*

Pub: Business Courier

Ed: Jon Newberry. **Description:** Duro Bag Manufacturing Company will expand capacity at its Florence, Kentucky plant and will add around 130 jobs over the next few years. The state of Kentucky has given preliminary approval for up to $1 million in tax incentives over 10 years, tied to the creation of new jobs. The company's investment will include new production and packaging equipment and building improvements.

35326 ■ *"Eclipse to Hire 50 for Airp;ort Hangar" in Business Review, Albany New York (Vol. 34, November 9, 2007, No. 32, pp. 3)*

Pub: American City Business Journals, Inc.

Ed: Robin K. Cooper. **Description:** Eclipse Aviation, a jet manufacturer will hire fifty workers who will operate its new maintenance hangar at Albany International Airport. The company was expected to hire around twenty-five employees after it announced its plan to open one of the seven U.S. Factory Service Centers in 2005. Denise Zieske, the airport Economic Development Manager, expects the hangar construction to be completed by December 2007.

35327 ■ *"Empathy: An Entrepreneur's Killer App" in Women Entrepreneur (February 3, 2009)*

Pub: Entrepreneur Media Inc.

Ed: Kristi Hedges. **Description:** It is just as important to treat employees with courtesy and respect during bad economic times as it is in a good economy. Employers sometimes take advantage of such bad economic times since they realize that employees are grateful to have a job and cannot just quit and easily find work elsewhere. The importance of empathy in a company's leadership personnel is discussed.

35328 ■ *"Employers Plan to Fill Jobs" in Philadelphia Business Journal (Vol. 28, February 5, 2010, No. 51, pp. 1)*

Pub: American City Business Journals

Ed: Peter van Allen. **Description:** Philadelphia, Pennsylvania's largest employers have openings for at least 6,000 jobs. But businesses remain cautious and are selective in hiring or waiting to see what happens to federal policy changes.

35329 ■ *"End of an Era" in Barron's (Vol. 88, July 7, 2008, No. 27, pp. 3)*

Pub: Dow Jones & Co., Inc.

Ed: Alan Abelson. **Description:** June 2008 was a very bad month for US stocks, with investors losing as much as 41.9 percent in the first half of 2008 signaling an end to the financial environment that prevailed around the world since the 1980's. The US job market lost 62,000 jobs in June 2008.

35330 ■ *"Energy Sparks Job Growth" in The Business Journal-Serving Greater Tampa Bay (Vol. 28, August 8, 2008, No. 33, pp. 1)*

Pub: American City Business Journals, Inc.

Ed: Margie Manning. **Description:** Energy infrastructure projects in Tampa Bay, Florida, are increasing the demand for labor in the area. Energy projects requiring an increase in labor include TECO Energy Inc.'s plan for a natural gas pipeline in the area and the installation of energy management system in Bank of America's branches in the area.

35331 ■ *The Entrepreneur's Guide to Managing Growth and Handling Crisis*

Pub: Greenwood Publishing Group, Inc.

Ed: Theo J. Van Dijk. **Released:** December 2007. **Price:** $39.95. **Description:** The author explains how entrepreneurs can overcome crisis by changing the way they handle customers, by putting new processes and procedures in place, and managing employees in a professional manner. The book includes appendices with tips for hiring consultants, creating job descriptions, and setting up systems to chart cash flow as well as worksheets, tables and figures and a listing of resources.

35332 ■ *"Evaluating the 1996-2006 Employment Projections" in Montly Labor Review (Vol. 133, September 2010, No. 9, pp. 33)*

Pub: Bureau of Labor Statistics

Description: Bureau of Labor Statistics employment projections outperformed alternative naive models, but not projecting the housing bubble or the rise in oil prices caused some inaccuracies in the projects. These projections are used by policymakers, economists, and students.

35333 ■ *"Even Money on Recession" in Barron's (Vol. 88, March 10, 2008, No. 10, pp. M9)*

Pub: Dow Jones & Company, Inc.

Ed: Gene Epstein. **Description:** Discusses the US unemployment rate which was steady in February 2008 at 4.8 percent, while nonfarm payroll employment decreased by 63,000 in the same month, with the private sector losing 101,000 jobs. The economic indicators showed mixed signals on whether or not the US economy is in a recession.

35334 ■ *"Every Resume Tells a Story" in Women In Business (Vol. 62, September 2010, No. 3, pp. 26)*

Pub: American Business Women's Association

Ed: Kathleen Leighton. **Description:** Ways in which job applicants can write a good resume and promote themselves are discussed. It is believed that applicants should be proud of their accomplishments and they need to add details that will make them stand out. The importance of including a professional narrative in the resume is also explained.

35335 ■ *"Exit Strategy" in Barron's (Vol. 89, July 6, 2009, No. 27, pp. 3)*

Pub: Dow Jones & Co., Inc.

Ed: Alan Abelson. **Description:** US Federal Reserve is not likely to change its easy-money strategy in the short term. States such as California are suffering from spiraling costs and declining revenues and are struggling to balance their budgets. The US unemployment rate climbed to 9.5 percent in June 2009.

35336 ■ *"Face Issues if Elder Care, Unemployment Collide" in Atlanta Journal-Constitution (December 26, 2010, pp. G1)*

Pub: Atlanta Journal-Constitution

Ed: Amy Lindgren. **Description:** More issues arise during holiday for families with older members requiring care, including the issue of employment for those doing the caregiving.

35337 ■ *The Facebook Era: Tapping Online Social Networks to Build Better Products, Reach New Audiences, and Sell More Stuff*
Pub: Prentice Hall
Ed: Clara Shih. **Price:** $24.99. **Description:** The '90s were about the World Wide Web of information and the power of linking Web pages. Today it's about the World Wide Web of people and the power of the social graph. Online social networks are fundamentally changing the way we live, work, and interact. They offer businesses immense opportunities to transform customer relationships for profit: opportunities that touch virtually every business function, from sales and marketing to recruiting, collaboration to executive decision-making, product development to innovation.

35338 ■ *"Filling the Business Gap" in Hispanic Business (December 2010)*
Pub: Hispanic Business
Ed: Richard Larsen. **Description:** New York group seeks to increase state diversity supplier spending to help create jobs and boost the economy. According to a recent study, six out of 10 small business owners will increase capital spending but delay hiring in 2011. However, potential job creation is good among businesses owned by women and minorities.

35339 ■ *"Firms Upbeat About Future, Survey Shows" in Globe & Mail (January 17, 2006, pp. B4)*
Pub: CTVglobemedia Publishing Inc.
Ed: Heather Scoffield. **Description:** The issue of labor shortage for manufacturing sector, in Canada, is discussed. The survey results of Bank of Canada are presented.

35340 ■ *"FirstMerit's Top Executive Turns Around Credit Quality" in Crain's Cleveland Business (Vol. 28, October 15, 2007, No. 41, pp. 3)*
Pub: Crain Communications, Inc.
Ed: Shawn A. Turner. **Description:** Discusses the ways in which chairman and CEO Paul Greig has been able to improve FirstMerit Corp.'s credit quality and profit margin. Strategies included selling more than $70 million in bad loans, hiring a new chief credit officer and redirecting its focus on cross-selling its wealth and investment services to its commercial customers. Statistical data included.

35341 ■ *"Fresh Direct's Crisis" in Crain's New York Business (Vol. 24, January 14, 2008, No. 2, pp. 3)*
Pub: Crain Communications, Inc.
Ed: Lisa Fickenscher. **Description:** Freshdirect, an Internet grocery delivery service, finds itself under siege from federal immigration authorities, customers and labor organizations due to its employment practice of hiring illegals. At stake is the grocer's reputation as well as its ambitious growth plans, including an initial public offering of its stock.

35342 ■ *"Furniture Chain Moving to Harford" in Baltimore Business Journal (Vol. 27, January 22, 2010, No. 38, pp. 1)*
Pub: American City Business Journals
Ed: David J. Sernovitz. **Description:** Manchester, Connecticut-based Bob's Discount Furniture signed a lease for 672,000 square feet of space in Harford County, Maryland. The site will become the discount furniture retailer's distribution center in mid-Atlantic US. As many as 200 jobs could be generated when the center opens.

35343 ■ *"The Future Is Another Country; Higher Education" in The Economist (Vol. 390, January 3, 2009, No. 8612, pp. 43)*
Pub: The Economist Newspaper Inc.
Description: Due to the growth of the global corporation, more ambitious students are studying at universities abroad; the impact of this trend is discussed.

35344 ■ *The Game-Changer: How Every Leader Can Drive Everyday Innovation*
Pub: Crown Business
Ed: A.G. Lafley, Ram Charan. **Price:** $27.50. **Description:** Management guru Charan and Proctor & Gamble CEO Lafley provide lessons to encourage innovation at all levels, including how to hire for and encourage an environment of communication and tangible work processes.

35345 ■ *"Generation Y Goes To Work; Management" in The Economist (Vol. 390, January 3, 2009, No. 8612, pp. 48)*
Pub: The Economist Newspaper Inc.
Description: Unemployment rates among people in their 20s has increased significantly and there is a lower turnover in crisis-hit firms, which has made it more difficult to simply find another job if one is unsatisfied with the management style of his or her company. Managers are adopting a more command-and-control approach which is the antithesis of the open, collaborative style that younger employees prefer.

35346 ■ *"Get Hired Now! A 28-Day Program for Landing the Job You Want" in Black Enterprise (Vol. 37, October 2006, No. 3, pp. 119)*
Pub: Earl G. Graves Publishing Co. Inc.
Ed: C.J. Hayden; Frank Traditi. **Description:** Finding a job can be a challenge. Surveys estimate that 74 to 85 percent of those available are never advertised. Tips for searching out employment opportunities and landing the job you desire are explored.

35347 ■ *"Getting Going on Going Green" in HRMagazine (Vol. 53, August 2008, No. 8, pp. 8)*
Pub: Society for Human Resource Management
Contact: Henry G. Jackson, President
E-mail: hjackson@shrm.org
Ed: Rita Zeidner. **Description:** Being eco-friendly can help recruit and retain workers. Resources to help firms create green initiatives are presented.

35348 ■ *"Give 'Em a Break" in Entrepreneur (Vol. 35, November 2007, No. 11, pp. 32)*
Pub: Entrepreneur Media Inc.
Ed: J.J. Ramberg. **Description:** Andy Walter and Peer Pedersen founded Blue Orchid Capital, a fund of hedge funds, and Steamboat Foundation a foundation that helps college students find high-profile summer internships. Details on the fund and the foundation are presented.

35349 ■ *"Give Us Your Skilled" in Canadian Business (Vol. 80, October 8, 2007, No. 20, pp. 78)*
Pub: Rogers Media
Ed: Zena Olijnyk. **Description:** Demand for skilled workers in Canada is discussed. Despite a strong demand, as evidenced by shortages in both skilled and unskilled labor, the country's immigration policy is affecting the recruitment process. Peter Veress, founder and president of Vermax Group, believes the country is wasting opportunities to take advantage of its attractiveness as a destination for foreign workers.

35350 ■ *"Grace Puma; Senior Vice-President of Strategic Sourcing, United Airlines" in Crain's Chicago Business (May 5, 2008)*
Pub: Crain Communications, Inc.
Ed: John Rosenthal. **Description:** Profile of Grace Puma who is the senior vice-president of strategic sourcing at United Airlines and is responsible for cutting costs at the company in a number of ways including scheduling safety inspections at the same time as routine maintenance, thereby reducing the downtime of each aircraft by five days as well as replacing a third of her staff with outside talent.

35351 ■ *"The Great Fall" in Barron's (Vol. 88, March 10, 2008, No. 10, pp. 5)*
Pub: Dow Jones & Company, Inc.
Ed: Alan Abelson. **Description:** Discusses the US economy is considered to be in a recession, with the effects of the credit crisis expected to intensify as a result. Inflation is estimated at 4.3 percent in January 2008, while 63,000 jobs were lost in February 2008.

35352 ■ *"The Green Industry Jobs Gap" in Green Industry Pro (Vol. 23, October 2011)*
Pub: Cygnus Business Media
Ed: Gregg Wartgow. **Description:** According to the U.S. Bureau of Labor Statistics, the landscaping industry employs over 829,000 workers. According to another private study, the industry would employ more if they were able to find more people interested in performing the required work.

35353 ■ *"Green Light" in The Business Journal-Portland (Vol. 25, July 11, 2008, No. 18, pp. 1)*
Pub: American City Business Journals, Inc.
Ed: Erik Siemers. **Description:** Ecos Consulting, a sustainability consulting company based in Portland, Oregon, is seeing a boost in revenue as more businesses turn to sustainable practices. The company's revenue rose by 50 percent in 2007 and employees increased from 57 to 150. Other details about Ecos' growth are discussed.

35354 ■ *"Guidance On Career Guidance for Offender Reentry" in Occupational Outlook Quarterly (Vol. 54, Fall 2010, No. 3, pp. 24)*
Pub: U.S. Bureau of Labor Statistics
Description: Stable employment is a key factor in the successful rehabilitation of law offenders. The National Institute of Corrections hopes to improve offenders' long-term employment prospects.

35355 ■ *"Help for Job Seekers" in Crain's Detroit Business (Vol. 26, January 4, 2010, No. 1, pp. 14)*
Pub: Crain Communications Inc.
Description: CareerWorks is weekly paper targeting readers who are in a career transition or are looking for new employment.

35356 ■ *"Help for Job Seekers" in Crain's Detroit Business (Vol. 26, January 18, 2010, No. 3, pp. 14)*
Pub: Crain Communications Inc.
Description: CareerWorks is aimed at helping those who are in career transition or are looking for new jobs; this weekly collection of news, advertising and information includes weekly stories, events and the highlighting of a person who has successfully made the transition from one profession to another. On the Website, readers are welcome to post an anonymous resume in order to attract employers.

35357 ■ *"'Help Wanted' Meets 'Buy It Now': Why More Companies Are Integrating Marketing and Recruiting" in Inc. (November 2007, pp. 50-52)*
Pub: Gruner & Jahr USA Publishing
Ed: Ryan McCarthy. **Description:** Five tips to merge marketing and recruiting together include: thinking every help wanted ad as a marketing opportunity, treating every job candidate as a potential customer, involving the youngest employees in the interview process, look for way to promote recruiting events, and to sponsor community-oriented events.

35358 ■ *"Hickory Unemployment Stays Steady" in Charlotte Observer (February 2, 2007)*
Pub: Knight-Ridder/Tribune Business News
Ed: Jen Aronoff. **Description:** Unemployment rates remained unchanged in Hickory, North Carolina area; the region reported 6.1 percent unemployment.

35359 ■ *"High-Tech Job-Apalooza!" in Orlando Business Journal (Vol. 26, January 15, 2010, No. 33, pp. 1)*
Pub: American City Business Journals
Ed: Christopher Boyd. **Description:** Science Applications International Corporation, Saab Training USA LLC, CAE USA, and Pelliconi &C.SPA attempt to obtain $939,000 in tax incentives to generate 222 technology and defense-related jobs in Orange County, Florida. Each job will provide an average salary of $67,000. Future plans of each technology and defense firm are also presented.

35360 ■ *"Hire Education" in Canadian Business (Vol. 79, September 11, 2006, No. 18, pp. 114)*
Pub: Rogers Media
Ed: Erin Pooley. **Description:** Study results showing the perceptions of students while considering full-time employment and the attributes they look for in their future employers are presented.

35361 ■ *"HireDiversity: Some Companies Developing Affinity for Employee Groups" in Hispanic Business (October 2007, pp. 86-87)*
Pub: Hispanic Business
Ed: Hildy Medina. **Description:** Affinity groups, also known as employee resource networks, help companies identify and recruit candidates.

35362 ■ *"Hold the McJobs: Canada's High-End Employment Boom" in Globe & Mail (February 17, 2006, pp. B1)*
Pub: CTVglobemedia Publishing Inc.
Ed: Heather Scoffield. **Description:** A focus the increasing rate of high-end or professional jobs Canada and its negative influence on low-end and middle level jobs is presented.

35363 ■ *"Hospital Jobs" in Baltimore Business Journal (Vol. 28, June 25, 2010, No. 7, pp. 1)*
Pub: Baltimore Business Journal
Ed: Scott Graham. **Description:** Greater Baltimore, Maryland has four hospitals that are in the middle of transforming their campuses with new facilities for treating various patients. Construction at Mercy Medical Center, Johns Hopkins Hospital, Franklin Square Hospital and Anne Rundle Hospital has helped bring the construction industry back to life. Insights into the hiring plans of these hospitals are also included.

35364 ■ *"Hospital Moves Toward Self-Rule" in Business Courier (Vol. 24, December 7, 2008, No. 34, pp. 1)*
Pub: American City Business Journals, Inc.
Ed: James Ritchie. **Description:** Christ Hospital is planning on hiring 100 employees that will work on its newly leased facility located in Eden Park Drive.

35365 ■ *"How to Attract Big-City Talent to Small Towns" in Advertising Age (Vol. 79, July 7, 2008, No. 26, pp. 24)*
Pub: Crain Communications, Inc.
Ed: Joe Erwin. **Description:** Advice concerning ways in which to attract talent to mid-market agencies is given and innovative techniques that have worked for some firms are discussed.

35366 ■ *How to Become a Great Boss: The Rules for Getting and Keeping the Best Employees*
Pub: Hyperion Special Markets
Ed: Jeffrey J. Fox. **Released:** May 15, 2002. **Price:** $16.95. **Description:** The book offers valuable advice to any manager or entrepreneur to improve leadership and management skills. Topics covered include: hiring, managing, firing, partnership and competition, self and organization, employee performance, attitude, and priorities.

35367 ■ *How to Hire, Train, and Keep the Best Employees for Your Small Business*
Pub: Atlantic Publishing Company
Ed: Dianna Podmoroff. **Released:** June 2004. **Price:** $29.95. **Description:** Costs of hiring, training, and lost productivity costs related to losing employees.

35368 ■ *How to Make Money While You Look for a Job*
Pub: Booklocker.com, Incorporated
Ed: Donna Boyette. **Released:** March 2005. **Price:** $11.95. **Description:** Six steps to make money while searching for employment are outlined, from setting up a home-based office to selling a service.

35369 ■ *"How to Pick an All-Star" in Canadian Business (Vol. 79, October 9, 2006, No. 20, pp. 15)*
Pub: Rogers Media
Ed: Andy Holloway. **Description:** Factors that determine the competency levels o f individuals are discussed. The need for firms to take into consideration the right selection factors while hiring an employee is presented.

35370 ■ *"How to Protect Your Job in a Recession" in Harvard Business Review (Vol. 86, September 2008, No. 9, pp. 113)*
Pub: Harvard Business School Press
Ed: Janet Banks; Diane Coutu. **Description:** Strategies are presented for enhancing one's job security. These include being a team player, empathizing with management, preserving optimism, and concentrating on the customer.

35371 ■ *"How to Secure U.S. Jobs" in Gallup Management Journal (October 27, 2011)*
Pub: Gallup
Ed: Jim Clifton. **Description:** If America doubled its number of engaged customers globally, it could triple exports, which would create more good jobs and put the US economy back on track.

35372 ■ *How to Start a Home-Based Senior Care Business: Develop a Winning Business Plan*
Pub: Globe Pequot Press
Ed: James L. Ferry. **Released:** January 10, 2010. **Price:** $18.95. **Description:** Everything needed to know in order to start and run a profitable, ethical, and satisfying senior care business from your home. Information covers writing a good business plan, marketing services to families, creating a fee structure, and developing a network of trusted caregivers and service providers.

35373 ■ *Hug Your Customers*
Pub: Hyperion Books
Ed: Jack Mitchell. **Price:** $19.95. **Description:** The CEO of Mitchells/Roberts, two very successful clothing stores, professes his belief in showering customers with attention. His secrets for long-term business success include advice about attracting a good staff, lowering marketing costs, and maintaining higher gross margins and revenues.

35374 ■ *"If Just One Person Applies, Are You Required to Hire Him?" in HR Specialist (Vol. 8, September 2010, No. 9, pp. 7)*
Pub: Capitol Information Group Inc.
Description: It is legal to decline hiring an applicant, or even promoting a current employee, if they are the only applicant for a particular position. It may be good choice to wait for more applicants or to change recruiting strategy.

35375 ■ *"Illinois Bets On Recycling Program" in Chicago Tribune (November 29, 2008)*
Pub: McClatchy-Tribune Information Services
Ed: Joel Hood. **Description:** Traditionally the holiday gift-giving season is one of the most wasteful times of year and the state of Illinois is granting $760,000 to small businesses and cities in an attempt to expand curbside recycling programs and hire additional workers to address electronic waste.

35376 ■ *"IMRA's Ultrafast Lasers Bring Precision, profits; Ann Arbor Company Eyes Expansion" in Crain's Detroit Business (March 10, 2008)*
Pub: Crain Communications, Inc.
Ed: Tom Henderson. **Description:** IMRA America Inc. plans to expand its headquarters and has applied for permits to build a fourth building that will house research and development facilities and allow the company more room for manufacturing; the company plans to add about 20 more employees that would include research scientists, manufacturing and assembly workers, engineers and salespeople. The growth is due mainly to a new technology of ultrafast fiber lasers that reduce side effects for those getting eye surgeries and help manufacturers of computer chips to reduce their size and cost.

35377 ■ *"The Ins and Outs of Unemployment in Canada, 1976-2008" in Canadian Journal of Economics (Vol. 44, November 2011, No. 4, pp. 1331)*
Pub: Blackwell Publishers Ltd.
Ed: Michele Campolieti. **Description:** Flows into and out of unemployment in Canada at an aggregate and a number of disaggregated levels are studied.

35378 ■ *"Inside the New Nortel" in Canadian Business (Vol. 79, November 6, 2006, No. 22, pp. 93)*
Pub: Rogers Media
Ed: Andrew Wahl. **Description:** The team plans of Nortel Networks to improve its technology market by appointing new team are analyzed.

35379 ■ *"Insuraprise Growing Fast" in Austin Business Journal (Vol. 31, April 22, 2011, No. 7, pp. 1)*
Pub: American City Business Journals Inc.
Ed: Sandra Zaragoza. **Description:** Austin, Texas-based Insuraprise Inc. is finalizing the purchase of a 24,000-square-foot office at 12116 Jekel Circle. The firm, with 23 salespeople and sales that are growing nearly 300 percent over the past 18 months, will now have room to grow. Insuraprise plans to hire 35 new salespersons for its call center.

35380 ■ *"Interbrand's Creative Recruiting" in Business Courier (Vol. 27, November 12, 2010, No. 28, pp. 1)*
Pub: Business Courier
Ed: Dan Monk. **Description:** Global brand consulting firm Interbrand uses a creative recruitment agency to attract new employees into the company. Interbrand uses themed parties to attract prospective employees. The 'Alice In Wonderland' tea party for example, allowed the company to hire five new employees.

35381 ■ *"Interest in 'Encore Careers' is Growing" in HRMagazine (Vol. 53, November 2008, No. 11, pp. 22)*
Pub: Society for Human Resource Management
Contact: Henry G. Jackson, President
E-mail: hjackson@shrm.org
Description: Unexpectedly large numbers of baby boomers are looking for jobs that can provide them with 'means and meaning', according to a survey by MetLife and Civic Ventures. They can find those jobs in encore careers, an opportunity to do work that has a social impact and personal meaning.

35382 ■ *"Job-Hopping to the Top and Other Career Fallacies" in Harvard Business Review (Vol. 88, July-August 2010, No. 7-8, pp. 154)*
Pub: Harvard Business School Publishing
Ed: Monika Hamori. **Description:** Fallacies identified and discussed include the belief that a career move should always be a move up, that industry and career switches are penalized, and that large corporations are the only loci for reaping large rewards.

35383 ■ *"Job Losses and Budget Shortfall Adding to Economic Woes" in Sacramento Business Journal (Vol. 25, July 11, 2008, No. 19, pp. 1)*
Pub: American City Business Journals, Inc.
Ed: Kathy Robertson. **Description:** Budget cuts in California have been approved amid rising unemployment in a slowing economy. Statistics show that total industry employment in the Sacramento region decreased by 3,700 jobs from May 2007 to May 2008. Governor Arnold Schwarzenegger has ordered a 10 percent budget cut for state departments, but this cut will likely mean few layoffs.

35384 ■ *"Job Seeker's Readiness Guide: Unemployment's High and Competition is Tough" in Black Enterprise (Vol. 40, July 2010, No. 12, pp. 83)*
Pub: Earl G. Graves Publishing Co. Inc.
Description: Five key areas to help someone seeking employment gain the competitive edge are listed.

35385 ■ *"Jobs Data Show A Slow Leak" in Barron's (Vol. 88, July 7, 2008, No. 27, pp. 34)*
Pub: Dow Jones & Co., Inc.
Ed: Gene Epstein. **Description:** In June 2008, the United States manufacturing sector showed an expansion, with the purchasing managers' index rising to 50.2 from 49.6; the unemployment rate in the US, which stayed steady at 5.5 percent in June 2008 is also discussed. Statistical data included.

35386 ■ *"Jobs Data Show Wild Card" in Barron's (Vol. 90, September 6, 2010, No. 36, pp. M12)*
Pub: Barron's Editorial & Corporate Headquarters
Ed: Gene Epstein. **Description:** August 2010 jobs report revealed a 54,000 decline in non-farm payrolls and that the unemployment rate remains unchanged at 9.6 percent. The report also shows a welcome rise of 848,999 in the household-data category. The

unemployment rate shows a reversed trend where men's 10.6 percent unemployment is higher than women's 8.6 percent rate.

35387 ■ *"The Jobs Man" in Business Courier (Vol. 26, December 25, 2009, No. 35, pp. 1)*
Pub: American City Business Journals, Inc.

Ed: Lucy May. **Description:** Entrepreneur Bob Messer, a volunteer for Jobs Plus Employment Network in Cincinnati's Over-the-Rhine neighborhood, regularly conducts a seminar that aims to help attendees prepare for employment. Jobs Plus founder Burr Robinson asked Messer to create the seminar in order to help unemployed jobseekers. So far, the program has helped 144 individuals with full time jobs in 2009.

35388 ■ *"Know It All Finds Applicants are Stretching the Truth" in Philadelphia Business Journal (Vol. 28, September 11, 2009, No. 30, pp. 1)*
Pub: American City Business Journals

Ed: Athena D. Merritt. **Description:** Know It All Background Research Services has reported that discrepancies in background checks reached 19.8 percent in 2009. Reports show that 42 percent of the discrepancies involve lying about previous employment, and 37 percent involve education information. Marc Bourne, the company's vice president, believes that employers have cause to be concerned.

35389 ■ *"Kodiak Bucks Bear Market" in Austin Business JournalInc. (Vol. 29, December 18, 2009, No. 41, pp. 1)*
Pub: American City Business Journals

Ed: Kate Harrington. **Description:** Austin, Texas-based Kodiak Assembly Solutions LLC, a company that installs components into printed circuit boards for product or evaluation tool kit prototyping purposes, will expand despite the recession. It will relocate from a 28,000 square foot space to a 42,000 square foot space in North Austin. The firm will also increase its workforce by 20 employees.

35390 ■ *"The Labor Crunch is Coming" in Canadian Business (Vol. 80, December 25, 2006, No. 1, pp. 74)*
Pub: Rogers Media

Description: The need for skilled and educated workforce to meet labor shortage in future in Canada is discussed.

35391 ■ *"Labor Force Data" in Montly Labor Review (Vol. 133, September 2010, No. 9, pp. 89)*
Pub: Bureau of Labor Statistics

Description: Employment status of the population of the U.S. by sex, age, race and origin is presented.

35392 ■ *"Labor Pains" in Canadian Business (Vol. 79, August 14, 2006, No. 16-17, pp. 80)*
Pub: Rogers Media

Description: Canada's employment insurance is analyzed in view of the growing shortage of labor.

35393 ■ *"LaSalle Street Firms Cherry-Pick Talent As Wall Street Tanks" in Crain's Chicago Business (Vol. 31, November 17, 2008, No. 46)*
Pub: Crain Communications, Inc.

Ed: H. Lee Murphy. **Description:** Many local businesses are taking advantage of the lay offs that many major Wall Street firms are undergoing in their workforces; these companies see the opportunity to woo talent and expand their staff with quality executives.

35394 ■ *"Last Founder Standing" in Conde Nast Portfolio (Vol. 2, June 2008, No. 6, pp. 124)*
Pub: Conde Nast Publications
Contact: David Carey, President

Ed: Kevin Maney. **Description:** Interview with Amazon CEO Jeff Bezos in which he discusses the economy, the company's new distribution center and the hiring of employees for it, e-books, and the overall vision for the future of the firm.

35395 ■ *"Laying the Groundwork: In Developing Personnel, the Work Takes Place Beforehand" in Black Enterprise (February 2008)*
Pub: Earl G. Graves Publishing Co. Inc.

Ed: Tamara E. Holmes. **Description:** Small business owners know the devastation of hiring the wrong employee for a position. Steps to improve hiring using a long-term plan are outlined.

35396 ■ *"Leading Ohio Internet Marketing Firm Announces Growth in September" in Marketing Weekly News (September 26, 2009, pp. 24)*
Pub: Investment Weekly News

Description: Despite a poor economy, Webbed Marketing, a leading social media marketing and search engine optimization firm in the Midwest, has added five additional professionals to its fast-growing team. The company continues to win new business, provide more services and hire talented employees.

35397 ■ *"Legalities of Diversity" in Hispanic Business (September 2007, pp. 26)*
Pub: Hispanic Business

Ed: Francisco Ramos Jr., Bill Krutzen. **Description:** Most companies in America have diversity programs, however, critics believe diversity can be used as reverse discrimination because minorities are getting preferential treatment in hiring, promotion, and admissions.

35398 ■ *The Logic of Life: The Rational Economics of an Irrational World*
Pub: Random House

Ed: Tim Harford. **Released:** February 2009. **Price:** $15.00 paperback. **Description:** Harford excels at making economists' studies palatable for discerning but non-expert readers. The uses hard data to show why promiscuous teens are actually health-conscious, divorce hasn't gotten a fair shake, corporate bosses will always be overpaid and job prospects for minorities continue to be grim.

35399 ■ *"Looking To Hire Young? Be Careful" in Boston Business Journal (Vol. 30, November 19, 2010, No. 43, pp. 1)*
Pub: Boston Business Journal

Ed: Lisa van der Pool. **Description:** The Massachusetts Commission Against Discrimination (MCAD) has been using undercover job applicants to expose discrimination. Cabot's Ice Cream and Restaurant has been accused of denying older workers equal employment opportunities. MCAD has discovered unfair hiring practices such as hiring high school and college students.

35400 ■ *"Losing the Top Job - And Winning It Back" in Harvard Business Review (Vol. 88, October 2010, No. 10, pp. 136)*
Pub: Harvard Business School Publishing

Ed: Alison Beard. **Description:** Michael Mack chronicles the changes in perspectives that occurred when he was fired from Garden Fresh, a restaurant firm he co-owned. Once again at the company helm, he is now more receptive to outside input and acknowledges the importance of work-life balance.

35401 ■ *"Managing the Facebookers; Business" in The Economist (Vol. 390, January 3, 2009, No. 8612, pp. 10)*
Pub: Economist Newspaper Ltd.

Description: According to a report from PricewaterhouseCoopers, a business consultancy, workers from Generation Y, also known as the Net Generation, are more difficult to recruit and integrate into companies that practice traditional business acumen. 61 percent of chief executive managers say that they have trouble with younger employees who tend to be more narcissistic and more interested in personal fulfillment with a need for frequent feedback and an overprecise set of objectives on the path to promotion which can be hard for managers who are used to a different relationship with their subordinates. Older bosses should prepare to make some concessions to their younger talent since some of the issues that make them happy include cheaper online ways to communicate and additional coaching, both of which are good for business.

35402 ■ *Managing the Older Worker: How to Prepare for the New Organizational Order*
Pub: Harvard Business Press

Ed: Peter Cappelli, Bill Novelli. **Price:** $29.95. **Description:** Your organization needs older workers more than ever: They transfer knowledge between generations, transmit your company's values to new hires, make excellent mentors for younger employees, and provide a 'just in time' workforce for special projects.

35403 ■ *"A Manufacturing Revival" in Boston Business Journal (Vol. 31, May 27, 2011, No. 18, pp. 1)*
Pub: Boston Business Journal

Ed: Kyle Alspach. **Description:** Massachusetts' manufacturing sector has grown despite the high cost of labor, real estate and electricity. Manufacturing jobs in the state have increased to 2,800 in April 2011.

35404 ■ *"Meet the Gatekeepers" in Crain's Chicago Business (Vol. 30, February 2007, No. 6, pp. 40)*
Pub: Crain Communications, Inc.

Ed: Kate Ryan. **Description:** Recruiters at big investment banking firms agree that the way to get your foot in the door requires common sense issues such as not answering your phone in the middle of an interview, proofreading your cover letter, and research. Interviews with three top executives give more insight and advice.

35405 ■ *"Microsoft Clicks Into High Speed" in Hispanic Business (Vol. 30, July-August 2008, No. 7-8, pp. 54)*
Pub: Hispanic Business, Inc.

Ed: Derek Reveron. **Description:** Microsoft's diversity hiring and vendor diversity program to capture more Hispanic consumer and business-to-business market is described. One of the main goals of these programs is to hire more Hispanic executives and managers who will help the company develop and market products and services that will appeal and benefit Hispanic consumers.

35406 ■ *"Mission: Recruitment" in HRMagazine (Vol. 54, January 2009, No. 1, pp. 42)*
Pub: Society for Human Resource Management
Contact: Henry G. Jackson, President
E-mail: hjackson@shrm.org

Ed: Theresa Minton-Eversole. **Description:** Due to the hiring challenges faced by Army recruiters, they are partnering with employers in order to establish connections to high quality, Army-trained individuals when they separate from active duty.

35407 ■ *"A Model Development" in Crain's Cleveland Business (Vol. 28, October 1, 2007, No. 39, pp. 12)*
Pub: Crain Communications, Inc.

Description: Profile a Forest City Enterprises Inc., a firm that is developing a project in New Mexico called Mesa del Sol. The Albuquerque development is being seen as the vanguard of master-planned communities with its high-tech economic development center which is expected to become the site of 60,000 jobs, 38,000 homes and a town center.

35408 ■ *"The Money Train: How Public Projects Shape Our Economic Future" in Hawaii Business (Vol. 54, September 2008, No. 3, pp. 31)*
Pub: Hawaii Business Publishing

Ed: Jason Ubay. **Description:** Public projects impact the construction industry as such projects create jobs and new infrastructure that can lead to private developments. Details on the government contracts and construction projects in Hawaii and their rising costs and impact on the state's economy are discussed.

35409 ■ *"More than Able" in Entrepreneur (Vol. 36, March 2008, No. 3, pp. 81)*
Pub: Entrepreneur Media Inc.

Ed: Mark Henricks. **Description:** Disabled workers are motivated employees and work longer hours. A study shows that accommodating disabled workers is very low cost and provides benefits to employers, such as improved employee retention and increased customer base. Other details about hiring disabled workers are discussed.

35410 ■ *"More Jobs Heading to Suburb" in Austin Business JournalInc. (Vol. 29, November 20, 2009, No. 37, pp. 1)*
Pub: American City Business Journals
Ed: Kate Harrington. **Description:** Site of Advanced Integration Technologies (AIT) in Pflugerville, Texas might increase its workforce to 80 employees in the next six months due to the creation of an incentive package. Funds from the Pflugerville Community Development Corporation have been helping AIT's initiative to hire more workers. The firm receives $2,000 from the plan for every new employee it hires.

35411 ■ *"More Mexican Labor Needed in Oil Patch, Executives Say" in Globe & Mail (February 23, 2007, pp. B1)*
Pub: CTVglobemedia Publishing Inc.
Ed: Steven Chase. **Description:** The plans of top North American chief executive officers to recommend the employment of temporary workers from Mexico for the development of oil sands in Alberta, Canada, are discussed.

35412 ■ *"A Motorola Spinoff Is No Panacea" in Barron's (Vol. 88, March 31, 2008, No. 13, pp. 19)*
Pub: Dow Jones & Company, Inc.
Ed: Mark Veverka. **Description:** Motorola's plan to try and spinoff their handset division is bereft of details as to how or specifically when in 2009 the spinoff would occur. There's no reason to buy the shares since there's a lot of execution risk to the plan. Motorola needs to hire a proven cellphone executive and develop a compelling new cellphone platform.

35413 ■ *"The Myth of the Overqualified Worker" in Harvard Business Review (Vol. 88, December 2010, No. 12, pp. 30)*
Pub: Harvard Business School Publishing
Ed: Andrew O'Connell. **Description:** It is recommended to seriously consider job candidates with qualifications exceeding the position being recruited because research shows these individuals work harder, but do not quit any sooner than those whose qualifications more closely match the position.

35414 ■ *"NASA Taps Younger Talent Pool to Supplement Aging Work Force" in Crain's Cleveland Business (Vol. 30, June 22, 2009, No. 24, pp. 1)*
Pub: Crain Communications, Inc.
Ed: Chuck Soder. **Description:** NASA's Glenn Research Center has reversed the trend towards hiring older workers with more experience by recruiting for entry-level positions as part of a pilot program to attract younger talent.

35415 ■ *"NEMRA Announces Headquarters Move" in Agency Sales Magazine (Vol. 39, September-October 2009, No. 9, pp. 53)*
Pub: MANA
Description: NEMRA, the National Electrical Manufacturers' Representatives Association is moving their headquarters to 28 Deer Street, Suite 302, Portsmouth, New Hampshire. The association has also added Michelle Rivers-Jameson as their manager of operations and Kirsty Stebbins as their manager of marketing and member services.

35416 ■ *"Networking Web Sites: a Two-Edged Sword" in Contractor (Vol. 56, October 2009, No. 10, pp. 52)*
Pub: Penton Media, Inc.
Ed: H. Kent Craig. **Description:** People need to be careful about the information that they share on social networking Web sites. They should realize that future bosses, coworkers, and those that might want to hire them might read those information. Posting on these sites can cost career opportunities and respect.

35417 ■ *"Never Boring: Ad Agencies' Big Changes" in Business Courier (Vol. 24, February 8, 2008, No. 44, pp. 1)*
Pub: American City Business Journals, Inc.
Ed: Dan Monk. **Description:** Many changes are occurring in Cincinnati's advertising industry, including new clients, acquisitions, and market leaders, and an increase in employment. Bridge Worldwide passed Northlich LLC as the city's largest advertising agency.

35418 ■ *"New Boss at Nortel Mines GE for New Executives" in Globe & Mail (February 6, 2006, pp. B1)*
Pub: CTVglobemedia Publishing Inc.
Ed: Catherine McLean. **Description:** Chief executive officer Mike Zafirovski of Nortel Networks Corp. appoints executives Dennis Carey, Joel Hackney and Don McKenn of GE Electric Co. The managerial abilities of Mike are discussed.

35419 ■ *"A New Breed of Entrepreneurs" in Black Enterprise (Vol. 37, November 2006, No. 4, pp. 16)*
Pub: Earl G. Graves Publishing Co. Inc.
Description: Black entrepreneurs are an important part of the chain for providing economic opportunities within the community. Many black business owners are more likely to hire black employees and apply innovative strategies in building their businesses rather than taking the traditional route.

35420 ■ *The New Job Security: The 5 Best Strategies for Taking Control of Your Career*
Pub: Crown Business Books
Ed: Pam Lassiter. **Released:** September 7, 2010. **Price:** $14.99. **Description:** This book will help individuals to uncover interesting alternative jobs, generate multiple income streams, shape their job to reflect values and goals, move successfully through the company, and plan for career transitions to keep them in control. Online resources, real-life examples, practical exercises and a no-nonsense approach will aid in job stability.

35421 ■ *"New Jobless Claims Filed in December Soar" in Baltimore Business Journal (Vol. 27, January 29, 2010, No. 39, pp. 1)*
Pub: American City Business Journals
Ed: Scott Dance. **Description:** Maryland received 48,693 new claims for unemployment benefits in December 2009, reaching its highest monthly total since 1974. The number of claims was up 49 percent from November and 13 percent from the same period in 2008. Labor officials and economists discuss this trend.

35422 ■ *"No Time to Grieve" in Women In Business (Vol. 63, Fall 2011, No. 3, pp. 22)*
Pub: American Business Women's Association
Ed: Diane Stafford. **Description:** Individuals who have experienced job loss must go through the emotional stages related to this event in order to gain the best re-employment opportunities. The first step towards re-employment is to make the job search public. Tips for improving one's online footprint are also given.

35423 ■ *"Nonprofit to Grow" in Austin Business JournalInc. (Vol. 29, January 22, 2010, No. 46, pp. 1)*
Pub: American City Business Journals
Ed: Sandra Zaragoza. **Description:** Southwest Key Programs Inc. received a $2.1 million grant from the U.S. Economic Development Administration to help finance the building of a $3.6 million 'Social Enterprise Complex'. The complex is expected to create at least 100 jobs in East Austin, Texas. Details of the plan for the complex are presented.

35424 ■ *"Northern Kentucky Adds 1,355 Jobs in '07" in Business Courier (Vol. 24, February 15, 2008, No. 45, pp. 3)*
Pub: American City Business Journals, Inc.
Ed: Lucy May. **Description:** Jobs generated by new and expanding businesses in Northern Kentucky in 2007 totaled to 1,355, which boosted total business sales to $410 million. The ripple effects of the businesses are expected to create 5,432 new jobs and increase business sales to more than $888 million.

35425 ■ *"Numbers Game" in Baltimore Business Journal (Vol. 27, February 6, 2010, No. 40, pp. 1)*
Pub: American City Business Journals
Ed: Scott Dance. **Description:** Doubts are being raised regarding the impact of the federal stimulus spending in addressing unemployment in Maryland, which has experienced 1,800 jobs created so far. Details on the view of companies and the insufficient amount of contracts that lead to the fewer number of workers being hired are discussed.

35426 ■ *"NYC Tops Hub in Tech VC Dollars" in Boston Business Journal (Vol. 31, August 5, 2011, No. 28, pp. 1)*
Pub: Boston Business Journal
Ed: Kyle Alspach. **Description:** New York City has been outdoing Boston in terms of venture capital for technology firms since second quarter 2010. New York tech firms raised $865 million during the first two quarters of 2011 against Boston techs' $682 million. Boston has the edge, though, when it comes to hiring engineering talent as it is home to the Massachusetts Institute of Technology.

35427 ■ *"Oakland County to Survey Employers on Needed Skills" in Crain's Detroit Business (Vol. 24, April 14, 2008, No. 15, pp. 30)*
Pub: Crain Communications Inc.
Ed: Chad Halcom. **Description:** In an attempt to aid educators and attract talent, Oakland County plans to collect data from 1,000 local employers on workforce skills they need now or will need soon.

35428 ■ *"Old Ford Plant to Sign New Tenants" in Business Courier (Vol. 27, August 13, 2010, No. 15, pp. 1)*
Pub: Business Courier
Ed: Dan Monk. **Description:** Ohio Realty Advisors LLC, a company handling the marketing of the 1.9 million-square-foot former Ford Batavia plant is on the brink of landing one distribution and three manufacturing firms as tenants. These tenants are slated to occupy about 20 percent of the facility and generate as many as 250 jobs in Ohio.

35429 ■ *"On the Clock" in Canadian Business (Vol. 82, April 27, 2009, No. 7, pp. 28)*
Pub: Rogers Media
Ed: Sarka Halas. **Description:** Survey of 100 Canadian executives found that senior managers can be out of a job for about nine months before their careers are adversely affected. The nine month mark can be avoided if job seekers build networks even before they lose their jobs. Job seekers should also take volunteer work and training opportunities to increase their changes of landing a job.

35430 ■ *"On Hire Ground" in Entrepreneur (Vol. 36, February 2008, No. 2, pp. 19)*
Pub: Entrepreneur Media Inc.
Description: ADP Small Business Services, an economic consulting firm, showed that small businesses had increased employment rates in 2007 and added 77,000 jobs in November 2007. Entrepreneurial employment and data showing the contribution of small businesses to job growth are presented.

35431 ■ *"Online Tools for Jobseekers" in Occupational Outlook Quarterly (Vol. 55, Fall 2011, No. 3, pp. 20)*
Pub: U.S. Bureau of Labor Statistics
Description: U.S. Department of Labor's CareerOneStop provides a collection of Web-based tools serving students, jobseekers, employers, and the workforce. The top six categories for job listings nationwide include general job boards, niche job boards, career planning tools, career explorations sites, social media job search sites, and other tools which include interview preparation tools and training grants.

35432 ■ *"Orders Up; Jobs Below Forecast" in Charlotte Observer (February 2, 2007)*
Pub: Knight-Ridder/Tribune Business News
Ed: Kerry Hall. **Description:** U.S. Labor Department reported unemployment rates at 4.6 percent, up one-tenth of a percent. Economists had predicted 170,000 new jobs, but only 111,000 were created.

35433 ■ *"Out to Draw Work, Talent" in Crain's Detroit Business (Vol. 24, April 14, 2008, No. 15, pp. 3)*
Pub: Crain Communications, Inc.
Ed: Bill Shea. **Description:** Profile of Southfield-based Kinetic Post Inc., a growing post-production house that offers video, audio, animation, print, online and related services to corporations and advertising agencies.

35434 ■ *"Outlook 2007" in Canadian Business (Vol. 80, December 25, 2006, No. 1, pp.)*
Pub: Rogers Media
Ed: David Wolf. **Description:** Economists' 2007 forecast on global economy, particularly about Canada's housing and labor market among other sectors, is discussed.

35435 ■ *"Overseas Overtures" in Business Journal-Portland (Vol. 24, October 26, 2007, No. 35, pp. 1)*
Pub: American City Business Journals, Inc.
Ed: Robin J. Moody. **Description:** Oregon has a workforce shortage, specifically for the health care industry. Recruiting agencies, such as the International Recruiting Network Inc., answers the high demand for workforce by recruiting foreign employees. The difficulties recruiting companies experience with regards to foreign labor laws are investigated.

35436 ■ *"Part-Time Assignments" in Black Enterprise (Vol. 37, December 2006, No. 5, pp. 70)*
Pub: Earl G. Graves Publishing Co. Inc.
Description: During critical change initiatives interim management, an employment model which uses senior-level executives to manage a special project or specific business function on a temporary basis, can have many benefits.

35437 ■ *"Pay Me! How to Get the Money You're Owed When No One Seems to Have Any" in Entrepreneur (Vol. 37, July 2009, No. 7, pp. 49)*
Pub: Entrepreneur Media, Inc.
Ed: Randy B. Hecht. **Description:** How certain collections scenarios with clients, who have already fallen behind on their payments, should be handled is discussed. During a down economy, business owners should properly manage collection and billing because this can actually strengthen client relationships. Insights on hiring a collections agency are also presented.

35438 ■ *"The People Puzzle; Re-Training America's Workers" in The Economist (Vol. 390, January 3, 2009, No. 8612, pp. 32)*
Pub: The Economist Newspaper Inc.
Description: With thousands of workers losing their jobs, America is now facing the task of getting them back to work. With an overall unemployment rate of 6.7 percent, the federal government has three main ways for leading workers back to employment: training them for new jobs, providing unemployment insurance in order to replace lost wages during the period of job-hunting; and matching employers who desire a skill with workers who have that skill. Specialized staffing agencies provide employers and potential employees with the help necessary to find a job in some of the more niche markets.

35439 ■ *"Perspective: Borderline Issues" in Entrepreneur (Vol. 35, October 2007, No. 10, pp. 48)*
Pub: Entrepreneur Media Inc.
Ed: Joshua Kurlantzick. **Description:** Failure of the immigration reform bill is expected to result in increased difficulty in finding workers that would take on the dirty and perilous jobs, which are usually taken by immigrants. Regularizing immigration on the other hand will cost business owners money by making them spend for the legality of their employees' stay in the U.S. Other effects of immigration laws on entrepreneurs are discussed.

35440 ■ *"A Piece of the Action" in Black Enterprise (Vol. 38, January 2008, No. 6, pp. 42)*
Pub: Earl G. Graves Publishing Co. Inc.
Ed: Alan Hughes. **Description:** Andre Williams, owner of Kaze Sushi restaurant, offered generous incentive plan-equity in the business in order to acquire Chef Kaze Chan and Chef Hari Chan. Williams' entrepreneurial pursuits are discussed.

35441 ■ *"Pitch for SPX Expansion was Full of Energy" in Charlotte Business Journal (Vol. 25, November 19, 2010, No. 35, pp. 1)*
Pub: Charlotte Business Journal
Ed: John Downey. **Description:** SPX Corporation announced that it will expand their headquarters in Ballantyne after Charlotte and North Carolina leaders made an aggressive push to retain the company. SPX Corporation is expected to invest $70 million for the expansion, which would mean 180 new jobs in Charlotte.

35442 ■ *"Plan Your Future with My Next Move" in Occupational Outlook Quarterly (Vol. 55, Summer 2011, No. 2, pp. 22)*
Pub: U.S. Bureau of Labor Statistics
Description: My Next Move, an online tool offering a variety of user-friendly ways to browse more than 900 occupations was created by the National Center for O NET Development for the US Department of Labor's Employment and Training Administration. Clicking on an occupation presents a one-page profile summarizing key information for specific careers.

35443 ■ *"Prescription for Health: Choosing the Best Healthcare Plan" in Black Enterprise (Vol. 38, July 2008, No. 12, pp. 48)*
Pub: Earl G. Graves Publishing Co. Inc.
Ed: Tamara E. Holmes. **Description:** According to a survey of small-business owners conducted by SurePayroll Inc., 20 percent of respondents have had a prospective employee refuse a job offer because healthcare benefits did not come with it. Cost is not the only reason many small-business owners do not offer these benefits. Guidelines to help take some of the confusion out of the guesswork that comes with trying to find the proper fit concerning healthcare benefits are outlined.

35444 ■ *"Prichard the Third" in Canadian Business (Vol. 83, October 12, 2010, No. 17, pp. 34)*
Pub: Rogers Media Ltd.
Ed: Thomas Watson. **Description:** Robert Prichard, the new chair of international business law firm Torys, talks about his current role; his job involved advising clients, representing the firm, being part of the leadership team, and recruiting talent. He considers 'Seven Days in Tibet' as the first book to have an influence on his world view.

35445 ■ *"The Profitability of Mobility" in Entrepreneur (Vol. 37, September 2009, No. 9, pp. 98)*
Pub: Entrepreneur Media, Inc.
Ed: John Daley. **Description:** Wireless Zone franchisee Jonah Engler says he manages the business by hiring managers that could do the job. He has given his employees small equity ownership in the company. He also says great service and referrals have contributed to his business' growth.

35446 ■ *"Project Could Forge Path to Jobs, Growth" in Business Courier (Vol. 26, September 11, 2009, No. 20, pp. 1)*
Pub: American City Business Journals, Inc.
Ed: Lucy May. **Description:** The planned 13.5 mile Mill Creek Greenway Trail extension could create 445 jobs and bring $52 million to the economy of Cincinnati, Ohio. The trail extension would cost $24 million and would be used for recreational purposes.

35447 ■ *"A Proper Welcome" in Canadian Business (Vol. 79, July 17, 2006, No. 14-15, pp. 67)*
Pub: Rogers Media
Ed: Graham Lowe. **Description:** New-employee orientation programs of various companies are highlighted. Useful practices to create a comfortable ambiance for new recruits are elucidated as well.

35448 ■ *"Protecting Company Secrets" in Inc. (February 2008, pp. 38-39)*
Pub: Gruner & Jahr USA Publishing
Ed: Scott Westcott. **Description:** A legal guide for noncompete clauses when hiring new employees is outlined, stressing how each state has its own set of laws.

35449 ■ *"Prudential Courts Hispanics" in Hispanic Business (March 2008, pp. 38, 40)*
Pub: Hispanic Business
Ed: Melinda Burns. **Description:** Prudential Financial Inc. is reaching out to Hispanic Chambers of Commerce in an effort to hire and do business with the Hispanic community in the U.S.

35450 ■ *"Putting Vets to Work" in Business Week (September 22, 2008, No. 4100, pp. 18)*
Pub: McGraw-Hill Companies, Inc.
Ed: Deborah Stead. **Description:** Advice is provided by former Marine Sal Cepeda, a consultant who advises employers on hiring veterans, for former military personnel coming back into the workforce.

35451 ■ *"Quick Earnings Revival Unlikely" in Barron's (Vol. 88, June 30, 2008, No. 26, pp. 31)*
Pub: Dow Jones & Co., Inc.
Ed: Johanna Bennett. **Description:** Analysts are pushing back their prediction of a U.S. economy turnaround to 2009. A recession in the first half of 2008 may not have happened but unemployment is rising and house prices continue to fall.

35452 ■ *"Quits Versus Layoffs" in Occupational Outlook Quarterly (Vol. 55, Fall 2011, No. 3, pp. 36)*
Pub: U.S. Bureau of Labor Statistics
Description: Data from the U.S. Bureau of Labor Statistics provides data from the Job Openings and Labor Turnover Survey regarding quits and layoffs.

35453 ■ *"Race and Gender Diversity" in Business Horizons (November-December 2007, pp. 445)*
Pub: Elsevier Technology Publications
Ed: James C. Wimbush. **Description:** Research conducted on diversity building, employee recruitment, gender issues in management, and pay inequality from 2006 through present are discussed. Diversity conditions and attitudes toward it are slowly improving based on these findings.

35454 ■ *"Recruiters Look Beyond Backyard to Find Gen Y Workers" in HRMagazine (Vol. 53, November 2008, No. 11, pp. 22)*
Pub: Society for Human Resource Management
Contact: Henry G. Jackson, President
E-mail: hjackson@shrm.org
Description: More than two-thirds of recent college graduates would relocate for a job, and 70 percent would be willing to move for an employer, according to the 2008 Hot Cities Survey; New York, Washington DC, and Chicago top the list of most desirable cities for relocation.

35455 ■ *"Recruiting 2.0" in Entrepreneur (Vol. 35, November 2007, No. 11, pp. 100)*
Pub: Entrepreneur Media Inc.
Ed: Andrea Cooper. **Description:** Technology is becoming a tool to help small companies find the best employees. Firms can look into social networking sites to see recommendations from the applicants' colleagues. Tips on how to select the employees online are listed.

35456 ■ *"Regional Talent Network Unveils Jobs Web Site" in Crain's Cleveland Business (Vol. 30, June 1, 2009, No. 21, pp. 11)*
Pub: Crain Communications, Inc.
Description: Regional Talent Network launched WhereToFindHelp.org, a Website designed to act as a directory of all Northeast Ohio resources that can help employers recruit and job seekers look for positions. The site also lists organizations offering employment and training services.

35457 ■ *"Reps Have Needs Too!" in Agency Sales Magazine (Vol. 39, December 2009, No. 11, pp. 16)*
Pub: MANA
Ed: Bill Heyden. **Description:** There is common information that a sales representatives needs to know prior to choosing a manufacturer to represent. Both parties must keep promises made to customers and prospects. Reps also need the support from the

manufacturers and to clear matters regarding their commission. Interviewing tips for representatives to get this vital information are presented.

35458 ■ *"Reps Vs. Factory Direct Sales Force..Which Way to Go?" in Agency Sales Magazine (Vol. 39, September-October 2009, No. 9, pp. 28)*
Pub: MANA
Ed: Eric P. Johnson. **Description:** Hiring independent manufacturers' sales representative is a cost-effective alternative to a direct sales force. Sales reps have predictable sales costs that go up and down with sales, stronger local relationships and better market intelligence.

35459 ■ *"Reps Vs. Factory Direct Sales Force..Which Way to Go?" in Agency Sales Magazine (Vol. 39, September-October 2009, No. 9, pp. 28)*
Pub: MANA
Ed: Eric P. Johnson. **Description:** Hiring independent manufacturers' sales representative is a cost-effective alternative to a direct sales force. Sales reps have predictable sales costs that go up and down with sales, stronger local relationships and better market intelligence.

35460 ■ *The Restaurant Manager's Handbook: How to Set Up, Operate, and Manage a Financially Successful Food Service Operation*
Pub: Atlantic Publishing Company
Released: September 25, 2007. **Price:** $79.95. **Description:** Insight is offered on running a successful food service business. Nine new chapters detail restaurant layout, new equipment, principles for creating a safer work environment, and new effective techniques to interview, hire, train, and manage employees.

35461 ■ *"'Resume Mining' Services Can Save Time, Money" in HR Specialist (Vol. 8, September 2010, No. 9, pp. 7)*
Pub: Capitol Information Group Inc.
Description: Low-cost resume mining services can help human resource departments save time and money by searching online resume databases for candidates matching specific job qualifications.

35462 ■ *"Retiring Baby Boomers and Dissatisfied Gen-Xers Cause..Brain Drain" in Agency Sales Magazine (Vol. 39, November 2009, No. 10)*
Pub: MANA
Ed: Denise Kelly. **Description:** Due to the impending retirement of the baby boomers a critical loss of knowledge and experience in businesses will result. Creating a plan to address this loss of talent centered on the development of the younger generation is discussed.

35463 ■ *"Ronald Taketa" in Hawaii Business (Vol. 54, September 2008, No. 3, pp. 28)*
Pub: Hawaii Business Publishing
Ed: Shara Enay. **Description:** Interview with Ronald Taketa of the Hawaii Carpenters Union who states that the economic downturn has affected the construction industry as 20 percent of the union's 7,800 members are unemployed. He shares his thoughts about the industry's economic situation, the union's advertisements, and his role as a leader of the union.

35464 ■ *"The Rypple Effect; Performance Management" in The Economist (Vol. 390, January 3, 2009, No. 8612, pp. 48)*
Pub: The Economist Newspaper Inc.
Description: New companies such as Rypple, a new, web-based service, claim that they can satisfy the Net Generation's need for frequent assessments while easing the burden this creates for management.

35465 ■ *"A Safety Net in Need of Repair" in The Economist (Vol. 390, January 3, 2009, No. 8612, pp. 33)*
Pub: The Economist Newspaper Inc.
Description: America's unemployment-insurance scheme is outdated and skimpy compared to other industrialized countries despite the fact that Americans tend to work harder at returning to the job market; the benefits are lower and available for a smaller amount of time and less unemployed workers are even able to collect these benefits. Statistical data included.

35466 ■ *"Samsung's Metamorphosis" in Austin Business Journal (Vol. 31, May 20, 2011, No. 11, pp. 1)*
Pub: American City Business Journals Inc.
Ed: Christopher Calnan. **Description:** Samsung Austin Semiconductor LP, a developer of semiconductors for smartphones and tablet computers, plans to diversify its offerings to include niche products: flash memory devices and microprocessing devices. In light of this strategy, Samsung Austin will be hiring 300 engineers as part of a $3.6 billion expansion of its plant.

35467 ■ *"Scouting and Keeping Good Talent in the Workplace" in Hawaii Business (Vol. 53, January 2008, No. 7, pp. 50)*
Pub: Hawaii Business Publishing
Ed: Christie Dermegian. **Description:** Tips on improving employee selection and retention are presented. The strategies in choosing and keeping the right employees include identifying which type of people the company needs and improving the workplace environment.

35468 ■ *"Second Chance Counselor" in Business Courier (Vol. 27, July 2, 2010, No. 9, pp. 1)*
Pub: Business Courier
Ed: Lucy May. **Description:** Stephen Tucker, director of workforce development for the Urban League of Greater Cincinnati, is an example of how ex-offenders can be given chances for employment after service jail sentences. How the Urban Leagues' Solid Opportunities for Advancement job training program helped Tucker and other ex-offenders is discussed.

35469 ■ *"A Second Chance to Make a Living" in The Business Journal-Milwaukee (Vol. 25, September 19, 2008, No. 52, pp. A1)*
Pub: American City Business Journals, Inc.
Description: Unemployed workers and baby boomers are driving interest in purchasing small businesses. BizBuySell general manager Mike Handelsman reveals that the supply of small businesses for sale is decreasing due to the increased demand. The trends in the small business market are analyzed.

35470 ■ *"Second to None" in Crain's Detroit Business (Vol. 26, January 18, 2010, No. 3, pp. 9)*
Pub: Crain Communications Inc.
Ed: Nancy Kaffer. **Description:** Second-stage companies are beginning to attract more attention from government entities and the business community alike, due in part to their ability to create jobs more rapidly than their counterparts both smaller and larger. Second-stage companies have between 10-99 employees and consistently have supplied the most jobs, despite overall job declines in recent years.

35471 ■ *"Sign of the Times: Temp-To-Perm Attorneys" in HRMagazine (Vol. 54, January 2009, No. 1, pp. 24)*
Pub: Society for Human Resource Management
Contact: Henry G. Jackson, President
E-mail: hjackson@shrm.org
Ed: Bill Leonard. **Description:** A growing number of law firms are hiring professional staff on a temp-to-perm basis according to the president of Professional Placement Services in Florida. Firms can save money while testing potential employees on a temporary basis.

35472 ■ *"Sign Up To Grow Your Business, Generate Jobs" in Women Entrepreneur (November 25, 2008)*
Pub: Entrepreneur Media Inc.
Ed: Eve Gumpel. **Description:** Nell Merlino has announced the new Make Mine A Million-Dollar Race, which aims to encourage hundreds of thousands of women entrepreneurs to grow their business to revenue goals of $250,00, $500,000 or $1 million and more as well as create 800,000 new jobs in an attempt to stimulate the nation's economy.

35473 ■ *"Size Matters" in Entrepreneur (Vol. 36, April 2008, No. 4, pp. 44)*
Pub: Entrepreneur Media, Inc.
Ed: Robert Kiyosaki. **Description:** Entrepreneurs planning to expand their business face challenges when it comes to employing more people and addressing internal relationships, communications and procedures. People skills, organizational skills and leadership skills are some of the things to consider before adding employees.

35474 ■ *"Small Business Employment" in Small Business Economic Trends (April 2008, pp. 9)*
Pub: National Federation of Independent Business
Ed: William C. Dunkelberg, Holly Wade. **Description:** Four tables and a graph representing employment rates of small businesses in the U.S. are presented. The tables include figures on employment changes, number of qualified applicants, job openings, and hiring plans.

35475 ■ *"Small Business Employment" in Small Business Economic Trends (March 2008, pp. 9)*
Pub: National Federation of Independent Business
Ed: William C. Dunkelberg, Holly Wade. **Description:** Four tables and a graph that present employment rates of small businesses in the U.S. are provided. The tables include figures on employment changes, number of qualified applicants, job openings and hiring plans.

35476 ■ *"Small Business Employment" in Small Business Economic Trends (February 2008, pp. 9)*
Pub: National Federation of Independent Business
Ed: William C. Dunkelberg, Holly Wade. **Description:** Four tables and a graph that present employment rates of small businesses in the U.S. are provided. The tables include figures on employment changes, number of qualified applicants, job openings and hiring plans.

35477 ■ *"Small Business Employment" in Small Business Economic Trends (January 2008, pp. 9)*
Pub: National Federation of Independent Business
Description: Table from a survey of small businesses in the U.S. is given, representing actual employment changes from January 2002 to December 2007. A graph comparing planned employment and current job openings from January 1986 to December 2007 is also supplied. Tables showing job opening, hiring plans, and qualified applicants for job openings are also presented.

35478 ■ *"Small Business Employment" in Small Business Economic Trends (September 2010, pp. 9)*
Pub: National Federation of Independent Business
Ed: William C. Dunkelberg, Holly Wade. **Description:** A table from a survey of small businesses in the U.S. is given, representing actual employment changes from January 2005 to August 2010. A graph comparing planned employment and current job openings from January 1986 to August 2010 is also supplied. Tables showing job openings, hiring plans, and qualified applicants for job openings are also presented.

35479 ■ *"Small Business Employment" in Small Business Economic Trends (July 2010, pp. 9)*
Pub: National Federation of Independent Business
Description: A table from a survey of small businesses in the U.S. is given representing actual employment changes from January 2005 to June 2010. A graph comparing planned employment and current job openings from January 1986 to June 2010 is also supplied. Tables showing job openings, hiring plans, and qualified applicants for job openings are also presented.

35480 ■ *The Small Business Owner's Manual: Everything You Need to Know to Start Up and Run Your Business*

Pub: Career Press, Incorporated

Ed: Joe Kennedy. **Released:** June 2005. **Price:** $19.99 (US), $26.95 (Canadian). **Description:** Comprehensive guide for starting a small business, focusing on twelve ways to obtain financing, business plans, selling and advertising products and services, hiring and firing employees, setting up a Web site, business law, accounting issues, insurance, equipment, computers, banks, financing, customer credit and collection, leasing, and more.

35481 ■ *"Staffing Firm Grows by Following Own Advice-Hire a Headhunter" in Crain's Detroit Business (Vol. 24, October 6, 2008, No. 40, pp. 1)*

Pub: Crain Communications, Inc.

Ed: Sherri Begin. **Description:** Profile of Venator Holdings L.L.C., a staffing firm that provides searches for companies in need of financial-accounting and technical employees; the firm's revenue has increased from $1.1 million in 2003 to a projected $11.5 million this year due to a climate in which more people are exiting the workforce than are coming in with those particular specialized skills and the need for a temporary, flexible workforce for contract placements at companies that do not want to take on the legacy costs associated with permanent employees. The hiring of an external headhunter to find the right out-of-state manager for Venator is also discussed.

35482 ■ *"Star Power" in Small Business Opportunities (September 2008)*

Pub: Entrepreneur Press

Contact: Perlman Neil, President

Description: Employee retention is an important factor for corporate executives to consider because the impact of excessive turnovers can be devastating to a company causing poor morale, unemployment claims, hiring costs, lost production and customer loss. Although there is no specific formula for retaining employees, there are several things every organization can do to keep their workers happy and increase the chances that they will stay loyal and keep working for the company for years to come; tips aimed at management regarding good employee relationships are included.

35483 ■ *"Start Filling Your Talent Gap - Now" in Business Strategy Review (Vol. 21, Spring 2010, No. 1, pp. 56)*

Pub: Wiley-Blackwell

Ed: Alan Bird, Lori Flees, Paul Di Paola. **Description:** As businesses steer their way out of turbulence, they have a unique opportunity to identify their leadership supply and demand and then to close the talent gap in their organization. Authors explain how to take immediate steps to build the right team now and lay the groundwork for a long-term approach for nurturing talent within the organization.

35484 ■ *"Stimulus Effect Slow" in Baltimore Business Journal (Vol. 27, October 23, 2009, No. 24, pp. 1)*

Pub: American City Business Journals

Ed: Scott Dance. **Description:** Companies in Maryland have reported only 154 new jobs being created or saved in Greater Baltimore and 965 jobs overall in the state because of stimulus cash. The federal stimulus program was expected to create thousands of new jobs but statistics show its failure to reduce unemployment in the state.

35485 ■ *"The Story Of Diane Greene" in Barron's (Vol. 88, July 14, 2008, No. 28, pp. 31)*

Pub: Dow Jones & Co., Inc.

Ed: Mark Veverka. **Description:** Discusses the ousting of Diane Greene as a chief executive of VMWare, a developer of virtualization software, after the firm went public; in this case Greene, a brilliant engineer, should not be negatively impacted by the decision because it is common for companies to bring in new executive leadership that is more operations oriented after the company goes public.

35486 ■ *"Succeed at a New Job" in Canadian Business (Vol. 79, November 20, 2006, No. 23, pp. 65)*

Pub: Rogers Media

Ed: Claire Gagne. **Description:** Collections of questions that job-seekers can ask the interviewer during employment interviews are presented.

35487 ■ *"SunBank Plans Expansion Via Wall-Mart" in Business Journal-Serving Phoenix and the Valley of the Sun (Vol. 10, November 9, 2007)*

Pub: American City Business Journals, Inc.

Ed: Chris Casacchia. **Description:** SunBank plans to install 12 to 14 branches in Wal-Mart stores in Arizona and hire 100 bankers by the end of 2008. Wal-Mart also offers financial products at other stores through partnerships with other banks.

35488 ■ *"Talent Shows" in Canadian Business (Vol. 81, December 24, 2007, No. 1, pp. 14)*

Pub: Rogers Media

Ed: Megan Harman. **Description:** Canadian companies are increasingly turning to marketing to promote themselves as employers, as concerns on employee recruitment increase with the nearing retirement age of the baby boomers. Details on skills shortage, the potential advantage for the immigrant workforce, and employee retention are discussed.

35489 ■ *"Tata's Novi Unit Looks to Hire 200 Engineers" in Crain's Detroit Business (Vol. 26, January 18, 2010, No. 3, pp. 4)*

Pub: Crain Communications Inc.

Ed: Lindsay Chappell. **Description:** Indian conglomerate Tata Sons Ltd.'s Novi-based engineering subsidiary is expected to hire around 200 engineers in the next three months or so, in part due to a more sophisticated attitude about outsourcing vehicle engineering to other companies.

35490 ■ *"Testing Firm to Add Jobs" in Business Courier (Vol. 26, December 11, 2009, No. 33, pp. 1)*

Pub: American City Business Journals, Inc.

Ed: Dan Monk. **Description:** Cincinnati-based Q Laboratories announced plans to add dozens of jobs with the $1.6 million stimulus assisted expansion. The company hired Michael Lichtenberg & Sons Construction Co. to build a new 9,000 square foot laboratory building.

35491 ■ *"Three Steps to Follow when Job Hunting" in Contractor (Vol. 56, September 2009, No. 9, pp. 62)*

Pub: Penton Media, Inc.

Ed: H. Kent Craig. **Description:** Advice on how project managers in the United States plumbing industry should look for jobs in view of the economic crisis. Job seekers should consider relocating to places where there are an abundance of project management jobs. Resumes should also be revised to make an applicant stand out.

35492 ■ *"Tough Sell" in Black Enterprise (Vol. 37, October 2006, No. 3, pp. 92)*

Pub: Earl G. Graves Publishing Co. Inc.

Ed: Sonia Alleyne. **Description:** Career coaches can evaluate your talents and skills. In an era where more companies are downsizing a coach can help you decide if you are suited for your industry or should try switching careers.

35493 ■ *"Toyota Revs Up Plans for Ontario Plant" in Globe & Mail (February 7, 2006, pp. B1)*

Pub: CTVglobemedia Publishing Inc.

Ed: Greg Keenan. **Description:** The production output and workforce addition proposals of Toyota Motor Corp., at Ontario plant, are presented.

35494 ■ *"Trade Craft: Take Pride in Your Trade, Demand Excellence" in Contractor (Vol. 56, October 2009, No. 10, pp. 24)*

Pub: Penton Media, Inc.

Ed: Al Schwartz. **Description:** There is a need for teaching, developing, and encouraging trade craft. An apprentice plumber is not only versed in the mechanical aspects of the trade but he also has a working knowledge of algebra, trigonometry, chemistry, and thermal dynamics. Contractors should be demanding on their personnel regarding their trade craft and should only keep and train the very best people they can hire.

35495 ■ *"Tri-State Lags Peer Cities in Jobs, Human Capital, Study Says" in Business Courier (Vol. 27, September 24, 2010, No. 21, pp. 1)*

Pub: Business Courier

Ed: Dan Monk, Lucy May. **Description:** Greater Cincinnati, Ohio has ranked tenth overall in the 'Agenda 360/Vision 2015 Regional Indicators Project' report. The study ranked 12-city-peer groups in categories such as job indicators standing and people indicators standing. The ranking of jobs and human capital study is topped by Minneapolis, followed by Denver, Raleigh, and Austin.

35496 ■ *"Uncertain Labor Pool Troubles Businesses" in Business First-Columbus (October 19, 2007, pp. A1)*

Pub: American City Business Journals, Inc.

Ed: Kevin Kemper. **Description:** Businesses in Columbus, Ohio are having difficulty finding skilled workers and expect this trend to continue through 2010-2020. They are trying to recruit young workers to address the shortage in skilled labor.

35497 ■ *"Under Pressure" in Canadian Business (Vol. 81, July 21, 2008, No. 11, pp. 18)*

Pub: Rogers Media Ltd.

Ed: Joe Castaldo. **Description:** According to a survey conducted by COMPASS Inc., meeting revenue targets is the main cause of job stress for chief executive officers. Staffing and keeping expenditures lower also contribute to the workplace stress experienced by business executives. Other results of the survey are presented.

35498 ■ *"Unemployment Rates" in The Economist (Vol. 390, January 3, 2009, No. 8612, pp. 75)*

Pub: The Economist Newspaper Inc.

Description: Countries that are being impacted the worst by rising unemployment rates are those that have also been suffering from the housing market crisis. Spain has been the hardest hit followed by Ireland. America and Britain are also seeing levels of unemployment that indicate too much slack in the economy.

35499 ■ *"Union Questions Patrick Cudahy Layoffs" in Business Journal-Milwaukee (Vol. 28, December 3, 2010, No. 9, pp. A1)*

Pub: Milwaukee Business Journal

Ed: Rich Ravito. **Description:** United Food and Commercial Workers Local 1473 is investigating Patrick Cudahy Inc.'s termination of 340 jobs. The union said the company has violated the law for failing to issue proper notice of a mass layoff.

35500 ■ *"U.S. Economy's Underlying Strengths Limit Recession Threat" in Hispanic Business (Vol. 30, April 2008, No. 4, pp. 14)*

Pub: Hispanic Business

Ed: Dr. Juan B. Solana. **Description:** Large and small businesses as well as consumers and policy-makers are attempting to identify the areas of risk and loss created by the economic crisis; analysts are now estimating that U.S. mortgage losses could reach the $380 to $400 billion mark. Also discusses the falling of wages and the rising of unemployment. Statistical data included.

35501 ■ *"Use a Benefits Checklist to Ease New-Hire Onboarding" in HR Specialist (Vol. 8, September 2010, No. 9, pp. 4)*

Pub: Capitol Information Group Inc.

Description: Checklist to help employees enroll in a company's benefit offerings is provided, courtesy of Wayne State University in Detroit, Michigan.

35502 ■ *"VC Boosts WorkForce; Livonia Software Company to Add Sales, Marketing Staff" in Crain's Detroit Business (March 24, 2008)*
Pub: Crain Communications, Inc.
Ed: Tom Henderson. **Description:** WorkForce Software Inc., a company that provides software to manage payroll processes and oversee compliance with state and federal regulations and with union rules, plans to use an investment of $5.5 million in venture capital to hire more sales and marketing staff.

35503 ■ *"Verizon Comes Calling With 500 Jobs" in Business First Columbus (Vol. 25, September 15, 2008, No. 4, pp. 1)*
Pub: American City Business Journals
Ed: Brian R. Ball. **Description:** Hilliard, Ohio offered Verizon Wireless a 15-year incentive package worth $3.4 million for the company to move 300 customer financial services jobs to the city in addition to the 200 jobs from their facility in Dublin, Ohio. The incentives include a return of 15 percent of the income tax generated by the jobs.

35504 ■ *"Wal-Mart Sharpens Focus on Roxbury" in Boston Business Journal (Vol. 31, July 8, 2011, No. 24, pp. 1)*
Pub: Boston Business Journal
Ed: Mary Moore. **Description:** Wal-Mart Stores is boosting its search for a possible location in the Roxbury section of Boston, Massachusetts. The search is focused on underserved communities in terms of jobs and access to reasonably-priced merchandise. The extent Boston's African American community has clashed with Mayor Thomas M. Memino over the accommodations of the retailer in Roxbury is discussed.

35505 ■ *"Walker Seeks More Business Participation" in Business Journal-Milwaukee (Vol. 28, December 10, 2010, No. 10, pp. A1)*
Pub: Milwaukee Business Journal
Ed: Rich Kirchen. **Description:** Wisconsin governor Scott Walker is seeking the aid of Milwaukee business leaders to participate in resolving the challenges posed by the economic crisis. Walker is aiming to create 250,000 jobs. He is also planning to call a special session of the legislature to enact strategies to jumpstart the economy.

35506 ■ *The Wall Street Journal. Complete Small Business Guidebook*
Pub: Three Rivers Press
Ed: Colleen DeBaise. **Released:** December 29, 2009. **Price:** $15.00. **Description:** The mechanics of building, running and growing a profitable business are outlined, teaching how to write a business plan, ways to finding money during lean years, how to keep stress in check, time management, investment in technology, hiring, marketing, management basics, angel investing and venture capital, as well as an exit strategy.

35507 ■ *"Wanted: African American Professional for Hire" in Black Enterprise (Vol. 37, November 2006, No. 4, pp. 93)*
Pub: Earl G. Graves Publishing Co. Inc.
Ed: Joe Watson. **Description:** Excerpt from the book, Without Excuses: Unleash the Power of Diversity to Build Your Business, speaks to the lack of diversity in the corporate arena and why executives, recruiters, and HR professionals claim they are unable to find qualified individuals of different races when hiring.

35508 ■ *"The War for Good Jobs; The World Will IBe Led with Economic Force" in Gallup Management Journal (September 7, 2011)*
Pub: Gallup
Ed: Jim Clifton. **Description:** Gallup's chairman believes the next world war will be for good jobs and the winner will triumph with economic force, driven primarily by job creation and quality GDP growth.

35509 ■ *"The War for Talent" in Canadian Business (Vol. 80, January 29, 2007, No. 3, pp. 60)*
Pub: Rogers Media
Ed: Erin Pooley. **Description:** The recruitment policies of Canadian businesses are described. The trends pertaining to the growth of executive salaries in Canada are discussed.

35510 ■ *"Water Company Eyeing Region for a New Plant" in Charlotte Business Journal (Vol. 25, December 10, 2010, No. 38, pp. 1)*
Pub: Charlotte Business Journal
Ed: Ken Elkins. **Description:** California-based Niagara Bottling Company is hoping to find a site in Charlotte, North Carolina where it can build a water bottling plant that would employ 70 workers. The investment is expected to cost about $25 million to $40 million.

35511 ■ *"Wattles Plugs Back Into State" in Business Journal Portland (Vol. 27, November 19, 2010, No. 38, pp. 1)*
Pub: Portland Business Journal
Ed: Wendy Culverwell. **Description:** Denver, Colorado-based Ultimate Electronics Inc.'s first store in Oregon was opened in Portland and the 46th store in the chain of electronic superstores is expected to employ 70-80 workers. The venture is the latest for Mark Wattles, one of Oregon's most successful entrepreneurs, who acquired Ultimate from bankruptcy.

35512 ■ *"Waugh Chapel to Expand" in Baltimore Business Journal (Vol. 28, August 27, 2010, No. 16, pp. 1)*
Pub: Baltimore Business Journal
Ed: Daniel J. Sernovitz. **Description:** Developer Greenberg Gibbons Corporation has broken ground on a $275 million, 1.2 million-square-foot addition to its Village at the Waugh Chapel mixed-use complex. Aside from creating 2,600 permanent jobs, the addition, named Village South, is expected to lure Target and Wegmans Food Markets to Crofton, Maryland. Funding for this project is discussed.

35513 ■ *"Wayne, Oakland Counties Create Own 'Medical Corridor'" in Crain's Detroit Business (Vol. 24, October 6, 2008, No. 40, pp. 8)*
Pub: Crain Communications, Inc.
Ed: Jay Greene. **Description:** Woodward Medical Corridor that runs along Woodward Avenue and currently encompasses twelve hospitals and is rapidly growing with additional physician offices, advanced oncology centers and new hospitals. Beaumont Hospital is building a $160 million proton-beam therapy cancer center on its Royal Oak campus in a joint venture with Procure Treatment Centers of Bloomington Ind. That is expected to open in 2010 and will employ approximately 145 new workers.

35514 ■ *"Wealth and Jobs: the Broken Link" in Harvard Business Review (Vol. 88, November 2010, No. 11, pp. 44)*
Pub: Harvard Business School Publishing
Ed: Nitin Nohria. **Description:** Rebuilding the link between business and job creation to shore up the middle class is advocated. A blend of government policies and business strategies that foster entrepreneurship and innovation are essential.

35515 ■ *"Web Site Design, Content Can Boost Diversity" in HRMagazine (Vol. 53, August 2008, No. 8, pp. 20)*
Pub: Society for Human Resource Management
Contact: Henry G. Jackson, President
E-mail: hjackson@shrm.org
Description: Design and content of an employer's Website influences prospective young job candidates, especially young black job seekers, a new academic study has found. The findings appear in Black and White and Read All Over: Race Differences in Reactions To Recruitment Web Sites, published in the summer 2008 issue of the Human Resource Management Journal.

35516 ■ *"Web Site Focuses on Helping People Find Jobs, Internships with Area Businesses" in Crain's Detroit Business (Vol. 26, Jan. 4, 2010)*
Pub: Crain Communications Inc.
Ed: Dustin Walsh. **Description:** DetroitIntern.com, LLC is helping metro Detroit college students and young professionals find career-advancing internships or jobs with local businesses.

35517 ■ *The Well-Timed Strategy: Managing Business Cycle for Competitive Advantage*
Pub: Wharton School Publishing
Ed: Peter Navarro. **Released:** January 23, 2006. **Price:** $34.99. **Description:** An overview of business cycles and risks is presented. Recession is a good time to find key personnel for a small business. Other issues addressed include investment, production, and marketing in order to maintain a competitive edge.

35518 ■ *"What Businesses Can Do: Growing the Supply of Highly Skilled Graduates" in Canadian Business (Vol. 81, October 27, 2008, No. 18)*
Pub: Rogers Media Ltd.
Description: Employers in Canada have expressed concerns over the findings of various studies that revealed current and projected labor shortages in the country. A low birthrate and an aging population is contributing to the problem. Ways businesses can increase the supply of highly skilled workers in Canada is presented.

35519 ■ *"What You Look Like Online" in Black Enterprise (Vol. 37, January 2007, No. 6, pp. 56)*
Pub: Earl G. Graves Publishing Co. Inc.
Ed: Marcia A. Reed-Woodard. **Description:** Of 100 executive recruiters 77 percent stated that they use search engines to check the backgrounds of potential job candidates, according to a survey conducted by ExecuNet. Of those surveyed 35 percent stated that they eliminate potential candidates based on information they find online so it is important to create a positive Web presence which highlights professional image qualities.

35520 ■ *"What You Should Know About Signing Bonuses" in Black Enterprise (Vol. 38, October 2007, No. 3, pp. 70)*
Pub: Earl G. Graves Publishing Co. Inc.
Ed: Marcia Reed-Woodard. **Description:** High-level corporate executives are receiving sign-on bonuses. According to a study conducted by World@Work, nearly 70 percent of employers signing bonuses attract key employees.

35521 ■ *"What's Working Now: In Providing Jobs for North Carolinians" in Business North Carolina (Vol. 28, February 2008, No. 2, pp. 16)*
Pub: Business North Carolina
Ed: Edward Martin, Frank Maley. **Description:** Individuals previously employed in the furniture, tobacco, or textile manufacturing sectors have gone back to school to be trained in new sectors in the area such as life sciences, finances and other emerging sectors.

35522 ■ *"When You Need Strong Millennials in Your Workplace" in Agency Sales Magazine (Vol. 39, November 2009, No. 10, pp. 22)*
Pub: MANA
Ed: Joanne G. Sujansky. **Description:** Millennials are bringing a new set of skills and a different kind of work ethics to the workplace. This generation is used to receiving a great deal of positive feedback and they expect to continue receiving this on the job. Expectations should be made clear to this generation and long-term career plans and goals should also be discussed with them.

35523 ■ *"Why Entrepreneurs Matter More Than Innovators" in Gallup Management Journal (November 22, 2011)*
Pub: Gallup
Ed: Jim Clifton. **Description:** In the race to create good jobs, leaders are not paying enough attention to cultivating talented entrepreneurs, rather they invest too much attention on innovation.

35524 ■ *"Why Is It So Hard To Find Good People? The Problem Might Be You" in Inc. (Vol. 33, November 2011, No. 9, pp. 100)*
Pub: Inc. Magazine
Ed: April Joyner. **Description:** Entrepreneurs sometimes struggle to find good workers. A recent survey shows hiring as their top concern. Four common mistakes that can occur during the hiring process our outlined.

35525 ■ *"Winburn's Big Idea" in Business Courier (Vol. 27, October 8, 2010, No. 23, pp. 1)*
Pub: Business Courier
Ed: Dan Monk, Lucy May. **Description:** Cincinnati Councilman Charlie Winburn proposed the creation of Cincinnati Competitive Edge Division and to remake a small-business division of the city in order to start a job-creation program. The new division will monitor compliance to the city's small business inclusion regulations, as well as to help small business owners grow.

35526 ■ *"Work To Do" in Canadian Business (Vol. 81, July 22, 2008, No. 12-13, pp. 22)*
Pub: Rogers Media Ltd.
Ed: Jane Bao. **Description:** Recruiting firm Manpower revealed that 36 percent of Canadian employers had trouble filling positions in 2007, highlighting the labor shortage and the need to bring in more workers. Underemployment of immigrants costs up to $6 billion to Canada's economy every year. Other views regarding Canada's labor shortage and on its economic impact are presented.

35527 ■ *The Worst-Case Scenario Business Survival Guide*
Pub: John Wiley & Sons, Inc.
Released: September 28, 2009. **Price:** $17.95. **Description:** Since 1999, the Worst-Case Scenario survival handbooks have provided readers with real answers for the most extreme situations. Now, in a time of economic crisis, the series returns with a new, real-world guide to avoiding the worst business cataclysms.

35528 ■ *"You Are What They Click" in Entrepreneur (Vol. 37, July 2009, No. 7, pp. 43)*
Pub: Entrepreneur Media, Inc.
Ed: Mikal Belicove. **Description:** Hiring the right website design firm is the first stage in building an online business, and this involves various factors such as price, technical expertise, and talent. Writing a request for proposal (RFP) detailing the website's details, which include purpose, budget and audience, is the first step the process. Other tips in finding the right web designer are given.

35529 ■ *"Your First 100 Days on Your New Job" in Women In Business (Vol. 63, Spring 2011, No. 1, pp. 28)*
Pub: American Business Women's Association
Ed: Diane Stafford. **Description:** The first 100 days on the job are crucial if the person's permanent hiring is conditional on surviving a probationary period. The new hire must do more than just master the job's technical details to maximize the chance of success. Details of some basic tips to fit into the corporate culture and get along with coworkers are also discussed.

35530 ■ *"Youth Employment in the Summer of 2010" in Montly Labor Review (Vol. 133, September 2010, No. 9, pp. 2)*
Pub: Bureau of Labor Statistics
Description: The number of youth 16 to 24 years old rose by 1.8 million from April to July 2010. Statistical data included.

35531 ■ *"ZF Revving Up Jobs, Growth" in Business Courier (Vol. 26, November 6, 2009, No. 28, pp. 1)*
Pub: American City Business Journals, Inc.
Ed: Jon Newberry. **Description:** Proposed $96 million expansion of German-owned automotive supplier ZF Steering systems LLC is anticipated to generate 299 jobs in Boone County, Kentucky. ZF might invest $90 million in equipment, while the rest will go to building and improvements.

TRADE PERIODICALS

35532 ■ *Insight into Diversity: The EEO Recruitment Publication*
Pub: INSIGHT Into Diversity
URL(s): www.insightintodiversity.com. **Ed:** Michael Rainey. **Released:** Monthly

VIDEOCASSETTES/ AUDIOCASSETTES

35533 ■ *Brief Encounters*
Excellence in Training Corp.
c/o ICON Training
804 Roosevelt St.
Polk City, IA 50226
Free: 800-609-0479
Co. E-mail: info@icontraining.com
URL: http://www.icontraining.com
Released: 1991. **Price:** $695.00. **Description:** A presentation on 10 techniques to help interviewers select the best-qualified job applicant. **Availability:** VHS; 3/4 U; Special order formats.

35534 ■ *Chinese for Affirmative Action*
Chinese for Affirmative Action (CAA)
17 Walter U. Lum Pl.
San Francisco, CA 94108
Ph: (415)274-6750
Fax: (415)397-8770
Co. E-mail: info@caasf.org
URL: http://www.caasf.org
Contact: Andy Wong, Director
Released: 1974. **Description:** "Chinese for Affirmative Action" is a promotional program about the civil rights organization based in San Francisco's Chinatown. **Availability:** 3/4 U.

35535 ■ *Communication Series: Interviewing*
Michigan State University
Media Services
126 Instructional Media Center
East Lansing, MI 48824-2121
Ph: (517)353-3960
Fax: (517)353-1817
Co. E-mail: jowett@msu.edu
URL: http://imc.msu.edu/
Released: 1981. **Description:** Mike Wallace, George Gallup and John Shingleton are interviewed about the techniques they use for interviewing. **Availability:** VHS; 3/4 U.

35536 ■ *The Effective Manager*
Nightingale-Conant Corp.
6245 W. Howard St.
Niles, IL 60714
Ph: (847)647-0300
Free: 800-560-6081
URL: http://www.nightingale.com
Released: 19??. **Price:** $95.00. **Description:** A series of award-winning programs designed to promote effective management and help increase sales. Audio tapes and booklets are included, and the series can be purchased individually or as a set. **Availability:** VHS.

35537 ■ *Equal Treatment/Equal Opportunity*
Gulf Publishing Co.
2 Greenway Plz., Ste. 1020
Houston, TX 77046-0208
Ph: (713)529-4301
Free: 800-231-6275
Fax: (713)520-4433
Co. E-mail: advertising@gulfpub.com
URL: http://www.gulfpub.com
Contact: John Royall, President
Released: 1984. **Price:** $375.00. **Description:** This program is designed to help the workforce to understand what comprises discrimination. **Availability:** VHS; 3/4 U.

35538 ■ *Man Hunt*
Video Arts, Inc.
c/o Aim Learning Group
8238-40 Lehigh
Morton Grove, IL 60053-2615
Free: 877-444-2230
Fax: (416)252-2155
Co. E-mail: service@aimlearninggroup.com
URL: http://www.aimlearninggroup.com
Released: 1974. **Price:** $790.00. **Description:** Often, managers feels that they know the person they want for a job just by seeing them. The purpose of this program is to make managers realize this is not so. It shows where and how the principal faults occur: failure to prepare for the interview, failure to draw the candidate out and get him to talk freely, and failure to come out with direct, probing questions. **Availability:** VHS; 8 mm; 3/4 U; Special order formats.

35539 ■ *Managing Frontline Service*
Video Arts, Inc.
c/o Aim Learning Group
8238-40 Lehigh
Morton Grove, IL 60053-2615
Free: 877-444-2230
Fax: (416)252-2155
Co. E-mail: service@aimlearninggroup.com
URL: http://www.aimlearninggroup.com
Released: 1989. **Price:** $730.00. **Description:** Through case studies in two highly successful corporations, this video shows how to improve performance by selecting, training, and motivating the right people. **Availability:** VHS; 8 mm; 3/4 U; Special order formats.

35540 ■ *More Than a Gut Feeling 2*
American Media, Inc.
4621 121st St.
Urbandale, IA 50323-2311
Ph: (515)224-0919
Free: 888-776-8268
Fax: (515)327-2555
Co. E-mail: custsvc@ammedia.com
URL: http://www.ammedia.com
Released: 1991. **Price:** $695.00. **Description:** This follow-up to "More Than a Gut Feeling" shows how to gauge a job candidate's future performance by getting her or him talk about past job experience. A leader's guide, desk reminder card, and charts of legal and illegal questions are included. **Availability:** VHS; 3/4 U; Special order formats.

CONSULTANTS

35541 ■ Barada Associates Inc.
130 E 2nd St.
Rushville, IN 46173
Ph: (765)932-5917
Fax: (765)932-2938
Co. E-mail: info@baradainc.com
URL: http://www.baradainc.com
Contact: William C. Barada, President
E-mail: will@baradainc.com
Scope: Professional employment screening services provides client companies within dependent and objective reference reports on candidates for salaried and hourly employment. **Founded:** 1979. **Publications:** "Reference Checking for Everyone," 2004; "Reference Checking is More Than Ever," Human Resource Magazine, 1996; "The Paper Chase," Indianapolis Monthly, 1995; "Check it Out-Hiring? What You Don't Know Could Hurt You," the American School Board Journal, 1994; "Reference Checking: Increased Necessity to Exercise Reasonable Care," Kin cannon & Reed, 1994; "Reference Checking More Critical Than Ever," Association of Executive Search Consultants Inc, Dec, 1993; "Honest References," Human Resource Executive, Sep, 1993; "Check References with Care," Nation's Business, May, 1993; "Don't Overlook Reference Checks," the School Administrator, May, 1992. **Telecommunication Services:** sales@baradainc.com.

35542 ■ Gately Consulting
115 Dutcher St.
Hopedale, MA 01747-1006
Ph: (508)473-0955
URL: http://www.gatelyconsulting.com
Contact: Robert F. Gately, Owner
E-mail: bobgately@csi.com
Scope: Provides the PofileXT assessment, an innovative assessment technology, for personnel and pre-employment evaluations, and ensuring success in matching people to jobs and 360's. **Founded:** 1992. **Publications:** "The Employer's Advantage Newsletter". **Seminars:** The New Art of Hiring Smart.

35543 ■ Edward M. Hepner & Associates
4667 Macarthur Blvd., Ste. 405
Newport Beach, CA 92660
Ph: (714)250-0818

Fax: (714)553-8437
Contact: Edward M. Hepner, President
Scope: An immigration consultant and labor certification specialist. Assists in obtaining visa for work, immigration and business development within the United States and Canada.

COMPUTERIZED DATABASES

35544 ■ *ABI/INFORM®*
789 E Eisenhower Pkwy.
Ann Arbor, MI 48106-1346
Ph: (734)761-4700
Free: 800-521-0600
Co. E-mail: info@il.proquest.com
URL: http://www.il.proquest.com
Contact: Matt Dunie, President
Availability: Online: ProQuest Co.; ProQuest LLC-Dialog; ProQuest LLC - Dialog; LexisNexis Group; STN International; Wolters Kluwer Health - Ovid.
Type: Full-text; Bibliographic; Image.

START-UP INFORMATION

35545 ■ *101 Businesses You Can Satrt at with Less Thank One Thousand Dollars: For Retirees*
Pub: Atlantic Publishing Company
Ed: Christina Bultinck. **Released:** December 2006. **Price:** $21.95. **Description:** Business ideas to help retirees start a home-based business on a low budget.

35546 ■ *101 Businesses You Can Start at with Less Than One Thousand Dollars: For Stay-At-Home Moms and Dads*
Pub: Atlantic Publishing Company
Ed: Christina Bultinck. **Released:** December 2006. **Price:** $21.95. **Description:** Business ideas to help stay-at-home moms and dads start a home-based business on a low budget.

35547 ■ *101 Businesses You Can Start with Less Than One Thousand Dollars: for Stay-at-Home Moms and Dads*
Pub: Atlantic Publishing Company
Ed: Heather Lee Shepherd. **Released:** October 2007. **Price:** $21.95. **Description:** Over 100 business ideas are detailed to help stay-at-home parents earn extra money to add to the family income. These businesses can be started with minimum training and investment and most can be easily operated by one person and eventually be sold for an additional profit; many are started with less than one hundred dollars and can be run from home.

35548 ■ *101 Internet Businesses You Can Start from Home: How to Choose and Build Your Own Successful E-Business*
Pub: Maximum Press
Ed: Susan Sweeney. **Released:** June 2006. **Price:** $29.95. **Description:** Guide for starting and growing an Internet business; information for developing a business plan, risk levels, and promotional techniques are included.

35549 ■ *Breaking Free: How to Work at Home with the Perfect Small Business Opportunity*
Pub: Lulu.com
Ed: Brian Armstrong. **Released:** June 2007. **Price:** $24.95. **Description:** Three ways to smooth the transition from working for someone else to starting your own business are outlined. Seven exercises to help discover the type of business you should start, how to incorporate, get important tax benefits, and start accepting payments immediately are examined.

35550 ■ *"Caring Concern" in Small Business Opportunities (September 2010)*
Pub: Harris Publications Inc.
Description: Profile of Joshua Hoffman, founder and CEO of HomeWell Senior Care, Inc., provider of non-medical live-in and hourly personal care, companionship and homemaker services for seniors so they can remain in their own homes.

35551 ■ *The Complete Guide to Making Money at Home: Everything You Need to Know to Earn Riches at Home*
Pub: Ridgewood Press
Ed: Gary J. Fuller. **Released:** January 2006. **Price:** $19.95. **Description:** Guide for starting and running an at-home business.

35552 ■ *The Craft Business Answer Book: Starting, Managing, and Marketing a Home-Based Art, Crafts, Design Business*
Pub: M. Evans and Company, Incorporated
Ed: Barbara Brabec. **Released:** August 2006. **Price:** $16.95. **Description:** Expert advice for starting a home-based art or crafts business is offered.

35553 ■ *Earn Cash Crafting at Home: An MBA At-Home Mom Explains Step-by-Step Her Fun, Proven, Money-Making, Own-Your-Own Business Formula*
Pub: Dark Horse, Incorporated
Ed: Maria Colman. **Released:** March 2006. **Price:** $10.00. **Description:** Manual offering advice to start and run an at-home craft business.

35554 ■ *"Fast-Forward Fortune" in Small Business Opportunities (July 2010)*
Pub: Harris Publications Inc.
Description: Profile of Steve Dalbec and his home-based Home Video Studio where he earns income by offering a wide variety of video services to clients from duplicating CDs, video to DVD transfer, sports videos and more. Dalbec believes this is the perfect home-based business.

35555 ■ *"Five Low-Cost Home Based Startups" in Women Entrepreneur (December 16, 2008)*
Pub: Entrepreneur Media Inc.
Ed: Lesley Spencer Pyle. **Description:** During tough economic times, small businesses have an advantage over large companies because they can adjust to economic conditions more easily and without having to go through corporate red tape that can slow the implementation process. A budding entrepreneur may find success by taking inventory of his or her skills, experience, expertise and passions and utilizing those qualities to start a business. Five low-cost home-based startups are profiled. These include starting an online store, a virtual assistant service, web designer, sales representative and a home staging counselor.

35556 ■ *Getting Rich In Your Underwear: How To Start and Run a Profitable Home-Based Business*
Pub: HCM Publishing
Ed: Peter I. Hupalo. **Released:** April 1, 2005. **Price:** $17.95. **Description:** Book offers insight into starting a home-based business. Entrepreneurs will learn about business models and the home business; distribution and fulfillment of product or service; marketing and sales; how to overcome the fear of starting a business; personal success characteristics; naming a business; zoning and insurance; intellectual capital; copyrights, trademarks, and patents; limited liability companies and S-corporations; business expenses and accounting; taxes; fifteen basic steps for starting a home-based business, state resources for starting a home company; and seven home-based business ideas.

35557 ■ *Going Solo: Developing a Home-Based Consulting Business from the Ground Up*
Pub: McGraw-Hill Companies Inc.
Contact: Deven Sharma, President
Ed: William J. Bond. **Released:** January 1997. **Description:** Ways to turn specialized knowledge into a home-based successful consulting firm, focusing on targeting client needs, business plans, and growth.

35558 ■ *"Green Clean Machine" in Small Business Opportunities (Winter 2010)*
Pub: Harris Publications Inc.
Description: Eco-friendly maid franchise plans to grow its $62 million sales base. Profile of Maid Brigade, a green-cleaning franchise is planning to expand across the country.

35559 ■ *Home-Based Business for Dummies*
Pub: John Wiley and Sons, Inc.
Ed: Paul Edwards, Sarah Edwards, Peter Economy. **Released:** February 25, 2005. **Price:** $19.99. **Description:** Provides all the information needed to start and run a home-based business. Topics include: selecting the right business; setting up a home office; managing money, credit, and financing; marketing; and ways to avoid distractions while working at home.

35560 ■ *Home-Based Travel Agent, 5th Edition*
Pub: The Intrepid Traveler
Ed: Kelly Monaghan. **Released:** March 2006. **Price:** $59.95. **Description:** Advice for starting and running a home-based travel agency is given.

35561 ■ *"Home Work" in Black Enterprise (Vol. 37, October 2006, No. 3, pp. 78)*
Pub: Earl G. Graves Publishing Co. Inc.
Ed: James C. Johnson. **Description:** Information on starting a resume-writing service is profiled.

35562 ■ *How to Make Money While You Look for a Job*
Pub: Booklocker.com, Incorporated
Ed: Donna Boyette. **Released:** March 2005. **Price:** $11.95. **Description:** Six steps to make money while searching for employment are outlined, from setting up a home-based office to selling a service.

35563 ■ *How to Open and Operate a Financially Successful Landscaping, Nursery or Lawn Service Business: With Companion CD-ROM*
Pub: Atlantic Publishing Company
Ed: Lynn Wasnak. **Released:** June 1, 2009. **Price:** $39.95. **Description:** Guide provides understanding of the basic concepts of starting and running a service business, focusing on the operation of a small nursery, landscaping, or lawn service or combining the three operations. It also offers tips for running the business from the home.

35564 ■ *How to Start a Home-Based Consulting Business: Define Your Specialty Build a Client Base Make Yourself Indispensable*
Pub: Globe Pequot Press
Ed: Bert Holtje. **Released:** January 10, 2010. **Price:** $18.95. **Description:** Everything needed for starting and running a successful consulting business from home.

35565 ■ *How to Start a Home-Based Craft Business, 5th Ed.*
Pub: Globe Pequot Press
Ed: Kenn Oberrecht. **Released:** July 2007. **Price:** $18.95. **Description:** Step-by-step guide for starting and growing a home-based craft business.

35566 ■ *How to Start a Home-Based Craft Business, 5th Edition*
Pub: Globe Pequot Press
Ed: Kenn Oberrecht. **Released:** July 2007. **Price:** $18.95. **Description:** Advice for starting a home-based craft business is given, including sources for finding supplies on the Internet, writing a business plan, publicity, zoning ordinances, and more.

35567 ■ *How to Start a Home-Based Event Planning Business*
Pub: Globe Pequot Press
Ed: Jill Moran. **Released:** July 2007. **Price:** $18.95. **Description:** Guide to starting and growing a business planning events from a home-based firm.

35568 ■ *How to Start a Home-Based Interior Design Business*
Pub: Globe Pequot Press
Ed: Nita Phillips. **Released:** January 2006.

35569 ■ *How to Start a Home-Based Landscaping Business*
Pub: Globe Pequot Press
Ed: Owen E. Dell. **Released:** December 2005. **Price:** $18.95. **Description:** Guide to starting and running a home-based landscaping business.

35570 ■ *How to Start a Home-Based Mail Order Business*
Pub: Globe Pequot Press
Ed: Georganne Fiumara. **Released:** January 2005. **Price:** $17.95. **Description:** Step-by-step guide for starting and growing a home-based mail order business. Information about equipment, pricing, online marketing, are included along with worksheets and checklists for planning.

35571 ■ *How to Start a Home-Based Online Retail Business*
Pub: Globe Pequot Press
Ed: Jeremy Shepherd. **Released:** February 2007. **Price:** $18.95. **Description:** Information for starting an online retail, home-based business is shared.

35572 ■ *How to Start a Home-Based Personal Chef Business*
Pub: Globe Pequot Press
Ed: Denise Vivaldo. **Released:** December 2006. **Price:** $18.95. **Description:** Everything needed to know to start a personal chef business is featured.

35573 ■ *How to Start a Home-Based Professional Organizing Business*
Pub: Globe Pequot Press
Ed: Dawn Noble. **Released:** March 2007. **Price:** $18.95. **Description:** Tips for starting a home-based professional organizing business are presented.

35574 ■ *How to Start a Home-Based Senior Care Business: Develop a Winning Business Plan*
Pub: Globe Pequot Press
Ed: James L. Ferry. **Released:** January 10, 2010. **Price:** $18.95. **Description:** Everything needed to know in order to start and run a profitable, ethical, and satisfying senior care business from your home. Information covers writing a good business plan, marketing services to families, creating a fee structure, and developing a network of trusted caregivers and service providers.

35575 ■ *How to Start a Home-Based Web Design Business, 4th Edition*
Pub: Globe Pequot Press
Ed: Jim Smith. **Released:** July 1, 2010. **Price:** $18.95. **Description:** Comprehensive guide contains all the necessary tools and strategies required to successfully launch and grow a Web design business.

35576 ■ *How to Start and Run a Home-Based Landscaping Business*
Pub: Globe Pequot Press
Ed: Owen E. Dell. **Released:** December 2005. **Price:** $18.95. **Description:** Guide to starting and running a successful home-based landscaping business, including tips for marketing on the Internet.

35577 ■ *Interior Design Business*
Pub: Globe Pequot Press
Ed: Suzanne DeWalt; Nita B. Phillips. **Released:** January 2006. **Price:** $18.95. **Description:** Tips for starting and running a home-based interior design business are given.

35578 ■ *"Legendary Success" in Small Business Opportunities (November 2010)*
Pub: Harris Publications Inc.
Description: Von Schrader is famous in the cleaning industry and more than 50,000 individuals have started their own professional cleaning service businesses using the company's air cell technology cleaning systems along with their proven business systems. This is a perfect business for anyone wishing to start and run it from their home.

35579 ■ *"Road Map To Riches" in Small Business Opportunities (September 2010)*
Pub: Harris Publications Inc.
Description: Profile of Philip Nenadov who launched The Transportation Network Group during the recession. This franchise is low cost and can earn six figures while working from home by becoming a trucking agent.

35580 ■ *Scrapbooking for Profit: Cashing in on Retail, Home-Based and Internet Opportunities*
Pub: Allworth Press
Ed: Rebecca Pittman. **Released:** June 2005. **Price:** $19.95 (US), $22.95 (Canadian). **Description:** Eleven strategies for starting a scrapbooking business, including brick-and-mortar stores, home-based businesses, and online retail and wholesale outlets.

35581 ■ *Start and Run a Home-Based Food Business*
Pub: Self-Counsel Press, Inc.
Ed: Mimi Shotland Fix. **Released:** January 10, 2010. **Price:** $21.95. **Description:** Information is shared to help start and run a home-based food business, selling your own homemade foods.

35582 ■ *Start Your Own Fashion Accessories Business*
Pub: Entrepreneur Press
Contact: Perlman Neil, President
Released: March 1, 2009. **Price:** $17.95. **Description:** Entrepreneurs wishing to start a fashion accessories business will find important information for setting up a home workshop and office, exploring the market, managing finances, publicizing and advertising the business and more.

35583 ■ *"This Biz Is Booming" in Small Business Opportunities (Winter 2010)*
Pub: Harris Publications Inc.
Description: Non-medical home care is a $52 billion industry. Advice to start a non-medical home care business is provided, focusing on franchise FirstLight HomeCare, but showing that independent home care agencies are also successful.

35584 ■ *Ultimate Homebased Business Handbook: How to Start, Run, and Grow Your Own Profitable Business*
Pub: Entrepreneur Press
Ed: James Stephenson. **Released:** June 2008. **Price:** $29.95 (US), $34.95 (Canadian). **Description:** Detailed information for anyone wanting to start a home-based business. Topics include how-to tips, ideas, tools, and print and online resources.

35585 ■ *Web Design Business*
Pub: Globe Pequot Press
Ed: Jim Smith. **Released:** January 2007. **Price:** $18.95. **Description:** Information for starting a home-based Web design firm is given.

35586 ■ *Work at Home Now*
Pub: Career Press, Inc.
Ed: Christine Durst, Michael Haaren. **Released:** October 9, 2010. **Price:** $14.99. **Description:** There are legitimate home-based jobs and projects that can be found on the Internet, but trustworthy guidance is scarce. There is a 58 to 1 scam ratio in work at-home advertising filled with fraud.

35587 ■ *Work@home: A Practical Guide for Women Who Want to Work from Home*
Pub: Woman's Missionary Union
Contact: Debby Akerman, President
Ed: Glynnis Whitwer. **Released:** March 2007. **Price:** $15.99. **Description:** Fifty-three percent of all small business are home-based. The book provides tips to women for starting a home-based business.

ASSOCIATIONS AND OTHER ORGANIZATIONS

35588 ■ American Home Business Association (AHBA)
965 E 4800, Ste. 3C
Salt Lake City, UT 84117
Ph: (801)273-2350
Free: 866-396-7773
Fax: (866)396-7773
Co. E-mail: info@homebusinessworks.com
URL: http://www.homebusinessworks.com
Description: Offers benefits and services dedicated to supporting the needs of home business, small business and entrepreneurs. Benefits include health-auto-home insurance, legal, low long distance and 800 numbers, business line of credit, merchant accounts, tax programs, office supply and travel discounts and more. Seeks to provide members access to the best traditional benefits and timely information that is critical to conduct a successful home, small or Internet business. **Founded:** 1994. **Publications:** *AHBA Hotline Newsletter* (Bimonthly). **Telecommunication Services:** info@homebusiness.com.

35589 ■ Canadian Federation of Independent Business (CFIB)—Federation Canadienne de l'Entreprise Independante
401-4141 Yonge St., Ste. 401
Toronto, ON, Canada M2P 2A6
Ph: (416)222-8022
Free: 888-234-2232
Fax: (416)222-6103
Co. E-mail: cfib@cfib.ca
URL: http://www.cfib-fcei.ca/english/index.html
Contact: Danny Kelly, President
Description: Independent businesses. Promotes economic well-being of members and seeks to maintain a healthy domestic business climate. Represents members' interests before government agencies, labor and industrial organizations, and the public. **Scope:** entrepreneurship, economic policy, small business, public policy. **Founded:** 1971. **Subscriptions:** 4000 books periodicals reports. **Publications:** *Mandate* (Quarterly); *Quarterly Business Barometer* (3/year). **Awards:** Canada Awards for Excellence.

35590 ■ *Mandate*
401-4141 Yonge St., Ste. 401
Toronto, ON, Canada M2P 2A6
Ph: (416)222-8022
Free: 888-234-2232
Fax: (416)222-6103
Co. E-mail: cfib@cfib.ca
URL: http://www.cfib-fcei.ca/english/index.html
Contact: Danny Kelly, President
Released: Quarterly

35591 ■ National Association for Business Organizations (NAFBO)
5432 Price Ave.
Baltimore, MD 21215

Ph: (410)367-5309
Co. E-mail: nahbb@msn.com
URL: http://www.ameribizs.com/global
Contact: Rudolph Lewis, President
Description: Business organizations that develop and support small businesses that have the capability to provide their products or services on a national level. Promotes small business in a free market system; represents the interests of small businesses to government and community organizations on small business affairs; monitors and reviews laws that affect small businesses; promotes a business code of ethics. Supplies members with marketing and management assistance; encourages joint marketing services between members. Operates a Home Based Business Television Network that provides an affordable audio/visual media for small and home based businesses. **Founded:** 1986. **Awards:** Entrepreneur Certificate.

35592 ■ National Association of Home Based Businesses (NAHBB)
5432 Price Ave.
Baltimore, MD 21215
Ph: (410)367-5308
Fax: (410)356-1672
Co. E-mail: nahbb@msn.com
URL: http://www.usahomebusiness.com
Contact: Rudolph Lewis, President
Description: Provides support and development services to home-based businesses. Offers business models and franchise development and marketing services. **Founded:** 1984. **Publications:** *National Register of U.S. Home Based Business* (Annual). **Educational Activities:** National Home Based Business Convention (Annual); National Association of Home Based Businesses Convention (Annual). **Awards:** Best Home Based Business (Annual).

35593 ■ *Quarterly Business Barometer*
401-4141 Yonge St., Ste. 401
Toronto, ON, Canada M2P 2A6
Ph: (416)222-8022
Free: 888-234-2232
Fax: (416)222-6103
Co. E-mail: cfib@cfib.ca
URL: http://www.cfib-fcei.ca/english/index.html
Contact: Danny Kelly, President
Released: 3/year

REFERENCE WORKS

35594 ■ *The 30-Second Commute*
Pub: McGraw-Hill
Ed: Beverley Williams; Don Cooper. **Released:** 2004. **Price:** $19.95. **Description:** Home-based business owners explain how entrepreneurs can avoid long commutes and high costs of working outside the home by starting a home-based company. Essential steps for launching a successful home-based business are covered, including type of business, legal issues, and writing a business plan.

35595 ■ *201 Great Tips for Your Small Business: Increase Your Profit and Joy in Your Work*
Pub: Dundren Press Limited
Ed: Julie V. Watson. **Released:** April 2006. **Price:** $24.99. **Description:** Tips and hints for home-based, micro, and small businesses are presented.

35596 ■ *Being Self-Employed: How to Run a Business Out of Your Home, Claim Travel and Depreciation and Earn a Good Income Well into Your 70s or 80s*
Pub: Allyear Tax Guides
Ed: Holmes F. Crouch, Irma Jean Crouch, Barbara J. MacRae. **Released:** September 2004. **Price:** $24.95 (US), $37.95 (Canadian). **Description:** Guide for small business to keep accurate tax records.

35597 ■ *Business Know-How: An Operational Guide for Home-Based and Micro-Sized Businesses with Limited Budgets*
Pub: Adams Media Corporation
Ed: Janet Attard. **Price:** $17.95.

35598 ■ *Careers for Homebodies and Other Independent Souls*
Pub: McGraw-Hill
Ed: Jan Goldberg. **Released:** March 2007. **Price:** $13.95. **Description:** The books offers insight into choosing the right career for individuals. Jobs range from office to outdoors, job markets, and levels of education requirements.

35599 ■ *"Daddy's Home! Fathers Stay Home To Watch the Kids and Build Businesses To Suit Their Values" in Black Enterprise (October 2007)*
Pub: Earl G. Graves Publishing Co. Inc.
Ed: George Alexander. **Description:** Fathers are staying home and running home-based businesses in order to spend more time with their families.

35600 ■ *"Floral-Design Kiosk Business in Colorado Springs Blossoming" in Colorado Springs Business Journal (September 24, 2010)*
Pub: Dolan Media Newswires
Ed: Monica Mendoza. **Description:** Profile of Shellie Greto and her mother Jackie Martin who started a wholesale flower business in their garage. The do-it-yourself floral arrangement firm started a kiosk business in supermarkets called Complete Design.

35601 ■ *Greater Phoenix Chamber Membership List--Home-Based Businesses*
Pub: Greater Phoenix Chamber of Commerce
Contact: Todd Sanders, President
URL(s): www.phoenixchamber.com/. **Price:** $13, Members; $15, Nonmembers; $15, Members diskette; $17, Nonmembers diskette; all prices include shipping. **Covers:** 67 home-based businesses in the greater Phoenix, Arizona area. **Entries include:** Contact details.

35602 ■ *Home Business Tax Deductions: Keep What You Earn*
Pub: NOLO
Ed: Stephen Fishman. **Released:** November 2006. **Price:** $34.99. **Description:** Home business tax deductions are outlined. Basic information on the ways various business structures are taxed and how deductions work is included.

35603 ■ *Homemade Money: How to Select, Start, Manage, Market and Multiply the Profits of a Business at Home*
Pub: M. Evans & Company Inc.
Contact: William Fryer, Manager
URL(s): www.rlpgtrade.com. **Released:** Published in two volumes. **Price:** $24.95, Individuals book 1 and 2. **Publication includes:** A special 76 page, updated "A-Z Crash Course" on business basics and a directory of 300 listings. **Entries include:** Supplier name, address, description of information, price, order information. Principal content of the book is editorial matter on beginning and developing a home-based business. **Arrangement:** Classified by subject. **Indexes:** Alphabetical.

35604 ■ *Housecleaning Business: Organize Your Business - Get Clients and Referrals - Set Rates and Services*
Pub: Globe Pequot Press
Ed: Laura Jorstad, Melinda Morse. **Released:** June 1, 2009. **Price:** $18.95. **Description:** This book shares insight into starting a housecleaning businesses. It shows how to develop a service manual, screen clients, serve customers, select cleaning products, competition, how to up a home office, using the Internet to grow the business and offering green cleaning options to clients.

35605 ■ *How to Create an Unlimited Income Sitting at Home in Your Pajamas*
Pub: PublishAmerica, Incorporated
Ed: Michael Klisouris. **Released:** April 2006. **Price:** $19.95. **Description:** Step-by-step guide for starting, operating and expanding a home-based business is featured.

35606 ■ *"How to Set Up an Effective Home Office" in Women Entrepreneur (August 22, 2008)*
Pub: Entrepreneur Media Inc.
Ed: Laura Stack. **Description:** Checklist provides ways in which one can arrange their home office to provide the greatest efficiency which will allow maximum productivity and as a result the greater the chance of success.

35607 ■ *How to Start a Home-Based Senior Care Business: Check-in-Care, Transportation Services, Shopping and Cooking*
Pub: Globe Pequot Press
Ed: James L. Ferry. **Released:** January 1, 2010. **Price:** $18.95. **Description:** Information is provided to start a home-based senior care business.

35608 ■ *How to Start a Home-Based Writing Business, 5th Edition*
Pub: Globe Pequot Press
Ed: Lucy Parker. **Released:** December 2007. **Price:** $18.95. **Description:** Guide for starting and running a home-based writing business.

35609 ■ *"Is It Time to Move to a Real Office?" in Women Entrepreneur (December 30, 2008)*
Pub: Entrepreneur Media Inc.
Ed: Aliza Sherman. **Description:** Before moving a company from a home-office to a real office it is important to make sure that the additional overhead that will be incurred by the move is comfortably covered and that the move is being done for the right reasons. Several women entrepreneurs who have moved their businesses from their homes to an actual rental space are profiled.

35610 ■ *Make Your Business Survive and Thrive! 100+ Proven Marketing Methods to Help You Beat the Odds*
Pub: John Wiley & Sons, Incorporated
Ed: Priscilla Y. Huff. **Released:** December 2006. **Price:** $19.95. **Description:** One hundred proven methods to successfully run a small home-based business are outlined.

35611 ■ *Make Your Business Survive and Thrive! 100+ Proven Marketing Methods to Help You Beat the Odds*
Pub: John Wiley & Sons, Incorporated
Ed: Priscilla Y. Huff. **Released:** December 2006. **Price:** $19.95. **Description:** Small business and entrepreneurial expert gives information to help small and home-based businesses grow.

35612 ■ *More Than a Pink Cadillac*
Pub: McGraw-Hill
Ed: Jim Underwood. **Released:** 2002. **Price:** $23.95. **Description:** Profile of Mary Kay Ash who turned her $5,000 investment into a billion-dollar corporation. Ash's nine principles that form the foundation of her company's global success are outlined. Stories from her sales force leaders share ideas for motivating employees, impressing customers and building a successful company. The book emphasizes the leadership skills required to drive performance in any successful enterprise.

35613 ■ *My So-Called Freelance Life: How to Survive and Thrive as a Creative Professional for Hire*
Pub: Seal Press
Contact: Charlie Winton, Manager
Ed: Michelle Goodman. **Released:** October 1, 2008. **Price:** $15.95. **Description:** Guidebook for women wishing to start a freelancing business; tips, advice, how-to's and all the information needed to survive working from home are included.

35614 ■ *No Place Like Home: Organizing Home-Based Labor in the Era of Structural Adjustment*
Pub: Routledge Inc.
Ed: David Staples. **Released:** November 2006. **Price:** $70.00. **Description:** The book examines the role of home-based women workers in contemporary capitalism.

35615 ■ *101 Best Home-Based Success Secrets for Women*
Pub: Prima Publishing
Ed: Priscilla Y. Huff. **Released:** 1999.

35616 ■ *"Opportunity Knocks" in Small Business Opportunities (September 2008)*
Pub: Entrepreneur Media Inc.
Description: Profile of YourOffice USA, a franchise that provides home-based and small businesses cost-effective and efficient support through 'virtual' offices that are available as much or as little as the client needs it; they also supply necessary tools such as a professional business address, private mailbox service, personalized telephone answering and more that supports clients who want to look, act and operate with an advanced business image.

35617 ■ *Save $2000 to $8000 in Taxes with a Home-Based Business*
Pub: TKG Publishing
Ed: Greco Garcia. **Released:** February 2007. **Price:** $16.99. **Description:** Tax advice for a home-based business is given.

35618 ■ *Shedworking: The Alternative Workplace Revolution*
Pub: Frances Lincoln Limited
Ed: Alex Johnson. **Released:** June 10, 2010. **Price:** $29.95. **Description:** Shedworking is an alternative office space for those working at home. The book features shedworkers and shedbuilders from around the world who are leading this alternative workplace revolution and why this trend is working.

35619 ■ *Smart Tax Write-Offs, 5th Ed.*
Pub: Rayve Productions, Inc.
Ed: Norm Ray. **Released:** February 2008. **Price:** $15.95. **Description:** Guidebook to help small business owners take advantage of legitimate tax deductions for home-based and other entrepreneurial businesses.

35620 ■ *"Teleworkers Confess Biggest At-Home Distractions" in Employee Benefit News (Vol. 25, November 1, 2011, No. 14, pp. 7)*
Pub: SourceMedia Inc.
Ed: Kelley M. Butler. **Description:** Telecommuting can actually make some workers more efficient and productive versus working inside the office.

35621 ■ *The Travel Agent's Complete Desk Reference, 5th Edition*
Pub: The Intrepid Traveler
Ed: Kelly Monaghan. **Released:** August 25, 2009. **Price:** $39.95. **Description:** Reference book that provides essential information to the home-based travel agent.

35622 ■ *"TW Trade Shows to Offer Seminars On Niche Selling, Social Media" in Travel Weekly (Vol. 69, October 4, 2010, No. 40, pp. 9)*
Pub: NorthStar Travel Media LLC
Description: Travel Weekly's Leisure World 2010 and Fall Home Based Travel Agent Show focused on niche selling, with emphasis on all-inclusives, young consumers, groups, incentives, culinary vacations, and honeymoon or romance travel.

35623 ■ *"The Ultimate Home Shopping Network" in Austin Business JournalInc. (Vol. 28, October 17, 2008, No. 31, pp. A1)*
Pub: American City Business Journals
Ed: Sandra Zaragoza. **Description:** New York-based Etcetera sells their clothing through more than 850 fashion consultants in the U.S. Central Texas is one of the company's top markets and the company is looking to increase its fashion consultants in the area from five to about 20 since they believe there is plenty of room to expand their customer base in the area.

35624 ■ *What Losing Taught Me about Winning: The Ultimate Guide for Success in Small and Home-Based Business*
Pub: Fireside Publishing
Ed: Fran Tarkenton; Wes Smith. **Released:** April 7, 1999. **Price:** $17.95. **Description:** Provides insight into running a successful small business.

35625 ■ *Work From Home Jobs Directory*
Pub: Lulu.com
Ed: Debra Mundell. **Released:** May 2006. **Price:** $18.00. **Description:** Resources for starting and growing a home-based business are listed.

35626 ■ *Working for Yourself: Law and Taxes for Independent Contractors, Freelancers and Consultants*
Pub: NOLO Publications
Ed: Stephen Fishman. **Released:** March 2008. **Price:** $39.99 paperback. **Description:** In-depth information is shared for contractors, freelancers and consultants involving business law and small business taxes.

TRADE PERIODICALS

35627 ■ *At-Home Dad*
Pub: Peter Baylies
Contact: Peter Baylies, Editor
Released: Monthly. **Price:** $15, U.S.; $18, Canada; $24, elsewhere. **Description:** Promotes the concept of fathers staying home to raise the children. Includes stories from at-home-dads, home business stories, recipes, lists of resources, and playgroups to join. Recurring features include letters to the editor, interviews, news of research, book reviews, notices of publications available, and a column titled Dr. Bob.

35628 ■ *Home-Based Working Moms*
Pub: Home-Based Working Moms
Ed: Lesley Spencer, Editor, lesley@hbwm.com. **Released:** Monthly. **Price:** $49; $54, Canada; $65, other countries. **Description:** Directed toward parents working at home and those interested in doing so. Designed to provide support, networking, and information related to working at home with children. Recurring features include interviews, job listings, marketing tips, and a column titled Home Business Ideas.

35629 ■ *The Home Business Report*
Pub: The Kerner Group Inc.
Ed: Rick Kerner, Editor. **Released:** Monthly. **Description:** Provides information on how to operate a home-based business or work from home. Features real life success stories, how-to articles on marketing, and strategies to keep focused on goals. Recurring features include letters to the editor, interviews, news of research, job listings, book reviews, and notices of publications available.

35630 ■ *Our Place*
Pub: Home-Based Working Moms
Ed: Lesley Spencer, Editor, lesley@hbwm.com. **Released:** Biweekly, 10/year. **Price:** $49, U.S.; $54, Canada; $65, elsewhere. **Description:** Advocates home employment and home businesses to allow parents more time with their children. Offers ideas, marketing tips, member profiles to promote successful employment at home. Recurring features include interviews, job listings, and book reviews.

VIDEOCASSETTES/ AUDIOCASSETTES

35631 ■ *Alternate Work Sites: At Home, at Work*
Encyclopedia Britannica
331 N. LaSalle St.
Chicago, IL 60654
Ph: (312)347-7159
Free: 800-323-1229
Fax: (312)294-2104
URL: http://www.britannica.com
Released: 1988. **Price:** $395.00. **Description:** This film features Control Data Corporation of Minneapolis and workers in an Alpine Swiss village showing how to create a work site. **Availability:** VHS; 3/4 U.

35632 ■ *American Institute of Small Business: Setting Up a Home-Based Business*
American Institute of Small Business
23075 Highway 7, Ste. 200
Shorewood, MN 55331
Ph: (952)545-7001
Free: 800-328-2906
Fax: (952)545-7020
Co. E-mail: judy@aisb.biz
URL: http://www.pfa.com/AISB.htm
Released: 199?. **Price:** $69.95. **Description:** Step-by-step guide to operating a business out of your home. **Availability:** VHS.

35633 ■ *Inc. Magazine Business Success Programs*
Cambridge Educational
c/o Films Media Group
132 West 31st Street, 17th Floor
Ste. 124
New York, NY 10001
Free: 800-257-5126
Fax: (609)671-0266
Co. E-mail: custserve@films.com
URL: http://www.cambridgeol.com
Released: 1987. **Price:** $99.95. **Description:** These four programs contain a step-by-step explanation of what must be done to succeed in business. **Availability:** VHS; CC.

TRADE SHOWS AND CONVENTIONS

35634 ■ National Association of Home Based Businesses Convention
National Association of Home Based Businesses (NAHBB)
5432 Price Ave.
Baltimore, MD 21215
Ph: (410)367-5308
Fax: (410)356-1672
Co. E-mail: nahbb@msn.com
URL: http://www.usahomebusiness.com
Contact: Rudolph Lewis, President
URL(s): www.usahomebusiness.com. **Frequency:** Annual. **Audience:** Trade buyers and general public. **Principal Exhibits:** Home based business products and services, support associations, trade supplies, and related equipment.

CONSULTANTS

35635 ■ Joanne H. Pratt Associates
3520 Routh St.
Dallas, TX 75219-4730
Ph: (214)528-6540
Fax: (214)528-5730
Co. E-mail: joannepratt@post.harvard.edu
Contact: John A. Davis, Manager
Scope: Performs market research and advising on the virtual office, including telecommuting and home based businesses. Helps organizations implement teleworking and telecommuting. Recent emphasis on related topics such as e commerce and personnel productivity. Also helps employees obtain permission to telework. Serves private industries as well as government agencies worldwide. **Founded:** 1981. **Publications:** "The Impact of Location on Net Income: A Comparison of Home based and Non-home based Sole Proprietors," 2006; "Telework: The Latest Figures and what they Mean," 2005; "Teleworking Comes of Age with Broadband," Apr, 2003; "Telework Trends in the United States," 2003; "Strategies for Small Business Success," 2002; "Teleworkers, Trips and Telecommunications: Technology drives telework-but does it reduce trips?," 2002; "Telework and Society-Implications for Corporate and Societal Cultures, in Telework: The New Workplace of the 21st Century," Oct, 2000. **Seminars:** The Connected Home: Paradise or Poison; Equipping for Telework Success; Myths and Realities of Working at Home; Using Telemanagement to Increase Staff Productivity; Meet Your Home Office Customers; Telecommuting: What is it? Will it Work for Me?; Telemanaging a Remote Workforce.

FRANCHISES AND BUSINESS OPPORTUNITIES

35636 ■ CMIT Solutions
500 N Capital of TX Highway, Bldg. 6, Ste. 200
Austin, TX 78746

Ph: (512)477-6667
Free: 800-710-2648
Fax: (512)692-3711
URL: http://www.cmitsolutions.com
Description: Offers IT service and computer support to small businesses. Franchise can be home-based, as we service the client at their place of business. **No. of Franchise Units:** 137. **Founded:** 1994.. **Franchised:** 1998. **Equity Capital Needed:** $124,800-$150,950 total investment. **Franchise Fee:** $49,500. **Royalty Fee:** 6%. **Financial Assistance:** Limited third party financing available. **Training:** Offers 3 weeks training at headquarters, 1 week onsite with ongoing support.

35637 ■ Crock A Doodle
299 Wayne Gretzy Pkwy.
Brantford, ON, Canada N3R 8A5
Ph: (519)752-8080
Co. E-mail: franchise@crockadoodle.com
URL: http://www.imaginelovingwhatyoudo.com
Description: Provides a variety of pottery painting events and activities for groups of all kinds. For women, we offer a calendar full of pottery-painting workshops and classes, as well as creative activities for girls' nights, bridal showers and special occasions. For children, we offer birthday parties, seasonal events and pottery-painting classes, as well as creative programming for camps, schools, teams and groups. The opportunity extends throughout the community to corporate team builders, fundraisers and community events of all kinds. **No. of Franchise Units:** 10. **No. of Company-Owned Units:** 2. **Founded:** 2002. **Franchised:** 2004. **Equity Capital Needed:** Total investment from $75,000. **Franchise Fee:** $20,000. **Training:** Provides 2 weeks plus ongoing support.

35638 ■ DEI Franchise Systems
PO Box 20169
Cincinnati, OH 45230
Ph: (212)581-7390
Free: 800-224-2140
Fax: (212)245-7897
Co. E-mail: franchise@dei-sales.com
URL: http://www.dei-sales.com
Description: Sales training industry. **No. of Franchise Units:** 32. **No. of Company-Owned Units:** 1. **Founded:** 1979.. **Franchised:** 2003. **Equity Capital Needed:** $60,000-$75,000. **Franchise Fee:** $50,000. **Royalty Fee:** 7%. **Training:** Offers 2 weeks home-based training and 2 weeks at headquarters with ongoing support.

35639 ■ DNA Services of America
130 Fifth Ave., 10th Fl.
New York, NY 10011-4399
Ph: (212)242-4399
Description: Own a high-demand, innovative business that serves the growing needs of Americans by offering members of your community peace of mind through evidence provided by DNA identification test results for paternity, family relationship establishment, infidelity testing and forensic DNA. **Equity Capital Needed:** $49,175-$97,100 total investment. **Training:** Offers a complete, proven business system, ongoing support, and thorough training.

35640 ■ Home Video Studio
8148 Raven Rock Dr.
Indianapolis, IN 46256
Ph: (317)964-8048
Free: 800-464-8220
Fax: (317)577-1522
Description: Home based video studio. **No. of Franchise Units:** 70. **No. of Company-Owned Units:** 2. **No. of Operating Units:** 75. **Founded:** 1991.. **Franchised:** 2006. **Equity Capital Needed:** $69,050-$97,300. **Franchise Fee:** $25,000. **Royalty Fee:** 7%. **Financial Assistance:** Limited third party financing available. **Training:** Yes.

35641 ■ Interiors by Decorating Den
8659 Commerce Dr.
Easton, MD 21601
Ph: (800)332-3367
Fax: (410)820-5131
Co. E-mail: decden@decoratingden.com
URL: http://www.decoratingden.com
Description: Interiors by Decorating is one of the oldest, international, shop-at-home interior decorating franchises in the world. Our company-trained interior decorators bring 1000's of samples including window coverings, wall coverings, floor coverings, furniture and accessories to their customer's home in our uniquely equipped ColorVan. Special business features include: home-based, marketing systems, business systems, training, support, and complete sampling. **No. of Franchise Units:** 501. **Founded:** 1969. **Franchised:** 1970. **Equity Capital Needed:** $25,000. **Franchise Fee:** $29,900. **Training:** Training combines classroom work, home study, meetings, seminars and on-the-job experience including working with an experienced interior decorator. Secondary, advanced and graduate certification training continue throughout the franchise owner's career with Interiors by Decorating Den.

35642 ■ The LiceSquad Inc.
Lice Squad Canada Inc.
3A King St.
Cookstown, ON, Canada L0L 1L0
Ph: (705)458-4448
Free: 888-542-3778
Fax: (705)458-8887
Co. E-mail: franchiseinfo@licesquad.com
URL: http://www.licesquad.com
Description: Join Canada's leading head lice removal and Education Company. Low start up costs and proven potential. Perfect for those in the nursing, hairdressing and child care fields. Our clients include schools, families, camps and other child care organizations. Our home-based business model allows flexibility. Enjoy both family and career. 15 successful LiceSquad franchises operating in Ontario with master franchises available. **No. of Franchise Units:** 9. **No. of Company-Owned Units:** 20. **Founded:** 2001. **Franchised:** 2002. **Equity Capital Needed:** $42,000-$85,000 investment required; start-up capital required $25,000-$35,000. **Franchise Fee:** $20,000. **Training:** Provides training (excluding travel/hotel costs).

35643 ■ Liquid Capital Canada Corp.
5734 Yonge St., Ste. 400
Toronto, ON, Canada M2M 4E7
Ph: (416)342-8199
Free: 866-272-3704
Fax: (866)611-8886
URL: http://www.lcfranchise.com
Description: Operation of home-based B2B providing account receivable financing to small business. **No. of Franchise Units:** 27. **No. of Company-Owned Units:** 1. **Founded:** 1999.. **Franchised:** 2000. **Equity Capital Needed:** $200,000. **Franchise Fee:** $50,000. **Training:** Yes.

35644 ■ On Track Power Window Repair
On Track Franchising, LLC
4616 Popular Level Rd.
Louisville, KY 40213
Ph: (502)777-0114
Fax: (502)962-6250
Co. E-mail: john@ontrackrepair.com
URL: http://www.OnTrackRepair.com
Description: Power window repair. This is virtually an untapped multi-billion dollar market. There is a continuous supply of window systems to repair. **No. of Company-Owned Units:** 1. **Founded:** 2002.. **Franchised:** 2007. **Equity Capital Needed:** $64,200-$77,900. **Franchise Fee:** $32,000. **Royalty Fee:** 7%. **Training:** Provides 2 weeks hands on training and in depth technical instruction as it relates to power and manual window, door locks, mirrors, latches and door handles.

35645 ■ The Original Basket Boutique
363 Sioux Rd., Ste. 140
Sherwood Park, AB, Canada T8A 4W7
Ph: (780)416-2530
Free: 877-622-8008
Fax: (780)416-2531
Co. E-mail: info@originalbasketboutique.com
URL: http://www.originalbasketboutique.com
Description: The Original Basket Boutique, Canada's exclusive custom gift basket franchise. **No. of Franchise Units:** 26. **No. of Operating Units:** 38. **Founded:** 1989. **Franchised:** 1989. **Equity Capital Needed:** $47,500-$59,000. **Franchise Fee:** $35,000. **Royalty Fee:** $225/month. **Financial Assistance:** Financial assistance available with franchise fee. **Training:** Offers 3-4 days training at headquarters with ongoing support.

35646 ■ Padgett Business Services (Oakville, Canada)
3100 boul le Carrefour, Ste. 554
Laval, QC, Canada H7T 2K7
Ph: (888)723-4388
Fax: (877)231-4911
URL: http://www.padgetfranchises.ca
Description: Supplier of small business services including accounting, tax preparation and consultation, payroll services and business advice. **No. of Franchise Units:** 120. **Founded:** 1966.. **Franchised:** 1975. **Equity Capital Needed:** $40,000-$48,000 investment required; $30,000-$50,000 start-up capital required. **Franchise Fee:** $25,000. **Training:** Complete program of training and support.

35647 ■ Par-T-Perfect Party Planners
T-20 Bowen Bay Rd.
Bowen Island, BC, Canada V0N 1G0
Ph: (604)947-0274
Co. E-mail: info@par-t-perfect.com
URL: http://www.par-t-perfect.com
Description: Par-T-Perfect is a unique children's party and event service. A great home-based business opportunity!. **No. of Franchise Units:** 21. **No. of Company-Owned Units:** 2. **Founded:** 1988. **Franchised:** 2001. **Equity Capital Needed:** $10,000-$20,000 including franchise fee. **Franchise Fee:** $15,000-$24,500. **Training:** 2 weeks and ongoing.

35648 ■ Suburban Cylinder Express
Suburban Franchising, Inc.
240 Rte. 10 W
Whippany, NJ 07981
Ph: (770)518-9948
Free: 866-218-7026
Co. E-mail: dzabkar@suburbanpropane.com
URL: http://www.suburbancylinderexpress.com
Description: The franchise is a home-based business opportunity center. It provides propane cylinders to residential and commercial customers. **No. of Company-Owned Units:** 21. **Founded:** 2001.. **Franchised:** 2002. **Equity Capital Needed:** $63,450-$123,200. **Franchise Fee:** $34,900. **Training:** Provides initial start-up training, ongoing business consultation, customized business software, scheduling and route optimization software, national phone customer sales center, technology help desk, a consumer website, brochures, flyers, coupons and other direct mail and mass marketing tools and materials.

35649 ■ Travel Lines Express Franchise Group
9858 Glades Rd.
Boca Raton, FL 33434
Ph: (561)482-9557
Description: Full service home based travel agency. **No. of Franchise Units:** 50. **No. of Company-Owned Units:** 1. **Founded:** 1980.. **Franchised:** 2003. **Equity Capital Needed:** $1,000-$3,000. **Franchise Fee:** $300. **Training:** Yes.

35650 ■ Two Blonds & A Brunette Gift Co.
201 Park Pl. E
Winnipeg, MB, Canada R3P 2E4
Ph: (204)792-9800
URL: http://www.twoblondsandabrunettegiftco.com
Description: Initial home-based gift-giving business. **No. of Franchise Units:** 10. **Founded:** 2002.. **Franchised:** 2006. **Equity Capital Needed:** Franchise fee plus $1,000 set-up fee. **Franchise Fee:** $15,000 plus, includes inventory, training, and materials. **Training:** 3 days; airfare and hotel paid.

ASSOCIATIONS AND OTHER ORGANIZATIONS

35651 ■ ASTD—American Society for Training and Development (ASTD)
1640 King St.
Alexandria, VA 22314-2746
Ph: (703)683-8100
Free: 800-628-2783
Fax: (703)683-1523
Co. E-mail: customercare@astd.org
URL: http://www.astd.org
Contact: Tony Bingham, President
E-mail: tbingham@astd.org
Description: Represents workplace learning and performance professionals. **Scope:** training and development, workplace performance. **Founded:** 1943. **Subscriptions:** 5000. **Publications:** *TD Magazine*; *ASTD Buyer's Guide* (Annual); *ASTD Buyer's Guide* (Annual); *Info-Line: Tips, Tools, and Intelligence for Trainers* (Monthly); *Learning Circuits* (Monthly); *T and D Magazine*; *TD Magazine* (Monthly); *Member Information Exchange (MIX)*; *TRAINET*; *Training Resources: ASTD Buyer's Guide* (Annual); *Buyer's Guide & Consultant Directory*; *American Society for Training and Development--Training Video Directory*; *ASTD Buyer's Guide and Consultants Directory*; *Who's Who in Training and Development* (Annual); *ASTD Buyer's Guide and Consultants Directory*; *American Society Training and Development Buyer's Guide and Consultant Directory* (Annual); *Technical Training: Learning Technology for Performance Improvement*; *ASTD Buyer's Guide & Consultant Directory* (Annual); *Infoline Plus* (Monthly). **Educational Activities:** International Exposition (Annual); TechKnowledge Conference & Exposition (Annual); American Society for Training and Development Conference; TechKnowledge Conference and Exposition (Annual). **Awards:** ASTD BEST Award; Awards in the Advancing ASTD's Vision; Awards in the Advancing Workplace Learning and Performance; Excellence in Practice; Dissertation Award; Torch Award; Gordon M. Bliss Memorial Award; Distinguished Contribution to Workplace Learning and Performance Award. **Telecommunication Services:** subscriberservice@astd.org.

35652 ■ *Canadian Learning Journal*
720 Spadina Ave., Ste. 315
Toronto, ON, Canada M5S 2T9
Ph: (416)367-5900
Free: 866-257-4275
Fax: (416)367-1642
Co. E-mail: info@cstd.ca
URL: http://www.cstd.ca
Contact: Lynn Johnston, President
Released: Semiannual **Price:** included in membership dues.

35653 ■ Canadian Society for Training and Development (CSTD)—Societe Canadienne pour la Formation et le Perfectionnement
720 Spadina Ave., Ste. 315
Toronto, ON, Canada M5S 2T9
Ph: (416)367-5900
Free: 866-257-4275
Fax: (416)367-1642
Co. E-mail: info@cstd.ca
URL: http://www.cstd.ca
Contact: Lynn Johnston, President
Description: Works for the profession of training, workplace learning and human resources development. **Founded:** 2003. **Publications:** *Canadian Learning Journal* (Semiannual). **Awards:** President's Award; Volunteer Recognition Award; President's Award (Annual); Volunteer Award (Annual).

35654 ■ HR People and Strategy (HRPS)
401 N Michigan Ave., Ste. 2200
Chicago, IL 60611
Ph: (312)321-6805
Fax: (312)673-6944
Co. E-mail: info@hrps.org
URL: http://www.hrps.org
Contact: Kevin Rubens, Chairperson
Description: Human resource planning professionals representing 160 corporations and 3,000 individual members, including strategic human resources planning and development specialists, staffing analysts, business planners, line managers, and others who function as business partners in the application of strategic human resource management practices. Seeks to increase the impact of human resource planning and management on business and organizational performance. Sponsors program of professional development in human resource planning concepts, techniques, and practices. Offers networking opportunities. **Founded:** 1977. **Publications:** *People and Strategy* (Quarterly); *People & Strategy* (Quarterly); *Human Resource Planning Society--Membership Directory* (Annual).

35655 ■ Human Resources Research Organization (HumRRO)
66 Canal Center Plz., Ste. 700
Alexandria, VA 22314-1591
Ph: (703)549-3611
Fax: (703)548-5574
URL: http://www.humrro.org
Contact: Dr. William J. Strickland, President
Description: Behavioral and social science researchers seeking to improve human performance, particularly in organizational settings, through behavioral and social science research, development, consultation and instruction. Promotes research and development to solve specific problems in: training and education; development, refinement, and instruction in the technology of training and education; studies and development of techniques to improve the motivation of personnel in training and on the job; research of leadership and management, and development of leadership programs; criterion development, individual assessment, and program evaluation in training and operating systems; measurement and evaluation of human performance under varying circumstances; organizational development studies, including performance counseling, group decision-making, and factors that affect organizational competence; development of manpower information systems and the application of management science on personnel systems. Encourages use of high technology for instructional purposes by means of computer assisted instruction, interactive video, and computer literacy. Offers technical publication services including data analysis and editorial, word processing, production, and printing services. **Scope:** An independent, nonprofit corporation which strives to improve human performance (primarily in organizational settings) through behavioral and social science research, product development, consultation, and instruction. Active in the fields of education and training, testing and assessment, survey research, program evaluation, and human factors engineering. **Founded:** 1951. **Awards:** Meredith P. Crawford Fellowships in I/O Psychology; Meredith P. Crawford Fellowship in I/O Psychology (Annual). **Seminars:** An examination of the properties of local dependence measures when applied to adaptive data, Computing and communicating test accuracy for high-stakes decisions, Development of cross-cultural perspective taking skills, Developing, implementing, and scoring valid job simulations, Executive and senior leader development: A best practices review, Integrating reliability and validity based perspectives on error in performance ratings, Job incumbent perceptions of faking on noncognitive inventories, Modeling the psychometric properties of multisource ratings: CFA vs. GLMM, Performance level descriptions: Similarities and differences among select states, Reducing bias through propensity scoring: A study of SAT coaching, Retaining personality measures after failure: Changes in scores and strategies, Review of information and communication technology literacy measures, Self-presentation on personality measures: A meta-analysis, Using cases as a proxy for experience in leadership development, Using patterns to understand the dynamics of leader behavior, Verification testing in unproctored internet testing programs, A cross-cultural look at items of logic-based reasoning, An overlooked problem with standard practices for analyzing ratings data from ill-structured measurement designs, Context effects in internet testing: A literature review, Differentiating in the Upper Tail: Selecting Among High-Scoring Applicants, Gaining insight into situational judgment test functioning via spline regression, Ill-Structured measurement designs and reliability: The tale of a HumRRO IR&D project, Influence of subject matter expert (SME) personality on job analysis ratings, Modeling intraindividual change in soldiers attitudes and values during the first term of enlistment SES and admissions test validity: Within race analyses, The Feasibility of using O NET to study skill changes, Validation of a person organization personality hybrid measure, Validating psychological screening examinations and background investigations for applicant screening.

35656 ■ International Personnel Management Association - Canada (IPMA)—L'Association internationale de la gestion du personnel - Canada
21 Midland Crescent, Unit 74
Ottawa, ON, Canada K2H 8P6
Ph: (613)226-2297
Free: 888-226-5002
Fax: (613)226-2298
Co. E-mail: info@ipma-aigp.ca
URL: http://www.ipma-aigp.ca
Contact: Carol Hopkins, Executive Director
Description: Human resources professionals employed by public agencies. Seeks to advance the

practice of personnel management. Facilitates ongoing professional development of members; sponsors research and educational programs. **Awards:** Gold Star Agency Award (Annual). **Telecommunication Services:** national@ipma-aigp.ca.

35657 ■ Public Risk Management Association (PRIMA)
700 S Washington St., Ste. 218
Alexandria, VA 22314
Ph: (703)528-7701
Fax: (703)739-0200
Co. E-mail: info@primacentral.org
URL: http://www.primacentral.org
Contact: Marshall Davies, Executive Director
Description: Public agency risk, insurance, human resources, attorneys, and/or safety managers from cities, counties, villages, towns, school boards, and other related areas. Provides an information clearinghouse and communications network for public risk managers to share resources, ideas, and experiences. Offers information on risk, insurance, and safety management. Monitors state and federal legislative actions and court decisions that deal with immunity, tort liability, and intergovernmental risk pools. Maintains library containing current reports from governmental units on their insurance procedures, self-insurance plans, and loss control and safety programs; and copies of policy statements, job descriptions, contractual arrangements, and indemnification clauses. **Scope:** risk management, public health and safety, varied RFPs, job descriptions. **Founded:** 1978. **Subscriptions:** 3000 business records papers reports video recordings. **Publications:** *PRIMA Public Risk* (10/year). **Educational Activities:** Conference for Public Agencies (Annual); Government Risk Management Seminar (Annual); Annual Conference for Public Agencies (Annual). **Awards:** Outstanding Achievement Awards; Public Risk Manager of the Year Award; Public Sector Risk Manager of the Year (Annual).

EDUCATIONAL PROGRAMS

35658 ■ Advanced Diversity Strategies (Onsite)
Seminar Information Service, Inc.
20 Executive Park, Ste. 120
Irvine, CA 92614
Ph: (949)261-9104
Free: 877-SEM-INFO
Fax: (949)261-1963
Co. E-mail: info@seminarinformation.com
URL: http://www.seminarinformation.com
Price: $1,395.00. **Description:** Covers the fundamentals of carrying out an evaluation and the acknowledging and rewarding progress, including best practices for senior managers, line managers, and employees. **Dates and Locations:** New York, NY.

35659 ■ Advanced Employee Complaint Handling (Onsite)
Seminar Information Service, Inc.
20 Executive Park, Ste. 120
Irvine, CA 92614
Ph: (949)261-9104
Free: 877-SEM-INFO
Fax: (949)261-1963
Co. E-mail: info@seminarinformation.com
URL: http://www.seminarinformation.com
Price: $1,595.00. **Description:** Advanced skills needed to handle complex employee internal complaints and investigations. **Dates and Locations:** New York, NY.

35660 ■ Advanced Issues in EEO Law
Seminar Information Service, Inc.
20 Executive Park, Ste. 120
Irvine, CA 92614
Ph: (949)261-9104
Free: 877-SEM-INFO
Fax: (949)261-1963
Co. E-mail: info@seminarinformation.com
URL: http://www.seminarinformation.com
Price: $1,195.00. **Description:** Interactive workshop provides advanced skills needed to identify and address more complex issues in Equal Opportunity Law and procedure. **Dates and Locations:** New York, NY.

35661 ■ Affirmative Action Plan Workshop (Onsite)
Seminar Information Service, Inc.
20 Executive Park, Ste. 120
Irvine, CA 92614
Ph: (949)261-9104
Free: 877-SEM-INFO
Fax: (949)261-1963
Co. E-mail: info@seminarinformation.com
URL: http://www.seminarinformation.com
Price: $1,050.00. **Description:** Learn how to write an affirmative action plan, including the preparation statistical analysis. **Dates and Locations:** Palatine, IL; and Waukesha, WI.

35662 ■ Applying Diversity Management to Innovation, Decision Making, Complex Problem Solving and Business Results (Onsite)
Seminar Information Service, Inc.
20 Executive Park, Ste. 120
Irvine, CA 92614
Ph: (949)261-9104
Free: 877-SEM-INFO
Fax: (949)261-1963
Co. E-mail: info@seminarinformation.com
URL: http://www.seminarinformation.com
Price: $995.00. **Description:** Learn to look at diversity to create value and results versus recruiting and retention, including how to determine 'true diversity' based on perspectives, interpretations, and predictive models, how to use diversity as a trigger for innovation, and examples of how diversity produces performance, productivity, creativity, quality decisions, and commercial value.

35663 ■ Bob Pike's Train-the-Trainer Boot Camp (Onsite)
Seminar Information Service, Inc.
20 Executive Park, Ste. 120
Irvine, CA 92614
Ph: (949)261-9104
Free: 877-SEM-INFO
Fax: (949)261-1963
Co. E-mail: info@seminarinformation.com
URL: http://www.seminarinformation.com
Price: $1,495.00. **Description:** Gives you the powerful high content, high involvement skills you'll need to add new energy and excitement to your own training sessions. **Dates and Locations:** Cities throughout the United States.

35664 ■ The Complete Course on Interviewing People (Onsite)
Padgett-Thompson Seminars
Rockhurst University CEC
14502 W. 105th St.
Lenexa, KS 66215
Free: 800-349-1935
URL: http://www.findaseminar.com/tpd/Padgett-Thompson-Seminars.asp
Price: $199.00. **Description:** A one-day seminar that teaches insider techniques for going beyond the basics to master the art of interviewing people. **Dates and Locations:** Baltimore, MD; Denver, CO; Phoenix, AZ.

35665 ■ Creative Problem Solving and Strategic Thinking (Onsite)
Fred Pryor Seminars & CareerTrack
5700 Broadmoor St., Ste. 300
Mission, KS 66202
Free: 800-780-8476
Fax: (913)967-8849
Co. E-mail: customerservice@pryor.com
URL: http://www.pryor.com
Price: $199.00; $189.00 for groups of 5 or more. **Description:** Learn to think beyond traditional thinking patterns and behaviors gaining a new set of skills for developing strategies that generate results. **Dates and Locations:** Cities throughout the United States.

35666 ■ The Essentials of HR Law 2012 (Onsite) (Canada)
Fred Pryor Seminars & CareerTrack
5700 Broadmoor St., Ste. 300
Mission, KS 66202
Free: 800-780-8476
Fax: (913)967-8849
Co. E-mail: customerservice@pryor.com
URL: http://www.pryor.com
Price: $149.00; $139.00 for groups of 3 or more. **Description:** Learn what you need to know to handle the legal issues and gray areas you face every day keeping your organization compliant . **Dates and Locations:** Cities throughout the United States.

35667 ■ The Essentials of Human Resources Law (Onsite)
Fred Pryor Seminars & CareerTrack
5700 Broadmoor St., Ste. 300
Mission, KS 66202
Free: 800-780-8476
Fax: (913)967-8849
Co. E-mail: customerservice@pryor.com
URL: http://www.pryor.com
Price: $149.00; $139.00 for groups of 5 or more. **Description:** How to keep your organization legally sound and compliant while learning how to think like a lawyer, so you can anticipate problems before they arise. **Dates and Locations:** Cities throughout the United States.

35668 ■ Essentials for Personnel and HR Assistants (Onsite)
Padgett-Thompson Seminars
Rockhurst University CEC
14502 W. 105th St.
Lenexa, KS 66215
Free: 800-349-1935
URL: http://www.findaseminar.com/tpd/Padgett-Thompson-Seminars.asp
Price: $249.00. **Description:** A one-day seminar that covers the important trends and changes facing HR professionals today. **Dates and Locations:** Hartford, CT; Arlington, VA.

35669 ■ FMLA Compliance (Onsite)
Padgett-Thompson Seminars
Rockhurst University CEC
14502 W. 105th St.
Lenexa, KS 66215
Free: 800-349-1935
URL: http://www.findaseminar.com/tpd/Padgett-Thompson-Seminars.asp
Price: $249.00. **Description:** Seminar covers the top five issues that land companies in the courtroom over FMLA disputes. **Dates and Locations:** Oklahoma City, OK.

35670 ■ Fundamentals of Employee Benefits (Onsite)
Seminar Information Service, Inc.
20 Executive Park, Ste. 120
Irvine, CA 92614
Ph: (949)261-9104
Free: 877-SEM-INFO
Fax: (949)261-1963
Co. E-mail: info@seminarinformation.com
URL: http://www.seminarinformation.com
Price: $1,395.00. **Description:** Course will provide a comprehensive overview of the full-range of benefits responsibilities, as well as an in-depth look at the key aspects of benefits, alternatives for your organization and approaches for containing costs.

35671 ■ Fundamentals of Human Resources Management (Onsite) (Canada)
Canadian Management Centre (CMC)
150 York St., 5th Fl.
Toronto, ON, Canada M5H 3S5
Ph: (416)214-5678
Free: 877-262-2519

Fax: (416)313-4985
Co. E-mail: cmcinfo@cmctraining.org
URL: http://www.cmctraining.org
Contact: John Wright, President
Price: $2,395.00 Canadian for non-members; $2,195.00 Canadian for CMC members. **Description:** Covers HR planning and administration, staffing, training, technology, compensation, and legal issues. **Dates and Locations:** Toronto, ON.

35672 ■ HR Administration and the Law (Onsite)
Seminar Information Service, Inc.
20 Executive Park, Ste. 120
Irvine, CA 92614
Ph: (949)261-9104
Free: 877-SEM-INFO
Fax: (949)261-1963
Co. E-mail: info@seminarinformation.com
URL: http://www.seminarinformation.com
Price: $370.00. **Description:** Offers practical compliance suggestions for the most common employment law-related issues faced today. **Dates and Locations:** Waukesha, WI; and Palatine, IL.

35673 ■ Human Resources for Anyone with Newly Assigned HR Responsibilities (Onsite)
Fred Pryor Seminars & CareerTrack
5700 Broadmoor St., Ste. 300
Mission, KS 66202
Free: 800-780-8476
Fax: (913)967-8849
Co. E-mail: customerservice@pryor.com
URL: http://www.pryor.com
Price: $199.00; $189.00 for groups of 5 or more. **Description:** A comprehensive primer on all the issues including recordkeeping, hiring, firing, discrimination, and more. **Dates and Locations:** Cities throughout the United States.

35674 ■ Human Resources and the Law (Onsite)
Seminar Information Service, Inc.
20 Executive Park, Ste. 120
Irvine, CA 92614
Ph: (949)261-9104
Free: 877-SEM-INFO
Fax: (949)261-1963
Co. E-mail: info@seminarinformation.com
URL: http://www.seminarinformation.com
Price: $1,995.00. **Description:** Provides the human resources professional with an understanding of the laws that obligate employers, recent legislation and court cases defining employer/employee rights and obligations, legal and business considerations bearing on employer decisions, practical implications of the laws in day-to-day human resources operations, impact of the laws on the development of policies and procedures, and alternatives for minimizing the company's exposure to employee lawsuits and administrative charges. **Dates and Locations:** New York, NY.

35675 ■ Human Resources for Professionals who've Recently Assumed HR Responsibilities (Onsite)
Seminar Information Service, Inc.
20 Executive Park, Ste. 120
Irvine, CA 92614
Ph: (949)261-9104
Free: 877-SEM-INFO
Fax: (949)261-1963
Co. E-mail: info@seminarinformation.com
URL: http://www.seminarinformation.com
Price: $199.00. **Description:** Fast-paced and information-rich, this program condenses the most important of the most important HR basics into clear, concise, easy-to-understand training.

35676 ■ Human Resources for Professionals Who've Recently Assumed HR Responsibilities (Onsite)
Padgett-Thompson Seminars
Rockhurst University CEC
14502 W. 105th St.
Lenexa, KS 66215
Free: 800-349-1935
URL: http://www.findaseminar.com/tpd/Padgett-Thompson-Seminars.asp
Price: $199.00. **Description:** Workshop provides the information and confidence needed to meet tough HR challenges. **Dates and Locations:** Cities throughout the United States.

35677 ■ Instructional Design for Participant-Centered Training (Onsite)
Seminar Information Service, Inc.
20 Executive Park, Ste. 120
Irvine, CA 92614
Ph: (949)261-9104
Free: 877-SEM-INFO
Fax: (949)261-1963
Co. E-mail: info@seminarinformation.com
URL: http://www.seminarinformation.com
Price: $1,795.00. **Description:** Learn to apply the eight step design process to create a training course from nothing or enhance an existing program. **Dates and Locations:** Minneapolis, MN.

35678 ■ Instructional Design for Trainers (Onsite)
Seminar Information Service, Inc.
20 Executive Park, Ste. 120
Irvine, CA 92614
Ph: (949)261-9104
Free: 877-SEM-INFO
Fax: (949)261-1963
Co. E-mail: info@seminarinformation.com
URL: http://www.seminarinformation.com
Price: $2,345.00. **Description:** Applications-based workshop where you will prepare a training plan designed to meet your company's every need. **Dates and Locations:** New York, NY; and Arlington, VA.

35679 ■ Introduction to Human Resources Law
Seminar Information Service, Inc.
20 Executive Park, Ste. 120
Irvine, CA 92614
Ph: (949)261-9104
Free: 877-SEM-INFO
Fax: (949)261-1963
Co. E-mail: info@seminarinformation.com
URL: http://www.seminarinformation.com
Price: $995.00. **Description:** Overview of the legal issues associated with day-to-day employment-related decisions and actions. **Dates and Locations:** New York, NY.

35680 ■ Recruiting, Interviewing and Selecting Employees (Onsite)
American Management Association
600 AMA Way
Saranac Lake, NY 12983-5534
Ph: (212)586-8100
Free: 877-566-9441
Fax: (518)891-0368
Co. E-mail: customerservice@amanet.org
URL: http://www.amaseminars.org
Price: $2,345.00 for non-members; $2,095.00 for AMA members; and $1,794.00 for General Services Administration (GSA) members. **Description:** Covers recruitment sources, filtering applicants, interview techniques and questions, and EEO and affirmative action guidelines. **Dates and Locations:** Chicago, IL; Los Angeles, CA; and New York, NY.

35681 ■ Succession Planning: Developing Leaders from Within (Onsite)
American Management Association
600 AMA Way
Saranac Lake, NY 12983-5534
Ph: (212)586-8100
Free: 877-566-9441
Fax: (518)891-0368
Co. E-mail: customerservice@amanet.org
URL: http://www.amaseminars.org
Price: $2,195.00 for non-members; $1,995.00 for AMA members; and $1,708.00 for General Services Administration (GSA) members. **Description:** Learn to implement a succession plan to minimize gaps in leadership. **Dates and Locations:** Atlanta, GA; and New York, NY.

35682 ■ Train the Trainer: Facilitation Skills Workshop (Onsite) (Canada)
Canadian Management Centre (CMC)
150 York St., 5th Fl.
Toronto, ON, Canada M5H 3S5
Ph: (416)214-5678
Free: 877-262-2519
Fax: (416)313-4985
Co. E-mail: cmcinfo@cmctraining.org
URL: http://www.cmctraining.org
Contact: John Wright, President
Price: $1,995.00 members; $2,195.00 non-members Canadian. **Description:** Gain practical, proven techniques and strategies for facilitating high impact learning experiences. **Dates and Locations:** Toronto, ON.

35683 ■ Training for Impact
Seminar Information Service, Inc.
20 Executive Park, Ste. 120
Irvine, CA 92614
Ph: (949)261-9104
Free: 877-SEM-INFO
Fax: (949)261-1963
Co. E-mail: info@seminarinformation.com
URL: http://www.seminarinformation.com
Price: $1,895.00. **Description:** Designed for those accountable for delivering face-toface training programs. **Dates and Locations:** New York, NY.

35684 ■ The Workshop for Personnel/HR Assistants (Onsite)
Seminar Information Service, Inc.
20 Executive Park, Ste. 120
Irvine, CA 92614
Ph: (949)261-9104
Free: 877-SEM-INFO
Fax: (949)261-1963
Co. E-mail: info@seminarinformation.com
URL: http://www.seminarinformation.com
Price: $399.00. **Description:** Learn the essentials of accepted human resources procedures, as well as a clear understanding of current employment law, rules and regulations. **Dates and Locations:** Cities throughout the United States.

REFERENCE WORKS

35685 ■ *The 4-Hour Workweek*
Pub: Crown Publishing/Random House
Ed: Timothy Ferris. **Released:** April 24, 2007. **Price:** $19.95. **Description:** Examination of ways to cut the hours you work and find more enjoyment in your life.

35686 ■ *"16 Creative and Cheap Ways to Say 'Thank You" in HR Specialist (Vol. 8, September 2010, No. 9, pp. 8)*
Pub: Capitol Information Group Inc.
Description: Tips for starting an employee appreciation program for a small company are presented.

35687 ■ *30 Reasons Employees Hate Their Managers: What Your People May Be Thinking and What You Can Do About It*
Pub: AMACOM
Ed: Bruce L. Katcher, with Adam Snyder. **Released:** March 7, 2007. **Price:** $21.95. **Description:** Thirty reasons why American employees are unhappy in their jobs are outlined. Each chapter is opened with a reason, an examination of how it creates work difficulties, and makes suggestions to managers on how to best address each issue.

35688 ■ *365 Answers about Human Resources for the Small Business Owner: What Every Manager Needs to Know about Work Place Law*
Pub: Atlantic Publishing Company
Ed: Mary Holihan. **Released:** June 2006. **Price:** $21. 95. **Description:** Common questions employers ask about employees and the law are answered.

35689 ■ *"2010 Book of Lists" in Tampa Bay Business Journal (Vol. 30, December 22, 2009, No. 53, pp. 1)*
Pub: American City Business Journals
Description: Rankings of companies and organizations within the human resources, banking and finance, business services, healthcare, real estate,

technology, hospitality and travel, and education industries in the Greater Tampa Bay area are presented. Rankings are based on sales, business size, and more.

35690 ■ *Achieving Planned Innovation: A Proven System for Creating Successful New Products and Services*
Pub: Simon and Schuster

Ed: Frank R. Bacon. **Released:** August 2007. **Price:** $16.95. **Description:** Planned innovation is a disciplined and practical step-by-step sequence of procedures for reaching the intended destination point: successful products. This easy-to-read book explains the system along with an action-oriented program for continuous success in new-product innovations. Five steps outlined include: a disciplined reasoning process; lasting market orientation; proper selection criteria that reflect both strategic and tactical business objectives and goals along with dynamic matching of resources to present and future opportunities, and positive and negative requirements before making major expenditures; and proper organizational staffing. The author explains what to do and evaluating the potential of any new product or service, ranging from ventures in retail distribution to the manufacture of goods as diverse as bicycles, motorcycles, aerospace communication and navigation equipment, small business computers, food packaging, and medical products.

35691 ■ *"Advancing the Ball" in Inside Healthcare (Vol. 6, December 2010, No. 7, pp. 31)*
Pub: RedCoat Publishing Inc.

Ed: Michelle McNickle. **Description:** Profile of Medicalodges an elder-care specialty company that provides both patient care and technology development. President and CEO of the firm believes that hiring good employees is key to growth for any small business.

35692 ■ *Aging and Working in the New Economy: Changing Career Structures in Small IT Firms*
Pub: Edward Elgar Publishing, Inc.

Ed: Julie McMullin, Victor W. Marshall. **Released:** March 1, 2010. **Price:** $110.00. **Description:** Case studies and analyses provide insight into the structural features of small- and medium-sized firms in the information technology sector, and the implications of these features for the careers of people employed by them.

35693 ■ *American Bar Association Legal Guide for Small Business: Everything You Need to Know About Small Business*
Pub: Random House Information Group
Contact: Markus Dohle, Accountant

Ed: American Bar Association. **Released:** June 10, 2010. **Description:** The American Bar Association provides insight into financial, health and family issues affecting small business, including start up issues, employment laws, financing a business, and selling a business.

35694 ■ *"American Chemistry Council Launches Flagship Blog" in Ecology,Environment & Conservation Business (October 29, 2011, pp. 5)*
Pub: HighBeam Research

Description: American Chemistry Council (ACC) launched its blog, American Chemistry Matters, where interactive space allows bloggers to respond to news coverage and to discuss policy issues and their impact on innovation, competitiveness, job creation and safety.

35695 ■ *"Amount Md. Pays to Unemployed Dips to Lowest Level Since '08" in Baltimore Business Journal (Vol. 28, November 12, 2010, No. 27)*
Pub: Baltimore Business Journal

Ed: Scott Dance. **Description:** Maryland paid out $50 million for unemployment benefits in September 2010 for its lowest payout since 2008. The drop in unemployment payout could mean lower taxes for employers who pay for the benefits. The unemployment rate in Maryland, however, increased to 7.5 percent.

35696 ■ *"The Anatomy of a High Potential" in Business Strategy Review (Vol. 21, Autumn 2010, No. 3, pp. 52)*
Pub: Blackwell Publishers Ltd.

Ed: Doug Ready, Jay Conger, Linda Hill, Emily Stecker. **Description:** Companies have long been interested in identifying high potential employees, but few firms know how to convert top talent into game changers, or people who can shape the future of the business. The authors have found the 'x factors' that can make a high-potential list into a strong competitive advantage.

35697 ■ *"The Anatomy of a High Potential" in Business Strategy Review (Vol. 21, Autumn 2010, No. 3, pp. 52)*
Pub: Wiley-Blackwell

Ed: Doug Ready, Jay Conger, Linda Hill, Emily Stecker. **Description:** Companies have long been interested in identifying high-potential employees, but few firms know how to convert top talent into game changers - people who can shape the future of the business. The authors have found the x-factors that can make the high-potential list into a strong competitive advantage.

35698 ■ *"Apprenticeship: Earn While You Learn" in Occupational Outlook Quarterly (Vol. 54, Fall 2010, No. 3, pp. 24)*
Pub: U.S. Bureau of Labor Statistics

Description: Paid training, or apprenticeships, are examined. Registered apprenticeship programs conform to certain guidelines and industry-established training standards and may be run by businesses, trade or professional associations, or partnerships with business and unions.

35699 ■ *"Ask Inc." in Inc. (November 2007, pp. 69)*
Pub: Gruner & Jahr USA Publishing

Description: The best time to terminate an employee is discussed.

35700 ■ *"At Your Service: Corporate Concierges Come in Three Varieties" in Incentive (August 25, 2008)*
Pub: Nielson Business Media

Ed: Nathan Adkisson. **Description:** Companies are offering corporate concierge services to handle tasks for new employees as a sign-on benefit. Concierge of Boston has six employees that focus on fulfilling the needs of individuals.

35701 ■ *Atiyah's Accidents, Compensation and the Law*
Pub: Cambridge University Press
Contact: Richard Ziemacki, President
E-mail: rziemacki@cambridge.org

Ed: Peter Cane, Patrick Atiyah. **Released:** January 22, 2010. **Price:** $56.00. **Description:** Leading authority on the law of personal injuries compensation and the social, political and economic issues surrounding it.

35702 ■ *"Austin on Verge of Losing 7,500 Jobs" in Austin Business Journal (Vol. 31, May 6, 2011, No. 9, pp. 1)*
Pub: American City Business Journals Inc.

Ed: Jacob Dirr. **Description:** Proposed state budget cuts are seen to result in the loss of as many as 7,500 public and private sector jobs in Austin, Texas, with the private sector losing the majority of workers. Comments from analysts are included.

35703 ■ *"Bar Hopping: Your Numbers At a Glance" in Inc. (January 2008, pp. 44-45)*
Pub: Gruner & Jahr USA Publishing

Ed: Michael Fitzgerald. **Description:** Software that helps any company analyze data include Crystal Xcelsius, a program that takes data from Excel documents and turns them into animated gauges, charts and graphs; CashView, a Web-based application that tracks receivables and payables; iDashboards, a Web-based programs that produces animated gauges, maps, pie charts and graphs; Corda Human Capital Management, that transforms stats like head count, productivity, and attrition into graphs and dials; NetSuite, a Web-based application that tracks key indicators; and Cognos Now, that gauges, dials, and graphs data.

35704 ■ *"Battling Back from Betrayal" in Harvard Business Review (Vol. 88, December 2010, No. 12, pp. 130)*
Pub: Harvard Business School Publishing

Ed: Daniel McGinn. **Description:** Stephen Greer's scrap metal firm, Hartwell Pacific, lost several million dollars due to a lack of efficient and appropriate inventory audits, accounting procedures, and new-hire reference checks for his foreign operations. Greer believes that balancing growth with control is a key component of success.

35705 ■ *"BETC Backers Plot Future" in Business Journal Portland (Vol. 27, December 10, 2010, No. 41, pp. 1)*
Pub: Portland Business Journal

Ed: Erik Siemers. **Description:** A coalition of clean energy groups and industrial manufacturers have spearheaded a campaign aimed at persuading Oregon legislators that the state's Business Energy Tax Credit (BETC) is vital in job creation. Oregon's BETC grants tax credits for 50 percent of an eligible renewable or clean energy project's cost. However, some legislators propose BETC's abolition.

35706 ■ *"Beyond Auto; Staffing Firm Malace Grabs Revenue Jump" in Crain's Detroit Business (Vol. 26, January 18, 2010, No. 3, pp. 3)*
Pub: Crain Communications Inc.

Ed: Sherri Welch. **Description:** Malace & Associates Inc., the Troy-based human resources management company, expects its diversification into nonautomotive industries to help double its revenues this year. Due to the automotive downturn, between October 2008 and March 2009 the company lost approximately 48 percent of its business.

35707 ■ *"Big Paychecks for Hospital CEOs" in Sacramento Business Journal (Vol. 28, April 8, 2011, No. 6, pp. 1)*
Pub: Sacramento Business Journal

Ed: Kathy Robertson. **Description:** Hospital chief executives in Sacramento, California have been receiving large salaries, tax records show. The huge salaries reflect the high demand for successful hospital chief executives. Statistical data included.

35708 ■ *"BofA Cutting 70 Charlotte Tech Jobs" in Charlotte Observer (January 31, 2007)*
Pub: Knight-Ridder/Tribune Business News

Ed: Rick Rothacker. **Description:** Bank of America announced the elimination of 70 technology positions at their Charlotte, North Carolina facility. The move is part of the company's effort to increase efficiency.

35709 ■ *"Boosting Corporate Entrepreneurship Through HRM Practices" in Human Resource Management (Vol. 49, July-August 2010, No. 4)*
Pub: John Wiley

Ed: Ralf Schmelter, Rene Mauer, Christiane Borsch, Malte Brettel. **Description:** A study was conducted to determine which human resource management (HRM) practices promote corporate entrepreneurship (CE) in small and medium-sized enterprises (SMEs). Findings indicate that staff selection, staff development, training, and staff rewards on CE have a strong impact on SMEs.

35710 ■ *"Boosting Strategy With An Online Community" in Business Strategy Review (Vol. 21, Spring 2010, No. 1, pp. 40)*
Pub: Wiley-Blackwell

Ed: Lynda Gratton, Joel Casse. **Description:** A program that merged online communities with strategic development and implementation at Nokia has provided valuable lessons about new ways employees are able to engage and interact.

35711 ■ *"Both Eyes on the Prize" in Canadian Business (Vol. 83, September 14, 2010, No. 15, pp. 42)*
Pub: Rogers Media Ltd.
Ed: Jacqueline Nelson. **Description:** North American executive compensation has fundamentally shifted partly due to pressure from the US government and recent adjustments in the way CEO pay packages are structured. The changes have also become common practice in Canada and helped in scrutinizing the executive pay.

35712 ■ *"Bracing for More Layoffs" in Sacramento Business Journal (Vol. 28, September 30, 2011, No. 31, pp. 1)*
Pub: Sacramento Business Journal
Ed: Melanie Turner. **Description:** Sacramento, California workers are preparing for a fresh wave of layoffs. The weak economy is seen to drive the development.

35713 ■ *"Brad Wall" in Canadian Business (Vol. 82, April 27, 2009, No. 7, pp. 9)*
Pub: Rogers Media
Ed: Joe Castaldo. **Description:** Saskatchewan Premier Brad Wall believes that the mood in the province is positive, as its economy is one of the few that is expected to post growth in 2009. Wall actively promotes the province in job fairs, offering $20,000 in tuition for recent college and university graduates that relocate in the province for seven years. Wall's views on the province's economy and challenges are presented.

35714 ■ *"Breaking Bad: Rid Yourself of Negative Habits" in Black Enterprise (Vol. 40, July 2010, No. 12, pp. 104)*
Pub: Earl G. Graves Publishing Co. Inc.
Ed: Renita Burns. **Description:** Tardiness, procrastination, chronic complaining are among the bad habits that can make people bad employees; tips for breaking these habits are outlined.

35715 ■ *"Bridging the Worlds" in Academy of Management Journal (Vol. 50, No. 5, October 2007, pp. 1043)*
Pub: Academy of Management
Contact: Ming-Jer Chen, President
Ed: Lise Saari. **Description:** Need to transfer human resource research information published in journals to practitioners and organizations is investigated, along with suggestions on ways of achieving this goal.

35716 ■ *"Brief: Janitorial Company Must Pay Back Wages" in Buffalo News (September 24, 2011)*
Pub: The Buffalo News
Ed: Jonathan D. Epstein. **Description:** Knights Facilities Management, located in Michigan, provides grounds maintenance and janitorial services at the Ralph Wilson Stadium in Buffalo, New York. The US Department of Labor ordered the firm to pay $22,000 in back wages and damages to 26 employees for overtime and minimum wage compensation. Details of the company's violation of the Fair Labor Standards Act are included.

35717 ■ *Business Black Belt: Develop the Strength, Flexibility and Agility to Run Your Company*
Pub: Career Press, Inc.
Ed: Burke Franklin. **Released:** November 1, 2010. **Price:** $15.99. **Description:** Manual offering insights that will enable anyone to become successful in small business. Seventy short chapters included topics such as attitude, management, marketing, selling, employees, money, MBAs, lawyers, consultants, and investors.

35718 ■ *Business Warrior: Strategy for Entrepreneurs*
Pub: Clearbridge Publishing
Ed: Sun Tzu. **Released:** September 2006. **Price:** $19.95. **Description:** Advice to help entrepreneurs understand competitive strategies in order to succeed, focusing on sales, marketing, and personnel management.

35719 ■ *"Businesses Need to Know State, Federal Laws for Employing Minors" in Crain's Detroit Business (Vol. 25, June 15, 2009, No. 24)*
Pub: Crain Communications Inc. - Detroit
Ed: Nancy Kaffer. **Description:** Small business owners must know the law before employing minors. According to Steven Fishman, partner with Bodman LLP, who practices workplace law, most small business owners are not aware of laws regarding employment of minors.

35720 ■ *"Calling All Recruiters: Agent HR Puts Staffing Agents In Charge" in Black Enterprise (Vol. 38, December 2007, No. 5, pp. 72)*
Pub: Earl G. Graves Publishing Co. Inc.
Ed: Chana Garcia. **Description:** Recruiting and staffing agencies are seeing a drop in services due to slow economic growth. AgentHR partners with full-service recruiters who have three to five year's experience-specialists soliciting their own clients, provide staffing services, and manage their own accounts, thus combining the roles of recruiter and salesperson.

35721 ■ *"Capital Position" in Business Journal-Milwaukee (Vol. 28, December 24, 2010, No. 12, pp. A1)*
Pub: Milwaukee Business Journal
Ed: Rich Kirchen. **Description:** Canada-based BMO Financial Group has purchased Marshall and Isley Corporation (M and I), which dominated lending among Wisconsin businesses for decades. The sale of M and I will enable other banks to recruit M and I's customers but BMO Financial remains a stronger competitor since it possesses a more potent capital position.

35722 ■ *"Cautious Hiring in January Report" in Charlotte Observer (February 3, 2007)*
Pub: Knight-Ridder/Tribune Business News
Ed: Kerry Hall. **Description:** U.S. Labor Department released a report that shows 111,000 new positions in January 2007, compared to 206,000 in December 2006. Employers remain cautious about hiring.

35723 ■ *"CEO Pay: Best Bang for Buck" in Philadelphia Business Journal (Vol. 30, September 30, 2011, No. 33, pp. 1)*
Pub: American City Business Journals Inc.
Ed: Jeff Blumenthal. **Description:** A study by Strategic Research Solutions on the compensation of chief executive officers in Philadelphia, Pennsylvania-based public companies reveals that only a few of them performed according to expectations. These include Brian Roberts of Comcast, John Conway of Crown Holdings, and Frank Hermance of Ametek Inc.

35724 ■ *"CEO Pay: The Details" in Crain's Detroit Business (Vol. 25, June 22, 2009, No. 25, pp.)*
Pub: Crain Communications Inc. - Detroit
Description: Total compensation packages for CEOs at area companies our outlined. These packages include salary, bonuses, stock awards, and options.

35725 ■ *"CEOs Split on Migrant Workers" in Canadian Business (Vol. 83, September 14, 2010, No. 15, pp. 23)*
Pub: Rogers Media Ltd.
Ed: Jacqueline Nelson. **Description:** A survey of Canadian CEOs shows that 49 percent of the respondents believe it was wrong to suspend the immigration programs and companies should be allowed to hire the most skilled workers regardless of citizenship. However, 42 percent believe the suspension was right because employment of Canadians must take precedence.

35726 ■ *"CEOs With a Functional Background in Operations" in Human Resource Management (Vol. 49, September-October 2010, No. 5)*
Pub: John Wiley
Ed: Burak Koyuncu, Shainaz Firfiray, Bjorn Claes, Monika Hamori. **Description:** A study was conducted to determine whether companies that appoint chief executive officers (CEOs) with an operations background exhibit better post-succession financial performance relative to organizations that appoint CEOs with other functional backgrounds. A total of 437 CEOs from U.S. firms in eight industries were included in the study.

35727 ■ *"City Consults Executives on Police Hire" in Business Courier (Vol. 27, August 27, 2010, No. 17, pp. 1)*
Pub: Business Courier
Ed: Lucy May, Dan Monk. **Description:** The City of Cincinnati, Ohio has begun a selection process for the new police chief by consulting the city's business executives. The city charter amendment known as Issue 5 has removed civil service protection from the chief's post and enables City Manager Milton Dohoney to hire a chief from outside the department.

35728 ■ *"The Classless Workplace: The Digerati and the New Spirit of Technocapitalism" in WorkingUSA (Vol. 11, June 2008, No. 2, pp. 181)*
Pub: Blackwell Publishers Ltd.
Ed: Eran Fisher. **Description:** Article argues the formation of a new type of economic actor at the intersection of a new capitalism and a new technology: The Dierati. The discourse in based on the analysis of the popular magazine Wired, which registers the culture of contemporary technocapitalism. The suggestion that the new persona of the digerati is constructed as a rejection of the ethics, which dominated the Fordist workplace and Fordist society: Hierarchy and differentiation between workers, on the one hand and capitalists and managers, on the other hand. The transformation of these two categories, workers and capitalists into the digerati worker and the digerati entrepreneur, is described. Set within the context of the structural transformations of capitalism from Fordism to post-Fordism, the article shows the ideological fit of the new ethics of the digerati to the new working arrangements of post-Fordist capitalism, characterized by more privatizes, flexible, and precarious working arrangements.

35729 ■ *"Collateral Damage" in Business Courier (Vol. 26, October 16, 2009, No. 25, pp. 1)*
Pub: American City Business Journals, Inc.
Ed: Jon Newberry. **Description:** Non-union construction firms representing Ohio Valley Associated Builders and Contractors Inc. have filed cases against unionized shops claiming violations of wage law in Ohio. Defendants say the violations are minor, however, they believe they are caught in the middle of the group's campaign to change the state's wage law.

35730 ■ *"Combat Mission: Rebuffed, BAE Systems Fights Army Contract Decision" in Business Courier (Vol. 26, September 25, 2009)*
Pub: American City Business Journals, Inc.
Ed: Jon Newberry. **Description:** BAE Systems filed a complaint with the US Government Accountability Office after the US Army issued an order to BAE's competitor for armoured trucks which is potentially worth over $3 billion. Hundreds of jobs in Butler County, Ohio hinge on the success of the contract protest.

35731 ■ *"Commentary" in Small Business Economic Trends (September 2010, pp. 3)*
Pub: National Federation of Independent Business
Ed: William C. Dunkelberg, Holly Wade. **Description:** A commentary on the economic trends for small businesses in the U.S. is presented. An analysis of the unemployment rate and inflation is given. Economic growth is also expected to remain sub-par for some time, unless new policies are introduced.

35732 ■ *"Commentary. On Federal Reserve's Cut of Interest Rates" in Small Business Economic Trends (January 2008, pp. 3)*
Pub: National Federation of Independent Business
Description: Federal Reserve cut interest rates and announced its economic outlook on September 18, 2007 to stimulate spending. The cut in interest rates, however, may not help in supporting consumer

spending because savers may lose interest income. The expected economic impact of the interest rate cuts and the U.S. economic outlook are also discussed.

35733 ■ *"Commentary. Small Business Economic Trends" in Small Business Economic Trends (March 2008, pp. 3)*
Pub: National Federation of Independent Business
Ed: William C. Dunkelberg, Holly Wade. **Description:** Commentary on the economic trends for small businesses in the U.S. is presented. Analysis of the labor market and low interest rates is given. The effect of the Federal Reserve's policy announcement on small business owner optimism is also discussed.

35734 ■ *"Commentary. Small Business Economic Trends" in Small Business Economic Trends (February 2008, pp. 3)*
Pub: National Federation of Independent Business
Ed: William C. Dunkelberg, Holly Wade. **Description:** Commentary on the economic trends for small businesses in the U.S. is presented. Analysis of the U.S. Federal Reserve Board's efforts to prevent a recession is given. Reduction in business inventories is also discussed.

35735 ■ *"Comparative Indicators" in Montly Labor Review (Vol. 133, September 2010, No. 9, pp. 87)*
Pub: Bureau of Labor Statistics
Description: Labor market indicators for years 2008 and 2009 are given. Statistical data included.

35736 ■ *"Competing for Jobs" in Women In Business (Vol. 63, Summer 2011, No. 2, pp. 37)*
Pub: American Business Women's Association
Ed: Leigh Elmore. **Description:** Job hunting tips for women in the US in relation to generation demographic groups are presented. Effective communications and positive interactions are essential to career development. Generation groups' strengths and weaknesses as job seekers are also given.

35737 ■ *"Competing on Talent Analytics" in Harvard Business Review (Vol. 88, October 2010, No. 10, pp. 52)*
Pub: Harvard Business School Publishing
Ed: Thomas H. Davenport, Jeanne Harris, Jeremy Shapiro. **Description:** Six ways to use talent analytics to obtain the highest level of value from employees are listed. These include human-capital investment analysis, talent value models, workforce forecasts, and talent supply chains.

35738 ■ *"Complaints, Workforce Composition, Productivity, Organizational Values" in HRMagazine (Vol. 54, January 2009, No. 1, pp. 29)*
Pub: Society for Human Resource Management
Contact: Henry G. Jackson, President
E-mail: hjackson@shrm.org
Ed: Amy Maingault, Regan Halvorsen, Rue Dooley, Liz Petersen. **Description:** Workforce composition trends that management should monitor are outlined. A goal-development process is discussed.

35739 ■ *Complete Employee Handbook: A Step-by-Step Guide to Create a Custom Handbook That Protects Both the Employer and the Employee*
Pub: Moyer Bell
Ed: Michael A. Holzschu. **Released:** August 2007. **Price:** $39.95. **Description:** Comprehensive guide for employers deal with personnel issues; CD-ROM contains sample employee handbooks, federal regulations and laws, forms for complying with government programs and worksheets for assessing personnel needs and goals.

35740 ■ *"Compulsory Proportional Representation: Allaying Potential Concerns" in WorkingUSA (Vol. 11, September 2008, No. 3, pp. 349)*
Pub: Blackwell Publishers Ltd.
Ed: Mark Harcourt, Helen Lam. **Description:** Present union certification system has many faults, the most important of which is its failure to deliver employee representation to all but a small and declining minority of workers. As an alternative, compulsory proportional representation (CPR) would have many advantages, particularly when compared with other reform proposals, most of which are designed to only reinvigorate, modify, or supplement the existing system.

35741 ■ *"Condensed Capitalism" in Human Resource Management (Vol. 49, September-October 2010, No. 5, pp. 965-968)*
Pub: John Wiley
Ed: Matthew M. Bodah. **Description:** Review of the book, 'Condensed Capitalism: Campbell Soup and the Pursuit of Cheap Production in the Twentieth Century'.

35742 ■ *"Connecting the Dots Between Wellness and Elder Care" in Benefits and Compensation Digest (Vol. 47, August 2010, No. 8, pp. 18)*
Pub: International Foundation of Employee Benefit Plans
Contact: Richard Lyall, President
Ed: Sandra Timmermann. **Description:** Employees caring for aged and infirm parents deal with time and financial issues and other stresses. The connection between health status of caregivers and employers' health care costs could be aided by linking programs and benefits with wellness and caregiving.

35743 ■ *"The Consequences of Tardiness" in Modern Machine Shop (Vol. 84, August 2011, No. 3, pp. 34)*
Pub: Gardner Business Media, Inc.
Contact: Richard G. Kline, President
E-mail: rkline@gardnerweb.com
Ed: Wayne S. Chaneski. **Description:** Five point addressing motivating factors behind employees who are tardy and those who choose to be on time in the workplace are shared.

35744 ■ *"A Conversation with; Renea Butler, Real Estate One Inc." in Crain's Detroit Business (Vol. 25, June 8, 2009, No. 23, pp. 12)*
Pub: Crain Communications Inc. - Detroit
Ed: Ryan Beene. **Description:** Renea Butler, vice president of administration and human resources for Real Estate One Inc. in Southfield as well as vice president for public relations for the Human Resource Association of Greater Detroit, talks about how the economy has affected human resource services.

35745 ■ *"Corporate Responsibility" in Professional Services Close-Up (July 2, 2010)*
Pub: Close-Up Media
Description: List of firms awarded the inaugural Best Corporate Citizens in Government Contracting by the Corporate Responsibility Magazine is presented. The list is based on the methodology of the Magazine's Best Corporate Citizen's List, with 324 data points of publicly-available information in seven categories which include: environment, climate change, human rights, philanthropy, employee relations, financial performance, and governance.

35746 ■ *Create Your Own Employee Handbook: A Legal and Practical Guide*
Pub: NOLO
Ed: Amy DelPo, Lisa Guerin. **Released:** June 2009. **Price:** $49.99. **Description:** Information for business owners to develop an employee handbook that covers company benefits, policies, procedures, and more.

35747 ■ *"Creating Your Personal Succession Plan" in Black Enterprise (Vol. 38, December 2007, No. 5, pp. 86)*
Pub: Earl G. Graves Publishing Co. Inc.
Ed: Marcia Reed-Woodard. **Description:** Society for Human Resource Management's Succession Planning Survey Report shows that over 58 percent of companies surveyed use succession plans for employees preparing to transition to higher-level positions.

35748 ■ *The Creative Business Guide to Running a Graphic Design Business*
Pub: W.W. Norton & Company, Incorporated
Ed: Cameron S. Foote. **Released:** April 2004. **Price:** $23.10. **Description:** Advice for running a graphic design firm, focusing on organizations, marketing, personnel and operations.

35749 ■ *"Creative In-Sourcing Boosts Franchisee Performance" in Franchising World (Vol. 42, September 2010, No. 9, pp. 16)*
Pub: International Franchise Association
Ed: Daniel M. Murphy. **Description:** Operational training and support is usually provided by franchisors. To be successful in this process it is important to balance the reality of limited financial and human resources.

35750 ■ *"A Crowd for the Cloud" in CIO (Vol. 24, October 2, 2010, No. 1, pp. 16)*
Pub: CIO
Ed: Stephanie Overby. **Description:** Information about a project which aimed to implement a cloud-based crowdsourcing platform and innovation-management process is provided. Chubb Group of Insurance Companies wanted to mine revenue-generating ideas from its 10,400 employees and hundreds of thousands of external agents. The company hosted its first innovation event using its new system in October 2008.

35751 ■ *"CSX Transportation: Supplier Diversity on the Right Track" in Hispanic Business (July-August 2009, pp. 34)*
Pub: Hispanic Business
Description: CSX Transportation is a leader in delivering essential products, operating as many as 1,200 trains and a fleet of more than 100,000 freight cars. CSX attributes its success by valuing diversity in both hiring and supplier contracts.

35752 ■ *"Custom Fit" in Canadian Business (Vol. 80, November 19, 2007, No. 23, pp. 42)*
Pub: Rogers Media
Ed: Andy Holloway. **Description:** Proper employee selection will help ensure a company has the people with the skills it really needs. Employee development is integral in coping with changes in the company. The importance of hiring the right employee and developing his skills is examined.

35753 ■ *"Cutting Health Care Costs: the 3-Legged Stool" in HR Specialist (Vol. 8, September 2010, No. 9, pp. 1)*
Pub: Capitol Information Group Inc.
Description: Employer spending on health insurance benefits to employees is investigated.

35754 ■ *"Debt-Collection Agency to Lay Off 368 in Hampton Center" in Virginian-Pilot (December 4, 2010)*
Pub: Virginian-Pilot
Ed: Tom Shean. **Description:** NCO Financial Systems Inc., provider of debt-collection and outsourcing services will permanently lay off 368 workers at its Hampton call center in 2011.

35755 ■ *"Delta Looks at Downtown Departure" in Business Courier (Vol. 27, October 1, 2010, No. 22, pp. 1)*
Pub: Business Courier
Ed: Dan Monk. **Description:** Delta Air Lines Inc. has been looking for a smaller office for its reservations center in downtown Cincinnati, Ohio. Delta has informed the city of its plan to seek proposals on office space alternatives in advance of the 2011 lease expiration. Insights on the current employment status at the reservations center are also given.

35756 ■ *The Department of Labor's Overtime Regulations Effect on Small Business: Congressional Hearing*
Pub: DIANE Publishing Company
Ed: W. Todd Akin. **Released:** April 2006. **Price:** $20.00. **Description:** An overview of the Congressional hearing regarding the Department of Labor's regulations governing overtime and how they impact small business.

35757 ■ *"Developing the Next Generation of Rosies" in Employee Benefit News (Vol. 25, November 1, 2011, No. 14, pp. 36)*
Pub: SourceMedia Inc.
Ed: Kathleen Koster. **Description:** According to the research group Catalyst, women made up 46.7 percent of the American workforce in 2010, however only 14.4 percent was Fortune 500 executive officers and 15.7 percent held Fortune 500 board seats. Statistical data included.

35758 ■ *"DHS Finalizes Rules Allowing Electronic I-9s" in HR Specialist (Vol. 8, September 2010, No. 9, pp. 5)*
Pub: Capitol Information Group Inc.
Description: U.S. Department of Homeland Security issued regulations that give employers more flexibility to electronically sing and store I-9 employee verification forms.

35759 ■ *The Diversity Code: Unlocking the Secrets to Making Differences Work in the Real World*
Pub: AMACOM
Ed: Michelle T. Johnson. **Released:** September 8, 2010. **Price:** $19.95. **Description:** The most diligent compliance with laws and regulations can't foster true work place diversity. The best organizations have become genuine cross-cultural communities that believe equality in reconciling difference and valuing them. The book promotes understanding by answering many of the toughest questions that professionals and their employers are afraid to ask.

35760 ■ *"DOL Sets Stiff New Child Labor Penalties" in HR Specialist (Vol. 8, September 2010, No. 9, pp. 2)*
Pub: Capitol Information Group Inc.
Description: U.S. Department of Labor (DOL) will impose new penalties for employers that violate U.S. child labor laws. Details of the new law are included.

35761 ■ *"Downturn Tests HCL's Pledge to Employees" in Workforce Management (Vol. 88, November 16, 2009, No. 12, pp. 23)*
Pub: Crain Communications Inc.
Ed: Ed Frauenheim. **Description:** HCL Technologies has kept its promise to keep from laying any employees off during the recession which served as a test for the tech firm's Employee First program, which seeks to give workers greater income security as well as a stronger voice in the firm.

35762 ■ *"Dynamic Supply Chain Alignment" in Human Resource Management (Vol. 49, September-October 2010, No. 5, pp. 969-973)*
Pub: John Wiley
Ed: Kim Sundtoft Hald. **Description:** Review of the book, 'Dynamic Supply Chain Alignment: A New Business Model for Peak Performance in Enterprise Supply Chains Across All Geographies'.

35763 ■ *"Elder Care At Work" in HRMagazine (Vol. 53, September 2008, No. 9, pp. 111)*
Pub: Society for Human Resource Management
Contact: Henry G. Jackson, President
E-mail: hjackson@shrm.org
Ed: Pamela Babcock. **Description:** Many employers are helping workers who face sudden, short-term elder care needs.

35764 ■ *"Employee Called for Jury Duty" in Business Owner (Vol. 35, March-April 2011, No. 2, pp. 14)*
Pub: DL Perkins Company
Description: State laws govern small business rights and obligations regarding employee jury duty obligations. All states do require that employers allow employees to fulfill their jury duty obligations and retaliation, demotion, discipline or termination resulting from jury duty is illegal.

35765 ■ *Employee Management for Small Business*
Pub: Self-Counsel Press, Incorporated
Ed: Lin Grensing-Pophal. **Released:** November 2009. **Price:** $20.95. **Description:** Management tools to help entrepreneurs maintain an effective human resources plan for a small company.

35766 ■ *"Employees Can't Be Punished for Refusing to Work Due to Safety Concerns" in HR Specialist (Vol. 8, September 2010, No. 9, pp. 1)*
Pub: Capitol Information Group Inc.
Description: Whistle-blower provisions in several federal laws make it illegal for employers to retaliate against employees who raise safety concerns to their employer or the government.

35767 ■ *"Employees Change Clothes at Work? Heed New Pay Rules" in HR Specialist (Vol. 8, September 2010, No. 9, pp. 1)*
Pub: Capitol Information Group Inc.
Description: U.S. Department of Labor issued a new interpretation letter that states times spent changing in and out of 'protective clothing' (e.g., helmets, smocks, aprons, gloves, etc.) is considered paid time. It also says time spent changing 'ordinary clothes' (i. e., uniform) may not be compensable itself, but could start the clock on the workday, meaning all activities after - such as walking to the workstation - would be paid time. More details and a link to the DOL are included.

35768 ■ *Employer Legal Forms Simplified*
Pub: Nova Publishing Company
Ed: Daniel Sitarz. **Released:** August 2007. **Price:** $24.95. **Description:** Business reference containing the following forms needed to handle employees in any small business environment: application, notice, confidentiality, absence, federal employer forms and notices, and many payroll forms. All forms are included on a CD that comes in both PDF and text formats. Adobe Acrobat Reader software is also included on the CD. The forms are valid in all fifty states and Washington, DC.

35769 ■ *"Encouraging Study in Critical Languages" in Occupational Outlook Quarterly (Vol. 55, Summer 2011, No. 2, pp. 23)*
Pub: U.S. Bureau of Labor Statistics
Description: Proficiency in particular foreign languages is vital to the defense, diplomacy, and security of the United States. Several federal programs provide scholarships and other funding to encourage high school and college students to learn languages of the Middle East, China, and Russia.

35770 ■ *"The End of Clock-Punching" in Canadian Business (Vol. 83, September 14, 2010, No. 15, pp. 96)*
Pub: Rogers Media Ltd.
Ed: Lyndsie Bourgon. **Description:** Workplace consultant Peter Hadwen is pushing for the transformation of Canada's government departments into results-only work environments (ROWE). ROWE does not require employees to show up to work at a certain time as long as they are meeting goals and achieving results in their jobs. Details of studies regarding ROWE in US companies are examined.

35771 ■ *"Entrepreneurial Human Resource Leadership" in Human Resource Management (Vol. 49, July-August 2010, No. 4, pp. 793-804)*
Pub: John Wiley
Ed: David C. Strubler, Benjamin W. Redekop. **Description:** Dwight Carlson, a visionary entrepreneur, talks about his main role as a leader. He believes that experience can help in making choices between difficult alternatives. He also thinks that leaders do not really motivate people, they actually create an environment where they motivate themselves.

35772 ■ *The Entrepreneur's Guide to Managing Growth and Handling Crisis*
Pub: Greenwood Publishing Group, Inc.
Ed: Theo J. Van Dijk. **Released:** December 2007. **Price:** $39.95. **Description:** The author explains how entrepreneurs can overcome crisis by changing the way they handle customers, by putting new processes and procedures in place, and managing employees in a professional manner. The book includes appendices with tips for hiring consultants, creating job descriptions, and setting up systems to chart cash flow as well as worksheets, tables and figures and a listing of resources.

35773 ■ *"Evaluating the 1996-2006 Employment Projections" in Montly Labor Review (Vol. 133, September 2010, No. 9, pp. 33)*
Pub: Bureau of Labor Statistics
Description: Bureau of Labor Statistics employment projections outperformed alternative naive models, but not projecting the housing bubble or the rise in oil prices caused some inaccuracies in the projects. These projections are used by policymakers, economists, and students.

35774 ■ *"Every Resume Tells a Story" in Women In Business (Vol. 62, September 2010, No. 3, pp. 26)*
Pub: American Business Women's Association
Ed: Kathleen Leighton. **Description:** Ways in which job applicants can write a good resume and promote themselves are discussed. It is believed that applicants should be proud of their accomplishments and they need to add details that will make them stand out. The importance of including a professional narrative in the resume is also explained.

35775 ■ *"Evidence-Based Management and the Marketplace For Ideas" in Academy of Management Journal (Vol. 50, No. 5, October 2007, pp. 1009)*
Pub: Academy of Management
Contact: Ming-Jer Chen, President
Ed: Wayne F. Cascio. **Description:** Study examines the relevance of material to actual usage in human resource management. Results reveal that it is important to design modules with execution in mind in seeking advice from professionals in relevant organizations.

35776 ■ *"Executives Exit at Wal-Mart in China" in Wall Street Journal Eastern Edition (October 17 , 2011, pp. B3)*
Pub: Dow Jones & Company Inc.
Ed: Laurie Burkitt. **Description:** Woes for Wal-Mart Inc.'s subsidiary in China are adding up as Wal-Mart China president and chief executive Ed Chan stepped down, as well as the company's senior vice president for human resources, Clara Wong. The company has been charged by regulators with mislabeling pork products, the result which has forced stores to close. Sales in China have been slow at the retail stores.

35777 ■ *"Face Issues if Elder Care, Unemployment Collide" in Atlanta Journal-Constitution (December 26, 2010, pp. G1)*
Pub: Atlanta Journal-Constitution
Ed: Amy Lindgren. **Description:** More issues arise during holiday for families with older members requiring care, including the issue of employment for those doing the caregiving.

35778 ■ *The Facebook Era: Tapping Online Social Networks to Build Better Products, Reach New Audiences, and Sell More Stuff*
Pub: Prentice Hall
Ed: Clara Shih. **Price:** $24.99. **Description:** The '90s were about the World Wide Web of information and the power of linking Web pages. Today it's about the World Wide Web of people and the power of the social graph. Online social networks are fundamentally changing the way we live, work, and interact. They offer businesses immense opportunities to transform customer relationships for profit: opportunities that touch virtually every business function, from sales and marketing to recruiting, collaboration to executive decision-making, product development to innovation.

35779 ■ *"Falling Local Executive Pay Could Suggest a Trend" in Tampa Bay Business Journal (Vol. 30, January 15, 2010, No. 4, pp. 1)*
Pub: American City Business Journals
Ed: Margie Manning. **Description:** Tampa Bay, Florida-based Raymond James Financial Inc. and MarineMax Inc.'s proxy statements have shown the decreasing compensation of the companies' highest paid executives. The falling trend in executive compensation was a result of intensified shareholder scrutiny and the economy.

35780 ■ *Fast-Track Business Start-Up Kit: California*
Pub: DP Group, Incorporated

Ed: Carolyn Usinger. **Released:** September 2006. **Price:** $29.00. **Description:** Step-by-step guide for starting and running a business in California, including information on sole proprietors, partnerships, limited liability companies, S and C corporations, as well as details concerning business entities, sales taxes, environmental issues, human resources, and more.

35781 ■ *"Filling the Business Gap" in Hispanic Business (December 2010)*
Pub: Hispanic Business

Ed: Richard Larsen. **Description:** New York group seeks to increase state diversity supplier spending to help create jobs and boost the economy. According to a recent study, six out of 10 small business owners will increase capital spending but delay hiring in 2011. However, potential job creation is good among businesses owned by women and minorities.

35782 ■ *"First Franchising Census Report Highlights Industry's Economic Role" in Franchising World (Vol. 42, November 2010, No. 11, pp. 41)*
Pub: International Franchise Association

Ed: John Reynolds. **Description:** Franchise businesses accounted for 10.5 percent of businesses with paid employees in the year 2007.

35783 ■ *"Fitness: Dispelling Rocky Mountain Myths Key to Wellness" in Employee Benefit News (Vol. 25, November 1, 2011, No. 14, pp. 12)*
Pub: SourceMedia Inc.

Ed: Andrea Davis. **Description:** Andrew Sykes, chairman of Health at Work Wellness Actuaries, states that it is a myth that Colorado is ranked as the healthiest state in America. Sykes helped implement a wellness programs at Brighton School District in the Denver area.

35784 ■ *"Future Autoworkers will Need Broader Skills" in Crain's Detroit Business (Vol. 25, June 8, 2009, No. 23, pp. 13)*
Pub: Crain Communications Inc. - Detroit

Ed: Ryan Beene. **Description:** Auto industry observers report that new workers in the industry will need advanced skills and educational backgrounds in engineering and technical fields because jobs in the factories will become more technology-based and multidisciplinary.

35785 ■ *"The Future of Work" in Black Enterprise (Vol. 41, August 2010, No. 1, pp. 65)*
Pub: Earl G. Graves Publishing Co. Inc.

Ed: Annya M. Lott. **Description:** Technology, globalization, and outsourcing will continue to shape the future of work. Social media is a means for small companies to market goods and services.

35786 ■ *"The Future of Work" in Business Strategy Review (Vol. 21, Autumn 2010, No. 3, pp. 16)*
Pub: Wiley-Blackwell

Ed: Lynda Gratton. **Description:** Work is universal. Buy, how, why, where and when we work has never been so open to individual interpretation. The certainties of the past have been replaced by ambiguity, questions and the steady hum of technology. Research covering 21 global companies and more than 200 executives covers the future of work.

35787 ■ *"Generation Y: Engaging the Invincibles" in Employee Benefit News (Vol. 25, November 1, 2011, No. 14, pp. 22)*
Pub: SourceMedia Inc.

Ed: Bremma Shebel, Dannel Dan. **Description:** Employers will need to engage younger workers about healthcare decisions and lifestyle improvement as they become the majority worker as boomers retire.

35788 ■ *"Get Prepared for New Employee Free Choice Act" in HRMagazine (Vol. 53, December 2008, No. 12, pp. 22)*
Pub: Society for Human Resource Management
Contact: Henry G. Jackson, President
E-mail: hjackson@shrm.org

Ed: Allen Smith. **Description:** According to the director of global labor and employee relations with Ingersoll Rand Company, unions may have started having employees signing authorization cards in anticipation of the Employee Free Choice Act. Once signed, the cards are good for one year and employers would have only ten days in which to prepare for bargaining with unions over the first labor contract. The Act also requires these negotiations be subject to mandatory arbitration if a contract is not reached within 120 days of negotiations with unions, resulting in employers' wage rates, health insurance, retirement benefits and key language about flexibility would be determined by an arbitrator with no vested interest in the success of the company.

35789 ■ *"Getting Going on Going Green" in HRMagazine (Vol. 53, August 2008, No. 8, pp. 8)*
Pub: Society for Human Resource Management
Contact: Henry G. Jackson, President
E-mail: hjackson@shrm.org

Ed: Rita Zeidner. **Description:** Being eco-friendly can help recruit and retain workers. Resources to help firms create green initiatives are presented.

35790 ■ *"Give 'Em a Break" in Entrepreneur (Vol. 35, November 2007, No. 11, pp. 32)*
Pub: Entrepreneur Media Inc.

Ed: J.J. Ramberg. **Description:** Andy Walter and Peer Pedersen founded Blue Orchid Capital, a fund of hedge funds, and Steamboat Foundation a foundation that helps college students find high-profile summer internships. Details on the fund and the foundation are presented.

35791 ■ *"Give Us Your Skilled" in Canadian Business (Vol. 80, October 8, 2007, No. 20, pp. 78)*
Pub: Rogers Media

Ed: Zena Olijnyk. **Description:** Demand for skilled workers in Canada is discussed. Despite a strong demand, as evidenced by shortages in both skilled and unskilled labor, the country's immigration policy is affecting the recruitment process. Peter Veress, founder and president of Vermax Group, believes the country is wasting opportunities to take advantage of its attractiveness as a destination for foreign workers.

35792 ■ *"The Global Talent Hunt" in Business Strategy Review (Vol. 21, Spring 2010, No. 1, pp. 78)*
Pub: Wiley-Blackwell

Ed: Richard Emerton. **Description:** Richard Emerton explains how the new 'triple context' of economy, environment and society will have profound implications for human resource practices. He suggests that viewing talent as abundant is the right perspective for a manager.

35793 ■ *"Glossary of Health Benefit Terms" in HRMagazine (Vol. 53, August 2008, No. 8, pp. 78)*
Pub: Society for Human Resource Management
Contact: Henry G. Jackson, President
E-mail: hjackson@shrm.org

Description: Glossary of health benefit terms is presented to help when choosing a health benefits package.

35794 ■ *The Green Collar Economy: How One Solution Can Fix Our Two Biggest Problems*
Pub: HarperCollins Publishers

Ed: Van Jones. **Released:** November 1, 2009. **Price:** $14.99. **Description:** This book offers insight into rebuilding the nation's infrastructure and creating alternative energy sources that could boost the economy through increased employment and higher wages while decreasing our dependence on fossil fuels.

35795 ■ *"The Green Industry Jobs Gap" in Green Industry Pro (Vol. 23, October 2011)*
Pub: Cygnus Business Media

Ed: Gregg Wartgow. **Description:** According to the U.S. Bureau of Labor Statistics, the landscaping industry employs over 829,000 workers. According to another private study, the industry would employ more if they were able to find more people interested in performing the required work.

35796 ■ *"Grooming Your Online Persona" in Women In Business (Vol. 62, June 2010, No. 2, pp. 36)*
Pub: American Business Women's Association

Ed: Diane Stafford. **Description:** Employees' use of online social networks could become a basis on how their employers, clients, or business partners would judge them. Personal details, pictures and other online data should be filtered to avoid inappropriate or uncomfortable situations and distinguish personal from professional or work life.

35797 ■ *"Guidance On Career Guidance for Offender Reentry" in Occupational Outlook Quarterly (Vol. 54, Fall 2010, No. 3, pp. 24)*
Pub: U.S. Bureau of Labor Statistics

Description: Stable employment is a key factor in the successful rehabilitation of law offenders. The National Institute of Corrections hopes to improve offenders' long-term employment prospects.

35798 ■ *"Health Job Shift Looms" in Boston Business Journal (Vol. 31, June 3, 2011, No. 19, pp. 3)*
Pub: Boston Business Journal

Ed: Julie M. Donnelly. **Description:** Pending health care payment reform in Massachusetts is seen to adversely impact hospital staff. Hospitals are also seen to serve more patients once the bill is approved.

35799 ■ *"Hickory Unemployment Stays Steady" in Charlotte Observer (February 2, 2007)*
Pub: Knight-Ridder/Tribune Business News

Ed: Jen Aronoff. **Description:** Unemployment rates remained unchanged in Hickory, North Carolina area; the region reported 6.1 percent unemployment.

35800 ■ *"High-Tech Job-Apalooza!" in Orlando Business Journal (Vol. 26, January 15, 2010, No. 33, pp. 1)*
Pub: American City Business Journals

Ed: Christopher Boyd. **Description:** Science Applications International Corporation, Saab Training USA LLC, CAE USA, and Pelliconi &C.SPA attempt to obtain $939,000 in tax incentives to generate 222 technology and defense-related jobs in Orange County, Florida. Each job will provide an average salary of $67,000. Future plans of each technology and defense firm are also presented.

35801 ■ *"Hire Power" in Entrepreneur (Vol. 35, November 2007, No. 11, pp. 105)*
Pub: Entrepreneur Media Inc.

Ed: Mark Henricks. **Description:** Companies with big resources may hire human resource (HR) consultants to help with writing manuals, drafting policies and designing benefits for employees. HR consultants may also be hired to assist with specific functions or other strategic aspects.

35802 ■ *"HireDiversity: Some Companies Developing Affinity for Employee Groups" in Hispanic Business (October 2007, pp. 86-87)*
Pub: Hispanic Business

Ed: Hildy Medina. **Description:** Affinity groups, also known as employee resource networks, help companies identify and recruit candidates.

35803 ■ *"Holiday Cheer" in Business Journal-Serving Phoenix & the Valley of the Sun (Vol. 31, December 3, 2010, No. 13, pp. 1)*
Pub: Phoenix Business Journal

Ed: Lynn Ducey, Mike Sunnucks. **Description:** Results of a study conducted by Challenger, Gray & Christmas Inc., shows that 68 percent of companies are planning holiday parties in 2010, up slightly from 62 percent in 2009. About 53 percent of those having holiday parties are holding them on company premises.

35804 ■ *"Hospital Jobs" in Baltimore Business Journal (Vol. 28, June 25, 2010, No. 7, pp. 1)*
Pub: Baltimore Business Journal
Ed: Scott Graham. **Description:** Greater Baltimore, Maryland has four hospitals that are in the middle of transforming their campuses with new facilities for treating various patients. Construction at Mercy Medical Center, Johns Hopkins Hospital, Franklin Square Hospital and Anne Rundle Hospital has helped bring the construction industry back to life. Insights into the hiring plans of these hospitals are also included.

35805 ■ *"Hospitals Mandate Shots" in Business Courier (Vol. 27, November 19, 2010, No. 29, pp. 1)*
Pub: Business Courier
Ed: James Ritchie. **Description:** TriHealth has mandated that employees who refuse to get the vaccination shot for 2010 could be penalized with unpaid administrative leave. Other hospital employers, such as University Hospital and Cincinnati Children's Hospital and Medical Center have fired employees for forgoing flu shots. Vaccination rates among hospital employees are given.

35806 ■ *"Hourly Payment and Volunteering" in Academy of Management Journal (August 2007)*
Pub: Academy of Management
Contact: Ming-Jer Chen, President
Ed: Sanford E. DeVoe, Jeffrey Pfeffer. **Description:** Brief description about theoretically important class of work, which is freely undertaken without remuneration, is presented.

35807 ■ *How to Become a Great Boss: The Rules for Getting and Keeping the Best Employees*
Pub: Hyperion Special Markets
Ed: Jeffrey J. Fox. **Released:** May 15, 2002. **Price:** $16.95. **Description:** The book offers valuable advice to any manager or entrepreneur to improve leadership and management skills. Topics covered include: hiring, managing, firing, partnership and competition, self and organization, employee performance, attitude, and priorities.

35808 ■ *"How Hard Could It Be? The Four Pillars of Organic Growth" in Inc. (January 2008, pp. 69-70)*
Pub: Gruner & Jahr USA Publishing
Ed: Joel Spolsky. **Description:** Revenue, head count, public relations, and quality are the four most important aspects of any growing business.

35809 ■ *How to Start and Run Your Own Corporation: S-Corporations For Small Business Owners*
Pub: HCM Publishing
Ed: Peter I. Hupalo. **Released:** March 6, 2003. **Price:** $22.95. **Description:** Basics of corporate business structure are explained. Topics include discovering the best business structure for your company; how to decided between an S-Corporation and LLC; choosing the state in which to incorporate, how to form a corporation, angel investing, special issues for one-person corporations, the role of bylaws and corporate minutes, board of directors, taxes, workers' compensation issues, retirement plans, and more.

35810 ■ *"How to Turn Employee Conflict Into a Positive, Productive Force" in HR Specialist (Vol. 8, September 2010, No. 9, pp. 6)*
Pub: Capitol Information Group Inc.
Description: Ways to help manage a team of workers are presented, focusing on ways to avoid conflict within the group are discussed.

35811 ■ *HRD in Small Organizations: Research and Practice*
Pub: Routledge
Ed: Jim Steward, Graham Beaver. **Released:** February 2004. **Price:** $190.00. **Description:** Approaches to human resource development in small organizations are evaluated.

35812 ■ *"Human Capital: When Change Means Terminating an Employee" in Black Enterprise (Vol. 41, November 2010, No. 4, pp. 40)*
Pub: Earl G. Graves Publishing Co. Inc.
Ed: Tamara E. Holmes. **Description:** Covering successful business change strategies, this article focuses on how the law and nondiscrimination policies can affect this aspect of the workplace.

35813 ■ *"The Human Element" in Canadian Business (Vol. 80, April 23, 2007, No. 9, pp. 78)*
Pub: Rogers Media
Ed: Jeff Sanford. **Description:** The effects of human resource programs on stocks and investor relations are presented.

35814 ■ *Human Resource Executive's Market Resource*
Pub: LRP Publications
Contact: Kenneth Kahn, President
E-mail: kKahn@lrp.com
URL(s): www.lrp.com. **Released:** Annual; November. **Covers:** Approximately 100 vendor companies and associations serving all aspects of human resources administration, including benefits, consulting and information services, software, employee assistance programs, health care, meeting and conference facilities, out placement and recruitment services, pension and retirement, recognition awards and incentives, relocation services, safety and security, temporary services, testing and assessment, training and development, and other services. **Entries include:** Company name, address, phone, product/service, company philosophy, facilities, literature available, etc. **Database includes:** Human resources calendar of events; new literature review. **Arrangement:** Classified by product/service. **Indexes:** Name.

35815 ■ *"Human Resource Management: Challenges for Graduate Education" in Business Horizons (Vol. 51, March-April 2008, No. 2, pp. 151)*
Pub: Elsevier Advanced Technology Publications
Ed: James C. Wimbush. **Description:** Human resource management education at the master's and doctoral degree levels is discussed. There is an ever-increasing need to produce human resource managers who understand the value of human resource management as a strategic business contributor. uman.

35816 ■ *Human Resources for Small Business Made Easy*
Pub: Skilled Learning Incorporated
Ed: Ruth Zimmerman. **Released:** November 2006. **Description:** Guide for human resource development for small businesses.

35817 ■ *"If Just One Person Applies, Are You Required to Hire Him?" in HR Specialist (Vol. 8, September 2010, No. 9, pp. 7)*
Pub: Capitol Information Group Inc.
Description: It is legal to decline hiring an applicant, or even promoting a current employee, if they are the only applicant for a particular position. It may be good choice to wait for more applicants or to change recruiting strategy.

35818 ■ *"Inch by Inch, Employees Lose Ground" in Business Courier (Vol. 26, November 13, 2009, No. 29, pp. 1)*
Pub: American City Business Journals, Inc.
Ed: James Ritchie. **Description:** Employees in Ohio who retained their jobs have suffered losses in salary and other benefits, as companies exert efforts to save money. Thirty-four percent of employees experienced pay cuts. Statistical data included.

35819 ■ *"Injury and Illness Data" in Montly Labor Review (Vol. 133, September 2010, No. 9, pp. 147)*
Pub: Bureau of Labor Statistics
Description: Occupational injury and illness rates by industry in the U.S. are presented.

35820 ■ *"The Ins and Outs of Unemployment in Canada, 1976-2008" in Canadian Journal of Economics (Vol. 44, November 2011, No. 4, pp. 1331)*
Pub: Blackwell Publishers Ltd.
Ed: Michele Campolieti. **Description:** Flows into and out of unemployment in Canada at an aggregate and a number of disaggregated levels are studied.

35821 ■ *"Interbrand's Creative Recruiting" in Business Courier (Vol. 27, November 12, 2010, No. 28, pp. 1)*
Pub: Business Courier
Ed: Dan Monk. **Description:** Global brand consulting firm Interbrand uses a creative recruitment agency to attract new employees into the company. Interbrand uses themed parties to attract prospective employees. The 'Alice In Wonderland' tea party for example, allowed the company to hire five new employees.

35822 ■ *"Interest in 'Encore Careers' is Growing" in HRMagazine (Vol. 53, November 2008, No. 11, pp. 22)*
Pub: Society for Human Resource Management
Contact: Henry G. Jackson, President
E-mail: hjackson@shrm.org
Description: Unexpectedly large numbers of baby boomers are looking for jobs that can provide them with 'means and meaning', according to a survey by MetLife and Civic Ventures. They can find those jobs in encore careers, an opportunity to do work that has a social impact and personal meaning.

35823 ■ *"International Benefits Roundup" in Employee Benefit News (Vol. 25, December 1, 2011, No. 15)*
Pub: SourceMedia Inc.
Description: Employee contributions to an employer-sponsored defined contribution plan in Japan will allowed on a tax-deductible basis; however, currently employee contributions are not allowed. The defined contribution plan is outlined for better understanding.

35824 ■ *"International Comparisons Data" in Montly Labor Review (Vol. 133, September 2010, No. 9, pp. 143)*
Pub: Bureau of Labor Statistics
Description: Unemployment rates adjusted to U.S. concepts and ten countries are presented.

35825 ■ *International Handbook of Entrepreneurship and HRM*
Pub: Edward Elgar Publishing, Inc.
Ed: Rowena Barrett, Susan Mayson. **Released:** March 10, 2010. **Price:** $235.00. **Description:** Conceived on the basis that there is a growing recognition of the interplay between human resource management and entrepreneurship, this volume offers insights into the role of HRM and entrepreneurial firms.

35826 ■ *"Is It Time to Ban Swearing at Work?" in HR Specialist (Vol. 8, September 2010, No. 9, pp. 2)*
Pub: Capitol Information Group Inc.
Description: Screening software has been developed to identify profanity used in business correspondence.

35827 ■ *"Is Your Employees' BMI Your Business?" in Canadian Business (Vol. 83, September 14, 2010, No. 15, pp. 98)*
Pub: Rogers Media Ltd.
Ed: Jacqueline Nelson. **Description:** Canada's Public Health Agency's research shows that there is a solid business case for companies to promote active living to their employees. However, employers must toe the line between being helpful and being invasive. Insights into the issues faces by companies when introducing health programs are discussed.

35828 ■ *"Job Corps Center Remains Vacant After Operator is Booted" in Tampa Bay Business Journal (Vol. 30, January 15, 2010, No. 4, pp. 1)*
Pub: American City Business Journals
Ed: Jane Meinhardt. **Description:** Pinellas County, Florida Job Corps Center has remained vacant due to a conflict over the $16 million contract awarded to

Res-Care Inc. by the US Department of Labor (DOL) The DOL has ordered Res-Care to stop operation at the center and it is uncertain when it will open or what company will operate it.

35829 ■ *"Job-Hopping to the Top and Other Career Fallacies" in Harvard Business Review (Vol. 88, July-August 2010, No. 7-8, pp. 154)*
Pub: Harvard Business School Publishing
Ed: Monika Hamori. **Description:** Fallacies identified and discussed include the belief that a career move should always be a move up, that industry and career switches are penalized, and that large corporations are the only loci for reaping large rewards.

35830 ■ *"Job Reviews: Annual Assessments Still the Norm" in HR Specialist (Vol. 8, September 2010, No. 9, pp. 1)*
Pub: Capitol Information Group Inc.
Description: An OfficeTeam survey of 500 HR professionals asked how their organizations conduct formal performance appraisals. Responses to the questions are examined.

35831 ■ *"Job Seeker's Readiness Guide: Unemployment's High and Competition is Tough" in Black Enterprise (Vol. 40, July 2010, No. 12, pp. 83)*
Pub: Earl G. Graves Publishing Co. Inc.
Description: Five key areas to help someone seeking employment gain the competitive edge are listed.

35832 ■ *"Jobs Data Show Wild Card" in Barron's (Vol. 90, September 6, 2010, No. 36, pp. M12)*
Pub: Barron's Editorial & Corporate Headquarters
Ed: Gene Epstein. **Description:** August 2010 jobs report revealed a 54,000 decline in non-farm payrolls and that the unemployment rate remains unchanged at 9.6 percent. The report also shows a welcome rise of 848,999 in the household-data category. The unemployment rate shows a reversed trend where men's 10.6 percent unemployment is higher than women's 8.6 percent rate.

35833 ■ *"The Jobs Man" in Business Courier (Vol. 26, December 25, 2009, No. 35, pp. 1)*
Pub: American City Business Journals, Inc.
Ed: Lucy May. **Description:** Entrepreneur Bob Messer, a volunteer for Jobs Plus Employment Network in Cincinnati's Over-the-Rhine neighborhood, regularly conducts a seminar that aims to help attendees prepare for employment. Jobs Plus founder Burr Robinson asked Messer to create the seminar in order to help unemployed jobseekers. So far, the program has helped 144 individuals with full time jobs in 2009.

35834 ■ *"Know It All Finds Applicants are Stretching the Truth" in Philadelphia Business Journal (Vol. 28, September 11, 2009, No. 30, pp. 1)*
Pub: American City Business Journals
Ed: Athena D. Merritt. **Description:** Know It All Background Research Services has reported that discrepancies in background checks reached 19.8 percent in 2009. Reports show that 42 percent of the discrepancies involve lying about previous employment, and 37 percent involve education information. Marc Bourne, the company's vice president, believes that employers have cause to be concerned.

35835 ■ *"Labor Force Data" in Montly Labor Review (Vol. 133, September 2010, No. 9, pp. 89)*
Pub: Bureau of Labor Statistics
Description: Employment status of the population of the U.S. by sex, age, race and origin is presented.

35836 ■ *"Laying the Groundwork: In Developing Personnel, the Work Takes Place Beforehand" in Black Enterprise (February 2008)*
Pub: Earl G. Graves Publishing Co. Inc.
Ed: Tamara E. Holmes. **Description:** Small business owners know the devastation of hiring the wrong employee for a position. Steps to improve hiring using a long-term plan are outlined.

35837 ■ *"Layoffs Continue to Be a Drag on Region's Recovery" in Philadelphia Business Journal (Vol. 28, January 22, 2010, No. 49, pp. 1)*
Pub: American City Business Journals
Ed: Athena D. Merritt. **Description:** Mass layoffs continue to hamper Pennsylvania's economic recovery. Job losses are predicted to decline in 2010.

35838 ■ *"Leave Policies: How to Avoid Leave-Related Lawsuits" in Employee Benefit News (Vol. 25, December 1, 2011, No. 15, pp. 12)*
Pub: SourceMedia Inc.
Ed: John F. Galvin. **Description:** Tips for employers when adding disability and maternity leave benefits to workers are outlined, with focus on ways to avoid leave-related lawsuits.

35839 ■ *"Legalities of Diversity" in Hispanic Business (September 2007, pp. 26)*
Pub: Hispanic Business
Ed: Francisco Ramos Jr., Bill Krutzen. **Description:** Most companies in America have diversity programs, however, critics believe diversity can be used as reverse discrimination because minorities are getting preferential treatment in hiring, promotion, and admissions.

35840 ■ *"Legislature to Tackle Crisis in Jobless Fund" in Baltimore Business Journal (Vol. 27, December 18, 2009, No. 32, pp. 1)*
Pub: American City Business Journals
Ed: Scott Dance. **Description:** Maryland's General Assembly is set to finalize changes to the state's unemployment insurance system as soon as it convenes for the 2010 session. The move was aimed to draw $127 million in stimulus money that can support the nearly depleted fund of unemployment benefits within 45 days.

35841 ■ *"Less Than Zero" in Canadian Business (Vol. 80, November 5, 2007, No. 22, pp. 36)*
Pub: Rogers Media
Ed: Andy Holloway. **Description:** Zero-tolerance policy with regards to discrimination and harassment at the workplace has been adopted by many companies. However, employers must exercise caution in terminating employees based on zero-tolerance policies since there are laws governing illegal dismissals. Important considerations employers should make in dismissing workers, such as proof of willful misconduct, are discussed.

35842 ■ *"Linking Human Capital to Competitive Advantages" in Human Resource Management (Vol. 49, September-October 2010, No. 5)*
Pub: John Wiley
Ed: Yan Jin, Margaret M. Hopkins, Jenell L.S. Wittmer. **Description:** A study was conducted to confirm the links among human capital, firm flexibility, and firm performance. The study also examines the emerging role of flexibility for a company's performance. A total of 201 senior supply chain management professionals from several manufacturing companies were included in the study.

35843 ■ *"Location, Location" in Black Enterprise (Vol. 38, February 2008, No. 7, pp. 64)*
Pub: Earl G. Graves Publishing Co. Inc.
Ed: Marcia Reed-Woodard. **Description:** Overseas work assignments are increasing, especially for workers in the U.S., Canada and Latin America.

35844 ■ *"Looking To Hire Young? Be Careful" in Boston Business Journal (Vol. 30, November 19, 2010, No. 43, pp. 1)*
Pub: Boston Business Journal
Ed: Lisa van der Pool. **Description:** The Massachusetts Commission Against Discrimination (MCAD) has been using undercover job applicants to expose discrimination. Cabot's Ice Cream and Restaurant has been accused of denying older workers equal employment opportunities. MCAD has discovered unfair hiring practices such as hiring high school and college students.

35845 ■ *"Losing the Top Job - And Winning It Back" in Harvard Business Review (Vol. 88, October 2010, No. 10, pp. 136)*
Pub: Harvard Business School Publishing
Ed: Alison Beard. **Description:** Michael Mack chronicles the changes in perspectives that occurred when he was fired from Garden Fresh, a restaurant firm he co-owned. Once again at the company helm, he is now more receptive to outside input and acknowledges the importance of work-life balance.

35846 ■ *"Make a Resolution: ADA Training" in HRMagazine (Vol. 54, January 2009, No. 1, pp. 81)*
Pub: Society for Human Resource Management
Contact: Henry G. Jackson, President
E-mail: hjackson@shrm.org
Ed: Victoria Zellers. **Description:** Americans with Disabilities Act (ADA) Amendments Act took effect January 1, 2009. The ADA Amendments Act means that more applicants and employees are eligible for reasonable accommodations and that employers need to develop a new ADA compliance strategy.

35847 ■ *Managing the Older Worker: How to Prepare for the New Organizational Order*
Pub: Harvard Business Press
Ed: Peter Cappelli, Bill Novelli. **Price:** $29.95. **Description:** Your organization needs older workers more than ever: They transfer knowledge between generations, transmit your company's values to new hires, make excellent mentors for younger employees, and provide a 'just in time' workforce for special projects.

35848 ■ *"M&I Execs May Get Golden Parachutes" in Business Journal-Milwaukee (Vol. 28, December 31, 2010, No. 14, pp. A3)*
Pub: Milwaukee Business Journal
Ed: Rich Kirchen. **Description:** Marshall and Isley Corporation's top executives have a chance to receive golden-parachute payments it its buyer, BMO Financial Group, repays the Troubled Asset Relief Program (TARP) loan on behalf of the company. One TARP rule prevents golden-parachute payments to them and the next five most highly paid employees of TARP recipients.

35849 ■ *"A Manufacturing Revival" in Boston Business Journal (Vol. 31, May 27, 2011, No. 18, pp. 1)*
Pub: Boston Business Journal
Ed: Kyle Alspach. **Description:** Massachusetts' manufacturing sector has grown despite the high cost of labor, real estate and electricity. Manufacturing jobs in the state have increased to 2,800 in April 2011.

35850 ■ *"Mapping Out a Career" in Occupational Outlook Quarterly (Vol. 54, Fall 2010, No. 3, pp. 12)*
Pub: U.S. Bureau of Labor Statistics
Ed: Audrey Watson. **Description:** Geographic distribution of occupations is studied, along with lifestyle considerations when choosing a career.

35851 ■ *"Market Recoups Its Losses - And Its Optimism" in Barron's (Vol. 89, July 20, 2009, No. 29, pp. M3)*
Pub: Dow Jones & Co., Inc.
Ed: Kopin Tan. **Description:** US stock markets gained heavily in the third week of July 2009, rising by about 7 percent during the week. The shares of human resource management companies could be overpriced as they are trading at very high price-earnings multiples. Baxter International faces a class-action suit due to its alleged conspiracy with CSL to fix blood-plasma product prices.

35852 ■ *"May I Handle That For You?" in Inc. (March 2008, pp. 40, 42)*
Pub: Gruner & Jahr USA Publishing
Ed: Taylor Mallory. **Description:** According to a recent survey, 53 percent of all companies outsource a portion of their human resources responsibilities. Ceridian, Administaff, Taleo, KnowledgeBank, and CheckPoint HR are among the companies profiled.

35853 ■ *"Mayor Unveils Business Plan" in Boston Business Journal (Vol. 29, September 16, 2011, No. 19, pp. 1)*
Pub: American City Business Journals Inc.
Ed: Gary Haber. **Description:** Mayor Stephanie Rawlings-Blake of Baltimore, Maryland unveiled her plan to push the economy forward. Her key objectives include giving more support for the city's technology companies and refocusing the Baltimore Development Corporation on job creation and retention.

35854 ■ *MBA In a Day*
Pub: John Wiley and Sons, Inc.
Ed: Steven Stralser, PhD. **Released:** 2004. **Price:** $34.95. **Description:** Management professor presents important concepts, business topics and strategies that can be used by anyone to manage a small business or professional practice. Topics covered include: human resources and personal interaction, ethics and leadership skills, fair negotiation tactics, basic business accounting practices, project management, and the fundamentals of economics and marketing.

35855 ■ *"Meet Rebecca. She's Here to Fire You" in Inc. (November 2007, pp. 25-26)*
Pub: Gruner & Jahr USA Publishing
Ed: Max Chafkin. **Description:** Amid liability concerns as well as CEO guilt, more and more firms are using consulting companies to fire workers. These outsourced firms help small companies structure severance and document information in order to limit legal liability when firing an employee.

35856 ■ *"Meetings Go Virtual" in HRMagazine (Vol. 54, January 2009, No. 1, pp. 74)*
Pub: Society for Human Resource Management
Contact: Henry G. Jackson, President
E-mail: hjackson@shrm.org
Ed: Elizabeth Agnvall. **Description:** Microsoft Office Live Meeting conferencing software allows companies to schedule meetings from various company locations, thus saving travel costs.

35857 ■ *"Mind the Gap" in Canadian Business (Vol. 80, November 5, 2007, No. 22, pp. 21)*
Pub: Rogers Media
Ed: Matthew McCleam. **Description:** The average difference in median wages between men and women who have full-time jobs, according to the Organization Co-operation and Development is over 15 percent and that number is above 20 percent in Canada. The difference in earnings has become smaller since the 1960s, as more women have joined the labor market. The reasons for the wage gap are examined.

35858 ■ *"Mismanaging Pay and Performance" in Business Strategy Review (Vol. 21, Summer 2010, No. 2, pp. 54)*
Pub: Wiley-Blackwell
Ed: Rupert Merson. **Description:** Understanding the relationship between performance measurement and desired behaviors is an important element of a company's talent management.

35859 ■ *"Mission: Recruitment" in HRMagazine (Vol. 54, January 2009, No. 1, pp. 42)*
Pub: Society for Human Resource Management
Contact: Henry G. Jackson, President
E-mail: hjackson@shrm.org
Ed: Theresa Minton-Eversole. **Description:** Due to the hiring challenges faced by Army recruiters, they are partnering with employers in order to establish connections to high quality, Army-trained individuals when they separate from active duty.

35860 ■ *"Monitor Work Productivity" in Business Owner (Vol. 35, July-August 2011, No. 4, pp. 4)*
Pub: DL Perkins Company
Description: Tips for tracking employee productivity are explained.

35861 ■ *"More than Able" in Entrepreneur (Vol. 36, March 2008, No. 3, pp. 81)*
Pub: Entrepreneur Media Inc.
Ed: Mark Henricks. **Description:** Disabled workers are motivated employees and work longer hours. A study shows that accommodating disabled workers is very low cost and provides benefits to employers, such as improved employee retention and increased customer base. Other details about hiring disabled workers are discussed.

35862 ■ *"More Jobs Heading to Suburb" in Austin Business Journallnc. (Vol. 29, November 20, 2009, No. 37, pp. 1)*
Pub: American City Business Journals
Ed: Kate Harrington. **Description:** Site of Advanced Integration Technologies (AIT) in Pflugerville, Texas might increase its workforce to 80 employees in the next six months due to the creation of an incentive package. Funds from the Pflugerville Community Development Corporation have been helping AIT's initiative to hire more workers. The firm receives $2,000 from the plan for every new employee it hires.

35863 ■ *"More Small Businesses Willing to Fund Employees' Benefits" in Baltimore Business Journal (Vol. 28, June 18, 2010, No. 6, pp. 1)*
Pub: Baltimore Business Journal
Ed: Scott Graham. **Description:** An increasing number of small businesses in Maryland are tapping into potentially cheaper self-funded health plans instead of providing fully insured benefits to employees through traditional health plans. Self-funded health plans charge employers for health care up to a specified level. Economic implications of self-funded plans to small businesses are discussed.

35864 ■ *"The Myth of the Overqualified Worker" in Harvard Business Review (Vol. 88, December 2010, No. 12, pp. 30)*
Pub: Harvard Business School Publishing
Ed: Andrew O'Connell. **Description:** It is recommended to seriously consider job candidates with qualifications exceeding the position being recruited because research shows these individuals work harder, but do not quit any sooner than those whose qualifications more closely match the position.

35865 ■ *"NASA Taps Younger Talent Pool to Supplement Aging Work Force" in Crain's Cleveland Business (Vol. 30, June 22, 2009, No. 24, pp. 1)*
Pub: Crain Communications, Inc.
Ed: Chuck Soder. **Description:** NASA's Glenn Research Center has reversed the trend towards hiring older workers with more experience by recruiting for entry-level positions as part of a pilot program to attract younger talent.

35866 ■ *"New Career Center Opens at Right Time: Laid-Off Freightliner Workers Will Need Help" in Charlotte Observer (February 1, 2007)*
Pub: Knight-Ridder/Tribune Business News
Ed: Gail Smith-Arrants. **Description:** Rowan-Cabarrus Community College announced the opening of its new career development center that will help area workers train for new careers.

35867 ■ *The New Job Security: The 5 Best Strategies for Taking Control of Your Career*
Pub: Crown Business Books
Ed: Pam Lassiter. **Released:** September 7, 2010. **Price:** $14.99. **Description:** This book will help individuals to uncover interesting alternative jobs, generate multiple income streams, shape their job to reflect values and goals, move successfully through the company, and plan for career transitions to keep them in control. Online resources, real-life examples, practical exercises and a no-nonsense approach will aid in job stability.

35868 ■ *"New Jobless Claims Filed in December Soar" in Baltimore Business Journal (Vol. 27, January 29, 2010, No. 39, pp. 1)*
Pub: American City Business Journals
Ed: Scott Dance. **Description:** Maryland received 48,693 new claims for unemployment benefits in December 2009, reaching its highest monthly total since 1974. The number of claims was up 49 percent from November and 13 percent from the same period in 2008. Labor officials and economists discuss this trend.

35869 ■ *The No Asshole Rule*
Pub: Warner Books Inc.
Ed: Robert I. Sutton PhD. **Released:** February 22, 2007. **Price:** $22.99. **Description:** Problem employees are more than just a nuisance they are a serious and costly threat to corporate success and employee health.

35870 ■ *"No Time to Grieve" in Women In Business (Vol. 63, Fall 2011, No. 3, pp. 22)*
Pub: American Business Women's Association
Ed: Diane Stafford. **Description:** Individuals who have experienced job loss must go through the emotional stages related to this event in order to gain the best re-employment opportunities. The first step towards re-employment is to make the job search public. Tips for improving one's online footprint are also given.

35871 ■ *Non-Standard Employment under Globalization*
Pub: Palgrave Macmillan
Ed: Koichi Usami. **Released:** January 19, 2010. **Price:** $100.00. **Description:** Expansion of non-standard employment under globalization is being recognized in all of the newly industrialized countries. The book examines deregulation of labor markets, social protection for nonstandard workers, and social security reforms in accordance with the transformation of employment.

35872 ■ *"Notes on Current Labor Statistics" in Montly Labor Review (Vol. 133, September 2010, No. 9, pp. 75)*
Pub: Bureau of Labor Statistics
Description: Principal statistics and calculated by the Bureau of Labor Statistics are presented. The series includes statistics on labor force; employment; unemployment; labor compensation; consumer, producer, and international prices; productivity; international comparisons; and injury and illness statistics.

35873 ■ *"Numbers Game" in Baltimore Business Journal (Vol. 27, February 6, 2010, No. 40, pp. 1)*
Pub: American City Business Journals
Ed: Scott Dance. **Description:** Doubts are being raised regarding the impact of the federal stimulus spending in addressing unemployment in Maryland, which has experienced 1,800 jobs created so far. Details on the view of companies and the insufficient amount of contracts that lead to the fewer number of workers being hired are discussed.

35874 ■ *Off-Ramps and On-Ramps: Keeping Talented Women on the Road to Success*
Pub: Harvard Business School Press
Ed: Sylvia Ann Hewlett. **Price:** $29.95. **Description:** Hewlett (founding president for the Center for Work-Life Policy) examines why many women exit their careers, taking 'off-ramps' (leaving altogether) or 'scenic routes' (opting to work part-time), often during critical, competitive times. She also provides valuable suggestions for companies hoping to retain talented employees of any gender.

35875 ■ *"Olympus is Urged to Revise Board" in Wall Street Journal Eastern Edition (November 28, 2011, pp. B3)*
Pub: Dow Jones & Company Inc. Enterprise Media Group
Contact: Clare Hart, President
Ed: Phred Dvorak. **Description:** Koji Miyata, once a director on the board of troubled Japanese photographic equipment company, is urging the company to reorganize its board, saying the present group should resign their board seats but keep their management positions. The company has come under scrutiny for its accounting practices and costly acquisitions.

35876 ■ *"On the Clock" in Canadian Business (Vol. 82, April 27, 2009, No. 7, pp. 28)*
Pub: Rogers Media
Ed: Sarka Halas. **Description:** Survey of 100 Canadian executives found that senior managers can be out of a job for about nine months before their careers are adversely affected. The nine month mark can be avoided if job seekers build networks even before they lose their jobs. Job seekers should also take volunteer work and training opportunities to increase their changes of landing a job.

35877 ■ *"On Hire Ground" in Entrepreneur (Vol. 36, February 2008, No. 2, pp. 19)*
Pub: Entrepreneur Media Inc.
Description: ADP Small Business Services, an economic consulting firm, showed that small businesses had increased employment rates in 2007 and added 77,000 jobs in November 2007. Entrepreneurial employment and data showing the contribution of small businesses to job growth are presented.

35878 ■ *One Foot Out the Door: How to Combat the Psychological Recession That's Alienating Employees and Hurting American Business*
Pub: AMACOM
Ed: Judith M. Bardwick. **Released:** October 31, 2007. **Price:** $24.95. **Description:** Drawing on research that indicates Generation X and younger baby boomers feel disconnected from their jobs, the author explores the causes (bad management) of that disengagement. Her pragmatic suggestions about how companies can prove their commitment to employees is beneficial.

35879 ■ *"One Workforce - Many Languages" in HRMagazine (Vol. 54, January 2009, No. 1, pp. 32)*
Pub: Society for Human Resource Management
Contact: Henry G. Jackson, President
E-mail: hjackson@shrm.org
Ed: Rita Zeidner. **Description:** Many U.S. employers are investing in English classes to upgrade their immigrant workers' skills on the job.

35880 ■ *"Online Tools for Jobseekers" in Occupational Outlook Quarterly (Vol. 55, Fall 2011, No. 3, pp. 20)*
Pub: U.S. Bureau of Labor Statistics
Description: U.S. Department of Labor's CareerOneStop provides a collection of Web-based tools serving students, jobseekers, employers, and the workforce. The top six categories for job listings nationwide include general job boards, niche job boards, career planning tools, career explorations sites, social media job search sites, and other tools which include interview preparation tools and training grants.

35881 ■ *"Open Enrollment: Staying Healthy During Enrollment Season" in Employee Benefit News (Vol. 25, November 1, 2011, No. 14, pp. 41)*
Pub: SourceMedia Inc.
Ed: Shana Sweeney. **Description:** Tips for staying healthy during your benefit open enrollment period are outlined.

35882 ■ *"Optimism Index" in Black Enterprise (Vol. 41, September 2010, No. 2, pp. 24)*
Pub: Earl G. Graves Publishing Co. Inc.
Description: According to a Pew Research Center report, 81 percent of African Americans expect to improve their finances in 2011. Blacks have carried a disproportionate share of job losses and housing foreclosures in the recession that began in 2007.

35883 ■ *"Orders Up; Jobs Below Forecast" in Charlotte Observer (February 2, 2007)*
Pub: Knight-Ridder/Tribune Business News
Ed: Kerry Hall. **Description:** U.S. Labor Department reported unemployment rates at 4.6 percent, up one-tenth of a percent. Economists had predicted 170,000 new jobs, but only 111,000 were created.

35884 ■ *"Organization Redesign and Innovative HRM" in Human Resource Management (Vol. 49, July-August 2010, No. 4, pp. 809-811)*
Pub: John Wiley
Ed: Pat Lynch. **Description:** An overview of the book, 'Organization Redesign and Innovative HRM' is presented.

35885 ■ *Organizations Alive!: Six Things That Challenge - Seven That Bring Success*
Pub: Yuill & Associates
Ed: Jan Yuill. **Released:** January 2005. **Price:** $35.12 for book and guide. **Description:** New insight into understanding how organizations function as individuals is presented by an international consultant. Customer service, resource management, outsourcing, and management are among the issues covered.

35886 ■ *"Outplacement Services" in Black Enterprise (Vol. 38, March 2008, No. 8, pp. 60)*
Pub: Earl G. Graves Publishing Co. Inc.
Ed: Marcia Reed Woodard. **Description:** Tips to use while in career-transition are offered. Many times outplacement services are provided as part of a severance package to employees.

35887 ■ *"Over and Out" in Entrepreneur (Vol. 36, February 2008, No. 2, pp. 25)*
Pub: Entrepreneur Media Inc.
Ed: Julie Moline. **Description:** Ben Wolin, owner of Waterfront Media that operates wellness and health Websites, had employed the services of human resource consulting firm to advise him in regard to overtime pay. Guidelines on how to avoid overtime pay violations are presented.

35888 ■ *"Pack Mentality" in Crain's Chicago Business (Vol. 31, April 21, 2008, No. 16, pp. 31)*
Pub: Crain Communications, Inc.
Ed: Sarah A. Klein. **Description:** Jill Smart, the head of human resources for a company with 170,000 employees worldwide, frequently travels to India, London and Singapore; Ms. Smart provides advice concerning efficiency, time management and avoiding jet-lag.

35889 ■ *"Paid to Persuade: Careers in Sales" in Occupational Outlook Quarterly (Vol. 55, Summer 2011, No. 2, pp. 24)*
Pub: U.S. Bureau of Labor Statistics
Ed: Ilka Maria Torpey. **Description:** Sales workers are paid to persuade others to buy goods and services. There were over 13 million wage and salary sales workers in the US in 2010. Wages in sales careers can vary and some become lucrative, lifelong career positions. Seven sales occupations with annual wages higher than $33,000 are profiled.

35890 ■ *"Pay Fell for Many Local Execs in '09" in Baltimore Business Journal (Vol. 28, July 2, 2010, No. 8, pp. 1)*
Pub: Baltimore Business Journal
Ed: Gary Haber. **Description:** Compensation for the 100 highest-paid executives in the Baltimore, Maryland area decreased in 2009, compared with 2008. At least $1 million were received by 59 out of 100 executives in 2009, while 75 earned the said amount in 2008. Factors that contributed to the executives' decisions to take pay cuts are discussed.

35891 ■ *"Paychecks of Some Bank CEOs Have a Pre-Recession Look" in Boston Business Journal (Vol. 29, May 13, 2011, No. 1, pp. 1)*
Pub: American City Business Journals Inc.
Ed: Gary Haber. **Description:** The salaries of United States-based bank chief executive officers have increased to pre-recession levels. Wells Fargo and Company's John G. Stumpf received $17.6 million in 2010. Community bank executives, on the other hand, have seen minimal increases.

35892 ■ *"Perks Still Popular: Jets May be Out, but CEO Benefits Abound" in Crain's Detroit Business (Vol. 25, June 22, 2009)*
Pub: Crain Communications Inc. - Detroit
Ed: Ryan Beene. **Description:** Benefits packages of local CEOs are outlined. Statistical data included.

35893 ■ *"Perspective: Borderline Issues" in Entrepreneur (Vol. 35, October 2007, No. 10, pp. 48)*
Pub: Entrepreneur Media Inc.
Ed: Joshua Kurlantzick. **Description:** Failure of the immigration reform bill is expected to result in increased difficulty in finding workers that would take on the dirty and perilous jobs, which are usually taken by immigrants. Regularizing immigration on the other hand will cost business owners money by making them spend for the legality of their employees' stay in the U.S. Other effects of immigration laws on entrepreneurs are discussed.

35894 ■ *Pink Slip Power!: Recover and Succeed It's Up To You!*
Pub: Infinity Publishing
Ed: Wade J. Wnuk. **Released:** March 2004. **Price:** $9.95. **Description:** Advice is given to those facing loss of employment. The book discusses issues such as: restraining emotions before reacting to a severance package ceasing to brood on the past, focusing on the future, networking and looking for hidden job opportunities, preparing resumes, and gearing up for interviews. Four chapters cover ideas for facing reality, formulating a plan, promoting one's self, and persisting in the face of adversity.

35895 ■ *"Plan Your Future with My Next Move" in Occupational Outlook Quarterly (Vol. 55, Summer 2011, No. 2, pp. 22)*
Pub: U.S. Bureau of Labor Statistics
Description: My Next Move, an online tool offering a variety of user-friendly ways to browse more than 900 occupations was created by the National Center for O NET Development for the US Department of Labor's Employment and Training Administration. Clicking on an occupation presents a one-page profile summarizing key information for specific careers.

35896 ■ *Prepare for the Worst, Plan for the Best: Disaster Preparedness and Recovery for Small Businesses*
Pub: John Wiley & Sons, Incorporated
Ed: Donna R. Childs. **Released:** July 2009. **Price:** $24.95. **Description:** Guide to help small businesses protect themselves from disasters. New information is presented on Redundant Arrays of Independent Disk (RAID) hardware backups, calling trees and the Internet, power outages and suppliers, as well as wireless networks.

35897 ■ *"Privacy Concern: Are 'Group' Time Sheets Legal?" in HR Specialist (Vol. 8, September 2010, No. 9, pp. 4)*
Pub: Capitol Information Group Inc.
Description: Under the Fair Labor Standards Act (FLSA) employers are required to maintain and preserve payroll or other records, including the number of hours worked, but it does not prescribe a particular order or form in which these records must be kept.

35898 ■ *"Productivity Data" in Montly Labor Review (Vol. 133, September 2010, No. 9, pp. 137)*
Pub: Bureau of Labor Statistics
Description: Productivity data is presented through indexes of productivity, hourly compensation and unit costs in 2007.

35899 ■ *"Project Could Forge Path to Jobs, Growth" in Business Courier (Vol. 26, September 11, 2009, No. 20, pp. 1)*
Pub: American City Business Journals, Inc.
Ed: Lucy May. **Description:** The planned 13.5 mile Mill Creek Greenway Trail extension could create 445 jobs and bring $52 million to the economy of Cincinnati, Ohio. The trail extension would cost $24 million and would be used for recreational purposes.

35900 ■ *"Protecting Company Secrets" in Inc. (February 2008, pp. 38-39)*
Pub: Gruner & Jahr USA Publishing
Ed: Scott Westcott. **Description:** A legal guide for noncompete clauses when hiring new employees is outlined, stressing how each state has its own set of laws.

35901 ■ *"Prudential Courts Hispanics" in Hispanic Business (March 2008, pp. 38, 40)*
Pub: Hispanic Business
Ed: Melinda Burns. **Description:** Prudential Financial Inc. is reaching out to Hispanic Chambers of Commerce in an effort to hire and do business with the Hispanic community in the U.S.

35902 ■ *"Putting an End to End-of-Year Reviews" in Inc. (December 2007, pp. 58, 61)*
Pub: Gruner & Jahr USA Publishing
Ed: Scott Westcott. **Description:** Performance assessments can be used in place of blunt employee reviews in order to create effective annual reviews.

35903 ■ *"Quits Versus Layoffs" in Occupational Outlook Quarterly (Vol. 55, Fall 2011, No. 3, pp. 36)*
Pub: U.S. Bureau of Labor Statistics
Description: Data from the U.S. Bureau of Labor Statistics provides data from the Job Openings and Labor Turnover Survey regarding quits and layoffs.

35904 ■ *Race and Entrepreneurial Success: Black-, Asian-, and White-Owned Businesses in the United States*
Pub: The MIT Press
Contact: Ellen W. Faran, Director
E-mail: ewfaran@mit.edu
Ed: Robert W. Fairlie. **Released:** September 30, 2008. **Price:** $35.00. **Description:** Trends in minority small business ownership are explored, focusing on the importance of human capital, financial capital, and family business background in successful business ownership.

35905 ■ *"Race and Gender Diversity" in Business Horizons (November-December 2007, pp. 445)*
Pub: Elsevier Technology Publications
Ed: James C. Wimbush. **Description:** Research conducted on diversity building, employee recruitment, gender issues in management, and pay inequality from 2006 through present are discussed. Diversity conditions and attitudes toward it are slowly improving based on these findings.

35906 ■ *Reality-Based Leadership: Ditch the Drama, Restore Sanity to the Workplace*
Pub: Jossey-Bass
Ed: Cy Wakeman. **Price:** $27.95. **Description:** Recent polls show that 71 percent of workers think about quitting their jobs every day. That number would be shocking if people actually were quitting. Worse, they go to work, punching time clocks and collecting pay checks, while checked out emotionally. Cy Wakeman reveals how to be the kind of leader who changes the way people think about and perceive their circumstances, one who deals with the facts, clarifies roles, gives clean and direct feedback, and insists that everyone do the same without drama or defensiveness.

35907 ■ *"Recession Drags Down CEO Pay; Full Impact May Not Have Played Out" in Crain's Detroit Business (Vol. 25, June 22, 2009, No. 25)*
Pub: Crain Communications Inc. - Detroit
Ed: Ryan Beene. **Description:** Median overall compensation package for Detroit's top-compensated 50 CEOs was down 10.67 percent from $2.3 million in 2007 to $2.06 million in 2008. Statistical data included.

35908 ■ *"Recruiters Look Beyond Backyard to Find Gen Y Workers" in HRMagazine (Vol. 53, November 2008, No. 11, pp. 22)*
Pub: Society for Human Resource Management
Contact: Henry G. Jackson, President
E-mail: hjackson@shrm.org
Description: More than two-thirds of recent college graduates would relocate for a job, and 70 percent would be willing to move for an employer, according to the 2008 Hot Cities Survey; New York, Washington DC, and Chicago top the list of most desirable cities for relocation.

35909 ■ *"Recruiting 2.0" in Entrepreneur (Vol. 35, November 2007, No. 11, pp. 100)*
Pub: Entrepreneur Media Inc.
Ed: Andrea Cooper. **Description:** Technology is becoming a tool to help small companies find the best employees. Firms can look into social networking sites to see recommendations from the applicants' colleagues. Tips on how to select the employees online are listed.

35910 ■ *"Regional Talent Network Unveils Jobs Web Site" in Crain's Cleveland Business (Vol. 30, June 1, 2009, No. 21, pp. 11)*
Pub: Crain Communications, Inc.
Description: Regional Talent Network launched WhereToFindHelp.org, a Website designed to act as a directory of all Northeast Ohio resources that can help employers recruit and job seekers look for positions. The site also lists organizations offering employment and training services.

35911 ■ *"Remind Managers to Avoid Talk of Employee Longevity" in HR Specialist (Vol. 8, September 2010, No. 9, pp. 3)*
Pub: Capitol Information Group Inc.
Description: Supervisors need to understand that casual conversations can be used against an organization in law suits.

35912 ■ *"Renren Partnership With Recruit to Launch Social Wedding Services" in Benzinga.com (June 7, 2011)*
Pub: Benzinga.com
Ed: Benzinga Staff. **Description:** Renren Inc., the leading real name social networking Internet platform in China has partnered with Recruit Company Limited, Japan's largest human resource and classified media group to form a joint venture to build a wedding social media catering to the needs of engaged couples and newlyweds in China.

35913 ■ *"Research in Personnel and Human Resources Management, Vol. 28" in Human Resource Management (Vol. 49, July-August 2010, No. 4)*
Pub: John Wiley
Ed: Mukta Kulkarni. **Description:** An overview of the book, 'Research in Personnel and Human Resources Management', Vol. 28 is presented.

35914 ■ *"'Resume Mining' Services Can Save Time, Money" in HR Specialist (Vol. 8, September 2010, No. 9, pp. 7)*
Pub: Capitol Information Group Inc.
Description: Low-cost resume mining services can help human resource departments save time and money by searching online resume databases for candidates matching specific job qualifications.

35915 ■ *"Retailers, City Clash Over Wages" in Baltimore Business Journal (Vol. 28, July 9, 2010, No. 9, pp. 1)*
Pub: Baltimore Business Journal
Ed: Daniel J. Sernovitz. **Description:** A bill pending before the City Council of Baltimore, Maryland would mandate the city's major retailers to pay their employees at least $10.57 per hour, $3 higher than was state law requires. Major retailers, as defined in the said bill by Councilwoman Mary Pat Clarke, have gross sales of at least $10 million. Reactions of the retailers affected are presented.

35916 ■ *"Retirement Barriers: Lowering Retirement System Barriers for Women" in Employee Benefit News (Vol. 25, December 1, 2011, No. 15)*
Pub: SourceMedia Inc.
Ed: Mary Nell Billings. **Description:** Challenges faced by small business for lowering retirement benefits barriers for women and minorities, which is difficult to put into practice, is discussed.

35917 ■ *"Retirement Plan Disclosures: Prepare Now for Fiduciary Rules" in Employee Benefit News (Vol. 25, November 1, 2011, No. 14, pp. 24)*
Pub: SourceMedia Inc.
Ed: Brian M. Pinheiro, Kurt R. Anderson. **Description:** Department of Labor has delayed the deadlines on new affirmative obligations for fiduciaries of retirement plans subject to the Employee Retirement Income Security Act. Details included.

35918 ■ *"Risk Management Starts at the Top" in Business Strategy Review (Vol. 21, Spring 2010, No. 1, pp. 18)*
Pub: Wiley-Blackwell
Ed: Paul Strebel, Hongze Lu. **Description:** Authors question why, at the end of 2008, Citigroup, Merrill Lynch and UBS had well over $40 billion in sub-prime write-downs and credit losses, while some of their competitors were much less exposed. Their research into the situation revealed correlations of great import to today's firms.

35919 ■ *"A Say on Pay" in Canadian Business (Vol. 82, April 27, 2009, No. 7, pp. 14)*
Pub: Rogers Media
Ed: Joe Castaldo. **Description:** A COMPAS Inc. survey of 134 Canadian chief executive officers found that 44 percent agree that CEO compensation should be subject to a non-binding vote. The respondents were also divided on whether to allow shareholders to exercise retroactive clawbacks on executive compensation if firm performance turns out to be worse than projected.

35920 ■ *"Second Chance Counselor" in Business Courier (Vol. 27, July 2, 2010, No. 9, pp. 1)*
Pub: Business Courier
Ed: Lucy May. **Description:** Stephen Tucker, director of workforce development for the Urban League of Greater Cincinnati, is an example of how ex-offenders can be given chances for employment after service jail sentences. How the Urban Leagues' Solid Opportunities for Advancement job training program helped Tucker and other ex-offenders is discussed.

35921 ■ *Six SIGMA for Small Business*
Pub: Entrepreneur Press
Ed: Greg Brue. **Released:** October 2005. **Price:** $19.95 (US), $26.95 (Canadian). **Description:** Jack Welch's Six SIGMA approach to business covers accounting, finance, sales and marketing, buying a business, human resource development, and new product development.

35922 ■ *"Small Business Employment" in Small Business Economic Trends (April 2008, pp. 9)*
Pub: National Federation of Independent Business
Ed: William C. Dunkelberg, Holly Wade. **Description:** Four tables and a graph representing employment rates of small businesses in the U.S. are presented. The tables include figures on employment changes, number of qualified applicants, job openings, and hiring plans.

35923 ■ *"Small Business Employment" in Small Business Economic Trends (March 2008, pp. 9)*
Pub: National Federation of Independent Business
Ed: William C. Dunkelberg, Holly Wade. **Description:** Four tables and a graph that present employment rates of small businesses in the U.S. are provided. The tables include figures on employment changes, number of qualified applicants, job openings and hiring plans.

35924 ■ *"Small Business Employment" in Small Business Economic Trends (February 2008, pp. 9)*
Pub: National Federation of Independent Business
Ed: William C. Dunkelberg, Holly Wade. **Description:** Four tables and a graph that present employment rates of small businesses in the U.S. are provided. The tables include figures on employment changes, number of qualified applicants, job openings and hiring plans.

35925 ■ *"Small Business Employment" in Small Business Economic Trends (January 2008, pp. 9)*
Pub: National Federation of Independent Business
Description: Table from a survey of small businesses in the U.S. is given, representing actual employment changes from January 2002 to December 2007. A graph comparing planned employment and current job openings from January 1986 to December 2007 is also supplied. Tables showing job opening, hiring plans, and qualified applicants for job openings are also presented.

35926 ■ *"Small Business Employment" in Small Business Economic Trends (September 2010, pp. 9)*
Pub: National Federation of Independent Business
Ed: William C. Dunkelberg, Holly Wade. **Description:** A table from a survey of small businesses in the U.S. is given, representing actual employment changes from January 2005 to August 2010. A graph comparing planned employment and current job openings from January 1986 to August 2010 is also supplied. Tables showing job openings, hiring plans, and qualified applicants for job openings are also presented.

35927 ■ *"Small Business Employment" in Small Business Economic Trends (July 2010, pp. 9)*
Pub: National Federation of Independent Business
Description: A table from a survey of small businesses in the U.S. is given representing actual employment changes from January 2005 to June 2010. A graph comparing planned employment and current job openings from January 1986 to June 2010 is also supplied. Tables showing job openings, hiring plans, and qualified applicants for job openings are also presented.

35928 ■ *"Something Different in the Air? The Collapse of the Schwarzenegger Health Plan in Calfornia" in WorkingUSA (June 2008)*
Pub: Blackwell Publishers Ltd.
Ed: Daniel J.B. Mitchell. **Description:** In January 2007, California Governor Arnold Schwarzenegger proposed a state universal health care plan modeled after the Massachusetts individual mandate program. A year later, the plan was dead. Although some key interest groups eventually backed the plan, it was overwhelmed by a looming state budget crisis and a lack of gubernatorial focus. Although much acclaimed for his stance on greenhouse gases, stem cells, hydrogen highways, and other Big Ideas, diffused gubernatorial priorities and a failure to resolve California's chronic fiscal difficulties let the clock run out on universal health care.

35929 ■ *"Sometimes You Have to Ignore the Rule Book" in Canadian Business (Vol. 83, September 14, 2010, No. 15, pp. 13)*
Pub: Rogers Media Ltd.
Ed: Richard Branson. **Description:** The rule book has provided a clear framework for employees particularly when cash and accounting are at issue. However, sometimes rules were made to be broken and the rule book should not become an excuse for poor customer service or hinder great service. How Virgin Atlantic practices this type of corporate culture is discussed.

35930 ■ *"Start Filling Your Talent Gap - Now" in Business Strategy Review (Vol. 21, Spring 2010, No. 1, pp. 56)*
Pub: Wiley-Blackwell
Ed: Alan Bird, Lori Flees, Paul Di Paola. **Description:** As businesses steer their way out of turbulence, they have a unique opportunity to identify their leadership supply and demand and then to close the talent gap in their organization. Authors explain how to take immediate steps to build the right team now and lay the groundwork for a long-term approach for nurturing talent within the organization.

35931 ■ *"Startup on Cusp of Trend" in Austin Business JournalInc. (Vol. 29, January 8, 2010, No. 44, pp. 1)*
Pub: American City Business Journals
Ed: Christopher Calnan. **Description:** Austin-based Socialware Inc. introduced a new business called social middleware, which is a software that is layered between the company network and social networking Website used by workers. The software was designed to give employers a measure of control over content while allowing workers to continue using online social networks.

35932 ■ *"Streaming Hot Currie" in Canadian Business (Vol. 80, April 23, 2007, No. 9, pp. 10)*
Pub: Rogers Media
Ed: Paul Brent. **Description:** The views of Richard Currie, former president of Loblow Cos. Ltd., on the human resource policy of the company are presented.

35933 ■ *"Stung by Recession, Hemmer Regroups with New Strategy" in Business Courier (Vol. 27, June 4, 2010, No. 5, pp. 1)*
Pub: Business Courier
Ed: Lucy May. **Description:** Paul Hemmer Companies reduced its work force and outsourced operations such as marketing and architecture, in order for the commercial and construction firm to survive the recession. Hammer's total core revenue in 2009 dropped to less than $30 million forcing the closure of its Chicago office.

35934 ■ *"Surprise Package" in Business Courier (Vol. 27, June 25, 2010, No. 8, pp. 1)*
Pub: Business Courier
Ed: Dan Monk, Jon Newberry, Steve Watkins. **Description:** More than 60 percent of the chief executive officers (CEOs) in Greater Cincinnati's 35 public companies took a salary cut in 2009, but stock grants resulted in large paper gains for the CEOs. The salary cuts show efforts of boards of directors to observe austerity. Statistics on increased values of stock awards for CEOs, median pay for CEOs, and median shareholder return are also presented.

35935 ■ *"Survey Profile" in Small Business Economic Trends (September 2010, pp. 19)*
Pub: National Federation of Independent Business
Ed: William C. Dunkelberg, Holly Wade. **Description:** Two graphs and a table presenting the profile of small businesses that participated in the National Federation of Independent Business (NFIB) survey are provided. The actual number of firms, their industry types, and the number of full and part-time employees are presented.

35936 ■ *"Swimming Against the Tide" in Human Resource Management (Vol. 49, July-August 2010, No. 4, pp. 575-598)*
Pub: John Wiley
Ed: David G. Collings, Anthony McDonnell, Patrick Gunnigle, Jonathan Lavelle. **Description:** A study was conducted to provide a benchmark of outward flows of international assignees from the Irish subsidiaries of foreign-owned multinational enterprises (MNEs) to corporate headquarters and other worldwide operations. Findings indicate that almost half of all MNEs use some form of outward staffing flows.

35937 ■ *"Swinging For the Fences" in Academy of Management Journal (October 2007, pp. 1055)*
Pub: Academy of Management
Contact: Ming-Jer Chen, President
Ed: William Gerard Sanders, Donald C. Hambrick. **Description:** Study examines managerial risk-taking vis-a-vis stock options of the company; results reveal that stock options instigate CEOs to take unwise risks that could bring huge losses to the company.

35938 ■ *Tactical Entrepreneur: The Entrepreneur's Game Plan*
Pub: Sortis Publishing
Ed: Brian J. Hazelgren. **Released:** September 2005. **Price:** $14.95. **Description:** A smart, realistic business plan is essential for any successful entrepreneur. Besides offering products or services, small business owners must possess skills in accounting, planning, human resources management, marketing, and information technology.

35939 ■ *The Talent Masters: Why Smart Leaders Put People Before Numbers*
Pub: Crown Business Books
Ed: Bill Conaty, Ram Charan. **Released:** November 9, 2010. **Price:** $27.50. **Description:** This book helps leaders recognize talent in their employees, and to put that talent to work to help achieve business success.

35940 ■ *"Talent Shows" in Canadian Business (Vol. 81, December 24, 2007, No. 1, pp. 14)*
Pub: Rogers Media
Ed: Megan Harman. **Description:** Canadian companies are increasingly turning to marketing to promote themselves as employers, as concerns on employee recruitment increase with the nearing retirement age of the baby boomers. Details on skills shortage, the potential advantage for the immigrant workforce, and employee retention are discussed.

35941 ■ *"Teleworkers Confess Biggest At-Home Distractions" in Employee Benefit News (Vol. 25, November 1, 2011, No. 14, pp. 7)*
Pub: SourceMedia Inc.
Ed: Kelley M. Butler. **Description:** Telecommuting can actually make some workers more efficient and productive versus working inside the office.

35942 ■ *"The Ten Commandments of Legal Risk Management" in Business Horizons (Vol. 51, January-February 2008, No. 1, pp. 13)*
Pub: Elsevier Advanced Technology Publications
Ed: Michael B. Metzger. **Description:** Effective legal risk management is tightly linked with ethical and good management, and managers' behaviors have to be professional and based on ethically defensible principles of action. Basic human tendencies cannot be used in justifying questionable decisions in court. Guidelines for legal risk management are presented.

35943 ■ *"This Just In" in Crain's Detroit Business (Vol. 25, June 22, 2009, No. 25, pp. 1)*
Pub: Crain Communications Inc. - Detroit
Description: Yamasaki Associates, an architectural firm has been sued for non payment of wages to four employees. Yamasaki spokesperson stated the economy has affected the company and it is focusing marketing efforts on areas encouraged by recovery funding.

35944 ■ *"'Tone-Deaf' Suitor or True Harasser: How to Tell" in HR Specialist (Vol. 8, September 2010, No. 9, pp. 1)*
Pub: Capitol Information Group Inc.
Description: Details are critical to any harassment charge in the workplace. Courts now list factors employers should consider when trying to determine whether an employee has been sexually harassed at work.

35945 ■ *"Tri-State Lags Peer Cities in Jobs, Human Capital, Study Says" in Business Courier (Vol. 27, September 24, 2010, No. 21, pp. 1)*
Pub: Business Courier
Ed: Dan Monk, Lucy May. **Description:** Greater Cincinnati, Ohio has ranked tenth overall in the 'Agenda 360/Vision 2015 Regional Indicators Project' report. The study ranked 12-city-peer groups in categories such as job indicators standing and people indicators standing. The ranking of jobs and human capital study is topped by Minneapolis, followed by Denver, Raleigh, and Austin.

35946 ■ *"Trust But Verify: FMLA Software Isn't Foolproof, So Apply a Human Touch" in HR Specialist (Vol. 8, September 2010, No. 9, pp. 3)*
Pub: Capitol Information Group Inc.
Description: Employers are using software to track FMLA information, however, it is important for employers to review reasons for eligibility requirements, particularly when an employee is reportedly overstepping the bounds within leave regulations due to software error.

35947 ■ *"Types of Health Plans" in HRMagazine (Vol. 53, August 2008, No. 8, pp. 72)*
Pub: Society for Human Resource Management
Contact: Henry G. Jackson, President
E-mail: hjackson@shrm.org
Description: Definitions are given for various types of health care coverage available. Fee-for-service

(FFS), health maintenance organization (HMO), preferred provider organization (PPO), point of service (POS) and consumer-directed health plan (CDHP) are outlined.

35948 ■ *"Uncashed Checks: Retirement Plans in a Quandry" in Employee Benefit News (Vol. 25, December 1, 2011, No. 15, pp. 18)*
Pub: SourceMedia Inc.
Ed: Terry Dunne. **Description:** Complex issues arise when employees don't cash their 401(k) balance checks. The US Department of Labor permits plans to cash out accounts of former employees with less than $1,000 to reduce the cost and time required to manage them.

35949 ■ *"Uncertain Labor Pool Troubles Businesses" in Business First-Columbus (October 19, 2007, pp. A1)*
Pub: American City Business Journals, Inc.
Ed: Kevin Kemper. **Description:** Businesses in Columbus, Ohio are having difficulty finding skilled workers and expect this trend to continue through 2010-2020. They are trying to recruit young workers to address the shortage in skilled labor.

35950 ■ *"Unfair Distraction of Employees" in Business Owner (Vol. 35, March-April 2011, No. 2, pp. 8)*
Pub: DL Perkins Company
Description: Fair Credit Collection Practices Act makes it illegal for collectors to contact a debtor at his or her place of employment if the collector is made aware that it is against personnel policy of the employer for the worker to take such a call.

35951 ■ *"Union Ethics Training: Building the Legitimacy and Effectiveness of Organized Labor" in WorkingUSA (Vol. 11, September 2008, No. 3)*
Pub: Blackwell Publishers Ltd.
Ed: Maggie Cohen. **Description:** Arguments are presented for the implementation of serious ethics training at all levels of labor unions and their contribution to union effectiveness by enhancing union legitimacy-understood as an amalgam of legal, pragmatic, and moral legitimacy and by paving the way to stable recognition of the labor movement as an integral part of American society, necessary to economic prosperity and the realization of fundamental American moral and social values.

35952 ■ *"Union Questions Patrick Cudahy Layoffs" in Business Journal-Milwaukee (Vol. 28, December 3, 2010, No. 9, pp. A1)*
Pub: Milwaukee Business Journal
Ed: Rich Ravito. **Description:** United Food and Commercial Workers Local 1473 is investigating Patrick Cudahy Inc.'s termination of 340 jobs. The union said the company has violated the law for failing to issue proper notice of a mass layoff.

35953 ■ *"Use a Benefits Checklist to Ease New-Hire Onboarding" in HR Specialist (Vol. 8, September 2010, No. 9, pp. 4)*
Pub: Capitol Information Group Inc.
Description: Checklist to help employees enroll in a company's benefit offerings is provided, courtesy of Wayne State University in Detroit, Michigan.

35954 ■ *"The Value of Human Resource Management for Organizational Performance" in Business Horizons (November-December 2007, pp. 503)*
Pub: Elsevier Technology Publications
Ed: Yongmei Liu, James G. Combs, David J. Ketchen, R. Duane Ireland. **Description:** Benefits of human resource management for business are studied using date from 19,000 organizations. Human resource management adds value to business, especially when it is integrated with business strategy and when human resource systems are emphasized.

35955 ■ *"Walker Seeks More Business Participation" in Business Journal-Milwaukee (Vol. 28, December 10, 2010, No. 10, pp. A1)*
Pub: Milwaukee Business Journal
Ed: Rich Kirchen. **Description:** Wisconsin governor Scott Walker is seeking the aid of Milwaukee business leaders to participate in resolving the challenges posed by the economic crisis. Walker is aiming to create 250,000 jobs. He is also planning to call a special session of the legislature to enact strategies to jumpstart the economy.

35956 ■ *"Wanted: African American Professional for Hire" in Black Enterprise (Vol. 37, November 2006, No. 4, pp. 93)*
Pub: Earl G. Graves Publishing Co. Inc.
Ed: Joe Watson. **Description:** Excerpt from the book, Without Excuses: Unleash the Power of Diversity to Build Your Business, speaks to the lack of diversity in the corporate arena and why executives, recruiters, and HR professionals claim they are unable to find qualified individuals of different races when hiring.

35957 ■ *"The War for Good Jobs; The World Will IBe Led with Economic Force" in Gallup Management Journal (September 7, 2011)*
Pub: Gallup
Ed: Jim Clifton. **Description:** Gallup's chairman believes the next world war will be for good jobs and the winner will triumph with economic force, driven primarily by job creation and quality GDP growth.

35958 ■ *"Waugh Chapel to Expand" in Baltimore Business Journal (Vol. 28, August 27, 2010, No. 16, pp. 1)*
Pub: Baltimore Business Journal
Ed: Daniel J. Sernovitz. **Description:** Developer Greenberg Gibbons Corporation has broken ground on a $275 million, 1.2 million-square-foot addition to its Village at the Waugh Chapel mixed-use complex. Aside from creating 2,600 permanent jobs, the addition, named Village South, is expected to lure Target and Wegmans Food Markets to Crofton, Maryland. Funding for this project is discussed.

35959 ■ *"We Have a Budget, Too" in Entrepreneur (Vol. 37, October 2009, No. 10, pp. 89)*
Pub: Entrepreneur Media, Inc.
Ed: Craig Matsuda. **Description:** One human resources executive at a financial services company claims that health care issues are as costly and irritating for companies as they are for the employees. Health care vendors and insurers try as much as possible to maximize profits, while companies exert much effort to maximize benefits for their workers.

35960 ■ *"Wealth and Jobs: the Broken Link" in Harvard Business Review (Vol. 88, November 2010, No. 11, pp. 44)*
Pub: Harvard Business School Publishing
Ed: Nitin Nohria. **Description:** Rebuilding the link between business and job creation to shore up the middle class is advocated. A blend of government policies and business strategies that foster entrepreneurship and innovation are essential.

35961 ■ *"Web Site Design, Content Can Boost Diversity" in HRMagazine (Vol. 53, August 2008, No. 8, pp. 20)*
Pub: Society for Human Resource Management
Contact: Henry G. Jackson, President
E-mail: hjackson@shrm.org
Description: Design and content of an employer's Website influences prospective young job candidates, especially young black job seekers, a new academic study has found. The findings appear in Black and White and Read All Over: Race Differences in Reactions To Recruitment Web Sites, published in the summer 2008 issue of the Human Resource Management Journal.

35962 ■ *"Well Done!" in Canadian Business (Vol. 80, April 23, 2007, No. 9, pp. 47)*
Pub: Rogers Media
Ed: Joe Castaldo. **Description:** The human resource management methods applied by different companies like Deloitte & Touche LLP are presented.

35963 ■ *The Well-Timed Strategy: Managing Business Cycle for Competitive Advantage*
Pub: Wharton School Publishing
Ed: Peter Navarro. **Released:** January 23, 2006. **Price:** $34.99. **Description:** An overview of business cycles and risks is presented. Recession is a good time to find key personnel for a small business. Other issues addressed include investment, production, and marketing in order to maintain a competitive edge.

35964 ■ *"What 17th Century Pirates Can Teach Us About Job Design" in Harvard Business Review (Vol. 88, October 2010, No. 10, pp. 44)*
Pub: Harvard Business School Publishing
Ed: Hayagreeva Rao. **Description:** Ways in which pirates typify the importance of separating star tasks, or strategic work, from guardian tasks, or the operational work are outlined.

35965 ■ *"What Businesses Can Do: Growing the Supply of Highly Skilled Graduates" in Canadian Business (Vol. 81, October 27, 2008, No. 18)*
Pub: Rogers Media Ltd.
Description: Employers in Canada have expressed concerns over the findings of various studies that revealed current and projected labor shortages in the country. A low birthrate and an aging population is contributing to the problem. Ways businesses can increase the supply of highly skilled workers in Canada is presented.

35966 ■ *"What Employees Worldwide Have in Common" in Gallup Management Journal (September 22, 2011)*
Pub: Gallup
Ed: Steve Crabtree. **Description:** According to a Gallup study, workplace conditions are strongly tied to personal wellbeing, regardless of geographic region. The employee study covered 116 countries.

35967 ■ *"What to Pay Your Top Team" in Inc. (March 2008, pp. 108-112, 114)*
Pub: Gruner & Jahr USA Publishing
Ed: Jennifer Gill. **Description:** In-depth examination to help business owners decide if they paying their executives properly. A guide to executive salaries at private companies is presented. Statistical data included.

35968 ■ *"What Recovery?" in Canadian Business (Vol. 82, April 27, 2009, No. 7, pp. 18)*
Pub: Rogers Media
Ed: Rachel Pulfer. **Description:** U.S. markets have rallied on the end of March 2009 but experts and analysts believe that it could be short-lived. Market rallies were found to be common during recessions and are not indicative of economic recovery. Meanwhile, it is believed that employment will be a key factor that will determine the U.S. economic recovery.

35969 ■ *"What You Should Know About Signing Bonuses" in Black Enterprise (Vol. 38, October 2007, No. 3, pp. 70)*
Pub: Earl G. Graves Publishing Co. Inc.
Ed: Marcia Reed-Woodard. **Description:** High-level corporate executives are receiving sign-on bonuses. According to a study conducted by World@Work, nearly 70 percent of employers signing bonuses attract key employees.

35970 ■ *"What's Working Now: In Providing Jobs for North Carolinians" in Business North Carolina (Vol. 28, February 2008, No. 2, pp. 16)*
Pub: Business North Carolina
Ed: Edward Martin, Frank Maley. **Description:** Individuals previously employed in the furniture, tobacco, or textile manufacturing sectors have gone back to school to be trained in new sectors in the area such as life sciences, finances and other emerging sectors.

35971 ■ *"When R&D Spending Is Not Enough" in Human Resource Management (Vol. 49, July-August 2010, No. 4, pp. 767-792)*
Pub: John Wiley
Ed: Sheng Wang, Rebecca M. Guidice, Judith W. Tansky, Zhong-Ming Wang. **Description:** A study was conducted to examine the effect of contextual contingencies on innovation. Findings indicate that Chinese manufacturers with cultures emphasizing innovation

and teamwork more effectively utilize financial resources in the innovation process. Results also show that a culture emphasizing outcomes and stability leads to lower levels innovation irrespective of investments.

35972 ■ *"Why Did We Ever Go Into HR?" in Harvard Business Review (Vol. 86, July-August 2008, No. 8, pp. 39)*
Pub: Harvard Business School Press
Ed: Matthew D. Breitfelder; Daisy Wademan Dowling. **Description:** Examines the role of human resource directors and how their jobs foster new ideas and generate optimism.

35973 ■ *"Why HR Practices Are Not Evidence-Based" in Academy of Management Journal (Vol. 50, No. 5, October 2007, pp. 1033)*
Pub: Academy of Management
Contact: Ming-Jer Chen, President
Ed: Denise M. Rousseau. **Description:** A suggestion that an Evidence-Based Management Collaboration (EBMC) can be established to facilitate effective transfer of ideas between science and practice is presented.

35974 ■ *"Why Is It So Hard To Find Good People? The Problem Might Be You" in Inc. (Vol. 33, November 2011, No. 9, pp. 100)*
Pub: Inc. Magazine
Ed: April Joyner. **Description:** Entrepreneurs sometimes struggle to find good workers. A recent survey shows hiring as their top concern. Four common mistakes that can occur during the hiring process our outlined.

35975 ■ *"Why Men Still Get More Promotions Than Women" in Harvard Business Review (Vol. 88, September 2010, No. 9, pp. 80)*
Pub: Harvard Business School Publishing
Ed: Herminia Ibarra, Nancy M. Carter, Christine Silva. **Description:** Sponsorship, rather than mentoring, is identified as the main difference in why men still receive more promotions than women. Active executive sponsorship is key to fostering career advancement.

35976 ■ *"Will Workers Be Left To Build It Here?" in Boston Business Journal (Vol. 31, June 3, 2011, No. 19, pp. 1)*
Pub: Boston Business Journal
Ed: Kyle Alspach. **Description:** Lack of skilled workers has resulted in delayed expansion of local manufacturing operations in Massachusetts. Acme Packet Inc. expects to add only 10 jobs by the end of 2011.

35977 ■ *"Winburn's Big Idea" in Business Courier (Vol. 27, October 8, 2010, No. 23, pp. 1)*
Pub: Business Courier
Ed: Dan Monk, Lucy May. **Description:** Cincinnati Councilman Charlie Winburn proposed the creation of Cincinnati Competitive Edge Division and to remake a small-business division of the city in order to start a job-creation program. The new division will monitor compliance to the city's small business inclusion regulations, as well as to help small business owners grow.

35978 ■ *"Work Force: In the Mix" in Entrepreneur (Vol. 35, October 2007, No. 10, pp. 109)*
Pub: Entrepreneur Media Inc.
Ed: Mark Henricks. **Description:** A study of 708 companies' diversity programs shows that diversity training alone is not the most effective way of increasing diversity in management. It was found that one effective way of putting minorities and women in management teams is to give a team or a person the task of improving diversity in the company. The reason why accountability succeeds in diversifying the workforce is discussed.

35979 ■ *"Working For Pennies? Huge Pay Gap Between Top Executives and Black Employees" in Black Enterprise (Vol. 38, March 2008, No. 8)*
Pub: Earl G. Graves Publishing Co. Inc.
Ed: Cliff Hocker, Wendy Isom. **Description:** CEO pay is out of control because most board members approving high salaries and compensation packages are often executives at other firms. According to a study conducted by the Institute for Policy Studies, CEOs earn more than 1,085 times the average full-time black worker's median earnings.

35980 ■ *"The Workplace Generation Gaps" in Women In Business (Vol. 62, June 2010, No. 2, pp. 8)*
Pub: American Business Women's Association
Ed: Leigh Elmore. **Description:** Generation gaps among baby boomers, Generation X and Generation Y in the workplace are attributed to technological divides and differences in opinions. These factors could lead to workplace misunderstandings, employee turnover and communication difficulties. Details on managing such workplace gaps are discussed.

35981 ■ *The Worst-Case Scenario Business Survival Guide*
Pub: John Wiley & Sons, Inc.
Released: September 28, 2009. **Price:** $17.95. **Description:** Since 1999, the Worst-Case Scenario survival handbooks have provided readers with real answers for the most extreme situations. Now, in a time of economic crisis, the series returns with a new, real-world guide to avoiding the worst business cataclysms.

35982 ■ *"Your First 100 Days on Your New Job" in Women In Business (Vol. 63, Spring 2011, No. 1, pp. 28)*
Pub: American Business Women's Association
Ed: Diane Stafford. **Description:** The first 100 days on the job are crucial if the person's permanent hiring is conditional on surviving a probationary period. The new hire must do more than just master the job's technical details to maximize the chance of success. Details of some basic tips to fit into the corporate culture and get along with coworkers are also discussed.

35983 ■ *"Youth Employment in the Summer of 2010" in Montly Labor Review (Vol. 133, September 2010, No. 9, pp. 2)*
Pub: Bureau of Labor Statistics
Description: The number of youth 16 to 24 years old rose by 1.8 million from April to July 2010. Statistical data included.

TRADE PERIODICALS

35984 ■ *Employee Benefit Plan Review*
Pub: Aspen Publishers, Inc.
Contact: Robert Becker, President
URL(s): www.aspenpublishers.com/product.asp?catalog_name=Aspen&product_id=SS00136808. **Released:** Monthly **Price:** $315, Individuals.

35985 ■ *Employee Terminations Law Bulletin*
Pub: Quinlan Publishing Co.

35986 ■ *FERA--Focus*
Pub: FERA Inc.
Ed: John A. Seeley, Editor. **Released:** 3/year. **Price:** Free. **Description:** Discusses consulting work and research on evaluation of corporate training, human resource development programs, community-based social services, and educational programs.

35987 ■ *HRMagazine: On Human Resource Management*
Pub: Society for Human Resource Management
Contact: Henry G. Jackson, President
E-mail: hjackson@shrm.org
URL(s): www.shrm.org/Publications/hrmagazine/Pages/default.aspx. **Ed:** Nancy M. Davis. **Released:** Monthly **Price:** $70, Individuals; $90, Canada.

35988 ■ *Human Factors in Ergonomics and Manufacturing*
Pub: John Wiley & Sons Inc.
Contact: Stephen M. Smith, President
URL(s): onlinelibrary.wiley.com/journal/10.1002/(-ISSN)1520-6564. **Ed:** Waldemar Karwoski, Gavriel Salvendy. **Released:** Bimonthly **Price:** $1427, Institutions print & online; $1553, Institutions, other countries print & online; $1240, Institutions print only; $1240, Institutions, Canada and Mexico print only; $1366, Institutions, other countries print only.

35989 ■ *Human Resources Management: Ideas and Trends Newsletter*
Pub: CCH Inc.
Contact: Mike Sabbatis, President
Released: Biennial. **Price:** $339. **Description:** Covers general human resources management issues.

35990 ■ *Journal of Workplace Rights*
Pub: Baywood Publishing Company Inc.
Contact: Stuart Cohen, President
URL(s): baywood.com/journals/previewjournals.asp?id=jwr. **Ed:** Joel Rudin. **Released:** 4/yr. **Price:** $349, Institutions; $331, Institutions online.

35991 ■ *Supervisor's Guide to Employment Practices*
Pub: Clement Communications Inc.
Contact: Robi L. Garthwait, Managing Editor
Released: Biweekly. **Price:** $195, single issue. **Description:** Provides information to managers and supervisors regarding sensitive human resource issues.

35992 ■ *What's Working in Human Resources*
Pub: Progressive Business Publications
Contact: Ron McRae, Editor-in-Chief
Released: Semimonthly. **Price:** $299, individuals. **Description:** Reports on the latest trends in Human Resources, including the latest employment law rulings. Recurring features include interviews, news of research, a calendar of events, news of educational opportunities, and a column titlted Sharpen Your Judgment.

VIDEOCASSETTES/ AUDIOCASSETTES

35993 ■ *Conducting an Effective Job Interview*
Phoenix Learning Group
2349 Chaffee Dr.
Saint Louis, MO 63146-3306
Ph: (314)569-0211
Free: 800-221-1274
Fax: (314)569-2834
URL: http://www.phoenixlearninggroup.com
Released: 1988. **Price:** $450.00. **Description:** This video teaches you how to interview effectively. **Availability:** VHS; 8 mm; 3/4 U.

35994 ■ *Conflicts, Conflicts!*
University of Washington Educational Media Collection
Kane Hall, Rm. 35
Campus Box 353095
Seattle, WA 98195
Ph: (206)543-9907
Fax: (206)616-6501
URL: http://www.css.washington.edu/emc
Released: 1985. **Description:** This is a management training film demonstrating techniques for avoiding conflicts. **Availability:** VHS; 3/4 U.

35995 ■ *Creating Effective Workshops: The Design Doctor Is In*
ASTD
1640 King St.
Alexandria, VA 22314-2746
Ph: (703)683-8100
Free: 800-628-2783

Fax: (703)683-1523
Co. E-mail: customercare@astd.org
URL: http://www.astd.org
Contact: Tony Bingham, President
E-mail: tbingham@astd.org

Released: 1989. **Description:** The successes and failures of others can help you plan your next training sessions. From start to finish, expert trainer and Human Resource Development manager Susan Warshauer shows how to control fears associated with learning new skills, how to ensure new skills make it back to the workplace, and how to move smoothly through a variety of topics. **Availability:** VHS; 3/4 U.

35996 ■ *Fair & Effective Discipline*
Business & Legal Resources, Inc. (BLR)
141 Mill Rock Rd., E
Old Saybrook, CT 06475
Ph: (860)510-0100
Free: 800-454-0404
Fax: (860)510-7220
Co. E-mail: service@blr.com
URL: http://www.blr.com
Contact: Robert Brady, President

Released: 1986. **Description:** A training film for managers in handling employee problems-absenteeism, poor performance, etc. **Availability:** VHS; 3/4 U.

35997 ■ *Flexible Working Time: More Time to Live*
Encyclopedia Britannica
331 N. LaSalle St.
Chicago, IL 60654
Ph: (312)347-7159
Free: 800-323-1229
Fax: (312)294-2104
URL: http://www.britannica.com

Released: 1988. **Price:** $395.00. **Description:** A look at the Dutch postal service and a German department store, two places where the employees have flexible working hours. **Availability:** VHS; 3/4 U.

35998 ■ *Hiring and Firing*
Aspen Publishers, Inc.
7201 McKinney Cir.
Frederick, MD 21704
Ph: (301)698-7100
Free: 800-234-1660
Fax: (800)901-9075
Co. E-mail: customerservice@aspenpublisher.com
URL: http://www.aspenpublishers.com
Contact: Robert Becker, President

Released: 1985. **Description:** For business supervisors, a film on how to decide when to terminate and hire personnel. **Availability:** VHS; 3/4 U; Special order formats.

35999 ■ *How to Interview Clients Effectively*
American Law Institute
American Bar Association Committee on Continuing Education
4025 Chestnut St.
Philadelphia, PA 19104
Ph: (215)243-1600
Free: 800-CLENEWS
Fax: (215)243-1636
Co. E-mail: custserv@ali-aba.org
URL: http://www.ali.org

Released: 1993. **Price:** $95. **Description:** Studies the interviewing process, offering advice on opening the interview, probing for details, testing theories, and closing the interview. Includes study guide. **Availability:** VHS.

36000 ■ *The Power of Positive and Effective Communication*
Aspen Publishers, Inc.
7201 McKinney Cir.
Frederick, MD 21704
Ph: (301)698-7100
Free: 800-234-1660
Fax: (800)901-9075
Co. E-mail: customerservice@aspenpublisher.com
URL: http://www.aspenpublishers.com
Contact: Robert Becker, President

Released: 1987. **Price:** $495.00. **Description:** A program which teaches supervisors how to be sure to give clear instructions to their subordinates. **Availability:** VHS; 3/4 U; Special order formats.

36001 ■ *The Trouble with Words*
Film Library/National Safety Council California Chapter
4553 Glencoe Ave., Ste. 150
Marina Del Rey, CA 90292
Ph: (310)827-9781
Free: 800-421-9585
Fax: (310)827-9861
Co. E-mail: California@nsc.org
URL: http://www.nsc.org/nsc_near_you/FindYourLocalChapter/Pages/California.aspx

Released: 198?. **Description:** Provides some suggestions for creating better communication and higher productivity among employees. **Availability:** VHS; 3/4 U.

36002 ■ *Understanding EEOC, Part 1-3*
RMI Media
1365 N. Winchester St.
Olathe, KS 66061-5880
Ph: (913)768-1696
Free: 800-745-5480
Fax: (800)755-6910
Co. E-mail: actmedia@act.org
URL: http://www.actmedia.com

Released: 1987. **Price:** $80.00. **Description:** In this three-part series, equal employment opportunity laws are explained and followed by suggestions for companies seeking to develop practices, policies, and procedures in this area. **Availability:** VHS; 3/4 U.

36003 ■ *Who Wants to Play God?*
Film Library/National Safety Council California Chapter
4553 Glencoe Ave., Ste. 150
Marina Del Rey, CA 90292
Ph: (310)827-9781
Free: 800-421-9585
Fax: (310)827-9861
Co. E-mail: California@nsc.org
URL: http://www.nsc.org/nsc_near_you/FindYourLocalChapter/Pages/California.aspx

Released: 198?. **Description:** This is an examination of why many performance reviews fail to increase employee effectiveness. **Availability:** VHS; 3/4 U.

CONSULTANTS

36004 ■ Advanced Benefits & Human Resources
9350-F Snowden River Pkwy., Ste. 222
Columbia, MD 21045
Ph: (410)290-9037
Fax: (410)740-2568
Co. E-mail: hrb@abhr.com
Contact: Linda Polacek, President

Scope: Provides human resource consulting to high technology businesses. Offers services in the areas of human resources, benefits, and training. Creates, maintains, or updates current human resource functions. **Founded:** 1996.

36005 ■ Arnold Consulting Group Inc. (ACG)
7839 Main St., Ste. 683
Fishers, NY 14453-9800
Ph: (585)507-4259
Co. E-mail: acg4u@aol.com
URL: http://www.arnoldconsultinggroup.com
Contact: Brian C. Arnold, President

Scope: It is a management consulting firm dedicated to partnering with companies to create, design, and implement leadership and organizational solutions aligned with their business strategies. Given the changing organizational dynamics, new technology, government scrutiny, and global competition, the challenges facing business leaders are daunting. ACG understands leaders of effective organizations need continuously updated skills, keener insight and increased creativity to compete effectively in the global marketplace. **Founded:** 1992. **Seminars:** Negotiation Strategies; Leadership Development; Competency Design; High Performance Teams Development; Management of Conflict; Employee Empowerment; Team Building; Job Search.

36006 ■ Barker & Associates
1974 Wexford Cir.
Wheaton, IL 60187-6166
Ph: (630)260-9927
Fax: (630)260-9928
Contact: Patricia D. Barker, President

Scope: Consulting, training, and coaching firm specializing in providing human resource assessment, selection and development services focused primarily on people skills. Serves small, mid, and large-size organizations in both private industry and not-for-profit associations. **Founded:** 1982. **Seminars:** Strategic Marketing; Consultative Selling and Customer Service; From Hiring to Appraising - Developing Your Employees; Increased Productivity Through Managed Stress; Producing People Results Through Team building; Conflict Management; Communications, Managing Transition and Change; Creative Problem Solving.

36007 ■ BeamPines Inc.
232 Madison Ave., 10th Fl.
New York, NY 10016
Ph: (212)476-4100
Fax: (212)986-7798
Co. E-mail: info@beamgroup.com
URL: http://www.beampines.com
Contact: Jonathan B. Santamaria, President
E-mail: jsantamaria@beampines.com

Scope: A human resource consultancy with expertise in employment and employee development. Serves businesses in the United States Provides comprehensive talent management services to help organizations attract, retain and continuously develop the best people. **Founded:** 1981. **Publications:** "Ontarios Green Energy and Green Economy Act," 2009; "Citizens Guide to Pollution Prevention,"; "Le Guide du citoyen pour la prevention de la pollution," Mar, 2005; "Ontarios Industrial Emissions Reduction Plan," 2005; "Ensuring Green Power Supplies in Ontario Responding to Perverse Subsidies and Other Market Inequities," Oct, 2003; "A Municipal Guide to Wind Power Development in Ontario," Apr, 2003; "Green Power Opportunities for Ontario," 2002; "Third Annual Green Power Trade Show," 2002; "Sixth Annual Report on Ontarios Environment" 2002; "Ontarios Environment and the Common Sense Revolution: A Fifth Year Report," 2000; "The Quality of Air," Mar, 1999. **Seminars:** Executive Development Counseling®.

36008 ■ Benefit Partners Inc.
2140 Regent St., Ste. 1
Sudbury, ON, Canada P3E 5S8
Ph: (705)524-1559
Free: 800-461-6326
Fax: (705)524-5553
Co. E-mail: info@benefitpartners.com
URL: http://www.benefitpartners.com
Contact: Bruce Frick, Managing Director
E-mail: bruce.frick@benefitpartners.com

Scope: Services include employee benefits, pension, executive compensation, human resources and financial management. Industries served: Corporate and personal insurance planning and private wealth management. **Telecommunication Services:** denise.marshall@benefitpartners.com.

36009 ■ Benefits Dynamics Inc. (BDI)
89 N Haddon Ave., Ste. D
Haddonfield, NJ 08033-2473
Ph: (856)616-1400
Fax: (856)616-1401
Co. E-mail: benefit@benefitdynamics.com
Contact: JoAnn Massanova, President
E-mail: joannm@benefitdynamics.com

Scope: A full service employee benefit, record keeping consultant and outsourcing organization. Provides pension consulting, administration and actuarial services, cafeteria and flexible benefit plans, human resource systems outsourcing, interactive voice-response systems, electronic employee benefit enrollment and transportation plans. **Founded:** 1979.

36010 ■ Bijan International Inc.
11776 Jollyville Rd., Ste. 250
Austin, TX 78759-3900
Ph: (512)923-6932
Fax: (512)219-0383
Co. E-mail: info@bijanintl.com
URL: http://www.bijanintl.com
Contact: Bijan Afkami, President
E-mail: bijan@bijanintl.com
Scope: A leadership development consulting and training firm. Offers leadership training workshops, seminars and programs, corporate training, and executive coaching. Consultants interact with senior management to conduct assessment processes; facilitate motivation within groups to accelerate the learning process; implement customized and exciting training programs; design long range initiatives and incentive programs; and create improvements in individual and team performance. **Founded:** 1993. **Publications:** "Coaching firm Rallies Businesses," Jan, 2003; "A Journey of 1000 Miles". **Seminars:** Emotional Intelligence; Discovering Diversity; Empowered Women; High-Velocity Change; The Positive Power of Feed back; Team work; Customer Service; Sexual Harassment; Leaders In Sales; Body Therapy; Personal Effectiveness; Teamwork Skills; Leadership Abilities.

36011 ■ Blankinship & Associates Inc.
322 C St.
Davis, CA 95616
Ph: (530)757-0941
Fax: (530)757-0940
Co. E-mail: blankinship@envtox.com
URL: http://www.h2osci.com
Contact: Michael Blankinship, President
E-mail: mike@envtox.com
Scope: Specializes in assisting water resource and conveyance, golf and production, protection and enhancement of natural resources. **Founded:** 2000. **Publications:** "Air Blast Sprayer Calibration and Chlorpyrifos Irrigation Study," Oct, 2007; "How Green is your golf course," Prosper Magazine, 2007. **Seminars:** CDFG Wildlands IPM Seminar, Oct, 2009.

36012 ■ Brown Associates Inc.
65 Birch Hill Rd.
Belmont, MA 02478-1730
Ph: (617)489-2500
Fax: (617)484-6611
Co. E-mail: axlex3@aol.com
Contact: Floyd Brown, Chief Executive Officer
Scope: Provider of outsourced human resources consulting and training services to business, educational, and municipal clients. It is also engaged in staffing, manpower planning, compensation, and performance evaluation solutions. **Founded:** 1967. **Publications:** "The Legal Evolution of Sexual Harassment"; "Top 10 Human Resource Mistakes and How to Avoid Them"; "Do You Need a Consultant?". **Seminars:** Preventing Sexual Harassment in the Workplace; Employment Law: All You Need to Know From A to Z; Selecting and Preparing Employees for International Assignments; Outplacement-How to Humanely Handle a Reduction in Force.

36013 ■ Carelli & Associates
17 Reid Pl.
Delmar, NY 12054
Ph: (518)439-0233
Fax: (518)439-3006
Co. E-mail: truthaboutsupervision@yahoo.com
URL: http://www.carelli.com
Contact: Anne O Brien Carelli, Owner
E-mail: anneobriencarelli@yahoo.com
Scope: Provider of writing and editing services to industry and businesses, health care and educational institutions, and government agencies. Also provides program management in creating and disseminating publications and in implementing related training. Assists organizations in designing and implementing team-based management. Offers supervisory skills training and problem-solving work sessions for managers. Individual Consultation are provided for managers, CEOs, potential supervisors including 360 degree assessments. **Founded:** 1988. **Publications:** "The Truth About Supervision: Coaching, Teamwork, Interviewing, Appraisals, 360 degree Assessments, and Recognition". **Seminars:** Supervisory Skills Training Series; Problem-Solving Work Sessions for Managers; Effective Leadership.

36014 ■ The Center for Organizational Excellence Inc.
15204 Omega Dr., Ste. 300
Rockville, MD 20850
Ph: (301)948-1922
Free: 877-674-3923
Fax: (301)948-2158
Co. E-mail: results@center4oe.com
URL: http://www.center4oe.com
Contact: Stephen Goodrich, President
E-mail: sgoodrich@center4oe.com
Scope: An organizational effectiveness consulting firm specializing in helping organizations achieve results through people, process, and performance. Service areas include organizational performance systems, leadership systems, customer systems, and learning systems. **Founded:** 1984.

36015 ■ CFI Group USA L.L.C.—Claes Fornell International
625 Avis Dr.
Ann Arbor, MI 48108-9649
Ph: (734)930-9090
Free: 800-930-0933
Fax: (734)930-0911
Co. E-mail: askcfi@cfigroup.com
URL: http://www.cfigroup.com
Contact: Sheri Teodoru, Chief Executive Officer
E-mail: steodoru@mail.cfigroup.com
Scope: Management consulting firm that helps its clients worldwide to maximize shareholder value by optimizing customer and employee satisfaction. Clients span a variety of industries, including manufacturing, telecommunications, retail and government. **Founded:** 1988. **Publications:** "Customer Satisfaction and Stock Prices: High Returns, Low Risk," American Marketing Association, Jan, 2006; "Customer Satisfaction Index Climbs," The Wall Street Journal, Feb, 2004; "What's Next? Customer Service is Key to Post-Boom Success," The Bottom Line, Mar, 2003; "Boost Stock Performance, Nation's Economy," Quality Progress, Feb, 2003.

36016 ■ Cole Financial Service Inc.
3170 E, Lafayette Blvd.
Detroit, MI 48207-4378
Ph: (313)962-7055
Free: 877-972-7055
Fax: (313)962-7815
Co. E-mail: jason.a.cole@colefinancial1.net
URL: http://www.colefinancial1.net
Contact: Patricia Allen Cole, President
E-mail: Patricia.a.cole@colefinancial1.net
Scope: A full service human capital development firm providing services in recruiting, coaching, retaining, developing and retiring. Works with front line staff, managers and executive level decision makers that set strategy. Industries served: Engineering, construction, government and other business entities. **Founded:** 1983. **Seminars:** How to Run Your Own Business; 25Ways to stay in Business 25Years; How to Tap Your Potential and Discover Your GENIUS; The Job Ladder Steps to SUCCESS; Making and Keeping a Budget; Records Retention and Disposal; Take Control of Your Life; Time and Priority Management; TQM - Total Quality Management; Leadership 101; Leadership 201; Diversity Agent or Opponent A Personal Development Workshop; Coaching in a Diverse Workplace.

36017 ■ Consulting & Conciliation Service (CCS)
2219 H St., Ste. 1
Sacramento, CA 95816
Ph: (916)396-0480
Free: 888-898-9780
Fax: (916)441-2828
Co. E-mail: service@azurewings.net
Contact: Jane A. McCluskey, Principal
E-mail: service@azurewings.net
Scope: Offers consulting and conciliation services. Provides pre-mediation counseling, training and research on preparing for a peaceful society, mediation and facilitation, and preparation for shifts in structure, policy and personnel. Offers sliding scale business rates and free individual consultation. **Publications:** "Native America and Tracking Shifts in US Policy"; "Biogenesis: A Discussion of Basic Social Needs and the Significance of Hope". **Seminars:** Positive Approaches to Violence Prevention: Peace building in Schools and Communities.

36018 ■ Controlled Resources
1021 E 1st Ave., Apt. 822
Broomfield, CO 80020
Ph: (708)798-2978
Fax: (727)532-3955
Co. E-mail: lwightman@mindspring.com
Scope: Firm offers business and management consultancy services.

36019 ■ CoStaff Services L.L.C.
29100 NW Highway, Ste. 240
Southfield, MI 48034
Ph: (248)671-1400
Free: 866-426-7823
Fax: (248)692-0816
Co. E-mail: info@costaffservices.com
URL: http://www.costaffservices.com
Contact: Michael Bulgarelli, President
E-mail: mbulfarelli@costaffservices.com
Scope: A PEO (Professional Employer Organization) and HRO (Human Resource Outsource) firm that provides outsourced human resource services to small and medium size businesses. Hires the employees of the client company to the PEO payroll and then leases these same employees back to the client company. Seeks to reduce the time spent on payroll administration, benefits administration, risk and liability management, and governmental compliance. **Founded:** 2000. **Telecommunication Services:** sales@costaffservices.com.

36020 ■ The Devine Group Inc.
7755 Montgomery Rd., Ste. 180
Cincinnati, OH 45236
Ph: (513)792-7500
Free: 866-792-7500
Fax: (513)793-8535
Co. E-mail: sales@devinegroup.com
URL: http://www.devinegroup.com
Contact: David C. Devine, Chief Executive Officer
E-mail: david@devinegroup.com
Scope: A human resource consulting company devoted to providing reliable and responsive information focusing on performance issues and answers. Dedicated to analyzing and enhancing job performance. Custom design and implement programs and workshops that will result in demonstrable behavior change on the job. Assist clients enhance their productivity via behavior analysis. **Founded:** 1970. **Publications:** "Leveraging Assessments for Enterprise Improvement," Oct, 2006; "Evaluation of Assessment Tools: The Five Criteria," Oct, 2006; "People Improvement Using Behavior Assessment," Aug, 2005; "Measuring Personality: The Good, the Bad and the Ugly". **Special Services:** The Devine Inventory®.

36021 ■ DiversityWorks
800 Heinz Ave., Ste. 14
Berkeley, CA 94710
Ph: (510)540-7008
Fax: (510)540-6976
Co. E-mail: mail@diversityworks.org
URL: http://www.diversityworks.org
Contact: Moses J. Ceaser, President
Scope: Offers diversity consulting to businesses, schools, youth groups, and a variety of organizations. Designs programs to suit to individual clients' needs. Areas of expertise include: Community-building (and team-building), consciousness-raising, skill building (leadership development, popular education, facilitation) and taking action. **Founded:** 1998. **Publications:** "Diversity Words"; "A Woman's Beauty"; "Youth Violence"; "Modern Day Minstrels"; "Love Makes the World Go Round"; "Glorification of White Supremacy through Movies".

36022 ■ DJT Consulting Group L.L.C.
PO Box 8595
San Jose, CA 95155

Ph: (408)280-1153
Co. E-mail: info@djtconsulting.com
URL: http://www.djtconsulting.com
Contact: Sherry V. Bruning, Principal
Scope: Offers a range of grant management services including contract monitoring, research, grant writing, evaluation and project management. Specializes in grant proposal writing, project management and program development. Assists enhance financial resources, programs and services. **Founded:** 2000. **Seminars:** Finding and Winning Government Grants. **Telecommunication Services:** sherry@djtconsulting.com.

36023 ■ Dorn & Associates Inc.
8506 Bass Lake Rd.
Minneapolis, MN 55428-5304
Ph: (763)533-7689
Fax: (763)533-1143
Contact: John L. Dorn, President
Scope: Services include accounting, marketing, employment partnership, new doctor agreements, personnel issues and human resources assessment, practice management, practice merger acquisition sale and liquidation, practice surveys and valuation, staff development and training. **Founded:** 2000.

36024 ■ Eastern Point Consulting Group Inc.
36 Glen Ave.
Newton, MA 02464
Ph: (617)965-4141
Fax: (617)965-4172
Co. E-mail: info@eastpt.com
URL: http://www.eastpt.com
Contact: Katherine A. Herzog, President
E-mail: kherzog@eastpt.com
Scope: Specializes in bringing practical solutions to complex challenges. Provides consulting and training in managing diversity; comprehensive sexual-harassment policies and programs; organizational development; benchmarks 360 skills assessment; executive coaching; strategic human resource planning; team building; leadership development for women; mentoring programs; and gender issues in the workplace. **Founded:** 1995. **Seminars:** Leadership Development for Women.

36025 ■ Effective Compensation Inc. (ECI)
30792 Southview Dr., Ste. 101
Evergreen, CO 80439
Ph: (303)854-1000
Free: 877-746-4324
Fax: (303)854-1030
Co. E-mail: eci@effectivecompensation.com
URL: http://www.effectivecompensation.com
Contact: Terry L. Isselhardt, Chief Executive Officer
E-mail: tisselhardt@effectivecompensation.com
Scope: Independent compensation consulting firm specializing in working with clients on a collaborative basis to improve their organization's efficiency through competitive, focused total compensation processes. Helps organizations determine how to competitively pay their employees. Provides quality, culture sensitive, compensation consulting assistance to all types of employers. Specializes in surveys like drilling industry compensation surveys, environmental industry compensation surveys, liquid pipeline round table compensation surveys; and oil and gas E and P industry compensation surveys. **Founded:** 1991. **Publications:** "Alternative Job Evaluation Approaches"; "Broad Banding: A Management Overview"; "Job Evaluation: Understanding the Issues"; "Industry Compensation Surveys"; "Skill Based Pay"; "Four Levels of Team Membership"; "Factors in Designing an Incentive Plan"; "Key Stock Allocation Issues"; "Stock Plans Primer". **Seminars:** Alternative Job Evaluation Approaches; Broad Banding: A Management Overview; Skill Based Pay; Job Evaluation: Understanding the Issues; Designing Compensation Programs that Motivate Employees; Master the Compensation Maze; Base Salary Administration Manual.

36026 ■ Effective Resources Inc. (ERI)
118 N Peters Rd., Ste. 171
Knoxville, TN 37923
Ph: (865)622-7138
Free: 800-288-6044
Fax: (800)409-2812
Co. E-mail: customerservice@effectiveresources.com
URL: http://www.effectiveresources.com
Contact: Barry L. Brown, Principal
E-mail: barry@effectiveresources.com
Scope: Human resource consulting firm helping clients in all aspects of planning and implementation, to assure the program meets their objectives and budget considerations. Can work with clients on an interim basis or as consultants on short term assignment. Products and services include salary and benefits surveys, employee satisfaction surveys, performance management, compensation administration, compliance assistance and personality profile testing. Specializes in compensation and incentive plans, performance appraisals, team building and personnel policies and procedures, affirmative action plan preparation. **Founded:** 1988. **Special Services:** DiSC® Personality Profile.

36027 ■ Executive Directions International Inc.
1536 NW 97th St.
Clive, IA 50325-6402
Ph: (515)457-9300
Co. E-mail: culp@workwise.net
URL: http://www.workwise.net
Contact: Dr. Mildred L. Culp, President
E-mail: culp@workwise.net
Scope: Developer of customized contents. It also addresses the needs of print and online editors in newspaper groups and their independent counterparts. **Founded:** 1981. **Publications:** "Be Work Wise: Re-tooling your work for the 21st century," Executive Directions International, 1994; "After belief," 1976. **Seminars:** Getting the Right Media Attention. **Special Services:** WorkWise; WorkWise Interactive™; WorkWise Advice™.

36028 ■ The Executive Group
1645 Parkhill Dr., Ste. 4
Billings, MT 59102
Ph: (406)252-7770
Free: 800-755-5161
Fax: (406)255-7478
Co. E-mail: exgzinfo@wtp.net
Contact: Bill Crago, President
E-mail: bill@exegrp.net
Scope: The company provides executive recruitment. Services include geographic searches, interviewing assistance, screening/referencing, travel arrangements, final offer negotiation, company and candidate Follow-Up. **Founded:** 1985.

36029 ■ Fox Lawson & Associates L.L.C.
1335 County Road D, Cir. E
Saint Paul, MN 55109-5260
Ph: (651)635-0976
Free: 800-383-0976
Fax: (651)635-0980
Co. E-mail: jfox@foxlawson.com
URL: http://www.foxlawson.com
Contact: James C. Fox, Partner
E-mail: jfox@foxlawson.com
Scope: A compensation and human resources consulting firm, provides services to businesses of all sizes including finance, manufacturing, high tech, software development, food, retail, wholesale trade, communications, transportation, service, not-for-profit and education. **Founded:** 1995. **Seminars:** Compensation Strategies - Not Having a Plan Could Break the Bank.

36030 ■ Stephen J. Gill Consulting
3051 Geddes Ave.
Ann Arbor, MI 48104
Ph: (734)665-7728
Fax: (734)665-7864
Co. E-mail: sjgill@stephenjgill.com
URL: http://www.stephenjgill.com
Contact: Dr. Stephen J. Gill, Owner
E-mail: sjgill@stephenjgill.com
Scope: A consultant for human performance improvement, provides needs analysis, program evaluation and impact assessment services. Assists companies in planning effective learning programs. Industries served: Automobile manufacturing, furniture manufacturing, software development, healthcare, utilities, colleges, universities, nonprofits and philanthropic foundations. **Founded:** 1993. **Publications:** "Communication in High Performance Organizations: Principles and Best Practices," Kindle, 2011; "Developing a Learning Culture in Nonprofit Organizations," Sage, 2010; "The 5As Framework," RealTime Performance, 2009; "Myth and Reality of E-Learning," Nov, 2003; "The Manager's Pocket Guide to Organizational Learning," HRD Press, Sep, 2000; "The Learning Alliance: Systems Thinking in Human Resource Development," Jossey-Bass, Aug, 1994; "Developing a Learning Culture in Non profit Organizations". **Seminars:** Organizational Learning; High Impact Training; Training Evaluation; Survey Design; Outcomes and Impact Assessment.

36031 ■ Global Business Consultants (GBC)
200 Lake Hills Rd.
Pinehurst, NC 28374-0776
Ph: (910)295-5991
Fax: (910)295-5991
Co. E-mail: gbc@pinehurst.net
Contact: Nan S. Leaptrott, President
E-mail: nan@yourculturecoach.com
Scope: Firm specializes in human resources management; project management; software development; and international trade. Offers litigation support. **Founded:** 1987. **Publications:** "Culture to Culture: Mission Trip Do's and Don'ts," Jul, 2005; "Rules of the Game: Global Business Protocol". **Seminars:** Cross-Cultural Training.

36032 ■ Goren & Associates Inc.
32000 Northwestern Hwy., Ste. 128
Farmington Hills, MI 48334-1565
Ph: (248)851-0824
Free: 800-851-0824
Fax: (248)851-8751
Co. E-mail: info@gorentrain.com
URL: http://www.gorentrain.com
Contact: Bill Berris, President
Scope: Provider of customized, organizational, and human resources development and training programs. Industries served: primarily manufacturing. **Founded:** 1981. **Publications:** "The healthy child cookbook: 146 healthy snacks, meals, and desserts," The wellness institute; "Why is my child so overweight". **Seminars:** Instituting Change; Adjusting to Stress and Change; Initiating and Managing Change For Leaders; Deterring Sexual Harassment; Deterring Workplace Violence; Diversity in the Workplace; Collaborative Negotiation; Customizing our Service, Servicing our Customers; Dealing with Difficult Customers; Stress Management; Conducting Successful Meetings; How to Deliver a Dynamic Presentation; Creating a Motivating Team; Coaching Skills for Leaders.

36033 ■ Pamela K. Henry & Associates
13329 Kingman Dr., Ste. B
Austin, TX 78729-4908
Ph: (512)335-1237
Fax: (512)335-1237
Co. E-mail: info@pamelakhenry.com
URL: http://www.pamelakhenry.com
Contact: Pamela K. Henry, Principal
Scope: Specializes in career transition skills consulting. Services in resume development and interview coaching. Also offers consulting in workplace diversity and sexual harassment prevention. **Publications:** "Diversity and the Bottom Line: Prospering in the Global Economy". **Seminars:** Competency-based Interviewing; Executive Interviewing; Selection Best Practices; Career Transitioning; Effectively Recruiting a Diverse Workforce; Creating Cultural Competence & Inclusion on Teams; Preventing Sexual Harassment.

36034 ■ Edward M. Hepner & Associates
4667 Macarthur Blvd., Ste. 405
Newport Beach, CA 92660
Ph: (714)250-0818
Fax: (714)553-8437
Contact: Edward M. Hepner, President
Scope: An immigration consultant and labor certification specialist. Assists in obtaining visa for work, immigration and business development within the United States and Canada.

36035 ■ C. W. Hines and Associates Inc.—C&W Associates Inc.
344 Churchill Cir., Sanctuary Bay
White Stone, VA 22578
Ph: (804)435-8844
Fax: (804)435-8855
Co. E-mail: turtlecwh@aol.com
URL: http://www.cwhinesassociates.org
Contact: Dr. Carolyn C.W. Hines, President
Scope: Management consultants with expertise in the following categories: advertising and public relations; health and human resources; management sciences; organizational development; computer sciences; financial management; behavioral sciences; environmental design; technology transfer; project management; facility management; program evaluation; and business therapy. Also included are complementary areas such as sampling procedures; job training; managerial effectiveness; corporate seminars; gender harassment; training for trainers and leadership and management skills development. **Founded:** 1979. **Publications:** "Money Muscle, 120 Exercises To Build Spiritual And Financial Strength," 2004; "Inside Track: Executives Coaching Executives"; "Money Muscle: 122 Exercises to Build Financial Strength"; "Nuts and Bolts of Work Force Diversity"; "Legal Issues, published in the Controllers Business Advisor"; "Identifying Racism: Specific Examples"; "BOSS Spelled Backwards is double SSOB! Or is it?"; "A No-Nonsense Guide to Being Stressed". **Seminars:** Career Development; Coaching and Counseling for Work Success; Communicating More Effectively in a Diverse Work Environment; Communications 600: Advanced Skills for Relationship Building; Customer Service: Building a Caring Culture.

36036 ■ HR Advice.com
PO Box 313
Mountain Lakes, NJ 07046
Ph: (973)331-9809
Free: 877-854-0469
Co. E-mail: hrpro@hradvice.com
URL: http://www.hradvice.com
Contact: Susan Gordon, Manager
Scope: Specializes in the areas of employee relations, business planning and strategy, recruiting, human resources policy, compensation and benefits, training, development and performance systems. Provides services including human resources and business planning, resolves challenging workplace issues, defines organizational culture and creates or modifies human resources policies and programs. Also provides guidance to salary, benefits and incentive in the workplace.

36037 ■ HR Answers Inc.
7659 SW Mohawk St.
Tualatin, OR 97062
Ph: (503)885-9815
Free: 877-287-4476
Fax: (503)885-8614
Co. E-mail: info@hranswers.com
URL: http://www.hranswers.com
Contact: Judith Clark, President
E-mail: jclark@hranswers.com
Scope: Provider of all types of human resource management consulting services, either on a retained or project basis. Services include compensation program design or support, benefit plan assessment, policy and procedure development, AAP and EEO/OFCCP compliance, human resource function audits, supervisory, managerial and employee training, employee relation issues/assistance, employment law compliance, employee handbooks, risk management, performance management design and information and organizational development and transition strategies. **Founded:** 1985. **Seminars:** Creating Your Safety Committee, Oct, 2006; Top Ten Best Practicesforl-9's, Oct, 2006; Sailing the Rough C's - Communication, Counseling & Conflict Resolution; Breaking the Secret Codes of Communication; Can We Talk; Coach or Discipline - What Action is Appropriate; Catch Your Employees Doing Something Right; The Future of Human Resources.

36038 ■ The HR Dept.
22 W Pennsylvania Ave.
Bel Air, MD 21014
Ph: (410)893-0901
Fax: (410)893-0901
Co. E-mail: ghr@hrdept.com
URL: http://www.hrdept.com
Contact: Gerald H. Reynolds, Jr., President
E-mail: ghr@hrdept.com
Scope: Provides human resources management support to small business employers on a part-time basis. Standard support services include the review of the human resources functions, compliance issues, performance appraisal programs, handbooks and policy manuals, annual human resources calendar, quarterly human resources reports, formal compensation structure, benefit plans analysis, manager training, human resources training, day to day employee issues, and human resources advice, and augmenting functioning HR departments. **Founded:** 1998.

36039 ■ Human Networks Inc.
210 Crest St.
Ann Arbor, MI 48103-4316
Ph: (734)665-1220
Fax: (734)665-1220
Co. E-mail: mbmurphy-aa@excite.com
Contact: Michael Murphy, Principal Owner
E-mail: mbmurphy-aa@excite.com
Scope: Provider of the following consulting services: training in the areas of stress management, team building, supervisory skills, and leadership skills; and consultation regarding organizational climate assessment and improvement. Industries served include automotive, banking, small business, school, universities, and human service agencies. **Founded:** 1983. **Publications:** "Grassroot Development: Establishing Successful Microenterprises". **Seminars:** Mind Over Matter; How Things Work at Work; The Internal Consultant: Special Skills; The External Consultant: Skills.

36040 ■ Human Resource Specialties Inc.
3 Monroe Pky., Ste. 900
Lake Oswego, OR 97035
Ph: (503)697-3329
Free: 800-354-3512
Fax: (503)636-1594
Co. E-mail: info@hrspecialties.com
URL: http://www.hrspecialties.com
Contact: Sandy Henderson, President
E-mail: sandyh@hrspecialties.com
Scope: Provider of human resources assistance to organizations. Offers preparation of affirmative action plans, support documents, and adverse impact studies of personnel activities. Also offers customized consultations in small business services, diversity and discrimination, and investigations, complaints and grievances. Provides investigations, including allegations of unfair treatment, equal employment opportunity (EEO) and racial or sexual harassment. Offers customized web-based training (webinars) on a variety of HR, EEO and AAP-related topics. **Founded:** 1984.

36041 ■ I.H.R. Solutions
3333 E Bayaud Ave., Ste. 219
Denver, CO 80209
Ph: (303)588-4243
Fax: (303)978-0473
Co. E-mail: dhollands@ihrsolutions.com
Contact: Deborah Hollands, Owner
E-mail: dhollands@ihrsolutions.com
Scope: Provides joint-venture and start-up human resource consulting services as well as advice on organization development for international human capital. Industries served: high-tech and telecommunications. **Founded:** 1997.

36042 ■ In Plain English—R.H. Wohl & Associates Inc.
14501 Antigone Dr.
Gaithersburg, MD 20885-3300
Ph: (301)340-2821
Free: 800-274-9645
Fax: (301)279-0115
Co. E-mail: rwohl@inplainenglish.com
URL: http://www.inplainenglish.com
Contact: Ronald H. Wohl, President
E-mail: rwohl@inplainenglish.com
Scope: Management consultants helping government and businesses research, design, write and produce user oriented management information for human resources, employee benefits, business process, corporate and marketing needs. Services include: GSA mob is schedule for consulting to the government; employee benefit communications, plain English business writing workshops for print and electronic media; communicating strategy and tactics; marketing research, business planning and communications; readability testing; usability testing and monitoring strategy. **Founded:** 1977. **Publications:** "The Benefits Communication"; "The Employee Benefits Communication ToolKit," Commerce Clearinghouse; "Benefits Communication," Business and Legal Reports. **Seminars:** Plain English Writing Training; Summary Plan Description Compliance workshops; Re-Humanizing the Corporation, Human Resources and Employee Benefits Communication Workshop; 21 Writing Tips for the 21st Century; Make the Write Impression; Writing to Inform and Instruct; The Dreaded Nuts and Bolts; Writing to Persuade; Writing Policy and Procedure Manuals In Plain English; Writing for Accountants and Auditors In Plain English. **Special Services:** In Plain English®.

36043 ■ Incentive Solutions Inc. (ISI)
2337 Perimeter Park Dr., Ste. 220
Atlanta, GA 30341
Ph: (770)457-4597
Free: 800-463-5836
Fax: (770)457-4994
Co. E-mail: info@incentivesolutions.com
URL: http://www.incentivesolutions.com
Contact: Mark Herbert, President
E-mail: mherbert@incentivesolutions.com
Scope: Corporate incentive and motivation programs from group travel to incentive debit cards and merchandise gift certificates. Specializes in business meeting planning, audio/visual services, and Internet development to support business communications. **Founded:** 1994. **Special Services:** RewardTrax®.

36044 ■ KEYGroup
1800 St. Claire Plz., 1121 Boyce Rd.
Pittsburgh, PA 15241-3918
Ph: (724)942-7900
Free: 800-456-5790
Fax: (724)942-4648
URL: http://www.keygrp.com
Contact: Jan Ferri-Reed, President
Scope: A management consulting and training firm providing expertise in the areas of creativity, influencing skills, leadership, teambuilding, assessment and organizational effectiveness. Industries served: Fortune 500executives, healthcare administrators, manufacturing managers, government/military supervisors, insurance, financial and service industry managers, educational administrators, small business owners and community leaders. **Founded:** 1980. **Publications:** "Keeping the Millennials"; "Leading a Multi-Generational Workforce"; "Keys That Open Doors to Success - Key Words for Leaders"; "The Power of Partnering"; "The Keys to Conquering Change: 100 Tales of Success"; "The Keys to Putting Change in Your Pocket"; "The Keys to Mastering Leadership"; "Training Games for Managing Change"; "Private Sector: We Get You! Make Work Cultures Fit the Needs and Aspirations of Young Adults, and They Will Stay Here," Sep, 2005. **Seminars:** Performance Management, Enhancing Creativity Leading Others; Coaching for Improved Performance; Team-Building; Supervisory Development; Train-the-Trainer; Stress Management; Presentation Skills; Think-on-Your-Feet; Communicating Your BEST; leadership training team building. **Special Services:** KEYGroup®.

36045 ■ William E. Kuhn & Associates
234 Cook St.
Denver, CO 80206-5305
Ph: (303)322-8233

Fax: (303)331-9032
Co. E-mail: billkuhn1@cs.com
Contact: William E. Kuhn, Owner
E-mail: billkuhn1@cs.com
Scope: Firm specializes in strategic planning; profit enhancement; small business management; mergers and acquisitions; joint ventures; divestitures; human resources management; performance appraisals; team building; sales management; appraisals and valuations. **Founded:** 1980. **Publications:** "Creating a High-Performance Dealership," Office SOLUTIONS & Office DEALER, Jul-Aug, 2006.

36046 ■ LRP Publications
lrp.com Technology Contacts
747 Dresher Rd., Ste. 500
Horsham, PA 19044
Ph: (215)784-0860
Free: 800-341-7874
Fax: (215)784-9639
Co. E-mail: techsup@lrp.com
URL: http://www.lrp.com
Contact: Kenneth Kahn, President
E-mail: kKahn@lrp.com
URL(s): www.dartnellcorp.com. **Description:** Description: Publishes legal loose-leaf and information in the areas of workers 'compensation, federal government employee relations, labor arbitration, bankruptcy and education law and state and local employment law. Offers online employment litigation tracking service and arbitration searches. Accepts unsolicited manuscripts. Reaches market through direct mail and telephone sales. **Scope:** Multi-faceted publisher of business-to-business newsletters, magazines, loose-leaf publications, videos, software and on-line services covering various professional markets, such as human resources, education, employment law, federal-sector employment, bankruptcy, health, disability, elder care, workers' compensation and personal injury verdicts and settlements. Offers training and professional development in national conferences and trade shows. **Founded:** 1977. **Holdings:** 5000 books; 1000 bound periodical volumes. **Publications:** *Instant Computer Arbitration Search*; *Risk and Insurance*; *Human Resource Executive*; *CTD News*; *Counterpoint* (Quarterly); *Disability Compliance Bulletin* (Biweekly); *Workers' Compensation Monitor*; *Workplace Substance Abuse Advisor*; *Risk & Insurance Magazine*; *Today's School Psychologist*; *Risk & Insurance* (Monthly); *Team Leader*; *Human Resource Executive's Market Resource* (Annual); *AIDS Policy and Law*; *The AIDS Directory*; *Pennsylvania Workers' Compensation Law Reporter* (Semimonthly); *Missouri Workers' Compensation Law Reporter* (Monthly); *Federal Equal Opportunity Reporter* (Semimonthly); *New York Workers' Compensation Law Reporter* (Semimonthly); *Michigan Workers' Compensation Law Reporter* (Semimonthly); *Current Award Trends in Personal Injury* (Annual); *Early Childhood Law and Policy Reporter* (Monthly); *Federal Human Resources Week: News, Strategies and Best Practices for the HR Professional*; *AIDS Policy and Law: The Biweekly Newsletter on Legislation, Regulation, and Litigation Concerning AIDS*. **Telecommunication Services:** custserve@lrp.com; custserv@lrp.com.

36047 ■ Lubin Schwartz & Goldman Inc.
2369 Franklin Rd.
Bloomfield Hills, MI 48302
Ph: (248)332-3100
Fax: (248)332-6396
Co. E-mail: info@lsgip.com
Contact: Jay Schreibman, President
Scope: Firm specializes in property and casualty insurance, employee health and welfare programs, and financial services. Offers strategic consulting services. **Founded:** 1967.

36048 ■ JG Manley and Associates
1403 Sneed Rd. W
Franklin, TN 37069-6932
Ph: (615)309-6999
Fax: (615)309-8874
Co. E-mail: manleyjg@aol.com
Contact: John G. Manley, President
E-mail: manleyjg@aol.com
Scope: Consulting firm whose services include labor relations and law, collective bargaining, employment law, benefits and compensation, and training for businesses. Specializes in labor relations, employment law, organizational planning, administration, health-care and employee benefit plans, compensation, training, safety, and human resources.

36049 ■ McCreight & Company Inc.
36 Grove St.
New Canaan, CT 06840
Ph: (203)801-5000
Fax: (866)646-8339
Co. E-mail: roc@implementstrategy.com
URL: http://www.implementstrategy.com
Contact: John A. McCreight, President
E-mail: jmc@implementstrategy.com
Scope: Assist the global clients with strategy implementation involving large scale change, including mergers, divestitures, alliances and new business launches. **Founded:** 1983. **Publications:** "The Board's Role in Strengthening M and A Success," Boardroom Briefing, 2008; "Creating the Future," Ask Magazine, 2007; "Strategy Implementation Insights," Mccreight and Company Inc, Oct, 2007; "Sustaining Growth," Deloitte and Ct Technology Council, Jul, 2006; "A Four Phase Approach to Succession Planning," Southern Connecticut Newspapers Inc, 2005. **Seminars:** Successful Mergers and Acquisitions-An Implementation Guide; Global 100One-Face-to-the-Customer; Implementation of Strategic Change.

36050 ■ Harvey A. Meier Co. (HAM)
410 W Nevada St.
Ashland, OR 97520-1043
Ph: (509)458-3210
Fax: (541)488-7905
Co. E-mail: harvey@harveymeier.com
URL: http://www.harveymeier.com
Contact: Dr. Harvey A. Meier, President
E-mail: harvey@harveymeier.com
Scope: Provider of service to chief executive officers and board of directors. Specializes in interim management, strategic planning, financial planning and organization governance. **Publications:** "The D'Artagnan Way".

36051 ■ Michigan CFO Associates Inc.
12900 Hall Rd., Ste. 455
Sterling Heights, MI 48313
Ph: (586)580-3285
Fax: (586)580-3287
Co. E-mail: info@michigancfoservices.com
URL: http://www.michiganCFOservices.com
Contact: Erica Johnson, Analyst
Scope: Firm that provides part-time Chief Financial Officer expertise on a long-term basis. **Publications:** "Is the Flight Attendant Flying the Plane? Mismatching Skills Causes Many Businesses to Crash"; "Are You Worth $15/per hour? Getting Maximum Value Out of YOUR Time"; "CFO Insider Tools: Flexible Budgets". **Seminars:** 10 Keys to a Healthy Business.

36052 ■ Dawn Miller and Associates
1486 Bonniebrook Heights Rd.
Gibsons, BC, Canada V0N 1V5
Ph: (604)886-8278
Fax: (604)886-5313
Contact: Dawn Miller, Chief Executive Officer
E-mail: dawn_miller@dccnet.com
Scope: Provides human resources development, planning, consulting and training for small businesses. **Founded:** 1987. **Publications:** "10 Keys to Thriving in Changing Times".

36053 ■ R.E. Moulton Inc.
50 Doaks Ln.
Marblehead, MA 01945
Ph: (781)631-1325
Fax: (781)631-2165
Co. E-mail: mike_lee@remoultoninc.com
URL: http://www.oneamerica.com/wps/wcm/connect/REMoulton
Contact: Willard A. Knarr, Jr., President
Scope: Offers underwriting services, marketing solutions, claims administration and adjudication; policy and commission administration; and risk management solutions to clients. Supplementary service s include risk management and employee assistance. Clients include individuals, business men, employers and finance professionals. **Founded:** 1976.

36054 ■ The Murdock Group Holding Corp.
4084 South 300 West
Salt Lake City, UT 84107
Ph: (801)268-3232
Free: 888-888-0892
Fax: (801)268-3289
Contact: K. C. Holmes, President
Scope: Specializes in providing full service career services and seminars for individuals and companies, including out-placements, 'The Hiring Series' and career expos. **Founded:** 1997. **Publications:** "The Job Seekers Bible". **Seminars:** Networking; Interviewing, Negotiating; Marketing Yourself, Effective Hiring Fundamentals On-site Training Topics.

36055 ■ New England Human Resource Group
36 Cedar Pond Dr.
Warwick, RI 02886
Ph: (401)826-2137
Contact: Ronald G. Snyder, President
Scope: Firm specializes in compensation systems, benefits, legal compliance, personnel policies, resources, employee relations law, safety and risk management, training and development, continuous improvement, career management, organizational change, strategic planning, human resource audits, ISO 9000 and QS 9000, professional development, financial planning, staffing, and executive development. **Founded:** 1985.

36056 ■ Nightingale Associates
7445 Setting Sun Way
Columbia, MD 21046
Ph: (410)381-4280
Fax: (410)381-4280
Co. E-mail: fredericknightingale@nightingaleassociates.net
URL: http://www.nightingaleassociates.net
Contact: Frederick C. Nightingale, Managing Director
E-mail: fredericknightingale@nightingaleAssociates.net
Scope: Management training and consulting firm offering the following skills: productivity and accomplishment; leadership skills for the experienced manager; management skills for the new manager; leadership and teambuilding; supervisory development; creative problem solving; real strategic planning; providing superior customer service; international purchasing and supply chain management; negotiation skills development and fundamentals of purchasing. **Founded:** 1984. **Seminars:** Productivity and Accomplishment Management Skills for the New Manager; Leadership and Team building; Advanced Management; Business Process Re engineering; Strategic Thinking; Creative Problem Solving; Customer Service; International Purchasing and Materials Management; Fundamentals of Purchasing; Negotiation Skills Development; Providing superior customer service; Leadership skills for the experienced manager.

36057 ■ Organizational Synergies
10497 Town & Country Way, Ste. 950
Houston, TX 77024-1117
Ph: (713)461-2203
Fax: (713)461-5024
Contact: Darlene Underwood, President
Scope: Offers services in organizational effectiveness, outplacement and outsourcing. Specific services include employee development, business effectiveness analysis, business plans, climate analysis, corporate culture, departmental effectiveness analysis, management assessment, organizational effectiveness, organizational planning/design, strategic planning/direction, succession planning, work process analysis, visioning, measuring employee and management perceptions, management planning for shared vision and purpose, strategic planning/business unit planning, structure and work flow process analysis, management assessment and support services, skill and competency assessment, staff selection, alternative work arrangements, culture analysis compensation, and employee benefit plan analysis.

36058 ■ Palmetto Business Group Inc. (PBG)
1531 Blanding St., Ste. 2
Columbia, SC 29201

Ph: (803)252-4411
Fax: (803)252-3080
Co. E-mail: tchaffin_pbg@bellsouth.net
URL: http://www.palmettobusinessgroup.com
Contact: Wendel T. Chaffin, President
E-mail: tchaffin@palmettobusinessgroup.com
Scope: Provides human resources consulting services; specializes in the areas: Accident prevention, affirmative action plans, drug free workplace, EEOC compliance, employee training, interviewing, leadership, search, management recruiting, outplacement, performance appraisals, safety and health administration, strategic planning, teambuilding, and wage and benefit administration. **Telecommunication Services:** tchaffin@palmettobusinessgroup.com.

36059 ■ Papa and Associates Inc.
200 Consumers Rd., Ste. 305
Toronto, ON, Canada M2J 4R4
Ph: (416)512-7272
Fax: (416)512-2016
Co. E-mail: ppapa@papa-associates.com
URL: http://www.papa-associates.com
Contact: Peter Papakostantinu, President
E-mail: ppapa@papa-associates.com
Scope: Provider of broad based management consulting services in the areas of quality assurance, environmental, health and safety and integrated management systems. **Founded:** 1989.

36060 ■ PATH Associates
19 Coldwater Ct., Ruxton Crossing
Towson, MD 21204
Ph: (410)821-0538
Fax: (410)821-0538
Co. E-mail: pathassoc@aol.com
URL: http://www.pathassociatesonline.com
Contact: Robert Younglove, President
E-mail: robert_younglove@pathassociatesonline.com
Scope: Provider of keynote talks and workshops to associations, corporations, high growth industries, hospitals, and government agencies. Emphasis is on effective programs to prevent stress and develop mental potential to increase effectiveness on the job and in life management. Also active in the areas of management training, health education, human energy and power, and youth leadership development. Offers individual consultation and coaching sessions on motivation, career goals and stress management. **Founded:** 1974. **Publications:** "Speaking of Success," Volume 5, Insight Publishing, 2007; "Self-Confidence on the Job Survey," 2007; "Prioritize Your Values"; "Don't Let Kids Push Your Hot Button"; "When will you get a Round Tuit?"; "Sponsor Success, A Workbook for Turning Good Intentions Into Positive Results". **Seminars:** Staying Healthy in Times of Change; Dealing with People in Difficult Situations; Coaching for Performance Improvement and Influence Management; Sharpen Your Skills at Positively Influencing Children and Teens.

36061 ■ Norman Peterson & Associates (NPA)—OUR System
526 Washington St., Ste. 1
Ashland, OR 97520
Ph: (541)488-0162
Free: 800-497-1368
Fax: (541)488-5408
Co. E-mail: info@returntowork.com
URL: http://www.returntowork.com
Contact: Norman A. Peterson, President
E-mail: shollingsworth@returntowork.com
Scope: A workers' compensation consulting firm that assists organizations in addressing workers compensation and ADA issues. Primary service is implementation of a copyrighted transitional work program, which documents productive temporary assignments for injured employees. Industries served: Governmental units, hospitals, school districts, manufacturers, food and beverage distribution, construction, printing and others. **Founded:** 1985. **Publications:** "Planning Pays Off in Back to Work Programs," Ohio Association of School Business Officials Chronicle; "Diving into a pool Return-to-Work program," Public Risk Magazine. **Special Services:** OUR®; BridgIt.

36062 ■ Pitts - Aldrich Associates (PAA)
1501 Oxford Rd.
Grosse Pointe Woods, MI 48236-1848
Ph: (313)881-3433
Co. E-mail: christina@pittsaldrichassociates.com
URL: http://www.pittsaldrichassociates.com
Contact: Christina Pitts, President
E-mail: christina@pittsaldrichassociates.com
Scope: Firm offers consulting, facilitations, coaching, and training in strategic planning, change and transitions, culture and diversity, performance goals, project management, leader development, team effectiveness, retention/succession, coaching, board governance, fund development and corporate citizenship. **Founded:** 1990. **Publications:** "At the Podium/In the Press: Optimize 5"; "Leadership Basics"; "Managing Change"; "A Gift of the Four-Legs: Presence, Trust, Vulnerability and...; "Leadership Has Gone to the Horses'; "Brown Paper Bag"; "The Phoenix Challenge: Rising to Fulfillment"; "Navigating the Badlands- Leadership in the New Century," 2009; "Color Me Purple- Embracing Differences to Optimize Performance"; "The End of Work & Rise of the Nonprofit Sector"; "Building Mentoring Inside Your Organization". **Seminars:** Journey to Authencity; Optimize5-From the World of Horses - Practical Wisdom for Success; The Phoenix Challenge: Rising to Fulfillment; Optimizing Relationship, Partnership & Teamwork; Change: Your Ally For Success.

36063 ■ The Plotkin Group
5650 El Camino Real, Ste. 223
Carlsbad, CA 92008-7146
Ph: (760)603-8791
Free: 800-877-5685
Fax: (760)603-8570
Co. E-mail: info@plotkingroup.com
URL: http://www.plotkingroup.com
Contact: James Plotkin, President
E-mail: jim@plotkingroup.com
Scope: Employee testing and training organization offering pre-employment honesty, altitude, aptitude and skills tests; and past employment, 360degree assessments, behavior, style and communication tests by phone, paper and pencil, computers, the web, employee attitude surveys, customer service, sales, and management training. **Founded:** 1968. **Publications:** "Building a Winning Team"; "Achieving Above and Beyond Service"; "American Businesses Face Mountain of Problems"; "Appreciating the Richness of Cultural Diversity"; "Attitude is Everything"; "Club members spems are Driving Us All Crazy"; "Credibility and Trust"; "Crime Prevention: The Integrity Business"; "Employee Theft: Hidden Enemy"; "Empowering Employees Without Losing Control"; "How to Build Customer Loyalty"; "Hr Issues of the Millennium"; "Just the Facts (Honesty Testing)"; "Nation's Jobless Must Be Retrained, Put to Work"; "Phone Answering Systems: A Blessing Or a Curse?"; "Strive to Convert Poor Service Into Good Service"; "Tests are Best for Picking Best Worker for the Job"; "The Pre-Interview Hiring Process"; "Time Management"; "What Do Members Want"; "Who to Promote"; "You Can't Turn a Frog Into a Prince"; "Club members speak out about their dining room"; "Companies should stress attitudes over skills (SUN)"; "Companies will always need honest and dependable workers (SUN)"; "Dealing with the angry member"; "Employee selection: A key to member retention"; "Good customer service is the best route to profits (SUN)"; "Hiring, the key to profitability (SUN)"; "Honesty tests are legitimate tool for finding good employees (SUN)"; "How not to handle a crisis"; "How not to open a theater"; "How to determine an applicant's attitude"; "How to identify and develop leadership traits in employees"; "How to introduce pre-employment testing into an organization"; "Integrity among youth is on decline (SUN)"; "Issues of concern for owners"; "Issues of concern for golf companies"; "Ownership and empowerment"; "Road to success paved with customer satisfaction (SUN)"; "Screen applicants to weed out thieves (SUN)"; "When the going gets tough". **Seminars:** Building a Winning Team; Above and Beyond Customer Service Training; Taking the Guess Work Out of Hiring and Promoting.

36064 ■ Shannon Staffing Inc.
636 Chestnut St.
Coshocton, OH 43812
Ph: (740)622-2600
Fax: (740)622-9638
Co. E-mail: coshocton@shannonstaffing.com
Contact: Edward A. Seitz, President
E-mail: eseitz@shannonstaffing.com
Scope: Serving broad range of industries and public sector organizations and foundations. Specializing in human resources recruiting and outplacement counseling on international scale for businesses of all sizes. Offers expertise in human resources policies and procedures, supervisor development, manager leadership style development, interview training, etc. Provides consulting to small business in human resources, advertising, marketing, sales, public relations and community relations. **Founded:** 1985. **Publications:** "Powells Rules for Picking People". **Seminars:** Time Management workshop.

36065 ■ Siebrand-Wilton Associates Inc.
PO Box 369
Marlboro, NJ 07746-0369
Ph: (732)917-0239
Fax: (732)972-0214
Co. E-mail: clientsvcs@s-wa.com
URL: http://www.s-wa.com
Contact: John S. Sturges, President
E-mail: bencomp@s-wa.com
Scope: Assesses, plans and implements human resources aspects of mergers and acquisitions. Offers human resources consulting in compensation and benefit plan design, mergers and acquisitions (HR aspects), business ethics assessment and development, editing, writing and association management services, and contract professionals and interim executives. **Founded:** 1986. **Publications:** "Should Government or Business Try to Save Medicare," HR News; "Executive Temping," HR Horizons; "When is an Employee Truly an Employee," HR Magazine; "Examining Your Insurance Carrier," HR Magazine.

36066 ■ Ted Smith Associates (TSA)
PO Box 4217
Austin, TX 78765-4217
Ph: (512)627-0951
Fax: (512)453-4551
Contact: Dr. Edward Smith, Principal
Scope: Business and technical communication training consultant. Consulting services include curriculum development and editing, technical writing and editing, business writing and editing, and voice over talent. Also provides writing coaching, executive writing coaching, and presentation coaching. **Founded:** 1985. **Publications:** "Writing at Work: Professional Writing Skills for People on the Job". **Seminars:** Business Communication and Technical Communication Training.

36067 ■ Speech Coach for Executives
2186 Mountain Grove Ave., Ste. 171
Burlington, ON, Canada L7R 1L2
Ph: (905)335-1997
Free: 800-304-1861
Fax: (905)335-2176
Co. E-mail: coach@torok.com
URL: http://www.SpeechCoachforExecutives.com
Contact: George Torok, Principal
E-mail: george@torok.com
Scope: Consultant provides speaking and presentation skills coaching and training for executives, business professionals, and sales leaders. **Publications:** "Too much information: not enough time"; "Establish Your Believability"; "Smile: say cheese"; "Master the pause: it will make you a master"; "Presentation Power does not come from PowerPoint"; "Boardroom Presentations: Sweat Like a Horse"; "Presentation Skills Success"; "How to write your speech in five minutes"; "10 Power Tips for Presentations with Computer Projection". **Special Services:** Power Presentations™.

36068 ■ STAR Associates Inc.—Strategies, Tactics and Results Associates Inc.
The BeuMar Bldg., 12 W Montgomery St.
Baltimore, MD 21230
Ph: (410)727-1558
Free: 877-708-7827

Fax: (410)752-2579
Co. E-mail: barbara@starassociatesinc.com
URL: http://www.starassociatesinc.com
Contact: Barbara A. Robinson, President
E-mail: barbara@starassociates.com
Scope: Provide in-home aide health care to the senior population. Also provide transportation services for the department of aging. Provide training for all related health care industry needs. Provide residential group homes for youth between the ages of 13 and 18 years. Diversity and leadership training and development programs for women. **Founded:** 1985. **Publications:** "Eyes of the Beholder," Jun, 2000; "And Still, I Cry," 1993; "Yes You Can". **Seminars:** Supervisory or Management Practices; Team Playing and Group Dynamics; Time and Stress Management; Effective Communication: One Minute Management; Progressive Discipline; Project Management; Creative Decision Making and Problem Solving; Leadership Development; Absenteeism Reduction; Sales Training; Marketing Strategies; Making the leap from worker to supervisor; How to make things happen-boosting worker productivity, enthusiasm and commitment; Personal self-leadership as an essential ingredient; Who am I.

36069 ■ Stier Associates
4 Dunellen
Cromwell, CT 06416-2702
Ph: (860)635-1590
Fax: (860)635-1591
Co. E-mail: sstier7@comcast.net
Contact: Dr. Suzanne Stier, President
Scope: Offers personal development consulting. Services include: succession planning, executive coaching, strategic management, team building, and board development. Consulting services for public companies include: process consulting, team building, executive coaching, diversity management, strategic management and religious institutions. **Founded:** 1981.

36070 ■ Sylvia M. Sultenfuss
3317 Alden Pl. Dr.
Atlanta, GA 30319
Ph: (404)237-7130
Co. E-mail: sylvia@joyofadulthood.com
URL: http://www.joyofadulthood.com
Scope: Offers organizational consultation and programs such as specialized management training, excellence in productivity, stress management program, teambuilding, working together with different styles of communication, stress reduction program, leadership effectiveness, conflict resolution, corporate wellness programs, and employee assistance programs. The focus is on small businesses or divisions where personnel issues and development are the target need. Serves private industries as well as government agencies. **Founded:** 1980. **Publications:** "Take the time to make time for yourself," AJC Pulse, May, 2005; "The Joy of Adulthood: A Crash Course in Designing the Life You Want," Palladium Productions, 2004; "Wake Up and Live the Life You Love: Finding Your Life's Passion," Little Seed Publishing, 2004; "Going Home for the Holidays," Labrys Atlanta, Dec, 2004; "Strategies to help resolve conflicts that arise," AJC Pulse, Feb, 2003; "On forgiveness," AJC Pulse, May, 2002; "The healer's grief: Learning to let go, say goodbye," AJC Pulse, Dec, 2001; "A way toward healing of the nation's post-traumatic grief," AJC Pulse, Dec, 2001; "The Joy Of Adulthood: A Crash Course In Designing The Life You Want". **Seminars:** Leadership: What it Is and Isn't; Bringing Passion and Spirit to Leadership; Mentoring for Success; Gender Communication in the Workplace: The Hormones Do Make a Difference; Designing and Sustaining a Conscious Adult Being; Communicating with Difficult People; Having What You Want Without Controlling Life; Sustaining Balance in the Midst of Chaos; Who's Speaking? Who's Listening Bring Power to Your Communication; Breaking the Love Patterns that Bind; Discovering, Sustaining and Building your Spiritual Relationships; Healing Significant Woundings of Life; Living Life Like it Matters; Love and Honor; Trust and Forgiveness; The Next Step.

36071 ■ Vaccari & Associates Inc.
17 Cypress St. 1
Marblehead, MA 01945-1925
Ph: (781)639-0946
Fax: (781)639-0946
Co. E-mail: rvaccari1@verizon.net
Contact: Ralph J. Vaccari, President
E-mail: rvaccari@rcn.com
Scope: A provider of appraisals for primary and secondary mortgages, mortgage refinancing, employee relocation, private mortgage insurance removal, estate planning and divorce settlement. **Founded:** 1996.

36072 ■ Verbit & Co.
19 Bala Ave.
Bala Cynwyd, PA 19004-3202
Ph: (610)668-9840
Co. E-mail: verbitcompany@earthlink.net
Contact: Alan C. Verbit, President
Scope: Management consulting firm to assist executives and managers fulfill their mission and to assure that adequate planning of day-to-day operations occurs; that controls sufficient to safeguard valuable resources; and that results of decisions reviewed in sufficient time to effect continuing action. Financial planning and control-to develop accounting, budgeting, forecasting and other information systems for the management of resources and evaluation of strategies. Services also include: Evaluation of desk-top computer systems for small firms; CAD/CAM implementation plan and orderly introduction of CAD/CAM. Industries served: manufacturing, distribution, metals casting, equipment and components, professional services, health care, retail, nonprofit and government. **Founded:** 1981. **Seminars:** Integrating Manufacturing Management Systems with Business Systems; Negotiating Information Systems Agreements with Suppliers.

36073 ■ Wheeler & Associates
13902 N Dale Mabry Hwy.
Tampa, FL 33618
Ph: (813)264-4977
Contact: S. Earl Wheeler, President
Scope: Provider of services in career and vocational counseling, human resource development and training and managerial development assistance for all levels of management. Offers organizational effectiveness studies and organizational design assistance for private and public enterprises. Industries served include educational institutions and training schools, small businesses, and engineering firms. **Founded:** 1985.

36074 ■ Workplace Dimensions Inc.
7004 Lakewood Dr.
Richmond, VA 23229-6934
Ph: (804)673-8777
Fax: (804)673-8178
Co. E-mail: hr@workplacedimensions.com
URL: http://www.workplacedimensions.com
Contact: Carol R. Losee, Principal
Scope: Offers human resources services including designing salary programs and performance management systems, customizing employee handbooks and personnel policy manuals, conducting employee and management training on harassment prevention and other relevant topics, and reviewing business practices for compliance. **Founded:** 1995. **Special Services:** Interviewer's Toolkit; Employer's Toolkit.

COMPUTERIZED DATABASES

36075 ■ *Human Resources Report*
1801 S Bell St.
Arlington, VA 22202
Free: 800-372-1033
Co. E-mail: customercare@bna.com
URL: http://www.bna.com
Availability: Online: Bloomberg LP-Bloomberg BNA. **Type:** Full-text.

LIBRARIES

36076 ■ American Society for Training and Development - Information Center
1640 King St.
Alexandria, VA 22313-2043
Ph: (703)683-8100
Free: 800-628-2783
Fax: (703)683-1523
Co. E-mail: customercare@astd.org
URL: http://www.astd.org
Scope: Human resource development - general, management, training, career development, Organization development, consulting skills. **Services:** Library open to national members of the Society. **Founded:** 1984. **Holdings:** 3000 bound volumes. **Subscriptions:** 60 journals and other serials.

36077 ■ Walt Disney World - Global Business Technology Strategy Library
Team Disney 336-N
1375 Buena Vista Dr.
Lake Buena Vista, FL 32830-1000
Ph: (407)828-4250
Fax: (407)827-8260
Co. E-mail: david.w.hartman@disney.com
URL: http://disneyworld.disney.go.com/wdw
Contact: David Hartman, Librarian
Scope: Computer science, human resources, general business. **Services:** Center not open to the public. **Founded:** 1986. **Holdings:** 4000 books, videos, DVDs, and CDs; 100 AV equipment. **Subscriptions:** 200 journals and other serials; 3 newspapers.

36078 ■ Towers Perrin - Western Canada Information Centre
3700, 150 - 6 Ave., SW
Calgary, AB, Canada T2P 3Y7
Ph: (403)261-1432
Fax: (403)237-6733
Co. E-mail: val.ward@towers.com
Contact: Val Ward
Scope: Human resource management, total rewards, pensions, employee benefits, executive compensation, employee communications, pension and benefits administration services, pension fund asset management. **Services:** Interlibrary loan. **Founded:** 1984. **Holdings:** 1000 books. **Subscriptions:** 100 journals and other serials; 4 newspapers.

36079 ■ Towers Watson Information Centre
1100 Melville St., Ste. 1600
Vancouver, BC, Canada V6E 4A6
Ph: (604)691-1000
Fax: (604)691-1062
URL: http://www.towerswatson.com/
Scope: Actuarial science, employee benefits, compensation, human resources. **Holdings:** Figures not available.

36080 ■ Walgreen Performance Development Library
200 Wilmot Rd.
Deerfield, IL 60015
Ph: (847)914-2500
Free: 877-250-5823;
URL: http://www.walgreens.com
Scope: Human resources, performance technology. **Services:** Library not open to the public. **Holdings:** 1000 books; 200 archival items. **Subscriptions:** 80 journals and other serials.

RESEARCH CENTERS

36081 ■ University of British Columbia - Bureau for Research on Applications of Information Technology (BRITE)
2053 Main Mall
Faculty of Commerce & Business Administration
Vancouver, BC, Canada V6T 1Z2
Ph: (604)822-8390
Fax: (604)822-0045
Co. E-mail: carson.woo@ubc.ca
URL: http://www.sauder.ubc.ca/Faculty/Research_Centres/Bureau_for_Research_on_Applicati ons_of_IT
Contact: Prof. Carson Woo, Director

REFERENCE WORKS

36082 ■ ***Choosing the Right Legal Form of Business: The Complete Guide to Becoming a Sole Proprietor, Partnership, LLC, or Corporation***
Pub: Atlantic Publishing Company

Ed: Pat Mitchell. **Released:** January 1, 2009. **Price:** $24.95. **Description:** According to the U.S. Small Business Administration, nearly 250,000 new businesses start up annually; currently there are over nine million small companies in the nation. The importance of choosing the proper legal form of business is stressed.

36083 ■ ***"Coca-Cola Bottler Up for Sale: CEO J. Bruce Llewellyn Seeks Retirement" in Black Enterprise (Vol. 37, December 2006, No. 5, pp. 31)***
Pub: Earl G. Graves Publishing Co. Inc.
Ed: Marcia A. Wade. **Description:** J. Bruce Llewellyn of Brucephil Inc., the parent company of the Philadelphia Coca-Cola Bottling Co. has agreed to sell its remaining shares to Coca-Cola Co., which previously owned 31 percent of Philly Coke. Analysts believe that Coca-Cola will eventually sell its shares to another bottler.

36084 ■ ***"Protect Your Assets" in Black Enterprise (Vol. 38, January 2008, No. 6, pp. 38)***
Pub: Earl G. Graves Publishing Co. Inc.
Ed: Trevor Delaney. **Description:** Owner of rental properties seeks advice for incorporating versus getting an LLC for the business.

36085 ■ ***"SoBran Partners with U.S. Navy" in Black Enterprise (Vol. 37, October 2006, No. 3, pp. 38)***
Pub: Earl G. Graves Publishing Co. Inc.
Ed: Glenn Townes. **Description:** SoBran Inc., partnered with Lockheed Martin and signed a three-Tear production service contract with the Naval Aviation Depot in Jacksonville, Florida. The $44 million contract will allow SoBran to transport and warehouse materials for Navy facilities.

36086 ■ ***"World Wide Technology Expands" in Black Enterprise (Vol. 37, December 2006, No. 5, pp. 34)***
Pub: Earl G. Graves Publishing Co. Inc.
Ed: Marcia A. Wade. **Description:** World Wide Technology Inc. opened a streamlined, higher capacity 12,000-square-foot Integration Technology Center near its corporate headquarters in St. Louis. The new venture will transfer lower costs to customers.

Incubators

START-UP INFORMATION

36087 ■ *"The New Orleans Saints" in Entrepreneur (Vol. 37, August 2009, No. 8, pp. 40)*
Pub: Entrepreneur Media, Inc.
Ed: Jason Meyers. **Description:** Idea Village is a nonprofit group that fosters entrepreneurship in New Orleans, Louisiana. Entrepreneurship is indeed growing in the city during a time when the city is still recovering from the damage of hurricane Katrina.

36088 ■ *"The New Orleans Saints" in Entrepreneur (Vol. 37, August 2009, No. 8, pp. 40)*
Pub: Entrepreneur Media, Inc.
Ed: Jason Meyers. **Description:** Idea Village is a nonprofit group that fosters entrepreneurship in New Orleans, Louisiana. Entrepreneurship is indeed growing in the city during a time when the city is still recovering from the damage of hurricane Katrina.

36089 ■ *"Rehab Will Turn Hospital Into Incubator" in The Business Journal-Serving Metropolitan Kansas City (Vol. 26, September 12, 2008)*
Pub: American City Business Journals, Inc.
Ed: Rob Roberts. **Description:** Independence Regional Health Center will be purchased by CEAH Realtors and be converted into the Independence Regional Entrepreneurial Center, a business incubator that will house startups and other tenants. Other details about the planned entrepreneurial center are provided.

36090 ■ *"Victoria Colligan; Co-Founder, Ladies Who Launch Inc., 38" in Crain's Cleveland Business (Vol. 28, November 19, 2007, No. 46)*
Pub: Crain Communications, Inc.
Ed: Jay Miller. **Description:** Profile of Victoria Colligan who is the co-founder of Ladies Who Launch Inc., an organization with franchises in nearly 50 cities; the company offers women entrepreneurs workshops and a newsletter to help women balance their businesses with other aspects of their lives. Ms. Colligan found that women were learning about being business owners differently than men and she felt that there was a need to create opportunities for networking for women launching businesses that had more of a lifestyle purpose.

REFERENCE WORKS

36091 ■ *"Biz Assesses 'Textgate' Fallout; Conventions, Smaller Deals Affected' in Crain's Detroit Business (Vol. 24, March 31, 2008)*
Pub: Crain Communications, Inc.
Ed: Tom Henderson. **Description:** Businesspeople who were trying to measure the amount of economic damage is likely to be caused due to Mayor Kwame Kilpatrick's indictment on eight charges and found that: automotive and other large global deals are less likely to be affected than location decisions by smaller companies and convention site decisions. Also being affected are negotiations in which Mexican startup companies were planning a partnership with the TechTown incubator to pursue opportunities in the auto sector; those plans are being put on hold while they look at other sites.

36092 ■ *"The Business of Activism" in Entrepreneur (Vol. 37, September 2009, No. 9, pp. 43)*
Pub: Entrepreneur Media, Inc.
Ed: Mary Catherine O'Connor. **Description:** San Francisco, California-based business incubator Virgance has been promoting sustainable projects by partnering with businesses. The company has launched campaigns which include organizing homeowners in negotiating with solar installers. The company is also planning to expand its workforce.

36093 ■ *"Henry Ford Health Leases Lab Space at TechTown" in Crain's Detroit Business (Vol. 24, March 31, 2008, No. 13, pp. 5)*
Pub: Crain Communications, Inc.
Ed: Tom Henderson. **Description:** Henry Ford Health System has signed a seven-year lease at TechTown, the high-tech incubator and research park affiliated with Wayne State University, to take over 14,000 square feet of space for four research groups and laboratories. Construction has already begun and Henry Ford officials hope to take occupancy as early as June 1.

36094 ■ *"Mexican Companies to Rent Space in TechTown, Chinese Negotiating" in Crain's Detroit Business (Vol. 24, September 29, 2008, No. 39)*
Pub: Crain Communications Inc.
Ed: Tom Henderson. **Description:** Wayne State University's TechTown, the business incubator and research park, has signed an agreement with the Mexican government that will provide temporary office space to 25 Mexican companies looking to find customers or establish partnerships in Michigan. TechTown's executive director is negotiating with economic development officials from China. To accommodate foreign visitors the incubator is equipping offices with additional equipment and resources.

36095 ■ *"Spread Your Wings" in Canadian Business (Vol. 81, March 17, 2008, No. 4, pp. 31)*
Pub: Rogers Media
Ed: Megan Harman. **Description:** Financing from angel investors is one avenue that should be explored by startups. Angel investors are typically affluent individuals who invest their own money. Angel investors usually want at least 10 times their initial investment within eight years but they benefit the businesses through their help in decision-making and the industry expertise they provide.

36096 ■ *"STAR TEC Incubator's Latest Resident Shows Promise" in The Business Journal-Serving Greater Tampa Bay (August 8, 2008)*
Pub: American City Business Journals, Inc.
Ed: Jane Meinhardt. **Description:** Field Forensics Inc., a resident of the STAR Technology Enterprise Center, has grown after being admitted into the business accelerator. The producer of defense and security devices and equipment has doubled 2007 sales as of 2008.

36097 ■ *"TechLift Strives to Fill in Gaps in Entrepreneurial Support Efforts" in Crain's Cleveland Business (November 12, 2007)*
Pub: Crain Communications, Inc.
Ed: Marsha Powers. **Description:** Profile of the program, TechLift, a new business model launched by NorTech, that is aiming to provide assistance to technology-based companies that may not be a good fit for other entrepreneurial support venues.

36098 ■ *"The Union of Town and Gown" in Entrepreneur (Vol. 37, October 2009, No. 10, pp. 47)*
Pub: Entrepreneur Media, Inc.
Ed: Jason Daley. **Description:** Ten of the best entrepreneurial initiatives involving cities and local universities in the US are described. Cities and universities are joining up for these efforts to strengthen local economies and stop brain drain.

START-UP INFORMATION

36099 ■ *"Docs Prop Up Health Insurer" in Business First-Columbus (December 14, 2007, pp. A1)*
Pub: American City Business Journals, Inc.
Ed: Carrie Ghose. **Description:** Doctors and executives supporting Physicians Assurance Corporation, a startup health insurer in Central Ohio, were required to raise $2.5 million before they could apply for a license from the state Department of Insurance. The company, which hopes to acquire its license by January 2007, will focus on doctor's offices and businesses with two to ninety-nine employees.

36100 ■ *"Startup Makes Attempt to 'Reform' Health Insurance" in Austin Business JournalInc. (Vol. 29, January 15, 2010, No. 45, pp. 1)*
Pub: American City Business Journals
Ed: Sandra Zaragoza. **Description:** Health insurance provider ETMG LLC of Austin, Texas plans to act as a managing general agent and a third-party administrator that can facilitate customized plans for small businesses and sole proprietors. According to CEO Mark Adams, profitability is expected for ETMG, which have also clinched $1.5 million worth of investments. Entities that have agreed to do business with ETMG are presented.

ASSOCIATIONS AND OTHER ORGANIZATIONS

36101 ■ National Council of Self-Insurers (NCSI)
1253 Springfield Ave.
PMB 345
New Providence, NJ 07974
Ph: (908)665-2152
Fax: (908)665-4020
Co. E-mail: natcouncil@aol.com
URL: http://www.natcouncil.com
Contact: David Kaplan, President
Description: State associations, individual companies, associate members, and professional members concerned with self-insurance under the workmen's compensation laws. Promotes and protects, at all governmental levels, the interests of self-insurers or legally non-insured employers and their employees in matters of legislative and administrative activity affecting workmen's compensation; assists, advises, and uses its resources in developing and implementing common objectives among self-insurers. Current goals are: a workmen's compensation program that is just, both to the individual and to the employer; equitable distribution of the compensation dollar; strong vocational rehabilitation incentives for the injured employee. **Founded:** 1946. **Publications:** *Self-Insurance Requirements of the States* (Periodic). **Educational Activities:** National Council of Self-Insurers Meeting (Annual).

EDUCATIONAL PROGRAMS

36102 ■ AMA's Insurance and Risk Management Workshop (Onsite)
American Management Association
600 AMA Way
Saranac Lake, NY 12983-5534
Ph: (212)586-8100
Free: 877-566-9441
Fax: (518)891-0368
Co. E-mail: customerservice@amanet.org
URL: http://www.amaseminars.org
Price: $2,195.00 for non-members; $1,995.00 for AMA members; and $1,708.00 for General Services Administration (GSA) members. **Description:** Covers everything from coverage and cost to liability limits, retention and broker services. **Dates and Locations:** New York, NY; and San Francisco, CA.

REFERENCE WORKS

36103 ■ *"2010 Book of Lists" in Austin Business JournalInc. (Vol. 29, December 25, 2009, No. 42, pp. 1)*
Pub: American City Business Journals
Description: Rankings of companies and organizations within the business services, finance, healthcare, hospitality and travel, insurance, marketing and media, professional services, real estate, education and technology industries in Austin, Texas are presented. Rankings are based on sales, business size, and other statistics.

36104 ■ *"Abroad, Not Overboard" in Entrepreneur (Vol. 36, April 2008, No. 4, pp. 68)*
Pub: Entrepreneur Media, Inc.
Ed: Crystal Detamore-Rodman. **Description:** Export-Import Bank is an agency created by the U.S. government to help exporters get credit insurance and capital loans by providing them with loan guarantees. The bank, being criticized as supporting more the bigger exporters, has allotted to smaller businesses a bigger portion of the annual credit being approved.

36105 ■ *"All-Star Advice 2010" in Black Enterprise (Vol. 41, October 2010, No. 3, pp. 97)*
Pub: Earl G. Graves Publishing Co. Inc.
Ed: Renita Burns, Sheiresa Ngo, Marcia Wade Talbert. **Description:** Financial experts share tips on real estate, investing, taxes, insurance and debt management.

36106 ■ *"The Annual Entitlement Lecture: Trustees of Medicare and Social Security Issue Another Dismal Report" in Barron's (March 31, 2008)*
Pub: Dow Jones & Company, Inc.
Ed: Thomas G. Donlan. **Description:** Expenditures on Medicare hospital insurance and the revenues available to pay for it have led to a gap of capital valued at $38.6 trillion. Slashing the benefits or raising taxes will not solve the gap which exists unless the government saves the money and invests it in private markets.

36107 ■ *"Anthem Leading the Way in Social Tech Revolution" in Inside Business (Vol. 13, September-October 2011, No. 5, pp. 1B3)*
Pub: Great Lakes Publishing Co.
Ed: Ryan Clark. **Description:** Anthem Blue Cross and Blue Shield is leading the way in social technology. The firm's social media initiatives to promote itself are outlined.

36108 ■ *"An Apple a Day" in Entrepreneur (Vol. 36, February 2008, No. 2, pp. 19)*
Pub: Entrepreneur Media Inc.
Ed: Mark Henricks. **Description:** Businesses are handling rising health coverage costs by providing employees with wellness programs, which include smoking-cessation programs, consumer-directed plans for savings on premiums, and limited medical care plans. Details on the growing trend regarding employee health coverage are discussed.

36109 ■ *"Are Prepaid Legal Services Worthwhile?" in Contractor (Vol. 56, December 2009, No. 12, pp. 31)*
Pub: Penton Media, Inc.
Ed: Susan Linden McGreevy. **Description:** Companies' provision of legal insurance as an employee benefit in the United States is discussed. Stoppage of premium payment halts employee coverage. It also does not cover all kinds of personal issues.

36110 ■ *"Are You Overinsured? Some Policies May Not Offer Much Additional Benefit" in Black Enterprise (Vol. 38, March 2008, No. 8, pp. 126)*
Pub: Earl G. Graves Publishing Co. Inc.
Ed: Tamara E. Holmes. **Description:** Travel insurance, identity-theft insurance, specific disease or health condition insurance policies are described. Advice is given to help determine if you are over-insured.

36111 ■ *"Baldwin Connelly Partnership Splits" in Business Journal Serving Greater Tampa Bay (Vol. 30, November 19, 2010, No. 48, pp. 1)*
Pub: Tampa Bay Business Journal
Ed: Alexis Muellner. **Description:** The fast-growing insurance brokerage Baldwin Connelly is now breaking up after five years. Two different entrepreneurial visions have developed within the organization and founders Lowry Baldwin and John Connell will not take separate tracks. Staffing levels in the firm are expected to remain the same.

36112 ■ *"Bank Forces Brooke Founder To Sell His Holdings" in The Business Journal-Serving Metropolitan Kansas City (October 10, 2008)*
Pub: American City Business Journals, Inc.
Ed: James Dornbrook. **Description:** Robert Orr who is the founder of Brooke Corp., a franchise of insurance agencies, says that he was forced to sell virtually all of his stocks in the company by creditors. First United Bank held the founder's stock as collateral for two loans worth $5 million and $7.9 million, which were declared in default in September 2008. Details of the selling of the company's stocks are provided.

36113 ■ *"Bills Raise Blues Debate; An Unfair Edge or Level Playing Field?" in Crain's*

Detroit Business (Vol. 24, January 21, 2008, No. 3)
Pub: Crain Communications Inc. - Detroit
Ed: Sherri Begin. **Description:** Changes in Michigan state law would change the way health insurance can be sold to individuals. Michigan Blue Cross Blue Shield is working to keep its tax-exempt status while staying competitive against for-profit insurers and nonprofit HMOs.

36114 ■ *"Blue Cross Confronts Baby Blues" in Marketing to Women (Vol. 21, March 2008, No. 3, pp. 3)*
Pub: EPM Communications Inc.
Contact: Ira Mayer, President
E-mail: imayer@epmcom.com
Description: Blue Cross of California has launched a Maternity Depression Program aimed at educating mothers suffering from postpartum depression.

36115 ■ *"Blue Cross to Put Kiosk in Mall" in News & Observer (November 9, 2010)*
Pub: News & Observer
Ed: Alan M. Wolf. **Description:** Blue Cross and Blue Shield of North Carolina has placed a kiosk in Durham's Streets of Southpoint in order to market its health insurance.

36116 ■ *Business Insurance--Agent/Broker Profiles Issue*
Pub: Business Insurance
URL(s): www.businessinsurance.com. **Ed:** Regis J. Coccia. **Released:** Annual; Latest edition 2008. **Publication includes:** List of top 10 insurance agents/brokers worldwide specializing in commercial insurance. **Entries include:** Firm name, address, phone, fax, branch office locations, year established, names of subsidiaries, gross revenues, premium volume, number of employees, principal officers, percent of revenue generated by commercial retail brokerage, acquisitions. **Arrangement:** Alphabetical by company. **Indexes:** Geographical.

36117 ■ *"Businesses Balk at 1099 Provision in Health Reform Law" in Baltimore Business Journal (Vol. 28, August 13, 2010, No. 14, pp. 1)*
Pub: Baltimore Business Journal
Ed: Scott Dance. **Description:** Small business advocates and accountants have criticized the Internal Revenue Service Form 1099 provision in the health care reform law as not worth the cost of time and money. Critics believe the policy would create a deluge of the documents that is too much for the companies or the IRS to handle. Details of the provision are also discussed.

36118 ■ *"Businesses Keep a Watchful Eye on Worker's Comp" in The Business Journal-Serving Greater Tampa Bay (September 5, 2008)*
Pub: American City Business Journals, Inc.
Ed: Jane Meinhardt. **Description:** Pending a ruling from the Florida Supreme Court that could uphold the 2003 changes on workers' compensation law, the outcome would include restrictions on claimant attorneys' fees and allow the competitive workers' compensation insurance rates to remain low. However, insurance rates are expected to go up if the court overturns the changes.

36119 ■ *"Cerner Works the Business Circuit" in Business Journal-Serving Metropolitan Kansas City (Vol. 26, October 5, 2007, No. 4, pp. 1)*
Pub: American City Business Journals, Inc.
Ed: Rob Roberts. **Description:** Cerner Corporation is embracing the coming of the electronic medical record exchange by creating a regional health information organization (RHIO) called the CareEntrust. The RHIO convinced health insurers to share claims data with patients and clinicians. At the Center Health Conference, held October 7 to 10, Cerner will demonstrate the software it developed for CareEntrust to the 40,000 healthcare and information technology professionals.

36120 ■ *"Changes Sought to Health Law" in Baltimore Business Journal (Vol. 28, July 30, 2010, No. 12, pp. 1)*
Pub: Baltimore Business Journal
Ed: Kent Hoover. **Description:** Business groups that opposed health care reform are working to undo parts of the new laws even before they go into effect. Business groups are gaining support for one legislative fix, which is repealing the law's provision that requires all businesses to file 1099 forms with the IRS any time they pay more than $600 a year to another business.

36121 ■ *"CNinsure Offers Safety in Numbers" in Barron's (Vol. 90, September 13, 2010, No. 37, pp. 29)*
Pub: Barron's Editorial & Corporate Headquarters
Ed: Teresa Rivas. **Description:** China's insurance holding company CNinsure has a long growth future due to the nascent insurance market in the country. It has also been diversifying its offerings and it has a broad network in the nation. The shares of the company are trading cheaply at nearly 14 times its 2011 earnings, and is considered a good point for investors.

36122 ■ *"Connecting the Dots Between Wellness and Elder Care" in Benefits and Compensation Digest (Vol. 47, August 2010, No. 8, pp. 18)*
Pub: International Foundation of Employee Benefit Plans
Contact: Richard Lyall, President
Ed: Sandra Timmermann. **Description:** Employees caring for aged and infirm parents deal with time and financial issues and other stresses. The connection between health status of caregivers and employers' health care costs could be aided by linking programs and benefits with wellness and caregiving.

36123 ■ *"Consulting Firm Goes Shopping" in Crain's Chicago Business (Vol. 31, April 28, 2008, No. 17, pp. 45)*
Pub: Crain Communications, Inc.
Ed: Phuong Ly. **Description:** Clark & Wamberg LLC was created last year after the merger of Clark Inc. to a Dutch insurance conglomerate. Clark Inc. was a life insurance and benefits consultancy which had been on a downslide, returning just 5.6 percent a year to shareholders. In contrast Clark & Wamberg posted first-year revenue of $106.8 million, fueled by business from its executive compensation and health care clients.

36124 ■ *"Continuously Monitoring Workers' Comp Can Limit Costs" in Crain's Cleveland Business (Vol. 28, October 8, 2007, No. 40, pp. 21)*
Pub: Crain Communications, Inc.
Ed: Michael Lagnoni. **Description:** When operating without a plan for managing its workers' compensation program, a company risks losing money. For most companies workers' compensation insurance premiums are often reduced to an annual budget entry but employers who are actively involved in the management of their programs are more likely to experience reductions in premiums and limit indirect costs associated with claims.

36125 ■ *"Controversial Bill Could Raise Rates for Homeowners" in Orlando Business Journal (Vol. 26, January 22, 2010, No. 34, pp. 1)*
Pub: American City Business Journals
Ed: Oscar Pedro Musibay; Christopher Boyd. **Description:** Florida Senate Bill 876 and its companion House Bill 447 are pushing for the deregulation of rates in the state's home insurance market. The bill is being opposed by consumer advocates as it could mean higher rates for homeowner insurance policies.

36126 ■ *"Cost of Md. Health Plan Not Known" in Baltimore Business Journal (Vol. 28, September 3, 2010, No. 17, pp. 1)*
Pub: Baltimore Business Journal
Ed: Emily Mullin. **Description:** United States health reform is seen to result in increased health insurance prices in Maryland. However, health care reform advocates claim a new marketplace and increased competition will help keep costs down.

36127 ■ *"Courting Canadian Customers Confounds Car Dealers" in Business First Buffalo (November 9, 2007, pp. 1)*
Pub: American City Business Journals, Inc.
Ed: James Fink. **Description:** Strength of the Canadian dollar has led to an influx of potential customers for the Western New York automobile industry, but franchising restrictions and licensing as well as insurance issues have limited the potential of having larger sales figures. Border and trade issues that affect the car industry in WNY are also discussed.

36128 ■ *"CreFirst To Reward Doctors for Reducing Costs, Improving Care" in Baltimore Business Journal (Vol. 28, June 4, 2010, No. 4, pp. 1)*
Pub: Baltimore Business Journal
Ed: Scott Graham. **Description:** CareFirst Blue Cross Blue Shield plans to introduce a program that dangles big financial rewards to physicians who change the way they deliver primary care by improving the health of their sickest patients while reducing costs. The company will soon begin recruiting primary care physicians in Maryland, Washington DC, and Northern Virginia.

36129 ■ *"Crop Insurance Harvest Prices in 2011" in Farm Industry News (November 9, 2011)*
Pub: Penton Business Media Inc.
Ed: Gary Schnitkey. **Description:** Risk Management Agency (RMA) reported harvest prices for corn and soybean grown in the Midwest with corn at $6.32 per bushel, 31 cents higher than the project $6.01; soybeans were at $12.14 per bushel, down $1.35 from the projected price of $13.49.

36130 ■ *"Cutting Health Care Costs: the 3-Legged Stool" in HR Specialist (Vol. 8, September 2010, No. 9, pp. 1)*
Pub: Capitol Information Group Inc.
Description: Employer spending on health insurance benefits to employees is investigated.

36131 ■ *"Diana Bonta: Keeping People Healthy and Thriving" in Hispanic Business (Vol. 30, April 2008, No. 4, pp. 30)*
Pub: Hispanic Business
Ed: Leanndra Martinez. **Description:** Diana Bonta serves as vice president of public affairs for Kaiser Permanente and is a strong advocate for health reform and improving access to health care. In order to better serve the underinsured and uninsured, she directs Kaiser's Community Benefit division that devoted $369 million last year to this cause.

36132 ■ *Dictionary of Real Estate Terms*
Pub: Barron's Educational Series Inc.
Contact: Alex Holtz, President
E-mail: aholtz@berronseduc.com
Ed: Jack P. Friedman, Jack C. Harris, J. Bruce Lindeman. **Released:** October 2008. **Price:** $13.99. **Description:** More than 2,500 real estate terms relating to mortgages and financing, brokerage law, architecture, rentals and leases, property insurance, and more.

36133 ■ *"Discovery Communications" in Workforce Management (Vol. 88, December 14, 2009, No. 13, pp. 17)*
Pub: Crain Communications Inc.
Ed: Jeremy Smerd. **Description:** Discovery Communications provides its employees a wealth of free health services via a comprehensive work-site medical clinic that is available to its employees and their dependents. Overview of the company's innovative approach to healthcare is presented.??.

36134 ■ *"Doctors Eye Rating Plan With Caution" in The Business Journal-Portland (Vol. 25, July 4, 2008, No. 17, pp. 1)*
Pub: American City Business Journals, Inc.
Ed: Robin J. Moody. **Description:** Doctors in Portland, Oregon are wary of a new Providence Health Plan system that rates their performance on patients with certain medical conditions. The system is expected to discourage wasteful procedures, thereby, saving employers' money. Other mechanics of the rating system are also discussed.

36135 ■ *"Doctors, Health Insurers Squabble Over Who Sends Patients the Bill" in Baltimore Business Journal (Vol. 27, February 6, 2010)*
Pub: American City Business Journals
Ed: Scott Graham. **Description:** Issue of allowing patients to send reimbursement checks to physicians who are not part of their health insurer's provider network is being debated in Maryland. Details on the proposed Maryland bill and the arguments presented by doctors and insurers are outlined.

36136 ■ *"Doctor's Orders" in Canadian Business (Vol. 79, November 20, 2006, No. 23, pp. 73)*
Pub: Rogers Media
Ed: Jeff Sanford. **Description:** George Cohon, the founder of McDonald's in Canada and Russia, speaks about the Canadian market and the experience of starting McDonald's in Canada.

36137 ■ *"Doctors Warn of Problems" in Austin Business JournalInc. (Vol. 29, December 4, 2009, No. 39, pp. 1)*
Pub: American City Business Journals
Ed: Sandra Zaragoza. **Description:** Texas physicians have voiced their concern regarding the potential cuts in Medicare reimbursement rates due to the 21 percent cut imposed by Centers for Medicare and Medicaid at the start of 2010. Experts believe the large cuts would result in the closure of some physician practices. Details of the Texas Medical Association's stand on the health reform bill are examined.

36138 ■ *"Doing Without" in Baltimore Business Journal (Vol. 28, June 11, 2010, No. 5, pp. 1)*
Pub: Baltimore Business Journal
Ed: Scott Graham. **Description:** Maryland Health Care Commission report figures have shown only 47,661 small businesses provided some level of health coverage to 381,517 employees in 2009. These numbers are down from 51,283 employers who offered benefits to 407,983 employees in 2008 to highlight a disturbing trend in Maryland's small-group insurance market. Reasons for the drop are discussed.

36139 ■ *"E-Medical Records Save Money, Time in Ann Arbor" in Crain's Detroit Business (Vol. 24, January 21, 2008, No. 3, pp. 6)*
Pub: Crain Communications Inc. - Detroit
Ed: Jay Greene. **Description:** Ann Arbor Area Health Information Exchange is improving patient outcomes by sharing clinical and administrative data in electronic medical record systems.

36140 ■ *"Elder Care Costs Surge" in National Underwriter Life & Health (Vol. 114, November 8, 2020, No. 21, pp. 25)*
Pub: Summit Business Media
Ed: Trevor Thomas. **Description:** Nursing home and assisted living rates rose from 2009 to 2010, according to MetLife Mature Market Institute. Statistical data included.

36141 ■ *"Employer Jobless Tax Could Rise" in Sacramento Business Journal (Vol. 28, May 27, 2011, No. 13, pp. 1)*
Pub: Sacramento Business Journal
Ed: Kathy Robertson. **Description:** The government of California is facing an estimated $16 billion deficit in its unemployment insurance fund. Unemployment insurance spending has exceeded employer contributions to the fund. Statistics on unemployment insurance is included.

36142 ■ *"Employers Tied in Knots" in Sacramento Business Journal (Vol. 25, August 15, 2008, No. 24, pp. 1)*
Pub: American City Business Journals, Inc.
Ed: Kathy Robertson. **Description:** Conflicting laws on same sex marriage have been posing problems for companies, and insurers in California. The court ruling that allowed gay marriages has created differences between state and federal laws. Federal laws on same-sex spouse taxation are also seen to complicate the issue.

36143 ■ *"Employers Waking Up to Effects of Workers' Sleep Problems" in Crain's Cleveland Business (Vol. 28, December 3, 2007, No. 48, pp. 18)*
Pub: Crain Communications, Inc.
Ed: Jennifer Keirn. **Description:** Employers are beginning to realize that poor sleep quality can impact their bottom lines with higher health care costs and more lost-time accidents. The National Institutes of Health estimates that sleep deprivation, sleep disorders and excessive daytime sleepiness add about $15 billion to our national health care bill and cost employers $50 billion in lost productivity.

36144 ■ *"Experts Take the Temp of Obama Plan" in The Business Journal-Serving Metropolitan Kansas City (Vol. 27, November 14, 2008, No. 10)*
Pub: American City Business Journals, Inc.
Ed: Rob Roberts. **Description:** Kansas City, Missouri-based employee benefits experts say president-elect Barack Obama's health care reform plan is on track. Insurance for children and capitalization for health information technology are seen as priority areas. The plan is aimed at reducing the number of uninsured people in the United States.

36145 ■ *"Export Initiative Launched" in Philadelphia Business Journal (Vol. 28, December 11, 2009, No. 43, pp. 1)*
Pub: American City Business Journals
Ed: Athena D. Merritt. **Description:** The first initiative that came out of the partnership between the Export-Import Bank of the US, the city of Philadelphia, and the World Trade Center of Greater Philadelphia is presented. A series of export finance workshops have featured Ex-Im Bank resources that can provide Philadelphia businesses with working capital, insurance protection and buyer financing.

36146 ■ *"Firms Sue Doracon to Recoup More Than $1M in Unpaid Bills" in Baltimore Business Journal (Vol. 28, July 9, 2010, No. 9, pp. 1)*
Pub: Baltimore Business Journal
Ed: Scott Dance. **Description:** Concrete supplier Paul J. Rach Inc., Selective Insurance Company, and equipment leasing firm Colonial Pacific Leasing Corporation intend to sue Baltimore, Maryland-based Doracon Contracting Inc. for $1 million in unpaid bills. Doracon owed Colonial Pacific $794,000 and the equipment is still in Doracon's possession. Selective Insurance and Paul J. Rach respectively seek $132,000 and $88,000.

36147 ■ *"For All It's Worth" in Entrepreneur (Vol. 36, April 2008, No. 4, pp. 46)*
Pub: Entrepreneur Media, Inc.
Ed: Farnoosh Torabi. **Description:** Discusses the federal estate tax system requires that 45 percent of the money beyond $2 million be given to the government. Ways on how to minimize the effects of estate tax on assets include: creating bypass trusts for married couples; setting up an irrevocable life insurance trust to avoid taxation of estate for insurance benefactors; and having annual gift tax exclusion.

36148 ■ *"Generational Savvy" in Hawaii Business (Vol. 54, August 2008, No. 2, pp. 135)*
Pub: Hawaii Business Publishing
Ed: Jolyn Okimoto Rosa. **Description:** Lawrence Takeo Kagawa founded Security Insurance Agency, later renamed Occidental Underwriters of Hawaii Ltd., in 1933 to provide insurance to Asian-Americans in Hawaii at lower premiums. Details on the company's history, growth investment products and Transamerica Life products and 75 years of family-run business are discussed.

36149 ■ *Green Your Small Business: Profitable Ways to Become an Ecopreneur*
Pub: McGraw-Hill
Ed: Scott Cooney. **Released:** November 7, 2008. **Price:** $19.95 paperback. **Description:** Advice and guidance is given to help any entrepreneur start, build or grow a green business, focusing on green business basics, market research and financing, as well as handling legal and insurance issues.

36150 ■ *"Greenberg Sues U.S. Over AIG Rescue" in Wall Street Journal Eastern Edition (November 22 , 2011, pp. C3)*
Pub: Dow Jones & Company Inc.
Ed: Liam Pleven, Serena Ng. **Description:** Former Chief Executive Officer of American International Group Inc., Maurice R. 'Hank' Greenberg, has filed a lawsuit against the United States and the Federal Reserve Bank of New York on behalf of shareholders and his company, Starr International Company Inc., claiming that the government was wrong in taking control of the insurance giant and used it to move tens of millions of dollars to the trading partners of AIG.

36151 ■ *"Harleysville Eyes Growth After Nationwide Deal" in Philadelphia Business Journal (Vol. 30, October 7, 2011, No. 34, pp. 1)*
Pub: American City Business Journals Inc.
Ed: Jeff Blumenthal. **Description:** Harleysville Group announced growth plans after the company was sold to Columbus, Ohio-based Nationwide Mutual Insurance Company for about $1.63 billion. Nationwide gained an independent agency platform in 32 states with the Harleysville deal.

36152 ■ *"Health Alliance Could Sell Group" in Business Courier (Vol. 27, June 18, 2010, No. 7, pp. 1)*
Pub: Business Courier
Ed: James Ritchie. **Description:** Health Alliance could sell the 31-doctor Greater Cincinnati Associated Physicians Group. The group has seen several members withdraw ever since the group filed a complaint asking to be released from services to Health Alliance.

36153 ■ *"Health Care Braces for Federal Cuts" in Boston Business Journal (Vol. 29, August 19, 2011, No. 15, pp. 1)*
Pub: American City Business Journals Inc.
Ed: Scott Dance. **Description:** The healthcare industry in Baltimore is expecting negative effects from the federal debt ceiling on Medicare and Medicaid spending. Medicare funds are expected to be slashed and could impact hospitals and doctors.

36154 ■ *"Health Care of the Future" in Business Journal Serving Greater Tampa Bay (Vol. 30, November 19, 2010, No. 48, pp. 1)*
Pub: Tampa Bay Business Journal
Ed: Margie Manning. **Description:** Information about accountable care organizations (ACO), which are integrated care systems with doctors and hospitals working closely together to handle patient care, is provided. The Patient Protection and Affordable Care Act paved the way for ACOs as Medicare demonstration projects.

36155 ■ *"Health Centers Plan Expansion" in Crain's Detroit Business (Vol. 25, June 15, 2009, No. 24, pp. 3)*
Pub: Crain Communications Inc. - Detroit
Ed: Jay Greene. **Description:** Detroit has five federally qualified health centers that plan to receive over $3 million in federal stimulus money that will be used to expand projects that will care for uninsured patients.

36156 ■ *"Health Insurance Dilemmas" in Hispanic Business (January-February 2008, pp. 58)*
Pub: Hispanic Business
Ed: Anna Davison. **Description:** Small business owners discussed the challenges they face providing health insurance to employees.

36157 ■ *"Health IT Regulations Generate Static Among Providers" in Philadelphia Business Journal (Vol. 28, January 29, 2010, No. 50, pp. 1)*
Pub: American City Business Journals
Ed: John George. **Description:** US Centers for Medicaid and Medicare Services and the Office of the National Coordinator for Health Information

Technology have proposed rules regarding the meaningful use of electronic health records. The rules must be complied with by hospitals and physicians to qualify for federal stimulus funds.

36158 ■ *"Health Reform Could Expand HSA-Based Plans" in Workforce Management (Vol. 88, December 14, 2009, No. 13, pp. 6)*
Pub: Crain Communications Inc.
Ed: Jeremy Smerd. **Description:** HSA-qualified plans are the cheapest insurance plans on the market as they have a higher deductible but cost less upfront. If health care reform passes, HSA-qualified plans should benefit greatly.

36159 ■ *"Health Reform How-To" in Business Courier (Vol. 26, December 11, 2009, No. 33, pp. 1)*
Pub: American City Business Journals, Inc.
Ed: James Ritchie. **Description:** Greater Cincinnati health care leaders shared views about the health care reform bill. Respondents included the Cincinnati Visiting Nurse's Wallen Falberg, healthcare consultant Hirsch Cohen, Greater Cincinnati Health Council's Coleen O'Toole, Employer Health Care Alliance's Sharron DiMario, Legal Aid Society of Greater Cincinnati's Col Owens, Christ Hospital's Susan Croushore, and Humana of Ohio's Tim Cappel.

36160 ■ *"Healthcare: How To Get a Better Deal" in Inc. (November 2007, pp. 34)*
Pub: Gruner & Jahr USA Publishing
Ed: Sarah Goldstein. **Description:** Things to consider when choosing an insurance carrier for your employees are explored.

36161 ■ *"Here's How Buffett Spent 2007" in Barron's (Vol. 88, March 10, 2008, No. 10, pp. 48)*
Pub: Dow Jones & Company, Inc.
Ed: Andrew Bary. **Description:** Earnings of Berkshire Hathaway may decline in 2008 due to a tighter insurance market, but its portfolio is expected to continue growing. Warren Buffett purchased $19.1 billion worth of stocks in 2007.

36162 ■ *"Home Sweet Home" in Canadian Business (Vol. 79, October 9, 2006, No. 20, pp. 22)*
Pub: Rogers Media
Ed: Peter Shawn Taylor. **Description:** Changes being made in the management of mortgage insurance business in Canada are critically analyzed.

36163 ■ *"Hospital Fighting for Its Life; Board of St. Anthony Scrambles to Stem Losses" in Crain's Chicago Business (April 28, 2008)*
Pub: Crain Communications, Inc.
Ed: Mike Colias. **Description:** Chicago's Catholic health chain was looking to sell the money-losing hospital St. Anthony Hospital on the West Side but with the financial picture improving and no merger offers in the works the investment bank hired to shop the hospital is hoping to operate the 111-year-old facility as an independent entity. St. Anthony serves as a 'safety net' for the region since an increasing number of its patients are uninsured or on public aid, which pays far less than commercial insurers.

36164 ■ *"Hospitals See Major Shift To Outpatient Care" in The Business Journal-Milwaukee (Vol. 25, September 12, 2008, No. 51, pp. A1)*
Pub: American City Business Journals, Inc.
Ed: Corrinne Hess. **Description:** Statistics show that the revenue of Wisconsin hospitals from outpatient medical care is about to surpass revenue from hospital patients who stay overnight. This revenue increase is attributed to new technology and less-invasive surgery. Trends show that the shift toward outpatient care actually started in the late 1980s and early 1990s.

36165 ■ *"How to Maximize Your Investment Income" in Contractor (Vol. 56, December 2009, No. 12, pp. 33)*
Pub: Penton Media, Inc.
Ed: Irv Blackman. **Description:** Private placement life insurance (PPLI) can minimize taxes and protect assets. PPLI is a form of variable universal insurance that is offered privately. Risk of insurance company illiquidity is avoided as investments are placed in separate accounts.

36166 ■ *How to Start a Home-Based Senior Care Business: Check-in-Care, Transportation Services, Shopping and Cooking*
Pub: Globe Pequot Press
Ed: James L. Ferry. **Released:** January 1, 2010. **Price:** $18.95. **Description:** Information is provided to start a home-based senior care business.

36167 ■ *"How a Unique Culture Proposition Became a USP" in Business Strategy Review (Vol. 21, Spring 2010, No. 1, pp. 52)*
Pub: Wiley-Blackwell
Ed: Adam Kingl. **Description:** How can you transform the way you do things into a compelling sales proposition? Zurich Insurance has created a Unique Culture Proposition which may be its Unique Selling Point.

36168 ■ *"Humana: Take Pay Cut or Get Out" in Business Courier (Vol. 24, February 1, 2008, No. 43, pp. 1)*
Pub: American City Business Journals, Inc.
Ed: James Ritchie. **Description:** Insurer Humana Inc. is removing some surgery centers from its network for refusing to welcome the new payment system. Evendale Surgery Center and the Surgery Center of Cincinnati will be removed from the network because they resist the newly imposed lower rates. Speculations over Humana's decision are discussed.

36169 ■ *"IBC Reverses Member Slide" in Philadelphia Business Journal (Vol. 30, September 23, 2011, No. 32, pp. 1)*
Pub: American City Business Journals Inc.
Ed: John George. **Description:** Health insurer Independence Blue Cross (IBC) added more than 40,000 members across all product lines since the start of 2011. It has 2.2 million members in Pennsylvania's Philadelphia region and 3.1 million members across the U.S. Services and other growth-related plans of IBC are covered.

36170 ■ *"Impressive Numbers: Companies Experience Substantial Increases in Dollars, Employment" in Hispanic Business (July-August 2007)*
Pub: Hispanic Business
Ed: Derek Reveron. **Description:** Profiles of five fastest growing Hispanic companies reporting increases in revenue and employment include Brightstar, distributor of wireless products; Greenway Ford Inc., a car dealership; Fred Loya Insurance, auto insurance carrier; and Group O, packaging company; and Diverse Staffing, Inc., an employment and staffing firm.

36171 ■ *"Injured Workers Caught in the Middle" in Sacramento Business Journal (Vol. 28, June 10, 2011, No. 15, pp. 1)*
Pub: Sacramento Business Journal
Ed: Kelly Johnson. **Description:** A bill that would extend the cap on disability payments to nearly five years is in the works, but employers and insurance companies fear it would increase their costs. Proponents of the bill say, however, that it would correct unfairness suffered by the employees. Features of the bill are discussed as well as its effects on both parties and the State of California.

36172 ■ *"Insurance Firm Consolidates Offices; Integro Finds the Right Price Downtown" in Crain's New York Business (January 14, 2008)*
Pub: Crain Communications, Inc.
Description: Integro insurance brokers is relocating its headquarters to 1 State Street Plaza, where it will consolidate its operations in March. The firm feels that the upscale design will provide an appropriate setting for entertaining clients and an engaging work environment for employees.

36173 ■ *"Insurance: Marathon Effort" in Canadian Business (Vol. 80, January 29, 2007, No. 3, pp. 11)*
Pub: Rogers Media
Ed: Jeff Sanford. **Description:** The efforts of the insurance firm ING Canada Inc. to manage its relations with its customers are described. The enhancement of the insurance services provided by the company is discussed.

36174 ■ *"An Insurance Roll-Up In Danger of Unraveling" in Barron's (Vol. 88, March 17, 2008, No. 11, pp. 51)*
Pub: Dow Jones & Company, Inc.
Ed: Bill Alpert. **Description:** Shares of National Financial Partners have fallen below their initial offering price as sputtering sales and management turnover leave many investors wondering. One of the company's star brokers is being sued for their 'life settlement' contracts while another broker is being pursued by the IRS for unpaid taxes.

36175 ■ *"Insuraprise Growing Fast" in Austin Business Journal (Vol. 31, April 22, 2011, No. 7, pp. 1)*
Pub: American City Business Journals Inc.
Ed: Sandra Zaragoza. **Description:** Austin, Texas-based Insuraprise Inc. is finalizing the purchase of a 24,000-square-foot office at 12116 Jekel Circle. The firm, with 23 salespeople and sales that are growing nearly 300 percent over the past 18 months, will now have room to grow. Insuraprise plans to hire 35 new salespersons for its call center.

36176 ■ *"Insurer Buys Foundation's Uptown HQ" in Charlotte Business Journal (Vol. 25, December 17, 2010, No. 39, pp. 1)*
Pub: Charlotte Business Journal
Ed: Will Boye. **Description:** Charlotte, North Carolina-based Synergy Coverage Solutions has purchased the three-story building owned by Foundations For the Carolinas for slightly more than $3 million. Synergy plans to relocate its operation in the uptown building by August 2011.

36177 ■ *"Insurers No Longer Paying Premium for Advertising" in Brandweek (Vol. 49, April 21, 2008, No. 16, pp. SR3)*
Pub: VNU Business Media, Inc.
Ed: Eric Newman. **Description:** Insurance companies are cutting their advertising budgets after years of accelerated double-digit growth in spending due to the economic downturn, five years of record-breaking ad spend and a need to cut expenditures as claims costs rise and a competitive market keeps premiums in place. Statistical data included.

36178 ■ *"Insurers Warn Brokers" in Sacramento Business Journal (Vol. 25, August 22, 2008, No. 25, pp. 1)*
Pub: American City Business Journals, Inc.
Ed: Kathy Robertson. **Description:** Sacramento, California-based health plans have warned insurance brokers not to combine two different kinds of insurance products or they will be stricken from the sales network. The health plans also asked employers to promise not to combine plans with self-insurance. Such schemes are seen to destroy lower-premium health products.

36179 ■ *"Internet Marketing 2.0: Closing the Online Chat Gap" in Agent's Sales Journal (November 2009, pp. 14)*
Pub: Summit Business Media
Ed: Jeff Denenholz. **Description:** Advice regarding the implementation of an Internet marketing strategy for insurance agencies includes how and why to incorporate a chat feature in which a sales agent can communicate in real-time with potential or existing customers. It is important to understand if appropriate response mechanisms are in place to convert leads into actual sales.

36180 ■ *"Is Hawaii Ready for Universal Health Care?" in Hawaii Business (Vol. 53, February 2008, No. 8, pp. 26)*
Pub: Hawaii Business Publishing
Description: Representative Lyn Finnegan does not believe that a universal health is good for Hawaii as health insurance for everyone will be difficult to achieve. Representative John M. Mizuno says that

House Bill 1008 introduced in the state was a landmark for Hawaii as it will provide the people with health care insurance. Other details about their opinion on the topic are presented.

36181 ■ *"Is There a Doctor In the House?" in Black Enterprise (Vol. 41, December 2010, No. 5, pp. 42)*
Pub: Earl G. Graves Publishing Co. Inc.

Ed: Renita Burns. **Description:** Health insurance premiums have increased between 15 percent and 20 percent for small business owners, making it one of the most expensive costs. Ways to evaluate a health plan's costs and effectiveness are examined.

36182 ■ *"The Keeper of Records" in Black Enterprise (Vol. 41, December 2010, No. 5, pp. 54)*
Pub: Earl G. Graves Publishing Co. Inc.

Ed: Denise Campbell. **Description:** Medical billing and coding, submission of claims to health insurance companies and Medicare or Medicaid for payment is one of the fastest growing disciplines in healthcare.

36183 ■ *King of Capital*
Pub: John Wiley and Sons, Inc.

Ed: Amey Stone; Mike Brewster. **Released:** 2004. **Price:** $16.95. **Description:** Biography of Sandy Weill describes how he became a billionaire business giant by creating successful companies from smaller, sometimes failing firms; creating successful new products where none previously existed; and making deals no one thought possible. He is also responsible for changing the landscape of the banking industry and insurance business when he created Citigroup in 1998, the world's largest financial services firm.

36184 ■ *"Labor Pains" in Canadian Business (Vol. 79, August 14, 2006, No. 16-17, pp. 80)*
Pub: Rogers Media

Description: Canada's employment insurance is analyzed in view of the growing shortage of labor.

36185 ■ *"Law Allows Captive Insurance Companies to Form in State" in Crain's Detroit Business (Vol. 24, March 31, 2008, No. 13, pp. 29)*
Pub: Crain Communications, Inc.

Description: Discusses new legislation allowing the formation of captive insurance companies in the state of Michigan; these companies are subsidiaries of non-insurers that are formed primarily to insure some or all of the risks of its parent company.

36186 ■ *"Leave Policies: How to Avoid Leave-Related Lawsuits" in Employee Benefit News (Vol. 25, December 1, 2011, No. 15, pp. 12)*
Pub: SourceMedia Inc.

Ed: John F. Galvin. **Description:** Tips for employers when adding disability and maternity leave benefits to workers are outlined, with focus on ways to avoid leave-related lawsuits.

36187 ■ *"Lifetime Planning with a Twist" in Contractor (Vol. 56, July 2009, No. 7, pp. 40)*
Pub: Penton Media, Inc.

Ed: Irv Blackman. **Description:** Private Placement Life Insurance lets wealthy investors make their investment gains tax-free and can be set up so investors can make tax-free loans from the policy. This can be used on a younger member of the family as a wealth-building strategy if the investor is uninsurable.

36188 ■ *"Local Hospitals Wage Wars on 'Bounce-Backs" in Business Courier (Vol. 27, July 30, 2010, No. 13, pp. 1)*
Pub: Business Courier

Ed: James Ritchie. **Description:** Health care organizations in Greater Cincinnati area have tried a number of care and follow up programs, primarily focused on congestive heart failure to prevent readmissions to hospitals. Hospital administrators have made the averting of bounce-backs a priority due to new federal government plans on reimbursement.

36189 ■ *Managing Health Benefits in Small and Mid-Sized Organizations*
Pub: Amacom

Ed: Patricia Halo. **Released:** July 1999. **Description:** Comprehensive guide for developing health care plans for companies employing between 50 and 5,000 employees in order to provide employees with better health care at lower prices.

36190 ■ *"Manulife Posts Billion-Dollar Profit" in Globe & Mail (February 14, 2007, pp. B7)*
Pub: CTVglobemedia Publishing Inc.

Ed: Andrew Willis. **Description:** Manulife Financial Corp., Canada's largest insurer, reported $1.1 billion profit in the fourth quarter of 2006. The financial results of Manulife reflected a 39 percent rise in quarterly profit at the nation's wealth management division.

36191 ■ *"Markel American Insurance Company Announces Wedding and Special Event Insurance for Consumers" in Benzinga.com (February 16, 2011)*
Pub: Benzinga.com

Ed: Benzinga Staff. **Description:** Markel American Insurance Company, headquartered in Waukesha, Wisconsin has launched its new special event insurance and wedding insurance to protect both liabilities and cancellations associated with these events.

36192 ■ *"Maryland Hospitals Cope with Rare Drop in Patient Admissions" in Boston Business Journal (Vol. 29, September 23, 2011, No. 20, pp. 1)*
Pub: American City Business Journals Inc.

Ed: Scott Dance. **Description:** Admissions to Maryland hospitals have dropped to less than 700,000 in fiscal year 2010 and initial figures for fiscal 2011 show in-patient admissions are now nearing 660,000. The decline can be partly attributed to new ways health insurers are paying hospitals for care and to the financial reward hospitals get for cutting back on admissions.

36193 ■ *"The Massachusetts Mess: Good Health Care Is Expensive" in Barron's (Vol. 89, July 27, 2009, No. 30, pp. 39)*
Pub: Dow Jones & Co., Inc.

Ed: Thomas G. Donlan. **Description:** Massachusetts' mandatory health insurance has produced the highest rate of insurance coverage among the states but the state is now unable to afford its dream of universal coverage just three years after they enacted it. This supposed model for federal health-care reform is turning out to be a joke.

36194 ■ *"Meadowbrook CEO Sees 20 Percent Growth With New Acquisition" in Crain's Detroit Business (Vol. 24, March 10, 2008, No. 10, pp. 4)*
Pub: Crain Communications, Inc.

Ed: Jay Greene. **Description:** Discusses the major turnaround of Meadowbrook Insurance Group after Robert Cubbin became CEO and implemented a new business strategy.

36195 ■ *"Meadowbrook To Acquire ProCentury in $272.6 Million Deal" in Crain's Detroit Business (Vol. 24, February 25, 2008, No. 8, pp. 4)*
Pub: Crain Communications Inc. - Detroit

Description: Meadowbrook Insurance Group, based in Southfield, Michigan reports its proposed acquisition of ProCentury Corporation based in Columbus, Ohio. Meadowbrook provides risk-management to agencies, professional and trade associations and small-to-midsize businesses.

36196 ■ *"Medicaid Insurers See Growth in Small Business Market" in Boston Business Journal (Vol. 31, July 15, 2011, No. 25, pp. 1)*
Pub: Boston Business Journal

Ed: Julie M. Donnelly. **Description:** BMC HealthNet Plan announced plans to launch small business products to serve small businesses that are priced out of rising premium rates at large Massachusetts insurers. BMC joined competitors CeltiCare Health Plan and Neighborhood Health Plan in augmenting its core business.

36197 ■ *"Medicare Plans Step Up Battle for Subscribers" in Sacramento Business Journal (Vol. 28, October 21, 2011, No. 34, pp. 1)*
Pub: Sacramento Business Journal

Ed: Kathy Robertson. **Description:** California's market for health plans have become increasingly competitive as more than 313,000 seniors try to figure out the best plans to meet their needs for 2012. Health plans are rated on Medicare materials to help consumers distinguish among the Medicare health maintenance organizations (HMOs).

36198 ■ *"The Moody Blues" in Entrepreneur (Vol. 36, April 2008, No. 4, pp. 87)*
Pub: Entrepreneur Media, Inc.

Ed: Mark Henricks. **Description:** Depression among employees can affect their productivity and cost the company. Businesses with a workforce that is likely to have depression should inform their employees about the health benefits covered by insurance. Other details on how to address depression concerns among employees are discussed.

36199 ■ *"More Businesses Will Shift Health Costs to Workers" in Business Review, Albany New York (Vol. 34, November 16, 2007, No. 33, pp. 1)*
Pub: American City Business Journals, Inc.

Ed: Barbara Pinckney. **Description:** Survey conducted by consulting firm Benetech Inc. showed that sixty percent of employers are planning to increase payroll deductions to pay for health insurance premiums. More than ninety percent of the employers prefer HMO plans, followed by Preferred Provider Organizations. Other details of the survey are discussed.

36200 ■ *"More Small Businesses Willing to Fund Employees' Benefits" in Baltimore Business Journal (Vol. 28, June 18, 2010, No. 6, pp. 1)*
Pub: Baltimore Business Journal

Ed: Scott Graham. **Description:** An increasing number of small businesses in Maryland are tapping into potentially cheaper self-funded health plans instead of providing fully insured benefits to employees through traditional health plans. Self-funded health plans charge employers for health care up to a specified level. Economic implications of self-funded plans to small businesses are discussed.

36201 ■ *"Most States Have High-Risk Health Insurance Pools" in Crain's Detroit Business (Vol. 24, March 24, 2008, No. 12, pp. 31)*
Pub: Crain Communications, Inc.

Ed: Jay Greene. **Description:** High-risk health insurance pools, designed to cover individuals with medical conditions that essentially make them otherwise uninsurable, are being debated by the Senate Health Policy Committee; the pool concept is supported by Blue Cross Blue Shield of Michigan and contested by a number of consumer groups and competing health insurers.

36202 ■ *"Nationwide Bank Ready for December Conversion" in Business First-Columbus (October 12, 2007, pp. A1)*
Pub: American City Business Journals, Inc.

Ed: Adrian Burns. **Description:** Nationwide Bank will increase marketing to its customers, including the 45,000 that came from the acquisition of Nationwide Federal Credit Union in December 2006. Upgrading its online banking system and Website will bring the company and its services closer to clients. The influence of the insurance industry on the bank's marketing strategy is also examined.

36203 ■ *"New Database Brings Doctors Out of the Dark" in Business Courier (Vol. 26, October 23, 2009, No. 26, pp. 1)*
Pub: American City Business Journals, Inc.

Ed: James Ritchie. **Description:** A database created by managed care consulting firm Praesentia allows doctors in Cincinnati to compare average reimbursements from health insurance companies to doctors in different areas. Specialist doctors in the city are paid an average of $172.25 for every office consultation.

36204 ■ *"New Health Law, Lack of Docs Collide on Cape Cod" in Boston Business Journal (Vol. 27, October 12, 2007, No. 37, pp. 1)*
Pub: American City Business Journals Inc.
Ed: Mark Hollmer. **Description:** There is a shortage of primary care providers at Outer Cape Health Services in Massachusetts, with the isolation of the area and as physicians look for higher paying careers in specialty positions. The Commonwealth Health Insurance Connector Authority is pushing for a new health insurance law and is working with Cape Cod Chamber of Commerce to conduct outreach programs.

36205 ■ *"Nixon Assails Insurance Rules" in Globe & Mail (March 4, 2006, pp. B5)*
Pub: CTVglobemedia Publishing Inc.
Ed: Sinclair Stewart. **Description:** The opinions of chief executive officer Gordon Nixon of Royal Bank of Canada on the need to amend banking regulations, in order to provide insurance services, are presented.

36206 ■ *"North American Pet Health Insurance Market Poised for Growth" in Pet Product News (Vol. 64, December 2010, No. 12, pp. 4)*
Pub: BowTie Inc.
Ed: David Lummis. **Description:** The pet health insurance market is expected to further grow after posting about $350 million in sales in 2009, a gain of more than $40 million. Pet insurance firms have offered strategies such as product humanization in response to this growth forecast. Meanwhile, pet insurance shoppers have been provided more by insurance firms with wider choices.

36207 ■ *"Norvax University Health Insurance Sales Training and Online Marketing Conference" in Internet Wire (January 27, 2010)*
Pub: Comtex News Network, Inc.
Description: Overview of the Norvax University Marketing and Sales Success Conference Tour which includes insurance sales training seminars, proven and innovative online marketing techniques and a host of additional information and networking opportunities.

36208 ■ *"Now the Real Work Begins" in Baltimore Business Journal (Vol. 28, October 15, 2010, No. 23, pp. 1)*
Pub: Baltimore Business Journal
Ed: Emily Mullin. **Description:** The Henry J. Kaiser Family Foundation's survey shows nearly 53 percent of Americans remain confused about health care reform and it was up to the states to educate the people. However, Maryland is still trying to figure out how to conduct the campaign without guidance or funding from the Federal government.

36209 ■ *"Open Enrollment: Staying Healthy During Enrollment Season" in Employee Benefit News (Vol. 25, November 1, 2011, No. 14, pp. 41)*
Pub: SourceMedia Inc.
Ed: Shana Sweeney. **Description:** Tips for staying healthy during your benefit open enrollment period are outlined.

36210 ■ *"Passing It On: Using Life Insurance as an Estate Planning Tool" in Inc. (October 2007, pp. 47-49)*
Pub: Gruner & Jahr USA Publishing
Ed: Elaine Appleton Grant. **Description:** Permanent life insurance policies can be used to cover estate taxes for heirs inheriting large estates, while allowing them time to sell any small business. Six tips are included to assist in choosing the right policy.

36211 ■ *"Patients to Elect to Cut Care" in The Business Journal-Serving Metropolitan Kansas City (Vol. 27, November 21, 2008, No. 11, pp. 1)*
Pub: American City Business Journals, Inc.
Ed: Rob Roberts. **Description:** Patients in Kansas City, Missouri are cutting down on health care services due to the economic crisis. A decline in diagnostic procedures has been observed at Northland Cardiology. Elective reconstructive procedures have also been reduced by 25 percent. Additional information and statistics regarding the healthcare sector is included.

36212 ■ *"Patricia Hemingway Hall; President, Chief Operating Officer, Health Care Service Corp." in Crain's Chicago Business (May 5, 2008)*
Pub: Crain Communications, Inc.
Ed: Mike Colias. **Description:** Profile of Patricia Hemingway Hall who is the president and chief operating officer of Health Care Service Corp., a new strategy launched by Blue Cross & Blue Shield of Illinois; the new endeavor will emphasize wellness rather than just treatment across its four health plans.

36213 ■ *"PCH Gets Trauma Center Status" in The Business Journal - Serving Phoenix and the Valley of the Sun (Vol. 28, July 11, 2008, No. 45)*
Pub: American City Business Journals, Inc.
Ed: Angela Gonzales. **Description:** Phoenix Children's Hospital has been allowed by the Arizona Department of Health Services to launch the state's first trauma center for children. The trauma center is expected to cost the hospital $7 million a year.

36214 ■ *"The People Puzzle; Re-Training America's Workers" in The Economist (Vol. 390, January 3, 2009, No. 8612, pp. 32)*
Pub: The Economist Newspaper Inc.
Description: With thousands of workers losing their jobs, America is now facing the task of getting them back to work. With an overall unemployment rate of 6.7 percent, the federal government has three main ways for leading workers back to employment: training them for new jobs, providing unemployment insurance in order to replace lost wages during the period of job-hunting; and matching employers who desire a skill with workers who have that skill. Specialized staffing agencies provide employers and potential employees with the help necessary to find a job in some of the more niche markets.

36215 ■ *"Planning a Wedding Fit for a Royal? Read This First, Urge Legal and General" in Benzinga.com (April 21, 2011)*
Pub: Benzinga.com
Ed: Benzinga Staff. **Description:** When planning a wedding, the author suggests checking life insurance to be sure you are covered for any situations that may arise.

36216 ■ *"Prescription for Health: Choosing the Best Healthcare Plan" in Black Enterprise (Vol. 38, July 2008, No. 12, pp. 48)*
Pub: Earl G. Graves Publishing Co. Inc.
Ed: Tamara E. Holmes. **Description:** According to a survey of small-business owners conducted by SurePayroll Inc., 20 percent of respondents have had a prospective employee refuse a job offer because healthcare benefits did not come with it. Cost is not the only reason many small-business owners do not offer these benefits. Guidelines to help take some of the confusion out of the guesswork that comes with trying to find the proper fit concerning healthcare benefits are outlined.

36217 ■ *"The Price of Citizenship" in Canadian Business (Vol. 79, August 14, 2006, No. 16-17, pp. 13)*
Pub: Rogers Media
Ed: Jack Mintz. **Description:** Safety and insurance benefits provided by the Canadian government to Canadian passport holders returning from Lebanon, is discussed.

36218 ■ *"Public Health Care Funding and the Montana Economy" in Montana Business Quarterly (Vol. 49, Spring 2011, No. 1, pp. 23)*
Pub: Bureau of Business & Economic Research
Ed: Gregg Davis. **Description:** Montana has more baby boomers and veterans per capita than any other state in the nation. The role of public health in the state is a crucial part of the state's economy.

36219 ■ *"Recovery on Tap for 2010?" in Orlando Business Journal (Vol. 26, January 1, 2010, No. 31, pp. 1)*
Pub: American City Business Journals
Ed: Melanie Stawicki Azam, Richard Bilbao, Christopher Boyd, Anjali Fluker. **Description:** Economic forecasts for Central Florida's leading business sectors in 2010 are presented. These sectors include housing, film and TV, sports business, law, restaurants, aviation, tourism and hospitality, banking and finance, commercial real estate, retail, health care, insurance, higher education, and manufacturing. According to some local executives, Central Florida's economy will slowly recover in 2010.

36220 ■ *"Rich or Poor, Hospitals Must Work Together" in Crain's Chicago Business (Vol. 31, April 28, 2008, No. 17, pp. 22)*
Pub: Crain Communications, Inc.
Description: Chicago=area safety-net hospitals that serve the poor, uninsured and underinsured are struggling to stay open while wealthier areas compete to build advanced facilities for the expensive surgical procedures their privately insured patients can afford. If these safety-net hospitals close, their patients, many of them in ambulances, will show up at the remaining hospitals resulting in a strain that will test the ability of hospitals across the region to care for all of their patients. Hospitals need to address the threats to the local health care system before it slips into crisis since the current every-hospital-for-itself approach that pays off big for some will eventually will make losers of everyone.

36221 ■ *"RPA Preps for Building Radiant Conference, Show" in Contractor (Vol. 57, January 2010, No. 1, pp. 5)*
Pub: Penton Media, Inc.
Description: Radiant Panel Association is accepting registrations for its Building Radiant 2010 Conference and Trade Show. The conference will discuss radiant heating as well as insurance and other legal matters for mechanical contractors.

36222 ■ *"A Safety Net in Need of Repair" in The Economist (Vol. 390, January 3, 2009, No. 8612, pp. 33)*
Pub: The Economist Newspaper Inc.
Description: America's unemployment-insurance scheme is outdated and skimpy compared to other industrialized countries despite the fact that Americans tend to work harder at returning to the job market; the benefits are lower and available for a smaller amount of time and less unemployed workers are even able to collect these benefits. Statistical data included.

36223 ■ *"Sluggish Market Gives Hospitals the Financial Chills" in The Business Journal-Serving Greater Tampa Bay (Vol. 28, August 1, 2008)*
Pub: American City Business Journals, Inc.
Ed: Margie Manning. **Description:** Operating margins for hospitals in the Tampa Bay, Florida area have been reduced from 2 percent in 2006 to 0.8 percent in 2007 due to a weaker US economy. Total margins, on the other hand, rose from 2.9 percent to 3.3 percent in the same period.

36224 ■ *"Small Biz Owners Are Tapping Into Health Savings Plans" in Small Business Opportunities (Fall 2007)*
Pub: Harris Publications Inc.
Ed: Michael L. Corne. **Description:** Health savings accounts were developed by Golden Rule, a United Healthcare company. Today, more than 40 percent of the company's customers are covered by health savings account plans.

36225 ■ *Small Business Access and Alternatives to Health Care: Congressional Hearing*
Pub: DIANE Publishing Company
Ed: Donald A. Manzullo. **Released:** July 2006. **Price:** $35.00. **Description:** Congressional hearings regarding the health care crisis facing America's small businesses is discussed.

36226 ■ *Small Business Desk Reference*
Pub: Penguin Books USA Inc.
Ed: Gene Marks. **Released:** December 2004. **Description:** Comprehensive guide for starting or running a successful small business, focusing on buying a business or franchise, writing a business plan, financial management, accounting, legal issues, human resources management, operations, marketing, sales, customer service, taxes, insurance, and ethics. Information for launching a restaurant, property management firm, retail outlet, consulting firm, and service business is included.

36227 ■ *"Small Businesses Changing Their Health Plan Preferences" in Boston Business Journal (Vol. 29, June 24, 2011, No. 7, pp. 1)*
Pub: American City Business Journals Inc.
Ed: Scott Dance. **Description:** Small businesses in Maryland are shifting from traditional health plans to the consumer-oriented health savings accounts or HSAs. Health insurance industry experts say the change is indicative of the insurance buyers' desire to be more thrifty and discerning in their health care purchases.

36228 ■ *"Small, But Mighty" in Employee Benefit News (Vol. 25, November 1, 2011, No. 14, pp. 32)*
Pub: SourceMedia Inc.
Ed: Andrea Davis. **Description:** Three consulting firms are facing the challenge of helping clients understand the new health care reform in a tight economy.

36229 ■ *"The Smell of Fear: Is a Bottom Near?" in Barron's (Vol. 88, March 17, 2008, No. 11, pp. M3)*
Pub: Dow Jones & Company, Inc.
Ed: Kopin Tan. **Description:** Liquidity problems at Bear Stearns frightened investors in markets around the world due to the fear of the prospects of a big bank's failure. Shares of health maintenance organizations got battered led by WellPoint, and Humana but longer-term investors who could weather short-term volatility may find value here. The value of J. Crew shares is also discussed.

36230 ■ *Starting and Running Your Own Horse Business*
Pub: Storey Publishing, LLC
Ed: Mary Ashby McDonald. **Released:** November 1, 2009. **Price:** $19.95. **Description:** Insight into starting and running a successful equestrian business is given. The book covers safety, tips for operating a riding school or horse camp, strategies for launching a carriage business, along with tax and insurance advice.

36231 ■ *"Steeling for Battle" in Crain's Chicago Business (Vol. 31, April 21, 2008, No. 16, pp. 3)*
Pub: Crain Communications, Inc.
Ed: Bob Tita. **Description:** Discusses contract negotiations between the United Steelworkers union and ArcelorMittal USA Inc., the nation's largest steelmaker, and U.S. Steel Corp., the third-largest; the union sees these negotiations as the best chance in two decades to regain lost ground but industry experts predict the companies will try to reduce benefits, demand a separate, lower wage scale for new hires and look for relief from the rising costs for retirees' health insurance coverage.

36232 ■ *"Struggling States Slashing Health Care For Poor" in Chicago Tribune (January 15, 2009)*
Pub: McClatchy-Tribune Information Services
Ed: Noam N. Levey. **Description:** Health officials warn that even the huge federal rescue plan may not be enough to restore health services being eliminated due to the economic crisis.

36233 ■ *"Survivorship Policies: Planning a Policy for Two" in Employee Benefit News (Vol. 25, November 1, 2011, No. 14, pp. 20)*
Pub: SourceMedia Inc.
Ed: Marli D. Riggs. **Description:** Survivorship insurance is becoming an added benefit high net worth individuals and executives should consider when evaluating life insurance policies.

36234 ■ *"Sutter, CHW Reject Blue Cross Deal" in Sacramento Business Journal (Vol. 25, August 15, 2008, No. 24, pp. 1)*
Pub: American City Business Journals, Inc.
Ed: Kathy Robertson. **Description:** California-based Sutter Health and Catholic Healthcare West have rejected the $11.8 million class action settlement in connection with contract rescissions between California hospitals and Anthem Blue Cross. Blue Cross can halt the settlement if not enough hospitals accept it. The deal covers all hospitals that owe money due to rescinded Blue Cross coverage.

36235 ■ *"Symbility Solutions Joins Motion Computing Partner Program" in Canadian Corporate News (May 14, 2007)*
Pub: Comtex News Network Inc.
Description: Symbility Solutions Inc., a wholly owned subsidiary of Automated Benefits Corp., announced an agreement with Alliance Partner of Motion Computing, a leader in wireless communications and mobile computing, in which both companies will invest in a sales and marketing strategy that focuses specifically on the insurance market.

36236 ■ *"Taking Full Advantage: What You Need To Know During Open-Enrollment Season" in Black Enterprise (Vol. 38, November 2007, No. 4)*
Pub: Earl G. Graves Publishing Co. Inc.
Ed: Donald Jay Korn. **Description:** Employees can change or enroll in new insurance benefits during the fall season. It is important to assess each plan offered and to determine your deductible. Statistical data included.

36237 ■ *"Tenacious Trailblazer" in Hispanic Business (Vol. 30, April 2008, No. 4, pp. 26)*
Pub: Hispanic Business
Ed: Melinda Burns. **Description:** Dr. Sandra Hernandez has been named as Hispanic Business Woman of the Year for her pioneering work in health care reform. Dr. Hernandez is the first Hispanic and the first woman to serve as public health director for the city and county of San Francisco.

36238 ■ *"Thousands Balk at Health Law Sign-Up Mandate" in Boston Business Journal (Vol. 27, November 9, 2007, No. 41, pp. 1)*
Pub: American City Business Journals Inc.
Ed: Mark Hollmer. **Description:** About 100,000 Massachusetts residents have not signed up for insurance plans created as part of the state's health care reform law. Insurers have underestimated the number of new customers signing up for insurance and come close to risking penalties if they do not get insurance by the end of 2007. The Commonwealth Health Insurance Connector Authority's deadline to buy insurance before penalties kick in is November 15, 2007.

36239 ■ *"Top 50 In Total Revenue" in Canadian Business (Vol. 81, Summer 2008, No. 9, pp. 119)*
Pub: Rogers Media Ltd.
Description: Table showing the top 50 Canadian companies in terms of total revenue is presented. Manulife Financial Corp. topped the list with revenue of 34.5 billion. The financial services firm is the 6th largest provider of life insurance in the world and the second largest in North America.

36240 ■ *"United Insurance To Grow St. Pete's Corporate Base" in The Business Journal-Serving Greater Tampa Bay (August 29, 2008)*
Pub: American City Business Journals, Inc.
Ed: Margie Manning. **Description:** United Insurance Holdings LC is on its way to becoming a public company by agreeing in a reverse merger with FMG Acquisition Corp. The $104.3 million agreement will provide the company's St. Petersburg operations the opportunity to grow. The other impacts of the proposed reverse merger are examined.

36241 ■ *"UnitedHealthcare Resists Prognosis" in The Business Journal-Serving Metropolitan Kansas City (Vol. 26, August 29, 2008, No. 51)*
Pub: American City Business Journals, Inc.
Ed: Rob Roberts. **Description:** Saint Luke's Hospital Systems terminated UnitedHealthcare from its insurance provider network on July 25, 2008. Negotiators with both parties have stopped speaking, and employees under UnitedHealthcare plans will have to pay higher bills unless Saint Luke's reconsiders its decision. The parties' previous negotiations are discussed.

36242 ■ *"VPA to Pay $9.5 Million to Settle Whistle-Blower Lawsuits" in Crain's Detroit Business (Vol. 26, January 11, 2010, No. 2, pp. 13)*
Pub: Crain Communications Inc.
Ed: Jay Greene. **Description:** According to Terrence Berg, first assistant with the U.S. Attorney's Office in Detroit, Voluntary Physicians Association, a local home health care company, has agreed to pay $9.5 million to settle four whistle-blower lawsuits; the agreement settles allegations that VPA submitted claims to TriCare, the Michigan Medicaid program and Medicare for unnecessary home visits, tests and procedures.

36243 ■ *"W&S to Trim Rich Retirement Plan" in Business Courier (Vol. 27, October 15, 2010, No. 24, pp. 1)*
Pub: Business Courier
Ed: Dan Monk. **Description:** Insurance firm Western & Southern Financial Group announced that it will reduce the pension benefits of its 4,000 associates by more than 30 percent starting January 1, 2011. The move is expected to reduce annual retirement payments by several thousand dollars per associate. Western is a Fortune 500 company and has $34 billion in total assets.

36244 ■ *"We Have a Budget, Too" in Entrepreneur (Vol. 37, October 2009, No. 10, pp. 89)*
Pub: Entrepreneur Media, Inc.
Ed: Craig Matsuda. **Description:** One human resources executive at a financial services company claims that health care issues are as costly and irritating for companies as they are for the employees. Health care vendors and insurers try as much as possible to maximize profits, while companies exert much effort to maximize benefits for their workers.

36245 ■ *"Week on the Web" in Crain's Detroit Business (Vol. 25, June 22, 2009, No. 25, pp. 19)*
Pub: Crain Communications Inc. - Detroit
Description: Blue Cross Blue Shield of Michigan, in a class-action lawsuit, will pay about 100 families whose children were either denied coverage for autism treatment or paid for treatment out of pocket. The settlement is worth about $ million.

36246 ■ *"What Choice Did I Have?" in Entrepreneur (Vol. 37, October 2009, No. 10, pp. 88)*
Pub: Entrepreneur Media, Inc.
Ed: Craig Matsuda. **Description:** Profile of a worker at a financial services company who acquired first hand knowledge concerning the relationship between health insurance costs and coverage. The worker's son got severely ill, forcing the worker to spend above what is covered by health insurance.

36247 ■ *"Work At It!" in Hawaii Business (Vol. 53, October 2007, No. 4, pp. 44)*
Pub: Hawaii Business Publishing
Ed: Cathy S. Cruz-George. **Description:** Employers in Hawaii are mitigating the effects of rising health-care costs by giving their employees health insurance and offering wellness programs. Employer-based health insurance has increases by 87 percent in the United States over the 2000-2006 period. Wellness programs that address different aspects of employees' health, such as food consumption, drug compliance and smoking habits, are discussed.

36248 ■ *"The Worst-Run Industry in Canada: Health Care" in Canadian Business (Vol. 83, October 12, 2010, No. 17, pp. 39)*
Pub: Rogers Media Ltd.
Ed: Rachel Mendleson. **Description:** Most Canadians believe that the problem of the country's health care system is rooted in insufficient funding, demo-

graphic overload, or corporate profiteering. However, health economists and policy analysts think the real issues is mismanagement, as the pervasive inefficiency is affecting the system's structure.

36249 ■ *"Year-End Tax Tips" in Hawaii Business (Vol. 53, December 2007, No. 6, pp. 136)*
Pub: Hawaii Business Publishing
Ed: Kathleen Bryan. **Description:** Tax planning tips for the end of 2007, in relation to the tax breaks that are scheduled to expire, are presented. Among the tax breaks that will be expiring at the 2007 year-end are sales tax deduction in the state and local level, premiums on mortgage insurance, and deduction on tuition. The impacts of these changes are discussed.

36250 ■ *"Young Adults Choose to go Without Health Insurance" in Business Review, Albany New York (Vol. 34, November 30, 2007, No. 35, pp. 1)*
Pub: American City Business Journals, Inc.
Ed: Barbara Pinckney. **Description:** U.S. Census Bureau revealed that in 2006, 19 million people between the ages of 18 and 34 were without health insurance, or 40 percent of the uninsured individuals in the country. College graduation usually means the end of health coverage, since most fresh graduates opt to not get any health insurance plan. Solutions to this growing issue are also addressed.

TRADE PERIODICALS

36251 ■ *The John Liner Letter*
Pub: Standard Publishing Corp.
Contact: John Cross, President
Ed: Robert Montgomery, Editor. **Released:** Monthly. **Price:** $262, U.S.; $340.60, elsewhere. **Description:** Provides risk management and technical insurance advice for business firms, such as broadening coverage, cutting costs, and anticipating special insurance problems.

36252 ■ *Risk & Insurance Magazine*
Pub: LRP Publications
Contact: Kenneth Kahn, President
E-mail: kKahn@lrp.com
Ed: Cyril Tuohy, Managing Editor. **Released:** Monthly and semi-monthly in April, September and October. **Description:** Provides business executives and insurance professionals with the insight, information and strategies they need to mitigate challenging business risks. Discusses a wide variety of business risks and mitigation strategies from insurance, employee benefits and alternative risk transfer to emerging risks and the strategies for addressing them.

36253 ■ *Unemployment Insurance Reports with Social Security*
Pub: CCH Inc.
Contact: Mike Sabbatis, President
Released: Monthly. **Price:** $4,849, individuals CD-ROM. **Description:** Issues of CCH's Unemployment Insurance Reports with Social Security provide timely information on social security and federal/state unemployment insurance taxes, coverage, and benefits. Pertinent federal and state laws are reported promptly and reflected in place in the explanatory guides, as are regulations, judicial and administrative decisions, rulings, releases, and forms. Explanatory guides include examples showing how rules apply and offer practical information regarding the tax management, coverage, and benefit aspects of the social security and unemployment insurance systems. Each issue starts off with an informative Report Letter summarizing recent developments in these areas.

VIDEOCASSETTES/ AUDIOCASSETTES

36254 ■ *Going Bare: Crisis in Insurance*
New Jersey Network (NJN)
25 S Stockton St.
Trenton, NJ 08625-0777
Ph: (609)777-5273
Free: 800-792-8645
Fax: (609)643-4004
Co. E-mail: productioncenter@njn.org
URL: http://www.njn.net
Contact: Janice Selinger, Director
Released: 1988. **Description:** Examines the history of the insurance industry, price wars between insurance companies, and small businesses who are without liability insurance because of extremely high premiums. **Availability:** VHS; 3/4 U.

CONSULTANTS

36255 ■ A.E. Roberts Co.
11490 Xeon St. NW, Ste. 200
Coon Rapids, MN 55448-3111
Ph: (763)757-5119
Free: 800-486-4585
Fax: (413)215-6877
Scope: Specializes in compliance training, focusing on regulatory compliance and human resource management issues. **Founded:** 1989. **Seminars:** ADA Seminar; COBRA Seminar; FMLA Seminar; HIPAA Privacy Seminar; HIPAA Portability Seminar; Section 125 Cafeteria Plans Seminar.

36256 ■ Leonard R. Friedman Risk Management Inc. (LRF/RM)
170 Great Neck Rd., Ste. 140
Great Neck, NY 11021-3337
Ph: (516)466-0750
Fax: (516)466-0997
Co. E-mail: info@lrfrm.com
URL: http://www.lrfrm.com
Contact: Rachel L. Efrati, Vice President
E-mail: refrati@lrfrm.com
Scope: Provider of risk and insurance management and safety and claims managements services to corporations across the country. Analyzes exposure to loss, audits insurance contracts, structures competitive bidding, reviews contracts and leases, implements and monitors safety and claims management programs and recommends risk transfer programs to reduce exposure to loss. Industries served: profit and nonprofit companies engaged in retail, manufacturing, distributing, hospitality, real estate and service. **Founded:** 1974.

36257 ■ Health Insurance Specialists Inc. (HISI)
17620-B Redland Rd.
Rockville, MD 20855
Ph: (301)590-0006
Fax: (301)590-0661
Co. E-mail: info@his-inc.com
URL: http://www.his-inc.com
Contact: Jon S. Belinkie, President
E-mail: jbelinkie@his-inc.com
Scope: Serves a wide variety of businesses and individuals by designing comprehensive insurance packages and benefit plans, full service insurance and financial services firm, third party administration, human resources outsourcing. **Founded:** 1982.

36258 ■ Siver Insurance Consultants—E W Siver & Associates Inc.
805 Executive Center Dr. W, Ste. 110
Saint Petersburg, FL 33702
Ph: (727)577-2780
Fax: (727)579-8692
Co. E-mail: gerickson@siver.com
URL: http://www.siver.com
Contact: George W. Erickson, President
E-mail: gerickson@siver.com
Scope: Provider of advice and counsel (no sales) on matters involving insurance, including property, casualty, life, disability, health and title insurance plus risk management, employee welfare benefits and managed care. **Founded:** 1970. **Seminars:** Third Party Administrators Performance Audit: Self Funded Group Medical Programs; Self Funded Workers Compensation Programs.

36259 ■ United Insurance Consultants Inc.—UIC Inc.
1 Park Way, 3rd Fl.
Upper Saddle River, NJ 07458
Ph: (201)661-5010
Fax: (201)221-7529
Co. E-mail: info@uici.com
URL: http://www.uici.com
Contact: Thomas A. Kovatch, President
Scope: An independent insurance consulting firm that informs and educates clients of the importance of properly protecting the value of their business. Helps companies understand their insurance contracts, costs involved in properly protecting their assets and liability exposures. **Founded:** 1978.

FRANCHISES AND BUSINESS OPPORTUNITIES

36260 ■ Paul Davis Restoration
One Independent Dr., Ste. 2300
Jacksonville, FL 32202
Ph: (800)722-5066
Fax: (904)899-6217
URL: http://www.pdrestoration.com
Description: Computerized contracting and cleaning services to the insurance industry. **No. of Franchise Units:** 230. **Founded:** 1966.. **Franchised:** 1971. **Equity Capital Needed:** $45,000-$144,000 emergency service; $180,000-$240,000 restoration. **Franchise Fee:** $29,000 or $75,000. **Financial Assistance:** Yes. **Training:** 4 week training at corporate headquarters, followed by 1 week of onsite training at new franchise location.

36261 ■ Paul's Professional Window Washing Franchise Inc.
Paul's Prof. Window Washing Inc.
2707 Foothill Blvd.
La Cresenta, CA 91214
Ph: (818)249-7917
Fax: (818)249-7806
Description: Residential window cleaning company. **No. of Company-Owned Units:** 1. **Founded:** 1981.. **Franchised:** 2004. **Equity Capital Needed:** $42,500-$76,000 initial investment. **Franchise Fee:** $17,500. **Training:** Yes.

36262 ■ Puroclean - The Paramedics of Property Damage
PuroSystems, Inc.
6001 Hiatus Rd., Ste. 13
Tamarac, FL 33321
Free: 800-775-PURO
Fax: (800)995-8527
Co. E-mail: sales@puroclean.com
URL: http://www.purocleanopportunity.com
Description: Property damage restoration. **No. of Franchise Units:** 275. **Founded:** 1989.. **Franchised:** 1990. **Equity Capital Needed:** $74,710-$99,825. **Franchise Fee:** $45,000. **Financial Assistance:** Yes. **Training:** Provides 3 weeks at corporate training center & 1 week field training covering customer service, marketing/advertising, computer software, product knowledge, management, & hands-on application with ongoing 24 hour support.

COMPUTERIZED DATABASES

36263 ■ *Business Insurance*
1155 Gratiot Ave.
Detroit, MI 48207
Ph: (313)446-6000
Free: 800-678-2427
Fax: (313)446-1616
Co. E-mail: info@crain.com
URL: http://www.crain.com
Availability: Online: ProQuest LLC - Dialog; LexisNexis Group; Crain Communications Inc. **Type:** Full-text.

LIBRARIES

36264 ■ Anderson, Kill & Olick - Library
1717 Pennsylvania Ave. NW, Ste. 200
Washington, DC 20006
Ph: (202)416-6500

Fax: (202)416-6555
Co. E-mail: akodc@andersonkill.com
URL: http://www.andersonkill.com
Scope: Insurance - property, fire, medical disability, casualty; law - civil, insurance. **Services:** Interlibrary loan; library not open to the public. **Holdings:** Books and periodicals. **Subscriptions:** 15 journals and other serials; 4 newspapers.

36265 ■ Buffalo & Erie County Public Library - Business, Science & Technology
1 Lafayette Sq.
Buffalo, NY 14203
Ph: (716)858-8900
Fax: (716)858-6211
URL: http://www.buffalolib.org
Contact: Nancy Mueller, Division Manager
Scope: Investments, real estate, economics, marketing, engineering, computer science, technology, medical information for laymen, consumer information, automotive repair. **Services:** Interlibrary loan; copying; library open to the public. **Founded:** 1952. **Holdings:** 312,916 books; 60,516 bound periodical volumes; 600 periodical. **Subscriptions:** 2908 journals and other serials; 4 newspapers.

36266 ■ Long & Levit Library
465 California St., 5th Fl.
San Francisco, CA 94104
Ph: (415)397-2222
Fax: (415)397-6392
Co. E-mail: info@longlevit.com
URL: http://www.longlevit.com
Scope: Insurance, environmental, professional liability, construction. **Services:** Interlibrary loan; copying; library open to the public at librarian's discretion. **Founded:** 1927. **Holdings:** 10,000 books. **Subscriptions:** 75 journals and other serials; 4 newspapers.

36267 ■ National Association of Professional Insurance Agents Library
400 N. Washington St.
Alexandria, VA 22314
Ph: (703)836-9340
Fax: (703)836-1279
Co. E-mail: patbo@pianet.org
URL: http://www.pianet.com
Contact: Patricia A. Barowski, Senior Vice President
Scope: Anti-Semitism, insurance, insurance law. **Services:** Library not open to the public. **Holdings:** 1400 volumes; CD-ROMs.

International Trade

START-UP INFORMATION

36268 ■ *Canadian Small Business Kit for Dummies*
Pub: CDG Books Canada, Incorporated
Ed: Margaret Kerr, JoAnn Kurtz. **Released:** March 2007. **Price:** $37.99 (Canadian). **Description:** Entrepreneurial guide to starting and running a small business in Canada.

36269 ■ *The Canadian Small Business Survival Guide: How to Start and Operate Your Own Successful Business*
Pub: Dundurn Group
Ed: Benj Gallander. FRQ June 2002. **Price:** $26.99. **Description:** Ideas for starting and running a successful small business. Topics include selecting a business, financing, government assistance, locations, franchises, and marketing ideas.

36270 ■ *International Entrepreneurship: Starting, Developing, and Managing a Global Venture*
Pub: SAGE Publications USA
Contact: Blaise R. Simqu, President
Ed: Robert D. Hisrich. **Released:** February 1, 2009. **Price:** $53.95. **Description:** International entrepreneurship combines the aspects of domestic entrepreneurship along with other disciplines, including anthropology, economics, geography, history, jurisprudence, and language.

36271 ■ *"Savvy Solutions" in Black Enterprise (Vol. 41, September 2010, No. 2, pp. 46)*
Pub: Earl G. Graves Publishing Co. Inc.
Ed: Tennille M. Robinson. **Description:** Insight is given to help start an import and export business.

ASSOCIATIONS AND OTHER ORGANIZATIONS

36272 ■ American Association of Exporters and Importers (AAEI)
1050 17th St. NW, Ste. 810
Washington, DC 20036
Ph: (202)857-8009
Fax: (202)857-7843
Co. E-mail: hq@aaei.org
URL: http://www.aaei.org
Contact: Steve Johnsen, Chairman
Description: Exporters and importers of goods, products, and raw materials; wholesalers and retailers; customs brokers and forwarders; banks; insurance underwriters; steamship companies; customs attorneys and others engaged directly or indirectly in dealing with exports and imports. Seeks fair and equitable conditions for world trade. Anticipates problems of interpretation of laws and regulations affecting members' businesses; gathers and disseminates data on world trade; supports and creates legislation promoting balanced international trade; works for fair administration of policy. Maintains liaison with government committees, agencies, and other trade policy groups. Testifies for exporters and importers before government and other official bodies. Studies problems concerning export and import; offers advice and support to members facing problems in their businesses; conducts forums and workshops on timely topics and developments; holds exporting and importing seminars. Operates extensive library of research information and government data, and records legal precedents. **Founded:** 1921. **Publications:** *International Trade Alert* (Weekly). **Awards:** Lifetime Achievement (Annual); Trade Warrior (Annual).

36273 ■ American Hellenic Institute (AHI)
1220 16th St. NW
Washington, DC 20036
Ph: (202)785-8430
Fax: (202)785-5178
Co. E-mail: nlarigakis@ahiworld.org
URL: http://www.ahiworld.org
Contact: Nick Larigakis, President
Description: Seeks to strengthen political, cultural, trade, commerce, and related matters between the U.S. and Greece, Cyprus, and the American Hellenic community. Conducts research on issues such as Turkish threats to the Aegean, Cyprus, the rule of law, and human rights. Sponsors internship program and seminars. **Founded:** 1974. **Publications:** *AHI Report* (3/year); *American Hellenic Who's Who*; *General News*; *Handbook on United States Relations with Greece and Cyprus*; *Rule of Law and Conditions on Foreign Aid to Turkey*. **Educational Activities:** Hellenic Heritage and National Public Service Awards Dinner (Annual).

36274 ■ American Indonesian Chamber of Commerce (AICC)
317 Madison Ave., Ste. 1619
New York, NY 10017
Ph: (212)687-4505
Fax: (212)867-5844
Co. E-mail: wayne@aiccusa.org
URL: http://www.aiccusa.org
Contact: Wayne Forrest, President
Description: Holds briefings on new trade policies in Indonesia and offers orientation workshops to company personnel traveling to Indonesia. **Founded:** 1949. **Publications:** *American Business Directory for Indonesia* (Periodic); *Executive Diary*; *Members Bulletin* (Periodic); *Outlook Indonesia* (Quarterly); *Sourcing Products in Indonesia: A Guide for Importers*. **Telecommunication Services:** aiccny@bigplanet.com.

36275 ■ American Israel Chamber of Commerce - Southeast Region (AICC)
400 Northridge Rd., Ste. 260
Atlanta, GA 30350
Ph: (404)843-9426
Fax: (404)843-1416
Co. E-mail: aiccse@aiccse.org
URL: http://www.aiccse.org
Contact: Tom Glaser, President
Description: American and Israeli companies. Promotes increased trade between Israel and the United States, with emphasis on increasing Israeli-American trade involving companies in the southeastern U.S. Facilitates networking and contact development involving Israeli and U.S. corporations; makes available trade mentoring and matchmaking services; sponsors educational programs. **Founded:** 1992. **Publications:** *Latest Southeast-Israel Business News* (Monthly).

36276 ■ American-Uzbekistan Chamber of Commerce (AUCC)
1300 Connecticut Ave. NW, Ste. 501
Washington, DC 20036
Ph: (202)223-1770
Co. E-mail: info@aucconline.com
URL: http://www.aucconline.com
Contact: Carolyn B. Lamm, Chairperson
Description: Brings together companies and individual professionals interested in promoting trade and investment between Uzbekistan and the United States. Represents business and industry to promote growth in interest of the U.S. business community in Uzbekistan. **Founded:** 1993. **Awards:** Statesmanship Award (Annual).

36277 ■ Australian Trade Commission (AUSTRADE)
150 E 42nd St., 34th Fl.
New York, NY 10017-5612
Ph: (646)344-8111
Fax: (212)867-7710
Co. E-mail: info@austrade.gov.au
URL: http://www.austrade.gov.au
Contact: Mr. Peter Grey, Chief Executive Officer
Description: Works in the promotion of Australian products and investments in the U.S. **Publications:** *Export Update* (Monthly).

36278 ■ Austrian Trade Commission (ATC)
120 W 45th St., 9th Fl.
New York, NY 10036
Ph: (212)421-5250
Fax: (212)421-5251
Co. E-mail: newyork@advantageaustria.org
URL: http://www.advantageaustria.org/us
Description: Promotes U.S.-Austrian trade with particular emphasis on Austrian exports to the U.S.; identifies Austrian trade sources to meet U.S. commercial demand. Handles inquiries related to trade between the two nations and deals with issues such as customs duties, trade laws, and licensing. Compiles statistics. Sponsors trade exhibits. **Founded:** 1950.

36279 ■ Austrian Trade Commissions in the United States (ATCUSC)
11601 Wilshire Blvd., Ste. 2420
Los Angeles, CA 90025
Ph: (310)477-9988
Fax: (310)477-1643
Co. E-mail: losangeles@advantageaustria.org
URL: http://www.advantageaustria.org/us
Contact: Rudolf Thaler, Commissioner
Description: Corporations in Austria, Canada and the United States. Promotes increased trade between the U.S., Canada, and Austria. Works to remove legislative barriers to international trade; represents

members before international trade organizations and agencies; facilitates establishment of joint ventures and other international business connections involving members.

36280 ■ Brazilian-American Chamber of Commerce (BACC)
509 Madison Ave., Ste. 304
New York, NY 10022
Ph: (212)751-4691
Fax: (212)751-7692
Co. E-mail: info@brazilcham.com
URL: http://www.brazilcham.com
Contact: John D. Landers, President
Description: Corporations, partnerships, financial institutions, and individuals either in the U.S. or Brazil interested in fostering two-way trade and investment between the countries. Compiles statistics and provides special mailings, press releases, information, and business contacts. Maintains files on business and trade information. Sponsors breakfast briefings, luncheons, seminars and gala dinners. **Founded:** 1968. **Publications:** *Brazilian-American Who's Who* (Irregular); *Brazilian-American Business Review/Directory* (Annual). **Awards:** Person of the Year (Annual).

36281 ■ Brazilian Government Trade Bureau of the Consulate General of Brazil in New York (BGTB)
1185 Ave. of the Americas, 21st Fl.
New York, NY 10036
Ph: (917)777-7777
Fax: (212)827-0225
URL: http://www.brazilny.org
URL(s): www.braziltradenet.gov.br. **Description:** Commercial Office of the Brazil Consulate in New York. Offers online match between Brazilian exporters of goods and services and U.S. importers. **Founded:** 1936.

36282 ■ British Trade Office at Consulate-General
845 3rd Ave.
New York, NY 10022
Ph: (212)745-0200
Fax: (212)754-3062
URL: http://www.uktradeinvestcanada.org
URL(s): www.britainusa.com/ny. **Description:** British government office that promotes trade with the U.S.; assists British companies selling in the U.S.; aids American companies that wish to import goods from or invest in Britain.

36283 ■ BritishAmerican Business Inc. of New York and London
52 Vanderbilt Ave., 20th Fl.
New York, NY 10017
Ph: (212)661-4060
Fax: (212)661-4074
Co. E-mail: nyinfo@babinc.org
URL: http://www.babinc.org
Contact: Richard Fursland, Chief Executive Officer
E-mail: nrosier@babinc.org
Description: Works to increase the trade and investment between the U.S. and the U.K. by offering member companies a full range of transatlantic business services, information, and contacts. **Publications:** *Network London* (Quarterly); *Network New York* (Quarterly); *American British Business Handbook* (Annual); *British American Business Handbook* (Annual); *BritishAmerican Business Inc. - Membership Directory* (Annual); *Investment News* (Monthly); *Issue Insight* (Bimonthly); *British American Business Inc.--Membership Directory* (Annual); *British-American Chamber of Commerce--UK and US Investment Directory* (Biennial); *The UK/USA Investment Directory & Business Resource* (Biennial); *UK & USA* (Quarterly); *UK and USA Directory of Investment* (Semimonthly).

36284 ■ Canada-United States Business Association (CUSBA)
600 Renaissance Ctr., Ste. 1100
Detroit, MI 48243
Ph: (313)446-7013
Fax: (313)567-2164
Co. E-mail: cheryl.clark@international.gc.ca
URL: http://www.canadainternational.gc.ca/detroit/commerce_can/ba-ab.aspx?lang=eng
Contact: Herold Deason, President
Description: Consists of supporters of business such as labor, banking, consulting, government, and academia. Promotes stronger business and trading lineages between the U.S. and Canada by providing a forum to exchange information and ideas and to build relationships. Conducts educational programs; maintains speakers' bureau, panels, and special events. **Founded:** 1992.

36285 ■ Canadian-American Business Council (CABC)
1900 K St. NW, Ste. 100
Washington, DC 20006
Ph: (202)496-7906
Fax: (202)496-7756
Co. E-mail: erigby@mckennalong.com
URL: http://www.canambusco.org
Contact: Ms. Emma Rigby, Deputy Director
Description: Individuals, corporations, institutions and organizations with an interest in trade between the United States and Canada. Promotes free trade. Gathers and disseminates information; maintains speakers' bureau. **Founded:** 1987. **Educational Activities:** Pharmaceuticals Conference (Periodic). **Awards:** Canadian-American Business Achievement Award (Annual).

36286 ■ Colombian American Association (CAA)
641 Lexington Ave., Ste. 1430
New York, NY 10022
Ph: (212)233-7776
Fax: (212)233-7779
Co. E-mail: programs@andean-us.com
URL: http://www.colombianamerican.org
Contact: Christian Murrle, President
Description: Facilitates commerce and trade between the Republic of Colombia and the U.S. Fosters and advances cultural relations and goodwill between the two nations. Encourages sound investments in Colombia by Americans and in the U.S. by Colombians. Disseminates information in the U.S. concerning Colombia. **Founded:** 1927. **Awards:** Paul E. Calvet Award.

36287 ■ Council of the Americas (CoA)
680 Park Ave.
New York, NY 10065
Ph: (212)628-3200
Fax: (212)517-6247
Co. E-mail: rmelzi@as-coa.org
URL: http://www.as-coa.org
Contact: Susan L. Segal, President
Description: Promotes on behalf of its members, policies and practices favoring free trade and investment, market economies and the rule of law in West Hemisphere. Provides a forum for its members to discuss economic, political and social issues relevant to the Hemisphere with public and private sector leaders. Represents the membership in public policy discussions. Assists members in the achievement of their business objectives in the region. **Founded:** 1965.

36288 ■ Council for International Tax Education (CITE)
PO Box 1012
White Plains, NY 10602
Ph: (914)328-5656
Free: 800-207-4432
Fax: (914)328-5757
Co. E-mail: info@citeusa.org
URL: http://www.citeusa.org
Contact: Diane Pastore, Executive Director
Description: Corporations, professional firms, and individual tax advisors. Works to maximize members' understanding of U.S. tax incentives and other offshore benefits available to exporters. Conducts educational programs for companies that generate tax incentives for the export of U.S. goods. Holds seminars on international tax, export and cross-border lease finance, and incentives offered companies that set up manufacturing or operating sites abroad. **Founded:** 1982. **Educational Activities:** CITE Conference.

36289 ■ Danish American Chamber of Commerce (DACC)
PO Box 2886
New York, NY 10163
Ph: (917)618-8060
Co. E-mail: daccny@daccny.com
URL: http://www.daccny.com
Contact: Peter Hessellund-Jensen, Chairman
Description: Danish and American business leaders; firms and institutions. Functions as an advisory board to support and promote commercial relations between the United States and Denmark, in both directions; makes itself available for consultation with the Danish diplomatic representatives in the U.S. and to the U.S. Department of Commerce, as well as to trade groups and members in Denmark and the U.S. Attempts to avoid duplication of governmental activities. **Founded:** 1974.

36290 ■ European-American Business Council (EABC)
919 18th St. NW, Ste. 220
Washington, DC 20006
Ph: (202)828-9104
Fax: (202)828-9106
URL: http://www.eabc.org
Contact: Michael C. Maibach, President
Description: Represents over 50 major European and North American companies with a focus on promoting trans-Atlantic growth, bilateral trade, and investment in order to foster prosperity and stability between the U.S. and Europe. Committed to fortifying EU-US economic integration, growth and competitiveness. **Founded:** 1989.

36291 ■ Federation of International Trade Associations (FITA)
172 Fifth Ave., No. 118
Brooklyn, NY 11217
Ph: (703)634-3482
Free: 888-491-8833
Co. E-mail: info@fita.org
URL: http://www.fita.org
Contact: Kimberly Park, President
Description: Fosters international trade by strengthening the role of local, regional, and national associations throughout the United States, Mexico, and Canada that have an international mission; affiliates are 450 independent international associations. **Founded:** 1984. **Publications:** *Directory of North American Trade Association* (Annual); *FITA's Really Useful Sites* (Biweekly). **Awards:** Really Useful Sites Award (Biweekly).

36292 ■ Finnish American Chamber of Commerce (FACC)
866 UN Plz., Ste. 250
New York, NY 10017
Ph: (212)821-0225
Fax: (212)750-4418
Co. E-mail: faccnyc@verizon.net
URL: http://www.facc-ny.com
Contact: Michael Student, President
Description: Maintains liaison with similar groups abroad; conducts seminars; arranges meetings with speakers. **Founded:** 1958. **Telecommunication Services:** info@finland.com.

36293 ■ French-American Chamber of Commerce (FACC)
1350 Broadway, Ste. 2101
New York, NY 10018
Ph: (212)867-0123
Fax: (212)867-9050
Co. E-mail: info@faccnyc.org
URL: http://www.faccnyc.org
Contact: Serge Bellanger, President
Description: Promotes trade between the U.S. and France and fosters economic, commercial and financial relations between the two countries. Functions in an advisory and informative capacity and assists in organizing business contacts for its members. Holds roundtable discussions, business card exchanges and other events. Sponsors educational programs. **Founded:** 1896. **Publications:** *French-*

American Chamber of Commerce--Membership Directory (Annual); *National Membership Directory of the French-American Chamber of Commerce* (Annual). **Awards:** Person of the Year (Annual).

36294 ■ Global Offset and Countertrade Association (GOCA)
818 Connecticut Ave. NW, 12th Fl.
Washington, DC 20006
Ph: (202)887-9011
Fax: (202)872-8324
Co. E-mail: goca@globaloffset.org
URL: http://www.globaloffset.org
Contact: Mary O. Fromyer, Executive Director
Description: Promotes trade and commerce between companies and their foreign customers who engage in reciprocal trade, including offset and countertrade, as a form of doing business. **Founded:** 1986.

36295 ■ Guam Chamber of Commerce
Ada Plaza Center
Hagatna, GU 96910
Ph: (671)472-6311
Fax: (671)472-6202
Co. E-mail: david.john@ascpac.com
URL: http://www.guamchamber.com.gu
Contact: Kaleo S. Moylan, Chairman
Description: Businesses and trade organizations. Promotes increased international trade and tourism. Gathers and disseminates information; conducts promotional activities; represents members' interests. **Founded:** 1924. **Publications:** *Directory of Members* (Annual); *President's Report* (Monthly); *Small Business Focus* (Quarterly); *Guam Chamber of Commerce--Directory of Members*; *The President's Report* (Monthly). **Educational Activities:** Guam Chamber of Commerce Meeting (Annual). **Awards:** Commerce Scholarship Award (Annual); Small Business Awards (Annual).

36296 ■ Hellenic-American Chamber of Commerce
370 Lexington Ave., 27th Fl.
New York, NY 10017
Ph: (212)629-6380
Fax: (212)564-9281
Co. E-mail: hellenicchamber-nyc@att.net
URL: http://www.hellenicamerican.cc
Contact: John C. Stratakis, Chairman
Description: Promotes commerce and trade; represents members' interests. **Founded:** 1947.

36297 ■ Hong Kong Trade Development Council (HKTDC)
219 E 46th St.
New York, NY 10017
Ph: (212)838-8688
Fax: (212)838-8941
Co. E-mail: new.york.office@hktdc.org
URL: http://www.hktdc.com
Description: Quasi-governmental body responsible for promoting Hong Kong trade with the rest of the world and creating a favorable image for Hong Kong as a trading partner and international trade center. Sponsors trade missions and participates in major trade shows around the world. Maintains library of trade publications in both Hong Kong and its North American offices. Compiles statistics. **Founded:** 1966. **Publications:** *Hong Kong Apparel* (Quarterly); *Hong Kong Electronics* (Semiannual); *Hong Kong Enterprise* (Monthly); *Hong Kong Gifts and Premiums* (Annual); *Hong Kong for the Business Visitor.* **Educational Activities:** Hong Kong Electronics Fair (Annual); Hong Kong Fashion Week for Fall/Winter (Annual); Hong Kong Toys and Games Fair (Annual); Hong Kong Watch and Clock Fair (Annual).

36298 ■ Innovation Norway - United States—Export Council of NorwayNorwegian Trade Council;
655 3rd Ave., Ste. 1810
New York, NY 10017-9111
Ph: (212)885-9700
Fax: (212)885-9710
Co. E-mail: newyork@innovationnorway.no
URL: http://www.innovasjonnorge.no/Kontorer-i-utlandet/usa-newyork/
Description: U.S. branch of the Export Council of Norway. Assists Norwegian companies in marketing their goods and services in the U.S. Provides information to Norwegian exporters on U.S. markets, tariffs and statistics, trade constraints, and distribution channels. Establishes contacts with U.S. authorities, marketing and manufacturing firms, local lawyers, accountants, banks, patent offices, advertising and public relations agencies, consultants, and credit and debt collection agencies. Aids in establishing Norwegian subsidiaries in the U.S. **Founded:** 1945.

36299 ■ Italian-American Chamber of Commerce (IACC)
500 N Michigan Ave., Ste. 506
Chicago, IL 60611
Ph: (312)553-9137
Fax: (312)553-9142
Co. E-mail: info@iacc-chicago.com
URL: http://www.iacc-chicago.com
Contact: Fulvio Calcinardi, Executive Director
Description: Promotes trade between Italy and the U.S. and aids Italian organizations and companies to promote their products and/or services in the U.S. Organizes trade missions to Italian trade shows and trade delegations of U.S. businesses in Italy to meet with companies and organizations. Represents CASIC-BIC Sardinia to promote foreign investments in the industrial area of Cagliari, Sardinia. **Founded:** 1907.

36300 ■ Italy-America Chamber of Commerce (IACC)
730 5th Ave., Ste. 600
New York, NY 10019
Ph: (212)459-0044
Fax: (212)459-0090
Co. E-mail: info@italchamber.org
URL: http://www.italchamber.org
Contact: Alberto Comini, President
Description: Brings together businesses ranging from individual entrepreneurs to large corporations. Advances the interests of its members through contacts and interaction with government agencies, trade associations and leading international organizations. **Founded:** 1887. **Publications:** *Trade with Italy* (Bimonthly); *IACCInform* (Monthly); *Trade With Italy* (Bimonthly); *Trade with Italy* (Biennial); *United States - Italy Trade Directory* (Annual). **Educational Activities:** Mifur - International Fur and Leather Exhibition (Annual). **Awards:** Business and Culture Award; Business and Culture Award (Annual); Golden Award (Annual).

36301 ■ Japan External Trade Organization (JETRO)
1221 Ave. of the Americas
McGraw Hill Bldg., 42nd Fl.
New York, NY 10020
Ph: (212)997-0400
Fax: (212)997-0464
Co. E-mail: masaki_fujihara@jetro.go.jp
URL: http://www.jetro.org
Contact: Masaki Fujihara, Director
Description: Supports foreign companies in export and/or investment to Japan-related business ventures. Disseminates comprehensive information on the Japanese economy and market through surveys, reports, publications, and newsletters. Conducts trade and investment promotion seminars and symposia. Sponsors trade shows and exhibitions. Provides professional business consultation services and handles trade-related inquiries and provides opportunities for international exchange. **Founded:** 1958.

36302 ■ Japanese Chamber of Commerce and Industry of New York (JCCINY)
145 W 57th St.
New York, NY 10019
Ph: (212)246-8001
Fax: (212)246-8002
Co. E-mail: info@jcciny.org
URL: http://www.jcciny.org
Contact: Seiei Ono, President
Description: Japanese and non-Japanese corporations. Fosters improved trade relations between the U.S. and Japan. Conducts seminars and surveys. **Founded:** 1932. **Publications:** *Japan's Industries and Trade: Profiles and Interrelationships with the United States*; *Joining In! A Handbook for Better Corporate Citizenship in the U.S.*.

36303 ■ Joint Industry Group (JIG)
111 Rockville Pike, Ste. 410
Rockville, MD 20850
Ph: (202)466-5490
Fax: (202)559-0131
Co. E-mail: jig@moinc.com
URL: http://www.jig.org
Contact: Megan Giblin, Chairperson
Description: Trade associations and business and professional firms engaged in international trade. Seeks to influence administration of customs and related trade laws to facilitate trade and encourage compliance. **Founded:** 1976. **Awards:** Excellence in Government Award (Annual).

36304 ■ Latin Chamber of Commerce of U.S.A.—Camara de Comercio Latina de los EEUU
1401 W Flagler St.
Miami, FL 33135
Ph: (305)642-3870
Fax: (305)642-0653
Co. E-mail: walexander@camacol.org
URL: http://www.camacol.org
Contact: Patricia Arias, Managing Director
Description: Provides placement services; compiles statistics. Maintains information and referral service. **Founded:** 1965. **Educational Activities:** Hemispheric Congress (Annual); CAMACOL Hemispheric Congress (Annual). **Telecommunication Services:** info@camacol.org.

36305 ■ Moroccan American Business Council (MABC)
1085 Commonwealth Ave., Ste. 194
Boston, MA 02215
Ph: (508)230-9943
Fax: (508)230-9943
Co. E-mail: moulay@usa-morocco.org
URL: http://www.usa-morocco.org
Contact: Moulay M. Alaoui, Chairman
Description: Promotes commerce and business between Morocco and the United States. **Founded:** 1995.

36306 ■ National Association of Export Companies (NEXCO)
Grand Central Station
New York, NY 10163
Free: 877-291-4901
Fax: (646)349-9628
Co. E-mail: director@nexco.org
URL: http://www.nexco.org
Contact: Barney Lehrer, President
Description: Established independent international trade firms, bilateral chambers of commerce, banks, law firms, accounting firms, trade associations, insurance companies, and product/service providers; export trading companies; export management companies. Promotes expansion of U.S. trade. Promotes the participation of members in international trade. Conducts educational programs. **Founded:** 1963.

36307 ■ National Association of Foreign-Trade Zones (NAFTZ)
1001 Connecticut Ave. NW, Ste. 350
Washington, DC 20036
Ph: (202)331-1950
Fax: (202)331-1994
Co. E-mail: info@naftz.org
URL: http://www.naftz.org
Contact: Willard M. Berry, President
Description: Foreign-trade zone grantees, operators, and users; law firms, automobile manufacturers, port authorities, customs brokers, industrial firms,

chambers of commerce, magazine and newspaper firms, development corporations, and concerned individuals. Aims to promote, stimulate, and improve foreign-trade zones and their utilization as integral and valuable tools in the international commerce of the U.S.; to encourage the establishment of foreign-trade zones to foster investment and the creation of jobs in the US. Sponsors seminars. **Founded:** 1973. **Publications:** *U.S. Foreign Trade Zones*; *Zones Report* (Periodic); *The Impact of Foreign Trade Zones on the 50 States and Puerto Rico*.

36308 ■ Netherlands Chamber of Commerce in the United States (NLCOC)
267 5th Ave., Ste. 908
New York, NY 10016
Ph: (212)265-6460
Fax: (212)265-6402
Co. E-mail: netherlandstrust@aol.com
URL: http://www.netherlands.org
Contact: Kersen J. De Jong, President
Description: Aims to maintain and expand business relations between The Netherlands and the United States. **Founded:** 1903. **Awards:** George Washington Vanderbilt Trophy (Periodic).

36309 ■ Norwegian-American Chamber of Commerce (NACC)
655 3rd Ave., Ste. 1810
New York, NY 10017
Ph: (212)885-9737
Co. E-mail: shipping@ntcny.org
URL: http://www.naccusa.org
Contact: Blaine Collins, President
Description: Promotes business and trade among members and between Norway and the United States. Provides networking opportunities and source information. **Founded:** 1915. **Publications:** *Norwegian American Chamber of Commerce--Membership Directory* (Biennial); *Norwegian American Commerce* (Quarterly). **Awards:** NACC Achievement Award (Annual); Trade Award (Annual).

36310 ■ Romanian-U.S. Business Council
15303 North Dallas Pkwy., 10th Flr.
Addison, TX 75001
Ph: (646)678-2905
Co. E-mail: info@usrobc.org
URL: http://usrobc.org
Description: Advocates American business interests with respect to U.S. Romanian trade and investments. Provides the American and Romanian business communities with a means of discussing bilateral trade and investment issues and the formulation of policy positions that will promote and expand economic relations between the two countries. Facilitates appropriate legislation and policies regarding trade between the U.S. and Romania. Has sponsored seminars on topics such as possibilities for cooperative commercial efforts in other countries and cooperation in energy development. **Founded:** 1974.

36311 ■ Society of International Business Fellows (SIBF)
191 Peachtree St. NE, Ste. 3950
Atlanta, GA 30303-1740
Ph: (404)525-7423
Fax: (404)525-5331
URL: http://www.sibf.org
Contact: Nancy Haselden, Executive Director
Description: Businesspeople active or with an interest in international trade. Promotes "enhancement of the international competitiveness and prosperity of its members and the growth of the South as a vital region for global business." Works to strengthen personal and professional relations among members; conducts educational programs in international business and trade. **Founded:** 1981.

36312 ■ Spain-United States Chamber of Commerce—Camera de Comercio Espana - Estados Unidos
Empire State Bldg.
350 5th Ave., Ste. 2600
New York, NY 10118
Ph: (212)967-2170
Fax: (212)564-1415
Co. E-mail: info@spainuscc.org
URL: http://www.spainuscc.org
Contact: Xavier Ruiz, Chairman
Description: Spanish and U.S. business persons dedicated to the expansion of Spanish-American trade and goodwill. **Founded:** 1959. **Publications:** *Business Directories*; *Visa and Work Permits for the USA*. **Educational Activities:** Gala Dinner (Annual); Tapas and Tarjetas (Quarterly). **Awards:** Business Leader of the Year (Annual); Business Leader of the Year Award.

36313 ■ Swedish Trade Council
150 N Michigan Ave., Ste. 1950
Chicago, IL 60601
Ph: (312)781-6222
Fax: (312)276-8606
Co. E-mail: usa@swedishtrade.se
URL: http://www.swedishtrade.se/english
Contact: James Armstrong, Associate
Description: Promotes Swedish exports and assists American companies in contacting Swedish suppliers. Performs market developments studies and research, partner searches, and project management. **Founded:** 1972. **Publications:** *Swedish Export Directory* (Annual). **Telecommunication Services:** james.armstrong@swedishtrade.se.

36314 ■ U.S. Austrian Chamber of Commerce
165 W 46th St., Ste. 1113
New York, NY 10036
Ph: (212)819-0117
Co. E-mail: office@usaustrianchamber.org
URL: http://usaustrianchamber.org
Contact: Johannes P. Hofer, President
Description: Hosts receptions and luncheons. Sponsors Viennese Opera Ball, panel discussions, and business assistance. **Founded:** 1946. **Educational Activities:** Viennese Opera Ball (Annual). **Awards:** Person of the Year.

36315 ■ United States Council for International Business (USCIB)
1212 Avenue of the Americas
New York, NY 10036
Ph: (212)354-4480
Fax: (212)575-0327
Co. E-mail: info@uscib.org
URL: http://www.uscib.org
Contact: Mr. Peter M. Robinson, President
Description: Serves as the U.S. National Committee of the International Chamber of Commerce. Enables multinational enterprises to operate effectively by representing their interests to intergovernmental and governmental bodies and by keeping enterprises advised of international developments having a major impact on their operations. Serves as: U.S. representative to the International Organization of Employers; national affiliate to the U.S.A. Business and Industry Advisory Committee to the BIAC. Operates ATA Carnet export service, which enables goods to be shipped overseas duty-free for demonstration and exhibition. Sponsors seminars and luncheon briefings. **Founded:** 1945. **Publications:** *United States Council Foundation: Occasional Paper*. **Awards:** International Leadership Award; International Leadership Award (Annual). **Telecommunication Services:** membership@uscib.org; probinson@uscib.org.

36316 ■ United States Mexico Chamber of Commerce (USMCOC)
PO Box 14414
Washington, DC 20004
Ph: (703)752-4751
Fax: (703)642-1088
Co. E-mail: news-hq@usmcoc.org
URL: http://www.usmcoc.org
Contact: Al Zapanta, President
Description: U.S. businessmen and chambers of commerce in Mexico representing 350,000 companies. Works to promote private sector trade and investment between the United States and Mexico. Offers advice on economic, legal, and trade issues; informs members of long-range advantages of alternative plant locations. Works with both governments on the executive, legislative, and federal levels. Monitors legislation and regulations concerning trade issues critical to business development in both countries. Conducts seminars and luncheons. **Founded:** 1973. **Publications:** *Chamber News* (Quarterly); *United States-Mexico Chamber of Commerce--Membership Directory and Resource Guide*; *United States-Mexico Chamber of Commerce--Regional Newsletters* (Periodic). **Educational Activities:** NFTA Update (Semiannual). **Awards:** Good Neighbor Award; Good Neighbor Award (Annual). **Telecommunication Services:** zapantaz@usmcoc.org.

36317 ■ U.S. Pan Asian American Chamber of Commerce (USPAACC)
1329 18th St. NW
Washington, DC 20036
Ph: (202)296-5221
Free: 800-696-7818
Fax: (202)296-5225
Co. E-mail: info@uspaacc.com
URL: http://www.uspaacc.com
Contact: Susan Au Allen, President
Description: Businesspersons and professionals united to promote contract, education and other opportunities for Asian American businesses and their partners in corporate America and government agencies. Promotes programs and activities to help members pursue owning and growing their business; enter mainstream society; and participate in procurement, commerce, trade, investment and employment opportunities in corporate America and government. Conducts educational and networking activities. Maintains scholarship fund. Holds business colloquies. Sponsors speakers' bureau. Conducts research and charitable programs. **Founded:** 1984. **Publications:** *East-West Report* (Quarterly); *East West Report* (Quarterly). **Educational Activities:** CelebrAsian Conference (Annual). **Awards:** Asian American Scholarships; Pepsico Scholarships; Excellence 200 Awards; Corporate of the Year (Annual); Government of the Year (Annual); USPAACC Scholarships (Annual); USPAACC/Wells Fargo Asian Business Award (Annual); Paul Shearman Allen and Associate Scholarships; Bruce Lee Scholarships; Ruth Mu-Lan and James S.C. Chao Scholarships; Philip Morris USA Scholarships; Drs. Poh Shien and Judy Young Scholarships; U.S. Pan Asian American Chamber of Commerce McDonald's Scholarships; U.S. Pan Asian American Chamber of Commerce UPS Scholarships.

36318 ■ U.S. Russia Business Council (USRBC)
1110 Vermont Ave. NW, Ste. 350
Washington, DC 20005-3544
Ph: (202)739-9180
Fax: (202)659-5920
Co. E-mail: verona@usrbc.org
URL: http://www.usrbc.org
Contact: Edward S. Verona, President
Description: U.S. corporations doing business in Russia. Promotes adoption of public policies conducive to international trade in both the United States and Russia. Conducts lobbying activities; facilitates establishment of joint ventures involving U.S. and Russian companies; maintains bank of job listings; compiles trade statistics. Gathers and disseminates information on political, economic, and social issues affecting trade with Russia. **Scope:** Russia, international trade. **Founded:** 1993. **Subscriptions:** books periodicals. **Publications:** *Russia Business Watch* (Quarterly).

36319 ■ U.S.A. - Business and Industry Advisory Committee to the OECD (USA-BIAC)
c/o United States Council for International Business
1212 Avenue of the Americas
New York, NY 10036
Ph: (212)354-4480
Fax: (212)575-0327
Co. E-mail: membership@uscib.org
URL: http://www.uscib.org
Contact: Harold McGraw, III, Chairman
Description: Sponsored by United States Council for International Business. Represents the United States on the Business and Industry Advisory Committee to the Organisation for Economic Co-Operation and Development. Acts as the official channel for conveying the views of the business community to the OECD

in the fields of economics, finance, international trade, industrial relations, information and telecommunications policy investment, and taxation. **Founded:** 1962.

36320 ■ Venezuelan American Association of the United States (VAAUS)
641 Lexington Ave., Ste. 1430
New York, NY 10022
Ph: (212)233-7776
Fax: (212)233-7779
Co. E-mail: info@andean-us.com
URL: http://www.venezuelanamerican.org
Contact: Clara Krivoy, President
Description: Financial institutions, businesses, organizations, and individuals interested in the expansion and improvement of trade and trade relations between Venezuela and the United States. Fosters cultural and commercial relations, facilitates investment between the U.S. and Venezuela, and promotes improved understanding between businesspersons of the two nations. Conducts informal meetings with speakers and discussions. **Founded:** 1936. **Publications:** *Venezuela News Bulletin* (Monthly).

EDUCATIONAL PROGRAMS

36321 ■ Creating a Positive, High-Energy Workplace (Onsite)
Padgett-Thompson Seminars
Rockhurst University CEC
14502 W. 105th St.
Lenexa, KS 66215
Free: 800-349-1935
URL: http://www.findaseminar.com/tpd/Padgett-Thompson-Seminars.asp
Price: $199.00. **Description:** A seminar for those who want to gain crucial insights into increasing their bottom line by fostering an energized climate where anything is possible. **Dates and Locations:** Boston, MA; Hartford, CT; Albany, NY.

36322 ■ Foreign Military Sales (Onsite)
Seminar Information Service, Inc.
20 Executive Park, Ste. 120
Irvine, CA 92614
Ph: (949)261-9104
Free: 877-SEM-INFO
Fax: (949)261-1963
Co. E-mail: info@seminarinformation.com
URL: http://www.seminarinformation.com
Price: $1,025.00. **Description:** Contractors who want to engage in international contracting successfully and profitably must be able to navigate a complex web of statutes, regulations and policies governing FRMS, FMF and U.S. export controls. **Dates and Locations:** Washington, DC.

REFERENCE WORKS

36323 ■ *"10 Trends That Are Shaping Global Media Consumption" in Advertising Age (Vol. 81, December 6, 2010, No. 43, pp. 3)*
Pub: Crain Communications, Inc.
Ed: Ann Marie Kerwin. **Description:** Ad Age offers the statistics from the TV penetration rate in Kenya to the number of World Cup watchers and more.

36324 ■ *"35-Year-Old Downtown Fabric Store Closes Doors" in The Times and Democrat (September 29, 2009)*
Pub: The Times and Democrat
Description: Warren's Fashion Fabrics Inc., a 35-year-old retail fabric, decor and sewing store, officially closed its doors due, in part, to the changing tide of the industry in which fewer women sew and products from countries such as China are so cheap.

36325 ■ *"2008: Year of the Rat Race" in Mergers & Acquisitions: The Dealmaker's Journal (March 1, 2008)*
Pub: SourceMedia, Inc.
Ed: Danelle Fugazy. **Description:** Although China still presents opportunities to Western investors, many are discovering that much more research needs to be done concerning doing business in that country before investing there becomes truly mainstream. According to one source, there are at least 300,000 small state-owned enterprises in China and millions of middle-market privately owned companies; the Chinese stock market can only handle about 50 to 70 IPOs a year and lists about 1,500 companies at a time.

36326 ■ *"ABB Could Still Engineer an Upside" in Barron's (Vol. 89, July 20, 2009, No. 29, pp. M6)*
Pub: Dow Jones & Co., Inc.
Ed: Goran Mijuk. **Description:** Swiss engineering company ABB can remain profitable as its power transmission and distribution activities continue to generate earnings. The company is also benefiting from increased exposure in emerging markets.

36327 ■ *"Abroad, Not Overboard" in Entrepreneur (Vol. 36, April 2008, No. 4, pp. 68)*
Pub: Entrepreneur Media, Inc.
Ed: Crystal Detamore-Rodman. **Description:** Export-Import Bank is an agency created by the U.S. government to help exporters get credit insurance and capital loans by providing them with loan guarantees. The bank, being criticized as supporting more the bigger exporters, has allotted to smaller businesses a bigger portion of the annual credit being approved.

36328 ■ *"According to the Chinese Zodiac, 2009 is the Year of the Ox" in Canadian Business (Vol. 81, December 8, 2008, No. 21, pp. 74)*
Pub: Rogers Media Ltd.
Ed: Zarka Halas. **Description:** Forecasts for China in 2009 are presented. China is expected to maintain an 8 percent growth rate to keep the current labor market. A total of 68,000 companies have collapsed in China in the first half of 2008, while 2.5 million workers are likely to lose jobs in the Pearl River Delta by the end of 2008.

36329 ■ *"Adidas' Brand Ambitions" in Business Journal Portland (Vol. 27, December 10, 2010, No. 41, pp. 1)*
Pub: Portland Business Journal
Ed: Erik Siemers. **Description:** Adidas AG, the second-largest sporting goods brand in the world, hopes to increase global revenue by 50 percent by 2015. The German company, which reported $14.5 billion sales, plans to improve its U.S. market. The U.S. is Adidas' largest, but also the most underperforming market for the firm.

36330 ■ *"Advances in Pump Technology - Part Two" in Contractor (Vol. 57, February 2010, No. 2, pp. 22)*
Pub: Penton Media, Inc.
Ed: Mark Eatherton. **Description:** Chinese and Japanese companies have come up with refrigerant based heat pump products that are air based which will significantly lower the installed cost of heat pump based systems. Some of these newer models have variable speed, soft start compressors and have the ability to perform high-efficiency heat pump operation on a modulating basis.

36331 ■ *"AF Expands in New Green Building in Gothenburg" in Ecology,Environment & Conservation Business (September 24, 2011, pp. 2)*
Pub: HighBeam Research
Description: AF signed a ten-year tenancy contract with Skanska for the premises of its new green building in Gothenburg, Sweden. AF offers qualified services and solutions for industrial processes, infrastructure projects and the development of products and IT systems.

36332 ■ *"Africa Rising" in Harvard Business Review (Vol. 86, September 2008, No. 9, pp. 36)*
Pub: Harvard Business School Press
Ed: John T. Landry. **Description:** Review of the book entitled, 'Africa Rising: How 900 Million African Consumers Offer More Than You Think' provides advice for marketing to those on the African continent.

36333 ■ *"Aggenix Completes Merger with German Giant" in Houston Business Journal (Vol. 40, December 25, 2009, No. 33, pp. 2)*
Pub: American City Business Journals
Ed: Mary Ann Azevedo. **Description:** Agennix Inc. has completed its transformation into a German company after Germany-based GPC Biotech merged into the former publicly traded Agennix AG. One quarter of Agennix's 60 employees will remain in Houston. Details on Agennix's drug trials are examined.

36334 ■ *"Airing It Out" in The Business Journal-Serving Greater Tampa Bay (Vol. 28, July 11, 2008, No. 29, pp. 1)*
Pub: American City Business Journals, Inc.
Ed: Jane Meinhardt. **Description:** Flanders Corp. is planning to expand its business in Europe and Southeast Asia. The St. Petersburg, Florida-based company has about 2,800 employees and manufactures air filtration products for industrial and residential applications.

36335 ■ *"All About The Benjamins" in Canadian Business (Vol. 81, September 29, 2008, No. 16, pp. 92)*
Pub: Rogers Media Ltd.
Ed: David Baines. **Description:** Discusses real estate developer Royal Indian Raj International Corp., a company that planned to build a $3 billion 'smart city' near the Bangalore airport; to this day nothing has ever been built. The company was incorporated in 1999 by Manoj C. Benjamin one investor, Bill Zack, has been sued by the developer for libel due to his website that calls the company a scam. Benjamin has had a previous case of fraud issued against him as well as a string of liabilities and lawsuits.

36336 ■ *"All For One, None for All?" in Canadian Business (Vol. 83, October 12, 2010, No. 17, pp. 60)*
Pub: Rogers Media Ltd.
Ed: Michael McCullogh. **Description:** The effect of the growth of Canada's overseas provincial trade offices on Canadian trade is discussed. Economic development commissions in the country have devised a single 'Consider Canada' campaign to pitch foreign investors. It is hoped that large cities will gain from banding together rather than competing against one another.

36337 ■ *"Alliance Offers to Help Italian Workers Settle In" in Crain's Detroit Business (Vol. 25, June 15, 2009, No. 24, pp. 21)*
Pub: Crain Communications Inc. - Detroit
Ed: Nancy Kaffer. **Description:** Italian American Alliance for Business and Technology will help workers arriving from Italy to transition to their new homes in the Detroit area.

36338 ■ *"Allied Brands Loses Baskin-Robbins Franchise Down Under" in Ice Cream Reporter (Vol. 23, November 20, 2010, No. 12, pp. 2)*
Pub: Ice Cream Reporter
Description: Dunkin Brands, worldwide franchisor of Baskin-Robbins, terminated the master franchise agreement for Australia held by the food marketer Allied Brands Services.

36339 ■ *"An Amazing Race" in Canadian Business (Vol. 81, March 3, 2008, No. 3, pp. 25)*
Pub: Rogers Media
Ed: Rachel Pulfer. **Description:** U.S. presidential candidates Barack Obama and Hilary Clinton lead the Democratic Part primaries while John McCain is a frontrunner at the Republican Party. These leading candidates have different plans for the U.S. economy which will affect Canada's own economy particularly concerning trade policies. The presidential candidates' proposals and the impacts of U.S. economic downturn on Canada are examined.

36340 ■ *American Chambers of Commerce Abroad*
Pub: U.S. Chamber of Commerce
Contact: Thomas J. Donohue, President
E-mail: tdonohue@uschamber.com
URL(s): www.uschamber.comwww.uschamber.com/international/directory/default. **Covers:** 112 American chambers of commerce in 99 countries. **Entries in-**

clude: Name, address, phone, fax, title, telex, E-mail and web addresses, geographical area served, and subsidiary and branch names and locations. **Arrangement:** Geographical.

36341 ■ *"The Americans Are Coming" in The Economist (Vol. 390, January 3, 2009, No. 8612, pp. 44)*
Pub: The Economist Newspaper Inc.
Description: Student recruitment consultancies, which help place international students at universities in other countries and offer services such as interpreting or translating guidelines, are discussed; American universities who have shunned these agencies in the past; the result has been that America underperforms in relation to its size with a mere 3.5 percent of students on its campuses that are from abroad.

36342 ■ *"Ampm Focus Has BP Working Overtime; New Convenience-Store Brand Comes to Chicago" in Crain's Chicago Business (April 28, 2008)*
Pub: Crain Communications, Inc.
Ed: John T. Slania. **Description:** Britian's oil giant BP PLC is opening its ampm convenience stores in the Chicago market and has already begun converting most of its 78 Chicago-area gas stations to ampms. The company has also started to franchise the stores to independent operators. BP is promoting the brand with both traditional and unconventional marketing techniques such s real or simulated 3D snacks embedded in bus shelter ads and an in-store Guitar Hero contest featuring finalists from a recent contest at the House of Blues.

36343 ■ *"And The Winner Is.." in Canadian Business (Vol. 81, March 3, 2008, No. 3, pp. 21)*
Pub: Rogers Media
Ed: Joe Castaldo. **Description:** Thirty out of 141 Canadian chief executive officers think that Hilary Clinton would be best for U.S.-Canada relations if elected as U.S. president. Findings also revealed that 60 respondents believe that presidential candidate John McCain would be best on handling issues of international military-security. Views on the candidates' performance and their ability to deal with the declining U.S. economy as well as international trade issues are also given.

36344 ■ *Animal Spirits: How Human Psychology Drives the Economy, and Why it Matters for Global Capitalism*
Pub: Princeton University Press
Ed: George A. Akerlof, Robert J. Shiller. **Released:** 2009. **Price:** $24.95. **Description:** Psychological factors that led to the depressed economy and how it may impede a turnaround.

36345 ■ *"Ann Alexander; Senior Attorney, Natural Resources Defense Council" in Crain's Chicago Business (Vol. 31, May 5, 2008, No. 18)*
Pub: Crain Communications, Inc.
Ed: Emily Stone. **Description:** Profile of Ann Alexander who is the senior attorney at the Natural Resources Defense Council and is known for her dedication to the environment and a career spent battling oil companies, steelmakers and the government to change federal regulations. One recent project aims to improve the Bush administration's fuel economy standards for SUVs. Past battles include her work to prevent permits from slipping through the cracks such as the proposal by London-based BP PLC to dump 54 percent more ammonia and 35 percent more suspended solids from its Whiting, Indiana refinery into Lake Michigan-the source of drinking water for Chicago and its surrounding communities.

36346 ■ *"Another Determinant of Entrepreneurship" in International Journal of Entrepreneurship and Small Business (Vol. 10, July 6, 2010)*
Pub: Publishers Communication Group
Ed: Felix Pauligard Ntep, Wilton Wilton. **Description:** Interviews were carried out with entrepreneurs of Douala, Cameroon. These entrepreneurs believe that witchcraft existed and could bring harm to them or their enterprises.

36347 ■ *"Arario Gallery Opens First American Space" in Art Business News (Vol. 34, November 2007, No. 11, pp. 14)*
Pub: Pfingsten Publishing, LLC
Description: Opening a new space in New York's Chelsea gallery district is Arario Gallery, a leader in the field of Asian contemporary art; the gallery will feature new works by Chinese artists at its opening.

36348 ■ *"Areva Diversifies Further Into Wind" in Wall Street Journal Eastern Edition (November 29, 2011, pp. B7)*
Pub: Dow Jones & Company Inc. Enterprise Media Group
Contact: Clare Hart, President
Ed: Max Colchester, Noemie Bisserbe. **Description:** French engineering company Areva SA is diversifying and moving away from nuclear energy projects. One sign of that is its recent discussion to construct 120 wind turbines to be located at two German wind farms. Such a deal, if signed, would be worth about US$1.59 billion.

36349 ■ *"Arizona Firms In Chicago Go For Gold With '08 Games" in The Business Journal - Serving Phoenix and the Valley of the Sun (Vol. 28, August 8, 2008, No. 49, pp. 1)*
Pub: American City Business Journals, Inc.
Ed: Patrick O'Grady. **Description:** More than 20 U.S. athletes will wear Arizona-based eSoles LLC's custom-made insoles to increase their performance at the 2008 Beijing Olympics making eSoles one of the beneficiaries of the commercialization of the games. Translation software maker Auralog Inc saw a 60 percent jump in sales from its Mandarin Chinese language applications.

36350 ■ *"Around the World" in Entrepreneur (Vol. 36, March 2008, No. 3, pp. 82)*
Pub: Entrepreneur Media Inc.
Ed: Gail Dutton. **Description:** Joining a global consortium can improve a business greater access to services and expertise from other members around the world. The goal is to develop the company to be able to reach to a wider customer base; other details on the benefits of joining a consortium are discussed.

36351 ■ *"Around the World in a Day" in Agency Sales Magazine (Vol. 39, August 2009, No. 8, pp. 36)*
Pub: MANA
Ed: Jack Foster. **Description:** Highlights of Manufacturer's Agents National Association (MANA) member Les Rapchak one-day visit to Basra, Iraq are presented. Rapchak completed the trip via Frankfurt, Germany and Kuwait with a stop afterwards in Istanbul, Turkey. His purpose for the trip was to take part in a seminar at the State Company for Petrochemical Industries.

36352 ■ *"Asia Breathes a Sigh of Relief" in Business Week (September 22, 2008, No. 4100, pp. 32)*
Pub: McGraw-Hill Companies, Inc.
Ed: Bruce Einhorn; Theo Francis; Chi-Chu Tschang; Moon Ihlwan; Hiroko Tashiro. **Description:** Foreign bankers, such as those in Asia, that had been investing heavily in the United States began to worry as the housing crisis deepened and the impact on Freddie Mac and Fannie Mae became increasingly clear. Due to the government bailout, however, central banks will most likely continue to buy American debt.

36353 ■ *"'The Asian Decade" in Hawaii Business (Vol. 53, January 2008, No. 7, pp. 19)*
Pub: Hawaii Business Publishing
Ed: Cathy S. Cruz-George. **Description:** Chaney Brooks, a Hawaiian real estate company, has affiliated with commercial real estate network NAI Global. The NAI partnership will improve Hawaii's international business, particularly its Asian investments. Hawaii's diverse workforce is evaluated, with regards to being an asset for international businesses.

36354 ■ *Asian Godfathers: Money and Power in Hong Kong and Southeast Asia*
Pub: Grove/Atlantic Inc.
Contact: Morgan Entrekin, President
E-mail: mentrekin@groveatlantic.com
Ed: Joe Studwell. **Released:** September 2008. **Price:** $15.00 paperback. **Description:** Expose of some of Southeast Asia's top business moguls is highlighted, along with a look into the region's economic and social cultures.

36355 ■ *"Au Revoir Or Goodbye?" in Barron's (Vol. 88, July 14, 2008, No. 28, pp. 5)*
Pub: Dow Jones & Co., Inc.
Ed: Alan Abelson. **Description:** Former Senator Phil Gramm's opinion that the U.S. is a 'nation of whiners' as they moan about recession is another example of the disconnection between Washington and Wall Street on one hand and the real world on the other. It would be a catastrophe for most of the world if Fannie Mae and Freddie Mac were to go under and take their trillions of mortgage debt with them.

36356 ■ *"AV Concept Expands Into Green Energy Storage" in Wireless News (January 25, 2010)*
Pub: Close-Up Media
Description: Electronics distributor and manufacturer AV Concept Holdings Limited announced a marketing partnership with Boston-Power, a provider of lithium-ion batteries, with a focus in the Chinese and Korean markets.

36357 ■ *"Awaiting a Call from Deutsche Telekom" in Barron's (Vol. 90, September 6, 2010, No. 36, pp. M5)*
Pub: Barron's Editorial & Corporate Headquarters
Ed: Vito J. Racanelli. **Description:** Deutsche Telekom's (DT) T-Mobile USA Unit has settled in the number four position in the market and the parent company will need to decide if it will hold onto the company in the next 12-18 months from September 2010. T-Mobile's rivals will make critical improvements during this time and DT has the option to upgrade T-Mobile at the cost of improvements to its other units.

36358 ■ *"B2B Commercial Collection Agency Accounts Fall" in Managing Credit, Receivables & Collections (November 2010, No. 10-11, pp. 9)*
Pub: Institute of Management & Administration
Description: A fall in the number of Business-To-Business collection accounts reflects the pace of the global economic recovery.

36359 ■ *"A Baby Step to the South" in Canadian Business (Vol. 81, July 22, 2008, No. 12-13, pp. 21)*
Pub: Rogers Media Ltd.
Ed: Jane Bao. **Description:** Canada's free trade agreement (FTA) with Colombia is seen as Canada's re-engagement with Latin America. Some politicians believe that the FTA is more of a political agreement than a trade agreement with Colombia. Key information on Canada's trade agreements, as well as trade with Colombia and Latin American countries, is presented.

36360 ■ *"Back in the Race" in Barron's (Vol. 88, March 17, 2008, No. 11, pp. 43)*
Pub: Dow Jones & Company, Inc.
Ed: Leslie P. Norton. **Description:** Katherine Schapiro was able to get Sentinel International Equity's Morningstar classification to blended fund from a value fund rating after joining Sentinel from her former jobs at Strong Overseas Fund. Schapiro aims to benefit from the global rebalancing as the U.S.'s share of the world economy shrinks.

36361 ■ *"Back on Track-Or Off the Rails?" in Business Week (September 22, 2008, No. 4100, pp. 22)*
Pub: McGraw-Hill Companies, Inc.
Ed: Peter Coy; Tara Kalwarski. **Description:** Discusses the possible scenarios the American economy may undergo due to the takeover of Fannie Mae and Freddie Mac. Statistical data included.

36362 ■ *Bad Samaritans: The Myth of Free Trade and the Secret History of Capitalism*
Pub: Bloomsbury USA

Ed: Ha-Joon Chang. **Released:** 2009. **Price:** $26.95. **Description:** Economist challenges open-market proponents and believes that free trade would do more harm than good.

36363 ■ *"Bargain Hunting In Vietnam" in Barron's (Vol. 88, July 14, 2008, No. 28, pp. M6)*
Pub: Dow Jones & Co., Inc.

Ed: Elliot Wilson. **Description:** Vietnam's economy grew by just 6.5 percent for the first half of 2008 and its balance of payments ballooned to $14.4 billion. The falling stock prices in the country is a boon for bargain hunters and investing in the numerous domestic funds is one way of investing in the country. Some shares that investors are taking an interest in are also discussed.

36364 ■ *"Bark and Bite" in Canadian Business (Vol. 81, March 31, 2008, No. 5, pp. 20)*
Pub: Rogers Media

Ed: Rachel Pulfer. **Description:** Hillary Clinton and Barack Obama both want to renegotiate NAFTA but the most job losses in the American manufacturing industry is caused by technological change and Asian competition than with NAFTA. The risk of protectionist trade policies has increased given the political atmosphere.

36365 ■ *"Baskin-Robbins Expanding in China and U.S." in Ice Cream Reporter (Vol. 21, August 20, 2008, No. 9, pp. 1)*
Pub: Ice Cream Reporter

Description: Baskin-Robbins will open its first store in Shanghai, China along with plans for 100 more shops in that country. They will also be expanding their market in the Dallas/Fort Worth, Texas area as well as Greater Cincinnati/Northern Kentucky regions.

36366 ■ *"Baskin-Robbins: New in U.S., Old in Japan" in Ice Cream Reporter (Vol. 23, August 20, 2010, No. 9, pp. 2)*
Pub: Ice Cream Reporter

Description: Baskin-Robbins is celebrating its first franchise in Japan.

36367 ■ *"Battling Back from Betrayal" in Harvard Business Review (Vol. 88, December 2010, No. 12, pp. 130)*
Pub: Harvard Business School Publishing

Ed: Daniel McGinn. **Description:** Stephen Greer's scrap metal firm, Hartwell Pacific, lost several million dollars due to a lack of efficient and appropriate inventory audits, accounting procedures, and new-hire reference checks for his foreign operations. Greer believes that balancing growth with control is a key component of success.

36368 ■ *"BayTSP, NTT Data Corp. Enter Into Reseller Pact to Market Online IP Monitoring" in Professional Services Close-Up (Sept. 11, 2009)*
Pub: Close-Up Media

Description: Due to incredible interest from distributors and content owners across Asia, NTT Data Corp. will resell BayTSP's online intellectual property monitoring, enforcement, business intelligence and monetization services in Japan.

36369 ■ *"Be a Better Manager: Live Abroad" in Harvard Business Review (Vol. 88, September 2010, No. 9, pp. 24)*
Pub: Harvard Business School Publishing

Ed: William W. Maddux, Adam D. Galinsky, Carmit T. Tadmor. **Description:** Interrelationship between international experience and entrepreneurship is discussed. Individuals with international experience are likelier to be promoted and to develop new products and businesses.

36370 ■ *"Beltway Monitor" in Mergers & Acquisitions: The Dealmaker's Journal (March 1, 2008)*
Pub: SourceMedia, Inc.

Description: Discusses in detail The Foreign Investment and National Security Act of 2007 which was put into legislation due to the initially approved acquisition of certain U.S. ports by Dubai Ports World which set off a firestorm of controversy.

36371 ■ *Benchmarking the Canadian Business Presence in East Asia*
Pub: University of Toronto Press Inc.

Ed: A.E. Safarian; Wendy Dobson. **Released:** October 27, 1995. **Price:** $19.00. **Description:** Covers Canadian trade with East Asian economies.

36372 ■ *"Best Growth Stocks" in Canadian Business (Vol. 81, Summer 2008, No. 9, pp. 61)*
Pub: Rogers Media Ltd.

Ed: Calvin Leung. **Description:** Table showing the one-year performance of growth stocks is presented. Edmonton-based Stantec Inc. expects to advance its sales and profits by 15 percent to 20 percent per year through tapping international markets and acquisitions. Analysts forecast a 17.1 percent growth rate annually over the next 3 to 5 years.

36373 ■ *"Best Turnaround Stocks" in Canadian Business (Vol. 82, Summer 2009, No. 8, pp. 32)*
Pub: Rogers Media

Ed: Calvin Leung. **Description:** Canadian companies that are believed to have the potential for the best turnaround stocks are presented. Suggested stocks include those of Migao Corporation, which is rated by most research firms as a Buy. Migao produces potash-based fertilizers for the Chinese market.

36374 ■ *"Bet on China" in Canadian Business (Vol. 80, November 5, 2007, No. 22, pp. 30)*
Pub: Rogers Media

Ed: Thomas Watson. **Description:** Former U.S. Federal Reserve Board head, Alan Greenspan, warns that contraction will happen in the Chinese market. However, the economic success of China does not seem to be at the point of ending, as the country remains the largest market for mobile telecommunications. Forecasts for Chinese trading and investments are provided.

36375 ■ *"Bet on the Subcontinent" in Canadian Business (Vol. 81, April 14, 2008, No. 6, pp. 27)*
Pub: Rogers Media

Ed: Calvin Leung. **Description:** Morgan Stanley Capital International India Index is down 28 percent for the first half of 2008 but this index rebounded 6 percent in 2002 then skyrocketed 65 percent in 2003. The economic reforms in the 1990's have created a growing middle class and households that can afford discretionary items will grow from eight million to 94 million by 2025. India's equity market could outperform developed markets if its economy grows at its current rate.

36376 ■ *"Betting On Volatile Materials" in Barron's (Vol. 88, July 14, 2008, No. 28, pp. M11)*
Pub: Dow Jones & Co., Inc.

Ed: John Marshall. **Description:** Economic slowdowns in the U.S., Europe and China could cause sharp short-term declines in the materials sector. The S&P Materials sector is vulnerable to shifts in the flow of funds. Statistical data included.

36377 ■ *"Beware this Chinese Export" in Barron's (Vol. 90, August 30, 2010, No. 35, pp. 21)*
Pub: Barron's Editorial & Corporate Headquarters

Ed: Bill Alpert, Leslie P. Norton. **Description:** A look at 158 China reverse-merger stocks in the U.S. reveal that the median underperformed the index of U.S. listed Chinese companies by 75 percent in their first three years. These reverse merger stocks also lagged the Russell 2000 index of small cap stocks by 66 percent.

36378 ■ *Billions of Entrepreneurs: How China and India Are Reshaping Their Futures and Yours*
Pub: Harvard Business School Press

Ed: Tarun Khanna. **Released:** 2009. **Price:** $29.95. **Description:** Various success strategies for success in both China and India are examined. Implications of the concurrent economic booms in both countries are cited.

36379 ■ *"Biz Assesses 'Textgate' Fallout; Conventions, Smaller Deals Affected" in Crain's Detroit Business (Vol. 24, March 31, 2008)*
Pub: Crain Communications, Inc.

Ed: Tom Henderson. **Description:** Businesspeople who were trying to measure the amount of economic damage is likely to be caused due to Mayor Kwame Kilpatrick's indictment on eight charges and found that: automotive and other large global deals are less likely to be affected than location decisions by smaller companies and convention site decisions. Also being affected are negotiations in which Mexican startup companies were planning a partnership with the TechTown incubator to pursue opportunities in the auto sector; those plans are being put on hold while they look at other sites.

36380 ■ *"Black Diamond Holdings Corp. Receives SEC Approval" in Canadian Corporate News (May 16, 2007)*
Pub: Comtex News Network Inc.

Description: Black Diamond Holdings, Corp., a British Columbia domiciled company and its two wholly owned subsidiaries are engaged in the bottling, importation, distribution, marketing, and brand creation of premium spirits and wines to worldwide consumers, announced that it has completed the SEC review process and has applied to list for trading in the United States on the OTC.BB.

36381 ■ *"Blood Diamonds are Forever" in Canadian Business (Vol. 83, August 17, 2010, No. 13-14, pp. 59)*
Pub: Rogers Media Ltd.

Ed: Matthew McClearn. **Description:** The failed case against Donald McKay who was found in possession of rough diamonds in a raid by Royal Canadian Mounted Police has raised doubts about Kimberley Process (KP) attempts to stop the illicit global trade in diamonds. KP has managed to reduce total global trade of blood diamonds by 1 percent in mid-2000.

36382 ■ *"Blues at the Toy Fair: Industry Reeling From Recalls, Lower Sales Volumes" in Crain's New York Business (February 18, 2008)*
Pub: Crain Communications Inc.

Ed: Elisabeth Cordova. **Description:** Over 1,500 toy developers and vendors will attend the American International Toy Fair, expected to be low-key due to recent recalls of toys not meeting American safety standards. Toy retailers and manufacturers, as well as the Chinese government, are promoting product testing to prevent toxic metals in toys.

36383 ■ *"BMW Makes Bet on Carbon Maker" in Wall Street Journal Eastern Edition (November 19 , 2011, pp. B3)*
Pub: Dow Jones & Company Inc.

Ed: Christoph Rauwald. **Description:** Eight months ago, Volkswagen AG acquired a 10 percent holding in carbon-fiber maker SGL Carbon SE. Its rival BMW AG is catching up by acquiring 15.2 percent stake in SGL as it seeks alliances like the rest of the industry in order to share industrial costs of new product development.

36384 ■ *"Boeing Scores $21.7 Billion Order in Indonesia" in Wall Street Journal Eastern Edition (November 18 , 2011, pp. B6)*
Pub: Dow Jones & Company Inc.

Ed: David Kesmodel, Laura Meckler. **Description:** Boeing has garnered a large contract to deliver Boeing 737 jets to Indonesia's Lion Air. There are those who are lobbying against the US government's practice of subsidizing foreign companies that make contracts with American aerospace companies.

36385 ■ *"Boosting Corporate Entrepreneurship Through HRM Practices" in Human Resource Management (Vol. 49, July-August 2010, No. 4)*
Pub: John Wiley
Ed: Ralf Schmelter, Rene Mauer, Christiane Borsch, Malte Brettel. **Description:** A study was conducted to determine which human resource management (HRM) practices promote corporate entrepreneurship (CE) in small and medium-sized enterprises (SMEs). Findings indicate that staff selection, staff development, training, and staff rewards on CE have a strong impact on SMEs.

36386 ■ *"Border Boletin: UA to Take Lie-Detector Kiosk to Poland" in Arizona Daily Star (September 14, 2010)*
Pub: Arizona Daily Star
Ed: Brady McCombs. **Description:** University of Arizona's National Center for Border Security and Immigration Research will send a team to Warsaw, Poland to show border guards from 27 European Union countries the center's Avatar Kiosk. The Avatar technology is designed for use at border ports and airports to assist Customs officers detect individuals who are lying.

36387 ■ *"Bottler Will Regain Its Pop" in Barron's (Vol. 88, March 17, 2008, No. 11, pp. 56)*
Pub: Dow Jones & Company, Inc.
Ed: Alexander Eule. **Description:** Discusses he 30 percent drop in the share price of PepsiAmericas Inc. from their 2007 high which presents an opportunity to buy into the company's dependable U.S. market and fast growing Eastern European business. The bottler's Eastern European operating profits in 2007 grew to $101 million from $21 million in 2006.

36388 ■ *"Bottom-Fishing and Speed-Dating in India" in Barron's (Vol. 88, March 24, 2008, No. 12, pp. M12)*
Pub: Dow Jones & Company, Inc.
Ed: Elliot Wilson. **Description:** Indian stocks have fallen hard in 2008, with Mumbai's Sensex 30 down 30 percent from its January 2008 peak of 21,000 to 14,995 in March. The India Private Equity Fair 2008 attracted 140 of the world's largest private equity firms and about 24 of India's fastest-growing corporations. Statistical data included.

36389 ■ *"Bountiful Barrels: Where to Find $140 Trillion" in Barron's (Vol. 88, July 14, 2008, No. 28, pp. 40)*
Pub: Dow Jones & Co., Inc.
Ed: Andrew Bary. **Description:** Surge in oil prices has caused a large transfer of wealth to oil-producing countries thereby reshaping the global economy. Oil reserves of oil exporting countries are now valued at $140 trillion. Economist Stephen Jen believes that this wealth will be transformed into paper assets as these countries invest in global stocks and bonds.

36390 ■ *Brazilian-American Business Review/Directory*
Pub: Brazilian-American Chamber of Commerce
Contact: John D. Landers, President
URL(s): www.brazilcham.com. **Released:** Annual; Latest edition 2009. **Price:** $80, for nonmembers in U.S.; $100, for nonmembers outside U.S.; $150, CD-ROM in U.S.; $200, CD-ROM outside U.S. **Covers:** Brazilian and American businesses interested in developing trade and investment between the two countries. **Entries include:** Company name, address, phone, fax, key personnel, Standard Industrial Classification (SIC) code. **Database includes:** Economic and business statistics; U.S. -Brazil business information.

36391 ■ *"Brazil's New King of Food" in Barron's (Vol. 89, July 13, 2009, No. 28, pp. 28)*
Pub: Dow Jones & Co., Inc.
Ed: Kenneth Rapoza. **Description:** Perdigao and Sadia's merger has resulted in the creation of Brasil Foods and the shares of Brasil Foods provides a play on both Brazil's newly energized consumer economy and its role as a major commodities exporter. Brasil Foods shares could climb as much as 36 percent.

36392 ■ *"Brewing a Love-Haiti Relationship" in The Business Journal - Serving Phoenix and the Valley of the Sun (Vol. 28, July 4, 2008, No. 44)*
Pub: American City Business Journals, Inc.
Ed: Yvonne Zusel. **Description:** Jean and Alicia Marseille have ventured into a coffee distribution company called Ka Bel LLC which markets Marabou brand of coffee imported from Haiti. Part of the proceeds of the business is donated to entrepreneurs from Jean's country, Haiti. Details of the Marseille's startup business and personal mission to help are discussed.

36393 ■ *"Brewing National Success" in Hawaii Business (Vol. 53, November 2007, No. 5, pp. 46)*
Pub: Hawaii Business Publishing
Ed: Alex Salkever. **Description:** Kona Brewing Co. (KBC) is already selling its brews in four cities in Florida and 17 other states and Japan as well. KBC is currently forming a deal with Red Hook to produce Longboard Lager and other KBC brews at Red Hooks' brewery in New Hampshire. KBC's chief executive officer Mattson Davis shares KBC's practices for success.

36394 ■ *"Broadband Reaches Access Limits in Europe" in Information Today (Vol. 26, February 2009, No. 2, pp. 22)*
Pub: Information Today, Inc.
Ed: Jim Ashling. **Description:** Eurostat (the Statistical Office of the European communities) reports results from is survey regarding Internet use by businesses throughout its 27-member states. Iceland, Finland and the Netherlands provide the most access at broadband speeds, followed by Belgium, Spain and France.

36395 ■ *"Buhler Versatile Launches Next Generation of Equipment" in Farm Industry News (November 23, 2011)*
Pub: Penton Business Media Inc.
Ed: Jodie Wehrspann. **Description:** Canadian owned Versatile is expanding its four-wheel drive tractor division with sprayers, tillage, and seeding equipment.

36396 ■ *Building Wealth in China: 36 True Stories of Chinese Millionaires and How They Made Their Fortunes*
Pub: Crown Business Books
Ed: Ling, Zhu. **Released:** April 27, 2010. **Price:** $15. 00. **Description:** Thirty-six of China's most successful and innovative entrepreneurs discuss valuable lessons for growing a business in China.

36397 ■ *Business Stripped Bare: Adventures of a Global Entrepreneur*
Pub: Virgin Books/Random House
Ed: Sir Richard Branson. **Released:** January 22, 2010. **Price:** $26.95. **Description:** Successful entrepreneur, Sir Richard Branson, shares the inside track on some of his greatest achievements in business and the lessons learned from setbacks.

36398 ■ *"Calendar" in Crain's Detroit Business (Vol. 26, January 11, 2010, No. 2, pp. 16)*
Pub: Crain Communications Inc.
Description: Listing of events includes seminars sponsored by the Detroit Economic Club as well as conferences dealing with globalization and graphic design.

36399 ■ *"Calendar" in Crain's Detroit Business (Vol. 26, January 18, 2010, No. 3, pp. 16)*
Pub: Crain Communications Inc.
Description: Listing of events includes seminars sponsored by the Detroit Economic Club as well as conferences dealing with globalization and marketing.

36400 ■ *"California Company Suing City's Lupin Over its Generic Diabetes Drug" in Baltimore Business Journal (Vol. 27, January 1, 2010)*
Pub: American City Business Journals
Ed: Gary Haber. **Description:** California-based Depomed Inc. is suing Baltimore, Maryland-based Lupin Pharmaceuticals Inc. and its parent company in India over the patents to a diabetes drug. Lupin allegedly infringed on Depomed's four patents for Glumetza when it filed for permission to sell its own version of the drug with the US Food and Drug Administration. Details on generic pharmaceutical manufacturer tactics are discussed.

36401 ■ *"Cambodia Calls" in Barron's (Vol. 89, July 27, 2009, No. 30, pp. M7)*
Pub: Dow Jones & Co., Inc.
Ed: Leslie P. Norton. **Description:** Interest in frontier markets could jump if enthusiasm about growth in the developed world gathers steam. Cambodia is the latest market to get attention where a handful of investors are trying to set up funds. One investor believes that Cambodia is back open for business but others are still cautious about investing in the country.

36402 ■ *"Can a Brazilian SUV Take On the Jeep Wrangler?" in Business Week (September 22, 2008, No. 4100, pp. 50)*
Pub: McGraw-Hill Companies, Inc.
Ed: Helen Walters. **Description:** Profile of the Brazilian company TAC as well as the flourishing Brazilian car market; TAC has launched a new urban vehicle, the Stark, which has won prizes for innovation; the company uses local technology and manufacturing expertise.

36403 ■ *"Canada Nears European Trade Treaty" in Globe & Mail (February 5, 2007, pp. B1)*
Pub: CTVglobemedia Publishing Inc.
Ed: Steven Chase. **Description:** The probable establishment of a treaty by Canada with Norway, Switzerland and Iceland for free-trade is discussed. The treaty will allow an annual business of $11 billion to take place in Canada.

36404 ■ *"Canada, Not China, Is Partner In Our Economic Prosperity" in Crain's Chicago Business (Vol. 31, April 14, 2008, No. 15, pp. 14)*
Pub: Crain Communications, Inc.
Ed: Paul O'Connor. **Description:** In 2005 more than $500 billion in two-way trade crossed the friendly border between the Great Lakes states and Canadian provinces and for decades Canada is every Great Lakes State's number one and growing export market.

36405 ■ *"Canada Wins Second NAFTA Decision on Softwood Tariffs" in Globe & Mail (March 18, 2006, pp. B2)*
Pub: CTVglobemedia Publishing Inc.
Ed: Steven Chase; Peter Kennedy. **Description:** Canada has won a second major North American Free Trade Agreement (NAFTA) victory in five years of legal battles over U.S. tariffs on softwood. Details of the controversy and ruling are presented.

36406 ■ *Canadian Entrepreneurship and Small Business Management*
Pub: McGraw-Hill Ryerson, Limited
Ed: D. Wesley Balderson. **Released:** February 2005. **Description:** Successful entrepreneurship and small business management is shown through the use of individual Canadian small business experiences.

36407 ■ *"Canadian Hydronics Businesses Promote 'Beautiful Heat" in Indoor Comfort Marketing (Vol. 70, September 2011, No. 9, pp. 20)*
Pub: Industry Publications Inc.
Description: Canadian hydronics companies are promoting their systems as beautiful heat. Hydronics is the use of water as the heat-transfer medium in heating and cooling system.

36408 ■ *Canadian Multinationals and International Finance*
Pub: International Specialized Books Services
Ed: Greg Marchildon. **Released:** October 1, 1992. **Price:** $190.00. **Description:** Seven stories that explore the role of Canadian multinational enterprise in world finance, trade and direct investment.

36409 ■ *"Canadian Patients Give Detroit Hospitals a Boost" in Crain's Detroit Business (Vol. 24, April 14, 2008, No. 15, pp. 10)*
Pub: Crain Communications Inc.
Ed: Jay Greene. **Description:** Each year thousands of Canadians travel to Detroit area hospitals seeking quicker solutions to medical problems or access to services that are limited or unavailable in Canada.

36410 ■ *"The Canadians Are Coming!" in Canadian Business (Vol. 80, October 22, 2007, No. 21, pp. 15)*
Pub: Rogers Media
Ed: Rachel Pulfer. **Description:** Toronto-Dominion Bank declared its acquisition of the New Jersey-based Commerce Bancorp for C$8.5 billion. Royal Bank of Canada has scooped up Trinidad-based Financial Group for C$2.2 billion. Details of the foreign acquisitions, as well as the impact of high Canadian dollars on the mergers are discussed.

36411 ■ *"Caterpillar to Expand Research, Production in China" in Chicago Tribune (August 27, 2008)*
Pub: McClatchy-Tribune Information Services
Ed: James P. Miller. **Description:** Caterpillar Inc., the Peoria-based heavy-equipment manufacturer, plans to establish a new research-and-development center at the site of its rapidly growing campus in Wuxi.

36412 ■ *"A Cautionary Tale for Emerging Market Giants" in Harvard Business Review (Vol. 88, September 2010, No. 9, pp. 99)*
Pub: Harvard Business School Publishing
Ed: J. Stewart Black, Allen J. Morrison. **Description:** Key factors that negatively affected Japan corporate growth and organizational effectiveness include: devotion to established path, isolated domestic markets, homogenous executive teams, and a non-contentious labor force. Solutions include leadership development programs, multicultural input, and cross-cultural training.

36413 ■ *"Cemex Paves a Global Road to Solid Growth" in Barron's (Vol. 88, March 10, 2008, No. 10, pp. 24)*
Pub: Dow Jones & Company, Inc.
Ed: Sandra Ward. **Description:** Shares of Cemex are expected to perform well with the company's expected strong performance despite fears of a US recession. The company has a diverse geographical reach and benefits from a strong worldwide demand for cement.

36414 ■ *"Cents and Sensibility" in Playthings (Vol. 107, January 1, 2009, No. 1, pp. 19)*
Pub: Reed Business Information
Contact: Jeff Greisch, President
Ed: Pamela Brill. **Description:** Recent concerns over safety, phthalate and lead paint and other toxic materials, as well as consumers going green, are issues discussed by toy manufacturers. Doll manufacturers also face increase labor and material costs and are working to design dolls that girls will love.

36415 ■ *"CEOs Decry Budget Taxation Change" in Globe & Mail (April 2, 2007, pp. B1)*
Pub: CTVglobemedia Publishing Inc.
Ed: Steven Chase. **Description:** The views of the chief executive officers of Canadian firms, on the changes in the country's policy governing the taxation of foreign deals, are presented.

36416 ■ *"Champion Enterprises Buys UK Company" in Crain's Detroit Business (Vol. 24, March 17, 2008, No. 11, pp. 4)*
Pub: Crain Communications, Inc.
Ed: Daniel Duggan. **Description:** With the acquisition of ModularUK Building Systems Ltd., a steel-frame modular manufacturer, Champion Enterprises has continued its expansion outside the United States.

36417 ■ *Change in SMEs: The New European Capitalism*
Pub: Palgrave Macmillan
Ed: Katharina Bluhm; Rudi Schmidt. **Released:** October 2008. **Price:** $95.00. **Description:** Effects of global change on corporate governance, management, competitive strategies and labor relations in small-to-medium sized enterprises in various European countries are discussed.

36418 ■ *"A Change Would Do You Good" in Canadian Business (Vol. 80, November 19, 2007, No. 23, pp. 15)*
Pub: Rogers Media
Ed: Geoff Kirbyson. **Description:** Western Glove Works will be manufacturing clothing offshore, including Sheryl Crow's jeans collection, in countries such as China and the Philippines. The company decided to operate offshore after 86 years of existence due to the high price of manufacturing jeans in Canada. Western Glove's focus on producing celebrity-endorsed goods is discussed.

36419 ■ *"Changing the Rules of the Accounting Game" in Canadian Business (Vol. 81, December 8, 2008, No. 21, pp. 19)*
Pub: Rogers Media Ltd.
Ed: Al Rosen. **Description:** Interference from world politicians in developing accounting standards is believed to have resulted in untested rules that are inferior to current standards. European lawmakers have recently asked to change International Financial Reporting Standards.

36420 ■ *"Charlotte Pipe Launches Satirical Campaign" in Contractor (Vol. 57, January 2010, No. 1, pp. 6)*
Pub: Penton Media, Inc.
Description: Charlotte Pipe and Foundry Co. launched an advertising campaign that uses social media and humor to make a point about how it can be nearly impossible to determine if imported cast iron pipes and fittings meet the same quality standards as what is made in the U.S. The campaign features 'pipe whisperers' and also spoofs pipe sniffing dogs.

36421 ■ *"The China Connection" in Crain's Chicago Business (Vol. 31, March 24, 2008, No. 12, pp. 26)*
Pub: Crain Communications, Inc.
Ed: Samantha Stainburn. **Description:** Interview with Ben Munoz who studied abroad in Beijing, China for three months to study international economics, e-commerce and global leadership.

36422 ■ *"China Pegs Surplus at $101.9 Billion" in Globe & Mail (January 12, 2006, pp. B1)*
Pub: CTVglobemedia Publishing Inc.
Ed: Barrie McKenna. **Description:** The reasons behind the trade surplus of $101.9 billion, in China, are presented.

36423 ■ *"The China Tax" in Forbes (Vol. 180, October 1, 2007, No. 6, pp. 35)*
Pub: Forbes Inc.
Ed: Robyn Meredith. **Description:** U.S. consumers can see a rise in prices for goods made in China due to growing pressure from Congress to ensure safe products from that country. Taxing products imported from China could be levied in five different forms listed.

36424 ■ *"China Trade Deficit Costs California Jobs" in Sacramento Business Journal (Vol. 25, August 8, 2008, No. 23, pp. 1)*
Pub: American City Business Journals, Inc.
Ed: Melanie Turner. **Description:** California topped the ranking of states with job losses because of the rising trade deficit with China, losing 325,800 jobs between 2001-2007. The U.S. has lost 2.3 million workers within the period. Other views and information on the job loses because of the trade deficit with China, are presented.

36425 ■ *"China Vs. the World: Whose Technology Is It?" in Harvard Business Review (Vol. 88, December 2010, No. 12, pp. 94)*
Pub: Harvard Business School Publishing
Ed: Thomas M Hout, Pankaj Ghemawat. **Description:** Examination of the regulation the Chinese government is implementing that require foreign corporations wishing to do business in the country to give up their new technologies. These regulations avoid World Trade Organization technology transfer provisions and complicate the convergence of socialism and capitalism.

36426 ■ *"China's Dagong Show" in Canadian Business (Vol. 83, August 17, 2010, No. 13-14, pp. 15)*
Pub: Rogers Media Ltd.
Ed: Matthew McClearn. **Description:** Beijing, China-based Dagong Global Credit Rating has downgraded US credit ratings, as well as other developed countries such as Canada, while granting higher ratings to China, Russia and Brazil. However, there is a perceived disconnection between Dagong's ratings and its official pronouncements.

36427 ■ *China's Rational Entrepreneurs: The Development of the New Private Business Sector*
Pub: Routledge
Ed: Barbara Krug. **Released:** March 2004. **Price:** $195.00 (US). **Description:** Difficulties faced by entrepreneurs in China are discussed, including analysis for understanding their behavior and relations with local governments in order to secure long-term business success.

36428 ■ *"China's Transition to Green Energy Systems" in Energy Policy (Vol. 39, October 2011, No. 10, pp. 5909-5919)*
Pub: Reed Elsevier Reference Publishing
Ed: Wei Li, Guojun Song, Melanie Beresford, Ben Ma. **Description:** The economics of home solar water heaters and their growing popularity in Dezhous City, China is discussed.

36429 ■ *Chinese Ethnic Business*
Pub: Routledge Inc.
Ed: Eric Fong; Chiu Ming Luk. **Released:** October 2006. **Description:** Impact of globalization on Chinese ethnic small businesses is covered, focusing on U.S., Australia, and Canada.

36430 ■ *Chinese Ethnic Business: Global and Local Perspectives*
Pub: Routledge
Ed: Eric Fong; Chiu Luk. **Released:** May 2009. **Price:** $39.95 paperback. **Description:** Globalization impacts on the development of Chinese businesses are analyzed, focusing on economic globalization of the United States, Australia, and Canada. Information is focused on economic globalization and Chinese community development, transnational linkages, local urban structures, homogenization and place attachment, as well as methodology such as ethnographic studies, historical analysis, geographic studies and statistical analysis.

36431 ■ *"Chinese Fund Loans $33.5 Million to Prestolite" in Crain's Detroit Business (Vol. 26, January 18, 2010, No. 3, pp. 1)*
Pub: Crain Communications Inc.
Ed: Ryan Beene. **Description:** Prestolite Electric Inc., a distributor of alternators and starter motors for commercial and heavy-duty vehicles, looked to China for fresh capital in order to fund new product launches.

36432 ■ *"Chinese Solar Panel Manufacturer Scopes Out Austin" in Austin Business JournalInc. (Vol. 29, October 30, 2009, No. 34, pp. 1)*
Pub: American City Business Journals
Ed: Jacob Dirr. **Description:** China's Yingli Green Energy Holding Company Ltd. is looking for a site in order to construct a $20 million photovoltaic panel plant. Both Austin and San Antonio are vying to house the manufacturing hub. The project could create about 300 jobs and give Austin a chance to become a player in the solar energy market. Other solar companies are also considering Central Texas as an option to set up shop.

36433 ■ *Cities from the Arabian Desert: The Building of Jubail and Yanbu in Saudi Arabia*
Pub: Turnaround Associates
Ed: Andrea H. Pampanini. **Released:** May 2005. **Price:** $35.00. **Description:** An overview of Saudi Arabia's government to take control of the nation's

natural resources and change the government, educational system, and its culture by evolving into a modern industrial society.

36434 ■ *"City Slickers" in Canadian Business (Vol. 81, March 31, 2008, No. 5, pp. 36)*
Pub: Rogers Media
Ed: Joe Castaldo. **Description:** Richard Florida believes that the creative class drives the economy and the prosperity of countries depends on attracting and retaining these people. Florida has brought attention to developing livable and economically vibrant cities thanks in part to his promotional skills. However, he has also drawn critics who see his data on his theories as flimsy and inadequate.

36435 ■ *"Clicks From Round the World: Simplifying International E-Commerce" in Inc. (Volume 32, December 2010, No. 10, pp. 146)*
Pub: Inc. Magazine
Ed: Ryan Underwood. **Description:** By 2014, global e-commerce spending is expected to increase more than 90 percent, with much of that growth coming from Latin America.

36436 ■ *"Closed Minds and Open Skies" in Barron's (Vol. 88, March 10, 2008, No. 10, pp. 50)*
Pub: Dow Jones & Company, Inc.
Ed: Thomas Donlan. **Description:** American politicians have closed minds when it comes to fair trade. The American government must not interfere with the country's manufacturing industries or worry about outsourcing defense contracts to European aerospace company Airbus.

36437 ■ *"CNinsure Offers Safety in Numbers" in Barron's (Vol. 90, September 13, 2010, No. 37, pp. 29)*
Pub: Barron's Editorial & Corporate Headquarters
Ed: Teresa Rivas. **Description:** China's insurance holding company CNinsure has a long growth future due to the nascent insurance market in the country. It has also been diversifying its offerings and it has a broad network in the nation. The shares of the company are trading cheaply at nearly 14 times its 2011 earnings, and is considered a good point for investors.

36438 ■ *"CO2 Emissions Embodied in China-US Trade" in Energy Policy (Vol. 39, October 2011, No. 10, pp. 5980-5987)*
Pub: Reed Elsevier Reference Publishing
Ed: Huibin Du, Guozhu Mao, Alexander M. Smith, Xuxu Wang, Yuan Wang, Jianghong Guo. **Description:** Input and output analysis based on the energy per dollar ratio for carbon dioxide emissions involved in China-United States trade is outlined.

36439 ■ *"Cold Stone Creamery" in Ice Cream Reporter (Vol. 22, January 20, 2009, No. 2, pp. 8)*
Pub: Ice Cream Reporter
Description: Franchise News reports that Cold Stone Creamery is looking for master franchisees to support its expansion into the North German market. The report notes that following its successful launch in Denmark, the firm is also preparing for expansion into France.

36440 ■ *"Coming: Cheaper Oil and a Stronger Buck" in Barron's (Vol. 88, March 24, 2008, No. 12, pp. 53)*
Pub: Dow Jones & Company, Inc.
Ed: Lawrence C. Strauss. **Description:** Carl C. Weinberg, the chief economist of High Frequency Economics, forecasts that Chinese economic growth will slow down and that oil prices will drop to $80 a barrel in 2008. He also believes that the US dollar will start rising the moment the Federal Reserve stops cutting interest rates.

36441 ■ *Competing in Emerging Markets*
Pub: Taylor & Francis Group
Contact: Peter Rigby, Chief Executive Officer
Ed: Hemant Merchant. **Released:** October 2007. **Price:** $62.95. **Description:** Understanding the perils and promises of emerging markets to the growth of companies is discussed. Readings and case studies focus on the strategic and operational challenges companies face while competing in emerging markets.

36442 ■ *"Competition At Last?" in Canadian Business (Vol. 81, July 22, 2008, No. 12-13, pp. 7)*
Pub: Rogers Media Ltd.
Description: Competition Policy Review Panel's 'Compete to Win' report revealed that Canada is being 'hollowed-out' by foreign acquisitions. The panel investigated competition and foreign investment policies in Canada. Key information on the report, as well as views on the Investment Canada Act and the Competition Act, is presented.

36443 ■ *"Confidence High, But Lenders More Cautious" in Farmer's Weekly (March 28, 2008, No. 320)*
Pub: Reed Business Information
Contact: Jeff Greisch, President
Description: Discusses the effect of the global credit crunch on farmers as well as recent auctions which were timed to beat changes to capital gains tax.

36444 ■ *"Coping With a Shrinking Planet" in Agency Sales Magazine (Vol. 39, December 2009, No. 11, pp. 46)*
Pub: MANA
Ed: Mark Young. **Description:** China and India are forcing big changes in the world and are posing a huge threat to U.S. manufacturers and their sales representatives. Reps may want to consider expanding into these territories. Helping sell American products out of the country presents an opportunity for economic expansion.

36445 ■ *"Copy Karachi?" in Barron's (Vol. 88, June 30, 2008, No. 26, pp. 5)*
Pub: Dow Jones & Co., Inc.
Ed: Randall W. Forsyth. **Description:** Karachi bourse had a historic 8.6 percent one-day gain because the bourse banned short-selling for a month and announced a 30 billion rupee fund to stabilize the market. The shares of General Motors are trading within the same values that it had in 1974. The reasons for this decline are discussed.

36446 ■ *"Corporate Governance Reforms in China and India: Challenges and Opportunities" in Business Horizons (January-February 2008)*
Pub: Elsevier Advanced Technology Publications
Ed: Nandini Rajagopalan, Yan Zhang. **Description:** The evolution of corporate governance reforms and the role of privatization and globalization in India and China are studied. Shortage of qualified independent directors and lack of incentives were found to be two of the major challenges in governance. The implications of and solutions to these challenges are highlighted.

36447 ■ *"Cost Remains Top Factor In Considering Green Technology" in Canadian Sailings (June 30, 2008)*
Pub: UBM Global Trade
Contact: Leonard J. Corallo, President
Ed: Julie Gedeon. **Description:** Improving its environmental performance remains a priority in the shipping industry; however, testing new technologies can prove difficult due to the harsh conditions that ships endure as well as installation which usually requires a dry dock.

36448 ■ *Country Studies in Entrepreneurship: A Historical Perspective*
Pub: Palgrave Macmillan
Ed: Ioanna Minoglou; Cassis Youssef. **Released:** July 2006. **Price:** $80.00. **Description:** Comparison of eight national entrepreneurial ventures, covering three continents, is discussed.

36449 ■ *"Courting Canadian Customers Confounds Car Dealers" in Business First Buffalo (November 9, 2007, pp. 1)*
Pub: American City Business Journals, Inc.
Ed: James Fink. **Description:** Strength of the Canadian dollar has led to an influx of potential customers for the Western New York automobile industry, but franchising restrictions and licensing as well as insurance issues have limited the potential of having larger sales figures. Border and trade issues that affect the car industry in WNY are also discussed.

36450 ■ *"CPR-CN Deal to Ease Vancouver Logjam" in Globe & Mail (January 27, 2006, pp. B4)*
Pub: CTVglobemedia Publishing Inc.
Ed: Brent Jang. **Description:** In a bid to lessen West coast port grid lock Canadian Pacific Railway Ltd and Canadian National Railway Co. has agreed to share tracks in the Vancouver region. This will allow the trains to operate more efficiently from the Vancouver Port.

36451 ■ *Creating Capitalism Joint-Stock Enterprise in British Politics and Culture, 1800-1870*
Pub: Royal Historical Society
Ed: James Taylor. **Released:** October 2006. **Price:** $80.00. **Description:** The growth of joint-stock business in Victorian Britain is discussed, particularly the resistance to it.

36452 ■ *"Creativity: A Key Link to Entrepreneurial Behavior" in Business Horizons (September-October 2007, pp. 365)*
Pub: Elsevier Technology Publications
Ed: Stephen Ko, John E. Butler. **Description:** Importance of creativity and its link to entrepreneurial behavior is examined. In a study of various entrepreneurs, studies concluded that a solid knowledge base, a well-developed social network, and a strong focus on identifying opportunities are relevant to entrepreneurial behavior.

36453 ■ *"Critics Target Bribery Law" in Wall Street Journal Eastern Edition (November 28, 2011, pp. B1)*
Pub: Dow Jones & Company Inc. Enterprise Media Group
Contact: Clare Hart, President
Ed: Joe Palazzuolo. **Description:** Concern about how the Foreign Corrupt Practices Act, the United States' anti-bribery law, is enforced has drawn the focus of corporate lobbyists. Corporations have paid some $4 billion in penalties in cases involving the law, which prohibits companies from paying foreign officials bribes. The US Chamber of Commerce believes amending the act should be a priority.

36454 ■ *Currency Internationalization: Global Experiences and Implications for the Renminbi*
Pub: Palgrave Macmillan
Ed: Wensheng Peng, Chang Shu. **Released:** January 5, 2010. **Price:** $100.00. **Description:** A collection of academic studies relating to the potential internationalization of China's remninbi. It also discusses the increasing use of China's remninbi currency in international trade and finance.

36455 ■ *D & B Principal International Businesses: The World Marketing Directory*
Pub: Dun and Bradstreet Corp.
Contact: David J. Emery, President
URL(s): dnb.com.au/Sales_and_Marketing/International_business_directories/Principal_International_Business_Directory. **Released:** Annual **Price:** $595, commercial & library price. **Covers:** approximately 55,000 leading businesses in all lines, outside of the U.S., in 143 countries. **Entries include:** Company name, address, phone, fax, D&B number, telex, up to six Standard Industrial Classification (SIC) code, line of business, sales volume (in U.S. currency), number of employees, parent company and location, executive name and title, year established, and import/export designation. **Arrangement:** Geographical. **Indexes:** Geographical, cross-referenced alphabetical, industry classification.

36456 ■ *"Darkness Falling.." in Barron's (Vol. 89, July 20, 2009, No. 29, pp. 13)*
Pub: Dow Jones & Co., Inc.
Description: Newsletter writer Arch Crawford believes that market indicators signal a possible downturn in US stock markets. High risk areas also include China and Japan .

36457 ■ *"Dealing With Dangers Abroad" in Financial Executive (Vol. 23, December 2007, No. 10, pp. 32)*
Pub: Financial Executives International
Ed: Jeffrey Marshall. **Description:** Clear processes and responsibilities for risk management for all companies going global are essential. U.S. toy manufacturer, Matel was put into crisis mode after its Chinese-made toys were recalled due to the use of lead-based paint or tiny magnets in its products.

36458 ■ *"Decline in Assets Is Costly for Advisers" in The Business Journal-Serving Metropolitan Kansas City (Vol. 27, October 24, 2008)*
Pub: American City Business Journals, Inc.
Ed: James Dornbrook. **Description:** Financial advisers in the Kansas City, Missouri area are forced to cut costs as their assets have decreased sharply due to the huge drop in stock prices. American Century Investments was forced to diversify into foreign assets and cut 90 jobs as its assets dropped to $84 billion. Diversification has softened the impact of the steep decline in stock prices for Waddell & Reed Financial Inc.

36459 ■ *"Deere to Open Technology Center in Germany" in Chicago Tribune (September 3, 2008)*
Pub: McClatchy-Tribune Information Services
Ed: James P. Miller. **Description:** Deere & Co. plans to open a technology and innovation center in Germany; details of the company's expansion plans are discussed.

36460 ■ *Democratization Without Representation: The Politics of Small Industry in Mexico*
Pub: Pennsylvania State University Press
Ed: Kenneth C. Shalden. **Released:** March 2006. **Price:** $31.95. **Description:** Opportunities for individuals to participate in Mexico's democracy and how it is affecting the way industries do business.

36461 ■ *"The Design of Tax Policy in Canada" in Canadian Journal of Economics (Vol. 44, November 2011, No. 4, pp. 1184)*
Pub: Blackwell Publishers Ltd.
Ed: Kevin Milligan. **Description:** Empirical evidence and tax policy design are presented by Richard Blundell.

36462 ■ *"Despite Hot Toys, Holiday Sales Predicted To Be Ho-Ho-Hum" in Drug Store News (Vol. 29, November 12, 2007, No. 14, pp. 78)*
Pub: Drug Store News
Ed: Doug Desjardins. **Description:** Summer toy recalls have retailers worried about holiday sales in 2007. Mattel was heavily impacted from the recall of millions of toys manufactured in China.

36463 ■ *"Destination Africa: A Look at How Tourism Could Change the Face and Economics of Africa" in Black Enterprise (February 2008)*
Pub: Earl G. Graves Publishing Co. Inc.
Ed: Sonia Alleyne. **Description:** Countries in Africa are experiencing high rates of growth in tourism than the worldwide average. Statistical data included.

36464 ■ *"Deutsche Bank Joins the Club" in Barron's (Vol. 88, March 31, 2008, No. 13, pp. M6)*
Pub: Dow Jones & Company, Inc.
Ed: Arindam Nag. **Description:** Deutsche Bank's tangible leverage has worsened sharply in the past year from 2.1 percent to 2.3 percent during 2002-2006 to only 1.6 percent. The bank has also been accumulating a lot of illiquid assets and its Level-3 assets are three times its tangible equity.

36465 ■ *Developmental Entrepreneurship: Adversity, Risk, and Isolation*
Pub: Elsevier Science and Technology Books
Ed: Craig Galbraith. **Released:** August 2006. **Price:** $99.95. **Description:** Volume five of the series, this book focuses on the fields of entrepreneurship, sociology, and economics. Fifteen articles related to entrepreneurship and small business development within a global environment are included.

36466 ■ *Digital Divide: Civic Engagement, Information Poverty, and the Internet Worldwide*
Pub: Cambridge University Press
Contact: Richard Ziemacki, President
E-mail: rziemacki@cambridge.org
Ed: Pippa Norris. **Released:** January 22, 2010. **Price:** $28.99. **Description:** The expansive growth of the Internet is intensifying existing inequalities between the information rich and poor. The book examines the evidence for access and use of the Internet in 179 countries and discusses the global divide that is evident between industrialized and developing societies.

36467 ■ *"Direct Recovery Associates Debt Collection Agency Beats Industry Record" in Internet Wire (June 24, 2010)*
Pub: Comtex
Description: Direct Recovery Associates Inc. was named as one of the highest collection records in the industry, which has consistently improved over 18 years. The firm is an international attorney-based debt collection agency.

36468 ■ *"Direct Recovery Associates, Inc. Debt Collection Agency Founder Featured in China Daily" in Internet Wire (November 9, 2010)*
Pub: Comtex
Description: Richard Hart, founder of Direct Recovery Associates, was featured in an article published in the China Daily. The article discussed the increased credit and debt collection demands involving the U.S. and China.

36469 ■ *Directory of American Firms Operating in Foreign Countries*
Pub: Uniworld Business Publications Inc.
Contact: M. Christopher Shimkin, President
E-mail: cshimkin@uniworldbp.com
URL(s): www.uniworldbp.com. **Ed:** Barbara D. Fiorito. **Released:** Biennial; latest edition 20th, March 2009. **Price:** $435, Individuals hardcover, plus shipping charges; $975, Individuals CD-ROM. **Covers:** About 4,300 American corporations with 125,000 subsidiaries or affiliates outside the United States. **Entries include:** Company name, address, phone; names and titles of key personnel; number of employees, annual sales, NAICS code, web address, locations and types of facilities in foreign countries, number of employees, product/service. Separate country editions also available. **Arrangement:** Alphabetical. **Indexes:** Foreign operation by country.

36470 ■ *"Disney Has High Hopes for Duffy" in Canadian Business (Vol. 83, October 12, 2010, No. 17, pp. 14)*
Pub: Rogers Media Ltd.
Ed: James Cowan. **Description:** The reintroduction of Duffy is expected to create a new, exclusive product line that distinguishes Disney's parks and stores from competitors. Duffy, a teddy bear, was first introduced at a Disney World store in Florida in 2002. The character was incorporated into the Disney mythology when its popularity grew in Japan.

36471 ■ *"Diversity Knocks" in Canadian Business (Vol. 83, October 12, 2010, No. 17, pp. 62)*
Pub: Rogers Media Ltd.
Ed: Angelina Chapin. **Description:** Canadian companies have a global edge because of their multicultural workforce. However, most of these organizations do not take advantage and avoid doing business abroad. Canadian firms could leverage their multicultural staff with language skills and knowledge of local customs.

36472 ■ *"Dividing to Conquer" in Barron's (Vol. 88, March 31, 2008, No. 13, pp. 22)*
Pub: Dow Jones & Company, Inc.
Ed: Andrew Bary. **Description:** Altria's spin off of Philip Morris International could unlock substantial value for both domestic and international cigarette concerns. The strong brands and ample payouts from both companies will most likely impress investors.

36473 ■ *"Doctors, Health Insurers Squabble Over Who Sends Patients the Bill" in Baltimore Business Journal (Vol. 27, February 6, 2010)*
Pub: American City Business Journals
Ed: Scott Graham. **Description:** Issue of allowing patients to send reimbursement checks to physicians who are not part of their health insurer's provider network is being debated in Maryland. Details on the proposed Maryland bill and the arguments presented by doctors and insurers are outlined.

36474 ■ *Doing Business Anywhere: The Essential Guide to Going Global*
Pub: John Wiley and Sons, Inc.
Ed: Tom Travis. **Released:** 2007. **Price:** $24.95. **Description:** Plans are given for new or existing businesses to organize, plan, operate and execute a business on a global basis. Trade agreements, brand protection and patents, ethics, security as well as cultural issues are among the issues addressed.

36475 ■ *"Dollar Daze: Canadian Businesses Must Adjust to a New Reality" in Canadian Business (Vol. 80, Winter 2007, No. 24, pp. 11)*
Pub: Rogers Media
Ed: Jeff Sanford. **Description:** Several Canadian businessmen lost massive amounts in the Canadian value of their investments due to the volatility of the U.S. dollar. The factors that weighed down the value of the U.S. dollar include the announcement by China to diversify their currency reserves away from the U.S. dollar and concerns about the price of oil.

36476 ■ *"Dollar Doldrums; How American Companies are Beating the Currency Crunch" in Inc. (March 2008, pp. 45-46)*
Pub: Gruner & Jahr USA Publishing
Ed: Sarah Goldstein. **Description:** Despite the low American dollar, some exporters are seeing a growth in their businesses, while other have had to relocate operations and switch to U.S. supplier. Four business owners tell how they are dealing with the current economic conditions.

36477 ■ *"Don't Bet Against The House" in Barron's (Vol. 88, July 14, 2008, No. 28, pp. 20)*
Pub: Dow Jones & Co., Inc.
Ed: Sandra Ward. **Description:** Shares of Nasdaq OMX have lost more than 50 percent of their value from November 2007 to July 2008 but the value of these shares could climb 50 percent on the strength of world security exchanges. Only 15 percent of the company's revenues come from the U.S. and the shares are trading at 12.5 times the amount expected for 2008.

36478 ■ *"Don't Tweak Your Supply Chain - Rethink It End to End" in Harvard Business Review (Vol. 88, October 2010, No. 10, pp. 62)*
Pub: Harvard Business School Publishing
Ed: Hau L. Lee. **Description:** Hong Kong apparel firm Esquel Apparel Ltd. is used to illustrate supply chain reorganization to improve a firm's sustainability. Discussion focuses on taking a broad approach rather than addressing individual steps or processes.

36479 ■ *"Dow Champions Innovative Energy Solutions for Auto Industry at NAIAS" in Business of Global Warming (January 25, 2010, pp. 7)*
Pub: Investment Weekly News
Description: This year's North American International Auto Show in Detroit will host the 'Electric Avenue' exhibit sponsored by the Dow Chemical Company. The display will showcase the latest in innovative energy solutions from Dow as well as electric vehicles and the technology supporting them. This marks the first time a non-automotive manufacturer is part of the main floor of the show.

36480 ■ *"Down Mexico Way" in Canadian Business (Vol. 79, September 25, 2006, No. 19, pp. 27)*
Pub: Rogers Media
Description: Presidential election in Mexico and its effects on its economy is discussed.

36481 ■ *"Dragon, but.." in Canadian Business (Vol. 81, December 8, 2008, No. 21, pp. 45)*
Pub: Rogers Media Ltd.
Ed: Matthew McLearn. **Description:** The greatest challenge in smooth trade relations between China and Canada is believed to be lukewarm relations with China over human rights issues. Australia on the other hand, has attracted huge Chinese outward direct investments because of strong trade relations.

36482 ■ *"Dreaming in Macau" in Canadian Business (Vol. 81, December 8, 2008, No. 21, pp. 65)*
Pub: Rogers Media Ltd.
Ed: Joe Chidley. **Description:** Key information, as well as views on the economic aspects of Macau are presented. Macau was once monopolized by Stanley Ho's Sociedad de Turismo e Diversoes de Macau, but the government transformed the area into a leisure-and-entertainment spot. Details about Cirque de Soleil are also presented.

36483 ■ *"Drilling Deep and Flying High" in Barron's (Vol. 88, June 30, 2008, No. 26, pp. 34)*
Pub: Dow Jones & Co., Inc.
Ed: Kenneth Rapoza. **Description:** Shares of Petrobras could rise another 25 percent if the three deep-water wells that the company has found proves as lucrative as some expect. Petrobras will become an oil giant if the reserves are proven.

36484 ■ *E-Commerce in Regional Small to Medium Enterprises*
Pub: Idea Group Publishing
Ed: Robert MacGregor. **Released:** July 2007. **Price:** $99.95. **Description:** Strategies small to medium enterprises (SMEs) need to implement in order to compete with larger, global businesses and the role electronic commerce plays in this process are outlined. Studies of e-commerce in multiple regional areas, focusing on the role of business size, business sector, market focus, gender of CEO, and education level of the CEO are discussed.

36485 ■ *"Easy to be Queasy" in Canadian Business (Vol. 81, December 24, 2007, No. 1, pp. 25)*
Pub: Rogers Media
Ed: Jack Mintz. **Description:** Canada could be facing a slowdown in economic growth for 2008 as the country's economy depends on the U.S. economy, which is still facing recession in the subprime market. Details on Canada's economic growth, the impact of the weak U.S. dollar, increase in the unemployment rate, and decline in tax revenue are explored.

36486 ■ *"easyhome Ltd. Discovers Employee Fraud at an Easyfinancial Kiosk Company" in Internet Wire (October 14, 2010)*
Pub: Comtex
Description: Canada's leading merchandise leasing company and provider of financial services, easyhome Ltd., reported employee fraud totaling $3.4 million that was perpetrated against the firm's easyfinancial services business.

36487 ■ *"EBay Finally Gaining Traction in China" in San Jose Mercury News (October 26, 2011)*
Pub: San Jose Mercury News
Ed: John Boudreau. **Description:** eBay has developed a new strategy in China that allows exporters of every type of merchandise to sell directly to eBays 97 million overseas users.

36488 ■ *EBay Income: How ANYONE of Any Age, Location, and/or Background Can Build a Highly Profitable Online Business with eBay*
Pub: Atlantic Publishing Company
Released: December 1, 2010. **Price:** $24.95. **Description:** A complete overview of eBay is given and guides any small company through the entire process of creating the auction and auction strategies, photography, writing copy, text and formatting, multiple sales, programming tricks, PayPal, accounting, creating marketing, merchandising, managing email lists, advertising plans, taxes and sales tax, best time to list items and for how long, sniping programs, international customers, opening a storefront, electronic commerce, buy-it now pricing, keywords, Google marketing and eBay secrets.

36489 ■ *"Economic Distance and the Survival of Foreign Direct Investments" in Academy of Management Journal (Vol. 50, No. 5, October 2007)*
Pub: Academy of Management
Contact: Ming-Jer Chen, President
Ed: Eric W.K. Tsang, Paul S.L. Yip. **Description:** Study was undertaken to assess the relationship between economic disparities of various countries and foreign direct investments, focusing on Singapore. Results revealed that economic distance has a definite impact on foreign direct investment hazard rates.

36490 ■ *The Economics and Management of Small Business: An International Perspective*
Pub: Routledge
Ed: Graham Bannock. **Released:** May 2005. **Price:** $65.00. **Description:** International perspectives on the economics and management of small business, featuring case studies and empirical research.

36491 ■ *"An Educated Play on China" in Barron's (Vol. 88, June 30, 2008, No. 26, pp. M6)*
Pub: Dow Jones & Co., Inc.
Ed: Mohammed Hadi. **Description:** New Oriental Education & Technology Group sells English-language courses to an increasingly competitive Chinese workforce that values education. The shares in this company have been weighed down by worries on the impact of the Beijing Olympics on enrollment and the Sichuan earthquake. These shares could be a great way to get exposure to the long-term growth in China.

36492 ■ *Effect of the Overvalued Dollar on Small Exporters: Congressional Hearing*
Pub: DIANE Publishing Company
Ed: Donald Manzullo. **Released:** September 2002. **Price:** $30.00. **Description:** Congressional hearing: Witnesses: Dr. Lawrence Chimerine, Economist; Tony Raimondo, President and CEO, Behlen Manufacturing Company; Robert J. Weskamp, President, Wes-Tech, Inc.; Wayne Dollar, President, Georgia Farm Bureau; and Vargese George, President and CEO, Westex International, Inc. Appendix includes correspondence sent to committee on the overvalued dollar.

36493 ■ *"Elastic Path Software Joins Canada in G20 Young Entrepreneur Summit" in Internet Wire (June 14, 2010)*
Pub: Comtex
Description: The Canadian Youth Business Foundation hosted the G20 Young Entrepreneur Summit and announced that Harry Chemko of British Columbia's Elastic Path Software will be a member of the Canadian delegation at the G20 Young Entrepreneur Summit. Details are included.

36494 ■ *Electronic Commerce*
Pub: Course Technology
Ed: Gary Schneider, Bryant Chrzan, Charles McCormick. **Released:** May 1, 2010. **Price:** $117.95. **Description:** E-commerce can open the door to more opportunities than ever before for small business. Packed with real-world examples and cases, the book delivers comprehensive coverage of emerging online technologies and trends and their influence on the electronic marketplace. It details how the landscape of online commerce is evolving, reflecting changes in the economy and how business and society are responding to those changes. Balancing technological issues with the strategic business aspects of successful e-commerce, the new edition includes expanded coverage of international issues, social networking, mobile commerce, Web 2.0 technologies, and updates on spam, phishing, and identity theft.

36495 ■ *The Elephant and the Dragon: The Rise of India and China and What It Means to All of Us*
Pub: W.W. Norton & Company
Ed: Robyn Meredith. **Released:** 2008. **Price:** $15.95. **Description:** The author illustrates how both China and India have followed their own economic path, and examines the countries' similarities and considers the repercussions of their growing involvement in the world market.

36496 ■ *Emerging Business Online: Global Markets and the Power of B2B Internet Marketing*
Pub: FT Press
Ed: Lara Fawzy, Lucas Dworksi. **Released:** October 1, 2010. **Price:** $49.99. **Description:** An introduction into ebocube (emerging business online), a comprehensive proven business model for Internet B2B marketing in emerging markets.

36497 ■ *"End of the Beginning" in Canadian Business (Vol. 81, November 10, 2008, No. 19, pp. 17)*
Pub: Rogers Media Ltd.
Ed: David Wolf. **Description:** The freeze in the money markets and historic decline in equity markets around the world finally forced governments into aggressive coordinated action. The asset price inflation brought on by cheap credit will now work in reverse and the tightening of credit will be difficult economically. Canada is exposed to the fallout everywhere, given that the U.S, the U.K. and Japan buy 30 percent of Canada's output.

36498 ■ *"Enforcer In Fantasyland" in Crain's New York Business (Vol. 24, February 25, 2008, No. 8, pp. 10)*
Pub: Crain Communications Inc.
Ed: Hilary Potkewitz. **Description:** Patent law, particularly in the toy and game industry, is recession-proof according to Barry Negrin, partner at Pryor Cashman. Negrin co-founded his patent practice group. Despite massive recalls of toys and the concern over toxic toys, legal measures are in place in this industry.

36499 ■ *Enterprising Women in Urban Zimbabwe: Gender, Microbusiness, and Globalization*
Pub: Indiana University Press
Contact: Janet Rabinowitch, Director
E-mail: jrabinow@indiana.edu
Ed: Mary Johnson Osirim. **Released:** April 1, 2009. **Price:** $39.95. **Description:** An investigation into the business and personal experiences of women entrepreneurs in the microenterprise sector in Zimbabwe. Many of these women work as market traders, crocheters, seamstresses, and hairdressers.

36500 ■ *The Entrepreneurial Culture Network Advantage Within Chinese and Irish Software Firms*
Pub: Edward Elgar Publishing, Incorporated
Ed: Tsang. **Released:** October 2006. **Price:** $95.00. **Description:** Ways national cultural heritage influences entrepreneurial ventures are discussed.

36501 ■ *Entrepreneurial Strategies: New Technologies and Emerging Markets*
Pub: Blackwell Publishing Inc.
Contact: Gordon Tibbitts, President
Ed: Arnold Cooper; Sharon Alvarez; Alejandro Carrera; Luiz Mesquita; Robert Vassolo. **Released:** August 2006. **Price:** $69.95. **Description:** Ideas to help a small business expand into emerging market economies (EMEs) are discussed. Despite the high failure rate, this book helps a small firm develop a successful plan.

36502 ■ *Entrepreneurship: Frameworks and Empirical Investigations from Forthcoming Leaders of European Research*
Pub: Elsevier Science and Technology Books
Ed: Johan Wiklund; Dimo Dimov; Jerome A. Katz; Dean Shepherd. **Released:** July 2006. **Price:** $99.95. **Description:** Entrepreneurial research and theory cover the early growth of research-based startups and the role of learning in international entrepreneurship, focusing on Europe.

36503 ■ *Entrepreneurship, Investment and Spatial Dynamics Lessons and Implications*

for an Enlarged EU
Pub: Edward Elgar Publishing, Incorporated
Ed: Nijkamp. **Released:** September 2006. **Price:** $100.00. **Description:** Understanding the impact and interaction between investment, knowledge and entrepreneurship with an expanding European Union.

36504 ■ *Entrepreneurship and Small Business*
Pub: Palgrave Macmillan
Ed: Paul Burns. **Released:** January 2007. **Price:** $74.95. **Description:** Entrepreneurial skills, focusing on good management practices are discussed. Topics include family businesses, corporate, international and social entrepreneurship.

36505 ■ *Entrepreneurship and Small Business Development in the Former Soviet Bloc*
Pub: Routledge
Ed: David Smallbone, Friederike Welter. **Released:** January 10, 2010. **Price:** $140.00. **Description:** Examination of entrepreneurship and small business in Russia and other key countries of Eastern Europe, showing how far small businesses have developed in the region.

36506 ■ *Entrepreneurship and SMEs in the Euro-Zone*
Pub: Imperial College Press
Ed: Dana. **Released:** May 2006. **Price:** $48.00. **Description:** Information regarding entrepreneurship and SMEs in Europe is presented.

36507 ■ *"ESolar Partners With Penglai on Landmark Solar Thermal Agreement for China" in Business of Global Warming (January 25, 2010, pp. 8)*
Pub: Investment Weekly News
Description: Penglai Electric, a privately-owned Chinese electrical power equipment manufacturer, and eSolar, a global provider of cost-effective and reliable solar power plants, announced a master licensing agreement in which eSolar will build at least 2 gigawatts of solar thermal power plants in China over the next 10 years.

36508 ■ *"European Stocks on Deck" in Barron's (Vol. 89, July 27, 2009, No. 30, pp. M7)*
Pub: Dow Jones & Co., Inc.
Ed: Vito J. Racanelli. **Description:** European stocks are cheap and these trade at a discount to U.S. equities rarely seen in the past 40 years. This represents an opportunity for Americans and trends show that Europe's stocks outperform when there is a discrepancy between the price to earnings ratio in European stocks versus U.S. stocks and when sentiment on European equities are downbeat.

36509 ■ *"Europe's Meltdown" in Canadian Business (Vol. 83, June 15, 2010, No. 10, pp. 76)*
Pub: Rogers Media Ltd.
Ed: Bryan Borzykowski. **Description:** As European countries such as Greece, Spain, and Portugal struggle with debt problems, it is worth noting that its equities trade at a 30 percent discount to the U.S. and that a 10 percent drop in the Euro translates to a 10 percent rise in profitability for exporters. Investors may also want to focus on business-to-business operations rather than consumer-focused ones.

36510 ■ *"Event Stresses Cross-Border Cooperation" in Crain's Detroit Business (Vol. 24, March 31, 2008, No. 13, pp. 5)*
Pub: Crain Communications, Inc.
Ed: Chad Halcom. **Description:** According to John Austin, a senior fellow of The Brookings Institution, open immigration policies, better transportation and trade across the border and a cleanup of the Great Lakes will bring economic resurgence to Midwestern states and Canadian provinces with manufacturing economies.

36511 ■ *"Everybody Wants To Save the World: But When You Start a Charity Overseas, Good Intentions Often Go Awry" in Inc. (December 2007)*
Pub: Gruner & Jahr USA Publishing
Ed: Dalia Fahmy. **Description:** Unique set of challenges faced by small businesses wanting to create a charity overseas. Five key issues to explore before starting a charity overseas are examined.

36512 ■ *"Executives Exit at Wal-Mart in China" in Wall Street Journal Eastern Edition (October 17 , 2011, pp. B3)*
Pub: Dow Jones & Company Inc.
Ed: Laurie Burkitt. **Description:** Woes for Wal-Mart Inc.'s subsidiary in China are adding up as Wal-Mart China president and chief executive Ed Chan stepped down, as well as the company's senior vice president for human resources, Clara Wong. The company has been charged by regulators with mislabeling pork products, the result which has forced stores to close. Sales in China have been slow at the retail stores.

36513 ■ *"Export Opportunity" in Business Journal-Portland (Vol. 24, October 12, 2007, No. 33, pp. 1)*
Pub: American City Business Journals, Inc.
Ed: Matthew Kish. **Description:** U.S. dollar is weak, hitting an all-time low against the Euro, while the Canadian dollar is also performing well it hit parity for the first time after more than thirty years. The weak U.S. dollar is making companies that sell overseas benefit as it makes their goods cheaper to buy.

36514 ■ *Export Sales and Marketing Manual*
Pub: Export Institute
Contact: Mr. John R. Jagoe, Director
URL(s): www.exportusa.comwww.exportinstitute.com/agora.cgi?page=products01.htm, www.exportinstitute.com. **Released:** Annual; Latest edition 24th; 2011. **Price:** $295, Individuals print or CD; $395, Other countries print & CD. **Publication includes:** List of approximately 4,000 international trade contacts, including World Trade Centers, U.S. Department of Commerce Trade Specialists and Country Desk Officers, State International Trade offices, small business development centers, U.S. Customs services, U.S. Port Authorities, U.S. embassies, foreign trade associations in the U.S., and chambers of commerce in foreign countries, and foreign embassies and chambers of commerce in the U.S. **Entries include:** Name, address, phone, fax, name and title of contact, geographical area served, products covered, description of services, and 1,200 internet addresses of export-related sites. Principal content of publication is a step-by-step program showing U.S. companies and entrepreneurs how to begin exporting or increase their existing overseas sales. **Arrangement:** Classified by product/service and export marketing functions. **Indexes:** General, international trade or export/import. Worksheets, graphs, flow charts, pricing and budgeting formats, international price quotations, export contracts, international shipping documents, samples of international correspondence, glossaries, index and illustrations.

36515 ■ *"Face Values: Responsibility Inc" in Business Strategy Review (Vol. 21, Summer 2010, No. 2, pp. 66)*
Pub: Wiley-Blackwell
Ed: John Connolly. **Description:** Investment and growth in emerging markets will bring new opportunities, but with them added responsibility. Will companies be able to rise to meet the new responsibility agenda?.

36516 ■ *"Face Values: Responsibility Inc." in Business Strategy Review (Vol. 21, Summer 2010, No. 2, pp. 66)*
Pub: Blackwell Publishers Ltd.
Ed: John Connolly. **Description:** Investment and growth in emerging markets will bring new opportunities, but added responsibility comes with it. Will companies be able to rise to meet the new responsibility agenda?.

36517 ■ *Facilitating Sustainable Innovation through Collaboration: A Multi-Stakeholder Perspective*
Pub: Springer
Ed: Joseph Sarkis, James J. Cordeiro, Diego Vazquez Brust. **Released:** March 10, 2010. **Price:** $169.00. **Description:** An international perspective of sustainable innovation with contributions from Australia, Europe, and North America, by prominent policy makers, scientific researchers and others.

36518 ■ *"Facing the Future" in Canadian Business (Vol. 81, March 31, 2008, No. 5, pp. 69)*
Pub: Rogers Media
Ed: John Gray. **Description:** Discusses a web poll of 122 Canadian CEOs which shows that these leaders are convinced that the U.S. economy is slowing but are split on the impact that this will have on the Canadian economy. The aging and retiring workforce and the strong Canadian dollar are other concerns by these leaders.

36519 ■ *Factory Girls: From Village to City in a Changing China*
Pub: Spiegel & Grau
Ed: Leslie T. Chang. **Released:** 2009. **Price:** $26.00. **Description:** Young women who flee the rural villages in China find exhausting work and social mobility working in factories.

36520 ■ *"Fair Play? China Cheats, Carney Talks and Rankin Walks; Here's the Latest" in Canadian Business (Vol. 81, March 17, 2008, No. 4)*
Pub: Rogers Media
Description: Discusses the World Trade Organization which says that China is breaking trade rules by taxing imports of auto parts at the same rate as foreign-made finished cars. Mark Carney first speech as the governor of the Bank of Canada made economists suspect a rate cut on overnight loans. Andre Rankin was ordered by the Ontario Securities Commission to pay $250,000 in investigation costs.

36521 ■ *False Economy: A Surprising Economic History of the World*
Pub: Riverhead Booksk
Ed: Alan Beattie. **Released:** 2009. **Price:** $26.95. **Description:** History shows that the choices made by countries, not luck, determine its economic fate.

36522 ■ *"Familiar Fun" in Crain's Cleveland Business (Vol. 28, October 22, 2007, No. 42, pp. 3)*
Pub: Crain Communications Inc.
Ed: John Booth. **Description:** Marketing for the 2007 holiday season has toy retailers focusing on American-made products because of recent recalls of toys produced in China that do not meet U.S. safety standards.

36523 ■ *"Fast Revival Unlikely For Indian 'Net Stocks" in Barron's (Vol. 88, July 7, 2008, No. 27, pp. 12)*
Pub: Dow Jones & Co., Inc.
Ed: Leslie P. Norton. **Description:** Shares of Indian Internet companies Rediff.com and Sify are not likely to stage a rebound due to weak financial results. Rediff.com shares have declined 39.2 percent in 2008, while Sify shares are down 35.8 percent.

36524 ■ *Faster Cheaper Better*
Pub: Crown Business Books
Ed: Michael Hammer. **Released:** December 28, 2010. **Price:** $27.50. **Description:** Nine levels for transforming work in order to achieve business growth are outlined. The book helps small business compete against the low-wage countries.

36525 ■ *"Fed May Ban Amphibian Trade" in Pet Product News (Vol. 64, November 2010, No. 11, pp. 13)*
Pub: BowTie Inc.
Description: U.S. Fish and Wildlife Service is seeking public input on a petition submitted by the conservation activist group Defenders of Wildlife. The petition involves possible classification of chytrid fungus-infected amphibians and amphibian eggs as 'injurious wildlife' under the Lacey Act. Interstate trading or importation of injurious wildlife into the U.S. is not allowed.

36526 ■ *Female Entrepreneurship in East and South-East Asia: Opportunities and Challenges*
Pub: Woodhead Publishing Ltd.
Ed: Philippe Debroux. **Released:** February 10, 2010. **Description:** A detailed study of female entrepreneurship in Asia, where public authorities are slowly realizing the importance of women as workers and entrepreneurs.

36527 ■ *"Fertilizer for Growth" in Canadian Business (Vol. 83, September 14, 2010, No. 15, pp. 76)*
Pub: Rogers Media Ltd.
Ed: Bryan Borzykowski. **Description:** Australian-based BHP Billiton launches a C$38.5 billion hostile takeover bid for Saskatchewan-based Potash Corporation and some investors immediately bought Potash stock at C$130. However, Potash has resisted BHP's offer and announced a plan to try to stop the deal.

36528 ■ *"Fight Against Fake" in The Business Journal-Portland (Vol. 25, July 18, 2008, No. 19, pp. 1)*
Pub: American City Business Journals, Inc.
Ed: Erik Siemers. **Description:** Companies, such as Columbia Sportswear Co. and Nike Inc., are fighting the counterfeiting of their sportswear and footwear products through the legal process of coordinating with law enforcement agencies to raid factories. Most of the counterfeiting factories are in China and India. Other details on the issue are discussed.

36529 ■ *"The Finance Function In A Global Corporation" in Harvard Business Review (Vol. 86, July-August 2008, No. 8, pp. 108)*
Pub: Harvard Business School Press
Ed: Mihir A. Desai. **Description:** Designing and implementing a successful finance function in a global setting is discussed. Additional topics include the internal capital market, managing risk and budgeting capital internationally.

36530 ■ *"Finding A Higher Gear" in Harvard Business Review (Vol. 86, July-August 2008, No. 8, pp. 68)*
Pub: Harvard Business School Press
Ed: Thomas A. Stewart; Anand P. Raman. **Description:** Anand G. Mahindra, the chief executive officer of Mahindra and Mahindra Ltd., discusses how his company fosters innovation, drawn from customer centricity, and how this will grow the company beyond India's domestic market.

36531 ■ *"Finding Life Behind the Numbers" in Crain's Chicago Business (Vol. 31, March 24, 2008, No. 12, pp. 25)*
Pub: Crain Communications, Inc.
Ed: Samantha Stainburn. **Description:** Interview with Phillip Capodice who is a graduate student at DePaul University's Kellstadt Graduate School of Business and studied abroad in Lima, Peru where he visited a number of companies including some who are trade partners with the United States.

36532 ■ *"Finding Your Place in the World: Global Diversity Has Become a Corporate Catchphrase" in Black Enterprise (November 2007)*
Pub: Earl G. Graves Publishing Co. Inc.
Ed: Wendy Harris. **Description:** Does the inclusion of workers from other countries mean exclusion of African American workers in the U.S.?.

36533 ■ *"Firm Takes 'Local' Worldwide" in Hispanic Business (July-August 2007, pp. 48)*
Pub: Hispanic Business
Ed: Keith Rosenblum. **Description:** Willy A. Bermello tells how he has expanded his architectural, engineering and construction firm globally.

36534 ■ *"Five-Ring Circus" in Entrepreneur (Vol. 35, November 2007, No. 11, pp. 76)*
Pub: Entrepreneur Media Inc.
Ed: Scott Bernard Nelson. **Description:** China's economy is growing and is expected to do well even after the 2008 Olympics, but growth could slow from eleven percent to eight or nine percent. Chinese portfolio concerns with regard to health and environmental records and bureaucratic fraud are discussed.

36535 ■ *"Flying the Unfriendly Skies" in Crain's Chicago Business (Vol. 31, April 21, 2008, No. 16, pp. 26)*
Pub: Crain Communications, Inc.
Ed: Sarah A. Klein. **Description:** Due to the number of Chicago companies and entrepreneurs who are traveling overseas more frequently in order to strengthen ties with customers, companies and oftentimes even business partners, the number of flights leaving O'Hare International Airport for destinations abroad has surged; In 2007, international passengers departing O'Hare totaled 5.7 million, up from 2.4 million in 1990.

36536 ■ *"For Baxter, A Lingering PR Problem; Ongoing Focus On Heparin Deaths Ups Heat On CEO" in Crain's Chicago Business (April 21, 2008)*
Pub: Crain Communications, Inc.
Ed: Mike Colias. **Description:** Baxter International Inc.'s recall of the blood-thinning medication heparin has exposed the company to costly litigation and put the perils of overseas drug manufacturing in the spotlight. Wall Street investors predict that an indefinite halt in production of the drug should not hurt the company's bottom line since heparin represents a tiny sliver of the business. Since Baxter began recalling the drug in January its shares have continued to outpace most other medical stocks.

36537 ■ *"For Bombardier, a Case of Deja Vu" in Canadian Business (Vol. 83, August 17, 2010, No. 13-14, pp. 28)*
Pub: Rogers Media Ltd.
Ed: Laura Cameron. **Description:** Foreign competitors have accused the Quebec government and the Societe de transport de Montreal of giving Bombardier preferential treatment when it bids for contract to replace Montreal metro's rail cars. Bombardier was in a similar situation in 1974 when it won the contract to build the metro's second generation rail cars.

36538 ■ *Forces of Fortune: The Rise of the New Muslim Middle Class and What It Will Mean for Our World*
Pub: Free Press Media Group Inc.
Ed: Vali Nasr. **Released:** September 10, 2009. **Price:** $26.00. **Description:** The author argues that entrepreneurial, religiously conservative contingents in such countries as Turkey, Pakistan, and Iran can propel the Middle East into democratic and prosperous times.

36539 ■ *"ForeSee Finds Satisfaction On Web Sites, Bottom Line" in Crain's Detroit Business (Vol. 24, February 25, 2008, No. 8, pp. 3)*
Pub: Crain Communications Inc. - Detroit
Ed: Tom Henderson. **Description:** Ann Arbor-based ForeSee Results Inc. evaluates user satisfaction on Web sites. The company expects to see an increase of 40 percent in revenue for 2008 with plans to expand to London, Germany, Italy and France by the end of 2009.

36540 ■ *"The Four Cheapest Plays in Emerging Markets" in Barron's (Vol. 89, July 27, 2009, No. 30, pp. 34)*
Pub: Dow Jones & Co., Inc.
Ed: Lawrence C. Strauss. **Description:** Portfolio manager Arjun Divecha of the GMO Emerging Markets III Fund says that the main thing in investing in emerging markets is getting the country right since getting it wrong makes it harder to add value. Divecha says that the four countries that they are positive on are Turkey, Russia, South Korea, and Thailand.

36541 ■ *"Franchise Law in China: Law, Regulations, and Guidelines" in Franchise Law Journal (Vol. 27, Summer 2007, No. 1, pp. 57)*
Pub: American Bar Association
Contact: Carolyn Lamm, President
Ed: Paul Jones, Erik Wulff. **Description:** Issues faced by foreign franchising are discussed, with a focus on China.

36542 ■ *"Freeing the Wheels of Commerce" in Hispanic Business (July-August 2007, pp. 50, 52, 54)*
Pub: Hispanic Business
Ed: Keith Rosenblum. **Description:** SecureOrigins, a border-based partnership with high-tech innovators is working to move goods faster, more efficiently, and securely.

36543 ■ *"Fries With That?" in Canadian Business (Vol. 81, September 29, 2008, No. 16, pp. 33)*
Pub: Rogers Media Ltd.
Ed: Calvin Leung. **Description:** Profile of Toronto-based New York Fries, which has four stores in South Korea, is planning to expand further as well as into Hong Kong and Macau; the company also has a licensee in the United Arab Emirates whom is also planning to expand.

36544 ■ *"From American Icon to Global Juggernaut" in Automotive News (Vol. 86, October 31, 2011, No. 6488, pp. S003)*
Pub: Crain Communications Inc.
Ed: Peter Brown. **Description:** Chevrolet celebrates its 100th Anniversary. The brand revolutionized its market with affordable cars that bring technology to the masses. Chevys have been sold in 140 countries and the company is responding to a broader market.

36545 ■ *"From Malls to Steel Plants" in Crain's Chicago Business (Vol. 31, April 28, 2008, No. 17, pp. 30)*
Pub: Crain Communications, Inc.
Ed: Samantha Stainburn. **Description:** Profile of the company Graycor Inc. which started out as a sand-blasting and concrete-breaking firm but has grown into four businesses due to innovation and acquisitions. Graycor's businesses include: Graycor Industrial Constructors Inc., which builds and renovates power plants and steel mills; Graycor Construction Co., which erects stores, medical centers and office buildings; Graycor Blasting Co., which uses explosives and blasts tunnels for industrial cleaning, and Graycor International Inc., which provides construction services in Mexico.

36546 ■ *"From War Zone to Franchise Zone" in Entrepreneur (Vol. 37, August 2009, No. 8, pp. 104)*
Pub: Entrepreneur Media, Inc.
Ed: Jason Daley. **Description:** Ross Paterson says that he realized that the material he used in the Growth Coach franchise could give the people of Afghanistan the systematic model they need. Paterson says that the Afghans are very business-oriented people but that they work in a different system than Americans.

36547 ■ *Fugitive Denim: A Moving Story of People and Pants in the Borderless World of Global Trade*
Pub: W.W. Norton & Company
Ed: Rachel Snyder. **Released:** April 2009. **Price:** $16.95. **Description:** In-depth study of the global production and processes of how jeans are designed, sewn, and transported as well as how the cotton for denim is grown, regulated, purchased and processed.

36548 ■ *"Furniture Making May Come Back--Literally" in Business North Carolina (Vol. 28, March 2008, No. 3, pp. 32)*
Pub: Business North Carolina
Description: Due to the weak U.S. dollar and the fact that lumber processors never left the country, foreign furniture manufacturers are becoming interested in moving manufacturing plants to the U.S.

36549 ■ *"Future of Diversity: Cultural Inclusion Is a Business Imperative" in Black Enterprise (Vol. 41, August 2010, No. 1, pp. 75)*
Pub: Earl G. Graves Publishing Co. Inc.
Ed: Annya M. Lott. **Description:** As globalization continues to make the world a smaller place, workforce diversity will be imperative to any small company in order to be sustainable.

36550 ■ *"The Future Is Another Country; Higher Education" in The Economist (Vol. 390, January 3, 2009, No. 8612, pp. 43)*
Pub: The Economist Newspaper Inc.
Description: Due to the growth of the global corporation, more ambitious students are studying at universities abroad; the impact of this trend is discussed.

36551 ■ *"The Future of Work" in Black Enterprise (Vol. 41, August 2010, No. 1, pp. 65)*
Pub: Earl G. Graves Publishing Co. Inc.
Ed: Annya M. Lott. **Description:** Technology, globalization, and outsourcing will continue to shape the future of work. Social media is a means for small companies to market goods and services.

36552 ■ *"The Future of Work" in Business Strategy Review (Vol. 21, Autumn 2010, No. 3, pp. 16)*
Pub: Blackwell Publishers Ltd.
Ed: Lynda Gratton. **Description:** Work is universal. But how, why, where and when we work has never been so open to individual interpretation. The certainties of the past have been replaced by ambiguity, questions and the steady hum of technology. Now, in a groundbreaking research project covering 21 global companies and more than 200 executives, the author is making sense of the future of work.

36553 ■ *"The Future of Work" in Business Strategy Review (Vol. 21, Autumn 2010, No. 3, pp. 16)*
Pub: Wiley-Blackwell
Ed: Lynda Gratton. **Description:** Work is universal. Buy, how, why, where and when we work has never been so open to individual interpretation. The certainties of the past have been replaced by ambiguity, questions and the steady hum of technology. Research covering 21 global companies and more than 200 executives covers the future of work.

36554 ■ *"G20 Young Entrepreneur Alliance Signs Charter Outlining Commitment to Entrepreneurship" in Internet Wire (November 10, 2010)*
Pub: Comtex
Description: G20 Young Entrepreneur Summit members created a charter document that outlines their support for the G20 process to include entrepreneurship on its agenda. Details of the Summit are included.

36555 ■ *"German Win Through Sharing" in Canadian Business (Vol. 83, September 14, 2010, No. 15, pp. 16)*
Pub: Rogers Media Ltd.
Ed: Jordan Timm. **Description:** German economic historian Eckhard Hoffner has a two-volume work showing how German's relaxed attitude toward copyright and intellectual property helped it catch up to industrialized United Kingdom. Hoffner's research was in response to his interest in the usefulness of software patents. Information on the debate regarding Canada's copyright laws is given.

36556 ■ *"Getting a Grip on the Saddle: Chasms or Cycles?" in Journal of Marketing (Vol. 75, July 2011, No. 4, pp. 21)*
Pub: American Marketing Association
Ed: Deepa Chandrasekaran, Gerald J. Tellis. **Description:** A study of the saddle's generality across products and countries is presented. The saddle is fairly pervasive based on empirical analysis of historical sales data from ten products across 19 countries. The results indicate chasms and technological cycles for information/entertainment products while business cycles and technological cycles affect kitchen/laundry products.

36557 ■ *"Getting Rid of Global Glitches: Choosing Software For Trade Compliance" in Black Enterprise (Vol. 41, September 2010, No. 2, pp. 48)*
Pub: Earl G. Graves Publishing Co. Inc.
Ed: Marcia Wade Talbert. **Description:** Compliance software for trading with foreign companies must be compatible with the U.S. Census Bureau's Automated Export System (www.aesdirect.gov). It has to be current with regulatory requirements for any country in the world. Whether owners handle their own compliance or hire a logistics company, they need to be familiar with this software in order to access reports and improve transparency and efficiency of theft supply chain.

36558 ■ *Global E-Commerce: Impacts of National Environment and Policy*
Pub: Cambridge University Press
Contact: Richard Ziemacki, President
E-mail: rziemacki@cambridge.org
Ed: Kenneth L. Kraemer; Jason Dedrick; Nigel P. Melville; Kevin Zhu. **Released:** August 2006. **Price:** $75.00. **Description:** Global assessment of the impact of e-business on companies as well as countries.

36559 ■ *Global Economic Crisis: Impact on Small Business*
Pub: Cengage South-Western
Ed: Global Economics Crisis Resource Center. **Released:** March 1, 2009. **Price:** $17.95. **Description:** A discussion of the historical context of the global economic crisis is presented, along with a discussion on the impact of this crisis on small businesses. It also provides learning goals, questions, key terms, and digital access to the Global Economic Crisis Resource Center.

36560 ■ *"The Global Economy, the Labor Force and Franchising's Future" in Franchising World (Vol. 42, September 2010, No. 9, pp. 35)*
Pub: International Franchise Association
Ed: Jeffrey A. Rosensweig. **Description:** Point forecasting and the methodology called scenario analysis are presented looking at the global economy and future of franchising in the U.S. and abroad.

36561 ■ *Global Electronic Business Research: Opportunities and Directions*
Pub: Idea Group Publishing
Ed: Nabeel A.Y. Al-Qirim. **Released:** December 2005. **Price:** $ 74.95. **Description:** Importance electronic commerce research plays in small to medium-sized enterprises in various countries.

36562 ■ *"The Global Environment Movement is Bjorn Again" in Canadian Business (Vol. 83, September 14, 2010, No. 15, pp. 11)*
Pub: Rogers Media Ltd.
Ed: Steve Maich. **Description:** Danish academic Bjorn Lomborg is in favor of decisive action to combat climate change in his new book and was given front page treatment by a London newspaper. Environmentalist groups see this as a victory since Lomborg had not previously considered climate change an immediate issue.

36563 ■ *"Global Imagery in Online Advertisements" in Business Communication Quarterly (December 2007, pp. 487)*
Pub: SAGE Publications USA
Contact: Blaise R. Simqu, President
Ed: Geraldine E. Hynes, Marius Janson. **Description:** Respondents from six countries were interviewed about their reactions to two online ads to determine cultural differences in understanding advertising elements. Universal appeals and cultural values determine the effectiveness of symbols in online advertising.

36564 ■ *"Global Market Could Be Silver Lining" in Hispanic Business (January-February 2008, pp. 14, 16, 18)*
Pub: Hispanic Business
Description: Economic slowdown in the U.S. is expected to continue through 2008. However, the export sector should hold steady during the same period.

36565 ■ *"Global-Preneuring: Tax Ramifications Can Make or Break a Worldwide Enterprise" in Small Business Opportunities (May 2008)*
Pub: Harris Publications Inc.
Description: It is imperative to consider the tax ramifications when starting or expanding a global enterprise.

36566 ■ *"Global: Put It on Autopilot" in Entrepreneur (Vol. 35, October 2007, No. 10, pp. 110)*
Pub: Entrepreneur Media Inc.
Ed: Laurel Delaney. **Description:** A business that aims to enter the global market must first streamline its global supply chain (GSC). A streamlined GSC can be achieved by laying out the company's processes and by automating it with supply chain management software. Advantages of GSC automation such as credibility are provided.

36567 ■ *"The Global Talent Hunt" in Business Strategy Review (Vol. 21, Spring 2010, No. 1, pp. 78)*
Pub: Wiley-Blackwell
Ed: Richard Emerton. **Description:** Richard Emerton explains how the new 'triple context' of economy, environment and society will have profound implications for human resource practices. He suggests that viewing talent as abundant is the right perspective for a manager.

36568 ■ *"Going the Distance" in Hispanic Business (July-August 2007, pp. 38-40, 42-43)*
Pub: Hispanic Business
Ed: Keith Rosenblum. **Description:** Top Hispanic export companies are discussed; charts with exporters by sector as well as a complete listing that includes company name, CEO, number of employees, revenue information, export sales, growth, products and services and destinations are included.

36569 ■ *"Golden Spoon Accelerates Expansion Here and Abroad" in Ice Cream Reporter (Vol. 22, December 20, 2008, No. 1, pp. 2)*
Pub: Ice Cream Reporter
Description: Golden Spoon frozen yogurt franchise chain is developing 35 more locations in the Phoenix, Arizona area along with plans to open a store in Japan.

36570 ■ *"Gordon Nixon" in Canadian Business (Vol. 80, November 5, 2007, No. 22, pp. 9)*
Pub: Rogers Media
Ed: Rachel Pulfer. **Description:** Royal Bank of Canada (RBC) CEO, Gordon Nixon, believes the Canadian financial services segment is heavily regulated. Nixon also feels that it has become difficult for local banks to enter the market since foreign banks can easily come in and compete with them. His views on RBC's success are provided.

36571 ■ *"Gordon Nixon Q&A" in Canadian Business (Vol. 80, November 5, 2007, No. 22, pp. 9)*
Pub: Rogers Media
Ed: Rachel Pulfer. **Description:** Royal Bank of Canada (RBC) chief executive officer Gordon Nixon believes that the Canadian financial services segment is heavily regulated. Nixon also feels that it has become difficult for local banks to enter the market since foreign banks can easily come in and compete with Canadian banks. His views on RBC's success are provided.

36572 ■ *Grassroots NGOs by Women for Women: The Driving Force of Development in India*
Pub: SAGE Publications USA
Contact: Blaise R. Simqu, President
Ed: Femida Handy; Meenaz Kassam; Suzanne Feeney; Bhagyashree Ranade. **Released:** July 2006. **Price:** $29.95. **Description:** Understanding the role of non-governmental organizations in women's development is offered through interviews with twenty women in India who have founded NGOs serving women.

36573 ■ *"The Great Cleanup" in Canadian Business (Vol. 81, April 14, 2008, No. 6, pp. 50)*
Pub: Rogers Media
Ed: Graham Silnicki. **Description:** China's rectification program includes the licensing of 100 percent of food producers and monitoring of 100 percent of raw materials for exports between August and December,

2007. There is a lot of money to be made for those who are willing to help China win its quality battle. PharmEng International Inc. is one of the companies that helps Chinese companies meet international quality standards.

36574 ■ *"Grin and Bear It" in Canadian Business (Vol. 81, March 3, 2008, No. 3, pp. 53)*
Pub: Rogers Media
Ed: Jeff Sanford. **Description:** Discusses the United States economic downturn, caused by the credit market crisis, which is expected to affect the Canadian economy, as Canada depend on the U.S. for 80 percent of its exports. Economist David Rosenberg thinks that in 2008, housing prices will decline by 15 percent and gross domestic product growth will slow to 0.8 percent. Other forecasts for Canadian economy are given.

36575 ■ *"Grote Company Puts Final Wrap on Sandwich-Making Line" in Business First-Columbus (October 26, 2007, pp. A1)*
Pub: American City Business Journals, Inc.
Ed: Dan Eaton. **Description:** Grote Company acquired Oxfordshire, England-based Advanced Food Technology Ltd., giving the Ohio-based food cutting equipment company a manufacturing base in Europe. This is the company's second deal in four months. Details on Grote Company's plan to tap into the prepared fresh sandwich market are discussed.

36576 ■ *Growth Oriented Women Entrepreneurs and Their Businesses: A Global Research Perspective*
Pub: Edward Elgar Publishing, Incorporated
Ed: Candida G. Brush. **Released:** June 2006. **Price:** $135.00. **Description:** Roles women play in entrepreneurship globally and their economic impact are examined.

36577 ■ *"Guts Not Included" in Canadian Business (Vol. 81, March 31, 2008, No. 5, pp. 46)*
Pub: Rogers Media
Ed: Andrew Wahl. **Description:** Executives need the vision to create a strategy that prepares for an uncertain future in light of growing global competition. Canadian business leaders have the right skills and education but do not have enough tolerance for risk.

36578 ■ *"A Hacker in India Hijacked His Website Design and Was Making Good Money Selling It" in Inc. (December 2007, pp. 77-78, 80)*
Pub: Gruner & Jahr USA Publishing
Ed: Darren Dahl. **Description:** John Anton, owner of an online custom T-shirt business and how a company in India was selling software Website templates identical to his firm's Website.

36579 ■ *"Half a World Away" in Tampa Bay Business Journal (Vol. 30, December 4, 2009, No. 50, pp. 1)*
Pub: American City Business Journals
Ed: Jane Meinhardt. **Description:** Enterprise Florida has offered four trade grants for Florida's marine industry businesses to give them a chance to tap into the Middle East market at the Dubai International Boat Show on March 9 to 13, 2010. The grants pay for 50 percent of the exhibition costs for the qualifying business.

36580 ■ *"H&M Offers a Dress for Less" in Canadian Business (Vol. 83, September 14, 2010, No. 15, pp. 20)*
Pub: Rogers Media Ltd.
Ed: Laura Cameron. **Description:** Swedish clothing company H&M has implemented loss leader strategy by pricing some dresses at extremely low prices. The economy has forced retailers to keep prices down despite the increasing cost of manufacturing, partly due to Chinese labor becoming more expensive. How the trend will affect apparel companies is discussed.

36581 ■ *"Hank Paulson On the Housing Bailout and What's Ahead" in Business Week (September 22, 2008, No. 4100, pp. 19)*
Pub: McGraw-Hill Companies, Inc.
Ed: Maria Bartiromo. **Description:** Interview with Treasury Secretary Henry Paulson in which he discusses the bailout of Fannie Mae and Freddie Mac as well as the potential impact on the American economy and foreign interests and investments in the country. Paulson has faith that the government's actions will help to stabilize the housing market.

36582 ■ *"Headwinds From the New Sod Slow Aer Lingus" in Barron's (Vol. 88, March 10, 2008, No. 10, pp. M6)*
Pub: Dow Jones & Company, Inc.
Ed: Sean Walters; Arindam Nag. **Description:** Aer Lingus faces a drop in its share prices with a falling US market, higher jet fuel prices, and lower long-haul passenger load factors. British media companies Johnston Press and Yell Group are suffering from weaker ad revenue and heavier debt payments due to the credit crunch.

36583 ■ *"Heavy Duty: The Case Against Packing Lightly" in Crain's Chicago Business (Vol. 31, April 21, 2008, No. 16, pp. 29)*
Pub: Crain Communications, Inc.
Ed: Sarah A. Klein. **Description:** Penelope Biggs, a Northern Trust executive who manages sales teams in North America, Europe and Asia gives advice on traveling abroad for business including time management skills, handling time-zone hops and avoiding jet-lag.

36584 ■ *"The High-Intensity Entrepreneur" in Harvard Business Review (Vol. 88, September 2010, No. 9, pp. 74)*
Pub: Harvard Business School Publishing
Ed: Anne S. Habiby, Deirdre M. Coyle Jr. **Description:** Examination of the role of small companies in promoting global economic growth is presented. Discussion includes identifying entrepreneurial capability.

36585 ■ *"Hola and Aloha" in Hawaii Business (Vol. 53, December 2007, No. 6, pp. 131)*
Pub: Hawaii Business Publishing
Ed: Jason Ubay. **Description:** Juan Carlos Bianchetti is the trilingual owner of Ole Tours Hawaii, a travel wholesaler that targets Portuguese and Spanish-speaking visitors. The competition for American and Japanese tourists is already tight, which is why Bianchetti opted to target a different segment of the Hawaii tourism market. Plans for the company's expansion in Kauai, Brazil, and Argentina, are mentioned.

36586 ■ *"The Hollow Debate" in Canadian Business (Vol. 81, March 3, 2008, No. 3, pp. 26)*
Pub: Rogers Media
Ed: Thomas Watson. **Description:** According to a report conducted by the Conference Board of Canada, the Canadian business community is not being hollowed out by acquisitions made by foreign companies. Findings further showed that local businesses are protected by dual shares and that the economy can benefit more from foreign acquisitions than local mergers. The need to relax foreign ownership restrictions and other recommendations are presented.

36587 ■ *"Hong Kong's Boom in IPO" in Barron's (Vol. 89, July 13, 2009, No. 28, pp. M7)*
Pub: Dow Jones & Co., Inc.
Ed: Nick Lord. **Description:** Hong Kong's IPO (initial public offering) market is booming with 13 Chinese IPOs already on the market for the year as July 2009. One of them is Bawang International which raised $214 million after generating $9 billion in order which makes it 42 times oversubscribed.

36588 ■ *"Hot For All The Wrong Reasons" in Canadian Business (Vol. 81, March 31, 2008, No. 5, pp. 19)*
Pub: Rogers Media
Ed: Andrea Jezovit. **Description:** Soaring platinum prices are due to South Africa's platinum mining industry's safety issues and power supply disruptions that exacerbate the metal's supply problems. South Africa supplies 80 percent of the world's platinum. South Africa's power utility has said that it cannot guarantee the industry's power needs until 2013.

36589 ■ *"How Bad Is It?" in Hawaii Business (Vol. 54, July 2008, No. 1, pp. 35)*
Pub: Hawaii Business Publishing
Ed: Jolyn Okimoto Rosa. **Description:** Donald G. Horner, chief executive officer of First Hawaiian Bank, says that the current Hawaiian economic situation is a cyclical slowdown. Maurice Kaya, an energy consultant, says the slowdown is due to overdependence on imported fuels. Other local leaders, such as Constance H. Lau, also discuss their view on the current economic situation in Hawaii.

36590 ■ *"How to Conquer New Markets With Old Skills" in Harvard Business Review (Vol. 88, November 2010, No. 11, pp. 118)*
Pub: Harvard Business School Publishing
Ed: Mauro F. Guillen, Esteban Garcia-Canal. **Description:** Exploration of business-networking factors that have helped lead to the success of Spain's multinational companies is provided. These include development of political skills, access to capabilities and resources, globalization partnerships, and speed of implementation.

36591 ■ *"How Dell Will Dial for Dollars" in Austin Business JournalInc. (Vol. 29, December 4, 2009, No. 39, pp. 1)*
Pub: American City Business Journals
Ed: Christopher Calnan. **Description:** Dell Inc. revealed plans to launch a Mini3i smartphone in China which could enable revenue sharing by bundling with wireless service subscription. Dell's smartphone plan is similar to the netbook business, which Dell sold with service provided by AT&T Inc.

36592 ■ *"How Exports Could Save America" in Barron's (Vol. 89, July 20, 2009, No. 29, pp. 15)*
Pub: Dow Jones & Co., Inc.
Ed: Jonathan R. Laing. **Description:** Increase in US exports should help drive up the nation's economic growth, according to Wells Capital Management strategist Jim Paulsen. He believes US gross domestic product could grow by 3-3.5 percent annually starting in 2010 due to a more favorable trade balance.

36593 ■ *"How Foreigners Could Disrupt U.S. Markets" in Barron's (Vol. 90, September 13, 2010, No. 37, pp. 30)*
Pub: Barron's Editorial & Corporate Headquarters
Ed: Jim McTague. **Description:** An informal meeting by the House Homeland Security Panel concluded that U.S. stock exchanges and related trading routes can be the subject of attacks from rogue overseas traders. A drop in funding for the U.S. Department of Defense is discussed.

36594 ■ *"How High Can Soybeans Fly?" in Barron's (Vol. 88, March 10, 2008, No. 10, pp. M14)*
Pub: Dow Jones & Company, Inc.
Ed: Kenneth Rapoza. **Description:** Prices of soybeans have risen to $14.0875 a bushel, up 8.3 percent for the week. Increased demand, such as in China and in other developing economies, and the investment-driven commodities boom are boosting prices.

36595 ■ *"How Not to Raise Bank Capital" in Barron's (Vol. 88, June 30, 2008, No. 26, pp. M6)*
Pub: Dow Jones & Co., Inc.
Ed: Sean Walters. **Description:** French bank Natixis wants to raise 1 billion euros from cash provided by their two major owners. Natixis will reimburse Banque Populaire and Caisses d'Epargne with hybrid securities so this move will not benefit Natixis' core Tier 1 ratio. This has also given the impression that the company is afraid of a full rights issue which could shake investors' faith in the bank.

36596 ■ *"How to Secure U.S. Jobs" in Gallup Management Journal (October 27, 2011)*
Pub: Gallup
Ed: Jim Clifton. **Description:** If America doubled its number of engaged customers globally, it could triple exports, which would create more good jobs and put the US economy back on track.

36597 ■ *"How Two Flourishing Exporters Did It" in Hispanic Business (Vol. 30, July-August 2008, No. 7-8, pp. 46)*
Pub: Hispanic Business, Inc.

Ed: Richard Kaplan. **Description:** Vigorous growth in export revenues posted by two Hispanic-owned export companies Compasa LLC and Ametza LLC is discussed; both firms have benefited from their closer locations to major Mexican markets, superior quality of their products, market knowledge and the relationships of trust developed with key business partners.

36598 ■ *"Ian Gordon" in Canadian Business (Vol. 81, Summer 2008, No. 9, pp. 10)*
Pub: Rogers Media Ltd.

Ed: Matthew McClearn. **Description:** Bolder Investment Partners' Ian Gordon discussed the economic theory promulgated by Russian economist Nikolai Kondratieff. The cycle begins with a rising economy then followed by deflationary depression. Details of his views on the Kondratieff cycle and its application to the current economy are presented.

36599 ■ *"Ideas at Work: Sparkling Innovation" in Business Strategy Review (Vol. 21, Summer 2010, No. 2, pp. 7)*
Pub: Blackwell Publishers Ltd.

Ed: Julian Birkinshaw, Peter Robbins. **Description:** GlaxoSmithKline faced a situation common to large global organizations: how to allocate marketing resources to smaller, regional brands. A report on the company's inventive approach to worldwide marketing that led to the development of a unique and productive network are explored.

36600 ■ *"Ideas at Work: Sparkling Innovation" in Business Strategy Review (Vol. 21, Summer 2010, No. 2, pp. 07)*
Pub: Wiley-Blackwell

Ed: Julian Birkinshaw, Peter Robbins. **Description:** GlaxoSmithKline faced a situation common to large global organizations: how to allocate marketing resources to smaller, regional brands. The company's approach to worldwide marketing that led to the development of a unique and productive network is outlined.

36601 ■ *"Ideas at Work: Total Communicator" in Business Strategy Review (Vol. 21, Autumn 2010, No. 3, pp. 10)*
Pub: Blackwell Publishers Ltd.

Ed: Stuart Crainer. **Description:** Vittorio Colao has been chief executive of Vodafone Group for two years. He brings to the company special experience as CEO of RCS MediaGroup in Milan, which publishes newspapers, magazines and books in Italy, Spain and France. Prior to RCS, he held other positions within Vodaphone. Colao shares his views on business, the global economy and leading Vodafone.

36602 ■ *"Ideas at Work: Total Communicator" in Business Strategy Review (Vol. 21, Autumn 2010, No. 3, pp. 10)*
Pub: Wiley-Blackwell

Ed: Stuart Crainer. **Description:** Vittorio Colao has been chief executive of Vodafone Group for two years. He brings to the company some special experience: from 2004-2006 he was CEO of RCS MediaGroup in Milan, which publishes newspapers, magazines and books in Italy, Spain and France. Colao shares his views on business, the global economy and leading Vodafone.

36603 ■ *"IFRS Monopoly: the Pied Piper of Financial Reporting" in Accounting and Business Research (Vol. 41, Summer 2011, No. 3, pp. 291)*
Pub: American Institute of Certified Public Accountants
Contact: Barry C. Melancon, President
E-mail: bmelancon@aicpa.org

Ed: Shyam Sunder. **Description:** The disadvantages of granting monopoly to the international financial reporting standards (IFRS) are examined. Results indicate that an IFRS monopoly removes the chances for comparing alternative practices and learning from them. An IFRS monopoly also eliminates customization of financial reporting to fit local differences in governance, business, economic, and legal conditions.

36604 ■ *"An Ill Wind: Icelandic Bank Failures Chill Atlantic Canada" in Canadian Business (Vol. 81, November 10, 2008, No. 19, pp. 10)*
Pub: Rogers Media Ltd.

Ed: Charles Mandel. **Description:** Bank failures in Iceland have put a stop to flights ferrying Icelanders to Newfoundland to purchase Christmas gifts, thereby threatening Newfoundland's tourism industry. The credit of Newfoundland's fisheries is also being squeezed since most of Atlantic Canadian seafood processors hold lines of credit from Icelandic banks.

36605 ■ *"Ill Winds; Cuba's Economy" in The Economist (Vol. 390, January 3, 2009, No. 8612, pp. 20)*
Pub: The Economist Newspaper Inc.

Description: Cuba's long-term economic prospects remain poor with the economy forecasted to grow only 4.3 percent for the year, about half of the original forecast, due in part to Hurricane Gustav which caused $10 billion in damage and disrupted the food-supply network and devastated farms across the region; President Raul Castro made raising agricultural production a national priority and the rise in global commodity prices hit the country hard. The only bright spot has been the rise in tourism which is up 9.3 percent over 2007.

36606 ■ *Imagining India: The Idea of a Renewed Nation*
Pub: Penguin Group USA Inc.

Ed: Nandan Nilekani. **Released:** 2009. **Price:** $29.95. **Description:** National technology leader, Nandan Nilekan warns of pitfalls, obstacles and the danger of letting down the people of India.

36607 ■ *"Immigration Issues Frustrate Owners From Overseas" in The Business Journal-Serving Greater Tampa Bay (Vol. 28, August 15, 2008)*
Pub: American City Business Journals, Inc.

Ed: Margie Manning. **Description:** Investors who availed the E-2 visa program believe that the tightened restrictions on the visa program has trapped them in the United States. The E-2 investor visa program was designed to attract investors into the U.S., but restrictions were tightened after the September 11, 2001 attacks. Other views and information on E-2 and its impact on investors are presented.

36608 ■ *"iMozi Integrates Esprida LiveControl for Advanced DVD Kiosk Hardware" in Wireless News (December 20, 2010)*
Pub: Close-Up Media Inc.

Description: Provider of self-service entertainment technology, iMozi Canada has partnered with Esprida to make its automated DVD Kiosk solutions Esprida-enabled. Esprida develops remote device management solutions and will offer enhanced capabilities and to improve customer experience for users.

36609 ■ *Import/Export for Dummies*
Pub: John Wiley and Sons, Inc.

Ed: John J. Capela. **Released:** June 2008. **Price:** $19.99. **Description:** Provides entrepreneurs and small- to medium-size businesses with information required to start exporting products globally and importing goods to the U.S. Topics covered include the ins and outs of developing or expanding operations to gain market share, with details on the top ten countries in which America trades, from Canada to Germany to China.

36610 ■ *"Importers Share Safety Liability" in Feedstuffs (Vol. 80, January 21, 2008, No. 3, pp. 19)*
Pub: Miller Publishing Company, Inc.

Description: Pet food and toys containing lead paint are among products from China being recalled due to safety concerns. American Society for Quality's list of measures that outsourcing companies can take to help ensure safer products being imported to the U.S.

36611 ■ *"In the Bag?" in Canadian Business (Vol. 81, March 3, 2008, No. 3, pp. 57)*
Pub: Rogers Media

Ed: Calvin Leung. **Description:** American stocks are beginning to appear cheap amidst the threat of a worldwide economic slowdown, United States economic crisis and declining stock portfolios. Investors looking for bargain stocks should study the shares of Apple and Oshkosh Corp. Evaluation of other cheap-looking stocks such as the shares of Coach and 3M is also given.

36612 ■ *"In China, Railways to Riches" in Barron's (Vol. 88, July 7, 2008, No. 27, pp. M9)*
Pub: Dow Jones & Co., Inc.

Ed: Assif Shameen. **Description:** Shares of Chinese railway companies look to benefit from multimillion-dollar investments aimed at upgrading the Chinese railway network. Investment in the sector is expected to reach $210 billion for the 2006-2010 period.

36613 ■ *"In India, A Gold-Price Threat?" in Barron's (Vol. 88, June 30, 2008, No. 26, pp. M12)*
Pub: Dow Jones & Co., Inc.

Ed: Melanie Burton. **Description:** Gold purchases in India are falling as record prices take its toll on demand. Gold imports to India fell by 52 percent in May 2008 from the previous year and local prices are higher by one-third from the previous year to 12,540 rupees for 10 grams.

36614 ■ *"In the Wake of Pet-Food Crisis, Iams Sales Plummet Nearly 17 Percent" in Advertising Age (Vol. 78, May 14, 2007, No. 18, pp. 3)*
Pub: Crain Communications, Inc.

Ed: Jack Neff. **Description:** Although the massive U.S. pet-food recall impacted more than 100 brands, Procter & Gamble Co.'s Iams lost more sales and market share than any other industry player. According to Information Resources Inc. data, the brand's sales dropped 16.5 percent in the eight-week period ended April 22. Many analysts feel that the company could have handled the crisis in a better manner.

36615 ■ *"In With the Good" in Canadian Business (Vol. 80, November 5, 2007, No. 22, pp. 22)*
Pub: Rogers Media

Ed: Jack Mintz. **Description:** Restriction on foreign direct investment in Canada is unlikely to materialize despite Minister of Industry Jim Prentice's opinion that new rules be set in Ottawa regarding foreign state-owned businesses. Reasons why governments would not unreasonably regulate foreign investments are investigated.

36616 ■ *"Indigenous Tourism Operators" in International Journal of Entrepreneurship and Small Business (Vol. 10, July 6, 2010, No. 4)*
Pub: Publishers Communication Group

Ed: Andrews Cardow, Peter Wiltshier. **Description:** Emergent enthusiasm for tourism as a savior for economic development in the Chatham Islands of New Zealand is highlighted.

36617 ■ *"The Influencers" in Entrepreneur (Vol. 36, March 2008, No. 3, pp. 66)*
Pub: Entrepreneur Media Inc.

Ed: Andrea Cooper. **Description:** Among the 25 people, events, and trends that will influence business in 2008 are: the 2008 U.S. presidential elections, climate change, China, weakening U.S. dollar, mortgage crisis, generational shift, Bill Drayton, and Bill Gates. Other 2008 influencers are presented.

36618 ■ *Innovate to Great: Re-Igniting Sustainable Innovation to Win in the Global Economy*
Pub: McGraw-Hill

Ed: Judy Estrin. **Released:** September 12, 2008. **Price:** $27.95. **Description:** The author explores innovation and creativity as a means for small companies to survive and expand in the global economy.

36619 ■ *"Innovating Globally" in Business Strategy Review (Vol. 21, Spring 2010, No. 1, pp. 24)*
Pub: Wiley-Blackwell
Ed: Costas Markides, Stuart Crainer. **Description:** Costas Markides has spent over two decades studying business strategy and innovation. Recently, he has been focusing on the bigger picture of how people can address major social problems. Can the techniques used by managers to create innovation inside organizations work with global change?.

36620 ■ *"Innovating Low-Cost Business Models" in Strategy and Leadership (Vol. 39, March-April 2011, No. 2, pp. 43)*
Pub: Emerald Group Publishing Inc.
Ed: Nicholas Kachaner, Zhenya Lindgardt, David Michael. **Description:** A process that can be used to implement low-cost innovation is presented. The process can be used to address the competitive challenges presented by multinationals' practice of presenting applications and price points that are intended for developing markets into developed markets. The process involves targeting large, and low-income segments of the market.

36621 ■ *"Innovators Critical in Technical Economy" in Crain's Cleveland Business (Vol. 28, November 5, 2007, No. 44, pp. 10)*
Pub: Crain Communications, Inc.
Ed: Peter Rea. **Description:** Discusses the importance to attract, develop and retain talented innovators on Ohio's economy. Also breaks down the four fronts on which the international battle for talent is being waged.

36622 ■ *"Insider" in Canadian Business (Vol. 81, March 3, 2008, No. 3, pp. 96)*
Pub: Rogers Media
Description: History of gold usage and gold trading is presented in a timeline. Gold was a symbol of power and wealth in 2500 B.C., and in 1500 B.C., it became the first currency to be recognized internationally. Other remarkable events in the gold industry and laws that covered gold are discussed.

36623 ■ *"International Benefits Roundup" in Employee Benefit News (Vol. 25, December 1, 2011, No. 15)*
Pub: SourceMedia Inc.
Description: Employee contributions to an employer-sponsored defined contribution plan in Japan will allowed on a tax-deductible basis; however, currently employee contributions are not allowed. The defined contribution plan is outlined for better understanding.

36624 ■ *"International Comparisons Data" in Montly Labor Review (Vol. 133, September 2010, No. 9, pp. 143)*
Pub: Bureau of Labor Statistics
Description: Unemployment rates adjusted to U.S. concepts and ten countries are presented.

36625 ■ *"International Dairy Queen" in Ice Cream Reporter (Vol. 23, October 20, 2010, No. 11, pp. 7)*
Pub: Ice Cream Reporter
Description: International Dairy Queen will open more than 100 new outlets in China in 2011, adding to the current level of more than 300 outlets in that country.

36626 ■ *International Entrepreneurship*
Pub: Edward Elgar Publishing, Incorporated
Ed: Oviatt. **Released:** March 2007. **Price:** $295.00. **Description:** Universities are focusing research efforts on international entrepreneurship. The book features critical articles on the topic.

36627 ■ *International Entrepreneurship Education Issues and Newness*
Pub: Edward Elgar Publishing, Incorporated
Ed: Fayolle. **Released:** August 2006. **Price:** $120.00. **Description:** Entrepreneurial education, focusing on economic, political and social needs of a changing world; ideas for reassessing, redeveloping, and renewing curricula and methods for teaching entrepreneurship are offered.

36628 ■ *International Entrepreneurship in Small and Medium Size Enterprises: Orientation, Environment and Strategy*
Pub: Edward Elgar Publishing, Incorporated
Ed: Hamid Etemad. **Released:** October 2004. **Price:** $130.00. **Description:** Issues involved in internationalizing small and medium sized (SME) businesses. Topics include an investigation into the emerging patterns of SME growth and international expansion in response to the changing competitive environment, dynamics of competitive behavior, entrepreneurial processes and a formulation of strategy.

36629 ■ *"International ETFs: Your Passport to the World" in Barron's (Vol. 89, July 13, 2009, No. 28, pp. L10)*
Pub: Dow Jones & Co., Inc.
Ed: John Hintze. **Description:** International exchange traded funds give investors more choices in terms of investment plays and there are 174 U.S. ETF listings worth $141 billion as of July 2009. Suggestions on how to invest in these funds based on one's conviction on how the global economy will unfold are presented.

36630 ■ *"International Growth" in Black Enterprise (Vol. 38, July 2008, No. 12, pp. 64)*
Pub: Earl G. Graves Publishing Co. Inc.
Ed: Marcia A. Reed-Woodard. **Description:** Becoming an increasingly smaller portion of the global business environment is the U.S. economy. Christopher Catlin, an associate with Booz Allen Hamilton, a technology management and strategy-consulting firm, shares what he has learned about the global market.

36631 ■ *International Growth of Small and Medium Enterprises*
Pub: Routledge
Ed: Nina Nummela. **Released:** February 10, 2010. **Price:** $110.00. **Description:** This volume focuses on how companies expand their operations across borders through opportunity exploration and exploitation, and identification and development of innovations.

36632 ■ *International Handbook of Women and Small Business Entrepreneurship*
Pub: Edward Elgar Publishing, Incorporated
Ed: Fielden. **Released:** December 2006. **Price:** $50.00. **Description:** Practical initiatives and strategies for women entering small business entrepreneurial ventures are examined.

36633 ■ *The Internationalization of Asset Ownership in Europe*
Pub: Cambridge University Press
Contact: Richard Ziemacki, President
E-mail: rziemacki@cambridge.org
Ed: Harry Huizinga, Lars Jonung. **Released:** November 2005. **Price:** $112.00. **Description:** Ten financial experts provide analysis of the growth and the implications of foreign ownership in Europe's financial markets.

36634 ■ *"Is Globalization Threatening U.S. Hispanic Progress?" in Hispanic Business (Vol. 30, September 2008, No. 9, pp. 16)*
Pub: Hispanic Business, Inc.
Ed: Jessica Haro. **Description:** Talented Hispanic employees are making progress within the increasingly diverse American corporate scenario. However, while some experts believe the induction of foreign professionals through globalization will not impact this progress, others feel it could hamper opportunities for American Hispanics.

36635 ■ *"Is the Sun Setting on Oil Sector's Heydey?" in Globe & Mail (January 25, 2007, pp. B3)*
Pub: CTVglobemedia Publishing Inc.
Ed: Shawn McCarthy. **Description:** The effects of fuel efficiency management policies of the United States on Canadian petroleum industry are discussed. Canada is the largest exporter of crude oil to America after the Middle East.

36636 ■ *"Is 'Tsunami' of Freight in our Future?" in Business Courier (Vol. 26, November 27, 2009, No. 31, pp. 1)*
Pub: American City Business Journals, Inc.
Ed: Dan Monk. **Description:** Freight companies are planning for cargo-container shipping facilities on the riverfront of Cincinnati in light of the completion of the $5 billion Panama Canal expansion in 2015. The city's capability to utilize the growth in freight has been under investigation by authorities.

36637 ■ *"Islamic Banks Get a 'Libor' of Their Own" in Wall Street Journal Eastern Edition (November 25 , 2011, pp. C4)*
Pub: Dow Jones & Company Inc. Enterprise Media Group
Contact: Clare Hart, President
Ed: Katy Burne. **Description:** The London interbank offered rate, or Libor, has been used by banks internationally for years. It is the rate at which banks lend money to each other. The rate has not been used by Islamic banks, but now sixteen banks have come up with the Islamic Interbank Benchmark Rate.

36638 ■ *"It May Be Cheaper to Manufacture At Home" in Harvard Business Review (Vol. 88, October 2010, No. 10, pp. 84)*
Pub: Harvard Business School Publishing
Ed: Suzanne de Treville, Lenos Trigeorgis. **Description:** Using a real options framework rather than a discounted cash flow model to assess and value supply chain processes is examined. This enables companies to assess costs for a variety of situations, not just ideal or normal circumstances, which can make the difference between domestic and foreign manufacturing decisions.

36639 ■ *"Itochu Joins KKR in Samson Buyout" in Wall Street Journal Eastern Edition (November 25 , 2011, pp. B7)*
Pub: Dow Jones & Company Inc. Enterprise Media Group
Contact: Clare Hart, President
Description: Samson Investment Company is the target of a $7.2 billion leveraged buyout by a consortium led by US investment firm Kohlberg Kravis Roberts & Company and Tokyo-based Itochu Corporation, part of the consortium is coming in on the deal for a 25 percent holding, for which it will pay $1.04 billion.

36640 ■ *"It's Time To Swim" in Canadian Business (Vol. 81, March 3, 2008, No. 3, pp. 37)*
Pub: Rogers Media
Ed: Megan Harman. **Description:** Canadian manufacturers should consider Asian markets such as India and the United Arab Emirates as the U.S. economic downturn continues. Canada's shortage in skilled labor is also expected to negatively affect manufacturing industries. Ontario's plans to assist manufacturers are also presented.

36641 ■ *"It's What You Know. It's Who You Know. It's China" in Inc. (Vol. 33, October 2011, No. 8, pp. 80)*
Pub: Inc. Magazine
Ed: David H. Freedman. **Description:** Michael Lee will be the first American entrepreneur to build big in China. The company is piloting two large commercial real estate developments, one in New York City the other in Nanjing, China.

36642 ■ *"Jobs, Export Surge Confirm Recovery" in Globe & Mail (March 10, 2007, pp. B5)*
Pub: CTVglobemedia Publishing Inc.
Ed: Heather Scoffield. **Description:** The increase in the number of jobs and exports that is forecast to reverse the slowdown in the Canadian economy is discussed.

36643 ■ *"Keeping Railcars 'Busy At All Times' At TTX" in Crain's Chicago Business (Vol. 31, April 28, 2008, No. 17, pp. 6)*
Pub: Crain Communications, Inc.
Ed: Bob Tita. **Description:** Profile of the president of Chicago railcar pool operator TTX Co. and his business plan for the company which includes improving fleet management and car purchasing through better use of data on railroad demand.

36644 ■ *"Kenyans Embrace Moving Money By Text Message" in Chicago Tribune (October 7, 2008)*
Pub: McClatchy-Tribune Information Services
Ed: Laurie Goering. **Description:** Cell phone banking services are becoming more common, especially for foreign residents; customers are able to establish a virtual cell phone bank account through companies such as M-Pesa which allows their customers to pay bills, withdraw cash, pay merchants or text money to relatives.

36645 ■ *"Kids, Computers and the Social Networking Evolution" in Canadian Business (Vol. 81, October 27, 2008, No. 18, pp. 93)*
Pub: Rogers Media Ltd.
Ed: Penny Milton. **Description:** Social networking was found to help educate students in countries like the U.S., Canada and Mexico. Schools that embrace social networking teach students how to use computers safely and responsibility in order to counter threats to children on the Internet.

36646 ■ *"Kinetico Exec Going Global to Increase Growth Flow" in Crain's Cleveland Business (Vol. 28, October 1, 2007, No. 39, pp. 5)*
Pub: Crain Communications, Inc.
Ed: David Bennett. **Description:** Shamus Hurley, the new CEO and president of Kinetico Inc., a manufacturer of water filtering and softening equipment for residential, commercial and municipal use, plans to expand the company to target markets overseas.

36647 ■ *Kocham Business Directory*
Pub: Korean Chamber of Commerce & Industry in USA Inc.
URL(s): kocham.org/business-directory. **Released:** Annual **Covers:** About 700 offices of leading Korean companies operated by Korean nationals located throughout the United States. Other Korean service firms (banks, trade organizations, etc.) are also listed. **Entries include:** Firm name, address, phone, cable address, telex, name of United States representative or president. Exporter listings include above information for headquarters' address and product line. Importer listings include products. **Arrangement:** Exporters and importers are alphabetical; service firms are classified by type of service.

36648 ■ *"Kroger Girds for Invasion of U.K. Chain" in Business Courier (Vol. 24, November 2, 2008, No. 29, pp. 1)*
Pub: American City Business Journals, Inc.
Ed: Jon Newberry. **Description:** Tesco PLC will be opening its first Fresh & Easy Neighborhood Markets in Southern California. The company has committed $500 million per year to get a share of the $500 billion US food retailing market and will be opening more stores in quick succession. Tesco's arrival can be difficult for Kroger because Kroger had obtained much of its success by using Tesco's UK model.

36649 ■ *"Land Agent Taken Over" in Farmer's Weekly (March 28, 2008, No. 320)*
Pub: Reed Business Information
Contact: Jeff Greisch, President
Description: Property business Smiths Gore will take over Cluttons' rural division, one of the oldest names in land agency. Cluttons said it had decided to sell its rural business as part of a strategic repositioning that would refocus the business on commercial, residential and overseas opportunities.

36650 ■ *"The Last Ingredient?" in Canadian Business (Vol. 81, October 13, 2008, No. 17, pp. 88)*
Pub: Rogers Media Ltd.
Ed: Rachel Pulfer. **Description:** Views and information on Cookie Jar Group's plan to acquire rights for Strawberry Shortcake and the Care Bears are discussed. The move would make Cookie Jar a major player in the global children's entertainment market. Cookie Jar chief executive, Michael Hirsh is believed to be securing funds for the planned $195 million acquisition.

36651 ■ *"The Latin Beat Goes On" in Barron's (Vol. 88, July 7, 2008, No. 27, pp. L5)*
Pub: Dow Jones & Co., Inc.
Ed: Tom Sullivan. **Description:** Latin American stocks have outperformed other regional markets due to rising commodities prices and favorable economic climate. Countries such as Brazil, Mexico, Chile, and Peru provide investment opportunities, while Argentina and Venezuela are tougher places to invest.

36652 ■ *"Leaks in the Pipeline" in Hispanic Business (September 2007, pp. 18, 20, 22, 24)*
Pub: Hispanic Business
Ed: Holly Ocasio Rizzo. **Description:** Graduate schools need to focus on domestic diversity in order to attract Hispanic students in a growing global economy.

36653 ■ *"Leasing Midway; Look for Higher Parking Fees, More Retail Under Private Airport Operator" in Crain's Chicago Business (May 5, 2008)*
Pub: Crain Communications, Inc.
Ed: Paul Merrion. **Description:** According to experts, bids for the first privatization of a major U.S. airport could run as high as $3.5 billion. Information-gathering and negotiations will soon get under way with some or all of the six major international investor groups that recently expressed interest in running Midway.

36654 ■ *"Let Emerging Market Customers Be Your Teachers" in Harvard Business Review (Vol. 88, December 2010, No. 12, pp. 115)*
Pub: Harvard Business School Publishing
Ed: Guillermo D'Andrea, David Marcotte, Gwen Dixon Morrison. **Description:** Examination of effective strategies for emerging markets is presented. These include helping educate customers as well as selling to them, adapting to customers' habits, and focusing brands appropriately. Magazine Luiza, a chain store in Brazil, is used to illustrate these points.

36655 ■ *"Lightening the Load" in Crain's Cleveland Business (Vol. 28, October 8, 2007, No. 40, pp. 3)*
Pub: Crain Communications, Inc.
Ed: Jay Miller. **Description:** Companies reliant on barge deliveries are running well below capacity due to both the building up of silt at the bottom of the Cuyahoga River as well as the lower water levels which are causing a number of problems for the barges and big boats that deliver goods to the region.

36656 ■ *"Li'l Guy Rolls Up Into Bigger Company" in The Business Journal-Serving Metropolitan Kansas City (Vol. 26, September 12, 2008)*
Pub: American City Business Journals, Inc.
Ed: Suzanna Stagemeyer. **Description:** Li'l Guy Foods, a Mexican food company in Kansas City, Missouri, has merged with Tortilla King Inc. Li'l Guy's revenue in 2007 was $3.3 million, while a newspaper report said that Tortilla King's revenue in 2001 was $7.5 million. Growth opportunities for the combined companies and Li'l Guy's testing of the Wichita market are discussed.

36657 ■ *Local Enterprises in the Global Economy: Issues of Governance and Upgrading*
Pub: Edward Elgar Publishing, Incorporated
Ed: Hubert Schmitz. **Released:** November 2004. **Price:** $35.00 (soft cover), $110.00 (hard bound). **Description:** Examination of the relationships between globalization, corporate governance, and the economic performance of small businesses and local enterprises.

36658 ■ *"Local Manufacturers See Tax Proposal Hurting Global Operations" in Crain's Cleveland Business (Vol. 30, May 18, 2009, No. 20)*
Pub: Crain Communications, Inc.
Ed: Dan Shingler. **Description:** New tax laws proposed by the Obama Administration could hinder the efforts of some Northeast Ohio industrial companies from expanding their overseas markets. The law is designed to prevent companies from moving jobs overseas.

36659 ■ *"Location, Location" in Black Enterprise (Vol. 38, February 2008, No. 7, pp. 64)*
Pub: Earl G. Graves Publishing Co. Inc.
Ed: Marcia Reed-Woodard. **Description:** Overseas work assignments are increasing, especially for workers in the U.S., Canada and Latin America.

36660 ■ *"Lofty Ambitions" in Canadian Business (Vol. 80, October 22, 2007, No. 21, pp. 26)*
Pub: Rogers Media
Ed: Thomas Watson. **Description:** Canada has made its first trade deal in six years through the European Free Trade Agreement. This is a boost to the Canadian economy, but focus must be made on taking out internal barriers to inter-provincial trade and from third-party trade liberalization.

36661 ■ *"Look, Leap, and License" in Retail Merchandiser (Vol. 51, July-August 2011, No. 4, pp. 16)*
Pub: Phoenix Media Corporation
Description: Toys highlighting the Licensing International Expo 2011 included a life-sized Cookie Monster, Papa Smurf, Power Rangers, Transformer, and margarita wrestlers. Taking licensed properties international was a common theme at this year's show.

36662 ■ *"Loonie Tunes: When Will the Dollar Rise Again?" in Canadian Business (Vol. 81, November 10, 2008, No. 19, pp. 62)*
Pub: Rogers Media Ltd.
Ed: Joe Castaldo. **Description:** The Canadian dollar has weakened against the U.S. Dollar as the U.S. financial crisis rocked global markets. A currency strategist says that the strength of the U.S. dollar is not based on people's optimism on the U.S. economy but on a structural demand where U.S. non-financial corporations have been repatriating greenbacks from foreign subsidiaries.

36663 ■ *Macrowikinomics: Rebooting Business and the World*
Pub: Portfolio Hardcover
Ed: Don Tapscott, Anthony D. Williams. **Released:** September 28, 2010. **Price:** $27.95. **Description:** Wikinomics Don Tapscott and Anthony Williams showed how mass collaboration was changing the way businesses communicate, create value,, and compete in the new global marketplace in 2007. Now, in the wake of the global financial crisis, the principles of wikinomics have become more powerful than ever.

36664 ■ *Made in China: Secrets of China's Dynamic Entrepreneurs*
Pub: John Wiley & Sons, Inc.
Ed: Winter Nie, Katherine Xin. **Released:** March 1, 2009. **Price:** $24.95. **Description:** Insight and analysis of the strategies leading to China's rapidly growing economy are profiled.

36665 ■ *"Magpower May Build Solar Panels Here" in Austin Business Journal (Vol. 31, May 13, 2011, No. 10, pp. A1)*
Pub: American City Business Journals Inc.
Ed: Christopher Calnan. **Description:** RRE Austin Solar LLC CEO Doven Mehta has revealed plans to partner with Portugal-based Magpower SA, only if Austin energy buys electricity from planned solar energy farm in Pflugerville. Austin Energy has received 100 bids from 35 companies to supply 200 megawatts of solar- and wind-generated electricity.

36666 ■ *"Making Factory Tours Count" in Playthings (Vol. 107, January 1, 2009, No. 1, pp. 14)*
Pub: Reed Business Information
Contact: Jeff Greisch, President
Ed: Malcolm Denniss. **Description:** The importance of touring an overseas toy supplier's manufacturing facility is stressed. Strategies for general factory visits are outlined in order to determine safety-related quality assurance issues in production.

36667 ■ *"Making It Stick" in Business Courier (Vol. 24, November 9, 2008, No. 30, pp. 1)*
Pub: American City Business Journals, Inc.
Ed: Lucy May. **Description:** Discusses a report by the Brookings Institution which shows the need for the U.S. government to offer greater support to the

country's metro areas in order to excel globally. Ohio, which has seven of the country's 100 largest metropolitan areas, does not receive enough funds, due to the need to finance less populated areas. Because of this, Ohio politicians have to spread less funding in order to cover more constituents.

36668 ■ *Managing Complexity and Change in SMEs Frontiers in European Research*
Pub: Edward Elgar Publishing, Incorporated
Ed: Christensen. **Released:** December 2006. **Price:** $120.00. **Description:** Complexities faced by entrepreneurs in an expanding marketplace are discussed.

36669 ■ *Managing Economies, Trade and International Business*
Pub: Palgrave Macmillan
Ed: Aidan O'Connor. **Released:** January 19, 2010. **Price:** $90.00. **Description:** An in-depth look at the areas that affect and influence international business, exploring specific issues businesses face in terms of economic development, trade law, and international marketing and management.

36670 ■ *Managing India's Small Industrial Economy: The Catalytic Role of Industrial Counselors and Policy Makers*
Pub: SAGE Publications USA
Contact: Blaise R. Simqu, President
Ed: V. Padmanand, V.G. Patel. **Released:** June 2004. **Price:** $35.95. **Description:** Case studies and methodology are used to discuss the areas where industrial consultants are influencing sustainability and growth of small businesses in India's industrial economy.

36671 ■ *"Manufacturing Behind the Great Wall: What Works, What Doesn't" in Canadian Electronics (Vol. 23, February 2008, No. 1, pp. 6)*
Pub: CLB Media Inc.
Ed: Michel Jullian. **Description:** Electronic component producers are increasingly transitioning their manufacturing operations to China in order to take advantage of the growing Chinese manufacturing industry. It is believed that manufacturers have to carefully consider whether their run sizes are appropriate for Chinese manufacturing before moving their operations.

36672 ■ *"Manufacturing in the Middle Kingdom" in Inc. (December 2007, pp. 54-57)*
Pub: Gruner & Jahr USA Publishing
Ed: Alex Salkever. **Description:** Tips for manufacturing any new product in China as well as marketing said product is examined; five key steps for successfully managing Chinese contractors are listed.

36673 ■ *"Mapping the Social Internet" in Harvard Business Review (Vol. 88, July-August 2010, No. 7-8, pp. 32)*
Pub: Harvard Business School Publishing
Description: Chart compares and contrasts online social networks in selected countries.

36674 ■ *"Marine Act Amendments Gain Parliamentary Approval" in Canadian Sailings (July 7, 2008)*
Pub: UBM Global Trade
Contact: Leonard J. Corallo, President
Ed: Alex Binkley. **Description:** Changes to the Canada Marine Act provides better borrowing deals as well as an ability to tap into federal infrastructure funding for environmental protection measures, security improvements and other site enhancements.

36675 ■ *"Market Gamble" in Business Journal-Serving Phoenix and the Valley of the Sun (Vol. 5, October 5, 2007, No. 28, pp. 1)*
Pub: American City Business Journals, Inc.
Ed: Mike Padgett. **Description:** Al-BSR LLC, an Israeli group believes the housing market will regain its strength within three years. The group plans to build its $385 million project, called One Phoenix. The condominiums start at $500,000, with units ranging from 800 to 2,000 square feet.

36676 ■ *"Market Watch" in Barron's (Vol. 88, March 24, 2008, No. 12, pp. M18)*
Pub: Dow Jones & Company, Inc.
Ed: Ashraf Laidi; Marc Pado; David Kotok. **Description:** Latest measures implemented by the Federal Reserve to address the credit crisis did not benefit the US dollar, with the Japanese yen and the euro recouping earlier losses against the dollar. Goldman Sachs reported earnings of $3.23 per share, claiming a stronger liquidity position. The US markets bottomed early on 22 January 2007, according to evidence.

36677 ■ *"Market Watch" in Barron's (Vol. 89, July 20, 2009, No. 29, pp. M10)*
Pub: Dow Jones & Co., Inc.
Ed: Peter Greene; Michael Darda; Ian Wyatt; Stephanie Pomboy. **Description:** Concerns about a possible increase in US inflation rates are overblown as the country remains in a deflationary environment. Goldman Sachs's second quarter 2009 earnings have already been priced in as its shares rose. Germany's plans of a possible dollar bond sale are in anticipation of a rise in the euro's value.

36678 ■ *"Maurice Strong" in Canadian Business (Vol. 81, December 8, 2008, No. 21, pp. 70)*
Pub: Rogers Media Ltd.
Ed: Andrew Wahl. **Description:** Peking University honorary professor Maurice Strong believes that a lot of Westerners, including Canadians, do not take time to understand the business culture in China.

36679 ■ *The Mechanics of Modernity in Europe and East Asia: Institutional Origins of Social Change and Stagnation*
Pub: Routledge
Ed: Erik Ringmar. **Released:** April 1, 2009. **Price:** $44.95. **Description:** Discussion of reasons why certain countries embarked on a path of sustained economic growth while others declined in Europe and East Asia.

36680 ■ *"Melamine Analytical Methods Released" in Feedstuffs (Vol. 80, October 6, 2008, No. 41, pp. 2)*
Pub: Miller Publishing Company
Description: Romer Labs has released new validations for its AgraQuant Melamine enzyme-linked immunosorbent assay. The test kit screens for melamine in feed and diary products, including pet foods, milk and milk powder. Melamine by itself is nontoxic in low doses, but when combined with cyanuric acid it can cause fatal kidney stones. The Chinese dairy industry is in the midst of a huge melamine crisis; melamine-contaminated dairy and food products from China have been found in more than 20 countries.

36681 ■ *"Merchant Cash-Advance Company Enters Canada" in Cardline (Vol. 8, February 29, 2008, No. 9, pp. 1)*
Pub: SourceMedia Inc.
Description: Merchant cash-advance company is expanding operations into Canada.

36682 ■ *"Mexican Companies to Rent Space in TechTown, Chinese Negotiating" in Crain's Detroit Business (Vol. 24, September 29, 2008, No. 39)*
Pub: Crain Communications Inc.
Ed: Tom Henderson. **Description:** Wayne State University's TechTown, the business incubator and research park, has signed an agreement with the Mexican government that will provide temporary office space to 25 Mexican companies looking to find customers or establish partnerships in Michigan. TechTown's executive director is negotiating with economic development officials from China. To accommodate foreign visitors the incubator is equipping offices with additional equipment and resources.

36683 ■ *"Micro-Finance Agencies and SMEs" in International Journal of Entrepreneurship and Small Business (Vol. 11, August 3, 2010)*
Pub: Publishers Communication Group
Ed: Patricia A. Rowe, Michael J. Christie, Frank Hoy. **Description:** Institutional preparedness of economic development agencies for developing small and medium-sized enterprises (SMEs) is discussed. The cases presented illustrate variations in the micro-finance lender agency-enterprise development of processes for sharing vision and interdependence.

36684 ■ *"Mine Woes Could Rouse Zinc" in Barron's (Vol. 88, July 7, 2008, No. 27, pp. M12)*
Pub: Dow Jones & Co., Inc.
Ed: Andrea Hotter. **Description:** Prices of zinc could increase due to supply problems in producing countries such as Australia and China. London Metal Exchange prices for the metal have dropped about 36 percent in 2008.

36685 ■ *"Minimizing Import Risks" in Canadian Sailings (July 7, 2008)*
Pub: UBM Global Trade
Contact: Leonard J. Corallo, President
Ed: Jack Kohane. **Description:** New food and product safety laws may be enacted by Canada's Parliament; importers, retailers and manufacturers could face huge fines if the new laws are passed.

36686 ■ *"Mission to China" in Canadian Business (Vol. 81, December 8, 2008, No. 21, pp. 28)*
Pub: Rogers Media Ltd.
Ed: Andrew Wahl. **Description:** Canada China Business Council and the Council of the Federation visited China for a three-city trade mission. The trade mission aims to re-establish the strong relationship between China and Canada.

36687 ■ *"Montreal Port Head Lands CP Ships Deal" in Globe & Mail (January 5, 2006, pp. B4)*
Pub: CTVglobemedia Publishing Inc.
Description: The opinions of president Dominic Taddeo, on the positive impact of TUI AG's acquisition of CP Ships Ltd. on operations at Port of Montreal, are presented.

36688 ■ *"The Mood of a Nation" in Canadian Business (Vol. 81, April 14, 2008, No. 6, pp. 56)*
Pub: Rogers Media
Ed: Joe Castaldo. **Description:** Independent Fish Harvesters Inc. processes more kilograms a year and has had to hire more workers but its managers worry about how a slowdown in the U.S. economy will affect his business. A planned shopping complex in Mirabel Quebec, the manufacturing industry in Kitchener, Ontario, and a cattle farming business in Sarnia, Ontario are discussed to provide a snapshot of the challenges that business in Canada are facing as recession looms.

36689 ■ *More Than a Pink Cadillac*
Pub: McGraw-Hill
Ed: Jim Underwood. **Released:** 2002. **Price:** $23.95. **Description:** Profile of Mary Kay Ash who turned her $5,000 investment into a billion-dollar corporation. Ash's nine principles that form the foundation of her company's global success are outlined. Stories from her sales force leaders share ideas for motivating employees, impressing customers and building a successful company. The book emphasizes the leadership skills required to drive performance in any successful enterprise.

36690 ■ *"Mover and Sheika" in Conde Nast Portfolio (Vol. 2, June 2008, No. 6, pp. 104)*
Pub: Conde Nast Publications
Contact: David Carey, President
Ed: John Arlidge. **Description:** Profile of Princess Sheika Lubna who is the first female foreign trade minister in the Middle East, the United Arab Emirates biggest business envoy, paving the way for billions in new investment, and also a manufacturer of her own perfume line.

36691 ■ *"A Muddle at Marks & Spencer" in Barron's (Vol. 88, July 7, 2008, No. 27, pp. M7)*
Pub: Dow Jones & Co., Inc.
Ed: Molly Neal. **Description:** British retail outfit Marks & Spencer is encountering turbulent financial conditions but remains confident in spending 900 mil-

lion pounds sterling. The company has not made a profit forecast for the first half of 2008 and is suffering from a shrinking cash flow.

36692 ■ *The Multinational Enterprise Revisited: The Essential Buckley and Casson*
Pub: Palgrave Macmillan
Ed: Peter J. Buckley, Mark Casson. **Released:** January 5, 2010. **Price:** $95.00. **Description:** A compilation of essays gathered from over thirty years discussing the future of the multinational enterprise, and includes a new introduction and conclusion to bond the pieces together in a comprehensive overview of the theory of the multinational enterprise.

36693 ■ *"Native Wisdom" in Canadian Business (Vol. 80, October 8, 2007, No. 20, pp. 121)*
Pub: Rogers Media
Ed: Bernd Christmas. **Description:** Roles of Canadian indigenous peoples in the country's economic development are discussed. It is believed that empowering Canadian natives to contribute to the country's economy will positively affect the country's future. The need for education in preparing natives for the global economy is also tackled.

36694 ■ *"Nat'l Instruments Connects with Lego" in Austin Business JournalInc. (Vol. 28, August 22, 2008, No. 23, pp. 1)*
Pub: American City Business Journals
Ed: Laura Hipp. **Description:** Austin-based National Instruments Corporation has teamed with Lego Group from Denmark to create a robot that can be built by children and can be used to perform tasks. Lego WeDo, their latest product, uses computer connection to power its movements. The educational benefits of the new product are discussed.

36695 ■ *"Needed: A Strategy; Banking In China" in The Economist (Vol. 390, January 3, 2009, No. 8612, pp. 54)*
Pub: The Economist Newspaper Inc.
Description: International banks are competing for a role in China but are finding obstacles in their paths such as a reduction in the credit their operations may receive from Chinese banks and the role they can play in the public capital markets which remain limited.

36696 ■ *"Nestle Acquires Waggin' Train Dog Treat Company" in Pet Product News (Vol. 64, November 2010, No. 11, pp. 7)*
Pub: BowTie Inc.
Description: Vevey, Switzerland-based Nestle has acquired South Carolina-based dog treat firm Waggin' Train LLC from private equity firm VMG Partners in September 2010. Waggin' Train LLC, which will be operated as a wholly owned subsidiary, is expected to fill a gap in Nestle's dog treat product portfolio.

36697 ■ *"A New Alliance For Global Change" in Harvard Business Review (Vol. 88, September 2010, No. 9, pp. 56)*
Pub: Harvard Business School Publishing
Ed: Bill Drayton, Valeria Budinich. **Description:** Collaboration between social organizations and for-profit firms through the development of hybrid value chains to target complex global issues is promoted. While social organizations offer links to communities and consumers, firms provide financing and scale expertise.

36698 ■ *"New Global Hot Spots: Look Beyond Shanghai for the Next Big Thing" in Inc. (October 2007, pp. 40-41)*
Pub: Gruner & Jahr USA Publishing
Description: The Chinese government is investing money to lure U.S. companies to start doing business in Chengdu, China. The government is upgrading Chengdu's infrastructure and establishing free trade zones in a less polluted environment. Other cities profiled in the article include: Yekaterinburg, Russia; Poznan, Poland; Ahmadabad and Kolkata, India; Suzhou, China; Belo Horizonte, Brazil; Ras Al Khaimah, United Arab Emirates; and Aguascalientes, Mexico.

36699 ■ *"New Institutional Accounting and IFRS" in Accounting and Business Research (Vol. 41, Summer 2011, No. 3, pp. 309)*
Pub: American Institute of Certified Public Accountants
Contact: Barry C. Melancon, President
E-mail: bmelancon@aicpa.org
Ed: Peter Wysocki. **Description:** A new framework for institutional accounting research is presented. It has five fundamental components — efficient versus inefficient results, interdependencies, causation, level of analysis, and institutional structure. The use of the framework for evaluation accounting institutions such as the international financial reporting standards is discussed.

36700 ■ *"New Institutional Accounting and IFRS" in Accounting and Business Research (Vol. 41, Summer 2011, No. 3, pp. 309)*
Pub: Routledge
Ed: Peter Wysocki. **Description:** A new framework for institutional accounting research is presented. It has five fundamental components: efficient versus inefficient results, interdependencies, causation, level of analysis, and institutional structure. The use of the framework for evaluation accounting institutions such as the international financial reports standards (IFRS) is discussed.

36701 ■ *"New King Top the Charts" in The Business Journal-Portland (Vol. 25, August 8, 2008, No. 22, pp. 1)*
Pub: American City Business Journals, Inc.
Ed: Andy Giegerich. **Description:** Spanish-language KRYP-FM station's spring 2008 ratings soared to 6.4 from 2.8 for the previous year. The station timing is flawless given the fact that one of every three new Portland-area residents between 2002 and 2007 were Latino.

36702 ■ *The New Role of Regional Management*
Pub: Palgrave Macmillan
Ed: Bjorn Ambos, Bodo B. Schlegelmilch. **Released:** January 19, 2010. **Price:** $95.00. **Description:** Regional management is becoming more important to companies as they expand globally. This book explores the challenges of European, United States and Asian companies and outlines how regional headquarters can develop into Dynamic Competence Relay centers to master these issues.

36703 ■ *New Technology-Based Firms in the New Millennium, Volume 6*
Pub: Elsevier Science & Technology Books
Ed: Ray Oakey, R. Oakey. **Released:** May 2008. **Price:** $149.00. **Description:** Collection of papers from the Annual International High Technology Firms (HTSFs) Conference cover issues of importance to governments as they develop technological program. Papers are grouped into three sections: theory, strategy and clustering, and spin-off firms.

36704 ■ *"New Thinking for a New Financial Order" in Harvard Business Review (Vol. 86, September 2008, No. 9, pp. 26)*
Pub: Harvard Business School Press
Ed: Diana Farell. **Description:** Factors driving the current global economy are analyzed with a focus on the influence of new public and private sectors and the impact of unregulated markets.

36705 ■ *"New Work Order" in Black Enterprise (Vol. 38, March 2008, No. 8, pp. 60)*
Pub: Earl G. Graves Publishing Co. Inc.
Description: Today's management challenges includes issues of more competition, globalization, outsourcing and technological advances. Suggestions to help create progressive leadership in small business that sustains a competitive edge are listed.

36706 ■ *"New Zealand Natural Co-Branding with Mrs. Fields" in Ice Cream Reporter (Vol. 23, November 20, 2010, No. 12, pp. 2)*
Pub: Ice Cream Reporter
Description: Mrs. Fields has partnered with a New Zealand firm to co-brand ice cream and cookies in Australian markets.

36707 ■ *"New Zealand Natural Ice Cream is Opening a Second U.S. Scoop Shop" in Ice Cream Reporter (Vol. 21, October 20, 2008, No. 11, pp. 7)*
Pub: Ice Cream Reporter
Description: New Zealand Natural Ice Cream is opening a second store in California. The company is a market leader in New Zealand and has gained distribution through 300 outlets in California.

36708 ■ *"The Next Waive" in Hawaii Business (Vol. 53, January 2008, No. 7, pp. 27)*
Pub: Hawaii Business Publishing
Ed: Cathy S. Cruz-George. **Description:** Only 40,000 Koreans took a visit to Hawaii in 2007, a decline from the pre-September averages of 123,000 visits. The number of Korean visitors in Hawaii could increase if the visa waiver proposal is passed. Efforts to improve Hawaiian tourism are presented.

36709 ■ *"No Shortage of Challenges for Cross-Border Trade" in Canadian Sailings (June 30, 2008)*
Pub: UBM Global Trade
Contact: Leonard J. Corallo, President
Ed: Kathlyn Horibe. **Description:** Pros and cons of the North American Free Trade Agreement are examined. The agreement between the U.S. and Canada concerning trade was an essential step toward securing economic growth for Canadian citizens. Two-way trade between the counties has tripled since the agreement and accounts for 7.1 million American and 3 million Canadian jobs.

36710 ■ *Non-Standard Employment under Globalization*
Pub: Palgrave Macmillan
Ed: Koichi Usami. **Released:** January 19, 2010. **Price:** $100.00. **Description:** Expansion of non-standard employment under globalization is being recognized in all of the newly industrialized countries. The book examines deregulation of labor markets, social protection for nonstandard workers, and social security reforms in accordance with the transformation of employment.

36711 ■ *"Not In My Backyard" in Entrepreneur (Vol. 36, May 2008, No. 5, pp. 42)*
Pub: Entrepreneur Media, Inc.
Ed: Farnoosh Torabi. **Description:** More investors are turning to overseas real estate investments as the U.S. market sees a slowdown. Analysts say that risk-averse investors opt for funds with record of strong returns and U.S. real estate investment trusts that partner with foreign businesses for transparency purposes. Other details about foreign real estate investments are discussed.

36712 ■ *"Now You See It.." in Canadian Business (Vol. 81, November 10, 2008, No. 19, pp. 20)*
Pub: Rogers Media Ltd.
Ed: Sharda Prashad. **Description:** Total return swaps were offered by Deutsche Bank AG and UBS AG to foreign investors for them to avoid paying taxes on the proceeds of their shares of Fording Canadian Coal Trust when Teck Cominco offered to buy the company. This means that the Canadian government is losing tax revenue from foreigners and it is argued that a simpler tax system would avoid this practice.

36713 ■ *"Olympus is Urged to Revise Board" in Wall Street Journal Eastern Edition (November 28, 2011, pp. B3)*
Pub: Dow Jones & Company Inc. Enterprise Media Group
Contact: Clare Hart, President
Ed: Phred Dvorak. **Description:** Koji Miyata, once a director on the board of troubled Japanese photographic equipment company, is urging the company to reorganize its board, saying the present group should resign their board seats but keep their management positions. The company has come under scrutiny for its accounting practices and costly acquisitions.

36714 ■ ***"OMERS Joins Bid for U.K. Port Giant" in Globe & Mail (March 28, 2006, pp. B1)***
Pub: CTVglobemedia Publishing Inc.
Ed: Paul Waldie. **Description:** The plans of Ontario Municipal Employees Retirement Board to partner with Goldman Sachs Group Inc., in order to acquire Associated British Ports PLC, are presented.

36715 ■ ***"On the Itinerary: Your Future" in Entrepreneur (Vol. 37, October 2009, No. 10, pp. 92)***
Pub: Entrepreneur Media, Inc.
Ed: Joel Holland. **Description:** Josh Hackler's Spanish Vines imports and distributes wines from Spain while using Spanish culture to help market the wines. The business was hatched after Hackler signed up for a study-abroad program in Spain.

36716 ■ ***On the Wealth of Nations: Books That Changed the World***
Pub: Grove/Atlantic Inc.
Contact: Morgan Entrekin, President
E-mail: mentrekin@groveatlantic.com
Ed: P.J. O'Rourke. **Released:** December 21, 2007. **Price:** $21.95. **Description:** Author defends the tenets of freedom of trade, the healthy pursuit of self-interest, and the importance of being a person who 'adheres, on all occasions, steadily and resolutely to his maxims.'.

36717 ■ ***"OPEC Exposed" in Hawaii Business (Vol. 54, September 2008, No. 3, pp. 2)***
Pub: Hawaii Business Publishing
Ed: Serena Lim. **Description:** Organization of the Petroleum Exporting Countries (OPEC) has said that their effort in developing an alternative energy source has driven prices up. The biofuel sector is criticizing the statement, saying that a research study found that biofuels push petroleum prices down by 15 percent. Details on the effect of rising petroleum prices are discussed.

36718 ■ ***"Open Skies: Opportunity, Challenge for Airlines" in Crain's Chicago Business (April 21, 2008)***
Pub: Crain Communications, Inc.
Ed: Paul Merrion. **Description:** Discusses the new aviation agreement between Europe and the United States known as Open Skies; the pact creates opportunities for U.S. carriers to fly to new destinations in Europe from more U.S. cities; it also allows carriers to fly between European cities, something they have not been able to do until now.

36719 ■ ***"Oracle: No Profit of Doom" in Barron's (Vol. 88, March 31, 2008, No. 13, pp. 40)***
Pub: Dow Jones & Company, Inc.
Ed: Mark Veverka. **Description:** Oracle's revenues grew by 21 percent but fell short of expectation and their profits came in at the low-end of expectations. The company's shares dropped 8 percent but investors are advised to pay more attention to the company's earnings expansion rather than revenue growth in a slow economy. Nokia's Rick Simonson points out that their markets in Asia and particularly India is growing so they are not as affected by the U.S. economic conditions.

36720 ■ ***"Ottawa to Push for Gas Deal Between Petrocan, Gazprom" in Globe & Mail (February 13, 2006, pp. B1)***
Pub: CTVglobemedia Publishing Inc.
Ed: Greame Smith. **Description:** Jim Flaherty, finance minister of Canada is negotiating a 1.3 billion dollar deal between state owned Petro-Canada and Russia's OAO Gazprom. This once again highlighted the country's increasing dependence on Russia for its energy requirements.

36721 ■ ***Outsourcing: Information Technology, Original Equipment Manufacturer, Leo, Oursourcing, Offshoring Research Network, Crowdsourcing***
Pub: General Books LLC
Released: May 1, 2010. **Price:** $14.14. **Description:** Chapters include information for outsourcing firms and how to maintain an outsourcing business.

36722 ■ ***"Overseas Marketing Key to Success of Chicago Spire" in Commercial Property News (March 17, 2008)***
Pub: Nielsen Company
Description: New construction of the Chicago Spire, a condominium project located on Lake Michigan's shore, is being marketed to would-be clients in Asia where Chicago is viewed as an emerging world city.

36723 ■ ***"Overseas Overtures" in Business Journal-Portland (Vol. 24, October 26, 2007, No. 35, pp. 1)***
Pub: American City Business Journals, Inc.
Ed: Robin J. Moody. **Description:** Oregon has a workforce shortage, specifically for the health care industry. Recruiting agencies, such as the International Recruiting Network Inc., answers the high demand for workforce by recruiting foreign employees. The difficulties recruiting companies experience with regards to foreign labor laws are investigated.

36724 ■ ***"An Overview of Energy Consumption of the Globalized World Economy" in Energy Policy (Vol. 39, October 2011, No. 10, pp. 5920-2928)***
Pub: Reed Elsevier Reference Publishing
Ed: Z.M. Chen, G.Q. Chen. **Description:** Energy consumption and its impact on the global world economy is examined.

36725 ■ ***"Ownership Form, Managerial Incentives, and the Intensity of Rivalry" in Academy of Management Journal (Vol. 50, No. 4, August 2007)***
Pub: Academy of Management
Contact: Ming-Jer Chen, President
Ed: Govert Vroom, Javier Gimeno. **Description:** Ways in which differences in ownership form between franchised and company-owned units alter managerial incentives and competitive pricing in different oligopolistic contexts, or following competitors into foreign markets, is presented.

36726 ■ ***"Pack Mentality" in Crain's Chicago Business (Vol. 31, April 21, 2008, No. 16, pp. 31)***
Pub: Crain Communications, Inc.
Ed: Sarah A. Klein. **Description:** Jill Smart, the head of human resources for a company with 170,000 employees worldwide, frequently travels to India, London and Singapore; Ms. Smart provides advice concerning efficiency, time management and avoiding jet-lag.

36727 ■ ***"Parent Firm's Global Reach, Stricter Air Quality Rules Have Stock Smiling" in Crain's Cleveland Business (October 15, 2007)***
Pub: Crain Communications, Inc.
Ed: David Bennett. **Description:** Since Stock Equipment Co., a firm that makes industrial pollution control equipment, was acquired by Schenck Process Group, a diversified global manufacturer based in Germany, the company's orders from abroad have been on the rise. The purchase has opened the doors to regions such as Eastern and Central Europe, Latin America and Australia.

36728 ■ ***"Paying for the Recession: Rebalancing Economic Growth" in Montana Business Quarterly (Vol. 49, Spring 2011, No. 1, pp. 2)***
Pub: Bureau of Business & Economic Research
Ed: Patrick M. Barkey. **Description:** Four key issues required to address in order to rebalance economic growth in America are examined. They include: savings rates, global trade imbalances, government budgets and most importantly, housing price correction.

36729 ■ ***"PBSJ Launches Internal Probe" in Tampa Bay Business Journal (Vol. 30, January 8, 2010, No. 3, pp. 1)***
Pub: American City Business Journals
Ed: Margie Manning. **Description:** Florida-based engineering firm PBSJ Corporation has started an internal investigation into possible violations of any laws, including the Foreign Corrupt Practices Act. Projects handled by subsidiary PBS&J International in foreign countries are the focus of the investigation.

36730 ■ ***The Perfect Scent: A Year Inside the Perfume Industry in Paris and New York***
Pub: Henry Holt and Co.
Contact: Michael Naumann, President
Ed: Chandler Burr. **Released:** 2009. **Price:** $25.00. **Description:** An insiders glimpse at the development of two new fragrances from Hermes and Coty.

36731 ■ ***"Pet-Food Industry Too Slow" in Advertising Age (Vol. 78, March 26, 2007, No. 13, pp. 29)***
Pub: Crain Communications, Inc.
Description: Many crisis-communications experts believe that the pet-food industry mishandled the problem by waiting almost a month to recall the 60 million 'wet-food' products after numerous consumer complaints. Experts site that the first 24 to 49 hours are the most important in dealing with a crisis of this nature.

36732 ■ ***Petty Capitalists and Globalization: Flexibility, Entrepreneurship, and Economic Development***
Pub: State University of New York Press
Ed: Alan Smart, Josephine Smart. **Released:** January 2006. **Price:** $26.95. **Description:** Investigation into ways small businesses in Europe, Asia, and Latin America are required to operate and compete in the fast-growing transnational economy.

36733 ■ ***"Phoenix Company Realizing Dream of Global Growth" in The Business Journal - Serving Phoenix and the Valley of the Sun (Vol. 28, July 18, 2008, No. 46, pp. 1)***
Pub: American City Business Journals, Inc.
Ed: Chris Casacchia. **Description:** Phoenix, Arizona-based lubricant maker DreamBrands Inc. is realizing global growth. The company, which has been generating interest from institutional investors, is seeking a second round of funding. Details of the company's products and marketing plans are also discussed.

36734 ■ ***"Pipe Show Finds a Way for Smokers to Light Up" in Crain's Chicago Business (Vol. 31, April 28, 2008, No. 17, pp. 57)***
Pub: Crain Communications, Inc.
Ed: H. Lee Murphy. **Description:** With the help of attorneys within its local membership of 150 pipe collectors, the Chicagoland Pipe Collectors Club will be allowed to smoke at its 13th International Pipe & Tobacciana Show at Pheasant Run Resort. The event is expected to draw 4,000 pipe enthusiasts from as far as China and Russia.

36735 ■ ***"A Place in the Sun" in Canadian Business (Vol. 81, July 22, 2008, No. 12-13, pp. 56)***
Pub: Rogers Media Ltd.
Description: Experts believe that it is the best time for Canadians to own a retirement home in the U.S., where real estate prices are up to 50 percent below their peak. Other views concerning the economic conditions occurring in the United States, as well as on the implications for Canadians planning to invest in the country are presented.

36736 ■ ***"Play It Safe" in Entrepreneur (Vol. 35, November 2007, No. 11, pp. 26)***
Pub: Entrepreneur Media Inc.
Ed: Gwen Moran. **Description:** U.S.-based toy manufacturers find opportunity from concerns regarding the recent recalls of toys that are made in China. The situation can provide better probability of parents buying toys made in the U.S. or Europe, where manufacturing standards are stricter.

36737 ■ ***"Political Environments and Business Strategy: Implications for Managers" in Business Horizons (Vol. 51, January-February 2008)***
Pub: Elsevier Advanced Technology Publications
Ed: Gerald D. Keim, Amy J. Hillman. **Description:** Various government bodies and business organizations work together in shaping new business op-

portunities and policies that arise from globalization. Presented is framework of public policy considerations for business managers. The framework is based on Nobel laureate Douglas North's work.

36738 ■ *"Port Metro Vancouver Unveiled" in Canadian Sailings (July 7, 2008)*
Pub: UBM Global Trade
Contact: Leonard J. Corallo, President
Description: Vancouver Fraser Port Authority is marketing the port as Port Metro Vancouver; Along with the new name the port has announced additional strategies for continued growth and launched a new logo.

36739 ■ *"Port in the Storm" in Canadian Business (Vol. 81, October 13, 2008, No. 17, pp. 101)*
Pub: Rogers Media Ltd.
Ed: Calvin Leung. **Description:** Interport Inc.'s state-of-the-art studio complex in Toronto is discussed. The strong Canadian dollar, along with disputes within the movie industry, are creating challenges for the studio to secure Hollywood projects. Interport plans to compete for Hollywood projects based on quality.

36740 ■ *"Potash Sale Must Be Blocked" in Canadian Business (Vol. 83, October 12, 2010, No. 17, pp. 24)*
Pub: Rogers Media Ltd.
Ed: Kasey Coholan. **Description:** Chief executive officers (CEOs) and corporate leaders in Canada are concerned about the possible sale of Potash Corporation to foreign buyers. A Compas Inc. poll recently asked CEOs whether the Canadian Government should step in to block the sale of the country's largest fertilizer firm.

36741 ■ *"Pressure Growing on Processors" in Farmer's Weekly (March 28, 2008, No. 320)*
Pub: Reed Business Information
Contact: Jeff Greisch, President
Description: Increasing milk prices may be inevitable in order to stop more farmers from leaving the industry and encourage them to produce more milk.

36742 ■ *"Private Equity Firms Shopping Valley For Deals" in The Business Journal - Serving Phoenix and the Valley of the Sun (Vol. 29, September 19, 2008, No. 3, pp. 1)*
Pub: American City Business Journals, Inc.
Ed: Mike Sunnucks. **Description:** Private equity firms from California, Boston, New York, and overseas are expected to invest in growth-oriented real estate markets that include Phoenix. Real estate experts revealed that privately held investment and acquisition firms are looking to invest in real estate markets hit by the housing crisis. Views and information on private equity firms' real estate investments are presented.

36743 ■ *"Procter & Gamble Boosts Bet on Exclusive Brands" in Business Courier (Vol. 27, July 9, 2010, No. 10, pp. 1)*
Pub: Business Courier
Ed: Jon Newberry. **Description:** Procter & Gamble is creating more special versions of its brands such as Pringles and Pampers exclusively for retail partners such as Tesco in the U.K. The greater push towards this direction is seen as a way to regain market share.

36744 ■ *"Public Media Works to Launch DVD Kiosk Operations in Toronto, Canada" in Internet Wire (November 15, 2010)*
Pub: Comtex
Description: Public Media Works Inc. along with its EntertainmentXpress Inc., have partnered with Spot Venture Distribution Inc. and Signifi Solutions Inc., both headquartered in Toronto, Canada, to manage and expand the Spot DVD movie and game kiosk business in greater Toronto and other Canadian locations.

36745 ■ *"Pulque with Flavor" in Canadian Business (Vol. , pp.)*
Pub: Rogers Media Ltd.
Ed: Augusta Dwyer. **Description:** Mexico-based Pulque Poliqhui, which has exported 20,000 bottles of Pulque into Canada in March 2008, plans to distribute in Ontario and Quebec. Pulque Poliqhui is introducing Cool Passion, a fruit-flavored version of pulque in Canada.

36746 ■ *"Putting the World at Your Fingertips" in Barron's (Vol. 88, July 7, 2008, No. 27, pp. L13)*
Pub: Dow Jones & Co., Inc.
Ed: Neil A. Martin. **Description:** Currency-traded exchange funds allow investors to diversify their assets and take advantage of investment opportunities such as speculation and hedging. Investors can use these funds to build positions in favor of or against the US dollar.

36747 ■ *"Que Pasa? A Canadian-Cuban Credit Card Crisis" in Canadian Business (Vol. 81, March 31, 2008, No. 5, pp. 10)*
Pub: Rogers Media
Ed: Geoff Kirbyson. **Description:** Discusses the acquisition of CUETS Financial Ltd. by the Bank of America which means that CUETS-issued credit cards in Cuba are worthless since U.S. laws prohibit transactions from Cuba and other sanctioned countries. CUETS members are advised to take multiple payment methods to Cuba.

36748 ■ *"R&R Launches Upscale Spoony's and Low Fat Dragon's Den" in Ice Cream Reporter (Vol. 23, August 20, 2010, No. 9, pp. 3)*
Pub: Ice Cream Reporter
Description: European ice cream manufacturer R&R has acquired French ice cream maker Rolland and will position itself as an upscale challenger to brands like Ben & Jerry's.

36749 ■ *Reading Financial Reports for Dummies*
Pub: John Wiley and Sons, Inc.
Ed: Lita Epstein. **Released:** January 2009. **Price:** $21.99. **Description:** This second edition contains more new and updated information, including new information on the separate accounting and financial reporting standards for private/small businesses versus public/large businesses; updated information reflecting 2007 laws on international financial reporting standards; new content to match SEC and other governmental regulatory changes over the last three years; new information about how the analyst-corporate connection has changed the playing field; the impact of corporate communications and new technologies; new examples that reflect the current trends; and updated Websites and resources.

36750 ■ *"Ready To Take Your Business Global?" in Black Enterprise (Vol. 41, August 2010, No. 1, pp. 89)*
Pub: Earl G. Graves Publishing Co. Inc.
Ed: Alan Hughes. **Description:** The 2010 Black Enterprise Entrepreneurs Conference held in May stressed the need for all small firms to promote a global agenda in order to stay competitive.

36751 ■ *"Recalls Cause Consumers to Put More Stock in Online Reviews" in Crain's Cleveland Business (Vol. 28, November 12, 2007, No. 45)*
Pub: Crain Communications, Inc.
Ed: Jack Neff. **Description:** Due to the string of product recalls over the last year, consumers are looking at online product reviews to help them make purchasing decisions which could reshape marketing for a wide range of products.

36752 ■ *"Red October" in Canadian Business (Vol. 81, December 8, 2008, No. 21, pp. 61)*
Pub: Rogers Media Ltd.
Ed: Mitch Moxley. **Description:** Analysts predict that Chinese stock market traders practice prudence amidst the challenging financial conditions in stock markets. The Chinese stock markets imploded in the last 12 months, losing two-thirds of its value.

36753 ■ *"Religious Revival" in Canadian Business (Vol. 81, December 8, 2008, No. 21, pp. 57)*
Pub: Rogers Media Ltd.
Ed: Paul Webster. **Description:** Canada-based lawyer Cyndee Todgham Cherniak believes that Canadians wishing to do business in China should have professional competence, as well as cultural and spiritual sensitivity. Chinese government officials also acknowledge the role of religion in China's economy.

36754 ■ *"Renren Partners With Recruit to Launch Social Wedding Services" in Benzinga.com (June 7, 2011)*
Pub: Benzinga.com
Ed: Benzinga Staff. **Description:** Renren Inc. and Recruit Company Ltd. partnered to build a wedding social media catering to engaged couples and newlyweds in China. The platform will integrate online wedding related social content and offline media such as magazine and wedding exhibitions.

36755 ■ *"Renren Partnership With Recruit to Launch Social Wedding Services" in Benzinga.com (June 7, 2011)*
Pub: Benzinga.com
Ed: Benzinga Staff. **Description:** Renren Inc., the leading real name social networking Internet platform in China has partnered with Recruit Company Limited, Japan's largest human resource and classified media group to form a joint venture to build a wedding social media catering to the needs of engaged couples and newlyweds in China.

36756 ■ *"Reportlinker Adds Report: Social Networks: Five Consumer Trends for 2009" in Wireless News (October 23, 2009)*
Pub: Close-Up Media
Description: 'Social Networks: Five Consumer Trends for 2009,' a new market research report by Reportlinker.com found that in the countries of Italy and Spain lag behind their European neighbors in Internet development. Since large numbers of consumers in these two countries remain offline, only a minimal portion of total advertising spending goes into Internet marketing, and those advertising campaigns are directed at the relatively young, affluent users. Statistical data included.

36757 ■ *"Reps Continue to Move to International Trade" in Agency Sales Magazine (Vol. 39, September-October 2009, No. 9, pp. 24)*
Pub: MANA
Ed: Jack Foster. **Description:** Sales representatives should get involved and look into international trade if they want to be successful in the future. The weak U.S. dollar, labor costs, and the low cost of transportation are factors that drive the trend towards international trade.

36758 ■ *"RES Stakes Its Claim in Area" in Philadelphia Business Journal (Vol. 28, January 29, 2010, No. 50, pp. 1)*
Pub: American City Business Journals
Ed: Peter Key. **Description:** RES Software Company Inc. of Amsterdam, Netherlands appointed Jim Kirby as president for the Americas and Klaus Besier as chairman in an effort to boost the firm's presence in the US. Brief career profiles of Kirby and Besier are included. RES develops software that allows management of information flow between an organization and its employees regardless of location.

36759 ■ *"Research and Markets Adds Report: Asian - Internet Market" in Health and Beauty Close-Up (January 19, 2010)*
Pub: Close-Up Media
Description: Overview of Research and Markets new report regarding Internet marketing and e-commerce in the Asian region; statistical data included.

36760 ■ *"Research and Markets Adds Report: Cyprus: Convergence, Broadband and Internet Market" in Wireless News (September 4, 2009)*
Pub: Close-Up Media
Description: Overview of a new report by Research and Markets entitled, 'Cyprus Convergence, Broadband and Internet Market - Overview, Statistics and Forecasts.' Highlights include information regarding broadband accounts which now account for the majority of household Internet connections.

36761 ■ *"Research and Markets Adds Report: Ghana: Convergence, Broadband and Internet Market" in Wireless News (September 4, 2009)*
Pub: Close-Up Media
Description: Overview of a new report by Research and Markets entitled, 'Ghana Convergence, Broadband and Internet Market - Overview, Statistics and Forecasts.' Ghana was among the first countries in Africa connected to the Internet and to introduce ADSL broadband services; however, only 30 of the 140 licensed ISP's are operational making the sector highly competitive.

36762 ■ *"Riding the Export Wave: How To Find a Good Distributor Overseas" in Inc. (January 2008, pp. 49)*
Pub: Gruner & Jahr USA Publishing
Ed: Sarah Goldstein. **Description:** Small companies should contact the U.S. embassy in foreign companies in order to connect with the U.S. Commercial Service's Gold Key program that is designed to work with small and midsize exporters.

36763 ■ *"Rising in the East; Research and Development" in The Economist (Vol. 390, January 3, 2009, No. 8612, pp. 47)*
Pub: The Economist Newspaper Inc.
Description: Impressive growth of the technological research and development in Asian countries is discussed. Statistical data included.

36764 ■ *"Risk and Reward" in Canadian Business (Vol. 81, October 13, 2008, No. 17, pp. 21)*
Pub: Rogers Media Ltd.
Ed: Calvin Leung. **Description:** Macro-economist and currency analyst Mark Venezia believes that stable financial institutions, free-market reforms, and the role of central banks in keeping inflation and exchange rates stable could make emerging-market bonds strong performers for better future returns. Venezia's other views on emerging-market bonds are discussed.

36765 ■ *"Rough Trade" in Canadian Business (Vol. 79, September 11, 2006, No. 18, pp. 31)*
Pub: Rogers Media
Ed: Christina Campbell. **Description:** The divergence between trade policy agreements entered into by Chile and the Canadian government are highlighted. Canada-Chile Free Trade Agreement and the myth around the big benefits to be reaped by bilateral trade policy agreements are discussed.

36766 ■ *"Russian Renaissance" in Chicago Tribune (September 22, 2008)*
Pub: McClatchy-Tribune Information Services
Ed: Alex Rodriguez. **Description:** Winemakers from Russia are returning to the craft and quality of winemaking now that they are free from Soviet restraints.

36767 ■ *"SABMiller Deal Hit by Tax Ruling" in Wall Street Journal Eastern Edition (November 21 , 2011, pp. B9)*
Pub: Dow Jones & Company Inc.
Ed: David Fickling, Simon Zekaria. **Description:** SABMiller PLC, the giant brewer in the United Kingdom, is acquiring Australian beer icon Foster's Group Ltd. for US$9.9 billion, but will have to come up with another A$582 million following a tax ruling by the Australian Taxation Office in order that shareholders of Foster's don't lose.

36768 ■ *Saudi Arabia: Moving Towards a Privatized Economy*
Pub: Turnaround Associates
Ed: Andrea H. Pampanini. **Released:** April 2005. **Price:** $30.00. **Description:** An overview of how Saudi Arabia took control of its natural resources and created change in the government, education, and culture of the country. Production of oil and natural gas is control entirely by the Saudi Government, however the book discusses the trend towards privatizing particular sectors of the nation in order to compete globally.

36769 ■ *"Saudi Overtures" in The Business Journal-Portland (Vol. 25, August 15, 2008, No. 23, pp. 1)*
Pub: American City Business Journals, Inc.
Ed: Aliza Earnshaw. **Description:** Saudi Arabia's huge revenue from oil is creating opportunities for Oregon companies as the country develops new cities, industrial zones, and tourism centers. Oregon exported only $46.8 million worth of goods to Saudi Arabia in 2007 but the kingdom is interested in green building materials and methods, renewable energy and water quality control, and nanotechnology all of which Oregon has expertise in.

36770 ■ *"Saving Face Time" in Canadian Business (Vol. 81, December 8, 2008, No. 21, pp. 21)*
Pub: Rogers Media Ltd.
Ed: Calvin Leung. **Description:** Landing business deals in China requires fostering informal relationships as well as avoiding offensive gestures. Canadians planning to do business in China should be aware of the Chinese concept of 'face'. Other tips for doing business in China are listed.

36771 ■ *"Say What?" in Entrepreneur (Vol. 35, November 2007, No. 11, pp. 106)*
Pub: Entrepreneur Media Inc.
Ed: Gail Dutton. **Description:** Business enterprises with units and employees in different parts of the world may encounter problems with culture clashes. The employees' different cultural backgrounds can cause misunderstanding that can affect a company's operations. So before doing business in a particular region, it is important to study the history and culture of the area.

36772 ■ *"Scorched Earth: Will Environmental Risks in China Overwhelm Its Opportunities?" in Harvard Business Review (Vol. 85, June 2007, No. 6)*
Pub: Harvard Business School Publishing
Ed: Elizabeth Economy, Kenneth Lieberthal. **Description:** Environmental risks for business in China include water supply access, energy needs, pollution, and soil erosion. However, the nation's government is investing money to develop green technology and alternative energy sources.

36773 ■ *"Scripps' Dinner Bell" in Business Courier (Vol. 24, October 19, 2008, No. 27, pp. 1)*
Pub: American City Business Journals, Inc.
Ed: Dan Monk. **Description:** Discusses the split of E.W. Scripps Co.'s Food Network into a separate publicly traded company Scripps Networks Interactive could produce expansion into Asia and Europe.

36774 ■ *"Sedo Keeps Trucking in Good Times and Bad" in Crain's Chicago Business (Vol. 31, April 28, 2008, No. 17, pp. 35)*
Pub: Crain Communications, Inc.
Ed: Samantha Stainburn. **Description:** Discusses Seko Worldwide Inc., an Itasca-based freight forwarder, and its complicated road to growth and expansion on a global scale.

36775 ■ *"Selling Michigan; R&D Pushed as Reason For Chinese To Locate In State" in Crain's Detroit Business (Vol. 24, January 14, 2008)*
Pub: Crain Communications Inc. - Detroit
Ed: Marti Benedetti. **Description:** Southeast Michigan Economic Development organizations are working to develop relationships with Chinese manufacturers so they will locate their automotive research and development operations in the state.

36776 ■ *"Selling Pressures Rise in China" in Barron's (Vol. 88, March 10, 2008, No. 10, pp. M9)*
Pub: Dow Jones & Company, Inc.
Ed: Mohammed Hadi. **Description:** There are about 1.6 trillion yuan worth of shares up for sale in Chinese stock markets in 2008, adding to the selling pressures in these markets. The Chinese government has imposed restrictions to prevent a rapid rise in selling stocks.

36777 ■ *"Sense and Consensus" in Canadian Business (Vol. 81, October 13, 2008, No. 17, pp. 22)*
Pub: Rogers Media Ltd.
Ed: David Wolf. **Description:** Stock analysts' agree that earning estimates are seen to be optimistic in relation to their global economic outlook. Analysts are expected to cut earnings projections by fall because it may negatively affect the Canadian stock market. Other view on market analysis are presented.

36778 ■ *"The Service Imperative" in Business Horizons (Vol. 51, January-February 2008, No. 1, pp. 39)*
Pub: Elsevier Advanced Technology Publications
Ed: Mary Jo Bitner, Stephen W. Brown. **Description:** The importance of services is growing in developing countries like India and China, but little attention is given to service research, education and innovation. The 'service imperative' seeks to promote the advancement of services. The scope, objectives and philosophy of the service imperative platform are outlined.

36779 ■ *"Setting Up Shop in a Political Hot Spot" in Harvard Business Review (Vol. 88, October 2010, No. 10, pp. 141)*
Pub: Harvard Business School Publishing
Ed: Patrick Chun, John Coleman, Nabil el-Hage. **Description:** A fictitious foreign operations scenario is presented, with contributors providing comments and advice. The scenario involves a politically charged North Korean-South Korean business venture; suggestions range from ensuring financial flexibility in case of adverse events to avoiding any business venture until political stability is achieved.

36780 ■ *"Shaky on Free Trade" in Canadian Business (Vol. 81, December 24, 2007, No. 1, pp. 29)*
Pub: Rogers Media
Ed: Rachel Pulfer. **Description:** Rhetoric at the U.S. presidential elections seems to be pointing toward a weaker free trade consensus, with Democratic candidates being against the renewal of free trade deals, while Republican candidates seem to be for free trade.

36781 ■ *"Shire Seeking New Digs for Headquarters" in Philadelphia Business Journal (Vol. 30, September 2, 2011, No. 29, pp. 1)*
Pub: American City Business Journals Inc.
Ed: Natalie Kostelni. **Description:** Dublin, Ireland-based Shire PLC announced plans to relocate its North American headquarters from Chesterbrook Corporate Center in Wayne, Pennsylvania and currently evaluating their options. The specialty biopharmaceutical firm is also considering a move to New Jersey or Delaware.

36782 ■ *"Shopped Out; Retailing Gloom" in The Economist (Vol. 390, January 3, 2009, No. 8612, pp. 26)*
Pub: The Economist Newspaper Inc.
Description: Economic volatility in the retail sector is having an impact on a number of countries around the globe. Europe is experiencing hard economic times as well and unless businesses have a strong business plan banks feel unable to lend the money necessary to tide the retailers over. The falling pound has increased the cost of imported goods and small to midsize retail chains may not be able to weather such an unforgiving economic climate.

36783 ■ *"Sign of Progress" in Playthings (Vol. 106, October 1, 2008, No. 9, pp. 4)*
Pub: Reed Business Information
Contact: Jeff Greisch, President
Ed: Cliff Annicelli. **Description:** The ramifications of the toy recalls in 2007 are discussed. Mandates for lead-free toys and other safety issues are having an impact on the American toy industry.

36784 ■ *"Six Leading Economists on What to Expect in the Year Ahead: David Wolf" in Canadian Business (Dec. 24, 2007)*
Pub: Rogers Media
Ed: David Wolf. **Description:** The Canadian dollar recently hit parity with the U.S. dollar, and the exchange rate is going fast and overvaluation of the

Canadian dollar could bring in competition from U.S. products. Details on the impact of the slowdown of the U.S. economy on the exchange rate speed are discussed.

36785 ■ *"Six Things You Can Do To Ride Out A Turbulent Market" in Hispanic Business (Vol. 30, March 2008, No. 3, pp. 20)*
Pub: Hispanic Business
Ed: Hildy Medina; Michael Bowker. **Description:** Top financial experts' views on managing investment portfolios during turbulent periods in the stock market are reported. Experts prefer investing in health care, short term investments, international bonds and preferred stocks or just maintain cash until such times as the market settles.

36786 ■ *"Size Does Matter" in International Journal of Globalisation and Small Business (Vol. 4, September 21, 2010, No. 1, pp. 61)*
Pub: Publishers Communication Group
Ed: Julia Cornnell, Ranjit Voola. **Description:** Examination of how members of an Australian-based manufacturing and engineering cluster share knowledge through networking as a means to improve competitive advantage.

36787 ■ *"A Slice of Danish; Fixing Finance" in The Economist (Vol. 390, January 3, 2009, No. 8612, pp. 55)*
Pub: The Economist Newspaper Inc.
Description: Denmark's mortgage-holders and the county's lending system is presented.

36788 ■ *"Slimmed-Down Supplier TI Automotive Relaunches" in Crain's Detroit Business (Vol. 26, January 11, 2010, No. 2, pp. 14)*
Pub: Crain Communications Inc.
Ed: Robert Sherefkin. **Description:** TI Automotive Ltd., one of the world's largest suppliers of fuel storage and delivery systems, has reorganized the company by splitting it into five global divisions and is relaunching its brand which is now more focused on new technology.

36789 ■ *"Small Firms Punch Ticket for Growth" in Houston Business Journal (Vol. 40, January 29, 2010, No. 38, pp. 1)*
Pub: American City Business Journals
Ed: Allison Wollam. **Description:** Independent ticket agencies anticipate growth as American and Canadian authorities approved a merger between Ticketmaster and concert promoter Live Nation. Expansion of service offerings and acquisition of venues have also been done by independent ticket agencies in light of the merger. Details of the merger are included.

36790 ■ *The Small-Mart Revolution: How Local Businesses Are Beating the Global Competition*
Pub: Berrett-Koehler Publishers, Incorporated
Ed: Michael H. Shuman. **Released:** July 2007. **Price:** $16.95. **Description:** Advice is given to help small businesses compete in a global environment.

36791 ■ *Small and Medium-Sized Enterprises in Countries in Transition*
Pub: United Nations Publications
Contact: Christopher Woodthrope, Director (Acting)
Released: January 2005. **Price:** $18.00. **Description:** Characteristics of small and medium enterprise (SME) sector in transition countries and emerging market economies.

36792 ■ *SME Cluster Development: A Dynamic View on Survival Clusters in Developing Countries*
Pub: Palgrave Macmillan
Ed: Mario Davide Parrilli. **Released:** April 2007. **Price:** $90.00. **Description:** Survival clustering in developing countries is discussed in order to increase effectiveness of policy-making and development operations in local contexts.

36793 ■ *Social Enterprise in Europe*
Pub: Routledge Inc.
Ed: Marthe Nyssens. **Released:** August 2006. **Price:** $145.00 hardcopy; $46.95 paperback. **Description:** Social enterprises in Europe are examined through three ideas: that they have a complex mixture of goals, that they mobilize various kinds of markets and non-market resources, and that they are embedded in the political context.

36794 ■ *"Solar Credit Lapse Spur Late Demand" in The Business Journal - Serving Phoenix and the Valley of the Sun (Vol. 28, July 18, 2008)*
Pub: American City Business Journals, Inc.
Ed: Patrick O'Grady. **Description:** Businesses looking to engage in the solar energy industry are facing the problems of taxation and limited solar panel supply. Solar panels manufacturers are focusing more on the European market. Political issues surrounding the federal tax credit policy on solar energy users are also discussed.

36795 ■ *"Some Relief Possible Following Painful Week" in Barron's (Vol. 88, July 14, 2008, No. 28, pp. M3)*
Pub: Dow Jones & Co., Inc.
Ed: Kopin Tan. **Description:** Dow Chemical is offering a 74 percent premium to acquire Rohm & Haas' coatings and electronics materials operations. Frontline amassed a 5.6 percent stake in rival Overseas Shipholding Group and a merger between the two would create a giant global fleet with pricing power. Highlights of the U.S. stock market during the week that ended in July 11, 2008 are discussed. Statistical data included.

36796 ■ *"Sound Advice From Dr. Sleep" in Crain's Chicago Business (Vol. 31, April 21, 2008, No. 16, pp. 30)*
Pub: Crain Communications, Inc.
Ed: Sarah A. Klein. **Description:** James K. Wyatt, the director of the Sleep Disorders Centers at Rush University Medical Center in Chicago, gives advice to business executives concerning what to eat, how to nap and which drugs to take or avoid in order to ease the strain of air travel, particularly on overseas flights.

36797 ■ *"South African Connections: Small Business Owners Work Toward Forming Strategic Alliances" in Black Enterprise (March 2008)*
Pub: Earl G. Graves Publishing Co. Inc.
Ed: Aisha Sylvester. **Description:** National Minority Supplier Development Council Inc. is working to create business partnerships between African American businesses and black-owned South African companies within the country's pharmaceutical supply industry.

36798 ■ *"Speaking In Tongues: Rosetta Stone's TOTALE Adds 'Social' To Language Learning" in Black Enterprise (Vol. 41, September 2010, No. 2)*
Pub: Earl G. Graves Publishing Co. Inc.
Ed: Sonya A. Donaldson. **Description:** As small businesses become more globalized, it is necessary to learn new languages in order to compete. Rosetta Stone's TOTALe is profiled.

36799 ■ *A Splendid Exchange: How Trade Shaped the World*
Pub: Atlantic Monthly Press
Ed: William J. Bernstein. **Released:** 2009. **Price:** $30.00. **Description:** Chronicle of how commerce defined cultures and shaped history.

36800 ■ *Start-Up Nation*
Pub: Twelve/Hatchette Book Group
Ed: Dan Senor, Paul Singer. **Released:** 2009. **Price:** $26.99. **Description:** Amid the turmoil in the Middle East, Israel's economy continues to thrive.

36801 ■ *"Stimulus 'Loser' Won't Build Plant in Mass." in Boston Business Journal (Vol. 30, November 5, 2010, No. 41, pp. 1)*
Pub: Boston Business Journal
Ed: Kyle Alspach. **Description:** Boston-Power Inc. no longer plans to build an electric vehicle battery plant in Massachusetts after it failed to obtain stimulus funds from the federal government. The company is instead looking to build a lithium-ion battery plant in China and possibly Europe.

36802 ■ *Stop Working: Start a Business, Globalize It, and Generate Enough Cash Flow to Get Out of the Rat Race*
Pub: Eye Contact Media
Ed: Rohan Hall. **Released:** November 2004. **Price:** $15.99. **Description:** Advice is given to small companies to compete in the global marketplace by entrepreneur using the same strategy for his own business.

36803 ■ *Studies of Entrepreneurship, Business and Government in Hong Kong: The Economic Development of a Small Open Economy*
Pub: Edwin Mellen Press
Ed: Fu-Lai Tony Yu. **Released:** November 2006. **Price:** $109.95. **Description:** Institutional and Austrian theories are used to analyze the transformation taking place in Hong Kong's economy.

36804 ■ *The Subprime Solution: How Today's Global Financial Crisis Happened, and What to Do About It*
Pub: Princeton University Press
Ed: Robert J. Shiller. **Released:** 2009. **Price:** $16.95. **Description:** Yale economist discusses the worldwide financial crisis and offers plans to reform the system.

36805 ■ *"The Superpower Dilemma" in Canadian Business (Vol. 83, August 17, 2010, No. 13-14, pp. 42)*
Pub: Rogers Media Ltd.
Description: Canada has been an energy superpower partly because it controls the energy source and the production means, particularly of fossil fuels. However, Canada's status as superpower could diminish if it replaces petroleum exports with renewable technology for using sources of energy available globally.

36806 ■ *"Suppliers May Follow Fiat" in Crain's Detroit Business (Vol. 25, June 15, 2009, No. 24, pp. 1)*
Pub: Crain Communications Inc. - Detroit
Ed: Ryan Beene. **Description:** Italian suppliers to Fiat SpA are looking toward Detroit after the formation of Chrysler Group LLC, the Chrysler-Fiat partnership created from Chrysler's bankruptcy. The Italian American Alliance for Business and Technology is aware of two Italy-based powertrain component suppliers that are considering a move to Detroit.

36807 ■ *"Supply Chain Visibility A Two-Way Street" in Canadian Sailings (July 7, 2008)*
Pub: UBM Global Trade
Contact: Leonard J. Corallo, President
Ed: Jack Kohane. **Description:** Canada is experiencing unprecedented market pressures due to globalization. Competition from foreign countries, demand for better and faster service from customers and shorter innovation cycles are some of the problems the country is facing regarding trade and the importing and exporting industry.

36808 ■ *"Survey Distorts Cost of Capitals" in Canadian Business (Vol. 83, October 12, 2010, No. 17, pp. 22)*
Pub: Rogers Media Ltd.
Ed: Matthew McClearn. **Description:** Swiss bank UBS publishes a study comparing the costs of goods and services in megalopolises every three years. The study ranked Toronto and Montreal outside the Top 30 in 2009, but the two cities jumped to eighth and ninth in a recent update. This change can be contributed to the conversion of prices into Euros before making comparisons.

36809 ■ *"A Survival Guide for Crazy Times" in Canadian Business (Vol. 81, March 3, 2008, No. 3, pp. 61)*
Pub: Rogers Media
Ed: David Wolf. **Description:** Investors should ensure that their portfolios are positioned defensively more than the average as the U.S. and Canadian markets face turbulent times. They should not assume that U.S. residential property is a good place to

invest only because prices have dropped and the Canadian dollar is showing strength. Other tips that investors can use during unstable periods are supplied.

36810 ■ *Swedish-American Chamber of Commerce of the United States--Membership Directory*
Pub: Swedish-American Chamber of Commerce
URL(s): www.saccny.org/publications/membership-directory. **Released:** Annual; Latest edition 2009. **Covers:** About 1,800 United States and 200 Swedish members of the chamber, concerned with promoting commercial relations between the two countries. **Entries include:** Company name, address, phone, fax. **Arrangement:** Separate alphabetical lists by country. **Indexes:** Classified.

36811 ■ *"Swimming Against the Tide" in Human Resource Management (Vol. 49, July-August 2010, No. 4, pp. 575-598)*
Pub: John Wiley
Ed: David G. Collings, Anthony McDonnell, Patrick Gunnigle, Jonathan Lavelle. **Description:** A study was conducted to provide a benchmark of outward flows of international assignees from the Irish subsidiaries of foreign-owned multinational enterprises (MNEs) to corporate headquarters and other worldwide operations. Findings indicate that almost half of all MNEs use some form of outward staffing flows.

36812 ■ *"Taiwan Technology Initiatives Foster Growth" in Canadian Electronics (Vol. 23, February 2008, No. 1, pp. 28)*
Pub: CLB Media Inc.
Description: A study conducted by the Market Intelligence Center shows that currently, Taiwan is the world's larges producer of information technology products such as motherboards, servers, and LCD monitors. In 2006, Taiwan's LED industry reached a production value of NTD 21 billion. This push into the LED sector shows the Ministry of Economic Affairs' plan to target industries that are environmentally friendly.

36813 ■ *"Taking the Over-the-Counter Route to US" in Barron's (Vol. 88, July 7, 2008, No. 27, pp. 24)*
Pub: Dow Jones & Co., Inc.
Ed: Eric Uhlfelder. **Description:** Many multinational companies have left the New York Stock Exchange and allowed their shares to trade over-the-counter. The companies have taken advantage of a 2007 SEC rule allowing publicly listed foreign companies to change trading venues if less than 5 percent of global trading volume in the past 12 months occurred in the US.

36814 ■ *"Talent Shows" in Canadian Business (Vol. 81, December 24, 2007, No. 1, pp. 14)*
Pub: Rogers Media
Ed: Megan Harman. **Description:** Canadian companies are increasingly turning to marketing to promote themselves as employers, as concerns on employee recruitment increase with the nearing retirement age of the baby boomers. Details on skills shortage, the potential advantage for the immigrant workforce, and employee retention are discussed.

36815 ■ *"Tales of the City" in Canadian Business (Vol. 81, December 8, 2008, No. 21, pp. 37)*
Pub: Rogers Media Ltd.
Ed: Joe Chidley. **Description:** Key information on doing business in Hong Kong are shared by an entrepreneur, a consultant, an exporter, and a financier who were from Canada. Hong Kong hosts about 3,900 regional headquarters or offices of international companies.

36816 ■ *"Tao of Downfall" in International Journal of Entrepreneurship and Small Business (Vol. 11, August 31, 2010, No. 2, pp. 121)*
Pub: Publishers Communication Group
Ed: Wenxian Zhang, Ilan Alon. **Description:** Through historical reviews and case studies, this research seeks to understand why some initially successful entrepreneurs failed in the economic boom of past decades. Among various factors contributing to their downfall are a unique political and business environment, fragile financial systems, traditional cultural influences and personal characteristics.

36817 ■ *"Tasti D-Lite Has Franchise Agreement for Australia" in Ice Cream Reporter (Vol. 23, November 20, 2010, No. 12, pp. 3)*
Pub: Ice Cream Reporter
Description: Tasti D-Lite signed an international master franchise agreement with Friezer Australia Pty. Ltd. and will open 30 units throughout Australia over the next five years.

36818 ■ *"The Tata Way" in Business Strategy Review (Vol. 21, Summer 2010, No. 2, pp. 14)*
Pub: Wiley-Blackwell
Description: Tata Motors is one of the world's most talked-about companies. Its new ultra-low-cost Nano car is being heralded as the people's car. Vice chairman, Ravi Kant, talks about India and its emerging markets.

36819 ■ *"A Team Sport" in Business Courier (Vol. 26, October 2, 2009, No. 23, pp. 1)*
Pub: American City Business Journals, Inc.
Ed: Lisa Biank Fasig. **Description:** Procter & Gamble (P&G) revised the way it works with marketing, design and public relations firms. Creative discussions will be managed by only two representatives, the franchise leader and the brand agency leader in order for P&G to simplify operations as it grows larger and more global.

36820 ■ *"Tempel Steel To Expand Its Chicago Plant" in Chicago Tribune (August 22, 2008)*
Pub: McClatchy-Tribune Information Services
Ed: James P. Miller. **Description:** Tempel Steel Co. is no longer considering transferring a Libertyville factory's production to Mexico; the company has responded to government incentives and will instead shift that work to its plant on Chicago's North Side.

36821 ■ *"Thai Ice Cream Cremo Expanding to Middle East" in Ice Cream Reporter (Vol. 23, September 20, 2010, No. 10, pp. 3)*
Pub: Ice Cream Reporter
Description: Thai-based frozen dessert manufacturer Chomthana, maker of Cremo brand ice cream, is expanding into the Middle East.

36822 ■ *"There's More Upside in Germany" in Barron's (Vol. 90, September 6, 2010, No. 36, pp. M7)*
Pub: Barron's Editorial & Corporate Headquarters
Ed: Jonathan Buck. **Description:** Germany's stocks have gone up since the beginning of 2010, and investors can still benefit. These stocks will benefit from Germany's stellar economic performance and the relative weakness of the Euro. The prospects of the shares of Daimler and Hochtief are discussed.

36823 ■ *"TheStree.com: Study Abroad" in Entrepreneur (Vol. 35, October 2007, No. 10, pp. 44)*
Pub: Entrepreneur Media Inc.
Ed: Farnoosh Torabi. **Description:** Businessmen who wish to pursue foreign investments should study the country in which they will operate. Some investors do their research by completely exposing themselves to their prospective country, while others prefer studying the market home-based. Details of how investors pick their country and the different ways of investing in foreign land are presented.

36824 ■ *"Things Will Improve, or Not: a Chartered Financial Analyst Explains It All" in Canadian Business (Vol. 81, November 10, 2008)*
Pub: Rogers Media Ltd.
Description: Myles Zyblock expects the global economic slowdown to deepen over the next six to nine months. Zyblock addressed the Toronto CFA Society at their annual dinner in October 2008. He stressed a tight correlation between the credit ratio and asset prices and predicts the S&P 500 to be up by 11 percent by October 2009.

36825 ■ *"Thomas and His Washington Friends" in CFO (Vol. 23, October 2007, No. 10, pp. 18)*
Pub: CFO Publishing Corporation
Ed: Alix Stuart. **Description:** Reliance on Chinese suppliers to America's toymakers may become quite costly as Congress considers legislation that would increase fines to as high as $50 million for companies selling tainted products. The legislation would also require independent mandatory testing for makers of products for children.

36826 ■ *"The Three Amigos" in Canadian Business (Vol. 81, March 17, 2008, No. 4, pp. 19)*
Pub: Rogers Media
Ed: Rachel Pulfer. **Description:** Mexican president Felipe Calderon said that Mexico exported 30 percent more to Europe and 25 percent more to other countries in Latin America in 2006 in light of the downturn in the U.S. economy. Calderon made this announcement in a speech at Harvard University while protestors marched outside protesting against NAFTA.

36827 ■ *"Tied to Home: Female Owned Businesses Export Less, And It's Not Just Because They're Smaller" in Canadian Business (April 14, 2008)*
Pub: Rogers Media
Ed: Lauren McKeon. **Description:** Only 12 percent of small and midsized enterprises that are run by women export their products and services. Government agencies can be more proactive in promoting the benefits of exporting by including women in case studies and recruiting women as mentors. Exporting provides great growth potential especially for the service sector where women have an advantage.

36828 ■ *"Time to Engage Europe" in Canadian Business (Vol. 79, June 19, 2006, No. 13, pp. 19)*
Pub: Rogers Media
Ed: Jack Mintz. **Description:** European and Canadian governments improved their trade and investment relations with the March 18, 2004 frame work to develop a Trade and Investment Enhancement Agreement. Still there is lot of opportunities to solve tax and trade issues.

36829 ■ *"Timken's Bearings Rolling in China, India" in Crain's Cleveland Business (Vol. 28, October 29, 2007, No. 43, pp. 14)*
Pub: Crain Communications, Inc.
Ed: David Bennett. **Description:** Canton-based Timken Co., a manufacturer of bearings and specialty metals, is seeing growing demand for its line of tapered roller bearings, which allow rail users to carry heavy car loads. The company is finding significant growth in China and India due to their rapidly growing rail markets.

36830 ■ *"To Keep Freight Rolling, Springfield Must Grease the Hub" in Crain's Chicago Business (Vol. 31, April 21, 2008, No. 16, pp. 22)*
Pub: Crain Communications, Inc.
Ed: Paul O'Connor. **Description:** Discusses the importance of upgrading Chicago's continental-hub freight rail system which is integral to moving international products as well as domestic ones. Global tonnage is expected to double by 2020 and unless more money is designated to upgrade the infrastructure the local and national economy will suffer.

36831 ■ *"To Offshore Or Not To Offshore?" in Converting (Vol. 25, October 1, 2007, No. 10, pp. 10)*
Pub: Reed Business Information Inc.
Ed: Mark Spaulding. **Description:** Offshore manufacturing and the issue of buying raw materials from foreign suppliers by American companies is discussed. Results of a study conducted by Cap Gemini and Pro Logis regarding offshore manufacturing, especially to China, are presented.

36832 ■ *"Too Much Precaution About Biotech Corn" in Barron's (Vol. 88, March 17, 2008, No. 11, pp. 54)*
Pub: Dow Jones & Company, Inc.
Ed: Mark I. Schwartz. **Description:** In the U.S., 90 percent of cultivated soybeans are biotech varietals as well as 60 percent of the corn. Farmers have significantly reduced their reliance on pesticides in the growing of biotech corn. Biotech cotton cultivation has brought hundreds of millions of dollars in net financial gains to farmers. The European Union has precluded the cultivation or sale of biotech crops within its border.

36833 ■ *"Top 50 Exporters" in Hispanic Business (Vol. 30, July-August 2008, No. 7-8, pp. 42)*
Pub: Hispanic Business, Inc.
Ed: Hildy Medina. **Description:** Increases in exports revenues reported by food exporters and green companies in a time of economic slowdown in the U.S are described. Food exporters have benefited from the growth of high-volume grocery stores in underdeveloped countries and the German government's' promotion of solar energy has benefited the U.S. solar heating equipment and solar panel manufactures.

36834 ■ *"Top Private Companies" in Baltimore Business Journal (Vol. 28, August 27, 2010, No. 16, pp. 1)*
Pub: Baltimore Business Journal
Ed: Gary Haber. **Description:** The combined revenue of the 100 largest private firms in Maryland's Baltimore region dropped from about $22.7 billion in 2008 to $21 billion in 2009, an annual decrease of more than 7 percent. To survive the recession's impact, these firms resorted to strategies such as government contracting and overseas expansion. How these strategies affected the revenue of some firms is described.

36835 ■ *"Toward a Political Conception of Corporate Responsibility" in Academy of Management Review (October 2007, pp. 1096)*
Pub: ScholarOne, Inc.
Ed: Andreas Georg Scherer, Guido Palazzo. **Description:** The limitations of studies on corporate social responsibility and a new theory based on Jurgen Habermas theory of democracy are highlighted. The key role played by the business firm in globalization of society is presented.

36836 ■ *"Toy Scares Drive Business" in Boston Business Journal (Vol. 27, November 23, 2007, No. 43, pp. 1)*
Pub: American City Business Journals, Inc.
Ed: Joan Goodchild. **Description:** Several Boston businesses have tapped into the lead content scare in toys and other products manufactured in China. ConRoy Corporation LLC launched Toy Recall Alert!, an online tool to alert consumers about new recalls while Hybrivet Systems introduced screening test kit, LeadCheck. Other new products pertaining to toy safety are discussed.

36837 ■ *"Toy Story" in Forbes (Vol. 180, October 15, 2007, No. 8, pp. 102)*
Pub: Forbes Inc.
Description: Three voluntary recalls of Chinese-made toys were announced by American toymakers, sending Mattel stocks plummeting.

36838 ■ *"Toy Story: U.S.-Made a Hot Seller" in Crain's Detroit Business (Vol. 23, December 17, 2007, No. 51, pp. 3)*
Pub: Crain Communications Inc. - Detroit
Ed: Chad Halcom. **Description:** American Plastic Toys, located in Walled Lake, Michigan reports all its toys are made in the U.S. and have passed all U.S. safety standards. Revenue for American Plastic Toys reached nearly $33 million in 2005, and the company expects to exceed that because of recent toy safety recalls of products produced in China.

36839 ■ *"Trade Winds" in Canadian Sailings (June 30, 2008)*
Pub: UBM Global Trade
Contact: Leonard J. Corallo, President
Ed: Peter Malkovsky. **Description:** Trade between Canada and the United States is discussed as well as legislation concerning foreign trade and the future of this trade relationship.

36840 ■ *Trading Places: SMEs in the Global Economy, A Critical Research Handbook*
Pub: Edward Elgar Publishing, Incorporated
Ed: Lloyd-Reason. **Released:** September 2006. **Price:** $110.00. **Description:** An overview of international research for small and medium-sized companies wishing to expand in the global economy.

36841 ■ *"Transborder Short-Sea Shipping: Hurdles Remain" in Canadian Sailings (June 30, 2008)*
Pub: UBM Global Trade
Contact: Leonard J. Corallo, President
Ed: Kathlyn Horibe. **Description:** Legislation that would exempt non-bulk commercial cargo by water in the Great Lakes region from U.S. taxation is discussed.

36842 ■ *"The Transparent Supply Chain" in Harvard Business Review (Vol. 88, October 2010, No. 10, pp. 76)*
Pub: Harvard Business School Publishing
Ed: Steve New. **Description:** Examination of the use of new technologies to create a transparent supply chain, such as next-generation 2D bar codes in clothing labels that can provide data on a garment's provenance.

36843 ■ *"Tri-State to Get New Headquarters" in Business Courier (Vol. 27, October 22, 2010, No. 25, pp. 1)*
Pub: Business Courier
Ed: James Ritchie. **Description:** Hong Kong-based corn processing firm Global Bio-Chem Technology is set to choose Greater Cincinnati, Ohio as a location of its North American headquarters. The interstate access, central location, and low labor and property costs might have enticed Global Bio-Chem to invest in the region. Statistics on Chinese direct investment in U.S. are also presented.

36844 ■ *"Trillium Turmoil" in Canadian Business (Vol. 81, December 8, 2008, No. 21, pp. 16)*
Pub: Rogers Media Ltd.
Ed: Jeff Sanford. **Description:** Ontario's manufacturing success in the past was believed to have been built by the 1965 Canada-U.S. automotive pact and by advantages such as low-cost energy. The loss of these advantages along with the challenging economic times has hurt Ontario's manufacturing industry.

36845 ■ *"Tweaking On-Board Activities, Equipment Saves Fuel, Reduces CO2" in Canadian Sailings (June 30, 2008)*
Pub: UBM Global Trade
Contact: Leonard J. Corallo, President
Description: Optimizing ship activities and equipment uses less fuel and therefore reduces greenhouse gas emissions. Ways in which companies are implementing research and development techniques in order to monitor ship performance and analyze data in an attempt to become more efficient are examined.

36846 ■ *"Twitter Hack: Made in Japan? User Says Attack Showed Security Flaw" in Houston Chronicle (September 24, 2010, pp. 3)*
Pub: Houston Chronicle
Ed: Tomoko A. Hosaka. **Description:** Details of the attack on Twitter caused by a Japanese computer hacker are revealed.

36847 ■ *"Uncle Volodya's Flagging Christmas Spirit; Russia" in The Economist (Vol. 390, January 3, 2009, No. 8612, pp. 22)*
Pub: The Economist Newspaper Inc.
Description: Overview of Russia's struggling economy as well as unpopular government decisions such as raising import duties on used foreign vehicles so as to protect Russian carmakers.

36848 ■ *"Uncovering Offshoring's Invisible Costs" in HRMagazine (Vol. 54, January 2009, No. 1, pp. 1)*
Pub: Society for Human Resource Management
Contact: Henry G. Jackson, President
E-mail: hjackson@shrm.org
Ed: Rita Zeidner. **Description:** Nearly half of all offshore service work fails, often due to the invisible costs of communication and cultural friction according to researchers. The challenges of offshore services are discussed.

36849 ■ *Understanding Exporting in the Small and Micro Enterprise*
Pub: Nova Science Publishers, Inc.
Ed: Densil A. Williams. **Released:** April 1, 2009. **Price:** $79.00. **Description:** An examination into the reasons why some small and micro locally-owned businesses choose to sell a portion of their goods abroad while others facing similar market conditions remain focused on the domestic market.

36850 ■ *"Unemployment Rates" in The Economist (Vol. 390, January 3, 2009, No. 8612, pp. 75)*
Pub: The Economist Newspaper Inc.
Description: Countries that are being impacted the worst by rising unemployment rates are those that have also been suffering from the housing market crisis. Spain has been the hardest hit followed by Ireland. America and Britain are also seeing levels of unemployment that indicate too much slack in the economy.

36851 ■ *"Unilever Acquiring EVGA's Ice Cream Brands in Greece" in Ice Cream Reporter (Vol. 23, October 20, 2010, No. 11, pp. 1)*
Pub: Ice Cream Reporter
Description: Unilever will acquire the ice cream brands and distribution network of the Greek frozen dessert manufacturer EVGA.

36852 ■ *"U.S. Enters BlackBerry Dispute Compromise Sought Over Security Issues" in Houston Chronicle (August 6, 2010)*
Pub: Houston Chronicle
Ed: Matthew Lee. **Description:** U.S. State Department is working for a compromise with Research in Motion, manufacturer of the BlackBerry, over security issues. The Canadian company makes the smartphones and foreign governments believe they pose a security risk.

36853 ■ *"U.S. Targets China's Exported Paper" in Globe & Mail (March 31, 2007, pp. B5)*
Pub: CTVglobemedia Publishing Inc.
Ed: Barrie McKenna. **Description:** The prospects of the rise in duties on goods imported into the United States, due to the levy of duties on imports of Chinese paper, are discussed.

36854 ■ *"U.S. Trade Body Clears Apple in Patent Case" in Wall Street Journal Eastern Edition (November 23 , 2011, pp. C1)*
Pub: Dow Jones & Company Inc. Enterprise Media Group
Contact: Clare Hart, President
Ed: Matt Jarzemsky, Paul Mozur. **Description:** HTC Corporation alleged in its patent-infringement case against Apple Inc. that Apple violated patents of S3 Graphics Inc., a company which was acquired by HTC Corporation. Now the International Trade Commission has issued a ruling saying that Apple did not violate the patents.

36855 ■ *"Up On The Farm" in Canadian Business (Vol. 81, March 31, 2008, No. 5, pp. 23)*
Pub: Rogers Media
Ed: John Gray. **Description:** Agricultural products have outperformed both energy and metal and even the prospect of a global economic slowdown does not seem to hinder its prospects. The Organization for Economic Cooperation and Development sees prices above historic equilibrium levels during the

next ten years given that fuel and fertilizers remain high and greater demand from India and China remain steady.

36856 ■ *"V&J Scores Partnership with Shaq" in Business Journal-Milwaukee (Vol. 25, October 12, 2007, No. 2, pp. A1)*
Pub: American City Business Journals, Inc.
Ed: Rich Kirchen. **Description:** O'Neal Franchise Group has agreed to a partnership with V&J Foods of Milwaukee to handle Auntie Anne's shops in New York, South Africa, Michigan, and the Caribbean. V&J O'Neal Enterprises will open six Auntie Anne's soft pretzel shops in Detroit towards the end of 2007. Planned international ventures of the partnership are presented.

36857 ■ *"Vicki Avril; Senior Vice-President of Tubular Division, Ipsco Inc." in Crain's Chicago Business (Vol. 31, May 5, 2008, No. 18)*
Pub: Crain Communications, Inc.
Ed: Miriam Gottfried. **Description:** Profile of Vicki Avril who is the senior vice-president of the tubular division at Ipsco Inc. where she supervises 2,800 employees and 13 mills throughout the United States and Canada.

36858 ■ *"Viva Brazil" in Business Strategy Review (Vol. 21, Autumn 2010, No. 3, pp. 24)*
Pub: Wiley-Blackwell
Ed: Georgina Peters. **Description:** Brazil's current status as a major emerging market with a boundless economic horizon is a radical shift from its place in the world in the late 1960s to the mid 1990s. Lessons Brazil can teach other countries are outlined.

36859 ■ *"Viva La Evolucion" in Canadian Business (Vol. 80, February 12, 2007, No. 4, pp. 63)*
Pub: Rogers Media
Ed: Denis Seguin. **Description:** The rise of Cuba as an importance source of oil and its significance for the Canadian economy is discussed.

36860 ■ *"Wake-Up Call" in Canadian Business (Vol. 80, October 8, 2007, No. 20, pp. 58)*
Pub: Rogers Media
Ed: Andrea Mandel-Campbell. **Description:** The need for Canadian companies to develop global marketing strategies is discussed. Thomas Caldwell, chairman of Caldwell Securities, believes the country's average performance in global markets should be a cause for alarm. The factors affecting the country's current economic state is also presented.

36861 ■ *"Want People to Save? Force Them" in Harvard Business Review (Vol. 88, September 2010, No. 9, pp. 36)*
Pub: Harvard Business School Publishing
Ed: Dan Ariely. **Description:** Contrasts in U.S. attitudes towards savings and government regulation with those of Chile, where all employees are required to save 11 percent of their salary in a retirement account, are highlighted.

36862 ■ *"'We Had to Won the Mistakes" in Harvard Business Review (Vol. 88, July-August 2010, No. 7-8, pp. 108)*
Pub: Harvard Business School Publishing
Ed: Adi Ignatius. **Description:** Interview with Howard Schultz, CEO of Starbucks, covers topics that include investment in retraining, the impact of competition, premium quality, authenticity, customer services, strategy development, work-and-life issues, and international presence.

36863 ■ *"Weaving a Stronger Fabric: Organizing a Global Sweat-Free Apparel Production Agreement" in WorkingUSA (Vol. 11, June 2008, No. 2)*
Pub: Blackwell Publishers Ltd.
Ed: Eric Dirnbach. **Description:** Tens of millions of workers working under terrible sweatshop conditions in the global apparel industry. Workers are employed at apparel contractors and have been largely unsuccessful in organizing and improving their working conditions. The major apparel manufacturers and retailers have the most power in this industry, and they have adopted corporate social responsibility programs as a false solution to the sweatshop problem. The major North American apparel unions dealt with similar sweatshop conditions a century ago by organizing the contractors and brands into joint association contracts that significantly raised standards. Taking inspiration from their example, workers and their anti-sweatshop allies need to work together to coordinate a global organizing effort that builds worker power and establishes a global production agreement that negotiates with both contractors and the brands for improved wages, benefits, and working conditions.

36864 ■ *"Wegmans Uses Database for Recall" in Supermarket News (Vol. 56, September 22, 2008, No. 38)*
Pub: Penton Business Media, Inc.
Ed: Carol Angrisani. **Description:** Wegmans used data obtained through its loyalty card that, in turn, sent automated telephone calls to every customer who had purchased tainted pet food when Mars Petcare recalled dog food products.

36865 ■ *"Welsh Meat Sales on the Rise" in Farmer's Weekly (March 28, 2008, No. 320)*
Pub: Reed Business Information
Contact: Jeff Greisch, President
Description: Due, in part, to marketing efforts, retail sales of Welsh lamb and beef rose significantly in the first two months of 2008.

36866 ■ *What Works: Success in Stressful Times*
Pub: Harper Press
Ed: Hamish McRae. **Released:** January 21, 2010. **Price:** $30.12. **Description:** Exploration of success stories from across the glove, and what Michelle Obama referred to as 'the flimsy difference between success and failure.' Why do some initiatives take off while others flounder? How have communities managed to achieve so much while others struggle? What distinguishes the good companies from the bad? What lessons can be learned from the well-ordered Mumbai community made famous by 'Slumdog Millionaire'? Why have Canadian manners helped Whistler become the most popular ski resort in North America?.

36867 ■ *"What'll You Have Tonight?" in Barron's (Vol. 88, July 4, 2008, No. 28, pp. 22)*
Pub: Dow Jones & Co., Inc.
Ed: Neil A. Martin. **Description:** Shares of Diageo could rise by 30 percent a year from June 2008 after it slipped due to U.S. sales worries. The company also benefits from the trend toward more premium alcoholic beverage brands worldwide especially in emerging markets.

36868 ■ *"Wheatfield First Choice for Canadian Manufacturer" in Business First Buffalo (November 23, 2007, pp. 1)*
Pub: American City Business Journals, Inc.
Ed: James Fink. **Description:** Niagara County Industrial Development Agency is preparing an enticement program that would lure automotive parts manufacturer Pop & Lock Corporation to shift manufacturing operations to Wheatfield, Niagara County, New York. The package includes job-training grants and assistance for acquiring new machinery. Details of the plan are included.

36869 ■ *"Where Canada Meets the World" in Canadian Business (Vol. 80, October 8, 2007, No. 20, pp. 86)*
Pub: Rogers Media
Ed: Zena Olijnyk. **Description:** An overview of facilities within Canada's borders that contributes to the country's economy is presented. The facilities include fishing vessels and seaports. Agencies that regulate the borders such as the Canada Border Services Agency and the Department of Fisheries and Oceans are also presented.

36870 ■ *"Where Next?" in Business Strategy Review (Vol. 21, Summer 2010, No. 2, pp. 20)*
Pub: Wiley-Blackwell
Description: The emergence of large, vibrant and seemingly unstoppable new markets has been the good news story of the past decade. Brazil, Russia, India and China (BRIC) are among those who have emerged blinking into the new economy.

36871 ■ *"Where Oil-Rich Nations Are Placing Their Bets" in Harvard Business Review (Vol. 86, September 2008, No. 9, pp. 119)*
Pub: Harvard Business School Press
Ed: Rawi Abdelal; Ayesha Khan; Tarun Khanna. **Description:** Investment strategies of the Gulf Cooperation Council nations are examined in addition to how these have impacted the global economy and capitalism.

36872 ■ *"Who Gets the Last Laugh?" in Barron's (Vol. 88, March 31, 2008, No. 13, pp. 17)*
Pub: Dow Jones & Company, Inc.
Ed: Leslie P. Norton. **Description:** Nord/LB will take a charge of 82.5 million euros to cover potential losses apparently related to Vatas' refusal to take the shares of Remote MDx Inc. after buying the shares. Remote MDx's main product is an ankle bracelet to monitor criminals; the firm has lost over half of its market cap due to the Nord/LB troubles and questions about its revenues.

36873 ■ *"Who Produces for Whom in the World Economy?" in Canadian Journal of Economics (Vol. 44, November 2011, No. 4, pp. 1403)*
Pub: Blackwell Publishers Ltd.
Ed: Guillaume Daudin, Christine Rifflart, Danielle Schweisguth. **Description:** For two decades, the share of trade in inputs, also called vertical trade, has been dramatically increasing. In reallocating trade flows to their original input-producing industries and countries, the article suggests a new measure of international trade: 'value-added trade' and makes it possible to answer the question, 'who produces for whom?'.

36874 ■ *Who's Your City? How the Creative Economy is Making Where to Live the Most Important Decision of Your Life*
Pub: Basic Books
Ed: Richard Florida. **Released:** 2009. **Price:** $26.95. **Description:** Richard Florida disagrees with the notion that under globalization, a leveling has taken away the economic advantages of any place in particular. Florida believes that globalization has also created higher-level economic activities such as innovation, design, finance, and media to cluster in a smaller number of locations.

36875 ■ *"Why Change?" in Canadian Business (Vol. 80, October 8, 2007, No. 20, pp. 9)*
Pub: Rogers Media
Ed: Joe Chidley. **Description:** The need for economic change in Canada is discussed. Despite the country's economic growth and low unemployment rate, economic reform is needed in order to maximize its economic potential in the future. Other reasons for the need to further develop its economy, such as the rise of manufacturing and service industries in Asia and the emergence of regional trade pacts in South America are also tackled.

36876 ■ *"Why Mumbai at 1PM is the Center of the Business World" in Harvard Business Review (Vol. 88, October 2010, No. 10, pp. 38)*
Pub: Harvard Business School Publishing
Ed: Michael Segalla. **Description:** A time zone chart is presented for assisting in the planning of international conference calls.

36877 ■ *"Why You Aren't Buying Venezuelan Chocolate." in Harvard Business Review (Vol. 88, December 2010, No. 12, pp. 25)*
Pub: Harvard Business School Publishing
Ed: Rohit Deshpande. **Description:** The concept of provenance paradox is defined as the preconceived notions consumers have about the country of origin of a given product, which can pose significant difficulties for emerging markets. Five strategies are presented for combating this problem, including building on historic events that have informed cultural perspectives.

36878 ■ *"The Wine Spectator" in Business Courier (Vol. 27, November 26, 2010, No. 30, pp. 1)*
Pub: Business Courier
Ed: Dan Monk. **Description:** Vintner Select, a wine distributor, will introduce an internationally known portfolio of more than 50 German and Austrian wines. The company now distributes about 900 different wine labels from 220 producers in 10 countries to smaller, independent retailers in Indiana, Kentucky and Ohio.

36879 ■ *"Winner: Caparo Group Plc" in Crain's Detroit Business (Vol. 24, March 24, 2008, No. 12, pp. 12)*
Pub: Crain Communications, Inc.
Ed: Brent Snavely. **Description:** London-based Caparo Group plc saw its acquisition of Voestalpine Polynorm as an opportunity to gain a foothold in the North American automotive industry. Caparo was impressed with the company's breadth of manufacturing capabilities and quality systems as well as with the management team.

36880 ■ *Winner Take All: How Competitiveness Shapes the Fate of Nations*
Pub: Basic Books
Ed: Richard J. Elkus Jr. **Released:** 2009. **Price:** $27. 00. **Description:** American government and misguided business practices has allowed the U.S. to fall behind other countries in various market sectors such as cameras and televisions, as well as information technologies. It will take a national strategy to for America to regain its lead in crucial industries.

36881 ■ *"Winning Gold" in The Business Journal-Milwaukee (Vol. 25, August 8, 2008, No. 46, pp. A1)*
Pub: American City Business Journals, Inc.
Ed: Rich Rovito. **Description:** Johnson Controls Inc. of Milwaukee, Wisconsin is taking part in the 2008 Beijing Olympics with the installation of its sustainable control equipment and technology that monitor over 58,000 points in 18 Olympic venues. Details of Johnson Controls' green products and sustainable operations in China are discussed.

36882 ■ *"With Whom Do You Trade? Defensive Innovation and the Skill-Bias" in Canadian Journal of Electronics (Vol. 43, November 2010)*
Pub: Journal of the Canadian Economics Association
Ed: Pushan Dutt, Daniel Traca. **Description:** Examination into whether increased trade with ineffective protection of intellectual property has contributed to the skill-deepening of the 1980s. An index of effective protection of intellectual property at the country level, combining data on protection of patents and rule of law are presented. An industry-specific version of this index is given using as weights each country's trade share in the total trade of the industry. A decline is seen in this trade-weighted index, owing to a rise in trade with countries with low effective protection of intellectual property, which explains 29 percent of the rise within-industry skill-intensity.

36883 ■ *"WNY Casing In On Loonie's Climb" in Business First Buffalo (November 23, 2007, pp. 1)*
Pub: American City Business Journals, Inc.
Ed: Scott Thomas. **Description:** Economy of Western New York has rebounded since the 9/11 recession and the rise of the Canadian dollar, which has contributed to the areas economic growth. Canadian shoppers are frequenting markets in the area due to the parity of the U.S. and Canadian dollar. Details of the cross-border shopping and its impact in WNY are discussed.

36884 ■ *"A World of Investors" in Entrepreneur (Vol. 35, November 2007, No. 11, pp. 72)*
Pub: Entrepreneur Media Inc.
Ed: Gail Dutton. **Description:** Information technology services company mPortal Inc. raised nearly $15 million in financing from venture capital company Friedli Corporate Finance. The biggest international investors are European companies, while the venture capital market is growing in Asia.

36885 ■ *"The World Is Your Hospital" in Canadian Business (Vol. 81, July 22, 2008, No. 12-13, pp. 62)*
Pub: Rogers Media Ltd.
Ed: Sharda Prashad. **Description:** Medical tourism is seen as a booming industry around the world and is expected to grow to around $40 billion in 2010. Key information regarding medical tourism and services are presented. Views on the possible impact of medical tourism on Canada's health care industry, as well as medical tourism opportunities in Canada, are also given.

36886 ■ *"The World Is Your Oyster" in Canadian Business (Vol. 80, October 22, 2007, No. 21, pp. 140)*
Pub: Rogers Media
Ed: Regan Ray. **Description:** Business graduates are not that keen on working abroad. Fortune 500 companies are requiring executives to have a multi-country focus. The skill required for jobs abroad, as well as employment opportunities are discussed.

36887 ■ *"A World of Opportunity: Foreign Markets Offer Diversity to Keen Investors" in Canadian Business (Vol. 81, Summer 2008, No. 9)*
Pub: Rogers Media Ltd.
Ed: Andrew Wahl. **Description:** International Monetary Fund projected in its 'World Economy Outlook' that there is a 25 percent chance that a global recession will occur in 2008 and 2009. Global growth rate is forecasted at 3.7 percent in 2008. Inflation in Asia emerging markets and forecasts on stock price indexes are presented.

36888 ■ *"The World is Their Classroom" in Crain's Chicago Business (Vol. 31, March 24, 2008, No. 12, pp. 24)*
Pub: Crain Communications, Inc.
Ed: Samantha Stainburn. **Description:** Due to globalization more business students are studying abroad; 89 percent of eligible students in its executive MBA program went overseas in 2007 compared to 15 percent ten years ago.

36889 ■ *"The World Tomorrow" in Canadian Business (Vol. 81, December 24, 2007, No. 1, pp. 35)*
Pub: Rogers Media
Ed: Zena Olijnyk. **Description:** Global economy is predicted to be in a difficult period as analysts expect a slowdown in economic growth. Germany's Deutsche Bank wrote in a report about 'growth recession' that the chances of the world growth falling below two percent being one in three. Forecasts on other global economic aspects are explored.

36890 ■ *"Wrigley's Newest Taste: Wolfberry" in Crain's Chicago Business (Vol. 31, March 31, 2008, No. 13, pp. 1)*
Pub: Crain Communications, Inc.
Ed: David Sterrett. **Description:** Wm. Wrigley Jr. Co. has introduced a gum line in China that touts the medicinal advantages of aloe vera to improve skin and wolfberry to boost energy in an attempt to keep the company positioned as the top candy firm in China.

36891 ■ *"Yao Ming Courts China's Wine Boom" in Wall Street Journal Eastern Edition (November 28, 2011, pp. B4)*
Pub: Dow Jones & Company Inc. Enterprise Media Group
Contact: Clare Hart, President
Ed: Jason Chow. **Description:** Yao Ming, the former NBA 7-foot 6-inch Chinese basketball star, is set to cash in on the market potential for wine in China. He has created his own winery in California, Yao Family Wines, which will produce wines solely for the Chinese market.

36892 ■ *"You Won't Go Broke Filling Up On These Stocks" in Barron's (Vol. 88, July 14, 2008, No. 28, pp. 38)*
Pub: Dow Jones & Co., Inc.
Ed: Assif Shameen. **Description:** Due to high economic growth, pro-business policies and a consumption boom, the Middle East is a good place to look for equities. The best ways in which to gain exposure to this market include investing in the real estate industry and telecommunications markets as well as large banks that serve corporations and consumers.

36893 ■ *"ZF Revving Up Jobs, Growth" in Business Courier (Vol. 26, November 6, 2009, No. 28, pp. 1)*
Pub: American City Business Journals, Inc.
Ed: Jon Newberry. **Description:** Proposed $96 million expansion of German-owned automotive supplier ZF Steering systems LLC is anticipated to generate 299 jobs in Boone County, Kentucky. ZF might invest $90 million in equipment, while the rest will go to building and improvements.

SOURCES OF SUPPLY

36894 ■ *Importers Manual USA: The Single Source Reference Encyclopedia for Importing to the United States*
World Trade Press
Contact: Roy Hinkelman, Manager
E-mail: roy@worldtradepress.com
URL(s): store.worldtradepress.com/Importers_Manual_USA.php. **Released:** Biennial; latest edition 4, 2003. **Price:** $145, Individuals Hardcover; $108. 75, Individuals Sale Price. **Publication includes:** Lists of trade fairs, embassies, chambers of commerce, banks, and other sources of information on various aspects of international trade. **Entries include:** Source name, address, phone, telex, description. Principal content of publication is information on importing to the U.S. , including coverage of U.S. Customs, banking, laws, shipping, and insurance. **Indexes:** Product/service, geographical, source name.

TRADE PERIODICALS

36895 ■ *Bacard's Global Investor*
Pub: Ferney Scribes Inc.
Ed: Andre Bacard, Editor. **Released:** Monthly. **Price:** $129, U.S.. **Description:** Provides monthly updates of select no-load global and international funds, model portfolios, foreign market graphs, monthly analysis and current recommendations. Recurring features include news of research and a column titled Mutual Fund in the Spotlight.

36896 ■ *CUBANEWS*
Pub: Target Research
Ed: Larry Luxner, Editor. **Released:** Monthly. **Price:** $429, individuals; $199 academic institutions. **Description:** Covers business and economic issues involving Cuba, including an economic overview, monthly developments, and industrial analysis.

36897 ■ *Global Voice*
Pub: Berlitz International Inc.
Ed: Erin Giordano, Editor, erin.giordano@berlitz.com. **Released:** Quarterly. **Price:** Free. **Description:** Carries information on the importance of language fluency and cross-cultural understanding in international business.

36898 ■ *The International Trade Journal: Western Hemispheric Studies*
Pub: Routledge Journals Taylor & Francis Group
URL(s): www.tandf.co.uk/journals/titles/08853908.asp. **Ed:** Tagi Sagafi-Nejad, Antonio J. Rodriguez. **Released:** Quarterly **Price:** $339, Individuals print only; $537, Institutions online only; $596, Individuals print and online.

36899 ■ *International Trade Reporter*
Pub: Bureau of National Affairs Inc.
Contact: Linda G. Botsford, Managing Editor
Released: Weekly. **Price:** $1,159. **Description:** Covers current international trade policies of the U.S. and of major U.S. trading partners. Topics include

bilateral negotiations, customs, export/import policy, foreign investment, standards, taxation, and other related issues. Recurring features include a calendar of events, reports of meetings, and notices of publications available.

36900 ■ *International Trade Reporter Decisions*
Pub: Bureau of National Affairs Inc.
Ed: Linda G. Botsford, Editor, lbotsford@bna.com. **Released:** Biweekly. **Price:** $1330. **Description:** Carries digested, classified, and indexed judicial and administrative decisions dealing with legal issues arising from U.S. trade law.

36901 ■ *Journal of Asia-Pacific Business*
Pub: Routledge Journals Taylor & Francis Group
URL(s): www.tandfonline.com/toc/wapb20/current. **Ed:** Riad A. Ajami. **Released:** Quarterly **Price:** $373, Institutions online only; $130, Individuals online only; $415, Institutions print & online; $144, Individuals print & online.

36902 ■ *Journal of East-West Business*
Pub: Routledge Journals Taylor & Francis Group
URL(s): www.tandfonline.com/loi/wjeb20. **Ed:** Erdener Kaynak. **Released:** Quarterly **Price:** $489, Institutions online only; $136, Individuals online only; $543, Institutions print & online; $147, Individuals print & online.

36903 ■ *Ottawa Letter*
Pub: CCH Canadian Ltd.
Contact: Ian Rhind, President
Released: Biweekly. **Price:** $920. **Description:** Reports on current events and topics of Canada, such as free trade, human rights, employment, and defense. Also provides statistics, lending, and foreign exchange rates.

36904 ■ *Political Risk Letter*
Pub: The PRS Group Inc.
Contact: Mary Lou O. Walsh, Chief Executive Officer
E-mail: mlw@prsgroup.com
Released: Monthly, 12/year. **Price:** $415, U.S. and Canada. **Description:** Offers concise political and economic forecasts for both 18 month and 5 year time spans. Provides country risk forecasts and analysis on 100 countries around the world and provides indepth coverage on 20 countries.

36905 ■ *Puerto Rico Business Review*
Pub: Government Development Bank for Puerto Rico
Ed: Maria Socorro Rosario-Claudio, Editor. **Released:** Quarterly. **Price:** Free. **Description:** Covers business and finance related to Puerto Rico. Carries research articles from government and business leaders and government agencies on the Puerto Rican economy. Reports on activity in agricultural industries, import and export trade, retail trade, banking, tourism, manufacturing, and other enterprises. Recurring features include a column titled In Focus and a supplement called Puerto Rico Mon. Economic Indicators.

36906 ■ *SACC In New York*
Pub: Swedish-American Chamber of Commerce
Released: Monthly. **Price:** Included in membership. **Description:** Concerned with developments in the Swedish and U.S. business communities: unemployment rates, industry plans and investments, exports, government measures to stimulate the economy, and similar subjects. Covers the membership activities of the SACC. Recurring features include interviews with Swedish and U.S. executives.

36907 ■ *Washington Tariff & Trade Letter*
Pub: Gilston-Kalin Communications, LLC
Ed: Samuel M. Gilston, Editor. **Released:** Weekly. **Price:** $597 print or electronic. **Description:** Reports on U.S. trade policies, negotiations, regulations, and legislation.

VIDEOCASSETTES/ AUDIOCASSETTES

36908 ■ *Building the Trans-National Team*
Learning Communications L.L.C.
5520 Trabuco Rd.
Irvine, CA 92620-5705
Free: 800-622-3610
Fax: (949)727-4323
Co. E-mail: sales@learncom.com
URL: http://www.learncom.com
Contact: Lloyd W. Singer, President
Released: 1994. **Price:** $495.00. **Description:** Underlines the difficulties of doing business with people of various nationalities including French, Spanish, German, and British. Focusses on cultural differences. Comes with guide. **Availability:** VHS.

36909 ■ *The Dollars and Sense of Exporting: How to Navigate the Global Market*
PBS Home Video
Catalog Fulfillment Center
Charlotte, NC 28275-1089
Ph: (800)531-4727
Free: 800-645-4PBS
Co. E-mail: info@pbs.org
URL: http://www.pbs.org
Released: 1989. **Price:** $300.00. **Description:** Helpful information for companies that wish to enter or expand in the international marketplace. Includes tips on assistance offered by various levels of government. **Availability:** VHS; 3/4 U.

CONSULTANTS

36910 ■ 2010 Fund 5
24351 Spartan St.
Mission Viejo, CA 92691-3920
Ph: (949)583-1992
Fax: (949)583-0474
Contact: Wally Eater, Principal
Scope: Funds in formation that will invest in technologies licensed from 30 universities. **Founded:** 1982.

36911 ■ Americas Consulting Group Inc.—Americas Project Management Services
741 Riversville Rd.
Greenwich, CT 06831-2626
Ph: (203)863-9168
Fax: (203)863-9161
Co. E-mail: contact@americaspms.com
Contact: Laurent Martinez, Managing Director
E-mail: l.martinez@americaspms.com
Scope: A consultant whose expertise is in assisting companies in developing growth strategies within the western hemisphere. Also expertise's in international business with a special focus on marketing, information acquisition and investigations. **Founded:** 1998.

36912 ■ Cohen & Associates
1625 Holly Ln.
Munster, IN 46321
Ph: (219)923-3133
Fax: (219)923-2622
Contact: Chaim J. Cohen, President
Scope: Domestic and international business development. Counsels companies from the start-up stage through the opening of foreign markets. Import/Export strategies, general management consulting, marketing planning, and business development. **Founded:** 1990.

36913 ■ Dubuc Lucke & Company Inc.—Adventa Global Intermediaries
120 W 5th St.
Cincinnati, OH 45202-2713
Ph: (513)579-8330
Fax: (513)241-6669
Contact: Kenneth E. Dubuc, President
Scope: Provides consulting services in the areas of profit enhancement; small business management; mergers and acquisitions; joint ventures; divestitures; interim management; crisis management; turnarounds; appraisals; valuations; due diligence; and international trade. **Founded:** 1999.

36914 ■ First Washington Associates Ltd.
1501 Lee Hwy., Ste. 102
Arlington, VA 22209-1047
Ph: (703)525-0966
Fax: (703)276-8851
Contact: Delio E. Gianturco, President
Scope: Provider of technical assistance in all aspects of international trade finance, small business development and related disciplines, including feasibility studies, market research, design and implementation of export credit, guarantee and insurance programs, formulation of policies, procedures and programs for public and private sector clients. **Founded:** 1977.

36915 ■ Global Business Consultants (GBC)
200 Lake Hills Rd.
Pinehurst, NC 28374-0776
Ph: (910)295-5991
Fax: (910)295-5991
Co. E-mail: gbc@pinehurst.net
Contact: Nan S. Leaptrott, President
E-mail: nan@yourculturecoach.com
Scope: Firm specializes in human resources management; project management; software development; and international trade. Offers litigation support. **Founded:** 1987. **Publications:** "Culture to Culture: Mission Trip Do's and Don'ts," Jul, 2005; "Rules of the Game: Global Business Protocol". **Seminars:** Cross-Cultural Training.

36916 ■ Great Lakes Consulting Group Inc.
54722 Little Flower Trl.
Mishawaka, IN 46545
Ph: (574)287-4500
Fax: (574)233-2688
Contact: James E. Schrager, President
Scope: Provides consulting services in the areas of strategic planning; feasibility studies; start-up businesses; small business management; mergers and acquisitions; joint ventures; divestitures; interim management; crisis management; turnarounds; business process re-engineering; venture capital; and international trade. **Founded:** 1989.

36917 ■ Intex Exhibit Systems L.L.C.
1846 Sequoia Ave.
Orange, CA 92868
Ph: (714)940-0369
Free: 800-331-6633
Fax: (714)935-0223
Co. E-mail: info@intexexhibits.com
URL: http://www.intexexhibits.com
Contact: Matthias D. Kemeny, President
E-mail: mdk@intexexhibits.com
Scope: Specializes in the design and production of exhibits, displays and pavilions for world fairs, tradeshows and similar events. Services include product design, industrial and engineering design for educational exhibits, museum exhibits and science and technology museology. Serves private industry as well as government agencies. **Founded:** 1979. **Publications:** "Trade Show Marketing," Sep, 2000; "Exhibitor Times," 1998. **Special Services:** Fastpack™; Panelflo™; affordable-1™; thegraphic arm™; Expression™; TigerMark™.

36918 ■ Nightingale Associates
7445 Setting Sun Way
Columbia, MD 21046
Ph: (410)381-4280
Fax: (410)381-4280
Co. E-mail: fredericknightingale@nightingaleassociates.net
URL: http://www.nightingaleassociates.net
Contact: Frederick C. Nightingale, Managing Director
E-mail: fredericknightingale@nightingaleAssociates.net
Scope: Management training and consulting firm offering the following skills: productivity and accomplishment; leadership skills for the experienced manager; management skills for the new manager; leadership and teambuilding; supervisory development; creative problem solving; real strategic planning; providing superior customer service; international purchasing and supply chain management; negotiation skills development and fundamentals of purchasing. **Founded:** 1984. **Seminars:** Productivity and Accomplishment Management Skills for the New Manager; Leadership and Team building; Advanced Management; Business Process Re engineering; Strategic Thinking; Creative Problem Solving; Customer Service; International Purchasing and Materials Management; Fundamentals of Purchasing; Negotiation Skills Development; Providing superior customer service; Leadership skills for the experienced manager.

36919 ■ Plans and Solutions Inc.
7823 Mistic View Ct.
Derwood, MD 20855
Ph: (301)947-8150
Fax: (240)525-5601
Co. E-mail: info@plansandsolutions.com
URL: http://www.plansandsolutions.com
Contact: Kenneth D. Weiss, President
E-mail: kw@plansandsolutions.com
Scope: Market research and competitive analysis; marketing and promotion planning, and executing promotion plans. Specializes in registration and problem solving services that include food canning establishment and process registration, registration under the terrorism act, assistance in case of detention of shipments, and on-site inspection of processing plants and records. Most clients are minority-owned businesses in the USA and companies overseas that want to begin or increase exports to the United States and Canada. **Founded:** 1996. **Publications:** "Building an Import/Export Business," John Wiley & Sons, 2002; "How to Conquer the U.S. Market"; "Going Global (Getting Started in International Trade)". **Seminars:** U.S. Import Regulations on Food Products.

36920 ■ Ralph J. Sigona Associates
1575 Center Ave.
Fort Lee, NJ 07024-4644
Ph: (201)461-3067
Contact: Ralph J. Sigona, President
Scope: International business consultants offering these services: Formulation and execution of commercial and marketing programs for imported and/or exported products in the United States, in Europe, and in other major world markets; search for and selection of importers and distributors for the introduction of manufactured products in foreign markets; market research and market intelligence services; evaluation and implementation of business and product opportunities on behalf of qualified clients. Serves private industries as well as government agencies. **Founded:** 1981. **Seminars:** How to Sell Overseas, International Marketing Procedures and Practices (annually).

COMPUTERIZED DATABASES

36921 ■ *Antitrust & Trade Regulation Report*
1801 S Bell St.
Arlington, VA 22202
Free: 800-372-1033
Co. E-mail: customercare@bna.com
URL: http://www.bna.com
Availability: Online: LexisNexis Group; Bloomberg LP-Bloomberg BNA; Thomson Reuters - Westlaw. **Type:** Full-text.

36922 ■ *Business Browser North America*
300 Baker Ave.
Concord, MA 01742
Ph: (978)318-4300
Fax: (978)318-4690
Co. E-mail: sales@onesource.com
URL: http://www.onesource.com
Availability: Online: Infogroup-OneSource Information Services Inc. **Type:** Directory; Numeric; Statistical; Full-text.

36923 ■ *EIU ViewsWire*
26 Red Lion Sq.
London WC1R 4HQ, United Kingdom
Ph: 20 7576 8181
Fax: 20 7576 8476
Co. E-mail: london@eiu.com
URL: http://www.eiu.com
Availability: Online: LexisNexis Group; Financial Times Ltd.; The Economist Group - Economist Intelligence Unit Ltd. **Type:** Full-text; Numeric.

36924 ■ *Global Business Browser*
300 Baker Ave.
Concord, MA 01742
Ph: (978)318-4300
Fax: (978)318-4690
Co. E-mail: sales@onesource.com
URL: http://www.onesource.com
Availability: Online: Infogroup-OneSource Information Services Inc. **Type:** Directory; Numeric; Statistical; Full-text.

36925 ■ *International Trade Reporter™*
1801 S Bell St.
Arlington, VA 22202
Free: 800-372-1033
Co. E-mail: customercare@bna.com
URL: http://www.bna.com
Availability: Online: Bloomberg LP-Bloomberg BNA; Thomson Reuters - Westlaw. **Type:** Full-text.

36926 ■ *United States International Trade in Goods and Services*
4600 Silver Hill Rd.
Washington, DC 20233-0001
Ph: (301)457-4100
Free: 800-923-8282
Fax: (301)457-4714
Co. E-mail: webmaster@census.gov
URL: http://www.census.gov
Availability: Online: U.S. Census Bureau. **Type:** Statistical.

36927 ■ *Ward's Business Directory of U.S. Private and Public Companies*
10650 Toebben Dr.
Independence, KY 41051
Free: 800-354-9706
Fax: (800)487-8488
Co. E-mail: investors@cengage.com
URL: http://www.gale.cengage.com
Contact: Ronald Dunn, President
URL(s): www.gale.cengage.com. **Released:** Annual; Latest edition 54th; June, 2011. **Price:** Edition 48 (2002): 8-vol. set, $3,075.00 (includes inter-edition supplement). Some individual volumes also sold separately.; $3627, Individuals five-volume set; $3205, Individuals four-volume set; $1697, Individuals volumes 5, 6, or 7; $1149, Individuals volume 8. **Covers:** Approximately 112,000 companies, 90% of which are privately owned, representing all industries. **Entries include:** Company name, address, phone, fax, toll-free, e-mail, URL, names and titles of up to five officers, up to four Standard Industrial Classification (SIC) codes, NAICS code, revenue figure, number of employees, year founded, ticker symbol, stock exchange, immediate parent, fiscal year end, import/export, type of company (public, private, subsidiary, etc.). In Vol. 4, lists of top 1,000 privately held companies ranked by sales vol., top 1,000 publicly held companies ranked by sales volume, and top 1,000 employers ranked by number of employees; analyses of public and private companies by state, revenue per employee for top 1,000 companies, public and private companies by SIC code and NAICS code. In volume 5, national Standard Industrial Classification (SIC) code rankings are listed, while volumes 6 and 7 lists Standard Industrial Classification (SIC) code rankings by state. In all volumes, guide to abbreviations, codes, and symbols; explanation of classification system; numerical and alphabetical listings of SIC and NAICS codes. In volume 8, NAICS rankings. In the supplement, 10,000 new listings not contained in the main edition are included. **Arrangement:** Volumes 1, 2, and 3, alphabetical; volume 4 is geographical by state, then ascending zip; volume 5 is classified by 4-digit SIC code, then ranked by sales; volumes 6 and 7 are classified by Standard Industrial Classification (SIC) code within state; volume 8 classified by NAICS, then ranked; supplement arranged alphabetical and Standard Industrial Classification (SIC) code. **Indexes:** Company name index in volumes 5, 7, and 8. **Availability:** Online: Cengage Learning Inc. CD-ROM: Cengage Learning Inc. **Type:** Directory; Numeric.

LIBRARIES

36928 ■ Canada Department of Foreign Affairs and International Trade - Main Library—Affaires Etrangeres et Commerce International Canada - Bibliotheque.
Lester B. Pearson Bldg.
125 Sussex Dr.
Ottawa, ON, Canada K1A 0G2
Ph: (613)992-6150
Fax: (613)944-0222
Co. E-mail: library-biblio.aiml@international.gc.ca
URL: http://www.dfait-maeci.gc.ca
Contact: Jo-Anne Valentine, Librarian
URL(s): www.international.gc.ca/library-bibliotheque. **Scope:** International relations, International law, International economics, trade, investment, International organizations. **Services:** Interlibrary loan; copying; Library open to the public with restrictions. **Founded:** 1909. **Holdings:** 50,000 monographs; 30,000 bound periodical volumes; 550,000 documents; 200,000 microforms; 800 maps.

36929 ■ Canadian International Trade Tribunal Library—Tribunal Canadien du Commerce Exterieur.
333 Laurier Ave. W., 15th Fl.
Ottawa, ON, Canada K1A 0G7
Ph: (613)990-2418
Fax: (613)990-2439
Co. E-mail: ursula.schultz@citt-tcce.gc.ca
URL: http://www.citt.gc.ca
Contact: Ursula Schultz, Librarian
URL(s): www.collectionscanada.gc.ca/6/30/s30-223-e.html. **Scope:** Trade, tariffs, customs and excise, Canadian law, commerce, economics. **Services:** Interlibrary loan; copying; library open to the public by appointment. **Founded:** 1989. **Holdings:** 6000 books; 1000 bound periodical volumes. **Subscriptions:** 300 journals and other serials; 12 newspapers. **Telecommunication Services:** secretary@citt-tcce.gc.ca.

36930 ■ Ontario Ministry of Economic Development and Trade - InfoSource
900 Bay St.
Hearst Block, 8th Fl.
Toronto, ON, Canada M7A 2E1
Ph: (416)325-6666
Fax: (416)325-6688
Co. E-mail: info@edt.gov.on.ca
URL: http://www.ontariocanada.com/ontcan/1medt/en/home_en.jsp
Scope: Trade, industry, small business, management, company information, economic development. **Services:** Copying; scanning. **Founded:** 1994. **Holdings:** 200 books; microfiche; 20 CD-ROMs.

36931 ■ Woodbury University Library
7500 Glenoaks Blvd.
Burbank, CA 91504-1052
Ph: (818)252-5201
Fax: (818)767-4534
Co. E-mail: jennifer.rosenfeld@woodbury.edu
URL: http://library.woodbury.edu
Contact: Nedra Peterson, Director
Scope: Business and management, International business, art, architecture, interior design, fashion marketing and design, psychology, animation. **Services:** Interlibrary loan; copying; Library open to the public for reference use only. **Founded:** 1884. **Holdings:** 65,000 books; 3070 bound periodical volumes; 17,401 slides; 2000 DVD/VHS. **Subscriptions:** 300 journals and other serials; 5 newspapers. **Telecommunication Services:** nedra.peterson@woodbury.edu.

RESEARCH CENTERS

36932 ■ Georgia Institute of Technology - Enterprise Innovation Institute
75th St. NW, Ste. 314
Atlanta, GA 30308
Ph: (404)894-6986
Fax: (404)894-1192
Co. E-mail: stephen.fleming@innovate.gatech.edu
URL: http://innovate.gatech.edu
Contact: Stephen Fleming, Vice President
Services: Market Analysis; Product Analysis; Quality Assessments; Re-engineering and Design Services; Standards Interpretation; Standards Updating Service. **Founded:** 1991. **Publications:** *European*

Market Bulletin; *Standards Newsletter*; *European Standards Directory* (Annual). **Educational Activities:** Seminars and workshops on standards-related topics; Training Seminars and Workshops.

36933 ■ University of Maryland at College Park - Center for Global Business Education (CGBE)
2410 Van Munching Hall
Robert H. Smith School of Business
College Park, MD 20742-1815
Ph: (301)405-0200
Fax: (301)314-9526
Co. E-mail: lbarnard@rhsmith.umd.edu
URL: http://www.rhsmith.umd.edu/global
Contact: Lisa Barnard, Director
Founded: 1990. **Educational Activities:** CGBE Conferences and workshops (Occasionally). **Telecommunication Services:** ogp@rhsmith.umd.edu.

36934 ■ University of Maryland at College Park - International Communications and Negotiations Simulations (ICONS)
0145 Tydings Hall
Department of Government & Politics
College Park, MD 20742
Ph: (301)405-4172
Fax: (301)314-9301
Co. E-mail: dfridl@umd.edu
URL: http://www.icons.umd.edu
Contact: Daniella Fridl, Director
Founded: 1982. **Telecommunication Services:** icons@gvpt.umd.edu.

Intrapreneurship

REFERENCE WORKS

36935 ■ *"Black Gold" in Canadian Business (Vol. 79, August 14, 2006, No. 16-17, pp. 57)*
Pub: Rogers Media
Ed: Erin Pooley. **Description:** A list of the top ten jobs in the petroleum industry in Canada along with pay and nature of jobs, is presented.

36936 ■ *"Diana Bonta: Keeping People Healthy and Thriving" in Hispanic Business (Vol. 30, April 2008, No. 4, pp. 30)*
Pub: Hispanic Business
Ed: Leanndra Martinez. **Description:** Diana Bonta serves as vice president of public affairs for Kaiser Permanente and is a strong advocate for health reform and improving access to health care. In order to better serve the underinsured and uninsured, she directs Kaiser's Community Benefit division that devoted $369 million last year to this cause.

36937 ■ *"Female Hispanic Professionals by the Number" in Hispanic Business (Vol. 30, April 2008, No. 4, pp. 8)*
Pub: Hispanic Business
Description: More executive opportunities are presenting themselves for future generations of Hispanic women who are more frequently being found in high-level positions. Statistical data included.

36938 ■ *"The Ten Worst Leadership Habits" in Canadian Business (Vol. 81, March 31, 2008, No. 5, pp. 63)*
Pub: Rogers Media
Ed: Michael Stern. **Description:** Ten leadership behaviors that aspiring leaders need to avoid are presented. These include expecting colleagues and subordinates to be like themselves, attending too many meetings, being miserly when it comes to recognition and praise, and giving an opinion often.

36939 ■ *"The Trusty Sidekick" in Canadian Business (Vol. 81, March 31, 2008, No. 5, pp. 33)*
Pub: Rogers Media
Ed: John Gray. **Description:** Being second-in-command is a good opportunity to be mentored by the boss and puts the executive in the position to see the whole organization and have influence to make changes. However, the chief operating officer has the unenviable task of trying to achieve unattainable goals. Executives who want to become the right hand man must go beyond their job description.

36940 ■ *"The Winner's Circle" in Hispanic Business (Vol. 30, April 2008, No. 4, pp. 20)*
Pub: Hispanic Business
Ed: Hildy Medina. **Description:** Although there has been progress concerning Hispanic women professionals who are growing in numbers in the upper echelons of the corporate arena, many still find that they face discrimination when it comes to pay and promotions. Statistical data included.

36941 ■ *"Young Giants" in Canadian Business (Vol. 79, August 14, 2006, No. 16-17, pp. 47)*
Pub: Rogers Media
Ed: Brad Purdy. **Description:** New generations of young chiefs of oil and gas companies in Canada, are featured.

VIDEOCASSETTES/ AUDIOCASSETTES

36942 ■ *Inspiring Innovation*
American Management Association (AMA)
1601 Broadway
New York, NY 10019-7420
Ph: (212)586-8100
Free: 877-566-9441
Fax: (212)903-8168
Co. E-mail: customerservice@amanet.org
URL: http://www.amanet.org
Contact: Charles R. Craig, Chairman
Released: 19??. **Price:** $545.00. **Description:** Contains information on how to get started with the idea of innovation. **Availability:** VHS; CC.

START-UP INFORMATION

36943 ■ *Entrepreneurship Strategy: Changing Patterns in New Venture Creation, Growth, and Reinvention*
Pub: SAGE Publications USA
Contact: Blaise R. Simqu, President
Ed: Lisa K. Gundry; Jill R. Kickul. **Released:** August 2006. **Price:** $69.95. **Description:** Entrepreneurial strategies that incorporate new venture emergence, early growth, and reinvention and innovation are examined.

36944 ■ *"Firefighter Wins ABC's American Inventor" in Hispanic Business (September 2007, pp. 94)*
Pub: Hispanic Business
Description: Greg Chavez, firefighter, won ABC televisions American Inventor award of $1 million for his Guardian Angel invention. The device makes Christmas trees safer.

36945 ■ *Mommy Millionaire: How I Turned My Kitchen Table Idea Into a Million Dollars and How You Can, Too!*
Pub: St. Martin's Press LLC
Ed: Kim Lavine. **Released:** February 19, 2008. **Price:** $14.95. **Description:** Advice, secrets and lessons for making a million dollars from a mom who turned her kitchen into a successful business; tools cover developing and patenting an idea, cold calling, trade shows, QVC, big retailers, manufacturing, and raising venture capital.

36946 ■ *The Mousedriver Chronicles*
Pub: Perseus Books Group
Ed: John Lusk; Kyle Harrison. **Released:** 2003. **Price:** $16.95. **Description:** Entrepreneurial voyage through the startup business of two ivy-league business school graduates and the lessons they learned while developing their idea of a computer mouse that looks like a golf driver into the marketplace. The book is an inspiration for those looking to turn an idea into a company.

36947 ■ *"Troy Patent Law Firm Launches Rent-Free Tech Incubator" in Crain's Detroit Business (Vol. 25, June 8, 2009, No. 23, pp. 4)*
Pub: Crain Communications Inc. - Detroit
Ed: Tom Henderson. **Description:** Young Basile Hanlon MacFarlane & Helmholdt PC, a patent law firm located in Troy, Michigan has created a small, rent-free technology incubator on site. The incubator will be called North Woodward Tech Incubator and has room for four or five startups. The incubator is for the earliest or pre-seed stage for entrepreneurs who have not yet gotten significant investment capital.

ASSOCIATIONS AND OTHER ORGANIZATIONS

36948 ■ American Society of Inventors (ASI)
PO Box 58426
Philadelphia, PA 19102
Ph: (215)546-6601
Co. E-mail: info@asoi.org
URL: http://www.asoi.org
URL(s): www.americaninventor.org. **Description:** Engineers, scientists, businessmen, and others who are interested in a cooperative effort to serve both the short- and long-term needs of the inventor and society. Works with government and industry to improve the environment for the inventor. Aims to encourage invention and innovation; help the independent inventor become self-sufficient. Establishes a networking system for inventors and businessmen to solve problems. Sponsors educational programs. **Founded:** 1953. **Publications:** *Inventors Digest* (Annual).

36949 ■ International Licensing Industry Merchandisers' Association (LIMA)
350 5th Ave., Ste. 4019
New York, NY 10118
Ph: (212)244-1944
Fax: (212)563-6552
Co. E-mail: info@licensing.org
URL: http://www.licensing.org
Contact: Charles M. Riotto, President
Description: Companies and individuals engaged in the marketing and servicing of licensed properties, both as agents and as property owners; manufacturers and retailers in the licensing business; supporters of the licensing industry. Professional association for the licensing industry worldwide. Objectives are to establish a standard reflecting a professional and ethical management approach to the marketing of licensed properties; to become the leading source of information in the industry; to communicate this information to members and others in the industry through publishing, public speaking, seminars, and an open line; to represent the industry in trade and consumer media and in relationships with the government, retailers, manufacturers, other trade associations, and the public. Conducts research programs. Compiles statistics; maintains hall of fame and placement service. **Founded:** 1985. **Publications:** *LIMA BottomLine* (Quarterly); *LIMA Worldwide Licensing Resource Directory* (Annual). **Educational Activities:** Licensing International and Licensing University (Annual). **Awards:** LIMA International Licensing Award (Annual).

36950 ■ International Trademark Association (INTA)
655 3rd Ave., 10th Fl.
New York, NY 10017-5617
Ph: (212)642-1700
Fax: (212)768-7796
Co. E-mail: info@inta.org
URL: http://www.inta.org
Contact: Gregg Marrazzo, President
Description: Trademark owners; associate members are lawyers, law firms, advertising agencies, designers, market researchers, and others in the trademark industries. Seeks to: protect the interests of the public in the use of trademarks and trade names; promote the interests of members and of trademark owners generally in the use of their trademarks and trade names; disseminate information concerning the use, registration, and protection of trademarks in the United States, its territories, and in foreign countries. Maintains job bank and speakers' bureau. **Scope:** trademarks. **Founded:** 1878. **Subscriptions:** 3000 books periodicals. **Publications:** *The Trademarker Reporter*, *International Trademark Association--Membership Directory*; *INTA Bulletin* (Biweekly); *The Trademark Reporter* (Bimonthly). **Educational Activities:** International Trademark Association Meeting (Annual). **Awards:** International Trademark Association-Ladas Memorial Awards.

36951 ■ Inventors Assistance League (IAL)
1053 Colorado Blvd., Ste. G1
Los Angeles, CA 90041
Ph: (818)246-6542
Free: 877-433-2246
Fax: (818)246-6546
URL: http://www.inventions.org
Contact: Rusty Ruscetta, Chief Executive Officer
Description: Inventors and manufacturers. Helps inventors get their products into the marketplace and assists manufacturers in finding new products to make and market. Brings together inventors and manufacturers for mutual benefit. Maintains speakers' bureau, small museum, and hall of fame. **Founded:** 1963. **Publications:** *Inventor's Advisory*.

36952 ■ National Inventors Foundation (NIF)
c/o Inventors Assistance League
1053 Colorado Blvd., Ste. G1
Los Angeles, CA 90041
Ph: (818)246-6542
Free: 877-433-2246
Fax: (818)246-6546
Co. E-mail: rustyr@earthlink.net
URL: http://www.inventions.org
Contact: Ted De Boer, President
Description: Independent inventors united to educate individuals regarding the protection and promotion of inventions and new products. Instructs potential inventors on patent laws and how to protect their inventions through methods developed by the foundation. Teaches advertising, sales and marketing techniques to get ideas into the marketplace to determine their commercial value. Assists individuals throughout the U.S. and in 44 other countries. Maintains speakers' bureau, hall of fame, and museum. **Scope:** patents, copyrights, trademarks, sales, advertising and marketing. **Founded:** 1963. **Subscriptions:** 1800.

REFERENCE WORKS

36953 ■ *"ABM Janitorial Services Receives Service Excellence Award from Jones Lang LaSalle" in Investment Weekly News (July 16, 2011, pp. 75)*
Pub: NewsRX
Description: ABM Janitorial Services was awarded the 2010 Jones Lang LaSalle Distinction award in the category of Service Excellence. LaSalle is a leading financial and professional services firm that specializes in real estate services and investment manage-

ment. The program recognizes supplier partners who play a vital role in LaSalle's aim to provide the highest quality of services, value and innovation to clients.

36954 ■ *The Accidental Entrepreneur: The 50 Things I Wish Someone Had Told Me About Starting a Business*
Pub: AMACOM
Ed: Susan Urquhart-Brown. **Released:** March 2008. **Price:** $17.95. **Description:** Advice is offered to any would-be entrepreneur, including eight questions to ask before launching a new business, ten traits of a successful entrepreneur, how to obtain licenses and selling permits, best way to create a business plan, ten ways to get referrals, six secrets of marketing, investment and financial information, ways to avoid burnout, and the seven biggest pitfalls to avoid.

36955 ■ *Achieving Planned Innovation: A Proven System for Creating Successful New Products and Services*
Pub: Simon and Schuster
Ed: Frank R. Bacon. **Released:** August 2007. **Price:** $16.95. **Description:** Planned innovation is a disciplined and practical step-by-step sequence of procedures for reaching the intended destination point: successful products. This easy-to-read book explains the system along with an action-oriented program for continuous success in new-product innovations. Five steps outlined include: a disciplined reasoning process; lasting market orientation; proper selection criteria that reflect both strategic and tactical business objectives and goals along with dynamic matching of resources to present and future opportunities, and positive and negative requirements before making major expenditures; and proper organizational staffing. The author explains what to do and evaluating the potential of any new product or service, ranging from ventures in retail distribution to the manufacture of goods as diverse as bicycles, motorcycles, aerospace communication and navigation equipment, small business computers, food packaging, and medical products.

36956 ■ *"All Indicators in Michigan Innovation Index Drop in 4Q" in Crain's Detroit Business (Vol. 25, June 22, 2009, No. 25, pp. 9)*
Pub: Crain Communications Inc. - Detroit
Ed: Ryan Beene. **Description:** Economic indicators that rate Michigan's innovation fell in the fourth quarter of 2008. The index of trademark applications, SBA loans, venture capital funding, new incorporations and other indicators traced dropped 12.6 points.

36957 ■ *"American Chemistry Council Launches Flagship Blog" in Ecology,Environment & Conservation Business (October 29, 2011, pp. 5)*
Pub: HighBeam Research
Description: American Chemistry Council (ACC) launched its blog, American Chemistry Matters, where interactive space allows bloggers to respond to news coverage and to discuss policy issues and their impact on innovation, competitiveness, job creation and safety.

36958 ■ *"Are You a Young Canadian Entrepreneur Looking for Recognition?" in CNW Group (November 10, 2010)*
Pub: Comtex
Description: Business Development Bank of Canada is looking for young Canadian entrepreneurs ages 19 to 35 for its 2011 Young Entrepreneur Awards. The awards pay tribute to remarkable young Canadian entrepreneurs for their creativity, innovative spirit and community development, as well as business success.

36959 ■ *"The Art of Rapid, Hands-On Execution Innovation" in Strategy and Leadership (Vol. 39, March-April 2011, No. 2, pp. 28)*
Pub: Emerald Group Publishing Inc.
Ed: Anssi Tuulenmaki, Liisa Valikangas. **Description:** A model of 'rapid execution innovation' that can be used to increase the chances of achieving innovations that develop into successful new business models is introduced. The model involves company experiments that inspire the radical rethinking business opportunities, and by continuing these experiments until the idea evolves into a product.

36960 ■ *"Auto Show Aims to Electrify" in Crain's Detroit Business (Vol. 26, January 11, 2010, No. 2, pp. 1)*
Pub: Crain Communications, Inc.
Ed: Ryan Beene. **Description:** Overview of the North American International Auto show include sixteen production and concept vehicles including eight from the Detroit 3. High-tech battery suppliers as well as hybrid and electric vehicles will highlight the show.

36961 ■ *"Auxilium Drug's New Use: Putting Squeeze On Cellulite" in Philadelphia Business Journal (Vol. 30, September 16, 2011, No. 31, pp. 1)*
Pub: American City Business Journals Inc.
Ed: John George. **Description:** Auxilium Pharmaceuticals and BioSpecifics Technologies are getting on with their plans of finding new uses for their drug Xiaflex, a possible treatment for cellulite. The two firms have dismissed their pending litigations and mapped out an amended licensing agreement for their search for the potential uses of the drug.

36962 ■ *"Avoiding Invention Scams" in Black Enterprise (Vol. 37, January 2007, No. 6, pp. 46)*
Pub: Earl G. Graves Publishing Co. Inc.
Ed: James C. Johnson. **Description:** Invention promotion firms provide inventors assistance in developing a prototype for product development. It is important to research these companies before making a commitment to work with them because there are a number of these firms that are not legitimate and have caused independent inventors to lose thousands of dollars by making false claims as to the market potential of the inventions.

36963 ■ *"Bankruptcy Claims Brooke, Gives Franchisees Hope" in The Business Journal-Serving Metropolitan Kansas City (October 31, 2008)*
Pub: American City Business Journals, Inc.
Ed: James Dornbrook; Steve Vockrodt. **Description:** Insurer Brooke Corp. was required to file for Chapter 11 bankruptcy for a deal to sell all of its assets to businessmen Terry Nelson and Lysle Davidson. The new Brooke plans to share contingency fees with franchisees. The impacts of the bankruptcy case on Brooke franchisees are discussed.

36964 ■ *"Be Innovative In Other Ways" in Green Industry Pro (Vol. 23, March 2011, No. 3, pp. 4)*
Pub: Cygnus Business Media
Ed: Rod Dickens. **Description:** Emphasis is put on the importance of putting the customer first in order to successfully market any product or service. Six marketing ideas are presented to promote a landscaping business.

36965 ■ *"Best Growth Stocks" in Canadian Business (Vol. 82, Summer 2009, No. 8, pp. 28)*
Pub: Rogers Media
Ed: Calvin Leung. **Description:** Canadian stocks that are considered as the best growth stocks, and whose price-earnings ratio is less than their earnings growth rate, are suggested. Suggestions include pharmaceutical firm Paladin Labs, which was found to have 13 consecutive years of revenue growth. Paladin Labs acquires or licenses niche drugs and markets them in Canada.

36966 ■ *"Blast from the Past" in Entrepreneur (Vol. 35, November 2007, No. 11, pp. 48)*
Pub: Entrepreneur Media Inc.
Ed: Robert Kiyosaki. **Description:** Entrepreneurs of today face the challenge of creating new ideas. Collaborating with younger employees provides new perspective, but it also has to be a partnership with old ideas and sharing experiences between the older and the younger to forecast the future.

36967 ■ *"Bloomberg Law Upgraded Its Online Legal Research Platform" in Information Today (Vol. 28, September 2011, No. 8, pp. 28)*
Pub: Information Today, Inc.
Description: Bloomberg Law upgraded its online legal research platform for law practices. The new services includes a redesigned interface, improved search capabilities, and expanded collaboration and workflow features, while maintaining it comprehensive law resources such as mergers and acquisitions, antitrust, and securities.

36968 ■ *"Born of Culture of Innovation" in Canadian Business (Vol. 81, October 27, 2008, No. 18, pp. 98)*
Pub: Rogers Media Ltd.
Description: MaRS, an independent nonprofit organization, aims to better capture the relevant commercial potential of Ontario's research and to connect the worlds of science, business, and capital as well as to stimulate a culture of innovation. Profile of MaRS and its 'MaRS Innovation' program is included.

36969 ■ *Borrowing Brilliance: The Six Steps to Business Innovation by Building on the Ideas of Others*
Pub: Gotham
Ed: David Kord Murray. **Price:** $26.00. **Description:** The author builds the case that cherry-picking the ideas of others is a vital part of the research and development process for any small firm.??.

36970 ■ *"Bridging the Talent Gap Through Partnership and Innovation" in Canadian Business (Vol. 81, October 27, 2008, No. 18, pp. 88)*
Pub: Rogers Media Ltd.
Description: Research revealed that North America is short by more than 60,000 qualified networking professionals. Businesses, educators and communities are collaborating in order to address the shortfall.

36971 ■ *"Brooke Agents Claim Mistreatment" in The Business Journal-Serving Metropolitan Kansas City (Vol. 27, October 24, 2008, No. 7, pp. 1)*
Pub: American City Business Journals, Inc.
Ed: James Dornbrook. **Description:** Franchisees of Brooke Corp., an insurance franchise, face uncertainty as their bills remain unpaid and banks threaten to destroy their credit. The company bundled and sold franchisee loans to different banks, but the credit crunch left the company with massive debts and legal disputes.

36972 ■ *"A Burning Issue: Lives Are at Stake Every Day" in Contractor (Vol. 56, October 2009, No. 10, pp. 29)*
Pub: Penton Media, Inc.
Ed: Julius A. Ballanco; Stanley Wolfson. **Description:** American Society of Plumbing Engineers has been accused of being biased for supporting rules that require residential fire sprinklers although the society's members will not receive any benefit from their installation. The organization trains and certifies plumbing engineers who design life-saving fire protection systems.

36973 ■ *"California Company Suing City's Lupin Over its Generic Diabetes Drug" in Baltimore Business Journal (Vol. 27, January 1, 2010)*
Pub: American City Business Journals
Ed: Gary Haber. **Description:** California-based Depomed Inc. is suing Baltimore, Maryland-based Lupin Pharmaceuticals Inc. and its parent company in India over the patents to a diabetes drug. Lupin allegedly infringed on Depomed's four patents for Glumetza when it filed for permission to sell its own version of the drug with the US Food and Drug Administration. Details on generic pharmaceutical manufacturer tactics are discussed.

36974 ■ *"Can America Invent Its Way Back?" in Business Week (September 22, 2008, No. 4100, pp. 52)*
Pub: McGraw-Hill Companies, Inc.
Description: Business leaders as well as economists agree that innovative new products, services and ways of doing business may be the only way in which America can survive the downward spiral of the

economy; innovation economics may be the answer and may even provide enough growth to enable Americans to prosper in the years to come.

36975 ■ *"Can He Win the Patent Game?" in Globe & Mail (February 20, 2006, pp. B1)*
Pub: CTVglobemedia Publishing Inc.
Ed: Simon Avery; Paul Waldie. **Description:** A profile on managerial abilities of chief executive officer Jim Balsillie of Research In Motion Ltd., who will face the patent case with NTP Inc., is presented.

36976 ■ *"Canadian Research Generates Innovation and Prosperity" in Canadian Business (Vol. 81, October 27, 2008, No. 18, pp. 87)*
Pub: Rogers Media Ltd.
Description: Universities play a key role in helping Canadians achieve prosperity, competitiveness, and quality of life by conducting more than a third of Canada's research. Research in universities help train graduates to apply sophisticated knowledge to real problems.

36977 ■ *"The Case for a Bright Future" in Canadian Business (Vol. 83, July 20, 2010, No. 11-12, pp. 58)*
Pub: Rogers Media Ltd.
Ed: Andrew Potter. **Description:** Writer Matt Ridley argues that trade is the determinant of development and that it is the reason why humans got rich. Ridley believes that the important innovations are often low-tech and is often processes rather than products.

36978 ■ *"Clash of the Titans" in Canadian Business (Vol. 80, March 12, 2007, No. 6, pp. 27)*
Pub: Rogers Media
Ed: Andrew Wahl. **Description:** The frequent allegations of Google Inc. and Microsoft Corp. against each other over copyright and other legal issues, with a view to taking away other's market share, is discussed.

36979 ■ *Clicking Through: A Survival Guide for Bringing Your Company Online*
Pub: Bloomberg Press
Ed: Jonathan I. Ezor. **Released:** October 1999. **Description:** Summary of legal compliance issues faced by small companies doing business on the Internet, including copyright and patent laws.

36980 ■ *"Clusters Last Stand?" in Canadian Electronics (Vol. 23, February 2008, No. 1, pp. 6)*
Pub: CLB Media Inc.
Description: Survival of technology clusters was the focus of Strategic Microelectronics Council's conference entitled, 'The Power of Community: Building Technology Clusters in Canada'. Clusters can help foster growth in the microelectronics sector, and it was recognized that government intervention is needed to maintain these clusters.

36981 ■ *"Code Name: Investors: Go From Golden Idea to Agent of Invention" in Black Enterprise (Vol. 41, November 2010, No. 4, pp. 78)*
Pub: Earl G. Graves Publishing Co. Inc.
Ed: Renita Burns. **Description:** Profile of Andre Woolery, inventor of a magnetic wristband that holds small nails, screws, drill bits, and small tools, allowing handymen to keep essential tools at hand while working.

36982 ■ *"Companies Must Innovate, Regardless of Economy" in Crain's Detroit Business (Vol. 25, June 1, 2009, No. 22, pp. M007)*
Pub: Crain Communications Inc. - Detroit
Ed: Sherri Begin Welch. **Description:** Despite the economy, leaders of Michigan's successful companies stress that small businesses must innovate in order to grow.

36983 ■ *"Connectors for Space, Mil/Aero and Medical Applications" in Canadian Electronics (Vol. 23, June-July 2008, No. 4, pp. 13)*
Pub: Action Communication Inc.
Ed: Gilles Parguey. **Description:** Product information on electrical connectors for use in space, military, aeronautics, and medical applications is provided. These connectors are built to withstand the extreme conditions offered by the harsh working environments in those applications.

36984 ■ *Content Rich: Writing Your Way to Wealth on the Web*
Pub: 124 S Mercedes Rd.
Ed: Jon Wuebben. **Released:** April 2008. **Price:** $19.95. **Description:** A definitive search engine optimization (SEO) copywriting guide for search engine rankings and sales conversion. It includes topics not covered in other books on the subject and targets the small to medium sized business looking for ways to maximize online marketing activities as well as designers and Web developers seeking to incorporate more SEO techniques into design and content.

36985 ■ *"Copyright Clearance Center (CCC) Partnered with cSubs" in Information Today (Vol. 28, November 2011, No. 10, pp. 14)*
Pub: Information Today, Inc.
Description: Copyright Clearance Center (CCC) partnered with cSubs to integrate CCC's point-of-content licensing solution RightsLink Basic directly into cSubs workflow. The partnership will allow cSubs' customers a user-friendly process for obtaining permissions. Csubs is a corporate subscription management service for books, newspapers, and econtent.

36986 ■ *"The Copyright Evolution" in Information Today (Vol. 28, November 2011, No. 10, pp. 1)*
Pub: Information Today, Inc.
Ed: Nancy Davis Kho. **Description:** For information professionals, issues surrounding copyright compliance have traditionally been on the consumption side. However, today, content consumption is only half the program because blogging, tweeting, and commenting is a vital part of more standard duties for workers as corporations aim to create authentic communications with customers.

36987 ■ *"Courting Canadian Customers Confounds Car Dealers" in Business First Buffalo (November 9, 2007, pp. 1)*
Pub: American City Business Journals, Inc.
Ed: James Fink. **Description:** Strength of the Canadian dollar has led to an influx of potential customers for the Western New York automobile industry, but franchising restrictions and licensing as well as insurance issues have limited the potential of having larger sales figures. Border and trade issues that affect the car industry in WNY are also discussed.

36988 ■ *Craft, Inc.*
Pub: Chronicle Books LLC
Ed: Meg Mateo Ilasco. **Released:** August 2007. **Price:** $16.95. **Description:** Business primer for entrepreneurial crafters wishing to turn their hobbies into a small business, including tips for developing products, naming the company, writing a business plan, applying for licenses, and paying taxes.

36989 ■ *"Craig Muhlhauser" in Canadian Business (Vol. 81, September 15, 2008, No. 14-15, pp. 6)*
Pub: Rogers Media Ltd.
Ed: Andrew Wahl. **Description:** Interview with Craig Muhlhauser who is the CEO of Celestica, a manufacturing company that provides services for the electronics sector; Muhlhauser discusses the company's restructuring program, which he feels was the secret to their surprising first-quarter results. Muhlhauser states that the company is operating with more forward visibility and that understanding the opportunities during the current economic situation presents the biggest challenge.

36990 ■ *"The Design of Things to Come" in Business Horizons (Vol. 51, January-February 2008, No. 1, pp. 74)*
Pub: Elsevier Advanced Technology Publications
Ed: Mimi Dollinger. **Description:** Review of the book that helps entrepreneurs develop and market new products, 'The Design of Things to Come: How Ordinary People Create Extraordinary Products'.

36991 ■ *Doing Business Anywhere: The Essential Guide to Going Global*
Pub: John Wiley and Sons, Inc.
Ed: Tom Travis. **Released:** 2007. **Price:** $24.95. **Description:** Plans are given for new or existing businesses to organize, plan, operate and execute a business on a global basis. Trade agreements, brand protection and patents, ethics, security as well as cultural issues are among the issues addressed.

36992 ■ *"Dropped Calls" in Canadian Business (Vol. 80, November 5, 2007, No. 22, pp. 34)*
Pub: Rogers Media
Ed: Andrew Wahl. **Description:** Control over Canada's telecommunications market by Telus, Rogers and Bell Canada has resulted in a small number of innovations. The pricing regimes of these carriers have also stifled innovations in the telecommunications industry. The status of Canada's telecommunications industry is further analyzed.

36993 ■ *Embedded Entrepreneurship: The Institutional Dynamics of Innovation*
Pub: Routledge
Ed: Alexander Ebner. **Released:** April 10, 2010. **Price:** $150.00. **Description:** In this book, Alexander Ebner reconstructs the theory of entrepreneurship from an institutional perspective.

36994 ■ *"Enforcer In Fantasyland" in Crain's New York Business (Vol. 24, February 25, 2008, No. 8, pp. 10)*
Pub: Crain Communications Inc.
Ed: Hilary Potkewitz. **Description:** Patent law, particularly in the toy and game industry, is recession-proof according to Barry Negrin, partner at Pryor Cashman. Negrin co-founded his patent practice group. Despite massive recalls of toys and the concern over toxic toys, legal measures are in place in this industry.

36995 ■ *Enlightened Leadership: Best Practice Guidelines and Time Tools for Easily Implementing Learning Organizations*
Pub: Learning House Publishing, Inc.
Ed: Ralph LoVuolo; Alan G. Thomas. **Released:** May 2006. **Price:** $79.99. **Description:** Innovation and creativity are essential for any successful small business. The book provides owners, managers, and team leaders with the tools necessary to produce 'disciplined innovation'.

36996 ■ *Enterprise, Entrepreneurship and Innovation: Concepts, Context and Commercialization*
Pub: Elsevier Science and Technology Books
Ed: Robin Lowe, Sue Marriott. **Released:** June 2006. **Price:** $39.95. **Description:** Application of enterprise, innovation and entrepreneurship are discussed to help companies grow.

36997 ■ *Enterprise Planning and Development: Small Business and Enterprise Start-Up Survival and Growth*
Pub: Elsevier Science and Technology Books
Ed: David Butler. **Released:** August 2006. **Price:** $42.95. **Description:** Innovation, intellectual property, and exit strategies are among the issues discussed in this book involving current entrepreneurship.

36998 ■ *"Entrepreneurial Orientation and Firm Performance" in Journal of Small Business and Entrepreneurship (Vol. 23, Winter 2010, No. 1)*
Pub: Canadian Council for Small Business and Entrepreneurship
Description: The article develops a theoretical model of the relationship between firm-level entrepreneurship and firm performance. This model is intended to further clarify the consequences of an 'entrepreneurial orientation', paying particular attention to the differential relationship that exists between the three sub-dimensions of entrepreneurial orientation and firm performance. Included in the theoretical model are other important variables (such as organizational structure and environmental characteristics) that may impact the EO-performance relationship. Propositions are developed regarding the various configura-

tions of the sub-dimensions of EO and organizational structure that would be most appropriate in a given environmental context. Future research may also benefit from considering the important role that organizational strategy and life cycle stage play in this model. The implications of this model for both researchers and managers are discussed.

36999 ■ *Entrepreneurship, Innovation and Economic Growth*
Pub: Edward Elgar Publishing, Incorporated
Ed: David B. Audretsch. **Released:** July 2006. **Price:** $145.00. **Description:** Links between entrepreneurship, innovation and economic growth are examined.

37000 ■ *The Facebook Era: Tapping Online Social Networks to Build Better Products, Reach New Audiences, and Sell More Stuff*
Pub: Prentice Hall
Ed: Clara Shih. **Price:** $24.99. **Description:** The '90s were about the World Wide Web of information and the power of linking Web pages. Today it's about the World Wide Web of people and the power of the social graph. Online social networks are fundamentally changing the way we live, work, and interact. They offer businesses immense opportunities to transform customer relationships for profit: opportunities that touch virtually every business function, from sales and marketing to recruiting, collaboration to executive decision-making, product development to innovation.

37001 ■ *"Facilitating and Rewarding Creativity During New Product Development" in Journal of Marketing (Vol. 75, July 2011, No. 4, pp. 53)*
Pub: American Marketing Association
Ed: James E. Burroughs, Darren W. Dahl, C. Page Moreau, Amitava Chattopadhay, Gerald J. Gorn. **Description:** A study to determine the effects of rewards to creativity in the process of new product development is presented. The findings show that the effect of rewards can be made positive if combined with appropriate creativity training.

37002 ■ *Facilitating Sustainable Innovation through Collaboration: A Multi-Stakeholder Perspective*
Pub: Springer
Ed: Joseph Sarkis, James J. Cordeiro, Diego Vazquez Brust. **Released:** March 10, 2010. **Price:** $169.00. **Description:** An international perspective of sustainable innovation with contributions from Australia, Europe, and North America, by prominent policy makers, scientific researchers and others.

37003 ■ *Fast Company's Greatest Hits: Ten Years of the Most Innovative Ideas in Business*
Pub: Penguin Group Incorporated
Ed: John Byrne; David Lidsky; Mark N. Vamos. **Released:** July 2006. **Price:** $24.95. **Description:** Offering of Fast Company's best articles covering business ideas and profiles of successful firms and their leaders.

37004 ■ *"Federal Fund Valuable Tool For Small-Biz Innovators" in Crain's Detroit Business (Vol. 24, September 29, 2008, No. 39, pp. 42)*
Pub: Crain Communications Inc.
Ed: Nancy Kaffer. **Description:** Grants from the Small Business Innovation Research Program, or SBIR grants, are federal funds that are set aside for 11 federal agencies to allocate to tech-oriented small-business owners. Firms such as Biotechnology Business Consultants help these companies apply for SBIR grants.

37005 ■ *"The Fences of a Patent" in Information Today (Vol. 26, February 2009, No. 2, pp. 13)*
Pub: Information Today, Inc.
Ed: George H. Pike. **Description:** Patent law is examined using the Blackboard course management software used by many colleges and universities as its example.

37006 ■ *"FinOvation 2009" in Farm Industry News (Vol. 42, January 1, 2009, No. 1)*
Pub: Penton Media Inc.
Contact: John French, President
Ed: Karen McMahon; David Hest; Mark Moore. **Description:** New and innovative products and technologies are presented.

37007 ■ *"Fledgling Brands May Take the Fall With Steve & Barry's" in Advertising Age (Vol. 79, July 7, 2008, No. 26, pp. 6)*
Pub: Crain Communications, Inc.
Ed: Natalie Zmuda. **Description:** Steve & Barry's, a retailer that holds licensing deals with a number of designers and celebrities, may have to declare bankruptcy; this leaves the fate of the retailer's hundreds of licensing deals and exclusive celebrity lines in question.

37008 ■ *"Flu is a Booster for Firms Here" in Philadelphia Business Journal (Vol. 28, September 25, 2009, No. 32, pp. 1)*
Pub: American City Business Journals
Ed: John George. **Description:** GlaxoSmithKline, AstraZeneca, CSL Biotherapies, and Sanofi Aventis were awarded contract by the US Government to supply swine flu vaccines. It is estimated that global sales of the vaccine could reach billions of dollars.

37009 ■ *"Flue Vaccines are Going Green" in Canadian Business (Vol. 83, September 14, 2010, No. 15, pp. 24)*
Pub: Rogers Media Ltd.
Ed: Angelia Chapman. **Description:** Quebec-based Medicago has found a solution to the bottleneck in the production of influenza vaccines by using plant-based processes instead of egg-based systems. Medicago's US Department of Defense funded research has produced the technology that speeds up the production time for vaccines by almost two-thirds. Insights into Medicago's patented process are also given.

37010 ■ *"Freeing the Wheels of Commerce" in Hispanic Business (July-August 2007, pp. 50, 52, 54)*
Pub: Hispanic Business
Ed: Keith Rosenblum. **Description:** SecureOrigins, a border-based partnership with high-tech innovators is working to move goods faster, more efficiently, and securely.

37011 ■ *"Fries With That?" in Canadian Business (Vol. 81, September 29, 2008, No. 16, pp. 33)*
Pub: Rogers Media Ltd.
Ed: Calvin Leung. **Description:** Profile of Toronto-based New York Fries, which has four stores in South Korea, is planning to expand further as well as into Hong Kong and Macau; the company also has a licensee in the United Arab Emirates whom is also planning to expand.

37012 ■ *From Concept To Consumer: How to Turn Ideas Into Money*
Pub: Pearson Education Inc.
Ed: Phil Baker. **Released:** 2009. **Price:** $24.99. **Description:** Renowned product developer Phil Baker explains how a great idea accounts for only 5 percent of all the factors of success and why the majority of success is dependent upon a myriad of other factors, including the time it takes to get to market, price, marketing and distribution. By being their own best competition, a small company can stay one step ahead of competitors.

37013 ■ *"Fueling Change" in Entrepreneur (Vol. 35, November 2007, No. 11, pp. 46)*
Pub: Entrepreneur Media Inc.
Ed: Carol Tice. **Description:** Creativity guru John Kao says the United States is complacent when it comes to business. He talks about how entrepreneurs should think innovatively in terms of big changes.

37014 ■ *"Full-Court Press for Apple" in Barron's (Vol. 88, March 24, 2008, No. 12, pp. 47)*
Pub: Dow Jones & Company, Inc.
Ed: Mark Veverka. **Description:** Apple Inc. is facing more intellectual property lawsuits in 2008, with 30 patent lawsuits filed compared to 15 in 2007 and nine in 2006. The lawsuits, which involve products such as the iPod and the iPhone, present some concern for Apple's shareholders.

37015 ■ *The Game-Changer: How You Can Drive Revenue and Profit Growth with Innovation*
Pub: Crown Business
Ed: A.G. Lafley, Ram Charan. **Released:** 2009. **Price:** $27.50. **Description:** Former Proctor and Gamble CEO A.G. Lafley outlines principles of innovation that turned the company around and shows how that strategy can work for any business.

37016 ■ *The Game Makers*
Pub: Harvard Business School Press
Ed: Philip E. Orbanes. **Released:** November 2003. **Price:** $29.95. **Description:** Profile of game expert and president of a specialty game company, author of books about games, Monopoly championship judge, senior vice president of research and development at Parker Brothers, and inventor of board and card games in highlighted.

37017 ■ *"GeckoSystems Reduces Sensor Fusion Costs Due to Elder Care Robot Trials" in Internet Wire (December 14, 2010)*
Pub: Comtex
Description: GeckoSystems International Corporation has been able to reduce the cost of its sensor fusion system while maintaining reliability and performance. The firm's ongoing first in-home elder care robot trials have sparked interest regarding its business model, technologies available for licensing, and joint domestic and international ventures.

37018 ■ *"German Win Through Sharing" in Canadian Business (Vol. 83, September 14, 2010, No. 15, pp. 16)*
Pub: Rogers Media Ltd.
Ed: Jordan Timm. **Description:** German economic historian Eckhard Hoffner has a two-volume work showing how German's relaxed attitude toward copyright and intellectual property helped it catch up to industrialized United Kingdom. Hoffner's research was in response to his interest in the usefulness of software patents. Information on the debate regarding Canada's copyright laws is given.

37019 ■ *"Getting Inventive With..Ed Spellman" in Crain's Cleveland Business (Vol. 28, October 22, 2007, No. 42, pp. 18)*
Pub: Crain Communications, Inc.
Ed: Kimberly Bonvissuto. **Description:** Profile featuring Ed Spellman, a mechanical engineer who decided to quit his job at Invacare Corp., a medical equipment manufacturer and distributor, in order to devote his full attention to promoting his numerous inventions, including the DV-Grip, a vehicle mount for portable DVD players.

37020 ■ *"Getting Inventive With..John Nottingham and John Spirk" in Crain's Cleveland Business (Vol. 28, October 22, 2007, No. 42, pp. 19)*
Pub: Crain Communications, Inc.
Ed: Kimberly Bonvissuto. **Description:** Profile featuring John Spirk and John Nottingham of the Cleveland-based firm, Nottingham-Spirk Design Associates; the company holds 486 issued and commercialized patents and has reported over $30 billion in new product sales.

37021 ■ *"Getting Inventive With..Richard Brindisi and Gregory Vittardi" in Crain's Cleveland Business (Vol. 28, October 22, 2007, No. 42)*
Pub: Crain Communications, Inc.
Ed: Kimberly Bonvissuto. **Description:** Profile of the SmartShopper, a handheld, voice-recognition device for dictating shopping and errand lists, and its creators, Richard G. Brindisi and Gregory Vittardi.

37022 ■ *"Getting the Word Out" in Modern Machine Shop (Vol. 84, September 2011, No. 4, pp. 16)*
Pub: Gardner Business Media, Inc.
Contact: Richard G. Kline, President
E-mail: rkline@gardnerweb.com
Ed: Derek Korn. **Description:** Many times machine shops create devices to streamline their own machin-

ing processes and find these devices can be used by other shops, thus developing a marketable product. Tips for this process are outlined.

37023 ■ *The Gridlock Economy: How Too Much Ownership Wrecks Markets, Stops Innovation, and Costs Lives*
Pub: Basic Books
Ed: Michael Heller. **Released:** 2009. **Price:** $26.00. **Description:** While private ownership generally creates wealth, the author believes that economic gridlock results when too many people own pieces of one thing, which results in too many people being able to block each other from creating or using a scarce source.

37024 ■ *"GTI Licenses TMC to Cannon Boiler Works" in Contractor (Vol. 56, December 2009, No. 12, pp. 6)*
Pub: Penton Media, Inc.
Description: Gas Technology Institute has licensed Cannon Boiler Works Inc. to use its transport membrane condenser technology. The technology can be applied to elevated-temperature industrial processes such as boilers. It allows the capture and beneficial use of latent waste heat and water vapor from exhaust/flue gas.

37025 ■ *"Harnessing the Wisdom of Crowds" in Entrepreneur (Vol. 37, September 2009, No. 9, pp. 74)*
Pub: Entrepreneur Media, Inc.
Ed: Mark Henricks. **Description:** Online customer service business Get Satisfaction has registered growth. The business enables customers to search for answers to common product questions. Customers use the service to post questions, complaints, and even product ideas.

37026 ■ *"The Hired Guns" in Business Courier (Vol. 26, November 13, 2009, No. 29, pp. 1)*
Pub: American City Business Journals, Inc.
Ed: Lisa Biank Fasig. **Description:** YourForce has nearly 6,000 retired scientists and researchers who work together in helping Procter & Gamble (P&G) and other companies in addressing various project needs. Operating as an online innovation community, YourEncore is a result of P&G's Connect Develop program.

37027 ■ *"Hispanic Executives Continue Their Rise to Prominence Amid a Shaky Economy" in Hispanic Business (January-February 2009, pp. 12-14)*
Pub: Hispanic Business
Ed: Michael Bowker. **Description:** Hispanic Business Media's 2009 Corporate Elite winners defied expectations and a tough economy and rose to the top of their industries; innovation being cited as key to growth of Hispanic-owned companies.

37028 ■ *"Honoring Creativity" in Playthings (Vol. 107, January 1, 2009, No. 1, pp. 28)*
Pub: Reed Business Information
Contact: Jeff Greisch, President
Ed: Cliff Annicelli. **Description:** Toy & Game Inventors Expo is held annually in conjunction with the Chicago Toy & Game Fair. The event honors toy inventors in the categories of Game Design, Toy Design and Rising Stars, plus a lifetime achievement award. Profile of the company, Toying With Games, founded by Joyce Johnson and Colleen McCarthy-Evans are included in the article.

37029 ■ *"How Hard Could It Be? Why the Most Important Innovations Are Often Those That Appear To Be Fatally Flawed" in Inc. (February 2008)*
Pub: Gruner & Jahr USA Publishing
Ed: Joel Spolsky. **Description:** Many times, things that seemed silly or impossible have become great innovations.

37030 ■ *"How Innovative Is Michigan? Index Aims To Keep Track" in Crain's Detroit Business (Vol. 24, February 4, 2008, No. 5, pp. 1)*
Pub: Crain Communications Inc. - Detroit
Ed: Chad Halcom. **Description:** Profile of the newly created 'Innovation Index', released by the University of Michigan-Dearborn. The report showed a combination of indicators that gauged innovation activity in the state slightly lower for second quarter 2007, but ahead of most levels for most of 2006. Statistical data included.

37031 ■ *"How to Save Good Ideas" in Harvard Business Review (Vol. 88, October 2010, No. 10, pp. 129)*
Pub: Harvard Business School Publishing
Ed: Jeff Kehoe. **Description:** Harvard Business School Professor John P. Kotter identifies situations that may hinder the development and implementation of ideas, and discusses effective ways to counter them.

37032 ■ *How to Start an Internet Sales Business*
Pub: Lulu.com
Ed: Dan Davis. **Released:** August 2005. **Price:** $19.95. **Description:** Small business guide for launching an Internet sales company. Topics include business structure, licenses, and taxes.

37033 ■ *How to Start and Run a Small Book Publishing Company: A Small Business Guide to Self-Publishing and Independent Publishing*
Pub: HCM Publishing
Ed: Peter I. Hupalo. **Released:** August 30, 2002. **Price:** $18.95. **Description:** The book teaches all aspects of starting and running a small book publishing company. Topics covered include: inventory accounting in the book trade, just-in-time inventory management, turnkey fulfillment solutions, tax deductible costs, basics of sales and use tax, book pricing, standards in terms of the book industry, working with distributors and wholesalers, cover design and book layout, book promotion and marketing, how to select profitable authors to publish, printing process, printing on demand, the power of a strong backlist, and how to value copyright.

37034 ■ *"Idea-Generation Program Creates Winning Programs" in Business Journal-Serving Metropolitan Kansas City (October 19, 2007)*
Pub: American City Business Journals, Inc.
Ed: James Dombrook. **Description:** Eureka Ranch has developed 'Eureka! Winning Ways', a program that helps companies create new ideas for their business. Brunson Instruments is the first Missouri manufacturer to engage in the program. The procedures in the new product idea generation program are supplied.

37035 ■ *"Ideas at Work: Sparkling Innovation" in Business Strategy Review (Vol. 21, Summer 2010, No. 2, pp. 7)*
Pub: Blackwell Publishers Ltd.
Ed: Julian Birkinshaw, Peter Robbins. **Description:** GlaxoSmithKline faced a situation common to large global organizations: how to allocate marketing resources to smaller, regional brands. A report on the company's inventive approach to worldwide marketing that led to the development of a unique and productive network are explored.

37036 ■ *"Ideas at Work: Sparkling Innovation" in Business Strategy Review (Vol. 21, Summer 2010, No. 2, pp. 07)*
Pub: Wiley-Blackwell
Ed: Julian Birkinshaw, Peter Robbins. **Description:** GlaxoSmithKline faced a situation common to large global organizations: how to allocate marketing resources to smaller, regional brands. The company's approach to worldwide marketing that led to the development of a unique and productive network is outlined.

37037 ■ *"Illinois Regulators Revoke Collection Agency's License" in Collections & Credit Risk (Vol. 15, August 1, 2010, No. 7, pp. 13)*
Pub: SourceMedia Inc.
Description: Creditors Service Bureau of Springfield, Illinois had its license revoked by a state regulatory agency and was fined $55,000 because the owner and president, Craig W. Lewis, did not turn over portions of collected funds to clients.

37038 ■ *"The Impact of Acquisitions On the Productivity of Inventors at Semiconductor Firms" in Academy of Management Journal (October 2007)*
Pub: Academy of Management
Contact: Ming-Jer Chen, President
Ed: Rahul Kapoor, Kwanghui Lim. **Description:** Study examined the relation between knowledge-based and incentive-based outlook in explaining the impact of acquisitions on the productivity of inventors at acquired semiconductor firms. Results showed a definite relation between the two perspectives.

37039 ■ *"In Search of the Next Big Thing: It's Out There - Just Waiting For You To Find It" in Inc. (Volume 32, December 2010, No. 10, pp. 34)*
Pub: Inc. Magazine
Ed: April Joyner. **Description:** Innovation is the future for small business. A new book, Inside Real Innovation: How the Right Approach Can Move Ideas from R&D to Market - And Get the Economy Moving helps to break down the process by which innovation occurs.

37040 ■ *Innov and Entrepren in Biotech*
Pub: Edward Elgar Publishing, Incorporated
Ed: Hine. **Released:** April 2006. **Price:** $100.00. **Description:** Innovation processes underlying successful entrepreneurship in the biotechnology sector are explored.

37041 ■ *Innovate to Great: Re-Igniting Sustainable Innovation to Win in the Global Economy*
Pub: McGraw-Hill
Ed: Judy Estrin. **Released:** September 12, 2008. **Price:** $27.95. **Description:** The author explores innovation and creativity as a means for small companies to survive and expand in the global economy.

37042 ■ *"Innovating Globally" in Business Strategy Review (Vol. 21, Spring 2010, No. 1, pp. 24)*
Pub: Wiley-Blackwell
Ed: Costas Markides, Stuart Crainer. **Description:** Costas Markides has spent over two decades studying business strategy and innovation. Recently, he has been focusing on the bigger picture of how people can address major social problems. Can the techniques used by managers to create innovation inside organizations work with global change?.

37043 ■ *"Innovating Low-Cost Business Models" in Strategy and Leadership (Vol. 39, March-April 2011, No. 2, pp. 43)*
Pub: Emerald Group Publishing Inc.
Ed: Nicholas Kachaner, Zhenya Lindgardt, David Michael. **Description:** A process that can be used to implement low-cost innovation is presented. The process can be used to address the competitive challenges presented by multinationals' practice of presenting applications and price points that are intended for developing markets into developed markets. The process involves targeting large, and low-income segments of the market.

37044 ■ *Innovation and Entrepreneurship*
Pub: Elsevier Science & Technology Books
Ed: Peter F. Drucker. **Released:** May 2007. **Price:** $27.95. **Description:** Profile of entrepreneurial innovation.

37045 ■ *Innovation and Entrepreneurship*
Pub: HarperInformation
Ed: Peter F. Drucker. **Released:** May 2006. **Price:** $16.99. **Description:** Innovation and entrepreneurship in America's new economy.

37046 ■ *Innovation and Entrepreneurship*
Pub: HarperCollins Publishers, Inc.
Ed: Peter F. Drucker. **Released:** May 2006. **Price:** $16.95. **Description:** Presentation of entrepreneurship and innovation and a purposeful and systematic discipline and the challenges and opportunities of the American entrepreneurial economy.

37047 ■ *Innovation and Its Discontents*
Pub: Princeton University Press

Ed: Josh Lerner, Adam B. Jaffe. **Released:** 2006. **Price:** $21.95 paperback. **Description:** According to the authors, America's patent system does not effectively serve as a generator and protector of patents and intellectual property.

37048 ■ *Innovation Methodologies in Enterprise Research*
Pub: Edward Elgar Publishing, Incorporated

Ed: Hine. **Released:** December 2006. **Price:** $75.00. **Description:** The importance of qualitative, interpretist research in the field of enterprise research is discussed. The book stresses how enterprise research is a new method and permits a wide scope for new and innovative research studies.

37049 ■ *Innovation Nation: How America Is Losing Its Innovation Edge, Why It Matters, and How We Can Get It Back*
Pub: Free Press/Simon & Schuster

Ed: John Kao. **Released:** October 2, 2007. **Price:** $26.00. **Description:** Diagnoses of the lack of innovation being seen in the United States today is examined by a former Harvard Business School professor. He explains how innovation works and puts forth a strategy proposal in an attempt to help America regain its edge on innovation.

37050 ■ *"Innovation Station" in Canadian Business (Vol. 80, October 8, 2007, No. 20, pp. 42)*
Pub: Rogers Media

Ed: Andrew Wahl. **Description:** Study and teaching of entrepreneurship at the University of Waterloo is discussed. Research projects in the university are expected to be influential in Canada's economic development. In spite of the success of these studies, financing is still a problem for the university, especially in technological innovations.

37051 ■ *"Innovation's Holy Grail" in Harvard Business Review (Vol. 88, July-August 2010, No. 7-8, pp. 132)*
Pub: Harvard Business School Publishing

Ed: C.K. Prahalad, R.A. Mashelkar. **Description:** Three forms of business innovation are presented, inspired by the tenets of Mahatma Gandhi. They are: changing organizational capabilities, sourcing or creating new capabilities, and disrupting conventional business models. Illustrations for these methods are also included.

37052 ■ *"Inside Out" in Playthings (Vol. 107, January 1, 2009, No. 1, pp. 3)*
Pub: Reed Business Information
Contact: Jeff Greisch, President

Description: Mattel signed on as the global master toy licensee for Cartoon Network's The Secret Saturdays while Toy Island signed a deal for wooden toys based on several leading Nick Jr. properties.

37053 ■ *International Growth of Small and Medium Enterprises*
Pub: Routledge

Ed: Nina Nummela. **Released:** February 10, 2010. **Price:** $110.00. **Description:** This volume focuses on how companies expand their operations across borders through opportunity exploration and exploitation, and identification and development of innovations.

37054 ■ *"Inventive Doctor New Venture Partner" in Houston Business Journal (Vol. 40, January 29, 2010, No. 38, pp. A2)*
Pub: American City Business Journals

Ed: Ford Gunter. **Description:** Dr. Billy Cohn, a surgeon from Houston, Texas has been named as venture partner for venture firm Sante Ventures LLC of Austin, Texas. Cohn will be responsible for seeing marketable developing technologies in the medical industry. The motivation for Cohn's naming as venture partner is his development of a minimally invasive therapy for end-stage renal disease.

37055 ■ *"Judge Gives RIM One Last Chance" in Globe & Mail (February 25, 2006, pp. B5)*
Pub: CTVglobemedia Publishing Inc.

Ed: Barrie McKenna; Paul Waldie. **Description:** United States District Court Judge James Spencer offers more time for Research In Motion Ltd. (RIM) to settle the patent infringement dispute with NTP Inc. RIM's shares increase by 6.2 percent following the decision.

37056 ■ *Jump Start Your Business Brain*
Pub: Brain Brew Books

Ed: Doug Hall, Tom Peters. **Released:** 2005. **Price:** $16.99 paperback. **Description:** Author focuses on helping small business owners to become more successful using simple tools that help them discover, develop, and identify great ideas.

37057 ■ *Jump Start Your Business Brain: Ideas, Advice and Insights for Immediate Marketing and Innovation Success*
Pub: Emmis Books
Contact: Richard Hunt, President
E-mail: rhunt@emmis.com

Ed: Doug Hall. **Released:** April 2005. **Price:** $23.99. **Description:** Strategies to improve sales, marketing, and business development.

37058 ■ *"Kaiser Permanente's Innovation on the Front Lines" in Harvard Business Review (Vol. 88, September 2010, No. 9, pp. 92)*
Pub: Harvard Business School Publishing

Ed: Lew McCreary. **Description:** Kaiser Permanente's human-centered model for organizational effectiveness emphasizes the roles of patients and providers as collaborators driving quality improvement and innovation.

37059 ■ *"Lawyers Sued Over Lapsed Lacrosse Patent" in Crain's Detroit Business (Vol. 25, June 8, 2009, No. 23, pp. 5)*
Pub: Crain Communications Inc. - Detroit

Ed: Chad Halcom. **Description:** Warrior Sports Inc., a manufacturer of lacrosse equipment located in Warren, Michigan is suing the law firm Dickinson Wright PLLC and two of its intellectual property lawyers over patent rights to lacrosse equipment.

37060 ■ *Life Entrepreneurs*
Pub: Jossey Bass

Ed: Christopher Gergen; Gregg Vanourek. **Released:** 2008. **Price:** $24.95. **Description:** Consultants Christopher Gergen and Gregg Vanourek present the basic principles for becoming a successful entrepreneur: recognizing opportunity, taking risks, and innovation.

37061 ■ *"Life's Work" in Harvard Business Review (Vol. 88, July-August 2010, No. 7-8, pp. 172)*
Pub: Harvard Business School Publishing

Ed: Alison Beard. **Description:** The founder of appliance company Dyson Ltd. discusses the role of making mistakes in learning and innovation, and emphasizes the importance of hands-on involvement to make a company successful.

37062 ■ *"The Little Insect" in Canadian Electronics (Vol. 23, June-July 2008, No. 4, pp. 6)*
Pub: Action Communication Inc.

Ed: Tim Gouldson. **Description:** Electronics designers should not be underestimated because they can manufacture technologies vital to saving lives and bringing peace. They have designed robots and other electronic equipment that are as small as insects.

37063 ■ *"Local Company Seeks Patent For Armored Trucks" in Crain's Detroit Business (Vol. 24, February 4, 2008, No. 5, pp. 10)*
Pub: Crain Communications Inc. - Detroit

Description: Profile of James LeBlanc Sr., mechanical engineer and defense contractor, discusses his eleven utility patents pending for a set of vehicles and subsystems that would work as countermeasures to explosively formed projectiles.

37064 ■ *"Look, Leap, and License" in Retail Merchandiser (Vol. 51, July-August 2011, No. 4, pp. 16)*
Pub: Phoenix Media Corporation
Description: Toys highlighting the Licensing International Expo 2011 included a life-sized Cookie Monster, Papa Smurf, Power Rangers, Transformer, and margarita wrestlers. Taking licensed properties international was a common theme at this year's show.

37065 ■ *"Look Out, Barbie, Bratz are Back" in Canadian Business (Vol. 83, August 17, 2010, No. 13-14, pp. 18)*
Pub: Rogers Media Ltd.
Ed: Joe Castaldo. **Description:** California-based MGA Entertainment has wrestled back control over Bratz from Mattel after a six-year legal battle. However, MGA owner Isaac Larian could still face legal hurdles if Mattel pursues a retrial. He now has to revive the brand which virtually disappeared from stores when Mattel won the rights for Bratz.

37066 ■ *"MaggieMoo's Ice Cream and Treatery" in Ice Cream Reporter (Vol. 23, September 20, 2010, No. 10, pp. 7)*
Pub: Ice Cream Reporter
Description: MaggieMoo's Ice Cream and Treatery has launched a new Website where visitors can learn about the brands newest ice cream innovations.

37067 ■ *Market Rebels: How Activists Make or Break Radical Innovations*
Pub: Princeton University Press
Ed: Hayagreeva Rao. **Released:** 2009. **Price:** $24.95. **Description:** Informal groups of enthusiasts could be the key to making a new product the next big thing to hit the marketplace.

37068 ■ *Medici Effect*
Pub: Harvard Business School Press
Ed: Frans Johansson. **Released:** October 30. 2006. **Price:** $16.00. **Description:** Examples of how ideas can be turned into path-breaking innovations.

37069 ■ *"Mentor Medical Device Maker's Partnerships Open New Opportunities" in Crain's Cleveland Business (Vol. 30, June 22, 2009, No. 24)*
Pub: Crain Communications, Inc.
Ed: Chuck Soder. **Description:** Frantz Medical Development Ltd. develops medical devices based on ideas from outside inventors. The company wants to manufacture the innovations at its Mentor campus.

37070 ■ *"Molycorp Funds Wind Energy Technology Company" in Manufacturing Close-Up (September 19, 2011)*
Pub: Close-Up Media
Description: Molycorp Inc., producer of rare earth oxides (REO) and a REO producer outside of China, announced it will invest in Boulder Wind Power, which has designed a rare earth magnet powered wind turbine generator. This new generator can produce electricity as low as $0.04 per Kilowatt Hour. Boulder Wind Power's patented wind turbine technology allows for use of rare earth permanent magnets that do not require dysprosium, which is relatively scarce.

37071 ■ *"Mosaid Grants First Wireless Parent License To Matsushita" in Canadian Electronics (Vol. 23, June-July 2008, No. 5, pp. 1)*
Pub: Action Communication Inc.
Description: Matsushita Electric Industrial Co. Ltd. has been granted a six-and-a-half-year license by Mosaid Technologies Inc. to manufacture the latter's products. The patent portfolio license agreement covers Mosaid's Wi-Fi, Wi-Max, CDMA-enabled notebook computers and other products.

37072 ■ *"The Natural Environment, Innovation, and Firm Performance" in Family Business Review (Vol. 19, December 2006, No. 4)*
Pub: Family Firm Institute
Contact: Judy L. Green, President
Ed: Justin Craig, Clay Dibrell. **Description:** Comparative study of the impact of firm-level natural environment-related policies on innovation and performance of family and non-family firms is presented.

37073 ■ *"New Approach Could Boost Ivory Tower Innovation" in Business Journal-Portland (Vol. 24, November 16, 2007, No. 37, pp. 1)*
Pub: American City Business Journals, Inc.
Ed: Aliza Earnshaw. **Description:** New approach which aims to help universities move to a corporate structure, secure funds, and find professional managers is being explored. Accelerator Corporation was able to help six companies through its funding. Joe Tanous who is behind Oregon's State University's enhanced commercialization, would like to apply the same approach Accelerator used to help Oregon State University, the University of Oregon, Portland State University and Oregon Health and Science University.

37074 ■ *The New Innovators: How Canadians are Shaping the Knowledge-Based Economy*
Pub: James Lorimer & Company Ltd.
Ed: Roger Voyer; Patti Ryan. **Released:** January 1, 1994. **Price:** $29.95. **Description:** Details are examined showing how the innovation process works and how ideas are successfully translated into marketable products.

37075 ■ *"New Life for Old Chemistries" in Farm Industry News (Vol. 42, January 1, 2009, No. 1)*
Pub: Penton Media Inc.
Contact: John French, President
Ed: Mark Moore. **Description:** To expand the uses of familiar crop protection products, chemical companies are utilizing biotechnology research and development tools; many off-patent products are being rejuvenated with small changes to make the product even better than it was when originally conceived.

37076 ■ *"The Next Great Canadian Idea?" in Canadian Business (Vol. 81, July 21, 2008, No. 11, pp. 45)*
Pub: Rogers Media Ltd.
Ed: Sharda Prashad. **Description:** Thane Heins has invented a generator that produces energy in an isolated system which contradicts the law of conservation of energy. Perepiteia generator is referred to as a 'perpetual motion machine.' Other inventions slated for the Canadian invention competition include Rob Matthies' batteries and Frank Naumann's Smart Trap.

37077 ■ *"The Next Step in Patent Reform" in Information Today (Vol. 28, November 2011, No. 10, pp. 1)*
Pub: Information Today, Inc.
Ed: George H. Pike. **Description:** The Leahy-Smith America Invents Act was signed into law in September 2011. The new act reformed the previous US patent system. Information involving the new patent law process is discussed.

37078 ■ *"Nike's Next Splash" in The Business Journal-Portland (Vol. 25, August 22, 2008, No. 24, pp. 1)*
Pub: American City Business Journals, Inc.
Ed: Erik Siemers. **Description:** Business analysts expect Nike to bid for the endorsement services of swimmer Michael Phelps after the swimmer's contract with Speedo expires. The company, however, is a lightweight in the swimming apparel market and is not focusing on swimming as a growth sector.

37079 ■ *"No Lines, No Waiting" in The Business Journal-Serving Greater Tampa Bay (Vol. 28, August 15, 2008, No. 34, pp. 1)*
Pub: American City Business Journals, Inc.
Ed: Jane Meinhardt. **Description:** Voda LLC, which was founded to commercialize developments by David Fries, develops outdoor sensor networks used for environmental monitoring by markets like research, the security industry, and the government. Fries already licensed 12 technologies for clients for about $130,000 per technology. Other information on Voda LLC is presented.

37080 ■ *"Of Marks and Men" in Canadian Business (Vol. 80, March 12, 2007, No. 6, pp. 59)*
Pub: Rogers Media
Ed: Andy Holloway. **Description:** The importance on the part of business enterprises to register for trademarks to avoid any threat of litigation in future is discussed.

37081 ■ *"Organization Redesign and Innovative HRM" in Human Resource Management (Vol. 49, July-August 2010, No. 4, pp. 809-811)*
Pub: John Wiley
Ed: Pat Lynch. **Description:** An overview of the book, 'Organization Redesign and Innovative HRM' is presented.

37082 ■ *"Patent Pain" in Canadian Business (Vol. 80, November 19, 2007, No. 23, pp. 43)*
Pub: Rogers Media
Ed: Andrew Wahl. **Description:** James McBride of World Standard Fitness has prepared a patent for his invention, a rubberized lifting strap. The patent helped raid interest for the product, however other similar products have already been available in the market. Benefits of having an invention patented are examined.

37083 ■ *"Patently Absurd" in Globe & Mail (January 28, 2006, pp. B4)*
Pub: CTVglobemedia Publishing Inc.
Ed: Barrie McKenna; Paul Waldie; Simon Avery. **Description:** An overview of facts about patent dispute between Research In Motion Ltd. and NTP Inc. is presented.

37084 ■ *"Patently (Un)Clear" in Business Strategy Review (Vol. 21, Spring 2010, No. 1, pp. 28)*
Pub: Wiley-Blackwell
Ed: Markus Reitzig, Stefan Wagner. **Description:** After developing a great product or process, it's important to protect it. The benefits of using internal patent lawyers versus outsourcing the task are examined.

37085 ■ *Patent's Handbook: A Guide for Inventors and Researchers to Searching Patent Documents and Preparing and Making an Application*
Pub: McFarland & CPI, Publishers
Contact: Shelia Baldwin, Manager
E-mail: sbaldwin@mcfarlandpub.com
URL(s): www.mcfarlandpub.com. **Price:** $39.95, Individuals softcover. **Publication includes:** List of information sources for researching patents and inventorship. Principal content of publication is an overview of the patent system in the United States. **Database includes:** Diagrams, facsimiles, appendix. **Indexes:** Master.

37086 ■ *Payback: Reaping the Rewards of Innovation*
Pub: Harvard Business School Publishing
Ed: James P. Andrew; Harold L. Sirkin; John Butman. **Released:** January 9, 2007. **Price:** $29.95. **Description:** Three different business innovation models are presented: integration, orchestration, and serving as licensor.

37087 ■ *"PGA Tour: Course Management" in Retail Merchandiser (Vol. 51, September-October 2011, No. 5, pp. 38)*
Pub: Phoenix Media Corporation
Ed: Eric Slack. **Description:** PGA Tour must reach new customers and solidify relationships with its traditional base in order to continue its success. The PGA brand equity has translated into one of the largest retail licensing operations worldwide.

37088 ■ *"Pick A Trademark You Can Protect" in Women Entrepreneur (November 3, 2008)*
Pub: Entrepreneur Media Inc.
Ed: Nina L. Kaufman. **Description:** Provides information regarding trademarks, how to choose a name that will win approval from the U.S. Patent and Trademark Office, and how to choose a trademark that one can protect.

37089 ■ *"Pioneering Strategies for Entrepreneurial Success" in Business Horizons (Vol. 51, January-February 2008, No. 1, pp. 21)*
Pub: Elsevier Advanced Technology Publications
Ed: Candida G. Brush. **Description:** Entrepreneurs are known for new products, services, processes, markets and industries. In order to achieve success, they have to develop a clear vision, creatively manage finances, and use social skills to persuade others to commit to the venture. Pioneering strategies and their implementation are examined.

37090 ■ *"A Practical Approach to Addressing Holdover Ex-Franchisee Trademark Issues" in Franchise Law Journal (Vol. 27, Summer 2007, No. 1)*
Pub: American Bar Association
Contact: Carolyn Lamm, President
Ed: Christopher P. Bussert, William M. Bryner. **Description:** Franchisor-franchisee relationships can become legally complicated when they are terminated. Laws governing trademarks and other proprietary materials are examined.

37091 ■ *"Presidential Address: Innovation in Retrospect and Prospect" in Canadian Journal of Electronics (Vol. 43, November 2010, No. 4)*
Pub: Journal of the Canadian Economics Association
Ed: James A. Brander. **Description:** Has innovation slowed in recent decades? While there has been progress in information and communications technology, the recent record of innovation in agriculture, energy, transportation and healthcare sectors is cause for concern.

37092 ■ *"Probability Processing Chip: Lyric Semiconductor" in Inc. (Volume 32, December 2010, No. 10, pp. 52)*
Pub: Inc. Magazine
Ed: Christine Lagorio. **Description:** Lyric Semiconductor, a start up located in Cambridge, Massachusetts, has developed a computer chip that also uses values that fall between zero and one, resulting in a chip that can process information using probabilities, considering many possible answers that find the best fit.

37093 ■ *"Profile: Lynda Gratton" in Business Strategy Review (Vol. 21, Autumn 2010, No. 3, pp. 74)*
Pub: Wiley-Blackwell
Ed: Stuart Crainer. **Description:** The early 20th Century marked the dawn of modern enterprise management, and no one influenced its practice more than Frederick W. Taylor, inventor of 'scientific management'. This radical transformation of management and among the few thinkers most influencing this transformation is Lynda Gratton, London Business School Professor of Management Practice.

37094 ■ *"Providing Expertise Required to Develop Microsystems" in Canadian Electronics (Vol. 23, February 2008, No. 1, pp. 6)*
Pub: CLB Media Inc.
Ed: Ian McWalter. **Description:** CMC Microsystems, formerly Canadian Microelectronics Corporation, is focused on empowering microelectronics and Microsystems research in Canada. Microsystems offers the basis for innovations in the fields of science, environment, technology, automotives, energy, aerospace and communications technology. CMC's strategy in developing Microsystems in Canada is described.

37095 ■ *"The Quest for the Smart Prosthetic" in Canadian Business (Vol. 83, October 12, 2010, No. 17, pp. 26)*
Pub: Rogers Media Ltd.
Ed: Jacqueline Nelson. **Description:** Information about a two-year research project led by Southern Methodist University (SMU) and funded by the Defense Advance Research Projects Agency (DARPA) is provided. The agency aims to create a 'smart prosthetic' which will improve the lives of military amputees. The planned prosthetic will use a sensor that can carry nerve signals through synthetic channels.

37096 ■ *"Radiant Commences In-Lab Testing for US Air Mobility Command" in Canadian*

Corporate News (May 16, 2007)
Pub: Comtex News Network Inc.
Description: The Boeing Company will be conducting in-lab infrared material testing for the Radiant Energy Corporation, developer and marketer of InfraTek, the environmentally friendly, patented infrared pre-flight aircraft deicing system.

37097 ■ *"Realtors Signing Out" in The Business Journal-Serving Metropolitan Kansas City (Vol. 27, November 21, 2008, No. 11, pp. 1)*
Pub: American City Business Journals, Inc.
Ed: Rob Roberts. **Description:** The Kansas City Regional Association of Realtors has lost 1,000 of its members due to the downturn in the housing market. Applications for realtor licenses have dropped by 159 percent. Changes in Missouri's licensing requirements are seen as additional reasons for the declines.

37098 ■ *"Region to Be Named Innovation Hub" in Business Courier (Vol. 27, July 2, 2010, No. 9, pp. 1)*
Pub: Business Courier
Ed: Dan Monk. **Description:** The selection of Cincinnati's consumer-marketing cluster as a 'Hub of Innovation' by the Ohio Department of Development could boost Cincinnati's chances of receiving $100 million in grants from Ohio's Third Frontier program and other funding sources. Implications of the University of Cincinnati's designation as a Center of Excellence in Advanced Transportation and Aerospace are also discussed.

37099 ■ *"Regulators Revoke Mann Bracken's Collection Agency Licenses" in Collections & Credit Risk (Vol. 15, September 1, 2010, No. 8, pp. 19)*
Pub: SourceMedia Inc.
Description: Maryland regulators have revoked the collections licenses of defunct law firm Mann Bracken LLP.

37100 ■ *Remix: Making Art and Commerce Thrive in the Hybrid Economy*
Pub: Penguin Group USA Inc.
Ed: Lawrence Lessig. **Released:** 2009. **Price:** $25.95. **Description:** An examination of copyright laws in the digital age.

37101 ■ *"Rep. Loretta Sanchez Holds a Hearing on Small Business Cyber Security" in Political/Congressional Transcript Wire (July 29, 2010)*
Pub: CQ Roll Call
Description: U.S. House Committee on Armed Services, Subcommittee on Terrorism, Unconventional Threats and Capabilities held a hearing on small business cyber security innovation.

37102 ■ *"Rethinking the Organization" in Strategy & Leadership (Vol. 38, September-October 2010, No. 5, pp. 13-19)*
Pub: Emerald Inc.
Ed: Stephen Denning. **Description:** A study identifies the changes needed to be adopted by top managers to achieve game-changing innovation at an organization-wide level. Findings indicate that CEOs should practice pull management in order to nurture fruitful communication between employees and customers and achieve organizational involvement of customers.

37103 ■ *"RIM Says It's Willing to Cut a Check" in Globe & Mail (February 24, 2006, pp. B1)*
Pub: CTVglobemedia Publishing Inc.
Ed: Simon Avery. **Description:** The settlement terms proposed by Research In Motion Ltd. in a patent infringement case with NTP Inc. are presented.

37104 ■ *"RIM's Test of Faith" in Canadian Business (Vol. 80, April 9, 2007, No. 8, pp. 29)*
Pub: Rogers Media
Ed: Joe Castaldo. **Description:** The growth of Research In Motion Ltd. in terms of its sales and profits despite a patent suit on it and competition of rivals is discussed.

37105 ■ *Risk Takers and Innovators, Great Canadian Business Ventures Since 1950*
Pub: Altitude Publishing
Ed: Sandra Phinney. **Released:** June 15, 2004. **Price:** $7.95. **Description:** Successful business leaders share their creativity, technology skills, and entrepreneurship.

37106 ■ *"Safer Ammonium-Nitrate-Based Fertilizer" in Farm Industry News (Vol. 42, January 1, 2009, No. 1)*
Pub: Penton Media Inc.
Contact: John French, President
Description: Honeywell has patented a new technology which it will use to develop a highly effective, safer ammonium-nitrate-based fertilizer that has a significantly lower potential for explosion.

37107 ■ *"Second Cup?" in Canadian Business (Vol. 81, July 21, 2008, No. 11, pp. 50)*
Pub: Rogers Media Ltd.
Ed: Calvin Leung. **Description:** Profile of James Gosling who is credited as the inventor of the Java programming language; however, the 53-year-old software developer feels ambivalent for being credited as inventor since many people contributed to the language. Netscape and Sun Microsystems incorporation of the programming language into Java is presented.

37108 ■ *"Serials Solutions Launches 360 Resource Manager Consortium Edition" in Information Today (Vol. 26, February 2009, No. 2, pp. 32)*
Pub: Information Today, Inc.
Description: Serials Solutions new Serials Solutions 360 Resource Manager Consortium Edition helps consortia, groups and member libraries with their e-resource management services. The products allows users to consolidate e-resource metadata and acquisition information into one place, which enables groups to manage holdings, subscriptions, licensing, contacts, and cost information and to streamline delivery of information to members.

37109 ■ *"The Service Imperative" in Business Horizons (Vol. 51, January-February 2008, No. 1, pp. 39)*
Pub: Elsevier Advanced Technology Publications
Ed: Mary Jo Bitner, Stephen W. Brown. **Description:** The importance of services is growing in developing countries like India and China, but little attention is given to service research, education and innovation. The 'service imperative' seeks to promote the advancement of services. The scope, objectives and philosophy of the service imperative platform are outlined.

37110 ■ *"Shedding Light on Innovation" in Rental Product News (Vol. 33, June 2011)*
Pub: Cygnus Business Media
Ed: Rod Dickens. **Description:** Light tower manufacturers have introduced numerous new products that feature alternative power sources, LED lighting and a second generation of performance and value.

37111 ■ *"Sinai Doctor Seeks FDA OK for Drug" in Baltimore Business Journal (Vol. 28, July 16, 2010, No. 10, pp. 1)*
Pub: Baltimore Business Journal
Ed: Emily Mullin. **Description:** Paul Gurbel, Sinai Hospital Center for Thrombosis Research director, is seeking an FDA approval of Brilinta, a drug which he helped create and test. Gurbel says that the approval could bring the drug to market as early as December 2010. The drug is expected to rival Bristol-Myers' Plavix, which generated almost $6.2 billion in 2009.

37112 ■ *"Singapore Airlines' Balancing Act" in Harvard Business Review (Vol. 88, July-August 2010, No. 7-8, pp. 145)*
Pub: Harvard Business School Publishing
Ed: Loizos Heracleous, Jochen Wirtz. **Description:** Singapore Airlines is used as an illustration of organizational effectiveness. The article includes the firm's 4-3-3 rule of spending, its promotion of centralized as well as decentralized innovation, use of technology, and strategic planning.

37113 ■ *"The Sky's the Limit" in Retail Merchandiser (Vol. 51, July-August 2011, No. 4, pp. 64)*
Pub: Phoenix Media Corporation
Ed: John Capizzi. **Description:** Mars Retail Group (MRG) is the licensing division handling M&M's Brand Candies. Since taking over the brand they have expanded from 12 licensees to 50 licensees with new offerings.

37114 ■ *"Slick Science" in Canadian Business (Vol. 81, September 15, 2008, No. 14-15, pp. 55)*
Pub: Rogers Media Ltd.
Ed: Andrew Nikiforuk. **Description:** N-Solv Corp's John Nenniger has discovered a better alternative to steam-assisted gravity drainage methods for extracting bitumen. Nenniger's technique also relies on gravity but replaces steam with propane, which leaves behind impurities like asphaltenes and heavy metals that are too dirty to burn.

37115 ■ *Small Business: Innovation, Problems and Strategies*
Pub: Nova Science Publishers, Inc.
Ed: John E. Michaels, Leonardo F. Piraro. **Released:** April 1, 2009. **Price:** $89.00. **Description:** Innovation is a fundamental determinant of value creation in businesses and can also be a key to successful economic growth. The innovative process and innovative effort of small companies are examined and evaluated, along with alternative strategies.

37116 ■ *Small Business Legal Tool Kit*
Pub: Entrepreneur Press
Ed: Ira Nottonson; Theresa A. Pickner. **Released:** May 2007. **Price:** $36.95. **Description:** Legal expertise is provided by two leading entrepreneurial attorneys. Issues covered include forming and operating a business: taxes, contracts, leases, bylaws, trademarks, small claims court, etc.

37117 ■ *"A Sports Extravaganza - To Go" in Canadian Business (Vol. 79, June 19, 2006, No. 13, pp. 21)*
Pub: Rogers Media
Ed: Andy Holloway. **Description:** Television broadcasting industry in Canada utilizing advanced technologies like mobile television and internet protocol television in broadcasting major sports events. Large number of new technologies are being invented to support increasing demand.

37118 ■ *"Steve Meginniss Helped Reinvent the Toothbrush. Can He Do the Same Thing for Wheels?" in Inc. (February 2008, pp. 32)*
Pub: Gruner & Jahr USA Publishing
Ed: Dalia Fahmy. **Description:** Profile of Steve Meginniss, co-inventor of Sonicare Toothbrush and inventor of a two-gear wheel for wheelchairs. Mgeinniss discusses his need to raid $1 million to promote and cut manufacturing costs for this new product that helps reduce pain for users.

37119 ■ *"Stop the Innovation Wars" in Harvard Business Review (Vol. 88, July-August 2010, No. 7-8, pp. 76)*
Pub: Harvard Business School Publishing
Ed: Vijay Govindarajan, Chris Trimble. **Description:** Methods for managing conflicts between partners during the innovation initiative process are highlighted. These include dividing the labor, assembling a dedicated team, and mitigating likelihood for any potential conflict.

37120 ■ *"Street Beaters: How the Top Stock Earners on Our List Pulled It Off" in Canadian Business (Vol. 80, Winter 2007, No. 24, pp. 135)*
Pub: Rogers Media
Ed: Jeff Sanford. **Description:** Shares of Research in Motion Ltd. jumped 163 percent in 2007 after setting their patent dispute. ShawCor Ltd.'s stocks rose 99.6 percent while Onex Corporation's shares reached a high of $41.25 in 2007 from its $25 average in 2006.

37121 ■ *"Study Puts Hub On Top of the Tech Heap" in Boston Business Journal (Vol. 30, November 26, 2010, No. 44, pp. 1)*
Pub: Boston Business Journal
Ed: Galen Moore. **Description:** The Ewing Marion Kauffman Foundation ranked Massachusetts at the top in its evaluations of states' innovative industries, government leadership, and education. Meanwhile, research blog formDs.com also ranked Massachusetts number one in terms of venture-capital financings per capita.

37122 ■ *SuperCorp: How Vanguard Companies Create Innovation, Profits, Growth, and Social Good*
Pub: Crown Business
Ed: Rosabeth Moss Kanter. **Released:** 2009. **Price:** $27.50. **Description:** Harvard professor makes a persuasive case showing how social good is good for any company's bottom line.

37123 ■ *"The 'Supply Side' of the Auto Industry" in Montly Labor Review (Vol. 133, September 2010, No. 9, pp. 72)*
Pub: Bureau of Labor Statistics
Description: Restructuring and geographic change in the automobile industry is discussed.

37124 ■ *"Tastee-Freez Celebrates 60th Anniversary" in Ice Cream Reporter (Vol. 23, July 20, 2010, No. 8, pp. 2)*
Pub: Ice Cream Reporter
Description: Tastee-Freez founders, Leo Moranz (inventor) and Harry Axene, an inventor partnered to market the soft-serve pump and freezer for serving frozen treats back in 1950.

37125 ■ *Technological Entrepreneurship*
Pub: Edward Elgar Publishing, Incorporated
Ed: Donald Siegel. **Released:** October 2006. **Price:** $230.00. **Description:** Technological entrepreneurship at universities is discussed. The book covers four related topics: university licensing and patenting; science parks and incubators; university-based startups; and the role of academic science in entrepreneurship.

37126 ■ *"Think Disruptive! How to Manage In a New Era of Innovation" in Strategy & Leadership (Vol. 38, July-August 2010, No. 4, pp. 5-10)*
Pub: Emerald Inc.
Ed: Brian Leavy, John Sterling. **Description:** The views expressed by Scott Anthony, president of an innovation consultancy Innosight, on the need for corporate leaders to apply disruptive innovation in a recessionary environment are presented. His suggestion that disruptive innovation is the only way to survive during the economic crisis is discussed.

37127 ■ *"Time for a Leap Of Faith?" in Women Entrepreneur (November 18, 2008)*
Pub: Entrepreneur Media Inc.
Ed: Cynthia McKay. **Description:** Starting a new business, despite the downturn in the economy, can prove to be a successful endeavor if one has the time, energy and most importantly a good idea.

37128 ■ *The Tipping Point*
Pub: Back Bay/Little, Brown
Ed: Malcom Gladwell. **Price:** $14.95. **Description:** How and why certain products and ideas become fads.

37129 ■ *The Tipping Point: How Little Things Can Make a Big Difference*
Pub: Little Brown & Company
Ed: Malcolm Gladwell. **Released:** January 2002. **Price:** $14.95. **Description:** Correlation between societal changes and marketing and business trends.

37130 ■ *"Tool Time" in Entrepreneur (Vol. 36, March 2008, No. 3, pp. 90)*
Pub: Entrepreneur Media Inc.
Ed: Nichole A. Torres. **Description:** DaVinci Institute holds an annual event in Colorado to display new products and inventions. Innovative Design Engineering Animation is a consulting company that helps inventors develop product through various stages. NineSigma Inc. has an online marketplace where inventors can post ideas for clients needing new products.

37131 ■ *Trade-Off: The Ever-Present Tension Between Quality and Conscience*
Pub: Crown Business Books
Ed: Kevin Maney. **Released:** August 17, 2010. **Price:** $15.00. **Description:** The tension between fidelity (the quality of a consumer's experience) and convenience (the ease of getting and paying for a product) are shown to be the forces that determine the success or failure of new products and services in the marketplace.

37132 ■ *Trademarkscan--International Register*
Pub: Thomson CompuMark Americas
Contact: Richard J. Harrington, President
URL(s): compumark.thomson.com. **Released:** Semimonthly **Entries include:** Trademark word and/or design reference, current status, international class(-es), description of product/service, registration number, publication details, owner name/location. **Database covers:** Over 445,000 active registered trademarks on file at the World Intellectual Property Organization. Also included are inactive records from the last 3 years.

37133 ■ *"Under Armour Wants to Equip Athletes, Too" in Boston Business Journal (Vol. 29, July 8, 2011, No. 9, pp. 1)*
Pub: American City Business Journals Inc.
Ed: Ryan Sharrow. **Description:** Baltimore sportswear maker Under Armour advances plans to enter into the equipment field, aiming to strengthen its hold on football, basketball and lacrosse markets where it already has a strong market share. The company is now cooking up licensing deals to bolster the firm's presence among athletes.

37134 ■ *"U.S. Trade Body Clears Apple in Patent Case" in Wall Street Journal Eastern Edition (November 23 , 2011, pp. C1)*
Pub: Dow Jones & Company Inc. Enterprise Media Group
Contact: Clare Hart, President
Ed: Matt Jarzemsky, Paul Mozur. **Description:** HTC Corporation alleged in its patent-infringement case against Apple Inc. that Apple violated patents of S3 Graphics Inc., a company which was acquired by HTC Corporation. Now the International Trade Commission has issued a ruling saying that Apple did not violate the patents.

37135 ■ *"Universal Music Sues Grooveshark's Parent" in Wall Street Journal Eastern Edition (November 22 , 2011, pp. B5)*
Pub: Dow Jones & Company Inc.
Ed: Ethan Smith. **Description:** Escape Media Group Inc., the parent company of online-music service Grooveshark, and seven of its executives have been sued by Universal Music Group, which alleges patent infringement involving its sound recordings. The executives are alleged to have uploaded thousands of songs onto Grooveshark.

37136 ■ *"Unlicensed Utah Collection Agency Settles with Idaho Department of Finance" in Idaho Business Review, Boise (July 15, 2010)*
Pub: Idaho Business Review
Description: Federal Recovery Acceptance Inc., doing business as Paramount Acceptance in Utah, agreed to pay penalties and expenses after the firm was investigated by the state for improprieties. The firm was charged with conducting unlicensed collection activity.

37137 ■ *"The Valuation of Players" in Canadian Business (Vol. 80, October 22, 2007, No. 21, pp. 39)*
Pub: Rogers Media
Ed: Jeff Sanford. **Description:** Business professionals are supplementing their Masters in Business Administration degrees with CBV or chartered business valuator. CBVs are trained, not only in business tangibles, but also in business intangibles such as market position, reputation, intellectual property, and patent. Details of employment opportunities for chartered business valuators are discussed.

37138 ■ *"Viewing Ironman As Gold, R.I. Firm Buys Its Parent" in The Business Journal-Serving Greater Tampa Bay (Vol. 28, September 19, 2008)*
Pub: American City Business Journals, Inc.
Ed: Pete Williams. **Description:** Providence Equity Partners purchased World Triathlon Corp., parent company of the Ironman Triathlon, for an undisclosed sum. The acquisition means that the World Triathlon Headquarters will move to Tampa, Florida, and allows Providence Equity Partners to stage or license rights to Ironman and half-Ironman distance events.

37139 ■ *"Wall Street Is No Friend to Radical Innovation" in Harvard Business Review (Vol. 88, July-August 2010, No. 7-8, pp. 28)*
Pub: Harvard Business School Publishing
Ed: Julia Kirby. **Description:** Research indicates that investors are skittish about backing a business that proposes significant changes to its product or service status quo.

37140 ■ *"Water Distiller" in Canadian Business (Vol. 81, September 29, 2008, No. 16, pp. 52)*
Pub: Rogers Media Ltd.
Ed: Matthew McClearn. **Description:** Les Fairn's invention of a water distiller called a Solarsphere was recognized in the Great Canadian Invention Competition. Fairn's invention resembles a buoy that uses the sun's energy to vaporize dirty water then leaves the impurities behind in a sump. The invention has an application for producing potable water in impoverished countries.

37141 ■ *"What Players in the Midmarket Are Talking About" in Mergers & Acquisitions: The Dealmaker's Journal (March 1, 2008)*
Pub: SourceMedia, Inc.
Description: Sports Properties Acquisition Corp. went public at the end of January; according to the company's prospectus, it is not limiting its focus to just teams, it is also considering deals for stadium construction companies, sports leagues, facilities, sports-related advertising and licensing of products, in addition to other related segments.

37142 ■ *"When and How to Innovate Your Business Model" in Strategy & Leadership (Vol. 38, July-August 2010, No. 4, pp. 17-26)*
Pub: Emerald Inc.
Ed: Edward Giesen, Eric Riddleberger, Richard Christner, Ragna Bell. **Description:** A study uses survey data to identify factors that are considered by corporate leaders regarding when and how they should innovate their business model. Findings identify a set of characteristics called the 'Three A's, Namely, Aligned, Analytical and Adaptable, which corporate leaders use consistently to successfully design and execute business-model innovation.

37143 ■ *"When R&D Spending Is Not Enough" in Human Resource Management (Vol. 49, July-August 2010, No. 4, pp. 767-792)*
Pub: John Wiley
Ed: Sheng Wang, Rebecca M. Guidice, Judith W. Tansky, Zhong-Ming Wang. **Description:** A study was conducted to examine the effect of contextual contingencies on innovation. Findings indicate that Chinese manufacturers with cultures emphasizing innovation and teamwork more effectively utilize financial resources in the innovation process. Results also show that a culture emphasizing outcomes and stability leads to lower levels innovation irrespective of investments.

37144 ■ *"Where Good Ideas Come From: The Natural History of Innovation" in Business Owner (Vol. 35, July-August 2011, No. 4, pp. 6)*
Pub: DL Perkins Company
Description: A history of ideas, concepts, innovations and technologies that have created a successful small business environment are explored.

37145 ■ *"Where New Economy Initiative Grants Have Gone" in Crain's Detroit Business (Vol. 25, June 1, 2009, No. 22, pp. M014)*
Pub: Crain Communications Inc. - Detroit
Description: Listing of grants totaling $20.5 million focusing on talent development, attraction and retention; innovation and entrepreneurship; and shifting to a culture that values learning, work and innovation, is presented.

37146 ■ *"A Whiteboard that Peels and Sticks" in Inc. (Volume 32, December 2010, No. 10, pp. 58)*
Pub: Inc. Magazine
Ed: Issie Lapwosky. **Description:** Profile of an affordable adhesive whiteboard that can be restuck multiple times; the whiteboard was created by three college friends. The students share insight in the contacts they used in order to promote the sale of their invention.

37147 ■ *"Why Copyright Isn't Property" in Information Today (Vol. 26, February 2009, No. 2, pp. 18)*
Pub: Information Today, Inc.
Ed: K. Matthew Dames. **Description:** An overview of intellectual property is presented. Intellectual property refers to 'creations of the mind: inventions, literary and artistic works, and symbols, names, and designs used in commerce', according to the World Intellectual Property Organization (WIPO). WIPO divides intellectual property into two categories: industrial property consisting of patents, trademarks, and industrial designs; and copyright: literary, artistic, creative, and aesthetic works.

37148 ■ *"Why Entrepreneurs Matter More Than Innovators" in Gallup Management Journal (November 22, 2011)*
Pub: Gallup
Ed: Jim Clifton. **Description:** In the race to create good jobs, leaders are not paying enough attention to cultivating talented entrepreneurs, rather they invest too much attention on innovation.

37149 ■ *"With Whom Do You Trade? Defensive Innovation and the Skill-Bias" in Canadian Journal of Electronics (Vol. 43, November 2010)*
Pub: Journal of the Canadian Economics Association
Ed: Pushan Dutt, Daniel Traca. **Description:** Examination into whether increased trade with ineffective protection of intellectual property has contributed to the skill-deepening of the 1980s. An index of effective protection of intellectual property at the country level, combining data on protection of patents and rule of law are presented. An industry-specific version of this index is given using as weights each country's trade share in the total trade of the industry. A decline is seen in this trade-weighted index, owing to a rise in trade with countries with low effective protection of intellectual property, which explains 29 percent of the rise within-industry skill-intensity.

37150 ■ *"Working the Streets" in Baltimore Business Journal (Vol. 28, July 30, 2010, No. 12, pp. 1)*
Pub: Baltimore Business Journal
Ed: Amanda Pino. **Description:** Reports show that street vendors are popping up on new corners in Baltimore, Maryland, with city-inspected stainless steel food carts in tow. Applications for street vending licenses shot up at the end of 2009 and into this summer. It is believed that pinning down the exact number of vendors operating at any one point is difficult.

TRADE PERIODICALS

37151 ■ *BNA's Patent, Trademark & Copyright Journal*
Pub: Bureau of National Affairs Inc.
Contact: James D. Crowne, Managing Editor
Released: Weekly. **Price:** $1,289. **Description:** Monitors developments in the intellectual property field, including patents, trademarks, and copyrights. Covers proposed and enacted legislation, litigation, Patent and Trademark Office decisions, Copyright Office practices, activities of professional associations, government contracting, and international developments.

37152 ■ *Eureka! The Canadian Invention & Innovation Newsletter*
Pub: Canadian Innovation Centre
Ed: Carolyn Parks, Editor. **Released:** Quarterly. **Price:** Free. **Description:** Serves as a forum for Canadian inventors and innovators.

37153 ■ *United States Patents Quarterly*
Pub: Bureau of National Affairs Inc.
Contact: William R. McKey, Managing Editor
Released: Weekly. **Price:** $1,539. **Description:** Reports important decisions dealing with patents, trademarks, copyrights, unfair competition, trade secrets, and computer chip protection.

VIDEOCASSETTES/ AUDIOCASSETTES

37154 ■ *Entrepreneurs Series, Part 1: The Entrepreneurs*
Instructional Video
2219 C St.
Lincoln, NE 68502
Ph: (402)475-6570
Free: 800-228-0164
Fax: (402)475-6500
Co. E-mail: feedback@insvideo.com
URL: http://www.insvideo.com
Released: 19??. **Price:** $19.98. **Description:** Part one of the six-part Entrepreneurs Series. Profiles King Gillette, Wally Amos, John H. Johnson, Charles Darrow, Thomas Edison, and others. **Availability:** VHS.

37155 ■ *Entrepreneurs Series, Part 2: The Land & Its People*
Instructional Video
2219 C St.
Lincoln, NE 68502
Ph: (402)475-6570
Free: 800-228-0164
Fax: (402)475-6500
Co. E-mail: feedback@insvideo.com
URL: http://www.insvideo.com
Released: 19??. **Price:** $19.98. **Description:** Part 2 of the six-part Entrepreneurs Series. Profiles Cyrus McCormick, Harland Sanders, John D. Rockefeller, Gustavius Swift, and others. **Availability:** VHS.

37156 ■ *Entrepreneurs Series, Part 3: Expanding America*
Instructional Video
2219 C St.
Lincoln, NE 68502
Ph: (402)475-6570
Free: 800-228-0164
Fax: (402)475-6500
Co. E-mail: feedback@insvideo.com
URL: http://www.insvideo.com
Released: 19??. **Price:** $19.98. **Description:** Part three of the six-part Entrepreneurs Series. Profiles DeWitt Clinton, Henry Ford, Deke Slayton, James Hill, Charles Lindbergh, and others. **Availability:** VHS.

37157 ■ *Entrepreneurs Series, Part 4: Made in America*
Instructional Video
2219 C St.
Lincoln, NE 68502
Ph: (402)475-6570
Free: 800-228-0164
Fax: (402)475-6500
Co. E-mail: feedback@insvideo.com
URL: http://www.insvideo.com
Released: 19??. **Price:** $19.98. **Description:** Fourth part of the six-part Entrepreneurs Series. Profiles Andrew Carnegie, Eli Whitney, Samuel Colt, Henry Kaiser, and others. **Availability:** VHS.

37158 ■ *Entrepreneurs Series, Part 5: Giving 'Em What They Want*
Instructional Video
2219 C St.
Lincoln, NE 68502
Ph: (402)475-6570
Free: 800-228-0164
Fax: (402)475-6500
Co. E-mail: feedback@insvideo.com
URL: http://www.insvideo.com
Released: 19??. **Price:** $19.98. **Description:** Part five of the six-part Entrepreneurs Series. Profiles P.T. Barnum, Richard Sears, Lillian Vernon Katz, Victor Kiam, Lee Iacocca, and others. **Availability:** VHS.

37159 ■ *Entrepreneurs Series, Part 6: Instant America*
Instructional Video
2219 C St.
Lincoln, NE 68502
Ph: (402)475-6570
Free: 800-228-0164
Fax: (402)475-6500
Co. E-mail: feedback@insvideo.com
URL: http://www.insvideo.com
Released: 19??. **Price:** $19.98. **Description:** Part six of the six-part Entrepreneurs Series. Profiles Samuel Morse, Alexander Graham Bell, Adolph Zukor, David Sarnoff, George Eastman, and others. **Availability:** VHS.

37160 ■ *From Mind to Market: The Patent Process*
Instructional Video
2219 C St.
Lincoln, NE 68502
Ph: (402)475-6570
Free: 800-228-0164
Fax: (402)475-6500
Co. E-mail: feedback@insvideo.com
URL: http://www.insvideo.com
Released: 19??. **Price:** $34.95. **Description:** Outlines the patent process, covering ways to protect your ideas, innovation, disclosure documents, prototypes, patent types, patent searches, marketing, and inventor show information. **Availability:** VHS.

37161 ■ *Handling Trademark Registrations under the New Law*
American Law Institute
American Bar Association Committee on Continuing Education
4025 Chestnut St.
Philadelphia, PA 19104
Ph: (215)243-1600
Free: 800-CLENEWS
Fax: (215)243-1636
Co. E-mail: custserv@ali-aba.org
URL: http://www.ali.org
Released: 1989. **Price:** $95. **Description:** Discusses the result of the 1989 changes in the U.S. Trademark Law. Complete with study guide. **Availability:** VHS.

CONSULTANTS

37162 ■ Jordan Driks
284 Melrose Ave.
Merion Station, PA 19066
Ph: (610)664-0290
Fax: (610)664-0292
Scope: Extensive background in all phases of patent practice including negotiation and drafting of agreements, Preparation and prosecution of patent applications, negotiating with the government and designing licensing programs.

37163 ■ Invent Resources Inc. (IRI)
PO Box 548
Lexington, MA 02420-0005
Ph: (781)862-0200
Fax: (781)721-2300
Co. E-mail: pavelle@comcast.net
URL: http://www.weinvent.com
Contact: Dr. Richard Pavelle, President
E-mail: pavelle@comcast.net
Scope: Provider of consultancy services to provide support in developing and prototyping new, proprietary products. Offer inventory services on demand.

Assist clients who need innovations in product lines, have hit technical bottlenecks, or need improvements in manufacturing processes. Provide assistance to individuals and clients in obtaining, reviewing, and strengthening patents. **Founded:** 1991. **Telecommunication Services:** rp@theworld.com.

37164 ■ Margiloff & Associates
621 Royalview St.
Duarte, CA 91010-1346
Ph: (626)303-1266
Fax: (626)303-0127
Contact: Dorine Margiloff, Manager
Scope: Energy and water conservation studies, analysis of research and development, licensing, economics and project management. Projects involve development, training, utility review, cost analysis, manufacturing system improvement, process modeling and expert witness services. Clients include in the field of food, chemical, fermentation, energy, financial and legal services, government and general manufacturing fields. **Founded:** 1983.

37165 ■ Jerome W. McGee & Associates—Bruce W. McGee & Associates
7826 Eastern Ave. NW, Ste. 300
Washington, DC 20012
Ph: (202)726-7272
Fax: (202)726-2946
Contact: Bruce W. McGee, President
Scope: Business consultants experienced in office automation, small business management, invention and patent counseling, technology commercialization, loan packaging and business plan development. **Founded:** 1985. **Seminars:** Marketing Research for the High-Technology Business; Introduction to Microcomputers; Marketing Technological Products to Industry; How to Evaluate Your Technical Idea; Patenting Your Own Invention.

37166 ■ National Congress of Inventor Organizations (NCIO)
8306 Wilshire Blvd., Ste. 391
Beverly Hills, CA 90211
Ph: (323)878-6952
Free: 800-458-5624
Fax: (213)947-1079
Co. E-mail: ncio@inventionconvention.com
URL: http://www.inventionconvention.com/ncio
Contact: Stephen Paul Gnass, Executive Director
URL(s): inventionconvention.com/ncio. **Description:** Represents inventors' groups. Coordinates information relating to inventor education and programs such as wanted and available inventions and credible organizations offering development and marketing assistance. Offers children's services and educational programs. Maintains speakers' bureau. **Scope:** Offers group and one-on-one consultations to independent inventors and small companies to guide them towards self reliance and responsibility in getting products into the marketplace. Customized evaluation and strategy along with matchmaking, networking and support services are personalized to help companies and individuals speed up the process of launching new products and technologies into the marketplace. Industries served: independent inventors, engineers, research and development labs, invent-to-order job shops, innovation and technology centers, universities, as well as small businesses, legal professions, manufacturing, distributors, sales and marketing professionals, inventor groups, and government agencies. **Founded:** 1986. **Subscriptions:** books. **Publications:** "Inventors Idol"; "Invention Connections". **Educational Activities:** National Innovation Workshop. **Seminars:** Exhibitor Excellence, Boothmanship - Maximizing Tradeshow Performances; Masters of the Invention Process. **Special Services:** Invention Connection®.

37167 ■ Patent Attornies & Agents
1601 Market St., Ste. 2400
Philadelphia, PA 19103-2301
Ph: (215)563-4100
Fax: (215)563-4044
Contact: John S. Child, Jr., Principal
Scope: Provide solutions in the area of patent trademark and copyright laws. Technical area of specialization is chemistry. Involved in legal matters relating to trade secrets. **Founded:** 1974.

COMPUTERIZED DATABASES

37168 ■ *Canadian Patent Reporter Plus (CPR)*
1 Corporate Plz.
2075 Kennedy Rd.
Toronto, ON, Canada M1T 3V4
Ph: (416)609-3800
Free: 800-387-5351
Fax: (416)298-5082
URL: http://www.canadalawbook.ca
Availability: Online: Thomson Reuters Canada Ltd.-Carswell-Canada Law Book. CD-ROM: Thomson Reuters Canada Ltd.-Carswell-Canada Law Book. **Type:** Full-text.

37169 ■ *CLAIMS® Citation Database*
PO Box 1148
Madison, CT 06443
Ph: (203)779-5301
Fax: (203)583-4521
Co. E-mail: info@ificlaims.com
URL: http://www.ificlaims.com
Availability: Online: ProQuest LLC - Dialog. **Type:** Bibliographic.

37170 ■ *Health & Wellness InSite<svs>*
610 Opperman Dr.
Eagen, MN 55122
Free: 800-477-4300
Co. E-mail: gale.contentlicensing@cengage.com
URL: http://www.insite2.gale.com
Availability: Online: Cengage Learning Inc. - Gale - InSite2. **Type:** Full-text.

37171 ■ *Industrial Patent Activity in the United States Parts 1 and 2, 1974-1998 (IPA)*
Madison Bldgs. (East & West)
600 Dulany St.
Alexandria, VA 22314
Ph: (703)308-4357
Free: 800-786-9199
Fax: (703)306-2737
Co. E-mail: usptoinfo@uspto.gov
URL: http://www.uspto.gov
Availability: CD-ROM: U.S. Department of Commerce - Technology Administration - National Technical Information Service. **Type:** Patents/Trademarks.

37172 ■ *LexisNexis Patent & Trademark File History Services*
9443 Springboro Pke.
Dayton, OH 45342
Ph: (937)865-6800
Free: 800-227-4908
Co. E-mail: customerservice.customer.support@lexisnexis.com
URL: http://www.bender.com/
Contact: Michael Walsh, President
Availability: Online: LexisNexis Group. CD-ROM: LexisNexis Group. **Type:** Full-text.

37173 ■ *Patent, Trademark & Copyright Journal®*
1801 S Bell St.
Arlington, VA 22202
Free: 800-372-1033
Co. E-mail: customercare@bna.com
URL: http://www.bna.com
Availability: Online: Bloomberg LP-Bloomberg BNA; Thomson Reuters - Westlaw. **Type:** Full-text.

LIBRARIES

37174 ■ Chicago Public Library Central Library - Business/Science/Technology Division
Harold Washington Library Center
400 S. State St., 4th Fl.
Chicago, IL 60605
Ph: (312)747-4450
Fax: (312)747-4975
URL: http://www.chipublib.org/branch/details/library/harold-washington/p/Bst
Scope: Small business, marketing, technology, corporate reports, investments, management, personnel, patents, physical and biological sciences, medicine, health, computer science, careers, environmental information, gardening, cookbooks. **Services:** Interlibrary loan; copying; division open to the public. **Founded:** 1977. **Holdings:** 415,000 books; 52,100 bound periodical volumes; 33,000 reels of microfilm; Securities and Exchange Commission (SEC) reports; federal specifications and standards; American National Standards Institute standards; corporate Annual reports. **Subscriptions:** 4000 journals and other serials; 8 newspapers.

37175 ■ Finnegan, Henderson, Farabow, Garrett and Dunner Library
901 New York Ave., NW
Washington, DC 20001-4413
Ph: (202)408-4000
Fax: (202)408-4400
Co. E-mail: barbara.mccurdy@finnegan.com
URL: http://www.finnegan.com
Contact: Virginia McNitt, Director, Library Services
Scope: Patent law, trademark law, federal procedure. **Services:** Interlibrary loan; Library not open to the public. **Founded:** 1966. **Holdings:** 11,000 books; 200 bound periodical volumes. **Subscriptions:** 700 journals and other serials; 6 newspapers.

37176 ■ O'Melveny & Myers LLP Library
2 Embarcadero Ctr., 28th Fl.
San Francisco, CA 94111-3823
Ph: (415)984-8700
Fax: (415)984-8701
URL: http://www.omm.com
Contact: Michael Tubach, Partner
Scope: Law. **Services:** Library not open to the public. **Founded:** 1989. **Holdings:** 8000 books. **Subscriptions:** 75 journals and other serials; 10 newspapers.

37177 ■ Sentron Medical Inc. - Senmed Medical Ventures Library
4445 Lake Forest Dr., No. 600
Cincinnati, OH 45242-3798
Ph: (513)563-3240
Fax: (513)563-3261
URL: http://www.senmed.com/organization.htm
Contact: Rosanne Wohlwender
Scope: Biotechnology, medical devices and diagnostics, technology transfer, pharmaceuticals, venture capital, licensing. **Services:** Library not open to the public. **Founded:** 1987. **Holdings:** 800 books; 50 reports. **Subscriptions:** 100 journals and other serials; 2 newspapers.

RESEARCH CENTERS

37178 ■ Indiana State University - Office of Sponsored Programs (OSP)
Erickson Hall, Rm. 511
200 N 7th St.
Terre Haute, IN 47809-9989
Ph: (812)237-3088
Free: 800-468-6478
Fax: (812)237-3092
Co. E-mail: dawn.underwood@indstate.edu
URL: http://www.indstate.edu/osp
Contact: Dawn Underwood, Director
Services: Offers individual assistance: in the preparation and submission of proposals. **Publications:** *Creating a Grant Proposal Budget*; *Finding Money for Your Project*; *Preparing a Winning Grant Proposal*. **Educational Activities:** OSP Seminars and workshops. **Telecommunication Services:** osp@indstate.edu.

37179 ■ University of Wisconsin—Whitewater - Wisconsin Innovation Service Center (WISC)
1200 Hyland Hall
Whitewater, WI 53190
Ph: (262)472-1365
Fax: (262)472-1600
Co. E-mail: innovate@uww.edu
URL: http://wisc.uww.edu
Contact: Ronald (Bud) Gayhart, Director
Services: Market information to clients; Technical reviews. **Founded:** 1980.

Inventory

EDUCATIONAL PROGRAMS

37180 ■ Best Practices for Managing Inventories and Cycle Counts (Onsite)
Seminar Information Service, Inc.
20 Executive Park, Ste. 120
Irvine, CA 92614
Ph: (949)261-9104
Free: 877-SEM-INFO
Fax: (949)261-1963
Co. E-mail: info@seminarinformation.com
URL: http://www.seminarinformation.com
Price: $199.00. **Description:** Learn how to use specific techniques that will actually improve speed and accuracy when counting inventory. **Dates and Locations:** Cities throughout the United States.

37181 ■ How to Manage Inventories and Cycle Counts
Fred Pryor Seminars & CareerTrack
5700 Broadmoor St., Ste. 300
Mission, KS 66202
Free: 800-780-8476
Fax: (913)967-8849
Co. E-mail: customerservice@pryor.com
URL: http://www.pryor.com
Price: $199.00; $189.00 for groups of 5 or more. **Description:** Cost saving methods and time saving techniques to ensure accurate counts and inventories. **Dates and Locations:** Cities throughout the United States.

37182 ■ Inventory Management Techniques (Onsite)
Seminar Information Service, Inc.
20 Executive Park, Ste. 120
Irvine, CA 92614
Ph: (949)261-9104
Free: 877-SEM-INFO
Fax: (949)261-1963
Co. E-mail: info@seminarinformation.com
URL: http://www.seminarinformation.com
Price: $2,345.00; $2,095.00 for AMA members. **Description:** Learn how to assure less inventory where the product pipeline begins and greater customer satisfaction where it ends. **Dates and Locations:** Chicago, IL; New York, NY; Arlington, VA; and Atlanta, GA.

37183 ■ Managing Inventories and Cycle Counts (Onsite)
Padgett-Thompson Seminars
Rockhurst University CEC
14502 W. 105th St.
Lenexa, KS 66215
Free: 800-349-1935
URL: http://www.findaseminar.com/tpd/Padgett-Thompson-Seminars.asp
Price: $249.00. **Description:** One-day workshop focusing on methods to streamline processes and keep a warehouse running smoothly. **Dates and Locations:** Cities throughout the United States.

37184 ■ Successful Inventory Management (Onsite)
Fred Pryor Seminars & CareerTrack
5700 Broadmoor St., Ste. 300
Mission, KS 66202
Free: 800-780-8476
Fax: (913)967-8849
Co. E-mail: customerservice@pryor.com
URL: http://www.pryor.com
Price: $199.00; $189.00 for groups of 5 or more. **Description:** Learn proven cost saving methods that improve inventory and cycle count accuracy. **Dates and Locations:** Cities throughout the United States.

REFERENCE WORKS

37185 ■ *"Battling Back from Betrayal" in Harvard Business Review (Vol. 88, December 2010, No. 12, pp. 130)*
Pub: Harvard Business School Publishing
Ed: Daniel McGinn. **Description:** Stephen Greer's scrap metal firm, Hartwell Pacific, lost several million dollars due to a lack of efficient and appropriate inventory audits, accounting procedures, and new-hire reference checks for his foreign operations. Greer believes that balancing growth with control is a key component of success.

37186 ■ *"Beyond Zipcar: Collaborate Consumption" in Harvard Business Review (Vol. 88, October 2010, No. 10, pp. 30)*
Pub: Harvard Business School Publishing
Ed: Rachel Botsman, Roo Rogers. **Description:** Description of the rise of collaborative consumption, the sharing or redistributing of products, rather than the purchasing thereof is discussed.

37187 ■ *"ChemSW Software Development Services Available for Outsourcing" in Information Today (Vol. 26, February 2009, No. 2, pp. 30)*
Pub: Information Today, Inc.
Description: ChemSW software development services include requirements analysis, specification development, design, development, testing, and system documentation as an IT outsourcing solution. The company can also develop software tracking systems for satellite stockrooms, provide asset management integration solutions and more.

37188 ■ *"Commentary. On Federal Reserve's Cut of Interest Rates" in Small Business Economic Trends (January 2008, pp. 3)*
Pub: National Federation of Independent Business
Description: Federal Reserve cut interest rates and announced its economic outlook on September 18, 2007 to stimulate spending. The cut in interest rates, however, may not help in supporting consumer spending because savers may lose interest income. The expected economic impact of the interest rate cuts and the U.S. economic outlook are also discussed.

37189 ■ *"Commentary. Small Business Economic Trends" in Small Business Economic Trends (February 2008, pp. 3)*
Pub: National Federation of Independent Business
Ed: William C. Dunkelberg, Holly Wade. **Description:** Commentary on the economic trends for small businesses in the U.S. is presented. Analysis of the U.S. Federal Reserve Board's efforts to prevent a recession is given. Reduction in business inventories is also discussed.

37190 ■ *"Dean Foods" in Ice Cream Reporter (Vol. 23, September 20, 2010, No. 10, pp. 8)*
Pub: Ice Cream Reporter
Description: Dean Foods promoted Joseph Scalzo to President and Chief Operating Officer to oversee the firm's operational turnaround and near-term strategic initiatives as well as business units. Key functions will include worldwide supply chain and research and development.

37191 ■ *"Don't Tweak Your Supply Chain - Rethink It End to End" in Harvard Business Review (Vol. 88, October 2010, No. 10, pp. 62)*
Pub: Harvard Business School Publishing
Ed: Hau L. Lee. **Description:** Hong Kong apparel firm Esquel Apparel Ltd. is used to illustrate supply chain reorganization to improve a firm's sustainability. Discussion focuses on taking a broad approach rather than addressing individual steps or processes.

37192 ■ *"Dynamic Supply Chain Alignment" in Human Resource Management (Vol. 49, September-October 2010, No. 5, pp. 969-973)*
Pub: John Wiley
Ed: Kim Sundtoft Hald. **Description:** Review of the book, 'Dynamic Supply Chain Alignment: A New Business Model for Peak Performance in Enterprise Supply Chains Across All Geographies'.

37193 ■ *eBay Business the Smart Way*
Pub: AMACOM
Ed: Joseph T. Sinclair. **Released:** June 6, 2007. **Price:** $17.95. **Description:** eBay commands ninety percent of all online auction business. Computer and software expert and online entrepreneur shares information to help online sellers get started and move merchandise on eBay. Tips include the best ways to build credibility, find products to sell, manage inventory, create a storefront Website, and more.

37194 ■ *"Economic Trends for Small Business" in Small Business Economic Trends (April 2008, pp. 1)*
Pub: National Federation of Independent Business
Ed: William C. Dunkelberg, Holly Wade. **Description:** Summary of economic trends for small businesses in the U.S. is presented. Economic indicators such as capital spending, inventories and sales, inflation, and profits are given. Analysis of credit markets is also provided.

37195 ■ *"Energy Outfitter Wings Into Houston" in Houston Business Journal (Vol.*

40, December 4, 2009, No. 30, pp. 2A)
Pub: American City Business Journals
Ed: Ford Gunter. **Description:** Red Wing Shoe Company Inc. has launched its personal protective equipment (PPE) line for oil and gas industry crewmen in North America by opening a 13,000 square foot distribution hub in Houston, Texas. The Houston facility was created to supply directly the oil and gas industry and to carry inventory for select distributors.

37196 ■ *"Global: Put It on Autopilot" in Entrepreneur (Vol. 35, October 2007, No. 10, pp. 110)*
Pub: Entrepreneur Media Inc.
Ed: Laurel Delaney. **Description:** A business that aims to enter the global market must first streamline its global supply chain (GSC). A streamlined GSC can be achieved by laying out the company's processes and by automating it with supply chain management software. Advantages of GSC automation such as credibility are provided.

37197 ■ *"Hot Kicks, Cool Price" in Black Enterprise (Vol. 37, December 2006, No. 5, pp. 34)*
Pub: Earl G. Graves Publishing Co. Inc.
Ed: Topher Sanders. **Description:** Stephon Marbury of the New York Nicks introduced a new basketball shoe, the Starbury One, costing $14.98. The shoes are an addition to the Starbury clothing line and although the privately owned company would not disclose figures; stores sold out of a month's worth of inventory in merely three days.

37198 ■ *Housecleaning Business: Organize Your Business - Get Clients and Referrals - Set Rates and Services*
Pub: Globe Pequot Press
Ed: Laura Jorstad, Melinda Morse. **Released:** June 1, 2009. **Price:** $18.95. **Description:** This book shares insight into starting a housecleaning business. It shows how to develop a service manual, screen clients, serve customers, select cleaning products, competition, how to up a home office, using the Internet to grow the business and offering green cleaning options to clients.

37199 ■ *How to Start and Run a Small Book Publishing Company: A Small Business Guide to Self-Publishing and Independent Publishing*
Pub: HCM Publishing
Ed: Peter I. Hupalo. **Released:** August 30, 2002. **Price:** $18.95. **Description:** The book teaches all aspects of starting and running a small book publishing company. Topics covered include: inventory accounting in the book trade, just-in-time inventory management, turnkey fulfillment solutions, tax deductible costs, basics of sales and use tax, book pricing, standards in terms of the book industry, working with distributors and wholesalers, cover design and book layout, book promotion and marketing, how to select profitable authors to publish, printing process, printing on demand, the power of a strong backlist, and how to value copyright.

37200 ■ *"Inventory Glut" in Business Courier (Vol. 24, March 28, 2008, No. 51, pp. 1)*
Pub: American City Business Journals, Inc.
Ed: Laura Baverman. **Description:** Indian Hill and the downtown area have the highest monthly absorption rate for housing on a list of 42 Greater Cincinnati and Northern Kentucky neighborhoods. The two neighborhoods have 19 and 27 months of housing inventory respectively, which means home sellers need to either lower their prices or be very patient.

37201 ■ *"Is Your Supply Chain Sustainable?" in Harvard Business Review (Vol. 88, October 2010, No. 10, pp. 74)*
Pub: Harvard Business School Publishing
Description: Charts and models are presented to help a firm assess its sustainability.

37202 ■ *"It May Be Cheaper to Manufacture At Home" in Harvard Business Review (Vol. 88, October 2010, No. 10, pp. 84)*
Pub: Harvard Business School Publishing
Ed: Suzanne de Treville, Lenos Trigeorgis. **Description:** Using a real options framework rather than a discounted cash flow model to assess and value supply chain processes is examined. This enables companies to assess costs for a variety of situations, not just ideal or normal circumstances, which can make the difference between domestic and foreign manufacturing decisions.

37203 ■ *"Miller's Crossroad" in Canadian Business (Vol. 83, September 14, 2010, No. 15, pp. 58)*
Pub: Rogers Media Ltd.
Ed: Joe Castaldo. **Description:** Future Electronics founder and billionaire Robert Miller shares the secret of Future's unique operating model, which is based on inventory and market research. Miller attributes much of the company's success to its privately held status that enables quick movement against competitors.

37204 ■ *"Monaco Pay Cut Draws Attention" in The Business Journal-Portland (Vol. 25, August 8, 2008, No. 22, pp. 1)*
Pub: American City Business Journals, Inc.
Ed: Erik Siemers. **Description:** Monaco Coach Corp. cut the salaries of five top executives in an effort to reduce the company's $178 million worth of inventory. The executives can earn the lost salary back if the inventory is reduced by $58 million a year after August 2008.

37205 ■ *"Online Reverse Auctions: Common Myths Versus Evolving Reality" in Business Horizons (September-October 2007, pp. 373)*
Pub: Elsevier Technology Publications
Ed: Tobias Schoenherr, Vincent A. Mabert. **Description:** Common misconceptions about online reverse auctions are examined based on the data obtained from 30 case study companies. Strategies for maintaining a good buyer-supplier relationship and implications for firms and supply managers are presented.

37206 ■ *"Perfecting Customer Services" in Pet Product News (Vol. 64, November 2010, No. 11, pp. 18)*
Pub: BowTie Inc.
Description: Pet supply retailers are encouraged to emphasize customer experience and sales representatives' knowledge of the store's product offerings to foster repeat business. Employee protocols could be implemented to improve customer interaction. Other guidelines on developing a pet supply retail environment that advances repeat business are presented.

37207 ■ *"Sheets Makers Optimistic Amid Price, Delivery Issues" in Home Textiles Today (Vol. 31, May 24, 2011, No. 13, pp. 8)*
Pub: Reed Business Information
Contact: Jeff Greisch, President
Ed: Jill Rowen. **Description:** Retail sales of sheets and pillowcases dropped 4.7 percent in volume in 2009. Retailers pulled back inventory significantly in 2010. Statistical data included.

37208 ■ *"Small Business Inventories" in Small Business Economic Trends (April 2008, pp. 14)*
Pub: National Federation of Independent Business
Ed: William C. Dunkelberg, Holly Wade. **Description:** Three tables and a graph presenting the inventories of small businesses in the U.S. are provided. The tables include figures on actual inventory changes, inventory satisfaction, and inventory plans.

37209 ■ *"Small Business Inventories" in Small Business Economic Trends (March 2008, pp. 14)*
Pub: National Federation of Independent Business
Ed: William C. Dunkelberg, Holly Wade. **Description:** Three tables and a graph presenting the inventories of small businesses in the U.S. are given. The tables include figures on actual inventory changes, inventory satisfaction, and inventory plans.

37210 ■ *"Small Business Inventories" in Small Business Economic Trends (February 2008, pp. 14)*
Pub: National Federation of Independent Business
Ed: William C. Dunkelberg, Holly Wade. **Description:** Three tables and a graph presenting the inventories of small businesses in the U.S. are given. The tables include figures on actual inventory changes, inventory satisfaction, and inventory plans.

37211 ■ *"Small Business Inventories" in Small Business Economic Trends (January 2008, pp. 14)*
Pub: National Federation of Independent Business
Description: Graph representing actual and planned inventories among small businesses surveyed in the U.S. from January 1986 to December 2007 is presented. A graph comparing inventory satisfaction and inventory plans over the same time period is also given. Tables showing actual inventory changes, inventory satisfaction, and inventory plans are also supplied.

37212 ■ *"Small Business Inventories" in Small Business Economic Trends (September 2010, pp. 15)*
Pub: National Federation of Independent Business
Ed: William C. Dunkelberg, Holly Wade. **Description:** A graph representing actual and planned inventories among small businesses surveyed in the U.S. from January 1986 to August 2010 is presented. A graph comparing inventory satisfaction and inventory plans over the same time period is also given. Tables showing actual changes, inventory satisfaction and inventory plans are also supplied.

37213 ■ *"Small Business Inventories" in Small Business Economic Trends (July 2010, pp. 14)*
Pub: National Federation of Independent Business
Description: A graph representing actual and planned inventories among small businesses surveyed in the U.S. from January 1986 to June 2010 is presented. A graph comparing inventory satisfaction and inventory plans over the same time period is also given. Tables showing actual inventory changes, inventory satisfaction, and inventory plans are also supplied.

37214 ■ *Small Business Management*
Pub: John Wiley & Sons, Incorporated
Ed: Margaret Burlingame. **Released:** March 2007. **Price:** $44.95. **Description:** Advice for starting and running a small business as well as information on the value and appeal of small businesses, is given. Topics include budgets, taxes, inventory, ethics, e-commerce, and current laws.

37215 ■ *"The Suits Look Better Than the Shares" in Barron's (Vol. 88, March 31, 2008, No. 13, pp. 25)*
Pub: Dow Jones & Company, Inc.
Ed: Bill Alpert. **Description:** Jos. A. Bank's inventory has increased sharply raising questions about the company's growth prospects. The company's shares have already dropped significantly from 46 to 23 and could still continue its slide. The company is also battling a class action suit where plaintiffs allege that the Bank inventories were bloated.

37216 ■ *"Summary. Economic Trends for Small Business" in Small Business Economic Trends (March 2008, pp. 1)*
Pub: National Federation of Independent Business
Ed: William C. Dunkelberg, Holly Wade. **Description:** Summary of economic trends for small businesses in the U.S. is provided. Economic indicators such as capital spending, inventories and sales, inflation, and profits are given. Analysis of credit markets is also provided.

37217 ■ *"Summary. Economic Trends for Small Business" in Small Business Economic Trends (February 2008, pp. 1)*
Pub: National Federation of Independent Business
Ed: William C. Dunkelberg, Holly Wade. **Description:** Summary of economic trends for small businesses in the U.S. is provided. Economic indicators such as capital spending, inventories and sales, inflation, and profits are given. Analysis of credit markets is also provided.

37218 ■ *"The Sustainable Supply Chain" in Harvard Business Review (Vol. 88, October*

2010, No. 10, pp. 70)
Pub: Harvard Business School Publishing
Ed: Steven Prokesch. **Description:** Peter Senge, founder of the Society for Organizational Learning, emphasizes the importance of assessing the system as a whole under which one is operating, and learning how to work with individuals with which one has not worked previously. He also points to nongovernmental organizations to provide assistance and legitimacy.

37219 ■ *"Swagelok Boss" in Crain's Cleveland Business (Vol. 30, June 29, 2009, No. 25, pp. 4)*
Pub: Crain Communications, Inc.
Ed: Dan Shingler. **Description:** Swagelok Company president and CEO has not laid off an employee in its 65 years of existence and said at a recent convention that he plans to keep his 4,000 employees working and inventories at normal levels despite the recession.

37220 ■ *"Technology and Returnable Asset Management" in Canadian Electronics (Vol. 23, February 2008, No. 1, pp. 6)*
Pub: CLB Media Inc.
Ed: Mark Borkowski. **Description:** Peter Kastner, president of Vestigo Corporation, believes that public companies without an asset track, trace, and control system in place could face Sarbanes-Oakley liability if error-prone processes result to misstatements of asset inventory positions. He also thinks that the system can improve return on assets by increasing the utilization of returnables.

37221 ■ *"The Transparent Supply Chain" in Harvard Business Review (Vol. 88, October 2010, No. 10, pp. 76)*
Pub: Harvard Business School Publishing
Ed: Steve New. **Description:** Examination of the use of new technologies to create a transparent supply chain, such as next-generation 2D bar codes in clothing labels that can provide data on a garment's provenance.

37222 ■ *"An Unfair Knock on Nokia" in Barron's (Vol. 88, March 10, 2008, No. 10, pp. 36)*
Pub: Dow Jones & Company, Inc.
Ed: Mark Veverka. **Description:** Discusses the decision by the brokerage house Exane to recommend a Sell on Nokia shares, presumably due to higher inventories, which is unfounded. The news that the company's inventories are rising is not an indicator of falling demand for its products. The company is also benefiting from solid management and rising market share.

37223 ■ *"Weathering the Economic Storm" in Playthings (Vol. 107, January 1, 2009, No. 1, pp. 10)*
Pub: Reed Business Information
Contact: Jeff Greisch, President
Ed: J. Tol Broome Jr. **Description:** Six steps for toy companies to survive the economic turndown are outlined: Outline your business model; seek professional input; meet with your banker; cut your costs; manage your inventory; and use your trade credit.

VIDEOCASSETTES/ AUDIOCASSETTES

37224 ■ *Inventory Observation and Valuation*
SmartPros Ltd.
12 Skyline Dr.
Hawthorne, NY 10532-2133
Ph: (914)345-2620
Co. E-mail: admin@smartpros.com
URL: http://www.smartpros.com
Contact: Jack Fingerhut, President
Released: 1991. **Description:** A review of inventory observation for staff accountants. **Availability:** VHS; 3/4 U.

CONSULTANTS

37225 ■ R. J. Levulis & Associates
601 Sequoia Trl.
Roselle, IL 60172
Ph: (630)924-9494
Fax: (630)924-9507
Contact: Raymond J. Levulis, Principal
E-mail: rlevulis@msn.com
Scope: Aids manufacturing and distribution clients in securing lasting benefits through cost and investment containment, customer service improvement, cycle time reduction, factory and warehouse space layout, and similar operations and distribution activities. **Founded:** 1989. **Publications:** "Finite Scheduling"; "Warehouse Management Systems"; "Materials Handling an Overlooked Weapon"; "The Abc of Inventory Management". **Seminars:** World Class Manufacturing; Better Warehousing; Basic Principles of Commercial Activities.

37226 ■ Williamson Imagineering
621 NE 162nd Ave., Ste. 19
Portland, OR 97230-5750
Contact: Steve Williamson, Owner
Scope: Database developer specializing in retail quoting and inventory control applications in the PC environment. Provides system analysis of existing procedures and/or applications, and offers consultation for efficiency recommendations. Provides user training on developed applications as well as off-the-shelf software and operating systems. Industries served: small business, municipal, and light industrial. **Founded:** 1994. **Publications:** "Saving Money on Backpacking Food".

FRANCHISES AND BUSINESS OPPORTUNITIES

37227 ■ AccuTrak Inventory Specialists
PO Box 14782
Surfside Beach, SC 29587
Ph: (843)293-8274
Fax: (843)293-5075
Description: Inventory consultants. **No. of Franchise Units:** 28. **No. of Company-Owned Units:** 1. **Founded:** 1993.. **Franchised:** 2000. **Equity Capital Needed:** $49,000-$58,000. **Franchise Fee:** $32,500. **Royalty Fee:** 7%. **Training:** Provides 4 days at headquarters, 4 days at approved franchisee training site with ongoing support.

37228 ■ Bevinco
505 Consumers Rd., Ste. 510
Toronto, ON, Canada M2J 4V8
Ph: (416)490-6266
Fax: (416)490-6899
Co. E-mail: info@bevinco.com
URL: http://www.bevinco.com
Description: Liquor inventory control system for bars, restaurants, hotels, clubs, etc. **No. of Franchise Units:** 250. **No. of Company-Owned Units:** 1. **Founded:** 1987.. **Franchised:** 1991. **Equity Capital Needed:** $40,000. **Franchise Fee:** $40,000. **Financial Assistance:** Yes. **Training:** 7 days corporate training in Toronto, 5-10 days regional training with state master franchise.

COMPUTERIZED DATABASES

37229 ■ *Atlantic Provinces Reports (APR)*
PO Box 302
Fredericton, NB, Canada E3B 4Y9
Ph: (506)453-9921
Free: 800-561-0220
Fax: (506)453-9525
Co. E-mail: service@mlb.nb.ca
URL: http://www.mlb.nb.ca
Availability: Online: LexisNexis Canada Inc. **Type:** Bibliographic.

COMPUTER SYSTEMS/ SOFTWARE

37230 ■ *PCINV: Inventory Control*
Pembroke 5, Ste. 108
Virginia Beach, VA 23462
Ph: (757)499-8911
Fax: (757)490-5932
Co. E-mail: crsweb@crsva.com
URL: http://www.crsva.com
Description: Available for IBM computers. System provides inventory data management for various businesses.

ASSOCIATIONS AND OTHER ORGANIZATIONS

37231 ■ Strategic and Competitive Intelligence Professionals (SCIP)
1700 Diagonal Rd., Ste. 600
Alexandria, VA 22314
Ph: (703)739-0696
Fax: (703)739-2524
Co. E-mail: info@scip.org
URL: http://www.scip.org
Contact: Michel Bernaiche, Chief Executive Officer
Description: Acts as a forum for the exchange of news and ideas among professionals involved in competitive intelligence and analysis. Addresses legal and ethical concerns; provides opportunities for improving professional expertise. Conducts programs of interest to members. **Founded:** 1986. **Publications:** *Competitive Intelligence* (Bimonthly); *SCIP Online* (Biweekly); *Journal of Competitive Intelligence and Management* (Quarterly); *SCIP.ORG In-box* (Weekly). **Awards:** Catalyst Award; Faye Brill Award; Fellows Award; Meritorious Award; Catalyst Award (Annual); Faye Brill Award (Annual); Fellows Award (Annual); Meritorious Award (Annual).

REFERENCE WORKS

37232 ■ *"Ask Inc." in Inc. (December 2007, pp. 83-84)*
Pub: Gruner & Jahr USA Publishing
Ed: Ari Weinzweig. **Description:** Questions regarding knowledge management in the case of a retiring CFO, issues involved in opening a satellite office for a New York realtor, and information for hiring a multicultural workforce are all discussed.

37233 ■ *"Bridging the Worlds" in Academy of Management Journal (Vol. 50, No. 5, October 2007, pp. 1043)*
Pub: Academy of Management
Contact: Ming-Jer Chen, President
Ed: Lise Saari. **Description:** Need to transfer human resource research information published in journals to practitioners and organizations is investigated, along with suggestions on ways of achieving this goal.

37234 ■ *Conquering Information Chaos in the Growing Business: IBM Solutions for Managing Information in an On Demand World*
Pub: Maximum Press
Ed: Jim Hoskins. **Released:** April 2005. **Price:** $29. 95. **Description:** Information management is critical to any business.

37235 ■ *"Creativity: A Key Link to Entrepreneurial Behavior" in Business Horizons (September-October 2007, pp. 365)*
Pub: Elsevier Technology Publications
Ed: Stephen Ko, John E. Butler. **Description:** Importance of creativity and its link to entrepreneurial behavior is examined. In a study of various entrepreneurs, studies concluded that a solid knowledge base, a well-developed social network, and a strong focus on identifying opportunities are relevant to entrepreneurial behavior.

37236 ■ *Electronic Commerce: Technical, Business, and Legal Issues*
Pub: Prentice Hall PTR
Ed: Oktay Dogramaci; Aryya Gangopadhyay; Yelena Yesha; Nabil R. Adam. **Released:** August 1998. **Description:** Provides insight into the goals of using the Internet to grow a business in the areas of networking and telecommunication, security, and storage and retrieval; business areas such as marketing, procurement and purchasing, billing and payment, and supply chain management; and legal aspects such as privacy, intellectual property, taxation, contractual and legal settlements.

37237 ■ *Enterprise Planning and Development: Small Business and Enterprise Start-Up Survival and Growth*
Pub: Elsevier Science and Technology Books
Ed: David Butler. **Released:** August 2006. **Price:** $42.95. **Description:** Innovation, intellectual property, and exit strategies are among the issues discussed in this book involving current entrepreneurship.

37238 ■ *Entrepreneurship and Technology Policy*
Pub: Edward Elgar Publishing, Incorporated
Ed: Link. **Released:** August 2006. **Price:** $190.00. **Description:** Journal articles focusing how and the ways small businesses' technical contributions are affecting business. The book is divided into four parts: Government's Direct Support of R&D, Government's Leveraging of R&D, Government's Infrastructure Policies; and Knowledge Flows from Universities and Laboratories.

37239 ■ *"From the Battlefield to the Boardroom" in Business Horizons (Vol. 51, March-April 2008, No. 2, pp. 79)*
Pub: Elsevier Advanced Technology Publications
Ed: Catherine M. Dalton. **Description:** Effective intelligence gathering, a thorough understanding of the mission, efficient use of resources, and strategic leadership are vital to achieving success in business as well as in the battlefield. Examples of effective leadership in the battle of Gettysburg are cited.

37240 ■ *"German Win Through Sharing" in Canadian Business (Vol. 83, September 14, 2010, No. 15, pp. 16)*
Pub: Rogers Media Ltd.
Ed: Jordan Timm. **Description:** German economic historian Eckhard Hoffner has a two-volume work showing how German's relaxed attitude toward copyright and intellectual property helped it catch up to industrialized United Kingdom. Hoffner's research was in response to his interest in the usefulness of software patents. Information on the debate regarding Canada's copyright laws is given.

37241 ■ *Getting Rich In Your Underwear: How To Start and Run a Profitable Home-Based Business*
Pub: HCM Publishing
Ed: Peter I. Hupalo. **Released:** April 1, 2005. **Price:** $17.95. **Description:** Book offers insight into starting a home-based business. Entrepreneurs will learn about business models and the home business; distribution and fulfillment of product or service; marketing and sales; how to overcome the fear of starting a business; personal success characteristics; naming a business; zoning and insurance; intellectual capital; copyrights, trademarks, and patents; limited liability companies and S-corporations; business expenses and accounting; taxes; fifteen basic steps for starting a home-based business, state resources for starting a home company; and seven home-based business ideas.

37242 ■ *"How Business Intelligence Can Affect Bottomline" in Canadian Electronics (Vol. 23, February 2008, No. 1, pp. 6)*
Pub: CLB Media Inc.
Ed: Mark Borkowski. **Description:** Business intelligence has an important role in delivering the right information in a secured manner. However, coping with data volume, cost, workload, time, availability and compliance have been a problem for business intelligence projects. Ways to avoid problems in business intelligence projects and examples of business intelligence applications are provided.

37243 ■ *"The Impact of Acquisitions On the Productivity of Inventors at Semiconductor Firms" in Academy of Management Journal (October 2007)*
Pub: Academy of Management
Contact: Ming-Jer Chen, President
Ed: Rahul Kapoor, Kwanghui Lim. **Description:** Study examined the relation between knowledge-based and incentive-based outlook in explaining the impact of acquisitions on the productivity of inventors at acquired semiconductor firms. Results showed a definite relation between the two perspectives.

37244 ■ *Innovation and Its Discontents*
Pub: Princeton University Press
Ed: Josh Lerner, Adam B. Jaffe. **Released:** 2006. **Price:** $21.95 paperback. **Description:** According to the authors, America's patent system does not effectively serve as a generator and protector of patents and intellectual property.

37245 ■ *"Integrating Business Core Knowledge through Upper Division Report Composition" in Business Communication Quarterly (December 2007)*
Pub: SAGE Publications USA
Contact: Blaise R. Simqu, President
Ed: Joy Roach, Daniel Tracy, Kay Durden. **Description:** An assignment that integrates subjects and encourages the use of business communication report-writing skills is presented. This assignment is designed to complement business school curricula and help develop critical thinking and organizational skills.

37246 ■ *Know-Who Based Entrepreneurship from Knowledge Creation to Business Implementation*
Pub: Edward Elgar Publishing, Incorporated
Ed: Harryson. **Released:** August 2006. **Price:** $130.00. **Description:** Analysis of the knowledge and interconnected areas of entrepreneurship and networking across various levels is presented. Best practice companies are profiled.

37247 ■ *"Lawyers Sued Over Lapsed Lacrosse Patent" in Crain's Detroit Business (Vol. 25, June 8, 2009, No. 23, pp. 5)*
Pub: Crain Communications Inc. - Detroit
Ed: Chad Halcom. **Description:** Warrior Sports Inc., a manufacturer of lacrosse equipment located in Warren, Michigan is suing the law firm Dickinson Wright PLLC and two of its intellectual property lawyers over patent rights to lacrosse equipment.

37248 ■ *"Legislating the Cloud" in Information Today (Vol. 28, October 2011, No. 9, pp. 1)*
Pub: Information Today, Inc.
Description: Internet and telecommunications industry leaders are asking for legislation to address the emerging market in cloud computing. Existing communications laws do not adequately govern the modern Internet.

37249 ■ *Managing the Older Worker: How to Prepare for the New Organizational Order*
Pub: Harvard Business Press
Ed: Peter Cappelli, Bill Novelli. **Price:** $29.95. **Description:** Your organization needs older workers more than ever: They transfer knowledge between generations, transmit your company's values to new hires, make excellent mentors for younger employees, and provide a 'just in time' workforce for special projects.

37250 ■ *"The Metrics of Knowledge: Mechanisms for Preserving the Value of Managerial Knowledge" in Business Horizons (Nov.-Dec. 2007)*
Pub: Elsevier Technology Publications
Ed: Eliezer Geisler. **Description:** Mechanisms to reduce the loss of managerial knowledge, such as socialization, tutoring, mentoring, and continuous reporting are proposed. These informal mechanisms should become integral components of knowledge management or organizations.

37251 ■ *Organizations Alive!: Six Things That Challenge - Seven That Bring Success*
Pub: Yuill & Associates
Ed: Jan Yuill. **Released:** January 2005. **Price:** $35.12 for book and guide. **Description:** New insight into understanding how organizations function as individuals is presented by an international consultant. Customer service, resource management, outsourcing, and management are among the issues covered.

37252 ■ *"Perfecting Customer Services" in Pet Product News (Vol. 64, November 2010, No. 11, pp. 18)*
Pub: BowTie Inc.
Description: Pet supply retailers are encouraged to emphasize customer experience and sales representatives' knowledge of the store's product offerings to foster repeat business. Employee protocols could be implemented to improve customer interaction. Other guidelines on developing a pet supply retail environment that advances repeat business are presented.

37253 ■ *"Protect Your Trade Secrets" in Business Owner (Vol. 35, July-August 2011, No. 4, pp. 11)*
Pub: DL Perkins Company
Description: Every business has secret information which can include customer lists and contracts or secret formulas and methods used in production of goods vital to the operation. A list of things every small business owner should do to protect these secrets is outlined.

37254 ■ *"Protecting Company Secrets" in Inc. (February 2008, pp. 38-39)*
Pub: Gruner & Jahr USA Publishing
Ed: Scott Westcott. **Description:** A legal guide for noncompete clauses when hiring new employees is outlined, stressing how each state has its own set of laws.

37255 ■ *"Research Note" in International Journal of Globalisation and Small Business (Vol. 4, September 21, 2010, No. 1, pp. 92)*
Pub: Publishers Communication Group
Ed: Alexander Bode, Tobias B. Talmon l'Armee, Simon Alig. **Description:** The cluster concept has steadily increased its importance during the past years both from practitioners' and reearchers' points of view. Simultaneously, many corporate networks are established. Researchers from different areas (business management, economic social and geographical science) are trying to explain both phenomena.

37256 ■ *"Size Does Matter" in International Journal of Globalisation and Small Business (Vol. 4, September 21, 2010, No. 1, pp. 61)*
Pub: Publishers Communication Group
Ed: Julia Cornnell, Ranjit Voola. **Description:** Examination of how members of an Australian-based manufacturing and engineering cluster share knowledge through networking as a means to improve competitive advantage.

37257 ■ *"A Strategic Risk Approach to Knowledge Management" in Business Horizons (November-December 2007, pp. 523)*
Pub: Elsevier Technology Publications
Ed: Bruce E. Perrott. **Description:** Knowledge management practices of Ramsay Health Care are studied to investigate the issues facing effective knowledge management. A knowledge process model is developed and presented.

37258 ■ *Strategies for Growth in SMEs: The Role of Information and Information Systems*
Pub: Elsevier Science & Technology Books
Ed: Margi Levy, Philip Powell. **Released:** December 2004. **Price:** $62.95. **Description:** Role of information and information systems in the growth of small and medium-sized enterprises in the U.S.

37259 ■ *Successful Proposal Strategies for Small Business: Using Knowledge Management to Win Government, Private-Sector, and International Contracts, Fourth E*
Pub: Artech House, Incorporated
Ed: Robert S. Frey. **Released:** February 2008. **Price:** $129.00. **Description:** Front-end proposal planning and storyboarding, focusing on the customer mission in proposals, along with the development of grant proposals.

37260 ■ *"Valuation of Intangible Assets in Franchise Companies and Multinational Groups" in Franchise Law Journal (Winter 2008)*
Pub: American Bar Association
Contact: Carolyn Lamm, President
Ed: Bruce S. Schaeffer, Susan J. Robins. **Description:** Intangible assets, also known as intellectual properties are the most valuable assets for companies today. Legal intellectual property issues faced by franchises firms are discussed.

37261 ■ *"The Valuation of Players" in Canadian Business (Vol. 80, October 22, 2007, No. 21, pp. 39)*
Pub: Rogers Media
Ed: Jeff Sanford. **Description:** Business professionals are supplementing their Masters in Business Administration degrees with CBV or chartered business valuator. CBVs are trained, not only in business tangibles, but also in business intangibles such as market position, reputation, intellectual property, and patent. Details of employment opportunities for chartered business valuators are discussed.

37262 ■ *"Why Copyright Isn't Property" in Information Today (Vol. 26, February 2009, No. 2, pp. 18)*
Pub: Information Today, Inc.
Ed: K. Matthew Dames. **Description:** An overview of intellectual property is presented. Intellectual property refers to 'creations of the mind: inventions, literary and artistic works, and symbols, names, and designs used in commerce', according to the World Intellectual Property Organization (WIPO). WIPO divides intellectual property into two categories: industrial property consisting of patents, trademarks, and industrial designs; and copyright: literary, artistic, creative, and aesthetic works.

37263 ■ *"Why HR Practices Are Not Evidence-Based" in Academy of Management Journal (Vol. 50, No. 5, October 2007, pp. 1033)*
Pub: Academy of Management
Contact: Ming-Jer Chen, President
Ed: Denise M. Rousseau. **Description:** A suggestion that an Evidence-Based Management Collaboration (EBMC) can be established to facilitate effective transfer of ideas between science and practice is presented.

37264 ■ *"With Whom Do You Trade? Defensive Innovation and the Skill-Bias" in Canadian Journal of Electronics (Vol. 43, November 2010)*
Pub: Journal of the Canadian Economics Association
Ed: Pushan Dutt, Daniel Traca. **Description:** Examination into whether increased trade with ineffective protection of intellectual property has contributed to the skill-deepening of the 1980s. An index of effective protection of intellectual property at the country level, combining data on protection of patents and rule of law are presented. An industry-specific version of this index is given using as weights each country's trade share in the total trade of the industry. A decline is seen in this trade-weighted index, owing to a rise in trade with countries with low effective protection of intellectual property, which explains 29 percent of the rise within-industry skill-intensity.

CONSULTANTS

37265 ■ VenturEdge Corp.
4711 Yonge St., Ste. 1105
Toronto, ON, Canada M2N 6K8
Ph: (416)224-2000
Fax: (416)224-2376
Co. E-mail: info@venturedge.com
URL: http://www.venturedge.com
Contact: Morris Langer, President
E-mail: langer@venturedge.com
Scope: Provides services including strategy formulation; business planning; financial management; business coaching; performance improvement; information management; merger, acquisitions and divestitures; family succession planning; competitive intelligence. **Founded:** 1972. **Publications:** "Reputation," Harvard Business School Press, 1996; "Competing for the Future," Harvard Business School Press, 1994; "The Fifth Discipline," 1990.

START-UP INFORMATION

37266 ■ *Angel Financing: How to Find and Invest in Private Equity*
Pub: John Wiley and Sons, Inc.

Ed: Gerald A. Benjamin; Joel B. Margulis. **Price:** $65. 00. **Description:** The book provides a proven strategy to help entrepreneurs find angel investors. Interviews with angel investors as well as information about investors' hedging strategies, risk assessments, syndication orientation, financial return expectations, deal structuring preferences, monitoring investments, harvesting returns, and realist exit strategies are covered.

37267 ■ *The Art of the Start: The Time-Tested, Battle-Hardened Guide for Anyone Starting Anything*
Pub: Penguin Books USA Inc.

Ed: Guy Kawasaki. **Released:** September 2004. **Price:** $26.95. **Description:** Advice for someone starting a new business covering topics such as hiring employees, building a brand, business competition, and management.

37268 ■ *The Beermat Entrepreneur: Turn Your Good Idea Into a Great Business*
Pub: Pearson Education Ltd.
Contact: Rod Bristow, President

Ed: Mike Southon, Andrew Leigh, Chris West. **Released:** March 1, 2009. **Price:** $39.50. **Description:** Information to help start, maintain and grow a small business is given, along with suggestions for working with a bank.

37269 ■ *Building a Dream: A Canadian Guide to Starting Your Own Business*
Pub: McGraw-Hill Ryerson Ltd.

Ed: Walter S. Good. **Released:** 2005. **Description:** Topics covered include evaluating business potential, new business ideas, starting or buying a business, franchise opportunities, business organization, protecting an idea, arranging financing, and developing a business plan.

37270 ■ *The Canadian Small Business Survival Guide: How to Start and Operate Your Own Successful Business*
Pub: Dundurn Group

Ed: Benj Gallander. FRQ June 2002. **Price:** $26.99. **Description:** Ideas for starting and running a successful small business. Topics include selecting a business, financing, government assistance, locations, franchises, and marketing ideas.

37271 ■ *Cash In On Cash Flow*
Pub: Simon and Schuster Inc.
Contact: Carolyn Reidy, President
E-mail: carolyn.reidy@simonandschuster.com

Ed: Lawrence J. Pino. **Released:** July 2005. **Price:** $19.95. **Description:** Guide to assist entrepreneurs with starting a new business as a cash flow specialist.

37272 ■ *The Complete Idiot's Guide to Starting and Running a Thrift Store*
Pub: Alpha Publishing House

Ed: Ravel Buckley, Carol Costa. **Released:** January 5, 2010. **Price:** $18.95. **Description:** Thrift stores saw a 35 percent increase in sales during the falling economy in 2008. Despite the low startup costs, launching and running a thrift store is complicated. Two experts cover the entire process, including setting up a store on a nonprofit basis, choosing a location, funding, donations for saleable items, recruiting and managing staff, sorting items, pricing, and recycling donations.

37273 ■ *The Entrepreneur and Small Business Problem Solver*
Pub: John Wiley & Sons, Incorporated

Ed: William A. Cohen. **Released:** December 2005. **Price:** $24.95 (US), $31.99 (Canadian). **Description:** Revised edition of the resource for entrepreneurs and small business owners that covers everything from start-up financing and loans to new product promotion and more.

37274 ■ *"Entrepreneurs: Search Party" in Business Strategy Review (Vol. 21, Autumn 2010, No. 3, pp. 30)*
Pub: Wiley-Blackwell

Ed: Georgina Peters. **Description:** Entrepreneurs tend to be fixated on coming up with a foolproof idea for a new business and then raising money to start it. Raising startup funds is difficult, but it doesn't have to be that way. Search funds offers an innovative alternative, and the results are often impressive.

37275 ■ *Entrepreneurship*
Pub: John Wiley and Sons Inc.

Ed: William D. Bygrave; Andrew Zacharakis. **Released:** March 2007. **Price:** $115.95. **Description:** Information for starting a new business is shared, focusing on marketing and financing a product or service.

37276 ■ *"ETF Process May be Tweaked" in Austin Business Journallnc. (Vol. 28, December 26, 2008, No. 41, pp. 3)*
Pub: American City Business Journals

Ed: Christopher Calnan. **Description:** Some government officials are proposing for an adjustment of the Texas Emerging Technology Fund's (ETF) policies. The ETF was created to get startup companies capital to get off the ground. Reports show that the global recession had made it more difficult for startup companies to garner investment.

37277 ■ *"Home Grown" in Hawaii Business (Vol. 53, November 2007, No. 5, pp. 51)*
Pub: Hawaii Business Publishing

Ed: Jolyn Okimoto Rosa. **Description:** Discusses a program that focuses on Native Hawaiian entrepreneurs and offers business training at the Kapiolani Community College; upon completion of the program, participants may apply for a loan provided by the Office of Hawaiian Affairs (OHA) to help them start their business. OHA plans to present the restructured loan program in November 2007, with aims of shortening the loan process.

37278 ■ *How to Get the Financing for Your New Small Business: Innovative Solutions from the Experts Who Do It Every Day*
Pub: Atlantic Publishing Company

Ed: Sharon L. Fullen. **Released:** May 2006. **Price:** $39.95, includes companion CD-Rom. **Description:** Ready capital is essential for starting and expanding a small business. Topics include traditional financing methods, financial statements, and a good business plan.

37279 ■ *"Money Matters: Using Sound Resources, You Can Find Capital For Your Business" in Black Enterprise (Vol. 38, November 2007, No. 4)*
Pub: Earl G. Graves Publishing Co. Inc.

Ed: Carolyn M. Brown. **Description:** Profile of fashion designer Kara Saun who inspired an angel investor from Connecticut to help launch her Fall 2006 clothing line.

37280 ■ *Raising Capital*
Pub: Kiplinger Books and Tapes

Ed: Andrew J. Sherman. **Price:** $34.95. **Description:** Corporate attorney provides a comprehensive guide using in-depth, practical advice on raising money to start and grow a business. A 115-page appendix contains samples of financing agreements, forms and questionnaires.

37281 ■ *"SBA Streamlines Loans and Ramps Up Web Presence" in Hispanic Business (January-February 2008, pp. 64)*
Pub: Hispanic Business

Description: Federal government's Small Business Administration offers informational resources and tools to individuals wishing to start a new company as well as those managing existing firms. The site consists of over 20,000 pages with information, advice and tips on starting, financing and managing any small business. Free online courses are also provided.

37282 ■ *The Small Business Owner's Manual: Everything You Need to Know to Start Up and Run Your Business*
Pub: Career Press, Incorporated

Ed: Joe Kennedy. **Released:** June 2005. **Price:** $19.99 (US), $26.95 (Canadian). **Description:** Comprehensive guide for starting a small business, focusing on twelve ways to obtain financing, business plans, selling and advertising products and services, hiring and firing employees, setting up a Web site, business law, accounting issues, insurance, equipment, computers, banks, financing, customer credit and collection, leasing, and more.

37283 ■ *"State Fund That Aids New Companies Likely To Wither" in Crain's Detroit Business (Vol. 24, February 25, 2008,*

No. 8, pp. 16)
Pub: Crain Communications Inc. - Detroit
Ed: Tom Henderson. **Description:** Officials are committed to fighting to save funding for the statewide Strategic Economic Investment and Commercialization Board which provides pre-seed money to start-up firms.

37284 ■ *The Toilet Paper Entrepreneur: The Tell-It-Like-It-Is Guide to Cleaning Up In Business, Even If You Are At the End of Your Roll*
Pub: Obsidian Launch LLC
Ed: Mike Michalowicz. **Price:** $24.95. **Description:** The founder of three multimillion-dollar companies, including Obsidian Launch, a company that partners with first-time entrepreneurs to grow their concepts into industry leaders.

37285 ■ *Working for Yourself: An Entrepreneur's Guide to the Basics*
Pub: Kogan Page, Limited
Contact: Ben Glover, Director of Marketing
Ed: Jonathan Reuvid. **Released:** September 2006. **Description:** Guide for starting a new business venture, focusing on raising financing, legal and tax issues, marketing, information technology, and site location.

ASSOCIATIONS AND OTHER ORGANIZATIONS

37286 ■ Commercial Finance Association (CFA)
370 7th Ave., Ste. 1801
New York, NY 10001-3979
Ph: (212)792-9390
Fax: (212)564-6053
Co. E-mail: info@cfa.com
URL: http://www.cfa.com
Contact: John Fox, Chairman
Description: Organizations engaged in asset-based financial services including commercial financing and factoring and lending money on a secured basis to small- and medium-sized business firms. Acts as a forum for information and consideration about ideas, opportunities and legislation concerning asset-based financial services. Seeks to improve the industry's legal and operational procedures. Offers job placement and reference services for members. Sponsors School for Field Examiners and other educational programs. Compiles statistics; conducts seminars and surveys; maintains speakers' bureau and 21 committees. **Founded:** 1944. **Publications:** *The Secured Lender* (Bimonthly). **Educational Activities:** Commercial Finance Association Convention (Annual).

37287 ■ National Association of Development Companies (NADCO)
6764 Old McLean Village Dr.
McLean, VA 22101
Ph: (703)748-2575
Fax: (703)748-2582
Co. E-mail: chris@nadco.org
URL: http://www.nadco.org
Contact: Christopher L. Crawford, President
Description: Small Business Administration Section 504 certified development companies. Provides long-term financing to small and medium-sized businesses. Represents membership in negotiations with the SBA, Congress, and congressional staff members; negotiates changes in legislation, regulations, operation procedures, and other matters such as prepayments problems, reporting requirements, and loan servicing procedures. Provides technical assistance and information regarding special training programs, marketing techniques, audit checklists, and loan closing and processing procedures. Compiles statistics. **Founded:** 1981. **Publications:** *NADCO News* (Monthly). **Educational Activities:** Winter Board Meeting (Annual).

37288 ■ Risk Management Association (RMA)
1801 Market St., Ste. 300
Philadelphia, PA 19103-1613
Ph: (215)446-4000
Fax: (215)446-4101
Co. E-mail: RMAAR@rmahq.org
URL: http://www.rmahq.org
Contact: Kevin M. Blakey, President
URL(s): www.rmahq.org/RMA. **Description:** Commercial and savings banks, and savings and loan, and other financial services companies. Conducts research and professional development activities in areas of loan administration, asset management, and commercial lending and credit to increase professionalism. **Scope:** commercial lending and credit. **Founded:** 1914. **Subscriptions:** archival material books monographs periodicals. **Publications:** *Compare2*; *Member Roster* (Annual); *RMA Annual Statement Studies* (Annual); *The RMA Journal* (10/year); *Annual Statement Studies*; *Annual Statement Studies: Industry Default Probabilities and Cash Flow Measures*. **Educational Activities:** International Securities Lending (Annual); Loan Management Seminar (Annual); Lending and Credit Risk Management (Annual); RMA, The Risk Management Association Annual Conference of Lending and Credit Risk Management (Annual). **Awards:** Award for Journalistic Excellence (Annual); National Paper Writing Competition Award (Annual). **Telecommunication Services:** member@rmahq.org; customers@rmahq.org.

REFERENCE WORKS

37289 ■ *"Abroad, Not Overboard" in Entrepreneur (Vol. 36, April 2008, No. 4, pp. 68)*
Pub: Entrepreneur Media, Inc.
Ed: Crystal Detamore-Rodman. **Description:** Export-Import Bank is an agency created by the U.S. government to help exporters get credit insurance and capital loans by providing them with loan guarantees. The bank, being criticized as supporting more the bigger exporters, has allotted to smaller businesses a bigger portion of the annual credit being approved.

37290 ■ *"Advance America Closing All Pa. Stores" in American Banker (Vol. 172, December 20, 2007, No. 244, pp. 11)*
Pub: SourceMedia Inc.
Ed: William Launder. **Description:** Advance America Cash Advance Centers Inc. is closing its 66 locations in Pennsylvania while it awaits a state Supreme Court ruling about the excessively high fees it carries for loan products.

37291 ■ *"Affordable Financing for Acquisitions" in Franchising World (Vol. 42, September 2010, No. 9, pp. 47)*
Pub: International Franchise Association
Ed: Gene Cerrotti. **Description:** Acquisition pricing is reasonable and interest rates are low and quality franchised resale opportunities are priced 4.5 times EBITDA. Information about Small Business Administration loans is also included.

37292 ■ *"All Indicators in Michigan Innovation Index Drop in 4Q" in Crain's Detroit Business (Vol. 25, June 22, 2009, No. 25, pp. 9)*
Pub: Crain Communications Inc. - Detroit
Ed: Ryan Beene. **Description:** Economic indicators that rate Michigan's innovation fell in the fourth quarter of 2008. The index of trademark applications, SBA loans, venture capital funding, new incorporations and other indicators traced dropped 12.6 points.

37293 ■ *American Bar Association Legal Guide for Small Business: Everything You Need to Know About Small Business*
Pub: Random House Information Group
Contact: Markus Dohle, Accountant
Ed: American Bar Association. **Released:** June 10, 2010. **Description:** The American Bar Association provides insight into financial, health and family issues affecting small business, including start up issues, employment laws, financing a business, and selling a business.

37294 ■ *"Angel Investing 2009" in Inc. (Vol. 31, January-February 2009, No. 1, pp. 83)*
Pub: Mansueto Ventures LLC
Ed: Kasey Wehrum. **Description:** Tips for finding funding in tough economic times are presented, including secrets for closing second-round deals.

37295 ■ *"Angel Investments Tripled in 2009" in Austin Business JournalInc. (Vol. 29, January 8, 2010, No. 44, pp. 1)*
Pub: American City Business Journals
Ed: Christopher Calnan. **Description:** Central Texas Angel Network (CTAN) has invested $3.5 million in 12 ventures, which include 10 in Austin, Texas in 2009 to triple the amount it invested during 2008. The largest recipient of CTAN's investments is life sciences, which attracted 20 percent of the capital, while software investments fell to 18 percent. The new screening process that helps startups secure CTAN capital is explored.

37296 ■ *"Angel Investors Across State Collaborate" in Austin Business Journal (Vol. 31, May 20, 2011, No. 11, pp. 1)*
Pub: American City Business Journals Inc.
Ed: Christopher Calnan. **Description:** Texas' twelve angel investing groups are going to launch the umbrella organization Alliance of Texas Angel Networks (ATAN) to support more syndicated deals and boost investments in Texas. In 2010, these investing groups infused more than $24 million to startups in 61 deals.

37297 ■ *"Apartment Market Down, Not Out" in Crain's Detroit Business (Vol. 24, October 6, 2008, No. 40, pp. 9)*
Pub: Crain Communications, Inc.
Ed: Daniel Duggan. **Description:** Detroit's apartment market is considered to have some of the strongest fundamentals of any apartment market in the country with relatively low vacancy rates and a relatively low supply of new units compared with demand. Investors continue to show interest in the buildings but the national lending market is making it difficult to invest in the city.

37298 ■ *"Are We There Yet?" in Business Courier (Vol. 24, April 4, 2008, No. 52, pp. 1)*
Pub: American City Business Journals, Inc.
Ed: Lucy May; Dan Monk. **Description:** Groundbreaking for The Banks project happened in April 2, 2008, however, the future of the development remains uncertain due to some unresolved issues such as financing. Developers Harold A. Dawson Co. and Carter still have to pass final financing documents to Hamilton County and Cincinnati. The issue of financial commitment for the central riverfront project is examined.

37299 ■ *"Area VCs Take Praise, Lumps, on Web site" in Boston Business Journal (Vol. 27, October 26, 2007, No. 39, pp. 1)*
Pub: American City Business Journals Inc.
Ed: Jesse Noyes. **Description:** TheFunded.com is a social networking site that allows entrepreneurs to rate venture capitalists and post their comments. Information about venture capitalist firms such as size and the partners behind it are also provided.

37300 ■ *The Art of the Start*
Pub: Portfolio Publishing
Ed: Guy Kawasaki. **Price:** $26.95. **Description:** Apple's Guy Kawasaki offers information to help would-be entrepreneurs create new enterprises. As founder and CEO of Garage Technology Ventures, he has field-tested his ideas with newly hatched companies and he takes readers through every phase of creating a business, from the very basics of raising money and designing a business model through the many stages that eventually lead to success and thus giving back to society.

37301 ■ *"Asia Breathes a Sigh of Relief" in Business Week (September 22, 2008, No. 4100, pp. 32)*
Pub: McGraw-Hill Companies, Inc.
Ed: Bruce Einhorn; Theo Francis; Chi-Chu Tschang; Moon Ihlwan; Hiroko Tashiro. **Description:** Foreign bankers, such as those in Asia, that had been investing heavily in the United States began to worry as the housing crisis deepened and the impact on Freddie Mac and Fannie Mae became increasingly clear. Due to the government bailout, however, central banks will most likely continue to buy American debt.

37302 ■ *"Au Revoir Or Goodbye?" in Barron's (Vol. 88, July 14, 2008, No. 28, pp. 5)*
Pub: Dow Jones & Co., Inc.
Ed: Alan Abelson. **Description:** Former Senator Phil Gramm's opinion that the U.S. is a 'nation of whiners' as they moan about recession is another example of the disconnection between Washington and Wall Street on one hand and the real world on the other. It would be a catastrophe for most of the world if Fannie Mae and Freddie Mac were to go under and take their trillions of mortgage debt with them.

37303 ■ *"Back on Track-Or Off the Rails?" in Business Week (September 22, 2008, No. 4100, pp. 22)*
Pub: McGraw-Hill Companies, Inc.
Ed: Peter Coy; Tara Kalwarski. **Description:** Discusses the possible scenarios the American economy may undergo due to the takeover of Fannie Mae and Freddie Mac. Statistical data included.

37304 ■ *"Bad-Loan Bug Bites Mid-Tier Banks; More Pain, Tighter Lending Standards Ahead, CEOs Say" in Crain's Chicago Business (May 5, 2008)*
Pub: Crain Communications, Inc.
Ed: Steve Daniels. **Description:** Mid-sized commercial banks form the bedrock of Chicago's financial-services industry and they are now feeling the results of the credit crisis that has engulfed the nation's largest banks and brokerages. Commercial borrowers are seeing tighter terms on loans and higher interest rates while bank investors are unable to forecast lenders' earnings performance from quarter to quarter. Statistical data included.

37305 ■ *"Bad Loans Start Piling Up" in Crain's New York Business (Vol. 24, January 7, 2008, No. 1, pp. 2)*
Pub: Crain Communications, Inc.
Ed: Tom Fredrickson. **Description:** Problems in the subprime mortgage industry have extended to other lending activities as evidenced by bank charge-offs on bad commercial and industrial loans which have more than doubled in the third quarter.

37306 ■ *"Bailout May Force Cutbacks, Job Losses" in The Business Journal - Serving Phoenix and the Valley of the Sun (Vol. 29, September 26, 2008, No. 4, pp. 1)*
Pub: American City Business Journals, Inc.
Ed: Mike Sunnucks. **Description:** Economists say the proposed $700 billion bank bailout could affect Arizona businesses as banks could be forced to reduce the amount and number of loans it has thereby forcing businesses to shrink capital expenditures and then jobs. However, the plan could also stimulate the economy by taking bad loans off banks balance sheets according to another economist.

37307 ■ *"Bank Bullish on Austin" in Austin Business JournalInc. (Vol. 29, November 13, 2009, No. 36, pp. A1)*
Pub: American City Business Journals
Ed: Kate Harrington. **Description:** American Bank's presence in Austin, Texas has been boosted by new management and a new 20,000 square foot building. This community bank intends to focus on building relationship with commercial banking customers. American Bank also plans to extend investment banking, treasury management, and commercial lending services.

37308 ■ *"Bank Forces Brooke Founder To Sell His Holdings" in The Business Journal-Serving Metropolitan Kansas City (October 10, 2008)*
Pub: American City Business Journals, Inc.
Ed: James Dornbrook. **Description:** Robert Orr who is the founder of Brooke Corp., a franchise of insurance agencies, says that he was forced to sell virtually all of his stocks in the company by creditors. First United Bank held the founder's stock as collateral for two loans worth $5 million and $7.9 million, which were declared in default in September 2008. Details of the selling of the company's stocks are provided.

37309 ■ *"A Banking Play Without Banking Plagues" in Barron's (Vol. 88, March 31, 2008, No. 13, pp. 26)*
Pub: Dow Jones & Company, Inc.
Ed: Jack Willoughby. **Description:** Fiserv's shares have been dragged down by about 20 percent which presents an appealing entry point since the shares could rise by 30 percent or more by 2009. The company enables banks to post and open new checks and keeps track of loans which are not discretionary processes of banks.

37310 ■ *"Bankruptcies Shoot Up 68 Percent" in Sacramento Business Journal (Vol. 25, July 18, 2008, No. 20, pp. 1)*
Pub: American City Business Journals, Inc.
Ed: Kathy Robertson. **Description:** Personal bankruptcy in the Sacramento area rose by 88 percent for the first half of 2008 while business bankruptcies rose by 50 percent for the same period. The numbers of consumer bankruptcy reflects the effect of high debt, rising mortgage costs, and declining home values on U.S. households.

37311 ■ *"Bankruptcies Swell" in The Business Journal-Portland (Vol. 25, July 4, 2008, No. 17, pp. 1)*
Pub: American City Business Journals, Inc.
Ed: Andy Giegerich. **Description:** Individual and business bankruptcy filings in Portland, Oregon had increased. The rising gas and food prices, mortgage crisis and tightening lending standards are seen as causes of bankruptcies. Statistics on bankruptcy filings are also provided.

37312 ■ *"Bankruptcy Blowback" in Business Week (September 22, 2008, No. 4100, pp. 36)*
Pub: McGraw-Hill Companies, Inc.
Ed: Jessica Silver-Greenberg. **Description:** Changes to bankruptcy laws which were enacted in 2005 after banks and other financial institutions lobbied hard for them are now suffering the consequences of the laws which force more troubled borrowers to let their homes go into foreclosure; lenders suffer financially every time they have to take on a foreclosure and the laws in which they lobbied so hard to see enacted are now becoming a problem for these lending institutions. Details of the changes in the laws are outlined as are the affects on the consumer, the economy and the lenders.

37313 ■ *"Banks Beef Up Deposits, But Lending Lags" in Baltimore Business Journal (Vol. 28, October 29, 2010, No. 25, pp. 1)*
Pub: Baltimore Business Journal
Ed: Gary Haber. **Description:** Bank deposits in the Greater Baltimore area have increased but commercial loans have not. Small business owners complain that banks do not help them expand their businesses, but banks argue that they want to lend but the borrowers have to meet standard qualifications.

37314 ■ *"Banks Find Borrowers Off the Beaten Path" in Boston Business Journal (Vol. 30, December 3, 2010, No. 45, pp. 1)*
Pub: Boston Business Journal
Ed: Tim McLaughlin. **Description:** Banks in Boston have found unlikely applicants for bank loans in organizations such as the Dorchester Collegiate Academy. Dorchester is a charter school in its second year of operation, but qualified for $1.08 million to finance its own building. Other information, as well as views on the unexpected borrowers in Boston, is presented.

37315 ■ *"Banks Seeing Demand for Home Equity Loans Slowing" in Crain's Cleveland Business (Vol. 28, December 3, 2007, No. 48, pp. 1)*
Pub: Crain Communications, Inc.
Ed: Shawn A. Turner. **Description:** Discusses the reasons for the decline in demand for home equity loans and lines of credit. Statistical data included.

37316 ■ *"Basel3 Quick Fix Actually Neither" in Canadian Business (Vol. 83, October 12, 2010, No. 17, pp. 19)*
Pub: Rogers Media Ltd.
Ed: Thomas Watson. **Description:** Information about the so-called Basel 3 standards, which will require banks to hold top-quality capital totaling at least 7 percent of their risk-bearing assets is provided. The rules' supporters believe that a good balance has been reached between improving the Basel 2 framework and maintaining enough lending capital to stimulate an economic growth.

37317 ■ *"The Beauty of Banking's Big Ugly" in Barron's (Vol. 89, July 27, 2009, No. 30, pp. 31)*
Pub: Dow Jones & Co., Inc.
Ed: Andrew Bary. **Description:** Appeal of the shares of Citigroup comes from its sharp discount to its tangible book value and the company's positive attributes include a strong capital position, high loan-loss reserves, and their appealing global-consumer. The shares have the potential to generate nice profits and decent stock gains as the economy turns.

37318 ■ *"Best Turnaround Stocks" in Canadian Business (Vol. 81, Summer 2008, No. 9, pp. 65)*
Pub: Rogers Media Ltd.
Ed: Calvin Leung. **Description:** Share prices of Sierra Wireless Inc. and EXFO Electro Optical Engineering Inc. have fallen over the past year but have good chance at a rebound considering that the companies have free cash flow and no long-term debt. One-year stock performance analysis of the two companies is presented.

37319 ■ *"Beware the Ides of March" in Canadian Business (Vol. 81, April 14, 2008, No. 6, pp. 13)*
Pub: Rogers Media
Ed: Jeff Sanford. **Description:** Financial troubles of Bear Stearns in March, 2008 was part of the credit crunch that started in the summer of 2007 in the U.S. when subprime mortgages that were written for people who could barely afford the payments started defaulting. The bankruptcy protection given to 20 asset backed commercial paper trusts is being fought by the investors in these securities who could stand to lose 40 percent of their money under the agreement.

37320 ■ *"BofA Goes for Small Business" in Austin Business Journal (Vol. 31, July 22, 2011, No. 20, pp. A1)*
Pub: American City Business Journals Inc.
Ed: Christopher Calnan. **Description:** Bank of America is planning to target small businesses as new customers. The bank lost its number one market share in Austin, Texas in 2010.

37321 ■ *"Bracing for a Bear of a Week" in Barron's (Vol. 88, March 17, 2008, No. 11, pp. 24)*
Pub: Dow Jones & Company, Inc.
Ed: Jacqueline Doherty. **Description:** JPMorgan Chase and the Federal Reserve Bank of New York's opening of a line of credit to Bear Stearns cut the stock price of Bear Stearns by 47 percent to 30 followed by speculation of an imminent sale. JP Morgan may be the only potential buyer for the firm and some investors say Bears could be sold at $20 to $30. Bears prime assets include its enormous asset base worth $395 billion.

37322 ■ *Bridging the Equity Gap for Innovative SMEs*
Pub: Palgrave Macmillan
Ed: Elisabetta Gualandri. **Released:** December 1, 2009. **Price:** $85.00. **Description:** This book addresses the evaluation of financial constraints faced by innovative and startup companies and explores ways for bridging the financing and equity gap faced by small to medium business enterprises.

37323 ■ *"Burdened by Debt, Borders Group Suspends Dividends, May Be Sold" in Crain's Detroit Business (Vol. 24, March 24, 2008, No. 12)*
Pub: Crain Communications, Inc.
Ed: Nancy Kaffer. **Description:** Ann Arbor-based Borders Group Inc. is exploring its options and may put itself up for sale due to its declining stock price and mounting debt. The company's fiscal year was

capped by poor holiday sales and Borders does not have the cash on hand to meet the 2009 goals set in its strategic plan.

37324 ■ *"Cabela's Repays Incentives as Sales Lag" in Business Journal-Milwaukee (Vol. 28, November 19, 2010, No. 7, pp. A1)*
Pub: Milwaukee Business Journal
Ed: Stacy Vogel Davis. **Description:** Cabela's has given back $266,000 to the government of Wisconsin owing to its failure to meet projected revenue goals for its Richfield, Wisconsin store. It has also failed to meet sales tax and hiring projection. The company received $4 million in incentives from Washington County.

37325 ■ *"Can You Say $1 Million? A Language-Learning Start-Up Is Hoping That Investors Can" in Inc. (Vol. 33, November 2011, No. 9, pp. 116)*
Pub: Inc. Magazine
Ed: April Joyner. **Description:** Startup, Verbling is a video platform that links language learners and native speakers around the world. The firm is working to raise money to hire engineers in order to build the product and redesign their Website.

37326 ■ *"Can Your Business Still Land a Loan?" in Entrepreneur (Vol. 37, August 2009, No. 8, pp. 62)*
Pub: Entrepreneur Media, Inc.
Ed: Carol Tice. **Description:** Banks are now sticking to the rules before making business loans. A business's existing bank should be the first place they should go to for a loan but if this fails, they should then look to smaller community and regional banks.

37327 ■ *"Capital Position" in Business Journal-Milwaukee (Vol. 28, December 24, 2010, No. 12, pp. A1)*
Pub: Milwaukee Business Journal
Ed: Rich Kirchen. **Description:** Canada-based BMO Financial Group has purchased Marshall and Isley Corporation (M and I), which dominated lending among Wisconsin businesses for decades. The sale of M and I will enable other banks to recruit M and I's customers but BMO Financial remains a stronger competitor since it possesses a more potent capital position.

37328 ■ *"Cautions On Loans With Your Business" in Business Owner (Vol. 35, July-August 2011, No. 4, pp. 5)*
Pub: DL Perkins Company
Description: Caution must be used when borrowing from or lending to any small business. Tax guidelines for the borrowing and lending practice are also included.

37329 ■ *"Centerpoint Funding In Limbo" in The Business Journal - Serving Phoenix and the Valley of the Sun (Vol. 28, August 1, 2008, No. 48)*
Pub: American City Business Journals, Inc.
Ed: Jan Buchholz. **Description:** Avenue Communities LLC has threatened to file a case against Mortgages Ltd. over the finance of the Centerpoint development project in Tempe, Arizona. Avenue Communities want Mortgages Ltd. to file a motion with the U.S. Bankruptcy Court so that it can secure financing for the project. Other views and information on the finance of Centerpoint, are presented.

37330 ■ *"Centrue Sets Down New Roots in St. Louis; Bank Looks to Expand in Exurbs of Chicago" in Crain's Chicago Business (May 5, 2008)*
Pub: Crain Communications, Inc.
Ed: H. Lee Murphy. **Description:** Centrue Financial Corp. has moved its headquarters from Ottawa to suburban St. Louis in search of higher-growth markets. The banks acquisitions and expansion plans are also discussed.

37331 ■ *Chain of Blame: How Wall Street Caused the Mortgage and Credit Crisis*
Pub: John Wiley & Sons, Inc.
Ed: Paul Muolo, Mathew Padilla. **Released:** 2009. **Price:** $27.95. **Description:** The book describes how risky loans given irresponsibly put big investment banks at the center of the subprime crisis.

37332 ■ *"Channelside On the Blocks" in The Business Journal-Serving Greater Tampa Bay (Vol. 28, August 29, 2008, No. 36, pp. 1)*
Pub: American City Business Journals, Inc.
Ed: Michael Hinman. **Description:** In a bankruptcy auction for The Place, one of the more visible condominium projects at Channelside, the lowest bid is just below $73 a square foot. KeyBank National Association, the Key Developers Group LLC's lender, leads the auction planned for October 15, 2008. The reason behind the low minimum bid required to participate in the said action is discussed.

37333 ■ *"Chasing Credit" in Canadian Business (Vol. 81, November 10, 2008, No. 19, pp. 59)*
Pub: Rogers Media Ltd.
Ed: Joe Castaldo. **Description:** Small and medium sized companies are dealing with tightening credit because they appear riskier than usual. Some of these businesses are turning to private investors, but this is not easy since many have invested everything in the stock market. The sector is expected to weaken with the broader Canadian market in the next six months from October 2008.

37334 ■ *"Chinese Fund Loans $33.5 Million to Prestolite" in Crain's Detroit Business (Vol. 26, January 18, 2010, No. 3, pp. 1)*
Pub: Crain Communications Inc.
Ed: Ryan Beene. **Description:** Prestolite Electric Inc., a distributor of alternators and starter motors for commercial and heavy-duty vehicles, looked to China for fresh capital in order to fund new product launches.

37335 ■ *"City Eyeing Tax Breaks for Arena" in Boston Business Journal (Vol. 29, June 3, 2011, No. 4, pp. 1)*
Pub: American City Business Journals Inc.
Ed: Daniel J. Sernovitz. **Description:** Baltimore City is opting to give millions of dollars in tax breaks and construction loans to a group of private investors led by William Hackerman who is proposing to build a new arena and hotel at the Baltimore Convention Center. The project will cost $500 million with the state putting up another $400 million for the center's expansion.

37336 ■ *"Cleanup to Polish Plating Company's Bottom Line" in Crain's Cleveland Business (Vol. 28, October 29, 2007, No. 43, pp. 4)*
Pub: Crain Communications, Inc.
Ed: Jay Miller. **Description:** Barker Products Co, a manufacturer of nuts and bolts, is upgrading its aging facility which will allow them to operate at capacity and will save the company several hundred thousand dollars a year in operating costs. The new owners secured a construction loan from the county's new Commercial Redevelopment Fund which will allow them to upgrade the building which was hampered by years of neglect.

37337 ■ *"Clock Ticks On Columbia Sussex Debt" in Business Courier (Vol. 27, July 30, 2010, No. 13, pp. 1)*
Pub: Business Courier
Ed: Dan Monk. **Description:** Cincinnati, Ohio-based Columbia Sussex Corporation has made plans to restructure a $1 billion loan bundle that was scheduled to mature in October 2010. The privately held hotel has strived in a weak hotel market to keep pace with its $3 billion debt load.

37338 ■ *"Coming Soon: Bailouts of Fannie and Freddie" in Barron's (Vol. 88, July 14, 2008, No. 28, pp. 14)*
Pub: Dow Jones & Co., Inc.
Ed: Jonathan R. Laing. **Description:** Assurances from the government that Fannie Mae and Freddie Mac are adequately capitalized and able to carry on their duties as guarantors or owners of over $5 trillion of U.S. home mortgages are designed to keep both entities afloat until they attempt to raise $10 billion in new equity. The government would assume any losses in a bailout and owners of the banks' papers would profit as yields drop.

37339 ■ *The Commonsense Way to Build Wealth: One Entrepreneur Shares His Secrets*
Pub: Griffin Publishing Group
Ed: Jack Chou. **Released:** September 2004. **Price:** $19.95. **Description:** Entrepreneurial tips to accumulate wealth, select the proper business or franchise, choose and manage rental property, and how to negotiate a good lease.

37340 ■ *"Community Food Co-op Creates Revolving Loan Program for Local Farmers" in Bellingham Business Journal (Vol. February 2010, pp. 3)*
Pub: Sound Publishing Inc.
Description: Community Food Co-op's Farm Fund received a $12,000 matching grant from the Sustainable Whatcom Fund of the Whatcom Community Foundation. The Farm Fund will create a new revolving loan program for local farmers committed to using sustainable practices.

37341 ■ *The Complete Guide to Buying a Business*
Pub: NOLO
Ed: Fred S. Steingold. **Released:** November 2007. **Price:** $24.99. **Description:** Key steps in buying a business are highlighted, focusing on legal issues, tax considerations, approaches for valuing a business, financing, structuring the deal, along with forms and documents for taking ownership are included.

37342 ■ *"Compounding Opportunity" in Hispanic Business (October 2007, pp. 72, 74-75)*
Pub: Hispanic Business
Ed: Hildy Medina. **Description:** New banks are targeting Hispanic entrepreneurs.

37343 ■ *"Condominium Sales Fall to a Seven-Year Low" in Crain's Chicago Business (Vol. 31, November 10, 2008, No. 45, pp. 2)*
Pub: Crain Communications, Inc.
Ed: Alby Gallun. **Description:** Downtown Chicago condominium market is experiencing the lowest number of sales in years due to the tightening of the mortgage lending market, the Wall Street crisis and the downturn in the economy. The supply of new condos is soaring, the result of the building boom of 2005 and 2006; many developers are finding it difficult to pay off construction loans and fear foreclosure on their properties. Additional information and statistical data related to the downtown condominium market is provided.

37344 ■ *"Consumers Finding It Harder to Get and Keep Credit" in Chicago Tribune (January 10, 2009)*
Pub: McClatchy-Tribune Information Services
Ed: Susan Chandler. **Description:** Five tips to maintain a good credit rating in these economic times are outlined and discussed.

37345 ■ *"A Conversation With; Ron Gatner, Jones Lang LaSalle" in Crain's Detroit Business (Vol. 24, October 6, 2008, No. 40, pp. 9)*
Pub: Crain Communications, Inc.
Description: Interview with Ron Gatner who is a corporate real estate adviser with the real estate company Jones Lang LaSalle as well as the company's executive vice president and part of the tenant advisory team; Gatner speaks about the impact that the Wall Street crisis is having on the commercial real estate market in Detroit.

37346 ■ *"Cornered by Credit; As $1 Billion in Loans Come Due, Will Landlords Find Funds?" in Crain's Detroit Business (October 6, 2008)*
Pub: Crain Communications, Inc.
Ed: Daniel Duggan. **Description:** Conduit loans are used by many real estate investors and are normally issued in 7- to 10-year terms with balloon payments due at the end, requiring the full balance to be paid upon maturity. Many building owners may find their properties going into foreclosure as these loans mature next year since these loans cannot be extended like typical loans and the credit crisis along

with falling property values is making it more difficult to secure new sources of funding. Possible solutions to this problem are also explored.

37347 ■ *"Corus Eases Off Ailing Condo Market; Office Developers Get Majority of 1Q Loans" in Crain's Chicago Business (April 28, 2008)*
Pub: Crain Communications, Inc.
Ed: H. Lee Murphy. **Description:** Corus Bankshares Inc., a specialist in lending for the condominium high-rise construction market, is diversifying its portfolio by making loans to office developers and expects to be investing in hotels through the rest of the year. Corus' $7.57 billion loan portfolio is also discussed in detail as well as the company's earnings and share price. Statistical data included.

37348 ■ *"Crash Pads" in Business Courier (Vol. 24, November 2, 2008, No. 29, pp. 1)*
Pub: American City Business Journals, Inc.
Ed: Jon Newberry. **Description:** Francisca Webster accumulated $4 million in mortgage debt in about 2 months. She filed a lawsuit against her tax preparer and her mortgage broker contending that the defendants had breached their fiduciary duties to her and made fraudulent misrepresentations to her. The other details of the case are supplied.

37349 ■ *"The Credit Crisis Continues" in Barron's (Vol. 88, March 10, 2008, No. 10, pp. M12)*
Pub: Dow Jones & Company, Inc.
Ed: Randall W. Forsyth. **Description:** Short-term Treasury yields dropped to new cyclical lows in early March 2008, with the yield for the two-year Treasury note falling to 1.532 percent. Spreads of the mortgage-backed securities of Fannie Mae and Freddie Mac rose on suspicion of collapses in financing.

37350 ■ *"Credit Crisis Puts Market in Unprecedented Territory" in Crain's New York Business (Vol. 24, January 7, 2008, No. 1, pp. 14)*
Pub: Crain Communications, Inc.
Ed: Aaron Elstein. **Description:** Banks are being forced to take enormous losses due to investors who are refusing to buy anything linked to subprime mortgages and associated securities.

37351 ■ *"Credit Crunch Gives, Takes Away" in The Business Journal-Serving Metropolitan Kansas City (Vol. 27, October 17, 2008, No. 5, pp. 1)*
Pub: American City Business Journals, Inc.
Ed: Suzanna Stagemeyer. **Description:** Although many Kansas City business enterprises have been adversely affected by the U.S. credit crunch, others have remained relatively unscathed. Examples of how local businesses are being impacted by the crisis are provided including: American Trailer & Storage Inc., which declared bankruptcy after failing to pay a long-term loan; and NetStandard, a technology firm who, on the other hand, is being pursued by prospective lenders.

37352 ■ *"Credit Crunch Takes Bite Out Of McDonald's" in Advertising Age (Vol. 79, September 29, 2008, No. 36, pp. 1)*
Pub: Crain Communications, Inc.
Ed: Emily Bryson York. **Description:** McDonald's will delay its launch of coffee bars inside its restaurants due to the banking crisis which has prompted Bank of America to halt loans to the franchise chains.

37353 ■ *"Credit-Market Crisis Batters Origen Financial's Bottom Line" in Crain's Detroit Business (Vol. 24, March 31, 2008, No. 13, pp. 4)*
Pub: Crain Communications, Inc.
Description: Overview of the effect the credit-market crisis has had on Origen Financial Inc., a company that underwrites and services loans for manufactured housing. CEO Ronald Klein didn't think Origen would be affected by the collapse due to its sound operations but the company's share price dropped considerably causing its auditors to warn that the company's existence could be in jeopardy.

37354 ■ *"Credit Unions Buck Trend, Lend Millions More" in Saint Louis Business Journal (Vol. 32, September 9, 2011, No. 2, pp. 1)*
Pub: Saint Louis Business Journal
Ed: Greg Edwards. **Description:** St. Louis, Missouri-based credit unions have been making more loans despite the weak economy. Credit unions have made a total of $3.46 billion in outstanding loans as of June 30, 2011.

37355 ■ *"Critics: Efforts to Fix Loans Won't Stop Foreclosure Wave" in Business First Columbus (Vol. 25, November 14, 2008, No. 12, pp. A1)*
Pub: American City Business Journals
Ed: Adrian Burns. **Description:** Efforts by U.S. banks to help homeowners pay mortgages are seen to have little if any impact on foreclosures. Banks have announced plans to identify and aid troubled borrowers. Statistical data included.

37356 ■ *"Culture, Community and Chicken Fingers" in Entrepreneur (Vol. 37, July 2009, No. 7, pp. 96)*
Pub: Entrepreneur Media, Inc.
Ed: Jason Daley. **Description:** Raising Cane's Chicken Fingers founder Todd Graves shares his experiences in running the company - from getting funding to plans for company. Graves believes that the company wants franchisees to live and breathe the brand, and that the key to its success is doing one thing and doing it right. Cane's Pillar Program, a financial support program for franchisees, is also discussed.

37357 ■ *"The Deal - Rhymes With Steal - Of A Lifetime" in Barron's (Vol. 88, March 24, 2008, No. 12, pp. 24)*
Pub: Dow Jones & Company, Inc.
Ed: Andrew Bary. **Description:** JPMorgan Chase's impending acquisition of Bear Stearns for $2.50 a share is a huge steal for the former. JPMorgan is set to acquire a company with a potential annual earnings of $1 billion while the Federal Reserve funds Bear's illiquid assets by providing $30 billion in non-recourse loans.

37358 ■ *"Dealers Fight To Steer Course" in The Business Journal-Serving Metropolitan Kansas City (Vol. 27, November 7, 2008, No. 9, pp. 1)*
Pub: American City Business Journals, Inc.
Ed: Steve Vockrodt. **Description:** One local automobile dealer says that their sales are down by 30 to 40 percent and that car financing is now in the low 60 percentile from 85 to 88 percent. The National Automobile Dealers Association says that 700 dealerships are likely to be lost for 2008.

37359 ■ *"Death Spiral" in Business Journal Serving Greater Tampa Bay (Vol. 30, October 29, 2010, No. 45, pp. 1)*
Pub: Tampa Bay Business Journal
Ed: Margie Manning. **Description:** Bay Cities Bank has started working on the loan portfolio of its acquisition, Progress Bank of Florida. Regulators closed Progress Bank in October 2010 after capital collapsed due to charge-offs and increases in the provision for future loan losses.

37360 ■ *"Delinquent Properties on the Rise" in Business Courier (Vol. 27, June 11, 2010, No. 6, pp. 1)*
Pub: Business Courier
Ed: Dan Monk. **Description:** Reports show that Cincinnati now ranks in the U.S. Top 20 for its delinquency rate on securitized commercial real estate loans. In December 2009, the region ranked 28th out of 50 cities studied by Trepp LLC. As of May 30, 2010, more than $378 million in commercial mortgage-backed security loans were more than 60 days past due.

37361 ■ *"Developer Wins Bout with Bank in Roundabout Way" in Tampa Bay Business Journal (Vol. 30, January 29, 2010, No. 6, pp. 1)*
Pub: American City Business Journals
Ed: Janet Leiser. **Description:** Developer Donald E. Phillips of Phillips Development and Realty LLC won against the foreclosure filed by First Horizon National Corporation, which is demanding the company to fully pay its $2.9 million loan. Phillips requested that his company pay monthly mortgage and extend the loan's maturity date.

37362 ■ *"Do-Gooder Finance: How a New Crop of Investors Is Helping Social Entrepreneurs" in Inc. (February 2008, pp. 29-30)*
Pub: Gruner & Jahr USA Publishing
Ed: Nitasha Tiku. **Description:** Social venture firms are not seeking to sell companies as quickly as traditional venture companies. Four socially minded venture capital firms and banks profiled include, Underdog Venture, Island Pond, Vermont; Root Capital, Cambridge, Massachusetts; ShoreBank Pacific, Ilwaco, Washington; and TBL Capital, Sausalito, California.

37363 ■ *"Don't Count Your Millions Yet" in Business Courier (Vol. 24, January 11, 2008, No. 40, pp. 1)*
Pub: American City Business Journals, Inc.
Ed: Steve Watkins. **Description:** Merger and acquisition deals have been difficult to complete since 2007 largely due to a weaker economy and the credit crunch. Buyers have become more cautious because of the state of the economy and capital has become tougher to obtain because of the credit market crisis. The trends in mergers and acquisitions are analyzed further.

37364 ■ *"Don't Expect Quick Fix" in The Business Journal-Serving Metropolitan Kansas City (Vol. 27, October 3, 2008, No. 3, pp. 1)*
Pub: American City Business Journals, Inc.
Ed: James Dornbrook. **Description:** United States governmental entities cannot provide a quick fix solution to the current financial crisis. The economy requires a systemic change in the way people think about credit. The financial services industry should also focus on core lending principles.

37365 ■ *"EDF Ventures Dissolves Fund, Begins Anew On Investment" in Crain's Detroit Business (Vol. 24, February 25, 2008, No. 8, pp. 14)*
Pub: Crain Communications Inc. - Detroit
Ed: Tom Henderson. **Description:** EDF Ventures is Michigan's oldest venture capital firm and was part of the second round of investments by the state's 21st Century Investment Fund and the Venture Michigan Fund.

37366 ■ *"Emerging Tech Fund Strong in 2009" in Austin Business JournalInc. (Vol. 29, December 25, 2009, No. 42, pp. 1)*
Pub: American City Business Journals
Ed: Christopher Calnan. **Description:** Texas' Emerging Technology Fund (ETF) has seen an increase in applications from the state's technology companies in 2009. ETF received 87 applications in 2009 from Central Texas companies versus 50 during 2008 while $10.5 million was given to seven Texas companies compared with $10.6 million to ten companies in 2008.

37367 ■ *"Export Initiative Launched" in Philadelphia Business Journal (Vol. 28, December 11, 2009, No. 43, pp. 1)*
Pub: American City Business Journals
Ed: Athena D. Merritt. **Description:** The first initiative that came out of the partnership between the Export-Import Bank of the US, the city of Philadelphia, and the World Trade Center of Greater Philadelphia is presented. A series of export finance workshops have featured Ex-Im Bank resources that can provide Philadelphia businesses with working capital, insurance protection and buyer financing.

37368 ■ *"Fair Play? China Cheats, Carney Talks and Rankin Walks; Here's the Latest" in Canadian Business (Vol. 81, March 17, 2008, No. 4)*
Pub: Rogers Media
Description: Discusses the World Trade Organization which says that China is breaking trade rules by taxing imports of auto parts at the same rate as foreign-made finished cars. Mark Carney first speech as the governor of the Bank of Canada made economists suspect a rate cut on overnight loans. Andre Rankin was ordered by the Ontario Securities Commission to pay $250,000 in investigation costs.

37369 ■ *Family Limited Partnership Deskbook*
Pub: American Bar Association
Contact: Carolyn Lamm, President
Ed: David T. Lewis; Andrea C. Chomakos. **Released:** March 25, 2008. **Price:** $169.95. **Description:** Forming and funding a family limited partnership or limited liability company is complicated. In-depth analysis of all facets of this business entity are examined using detailed guidance on the basic principles of drafting, forming, funding, and valuing an FLP or LLC and also covers tax concerns. Examples and extensive sample forms are included on a CD-ROM included with the book.

37370 ■ *"Fannie and Freddie: How They'll Change" in Business Week (September 22, 2008, No. 4100, pp. 30)*
Pub: McGraw-Hill Companies, Inc.
Ed: Jane Sasseen. **Description:** Three possible outcomes of the fate of struggling mortgage giants Freddie Mac and Fannie Mae after the government bailout are outlined.

37371 ■ *"Fight Ensues Over Irreplaceable Gowns" in Tampa Bay Business Journal (Vol. 30, January 15, 2010, No. 4, pp. 1)*
Pub: American City Business Journals
Ed: Janet Leiser. **Description:** People's Princess Charitable Foundation Inc. founder Maureen Rorech Dunkel has sought Chapter 11 bankruptcy protection before a state court decides on the fate of the five of 13 Princess Diana Gowns. Dunkel and the nonprofit were sued by Patricia Sullivan of HRH Venture LLC who claimed they defaulted on $1.5 million in loans.

37372 ■ *"Financing for NNSA Plant Is a Work in Progress" in The Business Journal-Serving Metropolitan Kansas City (October 24, 2008)*
Pub: American City Business Journals, Inc.
Ed: Rob Roberts. **Description:** The Kansas City Council approved a development plan for a $500 million nuclear weapons parts plant in south Kansas City. The US Congress approved a $59 million annual lease payment to the plant's developer. Financing for the construction of the plant remains in question as the plant's developers have to shoulder construction costs.

37373 ■ *Financing Your Business: Get a Grip on Finding the Money*
Pub: Self-Counsel Press, Incorporated
Ed: Angie Mohr. **Released:** October 2004. **Price:** $14.95 (US), $19.95 (Canadian). **Description:** Recommendations to help raise capital for a new or expanding small company.

37374 ■ *Financing Your Small Business*
Pub: Barron's Educational Series Inc.
Contact: Alex Holtz, President
E-mail: aholtz@berronseduc.com
Ed: Robert Walter. **Released:** December 2003. **Description:** Tips for raising venture capital, dealing with bank officials, and initiating public offerings of stock shares for small business.

37375 ■ *"Find Private Money for FutureGen Plant" in Crain's Chicago Business (Vol. 34, September 12, 2011, No. 37, pp. 18)*
Pub: Crain Communications Inc.
Description: FutureGen is a clean-coal power plant being developed in Southern Illinois. The need for further funding is discussed.

37376 ■ *"Florin Car Dealers Drive Plan" in Sacramento Business Journal (Vol. 25, August 22, 2008, No. 25, pp. 1)*
Pub: American City Business Journals, Inc.
Ed: Melanie Turner. **Description:** Automobile dealers in Sacramento, California are working with the city and the business district in planning for future redevelopment in Florin Road. The move stemmed from pressure from the Elk Grove Auto Mall, high fuel prices and the credit crunch. The area has suffered business closures recently.

37377 ■ *"Former Mayor Driving $500 Million Real Estate Equity Fund" in The Business Journal - Serving Phoenix and the Valley of the Sun (Vol. 28, August 15, 2008, No. 50, pp. 1)*
Pub: American City Business Journals, Inc.
Ed: Jan Buchholz. **Description:** Paul John, the former mayor of Phoenix, is establishing a $500 million real estate asset management fund. The fund is dubbed Southwest Next Capital Management and has attracted three local partners, namely Joseph Meyer, Jay Michalowski, and James Mullany, who all have background in finance and construction.

37378 ■ *"Gateway Delays Start" in The Business Journal-Serving Metropolitan Kansas City (Vol. 27, October 31, 2008, No. 8, pp. 1)*
Pub: American City Business Journals, Inc.
Ed: Rob Roberts. **Description:** Economic problems caused, in part, by the Wall Street crisis has resulted in the setback of a proposed mixed-use redevelopment project, The Gateway. The $307 million project, which includes the Kansas Aquarium, will be delayed due to financing problems. Details of the project are given.

37379 ■ *"Going to Bat" in Canadian Business (Vol. 80, February 26, 2007, No. 5, pp. S7)*
Pub: Rogers Media
Description: Various strategies to make the business loan lending process simple and faster are presented.

37380 ■ *Golden States Financial Directory*
Pub: Accuity Inc.
Contact: Hugh M. Jones, IV, President
URL(s): store.accuitysolutions.com/order.html. **Released:** Semiannual; January and July. **Price:** $430, Individuals. **Covers:** Holding companies, head offices and branches of all commercial banks, savings and loans, and credit unions with assets over $5 million in Alaska, Arizona, California, Colorado, Hawaii, Idaho, Montana, New Mexico, Oregon, Utah, Washington, and Wyoming. **Entries include:** Name, address, phone, fax, key bank officers by functional title, directors, date established, detailed financial data, association's membership, correspondent banks, out-of-town branches, holding company affiliation, ABA Transit Number and Routing Symbol, MICR number with check digit, type of charter. **Arrangement:** Geographical. **Indexes:** Alphabetical.

37381 ■ *"A Good Step, But There's a Long Way to Go" in Business Week (September 22, 2008, No. 4100, pp. 10)*
Pub: McGraw-Hill Companies, Inc.
Ed: James C. Cooper. **Description:** Despite the historic action by the U.S. government to nationalize the mortgage giants Freddie Mac and Fannie Mae, rising unemployment rates may prove to be an even bigger roadblock to bringing back the economy from its downward spiral. The takeover is meant to restore confidence in the credit markets and help with the mortgage crisis but the rising rate in unemployment may make many households unable to take advantage of any benefits which arise from the bailout. Statistical data included.

37382 ■ *"Good Track Record Helps Developer Secure Construction Loan for Offices" in Miami Daily Business Review (March 26, 2008)*
Pub: ALM Media Inc.
Description: Luis Lamar, developer, has secured a $64.75 million construction loan to construct a Class A office building in Kendall, Florida. Details of the loan and proposed construction are presented.

37383 ■ *"Goodwill Haunts Local Companies; Bad Buyouts During Boom Times Producing Big Writedowns" in Crain's Chicago Business (Apr. 28, 2008)*
Pub: Crain Communications, Inc.
Ed: Ann Saphir. **Description:** Many companies are having to face the reality that they overpaid for acquisitions made in better economic times; investors often dismiss such one-time charges as mere accounting adjustments but writeoffs related to past acquisitions can signal future problems because they mean the expected profits that justified the purchase have not materialized. Writeoffs are particularly worrisome for firms with a lot of debt and whose banks require them to have enough assets to back up their borrowings.

37384 ■ *"Growing Field" in Crain's Detroit Business (Vol. 26, January 11, 2010, No. 2, pp. 3)*
Pub: Crain Communications Inc.
Description: Detroit's TechTown was awarded a combination loan and grant of $4.1 million from the U.S. Department of Housing and Urban Development to build a 15,000-square-foot stem cell center, a collection of laboratories that will be available to both for-profit companies and university researchers.

37385 ■ *"Hank Paulson On the Housing Bailout and What's Ahead" in Business Week (September 22, 2008, No. 4100, pp. 19)*
Pub: McGraw-Hill Companies, Inc.
Ed: Maria Bartiromo. **Description:** Interview with Treasury Secretary Henry Paulson in which he discusses the bailout of Fannie Mae and Freddie Mac as well as the potential impact on the American economy and foreign interests and investments in the country. Paulson has faith that the government's actions will help to stabilize the housing market.

37386 ■ *"Hard Times for Hard Money" in Sacramento Business Journal (Vol. 25, July 18, 2008, No. 20, pp. 1)*
Pub: American City Business Journals, Inc.
Ed: Michael Shaw. **Description:** Three private lenders who supplied $1 million sued VLD Realty, its associated companies and owners Volodymyr and Leonid Dubinsky accusing them of default after a plan to build two subdivisions fell through. Investigators are finding that borrowers and lenders ignored most rules on private investments on real estate.

37387 ■ *"Hayes Lemmerz Reports Some Good News Despite Losses" in Crain's Detroit Business (Vol. 24, April 14, 2008, No. 15, pp. 4)*
Pub: Crain Communications Inc.
Ed: Nancy Kaffer. **Description:** Hayes Lemmerz International Inc., a wheel manufacturer from Northville that has reported a positive free cash flow for the first time in years, a narrowed net loss in the fourth quarter and significant restructuring of the company's debt.

37388 ■ *"Health Care Leads Sectors Attracting Capital" in Hispanic Business (March 2008, pp. 14-16, 18)*
Pub: Hispanic Business
Ed: Scott Williams. **Description:** U. S. Hispanic healthcare, media, and food were the key industries in the U.S. gaining investors in 2007.

37389 ■ *"Health Providers Throw Lifeline to Clinics" in Sacramento Business Journal (Vol. 25, July 25, 2008, No. 21, pp. 1)*
Pub: American City Business Journals, Inc.
Ed: Kathy Robertson. **Description:** Health Net of California Inc., Catholic Healthcare West and Sutter Health are each providing up to $5 million in no-interest and low-interest loans to clinics in California, while the Sisters of Mercy of the Americas Burlingame Regional Community is offering $300,000. Other details on the short term loans are discussed.

37390 ■ *Home-Based Business for Dummies*
Pub: John Wiley and Sons, Inc.
Ed: Paul Edwards, Sarah Edwards, Peter Economy. **Released:** February 25, 2005. **Price:** $19.99. **Description:** Provides all the information needed to start

and run a home-based business. Topics include: selecting the right business; setting up a home office; managing money, credit, and financing; marketing; and ways to avoid distractions while working at home.

37391 ■ *"A Home of Her Own" in Hawaii Business (Vol. 53, October 2007, No. 4, pp. 51)*
Pub: Hawaii Business Publishing
Ed: Maria Torres-Kitamura. **Description:** It was observed that the number of single women in Hawaii purchasing their own home has increased, as that in the whole United States where the percentage has increased from 14 percent in 1995 to 22 percent in 2006. However, First Hawaiian Bank's Wendy Lum thinks that the trend will not continue in Hawaii due to lending restrictions. The factors that women consider in buying a home of their own are presented.

37392 ■ *"Homes Stall As Owners Resist Major Price Cuts" in Crain's Chicago Business (Vol. 31, April 21, 2008, No. 16, pp. 38)*
Pub: Crain Communications, Inc.
Ed: Kevin Davis. **Description:** Discusses the high-end housing market and the owners who are resisting major price cuts as well as the buyers who look at long market times as a sign that something is wrong with the property.

37393 ■ *"Hospitals Feel Pain from Slow Economy" in Business Courier (Vol. 27, September 3, 2010, No. 18, pp. 1)*
Pub: Business Courier
Ed: James Ritchie. **Description:** Hospitals in Cincinnati, Ohio have suffered from decreased revenues owing to the economic crises. Declining patient volumes and bad debt have also adversely impacted hospitals.

37394 ■ *How to Raise Capital: Techniques and Strategies for Financing and Valuing Your Small Business*
Pub: McGraw-Hill Companies Inc.
Contact: Deven Sharma, President
Ed: Jeffrey A. Timmons, Stephen Spinelli, Andrew Zacharakis. **Released:** May 2004. **Price:** $16.95 (US), $24.95 (Canadian). **Description:** Small business financing process is examined. Tips for identifying the financial life cycle of new ventures, developing a framework for financial strategies, and understanding an investor's prospective.

37395 ■ *How to Start and Run Your Own Corporation: S-Corporations For Small Business Owners*
Pub: HCM Publishing
Ed: Peter I. Hupalo. **Released:** March 6, 2003. **Price:** $22.95. **Description:** Basics of corporate business structure are explained. Topics include discovering the best business structure for your company; how to decided between an S-Corporation and LLC; choosing the state in which to incorporate, how to form a corporation, angel investing, special issues for one-person corporations, the role of bylaws and corporate minutes, board of directors, taxes, workers' compensation issues, retirement plans, and more.

37396 ■ *"How To Get a Loan the Web 2.0 Way" in Black Enterprise (Vol. 41, December 2010, No. 5, pp. 23)*
Pub: Earl G. Graves Publishing Co. Inc.
Ed: John Simons. **Description:** People are turning to online peer-to-peer network for personal loans as banks are lending less money.

37397 ■ *"If You Go Into the Market Today.." in Canadian Business (Vol. 82, Summer 2009, No. 8, pp. 18)*
Pub: Rogers Media
Ed: Jeff Sanford. **Description:** Opinions of experts and personalities who are known to have bear attitudes towards the economy were presented in the event 'A Night with the Bears' in Toronto in April 2009. Known bears that served as resource persons in the event were Nouriel Roubini, Eric Sprott, Ian Gordon, and Meredith Whitney. The bears were observed to have differences regarding consumer debt.

37398 ■ *"In the SBA's Face" in Hispanic Business (December 2010)*
Pub: Hispanic Business
Ed: Richard Larsen. **Description:** Lloyd Chapman uses the American Small Business League to champion small business. Statistical data included.

37399 ■ *"Industry Escalates Lobbying Efforts For Loan Program" in Crain's Detroit Business (Vol. 24, September 22, 2008, No. 38, pp. 22)*
Pub: Crain Communications Inc.
Ed: Jay Greene; Ryan Beene; Harry Stoffer. **Description:** Auto suppliers such as Lear Corp., which is best known for vehicle seating, also supplies high-voltage wiring for Ford hybrids and is developing other hybrid components. These suppliers are joining automakers in lobbying for the loan program which would promote the accelerated development of fuel-efficient vehicles.

37400 ■ *"Inside the Mind of an Investor: Lessons from Bill Draper" in Inc. (Volume 32, December 2010, No. 10, pp. 140)*
Pub: Inc. Magazine
Ed: Leigh Buchanan. **Description:** Profile of the three-generation Draper family, the first venture capital firm west of the Mississippi.

37401 ■ *"Insider" in Canadian Business (Vol. 81, March 31, 2008, No. 5, pp. 76)*
Pub: Rogers Media
Ed: John Gray. **Description:** Discusses a comparison of an average Canadian family's finances in 1990 with the data from 2007. The average family in 2007 has over $80,000 in debt compared to just under $52,000 in 1990. However, Canadians have also been accumulating solid assets such as homes and stocks. This means that Canadian debt load has fallen from 22 percent in 1990 to 20 percent in 2007 when taken as a percentage of total net worth.

37402 ■ *"Investment Bank Predicts Shakeup in Farm Equipment Industry" in Farm Industry News (November 16, 2011)*
Pub: Penton Business Media Inc.
Ed: Jodie Wehrspann. **Description:** Farming can expect to see more mergers and acquisitions in the agricultural equipment industry, as it appears to be in the early stages of growth over the next few years.

37403 ■ *"Islamic Banks Get a 'Libor' of Their Own" in Wall Street Journal Eastern Edition (November 25 , 2011, pp. C4)*
Pub: Dow Jones & Company Inc. Enterprise Media Group
Contact: Clare Hart, President
Ed: Katy Burne. **Description:** The London interbank offered rate, or Libor, has been used by banks internationally for years. It is the rate at which banks lend money to each other. The rate has not been used by Islamic banks, but now sixteen banks have come up with the Islamic Interbank Benchmark Rate.

37404 ■ *"Karen Case; President of Commercial Real Estate Lending, Privatebancorp Inc." in Crain's Chicago Business (May 5, 2008)*
Pub: Crain Communications, Inc.
Ed: Dee Gill. **Description:** Profile of Karen Case who was hired by PrivateBancorp Inc. to turn its minor share of the city's commercial real estate lending market into a major one.

37405 ■ *"Kenosha 'Lifestyle Center' Delayed" in The Business Journal-Milwaukee (Vol. 25, August 8, 2008, No. 46, pp. A1)*
Pub: American City Business Journals, Inc.
Ed: Rich Kirchen. **Description:** Quality Centers of Orlando, Florida has postponed construction plans for the Kenosha Town Center in Kenosha County, Wisconsin to 2009 due to the economic downturn and lending concerns. The $200-million, 750,000-square-foot retail and residential center will be located near the corner of Wisconsin Highway 50 and I-94.

37406 ■ *"Kerry Steel to Sell Inventory, Close Business After 30 Years" in Crain's Detroit Business (Vol. 24, March 17, 2008, No. 11, pp. 26)*
Pub: Crain Communications, Inc.
Ed: Brent Snavely. **Description:** Kerry Steel Inc. has confirmed that it is selling all of its inventory and equipment and is going out of business; the company, which was once one of the largest steel service centers in the Midwest, has sustained financial losses and is in violation of its loan agreements.

37407 ■ *"Kimball Hill Files for Chapter 11" in Crain's Chicago Business (Vol. 31, April 28, 2008, No. 17, pp. 12)*
Pub: Crain Communications, Inc.
Description: Homebuilder Kimball Hill filed for Chapter 11 bankruptcy protection after months of negotiations with lenders. The firm plans to continue operations as it restructures its debt.

37408 ■ *"Know Your Numbers" in Inc. (Volume 32, December 2010, No. 10, pp. 39)*
Pub: Inc. Magazine
Ed: Norm Brodsky. **Description:** Ways to maximize profit and minimize tax burden are presented.

37409 ■ *"Lack of Support Drives Scientists Away from Valley" in The Business Journal - Serving Phoenix and the Valley of the Sun (Vol. 28, August 1, 2008, No. 48, pp. 1)*
Pub: American City Business Journals, Inc.
Ed: Angela Gonzales. **Description:** Lack of support for scientists has caused scientists like Dietrich Stephan to depart from the city. Stephan is expected to relocate to California where he has found funding for his company Navigenics. Other views and information on the rising rate of the departure of scientists are presented.

37410 ■ *"Laugh or Cry?" in Barron's (Vol. 88, March 24, 2008, No. 12, pp. 7)*
Pub: Dow Jones & Company, Inc.
Ed: Alan Abelson. **Description:** Discusses the American economy which is just starting to feel the effect of the credit and housing crises. JPMorgan Chase purchased Bear Stearns for $2 a share, much lower than its share price of $60, while quasi-government entities Fannie Mae and Freddie Mac are starting to run into trouble.

37411 ■ *"Law Firms See Improvement in Financing Climate" in Sacramento Business Journal (Vol. 28, October 14, 2011, No. 33, pp. 1)*
Pub: Sacramento Business Journal
Ed: Kathy Robertson. **Description:** Sacramento, California-based Weintraub Genshlea Chediak Law Corporation has helped close 26 financing deals worth more than $1.6 billion in 2010, providing indication of improvement in Sacramento's economy. Lawyers have taken advantage of low interest rates to make refinancing agreements and help clients get new funds.

37412 ■ *"Leaning Tower" in Business Courier (Vol. 27, June 4, 2010, No. 5, pp. 1)*
Pub: Business Courier
Ed: Jon Newberry. **Description:** New York-based developer Armand Lasky, owner of Tower Place Mall in downtown Cincinnati, Ohio has sued Birmingham, Alabama-based Regions Bank to prevent the bank's foreclosure on the property. Regions Bank claims Lasky was in default on an $18 million loan agreement. Details on the mall's leasing plan is also discussed.

37413 ■ *"Lehman's Hail Mary Pass" in Business Week (September 22, 2008, No. 4100, pp. 28)*
Pub: McGraw-Hill Companies, Inc.
Ed: Matthew Goldstein; David Henry; Ben Levison. **Description:** Overview of Lehman Brothers' CEO Richard Fuld's plan to keep the firm afloat and end the stock's plunge downward; Fuld's strategy calls for selling off a piece of the firm's investment management business.

37414 ■ *"Lenders" in The Business Journal - Serving Phoenix and the Valley of the Sun (Vol. 28, July 25, 2008, No. 47, pp. 1)*
Pub: American City Business Journals, Inc.
Ed: Jan Buchholz. **Description:** Private equity lender Investor Mortgage Holdings Inc. has continued growing despite the crisis surrounding the real estate and financial industries and has accumulated a $700 million loan portfolio. Private lending has become increasingly important in financing real estate deals as commercial credit has dried up.

37415 ■ *"Lenders Get Boost from Low Rates" in Saint Louis Business Journal (Vol. 32, September 9, 2011, No. 2, pp. 1)*
Pub: Saint Louis Business Journal
Ed: Greg Edwards. **Description:** St. Louis, Missouri-based lenders have benefitted from record low mortgage interest rates. Housing loan applications have increased in view of the development.

37416 ■ *"Lending Door Slams" in Puget Sound Business Journal (Vol. 29, October 24, 2008, No. 27, pp. 1)*
Pub: American City Business Journals
Ed: Jeanne Lang Jones, Kirsten Grind. **Description:** KeyBank's closure of its Puget Sound unit that services single-family homebuilders is part of a nationwide shutdown that includes similar closures in other cities. Bank of America is adopting more conservative terms for homebuilding loans while Union Bank of California is still offering credit for market rate housing.

37417 ■ *"Lending Idea Gets Mixed Review" in Tampa Bay Business Journal (Vol. 29, October 30, 2009, No. 45, pp. 1)*
Pub: American City Business Journals
Ed: Kent Hoover, Margie Manning. **Description:** Tampa Bay area, Florida's community banks have expressed disapproval to the proposal of President Obama to increase lending to small business, wherein the government will provide cheap capital through US Treasury Troubled Asset Relief Program (TARP). The banks were hesitant on the plan because of the strings attached to TARP.

37418 ■ *"Lending Stays Down at Local Banks" in Business Courier (Vol. 27, October 1, 2010, No. 22, pp. 1)*
Pub: Business Courier
Ed: Steve Watkins. **Description:** Greater Cincinnati's largest banks have experienced decreases in loans in the past year due to weak economy and sagging loan demands. Analysis of mid-year data has shown that loans drop by a total of $3.6 billion or 4 percent at the ten largest banks as of June 30, 2010 compared to same period in 2009.

37419 ■ *"A Limited Sphere of Influence" in Mergers & Acquisitions: The Dealmaker's Journal (March 1, 2008)*
Pub: SourceMedia, Inc.
Ed: Ken MacFadyen. **Description:** Changes to the interest rate has had little impact on the mergers and acquisitions market since the federal funds rate does not link directly to the liquidity available to the M&A market; lenders are looking at cash flows and are likely to remain cautious due to other factors impacting the market.

37420 ■ *"The Loan Arranger" in Canadian Business (Vol. 80, October 22, 2007, No. 21, pp. 15)*
Pub: Rogers Media
Ed: Rachel Pulfer. **Description:** Muhammad Yunus received the Nobel Prize in 2006 for the organization that he founded, the Grameen Bank. The bank has helped women in developing countries and has also begun helping millions of individuals to make loans in the U.S. through the Grameen Bank. An evaluation of the Grameen model is provided.

37421 ■ *"Loan Dollars Sit Idle for Energy Plan" in Baltimore Business Journal (Vol. 28, September 10, 2010, No. 18, pp. 1)*
Pub: Baltimore Business Journal
Ed: Scott Dance. **Description:** The Maryland Energy Administration has millions of dollars in Federal stimulus and state energy efficiency cash sitting idle and might be lost once the window for stimulus spending is gone. However, businesses have no interest in betting on renewable energy because some cannot afford to take out more loans. Other challenges faced by these businesses are presented.

37422 ■ *"Local Commercial Real Estate Foreclosures Continue to Rise" in Baltimore Business Journal (Vol. 28, October 1, 2010, No. 21, pp. 1)*
Pub: Baltimore Business Journal
Ed: Daniel J. Sernovitz. **Description:** Foreclosures of commercial real estate across the Greater Baltimore area have continued to rise. The region is now host to about $2 billion worth of commercial properties that carry a maturing debt or have been foreclosed. Commercial real estate owners are unable to finance their debts because banks have become stricter in passing out loans.

37423 ■ *"Local Firms Will Feel Impact Of Wall St. Woes" in The Business Journal-Milwaukee (Vol. 25, September 19, 2008, No. 52, pp. A1)*
Pub: American City Business Journals, Inc.
Ed: Rich Kirchen. **Description:** Wall Street's crisis is expected to affect businesses in Wisconsin, in terms of decreased demand for services and products and increased financing costs. Businesses in Milwaukee area may face higher interest rates and tougher loan standards. The potential impacts of the Wall Street crisis on local businesses are examined further.

37424 ■ *"Local Lending Tumbles $10 Billion Since '08" in Saint Louis Business Journal (Vol. 31, August 26, 2011, No. 53, pp. 1)*
Pub: Saint Louis Business Journal
Ed: Greg Edwards. **Description:** St. Louis, Missouri-based banks lending fell by more than 30 percent in less than three years, from about $30 billion in third and fourth quarters 2008 to about $20 billion in the most recent quarter. However, community banks revealed that they want to lend but there is no loan demand.

37425 ■ *"Local M&A Activity Sputters in 1Q" in Crain's Chicago Business (Vol. 31, April 21, 2008, No. 16, pp. 20)*
Pub: Crain Communications, Inc.
Ed: H. Lee Murphy. **Description:** Local mergers-and-acquisitions activity is down by 34 percent in the first quarter compared to the fourth quarter of last year due to the credit crisis making financing harder to obtain.

37426 ■ *"Lotus Starts Slowly, Dodges Subprime Woes" in Crain's Detroit Business (Vol. 24, April 14, 2008, No. 15, pp. 3)*
Pub: Crain Communications, Inc.
Ed: Tom Henderson. **Description:** Discusses Lotus Bancorp Inc. and their business plan, which although is not right on target due to the subprime mortgage meltdown, is in a much better position than its competitors due to the quality of their loans.

37427 ■ *"Making Waves" in Business Journal Portland (Vol. 27, November 26, 2010, No. 39, pp. 1)*
Pub: Portland Business Journal
Ed: Erik Siemers. **Description:** Corvallis, Oregon-based Columbia Power Technologies LLC is about to close a $2 million Series A round of investment initiated by $750,000 from Oregon Angel Fund. The wave energy startup company was formed to commercialize the wave buoy technology developed by Oregon State University researchers.

37428 ■ *"M&I Execs May Get Golden Parachutes" in Business Journal-Milwaukee (Vol. 28, December 31, 2010, No. 14, pp. A3)*
Pub: Milwaukee Business Journal
Ed: Rich Kirchen. **Description:** Marshall and Isley Corporation's top executives have a chance to receive golden-parachute payments it its buyer, BMO Financial Group, repays the Troubled Asset Relief Program (TARP) loan on behalf of the company. One TARP rule prevents golden-parachute payments to them and the next five most highly paid employees of TARP recipients.

37429 ■ *"The Marathon Club: Building a Bridge to Wealth" in Hispanic Business (March 2008, pp. 24)*
Pub: Hispanic Business
Ed: Hildy Median. **Description:** Minority businesses find it more difficult to secure venture capital for entrepreneurial pursuits. Joe Watson, CEO of Without Excuses and Strategic Hire, suggests Hispanics and African Americans collaborate on issues of importance to minority entrepreneurs.

37430 ■ *"Marine Act Amendments Gain Parliamentary Approval" in Canadian Sailings (July 7, 2008)*
Pub: UBM Global Trade
Contact: Leonard J. Corallo, President
Ed: Alex Binkley. **Description:** Changes to the Canada Marine Act provides better borrowing deals as well as an ability to tap into federal infrastructure funding for environmental protection measures, security improvements and other site enhancements.

37431 ■ *"Market Watch: A Sampling of Advisory Opinion" in Barron's (Vol. 88, March 17, 2008, No. 11, pp. M10)*
Pub: Dow Jones & Company, Inc.
Ed: Paul Schatz; William Gibson; Michael Darda. **Description:** S&P 500 bank stocks were down 46 percent from their 2007 peak while the peak to through fall in 1989-1990 was just over 50 percent. This suggests that the bottom on the bank stocks could be near. The Federal Reserve Board announced they will lend up to $200 billion to primary lenders in exchange other securities.

37432 ■ *"A Matter of Interest" in Canadian Business (Vol. 79, July 17, 2006, No. 14-15, pp. 21)*
Pub: Rogers Media
Ed: Jeff Sanford. **Description:** With the steady decrease in savings, the need for growth in Canada's payloan industry is discussed. Also emphasized are the challenges faced by payloan operators.

37433 ■ *"Md. Bankers Say 'Devil Is In the Details' of New $30B Loan Fund" in Baltimore Business Journal (Vol. 28, October 8, 2010, No. 22)*
Pub: Baltimore Business Journal
Ed: Gary Haber. **Description:** Maryland community bankers have expressed doubts over a new federal loan program for small business. The new law will also earmark $80 billion for community banks. Comments from executives also given.

37434 ■ *"Measuring the Impact" in Mergers & Acquisitions: The Dealmaker's Journal (March 1, 2008)*
Pub: SourceMedia, Inc.
Ed: Ken MacFadyen. **Description:** Discusses a new study out of Europe which contends that the private equity market does not have as much impact on the overall economy as critics contend.

37435 ■ *"MEDC: Put Venture Funds to Work" in Crain's Detroit Business (Vol. 25, June 22, 2009, No. 25, pp. 1)*
Pub: Crain Communications Inc. - Detroit
Ed: Tom Henderson. **Description:** Michigan Strategic Fund board will finalize approval for ESP Holdings II LLC, Peninsula Capital Partners LLC, Triathlon Medical Ventures LLC and Arsenal Venture Partners Inc. are expected to share $35.5 million from the fund.

37436 ■ *"Merchant Cash-Advance Company Enters Canada" in Cardline (Vol. 8, February 29, 2008, No. 9, pp. 1)*
Pub: SourceMedia Inc.
Description: Merchant cash-advance company is expanding operations into Canada.

37437 ■ *"Micro-Finance Agencies and SMEs" in International Journal of Entrepreneurship and Small Business (Vol. 11, August 3, 2010)*
Pub: Publishers Communication Group
Ed: Patricia A. Rowe, Michael J. Christie, Frank Hoy. **Description:** Institutional preparedness of economic development agencies for developing small and medium-sized enterprises (SMEs) is discussed. The

cases presented illustrate variations in the microfinance lender agency-enterprise development of processes for sharing vision and interdependence.

37438 ■ *"Microlending Seen as Having a Major Impact" in Business Journal Serving Greater Tampa Bay (Vol. 30, November 26, 2010, No. 49, pp. 1)*
Pub: Tampa Bay Business Journal
Ed: Margie Manning. **Description:** There are several organizations that are planning to offer microlending services in Tampa Bay, Florida. These include the Children's Board of Hillsborough County, and OUR Microlending Florida LLC. Organizations that are already offering these services in the area include the Small Business Administration and the Tampa Bay Black Business Investment Corp.

37439 ■ *"Midwest Seeks Concessions From Creditors" in The Business Journal-Milwaukee (Vol. 25, July 25, 2008, No. 44, pp. A1)*
Pub: American City Business Journals, Inc.
Ed: Rich Rovito. **Description:** Midwest Airlines Inc. is turning to creditors and lease holders for the financial aspect of its restructuring, which involves going back to serving popular business destinations. Chief executive officer Timothy believes that the company can survive in a niche market as long as it provides quality service. He discusses Midwest's restructuring plan.

37440 ■ *"Millions Needed To Finish First Place" in The Business Journal-Milwaukee (Vol. 25, August 15, 2008, No. 47, pp. A1)*
Pub: American City Business Journals, Inc.
Ed: Rich Kirchen. **Description:** First Place on the River condominium project in Milwaukee, Wisconsin, needs $18.2 million before it can be completed. A total of $6.8 million have already been spent since the project went into receivership on 31 January 2008.

37441 ■ *"MoneyGram In Pact With Payday Lender" in American Banker (Vol. 173, March 7, 2008, No. 46, pp. 6)*
Pub: SourceMedia Inc.
Ed: William Launder. **Description:** Details of pact between MoneyGram International Inc. and Advance America Cash Advance Centers are examined.

37442 ■ *"More Contractors Unpaid" in Puget Sound Business Journal (Vol. 29, October 3, 2008, No. 24, pp. 1)*
Pub: American City Business Journals
Ed: Brad Berton. **Description:** An 80 percent rise in the filing of mechanics' liens was reported in Seattle, Washington. It is believed that financial problems are spreading to construction companies and contractors as home sales slide and builders default on construction loans. Delinquencies of single-family construction homes has increased.

37443 ■ *"Mortgage Securities Drop Hits Home" in The Business Journal-Serving Metropolitan Kansas City (Vol. 27, October 17, 2008, No. 5)*
Pub: American City Business Journals, Inc.
Ed: Rob Roberts. **Description:** Sale of commercial mortgage-backed securities (CMBS) in Kansas City, Missouri have declined. The area may avoid layoffs if the United States government succeeds in stabilizing the economy. Major CMBS players in the area include Midland Loan Services Inc. and KeyBank Real Estate Capital.

37444 ■ *"Mr. Deeds" in Canadian Business (Vol. 81, March 31, 2008, No. 5, pp. 24)*
Pub: Rogers Media
Ed: Thomas Watson. **Description:** Ron Sandler has the right experience to save Northern Rock PLC get through its liquidity problems. Sandler is known for saving Lloyd's of London in the mid-90's and he is not afraid to make enemies. Ron Sandler's assignment to help Northern Rock comes at a time when the health of the U.K. housing is not great.

37445 ■ *"Muddy Portfolio Raises a Question: Just What Is National City Worth?" in Crain's Detroit Business (Vol. 24, April 7, 2008, No. 14)*
Pub: Crain Communications, Inc.
Ed: Jay Miller. **Description:** National City Bank is looking at strategies to help it deal with its credit and loan problems which are reflected in its falling stock price. One possible solution is a merger with another bank, however most national banks are facing their own home-loan portfolio issues and may be unable to tackle another company's unresolved problems. Statistical data included.

37446 ■ *"Neighborhood Watch" in Baltimore Business Journal (Vol. 28, July 23, 2010, No. 11, pp. 1)*
Pub: Baltimore Business Journal
Ed: Daniel J. Sernovitz. **Description:** Maryland government and housing leaders are set to spend $100 million in federal funding to stem the increase in foreclosures in the area. The federal funding is seen as inadequate to resolve the problem of foreclosures.

37447 ■ *"NetSpend, Payday Firm in Pact" in American Banker (Vol. 173, February 22, 2008, No. 7, pp. 7)*
Pub: SourceMedia Inc.
Ed: Daniel Wolfe. **Description:** NetSpend Corporation of Austin, Texas is providing its prepaid cards to Advance America Cash Advance Centers Inc., a Spartanburg, South Carolina payday lender.

37448 ■ *"A New Kid on the Block" in Barron's (Vol. 88, March 17, 2008, No. 11, pp. 58)*
Pub: Dow Jones & Company, Inc.
Ed: Thomas G. Donlan. **Description:** Discusses the Federal Reserve which has offered to lend $100 billion in cash to banks and $200 billion in Treasuries to Wall Street investment banks that have problems with liquidity. The reluctance of the banks to lend money to meet a margin call on securities that could still depreciate is the reason why the agency is going into the direct loan business.

37449 ■ *"The Next Government Bailout?" in Barron's (Vol. 88, March 10, 2008, No. 10, pp. 21)*
Pub: Dow Jones & Company, Inc.
Ed: Jonathan Laing. **Description:** Fannie Mae may need a government bailout as it faces huge hits brought about by the effects of the housing crisis. The shares of the government-sponsored enterprise have dropped 65 percent since the housing crisis began.

37450 ■ *"No End to the Nightmare; America's Car Industry" in The Economist (Vol. 390, January 3, 2009, No. 8612, pp. 46)*
Pub: The Economist Newspaper Inc.
Description: Detroit's struggling auto industry and the government loan package is discussed as well as the United Auto Worker union, which is loathed by Senate Republicans.

37451 ■ *"Not Enough To Go Around" in The Business Journal-Milwaukee (Vol. 25, August 15, 2008, No. 47, pp. A1)*
Pub: American City Business Journals, Inc.
Ed: David Doege. **Description:** Most of the creditors of bankrupt real estate developer Scott Fergus are likely to remain unpaid as he only has an estimated $30,000 available for paying debts. Creditors, as of the 13 August 2008 deadline for filing claims, have filed a total of $79.1 million in claims.

37452 ■ *"A Novel Fix for the Credit Mess" in Barron's (Vol. 88, March 31, 2008, No. 13, pp. 10)*
Pub: Dow Jones & Company, Inc.
Ed: Michael Santoli. **Description:** Due to the common bank-leverage factor of 10, the $250 billion of lost bank capital would have supported $2.5 trillion in lending capacity. Jeffrey Lewis suggests onerous regulations on bank-holding companies that own 10 to 25 percent, as they are partly to blame. Statistical data included.

37453 ■ *"Ohio Commerce Draws Closer to Profitability" in Crain's Cleveland Business (Vol. 28, October 29, 2007, No. 43, pp. 14)*
Pub: Crain Communications, Inc.
Ed: Shawn A. Turner. **Description:** Overview of the business plan of Ohio Commerce Bank, a de novo, or startup bank that is close to turning the corner to profitability. The bank opened in November 2006 and focuses on dealing with small businesses totaling $5 million or less in annual revenues.

37454 ■ *"OK, Bring in the Lawyers" in Crain's Chicago Business (Vol. 31, November 17, 2008, No. 46, pp. 26)*
Pub: Crain Communications, Inc.
Ed: Daniel Rome Levine. **Description:** Bankruptcy attorneys are finding the economic and credit crisis a benefit for their businesses due to the high number of business owners and mortgage holders that are need of their services. One Chicago firm is handling ten times the number of cases they did the previous year and of that about 80 percent of their new clients are related to the real estate sector.

37455 ■ *"On Growth Path of Rising Star" in Boston Business Journal (Vol. 31, June 24, 2011, No. 22, pp. 3)*
Pub: Boston Business Journal
Ed: Kyle Alspach. **Description:** 1366 Technologies Inc. of Lexington, Massachusetts is considered a rising solar power technology company. The firm secured $150 million loan guarantee from the US Department of Energy that could go to the construction of a 1,000 megawatt solar power plant.

37456 ■ *"Past Due: $289 Million in Loans" in Saint Louis Business Journal (Vol. 32, September 23, 2011, No. 4, pp. 1)*
Pub: Saint Louis Business Journal
Ed: Evans Binns. **Description:** New York-based Trepp LLC research found about $289 million in local commercial mortgage-backed securities loans on 20 properties delinquent in payments by 30 days or more as of August 31, 2011. The report also placed the delinquency rate for St. Louis at that time at 9.64 percent.

37457 ■ *"Picture of Success" in Black Enterprise (Vol. 38, December 2007, No. 5, pp. 71)*
Pub: Earl G. Graves Publishing Co. Inc.
Ed: Sheiresa McRae. **Description:** Profile of Kenya Cagle, president and CEO of Caglevision Inc., an independent motion picture production company. Cagle, former off-Broadway child actor, kept his company afloat with financial backing and support from friends, employees, and business colleagues.

37458 ■ *"Placer Land Sells for $12 Million" in Sacramento Business Journal (Vol. 25, July 25, 2008, No. 21, pp. 1)*
Pub: American City Business Journals, Inc.
Ed: Michael Shaw; Celia Lamb. **Description:** Reynen & Bardis Communities Inc., a Sacramento, California-based homebuilder, has purchased the Antonio Mountain Ranch in Placer County, California shortly before the property's scheduled foreclosure on June 27, 2008. Placer County Recorder's data show that the purchase price of the 808-acre wetland-rich property is $12 million.

37459 ■ *"'Pre-Sale' for Planned Could Mich Tower" in Crain's Chicago Business (Vol. 31, March 24, 2008, No. 12, pp. 14)*
Pub: Crain Communications, Inc.
Ed: Eddie Baeb. **Description:** Condominium developer William Warman is planning to build a mixed-use tower at 300 North Michigan Avenue which would include a hotel, retail space, apartments and a parking garage. Mr. Warman is looking for investors to buy part or all of the space in order to make it easier to land financing.

37460 ■ *Prepare to Be a Teen Millionaire*
Pub: Health Communications, Inc.
Contact: Peter Vegso, President
Ed: Robyn Collins; Kimberly Spinks Burleson. **Released:** April 1, 2008. **Price:** $16.95. **Description:** Business reference for any teenager wishing to

become a successful entrepreneur; advice is given from successful teenage millionaires. Topics covered include: choosing a business name, type, and location; use of the Internet; legal issues; branding, sales, and marketing; funding and financial management; return on investment; retirement; development of a sound business plan; and certification for minority or women-owned companies.

37461 ■ *"Private Equity Firms Shopping Valley For Deals" in The Business Journal - Serving Phoenix and the Valley of the Sun (Vol. 29, September 19, 2008, No. 3, pp. 1)*
Pub: American City Business Journals, Inc.
Ed: Mike Sunnucks. **Description:** Private equity firms from California, Boston, New York, and overseas are expected to invest in growth-oriented real estate markets that include Phoenix. Real estate experts revealed that privately held investment and acquisition firms are looking to invest in real estate markets hit by the housing crisis. Views and information on private equity firms' real estate investments are presented.

37462 ■ *"Proposed Accounting Changes Could Complicate Tenant's Leases" in Baltimore Business Journal (Vol. 28, July 2, 2010, No. 8, pp. 1)*
Pub: Baltimore Business Journal
Ed: Daniel J. Sernovitz. **Description:** The Financial Accounting Standards Board has proposed that companies must indicate the value of real estate leases as assets and liabilities on balance sheets instead of expenses. The proposals could cause some companies to document millions of dollars in charges on their books or find difficulty in getting loans.

37463 ■ *Race and Entrepreneurial Success: Black-, Asian-, and White-Owned Businesses in the United States*
Pub: The MIT Press
Contact: Ellen W. Faran, Director
E-mail: ewfaran@mit.edu
Ed: Robert W. Fairlie. **Released:** September 30, 2008. **Price:** $35.00. **Description:** Trends in minority small business ownership are explored, focusing on the importance of human capital, financial capital, and family business background in successful business ownership.

37464 ■ *"Race, Not Income, Played Role in Subprime Loans" in Black Enterprise (Vol. 40, July 2010, No. 12, pp. 26)*
Pub: Earl G. Graves Publishing Co. Inc.
Ed: Deborah Creighton Skinner. **Description:** African Americans were 80 percent more likely than whites to receive a subprime loan and were almost 20 percent more likely to go into foreclosure, according to a study done by the National Community Reinvestment Coalition. Statistical data included.

37465 ■ *Raising Capital*
Pub: Raising Capital
Ed: Andrew J. Sherman. **Price:** $34.95.

37466 ■ *Raising Capital*
Pub: Greenwood Publishing Group, Inc.
Ed: David Nour. **Released:** March 1, 2009. **Price:** $39.95. **Description:** An overview to help entrepreneurs find capital for starting and maintaining a small business is presented. The author shows how to develop long-term relationships with financial partners and ways to attract financing to fund the startup and growth phases of any business. Entrepreneurs tell how they raised money from friends, family, angel investors, banks and venture capitalists and private equity firms.

37467 ■ *Raising Venture Capital for the Serious Entrepreneur*
Pub: McGraw-Hill Inc.
Ed: Dermot Berkery. **Released:** September 2007. **Price:** $49.95. **Description:** Sourcebook to help entrepreneurs secure venture capital from investors.

37468 ■ *"Ready for a Rally?" in The Economist (Vol. 390, January 3, 2009, No. 8612, pp. 54)*
Pub: The Economist Newspaper Inc.
Description: Analysts predict that the recession could end by 2010. The current economic crisis is presented in detail.

37469 ■ *"Real Estate Defaults Top $300M" in Business Courier (Vol. 26, January 15, 2010, No. 39, pp. 1)*
Pub: American City Business Journals, Inc.
Ed: Dan Monk. **Description:** Cincinnati commercial real estate owners defaulting in securitized loans reached $306 million at the end of 2009. The trend has lifted the region's default rate to nearly 9 percent. National average for commercial real estate default is examined.

37470 ■ *"Real Estate Woes Mount for State's Smaller Banks" in Boston Business Journal (Vol. 27, November 30, 2007, No. 44, pp. 1)*
Pub: American City Business Journals Inc.
Ed: Craig M. Douglas. **Description:** Massachusetts banking industry is facing a steep increase on loan defaults such as in home mortgages and condominium projects, contrary to public belief that the local industry is safe from the real estate meltdown. The dollar value of local banks' nonperforming loans doubled in 2007, and is rising statewide. Other banking issues in the state are discussed.

37471 ■ *"Recession-Proof Your Startup" in Crain's Chicago Business (Vol. 31, November 10, 2008, No. 45, pp. 24)*
Pub: Crain Communications, Inc.
Description: Detailed information concerning ways in which to start a business during an economic crisis is provided. Ways in which to find financing, the importance of a solid business plan, customer service, problem-solving and finding the right niche for the region are also discussed.

37472 ■ *"Refi Requests Soar, But New Rules May Mean Fewer Closings" in The Business Review Albany (Vol. 35, April 4, 2008, No. 53, pp. 1)*
Pub: The Business Review
Ed: Barbara Pinckney. **Description:** National refinancing applications grew by 82 percent in the week that ended March 21, 2008, due to the depressed real estate market and lower interest rates. Refinancing applicants, however, may be surprised with new rules on loan applications such as the required credit score of at least 720 in avoiding payment of extra fees. The developments in application standards for home loans are also examined.

37473 ■ *"Research Reports" in Barron's (Vol. 88, March 24, 2008, No. 12, pp. M10)*
Pub: Dow Jones & Company, Inc.
Description: Investors are recommending purchasing shares of Ampco Pittsburgh due to an expected surge in earnings. Deteriorating credit quality presents problems for the shares of BankAtlantic Bancorp, whose price targets have been lowered from $7 to $5 each. Shares of Helicos Biosciences are expected to move sideways from their $6 level. Statistical data included.

37474 ■ *"Restaurants Rewrite Menu to Get Financing" in Saint Louis Business Journal (Vol. 31, August 19, 2011, No. 52, pp. 1)*
Pub: Saint Louis Business Journal
Ed: Peter Solomont. **Description:** St. Louis, Missouri-based restaurants are finding new ways to secure financing. The weak economy has made it difficult for restaurants to secure bank financing.

37475 ■ *"Return to Wealth; Bank Strategy" in The Economist (Vol. 390, January 3, 2009, No. 8612, pp. 56)*
Pub: The Economist Newspaper Inc.
Description: UBS' strategy to survive these trying economic times is presented. Statistical data included. UBS has a stronger balance-sheet than most of its investment-banking peers and has reduced its portfolio.

37476 ■ *"Running the Numbers" in Entrepreneur (Vol. 37, July 2009, No. 7, pp. 87)*
Pub: Entrepreneur Media, Inc.
Ed: Carol Tice. **Description:** Ways in which entrepreneurs can assess if they are ready to be a multi-unit franchisee are presented. Choosing the right locations, knowing how much assistance they can get from the franchisor, and financing are the key considerations when planning additional franchise units. Examples of success in multi-unit operations and multi-unit terms are also presented.

37477 ■ *"Samsung 'Holding Breath" in Austin Business Journallnc. (Vol. 29, January 29, 2010, No. 47, pp. 1)*
Pub: American City Business Journals
Ed: Jacob Dirr. **Description:** Samsung Austin Semiconductor LLC entered into an incentives agreement with the State of Texas in 2005, which involved $230 million in tax breaks and public financing. Terms of the agreement have been met, but some are questioning whether the company will be able to meet its goals for the Austin operations in 2010.

37478 ■ *"Savvy Solutions" in Black Enterprise (Vol. 41, December 2010, No. 5, pp. 42)*
Pub: Earl G. Graves Publishing Co. Inc.
Ed: Tennille M. Robinson. **Description:** Individual asks for advice in launching a graphic design business, particularly grants available in a slow economy.

37479 ■ *"Savvy Solutions" in Black Enterprise (Vol. 41, October 2010, No. 3, pp. 52)*
Pub: Earl G. Graves Publishing Co. Inc.
Ed: Tennille M. Robinson. **Description:** Husband and wife team seek advice for expanding their catering business. They are also seeking funding resources.

37480 ■ *"SBA-Backed Lending Slides; Economy, Close Scrutiny of Applications Cited" in Crain's Detroit Business (March 10, 2008)*
Pub: Crain Communications, Inc.
Ed: Nancy Kaffer. **Description:** Due to the state of the economy and a closer scrutiny on applications, Small Business Administration-backed loans are down by a significant margin in one loan program and have decreased slightly across the board. Statistical data included.

37481 ■ *"SBA Can Improve Your Cash Flow" in Business Owner (Vol. 35, September-October 2011, No. 5, pp. 3)*
Pub: DL Perkins Company
Description: Federal assistance available to small business is examined. The Small Business Administration loan guarantee program is designed to improve availability and attractiveness of small business loans.

37482 ■ *"SBA Intervenes to Keep Cash Flowing" in Business First Columbus (Vol. 25, November 21, 2008, No. 14, pp. A1)*
Pub: American City Business Journals
Ed: Adrian Burns. **Description:** U.S. Small Business Administration's loan volumes fell as it tried to cushion the impact of the economic crisis on small businesses. Large investors have pulled back buying SBA loans due to declining profits, but demand for SBA loans are seen to resurge due to low risk.

37483 ■ *"SBA Lending Hits Record" in Saint Louis Business Journal (Vol. 32, September 30, 2011, No. 5, pp. 1)*
Pub: Saint Louis Business Journal
Ed: Rick Desloge. **Description:** US Small Business Administration loans have reached a record high of $200 million in 2011. The agency decreased the usual loan fees.

37484 ■ *"SBA Lending Jumps in May; Loan Guarantee Raised, Fee Axed" in Crain's Detroit Business (Vol. 25, June 8, 2009, No. 23, pp. 1)*
Pub: Crain Communications Inc. - Detroit
Ed: Nancy Kaffer. **Description:** U.S. Small Business Administration backed 102 loans through its 7(a) program in May. Statistical data included.

37485 ■ *SBA Loans: A Step-by-Step Guide*
Pub: John Wiley & Sons Inc.
Contact: Stephen M. Smith, President
URL(s): www.wiley.com/WileyCDA/WileyTitle/productCd-0471207527.html. **Released:** Latest edition 4th; Published May, 2002. **Price:** $27.95, Individuals paperback. **Publication includes:** A directory of Small Business Association field offices and a directory of services offered by the SBA. Principal content of publication is Step-by-step information of locating and securing a small business loan, including developing a business plan, researching finance options, recent lending statistics, eligibility requirements and other details.

37486 ■ *"SBA Reinvigorates Loan Program" in Crain's Cleveland Business (Vol. 30, June 29, 2009, No. 25, pp. 1)*
Pub: Crain Communications, Inc.
Ed: Arielle Kass. **Description:** U.S. Small Business Administration has changed its loan programs that encourage banks to lend and businesses to borrow. Details of the program are discussed.

37487 ■ *"Seeking Local SBA Loan?" in Business Courier (Vol. 26, October 16, 2009, No. 25, pp. 1)*
Pub: American City Business Journals, Inc.
Ed: Steve Watkins. **Description:** The largest banks in Greater Cincinnati reduced Small Business Administration (SBA) lending by 41 percent for the fiscal year ended September 2009. For the year, local SBA loans from all banks in the area declined 25 percent. The importance of SBA loans for growth of small business is examined.

37488 ■ *"Sense of Discovery" in Business Journal Portland (Vol. 27, November 19, 2010, No. 38, pp. 1)*
Pub: Portland Business Journal
Ed: Erik Siemers. **Description:** Tigard, Oregon-based Exterro Inc. CEO Bobby Balachandran announced plans to go public without the help of an institutional investor. Balachandran believes Exterro could grow to a $100 million legal compliance software company in the span of three years. Insights on Exterro's growth as market leader in the $1 billion legal governance software market are also given.

37489 ■ *"Sentiment Split on Financials" in Barron's (Vol. 88, March 24, 2008, No. 12, pp. M14)*
Pub: Dow Jones & Company, Inc.
Ed: Steven M. Sears. **Description:** Experts in the financial sector are split as to whether or not the worst of the financial crisis brought on by the credit crunch is over. Some options traders are trading on are defensive puts, expecting the worst, while investors buying calls are considered as bullish.

37490 ■ *"Sharing the Micro Wealth" in Entrepreneur (Vol. 37, July 2009, No. 7, pp. 46)*
Pub: Entrepreneur Media, Inc.
Ed: Jennie Dorris. **Description:** Step-by-step guide is presented on how Kiva.org, a website which allows people to make microloans to entrepreneurs across the world, works. The website, founded by Matt Flannery, raises $1 million weekly and it will add U.S. entrepreneurs to its list of loan recipients in June 2010. Other features of Kiva.org are discussed.

37491 ■ *"Shopped Out; Retailing Gloom" in The Economist (Vol. 390, January 3, 2009, No. 8612, pp. 26)*
Pub: The Economist Newspaper Inc.
Description: Economic volatility in the retail sector is having an impact on a number of countries around the globe. Europe is experiencing hard economic times as well and unless businesses have a strong business plan banks feel unable to lend the money necessary to tide the retailers over. The falling pound has increased the cost of imported goods and small to midsize retail chains may not be able to weather such an unforgiving economic climate.

37492 ■ *"'Short Sales,' A Sign of Housing Troubles, Start Popping Up" in The Business Review Albany (Vol. 35, April 11, 2008, No. 1, pp. 1)*
Pub: The Business Review
Ed: Michael DeMasi. **Description:** Discusses the number of short sales, where homeowners ask banks to forgive part of their mortgages to sell the properties, which is starting to increase in the Albany, New York area. Real estate agents in the area are taking up crash courses in short selling.

37493 ■ *"A Slice of Danish; Fixing Finance" in The Economist (Vol. 390, January 3, 2009, No. 8612, pp. 55)*
Pub: The Economist Newspaper Inc.
Description: Denmark's mortgage-holders and the county's lending system is presented.

37494 ■ *"Small Business Credit Conditions" in Small Business Economic Trends (April 2008, pp. 12)*
Pub: National Federation of Independent Business
Ed: William C. Dunkelberg, Holly Wade. **Description:** Graphs and tables that present the credit conditions of small businesses in the U.S. are provided. The tables include figures on availability of loans, interest rates, and expected credit conditions.

37495 ■ *"Small Business Credit Conditions" in Small Business Economic Trends (February 2008, pp. 12)*
Pub: National Federation of Independent Business
Ed: William C. Dunkelberg, Holly Wade. **Description:** Graphs and tables that present the credit conditions of small businesses in the U.S. are provided. The tables include figures on availability of loans, interest rates, and expected credit conditions.

37496 ■ *"Small Business Credit Conditions" in Small Business Economic Trends (January 2008, pp. 12)*
Pub: National Federation of Independent Business
Description: Graphs representing loan availability and interest rates among U.S. small businesses surveyed from January 1986 to December 2007 are given. Tables showing regular borrowers, availability of loans, satisfied borrowing needs, expected credit conditions, relative interest rate paid by regular borrowers, and actual interest rate paid on short-term loans by borrowers are also presented.

37497 ■ *"Small Business Credit Conditions" in Small Business Economic Trends (September 2010, pp. 12)*
Pub: National Federation of Independent Business
Ed: William C. Dunkelberg, Holly Wade. **Description:** Graphs representing loan availability and interest rates among U.S. small businesses surveyed from January 1986 to August 2010 are given. Tables showing regular borrowers, availability of loans, satisfied borrowing needs, expected credit conditions, relative interest rate paid by regular borrowers, and actual interest rate paid on short-term loans by borrowers are also presented.

37498 ■ *"Small Business Credit Conditions" in Small Business Economic Trends (July 2010, pp. 12)*
Pub: National Federation of Independent Business
Description: Graphs representing loan availability and interest rates among U.S. small businesses surveyed from January 1986 to June 2010 are given. Tables showing regular borrowers, availability of loans, satisfied borrowing needs, expected credit conditions, relative interest rate paid by regular borrowers, and actual interest rate paid on short-term loans by borrowers are also presented.

37499 ■ *Small Business Loan Program Kit*
Pub: International Wealth Success, Inc.
Ed: Tyler G. Hicks. **Released:** 2006. **Price:** $100.00. **Description:** Guide to the Small Business Loan Program that offers loans to small and minority-owned companies doing work for government agencies, large corporations, hospitals, universities, and similar organizations.

37500 ■ *Small Business Management*
Pub: John Wiley and Sons Inc.
Ed: Margaret Burlingame; Don Gulbrandsen; Richard M. Hodgetts; Donald F. Kuratko. **Released:** March 2007. **Price:** $44.95. **Description:** Tips for starting and running a successful small business are given, including advice on writing a business plan, financing, and the law.

37501 ■ *"Soldiering On to Remake the SBA" in Inc. (February 2008, pp. 21)*
Pub: Gruner & Jahr USA Publishing
Description: Steven Preston discusses efforts to improve the Small Business Administration's processes to improve services to small businesses. Topics covered include customer service issues, loans, and fraud.

37502 ■ *Southwestern Financial Directory: 11th Fed, Dallas*
Pub: Accuity Inc.
Contact: Hugh M. Jones, IV, President
URL(s): store.accuitysolutions.com/order.html. **Released:** Semiannual; January and July. **Price:** $325, Individuals. **Covers:** Holding companies, head offices and branches of every commercial bank, Savings & Loan, and credit union over $5 million in the states of Arkansas, Louisiana, New Mexico, Oklahoma, and Texas. **Entries include:** Name, address, phone, fax, key bank officers by functional title, directors, date established, detailed financial data, association's membership, correspondent banks, out-of-town branches, holding company affiliation, ABA Transit Number and Routing Symbol, MICR number with check digit, type of charter. **Arrangement:** Geographical. **Indexes:** Alphabetical.

37503 ■ *"State Budget Woes Hurt Many Vendors, Senior Services" in Sacramento Business Journal (Vol. 25, August 15, 2008, No. 24, pp. 1)*
Pub: American City Business Journals, Inc.
Ed: Melanie Turner. **Description:** Delays in the passage of the California state budget have adversely affected the health care industry. The Robertson Adult Day Health Care had taken out loans to keep the business afloat. The state Legislature has reduced Medi-Cal reimbursement to health care providers by 10 percent.

37504 ■ *"State Investment Goes Sour" in Business Journal Portland (Vol. 26, December 4, 2009, No. 39, pp. 1)*
Pub: American City Business Journals Inc.
Ed: Erik Siemers. **Description:** Oregon might recoup only $500,000 of a $20 million loan to Vancouver-based Cascade Grain Products LLC. Cascade Grain's ethanol plant in Clatskanie, OR will be put into auction under the supervision of a bankruptcy court.

37505 ■ *"State VC Fund To Get At Least $7.5 Million" in Crain's Detroit Business (Vol. 24, February 25, 2008, No. 8, pp. 14)*
Pub: Crain Communications Inc. - Detroit
Description: Michigan's 21st Century Investment Fund is expected to receive $7.5 million, financed by tobacco-settlement money. The Michigan Strategic Fund Board will determine which firms will receive venture capital, which is mandated by legislation to invest the fund within three years.

37506 ■ *"State Wants to Add Escape Clause to Leases" in Sacramento Business Journal (Vol. 28, October 14, 2011, No. 33, pp. 1)*
Pub: Sacramento Business Journal
Ed: Michael Shaw. **Description:** California Governor Jerry Brown's administration has decided to add escape clauses to new lease agreements, which created new worry for building owners and brokers in Sacramento, California. Real estate brokers believe the appropriation of funds clauses have been making the lenders nervous and would result in less competition.

37507 ■ *"Sterotaxis Needs $10 Million in 60 Days" in Saint Louis Business Journal (Vol. 32, October 7, 2011, No. 6, pp. 1)*
Pub: Saint Louis Business Journal
Ed: E.B. Solomont. **Description:** Medical device firm Stereotaxis signed a loan modification deal with Silicon Valley Bank. The company suffered massive

losses during second quarter 2011. Under the deal, the company waived the minimum tangible net work covenant of the original loan in exchange for reduction in its credit line.

37508 ■ *"Still No Arena Financing Plan" in Sacramento Business Journal (Vol. 28, May 27, 2011, No. 13, pp. 1)*
Pub: Sacramento Business Journal
Ed: Kelly Johnson. **Description:** The government of Sacramento, California has yet to devise a plan to finance the construction of a proposed stadium. The arena is estimated to cost $387 million. A brief description of the facility is also included.

37509 ■ *"Struggling Community Banks Find Little Help In Wall Street Bailout" in Crain's Detroit Business (Vol. 24, September 29, 2008)*
Pub: Crain Communications Inc.
Ed: Tom Henderson. **Description:** Both public and private Michigan bands have been hit hard by poorly performing loan portfolios and although their problems were not caused by high-risk securities but by a longtime statewide recession and a housing slump, these community banks have little hope of seeing any of the bailout money that has been allotted for the larger institutions.

37510 ■ *"Stuck With Two Mortgages; The Nightmare When Buyers Upgrade" in Crain's Chicago Business (Vol. 31, April 21, 2008, No. 16)*
Pub: Crain Communications, Inc.
Ed: Darci Smith. **Description:** Discusses the problem a number of people are facing due to the slump in the housing market: being stuck with two mortgages when they move because their former homes have not sold. Many thought they could afford to move to a larger home, anticipating significant equity appreciation that did not occur; now they are left with lowering their price and competing with the host of new developments.

37511 ■ *"Sunwest Vies To Stave Off Bankruptcy" in The Business Journal-Portland (Vol. 25, August 15, 2008, No. 23, pp. 1)*
Pub: American City Business Journals, Inc.
Ed: Robin J. Moody. **Description:** Sunwest Management Inc. is teetering on the edge of bankruptcy as creditors start foreclosure on nine of their properties. This could potentially displace residents of the assisted living operator. Sunwest is trying to sell smaller packages of properties to get a $100 million bridge loan to maintain operations.

37512 ■ *"Survival Guide: There Can Be an Upside to Managing a Downturn" in Canadian Business (Vol. 81, November 10, 2008, No. 19, pp. 54)*
Pub: Rogers Media Ltd.
Ed: Sharda Prashad. **Description:** Canada-based Foxy is already limiting its exposure to retailers who could be a credit problem in case of recession. Retirement Life Communities is entering into fixed-rate and fixed-term loans for them to have sufficient financing to grow. Business owners need to realize that customers want more for less.

37513 ■ *"Tech Godfather Steve Walker Winding Down Howard Venture Fund" in Baltimore Business Journal (Vol. 27, December 11, 2009, No. 31)*
Pub: American City Business Journals
Ed: Scott Dance. **Description:** Steve Walker, president of venture capital fund firm Walker Ventures, will be closing the Howard County, Maryland-based firm as the economic situation is finding it difficult to recover investor's money. According to Walker, the economy also constrained investors from financing venture funds. Despite the closure, Walker will continue his work in the local angel investing community.

37514 ■ *"This Just In" in Crain's Detroit Business (Vol. 25, June 1, 2009, No. 22, pp. 1)*
Pub: Crain Communications Inc. - Detroit
Description: Three veterans of the auto industry have partnered to create, Revitalizing Michigan, a nonprofit dedicated to help manufacturers improve their processes. The firm is seeking federal, state and private grants to fund the mission.

37515 ■ *"THL Credit Is Hunting In Middle Market" in Boston Business Journal (Vol. 30, October 22, 2010, No. 39, pp. 1)*
Pub: Boston Business Journal
Ed: Tim McLaughlin. **Description:** THL Credit has been supplying capital to middle market companies in Massachusetts. The company has reported investment income of $2.44 million at the end of June 2010.

37516 ■ *Thomson World Bank Directory: International Edition*
Pub: Accuity Inc.
Contact: Hugh M. Jones, IV, President
URL(s): www.accuitysolutions.comwww.tfp.com. **Released:** Annual; Published September. **Price:** $685, Individuals. **Covers:** Over 10,000 international banks and their branches in around 200 countries around the globe, including the top 1,000 U.S. Banks. **Entries include:** Institution name, address, phone, fax, key banking officers by functional title, directors, data established, expanded statement of condition, including a profit and loss account and historic performance ratios. **Arrangement:** Geographical. **Indexes:** Alphabetical.

37517 ■ *"TMC Development Closes $1.1 Million Real Estate Purchase" in Internet Wire (September 17, 2009)*
Pub: Comtex News Network, Inc.
Description: TMC Development announced the closing of a $1.1 million real estate purchase for Mansa, LLC dba Kwikee Mart, a Napa-based convenience store; TMC helped the company secure a Small Business Administration 504 loan in order to purchase the acquisition of a 3,464 square foot building. SBA created the 504 loan program to provide financing for growing small and medium-sized businesses.

37518 ■ *"Today's Business Sale Climate" in Business Owner (Vol. 35, September-October 2011, No. 5, pp. 10)*
Pub: DL Perkins Company
Description: Despite the weak economy, there is a surplus of individuals wanting to purchase a small business. The Small Business Administration loan guarantees program helps with its loans for purchase/sale of business assistance.

37519 ■ *"Too Much Information?" in Black Enterprise (Vol. 37, December 2006, No. 5, pp. 59)*
Pub: Earl G. Graves Publishing Co. Inc.
Ed: James C. Johnson. **Description:** African American business owners often face the dilemma of whether or not to divulge their minority status when soliciting new customers and financial institutions. The quality of the products or services is always the key factor and race should never define one's business; however, it is appropriate to market oneself as a minority or women-owned business, especially if the company is in an industry where those clients are offered top-tier contracts.

37520 ■ *"Training Center Wants to be College" in Austin Business JournalInc. (Vol. 29, November 13, 2009, No. 36, pp. A1)*
Pub: American City Business Journals
Ed: Sandra Zaragoza. **Description:** Texas-based CyberTex Institute, a job training center, has established technical careers in an effort to obtain federal accreditation as a college. A college status would allow CyperTex to extend financial assistance to students. Aside from potentially having an enlarged student body and expanded campus, CyberTex would be allowed to engage in various training programs.

37521 ■ *"Triad, Fortune Dump TARP Cut Costs, Boost Lending" in Saint Louis Business Journal (Vol. 32, October 7, 2011, No. 6, pp. 1)*
Pub: Saint Louis Business Journal
Ed: Greg Edwards. **Description:** St. Louis, Missouri-based Triad Bank and Fortune Bank have been using an alternative federal loan program to pay back financing from the Troubled Asset Relief Program. Triad got a $5 million loan at one percent interest rate from the US Small Business Lending Fund.

37522 ■ *"Troubled Project In Court" in The Business Journal-Portland (Vol. 25, July 25, 2008, No. 20, pp. 1)*
Pub: American City Business Journals, Inc.
Ed: Wendy Culverwell. **Description:** Views and information on Salpare Bay's Hayden Island project, as well as on financing problems and cases associated with the project, are presented. Construction of luxurious waterside condominiums stopped last fall, after the discovery of financing problems and subcontractors and other parties started filing claims and counterclaims.

37523 ■ *"Try, Try Again" in Baltimore Business Journal (Vol. 28, August 20, 2010, No. 15, pp. 1)*
Pub: Baltimore Business Journal
Ed: Gary Haber. **Description:** Customers' refinancing of mortgages has boosted Baltimore, Maryland mortgage banking business. The housing decline has resulted in a decrease in the number of people looking for new mortgages.

37524 ■ *"Turmoil Means Changes For Retailers" in The Business Journal-Serving Metropolitan Kansas City (Vol. 27, October 10, 2008, No. 4)*
Pub: American City Business Journals, Inc.
Ed: Suzanna Stagemeyer. **Description:** Impacts of the financial crisis on Kansas Metropolitan Area retailers are varied. Rob Dalzell, for instance, found it difficult to secure a loan for his new self-serve yogurt store Yummo. The trends in retailing in the area are examined further as well as ways in which local businesses are changing in an attempt to stay solvent during the economic downturn.

37525 ■ *"U-Swirl Added to SBA's Franchise Registry" in Ice Cream Reporter (Vol. 23, September 20, 2010, No. 10, pp. 1)*
Pub: Ice Cream Reporter
Description: Healthy Fast Food Inc., parent to the U-SWIRL Frozen Yogurt cafe chain announced that the U.S. Small Business Administration listed U-SWIRL Frozen Yogurt on its official franchise registry. This move will allow U-SWIRL the benefits of a streamlined review process for SBA financing.

37526 ■ *"U.S. Economy's Underlying Strengths Limit Recession Threat" in Hispanic Business (Vol. 30, April 2008, No. 4, pp. 14)*
Pub: Hispanic Business
Ed: Dr. Juan B. Solana. **Description:** Large and small businesses as well as consumers and policymakers are attempting to identify the areas of risk and loss created by the economic crisis; analysts are now estimating that U.S. mortgage losses could reach the $380 to $400 billion mark. Also discusses the falling of wages and the rising of unemployment. Statistical data included.

37527 ■ *"Valenti: Roots of Financial Crisis Go Back to 1998" in Crain's Detroit Business (Vol. 24, October 6, 2008, No. 40, pp. 25)*
Pub: Crain Communications, Inc.
Ed: Tom Henderson; Nathan Skid. **Description:** Interview with Sam Valenti III who is the chairman and CEO of Valenti Capital L.L.C., a wealth-management firm; Valenti discusses in detail the history that led up to the current economic crisis as well as his prediction for the future of the country.

37528 ■ *"VC Money Down In State, Number of Deals Up" in Crain's Detroit Business (Vol. 24, January 28, 2008, No. 4, pp. 18)*
Pub: Crain Communications Inc. - Detroit
Ed: Tom Henderson. **Description:** Despite the amount of money invested by venture capitalists in Michigan is down, the number of deals rose according to the annual Money Tree report. Venture capital firms invested a combined $105.4 million in 22 deals that involved 19 companies in the state.

37529 ■ *The Wall Street Journal. Complete Small Business Guidebook*
Pub: Three Rivers Press
Ed: Colleen DeBaise. **Released:** December 29, 2009. **Price:** $15.00. **Description:** The mechanics of building, running and growing a profitable business are outlined, teaching how to write a business plan, ways to finding money during lean years, how to keep stress in check, time management, investment in technology, hiring, marketing, management basics, angel investing and venture capital, as well as an exit strategy.

37530 ■ *"Wanted: Angels in the Country" in Austin Business JournalInc. (Vol. 28, July 18, 2008, No. 18, pp. 1)*
Pub: American City Business Journals
Ed: Laura Hipp. **Description:** A proposal is being pushed forward by managers of Texas' Emerging Technology Fund to create an angel investors' network. The proposal is asking that tax credits for those who invest in research and development projects be granted in order to boost the number of technology companies in the state.

37531 ■ *"Welcome Back" in Canadian Business (Vol. 82, April 27, 2009, No. 7, pp. 25)*
Pub: Rogers Media
Ed: Sarka Halas. **Description:** Some Canadian companies such as Gennum Corporation have taken advantage of corporate sale-leasebacks to raise money at a time when credit is hard to acquire. Corporate sale-leasebacks allow companies to sell their property assets while remaining as tenants of the building. Sale-leasebacks allow firms to increase capital while avoiding the disruptions that may result with moving.

37532 ■ *"What's In a Name?" in Barron's (Vol. 88, March 17, 2008, No. 11, pp. 7)*
Pub: Dow Jones & Company, Inc.
Ed: Alan Abelson. **Description:** Eliot Spitzer's resignation incidentally caused the stock market to go up by 400 points. The Federal Reserve Board's new Term Securities Lending Facility provides liquidity to the big lenders by funneling $200 billion in the form of 28-day loans of Treasuries. The analysis of Paul Brodsky and Lee Quaintance of QB Partners on the demand for commodities is also discussed.

37533 ■ *"What's In a Relationship? The Case of Commercial Lending" in Business Horizons (Vol. 51, March-April 2008, No. 2, pp. 93)*
Pub: Elsevier Advanced Technology Publications
Description: Academic literature on relationship lending and banking to small and medium enterprises is analyzed. This practice is best suited to some SME types but creates special challenges for bank managers. Relationship lending may also be better delivered by community banks.

37534 ■ *"Where the Loans Are" in Boston Business Journal (Vol. 30, October 22, 2010, No. 39, pp. 1)*
Pub: Boston Business Journal
Ed: Craig M. Douglas. **Description:** Massachusetts-based community banks have been investing in multifamily apartment projects. Lending has decline during the first half of 2010. A $264 million increase in multifamily loans has also been observed.

37535 ■ *"Where to Stash Your Cash" in Barron's (Vol. 88, March 17, 2008, No. 11, pp. 41)*
Pub: Dow Jones & Company, Inc.
Ed: Mike Hogan. **Description:** Investors are putting their money in money-market mutual funds seeking fractionally better yields and a safe haven from the uncertainties that was brought about by subprime lending. These funds, however, are hovering near 3.20 percent which is less than the 4 percent inflation rate.

37536 ■ *"Wobbling Economy" in The Business Journal-Serving Metropolitan Kansas City (Vol. 27, September 26, 2008, No. 2, pp. 1)*
Pub: American City Business Journals, Inc.
Ed: Rob Roberts. **Description:** Real estate developers in Kansas City Metropolitan Area are worried of the possible impacts of the crisis at Wall Street. They expect tightening of the credit market, which will result in difficulty of financing their projects. The potential effects of the Wall Street crisis are examined further.

37537 ■ *"Woes Portend Consumer Shift" in The Business Journal-Serving Metropolitan Kansas City (Vol. 27, September 26, 2008, No. 2, pp. 1)*
Pub: American City Business Journals, Inc.
Ed: Suzanna Stagemeyer. **Description:** Black Bamboo owner Tim Butt believes that prolonged tightening of the credit market will result in consumer spending becoming more cash-driven that credit card driven. The financial crisis has already constricted spending among consumers. Forecasts for the US economy are provided.

37538 ■ *Women Entrepreneurs*
Pub: Edward Elgar Publishing, Incorporated
Ed: Andrea Smith-Hunter. **Released:** October 2006. **Price:** $120.00. **Description:** Focus is on women entrepreneurs; information includes human capital, network structures and financial capital, with comparative analysis across racial lines.

37539 ■ *"Women: Send Me An Angel" in Entrepreneur (Vol. 35, October 2007, No. 10, pp. 38)*
Pub: Entrepreneur Media Inc.
Ed: Aliza Sherman. **Description:** Golden Seeds has invested in Enter Artemis Woman LLC when the latter decided to put its products into Wal-Mart. Golden Seeds was formed by angel investors who aim to help women build their own businesses. Tips on how to approach angel investors and getting angel funding are given.

37540 ■ *"The Worst Lies Ahead for Wall Street; More Losses Certain" in Crain's New York Business (Vol. 24, January 21, 2008, No. 3, pp. 1)*
Pub: Crain Communications, Inc.
Ed: Aaron Elstein. **Description:** Due to the weakening economy, many financial institutions will face further massive losses forcing them to borrow more at higher interest rates and dragging down their earnings for years to come. The effects on commercial real estate and credit card loans are also discussed as well as the trend to investing in Asia and the Middle East.

37541 ■ *"The Wrong Tune" in The Business Journal-Portland (Vol. 25, July 25, 2008, No. 20, pp. 1)*
Pub: American City Business Journals, Inc.
Ed: Robin J. Moody. **Description:** Views and information on turnaround management and recovery plans of the Oregon Symphony, are presented. The nonprofit organization has lost a total of $5.1 million between 2002 and 2008, and $400,000 annual interest payments for a $7 million bank loan. Increased ticket sales, as well as cost cutting measures, are helping improve the finance of the organization.

37542 ■ *"You Better Shop Around: Four Steps to Getting the Best Deal On a Home Loan" in Black Enterprise (Vol. 40, July 2010, No. 12, pp. 78)*
Pub: Earl G. Graves Publishing Co. Inc.
Ed: Tara-Nicholle Nelson. **Description:** Four steps to help anyone seeking a mortgage for a home purchase are listed.

37543 ■ *"Your Exposure to Bear Stearns" in Barron's (Vol. 88, March 17, 2008, No. 11, pp. 45)*
Pub: Dow Jones & Company, Inc.
Ed: Tom Sullivan; Jack Willoughby. **Description:** Bear Stearns makes up 5.5 percent of Pioneer Independence's portfolio, 1.4 percent of Vanguard Windsor II's portfolio, 1.2 percent of Legg Mason Value Trust, about 1 percent of Van Kampen Equity & Income, and 0.79 percent of Putnam Fund for Growth & Income. Ginnie Mae securities are now trading at 1.78 percentage points over treasuries due to the mortgage crises.

37544 ■ *Your Guide to Arranging Bank and Debt Financing for Your Own Business in Canada*
Pub: Productive Publications
Ed: Iain Williamson. **Released:** December 31, 2000. **Description:** Bank financing for small businesses in Canada is discussed.

37545 ■ *Your Guide to Canadian Export Financing: Successful Techniques for Financing Your Exports from Canada*
Pub: Productive Publications
Ed: Iain Williamson. **Released:** December 31, 2000. **Description:** Canadian export financing is covered.

37546 ■ *Your Guide to Preparing a Plan to Raise Money for Your Own Business*
Pub: Productive Publications
Ed: Iain Williamson. **Released:** June 1991. **Description:** A good business plan is essential for raising money for any small business.

TRADE PERIODICALS

37547 ■ *Mortgage Technology*
Pub: SourceMedia Inc.
Contact: Douglas J. Manoni, Chief Executive Officer
E-mail: doug.manoni@sourcemedia.com
URL(s): www.nationalmortgagenews.com/technology/. **Released:** Monthly **Price:** $88, U.S.; $108, Canada; $108, Other countries.

CONSULTANTS

37548 ■ Pioneer Business Consultants
9042 Garfield Ave., Ste. 211
Huntington Beach, CA 92646
Ph: (714)964-7600
Fax: (714)962-6585
Contact: John J. Collins, President
Scope: Offers general management consulting specializing in business acquisitions, tax and business planning, cash flow analyses, business valuations and business sales and expert witness court testimony regarding business sales, valuations and accounting. **Founded:** 1980.

FRANCHISES AND BUSINESS OPPORTUNITIES

37549 ■ Stop 'N' Cash
Stop 'N' Cash 5000 Inc.
809 Victoria St. N
Kitchener, ON, Canada N2B 3C3
Ph: (519)896-8088
Fax: (519)576-8853
Co. E-mail: Stnc1020@stopncash.com
URL: http://www.stopncash.com
Description: The franchise provides a payday loan scheme and a solid investment return. **No. of Franchise Units:** 64. **No. of Company-Owned Units:** 9. **Founded:** 1998.. **Franchised:** 1999. **Equity Capital Needed:** $150,000-$200,000. **Franchise Fee:** $30,000. **Training:** 1 week of in-house in Kitchener, and ongoing support.

RESEARCH CENTERS

37550 ■ University of Nebraska—Kearney - Nebraska Business Development Center (NBDC)
W Ctr. Bldg., Rm. 135
1917 W 24th St.
Kearney, NE 68849-4440
Ph: (308)865-8344

Fax: (308)865-8153
Co. E-mail: nbdcunk@unk.edu
URL: http://www.unk.edu/academics/nbdc.aspx?id=1936
Contact: Odee Ingersoll, Director
Services: Consulting. **Founded:** 1977. **Publications:** *NBDC Business Calendar* (Quarterly). **Educational Activities:** Continuing education programs. **Telecommunication Services:** ingersollo@unk.edu.

START-UP INFORMATION

37551 ■ *Effective Small Business Management: An Entrepreneurial Approach*
Pub: Prentice Hall Higher Education
Ed: Norman M. Scarborough; Thomas W. Zimmerer; Douglas L. Wilson. **Released:** March 2006. **Price:** $178.33. **Description:** Provides undergraduate and graduate entrepreneurship and/or small business management courses with information to successfully launch a new company. The books offers entrepreneurs the tools required to develop staying power to succeed and grow their new business.

37552 ■ *Essentials of Entrepreneurship and Small Business Management*
Pub: Prentice Hall PTR
Ed: Thomas W. Zimmerer; Norman M. Scarborough; Doug Wilson. **Released:** February 2007. **Price:** $106. 67. **Description:** New venture creation and the knowledge required to start a new business are shared. The challenges of entrepreneurship, business plans, marketing, e-commerce, and financial considerations are explored.

37553 ■ *Small Business Management*
Pub: John Wiley & Sons, Incorporated
Ed: Margaret Burlingame. **Released:** March 2007. **Price:** $44.95. **Description:** Advice for starting and running a small business as well as information on the value and appeal of small businesses, is given. Topics include budgets, taxes, inventory, ethics, e-commerce, and current laws.

37554 ■ *Small Business Management: Launching and Managing New Ventures*
Pub: Nelson Thomson Learning
Ed: Justin G. Longenecker. **Released:** March 2006. **Price:** $78.95. **Description:** Tips for starting and running a successful new company are provided.

37555 ■ *Small Business Tool Kit*
Pub: Lessons Professional Publishing
Ed: Linda M. Magoon. **Released:** April 10, 2010. **Price:** $40.00. **Description:** When starting a business, new managers and entrepreneurs require many resources to get the company up and running successfully. This book covers a wide range of topics that are critical for any new business owner.

ASSOCIATIONS AND OTHER ORGANIZATIONS

37556 ■ American Management Association (AMA)
1601 Broadway
New York, NY 10019-7420
Ph: (212)586-8100
Free: 877-566-9441
Fax: (212)903-8168
Co. E-mail: customerservice@amanet.org
URL: http://www.amanet.org
Contact: Charles R. Craig, Chairman
URL(s): www.amanet.org/books. **Description:** Provides educational forums worldwide where members and their colleagues learn superior, practical business skills and explore best practices of world-class organizations through interaction with each other and expert faculty practitioners. Maintains a publishing program providing tools individuals use to extend learning beyond the classroom in a process of lifelong professional growth and development through education. **Founded:** 1923. **Publications:** *HR Focus* (Monthly); *Management Review* (Monthly); *The Take-Charge Assistant* (Monthly); *The Take-Charge Assistant*; *Organizational Dynamics: A Quarterly Review of Organizational Behavior for Management Executives*; *Small Business Reports: For Decision Makers in America's Small and Mid-Size Companies* (Monthly); *Organizational Dynamics: A Quarterly Review of Organizational Behavior for Professional Managers* (Quarterly); *AMA's Directory of Human Resource Products and Services*; *Make Your Contacts Count*. **Educational Activities:** Effective Technical Writing (Onsite); Conference for Executive Secretaries and Administrative Assistants (Annual); Conference for Executive Secretaries and Administrative Assistants (Annual). **Telecommunication Services:** membership@amanet.org; cust-serv@amanet.org.

37557 ■ Association for Corporate Growth - Toronto Chapter (ACG)—Canadian Angus Association
720 Spadina Ave., Ste. 202
Toronto, ON, Canada M5S 2T9
Ph: (416)868-1881
Fax: (416)391-3633
Co. E-mail: acgtoronto@acg.org
URL: http://www.acg.org/toronto/default.aspx
Contact: Stephen B. Smith, President
Description: Professionals with a leadership role in strategic corporate growth. Seeks to facilitate the professional advancement of members, and the practice of corporate growth management. Fosters communication and cooperation among members; conducts continuing professional education programs. **Founded:** 1973. **Publications:** *Mergers & Acquisitions - The Dealmaker's Journal* (Monthly). **Educational Activities:** Association for Corporate Growth - Toronto Chapter Board meeting (Monthly); Capital Connection (Annual). **Awards:** Toronto Chapter Leadership Award (Annual).

37558 ■ Business Modeling and Integration Domain Task Force (BMIDTF)
140 Kendrick St., Bldg. A, Ste. 300
Needham, MA 02494
Ph: (781)444-0404
Fax: (781)444-0320
Co. E-mail: fred.a.cummins@gmail.com
URL: http://bmi.omg.org
Contact: Mr. Fred A. Cummins, Co-Chairman
Description: Aims to empower all companies, across all industries, to develop and operate business processes that span multiple applications and business partners, behind the firewall and over the Internet. **Scope:** business process management. **Founded:** 2000. **Subscriptions:** articles papers.

37559 ■ Canadian Institute of Management (CIM)—Institut Canadien de Gestion
15 Collier St., Lower Level
Barrie, ON, Canada L4M 1G5
Ph: (705)725-8926
Free: 800-387-5774
Fax: (705)725-8196
Co. E-mail: office@cim.ca
URL: http://www.cim.ca
Contact: Paul Markle, President
Description: Management personnel. Seeks to advance the practice of business management; promotes continuing professional development of members. Serves as a clearinghouse on management and related topics; facilitates exchange of information among members; makes available educational and training programs. **Founded:** 1942. **Publications:** *Canadian Manager* (Quarterly); *Canadian Manager: The Magazine for Managers* (Quarterly).

37560 ■ Canadian Management Centre (CMC)
150 York St., 5th Fl.
Toronto, ON, Canada M5H 3S5
Ph: (416)214-5678
Free: 877-262-2519
Fax: (416)313-4985
Co. E-mail: cmcinfo@cmctraining.org
URL: http://www.cmctraining.org
Contact: John Wright, President
Description: Managers of corporations and organizations. Promotes excellence in management. Conducts educational and training programs for management personnel. **Scope:** Provides courses in areas such as general management, communications, marketing, sales, project management and finance. Specialized services include customized on-site training and programs tailored for the government sector. **Founded:** 1963. **Publications:** "The Seven-Second Advantage"; "Stress and Coaching"; "Great Managers Attract (and Keep) Great Talent"; "Why Aren't There More Good Managers?"; "Don't Delegate More - Delegate More Effectively"; "Managing in Uncertain Times: Transforming Employees from "Comfeartable" to Courageous"; "Ten Obstacles to Successful Decision Making"; "How to Be a Super Supervisor"; "The Evolution of Diversity: From 'The Right Thing' to Business Strategy"; "Okay, Okay, We Get It About Talent Management, But Do We Really"; "What High-Performing Companies Are Doing Now to Retain Talent Later"; "How Do You Want To Be Treated"; "The Ethics Dilemma"; "Understanding And Coping With Difficult Managers"; "Great Managers Lead Differently"; "Time Management for the Hurried and the Harried Professional"; "Well-Trained People Are Priceless"; "What Should We Be Measuring-Satisfaction or Engagement". **Educational Activities:** Communicating Change; Getting Better Results Through Conversations; Managing Difficult and Sensitive Conversations (Onsite); Exceptional Customer Service Leadership; Financial Modeling and Forecasting; High-Impact Decision Making (Onsite); Framework for Excellence (Course on Request); Introduction to Process Mapping (Course on Request); Organizational Excellence Assessment (Course on Request); Quest for a Healthy Workplace (Course on Request); PMP Exam Prep Workshop (Onsite); The Comprehensive Project Management Workshop (Onsite); Creating Customer Value Through Competitive Advantage; Sales in Turbulent Times; Strategy Execution: Getting it Done (Onsite);

Developing Executive Leadership; Canadian Management Centre's 5-Day "MBA"(Canada) (Onsite); Stepping Up to Leadership; The Project Planning Workshop; Negotiating to Win (Onsite); High Performance Business Writing (Onsite); Maximum Performance Leadership; Assertiveness Training for Managers (Onsite); Assertiveness Training for Women in Business; Interpersonal Skills for Managers (Onsite); Fundamentals of Purchasing; CMC's Course on Financial Analysis (Onsite); Leadership Skills for Supervisors (Onsite); Dealing with Competing Demands; Successfully Managing People (Onsite) ; Improving Your Managerial Effectiveness (Course on Request); The Effective Facilitator; Getting Results Without Authority (Onsite); Senior Project Management (Onsite); Technical Project Management; Strategic Planning (Onsite); Fundamentals of Human Resources Management (Onsite); Strategic Agility and Resilience: Embracing Change to Drive Growth; Moving Ahead: Breaking Behaviour Patterns That Hold You Back (Onsite); Debits and Credits: How Accounting Really Works; Coaching for Business Results: A Hands-On Practical Workshop (Onsite); Improving Performance of Remote and Virtual Workers (Onsite); Making the Transition to Supervising and Managing Others (Onsite); Management Skills for New Supervisors and Managers (Onsite); Quest for Quality Process Improvement Tools (Course on Request); Business Skills for Project Managers: Improve Your Focus, Credibility and Success; Project Cost Management: Estimating, Budgeting and Earned Value Analysis (Onsite); Train the Trainer: Facilitation Skills Workshop (Onsite); Confronting the Tough Stuff: Turning Managerial Challenges into Positive Results (Onsite); Process Management: Applying Process Mapping to Analyze and Improve Your Operation (Onsite); Leadership and Team Development for Managerial Success (Onsite); Fundamentals of Marketing: Your Action Plan for Success (Onsite); Preparing for Leadership: What It Takes to Take the Lead (Onsite); Responding to Conflict: Strategies for Improved Communication (Onsite); Communication and Interpersonal Skills for IT & Technical Professionals (Onsite); Improving Your Project Management Skills: The Basics for Success (Onsite); Coaching: A Strategic Tool for Effective Leadership (Onsite); Communicating Up, Down and Across the Organization (Onsite); How to Communicate with Diplomacy, Tact and Credibility (Onsite). **Seminars:** Skills Plus: Selling Different Clients Differently, Toronto, May, 2007; Management Skills for New Managers, Calgary, May, 2007; Time and Territory Management for Salespeople, Toronto, May, 2007; Developing Executive Leadership, Toronto, Apr, 2007; Building Business Acumen for Learning Professionals, Toronto, Apr, 2007; Communicating Up, Down and Across the Organization, Toronto, Mar, 2007; Managing Customer Conflict, Toronto, Feb, 2007; Negotiating to Win, Toronto, Jan, 2007.

37561 ■ *Canadian Manager*
15 Collier St., Lower Level
Barrie, ON, Canada L4M 1G5
Ph: (705)725-8926
Free: 800-387-5774
Fax: (705)725-8196
Co. E-mail: office@cim.ca
URL: http://www.cim.ca
Contact: Paul Markle, President
Released: Quarterly **Price:** free for members.

37562 ■ International Council for Small Business (ICSB)
GWU School of Business
Washington, DC 20052
Ph: (202)994-0704
Fax: (202)994-4930
Co. E-mail: icsb@gwu.edu
URL: http://www.icsb.org
Contact: Sylvio Rosa, Jr., President
E-mail: srosa@parqtec.com.br
Description: Management educators, researchers, government officials and professionals in 80 countries. Fosters discussion of topics pertaining to the development and improvement of small business management. **Founded:** 1955. **Publications:** *Journal of Small Business Management* (Quarterly). **Telecommunication Services:** aymanelt@icsb.org.

37563 ■ Machinery Information Management Open Systems Alliance (MIMOSA)
204 Marina Dr., Ste. 100
Tuscaloosa, AL 35406
Ph: (949)625-8616
Fax: (949)625-8616
Co. E-mail: info@mimosa.org
URL: http://www.mimosa.org
Contact: Alan T. Johnston, President
Description: Develops and encourages the adoption of open information standards for Operations and Maintenance and Collaborative Asset Lifecycle Management in commercial and military applications. Provides a forum for the members, bringing together subject matter experts in cross disciplinary technologies, to enable complex solutions for Equipment Operators, Maintainers and Fleet Managers.

37564 ■ *Mergers & Acquisitions - The Dealmaker's Journal*
720 Spadina Ave., Ste. 202
Toronto, ON, Canada M5S 2T9
Ph: (416)868-1881
Fax: (416)391-3633
Co. E-mail: acgtoronto@acg.org
URL: http://www.acg.org/toronto/default.aspx
Contact: Stephen B. Smith, President
Released: Monthly **Price:** included in membership dues.

37565 ■ National Management Association (NMA)
2210 Arbor Blvd.
Dayton, OH 45439
Ph: (937)294-0421
Fax: (937)294-2374
Co. E-mail: nma@nma1.org
URL: http://www.nma1.org
Contact: Melinda M. Hester, Chairwoman
Description: Business and industrial management personnel; membership comes from supervisory level, with the remainder from middle management and above. Seeks to develop and recognize management as a profession and to promote the free enterprise system. Prepares chapter programs on basic management, management policy and practice, communications, human behavior, industrial relations, economics, political education, and liberal education. Maintains speakers' bureau and hall of fame. Maintains educational, charitable, and research programs. Sponsors charitable programs. **Founded:** 1925. **Publications:** *Manage* (Quarterly); *Manage* (Quarterly); *National Speakers' Directory* (Periodic). **Awards:** American Enterprise Speech Contest Award (Annual); Executive of the Year Award (Annual); The McFeely Award (Annual).

37566 ■ Organization Design Forum (ODF)
5016 E Mulberry Dr.
Phoenix, AZ 85018
Ph: (602)510-9105
Co. E-mail: info@organizationdesignforum.org
URL: http://www.organizationdesignforum.org
Contact: Tanya Spelts, Administrator
Description: Academics, practitioners, consultants, and human resource professionals. Works to promote the knowledge and practice of organizational design. Focuses on the effect organization structure and processes have on the performance of individuals, groups, and the organization itself. Offers basic and advanced training in organization design techniques. **Scope:** recipients of Crystal Apple Award presentation. **Founded:** 1989. **Subscriptions:** 3 video recordings. **Publications:** *Organization Design*. **Awards:** Crystal Apple (Annual).

37567 ■ SCORE
1175 Herndon Pkwy., Ste. 900
Herndon, VA 20170
Free: 800-634-0245
Co. E-mail: help@score.org
URL: http://www.score.org
Contact: Kenneth W. Yancey, Jr., Chief Executive Officer
Description: Serves as volunteer program sponsored by U.S. Small Business Administration in which working and retired business management professionals provide free business counseling to men and women who are considering starting a small business, encountering problems with their business, or expanding their business. Offers free one-on-one counseling, online counseling and low cost workshops on a variety of business topics. **Scope:** business. **Founded:** 1964. **Subscriptions:** books clippings periodicals. **Publications:** *SCORE eNews* (Monthly); *SCORE Today* (Monthly). **Awards:** Outstanding Woman-owned Business Award (Annual); SCORE Chapter of the Year Award (Annual).

37568 ■ Society for Advancement of Management (SAM)
6300 Ocean Dr.
OCNR 330, Unit 5807
Corpus Christi, TX 78412
Ph: (361)825-6045
Free: 888-827-6077
Fax: (361)825-2725
Co. E-mail: sam@samnational.org
URL: http://www.samnational.org
Contact: Dr. Moustafa H. Abdelsamad, President
URL(s): www.cob.tamucc.edu/sam/, www.enterprise.tamucc.edu/sam. **Description:** Represents management executives in industry commerce, government, and education. Fields of interest include management education, policy and strategy, MIS, international management, administration, budgeting, collective bargaining, distribution, incentives, materials handling, quality control, and training. **Founded:** 1912. **Publications:** *Advanced Management Journal* (Quarterly); *SAM Advanced Management Journal* (Quarterly); *SAM Management In Practice* (Quarterly); *The SAM News International* (Quarterly); *Society for Advancement of Management--International Business Conference Proceedings* (Annual). **Educational Activities:** Society for Advancement of Management Meeting (Annual); Business Conference (Annual).

37569 ■ Women in Management (WIM)
PO Box 6690
Elgin, IL 60121-6690
Ph: (708)386-0496
Free: 877-946-6285
Fax: (847)683-3751
Co. E-mail: nationalwim@wimonline.org
URL: http://www.wimonline.org
Contact: Katrina Laflin, President
Description: Supports network of women in professional and management positions that facilitate the exchange of experience and ideas. Promotes self-growth in management; provides speakers who are successful in management; sponsors workshops and special interest groups to discuss problems and share job experiences. **Founded:** 1976. **Publications:** *Women in Management--National Directory* (Annual). **Awards:** Charlotte Danstrom Awards.

37570 ■ World Confederation of Productivity Science (WCPS)
c/o Ms. Linda Carbone, Exec. Sec.
500 Sherbrooke St. W, Ste. 900
Montreal, QC, Canada H3A 3C6
Co. E-mail: secretariat@wcps.info
URL: http://www.wcps.info
Contact: Mr. Jean-Claude Lauzon, Chairman
Description: Fraternal association of manufacturing and commercial enterprises and employees, government agencies, professional institutions, and researchers. Goals are to promote productivity science, advance management techniques, and improve the quality of working life and environment. **Founded:** 1969. **Subscriptions:** 3000. **Educational Activities:** World Productivity Congress (Biennial).

EDUCATIONAL PROGRAMS

37571 ■ The 8th Habit: From Effectiveness to Greatness
American Management Association
600 AMA Way
Saranac Lake, NY 12983-5534
Ph: (212)586-8100
Free: 877-566-9441

Fax: (518)891-0368
Co. E-mail: customerservice@amanet.org
URL: http://www.amaseminars.org

Price: $2,195.00 for non-members; $1,995.00 for AMA members; and $1,708.00 for General Services Administration (GSA) members. **Description:** Learn to reach your full potential and inspire others through the teachings of Dr. Stephen R. Covey of Franklin-Covey. **Dates and Locations:** New York, NY; Las Vegas, NV; and Atlanta, GA.

37572 ■ Achieving Leadership Success Through People (Onsite)
AMA
600 AMA Way
Saranac Lake, NY 12983-5534
Ph: (212)586-8100
Free: 877-566-9441
Fax: (518)891-0368
Co. E-mail: customerservice@amanet.org
URL: http://www.amaseminars.org

Price: $2,645.00 for non-members; $2,395.00 for AMA members; and $2,051.00 for General Services Administration (GSA) members. **Description:** Learn to lead more effectively by creating rapport, synergy, and two-way trust in this two-day course. **Dates and Locations:** New York, NY; Dallas, TX; San Francisco, CA; Lake Buena Vista, FL; Washington, DC; Atlanta, GA; and Arlington, VA.

37573 ■ Advanced Issues in Employee Relations
Seminar Information Service, Inc.
20 Executive Park, Ste. 120
Irvine, CA 92614
Ph: (949)261-9104
Free: 877-SEM-INFO
Fax: (949)261-1963
Co. E-mail: info@seminarinformation.com
URL: http://www.seminarinformation.com

Price: $1,495.00. **Description:** Key topics include coaching managers to more effectively manage high performing employees who consistently demonstrate one serious performance failing, collaborating with managers to assist them in focusing on performance issues without being influenced by employees' personal circumstances, working with managers on dealing more effectively with strong negative employee reactions to direction or feedback, and addressing managers' behavior that is inappropriate and potentially high risk. **Dates and Locations:** New York, NY.

37574 ■ Advanced IT Audit School (Onsite)
Seminar Information Service, Inc.
20 Executive Park, Ste. 120
Irvine, CA 92614
Ph: (949)261-9104
Free: 877-SEM-INFO
Fax: (949)261-1963
Co. E-mail: info@seminarinformation.com
URL: http://www.seminarinformation.com

Price: $3,095.00. **Description:** This advanced hands-on workshop will show you how to use software tools to identify and test key control points in your organization's network infrastructure.

37575 ■ AMA's 5-Day MBA Workshop (Onsite)
American Management Association
600 AMA Way
Saranac Lake, NY 12983-5534
Ph: (212)586-8100
Free: 877-566-9441
Fax: (518)891-0368
Co. E-mail: customerservice@amanet.org
URL: http://www.amaseminars.org

Price: $3,545.00 for non-members; $3,195.00 for AMA members; and $2,736.00 for General Services Administration (GSA) members. **Description:** Five-day seminar; covers a broad overview of business concepts typically covered in university-level MBA programs. **Dates and Locations:** Cities throughout the United States.

37576 ■ AMA's Advanced Executive Leadership Program (Onsite)
American Management Association
600 AMA Way
Saranac Lake, NY 12983-5534
Ph: (212)586-8100
Free: 877-566-9441
Fax: (518)891-0368
Co. E-mail: customerservice@amanet.org
URL: http://www.amaseminars.org

Price: $2,645.00 for non-members; $2,395.00 for AMA members; and $2,051.00 for General Services Adminstration (GSA) members. **Description:** An intensive three day seminar focusing on executive leadership. **Dates and Locations:** Scotsdale, AZ; and New York, NY.

37577 ■ AMA's Comprehensive Project Management Workshop (Onsite)
American Management Association
600 AMA Way
Saranac Lake, NY 12983-5534
Ph: (212)586-8100
Free: 877-566-9441
Fax: (518)891-0368
Co. E-mail: customerservice@amanet.org
URL: http://www.amaseminars.org

Price: $3,095.00 for non-members; $2,795.00 for AMA members; and $2,393.00 for General Services Administration (GSA) members. **Description:** Five-day seminar examining the framework, reviewing project management body of knowledge, initiating the project, planning the project, executing project plan, monitoring and controlling project and closing the project. **Dates and Locations:** New York, NY; Arlington, VA; Washigton, DC; San Francisco, CA: and Los Angeles, CA.

37578 ■ AMA's Leading with Emotional Intelligence (Onsite)
American Management Association
600 AMA Way
Saranac Lake, NY 12983-5534
Ph: (212)586-8100
Free: 877-566-9441
Fax: (518)891-0368
Co. E-mail: customerservice@amanet.org
URL: http://www.amaseminars.org

Price: $2,545.00 for non-members; $2,295.00 for AMA members; and $1,965.00 for General Services Administration (GSA) members. **Description:** Covers the importance of emotional intelligence in the workplace, and developing a style to effectively communicate and use emotions positively. **Dates and Locations:** Cities throughout the United States.

37579 ■ The Art of Coaching Employees to Excel (Onsite)
Padgett-Thompson Seminars
Rockhurst University CEC
14502 W. 105th St.
Lenexa, KS 66215
Free: 800-349-1935
URL: http://www.findaseminar.com/tpd/Padgett-Thompson-Seminars.asp

Price: $199.00. **Description:** Teaches managers how to approach performance issues, set morale, and create self-esteem in the workplace. **Dates and Locations:** Albuquerque, NM; Las Vegas, NV; San Diego, CA.

37580 ■ Assertive Management (Onsite)
Seminar Information Service, Inc.
20 Executive Park, Ste. 120
Irvine, CA 92614
Ph: (949)261-9104
Free: 877-SEM-INFO
Fax: (949)261-1963
Co. E-mail: info@seminarinformation.com
URL: http://www.seminarinformation.com

Price: Contact for fees. **Description:** Develop the qualities necessary for successful, assertive management. Participants gain confidence and skill in being 'pro-active' in communicating with others, including how to use positive, win-win approaches and to defuse emotionally charged situations in order to work more effectively with their fellow workers, supervisors and subordinates.

37581 ■ Assertiveness Skills: Communicating with Authority and Impact (Onsite)
Seminar Information Service, Inc.
20 Executive Park, Ste. 120
Irvine, CA 92614
Ph: (949)261-9104
Free: 877-SEM-INFO
Fax: (949)261-1963
Co. E-mail: info@seminarinformation.com
URL: http://www.seminarinformation.com

Price: $1,890.00. **Description:** Learn how to develop a positive assertive style, including how to respond productively to challenging behavior patterns in others, react positively in demanding situations, and improve your relationships through a productive and powerful attitude. **Dates and Locations:** Rockville, MD; Reston, VA; New York, NY; Toronto, CN; and Ottawa, CN.

37582 ■ Assertiveness Skills for Managers and Supervisors (Onsite)
Padgett-Thompson Seminars
Rockhurst University CEC
14502 W. 105th St.
Lenexa, KS 66215
Free: 800-349-1935
URL: http://www.findaseminar.com/tpd/Padgett-Thompson-Seminars.asp

Price: $199.00. **Description:** Attendees will gain assertiveness skills they need to achieve the recognition they deserve. **Dates and Locations:** Baltimore, MD.

37583 ■ Assertiveness Training for Managers (Onsite)
American Management Association
600 AMA Way
Saranac Lake, NY 12983-5534
Ph: (212)586-8100
Free: 877-566-9441
Fax: (518)891-0368
Co. E-mail: customerservice@amanet.org
URL: http://www.amaseminars.org

Price: $2,345.00 for non-members; $2,095.00 for AMA members; and $1,794.00 for General Services Administration (GSA) members. **Description:** Learn how your behavior impacts your performance and how to take control without isolating others. **Dates and Locations:** New York, NY; Atlanta, GA; and San Francisco, CA.

37584 ■ Become a World Class Assistant (Onsite)
Seminar Information Service, Inc.
20 Executive Park, Ste. 120
Irvine, CA 92614
Ph: (949)261-9104
Free: 877-SEM-INFO
Fax: (949)261-1963
Co. E-mail: info@seminarinformation.com
URL: http://www.seminarinformation.com

Price: $1,995.00. **Description:** How to partner strategically for business success. **Dates and Locations:** Las Vegas, NV.

37585 ■ Best Practices for the Multi-project Manager (Onsite)
American Management Association
600 AMA Way
Saranac Lake, NY 12983-5534
Ph: (212)586-8100
Free: 877-566-9441
Fax: (518)891-0368
Co. E-mail: customerservice@amanet.org
URL: http://www.amaseminars.org

Price: $2,095.00 for non-members; $1,895.00 for AMA members; and $1,623.00 for General Services Administration (GSA) members. **Description:** Covers balancing work load, reducing risk and conflict, time management, prioritizing, and monitoring and reporting on multiple projects. **Dates and Locations:** New York, NY; Washington, DC; Chicago, IL; San Francisco, CA; and Arlington, VA.

37586 ■ Building a Positive, Motivated and Cooperative Team (Onsite)
Seminar Information Service, Inc.
20 Executive Park, Ste. 120
Irvine, CA 92614
Ph: (949)261-9104
Free: 877-SEM-INFO
Fax: (949)261-1963
Co. E-mail: info@seminarinformation.com
URL: http://www.seminarinformation.com
Price: $199.00. **Description:** Learn to create positive and productive results within the workplace utilizing real world examples. **Dates and Locations:** Cities throughout the United States.

37587 ■ Building a Successful Business Analysis Work Plan
Learning Tree International Inc.
1805 Library St.
Reston, VA 20190-5660
Ph: (703)709-9119
Free: 800-843-8733
Fax: (703)709-6405
Co. E-mail: uscourses@learningtree.com
URL: http://www.learningtree.com
Contact: Nick Schacht, President
Price: $2,490.00. **Description:** Learn to develop and execute a work plan using practical project management tools, methods, and techniques. **Dates and Locations:** New York, NY; Washington, DC; Reston, VA; Ottawa, ON; and Toronto, ON.

37588 ■ Building a Successful Business Analysis Work Plan: Effective Project Management Skills for Business Analysts (Onsite)
Seminar Information Service, Inc.
20 Executive Park, Ste. 120
Irvine, CA 92614
Ph: (949)261-9104
Free: 877-SEM-INFO
Fax: (949)261-1963
Co. E-mail: info@seminarinformation.com
URL: http://www.seminarinformation.com
Price: $2,490.00. **Description:** Learn practical project management methods, tools and techniques to adapt a work plan to the needs of the project and its stakeholders.

37589 ■ Business Analysis Essentials (Onsite)
Seminar Information Service, Inc.
20 Executive Park, Ste. 120
Irvine, CA 92614
Ph: (949)261-9104
Free: 877-SEM-INFO
Fax: (949)261-1963
Co. E-mail: info@seminarinformation.com
URL: http://www.seminarinformation.com
Price: $2,195.00. **Description:** Learn to define the scope of work and master requirements-gathering techniques that will work for a variety of projects and audiences. **Dates and Locations:** New York, NY; Dallas, TX; and Orlando, FL.

37590 ■ Business Process Analysis
Seminar Information Service, Inc.
20 Executive Park, Ste. 120
Irvine, CA 92614
Ph: (949)261-9104
Free: 877-SEM-INFO
Fax: (949)261-1963
Co. E-mail: info@seminarinformation.com
URL: http://www.seminarinformation.com
Price: $2,395.00. **Description:** Learn to model business processes as they are currently enacted, assess the quality of those business processes, and collaborate with the stakeholders to identify improvements. **Dates and Locations:** Cities throughout Canada.

37591 ■ Business Skills for Project Managers: Improve Your Focus, Credibility and Success
Canadian Management Centre (CMC)
150 York St., 5th Fl.
Toronto, ON, Canada M5H 3S5
Ph: (416)214-5678
Free: 877-262-2519
Fax: (416)313-4985
Co. E-mail: cmcinfo@cmctraining.org
URL: http://www.cmctraining.org
Contact: John Wright, President
Price: $2,195.00 for members; $2,395.00 for non-members. **Description:** This intermediate level course goes beyond the basics of project management. Learn to treat projects like profit-driven businesses. **Dates and Locations:** Toronto, ON.

37592 ■ Canadian Management Centre's 5-Day "MBA"(Canada) (Onsite)
Canadian Management Centre (CMC)
150 York St., 5th Fl.
Toronto, ON, Canada M5H 3S5
Ph: (416)214-5678
Free: 877-262-2519
Fax: (416)313-4985
Co. E-mail: cmcinfo@cmctraining.org
URL: http://www.cmctraining.org
Contact: John Wright, President
Price: $3,195.00 Canadian for non-members; $2,945.00 Canadian for CMC members. **Description:** Seminar that covers how the various components of a business must be linked, aligned and integrated into a successful business system, including business competencies, finance and accounting, marketing strategies, and leadership. **Dates and Locations:** Toronto, ON; Ottawa, ON; and Calgary, AB.

37593 ■ Coaching: A Strategic Tool for Effective Leadership (Onsite) (Canada)
Canadian Management Centre (CMC)
150 York St., 5th Fl.
Toronto, ON, Canada M5H 3S5
Ph: (416)214-5678
Free: 877-262-2519
Fax: (416)313-4985
Co. E-mail: cmcinfo@cmctraining.org
URL: http://www.cmctraining.org
Contact: John Wright, President
Price: $2,395.00 Canadian for non-members; $2,195.00 Canadian for CMC members. **Description:** Covers creating a successful environment, problem resolution, teamwork, soliciting valuable feedback, and models for successful coaching. **Dates and Locations:** Toronto, ON.

37594 ■ Coaching for Business Results: A Hands-On Practical Workshop (Onsite)
Canadian Management Centre (CMC)
150 York St., 5th Fl.
Toronto, ON, Canada M5H 3S5
Ph: (416)214-5678
Free: 877-262-2519
Fax: (416)313-4985
Co. E-mail: cmcinfo@cmctraining.org
URL: http://www.cmctraining.org
Contact: John Wright, President
Price: $495.00 for members; $545.00 for non-members. **Description:** This half-day workshop offers a concentrated blast of practical knowledge on coaching and motivating.

37595 ■ Coaching and Counseling for Outstanding Job Performance (Onsite)
American Management Association
600 AMA Way
Saranac Lake, NY 12983-5534
Ph: (212)586-8100
Free: 877-566-9441
Fax: (518)891-0368
Co. E-mail: customerservice@amanet.org
URL: http://www.amaseminars.org
Price: $2,195.00 for non-members; $1,995.00 for AMA members; and $1,708.00 for General Services Administration (GSA) members. **Description:** Covers creating a successful environment, problem resolution, teamwork, soliciting valuable feedback, and models for successful coaching. **Dates and Locations:** Arlington, VA; San Francisco, CA; and Washington, DC.

37596 ■ Coaching, Mentoring & Team-Building Skills (Onsite)
Seminar Information Service, Inc.
20 Executive Park, Ste. 120
Irvine, CA 92614
Ph: (949)261-9104
Free: 877-SEM-INFO
Fax: (949)261-1963
Co. E-mail: info@seminarinformation.com
URL: http://www.seminarinformation.com
Price: $299.00. **Description:** Learn how to motivate, inspire and guide people to success, including tools for improving cooperation, communication, and a high-energy environment that fosters teamwork. **Dates and Locations:** Madison, WI; and Anaheim, CA.

37597 ■ Collaborative Leadership Skills for Managers (Onsite)
American Management Association
600 AMA Way
Saranac Lake, NY 12983-5534
Ph: (212)586-8100
Free: 877-566-9441
Fax: (518)891-0368
Co. E-mail: customerservice@amanet.org
URL: http://www.amaseminars.org
Price: $2,195.00 for non-members; $1,995.00 for AMA members; and $1,708.00 for General Services Administration (GSA) members. **Description:** Learn to develop a collaborative style to build a mutual trust with your team and other departments. **Dates and Locations:** New York, NY; Chicago, IL; Atlanta, GA; Arlington, VA; and Washington, DC.

37598 ■ The Comprehensive Project Management Workshop (Onsite)
Canadian Management Centre (CMC)
150 York St., 5th Fl.
Toronto, ON, Canada M5H 3S5
Ph: (416)214-5678
Free: 877-262-2519
Fax: (416)313-4985
Co. E-mail: cmcinfo@cmctraining.org
URL: http://www.cmctraining.org
Contact: John Wright, President
Price: $2,995.00 for members; $2,745.00 for non-members. **Description:** Promotes project management expertise and prepares participants for PMP certification in this five-day seminar. **Dates and Locations:** Toronto, ON.

37599 ■ Conducting Employee Performance Evaluations (Onsite)
Padgett-Thompson Seminars
Rockhurst University CEC
14502 W. 105th St.
Lenexa, KS 66215
Free: 800-349-1935
URL: http://www.findaseminar.com/tpd/Padgett-Thompson-Seminars.asp
Price: $249.00. **Description:** For managers and supervisors who want to learn more about conducting fair, legal evaluations and make the review process an integral part of improving employee performance. **Dates and Locations:** New York, NY; Boston, MA.

37600 ■ Confronting the Tough Stuff: Advanced Management Skills for Supervisors (Onsite)
American Management Association
600 AMA Way
Saranac Lake, NY 12983-5534
Ph: (212)586-8100
Free: 877-566-9441
Fax: (518)891-0368
Co. E-mail: customerservice@amanet.org
URL: http://www.amaseminars.org
Price: $1,995.00 for non-members; $1,795.00 for AMA members; and $1,537.00 for General Services Administration (GSA) members. **Description:** Covers diffusing potential legal situations, dealing with challenges, writing performance evaluations, enhancing productivity, and managing diversity. **Dates and Locations:** Arlington, VA; Washington, DC; Chicago, IL; and New York, NY.

37601 ■ Confronting the Tough Stuff: Turning Managerial Challenges into Positive Results (Onsite) (Canada)
Canadian Management Centre (CMC)
150 York St., 5th Fl.
Toronto, ON, Canada M5H 3S5
Ph: (416)214-5678
Free: 877-262-2519
Fax: (416)313-4985
Co. E-mail: cmcinfo@cmctraining.org
URL: http://www.cmctraining.org
Contact: John Wright, President
Price: $1,995.00 Canadian for non-members; $1,845.00 Canadian for CMC members. **Description:** Seminar that covers the challenges and the problem-solving skills in the workplace, including coaching uncooperative employees, constructive and destructive conflict, techniques for using conflict to increase cohesion, four stages of mediation and techniques to mediate disputes between employees, and avoid potentially litigious situations. **Dates and Locations:** Mississauga, ON; Toronto, ON.

37602 ■ Creative Leadership for Managers, Supervisors, and Team Leaders (Onsite)
Fred Pryor Seminars & CareerTrack
5700 Broadmoor St., Ste. 300
Mission, KS 66202
Free: 800-780-8476
Fax: (913)967-8849
Co. E-mail: customerservice@pryor.com
URL: http://www.pryor.com
Price: $179.00; $169.00 for groups of 5 or more. **Description:** Learn techniques that increase your leadership skills and get employees on track in performance and productivity including, why traditional management models just don't measure up in today's workplace and what to use instead. **Dates and Locations:** Cities throughout the United States.

37603 ■ The Creative Leadership Workshop
Seminar Information Service, Inc.
20 Executive Park, Ste. 120
Irvine, CA 92614
Ph: (949)261-9104
Free: 877-SEM-INFO
Fax: (949)261-1963
Co. E-mail: info@seminarinformation.com
URL: http://www.seminarinformation.com
Price: $299.00. **Description:** Learn a bold new approach to motivate employees for greater productivity, stronger teamwork and improved morale in today's complex workforce. **Dates and Locations:** Cities throughout the United States.

37604 ■ The Creative Team-Building Workshop (Onsite)
Seminar Information Service, Inc.
20 Executive Park, Ste. 120
Irvine, CA 92614
Ph: (949)261-9104
Free: 877-SEM-INFO
Fax: (949)261-1963
Co. E-mail: info@seminarinformation.com
URL: http://www.seminarinformation.com
Price: $99.00. **Description:** Update your leadership skills through new creative ideas to inspire for results. **Dates and Locations:** King of Prussia, PA; Mount Laurel, NJ; Wilmington, DE; Allentown, PA; and Scranton, PA.

37605 ■ Creativity and Innovation (Onsite)
Seminar Information Service, Inc.
20 Executive Park, Ste. 120
Irvine, CA 92614
Ph: (949)261-9104
Free: 877-SEM-INFO
Fax: (949)261-1963
Co. E-mail: info@seminarinformation.com
URL: http://www.seminarinformation.com
Price: $2,095.00. **Description:** Develop creative thinking methods to generate ideas and solutions and learn how to align your ideas with corporate needs to add value and increase recognition. **Dates and Locations:** New York, NY; and Arlington, VA.

37606 ■ Critical Thinking: A New Paradigm for Peak Performance (Onsite)
Seminar Information Service, Inc.
20 Executive Park, Ste. 120
Irvine, CA 92614
Ph: (949)261-9104
Free: 877-SEM-INFO
Fax: (949)261-1963
Co. E-mail: info@seminarinformation.com
URL: http://www.seminarinformation.com
Price: $2,345.00.; $2,095.00 for AMA members. **Description:** Learn different styles of thinking and identify your personal preferences, including how to challenge assumptions and expand perceptions about situations. **Dates and Locations:** Arlington, VA; Chicago, IL; New York, NY; and Houston, TX.

37607 ■ Criticism & Discipline Skills for Managers and Supervisors (Onsite)
Fred Pryor Seminars & CareerTrack
5700 Broadmoor St., Ste. 300
Mission, KS 66202
Free: 800-780-8476
Fax: (913)967-8849
Co. E-mail: customerservice@pryor.com
URL: http://www.pryor.com
Price: $249.00; $229.00 for groups of 5 or more. **Description:** Learn proven techniques for managing difficult employees without incurring resentment, making enemies, or destroying relationships, including how to discipline employees who have a bad attitude, are chronically tardy, miss work often, refuse to take responsibility and challenge your authority. **Dates and Locations:** Cities throughout the United States.

37608 ■ Developing Executive Leadership (Canada)
Canadian Management Centre (CMC)
150 York St., 5th Fl.
Toronto, ON, Canada M5H 3S5
Ph: (416)214-5678
Free: 877-262-2519
Fax: (416)313-4985
Co. E-mail: cmcinfo@cmctraining.org
URL: http://www.cmctraining.org
Contact: John Wright, President
Price: $2,195.00 Canadian for non-members; $1,995.00 Canadian for CMC members. **Description:** Seminar that covers leadership in today's business environment, including techniques to improve effectiveness, leading individuals and groups, keys to developing influence, and how to create your own leadership development plan. **Dates and Locations:** Toronto, ON.

37609 ■ Developing Into a Powerful Leader (Onsite)
Seminar Information Service, Inc.
20 Executive Park, Ste. 120
Irvine, CA 92614
Ph: (949)261-9104
Free: 877-SEM-INFO
Fax: (949)261-1963
Co. E-mail: info@seminarinformation.com
URL: http://www.seminarinformation.com
Price: $1,595.00. **Description:** Enhance your ability to lead others and have them feel good about the process. **Dates and Locations:** Boston, MA.

37610 ■ Developing Your Emotional Intelligence (Onsite)
Padgett-Thompson Seminars
Rockhurst University CEC
14502 W. 105th St.
Lenexa, KS 66215
Free: 800-349-1935
URL: http://www.findaseminar.com/tpd/Padgett-Thompson-Seminars.asp
Price: $199.00. **Description:** Seminar provides skills to the eliminate stress and frustration brought on by others in the workplace. **Dates and Locations:** Buffalo, NY; Southfield, MI.

37611 ■ The Difference Between Good and Great Supervisors
Padgett-Thompson Seminars
Rockhurst University CEC
14502 W. 105th St.
Lenexa, KS 66215
Free: 800-349-1935
URL: http://www.findaseminar.com/tpd/Padgett-Thompson-Seminars.asp
Price: $249.00. **Description:** Workshop presents positive solutions, real-world tips, and strategies for managers and supervisors. **Dates and Locations:** Columbus, OH; Milwaukee, WI; Chicago, IL.

37612 ■ Driving Innovation: Proven Processes, Tools and Strategies for Growth (Onsite)
Seminar Information Service, Inc.
20 Executive Park, Ste. 120
Irvine, CA 92614
Ph: (949)261-9104
Free: 877-SEM-INFO
Fax: (949)261-1963
Co. E-mail: info@seminarinformation.com
URL: http://www.seminarinformation.com
Price: $1,495.00. **Description:** Learn to use proven processes and tools to imagine and execute new innovation opportunities, regardless of your creative disposition or your role in the organization.

37613 ■ Earned Value Management Systems (EVMS) for Project Managers
EEI Communications
66 Canal Ctr. Plz., Ste. 200
Alexandria, VA 22314-5507
Ph: (703)683-7453
Free: 888-253-2762
Fax: (703)683-7310
Co. E-mail: train@eeicom.com
URL: http://www.eeicom.com/training
Price: $745.00. **Description:** Seminar based on ANSI/EIA-748-A, Earned Value Management Systems, and the Project Management Institute's (PMI) Project Management Body of Knowledge (PMBOK) that covers resource planning and estimating, project budgeting, EVM (Earned Value Management) performance metrics, variance analyses, and EVMS reports. **Dates and Locations:** Silver Spring, MD; Alexandria, VA; Hunt Valley, MD; and Columbia, MD.

37614 ■ Effective Meeting Management (Onsite)
Seminar Information Service, Inc.
20 Executive Park, Ste. 120
Irvine, CA 92614
Ph: (949)261-9104
Free: 877-SEM-INFO
Fax: (949)261-1963
Co. E-mail: info@seminarinformation.com
URL: http://www.seminarinformation.com
Price: Contact for fees. **Description:** Learn how to keep control throughout the meeting, while creating a receptive, engaging, and energetic atmosphere. **Dates and Locations:** New York, NY.

37615 ■ Effective Negotiating
Karrass USA Ltd.
8370 Wilshire Blvd.
Beverly Hills, CA 90211-2333
Ph: (323)866-3800
Free: 800-232-8000
Co. E-mail: mail@karrass.com
URL: http://www.karrass.com
Price: $998.00. **Description:** Seminar topics include, sticking to your own game plan, what people forget to do, you have more power than you think, and using hidden leverage. **Dates and Locations:** Cities throughout the United States and Canada.

37616 ■ Effective Project Communications, Negotiations and Conflict (Onsite)
EEI Communications
8945 Guilford ., Ste. 145
Columbia, MD 21046
Ph: (410)309-8200
Free: 888-253-2762

Fax: (410)630-3980
Co. E-mail: train@eeicom.com
URL: http://www.eeicom.com/eei-training-services
Price: $1,065.00. **Description:** Learn what you need to know to lead projects through their initiation, planning, execution, and control phases, including the skills needed to find common ground, overcome resistance, resolve disputes, and gain commitment to project management efforts. **Dates and Locations:** Silver Spring, MD; Hunt Valley, MD; Columbia, MD; and Alexandria, VA.

37617 ■ Effective Training Techniques for Group Leaders (Onsite)
Seminar Information Service, Inc.
20 Executive Park, Ste. 120
Irvine, CA 92614
Ph: (949)261-9104
Free: 877-SEM-INFO
Fax: (949)261-1963
Co. E-mail: info@seminarinformation.com
URL: http://www.seminarinformation.com
Price: $370.00 for non-members; $275.00 for The Management Association, Inc. **Description:** Provides group leaders precise and practical methods to train their employees. Leaders also learn to spot worker training needs and provide effective on-the-job training. **Dates and Locations:** Palatine, IL; and Waukesha, WI.

37618 ■ Emotional Intelligence for Administrative Professionals (Onsite)
AMA
600 AMA Way
Saranac Lake, NY 12983-5534
Ph: (212)586-8100
Free: 877-566-9441
Fax: (518)891-0368
Co. E-mail: customerservice@amanet.org
URL: http://www.amaseminars.org
Price: $1,545.00 for non-members; $1,395.00 for AMA members; and $1,195.00 for General Services Administration (GSA) members. **Description:** A two-day course for administrative professionals to learn to keep their emotions in check in order to achieve lasting career success.

37619 ■ Enhancing Your Management Skills (Onsite)
Seminar Information Service, Inc.
20 Executive Park, Ste. 120
Irvine, CA 92614
Ph: (949)261-9104
Free: 877-SEM-INFO
Fax: (949)261-1963
Co. E-mail: info@seminarinformation.com
URL: http://www.seminarinformation.com
Price: $1,995.00. **Description:** Learn the critical success factors for driving results through goal alignment, coaching for performance, building trust, and driving committed action through stronger leadership. Receive practical, state-of-the-art tools and techniques for holding conversations that set clear expectations, provide focused feedback, create a motivational environment, and build commitment for needed change.

37620 ■ The Essential Administrative Professional: The Skills and Know-How to Make You Invaluable (Onsite)
AMA
600 AMA Way
Saranac Lake, NY 12983-5534
Ph: (212)586-8100
Free: 877-566-9441
Fax: (518)891-0368
Co. E-mail: customerservice@amanet.org
URL: http://www.amaseminars.org
Price: $1,795.00 for non-members; $1,595.00 for AMA members; and $1,366.00 for General Services Administration (GSA) members. **Description:** Learn to empower yourself by gaining the know-how that brings the acknowledgement you deserve in this two-day course.

37621 ■ Essential Coaching and Mentoring Skills for Managers, Supervisors and Team Leaders (Onsite)
Padgett-Thompson Seminars
Rockhurst University CEC
14502 W. 105th St.
Lenexa, KS 66215
Free: 800-349-1935
URL: http://www.findaseminar.com/tpd/Padgett-Thompson-Seminars.asp
Price: $199.00. **Description:** Seminar provides solutions to the toughest leadership problems. **Dates and Locations:** Cities throughout the United States.

37622 ■ Essential Facilitation (Onsite)
Interaction Associates
70 Fargo St., Ste. 908
Boston, MA 02210
Ph: (617)535-7000
Free: 800-347-8352
Fax: (617)535-7099
Co. E-mail: workshops@interactionassociates.com
URL: http://www.interactionassociates.com
Price: $2,395.00. **Description:** This seminar will show you how to effectively facilitate meetings and group processes. Addresses content, conflict, and context within meetings. **Dates and Locations:** Luling, LA; Arlington, VA; San Francisco CA;Boston, MA; and Dallas, TX.

37623 ■ Essentials of Project Management for the Nonproject Manager (Onsite)
AMA
600 AMA Way
Saranac Lake, NY 12983-5534
Ph: (212)586-8100
Free: 877-566-9441
Fax: (518)891-0368
Co. E-mail: customerservice@amanet.org
URL: http://www.amaseminars.org
Price: $2,095.00 for non-members; $1,895.00 for AMA members; and $1,623.00 for General Services Administration (GSA) members. **Description:** Learn and apply basic elements of project management to your job. **Dates and Locations:** Cities throughout the United States.

37624 ■ Excelling as A Manager or Supervisor (Onsite)
Seminar Information Service, Inc.
20 Executive Park, Ste. 120
Irvine, CA 92614
Ph: (949)261-9104
Free: 877-SEM-INFO
Fax: (949)261-1963
Co. E-mail: info@seminarinformation.com
URL: http://www.seminarinformation.com
Price: $149.00; $139.00 for four or more. **Description:** Offers solutions to help you fully achieve your potential as a true leader. **Dates and Locations:** Cities throughout the United States.

37625 ■ Excelling as a Highly Effective Team Leader (Onsite)
Seminar Information Service, Inc.
20 Executive Park, Ste. 120
Irvine, CA 92614
Ph: (949)261-9104
Free: 877-SEM-INFO
Fax: (949)261-1963
Co. E-mail: info@seminarinformation.com
URL: http://www.seminarinformation.com
Price: $399.00; $349.00 for four or more. **Description:** Learn the personal leadership characteristics and skills that create energy and enthusiasm increasing productivity and performance. **Dates and Locations:** Cities throughout the United States.

37626 ■ Exceptional Management Skills (Onsite)
Baker Communications Inc. (BCI)
10101 SW Fwy., Ste. 630
Houston, TX 77074
Ph: (713)627-7700
Fax: (713)587-2051
Co. E-mail: information@bakercommunications.com
URL: http://www.bakercommunications.com
Contact: Walter Rogers, President
Price: Contact for fees. **Description:** This two-day interactive workshop will provide the tools to make the most of interactions with subordinates. **Dates and Locations:** Cities throughout the United States.

37627 ■ Facilitation Skills (Onsite)
Seminar Information Service, Inc.
20 Executive Park, Ste. 120
Irvine, CA 92614
Ph: (949)261-9104
Free: 877-SEM-INFO
Fax: (949)261-1963
Co. E-mail: info@seminarinformation.com
URL: http://www.seminarinformation.com
Price: $2,490.00. **Description:** Learn how to facilitate goal-oriented results through planning, collaboration and consensus; Maintain facilitative focus by adopting the right frame of mind; Create a targeted agenda to make meetings productive; Start-up, manage and close effective meetings; Resolve disagreement using a range of consensus-building techniques; Develop and implement a facilitative action plan. **Dates and Locations:** Toronto and Ottawa, CN.

37628 ■ Facilitative Leadership (Onsite)
Interaction Associates
70 Fargo St., Ste. 908
Boston, MA 02210
Ph: (617)535-7000
Free: 800-347-8352
Fax: (617)535-7099
URL: http://www.interactionassociates.com
Price: $1,950.00. **Description:** Two-day seminar that offers seven principles to form a strategic framework for leadership. **Dates and Locations:** Arlington, VA.

37629 ■ Facilities Management (Onsite)
Fred Pryor Seminars & CareerTrack
5700 Broadmoor St., Ste. 300
Mission, KS 66202
Free: 800-780-8476
Fax: (913)967-8849
Co. E-mail: customerservice@pryor.com
URL: http://www.pryor.com
Price: $399.00; $379.00 for groups of 3 or more. **Description:** Covers techniques used by leading facilities managers to run a safe, cost-effective, and employee friendly environment. **Dates and Locations:** Cities throughout the United States.

37630 ■ Finance for Non-Financial Managers - Improving Financial Literacy (Onsite)
Learning Tree International Inc.
1805 Library St.
Reston, VA 20190-5660
Ph: (703)709-9119
Free: 800-843-8733
Fax: (703)709-6405
Co. E-mail: uscourses@learningtree.com
URL: http://www.learningtree.com
Contact: Nick Schacht, President
Price: $2,490.00. **Description:** Learn to integrate financial concepts and policies into management decisions and budgeting processes. **Dates and Locations:** Reston, VA; New York, NY; Rockville, MD; and Toronto, CN.

37631 ■ Foundation for Leading Teams (Onsite)
Seminar Information Service, Inc.
20 Executive Park, Ste. 120
Irvine, CA 92614
Ph: (949)261-9104
Free: 877-SEM-INFO
Fax: (949)261-1963
Co. E-mail: info@seminarinformation.com
URL: http://www.seminarinformation.com
Price: $370.00; $275.00 for MRA members. **Description:** learn to develop a clear understanding of effective team behaviors. **Dates and Locations:** Waukesha, WI.

37632 ■ Framework for Excellence (Course on Request)
Canadian Management Centre (CMC)
150 York St., 5th Fl.
Toronto, ON, Canada M5H 3S5
Ph: (416)214-5678
Free: 877-262-2519
Fax: (416)313-4985
Co. E-mail: cmcinfo@cmctraining.org
URL: http://www.cmctraining.org
Contact: John Wright, President
Price: $971.00 for members; $1,295.00 for non-members. **Description:** This course provides participants with a clear understanding of the scope and intent of the National Quality Institute's (NQI) Framework for Excellence.

37633 ■ Fundamentals of Project Management (Onsite)
Fred Pryor Seminars & CareerTrack
5700 Broadmoor St., Ste. 300
Mission, KS 66202
Free: 800-780-8476
Fax: (913)967-8849
Co. E-mail: customerservice@pryor.com
URL: http://www.pryor.com
Price: $299.00; $279.00 for groups of 5 or more. **Description:** Learn to plan, budget and schedule project in on time and within a budget. **Dates and Locations:** Cities throughout the United States.

37634 ■ Fundamentals of Successful Project Management (Onsite)
Seminar Information Service, Inc.
20 Executive Park, Ste. 120
Irvine, CA 92614
Ph: (949)261-9104
Free: 877-SEM-INFO
Fax: (949)261-1963
Co. E-mail: info@seminarinformation.com
URL: http://www.seminarinformation.com
Price: $399.00; $349.00 for four or more. **Description:** How to create a plan, implement it, monitor progress, correct as necessary and deliver as promised. **Dates and Locations:** Huntsville, AL.

37635 ■ Getting Results Without Authority (Onsite) (Canada)
Canadian Management Centre (CMC)
150 York St., 5th Fl.
Toronto, ON, Canada M5H 3S5
Ph: (416)214-5678
Free: 877-262-2519
Fax: (416)313-4985
Co. E-mail: cmcinfo@cmctraining.org
URL: http://www.cmctraining.org
Contact: John Wright, President
Price: $2,395.00 Canadian for non-members; $2,195.00 Canadian for CMC members. **Description:** Covers how to achieve results via other employees despite not having direct authority over them. **Dates and Locations:** Vancouver, BC; Toronto, ON; Edmonton, AB; Calgary, AB and Mississauga, ON.

37636 ■ Global Competencies for Diversity Leaders (Onsite)
Seminar Information Service, Inc.
20 Executive Park, Ste. 120
Irvine, CA 92614
Ph: (949)261-9104
Free: 877-SEM-INFO
Fax: (949)261-1963
Co. E-mail: info@seminarinformation.com
URL: http://www.seminarinformation.com
Price: $995.00. **Description:** Through the use of case studies, exercises, discussion with peers, and guidance from experts in the field, participants will develop a toolkit of competencies to achieve success, including why a global diversity strategy is essential, differences between U.S. and multinational diversity implementation, and key steps in creating a global diversity strategy. **Dates and Locations:** New York, NY.

37637 ■ High-Impact Decision Making (Onsite)
Canadian Management Centre (CMC)
150 York St., 5th Fl.
Toronto, ON, Canada M5H 3S5
Ph: (416)214-5678
Free: 877-262-2519
Fax: (416)313-4985
Co. E-mail: cmcinfo@cmctraining.org
URL: http://www.cmctraining.org
Contact: John Wright, President
Price: $1,995.00 for members; $1,845.00 for non-members. **Description:** Learn to make the best decision every time by reducing risks and maximizing results. **Dates and Locations:** Toronto, ON.

37638 ■ How to Be a Highly Successful Team Leader (Onsite)
Seminar Information Service, Inc.
20 Executive Park, Ste. 120
Irvine, CA 92614
Ph: (949)261-9104
Free: 877-SEM-INFO
Fax: (949)261-1963
Co. E-mail: info@seminarinformation.com
URL: http://www.seminarinformation.com
Price: $299.00. **Description:** Intensive two-day workshop that teaches the many dimensions of effective leadership and develop the skills needed to lead your team to maximum performance.

37639 ■ How to Be a Highly Successful Team Leader (Onsite)
Padgett-Thompson Seminars
Rockhurst University CEC
14502 W. 105th St.
Lenexa, KS 66215
Free: 800-349-1935
URL: http://www.findaseminar.com/tpd/Padgett-Thompson-Seminars.asp
Price: $299.00. **Description:** Two-day workshop to help explore the many dimensions of effective leadership and develop the skills needed to lead a team to peak performance. **Dates and Locations:** Boise, ID; Oak Brook, IL; Indianapolis, IN.

37640 ■ How to Create a Compelling Business Case
AMA
600 AMA Way
Saranac Lake, NY 12983-5534
Ph: (212)586-8100
Free: 877-566-9441
Fax: (518)891-0368
Co. E-mail: customerservice@amanet.org
URL: http://www.amaseminars.org
Price: $1,995.00 for non-members; $1,795.00 for AMA members. **Description:** Develop and present the strongest business case to get your projects approved in this two-day course. **Dates and Locations:** New York, NY; San Francisco, CA; and Chicago, IL.

37641 ■ How to Deal with Unacceptable Employee Behavior (Onsite)
Fred Pryor Seminars & CareerTrack
5700 Broadmoor St., Ste. 300
Mission, KS 66202
Free: 800-780-8476
Fax: (913)967-8849
Co. E-mail: customerservice@pryor.com
URL: http://www.pryor.com
Price: $179.00; $169.00 for groups of 5 or more. **Description:** Learn effective management techniques for dealing with problem employees, and how to tailor an individual approach for each employee's situation. **Dates and Locations:** Cities throughout the United States.

37642 ■ How to Effectively Manage Multiple Locations (Onsite)
Seminar Information Service, Inc.
20 Executive Park, Ste. 120
Irvine, CA 92614
Ph: (949)261-9104
Free: 877-SEM-INFO
Fax: (949)261-1963
Co. E-mail: info@seminarinformation.com
URL: http://www.seminarinformation.com
Price: $399.00; $349.00 for four or more. **Description:** Gain critical know-how for realizing full potential as a manager and a leader in one of the most challenging situations any manager could find themselves in. **Dates and Locations:** Cities throughout the United States.

37643 ■ How to Effectively Supervise People: Fundaments of Leading With Success! (Onsite)
Seminar Information Service, Inc.
20 Executive Park, Ste. 120
Irvine, CA 92614
Ph: (949)261-9104
Free: 877-SEM-INFO
Fax: (949)261-1963
Co. E-mail: info@seminarinformation.com
URL: http://www.seminarinformation.com
Price: $199.00. **Description:** This seminar teaches the fundamentals of leading with success, including what's expected of you and how to deal with various personalities and problem employees. **Dates and Locations:** Cities throughout the United States.

37644 ■ How to Excel at Managing and Supervising People (Onsite)
Seminar Information Service, Inc.
20 Executive Park, Ste. 120
Irvine, CA 92614
Ph: (949)261-9104
Free: 877-SEM-INFO
Fax: (949)261-1963
Co. E-mail: info@seminarinformation.com
URL: http://www.seminarinformation.com
Price: $299.00; $269.00 for 4 or more. **Description:** Learn skills to manage change, motivate, discipline, delegate, including problem solving for success. **Dates and Locations:** Cities throughout the United States.

37645 ■ How to Gather and Document User Requirements (Onsite)
Seminar Information Service, Inc.
20 Executive Park, Ste. 120
Irvine, CA 92614
Ph: (949)261-9104
Free: 877-SEM-INFO
Fax: (949)261-1963
Co. E-mail: info@seminarinformation.com
URL: http://www.seminarinformation.com
Price: $2,295.00. **Description:** Introduces the roles of the business analyst as they relate to the analysis and documentation requirements. **Dates and Locations:** Boston, MA; Ottawa, CN; Washington, DC; Orlando, FL; and Las Vegas, NV.

37646 ■ How to Get More Organized (Onsite)
Padgett-Thompson Seminars
Rockhurst University CEC
14502 W. 105th St.
Lenexa, KS 66215
Free: 800-349-1935
URL: http://www.findaseminar.com/tpd/Padgett-Thompson-Seminars.asp
Price: $169.00. **Description:** Seminar will teach how to meet deadlines by getting more done in less time. **Dates and Locations:** Phoenix, AZ; San Francisco, CA.

37647 ■ How to Handle Conflict and Confrontation (Onsite)
Padgett-Thompson Seminars
Rockhurst University CEC
14502 W. 105th St.
Lenexa, KS 66215
Free: 800-349-1935
URL: http://www.findaseminar.com/tpd/Padgett-Thompson-Seminars.asp
Price: $199.00. **Description:** A change management seminar that shows participants how to find positive solutions to negative situations. **Dates and Locations:** Cities throughout the United States.

37648 ■ How to Manage Emotions and Excel Under Pressure (Onsite)
Padgett-Thompson Seminars
Rockhurst University CEC
14502 W. 105th St.
Lenexa, KS 66215
Free: 800-349-1935
URL: http://www.findaseminar.com/tpd/Padgett-Thompson-Seminars.asp
Price: $199.00. **Description:** Workshop teaches the skills required to maintain emotional control in the workplace. **Dates and Locations:** Wilmington, DE.

37649 ■ How to Supervise People (Onsite)
Seminar Information Service, Inc.
20 Executive Park, Ste. 120
Irvine, CA 92614
Ph: (949)261-9104
Free: 877-SEM-INFO
Fax: (949)261-1963
Co. E-mail: info@seminarinformation.com
URL: http://www.seminarinformation.com
Price: $149.00; $139.00 for five or more. **Description:** Participants learn how to rate performance, relate to former peers, maintain a positive motivational climate, and handle conflicts. **Dates and Locations:** Cities throughout the United States.

37650 ■ Improving Performance of Remote and Virtual Workers (Onsite)
Canadian Management Centre (CMC)
150 York St., 5th Fl.
Toronto, ON, Canada M5H 3S5
Ph: (416)214-5678
Free: 877-262-2519
Fax: (416)313-4985
Co. E-mail: cmcinfo@cmctraining.org
URL: http://www.cmctraining.org
Contact: John Wright, President
Price: $495.00 for members; $545.00 for non-members. **Description:** Learn some of the practical strategies to build a performance-based team and to utilize technology to apply virtual management techniques. **Dates and Locations:** Toronto, ON.

37651 ■ Improving Your Managerial Effectiveness (Course on Request) (Canada)
Canadian Management Centre (CMC)
150 York St., 5th Fl.
Toronto, ON, Canada M5H 3S5
Ph: (416)214-5678
Free: 877-262-2519
Fax: (416)313-4985
Co. E-mail: cmcinfo@cmctraining.org
URL: http://www.cmctraining.org
Contact: John Wright, President
Price: $2,395.00 Canadian for non-members; $2,195.00 Canadian for CMC members. **Description:** Addresses issues faced by most management professionals, including personal, operational, organizational, and interpersonal effectiveness in today's workplace. **Dates and Locations:** Toronto, ON.

37652 ■ Improving Your Project Management Skills: The Basics for Success (Onsite)
American Management Association
600 AMA Way
Saranac Lake, NY 12983-5534
Ph: (212)586-8100
Free: 877-566-9441
Fax: (518)891-0368
Co. E-mail: customerservice@amanet.org
URL: http://www.amaseminars.org
Price: $2,195.00 for non-members; $1,995.00 for AMA members; and $1,708.00 for General Services Administration (GSA) members. **Description:** Covers the basic principles of project management, including setting goals and schedules, managing a project plan, estimating, and budgeting. **Dates and Locations:** Cities throughout the United States.

37653 ■ Improving Your Project Management Skills: The Basics for Success (Onsite) (Canada)
Canadian Management Centre (CMC)
150 York St., 5th Fl.
Toronto, ON, Canada M5H 3S5
Ph: (416)214-5678
Free: 877-262-2519
Fax: (416)313-4985
Co. E-mail: cmcinfo@cmctraining.org
URL: http://www.cmctraining.org
Contact: John Wright, President
Price: $2,395.00 Canadian for non-members; $2,195.00 Canadian for CMC members. **Description:** Topics include understanding project management, project planning and scheduling, documentation and reporting, and quality control. **Dates and Locations:** Edmonton, AB; Calgary, AB; Vaughan, ON; Ottawa, ON; Mississauga, ON; Vancouver, BC; and Toronto, ON.

37654 ■ Information Technology Project Management (Onsite)
American Management Association
600 AMA Way
Saranac Lake, NY 12983-5534
Ph: (212)586-8100
Free: 877-566-9441
Fax: (518)891-0368
Co. E-mail: customerservice@amanet.org
URL: http://www.amaseminars.org
Price: $2,195.00 for non-members; $1,995.00 for AMA members; and $1,708.00 for General Services Administration (GSA) members. **Description:** Covers the entire information systems process from start to finish, including budgeting, software tools, and scheduling. **Dates and Locations:** New York, NY; Arlington, VA; Washington, DC; Chicago, IL; and San Francisco, CA.

37655 ■ Interpersonal Skills for Managers (Onsite)
American Management Association
600 AMA Way
Saranac Lake, NY 12983-5534
Ph: (212)586-8100
Free: 877-566-9441
Fax: (518)891-0368
Co. E-mail: customerservice@amanet.org
URL: http://www.amaseminars.org
Price: $2,345.00 for non-members; $2,095.00 for AMA members; and $1,794.00 for General Services Administration (GSA) members. **Description:** Covers organizational change, diversity and electronic communication channels in the workplace. **Dates and Locations:** San Francisco, CA; Washington, DC; Chicago, IL; New York, NY; and Arlington, VA.

37656 ■ Introduction to Process Mapping (Course on Request)
Canadian Management Centre (CMC)
150 York St., 5th Fl.
Toronto, ON, Canada M5H 3S5
Ph: (416)214-5678
Free: 877-262-2519
Fax: (416)313-4985
Co. E-mail: cmcinfo@cmctraining.org
URL: http://www.cmctraining.org
Contact: John Wright, President
Price: $521.00 for members; $695.00 for non-members. **Description:** A one-day course examining process mapping and its efficiency within your organization.

37657 ■ Introduction to Project Management (Onsite)
EEI Communications
8945 Guilford Rd., Ste. 145
Columbia, MD 21046
Ph: (410)309-8200
Free: 888-253-2762
Fax: (410)630-3980
Co. E-mail: train@eeicom.com
URL: http://www.eeicom.com/eei-training-services
Price: $745.00. **Description:** Topics include understanding project management, characteristics of an effective manager, documentation, and quality control. **Dates and Locations:** Silver Spring, MD; Alexandria, VA; Hunt Valley, MD; and Columbia, MD.

37658 ■ IT Relationship Management: Aligning IT with the Business (Onsite)
Seminar Information Service, Inc.
20 Executive Park, Ste. 120
Irvine, CA 92614
Ph: (949)261-9104
Free: 877-SEM-INFO
Fax: (949)261-1963
Co. E-mail: info@seminarinformation.com
URL: http://www.seminarinformation.com
Price: $2,490.00. **Description:** Learn the best practices of an IT Relationship Manager (ITRM) for facilitating IT solutions that provide value to the business and satisfy the needs of business stakeholders. **Dates and Locations:** Rockville, MD; New York, NY; Reston, VA; and Toronto, CN.

37659 ■ Keys to Effectively Supervising People (Onsite)
Padgett-Thompson Seminars
Rockhurst University CEC
14502 W. 105th St.
Lenexa, KS 66215
Free: 800-349-1935
URL: http://www.findaseminar.com/tpd/Padgett-Thompson-Seminars.asp
Price: $249.00. **Description:** One-day seminar that immerses participants in the supervisory techniques, tools, and solutions needed to be more effective. **Dates and Locations:** Cities throughout the United States and Canada.

37660 ■ Leadership for Group Leaders II: Communication Skills for Group Leaders (Onsite)
Seminar Information Service, Inc.
20 Executive Park, Ste. 120
Irvine, CA 92614
Ph: (949)261-9104
Free: 877-SEM-INFO
Fax: (949)261-1963
Co. E-mail: info@seminarinformation.com
URL: http://www.seminarinformation.com
Price: $275.00 for MRA members; $370.00 for non-members. **Description:** Participants gain effective listening skills and the ability to give and receive feedback. **Dates and Locations:** Waukesha, WI; and Palatine, IL.

37661 ■ Leadership Skills: Building Success Through Teamwork (Onsite)
Seminar Information Service, Inc.
20 Executive Park, Ste. 120
Irvine, CA 92614
Ph: (949)261-9104
Free: 877-SEM-INFO
Fax: (949)261-1963
Co. E-mail: info@seminarinformation.com
URL: http://www.seminarinformation.com
Price: $2,490.00. **Description:** Learn how to: Develop your teams to maximize their strengths and enhance productivity; Optimize organization and work design for success in service delivery teams; Motivate your team with effective performance measurement; Integrate your role as a leader into your management style; Leverage the complementary skills and styles of your team; Eliminate barriers and chokepoints that block teamwork; Apply a diverse and multilevel approach to minimize communication breakdowns. **Dates and Locations:** Toronto, CN.

37662 ■ Leadership Skills: Building Success Through Teamwork (Onsite)
Learning Tree International Inc.
1805 Library St.
Reston, VA 20190-5660
Ph: (703)709-9119
Free: 800-843-8733
Fax: (703)709-6405
Co. E-mail: uscourses@learningtree.com
URL: http://www.learningtree.com
Contact: Nick Schacht, President
Price: $2,490.00. **Description:** Learn to develop teams to maximize their strengths and enhance productivity. **Dates and Locations:** Toronto, ON.

37663 ■ Leadership Skills for Supervisors (Onsite) (Canada)
Canadian Management Centre (CMC)
150 York St., 5th Fl.
Toronto, ON, Canada M5H 3S5
Ph: (416)214-5678
Free: 877-262-2519

Fax: (416)313-4985
Co. E-mail: cmcinfo@cmctraining.org
URL: http://www.cmctraining.org
Contact: John Wright, President
Price: $2,395.00 Canadian for non-members; $2,195.00 Canadian for CMC members. **Description:** Covers empowering supervisors and staff; using flow chart techniques as a means of assessing work flow and streamlining processes; coaching, mentoring, and providing feedback; organizing and leading productive meetings; and using brainstorming to cultivate ideas. **Dates and Locations:** Toronto, ON.

37664 ■ Leadership Skills and Team Development for IT and Technical Professionals (Onsite)
Seminar Information Service, Inc.
20 Executive Park, Ste. 120
Irvine, CA 92614
Ph: (949)261-9104
Free: 877-SEM-INFO
Fax: (949)261-1963
Co. E-mail: info@seminarinformation.com
URL: http://www.seminarinformation.com
Price: $2,345.00 for AMA members; $2,095.00 for non-members. **Description:** Interactive seminar provides hands-on exercises designed to help technical professionals build and lead a team, evaluate the team's performance, and develop an action plan for leadership success. **Dates and Locations:** New York, NY; San Francisco, CA; and Atlanta, GA.

37665 ■ Leadership and Supervisory Skills for Women (Onsite)
Padgett-Thompson Seminars
Rockhurst University CEC
14502 W. 105th St.
Lenexa, KS 66215
Free: 800-349-1935
URL: http://www.findaseminar.com/tpd/Padgett-Thompson-Seminars.asp
Price: $199.00. **Description:** A one-day workshop to learn strategies for effective leadership at all levels. **Dates and Locations:** Indianapolis, IN.

37666 ■ Leadership and Team Development for Managerial Success (Onsite)
American Management Association
600 AMA Way
Saranac Lake, NY 12983-5534
Ph: (212)586-8100
Free: 877-566-9441
Fax: (518)891-0368
Co. E-mail: customerservice@amanet.org
URL: http://www.amaseminars.org
Price: $2,095.00 for non-members; $1,895.00 for AMA members; and $1,623.00 for General Services Administration (GSA) members. **Description:** Covers the difference between managing and leading, developing and communicating goals, motivating a team, and various team concepts. **Dates and Locations:** San Diego, CA; Chicago, IL; Arlington, VA; and Washington, DC.

37667 ■ Leading Effective Teams II - Communicating with Your Teammates (Onsite)
Seminar Information Service, Inc.
20 Executive Park, Ste. 120
Irvine, CA 92614
Ph: (949)261-9104
Free: 877-SEM-INFO
Fax: (949)261-1963
Co. E-mail: info@seminarinformation.com
URL: http://www.seminarinformation.com
Price: $350.00 for non-members; $275.00 for MRA members. **Description:** Leaders learn their communication style and how it relates to their team members, as well as how to motivate through communication. **Dates and Locations:** Waukesha, WI.

37668 ■ Leading High-Performance Project Teams
Seminar Information Service, Inc.
20 Executive Park, Ste. 120
Irvine, CA 92614
Ph: (949)261-9104
Free: 877-SEM-INFO
Fax: (949)261-1963
Co. E-mail: info@seminarinformation.com
URL: http://www.seminarinformation.com
Price: $1,995.00. **Description:** Fast-paced, highly engaging workplace simulation enables you to integrate and apply five practices of exemplary leaders, and eight dimensions of high-performing teams, becoming a confident and competent leader. **Dates and Locations:** Cities throughout the United States.

37669 ■ Leading High Performance Teams
Seminar Information Service, Inc.
20 Executive Park, Ste. 120
Irvine, CA 92614
Ph: (949)261-9104
Free: 877-SEM-INFO
Fax: (949)261-1963
Co. E-mail: info@seminarinformation.com
URL: http://www.seminarinformation.com
Price: $1,495.00. **Description:** Builds awareness and skill in the areas of team dynamics, group problem solving, and group decision making. You will develop leadership skills applicable to many areas, but especially suited to self-directed work teams, employee participation teams, interdepartmental task groups, and other group situations where combined efforts are needed to reach optimal performance levels. **Dates and Locations:** New York, NY.

37670 ■ Leading Project Managers: A Guide to Success (Onsite)
Seminar Information Service, Inc.
20 Executive Park, Ste. 120
Irvine, CA 92614
Ph: (949)261-9104
Free: 877-SEM-INFO
Fax: (949)261-1963
Co. E-mail: info@seminarinformation.com
URL: http://www.seminarinformation.com
Price: $1,645.00. **Description:** Gain perspectives and review best practices on issues critical to those who manage project managers. **Dates and Locations:** Cities throughout the United States.

37671 ■ Leading Virtual and Remote Teams (Onsite)
American Management Association
600 AMA Way
Saranac Lake, NY 12983-5534
Ph: (212)586-8100
Free: 877-566-9441
Fax: (518)891-0368
Co. E-mail: customerservice@amanet.org
URL: http://www.amaseminars.org
Price: $2,545.00 for non-members; $2,295.00 for AMA members; and $1,965.00 for General Services Administration (GSA) members. **Description:** Covers leadership models, communication between teams, virtual team development, measuring performance, and utilizing technology effectively. **Dates and Locations:** Chicago, IL; Arlington, VA; Washington, DC; San Francisco, CA; Dallas, TX; New York, NY; and Las Vegas, CA..

37672 ■ Legal Issues for Managers (Onsite)
Seminar Information Service, Inc.
20 Executive Park, Ste. 120
Irvine, CA 92614
Ph: (949)261-9104
Free: 877-SEM-INFO
Fax: (949)261-1963
Co. E-mail: info@seminarinformation.com
URL: http://www.seminarinformation.com
Price: $1,990.00. **Description:** Using a case study, practical examples, and discussions participants will explore the law as it relates to making nondiscriminatory employment decisions, compliance with wage and hour laws, safety and health rights and responsibilities, required versus discretionary leaves of absence, managing employees covered by labor agreements, and individual rights and wrongful discharge.

37673 ■ Making Successful Business Decisions: Getting It Right the First Time (Onsite)
Learning Tree International Inc.
1805 Library St.
Reston, VA 20190-5660
Ph: (703)709-9119
Free: 800-843-8733
Fax: (703)709-6405
Co. E-mail: uscourses@learningtree.com
URL: http://www.learningtree.com
Contact: Nick Schacht, President
Price: $2,490.00. **Description:** Seminar for anyone in a decision-making capacity who would like to learn how to make successfull business decisions, including managers, business analysts, department heads, and team leaders. **Dates and Locations:** Rockville, MD; Alexandria, VA; Schaumburg, IL; and Reston, VA.

37674 ■ Making Successful Business Decisions: Getting it Right the First Time (Onsite)
Seminar Information Service, Inc.
20 Executive Park, Ste. 120
Irvine, CA 92614
Ph: (949)261-9104
Free: 877-SEM-INFO
Fax: (949)261-1963
Co. E-mail: info@seminarinformation.com
URL: http://www.seminarinformation.com
Price: $2,490.00. **Description:** Learn how to make intelligent decisions with limited time and information, how to convert conflicting opinions into useful insights, foster efficient and effective group decision making, and ensure decisions are implemented by the organization.

37675 ■ Making the Transition to Management (Onsite)
American Management Association
600 AMA Way
Saranac Lake, NY 12983-5534
Ph: (212)586-8100
Free: 877-566-9441
Fax: (518)891-0368
Co. E-mail: customerservice@amanet.org
URL: http://www.amaseminars.org
Price: $1,995.00 for non-members; $1,795.00 for AMA members; and $1,537.00 for General Services Administration (GSA) members. **Description:** Covers various aspects of the transition to manager, understanding what managers do, effective communication and coaching skills, setting attainable goals, and creating a positive atmosphere. **Dates and Locations:** Cities throughout the United States.

37676 ■ Making the Transition from Staff Member to Supervisor (Onsite)
American Management Association
600 AMA Way
Saranac Lake, NY 12983-5534
Ph: (212)586-8100
Free: 877-566-9441
Fax: (518)891-0368
Co. E-mail: customerservice@amanet.org
URL: http://www.amaseminars.org
Price: $1,895.00 for non-members; $1,695.00 for AMA members; and $1,451.00 for General Services Administration (GSA) members. **Description:** Covers various aspects of taking on a management position, setting goals, motivation, behavior styles, and time management. **Dates and Locations:** Cities throughout the United States.

37677 ■ Making the Transition to Supervising and Managing Others (Onsite) (Online)
Canadian Management Centre (CMC)
150 York St., 5th Fl.
Toronto, ON, Canada M5H 3S5
Ph: (416)214-5678
Free: 877-262-2519

Fax: (416)313-4985
Co. E-mail: cmcinfo@cmctraining.org
URL: http://www.cmctraining.org
Contact: John Wright, President
Price: $1,845.00 for members; $1,995.00 for non-members. **Description:** This seminar prepares you for a complete change of responsibilities and helps eliminate the anxiety that can accompany it. **Dates and Locations:** Montreal, PQ; Ottawa, ON; Regina, SK; Toronto, ON; Calgary, AB; Edmonton, AB; Vaughan, ON; Mississauga, ON; and Vancouver, BC.

37678 ■ Management and Leadership Skills for First-Time Supervisors and Managers (Onsite)
Padgett-Thompson Seminars
Rockhurst University CEC
14502 W. 105th St.
Lenexa, KS 66215
Free: 800-349-1935
URL: http://www.findaseminar.com/tpd/Padgett-Thompson-Seminars.asp
Price: $299.00. **Description:** An intensive two-day workshop for new supervisors who want to develop their management skills quickly. **Dates and Locations:** Salem, VA; Greensboro, NC; Raleigh, NC; and Charlotte, NC.

37679 ■ Management Skills for Administrative Professionals (Onsite)
American Management Association
600 AMA Way
Saranac Lake, NY 12983-5534
Ph: (212)586-8100
Free: 877-566-9441
Fax: (518)891-0368
Co. E-mail: customerservice@amanet.org
URL: http://www.amaseminars.org
Price: $1,895.00 for non-members; $1,695.00 for AMA members; and $1,451.00 for General Services Administration (GSA) members. **Description:** Geared towards the experienced administrative professional, this seminar covers effective communication skills, conflict resolution, organizational skills, partnering with your boss, and setting attainable goals. **Dates and Locations:** Arlington, VA; Washington, DC; Chicago, IL; San Francisco, CA; New York, NY; and Dallas, TX.

37680 ■ Management Skills: Building Performance and Productivity (Onsite)
Seminar Information Service, Inc.
20 Executive Park, Ste. 120
Irvine, CA 92614
Ph: (949)261-9104
Free: 877-SEM-INFO
Fax: (949)261-1963
Co. E-mail: info@seminarinformation.com
URL: http://www.seminarinformation.com
Price: $2,890.00. **Description:** Learn how to: Develop the vision and skills that result in real team commitment; Build and lead empowered and motivated teams; Delegate tasks and authority while maintaining control; Communicate effectively at all levels; Create world-class team performance; Become a skilled and effective leader. **Dates and Locations:** Reston, VA; New York, NY; Rockville, MD; Toronto,CN; and Ottawa, CN.

37681 ■ Management Skills: Building Performance and Productivity (Onsite)
Learning Tree International Inc.
1805 Library St.
Reston, VA 20190-5660
Ph: (703)709-9119
Free: 800-843-8733
Fax: (703)709-6405
Co. E-mail: uscourses@learningtree.com
URL: http://www.learningtree.com
Contact: Nick Schacht, President
Price: $2,890.00. **Description:** The course is valuable for both new and experienced managers. Provides information on how to become a skilled and effective leader. **Dates and Locations:** Reston, VA; New York, NY; Rockville, MD; Toronto, CN; Ottawa, CN.

37682 ■ Management Skills for First-Time Supervisors (Onsite)
Padgett-Thompson Seminars
Rockhurst University CEC
14502 W. 105th St.
Lenexa, KS 66215
Free: 800-349-1935
URL: http://www.findaseminar.com/tpd/Padgett-Thompson-Seminars.asp
Price: $179.00. **Description:** Through accelerated learning techniques, teaches skills and supervisory how-to's. **Dates and Locations:** Spokane, WA.

37683 ■ Management Skills for an IT Environment (Onsite)
Seminar Information Service, Inc.
20 Executive Park, Ste. 120
Irvine, CA 92614
Ph: (949)261-9104
Free: 877-SEM-INFO
Fax: (949)261-1963
Co. E-mail: info@seminarinformation.com
URL: http://www.seminarinformation.com
Price: $2,890.00. **Description:** Learn how to apply a proven management model for leading technical staff to excellence; identify key success criteria for leadership in an IT environment; leverage emotion to optimize communication and performance; motivate and empower technical professionals to achieve results; delegate proactively to focus on strengths of IT teams and build accountability. **Dates and Locations:** Reston, VA; Ottawa, CN; Schaumburg, IL; Los Angeles, CA; Philadelphia, PA; Toronto, CN; New York, NY; Alexandria, VA; and Rockville, MD.

37684 ■ Management Skills for New Supervisors and Managers (Onsite)
Canadian Management Centre (CMC)
150 York St., 5th Fl.
Toronto, ON, Canada M5H 3S5
Ph: (416)214-5678
Free: 877-262-2519
Fax: (416)313-4985
Co. E-mail: cmcinfo@cmctraining.org
URL: http://www.cmctraining.org
Contact: John Wright, President
Price: $2,195.00 for members; $2,395.00 for non-members. **Description:** Learn the tools to plan, organize, communicate, and monitor every situation effectively. **Dates and Locations:** Calgary, AB; Montreal, PQ; Vancouver, BC; Halifax, NS; Regina, SK;Ottawa, ON; and Toronto, ON.

37685 ■ Management Skills for Secretaries, Administrative Assistants, and Support Staff (Onsite)
Fred Pryor Seminars & CareerTrack
5700 Broadmoor St., Ste. 300
Mission, KS 66202
Free: 800-780-8476
Fax: (913)967-8849
Co. E-mail: customerservice@pryor.com
URL: http://www.pryor.com
Price: $99.00; $89.00 for groups of 5 or more. **Description:** Learn how to make decisions, manage change, solve problems, and negotiate what you need. **Dates and Locations:** Cities throughout the United States.

37686 ■ Managerial Skills of the New Supervisors
1601 Broadway
New York, NY 12983
Ph: (518)891-1500
Free: 800-262-9699
Fax: (518)891-0368
Co. E-mail: customerservice@amanet.org
URL: http://www.amanet.org
Description: Program topics include handling managerial responsibilities; utilizing leadership style; facilitating communication; motivating staff; coaching staff; delegating responsibilities; doing performance appraisals; and time management.

37687 ■ Managerial and Team-building Skills for Project Managers
American Management Association
600 AMA Way
Saranac Lake, NY 12983-5534
Ph: (212)586-8100
Free: 877-566-9441
Fax: (518)891-0368
Co. E-mail: customerservice@amanet.org
URL: http://www.amaseminars.org
Price: $1,895.00 for non-members; $1,695.00 for AMA members. **Description:** Covers improving people skills in order to create a powerful, cooperative project team. **Dates and Locations:** Atlanta, GA; and New York, NY.

37688 ■ Managing Change: People and Process (Onsite)
Seminar Information Service, Inc.
20 Executive Park, Ste. 120
Irvine, CA 92614
Ph: (949)261-9104
Free: 877-SEM-INFO
Fax: (949)261-1963
Co. E-mail: info@seminarinformation.com
URL: http://www.seminarinformation.com
Price: $3,190.00. **Description:** Learn how to manage change through the total integration of people and process, design and implement a framework for managing change, evaluate best practice approaches to people and process for delivering successful change, reduce the impact of risk while maximizing the benefit of change, overcome resistance to change, and assemble a practical toolkit tailored to the needs of your organization. **Dates and Locations:** Toronto, CN.

37689 ■ Managing Chaos: Dynamic Time Management, Recall, Reading, and Stress Management Skills for Administrative Professionals (Onsite)
American Management Association
600 AMA Way
Saranac Lake, NY 12983-5534
Ph: (212)586-8100
Free: 877-566-9441
Fax: (518)891-0368
Co. E-mail: customerservice@amanet.org
URL: http://www.amaseminars.org
Price: $1,645.00 for non-members; $1,495.00 for AMA members; and $1,280.00 for General Services Administration (GSA) members. **Description:** Covers learning techniques, productive planning, setting goals, and methods of controlling stress. **Dates and Locations:** New York, NY; Arlington, VA; Washington, DC; and Atlanta, GA.

37690 ■ Managing Chaos: How to set Priorities and Make Decisions Under Pressure (Onsite)
American Management Association
600 AMA Way
Saranac Lake, NY 12983-5534
Ph: (212)586-8100
Free: 877-566-9441
Fax: (518)891-0368
Co. E-mail: customerservice@amanet.org
URL: http://www.amaseminars.org
Price: $1,995.00 for non-members; $1,795.00 for AMA members; and $1,537.00 for General Services Administration (GSA) members. **Description:** Covers practical tools to prepare for unpredictable demands and balance changing priorities. **Dates and Locations:** Cities throughout the United States.

37691 ■ Managing Chaos: Tools to Set Priorities and Make Decisions Under Pressure (Onsite)
American Management Association
600 AMA Way
Saranac Lake, NY 12983-5534
Ph: (212)586-8100
Free: 877-566-9441

Fax: (518)891-0368
Co. E-mail: customerservice@amanet.org
URL: http://www.amaseminars.org

Price: $1,995.00 for non-members; $1,795.00 for AMA members; and $1,537.00 for General Services Administration (GSA) members. **Description:** Two-day seminar where you will learn techniques to adjust to the shifting challenges and demands. **Dates and Locations:** Cities throughout the United States.

37692 ■ Managing Conflict, Difficult People, and Discipline (Onsite)

Seminar Information Service, Inc.
20 Executive Park, Ste. 120
Irvine, CA 92614
Ph: (949)261-9104
Free: 877-SEM-INFO
Fax: (949)261-1963
Co. E-mail: info@seminarinformation.com
URL: http://www.seminarinformation.com

Price: $580.00; $435.00 for MRA members. **Description:** Learn conflict resolution techniques that focus on counseling and problem solving while maintaining effective work relationships, and applying those techniques to their individual workplace situations. **Dates and Locations:** Waukesha, WI; and Palatine, IL.

37693 ■ Managing Information Overload: Techniques for Working Smarter (Onsite)

Seminar Information Service, Inc.
20 Executive Park, Ste. 120
Irvine, CA 92614
Ph: (949)261-9104
Free: 877-SEM-INFO
Fax: (949)261-1963
Co. E-mail: info@seminarinformation.com
URL: http://www.seminarinformation.com

Price: $1,890.00. **Description:** Learn how to increase your productivity with effective information management skills, apply creative strategies, including mind maps, for processing information, adopt speed-reading techniques to quickly digest reports, and develop advanced memory skills to retain important information. **Dates and Locations:** Reston, VA; and Rockland MD.

37694 ■ Managing Multiple Project, Competing Priorites and Tight Deadlines (Onsite)

Padgett-Thompson Seminars
Rockhurst University CEC
14502 W. 105th St.
Lenexa, KS 66215
Free: 800-349-1935
URL: http://www.findaseminar.com/tpd/Padgett-Thompson-Seminars.asp

Price: $199.00. **Description:** Seminar provides the skills needed to immediately and effectively deal with multiple projects. **Dates and Locations:** Cities throughout the United States.

37695 ■ Managing Multiple Projects and Priorities (Onsite)

Seminar Information Service, Inc.
20 Executive Park, Ste. 120
Irvine, CA 92614
Ph: (949)261-9104
Free: 877-SEM-INFO
Fax: (949)261-1963
Co. E-mail: info@seminarinformation.com
URL: http://www.seminarinformation.com

Price: $199.00. **Description:** Learn to gain control of your time, your projects and your priorities. **Dates and Locations:** Cities throughout the United States.

37696 ■ Managing Organizational Transition (Onsite)

Seminar Information Service, Inc.
20 Executive Park, Ste. 120
Irvine, CA 92614
Ph: (949)261-9104
Free: 877-SEM-INFO
Fax: (949)261-1963
Co. E-mail: info@seminarinformation.com
URL: http://www.seminarinformation.com

Price: $795.00. **Description:** Learn the critical elements for driving successful change and develop coaching skills to create a change-ready culture. **Dates and Locations:** Chicago, IL.

37697 ■ Managing People in Projects (Onsite)

Seminar Information Service, Inc.
20 Executive Park, Ste. 120
Irvine, CA 92614
Ph: (949)261-9104
Free: 877-SEM-INFO
Fax: (949)261-1963
Co. E-mail: info@seminarinformation.com
URL: http://www.seminarinformation.com

Price: Contact for fees. **Description:** Learn how to have people want to work on your projects and how to improve your project results by applying a powerful approach to managing the people who work on them. **Dates and Locations:** Princeton, NJ; and San Francisco, CA.

37698 ■ Managing Subcontracts (Onsite)

Seminar Information Service, Inc.
20 Executive Park, Ste. 120
Irvine, CA 92614
Ph: (949)261-9104
Free: 877-SEM-INFO
Fax: (949)261-1963
Co. E-mail: info@seminarinformation.com
URL: http://www.seminarinformation.com

Price: $995.00. **Description:** Examines effective management and administration of subcontracts and complex purchase orders, including tailoring of the terms and conditions.

37699 ■ Managing in Tough Times (Onsite)

Seminar Information Service, Inc.
20 Executive Park, Ste. 120
Irvine, CA 92614
Ph: (949)261-9104
Free: 877-SEM-INFO
Fax: (949)261-1963
Co. E-mail: info@seminarinformation.com
URL: http://www.seminarinformation.com

Price: $2,490.00. **Description:** Learn how to demonstrate authentic and strong leadership to create an atmosphere of confidence and trust in tough times, share your vision and display confidence that the problems your team currently faces will be solved, and minimize stress and maximize productivity and performance during difficult times.

37700 ■ Managing a World-Class IT Department (Onsite)

American Management Association
600 AMA Way
Saranac Lake, NY 12983-5534
Ph: (212)586-8100
Free: 877-566-9441
Fax: (518)891-0368
Co. E-mail: customerservice@amanet.org
URL: http://www.amaseminars.org

Price: $2,345.00 for non-members; $2,095.00 for AMA members; and $1,794.00 for General Services Administration (GSA) members. **Description:** Three-day seminar for new or prospective IT managers; covers leadership techniques, common challenges, budgeting, planning, testing, and decision making. **Dates and Locations:** New York, NY; and Atlanta, GA.

37701 ■ Master Organizational Politics, Influence and Alliances (Onsite)

American Management Association
600 AMA Way
Saranac Lake, NY 12983-5534
Ph: (212)586-8100
Free: 877-566-9441
Fax: (518)891-0368
Co. E-mail: customerservice@amanet.org
URL: http://www.amaseminars.org

Price: $2,195.00 for non-members; $1,995.00 for AMA members; and $1,708.00 for General Services Administration (GSA) members. **Description:** Three-day seminar for experienced supervisors; covers driving high performance, relationship management, coaching, delegating, and your political image. **Dates and Locations:** Atlanta, GA; and San Francisco, CA.

37702 ■ Maximum Performance Leadership (Canada)

Canadian Management Centre (CMC)
150 York St., 5th Fl.
Toronto, ON, Canada M5H 3S5
Ph: (416)214-5678
Free: 877-262-2519
Fax: (416)313-4985
Co. E-mail: cmcinfo@cmctraining.org
URL: http://www.cmctraining.org
Contact: John Wright, President

Price: $2,195.00 Canadian for non-members; $1,995.00 Canadian for CMC members. **Description:** Covers advanced leadership skills for managers with several years of experience. **Dates and Locations:** Toronto, ON.

37703 ■ Motivation and Trust Building for Group Leaders (Onsite)

Seminar Information Service, Inc.
20 Executive Park, Ste. 120
Irvine, CA 92614
Ph: (949)261-9104
Free: 877-SEM-INFO
Fax: (949)261-1963
Co. E-mail: info@seminarinformation.com
URL: http://www.seminarinformation.com

Price: $275.00 for MRA members; $370.00 for non-members. **Description:** A practical understanding of basic leadership skills, work values, and organizational responsibility. **Dates and Locations:** Waukesha, WI; and Palatine, IL.

37704 ■ Moving Ahead: Breaking Behaviour Patterns That Hold You Back (Onsite)

Canadian Management Centre (CMC)
150 York St., 5th Fl.
Toronto, ON, Canada M5H 3S5
Ph: (416)214-5678
Free: 877-262-2519
Fax: (416)313-4985
Co. E-mail: cmcinfo@cmctraining.org
URL: http://www.cmctraining.org
Contact: John Wright, President

Price: $1,845.00 for members; $1,995.00 for non-members. **Description:** Change your professional image by overcoming destructive workplace behavior. **Dates and Locations:** Toronto, ON.

37705 ■ Organizational Excellence Assessment (Course on Request)

Canadian Management Centre (CMC)
150 York St., 5th Fl.
Toronto, ON, Canada M5H 3S5
Ph: (416)214-5678
Free: 877-262-2519
Fax: (416)313-4985
Co. E-mail: cmcinfo@cmctraining.org
URL: http://www.cmctraining.org
Contact: John Wright, President

Price: $1,095.00 for members; $1,295.00 for non-members. **Description:** Assesses how an organization's management systems compare against the Canadian Framework for Excellence.

37706 ■ Performance Management, Leading Change, and Putting It All Together (Onsite)

Seminar Information Service, Inc.
20 Executive Park, Ste. 120
Irvine, CA 92614
Ph: (949)261-9104
Free: 877-SEM-INFO
Fax: (949)261-1963
Co. E-mail: info@seminarinformation.com
URL: http://www.seminarinformation.com

Price: $580.00 for non-members; $435.00 for The Management Association, Inc. **Description:** Participants will learn a performance management system including how to prepare for and conduct performance reviews, how to manage individual and group change and the manager's role in the organizational change process. **Dates and Locations:** Waukesha, WI; and Palatine, IL.

37707 ■ Personal Skills for Professional Excellence (Onsite)
Seminar Information Service, Inc.
20 Executive Park, Ste. 120
Irvine, CA 92614
Ph: (949)261-9104
Free: 877-SEM-INFO
Fax: (949)261-1963
Co. E-mail: info@seminarinformation.com
URL: http://www.seminarinformation.com
Price: $2,890.00. **Description:** Learn how to: Achieve maximum productivity and effectiveness in your organization; Build and leverage your professional reputation; Get results working with different and difficult personality types; Maintain focus in pressure situations; Work productively within the political environment of your organization; Build and present persuasive proposals; Make a balanced choice between professional and personal commitments. **Dates and Locations:** Ottawa, CN; Reston, VA; Rockville, MD; New York, NY; and Toronto, CN.

37708 ■ Persuasive Communications in Marketing and Public Relations
EEI Communications
8945 Guilford Rd., Ste. 145
Columbia, MD 21046
Ph: (410)309-8200
Free: 888-253-2762
Fax: (410)630-3980
Co. E-mail: train@eeicom.com
URL: http://www.eeicom.com/eei-training-service
Price: $1,065.00. **Description:** Course designed for department heads and project managers, as well as mid-level communications professionals who want to expand their public relations and marketing skills. **Dates and Locations:** Alexandria, VA.

37709 ■ Persuasive Leadership: Storytelling that Inspires (Onsite)
Seminar Information Service, Inc.
20 Executive Park, Ste. 120
Irvine, CA 92614
Ph: (949)261-9104
Free: 877-SEM-INFO
Fax: (949)261-1963
Co. E-mail: info@seminarinformation.com
URL: http://www.seminarinformation.com
Price: $1,499.00. **Description:** Participants develop their storytelling abilities and learn how to use humor to persuade and motivate others, as well as polish their existing speaking skills and develop powerful new ones.

37710 ■ Play to Your Strengths: Harnessing the Power of Your Personality (Onsite)
American Management Association
600 AMA Way
Saranac Lake, NY 12983-5534
Ph: (212)586-8100
Free: 877-566-9441
Fax: (518)891-0368
Co. E-mail: customerservice@amanet.org
URL: http://www.amaseminars.org
Price: $2,445.00 for non-members; $2,195.00 for AMA members; and $1,880.00 for General Services Administration (GSA) members. **Description:** Learn the strengths and weaknesses of your own personality for effective leadership. **Dates and Locations:** San Francisco, CA; Washington, DC; and Arlington, VA.

37711 ■ PMP Exam Prep Workshop (Onsite)
Canadian Management Centre (CMC)
150 York St., 5th Fl.
Toronto, ON, Canada M5H 3S5
Ph: (416)214-5678
Free: 877-262-2519
Fax: (416)313-4985
Co. E-mail: cmcinfo@cmctraining.org
URL: http://www.cmctraining.org
Contact: John Wright, President
Price: $1,995.00 for members; $2,195.00 for non-members. **Description:** This three-day, PMP certification exam prep seminar covers the Guide to the Project Management Body of Knowledge on which the exam is based. **Dates and Locations:** Toronto, ON.

37712 ■ Positive Assertive Management (Onsite)
Seminar Information Service, Inc.
20 Executive Park, Ste. 120
Irvine, CA 92614
Ph: (949)261-9104
Free: 877-SEM-INFO
Fax: (949)261-1963
Co. E-mail: info@seminarinformation.com
URL: http://www.seminarinformation.com
Price: $1,495.00. **Description:** Covers the meaning of assertiveness, how assertiveness can benefit you, using assertive behavior, constructive confrontation and assertive listening. **Dates and Locations:** Boston, MA.

37713 ■ A Practical Guide to Controls for IT Professionals (Onsite)
Seminar Information Service, Inc.
20 Executive Park, Ste. 120
Irvine, CA 92614
Ph: (949)261-9104
Free: 877-SEM-INFO
Fax: (949)261-1963
Co. E-mail: info@seminarinformation.com
URL: http://www.seminarinformation.com
Price: Contact for fees. **Description:** Designed to provide all levels of IT personnel with an understanding of what controls are and why they are critical to safeguarding information assets. Discover why it is important to have a business-process view of IT controls and review the critical role they play in providing for a smooth running, efficiently manager IT environment.

37714 ■ Preparing for Leadership: What It Takes to Take the Lead (Onsite) (Canada)
Canadian Management Centre (CMC)
150 York St., 5th Fl.
Toronto, ON, Canada M5H 3S5
Ph: (416)214-5678
Free: 877-262-2519
Fax: (416)313-4985
Co. E-mail: cmcinfo@cmctraining.org
URL: http://www.cmctraining.org
Contact: John Wright, President
Price: $1,995.00 Canadian for non-members; $1,845.00 Canadian for CMC members. **Description:** Covers leadership roles, the characteristics of leaders, dealing with organizational politics, and creating an action plan. **Dates and Locations:** Ottawa, ON; Calgary, AB; Vancouver, BC; Regina, SK; and Toronto, ON.

37715 ■ The Proactive Leader I: Develop an Effective Agenda, Build Support, and Gain Traction
Seminar Information Service, Inc.
20 Executive Park, Ste. 120
Irvine, CA 92614
Ph: (949)261-9104
Free: 877-SEM-INFO
Fax: (949)261-1963
Co. E-mail: info@seminarinformation.com
URL: http://www.seminarinformation.com
Price: $1,495.00. **Description:** Learn to identify and prioritize arenas where you can effect change in your organization, including the skills of political competence to take the next steps toward building support and gaining traction for your idea. **Dates and Locations:** New York, NY.

37716 ■ Problem Solving and Decision Making (Onsite)
Seminar Information Service, Inc.
20 Executive Park, Ste. 120
Irvine, CA 92614
Ph: (949)261-9104
Free: 877-SEM-INFO
Fax: (949)261-1963
Co. E-mail: info@seminarinformation.com
URL: http://www.seminarinformation.com
Price: $1,795.00. **Description:** Based on the principles of rational process and a systematic approach to problem solving and decision making pioneered by Drs. Benjamin Tregoe and Charles Kepner. Participants develop an in-depth understanding of systematic process through case study practice, and apply these principles to urgent job-related concerns. Focus is on immediate, practical results. **Dates and Locations:** Cities throughout the United States.

37717 ■ Process Management: Applying Process Mapping to Analyze and Improve Your Operation (Onsite) (Canada)
Canadian Management Centre (CMC)
150 York St., 5th Fl.
Toronto, ON, Canada M5H 3S5
Ph: (416)214-5678
Free: 877-262-2519
Fax: (416)313-4985
Co. E-mail: cmcinfo@cmctraining.org
URL: http://www.cmctraining.org
Contact: John Wright, President
Price: $2,095.00 Canadian for non-members; $2,295.00 Canadian for CMC members. **Description:** Seminar that covers process mapping techniques, and application and documentation of standard operation procedures, including work simplification analysis and value added versus non-value added activity analysis. **Dates and Locations:** Toronto, ON.

37718 ■ Project Change Management (Onsite)
EEI Communications
8945 Guilford Rd., Ste. 145
Columbia, MD 21046
Ph: (410)309-8200
Free: 888-253-2762
Fax: (410)630-3980
Co. E-mail: train@eeicom.com
URL: http://www.eeicom.com/eei-training-services
Price: $745.00. **Description:** Seminar based on the Project Management Institute's (PMI) Project Management Body of Knowledge (PMBOK) that covers the principles of change management as applied to project management and products, including change control system, configuration management, coordinating changes throughout the project, and change management and project closure. **Dates and Locations:** Silver Spring, MD; Alexandria, VA; Hunt Valley, MD; and Columbia, MD.

37719 ■ Project Leadership: Building High-Performance Teams (Onsite)
Seminar Information Service, Inc.
20 Executive Park, Ste. 120
Irvine, CA 92614
Ph: (949)261-9104
Free: 877-SEM-INFO
Fax: (949)261-1963
Co. E-mail: info@seminarinformation.com
URL: http://www.seminarinformation.com
Price: $2,890.00. **Description:** Learn how to: Develop the leadership skills to build and sustain high-performing project teams; Develop effective team performance through the Leadership Services Model; Build a strong team identity through vision, purpose and commitment; Foster positive and productive team communication and define ground rules; Protect the team and convert conflicts into advantages that promote high performance; Maximize your leadership abilities when you return to your organization. **Dates and Locations:** Cities throughout the United States and Toronto and Ottawa, CN.

37720 ■ Project Management for Administrative Professionals (Onsite)
American Management Association
600 AMA Way
Saranac Lake, NY 12983-5534
Ph: (212)586-8100
Free: 877-566-9441
Fax: (518)891-0368
Co. E-mail: customerservice@amanet.org
URL: http://www.amaseminars.org
Price: $1,895.00 for non-members; $1,695.00 for AMA members; and $1,451.00 for General Services Administration (GSA) members. **Description:** Covers methods for planning, controlling, organizing, and tracking projects; problem solving techniques; and time management. **Dates and Locations:** Boston, MA; Arlington, VA; New York, NY; and San Francisco, CA .

37721 ■ Project Management for Auditors (Onsite)
Seminar Information Service, Inc.
20 Executive Park, Ste. 120
Irvine, CA 92614
Ph: (949)261-9104
Free: 877-SEM-INFO
Fax: (949)261-1963
Co. E-mail: info@seminarinformation.com
URL: http://www.seminarinformation.com
Price: $2,050.00. **Description:** Learn improved cost control, resource utilization, and more timely conclusions with project management techniques that are applicable to internal audit. **Dates and Locations:** Chicago, IL.

37722 ■ Project Management: Skills for Success (Onsite)
Seminar Information Service, Inc.
20 Executive Park, Ste. 120
Irvine, CA 92614
Ph: (949)261-9104
Free: 877-SEM-INFO
Fax: (949)261-1963
Co. E-mail: info@seminarinformation.com
URL: http://www.seminarinformation.com
Price: $2,890.00. **Description:** Learn how to: Produce a project plan for successful delivery; Plan and run projects using best practices in a 6-step project management process; Implement risk management techniques and mitigation strategies; Estimate and schedule task work and duration with confidence; Implement monitoring tools and controls to keep you fully in command of the project; Recognize and practice the leadership skills needed to run a motivated team. **Dates and Locations:** Cities throughout the United States and Toronto and Ottawa, CN.

37723 ■ Project Management for Software Development - Planning and Managing Successful Projects (Onsite)
Seminar Information Service, Inc.
20 Executive Park, Ste. 120
Irvine, CA 92614
Ph: (949)261-9104
Free: 877-SEM-INFO
Fax: (949)261-1963
Co. E-mail: info@seminarinformation.com
URL: http://www.seminarinformation.com
Price: $2,890.00. **Description:** Learn how to: Deliver successful software projects that support your organization's strategic goals; Match organizational needs to the most effective software development model; Plan and manage projects at each stage of the software development life cycle (SDLC); Create project plans that address real-world management challenges; Develop the skills for tracking and controlling the project deliverables; Focus on key tasks for the everyday management of software projects; Build an effective and committed team and keep them motivated day to day. **Dates and Locations:** Alexandria, VA; Rockville, MD; New York, NY; Ottawa, CN; Toronto, CN; Los Angeles, CA; and Reston, VA.

37724 ■ Project Management for Streaming DVD, and Multimedia
EEI Communications
66 Canal Ctr. Plz., Ste. 200
Alexandria, VA 22314-5507
Ph: (703)683-7453
Free: 888-253-2762
Fax: (703)683-7310
Co. E-mail: train@eeicom.com
URL: http://www.eeicom.com/training
Price: $425.00. **Description:** Covers an overview of the steps involved in bringing a multimedia or CD-ROM project to completion, including audience and purpose analysis, information and graphic design, planning and resources, managing the creative process, scheduling and budgeting, quality control, and video and sound options. **Dates and Locations:** Silver Spring, MD; Alexandria, VA; Hunt Valley, MD; and Columbia, MD.

37725 ■ Project Management: The Human and Technical View (Onsite)
Seminar Information Service, Inc.
20 Executive Park, Ste. 120
Irvine, CA 92614
Ph: (949)261-9104
Free: 877-SEM-INFO
Fax: (949)261-1963
Co. E-mail: info@seminarinformation.com
URL: http://www.seminarinformation.com
Price: $580.00. **Description:** A systematic, practical approach to successful project management, including skills to handle problems with members who won't commit, who resist change, or who won't cooperate. **Dates and Locations:** Waukesha, WI; and Palatine, IL.

37726 ■ Project Management for Web Development (Onsite)
EEI Communications
8945 Guilford Rd., Ste. 145
Alexandria, MD 21046
Ph: (410)309-8200
Free: 888-253-2762
Fax: (410)630-3980
Co. E-mail: train@eeicom.com
URL: http://www.eeicom.com/eei-training-services
Price: $745.00. **Description:** Covers the basics of managing and maintaining the development of a website. **Dates and Locations:** Silver Spring, MD; Alexandria, VA; Hunt Valley, MD; and Columbia, MD.

37727 ■ Project Management Workshop (Onsite)
Fred Pryor Seminars & CareerTrack
5700 Broadmoor St., Ste. 300
Mission, KS 66202
Free: 800-780-8476
Fax: (913)967-8849
Co. E-mail: customerservice@pryor.com
URL: http://www.pryor.com
Price: $199.00; $189.00 for groups of 5 or more. **Description:** One-day seminar guaranteed to help you complete projects in a timely manner within a budget. **Dates and Locations:** Cities throughout the United States.

37728 ■ The Project Performance Management Workshop: Time, Cost and Budget (Onsite)
American Management Association
600 AMA Way
Saranac Lake, NY 12983-5534
Ph: (212)586-8100
Free: 877-566-9441
Fax: (518)891-0368
Co. E-mail: customerservice@amanet.org
URL: http://www.amaseminars.org
Price: $2,195.00 for non-members; $1,995.00 for AMA members; and $1,708.00 for. **Description:** Three-day seminar to improve the performance of your projects by constructing a 'Work Breakdown Structure (WBS),' converting to a network schedule, developing a budget, and track performance using 'Earned Value Management (EVM)'. **Dates and Locations:** Arlington, VA; New York, NY; Atlanta, GA; and San Francisco, CA.

37729 ■ Project Scope and Requirements Management (Onsite)
Seminar Information Service, Inc.
20 Executive Park, Ste. 120
Irvine, CA 92614
Ph: (949)261-9104
Free: 877-SEM-INFO
Fax: (949)261-1963
Co. E-mail: info@seminarinformation.com
URL: http://www.seminarinformation.com
Price: $2,095.00. **Description:** Learn how to achieve project success by mastering scope control. **Dates and Locations:** San Francisco, CA; New York, NY; and Chicago, IL.

37730 ■ Quality for Project Managers (Onsite)
Seminar Information Service, Inc.
20 Executive Park, Ste. 120
Irvine, CA 92614
Ph: (949)261-9104
Free: 877-SEM-INFO
Fax: (949)261-1963
Co. E-mail: info@seminarinformation.com
URL: http://www.seminarinformation.com
Price: $1,995.00. **Description:** Learn about the philosophy and principles of quality management and learn how to translate these concepts into specific actions that are key to successful improvement efforts. **Dates and Locations:** Ottawa, CN; Orlando, FL; Washington, DC; and Chicago, IL.

37731 ■ Quest for a Healthy Workplace (Course on Request)
Canadian Management Centre (CMC)
150 York St., 5th Fl.
Toronto, ON, Canada M5H 3S5
Ph: (416)214-5678
Free: 877-262-2519
Fax: (416)313-4985
Co. E-mail: cmcinfo@cmctraining.org
URL: http://www.cmctraining.org
Contact: John Wright, President
Price: $971.00 for members; $1,295.00 for non-members. **Description:** With this two-day course, learn how an organization can improve performance and become more successful by implementing the NQI Progressive Excellence Program for a Healthy Workplace.

37732 ■ Quest for Quality Process Improvement Tools (Course on Request)
Canadian Management Centre (CMC)
150 York St., 5th Fl.
Toronto, ON, Canada M5H 3S5
Ph: (416)214-5678
Free: 877-262-2519
Fax: (416)313-4985
Co. E-mail: cmcinfo@cmctraining.org
URL: http://www.cmctraining.org
Contact: John Wright, President
Price: $971.00 for members; $1,295.00 for non-members. **Description:** This two-day course introduces process management tools and techniques to help participants identify and close quality gaps in their organizations.

37733 ■ Risk Management (Onsite)
Seminar Information Service, Inc.
20 Executive Park, Ste. 120
Irvine, CA 92614
Ph: (949)261-9104
Free: 877-SEM-INFO
Fax: (949)261-1963
Co. E-mail: info@seminarinformation.com
URL: http://www.seminarinformation.com
Price: $1,995.00. **Description:** Learn how to evaluate and respond to risk at the project and task levels. **Dates and Locations:** Washington, DC; and San Francisco, CA.

37734 ■ Sales and Use Tax 2012 Workshop (Onsite)
Seminar Information Service, Inc.
20 Executive Park, Ste. 120
Irvine, CA 92614
Ph: (949)261-9104
Free: 877-SEM-INFO
Fax: (949)261-1963
Co. E-mail: info@seminarinformation.com
URL: http://www.seminarinformation.com
Price: $195.00; $185.00 for 5 or more. **Description:** Gain a better understanding of sales and use tax and how to apply it to keep your bottom line in check. **Dates and Locations:** Cities throughout the United States.

37735 ■ Senior Project Management (Onsite) (Canada)
Canadian Management Centre (CMC)
150 York St., 5th Fl.
Toronto, ON, Canada M5H 3S5
Ph: (416)214-5678
Free: 877-262-2519

Fax: (416)313-4985
Co. E-mail: cmcinfo@cmctraining.org
URL: http://www.cmctraining.org
Contact: John Wright, President
Price: $2,395.00 Canadian for non-members; $2,195.00 Canadian for CMC members. **Description:** Covers project management basics, measuring project accomplishments, trends, human factors, and automated and administrative project support. **Dates and Locations:** Toronto, ON.

37736 ■ Situational Leadership II Workshop (Onsite)
Seminar Information Service, Inc.
20 Executive Park, Ste. 120
Irvine, CA 92614
Ph: (949)261-9104
Free: 877-SEM-INFO
Fax: (949)261-1963
Co. E-mail: info@seminarinformation.com
URL: http://www.seminarinformation.com
Price: $2,195.00 for AMA members; $1,995.00 for non-members. **Description:** Diagnose the needs of an individual at any particular point in time, then be able to apply the leadership style that is most responsive an productive for the situation at hand. **Dates and Locations:** New York, NY; Chicago, IL; and San Francisco, CA.

37737 ■ Stepping Up to Leadership (Canada)
Canadian Management Centre (CMC)
150 York St., 5th Fl.
Toronto, ON, Canada M5H 3S5
Ph: (416)214-5678
Free: 877-262-2519
Fax: (416)313-4985
Co. E-mail: cmcinfo@cmctraining.org
URL: http://www.cmctraining.org
Contact: John Wright, President
Price: $2,195.00 Canadian for non-members; $1,995.00 Canadian for CMC members. **Description:** Seminar that covers the role of leadership, including attitudes and barriers that prevent you from taking a leadership role, create partnerships that get you the information you need, team leading without the authority, Emotional Intelligence (EI), and career development strategies. **Dates and Locations:** Toronto, ON.

37738 ■ Strategic Agility and Resilience: Embracing Change to Drive Growth
Canadian Management Centre (CMC)
150 York St., 5th Fl.
Toronto, ON, Canada M5H 3S5
Ph: (416)214-5678
Free: 877-262-2519
Fax: (416)313-4985
Co. E-mail: cmcinfo@cmctraining.org
URL: http://www.cmctraining.org
Contact: John Wright, President
Price: $1,845.00 for members; $1,995.00 for non-members. **Description:** Master the competencies of agile leadership. **Dates and Locations:** Toronto, ON.

37739 ■ Strategic Diversity Retention (Onsite)
Seminar Information Service, Inc.
20 Executive Park, Ste. 120
Irvine, CA 92614
Ph: (949)261-9104
Free: 877-SEM-INFO
Fax: (949)261-1963
Co. E-mail: info@seminarinformation.com
URL: http://www.seminarinformation.com
Price: $895.00. **Description:** Step-by-step approach to developing a diversity retention strategy and why it fails. **Dates and Locations:** New York, NY.

37740 ■ Successfully Managing People (Onsite)
American Management Association
600 AMA Way
Saranac Lake, NY 12983-5534
Ph: (212)586-8100
Free: 877-566-9441
Fax: (518)891-0368
Co. E-mail: customerservice@amanet.org
URL: http://www.amaseminars.org
Price: $2,345.00 for non-members; $2,095.00 for AMA members; and $1,794.00 for General Services Administration (GSA) members. **Description:** Three day seminar covering negotiation, motivation, confidence, leadership skills, and dealing with various types of employees. **Dates and Locations:** Cities throughout the United States.

37741 ■ Successfully Managing People (Onsite) (Canada)
Canadian Management Centre (CMC)
150 York St., 5th Fl.
Toronto, ON, Canada M5H 3S5
Ph: (416)214-5678
Free: 877-262-2519
Fax: (416)313-4985
Co. E-mail: cmcinfo@cmctraining.org
URL: http://www.cmctraining.org
Contact: John Wright, President
Price: $2,395.00 Canadian for non-members; $2,195.00 Canadian for CMC members. **Description:** Covers negotiation, motivation, confidence, leadership skills, and dealing with various types of employees. **Dates and Locations:** Toronto, ON; Calgary, AB; and Mississauga, ON.

37742 ■ Supporting Multiple Bosses (Onsite)
Seminar Information Service, Inc.
20 Executive Park, Ste. 120
Irvine, CA 92614
Ph: (949)261-9104
Free: 877-SEM-INFO
Fax: (949)261-1963
Co. E-mail: info@seminarinformation.com
URL: http://www.seminarinformation.com
Price: $1,545.00. **Description:** Learn to deal with multiple bosses with different agendas, priorities, styles, and expectations. **Dates and Locations:** New York, NY; and San Francisco, CA. .

37743 ■ Systems Thinking (Onsite)
Seminar Information Service, Inc.
20 Executive Park, Ste. 120
Irvine, CA 92614
Ph: (949)261-9104
Free: 877-SEM-INFO
Fax: (949)261-1963
Co. E-mail: info@seminarinformation.com
URL: http://www.seminarinformation.com
Price: $1,395.00. **Description:** Learn how to become a systems thinker so you can resolve complex, systematic business dilemmas in a practical manner. **Dates and Locations:** San Francisco, CA.

37744 ■ Taking on Greater Responsibility: Step-up Skills for Nonmanagers (Onsite)
American Management Association
600 AMA Way
Saranac Lake, NY 12983-5534
Ph: (212)586-8100
Free: 877-566-9441
Fax: (518)891-0368
Co. E-mail: customerservice@amanet.org
URL: http://www.amaseminars.org
Price: $1,795.00 for non-members; $1,595.00 for AMA members; and $1,366.00 for General Services Administration (GSA) members. **Description:** Two-day seminar for new or prospective managers; covers management responsibilities, aligning with other managers, building respect with your team, coaching, motivating, and delegating. **Dates and Locations:** Cities throughout the United States.

37745 ■ Team Leadership Effectiveness Program 'Team Top Gun' (Onsite)
Seminar Information Service, Inc.
20 Executive Park, Ste. 120
Irvine, CA 92614
Ph: (949)261-9104
Free: 877-SEM-INFO
Fax: (949)261-1963
Co. E-mail: info@seminarinformation.com
URL: http://www.seminarinformation.com
Price: $1,495.00. **Description:** Three-day seminar using psychological profiles, 360 degree feedback, extensive experiential simulations, and state of the art content relating to success in team based organizations. **Dates and Locations:** Orange County, CA; San Diego, CA; Cincinnati, OH; Herdon, VA; and San Diego, CA.

37746 ■ The Technical Management Program (Onsite)
Seminar Information Service, Inc.
20 Executive Park, Ste. 120
Irvine, CA 92614
Ph: (949)261-9104
Free: 877-SEM-INFO
Fax: (949)261-1963
Co. E-mail: info@seminarinformation.com
URL: http://www.seminarinformation.com
Price: $3,795.00. **Description:** Designed for engineers, scientists, and other professionals, the program provides a practical balance between the technical and managerial aspects of improving personal and organizational performance. **Dates and Locations:** Los Angeles, CA.

37747 ■ Technical Project Management (Canada)
Canadian Management Centre (CMC)
150 York St., 5th Fl.
Toronto, ON, Canada M5H 3S5
Ph: (416)214-5678
Free: 877-262-2519
Fax: (416)313-4985
Co. E-mail: cmcinfo@cmctraining.org
URL: http://www.cmctraining.org
Contact: John Wright, President
Price: $2,395.00 Canadian for non-members; $2,195.00 Canadian for CMC members. **Description:** Covers defining cost, time, and scope; project leadership; utilizing status reports; and technical project control systems. **Dates and Locations:** Toronto, ON.

37748 ■ Technical Project Management (Onsite)
American Management Association
600 AMA Way
Saranac Lake, NY 12983-5534
Ph: (212)586-8100
Free: 877-566-9441
Fax: (518)891-0368
Co. E-mail: customerservice@amanet.org
URL: http://www.amaseminars.org
Price: $2,195.00 for non-members; $1,995.00 for AMA members; and $1,708.00 for General Services Administration (GSA) members. **Description:** Covers defining cost, time, and scope; project leadership; utilizing status reports; and scheduling with milestones. **Dates and Locations:** New York, NY; Washington, DC; Chicago, IL; and Arlington, VA.

37749 ■ Thinking Outside the Lines for Managers and Supervisors (Onsite)
Seminar Information Service, Inc.
20 Executive Park, Ste. 120
Irvine, CA 92614
Ph: (949)261-9104
Free: 877-SEM-INFO
Fax: (949)261-1963
Co. E-mail: info@seminarinformation.com
URL: http://www.seminarinformation.com
Price: $199.00. **Description:** Techniques and solutions for daily real world problems, including speedy decision making and motivating for results. **Dates and Locations:** Cities throughout the United States.

37750 ■ Thinking Outside the Lines (Onsite)
Padgett-Thompson Seminars
Rockhurst University CEC
14502 W. 105th St.
Lenexa, KS 66215

Free: 800-349-1935
URL: http://www.findaseminar.com/tpd/Padgett-Thompson-Seminars.asp
Price: $199.00. **Description:** For executives, managers, and team leaders who do not want to follow the same old way of doing things. **Dates and Locations:** Cities throughout the United States.

37751 ■ The Ultimate Supervisor's Workshop (Onsite)
Padgett-Thompson Seminars
Rockhurst University CEC
14502 W. 105th St.
Lenexa, KS 66215
Free: 800-349-1935
URL: http://www.findaseminar.com/tpd/Padgett-Thompson-Seminars.asp
Price: $399.00. **Description:** A two-day workshop where leaders come for fresh ideas and proven strategies. **Dates and Locations:** Denver, CO; Des Moines, IA; Omaha, NE.

37752 ■ Uncovering Fraud in Core Business Functions (Onsite)
Seminar Information Service, Inc.
20 Executive Park, Ste. 120
Irvine, CA 92614
Ph: (949)261-9104
Free: 877-SEM-INFO
Fax: (949)261-1963
Co. E-mail: info@seminarinformation.com
URL: http://www.seminarinformation.com
Price: $2,050.00. **Description:** Pinpoint the areas most prone to internal fraud and identify key indicators of potential crime. **Dates and Locations:** New York, NY.

37753 ■ The Voice of Leadership: How Leaders Inspire, Influence, and Achieve Results (Onsite)
American Management Association
600 AMA Way
Saranac Lake, NY 12983-5534
Ph: (212)586-8100
Free: 877-566-9441
Fax: (518)891-0368
Co. E-mail: customerservice@amanet.org
URL: http://www.amaseminars.org
Price: $2,545.00 for non-members; $2,295.00 for AMA members; and $1,965.00 for General Services Administration (GSA) members. **Description:** Covers managing change, how to inspire and influence, effective communication skills, coaching, and addressing conflict. **Dates and Locations:** Cities throughout the United States.

37754 ■ Win-Win Negotiations Training (Onsite)
Baker Communications Inc. (BCI)
10101 SW Fwy., Ste. 630
Houston, TX 77074
Ph: (713)627-7700
Fax: (713)587-2051
Co. E-mail: information@bakercommunications.com
URL: http://www.bakercommunications.com
Contact: Walter Rogers, President
Price: $1,700.00. **Description:** In this hands-on workshop, participants learn through practice exercises how to strengthen their negotiation skills. **Dates and Locations:** Cities throughout the United States and Canada.

37755 ■ Women in Leadership
Seminar Information Service, Inc.
20 Executive Park, Ste. 120
Irvine, CA 92614
Ph: (949)261-9104
Free: 877-SEM-INFO
Fax: (949)261-1963
Co. E-mail: info@seminarinformation.com
URL: http://www.seminarinformation.com
Price: $1,995.00. **Description:** Provides the knowledge, network, and impetus necessary to thrive at work, at home, and within your community. **Dates and Locations:** New York, NY.

REFERENCE WORKS

37756 ■ *The 4 Routes to Entrepreneurial Success*
Pub: Berrett-Koehler Publishers
Ed: John B. Miner. **Price:** $18.95. **Description:** After researching one hundred successful entrepreneurs, the author discovered there are basically four personality types of entrepreneurs: the personal achiever, the super salesperson, the real manager, and the expert idea generator.

37757 ■ *"13D Filings" in Barron's (Vol. 88, March 24, 2008, No. 12, pp. M13)*
Pub: Dow Jones & Company, Inc.
Description: HealthCor Management called as problematic the plan of Magellan Health Services to use its high cash balances for acquisitions. Carlson Capital discussed with Energy Partners possible changes in the latter's board. Investor Carl Icahn suggested that Enzon Pharmaceuticals consider selling itself or divest some of its assets.

37758 ■ *"13D Filings" in Barron's (Vol. 88, March 10, 2008, No. 10, pp. M11)*
Pub: Dow Jones & Company, Inc.
Description: Barington Capital and Clinton Group sent a letter to Dillard's demanding a list of the company's stockholders. Elliott Associates announced that it is prepared to take over Packeteer for $5.50 a share. Strongbow capital suggested a change in leadership in Duckwall-ALCO Stores.

37759 ■ *"13D Filings: Investors Report to the SEC" in Barron's (Vol. 88, March 31, 2008, No. 13, pp. M10)*
Pub: Dow Jones & Company, Inc.
Description: Obrem Capital Management wants Micrel to rescind Micrel's shareholder-rights plan and to boost its board to six members from five. Patricia L. Childress plans to nominate herself to the board of Sierra Bancorp, and Luther King Capital Management may consider a competing acquisition proposal for Industrial Distribution Group.

37760 ■ *"13D Filings: Investors Report to the SEC" in Barron's (Vol. 88, July 4, 2008, No. 28, pp. M10)*
Pub: Dow Jones & Co., Inc.
Description: Robino Stortini Holdings will seek control of Investors Capital Holdings either alone or with members of the company's management. Discovery Group I will withhold its votes at the nomination of directors for TESSCO Technologies while JMB Capital Partners Master Fund plans to nominate a slate of candidates to the board of Maguire Properties.

37761 ■ *30 Reasons Employees Hate their Managers*
Pub: AMACOM
Ed: Bruce L. Katcher. **Released:** March 2007. **Price:** $21.95. **Description:** Issues involved in employee negative feelings towards managers are discussed; a survey of more than 50,000 employees in 65 organizations of all types and sizes cited 30 main causes for ill will.

37762 ■ *30 Reasons Employees Hate Their Managers: What Your People May Be Thinking and What You Can Do About It*
Pub: AMACOM
Ed: Bruce L. Katcher, with Adam Snyder. **Released:** March 7, 2007. **Price:** $21.95. **Description:** Thirty reasons why American employees are unhappy in their jobs are outlined. Each chapter is opened with a reason, an examination of how it creates work difficulties, and makes suggestions to managers on how to best address each issue.

37763 ■ *32 Ways to Be a Champion in Business*
Pub: Three Rivers Press
Ed: Earvin Magic Johnson. **Released:** December 29, 2009. **Price:** $18.94. **Description:** Earvin Johnson discusses his transition from athlete to entrepreneur and discusses the importance of hard work in order to pursue your dreams of starting and running a successful business.

37764 ■ *"The 100 Fastest-Growing Companies" in Hispanic Business (Vol. 30, July-August 2008, No. 7-8, pp. 22)*
Pub: Hispanic Business, Inc.
Ed: Michael Bowker. **Description:** CEO's of the five fastest growing Hispanic-owned companies discuss the success of their companies; most of them attribute their success to proper investment and diversification, effective innovations and seeing growth opportunities where others see roadblocks.

37765 ■ *365 Answers about Human Resources for the Small Business Owner: What Every Manager Needs to Know about Work Place Law*
Pub: Atlantic Publishing Company
Ed: Mary Holihan. **Released:** June 2006. **Price:** $21.95. **Description:** Common questions employers ask about employees and the law are answered.

37766 ■ *"The 2007 Black Book" in Hawaii Business (Vol. 53, December 2007, No. 6, pp. 43)*
Pub: Hawaii Business Publishing
Description: Brief biographies of 364 top executives in Hawaii are presented. Information on their educational achievement, membership in associations, hobbies, family, present position and the company they work for are supplied.

37767 ■ *"2007 Fittest CEOs" in Hawaii Business (Vol. 53, October 2007, No. 4, pp. 40)*
Pub: Hawaii Business Publishing
Description: Discusses the outcome of the fittest chief executive officers in Hawaii competition for 2007. Hawaii Capital Management's David Low leads the list while Group Pacific (Hawaii) Inc.'s Chip Doyle and Greater Good Inc.'s Kari Leong placed second and third, respectively. The CEO's routines, eating habits, and inspirations for staying fit are provided.

37768 ■ *"2008 Woman of the Year Gala" in Hispanic Business (Vol. 30, July-August 2008, No. 7-8, pp. 58)*
Pub: Hispanic Business, Inc.
Ed: Brynne Chappell. **Description:** Brief report on the sixth annual Women of the Year Awards gala which was held at JW Marriott Desert Ridge Resort and Spa is given; 20 women were honored with these awards for their professional contribution, commitment to the advancement of the Hispanic community and involvement with charitable organizations.

37769 ■ *"2009 Corporate Elite: Our Top 25 Executives" in Hispanic Business (January-February 2009, pp. 16, 18, 20, 22)*
Pub: Hispanic Business
Description: Profiles of Hispanic Business Media's 2009 Corporate Elite are presented.

37770 ■ *"A&E Networks" in Brandweek (Vol. 49, April 21, 2008, No. 16, pp. SR9)*
Pub: VNU Business Media, Inc.
Ed: Anthony Crupi. **Description:** Provides contact information for sales and marketing personnel for the A&E Networks as well as a listing of the station's top programming and an analysis of the current season and the target audience for those programs running in the current season. A&E has reinvented itself as a premium entertainment brand over the last five years and with its $2.5 million per episode acquisition of The Sopranos, the station signaled that it was serious about getting back into the scripted programming business. The acquisition also helped the network compete against other cable networks and led to a 20 percent increase in prime-time viewers.

37771 ■ *"ABC" in Brandweek (Vol. 49, April 21, 2008, No. 16, pp. SR6)*
Pub: VNU Business Media, Inc.
Ed: John Consoli. **Description:** Provides contact information for sales and marketing personnel for the ABC network as well as a listing of the station's top programming and an analysis of the current season and the target audience for those programs running in the current season.

37772 ■ *"The Accountability Lens: A New Way to View Management Issues" in Business Horizons (September-October 2007, pp. 405)*
Pub: Elsevier Technology Publications
Ed: Angela T. Hall, Michael G. Bowen, Gerald R. Ferris, M. Todd Royle, Dale E. Fitzgibbons. **Description:** Organizations are viewed through an accountability lens in terms of source, focus, salience, and intensity to explain issues on corporate governance and ethics. Accountability environment, the individual's immediate work environment that directly affects the subjective experience of felt accountability, and its four main aspects are discussed.

37773 ■ *"Achieving Greatness" in Black Enterprise (Vol. 38, January 2008, No. 6, pp. 50)*
Pub: Earl G. Graves Publishing Co. Inc.
Description: Randall Pinkett, winner of a reality show on television and chairman of BCT Partners, insists that a business cannot survive by doing just enough or more of the same. Pinkett's New Jersey company provides management, technology and consulting to other firms.

37774 ■ *"Actions to Implement Three Potent Post-Crisis Strategies" in Strategy & Leadership (Vol. 38, September-October 2010, No. 5)*
Pub: Emerald Inc.
Ed: Saul J. Berman, Richard Christner, Ragna Bell. **Description:** The need for organizations to design and implement strategies to cope with the possible situations in the post-economic crisis environment is emphasized. The plans that organizations should implement to successfully manage uncertainty and complexity and to foster their eventual growth are discussed.

37775 ■ *"Adapt or Die" in Black Enterprise (Vol. 38, July 2008, No. 12, pp. 27)*
Pub: Earl G. Graves Publishing Co. Inc.
Ed: Oguntoyinbo Lekan. **Description:** Turbulence in the domestic auto industry is hitting auto suppliers hard and black suppliers, the majority of whom contract with the Big Three, are just beginning to establish relationships with import car manufacturers. The more savvy CEOs are adopting new technologies in order to weather the downturn in the economy and in the industry as a whole.

37776 ■ *"Air Canada to Slash 600 Non-Union Jobs" in Globe & Mail (February 11, 2006, pp. B3)*
Pub: CTVglobemedia Publishing Inc.
Ed: Brent Jang. **Description:** The reasons behind workforce reduction by ACE Aviation Holdings Inc. at Air Canada are presented.

37777 ■ *Airline Without a Pilot: Lessons in Leadership*
Pub: Targetmark Books
Ed: Harry L. Nolan, Jr. **Released:** December 2005. **Price:** $24.95. **Description:** The events that destroyed Delta Air Lines are used to define the failures when solid leadership is not at the helm of a company.

37778 ■ *"Airlines Mount PR Push to Win Public Support Against Big Oil" in Advertising Age (Vol. 79, July 14, 2008, No. 7, pp. 1)*
Pub: Crain Communications, Inc.
Ed: Michael Bush. **Description:** Top airline executives from competing companies have banded together in a public relations plan in which they are sending e-mails to their frequent fliers asking for aid in lobbying legislators to put a restriction on oil speculation.

37779 ■ *"Akron Community Foundation Hires Help for CEO Search" in Crain's Cleveland Business (Vol. 28, October 29, 2007, No. 43, pp. 6)*
Pub: Crain Communications, Inc.
Ed: Shannon Mortland. **Description:** Waverly Partners LLC, an executive search firm, has been hired by the Akron Community Foundation to search for its next president and CEO as Jody Bacon, the company's current CEO, will retire on July 31, 2008.

37780 ■ *"Albert Schultz" in Canadian Business (Vol. 83, August 17, 2010, No. 13-14, pp. 71)*
Pub: Rogers Media Ltd.
Ed: Steve Maich. **Description:** Soulpepper Theater Company founder and actor/director Albert Schultz shares the key ingredient to his success both artistically and commercially. Schultz believes his success was a combination of passion and persistence, as well as team building. He believes his entrepreneurial impulse came when he began thinking of making opportunities instead of taking them.

37781 ■ *"All In Good Fun" in Entrepreneur (Vol. 36, May 2008, No. 5, pp. 22)*
Pub: Entrepreneur Media, Inc.
Ed: Christopher Percy Collier. **Description:** According to a study conducted in 2007, humor in the workplace helps people communicate effectively and improves camaraderie. Company leaders and entrepreneurs can also tell humorous stories about themselves, but must also set lines that should not be crossed. The humorous atmosphere in the company YouSendIt is presented.

37782 ■ *"Always Striving" in Women In Business (Vol. 61, December 2009, No. 6, pp. 28)*
Pub: American Business Women's Association
Ed: Kathleen Leighton. **Description:** Jennifer Mull discusses her responsibilities and how she attained success as CEO of Backwoods, a gear and clothing store founded by her father in 1973. She places importance on being true to one's words and beliefs, while emphasizing the capacity to tolerate risks in business. Mull defines success as an evolving concept and believes there must always be something to strive for.

37783 ■ *The AMA Handbook of Project Management*
Pub: AMACOM
Ed: Paul C Dinsmore, Jeannette Cabanis-Brewin. **Released:** September 15, 2010. **Price:** $79.95. **Description:** A comprehensive reference presenting the critical concepts and theories all project managers must master using essays and advice from the field's top professionals.

37784 ■ *"Analysts Not Too Sad Over Gemunder" in Business Courier (Vol. 27, August 6, 2010, No. 14, pp. 1)*
Pub: Business Courier
Ed: James Ritchie. **Description:** Analysts and investors do not understand why Omnicare chief executive officer (CEO) Joel Gemunder suddenly retired after nearly thirty years with the Covington, Kentucky company. They believe that new leadership might invigorate the firm, which provides pharmacy and related services to the long-term care industry.

37785 ■ *"The Anatomy of a High Potential" in Business Strategy Review (Vol. 21, Autumn 2010, No. 3, pp. 52)*
Pub: Blackwell Publishers Ltd.
Ed: Doug Ready, Jay Conger, Linda Hill, Emily Stecker. **Description:** Companies have long been interested in identifying high potential employees, but few firms know how to convert top talent into game changers, or people who can shape the future of the business. The authors have found the 'x factors' that can make a high-potential list into a strong competitive advantage.

37786 ■ *"Anatomy of a Rumor" in Entrepreneur (Vol. 37, September 2009, No. 9, pp. 18)*
Pub: Entrepreneur Media, Inc.
Ed: Jason Daley. **Description:** Progression and adverse effect of office rumors on businesses are discussed. The quality of someone's work, tenure and personnel changes are the most prevalent categories of rumors. Workers can lose trust in management and one another as a result of rumors.

37787 ■ *"Anja Carroll; Media Director-McDonald's USA" in Advertising Age (Vol. 79, November 17, 2008, No. 34, pp. 6)*
Pub: Crain Communications, Inc.
Ed: Emily Bryson York. **Description:** Profile of Anja Carroll who is the media director for McDonald's USA and has the challenge of choosing the right mix of media for the corporation.

37788 ■ *"Ann Alexander; Senior Attorney, Natural Resources Defense Council" in Crain's Chicago Business (Vol. 31, May 5, 2008, No. 18)*
Pub: Crain Communications, Inc.
Ed: Emily Stone. **Description:** Profile of Ann Alexander who is the senior attorney at the Natural Resources Defense Council and is known for her dedication to the environment and a career spent battling oil companies, steelmakers and the government to change federal regulations. One recent project aims to improve the Bush administration's fuel economy standards for SUVs. Past battles include her work to prevent permits from slipping through the cracks such as the proposal by London-based BP PLC to dump 54 percent more ammonia and 35 percent more suspended solids from its Whiting, Indiana refinery into Lake Michigan-the source of drinking water for Chicago and its surrounding communities.

37789 ■ *"Applying Continuous Process Improvement for Managing Customer Loyalty" in Agency Sales Magazine (Vol. 39, November 2009, No. 10)*
Pub: MANA
Ed: Bob Cicerone; Aaron Hekele; Jason Morado. **Description:** Steps in effective process improvement that reveals where opportunities exist to improve management practices and control customer loyalty are discussed. The process consists of thirteen factors grouped into three sets.

37790 ■ *"Are There Material Benefits To Social Diversity?" in Hispanic Business (Vol. 30, September 2008, No. 9, pp. 10)*
Pub: Hispanic Business, Inc.
Ed: Brigida Benitez. **Description:** Diversity in American colleges and universities, where students view and appreciate their peers as individuals and do not judge them on the basis of race, gender, or ethnicity is discussed. The benefits of diversity in higher education are also acknowledged by the U.S. Supreme Court and by leading American corporations.

37791 ■ *"Are Your Goals Hitting the Right Target?" in Business Strategy Review (Vol. 21, Autumn 2010, No. 3, pp. 46)*
Pub: Blackwell Publishers Ltd.
Ed: Alan Meekings, Steve Briault, Andy Neely. **Description:** Setting targets is normal in most organizations. The authors think such a practice can cause more harm than good and offer a better strategy.

37792 ■ *"The Art of Appreciation" in Business Horizons (November-December 2007, pp. 441)*
Pub: Elsevier Technology Publications
Ed: Catherine M. Dalton. **Description:** The art of appreciation is an art less and less practices by employees. Employers should lead by example and practice this art to inspire employees to do the same.

37793 ■ *"The Art of the Huddle: How To Run a Prompt, Productive, and Painless Morning Meeting" in Inc. (November 2007, pp. 40, 42-43)*
Pub: Gruner & Jahr USA Publishing
Ed: Leigh Buchanan. **Description:** Five CEOs describe the ways they use meetings to improve their companies: team building, coordinating, efficiency, motivation, and strategic planning.

37794 ■ *"The Art of Persuasion: How You Can Get the Edge You Need To Reach Every Goal" in Small Business Opportunities (November 2007)*
Pub: Harris Publications Inc.
Ed: Paul Endress. **Description:** Expert in the field of psychology to business in the areas of communication, hiring and retention discusses a unique approach to solving business problems.

37795 ■ *"The Art of War for Women" in Hawaii Business (Vol. 54, July 2008, No. 1, pp. 23)*
Pub: Hawaii Business Publishing
Description: Business consultant Chi-Ning Chu talks about her new book 'The Art of War for Women: Sun Tzu's Ancient Strategies and Wisdom for Winning at Work', which discusses how women can more effectively win in business. She also shares her thoughts about the advantages that women have, which they can use in businesses decisions.

37796 ■ *"Ask Inc." in Inc. (November 2007, pp. 69)*
Pub: Gruner & Jahr USA Publishing
Description: The best time to terminate an employee is discussed.

37797 ■ *"Atlific Adds Management of 4 Hotels to Its Portfolio in Fort McMurray" in Canadian Corporate News (May 16, 2007)*
Pub: Comtex News Network Inc.
Description: Atlific Hotels & Resorts took over management for Merit Inn & Suites, The Merit Hotel, The Nomad Hotel and The Nomad Suites in Fort McMurray. The company feels that they will be able to increase the hotels' abilities to promote their services through their vast network of sales personnel and marketing and e-commerce team.

37798 ■ *"avVaa World Health Care Products Rolls Out Internet Marketing Program" in Health and Beauty Close-Up (September 18, 2009)*
Pub: Close-Up Media
Description: avVaa World Health Care Products, Inc., a biotechnology company, manufacturer and distributor of nationally branded therapeutic, natural health care and skin products, has signed an agreement with Online Performance Marketing to launch of an Internet marketing campaign in order to broaden its presence online. The impact of advertising on the Internet to generate an increase in sales is explored.

37799 ■ *"Back in the Race" in Barron's (Vol. 88, March 17, 2008, No. 11, pp. 43)*
Pub: Dow Jones & Company, Inc.
Ed: Leslie P. Norton. **Description:** Katherine Schapiro was able to get Sentinel International Equity's Morningstar classification to blended fund from a value fund rating after joining Sentinel from her former jobs at Strong Overseas Fund. Schapiro aims to benefit from the global rebalancing as the U.S.'s share of the world economy shrinks.

37800 ■ *"Bad Client? Make Break Cleanly, Swiftly - and Based On Numbers" in Crain's Detroit Business (Vol. 23, November 19, 2007, No. 47)*
Pub: Crain Communications Inc. - Detroit
Ed: Sheena Harrison. **Description:** Firing a difficult customer can be hard to do, but the best way to do it is cleanly and amicably.

37801 ■ *"The Balanced Business" in Women In Business (Vol. 63, Spring 2011, No. 1, pp. 14)*
Pub: American Business Women's Association
Ed: Leigh Elmore. **Description:** The balance scoreboard has developed to a full strategic planning and management system from its early use as a simple performance measurement network. Executives are able to execute their strategies by using information from the balance scoreboard. Insights on Mayer Group Inc. executive Ken Mayer's view of the balance scorecard are also shared.

37802 ■ *Balls!: 6 Rules for Winning Today's Business Game*
Pub: John Wiley & Sons, Incorporated
Ed: Alexi Venneri. **Released:** January 2005. **Price:** $29.95. **Description:** In order to be successful business leaders must be brave, authentic, loud, lovable, and spunky and they need to lead their competition.

37803 ■ *"B&B Hopes to Appeal to Fiat Execs" in Crain's Detroit Business (Vol. 25, June 15, 2009, No. 24, pp. 21)*
Pub: Crain Communications Inc. - Detroit
Ed: Daniel Duggan. **Description:** Cobblestone Manor, a ten-room bed and breakfast in Auburn Hills, Michigan is hoping to provide rooms for Fiat executives. The owners have been working with travel organizations to promote the castle-like bed and breakfast which appeals to European visitors.

37804 ■ *"Bank Bullish on Austin" in Austin Business JournalInc. (Vol. 29, November 13, 2009, No. 36, pp. A1)*
Pub: American City Business Journals
Ed: Kate Harrington. **Description:** American Bank's presence in Austin, Texas has been boosted by new management and a new 20,000 square foot building. This community bank intends to focus on building relationship with commercial banking customers. American Bank also plans to extend investment banking, treasury management, and commercial lending services.

37805 ■ *"Banks Fret About Gist Of Bailout" in The Business Journal-Serving Metropolitan Kansas City (Vol. 27, September 26, 2008, No. 2)*
Pub: American City Business Journals, Inc.
Ed: James Dornbrook. **Description:** Banks from the Kansas City area hope that the proposed $700 billion bailout will not send the wrong message. UMB Financial Corp. chairman says that he hopes that the bailout would benefit companies that were more risk restrained and punish those that took outsized risk. Other bank executives' perceptions on the planned bailout are given.

37806 ■ *"Barbara West" in Crain's Cleveland Business (Vol. 30, June 29, 2009, No. 25, pp. 14)*
Pub: Crain Communications, Inc.
Ed: Shannon Mortland. **Description:** Profile of Barbara West, administrative director of emergency medicine at MetroHealth Medical Center in Ohio. Ms. West manages Metro Life Flight that uses helicopters to transport patients to MetroHealth. She discusses the challenges of taking care of patients when big emergencies occur.

37807 ■ *"Barnes Shakes Up Sara Lee Exec Suite" in Crain's Chicago Business (Vol. 31, April 21, 2008, No. 16, pp. 1)*
Pub: Crain Communications, Inc.
Ed: David Sterrett. **Description:** In an attempt to cut costs and boost profits, Sara Lee Corp.'s CEO Brenda Barnes is restructuring the company's management team.

37808 ■ *"Battling Back from Betrayal" in Harvard Business Review (Vol. 88, December 2010, No. 12, pp. 130)*
Pub: Harvard Business School Publishing
Ed: Daniel McGinn. **Description:** Stephen Greer's scrap metal firm, Hartwell Pacific, lost several million dollars due to a lack of efficient and appropriate inventory audits, accounting procedures, and new-hire reference checks for his foreign operations. Greer believes that balancing growth with control is a key component of success.

37809 ■ *"BC Forest Safety Council Unveils Supervisor Course to Respond to Industry Demands" in Canadian Corporate News (May 14, 2007)*
Pub: Comtex News Network Inc.
Description: BC Forest Safety Council launched the sector's first supervisor training program that will lead to certification of forest supervisors in response to an industry-wide demand for standardized safety training for supervisors.

37810 ■ *"Be a Better Manager: Live Abroad" in Harvard Business Review (Vol. 88, September 2010, No. 9, pp. 24)*
Pub: Harvard Business School Publishing
Ed: William W. Maddux, Adam D. Galinsky, Carmit T. Tadmor. **Description:** Interrelationship between international experience and entrepreneurship is discussed. Individuals with international experience are likelier to be promoted and to develop new products and businesses.

37811 ■ *Be the Elephant: Build a Bigger, Better Business*
Pub: Workman Publishing Company
Ed: Steve Kaplan. **Price:** $19.95. **Description:** Entrepreneur and author sets out an accessible, no-frills plan for business owners, managers, and other industrialists to grow their businesses into elephants: big and strong but also smart. Advice is given on fostering a growth mind-set, assessing risk, and creating unique selling propositions.

37812 ■ *Be the Hero: Three Powerful Ways to Overcome Challenges in Work and In Life*
Pub: Berrett-Koehler Publishers, Inc.
Ed: Noah Blumenthal. **Released:** August 1, 2009. **Price:** $19.95. **Description:** Details are given to help individuals perform at their best when challenges are the greatest. It shows how to turn self-defeating thoughts and behavior into heroic actions.

37813 ■ *"Being Emotional During Decision Making-Good or Bad?" in Academy of Management Journal (Vol. 50, No. 4, August 2007)*
Pub: Academy of Management
Contact: Ming-Jer Chen, President
Ed: Myeong-Gu Seo, Lisa Feldman Barrett. **Description:** Relationship between affective experience and decision-making performance is studied.

37814 ■ *"Best Companies for Diversity" in Black Enterprise (Vol. 38, July 2008, No. 12, pp. 12)*
Pub: Earl G. Graves Publishing Co. Inc.
Description: Maintaining excellence in a company's diversity efforts requires critical challenges such as recruiting, retaining and developing talent in the executive pipeline. Top young and diverse emerging executives in corporate America are featured.

37815 ■ *"The Best Execs in Canada" in Canadian Business (Vol. 79, October 9, 2006, No. 20, pp. 68)*
Pub: Rogers Media
Description: The annual list of the most outstanding and innovative business executives of Canada is presented.

37816 ■ *"Best Managed Companies" in Canadian Business (Vol. 81, Summer 2008, No. 9, pp. 71)*
Pub: Rogers Media Ltd.
Ed: Calvin Leung. **Description:** Table showing the five-year annualized growth rate and one-year stock performance of companies that have grown their cash flow per share at an annualized rate of 15 percent or more over the past five years. Analysts project that the cash flow trend will continue. Other details of the stock performance index are presented.

37817 ■ *"Best Managed Companies (Canada)" in Canadian Business (Vol. 82, Summer 2009, No. 8, pp. 38)*
Pub: Rogers Media
Ed: Calvin Leung. **Description:** Agrium Inc. and Barrick Gold Corporation are among those that are found to be the best managed companies in Canada. Best managed companies also include software firm Open Text Corporation, which has grown annual sales by 75 percent and annual profits by 160 percent since 1995. Open Text markets software that allow firms to manage word-based data, and has 46,000 customers in 114 countries.

37818 ■ *"Big Paychecks for Hospital CEOs" in Sacramento Business Journal (Vol. 28, April 8, 2011, No. 6, pp. 1)*
Pub: Sacramento Business Journal
Ed: Kathy Robertson. **Description:** Hospital chief executives in Sacramento, California have been receiving large salaries, tax records show. The huge salaries reflect the high demand for successful hospital chief executives. Statistical data included.

37819 ■ *"Big Shoes to Fill for New United Way Chairman" in Business Courier (Vol. 27, June 25, 2010, No. 8, pp. 4)*
Pub: Business Courier
Ed: Lucy May. **Description:** David Dougherty, chairman of the nonprofit United Way of Greater Cincinnati, explains how he can surpass the nonprofit's 2009 campaign kickoff that raised $62 million. For 2010, Dougherty has prepared a $2 million matching grant from a group of local individuals, corporations, and foundations. Dougherty also discusses what he learned from participating in the 2009 campaign.

37820 ■ *"BIM and LPS Improve Project Management" in Contractor (Vol. 57, January 2010, No. 1, pp. 56)*
Pub: Penton Media, Inc.
Ed: Dennis Sowards. **Description:** Building Information Modeling helps reduce workspace conflicts and construction problems that are not seen in typical design efforts for mechanical contractors. The Last Planner System in Lean Construction also helps improve productivity in project management.

37821 ■ *"BIM: The Risks You Need to Watch Out For" in Contractor (Vol. 57, February 2010, No. 2, pp. 28)*
Pub: Penton Media, Inc.
Ed: Susan Linden McGreevy. **Description:** Legal and risk management issues surrounding Building Information Modeling (BIM) can be divided into three categories namely; intellectual property, liability for content, and the responsibility for the inputs into the model. The agreement should be done in a way that protects the intellectual rights of the authors when using BIM.

37822 ■ *"Black Gold" in Canadian Business (Vol. 79, August 14, 2006, No. 16-17, pp. 57)*
Pub: Rogers Media
Ed: Erin Pooley. **Description:** A list of the top ten jobs in the petroleum industry in Canada along with pay and nature of jobs, is presented.

37823 ■ *"Black's Truth: Will a Prison Stay Change the Way Conrad Black Operates?" in Canadian Business (Vol. 81, March 31, 2008, No. 5)*
Pub: Rogers Media
Ed: Matthew McClearn. **Description:** Conrad Black will serve a 6 and a half years in prison but he asserts that his successors at Hollinger International and Hollinger Inc. grossly mismanaged and unjustly enriched themselves. Black also asserts that International violated the so-called November Agreement and that he is the aggrieved party. Black's assertions show a character flaw that cannot be corrected in prison.

37824 ■ *"Block Plans Office Park Along K-10 Corridor" in The Business Journal-Serving Metropolitan Kansas City (Vol. 27, October 3, 2008)*
Pub: American City Business Journals, Inc.
Ed: Rob Roberts. **Description:** Kansas City, Missouri-based Block and Co. is planning to build four office buildings at the corner of College Boulevard and Ridgeview Road in Olathe. Features of the planned development are provided. Comments from executives are also presented.

37825 ■ *The Board Book: An Insider's Guide for Directors and Trustees*
Pub: W.W. Norton & Company
Ed: William G. Bowen. **Released:** 2009. **Price:** $26. 95. **Description:** A primer for all directors and trustees that provides suggestions for getting back to good-governance basics in business.

37826 ■ *"The Board Shorts Executive" in Hawaii Business (Vol. 53, January 2008, No. 7, pp. 33)*
Pub: Hawaii Business Publishing
Ed: Mike Markrich. **Description:** Vans Triple Crown of Surfing executive director Randy Rarick believes that the surfing business requires knowledge of the sport and integity to the game's lifestyle and spirit. His organization manages surfing events, and has generated jobs for the locals. Plans for Vans Triple Crown are supplied.

37827 ■ *The Book of Hard Choices: Making the Right Decisions at Work without Losing Your Self-Respect*
Pub: Broadway Books
Contact: David Drake, Manager
E-mail: ddrake@randomhouse.com
Ed: Peter Roy; James A. Autry. **Released:** December 2006. **Price:** $23.95.

37828 ■ *"Book Smart" in Hawaii Business (Vol. 53, December 2007, No. 6, pp. 39)*
Pub: Hawaii Business Publishing
Ed: David K. Choo. **Description:** Different parts of a biography entry in the Black Book are examined in relation to their usage in starting a conversation with an executive. The second part, which is the educational background, is considered the most significant of all, due to the amount of information given. The importance of making connections in Hawaii is discussed.

37829 ■ *Bo's Lasting Lessons*
Pub: Business Plus
Ed: Bo Schembechler; John U. Bacon. **Price:** $13. 99. **Description:** Leadership skills are taught.

37830 ■ *"Both Eyes on the Prize" in Canadian Business (Vol. 83, September 14, 2010, No. 15, pp. 42)*
Pub: Rogers Media Ltd.
Ed: Jacqueline Nelson. **Description:** North American executive compensation has fundamentally shifted partly due to pressure from the US government and recent adjustments in the way CEO pay packages are structured. The changes have also become common practice in Canada and helped in scrutinizing the executive pay.

37831 ■ *Bottom-Line Training: Performance-Based Results*
Pub: Training Education Management
Ed: Donald J. Ford. **Released:** June 2005. **Price:** $29.99. **Description:** Training is critical to any successful enterprise. The key to any successful training program involves defining and constantly focusing on the desired results of the program. The author provides a training model based on five phases, known as ADDIE: analysis, design, development, implementation and evaluation.

37832 ■ *Bradford's International Directory of Marketing Research Agencies*
Pub: Business Research Services Inc.
Contact: Thomas D. Johnson, President
URL(s): www.bradfordsdirectory.com. **Released:** Biennial; Latest edition 30th. **Price:** $95, Individuals in-print; $95, Individuals CD-ROM; $125, Individuals in print and CD-ROM. **Covers:** Over 2,300 marketing research agencies worldwide. Includes domestic and international demographic data and professional association contacts. **Entries include:** Company name, address, phone, name and title of contact, date founded, number of employees, description of products or services, e-mail, URL. **Arrangement:** Geographical. **Indexes:** Alphabetical by company.

37833 ■ *"Brett Wilson" in Canadian Business (Vol. 81, July 22, 2008, No. 12-13, pp. 80)*
Pub: Rogers Media Ltd.
Ed: Michelle Magnan. **Description:** Interview with Brett Wilson who believes he became a 'capitalist with a heart' because he had a father who sold cars and a mother who was a social worker. He feels that being accelerated a grade was one of the biggest opportunities and challenges in his life. Brett Wilson's other views on business and on his family are presented.

37834 ■ *"Bringing Big Guns" in Business Courier (Vol. 24, January 18, 2008, No. 41, pp. 1)*
Pub: American City Business Journals, Inc.
Ed: Lucy May. **Description:** Chief executive officer of Nidland Co. John Hayden was assigend as Cincinnati USA Partnership chairman. Hayden will bring his expertise to help the partnership drive economic development in the Greater Cincinnati area. Details of the parntership's plans are suplied.

37835 ■ *"Bringing Manufacturing Concerns to Springfield" in Crain's Chicago Business (Vol. 31, March 31, 2008, No. 13, pp. 6)*
Pub: Crain Communications, Inc.
Ed: Paul Merrion. **Description:** Profile of the new executive vice-president of Tooling & Manufacturing Assn., Paul Merrion, a man who plans to grow TMA's membership with an aggressive legislative agenda in Springfield.

37836 ■ *"The Buck Stops Here" in Canadian Business (Vol. 81, November 10, 2008, No. 19, pp. 25)*
Pub: Rogers Media Ltd.
Ed: Sarka Halas. **Description:** Reputation strategist Leslie Gaines-Ross says that minimizing the damage followed by the identification of what went wrong are the first steps that companies need to take when trying to salvage their reputation. Gaines-Ross states that it is up to the CEO to ensure the company's speedy recovery and they need to be at the forefront of the process.

37837 ■ *"Budget Strategically to Stay on Course" in Entrepreneur (August 28, 2008)*
Pub: Entrepreneur Media Inc.
Ed: Tim Berry. **Description:** Budgeting is one of the most valuable tools in a manager's arsenal. The importance of budgeting is discussed and tips for surviving an economic recession are provided.

37838 ■ *"Building Alexian Brothers' Clinical Reputation" in Crain's Chicago Business (Vol. 31, May 5, 2008, No. 18, pp. 6)*
Pub: Crain Communications, Inc.
Ed: Mike Colias. **Description:** Profile of the CEO of Alexian Brothers Medical Center in Elk Grove Village who plans to stabilize Alexian Brothers' financial performance in part by eliminating $20 million in annual costs.

37839 ■ *Business Black Belt: Develop the Strength, Flexibility and Agility to Run Your Company*
Pub: Career Press, Inc.
Ed: Burke Franklin. **Released:** November 1, 2010. **Price:** $15.99. **Description:** Manual offering insights that will enable anyone to become successful in small business. Seventy short chapters included topics such as attitude, management, marketing, selling, employees, money, MBAs, lawyers, consultants, and investors.

37840 ■ *Business Diagnostics: The Canadian Edition 2nd Ed.*
Pub: Trafford Publishing
Ed: Michael Thompson; Richard Mimick. **Released:** July 6, 2006. **Price:** $70.00. **Description:** Business management skills are outlined.

37841 ■ *"Business Ethics, Strategic Decision Making, and Firm Performance" in Business Horizons (September-October 2007, pp. 353)*
Pub: Elsevier Technology Publications
Ed: Michael A. Hitt, Jaime D. Collins. **Description:** Strategic management and decision-making process are linked to business ethics. The Strengths, Weakness, Opportunities, and Threats (SWOT) analysis model is employed to design an effective strategy for companies.

37842 ■ *"Business Forecast: Stormy and Successful" in Women In Business (Vol. 62, June 2010, No. 2, pp. 12)*
Pub: American Business Women's Association
Ed: Kathleen Leighton. **Description:** Stormy Simon, vice president of customer service at Overstock.com is a self-made career woman who started out as a temporary employee in the company in 2001. She was not able to attend college because she had two sons to care for after her divorce. Simon got involved in advertising and media buying and shares her love for business.

37843 ■ *Business Management for Entrepreneurs*
Pub: Double Storey Books
Ed: Cecile Nieuwenhuizen. **Released:** March 1, 2009. **Price:** $35.95. **Description:** Lack of good management skills are usually the reason for any small company to fail. This book introduces entrepreneurs and managers of small to medium-sized firms to all functions required to manage successfully.

37844 ■ *Business Management for Tropical Dairy Farmers*
Pub: CSIRO Publishing
Ed: John Moran. **Released:** August 1, 2009. **Price:** $33.95. **Description:** Business management skills required for dairy farmers are addressed, focusing on financial management and ways to improve cattle housing and feeding systems.

37845 ■ *"Business Must Stand Up And Be Counted" in Crain's Detroit Business (Vol. 24, October 6, 2008, No. 40, pp. 6)*
Pub: Crain Communications, Inc.
Description: Discusses the challenges that the new mayor of Detroit faces concerning business, the state of the economy and the exceptionally tight budget the city is running on, which includes a lot of red ink. It is very likely that the city is going to see tax revenues fall substantially in the next few months and business leaders may find it in their favor to lend their support to the new mayor as well as provide him with the executive talent necessary to overcome some of these crucial issues.

37846 ■ *Business Stripped Bare: Adventures of a Global Entrepreneur*
Pub: Virgin Books/Random House
Ed: Sir Richard Branson. **Released:** January 22, 2010. **Price:** $26.95. **Description:** Successful entrepreneur, Sir Richard Branson, shares the inside track on some of his greatest achievements in business and the lessons learned from setbacks.

37847 ■ *"Business as Usual at RIM, Balsillie Says" in Globe & Mail (March 6, 2007, pp. B1)*
Pub: CTVglobemedia Publishing Inc.
Ed: Simon Avery. **Description:** The continuation of normal business at Research In Motion Ltd., after the resignation of Jim Balsillie from the chairman's post, is described. The investigation of securities fraud at Research In Motion Ltd., and the continuation of Jim Balsillie as the co-chief executive officer of the company is discussed.

37848 ■ *Business Warrior: Strategy for Entrepreneurs*
Pub: Clearbridge Publishing
Ed: Sun Tzu. **Released:** September 2006. **Price:** $19.95. **Description:** Advice to help entrepreneurs understand competitive strategies in order to succeed, focusing on sales, marketing, and personnel management.

37849 ■ *Busting the Myth of the Heroic CEO*
Pub: Cornell University Press
Contact: John G. Ackerman, Director
E-mail: jga4@cornell.edu
Ed: Michel Villette, Catherine Vuillermot. **Released:** 2010. **Price:** $24.95. **Description:** According to the authors, corporate leaders do not get ahead through productive risk-taking and innovation, but through ruthless exploitation of market imperfections and rivals.

37850 ■ *"Bye-Bye, Ol' Boys" in Canadian Business (Vol. 80, January 15, 2007, No. 2, pp. 16)*
Pub: Rogers Media
Ed: Michelle Magnan. **Description:** A profile of Kathy Sendall, senior vice-president of Petro-Canada of the North American division and chairperson of the Canadian Association of Petroleum Producers, is presented.

37851 ■ *"C. Andrew McCartney; President, Owner, Bowden Manufacturing Corp., 37" in Crain's Cleveland Business (November 19, 2007)*
Pub: Crain Communications, Inc.
Ed: David Bennett. **Description:** Profile of C. Andrew McCartney who was named president of Bowden Manufacturing Corp., a company that machines and fabricates metal and plastic parts for products ranging from airplanes to medical equipment; Mr. McCartney has since purchased the company, which posted $8 million in sales last year. He feels that part of his success is due to adherence to such policies such as gaining the employees trust and to avoid making promises to customers that Bowden cannot keep.

37852 ■ *"Can He Win the Patent Game?" in Globe & Mail (February 20, 2006, pp. B1)*
Pub: CTVglobemedia Publishing Inc.
Ed: Simon Avery; Paul Waldie. **Description:** A profile on managerial abilities of chief executive officer Jim Balsillie of Research In Motion Ltd., who will face the patent case with NTP Inc., is presented.

37853 ■ *"Can You Hear Me Now?" in Harvard Business Review (Vol. 86, July-August 2008, No. 8, pp. 23)*
Pub: Harvard Business School Press
Ed: Katharina Pick. **Description:** Tips for improving communication among boardroom members are presented. These include encouraging frankness via in-meeting leaders, and the ability of directors to meet without managers.

37854 ■ *Canadian Entrepreneurship and Small Business Management*
Pub: McGraw-Hill Ryerson, Limited
Ed: D. Wesley Balderson. **Released:** February 2005. **Description:** Successful entrepreneurship and small business management is shown through the use of individual Canadian small business experiences.

37855 ■ *The Carrot Principle: How the Best Managers Use Recognition to Engage Their Employees*
Pub: Free Press
Ed: Adrian Gostick; Chester Elton. **Released:** April 2009. **Price:** $22.95. **Description:** Book show ways that managers can fail to acknowledge special achievements of employees thereby risking alienating the best workers or losing them to competing firms.

37856 ■ *"The Case for Professional Boards" in Harvard Business Review (Vol. 88, December 2010, No. 12, pp. 50)*
Pub: Harvard Business School Publishing
Ed: Robert C. Pozen. **Description:** A professional directorship model can be applied to corporate governance. Suggestions for this include the reduction of board size to seven members in order to improve the effectiveness of decision making, along with the requirement that directors have industry expertise.

37857 ■ *"A Case Study: Real-Life Business Planning" in Entrepreneur (February 3, 2009)*
Pub: Entrepreneur Media Inc.
Ed: Tim Berry. **Description:** Provides a case study of a two-day planning meeting for Palo Alto Software in which the executives of the company met for their annual planning cycle and discussed ways in which the company needed to change in order to stay viable in today's tough economic climate.

37858 ■ *"A Cautionary Tale for Emerging Market Giants" in Harvard Business Review (Vol. 88, September 2010, No. 9, pp. 99)*
Pub: Harvard Business School Publishing
Ed: J. Stewart Black, Allen J. Morrison. **Description:** Key factors that negatively affected Japan corporate growth and organizational effectiveness include: devotion to established path, isolated domestic markets, homogenous executive teams, and a non-contentious labor force. Solutions include leadership development programs, multicultural input, and cross-cultural training.

37859 ■ *"CBS" in Brandweek (Vol. 49, April 21, 2008, No. 16, pp. SR6)*
Pub: VNU Business Media, Inc.
Ed: John Consoli. **Description:** Provides contact information for sales and marketing personnel for the CBS network as well as a listing of the station's top programming and an analysis of the current season and the target audience for those programs running in the current season.

37860 ■ *"CBS Television Distribution" in Brandweek (Vol. 49, April 21, 2008, No. 16, pp. SR13)*
Pub: VNU Business Media, Inc.
Ed: Marc Berman. **Description:** Provides contact information for sales and marketing personnel for CBS Television Distribution as well as a listing of the station's top programming and an analysis of the current season and the target audience for those programs running in the current season. Due to the unprecedented, decade-plus advantage of first-run leaders such as Wheel of Fortune, Oprah, Judge Judy and Entertainment Tonight, CBS is poised to remain a leader among the syndicates.

37861 ■ *"The Center of Success: Author Explores How Confidence Can Take You Further" in Black Enterprise (Vol. 38, March 2008, No. 8)*
Pub: Earl G. Graves Publishing Co. Inc.
Ed: Ayana Dixon. **Description:** Motivational speaker and author, Valorie Burton, provides a 50-question confidence quotient assessment to help business owners and managers develop confidence in order to obtain goals.

37862 ■ *"CEO Forecast" in Hispanic Business (January-February 2009, pp. 34, 36)*
Pub: Hispanic Business
Ed: Jessica Haro, Richard Kaplan. **Description:** As economic uncertainty fogs the future, executives turn to government contracts in order to boost business. Revenue sources, health care challenges, environmental consulting and remediation services, as well as technological strides are discussed.

37863 ■ *"CEO Pay: Best Bang for Buck" in Philadelphia Business Journal (Vol. 30, September 30, 2011, No. 33, pp. 1)*
Pub: American City Business Journals Inc.
Ed: Jeff Blumenthal. **Description:** A study by Strategic Research Solutions on the compensation of chief executive officers in Philadelphia, Pennsylvania-based public companies reveals that only a few of them performed according to expectations. These include Brian Roberts of Comcast, John Conway of Crown Holdings, and Frank Hermance of Ametek Inc.

37864 ■ *"CEO Pay: The Details" in Crain's Detroit Business (Vol. 25, June 22, 2009, No. 25, pp.)*
Pub: Crain Communications Inc. - Detroit
Description: Total compensation packages for CEOs at area companies our outlined. These packages include salary, bonuses, stock awards, and options.

37865 ■ *"CEO Tapped for Perrier, Poland Springs" in Black Enterprise (Vol. 38, February 2008, No. 7, pp. 30)*
Pub: Earl G. Graves Publishing Co. Inc.
Ed: Brenda Porter. **Description:** John J. Harris, newly appointed CEO, is hoping to increase market share of Nestle's bottled water products.

37866 ■ *"CEOs Decry Budget Taxation Change" in Globe & Mail (April 2, 2007, pp. B1)*
Pub: CTVglobemedia Publishing Inc.
Ed: Steven Chase. **Description:** The views of the chief executive officers of Canadian firms, on the changes in the country's policy governing the taxation of foreign deals, are presented.

37867 ■ *"CEOs Divided About Census" in Canadian Business (Vol. 83, August 17, 2010, No. 13-14, pp. 20)*
Pub: Rogers Media Ltd.
Ed: Jacqueline Nelson. **Description:** A Compass poll of Canadian CEOs on what the government should do with controversial long-form census is presented. The poll results show that 30 percent believe the government should remove any threat of punishment for failure to complete the survey. The CEOs also believe the law must be enforced by the government to encourage participation.

37868 ■ *"CEOs Gone Wild" in Canadian Business (Vol. 79, August 14, 2006, No. 16-17, pp. 15)*
Pub: Rogers Media
Ed: Thomas Watson. **Description:** Stock investment decisions of chief executive officers of metal companies in Canada, are discussed.

37869 ■ *"The CEO's New Armor" in Conde Nast Portfolio (Vol. 2, June 2008, No. 6, pp. 56)*
Pub: Conde Nast Publications
Contact: David Carey, President
Ed: John Cassidy. **Description:** Due to a new breed in C.E.O.'s contracts it is nearly impossible to fire them regardless of their performance. Despite the Sarbanes-Oxley Act in which attempted to codify C.E.O. responsibilities, corporate bosses responded

by quietly demanding individual contracts, which, in many cases, were drawn up by their own lawyers and accepted by company boards with no outside oversight or review.

37870 ■ *"CEOs Split on Migrant Workers" in Canadian Business (Vol. 83, September 14, 2010, No. 15, pp. 23)*
Pub: Rogers Media Ltd.
Ed: Jacqueline Nelson. **Description:** A survey of Canadian CEOs shows that 49 percent of the respondents believe it was wrong to suspend the immigration programs and companies should be allowed to hire the most skilled workers regardless of citizenship. However, 42 percent believe the suspension was right because employment of Canadians must take precedence.

37871 ■ *"CEOs With a Functional Background in Operations" in Human Resource Management (Vol. 49, September-October 2010, No. 5)*
Pub: John Wiley
Ed: Burak Koyuncu, Shainaz Firfiray, Bjorn Claes, Monika Hamori. **Description:** A study was conducted to determine whether companies that appoint chief executive officers (CEOs) with an operations background exhibit better post-succession financial performance relative to organizations that appoint CEOs with other functional backgrounds. A total of 437 CEOs from U.S. firms in eight industries were included in the study.

37872 ■ *"CEOs With Headsets" in Harvard Business Review (Vol. 88, September 2010, No. 9, pp. 21)*
Pub: Harvard Business School Publishing
Ed: Andrew Zimbalist. **Description:** Placing a salary cap on college coaches' compensation would not significantly affect coaching quality or an institution's ability to obtain talent. A salary growth rate comparison between coaches, university presidents, and full professors for the period 1986 to 2007 is also presented.

37873 ■ *"Certification Experts Germanischer Lloyd Wind Energy Assist NaiKun's Offshore Wind Project" in Canadian Corporate News (May 14, 2007)*
Pub: Comtex News Network Inc.
Description: Germanischer Lloyd Wind Energy (GL Wind) will examine, inspect, and provide quality management services for the engineering, design, and construction of the offshore wind project planned by NaiKun Wind Development Inc. in northwest British Columbia.

37874 ■ *"Challenges Await Quad in Going Public" in Milwaukee Business Journal (Vol. 27, January 29, 2010, No. 18, pp. A1)*
Pub: American City Business Journals
Ed: Rich Rovito. **Description:** Sussex, Wisconsin-based Quad/Graphics Inc.'s impending acquisition of rival Canadian World Color Press Inc. will transform it into a publicly held entity for the first time. Quad has operated as a private company for nearly 40 years and will need to adjust to changes, such as the way management shares information with Quad/Graphics' employees. Details of the merger are included.

37875 ■ *"Challenges, Responses and Available Resources" in Journal of Small Business and Entrepreneurship (Vol. 23, Winter 2010, No. 1)*
Pub: Canadian Council for Small Business and Entrepreneurship
Ed: Lynne Siemens. **Description:** Rural communities and their residents are exploring the potential of small business and entrepreneurship to address the economic changes they are facing. While these rural areas present many opportunities, business people in these areas face challenges which they must navigate to operate successfully.

37876 ■ *Change in SMEs: The New European Capitalism*
Pub: Palgrave Macmillan
Ed: Katharina Bluhm; Rudi Schmidt. **Released:** October 2008. **Price:** $95.00. **Description:** Effects of global change on corporate governance, management, competitive strategies and labor relations in small-to-medium sized enterprises in various European countries are discussed.

37877 ■ *"Characteristics of Great Salespeople" in Agency Sales Magazine (Vol. 39, November 2009, No. 10, pp. 40)*
Pub: MANA
Ed: Paul Pease. **Description:** Tips for managers in order to maximize the performance of their sales personnel are presented through several vignettes. Using performance based commission that rewards success, having business systems that support sales activity, and having an organizational culture that embraces sales as a competitive edge are some suggestions.

37878 ■ *The Checklist Manifesto: How to Get Things Right*
Pub: Metropolitan Books
Ed: Dr. Atul Gawande. **Price:** $24.50. **Description:** How tragic errors can be sharply reduced with a piece of paper, hand-drawn boxes, and a pencil.

37879 ■ *Chief Culture Officer: How to Create a Living, Breathing Corporation*
Pub: Basic Books
Ed: Grant McCracken. **Price:** $26.95. **Description:** Business consultant argues that corporations need to focus on 'reading' what's happening in the culture around them. Otherwise, companies will suffer the consequences, as Levi Strauss did when it missed out on the rise of hip-hop (and the baggy pants that are part of that lifestyle).

37880 ■ *"Choosing Strategies For Change" in Harvard Business Review (Vol. 86, July-August 2008, No. 8, pp. 130)*
Pub: Harvard Business School Press
Ed: John P. Kotter; Leonard A. Schlesinger. **Description:** Methods for implementing organizational change include identifying potential areas of resistance, providing the necessary skills and information to counteract resistance, and assessing situational factors that may influence results.

37881 ■ *"Citadel Hires Three Lehman Execs" in Chicago Tribune (October 2, 2008)*
Pub: McClatchy-Tribune Information Services
Ed: James P. Miller. **Description:** Citadel Investment Group LLC, Chicago hedge-fund operator, has hired three former senior executives of bankrupt investment banker Lehman Brothers Holding Inc. Citadel believes that the company's hiring spree will help them to further expand the firm's capabilities in the global fixed income business.

37882 ■ *"City Consults Executives on Police Hire" in Business Courier (Vol. 27, August 27, 2010, No. 17, pp. 1)*
Pub: Business Courier
Ed: Lucy May, Dan Monk. **Description:** The City of Cincinnati, Ohio has begun a selection process for the new police chief by consulting the city's business executives. The city charter amendment known as Issue 5 has removed civil service protection from the chief's post and enables City Manager Milton Dohoney to hire a chief from outside the department.

37883 ■ *"Class Management" in Canadian Business (Vol. 80, April 23, 2007, No. 9, pp. 64)*
Pub: Rogers Media
Ed: Erin Pooley. **Description:** The role of executive MBA programs in improving performance of employees is presented.

37884 ■ *"Clay Riddell" in Canadian Business (Vol. 80, February 12, 2007, No. 4, pp. 86)*
Pub: Rogers Media
Ed: Michelle Magnan. **Description:** Chief executive officer of Paramount Resources Clay Riddell shares his passion for oil and gas business.

37885 ■ *"The CMO of Consequence" in Business Strategy Review (Vol. 21, Autumn 2010, No. 3, pp. 42)*
Pub: Wiley-Blackwell
Ed: D. Eric Boyd, Rajesh K. Chandy, Marcus Cunha. **Description:** Do chief marketing officers matter? Some say that CMOs have limited effect on corporate performance and don't add significant value to the firm. The authors agree that the job in many firms is in great peril, but their research has uncovered why the contributions of some CMOs are invaluable.

37886 ■ *"CMO Nicholson Exits Pepsi as Share Declines" in Advertising Age (Vol. 79, July 7, 2008, No. 26, pp. 4)*
Pub: Crain Communications, Inc.
Ed: Natalie Zmuda. **Description:** Cie Nicholson, the chief marketing officer at Pepsi-Cola UK, is leaving the company at a time when its market share is down; the brand, which was known for its dynamic marketing, has diverted much of its attention from its core brands and shifted attention to the ailing Gatorade brand as well as Sobe Life Water and Amp.

37887 ■ *"CN Profit a Boon for Top Brass" in Globe & Mail (March 23, 2007, pp. B5)*
Pub: CTVglobemedia Publishing Inc.
Ed: Brent Jang. **Description:** Canadian National Railway Co., Montreal-based freight carrier, paid $7.3 million in compensation to its top five executives. The company has posted a record $2.1 billion profits in 2006.

37888 ■ *"CN to Webcast 2007 Analyst Meeting in Toronto May 23-24" in Canadian Corporate News (May 16, 2007)*
Pub: Comtex News Network Inc.
Description: Canadian National Railway Company (CN) broadcast its analyst meeting in Toronto with a webcast which focused on CN's opportunities, strategies, and financial outlook through the year 2010.

37889 ■ *"Cold Stone Creamery" in Ice Cream Reporter (Vol. 23, November 20, 2010, No. 12, pp. 6)*
Pub: Ice Cream Reporter
Description: Doug Ducey, former CEO of Cold Stone Creamery, was elected to the post of Arizona State Treasurer. Ducey was responsible for the firm's expansion to major brand status.

37890 ■ *"The Color of Success: ELC Focuses On Making Diversity Work" in Black Enterprise (Vol. 41, December 2010, No. 5, pp. 59)*
Pub: Earl G. Graves Publishing Co. Inc.
Ed: Sonia Alleyne. **Description:** CEOs and top ELC members at the annual recognition conference held in New York in October 2010 shared their perspective on corporate inclusion and advice for C-suite aspirants.

37891 ■ *"Comcast Networks" in Brandweek (Vol. 49, April 21, 2008, No. 16, pp. SR9)*
Pub: VNU Business Media, Inc.
Ed: Anthony Crupi. **Description:** Provides contact information for sales and marketing personnel for the Comcast networks as well as a listing of the station's top programming and an analysis of the current season and the target audience for those programs running in the current season. Experts believe Comcast will continue to acquire more stations into their portfolio.

37892 ■ *"Commitment Issues" in Workforce Management (Vol. 88, November 16, 2009, No. 12, pp. 20)*
Pub: Crain Communications Inc.
Ed: Ed Frauenheim. **Description:** Employee engagement refers to how committed workers are to their company and how much extra effort they are willing to put in on the job; firms could find that they are having a more difficult time coming out of the recession if they lack this important feature in workplace relations.

37893 ■ *"Competing on Talent Analytics" in Harvard Business Review (Vol. 88, October 2010, No. 10, pp. 52)*
Pub: Harvard Business School Publishing
Ed: Thomas H. Davenport, Jeanne Harris, Jeremy Shapiro. **Description:** Six ways to use talent analytics to obtain the highest level of value from employees are listed. These include human-capital investment analysis, talent value models, workforce forecasts, and talent supply chains.

37894 ■ *"The Competitive Imperative Of Learning" in Harvard Business Review (Vol. 86, July-August 2008, No. 8, pp. 60)*
Pub: Harvard Business School Press

Ed: Amy C. Edmondson. **Description:** Experimentation and reflection are important components for maintaining success in the business world and are the kind of character traits that can help one keep his or her competitive edge.

37895 ■ *"Complaints, Workforce Composition, Productivity, Organizational Values" in HRMagazine (Vol. 54, January 2009, No. 1, pp. 29)*
Pub: Society for Human Resource Management
Contact: Henry G. Jackson, President
E-mail: hjackson@shrm.org

Ed: Amy Maingault, Regan Halvorsen, Rue Dooley, Liz Petersen. **Description:** Workforce composition trends that management should monitor are outlined. A goal-development process is discussed.

37896 ■ *"Conference Calendar" in Marketing to Women (Vol. 21, March 2008, No. 3, pp. 7)*
Pub: EPM Communications Inc.
Contact: Ira Mayer, President
E-mail: imayer@epmcom.com

Description: Listing of current conferences and events aimed at women entrepreneurs and leaders.

37897 ■ *"Congratulations to the 2012 Top Ten Business Women of ABWA" in Women In Business (Vol. 63, Fall 2011, No. 3, pp. 14)*
Pub: American Business Women's Association

Description: Geri Bertram, Patti Bigger, and Susan Crowther are among the top ten businesswomen of the American Business Women's Association recognized for their contribution to the group, community involvement, and career achievements. Bertram is the manager for procurement planning control in Ingalls Shipbuilding while Bigger is Specialty Screw Corporation's corporate relations manager. Also on the list are Virginia DeGiorgi and Geanna Kincanon.

37898 ■ *"The Consequences of Tardiness" in Modern Machine Shop (Vol. 84, August 2011, No. 3, pp. 34)*
Pub: Gardner Business Media, Inc.
Contact: Richard G. Kline, President
E-mail: rkline@gardnerweb.com

Ed: Wayne S. Chaneski. **Description:** Five point addressing motivating factors behind employees who are tardy and those who choose to be on time in the workplace are shared.

37899 ■ *"Consulting Firm Goes Shopping" in Crain's Chicago Business (Vol. 31, April 28, 2008, No. 17, pp. 45)*
Pub: Crain Communications, Inc.

Ed: Phuong Ly. **Description:** Clark & Wamberg LLC was created last year after the merger of Clark Inc. to a Dutch insurance conglomerate. Clark Inc. was a life insurance and benefits consultancy which had been on a downslide, returning just 5.6 percent a year to shareholders. In contrast Clark & Wamberg posted first-year revenue of $106.8 million, fueled by business from its executive compensation and health care clients.

37900 ■ *"Contract Design as a Firm Capability" in Academy of Management Review (October 2007, pp. 1060)*
Pub: ScholarOne, Inc.

Ed: Nicholas Argyres, Kyle J. Mayer. **Description:** A firm's capabilities for designing detailed contracts and the role of managers, engineers, and lawyers in the design of such contracts is highlighted.

37901 ■ *"Convention Calendar" in Black Enterprise (Vol. 37, November 2006, No. 4, pp. 76)*
Pub: Earl G. Graves Publishing Co. Inc.

Description: Listing of conferences targeted at African American executives and business owners.

37902 ■ *"CoolBrands" in Canadian Business (Vol. 83, September 14, 2010, No. 15, pp. 25)*
Pub: Rogers Media Ltd.

Ed: Joe Castaldo. **Description:** CoolBrands International Inc.'s merger with Swisher International Inc., a US hygiene products and services company, has formally erased the last traces of the former ice cream company. CoolBrands began as a frozen yogurt stand in 1986 and flourished across the world. How the string of acquisitions and poor corporate governance led to its demise are cited.

37903 ■ *Corporate Crisis and Risk Management: Modeling, Strategies and SME Application*
Pub: Elsevier Science and Technology Books

Ed: M. Aba-Bulgu; S.M.N. Islam. **Released:** December 2006. **Price:** $115.00. **Description:** Methods and tools for handling corporate risk and crisis management are profiled for small to medium-sized businesses.

37904 ■ *"Corporate Diversity Driving Profits" in Hispanic Business (Vol. 30, September 2008, No. 9, pp. 12)*
Pub: Hispanic Business, Inc.

Ed: Michael Bowker. **Description:** U.S. businesses are beginning to appreciate the importance of diversity and are developing strategies to introduce a diverse workforce that reflects the cultural composition of their customers. The realization that diversity increases profits and the use of professional networks to recruit and retain skilled minority employees are two other new trends impacting corporate diversity in the U.S.

37905 ■ *"Corporate Elite Face Steep Challenges" in Hispanic Business (January-February 2008, pp. 20, 22, 24, 26, 28, 30, 32)*
Pub: Hispanic Business

Ed: Jonathan Higuera. **Description:** Hispanic men and women are moving up corporate ranks at leading companies in the U.S., including Ralph de la Vega, president and CEO of AT&T Mobility. Profiles of Vega and other Hispanic business leaders are included.

37906 ■ *Corporate Entrepreneurship: Top Managers and New Business Creation*
Pub: Cambridge University Press
Contact: Richard Ziemacki, President
E-mail: rziemacki@cambridge.org

Ed: Vijay Sathe. **Released:** February 2007. **Price:** $35.00. **Description:** Studies covering entrepreneurship and business growth are examined.

37907 ■ *"Corporate Governance Reforms in China and India: Challenges and Opportunities" in Business Horizons (January-February 2008)*
Pub: Elsevier Advanced Technology Publications

Ed: Nandini Rajagopalan, Yan Zhang. **Description:** The evolution of corporate governance reforms and the role of privatization and globalization in India and China are studied. Shortage of qualified independent directors and lack of incentives were found to be two of the major challenges in governance. The implications of and solutions to these challenges are highlighted.

37908 ■ *"Corporate Responsibility" in Professional Services Close-Up (July 2, 2010)*
Pub: Close-Up Media

Description: List of firms awarded the inaugural Best Corporate Citizens in Government Contracting by the Corporate Responsibility Magazine is presented. The list is based on the methodology of the Magazine's Best Corporate Citizen's List, with 324 data points of publicly-available information in seven categories which include: environment, climate change, human rights, philanthropy, employee relations, financial performance, and governance.

37909 ■ *"Corporate Social Responsibility: A Process Model of Sensemaking" in Academy of Management Review (January 2008, pp. 122)*
Pub: ScholarOne, Inc.

Ed: Kunal Basu, Guido Palazzo. **Description:** A novel process model of corporate social responsibility is presented. It uses organizational sensemaking to educate managers about elements of appropriate relationships with stakeholders and others.

37910 ■ *"Corporate Training" in Hawaii Business (Vol. 53, October 2007, No. 4, pp. 46)*
Pub: Hawaii Business Publishing

Ed: Cathy S. Cruz-George. **Description:** Kalani Pa, Mike Hann, and Li Si Yang are three of the fitness trainers who have worked with some of the participants at the Hawaii's Fittest CEO contest. Pa has trained Group Pacific Inc.'s Chip Doyle while Hann was Sharon Serene's trainer. Their insights on the profession of being a fitness trainer, and on working with executives are given.

37911 ■ *"Craig Muhlhauser" in Canadian Business (Vol. 81, September 15, 2008, No. 14-15, pp. 6)*
Pub: Rogers Media Ltd.

Ed: Andrew Wahl. **Description:** Interview with Craig Muhlhauser who is the CEO of Celestica, a manufacturing company that provides services for the electronics sector; Muhlhauser discusses the company's restructuring program, which he feels was the secret to their surprising first-quarter results. Muhlhauser states that the company is operating with more forward visibility and that understanding the opportunities during the current economic situation presents the biggest challenge.

37912 ■ *"Creating Your Personal Succession Plan" in Black Enterprise (Vol. 38, December 2007, No. 5, pp. 86)*
Pub: Earl G. Graves Publishing Co. Inc.

Ed: Marcia Reed-Woodard. **Description:** Society for Human Resource Management's Succession Planning Survey Report shows that over 58 percent of companies surveyed use succession plans for employees preparing to transition to higher-level positions.

37913 ■ *"Crisis Management" in Black Enterprise (Vol. 38, October 2007, No. 3, pp. 69)*
Pub: Earl G. Graves Publishing Co. Inc.

Ed: Faith Chukwudi. **Description:** Shirley W. Bridges, chief information officer for Delta Air Lines, discusses leadership skills that establish trust within an organization.

37914 ■ *"The Critical Need to Reinvent Management" in Business Strategy Review (Vol. 21, Spring 2010, No. 1, pp. 4)*
Pub: Wiley-Blackwell

Ed: Julian Birkinshaw. **Description:** The author believes that management is undervalued today - and for good reasons. Management, he says, has failed at the big-picture level and thinks it is time to reinvent the profession.

37915 ■ *"Cross Atlantic Commodities Launches National Internet Marketing Programs" in Manufacturing Close-Up (September 8, 2009)*
Pub: Close-Up Media

Description: Profile of the Internet campaign recently launched by Cross Atlantic Commodities, Inc., a manufacturer of specialty beauty and health products.

37916 ■ *"The Cult of Ralph" in Canadian Business (Vol. 79, September 25, 2006, No. 19, pp. 90)*
Pub: Rogers Media

Ed: Thomas Watson. **Description:** The contributions of Ralph Gilles to automobile manufacturing giant Daimler Chrysler AG are discussed.

37917 ■ *"Culture Club" in Canadian Business (Vol. 79, October 9, 2006, No. 20, pp. 115)*
Pub: Rogers Media

Ed: Calvin Leung. **Description:** Positive impacts of an effective corporate culture on the employees' productivity and the performance of the business are discussed.

37918 ■ *"Currency: I'm Otta Here" in Entrepreneur (Vol. 35, October 2007, No. 10, pp. 72)*
Pub: Entrepreneur Media Inc.

Ed: C.J. Prince. **Description:** Liberum Research revealed that 193 chief financial officers (CFOs) at small companies have either resigned or retired during the first half of 2007. A survey conducted by Tatum found that unreasonable expectations from the management and compliance to regulations are the main reasons why CFOs are leaving small firms. The chief executive officer's role in making CFOs stay is also discussed.

37919 ■ *"Custom Fit" in Canadian Business (Vol. 80, November 19, 2007, No. 23, pp. 42)*
Pub: Rogers Media

Ed: Andy Holloway. **Description:** Proper employee selection will help ensure a company has the people with the skills it really needs. Employee development is integral in coping with changes in the company. The importance of hiring the right employee and developing his skills is examined.

37920 ■ *"Customer Retention is Proportionate to Employee Retention" in Green Industry Pro (Vol. 23, September 2011)*
Pub: Cygnus Business Media

Description: Presented in a question-answer format, information is provided to help retain customers as well as keeping workers happy.

37921 ■ *"The CW" in Brandweek (Vol. 49, April 21, 2008, No. 16, pp. SR8)*
Pub: VNU Business Media, Inc.

Ed: John Consoli. **Description:** Provides contact information for sales and marketing personnel for the CW network as well as a listing of the station's top programming and an analysis of the current season and the target audience for those programs running in the current season. Purchases of advertising feel that Warner Bros. and CBS made a mistake merging The WB and UPN into the new CW rather than folding UPN into the more-established WB; compared to last season ratings are down more than 20 percent across the board.

37922 ■ *"David Low" in Hawaii Business (Vol. 53, October 2007, No. 4, pp. 38)*
Pub: Hawaii Business Publishing

Ed: Cathy S. Cruz-George. **Description:** Hawaii Capital Management managing director David Low ranked first in the 2007 competition for fittest male executives in Hawaii. This 5-foot-9 executive, who weighed 225 lbs. in 2003, weighs 150 lbs. in 2007. The activities that improved Low's fitness, such as weight training, swimming, biking, and running, are discussed.

37923 ■ *"Dean Foods" in Ice Cream Reporter (Vol. 23, September 20, 2010, No. 10, pp. 8)*
Pub: Ice Cream Reporter

Description: Dean Foods promoted Joseph Scalzo to President and Chief Operating Officer to oversee the firm's operational turnaround and near-term strategic initiatives as well as business units. Key functions will include worldwide supply chain and research and development.

37924 ■ *"Defensive Training" in Crain's Detroit Business (Vol. 24, September 22, 2008, No. 38, pp. 11)*
Pub: Crain Communications Inc.

Ed: Robert Ankeny. **Description:** Rising retaliation claims in regards to discrimination complaints are creating an atmosphere in which managers must learn how to avoid or deal with these lawsuits as well as the retaliation that often follows. Examples of cases are given as well as advice for dealing with such problems that may arise in the workplace.

37925 ■ *The Definitive Drucker: The Final Word from the Father of Modern Management*
Pub: McGraw-Hill

Ed: Elizabeth Haas Edersheim; A.G. Lafley. **Released:** December 2006. **Price:** $27.95.

37926 ■ *"Deja Vu" in Canadian Business (Vol. 81, July 22, 2008, No. 12-13, pp. 38)*
Pub: Rogers Media Ltd.

Ed: Joe Castaldo. **Description:** Laurent Beaudoin has retired as chief executive officer for Bombardier Inc.'s, a manufacturer of regional and business aircraft, but kept a role in the firm as a non-executive chairman. Beaudoin first resigned from the company in 1999, but had to return in 2004 to address challenging situations faced by the company. Beaudoin's views on management and the company are presented.

37927 ■ *"Demystifying Demotion" in Business Horizons (November-December 2007, pp. 455)*
Pub: Elsevier Technology Publications

Ed: Paula Phillips Carson, Kerry David Carson. **Description:** A model of employee demotion is developed after conducting personal interviews with more than 20 demotees. The effects of demotion, such as economic harm, lower well-being, underemployment, and grief reactions and identity crises are studied.

37928 ■ *Design Your Own Effective Employee Handbook: How to Make the Most of Your Staff with Companion CD-ROM*
Pub: Atlantic Publishing Company

Ed: Michelle Devon. **Released:** June 2006. **Price:** $39.95. **Description:** An employee handbook should include clearly written policies covering the rights and responsibilities of workers.

37929 ■ *"Designing Events Updates Online Suite" in Wireless News (October 25, 2009)*
Pub: Close-Up Media

Description: Designing Events, an outsourcing and consulting firm for conferences and meetings, announced the release of an update to its Designing Events Online suite of web-based management and marketing tools; features include enhanced versions of online registration and collaboration, content management, session development, social media and conference websites.

37930 ■ *"Developing the Next Generation of Rosies" in Employee Benefit News (Vol. 25, November 1, 2011, No. 14, pp. 36)*
Pub: SourceMedia Inc.

Ed: Kathleen Koster. **Description:** According to the research group Catalyst, women made up 46.7 percent of the American workforce in 2010, however only 14.4 percent was Fortune 500 executive officers and 15.7 percent held Fortune 500 board seats. Statistical data included.

37931 ■ *"DHR Hires Carr for Sports Group" in Crain's Detroit Business (Vol. 25, June 8, 2009, No. 23, pp. 5)*
Pub: Crain Communications Inc. - Detroit

Ed: Sherri Begin Welch. **Description:** Lloyd Carr, former head football coach for University of Michigan, has taken a position with DHR International in order to expand its searches for collegiate and professional sports organizations, recruit athletic directors, head coaches and other executives.

37932 ■ *"Diana Bonta: Keeping People Healthy and Thriving" in Hispanic Business (Vol. 30, April 2008, No. 4, pp. 30)*
Pub: Hispanic Business

Ed: Leanndra Martinez. **Description:** Diana Bonta serves as vice president of public affairs for Kaiser Permanente and is a strong advocate for health reform and improving access to health care. In order to better serve the underinsured and uninsured, she directs Kaiser's Community Benefit division that devoted $369 million last year to this cause.

37933 ■ *"Diana Sands; Vice-President of Investor Relations, Boeing Co." in Crain's Chicago Business (Vol. 31, May 5, 2008, No. 18, pp. 32)*
Pub: Crain Communications, Inc.

Ed: John Rosenthal. **Description:** Profile of Diana Sands who is the vice-president of investor relations at Boeing Co. which entails explaining the company's performance to securities analysts and institutional investors.

37934 ■ *"Dick Evans" in Canadian Business (Vol. 82, April 27, 2009, No. 7, pp. 78)*
Pub: Rogers Media

Ed: Sean Silcoff. **Description:** Former Rio Tinto Alcan chief executive officer Dick Evans believes that the 1982 downturn was worse than the current recession, at least for the mining sector. He also believes that while people are anxious, there is confidence that the economy will recover in two to three years. Key information on Evans, as well as his other views on being a CEO is presented.

37935 ■ *"Different Aspects of Project Management" in Contractor (Vol. 57, February 2010, No. 2, pp. 30)*
Pub: Penton Media, Inc.

Ed: H. Kent Craig. **Description:** There are differences when managing a two-man crew as a foreman and a 2,000 employee company as a corporate president. A project manager should have good skills in human psychology, accounting, and the knowledge of a mechanical engineer, architect, civil engineer, and also the meditative skills of a Zen master.

37936 ■ *"A Different Breed of Deal Maker is Emerging" in Globe & Mail (January 14, 2006, pp. B2)*
Pub: CTVglobemedia Publishing Inc.

Ed: Eric Reguly. **Description:** The managerial strategies of chief executive officers in business acquisitions of companies, such as Dofasco Inc., are presented.

37937 ■ *"Dirty Work Required" in Workforce Management (Vol. 88, November 16, 2009, No. 12, pp. 34)*
Pub: Crain Communications Inc.

Ed: John Hollon. **Description:** Due to salary freezes, pay cuts, layoffs, buyouts and a number of other stress factors brought about by the recession, employee engagement has been difficult to maintain by managers.

37938 ■ *"Discovery Networks" in Brandweek (Vol. 49, April 21, 2008, No. 16, pp. SR9)*
Pub: VNU Business Media, Inc.

Ed: Anthony Crupi. **Description:** Provides contact information for sales and marketing personnel for the Discovery networks as well as a listing of the station's top programming and an analysis of the current season and the target audience for those programs running in the current season. The networks flagship station returned to the top 10 in 2007, averaging 1.28 million viewers.

37939 ■ *"Disney-ABC Domestic Television Distribution" in Brandweek (Vol. 49, April 21, 2008, No. 16, pp. SR13)*
Pub: VNU Business Media, Inc.

Ed: Marc Berman. **Description:** Provides contact information for sales and marketing personnel for Disney-ABC Domestic Television Distribution as well as a listing of the station's top programming and an analysis of the current season and the target audience for those programs running in the current season.

37940 ■ *The Diversity Code: Unlocking the Secrets to Making Differences Work in the Real World*
Pub: AMACOM

Ed: Michelle T. Johnson. **Released:** September 8, 2010. **Price:** $19.95. **Description:** The most diligent compliance with laws and regulations can't foster true work place diversity. The best organizations have become genuine cross-cultural communities that believe equality in reconciling difference and valuing them. The book promotes understanding by answering many of the toughest questions that professionals and their employers are afraid to ask.

37941 ■ *"Do Something!" in Entrepreneur (Vol. 36, March 2008, No. 3, pp. 79)*
Pub: Entrepreneur Media Inc.

Ed: Chris Penttila. **Description:** Employers are addressing the cause of employee stress by adjusting work structure. Some of the actions taken to tackle the concern include examples such as the eCast executive having quick one-on-one talks with employees and GlaxoSmithKlline employees taking online stress assessment. Other details on reducing job/ employee stress are discussed.

37942 ■ *"Do You Need to Reinvent Your Managers?" in Rental Product News (Vol. 33, June 2011)*
Pub: Cygnus Business Media
Ed: Dick Detmer. **Description:** Rental business owners need to assess their management and be sure they perform as true leaders of the organization.

37943 ■ *"Do Your Really Know Your Problem: Entrepreneurs Have a Tendency To See What They Want To See" in Inc. (December 2007, pp. 95-96)*
Pub: Gruner & Jahr USA Publishing
Ed: Norm Brodsky. **Description:** Information is offered to help entrepreneurs diagnose and resolve company issues.

37944 ■ *"Does Rudeness Really Matter?" in Academy of Management Journal (October 2007, pp. 1181)*
Pub: Academy of Management
Contact: Ming-Jer Chen, President
Ed: Christine L. Porath, Amir Erez. **Description:** Study assessing the effect of impoliteness on performance and helpfulness showed rude behavior lowered performance levels and also decreased attitude of helpfulness.

37945 ■ *"Doing It Right" in Black Enterprise (Vol. 38, October 2007, No. 3, pp. 53)*
Pub: Earl G. Graves Publishing Co. Inc.
Ed: Sheiresa McRae. **Description:** One of the hardest things for every entrepreneur to do is delegate responsibility to employees; Anthony Samuels offers tips on the art of delegating.

37946 ■ *"Don't Hate the Cable Guy" in Saint Louis Business Journal (Vol. 31, August 5, 2011, No. 50, pp. 1)*
Pub: Saint Louis Business Journal
Ed: Angela Mueller. **Description:** Charter Communications named John Birrer as senior vice president of customer experience. The company experienced problems with its customer services.

37947 ■ *"Don't Leave Employees on the Outside Looking In" in Canadian Business (Vol. 83, July 20, 2010, No. 11-12, pp. 13)*
Pub: Rogers Media Ltd.
Ed: Richard Branson. **Description:** Managers should be careful with employee's tendencies to use the word 'they' when problems occur since this shows that employees are not associating themselves with their company. Employees should be involved in the development of the company and improving the flow of information is important in overcoming this communication challenge.

37948 ■ *"Don't Shoot the Messenger: A Wake-Up Call For Academics" in Academy of Management Journal (Vol. 50, No. 5, October 2007, pp. 1020)*
Pub: Academy of Management
Contact: Ming-Jer Chen, President
Ed: David E. Guest. **Description:** Author evaluates two well-known publications: HR Magazine and People Management, to emphasize the role of U.S. academics in communicating management practice.

37949 ■ *"The Downside of Self-Management" in Academy of Management Journal (August 2007)*
Pub: Academy of Management
Contact: Ming-Jer Chen, President
Ed: Claus W. Langfred. **Description:** Study reveals that self-managing teams might accidentally restructure themselves inefficiently in response to conflict, thus the possible structure-related effects are analyzed.

37950 ■ *"Downtowns Must Court Young, CEOs for Cities President Says" in Crain's Detroit Business (Vol. 24, October 6, 2008, No. 40, pp. 18)*
Pub: Crain Communications, Inc.
Ed: Amy Lane. **Description:** It is important to produce more college graduates, and keep them in Michigan, according to CEOs for Cities President Carol Coletta when she spoke to a session at the West Michigan Regional Policy Conference which was held in September in Grand Rapids. Ways in which city leaders can connect students to communities, resulting in employees who have vested interest in the region, are also discussed.

37951 ■ *"Downturn Tests HCL's Pledge to Employees" in Workforce Management (Vol. 88, November 16, 2009, No. 12, pp. 23)*
Pub: Crain Communications Inc.
Ed: Ed Frauenheim. **Description:** HCL Technologies has kept its promise to keep from laying any employees off during the recession which served as a test for the tech firm's Employee First program, which seeks to give workers greater income security as well as a stronger voice in the firm.

37952 ■ *"Dramatic Results: Making Opera (Yes, Opera) Seem Young and Hip" in Inc. (October 2007, pp. 61-62)*
Pub: Gruner & Jahr USA Publishing
Description: Profile of Peter Gelb, who turned New York's Metropolitan Opera into one of the most media-savvy organizations in the country, using a multifaceted marketing strategy through the media. Gelb used streaming audio and simulcasts on satellite radio and movie theaters to promote a message that opera is hip.

37953 ■ *The Dream Manager*
Pub: Hyperion
Ed: Matthew Kelly. **Price:** $19.95. **Description:** A business fable about the virtues of helping those working for and with you to achieve their dreams. Managers can boost morale and control turnover by adopting this policy.

37954 ■ *Driving With No Brakes: How a Bunch of Hooligans Built the Best Travel Company in the World*
Pub: Grand Circle Corporation
Ed: Alan and Harriet Lewis. **Price:** $19.95. **Description:** Inspirational book about how two courageous leaders built a remarkable company that can thrive in change and succeed in an unpredictable world. Important lessons for any business leader trying to create value in the 21st Century are included.

37955 ■ *"DST Turns to Banks for Credit" in The Business Journal-Serving Metropolitan Kansas City (Vol. 27, October 3, 2008, No. 3, pp. 1)*
Pub: American City Business Journals, Inc.
Ed: Rob Roberts. **Description:** Kansas City, Missouri-based DST Systems Inc., a company that provides sophisticated information processing, computer software services and business solutions, has secured a new five-year, $120 million credit facility from Enterprise Bank and Bank of the West. The deal is seen to reflect that the region and community-banking model remain stable. Comments from executives are also provided.

37956 ■ *The Dynamic Small Business Manager*
Pub: Lulu.com
Ed: Frank Vickers. **Released:** March 2006. **Price:** $39.99. **Description:** Practical advice is given to help small business owners successfully manage their company.

37957 ■ *E-Commerce in Regional Small to Medium Enterprises*
Pub: Idea Group Publishing
Ed: Robert MacGregor. **Released:** July 2007. **Price:** $99.95. **Description:** Strategies small to medium enterprises (SMEs) need to implement in order to compete with larger, global businesses and the role electronic commerce plays in this process are outlined. Studies of e-commerce in multiple regional areas, focusing on the role of business size, business sector, market focus, gender of CEO, and education level of the CEO are discussed.

37958 ■ *E-Myth Mastery: The Seven Essential Disciplines for Building a World Class Company*
Pub: HarperCollins Publishers Inc.
Ed: Michael E. Gerber. **Released:** March 2007. **Price:** $16.95. **Description:** Leadership, marketing, money, management, lead conversion, lead generation, client fulfillment are the seven keys to successful entrepreneurship.

37959 ■ *"The Early Bird Really Does Get the Worm" in Harvard Business Review (Vol. 88, July-August 2010, No. 7-8, pp. 30)*
Pub: Harvard Business School Publishing
Ed: Christoph Randler. **Description:** Research indicates that those who identify themselves as 'morning people' tend to be more proactive, and thus have a career-development advantage over those who identify themselves as 'night people'. Implications of the research are also discussed.

37960 ■ *Economic Freedom and the American Dream*
Pub: Palgrave Macmillan
Ed: Joseph Shaanan. **Released:** January 5, 2010. **Price:** $55.00. **Description:** An exploration into the effects of economic freedom on American in several areas such as markets, politics, and opportunities for would-be entrepreneurs.

37961 ■ *The Economics and Management of Small Business: An International Perspective*
Pub: Routledge
Ed: Graham Bannock. **Released:** May 2005. **Price:** $65.00. **Description:** International perspectives on the economics and management of small business, featuring case studies and empirical research.

37962 ■ *Ecopreneuring: Putting Purpose and the Planet Before Profits*
Pub: New Society Publishers
Ed: John Ivanko; Lisa Kivirist. **Released:** July 1, 2008. **Price:** $17.95 paperback. **Description:** Ecopreneurs in America are shifting profits and market share towards green living. The book provides a guideline for ecopreneurs in the areas of eco-business basics, purposeful management, marketing in the green economy, and running a lifestyle business.

37963 ■ *"El Paso Firm Rides Boom to the Top" in Hispanic Business (Vol. 30, July-August 2008, No. 7-8, pp. 28)*
Pub: Hispanic Business, Inc.
Ed: Jeremy Nisen. **Description:** VEMAC, a commercial construction management and general contracting firm that is experiencing success despite the plummeting construction market is discussed. VEMAC's success is attributed to the Pentagons' $5 billion investment in construction for the benefit of new personnel and their families to be transferred to Fort Bliss, a U.S. army base adjacent to El Paso.

37964 ■ *"The Emergence of Governance In an Open Source Community" in Academy of Management Journal (Vol. 50, No. 5, October 2007, pp. 1079)*
Pub: Academy of Management
Contact: Ming-Jer Chen, President
Ed: Siiobhan O'Mahony, Fabrizio Ferraro. **Description:** Study examined the method of self-governance among small communities producing collective goods, focusing on an open source software community. Results revealed that a combination of bureaucratic and democratic practices helped its governance system.

37965 ■ *"Empathy: An Entrepreneur's Killer App" in Women Entrepreneur (February 3, 2009)*
Pub: Entrepreneur Media Inc.
Ed: Kristi Hedges. **Description:** It is just as important to treat employees with courtesy and respect during bad economic times as it is in a good economy. Employers sometimes take advantage of such bad economic times since they realize that employees

are grateful to have a job and cannot just quit and easily find work elsewhere. The importance of empathy in a company's leadership personnel is discussed.

37966 ■ *Employee Management for Small Business*
Pub: Self-Counsel Press, Incorporated
Ed: Lin Grensing-Pophal. **Released:** November 2009. **Price:** $20.95. **Description:** Management tools to help entrepreneurs maintain an effective human resources plan for a small company.

37967 ■ *"Employee Motivation: A Powerful New Model" in Harvard Business Review (Vol. 86, July-August 2008, No. 8, pp. 78)*
Pub: Harvard Business School Press
Ed: Nitin Nohria; Boris Groysbert; Linda Eling Lee. **Description:** Four drives underlying employee motivation are discussed as well as processes for leveraging these drives through corporate culture, job design, reward systems, and resource-allocation priorities.

37968 ■ *"Empowered" in Harvard Business Review (Vol. 88, July-August 2010, No. 7-8, pp. 94)*
Pub: Harvard Business School Publishing
Ed: Josh Bernoff, Ted Schadler. **Description:** HERO concept (highly empowered and resourceful operative) which builds a connection between employees, managers, and IT is outlined. The resultant additional experience and knowledge gained by employees improves customer relationship management.

37969 ■ *"Energy Sparks Job Growth" in The Business Journal-Serving Greater Tampa Bay (Vol. 28, August 8, 2008, No. 33, pp. 1)*
Pub: American City Business Journals, Inc.
Ed: Margie Manning. **Description:** Energy infrastructure projects in Tampa Bay, Florida, are increasing the demand for labor in the area. Energy projects requiring an increase in labor include TECO Energy Inc.'s plan for a natural gas pipeline in the area and the installation of energy management system in Bank of America's branches in the area.

37970 ■ *Enlightened Leadership: Best Practice Guidelines and Time Tools for Easily Implementing Learning Organizations*
Pub: Learning House Publishing, Inc.
Ed: Ralph LoVuolo; Alan G. Thomas. **Released:** May 2006. **Price:** $79.99. **Description:** Innovation and creativity are essential for any successful small business. The book provides owners, managers, and team leaders with the tools necessary to produce 'disciplined innovation'.

37971 ■ *Enlightened Leadership: Best Practice Guidelines and Timesaving Tools for Easily Implementing Learning Organizations*
Pub: Learning House Publishing, Incorporated
Ed: Alan G. Thomas; Ralph L. LoVuolo; Jeanne C. Hillson. **Released:** September 2006, printable 3 times/year. **Price:** $21.00. **Description:** Book provides the tools required to create a learning organization management model along with a step-by-step guide for team planning and learning. The strategy works as a manager's self-help guide as well as offering continuous learning and improvement for company-wide success.

37972 ■ *Entrepreneurial Decision-Making Individuals, Tasks and Cognitions*
Pub: Edward Elgar Publishing, Incorporated
Ed: Gusfafsson. **Released:** December 2006. **Price:** $85.00. **Description:** Entrepreneurial decision-making is examined by comparing various individuals with differing levels of expertise and potential.

37973 ■ *"Entrepreneurial Orientation and Firm Performance" in Journal of Small Business and Entrepreneurship (Vol. 23, Winter 2010, No. 1)*
Pub: Canadian Council for Small Business and Entrepreneurship
Description: The article develops a theoretical model of the relationship between firm-level entrepreneurship and firm performance. This model is intended to further clarify the consequences of an 'entrepreneurial orientation', paying particular attention to the differential relationship that exists between the three sub-dimensions of entrepreneurial orientation and firm performance. Included in the theoretical model are other important variables (such as organizational structure and environmental characteristics) that may impact the EO-performance relationship. Propositions are developed regarding the various configurations of the sub-dimensions of EO and organizational structure that would be most appropriate in a given environmental context. Future research may also benefit from considering the important role that organizational strategy and life cycle stage play in this model. The implications of this model for both researchers and managers are discussed.

37974 ■ *Entrepreneurial Skills: 2nd Edition*
Pub: Double Storey Books
Ed: Cecile Nieuwenhuizen. **Released:** March 1, 2009. **Price:** $32.00. **Description:** Entrepreneurial skills are examined, showing how entrepreneurship differs from management mostly in attitude and approach.

37975 ■ *The Entrepreneur's Guide to Managing Growth and Handling Crisis*
Pub: Greenwood Publishing Group, Inc.
Ed: Theo J. Van Dijk. **Released:** December 2007. **Price:** $39.95. **Description:** The author explains how entrepreneurs can overcome crisis by changing the way they handle customers, by putting new processes and procedures in place, and managing employees in a professional manner. The book includes appendices with tips for hiring consultants, creating job descriptions, and setting up systems to chart cash flow as well as worksheets, tables and figures and a listing of resources.

37976 ■ *The Entrepreneur's Strategy Guide: Ten Keys for Achieving Marketplace Leadership*
Pub: Greenwood Publishing Group Inc.
Contact: Janann Sherman, Manager
Ed: Tom Cannon. **Released:** September 2006. **Price:** $44.95. **Description:** Ten principles of marketplace leadership are explored. The book provides a plan for small businesses, including diagnostics, checklists, and other interactive exercises to study both external and internal principles.

37977 ■ *"Everett Dowling" in Hawaii Business (Vol. 54, August 2008, No. 2, pp. 32)*
Pub: Hawaii Business Publishing
Ed: Jason Ubay. **Description:** Real estate developer Everett Dowling, president of Dowling Company Inc., talks about the company's sustainable management and services. The company's office has been retrofitted to earn a Leadership in Energy and Environmental Design (LEED) certification. Dowling believes that real estate development can be part of the sustainable solution.

37978 ■ *Everything I Know About Business I Learned at McDonald's: The 7 Leadership Principles that Drive Break Out Success*
Pub: The McGraw-Hill Companies
Ed: Paul Facella. **Released:** 2009. **Price:** $24.95. **Description:** McDonald's management philosophy is as simple as its menu, but don't underestimate the effectiveness of founder Ray Kroc's business plan.

37979 ■ *"Evidence-Based Management and the Marketplace For Ideas" in Academy of Management Journal (Vol. 50, No. 5, October 2007, pp. 1009)*
Pub: Academy of Management
Contact: Ming-Jer Chen, President
Ed: Wayne F. Cascio. **Description:** Study examines the relevance of material to actual usage in human resource management. Results reveal that it is important to design modules with execution in mind in seeking advice from professionals in relevant organizations.

37980 ■ *"The Evolution of Carolyn Elman" in Women In Business (Vol. 62, September 2010, No. 3, pp. 11)*
Pub: American Business Women's Association
Ed: Leigh Elmore. **Description:** Carolyn Elman, former executive director of the American Business Women's Association (ABWA), provides an overview of her career. Elman grew up with the Association, and it was part of her family's existence. She believes that the ABWA provides women the opportunity to learn and improve their skills in business.

37981 ■ *"The Evolution of Corporate Social Responsibility" in Business Horizons (November-December 2007, pp. 449)*
Pub: Elsevier Technology Publications
Ed: Philip L. Cochran. **Description:** Corporate social responsibility is now perceived as vital in enhancing the profitability of businesses while improving their reputation. It has changed business practices such as philanthropy, investment, and entrepreneurship.

37982 ■ *Execution: The Discipline of Getting Things Done*
Pub: Crown Publishing/Random House
Ed: Larry Bossidy, Ram Charan, Charles Burck. **Released:** June 15, 2002. **Price:** $27.50. **Description:** The book shows how to get things done and deliver results whether you are running an entire company or in your first management position.

37983 ■ *"The Executive Brain" in Canadian Business (Vol. 80, October 22, 2007, No. 21, pp. 41)*
Pub: Rogers Media
Ed: Rachel Pulfer. **Description:** Studies by Jordan Petersen, Frank Schmidt, and John Hunter show that leaders have highly evolved capacities to think using the prefrontal cortex of the brain. Inspirational leadership ability is located in the parietal lobe. Other details of the research are discussed.

37984 ■ *"Executive Decision: Just What the Doctor Ordered" in Globe & Mail (February 11, 2006, pp. B3)*
Pub: CTVglobemedia Publishing Inc.
Ed: Leonard Zehr. **Description:** The leadership ability of chief executive William Hunter of Angiotech Pharmaceuticals Inc., who acquired American Medical Instruments Holdings Inc. for $785 million, is discussed.

37985 ■ *"Executives Exit at Wal-Mart in China" in Wall Street Journal Eastern Edition (October 17 , 2011, pp. B3)*
Pub: Dow Jones & Company Inc.
Ed: Laurie Burkitt. **Description:** Woes for Wal-Mart Inc.'s subsidiary in China are adding up as Wal-Mart China president and chief executive Ed Chan stepped down, as well as the company's senior vice president for human resources, Clara Wong. The company has been charged by regulators with mislabeling pork products, the result which has forced stores to close. Sales in China have been slow at the retail stores.

37986 ■ *"Extreme Negotiations" in Harvard Business Review (Vol. 88, November 2010, No. 11, pp. 66)*
Pub: Harvard Business School Publishing
Ed: Jeff Weiss, Aram Donigian, Jonathan Hughes. **Description:** Examination of military negotiation skills that are applicable in business situations. Skills include soliciting others' perspectives, developing and proposing multiple solutions, and inviting others to assess them.

37987 ■ *The Facebook Era: Tapping Online Social Networks to Build Better Products, Reach New Audiences, and Sell More Stuff*
Pub: Prentice Hall
Ed: Clara Shih. **Price:** $24.99. **Description:** The '90s were about the World Wide Web of information and the power of linking Web pages. Today it's about the World Wide Web of people and the power of the social graph. Online social networks are fundamentally changing the way we live, work, and interact. They offer businesses immense opportunities to transform customer relationships for profit: opportunities that touch virtually every business function, from sales and marketing to recruiting, collaboration to executive decision-making, product development to innovation.

37988 ■ *"Facing the Future" in Canadian Business (Vol. 81, March 31, 2008, No. 5, pp. 69)*
Pub: Rogers Media
Ed: John Gray. **Description:** Discusses a web poll of 122 Canadian CEOs which shows that these leaders

are convinced that the U.S. economy is slowing but are split on the impact that this will have on the Canadian economy. The aging and retiring workforce and the strong Canadian dollar are other concerns by these leaders.

37989 ■ *"Falling Local Executive Pay Could Suggest a Trend" in Tampa Bay Business Journal (Vol. 30, January 15, 2010, No. 4, pp. 1)*
Pub: American City Business Journals
Ed: Margie Manning. **Description:** Tampa Bay, Florida-based Raymond James Financial Inc. and MarineMax Inc.'s proxy statements have shown the decreasing compensation of the companies' highest paid executives. The falling trend in executive compensation was a result of intensified shareholder scrutiny and the economy.

37990 ■ *"Familiar Face Aims to Rebuild Distributor's Once-Strong Local Ties" in Crain's Cleveland Business (December 3, 2007)*
Pub: Crain Communications, Inc.
Ed: David Bennett. **Description:** Phillips Contractors Supply, a tool distributor, has a new president and co-owner, James Beckett. Beckett was once vice president of operations so he knows the company well and has plans to re-establish the firm's presence in the region.

37991 ■ *Family Business*
Pub: Cengage South-Western
Ed: Ernesto J. Poza. **Released:** January 1, 2009. **Price:** $96.95. **Description:** Family-owned businesses face unique challenges in today's economy. This book provides the next generation of knowledge and skills required for profitable management and leadership in a family enterprise.

37992 ■ *Family Business Models*
Pub: Palgrave Macmillan
Ed: Alberto Gimeno. **Released:** June 10, 2010. **Price:** $45.00. **Description:** A unique new model for understanding family businesses gives readers the potential to build better managed and more stable family firms and to plan for a success future.

37993 ■ *"Family Governance and Firm Performance: Agency, Stewardship, and Capabilities" in Family Business Review (Vol. 19, March 2006)*
Pub: Family Firm Institute
Contact: Judy L. Green, President
Ed: Danny Miller, Isabelle Le Breton-Miller. **Description:** Study examining the effect of governance, agency perspective, and stewardship perspective on performances of major publicly-traded family-controlled businesses in the U.S. is presented.

37994 ■ *"Feeling the Heat: Effects of Stress, Commitment, and Job Experience On Job Performance" in Academy of Management Journal (Aug. 2007)*
Pub: Academy of Management
Contact: Ming-Jer Chen, President
Ed: Larry W. Hunter, Sherry M.B. Thatcher. **Description:** Links between bank branch employees' felt job stress, organizational commitment, job experience, and performance is analyzed. Results found are uniform with the attention view of stress.

37995 ■ *"Female Hispanic Professionals by the Number" in Hispanic Business (Vol. 30, April 2008, No. 4, pp. 8)*
Pub: Hispanic Business
Description: More executive opportunities are presenting themselves for future generations of Hispanic women who are more frequently being found in high-level positions. Statistical data included.

37996 ■ *Fierce Leadership*
Pub: Crown Business Books
Ed: Susan Scott. **Released:** January 11, 2011. **Price:** $15.00. **Description:** A bold alternative to the worst 'best' practices of business in the 21st Century.

37997 ■ *"Fifth Third CEO Kabat: A World of Difference" in Business Courier (Vol. 26, January 1, 2010, No. 37, pp. 1)*
Pub: American City Business Journals, Inc.
Ed: Steve Watkins. **Description:** CEO Kevin Kabat of Cincinnati-based Fifth Third Bancorp believes that the bank's assets of $111 billion and stock value of more than $10 indicate the recovery from the low stock prices posted in February 2009. He attributes the recovery from the federal government's stress test finding in May 2009 that Fifth Third needs to generate $1.1 billion.

37998 ■ *"Fighting the Good Fight" in Inc. (Vol. 33, October 2011, No. 8, pp. 8)*
Pub: Inc. Magazine
Ed: Eric Markowitz. **Description:** Rob Roy, former Navy SEAL, runs SOT-G a firm that offers an 80-hour leadership training course inspired by military combat preparations. Details of the program are outlined.

37999 ■ *Financial Times Guide to Business Start Up 2007*
Pub: Pearson Education, Limited
Contact: Steven A. Dowling, President
Ed: Sara Williams; Jonquil Lowe. **Released:** November 2006. **Price:** $52.50. **Description:** Guide for starting and running a new business is presented. Sections include ways to get started, direct marketing, customer relations, management and accounting.

38000 ■ *"Finding A Higher Gear" in Harvard Business Review (Vol. 86, July-August 2008, No. 8, pp. 68)*
Pub: Harvard Business School Press
Ed: Thomas A. Stewart; Anand P. Raman. **Description:** Anand G. Mahindra, the chief executive officer of Mahindra and Mahindra Ltd., discusses how his company fosters innovation, drawn from customer centricity, and how this will grow the company beyond India's domestic market.

38001 ■ *First, Break All the Rules: What the World's Greatest Managers Do Differently*
Pub: Simon and Schuster Inc.
Contact: Carolyn Reidy, President
E-mail: carolyn.reidy@simonandschuster.com
Ed: Marcus Buckingham, Curt Coffman. **Released:** May 1999. **Price:** $19.80. **Description:** Great managers break virtually every rule revered by conventional wisdom.

38002 ■ *The Five Dysfunctions of a Team: A Leadership Fable*
Pub: John Wiley & Sons, Incorporated
Ed: Patrick M. Lencioni. **Released:** April 2002. **Price:** $22.95. **Description:** Analysis of a hypothetical tale of the CEO of a struggling, high-profile firm with a dysfunctional executive team.

38003 ■ *"Five Steps to the Corner Office" in Canadian Business (Vol. 80, March 12, 2007, No. 6, pp. 36)*
Pub: Rogers Media
Ed: Marlene Rego. **Description:** Chief executive of Rona Retail Canada Inc., Robert Dutton, and chief executive of Sysco Food Services Winnipeg, Kim Doherty explain the way they reached the top of their careers.

38004 ■ *"Five Steps to an Effective Meeting" in Hawaii Business (Vol. 53, March 2008, No. 9, pp. 55)*
Pub: Hawaii Business Publishing
Ed: Jason Ubay. **Description:** Identifying goals and writing them down can help in knowing what needs get done. Engaging everyone is a way to get cooperation in reaching the goals set. Other tips on how to have an effective meeting are discussed.

38005 ■ *"Five Steps for Handling Independent Contractors" in Hawaii Business (Vol. 53, January 2008, No. 7, pp. 49)*
Pub: Hawaii Business Publishing
Ed: Jason Ubay. **Description:** Small companies should be cautious in dealing with independent contractors. They must understand that they cannot dictate specific operational procedures, job duties, standards of conduct and performance standards to the contractors, and they cannot interfere with the evaluation and training of the contractors' employees. Tips on negotiating with independent contractors are given.

38006 ■ *"Five Tips for New Managers" in Hawaii Business (Vol. 53, November 2007, No. 5, pp. 59)*
Pub: Hawaii Business Publishing
Ed: Jason Ubay. **Description:** New managers should remember to know what their roles are, learn from others, build an infrastructure according to the customer's needs, communicate professionally and have consideration.

38007 ■ *"Ford Executive Pay Could Fuel Tensions" in Globe & Mail (April 6, 2007, pp. B7)*
Pub: CTVglobemedia Publishing Inc.
Ed: John D. Stoll; Terry Kosdrosky; Chad Clinton. **Description:** The likely tension between workers and management over the $62 million offer of Ford Motor Co. to its top executives is discussed.

38008 ■ *"Former Mayor Driving $500 Million Real Estate Equity Fund" in The Business Journal - Serving Phoenix and the Valley of the Sun (Vol. 28, August 15, 2008, No. 50, pp. 1)*
Pub: American City Business Journals, Inc.
Ed: Jan Buchholz. **Description:** Paul John, the former mayor of Phoenix, is establishing a $500 million real estate asset management fund. The fund is dubbed Southwest Next Capital Management and has attracted three local partners, namely Joseph Meyer, Jay Michalowski, and James Mullany, who all have background in finance and construction.

38009 ■ *"Former Synthes Officers Receive Prison Sentences" in Wall Street Journal Eastern Edition (November 22 , 2011, pp. B4)*
Pub: Dow Jones & Company Inc.
Ed: Peter Loftus. **Description:** Michael D. Huggins, formerly chief operating officer of medical-device maker Synthes Ltd., and Thomas B. Higgins, formerly the president of Synthes spine unit, were given prison sentences of nine months while a third executive, John J. Walsh, formerly director of regulatory and clinical affairs in the spine division, was given a five-month sentence for their involvement in the promotion of the unauthorized use of a bone cement produced by the company.

38010 ■ *"Formulating Policy With a Parallel Organization" in Strategy & Leadership (Vol. 38, September-October 2010, No. 5, pp. 33-38)*
Pub: Emerald Inc.
Ed: Dale E. Zand, Thomas F. Hawk. **Description:** A study analyzes a case to examine the parallel organization concept and its successful implementation by a CEO to integrate independent divisions of a firm. Findings reveal that the implementation of the parallel organization improved the policy formulation, strategic planning profitability of the firm while also better integrating its independent divisions.

38011 ■ *"Forsys Metals Corporation Goes "Live" With Q4's On-Demand Disclosure Management Software" in Canadian Corporate News (May 16, 2007)*
Pub: Comtex News Network Inc.
Description: Forsys Metals Corp. selected Q4 Web Systems to automate its corporate website disclosure with Q4's software platform which also automates and simplifies many of the administrative tasks that Forsys was doing manually, allowing them to focus their internal resources on the business.

38012 ■ *"Four Lessons in Adaptive Leadership" in Harvard Business Review (Vol. 88, November 2010, No. 11, pp. 86)*
Pub: Harvard Business School Publishing
Ed: Michael Useem. **Description:** Four key factors to effective leadership are presented. These are establishing a personal link, making sound and timely

decisions, developing a common purpose while avoiding personal gain, and ensuring that objectives are clear without micromanaging those implementing them.

38013 ■ *"Fox" in Brandweek (Vol. 49, April 21, 2008, No. 16, pp. SR3)*
Pub: VNU Business Media, Inc.
Ed: John Consoli. **Description:** Provides contact information for sales and marketing personnel for the Fox network as well as a listing of the station's top programming and an analysis of the current season and the target audience for those programs running in the current season. In terms of upfront advertising dollars, it looks as if Fox will be competing against NBC for third place due to its success at courting the 18-49-year-old male demographic.

38014 ■ *"Fox Cable Entertainment Networks" in Brandweek (Vol. 49, April 21, 2008, No. 16, pp. SR10)*
Pub: VNU Business Media, Inc.
Ed: Anthony Crupi. **Description:** Provides contact information for sales and marketing personnel for the Fox Cable Entertainment networks as well as a listing of the station's top programming and an analysis of the current season and the target audience for those programs running in the current season.

38015 ■ *"Fraud Alleged at Norshield; Investors Out $215 Million" in Globe & Mail (March 8, 2007, pp. B1)*
Pub: CTVglobemedia Publishing Inc.
Ed: Paul Waldie. **Description:** The investigation of the diversion of $215 million in investors' money by the management of Norshield Asset Management (Canada) Ltd. is described.

38016 ■ *"Friendly Ice Cream Corporation" in Ice Cream Reporter (Vol. 23, August 20, 2010, No. 9, pp. 8)*
Pub: Ice Cream Reporter
Description: Friendly Ice Cream Corporation appointed Andrea M. McKenna as vice president of marketing and chief marketing officer.

38017 ■ *"Friends With Money" in Canadian Business (Vol. 81, Summer 2008, No. 9, pp. 22)*
Pub: Rogers Media Ltd.
Description: Two of the most well connected managers in Canadian capital markets Rob Farquharson and Brian Gibson will launch Panoply Capital Asset Management in June. The investment management company aims to raise a billion dollars from institutions and high-net worth individuals.

38018 ■ *"From the Battlefield to the Boardroom" in Business Horizons (Vol. 51, March-April 2008, No. 2, pp. 79)*
Pub: Elsevier Advanced Technology Publications
Ed: Catherine M. Dalton. **Description:** Effective intelligence gathering, a thorough understanding of the mission, efficient use of resources, and strategic leadership are vital to achieving success in business as well as in the battlefield. Examples of effective leadership in the battle of Gettysburg are cited.

38019 ■ *"Fuel for Thought" in Canadian Business (Vol. 81, April 14, 2008, No. 6, pp. 18)*
Pub: Rogers Media
Ed: John Gray. **Description:** Discusses a web poll of 133 CEOs and other business leaders that shows that they predict oil prices to increase to US $113 per barrel over the 2008 to 2010 timeframe. Most of the respondents did not favor cutting gas taxes but this group wants the government to cut taxes on fuel-efficient vehicles and increase subsidies to local transit systems.

38020 ■ *"The Future of Work" in Business Strategy Review (Vol. 21, Autumn 2010, No. 3, pp. 16)*
Pub: Blackwell Publishers Ltd.
Ed: Lynda Gratton. **Description:** Work is universal. But how, why, where and when we work has never been so open to individual interpretation. The certainties of the past have been replaced by ambiguity, questions and the steady hum of technology. Now, in a groundbreaking research project covering 21 global companies and more than 200 executives, the author is making sense of the future of work.

38021 ■ *"Gail Lissner; Vice-President, Appraisal Research Counselors" in Crain's Chicago Business (Vol. 31, May 5, 2008, No. 18, pp. 28)*
Pub: Crain Communications, Inc.
Ed: Phuong Ly. **Description:** Profile of Gail Lissner who is the vice-president of the Appraisal Research Counselors, a company that puts out the quarterly 'Residential Benchmark Report,' in which Ms. Lissner co-authors and is considered a must-read in the industry. Ms. Lissner has risen to become one of the most sought-after experts on the Chicago market considering real estate.

38022 ■ *"Gail Mukaihata Hannemann" in Hawaii Business (Vol. 53, January 2008, No. 7, pp. 24)*
Pub: Hawaii Business Publishing
Ed: Cathy S. Cruz-George. **Description:** Discusses the Girl Scouts of Hawaii which has altered its business model to become more appealing to young girls in the 21st century. Gail Mukaihata Hanneman, the chief executive officer of the nonprofit organization, states that the Girl Scouts has consolidated some of its operations to increase efficiency. Her views on what employers must learn about the youth and on the adults' roles in developing the younger generation are given.

38023 ■ *"A Gambling Man: Career Transitions that Put a Vegas Hotshot on Top" in Black Enterprise (Vol. 37, October 2006, No. 3, pp. 89)*
Pub: Earl G. Graves Publishing Co. Inc.
Ed: Laura Egodigwe. **Description:** Interview with Lorenzo Creighton, president and chief operating officer of MGM Mirage's New York-New York Hotel and Casino. Creighton talks about his history and the challenges he faced since he didn't come from the casino industry.

38024 ■ *"Game Changer" in Canadian Business (Vol. 83, June 15, 2010, No. 10, pp. 52)*
Pub: Rogers Media Ltd.
Ed: Jordan Timm. **Description:** Ubisoft chose Ontario to be the site for its new development studio and it has appointed Jade Raymond as its managing director. Raymond was born in Montreal in 1975 and studied computer science at McGill. Raymond is said to possess the understanding of the game industry's technical, art, and business components.

38025 ■ *The Game-Changer: How Every Leader Can Drive Everyday Innovation*
Pub: Crown Business
Ed: A.G. Lafley, Ram Charan. **Price:** $27.50. **Description:** Management guru Charan and Proctor & Gamble CEO Lafley provide lessons to encourage innovation at all levels, including how to hire for and encourage an environment of communication and tangible work processes.

38026 ■ *"A General's Pep Talk Taught Me That a Leader Can't Lose Sight of What It Means To Be a Grunt" in Inc. (March 2008, pp. 85-86)*
Pub: Gruner & Jahr USA Publishing
Ed: Joel Spolsky. **Description:** An Israeli general offers leadership advice to entrepreneurs.

38027 ■ *"Generation Y Goes To Work; Management" in The Economist (Vol. 390, January 3, 2009, No. 8612, pp. 48)*
Pub: The Economist Newspaper Inc.
Description: Unemployment rates among people in their 20s has increased significantly and there is a lower turnover in crisis-hit firms, which has made it more difficult to simply find another job if one is unsatisfied with the management style of his or her company. Managers are adopting a more command-and-control approach which is the antithesis of the open, collaborative style that younger employees prefer.

38028 ■ *"Get Back To Business Planning Fundamentals" in Entrepreneur (October 24, 2008)*
Pub: Entrepreneur Media Inc.
Ed: Tim Berry. **Description:** During a recession it is important to know what adjustment to make to your business plan. Some fundamentals to remember include: watching things more closely by tracking progress on cash, sales, new projects, customer satisfaction, ad spending and expenses; looking for built-in indicators such as what drives sales or expenses; watching what drives cash flow; and do not make mistakes such as laying off experienced employees too soon.

38029 ■ *Get in the Game: 8 Elements of Perseverance that Make the Difference*
Pub: Gotham/Penguin Group Incorporated
Ed: Cal Ripken, Jr.; Donald T. Phillips. **Released:** April 10, 2008. **Price:** $15.00. **Description:** Guidebook written by superstar athlete Cal Ripkin to help managers and entrepreneurs achieve success.

38030 ■ *"Get Online Quick in the Office Or in the Field" in Contractor (Vol. 56, October 2009, No. 10, pp. 47)*
Pub: Penton Media, Inc.
Ed: William Feldman; Patti Feldman. **Description:** Contractors can set up a web site in minutes using the www.1and1.com website. Verizon's Novatel MIFI 2372 HSPA personal hotspot device lets contractors go online in the field. The StarTech scalable business management system helps contractors manage daily operations.

38031 ■ *"Get Over Your Fear of Change" in Canadian Business (Vol. 83, June 15, 2010, No. 10, pp. 38)*
Pub: Rogers Media Ltd.
Ed: Michelle Magnan. **Description:** Organizational behavior professor Chip Heath says that resistance to change is based on the conflict between our analytical, rational side and our emotional side that is in love with comfort. Heath states that businesses tend to focus on the negatives during an economic crisis while they should be focusing on what is working and ways to do more of that.

38032 ■ *"Get Your Mojo Working" in Small Business Opportunities (March 2011)*
Pub: Harris Publications Inc.
Ed: Holly G. Green. **Description:** Ways to keep employees engaged and productive are discussed.

38033 ■ *"Getting Drowned Out by the Brainstorm" in Canadian Business (Vol. 83, June 15, 2010, No. 10, pp. 91)*
Pub: Rogers Media Ltd.
Ed: Joe Castaldo. **Description:** A study reveals that people generate more ideas when they do it alone rather than as part of a brainstorming group. The limited range of ideas is due to the fixation of group members on the first idea that gets offered.

38034 ■ *Getting to Innovation: How Asking the Right Questions Generates the Great Ideas Your Company Needs*
Pub: AMACOM
Ed: Arthur B. VanGundy. **Released:** July 2007. **Price:** $29.95. **Description:** Guide to achieving the critical first step in formulating creative and useful ideas that lead to results for any small company.

38035 ■ *Getting Things Done*
Pub: Warner Books Inc.
Ed: David Allen. **Released:** December 2002. **Price:** $16.00. **Description:** Methods for reducing stress and increasing performance are described.

38036 ■ *Getting Things Done: The Art of Stress-Free Productivity*
Pub: Penguin Books USA Inc.
Ed: David Allen. **Released:** December 2002. **Price:** $16.00. **Description:** Coach and management consultant recommends methods for stress-free performance under the premise that productivity is directly related to our ability to relax.

38037 ■ *Getting to Yes: Negotiating Agreement Without Giving In*
Pub: Penguin Books USA Inc.
Ed: Roger Fisher, William L. Ury, Bruce Patton. **Released:** December 1991. **Price:** $15.00. **Description:** Strategies for negotiating mutually acceptable agreements in all types of conflict.

38038 ■ *The Girl's Guide to Being a Boss (Without Being a Bitch): Valuable Lessons, Smart Suggestions, and True Stories for Succeeding*
Pub: Random Housing Publishing Group
Ed: Caitlin Friedman; Kimberly Yorio. **Released:** April 2006.

38039 ■ *"The Global Talent Hunt" in Business Strategy Review (Vol. 21, Spring 2010, No. 1, pp. 78)*
Pub: Wiley-Blackwell
Ed: Richard Emerton. **Description:** Richard Emerton explains how the new 'triple context' of economy, environment and society will have profound implications for human resource practices. He suggests that viewing talent as abundant is the right perspective for a manager.

38040 ■ *"GM Is On the Road Again" in Canadian Business (Vol. 83, September 14, 2010, No. 15, pp. 14)*
Pub: Rogers Media Ltd.
Ed: Thomas Watson. **Description:** Former General Motors CEO Rick Wagoner has been credited for single-handedly putting the automaker back on track before he was forced to resign and GM was restructured by the government. GM earned $2.19 billion the first half of 2010 after losing more than $80 billion in the three years leading up to its failure. GM's comeback is discussed.

38041 ■ *"Go East" in Canadian Business (Vol. 80, February 26, 2007, No. 5, pp. 21)*
Pub: Rogers Media
Ed: Claire Gagne. **Description:** The managerial strategies followed by Doug Doust, who left Wal-Mart to take over the position of senior vice-president of supply chain at the struggling Seiyu of Japan are presented.

38042 ■ *Go Put Your Strengths to Work*
Pub: Free Press/Simon & Schuster
Ed: Marcus Buckingham. **Price:** $30.00. **Description:** A guide to being more productive, focused and creative at work.

38043 ■ *"Go Team? Why Building a Cohesive Organization Is a Necessary Exercise" in Black Enterprise (Vol. 38, February 2008, No. 7, pp. 66)*
Pub: Earl G. Graves Publishing Co. Inc.
Ed: Angeli Rasbury. **Description:** Tips to help manage successful as well as productive teams are outlined for small business managers.

38044 ■ *"Going for the APEX" in Women In Business (Vol. 62, September 2010, No. 3, pp. 28)*
Pub: American Business Women's Association
Description: Information about the American Business Women's Association (ABWA) professional development tools, which keep members focused on personal excellence, is presented. The organization recently launched the APEX (Achieving Personal Excellence) Award to honor women who are making a commitment to themselves.

38045 ■ *"Gold Medal" in Canadian Business (Vol. 79, October 9, 2006, No. 20, pp. 57)*
Pub: Rogers Media
Ed: Andrew Wahl. **Description:** Creativity skills and management strategies of Rob McEwen, founder and chief executive officer of Goldcorp Inc., are presented.

38046 ■ *"Good Decisions. Bad Outcomes" in Harvard Business Review (Vol. 88, December 2010, No. 12, pp. 40)*
Pub: Harvard Business School Publishing
Ed: Dan Ariely. **Description:** Suggestions are provided for developing and implementing improved reward systems that in turn produce better decision-making processes. These include documenting critical assumptions and changing mind sets.

38047 ■ *Good to Great: Why Some Companies Make the Leap..and Others Don't*
Pub: HarperInformation
Ed: Jim Collins. **Released:** October 2001. **Price:** $29.99. **Description:** Management styles for growing a modern business.

38048 ■ *"Goodbye, Locker Room: Hello, Boardroom" in Inc. (Vol. 33, October 2011, No. 8, pp. 30)*
Pub: Inc. Magazine
Ed: Issie Lapowsky, Kasey Wehrum. **Description:** In 2005, the National Football League started the NFL Business Management and Entrepreneurial Program. Since the onset of the program, 700 players have participated in the program which takes place at the business schools of Harvard, the University of Pennsylvania, Northwestern and Stanford.

38049 ■ *"Goodwill Haunts Local Companies; Bad Buyouts During Boom Times Producing Big Writedowns" in Crain's Chicago Business (Apr. 28, 2008)*
Pub: Crain Communications, Inc.
Ed: Ann Saphir. **Description:** Many companies are having to face the reality that they overpaid for acquisitions made in better economic times; investors often dismiss such one-time charges as mere accounting adjustments but writeoffs related to past acquisitions can signal future problems because they mean the expected profits that justified the purchase have not materialized. Writeoffs are particularly worrisome for firms with a lot of debt and whose banks require them to have enough assets to back up their borrowings.

38050 ■ *"Grace Puma; Senior Vice-President of Strategic Sourcing, United Airlines" in Crain's Chicago Business (May 5, 2008)*
Pub: Crain Communications, Inc.
Ed: John Rosenthal. **Description:** Profile of Grace Puma who is the senior vice-president of strategic sourcing at United Airlines and is responsible for cutting costs at the company in a number of ways including scheduling safety inspections at the same time as routine maintenance, thereby reducing the downtime of each aircraft by five days as well as replacing a third of her staff with outside talent.

38051 ■ *"Great Canadian's President Folds His Cards" in Globe & Mail (February 21, 2006, pp. B4)*
Pub: CTVglobemedia Publishing Inc.
Ed: Peter Kennedy. **Description:** The reasons behind the resignation of Anthony Martin as president of Great Canadian Gaming Corp. are presented.

38052 ■ *"The Green Conversation" in Harvard Business Review (Vol. 86, September 2008, No. 9, pp. 58)*
Pub: Harvard Business School Press
Description: Six guidelines are presented for addressing and benefiting from environmentally conscious corporate decision making and practices. Topics covered include marketing, supply chain, and leadership.

38053 ■ *"Grooming Your Online Persona" in Women In Business (Vol. 62, June 2010, No. 2, pp. 36)*
Pub: American Business Women's Association
Ed: Diane Stafford. **Description:** Employees' use of online social networks could become a basis on how their employers, clients, or business partners would judge them. Personal details, pictures and other online data should be filtered to avoid inappropriate or uncomfortable situations and distinguish personal from professional or work life.

38054 ■ *Groundswell: Winning in a World Transformed by Social Technologies*
Pub: Harvard Business School Press
Ed: Charlene Li, Josh Bernoff. **Released:** 2008. **Price:** $29.95. **Description:** Corporate executives are struggling with a new trend: people using online social technologies (blogs, social networking sites, YouTube, podcasts) to discuss products and companies, write their own news, and find their own deals.

38055 ■ *Group Genius: The Creative Power of Collaboration*
Pub: Basic Books/Perseus Books Group
Ed: Keith Sawyer. **Released:** March 2008. **Price:** $16.95 paperback. **Description:** Organizations can foster creativity and innovation through discussion, argumentation and group activities.

38056 ■ *Groups in Context: Leadership and Participation in Small Groups*
Pub: McGraw-Hill Companies Inc.
Contact: Deven Sharma, President
Ed: Gerald L. Wilson. **Released:** June 2004. **Price:** $62.98. **Description:** Small group communication skills for the workplace, in churches, social groups, or civic organizations.

38057 ■ *Growing Business Handbook: Inspirational Advice from Successful Entrepreneurs and Fast-Growing UK Companies*
Pub: Kogan Page, Limited
Contact: Ben Glover, Director of Marketing
Ed: Adam Jolly. **Released:** February 2007. **Price:** $49.95. **Description:** Tips for growing and running a successful business are covered, focusing on senior managers in middle market and SME companies.

38058 ■ *Growing and Managing a Small Business: An Entrepreneurial Perspective*
Pub: Houghton Mifflin College Division
Ed: Kathleen R. Allen. **Released:** July 2006. **Price:** $105.27. **Description:** Introduction to business ownership and management from startup through growth.

38059 ■ *"Growing Pains" in Canadian Business (Vol. 80, November 19, 2007, No. 23, pp. 41)*
Pub: Rogers Media
Ed: Lauren McKeon. **Description:** Employee promotions must be done with consideration to the effects of ill-prepared leadership, which include high worker turnover, low morale, and ineffective management. Organizations must handle the transition period involved in promotion by setting clear expectations, providing guidelines on approaching different situations, and by welcoming the promoted employees; impacts are further analyzed.

38060 ■ *A Guide to the Project Management Body of Knowledge*
Pub: Project Management Institute
Contact: Peter Monkhouse, Chairman
Ed: Project Management Institute. **Released:** July 31, 2009. **Price:** $65.95. **Description:** A guide for project management using standard language, with new data flow diagrams; the Identify Stakeholders and Collect Requirements processes defined; and with greater attention placed on how knowledge areas integrate in the context of initiating, planning, executing, monitoring and controlling, and closing process groups.

38061 ■ *"Guidelines For Family Business Boards of Directors" in Family Business Review (Vol. 19, June 2006, No. 2, pp. 147)*
Pub: Family Firm Institute
Contact: Judy L. Green, President
Ed: Suzanne Lane. **Description:** Effective corporate governance standards for boards of directors of family businesses are examined.

38062 ■ *"Guts Not Included" in Canadian Business (Vol. 81, March 31, 2008, No. 5, pp. 46)*
Pub: Rogers Media
Ed: Andrew Wahl. **Description:** Executives need the vision to create a strategy that prepares for an uncertain future in light of growing global competition. Canadian business leaders have the right skills and education but do not have enough tolerance for risk.

38063 ■ *"Halls Give Hospital Drive $11 Million Infusion" in The Business Journal-Serving Metropolitan Kansas City (Vol. 26, July 18, 2008)*
Pub: American City Business Journals, Inc.
Ed: Rob Roberts. **Description:** Don Hall, chairman of Hallmark Cards Inc., and eight family members have announced that they will give $11 million to

Children's Mercy Hospitals and Clinics for its $800 million expansion plan. Hall Family Foundation president Bill Hall that contributions such as that for Children's Mercy reflect the charitable interests of the foundation's board and founders. The possible impacts of the Hall's donation are analyzed.

38064 ■ *The Halo Effect: And the Eight Other Business Delusions That Deceive Managers*
Pub: Free Press/Simon & Schuster Inc.
Ed: Phil Rosenzweig. **Released:** January 6, 2009. **Price:** $16.00 paperback. **Description:** Nine common business delusions, including the halo effect (which the author describes as the need to attribute positive qualities to successful individuals and companies), are illustrated using case studies of Lego, Cisco, and Nokia to show how adhering to myths can be bad for any business.

38065 ■ *"Handle With Care" in Hawaii Business (Vol. 53, October 2007, No. 5, pp. 66)*
Pub: Hawaii Business Publishing
Ed: Kenneth Sheffield. **Description:** Discusses a fiduciary, who may be a board member, business owner, or a trustee, and is someone who supervises and manages the affairs and the resources of a principal. Fiduciary duties, which include accounting, cost review and risk management, must be served with the benefit of the principal as the priority. Ways of breaching fiduciary duties and how to avoid them are discussed.

38066 ■ *"Harding Brews Success at Anheuser-Busch" in Black Enterprise (Vol. 37, February 2007, No. 7, pp. 1)*
Pub: Earl G. Graves Publishing Co. Inc.
Ed: Mashaun D. Simon. **Description:** Profile of Michael S. Harding, president and CEO of Anheuser-Busch packaging Group. Harding oversees five business units, 15 facilities, and over 2,300 workers.

38067 ■ *"HBC Enlists IBM to Help Dress Up Its On-Line Shopping" in Globe & Mail (February 7, 2006, pp. B3)*
Pub: CTVglobemedia Publishing Inc.
Ed: Simon Avery. **Description:** The details of management contract between Hudson's Bay Co. and International Business Machines Corp. are presented.

38068 ■ *"He Said, She Said: Stay Clear of Gossip In the Workplace With a Mature Attitude" in Black Enterprise (February 2008)*
Pub: Earl G. Graves Publishing Co. Inc.
Ed: Akoto Ofori-Atta. **Description:** It is important for employees to avoid gossip in the workplace because of the negative impact; it is recommended focusing on conversations that will help an individual's professional goals.

38069 ■ *"Health Nuts and Bolts" in Entrepreneur (Vol. 36, April 2008, No. 4, pp. 24)*
Pub: Entrepreneur Media, Inc.
Ed: Jacquelyn Lynn. **Description:** Encouraging employees to develop good eating habits can promote productivity at work. Ways on how to improve employee eating habits include employers setting a good example themselves and offering employees healthy options. Other details about the topic are discussed.

38070 ■ *"Heavy Duty: The Case Against Packing Lightly" in Crain's Chicago Business (Vol. 31, April 21, 2008, No. 16, pp. 29)*
Pub: Crain Communications, Inc.
Ed: Sarah A. Klein. **Description:** Penelope Biggs, a Northern Trust executive who manages sales teams in North America, Europe and Asia gives advice on traveling abroad for business including time management skills, handling time-zone hops and avoiding jet-lag.

38071 ■ *"Help, For Some" in Canadian Business (Vol. 81, December 8, 2008, No. 21, pp. 10)*
Pub: Rogers Media Ltd.
Ed: Joe Castaldo. **Description:** Over 80 percent of Canadian chief executives believe that government bailouts merely reward mediocre management and encourages companies to take risks because they know the government will help prevent their bankruptcy. Respondents to a COMPAS online survey believe bailouts are unfair for properly managed companies.

38072 ■ *"Henry Mintzberg: Still the Zealous Skeptic and Scold" in Strategy and Leadership (Vol. 39, March-April 2011, No. 2, pp. 4)*
Pub: Emerald Group Publishing Inc.
Ed: Robert J. Allio. **Description:** Henry Mintzberg, professor at the McGill University in Montreal, Canada, shares his thoughts on issues such as inappropriate methods in management education and on trends in leadership and management. Mintzberg believes that US businesses are facing serious management and leadership challenges.

38073 ■ *"The Hidden Advantages of Quiet Bosses" in Harvard Business Review (Vol. 88, December 2010, No. 12, pp. 28)*
Pub: Harvard Business School Publishing
Ed: Adam M. Grant, Francesca Gino, David A. Hofmann. **Description:** Research on organizations behavior indicates that, while extroverts most often become managers, introvert managers paired with proactive employees make a highly efficient and effective combination.

38074 ■ *"High Energy: Gaurdie Banister Joins Aera As President and CEO" in Black Enterprise (Vol. 38, July 2008, No. 12, pp. 30)*
Pub: Earl G. Graves Publishing Co. Inc.
Ed: Brenda Porter. **Description:** Gaurdie Banister Jr. has been appointed president and CEO of Aera Energy L.L.C., becoming one of the first African Americans in the nation to run a major energy corporation. His plans for the firm include utilizing new, sophisticated technologies in order to unlock the 3-1/2 billion barrels of resources the company has on their books in a safe and environmentally friendly way. He also hopes to increase production and maintain cost leadership.

38075 ■ *High Performance with High Integrity*
Pub: Harvard Business School Press
Ed: Ben W. Heineman Jr. **Released:** May 28, 2008. **Price:** $18.00. **Description:** The dark side of today's free-market capitalist system is examined. Under intense pressure to make the numbers, executives and employees are tempted to cut corners, falsify accounts, or worse. In today's unforgiving environment that can lead to catastrophe for a small company.

38076 ■ *"Higher Education" in Canadian Business (Vol. 79, October 23, 2006, No. 21, pp. 129)*
Pub: Rogers Media
Ed: Erin Pooley; Laura Bogomolny; Joe Castaldo; Michelle Magnan. **Description:** Details of some Canadian business schools, where students can simultaneously pursue a master of business administration degree and also be employed on a part time basis, are presented.

38077 ■ *"His Brother's Keeper: a Mentor Learns the True Meaning of Leadership" in Black Enterprise (Vol. 37, December 2006, No. 5, pp. 69)*
Pub: Earl G. Graves Publishing Co. Inc.
Ed: Laura Egodigwe. **Description:** Interview with Keith R. Wyche of Pitney Bowes Management Services which discusses the relationship between a mentor and mentee as well as sponsorship.

38078 ■ *"The Hispanic Business 100 Most Influential Hispanics" in Hispanic Business (October 2007, pp. 30)*
Pub: Hispanic Business
Description: Profiles of the one hundred Hispanic business leaders are presented.

38079 ■ *"Hispanic Executives Continue Their Rise to Prominence Amid a Shaky Economy" in Hispanic Business (January-February 2009, pp. 12-14)*
Pub: Hispanic Business
Ed: Michael Bowker. **Description:** Hispanic Business Media's 2009 Corporate Elite winners defied expectations and a tough economy and rose to the top of their industries; innovation being cited as key to growth of Hispanic-owned companies.

38080 ■ *"Hispanics Take Seats in America's Boardrooms" in Hispanic Business (January-February 2009, pp. 24, 28)*
Pub: Hispanic Business
Ed: Joshua Molina. **Description:** Three percent of those serving as directors of Fortune 500 companies in America are Hispanic. A listing of forty of these directors is included.

38081 ■ *"Holiday Cheer" in Business Journal-Serving Phoenix & the Valley of the Sun (Vol. 31, December 3, 2010, No. 13, pp. 1)*
Pub: Phoenix Business Journal
Ed: Lynn Ducey, Mike Sunnucks. **Description:** Results of a study conducted by Challenger, Gray & Christmas Inc., shows that 68 percent of companies are planning holiday parties in 2010, up slightly from 62 percent in 2009. About 53 percent of those having holiday parties are holding them on company premises.

38082 ■ *"Holidays Should Foster Mutual Respect" in Women In Business (Vol. 61, October-November 2009, No. 5, pp. 33)*
Pub: American Business Women's Association
Ed: Diane Stafford. **Description:** Workplaces have modified the way year-end holiday celebrations are held in an effort to promote mutual respect. The workers' varying religious beliefs, political affiliations, and other differences have brought about the modifications. The importance of developing mutual understanding is emphasized as a mechanism to stimulate successful business ties.

38083 ■ *"Hourly Payment and Volunteering" in Academy of Management Journal (August 2007)*
Pub: Academy of Management
Contact: Ming-Jer Chen, President
Ed: Sanford E. DeVoe, Jeffrey Pfeffer. **Description:** Brief description about theoretically important class of work, which is freely undertaken without remuneration, is presented.

38084 ■ *"How Anger Poisons Decision Making" in Harvard Business Review (Vol. 88, September 2010, No. 9, pp. 26)*
Pub: Harvard Business School Publishing
Ed: Jennifer S. Lerner, Katherine Shonk. **Description:** Importance of accountability in mitigating the negative effects of anger on the decision making process is stressed.

38085 ■ *How to Become a Great Boss: The Rules for Getting and Keeping the Best Employees*
Pub: Hyperion Special Markets
Ed: Jeffrey J. Fox. **Released:** May 15, 2002. **Price:** $16.95. **Description:** The book offers valuable advice to any manager or entrepreneur to improve leadership and management skills. Topics covered include: hiring, managing, firing, partnership and competition, self and organization, employee performance, attitude, and priorities.

38086 ■ *"How Fast Can This Thing Go Anyway?" in Inc. (March 2008, pp. 94-101)*
Pub: Gruner & Jahr USA Publishing
Ed: Stephanie Clifford. **Description:** Founder of Zipcar, an auto rental company, tell how he brought a new CEO into the company to boost revenue. The new CEO instituted a seven-step strategy to increase business.

38087 ■ *"How the Generation Gap Can Hurt Your Business" in Agency Sales Magazine (Vol. 39, November 2009, No. 10, pp. 16)*
Pub: MANA
Ed: Jack Foster. **Description:** Now that there are four generations of people in the workplace, there is a need to add flexibility to communications for

independent manufacturers representatives. Managers can encourage the younger generations to do the research and the boomers to process information and let each side report to the other.

38088 ■ *"How Has City Golf Privatization Played?" in Business Courier (Vol. 27, September 10, 2010, No. 19, pp. 1)*
Pub: Business Courier
Ed: Dan Monk. **Description:** It was reported that private contractors are getting more revenue from fewer golfers on city-owned courses in Cincinnati, Ohio. In 1998, the city handed over seven municipal courses to private management. However, some believe that the city has escalated a price war among the region's golf courses.

38089 ■ *"How Hierarchy Can Hurt Strategy Execution" in Harvard Business Review (Vol. 88, July-August 2010, No. 7-8, pp. 74)*
Pub: Harvard Business School Publishing
Description: A series of charts illustrate Harvard Business Review's Advisory Council survey results regarding perceptions of strategy development and execution identifying obstacles and key factors affecting implementation.

38090 ■ *"How In the World?" in Business Strategy Review (Vol. 21, Spring 2010, No. 1, pp. 12)*
Pub: Wiley-Blackwell
Ed: Stuart Crainer. **Description:** We may think of management as a recent phenomenon, but its roots lie in the first organizing activities of our ancestors. The author looks a the emergence of management as a profession. He finds that the road to modern management leads to a paradox and questions ways to change that.

38091 ■ *"How Investors React When Women Join Boards" in Harvard Business Review (Vol. 88, July-August 2010, No. 7-8, pp. 24)*
Pub: Harvard Business School Publishing
Ed: Andrew O'Connell. **Description:** Research reveals a cognitive bias in blockholders regarding the presence of women on boards of directors despite evidence showing that diversity improves results.

38092 ■ *How to Make Money with Social Media: Using New and Emerging Media to Grow Your Business*
Pub: FT Press
Ed: Jamie Turner, Reshma Shah. **Released:** October 1, 2010. **Price:** $24.99. **Description:** Marketers, executives, entrepreneurs are shown more effective ways to utilize Internet social media to make money. This guide brings together both practical strategies and proven execution techniques for driving maximum value from social media marketing.

38093 ■ *"How to Not Get Fired" in Entrepreneur (Vol. 37, September 2009, No. 9, pp. 62)*
Pub: Entrepreneur Media, Inc.
Ed: Brad Feld. **Description:** Advice on how chief executive officers (CEO) of venture capital funded firms can avoid being replaced is presented. A CEO should not be defensive of the prospect of being replaced. The CEO may also work with the investors and the board for a smooth transition.

38094 ■ *"How to Protect Your Job in a Recession" in Harvard Business Review (Vol. 86, September 2008, No. 9, pp. 113)*
Pub: Harvard Business School Press
Ed: Janet Banks; Diane Coutu. **Description:** Strategies are presented for enhancing one's job security. These include being a team player, empathizing with management, preserving optimism, and concentrating on the customer.

38095 ■ *How to Recognize and Reward Employees: 150 Ways to Inspire Peak Performance*
Pub: American Management Association
Contact: Charles R. Craig, Chairman
Ed: Donna Deeprose. **Released:** 2006. **Price:** $13.95.

38096 ■ *How Remarkable Women Lead: A Breakthrough Model for Work and Life*
Pub: Crown Business
Ed: Joanna Barsh, Susie Cranston. **Released:** September 24, 2009. **Price:** $27.50. **Description:** An introduction to remarkable women, from Time Inc.'s Ann Moore to Xerox's Anne Mulcahy, who recount their inspiring struggles.

38097 ■ *"How To Turn Your Efforts Into Results" in Green Industry Pro (Vol. 23, September 2011)*
Pub: Cygnus Business Media
Ed: Bob Coulter. **Description:** Working Smarter Training Challenge teaches that leaders are able to carry out solutions directly into their organization, develop skills and drive business results in key areas by creating a culture of energized workers who are able to take ownership of their performance as well as the performance of the company as a whole.

38098 ■ *"How to Turn Employee Conflict Into a Positive, Productive Force" in HR Specialist (Vol. 8, September 2010, No. 9, pp. 6)*
Pub: Capitol Information Group Inc.
Description: Ways to help manage a team of workers are presented, focusing on ways to avoid conflict within the group are discussed.

38099 ■ *How We Decide*
Pub: Houghton Mifflin Harcourt
Contact: Barry O'Callaghan, President
Ed: Jonah Lehrer. **Released:** February 2009. **Price:** $25.00. **Description:** Insights for entrepreneurs to help with decision making; the book describes potential traps such as negative information and how it carries more weight than positive information.

38100 ■ *How to Win Friends and Influence People*
Pub: Simon and Schuster Inc.
Contact: Carolyn Reidy, President
E-mail: carolyn.reidy@simonandschuster.com
Ed: Dale Carnegie. **Released:** February 15, 1990. **Price:** $7.99. **Description:** First published in 1937, this book helps people to understand human nature. The book teaches skills through underlying principles of dealing with people so that they feel important and appreciated.

38101 ■ *How to Write a Great Business Plan for Your Small Business in 60 Minutes or Less*
Pub: Atlantic Publishing
Ed: Sharon L. Fullen. **Released:** January 2006. **Price:** $39.95 includes CD-Rom. **Description:** A good business plan outlines goals and works as a company's resume to obtain funding, credit from suppliers, management of the operations and finances, promotion and marketing, and more.

38102 ■ *"How Yamana CEO First Struck Gold With Desert Sun" in Globe & Mail (February 27, 2006, pp. B3)*
Pub: CTVglobemedia Publishing Inc.
Ed: Andrew Willis. **Description:** The role of chief executive officer Peter Marronne of Yamana Gold Inc. in the acquisition of Desert Sun Mining Corp. is discussed.

38103 ■ *"HR Tech on the Go" in Workforce Management (Vol. 88, November 16, 2009, No. 12, pp. 1)*
Pub: Crain Communications Inc.
Ed: Ed Frauenheim. **Description:** Examination of the necessity of mobile access of human resources software applications that allow managers to recruit, schedule and train employees via their mobile devices; some industry leaders believe that mobile HR applications are vital while others see this new technology as hype.

38104 ■ *"Huberman Failing to Keep CTA on Track" in Crain's Chicago Business (Vol. 31, April 21, 2008, No. 16, pp. 22)*
Pub: Crain Communications, Inc.
Description: Discusses the deplorable service of CTA, the Chicago Transit Authority, as well as CTA President Ron Huberman who, up until last week had riders hoping he had the management skills necessary to fix the system's problems; Tuesday's event left hundreds of riders trapped for hours and thousands standing on train platforms along the Blue Line waiting for trains that never came.

38105 ■ *"Human Resource Management: Challenges for Graduate Education" in Business Horizons (Vol. 51, March-April 2008, No. 2, pp. 151)*
Pub: Elsevier Advanced Technology Publications
Ed: James C. Wimbush. **Description:** Human resource management education at the master's and doctoral degree levels is discussed. There is an ever-increasing need to produce human resource managers who understand the value of human resource management as a strategic business contributor. uman.

38106 ■ *"Hydronicahh - Everything in Modulation" in Contractor (Vol. 56, December 2009, No. 12, pp. 24)*
Pub: Penton Media, Inc.
Ed: Mark Eatherton. **Description:** Management and the environmental impact of a home hydronic system are discussed. Radiant windows have the potential to reduce energy consumption. A variable speed delta T pump is required for the construction of a hydronic wood pit.

38107 ■ *I Can't Believe I Get Paid to Do This*
Pub: Gold Leaf Publishing
Ed: Stacey Mayo. **Released:** October 2004. **Description:** This book is targeted to anyone unhappy in their current position. It is designed to help everyone feel good about their job.

38108 ■ *"Ian Delaney" in Canadian Business (Vol. 81, Summer 2008, No. 9, pp. 168)*
Pub: Rogers Media Ltd.
Ed: Joe Castaldo. **Description:** Interview with Ian Delaney who is the executive chairman of chemical company Sherritt International Corp.; Delaney previously worked as chief executive for a holding company owned by Peter Munk. Details of his beliefs, profession and family life are discussed.

38109 ■ *"IBM's Best-Kept Secret" in Canadian Business (Vol. 79, September 25, 2006, No. 19, pp. 19)*
Pub: Rogers Media
Ed: Andrew Wahl. **Description:** The contribution of IBM vice-president Steve Mills in company's development is discussed.

38110 ■ *"The Idea That Saved My Company" in Inc. (October 2007, pp. 42)*
Pub: Gruner & Jahr USA Publishing
Description: Profile of Chip Conley, founder of seventeen boutique hotels in the San Francisco, California Bay Area. Conley learned to overcome depression and regain his entrepreneurial inspiration, which in turn saved his company. Abraham Maslow, author of 'Toward of Psychology of Being' promoted Conley to write his own book, 'Peak: How Great Companies Get Their Mojo From Maslow'.

38111 ■ *"Ideas at Work: Total Communicator" in Business Strategy Review (Vol. 21, Autumn 2010, No. 3, pp. 10)*
Pub: Blackwell Publishers Ltd.
Ed: Stuart Crainer. **Description:** Vittorio Colao has been chief executive of Vodafone Group for two years. He brings to the company special experience as CEO of RCS MediaGroup in Milan, which publishes newspapers, magazines and books in Italy, Spain and France. Prior to RCS, he held other positions within Vodaphone. Colao shares his views on business, the global economy and leading Vodafone.

38112 ■ *"Ideas at Work: Total Communicator" in Business Strategy Review (Vol. 21, Autumn 2010, No. 3, pp. 10)*
Pub: Wiley-Blackwell
Ed: Stuart Crainer. **Description:** Vittorio Colao has been chief executive of Vodafone Group for two years. He brings to the company some special experience: from 2004-2006 he was CEO of RCS MediaGroup in Milan, which publishes newspapers, maga-

zines and books in Italy, Spain and France. Colao shares his views on business, the global economy and leading Vodafone.

38113 ■ *If Harry Potter Ran General Electric*
Pub: Doubleday Broadway Publishing Group
Ed: Tom Morris PhD. **Released:** May 16, 2006. **Price:** $26.00. **Description:** The values and timeless truths that underlie J.K. Rowling's popular Harry Potter books are discussed showing the lessons they offer to all individuals in their careers and daily lives.

38114 ■ *"I'll Be Back: For Entrepreneurs, Retirement Doesn't Mean Forever" in Inc. (February 2008, pp. 35-36)*
Pub: Gruner & Jahr USA Publishing
Ed: Leigh Buchanan. **Description:** Many entrepreneurs return to business after selling their companies and retiring. Advice is given to company owners for retirement planning.

38115 ■ *"In the Mobikey of Life" in Canadian Business (Vol. 81, July 21, 2008, No. 11, pp. 42)*
Pub: Rogers Media Ltd.
Ed: John Gray. **Description:** Toronto-based Route1 has created a data security software system that allows employees to access files and programs stored in the head office without permanently transferring data to the actual computer being used. Mobikey technology is useful in protecting laptops of chief executive officers, which contain confidential financial and customer data.

38116 ■ *"Increasing Building Work at Ryan Cos." in Crain's Chicago Business (Vol. 34, May 23, 2011, No. 21, pp. 6)*
Pub: Crain Communications Inc.
Ed: Eddie Baeb. **Description:** Profile of Tim Hennelly, who is working to make Ryan Company known as a pure builder rather than a developer-builder.

38117 ■ *Influence without Authority*
Pub: John Wiley and Sons Inc.
Ed: Allan R. Cohen; David L. Bradford. **Released:** March 2005. **Price:** $29.95.

38118 ■ *Instant Profit: Successful Strategies to Boost Your Margin and Increase the Profitability of Your Business*
Pub: McGraw-Hill Companies Inc.
Contact: Deven Sharma, President
Ed: Bradley J. Sugars. **Released:** December 2005. **Price:** $16.95 (US), $22.95 (Canadian). **Description:** Advice on management, money, marketing, and merchandising a successful small business is offered.

38119 ■ *"An Integrative Model of Experiencing and Responding to Mistreatment at Work" in Academy of Management Review (January 2008, pp. 76)*
Pub: ScholarOne, Inc.
Ed: Julie B. Olson-Buchanan, Wendy R. Boswell. **Description:** Integrative model with theoretical framework is presented to increase understanding of the effects of an individual's perceived experience of workplace mistreatment in dispute resolutions and the person's response to it.

38120 ■ *"Internationalization of Australian Family Businesses" in Family Business Review (Vol. 19, September 2006)*
Pub: Family Firm Institute
Contact: Judy L. Green, President
Ed: Chris Graves, Jill Thomas. **Description:** Concept that managerial capabilities of family firms lag behind those of non-family counterparts as they expand is discussed.

38121 ■ *"The Interplay Between Theory and Method" in Academy of Management Review (October 2007, pp. 1145)*
Pub: ScholarOne, Inc.
Ed: John Van Maanen, Jesper B. Sorensen, Terence R. Mitchell. **Description:** Discussion about the role of theory and method in particular organization and management studies, stressing the importance of balancing primacy of theory and evidence for better research results.

38122 ■ *"Into the Wild" in Inc. (October 2007, pp. 116-120, 122, 124, 126)*
Pub: Gruner & Jahr USA Publishing
Ed: Alison Stein Wellner. **Description:** Perry Klebahn, CEO of Timbuk2, manufacturer of messenger bags, tells how he took his top executives into the deep Wyoming wilderness in order to build employee team work skills. Other options for this type of team-building include cooking courses, changing a tire together, solving a kidnapping, or discussing ways to survive a nuclear winter.

38123 ■ *"Investing in the IT that Makes a Competitive Difference" in Harvard Business Review (Vol. 86, July-August 2008, No. 8, pp. 98)*
Pub: Harvard Business School Press
Ed: Andrew McAfee; Erik Brynjolfsson. **Description:** Components of a successful information technology management strategy are examined. These techniques are broad in spectrum, produce immediate results, are consistent and precise, facilitate monitoring, and promote enforceability.

38124 ■ *"Investors Finding Bay Area Deals" in Tampa Bay Business Journal (Vol. 29, November 6, 2009, No. 46, pp. 1)*
Pub: American City Business Journals
Ed: Margie Manning. **Description:** Private equity investors have found dozens of privately held companies in Tampa Bay area in Florida in which to invest $84 million fresh equity. Revenue generation, growth, solid management teams are some of the factors found by the investors on these companies which span a range of sizes and industries.

38125 ■ *"Irene Rosenfeld; Chairman and CEO, Kraft Foods Inc." in Crain's Chicago Business (Vol. 31, May 5, 2008, No. 18, pp. 31)*
Pub: Crain Communications, Inc.
Ed: David Sterrett. **Description:** Profile of Irene Rosenfeld who is the chairman and CEO of Kraft Foods Inc. and is entering the second year of a three-year plan to boost sales of well-known brands such as Oreo, Velveeta and Oscar Mayer while facing soaring commodity costs and a declining market-share. Ms. Rosenfeld's turnaround strategy also entails spending more on advertising and giving managers more control over their budgets and product development.

38126 ■ *"Is Business Ethics Getting Better? A Historical Perspective" in Business Ethics Quarterly (Vol. 21, April 2011, No. 2, pp. 335)*
Pub: Society for Business Ethics
Ed: Joanne B. Ciulla. **Description:** The question 'Is Business Ethics Getting Better?' as a heuristic for discussing the importance of history in understanding business and ethics is answered. The article uses a number of examples to illustrate how the same ethical problems in business have been around for a long time. It describes early attempts at the Harvard School of Business to use business history as a means of teaching students about moral and social values. In the end, the author suggests that history may be another way to teach ethics, enrich business ethics courses, and develop the perspective and vision in future business leaders.

38127 ■ *"Is Globalization Threatening U.S. Hispanic Progress?" in Hispanic Business (Vol. 30, September 2008, No. 9, pp. 16)*
Pub: Hispanic Business, Inc.
Ed: Jessica Haro. **Description:** Talented Hispanic employees are making progress within the increasingly diverse American corporate scenario. However, while some experts believe the induction of foreign professionals through globalization will not impact this progress, others feel it could hamper opportunities for American Hispanics.

38128 ■ *It's Not Just Who You Know: Transform Your Life (and Your Organization) by Turning Colleagues and Contacts into Lasting Relationships*
Pub: Crown Business Books
Ed: Tommy Spaulding. **Released:** August 10, 2010. **Price:** $23.00. **Description:** Tommy Spaulding teaches the reader how to reach out to others in order to create lasting relationships that go beyond superficial contacts.

38129 ■ *"It's Not 'Unprofessional' To Gossip At Work" in Harvard Business Review (Vol. 88, September 2010, No. 9, pp. 28)*
Pub: Harvard Business School Publishing
Ed: Joe Labianca. **Description:** Gossip can be of value to a company as an exchange of information and its use as a diagnostic tool can enable managers to address problems promptly and even head them off.

38130 ■ *"It's Time to Take Full Responsibility" in Harvard Business Review (Vol. 88, October 2010, No. 10, pp. 42)*
Pub: Harvard Business School Publishing
Ed: Rosabeth Moss Kanter. **Description:** A case for corporate responsibility is cited, focusing on long-term impact and the effects of public accountability.

38131 ■ *It's Your Ship*
Pub: Warner Books Inc.
Ed: Michael Abrashoff. **Released:** May 1, 2002. **Price:** $24.95. **Description:** Naval Captain D. Michael Abrashoff shares management principles he used to shape his ship, the U.S.S. Benfold, into a model of progressive leadership. Abrashoff revolutionized ways to face the challenges of excessive costs, low morale, sexual harassment, and constant turnover.

38132 ■ *"Janet Froetscher, CEO, United Way of Metropolitan Chicago" in Crain's Chicago Business (Vol. 31, May 5, 2008, No. 18, pp. 26)*
Pub: Crain Communications, Inc.
Ed: Emily Stone. **Description:** Profile of Janet Froetscher who is the CEO of United Way of Metropolitan Chicago who organized the country's largest-ever merger of non-profits with 53 smaller suburban chapters consolidating with the Chicago one. The consolidation saves $4 million a year with departments such as finance, information technology and communications which allows that money be spent funding job training, after-school programs and aid for 7,000 Hurricane Katrina evacuees living in the Chicago area.

38133 ■ *"Job Reviews: Annual Assessments Still the Norm" in HR Specialist (Vol. 8, September 2010, No. 9, pp. 1)*
Pub: Capitol Information Group Inc.
Description: An OfficeTeam survey of 500 HR professionals asked how their organizations conduct formal performance appraisals. Responses to the questions are examined.

38134 ■ *"Job Search Made Easy" in Black Enterprise (Vol. 38, January 2008, No. 6, pp. 54)*
Pub: Earl G. Graves Publishing Co. Inc.
Description: Profile of The Marquin Group's job portal called DiversityTalent.com. Marquin considered the challenges faced by corporations when recruiting senior executives; salaries, mortgage and relocation calculators for particular cities are provided.

38135 ■ *"Jobs Data Show A Slow Leak" in Barron's (Vol. 88, July 7, 2008, No. 27, pp. 34)*
Pub: Dow Jones & Co., Inc.
Ed: Gene Epstein. **Description:** In June 2008, the United States manufacturing sector showed an expansion, with the purchasing managers' index rising to 50.2 from 49.6; the unemployment rate in the US, which stayed steady at 5.5 percent in June 2008 is also discussed. Statistical data included.

38136 ■ *"Joe Wikert, General Manager, O'Reilly Technology Exchange" in Information Today (Vol. 26, February 2009, No. 2, pp. 21)*
Pub: Information Today, Inc.
Ed: Jamie Babbitt. **Description:** Joe Wikert, general manager of O'Reilly Technology Exchange discusses his plans to develop a free content model that will evolve with future needs. O'Reilly's major competitor is Google. Wikert plans to expand the firm's publishing program to include print, online, and in-person products and services.

38137 ■ *John F. Kennedy on Leadership: The Lessons and Legacy of a President*
Pub: AMACOM
Ed: John A. Barnes. **Released:** May 30, 2007. **Price:** $16.00 paperback. **Description:** The author provides concept-based chapters on the life and presidency of John F. Kennedy and his visions. Using his inaugural address, Barnes reflects on JFKs vision and his relationship with his staff.

38138 ■ *"John Risley" in Canadian Business (Vol. 80, February 26, 2007, No. 5, pp. 70)*
Pub: Rogers Media
Ed: Calvin Leung. **Description:** John Risley, co-founder of Clearwater Fine Foods, shares few managerial strategies that helped him to achieve success in various businesses.

38139 ■ *"Julie Holzrichter; Managing Director of Operations, CME Group Inc." in Crain's Chicago Business (Vol. 31, May 5, 2008, No. 18)*
Pub: Crain Communications, Inc.
Ed: Ann Saphir. **Description:** Profile of Julie Holzrichter who works as the managing director of operations for CME Group Inc. and is known as a decisive leader able to intercept and solve problems.

38140 ■ *Jump Start Your Business Brain: Ideas, Advice and Insights for Immediate Marketing and Innovation Success*
Pub: Emmis Books
Contact: Richard Hunt, President
E-mail: rhunt@emmis.com
Ed: Doug Hall. **Released:** April 2005. **Price:** $23.99. **Description:** Strategies to improve sales, marketing, and business development.

38141 ■ *"Junior Executives Need Hugs Too" in Canadian Business (Vol. 83, October 12, 2010, No. 17, pp. 87)*
Pub: Rogers Media Ltd.
Ed: James Cowan. **Description:** Psychology professor Mark Frame believes that sensitive men fail to meet perceptions of how a chief executive officer (CEO) should act. The results of a study show that communal qualities are highly valued in first-line and middle managers, but these qualities become less important when employees move closer to senior executive roles.

38142 ■ *"Just Be Nice" in Canadian Business (Vol. 79, October 9, 2006, No. 20, pp. 141)*
Pub: Rogers Media
Ed: Joe Castaldo. **Description:** The customer relationship management strategies on customer retention and satisfaction adopted by WestJet are discussed.

38143 ■ *"Just Shut The Hell Up" in Canadian Business (Vol. 81, July 22, 2008, No. 12-13, pp. 33)*
Pub: Rogers Media Ltd.
Ed: Jane Bao. **Description:** Employees desire better communication as opposed to more communication from their managers. Advice regarding managing communication in the workplace is given including ways in which speakers can say more with fewer words.

38144 ■ *"Karen Case; President of Commercial Real Estate Lending, Privatebancorp Inc." in Crain's Chicago Business (May 5, 2008)*
Pub: Crain Communications, Inc.
Ed: Dee Gill. **Description:** Profile of Karen Case who was hired by PrivateBancorp Inc. to turn its minor share of the city's commercial real estate lending market into a major one.

38145 ■ *"Kari Leong" in Hawaii Business (Vol. 53, October 2007, No. 4, pp. 39)*
Pub: Hawaii Business Publishing
Ed: Cathy S. Cruz-George. **Description:** Greater Good Inc. president Kari Leong is the number 1 fittest female executive in Hawaii for 2007. Leong exercises at the gym and at her home, and carries her two children for strength training. The physical activities she had undergone during her college life at the Gonzaga University are discussed.

38146 ■ *"Keeping Railcars 'Busy At All Times' At TTX" in Crain's Chicago Business (Vol. 31, April 28, 2008, No. 17, pp. 6)*
Pub: Crain Communications, Inc.
Ed: Bob Tita. **Description:** Profile of the president of Chicago railcar pool operator TTX Co. and his business plan for the company which includes improving fleet management and car purchasing through better use of data on railroad demand.

38147 ■ *"Kelvin Taketa" in Hawaii Business (Vol. 53, October 2007, No. 4, pp. 30)*
Pub: Hawaii Business Publishing
Ed: Scott Radway. **Description:** Hawaii Community Foundation chief executive officer Kelvin Taketa believes that the leadership shortage for nonprofit sector in Hawaii is a result of leaders retiring or switching to part-time work. Taketa adds that the duties of a nonprofit organization leader are very challenging, with the organizations being usually thinly staffed. His opinion on the prospects of young leadership in Hawaii is also given.

38148 ■ *"Key Budgeting Tips: For Your Management Team" in Agency Sales Magazine (Vol. 39, December 2009, No. 11, pp. 49)*
Pub: MANA
Ed: Gene Siciliano. **Description:** Constructing a budget must be the result of coordinated input and effort. Practice is also important in creating a budget and accurately predicting actual results is not the objective but giving the company a direction for course correction.

38149 ■ *"Kid Rock" in Canadian Business (Vol. 81, Summer 2008, No. 9, pp. 54)*
Pub: Rogers Media Ltd.
Ed: John Gray. **Description:** Damien Reynolds is the founder, chairman and chief executive officer of Vancouver-based Longview Capital Partners. The investment bank, founded in 2005, is one of the fastest-growing companies in British Columbia. The recent economic downturn has battered the stocks of the company and its portfolio of junior miners.

38150 ■ *The Kindess Revolution: The Company-Wide Culture Shift That Inspires Phenomenal Customer Service*
Pub: American Management Association
Contact: Charles R. Craig, Chairman
Ed: Ed Horrell. **Released:** 2006. **Price:** $23.00.

38151 ■ *"Kinetico Exec Going Global to Increase Growth Flow" in Crain's Cleveland Business (Vol. 28, October 1, 2007, No. 39, pp. 5)*
Pub: Crain Communications, Inc.
Ed: David Bennett. **Description:** Shamus Hurley, the new CEO and president of Kinetico Inc., a manufacturer of water filtering and softening equipment for residential, commercial and municipal use, plans to expand the company to target markets overseas.

38152 ■ *Kiss Theory Good Bye: Five Proven Ways to Get Extraordinary Results in Any Company*
Pub: Gold Pen Publishing
Ed: Bob Prosen. **Released:** August 2006. **Price:** $21. 95. **Description:** Author provides wisdom from his career as a high-level executive at AT&T Global Information Solutions, Sabre, and Hitachi, as well as his consulting firm. The book focuses on business execution rather than processes or theory of business management and provides step-by-step instructions allowing organizations to maximize profitability and results.

38153 ■ *Know-How: The 8 Skills That Separate People Who Perform from Those Who Don't*
Pub: Crown Publishing Group
Ed: Ram Charan. **Released:** January 2, 2007. **Price:** $27.50. **Description:** Know-how is what separates leaders who perform and deliver good results from those who don't.

38154 ■ *"Know Your Bones: Take Your Bone Health Seriously" in Women In Business (Vol. 62, June 2010, No. 2, pp. 40)*
Pub: American Business Women's Association
Description: Bone health for women with postmenopausal osteoporosis is encouraged to help create an appropriate health plan that includes exercise, diet and medication. Questions to consider when discussing possible plans with health care providers are presented.

38155 ■ *"Knowledge Workers" in Canadian Business (Vol. 79, October 9, 2006, No. 20, pp. 59)*
Pub: Rogers Media
Ed: Doug Cooper. **Description:** Knowledge workers as an integral part of organizations and the need for business leaders to effectively manage and recognize the talent of knowledge workers is discussed.

38156 ■ *"Kraft Taps Cheese Head; Jordan Charged With Fixing Foodmaker's Signature Product" in Crain's Chicago Business (April 14, 2008)*
Pub: Crain Communications, Inc.
Ed: David Sterrett. **Description:** Kraft Foods Inc. has assigned Rhonda Jordan, a company veteran, to take charge of the cheese and dairy division which has been losing market shares to cheaper store-brand cheese among cost-sensitive shoppers as Kraft and its competitors raise prices to offset soaring dairy costs.

38157 ■ *"Labor and Management: Working Together for a Stable Future" in Alaska Business Monthly (Vol. 27, October 2011, No. 10, pp. 130)*
Pub: Alaska Business Publishing Company
Ed: Nicole A. Bonham Colby. **Description:** Alaska unions and employers are working to ensure a consistent flow of skilled Alaska workers as current the current workforce reaches retirement age.

38158 ■ *"Laced Up and Ready to Run" in Barron's (Vol. 89, July 6, 2009, No. 27, pp. 12)*
Pub: Dow Jones & Co., Inc.
Ed: Christopher C. Williams. **Description:** Shares of Foot Locker could raise from $10 to about $15 a share with the improvement of the economy. The company has benefited from prudent management and merchandising as well as better cost cutting, allowing it to better survive in a recession.

38159 ■ *"Lafley Gives Look At His Game Plan" in Business Courier (Vol. 24, March 21, 2008, No. 50, pp. 1)*
Pub: American City Business Journals, Inc.
Ed: Lisa Biank Fasig. **Description:** Overview of A.G. Lafley's book entitled 'The Game-Changer', is presented. Lafley, Procter & Gamble Co.'s chief executive officer, documented his philosophy and strategy in his book. His work also includes Procter & Gamble's hands-on initiatives such as mock-up grocery stores and personal interviews with homeowners.

38160 ■ *"Land on Boardwalk" in Canadian Business (Vol. 82, April 27, 2009, No. 7, pp. 19)*
Pub: Rogers Media
Ed: Calvin Leung. **Description:** Boardwalk REIT remains as one of the most attractive real estate investment trusts in Canada, with 73 percent of analysts rating the firm a Buy. Analyst Neil Downey believes that good management, as well as a good business model, makes Boardwalk a good investment. Downey is concerned however, that a worsening of Alberta's economy could significantly impact Boardwalk.

38161 ■ *"LaSalle Street Firms Cherry-Pick Talent As Wall Street Tanks" in Crain's Chicago Business (Vol. 31, November 17, 2008, No. 46)*
Pub: Crain Communications, Inc.
Ed: H. Lee Murphy. **Description:** Many local businesses are taking advantage of the lay offs that many major Wall Street firms are undergoing in their workforces; these companies see the opportunity to woo talent and expand their staff with quality executives.

38162 ■ *"Last Founder Standing" in Conde Nast Portfolio (Vol. 2, June 2008, No. 6, pp. 124)*
Pub: Conde Nast Publications
Contact: David Carey, President
Ed: Kevin Maney. **Description:** Interview with Amazon CEO Jeff Bezos in which he discusses the economy, the company's new distribution center and the hiring of employees for it, e-books, and the overall vision for the future of the firm.

38163 ■ *"Lathrop Finds Partner In LA" in The Business Journal-Serving Metropolitan Kansas City (Vol. 27, November 21, 2008, No. 11, pp. 1)*
Pub: American City Business Journals, Inc.
Ed: Steve Vockrodt. **Description:** Kansas, Missouri-based Lathrop and Gage LLP is planning to merge with Spillane Shaeffer Aronoff Bandlow LLP. The merging of the business law firms will add entertainment clients to Lathrop's fold. Comments from executives are also presented.

38164 ■ *The Leader of the Future 2*
Pub: Jossey Bass
Ed: Frances Hesselbein; Marshall Goldsmith. **Released:** September 18, 2006. **Price:** $27.95. **Description:** Wisdom is lent to any small business owner or leader of a nonprofit organization.

38165 ■ *"Leaders in Denial" in Harvard Business Review (Vol. 86, July-August 2008, No. 8, pp. 18)*
Pub: Harvard Business School Press
Ed: Richard S. Tedlow. **Description:** Identifying denial in the corporate arena is discussed, along with its impact on business and how to prevent it from occurring.

38166 ■ *Leadership 101: What Every Leader Needs to Know*
Pub: Nelson Business
Ed: John C. Maxwell. **Released:** September 2002. **Price:** $9.99. **Description:** Ways to enhance leadership skills focusing on following a vision and bringing others along.

38167 ■ *"Leadership Behavior and Employee Voice: Is the Door Really Open?" in Academy of Management Journal (August 2007)*
Pub: Academy of Management
Contact: Ming-Jer Chen, President
Ed: James R. Detert, Ethan R. Burris. **Description:** Relationships between two types of change-oriented leadership and subordinate improvement-oriented voice in a two-phase study are presented.

38168 ■ *The Leadership Challenge*
Pub: Jossey-Bass Publishers
Ed: James M. Kouzes, Barry Z. Posner. **Released:** June 30, 1995. **Price:** $22.00. **Description:** According to research by the authors, people can make extraordinary things happen by liberating the leader within everyone around them. This handbook gives practical tips to aspire leaders in retail, manufacturing, government, community, church and school settings.

38169 ■ *"Leadership Counts" in Hispanic Business (January-February 2008, pp. 60, 62)*
Pub: Hispanic Business
Ed: Frank Nelson. **Description:** Small business leaders discuss the importance of including diversity initiatives into any plan.

38170 ■ *Leadership in the Era of Economic Uncertainty: Managing in a Downturn*
Pub: The McGraw-Hill Companies
Ed: Ram Charan. **Released:** December 2008. **Price:** $22.95. **Description:** Management consultant gives advice on how to weather the economic storm, focusing on cash flow and foregoing expansion.

38171 ■ *"Leadership in Flight" in Women In Business (Vol. 63, Fall 2011, No. 3, pp. 24)*
Pub: American Business Women's Association
Ed: Leigh Elmore. **Description:** Flight attendants in major airlines are trained to keep passengers comfortable and to calmly deal with emergencies. They also have a significant role in brand image and customer loyalty as they interact with the customers directly. Examples of teamwork leadership for flight attendants are given.

38172 ■ *The Leadership Secrets of Colin Powell*
Pub: McGraw-Hill Companies Inc.
Contact: Deven Sharma, President
Ed: Oren Harari. **Released:** July 2003. **Price:** $18. 95. **Description:** Profile of Colin Powell, stressing his abilities as a world leader.

38173 ■ *"Leadership: The Couch in the Corner Office: Surveying the Landscape of the CEO Psyche" in Inc. (January 2008, pp. 33-34)*
Pub: Gruner & Jahr USA Publishing
Description: Profile of Leslie G. Mayer, founder of the Leadership Group, a firm that provides assistance to CEOs of firms by offering a deep understanding of the relationships, insecurities, and blind spots that can weaken strong leadership.

38174 ■ *"Leadership Training" in Black Enterprise (Vol. 37, January 2007, No. 6, pp. 56)*
Pub: Earl G. Graves Publishing Co. Inc.
Ed: Sonia Alleyne. **Description:** Profile of Theopolis Holman, Group Vice-President of Duke Energy, who discusses how he prepared for the merger between Duke Energy and Cinergy. Holman oversees a division of 9,000 service contractors and employees.

38175 ■ *Leading with Character: Stories of Valor and Virtue and the Principles They Teach*
Pub: Information Age Publishing
Ed: John J. Sosik. **Released:** July 24, 2006. **Price:** $39.99. **Description:** Examination of the kind of character that leaders develop in themselves and others in order to create and sustain extraordinary organizational growth and performance.

38176 ■ *Leading the Charge*
Pub: Palgrave Macmillan
Ed: Tony Zinni, Tony Koltz. **Released:** July 16, 2009. **Price:** $25.00. **Description:** General Anthony Zinni recalls a lifetime of competition on the battlefield and in corporate boardrooms and is leading the call to action to restore American leadership and greatness.

38177 ■ *Leading at a Higher Level*
Pub: FT Press
Ed: Ken Blanchard. **Released:** November 2006. **Price:** $26.99. **Description:** Tips, advice and techniques from a management consultant to help entrepreneurs create a vision for their company; includes information on manager-employee relationships.

38178 ■ *Lean Six Sigmas That Works: A Powerful Action Plan for Dramatically Improving Quality, Increasing Speed, and Reducing Waste*
Pub: American Management Association
Contact: Charles R. Craig, Chairman
Ed: Bill Carreira; Bill Trudell. **Released:** 2006. **Price:** $21.95.

38179 ■ *"Legg's Compensation Committee Chair Defends CEO Fetting's Pay" in Boston Business Journal (Vol. 29, July 22, 2011, No. 11, pp. 1)*
Pub: American City Business Journals Inc.
Ed: Gary Haber. **Description:** Legg Mason Inc. CEO Mark R. Fetting has been awarded $5.9 million pay package and he expects to receive questions regarding it in the coming shareholders meeting. However, Baltimore, Maryland-based RKTL Associates chairman emeritus Harold R. Adams believes Fetting has done a tremendous job in bringing Legg's through a tough market.

38180 ■ *"Lehman's Hail Mary Pass" in Business Week (September 22, 2008, No. 4100, pp. 28)*
Pub: McGraw-Hill Companies, Inc.
Ed: Matthew Goldstein; David Henry; Ben Levison. **Description:** Overview of Lehman Brothers' CEO Richard Fuld's plan to keep the firm afloat and end the stock's plunge downward; Fuld's strategy calls for selling off a piece of the firm's investment management business.

38181 ■ *"Lessons Learned from Instructional Design Theory" in Business Communication Quarterly (December 2007, pp. 414)*
Pub: SAGE Publications USA
Contact: Blaise R. Simqu, President
Ed: Lisa A. Burke. **Description:** Instructors should present course information to business students in a way that enhances understanding and should use presentation techniques that students may eventually use; course materials should be kept relevant and simple.

38182 ■ *"Lessons from Turnaround Leaders" in Strategy and Leadership (Vol. 39, May-June 2011, No. 3, pp. 36-43)*
Pub: Emerald Group Publishing Inc.
Ed: David P. Boyd. **Description:** A study analyzes the cases of some successful turnaround leaders to present a strategic model to help firms tackle challenges such as employee inertia, competition and slow organizational renewal. It describes a change model consisting of five major steps to be followed by firms with environmental uncertainty for the purpose.

38183 ■ *"Let the Insults Fly: Want to Learn What Your Employees Really Think?" in Inc. (Vol. 33, October 2011, No. 8, pp. 36)*
Pub: Inc. Magazine
Ed: Jason Fried. **Description:** A company that hosts a Comedy Central-style celebrity roast of its top-selling product was able to improve their business.

38184 ■ *Liespotting: Proven Techniques to Detect Deception*
Pub: St. Martins Press/Macmillan
Ed: Pamela Meyer. **Released:** July 20, 2010. **Price:** $24.99. **Description:** Liespotting links three disciplines: facial recognition training, interrogation training, and a comprehensive survey of research in the field - into a specialized body of information developed specifically to help business leaders detect deception and get the information they need to successfully conduct their most important interactions and transactions.

38185 ■ *"Lifebank Grants Stock Options" in Canadian Corporate News (May 16, 2007)*
Pub: Comtex News Network Inc.
Description: Lifebank, a biomedical service company that provides processing cryogenic storage of umbilical cord blood stem cells, announced that, under its stock option plan, it has granted incentive stock options to directors, officers, and consultants of the company.

38186 ■ *"Life's Work: Ben Bradlee" in Harvard Business Review (Vol. 88, September 2010, No. 9, pp. 128)*
Pub: Harvard Business School Publishing
Ed: Alison Beard. **Description:** Newspaper publisher Ben Bradlee discusses factors that lead to success, including visible supervisors, enthusiasm, appropriate expansion, and the importance in truth in reporting.

38187 ■ *"Life's Work: Oliver Sacks" in Harvard Business Review (Vol. 88, November 2010, No. 11, pp. 152)*
Pub: Harvard Business School Publishing
Ed: Lisa Burrell. **Description:** Neurologist and author Oliver Sacks discusses whether different types of minds tend toward certain skills, physician-patient communication, and his own perspectives from being a patient himself.

38188 ■ *"Lifetime Networks" in Brandweek (Vol. 49, April 21, 2008, No. 16, pp. SR10)*
Pub: VNU Business Media, Inc.
Ed: Anthony Crupi. **Description:** Provides contact information for sales and marketing personnel for the ABC network as well as a listing of the station's top programming and an analysis of the current season and the target audience for those programs running in the current season. Lifetime will still produce its

original signature movies but will now focus its emphasis more clearly on series development in order to appeal to a younger, hipper female demographic.

38189 ■ *Linchpin: Are you Indispensable?*
Pub: Portfolio
Ed: Seth Godin. **Released:** January 26, 2010. **Price:** $25.95. **Description:** The best way to get what you're worth, according to the author, is to exert emotional labor, to be seen as indispensable, and to produce interactions that organizations and people care about.

38190 ■ *Lincoln on Leadership: Executive Strategies for Tough Times*
Pub: Grand Central Publishing
Ed: Donald T. Phillips. **Released:** February 1, 1993. **Price:** $14.99 (paperback). **Description:** Using President Abraham Lincoln's example of leadership, the author sets out to help business leaders adopt winning strategies.

38191 ■ *"Lines of Communication" in Entrepreneur (Vol. 37, October 2009, No. 10, pp. 80)*
Pub: Entrepreneur Media, Inc.
Ed: Brad Feld. **Description:** Entrepreneurial companies should establish a clear and open communication culture between their management teams and their venture capital backers. Chief executive officers should trust their leadership teams when it comes to communicating with venture capitalists.

38192 ■ *Local Enterprises in the Global Economy: Issues of Governance and Upgrading*
Pub: Edward Elgar Publishing, Incorporated
Ed: Hubert Schmitz. **Released:** November 2004. **Price:** $35.00 (soft cover), $110.00 (hard bound). **Description:** Examination of the relationships between globalization, corporate governance, and the economic performance of small businesses and local enterprises.

38193 ■ *The Logic of Life: The Rational Economics of an Irrational World*
Pub: Random House
Ed: Tim Harford. **Released:** February 2009. **Price:** $15.00 paperback. **Description:** Harford excels at making economists' studies palatable for discerning but non-expert readers. The uses hard data to show why promiscuous teens are actually health-conscious, divorce hasn't gotten a fair shake, corporate bosses will always be overpaid and job prospects for minorities continue to be grim.

38194 ■ *"Looking For Financing?" in Hispanic Business (Vol. 30, July-August 2008, No. 7-8, pp. 16)*
Pub: Hispanic Business, Inc.
Ed: Frank Nelson. **Description:** Investment firms want to know about businesses that need funding for either expansion or acquisition; companies fitting this profile are interviewed and their perceptions are discussed. Investment firms need businesses to be realistic in their expectations and business plans which show spending of funds and expected benefits, long term goals, track record and strong management teams.

38195 ■ *"The Lords of Ideas" in Business Strategy Review (Vol. 21, Autumn 2010, No. 3, pp. 57)*
Pub: Blackwell Publishers Ltd.
Ed: Stuart Crainer. **Description:** True originators of modern strategy are profiled.

38196 ■ *"Loseley Dairy Ice Cream" in Ice Cream Reporter (Vol. 23, November 20, 2010, No. 12, pp. 8)*
Pub: Ice Cream Reporter
Description: Neil Burchell has been named managing director of Loseley Dairy Ice Cream, one of the UK's largest independent producers. Burchell, with over 30 years experience in the food industry, was recently managing director of Rachel's, the leading organic dairy foods company in the UK, where he is credited with driving a sixfold increase in sales.

38197 ■ *"Losing the Top Job - And Winning It Back" in Harvard Business Review (Vol. 88, October 2010, No. 10, pp. 136)*
Pub: Harvard Business School Publishing
Ed: Alison Beard. **Description:** Michael Mack chronicles the changes in perspectives that occurred when he was fired from Garden Fresh, a restaurant firm he co-owned. Once again at the company helm, he is now more receptive to outside input and acknowledges the importance of work-life balance.

38198 ■ *"Lots More Mr. Nice Guy" in Canadian Business (Vol. 80, October 22, 2007, No. 21, pp. 58)*
Pub: Rogers Media
Ed: Zena Olijnyk. **Description:** Galen Weston Jr., executive chairman of Loblaw and heir to the Weston family business, has his hands full running the company. Details of his turnaround strategies and ambitious plans to increase profitability of the business are discussed.

38199 ■ *"Lots of Qualified Women, But Few Sit on Boards" in Globe & Mail (March 2, 2006, pp. B1)*
Pub: CTVglobemedia Publishing Inc.
Ed: Virginia Galt. **Description:** The findings of Catalyst Canada survey on the rise in women executives on boards of directors are presented.

38200 ■ *"Macho Men" in Canadian Business (Vol. 81, November 10, 2008, No. 19, pp. 23)*
Pub: Rogers Media Ltd.
Ed: Sharda Prashad. **Description:** Professors Robin Ely and Debra Meyerson found that oil rigs decreased accidents and increased productivity when they focused on improving safety and admitting errors rather than on a worker's individual strength. Professor Jennifer Berdahl shows there is pressure for men to be seen as masculine at work, which makes them avoid doing 'feminine' things such as parental leaves.

38201 ■ *Made to Stick: Why Some Ideas Survive and Others Die*
Pub: Doubleday Broadway Publishing Group
Ed: Chip Heath; Dan Heath. **Released:** January 2, 2007. **Price:** $26.00. **Description:** Entertaining, practical guide to effective business communication; information is derived form psychosocial studies on memory, emotion and motivation.

38202 ■ *"Madeleine Paquin" in Canadian Business (Vol. 81, March 3, 2008, No. 3, pp. 92)*
Pub: Rogers Media
Ed: Regan Ray. **Description:** Madeleine Paquin, chief executive officer and president of Logistec Corp., talks about how she balanced her career and her life as a mother to two girls. Paquin thinks that working mothers need to focus on some things instead of trying to do everything. Her career in the marine cargo handling industry is also discussed.

38203 ■ *"Magna Wants to Help Chrysler, but a Takeover's Not on the Cards" in Globe & Mail (March 1, 2007, pp. B1)*
Pub: CTVglobemedia Publishing Inc.
Ed: Greg Keenan. **Description:** The plans of Magna International Inc. to help Chrysler Corp. to overcome its financial problems are discussed. The appointment of Michael Neuman as the chief executive officer of Magna International Inc. is described.

38204 ■ *"Magnus Carlsen" in Canadian Business (Vol. 83, October 12, 2010, No. 17, pp. 79)*
Pub: Rogers Media Ltd.
Description: Magnus Carlsen, chess prodigy, talks about the importance of having a good feel for the game. He thinks that there are some similarities between chess and business, as both are about making good decisions in a limited amount of time. His views about motivation are also discussed.

38205 ■ *"The Mailman" in Canadian Business (Vol. 80, April 9, 2007, No. 8, pp. 14)*
Pub: Rogers Media
Ed: Zena Olijnyk. **Description:** Chief executive officer of Pitney Bowes Inc. Murray Martin's entrepreneurial skills in managing the company and his personal career are discussed.

38206 ■ *"Make It Easy" in Entrepreneur (Vol. 36, May 2008, No. 5, pp. 49)*
Pub: Entrepreneur Media, Inc.
Ed: Mike Hogan. **Description:** Zoho has a Planner that keep contacts, notes and reminders and a DB & Reports feature for reports, data analysis and pricing comparisons. WebEx WebOffice Workgroup supports document management and templates for contacts lists, time sheets and sales tracking. Other online data manages are presented.

38207 ■ *Making Difficult Decisions: How to Be Decisive and Get the Business Done*
Pub: John Wiley and Sons, Inc.
Ed: Peter Shaw. **Released:** August 2008. **Price:** $29. 95. **Description:** Experience of others can help entrepreneurs and managers make difficult business decisions. The strategies set forth in this book have been used successfully in public, private and voluntary sectors.

38208 ■ *"Making Diverse Teams Click" in Harvard Business Review (Vol. 86, July-August 2008, No. 8, pp. 20)*
Pub: Harvard Business School Press
Ed: Jeffrey T. Polzer. **Description:** 360-degree feedback to increase the efficacy of diverse-member workplace teams, which involves each member providing feedback to the others on the team is discussed.

38209 ■ *Making People Your Competitive Advantage*
Pub: Jossey Bass
Ed: Edward E. Lawler III. **Released:** 2008. **Price:** $29.95. **Description:** Competitive advantage in most organizations has shifted from reliability to innovation and flexibility. Organizations must combine the right structure with the right people to make it work.

38210 ■ *"Making the Tough Call: Great Leaders Recognize When Their Values Are On the Line" in Inc. (November 2007, pp. 36, 38)*
Pub: Gruner & Jahr USA Publishing
Ed: Noel M. Tichy, Warren G. Bennis. **Description:** Good judgment by company leaders is a process involving preparation, making the call, and executing the process. Character provides a moral compass for these decision makers.

38211 ■ *Management Lessons from Mayo Clinic*
Pub: McGraw-Hill
Ed: Leonard L. Berry; Kent D. Seltman. **Released:** June 6, 2008. **Price:** $27.95. **Description:** Management practices employed by the Mayo Clinic are examined to show why it is one of the world's most successful health care facilities.

38212 ■ *"Management Matters with Mike Myatt: Are You Creating Growth in a Down Economy?" in Commercial Property News (March 17, 2008)*
Pub: Nielsen Company
Ed: Mike Myatt. **Description:** Senior executives are expected to create growth for their company regardless of recession, economic slowdown, inflation, or tight credit and capital markets.

38213 ■ *The Management Myth: Why the "Experts" Keep Getting It Wrong*
Pub: W.W. Norton & Company
Ed: Matthew Stewart. **Released:** August 10, 2009. **Price:** $27.95. **Description:** An insider's perspective on the management consulting industry, which reveals the high fees and incompetent consultants.

38214 ■ *Management Rewired: Why Feedback Doesn't Work and Other Surprising Lessons from the Latest Brain Science*
Pub: Portfolio
Ed: Charles S. Jacobs. **Released:** 2009. **Price:** $25. 95. **Description:** According to the author, human psychology works better than feedback, praise or criticism when managing employees.

38215 ■ *The Management of Small and Medium Enterprises*
Pub: Routledge
Ed: Matthias Fink. **Released:** April 1, 2009. **Price:** $140.00. **Description:** Investigation into the underlying mechanisms and practices of management within small and medium enterprises is provided.

38216 ■ *"Managerial Rudeness: Bad Attitudes Can Demoralize Your Staff" in Black Enterprise (Vol. 37, January 2007, No. 6, pp. 58)*
Pub: Earl G. Graves Publishing Co. Inc.
Ed: Chauntelle Folds. **Description:** Positive leadership in the managerial realm leads to a more productive workplace. Managers who are negative, hostile, arrogant, rude or fail to accept any responsibility for their own mistakes find that employees will not give their all on the job.

38217 ■ *The Manager's Guide to Rewards: What You Need to Know to Get the Best of-and-from-Your Employees*
Pub: American Management Association
Contact: Charles R. Craig, Chairman
Ed: Doug Jensen; Tom McMullen; Mel Stark. **Released:** 2006. **Price:** $24.95.

38218 ■ *"Managers and Their Not-So Rational Decisions" in Business Horizons (Vol. 51, March-April 2008, No. 2, pp. 113)*
Pub: Elsevier Advanced Technology Publications
Ed: S. Trevis Certo, Brian L. Connelly, Laszlo Tihanyi. **Description:** Two cognitive systems influencing the decision making of managers are described. One is a fast, effortless, and intuitive process, while the other is slow, controlled, and rule-governed and the two systems interact with each other.

38219 ■ *"Managers as Visionaries: a Skill That Can Be Learned" in Strategy and Leadership (Vol. 39, September-October 2011, No. 5, pp. 56-58)*
Pub: Emerald Group Publishing Inc.
Ed: Stephen M. Millett. **Description:** A study uses research findings to examine whether visionary management can be learned. Results conclude that managers can learn visionary management through intuitive pattern recognition of trends and by using scenarios for anticipating and planning for likely future occurrences.

38220 ■ *Managing Business Growth: Get a Grip on the Numbers That Count*
Pub: Self-Counsel Press, Incorporated
Ed: Angie Mohr. **Released:** October 2004. **Price:** $14.95. **Description:** Fourth book in the Numbers 101 for Small Business Series, teaches how small company owners can expand their businesses using sound financial planning.

38221 ■ *Managing Economies, Trade and International Business*
Pub: Palgrave Macmillan
Ed: Aidan O'Connor. **Released:** January 19, 2010. **Price:** $90.00. **Description:** An in-depth look at the areas that affect and influence international business, exploring specific issues businesses face in terms of economic development, trade law, and international marketing and management.

38222 ■ *"Managing the Facebookers; Business" in The Economist (Vol. 390, January 3, 2009, No. 8612, pp. 10)*
Pub: Economist Newspaper Ltd.
Description: According to a report from PricewaterhouseCoopers, a business consultancy, workers from Generation Y, also known as the Net Generation, are more difficult to recruit and integrate into companies that practice traditional business acumen. 61 percent of chief executive managers say that they have trouble with younger employees who tend to be more narcissistic and more interested in personal fulfillment with a need for frequent feedback and an overprecise set of objectives on the path to promotion which can be hard for managers who are used to a different relationship with their subordinates. Older bosses should prepare to make some concessions to their younger talent since some of the issues that make them happy include cheaper online ways to communicate and additional coaching, both of which are good for business.

38223 ■ *Managing Labour in Small Firms*
Pub: Routledge
Ed: Susan Marlow. **Released:** December 2004. **Price:** $170.00. **Description:** Essays addressing conditions of workers in small business.

38224 ■ *Managing the Older Worker: How to Prepare for the New Organizational Order*
Pub: Harvard Business Press
Ed: Peter Cappelli, Bill Novelli. **Price:** $29.95. **Description:** Your organization needs older workers more than ever: They transfer knowledge between generations, transmit your company's values to new hires, make excellent mentors for younger employees, and provide a 'just in time' workforce for special projects.

38225 ■ *Managing for Results*
Pub: HarperCollins Publishers, Inc.
Ed: Peter F. Drucker. **Released:** October 2006. **Price:** $16.95. **Description:** Entrepreneurs running successful small companies focus on opportunity rather than problems.

38226 ■ *Managing a Small Business Made Easy*
Pub: Entrepreneur Press
Ed: Martin E. Davis. **Released:** September 2005. **Price:** $19.95 (US), $26.95 (Canadian). **Description:** Examination of the essential elements for an entrepreneur running a business, including advice on leadership, customer service, financials, and more.

38227 ■ *Managing for Success: The Latest in Management Thought and Practice from Canada's Premier Business School*
Pub: Harperaudio
Contact: Catherine MacGregor, Director
E-mail: catherine.macgregor@harpercollins.com
Ed: Monica Fleck. **Released:** December 2000. **Description:** Canadian business school offers insight into the latest management skills of the nation's business leaders.

38228 ■ *"Managing in Times of Uncertainty; What Leaders Can Learn From the Tumultuous Past Decade" in Gallup Management Journal (June 1, 2011)*
Pub: Gallup
Description: Executives and managers have been facing a global financial meltdown for the past 10 years along with ongoing wars, an increase in terrorism, and epic natural disasters. The leadership lessons learned over this time are examined.

38229 ■ *"M&I Execs May Get Golden Parachutes" in Business Journal-Milwaukee (Vol. 28, December 31, 2010, No. 14, pp. A3)*
Pub: Milwaukee Business Journal
Ed: Rich Kirchen. **Description:** Marshall and Isley Corporation's top executives have a chance to receive golden-parachute payments it its buyer, BMO Financial Group, repays the Troubled Asset Relief Program (TARP) loan on behalf of the company. One TARP rule prevents golden-parachute payments to them and the next five most highly paid employees of TARP recipients.

38230 ■ *"The Many Hats and Faces of NAOHSM" in Indoor Comfort Marketing (Vol. 70, May 2011, No. 5, pp. 8)*
Pub: Industry Publications Inc.
Description: Profile of the National Association of Oil Heating Service Managers, and its role in the industry, is presented.

38231 ■ *The Martha Rules: 10 Essentials for Achieving Success as You Start, Build, or Manage a Business*
Pub: Rodale Inc.
Contact: Maria Rodale, Chief Executive Officer
Ed: Martha Stewart. **Released:** October 2006. **Price:** $15.95. **Description:** Martha Stewart offers insight into starting, building and managing a successful business.

38232 ■ *The Martha Rules: 10 Essentials for Achieving Success as You Start, Grow, or Manage a Business*
Pub: Rodale Press, Inc.
Ed: Martha Stewart. **Released:** October 2005.

38233 ■ *Mastering Business Negotiation: A Working Guide to Making Deals and Resolving Conflict*
Pub: Jossey-Bass Publishers
Ed: Roy J. Lewicki; Alexander Hiam. **Released:** July 21, 2006. **Price:** $24.95. **Description:** Provides extensive insight into practical strategies and ideas for conducting business negotiations.

38234 ■ *"MBA Guide 2008" in Canadian Business (Vol. 81, November 10, 2008, No. 19, pp. 92)*
Pub: Rogers Media Ltd.
Ed: Sharda Prashad. **Description:** Escalating tuition costs for an MBA degree means that the return on investment could take longer. One study found that MBA degree holders who graduated during recessionary times earned less than those who graduated during good economic times.

38235 ■ *MBA In a Day*
Pub: John Wiley and Sons, Inc.
Ed: Steven Stralser, PhD. **Released:** 2004. **Price:** $34.95. **Description:** Management professor presents important concepts, business topics and strategies that can be used by anyone to manage a small business or professional practice. Topics covered include: human resources and personal interaction, ethics and leadership skills, fair negotiation tactics, basic business accounting practices, project management, and the fundamentals of economics and marketing.

38236 ■ *"MBAs Plus Designers Equals New Life for Business" in Globe & Mail (April 24, 2007, pp. B1)*
Pub: CTVglobemedia Publishing Inc.
Ed: Gordon Pitts. **Description:** The need for Canadian companies to combine the skills of management graduates and designers to achieve corporate growth is discussed.

38237 ■ *"Meadowbrook CEO Sees 20 Percent Growth With New Acquisition" in Crain's Detroit Business (Vol. 24, March 10, 2008, No. 10, pp. 4)*
Pub: Crain Communications, Inc.
Ed: Jay Greene. **Description:** Discusses the major turnaround of Meadowbrook Insurance Group after Robert Cubbin became CEO and implemented a new business strategy.

38238 ■ *"MEDC: Put Venture Funds to Work" in Crain's Detroit Business (Vol. 25, June 22, 2009, No. 25, pp. 1)*
Pub: Crain Communications Inc. - Detroit
Ed: Tom Henderson. **Description:** Michigan Strategic Fund board will finalize approval for ESP Holdings II LLC, Peninsula Capital Partners LLC, Triathlon Medical Ventures LLC and Arsenal Venture Partners Inc. are expected to share $35.5 million from the fund.

38239 ■ *"Meetings Go Virtual" in HRMagazine (Vol. 54, January 2009, No. 1, pp. 74)*
Pub: Society for Human Resource Management
Contact: Henry G. Jackson, President
E-mail: hjackson@shrm.org
Ed: Elizabeth Agnvall. **Description:** Microsoft Office Live Meeting conferencing software allows companies to schedule meetings from various company locations, thus saving travel costs.

38240 ■ *"Mentoring Support" in Black Enterprise (Vol. 38, July 2008, No. 12, pp. 64)*
Pub: Earl G. Graves Publishing Co. Inc.
Description: With his relocation from his multicultural team in New York to the less diverse Scripps Networks' headquarters in Knoxville, Earl Cokley has made it a top priority to push for more diversity and mentoring opportunities within the management of the media and marketing company.

38241 ■ *"Methodological Fit in Management Field Research" in Academy of Management Review (October 2007, pp. 1155)*
Pub: ScholarOne, Inc.
Ed: Amy C. Edmondson, Stacy E. McManus. **Description:** The importance of methodological fit in management field research is investigated in order to produce high quality results.

38242 ■ *"The Metrics of Knowledge: Mechanisms for Preserving the Value of Managerial Knowledge" in Business Horizons (Nov.-Dec. 2007)*
Pub: Elsevier Technology Publications
Ed: Eliezer Geisler. **Description:** Mechanisms to reduce the loss of managerial knowledge, such as socialization, tutoring, mentoring, and continuous reporting are proposed. These informal mechanisms should become integral components of knowledge management or organizations.

38243 ■ *Microfinance*
Pub: Palgrave Macmillan
Ed: Mario La Torre; Gianfranco A. Vento; Philip Molyneux. **Released:** October 2006. **Price:** $80.00. **Description:** Microfinance involves the analysis of operational, managerial and financial aspects of a small business.

38244 ■ *"Microsoft Clicks Into High Speed" in Hispanic Business (Vol. 30, July-August 2008, No. 7-8, pp. 54)*
Pub: Hispanic Business, Inc.
Ed: Derek Reveron. **Description:** Microsoft's diversity hiring and vendor diversity program to capture more Hispanic consumer and business-to-business market is described. One of the main goals of these programs is to hire more Hispanic executives and managers who will help the company develop and market products and services that will appeal and benefit Hispanic consumers.

38245 ■ *"The Middle Ages" in Hawaii Business (Vol. 53, October 2007, No. 4, pp. 42)*
Pub: Hawaii Business Publishing
Ed: Cathy S. Cruz-George. **Description:** Starcom Builders Inc.'s Theodore 'Ted' Taketa, School Kine Cookies' Steven Gold And Sharon Serene of Sharon Serene Creative are among the participants in Hawaii's Fittest CEO competition for executives over 50 years old. Taketa takes yoga classes, and also goes to the gym while Serne has Mike Hann as her professional trainer. Eating habits of the aforementioned executives are also described.

38246 ■ *"Miller's Crossroad" in Canadian Business (Vol. 83, September 14, 2010, No. 15, pp. 58)*
Pub: Rogers Media Ltd.
Ed: Joe Castaldo. **Description:** Future Electronics founder and billionaire Robert Miller shares the secret of Future's unique operating model, which is based on inventory and market research. Miller attributes much of the company's success to its privately held status that enables quick movement against competitors.

38247 ■ *"Mini Melts" in Ice Cream Reporter (Vol. 23, August 20, 2010, No. 9, pp. 8)*
Pub: Ice Cream Reporter
Description: Mini Melts appointed David S. Tade to position of director of sales USA in order to cultivate existing distributors and add new partners to its distribution network.

38248 ■ *"Mining Executive Telfer Pocketed Millions" in Globe & Mail (April 5, 2007, pp. B4)*
Pub: CTVglobemedia Publishing Inc.
Ed: Andy Hoffman. **Description:** The issue of huge compensation for former executive of both Goldcorp Inc. and UrAsia Energy Ltd., Ian Telfer, for his efficient management of stock options is discussed.

38249 ■ *The Mirror Test: How to Breathe New Life Into Your Business*
Pub: Grand Central Publishing
Ed: Jeffrey W. Hayzlett. **Released:** May 10, 2010. **Price:** $24.99. **Description:** Consultant and author, Jeffrey Hayzlett, explains why a business is not doing well and asks the questions that most business managers are afraid to ask.

38250 ■ *"Mismanaging Pay and Performance" in Business Strategy Review (Vol. 21, Summer 2010, No. 2, pp. 54)*
Pub: Blackwell Publishers Ltd.
Ed: Rupert Merson. **Description:** Understanding the relationship between performance and desired behaviors is an important element of a company's talent management.

38251 ■ *"Mismanaging Pay and Performance" in Business Strategy Review (Vol. 21, Summer 2010, No. 2, pp. 54)*
Pub: Wiley-Blackwell
Ed: Rupert Merson. **Description:** Understanding the relationship between performance measurement and desired behaviors is an important element of a company's talent management.

38252 ■ *"Mitch D'Olier" in Hawaii Business (Vol. 53, November 2007, No. 5, pp. 27)*
Pub: Hawaii Business Publishing
Ed: Cathy S. Cruz-George. **Description:** Mitch D'Olier chief executive officer of Kaneohe Ranch/ Harold K.L. Castle Foundation thinks that achievement gaps are a nationwide problem and that the Knowledge is Power Program is one of the programs that focuses on achievement gaps in some communities across the US. He also provides his insights on education in Hawaii and the current shortage of teachers.

38253 ■ *"Monaco Pay Cut Draws Attention" in The Business Journal-Portland (Vol. 25, August 8, 2008, No. 22, pp. 1)*
Pub: American City Business Journals, Inc.
Ed: Erik Siemers. **Description:** Monaco Coach Corp. cut the salaries of five top executives in an effort to reduce the company's $178 million worth of inventory. The executives can earn the lost salary back if the inventory is reduced by $58 million a year after August 2008.

38254 ■ *"Monitor Work Productivity" in Business Owner (Vol. 35, July-August 2011, No. 4, pp. 4)*
Pub: DL Perkins Company
Description: Tips for tracking employee productivity are explained.

38255 ■ *"The Moody Blues" in Entrepreneur (Vol. 36, April 2008, No. 4, pp. 87)*
Pub: Entrepreneur Media, Inc.
Ed: Mark Henricks. **Description:** Depression among employees can affect their productivity and cost the company. Businesses with a workforce that is likely to have depression should inform their employees about the health benefits covered by insurance. Other details on how to address depression concerns among employees are discussed.

38256 ■ *"More Important than Results" in Business Strategy Review (Vol. 21, Summer 2010, No. 2, pp. 81)*
Pub: Blackwell Publishers Ltd.
Ed: Bert De Reyck, Zeger Degraeve. **Description:** Managing only for results leads to crises. It is important to reward people for the decisions they make, not just for the results they create.

38257 ■ *"More Important than Results" in Business Strategy Review (Vol. 21, Summer 2010, No. 2, pp. 81)*
Pub: Wiley-Blackwell
Ed: Bert De Reyck, Zeger Degraeve. **Description:** Managing only for results leads to crises. Reward people for decisions they make, not just for the results they create.

38258 ■ *"More Mexican Labor Needed in Oil Patch, Executives Say" in Globe & Mail (February 23, 2007, pp. B1)*
Pub: CTVglobemedia Publishing Inc.
Ed: Steven Chase. **Description:** The plans of top North American chief executive officers to recommend the employment of temporary workers from Mexico for the development of oil sands in Alberta, Canada, are discussed.

38259 ■ *"A Motorola Spinoff Is No Panacea" in Barron's (Vol. 88, March 31, 2008, No. 13, pp. 19)*
Pub: Dow Jones & Company, Inc.
Ed: Mark Veverka. **Description:** Motorola's plan to try and spinoff their handset division is bereft of details as to how or specifically when in 2009 the spinoff would occur. There's no reason to buy the shares since there's a lot of execution risk to the plan. Motorola needs to hire a proven cellphone executive and develop a compelling new cellphone platform.

38260 ■ *"Mr. Deeds" in Canadian Business (Vol. 81, March 31, 2008, No. 5, pp. 24)*
Pub: Rogers Media
Ed: Thomas Watson. **Description:** Ron Sandler has the right experience to save Northern Rock PLC get through its liquidity problems. Sandler is known for saving Lloyd's of London in the mid-90's and he is not afraid to make enemies. Ron Sandler's assignment to help Northern Rock comes at a time when the health of the U.K. housing is not great.

38261 ■ *"MTV Networks" in Brandweek (Vol. 49, April 21, 2008, No. 16, pp. SR10)*
Pub: VNU Business Media, Inc.
Ed: Anthony Crupi. **Description:** Provides contact information for sales and marketing personnel for the MTV networks as well as a listing of the station's top programming and an analysis of the current season and the target audience for those programs running in the current season. MTV networks include MTV, VH1, Nickelodeon and Comedy Central.

38262 ■ *"Murdock Lifer Mans Main Street Journal" in Advertising Age (Vol. 79, July 7, 2008, No. 26, pp. 1)*
Pub: Crain Communications, Inc.
Ed: Nat Ives. **Description:** Profile of Les Hinton, the U.K. executive who was chosen by Rupert Murdoch to run Dow Jones and The Wall Street Journal; Hinton discusses The Wall Street Journal's unique spot in American business which has helped it survive a dwindling newspaper industry.

38263 ■ *"My Bad: Sometimes, Even CEOs Have to Say They're Sorry" in Inc. (October 2007, pp. 37-38)*
Pub: Gruner & Jahr USA Publishing
Ed: Donna Fenn. **Description:** A leader's stature with his employees can be elevated if he can admit a mistake simply with sincerity. Unfortunately for large companies these blunders make the news.

38264 ■ *"My Inglorious Road to Success" in Harvard Business Review (Vol. 88, July-August 2010, No. 7-8, pp. 38)*
Pub: Harvard Business School Publishing
Ed: Warren Bennis. **Description:** The author discusses the intersection of fortune and opportunity in his career success, and emphasizes the important role of awareness when taking advantage of both.

38265 ■ *"The Myth of the Overqualified Worker" in Harvard Business Review (Vol. 88, December 2010, No. 12, pp. 30)*
Pub: Harvard Business School Publishing
Ed: Andrew O'Connell. **Description:** It is recommended to seriously consider job candidates with qualifications exceeding the position being recruited because research shows these individuals work harder, but do not quit any sooner than those whose qualifications more closely match the position.

38266 ■ *"Natalie Peterson; Corporate Counsel, Steris Corp., 39" in Crain's Cleveland Business (Vol. 28, November 19, 2007, No. 46, pp. F-14)*
Pub: Crain Communications, Inc.
Ed: Chuck Soder. **Description:** Profile of Natalie Peterson, corporate counsel for Steris Corp., a manufacturer of sterilization products; Peterson's blue-collar background did not detour her from her collegiate goals although she hardly knew how to fill out a college application. After graduating from Stanford Law School in 1997, she opted to return to Cleveland in lieu of more lucrative job offers in San Francisco. She has joined the school board and has

participated in the 3Rs program, in which lawyers visit public schools in Cleveland to get students thinking about career choices and talk about constitutional law.

38267 ■ *"Nation of Islam Businessman Who Became Manager for Muhanmmad Ali Dies" in Chicago Tribune (August 28, 2008)*
Pub: McClatchy-Tribune Information Services

Ed: Trevor Jensen. **Description:** Profile of Jabir Herbert Muhammad who died on August 25, after heart surgery; Muhammad lived nearly all his life on Chicago's South Side and ran a number of small businesses including a bakery and a dry cleaners before becoming the manager to famed boxer Mohammad Ali.

38268 ■ *"NBC" in Brandweek (Vol. 49, April 21, 2008, No. 16, pp. SR6)*
Pub: VNU Business Media, Inc.

Ed: John Consoli. **Description:** Provides contact information for sales and marketing personnel for the NBC network as well as a listing of the station's top programming and an analysis of the current season and the target audience for those programs running in the current season. NBC also devised a new strategy of announcing its prime-time schedule 52 weeks in advance which was a hit for advertisers who felt this gave them a better opportunity to plan for product placement. Even with the station's creative sales programs, they could face a challenge from Fox in terms of upfront advertisement purchases.

38269 ■ *"NBC Universal Cable" in Brandweek (Vol. 49, April 21, 2008, No. 16, pp. SR11)*
Pub: VNU Business Media, Inc.

Ed: Anthony Crupi. **Description:** Provides contact information for sales and marketing personnel for the NBC Universal Cable networks as well as a listing of the station's top programming and an analysis of the current season and the target audience for those programs running in the current season. The network's stations include USA, Sci Fi and Bravo. Ad revenue for the network grew 30 percent in the first quarter.

38270 ■ *"NBC Universal Domestic Television Distribution" in Brandweek (Vol. 49, April 21, 2008, No. 16, pp. SR13)*
Pub: VNU Business Media, Inc.

Ed: Marc Berman. **Description:** Provides contact information for sales and marketing personnel for NBC Universal Domestic Television Distribution as well as a listing of the station's top programming and an analysis of the current season and the target audience for those programs running in the current season.

38271 ■ *"Need a Course Correction? Let ABWA Be Your Navigator" in Women In Business (Vol. 62, September 2010, No. 3, pp. 6)*
Pub: American Business Women's Association

Ed: Rene Street. **Description:** It is believed that the American Business Women's Association (ABWA) has the ability to help women in their quest for greater success. The organization also has the energy needed to move on to the next stage for women in business. ABWA's members have taken the initiative to embrace the group's potential.

38272 ■ *"Negotiating Tips" in Black Enterprise (Vol. 37, December 2006, No. 5, pp. 70)*
Pub: Earl G. Graves Publishing Co. Inc.

Description: Sekou Kaalund, head of strategy, mergers & acquisitions at Citigroup Securities & Fund Services, states that 'Negotiation skills are paramount to success in a business environment because of client, employee, and shareholder relationships'. He discusses how the book by George Kohlrieser, Hostage at the Table: How Leaders Can Overcome Conflict, Influence Others, and Raise Performance, has helped him negotiate more powerfully and enhance his skills at conflict-resolution.

38273 ■ *"NEMRA Announces Headquarters Move" in Agency Sales Magazine (Vol. 39, September-October 2009, No. 9, pp. 53)*
Pub: MANA

Description: NEMRA, the National Electrical Manufacturers' Representatives Association is moving their headquarters to 28 Deer Street, Suite 302, Portsmouth, New Hampshire. The association has also added Michelle Rivers-Jameson as their manager of operations and Kirsty Stebbins as their manager of marketing and member services.

38274 ■ *Never Eat Alone: And Other Secrets to Success, One Relationship at a Time*
Pub: Doubleday Broadway Publishing Group

Ed: Keith Ferrazzi, Tahl Raz. **Released:** February 2005. **Description:** Business networking strategies are offered.

38275 ■ *"The New Arsenal of Risk Management" in Harvard Business Review (Vol. 86, September 2008, No. 9, pp. 92)*
Pub: Harvard Business School Press

Ed: Kevin Bueler; Andrew Freeman; Ron Hulme. **Description:** Goldman Sachs Group Inc. is used to illustrate methods for successful risk management. The investment bank's business principles, partnerships, and oversight practices are discussed.

38276 ■ *"New BMO Boss Set to Cut 1,000 Jobs" in Globe & Mail (February 1, 2007, pp. B3)*
Pub: CTVglobemedia Publishing Inc.

Ed: Andrew Willis. **Description:** The decision of the new chief executive officer of the Bank of Montreal, Bill Downe, to cut down 1,000 jobs, to boost the company's performance is discussed.

38277 ■ *"New Boss at Nortel Mines GE for New Executives" in Globe & Mail (February 6, 2006, pp. B1)*
Pub: CTVglobemedia Publishing Inc.

Ed: Catherine McLean. **Description:** Chief executive officer Mike Zafirovski of Nortel Networks Corp. appoints executives Dennis Carey, Joel Hackney and Don McKenn of GE Electric Co. The managerial abilities of Mike are discussed.

38278 ■ *"New CEO For Friendly's" in Ice Cream Reporter (Vol. 23, September 20, 2010, No. 10, pp. 1)*
Pub: Ice Cream Reporter

Description: Friendly Ice Cream Corporation named Harsha V. Agadi as new chief executive officer. Agadi has 24 years experience in food service, most recently serving as CEO of Church's Chicken.

38279 ■ *The New Role of Regional Management*
Pub: Palgrave Macmillan

Ed: Bjorn Ambos, Bodo B. Schlegelmilch. **Released:** January 19, 2010. **Price:** $95.00. **Description:** Regional management is becoming more important to companies as they expand globally. This book explores the challenges of European, United States and Asian companies and outlines how regional headquarters can develop into Dynamic Competence Relay centers to master these issues.

38280 ■ *"The New Schools" in Black Enterprise (February 2008)*
Pub: Earl G. Graves Publishing Co. Inc.

Ed: Kinsley Kanu, Jr. **Description:** Ten educational programs to help top executives keep pace with the ever-changing market trends while gaining perspective on innovation and new ideas are examined.

38281 ■ *"A New Will to Win" in Harvard Business Review (Vol. 88, September 2010, No. 9, pp. 110)*
Pub: Harvard Business School Publishing

Ed: Daniel McGinn. **Description:** Importance of succession and contingency planning are emphasized in this account of Rick Hendrick's response to business loss coupled with personal tragedy. Focus and determination in leadership are also discussed.

38282 ■ *"New Work Order" in Black Enterprise (Vol. 38, March 2008, No. 8, pp. 60)*
Pub: Earl G. Graves Publishing Co. Inc.

Description: Today's management challenges includes issues of more competition, globalization, outsourcing and technological advances. Suggestions to help create progressive leadership in small business that sustains a competitive edge are listed.

38283 ■ *"Nexstar Super Meeting Breaks Business Barriers" in Contractor (Vol. 56, November 2009, No. 11, pp. 3)*
Pub: Penton Media, Inc.

Ed: Candace Roulo. **Description:** Around 400 Nexstar members met to discuss the trends in the HVAC industry and the economic outlook for 2010. Former lead solo pilot John Foley for the Blue Angels made a presentation on how a business can increase overall productivity based on the culture of the Blue Angels. Some breakout sessions tackled how to optimize workflow and marketing.

38284 ■ *"Nine Paradoxes of Problem Solving" in Strategy and Leadership (Vol. 39, May-June 2011, No. 3, pp. 25-31)*
Pub: Emerald Group Publishing Inc.

Ed: Alex Lowy. **Description:** Nine frequently-occurring inherent paradoxes in corporate decision making for solving complex problems are identified. The methods with which these paradoxes and their influence can be recognized and dealt with for firm leaders and management team members to better understand and solve the problems are discussed.

38285 ■ *The No Asshole Rule*
Pub: Warner Books Inc.

Ed: Robert I. Sutton PhD. **Released:** February 22, 2007. **Price:** $22.99. **Description:** Problem employees are more than just a nuisance they are a serious and costly threat to corporate success and employee health.

38286 ■ *"No, Management Is Not a Profession" in Harvard Business Review (Vol. 88, July-August 2010, No. 7-8, pp. 52)*
Pub: Harvard Business School Publishing

Ed: Richard Barker. **Description:** An argument is presented that management is not a profession, as it is less focused on mastering a given body of knowledge than it is on obtaining integration and collaboration skills. Implications for teaching this new approach are also examined.

38287 ■ *"No Secrets; Businesses Find It Pays to Open Books to Employees" in Crain's Detroit Business (Vol. 26, January 18, 2010, No. 3)*
Pub: Crain Communications Inc.

Ed: Dustin Walsh. **Description:** Many businesses are finding that practicing an open-book management wherein employees share financial and decision-making duties that are usually left up to executives of firms creates a transparency within a company that eliminates the us versus them mentality between management and employees. Another benefit to this business model is that employees get to really participate in the business, learning to manage money and run a business entity.

38288 ■ *"Nobel Winners Provide Insight on Outsourcing, Contract Work" in Workforce Management (Vol. 88, November 16, 2009, No. 12, pp. 11)*
Pub: Crain Communications Inc.

Ed: Jeremy Smerd. **Description:** Insights into such workforce management issues as bonuses, employee contracts and outsourcing has been recognized by the Nobel Prize winners in economics whose research sheds a light on the way economic decisions are made outside markets.

38289 ■ *"Nobody Knows What To Do" in Barron's (Vol. 88, March 17, 2008, No. 11, pp. 40)*
Pub: Dow Jones & Company, Inc.

Ed: Mark Veverka. **Description:** Attendees of the South by Southwest Interactive conference failed to get an insight on how to make money on the Web from former Walt Disney CEO Michael Eisner when

Eisner said there's no proven business model for financing projects. Eisner said he finances his projects with the help of his connections to get product-placement deals.

38290 ■ *Non-Standard Employment under Globalization*
Pub: Palgrave Macmillan

Ed: Koichi Usami. **Released:** January 19, 2010. **Price:** $100.00. **Description:** Expansion of non-standard employment under globalization is being recognized in all of the newly industrialized countries. The book examines deregulation of labor markets, social protection for nonstandard workers, and social security reforms in accordance with the transformation of employment.

38291 ■ *"Nortel Makes Customers Stars in New Campaign" in Brandweek (Vol. 49, April 21, 2008, No. 16, pp. 8)*
Pub: VNU Business Media, Inc.

Ed: Mike Beirne. **Description:** Nortel has launched a new television advertising campaign in which the business-to-business communications technology provider cast senior executives in 30-second TV case studies that show how Nortel's technology helped their businesses innovate.

38292 ■ *"Not Just for Kids: ADHD can be Debilitating for an Employee, and Frustrating for Bosses" in Canadian Business (April 14, 2008)*
Pub: Rogers Media

Ed: Andy Holloway. **Description:** Up to four percent of North American adults continue to feel the effects of Attention Deficit Hyperactivity Disorder or Attention Deficit Disorder. Explaining the value of the task at hand to people who are afflicted with these conditions is one way to keep them engaged in the workplace. Giving them opportunities to create their own working structure is another strategy to manage these people.

38293 ■ *Now, Discover Your Strengths*
Pub: Free Press/Simon & Schuster

Ed: Marcus Buckingham; Donald O. Clifton. **Price:** $30.00. **Description:** How to identify and develop your talents and those of your employees.

38294 ■ *Nudge*
Pub: Penguin Group USA Inc.

Ed: Richard H. Thaler, Cass R. Sunstein. **Description:** Advice is given to help improve the decision-making process in order to become a successful entrepreneur.

38295 ■ *"The Office: Do Not Disturb" in Inc. (November 2007, pp. 144)*
Pub: Gruner & Jahr USA Publishing

Ed: Leigh Buchanan. **Description:** The importance for any CEO to be accessible to his employees is stressed.

38296 ■ *"The Office: Good to Great" in Inc. (October 2007, pp. 140)*
Pub: Gruner & Jahr USA Publishing

Ed: Leigh Buchanan. **Description:** Qualities that make a good manager great are explored. Great bosses make their employees feel smart, they know who performs what job, know when to step back, and remember things about each employee such as their families' names.

38297 ■ *"Office Pests" in Canadian Business (Vol. 79, October 9, 2006, No. 20, pp. 122)*
Pub: Rogers Media

Ed: Calvin Leung. **Description:** Personality traits of employees and strategies for managers to effectively handle them are discussed.

38298 ■ *"The Office: The Bad and the Ugly" in Inc. (January 2008, pp. 120)*
Pub: Gruner & Jahr USA Publishing

Ed: Leigh Buchanan. **Description:** Seven signs that you are a bad boss are outlined to help managers improve their skills.

38299 ■ *The Official Guide for GMAT Verbal Review, 2nd Edition*
Pub: John Wiley & Sons, Inc.

Ed: Graduate Management Admissions Council. **Released:** August 17, 2009. **Price:** $17.95. **Description:** The only official verbal review for the GMAT from the creators of the test. The guide provides questions, answers, and explanations and targets study and helps improve verbal skills by focusing on the ability to read and comprehend written material, to reason and evaluate arguments, and to correct written material to conform to Standard English.

38300 ■ *"Olympus is Urged to Revise Board" in Wall Street Journal Eastern Edition (November 28, 2011, pp. B3)*
Pub: Dow Jones & Company Inc. Enterprise Media Group
Contact: Clare Hart, President

Ed: Phred Dvorak. **Description:** Koji Miyata, once a director on the board of troubled Japanese photographic equipment company, is urging the company to reorganize its board, saying the present group should resign their board seats but keep their management positions. The company has come under scrutiny for its accounting practices and costly acquisitions.

38301 ■ *"OMERS Labors With Troubles at the Top" in Globe & Mail (February 26, 2007, pp. B3)*
Pub: CTVglobemedia Publishing Inc.

Ed: Elizabeth Church. **Description:** The trouble over fund management and leadership change in the Ontario Municipal Employees Retirement System is discussed.

38302 ■ *"On the Clock" in Canadian Business (Vol. 82, April 27, 2009, No. 7, pp. 28)*
Pub: Rogers Media

Ed: Sarka Halas. **Description:** Survey of 100 Canadian executives found that senior managers can be out of a job for about nine months before their careers are adversely affected. The nine month mark can be avoided if job seekers build networks even before they lose their jobs. Job seekers should also take volunteer work and training opportunities to increase their changes of landing a job.

38303 ■ *On the Make: Clerks and the Quest for Capital in Nineteenth-Century America*
Pub: New York University Press
Contact: Steve Maikowski, Director
E-mail: steve.maikowski@nyu.edu

Ed: Brian Luskey. **Released:** January 1, 2010. **Price:** $48.00. **Description:** Through exploration into the diaries, newspapers, credit reports, census data, advice literature and fiction, the book presents the origins of the white collar culture, the antebellum clerk.

38304 ■ *"On Managerial Relevance" in Journal of Marketing (Vol. 75, July 2011, No. 4, pp. 211)*
Pub: American Marketing Association

Ed: Bernard J. Jaworski. **Description:** A study to define and clarify managerial relevance, in order to act as a catalyst for debate, disagreement and future scholarship, is presented. The role of chief marketing officer (CMO) is examined to identify areas of inquiry that are both novel and high managerially relevant. The analysis reveals the seven core tasks necessary to perform the CMO role.

38305 ■ *"On a Mission: Ginch Gonch Wants You to Get Rid of Your Tighty Whities" in Canadian Business (Vol. 81, September 29, 2008, No. 16)*
Pub: Rogers Media Ltd.

Ed: Michelle Magnan. **Description:** New Equity Capital acquired underwear maker Ginch Gonch in July 2008; founder Jason Sutherland kept his position as creative director of the company and will retain his title as 'director of stitches and inches'. The company is known for its products, which are reminiscent of the days when people wore underwear covered in cowboys and stars as kids. The company also claims that Nelly, Justin Timberlake, and Hilary Duff have worn their products.

38306 ■ *"On a Roll" in Canadian Business (Vol. 79, October 9, 2006, No. 20, pp. 51)*
Pub: Rogers Media

Ed: Joe Castaldo. **Description:** Corporate management strategies of Denis Turcotte, chief executive officer of Algoma Steel Inc., are presented.

38307 ■ *"On Track" in Canadian Business (Vol. 79, July 17, 2006, No. 14-15, pp. 51)*
Pub: Rogers Media

Ed: John Gray. **Description:** Results of the annual survey conducted by CanadaEs boards, to measure the levels of corporate governance of firms in Canada, which are presented.

38308 ■ *One Foot Out the Door: How to Combat the Psychological Recession That's Alienating Employees and Hurting American Business*
Pub: AMACOM

Ed: Judith M. Bardwick. **Released:** October 31, 2007. **Price:** $24.95. **Description:** Drawing on research that indicates Generation X and younger baby boomers feel disconnected from their jobs, the author explores the causes (bad management) of that disengagement. Her pragmatic suggestions about how companies can prove their commitment to employees is beneficial.

38309 ■ *"One Hundred Years of Excellence in Business Education: What Have We Learned?" in Business Horizons (January-February 2008)*
Pub: Elsevier Advanced Technology Publications

Ed: Frank Acito, Patricia M. McDougall, Daniel C. Smith. **Description:** Business schools have to be more innovative, efficient and nimble, so that the quality of the next generation of business leaders is improved. The Kelley School of Business, Indiana University ahs long been a leader in business education. The trends that influence the future of business education and useful success principles are discussed.

38310 ■ *The One Minute Manager*
Pub: William Morrow

Ed: Kenneth H. Blanchard, Spencer Johnson. **Released:** September 1, 1982. **Price:** $21.95. **Description:** Managers of small businesses as well as Fortune 500 companies have been following the management techniques described in this book. Results have shown increased productivity, job satisfaction, and personal prosperity.

38311 ■ *"One-Time Area Trust Executive Finds Trouble in N.H." in The Business Journal-Serving Metropolitan Kansas City (September 12, 2008)*
Pub: American City Business Journals, Inc.

Ed: Steve Vockrodt. **Description:** About 200 investors, some from Missouri's Kansas City area, claim that they had conducted business with Noble Trust Co. The trust company was placed under New Hampshire Banking Department's conservatorship after $15 million was discovered to be missing from its account. It is alleged that the money was lost in a Colorado Ponzi scheme.

38312 ■ *The Opposable Mind: How Successful Leaders Win Through Integrative Thinking*
Pub: Harvard Business School Press

Ed: Roger Martin. **Released:** December 2007. **Description:** The importance of integrative thinking for successful management is discussed.

38313 ■ *The Orange Revolution*
Pub: Free Press

Ed: Adrian Gostick, Chester Elton. **Released:** September 21, 2010. **Price:** $25.00. **Description:** Based on a 350,000-person study by the Best Companies Group, as well as research into exceptional teams at leading companies, including Zappos.com, Pepsi Beverages Company, and Madison Square Garden, the authors have determined a key set of characteristics displayed by members of breakthrough teams, and have identified a set of rules great teams live by, which generate a culture of positive teamwork and led to extraordinary results. Using specific stories from the teams they studied, they reveal in detail how these teams operate and how managers can transform their own teams into such high performers by fostering: stronger clarity of goals, greater trust among team members, more open and honest dialogue, stronger accountability for all team members, and purpose-based recognition of team member contributions.

38314 ■ *"Organizing for Disaster: Lessons from the Military" in Business Horizons (November-December 2007, pp. 479)*
Pub: Elsevier Technology Publications
Ed: Michael R. Weeks. **Description:** Design of resilient and robust organizational structures for disaster management is discussed. These structures must be planned before disasters in order to be more effective and efficient.

38315 ■ *Other Essentials of Business Ownership*
Pub: PublishAmerica, Incorporated
Ed: Charles Shaw. **Released:** May 2006. **Price:** $19. 95. **Description:** Things a business owner, entrepreneur, or manager must be aware of in order to successfully manage a small business.

38316 ■ *Our Iceberg is Melting*
Pub: St. Martin's Press
Contact: Sally Richardson, President
E-mail: sally.richardson@stmartins.com
Ed: John Kotter; Holger Rathgeber. **Released:** September 2006. **Price:** $19.95. **Description:** A fable about how to bring about change in a group.

38317 ■ *Out of the Comfort Zone: Learning to Expect the Unexpected*
Pub: Morgan & Claypool Publishers
Ed: Lisbeth Borbye. **Released:** May 10, 2010. **Price:** $35.00. **Description:** A collection of lectures covering technology, management and entrepreneurship.

38318 ■ *"The Outcome of an Organization Overhaul" in Black Enterprise (Vol. 41, December 2010, No. 5)*
Pub: Earl G. Graves Publishing Co. Inc.
Ed: Tamara E. Holmes. **Description:** Savvy business owners understand the need for change in order to stay competitive and be successful. This article examines how to manage change as well as what strategies can help employees to get with the program faster.

38319 ■ *Outsmart! How to Do What Your Competitors Can't*
Pub: FT Press
Ed: Jim Champy. **Released:** March 7, 2008. **Price:** $22.99. **Description:** Small business growth can be achieved through outsmarting your competition. The author identifies eight powerful ways to compete in the toughest marketplace.

38320 ■ *Overcoming the Five Dysfunctions of a Team: A Field Guide for Leaders, Manager, and Facilitators*
Pub: John Wiley and Sons, Inc.
Ed: Patrick M. Lencioni. **Released:** March 2005. **Price:** $26.95. **Description:** Tools, exercises, assessment, and real-world examples for overcoming the five dysfunctions of a team.

38321 ■ *"Owning the Right Risks" in Harvard Business Review (Vol. 86, September 2008, No. 9, pp. 102)*
Pub: Harvard Business School Press
Ed: Kevin Bueler; Andrew Freeman; Ron Hulme. **Description:** TXU Corp. is used to illustrate methods for successful risk management. The electric utility's practices include determining which risks are natural, embedding risk in all processes and decisions, and organizing corporate governance around risk.

38322 ■ *"Pack Mentality" in Crain's Chicago Business (Vol. 31, April 21, 2008, No. 16, pp. 31)*
Pub: Crain Communications, Inc.
Ed: Sarah A. Klein. **Description:** Jill Smart, the head of human resources for a company with 170,000 employees worldwide, frequently travels to India, London and Singapore; Ms. Smart provides advice concerning efficiency, time management and avoiding jet-lag.

38323 ■ *"Part-Time Assignments" in Black Enterprise (Vol. 37, December 2006, No. 5, pp. 70)*
Pub: Earl G. Graves Publishing Co. Inc.
Description: During critical change initiatives interim management, an employment model which uses senior-level executives to manage a special project or specific business function on a temporary basis, can have many benefits.

38324 ■ *A Passion for Planning: Financials, Operations, Marketing, Management, and Ethics*
Pub: University Press of America Inc.
Contact: Kelly Rogers, Director
URL(s): rowman.com. **Price:** $60.99, Individuals Paperback; £37.95, Individuals Paperback. **Covers:** Small business topics, including growth, manufacturing, technology, sales, distribution, services, resources, networking, and business ethics. **Entries include:** Contact details, Web sites.

38325 ■ *"Passionate About Empowering Women" in Women In Business (Vol. 63, Spring 2011, No. 1, pp. 24)*
Pub: American Business Women's Association
Ed: Leigh Elmore. **Description:** Krazy Coupon Ladies cofounder Joanie Demer shares her views about her book, 'Pick Another Checkout Lane, Honey', which she coauthored with Heather Wheeler. Demer believes using coupons is for everyone who wants to save money. She also believes that extreme couponing is not an exercise for those who lack organizational ability since it requires planning and discipline.

38326 ■ *"Patience May Pay Off" in Barron's (Vol. 89, July 13, 2009, No. 28, pp. 30)*
Pub: Dow Jones & Co., Inc.
Ed: Johanna Bennett. **Description:** New CEO Craig Herkert can turn around Supervalu and their shares could double to $30 in three years from June 2009 according to one investment officer. Herkert knows how to run a lean and tight operation since he has worked for Albertsons and Wal-Mart in the past.

38327 ■ *"Patricia Hemingway Hall; President, Chief Operating Officer, Health Care Service Corp." in Crain's Chicago Business (May 5, 2008)*
Pub: Crain Communications, Inc.
Ed: Mike Colias. **Description:** Profile of Patricia Hemingway Hall who is the president and chief operating officer of Health Care Service Corp., a new strategy launched by Blue Cross & Blue Shield of Illinois; the new endeavor will emphasize wellness rather than just treatment across its four health plans.

38328 ■ *"Pau Hana" in Hawaii Business (Vol. 53, December 2007, No. 6, pp. 118)*
Pub: Hawaii Business Publishing
Ed: Cathy Cruz-George. **Description:** Presented are the hobbies of four Hawaii executives as well as the reason these hobbies are an important part of their lives and add to their ability to manage effectively. Mike Wilkins, for example, is not only Turtle Bay Resort's director of sales and marketing, but is also a glider pilot, while Aubrey Hawk Public Relations president Aubrey Hawk loves baking. The interests of Queen Liliuokalani Trust's Thomas K. Kaulukukui Jr., Reyn Spooner's Tim McCullough, and Heide and Cook Ltd.'s Dexter S. Kekua, are discussed.

38329 ■ *"Pay Fell for Many Local Execs in '09" in Baltimore Business Journal (Vol. 28, July 2, 2010, No. 8, pp. 1)*
Pub: Baltimore Business Journal
Ed: Gary Haber. **Description:** Compensation for the 100 highest-paid executives in the Baltimore, Maryland area decreased in 2009, compared with 2008. At least $1 million were received by 59 out of 100 executives in 2009, while 75 earned the said amount in 2008. Factors that contributed to the executives' decisions to take pay cuts are discussed.

38330 ■ *Payback: Reaping the Rewards of Innovation*
Pub: Harvard Business School Publishing
Ed: James P. Andrew; Harold L. Sirkin; John Butman. **Released:** January 9, 2007. **Price:** $29.95. **Description:** Three different business innovation models are presented: integration, orchestration, and serving as licensor.

38331 ■ *"Paychecks of Some Bank CEOs Have a Pre-Recession Look" in Boston Business Journal (Vol. 29, May 13, 2011, No. 1, pp. 1)*
Pub: American City Business Journals Inc.
Ed: Gary Haber. **Description:** The salaries of United States-based bank chief executive officers have increased to pre-recession levels. Wells Fargo and Company's John G. Stumpf received $17.6 million in 2010. Community bank executives, on the other hand, have seen minimal increases.

38332 ■ *"Penny Chapman" in Canadian Business (Vol. 79, July 17, 2006, No. 14-15, pp. 75)*
Pub: Rogers Media
Ed: Erin Pooley. **Description:** Interview with Penny Chapman, president of Chapman's Ice Cream, who speaks about her journey from rags to riches.

38333 ■ *"Penny Chief Shops For Shares" in Barron's (Vol. 88, July 7, 2008, No. 27, pp. 29)*
Pub: Dow Jones & Co., Inc.
Ed: Teresa Rivas. **Description:** Myron Ullman III, chairman and chief executive officer of J.C. Penney, purchased $1 million worth of shares of the company. He now owns 393,140 shares of the company and an additional 1,282 on his 401(k) plan.

38334 ■ *"The People Who Influence You the Most - Believe In You" in Women In Business (Vol. 62, September 2010, No. 3, pp. 9)*
Pub: American Business Women's Association
Description: The president of the American Business Women's Association (ABWA) talks about her experiences in the organization. She believes that the dynamic women with whom she worked with helped her shape the organization into one that her predecessors believed it could become. The importance of dealing with challenges while making each experience an opportunity to learn is also discussed.

38335 ■ *"Pep Talk" in Black Enterprise (Vol. 40, July 2010, No. 12, pp. 104)*
Pub: Earl G. Graves Publishing Co. Inc.
Ed: Tennille M. Robinson. **Description:** Advice for maintaining motivation in any small business is given.

38336 ■ *"Perfecting the Process: Creating a Move Efficient Organization On Your Terms" in Black Enterprise (Vol. 41, October 2010, No. 3)*
Pub: Earl G. Graves Publishing Co. Inc.
Ed: Tamara E. Holmes. **Description:** More than ever, entrepreneurs need to identify new ways of doing business in a cost-effective manner in order to expand their companies, while remaining true to their customer demands.

38337 ■ *"Perks Still Popular: Jets May be Out, but CEO Benefits Abound" in Crain's Detroit Business (Vol. 25, June 22, 2009)*
Pub: Crain Communications Inc. - Detroit
Ed: Ryan Beene. **Description:** Benefits packages of local CEOs are outlined. Statistical data included.

38338 ■ *"Personal File: Esther Colwill" in Canadian Business (Vol. 80, April 23, 2007, No. 9, pp. 48)*
Pub: Rogers Media
Description: A brief profile of Esther Colwill, senior manager at Deloitte & Touche LLP, including her achievements which are also presented.

38339 ■ *"Personal File: Malcolm Smillie" in Canadian Business (Vol. 80, April 23, 2007, No. 9, pp. 44)*
Pub: Rogers Media
Description: A brief profile of Malcolm Smillie, marketing manager of 1-800-Got-Junk?, including his achievements which are also presented.

38340 ■ *"Peter Bynoe Trades Up" in Black Enterprise (Vol. 38, July 2008, No. 12, pp. 30)*
Pub: Earl G. Graves Publishing Co. Inc.
Ed: Alexis McCombs. **Description:** Chicago-based Loop Capital Markets L.L.C. has named Peter Bynoe managing director of corporate finance. Bynoe was previously a senior partner at the law firm DLA Piper U.S. L.L.P., where he worked on stadium deals.

38341 ■ *"Peter Gilgan" in Canadian Business (Vol. 82, April 27, 2009, No. 7, pp. 58)*
Pub: Rogers Media
Ed: Calvin Leung. **Description:** Mattamy Homes Ltd. president and chief executive officer Peter Gilgan believes that their business model of building communities in an organized way brings advantages to the firm and for their customers. He also believes in adopting their product prices to new market realities. Gilgan considers the approvals regime in Ontario his biggest challenge in the last 20 years.

38342 ■ *Pink Slip Power!: Recover and Succeed It's Up To You!*
Pub: Infinity Publishing
Ed: Wade J. Wnuk. **Released:** March 2004. **Price:** $9.95. **Description:** Advice is given to those facing loss of employment. The book discusses issues such as: restraining emotions before reacting to a severance package ceasing to brood on the past, focusing on the future, networking and looking for hidden job opportunities, preparing resumes, and gearing up for interviews. Four chapters cover ideas for facing reality, formulating a plan, promoting one's self, and persisting in the face of adversity.

38343 ■ *"Play It Safe or Take a Stand?" in Harvard Business Review (Vol. 88, November 2010, No. 11, pp. 139)*
Pub: Harvard Business School Publishing
Ed: Trish Gorman Clifford, Jay Barney. **Description:** A fictitious leadership scenario is presented, with contributors providing comments and recommendations. A female executive ponders whether to assert a point of view on a new venture. Both experts agree that after providing careful analysis of pros and cons, the executive should come to a well-informed conclusion.

38344 ■ *"The Play's the Thing" in Business Strategy Review (Vol. 21, Summer 2010, No. 2, pp. 58)*
Pub: Blackwell Publishers Ltd.
Ed: Michael G. Jacobides. **Description:** Those who study and plan strategies risk falling into the traps that maps, graphs, charts and matrices present. A better strategy might be using a playscript that can reveal the unfolding plots of business far better than traditional strategic tools as the landscapes shifts.

38345 ■ *"Political Environments and Business Strategy: Implications for Managers" in Business Horizons (Vol. 51, January-February 2008)*
Pub: Elsevier Advanced Technology Publications
Ed: Gerald D. Keim, Amy J. Hillman. **Description:** Various government bodies and business organizations work together in shaping new business opportunities and policies that arise from globalization. Presented is framework of public policy considerations for business managers. The framework is based on Nobel laureate Douglas North's work.

38346 ■ *The Portable MBA in Entrepreneurship*
Pub: John Wiley & Sons, Inc.
Ed: Andrew Zacharakis, William D. Bygrave. **Released:** December 9, 2010. **Price:** $34.95. **Description:** An updated and revised new edition of the comprehensive guide to modern entrepreneurship that tracks the core curriculum of leading business schools.

38347 ■ *"Positive Transformational Change" in Indoor Comfort Marketing (Vol. 70, April 2011, No. 4, pp. 30)*
Pub: Industry Publications Inc.
Ed: Blaine Fox. **Description:** Management changes taking place at Shark Bites HVAC firm are discussed.

38348 ■ *"Potash Sale Must Be Blocked" in Canadian Business (Vol. 83, October 12, 2010, No. 17, pp. 24)*
Pub: Rogers Media Ltd.
Ed: Kasey Coholan. **Description:** Chief executive officers (CEOs) and corporate leaders in Canada are concerned about the possible sale of Potash Corporation to foreign buyers. A Compas Inc. poll recently asked CEOs whether the Canadian Government should step in to block the sale of the country's largest fertilizer firm.

38349 ■ *"The Power of ABWA" in Women In Business (Vol. 62, September 2010, No. 3, pp. 36)*
Pub: American Business Women's Association
Ed: Leigh Elmore. **Description:** Information about the internship received by Erica Rockley at American Business Women's Association (ABWA) headquarters is presented. Rockley received heartfelt professional advice the days she spent at the office. She also learned the importance of networking.

38350 ■ *Power Ambition Glory*
Pub: Crown Business
Ed: Steve Forbes, John Prevas. **Released:** June 16, 2009. **Price:** $26.00. **Description:** An examination into the lives of the ancient world's greatest leaders and the lessons they have for today's business leaders.

38351 ■ *The Power of Full Engagement: Managing Energy, Not Time, is the Key to High Performance and Personal Renewal*
Pub: Free Press/Simon & Schuster
Ed: Jim Loehr; Tony Schwartz. **Released:** December 21, 2004. **Price:** $15.95 paperback. **Description:** The book presents a program to help stressed individuals find more purpose in their work and ways to better handle overburdened relationships.

38352 ■ *"Power In the Boardroom" in Black Enterprise (Vol. 38, February 2008, No. 7, pp. 112)*
Pub: Earl G. Graves Publishing Co. Inc.
Ed: Derek T. Dingle. **Description:** Comprehensive list of Black corporate directors for 250 of the largest companies in the U.S.; these leaders play a critical role in business development.

38353 ■ *"Power Play" in Harvard Business Review (Vol. 88, July-August 2010, No. 7-8, pp. 84)*
Pub: Harvard Business School Publishing
Ed: Jeffrey Pfeffer. **Description:** Guidelines include in-depth understanding of resources at one's disposal, relentlessness that still provides opponents with opportunities to save face, and a determination not to be put off by the processes of politics.

38354 ■ *The Power of a Positive No: How to Say No and Still Get to Yes*
Pub: Random Housing Publishing Group
Ed: William Ury. **Released:** December 2007. **Price:** $16.00. **Description:** According to the author, a positive no begins with yes and ends with yes.

38355 ■ *The Power of Pull: How Small Moves, Smartly Made, Can Set Big Things in Motion*
Pub: Basic Books
Ed: John Hagel III, Seely Brown, Lang Divison. **Released:** April 13, 2010. **Description:** Examination of how we can effectively address the most pressing challenges in a rapidly changing and increasingly interdependent world is addressed. New ways in which passionate thinking, creative solutions, and committed action can and will make it possible for small businesses owners to seize opportunities and remain in step with change.

38356 ■ *"Powerlessness Corrupts" in Harvard Business Review (Vol. 88, July-August 2010, No. 7-8, pp. 36)*
Pub: Harvard Business School Publishing
Ed: Rosabeth Moss Kanter. **Description:** Studies show that individuals who perceive that they are being treated poorly and denied sufficient freedom for a certain level of autonomy are more likely to act negatively.

38357 ■ *Predictable Results in Unpredictable Times*
Pub: RosettaBooks LLC
Ed: Stephen R. Covey, Bob Whitman, Breck England. **Released:** August 7, 2009. **Price:** $9.99. **Description:** Four essentials for getting great performance in good times and bad are outlined for any small business.

38358 ■ *"Prevent Disasters In Design Outsourcing" in Harvard Business Review (Vol. 86, September 2008, No. 9, pp. 30)*
Pub: Harvard Business School Press
Ed: Jason Amaral; Geoffrey Parker. **Description:** Factors that could compromise the quality and success of product platform outsourcing are examined including misaligned objectives and inadequate version control.

38359 ■ *"Price War: Managerial Salaries Are Beating the National Average, But Maybe Not for Long" in Canadian Business (March 31, 2008)*
Pub: Rogers Media
Ed: Megan Harman. **Description:** Real average hourly earnings of managers increase by 20 percent in ten years as companies increase wages to avoid the risk of losing key managers to the competition and in preparation for the retirement of baby boomers. Tough market conditions affect management more since their incentives are tied to individual and corporate performance.

38360 ■ *"Prichard the Third" in Canadian Business (Vol. 83, October 12, 2010, No. 17, pp. 34)*
Pub: Rogers Media Ltd.
Ed: Thomas Watson. **Description:** Robert Prichard, the new chair of international business law firm Torys, talks about his current role; his job involved advising clients, representing the firm, being part of the leadership team, and recruiting talent. He considers 'Seven Days in Tibet' as the first book to have an influence on his world view.

38361 ■ *"Profile" in Business Strategy Review (Vol. 21, Summer 2010, No. 2, pp. 86)*
Pub: Blackwell Publishers Ltd.
Description: In a new series, profiles of a major thinker who has made a significant difference in how organizations are managed and how business careers are shaped are presented.

38362 ■ *"Profile: Lynda Gratton" in Business Strategy Review (Vol. 21, Autumn 2010, No. 3, pp. 74)*
Pub: Blackwell Publishers Ltd.
Ed: Stuart Crainer. **Description:** The early 20th Century marked the dawn of modern enterprise management and no one influenced its practice more than Frederick W. Taylor, inventor of 'scientific management'. The early 21st Century marks a radical transformation of management.

38363 ■ *"Profile: Lynda Gratton" in Business Strategy Review (Vol. 21, Autumn 2010, No. 3, pp. 74)*
Pub: Wiley-Blackwell
Ed: Stuart Crainer. **Description:** The early 20th Century marked the dawn of modern enterprise management, and no one influenced its practice more than Frederick W. Taylor, inventor of 'scientific management'. This radical transformation of management and among the few thinkers most influencing this transformation is Lynda Gratton, London Business School Professor of Management Practice.

38364 ■ *"The Profitability of Mobility" in Entrepreneur (Vol. 37, September 2009, No. 9, pp. 98)*
Pub: Entrepreneur Media, Inc.
Ed: John Daley. **Description:** Wireless Zone franchisee Jonah Engler says he manages the business by hiring managers that could do the job. He has given his employees small equity ownership in the company. He also says great service and referrals have contributed to his business' growth.

38365 ■ *Project Management for Small Business Made Easy*
Pub: Entrepreneur Press
Ed: Sid Kemp. **Released:** April 2006. **Price:** $26.95. **Description:** Strategies for implementing project management for small business are offered.

38366 ■ *"Project Managers' Creed: Learn It, Live It" in Contractor (Vol. 56, November 2009, No. 11, pp. 46)*
Pub: Penton Media, Inc.
Ed: Kent Craig. **Description:** Project managers should take the health and safety of their subordinates above all else. A manager should deal with the things that distract him from his job before starting a day on the site. The manager should maintain a comfortable and relaxed attitude with his employees.

38367 ■ *"Public Opinion" in Entrepreneur (Vol. 36, April 2008, No. 4, pp. 28)*
Pub: Entrepreneur Media, Inc.
Ed: Aliza Sherman. **Description:** According to a 2007 report from Group and Organization Management, women in top positions can lead publicly traded companies to stock price and earnings growth. Some women business owners say that going public has provided them with the capital to grow. Details on the potential of women-managed publicly traded companies are discussed.

38368 ■ *"Putting an End to End-of-Year Reviews" in Inc. (December 2007, pp. 58, 61)*
Pub: Gruner & Jahr USA Publishing
Ed: Scott Westcott. **Description:** Performance assessments can be used in place of blunt employee reviews in order to create effective annual reviews.

38369 ■ *"The Puzzle of Our Productivity" in Canadian Business (Vol. 83, September 14, 2010, No. 15, pp. 22)*
Pub: Rogers Media Ltd.
Ed: Rachel Madison. **Description:** Industry Canada economist Annette Ryan revealed in a presentation to the Canadian Association for Business Economics that growth in Canadian labor productivity has steadily declined since the 1980s. Ryan believes that business decisions have played an important role in the poor productivity results. Other details of the findings are presented.

38370 ■ *"Q&A Patrick Pichette" in Canadian Business (Vol. 81, October 13, 2008, No. 17, pp. 6)*
Pub: Rogers Media Ltd.
Ed: Andrew Wahl. **Description:** Patrick Pichette finds challenge in taking over the finances of an Internet company that has a market cap of about $140 billion. He feels, however, that serving as Google's chief financial officer is nothing compared to running Bell Canada Enterprises (BCE). Pichette's other views on Google and BCE are presented.

38371 ■ *"QuikTrip Makes Fortune 'Best' List" in Tulsa World (January 22, 2010)*
Pub: Tulsa World
Ed: Kyle Arnold. **Description:** According to a list released by Fortune Magazine, QuikTrip Corp. is once again ranked among the best companies in the country to work for due to the core values and culture held by the company's management.

38372 ■ *"Race and Gender Diversity" in Business Horizons (November-December 2007, pp. 445)*
Pub: Elsevier Technology Publications
Ed: James C. Wimbush. **Description:** Research conducted on diversity building, employee recruitment, gender issues in management, and pay inequality from 2006 through present are discussed. Diversity conditions and attitudes toward it are slowly improving based on these findings.

38373 ■ *"Randy Perreira" in Hawaii Business (Vol. 53, February 2008, No. 8, pp. 28)*
Pub: Hawaii Business Publishing
Ed: David K. Choo. **Description:** Randy Perreira is recently named executive director of Hawaii Government Employees Association. He talks about how he was shaped growing up with a father who was a labor leader and how the challenges in 2008 compare with those in the time of his father. He also shares his thoughts about the importance of employees fighting for their rights.

38374 ■ *"The RBC Dynasty Continues" in Globe & Mail (January 30, 2006, pp. B1)*
Pub: CTVglobemedia Publishing Inc.
Ed: Gordon Pitts. **Description:** The details on business growth of Royal Bank of Canada, under chief executive officer Gordon Nixon, are presented.

38375 ■ *"The Real Job of Boards" in Business Strategy Review (Vol. 21, Autumn 2010, No. 3, pp. 36)*
Pub: Wiley-Blackwell
Ed: Harry Korine, Macrus Alexander, Pierre-Yves Gomez. **Description:** Widely seen as the key for ensuring quality in corporate governance, the board of directors has been a particular focal point for reform. The authors believe that more leadership at board level could avert many corporate crises in the future.

38376 ■ *"Real-Life Coursework for Real-Life Business People" in Women In Business (Vol. 63, Summer 2011, No. 2, pp. 22)*
Pub: American Business Women's Association
Ed: Leigh Elmore. **Description:** American Business Women's Association National Women's Leadership Conference provides members with academic business training courses. Members can take a variety of MBA-level courses that are taught by University of Kansas School of Business professors. Courses include marketing, management, leadership and communication and decision making.

38377 ■ *Reality-Based Leadership: Ditch the Drama, Restore Sanity to the Workplace*
Pub: Jossey-Bass
Ed: Cy Wakeman. **Price:** $27.95. **Description:** Recent polls show that 71 percent of workers think about quitting their jobs every day. That number would be shocking if people actually were quitting. Worse, they go to work, punching time clocks and collecting pay checks, while checked out emotionally. Cy Wakeman reveals how to be the kind of leader who changes the way people think about and perceive their circumstances, one who deals with the facts, clarifies roles, gives clean and direct feedback, and insists that everyone do the same without drama or defensiveness.

38378 ■ *Reality Check: The Irreverent Guide to Outsmarting, Outmanaging, and Outmarketing Your Competition*
Pub: Penguin Group USA Inc.
Ed: Guy Kawasaki. **Price:** $29.95. **Description:** Marketing guru and entrepreneur, Guy Kawasaki, provides a compilation of his blog posts on all aspects of starting and operating a business.

38379 ■ *"Recession Drags Down CEO Pay; Full Impact May Not Have Played Out" in Crain's Detroit Business (Vol. 25, June 22, 2009, No. 25)*
Pub: Crain Communications Inc. - Detroit
Ed: Ryan Beene. **Description:** Median overall compensation package for Detroit's top-compensated 50 CEOs was down 10.67 percent from $2.3 million in 2007 to $2.06 million in 2008. Statistical data included.

38380 ■ *"The Recession: Problem or Opportunity" in Women In Business (Vol. 61, October-November 2009, No. 5, pp. 34)*
Pub: American Business Women's Association
Ed: J. Douglas Bate. **Description:** Business organizations' success during a recession is based on how management views the economic situation. The recession may be deemed as a setback or may be visualized as an opportunity that has to be grabbed for the organization. Suggestions on what management should do in the opportunity-creating or proactive approach are also highlighted.

38381 ■ *"Redefining Failure" in Harvard Business Review (Vol. 88, September 2010, No. 9, pp. 34)*
Pub: Harvard Business School Publishing
Ed: Seth Godin. **Description:** Specific forms of failure, including design failure, failure of priorities, failure of opportunity, and failure to quit are examined. The negative implications of maintaining the status quo are discussed.

38382 ■ *"Reduce the Risk of Failed Financial Judgments" in Harvard Business Review (Vol. 86, July-August 2008, No. 8, pp. 24)*
Pub: Harvard Business School Press
Ed: Robert G. Eccles; Edward J. Fiedl. **Description:** Utilization of business consultants, evaluators, appraisers, and actuaries to decrease financial management risks is discussed.

38383 ■ *"Reinventing Management" in Harvard Business Review (Vol. 88, July-August 2010, No. 7-8, pp. 167)*
Pub: Harvard Business School Publishing
Ed: Roberta Fusaro. **Description:** Review of the book, 'Reinventing Management' is presented.

38384 ■ *"The Reinvention of Management" in Strategy and Leadership (Vol. 39, March-April 2011, No. 2, pp. 9)*
Pub: Emerald Group Publishing Inc.
Ed: Stephen Denning. **Description:** An examination found that critical changes in management practice involves five shifts. These shifts involve the firm's goals, model of coordination, the role of managers and values practiced. Other findings of the study are discussed.

38385 ■ *"The Relationship Between Boards and Planning In Family Businesses" in Family Business Review (Vol. 19, March 2006, No. 1, pp. 65)*
Pub: Family Firm Institute
Contact: Judy L. Green, President
Ed: Timothy Blumentritt. **Description:** Study determining the extent of control exercised by board of directors and advisory boards on business planning within family-owned businesses is covered.

38386 ■ *"Relocation, Relocation, Relocation" in Conde Nast Portfolio (Vol. 2, June 2008, No. 6, pp. 36)*
Pub: Conde Nast Publications
Contact: David Carey, President
Ed: Michelle Leder. **Description:** Perks regarding executive relocation are discussed.

38387 ■ *Remarkable Leadership*
Pub: Jossey Bass
Ed: Kevin Eikenberry. **Released:** August 30, 2007. **Price:** $27.95. **Description:** Handbook for anyone wishing to be an outstanding business leader; the framework and a mechanism for learning new things and applying current knowledge in a practical to any business situation is outlined.

38388 ■ *"Remind Managers to Avoid Talk of Employee Longevity" in HR Specialist (Vol. 8, September 2010, No. 9, pp. 3)*
Pub: Capitol Information Group Inc.
Description: Supervisors need to understand that casual conversations can be used against an organization in law suits.

38389 ■ *"Research Highlights Disengaged Workforce" in Workforce Management (Vol. 88, November 16, 2009, No. 12, pp. 22)*
Pub: Crain Communications Inc.
Ed: Ed Frauenheim. **Description:** Most researchers have documented a drop in employee engagement during the recession due to such factors as layoffs, restructuring and less job security.

38390 ■ *"Research Note" in International Journal of Globalisation and Small Business (Vol. 4, September 21, 2010, No. 1, pp. 92)*
Pub: Publishers Communication Group
Ed: Alexander Bode, Tobias B. Talmon l'Armee, Simon Alig. **Description:** The cluster concept has steadily increased its importance during the past years both from practitioners' and reearchers' points of view. Simultaneously, many corporate networks are established. Researchers from different areas (business management, economic social and geographical science) are trying to explain both phenomena.

38391 ■ *"Research in Personnel and Human Resources Management, Vol. 28" in Human Resource Management (Vol. 49, July-August 2010, No. 4)*
Pub: John Wiley
Ed: Mukta Kulkarni. **Description:** An overview of the book, 'Research in Personnel and Human Resources Management', Vol. 28 is presented.

38392 ■ *The Restaurant Manager's Handbook: How to Set Up, Operate, and Manage a Financially Successful Food Service Operation*
Pub: Atlantic Publishing Company
Released: September 25, 2007. **Price:** $79.95. **Description:** Insight is offered on running a successful food service business. Nine new chapters detail restaurant layout, new equipment, principles for creating a safer work environment, and new effective techniques to interview, hire, train, and manage employees.

38393 ■ *"Rethinking the Organization" in Strategy & Leadership (Vol. 38, September-October 2010, No. 5, pp. 13-19)*
Pub: Emerald Inc.
Ed: Stephen Denning. **Description:** A study identifies the changes needed to be adopted by top managers to achieve game-changing innovation at an organization-wide level. Findings indicate that CEOs should practice pull management in order to nurture fruitful communication between employees and customers and achieve organizational involvement of customers.

38394 ■ *"Retiring Baby Boomers and Dissatisfied Gen-Xers Cause..Brain Drain" in Agency Sales Magazine (Vol. 39, November 2009, No. 10)*
Pub: MANA
Ed: Denise Kelly. **Description:** Due to the impending retirement of the baby boomers a critical loss of knowledge and experience in businesses will result. Creating a plan to address this loss of talent centered on the development of the younger generation is discussed.

38395 ■ *"Risk Management Starts at the Top" in Business Strategy Review (Vol. 21, Spring 2010, No. 1, pp. 18)*
Pub: Wiley-Blackwell
Ed: Paul Strebel, Hongze Lu. **Description:** Authors question why, at the end of 2008, Citigroup, Merrill Lynch and UBS had well over $40 billion in sub-prime write-downs and credit losses, while some of their competitors were much less exposed. Their research into the situation revealed correlations of great import to today's firms.

38396 ■ *"Robert S. McNamara and the Evolution of Modern Management" in Harvard Business Review (Vol. 88, December 2010, No. 12, pp. 86)*
Pub: Harvard Business School Publishing
Ed: Phil Rosenzweig. **Description:** A chronicle of the emergence and development of Robert S. McNamara's management skills and perspectives, focusing on the role of his idealism. Lessons learned during the course of the Vietnam Ware are also delineated.

38397 ■ *"The Role of Human and Financial Capital in the Profitability and Growth of Women-Owned Small Firms" in Journal of Small Business Management*
Pub: Blackwell Publishing Inc.
Contact: Gordon Tibbitts, President
Ed: Susan Coleman. **Description:** Examines the relationship between the human and financial capital in both men and women-owned businesses and firm performance in the service and retail sectors.

38398 ■ *The Role of the Non-Executive Director in the Small to Medium-Sized Business*
Pub: Palgrave Macmillan
Ed: John Smithson. **Released:** March 2004. **Price:** $95.00. **Description:** The role of the non-executive director in a small to medium-sized business is examined.

38399 ■ *"Ron Carpenter" in Crain's Cleveland Business (Vol. 30, June 29, 2009, No. 25, pp. 12)*
Pub: Crain Communications, Inc.
Ed: Dan Shingler. **Description:** Profile of Ron Carpenter, owner of Production Tool Company located in Twinsburg, Ohio. Carpenter was forced to lay off half of his staff of 14 workers after the auto business tanked. He believes it was the single most difficult decision he had to make as a manager.

38400 ■ *"The Rypple Effect; Performance Management" in The Economist (Vol. 390, January 3, 2009, No. 8612, pp. 48)*
Pub: The Economist Newspaper Inc.
Description: New companies such as Rypple, a new, web-based service, claim that they can satisfy the Net Generation's need for frequent assessments while easing the burden this creates for management.

38401 ■ *"Safety Managers Need to Be Safety Experts" in Indoor Comfort Marketing (Vol. 70, May 2011, No. 5, pp. 10)*
Pub: Industry Publications Inc.
Ed: Mike Hodge. **Description:** It is imperative to have a good safety manager in place for all heating and cooling firms.

38402 ■ *"St. Rose Professor Builds Contractors and Micro-Doctors" in Business Review, Albany New York (Vol. 34, December 28, 2007, No. 39)*
Pub: American City Business Journals, Inc.
Ed: Robin K. Cooper. **Description:** Mike Mathews is an associate professor at the College of Saint Rose School of Business and one of the founders of the Center for Micro Enterprises Development, which provides training programs on business planning and management. Details of the business school's curricula and foundations are discussed.

38403 ■ *"Salary Hike for Managers Reflects Demand" in Farmer's Weekly (March 28, 2008, No. 320)*
Pub: Reed Business Information
Contact: Jeff Greisch, President
Description: Discusses the Institute of Agricultural Management and its survey of farm managers' pay and conditions; farm managers are getting paid 25 percent more than in 2003.

38404 ■ *Salesforce.com Secrets of Success: Best Practices for Growth and Profitability*
Pub: Prentice Hall Business Publishing
Contact: Jerome Grant, President
Ed: David Taber. **Released:** May 15, 2009. **Price:** $34.99. **Description:** Guide for using Salesforce.com; it provides insight into navigating through user groups, management, sales, marketing and IT departments in order to achieve the best results.

38405 ■ *"Sandi Jackson; Alderman, 7th Ward, City of Chicago" in Crain's Chicago Business (Vol. 31, May 5, 2008, No. 18, pp. 31)*
Pub: Crain Communications, Inc.
Ed: Sarah A. Klein. **Description:** Profile of Sandi Jackson who is an alderman of the 7th ward of the city of Chicago and is addressing issues such as poverty and crime as well as counting on a plan to develop the former USX Corp. steel mill to revitalize the area's economic climate.

38406 ■ *Sarbanes-Oxley for Dummies, 2nd Ed.*
Pub: John Wiley and Sons, Inc.
Ed: Jill Gilbert Welytok. **Released:** February 2008. **Price:** $21.99. **Description:** Provides the latest Sarbanes-Oxley (SOX) legislation with procedures to safely and effectively reduce compliance costs. Topics include way to: establish SOX standards for IT professionals, minimize compliances costs for every aspect of a business, survive a Section 404 audit, avoid litigation under SOX, anticipate future rules and trends, create a post-SOX paper trail, increase a company's standing and reputation, work with SOX in a small business, meet new SOX standards, build a board that can't be bought, and to comply with all SOX management mandates.

38407 ■ *"Save the Date" in Barron's (Vol. 90, September 13, 2010, No. 37, pp. 35)*
Pub: Barron's Editorial & Corporate Headquarters
Ed: Mark Veverka. **Description:** Mark Hurd is the new Co-President of Oracle after being forced out at Hewlett-Packard where he faced a harassment complaint. HP fired Hurd due to expense account malfeasance. Hurd is also set to speak at an Oracle trade show in San Francisco on September 20, 2010.

38408 ■ *"Savvas Chamberlain" in Canadian Business (Vol. 81, March 17, 2008, No. 4, pp. 92)*
Pub: Rogers Media
Ed: Andrew Wahl. **Description:** Savvas Chamberlain says he feels cheated during his teenage years because life was not normal for him growing up in Cyprus with all the uprisings against Britain. Chamberlain says he runs Dalsa like he plays chess because all his positions are shown all the time but he keeps his strategy to himself.

38409 ■ *"A Say on Pay" in Canadian Business (Vol. 82, April 27, 2009, No. 7, pp. 14)*
Pub: Rogers Media
Ed: Joe Castaldo. **Description:** A COMPAS Inc. survey of 134 Canadian chief executive officers found that 44 percent agree that CEO compensation should be subject to a non-binding vote. The respondents were also divided on whether to allow shareholders to exercise retroactive clawbacks on executive compensation if firm performance turns out to be worse than projected.

38410 ■ *"Scholarships for Minority Students" in Occupational Outlook Quarterly (Vol. 54, Fall 2010, No. 3, pp. 25)*
Pub: U.S. Bureau of Labor Statistics
Description: Gates Millennium Scholars scholarship is awarded to minority students with leadership skills, a good GPA, and college aspirations.

38411 ■ *Science Lessons: What the Business of Biotech Taught Me About Management*
Pub: Harvard Business School Press
Ed: Gordon Binder, Philip Bashe. **Released:** 2009. **Price:** $29.95. **Description:** Former CFO of biotechnology startup Amgen and veteran of Ford Motor Company provides a universal guide to management based on some of the same scientific principles used to create new drugs.

38412 ■ *"Scouting and Keeping Good Talent in the Workplace" in Hawaii Business (Vol. 53, January 2008, No. 7, pp. 50)*
Pub: Hawaii Business Publishing
Ed: Christie Dermegian. **Description:** Tips on improving employee selection and retention are presented. The strategies in choosing and keeping the right employees include identifying which type of people the company needs and improving the workplace environment.

38413 ■ *"Scripps Networks" in Brandweek (Vol. 49, April 21, 2008, No. 16, pp. SR12)*
Pub: VNU Business Media, Inc.
Ed: Anthony Crupi. **Description:** Provides contact information for sales and marketing personnel for the Scripps networks as well as a listing of the station's top programming and an analysis of the current season and the target audience for those programs running in the current season. Scripps networks include HGTV and the Food Network. HGTV boasts on of the industry's best commercial-retention averages, keeping nearly 97 percent of its viewers during advertising breaks.

38414 ■ *"SEC Doesn't Buy Biovail's Claims" in Barron's (Vol. 88, March 31, 2008, No. 13, pp. 20)*
Pub: Dow Jones & Company, Inc.
Ed: Bill Alpert. **Description:** Overstatement of earnings and chronic fraudulent conduct has led the SEC to file a stock fraud suit against Biovail, Eugene Mel-

nyk and three others present or former employees of Biovail. Melnyk had the firm file suit in 2006 that blames short-sellers and stock researchers for the company's drop in share price.

38415 ■ *"Segmenting When It Matters" in Business Strategy Review (Vol. 21, Spring 2010, No. 1, pp. 46)*
Pub: Wiley-Blackwell
Ed: Andreas Birnik, Richard Moat. **Description:** Authors argue that business complexity is directly linked to the degree of segmentation implemented by a company. They propose an approach to map business activities at the segment level to make sure that complexity is only introduced when it really matters.

38416 ■ *"The Self-Destructive Habits of Good Companies, and How to Break Them" in Harvard Business Review (Vol. 85, July-August 2007, No. 7-8)*
Pub: Harvard Business School Publishing
Ed: John T. Landry. **Description:** Review of the book that helps companies break bad habits and develop new ones for growth and success.

38417 ■ *"Selling a Job When There's Buyer's Remorse" in Contractor (Vol. 56, December 2009, No. 12, pp. 37)*
Pub: Penton Media, Inc.
Ed: H. Kent Craig. **Description:** Advice on how contractors should manage low-profit jobs in the United States are presented. Efforts should be made to try and find at least one quality field foreman or superintendent. Contractors should also try to respectfully renegotiate the terms of the job.

38418 ■ *"A Set-Theoretic Approach to Organizational Configurations" in Academy of Management Review (October 2007, pp. 1180)*
Pub: ScholarOne, Inc.
Ed: Peer C. Fiss. **Description:** The author argues about the mismatch between theory and methods that have led to decline in research on organizational configurations. He suggests adoption of set-theoretic methods to overcome this mismatch.

38419 ■ *"Shared Leadership In Teams: An Investigation of Antecedent Conditions and Performance" in Academy of Management Journal (Oct. 2007)*
Pub: Academy of Management
Contact: Ming-Jer Chen, President
Ed: Jay B. Carson, Paul E. Tesluk, Jennifer A. Marrone. **Description:** Study assessed the advantages of distribution of leadership among team members rather than on a single person revealed advantages that ranged from support and shared functions along with higher ratings from clients on their performance.

38420 ■ *"Siemens Boss on Big Scandals, Bullet-Proof Limos" in Globe & Mail (March 5, 2007, pp. B11)*
Pub: CTVglobemedia Publishing Inc.
Description: Interview with Klaus Kleinfeld, the chief executive officer of Siemens AG, in which he shares his views on the job challenges faced by him.

38421 ■ *Silos, Politics and Turf Wars: A Leadership Fable about Destroying the Barriers That Turn Colleagues Into Competitors*
Pub: Jossey Bass
Ed: Patrick M. Lencioni. **Released:** February 17, 2006. **Price:** $24.95. **Description:** The author addresses management problems through a fable that revolves around a self-employed consultant who has to dismantle silos at an upscale hotel, a technology company and a hospital. The story explains how organizations can use a collective operational vision in order to overcome pride, greed, and tribalism and work as a team with the same goal in mind.

38422 ■ *"Six Sears Board Members to Resign in April" in Globe & Mail (March 1, 2006, pp. B1)*
Pub: CTVglobemedia Publishing Inc.
Ed: Marina Strauss. **Description:** The reasons behind the departure of six board members of Sears Canada Inc. are presented.

38423 ■ *"Size Matters" in Entrepreneur (Vol. 36, April 2008, No. 4, pp. 44)*
Pub: Entrepreneur Media, Inc.
Ed: Robert Kiyosaki. **Description:** Entrepreneurs planning to expand their business face challenges when it comes to employing more people and addressing internal relationships, communications and procedures. People skills, organizational skills and leadership skills are some of the things to consider before adding employees.

38424 ■ *"Skinner's No Drive-Thru CEO" in Crain's Chicago Business (Vol. 31, April 28, 2008, No. 17, pp. 1)*
Pub: Crain Communications, Inc.
Ed: David Sterrett. **Description:** Profile of James Skinner who was named CEO for McDonald's Corp. in November 2004 and has proved to be a successful leader despite the number of investors who doubted him when he came to the position. Mr. Skinner has overseen three years of unprecedented sales growth and launched the biggest menu expansion in 30 years.

38425 ■ *Small Business Clustering Technology: Applications in Marketing, Management, Finance, and IT*
Pub: Idea Group Publishing
Ed: Robert C. MacGregor; Ann Hodgkinson. **Released:** June 2006. **Description:** An overview of the development and role of small business clusters in disciplines that include economics, marketing, management and information systems.

38426 ■ *Small Business for Dummies, 3rd Ed.*
Pub: John Wiley and Sons, Inc.
Ed: Eric Tyson; Jim Schell. **Released:** March 2008. **Price:** $21.99. **Description:** Guidebook for anyone wanting to start or grow a small business; topics include information financing, budgeting, marketing, management and more.

38427 ■ *Small Business Management*
Pub: John Wiley and Sons Inc.
Ed: Margaret Burlingame; Don Gulbrandsen; Richard M. Hodgetts; Donald F. Kuratko. **Released:** March 2007. **Price:** $44.95. **Description:** Tips for starting and running a successful small business are given, including advice on writing a business plan, financing, and the law.

38428 ■ *Small Business Management in Canada*
Pub: McGraw-Hill Companies Inc.
Contact: Deven Sharma, President
Ed: Robert M. Knight. **Released:** June 1981. **Description:** Small business management in Canada.

38429 ■ *Small-Business Management Guide: Advice from the Brass-Tacks Entrepreneur*
Pub: Henry Holt & Company
Ed: Jim Schell. **Released:** October 1995. **Description:** Entrepreneurs offer advice for managing a small business.

38430 ■ *Small-Business Management Guide: Advice from the Brass-Tacks Entrepreneur*
Pub: BookSurge LLC
Ed: Jim Schell. **Released:** 1995. **Description:** Collection of stories, tales and snippets from the perspective of a small business owner.

38431 ■ *The Small Business Owner's Manual: Everything You Need to Know to Start Up and Run Your Business*
Pub: Career Press, Incorporated
Ed: Joe Kennedy. **Released:** June 2005. **Price:** $19.99 (US), $26.95 (Canadian). **Description:** Comprehensive guide for starting a small business, focusing on twelve ways to obtain financing, business plans, selling and advertising products and services, hiring and firing employees, setting up a Web site, business law, accounting issues, insurance, equipment, computers, banks, financing, customer credit and collection, leasing, and more.

38432 ■ *Small Business Start-Up Workbook: A Step-by-Step Guide to Starting the Business You've Dreamed Of*
Pub: How To Books
Ed: Cheryl D. Rickman. **Released:** February 2006. **Price:** $24.75. **Description:** Book provides practical exercises for starting a small business, including marketing and management strategies.

38433 ■ *"Sobering Consequences" in The Business Journal-Milwaukee (Vol. 25, July 11, 2008, No. 42, pp. A1)*
Pub: American City Business Journals, Inc.
Ed: Rich Rovito. **Description:** Milwaukee Mayor Tom Barrett and Wisconsin Governor Jim Doyle met with MillerCoors management in an effort to convince the company to locate its corporate headquarters in the city. The company is expected to announce its decision by mid-July 2008. It was revealed that the decision-making process is focusing on determining an optimal location for the headquarters.

38434 ■ *"Social Intelligence and the Biology of Leadership" in Harvard Business Review (Vol. 86, September 2008, No. 9, pp. 74)*
Pub: Harvard Business School Press
Ed: Daniel Goleman; Richard Boyatzis. **Description:** Social intelligence within the framework of corporate leadership is defined and described. Guidelines for assessing one's own capabilities as a socially intelligent leader include empathy, teamwork, inspiration, and influence.

38435 ■ *"Social Media, E-Mail Remain Challenging for Employees" in Workforce Management (Vol. 88, December 14, 2009, No. 13, pp. 4)*
Pub: Crain Communications Inc.
Ed: Ed Frauenheim. **Description:** Examining the impact of Internet social networking and the workplace; due to the power of these new technologies, it is important that companies begin to set clear policies regarding Internet use and employee privacy.

38436 ■ *"Social Networkers for Hire" in Black Enterprise (Vol. 40, December 2009, No. 5, pp. 56)*
Pub: Earl G. Graves Publishing Co., Inc.
Ed: Brittany Hutson. **Description:** Companies are utilizing social networking sites in order to market their brand and personally connect with consumers and are increasingly looking to social media specialists to help with this task. Aliya S. King is one such web strategist, working for ICED Media by managing their Twitter, Facebook, YouTube and Flickr accounts for one of their publicly traded restaurant clients.

38437 ■ *"Social Networks in the Workplace" in Strategy & Leadership (Vol. 38, July-August 2010, No. 4, pp. 50-53)*
Pub: Emerald Inc.
Ed: Daniel Burrus. **Description:** The opinions of futurist Daniel Burrus on a novel trend called 'Business 2.0', which involves the use of social networking applications as business tools, are presented. His suggestion that personal social networking technology can be used by businesses to improve collaboration, problem solving, and leadership communications to achieve continuous value innovation is discussed.

38438 ■ *"Sometimes, Second Impressions Count Most" in Canadian Business (Vol. 83, October 12, 2010, No. 17, pp. 11)*
Pub: Rogers Media Ltd.
Ed: Richard Branson. **Description:** Developing a favorable impression at the first point of contact is imperative for businesses. Managers who want their organizations to make positive first and second impressions need to learn to balance the Web's labor-saving efficiencies with human assistants. The importance of considering the customer relations value in company Websites is also explained.

38439 ■ *"Sony Pictures Television" in Brandweek (Vol. 49, April 21, 2008, No. 16, pp. SR13)*
Pub: VNU Business Media, Inc.
Ed: Marc Berman. **Description:** Provides contact information for sales and marketing personnel for Sony Pictures Television Distribution as well as a list-

ing of the station's top programming and an analysis of the current season and the target audience for those programs running in the current season.

38440 ■ *"Sophia Siskel; CEO, Chicago Botanic Garden" in Crain's Chicago Business (Vol. 31, May 5, 2008, No. 18, pp. 36)*
Pub: Crain Communications, Inc.
Ed: John Rosenthal. **Description:** Profile of Sophia Siskel who is the CEO of the Chicago Botanic Garden and is overseeing the $100 million expansion which will put the Botanic Garden at the forefront of plant conservation science; Ms. Siskel is also an efficient marketer and researcher.

38441 ■ *"Sources" in Canadian Electronics (Vol. 23, August 2008, No. 5, pp. 12)*
Pub: Action Communication Inc.
Description: Directory of electronic manufacturers, distributors and representatives in Canada is provided. The list presents distributors and representatives under each manufacturer.

38442 ■ *"Spend Wisely on Managing Your Hedgerows" in Farmer's Weekly (March 28, 2008, No. 320)*
Pub: Reed Business Information
Contact: Jeff Greisch, President
Ed: Richard Winspear. **Description:** Discusses the importance of a well-managed hedge which should gradually grow upwards and outwards where eventually it would reach the point when rejuvenation by coppicing or laying was needed to restart the cycle.

38443 ■ *"Spotlight; 'Classroom Focus' at Encyclopaedia Britannica" in Crain's Chicago Business (Vol. 34, October 24, 2011, No. 42, pp. 6)*
Pub: Crain Communications Inc.
Ed: Paul Merrion. **Description:** Profile of Gregory Healy, product officer for Encyclopaedia Britannica is presented. Healy took the position in May 2010 and is focused on online offerings of their publication and to make them more useful to teachers.

38444 ■ *"Staffing Firm Grows by Following Own Advice-Hire a Headhunter" in Crain's Detroit Business (Vol. 24, October 6, 2008, No. 40, pp. 1)*
Pub: Crain Communications, Inc.
Ed: Sherri Begin. **Description:** Profile of Venator Holdings L.L.C., a staffing firm that provides searches for companies in need of financial-accounting and technical employees; the firm's revenue has increased from $1.1 million in 2003 to a projected $11.5 million this year due to a climate in which more people are exiting the workforce than are coming in with those particular specialized skills and the need for a temporary, flexible workforce for contract placements at companies that do not want to take on the legacy costs associated with permanent employees. The hiring of an external headhunter to find the right out-of-state manager for Venator is also discussed.

38445 ■ *"A Stalled Culture Change?" in Workforce Management (Vol. 88, December 14, 2009, No. 13, pp. 1)*
Pub: Crain Communications Inc.
Ed: Jeremy Smerd. **Description:** General Motors CEO Fritz Henderson's abrupt resignation shocked employees and signaled that Henderson had not done enough to change the company's culture, especially in dealing with its top management.

38446 ■ *"Star Power" in Small Business Opportunities (September 2008)*
Pub: Entrepreneur Press
Contact: Perlman Neil, President
Description: Employee retention is an important factor for corporate executives to consider because the impact of excessive turnovers can be devastating to a company causing poor morale, unemployment claims, hiring costs, lost production and customer loss. Although there is no specific formula for retaining employees, there are several things every organization can do to keep their workers happy and increase the chances that they will stay loyal and keep working for the company for years to come; tips aimed at management regarding good employee relationships are included.

38447 ■ *The Starbucks Experience*
Pub: McGraw-Hill
Ed: Joseph A. Michelli. **Released:** September 14, 2006. **Price:** $24.95. **Description:** Boardroom strategies, employee motivation tips, community involvement, and customer satisfaction are issues addressed, using Starbucks as a model.

38448 ■ *The Starfish and the Spider: The Unstoppable Power of Leaderless Organizations*
Pub: Portfolio Publishing
Ed: Ori Brafman; Rod A. Beckstrom. **Released:** 2008. **Price:** $15.00 paperback. **Description:** Through their experiences promoting peace and economic development through decentralizing networking, the authors offer insight into ways that decentralizing can change organizations. Three techniques for combating a decentralized competitor are examined.

38449 ■ *"The Stars Align: Trail Blazers, Headline Makers on 2007 List Set Example for Others" in Hispanic Business (October 2007, pp. 22)*
Pub: Hispanic Business
Description: Top one hundred most influential Hispanic business leaders comprise of 66 percent men and 34 percent women, distributed by 27 percent in government, 42 percent corporate, 11 percent education, five percent art and entertainment, and 15 percent in other sectors. Statistical data included.

38450 ■ *"Start Filling Your Talent Gap - Now" in Business Strategy Review (Vol. 21, Spring 2010, No. 1, pp. 56)*
Pub: Wiley-Blackwell
Ed: Alan Bird, Lori Flees, Paul Di Paola. **Description:** As businesses steer their way out of turbulence, they have a unique opportunity to identify their leadership supply and demand and then to close the talent gap in their organization. Authors explain how to take immediate steps to build the right team now and lay the groundwork for a long-term approach for nurturing talent within the organization.

38451 ■ *"State's Glass Ceiling Gets Higher" in Business Journal-Milwaukee (Vol. 25, October 5, 2007, No. 1, pp. A1)*
Pub: American City Business Journals, Inc.
Ed: Jennifer Batog. **Description:** Report showed that more than a third of Wisconsin's fifty largest companies have no female executive officers, and the number of companies with at least one woman at top departments has also decreased since 2005. Companies lacking women at upper management levels risk jeopardizing their firms' vitality as diversity in executive offices leads to diverse ideas that can help in relating better to customers and clients.

38452 ■ *"Stay in School: Economy Got You Down?" in Canadian Business (Vol. 81, November 10, 2008, No. 19, pp. 98)*
Pub: Rogers Media Ltd.
Ed: Graham F. Scott, Jane Bao. **Description:** A guide to Canadian MBA programs is presented. The tuition and length of each program is provided along with each school. Details on whether the universities offer part-time options, diversity, and co-op/internships are also given.

38453 ■ *"Staying Engaged" in Black Enterprise (Vol. 38, February 2008, No. 7, pp. 64)*
Pub: Earl G. Graves Publishing Co. Inc.
Ed: Sonia Alleyne. **Description:** Rules to help business leaders construct networking contacts in order to maximize professional success are outlined.

38454 ■ *"A Step Up" in Black Enterprise (Vol. 38, January 2008, No. 6, pp. 53)*
Pub: Earl G. Graves Publishing Co. Inc.
Description: Professional black women can get advice from a nonprofit program called ASCENT: Leading Multicultural Women to the Top. ASCENT's sessions last six months and are held at both Tuck School of Business at Dartmouth and UCLA Anderson School of Management.

38455 ■ *"Stone to Run Hickory Farmer's Market" in Charlotte Observer (January 31, 2007)*
Pub: Knight-Ridder/Tribune Business News
Ed: Jen Aronoff. **Description:** Betty Stone has been hired to manage the Downtown Hickory Farmers Market. The market will run from May 5 through October 6, 2007.

38456 ■ *"Stop the Innovation Wars" in Harvard Business Review (Vol. 88, July-August 2010, No. 7-8, pp. 76)*
Pub: Harvard Business School Publishing
Ed: Vijay Govindarajan, Chris Trimble. **Description:** Methods for managing conflicts between partners during the innovation initiative process are highlighted. These include dividing the labor, assembling a dedicated team, and mitigating likelihood for any potential conflict.

38457 ■ *"The Story Of Diane Greene" in Barron's (Vol. 88, July 14, 2008, No. 28, pp. 31)*
Pub: Dow Jones & Co., Inc.
Ed: Mark Veverka. **Description:** Discusses the ousting of Diane Greene as a chief executive of VMWare, a developer of virtualization software, after the firm went public; in this case Greene, a brilliant engineer, should not be negatively impacted by the decision because it is common for companies to bring in new executive leadership that is more operations oriented after the company goes public.

38458 ■ *"Strategic Issue Management as Change Catalyst" in Strategy and Leadership (Vol. 39, September-October 2011, No. 5, pp. 20-29)*
Pub: Emerald Group Publishing Inc.
Ed: Bruce E. Perrott. **Description:** A study analyzes the case of a well-known Australian healthcare organization to examine how a company's periodic planning cycle is supplemented with a dynamic, real-time, strategic-issue-management system under high turbulence conditions. Findings highlight the eight steps that a company's management can use in its strategic issue management (SIM) process to track, monitor and manage strategic issues so as to ensure that the corporate, strategy, and capability are aligned with one another in turbulent times.

38459 ■ *"A Strategic Risk Approach to Knowledge Management" in Business Horizons (November-December 2007, pp. 523)*
Pub: Elsevier Technology Publications
Ed: Bruce E. Perrott. **Description:** Knowledge management practices of Ramsay Health Care are studied to investigate the issues facing effective knowledge management. A knowledge process model is developed and presented.

38460 ■ *"Strategy: Hurry Up and Wait" in Business Courier (Vol. 24, February 1, 2008, No. 43, pp. 50)*
Pub: American City Business Journals, Inc.
Ed: Dan Monk. **Description:** It has taken years for Enerfab Inc. chairman Dave Herche to develop new product lines, form an expert management group and come up with a strategic-planning approach. However, his patience has paid off since Enerfab's revenue has grown by 93 percent since 2005. Herche's strategy for Enerfab and its impacts on the company are analyzed further.

38461 ■ *Streetwise Motivating and Rewarding Employees: New and Better Ways to Inspire Your People*
Pub: Adams Media Corporation
Contact: Gary Krebs, Director
E-mail: swatrous@adamsmedia.com
Ed: Alexander Hiam. **Released:** March 1999. **Description:** Ways for employers and business managers to motivate difficult employees.

38462 ■ *Strengths Based Leadership*
Pub: Gallup Press
Ed: Tom Rath, Barry Conchie. **Description:** Three keys to being a more effective leader.

38463 ■ *Strengthsfinder 2.0*
Pub: Gallup Press
Ed: Tom Rath. **Released:** 2007. **Price:** $22.95. **Description:** Author helps people uncover their talents in order to achieve their best each day.

38464 ■ *"Stress-Test Your Strategy: the 7 Questions to Ask" in Harvard Business Review (Vol. 88, November 2010, No. 11, pp. 92)*
Pub: Harvard Business School Publishing
Ed: Robert Simons. **Description:** Seven questions organizations should use to assess crisis management capabilities are: who is the primary customer, how do core values prioritize all parties, what performance variables are being tracked, what strategic boundaries have been set, how is creative tension being produced, how committed are workers to assisting each other, and what uncertainties are causing worry?.

38465 ■ *"Stymiest's RBC Compensation Triggers Shareholder Outrage" in Gl obe & Mail (January 28, 2006, pp. B3)*
Pub: CTVglobemedia Publishing Inc.
Ed: Sinclair Stewart. **Description:** The concerns of shareholders over the issue of Royal Bank of Canada's $6.6 million pay package for chief executive officer Barbara Stymiest, in 2004, are presented.

38466 ■ *"Succeeding at Succession" in Harvard Business Review (Vol. 88, November 2010, No. 11, pp. 29)*
Pub: Harvard Business School Publishing
Ed: James M. Citrin, Dayton Ogden. **Description:** Analysis of various executive succession scenarios is given. The article compares insider vs. outsider performance and the effectiveness of board members assuming the CEO position.

38467 ■ *Success Built to Last: Creating a Life That Matters*
Pub: Penguin Group Incorporated
Ed: Jerry Porras; Stewart Emery; Mark Thompson. **Released:** August 28, 2007. **Price:** $15.00. **Description:** Interviews with successful individuals are presented to help any entrepreneur or manager.

38468 ■ *A Successful Family Business*
Pub: Penguin Group USA Inc.
Ed: Neil Pahel, Janis Raye. **Released:** August 1, 2009. **Price:** $18.95. **Description:** Guide to running a family business includes information for expanding beyond the original family firm and family versus hired management.

38469 ■ *"Sullivan Led Bucyrus through Unforgettable Year" in Business Journal-Milwaukee (Vol. 28, December 17, 2010, No. 11, pp. A1)*
Pub: Milwaukee Business Journal
Ed: Rich Rovito. **Description:** Bucyrus International's president and CEO, Tim Sullivan, was chosen as Milwaukee, Wisconsin's Executive of the Year for 2010. Sullivan led Bucyrus through a year of dramatic change which started with the acquisition of the mining business of Terex Corporation and culminating with a deal to sell Caterpillar Inc.

38470 ■ *"The Superfluous Position" in Entrepreneur (Vol. 37, July 2009, No. 7, pp. 62)*
Pub: Entrepreneur Media, Inc.
Description: Profile of an anonymous editor at a multimedia company that publishes tourism guides who shares his experiences in dealing with an office-mate who was promoted as creative manager of content. Everyone was irritated by this person, who would constantly do something to justify his new title. The biggest problem was the fact that this person didn't have a clear job description.

38471 ■ *"Surprise Package" in Business Courier (Vol. 27, June 25, 2010, No. 8, pp. 1)*
Pub: Business Courier
Ed: Dan Monk, Jon Newberry, Steve Watkins. **Description:** More than 60 percent of the chief executive officers (CEOs) in Greater Cincinnati's 35 public companies took a salary cut in 2009, but stock grants resulted in large paper gains for the CEOs. The salary cuts show efforts of boards of directors to observe austerity. Statistics on increased values of stock awards for CEOs, median pay for CEOs, and median shareholder return are also presented.

38472 ■ *"Survey Finds State Execs Cool On Climate Change" in The Business Journal-Milwaukee (Vol. 25, August 8, 2008, No. 46, pp. A1)*
Pub: American City Business Journals, Inc.
Ed: David Doege. **Description:** According to a survey of business executives in Wisconsin, business leaders do not see climate change as a pressing concern, but businesses are moving toward more energy-efficient operations. The survey also revealed that executives believe that financial incentives can promote energy conservation. Other survey results are provided.

38473 ■ *"Survive the Small-to-Big Transition" in Entrepreneur (November 4, 2008)*
Pub: Entrepreneur Media Inc.
Ed: Elizabeth Wilson. **Description:** Transitioning a small company to a large company can be a challenge, especially during the time when it is too big to be considered small and too small to be considered big. Common pitfalls during this time are discussed as well as techniques business owners should implement when dealing with this transitional period.

38474 ■ *"Survivorship Policies: Planning a Policy for Two" in Employee Benefit News (Vol. 25, November 1, 2011, No. 14, pp. 20)*
Pub: SourceMedia Inc.
Ed: Marli D. Riggs. **Description:** Survivorship insurance is becoming an added benefit high net worth individuals and executives should consider when evaluating life insurance policies.

38475 ■ *"Swinging For the Fences" in Academy of Management Journal (October 2007, pp. 1055)*
Pub: Academy of Management
Contact: Ming-Jer Chen, President
Ed: William Gerard Sanders, Donald C. Hambrick. **Description:** Study examines managerial risk-taking vis-a-vis stock options of the company; results reveal that stock options instigate CEOs to take unwise risks that could bring huge losses to the company.

38476 ■ *Switch: How to Change Things When Change Is Hard*
Pub: Broadway Books
Contact: David Drake, Manager
E-mail: ddrake@randomhouse.com
Ed: Chip Heath, Dan Heath. **Released:** February 16, 2010. **Price:** $26.00. **Description:** Change is difficult for everyone. This book helps business leaders to motivate employees as well as to help everybody motive themselves and others.

38477 ■ *"A System for Continuous Organization Renewal" in Strategy & Leadership (Vol. 38, July-August 2010, No. 4, pp. 34-41)*
Pub: Emerald Inc.
Ed: Oliver Sparrow, Gill Ringland. **Description:** A study presents a unique system to facilitate continuous organizational renewal. An analysis indicates that the system is effective when organizations implement all its parts to achieve organizational renewal.

38478 ■ *Take Back Your Time: How to Regain Control of Work, Information and Technology*
Pub: St. Martin's Press LLC
Ed: Jan Jasper. **Released:** November 1999. **Price:** $16.99. **Description:** Strategies to become more organized and productive.

38479 ■ *"Taking on the World" in Canadian Business (Vol. 79, November 20, 2006, No. 23, pp. 43)*
Pub: Rogers Media
Description: The rankings of the top Canadian business executives are presented.

38480 ■ *The Talent Masters: Why Smart Leaders Put People Before Numbers*
Pub: Crown Business Books
Ed: Bill Conaty, Ram Charan. **Released:** November 9, 2010. **Price:** $27.50. **Description:** This book helps leaders recognize talent in their employees, and to put that talent to work to help achieve business success.

38481 ■ *"Tauri Group Partner Joining Homeland Security and Defense" in Wireless News (December 15, 2009)*
Pub: Close-Up Media
Description: Managing partner Cosmo DiMaggio III of the Tauri Group, a provider of analytic consulting for homeland security, defense and space clients, has been elected to the Board of Directors at Homeland Security and Defense Business Council.

38482 ■ *"The Tea Bag Test" in Canadian Business (Vol. 79, October 23, 2006, No. 21, pp. 83)*
Pub: Rogers Media
Ed: Clive Mather. **Description:** Tips for business executives, on how to manage leadership skills to attain optimal business growth, are presented.

38483 ■ *"Team Bonding for Fun and Profit" in Women Entrepreneur (December 3, 2008)*
Pub: Entrepreneur Media Inc.
Ed: Eve Gumpel. **Description:** Discusses the benefits that competitions such as the 2008 BG U.S. Challenge in Lake Placid, New York, can offer in terms of team building and employee motivation as well as networking and the development of a positive working relationship with partners and competitors alike.

38484 ■ *"Team Implicit Coordination Processes: A Team Knowledge-based Approach" in Academy of Management Review (January 2008, pp. 163)*
Pub: ScholarOne, Inc.
Ed: Ramon Rico, Miriam Sanchez-Manzanares, Francisco Gil, Cristina Gibson. **Description:** An integrated theoretical framework is developed to enhance understanding of the functioning of work teams and implicit coordination behaviors; the implications for team coordination theory and effective management of work teams is discussed.

38485 ■ *"Tech Deal Couples Homegrown Firms" in The Business Journal-Serving Greater Tampa Bay (Vol. 28, July 4, 2008, No. 28, pp. 1)*
Pub: American City Business Journals, Inc.
Ed: Michael Hinman. **Description:** Tampa Bay, Florida-based Administrative Partners Inc. was acquired by Tribridge Inc. resulting in the strengthening of the delivery of Microsoft products to clients. Other details of the merger of the management consulting services companies are presented.

38486 ■ *"Technology to the Rescue" in Contractor (Vol. 56, July 2009, No. 7, pp. 22)*
Pub: Penton Media, Inc.
Ed: Candace Ruolo. **Description:** Features of several products that will make the job of a mechanical contractor easier are discussed. These include Ridgid's line of drain and sewer inspection cameras and monitors, Motion Computing's Motion F5 tablet rugged tablet PC, the JobClock from Exaktime, and the TeleNav Track tool for mobile workforce management.

38487 ■ *"Telemundo" in Brandweek (Vol. 49, April 21, 2008, No. 16, pp. SR8)*
Pub: VNU Business Media, Inc.
Ed: John Consoli. **Description:** Provides contact information for sales and marketing personnel for the Telemundo network as well as a listing of the station's

top programming and an analysis of the current season and the target audience for those programs running in the current season.

38488 ■ *"Tempering Urgency Within Your Shop" in Modern Machine Shop (Vol. 84, October 2011, No. 5, pp. 16)*
Pub: Gardner Business Media, Inc.
Contact: Richard G. Kline, President
E-mail: rkline@gardnerweb.com
Ed: Derek Korn. **Description:** Because machine shops operate under an environment of urgency, patience can commingle with the pressure to produce products efficiently and timely.

38489 ■ *"Temporary Theory" in Canadian Business (Vol. 80, November 5, 2007, No. 22, pp. 33)*
Pub: Rogers Media
Ed: Joe Castaldo. **Description:** Employing a temporary manager is ideal for companies working on a strict budget and limited time. The strategy will provide the company with the skills of an expert manager for a cost that is less than that of hiring a full-time manager. The usage of interim managers, specifically in short-term projects, is discussed.

38490 ■ *"The Ten Commandments of Legal Risk Management" in Business Horizons (Vol. 51, January-February 2008, No. 1, pp. 13)*
Pub: Elsevier Advanced Technology Publications
Ed: Michael B. Metzger. **Description:** Effective legal risk management is tightly linked with ethical and good management, and managers' behaviors have to be professional and based on ethically defensible principles of action. Basic human tendencies cannot be used in justifying questionable decisions in court. Guidelines for legal risk management are presented.

38491 ■ *"The Ten Worst Leadership Habits" in Canadian Business (Vol. 81, March 31, 2008, No. 5, pp. 63)*
Pub: Rogers Media
Ed: Michael Stern. **Description:** Ten leadership behaviors that aspiring leaders need to avoid are presented. These include expecting colleagues and subordinates to be like themselves, attending too many meetings, being miserly when it comes to recognition and praise, and giving an opinion often.

38492 ■ *"Think Again: What Makes a Leader?" in Business Strategy Review (Vol. 21, Autumn 2010, No. 3, pp. 64)*
Pub: Wiley-Blackwell
Ed: Rob Goffee, Gareth Jones. **Description:** Leadership cannot be faked and all the self-help books in the world won't make you a leader - but there are four characteristics any leader must possess and they are outlined.

38493 ■ *"Think Disruptive! How to Manage In a New Era of Innovation" in Strategy & Leadership (Vol. 38, July-August 2010, No. 4, pp. 5-10)*
Pub: Emerald Inc.
Ed: Brian Leavy, John Sterling. **Description:** The views expressed by Scott Anthony, president of an innovation consultancy Innosight, on the need for corporate leaders to apply disruptive innovation in a recessionary environment are presented. His suggestion that disruptive innovation is the only way to survive during the economic crisis is discussed.

38494 ■ *"The Thinker" in Canadian Business (Vol. 81, March 31, 2008, No. 5, pp. 52)*
Pub: Rogers Media
Ed: Andrew Wahl. **Description:** Mihnea Moldoveanu provides much of the academic rigor that underpins Roger Martin's theories on how to improve the way business leaders think. Moldoveanu is also a classically trained pianist and founder of Redline Communications and has a mechanical engineering degree from MIT on top of his astounding knowledge on many academic fields.

38495 ■ *"Thinking Aloud" in Business Strategy Review (Vol. 21, Summer 2010, No. 2, pp. 47)*
Pub: Wiley-Blackwell
Ed: Yiorgos Mylonadis. **Description:** In each issue we ask an academic to explain the big question on which their research hopes to shed light. Yiorgos Mylonadis looks at how people define and solve problems.

38496 ■ *"Thinking Aloud: Julian Franks" in Business Strategy Review (Vol. 21, Autumn 2010, No. 3, pp. 35)*
Pub: Blackwell Publishers Ltd.
Ed: Stuart Crainer. **Description:** Julian Franks is Academic Director of the Centre for Corporate Governance at London Business School and lead investigator for a 1.4 million (sterling pounds) grand for research into corporate governance.

38497 ■ *"Thinking Aloud: Julian Franks" in Business Strategy Review (Vol. 21, Autumn 2010, No. 3, pp. 35)*
Pub: Wiley-Blackwell
Ed: Stuart Crainer. **Description:** Julian Franks is academic director of the Centre for Corporate Governance at London Business School and lead investigator for a (pounds sterling) 1.4 million grant for research into corporate governance.

38498 ■ *"Thomas D'Aquino" in Canadian Business (Vol. 80, November 19, 2007, No. 23, pp. 92)*
Pub: Rogers Media
Ed: Calvin Leung. **Description:** Thomas D'Aquino is the CEO and president of the Canadian Council of Chief Executives since 1981. D'Aquino thinks he has the best job in Canada because he can change the way policies are made and the way people think. Details of his career as a lawyer and CEO and his views on Canada's economy are provided.

38499 ■ *Three Moves Ahead*
Pub: John Wiley and Sons, Inc.
Ed: Bob Rice. **Released:** March 30, 2008. **Price:** $24.95. **Description:** Things the game of chess can teach about business are explored.

38500 ■ *"Tim Armstrong" in Canadian Business (Vol. 81, July 21, 2008, No. 11, pp. 10)*
Pub: Rogers Media Ltd.
Ed: Calvin Leung. **Description:** Interview with Tim Armstrong who is the president of advertising and commerce department of Google Inc. for North America; the information technology company executive talked about the emerging trends and changes to YouTube made by the company since its acquisition in 2006.

38501 ■ *"A Timely Matter" in Canadian Business (Vol. 81, March 31, 2008, No. 5, pp. 12)*
Pub: Rogers Media
Description: Discusses the committee responsible for restructuring $33 billion of asset-backed commercial paper which has moved back their implementation plan by a month citing complexities. British Columbia has surpassed the $1 billion mark in fiscal '07-'08 from their oil and gas rights. Biovail Corp. founder Eugene Melnyk said he had lost confidence in the management of the company.

38502 ■ *"To JM On Its 75th Anniversary" in Journal of Marketing (Vol. 75, July 2011, No. 4, pp. 129)*
Pub: American Marketing Association
Ed: Ruth M. Bolton. **Description:** How the Journal of Marketing influenced the marketing science and practice is presented. The Marketing Science Institute's 50th anniversary coincides with the journal's 75th anniversary and both have collaborated to tackle important marketing issues identified in MSI's priorities. The mind-set of managers worldwide was also influenced by ideas in the journal's articles.

38503 ■ *"Tom Gaglardi" in Canadian Business (Vol. 82, April 27, 2009, No. 7, pp. 56)*
Pub: Rogers Media
Ed: Calvin Leung. **Description:** Northland Properties Corporation president Tom Gaglardi believes that their business model of keeping much of operations in-house allows the firm to crate assets at a lesser price while commanding higher margins than their competitors. He believes that it is an ideal time to invest in the hospitality industry because of opportunities to purchase properties at low prices.

38504 ■ *Tough Choices: A Memoir*
Pub: Penguin Group
Ed: Carly Florina. **Released:** October 2006. **Price:** $24.95. **Description:** Former woman CEO at Hewlett-Packard is profiled.

38505 ■ *"Tough Times for the Irving Clan" in Canadian Business (Vol. 83, August 17, 2010, No. 13-14, pp. 14)*
Pub: Rogers Media Ltd.
Ed: Dean Jobb. **Description:** The death of John E. Irving and reported health problems of his nephew Kenneth Irving was a double blow to the billionaire Irving clan. Kenneth suddenly left his job as CEO of Fort Reliance, holding company for Irving Oil and new energy ventures, wherein the explanation was for personal reasons.

38506 ■ *"Tracking Your Fleet Can Increase Bottom Line" in Contractor (Vol. 56, November 2009, No. 11, pp. 26)*
Pub: Penton Media, Inc.
Ed: Candace Roulo. **Description:** GPS fleet management system can help boost a contractor's profits, employee productivity, and efficiency. These are available as a handheld device or a cell phone that employees carry around or as a piece of hardware installed in a vehicle. These lets managers track assets and communicate with employees about jobs.

38507 ■ *"Transcendent Leadership" in Business Horizons (Vol. 51, March-April 2008, No. 2, pp. 131)*
Pub: Elsevier Advanced Technology Publications
Ed: Mary Crossan, Daina Mazutis. **Description:** Transcendent leadership is framework integrating the leadership of self, others, and organizations. Much of the discourse regarding leadership has focused on leadership of others and the organization, while leadership of self is rarely tackled. Successful leaders are able to integrate these three levels of leadership.

38508 ■ *"Trend: Tutors to Help You Pump Up the Staff" in Business Week (September 22, 2008, No. 4100, pp. 45)*
Pub: McGraw-Hill Companies, Inc.
Ed: Reena Janaj. **Description:** High-level managers are turning to innovation coaches in an attempt to obtain advice on how to better sell new concepts within their companies. Individuals as well as consulting firms are now offering this service.

38509 ■ *"Trial of Enron Ex-Bosses to Begin Today" in Globe & Mail (January 30, 2006, pp. B1)*
Pub: CTVglobemedia Publishing Inc.
Ed: Shawn McCarthy. **Description:** The details of the case against former executives Kenneth L. Lay and Jeffrey Skilling of Enron Corp. are presented.

38510 ■ *"Trib TV Station Switching to Fox" in Crain's Chicago Business (Vol. 31, March 31, 2008, No. 13, pp. 14)*
Pub: Crain Communications, Inc.
Ed: Michelle Greppi. **Description:** Signaling the new Tribune owner Sam Zell's divergence from previous management is the company's shift of its KSWB-TV station in San Diego to News Corp.'s Fox from CW Television Network.

38511 ■ *"Trinity Western University Offers Project Management Course" in Bellingham Business Journal (Vol. February 2010, pp. 4)*
Pub: Sound Publishing Inc.
Description: Trinity Western University in Bellinham, Washington is offering a new certification program in project management. Students who take and pass the certification examination of the International Project Management Institutes will lead to positions in many industries. Details of the program are provided.

38512 ■ *True to Yourself: Leading a Values-Based Business*
Pub: Berrett-Koehler Publishers, Incorporated
Ed: Mark S. Albion. **Released:** June 2006. **Price:** $14.95. **Description:** Pressures faced by entrepreneurs running small companies are discussed. Advice is offered to help grow and maintain a profitable business.

38513 ■ *"The Trusty Sidekick" in Canadian Business (Vol. 81, March 31, 2008, No. 5, pp. 33)*
Pub: Rogers Media
Ed: John Gray. **Description:** Being second-in-command is a good opportunity to be mentored by the boss and puts the executive in the position to see the whole organization and have influence to make changes. However, the chief operating officer has the unenviable task of trying to achieve unattainable goals. Executives who want to become the right hand man must go beyond their job description.

38514 ■ *The Truth About Middle Managers: Who They Are, How They Work, Why They Matter*
Pub: Harvard Business School Publishing
Ed: Paul Osterman. **Released:** 2009. **Price:** $35.00. **Description:** The alienation of middle managers is bad for a company.

38515 ■ *"Turner Broadcasting System" in Brandweek (Vol. 49, April 21, 2008, No. 16, pp. SR13)*
Pub: VNU Business Media, Inc.
Ed: Anthony Crupi. **Description:** Provides contact information for sales and marketing personnel for the Turner Broadcasting System networks as well as a listing of the station's top programming and an analysis of the current season and the target audience for those programs running in the current season. Recent acquisitions are also discussed.

38516 ■ *"Twentieth Television" in Brandweek (Vol. 49, April 21, 2008, No. 16, pp. SR16)*
Pub: VNU Business Media, Inc.
Ed: Marc Berman. **Description:** Provides contact information for sales and marketing personnel for Twentieth Television as well as a listing of the station's top programming and an analysis of the current season and the target audience for those programs running in the current season.

38517 ■ *"Twenty Years of Advocacy and Education" in Women Entrepreneur (January 18, 2009)*
Pub: Entrepreneur Media Inc.
Ed: Eve Gumpel. **Description:** Profile of Sharon Hadary who served as executive director of the Center for Women's Business Research for two decades; Hadary discusses what she has learned about women business owners, their impact on the economy and what successful business owners share in common.

38518 ■ *Ubuntu!: An Aspiring Story About an African Tradition of Teamwork and Collaboration*
Pub: Broadway Books
Contact: David Drake, Manager
E-mail: ddrake@randomhouse.com
Ed: Bob Nelson, Stephen Lundin. **Released:** March 30, 2010. **Price:** $19.99. **Description:** The African tradition of teamwork and collaboration is used to demonstrate these skills to small business leaders.

38519 ■ *"UC's Goering Center to Get New Director" in Business Courier (Vol. 24, February 15, 2008, No. 45, pp. 3)*
Pub: American City Business Journals, Inc.
Ed: Dan Monk. **Description:** Kent Lutz, director of University of Cincinnati Goering (UC) Center for Family & Private Business is to leave the resource center in June 2008 after nine years of service. Changes in the UC-affiliated institute include the expansion of the board from three to seven members and developing new programs related to family businesses.

38520 ■ *The Ultimate Competitive Advantage*
Pub: Berrett-Koehler Publishers
Ed: Donald Mitchell; Carol Coles; B. Thomas Golisano. **Released:** March 12, 2003. **Price:** $36.95. **Description:** Results of a ten year study of companies that experienced fast growth over a three year period shows that while unsuccessful companies apply outdated business models, the successful ones improve their business models every two to four years.

38521 ■ *Ultimate Guide to Project Management*
Pub: Entrepreneurial Press
Ed: Sid Kemp. **Released:** October 2005. **Price:** $29.95 (US), $39.95 (Canadian). **Description:** Project management strategies including writing a business plan and developing a good advertising campaign.

38522 ■ *"The Uncompromising Leader" in Harvard Business Review (Vol. 86, July-August 2008, No. 8, pp. 50)*
Pub: Harvard Business School Press
Ed: Russell A. Eisenstat; Michael Beer; Nathaniel Foote; Tobias Fredburg; Flemming Norrgren. **Description:** Advice regarding how to drive performance without sacrificing commitment to people is given. Topics include development of shared purpose, organizational engagement, the fostering of collective leadership capability, and maintaining perspective.

38523 ■ *"Under Pressure" in Canadian Business (Vol. 81, July 21, 2008, No. 11, pp. 18)*
Pub: Rogers Media Ltd.
Ed: Joe Castaldo. **Description:** According to a survey conducted by COMPASS Inc., meeting revenue targets is the main cause of job stress for chief executive officers. Staffing and keeping expenditures lower also contribute to the workplace stress experienced by business executives. Other results of the survey are presented.

38524 ■ *"An Unfair Knock on Nokia" in Barron's (Vol. 88, March 10, 2008, No. 10, pp. 36)*
Pub: Dow Jones & Company, Inc.
Ed: Mark Veverka. **Description:** Discusses the decision by the brokerage house Exane to recommend a Sell on Nokia shares, presumably due to higher inventories, which is unfounded. The news that the company's inventories are rising is not an indicator of falling demand for its products. The company is also benefiting from solid management and rising market share.

38525 ■ *"Unify Corp. Back in the Black, Poised to Grow" in Sacramento Business Journal (Vol. 25, August 29, 2008, No. 26, pp. 1)*
Pub: American City Business Journals, Inc.
Ed: Melanie Turner. **Description:** It was reported that Unify Corp. returned to profitability in the fiscal year ended April 30, 2008 with a net income of $1.6 million, under the guidance of Todd Wille. Wille, who took over as the company's chief executive officer in October 2000, was named as Turnaround CEO of the Year in June 2008 for his efforts.

38526 ■ *"Unilever's CMO Finally Gets Down To Business" in Advertising Age (Vol. 79, July 7, 2008, No. 26, pp. 11)*
Pub: Crain Communications, Inc.
Ed: Jack Neff. **Description:** Overview of Unilever's chief marketing officer Simon Clift's strategy for promoting its products; now that the company has restructured, Clift is able to focus all of his energy on the challenges of the new-media climate that marketers are having to face.

38527 ■ *"Univision" in Brandweek (Vol. 49, April 21, 2008, No. 16, pp. SR8)*
Pub: VNU Business Media, Inc.
Ed: John Consoli. **Description:** Provides contact information for sales and marketing personnel for the Univision network as well as a listing of the station's top programming and an analysis of the current season and the target audience for those programs running in the current season. Univision is the No. 1 network on Friday nights in the 18-34 demographic, beating all English-language networks.

38528 ■ *"Unlimited Priorities Strengthens Executive Team" in Entertainment Close-Up (November 1, 2011)*
Pub: Close-Up Media
Description: Founder and president of Unlimited Priorities Corporation, Iris L. Hanney, added two executive level professionals to her team. The new employees will help increase the firm's capabilities in social media and information technology.

38529 ■ *"Unmasking Manly Men" in Harvard Business Review (Vol. 86, July-August 2008, No. 8, pp. 20)*
Pub: Harvard Business School Press
Ed: Robin J. Ely; Debra Meyerson. **Description:** Oil rig work is used to explore how focusing on job requirements and performance successfully challenged stereotypical views of masculinity and competence.

38530 ■ *"Unseen Injustice: Incivility as Modern Discrimination in Organizations" in Academy of Management Review (January 2008, pp. 55)*
Pub: ScholarOne, Inc.
Ed: Lilia M. Cortina. **Description:** Analysis of social psychological research on modern discrimination to explain the theory of incivility used as part of sexism and racism in organizations. The selective incivility observed is discussed, as well as its implications and efforts to eliminate it.

38531 ■ *"USAmeriBank Deals for Growth" in The Business Journal-Serving Greater Tampa Bay (Vol. 28, September 26, 2008, No. 40, pp. 1)*
Pub: American City Business Journals, Inc.
Ed: Margie Manning. **Description:** It is believed that the pending $14.9 million purchase of Liberty Bank by USAmeriBank could be at the forefront of a trend. Executives of both companies expect the deal to close by the end of 2008. USAmeriBank will have $430 million in assets and five offices in Pinellas, Florida once the deal is completed.

38532 ■ *"Used to Being Courted" in Business Courier (Vol. 24, March 14, 2008, No. 49, pp. 1)*
Pub: American City Business Journals, Inc.
Ed: Dan Monk. **Description:** College basketball coach Sean Miller is reported to be earning up to $900,000 a year. A look into the contract at regional universities show Thad Matta makes over $2 million in a year and that UK's Billy Gillispie makes over $2.7 million.

38533 ■ *"The Value of Conversations With Employees; Talk Isn't Cheap" in Gallup Management Journal (June 30, 2011)*
Pub: Gallup
Ed: Jessica Tyler. **Description:** When managers have meaningful exchanges with their employees, they don't only show they care, they also add value to their organization's bottom line.

38534 ■ *"VC Boosts WorkForce; Livonia Software Company to Add Sales, Marketing Staff" in Crain's Detroit Business (March 24, 2008)*
Pub: Crain Communications, Inc.
Ed: Tom Henderson. **Description:** WorkForce Software Inc., a company that provides software to manage payroll processes and oversee compliance with state and federal regulations and with union rules, plans to use an investment of $5.5 million in venture capital to hire more sales and marketing staff.

38535 ■ *"Vicki Avril; Senior Vice-President of Tubular Division, Ipsco Inc." in Crain's Chicago Business (Vol. 31, May 5, 2008, No. 18)*
Pub: Crain Communications, Inc.
Ed: Miriam Gottfried. **Description:** Profile of Vicki Avril who is the senior vice-president of the tubular division at Ipsco Inc. where she supervises 2,800 employees and 13 mills throughout the United States and Canada.

38536 ■ *"Virginia Albanese: President and CEO" in Inside Business (Vol. 13, September-October 2011, No. 5, pp. NC4)*
Pub: Great Lakes Publishing Co.
Ed: Jeannie Roberts. **Description:** Profile of Virginia Albanese, CEO of FedEx's Custom Critical Division in Akron, Ohio. Albanese discusses her philosophy on business leadership.

38537 ■ *"Voices: Climategate Leads Nowhere" in Business Strategy Review (Vol. 21, Summer 2010, No. 2, pp. 76)*
Pub: Blackwell Publishers Ltd.
Ed: Mick Blowfield. **Description:** An examination of the recent Climategate scandal that explores the damage caused by managers who are too easily mystified or misled.

38538 ■ *Wake Up and Smell the Zeitgeist*
Pub: Basic Books
Ed: Grand McCracken. **Released:** 2010. **Price:** $26. 95. **Description:** Insight is given into an element of corporate success that's often overlooked and valuable suggestions are offered for any small business to pursue.

38539 ■ *The Wall Street Journal. Complete Small Business Guidebook*
Pub: Three Rivers Press
Ed: Colleen DeBaise. **Released:** December 29, 2009. **Price:** $15.00. **Description:** The mechanics of building, running and growing a profitable business are outlined, teaching how to write a business plan, ways to finding money during lean years, how to keep stress in check, time management, investment in technology, hiring, marketing, management basics, angel investing and venture capital, as well as an exit strategy.

38540 ■ *"Wanted: African American Professional for Hire" in Black Enterprise (Vol. 37, November 2006, No. 4, pp. 93)*
Pub: Earl G. Graves Publishing Co. Inc.
Ed: Joe Watson. **Description:** Excerpt from the book, Without Excuses: Unleash the Power of Diversity to Build Your Business, speaks to the lack of diversity in the corporate arena and why executives, recruiters, and HR professionals claim they are unable to find qualified individuals of different races when hiring.

38541 ■ *"The War for Talent" in Canadian Business (Vol. 80, January 29, 2007, No. 3, pp. 60)*
Pub: Rogers Media
Ed: Erin Pooley. **Description:** The recruitment policies of Canadian businesses are described. The trends pertaining to the growth of executive salaries in Canada are discussed.

38542 ■ *"Warner Bros. Domestic Television Distribution" in Brandweek (Vol. 49, April 21, 2008, No. 16, pp. SR16)*
Pub: VNU Business Media, Inc.
Ed: Marc Berman. **Description:** Provides contact information for sales and marketing personnel for Warner Bros. Domestic Television Distribution as well as a listing of the station's top programming and an analysis of the current season and the target audience for those programs running in the current season.

38543 ■ *We Are Smarter Than Me: How to Unleash the Power of Crowds in Your Business*
Pub: Wharton School Publishing
Ed: Barry Libert; Jon Spector; Don Tapscott. **Released:** October 5, 2007. **Price:** $21.99. **Description:** Ways to use social networking and community in order to make decisions and plan your business, with a focus on product development, manufacturing, marketing, customer service, finance, management, and more.

38544 ■ *"Wear More Hats" in Canadian Business (Vol. 80, March 12, 2007, No. 6, pp. 39)*
Pub: Rogers Media
Ed: Michael Stern. **Description:** The need on the part of managers to volunteer to accept more responsibilities for their growth as well as that of company's is discussed.

38545 ■ *"Web-Based Solutions Streamline Operations" in Contractor (Vol. 56, December 2009, No. 12, pp. 28)*
Pub: Penton Media, Inc.
Ed: William Feldman; Patti Feldman. **Description:** Sage Project Lifecycle Management is a Web-based service platform for plumbing and HVAC contractors. It enables effective workflow and document management. Projectmates, on the other hand, is a Web-based enterprise-wide solution for managing both commercial plumbing and HVAC projects.

38546 ■ *"Web Site Focuses on Helping People Find Jobs, Internships with Area Businesses" in Crain's Detroit Business (Vol. 26, Jan. 4, 2010)*
Pub: Crain Communications Inc.
Ed: Dustin Walsh. **Description:** DetroitIntern.com, LLC is helping metro Detroit college students and young professionals find career-advancing internships or jobs with local businesses.

38547 ■ *"Well Done!" in Canadian Business (Vol. 80, April 23, 2007, No. 9, pp. 47)*
Pub: Rogers Media
Ed: Joe Castaldo. **Description:** The human resource management methods applied by different companies like Deloitte & Touche LLP are presented.

38548 ■ *The Well-Timed Strategy: Managing Business Cycle for Competitive Advantage*
Pub: Wharton School Publishing
Ed: Peter Navarro. **Released:** January 23, 2006. **Price:** $34.99. **Description:** An overview of business cycles and risks is presented. Recession is a good time to find key personnel for a small business. Other issues addressed include investment, production, and marketing in order to maintain a competitive edge.

38549 ■ *"Wendy Turner; Vice-President and General Manager, Vocalo.org" in Crain's Chicago Business (Vol. 31, May 5, 2008, No. 18, pp. 22)*
Pub: Crain Communications, Inc.
Ed: Kevin McKeough. **Description:** Profile of Wendy Turner who is a leader at Vocalo, a combination of talk radio and Web site, where listeners can set up profile pages similar to those on Facebook.

38550 ■ *"WestJet Hires a New CFO After Lengthy Search" in Globe & Mail (January 23, 2007, pp. B8)*
Pub: CTVglobemedia Publishing Inc.
Ed: Brent Jang. **Description:** Vito Culmone, formerly vice of Malson Canada, is appointed as chief financial officer.

38551 ■ *"Weyerhaeuser's REIT Decision Shouldn't Scare Investors Away" in Barron's (Vol. 88, June 30, 2008, No. 26, pp. 18)*
Pub: Dow Jones & Co., Inc.
Ed: Christopher Williams. **Description:** Weyerhaeuser Co.'s management said that a conversion to a real estate investment trust was not likely in 2009 since the move is not tax-efficient as of the moment and would overload its non-timber assets with debt. The company's shares have fallen by 19.5 percent. However, the company remains an asset-rich outfit and its activist shareholder is pushing for change.

38552 ■ *A Whack on the Side of the Head*
Pub: Business Plus
Ed: Roger von Oech. **Released:** May 2008. **Price:** $16.99. **Description:** The author, a consultant, shares insight into increasing entrepreneurial creativity.

38553 ■ *"What 17th Century Pirates Can Teach Us About Job Design" in Harvard Business Review (Vol. 88, October 2010, No. 10, pp. 44)*
Pub: Harvard Business School Publishing
Ed: Hayagreeva Rao. **Description:** Ways in which pirates typify the importance of separating star tasks, or strategic work, from guardian tasks, or the operational work are outlined.

38554 ■ *"What Brain Science Tells Us About How to Excel" in Harvard Business Review (Vol. 88, December 2010, No. 12, pp. 123)*
Pub: Harvard Business School Publishing
Ed: Edward M. Hallowell. **Description:** Relevant discoveries in brain research as they apply to boosting employee motivation and organizational effectiveness are explained. Included is a checklist of 15 items for use in assessing the fitness of a person for a particular job, focusing on the intersection of what one likes to do, what one does best, and what increases organizational value.

38555 ■ *"What CEOs Will Admit Out of the Office" in Inc. (November 2007, pp. 30)*
Pub: Gruner & Jahr USA Publishing
Ed: Sarah Goldstein. **Description:** Thirty CEOs from the fastest growing companies in the U.S. answer questions about their firms.

38556 ■ *What Got You Here Won't Get You There*
Pub: Hyperion Books
Ed: Marshall Goldsmith; Mark Reiter. **Released:** January 9, 2007. **Price:** $24.95. **Description:** Executive coach teaches how to climb the ladder to upper levels of management.

38557 ■ *"What It Takes to Be an Effective Leader" in Black Enterprise (Vol. 41, December 2010, No. 5, pp. 62)*
Pub: Earl G. Graves Publishing Co. Inc.
Ed: Sonia Alleyne. **Description:** Redia Anderson and Lenora Billings-Harris have partnered to write the book, 'Trailblazers: How Top Business Leaders Are Accelerating Results Through Inclusion and Diversity'. The book offers insight into best practices demonstrated by some of the most influential chief diversity officers in business.

38558 ■ *"What Your Employees Need to Know; They Probably Don't Know How They're Performing" in Gallup Management Journal (April 13, 2011)*
Pub: Gallup
Ed: Steve Crabtree. **Description:** Personalized feedback and recognition aren't just extras that make workers feel good about themselves they are critical predictors of positive performance.

38559 ■ *"When Emotional Reasoning Trumps IQ" in Harvard Business Review (Vol. 88, September 2010, No. 9, pp. 27)*
Pub: Harvard Business School Publishing
Ed: Roderick Gilkey, Ricardo Caceda, Clinton Kilts. **Description:** Strategic reasoning was found to be linked more closely to areas of the brain associated with intuition and emotion, rather than the prefrontal cortex, which is typically thought to be the center of such activity. Implications for management skills are discussed.

38560 ■ *When Growth Stalls: How It Happens, Why You're Stuck, and what To Do About It*
Pub: John Wiley & Sons, Inc.
Ed: Steve McKee. **Released:** March 1, 2009. **Price:** $27.95. **Description:** Marketing expert presents evidence that demonstrates that slow growth experienced by a firm is usually not the cause of mismanagement or blundering, but by natural market forces and destructive internal dynamics that are often unrecognized.

38561 ■ *"When and How to Innovate Your Business Model" in Strategy & Leadership (Vol. 38, July-August 2010, No. 4, pp. 17-26)*
Pub: Emerald Inc.
Ed: Edward Giesen, Eric Riddleberger, Richard Christner, Ragna Bell. **Description:** A study uses survey data to identify factors that are considered by corporate leaders regarding when and how they should innovate their business model. Findings identify a set of characteristics called the 'Three A's, Namely, Aligned, Analytical and Adaptable, which corporate leaders use consistently to successfully design and execute business-model innovation.

38562 ■ *"When the Longtime Star Fades" in Harvard Business Review (Vol. 88, September 2010, No. 9, pp. 117)*
Pub: Harvard Business School Publishing
Ed: Jimmy Guterman. **Description:** A fictitious aging employee scenario is presented, with contributors offering advice. The scenarios focuses on an older employee's match with a rapidly changing industry; suggestions include consolidating a niche business around the employee, and also engaging the older employee in solving the productivity issue.

38563 ■ *"When You Need Strong Millennials in Your Workplace" in Agency Sales Magazine (Vol. 39, November 2009, No. 10, pp. 22)*
Pub: MANA
Ed: Joanne G. Sujansky. **Description:** Millennials are bringing a new set of skills and a different kind of work ethics to the workplace. This generation is used to receiving a great deal of positive feedback and they expect to continue receiving this on the job. Expectations should be made clear to this generation and long-term career plans and goals should also be discussed with them.

38564 ■ *"Where Are They Now?" in Canadian Business (Vol. 79, October 9, 2006, No. 20, pp. 71)*
Pub: Rogers Media
Description: The profile of the top chief executive officers of Canada for the year 2005 is discussed.

38565 ■ *"Where to Buy the Right MBA" in Canadian Business (Vol. 79, October 23, 2006, No. 21, pp. 99)*
Pub: Rogers Media
Ed: Erin Pooley; Laura Bogomolny; Joe Castaldo; Michelle Magnan; Claire Gagne. **Description:** Details of Canadian graduate business schools offering Master of business administration degree are presented.

38566 ■ *Where Have All the Leaders Gone?*
Pub: Scribner Educational Publishers
Contact: Jack Romanos, President
Ed: Lee Iacocca. **Released:** April 2007. **Description:** Lee Iacocca discusses the principles of great leadership.

38567 ■ *"Whistleblower or Manipulator?" in Canadian Business (Vol. 81, July 22, 2008, No. 12-13, pp. 11)*
Pub: Rogers Media Ltd.
Ed: John Gray. **Description:** Discusses Maria Messina who is portrayed by prosecutors of the Livent Inc. trial as a whistleblower, while defense lawyers insist that she is a manipulator. Defense lawyers allege that Messina, who was Livent's chief financial officer, is a character assassin that made money out of Livent's bankruptcy. Other views on Messina, as well as information on the case, are presented.

38568 ■ *"Why Did We Ever Go Into HR?" in Harvard Business Review (Vol. 86, July-August 2008, No. 8, pp. 39)*
Pub: Harvard Business School Press
Ed: Matthew D. Breitfelder; Daisy Wademan Dowling. **Description:** Examines the role of human resource directors and how their jobs foster new ideas and generate optimism.

38569 ■ *"Why HR Practices Are Not Evidence-Based" in Academy of Management Journal (Vol. 50, No. 5, October 2007, pp. 1033)*
Pub: Academy of Management
Contact: Ming-Jer Chen, President
Ed: Denise M. Rousseau. **Description:** A suggestion that an Evidence-Based Management Collaboration (EBMC) can be established to facilitate effective transfer of ideas between science and practice is presented.

38570 ■ *"Why It Pays to be in the Boardroom" in Globe & Mail (January 16, 2006, pp. B1)*
Pub: CTVglobemedia Publishing Inc.
Ed: Janet McFarland. **Description:** The reasons behind higher stock compensation for board directors, in Canada, are presented. The survey is conducted by Patrick O'Callaghan & Associates and Korn/Ferry International.

38571 ■ *"Why Men Still Get More Promotions Than Women" in Harvard Business Review (Vol. 88, September 2010, No. 9, pp. 80)*
Pub: Harvard Business School Publishing
Ed: Herminia Ibarra, Nancy M. Carter, Christine Silva. **Description:** Sponsorship, rather than mentoring, is identified as the main difference in why men still receive more promotions than women. Active executive sponsorship is key to fostering career advancement.

38572 ■ *Why Work Sucks and How To Fix It*
Pub: Portfolio Publishing
Ed: Cali Ressler; Jody Thompson. **Released:** May 1, 2008. **Price:** $23.95. **Description:** Results-Only Work Environments (ROWE) not only make employees happier, it also delivers better results. ROWE allows employees to do whatever they want, whenever they want as long as business objectives are met. No more pointless meetings, fighting traffic to be to work on time, or asking for permission for time off.

38573 ■ *"The Wiki-Powered Workplace" in Workforce Management (Vol. 88, November 16, 2009, No. 12, pp. 8)*
Pub: Crain Communications Inc.
Description: Many organizations are successfully using wikis inside the corporate structure for business communications and knowledge sharing. Wikis can be a very powerful tool due to the inherent transparency that comes with allowing everything to be edited with the accountability of seeing who is doing the editing. A brilliant employee may be noticed sooner because they are doing work in the wiki and the work is being judged on its own merit.

38574 ■ *"Winner: Caparo Group Plc" in Crain's Detroit Business (Vol. 24, March 24, 2008, No. 12, pp. 12)*
Pub: Crain Communications, Inc.
Ed: Brent Snavely. **Description:** London-based Caparo Group plc saw its acquisition of Voestalpine Polynorm as an opportunity to gain a foothold in the North American automotive industry. Caparo was impressed with the company's breadth of manufacturing capabilities and quality systems as well as with the management team.

38575 ■ *"The Winner's Circle" in Hispanic Business (Vol. 30, April 2008, No. 4, pp. 20)*
Pub: Hispanic Business
Ed: Hildy Medina. **Description:** Although there has been progress concerning Hispanic women professionals who are growing in numbers in the upper echelons of the corporate arena, many still find that they face discrimination when it comes to pay and promotions. Statistical data included.

38576 ■ *"Winners and Losers" in Crain's Detroit Business (Vol. 25, June 22, 2009, No. 25, pp. 18)*
Pub: Crain Communications Inc. - Detroit
Description: Rankings for Detroit's 50 top-compensated CEOs has changed due to the economic recession. The biggest changes are discussed.

38577 ■ *"Wisdom from the Mountaintops" in Canadian Business (Vol. 83, October 12, 2010, No. 17, pp. 91)*
Pub: Rogers Media Ltd.
Ed: Matthew McClearn. **Description:** Techniques used to save lives on the world's highest mountains could make companies more creative. Mountaineers have time to talk to one another, and the resulting flow of ideas help climbers reach the summit. Organizations are expected to foster communication both internally and externally.

38578 ■ *"A Woman's Advantage" in Black Enterprise (Vol. 38, December 2007, No. 5, pp. 86)*
Pub: Earl G. Graves Publishing Co. Inc.
Ed: Marcia Reed-Woodard. **Description:** Leadership development is essential for any small business. Simmons College's Strategic Leadership for Women educational course offers a five-day program for professional women teaching powerful strategies to perform, compete, and win in the workplace.

38579 ■ *"Women as 21st Century Leaders" in Women In Business (Vol. 63, Summer 2011, No. 2, pp. 26)*
Pub: American Business Women's Association
Ed: Leigh Elmore. **Description:** American Business Women's Association and Park University have partnered to provide a leadership training program to attendees of the 2011 National Women's Leadership Conference. The courses will incorporate introduction to concepts, development of critical thinking skills and direct application through exercises. Comments from executives are also included.

38580 ■ *"Women Board Number Stagnates" in Boston Business Journal (Vol. 30, November 26, 2010, No. 44, pp. 1)*
Pub: Boston Business Journal
Ed: Mary Moore. **Description:** The 2010 data in 'Census of Women Directors and Executive Officers of Massachusetts Public Companies' showed little change in the number of executive officers and board members in the state's top 100 firms. The data was compiled by Bentley University, The Boston Club, and Mercer. Key information on 2010 Women on Boards is also provided.

38581 ■ *"Women Inch Forward on Corporate Boards" in Marketing to Women (Vol. 21, April 2008, No. 4, pp. 6)*
Pub: EPM Communications Inc.
Contact: Ira Mayer, President
E-mail: imayer@epmcom.com
Description: According to the latest study by Inter-Organization Network, few huge leaps of progress and in some cases backsliding has taken place in regards to gender diversity on corporate boards. Statistical data included.

38582 ■ *"Work Force: In the Mix" in Entrepreneur (Vol. 35, October 2007, No. 10, pp. 109)*
Pub: Entrepreneur Media Inc.
Ed: Mark Henricks. **Description:** A study of 708 companies' diversity programs shows that diversity training alone is not the most effective way of increasing diversity in management. It was found that one effective way of putting minorities and women in management teams is to give a team or a person the task of improving diversity in the company. The reason why accountability succeeds in diversifying the workforce is discussed.

38583 ■ *"Work Pray Love" in Harvard Business Review (Vol. 88, December 2010, No. 12, pp. 38)*
Pub: Harvard Business School Publishing
Ed: Rosabeth Moss Kanter. **Description:** It is recommended to reinvest in values in order to promote better employee-company engagement and performance.

38584 ■ *"Working For Pennies? Huge Pay Gap Between Top Executives and Black Employees" in Black Enterprise (Vol. 38, March 2008, No. 8)*
Pub: Earl G. Graves Publishing Co. Inc.
Ed: Cliff Hocker, Wendy Isom. **Description:** CEO pay is out of control because most board members approving high salaries and compensation packages are often executives at other firms. According to a study conducted by the Institute for Policy Studies, CEOs earn more than 1,085 times the average full-time black worker's median earnings.

38585 ■ *"The Workplace Generation Gaps" in Women In Business (Vol. 62, June 2010, No. 2, pp. 8)*
Pub: American Business Women's Association
Ed: Leigh Elmore. **Description:** Generation gaps among baby boomers, Generation X and Generation Y in the workplace are attributed to technological divides and differences in opinions. These factors could lead to workplace misunderstandings, employee turnover and communication difficulties. Details on managing such workplace gaps are discussed.

38586 ■ *"The World Is Your Oyster" in Canadian Business (Vol. 80, October 22, 2007, No. 21, pp. 140)*
Pub: Rogers Media
Ed: Regan Ray. **Description:** Business graduates are not that keen on working abroad. Fortune 500 companies are requiring executives to have a multi-country focus. The skill required for jobs abroad, as well as employment opportunities are discussed.

38587 ■ *"World's Best CEOs" in Barron's (Vol. 88, March 24, 2008, No. 12, pp. 33)*
Pub: Dow Jones & Company, Inc.
Ed: Andrew Bary. **Description:** Listing of the 30 best chief executive officers worldwide which was compiled through interviews with investors and analysts, analysis of financial and stock market performance, and leadership and industry stature.

38588 ■ *The Worst-Case Scenario Business Survival Guide*
Pub: John Wiley & Sons, Inc.
Released: September 28, 2009. **Price:** $17.95. **Description:** Since 1999, the Worst-Case Scenario survival handbooks have provided readers with real answers for the most extreme situations. Now, in a time of economic crisis, the series returns with a new, real-world guide to avoiding the worst business cataclysms.

38589 ■ *"Worth His Salt" in Hawaii Business (Vol. 53, January 2008, No. 7, pp. 45)*
Pub: Hawaii Business Publishing
Ed: Jolyn Okimoto Rosa. **Description:** Bryan Zada owns three PretzelMaker franchises, whose total loss amounted to $40,000 in 2003. Zada believes that listening to employees was one of the key steps in turning the business around. The efforts made to improve the franchises' products are also given.

38590 ■ *"Wrap It Up" in Entrepreneur (Vol. 36, April 2008, No. 4, pp. 84)*
Pub: Entrepreneur Media, Inc.
Ed: Barry Farber. **Description:** Tips on how to manage and get through the closing of a business sale are presented. Focus on what solutions you can bring and not on emotional attachments that can show your eagerness for the sale. Having a track of positive accomplishments can also help.

38591 ■ *"Wrigley's a Rich Meal for Mars" in Crain's Chicago Business (Vol. 31, May 5, 2008, No. 18, pp. 2)*
Pub: Crain Communications, Inc.
Ed: Steven R. Strahler. **Description:** Mars Inc. will have to manage wisely in order to make their acquisition of Wm. Wrigley Jr. Co. profitable due to the high selling price of Wrigley which far exceeds the industry norm. Statistical data included.

38592 ■ *"The Wrong Tune" in The Business Journal-Portland (Vol. 25, July 25, 2008, No. 20, pp. 1)*
Pub: American City Business Journals, Inc.
Ed: Robin J. Moody. **Description:** Views and information on turnaround management and recovery plans of the Oregon Symphony, are presented. The non-profit organization has lost a total of $5.1 million between 2002 and 2008, and $400,000 annual interest payments for a $7 million bank loan. Increased ticket sales, as well as cost cutting measures, are helping improve the finance of the organization.

38593 ■ *"Xerox's Former CEO On Why Succession Shouldn't Be a Horse Race" in Harvard Business Review (Vol. 88, October 2010, No. 10, pp. 47)*
Pub: Harvard Business School Publishing
Ed: Anne Mulcahy. **Description:** The importance of beginning talks between chief executive officers and boards of directors as early as possible to ensure a smooth transition is stressed. This can also prevent turning successions into competitions, with the resultant loss of talent when other candidates 'lose'.

38594 ■ *"Yates Helps Turn Log Home Green" in Contractor (Vol. 56, December 2009, No. 12, pp. 40)*
Pub: Penton Media, Inc.
Description: Upgrading and greening of a log home's HVAC system in Pennsylvania is discussed. F. W. Behler Inc. president Dave Yates was chosen to manage the project. A large coil of R-flex was used to connect the buffer tank to the garage's radiant heat system.

38595 ■ *"You Have to Lead From Everywhere" in Harvard Business Review (Vol. 88, November 2010, No. 11, pp. 76)*
Pub: Harvard Business School Publishing
Ed: Scott Berinato. **Description:** U.S. Coast Guard Admiral Thad W. Allen discusses effective leadership in successful crises management. Topics include influence of media and public perspective, the applicability of military training to the business arena, and the responsibility of a leader to set morale.

38596 ■ *"Young Giants" in Canadian Business (Vol. 79, August 14, 2006, No. 16-17, pp. 47)*
Pub: Rogers Media
Ed: Brad Purdy. **Description:** New generations of young chiefs of oil and gas companies in Canada, are featured.

38597 ■ *"Young-Kee Kim; Deputy Director, Fermi National Accelerator Laboratory" in Crain's Chicago Business (Vol. 31, May 5, 2008, No. 18)*
Pub: Crain Communications, Inc.
Ed: Phuong Ly. **Description:** Profile of Young-Kee Kim who is the deputy director of Fermilab, a physics lab where scientists study the smallest particles in the universe; Ms. Kim was a researcher at Fermilab before becoming deputy director two years ago; Fermilab is currently home to the most powerful particle accelerator in the world and is struggling to compete with other countries despite cuts in federal funding.

38598 ■ *"Your First 100 Days on Your New Job" in Women In Business (Vol. 63, Spring 2011, No. 1, pp. 28)*
Pub: American Business Women's Association
Ed: Diane Stafford. **Description:** The first 100 days on the job are crucial if the person's permanent hiring is conditional on surviving a probationary period. The new hire must do more than just master the job's technical details to maximize the chance of success. Details of some basic tips to fit into the corporate culture and get along with coworkers are also discussed.

TRADE PERIODICALS

38599 ■ *Human Factors in Ergonomics and Manufacturing*
Pub: John Wiley & Sons Inc.
Contact: Stephen M. Smith, President
URL(s): onlinelibrary.wiley.com/journal/10.1002/(ISSN)1520-6564. **Ed:** Waldemar Karwoski, Gavriel Salvendy. **Released:** Bimonthly **Price:** $1427, Institutions print & online; $1553, Institutions, other countries print & online; $1240, Institutions print only; $1240, Institutions, Canada and Mexico print only; $1366, Institutions, other countries print only.

38600 ■ *Innovative Leader*
Pub: Winston J. Brill & Associates
Released: Monthly. **Price:** Free. **Description:** Serves as a resource for managers on creativity and productivity.

38601 ■ *Journal of Economics and Management Strategy*
Pub: Blackwell Publishing Inc.
Contact: Gordon Tibbitts, President
URL(s): as.wiley.com/WileyCDA/WileyTitle/productCd-JEMS.html. **Ed:** Daniel F. Spulber, Jeffrey L. Coles, Zhiqi Chen, Luis M.B. Cabral, Esther Gal-Or. **Released:** Quarterly **Price:** $62, Individuals print & online; €91, Individuals print & online; £61, Other countries print & online; $59, Individuals online; €87, Individuals online; £57, Other countries online; $466, Institutions print & online; €466, Institutions print & online; $717, Institutions, other countries print & online.

38602 ■ *The Journal for Quality and Participation*
Pub: American Society for Quality
Contact: Paul E. Borawski, Chief Executive Officer
URL(s): www.asq.org/pub/jqp/. **Released:** 4/yr. **Price:** $52, Members domestic, individuals; $82, Members international, individuals; $75, Members includes GST individual, Canada; $87, Nonmembers domestic, individuals; $98, Nonmembers international, individuals; $98, Nonmembers Canadian, includes GST individual.

38603 ■ *Make It A Winning Life*
Pub: Wolf Rinke Associates,Inc.
Ed: Wolf J. Rinke, Ph.D., Editor, wolfrinke@aol.com. **Released:** Bimonthly. **Price:** Free. **Description:** Features ideas and strategies to help individuals succeed faster and improve the quality of their life. Remarks: America Online, Inc.

38604 ■ *Management Report for Nonunion Organizations*
Pub: John Wiley and Sons Inc.
Ed: Sarah Magee, Editor. **Released:** Monthly. **Price:** $995, U.S.; $995, Canada and Mexico; $1067, elsewhere. **Description:** Features news on current activities; employers' responses; NLRB rulings; court cases; pending legislation; government policies; and advice and opinions from Alfred T. DeMaria, "one of the country's foremost labor lawyers" representing management. Includes information on preventive tactics on how to handle human resources and labor issues without risking unionization, a campaign workshop on what the laws and regulations mean in terms of day-to-day management, white-collar organizing, and questions and answers on common problems.

38605 ■ *The Navigator*
Pub: Chart Your Course International Inc.
Contact: Gregory P. Smith, President
E-mail: greg@chartcourse.com
Released: Quarterly. **Price:** Free. **Description:** Publishes advice, how-to tips, and trends in business, including management, TQM, leadership, customer service. Recurring features include news of research, a calendar of events, and a column titled Improving Productivity.

38606 ■ *Quality Management Journal*
Pub: American Society for Quality
Contact: Paul E. Borawski, Chief Executive Officer
URL(s): asq.org/pub/qmj/. **Ed:** Barbara Flynn. **Released:** Quarterly **Price:** $59, U.S. members; $92, Canada members; $86, Other countries members; $87, U.S. non-members; $110, Canada non-members; $105, Other countries non-members.

38607 ■ *Quality Manager's Alert*
Pub: Progressive Business Publications
Ed: Jim Giuliano, Editor. **Released:** Semimonthly. **Price:** $299, individuals. **Description:** Communicates the latest information on changing quality standards and how companies get buy-in on quality from employees. Recurring features include interviews, news of research, a calendar of events, news of educational opportunities, and a column titled Sharpen Your Judgment.

38608 ■ *Self Employment Update*
Pub: Update Publicare Co.
Ed: A.C. Doyle, Editor. **Released:** Annual. **Description:** Introduces readers to the broad interest of self-employment. Carries news of relevant books. Recurring features include news of research and ideas for small businesses.

38609 ■ *Small Business Taxes and Management*
Pub: A/N Group Inc.
Contact: Steven A. Hopfenmuller, President
Released: Semimonthly, Daily (Mon. thru Fri.). **Price:** $49.95. **Description:** Offers current tax news, reviews of recent cases, tax saving tips, and personal financial planning for small business owners. Includes articles on issues such as finance and management. Remarks: Available online only.

38610 ■ *Small Farm News*
Pub: Small Farm Center
Ed: Susan McCue, Editor, semccue@ucdavis.edu. **Released:** Quarterly, 4/year. **Price:** Free. **Description:** Covers topics of interest to small farmers. Includes farmer profiles, government actions and crop information. Recurring features include letters to the editor, interviews, news of research, a calendar of events, notices of publications available, Directors' Column, resources section, news notes, and program news.

38611 ■ *Supervisors Legal Update*
Pub: Progressive Business Publications
Contact: Ron McRae, Editor-in-Chief
Ed: Thomas J. Gorman, IV, Editor. **Released:** Semimonthly. **Price:** $94.56, individuals. **Description:** Supplies brief updates on employment law for supervisors. Review a column titled Sharpen Your Judgment.

38612 ■ *Utility Automation*
Contact: Kathleen Wackowski, Regional Manager
E-mail: kathleenw@pennwell.com
URL(s): uaelp.pennnet.com. **Released:** Monthly **Price:** $85, Individuals; $94, Individuals Mexico/Canada; $225, Other countries; $145, Two years; $160, Two years Mexico/Canada; $403, Other countries 2 years.

VIDEOCASSETTES/ AUDIOCASSETTES

38613 ■ *American Business Management Series*
Instructional Video
2219 C St.
Lincoln, NE 68502
Ph: (402)475-6570
Free: 800-228-0164
Fax: (402)475-6500
Co. E-mail: feedback@insvideo.com
URL: http://www.insvideo.com
Released: 19??. **Description:** Management training series offers instruction on many of today's business and management issues. **Availability:** VHS.

38614 ■ *Anticipation: Rx for Crisis Management*
Aspen Publishers, Inc.
7201 McKinney Cir.
Frederick, MD 21704
Ph: (301)698-7100
Free: 800-234-1660
Fax: (800)901-9075
Co. E-mail: customerservice@aspenpublisher.com
URL: http://www.aspenpublishers.com
Contact: Robert Becker, President
Released: 1991. **Price:** $495.00. **Description:** A guide for supervisors on analyzing daily work situations in order to avoid trouble before it happens. **Availability:** VHS; 3/4 U.

38615 ■ *The Art of Negotiating*
Aspen Publishers, Inc.
7201 McKinney Cir.
Frederick, MD 21704
Ph: (301)698-7100
Free: 800-234-1660
Fax: (800)901-9075
Co. E-mail: customerservice@aspenpublisher.com
URL: http://www.aspenpublishers.com
Contact: Robert Becker, President
Released: 1991. **Price:** $495.00. **Description:** Supervisors and managers will learn how to get what they want with seven basic strategies in the fine art of negotiation. Hosted by master negotiator and world renowned counselor Gerard Nierenberg. **Availability:** VHS; 3/4 U.

38616 ■ *Beyond Start-Up: Management Lessons for Growing Companies*
Video Arts, Inc.
c/o Aim Learning Group
8238-40 Lehigh
Morton Grove, IL 60053-2615
Free: 877-444-2230
Fax: (416)252-2155
Co. E-mail: service@aimlearninggroup.com
URL: http://www.aimlearninggroup.com
Released: 1989. **Price:** $395.00. **Description:** Don't settle for being a small company—find out what it takes to expand your business. **Availability:** VHS; 3/4 U.

38617 ■ *Center on Profit*
International Dairy-Deli-Bakery Association (IDDBA)
PO Box 5528
Madison, WI 53705-0528
Ph: (608)310-5000
Fax: (608)238-6330
Co. E-mail: iddba@iddba.org
URL: http://www.iddba.org
Contact: Steve Beekhuizen, President
Released: 19??. **Price:** $160.00. **Description:** Teaches managers how to reduce unknown shrink, write effective orders and schedules, plus calculate deli items' profit and gross margin contribution to margin. **Availability:** VHS.

38618 ■ *Days of Reckoning*
Film Library/National Safety Council California Chapter
4553 Glencoe Ave., Ste. 150
Marina Del Rey, CA 90292
Ph: (310)827-9781
Free: 800-421-9585
Fax: (310)827-9861
Co. E-mail: California@nsc.org
URL: http://www.nsc.org/nsc_near_you/FindYourLocalChapter/Pages/California.aspx
Released: 198?. **Description:** This film chronicles the fables of managing a small business. **Availability:** VHS; 3/4 U.

38619 ■ *Dealing with Difficult People Volume Two*
RMI Media
1365 N. Winchester St.
Olathe, KS 66061-5880
Ph: (913)768-1696
Free: 800-745-5480
Fax: (800)755-6910
Co. E-mail: actmedia@act.org
URL: http://www.actmedia.com
Released: 1993. **Price:** $99.00. **Description:** Ed Greif explains how to handle very difficult problems with people. **Availability:** VHS.

38620 ■ *Delegating Responsibility*
1st Financial Training Services
1515 E. Woodfield Rd., Ste. 345
Schaumburg, IL 60173
Ph: (847)969-0900
Free: 800-442-8662
Fax: (847)969-0521
URL: http://www.1stfinancialtraining.com
Released: 1987. **Price:** $150.00. **Description:** A primer for managers in dispersing and assigning work to employees. **Availability:** VHS; 3/4 U.

38621 ■ *Discipline: A Matter of Judgment*
Encyclopedia Britannica
331 N. LaSalle St.
Chicago, IL 60654
Ph: (312)347-7159
Free: 800-323-1229
Fax: (312)294-2104
URL: http://www.britannica.com
Released: 1989. **Description:** This video teaches that discipline must educate, not humiliate, and urges fair, prompt, and consistent disciplinary action. **Availability:** VHS; 3/4 U.

38622 ■ *Don't Keep It To Yourself*
Instructional Video
2219 C St.
Lincoln, NE 68502
Ph: (402)475-6570
Free: 800-228-0164
Fax: (402)475-6500
Co. E-mail: feedback@insvideo.com
URL: http://www.insvideo.com
Released: 19??. **Price:** $150.00. **Description:** Part of the Super Vision for the '90s management training series. Discusses the importance of communication between supervisor and employees. Also provides information on how to increase productivity and decrease tension. **Availability:** VHS.

38623 ■ *Empowerment: The Attitude Opportunity*
International Training Consultants, Inc.
1838 Park Oaks
Kemah, TX 77565
Free: 800-998-8764
Co. E-mail: itc@trainingitc.com
URL: http://www.trainingitc.com
Released: 19??. **Price:** $495.00. **Description:** Part of the "Empowerment: The Employee Development Series." Teaches employees to accept responsibility for their attitude problems, seeing them as opportunities for improvement, and offers them tips on how to make the transition from attitude problem to attitude opportunity. Also provides information on how to monitor and reward their progress. Comes with leader's guide, self-study instructions, and five participant booklets. **Availability:** VHS.

38624 ■ *Everything You Always Wanted to Know about Management*
American Media, Inc.
4621 121st St.
Urbandale, IA 50323-2311
Ph: (515)224-0919
Free: 888-776-8268
Fax: (515)327-2555
Co. E-mail: custsvc@ammedia.com
URL: http://www.ammedia.com
Released: 1995. **Price:** $595. **Description:** Outlines the essentials of good management, including the six steps of delegation, employee empowerment, communication, feedback, and goal achievement. Includes course guide with participant exercises and case studies. **Availability:** VHS; CC.

38625 ■ *Leadership Skills by Aaron Alejandro*
Cambridge Educational
c/o Films Media Group
132 West 31st Street, 17th Floor
Ste. 124
New York, NY 10001
Free: 800-257-5126
Fax: (609)671-0266
Co. E-mail: custserve@films.com
URL: http://www.cambridgeol.com
Released: 1991. **Price:** $79.95. **Description:** Fast-paced leadership workshop designed to develop and sharpen leadership skills. **Availability:** VHS.

38626 ■ *Looking at It from Every Angle*
American Management Association (AMA)
1601 Broadway
New York, NY 10019-7420
Ph: (212)586-8100
Free: 877-566-9441
Fax: (212)903-8168
Co. E-mail: customerservice@amanet.org
URL: http://www.amanet.org
Contact: Charles R. Craig, Chairman
Released: 1985. **Description:** An analysis of proper business training in terms of management decision-making, problem-solving efficiency and department use. **Availability:** VHS; 3/4 U.

38627 ■ *Management Action Program*
Video Arts, Inc.
c/o Aim Learning Group
8238-40 Lehigh
Morton Grove, IL 60053-2615
Free: 877-444-2230
Fax: (416)252-2155
Co. E-mail: service@aimlearninggroup.com
URL: http://www.aimlearninggroup.com
Released: 1986. **Price:** $680.00. **Description:** A series of videos that look at customer service, innovation and productivity. **Availability:** VHS; 8 mm; 3/4 U; Special order formats.

38628 ■ *Management 1*
MR Communication Consultants
5000 Yonge St., Ste. 1705
Toronto, ON, Canada M2N 7E9
Ph: (416)506-9520

Free: 800-263-8326
Fax: (416)539-9604
Co. E-mail: info@mrcomm.com
URL: http://www.mrcomm.com
Released: 1980. **Description:** A course intended to teach supervisors the fundamental skills to apply to their work situation. **Availability:** VHS; 3/4 U.

38629 ■ *Management Techniques That Work*
Instructional Video
2219 C St.
Lincoln, NE 68502
Ph: (402)475-6570
Free: 800-228-0164
Fax: (402)475-6500
Co. E-mail: feedback@insvideo.com
URL: http://www.insvideo.com
Released: 19??. **Price:** $89.95. **Description:** Three management experts discuss techniques to improve productivity while also improving the workplace environment. Also looks at participative management and other techniques. **Availability:** VHS.

38630 ■ *The Management of Work*
Resources for Education & Management, Inc.
1804 Montreal Ct., Ste. A
Tucker, GA 30084
Released: 19??. **Description:** A series intended to show managers how to build the key skills of organizing, planning, directing, and controlling. **Availability:** VHS; 3/4 U.

38631 ■ *MBA—Management Basics in Action*
Phoenix Learning Group
2349 Chaffee Dr.
Saint Louis, MO 63146-3306
Ph: (314)569-0211
Free: 800-221-1274
Fax: (314)569-2834
URL: http://www.phoenixlearninggroup.com
Released: 1985. **Description:** A program library for management of business. **Availability:** VHS.

38632 ■ *Nobody's Perfect: Managing the Team*
Video Arts, Inc.
c/o Aim Learning Group
8238-40 Lehigh
Morton Grove, IL 60053-2615
Free: 877-444-2230
Fax: (416)252-2155
Co. E-mail: service@aimlearninggroup.com
URL: http://www.aimlearninggroup.com
Released: 1991. **Price:** $790.00. **Description:** How to put the right people in the right position on a team, enhancing win potential and covering weak spots. **Availability:** VHS; 8 mm; 3/4 U; Special order formats.

38633 ■ *One Small Step*
Film Library/National Safety Council California Chapter
4553 Glencoe Ave., Ste. 150
Marina Del Rey, CA 90292
Ph: (310)827-9781
Free: 800-421-9585
Fax: (310)827-9861
Co. E-mail: California@nsc.org
URL: http://www.nsc.org/nsc_near_you/FindYourLocalChapter/Pages/California.aspx
Released: 198?. **Description:** This film looks at how managers can improve their work environments through better communication with their employees. **Availability:** VHS; 3/4 U.

38634 ■ *Performance Management: The Road to Excellence*
Aspen Publishers, Inc.
7201 McKinney Cir.
Frederick, MD 21704
Ph: (301)698-7100
Free: 800-234-1660
Fax: (800)901-9075
Co. E-mail: customerservice@aspenpublisher.com
URL: http://www.aspenpublishers.com
Contact: Robert Becker, President
Released: 1985. **Price:** $495.00. **Description:** Employee work levels tend to increase when positive attributes and contributions are stressed. Learn how to implement this performance plan with these helpful tips. **Availability:** VHS; 3/4 U; Special order formats.

38635 ■ *Principles of Management*
RMI Media
1365 N. Winchester St.
Olathe, KS 66061-5880
Ph: (913)768-1696
Free: 800-745-5480
Fax: (800)755-6910
Co. E-mail: actmedia@act.org
URL: http://www.actmedia.com
Released: 1987. **Description:** These videos describe the basic skills needed for effective management. **Availability:** VHS; 3/4 U.

38636 ■ *Problem Solving: A Process for Managers*
Encyclopedia Britannica
331 N. LaSalle St.
Chicago, IL 60654
Ph: (312)347-7159
Free: 800-323-1229
Fax: (312)294-2104
URL: http://www.britannica.com
Released: 1989. **Description:** This program introduces managers to a practical, efficient six-step problem solving method applicable to most management problems. **Availability:** 3/4 U.

38637 ■ *Training Needs Assessment*
Aspen Publishers, Inc.
7201 McKinney Cir.
Frederick, MD 21704
Ph: (301)698-7100
Free: 800-234-1660
Fax: (800)901-9075
Co. E-mail: customerservice@aspenpublisher.com
URL: http://www.aspenpublishers.com
Contact: Robert Becker, President
Released: 1986. **Price:** $495.00. **Description:** Supervisor Dave Eppinger explains the process of training needs assessment and discusses the characteristics necessary for a completely efficient system. **Availability:** VHS; 3/4 U.

38638 ■ *What Went Wrong?*
Aspen Publishers, Inc.
7201 McKinney Cir.
Frederick, MD 21704
Ph: (301)698-7100
Free: 800-234-1660
Fax: (800)901-9075
Co. E-mail: customerservice@aspenpublisher.com
URL: http://www.aspenpublishers.com
Contact: Robert Becker, President
Released: 1985. **Price:** $495.00. **Description:** An instructional seminar in the art of decision-making and problem-solving in business. **Availability:** VHS; 3/4 U.

38639 ■ *Where There's a Will. . .: Leadership and Motivation*
Video Arts, Inc.
c/o Aim Learning Group
8238-40 Lehigh
Morton Grove, IL 60053-2615
Free: 877-444-2230
Fax: (416)252-2155
Co. E-mail: service@aimlearninggroup.com
URL: http://www.aimlearninggroup.com
Released: 1988. **Price:** $790.00. **Description:** Find out how you can motivate your workers to a higher productivity level. **Availability:** VHS; 8 mm; 3/4 U; Special order formats.

38640 ■ *Who Does What?*
Aspen Publishers, Inc.
7201 McKinney Cir.
Frederick, MD 21704
Ph: (301)698-7100
Free: 800-234-1660
Fax: (800)901-9075
Co. E-mail: customerservice@aspenpublisher.com
URL: http://www.aspenpublishers.com
Contact: Robert Becker, President
Released: 1989. **Price:** $495.00. **Description:** Supervisors will learn how to delegate authority and maximize employee productivity and time management by implementing a nine step checklist, demonstrated through a variety of workplace dramatizations. **Availability:** VHS; 3/4 U.

38641 ■ *Winning Entrepreneurial Style*
MGM/UA
MGM
10250 Constellation Blvd.
Los Angeles, CA 90067
Ph: (310)449-3000
URL: http://www.mgm.com
Released: 1986. **Description:** A bevy of nationwide entrepreneurs share their secrets for financial success. **Availability:** VHS; CC.

TRADE SHOWS AND CONVENTIONS

38642 ■ Alliance Texas
Showorks Inc.
1205 N. Napa St.
Spokane, WA 99202
Ph: (509)838-8755
Fax: (509)838-2838
Co. E-mail: showorks@showorksinc.com
URL: http://www.showorksinc.com
URL(s): www.allianceforbiz.com. **Price:** $140, registered before early bird date; $165, registered through early bird date; $195, Onsite. **Audience:** Buyers and contracting officers from military bases. **Principal Exhibits:** Small business procurement opportunities.

CONSULTANTS

38643 ■ 108 Ideaspace Inc.
108 Dundas St. W, Ste. 201
Toronto, ON, Canada M6B 2H8
Ph: (416)256-7773
Fax: (416)256-7763
Co. E-mail: request@108ideaspace.com
URL: http://www.ptadvisors.com
Contact: Randall M. Craig, President
E-mail: randall@108ideaspace.com
Scope: Organizational advisors to senior management in service- or information-based businesses: professional service firms, education and publishing and financial services. Services in management counsel (including investor/acquisition due diligence, executive coaching, risk assessment and facilitation, planning and leadership), marketing (including branding), technology and human resources. **Founded:** 1994. **Publications:** "Leaving the Mother Ship"; "The Working Resume". **Seminars:** No Job, Now What; Social Media Executive Briefing; Career Networking for Success; Development; Work-Life Balance; Integrated marketing planning workshop.

38644 ■ ABA Inc.
411-24 Wellesley St.
Toronto, ON, Canada M4Y 2X6
Ph: (416)219-8447
Fax: (416)924-4664
Contact: Ray Belanger, Vice President
E-mail: raybel2@home.com
Scope: Firm provides management consultation to emerging and growth oriented companies in the Internet, film and television, and multimedia industries. Areas of expertise include planning and developing practices in strategy, finance, marketing, HR, and operations. Services range from full strategy papers to business/marketing plans, and financial performance reviews. **Founded:** 1999. **Seminars:** Reduces Cycle Time; Cuts Costs; Improves Learning; Facilitates Accountability.

38645 ■ Advanced Benefits & Human Resources
9350-F Snowden River Pkwy., Ste. 222
Columbia, MD 21045
Ph: (410)290-9037

Fax: (410)740-2568
Co. E-mail: hrb@abhr.com
Contact: Linda Polacek, President
Scope: Provides human resource consulting to high technology businesses. Offers services in the areas of human resources, benefits, and training. Creates, maintains, or updates current human resource functions. **Founded:** 1996.

38646 ■ Advisory Management Services Inc.
9600 E 129th St., Ste. B
Kansas City, MO 64149-1025
Ph: (816)765-9611
Fax: (816)765-7447
Contact: Hal Wood, President
Scope: A management consulting and training firm specializing in employee relations, management and staff training, organizational development, strategic planning, and continuous quality improvement. **Founded:** 1979.

38647 ■ Charles J. Allen and Associates
2668 Foxglove St.
Woodridge, IL 60517
Ph: (630)963-1444
Contact: Charles J. Allen, President
Scope: Specializes in marketing, communication, advertising and promotional consulting. Also serves as business management consultants on a continuing basis. **Founded:** 1970.

38648 ■ The Alliance Management Group Inc.
38 Old Chester Rd., Ste. 300
Gladstone, NJ 07934
Ph: (908)234-2344
Fax: (908)234-0638
Co. E-mail: kathy@strategicalliance.com
URL: http://www.strategicalliance.com
Contact: Gene Slowinski, Director
E-mail: gene@strategicalliance.com
Scope: The firm enables leading companies to maximize the value of their strategic alliances, mergers and acquisitions. Offers services in partner evaluation process, a planning and negotiating program, mergers and acquisition integration, management issues, the turnaround or termination of poorly performing alliances, and a competitive strategic analysis program. **Publications:** "Effective Practices For Sourcing Innovation," Jan-Feb, 2009; "Intellectual Property Issues in Collaborative Research Agreements," Nov-Dec, 2008; "Building University Relationships in China," Sep-Oct, 2008; "Reinventing Corporate Growth: Implementing the Transformational Growth Model"; "The Strongest Link"; "Allocating Patent Rights in Collaborative Research Agreements"; "Protecting Know-how and Trade Secrets in Collaborative Research Agreements," Aug, 2006; "Sourcing External Technology for Innovation," Jun, 2006. **Special Services:** "Want, Find, Get, Manage" Model®; "Want, Find, Get, Manage" Framework®; WFGM Framework®; The Alliance Implementation Program®; WFGM Paradigm®; WFGM Model®; "Want, Find, Get, Manage" Paradigm®, Transformational Growth®; T-growth®.

38649 ■ Alliance Management International Ltd.
PO Box 470691
Cleveland, OH 44147-0691
Ph: (440)838-1922
Co. E-mail: bob@bgruss.com
Contact: Ashok Vasudevan, Director
Scope: A consulting company that helps to form national and international strategic alliances. Handles alliances between companies forming joint ventures. Staff specialized in small company-large company alliance, alliance assessment and analysis, and alliance strategic planning. **Seminars:** Joint Business Planning; Developing a Shared Vision; Current and New/Prospective Partner Assessment; Customer Service; Sales Training; Leader and Management Skills.

38650 ■ Allsup Inc.
300 Allsup Pl.
Belleville, IL 62223
Ph: (618)234-8434
Free: 800-854-1418
Fax: (618)236-5778
Co. E-mail: info@allsupinc.com
URL: http://www.allsup.com
Contact: Jim Allsup, President
Scope: Social Security disability claims services company understanding the specialized needs of those with disabilities. **Founded:** 1984. **Publications:** "The Alls up Alternative".

38651 ■ Anderson/Roethle Inc.
700 N Water St., Ste. 325
Milwaukee, WI 53202-4221
Ph: (414)276-0070
Fax: (414)276-4364
Co. E-mail: info@anderson-roethle.com
URL: http://www.anderson-roethle.com
Contact: Stanley C. Johnson, President
E-mail: scj@anderson-roethle.com
Scope: Provider of merger, acquisition and divestiture advisory services. Offers strategic planning, valuations and specialized M and A advisory services. **Founded:** 1963.

38652 ■ Apex Innovations Inc.
19951 W 162nd St.
Olathe, KS 66062
Ph: (913)254-0250
Fax: (913)254-0320
Co. E-mail: sales@apex-innovations.com
URL: http://www.apex-innovations.com
Contact: Wayne Abrams, President
E-mail: wayne.abrams@apex-innovations.com
Scope: A firm of business operations and technology professionals providing solutions nationwide for business needs. Provides a bridge between operations and technology for clients in manufacturing, insurance, banking and government. Offers services in business planning, assessment, education, business performance improvement, change management and the planning, and implementation management of solutions. **Founded:** 2002. **Special Services:** i-INFO. EPR™; i-INFO.WORKS™; i-INFO Classes™.

38653 ■ Aurora Management Partners Inc.
4485 Tench Rd., Ste. 340
Suwanee, GA 30024
Ph: (770)904-5209
Fax: (770)904-5226
Co. E-mail: rturcotte@auroramp.com
URL: http://www.auroramp.com
Contact: William A. Barbee, Director
E-mail: abarbee@auroramp.com
Scope: Specializes in turnaround management and reorganization consulting. Firm develop strategic initiatives, organize and analyze solutions, deal with creditor issues, review organizational structure and develop time frames for decision making. Turnaround services offered include Recovery plans and their implementation, Viability analysis, Crisis management, Financial restructuring, Corporate and organizational restructuring, Facilities rationalization, Liquidation management, Loan workout, Litigation support and Expert testimony, Contract renegotiation, Sourcing loan refinancing and Sourcing equity investment. **Founded:** 2005. **Publications:** "TMA Turnaround of the Year Award, Small Company, Honorable Mention," Nov, 2005; "Back From The Brink - Bland Farms," Progressive Farmer, Oct, 2004; "New Breed of Turnaround Managers," Catalyst Magazine, Aug, 2004; "Key Performance Drivers - Bland Farms," The Produce News, Apr, 2004; "Corporate Governance: Averting Crisis's Before They Happen," ABJ journal, Feb, 2004.

38654 ■ Avery, Cooper & Co.
4918-50th St.
Yellowknife, NT, Canada X1A 2P2
Ph: (867)873-3441
Free: 800-661-0787
Fax: (867)873-2353
Co. E-mail: gerry@averyco.nt.ca
URL: http://www.averycooper.com
Contact: Bernie H. Bauhaus, Manager
E-mail: bernieb@averyco.nt.ca
Scope: Accounting and management consulting firm. **Founded:** 1969. **Seminars:** Sage Software Training. **Special Services:** ACCPAC Plus; Sage Accpac ERP.

38655 ■ Bahr International Inc.
PO Box 795
Gainesville, TX 76241
Ph: (940)665-2344
Fax: (940)665-2359
Co. E-mail: info@bahrintl.com
URL: http://www.bahrintl.com
Contact: C. Charles Bahr, III, Chairman of the Board
Scope: Offers consulting in general management, corporate polices and culture, and strategic and long-range planning. Provides management audits and reports and profit improvement programs. High level strategic marketing, advertising strategy/tactics, turnaround consulting and management. **Founded:** 1978.

38656 ■ Melvin E. Barnette & Associates Inc.
805 Hopkins Ave.
Pendleton, SC 29670
Ph: (864)646-7622
Fax: (626)296-5113
Co. E-mail: melvin@mbarnette.com
URL: http://www.mbarnette.com
Contact: Melvin E. Barnette, President
Scope: Management consulting firm specializing in higher education and public sector consulting services. Offers services including higher education administrative, business and financial operations studies; structuring of upper-level management organizations; state government operations; legislative liaison; personnel evaluation; crisis resolution and management; and management training. **Founded:** 1986.

38657 ■ Bayer Center for Nonprofit Management (BCNM)
Robert Morris University, 6001 University Blvd.
Moon Township, PA 15219-3099
Ph: (412)397-6814
Free: 800-762-0097
Fax: (412)397-4097
Co. E-mail: bcnm@rmu.edu
URL: http://www.rmu.edu/bcnm
Contact: Cindy Bahn, Director
E-mail: bahn@rmu.edu
Scope: Center offers consulting services in: Board development, business planning, collaboration and alliances, financial management, fund development, organizational effectiveness, and technology planning. Also provides information and referral services, conducts applied research, and serves to convene in depth discussions on the problems of society addressed by nonprofit organizations. **Founded:** 1999. **Seminars:** A Starfish Can Grow a New Arm, Why Cant I?; Carnegie Science Centers SuperFun Science Fest; Disc Driving the Electronic Mall; Steady Hand Game; Planning an Accessible World.

38658 ■ Beacon Management - Management Consultants
1000 W McNab Rd.
Pompano Beach, FL 33069
Ph: (954)782-1119
Free: 800-771-8721
Fax: (954)969-2566
Co. E-mail: md@beaconmgmt.com
URL: http://www.beaconmgmt.com
Contact: Joyce Slencak, Manager
Scope: Specializes in change management, organized workplaces, multicultural negotiations and dispute resolutions and internet based decision making. **Founded:** 1985. **Publications:** "Sun-Sentinel Article," Oct, 2012.

38659 ■ Don L. Beck Associates Inc.
10050 N Foothill Blvd.
Cupertino, CA 95014-5601
Ph: (408)973-8688
Fax: (408)973-8714
Co. E-mail: dbeck@dlba.com
Contact: Don L. Beck, President
Scope: A management consulting firm specializing in building facilities planning and management worldwide. **Founded:** 1981.

38660 ■ Benchmark Consulting Group Inc.—Benchmark Advisors
283 Franklin St., Ste. 400
Boston, MA 02110-3100

Ph: (617)482-7661
Fax: (617)423-2158
Contact: Walter E. Robb, III, President
E-mail: werobb35@aol.com
Scope: Provides financial and management services to companies. Helps companies grow through debt, equity sourcing and restructuring, business valuation, acquisition and divestiture, computer information systems and improved operation profitability. **Founded:** 1978.

38661 ■ Better Bottom Lines
2365 Rebel Rd.
Cumming, GA 30041
Ph: (770)887-3450
Fax: (770)887-3450
Co. E-mail: skipgundlach@earthlink.net
Contact: Skip Gundlach, President
E-mail: skipgundlach@earthlink.net
Scope: Firm conducts management and marketing consulting. It serves all small businesses, with a concentration on electromechanical sales, service and installation companies in the U.S. and Canada. **Founded:** 1986.

38662 ■ Biomedical Management Resources (BMR)
PO Box 521125
Salt Lake City, UT 84152-1125
Ph: (801)272-4668
Fax: (801)277-3290
Co. E-mail: SeniorManagement@BiomedicalManagement.com
URL: http://www.biomedicalmanagement.com
Contact: Ping Fong, Jr., President
E-mail: pingfong@biomedicalmanagement.com
Scope: Provides business development, interim management, and executive search services. Assists companies in strategic alliances, corporate partnering, business acquisition. Demonstrated success in identifying recruiting, and placing key managers in difficult to hire positions. **Founded:** 1993.

38663 ■ Blackford Associates
30 George Rd.
Contoocook, NH 03229
Ph: (603)225-2228
Fax: (603)225-2228
Contact: John M. Blackford, Owner
Scope: Provider of general management consulting to smaller manufacturing companies. Counsels chief executive officers and presidents on strategy, organization, finances and operations. Areas of expertise include the following: new products, services or markets; problems of expansion or retrenchment; financing and bank relations; morale, organization and training; budgeting and business plans; factory flow and inventory control; quality control and methods; cash flow problems; and financial information and controls. **Founded:** 1984.

38664 ■ Blankinship & Associates Inc.
322 C St.
Davis, CA 95616
Ph: (530)757-0941
Fax: (530)757-0940
Co. E-mail: blankinship@envtox.com
URL: http://www.h2osci.com
Contact: Michael Blankinship, President
E-mail: mike@envtox.com
Scope: Specializes in assisting water resource and conveyance, golf and production, protection and enhancement of natural resources. **Founded:** 2000. **Publications:** "Air Blast Sprayer Calibration and Chlorpyrifos Irrigation Study," Oct, 2007; "How Green is your golf course," Prosper Magazine, 2007. **Seminars:** CDFG Wildlands IPM Seminar, Oct, 2009.

38665 ■ Blue Garnet Associates L.L.C.
8055 W Manchester Ave., Ste. 430
Los Angeles, CA 90293
Ph: (310)439-1930
Fax: (310)388-1657
URL: http://www.bluegarnet.net
Contact: Amanda Green, Principal
Scope: Provides expertise in organizational visioning, strategic and business planning, market opportunity and growth strategy, impact assessment, and leadership and governance. **Founded:** 2002.

38666 ■ C. Clint Bolte & Associates
809 Philadelphia Ave.
Chambersburg, PA 17201
Ph: (717)263-5768
Fax: (717)263-8954
Co. E-mail: clint@clintbolte.com
URL: http://www.clintbolte.com
Contact: C. Clint Bolte, Principal
E-mail: cbolte3@comcast.net
Scope: Provider of management consulting services to firms involved with the printing industry. Services include outsourcing studies, graphics supply chain management studies, company and equipment valuations, plant layout services, litigation support, fulfillment warehouse consulting and product development services. **Founded:** 1989. **Seminars:** How to compete with the majors.

38667 ■ Lisa Boyd Consulting L.L.C.
126 Clark Ave.
Ocean Grove, NJ 07756-1028
Ph: (732)774-4420
Fax: (732)774-2862
Co. E-mail: lisaboyd@earthlink.net
Contact: Ivan D. Armstrong, Principal
Scope: Provides professional housing development services. Assists with business plans, capacity building, project management, and property management assessment. **Founded:** 1996.

38668 ■ BPT Consulting Associates Ltd.
12 Parmenter Rd., Ste. B-6
Londonderry, NH 03053
Ph: (603)437-8484
Free: 888-278-0030
Fax: (603)434-5388
Contact: John Kuczynski, Managing Director
Scope: Provides management consulting expertise and resources to cross-industry clients with services for: Business Management consulting, People/Human Resources Transition and Training programs, and a full cadre of multi-disciplined Technology Computer experts. Virtual consultants with expertise in e-commerce, supply chain management, organizational development, and business application development consulting. **Founded:** 1991.

38669 ■ Chip Bradley Management Advisor
543 Delaware Ave., Ste. 11
Delmar, NY 12054-2835
Ph: (518)475-0152
Fax: (518)475-0152
Contact: Charles C. Bradley, President
Scope: Management training firm specializing in personal and interpersonal skills development. Offers problem-solving programs and products to meet productivity and profitability challenges. Industries served include colleges, universities, adult education centers; professional and trade associations; not-for-profit organizations; home-based entrepreneurs and independent consultants. **Founded:** 1989. **Seminars:** How to Begin and Build a Successful Consulting Practice; Managing Multiple Priorities in Your Work Unit; Making Time Count: How to Become a Better Manager of Yourself and Your Time; Supervisory Skills for New and Prospective Managers.

38670 ■ BrightMagnet
31339 Pacific Coast Hwy.
Malibu, CA 90265
Ph: (310)457-0444
Fax: (310)457-0444
Co. E-mail: info@brightmagnet.com
Contact: Jean Marie Bonthous, Owner
E-mail: jmb@leonardo.net
Scope: Boutique consultancy providing strategic counsel to organizations facing significant change or reputation. **Publications:** "Bibliography of Business/Competitive Intelligence and Benchmarking Literature," Aug, 1994. **Seminars:** Benchmarking; Developing Organizational Intelligence Capabilities; Coaching Skills for Managers; Effective Strategic Thinking; Competitive Analysis Techniques; Learning to Learn; Learning from Work.

38671 ■ BroadVision Inc.
1600 Seaport Blvd., Ste. 550, North Bldg.
Redwood City, CA 94063-5589
Ph: (650)295-0716
Free: 866-287-6669
Fax: (650)364-3425
Co. E-mail: info@broadvision.com
URL: http://www.broadvision.com
Contact: Dr. Pehong Chen, President
Scope: Firm delivers a combination of technologies and services in to the global market that enable its customers to power mission-critical web initiatives that ultimately deliver high-value to their bottom line. Areas of expertise include strategic services, interactive services, content and creative services and client services. Services include business planning, application strategy, ROI analysis, organization and business process consulting, building and deploying applications, content management, sourcing and workflow processes. **Founded:** 1993. **Publications:** *One-to-One Enterprise*; *One-to-One Knowledge*; *One-to-One Financial*; *One-to-One Retail Commerce*; *One-to-One Business Commerce*; *One-To-One Command Center*; *One-To-One Publishing Center*; *One-To-One Design Center*; *Onte-To-One Instant Publisher*; *One-To-One Billing*; *Retail Commerce Suite*; *MarketMaker*.

38672 ■ Business Education Associates (BEA)—Ashford Group Inc.
4 Long Hill Rd.
Bethel, CT 06801
Ph: (203)798-6035
Contact: Robert J. Popp, President
E-mail: bob@ashfordgrp.com
Scope: Offers tailored management education programs. Has been designed to meet the business education needs of companies implementing new systems and companies to re-educate users of existing systems. **Founded:** 1984. **Publications:** "The Ashford Group and TQuist Partner to Provide High Impact Manufacturing Solutions"; "The Future of ERP"; "Winning the Implementation Game". **Special Services:** Building Manufacturing Excellence.

38673 ■ Business Improvement Architects (BIA)
33 Riderwood Dr.
Toronto, ON, Canada M2L 2X4
Ph: (416)444-8225
Free: 866-346-3242
Fax: (416)444-6743
Co. E-mail: info@bia.ca
URL: http://www.bia.ca
Contact: Michael Stanleigh, Chief Executive Officer
E-mail: mstanleigh@bia.ca
Scope: Provider of the following services: strategic planning, leadership development, innovation and project and quality management. Specialize in strategic planning, change management, leadership assessment, and development of skills. **Founded:** 1989. **Publications:** "Avoiding Pit falls to Innovation"; "Create a New Dimension of Performance with Innovation"; "The Power of Appreciation in Leadership"; "Why It Makes Sense To Have a Strategic Enterprise Office"; "Burning Rubber at the Start of Your Project"; "Accounting for Quality"; "How Pareto Charts Can Help You Improve the Quality of Business Processes"; "Managing Resistance to Change". **Seminars:** The Innovation Process. . .From Vision to Reality, San Diego, Oct, 2007; Critical Thinking, Kuala Lump or, Sep, 2007; Critical Thinking, Brunei, Sep, 2007; Delivering Project Assurance, Auckland, Jun, 2007; From Crisis to Control: A New Era in Strategic Project Management, Prague, May, 2007; What Project Leaders Need to Know to Help Them Sleep Better At Night, London, May, 2007; Innovation Process. . .From Vision To Reality, Orlando, Apr, 2007. **Special Services:** Project Planning Tool™.

38674 ■ Business Ventures Corp.
1650 Oakbrook Dr., Ste. 405
Norcross, GA 30093-1881
Ph: (770)729-8000
Fax: (770)729-8028
Co. E-mail: info@bventures.com
Contact: Ruth A. King, President
E-mail: ruthking@bventures.com
Scope: Business development consultants specializing in construction industry. Works with HVAC, plumbing, and electrical contraction who need assistance in marketing, sales and promotion, operations management or finance. Also plan, execute,

and monitor the marketing, sales, and promotional activities for new product introductions. Firm also writes business plans, monitors financial health of businesses, and performs operations management. **Founded:** 1981. **Publications:** "The Ugly Truth about Managing People," 2007; "The Ugly Truth about Small Business," 2006; "How to Write a Business Plan," Atlanta Business Chronicle; "Ask 10 Questions Before You Begin Your Business," Income Opportunities "HVAC Bookkeeping and Financial Statements"; "Service Manager's Guide to Running a Profitable Service Department"; "HVAC Career Training Manual"; "Technician's Procedures Manual"; "HVAC Residential Pricing Manual"; "21 Ways to Keep the Honest People Honest Manual"; "Keeping Score: Financial Management for Entrepreneurs"; "Keeping Score: Improving Contractor Productivity and Profitability"; "Keeping Score: Financial Management for Contractors". **Seminars:** The Seven Rules for Business Success; The Seven Greatest Lies of Small Business; Understanding the Financial Side of Business; Small Business Marketing; Strategic Business Planning.

38675 ■ ByrneMRG Corp.
22 Isle of Pines Dr.
Hilton Head Island, SC 29928
Ph: (215)630-7411
Free: 888-816-8080
Co. E-mail: info@byrnemrg.com
URL: http://www.byrnemrg.com
Contact: Patrick J. Boyle, President
E-mail: pjboyle@byrnemrg.com
Scope: Specializes in management consulting, including department management, equipment evaluation and selection, project management, research and development planning; and database design and management. **Founded:** 1972. **Publications:** "Implementing Solutions to Everyday Issues". **Telecommunication Services:** pjboyle@byrnemrg.com.

38676 ■ Carelli & Associates
17 Reid Pl.
Delmar, NY 12054
Ph: (518)439-0233
Fax: (518)439-3006
Co. E-mail: truthaboutsupervision@yahoo.com
URL: http://www.carelli.com
Contact: Anne O Brien Carelli, Owner
E-mail: anneobriencarelli@yahoo.com
Scope: Provider of writing and editing services to industry and businesses, health care and educational institutions, and government agencies. Also provides program management in creating and disseminating publications and in implementing related training. Assists organizations in designing and implementing team-based management. Offers supervisory skills training and problem-solving work sessions for managers. Individual Consultation are provided for managers, CEOs, potential supervisors including 360 degree assessments. **Founded:** 1988. **Publications:** "The Truth About Supervision: Coaching, Teamwork, Interviewing, Appraisals, 360 degree Assessments, and Recognition". **Seminars:** Supervisory Skills Training Series; Problem-Solving Work Sessions for Managers; Effective Leadership.

38677 ■ Casino, Hotel & Resort Consultants L.L.C.
4825 Quality Ct., Ste. B
Las Vegas, NV 89103
Ph: (702)528-9537
Co. E-mail: info@hraba.com
URL: http://www.hraba.com
Contact: John S. Hraba, President
E-mail: jshraba@aol.com
Scope: Casino and hospitality industry consultants. Firm specializes in developing and implementing customized forecast and labor management control systems that deliver immediate, positive impact to the company's bottom line. Involved in production planning, employ surveys and communication, inventory management, business process reviews, audits, development and implementation of key management reports. **Founded:** 1989. **Seminars:** Payroll Cost Control; Effective Staff Scheduling. **Telecommunication Services:** john.hraba@hraba.com.

38678 ■ CBIZ Inc.
6050 Oak Tree Blvd. S, Ste. 500
Cleveland, OH 44131-6951
Ph: (216)447-9000
Fax: (216)447-9007
URL: http://www.cbizinc.com
Contact: Jerome P. Grisko, President
URL(s): www.cbiz.com. **Scope:** A business consulting and tax services firm providing financial, consulting, tax and business services through seven groups: Financial management, tax advisory, construction and real estate, health-care, litigation support, capital resource and CEO outsource. **Founded:** 1996. **Publications:** "FAS 154: Changes in the Way We Report Changes," 2006; "Equity-Based Compensation: How Much Does it Really Cost Your Business," 2006; "Preventing Fraud - Tips for Nonprofit Organizations"; "Today's Workforce and Nonprofit Organizations: Meeting a Critical Need"; "IRS Highlights Top Seven Form 990 Errors". **Seminars:** Health Care - What the Future Holds; Consumer Driven Health Plans; Executive Plans; Health Savings Accounts; Healthy Wealthy and Wise; Legislative Update; Medicare Part D; Retirement Plans.

38679 ■ C.C. Comfort Consulting
3370 N Hayden Rd., Ste. 123-127
Scottsdale, AZ 85251
Ph: (480)483-8364
Contact: Clifton C. Comfort, Jr., Principal
Scope: Evaluates, develops and implements financial, operational and compliance management systems strategies, programs and practices. Has professional recognition as certified public accountant, internal auditor, cost analyst and fraud examiner plus investigatory, law enforcement, and court experience ensure confidential handling of sensitive and legal matters. Works with management, audit, legal, security and outside personnel to evaluate and improve compliance, efficiency and effectiveness. **Founded:** 1983.

38680 ■ CEA Investments Corp.
301-2210 W 40th Ave.
Vancouver, BC, Canada V6M 1W6
Ph: (604)689-5547
Co. E-mail: info@ceainvestment.com
Contact: Emmanuel B. Nicolas, Principal
Scope: Specializes in strategic planning, mergers and acquisitions, and operations consulting, to midsized corporations. Areas of expertise include corporate planning, financial engineering, joint venture structuring, international corporate networking, identifying acquisition opportunities, locating investment partners, corporate evaluations, negotiating buy/sell agreements, business planning, markets studies and products evaluation, and outsourcing. **Founded:** 1988.

38681 ■ Cencir Inc.
24124 Lakeside Trl.
Crete, IL 60417
Ph: (708)672-3957
Fax: (708)672-4473
Co. E-mail: vevstad@cencir.com
URL: http://www.cencir.com
Contact: Vegard Vevstad, President
E-mail: vevstad@cencir.com
Scope: Firm seeks to transform entrepreneurial ventures into global enterprises using profitability audits and experience in highly distributed enterprises, including commercial chains selling or renting their products, services, or intellectual property through company branches, dealers, distributors, franchises, licenses, and Internet affiliates. Offers seminars and consultation with topics that include strategic decision-making, integrating entry and exit options, positioning, pricing, diversification, new ventures, vertical integration, distribution, organizational structures, and technology. Offers tools to improve recognition of key strategic issues; sell your strategy internally; identify and value core competencies; systemize and coordinate activities; select and implement dynamic IT strategy; improve asset utilization through innovation; avoid classic mistakes through continuous learning; use history of firm to affect change; apply seven forces to organization; recognize sustainable competitive advantages; predict market and competitive responses; use scenario analysis to model around uncertainty; and determine organizational requirements and adapt them. **Founded:** 1999. **Seminars:** Focus, Save Time, Learn, and Ask Questions of the Preeminent Channels of Distribution Experts.

38682 ■ The Center for Organizational Excellence Inc.
15204 Omega Dr., Ste. 300
Rockville, MD 20850
Ph: (301)948-1922
Free: 877-674-3923
Fax: (301)948-2158
Co. E-mail: results@center4oe.com
URL: http://www.center4oe.com
Contact: Stephen Goodrich, President
E-mail: sgoodrich@center4oe.com
Scope: An organizational effectiveness consulting firm specializing in helping organizations achieve results through people, process, and performance. Service areas include organizational performance systems, leadership systems, customer systems, and learning systems. **Founded:** 1984.

38683 ■ CFI Group USA L.L.C.—Claes Fornell International
625 Avis Dr.
Ann Arbor, MI 48108-9649
Ph: (734)930-9090
Free: 800-930-0933
Fax: (734)930-0911
Co. E-mail: askcfi@cfigroup.com
URL: http://www.cfigroup.com
Contact: Sheri Teodoru, Chief Executive Officer
E-mail: steodoru@mail.cfigroup.com
Scope: Management consulting firm that helps its clients worldwide to maximize shareholder value by optimizing customer and employee satisfaction. Clients span a variety of industries, including manufacturing, telecommunications, retail and government. **Founded:** 1988. **Publications:** "Customer Satisfaction and Stock Prices: High Returns, Low Risk," American Marketing Association, Jan, 2006; "Customer Satisfaction Index Climbs," The Wall Street Journal, Feb, 2004; "What's Next? Customer Service is Key to Post-Boom Success," The Bottom Line, Mar, 2003; "Boost Stock Performance, Nation's Economy," Quality Progress, Feb, 2003.

38684 ■ Chamberlain & Cansler Inc.
2251 Perimeter Park Dr.
Atlanta, GA 30341
Ph: (770)457-5699
Contact: Charles L. Cansler, Owner
Scope: Firm specializes in strategic planning; profit enhancement; small business management; interim management; crisis management; turnarounds. **Founded:** 1986.

38685 ■ Chartered Management Co.
10 S Riverside Plz., Ste. 1800
Chicago, IL 60606
Ph: (312)214-2575
Contact: William B. Avellone, President
Scope: Operations improvement consultants. Specializes in strategic planning; feasibility studies; management audits and reports; profit enhancement; start-up businesses; mergers and acquisitions; joint ventures; divestitures; interim management; crisis management; turnarounds; business process reengineering; venture capital; and due diligence. **Founded:** 1985.

38686 ■ Claremont Consulting Group
4525 Castle Ln.
La Canada, CA 91011-1436
Ph: (818)249-0584
Fax: (818)249-5811
Contact: Donald S. Remer, Partner
Scope: Consulting, coaching, training, and litigation support in project management, engineering management, system engineering and cost estimating. **Founded:** 1979. **Publications:** "What Every Engineer Should Know About Project Management"; "100% product-oriented work breakdown structures and their importance to system engineering". **Seminars:** Project Management, System Engineering and Cost Estimating.

38687 ■ BJ Cockrell Real Estate Appraisal & Consulting
17 Tucker St.
Milton, MA 02186
Ph: (617)698-6618
Fax: (617)698-6618
Contact: Beatrice James-Cockrell, Principal
E-mail: beajcockrell@comcast.net
Scope: Consultancy performs marketability studies, market studies, asset management analyses and disposition analyses for affordable housing market interests. Focuses on housing market studies and using valuation analysis skills for acquisition and disposition advisory assignments.

38688 ■ Colmen Menard Company Inc. (CMCI)
The Woods, 994 Old Eagle School Rd., Ste. 1000
Wayne, PA 19087
Ph: (484)367-0300
Fax: (484)367-0305
Co. E-mail: cmci@colmenmenard.com
URL: http://www.colmenmenard.com
Contact: David W. Menard, President
E-mail: dmenard@colmenmenard.com
Scope: Merger and acquisition corporate finance and business advisory services for public and private companies located in North America. **Founded:** 1982. **Publications:** "Success in Selling a Troubled Company," Nov, 2002; "Savvy Dealmakers," May, 2001; "Success in Selling a Troubled Company feature article from The Technology Times bimonthly newspaper," Apr, 2002; "Truisms," M&A Today, Nov, 2000.

38689 ■ Comer & Associates L.L.C.—Energy Alliance Group
5255 Holmes Pl.
Boulder, CO 80303
Ph: (303)786-7986
Free: 888-950-3190
Fax: (303)895-2347
Co. E-mail: jerry@comerassociates.com
URL: http://www.comerassociates.com
Contact: Jerry C. Comer, President
E-mail: jerry@comerassociates.com
URL(s): www.energyalliance.biz. **Scope:** Specialize in developing markets and businesses. Marketing support includes: Developing and writing strategic and tactical business plans; developing and writing focused, effective market plans; researching market potential and competition; implementing targeted marketing tactics to achieve company objectives; conducting customer surveys to determine satisfaction and attitudes toward client. Organization development support includes: Executive management training programs; executive coaching; team building; developing effective organization structures; and management of change in dynamic and competitive environments; individual coaching for management and leadership effectiveness. **Founded:** 1993. **Seminars:** Developing a Strategic Market Plan; Market Research: Defining Your Opportunity; Management and Leadership Effectiveness; Team Building; Developing a Business Plan; How to Close; Using Questions to Sell; Sales System Elements and Checklist; Working With Independent Reps; Features vs. Benefits; Overcoming Objections; Sales Force Automation.

38690 ■ Consulting & Conciliation Service (CCS)
2219 H St., Ste. 1
Sacramento, CA 95816
Ph: (916)396-0480
Free: 888-898-9780
Fax: (916)441-2828
Co. E-mail: service@azurewings.net
Contact: Jane A. McCluskey, Principal
E-mail: service@azurewings.net
Scope: Offers consulting and conciliation services. Provides pre-mediation counseling, training and research on preparing for a peaceful society, mediation and facilitation, and preparation for shifts in structure, policy and personnel. Offers sliding scale business rates and free individual consultation. **Publications:** "Native America and Tracking Shifts in US Policy"; "Biogenesis: A Discussion of Basic Social Needs and the Significance of Hope". **Seminars:** Positive Approaches to Violence Prevention: Peace building in Schools and Communities.

38691 ■ The Consulting Exchange
1770 Mass Ave., Ste. 288
Cambridge, MA 02140
Ph: (617)576-2100
Free: 800-824-4828
Co. E-mail: gday@consultingexchange.com
Contact: Geoffrey Day, President
E-mail: gday@consultingexchange.com
Scope: A consultant referral service for management and technical consultants. Serves a local, regional and international client base. **Founded:** 1982. **Publications:** "Looking for a Consultant? Success Points for Finding the Right One," Boston Business Journal, Jun, 2001; "Getting Full Value From Consulting is in Your Hands," Mass High Tech, May, 1998; "Developing Knowledge-Based Client Relationships, The Future of Professional Services"; "The Consultant's Legal Guide"; "The Business of Consulting: The Basics and Beyond".

38692 ■ The Corlund Group L.L.C. (CG)
101 Federal St., Ste. 310
Boston, MA 02110
Ph: (617)423-9364
Fax: (617)423-9371
Co. E-mail: info@corlundgroup.com
URL: http://www.corlundgroup.com
Contact: Wilmot J. Gravenslund, Director
E-mail: wgravenslund@corlundgroup.com
Scope: Boutique firm offering services in the areas of leadership, governance, and change with a particular focus on CEO and senior executive succession planning, including assessment, development, and orchestrating succession processes with management and Boards of Directors. Also Board governance effectiveness. **Founded:** 1996. **Publications:** "Are You Rolling the Dice on CEO Succession?" Center for Healthcare Governance, 2006; "Leadership Due Diligence: The Neglected Governance Frontier," Directorship, Sep, 2001; "Leadership Due Diligence: Managing the Risks," The Corporate Board, Aug, 2001; "Succession: The need for detailed insight," Directors and Boards, 2001; "CEO Succession: Who's Doing Due Diligence?," 2001. **Telecommunication Services:** corlund@corlundgroup.com.

38693 ■ Corporate Consulting Inc.
3333 Belcaro Dr.
Denver, CO 80209-4912
Ph: (303)698-9292
Fax: (303)698-9292
Co. E-mail: corpcons@compuserve.com
Contact: Devereux C. Josephs, President
Scope: Specializes in feasibility studies, organizational development, small business management, mergers and acquisitions, joint ventures, divestitures, interim management, crisis management, turnarounds, financing, appraisals valuations and due diligence studies. **Founded:** 1983.

38694 ■ Corporate Impact
33326 Bonnieview, Ste. 200
Avon Lake, OH 44012-1230
Ph: (440)930-2477
Fax: (440)930-2525
URL: http://www.corpimpact.com
Contact: Karl Busch, Principal
Scope: Provider of coaching, consultation, facilitation and training services to help you develop, a business that delivers sustained shareholder value and growth. Supports the development of the skills and implementation of the change programs learned in the workshop. Also, for small businesses, firm provides general consulting in the areas of strategic planning, marketing, and product and sales strategy. Industries served all except government and nonprofit. **Founded:** 1984. **Publications:** "8 Lies of Teamwork". **Seminars:** Personal Productivity Management; The Challenge of Leadership; Collaborative Problem Solving; The Creative Side of Enterprise; Teamwork and Peak Performance; Winning Customers; Conflict Resolution.

38695 ■ Morton Cotlar
700 Richards St.
Honolulu, HI 96813
Ph: (808)956-8732
Co. E-mail: morton@uhunix.uhcc.hawaii.edu
Contact: Morton Cotlar, Director
E-mail: morton@uhunix.uhcc.hawaii.edu
Scope: Provider of organizational management counsel including surveys of effectiveness in operations; training and development seminars for managers; consulting in organizational operations; development of expert systems for strategic planning and operations, and assistance with implementation. Serves private industries as well as government agencies. **Founded:** 1972. **Telecommunication Services:** morton@uhunix.bit.net.

38696 ■ Crystal Clear Communications Inc.
1633 W Winslow Dr., Ste. 210
Mequon, WI 53092
Ph: (262)240-0072
Fax: (262)240-0073
Co. E-mail: contact@crystalclear1.com
URL: http://www.crystalclear1.com
Contact: Barry J. Moze, Partner
E-mail: barrymoze@crystalclearl.com
Scope: Specialize in helping executives identify impediments to success, and then develop strategies to surmount them. Serves to identify core problems, suggest appropriate business changes, work with the organization to support these changes, and help executives articulate the behavior that will uphold these changes. Specializes in strategic planning; organizational development; small business management; executive coaching. **Founded:** 1986. **Publications:** "Weakest Link"; "Aware Leadership"; "Integrity"; "When Your Plate is Full"; "Problem Solving"; "Strategic Thinking".

38697 ■ Dare Mighty Things
901 N Glebe Rd., Ste. 1005
Arlington, VA 22203
Ph: (703)752-4331
Fax: (703)752-4332
Co. E-mail: info@daremightythings.com
URL: http://www.daremightythings.com
Contact: David van Patten, President
Scope: Provides management consulting services that help clients implement social solutions. Specializes in the development of large scale programs that impact high risk populations. Clients are government agencies, foundations, and non-profit organizations. Supports clients through the research and design of outcome-based social programs; the development of business plans and case statements; the delivery of performance-based training and technical assistance; and guidance in fund development and program sustainability. **Founded:** 1991.

38698 ■ The Decision Group (TDG)
7204 Penny Rd.
Raleigh, NC 27606
Ph: (919)851-9679
Fax: (919)851-9679
Co. E-mail: decisiongroup@nc.rr.com
Contact: Wilfred J. Kaydos, President
E-mail: willkaydos@nc.rr.com
Scope: Provider of comprehensive consulting services to manufacturing, distribution, and service companies in the areas of: productivity and quality improvement, performance measurement, information systems design, and operations management. Serves private industries as well as government agencies. **Founded:** 1982. **Publications:** "Measuring, Managing, and Maximizing Performance," Productivity Press; "Operational Performance Measurement: Increasing Total Productivity," St.Lucie Press; "Implementing Manufacturing Performance Measures-a Case Study". **Seminars:** Quality Improvement Made Simple; Measuring Performance to Increase Total Productivity.

38699 ■ Del Technology Inc.
7407 E Via Estrella Ave., Ste. 10
Scottsdale, AZ 85258-1006
Ph: (480)483-7588

Fax: (480)483-7533
Co. E-mail: ddonahoe@qwest.net
Contact: Georgine Donahoe, President
Scope: Provides services including management consulting, information technology and micro business. Focuses on organizational assessment, business process reengineering, quality assurance program development, hardware software evaluation and acquisition, applications software development and systems integration. **Founded:** 1990. **Publications:** "Standards for Information Systems Development and Project Administration". **Seminars:** Organization for Future Technology; Business Reengineering; Managing Successful Projects; Planning and Implementing the Information Systems Architecture; Successfully Managing the Information Resource.

38700 ■ Delohery Associates
3214 Cedar Bluff Dr. NE
Marietta, GA 30062
Ph: (770)977-3197
Fax: (770)977-9509
Contact: Pat D. Delohery, President
Scope: Offers total quality management, business process and procedure analysis and design using current contemporary quality techniques.

38701 ■ Denison Consulting
121 W Washington St., Ste. 201
Ann Arbor, MI 48104
Ph: (734)302-4002
Fax: (734)302-4023
Co. E-mail: mgillespie@denisonculture.com
URL: http://www.denisonculture.com
Contact: Bryan Adkins, Sr., President
E-mail: badkins@denisonculture.com
Scope: Organizational culture and leadership management firm. Consulting services include planning a survey program, providing feedback, linking survey results to strategic planning, leadership coaching, planning and implementing change interventions, and facilitating mergers and acquisitions. **Publications:** "Executive Coaching: Does leader behavior change with feedback and coaching," 2009; "Engagement Surveys: Gallup and Best Companies Face Criticism," 2009; "Managing Expectations-of You," 2006; "Out of the Blue," 2006; "Organizational Culture: Measuring and Developing It in Your Organization," 2005; "Riding the Tiger of Culture Change," 2004; "Like it or not, Culture Matters," 2000; "Why Mission Matters," 2000; "Ready Or Not, Here I Learn," 2000. **Seminars:** Building High Performance Organizations; Organizational Culture & Diagnosis; Managing Thought.

38702 ■ Development Resource Consultants (DRC)
PO Box 118
Rancho Cucamonga, CA 91729
Ph: (909)902-7655
Fax: (909)476-6942
Co. E-mail: drc@gotodrc.com
URL: http://www.gotodrc.com
Contact: Jerry R. Frey, Business Manager
E-mail: jfrey@gotodrc.com
Scope: Specializes in office re-organization, employee training in office organization, communication skills, sales training and career counseling. **Founded:** 1985. **Publications:** "Institute of Management Consultants Southern California Chapter," Jan, 2006.

38703 ■ Directions Ltd.
4021 Albert Dr.
Nashville, TN 37204-4009
Ph: (615)269-4043
Fax: (615)385-9559
Co. E-mail: scheuerm@bellsouth.net
Contact: Eddie Scheuerman, President
Scope: Works with Chief Executive Officers and companies trying to resolve problems that management and leadership have not had the time to solve due to other priorities. Areas of interest: management and leadership problems; resolving problems associated with profitability, growth, change and resources; strategic issues, under-performance issues and boards of directors issues. Experience is with publicly traded or privately owned companies in various industries. **Founded:** 1980.

38704 ■ donphin.com Inc.
1001 B Ave., Ste. 200
Coronado, CA 92118
Ph: (619)550-3533
Free: 800-234-3304
Fax: (619)600-0096
Co. E-mail: inquiry@donphin.com
URL: http://www.donphin.com
Contact: Vito Tanzi, President
Scope: Offers a comprehensive approach to understanding and applying a broad range of business principles: legal compliance issues, management concerns, health and safety, customer service, marketing, information management. Industries served: All developing small businesses. **Publications:** "Doing Business Right!"; "HR That Works!"; "Lawsuit Free! How to Prevent Employee Lawsuits"; "Building Powerful Employment Relationships!"; "Victims, Villains and Heroes: Managing Emotions in The Workplace". **Seminars:** Doing Business Right!; HR That Works!; Building Powerful Employment Relationships; Lawsuit Free!.

38705 ■ Dorn & Associates Inc.
8506 Bass Lake Rd.
Minneapolis, MN 55428-5304
Ph: (763)533-7689
Fax: (763)533-1143
Contact: John L. Dorn, President
Scope: Services include accounting, marketing, employment partnership, new doctor agreements, personnel issues and human resources assessment, practice management, practice merger acquisition sale and liquidation, practice surveys and valuation, staff development and training. **Founded:** 2000.

38706 ■ DRI Consulting (DRIC)
2 Otter Ln.
Saint Paul, MN 55127-6436
Ph: (651)415-1400
Free: 866-276-4600
Fax: (651)415-9968
Co. E-mail: dric@dric.com
URL: http://www.dric.com
Contact: Megan Brogger, Principal
E-mail: meganbrogger@dric.com
Scope: Provides high-quality, research-based services and training in leadership, team processes, supervision, and management, and organizational development, clients with direct and substantial impact on individual and team performance and on organizational success through proven processes for selecting, developing and deploying leaders. **Founded:** 1991.

38707 ■ Dubuc Lucke & Company Inc.—Adventa Global Intermediaries
120 W 5th St.
Cincinnati, OH 45202-2713
Ph: (513)579-8330
Fax: (513)241-6669
Contact: Kenneth E. Dubuc, President
Scope: Provides consulting services in the areas of profit enhancement; small business management; mergers and acquisitions; joint ventures; divestitures; interim management; crisis management; turnarounds; appraisals; valuations; due diligence; and international trade. **Founded:** 1999.

38708 ■ The DuMond Group
5282 Princeton Ave.
Westminster, CA 92683-2753
Ph: (714)373-0610
Contact: Adrianne H. Geiger-Dumond, President
Scope: Human resources and executive search consulting firm that specializes in organizational development; small business management; employee surveys and communication; performance appraisals; and team building. **Founded:** 1992.

38709 ■ Dunelm International
437 Colebrook Ln.
Bryn Mawr, PA 19010-3216
Ph: (610)989-0144
Fax: (610)964-9524
Co. E-mail: jecdunelm@worldnet.att.net
Contact: John E. Crowther, President
E-mail: Jecdunelm@dunelm.org.uk
Scope: Firm specializes in feasibility studies; start-up businesses; interim management; crisis management; turnarounds; business process re-engineering; sales forecasting; supply chain solution and project management. **Founded:** 1988.

38710 ■ Dynamic Firm Management Inc.
4570 Campus Dr., Ste. 60
Newport Beach, CA 92660
Ph: (949)640-2220
Co. E-mail: info@dynamicfirm.com
URL: http://www.dynamicfirm.com
Contact: Dennis McCue, Principal
E-mail: mccue@dynamicfirm.com
Scope: Management consulting to law firms, accounting firms and other professional service providers. Emphasis on partnership relations, compensation, strategic planning, increasing revenues, profitable firm operations and effective management and team building. Initial work includes the determination of client's objectives; quantifying measurable accomplishments and outlining the consulting requirements. Industries served: law firms, attorneys, professional service. **Founded:** 1987. **Publications:** "Workflow Management," C2M: Consulting to Management - The Journal of Management Consulting, Jun, 2006; "Why Good Partnerships Go Bad," The Journal of Law Office Economics and Management, Feb, 2006; "The Wisdom of Ambulance Chasers," LACBA Update, Feb, 2005; "7 Components to Building A Successful Firm," LACBA Update, Nov, 2004; "Maximize the Productivity of Your Support Team," LACBA Update, Mar, 2004; "Perfect Union," Daily Journal, Mar, 2004; "Future Perfect," Daily Journal, Dec, 2003.

38711 ■ Effective Resources Inc. (ERI)
118 N Peters Rd., Ste. 171
Knoxville, TN 37923
Ph: (865)622-7138
Free: 800-288-6044
Fax: (800)409-2812
Co. E-mail: customerservice@effectiveresources.com
URL: http://www.effectiveresources.com
Contact: Barry L. Brown, Principal
E-mail: barry@effectiveresources.com
Scope: Human resource consulting firm helping clients in all aspects of planning and implementation, to assure the program meets their objectives and budget considerations. Can work with clients on an interim basis or as consultants on short term assignment. Products and services include salary and benefits surveys, employee satisfaction surveys, performance management, compensation administration, compliance assistance and personality profile testing. Specializes in compensation and incentive plans, performance appraisals, team building and personnel policies and procedures, affirmative action plan preparation. **Founded:** 1988. **Special Services:** DiSC® Personality Profile.

38712 ■ EGL Holdings Inc.—EGL Holdings
3495 Piedmont Rd, Ste. 412, Piedmont Center 11
Atlanta, GA 30305-1773
Ph: (404)949-8300
Fax: (404)949-8311
Co. E-mail: info@eglholdings.com
URL: http://www.eglholdings.com
Contact: Arnold G. Schumacher, Senior Vice President
E-mail: agschumacher@eglholdings.com
Scope: A management consulting team that specializes in solving the financial problems of medium sized businesses and in helping the management capitalize on business opportunities. Designs and implements remedies for shortage of working capital and low profitability. Services include strategic corporate planning, cost reduction, profit improvement, acquisition analysis, divestiture and financing. Long term and short term analysis of business opportunities. **Founded:** 1988.

38713 ■ EMS Network International—EMS Consultants
858 Longview Rd.
Burlingame, CA 94010-6974
Ph: (650)342-5259
Fax: (650)344-5005
Co. E-mail: ems@emsnetwork.com
URL: http://www.emsnetwork.com
Contact: Michael E. Shays, President
E-mail: ems@atsemsnetwork.com
Scope: Helping teams to develop and implement breakthrough solutions through purpose expansion, solution-after-next, technology fiction, people participation and change management. Serves clients in all industries. **Founded:** 1987. **Publications:** "How to Get Value from a Management Consultant"; "Code Of Professional Conduct"; "Obedience to the Unenforceable"; "Controlling the Future"; "Seven Principles of Breakthrough Thinking"; "Ethical Fitness"; "Succession Planning"; "Case Study - Old & New Management"; "Case Study - Two Sales Staffs"; "Case Study - Administration & Faculty"; "Cartoons about Consulting". **Seminars:** Facilitation skills; basic skills for internal consultants; entrepreneurs and champions; breakthrough thinking, building decision skills and ethical fitness; How to resolve conflict and manage transitions; The Purpose-Target-Results approach to solving problems and leveraging opportunities; Sponsoring and mentoring innovators and intrapreneurs in your company; Advanced practices for management consultants; Sponsoring and mentoring innovators and entrepreneurs in your company; Eliminating Waste In Management Decision Making; Bringing Out the Itrapreneurs in Your Company; The Consultant's Role in Mastering Change; Closing The Sale. **Special Services:** Ethical Fitness®; How Good People Make Tough Decisions®; How to apply Breakthrough Thinking®.

38714 ■ Espionage Research Institute (ERI)
10903 Indian Head Hwy., Ste. 304
Fort Washington, MD 20744
Ph: (301)535-8326
Fax: (301)292-4635
Contact: Glenn H. Whidden, President
Scope: Dedicated to collect and promulgate information on hostile espionage activity. It attempts to keep all informed on hostile espionage activity that is directed against business and industry. **Founded:** 2001. **Publications:** "A Guidebook For Beginning Sweepers"; "The Ear Volume"; "The Attack on Axnan Headquarters"; "The TSCM Threat Book"; "The Russian Eavesdropping Threat As Of 1993".

38715 ■ Family Business Institute Inc.—Family Business Experts
904 Steffi Ct.
Lawrenceville, GA 30044-6933
Ph: (770)952-4085
Fax: (770)432-6660
Co. E-mail: asktheexpert@family-business-experts.com
URL: http://www.family-business-experts.com
Contact: Wayne Rivers, President
Scope: Assists families in business to achieve personal, family, and organizational goals by meeting challenges that are unique to family-owned businesses. Provides coordinated and integrated assessments and solutions for family issues and needs; for company finance and for human resource and operational requirements. **Founded:** 1985. **Publications:** "Professional Intervention in the Family Owned Business"; "Building Consensus in a Family Business"; "Professionalizing Family Business Management"; "Recognizing generations - know them by their weekends"; "Succession planning tactics"; "Succession Planning Obstacles in Family Business"; "Succession: three ways to ease the transition"; "Pruning the family business tree"; "Responsibility diffusion - the most critical impediment to successfully growing any kind of business"; "Breaking Up is Hard to Do: Divorce in the Family Business".

38716 ■ FCP Consulting
500 Sutter St., Ste. 507
San Francisco, CA 94102-1114
Ph: (415)956-5558
Fax: (415)956-5722
Contact: Cox Ferrall, President
Scope: Management consulting in Business-To-Business sales. **Founded:** 1986.

38717 ■ Firemark Investments
200 W DeVargas St., Ste. 9
Santa Fe, NM 87501
Ph: (505)989-8384
Free: 800-530-0786
Fax: (505)989-8316
Contact: Joanne Stone Morrissey, President
E-mail: jsm@firemarkinv.com
Scope: Firm provides management consulting, investment advice and fund management. **Founded:** 1983.

38718 ■ First Strike Management Consulting Inc.—FSMC Inc.
4001 Loblolly Ave.
Little River, SC 29566-1188
Ph: (843)385-6338
Fax: (843)390-1004
Co. E-mail: info@fsmc.com
URL: http://www.fsmc.com
Contact: J. D. Lewis, Chief Executive Officer
E-mail: jd.lewis@fsmc.com
Scope: Offers proposal management and program management services. Specializes in enterprise systems, management systems, and staff augmentation. Serves the following industries: Nuclear/Fossil Power, Petro-Chemical, Aerospace and Defense, Telecommunications, Engineering and Construction, Information Technology, Golf Course Construction/Management, Utility Engineering/Construction, Civil Works, and Housing Development. **Founded:** 1991. **Publications:** "Project Management for Executives"; "Project Risk Management"; "Project Communications Management"; "Winning Proposals, Four Computer Based Training (CBT) courses"; "Principles of Program Management". **Seminars:** Preparing Winning Proposals in Response to Government RFPs.

38719 ■ Foresight Management Group
14 Macintosh Cres.
Saint Catharines, ON, Canada L2N 7M2
Free: 800-851-6676
Fax: (519)748-4478
Contact: Ed Brooker, Principal
E-mail: ed@foresight-management.com
Scope: Consultants in camp ground design and planning, RV park design and planning and RV resort design and planning. Assists public agencies and private entrepreneurs with feasibility studies, development strategies and marketing plans including destination branding. **Publications:** "One Canadian's Perspective on the Country's Recent Decrease in Tourism," Dec, 2007; "The Future Looks Promising But Not Guaranteed"; "Profitable Parks"; "Strategic Marketing"; "What's the value of a penny?"; "Signs of the Time"; "Effective and Efficient Campground Development"; "We need MORE foresight and innovation! FAST!"; "Effective & Efficient Campground Development"; "Inspiration From an Unlikely Source"; "Test and Measure"; "Go Figure". **Seminars:** Marketing - Big Dollars, Small Dollars; Marketing for RV Parks; Marketing for Small Business; Branding As A Key Component Of A Marketing Strategy; How to get into the campground business; Thinking Out of the Box; Developing Underutilized Campgrounds; How to determine rates; Ecotourism: A Natural Branding Strategy; Capitalizing on Ecotourism; Stress Management; US Trends in the RV Park Industry; US Trends in the RV Industry; US Trends in the Tourism Industry; Innovation in Tourist Parks.

38720 ■ The Foster Group Inc.
180 N Stetson, Ste. 3470
Chicago, IL 60601
Ph: (312)609-1009
Fax: (312)609-1109
Co. E-mail: info@thefostergroup.com
URL: http://www.thefostergroup.com
Contact: John L. Foster, Jr., Managing Partner
E-mail: rpike@thefostergroup.com
Scope: Offers information systems and data security, financial accounting services, and management consulting. **Founded:** 1986.

38721 ■ Freese & Associates Inc.
PO Box 814
Chagrin Falls, OH 44022-0814
Ph: (440)564-9183
Fax: (440)564-7339
Co. E-mail: tfreese@freeseinc.com
URL: http://www.freeseinc.com
Contact: Duane L. Hile, Manager
Scope: A management consulting firm offering advice in all forms of business logistics. Consulting services are in the areas of strategic planning; network analysis, site selection, facility layout and design, outsourcing, warehousing, transportation and customer service. Typical projects include 3PL marketing surveys; third party outsourcing selection; operational audits; competitive analysis; inventory management; due diligence; and implementation project management. **Founded:** 1987. **Publications:** "Building Relationships is Key to Motivation," Distribution Center Management, Apr, 2006; "Getting Maximum Results from Performance Reviews," WERC Sheet, Oct, 2003; "SCM: Making the Vision a Reality," Supply Chain Management Review, Oct, 2003; "Contents Under Pressure," DC Velocity, Aug, 2003; "When Considering Outsourcing, It's Really a Financial Decision," Inventory Management Report, Mar, 2003. **Seminars:** WERC/CAWS Warehousing in China Conference, Sep, 2008; CSCMP Annual Conference, Denver, Oct, 2008; Keys to Retaining and Motivating Your Associates, Dallas, Mar, 2006; The Value and Challenges of Supply Chain Management, Dubai, Feb, 2006; Best Practices in Logistics in China, Jun, 2005; Keys to Motivating Associates, Dallas, May, 2005; The Goal and the Way of International Cooperation in Logistics, Jenobuk, Apr, 2005.

38722 ■ Max Freund
246 W Green St.
Claremont, CA 91711
Ph: (909)632-1247
Co. E-mail: max.freund@cgu.edu
URL: http://www.lfleadership.com
Contact: Natasha Wilder, Associate
Scope: Consultants and coaches provide training on leadership and success for individuals and organizations. Consults with organizations, teams, and communities on leadership, economic development, strategy, organizational learning, and team effectiveness. Other core practice areas are coaching groups and individuals, facilitating groups, training leaders and teams in skills to communicate effectively. Consultants also speak on social leadership, community economic development, change and transition management, diversity, and conflict transformation. **Seminars:** High Desert Resource Network Fundraising Academy for Grassroots Nonprofits, Aug, 2009; Developing the Next Generation of Leaders, Sep, 2008; Coaching Skills for Staff Development and Retention, Sep, 2008; Developing Funds, Transforming Leadership, San Bernardino County Grants Office, Jun, 2008; Developing Funds, Developing Leadership, High Desert Resource Network, Apr, 2008; Executive Coaching Skills; Fundraising Fundamentals for Non-profits.

38723 ■ George S. May International Co.
303 S Northwest Hwy.
Park Ridge, IL 60068-4255
Ph: (847)825-8806
Free: 800-955-0200
Fax: (847)825-7937
Co. E-mail: info@georgesmay.com
URL: http://www.georgesmay.com
Contact: Kerry Sam Jacobs, President
Scope: Management consulting firm addressing the concerns of medium and small-sized companies. Offers services in human capital management, customer relations management, profit and expense control, quality management, production control and technology management. Serves manufacturing, wholesale, retail, service, and healthcare businesses. **Founded:** 1925. **Seminars:** Break Even Analysis and Its Impact on Pricing; Health Care Facility Management; Your Managers and Supervisors Can be Outstanding Leaders.

38724 ■ Global Business Consultants (GBC)
200 Lake Hills Rd.
Pinehurst, NC 28374-0776

Ph: (910)295-5991
Fax: (910)295-5991
Co. E-mail: gbc@pinehurst.net
Contact: Nan S. Leaptrott, President
E-mail: nan@yourculturecoach.com
Scope: Firm specializes in human resources management; project management; software development; and international trade. Offers litigation support. **Founded:** 1987. **Publications:** "Culture to Culture: Mission Trip Do's and Don'ts," Jul, 2005; "Rules of the Game: Global Business Protocol". **Seminars:** Cross-Cultural Training.

38725 ■ Global Technology Transfer L.L.C.
1500 Dixie Hwy.
Park Hills, KY 41011-2819
Ph: (859)431-1262
Fax: (859)431-5148
Contact: Anthony Zembrodt, President
Scope: Firm specializes in product development; quality assurance; new product development; and total quality management focusing on household chemical specialties, especially air fresheners. Utilizes latest technology from global resources. Specializes in enhancement products for home and automobile. **Founded:** 1992.

38726 ■ Glynn Law Offices
49 Locust St.
Falmouth, MA 02540
Ph: (508)548-8282
Fax: (508)548-9075
Co. E-mail: pcg@glynnlawoffices.com
URL: http://www.glynnlawfirm.com
Contact: Suzanne Fay Glynn, Partner
E-mail: sfg@glynnlawoffices.com
Scope: A full service law firm specializing in affordable housing development and estate and business planning with a focus on taxation. **Founded:** 1982.

38727 ■ Arnold S. Goldin & Associates Inc.
5030 Champion Blvd., Ste. G-6231
Boca Raton, FL 33496
Ph: (561)994-5810
Fax: (561)994-5860
Co. E-mail: arnold@goldin.com
URL: http://www.goldin.com
Contact: Arnold S. Goldin, Principal
E-mail: arnold@goldin.com
Scope: An accounting and management consulting firm. Serves clients worldwide. Provides management services. Handles monthly write-ups and tax returns. **Founded:** 1978.

38728 ■ Goldore Consulting Inc.
120-5 St. NW, Ste. 1
Linden, AB, Canada T0M 1J0
Ph: (403)546-4208
Fax: (403)546-4208
Co. E-mail: goldore@leadershipessentials.com
Contact: Robert A. Orr, President
E-mail: orr@leadershipessentials.com
Description: Description: Publishes materials on leadership and management skills for churches and charitable organizations that provide services to developing countries. Also publishes in Spanish and Portuguese. Does not accept unsolicited manuscripts. Reaches market through direct mail and wholesalers and distributors, including Leadership Training Ministry Foundation, Inc. **Scope:** Provides consulting service in leadership and management skills. Industries served: primarily charities, non-profits; some businesses. **Founded:** 1990. **Seminars:** The Challenge Of Leadership.

38729 ■ Gordian Concepts & Solutions
16 Blueberry Ln.
Lincoln, MA 01773
Ph: (617)259-8341
Contact: Stephen R. Low, President
Scope: Engineering and management consultancy offering general, financial, and valuation services, civil and tax litigation support. Assists clients in entering new businesses, planning new products and services, and evaluating feasibility. Targets industrial concerns engaged in manufacturing, assembly, warehousing, energy production, process systems and biotechnology, steel, paper, and electronics. Serves businesses such as retailing, financial services, health care, satellite broadcasting and cable television, outdoor advertising and professional practices. **Founded:** 1990. **Publications:** "Establishing Rural Cellular Company Values," Cellular Business.

38730 ■ Great Lakes Consulting Group Inc.
54722 Little Flower Trl.
Mishawaka, IN 46545
Ph: (574)287-4500
Fax: (574)233-2688
Contact: James E. Schrager, President
Scope: Provides consulting services in the areas of strategic planning; feasibility studies; start-up businesses; small business management; mergers and acquisitions; joint ventures; divestitures; interim management; crisis management; turnarounds; business process re-engineering; venture capital; and international trade. **Founded:** 1989.

38731 ■ Great Western Association Management Inc.
7995 E Prentice Ave., Ste. 100
Greenwood Village, CO 80111
Ph: (303)770-2220
Fax: (303)770-1614
Co. E-mail: info83@gwami.com
URL: http://www.gwami.com
Contact: Karen M. Wojdyla, President
E-mail: kwojdyla@gwami.com
Scope: Provider of clients with products and services to effectively manage existing and startup, for- and not-for-profit organizations. Clients select from a menu of services including association development and public relations, conferences and seminars, financial management, membership communications, and governance. Expertise also includes association strategic planning, compliance, lobbying, meeting planning, fundraising, marketing and communications. Serves national, regional and state organizations. **Founded:** 1983. **Seminars:** Site selection; Creative program development; Contract negotiations; On-site conference management; Trade show management; Travel and logistics.

38732 ■ Joel Greenstein & Associates (JGA)
6212 Nethercombe Ct.
McLean, VA 22101
Ph: (703)893-1888
Co. E-mail: jgreenstein@contractmasters.com
Contact: Joel Greenstein, Principal
E-mail: jgreenstein@contractmasters.com
Scope: Provides services to minority and women-owned businesses and government agencies. Specializes in interpreting federal, agency-specific acquisition regulations and contract terms and conditions. Offers assistance with preparing technical, cost proposals and sealed bids.

38733 ■ Grimmick Consulting Services (GCS)
455 Donner Way
San Ramon, CA 94582
Ph: (925)735-1036
Fax: (925)735-1100
Co. E-mail: hank@grimmickconsulting.com
URL: http://www.grimmickconsulting.com
Contact: Henry Grimmick, President
E-mail: hank@grimmickconsulting.com
Scope: Provider of consulting services in the areas of strategic planning; organizational assessment; organizational development; leadership and management development Baldridge criteria, process improvement and balanced scorecards and team dynamics. **Founded:** 1993.

38734 ■ Harding & Co.
511 Harvard Ave.
Swarthmore, PA 19081
Ph: (610)544-9005
Fax: (973)763-9347
Co. E-mail: fharding@hardingco.com
URL: http://www.hardingco.com
Contact: Mimi Spangler, President
E-mail: mspangler@hardingco.com
Scope: Specializes in sales management, client development and employee training. **Founded:** 1993. **Publications:** "Cross-Selling Success: A Rainmakers Guide to Professional Account Development," Aug, 2002; "Rain Making: The Professional's Guide to Attracting New Clients"; "Creating Rainmakers: The Managers Guide to Training Professionals to Attract New Clients". **Telecommunication Services:** mspangler@hardingco.com.

38735 ■ Claude Hayes & Associates
9259 Hunterboro Dr.
Brentwood, TN 37027-6118
Ph: (615)370-8106
Fax: (615)370-8106
Contact: Claude W. Hayes, Jr., Owner
Scope: Provides services in the areas of turnarounds, reengineering, restructuring, reorganization, startups, high profile growth, acquisitions, divestitures, due diligence, strategic/business (marketing/sales) plans, inventory control and management, cost pricing and control, market management, demand forecasting. **Founded:** 1994.

38736 ■ Hewitt Development Enterprises (HDE)
1717 N Bayshore Dr., Ste. 2154
Miami, FL 33132
Ph: (305)372-0941
Fax: (305)372-0941
Co. E-mail: info@hewittdevelopment.com
URL: http://www.hewittdevelopment.com
Contact: Robert G. Hewitt, Principal
E-mail: bob@hewittdevelopment.com
Scope: Specializes in strategic planning; profit enhancement; start-up businesses; interim management; crisis management; turnarounds; production planning; just-in-time inventory management; and project management. Serves senior management (CEOs, CFOs, division presidents, etc.) and acquirers of distressed businesses. **Founded:** 1985.

38737 ■ Hickey & Hill Inc.
1009 Oak Hill Rd., Ste. 201
Lafayette, CA 94549-3812
Ph: (925)906-5331
Contact: Edwin L. Hill, Chief Executive Officer
Scope: Firm provides management consulting services to companies in financial distress. Expertise area: Corporate restructuring and turnaround. **Founded:** 1984.

38738 ■ hightechbiz.com—Leahy & Associates Inc.
4209 Santa Monica Blvd., Ste. 201
Los Angeles, CA 90029-3027
Ph: (323)913-3355
Free: 877-648-4753
Fax: (323)913-3355
URL: http://www.hightechbiz.com
Contact: Steven L. Hayes, Principal
Scope: A full service marketing agency specializing in integrated marketing solutions. Services include: marketing surveys; positioning surveys; strategic and tactical plans; implementation plans; management consulting; product brochures; product catalogs; product packaging; product data sheets; direct mail programs; media research; competitive research; complete creative; production and film; media placement; corporate identity; in-house creative; public relations. **Founded:** 1980.

38739 ■ C. W. Hines and Associates Inc.—C&W Associates Inc.
344 Churchill Cir., Sanctuary Bay
White Stone, VA 22578
Ph: (804)435-8844
Fax: (804)435-8855
Co. E-mail: turtlecwh@aol.com
URL: http://www.cwhinesassociates.org
Contact: Dr. Carolyn C.W. Hines, President
Scope: Management consultants with expertise in the following categories: advertising and public relations; health and human resources; management sciences; organizational development; computer sciences; financial management; behavioral sciences; environmental design; technology transfer; project management; facility management; program evaluation; and business therapy. Also included are complementary areas such as sampling procedures; job training; managerial effectiveness; corporate seminars; gender harassment; training for trainers and leadership and management skills development. **Founded:** 1979. **Publications:** "Money Muscle, 120

Exercises To Build Spiritual And Financial Strength," 2004; "Inside Track: Executives Coaching Executives"; "Money Muscle: 122 Exercises to Build Financial Strength"; "Nuts and Bolts of Work Force Diversity"; "Legal Issues, published in the Controllers Business Advisor"; "Identifying Racism: Specific Examples"; "BOSS Spelled Backwards is double SSOB! Or is it?"; "A No-Nonsense Guide to Being Stressed". **Seminars:** Career Development; Coaching and Counseling for Work Success; Communicating More Effectively in a Diverse Work Environment; Communications 600: Advanced Skills for Relationship Building; Customer Service: Building a Caring Culture.

38740 ■ Holt Capital
1916 Pike Pl., Ste. 12-344
Seattle, WA 98101
Ph: (206)484-0403
Fax: (206)789-8034
Co. E-mail: info@holtcapital.com
URL: http://www.holtcapital.com
Contact: Marilyn J. Holt, Chief Executive Officer
E-mail: mjholt@holtcapital.com
Scope: Registered investment advisory firm. Services include: Debt planning, private equity, mergers, divestitures and acquisitions, transaction support services. Connects companies with capital. **Founded:** 1980. **Publications:** "Early Sales Key to Early-Stage Funding"; "Financial Transactions: Who Should Be At Your Table"; "Get the Deal Done: The Four Keys to Successful Mergers and Acquisitions"; "Is Your First Paragraph a Turn-off"; "Bubble Rubble: Bridging the Price Gap for an Early-Stage Business"; "Are You Ready For The new Economy"; "Could I Get Money or Jail Time With That The Sarbanes-Oxley Act Of 2002 gives early-stage companies More Risks". **Seminars:** Attracting Private Investors; Five Proven Ways to Finance Your Company; How to Get VC Financing; Venture Packaging; How to Finance Company Expansion.

38741 ■ Human Resource Specialties Inc.
3 Monroe Pky., Ste. 900
Lake Oswego, OR 97035
Ph: (503)697-3329
Free: 800-354-3512
Fax: (503)636-1594
Co. E-mail: info@hrspecialties.com
URL: http://www.hrspecialties.com
Contact: Sandy Henderson, President
E-mail: sandyh@hrspecialties.com
Scope: Provider of human resources assistance to organizations. Offers preparation of affirmative action plans, support documents, and adverse impact studies of personnel activities. Also offers customized consultations in small business services, diversity and discrimination, and investigations, complaints and grievances. Provides investigations, including allegations of unfair treatment, equal employment opportunity (EEO) and racial or sexual harassment. Offers customized web-based training (webinars) on a variety of HR, EEO and AAP-related topics. **Founded:** 1984.

38742 ■ ICOP, Business Management Consultant—ICOP Investigations
5c-17/5d-4 Estate Santa Maria
Saint Thomas, VI 00803-5396
Ph: (340)776-0581
Fax: (340)776-3519
Co. E-mail: krim@thelastnegro.com
URL: http://www.thelastnegro.com
Contact: Rosalie Ballentine, Principal
Scope: Consultant in human relations dealing with attitudes and behavior. Also consults on racism, workplace violence, domestic violence, child abuse, sexism and philosophical attitudes to include religion. **Founded:** 1984. **Publications:** "The Simplistic Philosopher and Krim's Simplistic Philosophies," Vantage Press, W4, 1988.

38743 ■ I.H.R. Solutions
3333 E Bayaud Ave., Ste. 219
Denver, CO 80209
Ph: (303)588-4243
Fax: (303)978-0473
Co. E-mail: dhollands@ihrsolutions.com
Contact: Deborah Hollands, Owner
E-mail: dhollands@ihrsolutions.com
Scope: Provides joint-venture and start-up human resource consulting services as well as advice on organization development for international human capital. Industries served: high-tech and telecommunications. **Founded:** 1997.

38744 ■ IMC Consulting & Training
901 McHenry Ave., Ste. A
Modesto, CA 95350
Ph: (209)572-2271
Fax: (209)572-2862
Co. E-mail: info@imc-1.net
URL: http://www.imc-1.net
Contact: Michael J. Loschke, President
E-mail: michael@imc-1.net
Scope: Helps businesses and professionals identify, develop and market their selling proposition to increase profits. Services include B-to-B surveys, direct marketing, media relations, planning and strategy, sales management, training and leadership coaching. **Founded:** 1994. **Publications:** "Consultant Earns Advanced Certificate," Hccsc Business Review, Dec, 2004; "Adapting to Change - the New Competitive Advantage," Business Journal, Jul, 2004; "Loyalty Marketing Can Divide New Business," Jun, 2004; "Eleven Major Marketing Mistakes," Jul, 2003; "Planning to Win or Racing to Fail," Jun, 2003. **Seminars:** Negotiating High Profit Sales; How to Write Winning Proposals, Modesto Chamber of Commerce, Oct, 2007; Winning the 2nd Half: A 6-month Plan to Score New Customers and Profits. **Telecommunication Services:** imcinfo@imc-1.net.

38745 ■ The Impact Group L.L.C.
18 Stonewall Dr.
West Granby, CT 06090-1618
Ph: (860)653-0757
Fax: (928)396-2279
Co. E-mail: info@groupimpact.com
URL: http://www.groupimpact.com
Contact: Elaine A. Pullen, Principal
Scope: Firm specializes in business operations improvement and TQM consulting initiatives. **Founded:** 1997.

38746 ■ In Plain English—R.H. Wohl & Associates Inc.
14501 Antigone Dr.
Gaithersburg, MD 20885-3300
Ph: (301)340-2821
Free: 800-274-9645
Fax: (301)279-0115
Co. E-mail: rwohl@inplainenglish.com
URL: http://www.inplainenglish.com
Contact: Ronald H. Wohl, President
E-mail: rwohl@inplainenglish.com
Scope: Management consultants helping government and businesses research, design, write and produce user oriented management information for human resources, employee benefits, business process, corporate and marketing needs. Services include: GSA mob is schedule for consulting to the government; employee benefit communications, plain English business writing workshops for print and electronic media; communicating strategy and tactics; marketing research, business planning and communications; readability testing; usability testing and monitoring strategy. **Founded:** 1977. **Publications:** "The Benefits Communication"; "The Employee Benefits Communication ToolKit," Commerce Clearinghouse; "Benefits Communication," Business and Legal Reports. **Seminars:** Plain English Writing Training; Summary Plan Description Compliance workshops; Re-Humanizing the Corporation, Human Resources and Employee Benefits Communication Workshop; 21 Writing Tips for the 21st Century; Make the Write Impression; Writing to Inform and Instruct; The Dreaded Nuts and Bolts; Writing to Persuade; Writing Policy and Procedure Manuals In Plain English; Writing for Accountants and Auditors In Plain English. **Special Services:** In Plain English®.

38747 ■ The Institute for Management Excellence
PO Box 5459
Lacey, WA 98509-5459
Ph: (360)412-0404
Co. E-mail: pwoc@itstime.com
URL: http://www.itstime.com
Contact: Michael Anthony, Director
Scope: Management consulting and training focuses on improving productivity, using practices and creative techniques. Practices based on the company's theme: It's time for new ways of doing business. Industries served: public sector, law enforcement, finance or banking, non profit, computers or high technology, education, human resources, utilities. **Founded:** 1995. **Publications:** "Income Without a Job," 2008; "The Other Side of Midnight, 2000: An Executive Guide to the Year 2000 Problem"; "Concordance to the Michael Teachings"; "Handbook of Small Business Advertising"; "The Personality Game"; "How to Market Yourself for Success". **Seminars:** The Personality Game; Power Path Seminars; Productivity Plus; Sexual Harassment and Discrimination Prevention; Worker's Comp Cost Reduction; Americans with Disabilities Act; In Search of Identify: Clarifying Corporate Culture.

38748 ■ Interax Corp.
4524 S Michigan St.
South Bend, IN 46680-2287
Ph: (574)299-0660
Free: 800-560-4489
Fax: (574)299-0683
Co. E-mail: info@interaxcorp.com
URL: http://www.interaxcorp.com
Contact: T. Arthur Stump, President
Scope: Company provides management consulting services, including training, organizational group facilitation, total quality management, participative management, and human technology interaction management. Serves all industries worldwide. **Founded:** 1986. **Publications:** "Eye of the storm: Compaq executive turmoil traced to Pfeiffer's inner circle," May, 1999; "The Transformational Leader"; "Leading Change"; "The Human Side of Change: A practical guide to organization redesign"; "People, Performance, & Pay: Dynamic Compensation for Changing Organizations"; "Leadership is an Art"; "Managing Disagreement Constructively: Conflict Management in Organizations"; "Facilitation...From Discussion to Decision".

38749 ■ Interminds & Federer Resources Inc.
106 E 6th St., Ste. 310
Austin, TX 78701-3659
Ph: (512)476-8800
Fax: (512)476-8811
Co. E-mail: yesyoucan@interminds.com
URL: http://www.interminds.com
Contact: Frank Federer, President
E-mail: ffederer@integra100.com
Scope: Specializes in feasibility studies; startup businesses; small business management; mergers and acquisitions; joint ventures; divestitures; interim management; crisis management; turnarounds; production planning; team building; appraisals and valuations. **Founded:** 1985. **Publications:** "Yes You Can: How To Be A Success No Matter Who You Are Or Where You're From".

38750 ■ Interpersonal Coaching & Consulting (ICC)
1516 W Lake St., Ste. 2000S
Minneapolis, MN 55408
Ph: (612)381-2494
Fax: (612)381-2494
Co. E-mail: mail@interpersonal-coaching.com
URL: http://www.interpersonal-coaching.com
Contact: Mary Belfry, Partner
Scope: Provider of coaching and consulting to businesses and organizations. Assesses the interpersonal workplace through interviews, assessment instruments and individual group settings. Experienced as a therapist for over a decade. **Publications:** "Sexual Harassment In The Workplace For Newspapers". **Seminars:** More On Relationships; Sexual harassment and discrimination issues.

38751 ■ Johnston Co.
78 Bedford St.
Lexington, MA 02420
Ph: (781)862-7595
Fax: (781)862-9066
Co. E-mail: info@johnstoncompany.com
URL: http://www.johnstoncompany.com
Contact: Claire Sehringer, Manager
Scope: Specializes in management audits and reports; start-up businesses; small business management; mergers and acquisitions; joint ventures; divestitures; interim management; crisis management; turnarounds; cost controls; financing; venture capital; controller services; financial management, strategic and advisory services. **Founded:** 1987. **Publications:** "Why are board meetings such a waste of time," Boston Business Journal, Apr, 2004.

38752 ■ K & T Training—K & T Consulting
103 Greenville St.
Newnan, GA 30263
Ph: (770)253-5870
Fax: (770)253-8866
Contact: J. R. Tumperi, President
Scope: Specializes in strategic planning; profit enhancement; organizational development; start-up businesses; interim management; crisis management; turnarounds; business process re-engineering; team building; cost controls. **Founded:** 1983.

38753 ■ Kaiser Group Inc.
237 South St.
Waukesha, WI 53186
Ph: (262)544-4971
Fax: (262)544-6271
Co. E-mail: jnitz@kaisergrp.com
URL: http://www.kaisergrp.com
Contact: J. Wyatt Pope, President
Scope: Management support consultants with an emphasis on service to capital and consumer goods manufacturers of under twenty million in sales. Current activity is concentrated on startup and turnaround management, executive and supervisory development, marketing and sales strategies and planning, development of capital and loan formation packages, modular housing and real estate development, employment and training activities, participative management implementation, product and service costing, active market research programs and employee involvement programs. Serves private industries as well as government agencies. **Founded:** 1979. **Publications:** "A Comprehensive Resource Guide for Workforce Board Staff"; "Guide to Effective Work groups and Meetings"; "From Research to Reality"; "Business Services Team Development Guide". **Seminars:** Job Readiness and Assessment Strategies; Career Advising; Understanding Motivation; Customer Service Strategies; Developing Leadership for Supervisors; Case Management Interventions; Team Development.

38754 ■ Keiei Senryaku Corp.
19191 S Vermont Ave., Ste. 530
Torrance, CA 90502-1049
Ph: (310)366-3331
Free: 800-951-8780
Fax: (310)366-3330
Co. E-mail: takenakaes@earthlink.net
Contact: Kurt Miyamoto, President
Scope: Offers consulting services in the areas of strategic planning; feasibility studies; profit enhancement; organizational development; start-up businesses; mergers and acquisitions; joint ventures; divestitures; executive searches; sales management; and competitive analysis. **Founded:** 1989.

38755 ■ Kostka & Company Inc.
9 Wild Rose Ct.
Cromwell, CT 06416
Ph: (860)257-1045
Contact: Peter Kostka, Managing Partner
E-mail: peterpk@gmail.com
Scope: Areas of expertise: management consulting, global technology sourcing, complex project management, SKU management and new product introduction, application development, medical point-of-sale, multi-touch user interface, made-to-order management systems and Smartphone ERP connectivity. Clients include global fortune 500 companies as well as small and medium-sized businesses and startups. **Founded:** 1994.

38756 ■ William E. Kuhn & Associates
234 Cook St.
Denver, CO 80206-5305
Ph: (303)322-8233
Fax: (303)331-9032
Co. E-mail: billkuhn1@cs.com
Contact: William E. Kuhn, Owner
E-mail: billkuhn1@cs.com
Scope: Firm specializes in strategic planning; profit enhancement; small business management; mergers and acquisitions; joint ventures; divestitures; human resources management; performance appraisals; team building; sales management; appraisals and valuations. **Founded:** 1980. **Publications:** "Creating a High-Performance Dealership," Office SOLUTIONS & Office DEALER, Jul-Aug, 2006.

38757 ■ Leadership Development Center (LDC)
155 Edgewood Ave. S
Jacksonville, FL 32254
Ph: (904)387-0110
Free: 800-659-1720
Fax: (904)246-9270
Co. E-mail: jbleech@no-excuses.com
URL: http://www.no-excuses.com
Contact: James M. Bleech, President
E-mail: jbleech@no-excuses.com
Scope: Management consulting firm offering development of leadership skills for CEOs and senior management. Specializes in issues of corporate culture and strategic planning. Industries served: all. **Founded:** 1989. **Publications:** "Knockdown," Jul, 2002; "Let's Get Results Not Excuses," Lifetime Books; "The On Purpose Person"; "When the Other Guy's Price Is Lower," Lifetime Books. **Seminars:** Let's Get Results!; Corporate Culture and Values: Establishing the Center; The X Predicament: Maximizing Profits through Sales Department Design.

38758 ■ Liberty Business Strategies Ltd.
The Times Bldg., Ste. 400, Suburban Sq.
Ardmore, PA 19003
Ph: (610)649-3800
Fax: (610)649-0408
Co. E-mail: info@libertystrategies.com
URL: http://www.libertystrategies.com
Contact: Emmy S. Miller, President
E-mail: emmym@libertystrategies.com
Scope: Management consulting firm working with clients to gain speed and agility in driving their business strategy. The consulting model builds the alignment of strategy, organization commitment, and technology. Provides senior leader coaching and team development coaching. **Founded:** 1980. **Seminars:** Winning with Talent, Morison Annual Conference, Jul, 2009.

38759 ■ Lupfer & Associates (L&A)
92 Glen St.
Natick, MA 01760-5646
Ph: (508)655-3950
Fax: (508)655-7826
Co. E-mail: donlupfer@aol.com
Contact: Donald Lupfer, Owner
E-mail: don.lupfer@lupferassociates.com
Scope: Assists off shore hi-tech companies in entering United States markets and specializes in channel development for all sorts of products. Perform MARCOM support for hi-tech United States clients. **Founded:** 1988. **Publications:** "What's Next For Distribution-Feast or Famine"; "The Changing Global Marketplace"; "Making Global Distribution Work". **Seminars:** How to do Business in the United States.

38760 ■ Management Growth Institute (MGI)
27 Chelmsford Rd.
Rochester, NY 14618
Ph: (585)461-1353
Fax: (585)461-5266
Co. E-mail: kbalbertini@managementgrowth.com
URL: http://www.managementgrowth.com
Contact: Kathleen B. Albertini, Chief Executive Officer
E-mail: kbalbertini@managementgrowth.com
Scope: Offers assistance in the specification, design, and implementation of management development programs. Clients include individuals, small businesses, national trade associations, and government agencies. **Founded:** 1961. **Publications:** "Cost Reduction Is Your Company the Target," InFocus Magazine, Apr, 2010; "Fall-I hired this great person," The Canadian Mover, Dec, 2009; "Profit Strategies," Direction Magazine, Jul, 2009; "Customer Loyalty," InFocus Magazine, Jul, 2009; "Cash Management," The Portal Magazine, Jul, 2009; "What is Customer Loyalty," In FOCUS Magazine, Dec, 2008; "Strategies to Improve Profits," Aug, 2008; "A Question of Management," Moving World. **Seminars:** Profit Enhancement; Family-Owned Businesses; Strategic Planning; Survival and Growth in a Down Economy.

38761 ■ Management House Inc.
36422 Sidewinder Rd.
Carefree, AZ 85377-2708
Ph: (480)437-9023
Fax: (480)588-8905
Co. E-mail: info@managementhouse.com
URL: http://www.managementhouse.com
Contact: Dr. Clay Sherman, President
E-mail: drclay@managementhouse.com
Scope: Offers management consulting that emphasizes management education and human resources programming for health service, business, military, and academic organizations. This programming is based on needs analysis and can be presented as keynote addresses, half-day else full-day programs, multiple-day seminars and executive retreats. Programs is specifically developed to respond to needs analysis findings. **Founded:** 1980. **Publications:** "Raising Standards in American Healthcare"; "Creating the New American Hospital"; "Total Customer Satisfaction"; "From Losers to Winners"; "Managerial Performance & Promotability"; "Make Yourself Memorable Winning Strategies to Influence Others". **Seminars:** Offers the following in-house programs: The Uncommon Leader; The New American Organization; The New American Hospital; Productivity & Performance Improvement; Keys to Managerial Effectiveness; Creating Organizational Excellence; Managing Change & Conflict; Handling the Problem Employee; Gaining Power & Persuasion; Building a Winning Team; and Managing Stress, Strain, and Dis-Ease; Creating the New American Hospital: A Time For Greatness; Total Customer Satisfaction; Leading With Certainty in Uncertain Times; Raising Standards in American Health Care.

38762 ■ Management Methods Inc.
207 Johnston St. SE, Ste. 208
Decatur, AL 35602
Ph: (256)355-3896
Fax: (256)353-3140
Co. E-mail: davisw@managementmethods.com
URL: http://www.managementmethods.com
Contact: Davis M. Woodruff, President
E-mail: davisw@managementmethods.com
Scope: Management and manufacturing consultants who specialize in showing companies how to be the low cost, high quality producer in their industry. Services include general management consulting, total quality management, ISO-9000 or QS-9000, statistical process control, and other problem solving methods. Also a professional speaker for clients, trade associations, and professional groups. Clients include small businesses and Fortune 100 companies in the following industries: Automotive, chemicals, textiles, utilities, petroleum, plastics, and polymers, as well as government agencies. **Founded:** 1984. **Publications:** "A Manager's Guide to the 10 Essentials"; "A Manager's Guide to Tqm Success"; "Leading People and Managing Processes"; "Taking Care of the Basics, 101 Success Factors for Managers," 2005. **Seminars:** Statistical Process Control (SPC): Concepts and Applications; Advanced Statistical Methods; Team Problem Solving; Effective Management Methods; Measurement Systems SPC and ISO 9000; What To Do When Total Quality Manage-

ment Isn't Working; Seven Golden Rules for the Best Customer service; How To Make Quality Management a Success; Managing Without Unions; Five Techniques for Keeping Technical People From Failing as Managers; How To Stop the War Between Sales, Engineering and Manufacturing; Reengineer Your Company with Common Sense and Compassion; Having High Values in a Low Cost, High Quality Business.

38763 ■ Management Network Group Inc.—TMNG GlobalCambridge Strategic Management Group Inc.;
7300 College Blvd., Ste. 302
Overland Park, KS 66210-1879
Ph: (913)345-9315
Fax: (913)451-1845
URL: http://www.tmng.com
Contact: Micky K. Woo, President
E-mail: micky.woo@tmng.com
Scope: A provider of strategy, management, marketing, operational and technology consulting services to the global telecommunications industry. **Founded:** 1990. **Special Services:** Lexicon™; QBC™; QSA™.

38764 ■ Management Resource Partners
181 2nd Ave., Ste. 542
San Mateo, CA 94401
Ph: (650)401-5850
Fax: (650)401-5850
Contact: John C. Roberts, Owner
Scope: Firm specializes in strategic planning; small business management; mergers and acquisitions; joint ventures; divestitures; interim management; crisis management; turn around; venture capital; appraisals and valuations. **Founded:** 1981.

38765 ■ Management Strategies
1000 S Old Woodward Ave., Ste. 105
Birmingham, MI 48009
Ph: (248)258-2756
Fax: (248)258-3407
Co. E-mail: bob@hois.com
Contact: Robert E. Hoisington, President
E-mail: bob@hois.com
Scope: Firm specializes in strategic planning; feasibility studies; profit enhancement; organizational studies; start up businesses; turnarounds; business process re engineering; industrial engineering; marketing; ecommerce. **Founded:** 1985.

38766 ■ Management Technology Associates Ltd.
2768 SW Sherwood Dr., Ste. 105
Portland, OR 97201-2251
Ph: (503)224-5220
Fax: (503)224-5334
Co. E-mail: lcuster@mta-ltd.com
Contact: Lawrence R. Custer, President
E-mail: lcuster@mta-ltd.com
Scope: Offers troubled company turn arounds, strategic business planning, productivity improvement, information systems, business mediation and business valuations. Industries served: manufacturing, wholesale distribution, forest products, transportation, construction, retailing, health care, and government. **Founded:** 1982. **Publications:** "What it Takes to Manage in the '90's," Business Journal; "Bringing Management Techniques to Small Business Clients"; "How to Value and Sell Your Company". **Seminars:** Strategic Business Planning; Management Control Systems, Business Dispute Resolution; Management Techniques for Small Business Clients.

38767 ■ Market Focus
12 Maryland Rd.
Maplewood, NJ 07040
Ph: (973)378-2470
Fax: (973)378-2470
Co. E-mail: mcss66@marketfocus.com
Contact: Daniel A. Zaslow, President
E-mail: dakaslow@comcast.net
Scope: Offers advisory services to executives of corporate business units and mid-sized companies in the development and implementation of corporate and market strategies. Studies relate to business planning, new market/product entry, acquisitions and industry/competitive profiles for firms in advanced technology, business and financial services and basic industry. Projects focus on practical, effective approaches to maximizing the potential of existing operations and exploiting future growth opportunities. Practice philosophy emphasizes close client relationships, active management participation and senior consultant involvement. **Founded:** 1980. **Publications:** "Surviving in Hard Times," NJ Contractor. **Seminars:** Charting a Course for Future Company Growth; Marketing Planning; Construction Marketing in the 90's; Marketing and The CFO.

38768 ■ Stuart Matlins Associates
4 Sunset Farms, Rte. 4
Woodstock, VT 05091-0237
Ph: (802)457-4000
Free: 800-962-4544
Fax: (802)457-4004
Co. E-mail: sales@jewishlights.com
URL: http://www.jewishlights.com
Contact: Stuart M. Matlins, President
Scope: Provider of management consulting and research services to private and public sector clients. Services include: profit improvement; growth management; planning and organization; financial, economic and market feasibility; financial management and control; negotiations for new ventures, joint ventures and licensing of products/processes; and management training. **Founded:** 1974.

38769 ■ McDonald Consulting Group Inc.
1900 W Park Dr., Ste. 280
Westborough, MA 01581
Co. E-mail: info@mcdonaldconsultinggroup.com
URL: http://www.mcdonaldconsultinggroup.com
Contact: Ron A. McDonald, President
E-mail: rmcdonald@mcdonaldconsultinggroup.com
Scope: A management consulting firm specializing in assisting insurance companies improve operations. Provides services in the areas of strategic planning; profit enhancement; organizational development; interim management; crisis management; turnarounds; business process re-engineering; benefits and compensation planning and total quality management. **Founded:** 1993. **Publications:** "Improving Customer Focus through Organizational Structure," AASCIF News; "Changing Strategies in Hard Markets," The National Underwriter; "Moving Beyond Management 101: Postgraduate Time Management for Executives," The National Underwriter; "A New Attitude: 3 Clients Improved Results Through Our Fundamental Change Process," Bests Review; "How to Organize Your Company Around Your Customers," Bests Review. **Seminars:** How to establish "expense allowable"; How to design an incentive compensation plan around a units core success measures.

38770 ■ Jerome W. McGee & Associates—Bruce W. McGee & Associates
7826 Eastern Ave. NW, Ste. 300
Washington, DC 20012
Ph: (202)726-7272
Fax: (202)726-2946
Contact: Bruce W. McGee, President
Scope: Business consultants experienced in office automation, small business management, invention and patent counseling, technology commercialization, loan packaging and business plan development. **Founded:** 1985. **Seminars:** Marketing Research for the High-Technology Business; Introduction to Microcomputers; Marketing Technological Products to Industry; How to Evaluate Your Technical Idea; Patenting Your Own Invention.

38771 ■ MCR Capital Advisors L.L.P.
535 W 20th St., Ste. 100
Houston, TX 77028
Ph: (713)623-6778
Fax: (713)426-4601
Co. E-mail: magillp@mcrcapitaladvisors.com
URL: http://www.mcrcapitaladvisors.com
Contact: Patrick J. Magill, Partner
Scope: Valuations and strategy for mergers and acquisitions, workout agreements and development of strategic partnerships, direct business advisors to senior management and board of directors utilizing industry experience and business acumen, accounting and financial consulting for debt restructuring, outsourcing of top side accounting services and preparation for significant financing or IPO, and consulting for IT vendor evaluations, organizational design, human performance optimization and customer relationship management strategy. Serves the unique needs of small and mid size companies. **Founded:** 2001.

38772 ■ McShane Group Inc.
2345 York Rd., Ste. 102
Timonium, MD 21093
Ph: (410)560-0077
Fax: (410)560-2718
Co. E-mail: tmcshane@mcshanegroup.com
URL: http://www.mcshanegroup.com
Contact: Thomas P. McShane, President
E-mail: tmcshane@mcshanegroup.com
Scope: Turnaround consulting and crisis management firm. Specializes in due diligence services, interim management, strategic business realignments, business sale and asset depositions and debt restructuring. Industries served: technology, financial, retail, distribution, medical, educational, manufacturing, contracting, environmental and health care. **Founded:** 1987.

38773 ■ Medema Consulting Associates L.L.C.
2342 Paris Ave., SE
Grand Rapids, MI 49507-3112
Ph: (616)235-0554
Fax: (616)988-3104
Co. E-mail: dmedema@medemaconsulting.com
Contact: David Luke Medema, President
Scope: Firm creates and delivers customized training and consulting services in the areas of board governance and leadership development, diversity assessment and training, fund raising, human resources, meeting facilitation, performance improvement, strategic thinking, planning, evaluation, team building and workshops. **Founded:** 1999.

38774 ■ Medical Imaging Consultants Inc. (MIC)
1037 US Highway 46, Ste. G-2
Clifton, NJ 07013-2445
Ph: (973)574-8000
Free: 800-589-5685
Fax: (973)574-8001
Co. E-mail: info@micinfo.com
URL: http://www.micinfo.com
Contact: Dr. Philip A. Femano, President
E-mail: phil@micinfo.com
Scope: Provider of professional support services for radiology management and comprehensive continuing education programs for radiologic technologists. Management services include resource-critical database logistics; customer registration in educational programs; educational program development and Category A accreditation; national agency notification (e.g., ASRT, SNM-TS) of CE credits earned; meeting planning; manpower assessment; market research; expert witness; think-tank probes and executive summaries of industry issues. **Founded:** 1991. **Seminars:** Sectional Anatomy and Imaging Strategies; CT Cross-Trainer; CT Registry Review Program; MR Cross Trainer; MRI Registry Review Program; Digital Mammography Essentials for Technologists; Radiology Trends for Technologists.

38775 ■ Medical Outcomes Management Inc.
132 Central St., Ste. 215
Foxborough, MA 02035-2422
Ph: (508)543-0050
Fax: (508)543-1919
Co. E-mail: info@mom-inc.com
Contact: Alan F. Kaul, President
E-mail: alan@mom-inc.com
Scope: Management and technology consulting firm providing a specially focused group of services such as disease management programs and pharmacoeconomic studies. Services include clinical and educational projects, medical writing and editing, marketing and sales projects, disease registries, educational seminars, strategic planning projects, managed care organizations; and pharmaceutical and biotechnology companies. **Founded:** 1991. **Publications:** "Treatment of acute exacerbation's of chronic bronchitis in patients with chronic obstructive pulmonary disease: A retrospective cohort analysis logarith-

mically extended release vs. Azithromycin," 2003; "A retrospective analysis of cyclooxygenase-II inhibitor response patterns," 2002; "DUE criteria for use of regional urokinase infusion for deep vein thrombosis,"2002; "The formulary management system and decision-making process at Horizon Blue Cross Blue Shield of New Jersey," Pharmaco therapy, 2001. **Seminars:** Economic Modeling as a Disease Management Tool, Academy of Managed Care Pharmacy, Apr, 2005; Integrating Disease State Management and Economics, Academy of Managed Care Pharmacy, Oct, 2004; Clinical and economic outcomes in the treatment of peripheral occlusive diseases, Mar, 2003.

38776 ■ MHJ Associates
41 Coolidge St.
Brookline, MA 02446-2401
Ph: (617)232-7475
Fax: (617)879-1617
Co. E-mail: mhjassociates@rcn.com
Contact: Michael Jacobs, Owner
E-mail: m.jacobs@mhjassociates.com
Scope: Firm specializes in housing development and finance. Services include 40B permitting and financial analysis, project management, multifamily housing finance and feasibility analysis.

38777 ■ MIIX Healthcare Group
2 Princess Rd.
Lawrenceville, NJ 08648
Ph: (609)219-1111
Free: 800-234-6449
Fax: (609)219-6727
Contact: Daniel Goldberg, Chief Executive Officer
Scope: Firm provides comprehensive healthcare consulting services and unique products designed to assist physicians, and healthcare organizations meet the challenges of a managed care environment. Consulting services range from practice management to network formation and marketing, practice valuations, practice mergers and acquisitions, and compliance. **Founded:** 1996.

38778 ■ Miller/Cook & Associates Inc.
20 Marco Lake Dr., Ste. 12
Marco Island, FL 34145-3644
Ph: (239)394-5040
Free: 800-591-1141
Fax: (239)394-2652
Co. E-mail: info@millercook.com
URL: http://www.millercook.com
Contact: William B. Miller, President
Scope: Specializes in all areas of enrollment management, admissions and financial aid. Involves in institutional and enrollment analysis, strategic positioning/institutional image, enrollment integration/ operation, re-recruitment, financial aid and planning, integrated communications, training and workshops, and on-site management. **Founded:** 1988. **Publications:** "Capital gains: Surviving in an increasingly for profit world"; "Making steps to a brighter future". **Seminars:** Admissions: An overview of a changing profession; Admission practices: Managing the admissions office; Admission practices: Internal operations often make the difference; Effective communication and the enrollment process; Telemarketing or Tele counseling: How to use the telephone to effectively enroll and re-enroll students; Graduate and professional program recruitment: An overview Re-Recruitment: What is it? Is it necessary?; The effective use of electronic mediums in the recruitment process; The use of alumni to support and sustain your recruiting efforts.

38779 ■ Miller, Hellwig Associates
150 W End Ave.
New York, NY 10023-5713
Ph: (212)799-0471
Fax: (212)877-0186
Co. E-mail: millerhelwig@earthlink.net
Contact: Ernest C. Miller, President
Scope: Consulting services in the areas of start-up businesses; small business management; employee surveys and communication; performance appraisals; executive searches; team building; personnel policies and procedures; market research. Also involved in improving cross-cultural and multi-cultural relationships, particularly with Japanese clients. **Founded:** 1984. **Seminars:** Objectives and standards/recruiting for boards of directors.

38780 ■ Moats Kennedy Inc.
1155 W Madison St., Ste. 605
Chicago, IL 60607
Ph: (847)251-1661
Free: 800-728-1709
Fax: (847)251-5191
Co. E-mail: mkennedy@moatskennedy.com
URL: http://www.moatskennedy.com
Contact: Marilyn Moats Kennedy, Managing Partner
Scope: Provider of consulting services for a variety of associations and companies in the area of personnel and management. Speaks and consults on the following topics office politics, leadership skills, demographics workplace issues. Serves industry as well as government agencies in the U.S. **Founded:** 1975. **Publications:** "How to Prove Your Work Makes A Difference ," FOCUS: Journal for Respiratory Care & Sleep Medicine, 2005; "The Glamour Guide to Office Smarts"; "Salary Strategies: Everything You Need to Know to Get the Salary You Want"; "Career Knockouts: How to Battle Back,"; "Powerbase: How to Build It/How to Keep It"; "Office Warfare: Getting Ahead in the Aggressive 80s"; "The Glamour Guide to Office Smarts"; "In the Trenches"; "Job Strategies". **Seminars:** Managing Change: Understanding the Demographics of the Evolving Workforce; The Aging Workforce; Are You Giving Satisfaction or Just Service?; Management for the Millenium: Walking your talk.

38781 ■ R.E. Moulton Inc.
50 Doaks Ln.
Marblehead, MA 01945
Ph: (781)631-1325
Fax: (781)631-2165
Co. E-mail: mike_lee@remoultoninc.com
URL: http://www.oneamerica.com/wps/wcm/connect/REMoulton
Contact: Willard A. Knarr, Jr., President
Scope: Offers underwriting services, marketing solutions, claims administration and adjudication; policy and commission administration; and risk management solutions to clients. Supplementary service s include risk management and employee assistance. Clients include individuals, business men, employers and finance professionals. **Founded:** 1976.

38782 ■ Murray Dropkin & Associates—Dropkin Consulting
390 George St.
New Brunswick, NJ 08901
Ph: (732)828-3211
Fax: (732)828-4118
Co. E-mail: murray@dropkin.com
URL: http://www.dropkin.com
Contact: Murray Dropkin, President
E-mail: murray@dropkin.com
Scope: Specializes in feasibility studies; business management; business process re-engineering; and team building, health care and housing. **Founded:** 1969. **Publications:** "Bookkeeping for Nonprofits," Jossey Bass, 2005; "Guide to Audits of Nonprofit Organizations," PPC; "The Nonprofit Report," Warren, Gorham & Lamont; "The Budget Building Book for Nonprofits," Jossey-Bass; "The Cash Flow Management Book for Nonprofits," Jossey-Bass.

38783 ■ Navarro, Kim & Associates
529 N Charles St., Ste. 202
Baltimore, MD 21201-5043
Ph: (410)837-6317
Fax: (410)837-6294
Co. E-mail: bnavarro@sprynet.com
Contact: Beltran Navarro, Director
E-mail: bnavarro@sprynet.com
Scope: Specializes in bridging the gap between firms and non-traditional ethnic communities, especially in community development and institutional building. **Founded:** 1984.

38784 ■ New Commons
545 Pawtucket Ave., Studio 106A
Pawtucket, RI 02860
Ph: (401)351-7110
Fax: (401)351-7158
Co. E-mail: info@newcommons.com
URL: http://www.newcommons.com
Contact: Robert Leaver, Chief Executive Officer
E-mail: rleaver@newcommons.com
Scope: Builder of agile human networks to champion innovation and mobilize change; to pursue business opportunities; to custom design agile organizations and communities, to foster civic engagement. Clients include organizations on-profits, corporations, government agencies, educational institutions; networks-Trade/professional groups, IT services collaborations, service-sharing collectives; and communities- municipalities, states and statewide agencies, regional collaborations. **Founded:** 1982. **Publications:** "Plexus Imperative," Sep, 2005; "Creating 21st Century Capable Innovation Systems," Aug, 2004; "Call to Action: Building Providences Creative and Innovative Economy"; "Getting Results from Meetings"; "The Entrepreneur as Artist," Commonwealth Publications; "Leader and Agent of Change," Commonwealth Publications; "Achieving our Providence: Lessons of City-Building," Commonwealth Publications. **Seminars:** Introduction to Social Computing (Web 2.0), Jan, 2009; Every Company Counts, Jun, 2009; Facilitating for Results; Story-Making and Story-Telling. **Telecommunication Services:** inquiries@newcommons.com.

38785 ■ Nightingale Associates
7445 Setting Sun Way
Columbia, MD 21046
Ph: (410)381-4280
Fax: (410)381-4280
Co. E-mail: fredericknightingale@nightingaleassociates.net
URL: http://www.nightingaleassociates.net
Contact: Frederick C. Nightingale, Managing Director
E-mail: fredericknightingale@nightingaleAssociates.net
Scope: Management training and consulting firm offering the following skills: productivity and accomplishment; leadership skills for the experienced manager; management skills for the new manager; leadership and teambuilding; supervisory development; creative problem solving; real strategic planning; providing superior customer service; international purchasing and supply chain management; negotiation skills development and fundamentals of purchasing. **Founded:** 1984. **Seminars:** Productivity and Accomplishment Management Skills for the New Manager; Leadership and Team building; Advanced Management; Business Process Re engineering; Strategic Thinking; Creative Problem Solving; Customer Service; International Purchasing and Materials Management; Fundamentals of Purchasing; Negotiation Skills Development; Providing superior customer service; Leadership skills for the experienced manager.

38786 ■ Non-Profit Transitions L.L.C.
446 Main St.
Waltham, MA 02452
Ph: (617)501-5471
Fax: (617)527-7217
Co. E-mail: info@nptransitions.com
URL: http://www.nptransitions.com
Contact: Jeff Katz, Chief Executive Officer
Scope: Provides non-profit organizations with executive leadership and consulting during transition. Provides interim leaders, including chief executive officers, chief financial officers, and human resources directors. Change leadership services include executive coaching, governance and board performance evaluation, mediation and conflict resolution, strategic planning, search process leadership, and mergers and acquisitions. Other consulting services include organizational development, program performance, training and development, development and grant writing; and real estate project management. **Founded:** 2003. **Publications:** "Lessons from the Merger Culture War".

38787 ■ NOVUS L.L.C.
417 Main Ave., Ste. 209
Fargo, ND 58103
Ph: (701)238-0397

Fax: (701)298-3533
Co. E-mail: emonson@novusresults.com
Contact: Paul Smith, Manager
E-mail: psmith@novusresults.com
Scope: A full-service strategic business consulting group offering management services, including executive management, governance, human resources, operations management, financial management, information technology, and medical affairs.

38788 ■ Oakdales Olde Towne Veterinary Hospital
144 S 1st Ave.
Oakdale, CA 95361-3903
Ph: (209)847-9077
Fax: (209)847-4390
Co. E-mail: oakdalevet@aol.com
URL: http://www.oakdalevet.com
Contact: Mary Angela, Receptionist
Scope: Provider of diagnostic and therapeutic services for a pet's health care needs. Offers surgical services, anesthesia, radiology services, ultrasound services, electrocardiography services, dental services and dietary and behavioral counseling. **Founded:** 1948.

38789 ■ Organizational Consulting Services Inc.
230 S Bemiston Ave., Ste. 1107
Saint Louis, MO 63105-1907
Ph: (314)863-1200
Fax: (314)863-6718
Co. E-mail: rav@ocs-oe.com
URL: http://www.ocs-oe.com
Contact: Robert A. Vecchiotti, President
E-mail: rav@ocs-oe.com
Scope: Services include business assessment, planning, and restructuring; team building, executive assessment and development; financial analysis and cost accounting; market analysis and customer surveys. Consultants also serve as facilitators of planning retreats, offering guidance in strategy development and goal setting. The firm works with CEO's and senior executives of privately held companies and major corporations. **Founded:** 1980. **Seminars:** Leadership for Entrepreneurs, Missouri, Oct, 2006; The Integrated Executive seminars; Strategic Planning and Management; Change Management; Management Transitions; Team Building.

38790 ■ P2C2 Group Inc.
4101 Denfeld Ave.
Kensington, MD 20895-1514
Ph: (301)942-7985
Fax: (301)942-7986
Co. E-mail: info@p2c2group.com
URL: http://www.p2c2group.com
Contact: James E. Kendrick, President
E-mail: kendrick@p2c2group.com
Scope: Works with clients on the business side of federal program and project management. Services include program/project planning and optimization; acquisition strategy and work statements; IT Capital Planning and Investment Control (CPIC); business cases - new, revisions, critiques; budget analysis - cost benefits- alternatives; CPIC, SELC, and security documentation; research, metrics, analysis, and case studies. Consulting support helping to: Define or redefine programs; strengthen portfolio management; identify alternatives for lean budgets; improve capital planning and investment; develop better plans and documentation, and evaluate performance of existing program investments. **Founded:** 1994. **Publications:** "OMB 300s Go Online," Federal Sector Report, Mar, 2007; "Using Risk-Adjusted Costs for Projects," Federal Sector Report, Feb, 2007; "Make Better Decisions Using Case Studies," Federal Sector Report, Jan, 2007; "PMO Performance Measurement & Metrics"; "Executive Sponsors for Projects"; "ABCs of the Presidential Transition"; "Financial Systems and Enterprise Portfolio Management"; "The Future of CPIC"; "Critical Factors for Program and Project Success"; "Using Risk-Adjusted Costs for Projects"; "Tactics for a Successful Year of CPIC"; "Operational Analysis Reviews"; "Successful IT Strategic Planning"; "Information Technology Investment Management". **Seminars:** Requests For Information; Pre Solicitation Marketing; Qualifications Statement Support For The Capital Planning And Investment Control (cpic) Process; How To Hire A Management Consultant And Get The Results You Expect.

38791 ■ Papa and Associates Inc.
200 Consumers Rd., Ste. 305
Toronto, ON, Canada M2J 4R4
Ph: (416)512-7272
Fax: (416)512-2016
Co. E-mail: ppapa@papa-associates.com
URL: http://www.papa-associates.com
Contact: Peter Papakostantinu, President
E-mail: ppapa@papa-associates.com
Scope: Provider of broad based management consulting services in the areas of quality assurance, environmental, health and safety and integrated management systems. **Founded:** 1989.

38792 ■ Parker Consultants Inc.
230 Mason St.
Greenwich, CT 06830-6633
Ph: (203)861-6698
Contact: Donald L. Parker, President
Scope: Firm specializes in strategic planning; organizational development; small business management; performance appraisals; executive searches; team building; and customer service audits. **Founded:** 1988.

38793 ■ partnerTEL Inc.
5490 McGinnis Village Pl.
Alpharetta, GA 30005
Ph: (404)978-4400
Free: 800-864-8840
Fax: (404)531-0705
Co. E-mail: customersupport@partnertel.com
URL: http://www.partnertel.com
Contact: Dan Bommer, Chief Executive Officer
E-mail: dbommer@partnertel.com
Scope: A provider of telecom consulting, procurement and managed services. Assists businesses handle the strategic, operational, support and cost-containment challenges surrounding their communications services. Services in inventory and contract management, service management, A/Optimization, tax audits and wireless services. Helps business enterprises streamline their telecom procurement, management and expenditure processes and maximize their overall telecom savings rate and return on investment (ROI). Cost management services include business process outsourcing, hosted software solutions, cost containment consulting, bill auditing and recovery, spend analysis and reporting, business process analysis and outsourcing, carrier and product benchmarking, inventory management, order management, bill management and monitoring, invoice consolidation, electronic bill presentment and payment, trouble ticket management, PBX service, support and procurement, network management and monitoring, contract negotiation and procurement, SLA and contract compliance, rate plan optimization and vendor management.

38794 ■ Performance Consulting Associates Inc. (PCA)
3700 Crestwood Pky., Ste. 100
Duluth, GA 30096
Ph: (770)717-2737
Fax: (770)717-7014
Co. E-mail: info@pcaconsulting.com
URL: http://www.pcaconsulting.com
Contact: Richard A. Defazio, President
E-mail: defazio@pcaconsulting.com
Scope: Maintenance consulting and engineering firm specializing in production planning, project management, team building, and re-engineering maintenance. **Founded:** 1976. **Publications:** "Does Planning Pay," Plant Services, Nov, 2000; "Asset Reliability Coordinator," Maintenance Technology, Oct, 2000; "Know What it is You Have to Maintain," Maintenance Technology, May, 2000; "Does Maintenance Planning Pay," Maintenance Technology, Nov, 2000.; "What is Asset Management?"; "Implementing Best Business Practices".

38795 ■ Performance Consulting Group Inc.
8031 SW 35th Terr.
Miami, FL 33155-3443
Ph: (305)264-5577
Fax: (305)264-9079
Contact: Patrick J. O'Brien, President
Scope: Firm provides consulting services in the areas of strategic planning; profit enhancement; product development; and production planning. **Founded:** 1980.

38796 ■ Pioneer Business Consultants
9042 Garfield Ave., Ste. 211
Huntington Beach, CA 92646
Ph: (714)964-7600
Fax: (714)962-6585
Contact: John J. Collins, President
Scope: Offers general management consulting specializing in business acquisitions, tax and business planning, cash flow analyses, business valuations and business sales and expert witness court testimony regarding business sales, valuations and accounting. **Founded:** 1980.

38797 ■ Primavera Systems Inc.—Primavera SystemsOracle Primavera;
3 Bala Plz. W, Ste. 700
Bala Cynwyd, PA 19004-3481
Ph: (610)667-8600
Free: 800-423-0245
Fax: (610)667-7894
Co. E-mail: info@primavera.com
URL: http://www.primavera.com
Contact: Safra A. Catz, President
E-mail: safra.catz@oracle.com
Scope: Provider of comprehensive project portfolio management, control and execution software. **Founded:** 1983. **Publications:** *SureTrak Project Manager*; *Expedition*; *DataStore for Primavera*; *RA*; *Webster for Primavera*; *TeamPlay*; *Monte Carlo for Primavera*; *PEAK (Primavera Enterprise Access Kit)*; *Primavera Project Planner for the Enterprise (P3e)*; *Primavera Project Planner (P3)*. **Special Services:** PrimaveraP6®, Primavera ProSight®, Primavera®Contract Manager, Primavera Pertmaster®, Primavera®Cost Manager, Primavera Evolve®, Primavera®Contractor 6.1, Primavera Inspire®, PrimaveraProjectPlanner®3.1, SureTrak®Project Manager 3.0b.

38798 ■ PYA GatesMoore
33424 Peachtree Rd. NE, Monarch Twr., Ste. 700
Atlanta, GA 30326
Ph: (404)266-9876
Fax: (404)266-2669
Co. E-mail: info@pyagatesmoore.com
URL: http://www.pyagatesmoore.com
Contact: Ed Pershing, President
E-mail: epershing@pyapc.com
Scope: Firm provides management consulting and accounting services to medical practices, hospital owned practices, staff model managed care organizations, IPAs, MSOs, PO, and PHOs. Services include comprehensive operational assessments, managed care negotiations, practice start-ups and expansion, development of MSOs, strategic planning, mergers, cost accounting analysis, practice valuations, income division plans, medical record documentation and coding reviews, expert witness testimony, patient satisfaction surveys and corporate compliance planning. **Founded:** 1982. **Publications:** "Practicing Medicine in the 21st Century"; "Physicians, Dentists and Veterinarians"; "Insurance Portability and Accountability Act Privacy Manual"; "How To Guide for your Medical Practice and Health Insurance Portability and Accountability Act Security Manual"; "A How To Guide for your Medical Practice"; "Cost Analysis Made Simple: A Step by Step Guide to Using Cost Accounting to Ensure Practice Profitability"; "Cost Cutting Strategies for Medical Practices"; "Cost Cutting Strategies for Medical Practices"; "Getting the Jump on Year-End Tax Planning"; "New 401(k) Safe Harbor Option: Increased Opportunities for the Physician and Practice"; "Not All Tax News is Bad News"; "Shareholder Agreements: Identifying and Addressing Five Risk Areas"; "Surprise - Your Practice has a Deferred Income Tax Liability". **Seminars:** Documenting and Billing High Risk Codes, 2010; Current Challenges in Ob/Gyn Recruiting, 2010; Planning for Physician Wind-down & Retirement, 2010; HITECH "How To" - Opportunities & Risks, 2010; Pediatric Coding and Audits; Recruiting and Retaining Physicians; How to Prepare for the Recovery Audit Con-

tractors - RAC, 2010; Meaningful Use Rule, 2010; The Revenue Stream in Practice, Apr, 2008; Improving Efficiencies in a Small Family Medicine Practice, Oct, 2007; Using Compensation Models to Improve Performance, Sep, 2007; The Financial Side of Personnel Management, Sep, 2007; Pay for Performance-Is it Really Contracting for Quality?, New York State Ophthalmological Society, Sep, 2007; Beyond the Class Action Settlement Payments-Looking Prospectively at Managed Care Companies Behavior, New York State Ophthalmological Society, Sep, 2007; Protecting your clients from Embezzlement, Jun, 2007; What P4P Means to Your Medical Practice, May, 2007; Finance for the Practicing Physician, May, 2007; Trashing, Dipping and Ghosts in Medical Practices: Protecting your clients from Embezzlement, Apr, 2006.

38799 ■ Quality Specialists (QS)
13422 215th Ave. E
Sumner, WA 98390
Ph: (253)230-2886
Fax: (253)862-4937
Co. E-mail: inquiries@qualityspecialists.com
URL: http://www.qualityspecialists.com
Contact: John P. Wickern, President
E-mail: jwickern@qualityspecialists.com
Scope: Offers services in quality control, audit configuration control, and organizational culture change. **Publications:** "Audit Pigs"; "A Little Horse with Words"; "Don't Stiff Your Customers for a Measly $11"; "Grim Buck Tales"; "Health Care Reform"; "It's All How You Look At Things"; "Write to Express - Not Impress".

38800 ■ Research Applications Inc. (RAI)
414 Hungerford Dr., Ste. 220
Rockville, MD 20850-4125
Ph: (301)251-6717
Free: 888-311-6221
Fax: (301)251-6719
Contact: David H. Friedman, President
E-mail: dfriedman@resapplinc.com
Scope: A consulting firm provides specialized design, evaluation, testing and analytic services in the fields of social, computer and mathematical sciences. It brings to its customers a senior staff with strong theoretical and scientific backgrounds in areas of expertise, coupled with extensive practical knowledge and experience in contract research. The firm focuses on providing a group of interrelated services which include human resources support and improvement, computer programming support, direct mail services, and MOBIS. **Founded:** 1975. **Seminars:** Gender Awareness in the Workplace; Humor in the Workplace; Understanding and Using Assessments (Validity/Reliability); Diversity in the Workplace; Structured Interviews; Leadership; Leadership and Humor.

38801 ■ Rose & Crangle Ltd.
117 N 4th St.
Lincoln, KS 67455
Ph: (785)524-5050
Fax: (785)524-3130
Co. E-mail: rcltd@nckcn.com
URL: http://www.roseandcrangle.com
Contact: Robert D. Crangle, President
E-mail: rcltd@nckcn.com
Scope: Provider of evaluation, planning and policy analyzes for universities, associations, foundations, governmental agencies and private companies engaged in scientific, technological or educational activities. Special expertise in the development of new institutions. Special skills in providing planning and related group facilitation workshops. **Founded:** 1984. **Publications:** "Preface to Bulgarian Integration Into Europe and NATO: Issues of Science Policy And research Evaluation Practice," Ios Press, 2006; "Allocating Limited National Resources for Fundamental Research," 2005.

38802 ■ Rothschild Strategies Unlimited L.L.C.
19 Thistle Rd.
Norwalk, CT 06851-1909
Ph: (203)846-6898
Fax: (203)847-1426
Co. E-mail: bill@strategyleader.com
URL: http://www.strategyleader.com
Contact: Stephen M. Rothschild, President
Scope: Consults with senior management and business level strategy teams to develop overall strategic direction, set priorities and creates sustainable competitive advantages and differentiators. Enables organizations to enhance their own strategic thinking and leadership skills so that they can continue to develop and implement profitable growth strategies. **Founded:** 1983. **Publications:** "Putting It All Together-a guide to strategic thinking"; "Competitive Advantage"; "Ristaker, Caretaker, Surgeon & Undertaker four faces of strategic leadership"; "The Secret to GE's Success"; "Having the Right Strategic Leader and Team".

38803 ■ Sandler & Travis Trade Advisory Services Inc. (STTAS)—STTAS
1000 NW 57th Ct., Ste. 600
Miami, FL 33126
Ph: (305)267-9200
Fax: (305)267-5155
Co. E-mail: messages@strtrade.com
URL: http://www.strtrade.com
Contact: J. Nicole Bivens Collinson, President
E-mail: nbc@strtrade.com
Scope: An international trade and customs law firm concentrating in assisting clients with the movement of goods, personnel, and ideas across international borders. Customs and international trade consulting services include global customs modernization and compliance, customs department outsourcing and managed trade services, border security programs, tariff classification project management, valuation of merchandise, preference program project management, U.S. and Canadian customs compliance, duty drawback project management, temporary importation project management, and corporate responsibility in international sourcing. **Special Services:** STTAS™.

38804 ■ David G. Schantz
29 Wood Run Cir.
Rochester, NY 14612-2271
Ph: (716)723-0760
Fax: (716)723-8724
Co. E-mail: daveschantz@yahoo.com
URL: http://www.daveschantz.freeservers.com
Contact: David G. Schantz, Manager
Scope: Provider of industrial engineering services for photofinishing labs, including amateur-wholesale, professional, commercial, school, and package. **Founded:** 1992.

38805 ■ Schneider Consulting Group Inc.
50 S Steele St., Ste. 390
Denver, CO 80209-2834
Ph: (303)320-4413
Fax: (303)320-5795
Contact: Kim Schneider Malek, Vice President
E-mail: kim@scgfambus.com
Scope: Assists family-owned and privately-held business transition to the next generation and/or to a more professionally managed company, turn around consulting for small and medium size companies. **Founded:** 1987.

38806 ■ Scott Ashby Teleselling Inc.
1102 Ben Franklin Dr., Ste. 309
Sarasota, FL 34236
Ph: (941)388-4283
Fax: (941)388-5240
URL: http://www.scottashbyteleselling.com
Contact: R. Scott Ashby, President
E-mail: rscottashby@netscape.net
Scope: Provider of consulting services and customized training programs that emphasize consultative telephone selling techniques. **Founded:** 1979. **Publications:** "How Will the Internet Affect Teleselling Programs?"; "When is Telemarketing Really Not Telemarketing?"; "The Future of Account Management Telesales". **Seminars:** Start-Up Educational, Planning and Strategy Development; Existing Program Audit, Evaluation, State-of-the-Art Best Practices Comparison, Tracking and Measurement Review, Systems and Procedures Analysis, and Optional Selling Skills; Develop New or Revised Consultative Telephone Selling; Helping Clients Build Relationship and Grow Their Business by Phone.

38807 ■ Shealy & Associates
1100 Baker Lake Rd.
Guthrie, OK 73044-8977
Contact: Lon S. Shealy, Vice President
Scope: A network of consultants whose mission is to assist small-to-mid size organizations implement successful strategic management practices. Primarily engaged in the delivery of facilitating services to implement strategic renewal and planning. **Founded:** 1993. **Publications:** "Destiny by Design®"; "Metal Building Review," Industry Week; "Nation's Business and Building Systems". **Seminars:** Becoming a Leader.

38808 ■ Sklar and Associates Inc.
242 Laurel Bay Dr.
Murrells Inlet, SC 29576
Ph: (843)798-0412
Fax: (843)651-3090
Co. E-mail: sklarincdc@aol.com
URL: http://www.sklarinc.com
Contact: Tim Sklar, President
Scope: Provider of consulting services for business acquisitions, business development and project finance. Provides audit oversight services to listed corporations on Sarbanes-Oxley compliance. Services include: Due diligence analyses and corporate governance. Industries served: transportation sectors, energy sector and commercial real estate industries. **Seminars:** Financial Analysis in MBA; Emerging Company Finance; Due Diligence in Business Acquisition; Business Valuation.

38809 ■ Smart Ways to Work
1441 Franklin St., Ste. 301
Oakland, CA 94612-3219
Ph: (510)763-8482
Free: 800-599-8463
Fax: (510)763-0790
Co. E-mail: odette@smartwaystowork.com
URL: http://www.smartwaystowork.com
Contact: Odette Pollar, Owner
E-mail: odette@smartwaystowork.com
Scope: A management consulting firm specializing in the training of supervisors, managers and professional staff in the area of time management, problem solving, decision making and strategic planning. Assists businesses and corporations in developing and implementing programs for increased productivity, greater profit and improved employee morale. Serves private industries as well as government agencies. **Founded:** 1979. **Publications:** "Surviving Information Overload driving Information Overload: How to Find, Filter, and Focus on What's Important," Crisp Publications, Sep, 2003; "Take Back Your Life: Smart Ways to Simplify Daily Living," Conari Press, Apr, 1999; "365 Ways to Simplify Your Work Life," Kaplan Business, Aug, 1996; "Dynamics of Diversity: Strategic Programs for Your Organization," Crisp Publications, 1994; "Organizing Your Workspace: A Guide to Personal Productivity," Crisp Publications, May, 1992. **Seminars:** Managing Multiple Demands: Surviving Ground Zero; Defending Your Life: Balancing Work And Home; Desktop Sprawl: Conquer Your Paper Pile-Up; Getting It All Done: Breaking The Time Bind; To Give or Not To Give: The Delegation Dilemma; Information Happens: Don't Let It Happen On You; Take The Terror Out Of Talk: Secrets To Successful Speaking; To Give or Not To Give: The Delegation Dilemma; Managing Meetings.

38810 ■ Smith, Turner & Reeves P.A.
200 E Capital St., Ste. 100
Jackson, MS 39201-2200
Ph: (601)948-6700
Fax: (601)948-6000
Contact: Jon C. Turner, President
Scope: Offers services in business advisory, merger and acquisitions, physician practice management, financial management, turnaround and operational reviews. It also provides audit, tax and consulting services in the healthcare, utilities, telecommunications, insurance, government, lenders, manufacturing, retail/wholesale, construction, and law firm industries. **Founded:** 1974. **Publications:** "The Spirit

of Success". **Seminars:** Workshops for Lenders - Financial Statements; Troubled Borrowers; Asset Based Lending; Book keeping Workshops; Tax Law Updates.

38811 ■ Stalley Associates Inc.—Rodney E. Stalley & Associates Inc.
10635 James Cir.
Minneapolis, MN 55431-4157
Ph: (952)888-0617
Contact: Rodney E. Stalley, President
E-mail: rstalley@stalley.com
Scope: Advises management of companies in the areas of finance, administrative and general management, corporate objectives, policies and procedures, and management and organization audits. Firm has developed a particular expertise in advising management of young and growing companies. Advises in strategic planning, capital planning and financing strategies, securing private and public investment capital, establishing strategic alliances, management and staff organizational restructuring, working with board of directors, shareholders and serving as chief financial officer and chief operations officer on a contract basis. **Founded:** 1978. **Publications:** "Knowledge: The Key to Business Success"; "The Board of Directors: A Ceo's Source for Advice, Insight and Support"; "Controlling the Audit Expense".

38812 ■ Stillman H. Publishers Inc.
21405 Woodchuck Ln.
Boca Raton, FL 33428
Ph: (561)482-6343
Contact: Herbert Stillman, President
Scope: Offers consulting services in the following areas: management, start ups, profit maximization, world wide negotiating, interim management, corporate debt resolution. **Founded:** 1984.

38813 ■ Straightline Services Inc.
11 Centre St., Ste. 10
Salem, CT 06420-3845
Ph: (860)889-7929
Fax: (860)885-1894
Co. E-mail: straitln@aol.com
Contact: Wayne J. S. France, President
Scope: Design and implementation of organizational infrastructure, business plans and troubleshooting. Emphasizes on operations with a central and field or satellite offices. Industries served: Construction, resorts, Indian tribes, academies, small-medium sized business, mostly privately held. **Founded:** 1994.

38814 ■ Tamayo Consulting Inc.
169 Saxony Rd., Ste. 112
Encinitas, CA 92024-6779
Ph: (760)479-1352
Fax: (760)479-1465
Co. E-mail: info@tamayoconsulting.com
URL: http://www.tamayoconsulting.com
Contact: Jennifer Dreyer, President
E-mail: jdreyer@earthlink.net
Scope: It Provides training and consulting services. And also it specializes in leadership and team development. Industries served: private, non-profit, government, educational. **Founded:** 1986. **Seminars:** Presentation AdvantEdge Program; Lead point Development Program; Supervisor Development Programs.Identify Presentation Objectives; Implement 360-degree presentation assessment; conduct baseline-coaching session; Develop coaching plan; Staying connected.

38815 ■ The TEAM FOCUS Group
46 Pineridge Cres.
Saint Albert, AB, Canada T8N 4P4
Ph: (780)460-1625
Fax: (780)460-2003
Co. E-mail: mphillips@teamfocus.org
URL: http://www.teamfocus.org
Contact: Scot McClintock, Director
E-mail: smcclintock@teamfocus.org
Scope: An international consultancy group, specializing in the field of value and risk management, including project management, partnering and team alignment. Services include business program refocusing, strategy formulation, program planning, project definition, decision analysis, risk management, and team building. **Publications:** "VE Using Project Performance Criteria & Measures". **Seminars:** Sharpening The Performance Edge: Project Delivery Enhancement Through Value Assurance, Nov, 2003; Results Oriented Performance Using The Project Performance Enhancement Approach, Jun, 2002; Value Is In The Eye Of The Beholder, Part 1: A Framework For Smart Project Development And Service Enhancement, May, 2002; Accredited SAVE International Module I Basic Training Seminars; Team Building and Partnering training; Advanced Project Management training; Accredited SAVE International Module I Basic Training Seminars; Value Management Training Workshop; Risk Management Training Workshop.

38816 ■ Trendzitions Inc.
25691 Atlantic Ocean, Ste. B13
Lake Forest, CA 92630-8842
Ph: (949)727-9100
Free: 800-266-2767
Fax: (949)727-3444
Co. E-mail: ctooker@trendzitions.com
URL: http://www.trendzitions.com
Contact: Christian Tooker, President
E-mail: ctooker@trendzitions.com
Scope: Provider of services in the areas of communications consulting, project management, construction management, and furniture procurement. Offers information on spatial uses, building codes, ADA compliance and city ordinances. Also offers budget projections. **Founded:** 1986.

38817 ■ Turnaround Inc.
3415 A St. NW
Gig Harbor, WA 98335
Ph: (253)857-6730
Fax: (253)857-6344
Co. E-mail: info@turnround-inc.com
URL: http://www.turnaround-inc.com
Contact: Miles Stover, President
E-mail: mstover@turnaround-inc.com
Scope: Provider of interim executive management assistance and management advisory to small, medium and family-owned businesses that are not meeting their goals. Services include acting as an interim executive or on-site manager. Extensive practices in arena of bankruptcy management. **Founded:** 1997. **Publications:** "How to Identify Problem and Promising Management"; "How to Tell if Your Company is a Bankruptcy Candidate"; "Signs that Your Company is in Trouble"; "The Turnaround Specialist: How to File a Petition Under 11 USC 11". **Seminars:** Competitive Intelligence Gathering.

38818 ■ TWD & Associates—Thomas W. Dooley & Associates
431 S Patton Ave.
Arlington Heights, IL 60005-2253
Ph: (847)398-6410
Fax: (847)255-5095
Co. E-mail: tdoo@aol.com
Contact: Thomas W. Dooley, President
E-mail: twhdoo@yahoo.com
Scope: Consulting specialists in small business management particularly in the areas of personnel, training, marketing, franchising, sales, time management, budgeting, raising capital, and long-range planning. **Founded:** 1976. **Seminars:** Alternative Methods of Financing for Franchising; Effectiveness of Organizational Development Training Programs for Hourly-Hire Workers in Manufacturing Plants. **Special Services:** ABR®.

38819 ■ Tweed-Weber Inc. (TWI)
117 N 5th St.
Reading, PA 19601
Ph: (610)376-6615
Free: 800-999-6615
Fax: (610)376-9161
Co. E-mail: mail@tweedweber.com
URL: http://www.tweedweber.com
Contact: Alfred J. Weber, President
E-mail: alweber@tweedweber.com
Scope: A consulting firm specializing in customized market research and strategic planning. Expertise in strategic planning research and conducts customer satisfaction surveys; employee satisfaction surveys; market assessment customer satisfaction surveys. **Founded:** 1979.

38820 ■ ValueNomics Value Specialists
50 W San Fernando St., Ste. 600
San Jose, CA 95113
Fax: (408)200-6401
Co. E-mail: info@amllp.com
Contact: Gary E. Jones, Chief Executive Officer
Scope: Consulting is offered in the areas of financial management, process re-engineering, growth business services; governance, risk/compliance, SOX readiness and compliance, SAS 70, enterprise risk management, system security, operational and internal audit; business advisory services; valuation services; CORE assessment; contract assurance; transaction advisory services, IT solutions and litigation support services. **Founded:** 1993. **Publications:** "Dueling Appraisers: How Differences in Input and Assumptions May Control the Value," Apr, 2005; "The Business of Business Valuation and the CPA as an expert witness"; "The Business of Business Valuation," McGraw-Hill Professional Publishers Inc.

38821 ■ VenturEdge Corp.
4711 Yonge St., Ste. 1105
Toronto, ON, Canada M2N 6K8
Ph: (416)224-2000
Fax: (416)224-2376
Co. E-mail: info@venturedge.com
URL: http://www.venturedge.com
Contact: Morris Langer, President
E-mail: langer@venturedge.com
Scope: Provides services including strategy formulation; business planning; financial management; business coaching; performance improvement; information management; merger, acquisitions and divestitures; family succession planning; competitive intelligence. **Founded:** 1972. **Publications:** "Reputation," Harvard Business School Press, 1996; "Competing for the Future," Harvard Business School Press, 1994; "The Fifth Discipline," 1990.

38822 ■ Verbit & Co.
19 Bala Ave.
Bala Cynwyd, PA 19004-3202
Ph: (610)668-9840
Co. E-mail: verbitcompany@earthlink.net
Contact: Alan C. Verbit, President
Scope: Management consulting firm to assist executives and managers fulfill their mission and to assure that adequate planning of day-to-day operations occurs; that controls sufficient to safeguard valuable resources; and that results of decisions reviewed in sufficient time to effect continuing action. Financial planning and control-to develop accounting, budgeting, forecasting and other information systems for the management of resources and evaluation of strategies. Services also include: Evaluation of desk-top computer systems for small firms; CAD/CAM implementation plan and orderly introduction of CAD/CAM. Industries served: manufacturing, distribution, metals casting, equipment and components, professional services, health care, retail, nonprofit and government. **Founded:** 1981. **Seminars:** Integrating Manufacturing Management Systems with Business Systems; Negotiating Information Systems Agreements with Suppliers.

38823 ■ Via Nova Consulting
1228 Winburn Dr.
Atlanta, GA 30344
Ph: (404)761-7484
Fax: (404)762-7123
Scope: Consulting services in the areas of strategic planning; privatization; executive searches; market research; customer service audits; new product development; competitive intelligence; and Total Quality Management (TQM). **Founded:** 1994.

38824 ■ VIE Partners Inc. (VIE)
1973 Rte. 34, Ste. E-11
Wall, NJ 07719
Ph: (732)988-1066
Free: 888-484-3332
Fax: (732)988-4989
Co. E-mail: info@viepartners.com
URL: http://www.viepartners.com
Contact: Lisa T. Miller, President
E-mail: lmiller@viepartners.com
Scope: Expense management solutions firm specializing in expense analysis and review, procurement

strategies, revenue improvement techniques, and cost reduction strategies.

38825 ■ Vision Management
149 Meadows Rd.
Lafayette, NJ 07848-3120
Ph: (973)702-1116
Fax: (973)702-8311
Contact: Norman L. Naidish, President
Scope: Firm specializes in profit enhancement; strategic planning; business process reengineering; industrial engineering; facilities planning; team building; inventory management; and total quality management (TQM). **Founded:** 1984. **Publications:** "To increase profits, improve quality," Manufacturing Engineering, May, 2000.

38826 ■ Weich & Bilotti Inc.
600 Worcester Rd., 4th Fl.
Framingham, MA 01702
Ph: (508)663-1600
Fax: (508)663-1682
Co. E-mail: info@weich-bilotti.com
Contact: Mervyn D. Weich, Director
E-mail: mweich@weich-bilotti.com
Scope: Specializes in business plans, venture capital, computer information systems, turnaround/interim management, retail consulting, start-up process, college recruiting and IS and IT personnel. **Founded:** 1995.

38827 ■ Western Business Services Ltd.
1269 Lindsay St.
Regina, SK, Canada S4N 3B4
Ph: (306)522-1493
Fax: (306)522-9076
Contact: O'Neil Zuck, President
Scope: Provides marketing, financial and accounting services to individuals, on-profit organizations and commercial companies. **Founded:** 1992.

38828 ■ Westlife Consultants & Counsellors
95 October Ln.
Aurora, ON, Canada L4G 7A1
Ph: (905)867-0686
Fax: (416)799-5242
Co. E-mail: westlifeconsultant@hotmail.com
URL: http://www.westlifeconsultants.com
Contact: Dr. Syed N. Hussain, President
E-mail: westlifeconsultant@hotmail.com
Scope: Provider of entrepreneurs and businesses with a highly commercial and global perspectives on the international business development ideas under consideration. **Founded:** 1990. **Publications:** "Innovative Management"; "Team Building and Leadership"; "Financial Planning"; "Estate Planning"; "Risk Management"; "Export/Import Trade Finance Mechanics"; "Marketing and Sales Management"; "What Your Banker Needs to Know"; "Building A Successful Financial Plan".

38829 ■ What Makes You Smile
3552 Vancouver Ave.
San Diego, CA 92104-3822
Ph: (619)665-1432
Free: 888-787-0419
Co. E-mail: ginalinn.espinoza@gmail.com
URL: http://www.doctoralove.com
Contact: Gina Linn Espinoza-Price, President
E-mail: gina@whatmakesyousmile.com
Scope: Personal success coaching and life skill training. One on one, group seminars, critical thinking with executives, CEOs and business owners. **Founded:** 1997. **Seminars:** What Makes You Smile?; Smile Files, Have you left your distinctive mark on the world today?; Brainstorms For Sale, Is the Customer Always Right?; Make the best of your given talent; A smile is a lifetime of balance. **Telecommunication Services:** gina@doctoralove.com.

38830 ■ Wheeler and Young Inc.
33 Peter St.
Markham, ON, Canada L3P 2A5
Ph: (905)471-5709
Fax: (905)471-9989
Co. E-mail: wheeler@ericwheeler.ca
URL: http://www.ericwheeler.ca
Contact: Eric S. Wheeler, Managing Partner
E-mail: ewheeler@yorku.ca
Scope: Provider of consulting services to high-tech companies on the implementation of software development processes; quality management systems (including ISO 9000 compliance) and business management systems. Offers business management and knowledge-management services to organizations. Industries served: Knowledge-based industries, including software and hardware development, medical and legal professionals, information service providers. **Founded:** 1994.

38831 ■ Donald C. Wright CPA
3906 Lawndale Ln. N
Plymouth, MN 55446-2940
Ph: (763)478-6999
Co. E-mail: donaldwright@compuserve.com
URL: http://www.donaldwrightcpa.com
Contact: Donald C. Wright, President
E-mail: donaldwright@compuserve.com
Scope: Offers accounting, tax, and small business consulting services. Services include cash flow and budgeting analysis; financial forecast and projections; financial statements; reviews and compilations; tax planning, tax preparation; IRS and state/local representation; international taxation; estate, gift and trust tax return preparation; benefit plan services; business succession planning; estate planning; financial planning; management advisory services, pension and profit sharing plans, retirement planning, expert witness services and employee benefits plans. Serves individuals, corporations, partnerships, and non-profit organizations. **Founded:** 1968. **Seminars:** Qualified pension plans and employee welfare benefit plans.

38832 ■ Bruce D. Wyman Co.
6147 Poburn Landing Ct.
Burke, VA 22015-2535
Ph: (703)503-9753
Fax: (703)503-2091
Co. E-mail: bdwyman@bdwyman.com
URL: http://www.bdwyman.com
Contact: Bruce D. Wyman, President
E-mail: bdwyman@bdwyman.com
Scope: Provider of strategic business planning services to aid small and micro for-profit and nonprofit businesses and associations in identifying and handling challenges and opportunities in an environment of incomplete information. Services include business environmental scanning; mission, goal, and strategy identification and development; and development of integrated implementation plans to convert intentions into actions. Provide training in quality management tools, processes, and applications, as well as ASQ certification examination preparation. Industries served: All industries, with special emphasis on smaller firms and associations including micro businesses. **Founded:** 1988. **Publications:** "A New Acquisition Reform Culture for the Air Force," Program Manager, Feb, 1999. **Seminars:** The Best of Both Worlds: Combining Equity 3 and Integer Programming to Allocate Resources, Oct, 2004; Implementing Massive Change: Coordination, Communication, and Campaign Management, May, 2000; Strategic Business Planning for Small and Micro Businesses and Associations; quality management and processes consulting and training (CQMgr. and CQIA).

FRANCHISES AND BUSINESS OPPORTUNITIES

38833 ■ LMI Canada Inc.
205 Matheson Blvd. E, Unit 15
Mississauga, ON, Canada L4Z 3E3
Ph: (905)890-0504
Free: 877-857-4083
Co. E-mail: info@lmicanada.ca
URL: http://www.lmicanada.ca
Description: The franchise is a well-known personal, organizational and management development company, which enhances performance, productivity and profitability of their companies. **No. of Franchise Units:** 10. **No. of Company-Owned Units:** 1. **Founded:** 1980.. **Franchised:** 1998. **Franchise Fee:** $38,000. **Training:** Initial and ongoing support provided.

COMPUTERIZED DATABASES

38834 ■ *Corporate Governance Library®*
1801 S Bell St.
Arlington, VA 22202
Free: 800-372-1033
Co. E-mail: customercare@bna.com
URL: http://www.bna.com
Availability: Online: Bloomberg LP-Bloomberg BNA. **Type:** Full-text.

38835 ■ *Leadership and Management in Engineering*
1801 Alexander Bell Dr.
Reston, VA 20191-4400
Ph: (703)295-6300
Free: 800-548-2723
Fax: (703)295-6222
Co. E-mail: aei@asce.org
URL: http://content.aeinstitute.org
Contact: D. Wayne Klotz, President
Availability: Online: American Society of Civil Engineers-Architectural Engineering Institute. **Type:** Full-text.

38836 ■ *Stern's Management Review*
11260 Overland Ave., Ste. 16A
Culver City, CA 90230
Ph: (310)838-0551
Free: 800-773-0029
Fax: (310)838-2344
Co. E-mail: info@hrconsultant.com
URL: http://www.hrconsultant.com
Contact: Charlotte Page, Chief Executive Officer
Availability: Online: Stern & Associates. **Type:** Full-text.

LIBRARIES

38837 ■ Boston University - Frederick S. Pardee Management Library
595 Commonwealth Ave.
Boston, MA 02215
Ph: (617)353-4301
Fax: (617)353-4307
Co. E-mail: ajac@bu.edu
URL: http://www.bu.edu/library/management/
Contact: Arlyne A. Jackson, Director, Library Services
Scope: Management and management-related fields, healthcare management, public management, nonprofit management. **Services:** Library open to the public. **Founded:** 1997. **Holdings:** over 25,000 e-subscriptions (journals and databases); 91,541 volumes; 333,500 microforms. **Subscriptions:** 2357 journals and other serials.

38838 ■ Business Development Bank of Canada Research & Information Centre
5 Place Ville Marie, Ste. 300
Montreal, QC, Canada H3B 5E7
Ph: (514)283-7632
Free: 877-232-2269
Fax: (514)283-2304
URL: http://www.bdc.ca
Contact: Odette Lavoie, Specialist
Scope: Small business, management, Canadian business and industry, banking and finance, development banking. **Services:** Interlibrary loan; Library not open to the public. **Founded:** 1977. **Holdings:** 5000 books. **Subscriptions:** 100 journals and other serials; 7 newspapers.

38839 ■ Canada School of Public Service Library
373, Sussex Promenade
Ottawa, ON, Canada K1N 6Z2
Ph: (819)934-7702
Free: 866-703-9598

Fax: (819)953-1702
Co. E-mail: bibliast@csps-efpc.gc.ca
URL: http://www.csps-efpc.gc.ca/index-eng.asp
Contact: Darlene Nadeau, Director, Information Services
Scope: Management, government, public administration, coaching, leadership, diversity, language, training. **Services:** Interlibrary loan; copying; library open to public. **Founded:** 1990. **Holdings:** 10,000 books; 450 videos. **Subscriptions:** 65 serials. **Telecommunication Services:** publications@csps-efpc.gc.ca; info@csps-efpc.gc.ca.

38840 ■ Carnegie Library of Pittsburgh - Downtown & Business
612 Smithfield St.
Pittsburgh, PA 15222-2506
Ph: (412)281-7141
Fax: (412)471-1724
Co. E-mail: downtown@carnegielibrary.org
URL: http://www.carnegielibrary.org/locations/downtown
Contact: Karen Rossi, Department Head
Scope: Investments, small business, entrepreneurship, management, marketing, insurance, advertising, personal finance, accounting, real estate, job and career, International business. **Services:** Library open to the public. **Founded:** 1924. **Holdings:** 13,000 business volumes; VF materials; microfilm; looseleaf services; AV materials.

38841 ■ Chicago Public Library Central Library - Business/Science/Technology Division
Harold Washington Library Center
400 S. State St., 4th Fl.
Chicago, IL 60605
Ph: (312)747-4450
Fax: (312)747-4975
URL: http://www.chipublib.org/branch/details/library/harold-washington/p/Bst
Scope: Small business, marketing, technology, corporate reports, investments, management, personnel, patents, physical and biological sciences, medicine, health, computer science, careers, environmental information, gardening, cookbooks. **Services:** Interlibrary loan; copying; division open to the public. **Founded:** 1977. **Holdings:** 415,000 books; 52,100 bound periodical volumes; 33,000 reels of microfilm; Securities and Exchange Commission (SEC) reports; federal specifications and standards; American National Standards Institute standards; corporate Annual reports. **Subscriptions:** 4000 journals and other serials; 8 newspapers.

38842 ■ Comenius University - Faculty of Management Library
Odbojarov 10
820 05 Bratislava, Slovakia
Ph: 421 2 50117526
Fax: 421 2 50117527
Co. E-mail: sd@fm.uniba.sk
URL: http://www.fm.uniba.sk
Contact: Lydia Lackovicova, Director
Scope: Management. **Holdings:** 11,000 books.

38843 ■ Lappeenranta University of Technology Library—Lappeenrannan teknillinen yliopisto.
PO Box 20
FIN-53851 Lappeenranta, Finland
Ph: 358 5 294462111
Fax: 358 5 6212349
Co. E-mail: kirjasto@lut.fi
URL: http://www.lut.fi/en/library/Pages/Default.aspx
Contact: Anja Ukkola, Director, Library Services
Scope: Engineering, economics, management. **Founded:** 1969. **Holdings:** Books; journals.

38844 ■ Michigan Financial Independence Agency - Office of Training and Staff Development - Resource Library
Grand Tower, Ste. 301
235 S. Grand Ave.
Lansing, MI 48909
Ph: (517)335-4698
Fax: (517)241-7041
Contact: Ron Walters
Scope: Management, supervision, self-development. **Services:** Library open to governmental units, private children's agencies and private contractors. **Founded:** 1985. **Holdings:** 350 videotapes; 150 audiocassettes; 100 book summaries.

38845 ■ Nichols College - Conant Library
124 Center Rd.
Dudley, MA 01571
Ph: (508)213-2333
Free: 800-470-3379
Co. E-mail: reference@nichols.edu
URL: http://www.nichols.edu/academics/academics/Library
Contact: Jim Douglas, Director, Library Services
Scope: Management, advertising, finance and accounting, small business, marketing, taxation, economics, International trade, humanities. **Services:** Interlibrary loan; copying; information service to groups; document delivery; library open to Dudley and Webster residents. **Founded:** 1962. **Holdings:** 48,000 volumes; 1677 audio/visual titles; 3804 reels of microfilm. **Subscriptions:** 278 journals and electronic subscriptions. **Telecommunication Services:** jim.douglas@nichols.edu.

38846 ■ Ontario Ministry of Economic Development and Trade - InfoSource
900 Bay St.
Hearst Block, 8th Fl.
Toronto, ON, Canada M7A 2E1
Ph: (416)325-6666
Fax: (416)325-6688
Co. E-mail: info@edt.gov.on.ca
URL: http://www.ontariocanada.com/ontcan/1medt/en/home_en.jsp
Scope: Trade, industry, small business, management, company information, economic development. **Services:** Copying; scanning. **Founded:** 1994. **Holdings:** 200 books; microfiche; 20 CD-ROMs.

38847 ■ Southeastern University Library
501 I St., SW
Washington, DC 20024
Ph: (202)478-8225
Fax: (202)488-8093
Co. E-mail: library@seu.edu
URL: http://www.seuniversity.edu/library
Scope: Science, technology, humanities, health, social sciences. **Services:** Interlibrary loan; library open to the public. **Founded:** 1879. **Holdings:** 50,000 books.

38848 ■ Strategic Decisions Group Information Center
745 Emerson St.
Palo Alto, CA 94301
Ph: (650)475-4400
Fax: (650)854-6718
URL: http://www.sdg.com
Contact: Carl Spetzler, Chief Executive Officer
Scope: Business, management. **Services:** Interlibrary loan; copying; SDI; library open to the public at librarian's discretion. **Founded:** 1986. **Holdings:** 700 books. **Subscriptions:** 120 journals and other serials; 5 newspapers.

38849 ■ Touro College - Lander College for Men Library
75-31 150th St.
Kew Gardens Hills, NY 11367
Ph: (718)820-4894
Fax: (718)495-3824
Co. E-mail: joan.wagner2@touro.edu
URL: http://www.tourolib.org/about/libraries/kew-gardens-hills
Contact: Debora Duerksen, Librarian
Scope: Biology, business, computer science, management information science, political science, psychology, social sciences, Judaica. **Services:** Interlibrary loan; copying; library open to college staff and students. **Holdings:** Books; diskettes; audio and video tapes; CD-ROMs; DVDs; microfiche. **Telecommunication Services:** irene.cherry@touro.edu.

38850 ■ University of Gloucestershire - Learning and Information Services - Park Learning Centre
The Park
Cheltenham GL50 2RH, United Kingdom
Ph: 44 1242 714555
Co. E-mail: nquinton@glos.ac.uk
URL: http://insight.glos.ac.uk/departments/lis/lc/Pages/pklc.aspx
Contact: Neil Quinton, Assistant Manager
Scope: Business and management, computing, hospitality and tourism management, languages, information technology law, leisure, multimedia. **Holdings:** Books; journals. **Telecommunication Services:** librarypark@glos.ac.uk.

38851 ■ University of Massachusetts at Lowell - Lydon Library
North Campus
84 University Ave.
Lowell, MA 01854
Ph: (978)934-3205
Co. E-mail: margaret_manion@uml.edu
URL: http://libweb.uml.edu/Lydon.html
Contact: Margaret Manion, Librarian, Reference
Scope: Business, management, engineering, science. **Holdings:** Figures not available.

38852 ■ University of Southern Maine - Lewiston-Auburn College Library
51 Westminster St.
Lewiston, ME 04240
Ph: (207)753-6546
Fax: (207)753-6543
Co. E-mail: evelyng@usm.maine.edu
URL: http://library.usm.maine.edu/about/lac/index.php
Contact: Maureen Perry, Librarian, Reference
Scope: Social and behavioral studies, leadership, management, organizational studies, occupational therapy, nursing. **Services:** Interlibrary loan; Library open to the public. **Holdings:** 16,000 volumes; 450 videocassettes. **Subscriptions:** 200 journals and other serials. **Telecommunication Services:** libraryweb@usm.maine.edu.

38853 ■ US West Communications - Learning Systems/Employee Development Library
2626 W. Evans Ave.
Denver, CO 80219-5506
Ph: (303)763-1252
Fax: (303)985-6496
Contact: Gaylene Pepion, Librarian
Scope: Communications, management, economics, adult education, pluralism, computer technology. **Founded:** 1976. **Holdings:** 3000 books; Bell Company Practices; Bell technical journals. **Subscriptions:** 40 journals and other serials.

38854 ■ Woodbury University Library
7500 Glenoaks Blvd.
Burbank, CA 91504-1052
Ph: (818)252-5201
Fax: (818)767-4534
Co. E-mail: jennifer.rosenfeld@woodbury.edu
URL: http://library.woodbury.edu
Contact: Nedra Peterson, Director
Scope: Business and management, International business, art, architecture, interior design, fashion marketing and design, psychology, animation. **Services:** Interlibrary loan; copying; Library open to the public for reference use only. **Founded:** 1884. **Holdings:** 65,000 books; 3070 bound periodical volumes; 17,401 slides; 2000 DVD/VHS. **Subscriptions:** 300 journals and other serials; 5 newspapers. **Telecommunication Services:** nedra.peterson@woodbury.edu.

RESEARCH CENTERS

38855 ■ Bradley University - Center for Executive and Professional Development (CEPD)
Foster College of Business
1501 W Bradley Ave.
Peoria, IL 61625
Ph: (309)677-2253

Fax: (309)677-3374
Co. E-mail: aliberty@bradley.edu
URL: http://www.bradley.edu/fcba/community/cepd/index.shtml
Contact: Angie Liberty, Executive Director
Founded: 1991. **Educational Activities:** Customized workshops, to meet specific needs of businesses; Public seminars, on current business topics.

38856 ■ The Conference Board (TCB)
845 3rd Ave.
New York, NY 10022
Ph: (212)759-0900
Fax: (212)980-7014
Co. E-mail: nick.sutcliffe@conference-board.org
URL: http://www.conference-board.org
Contact: Jonathan Spector, Chief Executive Officer
Description: Corporations, government agencies, libraries, colleges, and universities. Fact-finding institution that conducts research and publishes studies on business economics and management experience. Holds more than 100 conferences, council meetings, and seminars per year in the U.S., Asia, and Europe where members exchange ideas and keep abreast of business trends and developments. Makes research available to secondary schools, colleges, and universities at minimum cost. Disseminates research data to the public. **Scope:** business operations, economics. **Founded:** 1916. **Subscriptions:** 6000 books periodicals. **Publications:** *Top Executive Compensation*; *The Conference Board Review* (Quarterly); *Consumer Confidence Survey* (Monthly); *International Economic Scoreboard*; *Across the Board*; *Business cycle indicators* (Monthly); *The Conference Board Review* (Bimonthly); *Consumer Confidence Survey* (Monthly); *E-mail Express* (Monthly); *Executive Action Series*; *The Conference Board, Inc. Research reports*; *StraightTalk* (10/year); *The Corporate Contributions Plan: From Strategy to Budget*; *HR Executive Review* (Quarterly); *Conference Board Briefing Charts* (Quarterly); *Multinational Register & Global Business Briefing*. **Educational Activities:** The Conference Board, Inc. Conferences; Forums and seminars on selected topics of business, professional, and academic interest.

38857 ■ Kansas State University - Center for Leadership
110 Calvin Hall
Department of Management
College of Business Administration
Manhattan, KS 66502
Ph: (785)532-7451
Fax: (785)532-1339
Co. E-mail: thomaswr@k-state.edu
Contact: Dr. Thomas Wright, Director
Founded: 1989. **Educational Activities:** Panel discussions, workshops, conferences, and seminars. **Awards:** Kauffman Internship in Entrepreneurism.

38858 ■ Organization Development Institute
11234 Walnut Ridge Rd.
Chesterland, OH 44026-1240
Ph: (440)729-7419
Fax: (440)729-9319
Co. E-mail: donwcole@aol.com
URL: http://www.odinstitute.org
Contact: Dr. Donald W. Cole, President
Services: Consulting. **Founded:** 1968. **Publications:** *Nonviolent Change Newsletter* (3/year); *Organization Development Journal* (Quarterly); *Organizations and Change* (Monthly); *International Registry of OD Professionals and the OD Handbook* (Annual). **Educational Activities:** Annual International Congress; Workshops for behavioral scientists and other interested parties; What's New in Organization Development and Human Resources Development Conference (Annual), in May; International, interorganizational, interdisciplinary Research/Study Team on Nonviolent Large Systems Change Meetings, in May. **Awards:** Jack Gibb Award, for the best presentation at the Annual Information Exchange, in the amount of $1000; Outstanding Organization Development Article of the Year; Outstanding Organization Development Project of the Year; Outstanding Organizational Development Consultant of the Year Award.

38859 ■ University of British Columbia - Centre for Operations Excellence (COE)
Sauder School of Business
2053 Main Mall
Vancouver, BC, Canada V6T 1Z2
Ph: (604)822-1800
Fax: (604)822-1544
Co. E-mail: info@coe.ubc.ca
URL: http://www.sauder.ubc.ca/coe
Contact: Annie Ko, Program Manager
Services: Industry Partners Program: partnership with leading companies to formulate and solve operations research problems using advanced management science methods (10/year). **Founded:** 1998.

START-UP INFORMATION

38860 ■ *Mommy Millionaire: How I Turned My Kitchen Table Idea Into a Million Dollars and How You Can, Too!*
Pub: St. Martin's Press LLC
Ed: Kim Lavine. **Released:** February 19, 2008. **Price:** $14.95. **Description:** Advice, secrets and lessons for making a million dollars from a mom who turned her kitchen into a successful business; tools cover developing and patenting an idea, cold calling, trade shows, QVC, big retailers, manufacturing, and raising venture capital.

38861 ■ *"The Ultimate Cure" in Conde Nast Portfolio (Vol. 2, June 2008, No. 6, pp. 110)*
Pub: Conde Nast Publications
Contact: David Carey, President
Ed: David Ewing Duncan. **Description:** Small upstarts as well as pharmaceutical giants are developing drugs for the neurotechnology industry; these firms are attempting to adapt groundbreaking research into the basic workings of the brain to new drugs for ailments ranging from multiple sclerosis to dementia to insomnia.

38862 ■ *"Well-Heeled Startup" in Business Journal Portland (Vol. 27, November 12, 2010, No. 37, pp. 1)*
Pub: Portland Business Journal
Ed: Erik Siemers. **Description:** Oh! Shoes LLC expects to receive about $1.5 million in funding from angel investors, while marketing a new line of high heel shoes that are comfortable, healthy, and attractive. The new line of shoes will use the technology of athletic footwear while having the look of an Italian designer. Oh! Shoes hopes to generate $35 million in sales by 2014.

ASSOCIATIONS AND OTHER ORGANIZATIONS

38863 ■ CAMUS International
c/o Terry Simpkins, Sec.-Treas.
45738 Northport Loop W
Fremont, CA 94538
Ph: (757)766-4559
Co. E-mail: info@camus.org
URL: http://www.camus.org
Contact: Terri Glendon Lanza, President
Description: Provides forum for manufacturing application users to interact with and learn from each other.

38864 ■ Canadian Plastics Industry Association (CPIA)—Association Canadienne de l'industrie des Plastiques
5955 Airport Rd., Ste. 125
Mississauga, ON, Canada L4V 1R9
Ph: (905)678-7748
Fax: (905)678-0774
URL: http://www.cpia.ca
Contact: Carol Hochu, President
Description: Plastics manufacturers, distributors, importers, and exporters in Canada. Encourages research and development programs. Represents and defends members' interests. **Founded:** 1942.

38865 ■ Canadian Tooling and Machining Association (CTMA)
140 McGovern Dr., Unit 3
Cambridge, ON, Canada N3H 4R7
Ph: (519)653-7265
Fax: (519)653-6764
Co. E-mail: info@ctma.com
URL: http://ctma.com
Contact: David Glover, President
Description: Aims to represent Canadian tooling manufacturing at all levels of governments, their departments, and agencies. **Founded:** 1963. **Publications:** *CTMA View*.

38866 ■ *CTMA View*
140 McGovern Dr., Unit 3
Cambridge, ON, Canada N3H 4R7
Ph: (519)653-7265
Fax: (519)653-6764
Co. E-mail: info@ctma.com
URL: http://ctma.com
Contact: David Glover, President

38867 ■ Forest Products Association of Canada (FPAC)—Association des Produits Forestiers du CanadaPublic Safety and Emergency Preparedness;
99 Bank St., Ste. 410
Ottawa, ON, Canada K1P 6B9
Ph: (613)563-1441
Fax: (613)563-4720
Co. E-mail: ottawa@fpac.ca
URL: http://www.fpac.ca/index.php/en/
Contact: Catherine Cobden, President
E-mail: ccobden@fpac.ca
URL(s): www.fpac.ca. **Description:** Forest products manufacturers. Lobbies government on legislation, taxation, and other policy matters. **Founded:** 1913. **Publications:** *Forest Products Association of Canada--Membership Directory*. **Educational Activities:** Paperweek (Annual); Paperweek (Annual).

38868 ■ LTD Shippers Association (LTD)
1230 Pottstown Pike, Ste. 6
Glenmoore, PA 19343
Ph: (610)458-3636
Fax: (610)458-8039
Co. E-mail: tomltd@aol.com
URL: http://www.ltdmgmt.com
Contact: Tom Craig, President
Description: Works to leverage the buying power of the members for lower ocean freight prices. Has scope that includes ocean rates from Asia to United States, to Canada, Mexico, Puerto Rico and many other destinations; also rates to the U.S. and Canada from Brazil, the Mediterranean, India and other origins. Aims to design, develop, negotiate, implement and manage logistics or transportation programs for members. **Founded:** 1994.

38869 ■ Manufacturing Jewelers and Suppliers of America (MJSA)
57 John L. Dietsch Sq.
Attleboro Falls, MA 02763
Ph: (401)274-3840
Free: 800-444-6572
Fax: (401)274-0265
Co. E-mail: info@mjsa.org
URL: http://www.mjsa.org
Contact: Dave Meleski, Chairman
Description: Represents American manufacturers and suppliers within the jewelry industry. Seeks to foster long-term stability and prosperity of the jewelry industry. Provides leadership in government affairs and industry education. **Founded:** 1903. **Publications:** *Buyers Guide* (Biennial); *MJSA Journal* (Monthly). **Awards:** American Vision Award (Annual); Education Foundation Scholarship Award (Annual).

38870 ■ National Association of Manufacturers (NAM)
733 10th St. NW
Washington, DC 20001
Ph: (202)637-3000
Free: 800-814-8468
Fax: (202)637-3182
Co. E-mail: manufacturing@nam.org
URL: http://www.nam.org
Contact: Mary Vermeer Andringa, Chairman of the Board
Description: Manufacturers and cooperating nonmanufacturers having a direct interest in or relationship to manufacturing. Represents industry's views on national and international problems to government. Maintains public affairs and public relations programs. Reviews current and proposed legislation, administrative rulings and interpretations, judicial decisions and legal matters affecting industry. Maintains numerous policy groups: Human Resources Policy; Small and Medium Manufacturers; Tax Policy; Resources & Environmental Policy; Regulation and Legal Reform Policy; International Economic Affairs. Affiliated with 150 local and state trade associations of manufacturers through National Industrial Council and 250 manufacturing trade associations through the Associations Council. **Founded:** 1895. **Publications:** *NAM Member Focus* (Monthly).

38871 ■ National Council for Advanced Manufacturing (NACFAM)
2025 M St. NW, Ste. 800
Washington, DC 20036
Ph: (202)367-1178
Fax: (202)367-2178
Co. E-mail: pattersonr@nacfam.org
URL: http://www.nacfam.org
Contact: Rusty Patterson, Chief Executive Officer
Description: Companies, university centers, laboratories, and manufacturing extension services, national trade associations, and national technical education associations. Seeks to "enhance the productivity, quality and competitiveness of all tiers of the U.S. domestic industrial base." Organizes public and private technology research and development

projects; serves as a network linking members; conducts workforce skills standards development programs. **Founded:** 1989. **Publications:** *NACFAM Weekly* (Weekly).

EDUCATIONAL PROGRAMS

38872 ■ Advanced Electric Motor/Generator/Actuator Design and Analysis for Automotive Applications (Onsite)
Seminar Information Service, Inc.
20 Executive Park, Ste. 120
Irvine, CA 92614
Ph: (949)261-9104
Free: 877-SEM-INFO
Fax: (949)261-1963
Co. E-mail: info@seminarinformation.com
URL: http://www.seminarinformation.com
Price: Contact for fees. **Description:** Provide extensive details on design and analysis of electric motors/generators, actuators using state-of-the-art techniques, including the fundamentals of electromagnetism and basic electric machine equations will be presented along with examples. **Dates and Locations:** Troy, MI.

38873 ■ Automotive Glazing Materials (Onsite)
Seminar Information Service, Inc.
20 Executive Park, Ste. 120
Irvine, CA 92614
Ph: (949)261-9104
Free: 877-SEM-INFO
Fax: (949)261-1963
Co. E-mail: info@seminarinformation.com
URL: http://www.seminarinformation.com
Price: $1,225.00; $1,130.00 for Society of Automotive Engineers members. **Description:** An overview of the different automotive glazing materials, past, present and future, including the laws that govern their use, and manufacture, installation, usage, testing, safety aspects and how they affect automotive performance. Topics include the chemical, physical and design issues of annealed, laminated, tempered, glass-plastic and plastic glazing materials. **Dates and Locations:** Troy, MI.

38874 ■ Automotive Lighting (Onsite)
Seminar Information Service, Inc.
20 Executive Park, Ste. 120
Irvine, CA 92614
Ph: (949)261-9104
Free: 877-SEM-INFO
Fax: (949)261-1963
Co. E-mail: info@seminarinformation.com
URL: http://www.seminarinformation.com
Price: $1,155.00; $1,035.00 for Society of Automotive Engineers members. **Description:** Provides broad information about automotive lighting systems with emphasis on lighting functions, effectiveness, and technologies, including the legal aspects and implications related to automotive lighting and examine safety measurements used with lighting functions and human factors costs. **Dates and Locations:** Detroit, MI.

38875 ■ A Familiarization of Drivetrain Components (Onsite)
Seminar Information Service, Inc.
20 Executive Park, Ste. 120
Irvine, CA 92614
Ph: (949)261-9104
Free: 877-SEM-INFO
Fax: (949)261-1963
Co. E-mail: info@seminarinformation.com
URL: http://www.seminarinformation.com
Price: $1,345.00; $1,184.00 for Society of Automotive Engineers members. **Description:** Learn to visualize both individual components and the entire drivetrain system without reference to complicated equations, with focus on the terms, functions, nomenclature, operating characteristics and effect on vehicle performance for each of the drivetrain components. **Dates and Locations:** Troy, MI.

38876 ■ OSHA Compliance and Workplace Safety
Padgett-Thompson Seminars
Rockhurst University CEC
14502 W. 105th St.
Lenexa, KS 66215
Free: 800-349-1935
URL: http://www.findaseminar.com/tpd/Padgett-Thompson-Seminars.asp
Price: $199.00. **Description:** This workshop offers the cost-effective solutions to keep the workplace safe and the OSHA inspectors away. **Dates and Locations:** Cities throughout the United States.

DIRECTORIES OF EDUCATIONAL PROGRAMS

38877 ■ Scott's Directories: National Manufacturers
Pub: Scott's Directories
Contact: Rabiya Shaikh, Manager
E-mail: rshaikh@scottsdirectories.com
URL(s): www.scottsinfo.comwww.scottsdirectories.com. **Ed:** Barbara Peard. **Released:** Annual; February; latest edition 2007 edition. **Price:** $899, Individuals CD; pinpointer; $1799, Individuals CD; profiler; $3499, Individuals CD; prospector; $849, Individuals online; pinpointer; $1699, Individuals online; profiler; $3299, Individuals online; prospector. **Covers:** 58,000 manufacturers throughout Canada. **Entries include:** Company name, address, phone, fax, telex, names and titles of key personnel, number of employees, parent or subsidiary companies, North American Standard Industrial (NAICS) code, product, export interest, and year established.

REFERENCE WORKS

38878 ■ "$3 Million in Repairs Prep Cobo for Auto Show" in Crain's Detroit Business (Vol. 26, January 4, 2010, No. 1, pp. 1)
Pub: Crain Communications Inc.
Ed: Nancy Kaffer. **Description:** Overview of the six projects priced roughly at $3 million which were needed in order to host the North American International Auto Show; show organizers stated that the work was absolutely necessary to keep the show in the city of Detroit.

38879 ■ "$49M Defense Contracts Hits Austin" in Austin Business JournalInc. (Vol. 28, August 8, 2008, No. 21, pp. A1)
Pub: American City Business Journals
Ed: Laura Hipp. **Description:** BAE Systems PLC has landed a $49 million contract to build thermal cameras, which are expected to be installed on tanks in 2009 and 2010. BAE is expected to land other defense contracts and is likely to add employees in order to meet production demands.

38880 ■ "The 490 Made Chevy a Bargain Player" in Automotive News (Vol. 86, October 31, 2011, No. 6488, pp. S22)
Pub: Crain Communications Inc.
Ed: David Phillips. **Description:** The first Chevrolet with the 490 engine was sold in 1913, but it was too expensive for masses. In 1914 the carmaker launched a lower-priced H-series of cars competitively priced. Nameplates such as Corvette, Bel Air, Camaro and Silverado have defined Chevrolet through the years.

38881 ■ "1914 Proved to Be Key Year for Chevy" in Automotive News (Vol. 86, October 31, 2011, No. 6488, pp. S18)
Pub: Crain Communications Inc.
Ed: Jamie Lareau. **Description:** Chevy Bow Tie emblem was born in 1914, creating the brand's image that has carried through to current days.

38882 ■ "A123-Fisker Deal May Mean 540 Jobs" in Crain's Detroit Business (Vol. 26, January 18, 2010, No. 3, pp. 4)
Pub: Crain Communications Inc.
Ed: Dustin Walsh. **Description:** Manufacturing plants in Livonia and Romulous may be hiring up to 540 skilled workers due to a contract that was won by A123 Systems Inc. that will result in the company supplying lithium-ion batteries to Fisker Automotive Inc. to be used in their Karma plug-in hybrid electric vehicle.

38883 ■ "AAAFCO Unveils Pet Food Resource" in Feedstuffs (Vol. 83, August 29, 2011, No. 35, pp. 15)
Pub: Miller Publishing Company
Description: The Association of American Feed Control Officials has launched a Website called The Business of Pet Food, which will address frequently asked questions about U.S. regulatory requirements for pet food. The site serves as an initial reference for anyone wishing to start a pet food business because it provides information and guidance.

38884 ■ "ABB Could Still Engineer an Upside" in Barron's (Vol. 89, July 20, 2009, No. 29, pp. M6)
Pub: Dow Jones & Co., Inc.
Ed: Goran Mijuk. **Description:** Swiss engineering company ABB can remain profitable as its power transmission and distribution activities continue to generate earnings. The company is also benefiting from increased exposure in emerging markets.

38885 ■ "Abraxis Bets On Biotech Hub" in Business Journal-Serving Phoenix and the Valley of the Sun (Vol. 10, November 9, 2007, No. 28)
Pub: American City Business Journals, Inc.
Ed: Angela Gonzales. **Description:** Abraxis BioScience Inc. purchased a 200,000 square foot manufacturing facility in Phoenix, Arizona from Watson Pharmaceuticals Inc. The company has the technology to allow chemotherapy drugs to be injected directly into tumor cell membranes. A human protein, albumin is used to deliver the chemotherapy.

38886 ■ Achieving Planned Innovation: A Proven System for Creating Successful New Products and Services
Pub: Simon and Schuster
Ed: Frank R. Bacon. **Released:** August 2007. **Price:** $16.95. **Description:** Planned innovation is a disciplined and practical step-by-step sequence of procedures for reaching the intended destination point: successful products. This easy-to-read book explains the system along with an action-oriented program for continuous success in new-product innovations. Five steps outlined include: a disciplined reasoning process; lasting market orientation; proper selection criteria that reflect both strategic and tactical business objectives and goals along with dynamic matching of resources to present and future opportunities, and positive and negative requirements before making major expenditures; and proper organizational staffing. The author explains what to do and evaluating the potential of any new product or service, ranging from ventures in retail distribution to the manufacture of goods as diverse as bicycles, motorcycles, aerospace communication and navigation equipment, small business computers, food packaging, and medical products.

38887 ■ "Ad Firms Stew Over Lost Car Biz; Diversifying Business Is Uphill Battle" in Crain's Detroit Business (Vol. 23, July 30, 2007, No. 31)
Pub: Crain Communications, Inc.
Ed: Jean Halliday. **Description:** Struggling Detroit automakers are breaking their tradition of loyalty and moving their advertising accounts to agencies in Los Angeles, San Francisco, and Boston; This has Detroit's advertising community very worried.

38888 ■ "Adapt or Die" in Black Enterprise (Vol. 38, July 2008, No. 12, pp. 27)
Pub: Earl G. Graves Publishing Co. Inc.
Ed: Oguntoyinbo Lekan. **Description:** Turbulence in the domestic auto industry is hitting auto suppliers hard and black suppliers, the majority of whom contract with the Big Three, are just beginning to establish relationships with import car manufacturers. The more savvy CEOs are adopting new technologies in order to weather the downturn in the economy and in the industry as a whole.

38889 ■ *"AdvacePierre Heats Up" in Business Courier (Vol. 27, October 29, 2010, No. 26, pp. 1)*
Pub: Business Courier
Ed: John Newberry. **Description:** Bill Toler, chief executive officer of AdvancePierre Foods, is aiming for more growth and more jobs. The company was formed after the merger of Pierre Foods with two Oklahoma-based food processing companies. Toler wants to expand production and is set to start adding employees in the next 6-12 months.

38890 ■ *"Aeronautics Seeking New HQ Site" in The Business Journal-Milwaukee (Vol. 25, September 5, 2008, No. 50, pp. 1)*
Pub: American City Business Journals, Inc.
Ed: Rich Kirchen. **Description:** Milwaukee, Wisconsin-based Aeronautics Corp. of America is planning to move its headquarters to a new site. The company has started to search for a new site. It also plans to consolidate its operations under one roof.

38891 ■ *"After Price Cuts, Competition GPS Makers Lose Direction" in Brandweek (Vol. 49, April 21, 2008, No. 16, pp. 16)*
Pub: VNU Business Media, Inc.
Ed: Steve Miller. **Description:** Garmin and TomTom, two of the leaders in portable navigation devices, have seen lowering revenues due to dramatic price cuts and unexpected competition from the broadening availability of personal navigation on mobile phones. TomTom has trimmed its sales outlook for its first quarter while Garmin's stock dropped 40 percent since February.

38892 ■ *"Aircraft Maker May Land Here" in Austin Business Journal (Vol. 31, April 15, 2011, No. 6, pp. 1)*
Pub: American City Business Journals Inc.
Ed: Jacob Dirr. **Description:** Icon Aircraft Inc. is planning to build a manufacturing facility in Austin, Texas. The company needs 100,000 square feet of space in a new or renovated plant. Executive comments are included.

38893 ■ *"Airing It Out" in The Business Journal-Serving Greater Tampa Bay (Vol. 28, July 11, 2008, No. 29, pp. 1)*
Pub: American City Business Journals, Inc.
Ed: Jane Meinhardt. **Description:** Flanders Corp. is planning to expand its business in Europe and Southeast Asia. The St. Petersburg, Florida-based company has about 2,800 employees and manufactures air filtration products for industrial and residential applications.

38894 ■ *Alaska Industrial Directory*
Pub: Harris InfoSource
Contact: Dennis Abrahams, President
E-mail: dennisa@harrisinfo.com
URL(s): www.harrisinfo.com. **Released:** Annual; latest edition 2010. **Price:** $495, Individuals Online. **Covers:** 6,200 manufacturing companies in Alaska. **Entries include:** Company name, address, county, phone, fax, web site address (on CD-ROM only), number of employees, names and titles of key executives, plant size, year established, parent company, annual sales, import/export information, Standard Industrial Classification (SIC) code, and product description. **Database includes:** Statistical data, trade show calendar. **Arrangement:** Geographical. **Indexes:** Geographical, alphabetical, SIC code, product.

38895 ■ *"Alberta's Runaway Train" in Canadian Business (Vol. 80, December 25, 2006, No. 1, pp. 17)*
Pub: Rogers Media
Ed: Andrew Nikiforuk. **Description:** The high revenue brought about by the growth in the number of oil sand plants in Canada and the simultaneous burden on infrastructure and housing is discussed.

38896 ■ *"Algoma Shares Soar on Growing Sale Rumors" in Globe & Mail (February 13, 2007, pp. B1)*
Pub: CTVglobemedia Publishing Inc.
Ed: Andrew Willis; Greg Keenan. **Description:** The stock prices of Algoma Steel Inc. have touched record high of $40 on the Toronto Stock Exchange. The growing rumors about the possible takeover bid is the major reason for the stock price growth.

38897 ■ *"All Options Open On Chrysler: Magna" in Globe & Mail (February 28, 2007, pp. B3)*
Pub: CTVglobemedia Publishing Inc.
Ed: Greg Keenan. **Description:** The 65 percent drop in the profits of Magna International Inc. and the plans of its chief executive officer Don Walker to make the company more competitive are discussed.

38898 ■ *"Alstom Launches te ECO 122 - 2.7MW Wind Turbine for Low Wind Sites" in CNW Group (September 28, 2011)*
Pub: CNW Group
Contact: Carolyn McGill-Davidson, President
Description: Alstom is launching its new ECO 122, a 2.7MW onshore wind turbine that combines high power and high capacity factor (1) to boost energy yield in low wind regions around the world. The ECO 122 will produce about 25 percent increased wind farm yield that current turbines and fewer turbines would be installed in areas.

38899 ■ *"Aluminium maker Novelis Soars on Indian Takeover Talk" in Globe & Mail (January 27, 2007, pp. B5)*
Pub: CTVglobemedia Publishing Inc.
Ed: Andy Hoffman. **Description:** The plans of India-based Kumar Mangalam Birla's Aditya Birla Group to bid for Atlanta-based rolled aluminium maker Novelis Inc. are discussed. The talks about the purchase have caused a rise in Novelis's share price.

38900 ■ *"American Axle Sues to Force Steelmaker to Resume Suspended Parts Shipment" in Crain's Detroit Business (Vol. 25, June 15, 2009)*
Pub: Crain Communications Inc. - Detroit
Ed: Robert Sherefkin. **Description:** American Axle & Manufacturing Holdings Inc. is facing a shutdown if a Michigan court does not force Republic Engineered Products Inc., a specialty steelmaker, to ship parts. If the parts are not shipped, it could cause assembly plants to shutdown.

38901 ■ *American Big Businesses Directory*
Pub: infoUSA Inc.
Contact: Rakesh Gupta, President
URL(s): www.infousa.com. **Released:** Annual **Price:** $295; $595, both print & CD-ROM. **Covers:** 218,000 U.S. businesses with more than 100 employees, and 500,000 key executives and directors. CD-ROM version contains 160,000 top firms and 431,000 key executives. **Entries include:** Name, address, phone, names and titles of key personnel, number of employees, sales volume, Standard Industrial Classification (SIC) codes, subsidiaries and parent company names, stock exchanges on which traded. **Arrangement:** Section 1: alphabetical by company name; Section 2: geographical by city; Section 3: classified by Standard Industrial Classification (SIC) code; Section 4: alphabetical by executive name. **Indexes:** Geographical, SIC, executive name.

38902 ■ *"Americhem to Shutter Maryland Operation" in Crain's Cleveland Business (Vol. 28, October 29, 2007, No. 43, pp. 14)*
Pub: Crain Communications, Inc.
Description: Americhem Inc., a manufacturer of colors and additives for polymer products has announced plans to expand two plants in Cuyahoga Falls while phasing out its operations in Salisbury, Maryland.

38903 ■ *"Amid Recession, Companies Still Value Supplier Diversity Programs" in Hispanic Business (July-August 2009, pp. 34)*
Pub: Hispanic Business
Ed: Joshua Molina. **Description:** The decline of traditionally strong industries, from automotive manufacturing to construction, has shaken today's economy and has forced small businesses, especially suppliers and minority-owned firms, turn to diversity programs in order to make changes.

38904 ■ *"Analysts: Intel Site May Be Last Major U.S.-Built Fab" in Business Journal-Serving Phoenix and the Valley of the Sun (Oct. 19, 2007)*
Pub: American City Business Journals, Inc.
Ed: Ty Young. **Description:** Intel's million-square-foot manufacturing facility, called Fab 32, is expected to open in 2007. The plant will mass-produce the 45-nanometer microchip. Industry analysts believe Fab 32 may be the last of its kind to be built in the U.S., as construction costs are higher in America than in other countries. Intel's future in Chandler is examined.

38905 ■ *"ANATURALCONCEPT" in Crain's Cleveland Business (Vol. 30, June 22, 2009, No. 24, pp. 1)*
Pub: Crain Communications, Inc.
Ed: Dan Shingler. **Description:** Cleveland-based Biomimicry Institute, led by Cleveland's Entrepreneurs for Sustainability and the Cuyahoga County Planning Commission, are using biomimicry to incorporate eco-friendliness with industry. Biomimicry studies nature's best ideas then imitates these designs and processes to solve human problems.

38906 ■ *"Ann Alexander; Senior Attorney, Natural Resources Defense Council" in Crain's Chicago Business (Vol. 31, May 5, 2008, No. 18)*
Pub: Crain Communications, Inc.
Ed: Emily Stone. **Description:** Profile of Ann Alexander who is the senior attorney at the Natural Resources Defense Council and is known for her dedication to the environment and a career spent battling oil companies, steelmakers and the government to change federal regulations. One recent project aims to improve the Bush administration's fuel economy standards for SUVs. Past battles include her work to prevent permits from slipping through the cracks such as the proposal by London-based BP PLC to dump 54 percent more ammonia and 35 percent more suspended solids from its Whiting, Indiana refinery into Lake Michigan-the source of drinking water for Chicago and its surrounding communities.

38907 ■ *"Aquatic Medications Engender Good Health" in Pet Product News (Vol. 64, November 2010, No. 11, pp. 47)*
Pub: BowTie Inc.
Ed: Madelaine Heleine. **Description:** Pet supply manufacturers and retailers have been exerting consumer education and preparedness efforts to help aquarium hobbyists in tackling ornamental fish disease problems. Aquarium hobbyists have been also assisted in choosing products that facilitate aquarium maintenance before disease attacks their pet fish.

38908 ■ *"Arizona Firms In Chicago Go For Gold With '08 Games" in The Business Journal - Serving Phoenix and the Valley of the Sun (Vol. 28, August 8, 2008, No. 49, pp. 1)*
Pub: American City Business Journals, Inc.
Ed: Patrick O'Grady. **Description:** More than 20 U.S. athletes will wear Arizona-based eSoles LLC's custom-made insoles to increase their performance at the 2008 Beijing Olympics making eSoles one of the beneficiaries of the commercialization of the games. Translation software maker Auralog Inc saw a 60 percent jump in sales from its Mandarin Chinese language applications.

38909 ■ *"Around the World in a Day" in Agency Sales Magazine (Vol. 39, August 2009, No. 8, pp. 36)*
Pub: MANA
Ed: Jack Foster. **Description:** Highlights of Manufacturer's Agents National Association (MANA) member Les Rapchak one-day visit to Basra, Iraq are presented. Rapchak completed the trip via Frankfurt, Germany and Kuwait with a stop afterwards in Istanbul, Turkey. His purpose for the trip was to take part in a seminar at the State Company for Petrochemical Industries.

38910 ■ *"AT&T Wins Networking Deal from GM Worth $1 Billion" in Globe & Mail*

(February 22, 2007, pp. B14)
Pub: CTVglobemedia Publishing Inc.
Description: AT&T Inc., the largest telephone company in the United States, won a $1 billion contract from General Motors Corp. to provide communications services to integrate the automaker's networks.

38911 ■ *"ATS Secures Investment From Goldman Sachs" in The Business Journal - Serving Phoenix and the Valley of the Sun (Vol. 29, September 26, 2008, No. 4, pp. 1)*
Pub: American City Business Journals, Inc.
Ed: Patrick O'Grady. **Description:** Goldman Sachs made an investment to American Traffic Solutions Inc. (ATS) which will allow it to gain two seats on the board of the red-light and speed cameras maker. The investment will help ATS maintain its rapid growth which is at 83 percent over the past 18 months leading up to September 2008.

38912 ■ *"Attorney Panel Tackles Contract Questions" in Agency Sales Magazine (Vol. 39, September-October 2009, No. 9, pp. 8)*
Pub: MANA
Ed: Jack Foster. **Description:** MANAfest conference tackled issues regarding a sales representative's contract. One attorney from the panel advised reps to go through proposed agreements with attorneys who are knowledgeable concerning rep laws. Another attorney advised reps to communicate with a company to ask about their responsibilities if that company is facing financial difficulty.

38913 ■ *"Auto Bankruptcies Could Weaken Defense" in Crain's Detroit Business (Vol. 25, June 8, 2009, No. 23, pp. 1)*
Pub: Crain Communications Inc. - Detroit
Ed: Chad Halcom. **Description:** Bankruptcy and supplier consolidation of General Motors Corporation and Chrysler LLC could interfere with the supply chains of some defense contractors, particularly makers of trucks and smaller vehicles.

38914 ■ *"Auto Sector's Outlook Dims, Survey Finds" in Globe & Mail (January 4, 2006, pp. B4)*
Pub: CTVglobemedia Publishing Inc.
Ed: Greg Keenan. **Description:** The findings of KPMG's survey, on the opinions of chief executives of automotive sector on the impact of higher gas prices, are presented.

38915 ■ *"Auto Show Aims to Electrify" in Crain's Detroit Business (Vol. 26, January 11, 2010, No. 2, pp. 1)*
Pub: Crain Communications, Inc.
Ed: Ryan Beene. **Description:** Overview of the North American International Auto show include sixteen production and concept vehicles including eight from the Detroit 3. High-tech battery suppliers as well as hybrid and electric vehicles will highlight the show.

38916 ■ *"Auto Supplier Stock Battered In Wake Of Wall Street Woes" in Crain's Detroit Business (Vol. 24, September 29, 2008, No. 39, pp. 4)*
Pub: Crain Communications Inc.
Ed: Ryan Beene. **Description:** Due to the volatility of the stock market and public perception of the $700 billion banking bailout, auto suppliers are now facing a dramatic drop in their shares. Statistical data included.

38917 ■ *"Autoline Goes West" in Michigan Vue (Vol. 13, July-August 2008, No. 4, pp. 6)*
Pub: Entrepreneur Media Inc.
Ed: Dave Gibbons. **Description:** Profile of Blue Sky Productions, a Detroit-based production company that produces the nationally syndicated television series 'Autoline', which traditionally probes inside the Detroit auto industry; the company recently decided to shoot in Southern California, an area that now has an immense auto industry but has been virtually ignored by the media. Blue Sky originally slated four shows but ended up producing eleven due to the immense amount of material they discovered concerning the state of California's auto market.

38918 ■ *"Automaker Foundations Run Leaner" in Crain's Detroit Business (Vol. 26, January 11, 2010, No. 2, pp. 1)*
Pub: Crain Communications Inc.
Ed: Sherri Welch. **Description:** Overview of the Detroit automobile industry includes restoring profitability, smarter marketing strategies and philanthropy. Each company comprising the Big 3 is examined, as is their vision for the future.

38919 ■ *"Automotive Trouble" in Canadian Business (Vol. 82, April 27, 2009, No. 7, pp. 11)*
Pub: Rogers Media
Ed: Thomas Watson. **Description:** The likely effects of a possible bailout of the U.S. automotive industry are examined. Some experts believe that a bailout will be good for the automotive industry and on the U.S. economy. Others argue however, that the nationalization may have a negative impact on the industry and on the economy.

38920 ■ *"AV Concept Expands Into Green Energy Storage" in Wireless News (January 25, 2010)*
Pub: Close-Up Media
Description: Electronics distributor and manufacturer AV Concept Holdings Limited announced a marketing partnership with Boston-Power, a provider of lithium-ion batteries, with a focus in the Chinese and Korean markets.

38921 ■ *"Bad News for Canada: U.S. New-Home Starts Sink" in Globe & Mail (February 17, 2007, pp. B7)*
Pub: CTVglobemedia Publishing Inc.
Ed: Tavia Grant. **Description:** The new-home construction in the United States dropped by 14.3 percent in January 2007. The sinking construction activity shows significant impact on the Canadian factories and lumber companies.

38922 ■ *"Baking Up Bigger Lance" in Charlotte Business Journal (Vol. 25, December 3, 2010, No. 37, pp. 1)*
Pub: Charlotte Business Journal
Ed: Ken Elkins. **Description:** Events that led to the merger between Charlotte, North Carolina-based snack food manufacturer Lance Inc. and Pennsylvania-based pretzel maker Snyder's of Hanover Inc. are discussed. The merger is expected to help Lance in posting a 70 percent increase in revenue, which reached $900 million in 2009. How the merger would affect Snyder's of Hanover is also described.

38923 ■ *"Bankruptcies" in Crain's Detroit Business (Vol. 24, September 29, 2008, No. 39, pp. 4)*
Pub: Crain Communications Inc.
Description: Current list of business that filed for Chapter 7 or 11 protection in U.S. Bankruptcy Court in Detroit include manufacturers, real estate companies, a printing company and a specialized staffing company.

38924 ■ *"Bark and Bite" in Canadian Business (Vol. 81, March 31, 2008, No. 5, pp. 20)*
Pub: Rogers Media
Ed: Rachel Pulfer. **Description:** Hillary Clinton and Barack Obama both want to renegotiate NAFTA but the most job losses in the American manufacturing industry is caused by technological change and Asian competition than with NAFTA. The risk of protectionist trade policies has increased given the political atmosphere.

38925 ■ *"Barnes Shakes Up Sara Lee Exec Suite" in Crain's Chicago Business (Vol. 31, April 21, 2008, No. 16, pp. 1)*
Pub: Crain Communications, Inc.
Ed: David Sterrett. **Description:** In an attempt to cut costs and boost profits, Sara Lee Corp.'s CEO Brenda Barnes is restructuring the company's management team.

38926 ■ *"Battered U.S. Auto Makers in Grip of Deeper Sales Slump" in Globe & Mail (April 4, 2007, pp. B1)*
Pub: CTVglobemedia Publishing Inc.
Ed: Greg Keenan. **Description:** The fall in Canadian sales and market share of Ford Motor Co., General Motors Corp. and Chrysler Group is discussed.

38927 ■ *"Bayer Job Cuts to Hit Canada" in Globe & Mail (March 3, 2007, pp. B7)*
Pub: CTVglobemedia Publishing Inc.
Description: Bayer AG, German drug maker, planned cut of 6,100 jobs as a part of their cost-cutting strategies. The company, which plans to save 700 million euros by the end of 2007, may eliminate some positions in Canadian branches.

38928 ■ *"Because He Is Always On the Accelerator: Jay Rogers: Local Motors, Chandler, Arizona" in Inc. (Volume 32, December 2010, No. 10)*
Pub: Inc. Magazine
Description: Profile of Jay Rogers, founder of Local Motors, who manufactures cars, including the Phoenix Rally Fighter made from lightweight composites rather than steel.

38929 ■ *"Beer Stocks Rally on Anheuser, InBev Report" in Globe & Mail (February 16, 2007, pp. B3)*
Pub: CTVglobemedia Publishing Inc.
Ed: Keith McArthur. **Description:** The stock prices of beer manufacturing industries have increased considerably after impressive profit reports from Anheuser Busch Cos Inc. and InBev SA. Complete analysis in this context is presented.

38930 ■ *"Behind the Scenes: Companies At the Heart of Everyday Life" in Inc. (February 2008, pp. 26-27)*
Pub: Gruner & Jahr USA Publishing
Ed: Athena Schindelheim. **Description:** Profiles of companies providing services to airports, making the environment safer and more efficient, as well as more comfortable for passengers and workers. Centerpoint Manufacturing provides garbage bins that can safely contain explosions producing thousands of pounds of pressure; Infax, whose software displays arrival and departure information on 19-foot-wide screens; Lavi Industries, whose products include security barricades, hostess stands, and salad-bar sneeze guards; and SATech maker of rubber flooring that helps ease discomfort for workers having to stand for long periods of time.

38931 ■ *"Bellingham Boatbuilder Norstar Yachts Maintains Family Tradition" in Bellingham Business Journal (Vol. February 2010, pp. 12)*
Pub: Sound Publishing Inc.
Ed: Isaac Bonnell. **Description:** Profile of Norstar Yachts and brothers Gary and Steve Nordtvedt who started the company in 1994. The company recently moved its operations to a 12,000 square foot space in the Fairhaven Marine Industrial Park.

38932 ■ *"Best Turnaround Stocks" in Canadian Business (Vol. 81, Summer 2008, No. 9, pp. 65)*
Pub: Rogers Media Ltd.
Ed: Calvin Leung. **Description:** Share prices of Sierra Wireless Inc. and EXFO Electro Optical Engineering Inc. have fallen over the past year but have good chance at a rebound considering that the companies have free cash flow and no long-term debt. One-year stock performance analysis of the two companies is presented.

38933 ■ *"The Best and Worst Economic Times" in Agency Sales Magazine (Vol. 39, December 2009, No. 11, pp. 22)*
Pub: MANA
Ed: Mark Young. **Description:** U.S. gross domestic product grew 3.5 percent and the stock market has improved but manufacturers are cutting commissions or dropping sales representatives. Despite these challenges, it can a good time for salespeople

because clients need them more than ever. Salesmen should find new ways to do business for their clients during this current challenging environment.

38934 ■ *"BETC Backers Plot Future" in Business Journal Portland (Vol. 27, December 10, 2010, No. 41, pp. 1)*
Pub: Portland Business Journal

Ed: Erik Siemers. **Description:** A coalition of clean energy groups and industrial manufacturers have spearheaded a campaign aimed at persuading Oregon legislators that the state's Business Energy Tax Credit (BETC) is vital in job creation. Oregon's BETC grants tax credits for 50 percent of an eligible renewable or clean energy project's cost. However, some legislators propose BETC's abolition.

38935 ■ *"Better Made's Better Idea: Diversify Despite Rising Costs" in Crain's Detroit Business (Vol. 24, September 22, 2008, No. 38, pp. 18)*
Pub: Crain Communications Inc.

Ed: Nathan Skid. **Description:** Better Made Snack Foods Inc. is planning to expand its product lines and market reach as well as boost manufacturing capability during a time in which the company is being buffeted by rising commodity and fuel costs. The company feels that diversification is the key to maintain sales and growth.

38936 ■ *"Betting On Volatile Materials" in Barron's (Vol. 88, July 14, 2008, No. 28, pp. M11)*
Pub: Dow Jones & Co., Inc.

Ed: John Marshall. **Description:** Economic slowdowns in the U.S., Europe and China could cause sharp short-term declines in the materials sector. The S&P Materials sector is vulnerable to shifts in the flow of funds. Statistical data included.

38937 ■ *"Beverage Brand Vies To Be the Latest Purple Prince" in Brandweek (Vol. 49, April 21, 2008, No. 16, pp. 20)*
Pub: VNU Business Media, Inc.

Ed: Becky Ebenkamp. **Description:** Profile on the new beverage product Purple and its founder, Ted Farnsworth; Purple is a drink that blends seven antioxidant-rich juices to create what Mr. Farnsworth calls a 'Cascade Effect' that boosts antioxidants' effectiveness. Mr. Farnsworth is marketing the brand's Oxygen Radical Absorbance Capability (ORAC) which is a value of 7,600 compared with orange juice's 1,200.

38938 ■ *"Beyond Auto; Staffing Firm Malace Grabs Revenue Jump" in Crain's Detroit Business (Vol. 26, January 18, 2010, No. 3, pp. 3)*
Pub: Crain Communications Inc.

Ed: Sherri Welch. **Description:** Malace & Associates Inc., the Troy-based human resources management company, expects its diversification into nonautomotive industries to help double its revenues this year. Due to the automotive downturn, between October 2008 and March 2009 the company lost approximately 48 percent of its business.

38939 ■ *"Big Boys Drawn Back to Play in Oil Sands" in Globe & Mail (March 7, 2006, pp. B2)*
Pub: CTVglobemedia Publishing Inc.

Ed: Deborah Yedlin. **Description:** The feasibility of companies such as Chevron Corp. in acquiring oil sands is discussed.

38940 ■ *"Birdcage Optimization" in Pet Product News (Vol. 64, November 2010, No. 11, pp. 54)*
Pub: BowTie Inc.

Description: Manufacturers have been emphasizing size, security, quality construction, stylish design, and quick cleaning when guiding consumers on making birdcage options. Selecting a birdcage is gaining importance considering that cage purchases have become the highest expense associated with owning a bird. Other avian habitat trends are also examined.

38941 ■ *"Biz Assesses 'Textgate' Fallout; Conventions, Smaller Deals Affected" in Crain's Detroit Business (Vol. 24, March 31, 2008)*
Pub: Crain Communications, Inc.

Ed: Tom Henderson. **Description:** Businesspeople who were trying to measure the amount of economic damage is likely to be caused due to Mayor Kwame Kilpatrick's indictment on eight charges and found that: automotive and other large global deals are less likely to be affected than location decisions by smaller companies and convention site decisions. Also being affected are negotiations in which Mexican startup companies were planning a partnership with the TechTown incubator to pursue opportunities in the auto sector; those plans are being put on hold while they look at other sites.

38942 ■ *"Black Diamond Holdings Corp. Receives SEC Approval" in Canadian Corporate News (May 16, 2007)*
Pub: Comtex News Network Inc.

Description: Black Diamond Holdings, Corp., a British Columbia domiciled company and its two wholly owned subsidiaries are engaged in the bottling, importation, distribution, marketing, and brand creation of premium spirits and wines to worldwide consumers, announced that it has completed the SEC review process and has applied to list for trading in the United States on the OTC.BB.

38943 ■ *"Black Gold" in Canadian Business (Vol. 79, August 14, 2006, No. 16-17, pp. 57)*
Pub: Rogers Media

Ed: Erin Pooley. **Description:** A list of the top ten jobs in the petroleum industry in Canada along with pay and nature of jobs, is presented.

38944 ■ *"Blast Blame" in The Business Journal-Milwaukee (Vol. 25, September 5, 2008, No. 50, pp. 1)*
Pub: American City Business Journals, Inc.

Description: Rexnord Industries LLC and J.M. Brennan Inc.'s property damage trial in connection with the explosion at the Falk Corp. plant in Menomonee Valley, Wisconsin is set to begin. Lawyers for the two companies have failed to reach a settlement. A leaking propane line was seen as the cause of the blast.

38945 ■ *"Blues at the Toy Fair: Industry Reeling From Recalls, Lower Sales Volumes" in Crain's New York Business (February 18, 2008)*
Pub: Crain Communications Inc.

Ed: Elisabeth Cordova. **Description:** Over 1,500 toy developers and vendors will attend the American International Toy Fair, expected to be low-key due to recent recalls of toys not meeting American safety standards. Toy retailers and manufacturers, as well as the Chinese government, are promoting product testing to prevent toxic metals in toys.

38946 ■ *"BMW Makes Bet on Carbon Maker" in Wall Street Journal Eastern Edition (November 19 , 2011, pp. B3)*
Pub: Dow Jones & Company Inc.

Ed: Christoph Rauwald. **Description:** Eight months ago, Volkswagen AG acquired a 10 percent holding in carbon-fiber maker SGL Carbon SE. Its rival BMW AG is catching up by acquiring 15.2 percent stake in SGL as it seeks alliances like the rest of the industry in order to share industrial costs of new product development.

38947 ■ *"BMW Revs Up for a Rebound" in Barron's (Vol. 89, July 13, 2009, No. 28, pp. M7)*
Pub: Dow Jones & Co., Inc.

Ed: Jonathan Buck. **Description:** Investors may like BMW's stocks because the company has maintained its balance sheet strength and has an impressive production line of new models that should boost sales in the next few years. The company's sales are also gaining traction, although their vehicle delivery was down 1.7 percent year on year on June 2009, this was still the best monthly sales figure for 2009.

38948 ■ *"Boeing Earns Its Wings With Strong Quarter" in Crain's Chicago Business (Vol. 31, April 28, 2008, No. 17, pp. 4)*
Pub: Crain Communications, Inc.

Ed: Daniel Rome Levine. **Description:** Interview with Michael A. Crowe, the senior managing director at Mesirow Financial Investment Management, who discusses highlights from the earnings season so far, his outlook for the economy and the stock market as well as what his company is purchasing. Mr. Crowe also recommends shares of five companies.

38949 ■ *"Boeing Scores $21.7 Billion Order in Indonesia" in Wall Street Journal Eastern Edition (November 18 , 2011, pp. B6)*
Pub: Dow Jones & Company Inc.

Ed: David Kesmodel, Laura Meckler. **Description:** Boeing has garnered a large contract to deliver Boeing 737 jets to Indonesia's Lion Air. There are those who are lobbying against the US government's practice of subsidizing foreign companies that make contracts with American aerospace companies.

38950 ■ *"Boeing's Next Flight May Well Be to the South" in Puget Sound Business Journal (Vol. 29, November 21, 2008, No. 31, pp.)*
Pub: American City Business Journals

Ed: Steve Wilhelm. **Description:** Southern states in the U.S. are luring Boeing Company to locate a new plant in their region which is experiencing a growing industrial base while offering permissive labor laws as selling points.

38951 ■ *"Bottler Will Regain Its Pop" in Barron's (Vol. 88, March 17, 2008, No. 11, pp. 56)*
Pub: Dow Jones & Company, Inc.

Ed: Alexander Eule. **Description:** Discusses he 30 percent drop in the share price of PepsiAmericas Inc. from their 2007 high which presents an opportunity to buy into the company's dependable U.S. market and fast growing Eastern European business. The bottler's Eastern European operating profits in 2007 grew to $101 million from $21 million in 2006.

38952 ■ *"Brewing National Success" in Hawaii Business (Vol. 53, November 2007, No. 5, pp. 46)*
Pub: Hawaii Business Publishing

Ed: Alex Salkever. **Description:** Kona Brewing Co. (KBC) is already selling its brews in four cities in Florida and 17 other states and Japan as well. KBC is currently forming a deal with Red Hook to produce Longboard Lager and other KBC brews at Red Hooks' brewery in New Hampshire. KBC's chief executive officer Mattson Davis shares KBC's practices for success.

38953 ■ *"A Bright Spot: Industrial Space in Demand Again" in Sacramento Business Journal (Vol. 28, October 21, 2011, No. 34, pp. 1)*
Pub: Sacramento Business Journal

Ed: Michael Shaw. **Description:** Sacramento, California's industrial sites have been eyed by potential tenants who are actively seeking space larger than 50,000 square feet.

38954 ■ *"Bringing Charities More Bang for Their Buck" in Crain's Chicago Business (Vol. 34, May 23, 2011, No. 21, pp. 31)*
Pub: Crain Communications Inc.

Ed: Lisa Bertagnoli. **Description:** Marcy-Newberry Association connects charities with manufacturers in order to use excess items such as clothing, janitorial and office supplies.

38955 ■ *"Bringing Manufacturing Concerns to Springfield" in Crain's Chicago Business (Vol. 31, March 31, 2008, No. 13, pp. 6)*
Pub: Crain Communications, Inc.

Ed: Paul Merrion. **Description:** Profile of the new executive vice-president of Tooling & Manufacturing Assn., Paul Merrion, a man who plans to grow TMA's membership with an aggressive legislative agenda in Springfield.

38956 ■ *"Brookfield Eyes 'New World" in Globe & Mail (February 6, 2007, pp. B1)*
Pub: CTVglobemedia Publishing Inc.
Ed: Sinclair Stewart; Elizabeth Church. **Description:** The efforts of Brookfield Asset Management Inc. to acquire American paper company, Longview Fibre Co., and Australian construction company Multiplex Ltd. are discussed.

38957 ■ *"Buhler Versatile Launches Next Generation of Equipment" in Farm Industry News (November 23, 2011)*
Pub: Penton Business Media Inc.
Ed: Jodie Wehrspann. **Description:** Canadian owned Versatile is expanding its four-wheel drive tractor division with sprayers, tillage, and seeding equipment.

38958 ■ *"Buick Prices Verano Below Rival Luxury Compacts" in Automotive News (Vol. 86, October 31, 2011, No. 6488, pp. 10)*
Pub: Crain Communications Inc.
Ed: Mike Colias. **Description:** General Motors's Verano will compete with other luxury compacts such as the Lexus IS 250 and the Acura TSX, but will be prices significantly lower coming in with a starting price of $23,470, about $6,000 to $10,000 less than those competitors.

38959 ■ *"Buying Chanel (All Of It)" in Conde Nast Portfolio (Vol. 2, June 2008, No. 6, pp. 34)*
Pub: Conde Nast Publications
Contact: David Carey, President
Ed: Willow Duttge. **Description:** Overview of the luxury company Chanel and an estimated guess as to what the company is worth.

38960 ■ *Buyology: Truth and Lies About Why We Buy*
Pub: Doubleday, a Division of Random House
Ed: Martin Lindstrom. **Released:** 2009. **Price:** $24.95. **Description:** Marketers study brain scans to determine how consumers rate Nokia, Coke, and Ford products.

38961 ■ *"C. Andrew McCartney; President, Owner, Bowden Manufacturing Corp., 37" in Crain's Cleveland Business (November 19, 2007)*
Pub: Crain Communications, Inc.
Ed: David Bennett. **Description:** Profile of C. Andrew McCartney who was named president of Bowden Manufacturing Corp., a company that machines and fabricates metal and plastic parts for products ranging from airplanes to medical equipment; Mr. McCartney has since purchased the company, which posted $8 million in sales last year. He feels that part of his success is due to adherence to such policies such as gaining the employees trust and to avoid making promises to customers that Bowden cannot keep.

38962 ■ *"Calendar" in Crain's Detroit Business (Vol. 24, October 6, 2008, No. 40, pp. 22)*
Pub: Crain Communications, Inc.
Description: Listing of events in the Detroit area include conferences addressing entrepreneurialism, economic development, manufacturing, marketing, the housing crisis and women business ownership.

38963 ■ *"California Company Suing City's Lupin Over its Generic Diabetes Drug" in Baltimore Business Journal (Vol. 27, January 1, 2010)*
Pub: American City Business Journals
Ed: Gary Haber. **Description:** California-based Depomed Inc. is suing Baltimore, Maryland-based Lupin Pharmaceuticals Inc. and its parent company in India over the patents to a diabetes drug. Lupin allegedly infringed on Depomed's four patents for Glumetza when it filed for permission to sell its own version of the drug with the US Food and Drug Administration. Details on generic pharmaceutical manufacturer tactics are discussed.

38964 ■ *"Can a Brazilian SUV Take On the Jeep Wrangler?" in Business Week (September 22, 2008, No. 4100, pp. 50)*
Pub: McGraw-Hill Companies, Inc.
Ed: Helen Walters. **Description:** Profile of the Brazilian company TAC as well as the flourishing Brazilian car market; TAC has launched a new urban vehicle, the Stark, which has won prizes for innovation; the company uses local technology and manufacturing expertise.

38965 ■ *"Capture New Markets" in Pet Product News (Vol. 64, December 2010, No. 12, pp. 12)*
Pub: BowTie Inc.
Ed: Ethan Mizer. **Description:** Flea and tick treatments are among the product categories that can be offered in order to clinch new markets. With the help of manufacturers, pet store retailers are encouraged to educate themselves about these products considering that capturing markets involves variations in customer perceptions. Retailers would then be deemed as resources and sources for these products.

38966 ■ *"Car Dealer Closings: Immoral, Slow-Death" in Crain's Detroit Business (Vol. 25, June 8, 2009, No. 23)*
Pub: Crain Communications Inc. - Detroit
Ed: Daniel Duggan. **Description:** Colleen McDonald discusses the closing of her two Chrysler dealerships located in Taylor and Livonia, Michigan, along with her Farmington Hills store, Holiday Chevrolet.

38967 ■ *"Car Trouble" in Canadian Business (Vol. 80, October 22, 2007, No. 21, pp. 27)*
Pub: Rogers Media
Ed: Thomas Watson. **Description:** Contract between General Motors Corporation and the United Auto Workers Union has created a competitive arm for the U.S. Big Three automakers. Data on the market and production data of car companies are presented.

38968 ■ *"Career Transition" in Crain's Detroit Business (Vol. 26, January 4, 2010, No. 1, pp. 14)*
Pub: Crain Communications Inc.
Description: Profile of Nicole Longhini-McElroy who has opted to radically change her career path from working in the manufacturing sector to becoming a self-published author of 'Charmed Adventures', a book series created to engage children in creative thought.

38969 ■ *"Catch the Wind to Hold Investor Update Conference Call on October 18, 2011" in CNW Group (October 4, 2011)*
Pub: CNW Group
Contact: Carolyn McGill-Davidson, President
Description: Catch the Wind Ltd., providers of laser-based wind sensor products and technology, held a conference call for analysts and institutional investors. The high-growth technology firm is headquartered in Manassas, Virginia.

38970 ■ *"Caterpillar to Expand Research, Production in China" in Chicago Tribune (August 27, 2008)*
Pub: McClatchy-Tribune Information Services
Ed: James P. Miller. **Description:** Caterpillar Inc., the Peoria-based heavy-equipment manufacturer, plans to establish a new research-and-development center at the site of its rapidly growing campus in Wuxi.

38971 ■ *"CAW Boss Troubled Over 'Vulnerable' Ford Plants" in Globe & Mail (January 19, 2006, pp. B6)*
Pub: CTVglobemedia Publishing Inc.
Ed: Greg Keenan. **Description:** The concerns of president Buzz Hargrove of Canadian Auto Workers on the impact of Ford Motor Co.'s restructuring efforts on closure of automotive plants in Canada, are presented.

38972 ■ *"CAW Hopes to Beat Xstrata Deadline" in Globe & Mail (January 30, 2007, pp. B3)*
Pub: CTVglobemedia Publishing Inc.
Ed: Andy Hoffman. **Description:** The decision of Canadian Auto Workers to strike work at Xstrata PLC over wage increase is discussed.

38973 ■ *"Cemex Paves a Global Road to Solid Growth" in Barron's (Vol. 88, March 10, 2008, No. 10, pp. 24)*
Pub: Dow Jones & Company, Inc.
Ed: Sandra Ward. **Description:** Shares of Cemex are expected to perform well with the company's expected strong performance despite fears of a US recession. The company has a diverse geographical reach and benefits from a strong worldwide demand for cement.

38974 ■ *"Cents and Sensibility" in Playthings (Vol. 107, January 1, 2009, No. 1, pp. 19)*
Pub: Reed Business Information
Contact: Jeff Greisch, President
Ed: Pamela Brill. **Description:** Recent concerns over safety, phthalate and lead paint and other toxic materials, as well as consumers going green, are issues discussed by toy manufacturers. Doll manufacturers also face increase labor and material costs and are working to design dolls that girls will love.

38975 ■ *"Centurion Signs Egypt Deal With Shell" in Globe & Mail (March 21, 2006, pp. B5)*
Pub: CTVglobemedia Publishing Inc.
Ed: Dave Ebner. **Description:** Centurion Energy International Inc., a Calgary-based natural gas producer in Egypt, has signed contract with Royal Dutch Shell PLC to explore about 320,000 hectares of land in Egypt. Details of the agreement are presented.

38976 ■ *"CEOs Gone Wild" in Canadian Business (Vol. 79, August 14, 2006, No. 16-17, pp. 15)*
Pub: Rogers Media
Ed: Thomas Watson. **Description:** Stock investment decisions of chief executive officers of metal companies in Canada, are discussed.

38977 ■ *"Champion Enterprises Buys UK Company" in Crain's Detroit Business (Vol. 24, March 17, 2008, No. 11, pp. 4)*
Pub: Crain Communications, Inc.
Ed: Daniel Duggan. **Description:** With the acquisition of ModularUK Building Systems Ltd., a steel-frame modular manufacturer, Champion Enterprises has continued its expansion outside the United States.

38978 ■ *"Change Is in the Air" in Agency Sales Magazine (Vol. 39, August 2009, No. 8, pp. 30)*
Pub: MANA
Ed: Jack Foster. **Description:** Highlights of the Power-Motion Technology Representatives Association (PTRA) 37th Annual Conference, which projected an economic upturn, are presented. Allan Bealulieu of the Institute for Trend Research gave the positive news while Manufacturer's Agents National Association (MANA) president Brain Shirley emphasized the need to take advantage of a turnaround.

38979 ■ *"A Change Would Do You Good" in Canadian Business (Vol. 80, November 19, 2007, No. 23, pp. 15)*
Pub: Rogers Media
Ed: Geoff Kirbyson. **Description:** Western Glove Works will be manufacturing clothing offshore, including Sheryl Crow's jeans collection, in countries such as China and the Philippines. The company decided to operate offshore after 86 years of existence due to the high price of manufacturing jeans in Canada. Western Glove's focus on producing celebrity-endorsed goods is discussed.

38980 ■ *"Charged Up for Sales" in Charlotte Business Journal (Vol. 25, October 15, 2010, No. 30, pp. 1)*
Pub: Charlotte Business Journal
Ed: Susan Stabley. **Description:** Li-Ion Motors Corporation is set to expand its production lines of electric cars in Sacramento, California. The plan is seen to create up to 600 jobs. The company's total investment is seen to reach $500 million.

38981 ■ *"Cheese Spread Whips Up a Brand New Bowl" in Brandweek (Vol. 49, April 21, 2008, No. 16, pp. 17)*
Pub: VNU Business Media, Inc.
Ed: Mike Beirne. **Description:** Mrs. Kinser's Pimento Cheese Spread is launching a new container for its product in order to attempt stronger brand marketing with a better bowl in order to win over the heads of households as young as in their 30s. The company also intends to begin distribution in Texas and the West Coast. Mrs. Kinser's is hoping that the new packaging will provide a more distinct branding and will help consumers distinguish what flavor they are buying.

38982 ■ *"Children's Products Maker Not the New Kid on the Block" in Crain's Cleveland Business (Vol. 28, November 26, 2007, No. 47, pp. 3)*
Pub: Crain Communications, Inc.
Ed: David Bennett. **Description:** Discusses the business model employed by Shamrock Industries Inc., a rising star in the competitive world of children's products; the company, which does business as Foundations Quality Children's Products, has expanded into a 63,000-square-foot distribution center which has boosted its local profile significantly.

38983 ■ *"Chinese Fund Loans $33.5 Million to Prestolite" in Crain's Detroit Business (Vol. 26, January 18, 2010, No. 3, pp. 1)*
Pub: Crain Communications Inc.
Ed: Ryan Beene. **Description:** Prestolite Electric Inc., a distributor of alternators and starter motors for commercial and heavy-duty vehicles, looked to China for fresh capital in order to fund new product launches.

38984 ■ *"Chinese Solar Panel Manufacturer Scopes Out Austin" in Austin Business JournalInc. (Vol. 29, October 30, 2009, No. 34, pp. 1)*
Pub: American City Business Journals
Ed: Jacob Dirr. **Description:** China's Yingli Green Energy Holding Company Ltd. is looking for a site in order to construct a $20 million photovoltaic panel plant. Both Austin and San Antonio are vying to house the manufacturing hub. The project could create about 300 jobs and give Austin a chance to become a player in the solar energy market. Other solar companies are also considering Central Texas as an option to set up shop.

38985 ■ *"Chrysler Unions Set Up Roadblocks to Private Equity" in Globe & Mail (March 20, 2007, pp. B3)*
Pub: CTVglobemedia Publishing Inc.
Ed: Greg Keenan. **Description:** The opposition of the Canadian Auto Workers union and the United Auto Workers to any proposal to sell Chrysler Group is discussed.

38986 ■ *"Clay Riddell" in Canadian Business (Vol. 80, February 12, 2007, No. 4, pp. 86)*
Pub: Rogers Media
Ed: Michelle Magnan. **Description:** Chief executive officer of Paramount Resources Clay Riddell shares his passion for oil and gas business.

38987 ■ *"Cleanup to Polish Plating Company's Bottom Line" in Crain's Cleveland Business (Vol. 28, October 29, 2007, No. 43, pp. 4)*
Pub: Crain Communications, Inc.
Ed: Jay Miller. **Description:** Barker Products Co, a manufacturer of nuts and bolts, is upgrading its aging facility which will allow them to operate at capacity and will save the company several hundred thousand dollars a year in operating costs. The new owners secured a construction loan from the county's new Commercial Redevelopment Fund which will allow them to upgrade the building which was hampered by years of neglect.

38988 ■ *"Closed Minds and Open Skies" in Barron's (Vol. 88, March 10, 2008, No. 10, pp. 50)*
Pub: Dow Jones & Company, Inc.
Ed: Thomas Donlan. **Description:** American politicians have closed minds when it comes to fair trade. The American government must not interfere with the country's manufacturing industries or worry about outsourcing defense contracts to European aerospace company Airbus.

38989 ■ *"CMO Nicholson Exits Pepsi as Share Declines" in Advertising Age (Vol. 79, July 7, 2008, No. 26, pp. 4)*
Pub: Crain Communications, Inc.
Ed: Natalie Zmuda. **Description:** Cie Nicholson, the chief marketing officer at Pepsi-Cola UK, is leaving the company at a time when its market share is down; the brand, which was known for its dynamic marketing, has diverted much of its attention from its core brands and shifted attention to the ailing Gatorade brand as well as Sobe Life Water and Amp.

38990 ■ *"Coca-Cola Bottler Up for Sale: CEO J. Bruce Llewellyn Seeks Retirement" in Black Enterprise (Vol. 37, December 2006, No. 5, pp. 31)*
Pub: Earl G. Graves Publishing Co. Inc.
Ed: Marcia A. Wade. **Description:** J. Bruce Llewellyn of Brucephil Inc., the parent company of the Philadelphia Coca-Cola Bottling Co. has agreed to sell its remaining shares to Coca-Cola Co., which previously owned 31 percent of Philly Coke. Analysts believe that Coca-Cola will eventually sell its shares to another bottler.

38991 ■ *"Coca-Cola Looks Ready to Pause" in Barron's (Vol. 88, March 10, 2008, No. 10, pp. 18)*
Pub: Dow Jones & Company, Inc.
Ed: Michael Santoli. **Description:** Shares of Coca-Cola are expected to turn sideways or experience a slight drop from $59.50 each to the mid-50 level. The company has seen its shares jump 40 percent since 2006, when it was in a series of measures to improve profitability.

38992 ■ *"The Code-Cracker" in Business Courier (Vol. 24, January 11, 2008, No. 40, pp. 1)*
Pub: American City Business Journals, Inc.
Ed: James Ritchie. **Description:** Michael Kennedy, a professor in the chemistry and biochemistry department at the Miami University, is a part of the Protein Structure Initiative, a project that is aimed at forming a catalog of three-dimensional protein structures. The initiative is a project of the Northeast Structural Genomics consortium, of which the Miami University is a member. The impacts of the research on drug development are discussed.

38993 ■ *"Combat Mission: Rebuffed, BAE Systems Fights Army Contract Decision" in Business Courier (Vol. 26, September 25, 2009)*
Pub: American City Business Journals, Inc.
Ed: Jon Newberry. **Description:** BAE Systems filed a complaint with the US Government Accountability Office after the US Army issued an order to BAE's competitor for armoured trucks which is potentially worth over $3 billion. Hundreds of jobs in Butler County, Ohio hinge on the success of the contract protest.

38994 ■ *"Coming Soon: Electric Tractors" in Farm Industry News (November 21, 2011)*
Pub: Penton Business Media Inc.
Ed: Jodie Wehrspann. **Description:** The agricultural industry is taking another look at electric farm vehicles. John Deere Product Engineering Center said that farmers can expect to see more diesel-electric systems in farm tractors, sprayers, and implements.

38995 ■ *"Compelling Opportunities" in Barron's (Vol. 88, March 10, 2008, No. 10, pp. 39)*
Pub: Dow Jones & Company, Inc.
Ed: Neil A. Martin. **Description:** Michael L. Reynal, portfolio manager of Principal International Emerging Markets Fund, is bullish on the growth prospects of stocks in emerging markets. He is investing big on energy, steel, and transportation companies.

38996 ■ *"Comtech's Winning Streak" in Crain's New York Business (Vol. 24, January 7, 2008, No. 1, pp. 3)*
Pub: Crain Communications, Inc.
Description: Comtech Telecommunications Corp., a designer and manufacturer of equipment that helps military track troops and vehicles on the field, has been one of the stock market's biggest winners over the past decade. Statistical data included.

38997 ■ *"Condensed Capitalism" in Human Resource Management (Vol. 49, September-October 2010, No. 5, pp. 965-968)*
Pub: John Wiley
Ed: Matthew M. Bodah. **Description:** Review of the book, 'Condensed Capitalism: Campbell Soup and the Pursuit of Cheap Production in the Twentieth Century'.

38998 ■ *"ContiTech Celebrates 100 Years" in American Printer (Vol. 128, July 1, 2011, No. 7)*
Pub: Penton Media Inc.
Description: ContiTech celebrated 100 years in business. The firm started in 1911 after developing the first elastic printing blanket. Other milestones for the firm include its manufacturing process for compressible printing blankets, the Conti-Air brand and climate-neutral printing blankets.

38999 ■ *"Contract Reveals Details of ACE Jet Deals" in Globe & Mail (January 24, 2006, pp. B3)*
Pub: CTVglobemedia Publishing Inc.
Ed: Brent Jang. **Description:** The details of contract between Boeing Co. and Air Canada are presented.

39000 ■ *"Contractors: Slots MBE Goal a Test" in Baltimore Business Journal (Vol. 27, November 20, 2009, No. 28, pp. 1)*
Pub: American City Business Journals
Ed: Scott Dance. **Description:** Slot machine manufacturers in Maryland have been searching minority business enterprises (MBEs) that will provide maintenance and delivery services to the machines. MBEs will also build the stands where the machines will be mounted.

39001 ■ *"A Conversation With Steven Hilfinger, Foley & Lardner L.L.P." in Crain's Detroit Business (Vol. 24, March 24, 2008, No. 12, pp. 1)*
Pub: Crain Communications, Inc.
Description: Interview with Steven Hilfinger who is a member of Foley & Lardner L.L.P.'s mergers and acquisitions practice and is co-chair of its automotive industry team. Hilfinger discusses such issues as the role a board of directors can play in the M&A process and the future of the auto market.

39002 ■ *"Coping With a Shrinking Planet" in Agency Sales Magazine (Vol. 39, December 2009, No. 11, pp. 46)*
Pub: MANA
Ed: Mark Young. **Description:** China and India are forcing big changes in the world and are posing a huge threat to U.S. manufacturers and their sales representatives. Reps may want to consider expanding into these territories. Helping sell American products out of the country presents an opportunity for economic expansion.

39003 ■ *"Copy Karachi?" in Barron's (Vol. 88, June 30, 2008, No. 26, pp. 5)*
Pub: Dow Jones & Co., Inc.
Ed: Randall W. Forsyth. **Description:** Karachi bourse had a historic 8.6 percent one-day gain because the bourse banned short-selling for a month and announced a 30 billion rupee fund to stabilize the market. The shares of General Motors are trading within the same values that it had in 1974. The reasons for this decline are discussed.

39004 ■ *"Craig Muhlhauser" in Canadian Business (Vol. 81, September 15, 2008, No. 14-15, pp. 6)*
Pub: Rogers Media Ltd.
Ed: Andrew Wahl. **Description:** Interview with Craig Muhlhauser who is the CEO of Celestica, a manufacturing company that provides services for the elec-

tronics sector; Muhlhauser discusses the company's restructuring program, which he feels was the secret to their surprising first-quarter results. Muhlhauser states that the company is operating with more forward visibility and that understanding the opportunities during the current economic situation presents the biggest challenge.

39005 ■ *"Credit-Market Crisis Batters Origen Financial's Bottom Line" in Crain's Detroit Business (Vol. 24, March 31, 2008, No. 13, pp. 4)*
Pub: Crain Communications, Inc.
Description: Overview of the effect the credit-market crisis has had on Origen Financial Inc., a company that underwrites and services loans for manufactured housing. CEO Ronald Klein didn't think Origen would be affected by the collapse due to its sound operations but the company's share price dropped considerably causing its auditors to warn that the company's existence could be in jeopardy.

39006 ■ *"Cruising In Choppy Water" in The Business Journal-Portland (Vol. 25, August 22, 2008, No. 24, pp. 1)*
Pub: American City Business Journals, Inc.
Ed: Erik Siemers. **Description:** Yacht builder Christensen Shipyards Inc. is experiencing robust business despite the slowing US economy, building four yachts a year as of 2008. The company expects revenues to hit $90 million and is opening a 500,000-square-foot plant in Tennessee.

39007 ■ *"The Cult of Ralph" in Canadian Business (Vol. 79, September 25, 2006, No. 19, pp. 90)*
Pub: Rogers Media
Ed: Thomas Watson. **Description:** The contributions of Ralph Gilles to automobile manufacturing giant Daimler Chrysler AG are discussed.

39008 ■ *"Cyclicals, Your Day Is Coming" in Barron's (Vol. 89, July 27, 2009, No. 30, pp. 24)*
Pub: Dow Jones & Co., Inc.
Ed: Dimitra DeFotis. **Description:** Cyclical stocks are likely to be big winners when the economy improves and 13 stocks that have improving earnings, decent balance sheets, and dividends are presented. These candidates include U.S. Steel, Alcoa, Allegheny Tech, Dow Chemical, and Nucor.

39009 ■ *"DaimlerChrysler Bears Down on Smart" in Globe & Mail (March 27, 2006, pp. B11)*
Pub: CTVglobemedia Publishing Inc.
Ed: Oliver Suess. **Description:** DaimlerChrysler AG, German automobile industry giant, is planning to cut down its workforce its Smart division. The Chrysler is also planning to stop the production of its four-seater models, to end losses at Smart division.

39010 ■ *"Danaher to Acquire Tectronix" in Canadian Electronics (Vol. 22, November-December 2007, No. 7, pp. 1)*
Pub: CLB Media Inc.
Description: Leading supplier of measurement, test and monitoring equipment Tektronix will be acquired by Danaher Corporation for $2.8 billion. Tektronix products are expected to complement Danaher's test equipment sector. The impacts of the deal on Tektronix shareholders and Danaher's operations are discussed.

39011 ■ *"Dealer Gets a Lift with Acquisitions at Year's End" in Crain's Detroit Business (Vol. 26, January 11, 2010, No. 2, pp. 3)*
Pub: Crain Communications, Inc.
Ed: Ryan Beene. **Description:** Alta Equipment Co., a forklift dealer, closed 2009 with a string of acquisitions expecting to double the firm's employee headcount and triple its annual revenue. Alta Lift Truck Services, Inc., as the company was known before the acquisitions, was founded in 1984 as Michigan's dealer for forklift manufacturer Yale Materials Handling Corp.

39012 ■ *"Dealing With Dangers Abroad" in Financial Executive (Vol. 23, December 2007, No. 10, pp. 32)*
Pub: Financial Executives International
Ed: Jeffrey Marshall. **Description:** Clear processes and responsibilities for risk management for all companies going global are essential. U.S. toy manufacturer, Matel was put into crisis mode after its Chinese-made toys were recalled due to the use of lead-based paint or tiny magnets in its products.

39013 ■ *"A Decent Proposal" in Hawaii Business (Vol. 53, March 2008, No. 9, pp. 52)*
Pub: Hawaii Business Publishing
Ed: Jacy L. Youn. **Description:** Bonnie Cooper and Brian Joy own Big Rock Manufacturing Inc., a stone manufacturing company, which sells carved rocks and bowls, lava benches, waterfalls, and Buddhas. Details about the company's growth are discussed.

39014 ■ *"Deere to Open Technology Center in Germany" in Chicago Tribune (September 3, 2008)*
Pub: McClatchy-Tribune Information Services
Ed: James P. Miller. **Description:** Deere & Co. plans to open a technology and innovation center in Germany; details of the company's expansion plans are discussed.

39015 ■ *"Defense Contractor May Expand Locally; BAE Systems Ramps Up Vehicle Prototypes" in Crain's Detroit Business (March 24, 2008)*
Pub: Crain Communications, Inc.
Ed: Chad Halcom. **Description:** Profile of BAE Systems, a defense contractor, that has built a prototype in the highly competitive Joint Light Tactical Vehicle project; the company has also completed its prototype RG33L Mine Resistant Recovery Maintenance Vehicle and has plans for expansion.

39016 ■ *"Deja Vu" in Canadian Business (Vol. 81, July 22, 2008, No. 12-13, pp. 38)*
Pub: Rogers Media Ltd.
Ed: Joe Castaldo. **Description:** Laurent Beaudoin has retired as chief executive officer for Bombardier Inc.'s, a manufacturer of regional and business aircraft, but kept a role in the firm as a non-executive chairman. Beaudoin first resigned from the company in 1999, but had to return in 2004 to address challenging situations faced by the company. Beaudoin's views on management and the company are presented.

39017 ■ *"Delaware Diaper Maker Wanting To Expand Less Than a Year After Move" in Business First-Columbus (December 7, 2007, pp. A6)*
Pub: American City Business Journals, Inc.
Ed: Dan Eaton. **Description:** Duluth, Georgia-based Associated Hygienic Products LLC is planning to expand its production operations by 20 percent and hire new workers. The diaper maker was awarded state incentives to facilitate its transfer from Marion to Delaware. Details are included.

39018 ■ *"Despite Gloom, Auto Sales Saw Gains in 2005" in Globe & Mail (January 5, 2006, pp. B1)*
Pub: CTVglobemedia Publishing Inc.
Ed: Greg Keenan. **Description:** An overview of positve automotive sales in Canada, for 2005, is presented.

39019 ■ *"Despite Hot Toys, Holiday Sales Predicted To Be Ho-Ho-Hum" in Drug Store News (Vol. 29, November 12, 2007, No. 14, pp. 78)*
Pub: Drug Store News
Ed: Doug Desjardins. **Description:** Summer toy recalls have retailers worried about holiday sales in 2007. Mattel was heavily impacted from the recall of millions of toys manufactured in China.

39020 ■ *"Detroit 3's Fall Would Be a Big One in Ohio" in Business First Columbus (Vol. 25, November 28, 2008, No. 14, pp. A1)*
Pub: American City Business Journals
Ed: Dan Eaton. **Description:** Ohio's economy will suffer huge negative effects in the event of a failure of one or more of the automotive companies, General Motors Corporation, Ford Motor Company, or Chrysler LLC. The state is home to 97,900 jobs in the automotive industry and is a vital link to the industry's supply network.

39021 ■ *"DeWind Delivering Turbines to Texas Wind Farm" in Professional Services Close-Up (September 25, 2011)*
Pub: Close-Up Media
Description: DeWind Company has begun shipment of turbines to the 20 MW Frisco Wind Farm located in Hansford County, Texas. DeWind is a subsidiary of Daewoo Shipbuilding and Marine Engineering Company. Details of the project are discussed.

39022 ■ *"Diana Sands; Vice-President of Investor Relations, Boeing Co." in Crain's Chicago Business (Vol. 31, May 5, 2008, No. 18, pp. 32)*
Pub: Crain Communications, Inc.
Ed: John Rosenthal. **Description:** Profile of Diana Sands who is the vice-president of investor relations at Boeing Co. which entails explaining the company's performance to securities analysts and institutional investors.

39023 ■ *"Digital Power Management and the PMBus" in Canadian Electronics (Vol. 23, June-July 2008, No. 4, pp. 8)*
Pub: Action Communication Inc.
Ed: Torbjorn Hohnberg. **Description:** PMBus is an interface that can be applied to a variety of devices including power management devices. Information on digital power management products using this interface are also provided.

39024 ■ *"Digital Printing Walks the Plank" in American Printer (Vol. 128, August 1, 2011, No. 8)*
Pub: Penton Media Inc.
Description: Digital print manufacturing is discussed.

39025 ■ *"Discount Beers Take Fizz Out Of Molson" in Globe & Mail (February 10, 2006, pp. B3)*
Pub: CTVglobemedia Publishing Inc.
Ed: Omar El Akkad. **Description:** The reasons behind the decline in profits by 60 percent for Molson Coors Brewing Co., during fourth quarter 2005, are presented.

39026 ■ *"The Dominance of Doubt" in Barron's (Vol. 89, July 13, 2009, No. 28, pp. M3)*
Pub: Dow Jones & Co., Inc.
Description: Five straight down days leading up to July 10, 2009 in the U.S. stock market reminds one strategist of 1982 when there was a feeling that things could never be the same again. One analyst is bullish on the stocks of Apple Inc. and sees the stocks rising to at least 180 in 12 months. The prospects of the shares of GM and Ford are also discussed.

39027 ■ *"The Doomsday Scenario" in Conde Nast Portfolio (Vol. 2, June 2008, No. 6, pp. 91)*
Pub: Conde Nast Publications
Contact: David Carey, President
Ed: Jeffrey Rothfeder. **Description:** Detroit and the U.S. auto industry are discussed as well as the ramifications of the demise of this manufacturing base. Similarities and differences between the downfall of the U.S. steel business and the impact it had on Pittsburg, Pennsylvania is also discussed.

39028 ■ *"Dow Champions Innovative Energy Solutions for Auto Industry at NAIAS" in Business of Global Warming (January 25, 2010, pp. 7)*
Pub: Investment Weekly News
Description: This year's North American International Auto Show in Detroit will host the 'Electric Avenue' exhibit sponsored by the Dow Chemical Company. The display will showcase the latest in innovative energy solutions from Dow as well as electric vehicles and the technology supporting them. This marks the first time a non-automotive manufacturer is part of the main floor of the show.

39029 ■ *"Dreyer's Grand Ice Cream" in Ice Cream Reporter (Vol. 23, September 20, 2010, No. 10, pp. 8)*
Pub: Ice Cream Reporter
Description: Dreyer's Grand Ice Cream will add one hundred new manufacturing jobs at its plant in Laurel, Maryland and another 65 new hires before the end of 2010 and another 35 in 2011.

39030 ■ *"Drilling Deep and Flying High" in Barron's (Vol. 88, June 30, 2008, No. 26, pp. 34)*
Pub: Dow Jones & Co., Inc.
Ed: Kenneth Rapoza. **Description:** Shares of Petrobras could rise another 25 percent if the three deepwater wells that the company has found proves as lucrative as some expect. Petrobras will become an oil giant if the reserves are proven.

39031 ■ *"Drop in the Bucket Makes a lot of Waves" in Globe & Mail (March 22, 2007, pp. B1)*
Pub: CTVglobemedia Publishing Inc.
Ed: Greg Keenan. **Description:** The concern of several auto makers in Canada over the impact of providing heavy rebates to customers buying energy-efficient cars is discussed.

39032 ■ *"Duro Bag to Expand, Add 130 Jobs" in Business Courier (Vol. 27, August 6, 2010, No. 14, pp. 1)*
Pub: Business Courier
Ed: Jon Newberry. **Description:** Duro Bag Manufacturing Company will expand capacity at its Florence, Kentucky plant and will add around 130 jobs over the next few years. The state of Kentucky has given preliminary approval for up to $1 million in tax incentives over 10 years, tied to the creation of new jobs. The company's investment will include new production and packaging equipment and building improvements.

39033 ■ *"The Dynamic DUO" in Canadian Electronics (Vol. 23, February 2008, No. 1, pp. 24)*
Pub: CLB Media Inc.
Description: Citronics Corporation not only aims to proved a good working environment for its employees, it also values the opinions of its personnel. Citronics had its employees test different workbenches before finally purchasing thirty-five of Lista's Align adjustable height workstation, which combines flexibility with aesthetics. The design of the Alin workbench is described.

39034 ■ *"Dynamic Duo" in Barron's (Vol. 88, March 10, 2008, No. 10, pp. 45)*
Pub: Dow Jones & Company, Inc.
Ed: Shirley A. Lazo. **Description:** General Dynamics, the world's sixth-largest military contractor, raised its dividend payout by 20.7 percent from 29 cents to 35 cents a share. Steel Dynamics, producer of structural steel and steel bar products, declared a 2-for-1 stock split and raised its quarterly dividend by 33 percent to a split-adjusted 10 cents a share.

39035 ■ *"Early Spring Halts Drilling Season" in Globe & Mail (March 14, 2007, pp. B14)*
Pub: CTVglobemedia Publishing Inc.
Ed: Norval Scott. **Description:** Decreased petroleum productivity in Canadian oil drilling rigs due to early spring season in western regions is discussed.

39036 ■ *"Eclipse to Hire 50 for Airp;ort Hangar" in Business Review, Albany New York (Vol. 34, November 9, 2007, No. 32, pp. 3)*
Pub: American City Business Journals, Inc.
Ed: Robin K. Cooper. **Description:** Eclipse Aviation, a jet manufacturer will hire fifty workers who will operate its new maintenance hangar at Albany International Airport. The company was expected to hire around twenty-five employees after it announced its plan to open one of the seven U.S. Factory Service Centers in 2005. Denise Zieske, the airport Economic Development Manager, expects the hangar construction to be completed by December 2007.

39037 ■ *"Effective Use of Field Time" in Agency Sales Magazine (Vol. 39, July 2009, No. 7, pp. 40)*
Pub: MANA
Description: Sales representatives need to consider the value of field visits to themselves and their customers ahead of time. Several anecdotes about field visits from the perspective of manufacturers and sale representatives are presented.

39038 ■ *"Electronics Assembly" in Canadian Electronics (Vol. 23, February 2008, No. 1, pp. 12)*
Pub: CLB Media Inc.
Description: I&J Fisnar Inc. has launched a new system of bench top dispensing robots while Vitronics Soltec and KIC have introduced a new reflow soldering machine. Teknek, on the other hand, has announced a new product, called the CM10, which an be used in cleaning large format substrates. Other new products and their description are presented.

39039 ■ *"EnCana Axes Spending on Gas Wells" in Globe & Mail (February 16, 2006, pp. B1)*
Pub: CTVglobemedia Publishing Inc.
Ed: Dave Ebner. **Description:** The reasons behind EnCana Corp.'s cost spending measures by $300 million on natural gas wells are presented. The company projects 2 percent cut in gas and oil sales for 2006.

39040 ■ *"The End of the Line for Line Extensions?" in Advertising Age (Vol. 79, July 7, 2008, No. 26, pp. 3)*
Pub: Crain Communications, Inc.
Description: After years of double-digit growth, some of the most heavily extended personal-care products have slowed substantially or even declined in the U.S. Unilever's Dove and P&G's Pantene and Olay are two such brands that have been affected. Statistical data included.

39041 ■ *"Energy Firms Face Stricter Definitions" in Globe & Mail (March 26, 2007, pp. B3)*
Pub: CTVglobemedia Publishing Inc.
Ed: David Ebner. **Description:** The Alberta Securities Commission has imposed strict securities regulations on oil and gas industries. Energy industries will have to submit revenue details to stake holders.

39042 ■ *"Energy Outfitter Wings Into Houston" in Houston Business Journal (Vol. 40, December 4, 2009, No. 30, pp. 2A)*
Pub: American City Business Journals
Ed: Ford Gunter. **Description:** Red Wing Shoe Company Inc. has launched its personal protective equipment (PPE) line for oil and gas industry crewmen in North America by opening a 13,000 square foot distribution hub in Houston, Texas. The Houston facility was created to supply directly the oil and gas industry and to carry inventory for select distributors.

39043 ■ *"Energy Slide Slows Fourth Quarter Profits" in Globe & Mail (April 13, 2007, pp. B9)*
Pub: CTVglobemedia Publishing Inc.
Ed: Angela Barnes. **Description:** The decrease in the fourth quarter profits of several companies across various industries in Canada, including mining and manufacturing, due to global decrease in oil prices, is discussed.

39044 ■ *"Enforcer In Fantasyland" in Crain's New York Business (Vol. 24, February 25, 2008, No. 8, pp. 10)*
Pub: Crain Communications Inc.
Ed: Hilary Potkewitz. **Description:** Patent law, particularly in the toy and game industry, is recession-proof according to Barry Negrin, partner at Pryor Cashman. Negrin co-founded his patent practice group. Despite massive recalls of toys and the concern over toxic toys, legal measures are in place in this industry.

39045 ■ *"Engineering Services Supplier Launches 'Robotic Renaissance'" in Modern Machine Shop (Vol. 84, September 2011, No. 4, pp. 46)*
Pub: Gardner Business Media, Inc.
Contact: Richard G. Kline, President
E-mail: rkline@gardnerweb.com
Description: Profile of Applied Manufacturing Technologies (AMT) new hiring initiative that supports continuing growth in the robotics industry. AMT is located in Orion, Michigan and supplies factory automation design, engineering and process consulting services.

39046 ■ *"Evaluate Your Process and Do It Better" in Modern Machine Shop (Vol. 84, October 2011, No. 5, pp. 34)*
Pub: Gardner Business Media, Inc.
Contact: Richard G. Kline, President
E-mail: rkline@gardnerweb.com
Ed: Wayne S. Chaneski. **Description:** In order to be more competitive, many machine shops owners are continually looking at their processes and procedures in order to be more competitive.

39047 ■ *"Event Stresses Cross-Border Cooperation" in Crain's Detroit Business (Vol. 24, March 31, 2008, No. 13, pp. 5)*
Pub: Crain Communications, Inc.
Ed: Chad Halcom. **Description:** According to John Austin, a senior fellow of The Brookings Institution, open immigration policies, better transportation and trade across the border and a cleanup of the Great Lakes will bring economic resurgence to Midwestern states and Canadian provinces with manufacturing economies.

39048 ■ *"Everyone Has a Story Inspired by Chevrolet" in Automotive News (Vol. 86, October 31, 2011, No. 6488, pp. S003)*
Pub: Crain Communications Inc.
Ed: Keith E. Crain. **Description:** Besides being a great ad slogan, 'Baseball, Hot Dogs, Apple Pie and Chevrolet', the brand conjures up memories for most everyone in our society. Louis Chevrolet had a reputation as a race car driver and lent his name to the car that has endured for 100 years.

39049 ■ *"Executive Decision: Damn the Profit Margins, Sleeman Declares War on Buck-a-Beer Foes" in Globe & Mail (January 28, 2006, pp. B3)*
Pub: CTVglobemedia Publishing Inc.
Ed: Andy Hoffman. **Description:** The cost savings plans of chief executive officer John Sleeman of Sleeman Breweries Ltd. are presented.

39050 ■ *"Executive Decision: Just What the Doctor Ordered" in Globe & Mail (February 11, 2006, pp. B3)*
Pub: CTVglobemedia Publishing Inc.
Ed: Leonard Zehr. **Description:** The leadership ability of chief executive William Hunter of Angiotech Pharmaceuticals Inc., who acquired American Medical Instruments Holdings Inc. for $785 million, is discussed.

39051 ■ *"Executive Decision: Lead a Double Life for Geac's Sake" in Globe & Mail (January 21, 2006, pp. B4)*
Pub: CTVglobemedia Publishing Inc.
Ed: Simon Avery. **Description:** The details of growth of Geac Computer Corporation Ltd., under chief executive officer Charles Jones, are presented.

39052 ■ *"Executive Interview: Arturo Elias" in Canadian Business (Vol. 80, January 29, 2007, No. 3, pp. 16)*
Pub: Rogers Media
Ed: Thomas Watson. **Description:** The views of Arturo Elias, the president of General Motors Canada Limited, on the prospects of the growth of the company revenues during the year 2007 are presented.

39053 ■ *"Expanding Middleby's Food Processing Biz" in Crain's Chicago Business (Vol. 31, April 21, 2008, No. 16, pp. 6)*
Pub: Crain Communications, Inc.
Ed: David Sterrett. **Description:** Profile of the executive vice-president of the food processing company, Middleby Corp, whose business plan is to develop new products, begin looking for acquisitions and simplify operations in order to expand the firm.

39054 ■ *"Experts Strive to Educate on Proper Pet Diets" in Pet Product News (Vol. 64, November 2010, No. 11, pp. 40)*
Pub: BowTie Inc.
Ed: John Hustace Walker. **Description:** Pet supply manufacturers have been bundling small mammal food and treats with educational sources to help retailers avoid customer misinformation. This action has been motivated by the customer's quest to seek proper nutritional advice for their small mammal pets.

39055 ■ *"Extra Rehab Time Boosts M-B's Off-Lease Profits" in Automotive News (Vol. 86, October 31, 2011, No. 6488, pp. 22)*
Pub: Crain Communications Inc.
Ed: Arlena Sawyers. **Description:** Mercedes-Benz Financial Services USA is holding on to off-lease vehicles in order to recondition them and the move is boosting profits for the company.

39056 ■ *"Exxon Braving the Danger Zones" in Globe & Mail (March 8, 2007, pp. B1)*
Pub: CTVglobemedia Publishing Inc.
Ed: Shawn McCarthy. **Description:** The plans of Exxon Mobil Corp. to increase its revenues through the expansion of its operations in Asia, Africa, and the Middle East are discussed.

39057 ■ *Factory Girls: From Village to City in a Changing China*
Pub: Spiegel & Grau
Ed: Leslie T. Chang. **Released:** 2009. **Price:** $26.00. **Description:** Young women who flee the rural villages in China find exhausting work and social mobility working in factories.

39058 ■ *"Fair Play? China Cheats, Carney Talks and Rankin Walks; Here's the Latest" in Canadian Business (Vol. 81, March 17, 2008, No. 4)*
Pub: Rogers Media
Description: Discusses the World Trade Organization which says that China is breaking trade rules by taxing imports of auto parts at the same rate as foreign-made finished cars. Mark Carney first speech as the governor of the Bank of Canada made economists suspect a rate cut on overnight loans. Andre Rankin was ordered by the Ontario Securities Commission to pay $250,000 in investigation costs.

39059 ■ *"Familiar Fun" in Crain's Cleveland Business (Vol. 28, October 22, 2007, No. 42, pp. 3)*
Pub: Crain Communications Inc.
Ed: John Booth. **Description:** Marketing for the 2007 holiday season has toy retailers focusing on American-made products because of recent recalls of toys produced in China that do not meet U.S. safety standards.

39060 ■ *"Feet on the Street: Reps Are Ready to Hit the Ground Running" in Agency Sales Magazine (Vol. 39, July 2009, No. 7, pp. 12)*
Pub: MANA
Ed: Jack Foster. **Description:** One of the major benefits to manufacturers in working with sales representatives is the concept of synergistic selling where the rep shows his mettle. The rep of today is a solution provider that anticipates and meets the customer's needs.

39061 ■ *"Fight Against Fake" in The Business Journal-Portland (Vol. 25, July 18, 2008, No. 19, pp. 1)*
Pub: American City Business Journals, Inc.
Ed: Erik Siemers. **Description:** Companies, such as Columbia Sportswear Co. and Nike Inc., are fighting the counterfeiting of their sportswear and footwear products through the legal process of coordinating with law enforcement agencies to raid factories. Most of the counterfeiting factories are in China and India. Other details on the issue are discussed.

39062 ■ *"Fighting Detroit" in Baltimore Business Journal (Vol. 27, January 22, 2010, No. 38, pp. 1)*
Pub: American City Business Journals
Ed: Daniel J. Sernovitz. **Description:** Baltimore, Maryland-based car dealers could retrieve their franchises from car manufacturers, Chrysler LLC and General Motors Corporation, through a forced arbitration. A provision in a federal budget mandates the arbitration. The revoking of franchises has been attributed to the car manufacturers' filing of bankruptcy protection.

39063 ■ *"Finalist: BlackEagle Partners L.L.C." in Crain's Detroit Business (Vol. 24, March 24, 2008, No. 12, pp. 12)*
Pub: Crain Communications, Inc.
Ed: Brent Snavely. **Description:** Overview of private-equity firm, BlackEagle Partners L.L.C., an upstart that acquired Rockford Products Corp. in order to improve the performance of the company who does business with several major tier-one automotive suppliers; Rockford manufactures highly engineered chassis and suspension components for automakers and the automotive aftermarket.

39064 ■ *"Finalist: Private Company, $100M-$1B" in Crain's Detroit Business (Vol. 25, June 22, 2009, No. 25)*
Pub: Crain Communications Inc. - Detroit
Ed: Chad Halcom. **Description:** Profile of U.S. Farathane Corporation, the Sterling Heights, Michigan-based automotive plastic components maker. The company's CFO discusses ways they are coping with the cutbacks at major automobile factories.

39065 ■ *"Financing for NNSA Plant Is a Work in Progress" in The Business Journal-Serving Metropolitan Kansas City (October 24, 2008)*
Pub: American City Business Journals, Inc.
Ed: Rob Roberts. **Description:** The Kansas City Council approved a development plan for a $500 million nuclear weapons parts plant in south Kansas City. The US Congress approved a $59 million annual lease payment to the plant's developer. Financing for the construction of the plant remains in question as the plant's developers have to shoulder construction costs.

39066 ■ *"Firms Upbeat About Future, Survey Shows" in Globe & Mail (January 17, 2006, pp. B4)*
Pub: CTVglobemedia Publishing Inc.
Ed: Heather Scoffield. **Description:** The issue of labor shortage for manufacturing sector, in Canada, is discussed. The survey results of Bank of Canada are presented.

39067 ■ *"First Impression of Robotic Farming Systems" in Farm Industry News (September 30, 2011)*
Pub: Penton Business Media Inc.
Ed: Jodie Wehrspann. **Description:** Farm Science Review featured tillage tools and land rollers, including John Deere's GPS system where a cart tractor is automatically controlled as well as a new line of Kinze's carts and a video of their robotic system for a driver-less cart tractor.

39068 ■ *"First Suzlon S97 Turbines Arrive in North America for Installation" in PR Newswire (September 28, 2011)*
Pub: United Business Media
Description: Suzlon Energy Ltd., the world's fifth largest manufacturer of wind turbines, will install its first S97 turbine at the Amherst Wind Farm Project. These turbines will be installed on 90-meter hub height towers and at full capacity, will generate enough electricity to power over 10,000 Canadian homes.

39069 ■ *"Five Reasons Why the Gap Fell Out of Fashion" in Globe & Mail (January 27, 2007, pp. B4)*
Pub: CTVglobemedia Publishing Inc.
Ed: Keith McArthur. **Description:** The five major market trends that have caused the decline of fashion clothing retailer Gap Inc.'s sales are discussed. The shift in brand, workplace fashion culture, competition, demographics, and consumer preferences have lead to the Gap's brand identity.

39070 ■ *"Florida's Bright Upside" in Tampa Bay Business Journal (Vol. 29, November 6, 2009, No. 46, pp. 1)*
Pub: American City Business Journals
Ed: Michael Hinman. **Description:** Florida's Public Service Commission (PSC) decision on a power purchase agreement that could add 25 megawatts of solar energy on Tampa Electric Company's offerings is presented. The decision could support the growing market for suppliers and marketers of renewable energy such as Jabil Circuit Inc., which manufactures photovoltaic modules. Details of the agreement are discussed.

39071 ■ *"Flying High?" in Canadian Business (Vol. 80, April 9, 2007, No. 8, pp. 42)*
Pub: Rogers Media
Ed: Thomas Watson. **Description:** The increase in Bombardier Inc.'s income by 30 percent to $112 million and increase in its share prices are discussed. The caution of analysts about its accounting methods that may adversely hit the company in future, too is discussed.

39072 ■ *"Foods for Thought" in Pet Product News (Vol. 64, December 2010, No. 12, pp. 16)*
Pub: BowTie Inc.
Ed: Maddy Heleine. **Description:** Manufacturers have been focused at developing species-specific fish foods due to consumer tendency to assess the benefits of the food they feed their fish. As retailers stock species-specific fish foods, manufacturers have provided in-store items and strategies to assist in efficiently selling these food products. Trends in fish food packaging and ingredients are also discussed.

39073 ■ *"For Baxter, A Lingering PR Problem; Ongoing Focus On Heparin Deaths Ups Heat On CEO" in Crain's Chicago Business (April 21, 2008)*
Pub: Crain Communications, Inc.
Ed: Mike Colias. **Description:** Baxter International Inc.'s recall of the blood-thinning medication heparin has exposed the company to costly litigation and put the perils of overseas drug manufacturing in the spotlight. Wall Street investors predict that an indefinite halt in production of the drug should not hurt the company's bottom line since heparin represents a tiny sliver of the business. Since Baxter began recalling the drug in January its shares have continued to outpace most other medical stocks.

39074 ■ *"For the Seasoned Buyer" in Inc. (Vol. 30, November 2008, No. 11, pp. 32)*
Pub: Mansueto Ventures LLC
Ed: Darren Dahl. **Description:** Dominick Fimiano shares his plans to sell his ten-year-old business that manufactures and sells frozen pizza dough and crusts as well as a variety of topped pizzas. Products are purchased by schools, hospitals, bowling alleys and amusement parks. The business sale includes the buyer's taking on Fimiano's son the firm's most senior employee.

39075 ■ *"Ford Canada's Edsel of a Year: Revenue Plummets 24 Percent in '05" in Globe & Mail (February 2, 2006, pp. B1)*
Pub: CTVglobemedia Publishing Inc.
Ed: Greg Keenan. **Description:** Ford Motor Company of Canada Ltd. posted 24% decline in revenues for 2005. The drop in earnings is attributed to plant shutdown in Oaksville, Canada.

39076 ■ *"Ford, Chrysler Dinged as Little Cars Rule Road" in Globe & Mail (March 2, 2007, pp. B3)*
Pub: CTVglobemedia Publishing Inc.
Ed: Greg Keenan. **Description:** The Ford Motor Co. and the Chrysler Group posted a decline in automobile sales in the first two months of 2007. The sales statistics of other automobile companies in Canada are also presented.

39077 ■ *"Ford Fix Requires 'Painful' Remedy" in Globe & Mail (January 9, 2006, pp. B1)*
Pub: CTVglobemedia Publishing Inc.
Ed: Greg Keenan. **Description:** The plans of Ford Motor Co. to streamline Canadian operations are presented.

39078 ■ *"Ford's $12.7 Billion Loss Signals End of an Era" in Globe & Mail (January 26, 2007, pp. B1)*
Pub: CTVglobemedia Publishing Inc.
Ed: Greg Keenan. **Description:** The loss of $12.7 billion incurred by Ford Motors Co., and its decision to close down several of its plants, cut thousands of jobs and focus on passenger cars, is discussed.

39079 ■ *"Formaspace Finds a Bigger Home" in Austin Business Journallnc. (Vol. 29, December 4, 2009, No. 39, pp. 1)*
Pub: American City Business Journals
Ed: Kate Harrington. **Description:** Formaspace Technical Furniture has signed a lease for 56,700 square feet in Harris Ridge Business Center at Northeast Austin, Texas, which represents one of the area's largest leases for 2009. The new lease enables Formaspace to hire new employees, invest in new equipment, and take advantage of a taxing designation created for manufacturers.

39080 ■ *"Former Chrysler Dealers Build New Business Model" in Crain's Detroit Business (Vol. 25, June 22, 2009, No. 25, pp. 3)*
Pub: Crain Communications Inc. - Detroit
Ed: Daniel Duggan. **Description:** Joe Ricci is one of 14 Detroit area dealerships whose franchises have been terminated. Ricci and other Chrysler dealers in the area are starting new businesses or switching to new franchises.= Ricci's All American Buyer's Service will be located in Dearborn and will sell only used cars.

39081 ■ *"Fraser and Neave Acquires King's Creameries" in Ice Cream Reporter (Vol. 23, November 20, 2010, No. 12, pp. 1)*
Pub: Ice Cream Reporter
Description: Fraser and Neave Ltd., a Singapore-based consumer products marketer, has entered a conditional agreement to acquire all outstanding shares of King's Creameries, the leading manufacturer and distributor of frozen desserts.

39082 ■ *"Frito Lay Plans to Spice Up Life With New Chips" in Globe & Mail (February 21, 2006, pp. B3)*
Pub: CTVglobemedia Publishing Inc.
Ed: Andy Hoffman. **Description:** The reasons behind the launch of potato chips by Frito Lay Canada Inc., subsidiary of PepsiCo. Inc., are presented.

39083 ■ *"From American Icon to Global Juggernaut" in Automotive News (Vol. 86, October 31, 2011, No. 6488, pp. S003)*
Pub: Crain Communications Inc.
Ed: Peter Brown. **Description:** Chevrolet celebrates its 100th Anniversary. The brand revolutionized its market with affordable cars that bring technology to the masses. Chevys have been sold in 140 countries and the company is responding to a broader market.

39084 ■ *"Fromm Family Foods Converts Old Feed Mill Into Factory for Gourmet Pet Food" in Wisconsin State Journal (August 3, 2011)*
Pub: Capital Newspapers
Ed: Barry Adams. **Description:** Fromm Family Foods, a gourmet cat and dog food company spent $10 million to convert an old feed mill into a pet food manufacturing facility. The owner forecasts doubling or tripling its production of 600 tons of feed per week in about five years.

39085 ■ *"Fuel King: The Most Fuel-Efficient Tractor of the Decade is the John Deere 8295R" in Farm Industry News (November 10, 2011)*
Pub: Penton Business Media Inc.
Description: Farm Industry News compiled a list of the most fuel-efficient tractors with help from the Nebraska Tractor Test Lab, with the John Deere 8295R PTO winner of the most fuel-efficient tractor of the decade.

39086 ■ *"Fuel for Thought" in Canadian Business (Vol. 81, April 14, 2008, No. 6, pp. 18)*
Pub: Rogers Media
Ed: John Gray. **Description:** Discusses a web poll of 133 CEOs and other business leaders that shows that they predict oil prices to increase to US $113 per barrel over the 2008 to 2010 timeframe. Most of the respondents did not favor cutting gas taxes but this group wants the government to cut taxes on fuel-efficient vehicles and increase subsidies to local transit systems.

39087 ■ *"Fuel for Thought; Canadian Business Leaders on Energy Policy" in Canadian Business (Vol. 81, September 15, 2008, No. 14-15, pp. 12)*
Pub: Rogers Media Ltd.
Ed: Joe Castaldo. **Description:** Most Canadian business leaders worry about the unreliability of the oil supply but feel that Canada is in a better position to benefit from the energy supply crisis than other countries. Many respondents also highlighted the need to invest in renewable energy sources.

39088 ■ *"Full-Court Press for Apple" in Barron's (Vol. 88, March 24, 2008, No. 12, pp. 47)*
Pub: Dow Jones & Company, Inc.
Ed: Mark Veverka. **Description:** Apple Inc. is facing more intellectual property lawsuits in 2008, with 30 patent lawsuits filed compared to 15 in 2007 and nine in 2006. The lawsuits, which involve products such as the iPod and the iPhone, present some concern for Apple's shareholders.

39089 ■ *"Furniture Making May Come Back--Literally" in Business North Carolina (Vol. 28, March 2008, No. 3, pp. 32)*
Pub: Business North Carolina
Description: Due to the weak U.S. dollar and the fact that lumber processors never left the country, foreign furniture manufacturers are becoming interested in moving manufacturing plants to the U.S.

39090 ■ *"Future Autoworkers will Need Broader Skills" in Crain's Detroit Business (Vol. 25, June 8, 2009, No. 23, pp. 13)*
Pub: Crain Communications Inc. - Detroit
Ed: Ryan Beene. **Description:** Auto industry observers report that new workers in the industry will need advanced skills and educational backgrounds in engineering and technical fields because jobs in the factories will become more technology-based and multidisciplinary.

39091 ■ *"The Game of Operation" in Crain's Chicago Business (Vol. 31, April 28, 2008, No. 17, pp. 26)*
Pub: Crain Communications, Inc.
Ed: Samantha Stainburn. **Description:** Revenue at Medline Industries Inc., a manufacturer of medical products, has risen 12 percent a year since 1976, reaching $2.81 billion last year. Growth at the company is due to new and increasingly sophisticated operations by surgeons which brings about the need for more specialized tools.

39092 ■ *"Gas Supplies Low Heading Into Summer Season" in Globe & Mail (April 13, 2007, pp. B6)*
Pub: CTVglobemedia Publishing Inc.
Ed: Shawn McCarthy. **Description:** The decrease in the supply of gas due to maintenance problems at refineries in the United States and Canada is discussed.

39093 ■ *"Gatorade Loses Its Competitive Edge; Upstart Rivals Undercut Its Domination of Game" in Crain's Chicago Business (April 28, 2008)*
Pub: Crain Communications, Inc.
Ed: Natalie Zmuda. **Description:** According to beverage-marketing experts, Gatorade is losing some of its market share to aggressive new rivals who are appealing to younger consumers.

39094 ■ *"GE Looking to Extend Hot Streak" in Business Courier (Vol. 24, January 25, 2008, No. 42, pp. 1)*
Pub: American City Business Journals, Inc.
Ed: John Newberry. **Description:** GE Aviation has enjoyed strong revenues and sales due to increase aircraft engine orders. It has an engine backlog order of $19 million as of the end of 2007. Data on the aviation company's revenues, operating profit and total engine orders for the year 2004 to 2007 are presented.

39095 ■ *"GE Milestone: 1,000th Wind Turbine Installed in Canada" in CNW Group (October 4, 2011)*
Pub: CNW Group
Contact: Carolyn McGill-Davidson, President
Description: GE installed its 1,000th wind turbine in Canada at Cartier Wind Energy's Gros Morne project in the Gaspesie Region of Quebec, Canada. As Canada continues to expand its use of wind energy, GE plans to have over 1,100 wind turbines installed in the nation by the end of 2011.

39096 ■ *"General Motors Can't Kick Incentives-But They Work" in Advertising Age (Vol. 79, July 7, 2008, No. 26, pp. 3)*
Pub: Crain Communications, Inc.
Ed: Jean Halliday. **Description:** General Motors Corp. was able to maintain their market share just as Toyota Motor Corp. was beginning to pass the manufacturer; GM lured in customers with a sales incentive that they heavily advertised and subsequently helped build demand; investors, however, were not impressed and GM shares were hammered to their lowest point in 50 years after analysts speculated the company might go bankrupt.

39097 ■ *"Getting Inventive With..Ed Spellman" in Crain's Cleveland Business (Vol. 28, October 22, 2007, No. 42, pp. 18)*
Pub: Crain Communications, Inc.
Ed: Kimberly Bonvissuto. **Description:** Profile featuring Ed Spellman, a mechanical engineer who decided to quit his job at Invacare Corp., a medical equipment manufacturer and distributor, in order to devote his full attention to promoting his numerous inventions, including the DV-Grip, a vehicle mount for portable DVD players.

39098 ■ *"Getting the Word Out" in Modern Machine Shop (Vol. 84, September 2011, No. 4, pp. 16)*
Pub: Gardner Business Media, Inc.
Contact: Richard G. Kline, President
E-mail: rkline@gardnerweb.com
Ed: Derek Korn. **Description:** Many times machine shops create devices to streamline their own machining processes and find these devices can be used by other shops, thus developing a marketable product. Tips for this process are outlined.

39099 ■ *"Give 'Em a Boost" in Entrepreneur (Vol. 36, April 2008, No. 4, pp. 120)*
Pub: Entrepreneur Media, Inc.
Ed: Kristen Henning. **Description:** Amir Levin of Kaboost Corp. markets a plastic booster system that attaches to the bottom of a regular chair and raises it. He thought of the idea of creating the product after seeing his young cousins refusing to sit in their booster seats. Levin started his company in 2006.

39100 ■ *"Global Pain: Alberta's Gain" in Canadian Business (Vol. 79, August 14, 2006, No. 16-17, pp. 60)*
Pub: Rogers Media
Ed: Jeff Sanford. **Description:** Political problems and conflicts in oil-rich countries like Iran, Venezuela, and Russia among others, which have benefited the petroleum industry in Alberta, is discussed.

39101 ■ *"Global Steel Makers Circle Stelco" in Globe & Mail (April 19, 2007, pp. B3)*
Pub: CTVglobemedia Publishing Inc.
Ed: Greg Keenan. **Description:** The details of the take over bids offered to Stelco Inc. are presented. Due to these bids the shares of Stelco Inc rose up to 70 percent.

39102 ■ *"GM Axing Prices; Kerkorian Calls for Crisis Plan" in Globe & Mail (January 11, 2006, pp. B1)*
Pub: CTVglobemedia Publishing Inc.
Ed: Greg Keenan. **Description:** The financial restructuring proposal of investor Kirk Kerkorian for General Motors Corp. is presented.

39103 ■ *"GM Canada Revved Up Over Camaro" in Globe & Mail (February 17, 2006, pp. B4)*
Pub: CTVglobemedia Publishing Inc.
Ed: Greg Keenan. **Description:** General Manager of General Motors Canada is planning to start the production of company's muscle car Camaro in Canadian facility. The car was exhibited at Canadian International Auto Show held in Toronto.

39104 ■ *"GM-Chrysler Merger Could Cull Dealerships From Coast to Coast" in Globe & Mail (February 20, 2007, pp. B17)*
Pub: CTVglobemedia Publishing Inc.
Ed: Greg Keenan. **Description:** General Motors Corp. is planning to acquire Chrysler Group. The challenges before the possible merger are presented.

39105 ■ *"GM-Chrysler Merger: Just a Bigger Mess?" in Globe & Mail (February 17, 2007, pp. B3)*
Pub: CTVglobemedia Publishing Inc.
Ed: Barrie McKenna; Greg Keenan. **Description:** The General Motors Corp. is negotiating talks to acquire DaimlerChrysler AG's Chrysler Group. The five reasons for the possible merger of the companies are presented.

39106 ■ *"GM Flexes Muscles With New Camaro Concept" in Globe & Mail (January 10, 2006, pp. B15)*
Pub: CTVglobemedia Publishing Inc.
Ed: Greg Keenan. **Description:** General Motors Corp., has displayed the new concept car Chevrolet Camaro, at the North American International Auto Show in Detroit. The features of this automobile manufactured at the company's assembly plant in Quebec are discussed.

39107 ■ *"GM Is On the Road Again" in Canadian Business (Vol. 83, September 14, 2010, No. 15, pp. 14)*
Pub: Rogers Media Ltd.
Ed: Thomas Watson. **Description:** Former General Motors CEO Rick Wagoner has been credited for single-handedly putting the automaker back on track before he was forced to resign and GM was restructured by the government. GM earned $2.19 billion the first half of 2010 after losing more than $80 billion in the three years leading up to its failure. GM's comeback is discussed.

39108 ■ *"GM Releases 2010 Product Guide, Ends Production of Medium-Duty Trucks" in Contractor (Vol. 56, July 2009, No. 7, pp. 5)*
Pub: Penton Media, Inc.
Ed: Candace Roulo. **Description:** General Motors will cease production of the Chevrolet Kodiak and GMC Topkick by July 31, 2009. Their 2010 Product Guide for the U.S. still has four remaining brands including the Buick, Cadillac, Chevrolet, and GMC.

39109 ■ *"GM's Decision to Boot Dealer Prompts Sale" in Baltimore Business Journal (Vol. 27, November 6, 2009, No. 26, pp. 1)*
Pub: American City Business Journals
Ed: Daniel J. Sernovitz. **Description:** General Motors Corporation's (GM) decision to strip Baltimore's Anderson Automotive Group Inc. of its GM franchise has prompted the owner, Bruce Mortimer, to close the automotive dealership and sell the land to a developer. The new project could make way for new homes, a shopping center and supermarket.

39110 ■ *"GM's Volt Woes Cast Shadow on E-Cars" in Wall Street Journal Eastern Edition (November 28, 2011, pp. B1)*
Pub: Dow Jones & Company Inc. Enterprise Media Group
Contact: Clare Hart, President
Ed: Sharon Terlep. **Description:** The future of electric cars is darkened with the government investigation by the National Highway Traffic Safety Administration into General Motor Company's Chevy Volt after two instances of the car's battery packs catching fire during crash tests conducted by the Agency.

39111 ■ *"Great Expectations" in Canadian Business (Vol. 81, April 14, 2008, No. 6, pp. 34)*
Pub: Rogers Media
Ed: Andy Holloway. **Description:** Therma Blades Inc. says that the reports that say their Therma Blade ice skates were not working properly were inaccurate. The major mistake of the company was to fail to manage the public's expectation when they touted the blades as revolutionary. Therma Blades Inc. has since tested the product with the help of 120 players and physiological testing done on elite level players show that there was a 10 percent improvement in energy efficiency.

39112 ■ *"Green Acres" in Hawaii Business (Vol. 54, September 2008, No. 3, pp. 48)*
Pub: Hawaii Business Publishing
Ed: Jan Tenbruggencate. **Description:** Bill Cowern's Hawaiian Mahogany is a forestry business that processes low-value trees to be sold as wood chips, which can be burned to create biodiesel. Cowern is planning to obtain certification to market carbon credits and is also working with Green Energy Hawaii for the permit of a biomass-fueled power plant. Other details about Cowern's business are discussed.

39113 ■ *"Green Energy Exec Hits State Policy" in Boston Business Journal (Vol. 30, December 3, 2010, No. 45, pp. 1)*
Pub: Boston Business Journal
Ed: Kyle Alspach. **Description:** American Superconductor Corporation President Dan McGahn believes that the state government of Massachusetts is not proactive enough to develop the state into a manufacturing hub for wind power technology. McGahn believes that while Governor Deval Patrick campaigned for wind turbines in the state, his administration does not have the focus required to build the turbines in the state.

39114 ■ *"Green Firm Scouts Sites in Tri-State" in Business Courier (Vol. 27, July 23, 2010, No. 12, pp. 1)*
Pub: Business Courier
Ed: Dan Monk. **Description:** CresaPartners is searching for a manufacturing facility in Cincinnati, Ohio. The company is set to tour about ten sites in the area.

39115 ■ *"Green Shift Sees Red" in Canadian Business (Vol. 81, September 29, 2008, No. 16)*
Pub: Rogers Media Ltd.
Ed: Jeff Sanford. **Description:** Green Shift Inc. is suing the Liberal Party of Canada in an $8.5 million lawsuit for using the phrase 'green shift' when they rolled out their carbon tax and climate change policy. The company has come to be recognized as a consultant and provider of green products such as non-toxic, biodegradable cups, plates, and utensils for events.

39116 ■ *"Greening the Auto Industry" in Business Journal-Serving Phoenix & the Valley of the Sun (Vol. 30, July 23, 2010, No. 46, pp. 1)*
Pub: Phoenix Business Journal
Ed: Patrick O'Grady. **Description:** Thermo Fluids Inc. has been recycling used oil products since 1993 and could become Arizona's first home for oil filter recycling after retrofitting its Phoenix facility to include a compaction machine. The new service could help establish Thermo Fluids as a recycling hub for nearby states.

39117 ■ *"Greg Stringham" in Canadian Business (Vol. 81, March 3, 2008, No. 3, pp. 8)*
Pub: Rogers Media
Ed: Michelle Magnan. **Description:** Canadian Association of Petroleum Producers' Greg Stringham thinks that the new royalty plan will result in companies pulling out their investments for Alberta's conventional oil and gas sector. Stringham adds that Alberta is losing its competitive advantage and companies must study their cost profiles to retrieve that advantage. The effects of the royalty system on Alberta's economy are examined further.

39118 ■ *"Grote Company Puts Final Wrap on Sandwich-Making Line" in Business First-Columbus (October 26, 2007, pp. A1)*
Pub: American City Business Journals, Inc.
Ed: Dan Eaton. **Description:** Grote Company acquired Oxfordshire, England-based Advanced Food Technology Ltd., giving the Ohio-based food cutting equipment company a manufacturing base in Europe. This is the company's second deal in four months. Details on Grote Company's plan to tap into the prepared fresh sandwich market are discussed.

39119 ■ *"Growth in Fits and Starts" in Canadian Business (Vol. 83, July 20, 2010, No. 11-12, pp. 18)*
Pub: Rogers Media Ltd.
Ed: James Cowan. **Description:** US home sales and manufacturing indicators have dropped and fears of a double-dip recession are widespread. However, a chief economist says that this is endemic to what can be seen after a recession caused by a financial crisis. In Canada, consumer optimism is rising and anxiety over losing one's job is waning.

39120 ■ *"GTI Licenses TMC to Cannon Boiler Works" in Contractor (Vol. 56, December 2009, No. 12, pp. 6)*
Pub: Penton Media, Inc.
Description: Gas Technology Institute has licensed Cannon Boiler Works Inc. to use its transport membrane condenser technology. The technology can be applied to elevated-temperature industrial processes such as boilers. It allows the capture and beneficial use of latent waste heat and water vapor from exhaust/flue gas.

39121 ■ *"Halls Give Hospital Drive $11 Million Infusion" in The Business Journal-Serving Metropolitan Kansas City (Vol. 26, July 18, 2008)*
Pub: American City Business Journals, Inc.
Ed: Rob Roberts. **Description:** Don Hall, chairman of Hallmark Cards Inc., and eight family members have announced that they will give $11 million to Children's Mercy Hospitals and Clinics for its $800 million expansion plan. Hall Family Foundation president Bill Hall that contributions such as that for Children's Mercy reflect the charitable interests of the foundation's board and founders. The possible impacts of the Hall's donation are analyzed.

39122 ■ *"H&M Offers a Dress for Less" in Canadian Business (Vol. 83, September 14, 2010, No. 15, pp. 20)*
Pub: Rogers Media Ltd.
Ed: Laura Cameron. **Description:** Swedish clothing company H&M has implemented loss leader strategy by pricing some dresses at extremely low prices. The economy has forced retailers to keep prices down despite the increasing cost of manufacturing, partly due to Chinese labor becoming more expensive. How the trend will affect apparel companies is discussed.

39123 ■ *"Happy New Year, Celestica?" in Canadian Business (Vol. 80, January 15, 2007, No. 2, pp. 25)*
Pub: Rogers Media
Ed: Andrew Wahl. **Description:** Speculations on the performance of the electronics manufacturing company Celestica Inc. in 2007, which has been labelled as a 'sick' company in recent times, are presented.

39124 ■ *"Have I Got a Deal For You" in Canadian Business (Vol. 83, October 12, 2010, No. 17, pp. 65)*
Pub: Rogers Media Ltd.
Ed: Bryan Borzykowski. **Description:** U.S. automobile market currently has more than three players, providing investors with a number of investment options. The sector is still mired in uncertainty, but people believe that these companies can only grow from this point forward. However, investors should use due diligence before jumping into the market.

39125 ■ *Hawaii Industrial Directory*
Pub: Harris InfoSource
Contact: Dennis Abrahams, President
E-mail: dennisa@harrisinfo.com
URL(s): www.harrisinfo.com. **Ed:** Fran Carlsen. **Released:** Annual; Latest edition 2010. **Price:** $495, Individuals Online. **Covers:** 9,400 manufacturing companies in Hawaii. **Entries include:** Company name, address, phone, fax, web site address (on CD-ROM only), toll-free, names and titles of key personnel, number of employees, geographical area served, financial data, descriptions of product/service, Standard Industrial Classification (SIC) code, year established, annual revenues, plant size, legal structure, export/import information. **Arrangement:** Classified by product/service, line of business. **Indexes:** Product/service, name, geographical.

39126 ■ *"Hayes Lemmerz Reports Some Good News Despite Losses" in Crain's Detroit Business (Vol. 24, April 14, 2008, No. 15, pp. 4)*
Pub: Crain Communications Inc.
Ed: Nancy Kaffer. **Description:** Hayes Lemmerz International Inc., a wheel manufacturer from Northville that has reported a positive free cash flow for the first time in years, a narrowed net loss in the fourth quarter and significant restructuring of the company's debt.

39127 ■ *"Heart Test No Boom for BG Medical" in Boston Business Journal (Vol. 31, June 17, 2011, No. 21, pp. 1)*
Pub: Boston Business Journal
Ed: Julie M. Donnelly. **Description:** The Galectin-3 test failed to boost stock prices of its manufacturer, BG Medicine, which has fallen to $6.06/share. The company hopes that its revenue will be boosted by widespread adoption of an automated and faster version of the test, which diagnoses for heart failure.

39128 ■ *"Heavy Industry" in Business North Carolina (Vol. 28, February 2008, No. 2, pp. 54)*
Pub: Business North Carolina
Ed: Arthur O. Murray. **Description:** Volvo Construction Equipment factory in Asheville, North Carolina expanded its factory that builds road-construction machinery.

39129 ■ *"Help in Wings for Aviation, Defense" in Globe & Mail (March 12, 2007, pp. B1)*
Pub: CTVglobemedia Publishing Inc.
Ed: Simon Tuck. **Description:** The creation of a corporate subsidy fund by the Canadian government, to facilitate the growth of the aerospace and defense industries, is described.

39130 ■ *"Helping Customers Fight Pet Waste" in Pet Product News (Vol. 64, November 2010, No. 11, pp. 52)*
Pub: BowTie Inc.
Ed: Sandy Robins. **Description:** Pet cleaning products manufacturers have been enjoying high sales figures by paying attention to changing pet ownership trends and environmental awareness. Meanwhile, the inclusion of user-friendly features in these products has also been boosted by the social role of pets and the media attention to pet waste. How manufacturers have been responding to this demand is explored.

39131 ■ *"Hey, You Can't Do That" in Green Industry Pro (Vol. 23, September 2011)*
Pub: Cygnus Business Media
Ed: Rod Dickens. **Description:** Manufacturers of landscape equipment are making better use of energy resources, such as the use of fuel-injection systems instead of carburetors, lightweight materials, better lubricants, advanced battery technology, and innovative engine designs.

39132 ■ *"High Marks; Parker Hannifin's Stock Lauded by Wall Street Journal" in Crain's Cleveland Business (Vol. 28, November 5, 2007, No. 44)*
Pub: Crain Communications, Inc.
Description: According to The Wall Street Journal, Parker Hannifin Corp., a manufacturer of motion and control equipment, is one of eight stocks that are attractively priced and continuously showing growth.

39133 ■ *"High-Yield Turns Into Road Kill" in Barron's (Vol. 88, July 7, 2008, No. 27, pp. M7)*
Pub: Dow Jones & Co., Inc.
Ed: Emily Barrett. **Description:** High-yield bonds have returned to the brink of collapse after profits have recovered from the shock brought about by the collapse of Bear Stearns. The high-yield bond market could decline again due to weakness in the automotive sector, particularly in Ford and General Motors.

39134 ■ *"Hispantelligence Report" in Hispanic Business (July-August 2007, pp. 18)*
Pub: Hispanic Business
Description: Presentation of the Hispanic Business Stock Index shows the current value of fifteen Hispanic companies from January 3 through July 6, 2007. Results of a survey covering Hispanic household spending on new automobiles are also included. Statistical data included.

39135 ■ *A History of Small Business in America*
Pub: University of North Carolina Press
Contact: Kate Douglas Torrey, Director
E-mail: kate_torrey@unc.edu
Ed: Mansel G. Blackford. **Released:** May 2003. **Price:** $22.95. **Description:** History of American small business from the colonial era to present, showing how it has played a role in the nation's economic, political, and cultural development across manufacturing, sales, services and farming.

39136 ■ *"Hot Air" in Canadian Business (Vol. 81, July 22, 2008, No. 12-13, pp. 16)*
Pub: Rogers Media Ltd.
Ed: Joe Castaldo. **Description:** Over half of 101 business leaders who were recently surveyed oppose Liberal leader Stephane Dion's carbon-tax proposal, saying that manufacturers in Canada are likely to suffer from the plan. Additional key results of the survey are presented.

39137 ■ *"How CoolBrand's Thrills Turned to Chills" in Globe & Mail (January 25, 2007, pp. B1)*
Pub: CTVglobemedia Publishing Inc.
Ed: Keith McArthur. **Description:** The key reasons behind the sudden share price fall of ice cream giant CoolBrands International Inc. are discussed.

39138 ■ *"How the Generation Gap Can Hurt Your Business" in Agency Sales Magazine (Vol. 39, November 2009, No. 10, pp. 16)*
Pub: MANA
Ed: Jack Foster. **Description:** Now that there are four generations of people in the workplace, there is a need to add flexibility to communications for independent manufacturers representatives. Managers can encourage the younger generations to do the research and the boomers to process information and let each side report to the other.

39139 ■ *"How Much Profit is Enough?" in Automotive News (Vol. 86, October 31, 2011, No. 6488, pp. 12)*
Pub: Crain Communications Inc.
Ed: Keith Crain. **Description:** Workers at the big three automobile companies are unhappy about the issues of class wealth, like the high compensations offered to CEOs.

39140 ■ *"How Our Picks Beat The Bear" in Barron's (Vol. 88, July 14, 2008, No. 28, pp. 18)*
Pub: Dow Jones & Co., Inc.
Ed: Andrew Bary. **Description:** Performance of the stocks that Barron's covered in the first half of 2008 is discussed; some of the worst picks and most rewarding pans have been in the financial sector while the best plays were in the energy, materials, and the transportation sectors.

39141 ■ *"How to Plan and Execute Effective Sales Meetings" in Agency Sales Magazine (Vol. 39, August 2009, No. 8, pp. 8)*
Pub: MANA
Ed: Jack Foster. **Description:** Basic guide to successful representative-manufacturer sales meetings based on effective planning is presented. The representative and the manufacturer will reap the benefits of a productive meeting only when they both focus on what's going to transpire before, during and after the event. Insights from industry players are also presented.

39142 ■ *"HP Eats Into Rival Dell Sales as Profits Soar" in Globe & Mail (February 21, 2007, pp. B15)*
Pub: CTVglobemedia Publishing Inc.
Ed: Connie Guglielmo. **Description:** The world's largest personal computer maker Hewlett Packard Co. has reported increased profits by 26 percent to $1.55 billion during the first quarter. The company has outpaced its competitor Dell Inc. by offering low priced personal computers during this period.

39143 ■ *"Husky Proceeds on Heavy-Oil Expansion" in Globe & Mail (March 21, 2006, pp. B1)*
Pub: CTVglobemedia Publishing Inc.
Ed: Patrick Brethour. **Description:** Canadian energy giant Husky Energy Inc. has started its $90 million engineering effort to determine the cost of the $2.3 billion heavy-oil up gradation expansion plan. Details of the project are elaborated upon.

39144 ■ *"Hybrid Popularity Pushes Automakers to Add to Offerings" in Crain's Cleveland Business (Vol. 28, November 12, 2007, No. 45, pp. 30)*
Pub: Crain Communications, Inc.
Ed: David Sedgwick. **Description:** Due in part to Toyota's innovative marketing, automotive hybrids have caught on with consumers thus forcing other automakers to add hybrids to their product plans.

39145 ■ *"Hyundai Enters Minivan Market" in Globe & Mail (February 15, 2006, pp. B7)*
Pub: CTVglobemedia Publishing Inc.
Ed: Greg Keenan. **Description:** The reasons behind the launch of minivan by Hyundai Auto Canada Inc. are presented.

39146 ■ *"Hyundai's Hitting Its Stride" in Barron's (Vol. 89, July 20, 2009, No. 29, pp. M7)*
Pub: Dow Jones & Co., Inc.
Ed: Assif Shameen. **Description:** Hyundai Motors has kept growing by producing better products, enabling it to increase its sales and market share despite the weaker automotive market. The shares of Hyundai and Kia are poised to rise due to their improved finances.

39147 ■ *"Ian Delaney" in Canadian Business (Vol. 81, Summer 2008, No. 9, pp. 168)*
Pub: Rogers Media Ltd.
Ed: Joe Castaldo. **Description:** Interview with Ian Delaney who is the executive chairman of chemical company Sherritt International Corp.; Delaney previously worked as chief executive for a holding company owned by Peter Munk. Details of his beliefs, profession and family life are discussed.

39148 ■ *"Idea-Generation Program Creates Winning Programs" in Business Journal-Serving Metropolitan Kansas City (October 19, 2007)*
Pub: American City Business Journals, Inc.
Ed: James Dombrook. **Description:** Eureka Ranch has developed 'Eureka! Winning Ways', a program that helps companies create new ideas for their business. Brunson Instruments is the first Missouri manufacturer to engage in the program. The procedures in the new product idea generation program are supplied.

39149 ■ *"Idea Nation" in Canadian Business (Vol. 80, December 25, 2006, No. 1, pp. 57)*
Pub: Rogers Media
Ed: Andy Holloway. **Description:** The potential of manufacturing companies and their innovations in the progress of the Canadian economy is discussed.

39150 ■ *"Importers Share Safety Liability" in Feedstuffs (Vol. 80, January 21, 2008, No. 3, pp. 19)*
Pub: Miller Publishing Company, Inc.
Description: Pet food and toys containing lead paint are among products from China being recalled due

to safety concerns. American Society for Quality's list of measures that outsourcing companies can take to help ensure safer products being imported to the U.S.

39151 ■ *"Imports Frothing Up Beer Market" in Globe & Mail (February 16, 2006, pp. B4)*
Pub: CTVglobemedia Publishing Inc.
Ed: Andy Hoffman. **Description:** The reasons behind the rise in market share of beer imports, in Canada, are presented.

39152 ■ *"IMRA's Ultrafast Lasers Bring Precision, profits; Ann Arbor Company Eyes Expansion" in Crain's Detroit Business (March 10, 2008)*
Pub: Crain Communications, Inc.
Ed: Tom Henderson. **Description:** IMRA America Inc. plans to expand its headquarters and has applied for permits to build a fourth building that will house research and development facilities and allow the company more room for manufacturing; the company plans to add about 20 more employees that would include research scientists, manufacturing and assembly workers, engineers and salespeople. The growth is due mainly to a new technology of ultrafast fiber lasers that reduce side effects for those getting eye surgeries and help manufacturers of computer chips to reduce their size and cost.

39153 ■ *"In the Bag?" in Canadian Business (Vol. 81, March 3, 2008, No. 3, pp. 57)*
Pub: Rogers Media
Ed: Calvin Leung. **Description:** American stocks are beginning to appear cheap amidst the threat of a worldwide economic slowdown, United States economic crisis and declining stock portfolios. Investors looking for bargain stocks should study the shares of Apple and Oshkosh Corp. Evaluation of other cheap-looking stocks such as the shares of Coach and 3M is also given.

39154 ■ *"Industrial Vacancies Hit High; Economic Downturn Taking Toll on Area's Demand for Space" in Crain's Chicago Business (Apr. 21, 2008)*
Pub: Crain Communications, Inc.
Ed: Alby Gallun. **Description:** Hitting its highest level in four years in the first quarter is the Chicago-area industrial vacancy rate, a sign that the slumping economy is depressing demand for warehouse and manufacturing space.

39155 ■ *"Insert Grade Coating Improves Tool Live" in Modern Machine Shop (Vol. 84, October 2011, No. 5, pp. 124)*
Pub: Gardner Business Media, Inc.
Contact: Richard G. Kline, President
E-mail: rkline@gardnerweb.com
Ed: Emily K. Tudor. **Description:** Profile of Sumitomo Electric Carbide's AC420K insert that is a CVD-coated carbide grade that features layers of TiCN and Al.sub.2 O.sub.3 for wear, chipping and heat resistance.

39156 ■ *"Intel Forges New Strategy With Chinese Fabrication Plant" in Globe & Mail (March 26, 2007, pp. B6)*
Pub: CTVglobemedia Publishing Inc.
Ed: Don Clark. **Description:** World's largest semiconductor manufacturing giant Intel Corp. is planning to construct a new chip fabrication plant in China. It will be investing an estimated $2.5 billion for this purpose.

39157 ■ *"Intel: Tax Breaks Key" in Business Journal Portland (Vol. 27, October 22, 2010, No. 34, pp. 1)*
Pub: Portland Business Journal
Ed: Erik Siemers. **Description:** Intel Corporation believes that state tax incentives will be critical, especially in the purchase of manufacturing equipment, as they build a new chip factory in Hillsboro, Oregon. The tax breaks would help Intel avoid paying 10 times more in property taxes compared to average Washington County firms. Critics argue that Intel has about $15 billion in cash assets, and can afford the factory without the tax breaks.

39158 ■ *"Into the Wild" in Inc. (October 2007, pp. 116-120, 122, 124, 126)*
Pub: Gruner & Jahr USA Publishing
Ed: Alison Stein Wellner. **Description:** Perry Klebahn, CEO of Timbuk2, manufacturer of messenger bags, tells how he took his top executives into the deep Wyoming wilderness in order to build employee team work skills. Other options for this type of team-building include cooking courses, changing a tire together, solving a kidnapping, or discussing ways to survive a nuclear winter.

39159 ■ *"Iogen in Talks to Build Ethanol Plant in Canada" in Globe & Mail (March 21, 2007, pp. B7)*
Pub: CTVglobemedia Publishing Inc.
Ed: Shawn McCarthy. **Description:** Ottawa based Iogen Corp. is planning to construct a cellulosic ethanol plant in Saskatchewan region. The company will be investing an estimated $500 million for this purpose.

39160 ■ *"Iogen, VW Look to Build Ethanol Plant" in Globe & Mail (January 9, 2006, pp. B3)*
Pub: CTVglobemedia Publishing Inc.
Ed: Simon Tuck. **Description:** Iogen Corp. and Volkswagen AG plan cellulose ethanol plant in Germany. The details of the project are presented.

39161 ■ *"Irene Rosenfeld; Chairman and CEO, Kraft Foods Inc." in Crain's Chicago Business (Vol. 31, May 5, 2008, No. 18, pp. 31)*
Pub: Crain Communications, Inc.
Ed: David Sterrett. **Description:** Profile of Irene Rosenfeld who is the chairman and CEO of Kraft Foods Inc. and is entering the second year of a three-year plan to boost sales of well-known brands such as Oreo, Velveeta and Oscar Mayer while facing soaring commodity costs and a declining marketshare. Ms. Rosenfeld's turnaround strategy also entails spending more on advertising and giving managers more control over their budgets and product development.

39162 ■ *"It May Be Cheaper to Manufacture At Home" in Harvard Business Review (Vol. 88, October 2010, No. 10, pp. 84)*
Pub: Harvard Business School Publishing
Ed: Suzanne de Treville, Lenos Trigeorgis. **Description:** Using a real options framework rather than a discounted cash flow model to assess and value supply chain processes is examined. This enables companies to assess costs for a variety of situations, not just ideal or normal circumstances, which can make the difference between domestic and foreign manufacturing decisions.

39163 ■ *"It's In the Bag" in Entrepreneur (Vol. 36, April 2008, No. 4, pp. 122)*
Pub: Entrepreneur Media, Inc.
Ed: Celeste Hoang. **Description:** Sandy Stein launched Alexx Inc in 2004, which markets keychains, called Finders Key Purse, with unique designs to help find keys easier inside the purse. Some of the key ring designs are hearts, sandals, and crowns. The company has approximately $6 million worth of sales in 2007.

39164 ■ *"It's Time To Swim" in Canadian Business (Vol. 81, March 3, 2008, No. 3, pp. 37)*
Pub: Rogers Media
Ed: Megan Harman. **Description:** Canadian manufacturers should consider Asian markets such as India and the United Arab Emirates as the U.S. economic downturn continues. Canada's shortage in skilled labor is also expected to negatively affect manufacturing industries. Ontario's plans to assist manufacturers are also presented.

39165 ■ *"ITT Places Its Bet With Defense Buy; Selling Equipment to Army Pays Off" in Crain's New York Business (Vol. 24, January 7, 2008)*
Pub: Crain Communications, Inc.
Description: ITT Corp.'s revenue has jumped by 20 percent in each of the past three years due to demand for the company's radio sets and night-vision goggles. The firm has acquired EDO Corp., which specializes in battlefield communications systems, in an attempt to expand its defense-industry division.

39166 ■ *"Ivorydale Looks to Clean Up" in Business Courier (Vol. 26, January 15, 2010, No. 39, pp. 1)*
Pub: American City Business Journals, Inc.
Ed: Jon Newberry. **Description:** Cincinnati-based St. Bernard Soap Company plans to focus on new services such as product development and logistics and to continue growth and put excess capacity to work. The unit of Ontario, Canada-based Trillium Health Care Products Inc. is the largest contract manufacturer of bar soap in North America.

39167 ■ *"Japan-Brand Shortages Will Linger Into '12" in Automotive News (Vol. 86, October 31, 2011, No. 6488, pp. 1)*
Pub: Crain Communications Inc.
Ed: Amy Wilson, Mark Rechtin. **Description:** Floods in Thailand and the tsunami in Japan have caused shortages of Japanese-brand vehicle parts. These shortages are expected to linger into 2012.

39168 ■ *"Jeans Draw a Global Following" in Marketing to Women (Vol. 21, April 2008, No. 4, pp. 6)*
Pub: EPM Communications Inc.
Contact: Ira Mayer, President
E-mail: imayer@epmcom.com
Description: According to a global study by Synovate of jeans and the women who wear them uncovered trends such as brand loyalty and if given a choice 45 percent of all respondents say that if given a choice, they would wear jeans every day.

39169 ■ *"Jet Sales Put Bombardier Back in Black" in Globe & Mail (March 30, 2006, pp. B1)*
Pub: CTVglobemedia Publishing Inc.
Ed: Bertrand Morotte. **Description:** The details on Bombardier Inc., which posted 20 percent rise in shares following $86 million profit for fourth quarter 2005, are presented.

39170 ■ *"Jobs Data Show A Slow Leak" in Barron's (Vol. 88, July 7, 2008, No. 27, pp. 34)*
Pub: Dow Jones & Co., Inc.
Ed: Gene Epstein. **Description:** In June 2008, the United States manufacturing sector showed an expansion, with the purchasing managers' index rising to 50.2 from 49.6; the unemployment rate in the US, which stayed steady at 5.5 percent in June 2008 is also discussed. Statistical data included.

39171 ■ *"Johnson's Taps Online Animation" in Marketing to Women (Vol. 21, April 2008, No. 4, pp. 3)*
Pub: EPM Communications Inc.
Contact: Ira Mayer, President
E-mail: imayer@epmcom.com
Description: Johnson's has launched a new integrated campaign for its baby lotion in an effort to appeal to the growing number of moms online.

39172 ■ *"Juicy Feud; Deal Caps Years of Rancor in Wrigley Gum Dynasty" in Crain's Chicago Business (Vol. 31, May 5, 2008, No. 18, pp. 1)*
Pub: Crain Communications, Inc.
Ed: David Sterrett. **Description:** Discusses the sale of Wm. Wrigley Jr. Co. to Mars Inc. and Warren Buffett for $23 billion as well as the intra-family feuding which has existed for nearly a decade since William Wrigley Jr. took over as CEO of the company following his father's death.

39173 ■ *"Just Add Water and Lily Pads" in Crain's Chicago Business (Vol. 31, April 28, 2008, No. 17, pp. 50)*
Pub: Crain Communications, Inc.
Ed: Phuong Ly. **Description:** Aquascape Inc., a major manufacturer of pond-building supplies, is using the recent drought in the South which hurt its business significantly to create a new product: an upscale, decorative version of the rain barrel which will collect rainwater to circulate through a pond or a fountain.

39174 ■ *"Kawasaki's New Top Gun" in Brandweek (Vol. 49, April 21, 2008, No. 16, pp. 18)*
Pub: VNU Business Media, Inc.
Description: Discusses Kawasaki's marketing plan which included designing an online brochure in which visitors could create a video by building their own test track on a grid and then selecting visual special effects and musical overlay. This engaging and innovative marketing technique generated more than 166,000 unique users within the first three months of being launched.

39175 ■ *"KC Plants Downshift" in The Business Journal-Serving Metropolitan Kansas City (Vol. 27, November 7, 2008, No. 9, pp. 1)*
Pub: American City Business Journals, Inc.
Ed: James Dornbrook. **Description:** Discusses Ford Motor Co. and General Motors' factories in the region; Ford Motor Co. removed the second shift on the F-150 line at the Kansas City Assembly Plant but added a shift to the production of the Ford Escape and Mercury Mariner in an attempt to avoid layoffs. One spokesman for General Motors, however, states that they cannot guarantee that they won't make any production cuts and layoffs in the future.

39176 ■ *"Keltic Gets Nod to Build N.S. Petrochemical Plant" in Globe & Mail (March 15, 2007, pp. B9)*
Pub: CTVglobemedia Publishing Inc.
Ed: Shawn McCarthy. **Description:** The government of Nova Scotia has awarded clearance to Keltic Inc. for the construction of new petrochemical plant in Goldboro region. Complete details in this context are discussed.

39177 ■ *"Kerkorian Shakes Up Chrysler Race" in Globe & Mail (April 6, 2007, pp. B1)*
Pub: CTVglobemedia Publishing Inc.
Ed: Greg Keenan. **Description:** The bid of Kirk Kerkorian's Tracinda Corp. to acquire DaimlerChrysler AG for $4.5 billion is discussed.

39178 ■ *"Kerry Steel to Sell Inventory, Close Business After 30 Years" in Crain's Detroit Business (Vol. 24, March 17, 2008, No. 11, pp. 26)*
Pub: Crain Communications, Inc.
Ed: Brent Snavely. **Description:** Kerry Steel Inc. has confirmed that it is selling all of its inventory and equipment and is going out of business; the company, which was once one of the largest steel service centers in the Midwest, has sustained financial losses and is in violation of its loan agreements.

39179 ■ *"Key FDA Approval Yanked for Avastin" in Wall Street Journal Eastern Edition (November 19 , 2011, pp. B1)*
Pub: Dow Jones & Company Inc.
Ed: Thomas M. Burton, Jennifer Corbett Dooren. **Description:** Avastin, a drug manufactured by Genetech Inc. and used in the treatment of metastatic breast cancer in women, has had its approval by the US Food and Drug Administration withdrawn by the agency, which says there is no evidence the widely-used drug is successful in increasing the longevity of breast cancer patients.

39180 ■ *"Kinetico Exec Going Global to Increase Growth Flow" in Crain's Cleveland Business (Vol. 28, October 1, 2007, No. 39, pp. 5)*
Pub: Crain Communications, Inc.
Ed: David Bennett. **Description:** Shamus Hurley, the new CEO and president of Kinetico Inc., a manufacturer of water filtering and softening equipment for residential, commercial and municipal use, plans to expand the company to target markets overseas.

39181 ■ *The King of Vodka: The Story of Pyotr Smirnov and the Upheaval of an Empire*
Pub: HarperCollins Publishers
Ed: Linda Himelstein. **Released:** 2009. **Price:** $29. 99. **Description:** Biography of Pyotr Smirnov and how his determination took him from serf to the head of Smirnov Vodka. Smirnov's marketing techniques are defined and show how he expanded the drink worldwide.

39182 ■ *"Kohler Building Earns LEED Silver Certification" in Contractor (Vol. 56, September 2009, No. 9, pp. 12)*
Pub: Penton Media, Inc.
Description: United States Green Building Council has awarded Kohler Co. with the Silver Leadership in Energy and Environmental Design Status. The award has highlighted the company's work to transform its building into a more environmentally efficient structure. A description of the facility is also provided.

39183 ■ *"Kraft Taps Cheese Head; Jordan Charged With Fixing Foodmaker's Signature Product" in Crain's Chicago Business (April 14, 2008)*
Pub: Crain Communications, Inc.
Ed: David Sterrett. **Description:** Kraft Foods Inc. has assigned Rhonda Jordan, a company veteran, to take charge of the cheese and dairy division which has been losing market shares to cheaper store-brand cheese among cost-sensitive shoppers as Kraft and its competitors raise prices to offset soaring dairy costs.

39184 ■ *"Late to Minivan Party, VW Hitches Ride With Daimler" in Globe & Mail (January 6, 2006, pp. B1)*
Pub: CTVglobemedia Publishing Inc.
Ed: Greg Keenan. **Description:** DaimlerChrysler AG and Volkswagen AG plans to manufacture minivan. The details of joint venture are presented.

39185 ■ *"Lawyers Sued Over Lapsed Lacrosse Patent" in Crain's Detroit Business (Vol. 25, June 8, 2009, No. 23, pp. 5)*
Pub: Crain Communications Inc. - Detroit
Ed: Chad Halcom. **Description:** Warrior Sports Inc., a manufacturer of lacrosse equipment located in Warren, Michigan is suing the law firm Dickinson Wright PLLC and two of its intellectual property lawyers over patent rights to lacrosse equipment.

39186 ■ *"Lead-Free Products must Meet Requirements" in Contractor (Vol. 56, September 2009, No. 9, pp. 30)*
Pub: Penton Media, Inc.
Ed: Robert Gottermeier. **Description:** United States Environmental Protection Agency's adoption of the Safe Drinking Water Act is aimed at lowering lead extraction levels from plumbing products. Manufacturers have since deleaded brass and bronze potable water products. Meanwhile, California and Vermont have passed a law limiting lead content for potable water conveying plumbing products.

39187 ■ *The Leadership Challenge*
Pub: Jossey-Bass Publishers
Ed: James M. Kouzes, Barry Z. Posner. **Released:** June 30, 1995. **Price:** $22.00. **Description:** According to research by the authors, people can make extraordinary things happen by liberating the leader within everyone around them. This handbook gives practical tips to aspire leaders in retail, manufacturing, government, community, church and school settings.

39188 ■ *"Lean Machine" in Crain's Detroit Business (Vol. 26, Jan. 11, 2010)*
Pub: Crain Communications Inc.
Ed: Jay Greene. **Description:** Reducing waste and becoming more efficient is a goal of many businesses involved in the health care industry. These firms are looking to the local manufacturing sector, comparing themselves in specifically to the auto industry, for ways in which to become more efficient.

39189 ■ *"Lean Machine; Health Care Follows Auto's Lead, Gears Up for Efficiency" in Crain's Detroit Business (Vol. 26, January 11, 2010)*
Pub: Crain Communications, Inc.
Ed: Jay Greene. **Description:** Reducing waste and becoming more efficient is a goal of many businesses involved in the health care industry. These firms are looking to the local manufacturing sector, comparing themselves in specifically to the auto industry, for ways in which to become more efficient.

39190 ■ *"Leapin' Lizards, Does SoBe Have Some Work To Do On Life Water" in Brandweek (Vol. 49, April 21, 2008, No. 16, pp. 32)*
Pub: VNU Business Media, Inc.
Ed: Amy Shea. **Description:** Discusses the competing marketing campaigns of both Vitaminwater, now owned by Coca-Cola, and SoBe Life Water which is owned by Pepsi; also looks at the repositioning of Life Water as a thirst-quencher, rather than a green product as well as the company's newest advertising campaign.

39191 ■ *"Learn New Ideas from Experienced Menu Makers" in Nation's Restaurant News (Vol. 45, June 27, 2011, No. 13, pp. 82)*
Pub: Penton Media Inc.
Contact: John French, President
Ed: Nancy Kruse. **Description:** National Restaurant Association Restaurant, Hotel-Motel Show featured the Food Truck Spot, a firm committed to all aspects of mobile catering, foodtruck manufacturers, leasers of fully equipped truck and a food-truck franchising group.

39192 ■ *Lethal Logic: Exploding the Myths that Paralyze American Gun Policy*
Pub: Potomac Books
Ed: Dennis A. Henigen. **Released:** 2009. **Price:** $29. 95. **Description:** Marketing tactics being used by gun manufacturers regarding possible new gun control laws are examined.

39193 ■ *"Li'l Guy Rolls Up Into Bigger Company" in The Business Journal-Serving Metropolitan Kansas City (Vol. 26, September 12, 2008)*
Pub: American City Business Journals, Inc.
Ed: Suzanna Stagemeyer. **Description:** Li'l Guy Foods, a Mexican food company in Kansas City, Missouri, has merged with Tortilla King Inc. Li'l Guy's revenue in 2007 was $3.3 million, while a newspaper report said that Tortilla King's revenue in 2001 was $7.5 million. Growth opportunities for the combined companies and Li'l Guy's testing of the Wichita market are discussed.

39194 ■ *"Linens 'N Things, Dyson in Dust-Up" in Crain's Chicago Business (Vol. 31, March 24, 2008, No. 12, pp. 12)*
Pub: Crain Communications, Inc.
Description: Linens 'N Things is being sued by vacuum-cleaner manufacturer Dyson who is alleging that it hasn't been paid some of the $1.3 million it says it is owed for merchandise.

39195 ■ *"Lining Up at the Ethanol Trough (Ethanol Production in Canada)" in Globe & Mail (January 25, 2007, pp. B2)*
Pub: CTVglobemedia Publishing Inc.
Ed: Eric Reguly. **Description:** The future of ethanol production in Canada is discussed, alternate fuel market is expected to reach 35 billion gallons by 2017.

39196 ■ *"Linking Human Capital to Competitive Advantages" in Human Resource Management (Vol. 49, September-October 2010, No. 5)*
Pub: John Wiley
Ed: Yan Jin, Margaret M. Hopkins, Jenell L.S. Wittmer. **Description:** A study was conducted to confirm the links among human capital, firm flexibility, and firm performance. The study also examines the emerging role of flexibility for a company's performance. A total of 201 senior supply chain management professionals from several manufacturing companies were included in the study.

39197 ■ *"The Lithium Deficit" in Canadian Business (Vol. 82, April 27, 2009, No. 7, pp. 17)*
Pub: Rogers Media
Ed: Joe Castaldo. **Description:** Experts are concerned that there may not be enough lithium available to support the expected rise in demand for the natural resource. Lithium is used in lithium ion batter-

ies, the standard power source for electric and hybrid vehicles. Experts believe that the demand for lithium can only be measured once the technology is out in the market.

39198 ■ *"The Little Insect" in Canadian Electronics (Vol. 23, June-July 2008, No. 4, pp. 6)*
Pub: Action Communication Inc.
Ed: Tim Gouldson. **Description:** Electronics designers should not be underestimated because they can manufacture technologies vital to saving lives and bringing peace. They have designed robots and other electronic equipment that are as small as insects.

39199 ■ *"Local Auto Suppliers Upbeat as Detroit 3's Prospects Trend Up" in Crain's Cleveland Business (Vol. 30, June 8, 2009, No. 22, pp. 1)*
Pub: Crain Communications, Inc.
Ed: Dan Shingler. **Description:** According to the Center for Automotive Research located in Ann Arbor, Michigan, if Detroit automakers can hold their market share, they will end up producing more vehicles as the market recovers.

39200 ■ *"Local Green Technology on Display" in Crain's Detroit Business (Vol. 26, January 18, 2010, No. 3, pp. 1)*
Pub: Crain Communications Inc.
Ed: Ryan Beene. **Description:** Detroit's 2010 North American International Auto Show put the newest, most innovative green technologies on display showing that the Southeast Michigan automobile industry is gaining traction with its burgeoning e-vehicle infrastructure. Think, a Norwegian electric city-car manufacturer is eyeing sites in Southeast Michigan in which to locate its corporate headquarters and technical center for its North American branch.

39201 ■ *"Local Industrial Vacancies Climb" in Crain's Chicago Business (Vol. 31, November 17, 2008, No. 46, pp. 18)*
Pub: Crain Communications, Inc.
Ed: Eddie Baeb. **Description:** Demand for local industrial real estate has declined dramatically as companies that use warehouse and factory space struggle to survive in an ailing economy. According to a report by Colliers Bennett & Kahnweiler Inc., a commercial real estate brokerage, the regional vacancy rate has risen to 9.86 percent in the third quarter, the fourth straight increase and the highest in the past 14 years.

39202 ■ *"Local Manufacturers See Tax Proposal Hurting Global Operations" in Crain's Cleveland Business (Vol. 30, May 18, 2009, No. 20)*
Pub: Crain Communications, Inc.
Ed: Dan Shingler. **Description:** New tax laws proposed by the Obama Administration could hinder the efforts of some Northeast Ohio industrial companies from expanding their overseas markets. The law is designed to prevent companies from moving jobs overseas.

39203 ■ *"Local Shops' Wares Sound Good To Boomers Needing Some Fun" in Crain's Cleveland Business (Vol. 30, May 18, 2009, No. 20, pp. 5)*
Pub: Crain Communications, Inc.
Ed: Dan Shingler. **Description:** Dr. Z Amplification, who makes amplifiers for guitars and SuperTrapp Performance Exhausts, producer of tunable exhausts for motorcycles, are seeing increased sales as baby boomers look to add enjoyment to their lives.

39204 ■ *"A Look Ahead Into 2007" in Canadian Business (Vol. 80, December 25, 2006, No. 1, pp. 40)*
Pub: Rogers Media
Description: The 2007 forecasts for various industrial sectors like telecom, information technology, manufacturing, retail, financial and energy among others is discussed.

39205 ■ *"A Look At Three Gas-Less Cars" in Hispanic Business (Vol. 30, September 2008, No. 9, pp. 90)*
Pub: Hispanic Business, Inc.
Ed: Daniel Soussa. **Description:** Three major car manufacturers, Chevrolet, BMW, and Honda, are giving market leader Toyota competition for the next generation of eco-friendly car. The latest and most advanced of the gasoline-less cars designed by the three firms, namely, the Chevrolet Volt, BMW's Hydrogen 7, and the Honda FCX Clarity, are reviewed.

39206 ■ *"The Lost Opportunity for a Canadian Steel Giant" in Globe & Mail (April 23, 2007, pp. B1)*
Pub: CTVglobemedia Publishing Inc.
Ed: Greg Keenan. **Description:** The efforts of Algoma Steel Inc. to create a Canadian steel manufacturer that could survive the global trends of consolidation in the steel industry are described. The company's efforts to acquire Stelco Inc., Ivaco Inc. and Slater Steel Inc. are discussed.

39207 ■ *"Lynn Johnson, President: Dowland-Bach" in Alaska Business Monthly (Vol. 27, October 2011, No. 10, pp. 11)*
Pub: Alaska Business Publishing Company
Ed: Peg Stomierowski. **Description:** Profile of Lynn C. Johnson cofounder of Dowland-Bach Corporation, a manufacturing and distribution company is presented. The firms primary products are wellhead control and chemical injection systems for corrosion control, UL industrial control panels, and specialty stainless steel sheet metal fabrication.

39208 ■ *"Made In Canada" in Canadian Business (Vol. 80, March 12, 2007, No. 6, pp. 11)*
Pub: Rogers Media
Ed: Ian Harvey. **Description:** The devision of Christie Digital Systems Canada Inc. to increase production of its DLP projectors, in view of high demand from the United States, is discussed.

39209 ■ *"Magna Nears Top of Auto Parts Heap" in Globe & Mail (May 1, 2007, pp. B4)*
Pub: CTVglobemedia Publishing Inc.
Ed: Greg Keenan. **Description:** Magna International Inc. is poised to become the largest automobile parts supplier in North America. The state of the automobile parts industry in Canada is also discussed.

39210 ■ *"Magna in Talks on Building Cars for DaimlerChrysler" in Globe & Mail (February 27, 2007, pp. B1)*
Pub: CTVglobemedia Publishing Inc.
Ed: Greg Keenan. **Description:** The plans of Magna International Inc. to purchase securities of Chrysler Corp. are discussed. The possibility of the manufacture of cars by Magna International Inc. for DaimlerChrysler AG is discussed.

39211 ■ *"Magna Wants to Help Chrysler, but a Takeover's Not on the Cards" in Globe & Mail (March 1, 2007, pp. B1)*
Pub: CTVglobemedia Publishing Inc.
Ed: Greg Keenan. **Description:** The plans of Magna International Inc. to help Chrysler Corp. to overcome its financial problems are discussed. The appointment of Michael Neuman as the chief executive officer of Magna International Inc. is described.

39212 ■ *"Major Tech Employers Pulling Out" in Sacramento Business Journal (Vol. 25, August 1, 2008, No. 22, pp. 1)*
Pub: American City Business Journals, Inc.
Ed: Celia Lamb. **Description:** Biotechnology company Affymetrix Inc. is planning to close its West Sacramento, California plant and lay off 110 employees. The company said it will expand a corporate restructuring plan. Affymetrix also plans to lease out or sell its building at Riverside Parkway.

39213 ■ *"Making Factory Tours Count" in Playthings (Vol. 107, January 1, 2009, No. 1, pp. 14)*
Pub: Reed Business Information
Contact: Jeff Greisch, President
Ed: Malcolm Denniss. **Description:** The importance of touring an overseas toy supplier's manufacturing facility is stressed. Strategies for general factory visits are outlined in order to determine safety-related quality assurance issues in production.

39214 ■ *Managing Complexity and Change in SMEs Frontiers in European Research*
Pub: Edward Elgar Publishing, Incorporated
Ed: Christensen. **Released:** December 2006. **Price:** $120.00. **Description:** Complexities faced by entrepreneurs in an expanding marketplace are discussed.

39215 ■ *"Manufacturers Become Part of Coalition" in Contractor (Vol. 56, July 2009, No. 7, pp. 40)*
Pub: Penton Media, Inc.
Description: Bradford White Water Heaters, Rheem Water Heating, Rinnai America Corp., and A.O. Smith Water Heaters have joined the Consortium for Energy Efficiency in the Coalition for Energy Star Water Heaters. The coalition seeks to increase the awareness of Energy Star water heaters.

39216 ■ *"Manufacturers Urged to Adapt to Defense" in Crain's Cleveland Business (Vol. 30, June 22, 2009, No. 24, pp. 3)*
Pub: Crain Communications, Inc.
Ed: Dan Shingler. **Description:** Manufacturers in Northeast Ohio are making products for the military from steel, polymers or composite materials. The U.S. Department of Defense is teaching companies to work with titanium and other advanced metals in order to further manufacture for the military.

39217 ■ *"Manufacturing Behind the Great Wall: What Works, What Doesn't" in Canadian Electronics (Vol. 23, February 2008, No. 1, pp. 6)*
Pub: CLB Media Inc.
Ed: Michel Jullian. **Description:** Electronic component producers are increasingly transitioning their manufacturing operations to China in order to take advantage of the growing Chinese manufacturing industry. It is believed that manufacturers have to carefully consider whether their run sizes are appropriate for Chinese manufacturing before moving their operations.

39218 ■ *"Manufacturing Jobs Go Begging in Downturn" in Puget Sound Business Journal (Vol. 29, December 26, 2008, No. 36, pp. 1)*
Pub: American City Business Journals
Ed: Steve Wilhelm. **Description:** Trends show that skilled jobs in aerospace and other technology manufacturing industries are in a state of decline as layoffs hit broad sectors of the economy. Too few people are entering the field, prompting companies to try to maintain these skilled workers, thus creating problems that could affect the sector's vitality.

39219 ■ *"Manufacturing in the Middle Kingdom" in Inc. (December 2007, pp. 54-57)*
Pub: Gruner & Jahr USA Publishing
Ed: Alex Salkever. **Description:** Tips for manufacturing any new product in China as well as marketing said product is examined; five key steps for successfully managing Chinese contractors are listed.

39220 ■ *"A Manufacturing Revival" in Boston Business Journal (Vol. 31, May 27, 2011, No. 18, pp. 1)*
Pub: Boston Business Journal
Ed: Kyle Alspach. **Description:** Massachusetts' manufacturing sector has grown despite the high cost of labor, real estate and electricity. Manufacturing jobs in the state have increased to 2,800 in April 2011.

39221 ■ *"Many Procter Products To Get Price Increase" in Business Courier (Vol. 24, November 16, 2008, No. 31, pp. 1)*
Pub: American City Business Journals, Inc.
Ed: Lisa Biank Fasig. **Description:** Procter & Gamble Co. is increasing the prices of its products as a means to offset the rising costs of gas, plastics and raw materials. The price increase will be somewhere between 3 to 12 percent, depending on the product.

39222 ■ *"Market Takes Shape for Emissions Credits" in Globe & Mail (April 16, 2007, pp. B3)*
Pub: CTVglobemedia Publishing Inc.
Ed: Shawn McCarthy. **Description:** The effort of Canadian companies to prepare for emissions trading after the government imposes climate change regulations is discussed.

39223 ■ *"Marketer Bets Big on U.S.'s Growing Canine Obsession" in Advertising Age (Vol. 79, April 14, 2008, No. 15, pp. 14)*
Pub: Crain Communications, Inc.
Ed: Emily Bryson York. **Description:** Overview of FreshPet, a New Jersey company that began marketing two brands of refrigerated dog food-Deli Fresh and FreshPet Select-which are made from fresh ingredients such as beef, rice and carrots. The company projects continued success due to the amount of money consumers spend on their pets as well as fears derived from the 2007 recalls that inspired consumers to look for smaller, independent manufacturers that are less likely to source ingredients from China.

39224 ■ *"Markets Defy the Doomsayers" in Barron's (Vol. 88, March 24, 2008, No. 12, pp. M5)*
Pub: Dow Jones & Company, Inc.
Ed: Leslie P. Norton. **Description:** US stock markets registered strong gains, with the Dow Jones Industrial Average rising 3.43 percent on the week to close at 12,361.32, in a rally that may be seen as short-covering. Shares of Hansen Natural are poised for further drops with a slowdown in the energy drink market.

39225 ■ *"The Market's (Very) Tender Spring Shoots" in Barron's (Vol. 88, March 31, 2008, No. 13, pp. M3)*
Pub: Dow Jones & Company, Inc.
Ed: Kopin Tan. **Description:** Expansion in price-earnings multiples and a lower credit-default risk index has encouraged fans of the spring-awakening theory. Shares of industrial truckers have gone up 32 percent in 2008 and some shares are pushing five-year highs brought on by higher efficiency and earnings from more load carried. The prospects of the shares of Foot Locker are also discussed.

39226 ■ *"Massive Ford Restructuring to Cut 1,200 More Canadian Jobs" in Globe & Mail (January 24, 2006, pp. B1)*
Pub: CTVglobemedia Publishing Inc.
Ed: Greg Keenan. **Description:** The details on streamlining of operations of Ford Motor Co., in Canada, are presented.

39227 ■ *"Maternity Wear Goes Green" in Marketing to Women (Vol. 21, March 2008, No. 3, pp. 3)*
Pub: EPM Communications Inc.
Contact: Ira Mayer, President
E-mail: imayer@epmcom.com
Description: Mother's Work Inc. has launched a series of environmentally-friendly products made from such sustainable fibers as organic cotton and bamboo.

39228 ■ *"Medical Connectors: Meeting the Demands of Reliability, Portability, Size and Cost" in Canadian Electronics (February 2008)*
Pub: CLB Media Inc.
Ed: Murtaza Fidaali, Ted Worroll. **Description:** Component manufacturers who serve the medical industry need to ensure component reliability in order to maintain patient safety. Because of this, connectors in medical equipment are becoming more versatile. It is concluded that these manufacturers are facing challenges meeting the medical industry standards or reliability, miniaturization, portability, and cost.

39229 ■ *"Medical Market a Healthy Alternative" in Crain's Cleveland Business (Vol. 30, June 1, 2009, No. 21, pp. 3)*
Pub: Crain Communications, Inc.
Ed: Dan Shingler. **Description:** Manufacturing for the Medical Market: Requirements for Supply Chain Entry, was an event held in Northeast Ohio. Representatives from various health systems addressed 250 area manufacturers about their future medical supply needs.

39230 ■ *"Mentor Medical Device Maker's Partnerships Open New Opportunities" in Crain's Cleveland Business (Vol. 30, June 22, 2009, No. 24)*
Pub: Crain Communications, Inc.
Ed: Chuck Soder. **Description:** Frantz Medical Development Ltd. develops medical devices based on ideas from outside inventors. The company wants to manufacture the innovations at its Mentor campus.

39231 ■ *"Menu Foods Seeks Answers in Death of Ten Pets" in Globe & Mail (March 19, 2007, pp. B2)*
Pub: CTVglobemedia Publishing Inc.
Ed: Thomas M. Burton. **Description:** The failure of Menu Foods Inc. to ascertain the cause of ten deaths of house pets, which were fed its food products, prompting the government to recall the products from the market, is discussed.

39232 ■ *"Mercury (1939-2010)" in Canadian Business (Vol. 83, June 15, 2010, No. 10, pp. 27)*
Pub: Rogers Media Ltd.
Ed: Steve Maich. **Description:** Ford's Mercury brand of cars began in 1939 and it was designed by Ford to attract a wealthier clientele. Mercury was mentioned in a 1949 song by K.C. Douglas and was driven in the movie, 'Rebel Without a Cause'. However, the brand was too expensive for the mass market and not exclusive enough through the years, so Ford Motor Company decided to discontinue the brand in 2010.

39233 ■ *"Minimizing Import Risks" in Canadian Sailings (July 7, 2008)*
Pub: UBM Global Trade
Contact: Leonard J. Corallo, President
Ed: Jack Kohane. **Description:** New food and product safety laws may be enacted by Canada's Parliament; importers, retailers and manufacturers could face huge fines if the new laws are passed.

39234 ■ *"Minority Auto Suppliers Get Help Diversifying" in Crain's Detroit Business (Vol. 26, January 11, 2010, No. 2, pp. 3)*
Pub: Crain Communications, Inc.
Ed: Sherri Welch. **Description:** Displaced minority auto suppliers are being given assistance by the Kauffman's Foundation Urban Entrepreneur Partnership Detroit program, a three-year effort to assist 150 of the region's suppliers into more diversified businesses.

39235 ■ *"A Model Machine for Titanium" in Modern Machine Shop (Vol. 84, October 2011, No. 5, pp. 84)*
Pub: Gardner Business Media, Inc.
Contact: Richard G. Kline, President
E-mail: rkline@gardnerweb.com
Ed: Peter Zelinski. **Description:** Researchers have developed a machine tool that controls vibration in order to mill titanium more productively. In-depth information on the machine tool as well as understanding the processes involved in milling titanium is covered.

39236 ■ *"Modular Home Center Opens in Arcadia" in Charlotte Observer (February 1, 2007)*
Pub: Knight-Ridder/Tribune Business News
Ed: John Lawhorne. **Description:** Arcadia Home Center features modular homes constructed on a steel frame; regulations regarding the manufacture and moving of these homes are included.

39237 ■ *"Monaco Pay Cut Draws Attention" in The Business Journal-Portland (Vol. 25, August 8, 2008, No. 22, pp. 1)*
Pub: American City Business Journals, Inc.
Ed: Erik Siemers. **Description:** Monaco Coach Corp. cut the salaries of five top executives in an effort to reduce the company's $178 million worth of inventory. The executives can earn the lost salary back if the inventory is reduced by $58 million a year after August 2008.

39238 ■ *"Montana's Manufacturing Industry" in Montana Business Quarterly (Vol. 49, Spring 2011, No. 1, pp. 29)*
Pub: Bureau of Business & Economic Research
Ed: Todd A. Morgan, Charles E. Keegan III, Colin B. Sorenson. **Description:** Manufacturing remains a vital part of Montana's economy despite the recession and decline in the production of wood products. Statistical data included.

39239 ■ *"The Mood of a Nation" in Canadian Business (Vol. 81, April 14, 2008, No. 6, pp. 56)*
Pub: Rogers Media
Ed: Joe Castaldo. **Description:** Independent Fish Harvesters Inc. processes more kilograms a year and has had to hire more workers but its managers worry about how a slowdown in the U.S. economy will affect his business. A planned shopping complex in Mirabel Quebec, the manufacturing industry in Kitchener, Ontario, and a cattle farming business in Sarnia, Ontario are discussed to provide a snapshot of the challenges that business in Canada are facing as recession looms.

39240 ■ *"More Manufacturers Scout Military Contracts As Auto Industry Lags" in Crain's Detroit Business (Vol. 24, September 29, 2008, No. 39)*
Pub: Crain Communications Inc.
Ed: Chad Halcom. **Description:** Many Michigan manufacturers are looking to grow with new military contracts now that the reality of the auto industry is becoming more clear; these companies see that the government contracts may be the only way in which they will be able to stay in business through these rough economic times.

39241 ■ *"More Pain" in Canadian Business (Vol. 81, December 24, 2007, No. 1, pp. 12)*
Pub: Rogers Media
Ed: Lauren McKeon. **Description:** Manufacturing sector in Canada is sinking with a forecast by as much as 23 percent for 2008, which can be offset as manufacturers say they plan to increase productivity by 25 percent. Details on the sector's competitiveness, workforce, importing of machinery from the U.S. and financial needs for research and development are examined.

39242 ■ *"Mosaid Grants First Wireless Parent License To Matsushita" in Canadian Electronics (Vol. 23, June-July 2008, No. 5, pp. 1)*
Pub: Action Communication Inc.
Description: Matsushita Electric Industrial Co. Ltd. has been granted a six-and-a-half-year license by Mosaid Technologies Inc. to manufacture the latter's products. The patent portfolio license agreement covers Mosaid's Wi-Fi, Wi-Max, CDMA-enabled notebook computers and other products.

39243 ■ *"Motorola's New Cell Phone Lineup Includes Green Effort" in Chicago Tribune (January 14, 2009)*
Pub: McClatchy-Tribune Information Services
Ed: Eric Benderoff. **Description:** Motorola Inc. introduced a new line of mobile phones at the Consumer Electronics Show in Las Vegas; the phones are made using recycled water bottles for the plastic housing.

39244 ■ *"Motors and Motion Control" in Canadian Electronics (Vol. 23, February 2008, No. 1, pp. 23)*
Pub: CLB Media Inc.
Description: A new version of MicroMo Electronics Inc.'s Smoovy Series 0303..B has been added to MicroMo's DC motor product line. United Electronic Industries, on the other hand, has introduced the new UEIPAC series of programmable automation controllers that can offer solutions to various applications such as unmanned vehicle controllers. Features and functions of other new motors and motion control devices are given.

39245 ■ *"Move South Could Bring Big Benefits" in Business Journal-Portland (Vol. 24, November 9, 2007, No. 36, pp. 1)*
Pub: American City Business Journals, Inc.
Ed: Matthew Kish. **Description:** Freightliner LLC has announced that it would move around one-tenth of its jobs to Fort Mill, South Carolina, but stated that im-

mediate plans for headquarters relocation have not been made. The relocation of its headquarters is expected to earn $100 million in economic incentives. The benefits of moving to the area, aside from the economic incentives, are discussed.

39246 ■ *"Mover and Sheika" in Conde Nast Portfolio (Vol. 2, June 2008, No. 6, pp. 104)*
Pub: Conde Nast Publications
Contact: David Carey, President
Ed: John Arlidge. **Description:** Profile of Princess Sheika Lubna who is the first female foreign trade minister in the Middle East, the United Arab Emirates biggest business envoy, paving the way for billions in new investment, and also a manufacturer of her own perfume line.

39247 ■ *"Myths of Deleveraging" in Barron's (Vol. 90, August 23, 2010, No. 34, pp. M14)*
Pub: Barron's Editorial & Corporate Headquarters
Ed: Gene Epstein. **Description:** The opposite is true against reports about deleveraging or the decrease in credit since inflation-adjusted-investment factories and equipment rose 7.8 percent in the first quarter of 2010. On consumer deleveraging, sales of homes through credit is weak but there is a trend towards more realistic homeownership and consumer spending on durable goods rose 8.8 percent.

39248 ■ *"Natalie Peterson; Corporate Counsel, Steris Corp., 39" in Crain's Cleveland Business (Vol. 28, November 19, 2007, No. 46, pp. F-14)*
Pub: Crain Communications, Inc.
Ed: Chuck Soder. **Description:** Profile of Natalie Peterson, corporate counsel for Steris Corp., a manufacturer of sterilization products; Peterson's blue-collar background did not detour her from her collegiate goals although she hardly knew how to fill out a college application. After graduating from Stanford Law School in 1997, she opted to return to Cleveland in lieu of more lucrative job offers in San Francisco. She has joined the school board and has participated in the 3Rs program, in which lawyers visit public schools in Cleveland to get students thinking about career choices and talk about constitutional law.

39249 ■ *"Natural Attraction: Bath and Body Products Maker Delivers Wholesome Goodness" in Black Enterprise (Vol. 38, November 2007, No. 4)*
Pub: Earl G. Graves Publishing Co. Inc.
Ed: Kaylyn Kendall Dines. **Description:** Profile of Dawn Fitch, creator of Pooka Inc., manufacturer of handmade bath and body products that contain no preservatives. Sales are expected to reach $750,000 for 2007.

39250 ■ *"Navistar, Cat Talk Truck Deal" in Crain's Chicago Business (Vol. 31, March 24, 2008, No. 12, pp. 1)*
Pub: Crain Communications, Inc.
Ed: Bob Tita. **Description:** Caterpillar Inc. and Navistar International Corp. are negotiating a partnership in which Navistar would build Cat-branded trucks with engines supplied by the Peoria-based equipment manufacturer, Caterpillar.

39251 ■ *"NEMRA Announces Headquarters Move" in Agency Sales Magazine (Vol. 39, September-October 2009, No. 9, pp. 53)*
Pub: MANA
Description: NEMRA, the National Electrical Manufacturers' Representatives Association is moving their headquarters to 28 Deer Street, Suite 302, Portsmouth, New Hampshire. The association has also added Michelle Rivers-Jameson as their manager of operations and Kirsty Stebbins as their manager of marketing and member services.

39252 ■ *Nevada Manufacturers Register*
Pub: Harris InfoSource
Contact: Dennis Abrahams, President
E-mail: dennisa@harrisinfo.com
URL(s): www.harrisinfo.com. **Released:** Annual; latest edition 2010. **Covers:** Approximately 2,800 manufacturers in Nevada plus names and titles of key executives. **Entries include:** Company name, address, parent name/location, telephone, fax and 800 numbers, Web site address (on CD-ROM only), number of employees, year established, annual revenue, plant size, business description, Standard Industrial Classification (SIC) codes, executive names/titles, public ownership, legal structure, import/export designators, female/minority ownership. **Arrangement:** Classified by product/service, line of business. **Indexes:** Product/service, alphabetical, geographical, international trade.

39253 ■ *"New Battle of Alberta: Pipelines" in Globe & Mail (February 3, 2006, pp. B1)*
Pub: CTVglobemedia Publishing Inc.
Ed: Dave Ebner. **Description:** The details on stiffening competition between Enbridge Inc. and TransCanada Corp., to build petroleum pipeline from Alberta to Wisconsin, are presented.

39254 ■ *"New Drug Could Revitalize Amgen" in Barron's (Vol. 88, July 7, 2008, No. 27, pp. 23)*
Pub: Dow Jones & Co., Inc.
Ed: Johanna Bennett. **Description:** Shares of the biotechnology company Amgen could receive a boost from the release of the anti-osteoporosis drug denosumab. The shares, priced at $48.84 each, are trading at 11 times expected earnings for 2008 and could also be boosted by cost cutting measures.

39255 ■ *"New Ethanol Plant Planned In Iowa to Use Corn Stover" in Farm Industry News (June 27, 2011)*
Pub: Penton Business Media Inc.
Ed: Lynn Grooms. **Description:** DuPont Danisco Cellulosic Ethanol (DDCE) will buy land next to the Lincolnway Energy corn-based ethanol plant in Nevada, Iowa in order to produce ethanol from corn stover at the location.

39256 ■ *"The New Frontier" in Crain's Detroit Business (Vol. 26, January 18, 2010, No. 3, pp. S025)*
Pub: Crain Communications Inc.
Ed: Richard Truett; Bradford Wernle. **Description:** Due to the changing consumer preference resulting from new fuel-efficiency standards, concern about climate change and higher gasoline prices, Detroit car designers are beginning to shift focus onto smaller vehicles.

39257 ■ *"New Life for Porsche's VW Dreams" in Barron's (Vol. 89, July 6, 2009, No. 27, pp. 9)*
Pub: Dow Jones & Co., Inc.
Ed: Vito J. Racanelli. **Description:** Porsche and Volkswagen moved closer to a merger after the Qatar Investment Authority offered to take a stake in Porsche. The QIA could take up to a 30 percent stake in Porsche and purchase all Volkswagen calls for up to $6 billion.

39258 ■ *"New Race Suit at Local Coke Plant" in Business Courier (Vol. 24, February 1, 2008, No. 43, pp. 1)*
Pub: American City Business Journals, Inc.
Ed: Jon Newberry. **Description:** Another racial harassment lawsuit has been filed against the Coca-Cola Enterprises Inc. plant in Madisonville by its 23 black workers. The lawsuit alleges that the working environment at the plant continues to be offensive, abusive, intimidating and hostile. Details of the class-action suit are provided.

39259 ■ *"Nexen, OPTI Boost Oil Sands Spending" in Globe & Mail (February 18, 2006, pp. B5)*
Pub: CTVglobemedia Publishing Inc.
Ed: Dave Ebner. **Description:** The reasons behind the decision of Nexen Inc. and OPTI Canada Inc., to allocate 10 percent more funding on oil sands, are presented.

39260 ■ *"Nike's Next Splash" in The Business Journal-Portland (Vol. 25, August 22, 2008, No. 24, pp. 1)*
Pub: American City Business Journals, Inc.
Ed: Erik Siemers. **Description:** Business analysts expect Nike to bid for the endorsement services of swimmer Michael Phelps after the swimmer's contract with Speedo expires. The company, however, is a lightweight in the swimming apparel market and is not focusing on swimming as a growth sector.

39261 ■ *"Nine Sectors to Watch: Automotive" in Canadian Business (Vol. 81, December 24, 2007, No. 1, pp. 47)*
Pub: Rogers Media
Ed: Thomas Watson. **Description:** Forecasts on the Canadian automotive sector for 2008 are presented. Details on contract concessions made by American unions, the industry's Big Three (General Motors, Chrysler, and Ford) operations in Canada, and Canadian Auto Workers demand for higher wages are also discussed.

39262 ■ *"Nine Sectors to Watch: Metals" in Canadian Business (Vol. 81, December 24, 2007, No. 1, pp. 46)*
Pub: Rogers Media
Ed: John Gray. **Description:** Forecasts on the Canadian metal industries for 2008 are discussed. Details on mine production and the rise in prices are also presented.

39263 ■ *"Nissan Unveils Family Concept Car" in Marketing to Women (Vol. 21, February 2008, No. 2, pp. 3)*
Pub: EPM Communications Inc.
Contact: Ira Mayer, President
E-mail: imayer@epmcom.com
Description: Nissan displayed its latest design for the ultimate family vehicle at the 2008 North American International Auto Show in Detroit. The Nissan Forum targets families with older children.

39264 ■ *"No End to the Nightmare; America's Car Industry" in The Economist (Vol. 390, January 3, 2009, No. 8612, pp. 46)*
Pub: The Economist Newspaper Inc.
Description: Detroit's struggling auto industry and the government loan package is discussed as well as the United Auto Worker union, which is loathed by Senate Republicans.

39265 ■ *"No Frills - And No Dodge" in Crain's Detroit Business (Vol. 24, September 22, 2008, No. 38, pp. 3)*
Pub: Crain Communications Inc.
Ed: Bradford Wernle. **Description:** Chrysler LLC is in the middle of a business plan known as Project Genesis, a five-year strategy in which the company will reduce the dealer count by combining its Jeep, Chrysler and Dodge brands under one rooftop wherever possible. Not every dealer will be able to arrange this deal because of the investment required to expand stores in which have low-overhead; many of these stores feel that low-overhead structures are more likely to survive difficult times than the larger stores in which the Genesis consolidation plan intends to implement.

39266 ■ *"Nonstop Round Baler Earns Top International Award for Krone" in Farm Industry News (November 18, 2011)*
Pub: Penton Business Media Inc.
Ed: Karen McMahon. **Description:** The new Ultima baler from Krone can make and net a bale in 40 seconds without stopping, thus producing 90 bales an hour. The new baler, still in test stage, won top honors at the Agritechnica farm equipment show in Hannover, Germany.

39267 ■ *"Not All Contracts a Good Fit for Fashion Reps" in Agency Sales Magazine (Vol. 39, September-October 2009, No. 9, pp. 10)*
Pub: MANA
Ed: Jack Foster. **Description:** Difficult situations regarding the relationship between sales representatives and their principals in the fashion industry are presented and suggestions on how to create contracts that seek to prevent potential problems are provided. Sales reps should make sure that manufacturer has a viable business that is well thought-out and adequately financed.

39268 ■ *"Now See This" in Entrepreneur (Vol. 36, April 2008, No. 4, pp. 53)*
Pub: Entrepreneur Media, Inc.
Ed: Mike Hogan. **Description:** New high definition (HD) products are to be introduced in 2008 at the Consumer Electronics Show and the Macworld Conference & Expo. HD lineup from companies such as Dell Inc. and Hewlett-Packard Co. are discussed.

39269 ■ *"Nuclear Plans May Stall on Uranium Shortage" in Globe & Mail (March 22, 2007, pp. B4)*
Pub: CTVglobemedia Publishing Inc.
Ed: Shawn McCarthy. **Description:** The poor investments in uranium production and enrichment despite growing demand for it for nuclear energy is discussed.

39270 ■ *"Nvidia Shares Clobbered After Gloomy Warning" in Barron's (Vol. 88, July 7, 2008, No. 27, pp. 25)*
Pub: Dow Jones & Co., Inc.
Ed: Eric J. Savitz. **Description:** Shares of graphics chip manufacturer Nvidia suffered a 30 percent drop in its share price after the company warned that revenue and gross margin forecasts for the quarter ending July 27, 2008 will be below expectations. Stan Glasgow, chief operating officer of Sony Electronics, believes the US economic slowdown will not affect demand for the company's products. Statistical data included.

39271 ■ *"Nvidia's Picture Brighter Than Stock Price Indicates" in Barron's (Vol. 88, March 24, 2008, No. 12, pp. 46)*
Pub: Dow Jones & Company, Inc.
Ed: Eric J. Savitz. **Description:** Shares of graphics chip maker Nvidia, priced at $18.52 each, do not indicate the company's strong position in the graphics chip market. The company's shares have dropped due to fears of slower demand for PCs, but the company is not as exposed to broader economic forces.

39272 ■ *"Oakland County Hopes Auto Suppliers Can Drive Medical Industry Growth" in Crain's Detroit Business (March 10, 2008)*
Pub: Crain Communications, Inc.
Ed: Chad Halcom. **Description:** Oakland County officials are hoping to create further economic development for the region by pairing health care companies and medical device makers with automotive suppliers in an attempt to discover additional crossover technology.

39273 ■ *"Ocean of Opportunity" in Hawaii Business (Vol. 53, October 2007, No. 4, pp. 61)*
Pub: Hawaii Business Publishing
Ed: Mike Markrich. **Description:** Brew Moon owner Marcus Bender and former Coca-Cola Enterprises Inc. executive Jim Stevens have introduced Kai Vodka in June 2007. The new drink is being marketed to professional women, the number of which is increasing based on a research by the Queens College Department of Sociology. The development process of the new product is also discussed.

39274 ■ *"Old Ford Plant to Sign New Tenants" in Business Courier (Vol. 27, August 13, 2010, No. 15, pp. 1)*
Pub: Business Courier
Ed: Dan Monk. **Description:** Ohio Realty Advisors LLC, a company handling the marketing of the 1.9 million-square-foot former Ford Batavia plant is on the brink of landing one distribution and three manufacturing firms as tenants. These tenants are slated to occupy about 20 percent of the facility and generate as many as 250 jobs in Ohio.

39275 ■ *"On a Mission: Ginch Gonch Wants You to Get Rid of Your Tighty Whities" in Canadian Business (Vol. 81, September 29, 2008, No. 16)*
Pub: Rogers Media Ltd.
Ed: Michelle Magnan. **Description:** New Equity Capital acquired underwear maker Ginch Gonch in July 2008; founder Jason Sutherland kept his position as creative director of the company and will retain his title as 'director of stitches and inches'. The company is known for its products, which are reminiscent of the days when people wore underwear covered in cowboys and stars as kids. The company also claims that Nelly, Justin Timberlake, and Hilary Duff have worn their products.

39276 ■ *"Ontario Keeps Bleeding Jobs as Michelin Closes Tire Plant" in Globe & Mail (February 3, 2006, pp. B1)*
Pub: CTVglobemedia Publishing Inc.
Ed: Greg Keenan; Heather Scoffield. **Description:** The reasons behind facility shutdown and workforce reduction by Michelin SA, in Ontario, are presented.

39277 ■ *"Options Abound in Winter Wares" in Pet Product News (Vol. 64, November 2010, No. 11, pp. 1)*
Pub: BowTie Inc.
Ed: Maggie M. Shein. **Description:** Pet supply manufacturers emphasize creating top-notch construction and functional design in creating winter clothing for pets. Meanwhile, retailers and pet owners seek human-inspired style, quality, and versatility for pets' winter clothing. How retailers generate successful sales of pets' winter clothing outside of traditional brand marketing is also examined.

39278 ■ *"The Oracle's Endgame; Wrigley Investment Isn't What Many Call a Classic Buffett Play" in Crain's Chicago Business (May 5, 2008)*
Pub: Crain Communications, Inc.
Ed: Ann Saphir. **Description:** Discusses Warren Buffett's deal with Mars Inc. to buy Wm. Wrigley Jr. Co., a move which would make Mr. Buffett a minority shareholder in a privately held company, a departure from his typical investment strategy. Mr. Buffett's Berkshire Hathaway Inc. agreed to provide $4.4 billion to help finance the $23 billion deal to pay another $2.1 billion for an equity stake in the company once it became a subsidiary of Mars.

39279 ■ *"O'Reilly Will Soup Up KC Warehouse" in The Business Journal-Serving Metropolitan Kansas City (Vol. 26, August 15, 2008, No. 49)*
Pub: American City Business Journals, Inc.
Ed: Rob Roberts. **Description:** O'Reilly Automotive Inc. plans to construct a 215,000-square foot warehouse in Kansas City. The move is expected to triple the size of the company's distribution center. Other views and information on the planned warehouse construction, are presented.

39280 ■ *"Our Gadget of the Week" in Barron's (Vol. 88, March 10, 2008, No. 10, pp. 36)*
Pub: Dow Jones & Company, Inc.
Ed: Jay Palmer. **Description:** Review of the $1,599 Fujitsu Lifebook T2010 tablet notebook which is a lightweight notebook offering a comfortable keyboard and a 12-inch screen illuminated by light emitting diodes. The notebook, however, also offers limited capability with its low-end processor and the lack of a built-in optical drive and a touchpad.

39281 ■ *"Out of Fashion" in Barron's (Vol. 88, March 17, 2008, No. 11, pp. 48)*
Pub: Dow Jones & Company, Inc.
Ed: Robin Goldwyn Blumenthal. **Description:** Shares of Perry Ellis International and G-III Apparel Group have taken some beating in the market despite good growth earnings prospects. Perry Ellis sees earnings growth of 8 to 11 percent for fiscal 2009, while G-III Apparel expects earnings growth of 25 percent.

39282 ■ *Outsourcing: Information Technology, Original Equipment Manufacturer, Leo, Oursourcing, Offshoring Research Network, Crowdsourcing*
Pub: General Books LLC
Released: May 1, 2010. **Price:** $14.14. **Description:** Chapters include information for outsourcing firms and how to maintain an outsourcing business.

39283 ■ *"Packaging Firm Wraps Up Remake; Overseas Plants Help Firm Fatten Margins" in Crain's New York Business (January 7, 2008)*
Pub: Crain Communications, Inc.
Description: Sealed Air Corp., a packaging manufacturer, has seen its share price fall nearly 20 percent over the past two years, making it one of the worst performers in the packaging sector.

39284 ■ *"Pain Ahead as Profit Pressure Increases" in Crain's Chicago Business (Vol. 31, May 5, 2008, No. 18, pp. 4)*
Pub: Crain Communications, Inc.
Ed: Daniel Rome Levine. **Description:** Interview with David Klaskin, the chairman and chief investment officer at Oak Ridge Investments LLC, who discusses the outlook for the economy and corporate earnings, particularly in the housing and auto industries, the impact of economic stimulus checks, the weakness of the dollar and recommendations of stocks that individual investors may find helpful.

39285 ■ *"Paradise Lost" in Inc. (February 2008, pp. 102-109)*
Pub: Gruner & Jahr USA Publishing
Ed: Bo Burlingham. **Description:** Profile of Bo Burlingham, founder of Precision Manufacturing, a firm cited in books, magazines and newspaper articles for its people-centered culture and success.

39286 ■ *"Parent Firm's Global Reach, Stricter Air Quality Rules Have Stock Smiling" in Crain's Cleveland Business (October 15, 2007)*
Pub: Crain Communications, Inc.
Ed: David Bennett. **Description:** Since Stock Equipment Co., a firm that makes industrial pollution control equipment, was acquired by Schenck Process Group, a diversified global manufacturer based in Germany, the company's orders from abroad have been on the rise. The purchase has opened the doors to regions such as Eastern and Central Europe, Latin America and Australia.

39287 ■ *"Patchy Oil Profits" in Canadian Business (Vol. 80, February 12, 2007, No. 4, pp. 89)*
Pub: Rogers Media
Ed: Michelle Magnan. **Description:** The fall in fourth-quarter earnings of several oil and gas companies in Canada, in view of rise in their expenditure, is discussed.

39288 ■ *"PCI Express Powers Machine Vision" in Canadian Electronics (Vol. 23, February 2008, No. 1, pp. 8)*
Pub: CLB Media Inc.
Ed: Inder Kohli. **Description:** PCI Express is an innovative peripheral bus that can be used in industrial computing. The peripheral bus delivers a high-bandwidth, scaleable, point-to-point path from peripheral cards to the computing core. Features and functions of PCI Express are described in detail.

39289 ■ *"Pepsi Co. Breaches the Walls of Coke Fortress McDonald's" in Globe & Mail (March 13, 2007, pp. B1)*
Pub: CTVglobemedia Publishing Inc.
Ed: Keith McArthur. **Description:** Soft drinks giant Pepsi Co. has entered an agreement with fast food chain McDonald's for offering its products in outlets across Canada. Earlier Coca-Cola Co. used to offer its exclusive products in these outlets.

39290 ■ *The Perfect Scent: A Year Inside the Perfume Industry in Paris and New York*
Pub: Henry Holt and Co.
Contact: Michael Naumann, President
Ed: Chandler Burr. **Released:** 2009. **Price:** $25.00. **Description:** An insiders glimpse at the development of two new fragrances from Hermes and Coty.

39291 ■ *"Pet Food Bank 'Shares the Love'" in Pet Product News (Vol. 64, December 2010, No. 12, pp. 6)*
Pub: BowTie Inc.
Description: Winston-Salem, North Carolina-based nonprofit Share the Love Pet Food Bank has donated 60,000 pounds of pet food since its establishment in 2009. It has been linking pet food manufacturers and

rescue groups to supply unsold pet food to needy animals. The nonprofit intends to reach out to more animal welfare groups by building more warehouses.

39292 ■ *"Pet-Food Industry Too Slow" in Advertising Age (Vol. 78, March 26, 2007, No. 13, pp. 29)*
Pub: Crain Communications, Inc.
Description: Many crisis-communications experts believe that the pet-food industry mishandled the problem by waiting almost a month to recall the 60 million 'wet-food' products after numerous consumer complaints. Experts site that the first 24 to 49 hours are the most important in dealing with a crisis of this nature.

39293 ■ *"Phoenix Company Realizing Dream of Global Growth" in The Business Journal - Serving Phoenix and the Valley of the Sun (Vol. 28, July 18, 2008, No. 46, pp. 1)*
Pub: American City Business Journals, Inc.
Ed: Chris Casacchia. **Description:** Phoenix, Arizona-based lubricant maker DreamBrands Inc. is realizing global growth. The company, which has been generating interest from institutional investors, is seeking a second round of funding. Details of the company's products and marketing plans are also discussed.

39294 ■ *"Pierre's Ice Cream" in Ice Cream Reporter (Vol. 23, October 20, 2010, No. 11, pp. 8)*
Pub: Ice Cream Reporter
Description: Pierre's Ice Cream has started work on its new $8 million manufacturing facility in Cleveland, Ohio.

39295 ■ *"A Pioneer of Paying With Plastic" in Crain's Chicago Business (Vol. 31, April 28, 2008, No. 17, pp. 39)*
Pub: Crain Communications, Inc.
Ed: Phuong Ly. **Description:** Profile of Perfect Plastic Printing Corp., a family-owned company which manufactures credit cards, bank cards and gift cards and whose sales hit $50.1 million last year, a 16 percent jump from 2006.

39296 ■ *"Pitch for SPX Expansion was Full of Energy" in Charlotte Business Journal (Vol. 25, November 19, 2010, No. 35, pp. 1)*
Pub: Charlotte Business Journal
Ed: John Downey. **Description:** SPX Corporation announced that it will expand their headquarters in Ballantyne after Charlotte and North Carolina leaders made an aggressive push to retain the company. SPX Corporation is expected to invest $70 million for the expansion, which would mean 180 new jobs in Charlotte.

39297 ■ *"Playing Defense" in Crain's Chicago Business (Vol. 31, November 10, 2008, No. 45, pp. 4)*
Pub: Crain Communications, Inc.
Ed: Monee Fields-White. **Description:** Chicago's money managers are increasingly investing in local companies such as Caterpillar Inc., a maker of construction and mining equipment, Kraft Foods Inc. and Baxter International Inc., a manufacturer of medical products, in an attempt to bolster their portfolios. These companies have a history of surviving tough economic times.

39298 ■ *"Porsche Raises VW Stake, Makes Bid for Firm" in Globe & Mail (March 26, 2007, pp. B5)*
Pub: CTVglobemedia Publishing Inc.
Ed: Chad Thomas. Jeremy Van Logan. **Description:** Automobile giant Porsche AG has increased its stake in Volkswagen AG to $54 billion recently. The company is planning a merger by claiming 30% stake under German law.

39299 ■ *"Powder River Reports First Quarter Revenues Over 5 Million" in Canadian Corporate News (May 16, 2007)*
Pub: Comtex News Network Inc.
Description: Financial report for Powder River Basin Gas Corp., a revenue generating producer, marketer, and acquirer of crude oil and natural gas properties. Statistical data included.

39300 ■ *"Precision Fertilizer Spreading Shown at Agritechnica" in Farm Industry News (November 23, 2011)*
Pub: Penton Business Media Inc.
Ed: Karen McMahon. **Description:** Rauch, the German firm, introduced a new system that precisely spreads fertilizer on crops. The new product was shown at Agritechnica.

39301 ■ *"Press Release: Revolver Grain Auger End from Mauer Manufacturing" in Farm Industry News (December 17, 2010)*
Pub: Penton Business Media Inc.
Description: Profile of the Revolver Grain Auger End from Mauer Manufacturing is presented. The new design eliminates grain loss/dribble, reduces grain in the next year's crop, and has a greater clearance for combine unloading auger.

39302 ■ *"Pricey Oil, High Dollar Wipe Out Jobs" in Globe & Mail (February 11, 2006, pp. B6)*
Pub: CTVglobemedia Publishing Inc.
Ed: Heather Scoffield. **Description:** The impact of higher oil prices and dollar value, on manufacturing jobs in Canada, is discussed.

39303 ■ *"Priority: In Memoriam" in Inc. (December 2007, pp. 25-26, 28, 30)*
Pub: Gruner & Jahr USA Publishing
Ed: Ryan McCarthy. **Description:** Profiles of entrepreneurs who died in 2007; these individuals helped to create some major business trends in the last fifty years, from the advent of socially responsible business to development of quality manufacturing.

39304 ■ *"Products and Services" in Canadian Electronics (Vol. 23, August 2008, No. 5, pp. 46)*
Pub: Action Communication Inc.
Description: Directory of companies under the alphabetical listing of electronic equipment and allied components that they offer is presented.

39305 ■ *"Providing Expertise Required to Develop Microsystems" in Canadian Electronics (Vol. 23, February 2008, No. 1, pp. 6)*
Pub: CLB Media Inc.
Ed: Ian McWalter. **Description:** CMC Microsystems, formerly Canadian Microelectronics Corporation, is focused on empowering microelectronics and Microsystems research in Canada. Microsystems offers the basis for innovations in the fields of science, environment, technology, automotives, energy, aerospace and communications technology. CMC's strategy in developing Microsystems in Canada is described.

39306 ■ *"PRWT Service Acquires Pharmaceutical Plant: Firm Wins Multimillion-Dollar Contract with Merck" in Black Enterprise (March 2008)*
Pub: Earl G. Graves Publishing Co. Inc.
Ed: Tamara E. Holmes. **Description:** PRWT Services Inc. expanded through its acquisition of a chemical manufacturing plant in New Jersey. The Whitehouse Station, part of Merck & Co. Inc. produces active pharmaceutical ingredients for antibiotics, making PRWT the first minority-owned company in the U.S. to manufacture active pharmaceutical ingredients.

39307 ■ *"Pulp Friction: Spin Off Mills to Boost Wood Products" in Globe & Mail (February 18, 2006, pp. B3)*
Pub: CTVglobemedia Publishing Inc.
Ed: Peter Kennedy. **Description:** The reasons behind the decision of chief executive officer Jim Shepherd of Canfor Corp. to sell pulp mills are presented.

39308 ■ *"Put It In Drive" in Entrepreneur (Vol. 36, April 2008, No. 4, pp. 31)*
Pub: Entrepreneur Media, Inc.
Ed: Jill Amadio. **Description:** Commercial vehicle models for 2008 are presented. These new models are more user- and environment-friendly. Features and prices of car models and tips to consider before purchasing are presented.

39309 ■ *"Putting 'Extra' in Extra-Silky Shampoo" in Crain's Chicago Business (Vol. 31, April 28, 2008, No. 17, pp. 37)*
Pub: Crain Communications, Inc.
Ed: Phuong Ly. **Description:** Profile of HallStar Co., a Chicago-based company which develops and manufactures specialty chemicals to upgrade existing products such as hair dye, lotion and deodorant. HallStar has seen its annual earnings rise more than 30 percent since 2002.

39310 ■ *"Q&A: David Labistour" in Canadian Business (Vol. 81, March 17, 2008, No. 4, pp. 10)*
Pub: Rogers Media
Ed: Lauren McKeon. **Description:** David Labistour says that the difference between being a co-op retailer and a corporate-owned retailer in the case of Mountain Equipment Co-op (MEC) is that the company is owned by their customers and not by shareholders. Labistour also says that MEC works with their factories to ensure that these maintain ethical standards in the manufacturing process.

39311 ■ *"Q&A Interview With Perrin Beatty" in Canadian Business (Vol. 80, October 8, 2007, No. 20, pp. 13)*
Pub: Rogers Media
Description: Perrin Beatty, president and chief executive officer of the Canadian Chamber of Commerce, talks about his move from the Canadian Manufacturers and Exporters to his current organization. He also discusses the state of Canada's economy, as well as the need for leadership.

39312 ■ *"Q&A: Joseph Ribkoff" in Canadian Business (Vol. 81, March 31, 2008, No. 5, pp. 4)*
Pub: Rogers Media
Ed: Zena Olijnyk. **Description:** Joseph Ribkoff started his career in the garment trade by sweeping floors and running deliveries for a dress manufacturer called Town & Country and earned $16 a week. Ribkoff says that the key to controlling costs in Canada is to invest in the latest equipment and technology to stay competitive.

39313 ■ *"Qualcomm Could Win Big as the IPhone 3G Calls" in Barron's (Vol. 88, July 4, 2008, No. 28, pp. 30)*
Pub: Dow Jones & Co., Inc.
Ed: Eric J. Savitz. **Description:** Apple iPhone 3G's introduction could widen the smartphone market thereby benefiting handset chipmaker Qualcomm in the process. Qualcomm Senior V.P., Bill Davidson sees huge potential for his company's future beyond phones with their Snapdragon processor. The prospects of Sun Microsystems' shares are also discussed.

39314 ■ *"The Quest for the Smart Prosthetic" in Canadian Business (Vol. 83, October 12, 2010, No. 17, pp. 26)*
Pub: Rogers Media Ltd.
Ed: Jacqueline Nelson. **Description:** Information about a two-year research project led by Southern Methodist University (SMU) and funded by the Defense Advance Research Projects Agency (DARPA) is provided. The agency aims to create a 'smart prosthetic' which will improve the lives of military amputees. The planned prosthetic will use a sensor that can carry nerve signals through synthetic channels.

39315 ■ *"The Question: Who Do You Think Is the Most Genuine?" in Advertising Age (Vol. 79, July 7, 2008, No. 26, pp. 4)*
Pub: Crain Communications, Inc.
Ed: Ken Wheaton. **Description:** According to a survey conducted by Harris Interactive Reputation Quotient, Johnson & Johnson was deemed the most genuine brand. Google came in second followed by UPS.

39316 ■ *"A Questionable Chemical Romance" in Barron's (Vol. 88, July 14, 2008, No. 28, pp. 28)*
Pub: Dow Jones & Co., Inc.
Ed: Andrew Bary. **Description:** Dow Chemical paid $78-a-share for the surprise takeover of Rohm &

Haas. The acquisition is reducing Dow Chemical's financial flexibility at a time when chemical companies are being affected by high costs and a weak U.S. economy.

39317 ■ *"R&R Ice Cream" in Ice Cream Reporter (Vol. 23, November 20, 2010, No. 12, pp. 8)*
Pub: Ice Cream Reporter
Description: R&R Ice Cream, the United Kingdom's largest ice cream manufacturer, has completed a private offering of senior secured notes that has raised 298 million (pounds sterling) to fund expansion and acquisitions.

39318 ■ *"R&R Launches Upscale Spoony's and Low Fat Dragon's Den" in Ice Cream Reporter (Vol. 23, August 20, 2010, No. 9, pp. 3)*
Pub: Ice Cream Reporter
Description: European ice cream manufacturer R&R has acquired French ice cream maker Rolland and will position itself as an upscale challenger to brands like Ben & Jerry's.

39319 ■ *"Recession Management" in Canadian Business (Vol. 81, March 3, 2008, No. 3, pp. 62)*
Pub: Rogers Media
Ed: Joe Castaldo. **Description:** Some companies such as Capital One Financial Corp. are managing their finances as if a recession has already taken place to prepare themselves for the looming economic downturn. Intel Corp., meanwhile shows how increasing its investments during a recession could be advantageous. Tips on how companies can survive a recession are provided.

39320 ■ *"Recovery on Tap for 2010?" in Orlando Business Journal (Vol. 26, January 1, 2010, No. 31, pp. 1)*
Pub: American City Business Journals
Ed: Melanie Stawicki Azam, Richard Bilbao, Christopher Boyd, Anjali Fluker. **Description:** Economic forecasts for Central Florida's leading business sectors in 2010 are presented. These sectors include housing, film and TV, sports business, law, restaurants, aviation, tourism and hospitality, banking and finance, commercial real estate, retail, health care, insurance, higher education, and manufacturing. According to some local executives, Central Florida's economy will slowly recover in 2010.

39321 ■ *"Red Diesel Cost Sparks a Move to Home-Grown Fuel" in Farmer's Weekly (March 28, 2008, No. 320)*
Pub: Reed Business Information
Contact: Jeff Greisch, President
Description: Due to the rising cost of red diesel, the idea of growing one's own tractor fuel has an undeniable attraction for many farmers. A growing pressure is weighing on engine manufacturers to produce designs that can run on both SVO as well as biodiesel.

39322 ■ *"Redcorp Ventures Ltd.: Tulsequah Camp Construction Begins" in Canadian Corporate News (May 16, 2007)*
Pub: Comtex News Network Inc.
Description: Redfern Reources Ltd., a subsidiary of Redcorp Ventures Ltd., announced that Modular Transportable Solutions LLC was selected to design and manufacture its prefabricated, modular construction camp, cookhouse, administration buildings, and mine dry at the Tulsequah Mine location in northwest British Columbia due to the virtually indestructible design of the units that withstand extreme weather conditions.

39323 ■ *"Region to Be Named Innovation Hub" in Business Courier (Vol. 27, July 2, 2010, No. 9, pp. 1)*
Pub: Business Courier
Ed: Dan Monk. **Description:** The selection of Cincinnati's consumer-marketing cluster as a 'Hub of Innovation' by the Ohio Department of Development could boost Cincinnati's chances of receiving $100 million in grants from Ohio's Third Frontier program and other funding sources. Implications of the University of Cincinnati's designation as a Center of Excellence in Advanced Transportation and Aerospace are also discussed.

39324 ■ *"Reinventing Your Rep Training Program" in Agency Sales Magazine (Vol. 39, August 2009, No. 8, pp. 40)*
Pub: MANA
Description: Tips on how to encourage manufacturer's representatives to attend scheduled training sessions are given. Manufacturers should learn the value of keeping the training program up-to-date and communicate with the sales team to know what needs to be revamped. Problems faced by representatives with inside sales staff should also be addressed by the manufacturer.

39325 ■ *"Relationship "Farming" Tools" in Agency Sales Magazine (Vol. 39, August 2009, No. 8, pp. 46)*
Pub: MANA
Ed: Terry L. Brock. **Description:** Manufacturer's representatives should spend time, money and effort in establishing and maintaining relationships; one tool to help is the new Fujitsu S1500 scanner. The scanner can accomplish critical tasks, quickly, easily and at low cost. Other suggestions to help build better business relationships are given.

39326 ■ *"Rental Demand Boosts Revenue for Sun Communities Inc." in Crain's Detroit Business (Vol. 24, March 24, 2008, No. 12, pp. 4)*
Pub: Crain Communications, Inc.
Ed: Daniel Duggan. **Description:** Despite the decline in sales of manufactured homes, demand for rental units and rent-to-own programs have brought Sun Communities Inc. increased revenue. The real estate investment trust, based in Southfield, owns, operates, finances and develops manufactured home communities in the Midwest and Southeast. Statistical data included.

39327 ■ *"Rep Contracts: Simple, Clear, Fair" in Agency Sales Magazine (Vol. 39, September-October 2009, No. 9, pp. 3)*
Pub: MANA
Ed: Bryan C. Shirley. **Description:** Things that a manufacturer and a sales representative needs to strive for when creating an Agreement for Representation includes an agreement that is simple and complete, one that covers all the needs of both parties and is fair, equitable, and balanced. Sales representatives need to make more sales calls and find new opportunities during this recession.

39328 ■ *"Rep Vs. Direct: Always an Interesting Story" in Agency Sales Magazine (Vol. 39, July 2009, No. 7, pp. 3)*
Pub: MANA
Ed: Bryan C. Shirley. **Description:** Manufacturers benefit from outsourcing their field sales to professional sales representatives in the areas of multi-line selling and customer knowledge and relationship. Some misperceptions about sales reps include the belief that they are an additional 'channel' in sales.

39329 ■ *"Rep Vs. Direct: Inside the Mind of One Manufacturer" in Agency Sales Magazine (Vol. 39, July 2009, No. 7, pp. 8)*
Pub: MANA
Ed: Jack Foster. **Description:** Fantech President Glenn Thompson believes that a commissioned representative sales force is the most effective means of going to market. Thompson also discusses the pros and cons of working with reps and the qualities to look for in a rep.

39330 ■ *"Report: McD's Pepsi Score Best With Young Hispanics" in Brandweek (Vol. 49, April 21, 2008, No. 16, pp. 8)*
Pub: VNU Business Media, Inc.
Ed: Della de Lafuente. **Description:** According to a new report, in order to reach Hispanic Gen Yers, marketing strategists need to understand this demographic's 'bi-dentity,' something which has proved an elusive task to many marketers. Another trend is the emergence of Latinas who have careers, as opposed to just jobs. There is an opportunity to tap this new, young and empowered female market with innovative messaging. Statistical data included.

39331 ■ *"Reports of Banks' Revival were Greatly Exaggerated" in Barron's (Vol. 88, July 7, 2008, No. 27, pp. L14)*
Pub: Dow Jones & Co., Inc.
Ed: Jack Willoughby. **Description:** Performance of mutual funds improved for the second quarter of 2008 compared to the previous quarter, registering an average gain of 0.13 percent; funds focusing on natural resources rose the highest, their value rising by an average of 24.50 percent.

39332 ■ *"Reps Have Needs Too!" in Agency Sales Magazine (Vol. 39, December 2009, No. 11, pp. 16)*
Pub: MANA
Ed: Bill Heyden. **Description:** There is common information that a sales representatives needs to know prior to choosing a manufacturer to represent. Both parties must keep promises made to customers and prospects. Reps also need the support from the manufacturers and to clear matters regarding their commission. Interviewing tips for representatives to get this vital information are presented.

39333 ■ *"Reps Vs. Factory Direct Sales Force..Which Way to Go?" in Agency Sales Magazine (Vol. 39, September-October 2009, No. 9, pp. 28)*
Pub: MANA
Ed: Eric P. Johnson. **Description:** Hiring independent manufacturers' sales representative is a cost-effective alternative to a direct sales force. Sales reps have predictable sales costs that go up and down with sales, stronger local relationships and better market intelligence.

39334 ■ *"Reps Vs. Factory Direct Sales Force..Which Way to Go?" in Agency Sales Magazine (Vol. 39, September-October 2009, No. 9, pp. 28)*
Pub: MANA
Ed: Eric P. Johnson. **Description:** Hiring independent manufacturers' sales representative is a cost-effective alternative to a direct sales force. Sales reps have predictable sales costs that go up and down with sales, stronger local relationships and better market intelligence.

39335 ■ *"Research Reports: How Analysts Size Up Companies" in Barron's (Vol. 88, July 14, 2008, No. 28, pp. M13)*
Pub: Dow Jones & Co., Inc.
Ed: Anita Peltonen. **Description:** Shares of Bankrate and AutoZone both get a 'Buy' rating from analysts while Zions Bancorporation's shares are downgraded from 'Outperform' to 'Neutral'. The shares of Jet Blue Airline and Deckers Outdoor, a manufacturer of innovative footwear, are also rated and discussed. Statistical data included.

39336 ■ *"Revisiting Rep Coping Strategies" in Agency Sales Magazine (Vol. 39, December 2009, No. 11, pp. 32)*
Pub: MANA
Ed: Jack Foster. **Description:** Independent manufacturers representatives should become a well-rounded and complete businessman with continued education. The new type of representative is a problem solver and the resource for answering questions. Employing the concept of synergistic selling is also important to salespeople.

39337 ■ *Risk-Free Entrepreneur*
Pub: Adams Media Corporation
Ed: Don Debelak. **Released:** June 2006. **Price:** $14.95. **Description:** Information is offered to help entrepreneurs to develop an idea for a product or service and have other companies provide the marketing, manufacturing and staff.

39338 ■ *"River Plan in Disarray" in Business Journal Portland (Vol. 26, December 4, 2009, No. 39, pp. 1)*
Pub: American City Business Journals Inc.
Ed: Andy Giegerich. **Description:** Portland's proposed rules on a waterfront development plan for the Willamette River calls for fees intended for river bank

preservation, a move that could drive industrial manufacturers away. The manufacturers, under the Working Waterfront Coalition, claim that the proposals could increase riverfront building costs by 15 percent.

39339 ■ *"Ron Carpenter" in Crain's Cleveland Business (Vol. 30, June 29, 2009, No. 25, pp. 12)*
Pub: Crain Communications, Inc.
Ed: Dan Shingler. **Description:** Profile of Ron Carpenter, owner of Production Tool Company located in Twinsburg, Ohio. Carpenter was forced to lay off half of his staff of 14 workers after the auto business tanked. He believes it was the single most difficult decision he had to make as a manager.

39340 ■ *"Ross: There's Still Money In the Auto Industry" in Crain's Detroit Business (Vol. 24, January 28, 2008, No. 4, pp. 12)*
Pub: Crain Communications Inc. - Detroit
Ed: Brent Snavely. **Description:** Wilbur Ross, chairman and CEO of WL Ross and Company LLC, a private equity firm, predicts U.S. vehicle sales will fall by about 750,000 in 2008, but continues to look for supplier bargains.

39341 ■ *"Rough Q1 Begs Question: Is the Crocs Craze Over?" in Brandweek (Vol. 49, April 21, 2008, No. 16, pp. 16)*
Pub: VNU Business Media, Inc.
Ed: Eric Newman. **Description:** Crocs, a rubber shoemaker, announced last week that it missed its expected first quarter revenues by 15 percent. The popular rubber sandals are suffering in sales due to a number of factors including a tougher economic environment, less expensive, knock-off brands, the cold weather delay of the spring season and fading consumer interest in plastic shoes.

39342 ■ *"Roundtable - The Auto Sector Shifts Gears" in Mergers & Acquisitions: The Dealmaker's Journal (March 1, 2008)*
Pub: SourceMedia, Inc.
Description: Industry professionals discuss the current state of the automotive sector as well as what they predict for the future of the industry; also provides information for investors about opportunities in the sector.

39343 ■ *"Royal Dutch's Grip Firm on Shell" in Globe & Mail (March 19, 2007, pp. B1)*
Pub: CTVglobemedia Publishing Inc.
Ed: David Ebner. **Description:** The proposed acquisition of Shell Canada Ltd. by Royal Dutch Shell PLC for $8.7 billion is discussed.

39344 ■ *"Rumors Kill Algoma Takeover Talks" in Globe & Mail (March 14, 2007, pp. B14)*
Pub: CTVglobemedia Publishing Inc.
Ed: Tara Perkins. **Description:** Canada-based steel manufacturing giant Salzgitter AG has dropped its acquisition negotiations with Algoma Steel Inc. The decision comes after the secret price quotation was leaked to competitors.

39345 ■ *"Russian Renaissance" in Chicago Tribune (September 22, 2008)*
Pub: McClatchy-Tribune Information Services
Ed: Alex Rodriguez. **Description:** Winemakers from Russia are returning to the craft and quality of winemaking now that they are free from Soviet restraints.

39346 ■ *"Rust Belt No More: The Demise of Manufacturing" in Crain's Chicago Business (Vol. 31, March 31, 2008, No. 13, pp. 52)*
Pub: Crain Communications, Inc.
Ed: Sarah A. Klein. **Description:** Discusses the history of manufacturing in the Chicago area as well as the history of manufacturer International Harvester Co.

39347 ■ *"Sale of Solo Cup Plant Pending" in Boston Business Journal (Vol. 29, June 17, 2011, No. 6, pp. 1)*
Pub: American City Business Journals Inc.
Ed: Daniel J. Sernovitz. **Description:** Baltimore developers Vanguard Equities Inc. and Greenberg Gibbons Commercial have contracted to buy the Solo Cup Company facility in Owing Mills and are now considering several plans for the property. Sale should be completed by September 2011 but no proposed sale terms are disclosed.

39348 ■ *"Sandi Jackson; Alderman, 7th Ward, City of Chicago" in Crain's Chicago Business (Vol. 31, May 5, 2008, No. 18, pp. 31)*
Pub: Crain Communications, Inc.
Ed: Sarah A. Klein. **Description:** Profile of Sandi Jackson who is an alderman of the 7th ward of the city of Chicago and is addressing issues such as poverty and crime as well as counting on a plan to develop the former USX Corp. steel mill to revitalize the area's economic climate.

39349 ■ *"Sandvik Expands Energy-Saving Program" in Modern Machine Shop (Vol. 84, September 2011, No. 4, pp. 48)*
Pub: Gardner Business Media, Inc.
Contact: Richard G. Kline, President
E-mail: rkline@gardnerweb.com
Description: Sandvik Coromant, based in Fair Lawn, New Jersey, expanded its Sustainable Manufacturing Program that originally was developed to help Japanese-based firms reduce electricity consumption by 15 percent after the recent earthquake that cause loss of electrical power. The program now provides energy reduction through the Sandvick cutting tool technology, application techniques and productivity increases.

39350 ■ *"Saratoga Eagle Project Quenches Thirst To Grow" in Business Review, Albany New York (Vol. 34, November 30, 2007, No. 35, pp. 3)*
Pub: American City Business Journals, Inc.
Ed: Robin K. Cooper. **Description:** Saratoga Eagle Sales and Service will be searching for contractors for the construction of its new beverage distribution center at the WJ Grande Industrial Park in Saratoga Springs, New York. The $8 million, 107,000 square foot facility is part of Saratoga Eagle's expansion plan. The company's growth in the Capital Region market and $1.3 million tax break are discussed.

39351 ■ *"Search Engine: GE Looks Around" in Business Courier (Vol. 24, March 7, 2008, No. 48, pp. 1)*
Pub: American City Business Journals, Inc.
Ed: Laura Baverman. **Description:** GE Aviation, an aircraft engine company, could move about 1,500 Tri-employees to its new office in West Chester, Liberty Township, Northern Kentucky, as its leases are set to expire in 2009 and 2010. The company revealed that developers are prompting the firm to send out a request-for-proposal to choose development companies in 2008.

39352 ■ *"SECO Manufacturing" in Point of Beginning (Vol. , 2008, No. , pp.)*
Pub: BNP Media
Contact: Al Reser, President
Description: Seco Manufacturing's 3015-Series lock features an all-metal tilting holder with an improved brass front locking lever for improved security for any building.

39353 ■ *"The Second Most Fuel-Efficient Tractor of the Decade: John Deere 8320R" in Farm Industry News (November 10, 2011)*
Pub: Penton Business Media Inc.
Description: John Deere's 8320R Tractor was ranked second in the Farm Industry News listing of the top 40 most fuel-efficient tractors of the decade, following the winner, John Deere's 8295R PTO tractor.

39354 ■ *"Sellers Shift Gears" in Crain's Detroit Business (Vol. 25, June 22, 2009, No. 25, pp. 3)*
Pub: Crain Communications Inc. - Detroit
Description: Of the 14 new car Chrysler dealerships in the Detroit area who had franchises terminated, Joe Ricci of Dearborn will sell used cars at his new business called All American Buyer's Service; Lochmoor Automotive Group in Detroit will focus on Mahindra & Mahindra trucks; Mt. Clemens Dodge, Clinton Township is also selling Mahindra & Mahindra trucks; and Monicatti Chrysler Jeep, Sterling Heights, will offer service along with selling used cars.

39355 ■ *"Selling Michigan; R&D Pushed as Reason For Chinese To Locate In State" in Crain's Detroit Business (Vol. 24, January 14, 2008)*
Pub: Crain Communications Inc. - Detroit
Ed: Marti Benedetti. **Description:** Southeast Michigan Economic Development organizations are working to develop relationships with Chinese manufacturers so they will locate their automotive research and development operations in the state.

39356 ■ *"Seven Tips for Continuous Improvement" in American Printer (Vol. 128, July 1, 2011, No. 7)*
Pub: Penton Media Inc.
Description: Seven tips are given to help any graphic arts or printing company improve by integrating lean manufacturing into operations.

39357 ■ *"Shedding Light on Innovation" in Rental Product News (Vol. 33, June 2011)*
Pub: Cygnus Business Media
Ed: Rod Dickens. **Description:** Light tower manufacturers have introduced numerous new products that feature alternative power sources, LED lighting and a second generation of performance and value.

39358 ■ *"Shell Profit Top $2 Billion as Oil Sands Output Surges" in Globe & Mail (January 26, 2006, pp. B6)*
Pub: CTVglobemedia Publishing Inc.
Ed: Patrick Brethour. **Description:** The reasons behind posting of $2 billion profits for 2005, by Shell Canada Ltd. are presented.

39359 ■ *"Shermag Plans Two Shutdowns, 300 More Layoffs" in Globe & Mail (February 13, 2007, pp. B5)*
Pub: CTVglobemedia Publishing Inc.
Ed: Bertrand Marotte. **Description:** Shermag Inc., Canada's largest publicly traded furniture company, is permanently closing two plants and eliminating 300 jobs. The mounting losses and deteriorating stock prices are stated as main reasons for plant shutdowns.

39360 ■ *"Sherwin-Williams Workers Forgo Travel for Virtual Trade Show" in Crain's Cleveland Business (Vol. 28, October 15, 2007, No. 41)*
Pub: Crain Communications, Inc.
Ed: John Booth. **Description:** Overview of CyberCoating 2007, a cutting-edge virtual three-dimensional trade show that exhibitors such as Sherwin-Williams Co.'s Chemical Coatings Division will take part in by chatting verbally or via text messages in order to exchange information and listen to pitches just like they would on an actual trade show floor.

39361 ■ *"Shipbuilding & Defence" in Canadian Sailings (July 7, 2008)*
Pub: UBM Global Trade
Contact: Leonard J. Corallo, President
Ed: Sharon Hobson. **Description:** Overview of the Joint Support Ship Project whose initial budget was set at $2.1 billion for the acquisition of the ships required for the Canadian navy; another $800 million was allotted for 20 years of in-service support. Four teams of competitors bid for the contract and the Department of National Defence decided to fund two teams for the project definition phase of the competition.

39362 ■ *"Shoe's On Other Foot" in Business Courier (Vol. 24, November 30, 2008, No. 33, pp. 1)*
Pub: American City Business Journals, Inc.
Description: Ronald Hummons was fresh out of prison for felony in 2000, and through the help of spiritual non-profit group the Lord's Gym he was able to turn his life around and start his own company Grapevine Ltd. LLC, which makes C-town athletic shoes.

39363 ■ *The Six Sigma for Small and Medium Businesses: What You Need to Know Explained Simply*
Pub: Atlantic Publishing Company
Ed: Marsha R. Ford. **Released:** January 1, 2009. **Price:** $24.95. **Description:** The Six Sigma set of practices used to systematically improve business practices by eliminating defects. To be Six Sigma compliant, a company must produce no more than 3.4 defects per one million products, and if achieved will save the firm millions of dollars. The two main methodologies of Six Sigma are outlined.

39364 ■ *"Size Does Matter" in International Journal of Globalisation and Small Business (Vol. 4, September 21, 2010, No. 1, pp. 61)*
Pub: Publishers Communication Group
Ed: Julia Cornnell, Ranjit Voola. **Description:** Examination of how members of an Australian-based manufacturing and engineering cluster share knowledge through networking as a means to improve competitive advantage.

39365 ■ *"Slimmed-Down Supplier TI Automotive Relaunches" in Crain's Detroit Business (Vol. 26, January 11, 2010, No. 2, pp. 14)*
Pub: Crain Communications Inc.
Ed: Robert Sherefkin. **Description:** TI Automotive Ltd., one of the world's largest suppliers of fuel storage and delivery systems, has reorganized the company by splitting it into five global divisions and is relaunching its brand which is now more focused on new technology.

39366 ■ *"Slimmer Interiros Make Small Cars Seem Big" in Automotive News (Vol. 86, October 31, 2011, No. 6488, pp. 16)*
Pub: Crain Communications Inc.
Ed: David Sedgwick. **Description:** Cost-conscious buyers want luxury car amenities in their smaller vehicles, so automakers are rethinking interiors. Style, efficiency and value could be the next trend in vehicles.

39367 ■ *"S.M. Whitney Co. (1868-2010)" in Canadian Business (Vol. 83, October 12, 2010, No. 17, pp. 27)*
Pub: Rogers Media Ltd.
Ed: Angelina Chapin. **Description:** A history of S.M. Whitney Company is presented. The cotton company was opened in 1868. The cotton is sold to textile manufacturers after crops have been picked, ginned and baled. The company closed down in 2010 after chief executive officer Barry Whitney decided to sell his last bale of cotton.

39368 ■ *"Small is the New Big in Autos" in Globe & Mail (February 16, 2006, pp. B3)*
Pub: CTVglobemedia Publishing Inc.
Ed: Greg Keenan. **Description:** The reasons behind the introduction of subcompact cars by companies such as Ford Motor Co. are presented. The automobiles were unveiled at Canadian International Auto Show in Toronto.

39369 ■ *"Smart Car Sales Take Big Hit in Recession" in Business Journal-Milwaukee (Vol. 28, December 10, 2010, No. 10, pp. A1)*
Pub: Milwaukee Business Journal
Ed: Stacey Vogel Davis. **Description:** Sales of smart cars in Milwaukee declined in 2010. Smart Center Milwaukee sold only 52 new cars through October 2010. Increased competition is seen as a reason for the decline in sales.

39370 ■ *Sneaker Wars: The Enemy Brothers Who Founded Adidas and Puma and the Family Feud that Forever Changed the Business of Sport*
Pub: Ecco
Ed: Barbara Smit. **Released:** 2009. **Price:** $26.95. **Description:** A history of Puma and Adidas shoes and the two German brothers who built the empires.

39371 ■ *"Sobering Consequences" in The Business Journal-Milwaukee (Vol. 25, July 11, 2008, No. 42, pp. A1)*
Pub: American City Business Journals, Inc.
Ed: Rich Rovito. **Description:** Milwaukee Mayor Tom Barrett and Wisconsin Governor Jim Doyle met with MillerCoors management in an effort to convince the company to locate its corporate headquarters in the city. The company is expected to announce its decision by mid-July 2008. It was revealed that the decision-making process is focusing on determining an optimal location for the headquarters.

39372 ■ *"Solar Credit Lapse Spur Late Demand" in The Business Journal - Serving Phoenix and the Valley of the Sun (Vol. 28, July 18, 2008)*
Pub: American City Business Journals, Inc.
Ed: Patrick O'Grady. **Description:** Businesses looking to engage in the solar energy industry are facing the problems of taxation and limited solar panel supply. Solar panels manufacturers are focusing more on the European market. Political issues surrounding the federal tax credit policy on solar energy users are also discussed.

39373 ■ *"Solidarity UAW Forever" in Crain's Detroit Business (Vol. 25, June 1, 2009, No. 22, pp. M001)*
Pub: Crain Communications Inc. - Detroit
Ed: Ryan Beene. **Description:** United Auto Workers union has made it difficult for certain businesses to move to Michigan. Discussion is made about the issues involved and changes that need to be made in the way labor and management do business.

39374 ■ *"The Solution" in Entrepreneur (Vol. 37, October 2009, No. 10, pp. 71)*
Pub: Entrepreneur Media, Inc.
Ed: Jennifer Wang. **Description:** Ford's 2010 Transit Connect is a compact commercial van developed specifically for small business owners. The compact van offers an integrated in-dash computer system providing a cellular broadband connection.

39375 ■ *"Somanetics to Buy Back Up to $15 Million of Common Shares" in Crain's Detroit Business (Vol. 24, April 7, 2008, No. 14, pp. 4)*
Pub: Crain Communications, Inc.
Ed: Tom Henderson. **Description:** Somanetics Corp., a company that manufactures and markets noninvasive devices for monitoring blood oxygen levels in the brain and elsewhere in the body during surgery, plans to buy back up to $15 million worth of its common shares. Statistical data included on the company's current and past earnings and stock prices as well as its plans to increase revenue.

39376 ■ *"Some Relief Possible Following Painful Week" in Barron's (Vol. 88, July 14, 2008, No. 28, pp. M3)*
Pub: Dow Jones & Co., Inc.
Ed: Kopin Tan. **Description:** Dow Chemical is offering a 74 percent premium to acquire Rohm & Haas' coatings and electronics materials operations. Frontline amassed a 5.6 percent stake in rival Overseas Shipholding Group and a merger between the two would create a giant global fleet with pricing power. Highlights of the U.S. stock market during the week that ended in July 11, 2008 are discussed. Statistical data included.

39377 ■ *"Sources" in Canadian Electronics (Vol. 23, August 2008, No. 5, pp. 12)*
Pub: Action Communication Inc.
Description: Directory of electronic manufacturers, distributors and representatives in Canada is provided. The list presents distributors and representatives under each manufacturer.

39378 ■ *"The Spark's Back in Sanyo" in Barron's (Vol. 88, March 31, 2008, No. 13, pp. M9)*
Pub: Dow Jones & Company, Inc.
Ed: Jay Alabaster. **Description:** Things are looking up for Sanyo Electric after its string of calamities that range from major losses brought on by earthquake damage to its semiconductor operations and its near collapse and bailout. The company looks poised for a rebound as they are on track for their first net profit since 2003 and could beat its earnings forecast for 2008.

39379 ■ *"Special Sector" in Crain's Cleveland Business (Vol. 28, November 5, 2007, No. 44, pp. 3)*
Pub: Crain Communications, Inc.
Ed: David Bennett. **Description:** Specialty Metals Processing Inc. is investing more than $6 million to amp up productions; the company believes this big investment will pay off due to the company's ability to process complex metal alloys, such as titanium, in a region where there is a small number of competitors.

39380 ■ *"Spectre of Iran War Spooks Oil Markets" in Globe & Mail (March 28, 2007, pp. B1)*
Pub: CTVglobemedia Publishing Inc.
Ed: Shawn McCarthy. **Description:** The increase in the price of crude oil by $5 a barrel to reach $68 in the United States following speculation over war against Iran, is discussed.

39381 ■ *"Spell It Out" in Entrepreneur (Vol. 36, April 2008, No. 4, pp. 123)*
Pub: Entrepreneur Media, Inc.
Ed: Emily Weisberg. **Description:** IM:It is an apparel and accessories company that markets products with instant messaging (IM) acronyms and emoticons. Examples of these are 'LOL' and 'GTG'. Other details on IM:It products are discussed.

39382 ■ *"Spending the Stimulus" in Crain's Cleveland Business (Vol. 30, June 29, 2009, No. 25, pp. 3)*
Pub: Crain Communications, Inc.
Ed: Dan Shingler. **Description:** Three of northeast Ohio's industrial firms will receive funding from the President's economic stimulus package. Eaton Corporation, Cleveland, Ohio; Parker Hannifin Corporation and Timken Company are expected to see higher revenues from the government spending plans.

39383 ■ *"A Stalled Culture Change?" in Workforce Management (Vol. 88, December 14, 2009, No. 13, pp. 1)*
Pub: Crain Communications Inc.
Ed: Jeremy Smerd. **Description:** General Motors CEO Fritz Henderson's abrupt resignation shocked employees and signaled that Henderson had not done enough to change the company's culture, especially in dealing with its top management.

39384 ■ *"STAR TEC Incubator's Latest Resident Shows Promise" in The Business Journal-Serving Greater Tampa Bay (August 8, 2008)*
Pub: American City Business Journals, Inc.
Ed: Jane Meinhardt. **Description:** Field Forensics Inc., a resident of the STAR Technology Enterprise Center, has grown after being admitted into the business accelerator. The producer of defense and security devices and equipment has doubled 2007 sales as of 2008.

39385 ■ *"State Democrats Push for Changes to Plant Security Law" in Chemical Week (Vol. 172, July 19, 2010, No. 17, pp. 8)*
Pub: Access Intelligence L.L.C.
Contact: Donald Pazour, President
Ed: Kara Sissell. **Description:** Legislation has been introduced to revise the existing U.S. Chemical Facility Anti-Terrorism Standards (CFATS) that would include a requirement for facilities to use inherently safer technology (IST). The bill would eliminate the current law's exemption of water treatment plants and certain port facilities and preserve the states' authority to establish stronger security standards.

39386 ■ *"Steeling for Battle" in Crain's Chicago Business (Vol. 31, April 21, 2008, No. 16, pp. 3)*
Pub: Crain Communications, Inc.
Ed: Bob Tita. **Description:** Discusses contract negotiations between the United Steelworkers union and ArcelorMittal USA Inc., the nation's largest steelmaker, and U.S. Steel Corp., the third-largest; the union sees these negotiations as the best chance in two decades to regain lost ground but industry experts predict the companies will try to reduce benefits, demand a separate, lower wage scale for new hires and look for relief from the rising costs for retirees' health insurance coverage.

39387 ■ *"Steering Toward Profitability" in Black Enterprise (Vol. 41, December 2010, No. 5, pp. 72)*
Pub: Earl G. Graves Publishing Co. Inc.
Ed: Alan Hughes. **Description:** Systems Electro Coating LLC had to make quick adjustments when

auto manufacturers were in a slump. The minority father-daughter team discuss their strategies during the auto industry collapse.

39388 ■ *"Steve Meginniss Helped Reinvent the Toothbrush. Can He Do the Same Thing for Wheels?" in Inc. (February 2008, pp. 32)*
Pub: Gruner & Jahr USA Publishing
Ed: Dalia Fahmy. **Description:** Profile of Steve Meginniss, co-inventor of Sonicare Toothbrush and inventor of a two-gear wheel for wheelchairs. Mgeinniss discusses his need to raid $1 million to promote and cut manufacturing costs for this new product that helps reduce pain for users.

39389 ■ *"Stimulus 'Loser' Won't Build Plant in Mass." in Boston Business Journal (Vol. 30, November 5, 2010, No. 41, pp. 1)*
Pub: Boston Business Journal
Ed: Kyle Alspach. **Description:** Boston-Power Inc. no longer plans to build an electric vehicle battery plant in Massachusetts after it failed to obtain stimulus funds from the federal government. The company is instead looking to build a lithium-ion battery plant in China and possibly Europe.

39390 ■ *"Stock Car Racing" in Canadian Business (Vol. 81, September 15, 2008, No. 14-15, pp. 29)*
Pub: Rogers Media Ltd.
Ed: Thomas Watson. **Description:** Some analysts predict a Chapter 11-style tune-up making GM and Ford a speculative turnaround stock. However, the price of oil could make or break the shares of the Big Three U.S. automobile manufacturers and if oil goes up too high then a speculative stock to watch is an electric car company called Zenn Motor Co.

39391 ■ *"Stronach Confirms Magna Eyeing Chrysler" in Globe & Mail (March 9, 2007, pp. B1)*
Pub: CTVglobemedia Publishing Inc.
Ed: Greg Keenan. **Description:** The decision of auto parts manufacturing firm Magna International Inc. to participate in the take-over bid for Chrysler Group, as announced by its founder Frank Stronach, is discussed.

39392 ■ *"Succeed With the Right Equipment" in Pet Product News (Vol. 64, November 2010, No. 11, pp. 42)*
Pub: BowTie Inc.
Ed: Sandi Cain. **Description:** Grooming shop owners have been focusing on obtaining ergonomic, durable, and efficient products such as restraints, tables, and tubs. These products enhance the way grooming tasks are conducted. Ways pet supply manufacturers have responded to this trend are examined.

39393 ■ *"Suitors Circling Chrysler as Sale Likely" in Globe & Mail (February 19, 2007, pp. B1)*
Pub: CTVglobemedia Publishing Inc.
Ed: Jason Singer. **Description:** DaimlerChrysler AG is planning to sell or spin-off the Chrysler Group, as a cost cutting strategy. Chrysler reported a 40 percent drop in fourth quarter profit because of the $1.5 billion operating loss.

39394 ■ *"Sullivan Led Bucyrus through Unforgettable Year" in Business Journal-Milwaukee (Vol. 28, December 17, 2010, No. 11, pp. A1)*
Pub: Milwaukee Business Journal
Ed: Rich Rovito. **Description:** Bucyrus International's president and CEO, Tim Sullivan, was chosen as Milwaukee, Wisconsin's Executive of the Year for 2010. Sullivan led Bucyrus through a year of dramatic change which started with the acquisition of the mining business of Terex Corporation and culminating with a deal to sell Caterpillar Inc.

39395 ■ *"Supplements Mix Nutrition With Convenience" in Pet Product News (Vol. 64, November 2010, No. 11, pp. 44)*
Pub: BowTie Inc.
Ed: Karen Shugart. **Description:** Pet supply manufacturers have been making supplements and enhanced foods that improve mineral consumption, boost bone density, and sharpen appetite in herps. Customers seem to enjoy the convenience as particular herps demands are being addressed by these offerings. Features of other supplements and enhanced foods for herps are described.

39396 ■ *"Suppliers Look to Rack Up Big Sales to Distributors" in The Business Journal-Serving Metropolitan Kansas City (August 15, 2008)*
Pub: American City Business Journals, Inc.
Ed: James Dornbrook. **Description:** Suppliers of shelving units, conveyor systems and other equipment used in distribution facilities are expecting new business opportunities along with the planned intermodal projects in the Kansas City area. Suppliers have already observed that small distributors have started to relocate to the city because of the intermodal projects. Demand for shelves and lifts have also increased.

39397 ■ *"Suppliers May Follow Fiat" in Crain's Detroit Business (Vol. 25, June 15, 2009, No. 24, pp. 1)*
Pub: Crain Communications Inc. - Detroit
Ed: Ryan Beene. **Description:** Italian suppliers to Fiat SpA are looking toward Detroit after the formation of Chrysler Group LLC, the Chrysler-Fiat partnership created from Chrysler's bankruptcy. The Italian American Alliance for Business and Technology is aware of two Italy-based powertrain component suppliers that are considering a move to Detroit.

39398 ■ *"The 'Supply Side' of the Auto Industry" in Montly Labor Review (Vol. 133, September 2010, No. 9, pp. 72)*
Pub: Bureau of Labor Statistics
Description: Restructuring and geographic change in the automobile industry is discussed.

39399 ■ *"Surfing's Next Safari" in Entrepreneur (Vol. 37, July 2009, No. 7, pp. 24)*
Pub: Entrepreneur Media, Inc.
Ed: Dennis Romero. **Description:** Profile of Firewire Surfboards, a San Diego-based maker of lightweight surfboards, aims to capture surfing enthusiasts' attention with its use of unusual and high-tech materials. Firewire's biggest challenge is the preference for old-school surfboards, but the company is determined to revolutionize how surfboards should be made. The company's various innovations and experiences are also discussed.

39400 ■ *"Suzlon S88-Powered Wind Farm in Minnesota Secures Long-Term Financing" in PR Newswire (September 21, 2011)*
Pub: United Business Media
Description: Suzlon Energy Limited is the world's fifth largest manufacturer of wind turbines. Owners of the Grant County Wind Farm in Minnesota have secured a long-term financing deal for the ten Suzlon S88 2.1 MW wind turbines that generate enough electricity to power 7,000 homes.

39401 ■ *"Swagelok Boss" in Crain's Cleveland Business (Vol. 30, June 29, 2009, No. 25, pp. 4)*
Pub: Crain Communications, Inc.
Ed: Dan Shingler. **Description:** Swagelok Company president and CEO has not laid off an employee in its 65 years of existence and said at a recent convention that he plans to keep his 4,000 employees working and inventories at normal levels despite the recession.

39402 ■ *"Taiwan Technology Initiatives Foster Growth" in Canadian Electronics (Vol. 23, February 2008, No. 1, pp. 28)*
Pub: CLB Media Inc.
Description: A study conducted by the Market Intelligence Center shows that currently, Taiwan is the world's larges producer of information technology products such as motherboards, servers, and LCD monitors. In 2006, Taiwan's LED industry reached a production value of NTD 21 billion. This push into the LED sector shows the Ministry of Economic Affairs' plan to target industries that are environmentally friendly.

39403 ■ *"Takeover Frenzy Stokes Steel Stocks" in Globe & Mail (February 7, 2006, pp. B1)*
Pub: CTVglobemedia Publishing Inc.
Description: The impact of merger speculations, on shares of steel companies such as Ipsco Inc., is discussed.

39404 ■ *"Taking on Intel" in Canadian Business (Vol. 79, October 23, 2006, No. 21, pp. 27)*
Pub: Rogers Media
Ed: Andrew Wahl. **Description:** The decision of ATI Technologies Inc., a Canadian computer peripherals company to acquire cash and stocks worth US$5.4-billion from American microprocessor maker Advanced Micro Devices Inc., is discussed.

39405 ■ *"The Tata Way" in Business Strategy Review (Vol. 21, Summer 2010, No. 2, pp. 14)*
Pub: Wiley-Blackwell
Description: Tata Motors is one of the world's most talked-about companies. Its new ultra-low-cost Nano car is being heralded as the people's car. Vice chairman, Ravi Kant, talks about India and its emerging markets.

39406 ■ *"Tate & Lyle to Sell Redpath Division to American Sugar" in Globe & Mail (February 15, 2007, pp. B15)*
Pub: CTVglobemedia Publishing Inc.
Description: American Sugar Refining has agreed to acquire the Canadian sugar unit of Tate & Lyle PLC for $301.9 million. Tate & Lyle PLC has been selling off businesses and closing plants in order to focus on starches and Splenda.

39407 ■ *"Taylor Tests Land Grant Program" in Austin Business Journal (Vol. 31, June 3, 2011, No. 13, pp. 1)*
Pub: American City Business Journals Inc.
Ed: Vicky Garza. **Description:** Taylor Economic Development Corporation implemented a land grant program called Build On Our Lot to lure businesses to Taylor City, Austin, Texas. They are targeting small businesses, especially those in the renewable energy, advanced manufacturing, technical services and food products. Program details are included.

39408 ■ *"Tech Investing: March's Long Road" in Canadian Business (Vol. 80, January 29, 2007, No. 3, pp. 67)*
Pub: Rogers Media
Ed: Calvin Leung. **Description:** The efforts of March Networks, a manufacturer of digital surveillance equipment, from the decline in the price of its shares at the beginning of the year 2007 are described.

39409 ■ *"Tecumseh Products to Begin Moving HQ" in Crain's Detroit Business (Vol. 24, March 31, 2008, No. 13, pp. 35)*
Pub: Crain Communications, Inc.
Ed: Chad Halcom. **Description:** Tecumseh Products Co., a manufacturer of compressor products, will transfer its headquarters to Pittsfield Township near Ann Arbor.

39410 ■ *"Ted Stahl: Executive Chairman" in Inside Business (Vol. 13, September-October 2011, No. 5, pp. NC6)*
Pub: Great Lakes Publishing Co.
Ed: Miranda S. Miller. **Description:** Profile of Ted Stahl, who started working in his family's business when he was ten years old is presented. The firm makes dies for numbers and letters used on team uniforms. Another of the family firms manufactures stock and custom heat-printing products, equipment and supplies. It also educates customers on ways to decorate garments with heat printing products and offers graphics and software for customers to create their own artwork.

39411 ■ *"Teeling and Gallagher: A Textbook for Success" in Agency Sales Magazine (Vol. 39, September-October 2009, No. 9, pp. 20)*
Pub: MANA
Ed: Jack Foster. **Description:** Profile of Teeling & Gallagher, a manufacturing firm that was founded in 1946 as the D.G. Teeling Company and continued as

a one-person agency until 1960 when Tom Gallagher joined the company. Tom Gallagher talks about how things have changed and his work with his son Bob in the agency.

39412 ■ *"Tempel Steel To Expand Its Chicago Plant" in Chicago Tribune (August 22, 2008)*
Pub: McClatchy-Tribune Information Services
Ed: James P. Miller. **Description:** Tempel Steel Co. is no longer considering transferring a Libertyville factory's production to Mexico; the company has responded to government incentives and will instead shift that work to its plant on Chicago's North Side.

39413 ■ *"Thai Ice Cream Cremo Expanding to Middle East" in Ice Cream Reporter (Vol. 23, September 20, 2010, No. 10, pp. 3)*
Pub: Ice Cream Reporter
Description: Thai-based frozen dessert manufacturer Chomthana, maker of Cremo brand ice cream, is expanding into the Middle East.

39414 ■ *"There's More Upside in Germany" in Barron's (Vol. 90, September 6, 2010, No. 36, pp. M7)*
Pub: Barron's Editorial & Corporate Headquarters
Ed: Jonathan Buck. **Description:** Germany's stocks have gone up since the beginning of 2010, and investors can still benefit. These stocks will benefit from Germany's stellar economic performance and the relative weakness of the Euro. The prospects of the shares of Daimler and Hochtief are discussed.

39415 ■ *"They Like It Cold" in Business Journal Portland (Vol. 27, October 15, 2010, No. 33, pp. 1)*
Pub: Portland Business Journal
Ed: Erik Siemers. **Description:** Ajinomoto Frozen Foods USA Inc. has been investing in its Portland, Oregon facility. The company has completed a new rice production line. It has also spent $1.2 million on a new packaging technology.

39416 ■ *"This Just In" in Crain's Detroit Business (Vol. 25, June 1, 2009, No. 22, pp. 1)*
Pub: Crain Communications Inc. - Detroit
Description: Three veterans of the auto industry have partnered to create, Revitalizing Michigan, a nonprofit dedicated to help manufacturers improve their processes. The firm is seeking federal, state and private grants to fund the mission.

39417 ■ *"Thomas and His Washington Friends" in CFO (Vol. 23, October 2007, No. 10, pp. 18)*
Pub: CFO Publishing Corporation
Ed: Alix Stuart. **Description:** Reliance on Chinese suppliers to America's toymakers may become quite costly as Congress considers legislation that would increase fines to as high as $50 million for companies selling tainted products. The legislation would also require independent mandatory testing for makers of products for children.

39418 ■ *"Thomas Industrial Network Unveils Custom SPEC" in Entertainment Close-Up (March 3, 2011)*
Pub: Close-Up Media
Description: Thomas Industrial Network assists custom manufacturers and industrial service providers a complete online program called Custom SPEC which includes Website development and Internet exposure.

39419 ■ *"Ticket Tiff Erupts Over Fund Ads" in Globe & Mail (January 31, 2007, pp. B1)*
Pub: CTVglobemedia Publishing Inc.
Description: The opposition of Cineplex Entertainment LP to Mackenzie Financial Corp.'s advertisement about high cost of movie ticket is discussed.

39420 ■ *"A Timely Matter" in Canadian Business (Vol. 81, March 31, 2008, No. 5, pp. 12)*
Pub: Rogers Media
Description: Discusses the committee responsible for restructuring $33 billion of asset-backed commercial paper which has moved back their implementation plan by a month citing complexities. British Columbia has surpassed the $1 billion mark in fiscal '07-'08 from their oil and gas rights. Biovail Corp. founder Eugene Melnyk said he had lost confidence in the management of the company.

39421 ■ *"Timken's Bearings Rolling in China, India" in Crain's Cleveland Business (Vol. 28, October 29, 2007, No. 43, pp. 14)*
Pub: Crain Communications, Inc.
Ed: David Bennett. **Description:** Canton-based Timken Co., a manufacturer of bearings and specialty metals, is seeing growing demand for its line of tapered roller bearings, which allow rail users to carry heavy car loads. The company is finding significant growth in China and India due to their rapidly growing rail markets.

39422 ■ *"To Be or Not To Be an S Corporation" in Modern Machine Shop (Vol. 84, September 2011, No. 4, pp. 38)*
Pub: Gardner Business Media, Inc.
Contact: Richard G. Kline, President
E-mail: rkline@gardnerweb.com
Ed: Irving L. Blackman. **Description:** The definitions of both C corporations and S corporations are defined to help any machine shop discover which best suits the owner's business plan.

39423 ■ *"To Offshore Or Not To Offshore?" in Converting (Vol. 25, October 1, 2007, No. 10, pp. 10)*
Pub: Reed Business Information Inc.
Ed: Mark Spaulding. **Description:** Offshore manufacturing and the issue of buying raw materials from foreign suppliers by American companies is discussed. Results of a study conducted by Cap Gemini and Pro Logis regarding offshore manufacturing, especially to China, are presented.

39424 ■ *"Toolmakers' New Tack" in Crain's Detroit Business (Vol. 25, June 8, 2009,)*
Pub: Crain Communications Inc. - Detroit
Ed: Ryan Beene, Amy Lane. **Description:** MAG Industrial Automation Systems LLC and Dowding Machining Inc. have partnered to advance wind-turbine technology. The goal is to cut costs of wind energy to the same level as carbon-based fuel.

39425 ■ *"Top 50 Exporters" in Hispanic Business (Vol. 30, July-August 2008, No. 7-8, pp. 42)*
Pub: Hispanic Business, Inc.
Ed: Hildy Medina. **Description:** Increases in exports revenues reported by food exporters and green companies in a time of economic slowdown in the U.S are described. Food exporters have benefited from the growth of high-volume grocery stores in underdeveloped countries and the German governments' promotion of solar energy has benefited the U.S. solar heating equipment and solar panel manufactures.

39426 ■ *"Top Design Award for Massey Ferguson 7624 Dyna-VT" in Farm Industry News (November 14, 2011)*
Pub: Penton Business Media Inc.
Description: Massey Ferguson won top honors for its MF 7624 Dyna-VT as the Golden Tractor for Design award in the 2012 Tractor of the Year competition. The award is presented annually by journalists from 22 leading farming magazines in Europe and manufacturers have to be nominated to enter.

39427 ■ *"Tory Green?" in Canadian Business (Vol. 80, January 15, 2007, No. 2, pp. 72)*
Pub: Rogers Media
Ed: Joe Chidley. **Description:** The need for the government to participate actively in protecting the environment through proper enforcement of the Tories Clean Air Act, is discussed.

39428 ■ *The Towering World of Jimmy Choo: A Story of Power, Profits, and the Pursuit of the Perfect Shoe*
Pub: Bloomsbury USA
Ed: Lauren Goldstein Crowe, Sagra Maceira de Rosen. **Released:** 2009. **Description:** Profile of Jimmy Choo and his pursuit to manufacture the perfect shoe.

39429 ■ *"Toy Scares Drive Business" in Boston Business Journal (Vol. 27, November 23, 2007, No. 43, pp. 1)*
Pub: American City Business Journals, Inc.
Ed: Joan Goodchild. **Description:** Several Boston businesses have tapped into the lead content scare in toys and other products manufactured in China. ConRoy Corporation LLC launched Toy Recall Alert!, an online tool to alert consumers about new recalls while Hybrivet Systems introduced screening test kit, LeadCheck. Other new products pertaining to toy safety are discussed.

39430 ■ *"Toy Story" in Forbes (Vol. 180, October 15, 2007, No. 8, pp. 102)*
Pub: Forbes Inc.
Description: Three voluntary recalls of Chinese-made toys were announced by American toymakers, sending Mattel stocks plummeting.

39431 ■ *"Toy Story: U.S.-Made a Hot Seller" in Crain's Detroit Business (Vol. 23, December 17, 2007, No. 51, pp. 3)*
Pub: Crain Communications Inc. - Detroit
Ed: Chad Halcom. **Description:** American Plastic Toys, located in Walled Lake, Michigan reports all its toys are made in the U.S. and have passed all U.S. safety standards. Revenue for American Plastic Toys reached nearly $33 million in 2005, and the company expects to exceed that because of recent toy safety recalls of products produced in China.

39432 ■ *"Toyota Expected to Construct Two N.A. Plants" in Globe & Mail (February 14, 2007, pp. B4)*
Pub: CTVglobemedia Publishing Inc.
Description: Toyota Motor Corp. is planning to construct two vehicle assembly plants in North America and one more plant in Canada. The company is also planning to sell 208,000 vehicles in 2007.

39433 ■ *"Toyota Marks Record Profit Sales" in Globe & Mail (February 7, 2007, pp. B10)*
Pub: CTVglobemedia Publishing Inc.
Ed: Martin Fackler. **Description:** The record quarterly sales and earnings reported by Japanese automaker Toyota Motor Corp. are discussed. The company sold 2.16 million vehicles during the quarter while registering 426.8 billion yen in profits.

39434 ■ *"Toyota Revs Up Plans for Ontario Plant" in Globe & Mail (February 7, 2006, pp. B1)*
Pub: CTVglobemedia Publishing Inc.
Ed: Greg Keenan. **Description:** The production output and workforce addition proposals of Toyota Motor Corp., at Ontario plant, are presented.

39435 ■ *"Toyota Tops GM in Global Sales" in Globe & Mail (April 25, 2007, pp. B1)*
Pub: CTVglobemedia Publishing Inc.
Ed: Greg Keenan. **Description:** The success of Toyota Motor Corp. in surpassing General Motors Corp. in its global sales is discussed.

39436 ■ *"Trading Down at the Supermarket" in Barron's (Vol. 88, July 14, 2008, No. 28, pp. 36)*
Pub: Dow Jones & Co., Inc.
Ed: Alexander Eule. **Description:** Shares of Ralcorp Holdings are cheap at around $49.95 after slipping 20 percent prior to their acquisition of Post cereals from Kraft. Some analysts believe its shares could climb over 60 percent to $80 as value-seeking consumers buy more private label products.

39437 ■ *"Training the Troops: Battlefield Simulations Bring Growth to UNITECH" in Black Enterprise (Vol. 38, February 2008, No. 7, pp. 30)*
Pub: Earl G. Graves Publishing Co. Inc.
Ed: Cliff Hocker. **Description:** Universal Systems and Technology (UNITECH) received a total of over $45 million U.S. Department of Defense orders during September and October 2007. UNITECH designs and manufactures battlefield simulation devices used to train troops in the Army and Marine Corps.

39438 ■ *"Trillium Turmoil" in Canadian Business (Vol. 81, December 8, 2008, No. 21, pp. 16)*
Pub: Rogers Media Ltd.
Ed: Jeff Sanford. **Description:** Ontario's manufacturing success in the past was believed to have been built by the 1965 Canada-U.S. automotive pact and by advantages such as low-cost energy. The loss of these advantages along with the challenging economic times has hurt Ontario's manufacturing industry.

39439 ■ *"The Trouble With $150,000 Wine" in Barron's (Vol. 88, July 7, 2008, No. 27, pp. 33)*
Pub: Dow Jones & Co., Inc.
Ed: Orley Ashenfelter. **Description:** Review of the book, 'The Billionaire's Vinegar: The Mystery of the World's Most Expensive Bottle of Wine,' which discusses vintners along with the marketing and distribution of wine as well as the winemaking industry as a whole.

39440 ■ *"Turnaround Plays: The Return of Wi-LAN" in Canadian Business (Vol. 80, January 29, 2007, No. 3, pp. 68)*
Pub: Rogers Media
Ed: Joe Castaldo. **Description:** The recovery of the wireless equipment manufacturing firm Wi-LAN from near-bankruptcy, under the leadership of Jim Skippen, is described.

39441 ■ *"Turning Green Ink to Black" in The Business Journal-Serving Metropolitan Kansas City (Vol. 26, August 8, 2008, No. 48, pp. 1)*
Pub: American City Business Journals, Inc.
Ed: James Dornbrook. **Description:** InkCycle has introduced grenk, a line of environmentally-friendly printer toner and ink cartridges. The cartridges are collected and recycled after use by the company, which separates them into their metal, cardboard, and plastic components.

39442 ■ *"Twice the Innovation, Half the Tears" in Business Courier (Vol. 24, March 7, 2008, No. 48, pp. 1)*
Pub: American City Business Journals, Inc.
Ed: Lisa Biank Fasig. **Description:** Procter & Gamble was able to develop a pant-style diaper called Pampers First Pants by creating a virtual, three-dimensional baby. The company was able to reduce the number of real mock-ups that it had to make by putting the diapers on the virtual baby first. Specifics about product designs were not revealed by the company.

39443 ■ *"UC May Expand into Old Ford Plant" in Business Courier (Vol. 26, December 25, 2009, No. 35, pp. 1)*
Pub: American City Business Journals, Inc.
Ed: Dan Monk. **Description:** Developer Stuart Lichter is planning to acquire University of Cincinnati (UC) as a tenant at a two-story office building on a 132-acre site where a vacant Ford transmission plant is located. Details of the transaction are outlined.

39444 ■ *"Uncle Volodya's Flagging Christmas Spirit; Russia" in The Economist (Vol. 390, January 3, 2009, No. 8612, pp. 22)*
Pub: The Economist Newspaper Inc.
Description: Overview of Russia's struggling economy as well as unpopular government decisions such as raising import duties on used foreign vehicles so as to protect Russian carmakers.

39445 ■ *"Unexpected Guest" in Business Journal-Milwaukee (Vol. 28, November 19, 2010, No. 7, pp. A1)*
Pub: Milwaukee Business Journal
Ed: Rich Rovito. **Description:** Caterpillar has agreed to purchase Bucyrus for $92 per share. The deal, which is subjected to a $200 million termination fee, is expected to close in mid-2011.

39446 ■ *"An Unfair Knock on Nokia" in Barron's (Vol. 88, March 10, 2008, No. 10, pp. 36)*
Pub: Dow Jones & Company, Inc.
Ed: Mark Veverka. **Description:** Discusses the decision by the brokerage house Exane to recommend a Sell on Nokia shares, presumably due to higher inventories, which is unfounded. The news that the company's inventories are rising is not an indicator of falling demand for its products. The company is also benefiting from solid management and rising market share.

39447 ■ *"Unilever Acquiring EVGA's Ice Cream Brands in Greece" in Ice Cream Reporter (Vol. 23, October 20, 2010, No. 11, pp. 1)*
Pub: Ice Cream Reporter
Description: Unilever will acquire the ice cream brands and distribution network of the Greek frozen dessert manufacturer EVGA.

39448 ■ *"Unilever's CMO Finally Gets Down To Business" in Advertising Age (Vol. 79, July 7, 2008, No. 26, pp. 11)*
Pub: Crain Communications, Inc.
Ed: Jack Neff. **Description:** Overview of Unilever's chief marketing officer Simon Clift's strategy for promoting its products; now that the company has restructured, Clift is able to focus all of his energy on the challenges of the new-media climate that marketers are having to face.

39449 ■ *"Union, Heal Thyself" in Canadian Business (Vol. 81, July 21, 2008, No. 11, pp. 9)*
Pub: Rogers Media Ltd.
Description: General Motors Corp. was offered by the federal government a $250 million fund after the company declared plans to close its facility in Ontario. The government move is geared towards supporting the workers who have refused to support the automotive company. Details of the labor contract between General Motors and the Canadian Auto Workers are presented.

39450 ■ *"U.S. Enters BlackBerry Dispute Compromise Sought Over Security Issues" in Houston Chronicle (August 6, 2010)*
Pub: Houston Chronicle
Ed: Matthew Lee. **Description:** U.S. State Department is working for a compromise with Research in Motion, manufacturer of the BlackBerry, over security issues. The Canadian company makes the smartphones and foreign governments believe they pose a security risk.

39451 ■ *"U.S. Firm to Acquire Manufacturer GSW" in Globe & Mail (January 21, 2006, pp. B4)*
Pub: CTVglobemedia Publishing Inc.
Ed: Gordon Pitts. **Description:** The details on A.O. Smith Corp.'s acquisition of GSW Inc. are presented.

39452 ■ *"U.S. Playing Card Might Shuffle HQ" in Business Courier (Vol. 24, March 21, 2008, No. 50, pp. 1)*
Pub: American City Business Journals, Inc.
Ed: Jon Newberry. **Description:** United States Playing Card Co. is considering the possibility of relocating. It is expected that the company will finalize its decision by June 2008. According to Phil Dolci, the company's president, the firm is looking at certain locations in Ohio, Kentucky, and Indiana. He also revealed that the plan to relocate was prompted by the desire to improve the company's manufacturing facilities.

39453 ■ *"U.S. Widens Rocket Field" in Wall Street Journal Eastern Edition (October 17 , 2011, pp. B4)*
Pub: Dow Jones & Company Inc. Enterprise Media Group
Contact: Clare Hart, President
Ed: Andy Pasztor. **Description:** An agreement has been reached between National Aeronautics and Space Administration, the Department of Defense and the Air Force that will assist small commercial space ventures in bidding for profitable contracts for government launching. The program will give those companies a chance to compete against larger corporations.

39454 ■ *Utah Manufacturers Register*
Pub: Harris InfoSource
Contact: Dennis Abrahams, President
E-mail: dennisa@harrisinfo.com
URL(s): www.harrisinfo.com. **Released:** Annual; latest edition 2010. **Covers:** Approximately 4,600 manufacturers in Utah, plus names of key executives. **Entries include:** Company name, address, parent name/location, telephone, fax and 800 numbers, Web site address (on CD-ROM only), number of employees, year established, annual revenue, plant size, business description, Standard Industrial Classification (SIC) codes, executive names/titles, public ownership, legal structure, import/export designators, female/minority ownership. **Arrangement:** Classified by product/service, line of business. **Indexes:** Product/service, alphabetical, geographical, international trade.

39455 ■ *"Versatile's Back" in Farm Industry News (Vol. 42, January 1, 2009, No. 1)*
Pub: Penton Media Inc.
Contact: John French, President
Ed: Jodie Wehrspann. **Description:** Overview of Winnipeg, Manitoba's tractor manufacturer Versatile's strategy to rebrand its tractor segment; the strategy comes a year after Russian Combine Factory Rostselmash Ltd. bought the majority share of common stock from the Canadian business.

39456 ■ *"Vicki Avril; Senior Vice-President of Tubular Division, Ipsco Inc." in Crain's Chicago Business (Vol. 31, May 5, 2008, No. 18)*
Pub: Crain Communications, Inc.
Ed: Miriam Gottfried. **Description:** Profile of Vicki Avril who is the senior vice-president of the tubular division at Ipsco Inc. where she supervises 2,800 employees and 13 mills throughout the United States and Canada.

39457 ■ *"A Virtual Jog Mode for CAM" in Modern Machine Shop (Vol. 84, November 2011, No. 6, pp. 22)*
Pub: Gardner Business Media, Inc.
Contact: Richard G. Kline, President
E-mail: rkline@gardnerweb.com
Ed: Edwin Gasparraj. **Description:** In many cases, CAM programming required a specific, user-defined path. Siemens PLMs Generic Motion Controller is an alternative that defines the tool path within CAM. The program is a virtual 'teach' mode that enables the user to capture cutter locations by jogging machines axes within CAM.

39458 ■ *"Walk This Way" in Barron's (Vol. 90, August 23, 2010, No. 34, pp. 13)*
Pub: Barron's Editorial & Corporate Headquarters
Ed: Christopher C. Williams. **Description:** Crocs and Skechers are selling very popular shoes and sales show no signs of winding down. The shares of both companies are attractively prices.

39459 ■ *"We All Scream for Ice Cream" in Crain's Chicago Business (Vol. 31, April 28, 2008, No. 17, pp. 48)*
Pub: Crain Communications, Inc.
Ed: Phuong Ly. **Description:** Profile of Oberweis' ice cream shops which has expanded its business by delivering dairy products to grocery stores.

39460 ■ *We Are Smarter Than Me: How to Unleash the Power of Crowds in Your Business*
Pub: Wharton School Publishing
Ed: Barry Libert; Jon Spector; Don Tapscott. **Released:** October 5, 2007. **Price:** $21.99. **Description:** Ways to use social networking and community in order to make decisions and plan your business, with a focus on product development, manufacturing, marketing, customer service, finance, management, and more.

39461 ■ *"Weaving a Stronger Fabric: Organizing a Global Sweat-Free Apparel Production Agreement" in WorkingUSA (Vol.*

11, June 2008, No. 2)
Pub: Blackwell Publishers Ltd.
Ed: Eric Dirnbach. **Description:** Tens of millions of workers working under terrible sweatshop conditions in the global apparel industry. Workers are employed at apparel contractors and have been largely unsuccessful in organizing and improving their working conditions. The major apparel manufacturers and retailers have the most power in this industry, and they have adopted corporate social responsibility programs as a false solution to the sweatshop problem. The major North American apparel unions dealt with similar sweatshop conditions a century ago by organizing the contractors and brands into joint association contracts that significantly raised standards. Taking inspiration from their example, workers and their anti-sweatshop allies need to work together to coordinate a global organizing effort that builds worker power and establishes a global production agreement that negotiates with both contractors and the brands for improved wages, benefits, and working conditions.

39462 ■ *"A Week of the Worst Kind of Selling" in Barron's (Vol. 88, June 30, 2008, No. 26, pp. M3)*
Pub: Dow Jones & Co., Inc.
Ed: Kopin Tan. **Description:** In the week that ended in June 27, 2008 the selloff in the U.S. stock market was brought on by mounting bank losses and the spread of economic slowdown on top of high oil prices. The 31 percent decrease in the share price of Ingersoll-Rand since October 2007 may have factored in most of its risks. The company has completed its acquisition of Trane to morph into a refrigeration-equipment company.

39463 ■ *"Weighing the Write-Off" in Baltimore Business Journal (Vol. 28, September 10, 2010, No. 18, pp. 1)*
Pub: Baltimore Business Journal
Ed: Daniel J. Sernovitz. **Description:** President Barrack Obama has proposed to let business write off their investments in plant and equipment upgrades under a plan aimed at getting the economy going. The plan would allow a company to write off 100 percent of the depreciation for their new investments at one time instead of over several years.

39464 ■ *"Wenzel Downhole Tools Ltd. Announces First Quarter Results for 2007" in Canadian Corporate News (May 14, 2007)*
Pub: Comtex News Network Inc.
Description: Wenzel Downhole Tools Ltd., a manufacturer, renter, and seller of drilling tools used in gas and oil exploration, announced its financial results for the first quarter ended March 31, 2007 which includes achieved revenues of $14.5 million. Statistical data included.

39465 ■ *"What Do Your ISO Procedures Say?" in Modern Machine Shop (Vol. 84, September 2011, No. 4, pp. 34)*
Pub: Gardner Business Media, Inc.
Contact: Richard G. Kline, President
E-mail: rkline@gardnerweb.com
Ed: Wayne S. Chaneski. **Description:** ISO 9000 certification can be time-consuming and costly, but it is a necessary step in developing a quality management system that meets both current and potential customer needs.

39466 ■ *"What Is In Your Company Library?" in Modern Machine Shop (Vol. 84, October 2011, No. 5, pp. 60)*
Pub: Gardner Business Media, Inc.
Contact: Richard G. Kline, President
E-mail: rkline@gardnerweb.com
Ed: Mike Lynch. **Description:** A good company library in any machine shop can help keep employees productive. Safety as well as information are critical to complete any task in a shop.

39467 ■ *"What Makes for an Effective, Production-Oriented VMC?" in Modern Machine Shop (Vol. 84, November 2011, No. 6, pp. 24)*
Pub: Gardner Business Media, Inc.
Contact: Richard G. Kline, President
E-mail: rkline@gardnerweb.com
Ed: Derek Korn. **Description:** When a machine shop's existing VMC only offers a modest spindle performance and slow, non-cutting functions, the latest VMC technology for high-volume production that minimizes cycle times and maximizes competitiveness could be helpful. Makino's new Production Standard (PS) series of VMCs provides not only a number of standard features to shrink cycle times, but also design elements that can effectively support a shops production elements are defined.

39468 ■ *"What's New" in Crain's Cleveland Business (Vol. 30, June 8, 2009, No. 22, pp. 23)*
Pub: Crain Communications, Inc.
Description: Air Technical Industries in Ohio has launched a new product called the Scorpion Aircraft Tug that includes a built-in crane lift and auxiliary power unit that enables a fixed-base operator aircraft mechanic to move and precisely position aircraft weight up to 15,000 pounds.

39469 ■ *"What's New" in Crain's Cleveland Business (Vol. 30, June 1, 2009, No. 21, pp. 19)*
Pub: Crain Communications, Inc.
Description: Profile of Precision Polymer Casting, a manufacturer located in Northeast Ohio. Precision has launched its new product, Castinite HCR polymer composite pump base castings that are base plates that are used to mount a pump and electric motor for various chemical pumping operations. Details of the pump are included.

39470 ■ *"What's Working Now: In Providing Jobs for North Carolinians" in Business North Carolina (Vol. 28, February 2008, No. 2, pp. 16)*
Pub: Business North Carolina
Ed: Edward Martin, Frank Maley. **Description:** Individuals previously employed in the furniture, tobacco, or textile manufacturing sectors have gone back to school to be trained in new sectors in the area such as life sciences, finances and other emerging sectors.

39471 ■ *"Wheatfield First Choice for Canadian Manufacturer" in Business First Buffalo (November 23, 2007, pp. 1)*
Pub: American City Business Journals, Inc.
Ed: James Fink. **Description:** Niagara County Industrial Development Agency is preparing an enticement program that would lure automotive parts manufacturer Pop & Lock Corporation to shift manufacturing operations to Wheatfield, Niagara County, New York. The package includes job-training grants and assistance for acquiring new machinery. Details of the plan are included.

39472 ■ *"When R&D Spending Is Not Enough" in Human Resource Management (Vol. 49, July-August 2010, No. 4, pp. 767-792)*
Pub: John Wiley
Ed: Sheng Wang, Rebecca M. Guidice, Judith W. Tansky, Zhong-Ming Wang. **Description:** A study was conducted to examine the effect of contextual contingencies on innovation. Findings indicate that Chinese manufacturers with cultures emphasizing innovation and teamwork more effectively utilize financial resources in the innovation process. Results also show that a culture emphasizing outcomes and stability leads to lower levels innovation irrespective of investments.

39473 ■ *"Where the Money Is" in Conde Nast Portfolio (Vol. 2, June 2008, No. 6, pp. 113)*
Pub: Conde Nast Publications
Contact: David Carey, President
Description: Revenue generated from treatments for common brain disorders that are currently on the market are listed.

39474 ■ *"Where Rubber Meets Road" in Canadian Business (Vol. 80, March 12, 2007, No. 6, pp. 15)*
Pub: Rogers Media
Ed: Michelle Magnan. **Description:** The partnership between Engineered Drilling Solutions Inc. and EnCana Corp. to build road from rubber wastes and follow environment-friendly methods in work is discussed.

39475 ■ *"Who Gets the Last Laugh?" in Barron's (Vol. 88, March 31, 2008, No. 13, pp. 17)*
Pub: Dow Jones & Company, Inc.
Ed: Leslie P. Norton. **Description:** Nord/LB will take a charge of 82.5 million euros to cover potential losses apparently related to Vatas' refusal to take the shares of Remote MDx Inc. after buying the shares. Remote MDx's main product is an ankle bracelet to monitor criminals; the firm has lost over half of its market cap due to the Nord/LB troubles and questions about its revenues.

39476 ■ *"The Whole Package" in Entrepreneur (Vol. 36, February 2008, No. 2, pp. 24)*
Pub: Entrepreneur Media Inc.
Description: Holy Bohn, owner of The Honest Statute, developed an environmentally-friendly packaging for her pet food products. The company hired a packaging consultant and spent $175,000. Big corporations also spend money and plunge into the latest trends in packaging ranging from lighter and flexible to temperature-sensitive labels.

39477 ■ *"Why Change?" in Canadian Business (Vol. 80, October 8, 2007, No. 20, pp. 9)*
Pub: Rogers Media
Ed: Joe Chidley. **Description:** The need for economic change in Canada is discussed. Despite the country's economic growth and low unemployment rate, economic reform is needed in order to maximize its economic potential in the future. Other reasons for the need to further develop its economy, such as the rise of manufacturing and service industries in Asia and the emergence of regional trade pacts in South America are also tackled.

39478 ■ *"Why the Ethanol King Loves Driving his SUV" in Globe & Mail (January 29, 2007, pp. B17)*
Pub: CTVglobemedia Publishing Inc.
Ed: Gordon Pitts. **Description:** Ken Field, chairman of Canada's leading ethanol manufacturer Green-Field Ethanol, talks about the cars he drives, the commercial use of cellulose, ethanol's performance as an alternative to gasoline and about the plans of his firm to go public.

39479 ■ *Why GM Matters: Inside the Race to Transform an American Icon*
Pub: Walker & Company
Ed: William J. Holstein. **Released:** 2009. **Price:** $26.00. **Description:** A timely examination of General Motors Corporation and the problems it is facing.

39480 ■ *"Why Intel Should Dump Its Flash-Memory Business" in Barron's (Vol. 88, March 10, 2008, No. 10, pp. 35)*
Pub: Dow Jones & Company, Inc.
Ed: Eric J. Savitz. **Description:** Intel Corp. must sell its NAND flash-memory business as soon as it possibly can to the highest bidder to focus on its PC processor business and take advantage of other business opportunities. Apple should consider a buyback of 10 percent of the company's shares to lift its stock.

39481 ■ *"Why Nestle Should Sell Alcon" in Barron's (Vol. 88, March 17, 2008, No. 11, pp. M12)*
Pub: Dow Jones & Company, Inc.
Ed: Sean Walters. **Description:** Nestle should sell Alcon because Nestle can't afford to be complacent as its peers have made changes to their portfolios to boost competitiveness. Nestle's stake in Alcon and L'Oreal have been ignored by investors and Nestle could realize better value by strengthening its nutrition division through acquisitions.

39482 ■ *"Will Workers Be Left To Build It Here?" in Boston Business Journal (Vol. 31, June 3, 2011, No. 19, pp. 1)*
Pub: Boston Business Journal
Ed: Kyle Alspach. **Description:** Lack of skilled workers has resulted in delayed expansion of local manufacturing operations in Massachusetts. Acme Packet Inc. expects to add only 10 jobs by the end of 2011.

39483 ■ *"William Barr III; President, Co-Founder, Universal Windows Direct, 33" in Crain's Cleveland Business (November 19, 2007)*
Pub: Crain Communications, Inc.
Ed: David Bennett. **Description:** Profile of William Barr III, the president and co-founder of Universal Windows Direct, a manufacturer of vinyl windows and siding, whose successful salesmanship and leadership has propelled his company forward.

39484 ■ *"Wing and a Prayer" in Canadian Business (Vol. 81, November 10, 2008, No. 19, pp. 70)*
Pub: Rogers Media Ltd.
Ed: Sean Silcoff. **Description:** The 61st Annual National Business Aviation Association convention in Orlando, Florida saw unabashed display of wealth and privilege, but the U.S. market meltdown and possible economic crash has raised questions on the industry's future. Statistical details included.

39485 ■ *"Winner: Caparo Group Plc" in Crain's Detroit Business (Vol. 24, March 24, 2008, No. 12, pp. 12)*
Pub: Crain Communications, Inc.
Ed: Brent Snavely. **Description:** London-based Caparo Group plc saw its acquisition of Voestalpine Polynorm as an opportunity to gain a foothold in the North American automotive industry. Caparo was impressed with the company's breadth of manufacturing capabilities and quality systems as well as with the management team.

39486 ■ *"With Algoma Steel Gone, Is Stelco Next?" in Globe & Mail (April 16, 2007, pp. B1)*
Pub: CTVglobemedia Publishing Inc.
Ed: Greg Keenan. **Description:** Speculation in Canadian steel industry over possible sale of Stelco Inc. too after the sale of Algoma Steel Inc. to Essar Global Ltd. is discussed.

39487 ■ *"Worry No. 1 at Auto Show" in Crain's Detroit Business (Vol. 24, January 21, 2008, No. 3, pp. 1)*
Pub: Crain Communications Inc. - Detroit
Ed: Brent Snavely. **Description:** Recession fears clouded activity at the 2008 Annual North American International Auto Show. Automakers are expecting to see a drop in sales due to slow holiday retail spending as well as fallout from the subprime lending crisis.

39488 ■ *"Wrigley's a Rich Meal for Mars" in Crain's Chicago Business (Vol. 31, May 5, 2008, No. 18, pp. 2)*
Pub: Crain Communications, Inc.
Ed: Steven R. Strahler. **Description:** Mars Inc. will have to manage wisely in order to make their acquisition of Wm. Wrigley Jr. Co. profitable due to the high selling price of Wrigley which far exceeds the industry norm. Statistical data included.

39489 ■ *"Xerox Diverts Waste from Landfills" in Canadian Electronics (Vol. 23, February 2008, No. 1, pp. 1)*
Pub: CLB Media Inc.
Description: Xerox Corporation revealed that it was able to divert more than two billion pounds of electronic waste from landfills through waste-free initiatives. The company's program, which was launched in 1991, covers waste avoidance in imaging supplies and parts reuse. Environmental priorities are also integrated into manufacturing operations.

39490 ■ *"Xstrata and CAW Get Tentative Deal" in Globe & Mail (February 2, 2007, pp. B3)*
Pub: CTVglobemedia Publishing Inc.
Ed: Andy Hoffman. **Description:** The agreement between Xstrata PLC and Canadian Auto Workers union over wage hike is discussed.

39491 ■ *"Young Giants" in Canadian Business (Vol. 79, August 14, 2006, No. 16-17, pp. 47)*
Pub: Rogers Media
Ed: Brad Purdy. **Description:** New generations of young chiefs of oil and gas companies in Canada, are featured.

39492 ■ *"Zakkamono Taps Growing Market for Collectibles" in Hawaii Business (Vol. 54, September 2008, No. 3, pp. 68)*
Pub: Hawaii Business Publishing
Ed: Casey Chin. **Description:** Profile of Zakkamono, a business that designs and sells designer toys, shirts and other collectibles; the first toys being Mousubi and Miao figurines. Owners Zakka and Rae Huo say that one of the business' challenges is finding manufacturing resources. Other details about Zakkamono are discussed.

39493 ■ *"Zebra's Changing Stripes" in Crain's Chicago Business (Vol. 31, November 17, 2008, No. 46, pp. 4)*
Pub: Crain Communications, Inc.
Ed: John Pletz. **Description:** Zebra Technologies Corp., the world's largest manufacturer of bar-code printers is profiled; the company's stock has plunged with shares declining 40 percent in the past three months grinding the firm's growth to a halt. Zebra's plans to regain revenue growth are also discussed.

39494 ■ *"ZF Revving Up Jobs, Growth" in Business Courier (Vol. 26, November 6, 2009, No. 28, pp. 1)*
Pub: American City Business Journals, Inc.
Ed: Jon Newberry. **Description:** Proposed $96 million expansion of German-owned automotive supplier ZF Steering systems LLC is anticipated to generate 299 jobs in Boone County, Kentucky. ZF might invest $90 million in equipment, while the rest will go to building and improvements.

STATISTICAL SOURCES

39495 ■ *RMA Annual Statement Studies*
Pub: Risk Management Association
Contact: Kevin M. Blakey, President
Released: Annual. **Price:** $175.00 2006-07 edition, $105.00. **Description:** Contains composite balance sheets and income statements for more than 360 industries, including the accounting, auditing, and bookkeeping industries. Also contains five years of comparative historical data for discerning trends. Includes 16 commonly used ratios, computed for most of the size groupings for nearly every industry.

TRADE PERIODICALS

39496 ■ *Automotive Plastics Newsletter*
Pub: Market Search Inc.
Released: Biweekly. **Price:** $498, individuals. **Description:** Reports on news of the automotive and plastics industry. Also includes forecasts.

39497 ■ *CAMM News*
Pub: Canadian Association of Moldmakers
Contact: David Palmer, Chairman
Ed: Patricia Papp, Editor. **Released:** Quarterly, 5-6/year. **Description:** Contains items of interest to members of the moldmaking industry. Recurring features include editorials, information on education and shows, letters to the editor, a calendar of events, reports of meetings, news of educational opportunities, and columns titled Technical Corner and Members in the News.

39498 ■ *Composites in Manufacturing*
Pub: Society of Manufacturing Engineers
Contact: Barbara M. Fossum, President
E-mail: bfossum@sme.org
Released: Quarterly. **Price:** $108, U.S. nonmembers; $120, Canada and Mexico nonmembers. **Description:** Covers composites and advanced composite materials from development through application. Recurring features include a calendar of events, news of educational opportunities, industry news, and notices of publications available.

39499 ■ *Compoundings*
Pub: Independent Lubricant Manufacturers Association
Contact: Todd Coady, President
Ed: Michael Cannizzaro, Editor, editor@ilma.org. **Released:** Monthly. **Price:** Included in membership; $150, nonmembers in the U.S. **Description:** Presents timely technical and marketing news about the lubricant manufacturing industry. Covers trends, new products, legislative, and regulatory information. Also focuses on Association members and events.

39500 ■ *Electrical Product News*
Pub: Business Marketing & Publishing Inc.
Ed: George B. Young, Editor, editor@epnweb.com. **Released:** Monthly. **Description:** Covers electrical products and distributor services. Provides information on new products, product applications, manufacturer programs supporting product sales, features added to existing products, special promotions and incentive programs, and marketing/sales news. Recurring features include letters to the editor, news of research, reports of meetings, and columns titled Telemarketing and Taxes.

39501 ■ *Human Factors in Ergonomics and Manufacturing*
Pub: John Wiley & Sons Inc.
Contact: Stephen M. Smith, President
URL(s): onlinelibrary.wiley.com/journal/10.1002/(-ISSN)1520-6564. **Ed:** Waldemar Karwoski, Gavriel Salvendy. **Released:** Bimonthly **Price:** $1427, Institutions print & online; $1553, Institutions, other countries print & online; $1240, Institutions print only; $1240, Institutions, Canada and Mexico print only; $1366, Institutions, other countries print only.

39502 ■ *Industrial Laser Solutions*
Pub: PennWell Publishing Co.
Ed: Laureen Belleville, Editor, laureenb@pennwell.com. **Released:** Bimonthly. **Price:** Free. **Description:** Devoted exclusively to the increased productivity and profitability of industrial lasers. Offers current information on the application of lasers in material processing, lasers on the production line, new systems and products, technical and economic analyses, company information, business news and more.

39503 ■ *Manufacturer's Mart*
Pub: Manufacturers' Mart Publications
URL(s): www.manufacturersmart.com. **Released:** Monthly

39504 ■ *Manufacturing and Technology News*
Pub: Publishers & Producers
Ed: Richard McCormack, Editor, richard@manufacturingnews.com. **Released:** Biweekly. **Price:** $395, individuals. **Description:** Relates breaking news on manufacturing programs and policies, electronic commerce, new manufacturing technologies, and techniques. Carries guest editorials. Recurring features include letters to the editor, interviews, news of research, reports of meetings, book reviews, and notices of publications available.

39505 ■ *Member Connections*
Pub: Fabricators and Manufacturers Association International
Contact: Dave Barber, Chairman of the Board
Ed: Kimberly Pollard, Editor. **Released:** Bimonthly. **Price:** Included in membership. **Description:** Provides members with the latest news about the Association, including benefits and educational activities, all revolving around the metal forming and fabricating industries. Recurring features include a calendar of events, news of educational opportunities, book review, and Q & A forum.

39506 ■ *The MFP Report*
Pub: Bissett Communications Corp.
Contact: Brian Bissett, Editor
E-mail: bbissett@ix.netcom.com
Released: Monthly. **Price:** $659, U.S.; $699, elsewhere. **Description:** Offers business intelligence on the latest multifunction peripherals business, market and technology issues, and their impact. Features standards, products, trade shows, and company features. Recurring features include interviews, news of research, and a collection.

39507 ■ *SEMA News*
Pub: Specialty Equipment Market Association
Contact: Chris Kersting, President
E-mail: chrisk@sema.org
Released: Monthly. **Price:** Included in membership. **Description:** Covers the automotive specialty, performance equipment, and accessory sectors.

Recurring features include news of government and legislative actions, new products, international markets, and member and Association activities.

39508 ■ *Storklink*
Pub: Stork Technimet Inc.
Released: 4/year. **Price:** Free. **Description:** Presents technical articles detailing the use of materials science to solve problems of manufacture or failure of components. Covers subjects such as machinability, weldability, and various failure mechanisms such as fatigue, corrosion, and brittle fracture.

39509 ■ *Teamwork*
Pub: Dartnell Publications
Released: Biweekly. **Price:** $197. **Description:** Focuses on successful teamwork in manufacturing and corporate businesses. Recurring features include columns titled What Would You Do?, Test Yourself and See, and Teamwork in Action.

VIDEOCASSETTES/ AUDIOCASSETTES

39510 ■ *Competing Through Manufacturing*
Video Arts, Inc.
c/o Aim Learning Group
8238-40 Lehigh
Morton Grove, IL 60053-2615
Free: 877-444-2230
Fax: (416)252-2155
Co. E-mail: service@aimlearninggroup.com
URL: http://www.aimlearninggroup.com
Released: 1989. **Price:** $2890.00. **Description:** These three 50-minute videos will help you make your company competitive through innovative manufacturing. **Availability:** VHS; 8 mm; 3/4 U; Special order formats.

39511 ■ *Concerns Quarterly with Footage from CBS News: General Business*
Harcourt Brace College Publishers
301 Commerce, Ste. 3700
Fort Worth, TX 76102
Ph: (817)334-7500
Free: 800-237-2665
Fax: (817)334-0947
Co. E-mail: info@harcourt.com
URL: http://www.hmhco.com
Released: 1995. **Price:** $80.00. **Description:** Video newsletter containing footage from such CBS programs as CBS Evening News, 48 Hours, Street Stories, and CBS This Morning. Provides information on such topics as ethical responsibilities in business, people in business, competition, manufacturing, and marketing. Comes with instructor's guide. Available at an annual subscription rate of $300.00. **Availability:** VHS.

39512 ■ *Manufacturing Control in the Small Plant*
SkillSoft
107 Northeastern Blvd.
Nashua, NH 03062
Ph: (603)324-3000
Free: 877-545-5763
Fax: (603)324-3009
Co. E-mail: information@skillsoft.com
URL: http://www.skillsoft.com
Contact: Chuck Moran, President
Released: 19??. **Description:** Part of an integrated course for anyone involved in the management and operation of a small company, or a small division of a large company. **Availability:** 3/4 U.

TRADE SHOWS AND CONVENTIONS

39513 ■ Design & Manufacturing Midwest
URL(s): www.canontradeshows.com/expo/dmmidwest11/conference.html. **Audience:** Trade professionals. **Principal Exhibits:** Process control/automation, compressors and air equipment, computers in manufacturing, fluid power, general manufacturing, lubrication, heat treatment, lasers in manufacturing, machine tools, weighing sensors and instrumentation, drives and controls, pumps and valves, safety equipment, welding equipment, design in engineering, engineering products and materials, assembly, automation and robotics.

39514 ■ Plant Maintenance and Design Engineering Show/Montreal (PMDS)
Canadian Fluid Power Association
2175 Sheppard Ave. E., Ste. 310
Toronto, ON, Canada M2J 1W8
Ph: (416)499-1416
Fax: (416)491-1670
URL: http://www.cfpa.ca
Frequency: Biennial. **Audience:** Trade professionals. **Principal Exhibits:** Original equipment manufacturing, and the aftermarket of maintenance, repair/overhaul and operating of industrial machinery and equipment. **Dates and Locations:** Place Bonaventure.

39515 ■ Wisconsin Manufacturing & Technology Show
Expo Productions Inc.
510 Hartbrook Dr.
Hartland, WI 53029
Ph: (262)367-5500
Free: 800-367-5520
Fax: (262)367-9956
Co. E-mail: expo@execpc.com
URL: http://www.expoproductionsinc.com
URL(s): www.expoproductionsinc.com/tool_home.htm. **Price:** $5. **Frequency:** Biennial. **Audience:** Purchasing agents, presidents and CEOs of companies, and plant engineers. **Principal Exhibits:** Metal working machinery and related manufacturing equipment, supplies, and services machine tools. **Telecommunication Services:** jill@epishows.com.

CONSULTANTS

39516 ■ AGH & Associates
69 E Alden Ln.
Lake Forest, IL 60045-1297
Ph: (847)295-9220
Contact: Arthur Helt, Jr., President
E-mail: aghelt@aol.com
Scope: Industrial consultants specializing in plant layout and design for warehouse, packing systems, cranes specifications, office layouts, and material handling and material flow systems. Additional equipment selection and appraisal, manpower assessment, order processing, and production scheduling and time motion studies. Industries served: steel service centers and manufacturing plants. **Founded:** 1983.

39517 ■ Albee-Campbell L.L.C.
2913 Windmill Rd.
Sinking Spring, PA 19608-9087
Ph: (610)678-3361
Free: 800-445-0586
Fax: (610)678-3528
Co. E-mail: office@albee-campbell.com
Contact: Thomas C. Reinhart, President
Scope: Provider of full range of marketing services to manufacturers and manufacturers' representative agencies. Specializes in promoting product lines in specific sales territories. **Founded:** 1938. **Seminars:** How to Succeed with Manufacturers' Representatives.

39518 ■ Anderson/Roethle Inc.
700 N Water St., Ste. 325
Milwaukee, WI 53202-4221
Ph: (414)276-0070
Fax: (414)276-4364
Co. E-mail: info@anderson-roethle.com
URL: http://www.anderson-roethle.com
Contact: Stanley C. Johnson, President
E-mail: scj@anderson-roethle.com
Scope: Provider of merger, acquisition and divestiture advisory services. Offers strategic planning, valuations and specialized M and A advisory services. **Founded:** 1963.

39519 ■ Blackford Associates
30 George Rd.
Contoocook, NH 03229
Ph: (603)225-2228
Fax: (603)225-2228
Contact: John M. Blackford, Owner
Scope: Provider of general management consulting to smaller manufacturing companies. Counsels chief executive officers and presidents on strategy, organization, finances and operations. Areas of expertise include the following: new products, services or markets; problems of expansion or retrenchment; financing and bank relations; morale, organization and training; budgeting and business plans; factory flow and inventory control; quality control and methods; cash flow problems; and financial information and controls. **Founded:** 1984.

39520 ■ Distribution Assistance
PO Box 1418
East Dennis, MA 02641-1418
Ph: (508)385-9802
Fax: (508)385-9802
Co. E-mail: atsilk@gis.net
URL: http://www.distributionassistance.com
Contact: Mildred T. Silk, Secretary Treasurer
Scope: Developer of management logistics consultant solutions. It serves the banking, consumer products, financial services, insurance, non-profit, paper, and public warehousing industries. **Founded:** 1985. **Publications:** "Improving Warehouse Operations"; "Fundamentals of Traffic Management"; "Advanced Transportation Management"; "Cost Effective Worldwide Product Delivery"; "Supply Chain Management". **Seminars:** Professional development Logistics and Supply Chain Operations Seminars; ECR/Quick Response High Efficiency Supply Chain Management and Supply Chain Management in the Nineties.

39521 ■ Obie Good & Associates
122 Lake Lure Dr.
Alma, GA 31510
Ph: (912)632-6208
Fax: (912)632-6208
Contact: Obie Good, President
Scope: Manufacturing consultant in metal working field for commercial and military products, manufacturing management and engineering.

39522 ■ Hewitt Development Enterprises (HDE)
1717 N Bayshore Dr., Ste. 2154
Miami, FL 33132
Ph: (305)372-0941
Fax: (305)372-0941
Co. E-mail: info@hewittdevelopment.com
URL: http://www.hewittdevelopment.com
Contact: Robert G. Hewitt, Principal
E-mail: bob@hewittdevelopment.com
Scope: Specializes in strategic planning; profit enhancement; start-up businesses; interim management; crisis management; turnarounds; production planning; just-in-time inventory management; and project management. Serves senior management (CEOs, CFOs, division presidents, etc.) and acquirers of distressed businesses. **Founded:** 1985.

39523 ■ Industrial Management Services
103 Woodmancy Ln.
Fayetteville, NY 13066-1534
Ph: (315)637-8966
Contact: Lawrence H. Wishart, Managing Director
Scope: Assists manufacturers in minimizing their manufacturing costs by maximizing the return on investments in and expenditures for facilities and labor. This is accomplished by determining where improvements can be made, evaluating the potentials in each selected area, and developing ways of causing the potential improvement to be accomplished. Specific areas include: Economic feasibility studies, labor utilization studies, work measurement, expense reduction studies, facilities planning, long range planning, management controls, profit improvement surveys, incentive systems, design of manufacturing systems, plant layout, cost improvement programs, and assistance with safety programs. **Founded:** 1954.

39524 ■ The Institute for Management Excellence
PO Box 5459
Lacey, WA 98509-5459

Ph: (360)412-0404
Co. E-mail: pwoc@itstime.com
URL: http://www.itstime.com
Contact: Michael Anthony, Director
Scope: Management consulting and training focuses on improving productivity, using practices and creative techniques. Practices based on the company's theme: It's time for new ways of doing business. Industries served: public sector, law enforcement, finance or banking, non profit, computers or high technology, education, human resources, utilities. **Founded:** 1995. **Publications:** "Income Without a Job," 2008; "The Other Side of Midnight, 2000: An Executive Guide to the Year 2000 Problem"; "Concordance to the Michael Teachings"; "Handbook of Small Business Advertising"; "The Personality Game"; "How to Market Yourself for Success". **Seminars:** The Personality Game; Power Path Seminars; Productivity Plus; Sexual Harassment and Discrimination Prevention; Worker's Comp Cost Reduction; Americans with Disabilities Act; In Search of Identify: Clarifying Corporate Culture.

39525 ■ The Manhattan Consulting Group Inc.
214 E 54th St., Ste. 600
New York, NY 10022-6207
Ph: (212)751-3000
Contact: Thomas H. Kieren, President
Scope: Specializes in industry and corporate performance studies. It serves the pharmaceuticals, food, fabricated products, government, and other related industrial, commercial, and process industries. **Founded:** 1983. **Publications:** "Customer Satisfaction in the Electronics and Electrical Industries," Connector Technology Magazine; "Customer Satisfaction in the Chemical Industry," Chemical Week Magazine; "Customer Satisfaction in the Food Industry," Part 1, Food Processing Magazine; "Organization Change Issues for the 90s," Business Age Magazine; "Assessing the Viability of the Manufacturing Company," Commercial Lending Review. **Seminars:** Seminars and workshop in corporate performance and customer satisfaction management for industrial manufacturing companies, acquisition candidate evaluations, viability analysis for LBO firms and banks, and business strategy for a variety of institutions within the manufacturing sector.

39526 ■ Northwest Trade Adjustment Assistance Center
1200 Westlake Ave. N, Ste. 802
Seattle, WA 98109
Ph: (206)622-2730
Free: 800-667-8087
Fax: (206)622-1105
Co. E-mail: nwtaac@nwtaac.org
URL: http://www.nwtaac.org
Contact: Gary Kuhar, Executive Director
Scope: Provider of up to 75 percent cost paid technical assistance to help manufacturers improve their competitive position relative to imported products. areas of expertise include website design, ISO 9000 certification, new market identification, new product introduction, business plans, marketing plans, upgrading of product design and packaging, improvement of distribution, use of new technology, inventory cost reduction, production cost reduction, development of employee incentive plans and preparation of loan applications, industries served, manufacturers and food processors. **Founded:** 1979.

39527 ■ The Walden Group
968 Main St., Ste. 8
Wakefield, MA 01880-3979
Ph: (781)246-7599
Fax: (781)245-7598
Co. E-mail: sales@thewaldengroup.com
URL: http://www.thewaldengroup.com
Contact: Don Harnson, Senior Partner
Scope: Provider of solutions for firms in the distribution and manufacturing arenas. Specializes in small to medium sized enterprises. Services include distribution and manufacturing operations, information system selection and implementation, and self managing team implementation. Industries served: all. **Founded:** 1986. **Seminars:** New Age Warehousing; How to Control Manufacturing Without Acronyms; Information Technology in Manufacturing Today; 7 Steps to a Successful Manufacturing System.

FRANCHISES AND BUSINESS OPPORTUNITIES

39528 ■ The Gutter Guys
The Gutter Guys Franchisor, Inc.
2547 Fire Rd., Ste. E-5
Egg Harbor Township, NJ 08234
Ph: (609)646-4888
Fax: (609)646-7283
URL: http://www.thegutterguys.com
Description: Seamless gutter manufacturing, installation and maintenance. **No. of Franchise Units:** 10. **No. of Company-Owned Units:** 4. **Founded:** 1988.. **Franchised:** 2000. **Equity Capital Needed:** $36,500 liquid; $90,000 total investment range. **Franchise Fee:** $15,000. **Training:** Yes.

39529 ■ Old Hippy Wood Products Inc.
2415 80 Ave.
Edmonton, AB, Canada T6P 1N3
Ph: (780)448-1163
Free: 888-464-9700
Fax: (780)435-5475
Co. E-mail: franchise@oldhippy.com
URL: http://www.oldhippy.com
Description: Manufacturers high quality solid wood furniture in Pine, Birch, Cherry, Maple and Oak. From the manufacturing centre in Edmonton, Old Hippy supplies Canadian franchise-store outlets and is proud to be an experienced exporter to Japan. Old Hippy furniture is destined to become a cherished antique. **No. of Franchise Units:** 8. **No. of Company-Owned Units:** 1. **Founded:** 1990.. **Franchised:** 1992. **Equity Capital Needed:** $125,000 required investment; $25,000 start-up capital required. **Franchise Fee:** $15,000. **Training:** Initial training and ongoing support provided.

RESEARCH CENTERS

39530 ■ California State Polytechnic University, Pomona - Apparel Technology and Research Center (ATRC)
3801 W Temple Ave., Rm. 45-123
Pomona, CA 91768
Ph: (909)869-2082
Fax: (909)869-4454
Co. E-mail: pkilduff@csupomona.edu
URL: http://www.csupomona.edu/~atrc/
Contact: Prof. Peter Kilduff, Director
Services: Consulting and technical assistance. **Founded:** 1992. **Educational Activities:** ATRC Seminars (Monthly). **Telecommunication Services:** atrc@csupomona.edu.

39531 ■ Grand Valley State University - Michigan Small Business and Technology Development Center (MI-SBTDC)
Seidman College of Business
401 W Fulton St.
Grand Rapids, MI 49504
Ph: (616)331-7480
Fax: (616)331-7485
Co. E-mail: sbtdchq@gvsu.edu
URL: http://misbtdc.org
Contact: Carol Lopucki, Director
Services: Business management consulting. **Founded:** 1983.

39532 ■ National Center for Manufacturing Sciences (NCMS)
3025 Boardwalk
Ann Arbor, MI 48108-3230
Free: 800-222-6267
Fax: (734)995-1150
URL: http://www.ncms.org/main.html
Contact: Richard B. Jarman, President
Founded: 1986. **Publications:** *NCMS at a Glance*. **Educational Activities:** Annual meetings with exhibits.

39533 ■ Ohio State University - Engineering Research Center for Net Shape Manufacturing (ERC/NSM)
339 Baker Systems
1971 Neil Ave.
Columbus, OH 43210-1271
Ph: (614)292-9267
Fax: (614)292-7219
Co. E-mail: altan.1@osu.edu
URL: http://www.cpforming.org
Contact: Dr. Taylan Altan, Director
Services: Consulting. **Founded:** 1986. **Publications:** *Technical papers and presentations*. **Educational Activities:** Continuing education courses.

39534 ■ Rochester Institute of Technology - Center for Integrated Manufacturing Studies (CIMS)
111 Lomb Memorial Dr.
Rochester, NY 14623-5608
Ph: (585)475-5101
Free: 866-490-4044
Fax: (585)475-5250
Co. E-mail: info@cims.rit.edu
URL: http://www.cims.rit.edu
Contact: Dr. Nabil Nasr, Director
Services: Extension services: for small businesses. **Founded:** 1992. **Educational Activities:** CIMS Training programs.

39535 ■ Society of Manufacturing Engineers (NAMRI/SME) - North American Manufacturing Research Institution
1 SME Dr.
Dearborn, MI 48128-2408
Ph: (313)425-3000
Free: 800-733-4763
Fax: (313)425-3400
Co. E-mail: membership@sme.org
URL: http://www.sme.org/namri
Contact: Dennis S. Bray, President
Description: A division of the Society of Manufacturing Engineers. Represents individuals engaged in manufacturing research and technology development. Works to promote and stimulate research, writing, publication, and dissemination of new manufacturing technology; works to coordinate efforts and cooperate with counterpart organizations worldwide; works to provide a forum for the active community of researchers whose work contributes in furthering manufacturing technology and productivity. **Scope:** manufacturing technology and research. **Founded:** 1973. **Subscriptions:** archival material books clippings periodicals. **Publications:** *Proceedings of the North American Manufacturing Research Institution of the Society of Manufacturing Engineers* (Annual). **Educational Activities:** Annual meeting and conference; International Forum (Annual); North American Manufacturing Research Conference (Annual), in June, collocated with ASME Manufacturing Science and Engineering Conference. **Awards:** Outstanding Paper Award (Annual); S.M. Wu Research Implementation Award. **Telecommunication Services:** mstratton@sme.org.

39536 ■ Tennessee Technological University - Center for Manufacturing Research (CMR)
PO Box 5077
Cookeville, TN 38505-0001
Ph: (931)372-3362
Fax: (931)372-6345
Co. E-mail: kcurrie@tntech.edu
URL: http://www.tntech.edu/cmr/home
Contact: Prof. Kenneth R. Currie, Director
Services: Material testing. **Founded:** 1984. **Publications:** *Executive Summary* (Annual); *CMR Research reports*; *CMR Annual report* (Annual). **Educational Activities:** CMR Conferences; Industrial Study-Work Program; Seminars, workshops, and short courses, for practicing engineers. **Awards:** CMR Stipends, to graduate research assistants. **Telecommunication Services:** mfgctr@tntech.edu.

START-UP INFORMATION

39537 ■ *The Canadian Small Business Survival Guide: How to Start and Operate Your Own Successful Business*
Pub: Dundurn Group
Ed: Benj Gallander. FRQ June 2002. **Price:** $26.99. **Description:** Ideas for starting and running a successful small business. Topics include selecting a business, financing, government assistance, locations, franchises, and marketing ideas.

39538 ■ *Entrepreneurship*
Pub: John Wiley and Sons Inc.
Ed: William D. Bygrave; Andrew Zacharakis. **Released:** March 2007. **Price:** $115.95. **Description:** Information for starting a new business is shared, focusing on marketing and financing a product or service.

39539 ■ *Getting Rich In Your Underwear: How To Start and Run a Profitable Home-Based Business*
Pub: HCM Publishing
Ed: Peter I. Hupalo. **Released:** April 1, 2005. **Price:** $17.95. **Description:** Book offers insight into starting a home-based business. Entrepreneurs will learn about business models and the home business; distribution and fulfillment of product or service; marketing and sales; how to overcome the fear of starting a business; personal success characteristics; naming a business; zoning and insurance; intellectual capital; copyrights, trademarks, and patents; limited liability companies and S-corporations; business expenses and accounting; taxes; fifteen basic steps for starting a home-based business, state resources for starting a home company; and seven home-based business ideas.

39540 ■ *Going Solo: Developing a Home-Based Consulting Business from the Ground Up*
Pub: McGraw-Hill Companies Inc.
Contact: Deven Sharma, President
Ed: William J. Bond. **Released:** January 1997. **Description:** Ways to turn specialized knowledge into a home-based successful consulting firm, focusing on targeting client needs, business plans, and growth.

39541 ■ *How to Start a Home-Based Mail Order Business*
Pub: Globe Pequot Press
Ed: Georganne Fiumara. **Released:** January 2005. **Price:** $17.95. **Description:** Step-by-step guide for starting and growing a home-based mail order business. Information about equipment, pricing, online marketing, are included along with worksheets and checklists for planning.

39542 ■ *"Hype: If You Build It.." in Entrepreneur (Vol. 35, October 2007, No. 10, pp. 138)*
Pub: Entrepreneur Media Inc.
Ed: John Jantsch. **Description:** Marketing strategy can be achieved by determining what a company's target market is, and how that company is unique in its industry. Narrowing the market will make promoting the company's products or services easier, and identifying the company's unique qualities will help in sending out a uniform message to the clients. Details of how to develop a marketing strategy are provided.

39543 ■ *Jan and Jeannie Levinson's Startup Guide to Guerilla Marketing: A Simple Battle Plan for Boosting Profits*
Pub: Entrepreneur Press
Ed: Jay Conrad Levinson; Jeannie Levinson. **Released:** January 2008. **Price:** $21.95. **Description:** Primer for marketing a new or existing business.

39544 ■ *Mommy Millionaire: How I Turned My Kitchen Table Idea Into a Million Dollars and How You Can, Too!*
Pub: St. Martin's Press LLC
Ed: Kim Lavine. **Released:** February 19, 2008. **Price:** $14.95. **Description:** Advice, secrets and lessons for making a million dollars from a mom who turned her kitchen into a successful business; tools cover developing and patenting an idea, cold calling, trade shows, QVC, big retailers, manufacturing, and raising venture capital.

39545 ■ *"Online Fortunes" in Small Business Opportunities (Fall 2008)*
Pub: Entrepreneur Media Inc.
Description: Fifty hot, e-commerce enterprises for the aspiring entrepreneur to consider are featured; virtual assistants, marketing services, party planning, travel services, researching, web design and development, importing as well as creating an online store are among the businesses featured.

39546 ■ *"Revel in Riches!" in Small Business Opportunities (May 2008)*
Pub: Harris Publications Inc.
Description: Profile of Proforma, a business-to-business franchise firm providing print and promotional products.

39547 ■ *Small Business for Dummies, 3rd Ed.*
Pub: John Wiley and Sons, Inc.
Ed: Eric Tyson; Jim Schell. **Released:** March 2008. **Price:** $21.99. **Description:** Guidebook for anyone wanting to start or grow a small business; topics include information financing, budgeting, marketing, management and more.

39548 ■ *The Small Business Owner's Manual: Everything You Need to Know to Start Up and Run Your Business*
Pub: Career Press, Incorporated
Ed: Joe Kennedy. **Released:** June 2005. **Price:** $19.99 (US), $26.95 (Canadian). **Description:** Comprehensive guide for starting a small business, focusing on twelve ways to obtain financing, business plans, selling and advertising products and services, hiring and firing employees, setting up a Web site, business law, accounting issues, insurance, equipment, computers, banks, financing, customer credit and collection, leasing, and more.

39549 ■ *Start Your Own Net Services Business*
Pub: Entrepreneur Press
Contact: Perlman Neil, President
Released: February 1, 2009. **Price:** $17.95. **Description:** Web design, search engine marketing, new-media online, and blogging, are currently the four most popular web services available. This book provides information to start a net service business.

39550 ■ *"Startup Aims to Cut Out Coupon Clipping" in The Business Journal-Serving Metropolitan Kansas City (Vol. 26, August 15, 2008, No. 49)*
Pub: American City Business Journals, Inc.
Ed: Suzanna Stagemeyer. **Description:** TDP Inc., who started operations 18 months ago, aims to transform stale coupon promotions using technology by digitizing the entire coupon process. The process is expected to enable consumers to hunt coupons online where they will be automatically linked to loyalty cards. Other views and information on TDP and its services are presented.

39551 ■ *The Unofficial Guide to Starting a Small Business*
Pub: John Wiley & Sons, Incorporated
Ed: Marcia Layton Turner. **Released:** October 2004. **Price:** $16.99. **Description:** Information and tools for starting a small business, covering the start-up process, from market research, to business plans, to marketing programs.

39552 ■ *What No One Ever Tells You About Starting Your Own Business: Real-Life Start-Up Advice from 101 Successful Entrepreneurs*
Pub: Kaplan Publishing
Ed: Jan Norman. **Released:** July 2004. **Price:** $18.95 (US), $28.95 (Canadian). **Description:** From planning to marketing, advice is given to entrepreneurs starting new companies. s.

39553 ■ *Working for Yourself: An Entrepreneur's Guide to the Basics*
Pub: Kogan Page, Limited
Contact: Ben Glover, Director of Marketing
Ed: Jonathan Reuvid. **Released:** September 2006. **Description:** Guide for starting a new business venture, focusing on raising financing, legal and tax issues, marketing, information technology, and site location.

ASSOCIATIONS AND OTHER ORGANIZATIONS

39554 ■ Advertising and Marketing International Network (AMIN)
3587 Northshore Dr.
Wayzata, MN 55391
Ph: (952)457-1116
Fax: (952)471-7752
Co. E-mail: jsundby@aminworldwide.com
URL: http://www.aminworldwide.com
Contact: Janna Sperry Sundby, Manager, Member Services
Description: Comprised of cooperative worldwide network of non-competing independent advertising

agencies organized to provide facilities and branch office services for affiliated agencies. **Founded:** 1932. **Educational Activities:** Advertising and Marketing International Network Seminar (Annual).

39555 ■ American Academy of Professional Coders (AAPC)
2480 S 3850 W, Ste. B
Salt Lake City, UT 84120
Ph: (801)236-2200
Free: 800-626-2633
Fax: (801)236-2258
Co. E-mail: info@aapc.com
URL: http://www.aapc.com
Contact: Reed Pew, Chairman
Description: Works to elevate the standards of medical coding by providing ongoing education, certification, networking and recognition. Promotes high standards of physician and outpatient facility coding through education and certification. **Scope:** medical coding. **Founded:** 1988. **Subscriptions:** archival material articles books clippings periodicals. **Publications:** *Physician Coding Book Bundle 1*. **Educational Activities:** Coding Conference (Annual). **Awards:** Coder of the Year (Annual); Networker of the Year (Annual).

39556 ■ American Marketing Association (AMA)
311 S Wacker Dr., Ste. 5800
Chicago, IL 60606
Ph: (312)542-9000
Free: 800-262-1150
Fax: (312)542-9001
Co. E-mail: info@ama.org
URL: http://www.marketingpower.com
Contact: Michael Kullman, Chairperson
Description: Serves as a professional society of marketing and market research executives, sales and promotion managers, advertising specialists, academics, and others interested in marketing. Fosters research; sponsors seminars, conferences, and student marketing clubs; provides educational placement service and doctoral consortium. **Scope:** marketing, marketing research. **Founded:** 1937. **Subscriptions:** 6000 archival material books clippings monographs periodicals. **Publications:** *American Marketing Association--Proceedings* (Annual); *Journal of Marketing* (Bimonthly); *Journal of Marketing Research* (Bimonthly); *Journal of Public Policy and Marketing* (Semiannual); *Marketing Academics at AMA* (Bimonthly); *Marketing Health Service* (Quarterly); *Marketing Matters* (Biweekly). **Educational Activities:** Institute for Marketing Communications and Strategy (Annual); Summer Marketing Educator's Conference (Annual); Winter Marketing Educators Conference (Annual). **Awards:** Harold H. Maynard Award; William O'Dell Award; Charles Coolidge Parlin Award; H. Paul Root Award; Explor Award (Annual); Harold H. Maynard Award (Annual); AMA/Irwin/McGraw-Hill Distinguished Marketing Educator Award; Wayne A. Lemburg Award for Distinguished Service.

39557 ■ Association of Directory Marketing (ADM)
1187 Thorn Run Rd., Ste. 630
Moon Township, PA 15108-3198
Ph: (412)269-0663
Fax: (412)269-0655
Co. E-mail: nmd@localsearchassociation.org
URL: http://www.admworks.org
Contact: Neg Norton, President
Description: Certified marketing representatives and agencies; directory publishers; suppliers. Promotes use of telephone directories in marketing. Provides support and services to marketers wishing to make use of print and internet directories, telephone directories. **Founded:** 1990. **Publications:** *ADM Flash*. **Telecommunication Services:** adm@admworks.org.

39558 ■ Center for Exhibition Industry Research (CEIR)
12700 Park Central Dr., Ste. 308
Dallas, TX 75251
Ph: (972)687-9242
Fax: (972)692-6020
Co. E-mail: info@ceir.org
URL: http://www.ceir.org
Contact: Carrie Freeman Parsons, Chairperson
Description: Promotes the growth, awareness and value of exhibitions and other face-to-face marketing events by producing and delivering research-based knowledge tools. Consists of exhibition organizers, service providers, exhibitors, CVBs and facilities. **Scope:** industry marketing, professional development, history, growth, trends. **Founded:** 1978. **Subscriptions:** 150 articles books clippings periodicals reports.

39559 ■ Direct Marketing Association (DMA)
1120 Ave. of the Americas
New York, NY 10036-6700
Ph: (212)768-7277
Fax: (212)302-6714
Co. E-mail: ceo@the-dma.org
URL: http://www.the-dma.org
Contact: Linda A. Woolley, Chief Executive Officer
Description: Manufacturers, wholesalers, public utilities, retailers, mail order firms, publishers, schools, clubs, insurance companies, financial organizations, business equipment manufacturers, paper and envelope manufacturers, list brokers, compilers, managers, owners, computer service bureaus, advertising agencies, letter shops, research organizations, printers, lithographers, creators and producers of direct mail and direct response advertising. Studies consumer and business attitudes toward direct mail and related direct marketing statistics. Offers Mail Preference Service for consumers who wish to receive less mail advertising, Mail Order Action Line to help resolve difficulties with mail order purchases and Telephone Preference Service for people who wish to receive fewer telephone sales calls. Maintains hall of fame; offers placement service; compiles statistics. Sponsors several three-day Basic Direct Marketing Institutes, Advanced Direct Marketing Institutes and special interest seminars and workshops. Maintains Government Affairs office in Washington, DC. Operates Direct Marketing Educational Foundation. **Scope:** direct marketing. **Founded:** 1917. **Subscriptions:** 700 articles books periodicals. **Publications:** *The DMA Insider* (Quarterly); *Politically Direct* (Quarterly); *DMA Politically Direct*. **Awards:** DMA Hall of Fame (Annual); International ECHO Awards (Annual); International ECHO Awards; USPS Gold Mailbox Award. **Telecommunication Services:** lrc@the-dma.org.

39560 ■ *E-Image News*
6700 Cote-de-Liesse, Ste. 100
St.-Laurent, QC, Canada H4T 2B5
Ph: (514)489-5359
Free: 866-450-7722
Fax: (514)489-7760
Co. E-mail: info@pppc.ca
URL: http://www.promocan.com
Contact: Edward Ahad, President
Released: Monthly

39561 ■ Electronic Retailing Association (ERA)
607 14th St. NW, Ste. 530
Washington, DC 20005
Ph: (703)841-1751
Free: 800-987-6462
Fax: (425)977-1036
Co. E-mail: webadmin@retailing.org
URL: http://www.retailing.org
Contact: Steven Feinberg, Chairman
Description: Serves companies that use the power of electronic media to sell goods and services to the public. Its global membership includes television, radio and Internet retailers, along with expert backend suppliers. **Founded:** 1991. **Publications:** *E-News Weekly* (Weekly); *Marketing, Meetings and Membership* (Monthly); *Retailing.org* (Bimonthly); *Retailing.org Daily* (Daily). **Educational Activities:** Asia Meeting (Annual); European Conference (Annual). **Awards:** ERA Awards (Annual).

39562 ■ *The Idea Book*
6700 Cote-de-Liesse, Ste. 100
St.-Laurent, QC, Canada H4T 2B5
Ph: (514)489-5359
Free: 866-450-7722
Fax: (514)489-7760
Co. E-mail: info@pppc.ca
URL: http://www.promocan.com
Contact: Edward Ahad, President
Released: Annual **Price:** C$3.75, for distributors.

39563 ■ *Images*
6700 Cote-de-Liesse, Ste. 100
St.-Laurent, QC, Canada H4T 2B5
Ph: (514)489-5359
Free: 866-450-7722
Fax: (514)489-7760
Co. E-mail: info@pppc.ca
URL: http://www.promocan.com
Contact: Edward Ahad, President
Released: Semiannual **Price:** C$1.

39564 ■ International Internet Marketing Association (IIMA)
349 W Georgia St.
Vancouver, BC, Canada V6B 3Z4
Ph: (778)373-8785
Co. E-mail: info@iimaonline.org
URL: http://www.iimaonline.org
Contact: James Richardson, President
Description: Encourages internet and traditional marketers to use the internet as a vital component of the marketing mix. Supports members by providing networking and educational events designed to keep members informed about internet trends, changes, opportunities, and career advancement. **Founded:** 1998. **Awards:** Active State Member of the Year (Annual).

39565 ■ Mailing and Fulfillment Service Association (MFSA)
1421 Prince St., Ste. 410
Alexandria, VA 22314-2806
Ph: (703)836-9200
Free: 800-333-6272
Fax: (703)548-8204
Co. E-mail: mfsa-mail@mfsanet.org
URL: http://www.mfsanet.org
Contact: Michael Kellogg, Chairman of the Board
Description: Commercial direct mail producers, letter shops, mailing list houses, fulfillment operations, and advertising agencies. Conducts special interest group meetings. Offers specialized education; conducts research programs. **Founded:** 1920. **Publications:** *Postscripts* (Monthly); *MFSA Wage Salary, and Fringe Benefit Survey* (Semiannual); *Performance Profiles: The Financial Ratios for the Mailing Service Industry* (Annual); *Who's Who: MASA's Buyers' Guide to Blue Ribbon Mailing Services* (Annual). **Educational Activities:** Mid-Winter Executive Conference (Annual). **Awards:** Leo G. Bill Bernheimer Award (Annual); Miles Kimball Medallion (Annual); Henry Hoke, Sr. Award; Miles Kimball Medallion; Mailing Industry Ingenuity Award; President's Plaque; John Howie Wright Cup; L.V. Luke Kaiser Educational Award (Annual); Robert M. Huse Chapter Achievement Award (Annual); Leo G. Bill Bernheimer, Jr. Award; L. U. "Luke" Kaiser Educational Award.

39566 ■ Multi-Level Marketing International Association (MLMIA)
119 Stanford Ct.
Irvine, CA 92612
Ph: (949)854-0484
Fax: (949)854-7687
Co. E-mail: info@mlmia.com
URL: http://www.mlmia.com
Contact: Doris Wood, Chairperson Founder
Description: Companies, support groups, and distributors. Seeks to strengthen and improve the Multi-Level Marketing (also known as Network Marketing) industry in the U.S. and abroad. (Multi-Level Marketing is a method of selling products directly, independently, and usually out of the home, without the medium of a retail outlet.) Provides educational services to consumers and law enforcement agencies. Serves as an information source for the industry. Offers recommendations for start-up companies; maintains speakers' bureau; conducts training programs. **Scope:** MLM industry, self-improvement, legal. **Founded:** 1985. **Subscriptions:** 100. **Publications:** *Connections and Dittos from*

Doris (Monthly). **Educational Activities:** Multi-Level Marketing International Association Convention (Quarterly). **Awards:** Distributor of the Year (Annual); Hall of Fame (Periodic); International Company (Periodic); Supplier of the Year (Annual); Distributor of the Year Award; MLM Company of the Year; MLM Company of the Year (Annual); Support Company of the Year (Annual).

39567 ■ Promotional Products Professionals of Canada (PPPC)—Professionels en Produits Promotionnels du Canada
6700 Cote-de-Liesse, Ste. 100
St.-Laurent, QC, Canada H4T 2B5
Ph: (514)489-5359
Free: 866-450-7722
Fax: (514)489-7760
Co. E-mail: info@pppc.ca
URL: http://www.promocan.com
Contact: Edward Ahad, President
Description: Studies, promotes, fosters, and develops the economic interests of the participants in the promotional products industry of Canada. **Founded:** 1956. **Publications:** *E-Image News* (Monthly); *The Idea Book* (Annual); *Images* (Semiannual); *promoVantage* (Semiannual); *promoXpert* (Semiannual). **Educational Activities:** Promotional Products Professionals of Canada Convention (Annual); "TOPS" - Traveling Optimum Promotional Show (Bimonthly). **Awards:** Image Award (Annual).

39568 ■ *promoVantage*
6700 Cote-de-Liesse, Ste. 100
St.-Laurent, QC, Canada H4T 2B5
Ph: (514)489-5359
Free: 866-450-7722
Fax: (514)489-7760
Co. E-mail: info@pppc.ca
URL: http://www.promocan.com
Contact: Edward Ahad, President
Released: Semiannual

39569 ■ *promoXpert*
6700 Cote-de-Liesse, Ste. 100
St.-Laurent, QC, Canada H4T 2B5
Ph: (514)489-5359
Free: 866-450-7722
Fax: (514)489-7760
Co. E-mail: info@pppc.ca
URL: http://www.promocan.com
Contact: Edward Ahad, President
Released: Semiannual

39570 ■ Trade Show Exhibitors Association (TSEA)
2301 S Lake Shore Dr., Ste. 1005
Chicago, IL 60616
Ph: (312)842-8732
Fax: (312)842-8744
Co. E-mail: tsea@tsea.org
URL: http://www.tsea.org
Contact: Margit B. Weisgal, President
Description: Exhibitors working to improve the effectiveness of trade shows as a marketing tool. Purposes are to promote the progress and development of trade show exhibiting; to collect and disseminate trade show information; conduct studies, surveys, and stated projects designed to improve trade shows; to foster good relations and communications with organizations representing others in the industry; to undertake other activities necessary to promote the welfare of member companies. Sponsors Exhibit Industry Education Foundation and professional exhibiting seminars; the forum series of educational programs on key issues affecting the industry. Maintains placement services; compiles statistics. **Publications:** *Trade Show Ideas Magazine* (Monthly); *Trade Show Ideas*; *Trade Show Exhibitors Association--Membership Directory and Industry Buyer's Guide* (Continuous). **Awards:** Focus Awards; President's Award (Annual); Chairman's Award (Annual); Distinguished Service Award (Annual).

39571 ■ Women's Regional Publications of America (WRPA)
c/o Jill Duval, VP/Membership Chair
PO Box 12955
Albuquerque, NM 87195
Ph: (505)247-9195
Free: 800-282-8749
Co. E-mail: kgreen@womsdigest.net
URL: http://www.womensyellowpages.org
Contact: Karen Green, President
Description: Provides a forum where publishers of women's publications and business directories share information and resources. Increases the visibility, authority, influence and status of women's business for the purpose of promoting growth and support of women. Educates the general public about the need to support women-owned businesses, including equal opportunity employers and contractors. **Founded:** 1986.

EDUCATIONAL PROGRAMS

39572 ■ Advertising Research (Onsite)
Burke Institute
500 W 7th St.
Cincinnati, OH 45203
Ph: (513)684-4999
Free: 800-543-8635
Fax: (513)684-7733
Co. E-mail: register@burkeinstitute.com
URL: http://www.burkeinstitute.com
Price: $1,895.00. **Description:** This seminar provides a practical and a comprehensive framework for classifying various advertising research methods.

39573 ■ AMA's Advanced Course in Strategic Marketing (Onsite)
American Management Association
600 AMA Way
Saranac Lake, NY 12983-5534
Ph: (212)586-8100
Free: 877-566-9441
Fax: (518)891-0368
Co. E-mail: customerservice@amanet.org
URL: http://www.amaseminars.org
Price: $2,345.00 for non-members; $2,095.00 for AMA members; and $1,794.00 for General Services Administration (GSA) members. **Description:** Three-day seminar focusing on strategic marketing tools to increase the spending of customers and acquire new ones. **Dates and Locations:** Washington, DC; New York, NY; San Francisco, CA; Chicago, IL; and Arlington, VA.

39574 ■ Applications of Marketing Research (Onsite)
Seminar Information Service, Inc.
20 Executive Park, Ste. 120
Irvine, CA 92614
Ph: (949)261-9104
Free: 877-SEM-INFO
Fax: (949)261-1963
Co. E-mail: info@seminarinformation.com
URL: http://www.seminarinformation.com
Price: $1,995.00. **Description:** Learn which research techniques are used (and misused) for providing management with practical information to make decisions in several specific areas including new and current products, promotion, claim justification, demand analysis, positioning and segmentation. **Dates and Locations:** San Francisco, CA.

39575 ■ Applications of Marketing Research (Onsite)
Burke Institute
500 W 7th St.
Cincinnati, OH 45203
Ph: (513)684-4999
Free: 800-543-8635
Fax: (513)684-7733
Co. E-mail: register@burkeinstitute.com
URL: http://www.burkeinstitute.com
Price: $1,995.00. **Description:** Participants in this seminar will learn which research techniques are used for providing management with practical information to make decisions. **Dates and Locations:** San Francisco, CA.

39576 ■ Comprehensive Email Marketing Strategies Seminar (Onsite)
Seminar Information Service, Inc.
20 Executive Park, Ste. 120
Irvine, CA 92614
Ph: (949)261-9104
Free: 877-SEM-INFO
Fax: (949)261-1963
Co. E-mail: info@seminarinformation.com
URL: http://www.seminarinformation.com
Price: $1,699.00. **Description:** Learn how to meet your acquisition and retention objectives through the power of email; comply with changing regulations; crank up response using the latest best practices; reach your target every time; determine true campaign ROI by analyzing the measurements of success that matter; and identify what's working and what isn't through testing and improve campaign performance.

39577 ■ Consultative Selling Skills Training (Onsite)
Baker Communications Inc. (BCI)
10101 SW Fwy., Ste. 630
Houston, TX 77074
Ph: (713)627-7700
Fax: (713)587-2051
Co. E-mail: information@bakercommunications.com
URL: http://www.bakercommunications.com
Contact: Walter Rogers, President
Price: $1,700.00. **Description:** This hands-on, exercise-driven workshop teaches skills that boost sales and profitability through an increased understanding and implementation of the need/satisfaction sales process. **Dates and Locations:** Cities throughout the United States and Canada.

39578 ■ Creating Customer Value Through Competitive Advantage
Canadian Management Centre (CMC)
150 York St., 5th Fl.
Toronto, ON, Canada M5H 3S5
Ph: (416)214-5678
Free: 877-262-2519
Fax: (416)313-4985
Co. E-mail: cmcinfo@cmctraining.org
URL: http://www.cmctraining.org
Contact: John Wright, President
Price: $1,645.00 for members; $1,795.00 for non-members. **Description:** Learn about competitive advantage and how important this is to help sustain business growth. **Dates and Locations:** Toronto, ON.

39579 ■ Customer Satisfaction and Loyalty Research (Onsite)
Burke Institute
500 W 7th St.
Cincinnati, OH 45203
Ph: (513)684-4999
Free: 800-543-8635
Fax: (513)684-7733
Co. E-mail: register@burkeinstitute.com
URL: http://www.burkeinstitute.com
Price: $2,495.00. **Description:** A two-day seminar teaching why assessing customer satisfaction is important and how to design a study to measure customer satisfaction. **Dates and Locations:** Chicago, IL.

39580 ■ Data Analysis for Marketing Research: The Fundamentals (Onsite)
Burke Institute
500 W 7th St.
Cincinnati, OH 45203
Ph: (513)684-4999
Free: 800-543-8635
Fax: (513)684-7733
Co. E-mail: register@burkeinstitute.com
URL: http://www.burkeinstitute.com
Price: $1,995.00. **Description:** Participants will learn how to summarize basic trends and relationships in marketing research. **Dates and Locations:** Cincinnati, OH.

39581 ■ Designing Effective Questionnaires: A Step By Step Workshop (Onsite)
Burke Institute
500 W 7th St.
Cincinnati, OH 45203
Ph: (513)684-4999
Free: 800-543-8635

Fax: (513)684-7733
Co. E-mail: register@burkeinstitute.com
URL: http://www.burkeinstitute.com
Price: $2,495.00. **Description:** Participants will learn how to phrase questions and design questionnaires that are responsive to management's information needs. **Dates and Locations:** Chicago, IL; and Philadelphia, PA.

39582 ■ Designing Effective Questionnaires: A Step by Step Workshop (Onsite)
Seminar Information Service, Inc.
20 Executive Park, Ste. 120
Irvine, CA 92614
Ph: (949)261-9104
Free: 877-SEM-INFO
Fax: (949)261-1963
Co. E-mail: info@seminarinformation.com
URL: http://www.seminarinformation.com
Price: $2,495.00. **Description:** Learn how to phrase questions and design questionnaires that are responsive to management's information needs; the why and how of planning and flowcharting a questionnaire to guide the overall logic; how to implement mail, telephone and in-person questionnaires to increase response rates and improve overall data quality. **Dates and Locations:** Chicago, IL; and philadelphia, PA.

39583 ■ Focus Group Moderator Training (Onsite)
Seminar Information Service, Inc.
20 Executive Park, Ste. 120
Irvine, CA 92614
Ph: (949)261-9104
Free: 877-SEM-INFO
Fax: (949)261-1963
Co. E-mail: info@seminarinformation.com
URL: http://www.seminarinformation.com
Price: $2,995.00. **Description:** Learn through hands-on experiences: how to moderate a focus group by participating in a series of skill-building workshops and personal feedback sessions; to assess their development by watching multiple videotapes of themselves moderating group sessions; and how to consult with clients from design to final results presentation. **Dates and Locations:** Cincinnati, OH.

39584 ■ Focus Group Moderator Training (Onsite)
Burke Institute
500 W 7th St.
Cincinnati, OH 45203
Ph: (513)684-4999
Free: 800-543-8635
Fax: (513)684-7733
Co. E-mail: register@burkeinstitute.com
URL: http://www.burkeinstitute.com
Price: $2,995.00. **Description:** A four-day seminar that teaches how to moderate a focus group by participating in a series of skill-building workshops and personal feedback sessions. **Dates and Locations:** Cincinnati, OH.

39585 ■ Fundamentals of Marketing: Your Action Plan for Success (Onsite)
American Management Association
600 AMA Way
Saranac Lake, NY 12983-5534
Ph: (212)586-8100
Free: 877-566-9441
Fax: (518)891-0368
Co. E-mail: customerservice@amanet.org
URL: http://www.amaseminars.org
Price: $2,095.00 for non-members; $1,895.00 for AMA members; and $1,623.00 for General Services Administration (GSA) members. **Description:** Three-day seminar for new marketing professionals and product managers; covers marketing tools, skills, and techniques. **Dates and Locations:** Chicago, IL; New York, NY; San Francisco, CA; Washington, DC; and Arlington, VA.

39586 ■ Fundamentals of Marketing: Your Action Plan for Success (Onsite) (Canada)
Canadian Management Centre (CMC)
150 York St., 5th Fl.
Toronto, ON, Canada M5H 3S5
Ph: (416)214-5678
Free: 877-262-2519
Fax: (416)313-4985
Co. E-mail: cmcinfo@cmctraining.org
URL: http://www.cmctraining.org
Contact: John Wright, President
Price: $2,395.00 Canadian for non-members; $2,195.00 for CMC members. **Description:** Three-day seminar for new marketing professionals and product managers; covers marketing tools, skills, and techniques. **Dates and Locations:** Toronto, ON.

39587 ■ How to Write a Killer Marketing Plan (Onsite)
American Management Association
600 AMA Way
Saranac Lake, NY 12983-5534
Ph: (212)586-8100
Free: 877-566-9441
Fax: (518)891-0368
Co. E-mail: customerservice@amanet.org
URL: http://www.amaseminars.org
Price: $2,095.00 for non-members; $1,895.00 for AMA members; and $1,623.00 for General Services Administration (GSA) members. **Description:** Develop a successful marketing plan from financials to research to media method. **Dates and Locations:** New York, NY; Arlington, VA; Washington, DC; and San Diego, CA.

39588 ■ Intensive Introduction to Copyediting (Onsite)
EEI Communications
8945 Guilford Rd., Ste. 145
Columbia, MD 21046
Ph: (410)309-8200
Free: 888-253-2762
Fax: (410)630-3980
Co. E-mail: train@eeicom.com
URL: http://www.eeicom.com/eei-training-services
Price: $1,097.00. **Description:** Covers basic editorial marks, style, spelling and grammar, and other details of copywriting and editing. **Dates and Locations:** Columbia, MD; and Alexandria, VA.

39589 ■ Linking Customer, Employee and Process Data to Drive Profitability (Onsite)
Seminar Information Service, Inc.
20 Executive Park, Ste. 120
Irvine, CA 92614
Ph: (949)261-9104
Free: 877-SEM-INFO
Fax: (949)261-1963
Co. E-mail: info@seminarinformation.com
URL: http://www.seminarinformation.com
Price: $1,895.00. **Description:** Learn the origins of the rational for linkage research and analysis, and why linkage research and analysis is an area of critical importance to marketers and marketing researchers.

39590 ■ Market Research: How To Get The Right Data to Make the Right Decisions (Onsite)
Seminar Information Service, Inc.
20 Executive Park, Ste. 120
Irvine, CA 92614
Ph: (949)261-9104
Free: 877-SEM-INFO
Fax: (949)261-1963
Co. E-mail: info@seminarinformation.com
URL: http://www.seminarinformation.com
Price: $1,995.00. **Description:** Learn how to use market research to determine your company's competitive position and enhance performance.

39591 ■ Market Segmentation and Positioning Research (Onsite)
Seminar Information Service, Inc.
20 Executive Park, Ste. 120
Irvine, CA 92614
Ph: (949)261-9104
Free: 877-SEM-INFO
Fax: (949)261-1963
Co. E-mail: info@seminarinformation.com
URL: http://www.seminarinformation.com
Price: $2,495.00. **Description:** Learn how to segment your markets and select the best target markets for your products and services, including how to design marketing research studies from start to finish to segment markets and which commercial data sources are available to help you segment your markets.

39592 ■ The Marketing Plus Social Media Conference (Onsite)
Seminar Information Service, Inc.
20 Executive Park, Ste. 120
Irvine, CA 92614
Ph: (949)261-9104
Free: 877-SEM-INFO
Fax: (949)261-1963
Co. E-mail: info@seminarinformation.com
URL: http://www.seminarinformation.com
Price: $249.00. **Description:** Learn how to reach your marketing potential guaranteeing results. **Dates and Locations:** Cities throughout the United States.

39593 ■ Measuring and Maximizing Marketing ROI (Onsite)
Seminar Information Service, Inc.
20 Executive Park, Ste. 120
Irvine, CA 92614
Ph: (949)261-9104
Free: 877-SEM-INFO
Fax: (949)261-1963
Co. E-mail: info@seminarinformation.com
URL: http://www.seminarinformation.com
Price: $2,195.00. **Description:** Learn how to use marketing ROI results to general more competitive corporate-wide product and service strategies, including the challenges, opportunities and roadblocks of marketing ROI today and how leading companies track and access marketing ROI. **Dates and Locations:** Atlanta, GA.

39594 ■ New Product Research: Laying the Foundation for New Product Success (Onsite)
Seminar Information Service, Inc.
20 Executive Park, Ste. 120
Irvine, CA 92614
Ph: (949)261-9104
Free: 877-SEM-INFO
Fax: (949)261-1963
Co. E-mail: info@seminarinformation.com
URL: http://www.seminarinformation.com
Price: $1,995.00. **Description:** Learn how to design and implement marketing research studies to guide the total product development and evaluation process. **Dates and Locations:** Los Angeles, CA.

39595 ■ Next Generation Qualitative Tools: Social Media, Online Communities & Virtual Research Platforms (Onsite)
Seminar Information Service, Inc.
20 Executive Park, Ste. 120
Irvine, CA 92614
Ph: (949)261-9104
Free: 877-SEM-INFO
Fax: (949)261-1963
Co. E-mail: info@seminarinformation.com
URL: http://www.seminarinformation.com
Price: $2,095.00. **Description:** Learn how social media is being used by qualitative research professionals to support data and enhance the ability to reach their target audience, and more. **Dates and Locations:** San Francisco, CA.

39596 ■ Online Marketing and Search Engine Optimization
EEI Communications
8945 Guilford Rd., Ste. 145
Columbia, MD 21046
Ph: (410)309-8200
Free: 888-253-2762

Fax: (410)630-3980
Co. E-mail: train@eeicom.com
URL: http://www.eeicom.com/eei-training-services
Price: $745.00. **Description:** Covers how to increase traffic to your online site to market your products and services using the Web, including creating and implementation of your plan, setting a budget, redesigning Web site for search engine optimization, tips and tricks, promotion hints, tips, and advice, and how to measure your Internet marketing results. **Dates and Locations:** Alexandria, VA.

39597 ■ Online Research Best Practices and Innovations (Onsite)
Seminar Information Service, Inc.
20 Executive Park, Ste. 120
Irvine, CA 92614
Ph: (949)261-9104
Free: 877-SEM-INFO
Fax: (949)261-1963
Co. E-mail: info@seminarinformation.com
URL: http://www.seminarinformation.com
Price: $1,995.00. **Description:** Get up to date with the most recent developments relating to Web surveys and other online marketing research, and learn when to consider online qualitative research, including in-depth interviews, bulletin board sessions and online focus groups. **Dates and Locations:** Baltimore, MD.

39598 ■ Online Research Best Practices and Innovations (Onsite)
Burke Institute
500 W 7th St.
Cincinnati, OH 45203
Ph: (513)684-4999
Free: 800-543-8635
Fax: (513)684-7733
Co. E-mail: register@burkeinstitute.com
URL: http://www.burkeinstitute.com
Price: $1,995.00. **Description:** A two-day seminar to help participants get up to date with the most recent developments relating to Web surveys and other online marketing. **Dates and Locations:** Baltimore, MD.

39599 ■ Planning and Developing New Products (Onsite)
Seminar Information Service, Inc.
20 Executive Park, Ste. 120
Irvine, CA 92614
Ph: (949)261-9104
Free: 877-SEM-INFO
Fax: (949)261-1963
Co. E-mail: info@seminarinformation.com
URL: http://www.seminarinformation.com
Price: $2,195.00; $1,995.00 for AMA members. **Description:** Covers how to take your new product from concept to profitability. **Dates and Locations:** San Francisco, CA.

39600 ■ Practical Conjoint Analysis and Discrete Choice Modeling (Onsite)
Seminar Information Service, Inc.
20 Executive Park, Ste. 120
Irvine, CA 92614
Ph: (949)261-9104
Free: 877-SEM-INFO
Fax: (949)261-1963
Co. E-mail: info@seminarinformation.com
URL: http://www.seminarinformation.com
Price: $2,495.00. **Description:** Topics include full profile conjoint analysis, hybrid conjoint analysis, and conducting DCM studies. **Dates and Locations:** Chicago, IL.

39601 ■ Practical Marketing Research (Onsite)
Burke Institute
500 W 7th St.
Cincinnati, OH 45203
Ph: (513)684-4999
Free: 800-543-8635
Fax: (513)684-7733
Co. E-mail: register@burkeinstitute.com
URL: http://www.burkeinstitute.com
Price: $2,495.00. **Description:** A user-oriented discussion of traditional and contemporary methods for research practitioners. **Dates and Locations:** Chicago, IL; and San Francisco, CA.

39602 ■ Practical Multivariate Analysis (Onsite)
Burke Institute
500 W 7th St.
Cincinnati, OH 45203
Ph: (513)684-4999
Free: 800-543-8635
Fax: (513)684-7733
Co. E-mail: register@burkeinstitute.com
URL: http://www.burkeinstitute.com
Price: $2,695.00. **Description:** Extends participants' understanding of data analysis beyond 'Tools and Techniques of Data Analysis.'. **Dates and Locations:** Cincinnati, OH; and San Francisco, CA.

39603 ■ Pricing Strategies: Capturing and Sustaining a Competitive Advantage (Onsite)
Seminar Information Service, Inc.
20 Executive Park, Ste. 120
Irvine, CA 92614
Ph: (949)261-9104
Free: 877-SEM-INFO
Fax: (949)261-1963
Co. E-mail: info@seminarinformation.com
URL: http://www.seminarinformation.com
Price: $1,995.00. **Description:** Gain unique tools and proven tactics to better assess your current pricing position and develop a pricing strategy that will increase your company's 'wallet share' and long-term customer loyalty.

39604 ■ Sales in Turbulent Times
Canadian Management Centre (CMC)
150 York St., 5th Fl.
Toronto, ON, Canada M5H 3S5
Ph: (416)214-5678
Free: 877-262-2519
Fax: (416)313-4985
Co. E-mail: cmcinfo@cmctraining.org
URL: http://www.cmctraining.org
Contact: John Wright, President
Price: $495.00 for members; $545.00 for non-members. **Description:** This half-day seminar will cover techniques to uncover why your customer or prospect values doing business with you and follow through actions to gain referrals and testimonials. **Dates and Locations:** Toronto, ON.

39605 ■ Secrets of Copywriting Seminar: Fundamentals for Direct Marketing (Onsite)
Seminar Information Service, Inc.
20 Executive Park, Ste. 120
Irvine, CA 92614
Ph: (949)261-9104
Free: 877-SEM-INFO
Fax: (949)261-1963
Co. E-mail: info@seminarinformation.com
URL: http://www.seminarinformation.com
Price: $1,699.00. **Description:** Learn how to write clear and compelling copy, for both in print and online.

39606 ■ Social Media Marketing (Onsite)
Seminar Information Service, Inc.
20 Executive Park, Ste. 120
Irvine, CA 92614
Ph: (949)261-9104
Free: 877-SEM-INFO
Fax: (949)261-1963
Co. E-mail: info@seminarinformation.com
URL: http://www.seminarinformation.com
Price: $199.00. **Description:** Learn how you can obtain social marketing success for your organization. **Dates and Locations:** Cities throughout the United States.

39607 ■ Specialized Moderator Skills for Qualitative Research Applications (Onsite)
Burke Institute
500 W 7th St.
Cincinnati, OH 45203
Ph: (513)684-4999
Free: 800-543-8635
Fax: (513)684-7733
Co. E-mail: register@burkeinstitute.com
URL: http://www.burkeinstitute.com
Price: $2,995.00. **Description:** A four-day workshop designed for the active focus moderator. **Dates and Locations:** Cincinnati, OH.

39608 ■ Strategy Execution: Getting it Done (Onsite)
Canadian Management Centre (CMC)
150 York St., 5th Fl.
Toronto, ON, Canada M5H 3S5
Ph: (416)214-5678
Free: 877-262-2519
Fax: (416)313-4985
Co. E-mail: cmcinfo@cmctraining.org
URL: http://www.cmctraining.org
Contact: John Wright, President
Price: $2,195.00 for members; $2,395.00 for non-members. **Description:** Learn techniques to help ensure that costly and risky organizational or corporate strategy initiatives succeed. **Dates and Locations:** Toronto, ON.

39609 ■ Successful Product Management (Onsite)
American Management Association
600 AMA Way
Saranac Lake, NY 12983-5534
Ph: (212)586-8100
Free: 877-566-9441
Fax: (518)891-0368
Co. E-mail: customerservice@amanet.org
URL: http://www.amaseminars.org
Price: $2,195.00 for non-members; $1,995.00 for AMA members; and $1,708.00 for General Services Administrtion (GSA) members,. **Description:** Covers Product Manager duties, finance, marketing techniques, new product development, and advertising. **Dates and Locations:** Arlington, VA; Washington, DC; and Chicago, IL.

39610 ■ Tools & Techniques of Data Analysis (Onsite)
Seminar Information Service, Inc.
20 Executive Park, Ste. 120
Irvine, CA 92614
Ph: (949)261-9104
Free: 877-SEM-INFO
Fax: (949)261-1963
Co. E-mail: info@seminarinformation.com
URL: http://www.seminarinformation.com
Price: $2,695.00. **Description:** Includes everything participants want to know about data analysis in marketing research using a series of specially developed how-to flowcharts and real world examples, including how to plan, execute, analyze, interpret, and communicate the results of an analysis plan to answer management's questions. **Dates and Locations:** San Francisco, CA.

39611 ■ Tools and Techniques of Data Analysis (Onsite)
Burke Institute
500 W 7th St.
Cincinnati, OH 45203
Ph: (513)684-4999
Free: 800-543-8635
Fax: (513)684-7733
Co. E-mail: register@burkeinstitute.com
URL: http://www.burkeinstitute.com
Price: $2,695.00. **Description:** A comprehensive seminar that packs everything participants want to know about data analysis in marketing research into flowcharts and real world experience. **Dates and Locations:** San Francisco, CA.

39612 ■ Web Marketing: Design. Navigation. Analytics. Understanding the Big Picture (Onsite)
Seminar Information Service, Inc.
20 Executive Park, Ste. 120
Irvine, CA 92614
Ph: (949)261-9104
Free: 877-SEM-INFO

Fax: (949)261-1963
Co. E-mail: info@seminarinformation.com
URL: http://www.seminarinformation.com

Price: $1,699.00. **Description:** Both the marketer and the programmer learn how to get the creative and technical sides of website development working together achieving the best results.

39613 ■ Writing and Presenting Actionable Marketing Research Reports (Onsite)
Burke Institute
500 W 7th St.
Cincinnati, OH 45203
Ph: (513)684-4999
Free: 800-543-8635
Fax: (513)684-7733
Co. E-mail: register@burkeinstitute.com
URL: http://www.burkeinstitute.com

Price: $2,495.00. **Description:** A three-day seminar to teach participants what decision-makers want from a marketing research study and how to apply the findings. **Dates and Locations:** Cincinnati, OH.

REFERENCE WORKS

39614 ■ *6 Steps to Free Publicity*
Pub: ReadHowYouWant.com, Ltd.

Ed: Marcia Yudkin. **Released:** July 9, 2010. **Price:** $15.99. **Description:** Six steps to help promote a small business are given. The history of the Internet and its use to help provide free publicity to small firms is outlined.

39615 ■ *10 Steps to Successful Social Networking for Business*
Pub: ASTD
Contact: Tony Bingham, President
E-mail: tbingham@astd.org

Ed: Darin Hartley. **Released:** July 1, 2010. **Price:** $19.95. **Description:** Designed for today's fast-paced, need-it-yesterday business environment and for the thousands of workers who find themselves faced with new assignments, responsibilities, and requirements and too little time to learn what they must know.

39616 ■ *"10 Trends That Are Shaping Global Media Consumption" in Advertising Age (Vol. 81, December 6, 2010, No. 43, pp. 3)*
Pub: Crain Communications, Inc.

Ed: Ann Marie Kerwin. **Description:** Ad Age offers the statistics from the TV penetration rate in Kenya to the number of World Cup watchers and more.

39617 ■ *31 Days to Greeting Card Marketing Mastery*
Pub: Desktop Wings Inc.

Ed: Bruce Brown. **Released:** February 19, 2010. **Price:** $17.95. **Description:** The use of simple greeting cards for marketing and increasing sales is explained.

39618 ■ *49 Marketing Secrets (That Work) to Grow Sales*
Pub: Morgan James Publishing, LLC

Ed: Ronald Finklestein. **Released:** October 2007. **Price:** $19.95/. **Description:** This book was written to fill the void on marketing books and is tailored to the small business owner. The author helps the small business owner to understand marketing and who they can trust while doing business. The book includes information to help entrepreneurs discover winning marketing strategies, branding and corporate image, media strategies, networking tips, technology-based marketing ideas, event strategies, and sales strategies.

39619 ■ *101 Internet Businesses You Can Start from Home: How to Choose and Build Your Own Successful E-Business*
Pub: Maximum Press

Ed: Susan Sweeney. **Released:** June 2006. **Price:** $29.95. **Description:** Guide for starting and growing an Internet business; information for developing a business plan, risk levels, and promotional techniques are included.

39620 ■ *101 Ways to Really Satisfy Your Customers: How to Keep Your Customers and Attract New Ones*
Pub: Allen & Unwin Pty., Limited

Ed: Andrew Griffiths. **Released:** April 2007. **Price:** $14.95. **Description:** Tips for providing excellent customer service that ensure loyalty and interest to a small business are examined.

39621 ■ *"352 Media Group Opens New Tampa Web Design and Digital Marketing Office" in Entertainment Close-Up (May 2, 2011)*
Pub: Close-Up Media

Description: 352 Media Group opened its newest office in Tampa, Florida in May 2011. The firm is noted for its achievements in Web design and digital marketing.

39622 ■ *"529.com Wins Outstanding Achievement in Web Development" in Investment Weekly (November 14, 2009, pp. 152)*
Pub: Investment Weekly News

Description: Web Marketing Association's 2009 WebAward for Financial Services Standard of Excellence and Investment Standard of Excellence was won by 529.com, the website from Upromise Investments, Inc., the leading administrator of 529 college savings plans.

39623 ■ *"1914 Proved to Be Key Year for Chevy" in Automotive News (Vol. 86, October 31, 2011, No. 6488, pp. S18)*
Pub: Crain Communications Inc.

Ed: Jamie Lareau. **Description:** Chevy Bow Tie emblem was born in 1914, creating the brand's image that has carried through to current days.

39624 ■ *"A&E Networks" in Brandweek (Vol. 49, April 21, 2008, No. 16, pp. SR9)*
Pub: VNU Business Media, Inc.

Ed: Anthony Crupi. **Description:** Provides contact information for sales and marketing personnel for the A&E Networks as well as a listing of the station's top programming and an analysis of the current season and the target audience for those programs running in the current season. A&E has reinvented itself as a premium entertainment brand over the last five years and with its $2.5 million per episode acquisition of The Sopranos, the station signaled that it was serious about getting back into the scripted programming business. The acquisition also helped the network compete against other cable networks and led to a 20 percent increase in prime-time viewers.

39625 ■ *"Abacast, Citadel Strike Radio Ad Deal" in Business Journal Portland (Vol. 27, December 31, 2010, No. 44, pp. 3)*
Pub: Portland Business Journal

Ed: Erik Siemers. **Description:** Software firm Abacast Inc. has partnered with Citadel Media to aid the latter's advertising sales. Citadel provides radio networks and syndicated programs to 4,200 affiliate stations.

39626 ■ *"ABB Could Still Engineer an Upside" in Barron's (Vol. 89, July 20, 2009, No. 29, pp. M6)*
Pub: Dow Jones & Co., Inc.

Ed: Goran Mijuk. **Description:** Swiss engineering company ABB can remain profitable as its power transmission and distribution activities continue to generate earnings. The company is also benefiting from increased exposure in emerging markets.

39627 ■ *"ABC" in Brandweek (Vol. 49, April 21, 2008, No. 16, pp. SR6)*
Pub: VNU Business Media, Inc.

Ed: John Consoli. **Description:** Provides contact information for sales and marketing personnel for the ABC network as well as a listing of the station's top programming and an analysis of the current season and the target audience for those programs running in the current season.

39628 ■ *The Accidental Entrepreneur: The 50 Things I Wish Someone Had Told Me About Starting a Business*
Pub: AMACOM

Ed: Susan Urquhart-Brown. **Released:** March 2008. **Price:** $17.95. **Description:** Advice is offered to any would-be entrepreneur, including eight questions to ask before launching a new business, ten traits of a successful entrepreneur, how to obtain licenses and selling permits, best way to create a business plan, ten ways to get referrals, six secrets of marketing, investment and financial information, ways to avoid burnout, and the seven biggest pitfalls to avoid.

39629 ■ *"Ace Every Introduction" in Women Entrepreneur (September 10, 2008)*
Pub: Entrepreneur Media Inc.

Ed: Cynthia McKay. **Description:** Making a powerful first impression is one of the most important marketing tools a business owner can possess. Advice about meeting new business contacts is given.

39630 ■ *"Acsys Interactive Announces Crowdsourcing Comes to the Hospital Industry" in Internet Wire (August 23, 2010)*
Pub: Comtex

Description: Hospital marketers are obtaining data through crowdsourcing as strategy to gain ideas and feedback. The Hospital Industry Crowdsourced Survey of Digital, Integrated and Emerging Marketing is the first initiative among hospitals.

39631 ■ *"Active Sales" in Green Industry Pro (Vol. 23, September 2011)*
Pub: Cygnus Business Media

Ed: Gregg Wartgow. **Description:** Craig den Hartog, owner of Emerald Magic Lawn Care located in Holtsville, New York, describes the various marketing tactics he has developed to increase sales in the current economic environment. Statistical data included.

39632 ■ *"Ad Firms Stew Over Lost Car Biz; Diversifying Business Is Uphill Battle" in Crain's Detroit Business (Vol. 23, July 30, 2007, No. 31)*
Pub: Crain Communications, Inc.

Ed: Jean Halliday. **Description:** Struggling Detroit automakers are breaking their tradition of loyalty and moving their advertising accounts to agencies in Los Angeles, San Francisco, and Boston; This has Detroit's advertising community very worried.

39633 ■ *"Adidas' Brand Ambitions" in Business Journal Portland (Vol. 27, December 10, 2010, No. 41, pp. 1)*
Pub: Portland Business Journal

Ed: Erik Siemers. **Description:** Adidas AG, the second-largest sporting goods brand in the world, hopes to increase global revenue by 50 percent by 2015. The German company, which reported $14.5 billion sales, plans to improve its U.S. market. The U.S. is Adidas' largest, but also the most underperforming market for the firm.

39634 ■ *Advanced Selling for Dummies*
Pub: John Wiley and Sons, Inc.

Ed: Ralph R. Roberts; Joe Kraynak (As told to). **Released:** September 2007. **Price:** $21.99. **Description:** This book explores topics such as: visualizing success (includes exercises), investing and reinvesting in your own success, harnessing media and multimedia outlets, calculating risks that stretch your limits, creating lasting relationships, finding balance to avoid burnout and more. This guide is for salespeople who have already read 'Selling for Dummies' and now want forward-thinking, advanced strategies for recharging and reenergizing their careers and their lives. Blogging, Internet leads and virtual assistants are also discussed.

39635 ■ *"Advertisers Don't Party With CBS's Swingers" in Advertising Age (Vol. 79, July 7, 2008, No. 26, pp. 1)*
Pub: Crain Communications, Inc.

Ed: Brian Steinberg. **Description:** Broadcast networks that are trying to air edgier programming such as CBS's 'Swingtown' but are running into problems with advertisers who are fearful of consumer complaints and backlash when running commercials during such fare.

39636 ■ *"Advertisers Hooked on Horns, their Playground" in Austin Business JournalInc. (Vol. 28, July 25, 2008, No. 19, pp. A1)*
Pub: American City Business Journals
Ed: Sandra Zaragoza. **Description:** Renovation of the D.K. Royal-Texas Memorial Stadium has increased its advertising revenue from $570,000 in 1993 to $10 in 2008. Sponsorship has grown in the past years due to the revenue-sharing agreement, a ten-year contract through 2015 between the University of Texas and IMG College Sports.

39637 ■ *"Africa Rising" in Harvard Business Review (Vol. 86, September 2008, No. 9, pp. 36)*
Pub: Harvard Business School Press
Ed: John T. Landry. **Description:** Review of the book entitled, 'Africa Rising: How 900 Million African Consumers Offer More Than You Think' provides advice for marketing to those on the African continent.

39638 ■ *"After Price Cuts, Competition GPS Makers Lose Direction" in Brandweek (Vol. 49, April 21, 2008, No. 16, pp. 16)*
Pub: VNU Business Media, Inc.
Ed: Steve Miller. **Description:** Garmin and TomTom, two of the leaders in portable navigation devices, have seen lowering revenues due to dramatic price cuts and unexpected competition from the broadening availability of personal navigation on mobile phones. TomTom has trimmed its sales outlook for its first quarter while Garmin's stock dropped 40 percent since February.

39639 ■ *"The Agency Model Is Bent But Not Broken" in Advertising Age (Vol. 79, July 7, 2008, No. 26, pp. 17)*
Pub: Crain Communications, Inc.
Ed: Stephen Fajen. **Description:** In the new-media environment, advertising agencies must change the way in which they do business and receive payment.

39640 ■ *"The Agency-Selection Process Needs Fixing Now" in Advertising Age (Vol. 79, July 7, 2008, No. 26, pp. 18)*
Pub: Crain Communications, Inc.
Ed: Avi Dan. **Description:** Marketers are facing increased challenges in this sagging economic climate and must realize the importance of choosing the correct advertising agency for their company in order to benefit from a more-stable relationship that yields better business results. Advice for marketers regarding the best way to choose an agency is included.

39641 ■ *"Aiming at a Moving Web Target" in Entrepreneur (Vol. 37, August 2009, No. 8, pp. 30)*
Pub: Entrepreneur Media, Inc.
Ed: Dan O'Shea. **Description:** Rapidly increasing numbers of businesspeople are web surfing on mobile phones. To make a website that is accessible to people on the move, the main page should be light on images and graphics and the most important information should be put near the top. A more intensive route is to create a separate mobile-specific website.

39642 ■ *"Airlines Mount PR Push to Win Public Support Against Big Oil" in Advertising Age (Vol. 79, July 14, 2008, No. 7, pp. 1)*
Pub: Crain Communications, Inc.
Ed: Michael Bush. **Description:** Top airline executives from competing companies have banded together in a public relations plan in which they are sending e-mails to their frequent fliers asking for aid in lobbying legislators to put a restriction on oil speculation.

39643 ■ *"Albert Schultz" in Canadian Business (Vol. 83, August 17, 2010, No. 13-14, pp. 71)*
Pub: Rogers Media Ltd.
Ed: Steve Maich. **Description:** Soulpepper Theater Company founder and actor/director Albert Schultz shares the key ingredient to his success both artistically and commercially. Schultz believes his success was a combination of passion and persistence, as well as team building. He believes his entrepreneurial impulse came when he began thinking of making opportunities instead of taking them.

39644 ■ *"All Bundled Up" in Entrepreneur (Vol. 35, November 2007, No. 11, pp. 104)*
Pub: Entrepreneur Media Inc.
Ed: Kim T. Gordon. **Description:** Bundling is a marketing strategy that combines a variety of features to present products and services as a whole. Tips on how to handle bundling are outlined.

39645 ■ *All You Need Is a Good Idea!: How to Create Marketing Messages that Actually Get Results*
Pub: John Wiley and Sons, Inc.
Ed: Jay Heyman. **Released:** May 2008. **Price:** $24. 95. **Description:** Advertising guru Jay Heyman offers advice to successfully market products and services. Heyman uses his years of experience and case histories to become creative with advertising campaigns.

39646 ■ *"Alliance Atlantis Takes a Cheekier Attitude to Life" in Globe & Mail (March 5, 2007, pp. B5)*
Pub: CTVglobemedia Publishing Inc.
Ed: Keith McArthur. **Description:** Alliance Atlantis Communications Inc. is re-branding its human life ministry Life Network specialty channel as Slice. The new channel is being promoted with an advertising campaign.

39647 ■ *"Allied Brands Loses Baskin-Robbins Franchise Down Under" in Ice Cream Reporter (Vol. 23, November 20, 2010, No. 12, pp. 2)*
Pub: Ice Cream Reporter
Description: Dunkin Brands, worldwide franchisor of Baskin-Robbins, terminated the master franchise agreement for Australia held by the food marketer Allied Brands Services.

39648 ■ *"Also Active in the Fight Against Cancer is Dreyer's Grand Ice Cream" in Ice Cream Reporter (Vol. 23, October 20, 2010, No. 11, pp. 8)*
Pub: Ice Cream Reporter
Description: Dreyer's Grand Ice Cream partnered with Experience Project's BroadCause.com to raise awareness around pediatric cancer research.

39649 ■ *"Alternative Energy Calls for Alternative Marketing" in Indoor Comfort Marketing (Vol. 70, June 2011, No. 6, pp. 8)*
Pub: Industry Publications Inc.
Ed: Richard Rutigliano. **Description:** Advice for marketing solar energy products and services is given.

39650 ■ *"Alto Ventures Retains Investor Relations Professional" in Canadian Corporate News (May 16, 2007)*
Pub: Comtex News Network Inc.
Description: Alto Ventures Ltd., a gold exploration and development company with a portfolio of eleven properties in the Canadian Shield, announced that it has engaged the consulting services of Mark Prosser in order to focus on increasing investor awareness and exposure to the investment community through the dissemination of corporate information to a network of North American and European institutions, retail brokerage firms, and private investors.

39651 ■ *American Marketing Association--The M Guide Services Directory*
Pub: American Marketing Association
Contact: Lucille Pointer, President
URL(s): www.marketingpower.com/_layouts/mguide/default.aspx. **Released:** Annual; Latest edition 2009. **Covers:** 26,500 individual members and about 1,000 paid listings for member research and service firms. **Entries include:** For individuals--Member name, position, home and office address, and phone numbers. For advertisers--Company name, address, phone, names of principal executives.

39652 ■ *"Ampm Focus Has BP Working Overtime; New Convenience-Store Brand Comes to Chicago" in Crain's Chicago Business (April 28, 2008)*
Pub: Crain Communications, Inc.
Ed: John T. Slania. **Description:** Britian's oil giant BP PLC is opening its ampm convenience stores in the Chicago market and has already begun converting most of its 78 Chicago-area gas stations to ampms. The company has also started to franchise the stores to independent operators. BP is promoting the brand with both traditional and unconventional marketing techniques such s real or simulated 3D snacks embedded in bus shelter ads and an in-store Guitar Hero contest featuring finalists from a recent contest at the House of Blues.

39653 ■ *"Anja Carroll; Media Director-McDonald's USA" in Advertising Age (Vol. 79, November 17, 2008, No. 34, pp. 6)*
Pub: Crain Communications, Inc.
Ed: Emily Bryson York. **Description:** Profile of Anja Carroll who is the media director for McDonald's USA and has the challenge of choosing the right mix of media for the corporation.

39654 ■ *"Anthem Leading the Way in Social Tech Revolution" in Inside Business (Vol. 13, September-October 2011, No. 5, pp. 1B3)*
Pub: Great Lakes Publishing Co.
Ed: Ryan Clark. **Description:** Anthem Blue Cross and Blue Shield is leading the way in social technology. The firm's social media initiatives to promote itself are outlined.

39655 ■ *"App Time: Smartphone Applications Aren't Just for Fun and Games Anymore" in Inc. (Volume 32, December 2010, No. 10, pp. 116)*
Pub: Inc. Magazine
Ed: Jason Del Rey. **Description:** Smart phone technology can help any small business market their products and services.

39656 ■ *"Apparel Apparatchic at Kmart" in Barron's (Vol. 88, March 17, 2008, No. 11, pp. 16)*
Pub: Dow Jones & Company, Inc.
Description: Kmart began a nationwide search for women to represent the company in a national advertising campaign. Contestants need to upload their photos to Kmart's website and winners will be chosen by a panel of celebrity judges. The contest aims to reverse preconceived negative notions about the store's quality and service.

39657 ■ *"Applying Continuous Process Improvement for Managing Customer Loyalty" in Agency Sales Magazine (Vol. 39, November 2009, No. 10)*
Pub: MANA
Ed: Bob Cicerone; Aaron Hekele; Jason Morado. **Description:** Steps in effective process improvement that reveals where opportunities exist to improve management practices and control customer loyalty are discussed. The process consists of thirteen factors grouped into three sets.

39658 ■ *"Are Offline Pushes Important to E-Commerce?" in DM News (Vol. 31, September 14, 2009, No. 23, pp. 10)*
Pub: Haymarket Media, Inc.
Description: With the importance of Internet marketing and the popularity of ecommerce increasing experts debate the relevance of more traditional channels of advertising.

39659 ■ *"Are You Ignoring Trends That Could Shake Up Your Business?" in Harvard Business Review (Vol. 88, July-August 2010, No. 7-8, pp. 124)*
Pub: Harvard Business School Publishing
Ed: Elie Ofek, Luc Wathieu. **Description:** Ways for firms to capitalize on trends that might otherwise negatively affect their business are spotlighted. These include using certain aspects of the trend to augment traditional product/service offerings, and combining the trend with the offerings to transcend its traditional category.

39660 ■ *"Are You Ready for a Transformation?" in Women Entrepreneur (November 28, 2008)*
Pub: Entrepreneur Media Inc.
Ed: Aliza Sherman. **Description:** Marlene J. Waldock, an expert in women's empowerment and reinvention, discusses brand modification and what a business owner should consider before attempting to change or modify their brand.

39661 ■ *"Arizona Firms In Chicago Go For Gold With '08 Games" in The Business Journal - Serving Phoenix and the Valley of the Sun (Vol. 28, August 8, 2008, No. 49, pp. 1)*
Pub: American City Business Journals, Inc.
Ed: Patrick O'Grady. **Description:** More than 20 U.S. athletes will wear Arizona-based eSoles LLC's custom-made insoles to increase their performance at the 2008 Beijing Olympics making eSoles one of the beneficiaries of the commercialization of the games. Translation software maker Auralog Inc saw a 60 percent jump in sales from its Mandarin Chinese language applications.

39662 ■ *"Ask Inc." in Inc. (October 2007, pp. 73-74)*
Pub: Gruner & Jahr USA Publishing
Description: An online marketing research firm investigates the use of online communities such as MySpace and Second life in order to recruit individuals to answer surveys.

39663 ■ *"Ask Inc." in Inc. (October 2007, pp. 74)*
Pub: Gruner & Jahr USA Publishing
Description: Promoting a new comedy club using television, radio and print advertising and tracking results is discussed.

39664 ■ *"Ask Inc." in Inc. (January 2008, pp. 61)*
Pub: Gruner & Jahr USA Publishing
Description: Information to help crafter of custom quilts made from old T-shirts, baby clothes, jeans, and neckties to market her items on a small budget.

39665 ■ *"Associations" in MarketingMagazine (Vol. 115, September 27, 2010, No. 13, pp. 76)*
Pub: Rogers Publishing Ltd.
Description: Market data covering associations in Canada is presented.

39666 ■ *"At 5-Year Mark, News 9 Makes Presence Felt in Competition for Ad Dollars" in Business Review, Albany New York (October 5, 2007)*
Pub: American City Business Journals, Inc.
Ed: Barbara Pinckney. **Description:** The 24-hour news channel Capital News 9 can be watched live by viewers on their cell phones beginning late 2007 or early 2008 as part of a deal between Time Warner Cable and Sprint Nextel Corporation to bring Sprint's Pivot technology. News 9 marked its fifth year and plans to continue expanding coverage and provide better services to viewers.

39667 ■ *"Atlific Adds Management of 4 Hotels to Its Portfolio in Fort McMurray" in Canadian Corporate News (May 16, 2007)*
Pub: Comtex News Network Inc.
Description: Atlific Hotels & Resorts took over management for Merit Inn & Suites, The Merit Hotel, The Nomad Hotel and The Nomad Suites in Fort McMurray. The company feels that they will be able to increase the hotels' abilities to promote their services through their vast network of sales personnel and marketing and e-commerce team.

39668 ■ *"Attention, Please" in Entrepreneur (Vol. 36, April 2008, No. 4, pp. 52)*
Pub: Entrepreneur Media, Inc.
Ed: Andrea Cooper. **Description:** Gurbaksh Chahal created his own company ClickAgents at the age of 16, and sold it two years later for $40 million to ValueClick. He then founded BlueLithium, an online advertising network on behavioral targeting, which Yahoo! Inc. bought in 2007 for $300 million. Chahal, now 25, talks about his next plans and describes how BlueLithium caught Yahoo's attention.

39669 ■ *"Attorney Internet Marketing Services Launched by SEO Advantage at SEOLegal.com" in Internet Wire (October 5, 2009)*
Pub: Comtex News Network, Inc.
Description: SEO Advantage, an Internet marketing and website designer firm, has extended its services to the legal industry.

39670 ■ *Attracting Investors: A Marketing Approach to Finding Funds for Your Business*
Pub: John Wiley and Sons, Inc.
Ed: Philip Kotler, Hermawan Kartajaya, S. David Young. **Released:** August 2004. **Price:** $29.95 (US), $42.99 (Canadian). **Description:** Marketing experts advise entrepreneurs in ways to find investors in order to raise capital for their companies.

39671 ■ *Authenticity: What Consumers Really Want*
Pub: Harvard Business School Press
Ed: James H. Gilmore. **Released:** September 24, 2007. **Price:** $26.95. **Description:** In today's marketplace, consumers tend to buy based on how authentic a company's offer appears. A company's identity is explored through case studies and advertising slogans. The authors write from the theory that most everything is artificial, manmade, and fake.

39672 ■ *"Auto Show Taps Moms" in Marketing to Women (Vol. 21, April 2008, No. 4, pp. 3)*
Pub: EPM Communications Inc.
Contact: Ira Mayer, President
E-mail: imayer@epmcom.com
Description: Teamed with Mother Proof, an online site which features automotive content aimed at moms, the Chicago Auto Show will present a full day of programming with the emphasis on mom.

39673 ■ *"Automaker Foundations Run Leaner" in Crain's Detroit Business (Vol. 26, January 11, 2010, No. 2, pp. 1)*
Pub: Crain Communications Inc.
Ed: Sherri Welch. **Description:** Overview of the Detroit automobile industry includes restoring profitability, smarter marketing strategies and philanthropy. Each company comprising the Big 3 is examined, as is their vision for the future.

39674 ■ *"Avoiding Invention Scams" in Black Enterprise (Vol. 37, January 2007, No. 6, pp. 46)*
Pub: Earl G. Graves Publishing Co. Inc.
Ed: James C. Johnson. **Description:** Invention promotion firms provide inventors assistance in developing a prototype for product development. It is important to research these companies before making a commitment to work with them because there are a number of these firms that are not legitimate and have caused independent inventors to lose thousands of dollars by making false claims as to the market potential of the inventions.

39675 ■ *"avVaa World Health Care Products Rolls Out Internet Marketing Program" in Health and Beauty Close-Up (September 18, 2009)*
Pub: Close-Up Media
Description: avVaa World Health Care Products, Inc., a biotechnology company, manufacturer and distributor of nationally branded therapeutic, natural health care and skin products, has signed an agreement with Online Performance Marketing to launch of an Internet marketing campaign in order to broaden its presence online. The impact of advertising on the Internet to generate an increase in sales is explored.

39676 ■ *"Back to Business" in Retail Merchandiser (Vol. 51, September-October 2011, No. 5, pp. 18)*
Pub: Phoenix Media Corporation
Ed: Eric Slack. **Description:** National Football League owners and players have reached a labor agreement for the next ten years. America's football league can once again focus on providing fans with a great product both on and off the field.

39677 ■ *"Bakugan Battle Brawlers" in Advertising Age (Vol. 79, November 17, 2008, No. 43, pp. S2)*
Pub: Crain Communications, Inc.
Ed: Kate Fitzgerald. **Description:** Spin Master toys has a new hit, Bakugan Battle Brawlers, an interactive game board with 106 characters that battle with one another in tournaments. Bakugan tournaments are being held at Toys 'R' Us stores.

39678 ■ *"Balancing Risk and Return in a Customer Portfolio" in Journal of Marketing (Vol. 75, May 2011, No. 3, pp. 1)*
Pub: American Marketing Association
Ed: Crina O. Tarasi, Ruth N. Bolton, Michael D. Hutt, Beth A. Walker. **Description:** A framework for reducing the vulnerability and volatility of cash flows in customer portfolios is presented. The efficient portfolios of firms are identified and tested against their current portfolios and hypothetical profit maximization portfolios.

39679 ■ *"Banking on Twitter" in Baltimore Business Journal (Vol. 27, February 6, 2010, No. 40, pp. 1)*
Pub: American City Business Journals
Ed: Gary Haber. **Description:** Ways that banks are using Twitter, Facebook and other social networking sites to provide customer services is discussed. First Mariner Bank is one of those banks that are finding the social media platform as a great way to reach customers. Privacy issues regarding this marketing trend are examined.

39680 ■ *"Banks Deposit Reassurance, Calm Customers" in The Business Journal-Serving Greater Tampa Bay (Vol. 28, August 22, 2008)*
Pub: American City Business Journals, Inc.
Ed: Margie Manning. **Description:** Community banks in the Tampa Bay Area are training tellers and other customer care workers to help reassure customers that their deposits are safe. Other measures to reassure depositors include joining a network that allows banks to share deposits. Additional information on moves community banks are making to reassure consumers is presented.

39681 ■ *"Bar Hopping: Your Numbers At a Glance" in Inc. (January 2008, pp. 44-45)*
Pub: Gruner & Jahr USA Publishing
Ed: Michael Fitzgerald. **Description:** Software that helps any company analyze data include Crystal Xcelsius, a program that takes data from Excel documents and turns them into animated gauges, charts and graphs; CashView, a Web-based application that tracks receivables and payables; iDashboards, a Web-based programs that produces animated gauges, maps, pie charts and graphs; Corda Human Capital Management, that transforms stats like head count, productivity, and attrition into graphs and dials; NetSuite, a Web-based application that tracks key indicators; and Cognos Now, that gauges, dials, and graphs data.

39682 ■ *"Bartering Takes Businesses Back to Basics: Broker's Exchange Helps Members to Reach New Customers" in Buffalo News (July 9, 2010)*
Pub: The Buffalo News
Ed: Dino Grandoni. **Description:** Bartering clubs can help small businesses reach new customers and to expand their business.

39683 ■ *"BayTSP, NTT Data Corp. Enter Into Reseller Pact to Market Online IP Monitoring" in Professional Services Close-Up (Sept. 11, 2009)*
Pub: Close-Up Media
Description: Due to incredible interest from distributors and content owners across Asia, NTT Data Corp. will resell BayTSP's online intellectual property monitoring, enforcement, business intelligence and monetization services in Japan.

39684 ■ *"BBB Hires Marketing Firm to Attract More Businesses" in Baltimore Business*

Journal (Vol. 27, January 1, 2010, No. 35, pp. 1)
Pub: American City Business Journals
Ed: Julekha Dash. **Description:** Better Business Bureau (BBB) of Greater Maryland hired Bystry Carson & Associates Ltd. to assist in its rebranding efforts in order to entice more businesses. Bystry Carson will promote BBB's new mission at lectures, seminars, and networking events, as well as educate businesses about the agency through blogs and Twitter. BBB's services are also outlined.

39685 ■ *"BBB Reworks Logo, Grading System" in Crain's Cleveland Business (Vol. 28, October 8, 2007, No. 40, pp. 5)*
Pub: Crain Communications, Inc.
Ed: John Booth. **Description:** During the next year, the Better Business Bureau will adopt a grading system that will establish performance minimums that will make it tougher for some types of businesses to become accredited; this nationwide rebranding effort is part of a campaign to sharpen the Better Business Bureau's image.

39686 ■ *"Be Innovative In Other Ways" in Green Industry Pro (Vol. 23, March 2011, No. 3, pp. 4)*
Pub: Cygnus Business Media
Ed: Rod Dickens. **Description:** Emphasis is put on the importance of putting the customer first in order to successfully market any product or service. Six marketing ideas are presented to promote a landscaping business.

39687 ■ *"Because Kids Need To Be Heard: Tina Wells: Buzz Marketing Group: Voorhees, New Jersey" in Inc. (Volume 32, December 2010)*
Pub: Inc. Magazine
Ed: Tamara Schweitzer. **Description:** Profile of Tina Wells, founder and CEO of Buzz Marketing Group, who writes a tween book series called Mackenzie Blue to reach young girls.

39688 ■ *"Become A Brand" in Women Entrepreneur (September 14, 2008)*
Pub: Entrepreneur Media Inc.
Ed: Suzy Girard-Ruttenberg. **Description:** Powerful brands are effective, innovative, exclusive or even socially conscious; it is important for small businesses to understand the power of becoming a brand since it is one of the best ways in which to position one's company and drive its growth.

39689 ■ *Behind the Cloud*
Pub: Jossey-Bass
Ed: Marc Benioff, Carlye Adler. **Released:** 2010. **Price:** $27.95. **Description:** Salesforce.com is the world's most successful business-to-business cloud-computing company that sells an online service that helps businesses manage sales, customer service, and marketing functions.

39690 ■ *"Being all a-Twitter" in Canadian Business (Vol. 81, December 8, 2008, No. 21, pp. 22)*
Pub: Rogers Media Ltd.
Ed: Andrew Wahl. **Description:** Marketing experts suggest that advertising strategies have to change along with new online social media. Companies are advised to find ways to incorporate social software because workers and customers are expected to continue its use.

39691 ■ *"Ben & Jerry" in Ice Cream Reporter (Vol. 21, August 20, 2008, No. 9, pp. 7)*
Pub: Ice Cream Reporter
Description: Ben & Jerry's created a limited-batch ice cream to honor singer Elton John when he performed in Vermont. The treat was called 'Goodbye Yellow Brick Road' and featured chocolate ice cream, peanut butter cookie dough, butter brickle, and white chocolate chunks.

39692 ■ *"Best Buy's CEO On Learning to Love Social Media" in Harvard Business Review (Vol. 88, December 2010, No. 12, pp. 43)*
Pub: Harvard Business School Publishing
Ed: Brian J. Dunn. **Description:** Effective utilization of online social networks to enhance brand identity, connect with consumers, and address bad publicity scenarios is examined.

39693 ■ *"Better Business: Get Ready (Marketing Strategies for Better Sales Performance)" in Entrepreneur (Vol. 35, October 2007, No. 10)*
Pub: Entrepreneur Media Inc.
Ed: Gwen Moran. **Description:** Good sales practice increases sales performance and revenue. Sales consultant Paul S. Goldner believes that salespeople should research prospective clients before negotiating with them, while another consultant, Chet Holmes thinks that companies should support their salespeople and set sales performance standards. Other proven effective marketing strategies are presented.

39694 ■ *"Better ROI Or Your Money Back, Says Buzz Agency" in Advertising Age (Vol. 79, July 14, 2008, No. 7, pp. 1)*
Pub: Crain Communications, Inc.
Ed: Michael Bush. **Description:** Word-of-mouth marketing is discussed as well as the impact on the advertising industry. Although many firms specializing in this form of marketing have opened over the past few years, many marketers are reluctant to try this route.

39695 ■ *"Better Than New" in Bellingham Business Journal (Vol. February 2010, pp. 16)*
Pub: Sound Publishing Inc.
Ed: Ashley Mitchell. **Description:** Profile of family owned Better Than New clothing store that sells overstock items from department stores and clothing manufacturers. The stores location makes it easy to miss and its only advertising is a large sign posted outside. This is the sixth store owned by the couple, Keijeo and Sirba Halmekanqas.

39696 ■ *"Beverage Brand Vies To Be the Latest Purple Prince" in Brandweek (Vol. 49, April 21, 2008, No. 16, pp. 20)*
Pub: VNU Business Media, Inc.
Ed: Becky Ebenkamp. **Description:** Profile on the new beverage product Purple and its founder, Ted Farnsworth; Purple is a drink that blends seven antioxidant-rich juices to create what Mr. Farnsworth calls a 'Cascade Effect' that boosts antioxidants' effectiveness. Mr. Farnsworth is marketing the brand's Oxygen Radical Absorbance Capability (ORAC) which is a value of 7,600 compared with orange juice's 1,200.

39697 ■ *Beyond Buzz: The Next Generation of Word-of-Mouth Marketing*
Pub: AMACOM
Ed: Lois Kelly. **Released:** March 2007. **Price:** $24. 95. **Description:** New marketing ideas to bring attention to any small business are showcased.

39698 ■ *"Beyond YouTube: New Uses for Video, Online and Off" in Inc. (October 2007, pp. 53-54)*
Pub: Gruner & Jahr USA Publishing
Ed: Leah Hoffmann. **Description:** Small companies are using video technology for embedding messages into email, broadcasting live interactive sales and training seminars, as well as marketing campaigns. Experts offer insight into producing and broadcasting business videos.

39699 ■ *"Bioheat - Alternative for Fueling Equipment" in Indoor Comfort Marketing (Vol. 70, May 2011, No. 5, pp. 14)*
Pub: Industry Publications Inc.
Ed: Gary Hess. **Description:** Profile of Worley and Obetz, supplier of biofuels used as an alternative for fueling industry equipment.

39700 ■ *"BK Franchisees Lose Sleep Over Late-Night Rule" in Advertising Age (Vol. 79, August 11, 2008, No. 31, pp. 1)*
Pub: Crain Communications, Inc.
Ed: Emily Bryson York. **Description:** Burger King's corporate headquarters mandates that franchisees remain open until at least 2 a.m. Three Miami operators have filed a lawsuit that alleges the extended hours can be dangerous, do not make money and overtax the workforce.

39701 ■ *"BK Menu Gives Casual Dining Reason to Worry" in Advertising Age (Vol. 79, November 17, 2008, No. 43, pp. 12)*
Pub: Crain Communications, Inc.
Ed: Emily Bryson York. **Description:** Burger King is beginning to compete with such casual dining restaurants as Applebees and the Cheesecake Factory with new premium menu items, including thicker burgers and ribs; statistical data regarding the casual dining segment which continues to fall and Burger King, whose sales continue to rise is included.

39702 ■ *"Black Diamond Holdings Corp. Receives SEC Approval" in Canadian Corporate News (May 16, 2007)*
Pub: Comtex News Network Inc.
Description: Black Diamond Holdings, Corp., a British Columbia domiciled company and its two wholly owned subsidiaries are engaged in the bottling, importation, distribution, marketing, and brand creation of premium spirits and wines to worldwide consumers, announced that it has completed the SEC review process and has applied to list for trading in the United States on the OTC.BB.

39703 ■ *"Blue Bell Touts Non-Shrinkage" in Ice Cream Reporter (Vol. 21, July 20, 2008, No. 8, pp. 1)*
Pub: Ice Cream Reporter
Description: Blue Bell Ice Cream is promoting its decision to keep their ice cream products in a full half-gallon container rather than downsizing the package. Thirty-second television ads contrast the move by other ice cream makers to offer less for the same money.

39704 ■ *"Blue Cross Confronts Baby Blues" in Marketing to Women (Vol. 21, March 2008, No. 3, pp. 3)*
Pub: EPM Communications Inc.
Contact: Ira Mayer, President
E-mail: imayer@epmcom.com
Description: Blue Cross of California has launched a Maternity Depression Program aimed at educating mothers suffering from postpartum depression.

39705 ■ *"Blue Cross to Put Kiosk in Mall" in News & Observer (November 9, 2010)*
Pub: News & Observer
Ed: Alan M. Wolf. **Description:** Blue Cross and Blue Shield of North Carolina has placed a kiosk in Durham's Streets of Southpoint in order to market its health insurance.

39706 ■ *"Blue Hill Tavern to Host Baltimore's First Cupcake Camp" in Daily Record (August 10, 2011)*
Pub: Dolan Company
Ed: Rachel Bernstein. **Description:** Cities joining the trend to host cupcake camps are listed. The camps are open to all individuals wishing to share and eat cupcakes in an open environment.

39707 ■ *"Boise-based Highway 12 Invests in Crowdsourcing Platform" in Idaho Business Review (September 24, 2010)*
Pub: Dolan Media Newswires
Ed: Simon Shifrin. **Description:** The only venture capital fund in Idaho, Highway 12 Ventures, is funding Kapost a new company that helps news Websites, blogs and other online venues to pull content from a larger network of writers.

39708 ■ *"Book of Lists 2010" in Philadelphia Business Journal (Vol. 28, December 25, 2009, No. 45, pp. 1)*
Pub: American City Business Journals
Description: Rankings of companies and organizations within the banking, biotechnology, economic development, healthcare, hospitality, law and accounting, marketing and media, real estate, and technology industries in the Philadelphia, Pennsylvania area are presented. Rankings are based on sales, business size, and more.

39709 ■ ***BOOM: Marketing to the Ultimate Power Consumer-The Baby-Boomer Woman***
Pub: American Management Association
Contact: Charles R. Craig, Chairman
Ed: Mary Brown; Carol Orsborn. **Released:** 2006. **Price:** $24.00.

39710 ■ ***"Booze Makers Battle Over Turkey Day" in Advertising Age (Vol. 78, October 29, 2007, No. 43, pp. 4)***
Pub: Crain Communications, Inc.
Ed: Jeremy Mullman. **Description:** Beer and wine marketers are jockeying for position in regards to the Thanksgiving holiday.

39711 ■ ***"Bottoms Up!" in Entrepreneur (Vol. 36, April 2008, No. 4, pp. 128)***
Pub: Entrepreneur Media, Inc.
Ed: Amanda C. Kooser. **Description:** Jill Bernheimer launched her online alcohol business Domaine547 in 2007, and encountered challenges as legal issues over the licensing and launching of the business took about seven months to finish. Domain547 features blog and forum areas. Marketing strategy that connects to the social community is one of the ways to reach out to customers.

39712 ■ ***Bradford's International Directory of Marketing Research Agencies***
Pub: Business Research Services Inc.
Contact: Thomas D. Johnson, President
URL(s): www.bradfordsdirectory.com. **Released:** Biennial; Latest edition 30th. **Price:** $95, Individuals in-print; $95, Individuals CD-ROM; $125, Individuals in print and CD-ROM. **Covers:** Over 2,300 marketing research agencies worldwide. Includes domestic and international demographic data and professional association contacts. **Entries include:** Company name, address, phone, name and title of contact, date founded, number of employees, description of products or services, e-mail, URL. **Arrangement:** Geographical. **Indexes:** Alphabetical by company.

39713 ■ ***"Branching Out" in Canadian Business (Vol. 79, July 17, 2006, No. 14-15, pp. 41)***
Pub: Rogers Media
Description: Visa selected this narrative in an attempt to show the company's usefulness.

39714 ■ ***"Brand Imaging" in Small Business Opportunities (November 2010)***
Pub: Harris Publications Inc.
Ed: Karen Harnesk. **Description:** Design and branding pro shares strategies and tips to help guide any small business' image development.

39715 ■ ***"Brand Police Keep the Lines Distinct at GM" in Automotive News (Vol. 86, October 31, 2011, No. 6488, pp. 3)***
Pub: Crain Communications Inc.
Ed: Mike Colias. **Description:** Joel Ewanick, marketing chief at General Motors, is working to keep General Motor's four brands distinct within their brands.

39716 ■ ***"Branding Specialist" in Black Enterprise (Vol. 38, July 2008, No. 12, pp. 1)***
Pub: Earl G. Graves Publishing Co. Inc.
Ed: Faith Chukwudi. **Description:** Interview with Wonya Lucas who is the chief marketing officer for Discovery Communications and is known for building strong brands by understanding her audience and generating buy-in throughout the organization; Lucas discusses her role in the corporation, guerilla marketing techniques, and what companies tend to overlook in marketing their products or services.

39717 ■ ***"Branding Your Way" in Canadian Business (Vol. 80, February 12, 2007, No. 4, pp. 31)***
Pub: Rogers Media
Ed: Erin Pooley. **Description:** The trend in involving consumers in brand marketing by seeking their views through contests or inviting them to produce and submit commercials through Internet is discussed.

39718 ■ ***"Brands' Mass Appeal" in ADWEEK (Vol. 51, June 14, 2010, No. 24)***
Pub: Nielsen Business Media Inc.
Ed: Lisa Thorell, James Sherret. **Description:** Engineering/science crowdsourced projects tend to result from posting and/or publishing interim results as well as from other talents building upon those results to produce even better results. However, the author does not see the same results in the creative world.

39719 ■ ***"Brewing Up a Brand" in Canadian Business (Vol. 80, February 26, 2007, No. 5, pp. 68)***
Pub: Rogers Media
Ed: Clavin Leung. **Description:** The marketing strategies adopted by Molson Coors Brewing Company, to improve customer loyalty to the Coors Light brand, are presented.

39720 ■ ***"Bridging the Academic-Practitioner Divide in Marketing Decision Models" in Journal of Marketing (Vol. 75, July 2011, No. 4, pp. 196)***
Pub: American Marketing Association
Ed: Gary L. Lilien. **Description:** A study to determine the reason for the relatively low level of practical use of the many marketing models is presented. Changing the incentive and reward systems for marketing academics, practitioners, and intermediaries can bring about adoption and implementation improvements. Those changes could be beneficial by bridging the academic-practitioner divide.

39721 ■ ***Briefs for Building Better Brands: Tips, Parables and Insight into Market Leaders***
Pub: AGCD Brandspa Books
Ed: Allan Gorman. **Released:** September 2004. **Description:** In today's marketplace, a company needs to gain consumer trust in order to build a brand. By gaining trust, the brand gets sold by word-of-mouth publicity. The author calls this type of marketing: guerrilla marketing, and he believes it to be more effective than traditional advertising.

39722 ■ ***"Bright Lights, Big Impact: Why Digital Billboards are Growing in Popularity" in Inc. (March 2008, pp. 61-62)***
Pub: Gruner & Jahr USA Publishing
Ed: Sarah Goldstein. **Description:** Clear Channel provides high tech digital billboards which allow companies to change advertising as often as necessary during a contract period. The Outdoor Advertising Association of America predicts the growth of digital billboards at several hundred per year over the next few years. CEO of Magic Media believes all billboards will eventually go digital.

39723 ■ ***"Brite-Strike Tactical Launches New Internet Marketing Initiatives" in Internet Wire (September 15, 2009)***
Pub: Comtex News Network, Inc.
Description: Brite-Strike Tactical Illumination Products, Inc. has enlisted the expertise of Internet marketing guru Thomas J. McCarthy to help revamp the company's Internet campaign. An outline of the Internet marketing strategy is provided.

39724 ■ ***"The British Aren't Coming" in Crain's Chicago Business (Vol. 34, October 24, 2011, No. 42, pp. 3)***
Pub: Crain Communications Inc.
Ed: Brigid Sweeney. **Description:** In a move to attract tourists back to Chicago, its Convention and Tourism Bureau is marketing in London, England, Mexico, and Canada, but not Germany or France because of budget constraints.

39725 ■ ***"Broadcast Commercial Acceptance" in MarketingMagazine (Vol. 115, September 27, 2010, No. 13, pp. 29)***
Pub: Rogers Publishing Ltd.
Description: Advertising rules for the broadcast commercial industry in Canada are reviewed.

39726 ■ ***"The Buck Stops Here" in Canadian Business (Vol. 81, November 10, 2008, No. 19, pp. 25)***
Pub: Rogers Media Ltd.
Ed: Sarka Halas. **Description:** Reputation strategist Leslie Gaines-Ross says that minimizing the damage followed by the identification of what went wrong are the first steps that companies need to take when trying to salvage their reputation. Gaines-Ross states that it is up to the CEO to ensure the company's speedy recovery and they need to be at the forefront of the process.

39727 ■ ***"Building a Better Twitter Brand: My Foray Into Social Analytics" in Inc. (Vol. , pp.)***
Pub: Inc. Magazine
Ed: John Brandon. **Description:** A small business using Twitter to research and promote the firm decided to test some Web-based dashboards that allow you to manage and analyze accounts on multiple social media networks including Facebook, Twitter, and LinkedIn.

39728 ■ ***Building Buzz to Beat the Big Boys***
Pub: Greenwood Publishing Group, Inc.
Ed: Steve O'Leary; Kim Sheehan. **Released:** March 30, 2008. **Price:** $39.95. **Description:** Seventy to eighty percent of small retail stores fail within the first five years of opening due to competition from big-box retailers and online stores. Service providers and small retailers should capitalize on the fact that they are local and can connect on a personal level with customers in a way the big stores cannot. Word of mouth marketing methods are very critical to any small retail or service company. This book is designed to help any small business compete against large competitors.

39729 ■ ***Building Buzz to Beat the Big Boys***
Pub: Greenwood Publishing Group Inc.
Contact: Janann Sherman, Manager
Ed: Steve O'Leary. **Released:** March 2008. **Price:** $39.95. **Description:** Marketing methods to help small retailers compete against big box stores are examined. It is important for local stores to create a strong customer base.

39730 ■ ***"Building Confidence" in Black Enterprise (Vol. 38, January 2008, No. 6, pp. 50)***
Pub: Earl G. Graves Publishing Co. Inc.
Ed: Marcia A. Reed-Woodard. **Description:** Patriot Management in Chicago offers courses at its Investment Management Training Academy for the institutional asset management and investment sector. Classes are designed to help build investor confidence amid the scandals that hit the financial, investment and asset management industry.

39731 ■ ***Business Black Belt: Develop the Strength, Flexibility and Agility to Run Your Company***
Pub: Career Press, Inc.
Ed: Burke Franklin. **Released:** November 1, 2010. **Price:** $15.99. **Description:** Manual offering insights that will enable anyone to become successful in small business. Seventy short chapters included topics such as attitude, management, marketing, selling, employees, money, MBAs, lawyers, consultants, and investors.

39732 ■ ***"Business Forecast: Stormy and Successful" in Women In Business (Vol. 62, June 2010, No. 2, pp. 12)***
Pub: American Business Women's Association
Ed: Kathleen Leighton. **Description:** Stormy Simon, vice president of customer service at Overstock.com is a self-made career woman who started out as a temporary employee in the company in 2001. She was not able to attend college because she had two sons to care for after her divorce. Simon got involved in advertising and media buying and shares her love for business.

39733 ■ ***Business Marketing Association--Membership & Resource Directory***
Pub: Business Marketing Association
Contact: Rick Kean, Executive Director
URL(s): marketing.org/i4a/pages/index.cfm?pageid=1. **Released:** Annual; January. **Covers:**

Over 4,500 member business communications professionals in fields of advertising, marketing communications, and marketing; their service and supply companies are listed in the "Marketing Resources" section. **Entries include:** For individuals--Name, title, company with which affiliated, address, phone. For companies--Name, address, phone, contact, description of products or services. **Arrangement:** Individuals are alphabetical within chapter; companies are classified by product or service. **Indexes:** Alpha, company, chapter.

39734 ■ *"The Business Value of Social Networks" in Agency Sales Magazine (Vol. 39, July 2009, No. 7, pp. 44)*
Pub: MANA
Ed: Daniel Burrus. **Description:** Personal and business uses of several Web 2.0 tools for salespeople are discussed. Leading questions which will guide salespeople in finding out if one particular tool will benefit them are presented.

39735 ■ *Business Warrior: Strategy for Entrepreneurs*
Pub: Clearbridge Publishing
Ed: Sun Tzu. **Released:** September 2006. **Price:** $19.95. **Description:** Advice to help entrepreneurs understand competitive strategies in order to succeed, focusing on sales, marketing, and personnel management.

39736 ■ *"BusinessOnLine Launches a New Web-Based Search Engine Optimization Tool" in Internet Wire (October 19, 2009)*
Pub: Comtex News Network, Inc.
Description: First Link Checker, a complimentary new search engine optimization tool that helps site owners optimize their on-page links by understanding which of those links are actually being counted in Google's relevancy algorithm, was developed by BusinessOnLine, a rapidly growing Internet marketing agency. This tool will make it easy for the average web master to ensure that their internal link structure is optimized.

39737 ■ *Busting the Myth of the Heroic CEO*
Pub: Cornell University Press
Contact: John G. Ackerman, Director
E-mail: jga4@cornell.edu
Ed: Michel Villette, Catherine Vuillermot. **Released:** 2010. **Price:** $24.95. **Description:** According to the authors, corporate leaders do not get ahead through productive risk-taking and innovation, but through ruthless exploitation of market imperfections and rivals.

39738 ■ *"Buy Local to Land Great Deals" in Inside Business (Vol. 13, September-October 2011, No. 5, pp. SS8)*
Pub: Great Lakes Publishing Co.
Description: Buy Lakewood! Loyalty Program offers residents great bargains for shopping at local retailers. Residents sign up online and the city mails them a letter of appreciations along with a key card. Showing the key card at any participating businesses listed on the Website will provide discounts.

39739 ■ *"Buy the Pants, Save the Planet?" in Globe & Mail (February 5, 2007, pp. B1)*
Pub: CTVglobemedia Publishing Inc.
Ed: Keith McArthur. **Description:** The marketing campaign of the clothing company Diesel S.p.A. is discussed. The company has based its latest collection of T-shirt designs on the problem of global warming.

39740 ■ *"Buying In" in Harvard Business Review (Vol. 86, September 2008, No. 9, pp. 36)*
Pub: Harvard Business School Press
Ed: Andrew O'Connell. **Description:** Review of the book entitled, 'Buying In: The Secret Dialogue between What We Buy and Who We Are' which offers tips that those in the field of marketing will find useful.

39741 ■ *Buying In: The Secret Dialogue Between What We Buy and Who We Are*
Pub: Random House
Ed: Rob Walker. **Released:** 2008. **Price:** $25.00. **Description:** The book offers a look at the state of advertising today and shows why even those who feel like they see through marketing feel attached to specific brands as a way to both project and foster their identities.

39742 ■ *"Buying Power of Hispanics Growing" in Austin Business JournalInc. (Vol. 29, November 27, 2009, No. 38, pp. 1)*
Pub: American City Business Journals
Ed: Sandra Zaragoza. **Description:** Hispanic Marketing Symposium presented a report stating that the buying power of Hispanics of Austin, Texas has grown by 54 percent in last five years to $9.4 billion in 2009. Details on the projected growth of the Hispanic market in the are is covered.

39743 ■ *Buyology: Truth and Lies About Why We Buy*
Pub: Doubleday, a Division of Random House
Ed: Martin Lindstrom. **Released:** 2009. **Price:** $24.95. **Description:** Marketers study brain scans to determine how consumers rate Nokia, Coke, and Ford products.

39744 ■ *"Buzz Marketing for Movies" in Business Horizons (September-October 2007, pp. 395)*
Pub: Elsevier Technology Publications
Ed: Iris Mohr. **Description:** Application of buzz marketing through the context of movie differentiation strategies such as cosmetic movie features, differentiation to reach market segments, growing a movie segment, positioning to support the movie image, positioning to extend the movie image, and differentiation via non-traditional channels are all discussed.

39745 ■ *"Calendar" in Crain's Detroit Business (Vol. 24, October 6, 2008, No. 40, pp. 22)*
Pub: Crain Communications, Inc.
Description: Listing of events in the Detroit area include conferences addressing entrepreneurialism, economic development, manufacturing, marketing, the housing crisis and women business ownership.

39746 ■ *"Calendar" in Crain's Detroit Business (Vol. 26, January 18, 2010, No. 3, pp. 16)*
Pub: Crain Communications Inc.
Description: Listing of events includes seminars sponsored by the Detroit Economic Club as well as conferences dealing with globalization and marketing.

39747 ■ *Call Me Ted*
Pub: Grand Central Publishing
Ed: Ted Turner. **Released:** 2008. **Price:** $30.00. **Description:** Media mogul, Ted Turner's biography is full of personal and business details from his careers in advertising and broadcasting.

39748 ■ *"Calling An Audible" in The Business Journal-Milwaukee (Vol. 25, August 1, 2008, No. 45, pp. A1)*
Pub: American City Business Journals, Inc.
Ed: David Dedge. **Description:** Tough economic conditions are forcing entertainment businesses in Milwaukee, Wisconsin, to try new business strategies to keep attracting customers. These strategies include keeping prices steady despite increasing costs and new sales promotions.

39749 ■ *"Campaigner Survey: 46 Percent of Small Businesses Use Email Marketing" in Wireless News (November 21, 2009)*
Pub: Close-Up Media
Description: Almost half (46 percent) of small businesses surveyed by Campaigner's 2009 State of Small Business Online Marketing, say that they rely on email marketing to help them find new customers, keep existing ones and grow their businesses. The survey also found that 36 percent of small businesses plan to begin using email marketing over the next year. The trend to utilize Internet marketing tools is allowing small businesses to grow faster and generate higher revenues than those that are not using these mediums.

39750 ■ *"Canadian Hydronics Businesses Promote 'Beautiful Heat" in Indoor Comfort Marketing (Vol. 70, September 2011, No. 9, pp. 20)*
Pub: Industry Publications Inc.
Description: Canadian hydronics companies are promoting their systems as beautiful heat. Hydronics is the use of water as the heat-transfer medium in heating and cooling system.

39751 ■ *"Canadian Market Data" in MarketingMagazine (Vol. 115, September 27, 2010, No. 13, pp. 6)*
Pub: Rogers Publishing Ltd.
Description: Canadian marketing statistics are outlined.

39752 ■ *"Canadians Love Their Magazines" in MarketingMagazine (Vol. 115, September 27, 2010, No. 13, pp. 42)*
Pub: Rogers Publishing Ltd.
Description: Market data covering magazine published or consumed in Canada is presented.

39753 ■ *"Canon Focuses on New Moms" in Marketing to Women (Vol. 21, January 2008, No. 1, pp. 3)*
Pub: EPM Communications Inc.
Contact: Ira Mayer, President
E-mail: imayer@epmcom.com
Description: Canon launches a photo contest aimed at spotlighting baby's first pictures in an attempt to connect with new mothers.

39754 ■ *"Capture New Markets" in Pet Product News (Vol. 64, December 2010, No. 12, pp. 12)*
Pub: BowTie Inc.
Ed: Ethan Mizer. **Description:** Flea and tick treatments are among the product categories that can be offered in order to clinch new markets. With the help of manufacturers, pet store retailers are encouraged to educate themselves about these products considering that capturing markets involves variations in customer perceptions. Retailers would then be deemed as resources and sources for these products.

39755 ■ *"Capturing Generation Y: Ready, Set, Transform" in Credit Union Times (Vol. 21, July 14, 2010, No. 27, pp. 20)*
Pub: Summit Business Media
Ed: Senthil Kumar. **Description:** The financial services sector recognizes that Generation Y will have a definite impact on the way business is conducted in the future. The mindset of Generation Y is social and companies need to use networking tools such as Facebook in order to reach this demographic.

39756 ■ *"CarTango Lauches Site for Women" in Marketing to Women (Vol. 21, April 2008, No. 4, pp. 5)*
Pub: EPM Communications Inc.
Contact: Ira Mayer, President
E-mail: imayer@epmcom.com
Description: CarTango.com is an Internet site that seeks to overcome what women say are dismissive or pushy salespeople by allowing the shoppers the chance to decide what they want before inviting dealers to compete for their business.

39757 ■ *"CBS" in Brandweek (Vol. 49, April 21, 2008, No. 16, pp. SR6)*
Pub: VNU Business Media, Inc.
Ed: John Consoli. **Description:** Provides contact information for sales and marketing personnel for the CBS network as well as a listing of the station's top programming and an analysis of the current season and the target audience for those programs running in the current season.

39758 ■ *"CBS Television Distribution" in Brandweek (Vol. 49, April 21, 2008, No. 16, pp. SR13)*
Pub: VNU Business Media, Inc.
Ed: Marc Berman. **Description:** Provides contact information for sales and marketing personnel for CBS Television Distribution as well as a listing of the station's top programming and an analysis of the current season and the target audience for those

programs running in the current season. Due to the unprecedented, decade-plus advantage of first-run leaders such as Wheel of Fortune, Oprah, Judge Judy and Entertainment Tonight, CBS is poised to remain a leader among the syndicates.

39759 ■ *"Cell Phone the Ticket on American Airlines" in Chicago Tribune (November 14, 2008)*
Pub: McClatchy-Tribune Information Services
Ed: Julie Johnsson. **Description:** American Airlines is testing a new mobile boarding pass at O'Hare International Airport. Travelers on American can board flights and get through security checkpoints by flashing a bar code on their phones. Passengers must have an Internet-enabled mobile device and an active e-mail address in order to utilize this service.

39760 ■ *"Change Agent; What Peter Francese Says You Need to Know" in Advertising Age (Vol. 79, July 7, 2008, No. 26, pp. 13)*
Pub: Crain Communications, Inc.
Ed: Peter Francese. **Description:** Advice for marketers on how to deal effectively with a changing consumer base is given.

39761 ■ *"The Changing Face of the U.S. Consumer" in Advertising Age (Vol. 79, July 7, 2008, No. 26, pp. 1)*
Pub: Crain Communications, Inc.
Ed: Peter Francese. **Description:** It is essential for marketers to examine demographic shifts when looking at ways in which to market brands. The average head-of-households is aging and marketers must not continue to ignore them. Statistical data included.

39762 ■ *"Changing Fuel Compositions: What It Means To You and Your Business" in Indoor Comfort Marketing (Vol. 70, June 2011, No. 6, pp. 30)*
Pub: Industry Publications Inc.
Ed: Paul Nazzaro. **Description:** Biofuels are outlined and the way it is changing the HVAC/R industry are discussed.

39763 ■ *"Charlotte Pipe Launches Satirical Campaign" in Contractor (Vol. 57, January 2010, No. 1, pp. 6)*
Pub: Penton Media, Inc.
Description: Charlotte Pipe and Foundry Co. launched an advertising campaign that uses social media and humor to make a point about how it can be nearly impossible to determine if imported cast iron pipes and fittings meet the same quality standards as what is made in the U.S. The campaign features 'pipe whisperers' and also spoofs pipe sniffing dogs.

39764 ■ *"Cheese Spread Whips Up a Brand New Bowl" in Brandweek (Vol. 49, April 21, 2008, No. 16, pp. 17)*
Pub: VNU Business Media, Inc.
Ed: Mike Beirne. **Description:** Mrs. Kinser's Pimento Cheese Spread is launching a new container for its product in order to attempt stronger brand marketing with a better bowl in order to win over the heads of households as young as in their 30s. The company also intends to begin distribution in Texas and the West Coast. Mrs. Kinser's is hoping that the new packaging will provide a more distinct branding and will help consumers distinguish what flavor they are buying.

39765 ■ *"Chesapeake Beach Resort and Spa Announces Dream Waterfront Wedding Giveaway" in Benzinga.com (October 29, 2011)*
Pub: Benzinga.com
Ed: Benzinga Staff. **Description:** Chesapeake Beach Resort and Spa will give away a Dream Waterfront Wedding to a lucky bride and groom in order to promote their resort as a wedding venue.

39766 ■ *"Chew On This: Soul Fans to 'Chew' Games' First Play" in Philadelphia Business Journal (Vol. 30, September 30, 2011, No. 33, pp. 3)*
Pub: American City Business Journals Inc.
Ed: John George. **Description:** Arena football team Philadelphia Soul extended its marketing partnership with Just Born Inc. The team's fans will enter a contest where the winner will be allowed to select the team's first play during a home game.

39767 ■ *"Chief Boo Boo Officer" in Marketing to Women (Vol. 21, February 2008, No. 2, pp. 1)*
Pub: EPM Communications Inc.
Contact: Ira Mayer, President
E-mail: imayer@epmcom.com
Ed: Ellen Neuborne. **Description:** Pharmaceutical companies are reaching out to women through innovative marketing techniques.

39768 ■ *"Chiefs Hope Renovations Score Big With Sponsors" in The Business Journal-Serving Metropolitan Kansas City (Vol. 26, July 11, 2008)*
Pub: American City Business Journals, Inc.
Ed: James Dornbrook. **Description:** Kansas City Chiefs officials expect to obtain 12 to 14 new major sponsors with the completion of the Arrowhead Stadium renovations. The new sponsorship opportunities will include naming rights for the stadium and practice facility. The team's marketing strategies are discussed.

39769 ■ *"City Slickers" in Canadian Business (Vol. 81, March 31, 2008, No. 5, pp. 36)*
Pub: Rogers Media
Ed: Joe Castaldo. **Description:** Richard Florida believes that the creative class drives the economy and the prosperity of countries depends on attracting and retaining these people. Florida has brought attention to developing livable and economically vibrant cities thanks in part to his promotional skills. However, he has also drawn critics who see his data on his theories as flimsy and inadequate.

39770 ■ *"Clean Bathrooms Are Big Key to Convenience Store's Success" in Marketing to Women (Vol. 23, January 2010, No. 1, pp. 3)*
Pub: EPM Communications Inc.
Contact: Ira Mayer, President
E-mail: imayer@epmcom.com
Description: Buc-ee's, a Texas-based convenience store chain, is attributing its large female consumer base to the cleanliness of its bathrooms. The chain actually markets itself specifically to female consumers.

39771 ■ *"ClickFuel Launches New Products to Help Small and Mid-Sized Businesses Bolster Their Brand Online" in Internet Wire (Dec. 3,2009)*
Pub: Comtex News Network, Inc.
Description: Boostability, a provider of Enterprise Search Engine Optimization (SEO) software technology, has partnered with ClickFuel, a firm that designs, tracks and manages Internet marketing campaigns in order to leverage Boostability's technology in order to deliver comprehensive SEO solutions to small and mid-size businesses; three new products will also become available for these business clients to help them manage all facets of their online presence.

39772 ■ *"ClickFuel Launches New Products to Help Small and Mid-Sized Businesses Bolster Their Brand Online" in Internet Wire (Dec. 3, 2009)*
Pub: Comtex News Network, Inc.
Description: Boostability, a provider of Enterprise Search Engine Optimization (SEO) software technology, has partnered with ClickFuel, a firm that designs, tracks and manages Internet marketing campaigns in order to leverage Boostability's technology in order to deliver comprehensive SEO solutions to small and mid-size businesses; three new products will also become available for these business clients to help them manage all facets of their online presence.

39773 ■ *"ClickFuel Unveils Internet Marketing Tools for Small Businesses" in Internet Wire (October 19, 2009)*
Pub: Comtex News Network, Inc.
Description: ClickFuel, a firm that manages, designs and tracks marketing campaigns has unveiled a full software suite of affordable services and technology solutions designed to empower small business owners and help them promote and grow their businesses through targeted Internet marketing campaigns.

39774 ■ *"Clicks For Cash: Earning More From Your Website" in Inc. (December 2007, pp. 64-65)*
Pub: Gruner & Jahr USA Publishing
Ed: Michael Fitzgerald. **Description:** Ways to use a company's Website to generate revenue are discussed. Free services for placing ads include Google AdSense, AdBrite, AuctionAds, Chitkia eMiniMalls, Vizu Answers, and Value Click; profiles of each service are presented.

39775 ■ *"Clinic to Use Medical Summit to Pump Up Cardiology Center" in Crain's Cleveland Business (Vol. 28, October 1, 2007, No. 39, pp. 6)*
Pub: Crain Communications, Inc.
Ed: Chuck Soder. **Description:** Overview of the Medical Innovation Summit, sponsored by the Cleveland Clinic and regional business recruitment group Team NEO, whose theme was cardiology. The goal for this year's summit went beyond finding companies for the cardiovascular center, it also looked to market the region to other industries with growth potential.

39776 ■ *"Closing the Marketing Capabilities Gap" in Journal of Marketing (Vol. 75, July 2011, No. 4, pp. 183)*
Pub: American Marketing Association
Ed: George S. Day. **Description:** A look at the growing gap between the demands of the market and the capacity of organizations is presented. New thinking about marketing capabilities is needed to close the gap between the accelerating complexities of their market needs. The adaptive capabilities needed are vigilant market learning, adaptive market experimentation, and open marketing.

39777 ■ *"The CMO of Consequence" in Business Strategy Review (Vol. 21, Autumn 2010, No. 3, pp. 42)*
Pub: Wiley-Blackwell
Ed: D. Eric Boyd, Rajesh K. Chandy, Marcus Cunha. **Description:** Do chief marketing officers matter? Some say that CMOs have limited effect on corporate performance and don't add significant value to the firm. The authors agree that the job in many firms is in great peril, but their research has uncovered why the contributions of some CMOs are invaluable.

39778 ■ *"CMO Nicholson Exits Pepsi as Share Declines" in Advertising Age (Vol. 79, July 7, 2008, No. 26, pp. 4)*
Pub: Crain Communications, Inc.
Ed: Natalie Zmuda. **Description:** Cie Nicholson, the chief marketing officer at Pepsi-Cola UK, is leaving the company at a time when its market share is down; the brand, which was known for its dynamic marketing, has diverted much of its attention from its core brands and shifted attention to the ailing Gatorade brand as well as Sobe Life Water and Amp.

39779 ■ *"Colores Origenes: Martha Kruse" in Advertising Age (Vol. 77, November 13, 2006, No. 46, pp. S12)*
Pub: Crain Communications, Inc.
Ed: Laurel Wentz. **Description:** Home Depot has created a range of Latin paint colors called Colores Origenes; the new line was originally intended to launch only at locations with heavily Hispanic patrons but the company decided to make the line available at all of their stores.

39780 ■ *"Comcast Networks" in Brandweek (Vol. 49, April 21, 2008, No. 16, pp. SR9)*
Pub: VNU Business Media, Inc.
Ed: Anthony Crupi. **Description:** Provides contact information for sales and marketing personnel for the Comcast networks as well as a listing of the station's top programming and an analysis of the current season and the target audience for those programs running in the current season. Experts believe Comcast will continue to acquire more stations into their portfolio.

39781 ■ *"Come One, Come All" in Black Enterprise (Vol. 38, October 2007, No. 3, pp. 58)*
Pub: Earl G. Graves Publishing Co. Inc.
Ed: Tennille M. Robinson. **Description:** Ways to market a restaurant are cited.

39782 ■ *"Come Together" in Pet Product News (Vol. 64, December 2010, No. 12, pp. 28)*
Pub: BowTie Inc.
Ed: Lizett Bond. **Description:** Pet supply retailers have posted improved sales and improved customer service by bundling their offerings. Bundling pertains to grouping related items such as collars and leashes into a single unit for marketing purposes. Aside from providing convenience and enhanced product information to customers, bundling has facilitated more efficient purchases.

39783 ■ *"Commensurate with Experience" in Entrepreneur (Vol. 37, October 2009, No. 10, pp. 84)*
Pub: Entrepreneur Media, Inc.
Ed: Carol Tice. **Description:** RingRevenue, a firm that specializes in pay-per-call technology that allows affiliate networks and advertising agencies to track purchases, began a funding round in June 2009 which it closed quickly after obtaining $3.5 million in venture capital. The round was closed earlier than the projections of its owners due to their track record.

39784 ■ *"A Comment on 'Balancing Risk and Return in a Customer Portfolio'" in Journal of Marketing (Vol. 75, May 2011, No. 3, pp. 18)*
Pub: American Marketing Association
Ed: Fred Selnes. **Description:** Issues regarding the use of approaches to managing customer portfolios are described. These are related to assumptions in modern financial portfolio theory and return and risk.

39785 ■ *"Commercials Make Us Like TV More" in Harvard Business Review (Vol. 88, October 2010, No. 10, pp. 36)*
Pub: Harvard Business School Publishing
Ed: Leif Nelson. **Description:** Research indicates that people prefer commercial interruption over uninterrupted shows due to the break creating a reactivation of the initial pleasure when beginning a desirable activity.

39786 ■ *"Community Newspapers" in MarketingMagazine (Vol. 115, September 27, 2010, No. 13, pp. 38)*
Pub: Rogers Publishing Ltd.
Description: Market data for the newspaper industry in Canada is presented.

39787 ■ *The Complete Guide to Google Adwords: Secrets, Techniques, and Strategies You Can Learn to Make Millions*
Pub: Atlantic Publishing Company
Released: December 1, 2010. **Price:** $24.95. **Description:** Google AdWords, when it launched in 2002 signaled a fundamental shift in what the Internet was for so many individuals and companies. Learning and understanding how Google AdWords operates and how it can be optimized for maximum exposure, boosting click through rates, conversions, placement, and selection of the right keywords, can be the key to a successful online business.

39788 ■ *"Conference Calendar" in Marketing to Women (Vol. 21, April 2008, No. 4, pp. 7)*
Pub: EPM Communications Inc.
Contact: Ira Mayer, President
E-mail: imayer@epmcom.com
Description: Listing of current conferences and events concerning women, marketing and business.

39789 ■ *"Conference Calendar" in Marketing to Women (Vol. 21, March 2008, No. 3, pp. 7)*
Pub: EPM Communications Inc.
Contact: Ira Mayer, President
E-mail: imayer@epmcom.com
Description: Listing of current conferences and events aimed at women entrepreneurs and leaders.

39790 ■ *"Conference Calendar" in Marketing to Women (Vol. 21, February 2008, No. 2, pp. 1)*
Pub: EPM Communications Inc.
Contact: Ira Mayer, President
E-mail: imayer@epmcom.com
Description: Listing of current conferences and events concerning women, marketing and business.

39791 ■ *"Conference Calendar" in Marketing to Women (Vol. 22, July 2009, No. 7, pp. 7)*
Pub: EPM Communications Inc.
Contact: Ira Mayer, President
E-mail: imayer@epmcom.com
Description: Listing of conferences and seminars targeting female entrepreneurs.

39792 ■ *"Conference Calendar" in Marketing to Women (Vol. 22, August 2009, No. 8, pp. 7)*
Pub: EPM Communications Inc.
Contact: Ira Mayer, President
E-mail: imayer@epmcom.com
Description: Listing of conferences and seminars targeting female entrepreneurs.

39793 ■ *"Connie Ozan; Founder, Design Director, Twist Creative, 37" in Crain's Cleveland Business (Vol. 28, November 19, 2007, No. 46)*
Pub: Crain Communications, Inc.
Ed: John Booth. **Description:** Profile of Connie Ozan, design director and founder of Twist Creative, an advertising agency that she runs with her husband, Michael; Ms. Ozan credits her husband's business sense in bringing a more strategic side to the company in which to complement her art direction.

39794 ■ *Consumer Behavior*
Pub: Prentice Hall Business Publishing
Contact: Jerome Grant, President
Ed: Leon Schiffman, Leslile Kanuk. **Released:** August 7, 2009. **Price:** $180.00. **Description:** Consumer behavior is central to the planning, development and implementation of marketing strategies.

39795 ■ *Content Rich: Writing Your Way to Wealth on the Web*
Pub: 124 S Mercedes Rd.
Ed: Jon Wuebben. **Released:** April 2008. **Price:** $19. 95. **Description:** A definitive search engine optimization (SEO) copywriting guide for search engine rankings and sales conversion. It includes topics not covered in other books on the subject and targets the small to medium sized business looking for ways to maximize online marketing activities as well as designers and Web developers seeking to incorporate more SEO techniques into design and content.

39796 ■ *"Contest Produce Ad Designs on a Dime" in San Diego Business Journal (Vol. 31, August 23, 2010, No. 31, pp. 1)*
Pub: San Diego Business Journal
Ed: Mike Allen. **Description:** San Diego-based Prova.fm runs design contests for clients such as the U.S. Postal Service. The client then chooses the best entry from the contest. Prova.fm relies on the Internet to deliver a range of possible graphic solutions and allowing the customer to make the right selection for its business through a process called crowdsourcing.

39797 ■ *"Convenience Store Deal for Cardtronics" in American Banker (Vol. 174, July 28, 2009, No. 143, pp. 12)*
Pub: SourceMedia, Inc.
Description: Royal Buying Group, Inc., a convenience store marketing company, has agreed to recommend automated teller machine services from Cardtronics Inc., to its clients.

39798 ■ *"Conversation: Historian Geoffrey Jones On Why Knowledge Stays Put" in Harvard Business Review (Vol. 86, July-August 2008, No. 8)*
Pub: Harvard Business School Press
Ed: Gardiner Morse. **Description:** Geoffrey Jones, Harvard Business School's professor of business history, discusses factors that cause knowledge to concentrate in particular regions, rather than disperse, such as the location of wealth.

39799 ■ *"Conversations with Customers" in Business Journal Serving Greater Tampa Bay (Vol. 31, December 31, 2010, No. 1, pp. 1)*
Pub: Tampa Bay Business Journal
Description: Tampa Bay, Florida-based businesses have been using social media to interact with customers. Forty percent of businesses have been found to have at least one social media platform to reach customers and prospects.

39800 ■ *"Conversations Need to Yield Actions Measured in Dollars" in Advertising Age (Vol. 79, July 7, 2008, No. 26, pp. 18)*
Pub: Crain Communications, Inc.
Ed: Jonathan Salem Baskin. **Description:** New ways in which to market to consumers are discussed.

39801 ■ *"Convert New Customers to Long Term Accounts" in Indoor Comfort Marketing (Vol. 70, February 2011, No. 2, pp. 22)*
Pub: Industry Publications Inc.
Description: Marketing to new customers and suggestions for retaining them is covered.

39802 ■ *"Coping with the Web" in Agency Sales Magazine (Vol. 39, December 2009, No. 11, pp. 52)*
Pub: MANA
Ed: Karen Saunders. **Description:** When branding your company on the Internet, strategy should first be discussed with the website designer and the target and niche audience should also be defined. Describing 'what' and 'how' the product or service is offering is also important. In addition, perception, the logo, and the tag line are some elements that are needed to create a brand.

39803 ■ *"The Copyright Evolution" in Information Today (Vol. 28, November 2011, No. 10, pp. 1)*
Pub: Information Today, Inc.
Ed: Nancy Davis Kho. **Description:** For information professionals, issues surrounding copyright compliance have traditionally been on the consumption side. However, today, content consumption is only half the program because blogging, tweeting, and commenting is a vital part of more standard duties for workers as corporations aim to create authentic communications with customers.

39804 ■ *"Counting on Cornhole: Popular Bean Bag Game Brings Crowds to Bars" in Boston Business Journal (Vol. 29, July 15, 2011, No. 10, pp. 1)*
Pub: American City Business Journals Inc.
Ed: Alexander Jackson. **Description:** Cornhole game is being used by bars to spur business as the games hikes beer and food sales on slow weekdays. The game is played with two cornhole boards facing each other and is played with one or two people on one team who try to place a bag on the board.

39805 ■ *The Craft Business Answer Book: Starting, Managing, and Marketing a Home-Based Art, Crafts, Design Business*
Pub: M. Evans and Company, Incorporated
Ed: Barbara Brabec. **Released:** August 2006. **Price:** $16.95. **Description:** Expert advice for starting a home-based art or crafts business is offered.

39806 ■ *Craft Inc: Turn Your Creative Hobby into a Business*
Pub: Chronicle Books LLC
Ed: Meg Mateo Ilasco. **Released:** September 2007. **Price:** $16.95. **Description:** Guide to help any crafter turn their hobby into a successful business. The book covers all aspects including pricing, sales and marketing, trade shows, as well as interviews with successful craft artisans Jonathan Adler, Lotta Jansdotter, Denyse Schmidt and Jill Bliss.

39807 ■ *Craft, Inc.*
Pub: Chronicle Books LLC
Ed: Meg Mateo Ilasco. **Released:** August 2007. **Price:** $16.95. **Description:** Business primer for entrepreneurial crafters wishing to turn their hobbies into a small business, including tips for developing products, naming the company, writing a business plan, applying for licenses, and paying taxes.

39808 ■ *"Crain's Makes Ad Sales, Custom Marketing Appointments" in Crain's Chicago Business (Vol. 34, October 24, 2011, No. 42, pp. 13)*
Pub: Crain Communications Inc.
Description: Crain's Chicago Business announced key appointments in its sales department: David Denor has been named first director of custom marketing services and Kate Van Etten will succeed Denor as advertising director.

39809 ■ *The Creative Business Guide to Running a Graphic Design Business*
Pub: W.W. Norton & Company, Incorporated
Ed: Cameron S. Foote. **Released:** April 2004. **Price:** $23.10. **Description:** Advice for running a graphic design firm, focusing on organizations, marketing, personnel and operations.

39810 ■ *"Creative Marketing: How to Cultivate a Network of Endless Referrals" in Agency Sales Magazine (Vol. 39, July 2009, No. 7, pp. 38)*
Pub: MANA
Ed: Bob Burg. **Description:** Tips on how a salesperson can build a network of people that will bring them referrals are presented. Asking a person about their business and re-introducing one's self to an earlier acquaintance while remembering their names are some elements in the process of building this network.

39811 ■ *"Credit Crunch Takes Bite Out Of McDonald's" in Advertising Age (Vol. 79, September 29, 2008, No. 36, pp. 1)*
Pub: Crain Communications, Inc.
Ed: Emily Bryson York. **Description:** McDonald's will delay its launch of coffee bars inside its restaurants due to the banking crisis which has prompted Bank of America to halt loans to the franchise chains.

39812 ■ *"Cross Atlantic Commodities Launches National Internet Marketing Programs" in Manufacturing Close-Up (September 8, 2009)*
Pub: Close-Up Media
Description: Profile of the Internet campaign recently launched by Cross Atlantic Commodities, Inc., a manufacturer of specialty beauty and health products.

39813 ■ *Crossing the Chasm: Marketing and Selling Disruptive Products to Mainstream Customers*
Pub: HarperInformation
Ed: Geoffrey A. Moore. **Released:** September 2002. **Price:** $17.95. **Description:** A guide for marketing in high-technology industries, focusing on the Internet.

39814 ■ *"A Crowd for the Cloud" in CIO (Vol. 24, October 2, 2010, No. 1, pp. 16)*
Pub: CIO
Ed: Stephanie Overby. **Description:** Information about a project which aimed to implement a cloud-based crowdsourcing platform and innovation-management process is provided. Chubb Group of Insurance Companies wanted to mine revenue-generating ideas from its 10,400 employees and hundreds of thousands of external agents. The company hosted its first innovation event using its new system in October 2008.

39815 ■ *"Crowdsourcing their Way into One Big Mess" in Brandweek (Vol. 51, October 25, 2010, No. 38, pp. 26)*
Pub: Nielsen Business Media, Inc.
Ed: Gregg S. Lipman. **Description:** The Gap, was counting on crowdsourcing to provide feedback for its new logo, but it did not prove positive for the retailer. However, a massive outcry of negative opinion, via crowdsourcing, may not always equal valid, constructive criticism.

39816 ■ *"The CW" in Brandweek (Vol. 49, April 21, 2008, No. 16, pp. SR8)*
Pub: VNU Business Media, Inc.
Ed: John Consoli. **Description:** Provides contact information for sales and marketing personnel for the CW network as well as a listing of the station's top programming and an analysis of the current season and the target audience for those programs running in the current season. Purchases of advertising feel that Warner Bros. and CBS made a mistake merging The WB and UPN into the new CW rather than folding UPN into the more-established WB; compared to last season ratings are down more than 20 percent across the board.

39817 ■ *"Cyber Thanksgiving Online Shopping a Growing Tradition" in Marketing Weekly News (December 12, 2009, pp. 137)*
Pub: Investment Weekly News
Description: According to e-commerce analysts, Thanksgiving day is becoming increasingly important to retailers in terms of online sales. Internet marketers are realizing that consumers are already searching for Black Friday sales and if they find deals on the products they are looking for, they are highly likely to make their purchase on Thanksgiving day instead of waiting.

39818 ■ *"Daily Newspapers" in MarketingMagazine (Vol. 115, September 27, 2010, No. 13, pp. 32)*
Pub: Rogers Publishing Ltd.
Description: Market data covering the newspaper industry in Canada is examined.

39819 ■ *"Dana Anderson's Celebrity Rules for Digital Marketing" in Advertising Age (Vol. 81, December 6, 2010, No. 43, pp. 4)*
Pub: Crain Communications, Inc.
Ed: Kunur Patel. **Description:** Things that can be learned from Hollywood in terms of marketing strategy and communications are outlined.

39820 ■ *"Datran Media Executives to Lead Industry Debates Across Q1 Conferences" in Internet Wire (January 22, 2010)*
Pub: Comtex News Network, Inc.
Description: Datran Media, an industry-leading digital marketing technology company, will be sending members of its management team to several conferences in the early part of the first quarter of 2010; discussions will include Internet marketing innovations, e-commerce and media distribution.

39821 ■ *"A Day Late and a Dollar Short" in Indoor Comfort Marketing (Vol. 70, March 2011, No. 3, pp. 30)*
Pub: Industry Publications Inc.
Ed: Philip J. Baratz. **Description:** A discussion involving futures options and fuel oil prices is presented.

39822 ■ *"DCAA-Compliant Accounting Solution Provider Intros Redesign of Website at sympaq.com" in Entertainment Close-Up (April 18, 2011)*
Pub: Close-Up Media
Description: Aldebaron Inc., developer of DCAA-compliant accounting solution SYMPAQ SQL, launched a new Website that will assist government contractors access information about their products and services.

39823 ■ *"Deals Still Get Done at Drake's Coq d'Or" in Crain's Chicago Business (Vol. 31, November 17, 2008, No. 46, pp. 35)*
Pub: Crain Communications, Inc.
Ed: Shia Kapos. **Description:** Chicago's infamous Coq d'Or, a restaurant and lounge located at the Drake Hotel, is still a favorite establishment for noted executives but the eatery is now trying to cater to younger professionals through marketing and offering new beverages that appeal to that demographic. Many find it the perfect environment in which to close deals, relax or network.

39824 ■ *"Dear Customer: Managing E-Mail Campaigns" in Inc. (March 2008, pp. 58-59)*
Pub: Gruner & Jahr USA Publishing
Ed: Ryan Underwood. **Description:** Internet services that help firms manage their online business including email marketing, to manage subscriber lists, comply with spam regulations, monitor bouncebacks, and track potential customers are profiled. Constant Contact, MobileStorm Stun, Campaign Monitor, Pop Commerce, Emma, and StrongMail E-mail Server are among software and services highlighted.

39825 ■ *"December 19 Is a Great Day to be Terrible" in Internet Wire (December 15, 2009)*
Pub: Comtex News Network, Inc.
Description: Overview of the plans to market the grand opening of the newest Terrible Herbst location in Las Vegas, Nevada. Terrible Herbst is a complete convenience destination offering a gas station, convenience store, car wash and lube center.

39826 ■ *"Decoding Demand Opportunities" in Business Strategy Review (Vol. 21, Spring 2010, No. 1, pp. 64)*
Pub: Wiley-Blackwell
Ed: Erich Joachimsthaler, Markus Pfeiffer. **Description:** Classic marketing techniques, such as the use of focus groups or ethnographies, miss the enormous opportunities that can be leveraged once companies commit to understanding consumers in the context of life experiences.

39827 ■ *"Denali Asks Consumers to Name Next Moose Tracks Flavor" in Ice Cream Reporter (Vol. 23, August 20, 2010, No. 9, pp. 4)*
Pub: Ice Cream Reporter
Description: Denali Flavors based in Michigan is inviting consumer to name its newest Moose Tracks version of ice cream flavors.

39828 ■ *Design and Launch Your Online Boutique in a Week*
Pub: Entrepreneur Press
Ed: Melissa Campanelli. **Released:** June 26, 2008. **Price:** $17.95. **Description:** Tips for starting an online boutique in a short amount of time are given. The books shows how to build the online boutique with designer goods or your own product, ways to create eye-catching content, online tools to handle payments and accept orders, marketing and advertising techniques, and customer service.

39829 ■ *"The Design of Things to Come" in Business Horizons (Vol. 51, January-February 2008, No. 1, pp. 74)*
Pub: Elsevier Advanced Technology Publications
Ed: Mimi Dollinger. **Description:** Review of the book that helps entrepreneurs develop and market new products, 'The Design of Things to Come: How Ordinary People Create Extraordinary Products'.

39830 ■ *"Designer is Walking Ad for TIBI Line" in Charlotte Observer (February 5, 2007)*
Pub: Knight-Ridder/Tribune Business News
Ed: Crystal Dempsey. **Description:** Profile of Amy Smilovic, mother of two children, and clothing designer. Smilovic wears what she designs, making her a great marketing tool for her clothing line TIBI.

39831 ■ *The Designer's Guide to Marketing and Pricing: How to Win Clients and What to Charge Them*
Pub: F and W Publications, Inc.
Ed: Ilise Benun. **Released:** March 2008. **Price:** $19.99. **Description:** Guide to running a creative services business teaches designers how to be more effective, attract new clients, wages, and how to accurately estimate a project.

39832 ■ *"Designing Events Updates Online Suite" in Wireless News (October 25, 2009)*
Pub: Close-Up Media
Description: Designing Events, an outsourcing and consulting firm for conferences and meetings, announced the release of an update to its Designing Events Online suite of web-based management and marketing tools; features include enhanced versions

of online registration and collaboration, content management, session development, social media and conference websites.

39833 ■ *"Designing Solutions Around Customer Network Identity Goals" in Journal of Marketing (Vol. 75, March 2011, No. 2, pp. 36)*
Pub: American Marketing Association
Ed: Amber M. Epp, Linda L. Price. **Description:** The role relational and collective goals in creating customer solutions is investigated using in-depth interviews with 21 families. Findings revealed four integration processes in customer networks, namely, offerings formed around individual coalitions, concurrent participation, alternate participation, and offerings formed around priority goals.

39834 ■ *"Deskside Story: As the Latest Buzzword Suggests, PR Firms Are Happy To Drop By" in Inc. (December 2007, pp. 70, 73)*
Pub: Gruner & Jahr USA Publishing
Ed: Nitasha Tiku. **Description:** Setting up a meeting between a company's CEO and a journalist is known as deskside and is becoming popular again whereby a publicist offers clients deskside visits, briefings and alerts to help promote public relations for a company.

39835 ■ *"Destination Wedding Giveaway!" in Benzinga.com (October 29, 2011)*
Pub: Benzinga.com
Ed: Benzinga Staff. **Description:** Eden Condominiums in Perdido Key, Florida will award a beach wedding to a couple in 2012. The event is a marketing tool to draw attention brides as a perfect wedding venue.

39836 ■ *"A Direct Approach" in Business Journal-Portland (Vol. 24, November 9, 2007, No. 36, pp. 1)*
Pub: American City Business Journals, Inc.
Ed: Matthew Kish. **Description:** Respond 2 LLC's annual revenue has increased from $14.2 million in 2004 to almost $50 million in 2007. The growth is attributed to a $100 million contract with Vonage. The role of the popularity of infomercials on the success of the Portland-based marketing company is evaluated.

39837 ■ *"Direct Marketing" in MarketingMagazine (Vol. 115, September 27, 2010, No. 13, pp. 74)*
Pub: Rogers Publishing Ltd.
Description: Direct marketing data is shared covering provinces in Canada.

39838 ■ *"Discovery Networks" in Brandweek (Vol. 49, April 21, 2008, No. 16, pp. SR9)*
Pub: VNU Business Media, Inc.
Ed: Anthony Crupi. **Description:** Provides contact information for sales and marketing personnel for the Discovery networks as well as a listing of the station's top programming and an analysis of the current season and the target audience for those programs running in the current season. The networks flagship station returned to the top 10 in 2007, averaging 1.28 million viewers.

39839 ■ *"Disney-ABC Domestic Television Distribution" in Brandweek (Vol. 49, April 21, 2008, No. 16, pp. SR13)*
Pub: VNU Business Media, Inc.
Ed: Marc Berman. **Description:** Provides contact information for sales and marketing personnel for Disney-ABC Domestic Television Distribution as well as a listing of the station's top programming and an analysis of the current season and the target audience for those programs running in the current season.

39840 ■ *"The Display Group Is Super-Sized" in Michigan Vue (Vol. 13, July-August 2008, No. 4, pp. 34)*
Pub: Entrepreneur Media Inc.
Description: Profile of the Display Group, located in downtown Detroit, this company provides custom designed mobile marketing displays as well as special event production services for trade show displays. The rental house and design service is also beginning to see more business due to the film initiative, which provides incentives for films that are shooting in Michigan.

39841 ■ *"Dividing to Conquer" in Barron's (Vol. 88, March 31, 2008, No. 13, pp. 22)*
Pub: Dow Jones & Company, Inc.
Ed: Andrew Bary. **Description:** Altria's spin off of Philip Morris International could unlock substantial value for both domestic and international cigarette concerns. The strong brands and ample payouts from both companies will most likely impress investors.

39842 ■ *"Diving Into Internet Marketing" in American Agent and Broker (Vol. 81, December 2009, No. 12, pp. 24)*
Pub: Summit Business Media
Ed: Steve Anderson. **Description:** Internet marketing is becoming an essential tool for most businesses; advice is provided regarding the social networking opportunities available for marketing one's product or service on the Internet.

39843 ■ *"Do the Math on Discounts" in Entrepreneur (Vol. 37, October 2009, No. 10, pp. 82)*
Pub: Entrepreneur Media, Inc.
Ed: Jennifer Lawler. **Description:** Small business owners should consider all effects of discounts before implementing them. Some entrepreneurs do not discount prices for fear of damaging brands or their company's reputation.

39844 ■ *"Dollar General Selects GSI Commerce to Launch Its eCommerce Business" in Benzinga.com (October 29, 2011)*
Pub: Benzinga.com
Ed: Benzinga Staff. **Description:** Dollar General Corporation chose GSI Commerce, a leading provider of ecommerce and interactive marketing solutions, to launch its online initiative. GSI Commerce is an eBay Inc. company.

39845 ■ *"Dots Sings To New Tune With Its Radio Station" in Crain's Cleveland Business (Vol. 30, June 15, 2009, No. 23, pp. 7)*
Pub: Crain Communications, Inc.
Description: Dots LLC, a women's clothing retailer, has launched an online radio station on its Website. The station plays the in-store music to customers while they are shopping online.

39846 ■ *"Down on the Boardwalk" in Retail Merchandiser (Vol. 51, September-October 2011, No. 5, pp. 56)*
Pub: Phoenix Media Corporation
Ed: Eric Slack. **Description:** Classic board game, Monopoly, continues to be the most recognized game brand while staying fresh by entering new markets and gaming platforms for all walks of life. Monopoly is available in over 100 countries, translated into 43 languages and played by more than 1 billion people since its introduction, and the game is tailored to each geographic market it enters.

39847 ■ *"Doyle: Domino's New Pizza Seasoned with Straight Talk" in Crain's Detroit Business (Vol. 26, January 11, 2010, No. 2, pp. 1)*
Pub: Crain Communications Inc.
Ed: Nathan Skid. **Description:** Interview with J. Patrick Doyle, the CEO of Domino's Pizza, Inc.; the company has launched a new marketing campaign that focuses on its bold new vision.

39848 ■ *"Dozens 'Come Alive' in Downtown Chicago" in Green Industry Pro (July 2011)*
Pub: Cygnus Business Media
Ed: Gregg Wartgow. **Description:** Highlights from the Come Alive Outside training event held in Chicago, Illinois July 14-15, 2011 are shared. Nearly 80 people representing 38 landscape companies attended the event that helps contractors review their services and find ways to sell them in new and various ways.

39849 ■ *"Dramatic Results: Making Opera (Yes, Opera) Seem Young and Hip" in Inc. (October 2007, pp. 61-62)*
Pub: Gruner & Jahr USA Publishing
Description: Profile of Peter Gelb, who turned New York's Metropolitan Opera into one of the most media-savvy organizations in the country, using a multifaceted marketing strategy through the media. Gelb used streaming audio and simulcasts on satellite radio and movie theaters to promote a message that opera is hip.

39850 ■ *"Drive Traffic To Your Blog" in Women Entrepreneur (January 13, 2009)*
Pub: Entrepreneur Media Inc.
Ed: Lesley Spencer Pyle. **Description:** Internet social networking has become a vital component to marketing one's business. Tips are provided on how to establish a blog that will attract attention to one's business and keep one's customers coming back for more.

39851 ■ *Duct Tape Marketing: The World's Most Practical Small Business Marketing Guide*
Pub: Thomas Nelson Inc.
Ed: John Jantsch. **Released:** May 2008. **Price:** $14. 99. **Description:** Small business owners are provided the tools and tactics necessary to market and grow a business.

39852 ■ *e-Riches 2.0: Next-Generation Marketing Strategies for Making Million Online*
Pub: AMACOM
Ed: Scott Fox. **Released:** May 27, 2009. **Price:** $25. 00. **Description:** Beginner's guide to using the Internet to help grow business, including the best ways to use email lists and newsletters, RSS feeds, online viral marketing, social networking, microblogging, online video and radio/podcasts, tele-seminars and webinars, search engine keyword advertising and affiliate program advertising.

39853 ■ *"Eagles Measure Suite Success" in Philadelphia Business Journal (Vol. 30, September 9, 2011, No. 30, pp. 1)*
Pub: American City Business Journals Inc.
Ed: John George. **Description:** Philadelphia Eagles have a new software program that helps suite holders keep track of how their suite is being used and whether they are getting a return on their investment. The software allows suite holders to better utilize and distribute their tickets.

39854 ■ *"Easy Answers? Hall No" in Charlotte Business Journal (Vol. 25, December 17, 2010, No. 39, pp. 1)*
Pub: Charlotte Business Journal
Ed: Erik Spanberg. **Description:** Charlotte, North Carolina-based NASCAR Hall of Fame has been trying to recover from its shaky start, but still bullish on the future as officials intensify promotions. Sports museums and halls of fame are mainly dependent on families and always search for new exhibits and great appearances to boost attendance.

39855 ■ *EBay Income: How ANYONE of Any Age, Location, and/or Background Can Build a Highly Profitable Online Business with eBay*
Pub: Atlantic Publishing Company
Released: December 1, 2010. **Price:** $24.95. **Description:** A complete overview of eBay is given and guides any small company through the entire process of creating the auction and auction strategies, photography, writing copy, text and formatting, multiple sales, programming tricks, PayPal, accounting, creating marketing, merchandising, managing email lists, advertising plans, taxes and sales tax, best time to list items and for how long, sniping programs, international customers, opening a storefront, electronic commerce, buy-it now pricing, keywords, Google marketing and eBay secrets.

39856 ■ *"Eco-Preneuring" in Small Business Opportunities (Jan. 2008)*
Pub: Harris Publications Inc.
Description: Iceland Naturally is a joint marketing effort among tourism and business interests hoping to

increase demand for Icelandic products including frozen seafood, bottled water, agriculture, and tourism in North America.

39857 ■ *"Economic Crises Calls For Better Marketing Plans" in Entrepreneur (October 1, 2008)*
Pub: Entrepreneur Media Inc.
Ed: Tim Berry. **Description:** Revising one's business plan is essential, especially during times of economic crisis; sales and marketing plans should be reviewed, analyzed and changed in an attempt to survive the economic downturn.

39858 ■ *"Economics at Play When Allocating Seats to Series" in Boston Business Journal (Vol. 27, October 26, 2007, No. 39, pp. 1)*
Pub: American City Business Journals Inc.
Ed: Jesse Noyes, Naomi R. Kooker. **Description:** Business executives are trying to obtain as many baseball tickets to the World Series as possible. Allocating corporate seats to the Series is about maintaining tight relationships and influence clients. It is a key to business relationships.

39859 ■ *Ecopreneuring: Putting Purpose and the Planet Before Profits*
Pub: New Society Publishers
Ed: John Ivanko; Lisa Kivirist. **Released:** July 1, 2008. **Price:** $17.95 paperback. **Description:** Ecopreneurs in America are shifting profits and market share towards green living. The book provides a guideline for ecopreneurs in the areas of eco-business basics, purposeful management, marketing in the green economy, and running a lifestyle business.

39860 ■ *"Elanco Challenges Bayer's Advantage, K9 Advantix Ad Claims" in Pet Product News (Vol. 64, November 2010, No. 11, pp. 11)*
Pub: BowTie Inc.
Description: Elanco Animal Health has disputed Bayer Animal Health's print and Web advertising claims involving its flea, tick, and mosquito control products Advantage and K9 Advantix. The National Advertising Division of the Council of Better Business Bureaus recommended the discontinuation of ads, while Bayer Animal Health reiterated its commitment to self-regulation.

39861 ■ *Electronic Commerce*
Pub: Course Technology
Ed: Gary Schneider, Bryant Chrzan, Charles McCormick. **Released:** May 1, 2010. **Price:** $117.95. **Description:** E-commerce can open the door to more opportunities than ever before for small business. Packed with real-world examples and cases, the book delivers comprehensive coverage of emerging online technologies and trends and their influence on the electronic marketplace. It details how the landscape of online commerce is evolving, reflecting changes in the economy and how business and society are responding to those changes. Balancing technological issues with the strategic business aspects of successful e-commerce, the new edition includes expanded coverage of international issues, social networking, mobile commerce, Web 2.0 technologies, and updates on spam, phishing, and identity theft.

39862 ■ *Electronic Commerce: Technical, Business, and Legal Issues*
Pub: Prentice Hall PTR
Ed: Oktay Dogramaci; Aryya Gangopadhyay; Yelena Yesha; Nabil R. Adam. **Released:** August 1998. **Description:** Provides insight into the goals of using the Internet to grow a business in the areas of networking and telecommunication, security, and storage and retrieval; business areas such as marketing, procurement and purchasing, billing and payment, and supply chain management; and legal aspects such as privacy, intellectual property, taxation, contractual and legal settlements.

39863 ■ *"Elements For Success" in Small Business Opportunities (November 2008)*
Pub: Entrepreneur Press
Contact: Perlman Neil, President
Description: Profile of Elements, a physical fitness club that approach a healthy lifestyle for women, which includes the components of body, beauty and mind; the network of upscale, boutique style health clubs differ from other providers in its 'balanced lifestyle' approach to a healthy lifestyle. This unique niche is gaining in popularity despite the faltering economy.

39864 ■ *"Emack & Bolio" in Ice Cream Reporter (Vol. 23, October 20, 2010, No. 11, pp. 8)*
Pub: Ice Cream Reporter
Description: Emack & Bolio's is engaging in scent marketing using various odors to help boost sales by attracting consumers with scents appropriate to their products.

39865 ■ *Email Marketing by the Numbers: How to Use the World's Greatest Marketing Tool to Take Any Organization to the Next Level*
Pub: John Wiley and Sons Inc.
Ed: Chris Baggott. **Released:** April 2007. **Price:** $29.99 (CND). **Description:** Tips for using email to market small business products and services are provided.

39866 ■ *Emerging Business Online: Global Markets and the Power of B2B Internet Marketing*
Pub: FT Press
Ed: Lara Fawzy, Lucas Dworksi. **Released:** October 1, 2010. **Price:** $49.99. **Description:** An introduction into ebocube (emerging business online), a comprehensive proven business model for Internet B2B marketing in emerging markets.

39867 ■ *"The Emerging Capital Market for Nonprofits" in Harvard Business Review (Vol. 88, October 2010, No. 10, pp. 110)*
Pub: Harvard Business School Publishing
Ed: Robert S. Kaplan, Allen S. Grossman. **Description:** Demonstration of how nonprofits can use intermediaries to grow their organizational structures, giving them improved scale and impact is offered. Some intermediaries play a mutual-fund role and conduct due diligence, while others act as venture capital funds and implement strategy.

39868 ■ *"Emotional Brand Attachment and Brand Personality" in Journal of Marketing (Vol. 75, July 2011, No. 4, pp. 35)*
Pub: American Marketing Association
Ed: Lucia Malar, Harley Krohmer, Wayne D. Hoyer, Bettin Nyffeneger. **Description:** A study on whether the brand's personality should match the consumer's actual self or ideal self is presented. Actual self-congruence is found to have the most impact on emotional brand attachment.

39869 ■ *"Empire of Pixels" in Entrepreneur (Vol. 37, September 2009, No. 9, pp. 50)*
Pub: Entrepreneur Media, Inc.
Ed: Jason Daley. **Description:** Entrepreneur Jack Levin has successfully grown Imageshack, an image-hosting Web service. The Website currently gets 50 million unique visitors a month. Levin has launched Y-Frog, an application that uses Imageshack to allow Twitter users to add images to their posts.

39870 ■ *"The Employee Brand: Is Yours an All-Star?" in Business Horizons (September-October 2007, pp. 423)*
Pub: Elsevier Technology Publications
Ed: W. Glynn Mangold, Sandra Jeanquart Miles. **Description:** Employees can influence the brand image either positively or negatively. The typology presented provides guidelines on how employees can reflect a company's brand image. Classifications of organizations into all-star rookies, injured reserves, or strike-out kings are also discussed.

39871 ■ *"The End of the Line for Line Extensions?" in Advertising Age (Vol. 79, July 7, 2008, No. 26, pp. 3)*
Pub: Crain Communications, Inc.
Description: After years of double-digit growth, some of the most heavily extended personal-care products have slowed substantially or even declined in the U.S. Unilever's Dove and P&G's Pantene and Olay are two such brands that have been affected. Statistical data included.

39872 ■ *"Entrepreneur Column" in Entrepreneur (September 24, 2009)*
Pub: Entrepreneur Media, Inc.
Ed: Allen Moon. **Description:** In an attempt to compete with Google, Microsoft and Yahoo have entered a partnership to merge their search services; advice on the best ways to get noticed on this new search engine entitled Bing, is provided.

39873 ■ *Essentials of Entrepreneurship and Small Business Management*
Pub: Prentice Hall PTR
Ed: Thomas W. Zimmerer; Norman M. Scarborough; Doug Wilson. **Released:** February 2007. **Price:** $106.67. **Description:** New venture creation and the knowledge required to start a new business are shared. The challenges of entrepreneurship, business plans, marketing, e-commerce, and financial considerations are explored.

39874 ■ *"Every Little Bit Helps" in Black Enterprise (Vol. 38, November 2007, No. 4, pp. 102)*
Pub: Earl G. Graves Publishing Co. Inc.
Ed: Tennille M. Robinson. **Description:** After a career in the cosmetics industry, Tricialee Riley is marketing and advertising her new venture, the Polish Bar, a salon offering manicures, pedicures, makeup application, and waxing.

39875 ■ *"Facebook: A Promotional Budget's Best Friend" in Women Entrepreneur (February 1, 2009)*
Pub: Entrepreneur Media Inc.
Ed: Tamara Monosoff. **Description:** Facebook began as a social networking website but has become a valuable marketing tool for all types of businesses, organizations and causes. Tips are provided for creating a Facebook account and growing one's network on Facebook.

39876 ■ *The Facebook Era: Tapping Online Social Networks to Build Better Products, Reach New Audiences, and Sell More Stuff*
Pub: Prentice Hall
Ed: Clara Shih. **Price:** $24.99. **Description:** The '90s were about the World Wide Web of information and the power of linking Web pages. Today it's about the World Wide Web of people and the power of the social graph. Online social networks are fundamentally changing the way we live, work, and interact. They offer businesses immense opportunities to transform customer relationships for profit: opportunities that touch virtually every business function, from sales and marketing to recruiting, collaboration to executive decision-making, product development to innovation.

39877 ■ *Facebook Marketing: Designing Your Next Marketing Campaign*
Pub: Que
Ed: Justin R. Levy. **Released:** May 1, 2010. **Price:** $24.99. **Description:** Detailed steps are given in order to develop, use, and create awareness for any business. The book provides detailed instructions, along with case studies from known brands, for launching marketing campaigns on Facebook.

39878 ■ *"Fair Exchange" in Food and Drink (Winter 2010, pp. 84)*
Pub: Schofield Media Group
Ed: Don Mardak. **Description:** Bartering can assist firms in the food and beverage industry to attract new customers, maximize resources, and reduce cash expenses.

39879 ■ *"Familiar Fun" in Crain's Cleveland Business (Vol. 28, October 22, 2007, No. 42, pp. 3)*
Pub: Crain Communications Inc.
Ed: John Booth. **Description:** Marketing for the 2007 holiday season has toy retailers focusing on American-made products because of recent recalls of toys produced in China that do not meet U.S. safety standards.

39880 ■ *"Far Out: Satellite Radio Finds New Way to Tally Listeners" in Globe & Mail (March 14, 2007, pp. B14)*
Pub: CTVglobemedia Publishing Inc.
Ed: Grant Robertson. **Description:** The marketing strategy adopted by satellite radio broadcasting firm XM Satellite Radio Inc. in Canada for increasing its subscriber based is discussed.

39881 ■ *Fashion & Print Directory*
Pub: Peter Glenn Publications
Contact: Gregory James Blount, President
E-mail: gjames@pgdirect.com
URL(s): www.pgdirect.com/fpintro.asp. **Ed:** Gregory James. **Released:** Annual; November; latest edition 47th. **Price:** $39.95, Individuals. **Covers:** Advertising agencies, PR firms, marketing companies, 1,000 client brand companies and related services in the U.S. and Canada. Includes photographers, marketing agency, suppliers, sources of props and rentals, fashion houses, beauty services, locations. **Entries include:** Company name, address, phone; paid listings numbering 5,000 include description of products or services, key personnel. **Arrangement:** Classified by line of business.

39882 ■ *"Fast Fact: Quality of Foods, Cost Top Factors in Determining Where to Grocery Shop" in Marketing to Women (Vol. 22, August 2009)*
Pub: EPM Communications Inc.
Contact: Ira Mayer, President
E-mail: imayer@epmcom.com
Description: Efficient check-outs, customer service and a wide variety of products were all less important to female shoppers than the quality of food and value, which were seen as the ultimate factors in a woman's decision as to which grocery store they decide to frequent.

39883 ■ *"Fast Fact: Women's Online Habits" in Marketing to Women (Vol. 22, July 2009, No. 7, pp. 1)*
Pub: EPM Communications Inc.
Contact: Ira Mayer, President
E-mail: imayer@epmcom.com
Description: Lists the Internet habits of women. Statistical data included.

39884 ■ *"Feedback From Payers Will Be Vital For Future Developments" in Farmer's Weekly (March 28, 2008, No. 320)*
Pub: Reed Business Information
Contact: Jeff Greisch, President
Description: Potato Council staff will carry on working with levy payers to retain the same high caliber of marketing, research and other activities.

39885 ■ *"Financo Panel Lauds Product, Online Marketing" in Home Textiles Today (Vol. 31, January 25, 2010, No. 3, pp. 1)*
Pub: Reed Business Information, Inc.
Ed: James Mammarella. **Description:** Overview of the Financo Annual Merchandising Industry Chief Executives Event during which there was much discussion on the merits of e-commerce, online marketing as well as the traditional methods of brand recognition and retailing.

39886 ■ *"Find Your Marketing Mojo" in Business Owner (Vol. 35, July-August 2011, No. 4, pp. 14)*
Pub: DL Perkins Company
Description: Marketing and branding a small business can be learned and implemented by following a process that begins with setting and creating the vision that every successful venture requires: a crystal-clear vision for who you are, what you stand for, and why customers will come to you rather than competitors.

39887 ■ *"Finding the Voice of the Marketplace" in Mergers & Acquisitions: The Dealmaker's Journal (March 1, 2008)*
Pub: SourceMedia, Inc.
Description: Companies oftentimes are unable to achieve their strategic goals through acquisition due, in part, to not understanding the target's market and its position in the marketplace.

39888 ■ *"First: Package Deal" in Entrepreneur (Vol. 35, October 2007, No. 10, pp. 114)*
Pub: Entrepreneur Media Inc.
Ed: Nichole L. Torres. **Description:** Unique packaging of Me! Bath's products proved to be an effective marketing strategy for the company, which has over $3 million dollar sales yearly. Their ice cream-looking bath products have become popular and are much appreciated by vendors. Details of how packaging can affect sales are presented.

39889 ■ *"Fitter from Twitter" in Boston Business Journal (Vol. 30, December 17, 2010, No. 47, pp. 1)*
Pub: Boston Business Journal
Ed: Lisa van der Pool. **Description:** Small businesses are increasing their use of the Twitter microblogging platform to attract and retain customers. Lisa Johnson, who owns Modern Pilates studios, managed to raise awareness of her personal brand nationally through the social media platform.

39890 ■ *"Five Distinct Divisions, One Collective Focus" in Green Industry Pro (Vol. 23, October 2011)*
Pub: Cygnus Business Media
Ed: Gregg Wartgow. **Description:** Profile of ACLS Inc., an amalgamation of All Commercial Landscape Service (commercial maintenance), All Custom Landscape Service (design/build), Fresno Tree Service, Certified Water Consulting (irrigation), and Tractor Service (disking and flailing services on everything from one-acre lots to hundreds of acres of open land). The firm discusses its rebranding effort in order to increase sales.

39891 ■ *"Florida's Bright Upside" in Tampa Bay Business Journal (Vol. 29, November 6, 2009, No. 46, pp. 1)*
Pub: American City Business Journals
Ed: Michael Hinman. **Description:** Florida's Public Service Commission (PSC) decision on a power purchase agreement that could add 25 megawatts of solar energy on Tampa Electric Company's offerings is presented. The decision could support the growing market for suppliers and marketers of renewable energy such as Jabil Circuit Inc., which manufactures photovoltaic modules. Details of the agreement are discussed.

39892 ■ *"For MySpace, A Redesign to Entice Generation Y" in The New York Times (October 27, 2010, pp. B3)*
Pub: The New York Times Company
Ed: Miguel Helft. **Description:** MySpace is redesigning its Website in order to attract individuals from the Generation Y group.

39893 ■ *"For Staying True: Bobby Flam: Jumbo's Restaurant, Miami" in Inc. (Volume 32, December 2010, No. 10, pp. 102)*
Pub: Inc. Magazine
Ed: Leigh Buchanan. **Description:** Profile of Bobby Flam, owner of Jumbo's Restaurant in Miami, Florida.

39894 ■ *"Fox" in Brandweek (Vol. 49, April 21, 2008, No. 16, pp. SR3)*
Pub: VNU Business Media, Inc.
Ed: John Consoli. **Description:** Provides contact information for sales and marketing personnel for the Fox network as well as a listing of the station's top programming and an analysis of the current season and the target audience for those programs running in the current season. In terms of upfront advertising dollars, it looks as if Fox will be competing against NBC for third place due to its success at courting the 18-49-year-old male demographic.

39895 ■ *"Fox Cable Entertainment Networks" in Brandweek (Vol. 49, April 21, 2008, No. 16, pp. SR10)*
Pub: VNU Business Media, Inc.
Ed: Anthony Crupi. **Description:** Provides contact information for sales and marketing personnel for the Fox Cable Entertainment networks as well as a listing of the station's top programming and an analysis of the current season and the target audience for those programs running in the current season.

39896 ■ *"A Framework for Conceptual Contributions in Marketing" in Journal of Marketing (Vol. 75, July 2011, No. 4, pp. 136)*
Pub: American Marketing Association
Ed: Deborah J. MacInnis. **Description:** A look at a new framework for thinking about conceptualization in marketing is presented. Conceptual advances are essential to the vitality of the marketing discipline but recent writings indicate that advancement is slowing. The types of conceptual contributions are described, including their similarities and difference, and their importance to the field of marketing.

39897 ■ *"Franchisees Lose Battle Against BK" in Advertising Age (Vol. 79, June 2, 2008, No. 22, pp. 46)*
Pub: Crain Communications, Inc.
Ed: Emily Bryson York. **Description:** Burger King has had continuing litigation with former franchisees from New York, Luan and Elizabeth Sadik, who claim that Burger King's double cheeseburger, along with additional problems, created the environment for their eventual insolvency. Burger King has since terminated its test of selling the double cheeseburger for $1, although the company declined to comment on the reason for this decision.

39898 ■ *"Free Speech Vs. Privacy in Data Mining" in Information Today (Vol. 28, September 2011, No. 8, pp. 22)*
Pub: Information Today, Inc.
Ed: George H. Pike. **Description:** The U.S. Constitution does not explicitly guarantee the right of privacy. Organizations and businesses that require obtaining and disseminating information can be caught in the middle of privacy rights. The long-term impact on data mining, Internet marketing, and Internet privacy issues are examined.

39899 ■ *Free: The Future of a Radical Price*
Pub: Hyperion
Ed: Chris Anderson. **Released:** 2009. **Price:** $26.99. **Description:** A new trend shows companies using giveaways as a means to attract business and increase profits.

39900 ■ *"Free Your Mind" in Entrepreneur (Vol. 37, October 2009, No. 10, pp. 24)*
Pub: Entrepreneur Media Inc.
Ed: Joe Robinson. **Description:** Writer Chris Anderson believes that firms in the digital age should allow products and services to initially be sold for free. These companies could then charge for premium versions of these products and services after the free versions have gained attention.

39901 ■ *"Friendly" in Ice Cream Reporter (Vol. 21, August 20, 2008, No. 9, pp. 8)*
Pub: Ice Cream Reporter
Description: Advertising Age presented Friendly's with the award, 'Ad of the Day' for its television commercial depicting a Norman Rockwell-esque family transported to a psychedelic wonderland.

39902 ■ *"Friendly Ice Cream Corporation" in Ice Cream Reporter (Vol. 23, August 20, 2010, No. 9, pp. 8)*
Pub: Ice Cream Reporter
Description: Friendly Ice Cream Corporation appointed Andrea M. McKenna as vice president of marketing and chief marketing officer.

39903 ■ *"Frito Lay Plans to Spice Up Life With New Chips" in Globe & Mail (February 21, 2006, pp. B3)*
Pub: CTVglobemedia Publishing Inc.
Ed: Andy Hoffman. **Description:** The reasons behind the launch of potato chips by Frito Lay Canada Inc., subsidiary of PepsiCo. Inc., are presented.

39904 ■ *From Concept To Consumer: How to Turn Ideas Into Money*
Pub: Pearson Education Inc.
Ed: Phil Baker. **Released:** 2009. **Price:** $24.99. **Description:** Renowned product developer Phil Baker explains how a great idea accounts for only 5 percent of all the factors of success and why the majority of success is dependent upon a myriad of other factors, including the time it takes to get to market, price,

marketing and distribution. By being their own best competition, a small company can stay one step ahead of competitors.

39905 ■ *"From Craft Biz To Wholesale Giant" in Women Entrepreneur (January 19, 2009)*
Pub: Entrepreneur Media Inc.
Ed: Maria Falconer. **Description:** Advice is given on how to turn a small craft business into a full-time venture; tips to help one transition from a part-time designer to a full-time wholesaler and brand are also included.

39906 ■ *"From OTC Sellers to Surgeons, Healthcare Marketers Target Women to Achieve Growth" in Marketing to Women (February 2008)*
Pub: EPM Communications Inc.
Contact: Ira Mayer, President
E-mail: imayer@epmcom.com
Description: Healthcare companies are targeting women with ad campaigns, new product development and new technology in order to reach and develop brand loyalty.

39907 ■ *"Frosted Flakes Goes For Gold" in Marketing to Women (Vol. 21, April 2008, No. 4, pp. 3)*
Pub: EPM Communications Inc.
Contact: Ira Mayer, President
E-mail: imayer@epmcom.com
Description: Kellogg is appealing to health-conscious moms with its new product Frosted Flakes Gold.

39908 ■ *"FTC Takes Aim At Foreclosure 'Rescue' Firm" in The Business Journal-Serving Greater Tampa Bay (Vol. 28, September 19, 2008, No. 39)*
Pub: American City Business Journals, Inc.
Ed: Michael Hinman. **Description:** United Home Savers LLP has been ordered to halt its mortgage foreclosure rescue services after the Federal Trade Commission accused it of deceptive advertising. The company is alleged to have charged customers $1,200 in exchange for unfulfilled promises to keep them in their homes.

39909 ■ *"Fueling Business" in The Business Journal-Milwaukee (Vol. 25, July 25, 2008, No. 44, pp. A1)*
Pub: American City Business Journals, Inc.
Ed: David Doege. **Description:** Several businesses in Wisconsin's Milwaukee area are offering gas cards in order to attract customers. Examples of this include apartment manager Nancy Randle offering a $400 gas card to new tenants with a 1 year lease and dentist Perry Sukowatey giving a $25 gas card after examining patients. Other details on gas card promotions are discussed.

39910 ■ *"Funbrain Launches Preschool Content" in Marketing to Women (Vol. 21, March 2008, No. 3, pp. 3)*
Pub: EPM Communications Inc.
Contact: Ira Mayer, President
E-mail: imayer@epmcom.com
Description: Funbrain.com launches The Moms and Kids Playground, a section of the website devoted to activities and games for moms and kids aged 2 to 6; content aims at building early computer skills and to teach basic concepts such as counting and colors.

39911 ■ *"Funds "Friend" Facebook" in Barron's (Vol. 89, July 27, 2009, No. 30, pp. 30)*
Pub: Dow Jones & Co., Inc.
Ed: Leslie P. Norton. **Description:** Mutual-fund companies are the latest entrants to the 'social media' space and several companies have already set up Facebook and Twitter pages. The use of this technology pose special challenges for compliance and regulators especially since the Financial Industry Regulatory Authority reminds companies that advertising, sales and literature are governed by regulations.

39912 ■ *"Funeral Directors Get Creative As Boomers Near Great Beyond" in Advertising Age (Vol. 79, October 13, 2008, No. 38, pp. 30)*
Pub: Crain Communications, Inc.
Ed: Lenore Skenazy. **Description:** Despite the downturn in the economy, the funeral business is thriving due to the number of baby boomers who realize the importance of making preparations for their death. Marketers are getting creative in their approach and many companies have taken into consideration the need for a more environmental friendly way to dispose of bodies and thus have created innovative businesses that reflect this need.

39913 ■ *"Funny Business" in Canadian Business (Vol. 82, April 27, 2009, No. 7, pp. 27)*
Pub: Rogers Media
Ed: Rachel Pulfer. **Description:** Companies are advised to use humor in marketing to drive more revenue. IBM Canada, for example, commissioned Second City Communications for a marketing campaign that involved humor. While IBM Canada declined to give sales or traffic figures, firm executives rank the marketing campaign as an overall success.

39914 ■ *"The Future of Work" in Black Enterprise (Vol. 41, August 2010, No. 1, pp. 65)*
Pub: Earl G. Graves Publishing Co. Inc.
Ed: Annya M. Lott. **Description:** Technology, globalization, and outsourcing will continue to shape the future of work. Social media is a means for small companies to market goods and services.

39915 ■ *"Gain the 'Come Alive Outside' Selling Edge" in Green Industry Pro (July 2011)*
Pub: Cygnus Business Media
Ed: Jim Paluch. **Description:** Marketing the 'Come Alive Outside' slogan can help landscapers to increase their market share by identifying and applying these elements to each customer as well as their workers.

39916 ■ *"Gatorade Loses Its Competitive Edge; Upstart Rivals Undercut Its Domination of Game" in Crain's Chicago Business (April 28, 2008)*
Pub: Crain Communications, Inc.
Ed: Natalie Zmuda. **Description:** According to beverage-marketing experts, Gatorade is losing some of its market share to aggressive new rivals who are appealing to younger consumers.

39917 ■ *"General Motors Can't Kick Incentives-But They Work" in Advertising Age (Vol. 79, July 7, 2008, No. 26, pp. 3)*
Pub: Crain Communications, Inc.
Ed: Jean Halliday. **Description:** General Motors Corp. was able to maintain their market share just as Toyota Motor Corp. was beginning to pass the manufacturer; GM lured in customers with a sales incentive that they heavily advertised and subsequently helped build demand; investors, however, were not impressed and GM shares were hammered to their lowest point in 50 years after analysts speculated the company might go bankrupt.

39918 ■ *"Geo-Marketing: Site Selection by the Numbers" in Franchising World (Vol. 42, September 2010, No. 9, pp.)*
Pub: International Franchise Association
Ed: Kellen Vaughan. **Description:** Site location is critical when starting a new franchise. Information to help franchisees choose the right location is included.

39919 ■ *"Get Back To Business Planning Fundamentals" in Entrepreneur (October 24, 2008)*
Pub: Entrepreneur Media Inc.
Ed: Tim Berry. **Description:** During a recession it is important to know what adjustment to make to your business plan. Some fundamentals to remember include: watching things more closely by tracking progress on cash, sales, new projects, customer satisfaction, ad spending and expenses; looking for built-in indicators such as what drives sales or expenses; watching what drives cash flow; and do not make mistakes such as laying off experienced employees too soon.

39920 ■ *Get Clients Now!, 2nd Edition: A 28-Day Marketing Program for Professionals, Consultants, and Coaches*
Pub: American Management Association
Contact: Charles R. Craig, Chairman
Ed: C.J. Hayden. **Released:** 2006. **Price:** $19.95.

39921 ■ *"Get Online or Be Left Behind" in Women In Business (Vol. 61, August-September 2009, No. 4, pp. 33)*
Pub: American Business Women's Association
Ed: Diane Stafford. **Description:** Technology's significance for the connectivity purposes among business people is discussed. Details on the use of wireless tools and online social media to boost technology IQ are presented.

39922 ■ *"Get Personal" in Entrepreneur (Vol. 36, April 2008, No. 4)*
Pub: Entrepreneur Media, Inc.
Ed: Romanus Wolter. **Description:** Customers appreciate personal contact, and communicating with them can help business owners' customer relations. Some ways on how to keep a personal touch with customers and improve business dealings include blending technology with personal interaction and knowing what the customers want. Other tips are provided.

39923 ■ *"Get Real" in Entrepreneur (Vol. 36, April 2008, No. 4, pp. 86)*
Pub: Entrepreneur Media, Inc.
Ed: Kim T. Gordon. **Description:** Selling points of a product or service must show real benefits to women. Provide detailed information as women look at details more deeply before purchasing. Other tips on how to market products designed for women consumers are provided.

39924 ■ *"Get Them Talking" in Entrepreneur (Vol. 36, February 2008, No. 2, pp. 50)*
Pub: Entrepreneur Media Inc.
Ed: Heather Clancy. **Description:** Yelp.com is an Internet search site that presents businesses across the U.S., sorted according to the number of customer reviews they have received. One to five stars are used by the reviewers, or yelpers, to rate businesses. Details on how the International Orange day spa benefited from Yelp are discussed.

39925 ■ *"Getting the Bioheat Word Out" in Indoor Comfort Marketing (Vol. 70, September 2011, No. 9, pp. 32)*
Pub: Industry Publications Inc.
Description: Ways to market advanced liquid fuels to the public are outlined.

39926 ■ *Getting Clients and Keeping Clients for Your Service Business*
Pub: Atlantic Publishing Company
Ed: Anne M. Miller; Gail Brett Levine. **Released:** August 28, 2008. **Price:** $24.95 paperback. **Description:** Tips are offered to help any small service business identify customers, brand and grow the business, as well as development of logos, brochures and Websites.

39927 ■ *"Getting a Grip on the Saddle: Chasms or Cycles?" in Journal of Marketing (Vol. 75, July 2011, No. 4, pp. 21)*
Pub: American Marketing Association
Ed: Deepa Chandrasekaran, Gerald J. Tellis. **Description:** A study of the saddle's generality across products and countries is presented. The saddle is fairly pervasive based on empirical analysis of historical sales data from ten products across 19 countries. The results indicate chasms and technological cycles for information/entertainment products while business cycles and technological cycles affect kitchen/laundry products.

39928 ■ *"Getting NORA reauthorized is high priority" in Indoor Comfort Marketing (Vol. 70, February 2011, No. 2, pp. 14)*
Pub: Industry Publications Inc.
Description: The importance of reauthorizing the National Oilheat Research Alliance is stressed.

39929 ■ *"Giants Now Admit They Roam Planet Earth; Time To Buy?" in Barron's (Vol. 88, March 31, 2008, No. 13, pp. 39)*
Pub: Dow Jones & Company, Inc.
Ed: Eric J. Savitz. **Description:** Oracle's third-quarter results showed that top-line growth fell short of expectations but the company is expected to fare better than most applications companies in the downturn. Google had a flat growth in the number of people who click their online ads. The time for investors in the tech sector with a long-term horizon has arrived.

39930 ■ *"Giovanni Sanfilippo" in Art Business News (Vol. 34, November 2007, No. 11, pp. 14)*
Pub: Pfingsten Publishing, LLC
Description: GSG Publishing is marketing a new release of Maestro Sanfilippo's 'Timida', in a limited edition.

39931 ■ *"Give This Pooch a Home" in Advertising Age (Vol. 78, August 13, 2007, No. 32, pp. 4)*
Pub: Crain Communications, Inc.
Ed: Kimberly D. Williams. **Description:** Overview of FlexPetz, a pet-sharing program that targets customers that live in metropolitan areas and travel frequently, who want to have a dog but cannot care for one on a full time basis.

39932 ■ *"Global Imagery in Online Advertisements" in Business Communication Quarterly (December 2007, pp. 487)*
Pub: SAGE Publications USA
Contact: Blaise R. Simqu, President
Ed: Geraldine E. Hynes, Marius Janson. **Description:** Respondents from six countries were interviewed about their reactions to two online ads to determine cultural differences in understanding advertising elements. Universal appeals and cultural values determine the effectiveness of symbols in online advertising.

39933 ■ *"GM Canada Revved Up Over Camaro" in Globe & Mail (February 17, 2006, pp. B4)*
Pub: CTVglobemedia Publishing Inc.
Ed: Greg Keenan. **Description:** General Manager of General Motors Canada is planning to start the production of company's muscle car Camaro in Canadian facility. The car was exhibited at Canadian International Auto Show held in Toronto.

39934 ■ *"GM Flexes Muscles With New Camaro Concept" in Globe & Mail (January 10, 2006, pp. B15)*
Pub: CTVglobemedia Publishing Inc.
Ed: Greg Keenan. **Description:** General Motors Corp., has displayed the new concept car Chevrolet Camaro, at the North American International Auto Show in Detroit. The features of this automobile manufactured at the company's assembly plant in Quebec are discussed.

39935 ■ *"Go Beyond Local Search With Hyper-Local" in Women Entrepreneur (October 30, 2008)*
Pub: Entrepreneur Media Inc.
Ed: Lena West. **Description:** According to Forrester Research, as much as $500 billion in local spending in 2007 was influenced by the Internet and industry analysts report that consumers spend approximately 80 percent of their income within 50 miles of their home. Discussion of ways in which to capitalize on the hyper-local trend that is being driven by greater Internet connectivity and use of the web to find information is provided.

39936 ■ *"Google, MySpace Deal Hits Snag" in Globe & Mail (February 7, 2007, pp. B11)*
Pub: CTVglobemedia Publishing Inc.
Ed: Julia Angwin; Kevin J. Delaney. **Description:** MySpace's intention to partner with eBay which is delaying the finalization of its $900 million online advertising deal signed with Google Inc. is discussed.

39937 ■ *"Google Places a Call to Bargain Hunters" in Advertising Age (Vol. 79, September 29, 2008, No. 36, pp. 13)*
Pub: Crain Communications, Inc.
Ed: Abbey Klaassen. **Description:** Google highlighted application developers who have created tools for its Android mobile phone in the device's unveiling; applications such as ShopSavvy and CompareEverywhere help shoppers to find bargains by allowing them to compare prices in their local areas and across the web.

39938 ■ *"Got Slogan? Guidelines for Creating Effective Slogans" in Business Horizons (September-October 2007, pp. 415)*
Pub: Elsevier Technology Publications
Ed: Chiranjeev Kohli, Lance Leuthesser, Rajneesh Suri. **Description:** Relevant case studies of industry publications are considered to determine the creation and utilization of effective slogans. The importance of branding as well as factors that contribute to memory and recall are discussed.

39939 ■ *"Graceful Landing" in Entrepreneur (Vol. 37, November 2009, No. 11, pp. 59)*
Pub: Entrepreneur Media, Inc.
Ed: Mikal E. Belicove. **Description:** Successful marketers regularly use Website landing pages to capture qualified leads and make sales. It is believed that an effective landing page devoted to a single product or service offering can significantly boost leads and conversion rates. Organizations can create a top-notch landing page by anticipating customer expectations and focusing on a clear call to action.

39940 ■ *"Grand Bohemian Hotel in Orlando, Fla. Takes Lead in Wedding Planning" in Benzinga.com (August 4, 2011)*
Pub: Benzinga.com
Ed: Benzinga Staff. **Description:** MAD-Marketing launched a newly-designed Website for the Grand Bohemian Hotel in Orlando, Florida. The site features the hotel's wedding vanity site to help target prospective couples planning their weddings.

39941 ■ *"The Green Conversation" in Harvard Business Review (Vol. 86, September 2008, No. 9, pp. 58)*
Pub: Harvard Business School Press
Description: Six guidelines are presented for addressing and benefiting from environmentally conscious corporate decision making and practices. Topics covered include marketing, supply chain, and leadership.

39942 ■ *"Green Counting" in Canadian Business (Vol. 81, October 13, 2008, No. 17, pp. 27)*
Pub: Rogers Media Ltd.
Ed: Joe Castaldo. **Description:** Procter and Gamble research revealed that only 10 percent of North American consumers are willing to accept trade-offs for a greener product. Three out of four North American consumers will not accept a higher price or a decrease in a product's performance for an environmental benefit. Details on green marketing are also discussed.

39943 ■ *GreenBook Worldwide--Directory of Marketing Research Companies and Services*
Pub: New York AMA Communication Services Inc.
Contact: Ruth Hurd, Manager
URL(s): www.greenbook.org. **Released:** Annual; Latest edition 49th; 2011. **Price:** $180, both volumes; $15, Individuals USC; $38, Other countries. **Covers:** 1,600 marketing research companies worldwide (computer services, interviewing services, etc.) of marketing research needs; international coverage. Includes a list of computer programs for marketing research. **Entries include:** Company name, address, phone, name of principal executive, products and services, branch offices. **Arrangement:** Alphabetical. **Indexes:** Geographical, principal executive name, research services, market/industry served, computer program name, trademark/servicemarks.

39944 ■ *Greening Your Small Business: How to Improve Your Bottom Line, Grow Your Brand, Satisfy Your Customers and Save the Planet*
Pub: Prentice Hall Press
Contact: Dame Marjorie M. Scardino, Chief Executive Officer
Ed: Jennifer Kaplan. **Released:** November 3, 2009. **Price:** $19.95. **Description:** A definitive resource for anyone who wants their small business to be cutting-edge, competitive, profitable, and eco-conscious. Stories from small business owners address every aspect of going green, from basics such as recycling waste, energy efficiency, and reducing information technology footprint, to more in-depth concerns such as green marketing and communications, green business travel, and green employee benefits.

39945 ■ *"'Groundhog Day' B & B Likely Will Be Converted Into One In Real Life" in Chicago Tribune (October 21, 2008)*
Pub: McClatchy-Tribune Information Services
Ed: Carolyn Starks. **Description:** Everton Martin and Karla Stewart Martin have purchased the Victorian house that was featured as a bed-and-breakfast in the 1993 hit move 'Groundhog Day'; the couple was initially unaware of the structure's celebrity status when they purchased it with the hope of fulfilling their dream of owning a bed-and-breakfast.

39946 ■ *Groundswell: Winning in a World Transformed by Social Technologies*
Pub: Harvard Business School Press
Ed: Charlene Li; Josh Bernoff. **Released:** April 21, 2008. **Price:** $29.95. **Description:** Individuals are using online social technologies such as blogs, social networking sites, YouTube, and podcasts to discuss products and companies, write their own news, and find their own deals. When consumers you've never met are rating your company's products in public forums with which you have no experience or influence, your company is vulnerable. This book teaches the tools and data necessary to turn this treat into an opportunity.

39947 ■ *Groundswell: Winning in a World Transformed by Social Technologies*
Pub: Harvard Business School Press
Ed: Charlene Li, Josh Bernoff. **Released:** 2008. **Price:** $29.95. **Description:** Corporate executives are struggling with a new trend: people using online social technologies (blogs, social networking sites, YouTube, podcasts) to discuss products and companies, write their own news, and find their own deals.

39948 ■ *"Growing Pains" in Canadian Business (Vol. 81, July 22, 2008, No. 12-13, pp. 35)*
Pub: Rogers Media Ltd.
Ed: Alex Mylnek. **Description:** Laughing Stock Vineyards' Cynthia Enns and David Enns plan to target young buyers by using social media. The Enns however, are concerned that targeting younger buyers may affect Laughing Stock's image as a premium brand. Additional information regarding the company's future plans is presented.

39949 ■ *Guerrilla Marketing, 4th Edition: Easy and Inexpensive Strategies for Making Big Profits from Your Small Business*
Pub: Houghton Mifflin Company
Ed: Jay Conrad Levinson. **Released:** May 2007. **Price:** $19.95. **Description:** Marketing strategies for small businesses is designed to revolutionize, expand and grow businesses. .

39950 ■ *Guerrilla Marketing During Tough Times*
Pub: Morgan James Publishing, LLC
Ed: Jay Conrad Levinson. **Released:** November 2005. **Price:** $14.00. **Description:** Ways to market a small business during slow economic times.

39951 ■ *Guerrilla Marketing Goes Green: Winning Strategies to Improve Your Profits and Your Planet*
Pub: John Wiley & Sons, Inc.
Ed: Jay Conrad Levinson, Shel Horowitz. **Released:** January 10, 2010. **Price:** $21.95. **Description:** The latest tips on green marketing and sustainable business strategies are shared.

39952 ■ *Guerrilla Marketing for the New Millennium*
Pub: Morgan James Publishing, LLC
Ed: Jay Conrad Levinson. **Released:** September 2005. **Price:** $14.00. **Description:** Steps to successfully market a small business on the Internet.

39953 ■ *Guerrilla Marketing: Put Your Advertising on Steroids*
Pub: Morgan James Publishing, LLC
Ed: Jay Conrad Levinson. **Released:** December 2005. **Price:** $14.00. **Description:** Marketing concepts to successfully advertise any Internet business, featuring the ten most successful advertising campaigns of the 20th Century.

39954 ■ *"Half of Canadian Firms to Boost Marketing Budgets" in Globe & Mail (January 22, 2007, pp. B1)*
Pub: CTVglobemedia Publishing Inc.
Ed: Keith McArthur. **Description:** The advertising and marketing spending plans of different companies are presented.

39955 ■ *"Happy Trails: RV Franchiser Gives Road Traveling Enthusiasts a Lift" in Black Enterprise (Vol. 38, July 2008, No. 12, pp. 47)*
Pub: Earl G. Graves Publishing Co. Inc.
Ed: Tamara E. Holmes. **Description:** Overview of Bates International Motor Home Rental Systems Inc., a growing franchise that gives RV owners the chance to rent out their big-ticket purchases to others when they are not using them; Sandra Williams Bate launched the company as a franchise in July 1997 and now has a fleet of 30 franchises across the country. She expects the company to reach 2.2 million for 2008 due to a marketing initiative that will expand the company's presence.

39956 ■ *"Harlequin Leads the Way" in Marketing to Women (Vol. 22, July 2009, No. 7, pp. 1)*
Pub: EPM Communications Inc.
Contact: Ira Mayer, President
E-mail: imayer@epmcom.com
Description: Although the publishing industry has been slow to embrace new media options, the Internet is now a primary source for reaching women readers. Harlequin has been eager to court their female consumers over the Internet and often uses women bloggers in their campaigns strategies.

39957 ■ *"Harley-Davidson Moves to Unconventional Marketing Plan" in Business Journal-Milwaukee (Vol. 28, November 26, 2010, No. 8, pp. A1)*
Pub: Milwaukee Business Journal
Ed: Rich Rovito. **Description:** Harley Davidson Inc. hired Boulder, Colorado-based Victors & Spoils, an agency that specializes in crowdsourcing, to implement a new creative marketing model. Under the plan, Harley Davidson will draw on the ideas of its brand enthusiasts to help guide the brand's marketing direction.

39958 ■ *"Harness the Internet to Boost Equipment Sales" in Indoor Comfort Marketing (Vol. 70, July 2011, No. 7, pp. 24)*
Pub: Industry Publications Inc.
Ed: Richard Rutigliano. **Description:** Advice is given to increase HVAC/R equipment sales using the Internet.

39959 ■ *"The Harris Teeter Grocery Chain Has Started a New Ice Cream Club for Shoppers" in Ice Cream Reporter (Vol. 21, July 20, 2008)*
Pub: Ice Cream Reporter
Description: Store loyalty cards are being issued to Harris Teeter customers to purchase any variety of Ben & Jerry's, Haagen-Dazs, Dove, Starbucks, Ciao Bella, Clemmy's, Purely Decadent, So Delicious, Harris Teeter Naturals, HT Traders, Hunter Farms or Denali Ice Cream. One point is earned for every dollar spent, 30 total points earns a $5 electronic coupon towards the next purchase.

39960 ■ *"HBC Enlists IBM to Help Dress Up Its On-Line Shopping" in Globe & Mail (February 7, 2006, pp. B3)*
Pub: CTVglobemedia Publishing Inc.
Ed: Simon Avery. **Description:** The details of management contract between Hudson's Bay Co. and International Business Machines Corp. are presented.

39961 ■ *Heads in Beds*
Pub: Prentice Hall PTR
Ed: Ivo Raza. **Released:** May 28, 2004. **Description:** Advice is given to help build brands, generate sales and grow profits through marketing for any hospitality or tourism business.

39962 ■ *"Headwinds From the New Sod Slow Aer Lingus" in Barron's (Vol. 88, March 10, 2008, No. 10, pp. M6)*
Pub: Dow Jones & Company, Inc.
Ed: Sean Walters; Arindam Nag. **Description:** Aer Lingus faces a drop in its share prices with a falling US market, higher jet fuel prices, and lower long-haul passenger load factors. British media companies Johnston Press and Yell Group are suffering from weaker ad revenue and heavier debt payments due to the credit crunch.

39963 ■ *"Help Customers Choose Full Service Over Discount" in Indoor Comfort Marketing (Vol. 70, September 2011, No. 9, pp. 10)*
Pub: Industry Publications Inc.
Ed: Richard Rutigliano. **Description:** Marketing strategies for HVAC/R firms to use in 2011 and 2012 heating seasons are outlined, focusing on oil heat.

39964 ■ *"Help for Job Seekers" in Crain's Detroit Business (Vol. 26, January 4, 2010, No. 1, pp. 14)*
Pub: Crain Communications Inc.
Description: CareerWorks is weekly paper targeting readers who are in a career transition or are looking for new employment.

39965 ■ *"'Help Wanted' Meets 'Buy It Now': Why More Companies Are Integrating Marketing and Recruiting" in Inc. (November 2007, pp. 50-52)*
Pub: Gruner & Jahr USA Publishing
Ed: Ryan McCarthy. **Description:** Five tips to merge marketing and recruiting together include: thinking every help wanted ad as a marketing opportunity, treating every job candidate as a potential customer, involving the youngest employees in the interview process, look for way to promote recruiting events, and to sponsor community-oriented events.

39966 ■ *"Helping Customers Fight Pet Waste" in Pet Product News (Vol. 64, November 2010, No. 11, pp. 52)*
Pub: BowTie Inc.
Ed: Sandy Robins. **Description:** Pet cleaning products manufacturers have been enjoying high sales figures by paying attention to changing pet ownership trends and environmental awareness. Meanwhile, the inclusion of user-friendly features in these products has also been boosted by the social role of pets and the media attention to pet waste. How manufacturers have been responding to this demand is explored.

39967 ■ *"Herrell's Launches New Corporate Identity at Fancy Food Show" in Ice Cream Reporter (Vol. 23, July 20, 2010, No. 8, pp. 3)*
Pub: Ice Cream Reporter
Description: Herrell's ice cream introduced a new corporate branding at the Summer 2010 Fancy Food Show last summer. Slightly Mad Communications advertising agency developed the new brand to reflect the era of the early 1970s.

39968 ■ *"High-Tech, Niche Options Change Sports Marketing" in Crain's Detroit Business (Vol. 24, March 17, 2008, No. 11, pp. 14)*
Pub: Crain Communications, Inc.
Ed: Leah Boyd. **Description:** Sports advertisers have an ever-increasing menu of high-tech or niche marketing options such as interactive campaigns through cell phones and electronic banners which can span arenas.

39969 ■ *"Hitting the Green" in Canadian Business (Vol. 81, July 22, 2008, No. 12-13, pp. 34)*
Pub: Rogers Media Ltd.
Ed: Andy Holloway. **Description:** RBC is sponsoring the Canadian Open golf tournament, which is the second-oldest event in the PGA Tour. RBC is expected to receive television exposure on CBS and the Golf Channel. Additional information relating to the sponsorship is presented.

39970 ■ *"Hold the IPhone" in Canadian Business (Vol. 80, January 15, 2007, No. 2, pp. 22)*
Pub: Rogers Media
Ed: Andrew Wahl. **Description:** The rise in the price of shares of Apple Inc. after the introduction of its new product, the iPhone, is discussed.

39971 ■ *Home-Based Business for Dummies*
Pub: John Wiley and Sons, Inc.
Ed: Paul Edwards, Sarah Edwards, Peter Economy. **Released:** February 25, 2005. **Price:** $19.99. **Description:** Provides all the information needed to start and run a home-based business. Topics include: selecting the right business; setting up a home office; managing money, credit, and financing; marketing; and ways to avoid distractions while working at home.

39972 ■ *"Home Improvement Marketers Target Women With New Products, New Campaigns and Plenty of Pink" in Marketing to Women (March 2008)*
Pub: EPM Communications Inc.
Contact: Ira Mayer, President
E-mail: imayer@epmcom.com
Description: From creating tools that fit a woman's ergonomics to designs that fit a woman's fashion sense, home improvement is finding new ways in which to market to women.

39973 ■ *"Hostess Reveals Grand Prize Winner of 'CupCake Jackpot' Promotion" in Entertainment Close-Up (August 19, 2011)*
Pub: Close-Up Media
Description: Tricia Botbyl was the grand prize winner of the Hostess 'CupCake Jackpot' promotion that asked consumers to 'spin' online to win $10,000. Consumers were asked to vote for their favorite Hostess Brand cupcake flavor.

39974 ■ *How to Advertise a Small Business: Step by Step Guide to Starting Your Own Business*
Pub: Lewis and Renn Associates
Ed: Leslie D. Renn; Jerre G. Lewis. **Released:** 2007. **Price:** $21.95. **Description:** Step-by-step guide to help small business owners advertise products and services.

39975 ■ *"How to Attract Big-City Talent to Small Towns" in Advertising Age (Vol. 79, July 7, 2008, No. 26, pp. 24)*
Pub: Crain Communications, Inc.
Ed: Joe Erwin. **Description:** Advice concerning ways in which to attract talent to mid-market agencies is given and innovative techniques that have worked for some firms are discussed.

39976 ■ *"How to Boost Your Super Bowl ROI" in Advertising Age (Vol. 80, December 7, 2009, No. 41, pp. 3)*
Pub: Crain's Communications
Ed: Abbey Klaassen. **Description:** Internet marketing is essential, even for the corporations that can afford to spend $3 million on a 30-second Super Bowl spot; last year, Super Bowl advertising reached an online viewership of 99.5 million while 98.7 million people watched the game on television validating the idea that public relations must go farther than a mere television ad campaign. Social media provides businesses with a longer shelf life for their ad campaigns. Advice is also given regarding ways in which to strategize a smart and well-thought plan for utilizing the online marketing options currently available.

39977 ■ *"How to Conquer New Markets With Old Skills" in Harvard Business Review (Vol. 88, November 2010, No. 11, pp. 118)*
Pub: Harvard Business School Publishing
Ed: Mauro F. Guillen, Esteban Garcia-Canal. **Description:** Exploration of business-networking factors that have helped lead to the success of Spain's multinational companies is provided. These include development of political skills, access to capabilities and resources, globalization partnerships, and speed of implementation.

39978 ■ *How Customers Think*
Pub: Harvard Business School Press
Ed: Gerald Zaltman. **Released:** February 21, 2003. **Price:** $32.95. **Description:** Despite marketing efforts and customer surveys, nearly eighty percent of all new products fail of fall short of prediction within the first six months after introduction. Consumer reactions to products and marketing programs are investigated.

39979 ■ *"How to Dominate in Residential Maintenance" in Green Industry Pro (Vol. 23, October 2011)*
Pub: Cygnus Business Media
Ed: Gregg Wartgow. **Description:** Lawn care services were ranked among the most expendable consumer expenditures, according to the National Retail Federation data accumulated in early 2011. This makes it critical for any landscape firm to target sales efforts toward higher-income households and higher-value homes.

39980 ■ *How to Get Rich on the Internet*
Pub: Morgan James Publishing, LLC
Ed: Ted Ciuba. **Released:** August 2004. **Price:** $19. 95. **Description:** Interviews with successful Internet entrepreneurs provide insight into marketing products and services online using minimal investment. The importance of a sound marketing ad campaign using the Internet is discussed; maintaining a database and Website will automatically carry out business transactions daily. Suggestions for various types of businesses to run online are given.

39981 ■ *"How Good Advice 'Online' Can Attract Customers" in Indoor Comfort Marketing (Vol. 70, August 2011, No. 8, pp. 20)*
Pub: Industry Publications Inc.
Ed: Richard Rutigilano. **Description:** Online marketing tips for heating and cooling small businesses are explained.

39982 ■ *"How Hard Could It Be? Adventures In Software Demol'ling" in Inc. (December 2007, pp. 99-100)*
Pub: Gruner & Jahr USA Publishing
Ed: Joel Spolsky. **Description:** Founder and CEO of Fog Creek Software, a New York City software developer shares insight into his software demo tour used to promote his firm's products.

39983 ■ *"How to Improve Your Mobile Marketing" in Contractor (Vol. 56, October 2009, No. 10, pp. 54)*
Pub: Penton Media, Inc.
Ed: Matt Michel. **Description:** Plumbers can improve their mobile advertising by making their logos as large as possible and positioning their logo on top of the truck so people can see it over traffic. They should also make the phone numbers small because people only take note of these when the truck is parked.

39984 ■ *How to Make Big Money in Your Own Small Business: Unexpected Rules Every Small Business Owner Needs to Know*
Pub: Hyperion Press
Ed: Jeffrey J. Fox. **Released:** May 2004. **Price:** $16. 95. **Description:** Former sales and marketing pro offers advice on growing a small business.

39985 ■ *"How to Make Marketing Work" in Agency Sales Magazine (Vol. 39, September-October 2009, No. 9, pp. 30)*
Pub: MANA
Ed: John Graham. **Description:** Marketing's core concept is to focus total attention on the customer. Marketers should stop trying to manipulate customers and recognize that getting people through the door does not make them customers. Customer satisfaction is also important since even the most compelling marketing messages are worthless without this vital relationship.

39986 ■ *How to Make Money with Social Media: Using New and Emerging Media to Grow Your Business*
Pub: FT Press
Ed: Jamie Turner, Reshma Shah. **Released:** October 1, 2010. **Price:** $24.99. **Description:** Marketers, executives, entrepreneurs are shown more effective ways to utilize Internet social media to make money. This guide brings together both practical strategies and proven execution techniques for driving maximum value from social media marketing.

39987 ■ *"How to Make Your Website Really Sell" in Entrepreneur (Vol. 37, September 2009, No. 9, pp. 79)*
Pub: Entrepreneur Media, Inc.
Ed: David Port. **Description:** Advice on how to succeed in Internet marketing is presented. Offering visitors purchase incentives on the home page is encouraged. Delivery of customized landing pages and content is also recommended.

39988 ■ *"How to Manage Successful Crowdsourcing Projects" in eWeek (September 29, 2010)*
Pub: Ziff Davis Enterprise
Description: The advantages, challenges and pitfalls faced when using crowdsourcing to improve a business are outlined. Crowdsourcing helps to eliminate the need to rely on an internal workforce and the need to forecast task volume.

39989 ■ *"How Marketers Can Tap the Web" in Sales and Marketing Management (November 12, 2009)*
Pub: Nielsen Business Media, Inc.
Description: Internet marketing strategies require careful planning and tools in order to track success. Businesses are utilizing this trend to attract new clients as well as keep customers they already have satisfied. Advice on website development and design is provided.

39990 ■ *"How Not to Build a Website" in Women Entrepreneur (December 24, 2008)*
Pub: Entrepreneur Media Inc.
Ed: Erica Ruback; Joanie Reisen. **Description:** Tips for producing a unique and functional Website are given as well as a number of lessons a pair of entrepreneurs learned while trying to launch their networking website, MomSpace.com.

39991 ■ *"How to Ramp Up Marketing in a Downturn" in Entrepreneur (Vol. 37, July 2009, No. 7, pp. 55)*
Pub: Entrepreneur Media, Inc.
Ed: Jeff Wuorio. **Description:** How businesses can save money while boosting their marketing efforts during a down economy is discussed. Using price-driven marketing, online social networks, and cause-driven marketing are among the suggested ways companies can attract more customers. Guarantees and warrantees, as well as contests, can also be used as marketing tools.

39992 ■ *How to Start a Home-Based Senior Care Business: Develop a Winning Business Plan*
Pub: Globe Pequot Press
Ed: James L. Ferry. **Released:** January 10, 2010. **Price:** $18.95. **Description:** Everything needed to know in order to start and run a profitable, ethical, and satisfying senior care business from your home. Information covers writing a good business plan, marketing services to families, creating a fee structure, and developing a network of trusted caregivers and service providers.

39993 ■ *How to Start and Run a Home-Based Landscaping Business*
Pub: Globe Pequot Press
Ed: Owen E. Dell. **Released:** December 2005. **Price:** $18.95. **Description:** Guide to starting and running a successful home-based landscaping business, including tips for marketing on the Internet.

39994 ■ *How to Start and Run a Small Book Publishing Company: A Small Business Guide to Self-Publishing and Independent Publishing*
Pub: HCM Publishing
Ed: Peter I. Hupalo. **Released:** August 30, 2002. **Price:** $18.95. **Description:** The book teaches all aspects of starting and running a small book publishing company. Topics covered include: inventory accounting in the book trade, just-in-time inventory management, turnkey fulfillment solutions, tax deductible costs, basics of sales and use tax, book pricing, standards in terms of the book industry, working with distributors and wholesalers, cover design and book layout, book promotion and marketing, how to select profitable authors to publish, printing process, printing on demand, the power of a strong backlist, and how to value copyright.

39995 ■ *"How Two Flourishing Exporters Did It" in Hispanic Business (Vol. 30, July-August 2008, No. 7-8, pp. 46)*
Pub: Hispanic Business, Inc.
Ed: Richard Kaplan. **Description:** Vigorous growth in export revenues posted by two Hispanic-owned export companies Compasa LLC and Ametza LLC is discussed; both firms have benefited from their closer locations to major Mexican markets, superior quality of their products, market knowledge and the relationships of trust developed with key business partners.

39996 ■ *How to Use the Internet to Advertise, Promote, and Market Your Business or Web Site: With Little or No Money*
Pub: Atlantic Publishing Company
Released: December 1, 2010. **Price:** $24.95. **Description:** Information is given to help build, promote, and make money from your Website or brick and mortar store using the Internet, with minimal costs.

39997 ■ *How to Write a Great Business Plan for Your Small Business in 60 Minutes or Less*
Pub: Atlantic Publishing
Ed: Sharon L. Fullen. **Released:** January 2006. **Price:** $39.95 includes CD-Rom. **Description:** A good business plan outlines goals and works as a company's resume to obtain funding, credit from suppliers, management of the operations and finances, promotion and marketing, and more.

39998 ■ *Hug Your Customers*
Pub: Hyperion Books
Ed: Jack Mitchell. **Price:** $19.95. **Description:** The CEO of Mitchells/Roberts, two very successful clothing stores, professes his belief in showering customers with attention. His secrets for long-term business success include advice about attracting a good staff, lowering marketing costs, and maintaining higher gross margins and revenues.

39999 ■ *"Hybrid Popularity Pushes Automakers to Add to Offerings" in Crain's Cleveland Business (Vol. 28, November 12, 2007, No. 45, pp. 30)*
Pub: Crain Communications, Inc.
Ed: David Sedgwick. **Description:** Due in part to Toyota's innovative marketing, automotive hybrids have caught on with consumers thus forcing other automakers to add hybrids to their product plans.

40000 ■ *"Hyundai Enters Minivan Market" in Globe & Mail (February 15, 2006, pp. B7)*
Pub: CTVglobemedia Publishing Inc.
Ed: Greg Keenan. **Description:** The reasons behind the launch of minivan by Hyundai Auto Canada Inc. are presented.

40001 ■ *"I Hear You're Interested In a.." in Inc. (January 2008, pp. 40-43)*
Pub: Gruner & Jahr USA Publishing
Ed: Leah Hoffmann. **Description:** Four tips to help any small business generate sales leads online are examined.

40002 ■ *I Love You More Than My Dog*
Pub: Portfolio
Ed: Jeanne Bliss. **Price:** $22.95. **Description:** Ways to win passionate, loyal and vocal customers in order to build a small business is outlined.

40003 ■ *"An Ice Boost in Revenue; Wings Score With Expanded Corporate Sales" in Crain's Detroit Business (Vol. 25, June 1, 2009, No. 22)*
Pub: Crain Communications Inc. - Detroit
Ed: Bill Shea. **Description:** Stanley Cup finals always boost business for the Detroit area, even during a recession. The Red Wings corporate office reported corporate sponsorship revenue luxury suite rentals, Legends Club seats and advertising were up 40 percent this year over 2008.

40004 ■ *"Ideas at Work: Sparkling Innovation" in Business Strategy Review (Vol. 21, Summer 2010, No. 2, pp. 7)*
Pub: Blackwell Publishers Ltd.
Ed: Julian Birkinshaw, Peter Robbins. **Description:** GlaxoSmithKline faced a situation common to large global organizations: how to allocate marketing resources to smaller, regional brands. A report on the company's inventive approach to worldwide marketing that led to the development of a unique and productive network are explored.

40005 ■ *"Ideas at Work: Sparkling Innovation" in Business Strategy Review (Vol. 21, Summer 2010, No. 2, pp. 07)*
Pub: Wiley-Blackwell
Ed: Julian Birkinshaw, Peter Robbins. **Description:** GlaxoSmithKline faced a situation common to large global organizations: how to allocate marketing resources to smaller, regional brands. The company's approach to worldwide marketing that led to the development of a unique and productive network is outlined.

40006 ■ *"If the Opportunity is There, Move Boldly" in Indoor Comfort Marketing (Vol. 70, March 2011, No. 3, pp.)*
Pub: Industry Publications Inc.
Ed: Rich Rutigliano. **Description:** Suggestions are offered to help improve air conditioning sales.

40007 ■ *"The Impact of Brand Quality on Shareholder Wealth" in Journal of Marketing (Vol. 75, September 2011, No. 5, pp. 88)*
Pub: American Marketing Association
Ed: Sundar G. Bharardwaj, Kapil R. Tuli, Andre Bonfrer. **Description:** The effects of brand quality on idiosyncratic risk, systematic risk, and stock returns are investigated. Findings reveal that unexpected changes in brand quality negatively associated with idiosyncratic risk changes and positively related to stock returns. However, unexpected changes in brand quality will reduce shareholder wealth due to positive relationship with changes n systematic risk.

40008 ■ *"The Impact of Incomplete Typeface Logos on Perceptions of the Firms" in Journal of Marketing (Vol. 75, July 2011, No. 4, pp. 86)*
Pub: American Marketing Association
Ed: Henrik Hagtvedt. **Description:** A study of the influence of incomplete typeface logos on consumer perceptions of the company is presented. The findings suggest that companies should avoid incomplete typeface logos if perceptions of trustworthiness are critical or if consumers are likely to have a prevention focus.

40009 ■ *"Impulse Buys Find Their Way Into Grocery Cart" in Marketing to Women (Vol. 23, November 2010, No. 11, pp. 6)*
Pub: EPM Communications Inc.
Contact: Ira Mayer, President
E-mail: imayer@epmcom.com
Description: Impulse purchases are made by 90 percent of grocery shoppers according to a recent study. The number of items shoppers buy impulsively during a typical trip to the grocery store in 2010 are outlined.

40010 ■ *"In Print and Online" in Marketing to Women (Vol. 22, August 2009, No. 8, pp. 3)*
Pub: EPM Communications Inc.
Contact: Ira Mayer, President
E-mail: imayer@epmcom.com
Description: Seventeen magazine is unifying its print and Online editions with complementary content, a strategy that seems to be working as every aspect of Seventeen drives the reader to another component.

40011 ■ *"In Puerto Rico, Slow and Steady Wins Race" in Globe & Mail (February 24, 2007, pp. B3)*
Pub: CTVglobemedia Publishing Inc.
Ed: Andrew Willis. **Description:** The plan of Scotiabank de Puerto Rico's chief executive officer Richard Waugh to improve its market presence using its international banking relations is discussed.

40012 ■ *"In the Wake of Pet-Food Crisis, Iams Sales Plummet Nearly 17 Percent" in Advertising Age (Vol. 78, May 14, 2007, No. 18, pp. 3)*
Pub: Crain Communications, Inc.
Ed: Jack Neff. **Description:** Although the massive U.S. pet-food recall impacted more than 100 brands, Procter & Gamble Co.'s Iams lost more sales and market share than any other industry player. According to Information Resources Inc. data, the brand's sales dropped 16.5 percent in the eight-week period ended April 22. Many analysts feel that the company could have handled the crisis in a better manner.

40013 ■ *"Indoor Air Quality - a Tribute to Efficiency" in Indoor Comfort Marketing (Vol. 70, August 2011, No. 8, pp. 8)*
Pub: Industry Publications Inc.
Ed: Matthew Maleske. **Description:** Efficiency of new HVAC/R equipment has helped improve indoor air quality.

40014 ■ *"Indulgent Parsimony: an Enduring Marketing Approach" in Strategy and Leadership (Vol. 39, March-April 2011, No. 2, pp. 36)*
Pub: Emerald Group Publishing Inc.
Ed: Kenneth Alan Grossberg. **Description:** Indulgent parsimony (IP), a marketing strategy employed on consumers that are affected by recession, is found to be a relevant and appropriate approach that can help encourage buying. IP involves the selling of cheaper goods and services that allow consumers experience comfort and relief from stress.

40015 ■ *"Industry Vet To Spread Glory's Word" in Business First-Columbus (November 9, 2007, pp. A1)*
Pub: American City Business Journals, Inc.
Ed: Dan Eaton. **Description:** Glory Foods, Inc. chose Jacqueline Neal as its new president in October 2007. Neal has eleven years experience in brand management and has worked with food industry leaders such as Mars Inc., Kraft Foods Inc., and Nabisco Holdings Corporation. Neil's plans for the company are presented.

40016 ■ *Influence: The Psychology of Persuasion*
Pub: HarperCollins Publishers
Ed: Robert B. Cialdini. **Released:** June 2, 2009. **Price:** $17.99. **Description:** Whether you are the consumer or the salesperson, this book will help you understand the psychological foundations of marketing.

40017 ■ *"Info Junkie" in Crain's Chicago Business (Vol. 34, October 24, 2011, No. 42, pp. 35)*
Pub: Crain Communications Inc.
Ed: Christina Le Beau. **Description:** Greg Colando, president of Flor Inc., an eco-friendly carpet company located I Chicago discusses his marketing program to increase sales.

40018 ■ *"InnoCentive Announces Next Generation Crowdsourcing Platform" in Internet Wire (June 15, 2010)*
Pub: Comtex
Description: InnoCentive, Inc., a world leader in open innovation, is launching InnoCentive@Work3, a third generation of its @Work enterprise platform for collaborative-driven innovation for companies. The product will help clients solve critical business and technical issues by tapping information both inside and outside of a company.

40019 ■ *"Innovation Can Be Imperative for Those in Hands-On Trades" in Crain's Cleveland Business (Vol. 28, November 12, 2007, No. 45)*
Pub: Crain Communications, Inc.
Ed: Harriet Tramer. **Description:** Discusses the importance of networking and innovative marketing concerning those in art and restoration trades.

40020 ■ *"Inside Intel's Effectiveness System for Web Marketing" in Advertising Age (Vol. 81, January 25, 2010, No. 4, pp. 4)*
Pub: Crain's Communications
Ed: Beth Snyder Bulik. **Description:** Overview of Intel's internally developed program called Value Point System in which the company is using in order to evaluate and measure online marketing effectiveness.

40021 ■ *Instant Cashflow: Hundreds of Proven Strategies to Win Customers, Boost Margins and Take More Money Home*
Pub: McGraw-Hill Companies Inc.
Contact: Deven Sharma, President
Ed: Bradley J. Sugars. **Released:** December 2005. **Price:** $17.95 (US), $22.95 (Canadian). **Description:** Nearly 300 proven marketing and sales strategies are shared by the author, a self-made millionaire. Advice on creating the proper mindset, generating new leads, boosting the conversion rate of leads to sales, maximizing the value of the average sale, and measuring results is included.

40022 ■ *Instant Income*
Pub: McGraw-Hill Inc.
Ed: Janet Switzer. **Released:** February 2007. **Price:** $30.95 (CND). **Description:** Book covers small business advertising techniques, marketing, joint ventures, and sales.

40023 ■ *Instant Profit: Successful Strategies to Boost Your Margin and Increase the Profitability of Your Business*
Pub: McGraw-Hill Companies Inc.
Contact: Deven Sharma, President
Ed: Bradley J. Sugars. **Released:** December 2005. **Price:** $16.95 (US), $22.95 (Canadian). **Description:** Advice on management, money, marketing, and merchandising a successful small business is offered.

40024 ■ *"Insurers No Longer Paying Premium for Advertising" in Brandweek (Vol. 49, April 21, 2008, No. 16, pp. SR3)*
Pub: VNU Business Media, Inc.
Ed: Eric Newman. **Description:** Insurance companies are cutting their advertising budgets after years of accelerated double-digit growth in spending due to the economic downturn, five years of record-breaking ad spend and a need to cut expenditures as claims costs rise and a competitive market keeps premiums in place. Statistical data included.

40025 ■ *Integration Marketing: How Small Businesses Become Big Businesses and Big Businesses Become Empires*
Pub: John Wiley & Sons, Inc.
Ed: Mark Joyner. **Released:** May 1, 2009. **Price:** $22.95. **Description:** Leading Internet marketing expert offers a marketing methodology to grow any business.

40026 ■ *"Interested in 12 Billion Dollars?" in Indoor Comfort Marketing (Vol. 70, March 2011, No. 3, pp. 18)*
Pub: Industry Publications Inc.
Ed: Matthew Maleske. **Description:** Trends in the indoor quality industry are cited, with insight into expanding an existing indoor heating and cooling business.

40027 ■ *"Internet Marketing 2.0: Closing the Online Chat Gap" in Agent's Sales Journal (November 2009, pp. 14)*
Pub: Summit Business Media
Ed: Jeff Denenholz. **Description:** Advice regarding the implementation of an Internet marketing strategy for insurance agencies includes how and why to incorporate a chat feature in which a sales agent can communicate in real-time with potential or existing customers. It is important to understand if appropriate response mechanisms are in place to convert leads into actual sales.

40028 ■ *"Internet Marketing Agency .Com Marketing Wins National Awards for Web Design and SEO" in Marketing Weekly News (Jan. 2, 2010)*
Pub: Investment Weekly News
Description: Internet marketing agency .Com Marketing has won two bronze awards for its exceptional quality web services; the company is a full-service interactive marketing and advertising agency that specializes in a variety of online services including web design, social media marketing and press releases.

40029 ■ *"Internet Marketing Agency .Com Marketing Wins National Awards for Web Design and SEO" in Marketing Weekly News (January 2, 2010)*
Pub: Investment Weekly News
Description: Internet marketing agency .Com Marketing has won two bronze awards for its exceptional quality web services; the company is a full-service interactive marketing and advertising agency that specializes in a variety of online services including web design, social media marketing and press releases.

40030 ■ *"Internet Marketing and Social Media Knowledge Vital for SMBs" in Internet Wire (November 24, 2009)*
Pub: Comtex News Network, Inc.
Description: Small and medium-size businesses must learn to market themselves over the Internet in order to succeed and grow in today's marketplace. Web Marketing Today offers the largest source of the most important information concerning doing business on the Internet including e-commerce, email marketing and social networking opportunities.

40031 ■ *"Internet and Mobile Media" in MarketingMagazine (Vol. 115, September 27, 2010, No. 13, pp. 60)*
Pub: Rogers Publishing Ltd.
Description: Market data covering the Internet and mobile media in Canada is given.

40032 ■ *"Into the Light: Making Our Way Through the Economic Tunnel" in Agency Sales Magazine (Vol. 39, August 2009, No. 8, pp. 26)*
Pub: MANA
Ed: Michael Dotson. **Description:** Ways in which to avoid business stagnation brought about by the economic downturn, is presented. Being different, being a puzzle solver, and knowing the competition are among the things marketing personnel should do in order to wade through the economic downturn. Marketing via direct mail and the Internet also recommended.

40033 ■ *"Inventive Doctor New Venture Partner" in Houston Business Journal (Vol. 40, January 29, 2010, No. 38, pp. A2)*
Pub: American City Business Journals
Ed: Ford Gunter. **Description:** Dr. Billy Cohn, a surgeon from Houston, Texas has been named as venture partner for venture firm Sante Ventures LLC of Austin, Texas. Cohn will be responsible for seeing marketable developing technologies in the medical industry. The motivation for Cohn's naming as venture partner is his development of a minimally invasive therapy for end-stage renal disease.

40034 ■ *"IPhone 3G" in Advertising Age (Vol. 79, November 17, 2008, No. 43, pp. 15)*
Pub: Crain Communications, Inc.
Ed: Beth Snyder Bulik. **Description:** Review of Apple's new iPhone 3G which includes the addition of smart-phone applications as well as a price drop; the new functionalities as well as the lower price seems to be paying off for Apple who reported sales of 6.9 million iPhones in its most recent quarter, in which the 3G hit store shelves.

40035 ■ *"IPod Killers?" in Canadian Business (Vol. 79, November 20, 2006, No. 23, pp. 68)*
Pub: Rogers Media
Ed: Gerry Blackwell. **Description:** The features of Apple iPod that distinguishes it from other MP3 players available in the market are discussed.

40036 ■ *"Irene Rosenfeld; Chairman and CEO, Kraft Foods Inc." in Crain's Chicago Business (Vol. 31, May 5, 2008, No. 18, pp. 31)*
Pub: Crain Communications, Inc.
Ed: David Sterrett. **Description:** Profile of Irene Rosenfeld who is the chairman and CEO of Kraft Foods Inc. and is entering the second year of a three-year plan to boost sales of well-known brands such as Oreo, Velveeta and Oscar Mayer while facing soaring commodity costs and a declining market-share. Ms. Rosenfeld's turnaround strategy also entails spending more on advertising and giving managers more control over their budgets and product development.

40037 ■ *"Israeli Spam Law May Have Global Impact" in Information Today (Vol. 26, February 2009, No. 2, pp. 28)*
Pub: Information Today, Inc.
Ed: David Mirchin. **Description:** Israels new law, called Amendment 40 of the Communications Law, will regulate commercial solicitations including those sent without permission via email, fax, automatic phone dialing systems, or short messaging technologies.

40038 ■ *"It's Back to Business for the Ravens" in Boston Business Journal (Vol. 29, July 29, 2011, No. 12, pp. 1)*
Pub: American City Business Journals Inc.
Ed: Scott Dance. **Description:** The Baltimore Ravens football team has been marketing open sponsorship packages following the end of the National Football League lockout. Team officials are working to get corporate logos and slogans on radio and television commercials and online advertisements.

40039 ■ *"It's a Hit" in Entrepreneur (Vol. 36, March 2008, No. 3, pp. 110)*
Pub: Entrepreneur Media Inc.
Ed: John Jantsch. **Description:** Entrepreneurs use the Web to market business and keeping relevant content in the Website is important to address questions from customers. Other considerations in marketing businesses online include: interacting with site visitors, using Web applications for project collaboration and file storage, and encouraging customers to post reviews.

40040 ■ *"It's a New Game: Killerspin Pushes Table Tennis to Extreme Heights" in Black Enterprise (Vol. 37, October 2006, No. 3, pp. 73)*
Pub: Earl G. Graves Publishing Co. Inc.
Ed: Bridget McCrea. **Description:** Profile of Robert Blackwell and his company Killerspin L.L.C., which is popularizing the sport of table tennis. Killerspin has hit $1 million in revenues due to product sales primarily generated through the company's website, magazines, DVDs, and event ticket sales.

40041 ■ *It's Not Who You Know - It's Who Knows You!: The Small Business Guide to Raising Your Profits by Raising Your Profile*
Pub: John Wiley & Sons, Inc.
Ed: David Avrin. **Released:** November 9, 2010. **Price:** $24.95. **Description:** When it comes to promoting a small business or a brand, it is essential to know how valuable high-profile attention can be. But for most small companies, the cost of hiring an outside firm to increase attention can be too expensive.

40042 ■ *"Jacksonville-based Interline Expanding in Janitorial-Sanitation Market" in Florida Times-Union (May 10, 2011)*
Pub: Florida Times-Union
Ed: Mark Basch. **Description:** Interline Brands Inc., located in Jacksonville, Florida, aims to grow its business with two recent acquisitions of firms that distribute janitorial and sanitation products. Interline markets and distributes maintenance, repair and operations products.

40043 ■ *"Jay Berkowitz to Present Making Social Media Money Seminar at Affiliate Summit West" in Entertainment Close-Up (January 15, 2010)*
Pub: Close-Up Media
Description: Highlights of Jay Berkowitz's conference, 'Making Social Media Make Money' include ways in which to develop Internet marketing strategies that will maximize Website traffic and convert that traffic to sales.

40044 ■ *"Jeans Draw a Global Following" in Marketing to Women (Vol. 21, April 2008, No. 4, pp. 6)*
Pub: EPM Communications Inc.
Contact: Ira Mayer, President
E-mail: imayer@epmcom.com
Description: According to a global study by Synovate of jeans and the women who wear them uncovered trends such as brand loyalty and if given a choice 45 percent of all respondents say that if given a choice, they would wear jeans every day.

40045 ■ *"Jo-Ann Launches Quilt Your Colors Contest to Celebrate National Sewing Month" in Internet Wire (September 10, 2010)*
Pub: Comtex
Description: Jo-Ann Fabric and Craft Stores featured a contest to create a quilt in order to promote National Sewing Month.

40046 ■ *"Johnny Royal of Luthier Society Unveils Archimedes 1.0 Trailer" in Internet Wire (October 22, 2009)*
Pub: Comtex News Network, Inc.
Description: Luthier Society, a social media and viral branding agency, has released the first viral video for the company's ROI weighted-value software platform named Archimedes 1.0; users of the software will be able to determine the depth of their outreach efforts, saturation rate, value of their Internet presence and the geo-spatial location of their audience; this will give a true, monetized value for ROI (Return on Investment) in social media marketing.

40047 ■ *"Johnson's Taps Online Animation" in Marketing to Women (Vol. 21, April 2008, No. 4, pp. 3)*
Pub: EPM Communications Inc.
Contact: Ira Mayer, President
E-mail: imayer@epmcom.com
Description: Johnson's has launched a new integrated campaign for its baby lotion in an effort to appeal to the growing number of moms online.

40048 ■ *Jump Start Your Business Brain: Ideas, Advice and Insights for Immediate Marketing and Innovation Success*
Pub: Emmis Books
Contact: Richard Hunt, President
E-mail: rhunt@emmis.com
Ed: Doug Hall. **Released:** April 2005. **Price:** $23.99. **Description:** Strategies to improve sales, marketing, and business development.

40049 ■ *"Kawasaki's New Top Gun" in Brandweek (Vol. 49, April 21, 2008, No. 16, pp. 18)*
Pub: VNU Business Media, Inc.
Description: Discusses Kawasaki's marketing plan which included designing an online brochure in which visitors could create a video by building their own test track on a grid and then selecting visual special effects and musical overlay. This engaging and innovative marketing technique generated more than 166,000 unique users within the first three months of being launched.

40050 ■ *"Keep Customers Out of the Yellow Pages" in Contractor (Vol. 56, November 2009, No. 11, pp. 47)*
Pub: Penton Media, Inc.
Ed: Matt Michel. **Description:** Mechanical contractors should keep customers away from the Yellow Pages where they could find their competition by putting stickers on the water heater or the front of the directory. Giving out magnets to customers and putting the company name on sink rings and invoices are other suggestions.

40051 ■ *The King of Madison Avenue: David Ogilvy and the Making of Modern Advertising*
Pub: Palgrave Macmillan

Ed: Kenneth Roman. **Released:** 2009. **Price:** $27.95. **Description:** The rise and fall of David Ogilvy, once the leader on Madison Avenue, is discussed.

40052 ■ *The King of Vodka: The Story of Pyotr Smirnov and the Upheaval of an Empire*
Pub: HarperCollins Publishers

Ed: Linda Himelstein. **Released:** 2009. **Price:** $29.99. **Description:** Biography of Pyotr Smirnov and how his determination took him from serf to the head of Smirnov Vodka. Smirnov's marketing techniques are defined and show how he expanded the drink worldwide.

40053 ■ *"Knowing Is Growing: Five Strategies To Develop You and Your Business" in Black Enterprise (Vol. 38, November 2007, No. 4, pp. 106)*
Pub: Earl G. Graves Publishing Co. Inc.

Ed: Erinn R. Johnson. **Description:** Five strategies for growing a small business are listed by Andrew Morrison, founder of the Small Business Camp. The camp provides training, coaching, and marketing services to entrepreneurs.

40054 ■ *"Kraft Not Alone" in Crain's Chicago Business (Vol. 30, February 2007, No. 6, pp. 8)*
Pub: Crain Communications, Inc.

Description: Consumer watchdog group, The Center for Science in the Public Interest, has been putting pressure on food companies to be more truthful on their product labels. Listing of companies who have had misleading claims on their products is included.

40055 ■ *"Kubicki Juggles Lineup at Vianda" in Business Courier (Vol. 26, December 11, 2009, No. 33, pp. 1)*
Pub: American City Business Journals, Inc.

Ed: Dan Monk. **Description:** Cincinnati real estate developer Chuck Kubicki replaced the management team of Vianda LLC and cancelled contracts with two vendors that caused a surge of customer complaints. Vianda is a direct-response marketing firm that sells and distributes dietary supplements for wellness and sexual performance.

40056 ■ *"Kuno Creative to Present B2B Social Media Campaign Webinar" in Entertainment Close-Up (August 25, 2011)*
Pub: Close-Up Media

Description: Kuno Creative, an inbound marketing agency, will host Three Steps of a Successful B2B Social Media Campaign. The firm is a provider of Website development, branding, marketing strategy, public relations, Internet marketing, and inbound marketing.

40057 ■ *Lateral Marketing: New Techniques for Finding Breakthrough Ideas*
Pub: John Wiley & Sons, Incorporated

Ed: Philip Kotler, Fernando Trias de Bes. **Released:** September 2003. **Price:** $34.95. **Description:** Lateral marketing complements traditional marketing by allowing marketers develop a new product for a wider audience.

40058 ■ *"Laterooms and Octopus Travel Top Greenlight's Integrated Search Report for the Hotel Sector" in Internet Wire (October 23, 2009)*
Pub: Comtex News Network, Inc.

Description: According to a research report conducted by Greenlight, the UK's leading independent Internet search marketing agency, the most visible hotel websites in natural search during June 2009 are premierinn.com, booking.com and laterooms.com; OctopusTravel.com generated the greatest share of the paid search section with 21 percent visibility. The report is focused on the hotel sector and covers the second quarter of 2009. Statistical data included.

40059 ■ *"LatinWorks Cozies Up to Chevy in Detroit" in Austin Business Journal (Vol. 31, August 12, 2011, No. 23, pp. A1)*
Pub: American City Business Journals Inc.

Ed: Sandra Zaragoza. **Description:** Hispanic marketing agency LatinWorks opened an office in Detroit to better serve its client Chevrolet and to potentially secure more contracts from its parent company General Motors, whose offices are located nearby.

40060 ■ *"Lavante, Inc. Joins Intersynthesis, Holistic Internet Marketing Company" in Internet Wire (November 5, 2009)*
Pub: Comtex News Network, Inc.

Description: Lavante, Inc., the leading provider of on-demand vendor information and profit recovery audit solutions for Fortune 1000 companies has chosen Intersynthesis, a new holistic Internet marketing firm, as a provider of pay for performance services. Lavante believes that Intersynthesis' expertise and knowledge combined with their ability to develop integrated strategies, will help them fuel more growth.

40061 ■ *"Leading Ohio Internet Marketing Firm Announces Growth in September" in Marketing Weekly News (September 26, 2009, pp. 24)*
Pub: Investment Weekly News

Description: Despite a poor economy, Webbed Marketing, a leading social media marketing and search engine optimization firm in the Midwest, has added five additional professionals to its fast-growing team. The company continues to win new business, provide more services and hire talented employees.

40062 ■ *"Leapin' Lizards, Does SoBe Have Some Work To Do On Life Water" in Brandweek (Vol. 49, April 21, 2008, No. 16, pp. 32)*
Pub: VNU Business Media, Inc.

Ed: Amy Shea. **Description:** Discusses the competing marketing campaigns of both Vitaminwater, now owned by Coca-Cola, and SoBe Life Water which is owned by Pepsi; also looks at the repositioning of Life Water as a thirst-quencher, rather than a green product as well as the company's newest advertising campaign.

40063 ■ *"LED Screen Technology Takes Centre Stage" in Canadian Electronics (Vol. 23, June-July 2008, No. 4, pp. 17)*
Pub: Action Communication Inc.

Ed: Ed Whitaker. **Description:** Display technologies based on light emitting diodes are becoming more popular due to their flexibility, versatility and reproducibility of displays. These are being increasingly used in different applications, such as advertising and concerts.

40064 ■ *"Legislation Introduced" in Indoor Comfort Marketing (Vol. 70, July 2011, No. 7, pp. 6)*
Pub: Industry Publications Inc.

Description: New industry legislation is examined by the National Oilheat Research Alliance.

40065 ■ *"Leinie's Charts National Craft Beer Rollout" in The Business Journal-Milwaukee (Vol. 25, August 29, 2008, No. 49, pp. A1)*
Pub: American City Business Journals, Inc.

Ed: Rich Rovito. **Description:** Jacob Leinenkugel Brewing Co. is expected to complete the national rollout of its craft beer brands, while the launch of a new beer is prepared for this fall. The rollout is will likely benefit MillerCoors LLC, and will leave Alaska as the only state without Leinenkugel beer. Other views and information on Leinenkugel's national rollout are presented.

40066 ■ *"Let Emerging Market Customers Be Your Teachers" in Harvard Business Review (Vol. 88, December 2010, No. 12, pp. 115)*
Pub: Harvard Business School Publishing

Ed: Guillermo D'Andrea, David Marcotte, Gwen Dixon Morrison. **Description:** Examination of effective strategies for emerging markets is presented. These include helping educate customers as well as selling to them, adapting to customers' habits, and focusing brands appropriately. Magazine Luiza, a chain store in Brazil, is used to illustrate these points.

40067 ■ *"Let the Online Games Begin" in Canadian Business (Vol. 80, January 29, 2007, No. 3, pp. 23)*
Pub: Rogers Media

Ed: Andy Holloway. **Description:** The trends pertaining to the promotion of the products and services of different Canadian companies on the internet are discussed.

40068 ■ *Lethal Logic: Exploding the Myths that Paralyze American Gun Policy*
Pub: Potomac Books

Ed: Dennis A. Henigen. **Released:** 2009. **Price:** $29.95. **Description:** Marketing tactics being used by gun manufacturers regarding possible new gun control laws are examined.

40069 ■ *"Lifetime Networks" in Brandweek (Vol. 49, April 21, 2008, No. 16, pp. SR10)*
Pub: VNU Business Media, Inc.

Ed: Anthony Crupi. **Description:** Provides contact information for sales and marketing personnel for the ABC network as well as a listing of the station's top programming and an analysis of the current season and the target audience for those programs running in the current season. Lifetime will still produce its original signature movies but will now focus its emphasis more clearly on series development in order to appeal to a younger, hipper female demographic.

40070 ■ *"Lights, Camera, Action: Tools for Creating Video Blogs" in Inc. (Volume 32, December 2010, No. 10, pp. 57)*
Pub: Inc. Magazine

Ed: John Brandon. **Description:** A video blog is a good way to spread company news, talk about products, and stand out among traditional company blogs. New editing software can create two- to four-minute blogs using a webcam and either Windows Live Essentials, Apple iLife 2011, Powerdirector 9 Ultra, or Adobe Visual Communicator 3.

40071 ■ *"Little Cheer in Holiday Forecast for Champagne" in Advertising Age (Vol. 88, November 17, 2008, No. 43, pp. 6)*
Pub: Crain Communications, Inc.

Ed: Jeremy Mullman. **Description:** Due to a weak economy that has forced consumers to trade down from the most expensive alcoholic beverages as well as a weak U.S. dollar that has driven already lofty Champagne prices higher, makers of the French sparkling wine are anticipating a brutally slow holiday season.

40072 ■ *"Loblaw's Apparel Guru No Average Joe" in Globe & Mail (March 13, 2006, pp. B1)*
Pub: CTVglobemedia Publishing Inc.

Ed: Marina Strauss. **Description:** The details on Loblaw Companies Ltd., which unveiled Joe Fresh Style line of clothing, are presented.

40073 ■ *"Local Firm Snaps up 91 Area Pizza Huts" in Orlando Business Journal (Vol. 26, January 8, 2010, No. 32, pp. 1)*
Pub: American City Business Journals

Ed: Alexis Muellner, Anjali Fluker. **Description:** Orlando, Florida-based CFL Pizza LLC bought the 91 Orlando-area Pizza Hut restaurants for $35 million from parent company Yum! Brands Inc. CFL Pizza plans to distribute parts of the business to Central Florida vendors and the first business up for grabs is the advertising budget.

40074 ■ *"Lombard Leaves Starbucks" in Black Enterprise (Vol. 38, July 2008, No. 12, pp. 28)*
Pub: Earl G. Graves Publishing Co. Inc.

Ed: Tamara E. Holmes. **Description:** Ken Lombard stepped down from his position as head of Starbuck's entertainment division; the company is restructuring its entertainment unit in an attempt to revitalize sales and reduce costs.

40075 ■ *"Looking Out for the Little Guys" in Black Enterprise (Vol. 38, October 2007, No. 3, pp. 58)*
Pub: Earl G. Graves Publishing Co. Inc.
Ed: Kaylyn Kendall Dines. **Description:** Biz TechConnect is a Web portal that offers free online and social networking, along with four modules that help small businesses with marketing and advertising, communications and mobility, financial management, and customer relationship management.

40076 ■ *"A Love of Likes" in Boston Business Journal (Vol. 31, July 8, 2011, No. 24, pp. 1)*
Pub: Boston Business Journal
Ed: Lisa van der Pool. **Description:** An increasing number of companies in Boston, Massachusetts have been keen on getting Facebook 'likes' from people. Business owners realize that Facebook 'likes' could generate sales and based on some studies, equate to specific dollar values.

40077 ■ *Low-Budget Online Marketing for Small Business*
Pub: International Self-Counsel Press, Limited
Ed: Holly Berkley. **Released:** July 2005. **Price:** $14. 95. **Description:** Low-cost, effective online marketing tips for small companies selling products or services over the Internet.

40078 ■ *Low-Budget Online Marketing for Small Business*
Pub: Self-Counsel Press, Incorporated
Ed: Holley Berkley. **Released:** July 2005. **Price:** $14. 95, CD-Rom. **Description:** Low-cost, effective online marketing tips for small companies selling products or services over the Internet.

40079 ■ *Low-Budget Online Marketing for Small Business*
Pub: Self-Counsel Press Inc.
Ed: Holly Berkley. **Released:** August 2006. **Price:** $14.95, include CD-ROM. **Description:** Low-budget advertising campaigns are presented to help market any small business.

40080 ■ *Lucrative List Building*
Pub: Morgan James Publishing, LLC
Ed: Glen Hopkins. **Released:** July 2006. **Price:** $13. 95. **Description:** List building guaranteed to double profits is outlined.

40081 ■ *"Lunch Box Maker Gives Back" in Marketing to Women (Vol. 23, November 2010, No. 11, pp. 5)*
Pub: EPM Communications Inc.
Contact: Ira Mayer, President
E-mail: imayer@epmcom.com
Description: Female entrepreneurs launched a new program called, 'Share Your Lunch Project' that encourages mothers to give back and replace their child's lunchbox with their eco-friendly lunch boxes, which are available at select retailers. All proceeds from the project will benefit the World Food Program USA, which feeds children in developing countries.

40082 ■ *"Luster Lost" in Saint Louis Business Journal (Vol. 32, September 16, 2011, No. 3, pp. 1)*
Pub: Saint Louis Business Journal
Ed: E.B. Solomont. **Description:** Express Cripts shares have plunged 22.71 percent since late July amid regulatory concerns, as the luster of the second-largest deal announced for 2011 wore off. Express Scripts has become the largest pharmacy benefit manager in the country after the $29 billion deal to take rival Medco Health Solutions.

40083 ■ *"Lux Coffees, Breads Push Chains to React" in Advertising Age (Vol. 77, June 26, 2006, No. 26, pp. S14)*
Pub: Crain Communications, Inc.
Ed: Kate MacArthur. **Description:** Fast-food giants such as McDonald's, Burger King, Dunkin' Donuts and Subway have adjusted their menus in order to become more competitive with gourmet coffee shops and bakeries like Panera Bread and Starbucks which have taken a large share in the market. Statistical data included.

40084 ■ *"Luxe Men Are In Style" in Brandweek (Vol. 49, April 21, 2008, No. 16, pp. 12)*
Pub: VNU Business Media, Inc.
Description: According to a recent survey by Unity Marketing, among 1,300 luxury shoppers found that men spent an average of $2,401 on fashion items over a three-month period which is nearly $1,000 more than women. Men also spring for more luxury items such as vehicles and memberships to exclusive clubs.

40085 ■ *"Macy's Seeks Balance in All Things Ad-Related" in Crain's Chicago Business (Vol. 31, March 31, 2008, No. 13, pp. 19)*
Pub: Crain Communications, Inc.
Ed: Natalie Zmuda. **Description:** Macy's Inc. is seeking to balance its national television campaign with locally tailored promotions and products.

40086 ■ *Made To Stick: Why Some Ideas Survive and Others Die*
Pub: Random House
Ed: Chip Heath; Dan Heath. **Released:** 2007. **Price:** $26.00. **Description:** Eight principles marketers can use to make their ideas and branding efforts resonate with consumers.

40087 ■ *MadScam: Kick-Ass Advertising Without the Madison Avenue Price Tag*
Pub: Entrepreneur Press
Ed: George Parker. **Released:** January 2007. **Price:** $19.95. **Description:** Effective advertising plans for small to medium-sized business on a small budget.

40088 ■ *MadScam: Kick-Ass Advertising Without the Madison Avenue Price Tag*
Pub: McGraw-Hill Ryerson Ltd.
Ed: George Parker. **Released:** November 2006. **Price:** $24.95. **Description:** Effective advertising strategies for small companies on a budget are presented.

40089 ■ *"MaggieMoo's Ice Cream and Treatery" in Ice Cream Reporter (Vol. 23, September 20, 2010, No. 10, pp. 7)*
Pub: Ice Cream Reporter
Description: MaggieMoo's Ice Cream and Treatery has launched a new Website where visitors can learn about the brands newest ice cream innovations.

40090 ■ *Mail Order in the Internet Age*
Pub: Morgan James Publishing, LLC
Ed: Ted Ciuba. **Released:** May 2004. **Price:** $19.95. **Description:** Direct response market, or mail order, for marketing and selling a product or service is discussed, with emphasis on how direct marketing compares favorably to other methods in terms of speed, ease, profitability, and affordability. Advice is given for writing ads; seminars to attend; and newsletters, mailing lists and magazines in which to subscribe.

40091 ■ *Make Your Business Survive and Thrive! 100+ Proven Marketing Methods to Help You Beat the Odds*
Pub: John Wiley & Sons, Incorporated
Ed: Priscilla Y. Huff. **Released:** December 2006. **Price:** $19.95. **Description:** One hundred proven methods to successfully run a small home-based business are outlined.

40092 ■ *Make Your Business Survive and Thrive! 100+ Proven Marketing Methods to Help You Beat the Odds*
Pub: John Wiley & Sons, Incorporated
Ed: Priscilla Y. Huff. **Released:** December 2006. **Price:** $19.95. **Description:** Small business and entrepreneurial expert gives information to help small and home-based businesses grow.

40093 ■ *"Making Headlines" in Entrepreneur (Vol. 36, April 2008, No. 4, pp. 126)*
Pub: Entrepreneur Media, Inc.
Ed: John Janstch. **Description:** Tips on how to get journalists to notice your business and your new product offerings are presented. These include making a list of journalists that might be interested in the industry you are in and writing comments on their blogs.

40094 ■ *"Making the Most of Milk to Revive a Falling Market" in Farmer's Weekly (March 28, 2008, No. 320)*
Pub: Reed Business Information
Contact: Jeff Greisch, President
Description: DairyCo, eight of whom are working dairy farmers, aim to promote a feeding campaign for better herd health, provide research into efficient labor use, and sponsor discussion groups to enhance business skills.

40095 ■ *"Making Sense of Ambiguous Evidence" in Harvard Business Review (Vol. 86, September 2008, No. 9, pp. 53)*
Pub: Harvard Business School Press
Ed: Lisa Burrell. **Description:** Documentary filmmaker Errol Morris emphasizes the role of perception in portraying objective reality, and how investigation and analysis enhance the accuracy of that portrayal.

40096 ■ *"Making Visitors Out Of Listeners" in Hawaii Business (Vol. 54, July 2008, No. 1, pp. 18)*
Pub: Hawaii Business Publishing
Ed: Casey Chin. **Description:** Japanese workers are subscribing to the Official Hawaii Podcast in iTunes, which offers a free 20-minute, Japanese-language audio content on different topics, such as dining reviews and music from local artists. The concept is a way to attract Japanese travelers to come to Hawaii.

40097 ■ *"Making Your Mark: Five Steps To Brand Your Success" in Black Enterprise (Vol. 38, November 2007, No. 4, pp. 106)*
Pub: Earl G. Graves Publishing Co. Inc.
Ed: Erinn R. Johnson. **Description:** Founder of Velvet Suite Marketing Consulting Group, Melissa D. Johnson, assists clients in building brands. Johnson offers tips to develop and build a sold brand in her new book, 'Brand Me! Make Your Mark: Turn Passion Into Profit'.

40098 ■ *Managing Economies, Trade and International Business*
Pub: Palgrave Macmillan
Ed: Aidan O'Connor. **Released:** January 19, 2010. **Price:** $90.00. **Description:** An in-depth look at the areas that affect and influence international business, exploring specific issues businesses face in terms of economic development, trade law, and international marketing and management.

40099 ■ *"Manufacturing in the Middle Kingdom" in Inc. (December 2007, pp. 54-57)*
Pub: Gruner & Jahr USA Publishing
Ed: Alex Salkever. **Description:** Tips for manufacturing any new product in China as well as marketing said product is examined; five key steps for successfully managing Chinese contractors are listed.

40100 ■ *"Marble Slab Creamery" in Ice Cream Reporter (Vol. 23, November 20, 2010, No. 12, pp. 7)*
Pub: Ice Cream Reporter
Description: Marble Slab Creamery is promoting its company by offering a New Year's Eve Sweepstakes.

40101 ■ *"Marketer Bets Big on U.S.'s Growing Canine Obsession" in Advertising Age (Vol. 79, April 14, 2008, No. 15, pp. 14)*
Pub: Crain Communications, Inc.
Ed: Emily Bryson York. **Description:** Overview of FreshPet, a New Jersey company that began marketing two brands of refrigerated dog food-Deli Fresh and FreshPet Select-which are made from fresh ingredients such as beef, rice and carrots. The company projects continued success due to the amount of money consumers spend on their pets as well as fears derived from the 2007 recalls that inspired consumers to look for smaller, independent manufacturers that are less likely to source ingredients from China.

40102 ■ *"Marketers Push for Mobile Tuesday as the New Black Friday" in Advertising Age (Vol. 79, December 1, 2008, No. 44, pp. 21)*
Pub: Crain Communications, Inc.
Ed: Natalie Zmuda. **Description:** Marketers are using an innovative approach in an attempt to stimulate business on the Tuesday following Thanksgiving by

utilizing consumer's cell phones to alert them of sales or present them with coupons for this typically slow retail business day; with this campaign both advertisers and retailers are hoping to start Mobile Tuesday, another profitable shopping day in line with Black Friday and Cyber Monday.

40103 ■ *Marketing 2.0: Bridging the Gap between Seller and Buyer through Social Media Marketing*
Pub: Wheatmark
Ed: Bernie Borges. **Released:** July 14, 2009. **Price:** $22.95. **Description:** Winning strategies to attract people to your company and your employees using social media site on the Internet are outlined.

40104 ■ *"Marketing in the Digital World: Here's How to Craft a Smart Online Strategy" in Black Enterprise (Vol. 40, July 2010, No. 12, pp. 47)*
Pub: Earl G. Graves Publishing Co. Inc.
Ed: Sonya A. Donaldson. **Description:** Social media is an integral part of any small business plan in addressing marketing, sales, and branding strategies.

40105 ■ *Marketing for Dummies*
Pub: John Wiley & Sons Inc.
Contact: Stephen M. Smith, President
URL(s): www.wiley.com/WileyCDA/WileyTitle/productCd-047050210X.html. **Ed:** Alexander Hiam. **Released:** latest edition 3rd; Published October, 2009. **Price:** $21.99, Individuals paperback. **Publication includes:** Marketing web sites, marketing consultants, trade associations, market researchers, and other experts. **Entries include:** Individual or company name, address, phone number, web site address (where applicable). Principal content of publication is articles on marketing strategies.

40106 ■ *Marketing for Entrepreneurs*
Pub: FT Press
Ed: Jurgen Wolff. **Released:** December 9, 2010. **Price:** $24.99. **Description:** This text identifies marketing as the entire process of researching, creating, distributing and selling a product or service. It isn't about theory and metrics, rather it is a practical guide that starts with the basics of all marketing aspects.

40107 ■ *"Marketing Management Analytics Announces MMA Digital" in Internet Wire (January 26, 2010)*
Pub: Comtex News Network, Inc.
Description: Innovator and pioneer in marketing effectiveness, Marketing Management Analytics, is offering a new service called MMA Digital; using this service companies will be able to more accurately measure the effects of digital media alongside other marketing tools in order to better understand and leverage the drivers of online marketing success.

40108 ■ *Marketing Outrageously: How to Increase Your Revenue by Staggering Amounts*
Pub: Bard Press
Ed: Jon Spoelstra. **Released:** July 25, 2001. **Price:** $24.95. **Description:** Creative marketing strategies are defined. The book shows how considering marketing problems as outrageously but consistently can benefit any small business. The author talks about his own experience when there were not adequate funds for marketing and advertising and the outrageous approach he created to promote sports teams.

40109 ■ *"Marketing Scholarship 2.0" in Journal of Marketing (Vol. 75, July 2011, No. 4, pp. 225)*
Pub: American Marketing Association
Ed: Richard J. Lutz. **Description:** A study of the implications of changing environment and newer collaborative models for marketing knowledge production and dissemination is presented. Crowdsourcing has become a frequently employed strategy in industry. Academic researchers should collaborate more as well as the academe and industry, to make sure that important problems are being investigated.

40110 ■ *"Marketing: 'Twill Be the Season" in Entrepreneur (Vol. 35, October 2007, No. 10, pp. 108)*
Pub: Entrepreneur Media Inc.
Ed: Kim T. Gordon. **Description:** Entrepreneurs should plan ahead in order to promote products for the holiday season, since it is peak sales time. They can unify their business theme, use customer incentives, advertise early using TV or radio, and reorganize the company Website. Other ways to market for the holiday season are provided.

40111 ■ *Marketing in a Web 2.0 World - Using Social Media, Webinars, Blogs, and More to Boost Your Small Business on a Budget*
Pub: Atlantic Publishing Company
Ed: Peter VanRysdam. **Released:** June 1, 2010. **Price:** $24.95. **Description:** Web 2.0 technologies have leveled the playing field for small companies trying to boost their presence by giving them an equal voice against larger competitors. Advice is given to help target your audience using social networking hubs.

40112 ■ *Marketing Without Money for Small and Midsize Businesses: 300 FREE and Cheap Ways to Increase Your Sales*
Pub: Halle House Publishing
Contact: Nicholas E. Bade, Publisher
Ed: Nicholas E. Bade. **Released:** July 2005. **Price:** $16.95. **Description:** Three hundred practical low-cost or no-cost strategies to increase sales, focusing on free advertising, free marketing assistance, and free referrals to the Internet.

40113 ■ *Marketing that Works: How Entrepreneurial Marketing Can Add Sustainable Value to Any Sized Company*
Pub: Wharton School Publishing
Ed: Leonard M. Lodish; Howard Morgan; Shellye Archambeau. **Released:** March 2007. **Price:** $36.99 (CND). **Description:** Entrepreneurial marketing techniques are shared in order to help a new company position and target products and services.

40114 ■ *Marketing Works: Unlock Big Company Strategies for Small Business*
Pub: Morgan James Publishing, LLC
Ed: Chris Lee; Daniele Lima. **Released:** May 2006. **Price:** $19.95. **Description:** Marketing strategies for any small business are outlined.

40115 ■ *"Marketing: You Are On the Air: Radio and TV Producers Are Looking For Shows Starring Smart CEOs" in Inc. (December 2007, pp. 67-69)*
Pub: Gruner & Jahr USA Publishing
Ed: Sarah Goldstein. **Description:** Many successful entrepreneurs are being hired to host television and radio shows in order to share business expertise.

40116 ■ *Marketing Your Product*
Pub: Self-Counsel Press, Incorporated
Ed: Donald Cyr, Douglas Gray. **Released:** September 2009. **Price:** $20.95. **Description:** Tips for marketing any product in today's competitive consumer environment. One chapter focuses on using the Internet as a marketing tool.

40117 ■ *Marketing Your Small Business for Big Profits*
Pub: Morgan James Publishing, LLC
Released: September 2006. **Price:** $12.95. **Description:** Successful marketing tip to grow a small business are presented.

40118 ■ *"Mars Advertising's Orbit Grows as Other Ad Segments Fall" in Crain's Detroit Business (Vol. 25, June 1, 2009, No. 22, pp. 10)*
Pub: Crain Communications Inc. - Detroit
Ed: Bill Shea. **Description:** An electrical fire burned at Mars Advertising's headquarters in Southfield, Michigan. The company talks about its plans for regrouping and rebuilding. The family firm specializes in in-store marketing that targets consumers already in the buying mode.

40119 ■ *"Martha Stewart Launches Macys Line" in Marketing to Women (Vol. 21, March 2008, No. 3, pp. 5)*
Pub: EPM Communications Inc.
Contact: Ira Mayer, President
E-mail: imayer@epmcom.com
Description: Martha Stewart launches an exclusive line of home decor called Wedgwood as part of her relationship with Macy's stores.

40120 ■ *"Mass Mailers Try to Lick Rising Postal Rates" in Crain's Detroit Business (Vol. 24, March 10, 2008, No. 10, pp. 6)*
Pub: Crain Communications, Inc.
Ed: Sherri Begin. **Description:** Discusses the ways in which companies are trying to mitigate the effect of rising postal costs.

40121 ■ *"Maternity Wear Goes Green" in Marketing to Women (Vol. 21, March 2008, No. 3, pp. 3)*
Pub: EPM Communications Inc.
Contact: Ira Mayer, President
E-mail: imayer@epmcom.com
Description: Mother's Work Inc. has launched a series of environmentally-friendly products made from such sustainable fibers as organic cotton and bamboo.

40122 ■ *"A Matter of Online Trust" in Entrepreneur (Vol. 37, August 2009, No. 8, pp. 35)*
Pub: Entrepreneur Media, Inc.
Ed: Mikal E. Belicove. **Description:** Startup websites should make their potential customers feel confident to do business with them. To build customer's trust, the website should have an attractive and professional design, clear and simple navigation, error-free copy, and physical address, telephone number, and e-mail address.

40123 ■ *"Maximize Your Marketing Results In a Down Economy" in Franchising World (Vol. 42, November 2010, No. 11, pp. 45)*
Pub: International Franchise Association
Ed: Loren Rakich. **Description:** Strategies to help any franchisee to maximize their marketing efforts in a slow economy are outlined.

40124 ■ *Maximum Marketing, Minimum Dollars: The Top 50 Ways to Grow Your Small Business*
Pub: Kaplan Books
Ed: Kim Gordon. **Released:** April 2006. **Price:** $24. 00. **Description:** Marketing tips to increase sales are presented. Small business owners will learn to maximize marketing with 50 innovative and affordable methods, including online marketing.

40125 ■ *MBA In a Day*
Pub: John Wiley and Sons, Inc.
Ed: Steven Stralser, PhD. **Released:** 2004. **Price:** $34.95. **Description:** Management professor presents important concepts, business topics and strategies that can be used by anyone to manage a small business or professional practice. Topics covered include: human resources and personal interaction, ethics and leadership skills, fair negotiation tactics, basic business accounting practices, project management, and the fundamentals of economics and marketing.

40126 ■ *"McD's Dollar-Menu Fixation Sparks Revolt" in Advertising Age (Vol. 79, June 2, 2008, No. 22, pp. 1)*
Pub: Crain Communications, Inc.
Ed: Emily Bryson York. **Description:** McDonald's franchisees say that low-cost dollar-menu offerings are impacting their bottom line and many have discontinued the dollar-menu altogether due to rising commodity costs, an increase in minimum wage and consumers trading down to the lower-price items.

40127 ■ *"McD's Tries to Slake Consumer Thirst for Wider Choice of Drinks" in*

Advertising Age (Vol. 79, June 9, 2008, No. 23, pp. 1)
Pub: Crain Communications, Inc.
Ed: Natalie Zmuda; Emily Bryson York. **Description:** McDonald's is testing the sale of canned and bottled drinks in about 150 locations in an attempt to offer more options to consumers who are going elsewhere for their beverage choices.

40128 ■ *"McD's Warms Up For Olympics Performance" in Advertising Age (Vol. 79, July 7, 2008, No. 26, pp. 8)*
Pub: Crain Communications, Inc.
Description: Overview of McDonald's marketing plans for the company's sponsorship of the Olympics which includes a website, an alternate-reality game, names featured on U.S. athletes and on-the-ground activities.

40129 ■ *"MEC, Churchill Downs Saddle Up in Racing Deal" in Globe & Mail (March 6, 2007, pp. B1)*
Pub: CTVglobemedia Publishing Inc.
Ed: Greg Keenan. **Description:** The formation of a company called TrackNet Media Group LLC by Magna Entertainment Corp. and Churchill Downs Inc. for the broadcast of horse races on television is discussed. The efforts of the two companies to revive public interest in horse racing are described.

40130 ■ *"Media Terminology" in MarketingMagazine (Vol. 115, September 27, 2010, No. 13, pp. 80)*
Pub: Rogers Publishing Ltd.
Description: Media terminology is provided.

40131 ■ *"Medicine Men" in Canadian Business (Vol. 80, February 12, 2007, No. 4, pp. 19)*
Pub: Rogers Media
Ed: Joe Castaldo. **Description:** The effort of HPI Health Products' owners Dong Pedersen and Kent Pedersen to popularize their pain reliever product 'Lakota' is discussed.

40132 ■ *"Men May Wear the Pants in the Family, But Women Retain the Power of the Purse" in Marketing to Women (Vol. 22, August 2009, No. 8)*
Pub: EPM Communications Inc.
Contact: Ira Mayer, President
E-mail: imayer@epmcom.com
Description: Nearly 8 in 10 women say that their opinion holds the most sway in the families' financial decisions. Significant factors that influence women's $100 or more purchases include Online reviews, the opinion of spouse or significant other and expert recommendations. Statistical data included.

40133 ■ *"Mentoring Support" in Black Enterprise (Vol. 38, July 2008, No. 12, pp. 64)*
Pub: Earl G. Graves Publishing Co. Inc.
Description: With his relocation from his multicultural team in New York to the less diverse Scripps Networks' headquarters in Knoxville, Earl Cokley has made it a top priority to push for more diversity and mentoring opportunities within the management of the media and marketing company.

40134 ■ *"Merger Brings New Force to Hispanic Marketing Industry" in Hispanic Business (July-August 2007, pp. 60)*
Pub: Hispanic Business
Description: Merger between Latin Force LLC, a marketing strategy firm and Geoscape International Inc., a consumer intelligence and data analytics company is discussed.

40135 ■ *"Microsoft Clicks Into High Speed" in Hispanic Business (Vol. 30, July-August 2008, No. 7-8, pp. 54)*
Pub: Hispanic Business, Inc.
Ed: Derek Reveron. **Description:** Microsoft's diversity hiring and vendor diversity program to capture more Hispanic consumer and business-to-business market is described. One of the main goals of these programs is to hire more Hispanic executives and managers who will help the company develop and market products and services that will appeal and benefit Hispanic consumers.

40136 ■ *"Midwest Test" in Crain's Cleveland Business (Vol. 28, November 26, 2007, No. 47, pp. 1)*
Pub: Crain Communications, Inc.
Ed: John Booth. **Description:** Provides an overview of the experimental Wal-Mart Supercenter in Elyria which researches consumer preferences with department layouts, new merchandise and even exterior architecture. Store manager Bob Butler said, 'We're trying to get out of that box-store look.'.

40137 ■ *"Milk Producers Target Moms" in Marketing to Women (Vol. 21, January 2008, No. 1, pp. 3)*
Pub: EPM Communications Inc.
Contact: Ira Mayer, President
E-mail: imayer@epmcom.com
Description: In an attempt to encourage moms to serve milk with meals, the American Dairy Association partners with the New York State Dietetic Association to promote milk via a new logo, website and contest.

40138 ■ *"MillerCoors Needs the Quickie Mart" in Crain's Chicago Business (Vol. 32, November 16, 2009, No. 46, pp. 2)*
Pub: Crain Communications, Inc.
Ed: David Sterrett. **Description:** Power Marts convenience store owner Sam Odeh says that Chicago-based MillerCoors LLC has done a poor job at promoting its brand, keeping its signs up to date and stocking the shelves at his stores. He complains that the company's service has been awful and the marketing pathetic. Convenience stores accounted for more than $14 billion in beer sales in the past year.

40139 ■ *"Mini Melts Offers 'Win an Ice Cream Business' Contest" in Ice Cream Reporter (Vol. 23, October 20, 2010, No. 11, pp. 3)*
Pub: Ice Cream Reporter
Description: Mini Melts USA launched a promotional program offering contestants the opportunity to win a Mini Melts ice cream business. The business is not a franchise and there are not royalty fees.

40140 ■ *"Mobile: Juanes Fans Sing for Sprint" in Advertising Age (Vol. 79, November 3, 2008, No. 41, pp. 22)*
Pub: Crain Communications, Inc.
Ed: Laurel Wentz. **Description:** Marketers are appealing to the Hispanic market since they are more prone to use their cell phones to respond to contests, download videos, ringtones, or other data activity. Sprint recently sponsored a contest inviting people to sing like Colombian megastar Juanes; the participants filmed and sent their videos using their cell phones rather than laptops or camcorders illustrating the Hispanic overindex on mobile-phone technology. The contest generated hundreds of thousands of dollars in additional fee revenue, as monthly downloads increased 63 percent.

40141 ■ *"Mobile Marketing Grows With Size of Cell Phone Screens" in Crain's Detroit Business (Vol. 24, January 14, 2008, No. 2, pp. 13)*
Pub: Crain Communications Inc. - Detroit
Ed: Bill Shea. **Description:** Experts are predicting increased marketing for cell phones with the inception of larger screens and improved technology.

40142 ■ *"Moet, Rivals Pour More Ad Bucks Into Bubbly" in Advertising Age (Vol. 88, September 3, 2007, No. 35, pp. 4)*
Pub: Crain Communications, Inc.
Ed: Jeremy Mullman. **Description:** In an attempt to revive sluggish sales, champagne companies are raising their advertising budgets, transforming themselves from light-spending seasonal players to year-round heavyweights in the advertising world.

40143 ■ *"Mom Insight on Family, Current Affairs, and the Economy" in Marketing to Women (Vol. 23, November 2010, No. 11, pp. 5)*
Pub: EPM Communications Inc.
Contact: Ira Mayer, President
E-mail: imayer@epmcom.com
Description: Statistics regarding the way moms feel about current events, family and the economy are shared.

40144 ■ *"Moms Are Still Shopping" in Marketing to Women (Vol. 21, February 2008, No. 2, pp. 1)*
Pub: EPM Communications Inc.
Contact: Ira Mayer, President
E-mail: imayer@epmcom.com
Description: According to a monthly poll by Parenting Magazine, although the economic signs worsen many moms are still shopping. Statistical data included.

40145 ■ *"Moms Dis Super Bowl Ads" in Marketing to Women (Vol. 21, March 2008, No. 3, pp. 6)*
Pub: EPM Communications Inc.
Contact: Ira Mayer, President
E-mail: imayer@epmcom.com
Description: According to a survey by the Marketing to Moms Coalition, although 80 percent of moms tune into the Super Bowl most complain that the advertisements are not appropriate for a family sports viewing experience.

40146 ■ *"Moms Give More Thought to Nutrition" in Marketing to Women (Vol. 21, February 2008, No. 2, pp. 8)*
Pub: EPM Communications Inc.
Contact: Ira Mayer, President
E-mail: imayer@epmcom.com
Description: Moms are thinking more about nutritional issues than they did in the past and spending more time reading labels in the grocery store. 74 percent of moms consider the nutritional content of foods purchased for their children more now than they did two years ago.

40147 ■ *"Moms Mull Money" in Marketing to Women (Vol. 21, February 2008, No. 2, pp. 6)*
Pub: EPM Communications Inc.
Contact: Ira Mayer, President
E-mail: imayer@epmcom.com
Description: According to a survey by Countrywide Bank, women, especially mothers, are more concerned about their financial fitness than men.

40148 ■ *"Moms Rely on Coupons, Specials to Lower Grocery Bills" in Marketing to Women (Vol. 23, November 2010, No. 11, pp. 8)*
Pub: EPM Communications Inc.
Contact: Ira Mayer, President
E-mail: imayer@epmcom.com
Description: Eighty-four percent of moms surveyed reported using coupons when grocery shopping in order to lower costs. They are also purchasing less snack foods, fewer brand name items, alcoholic beverages, organic items, meat and fresh fruits and vegetables.

40149 ■ *"Moosylvania Releases Latest XL Marketing Trends Report" in Wireless News (October 6, 2009)*
Pub: Close-Up Media
Description: Moosylvania, a digital promotion and branding agency that also has an on-site research facility, has released its 2nd XL Marketing Trends Report which focuses on digital video; the study defines the top digital video trends marketers must focus on now and well into the future and notes that in 2010, Mobile Web Devices, such as smart phones will outnumber computers in this country. Statistical data included.

40150 ■ *"More Leading Retailers Using Omniture Conversion Solutions to Boost Sales and Ecommerce Performance" in*

Internet Wire (Sept. 22,2009)
Pub: Comtex News Network, Inc.
Description: Many retailers are utilizing Omniture conversion solutions to improve the performance of their ecommerce businesses; recent enhancements to Omniture Merchandising and Omniture Recommendations help clients drive increased conversion to their Internet ventures.

40151 ■ *"More Leading Retailers Using Omniture Conversion Solutions to Boost Sales and Ecommerce Performance" in Internet Wire (Sept. 22,2009)*
Pub: Comtex News Network, Inc.
Description: Many retailers are utilizing Omniture conversion solutions to improve the performance of their ecommerce businesses; recent enhancements to Omniture Merchandising and Omniture Recommendations help clients drive increased conversion to their Internet ventures.

40152 ■ *"More Sales Leads, Please: Or, What Happened When Frontline Selling Started Practicing What It Preaches" in Inc. (November 2007)*
Pub: Gruner & Jahr USA Publishing
Description: Frontline Selling located in Oakland, New Jersey helps train sales teams to generate and convert sales leads. The consulting firm doubled their marketing budget to increase their own sales.

40153 ■ *The Mousedriver Chronicles*
Pub: Perseus Books Group
Ed: John Lusk; Kyle Harrison. **Released:** 2003. **Price:** $16.95. **Description:** Entrepreneurial voyage through the startup business of two ivy-league business school graduates and the lessons they learned while developing their idea of a computer mouse that looks like a golf driver into the marketplace. The book is an inspiration for those looking to turn an idea into a company.

40154 ■ *"Moving Pitchers" in Entrepreneur (Vol. 37, December 2009, No. 12, pp. 46)*
Pub: Entrepreneur Media, Inc.
Ed: Gwen Moran. **Description:** Online videos have become accessible for business development and marketing due to the decline in production costs and the growth in viewership. Research company comScore reveals that 153 million Internet users in the U.S. watched an online video in August 2009. The benefits of using online videos to further market one's company are explained.

40155 ■ *MRA Blue Book Research Services Directory*
Pub: Marketing Research Association
Contact: Joe Ottaviani, President
E-mail: joe.ottaviani@burke.com
URL(s): www.bluebook.org. **Released:** Annual; Latest edition 2012. **Price:** $170, Nonmembers; $100, Members. **Covers:** Over 1,200 marketing research companies and field interviewing services. **Entries include:** Company name, address, phone, names of executives, services, facilities, special interviewing capabilities. **Database includes:** Separate geographical listings for firms with one-way mirror facilities, focus group moderators and facilities, central telephone facilities, and permanent shopping mall locations. **Arrangement:** Geographical; business type. **Indexes:** Geographic and by specialty.

40156 ■ *"MTV Networks" in Brandweek (Vol. 49, April 21, 2008, No. 16, pp. SR10)*
Pub: VNU Business Media, Inc.
Ed: Anthony Crupi. **Description:** Provides contact information for sales and marketing personnel for the MTV networks as well as a listing of the station's top programming and an analysis of the current season and the target audience for those programs running in the current season. MTV networks include MTV, VH1, Nickelodeon and Comedy Central.

40157 ■ *"Multichannel Marketing: Mindset and Program Development" in Business Horizons (September-October 2007)*
Pub: Elsevier Technology Publications
Ed: Bruce D. Weinberg, Salvatore Parise, Patricia J. Guinan. **Description:** Organizations should develop a multichannel mindset and design multichannel marketing programs in order to increase profitability and enhance customer satisfaction. Creating a holistic strategy, crating metrics that measure the impacts and overall performance, and designing organizational structure and incentives are key factors in implementing the marketing program.

40158 ■ *"Murdock Lifer Mans Main Street Journal" in Advertising Age (Vol. 79, July 7, 2008, No. 26, pp. 1)*
Pub: Crain Communications, Inc.
Ed: Nat Ives. **Description:** Profile of Les Hinton, the U.K. executive who was chosen by Rupert Murdoch to run Dow Jones and The Wall Street Journal; Hinton discusses The Wall Street Journal's unique spot in American business which has helped it survive a dwindling newspaper industry.

40159 ■ *"Nationwide Bank Ready for December Conversion" in Business First-Columbus (October 12, 2007, pp. A1)*
Pub: American City Business Journals, Inc.
Ed: Adrian Burns. **Description:** Nationwide Bank will increase marketing to its customers, including the 45,000 that came from the acquisition of Nationwide Federal Credit Union in December 2006. Upgrading its online banking system and Website will bring the company and its services closer to clients. The influence of the insurance industry on the bank's marketing strategy is also examined.

40160 ■ *"Navigate to Better Direct Response Messaging Through Search Marketing" in DM News (Vol. 32, January 18, 2010, No. 2, pp. 26)*
Pub: Haymarket Media, Inc.
Ed: Mark Simon. **Description:** Important lessons to apply when utilizing Internet marketing schemes include telling your customers you have what they want to buy, provide them with discounts or ways to save additional money and drive them to a customized destination like an Online store.

40161 ■ *"NBC" in Brandweek (Vol. 49, April 21, 2008, No. 16, pp. SR6)*
Pub: VNU Business Media, Inc.
Ed: John Consoli. **Description:** Provides contact information for sales and marketing personnel for the NBC network as well as a listing of the station's top programming and an analysis of the current season and the target audience for those programs running in the current season. NBC also devised a new strategy of announcing its prime-time schedule 52 weeks in advance which was a hit for advertisers who felt this gave them a better opportunity to plan for product placement. Even with the station's creative sales programs, they could face a challenge from Fox in terms of upfront advertisement purchases.

40162 ■ *"NBC Universal Cable" in Brandweek (Vol. 49, April 21, 2008, No. 16, pp. SR11)*
Pub: VNU Business Media, Inc.
Ed: Anthony Crupi. **Description:** Provides contact information for sales and marketing personnel for the NBC Universal Cable networks as well as a listing of the station's top programming and an analysis of the current season and the target audience for those programs running in the current season. The network's stations include USA, Sci Fi and Bravo. Ad revenue for the network grew 30 percent in the first quarter.

40163 ■ *"NBC Universal Domestic Television Distribution" in Brandweek (Vol. 49, April 21, 2008, No. 16, pp. SR13)*
Pub: VNU Business Media, Inc.
Ed: Marc Berman. **Description:** Provides contact information for sales and marketing personnel for NBC Universal Domestic Television Distribution as well as a listing of the station's top programming and an analysis of the current season and the target audience for those programs running in the current season.

40164 ■ *"Net Connections" in Black Enterprise (Vol. 38, July 2008, No. 12, pp. 28)*
Pub: Earl G. Graves Publishing Co. Inc.
Ed: Anthony S. Calypso. **Description:** Marketers are making strategic partnerships with online social networks in an attempt to gain further market reach. The value of these networks appears to be on the rise forcing media companies to recalculate their strategies for delivering products to customers.

40165 ■ *"Net Profits: Get a Social Life" in Entrepreneur (Vol. 35, October 2007, No. 10, pp. 140)*
Pub: Entrepreneur Media Inc.
Ed: Amanda C. Kooser. **Description:** Social networking sites such as Facebook and MySpace have millions of users, a sign that social networking is a growing industry. One way to enter this industry is target marketing, like Med3Q, a site for health-conscious individuals had done. How Med3q is earning through online advertising and sponsors is explained.

40166 ■ *"Network Like A Boy Scout" in Women Entrepreneur (January 15, 2009)*
Pub: Entrepreneur Media Inc.
Ed: Merrily Orsini. **Description:** Marketing for businesses that provide products or services that people only seek during emergencies or natural disasters such as hurricanes can be a challenge; tips for branding such businesses, networking and establishing a strong customer base that will refer your business to others are given.

40167 ■ *"Network Marketing Strategies for Marketing Professionals" in Black Enterprise (Vol. 38, October 2007, No. 3, pp. 70)*
Pub: Earl G. Graves Publishing Co. Inc.
Description: Network marketing programs are redefining the sales business and leveraging opportunities in the ever-expanding global, highly networked, and ultra-specialized marketplace.

40168 ■ *"Networking Web Sites: a Two-Edged Sword" in Contractor (Vol. 56, October 2009, No. 10, pp. 52)*
Pub: Penton Media, Inc.
Ed: H. Kent Craig. **Description:** People need to be careful about the information that they share on social networking Web sites. They should realize that future bosses, coworkers, and those that might want to hire them might read those information. Posting on these sites can cost career opportunities and respect.

40169 ■ *"Never Boring: Ad Agencies' Big Changes" in Business Courier (Vol. 24, February 8, 2008, No. 44, pp. 1)*
Pub: American City Business Journals, Inc.
Ed: Dan Monk. **Description:** Many changes are occurring in Cincinnati's advertising industry, including new clients, acquisitions, and market leaders, and an increase in employment. Bridge Worldwide passed Northlich LLC as the city's largest advertising agency.

40170 ■ *"The New Basics of Marketing" in Inc. (February 2008, pp. 75-81)*
Pub: Gruner & Jahr USA Publishing
Ed: Leigh Buchanan. **Description:** New tools for marketing a business or service include updating or upgrading a Website, using email or texting, or advertising on a social Internet network.

40171 ■ *"A New Day is Dawning" in Indoor Comfort Marketing (Vol. 70, August 2011, No. 8, pp. 18)*
Pub: Industry Publications Inc.
Ed: Paul Nazzaro. **Description:** New trends in the HVAC/R industry regarding biofuels and bioheat are explored.

40172 ■ *"The New Face of Social Media" in Hispanic Business (December 2010)*
Pub: Hispanic Business
Ed: Gary D. Fackler. **Description:** Latina bloggers carve out a new niche in social media that helps preserve their unique cultural identities.

40173 ■ *"New IPhone Also Brings New Way of Mobile Marketing" in Advertising Age (Vol. 79, June 16, 2008, No. 24, pp. 23)*
Pub: Crain Communications, Inc.
Ed: Abbey Klaasen. **Description:** Currently there are two kinds of applications for the iPhone and other mobile devices: native applications that allow for richer experiences and take advantage of features that are built into a phone and web applications, those that allow access to the web through specific

platforms. Marketers are interested in creating useful experiences for customers and opening up the platforms which will allow them to do this.

40174 ■ *"New King Top the Charts" in The Business Journal-Portland (Vol. 25, August 8, 2008, No. 22, pp. 1)*
Pub: American City Business Journals, Inc.
Ed: Andy Giegerich. **Description:** Spanish-language KRYP-FM station's spring 2008 ratings soared to 6.4 from 2.8 for the previous year. The station timing is flawless given the fact that one of every three new Portland-area residents between 2002 and 2007 were Latino.

40175 ■ *"New Recession-Proof Internet Marketing Package Allows Businesses to Ramp Up Web Traffic and Profits" in PR Newswire (Jan. 25, 2010)*
Pub: PR Newswire Association, LLC
Description: Profile of Reel Web Design, a leading marketing firm in New York City that caters to small to medium sized businesses with smaller budgets that need substantial return on investment; Reel Web Design offers video production and submission, web design and maintenance and press release writing among additional services.

40176 ■ *"New Recession-Proof Internet Marketing Package Allows Businesses to Ramp Up Web Traffic and Profits" in PR Newswire (Jan. 25, 2010)*
Pub: PR Newswire Association, LLC
Description: Profile of Reel Web Design, a leading marketing firm in New York City that caters to small to medium sized businesses with smaller budgets that need substantial return on investment; Reel Web Design offers video production and submission, web design and maintenance and press release writing among additional services.

40177 ■ *"New Sony HD Ads Tout Digital" in Brandweek (Vol. 49, April 21, 2008, No. 16, pp. 5)*
Pub: VNU Business Media, Inc.
Description: Looking to promote Sony Electronics' digital imaging products, the company has launched another campaign effort known as HDNA, a play on the words high-definition and DNA; originally Sony focused the HDNA campaign on their televisions, the new ads will include still and video cameras as well and marketing efforts will consist of advertising in print, Online, television spots and publicity at various venues across the country.

40178 ■ *"New TurnHere Survey Reveals Online Video Trends" in Internet Wire (October 22, 2009)*
Pub: Comtex News Network, Inc.
Description: TurnHere, Inc., the leading online video marketing services company, released the findings of its recent survey regarding current and future trends in online video among marketing agencies and brand recognition; the report found that online video has and will continue to play a prominent role in the realm of marketing edging out both search and email marketing campaigns. Additional highlights and statistical data included.

40179 ■ *"The Next Dimension" in Entrepreneur (Vol. 35, November 2007, No. 11, pp. 62)*
Pub: Entrepreneur Media Inc.
Ed: Heather Clancy. **Description:** Entrepreneurs can make use of virtual worlds like Second Life to promote their products or services. Details and cautions on the use of virtual worlds are discussed.

40180 ■ *"Next Generation Audi TT Hits Canadian Streets" in Canadian Corporate News (May 16, 2007)*
Pub: Comtex News Network Inc.
Description: Audi Canada prepares for the launch of the highly anticipated 2008 Audi TT, recipient of the 2007 World Car Design of the Year due to its contemporary look, powerful engine, and innovative technology, with a multiple touch-point marketing campaign.

40181 ■ *"The Next Great Canadian Idea?" in Canadian Business (Vol. 81, July 21, 2008, No. 11, pp. 45)*
Pub: Rogers Media Ltd.
Ed: Sharda Prashad. **Description:** Thane Heins has invented a generator that produces energy in an isolated system which contradicts the law of conservation of energy. Perepiteia generator is referred to as a 'perpetual motion machine.' Other inventions slated for the Canadian invention competition include Rob Matthies' batteries and Frank Naumann's Smart Trap.

40182 ■ *"A Nice Consistency" in Inc. (Vol. 31, January-February 2009, No. 1, pp. 94)*
Pub: Mansueto Ventures LLC
Ed: Jason Del Rey. **Description:** PJ Madison spent almost a quarter of its revenue promoting its latest product, organic ice cream. The Texas-based firm saw sales increase dramatically.

40183 ■ *Niche and Grow Rich*
Pub: Entrepreneur Press
Ed: Jennifer Basye Sander; Peter Sander. **Released:** 2003. **Description:** Consultants share insight to entrepreneurs wishing to find a profitable niche market. Authors write that good niche businesses are easy to start and easy to defend from competitors. They also report that finding a successful niche can attract and maintain good customers who are willing to pay more for unique goods and services.

40184 ■ *"Nike's Next Splash" in The Business Journal-Portland (Vol. 25, August 22, 2008, No. 24, pp. 1)*
Pub: American City Business Journals, Inc.
Ed: Erik Siemers. **Description:** Business analysts expect Nike to bid for the endorsement services of swimmer Michael Phelps after the swimmer's contract with Speedo expires. The company, however, is a lightweight in the swimming apparel market and is not focusing on swimming as a growth sector.

40185 ■ *"Nissan Unveils Family Concept Car" in Marketing to Women (Vol. 21, February 2008, No. 2, pp. 3)*
Pub: EPM Communications Inc.
Contact: Ira Mayer, President
E-mail: imayer@epmcom.com
Description: Nissan displayed its latest design for the ultimate family vehicle at the 2008 North American International Auto Show in Detroit. The Nissan Forum targets families with older children.

40186 ■ *"No, Those Casino Rama Ads Aren't Running in NYC" in Globe & Mail (March 15, 2006, pp. B1)*
Pub: CTVglobemedia Publishing Inc.
Ed: Keith McArthur. **Description:** The reason Casino Rama did not advertise on New York Cabs is discussed.

40187 ■ *"Nobody Knows What To Do" in Barron's (Vol. 88, March 17, 2008, No. 11, pp. 40)*
Pub: Dow Jones & Company, Inc.
Ed: Mark Veverka. **Description:** Attendees of the South by Southwest Interactive conference failed to get an insight on how to make money on the Web from former Walt Disney CEO Michael Eisner when Eisner said there's no proven business model for financing projects. Eisner said he finances his projects with the help of his connections to get product-placement deals.

40188 ■ *"Nortel Makes Customers Stars in New Campaign" in Brandweek (Vol. 49, April 21, 2008, No. 16, pp. 8)*
Pub: VNU Business Media, Inc.
Ed: Mike Beirne. **Description:** Nortel has launched a new television advertising campaign in which the business-to-business communications technology provider cast senior executives in 30-second TV case studies that show how Nortel's technology helped their businesses innovate.

40189 ■ *"Norvax University Health Insurance Sales Training and Online Marketing Conference" in Internet Wire (January 27, 2010)*
Pub: Comtex News Network, Inc.
Description: Overview of the Norvax University Marketing and Sales Success Conference Tour which includes insurance sales training seminars, proven and innovative online marketing techniques and a host of additional information and networking opportunities.

40190 ■ *"Note to Marketers: A Viral Video Has a Life of Its Own" in Advertising Age (Vol. 80, October 5, 2009, No. 33, pp. 29)*
Pub: Crain's Communications
Ed: Ken Wheaton. **Description:** Internet marketers do not decide whether or not an online video goes viral. It is the audience that decides what online videos to spread and such fare is usually passed around due to its content being downright witty or creative or so laughably bad that the audience wants to share it.

40191 ■ *"Nowspeed and OneSource to Conduct Webinar" in Internet Wire (December 14, 2009)*
Pub: Comtex News Network, Inc.
Description: OneSource, a leading provider of global business information, and Nowspeed, an Internet marketing agency, will conduct a webinar titled 'How to Develop Social Media Content That Gets Results' in order to provide marketers insight into how to develop and optimize effective social media content to get consumer results that translate into purchases and lead generation.

40192 ■ *"Nowspeed's David Reske to Speak at SolidWorks World 2010 in Anaheim" in Internet Wire (January 7, 2010)*
Pub: Comtex News Network, Inc.
Description: David Reske, managing director at Nowspeed, an Internet marketing agency based in the Boston area, will be presenting at SolidWorks World 2010; the convention's presentation will focus on proven methodologies, practical tips and real-world case studies in order to help attendees leverage the powerful Internet marketing innovations that are proving effective for businesses.

40193 ■ *Obsessive Branding Disorder: The Illusion of Business and the Business of Illusion*
Pub: Public Affairs
Ed: Lucas Conley. **Released:** 2008. **Price:** $22.95. **Description:** The implications of brand-centric marketing shows how defenseless consumers are against advertising because they are assaulted with 3,000 to 5,000 ads and branding stratagems that subtly dictate all aspects of their lives.

40194 ■ *"Ocean of Opportunity" in Hawaii Business (Vol. 53, October 2007, No. 4, pp. 61)*
Pub: Hawaii Business Publishing
Ed: Mike Markrich. **Description:** Brew Moon owner Marcus Bender and former Coca-Cola Enterprises Inc. executive Jim Stevens have introduced Kai Vodka in June 2007. The new drink is being marketed to professional women, the number of which is increasing based on a research by the Queens College Department of Sociology. The development process of the new product is also discussed.

40195 ■ *"Old Spice Guy (Feb.-July 2010)" in Canadian Business (Vol. 83, August 17, 2010, No. 13-14, pp. 23)*
Pub: Rogers Media Ltd.
Ed: Andrew Potter. **Description:** Old Spice Guy was played by ex-football player and actor Isaiah Mustafa who made the debut in the ad for Old Spice Red Zone body wash that was broadcast during Super Bowl XLIV in February 2010. Old Spice Guy has become one of social marketing success but was cancelled in July when online viewership started to wane.

40196 ■ *"Omniture's Next Version of SearchCenter Delivers Landing Page*

Optimization" in Internet Wire (September 24, 2009)
Pub: Comtex News Network, Inc.
Description: Omniture, Inc., a leading provider of online business optimization software, has announced a new release of Omniture SearchCenter; this latest version will allow search engine marketers to test landing pages across campaigns and ad groups.

40197 ■ *"On Beyond Powerpoint: Presentations Get a Wake-Up Call" in Inc. (November 2007, pp. 58-59)*
Pub: Gruner & Jahr USA Publishing
Ed: Michael Fitzgerald. **Description:** New software that allows business presentations to be shared online are profiled, including ProfCast, audio podcasts for sales, marketing, and training; SmartDraw2008, software that creates professional graphics; Dimdim, an open-Web conferencing tool; Empressr, a hosted Web service for creating, managing, and sharing multimedia presentations; Zentation, a free tool that allows users to watch slides and a videos of presenter; Spresent, a Web-based presentation tool for remote offices or conference calls.

40198 ■ *"On Managerial Relevance" in Journal of Marketing (Vol. 75, July 2011, No. 4, pp. 211)*
Pub: American Marketing Association
Ed: Bernard J. Jaworski. **Description:** A study to define and clarify managerial relevance, in order to act as a catalyst for debate, disagreement and future scholarship, is presented. The role of chief marketing officer (CMO) is examined to identify areas of inquiry that are both novel and high managerially relevant. The analysis reveals the seven core tasks necessary to perform the CMO role.

40199 ■ *"On a Mission: Ginch Gonch Wants You to Get Rid of Your Tighty Whities" in Canadian Business (Vol. 81, September 29, 2008, No. 16)*
Pub: Rogers Media Ltd.
Ed: Michelle Magnan. **Description:** New Equity Capital acquired underwear maker Ginch Gonch in July 2008; founder Jason Sutherland kept his position as creative director of the company and will retain his title as 'director of stitches and inches'. The company is known for its products, which are reminiscent of the days when people wore underwear covered in cowboys and stars as kids. The company also claims that Nelly, Justin Timberlake, and Hilary Duff have worn their products.

40200 ■ *"On Target" in Canadian Business (Vol. 81, July 22, 2008, No. 12-13, pp. 45)*
Pub: Rogers Media Ltd.
Ed: Calvin Leung. **Description:** Companies such as LavalifePRIME, a dating website devoted to singles 45 and older, discuss the value of marketing and services aimed at Canada's older consumers. One-third of Canada's 33 million people are 50-plus, controlling 77 percent of the countries wealth.

40201 ■ *"On Your Marks, American Airlines, Now Vote!" in Benzinga.com (, 2011)*
Pub: Benzinga.com
Ed: Benzinga Staff. **Description:** Wedding planner, Aviva Samuels, owner of Kiss the Planner boutique wedding and event planning agency in Florida, says that winning this contest would help her increase her knowledge base and provide in-depth, personal experience offering more destination wedding destinations.

40202 ■ *"The One Thing You Must Get Right When Building a Brand" in Harvard Business Review (Vol. 88, December 2010, No. 12, pp. 80)*
Pub: Harvard Business School Publishing
Ed: Patrick Barwise, Sean Meehan. **Description:** Four uses for new media include: communicating a clearly defined customer promise, creating trust via delivering on the promise, regularly improving on the promise, and innovating past what is familiar.

40203 ■ *"Online Marketing and Promotion of Canadian Films via Social Media Tools" in CNW Group (January 27, 2010)*
Pub: Comtex News Network, Inc.
Description: Telefilm Canada announced the launch of a pilot initiative aimed at encouraging the integration of online marketing and the use of social media tools into means of distribution ahead of a films' theatrical release. During this pilot phase Web-Cine 360 will target French-language feature films.

40204 ■ *"Online Marketing: Puppy Power: Using a New Tool Called a Widget To Boost Your Brand" in Inc. (November 2007, pp. 55-56)*
Pub: Gruner & Jahr USA Publishing
Ed: Dan Brody. **Description:** Widgets look like small television screens posted on Websites, blogs or desktops with a company's brand or logo. It can display any type of information or image, including sports scores, news headlines, weather reports, animated graphics, or a slide show. Profiles of Car-Domain Network, Babystrology, DailyPuppy.com, AnchorBank and more are included.

40205 ■ *"Online Postings Really Influence Older Women" in Marketing to Women (Vol. 22, July 2009, No. 7, pp. 8)*
Pub: EPM Communications Inc.
Contact: Ira Mayer, President
E-mail: imayer@epmcom.com
Description: Women over the age of 55 are more likely to be swayed to purchase a product by referrals from others, including Online postings by strangers. Another key influence is associated with the brand's ability to address their lifestyle needs.

40206 ■ *"Options Abound in Winter Wares" in Pet Product News (Vol. 64, November 2010, No. 11, pp. 1)*
Pub: BowTie Inc.
Ed: Maggie M. Shein. **Description:** Pet supply manufacturers emphasize creating top-notch construction and functional design in creating winter clothing for pets. Meanwhile, retailers and pet owners seek human-inspired style, quality, and versatility for pets' winter clothing. How retailers generate successful sales of pets' winter clothing outside of traditional brand marketing is also examined.

40207 ■ *"Orbitz Adds Parent Panel" in Marketing to Women (Vol. 21, March 2008, No. 3, pp. 5)*
Pub: EPM Communications Inc.
Contact: Ira Mayer, President
E-mail: imayer@epmcom.com
Description: Orbitz introduces the Orbitz Parent Panel in an attempt to better connect with traveling families.

40208 ■ *"Ordering Pizza Hut From Your Facebook Page?" in Advertising Age (Vol. 79, November 10, 2008, No. 42, pp. 50)*
Pub: Crain Communications, Inc.
Ed: Emily Bryson York. **Description:** Fast-food chains are experimenting with delivery/takeout services via social networks such as Facebook and iPhone applications. This also allows the chains to build valuable databases of their customers.

40209 ■ *"Org to Moms: Eat Your Veggies" in Marketing to Women (Vol. 21, April 2008, No. 4, pp. 3)*
Pub: EPM Communications Inc.
Contact: Ira Mayer, President
E-mail: imayer@epmcom.com
Description: In order to increase the purchase and consumption of fruit and vegetables to moms, the non profit Produce for Better Health Foundation is launching a series of initiatives.

40210 ■ *Our Daily Meds: How the Pharmaceutical Companies Transformed Themselves into Slick Marketing Machines*
Pub: Farrar, Straus and Giroux
Ed: Melody Petersen. **Released:** 2009. **Price:** $26.00. **Description:** Petersen, using industry memos, transcripts of meetings, and other sources shows how some drug companies are more concerned with the bottom line than with helping patients. Some of these firms are actually inventing 'diseases' in order to sell marginal medicines.

40211 ■ *"Our World with Black Enterprise" in Black Enterprise (Vol. 37, February 2007, No. 7, pp. 145)*
Pub: Earl G. Graves Publishing Co. Inc.
Description: Our World with Black Enterprise is a television broadcast that features roundtable discussions and interviews with important African American figures.

40212 ■ *"Out to Draw Work, Talent" in Crain's Detroit Business (Vol. 24, April 14, 2008, No. 15, pp. 3)*
Pub: Crain Communications, Inc.
Ed: Bill Shea. **Description:** Profile of Southfield-based Kinetic Post Inc., a growing post-production house that offers video, audio, animation, print, online and related services to corporations and advertising agencies.

40213 ■ *"Out-Of-Home and Transit" in MarketingMagazine (Vol. 115, September 27, 2010, No. 13, pp. 53)*
Pub: Rogers Publishing Ltd.
Description: Out-of-home and transit marketing data covering Canada is presented.

40214 ■ *"Overheating Taking Place? Pay Attention to Details.." in Indoor Comfort Marketing (Vol. 70, March 2011, No. 3, pp.)*
Pub: Industry Publications Inc.
Ed: George R. Carey. **Description:** Boiler facts are outlined to help the small HVAC company when servicing customers.

40215 ■ *"Overseas Marketing Key to Success of Chicago Spire" in Commercial Property News (March 17, 2008)*
Pub: Nielsen Company
Description: New construction of the Chicago Spire, a condominium project located on Lake Michigan's shore, is being marketed to would-be clients in Asia where Chicago is viewed as an emerging world city.

40216 ■ *The Owners Manual for Small Business*
Pub: Planning Shop
Ed: Rhonda Abrams. **Released:** December 2005. **Price:** $19.95. **Description:** Reference book offering tips for starting a small business, low-cost marketing, and communicating effectively.

40217 ■ *"Packers Still Want Marketing Deal With Favre" in The Business Journal-Milwaukee (Vol. 25, August 15, 2008, No. 47, pp. A1)*
Pub: American City Business Journals, Inc.
Ed: Mark Kass. **Description:** The Green Bay Packers plan to offer a $20 million marketing agreement to quarterback Brett Favre, including a clothing, merchandise, and collectibles line. The team is pursuing the agreement despite trading Favre to the New York Jets on 6 August 2008.

40218 ■ *"Pagetender LLC Releases Website Design Package for HubSpot Users" in Internet Wire (September 30, 2009)*
Pub: Comtex News Network, Inc.
Description: Profile of Pagetender LLC, a Certified HubSpot partner, who announced a Website Design Package marketed specifically for HubSpot Owner and Marketer users. This packaged was developed for small to medium sized businesses that want a website designed or their current site redesigned on HubSpot's Content Management System. Companies that would like a more robust site have the option of adding Flash development, ecommerce and photo galleries.

40219 ■ *"P&G's Iams Finds Itself in a Pet-Food Dogfight" in Advertising Age (Vol. 78, March 5, 2007, No. 10, pp. 6)*
Pub: Crain Communications, Inc.
Ed: Jack Neff. **Description:** Proctor & Gamble Co.'s Iams has been slow to embrace the trend toward foods for pets that appear fit for human consumption. Competitors such as Nestle Purina have made big

gains with its colorful premium Beneful brand and dry nuggets that look like chunks of vegetables and meat. Statistical data included.

40220 ■ *"Paper Tigers" in Conde Nast Portfolio (Vol. 2, June 2008, No. 6, pp. 84)*
Pub: Conde Nast Publications
Contact: David Carey, President
Ed: Roger Lowenstein. **Description:** Newspapers are losing their advertisers and readers and circulation today is equal to that of 1950, a time when the U.S. population was half its present size.

40221 ■ *"Partnering for Success" in Art Business News (Vol. 36, October 2009, No. 10, pp. 4)*
Pub: Summit Business Media
Ed: Jennifer Dulin Wiley. **Description:** In such a volatile economy many savvy artists and gallery owners are turning to out-of-the-box partnerships for continued success; these partnerships are also pervading the Internet, especially with such social media networks as Facebook and Twitter where artists and businesses can develop a loyal following.

40222 ■ *"Pau Hana" in Hawaii Business (Vol. 53, December 2007, No. 6, pp. 118)*
Pub: Hawaii Business Publishing
Ed: Cathy Cruz-George. **Description:** Presented are the hobbies of four Hawaii executives as well as the reason these hobbies are an important part of their lives and add to their ability to manage effectively. Mike Wilkins, for example, is not only Turtle Bay Resort's director of sales and marketing, but is also a glider pilot, while Aubrey Hawk Public Relations president Aubrey Hawk loves baking. The interests of Queen Liliuokalani Trust's Thomas K. Kaulukukui Jr., Reyn Spooner's Tim McCullough, and Heide and Cook Ltd.'s Dexter S. Kekua, are discussed.

40223 ■ *"Pavilions Poised for Image Overhaul" in The Business Journal - Serving Phoenix and the Valley of the Sun (Vol. 28, August 22, 2008)*
Pub: American City Business Journals, Inc.
Ed: Jan Buchholz. **Description:** DeRitto Partners Inc. is expected to push through with plans for a major renovation of the 1.1 million-square foot Scottsdale Pavilions in Scottsdale, Arizona. An aggressive marketing campaign is planned to be included in the renovation, which aims to address high vacancy rates and competition. Views and information on the planned renovation are presented.

40224 ■ *"People/Calendar" in Brandweek (Vol. 49, April 21, 2008, No. 16, pp. 30)*
Pub: VNU Business Media, Inc.
Description: Listing of current conferences, tradeshows and events concerning the marketing industry.

40225 ■ *"People; E-Commerce, Online Games, Mobile Apps" in Advertising Age (Vol. 80, October 19, 2009, No. 35, pp. 14)*
Pub: Crain's Communications
Ed: Nat Ives. **Description:** Profile of People Magazine and the ways in which the publisher is moving its magazine forward by exploring new concepts in a time of declining newsstand sales and advertising pages; among the strategies are e-commerce such as the brand People Style Watch in which consumers are able highlight clothing and jewelry and then connect to retailers' sites and a channel on Taxi TV, the network of video-touch screens in New Your City taxis.

40226 ■ *"People; E-Commerce, Online Games, Mobile Apps: This Isn't Your Mom's People" in Advertising Age (Vol. 80, October 19, 2009, No. 35)*
Pub: Crain's Communications
Ed: Nat Ives. **Description:** Profile of People Magazine and the ways in which the publisher is moving its magazine forward by exploring new concepts in a time of declining newsstand sales and advertising pages; among the strategies are e-commerce such as the brand People Style Watch in which consumers are able highlight clothing and jewelry and then connect to retailers' sites and a channel on Taxi TV, the network of video-touch screens in New Your City taxis.

40227 ■ *"The Perfect Formula to Build Your Brand" in Entrepreneur (Vol. 37, July 2009, No. 7, pp. 70)*
Pub: Entrepreneur Media, Inc.
Ed: Susan J. Linder. **Description:** Combining a product with expertise and a promise is the formula in building a brand for startups. The product will not sell itself, so one must consider what makes the product truly unique. Meanwhile, establishing trust and a foundation for a brand can be achieved by making a promise to the consumer and fulfilling it.

40228 ■ *"Personal File: Malcolm Smillie" in Canadian Business (Vol. 80, April 23, 2007, No. 9, pp. 44)*
Pub: Rogers Media
Description: A brief profile of Malcolm Smillie, marketing manager of 1-800-Got-Junk?, including his achievements which are also presented.

40229 ■ *"Pet-Food Crisis a Boon to Organic Players" in Advertising Age (Vol. 78, April 9, 2007, No. 15, pp. 3)*
Pub: Crain Communications, Inc.
Ed: Jack Neff. **Description:** In the wake of the pet-food recall crisis, the natural-and-organic segment of the market is gaining recognition and sales; one such manufacturer, Blue Buffalo, has not only seen huge sale increases but also has witnessed a 50-60 percent increase in traffic to the brand's website which has led to the decision to move up the timetable for the brand's first national ad campaign.

40230 ■ *"Pet-Food Industry Too Slow" in Advertising Age (Vol. 78, March 26, 2007, No. 13, pp. 29)*
Pub: Crain Communications, Inc.
Description: Many crisis-communications experts believe that the pet-food industry mishandled the problem by waiting almost a month to recall the 60 million 'wet-food' products after numerous consumer complaints. Experts site that the first 24 to 49 hours are the most important in dealing with a crisis of this nature.

40231 ■ *"Phoenix Conference Reveals Opportunities are Coming" in Indoor Comfort Marketing (Vol. 70, March 2011, No. 3, pp. 24)*
Pub: Industry Publications Inc.
Ed: Paul J. Nazzaro. **Description:** Advanced liquid fuels were spotlighted at the Phoenix conference revealing the opportunities for using liquid fuels.

40232 ■ *"Pick A Name, Not Just Any Name" in Women Entrepreneur (December 17, 2008)*
Pub: Entrepreneur Media Inc.
Ed: Maria Falconer. **Description:** Craft business owners must choose a name that sounds personal since customers who buy hand-made products want to feel that they are buying from an individual rather than an institution. Tips for choosing a name are provided.

40233 ■ *"Pink Label: Victoria's Sales Secret" in Advertising Age (Vol. 79, July 7, 2008, No. 26, pp. 4)*
Pub: Crain Communications, Inc.
Ed: Natalie Zmuda. **Description:** Victoria Secret's Pink label accounted for roughly 17 percent of the retailer's total sales last year. The company is launching a Collegiate Collection which will be promoted by a campus tour program.

40234 ■ *"Planning Your Next Move in Ad Land" in Advertising Age (Vol. 81, January 4, 2009, No. 1, pp. 1)*
Pub: Crain's Communications
Description: Overview of the challenges that ad agencies face today and will face in the years to come; highlights include problems occurring in various industries, Internet marketing innovations and the social media landscape.

40235 ■ *"Play By Play: These Video Products Can Add New Life to a Stagnant Website" in Black Enterprise (Vol. 41, December 2010, No. 5)*
Pub: Earl G. Graves Publishing Co. Inc.
Ed: Marcia Wade Talbert. **Description:** Web Visible, provider of online marketing products and services, cites video capability as the fastest-growing Website feature for small business advertisers. Profiles of various devices for adding video to a Website are included.

40236 ■ *"Play It Safe" in Entrepreneur (Vol. 35, November 2007, No. 11, pp. 26)*
Pub: Entrepreneur Media Inc.
Ed: Gwen Moran. **Description:** U.S.-based toy manufacturers find opportunity from concerns regarding the recent recalls of toys that are made in China. The situation can provide better probability of parents buying toys made in the U.S. or Europe, where manufacturing standards are stricter.

40237 ■ *"Please Pass the Mayo" in Crain's Chicago Business (Vol. 31, April 28, 2008, No. 17, pp. 32)*
Pub: Crain Communications, Inc.
Ed: Samantha Stainburn. **Description:** Fort Dearborn Co. has come a long way since it started as on one-press print shop; the family-owned company was struggling to keep up with the technology of making consumer product labels for curvy bottles of products like V8 V-Fusion juice and in 2006 sold off to Genstar Capital LLC which has pushed for acquisitions; last year, Fort Derborn bought its biggest competitor, Renaissance Mark Inc., doubling its size and adding spirit and wine makers to its client roster.

40238 ■ *"Poisoning Relationships: Perceived Unfairness in Channels of Distribution" in Journal of Marketing (Vol. 75, May 2011, No. 3, pp. 99)*
Pub: American Marketing Association
Ed: Stephen A. Samaha, Robert W. Palmatier, Rajiv P. Dant. **Description:** The effects of perceived unfairness on the relationships among members of distribution channels are examined. Perceived unfairness is found to directly damage relationships, aggravate the negative effects of conflict and opportunism, and undermine the benefits of the contract.

40239 ■ *"PopCap Games Achieves Significant Increase in Return on Ad Spend With Omniture SearchCenter" in Internet Wire (September 15, 2009)*
Pub: Comtex News Network, Inc.
Description: PopCap Games, a leading computer games provider, is using Omniture SearchCenter together with Omniture SiteCatalyst to increase revenue from its search engine marketing campaign. Omniture, Inc. is a leading provider of Internet business optimization software.

40240 ■ *"Port Metro Vancouver Unveiled" in Canadian Sailings (July 7, 2008)*
Pub: UBM Global Trade
Contact: Leonard J. Corallo, President
Description: Vancouver Fraser Port Authority is marketing the port as Port Metro Vancouver; Along with the new name the port has announced additional strategies for continued growth and launched a new logo.

40241 ■ *"Positive Transformational Change" in Indoor Comfort Marketing (Vol. 70, April 2011, No. 4, pp. 30)*
Pub: Industry Publications Inc.
Ed: Blaine Fox. **Description:** Management changes taking place at Shark Bites HVAC firm are discussed.

40242 ■ *"Powder River Reports First Quarter Revenues Over 5 Million" in Canadian Corporate News (May 16, 2007)*
Pub: Comtex News Network Inc.
Description: Financial report for Powder River Basin Gas Corp., a revenue generating producer, marketer, and acquirer of crude oil and natural gas properties. Statistical data included.

40243 ■ *The Power of Nice: How to Conquer the Business World with Kindness*
Pub: Doubleday
Ed: Linda Kaplan Thaler; Robin Koval. **Released:** September 19, 2006. **Price:** $17.95. **Description:** The key principles to running a business through thoughtfulness and kindness are exhibited with the use of success stories.

40244 ■ *The Power of Social Networking: Using the Whuffie Factor to Build Your Business*
Pub: Crown Business Books
Ed: Tara Hunt. **Released:** May 4, 2010. **Price:** $15.00. **Description:** This book shows how any small business can harness its power by increasing whuffie, the store of social capital that is the currency of the digital world. Blogs and social networks such as Facebook and Twitter are used to help grow any small firm.

40245 ■ *"Powers Reels in Pinger" in Business Courier (Vol. 24, December 21, 2008, No. 36, pp. 1)*
Pub: American City Business Journals, Inc.
Ed: Lisa Biank Fasig. **Description:** Powers Agency has acquired Dan Pinger Public Relations Inc. after three years in planning. The new company is to be called 'Pinger PR at Powers'. Details of the deal and the new company are discussed.

40246 ■ *"PPC's Major Commitment to Biofuel Infrastructure" in Indoor Comfort Marketing (Vol. 70, April 2011, No. 4, pp. 6)*
Pub: Industry Publications Inc.
Description: Petroleum Products Corporation's commitment to the biofuel infrastructure is outlined.

40247 ■ *Predictably Irrational: The Hidden Forces That Shape Our Decisions*
Pub: HarperCollins Publishers
Ed: Dan Ariely. **Released:** 2009. **Price:** $25.95. **Description:** Behaviorists are bringing the economics profession around to realizing that human beings are impulsive, shortsighted and procrastinating in behavior. Economists are using this information to market products to consumers.

40248 ■ *Prepare to Be a Teen Millionaire*
Pub: Health Communications, Inc.
Contact: Peter Vegso, President
Ed: Robyn Collins; Kimberly Spinks Burleson. **Released:** April 1, 2008. **Price:** $16.95. **Description:** Business reference for any teenager wishing to become a successful entrepreneur; advice is given from successful teenage millionaires. Topics covered include: choosing a business name, type, and location; use of the Internet; legal issues; branding, sales, and marketing; funding and financial management; return on investment; retirement; development of a sound business plan; and certification for minority or women-owned companies.

40249 ■ *"Pressed for Time" in Marketing to Women (Vol. 21, March 2008, No. 3, pp. 1)*
Pub: EPM Communications Inc.
Contact: Ira Mayer, President
E-mail: imayer@epmcom.com
Description: Statistical data concerning the tools women use for time management which include gadgets as well as traditional media such as calendars.

40250 ■ *"The Price Is Right: What You Can Learn From the Wine Industry" in Advertising Age (Vol. 88, February 11, 2008, No. 6, pp. 14)*
Pub: Crain Communications, Inc.
Ed: Lenore Skenazy. **Description:** In California a wine study was conducted in which participants' brains were hooked up to an MRI so researchers could watch what was happening in both the taste centers as well as the pleasure centers; the participants were given three different wines but were told that the samples were from a variety of wines that differed radically in price; surprisingly, the differences did not affect the taste centers of the brain, however, when the participants were told that a sample was more expensive, the pleasure centers were greatly affected.

40251 ■ *"Prime-Time Exposure" in Inc. (March 2008, pp. 66, 68)*
Pub: Gruner & Jahr USA Publishing
Ed: Adam Bluestein. **Description:** Product placement in television shows has increase sales for many companies. Tips for placing products or services into TV shows are explained: consider hiring an agency, target efforts, dream up a plot point, be ready to go on short notice, and work the niches.

40252 ■ *Principled Profit: Marketing that Puts People First*
Pub: Accurate Writing & More
Ed: Shel Horowitz. **Price:** $17.50. **Description:** The importance for companies to market ethically and honestly is stressed. Quality marketing will build customer loyalty and that will translate into new customers and repeat business. A customer-retention strategy is outlined along with ideas to increase profits of any small business.

40253 ■ *"Pro Livestock Launches Most Comprehensive Virtual Sales Barn for Livestock and Breed Stock" in Benzinga.com (October 29, 2011)*
Pub: Benzinga.com
Ed: Benzinga Staff. **Description:** Pro Livestock Marketing launched the first online sales portal for livestock and breed stock. The firm has designed a virtual sales barn allowing individuals to purchase and sell cattle, swine, sheep, goats, horses, rodeo stock, show animals, specialty animals, semen and embryos globally. It is like an eBay for livestock and will help ranchers and farmers grow.

40254 ■ *"Pro Teams Shift Ad Budgets; Naming Rights Deals Near $1 Billion" in Brandweek (Vol. 49, April 21, 2008, No. 16, pp. 18)*
Pub: VNU Business Media, Inc.
Ed: Barry Janoff. **Description:** More and more professional sports marketers are spending less of their advertising budgets on traditional media outlets such as television, print and radio; the growing trend in sports marketing is in utilizing new media venues such as the Internet in which innovative means are used to encourage interaction with fans.

40255 ■ *"Procter Gambles on Wallpaper; Putting Paint On a Roll" in Advertising Age (Vol. 77, September 18, 2006, No. 38, pp. 4)*
Pub: Crain Communications, Inc.
Ed: Jack Neff. **Description:** Procter & Gamble Co. has launched a new line of textured paints that are already applied to a wallpaper-like roll that can be hung without paste or wallpaper tools.

40256 ■ *Professional Services Marketing: How the Best Firms Build Premier Brands*
Pub: John Wiley & Sons, Inc.
Ed: Mike Schultz, John Doerr. **Released:** July 27, 2009. **Price:** $27.95. **Description:** Research based on best practices and processes for the professional services industry is presented. The book covers five key areas: creating a custom marketing and growth strategy, establishing a brand, implementing a marketing communications program, developing a lead strategy, and winning new clients.

40257 ■ *"Promote Your Business Through New Media" in Business Week (November 5, 2009)*
Pub: McGraw-Hill Companies
Ed: Karen E. Klein. **Description:** Traditional public relations strategies are becoming more and more outdated due to the rapid shift in Internet marketing opportunities. Ideas for marketing your company online are presented.

40258 ■ *"Promotions Create a Path to Better Profit" in Pet Product News (Vol. 64, December 2010, No. 12, pp. 1)*
Pub: BowTie Inc.
Ed: Joan Hustace Walker. **Description:** Pet store retailers can boost small mammal sales by launching creative marketing and promotions such as social networking and adoption days.

40259 ■ *"Pssst! Buzz About Target" in Barron's (Vol. 89, July 27, 2009, No. 30, pp. 15)*
Pub: Dow Jones & Co., Inc.
Ed: Katherine Cheng. **Description:** Target rebutted the rumor that they will disassociate themselves from a line of clothing inspired by the television show 'Gossip Girl'. Target's spokesman says that the retailer intends to remain closely identified with the show. Target's sales should benefit from the hotly anticipated clothing line.

40260 ■ *"Psst..Spread the Word" in Boston Business Journal (Vol. 27, November 23, 2007, No. 43, pp. 1)*
Pub: American City Business Journals Inc.
Ed: Lisa van der Pool. **Description:** More and more Boston companies are using word-of-mouth marketing to boost sales, and spending on it rose to $981 million in 2006. It is projected that spending on word-of-mouth marketing will reach $1.4 billion in 2007, and marketing companies using this type of method are getting higher funding. Trends in word-of-mouth marketing are discussed.

40261 ■ *"Pumping in Africa" in Canadian Business (Vol. 79, October 23, 2006, No. 21, pp. 162)*
Pub: Rogers Media
Ed: Jeff Sanford. **Description:** EastCoast Energy Corp.'s business venture of opening a natural gas company based in Tanzania and marketing of natural gas to expanding markets in East Africa is discussed.

40262 ■ *"Put Power in Your Direct Mail Campaigns" in Contractor (Vol. 56, September 2009, No. 9, pp. 64)*
Pub: Penton Media, Inc.
Ed: Matt Michel. **Description:** Advice on how members of the United States plumbing industry should manage direct mail marketing campaigns are offered. Determining the purpose of a campaign is recommended. Focusing on a single message, product or service is also encouraged.

40263 ■ *"Put Your Data to Work in the Marketplace" in Harvard Business Review (Vol. 86, September 2008, No. 9, pp. 34)*
Pub: Harvard Business School Press
Ed: Thomas C. Redman. **Description:** Nine strategies are presented for data asset marketing including exploiting asymmetries, unbundling, repackaging, and offering new content.

40264 ■ *"Quantivo Empowers Online Media Companies to Immediately Expand Audiences and Grow Online Profits" in Internet Wire (Nov. 18, 2009)*
Pub: Comtex News Network, Inc.
Description: Quantivo, the leader in on-demand Behavioral Analytics, has launched a new solution that includes 22 of the most critical Internet audience behavior insights as out-of-the-box reports; Internet marketers need to understand their audience, what they want and how often to offer it to them in order to gain successful branding and campaigns online.

40265 ■ *"Quebecor Inc. Takes Hit on Slipping Ad Revenue" in Globe & Mail (February 21, 2007, pp. B7)*
Pub: CTVglobemedia Publishing Inc.
Ed: Catherine McLean. **Description:** Canada-based Quebecor Inc. has reported fourth quarter losses of $97.1 million with revenues of $847.8 million. Decreased advertisement revenues are said to be the key reason behind the loss.

40266 ■ *"The Question: Who Do You Think Is the Most Genuine?" in Advertising Age (Vol. 79, July 7, 2008, No. 26, pp. 4)*
Pub: Crain Communications, Inc.
Ed: Ken Wheaton. **Description:** According to a survey conducted by Harris Interactive Reputation Quotient, Johnson & Johnson was deemed the most genuine brand. Google came in second followed by UPS.

40267 ■ *"A Quick Guide to NATE" in Indoor Comfort Marketing (Vol. 70, February 2011, No. 2, pp. 12)*
Pub: Industry Publications Inc.
Description: Guide for training and certification in the North American Technician Excellence award.

40268 ■ *"Quiznos Franchisees Walloped by Recession" in Advertising Age (Vol. 79, October 20, 2008, No. 39, pp. 3)*
Pub: Crain Communications, Inc.
Ed: Emily Bryson York. **Description:** While the recession has taken a toll on the entire restaurant industry, a number of Quiznos franchisees claim to have been disproportionately affected due to lackluster marketing, higher-than-average commodity costs, competition with Subway and a premium-pricing structure that is incompatible with a tight economy.

40269 ■ *"Race-Week Schedule Filling Up With Galas, Nonprofit Fundraisers" in Boston Business Journal (Vol. 29, July 22, 2011, No. 11, pp. 1)*
Pub: American City Business Journals Inc.
Ed: Alexander Jackson. **Description:** Baltimore, Maryland-based businesses and nonprofit groups have been planning their own events to coincide with the Baltimore Grand Prix during the Labor Day weekend. They also plan to partner with others in hopes of drumming up new business, raising money or to peddle their brands.

40270 ■ *"Radiant - the Hottest Topic in .. Cooling" in Indoor Comfort Marketing (Vol. 70, February 2011, No. 2, pp. 8)*
Pub: Industry Publications Inc.
Description: Examination of radiant cooling systems, a new trend in cooling homes and buildings.

40271 ■ *"Radiant Commences In-Lab Testing for US Air Mobility Command" in Canadian Corporate News (May 16, 2007)*
Pub: Comtex News Network Inc.
Description: The Boeing Company will be conducting in-lab infrared material testing for the Radiant Energy Corporation, developer and marketer of InfraTek, the environmentally friendly, patented infrared pre-flight aircraft deicing system.

40272 ■ *"Radio" in MarketingMagazine (Vol. 115, September 27, 2010, No. 13, pp. 24)*
Pub: Rogers Publishing Ltd.
Description: Market data in the radio broadcasting industry in Canada is outlined.

40273 ■ *"R&D Will Remain a Key Priority" in Farmer's Weekly (March 28, 2008, No. 320)*
Pub: Reed Business Information
Contact: Jeff Greisch, President
Description: Executives as well as the board of the new Horticultural Development Company (HDC) remain committed to the efficient delivery of research and development, a promotional drive and communications over the coming year.

40274 ■ *"RBC Holds Inside Card With HBC Credit Assets" in Globe & Mail (January 25, 2006, pp. B1)*
Pub: CTVglobemedia Publishing Inc.
Ed: Marina Strauss; Sinclair Stewart. **Description:** Hudson's Bay Co. (HBC) signed co-branding credit card agreement with Royal Bank of Canada are presented. The significance of the deal for HBC is discussed.

40275 ■ *"Real-Life Coursework for Real-Life Business People" in Women In Business (Vol. 63, Summer 2011, No. 2, pp. 22)*
Pub: American Business Women's Association
Ed: Leigh Elmore. **Description:** American Business Women's Association National Women's Leadership Conference provides members with academic business training courses. Members can take a variety of MBA-level courses that are taught by University of Kansas School of Business professors. Courses include marketing, management, leadership and communication and decision making.

40276 ■ *Reality Check: The Irreverent Guide to Outsmarting, Outmanaging, and Outmarketing Your Competition*
Pub: Penguin Group USA Inc.
Ed: Guy Kawasaki. **Price:** $29.95. **Description:** Marketing guru and entrepreneur, Guy Kawasaki, provides a compilation of his blog posts on all aspects of starting and operating a business.

40277 ■ *"Reaping Social-Media Rewards" in Canadian Business (Vol. 83, July 20, 2010, No. 11-12, pp. 19)*
Pub: Rogers Media Ltd.
Ed: Lyndsie Bourgon. **Description:** Foursquare is a social network which provides benefits such as discounts to users who show loyalty to a business or a brand. One marketing executive believes Foursquare is a good platform for loyalty programs and is an inexpensive alternative to Aeroplan.

40278 ■ *"The Rebranding Game: If at First You Pick the Wrong Name, You Can Always Try, Try Again" in Inc. (Vol. 30, December 2008, No. 12)*
Pub: Mansueto Ventures LLC
Ed: Ryan McCarthy. **Description:** Many entrepreneurs discover their firm's name can be too limiting or outdated. The process for rebranding a company is outlined.

40279 ■ *"Recalls Cause Consumers to Put More Stock in Online Reviews" in Crain's Cleveland Business (Vol. 28, November 12, 2007, No. 45)*
Pub: Crain Communications, Inc.
Ed: Jack Neff. **Description:** Due to the string of product recalls over the last year, consumers are looking at online product reviews to help them make purchasing decisions which could reshape marketing for a wide range of products.

40280 ■ *"Red, Pink and More: Cause Marketing Surges as a Prime Tactic to Reach Female Customers" in Marketing to Women (April 2008)*
Pub: EPM Communications Inc.
Contact: Ira Mayer, President
E-mail: imayer@epmcom.com
Description: According to the American Marketing Association, forty percent of women say they are more likely to purchase a product or service if they know a certain amount of the price is being donated directly to a cause or campaign that they believe in supporting.

40281 ■ *"Rediscovering the Land of Opportunity" in Green Industry Pro (July 2011)*
Pub: Cygnus Business Media
Ed: Gregg Wartgow. **Description:** Landscape contractors need to discover new strategies that will generate leads and convert those leads into sales.

40282 ■ *"Region to Be Named Innovation Hub" in Business Courier (Vol. 27, July 2, 2010, No. 9, pp. 1)*
Pub: Business Courier
Ed: Dan Monk. **Description:** The selection of Cincinnati's consumer-marketing cluster as a 'Hub of Innovation' by the Ohio Department of Development could boost Cincinnati's chances of receiving $100 million in grants from Ohio's Third Frontier program and other funding sources. Implications of the University of Cincinnati's designation as a Center of Excellence in Advanced Transportation and Aerospace are also discussed.

40283 ■ *"Reinventing Marketing to Manage the Environmental Imperative" in Journal of Marketing (Vol. 75, July 2011, No. 4, pp. 132)*
Pub: American Marketing Association
Ed: Philip Kotler. **Description:** Marketers must now examine their theory and practices due to the growing recognition of finite resources and high environmental costs. Companies also need to balance more carefully their growth goals with the need to purse sustainability. Insights on the rise of demarketing and social marketing are also given.

40284 ■ *"Renewed Vision" in Hawaii Business (Vol. 54, August 2008, No. 2, pp. 49)*
Pub: Hawaii Business Publishing
Ed: Jason Ubay. **Description:** Saint Francis Healthcare System of Hawaii, ranked 81 in Hawaii's top 250 companies for 2008, has been rebranding to focus on senior community healthcare and sold some of its operations, which explains the decline in gross sales from $219.5M in 2006 to $122.7M in 2007. The system's senior services and home hospice service expansion are provided.

40285 ■ *"Reply! Grows at Unprecedented Rate, Rips Beta Off Its Marketplace" in Marketing Weekly News (September 19, 2009, pp. 149)*
Pub: Investment Weekly News
Description: Profile of Reply.com, a leader in locally-targeted Internet marketing, announced significant growth in terms of revenue, enhanced features and services and new categories since launching its beta Reply! Marketplace platform. Even in the face of an economic downturn, the company has posted over 50 percent revenue growth in the Real Estate and Automotive categories.

40286 ■ *"Report: McD's Pepsi Score Best With Young Hispanics" in Brandweek (Vol. 49, April 21, 2008, No. 16, pp. 8)*
Pub: VNU Business Media, Inc.
Ed: Della de Lafuente. **Description:** According to a new report, in order to reach Hispanic Gen Yers, marketing strategists need to understand this demographic's 'bi-dentity,' something which has proved an elusive task to many marketers. Another trend is the emergence of Latinas who have careers, as opposed to just jobs. There is an opportunity to tap this new, young and empowered female market with innovative messaging. Statistical data included.

40287 ■ *"Reportlinker Adds Report: Social Networks: Five Consumer Trends for 2009" in Wireless News (October 23, 2009)*
Pub: Close-Up Media
Description: 'Social Networks: Five Consumer Trends for 2009,' a new market research report by Reportlinker.com found that in the countries of Italy and Spain lag behind their European neighbors in Internet development. Since large numbers of consumers in these two countries remain offline, only a minimal portion of total advertising spending goes into Internet marketing, and those advertising campaigns are directed at the relatively young, affluent users. Statistical data included.

40288 ■ *"Reportlinker.com Adds Report: GeoWeb and Local Internet Markets: 2008 Edition" in Entertainment Close-Up (September 11, 2009)*
Pub: Close-Up Media
Description: Reportlinker.com is adding a new market research report that is available in its catalogue: GeoWeb and Local Internet Markets - 2008 Edition; highlights include the outlook for consumer mapping services and an examination of monetizing services and an analysis the development outlook for geospacial Internet market, also referred to as the Geoweb.

40289 ■ *"Research and Markets Adds Report: Asian - Internet Market" in Health and Beauty Close-Up (January 19, 2010)*
Pub: Close-Up Media
Description: Overview of Research and Markets new report regarding Internet marketing and e-commerce in the Asian region; statistical data included.

40290 ■ *"Research and Markets Adds Report: Cyprus: Convergence, Broadband and Internet Market" in Wireless News (September 4, 2009)*
Pub: Close-Up Media
Description: Overview of a new report by Research and Markets entitled, 'Cyprus Convergence, Broadband and Internet Market - Overview, Statistics and Forecasts.' Highlights include information regarding broadband accounts which now account for the majority of household Internet connections.

40291 ■ ***"Research and Markets Adds Report: Ghana: Convergence, Broadband and Internet Market" in Wireless News (September 4, 2009)***
Pub: Close-Up Media
Description: Overview of a new report by Research and Markets entitled, 'Ghana Convergence, Broadband and Internet Market - Overview, Statistics and Forecasts.' Ghana was among the first countries in Africa connected to the Internet and to introduce ADSL broadband services; however, only 30 of the 140 licensed ISP's are operational making the sector highly competitive.

40292 ■ ***"Research and Markets Adds Report: The U.S. Mobile Web Market" in Entertainment Close-Up (December 10, 2009)***
Pub: Close-Up Media
Description: Highlights of the new Research and Markets report 'The U.S. Mobile Web Market: Taking Advantage of the iPhone Phenomenon' include: mobile Internet marketing strategies; the growth of mobile web usage; the growth of revenue in the mobile web market; and a look at Internet business communications, social media and networking.

40293 ■ ***"Research and Markets Adds Report: USA - Internet Market - Analysis, Statistics and Forecasts" in Wireless News (January 15, 2010)***
Pub: Close-Up Media
Description: According to Research and Markets new report concerning the United State's Internet market, e-commerce and Online advertising are expected to recover strongly in 2010.

40294 ■ ***"Rest Easy, Retailers" in Pet Product News (Vol. 64, December 2010, No. 12, pp. S1)***
Pub: BowTie Inc.
Ed: Wendy Bedwell-Wilson. **Description:** Pointers on how retailers can market all-natural beds and bedding products for pets are provided. The demand for these pet beds and bedding products has been increasing as customers become aware of the benefits of natural rest and relaxation products.

40295 ■ ***Restaurant Marketing for Owners and Managers***
Pub: John Wiley & Sons, Incorporated
Ed: Patti J. Shock, John T. Bowen, John M. Stefanelli. **Released:** October 2003. **Price:** $30.00. **Description:** Tools for combining marketing theory to practice in a restaurant business are covered.

40296 ■ ***"Restaurants Dish Up Meal Deals To Attract Customers" in Crain's Detroit Business (Vol. 24, October 6, 2008, No. 40, pp. 1)***
Pub: Crain Communications, Inc.
Ed: Nathan Skid. **Description:** Restaurateurs are devising many creative and rewarding incentives to get customers to frequent their establishments during this economic crisis. Innovative ways in which even higher-end establishments are drawing in business are discussed.

40297 ■ ***"Retailers Pull Out All Stops to Combat Poor Projections" in Austin Business JournalInc. (Vol. 28, November 21, 2008, No. 36, pp. 1)***
Pub: American City Business Journals
Ed: Jean Kwon. **Description:** Report from Wachovia Economics Group reports that holiday sales for 2008 are expected to decline by 2 percent and local retailers are planning to boost holiday sales through marketing efforts, which include giving freebies to early shoppers. Details on marketing strategies of several retailers are provided.

40298 ■ ***"The Return of the Infomercial" in Canadian Business (Vol. 83, September 14, 2010, No. 15, pp. 19)***
Pub: Rogers Media Ltd.
Ed: James Cowan. **Description:** Infomercials or direct response ads have helped some products succeed in the marketplace. The success of infomercials is due to the cheap advertising rates, expansion into retail stores and the products' oddball appeal. Insights into the popularity of infomercial products on the Internet and on television are given.

40299 ■ ***"Ric Elis/Dan Feldstein" in Charlotte Business Journal (Vol. 25, December 31, 2010, No. 41, pp. 6)***
Pub: Charlotte Business Journal
Ed: Ken Elkins. **Description:** Charlotte, North Carolina-based Internet marketing firm Red Ventures has grown significantly. General Atlantic has purchased stakes in Red Ventures.

40300 ■ ***"Rich Returns: Media Master" in Entrepreneur (Vol. 35, October 2007, No. 10, pp. 42)***
Pub: Entrepreneur Media Inc.
Ed: Robert Kiyosaki. **Description:** Advertising is a powerful way of reaching clients, however, public relations is a less expensive method which is just as effective as advertising. Entrepreneurs must also be ready to try something new to be noticed by the public. Insights on how to master the use of media are given.

40301 ■ ***"Rise Interactive, Internet Marketing Agency, Now Offers Custom Google Analytics Installation" in Internet Wire (September 29, 2009)***
Pub: Comtex News Network, Inc.
Description: In order to optimize a client's return of investment, Rise Interactive, a full-service Internet marketing agency, now offers custom Google Analytics installation to its customers; the installation process includes identifying an Internet marketing campaign's unique key performance indicators, translating them to actions one will perform o n a website and configuring the analytical tool to ensure the customized advertising campaign goals are set and properly tracked.

40302 ■ ***"Rise Interactive, Internet Marketing Agency, Now Offers Social Media Training and Advisory Services" in Internet Wire (Nov. 4, 2009)***
Pub: Comtex News Network, Inc.
Description: Profile of Rise Interactive, a full-service Internet marketing agency which has recently added social media to its list of offerings; the agency touts that its newest service gives their clients the power to have ongoing communication with current and potential customers on the sites they are most actively visiting.

40303 ■ ***"The Rise of Pompei" in Retail Merchandiser (Vol. 51, September-October 2011, No. 5, pp. 13)***
Pub: Phoenix Media Corporation
Description: Soho creative consulting group follows its C3 philosophy to create an invigorated brand experience that transforms customers from consumers to empowered buyers. Pompei AD is a leading creative consultancy that specializes in design and branding for retail, museum, hospitality, and other sectors.

40304 ■ ***Risk-Free Entrepreneur***
Pub: Adams Media Corporation
Ed: Don Debelak. **Released:** June 2006. **Price:** $14. 95. **Description:** Information is offered to help entrepreneurs to develop an idea for a product or service and have other companies provide the marketing, manufacturing and staff.

40305 ■ ***"Roadside Attraction" in Hawaii Business (Vol. 53, January 2008, No. 7, pp. 39)***
Pub: Hawaii Business Publishing
Ed: Jason Ubay. **Description:** Businesses beside the Kamehameha Highway find ways to survive in a rural community. Sunshine Arts Hawaii, for instance, uses a bright-colored and huge mural to attract tourists who drive along the highway. Other techniques employed by businesses in the aforementioned are des cribed.

40306 ■ ***"Rock Hall Shifts Advertising to 'Significant Markets' in Region" in Crain's Cleveland Business (Vol. 28, July 23, 2007, No. 29, pp. 6)***
Pub: Crain Communications, Inc.
Ed: John Booth. **Description:** Cleveland's Rock and Roll Hall of Fame and Museum is attempting a different marketing strategy this year with aims of reaching a broader audience in the Midwest and Great Lakes regions.

40307 ■ ***"ROIonline Announces Streaming Video Products" in Marketing Weekly News (December 5, 2009, pp. 155)***
Pub: Investment Weekly News
Description: ROIonline LLC, an Internet marketing firm serving business-to-business and the industrial marketplace, has added streaming video options to the Internet solutions it offers its clients; due to the huge increase of broadband connections, videos are now commonplace on the Internet and can often convey a company's message in a must more efficient, concise and effective way that will engage a website's visitor thus delivering a high return on a company's investment.

40308 ■ ***"Ronald Taketa" in Hawaii Business (Vol. 54, September 2008, No. 3, pp. 28)***
Pub: Hawaii Business Publishing
Ed: Shara Enay. **Description:** Interview with Ronald Taketa of the Hawaii Carpenters Union who states that the economic downturn has affected the construction industry as 20 percent of the union's 7,800 members are unemployed. He shares his thoughts about the industry's economic situation, the union's advertisements, and his role as a leader of the union.

40309 ■ ***"Rough Q1 Begs Question: Is the Crocs Craze Over?" in Brandweek (Vol. 49, April 21, 2008, No. 16, pp. 16)***
Pub: VNU Business Media, Inc.
Ed: Eric Newman. **Description:** Crocs, a rubber shoemaker, announced last week that it missed its expected first quarter revenues by 15 percent. The popular rubber sandals are suffering in sales due to a number of factors including a tougher economic environment, less expensive, knock-off brands, the cold weather delay of the spring season and fading consumer interest in plastic shoes.

40310 ■ ***"Roundtable: Functional Foods and Treats" in Pet Product News (Vol. 64, December 2010, No. 12, pp. S1)***
Pub: BowTie Inc.
Description: Executives and business owners from the pet supplies industries deliberate on the role of functional foods in the retail sector. Functional foods pertain to foods with specified health benefits. Insight into marketing functional foods and convincing pet owners to make the transition to these products is examined.

40311 ■ ***"Rule of the Masses: Reinventing Fashion Via Crowdsourcing" in WWD (Vol. 200, July 26, 2010, No. 17, pp. 1)***
Pub: Conde Nast Publications
Contact: David Carey, President
Ed: Cate T. Corcoran. **Description:** Large apparel brands and retailers are crowdsourcing as a way to increase customer loyalty and to build their businesses.

40312 ■ ***"Rumor Has It" in Entrepreneur (Vol. 35, October 2007, No. 10, pp. 30)***
Pub: Entrepreneur Media Inc.
Ed: Chris Penttila. **Description:** Some entrepreneurs like Ren Moulton and Dan Scudder regard rumor sites and product blogs as great sources of market research. However, there are legal issues that must be studied before using these Internet sites in marketing and product development. The use and limitations of rumor sites and product blogs are provided.

40313 ■ ***"Sabathia Deal Makes Dollars and Sense" in The Business Journal-Milwaukee (Vol. 25, July 11, 2008, No. 42, pp. A1)***
Pub: American City Business Journals, Inc.
Ed: Mark Kass. **Description:** It was reported that the Milwaukee Brewers' acquisition of CC Sabathia will mean that the team will pick up an estimated $5 million in salary that Sabathia is owed for the remainder of the season. Because of this, the team will not make

a profit in 2008. The acquisition of Sabathia is expected to cause an increase in attendance and merchandise revenue over the remainder of the season.

40314 ■ *"Sage Advice" in Canadian Business (Vol. 80, October 22, 2007, No. 21, pp. 70)*
Pub: Rogers Media
Ed: John Gray. **Description:** Seymour Schulich, one of Canada's richest men and generous philanthropist, wrote the book, 'Get Smarter: Life and Business Lessons'. The business book sold more than 50,000 copies and now sits on Canada's bestseller's list. Its popularity is attributed to the marketing efforts of the entrepreneur and author.

40315 ■ *"St. Elizabeth Fights for Share at St. Lukes" in Business Courier (Vol. 27, November 12, 2010, No. 28, pp. 1)*
Pub: Business Courier
Ed: James Ritchie. **Description:** Key information on how St. Elizabeth Healthcare helps partner St. Luke's Hospitals increase market share in the healthcare industry are presented. Some of St. Luke's hospitals, such as the St. Elizabeth Fort Thomas in Kentucky, are struggling with low occupancy rates, prompting St. Elizabeth to invest about $24 million to help St. Luke's increase its market share.

40316 ■ *Salesforce.com Secrets of Success: Best Practices for Growth and Profitability*
Pub: Prentice Hall Business Publishing
Contact: Jerome Grant, President
Ed: David Taber. **Released:** May 15, 2009. **Price:** $34.99. **Description:** Guide for using Salesforce.com; it provides insight into navigating through user groups, management, sales, marketing and IT departments in order to achieve the best results.

40317 ■ *"Schipul Enhances Website Via Tendenci 5" in Entertainment Close-Up (March 30, 2011)*
Pub: Close-Up Media
Description: Schipul, Website marketing and design firm, upgraded their Website using Tendenci 5 which features capabilities that cater to the interests of the user. Tendenci 5 also powers Websites for Houston Technology Center, Discovery Green, Tendenci and YMCA Houston.

40318 ■ *Scorecasting*
Pub: Crown Business Books
Ed: Tobias Moskowitz, L. Jon Wertheim. **Released:** January 25, 2011. **Price:** $26.00. **Description:** Behavioral economist and veteran writer partner to write about research and studies revealing the hidden forces that shape how basketball, baseball, football and hockey games are played, won and lost.

40319 ■ *"Scripps Networks" in Brandweek (Vol. 49, April 21, 2008, No. 16, pp. SR12)*
Pub: VNU Business Media, Inc.
Ed: Anthony Crupi. **Description:** Provides contact information for sales and marketing personnel for the Scripps networks as well as a listing of the station's top programming and an analysis of the current season and the target audience for those programs running in the current season. Scripps networks include HGTV and the Food Network. HGTV boasts on of the industry's best commercial-retention averages, keeping nearly 97 percent of its viewers during advertising breaks.

40320 ■ *"Sean Durfy" in Canadian Business (Vol. 80, April 23, 2007, No. 9, pp. 14)*
Pub: Rogers Media
Ed: Michelle Magnan. **Description:** Sean Durfy, president of WestJet Airlines Ltd., feels that marketing is essential factor for growth of airline industry.

40321 ■ *"Search and Discover New Opportunities" in DM News (Vol. 31, December 14, 2009, No. 29, pp. 13)*
Pub: Haymarket Media, Inc.
Ed: Chantal Tode. **Description:** Although other digital strategies are gaining traction in Internet marketing, search marketing continues to dominate this advertising forum. Companies like American Greetings, which markets e-card brands online, are utilizing social networking sites and affiliates to generate a higher demand for their products.

40322 ■ *"The Seat-Of-The-Pants School of Marketing" in Brandweek (Vol. 49, April 21, 2008, No. 16, pp. 24)*
Pub: VNU Business Media, Inc.
Ed: David Vinjamuri. **Description:** Excerpt from the book 'Accidental Branding: How Ordinary People Build Extraordinary Brands,' by David Vinjamuri, discusses six shared principles for creating a brand that is unique and will be successful over the long-term.

40323 ■ *Secrets to Power Marketing*
Pub: Stoddart Publishing Company, Ltd.
Ed: Peter Urs Bender; George Torok. **Released:** 2000. **Description:** How-to marketing book provides information for putting personal into any marketing plan. The book also offers marketing strategies build around perceptions, relationships, the media, leverage and database marketing.

40324 ■ *The Secrets of Spiritual Marketing: A Complete Guide for Natural Therapists*
Pub: O Books
Ed: Lawrence Ellyard. **Released:** November 1, 2009. **Price:** $24.95. **Description:** Strategies for marketing and advertising a natural therapy business are examined.

40325 ■ *"Security Alert: Data Server" in Entrepreneur (Vol. 36, February 2008, No. 2, pp. 28)*
Pub: Entrepreneur Media Inc.
Ed: Amanda C. Kooser. **Description:** Michael Kogon is the founder of Definition 6, a technology consulting and interactive marking firm. He believes in the philosophy that the best way to keep sensitive data safe is not to store it. Details on the security policies of his firm are discussed.

40326 ■ *"Seed Funding" in Saint Louis Business Journal (Vol. 31, July 29, 2011, No. 49, pp. 1)*
Pub: Saint Louis Business Journal
Ed: Kelsey Volkmann. **Description:** Monsanto kicked off a new campaign, 'St. Louis Grown' to show its commitment to the St. Louis, Missouri region after spending millions of dollars in recent years on national advertising campaigns. Monsanto had a marketing budget totaling $839 million in 2010 for both brand and corporate marketing.

40327 ■ *The Self-Publishing Manual: How To Write, Print, and Sell Your Own Book*
Pub: Para Publishing
Ed: Dan Poynter. **Released:** 2007. **Price:** $19.95. **Description:** The book provides a complete course in writing, publishing, marketing, promoting, and distributing books. Poynter offers a step-by-step study of the publishing industry and explains various book-marketing techniques.

40328 ■ *"Sell: Going Zen" in Entrepreneur (Vol. 35, October 2007, No. 10, pp. 106)*
Pub: Entrepreneur Media Inc.
Ed: Barry Farber. **Description:** Principles of Zen can actually be used to improve selling skills. Some of the Zen values such as being prepared, keeping silent, and practicing open-mindedness are applicable in the marketing world. Details on what salespeople can learn from Zen are provided.

40329 ■ *Selling the Invisible: A Field Guide to Modern Marketing*
Pub: Business Plus
Ed: Harry Beckwith. **Price:** $22.95. **Description:** Tips for marketing and selling intangibles such as health care, entertainment, tourism, legal services, and more are provided.

40330 ■ *Selling Online: Canada's Bestselling Guide to Becoming a Successful E-Commerce Merchant*
Pub: John Wiley and Sons Canada Ltd.
Ed: Jim Carroll; Rick Broadhead. **Released:** September 6, 2002. **Description:** Helps individuals build online retail enterprises; this updated version includes current tools, information and success strategies, how to launch an online storefront, security, marketing strategies, and mistakes to avoid.

40331 ■ *"Senate OKs Funds for Promoting Tourism" in Crain's Detroit Business (Vol. 24, March 31, 2008, No. 13, pp. 6)*
Pub: Crain Communications, Inc.
Ed: Amy Lane. **Description:** Discusses the Senate proposal which allocates funds for Michigan tourism and business promotion as well as Michigan's No Worker Left Behind initiative, a program that provides free tuition at community colleges and other venues to train displaced workers for high-demand occupations.

40332 ■ *The Seven Principles of WOM and Buzz Marketing: Crossing the Tipping Point*
Pub: Springer
Ed: Panos Mourdoukoulas, George J. Siomkos. **Released:** October 9, 2010. **Price:** $119.00. **Description:** An examination into the reasons for some word-of-mouth marketing campaigns being effective while other fail, with a discussion about which group of consumers should be targeted, and how to turn a word-of-mouth campaign into buzz.

40333 ■ *"Shoestring-Budget Marketing" in Women Entrepreneur (January 5, 2009)*
Pub: Entrepreneur Media Inc.
Ed: Maria Falconer. **Description:** Pay-per-click search engine advertising is the traditional type of e-marketing that may not only be too expensive for certain kinds of businesses but also may not attract the quality customer base a business looking to grow needs to find. Social networking websites have become a mandatory marketing tool for business owners who want to see growth in their sales; tips are provided for utilizing these networking websites in order to gain more visibility on the Internet which can, in turn, lead to the more sales.

40334 ■ *"Should I or Shouldn't I?" in Indoor Comfort Marketing (Vol. 70, February 2011, No. 2, pp. 30)*
Pub: Industry Publications Inc.
Ed: Philip J. Baratz. **Description:** Investment tips are shared for investing in futures options.

40335 ■ *"Should You Invest in the Long Tail?" in Harvard Business Review (Vol. 86, July-August 2008, No. 8, pp. 88)*
Pub: Harvard Business School Press
Ed: Anita Elberse. **Description:** Relevance of the long tail, or the sustainability of sales after a given product's launch is examined. It is posited that niche sales are not as sustainable as those for products with broader appeal.

40336 ■ *"Shout and Devour" in Tulsa World (November 7, 2009)*
Pub: Tulsa World
Ed: Kyle Arnold. **Description:** Profile of convenience store Shout and Sack whose owners have distanced themselves from the corporate fray of the chain stores by offering homemade lunches served at a counter; the store recently gained national exposure that highlighted the popularity despite a market share heavily dominated by franchises and chains.

40337 ■ *"Show Me the Love" in Canadian Business (Vol. 79, November 6, 2006, No. 22, pp. 77)*
Pub: Rogers Media
Ed: Jeannette Hanna. **Description:** The strategies to improve brand image with relation to success of Tim Horton's brand are presented.

40338 ■ *"Show and Tell" in Entrepreneur (Vol. 36, May 2008, No. 5, pp. 54)*
Pub: Entrepreneur Media, Inc.
Ed: Heather Clancy. **Description:** FreshStart Telephone uses recorded video testimonials of customers, by using Pure Digital Flip Video that downloads content directly to the computer, and uploads it in the company's website to promote their wireless phone service.

40339 ■ *"Sick of Trends? You Should Be" in Brandweek (Vol. 49, April 21, 2008, No. 16, pp. 22)*
Pub: VNU Business Media, Inc.
Ed: Eric Zeitoun. **Description:** Eric Zeitoun, the president of Dragon Rouge, a global brand consultancy, discusses the importance of macrotrends as opposed to microtrends which he feels are often irrelevant, create confusion and cause marketers to lose site of the larger picture of their industry. Macrotrends, on the other hand, create a fundamental, societal shift that influences consumer attitudes over a long period of time.

40340 ■ *"A Side Project Threatens To Get Totally Out of Control and I Think, 'How Fun"' in Inc. (October 2007, pp. 81-82)*
Pub: Gruner & Jahr USA Publishing
Ed: Joel Spolsky. **Description:** Profile of Fog Creek Software, makers of project-management software for other software developers. Fog Creek's owner discusses his idea to create a new product for his firm.

40341 ■ *"Sign, Sign, Everywhere a Sign: How I Did It: Richard Schaps" in Inc. (October 2007, pp. 128)*
Pub: Gruner & Jahr USA Publishing
Ed: Stephanie Clifford. **Description:** Richard Schaps shares the story of selling his outdoor-advertising firm, Van Wagner for $170 million and sharing the wealth with his employees. Schaps then started another outdoor-sign company.

40342 ■ *"Silverpop Recognized for Email Marketing Innovations by Econsultancy" in Marketing Weekly News (January 23, 2010, pp. 124)*
Pub: Investment Weekly News
Description: Econsultancy, a respected source of insight and advice on digital marketing and e-commerce, recognized Silverpop, the world's only provider of both marketing automation solutions and email marketing specifically tailored to the unique needs of B2C and B2B marketers at Econsultancy's 2009 Innovation Awards.

40343 ■ *"Similac Introduces New Packaging" in Marketing to Women (Vol. 21, February 2008, No. 2, pp. 3)*
Pub: EPM Communications Inc.
Contact: Ira Mayer, President
E-mail: imayer@epmcom.com
Description: Baby formula brand Similac introduces a new ready to feed packaging which requires no mixing, measuring or preparation.

40344 ■ *"Simplifying Social Media for Optimum Results" in Franchising World (Vol. 42, August 2010, No. 8, pp. 12)*
Pub: International Franchise Association
Ed: Paul Segreto. **Description:** Keys to effective technology usage requires the development of an integrated plan, choosing the most complementary tools and implementing well-planned strategies.

40345 ■ *"Sites Set" in Entrepreneur (Vol. 35, November 2007, No. 11, pp. 112)*
Pub: Entrepreneur Media Inc.
Ed: Nichole L. Torres. **Description:** Marketing information online can be a good bui9sness if you know who to target. Partnering with other online companies to provide information services that cater to specific groups of people is also helpful.

40346 ■ *Six SIGMA for Small Business*
Pub: Entrepreneur Press
Ed: Greg Brue. **Released:** October 2005. **Price:** $19.95 (US), $26.95 (Canadian). **Description:** Jack Welch's Six SIGMA approach to business covers accounting, finance, sales and marketing, buying a business, human resource development, and new product development.

40347 ■ *"Size Obsession" in Marketing to Women (Vol. 22, August 2009, No. 8, pp. 2)*
Pub: EPM Communications Inc.
Contact: Ira Mayer, President
E-mail: imayer@epmcom.com
Description: Clothing size is becoming a marketing tool for retailers who wish to seize more of the female market share. Women are more likely to purchase an item in a smaller size.

40348 ■ *"Slimmed-Down Supplier TI Automotive Relaunches" in Crain's Detroit Business (Vol. 26, January 11, 2010, No. 2, pp. 14)*
Pub: Crain Communications Inc.
Ed: Robert Sherefkin. **Description:** TI Automotive Ltd., one of the world's largest suppliers of fuel storage and delivery systems, has reorganized the company by splitting it into five global divisions and is relaunching its brand which is now more focused on new technology.

40349 ■ *"Small Budget, Big Impact" in Small Business Opportunities (Summer 2010)*
Pub: Harris Publications Inc.
Ed: Hilary J.M. Topper. **Description:** Ways to use social media to get in from of a target audience for small businesses are examined.

40350 ■ *The Small Business Bible: Everything You Need to Know to Succeed in Your Small Business*
Pub: John Wiley and Sons, Inc.
Ed: Steven D. Strauss. **Released:** September 2008. **Price:** $19.95 (US), $28.99 (Canadian). **Description:** Comprehensive guide to starting and running a successful small business. Topics include bookkeeping and financial management, marketing, publicity, and advertising.

40351 ■ *Small Business Clustering Technology: Applications in Marketing, Management, Finance, and IT*
Pub: Idea Group Publishing
Ed: Robert C. MacGregor; Ann Hodgkinson. **Released:** June 2006. **Description:** An overview of the development and role of small business clusters in disciplines that include economics, marketing, management and information systems.

40352 ■ *Small Business Desk Reference*
Pub: Penguin Books USA Inc.
Ed: Gene Marks. **Released:** December 2004. **Description:** Comprehensive guide for starting or running a successful small business, focusing on buying a business or franchise, writing a business plan, financial management, accounting, legal issues, human resources management, operations, marketing, sales, customer service, taxes, insurance, and ethics. Information for launching a restaurant, property management firm, retail outlet, consulting firm, and service business is included.

40353 ■ *Small Business Marketing for Dummies*
Pub: John Wiley & Sons, Incorporated
Ed: Barbara Findlay Schenck. **Released:** February 2005. **Price:** $19.99 (US), $25.99 (Canadian). **Description:** Marketing strategies for every type of small business.

40354 ■ *Small Business Start-Up Workbook: A Step-by-Step Guide to Starting the Business You've Dreamed Of*
Pub: How To Books
Ed: Cheryl D. Rickman. **Released:** February 2006. **Price:** $24.75. **Description:** Book provides practical exercises for starting a small business, including marketing and management strategies.

40355 ■ *"Small Dutch Islands Saba, Statia Content With Low-Key Niche" in Travel Weekly (Vol. 69, August 16, 2010, No. 33, pp. 22)*
Pub: NorthStar Travel Media LLC
Ed: Gay Nagle Myers. **Description:** Small Caribbean islands market and promote their region for tourism by never competing with the bigger destinations. Saba and Statia are the two smallest islands in the Caribbean and rely on repeat guests, word-of-mouth recommendations and travel agents willing to promote them.

40356 ■ *"Small is the New Big in Autos" in Globe & Mail (February 16, 2006, pp. B3)*
Pub: CTVglobemedia Publishing Inc.
Ed: Greg Keenan. **Description:** The reasons behind the introduction of subcompact cars by companies such as Ford Motor Co. are presented. The automobiles were unveiled at Canadian International Auto Show in Toronto.

40357 ■ *The Social Media Bible: Tactics, Tools, and Strategies for Business Success*
Pub: John Wiley & Sons, Inc.
Ed: Lon Safko, David Brake. **Released:** June 17, 2009. **Price:** $29.95. **Description:** Information is given to build or transform a business into social media, where customers, employees, and prospects connect, collaborate, and champion products and services in order to increase sales and to beat the competition.

40358 ■ *"Social Media By the Numbers: Social-Media Marketing Is All the Rage" in Inc. (Vol. 33, November 2011, No. 9, pp. 70)*
Pub: Inc. Magazine
Ed: J.J. McCorvey, Issie Lapowsky. **Description:** Six strategies to help small businesses use social media sites such as Facebook and Twitter to promote their companies are presented.

40359 ■ *"Social Media: Communicate the Important Stuff" in Agency Sales Magazine (Vol. 39, November 2009, No. 10, pp. 52)*
Pub: MANA
Ed: Jack Foster. **Description:** Social media such as Twitter or Facebook allows businesses to communicate with their customers over great distances but this technology can take away from the personal touch. For those that want to implement these tools in their marketing plans, they should first find out which social media networks their target audience use and give their customers reasons to become fans.

40360 ■ *"Social Media, E-Mail Remain Challenging for Employees" in Workforce Management (Vol. 88, December 14, 2009, No. 13, pp. 4)*
Pub: Crain Communications Inc.
Ed: Ed Frauenheim. **Description:** Examining the impact of Internet social networking and the workplace; due to the power of these new technologies, it is important that companies begin to set clear policies regarding Internet use and employee privacy.

40361 ■ *"Social Networkers for Hire" in Black Enterprise (Vol. 40, December 2009, No. 5, pp. 56)*
Pub: Earl G. Graves Publishing Co., Inc.
Ed: Brittany Hutson. **Description:** Companies are utilizing social networking sites in order to market their brand and personally connect with consumers and are increasingly looking to social media specialists to help with this task. Aliya S. King is one such web strategist, working for ICED Media by managing their Twitter, Facebook, YouTube and Flickr accounts for one of their publicly traded restaurant clients.

40362 ■ *"Social Networking Site for Moms" in Marketing to Women (Vol. 21, March 2008, No. 3, pp. 3)*
Pub: EPM Communications Inc.
Contact: Ira Mayer, President
E-mail: imayer@epmcom.com
Description: The Cradle is a social networking site devoted to pregnancy and new parenthood.

40363 ■ *"Social Networks in the Workplace" in Strategy & Leadership (Vol. 38, July-August 2010, No. 4, pp. 50-53)*
Pub: Emerald Inc.
Ed: Daniel Burrus. **Description:** The opinions of futurist Daniel Burrus on a novel trend called 'Business 2.0', which involves the use of social networking applications as business tools, are presented. His suggestion that personal social networking technology can be used by businesses to improve collaboration, problem solving, and leadership communications to achieve continuous value innovation is discussed.

40364 ■ ***"A Software Company's Whimsical Widgets Were an Instant Hit. But Its Core Product Was Getting Overshadowed" in Inc. (Jan. 2008)***
Pub: Gruner & Jahr USA Publishing
Ed: Alex Salkever. **Description:** A widget designed as a marketing tool tuned into a hit on Facebook. Should ChipIn shift its focus?.

40365 ■ ***"Somanetics to Buy Back Up to $15 Million of Common Shares" in Crain's Detroit Business (Vol. 24, April 7, 2008, No. 14, pp. 4)***
Pub: Crain Communications, Inc.
Ed: Tom Henderson. **Description:** Somanetics Corp., a company that manufactures and markets noninvasive devices for monitoring blood oxygen levels in the brain and elsewhere in the body during surgery, plans to buy back up to $15 million worth of its common shares. Statistical data included on the company's current and past earnings and stock prices as well as its plans to increase revenue.

40366 ■ ***"Sony Pictures Television" in Brandweek (Vol. 49, April 21, 2008, No. 16, pp. SR13)***
Pub: VNU Business Media, Inc.
Ed: Marc Berman. **Description:** Provides contact information for sales and marketing personnel for Sony Pictures Television Distribution as well as a listing of the station's top programming and an analysis of the current season and the target audience for those programs running in the current season.

40367 ■ ***"Sophia Siskel; CEO, Chicago Botanic Garden" in Crain's Chicago Business (Vol. 31, May 5, 2008, No. 18, pp. 36)***
Pub: Crain Communications, Inc.
Ed: John Rosenthal. **Description:** Profile of Sophia Siskel who is the CEO of the Chicago Botanic Garden and is overseeing the $100 million expansion which will put the Botanic Garden at the forefront of plant conservation science; Ms. Siskel is also an efficient marketer and researcher.

40368 ■ ***"Sophistication in Research in Marketing" in Journal of Marketing (Vol. 75, July 2011, No. 4, pp. 155)***
Pub: American Marketing Association
Ed: Donald R. Lehmann, Leigh McAlister, Richard Staelin. **Description:** A look at the current imbalance in the research in marketing is presented. The level of analytical rigor has risen in articles published in marketing academic journals but other desirable characteristics, such as communicability, relevance, and simplicity have been downplayed.

40369 ■ ***"Sorrell Digs Deep to Snag TNS" in Advertising Age (Vol. 79, July 14, 2008, No. 7, pp. 1)***
Pub: Crain Communications, Inc.
Ed: Michael Bush. **Description:** Martin Sorrell's strategic vision for expansion in order to become the largest ad-agency holding company in the world is discussed.

40370 ■ ***"Space Shut Hot" in Canadian Business (Vol. 80, October 22, 2007, No. 21, pp. 28)***
Pub: Rogers Media
Ed: John Gray. **Description:** Scandium, a metal first developed by the Soviet military in missile and fighter jets, sells for $700 a kilogram. The pricey metal is beginning to generate some hype, although current demand is still low. Details for marketing growth opportunities are discussed.

40371 ■ ***"Speak Better: Five Tips for Polished Presentations" in Women Entrepreneur (September 19, 2008)***
Pub: Entrepreneur Media Inc.
Ed: Suzannah Baum. **Description:** Successful entrepreneurs agree that exemplary public speaking skills are among the core techniques needed to propel their business forward. A well-delivered presentation can result in securing a new distribution channel, gaining new customers, locking into a new referral stream or receiving extra funding.

40372 ■ ***"Spell It Out" in Entrepreneur (Vol. 36, April 2008, No. 4, pp. 123)***
Pub: Entrepreneur Media, Inc.
Ed: Emily Weisberg. **Description:** IM:It is an apparel and accessories company that markets products with instant messaging (IM) acronyms and emoticons. Examples of these are 'LOL' and 'GTG'. Other details on IM:It products are discussed.

40373 ■ ***"Sponsorship, Booths Available for Spring Business Showcase" in Bellingham Business Journal (Vol. February 2010, pp. 3)***
Pub: Sound Publishing Inc.
Description: Third Annual Spring Business Showcase still have space available for vendors and sponsors. The event gives local businesses the opportunity to increase their visibility and provides a means to increase sales and build relationships.

40374 ■ ***"Spotlight; 'Classroom Focus' at Encyclopaedia Britannica" in Crain's Chicago Business (Vol. 34, October 24, 2011, No. 42, pp. 6)***
Pub: Crain Communications Inc.
Ed: Paul Merrion. **Description:** Profile of Gregory Healy, product officer for Encyclopaedia Britannica is presented. Healy took the position in May 2010 and is focused on online offerings of their publication and to make them more useful to teachers.

40375 ■ ***"Start Connecting Today" in Indoor Comfort Marketing (Vol. 70, May 2011, No. 5, pp. 34)***
Pub: Industry Publications Inc.
Ed: Paul Nazzaro. **Description:** An in-depth discussion regarding the use of biofuels on bioheat use and dealership.

40376 ■ ***"Start Moving Toward Advanced Fuels" in Indoor Comfort Marketing (Vol. 70, March 2011, No. 3, pp. 4)***
Pub: Industry Publications Inc.
Ed: Michael L. SanGiovanni. **Description:** Commentary on advanced fuels is presented.

40377 ■ ***Start Your Own Blogging Business, Second Edition***
Pub: Entrepreneur Press
Contact: Perlman Neil, President
Released: July 1, 2010. **Price:** $17.95. **Description:** Interviews with professional bloggers from some of the most popular blogs on the Internet will help anyone interested in starting their own blogging business.

40378 ■ ***Start Your Own Fashion Accessories Business***
Pub: Entrepreneur Press
Contact: Perlman Neil, President
Released: March 1, 2009. **Price:** $17.95. **Description:** Entrepreneurs wishing to start a fashion accessories business will find important information for setting up a home workshop and office, exploring the market, managing finances, publicizing and advertising the business and more.

40379 ■ ***Starting an iPhone Application Business for Dummies***
Pub: Wiley Publishing Inc.
Contact: William J. Pesce, President
Ed: Aaron Nicholson, Joel Elad, Damien Stolarz. **Released:** October 26, 2009. **Price:** $24.99. **Description:** Ways to create a profitable, sustainable business developing and marketing iPhone applications are profiled.

40380 ■ ***Starting a Yahoo! Business for Dummies***
Pub: John Wiley & Sons, Incorporated
Ed: Rob Snell. **Released:** June 2006. **Price:** $24.99. **Description:** Rob Snell offers advice for turning online browsers into buyers, increase online traffic, and build an online store from scratch.

40381 ■ ***Starting a Yahoo! Business For Dummies***
Pub: John Wiley & Sons, Incorporated
Ed: Rob Snell. **Released:** May 27, 2006. **Price:** $24. 99. **Description:** Advice helps turn Web browsers into buyers, boost online traffic, and information to launch a profitable online business.

40382 ■ ***"State of the Unions" in Canadian Business (Vol. 81, December 8, 2008, No. 21, pp. 23)***
Pub: Rogers Media Ltd.
Ed: Sharda Prashad. **Description:** Companies planning on joint ventures should look for partners they can trust and respect and are also competent. Joint venture deals aim to bring existing products to a a new market or in acquiring a foreign product for an existing market.

40383 ■ ***"Staying Power" in Canadian Business (Vol. 79, November 6, 2006, No. 22, pp. 73)***
Pub: Rogers Media
Ed: John Gray. **Description:** The effects on brand image on customer choices are analyzed. The need of maintaining brand image is also emphasized.

40384 ■ ***Steal These Ideas!: Marketing Secrets That Will Make You a Star***
Pub: Bloomberg Press
Ed: Steve Cone. **Released:** September 13, 2005. **Price:** $18.95. **Description:** The book shares information to successfully market any product or service.

40385 ■ ***"Sticking to Stories; Havey Ovshinksy Changes Method, Keeps the Mission" in Crain's Detroit Business (Vol. 24, March 31, 2008)***
Pub: Crain Communications, Inc.
Ed: Daniel Duggan. **Description:** Profile of Harvey Ovshinsky, an award-winning documentary filmmaker who has reinvented his work with corporations who want to market themselves with the transition to digital media. His company, HKO Media, takes Ovshinsky's art of storytelling and enhances it through multimedia operations on the Internet through a joint venture with a man he once mentored, Bob Kernen.

40386 ■ ***"Strength In Numbers" in Black Enterprise (Vol. 38, January 2008, No. 6, pp. 53)***
Pub: Earl G. Graves Publishing Co. Inc.
Description: According to recent studies geared to advertisers, African Americans represent a demographic that drives style and consumer trends. The African American buying power is expected to increase to $1.1 trillion by 2011. Beyond Demographics helps clients identify ways to value and measure investments within the black community.

40387 ■ ***"Stretch Your Advertising Dollars" in Women Entrepreneur (January 27, 2009)***
Pub: Entrepreneur Media Inc.
Ed: Rosalind Resnick. **Description:** During such poor economic times, most businesses are having to cut their advertising budgets; tips for targeting your advertising dollars toward the customer base most likely to buy your product are given.

40388 ■ ***"Study: New Moms Build A Lot of Brand Buzz" in Brandweek (Vol. 49, April 21, 2008, No. 16, pp. 7)***
Pub: VNU Business Media, Inc.
Description: According to a new survey which sampled 1,721 pregnant women and new moms, this demographic is having 109 word-of-mouth conversations per week concerning products, services and brands. Two-thirds of these conversations directly involve brand recommendations. The Internet is driving these word-of-mouth, or W-O-M, conversations among this segment, beating out magazines, television and other forms of media.

40389 ■ ***"Stung by Recession, Hemmer Regroups with New Strategy" in Business Courier (Vol. 27, June 4, 2010, No. 5, pp. 1)***
Pub: Business Courier
Ed: Lucy May. **Description:** Paul Hemmer Companies reduced its work force and outsourced operations such as marketing and architecture, in order for the commercial and construction firm to survive the recession. Hammer's total core revenue in 2009 dropped to less than $30 million forcing the closure of its Chicago office.

40390 ■ *"Success a Big Seller: N. Carolina, Duke Coaches Cash in as Marketers' Dreams" in Charlotte Observer (February 7, 2007)*
Pub: Knight-Ridder/Tribune Business News
Ed: Ken Tysiac. **Description:** North Carolina sporting coaches are marketing goods and services in television commercials and print media.

40391 ■ *"Success Products" in Black Enterprise (Vol. 37, February 2007, No. 7, pp. 135)*
Pub: Earl G. Graves Publishing Co. Inc.
Ed: Tanisha A. Sykes. **Description:** Using innovative resources that are already at your fingertips instead of trying to reach out to companies first is a great way to discover whether you have a viable idea or product. Be motivated to start an e-newsletter letting people know about your products and attend conferences like The Motivation Show, the world's largest exhibition of motivational products and services related to performance in business.

40392 ■ *Success Secrets of Social Media Marketing Superstars*
Pub: Entrepreneur Press
Contact: Perlman Neil, President
Ed: Mitch Meyerson. **Released:** June 1, 2010. **Price:** $21.95. **Description:** Provides access to the playbooks of social media marketers who reveal their most valuable strategies and tactics for standing out in the new online media environment.

40393 ■ *"Sunbrella Engages Consumers Via Social Media" in Home Textiles Today (Vol. 31, May 24, 2011, No. 13, pp. 4)*
Pub: Reed Business Information
Contact: Jeff Greisch, President
Description: Performance fabric brand Sunbrella is marketing to social media, such as Facebook and Twitter, in order to boost consumer interest and retailer support.

40394 ■ *"Super Success" in Small Business Opportunities (November 2008)*
Pub: Entrepreneur Press
Contact: Perlman Neil, President
Description: Profile of PromoWorks LLC, a company founded by Michael Kent, that distributes samples of food at grocery stores for clients like Kraft Foods, Inc. and Kellogg Co. and also handles the logistics, provides the employees and tracks the products' sales.

40395 ■ *"The Sure Thing That Flopped" in Harvard Business Review (Vol. 86, July-August 2008, No. 8, pp. 29)*
Pub: Harvard Business School Press
Ed: Gerald Zaltman; Lindsay Zaltman. **Description:** Fictitious brand extension scenario is presented, with contributors providing suggestions and advice. The company's struggles with expanding the brand may be alleviated by improving consumer research, focusing on emotional responses to products and services.

40396 ■ *"Survey: More Buyers Expect to Spend Less in Most Media" in Advertising Age (Vol. 79, July 7, 2008, No. 26, pp. 3)*
Pub: Crain Communications, Inc.
Ed: Megan McIlroy. **Description:** Marketers are decreasing their budgets for advertising in television, radio, newspaper and outdoor due to the economic downturn. Statistical data concerning advertising agencies and marketers included.

40397 ■ *"Survey Points to Big Jump in 2006 Ad Budgets" in Globe & Mail (January 23, 2006, pp. B3)*
Pub: CTVglobemedia Publishing Inc.
Ed: Keith McArthur. **Description:** The findings of ICA Survey of Marketing Budgets on the advertising budgets of marketing executives, in 2006, are presented.

40398 ■ *"The Sweet Spot: A Sugar-Coated Pitch Paid Off Big Time" in Black Enterprise (Vol. 37, November 2006, No. 4, pp. 71)*
Pub: Earl G. Graves Publishing Co. Inc.
Ed: Laura Egodigwe. **Description:** In an interview with Debra Sandler, president of McNeil Nutritionals L.L.C., Sandler talks about the challenges of bringing a new product to the marketplace, how her personal experiences effect her business decisions, and the difficulties of re-entering the workforce.

40399 ■ *"Sweet Tea; Neil Golden" in Advertising Age (Vol. 79, November 17, 2008, No. 43, pp. 4)*
Pub: Crain Communications, Inc.
Ed: Emily Bryson York. **Description:** McDonald's launch of iced coffee and sweat tea, which were promoted via price cuts over the summer, helped to boost sales at the fast-food chain.

40400 ■ *"A Switch in the Kitchen" in Barron's (Vol. 88, March 24, 2008, No. 12, pp. 17)*
Pub: Dow Jones & Company, Inc.
Description: Men are doing more kitchen duties, with 18 percent of meals at home being made by men in 2007 compared to 11 percent four years previously. Young wives, however, choose to forgo work and stay at home.

40401 ■ *"Sylvie Collection Offers a Feminine Perspective and Voice in Male Dominated Bridal Industry" in Benzinga.com (October 29, 2011)*
Pub: Benzinga.com
Ed: Benzinga Staff. **Description:** Bridal jewelry designer Sylvie Levine has created over 1,000 customizable styles of engagement rings and wedding bands and is reaching out to prospective new brides through a new Website, interactive social media campaign and monthly trunk show appearances.

40402 ■ *"Symbility Solutions Joins Motion Computing Partner Program" in Canadian Corporate News (May 14, 2007)*
Pub: Comtex News Network Inc.
Description: Symbility Solutions Inc., a wholly owned subsidiary of Automated Benefits Corp., announced an agreement with Alliance Partner of Motion Computing, a leader in wireless communications and mobile computing, in which both companies will invest in a sales and marketing strategy that focuses specifically on the insurance market.

40403 ■ *"T3 Grows, Recovers Well After Losing Dell" in Austin Business JournalInc. (Vol. 28, September 19, 2008, No. 27)*
Pub: American City Business Journals
Ed: Sandra Zaragoza. **Description:** T3 Inc. an Austin, Texas-based advertising company is recovering from losing its Dell Inc. account with the addition of new clients, such as Taco Bell, ConocoPhillips, Robbins Brothers, and Intel. The country is projected to earn capitalized billings of $313 million for 2008. Details on the company's plans to consolidate its offices are discussed.

40404 ■ *"Taco Bell; David Ovens" in Advertising Age (Vol. 79, November 17, 2008, No. 43, pp. S2)*
Pub: Crain Communications, Inc.
Ed: Emily Bryson York. **Description:** Due to the addition of new products such as a low-calorie, low-fat Fresco menu; a fruity iced beverage; and a value initiative, Taco Bell now accounts for half of Yum Brands' profits. The chain has also benefited from a new chief marketing officer, David Ovens, who oversees ad support.

40405 ■ *Tactical Entrepreneur: The Entrepreneur's Game Plan*
Pub: Sortis Publishing
Ed: Brian J. Hazelgren. **Released:** September 2005. **Price:** $14.95. **Description:** A smart, realistic business plan is essential for any successful entrepreneur. Besides offering products or services, small business owners must possess skills in accounting, planning, human resources management, marketing, and information technology.

40406 ■ *"Take Out the Garbage" in Entrepreneur (Vol. 37, August 2009, No. 8, pp. 26)*
Pub: Entrepreneur Media, Inc.
Ed: Michael Port. **Description:** Canned 1-2-3 sales tactics should be ditched since consumers express their values with the products and services they buy. Sales people should instead work their call list and become a masterful permission marketer, make relevant sales offers proportionate to the trust they have earned, and build credibility with the people they are meant to serve.

40407 ■ *"Talent Shows" in Canadian Business (Vol. 81, December 24, 2007, No. 1, pp. 14)*
Pub: Rogers Media
Ed: Megan Harman. **Description:** Canadian companies are increasingly turning to marketing to promote themselves as employers, as concerns on employee recruitment increase with the nearing retirement age of the baby boomers. Details on skills shortage, the potential advantage for the immigrant workforce, and employee retention are discussed.

40408 ■ *"Tap Into Food Truck Trend to Rev Up Sales, Build Buzz" in Nation's Restaurant News (Vol. 45, February 7, 2011, No. 3, pp. 18)*
Pub: Penton Media, Inc.
Ed: Brian Sacks. **Description:** Food truck trend is growing, particularly in New York City, Philadelphia, Washington DC, and Los Angeles, California. Man entrepreneurs are using a mobile food component to market their food before opening a restaurant.

40409 ■ *"A Team Sport" in Business Courier (Vol. 26, October 2, 2009, No. 23, pp. 1)*
Pub: American City Business Journals, Inc.
Ed: Lisa Biank Fasig. **Description:** Procter & Gamble (P&G) revised the way it works with marketing, design and public relations firms. Creative discussions will be managed by only two representatives, the franchise leader and the brand agency leader in order for P&G to simplify operations as it grows larger and more global.

40410 ■ *"Teams Buy Into Screen Scene" in Business First Buffalo (October 5, 2007, pp. 1)*
Pub: American City Business Journals, Inc.
Ed: James Fink. **Description:** Buffalo Bills, Buffalo Sabres, University of Buffalo, and Buffalo Bisons have all purchased new ribbon informational boards and video scoreboards to enhance their marketing strategies and improve the experience of sports fans. Vision boards of University of Buffalo and Sabres were installed by Daktronics, while Bills bought a Mitsubishi Diamond Vision board. The features that make the new scoreboards good promotional tools are described.

40411 ■ *"Technically Speaking" in Black Enterprise (Vol. 38, February 2008, No. 7, pp. 64)*
Pub: Earl G. Graves Publishing Co. Inc.
Ed: Sonia Alleyne. **Description:** Marketing manager for Texas Instruments discusses the Strategic Marketing of Technology Products course offered at the California Institute of Technology. The course helps turn products into profits.

40412 ■ *"Technology Drivers to Boost Your Bottom Line" in Franchising World (Vol. 42, August 2010, No. 8, pp. 15)*
Pub: International Franchise Association
Ed: Dan Dugal. **Description:** Technological capabilities are expanding quickly and smart franchises should stay updated on all the new developments, including smart phones, global positioning systems, and social media networks.

40413 ■ *"Technology Protects Lottery" in Arkansas Business (Vol. 26, September 28, 2009, No. 39, pp. 1)*
Pub: Journal Publishing Inc.
Ed: George Waldon. **Description:** Arkansas Lottery Commission was initially criticized for what was seen as a major breach in security protocol by revealing the exact location of 26 million lottery tickets during a publicity stunt in which the media was invited to the main distribution center; however, due to the high-tech security that has been implemented the tickets are worthless until their status is changed after passing through multiple security scans.

40414 ■ *"Telemundo" in Brandweek (Vol. 49, April 21, 2008, No. 16, pp. SR8)*
Pub: VNU Business Media, Inc.
Ed: John Consoli. **Description:** Provides contact information for sales and marketing personnel for the Telemundo network as well as a listing of the station's top programming and an analysis of the current season and the target audience for those programs running in the current season.

40415 ■ *"Television Broadcasting" in MarketingMagazine (Vol. 115, September 27, 2010, No. 13, pp. 16)*
Pub: Rogers Publishing Ltd.
Description: Market statistics covering the Canadian television broadcasting industry are covered.

40416 ■ *"That Canadian Tire Couple Won't Be Annoying You Anymore" in Globe & Mail (March 10, 2006, pp. B3)*
Pub: CTVglobemedia Publishing Inc.
Ed: Keith McArthur. **Description:** The details pertaining to the rolling out of new advertisements by Canadian Tire Corp. Ltd. are presented. The commercials have been made by Taxi Advertising and Design, which has redesigned the previous ad of the tire maker.

40417 ■ *"This Just In" in Crain's Detroit Business (Vol. 25, June 22, 2009, No. 25, pp. 1)*
Pub: Crain Communications Inc. - Detroit
Description: Yamasaki Associates, an architectural firm has been sued for non payment of wages to four employees. Yamasaki spokesperson stated the economy has affected the company and it is focusing marketing efforts on areas encouraged by recovery funding.

40418 ■ *"This Week: McD's Eyes Ad Plan, Shifts Breakfast Biz" in Crain's Chicago Business (Vol. 30, February 2007, No. 6, pp. 1)*
Pub: Crain Communications, Inc.
Ed: Kate MacArthur. **Description:** McDonald's is moving its national breakfast ad account from DDB Chicago to Arnold Worldwide of Boston and Moroch of Dallas in an attempt to change its marketing strategy. It is also doing a study to keep abreast of consumer trends.

40419 ■ *"Thomas Industrial Network Unveils Custom SPEC" in Entertainment Close-Up (March 3, 2011)*
Pub: Close-Up Media
Description: Thomas Industrial Network assists custom manufacturers and industrial service providers a complete online program called Custom SPEC which includes Website development and Internet exposure.

40420 ■ *"Thomas Morley; President, The Lube Stop Inc., 37" in Crain's Cleveland Business (Vol. 28, November 19, 2007, No. 46, pp. F-12)*
Pub: Crain Communications, Inc.
Ed: David Bennett. **Description:** Profile of Thomas Morley, president of The Lube Stop Inc., who is dedicated to promoting the company's strong environmental record as an effective way to differentiate Lube Stop from its competition. Since Mr. Morley came to the company in 2004, Lube Stop has increased sales by 10 percent and has boosted its operating profits by 30 percent.

40421 ■ *"Three Weeks To Startup" in Entrepreneur (December 19, 2008)*
Pub: Entrepreneur Media Inc.
Ed: Tim Berry; Sabrina Parsons. **Description:** Breakdown for realistically starting a business in three weeks is provided in detail.

40422 ■ *"Tigers Put to Test; Can Team Win Back Fans, Advertisers?" in Crain's Detroit Business (Vol. 24, October 6, 2008, No. 40, pp. 1)*
Pub: Crain Communications, Inc.
Ed: Bill Shea. **Description:** Despite the enormous amount of money the Detroit Tigers' owner Mike Ilitch spent on player salaries, a record $137.6 million this season, the team finished in last-place; ticket sales and advertising dollars for next season are expected to fall dramatically. Additional speculation regarding the future of the ball team is included.

40423 ■ *"Tim Armstrong" in Canadian Business (Vol. 81, July 21, 2008, No. 11, pp. 10)*
Pub: Rogers Media Ltd.
Ed: Calvin Leung. **Description:** Interview with Tim Armstrong who is the president of advertising and commerce department of Google Inc. for North America; the information technology company executive talked about the emerging trends and changes to YouTube made by the company since its acquisition in 2006.

40424 ■ *"Tim Hortons Aims for Breakfast Breakout" in Globe & Mail (February 13, 2006, pp. B3)*
Pub: CTVglobemedia Publishing Inc.
Ed: Andy Hoffman. **Description:** Fast food chain Tim Hortons will be launching its new breakfast menu with more combinations that include bacons, eggs and coffee. Tim Horton is subsidiary of Wendy's International Inc and has 290 outlets in America.

40425 ■ *The Tipping Point: How Little Things Can Make a Big Difference*
Pub: Little Brown & Company
Ed: Malcolm Gladwell. **Released:** January 2002. **Price:** $14.95. **Description:** Correlation between societal changes and marketing and business trends.

40426 ■ *"Tips to Improve Your Direct Mail Results" in Contractor (Vol. 57, January 2010, No. 1, pp. 55)*
Pub: Penton Media, Inc.
Ed: Matt Michel. **Description:** Plumbers can improve their direct mail efforts by buying quality lists and writing good headlines. The mail should also tell a story and urge its readers to action.

40427 ■ *"Titan to Become New York's Largest Provider of Phone Kiosk Advertising" in Marketing Weekly News (September 11, 2010, pp. 150)*
Pub: VerticalNews
Description: Titan will acquire from Verizon 1,900 payphones at 1,300 phone kiosk locations in New York City, New York. This transaction will triple the firm's inventory of New York Phone Kiosk media to over 5,000 advertising faces. Details are included.

40428 ■ *"Title Creep: The Chief Revenue Officer" in Inc. (March 2008, pp. 28)*
Pub: Gruner & Jahr USA Publishing
Ed: The title, Chief Revenue Officer, is growing. The marketing function of the CRO is to oversee sales, new product development, and pricing.

40429 ■ *"TiVo, Domino's Team to Offer Pizza Ordering by DVR" in Advertising Age (Vol. 79, November 17, 2008, No. 43, pp. 48)*
Pub: Crain Communications, Inc.
Ed: Brian Steinberg. **Description:** Domino's Pizza and TiVo are teaming up to make it possible for customers to order from the restaurant straight from their DVR. The companies see that this kind of interactive television and consumer experience will only serve to generate more sales as the customer can be exposed to a fuller range of menu selections and will not have to interrupt their viewing, while workers can spend more time making the product.

40430 ■ *"To Be Seen Is to Be Successful" in Pet Product News (Vol. 64, December 2010, No. 12, pp. 12)*
Pub: BowTie Inc.
Ed: David Arvin. **Description:** Guidelines on how pet business retailers can boost customer visibility are described considering that complacency could hamper retailers' efforts to effectively market their businesses. To enhance customer base and stand out from competing businesses, being different, strategic, creative, and differentiated is emphasized.

40431 ■ *"To Blog, Or Not To Blog" in Canadian Business (Vol. 80, December 25, 2006, No. 1, pp. 15)*
Pub: Rogers Media
Ed: Andy Holloway. **Description:** The growing use of weblogs for internet marketing by business enterprises is discussed.

40432 ■ *"To Catch Up, Colgate May Ratchet Up Its Ad Spending" in Advertising Age (Vol. 81, December 6, 2010, No. 43, pp. 1)*
Pub: Crain Communications, Inc.
Ed: Jack Neff. **Description:** Colgate-Palmolive Company has been losing market share in the categories of toothpaste, deodorant, body wash, dish soap and pet food.

40433 ■ *"To Help Maintain an Adequate Blood Supply During the Summer Months" in Ice Cream Reporter (Vol. 21, August 20, 2008, No. 9, pp. 8)*
Pub: Ice Cream Reporter
Description: Friendly's and the American Red Cross have partnered to offer blood donors a coupon for one free carton of Friendly's ice cream in order to maintain an adequate supply during summer months.

40434 ■ *"To JM On Its 75th Anniversary" in Journal of Marketing (Vol. 75, July 2011, No. 4, pp. 129)*
Pub: American Marketing Association
Ed: Ruth M. Bolton. **Description:** How the Journal of Marketing influenced the marketing science and practice is presented. The Marketing Science Institute's 50th anniversary coincides with the journal's 75th anniversary and both have collaborated to tackle important marketing issues identified in MSI's priorities. The mind-set of managers worldwide was also influenced by ideas in the journal's articles.

40435 ■ *"Too Much Information?" in Black Enterprise (Vol. 37, December 2006, No. 5, pp. 59)*
Pub: Earl G. Graves Publishing Co. Inc.
Ed: James C. Johnson. **Description:** African American business owners often face the dilemma of whether or not to divulge their minority status when soliciting new customers and financial institutions. The quality of the products or services is always the key factor and race should never define one's business; however, it is appropriate to market oneself as a minority or women-owned business, especially if the company is in an industry where those clients are offered top-tier contracts.

40436 ■ *"The Top Mistakes of Social Media Marketing" in Agency Sales Magazine (Vol. 39, November 2009, No. 9, pp. 42)*
Pub: MANA
Ed: Pam Lontos; Maurice Ramirez. **Description:** One common mistake in social media marketing is having more than one image on the Internet because this ruins a business' credibility. Marketers need to put out messages that are useful to their readers and to keep messages consistent.

40437 ■ *"Tourism Bureau Seeks Hotel Tax Hike" in Baltimore Business Journal (Vol. 27, December 18, 2009, No. 32, pp. 1)*
Pub: American City Business Journals
Ed: Rachel Bernstein. **Description:** Baltimore, Maryland's tourism agency, Visit Baltimore, has proposed a new hotel tax that could produce $2 million annually for its marketing budget, fund improvements to the city's 30-year-old convention center and help it compete for World Cup soccer games. Baltimore hotel leaders discuss the new tax.

40438 ■ *Trade Shows Worldwide: An International Directory of Events, Facilities, and Suppliers*
Pub: Cengage Learning Inc.
Contact: Ronald Dunn, President
URL(s): www.gale.cengage.com. **Released:** Annual; Latest edition 30th, April 2012. **Price:** $645, Individuals. **Covers:** Over 10,000 trade shows and exhibitions, including those held at conferences, conventions, meetings, trade and industrial events, merchandise marts, and national expositions; 6,000

trade show sponsors and organizers; of trade show facilities, services, and information sources, approximately 5,900 conference and convention centers, about 600 visitor and convention bureaus, 400 World Trade Centers; sources of information for the trade show industry, including professional associations, consulting organizations, and publications; and 1,900 trade show industry service suppliers. **Entries include:** name, address, phone, fax, e-mail, website, toll-free, phone, fax, name and title of contact; show frequency; founding date; audience; number of attendees; price for display space; description of exhibits; registration fees; industry programs; social events; square feet/meters of exhibition space; number of meeting rooms needed; number of hotel rooms and nights needed; publications, dates and locations of future shows. **Database includes:** Ranked lists of events by amount of exhibit space needed and by number of hotel rooms needed. **Arrangement:** Separate sections for shows and exhibitions, for sponsors/organizers, and for trade show facilities, services, and information sources. **Indexes:** Chronological (show date), geographical (show location), subject, name and keyword.

40439 ■ *"Traits that Makes Blogs Attractive to Book Publishers" in Marketing to Women (Vol. 22, July 2009, No. 7, pp. 1)*
Pub: EPM Communications Inc.
Contact: Ira Mayer, President
E-mail: imayer@epmcom.com
Description: Book publishers are finding a beneficial relationship between themselves and women bloggers on the Internet. A high visitor count, frequent updates and active readership are criteria for identifying the blogs with the most clout and therefore providing the greatest benefit to publishers.

40440 ■ *"Transportation Enterprise" in Advertising Age (Vol. 79, June 9, 2008, No. 23, pp. S10)*
Pub: Crain Communications, Inc.
Ed: Jean Halliday. **Description:** Overview of Enterprise rent-a-car's plan to become a more environmentally-friendly company. The family-owned business has spent $1 million a year to plant trees since 2006 and has added more fuel-efficient cars, hybrids and flex-fuel models.

40441 ■ *"Trend: Tutors to Help You Pump Up the Staff" in Business Week (September 22, 2008, No. 4100, pp. 45)*
Pub: McGraw-Hill Companies, Inc.
Ed: Reena Janaj. **Description:** High-level managers are turning to innovation coaches in an attempt to obtain advice on how to better sell new concepts within their companies. Individuals as well as consulting firms are now offering this service.

40442 ■ *"The Trouble With $150,000 Wine" in Barron's (Vol. 88, July 7, 2008, No. 27, pp. 33)*
Pub: Dow Jones & Co., Inc.
Ed: Orley Ashenfelter. **Description:** Review of the book, 'The Billionaire's Vinegar: The Mystery of the World's Most Expensive Bottle of Wine,' which discusses vintners along with the marketing and distribution of wine as well as the winemaking industry as a whole.

40443 ■ *"Troy Complex has New Brand, New Leases" in Crain's Detroit Business (Vol. 24, April 14, 2008, No. 15, pp. 32)*
Pub: Crain Communications Inc.
Ed: Daniel Duggan. **Description:** Discusses the rebranding of the 1.2 million-square-foot collection of office buildings in Troy purchased by New York-based Emmes Co. The firm has also pledged more than $6 million in upgrades, hired a new leasing company and completed 67,000 square feet of leasing with another 100,000 in negotiations.

40444 ■ *TRUTH: The New Rules for Marketing in a Skeptical World*
Pub: AMACOM
Ed: Lynn B. Upshaw. **Released:** August 8, 2007. **Price:** $24.95. **Description:** Because consumers are more informed today, small business owners must find new ways to market products and services.

40445 ■ *"Try a Little Social Media" in American Printer (Vol. 128, June 1, 2011, No. 6)*
Pub: Penton Media Inc.
Description: Social media helps keep Ussery Printing on customers radar. Jim David, VP of marketing for the firm, states that 350 people following them on Facebook are from the local area.

40446 ■ *"Turner Broadcasting System" in Brandweek (Vol. 49, April 21, 2008, No. 16, pp. SR13)*
Pub: VNU Business Media, Inc.
Ed: Anthony Crupi. **Description:** Provides contact information for sales and marketing personnel for the Turner Broadcasting System networks as well as a listing of the station's top programming and an analysis of the current season and the target audience for those programs running in the current season. Recent acquisitions are also discussed.

40447 ■ *"Twentieth Television" in Brandweek (Vol. 49, April 21, 2008, No. 16, pp. SR16)*
Pub: VNU Business Media, Inc.
Ed: Marc Berman. **Description:** Provides contact information for sales and marketing personnel for Twentieth Television as well as a listing of the station's top programming and an analysis of the current season and the target audience for those programs running in the current season.

40448 ■ *"The Twittering Class" in Entrepreneur (Vol. 37, September 2009, No. 9, pp. 40)*
Pub: Entrepreneur Media, Inc.
Ed: Mikal E. Belicove. **Description:** Advice on how entrepreneurs can use online social networks to promote their businesses is presented. Facebook offers applications and advertising solutions to promote Websites, products and services. Twitter, on the other hand, provides instant messaging, which can be done through computer or cell phone.

40449 ■ *Twitterville: How Businesses Can Thrive in the New Global Neighborhoods*
Pub: Portfolio Hardcover
Ed: Shel Israel. **Price:** $23.95. **Description:** Twitter is the most rapidly adopted communication tool in history, going from zero to ten million users in just over two years. On Twitter, word can spread faster than wildfire. Companies no longer have the option of ignoring the conversation. Unlike other hot social media spaces, Twitterville is dominated by professionals, not students. And despite its size, it still feels like a small town. Twitter allows people to interact much the way they do face-to-face, honestly and authentically.

40450 ■ *"UAlbany on the Hunt for New Brand" in Business Review, Albany New York (Vol. 34, October 5, 2007, No. 27, pp. 1)*
Pub: American City Business Journals, Inc.
Ed: Richard A. D'Errico. **Description:** State University of New York at Albany is working on a new marketing and branding initiative to help communicate its message better. The initiative is for the school to better understand its target audiences and their perception of the university.

40451 ■ *The Ultimate Guide to Electronic Marketing for Small Business: Low-Cost/High Return Tools and Techniques That Really Work*
Pub: John Wiley & Sons, Incorporated
Ed: Tom Antion. **Released:** June 2005. **Price:** $19.95 (US), $25.99 (Canadian). **Description:** Online marketing techniques for small business to grow and increase sales.

40452 ■ *Ultimate Small Business Marketing Guide*
Pub: Entrepreneur Press
Ed: James Stephenson. **Released:** January 2007. **Price:** $24.95. **Description:** Comprehensive information is provided to help market a small business; more than 1,500 tips are included.

40453 ■ *The Ultimate Small Business Marketing Toolkit: All the Tips, Forms, and Strategies You'll Ever Need!*
Pub: McGraw-Hill Inc.
Ed: Beth Goldstein. **Released:** July 2007. **Price:** $27. 95. **Description:** An all-in-one sales and marketing resource for entrepreneurs to grow a business.

40454 ■ *"Ultra Green Energy Services Opens NJ Biodiesel Transload Facility" in Indoor Comfort Marketing (Vol. 70, June 2011, No. 6, pp. 35)*
Pub: Industry Publications Inc.
Description: Profile of Ultra Green Energy Services and the opening of their new biodiesel facility in New Jersey is discussed.

40455 ■ *"Ultra Low Sulfur Diesel: The Promise and the Reality" in Indoor Comfort Marketing (Vol. 70, July 2011, No. 7, pp. 22)*
Pub: Industry Publications Inc.
Ed: Ed Kitchen. **Description:** Impacts of ultra low sulfur diesel are examined.

40456 ■ *"Under Armour Wants to Equip Athletes, Too" in Boston Business Journal (Vol. 29, July 8, 2011, No. 9, pp. 1)*
Pub: American City Business Journals Inc.
Ed: Ryan Sharrow. **Description:** Baltimore sportswear maker Under Armour advances plans to enter into the equipment field, aiming to strengthen its hold on football, basketball and lacrosse markets where it already has a strong market share. The company is now cooking up licensing deals to bolster the firm's presence among athletes.

40457 ■ *"Unfilled Hotels Go All Out for Business Meetings" in Crain's Detroit Business (Vol. 25, June 8, 2009, No. 23, pp. 9)*
Pub: Crain Communications Inc. - Detroit
Ed: Daniel Duggan. **Description:** Hotels in Michigan are offering discounts to companies holding business meetings at their properties. Details of competition and plans are included.

40458 ■ *"Unilever's CMO Finally Gets Down To Business" in Advertising Age (Vol. 79, July 7, 2008, No. 26, pp. 11)*
Pub: Crain Communications, Inc.
Ed: Jack Neff. **Description:** Overview of Unilever's chief marketing officer Simon Clift's strategy for promoting its products; now that the company has restructured, Clift is able to focus all of his energy on the challenges of the new-media climate that marketers are having to face.

40459 ■ *"U.S. Retailer Eyes 'Tween' Market" in Globe & Mail (January 30, 2007, pp. B1)*
Pub: CTVglobemedia Publishing Inc.
Ed: Marina Strauss. **Description:** The decision of Tween Brands Inc. (Too Incorporated) to open 100 new stores in Canada as part of its expansion is discussed. The company's focus on targeting girls for its products is detailed.

40460 ■ *"Univision" in Brandweek (Vol. 49, April 21, 2008, No. 16, pp. SR8)*
Pub: VNU Business Media, Inc.
Ed: John Consoli. **Description:** Provides contact information for sales and marketing personnel for the Univision network as well as a listing of the station's top programming and an analysis of the current season and the target audience for those programs running in the current season. Univision is the No. 1 network on Friday nights in the 18-34 demographic, beating all English-language networks.

40461 ■ *"Unleashing the Power of Marketing" in Harvard Business Review (Vol. 88, October 2010, No. 10, pp. 90)*
Pub: Harvard Business School Publishing
Ed: Beth Comstock, Ranjay Gulati, Stephen Liguori. **Description:** Chronicle of the development of General Electric's marketing framework that focused on three key factors: Principles, people and process. GE determined that successful marketing fulfills four functions: instigating, innovating, implementing, and integrating.

40462 ■ ***"Urban Tree Service" in New Hampshire Business Review (Vol. 33, March 25, 2011, No. 6, pp. 35)***
Pub: Business Publications Inc.
Description: Urban Tree Service received the Professional Communications Award from the Tree Care Industry Association for excellence in marketing and communications.

40463 ■ ***"Use Social Media to Enhance Brand, Business" in Contractor (Vol. 56, December 2009, No. 12, pp. 14)***
Pub: Penton Media, Inc.
Ed: Elton Rivas. **Description:** Advice on how plumbing contractors should use online social networks to increase sales is presented including such issues as clearly defining goals and target audience. An additional advantage to this medium is that advertisements can easily be shared with other users.

40464 ■ ***"Utah Technology Council: Social Media Is Here to Stay; Embrace It" in Wireless News (December 14, 2009)***
Pub: Close-Up Media
Description: Social media outlets such as Facebook and Twitter are blurring the lines between advertising, public relations, branding and marketing; businesses must stop thinking in terms of traditional marketing versus Internet marketing if they want to succeed in today's marketing climate.

40465 ■ ***"Vanity Plates" in Canadian Business (Vol. 82, April 27, 2009, No. 7, pp. 26)***
Pub: Rogers Media
Ed: Andy Holloway. **Description:** Politicians in the U.S. called for the review of firms that availed of the bailout money but are under deals for naming rights of sports stadiums. Angus Reid's Corporate Reputation and Sponsorship Index found for example, that there is little correlation between sponsoring arenas on having a better brand image. It is suggested that firms who enter these deals build closer to people's homes.

40466 ■ ***"Verizon's Big Gamble Comes Down to the Wire" in Globe & Mail (February 3, 2007, pp. B1)***
Pub: CTVglobemedia Publishing Inc.
Ed: Catherine McLean. **Description:** The launch of a new broadband service by Verizon Communications Inc. based on fibre optic cable technology is discussed. The company has spent $23 billion for introducing the new service.

40467 ■ ***"Versatile's Back" in Farm Industry News (Vol. 42, January 1, 2009, No. 1)***
Pub: Penton Media Inc.
Contact: John French, President
Ed: Jodie Wehrspann. **Description:** Overview of Winnipeg, Manitoba's tractor manufacturer Versatile's strategy to rebrand its tractor segment; the strategy comes a year after Russian Combine Factory Rostselmash Ltd. bought the majority share of common stock from the Canadian business.

40468 ■ ***"A View to a Killer Business Model" in Black Enterprise (Vol. 40, December 2009, No. 5, pp. 50)***
Pub: Earl G. Graves Publishing Co., Inc.
Ed: Sonya A. Donaldson. **Description:** Profile of Gen2Media Corp., a production, technology and Internet marketing firm based in Florida with offices in New York; Gen2Media is utilizing the advances in technology to now include video in its online marketing offerings.

40469 ■ ***"Virgin America Flies with V&S on Web" in ADWEEK (Vol. 51, July 12 2010, No. 27, pp. 31)***
Pub: Nielsen Business Media Inc.
Description: Victors & Spoils, a crowdsourcing agency is examined.

40470 ■ ***"Virtus.com Wins 'Best of Industry' WebAward for Excellence in Financial Services" in Investment Weekly News (October 24, 2009)***
Pub: Investment Weekly News
Description: Web Marketing Association honored Virtus.com, the Website of Virtus Investment Partners, Inc., for Outstanding Achievement in Web Development and Acsys Interactive was awarded the Financial Services Standard of Excellence Award for developing the site. The site was part of a rebranding effort and is a one-stop portal for both financial advisors and their investors.

40471 ■ ***"Virtus.com Wins 'Best of Industry' WebAward for Excellence in Financial Services" in Investment Weekly News (Oct. 24, 2009, pp. 227)***
Pub: Investment Weekly News
Description: Web Marketing Association honored Virtus.com, the Website of Virtus Investment Partners, Inc., for Outstanding Achievement in Web Development and Acsys Interactive was awarded the Financial Services Standard of Excellence Award for developing the site. The site was part of a rebranding effort and is a one-stop portal for both financial advisors and their investors.

40472 ■ ***"Vistaprint Survey Indicates that Online Marketing Taking Hold Among Small Businesses" in Internet Wire (December 10, 2009)***
Pub: Comtex News Network, Inc.
Description: According to a comprehensive survey from Vistaprint N.V., small businesses are very likely to increase their use of Internet marketing strategies such as paid and organic search, email marketing, social media networking and custom websites over the next year. Trends continue to show that more small businesses are indeed adapting to the changing marketplace and are more willing to diversify their marketing strategies than ever before.

40473 ■ ***"Vonage V-Phone: Use Your Laptop to Make Calls Via the Internet" in Black Enterprise (Vol. 37, January 2007, No. 6, pp. 52)***
Pub: Earl G. Graves Publishing Co. Inc.
Ed: James C. Johnson. **Description:** Overview of the Vonage V-Phone, which is small flash drive device that lets you make phone calls through a high-speed Internet connection and plugs into any computer's USB port. Business travels may find this product to be a wonderful solution as it includes 250MB of memory and can store files, digital photos, MP3s, and more.

40474 ■ ***"VTech Targets Tots With a Wee Wii" in Advertising Age (Vol. 79, September 8, 2008, No. 33, pp. 14)***
Pub: Crain Communications, Inc.
Ed: Beth Snyder Bulik. **Description:** V-Motion is a video-game console targeting 3-to-7-year-olds and is manufactured by educational toy company VTech. The company is marketing the product as a kind of Wii for preschoolers and hopes to build a formidable brand presence in the kids' electronics market.

40475 ■ ***"Wake-Up Call" in Canadian Business (Vol. 80, October 8, 2007, No. 20, pp. 58)***
Pub: Rogers Media
Ed: Andrea Mandel-Campbell. **Description:** The need for Canadian companies to develop global marketing strategies is discussed. Thomas Caldwell, chairman of Caldwell Securities, believes the country's average performance in global markets should be a cause for alarm. The factors affecting the country's current economic state is also presented.

40476 ■ ***"Wal-Mart Relaunches Private Brand, Reimagines Stores Layout" in Marketing to Women (Vol. 22, July 2009, No. 7, pp. 5)***
Pub: EPM Communications Inc.
Contact: Ira Mayer, President
E-mail: imayer@epmcom.com
Description: Wal-Mart is focusing its strategies by centering on new store layouts that they believe will match their new branding of 'fast, friendly, and clean' and enable mothers to 'just get on with what they need to do.'.

40477 ■ ***The Wall Street Journal. Complete Small Business Guidebook***
Pub: Three Rivers Press
Ed: Colleen DeBaise. **Released:** December 29, 2009. **Price:** $15.00. **Description:** The mechanics of building, running and growing a profitable business are outlined, teaching how to write a business plan, ways to finding money during lean years, how to keep stress in check, time management, investment in technology, hiring, marketing, management basics, angel investing and venture capital, as well as an exit strategy.

40478 ■ ***"Want to Unleash the Next Best Seller? Think Like a Dog" in Advertising Age (Vol. 79, March 10, 2008, No. 10, pp. 14)***
Pub: Crain Communications, Inc.
Ed: Lenore Skenazy. **Description:** Cott Corp. has launched a new product, fortified water for pets, in flavors ranging from peanut butter to parsley to spearmint.

40479 ■ ***"Warner Bros. Domestic Television Distribution" in Brandweek (Vol. 49, April 21, 2008, No. 16, pp. SR16)***
Pub: VNU Business Media, Inc.
Ed: Marc Berman. **Description:** Provides contact information for sales and marketing personnel for Warner Bros. Domestic Television Distribution as well as a listing of the station's top programming and an analysis of the current season and the target audience for those programs running in the current season.

40480 ■ ***"Warning Lights Flashing for Air Canada: Carty's Back" in Globe & Mail (February 22, 2006, pp. B1)***
Pub: CTVglobemedia Publishing Inc.
Ed: Brent Jang. **Description:** Air Canada's rival, Donald Carty, former chief executive officer at American Airlines and new chairman of Toronto based Regco Holdings Inc., launches Porter Airlines Inc. out of Toronto City Center Airport this fall.

40481 ■ ***"'We Are Not a Marketing Company" in Boston Business Journal (Vol. 31, June 10, 2011, No. 20, pp. 1)***
Pub: Boston Business Journal
Ed: Julie M. Donnelly. **Description:** Vertex Pharmaceuticals Inc. is marketing its new Hepatitis C treatment, Incivek. The company hired people to connect patients to the drug. Vertex is also set to move to a new facility in Boston, Massachusetts.

40482 ■ ***We Are Smarter Than Me: How to Unleash the Power of Crowds in Your Business***
Pub: Wharton School Publishing
Ed: Barry Libert; Jon Spector; Don Tapscott. **Released:** October 5, 2007. **Price:** $21.99. **Description:** Ways to use social networking and community in order to make decisions and plan your business, with a focus on product development, manufacturing, marketing, customer service, finance, management, and more.

40483 ■ ***"Web-Based Marketing Excites, Challenges Small Business Use" in Colorado Springs Business Journal (January 20, 2010)***
Pub: Dolan Media Co.
Ed: Becky Hurley. **Description:** Business-to-business and consumer-direct firms alike are using the fast-changing Web technologies to increase sales, leads and track consumer behavior but once a company commits to an Online marketing plan, experts believe, they must be prepared to consistently tweak and overhaul content and distribution vehicles in order to keep up.

40484 ■ ***"Web Biz Brulant Surfing for Acquisition Candidates" in Crain's Cleveland Business (Vol. 28, December 3, 2007, No. 48, pp. 6)***
Pub: Crain Communications, Inc.
Ed: Chuck Soder. **Description:** Brulant Inc., a provider of web development and marketing services, is looking to acquire other companies after growing for five years straight. The company is one of the largest technology firms in Northeast Ohio.

40485 ■ *"Webadvertising" in MarketingMagazine (Vol. 115, September 27, 2010, No. 13, pp. 70)*
Pub: Rogers Publishing Ltd.
Description: Website advertising in Canada is examined.

40486 ■ *"Web.Preneuring: How Local TV Ads and Online Marketing Can Help You Win Big" in Small Business Opportunities (January 2008)*
Pub: Harris Publications Inc.
Ed: David Waxman. **Description:** Spot Runner, an Internet-based advertising agency offers low-cost local business television ads. The company secures the ad buy, places and tracks the ads, and analyzes viewership and demographics for clients.

40487 ■ *"Website Triples Traffic in Three Weeks Using Press Releases" in PR Newswire (January 5, 2010)*
Pub: PR Newswire Association, LLC
Description: Irbtrax, an Internet marketing firm, concluded a comprehensive study revealing that online press release submission services offer measurable Website traffic-building results.

40488 ■ *"Website for Women 50 Launches" in Marketing to Women (Vol. 21, April 2008, No. 4, pp. 5)*
Pub: EPM Communications Inc.
Contact: Ira Mayer, President
E-mail: imayer@epmcom.com
Description: Vibrantnation.com is an online community targeting women over age 50; members can share recommendations on a variety of topics such as vacation spots, retailers and financial issues.

40489 ■ *"Welch's Uses Taste Strips in Ads" in Marketing to Women (Vol. 21, April 2008, No. 4, pp. 3)*
Pub: EPM Communications Inc.
Contact: Ira Mayer, President
E-mail: imayer@epmcom.com
Description: Welch's is positioning its 139-year-old brand in a new and inventive way with a new marketing campaign in which print ads will feature a tamper-evident flavor pouch that contains a dissolving taste strip flavored with Welch's grape juice.

40490 ■ *"Well-Heeled Startup" in Business Journal Portland (Vol. 27, November 12, 2010, No. 37, pp. 1)*
Pub: Portland Business Journal
Ed: Erik Siemers. **Description:** Oh! Shoes LLC expects to receive about $1.5 million in funding from angel investors, while marketing a new line of high heel shoes that are comfortable, healthy, and attractive. The new line of shoes will use the technology of athletic footwear while having the look of an Italian designer. Oh! Shoes hopes to generate $35 million in sales by 2014.

40491 ■ *The Well-Timed Strategy: Managing Business Cycle for Competitive Advantage*
Pub: Wharton School Publishing
Ed: Peter Navarro. **Released:** January 23, 2006. **Price:** $34.99. **Description:** An overview of business cycles and risks is presented. Recession is a good time to find key personnel for a small business. Other issues addressed include investment, production, and marketing in order to maintain a competitive edge.

40492 ■ *"Welsh Meat Sales on the Rise" in Farmer's Weekly (March 28, 2008, No. 320)*
Pub: Reed Business Information
Contact: Jeff Greisch, President
Description: Due, in part, to marketing efforts, retail sales of Welsh lamb and beef rose significantly in the first two months of 2008.

40493 ■ *"Wendy Turner; Vice-President and General Manager, Vocalo.org" in Crain's Chicago Business (Vol. 31, May 5, 2008, No. 18, pp. 22)*
Pub: Crain Communications, Inc.
Ed: Kevin McKeough. **Description:** Profile of Wendy Turner who is a leader at Vocalo, a combination of talk radio and Web site, where listeners can set up profile pages similar to those on Facebook.

40494 ■ *"What to Do in an Economic Upswing Before It's too Late" in Agency Sales Magazine (Vol. 39, November 2009, No. 10, pp. 36)*
Pub: MANA
Ed: John Graham. **Description:** Some marketing suggestions for businesses as the economy recovers are presented. These include not waiting for the economy to change and telling your brand's story. Showing people what you can do for them and changing doubters into believers is also advised.

40495 ■ *"What Homes Do Retirees Want?" in Canadian Business (Vol. 79, July 17, 2006, No. 14-15, pp.)*
Pub: Rogers Media
Ed: Joe Cataldo. **Description:** The obstacles and challenges faced by homebuilders in Canada as well as the approach adopted by them to appeal to the mature homebuilders segment, is discussed.

40496 ■ *"What Moms Want" in Marketing to Women (Vol. 21, February 2008, No. 2, pp. 6)*
Pub: EPM Communications Inc.
Contact: Ira Mayer, President
E-mail: imayer@epmcom.com
Description: According to a survey conducted by Eureka's Spa, moms would rather have an experience gift than flowers or chocolate. The top five dream gifts include a spa day, a weekend getaway, maid service, a bathroom makeover or a getaway weekend with girlfriends.

40497 ■ *"What Most Banks Fail to See; New and Complex Financial Regulations Can be Daunting" in Gallup Management Journal (March 10, 2011)*
Pub: Gallup
Ed: Sean Williams, Daniel Porcelli. **Description:** New financial regulations are complicated and politically charged. But banks that move beyond the fear of those regulations will find a new opportunity to engage customers.

40498 ■ *What Self-Made Millionaires Really Think, Know and Do: A Straight-Talking Guide to Business Success and Personal Riches*
Pub: John Wiley & Sons, Incorporated
Ed: Richard Dobbins; Barrie Pettman. **Released:** September 2006. **Price:** $24.95. **Description:** Guide for understanding the concepts of entrepreneurial success; the book offers insight into bringing an idea into reality, marketing, time management, leadership skills, and setting clear goals.

40499 ■ *"What Women Watch on TV" in Marketing to Women (Vol. 21, February 2008, No. 2, pp. 6)*
Pub: EPM Communications Inc.
Contact: Ira Mayer, President
E-mail: imayer@epmcom.com
Description: According to BIGresearch, women are more likely to watch sports than they are soap operas. Statistical data included.

40500 ■ *"What You Look Like Online" in Black Enterprise (Vol. 37, January 2007, No. 6, pp. 56)*
Pub: Earl G. Graves Publishing Co. Inc.
Ed: Marcia A. Reed-Woodard. **Description:** Of 100 executive recruiters 77 percent stated that they use search engines to check the backgrounds of potential job candidates, according to a survey conducted by ExecuNet. Of those surveyed 35 percent stated that they eliminate potential candidates based on information they find online so it is important to create a positive Web presence which highlights professional image qualities.

40501 ■ *"What's In Your Toolbox" in Women In Business (Vol. 61, August-September 2009, No. 4, pp. 7)*
Pub: American Business Women's Association
Ed: Mimi Kopulos. **Description:** Business owners are increasingly turning to using social networking websites, such as Facebook, LinkedIn and Twitter, to promote their companies. The number of adult social media users has increased from 8 percent in 2005 to 35 percent in 2009.

40502 ■ *"What's Next, Pup Tents in Bryant Park?" in Advertising Age (Vol. 78, January 29, 2007, No. 5, pp. 4)*
Pub: Crain Communications, Inc.
Ed: Stephanie Thompson. **Description:** Designers such as Ralph Lauren, Juicy Couture, Burberry and Kiehl's have been expanding their businesses with new clothing lines for pets. Packaged Facts, a division of MarketResearch.com, predicts that pet expenditures will continue to grow in the years to come.

40503 ■ *"What's Your Personal Social Media Strategy?" in Harvard Business Review (Vol. 88, November 2010, No. 11, pp. 127)*
Pub: Harvard Business School Publishing
Ed: Soumitra Dutta. **Description:** Identification of four distinct sectors and how they interrelate to social media is given. The sectors are personal and private; professional and private; personal and public; and professional and public. Appropriate topics and types of social media are discussed for each.

40504 ■ *"What's Your Social Media Strategy?" in Black Enterprise (Vol. 41, November 2010, No. 4, pp. 75)*
Pub: Earl G. Graves Publishing Co. Inc.
Ed: Denise Campbell. **Description:** Advice for using social media sites such as Twitter, Facebook and LinkedIn as a professional networking tool is given.

40505 ■ *"Where the Future is Made" in Indoor Comfort Marketing (Vol. 70, May 2011, No. 5, pp. 48)*
Pub: Industry Publications Inc.
Description: Research being performed at Brookhaven National Laboratory, located in Upton, New York, is discussed, focusing on new energy sources for our nation.

40506 ■ *"Where Women Work" in Marketing to Women (Vol. 21, April 2008, No. 4, pp. 8)*
Pub: EPM Communications Inc.
Contact: Ira Mayer, President
E-mail: imayer@epmcom.com
Description: According to the U.S. Census Bureau, 60 percent of America's professional tax preparers are women. Also features additional trends concerning women in the workplace. Statistical data included.

40507 ■ *"While Competitors Shut Doors, Subway Is Still Growing" in Advertising Age (Vol. 79, July 21, 2008, No. 28, pp. 4)*
Pub: Crain Communications, Inc.
Ed: Emily Bryson York. **Description:** Subway, the largest fast-food chain, with 22,000 U.S. locations, is adding 800 this year, despite the economic downturn that has caused competitors such as Starbucks to close stores and McDonald's to focus its expansion abroad.

40508 ■ *"A Whiteboard that Peels and Sticks" in Inc. (Volume 32, December 2010, No. 10, pp. 58)*
Pub: Inc. Magazine
Ed: Issie Lapwosky. **Description:** Profile of an affordable adhesive whiteboard that can be restuck multiple times; the whiteboard was created by three college friends. The students share insight in the contacts they used in order to promote the sale of their invention.

40509 ■ *"Whopper; Russ Klein" in Advertising Age (Vol. 79, November 17, 2008, No. 43, pp. S10)*
Pub: Crain Communications, Inc.
Ed: Emily Bryson York. **Description:** Burger King has seen a double digit increase in the sales of its Whopper hamburger despite the economic recession that has hit many in the restaurant industry particularly hard. For most of the spring, U.S. same-store-sales gains beat McDonald's.

40510 ■ *"Why Some Get Shaften By Google Pricing" in Advertising Age (Vol. 79, July 14, 2008, No. 7, pp. 3)*
Pub: Crain Communications, Inc.

Ed: Abbey Klaassen. **Description:** Google's search advertising is discussed as well as the company's pricing structure for these ads.

40511 ■ *"Why Women Blog and What They Read" in Marketing to Women (Vol. 22, July 2009, No. 7, pp. 8)*
Pub: EPM Communications Inc.
Contact: Ira Mayer, President
E-mail: imayer@epmcom.com

Description: Listing of topics that are visited the most by female Internet users. Statistical data included.

40512 ■ *"Why You Aren't Buying Venezuelan Chocolate." in Harvard Business Review (Vol. 88, December 2010, No. 12, pp. 25)*
Pub: Harvard Business School Publishing

Ed: Rohit Deshpande. **Description:** The concept of provenance paradox is defined as the preconceived notions consumers have about the country of origin of a given product, which can pose significant difficulties for emerging markets. Five strategies are presented for combating this problem, including building on historic events that have informed cultural perspectives.

40513 ■ *"Why You Need a New-Media 'Ringmaster'" in Harvard Business Review (Vol. 88, December 2010, No. 12, pp. 78)*
Pub: Harvard Business School Publishing

Ed: Patrick Spenner. **Description:** The concept of ringmaster is applied to brand marketing. This concept includes integrative thinking, lean collaboration skills, and high-speed decision cycles.

40514 ■ *"Winning With Women" in Marketing to Women (Vol. 22, August 2009, No. 8, pp. 6)*
Pub: EPM Communications Inc.
Contact: Ira Mayer, President
E-mail: imayer@epmcom.com

Description: Women shoppers are buying more utilitarian categories despite the overall fall in consumer electronics sales. Among the top five purchases women will defer in the next three months are personal consumer electronics, such as MP3 players and digital cameras, as well as home entertainment items.

40515 ■ *"With Traffic Jam in Super Bowl, Can Any Auto Brand Really Win?" in Advertising Age (Vol. 81, December 6, 2010, No. 43, pp. 1)*
Pub: Crain Communications, Inc.

Ed: Rupal Parekh, Brian Steinberg. **Description:** Car marketers are doubling down for Super Bowl XLV in Arlington, Texas and asking their ad agencies to craft commercials unique enough to break through the clutter and to capture viewers' attention.

40516 ■ *"Women-Centric Events Can Captivate Consumers" in Crain's Cleveland Business (Vol. 28, November 12, 2007, No. 45, pp. 24)*
Pub: Crain Communications, Inc.

Ed: Kimberly Bonvissuto. **Description:** Discusses innovative ways that companies are targeting the female consumer market including arranging networking and social events.

40517 ■ *"Women Clicking to Earn Virtual Dollars" in Sales and Marketing Management (November 11, 2009)*
Pub: Nielsen Business Media, Inc.

Ed: Stacy Straczynski. **Description:** According to a new report from Internet marketing firm Q Interactive, women are increasingly playing social media games where they are able to click on an ad or sign up for a promotion to earn virtual currency. Research is showing that this kind of marketing may be a potent tool, especially for e-commerce and online stores.

40518 ■ *"Women Inch Forward on Corporate Boards" in Marketing to Women (Vol. 21, April 2008, No. 4, pp. 6)*
Pub: EPM Communications Inc.
Contact: Ira Mayer, President
E-mail: imayer@epmcom.com
Description: According to the latest study by Inter-Organization Network, few huge leaps of progress and in some cases backsliding has taken place in regards to gender diversity on corporate boards. Statistical data included.

40519 ■ *"Women Losing IT Ground" in Marketing to Women (Vol. 21, February 2008, No. 2, pp. 6)*
Pub: EPM Communications Inc.
Contact: Ira Mayer, President
E-mail: imayer@epmcom.com
Description: According to a study conducted by The National Center for Women & Information Technology, women in technology are losing ground. Statistical data included.

40520 ■ *"Women Prefer Cookbooks Over Word-Of-Mouth for Recipe Suggestions" in Marketing to Women (Vol. 23, November 2010, No. 11, pp. 6)*
Pub: EPM Communications Inc.
Contact: Ira Mayer, President
E-mail: imayer@epmcom.com
Description: Sixty-five percent of women surveyed enjoy a sit-down dinner at least five times a week according to Martha Steward Omni-media. Cookbooks, recipe Websites, food-focused magazines, and TV cooking shows are their primary source for new recipes.

40521 ■ *"Women Prioritize Luxury Spending" in Marketing to Women (Vol. 22, July 2009, No. 7, pp. 8)*
Pub: EPM Communications Inc.
Contact: Ira Mayer, President
E-mail: imayer@epmcom.com
Description: In 2008, women spent 7 percent less on luxury items than in the previous year, according to Unity Marketing. Some luxury items, such as facial care products, are faring better than others. Statistical data included.

40522 ■ *"Women See Special Interest, Review Sites as Most Brand-Friendly" in Marketing to Women (Vol. 23, November 2010, No. 11, pp. 4)*
Pub: EPM Communications Inc.
Contact: Ira Mayer, President
E-mail: imayer@epmcom.com
Description: Rather focusing on specific demographics, marketing and ad agencies should focus on women's core needs such as mom versus mom or Gen X versus Baby Boomer.

40523 ■ *"Women Take Care of a Home's Inside, Men Work on the Outside" in Marketing to Women (Vol. 23, November 2010, No. 11, pp. 2)*
Pub: EPM Communications Inc.
Contact: Ira Mayer, President
E-mail: imayer@epmcom.com
Description: Women spend more time doing housework, caring for children, and talking on the telephone; while men's time is spent working, participating in sports, watching TV, and lawn maintenance.

40524 ■ *"WordStream Announces a Pair of Firsts for SEO and PPC Keyword Research Tools" in Internet Wire (November 10, 2009)*
Pub: Comtex News Network, Inc.
Description: WordSteam, Inc., a provider of pay-per-click (PPC) and search engine optimization (SEO) solutions for continuously expanding and optimizing search marketing efforts has released two new features in their flagship Keyword Management solution; these tools will allow marketers to analyze data from paid search, organic search and estimated totals from keyword suggestion tools side-by-side.

40525 ■ *"Work/Family Balance Boosts Business" in Marketing to Women (Vol. 21, February 2008, No. 2, pp. 8)*
Pub: EPM Communications Inc.
Contact: Ira Mayer, President
E-mail: imayer@epmcom.com
Description: Flexibility in the workplace is becoming a more important issue to both women and men. Statistical data included.

40526 ■ *Work at Home Now*
Pub: Career Press, Inc.
Ed: Christine Durst, Michael Haaren. **Released:** October 9, 2010. **Price:** $14.99. **Description:** There are legitimate home-based jobs and projects that can be found on the Internet, but trustworthy guidance is scarce. There is a 58 to 1 scam ratio in work at-home advertising filled with fraud.

40527 ■ *"Wrigley's Newest Taste: Wolfberry" in Crain's Chicago Business (Vol. 31, March 31, 2008, No. 13, pp. 1)*
Pub: Crain Communications, Inc.
Ed: David Sterrett. **Description:** Wm. Wrigley Jr. Co. has introduced a gum line in China that touts the medicinal advantages of aloe vera to improve skin and wolfberry to boost energy in an attempt to keep the company positioned as the top candy firm in China.

40528 ■ *"XM Burning Through Cash to Catch Sirius" in Globe & Mail (April 17, 2007, pp. B5)*
Pub: CTVglobemedia Publishing Inc.
Ed: Grant Robertson. **Description:** The effort of XM Satellite Radio Holdings Inc. to spend about $45 million to increase sale of its radio in Canada is discussed.

40529 ■ *"XM Mulls Betting the Bank in Competitive Game of Subscriber Growth" in Globe & Mail (March 18, 2006, pp. B3)*
Pub: CTVglobemedia Publishing Inc.
Ed: Grant Robertson. **Description:** Canadian Satellite Radio Inc., XM Canada, president and Chief Operating Officer Stephen Tapp feel that establishing a profile in satellite radio to attract subscribers is a very big challenge. His views on the Canadian radio market are detailed.

40530 ■ *"Yahoo! - Microsoft Pact: Alive Again?" in Barron's (Vol. 89, July 27, 2009, No. 30, pp. 8)*
Pub: Dow Jones & Co., Inc.
Ed: Mark Veverka. **Description:** Yahoo! reported higher than expected earnings in the second quarter of 2009 under CEO Carol Bartz who has yet to articulate her long-term vision and strategy for turning around the company. The media reported that Yahoo! and Microsoft are discussing an advertising-search partnership which should benefit both companies.

40531 ■ *"Yes, No, and Somewhat Likely: Survey the World with Web Polls" in Inc. (October 2007, pp. 58-59)*
Pub: Gruner & Jahr USA Publishing
Ed: Don Steinberg. **Description:** Online tools for surveying customers, employees and the general public include Zoomergan zPro and Zoomerang Sample, software designed to send surveys and allows viewing results; SurveyMonkey software creates, administers and allows viewing online surveys and results; Vizu software places a one-question poll on a particular Website; and Vovici EFM Feedback, a subscription service providing ongoing surveys to customers or employees.

40532 ■ *"You Can Rebuild It" in Entrepreneur (Vol. 37, July 2009, No. 7, pp. 28)*
Pub: Entrepreneur Media, Inc.
Ed: Robert Kiyosaki. **Description:** Entrepreneurs, during tough times, should melt down old business strategies and start rebuilding the business. The business and its customers should be redefined in order to maximize marketing efforts and stay afloat when business slows down. Personal experiences in melting down a business and starting over are also given.

40533 ■ *"You Can't Beat Habit" in Entrepreneur (Vol. 37, July 2009, No. 7, pp. 61)*
Pub: Entrepreneur Media, Inc.
Ed: Neale Martin. **Description:** Customers are changing their spending behavior because of the financial meltdown, and this poses an opportunity for businesses to change their marketing practices in order to regain customers. Being flexible is one way to reestablish purchase behavior, along with paying attention to customer feedback.

40534 ■ *"You Lost Me at Hello" in Entrepreneur (Vol. 35, November 2007, No. 11, pp. 136)*
Pub: Entrepreneur Media Inc.
Ed: John Jantsch. **Description:** Managing your marketing materials by making them more informational is an effective tool to educate consumers about your product. Information that should be included in your marketing kit are outlined.

40535 ■ *"Young Adult, Childless May Help Fuel Post-Recession Rebound" in Pet Product News (Vol. 64, November 2010, No. 11, pp. 4)*
Pub: BowTie Inc.
Description: Pet industry retailers and marketers are encouraged to tap into the young adult and childless couple sectors to boost consumer traffic and sales to pre-recession levels. Among young adult owners, pet ownership increased from 40 percent in 2003 to 49 percent in 2009. Meanwhile, the childless couple sector represented 63 percent of all dog/cat owners in 2009.

40536 ■ *"Your Big Give" in Small Business Opportunities (September 2008)*
Pub: Entrepreneur Press
Contact: Perlman Neil, President
Ed: Michael Guld. **Description:** Cause related marketing is beneficial to businesses as well as the communities they inhabit; three small businesses that are elevating their standing in the community while at the same time increasing their customer base are profiled.

40537 ■ *"Your Booming Business: How You Can Align Sales and Marketing for Dynamic Growth" in Small Business Opportunities (Spring 2008)*
Pub: Harris Publications Inc.
Ed: Voss W. Graham. **Description:** Voss Graham, founder and CEO of Inneractive Consulting Group Inc., works with companies to develop and hire successful sales teams. A checklist from the American Bankers Association to help write a business plan is included.

40538 ■ *"Your Bottom Line: How To Bring In Dollars When Times Are Tough" in Small Business Opportunities (November 2007)*
Pub: Harris Publications Inc.
Description: Adding a new product or promoting a product in a new way can help any small business during hard economic times.

40539 ■ *Your First Year in Real Estate: Making the Transition from Total Novice to Successful Professional*
Pub: Crown Business Books
Ed: Dirk Zeller. **Released:** $August 3, 2010. **Price:** $20.00. **Description:** Zeller helps new realtors to select the right company, develop mentor and client relationships, using the Internet and social networking to stay ahead of competition, to set and reach career goals, to stay current in the market, and more.

40540 ■ *"Your Turn in the Spotlight" in Inc. (Volume 32, December 2010, No. 10, pp. 57)*
Pub: Inc. Magazine
Ed: John Brandon. **Description:** Examples of three video blogs created by entrepreneurs to promote their businesses and products are used to show successful strategies. Wine Library TV promotes a family's wine business; SHAMA.TV offers marketing tips and company news; and Will It Blend? promotes sales of a household blender.

40541 ■ *YouTube and Video Marketing: An Hour a Day*
Pub: Sybex
Ed: Greg Jarboe. **Released:** August 10, 2009. **Price:** $29.99. **Description:** The importance of online video marketing for businesses is stressed. Tips for developing and implementing video marketing are outlined.

40542 ■ *"Zappo's CEO On Going to Extremes for Customers" in Harvard Business Review (Vol. 88, July-August 2010, No. 7-8, pp. 41)*
Pub: Harvard Business School Publishing
Ed: Tony Hsieh. **Description:** Footwear firm Zappos.com Inc. improved corporate performance through enhanced customer service. Enhancements include highly visible phone numbers, avoidance of scripts, and viewing call centers as marketing departments.

40543 ■ *"Zen and the Art of Twitter Maintenance" in Agency Sales Magazine (Vol. 39, September-October 2009, No. 9, pp. 48)*
Pub: MANA
Ed: Terry Brock. **Description:** Online social networks such as Twitter, LinkedIn, and Facebook should be used to stay in touch with business relationships, especially customers. There should be a focus on making customers happy and building the bottom-line when using these tools.

TRADE PERIODICALS

40544 ■ *Accutips*
Pub: Accudata America
Released: Monthly. **Price:** Free. **Description:** Discusses promotion and marketing issues relevant to businesses.

40545 ■ *ADM Flash*
Pub: Association of Directory Marketing
Contact: Neg Norton, President
Ed: Nancy Augustine, Editor, naugustine@admworks.org. **Released:** 10/year. **Price:** Free. **Description:** Features information about marketing directories.

40546 ■ *Business Ideas Newsletter*
Pub: Dan Newman Co.
Ed: Dan Newman, Editor. **Released:** 10/year. **Price:** $50. **Description:** Publishes information for advertising and marketing executives to increase results, returns, and profits. Reports on and interprets developments affecting the business community, including issues such as legislative and regulatory activities and tax reform. Covers new product developments, employment strategies, advertising techniques, and direct marketing potential. Recurring features include news of research, reports of meetings, news of educational opportunities, and book reviews.

40547 ■ *The Gauge*
Pub: Delahaye Medialink
Contact: Katharine Delahaye Paine, Publisher
E-mail: kpaine@delahaye.com
Ed: William Teunis Paarlberg, Editor, wpaarlberg@aol.com. **Released:** Bimonthly. **Price:** $75. **Description:** Provides information on and evaluates marketing communications activities of companies. Recurring features include interviews, news of research, and a calendar of events.

40548 ■ *Guerilla Marketing Newsletter*
Pub: Jay Conrad Levinson
Ed: William Shea, Editor. **Released:** Bimonthly. **Description:** Explores marketing trends, tips, and technology. Recurring features include news of research.

40549 ■ *Internet Marketing Report*
Pub: Progressive Business Publications
Ed: Alan Field, Editor. **Released:** Semimonthly. **Price:** $299, individuals. **Description:** Communicates the latest news and trends in website marketing. g.

40550 ■ *Journal of Global Marketing*
Pub: Routledge Journals Taylor & Francis Group
URL(s): www.tandf.co.uk/journals/WGLO. **Ed:** Erdener Kaynak. **Released:** 5/yr. **Price:** $152, Individuals online only; $168, Individuals print & online; $853, Institutions online only; $947, Institutions print + online.

40551 ■ *Journal of International Consumer Marketing*
Pub: Routledge Journals Taylor & Francis Group
URL(s): www.tandf.co.uk/journals/wicm. **Released:** Quarterly **Price:** $154, Individuals online only; $171, Individuals print + online; $843, Institutions online only; $937, Institutions print + online.

40552 ■ *Journal of Marketing Channels: Distribution Systems, Strategy & Management*
Pub: Routledge Journals Taylor & Francis Group
URL(s): www.tandf.co.uk/journals/WJMC. **Ed:** Bert Rosenbloom. **Released:** Quarterly **Price:** $114, Individuals online only; $123, Individuals print + online; $516, Institutions online only; $573, Institutions print + online.

40553 ■ *Journal of Relationship Marketing*
Pub: Routledge Journals Taylor & Francis Group
URL(s): www.tandfonline.com/toc/wjrm20/current. **Ed:** David Bejou. **Released:** Quarterly **Price:** $114, Individuals online only; $123, Individuals print + online; $523, Institutions online only; $581, Institutions print + online.

40554 ■ *Larry Chase's Web Digest for Marketers (WDFM)*
Pub: Chase Online Marketing Strategies,Inc
Contact: Larry Chase, Executive Editor
E-mail: larry@wdfm.com
Ed: Mary Gillen, Editor. **Released:** Weekly. **Price:** Free. **Description:** Delivers 15 short reviews of business-related websites every issue. Remarks: America Online, Inc.

40555 ■ *Magnet Marketing & Sales*
Pub: Graham Communications
Ed: Michael Maynard, Editor, m_maynard@grahamcomm.com. **Released:** Quarterly. **Price:** Free. **Description:** Contains information and advice on marketing, sales, and public relations.

40556 ■ *Marketing News: Reporting on the Marketing Profession*
Pub: American Marketing Association
Contact: Lucille Pointer, President
URL(s): www.marketingpower.com/AboutAMA/Pages/AMA%20Publications/Marketing% 20News/MarketingNews.aspx. **Ed:** Elisabeth Sullivan. **Released:** 16/yr. **Price:** $35, Members; $100, Nonmembers; $130, Institutions libraries and corporations; $3, Single issue individuals; $5, Single issue institutions; $140, Institutions, other countries extra for air delivery.

40557 ■ *Meetings & Conventions: The Meeting & Incentive Planners Resource*
Pub: Northstar Travel Media L.L.C.
Contact: Thomas Kemp, Chief Executive Officer
E-mail: tkemp@ntmllc.com
URL(s): www.meetings-conventions.com. **Ed:** Loren G. Edelstein. **Released:** Monthly **Price:** $89, Individuals print; $119, Canada and Mexico print; $209, Other countries print; $41.50, Individuals online.

40558 ■ *PCS Direct Marketing Newsletter*
Pub: PCS Mailing List Company
Contact: Ed Nasser, Associate Editor
E-mail: ednasser@pcslist.com
Ed: Ann Guyer, Editor, aguyer@pcslist.com. **Released:** Bimonthly. **Price:** Free. **Description:** Offers research tools, publications, and other advice on legal, medical, financial & consumer, direct marketing. Also covers mailing lists, databases, and software to assist with direct mailings. Reports on news and conferences in this field as well. Recurring features include notices of publications available and book reviews.

40559 ■ *PROMO: Ideas. Connections. Brands*
Pub: Penton
Contact: Raymond E. Maloney, President
URL(s): promomagazine.com/. **Released:** Monthly

40560 ■ *Promotion Marketing Association--Outlook*
Pub: Promotion Marketing Association Inc.
Contact: Claire Rosenzweig, Executive Director
E-mail: crosenzw@pmalink.org
Released: QRT. **Price:** Included in membership. **Description:** Discusses issues and trends in the field of promotion marketing. Analyzes the merits of various types of promotion programs and marketing techniques. Carries the results of surveys and studies of industry groups and premium usage conducted by the Association. Recurring features include calendar of events. Remarks: Available online only.

40561 ■ *Proof*
Pub: Direct Marketing Club of New York
Released: 10/year. **Description:** Provides information concerning direct marketing to members of the Direct Marketing Club of New York. Recurring features include a calendar of events, news of members, news of educational opportunities, book reviews, and various columns on direct marketing techniques and advancements.

40562 ■ *The Publicity Hound*
Pub: Joan Stewart
Contact: Joan Stewart, Publisher
E-mail: jstewart@publicityhound.com
Released: Weekly. **Price:** Free internet service. **Description:** Provides techniques and strategies on self-promotion and inexpensive publicity. Recurring features include letters to the editor, interviews, news of research, book reviews, news of educational opportunities, notices of publications available, and columns titled Advice From Media People, Seasonal Story Ideas, Resource Page, Success Stories, and Media Insider Secrets. Does not report public relations agency staff changes.

40563 ■ *Research Alert*
Pub: EPM Communications Inc.
Contact: Ira Mayer, President
E-mail: imayer@epmcom.com
Ed: Barbara Perrin, Editor, bperrin@epmcom.com. **Released:** 24/year. **Price:** $389, individuals $369/year, U.S. and Canada; $429 elsewhere. **Description:** Summarizes the most current consumer marketing research reports. Includes complete contact, methodology, and price information.

40564 ■ *Signs of the Times*
Pub: ST Media Group International Inc.
Contact: Tedd Swormstedt, President
URL(s): www.stmediagroup.com/index.php3?d=pubs&p=stsignweb.com/. **Ed:** Wade Swormstedt. **Released:** 13/yr.

VIDEOCASSETTES/ AUDIOCASSETTES

40565 ■ *Concerns Quarterly with Footage from CBS News: General Business*
Harcourt Brace College Publishers
301 Commerce, Ste. 3700
Fort Worth, TX 76102
Ph: (817)334-7500
Free: 800-237-2665
Fax: (817)334-0947
Co. E-mail: info@harcourt.com
URL: http://www.hmhco.com
Released: 1995. **Price:** $80.00. **Description:** Video newsletter containing footage from such CBS programs as CBS Evening News, 48 Hours, Street Stories, and CBS This Morning. Provides information on such topics as ethical responsibilities in business, people in business, competition, manufacturing, and marketing. Comes with instructor's guide. Available at an annual subscription rate of $300.00. **Availability:** VHS.

40566 ■ *Finding a Niche: Determining Business Potential*
Instructional Video
2219 C St.
Lincoln, NE 68502
Ph: (402)475-6570
Free: 800-228-0164
Fax: (402)475-6500
Co. E-mail: feedback@insvideo.com
URL: http://www.insvideo.com
Released: 19??. **Price:** $99.00. **Description:** Outlines the process of selecting an appropriate market for your product, including profile development of potential customers and planning and implementing a feasability study. **Availability:** VHS.

40567 ■ *Marketing*
Coast Telecourses
11460 Warner Ave.
Fountain Valley, CA 92708-2597
Ph: (714)241-6109
Free: 800-547-4748
Fax: (714)241-6286
Co. E-mail: coastlearning@coastline.edu
URL: http://www.coastlearning.org
Released: 1992. **Description:** A video course in marketing. **Availability:** VHS; 3/4 U; Q.

40568 ■ *Marketing Perspectives*
RMI Media
1365 N. Winchester St.
Olathe, KS 66061-5880
Ph: (913)768-1696
Free: 800-745-5480
Fax: (800)755-6910
Co. E-mail: actmedia@act.org
URL: http://www.actmedia.com
Released: 1987. **Description:** Reviews the basic concepts of marketing. **Availability:** VHS; 3/4 U.

40569 ■ *The New Selling with Service*
RMI Media
1365 N. Winchester St.
Olathe, KS 66061-5880
Ph: (913)768-1696
Free: 800-745-5480
Fax: (800)755-6910
Co. E-mail: actmedia@act.org
URL: http://www.actmedia.com
Released: 1993. **Price:** $89.95. **Description:** Philip Wexler explains how to implement a marketing philosophy to maintain and increase customers. **Availability:** VHS.

40570 ■ *That's Show Business: The Rules of Exhibiting*
Video Arts, Inc.
c/o Aim Learning Group
8238-40 Lehigh
Morton Grove, IL 60053-2615
Free: 877-444-2230
Fax: (416)252-2155
Co. E-mail: service@aimlearninggroup.com
URL: http://www.aimlearninggroup.com
Released: 1991. **Price:** $790.00. **Description:** A sensible yet humorous approach to business exhibitions show the most common mistakes and how to avoid them. **Availability:** VHS; 8 mm; 3/4 U; Special order formats.

TRADE SHOWS AND CONVENTIONS

40571 ■ HSMAI - Affordable Meetings West
Hospitality Sales and Marketing Association International (HSMAI)
1760 Old Meadow Rd., Ste. 500
McLean, VA 22102
Ph: (703)506-3280
Free: 877-643-3511
Fax: (703)506-3266
Co. E-mail: info@hsmai.org
URL: http://www.hsmai.org
Contact: Robert A. Gilbert, President
E-mail: bgilbert@hsmai.org
URL(s): events.jspargo.com/AMW09/public/enter.aspx. **Frequency:** Annual. **Audience:** Trade professionals. **Principal Exhibits:** Equipment, supplies, and services for the hospitality and marketing industry. **Telecommunication Services:** affordablemeetings@jspargo.com.

CONSULTANTS

40572 ■ 22squared Inc.
401 E Jackson St., 36th Fl.
Tampa, FL 33602
Ph: (813)202-1200
Fax: (813)202-1264
Co. E-mail: curtis@22squared.com
URL: http://www.22squared.com
Contact: Richard Ward, Chief Executive Officer
Scope: Provider of advertising solutions. It serves consumers and business owners. **Founded:** 1922.

40573 ■ Sol Abrams Public Relations Counsel & Marketing Consultants
331 Webster Dr.
New Milford, NJ 07646
Ph: (201)262-4111
Fax: (201)262-7669
Contact: Sol Abrams, Owner
E-mail: solbabrams@aol.com
Scope: Independent consulting provides publicity, public relations and marketing counsel and services to management of private and public enterprises. Also serves as public relations consultants to other public relations consulting firms, advertising agencies and marketing companies. Provides expert witness services involving public relations. Also lectures, trains, teaches, and conducts seminars in public relations and marketing. Industries served: Corporate management, businesses large and small including real estate, construction, entertainment, food, fashion, fundraising, automotive, aviation, franchising, government agencies, and nonprofit organizations. **Founded:** 1962. **Seminars:** How to Select a Public Relations Firm; Publicity and Promotion for Small Business Owner; Expose Yourself - Don't Be a Secret Agent -Increase Your Sales, Incomes, Images, Publicity, Profits and Prestige via Professional Public Relations.

40574 ■ Aegis Communications Inc.
2 Greenwich Plz., Ste. 100
Greenwich, CT 06830-6353
Ph: (203)622-4944
Contact: David Bushko, President
Scope: Marketing firm specializing in using visualization tools to help clients define communication needs and develop communication strategies and plans. **Founded:** 1993.

40575 ■ Alden and Associates Marketing Research
2536 Via Sanchez
Palos Verdes Estates, CA 90274-2806
Ph: (310)544-6282
Free: 800-742-6076
Fax: (310)544-6285
Co. E-mail: info@aa-mr.com
URL: http://www.aa-mr.com
Contact: Dr. Scott D. Alden CPC, President
E-mail: scott.alden@aa-mr.com
Scope: Full-service marketing research firm specializing in custom, industrial and consumer research conducted by mailed or web-based survey, telephone and personal interview, or focus group in North America, Latin America, Europe and Asia and Oceania. Industries served: All. **Founded:** 1976.

40576 ■ Charles J. Allen and Associates
2668 Foxglove St.
Woodridge, IL 60517
Ph: (630)963-1444
Contact: Charles J. Allen, President
Scope: Specializes in marketing, communication, advertising and promotional consulting. Also serves as business management consultants on a continuing basis. **Founded:** 1970.

40577 ■ Anderson/Roethle Inc.
700 N Water St., Ste. 325
Milwaukee, WI 53202-4221
Ph: (414)276-0070

Fax: (414)276-4364
Co. E-mail: info@anderson-roethle.com
URL: http://www.anderson-roethle.com
Contact: Stanley C. Johnson, President
E-mail: scj@anderson-roethle.com
Scope: Provider of merger, acquisition and divestiture advisory services. Offers strategic planning, valuations and specialized M and A advisory services. **Founded:** 1963.

40578 ■ ARG & Associates
4615 E Colt Ct.
Inverness, FL 34452
Ph: (352)341-3222
Contact: Andrew R. Guzman, Managing Director
Scope: IS strategic planning and tactical implementation. **Founded:** 1988. **Publications:** "Managerial Social Types and Why Managers Fail"; "The Benefits of Organizational Diversity". **Seminars:** Offers specialized training seminars in: enterprise IT/IS Strategic Planning; Selecting and ERP solution and sales force automation.

40579 ■ Barker & Associates
1974 Wexford Cir.
Wheaton, IL 60187-6166
Ph: (630)260-9927
Fax: (630)260-9928
Contact: Patricia D. Barker, President
Scope: Consulting, training, and coaching firm specializing in providing human resource assessment, selection and development services focused primarily on people skills. Serves small, mid, and large-size organizations in both private industry and not-for-profit associations. **Founded:** 1982. **Seminars:** Strategic Marketing; Consultative Selling and Customer Service; From Hiring to Appraising - Developing Your Employees; Increased Productivity Through Managed Stress; Producing People Results Through Team building; Conflict Management; Communications, Managing Transition and Change; Creative Problem Solving.

40580 ■ Barson Marketing Inc.
RR. 9
Manalapan, NJ 07726
Ph: (732)446-3662
Fax: (732)446-5609
Co. E-mail: info@barsonmarketing.com
URL: http://www.barsonmarketing.com
Contact: Donna C. Barson, President
E-mail: barson@barsonmarketing.com
Scope: Specializes in the preparation of analytical market studies of various industries that is used as a basis for marketing intelligence programs. Services include marketing strategies, market research, business and competitive intelligence, marketing communications. Industries Served: Personal care, pharmaceutical and health, retail, consumer packaged goods. **Founded:** 1984. **Seminars:** Marketing Intelligence for the Cosmetic and Skincare Markets; Monitoring Consumer Purchasing Trends through Marketing Intelligence; Marketing for Professionals; Marketing is No Longer a Dirty Word; Marketing is Essential; Marketing - What's It All About; Targeting Your Target Market; Setting up a marketing intelligence program; Finding Hard to Find Information; Know Thy Competition.

40581 ■ Better Bottom Lines
2365 Rebel Rd.
Cumming, GA 30041
Ph: (770)887-3450
Fax: (770)887-3450
Co. E-mail: skipgundlach@earthlink.net
Contact: Skip Gundlach, President
E-mail: skipgundlach@earthlink.net
Scope: Firm conducts management and marketing consulting. It serves all small businesses, with a concentration on electromechanical sales, service and installation companies in the U.S. and Canada. **Founded:** 1986.

40582 ■ BIA/Kelsey
15120 Enterprise Ct.
Chantilly, VA 20151
Ph: (703)818-2425
Free: 800-331-5086
Fax: (703)803-3299
Co. E-mail: info@bia.com
URL: http://www.bia.com
Contact: Neal Polachek, President
E-mail: npolachek@kelseygroup.com
URL(s): www.kelseygroup.com. **Scope:** A provider of research and fact-based analysis focusing on local advertising and electronic commerce. **Founded:** 1983. **Publications:** "Penetration of Online Media Surpasses Traditional Media for First Time Among Small-Business Advertisers," Aug, 2009; "Rapid Adoption of Advanced Mobile Devices Driving Increased Mobile Local Search Activity, According to The Kelsey Group," Nov, 2008; "Online Consumer Generated Reviews Have Significant Impact on Offline Purchase Behavior," Nov, 2007. **Seminars:** Drilling Down on Local: Marketplaces, The Westin Seattle, Seattle, Washington, Apr, 2008; The Future of Local Search in Europe, London, Jun, 2007; DDC2006?Directory Driven Commerce Conference, Hyatt Century Plaza, LA, Sep, 2006; Drilling Down on Local: Targeting the On-Demand Marketplace, 2005. **Telecommunication Services:** tkg@kelseygroup.com.

40583 ■ Bitner Goodman
701 W Cypress Creek Rd., Ste. 204
Fort Lauderdale, FL 33309-2045
Ph: (954)730-7730
Fax: (954)730-7130
Co. E-mail: gary@bitnergoodman.com
URL: http://www.bitnergoodman.com
Contact: Gary Bitner, President
Scope: A public relations, advertising and marketing consultancy. Serves industries including: travel, technology, telecommunications, financial services, consumer products, health-care, government, automotive, real estate and retail. **Founded:** 1980. **Telecommunication Services:** info@bitnergoodman.com.

40584 ■ Bourget Research Group
West Hartford, CT 06127
Ph: (860)242-7665
Fax: (860)561-1771
Co. E-mail: info@bourgetresearch.com
URL: http://www.bourgetresearch.com
Contact: Charles A. Bourget, Jr., President
Scope: Offers market research and consulting service on both national and regional basis. Performs consumer and industrial research including advertising testing, market potential and market share sampling, product design tests, image studies, attitude and awareness tests and opinion polls. All qualitative and quantitative services including data processing and reports. Industries served: banking, insurance, government agencies, health care, utilities like gas, electric, telephone, and manufacturing. **Founded:** 1960.

40585 ■ Business Improvement Architects (BIA)
33 Riderwood Dr.
Toronto, ON, Canada M2L 2X4
Ph: (416)444-8225
Free: 866-346-3242
Fax: (416)444-6743
Co. E-mail: info@bia.ca
URL: http://www.bia.ca
Contact: Michael Stanleigh, Chief Executive Officer
E-mail: mstanleigh@bia.ca
Scope: Provider of the following services: strategic planning, leadership development, innovation and project and quality management. Specialize in strategic planning, change management, leadership assessment, and development of skills. **Founded:** 1989. **Publications:** "Avoiding Pit falls to Innovation"; "Create a New Dimension of Performance with Innovation"; "The Power of Appreciation in Leadership"; "Why It Makes Sense To Have a Strategic Enterprise Office"; "Burning Rubber at the Start of Your Project"; "Accounting for Quality"; "How Pareto Charts Can Help You Improve the Quality of Business Processes"; "Managing Resistance to Change". **Seminars:** The Innovation Process. . .From Vision to Reality, San Diego, Oct, 2007; Critical Thinking, Kuala Lump or, Sep, 2007; Critical Thinking, Brunei, Sep, 2007; Delivering Project Assurance, Auckland, Jun, 2007; From Crisis to Control: A New Era in Strategic Project Management, Prague, May, 2007; What Project Leaders Need to Know to Help Them Sleep Better At Night, London, May, 2007; Innovation Process. . .From Vision To Reality, Orlando, Apr, 2007. **Special Services:** Project Planning Tool™.

40586 ■ Camarro Research
345 Carroll Rd.
Fairfield, CT 06825
Fax: (203)331-0470
Contact: Kenneth D. Camarro, Owner
E-mail: kcamarro@snet.net
Scope: Provides consultation in the areas of marketing, product development, market research and user application consulting. Also offers office automation product development and market research services. **Founded:** 1983. **Publications:** "Fax machine designs to make current equipment obsolete - Facsimile," Communications News, Mar, 1991; "Multifunction Product and Market Trend"; "Fax Trend Report".

40587 ■ Elizabeth Capen
27 E 95th St., Apt. 5E
New York, NY 10128-0824
Ph: (212)427-7654
Fax: (212)876-3190
Scope: Focuses on strategic marketing planning and positioning. Identifies effective marketing tools; plans and reviews advertising and collateral materials; writes business plans; and performs secondary research and competitive analysis. Industries served: services, small businesses, and entrepreneurial ventures in northeastern and middle Atlantic regions. **Founded:** 1985. **Seminars:** Handling Issues of Growth; Using Published Information as a Marketing Tool.

40588 ■ Capstone Communications Group
15 Wilson St.
Markham, ON, Canada L3P 1M9
Ph: (905)472-2330
Fax: (905)294-9435
Co. E-mail: capstone@capstonecomm.com
URL: http://www.capstonecomm.com
Contact: Keith Thirgood, Principal
E-mail: keith@capstonecomm.com
Scope: Provider of communications and marketing design, copywriting and production. **Founded:** 1982. **Publications:** "Guide to finding the best keywords for your site"; "Seeking Help: Ideas on how to get out from under"; "Get your visitors to voluntarily give you their contact information"; "Where is 'King Content'"; "Is Blogging the Next Great Thing"; "Nice Guys Finish First: How the right kind of volunteering can help grow your business"; "Why should a business have a website"; "Too Dull, Too Sharp"; "Dialing for Dollars: Is fax marketing for you"; "Getting Paid to Promote Yourself"; "Why should a business have a website"; "Cave Paintings, Baseball and Connecting: There's no such thing as a captive audience"; "Marketing vs. Selling: What's the difference and why should you care"; "Selling Services"; "A New Opportunity"; "Improve Your Website"; "How to Price Right"; "A Questionnaire for Businesses"; "Web Report Card: How this site has been performing"; "At The Speed Of Light". **Seminars:** Your Image Your Message Your Market; Emotional Marketing; Developing a Marketing Mindset; Target Marketing; How to Create Marketing Materials That Work; Facing the Challenge of the Blank Page-A Design Workshop for Non-Designers, How to Create Web Sites that Work; The Service Sellers Masters Course; The Net writing Masters Course; The Pricing Masters Course; The Info Product Masters Course; The Net Auction Masters Course; The Affiliate Masters Course.

40589 ■ Frederick Chin
94 Condor St.
East Boston, MA 02128-1306
Ph: (617)567-8554
Contact: Frederick Chin, Director
Scope: Offers market research, strategic and technical development, and formation of business liaisons for both public and private sectors industries in the United States, New England and Eastern Asia. **Founded:** 1990.

40590 ■ Kelley Chunn & Associates (KCA)
184 Dudley St., Ste. 106
Boston, MA 02119
Ph: (617)427-0997
Fax: (617)427-3997
Co. E-mail: kc4info@aol.com
URL: http://www.kelleychunn.com
Contact: Kelley C. Chunn, President
E-mail: kcprmail@aol.com
Scope: Consulting firm that specializes in multicultural and cause-related public relations and marketing. Services include: Cause-related marketing, strategic planning, community relations, corporate communications, guerrilla marketing, event planning and management, public affairs, media relations and training. **Founded:** 1991. **Publications:** "The Tipping point of social marketing Color Magazine"; "Community Voices, Bay State Banner"; "Education: Inner City Slickers," 2006. **Seminars:** Crisis communications; Guerrilla marketing; Ethnic marketing.

40591 ■ Clayton/Curtis/Cottrell
1722 Madison Ct.
Louisville, CO 80027-1121
Ph: (303)665-2005
Contact: Robert Cottrell, President
Scope: Market research firm specializes in providing consultations for packaged goods, telecommunications, direct marketing and printing, and packaging industries. Services include strategic planning; profit enhancement; startup businesses; mergers and acquisitions; joint ventures; divestitures; interim management; crisis management; turnarounds; market size, segmentation and rates of growth; competitor intelligence; image and reputation, and competitive analysis. **Founded:** 1981. **Publications:** "Turn an attitude into a purchase," Jul, 1995; "Mixed results for private label; price assaults by the national brands are getting heavy, but there's still a place for private label," Jun, 1995; "In-store promotion goes high-tech: is the conventional coupon destined for obsolescence?," Jun, 1995.

40592 ■ Comer & Associates L.L.C.—Energy Alliance Group
5255 Holmes Pl.
Boulder, CO 80303
Ph: (303)786-7986
Free: 888-950-3190
Fax: (303)895-2347
Co. E-mail: jerry@comerassociates.com
URL: http://www.comerassociates.com
Contact: Jerry C. Comer, President
E-mail: jerry@comerassociates.com
URL(s): www.energyalliance.biz. **Scope:** Specialize in developing markets and businesses. Marketing support includes: Developing and writing strategic and tactical business plans; developing and writing focused, effective market plans; researching market potential and competition; implementing targeted marketing tactics to achieve company objectives; conducting customer surveys to determine satisfaction and attitudes toward client. Organization development support includes: Executive management training programs; executive coaching; team building; developing effective organization structures; and management of change in dynamic and competitive environments; individual coaching for management and leadership effectiveness. **Founded:** 1993. **Seminars:** Developing a Strategic Market Plan; Market Research: Defining Your Opportunity; Management and Leadership Effectiveness; Team Building; Developing a Business Plan; How to Close; Using Questions to Sell; Sales System Elements and Checklist; Working With Independent Reps; Features vs. Benefits; Overcoming Objections; Sales Force Automation.

40593 ■ Conor Environmental Services Inc.
4 Shoppers Ln.
Turnersville, NJ 08012-1400
Ph: (609)589-5475
Fax: (609)589-6037
Co. E-mail: consultces@usa.net
Scope: Firm provides a full range of environmental and engineering consulting services for both public and private organizations. Environmental company provides assessment, engineering, and remediation services, specializing in industrial and hazardous waste management. The integrated approach-combining scientific, engineering, and management services-provides cost-effective solutions to the complex scope of environmental problems, risk assessment and audit programs; and spill response management and planning services. Industries served: manufacturing, petroleum, power plants, utilities, wastewater treatment facilities, pipelines, landfills, banks, financial institutions, real estate developers, law firms, insurance companies, and government. **Founded:** 1995. **Seminars:** Beating the Competition: Winning with Better Information.

40594 ■ Corporate Expressions International Inc.
105 Main St.
Hackensack, NJ 07601-7103
Ph: (201)488-1660
Fax: (201)488-6973
Contact: Victoria Wilson, President
Scope: Conducts marketing research with a special emphasis on multicultural marketing and Seniors. Serves all industries nationwide, with a special focus on health-care, entertainment and consumer products industries. **Founded:** 1989. **Seminars:** Marketing to Seniors.

40595 ■ Coyne Associates
4010 E Lake St.
Minneapolis, MN 55406-2201
Ph: (612)724-1188
Fax: (612)722-1379
Contact: John T. Coyne, Chief Executive Officer
Scope: A marketing and public relations consulting firm that specializes in assisting architectural, engineering, and contractor/developer firms. Services include: marketing plains and audits, strategic planning, corporate identity, turnarounds, and sales training. **Founded:** 2008.

40596 ■ Customer Perspectives
213 W River Rd.
Hooksett, NH 03106-2628
Ph: (603)647-1300
Free: 800-277-4677
Fax: (603)647-0900
Co. E-mail: info@customerperspectives.com
URL: http://www.customerperspectives.com
Contact: Angie Deschenes, Vice President
Scope: A market research consultancy specializing in mystery shopping. **Founded:** 1983. **Special Services:** Customer Perspectives™.

40597 ■ Development Resource Consultants (DRC)
PO Box 118
Rancho Cucamonga, CA 91729
Ph: (909)902-7655
Fax: (909)476-6942
Co. E-mail: drc@gotodrc.com
URL: http://www.gotodrc.com
Contact: Jerry R. Frey, Business Manager
E-mail: jfrey@gotodrc.com
Scope: Specializes in office re-organization, employee training in office organization, communication skills, sales training and career counseling. **Founded:** 1985. **Publications:** "Institute of Management Consultants Southern California Chapter," Jan, 2006.

40598 ■ Devillier Communications Inc.
3315 Fessenden St., NW
Washington, DC 20008-2034
Ph: (202)362-4429
Fax: (202)966-5754
Co. E-mail: info@devillier.com
URL: http://www.devillier.com
Contact: Linda Devillier, President
Scope: Firm marketing consultancy. Firm develops innovative solutions for a wide range of extra ordinary clients. **Founded:** 1984.

40599 ■ Digital Deli Inc.
3145 Geary Blvd., Ste. 532
San Francisco, CA 94118-3316
Ph: (415)387-7653
Free: 800-557-3354
Fax: (415)387-7656
Co. E-mail: sales@thedeli.com
Contact: Antonio White, President
E-mail: white@theDeli.com
Scope: Specializes in interactive marketing development. Provides strategic and tactical planning for interactive media. Specializes in marketing communications. **Founded:** 1995.

40600 ■ donphin.com Inc.
1001 B Ave., Ste. 200
Coronado, CA 92118
Ph: (619)550-3533
Free: 800-234-3304
Fax: (619)600-0096
Co. E-mail: inquiry@donphin.com
URL: http://www.donphin.com
Contact: Vito Tanzi, President
Scope: Offers a comprehensive approach to understanding and applying a broad range of business principles: legal compliance issues, management concerns, health and safety, customer service, marketing, information management. Industries served: All developing small businesses. **Publications:** "Doing Business Right!"; "HR That Works!"; "Lawsuit Free! How to Prevent Employee Lawsuits"; "Building Powerful Employment Relationships!"; "Victims, Villains and Heroes: Managing Emotions in The Workplace". **Seminars:** Doing Business Right!; HR That Works!; Building Powerful Employment Relationships; Lawsuit Free!.

40601 ■ Drennan Communications—Drennan Literary Agency
6 Robin Ln.
East Kingston, NH 03827-2000
Ph: (603)642-8002
Fax: (603)642-8002
Contact: William D. Drennan, President
Scope: Marketing consultants specializing in the creation of names for new products, new companies, and new processes for organizations of all sizes and for individuals. Additionally provides manuscript consultation and analysis as well as substantive editing, rewriting, copy editing, and proofreading. Also offers original writing for organizations of all sizes, government agencies, and for individuals. **Founded:** 1980.

40602 ■ Duncan Direct Associates
16 Elm St.
Peterborough, NH 03458
Ph: (603)924-3121
Fax: (603)924-8511
URL: http://www.duncandirect.com
Contact: George Duncan, Owner
E-mail: gduncan@pobox.com
Scope: Provides copy, strategy consulting and creative support to a nationwide roster of business-to-business and consumer marketers, and solo entrepreneurs. Specializes in sales letters and brochures to complete lead generation campaigns. **Founded:** 1976. **Publications:** "Direct Mail Lead Questionnaire/Checklist"; "Ten Copy Do's and Don'ts"; "Streetwise Direct Marketing," Adams Media, Jan, 2001; "Website Dynamics: The Four C's of Stickiness"; "It's For You: Telemarketing Without the Hangups"; "Determining Your Package Format"; "Preparing to Write: Researching the Product and the Market"; "All About Benefits"; "Writing and Designing Response Advertising"; "Alternative Print Media: The low cost route to prospecting"; "Direct Mail and the Dynamics of Response". **Seminars:** Book Marketing.

40603 ■ Everest Marketing
957 Ashland Ave.
Saint Paul, MN 55104-7019
Ph: (612)581-1333
Fax: (651)221-1978
Contact: Rebecca Aistrup, President
Scope: Provides business-to-business marketing services including marketing plan development, marketing communications, market research and business intelligence. **Founded:** 1993. **Publications:** "Finding and Using Local Market Research To Improve Your Sales"; "Marketing to the Right People at the Right Time"; "Marketing in a Sales-Driven Environment"; "Money Well Spent! (Eight Steps to a successful consulting project)"; "Does this sound like

you?"; "Marketing Quickies". **Seminars:** Market Research Basics for Managers; Profiting from Your Customer Database; Developing Your Strategic Marketing Plan from the Ground Up; A Team Process for Developing Your Marketing Plan; Developing a Commercialization Plan for Your SBIR (Small Business Innovation Research)Proposal; Using Marketing Strategies to Jump-Start Your Sales; Marketing in a Sales-Driven Environment and Marketing in a Technology-Driven Environment.

40604 ■ Edgar Falk Communications
301 E 78th St.
New York, NY 10021
Ph: (212)628-3314
Fax: (212)628-7606
Contact: Edgar A. Falk, President
E-mail: edgarafalk@earthlink.net
Scope: Offers full marketing services for the smaller retailer by the author of1, 001 Ideas to create Retail Excitement as well as public relations and marketing services for consumer goods and services. **Founded:** 1981.

40605 ■ The Farnsworth Group
6640 Intech Blvd., Ste. 100, Intech Bldg. 10
Indianapolis, IN 46278
Ph: (317)241-5600
Fax: (317)227-3010
Co. E-mail: tfg@thefarnsworthgroup.com
URL: http://www.thefarnsworthgroup.com
Contact: Bradley T. Farnsworth, President
E-mail: bfarnsworth@thefarnsworthgroup.com
Scope: Research-based marketing consulting company. Serves the home improvement, construction and building materials industries. Services for manufacturers include product development, brand optimization, growth opportunity, category improvement and channel satisfaction improvement. Services for retailers and dealers include market position assessment, business function improvement, category positioning and strategy and category improvement. **Founded:** 1989. **Publications:** "Research Guides Hyde Tool's Rebranding," Jun, 2011. **Telecommunication Services:** info@thefarnsworthgroup.com.

40606 ■ John C. Faulkner
27 Nearwater Ln.
Darien, CT 06820-5614
Ph: (203)656-2196
Fax: (203)656-2196
Scope: Specializes in marketing of industrial/consumer products and services, strategic planning, general management studies, and acquisition planning. Also market research, incentive sales compensation and organization. Serves private industries. **Founded:** 1983.

40607 ■ Steven M. Ferguson & Associates
6212 Massachusetts Ave.
Bethesda, MD 20816
Ph: (301)229-8676
Fax: (301)320-4495
Co. E-mail: sfergus@erols.com
Contact: Steven M. Ferguson, Director
E-mail: sf8h@nih.gov
Scope: Performs general marketing consultations and writing services for small to medium-sized firms. Serves as business education advisor for entrepreneurial educational programs. Serves private industries as well as government agencies. **Founded:** 1986. **Publications:** "S. Ferguson, Starting and Operating a Business in West Virginia," Oasis Press, 1992; "Starting and Operating a Business in the District of Columbia," Oasis Press, 1992.

40608 ■ Flor & Associates
179 Schan Dr.
Churchville, PA 18966-1619
Ph: (215)355-7466
Fax: (215)355-7464
Co. E-mail: fredflor@msn.com
Contact: Frederick Flor, President
Scope: Offers business development consulting helping companies increase the value of their businesses. Services include: market development for technologies sand products; product positioning strategies; technology assessment; competitive intelligence and analysis; team augmentation and facilitation; business growth strategies including acquisitions, licensing, and partnerships.

40609 ■ Russ Fons Public Relations
7509 Turtle Dove Ct.
Las Vegas, NV 89129-6032
Ph: (702)658-7654
Free: 888-658-7654
Fax: (702)658-1349
Co. E-mail: russfons@cox.net
Contact: Russ Fons, Owner
E-mail: russfons@cox.net
Scope: Offers corporate counseling and image development; media relations; marketing communications and product publicity; event management and special promotions; and graphic design and production. Industries served: All worldwide. Licensing and merchandising, literary services, Hispanic communications. Revenue Sharing/PI Advertising. **Founded:** 1980. **Publications:** "The Executive Crisis Manager, a planning guide to surviving corporate crisis".

40610 ■ Freese & Associates Inc.
PO Box 814
Chagrin Falls, OH 44022-0814
Ph: (440)564-9183
Fax: (440)564-7339
Co. E-mail: tfreese@freeseinc.com
URL: http://www.freeseinc.com
Contact: Duane L. Hile, Manager
Scope: A management consulting firm offering advice in all forms of business logistics. Consulting services are in the areas of strategic planning; network analysis, site selection, facility layout and design, outsourcing, warehousing, transportation and customer service. Typical projects include 3PL marketing surveys; third party outsourcing selection; operational audits; competitive analysis; inventory management; due diligence; and implementation project management. **Founded:** 1987. **Publications:** "Building Relationships is Key to Motivation," Distribution Center Management, Apr, 2006; "Getting Maximum Results from Performance Reviews," WERC Sheet, Oct, 2003; "SCM: Making the Vision a Reality," Supply Chain Management Review, Oct, 2003; "Contents Under Pressure," DC Velocity, Aug, 2003; "When Considering Outsourcing, It's Really a Financial Decision," Inventory Management Report, Mar, 2003. **Seminars:** WERC/CAWS Warehousing in China Conference, Sep, 2008; CSCMP Annual Conference, Denver, Oct, 2008; Keys to Retaining and Motivating Your Associates, Dallas, Mar, 2006; The Value and Challenges of Supply Chain Management, Dubai, Feb, 2006; Best Practices in Logistics in China, Jun, 2005; Keys to Motivating Associates, Dallas, May, 2005; The Goal and the Way of International Cooperation in Logistics, Jenobuk, Apr, 2005.

40611 ■ Geibel Marketing & Public Relations
PO Box 611
Belmont, MA 02478-0005
Ph: (617)484-8285
Fax: (617)489-3567
Co. E-mail: webquery@geibelmarketing.com
URL: http://www.geibelpr.com
Contact: Jeffrey Geibel, Principal
E-mail: jgeibel@geibelpr.com
Scope: Supports clients with sales messaging, sales-based marketing programs and consulting services that is developed from a diagnosis of both successful sales and market environment. Additional services include public relations, custom market research based on executive-level interviews, customized marketing skills instruction, video development and production supervision for sales messaging and marketing support videos. **Founded:** 1982. **Publications:** "Internet Damage Control: How to Prevent and Defend Against a Web Mugging"; "The Sick Press Release," 2006; "Applications Software Marketing: A Field Manual for Success"; "CSI Marketing-Separating Fact from Fiction"; "Blog-Where's the beef"; "How Digital Tools and Audiences are Changing Public Relations for Technology Businesses"; "How to Develop Successful LEED Marketing"; "Business Development, Market Sizing and Territory Planning"; "How to Develop a Deep Case Study"; "Do-It-Yourself Consulting - Some Caveats"; "Painful Marketing Forums"; "Are You Sure You are On-message"; "CSI Marketing - Separating Fact from Fiction"; "Can Your Marketing Pass the Test"; "Law Firm Marketing: A Practical Approach"; "The Kennedy Curse". **Seminars:** How to Develop a Vertical Marketing Program for Software and Systems; Public Relations Techniques for Vertical Market Product Launches; new rules of PR. **Special Services:** The Sales Autopsy™.

40612 ■ The Handler Group Inc.
425 W End Ave., Apt. 3A
New York, NY 10024-5718
Ph: (212)873-1899
Contact: Mark Lambert Handler, President
E-mail: mlhandler@aol.com
Scope: Provider of marketing, communication planning, and design services, specializing in development of internal and external business communications. Develops corporate identity, corporate literature, employee communications, sales promotion materials, consumer product packaging and information, brochures, annual reports, and presentation materials. Industries served: Cable/television, technology software, business information, hospitality, and banking. **Founded:** 1976.

40613 ■ hightechbiz.com—Leahy & Associates Inc.
4209 Santa Monica Blvd., Ste. 201
Los Angeles, CA 90029-3027
Ph: (323)913-3355
Free: 877-648-4753
Fax: (323)913-3355
URL: http://www.hightechbiz.com
Contact: Steven L. Hayes, Principal
Scope: A full service marketing agency specializing in integrated marketing solutions. Services include: marketing surveys; positioning surveys; strategic and tactical plans; implementation plans; management consulting; product brochures; product catalogs; product packaging; product data sheets; direct mail programs; media research; competitive research; complete creative; production and film; media placement; corporate identity; in-house creative; public relations. **Founded:** 1980.

40614 ■ Hills Consulting Group Inc.
6 Partridge Ct.
Novato, CA 94945-1315
Ph: (415)898-3944
Contact: Michael R. Hills, President
Scope: Specializes in strategic planning; marketing surveys; market research; customer service audits; new product development; competitive analysis; and sales forecasting. **Founded:** 1985.

40615 ■ C. W. Hines and Associates Inc.—C&W Associates Inc.
344 Churchill Cir., Sanctuary Bay
White Stone, VA 22578
Ph: (804)435-8844
Fax: (804)435-8855
Co. E-mail: turtlecwh@aol.com
URL: http://www.cwhinesassociates.org
Contact: Dr. Carolyn C.W. Hines, President
Scope: Management consultants with expertise in the following categories: advertising and public relations; health and human resources; management sciences; organizational development; computer sciences; financial management; behavioral sciences; environmental design; technology transfer; project management; facility management; program evaluation; and business therapy. Also included are complementary areas such as sampling procedures; job training; managerial effectiveness; corporate seminars; gender harassment; training for trainers and leadership and management skills development. **Founded:** 1979. **Publications:** "Money Muscle, 120 Exercises To Build Spiritual And Financial Strength," 2004; "Inside Track: Executives Coaching Executives"; "Money Muscle: 122 Exercises to Build Financial Strength"; "Nuts and Bolts of Work Force Diversity"; "Legal Issues, published in the Controllers Business Advisor"; "Identifying Racism: Specific Examples"; "BOSS Spelled Backwards is double SSOB! Or is it?"; "A No-Nonsense Guide to Being Stressed". **Seminars:** Career Development; Coaching and Counseling for Work Success; Communicat-

ing More Effectively in a Diverse Work Environment; Communications 600: Advanced Skills for Relationship Building; Customer Service: Building a Caring Culture.

40616 ■ Holcomb Gallagher Adams Advertising Inc.—Holcomb Design
300 Marconi Blvd., Ste. 305
Columbus, OH 43215
Ph: (614)221-3343
Fax: (614)221-3367
Co. E-mail: radams@hgainc.com
URL: http://www.hgainc.com
Contact: Rick Adams, Partner
E-mail: radams@hgainc.com
Scope: Consults in strategic marketing planning, and new business, brand equity, creative strategy, and media strategy development. Industries served: Consumer goods and services, manufacturing, retail, business-to-business products and services, education, travel, and tourism. **Founded:** 1993.

40617 ■ Hornberger & Associates (H&A)
1966 Lombard St.
San Francisco, CA 94123
Ph: (415)346-2106
Fax: (415)346-9993
Co. E-mail: info@hornbergerassociates.com
URL: http://www.hornbergerassociates.com
Contact: Deborah Hornberger, President
E-mail: deborah@hornbergerassociates.com
Scope: Specialized services include wealth management, retirement programs, small business banking, personal trust, investment management, brokerage services, mutual funds, relationship management, private banking and employee banking. Help clients by offering strategic marketing plans, market segmentation/niche marketing, website strategies and development; product development and introduction; client communications; product, sales and referral training; client retention programs and project management. **Founded:** 1992. **Publications:** "Establishing a Mini-trust Product," Bank Marketing, Oct, 1997. **Seminars:** Building a Marketing Plan Directed at Emerging Wealth Baby Boomers, Strategy Institute conference, Jun, 1999.

40618 ■ Ilium Associates Inc.
600 108th Ave. NE, Ste. 660
Bellevue, WA 98004
Ph: (425)646-6525
Free: 800-874-6525
Fax: (425)646-6525
Co. E-mail: ilium@ilium.com
URL: http://www.ilium.com
Contact: Carolyn Perez Andersen, President
E-mail: carolyn@ilium.com
Scope: Marketing consultants active in market research and analysis, marketing planning, product and packaging design and graphics, as well as architectural design, graphics, signage, electronics. Industries served: transportation, real estate development, architecture, manufacturing, software publishing and government agencies worldwide. **Founded:** 1972.

40619 ■ IMC Consulting & Training
901 McHenry Ave., Ste. A
Modesto, CA 95350
Ph: (209)572-2271
Fax: (209)572-2862
Co. E-mail: info@imc-1.net
URL: http://www.imc-1.net
Contact: Michael J. Loschke, President
E-mail: michael@imc-1.net
Scope: Helps businesses and professionals identify, develop and market their selling proposition to increase profits. Services include B-to-B surveys, direct marketing, media relations, planning and strategy, sales management, training and leadership coaching. **Founded:** 1994. **Publications:** "Consultant Earns Advanced Certificate," Hccsc Business Review, Dec, 2004; "Adapting to Change - the New Competitive Advantage," Business Journal, Jul, 2004; "Loyalty Marketing Can Divide New Business," Jun, 2004; "Eleven Major Marketing Mistakes," Jul, 2003; "Planning to Win or Racing to Fail," Jun, 2003. **Seminars:** Negotiating High Profit Sales; How to Write Winning Proposals, Modesto Chamber of Commerce, Oct, 2007; Winning the 2nd Half: A 6-month Plan to Score New Customers and Profits. **Telecommunication Services:** imcinfo@imc-1.net.

40620 ■ In Plain English—R.H. Wohl & Associates Inc.
14501 Antigone Dr.
Gaithersburg, MD 20885-3300
Ph: (301)340-2821
Free: 800-274-9645
Fax: (301)279-0115
Co. E-mail: rwohl@inplainenglish.com
URL: http://www.inplainenglish.com
Contact: Ronald H. Wohl, President
E-mail: rwohl@inplainenglish.com
Scope: Management consultants helping government and businesses research, design, write and produce user oriented management information for human resources, employee benefits, business process, corporate and marketing needs. Services include: GSA mob is schedule for consulting to the government; employee benefit communications, plain English business writing workshops for print and electronic media; communicating strategy and tactics; marketing research, business planning and communications; readability testing; usability testing and monitoring strategy. **Founded:** 1977. **Publications:** "The Benefits Communication"; "The Employee Benefits Communication ToolKit," Commerce Clearinghouse; "Benefits Communication," Business and Legal Reports. **Seminars:** Plain English Writing Training; Summary Plan Description Compliance workshops; Re-Humanizing the Corporation, Human Resources and Employee Benefits Communication Workshop; 21 Writing Tips for the 21st Century; Make the Write Impression; Writing to Inform and Instruct; The Dreaded Nuts and Bolts; Writing to Persuade; Writing Policy and Procedure Manuals In Plain English; Writing for Accountants and Auditors In Plain English. **Special Services:** In Plain English®.

40621 ■ JF Robinson Research & Demographics
28200 Hwy. 189
Lake Arrowhead, CA 92352
Ph: (909)337-1484
Fax: (909)337-1484
Co. E-mail: jrobi60317@aol.com
Contact: Jerry Robinson, Owner
Scope: Firm specializes in target marketing for public and private agencies and businesses, targeting consumers and voters. Reports include projections, geo-demographics, market potential, and consumer lists for specific segments of the population. Also offers research and development of funding and grants for non-profits using targeting methods and government appropriations, competitive, market, and opponent intelligence about domestic and foreign competitors. **Founded:** 1993. **Seminars:** Offers seminars on grants and funding research for non-profits, preparation for a school bond election, and using demographics in marketing and small business development.

40622 ■ James O. Kennedy & Co.
515 Monroe Ave.
River Forest, IL 60305-1901
Contact: James O. Kennedy, President
E-mail: jimboken@aol.com
Scope: Offers general marketing communications consulting, advertising, and business writing for small business. Industries served: General business. **Founded:** 1980.

40623 ■ Kenneth Stone Consulting Economist
2208 Van Buren Ave.
Ames, IA 50010-4519
Ph: (515)232-7766
Fax: (515)294-1700
Co. E-mail: kstone@iastate.edu
Contact: Kenneth Eugene Stone, Owner
E-mail: kstone@iastate.edu
Scope: Conducts seminars on competing with the mass merchandisers and "Big Box" stores. Helps retailers develop strategies at the firm level and community level. **Publications:** "Encyclopedia of Rural America, the Land and People," ABC- CLIO Inc, 1998; "Competing With the Retail Giants" .

40624 ■ Koch Group Inc.
129 Fairfield Way, Ste. 219
Bloomingdale, IL 60108
Ph: (630)941-1100
Free: 800-470-7845
Fax: (630)941-3865
Co. E-mail: info@kochgroup.com
URL: http://www.kochgroup.com
Contact: Peter Koch, Manager
Scope: Provider of industrial marketing consulting services to small to mid-sized manufacturers. Primary assistance includes industrial market research and analysis, identification of potential markets, strategic planning and plan implementation, market planning, sales analysis, competitor analysis. Specializes in assisting manufacturers identify, recruit, and manage agents and reps and developing website for business promotion. **Founded:** 1967. **Seminars:** Niche Marketing; Regional Industrial Association Recruiting; Strategic Marketing for Manufacturers; Strategic Marketing; How To Identify, Screen, Interview and Select High Quality Agents; Basics of Industrial Market Research; Elements of Industrial Marketing; Trade Adjustment Assistance For Firms; Developing New Business; Selecting An Industrial Web Site Developer; Strategic Selling; Pick Your Customer; Strategic and Tactical Marketing.

40625 ■ Krantz Marketing Services L.L.C.
3 Wentworth Rd.
Bedminster, NJ 07921
Ph: (908)326-3518
Fax: (908)757-0466
Co. E-mail: info@krantzonline.com
Contact: Boris M. Krantz, President
E-mail: boris@krantzonline.com
Scope: Offers strategic planning for digital marketing and e-business, public relations, advertising, marketing, research, management consulting, telemarketing, and sales and management training for clients in business-to-business, and professional services. **Founded:** 1980. **Seminars:** Sales Management; Market Planning; Pricing; Entrepreneurial Marketing; High Technology Marketing - Creating Differentiation in Product and Services Marketing.

40626 ■ Kubba Consultants Inc.
1255 Montgomery Dr.
Deerfield, IL 60015
Ph: (847)867-0874
URL: http://www.kubbainc.com
Contact: Ed Kubba, President
E-mail: edkubba@aol.com
Scope: Industrial and business-to-business marketing research and consulting. Services include new product research, new market evaluation, competitor analysis and customer value analysis. **Founded:** 1987.

40627 ■ Jeffrey Lant Associates Inc.
50 Follen St., Ste. 507
Cambridge, MA 02138
Ph: (617)547-6372
Fax: (617)547-0061
URL: http://www.jeffreylant.com
Contact: Dr. Jeffrey L. Lant, President
E-mail: drjlant@worldprofit.com
Description: Description: Publishes technical assistance books for nonprofit organizations, consultants, independent professionals and small and home-based businesses. Offers audio cassettes, workshops and consultation services. Also publishes twice monthly Worlgram newsletter. Reaches market through commission representatives, direct mail, telephone sales and the Internet. Accepts unsolicited manuscripts. **Scope:** Sets up businesses online, design websites and assists with marketing. **Founded:** 1979. **Publications:** "E-mail El Dorado," JLA Publications, 1998; "Web Wealth: How to Turn the World Wide Web Into a Cash Hose for Your Business. Whatever You're Selling," 1997; "Multi-Level Money," JLA Publications, 1994; "No More Cold Calls," JLA Publications, 1997; "Cash Copy"; "How to make at least $100000 a year"; "E-Money". **Seminars:** Business and personal development, including Establishing and Operating Your Successful Consulting Business; Successfully Promoting Your Small Business and Professional Practice; Succeeding in Your Mail Order Business; Successfully Raising

Money for Your Nonprofit Organization from Foundations, Corporations and Individuals; Money Making Marketing: Finding the People Who Need What You're Selling and Making Sure They Buy It; Getting Corporations, Foundations, and Individuals to Give You the Money Your Nonprofit Organization Needs.

40628 ■ Liberty Business Strategies Ltd.
The Times Bldg., Ste. 400, Suburban Sq.
Ardmore, PA 19003
Ph: (610)649-3800
Fax: (610)649-0408
Co. E-mail: info@libertystrategies.com
URL: http://www.libertystrategies.com
Contact: Emmy S. Miller, President
E-mail: emmym@libertystrategies.com
Scope: Management consulting firm working with clients to gain speed and agility in driving their business strategy. The consulting model builds the alignment of strategy, organization commitment, and technology. Provides senior leader coaching and team development coaching. **Founded:** 1980. **Seminars:** Winning with Talent, Morison Annual Conference, Jul, 2009.

40629 ■ Lupfer & Associates (L&A)
92 Glen St.
Natick, MA 01760-5646
Ph: (508)655-3950
Fax: (508)655-7826
Co. E-mail: donlupfer@aol.com
Contact: Donald Lupfer, Owner
E-mail: don.lupfer@lupferassociates.com
Scope: Assists off shore hi-tech companies in entering United States markets and specializes in channel development for all sorts of products. Perform MARCOM support for hi-tech United States clients. **Founded:** 1988. **Publications:** "What's Next For Distribution-Feast or Famine"; "The Changing Global Marketplace"; "Making Global Distribution Work". **Seminars:** How to do Business in the United States.

40630 ■ Management Strategies
1000 S Old Woodward Ave., Ste. 105
Birmingham, MI 48009
Ph: (248)258-2756
Fax: (248)258-3407
Co. E-mail: bob@hois.com
Contact: Robert E. Hoisington, President
E-mail: bob@hois.com
Scope: Firm specializes in strategic planning; feasibility studies; profit enhancement; organizational studies; start up businesses; turnarounds; business process re engineering; industrial engineering; marketing; ecommerce. **Founded:** 1985.

40631 ■ Market Focus
12 Maryland Rd.
Maplewood, NJ 07040
Ph: (973)378-2470
Fax: (973)378-2470
Co. E-mail: mcss66@marketfocus.com
Contact: Daniel A. Zaslow, President
E-mail: dakaslow@comcast.net
Scope: Offers advisory services to executives of corporate business units and mid-sized companies in the development and implementation of corporate and market strategies. Studies relate to business planning, new market/product entry, acquisitions and industry/competitive profiles for firms in advanced technology, business and financial services and basic industry. Projects focus on practical, effective approaches to maximizing the potential of existing operations and exploiting future growth opportunities. Practice philosophy emphasizes close client relationships, active management participation and senior consultant involvement. **Founded:** 1980. **Publications:** "Surviving in Hard Times," NJ Contractor. **Seminars:** Charting a Course for Future Company Growth; Marketing Planning; Construction Marketing in the 90's; Marketing and The CFO.

40632 ■ Marketing Leverage Inc.
2022 Laurel Oak Ln.
Palm City, FL 34990
Ph: (772)878-6495
Free: 800-633-1422
Fax: (772)659-8664
Co. E-mail: lkelly@marketingleverage.com
Contact: Lynn C. Kelly, President
E-mail: lkelly@marketingleverage.com
Scope: Consulting and research firm focusing on the targeting, retention and satisfaction of customers. Consulting is offered for due diligence; marketing and customer retention strategy; program design and implementation. Research services offered help clients determine service improvements that increase customer loyalty; boosting sales through better understanding buyer motivations; increasing the odds of product acceptance through new product concept testing; and improving the effectiveness of advertising, collateral, publications through audience evaluation. Clients include top financial services, insurance, health care, technology and management services organizations. **Founded:** 1987. **Publications:** "Creating Strategic Leverage"; "Exploring Corporate Strategy"; "Competitive Advantage"; "Breakpoint and Beyond "; "Competitive Strategy ". **Seminars:** Best Practices in Brainstorming; Getting Results in the Real World; Finding the Leverage in Your Customer Strategy; The Role of Communications in Building Customer Loyalty; Building a Customer Centered Relationship and Making it Pay. **Special Services:** The Marketing Leverage Win/Loss Tracking System™.

40633 ■ Marketing Plus
10 Townview Ln.
Petaluma, CA 94952
Ph: (707)763-2162
Fax: (707)765-2162
Contact: Thomas S. Drew, Owner
E-mail: tomdrewmgb@aol.com
Scope: Provider of marketing and management consulting for small to medium sized businesses. The firm's services include market determination and goal setting, development of marketing plans and strategies, and sales training and management. A focus of the consultant's expertise is the management of concurrent growth. Industries served: predominately service industries. **Founded:** 1989. **Seminars:** Goal Setting; Niche Marketing; 10 Most Frequent Marketing Mistakes; Hiring Winners.

40634 ■ Marketing Resource Group
31 Valley Forge Way
Foxboro, MA 02035
Ph: (508)543-8452
Fax: (508)842-7252
Contact: Candace la Chapelle, Vice President
E-mail: candacemrg@aol.com
Scope: Customized sales skills and field training systems for sales people, sales managers, executives and non-selling staff. Curriculum can be developed and branded for in-house program to be used with future trainees and new hires. Offers prescreening of sales candidates and strategic consulting. **Founded:** 1995. **Seminars:** Basic Sales Skills; Consultative Selling; Relationship Selling; Networking to Maximize Your Business; Six Critical Steps for Every Sales Call; Selling Skills for the Non-Sales Professional; Effective Sales Management; Maximizing Revenue.

40635 ■ A. Marks & Associates (AMA)—Marketing Implementation Services Inc.
436 W Frontage Rd., Ste. 2D
Northfield, IL 60093
Ph: (847)784-9950
Fax: (847)784-9975
Co. E-mail: info@grow-business.com
Contact: Michael N. Bernberg, President
E-mail: mbernberg@grow-business.com
Scope: Provides marketing, sales and customer service expertise to small and medium size manufacturing, distribution and service businesses wishing to reach their full growth potential. Assists ISO and QS certified companies in measuring customer satisfaction. Develops lower cost marketing and sales strategic alternatives for companies wishing to improve their marketing productivity. **Founded:** 1981.

40636 ■ Maximum Response Marketing
PO Box 505, Sta. Central
Halifax, NS, Canada B3J 2R7
Ph: (902)444-9457
Fax: (902)444-9457
Co. E-mail: maxresponse@hotmail.com
Contact: Charles Salmon, President
E-mail: maxresponse@hotmail.com
Scope: Specialists in designing effective, results-driven, direct marketing programs that generate inquiries, orders or donations for business, consumer and not-for-profit. Services include campaign planning and implementation; project management; creative direction and package design; direct mail copywriting and copy editing; database analysis and segmentation; mailing list procurement and evaluation; developing privacy policies; print procurement and supplier liaison; email marketing strategy, copy and list; telemarketing, scripting and training. **Founded:** 1991. **Seminars:** Direct Mail Fundraising Communications and Fundraising, Mount Saint Vincent University, 2004; Federal Privacy Legislation, Atlantic Regional Meeting, United Way of Canada, 2003; DM Campaign Basics, United Way of Canada National Conference, 2002; Bayers Lake Business Seminar Service, 2002; Using DM to Group Your Business, Atlantic Regional Meeting, United Way of Canada, 2002; Tips, Tools and Techniques: DM Fundraising 101, Atlantic Philanthropy Conference, 1999; Direct Marketing Tips Tools and Techniques and A Strategic Approach to Direct Mail Creative, Dalhousie University; How to Use Direct Marketing to Build Your Business in the Export Marketplace, ACOA (Atlantic Canada Opportunities Agency)-Trade Outreach Sessions; How to Cultivate Your Customers Using Direct Marketing Tools, NS Dept. of Agriculture-Bi-Annual Conference.

40637 ■ Scott McGarvey Associates
345 N Canal St., Ste. 905
Chicago, IL 60606-1360
Ph: (312)648-6275
Contact: Scott McGarvey, President
E-mail: smcg@gsbalum.uchicago.edu
Scope: Builds marketing knowledge based encompassing market assessment, customer needs analysis, business environment, competitive vulnerabilities, and industry benchmarking. Defines marketing strategies and customer value proposition to enable clients to reach the customers that are most profitable for their business. Enables a more efficient sales pipeline with powerful suspecting or prospecting tools. Designs, tests and refines marketing approaches that integrate direct marketing, advertising, electronic marketing, and telephone canvassing. **Founded:** 1992. **Seminars:** How to Successfully Market Your Consulting Services; The Customer Value Proposition: How to Create a Marketing Theme that Distinguishes Your Enterprise from Competition Improving customer satisfaction, loyalty and retention; How to Build a Direct Channel while keeping the Peace with Intermediaries.

40638 ■ Medical Imaging Consultants Inc. (MIC)
1037 US Highway 46, Ste. G-2
Clifton, NJ 07013-2445
Ph: (973)574-8000
Free: 800-589-5685
Fax: (973)574-8001
Co. E-mail: info@micinfo.com
URL: http://www.micinfo.com
Contact: Dr. Philip A. Femano, President
E-mail: phil@micinfo.com
Scope: Provider of professional support services for radiology management and comprehensive continuing education programs for radiologic technologists. Management services include resource-critical database logistics; customer registration in educational programs; educational program development and Category A accreditation; national agency notification (e.g., ASRT, SNM-TS) of CE credits earned; meeting planning; manpower assessment; market research; expert witness; think-tank probes and executive summaries of industry issues. **Founded:** 1991. **Seminars:** Sectional Anatomy and Imaging Strategies; CT Cross-Trainer; CT Registry Review Program; MR Cross Trainer; MRI Registry Review Program; Digital Mammography Essentials for Technologists; Radiology Trends for Technologists.

40639 ■ Mefford, Knutson & Associates Inc. (MK)
6437 Lyndale Ave. S, Ste. 103
Richfield, MN 55423-1465
Ph: (612)869-8011
Free: 800-831-0228
Fax: (612)869-8004
Co. E-mail: info@mkaonline.net
URL: http://www.mkaonline.net
Contact: Jeanette Mefford, Director
E-mail: jmefford@mkaonline.com
Scope: A consulting and licensed business brokerage firm specializing in start-up businesses; strategic planning; mergers and acquisitions; joint ventures; divestitures; business process re-engineering; personnel policies and procedures; market research; new product development and cost controls. **Founded:** 1990.

40640 ■ James J. Prihoda & Associates
400 Island Way, Ste. 707
Clearwater Beach, FL 33767
Ph: (727)446-4082
Contact: James J. Prihoda, President
Scope: Specializes in marketing and sales.

40641 ■ Douglas F. Roberts
555 Kirkland Way, Ste. 304
Kirkland, WA 98033
Ph: (425)822-9718
Fax: (425)827-4473
Contact: Kathleen A. Roberts, Partner
Scope: Using a proactive approach to strategic planning, customer focus, effective sales and marketing plans, and technical training, the firm develops custom programs, providing a foundation for continued business success in the medical device industry. **Founded:** 1993. **Publications:** "Effective Respiratory Specimen Collections," On-Air Productions, 1995. **Seminars:** Proactive Marketing in a Managed Care Environment.

40642 ■ Gary Ruben Inc., Marketing Communications Consultants
931 E 86th St., Ste. 206
Indianapolis, IN 46240-1860
Ph: (317)251-5330
Contact: Gary A. Ruben, President
Scope: A communications and marketing consulting firm whose services include: advertising agency selection, advertising agency performance review, advertising program structuring, creative assistance, advertising program measurement, public relations program structuring, advertising department personnel development, in house agency structuring, and executive counseling. Industries served include supermarket chains, franchise systems, and retail products and services. **Founded:** 1976.

40643 ■ Sales Systems Specialists
3051 N Course Dr., Ste. 401
Pompano Beach, FL 33069-3347
Ph: (954)978-6665
Contact: William Wexler, President
Scope: Provider of advertising, marketing research, marketing and sales strategies for technical firms. Industries served: manufacturers of technical products. **Founded:** 1967.

40644 ■ The Sanderson Group Inc.
515 E 85 St., Ste. 4E
New York, NY 10028
Ph: (212)249-2556
Fax: (212)249-2557
URL: http://www.thesandersongroup.com
Contact: Robin Sanderson, President
E-mail: robin@thesandersongroup.com
Scope: Offers marketing consulting; communications and event/promotion marketing; develops objectives, establishes strategies and tactics to capitalize on the opportunities, and executes programs. Services provided include: strategic and marketing planning, target marketing with expertise in college or teen markets, integrated marketing programs, sampling, event marketing, new product development, corporate communications, strategic alliance formation, website strategic partnerships, website development and marketing, new business development, market research, sales and field force creation and management and customer acquisition. **Founded:** 1998.

40645 ■ SCG Promotions Ltd.—Saxton Communications Group Ltd.
124 E 40th St., Ste. 1102
New York, NY 10016-1723
Ph: (212)867-2210
Fax: (212)867-2539
Contact: Michael J. Enzer, President
Scope: Marketing promotion/communications and research consulting firm that offers a total service marketing program. Clients include consumer product and services with a database of over 4000 brands. Industries served: Food, beverage, health and beauty aids. **Founded:** 1993. **Seminars:** Strategic Trends in Sales Promotion; Selling-By-Seminar.

40646 ■ Shannon Staffing Inc.
636 Chestnut St.
Coshocton, OH 43812
Ph: (740)622-2600
Fax: (740)622-9638
Co. E-mail: coshocton@shannonstaffing.com
Contact: Edward A. Seitz, President
E-mail: eseitz@shannonstaffing.com
Scope: Serving broad range of industries and public sector organizations and foundations. Specializing in human resources recruiting and outplacement counseling on international scale for businesses of all sizes. Offers expertise in human resources policies and procedures, supervisor development, manager leadership style development, interview training, etc. Provides consulting to small business in human resources, advertising, marketing, sales, public relations and community relations. **Founded:** 1985. **Publications:** "Powells Rules for Picking People". **Seminars:** Time Management workshop.

40647 ■ Tom Shillock Consulting
5545 SW Windsor Ct.
Portland, OR 97221-2150
Ph: (503)291-7928
Fax: (503)221-2052
Co. E-mail: tomsh@qwest.net
Contact: Tom Shillock, Principal
E-mail: tomsh@qwest.net
Scope: Offers consulting services in marketing and communications including public relations and advertising. Industries served: high technology. **Founded:** 1988.

40648 ■ Harvey C. Skoog
7151 E Addis Ave.
Prescott Valley, AZ 86314
Ph: (928)772-1448
Scope: Firm has expertise in taxes, payroll, financial planning, budgeting, buy/sell planning, business start-up, fraud detection, troubled business consulting, acquisition, and marketing. Serves the manufacturing, construction, and retailing industries in Arizona. **Founded:** 1977.

40649 ■ Stratamar Inc.
5661 Seapine Rd.
Hilliard, OH 43026
Ph: (614)946-4614
Fax: (614)529-2945
Co. E-mail: info@stratamar.com
URL: http://www.stratamar.com
Contact: Nancy Brown, Owner
Scope: A full-spectrum strategic marketing consulting company. Areas of concentration include product development, product management, strategic planning, development and implementation of tactical marketing plans, and Internet marketing. The primary focus is upon maximizing the benefit, cost ratio of promotions through the use of direct marketing, low cost media, and the like. **Founded:** 1998. **Publications:** "Business Plans," Feb, 2006.

40650 ■ The Tactix Group
1619 N 102 St.
Omaha, NE 68114
Ph: (402)393-3800
Fax: (402)393-5151
Co. E-mail: info@thetactixgroup.com
URL: http://www.thetactixgroup.com
Contact: Douglas R. Little, President
E-mail: dlittle@tactixinc.com
Scope: Offers integrated marketing system design and implementation, for customer relationship management. Serves manufacturing, distributing, high-tech, banking, and executive benefit industries. **Founded:** 1987. **Special Services:** Saleslogix (Client Server) Sales Automation Software.

40651 ■ Ultimate Wealth Inc.
2533 N Carson St.
Carson City, NV 89706
Ph: (702)953-0264
Free: 800-541-3816
Fax: (702)932-8670
Co. E-mail: robert@ultimatewealth.com
URL: http://www.ultimatewealth.com
Contact: Robert Imbriale, President
E-mail: robert@ultimatewealth.com
Scope: Specializes in consulting and training services in the area of Internet marketing. Hosts regular seminars, teleclasses, and offers training products as well as full consulting services to businesses worldwide. **Founded:** 1999. **Publications:** "Motivational Marketing: How to Effectively Motivate Your Prospects"; "The New Rules of Marketing and PR"; "How to Create an Information Product in One Day or Less"; "No Money Down Marketing"; "The Astonishing Power of Emotions"; "Direct Mail Marketing Secrets"; "The Ultimate Marketing Plan: Find Your Hook. Communicate Your Message"; "Money, and the Law of Attraction: Learning to Attract Wealth, Health, and Happiness"; "Will Work for Fun: Three Simple Steps for Turning Any Hobby or Interest Into Cash". **Seminars:** How to Create Your Own Product in 1 Day, Apr, 2006; Motivational Wealth; Effortless Marketing in Action.

40652 ■ Viewtech Market Research & Analysis
2004 Glendora Dr.
District Heights, MD 20747
Ph: (301)350-1111
Fax: (301)350-1428
Contact: Annie B. Carter, Owner
Scope: Independent market or research firm offers management, administrative, and data processing support services. Additional services include: Conference planning, program evaluation, direct mailings, feasibility studies, advertising specialties, and workshops and seminars. Also conducts in-store and in-school testing. Industries served: retail trade, transportation operations, and management, as well as government agencies. **Founded:** 1984. **Publications:** "The Marketing Guide for the Non-Marketing Manager". **Seminars:** The Art of Marketing; Building on New Opportunities; Surviving and Training As Entrepreneurs in the 21st Century; Imagination, Courage and Integrity in Marketing Research; Marketing & Selling Your Day Care Center; New 2003 Venture.

40653 ■ Westlife Consultants & Counsellors
95 October Ln.
Aurora, ON, Canada L4G 7A1
Ph: (905)867-0686
Fax: (416)799-5242
Co. E-mail: westlifeconsultant@hotmail.com
URL: http://www.westlifeconsultants.com
Contact: Dr. Syed N. Hussain, President
E-mail: westlifeconsultant@hotmail.com
Scope: Provider of entrepreneurs and businesses with a highly commercial and global perspectives on the international business development ideas under consideration. **Founded:** 1990. **Publications:** "Innovative Management"; "Team Building and Leadership"; "Financial Planning"; "Estate Planning"; "Risk Management"; "Export/Import Trade Finance Mechanics"; "Marketing and Sales Management"; "What Your Banker Needs to Know"; "Building A Successful Financial Plan".

40654 ■ William Blades L.L.C.
101 North Regulator Dr.
Cambridge, MD 21613

Ph: (443)477-0061
Co. E-mail: wblades@aol.com
URL: http://www.williamblades.com
Contact: William H. Blades, President
E-mail: wblades@aol.com
Scope: A business consulting firm with expertise in marketing and sales. Presents seminars, workshops and keynotes on the following topics: re-energizing the organization; professional selling and marketing; corporate culture; proactive leadership; world-class customer service; creativity; great teamwork. **Founded:** 1988. **Publications:** "Selling-The Mother of All Enterprise"; "Leadership Defined"; "Why Do We Make Change So Hard"; "10 Crucial Steps for Sales Management Success"; "In Sales, it's all About Accountability"; "Conversations Of Success"; "Celebrate Selling"; "Vision: Help Your Mind"; "Leadership Defined"; "Managing to Improve: 10 Areas of Emphasis for Workplace Leaders"; "Creativity: Let the Juices Flow in the Workplace"; "Get Bill Blades Philosophy on Boot Camps"; "Great Leadership Grows From a Mixed Bag"; "Self Improvement - The Million Dollar Equation". **Seminars:** Sales Leadership Culture Creativity; Sales and Management; Coaching for Executives and Sales Managers; Sales and Marketing Action Plans.

40655 ■ The Women's Global Business Alliance L.L.C. (WGBA)
501 Westport Ave., Ste. 205
Norwalk, CT 06851-4411
Ph: (203)938-7475
Fax: (203)286-1112
Co. E-mail: administration@wgba-business.com
Contact: Dr. Claire Gaudiani, Director
Scope: Provider of information regarding advanced information to impact business operations. Builds high-level business connections and alliances among senior-executive corporate women worldwide to improve the performance of the companies they lead. Direct and personal dialogues with influential business and world leaders. Access to resources, experts and insights to promote direct, positive and responsible impact on the bottom-line. **Special Services:** Peer Counsel™.

40656 ■ Alan J. Zell
PO Box 69
Portland, OR 97207-0069
Ph: (503)241-1988
Fax: (503)241-1989
Co. E-mail: azell@aol.com
URL: http://www.sellingselling.com
Contact: Alan J. Zell, Owner
E-mail: azell@aol.com
Scope: An advisory service for those who sell their services, products or their organization's ideas, information, and skills through face-to-face and telephone conversations, printed materials, the media, electronic communications, schools, guilds, trade shows, and display presentations. Industries served: minority and woman-owned businesses; government and education; medicine, law, accounting, technology, manufacturers, distributors, and retailers; professional and trade associations; and nonprofit organizations. **Founded:** 1983. **Publications:** "Elements of Selling"; "An Unconventional Look at the Complex Subject of Selling"; "The Art Of Selling Art"; "Selling Situations"; "What Customers need to know"; "Turnover & Return on Investment"; "The Ultimate Business Oxymoron"; "Walkin The Aisles, Looking at the Booths, etc"; "Four Uses Of Internet". **Seminars:** Ambassador Of Selling; An Unconventional Look at the Complex Subject of Selling; Selling Change . . . Pain or Progress, Revolution or Evolution?; Giving GOOD SERVICE When Giving Good Service Is Not Good Enough; Two Sides Of A Trade Show; Selling For People Who Do Not Like To Sell; The Art Of Selling Art; Yes, Technically Trained People Can Learn To Sell; Beginning Business, How To Achieve Your Goals. **Telecommunication Services:** alan@sellingselling.com.

40657 ■ Zogby International
901 Broad St.
Utica, NY 13501
Ph: (315)624-0200
Free: 877-462-7655
Fax: (315)624-0210
Co. E-mail: marketing@zogby.com
URL: http://www.zogby.com
Contact: John Zogby, President
E-mail: john@zogby.com
Scope: Specializes in providing market research and analysis services. **Founded:** 1984. **Publications:** "Just who are you calling anyway"; "All of this leads to a very basic question". **Seminars:** The Research Authority, Oct, 2006; Christian Science Monitor Break fast, Oct, 2006.

FRANCHISES AND BUSINESS OPPORTUNITIES

40658 ■ America's Choice/Canada's Choice
America's Choice International
20 Northpointe Pky., Ste. 180
Buffalo, NY 14228
Ph: (716)691-0596
Free: 800-831-2493
Fax: (716)691-0650
Description: Flat fee real estate marketing service. **No. of Franchise Units:** 77. **Founded:** 1992.. **Franchised:** 1994. **Equity Capital Needed:** $9,900-$29,200, including franchise fee. **Franchise Fee:** $7,000-$16,000. **Training:** Yes.

40659 ■ Homes 4Sale By Owner Network
5761 Eagle Trace Dr.
Sylvania, OH 43560
Ph: (619)328-5988
Free: 877-615-5177
Fax: (619)749-3922
Description: Full service real estate marketing. **No. of Franchise Units:** 3. **No. of Company-Owned Units:** 1. **Founded:** 2002.. **Franchised:** 2006. **Equity Capital Needed:** $25,000-$35,000. **Franchise Fee:** $19,500. **Training:** Yes.

COMPUTERIZED DATABASES

40660 ■ *BtoB*
1155 Gratiot Ave.
Detroit, MI 48207
Ph: (313)446-6000
Free: 800-678-2427
Fax: (313)446-1616
Co. E-mail: info@crain.com
URL: http://www.crain.com
Availability: Online: Crain Communications Inc. **Type:** Full-text.

LIBRARIES

40661 ■ Boston Public Library - Kirstein Business Branch
700 Boylston St.
Boston, MA 02116
Ph: (617)859-2142
Co. E-mail: ask@bpl.org
URL: http://www.bpl.org/kbl
Contact: Laura Pattison, Librarian
Scope: Business administration, retailing, advertising, finance, marketing, real estate, insurance, banking, taxation, accounting, investments, economics, business law, small business. **Services:** Copying is available through the library's interlibrary loan department; reference faxing up to three pages. **Founded:** 1930. **Holdings:** Moody's Manuals (1935 to present in print; 1909-1997 in microfiche); Commercial and Financial Chronicle, 1957-1987; Bank and Quotation Record, 1928-1987; Standard and Poor's Daily Stock Price Record: New York and American Stock Exchanges, 1962 to present; over-the-counter stocks, 1968 to present; domestic and foreign trade directories; city directories; telephone directories for New England and U.S. cities with populations over 100,000 for New England cities and towns; Standard Stock Market Service, 1921-1922; Standard Stock Offerings, 1925-1939; National Stock Summary, 1927 to present; Standard & Poor's Stock Guide, 1943 to present; New York and American Stock Exchange companies Annual and 10K reports on microfiche (1987-1996); Wall Street Journal on microfilm (latest 10 years); Wall Street Transcript on microfilm (latest 5 years); D-U-N-S Business Identification Service (November 1973 -1995). **Subscriptions:** 700 journals and other serials; 13 newspapers. **Telecommunication Services:** kirstein@bpl.org.

40662 ■ Carnegie Library of Pittsburgh - Downtown & Business
612 Smithfield St.
Pittsburgh, PA 15222-2506
Ph: (412)281-7141
Fax: (412)471-1724
Co. E-mail: downtown@carnegielibrary.org
URL: http://www.carnegielibrary.org/locations/downtown
Contact: Karen Rossi, Department Head
Scope: Investments, small business, entrepreneurship, management, marketing, insurance, advertising, personal finance, accounting, real estate, job and career, International business. **Services:** Library open to the public. **Founded:** 1924. **Holdings:** 13,000 business volumes; VF materials; microfilm; looseleaf services; AV materials.

40663 ■ Chicago Public Library Central Library - Business/Science/Technology Division
Harold Washington Library Center
400 S. State St., 4th Fl.
Chicago, IL 60605
Ph: (312)747-4450
Fax: (312)747-4975
URL: http://www.chipublib.org/branch/details/library/harold-washington/p/Bst
Scope: Small business, marketing, technology, corporate reports, investments, management, personnel, patents, physical and biological sciences, medicine, health, computer science, careers, environmental information, gardening, cookbooks. **Services:** Interlibrary loan; copying; division open to the public. **Founded:** 1977. **Holdings:** 415,000 books; 52,100 bound periodical volumes; 33,000 reels of microfilm; Securities and Exchange Commission (SEC) reports; federal specifications and standards; American National Standards Institute standards; corporate Annual reports. **Subscriptions:** 4000 journals and other serials; 8 newspapers.

40664 ■ Newfoundland and Labrador Business Service Centre
West Block, Confederation Bldg.
St. John's, NL, Canada A1B 4J6
Ph: (709)729-7000
Fax: (709)729-0654
Co. E-mail: mike.howley@acoa-apeca.gc.ca
URL: http://www.intrd.gov.nl.ca/intrd/department/branches/sibd/cnlbsc.html
Contact: Mike Howley, Manager
Scope: Marketing, small business, economic and regional development. **Services:** Copying; SDI; centre open to the public. **Founded:** 1973. **Holdings:** 10,000 books; 20 VF drawers of subject files; Standard Industrial Classification (SIC) files. **Subscriptions:** 300 journals and other serials.

40665 ■ Philip Morris Corporate Library
100 Park Ave., 17th Fl.
New York, NY 10017
Ph: (917)663-3863
Fax: (917)663-5317
Co. E-mail: david.deschenes@us.pm.com
Contact: David Deschenes, Director
Scope: Business, marketing, finance, tobacco. **Services:** Library not open to the public. **Holdings:** 2000 books; microfiche; tobacco trade literature. **Subscriptions:** 160 journals and other serials; 20 newspapers.

40666 ■ University of Kentucky - Business & Economics Information Center
B&E Info. Ctr., Rm. 116
335-BA Gatton College of Business & Economics
Lexington, KY 40506-0034
Ph: (859)257-8936
Fax: (859)257-1333
Co. E-mail: mrazeeq@pop.uk.edu
URL: http://www.uky.edu//Provost/academicprograms.html
Contact: Michael A. Razeeq, Librarian, Business
URL(s): gatton.uky.edu/. **Scope:** Business, economics, business management, marketing, finance, accounting. **Services:** Library open to the public for

reference use only. **Founded:** 1993. **Telecommunication Services:** cber@uky.edu; klimar@pop.uky.edu; provost@email.uky.edu.

RESEARCH CENTERS

40667 ■ Cleveland Public Library - Cleveland Research Center (CRC)
325 Superior Ave.
Cleveland, OH 44114-1271
Ph: (216)623-2999
Fax: (216)623-6987
Co. E-mail: crc@cpl.org
URL: http://www.cpl.org/?q=node/11
Contact: Aaron Mason, Manager
Founded: 1987.

40668 ■ Marketing Research Association (MRA)
110 National Dr.
Glastonbury, CT 06033
Ph: (860)682-1000
Fax: (860)682-1050
Co. E-mail: david.almy@marketingresearch.org
URL: http://www.marketingresearch.org
Contact: David Almy, Chief Executive Officer
Founded: 1957. **Publications:** *Alert! magazine* (Monthly); *Blue Book Research Services Directory* (Annual); *MRA Update e-newsletter* (Biweekly). **Educational Activities:** MRA Conferences (3/year); Web Seminars (Biweekly). **Awards:** Betsy J. Peterson Award (Annual), enrollment funding given to individuals currently in the survey and opinion research profession or those interested in pursuing a career in this profession. **Telecommunication Services:** e-mail@marketingresearch.org.

40669 ■ Northwestern University - Center for Retail Management
Kellogg School of Management
2001 Sheridan Rd.
Evanston, IL 60208
Ph: (847)467-3600
Fax: (847)467-3620
Co. E-mail: r-blattberg@kellogg.northwestern.edu
URL: http://www.kellogg.northwestern.edu/research/retail/
Contact: Prof. Robert C. Blattberg, Executive Director
Founded: 1993.

40670 ■ Wayne State College - Nebraska Business Development Center (NBDC)
Gardner Hall 101
1111 Main St.
Wayne, NE 68787
Ph: (402)375-7575
Fax: (402)375-7574
Co. E-mail: nbdc@wsc.edu
URL: http://www.wsc.edu/nbdc
Contact: Loren Kucera, Director
Services: Consulting. **Founded:** 1977. **Publications:** *NBDC Brochure*; *NBDC Business Calendar* (Annual). **Educational Activities:** Continuing education program. **Telecommunication Services:** lokucer1@wsc.edu.

Minority-Owned Business

START-UP INFORMATION

40671 ■ *Advancing Research on Minority Entrepreneurship*
Pub: SAGE Publications USA
Contact: Blaise R. Simqu, President
Ed: James H. Johnson Jr.; Timothy Bates; William E. Jackson III; James H. Johnson; William E. Jackson. **Released:** September 2007. **Price:** $34.00. **Description:** Although minorities are more likely to engage in start-up businesses than others, minority entrepreneurs are less likely to get their enterprises off the ground or succeed in growing their businesses. The higher failure rates, lower sales and profits and less employment are among topics discussed.

40672 ■ *The Complete Startup Guide for the Black Entrepreneur*
Pub: Career Press
Ed: Bill Bourdreaux. **Price:** $15.99.

40673 ■ *"The Next Generation: African Americans Are Successfully Launching Businesses Earlier In Life" in Black Enterprise (January 2008)*
Pub: Earl G. Graves Publishing Co. Inc.
Ed: Tennille M. Robinson. **Description:** According to a survey conducted by OPEN, a team dedicated small business at American Express, Generation Y individuals are three times more likely to start their own company. Three African American individuals who did just that are profiled.

40674 ■ *"Savvy Solutions" in Black Enterprise (Vol. 40, July 2010, No. 12, pp. 44)*
Pub: Earl G. Graves Publishing Co. Inc.
Ed: Tennille M. Robinson. **Description:** Advice is offered to an African American interested in starting a franchise operation.

ASSOCIATIONS AND OTHER ORGANIZATIONS

40675 ■ American Islamic Chamber of Commerce (AICC)
PO Box 93033
Albuquerque, NM 87199-3033
Co. E-mail: islam@americanislam.org
URL: http://americanislam.org
Description: Individuals and organizations. Seeks to advance the interests of Islamic-owned businesses in the United States. Conducts business education programs; provides technical and management assistance to Islamic-owned businesses.

40676 ■ Asian Women in Business (AWIB)
42 Broadway, Ste. 1748
New York, NY 10004
Ph: (212)868-1368
Fax: (212)868-1373
Co. E-mail: info@awib.org
URL: http://www.awib.org
Contact: Bonnie Wong, President
Description: Asian-American women in business. Seeks to enable Asian-American women to achieve their entrepreneurial potential. Serves as a clearinghouse on issues affecting small business owners; provides technical assistance and other support to members; sponsors business and entrepreneurial education courses. **Scope:** women, business, Asian American. **Founded:** 1995. **Awards:** Entrepreneurial Leadership Award (Annual).

40677 ■ Caribbean American Chamber of Commerce and Industry (CACCI)
63 Flushing Ave.
Brooklyn Navy Yard, Bldg. No. 5, Unit 239
Brooklyn, NY 11205
Ph: (718)834-4544
Fax: (718)834-9774
Co. E-mail: info@caccitradecenter.com
URL: http://www.caribbeantradecenter.com
Contact: Roy A. Hastick, Sr., President
Description: Promotes economic development among Caribbean American, African American, Hispanic and other minority entrepreneurs. **Founded:** 1985. **Educational Activities:** Caribbean American Chamber of Commerce and Industry Roundtable.

40678 ■ Center for Economic Options (CEO)
910 Quarrier St., Ste. 206
Charleston, WV 25301
Ph: (304)345-1298
Fax: (304)342-0641
Co. E-mail: info@economicoptions.org
URL: http://www.centerforeconomicoptions.org
Contact: Pam Curry, Executive Director
Description: Seeks to improve the economic position and quality of life for women, especially low-income and minority women. Works to provide access to job training and employment options to women. Supports self-employed women and small business owners by offering training and technical assistance and information. Advocates women's legal right to employment, training, education, and credit. Seeks to inform the public on economic issues related to women; while activities are conducted on local and state levels, group cooperates with national and international organizations on issues relating to employment and economic justice for women. Maintains speakers' bureau and library. Compiles statistics; conducts research. **Founded:** 1979. **Publications:** *Women and Employment News*.

40679 ■ Cuban American National Council (CNC)
1223 SW 4th St.
Miami, FL 33135
Ph: (305)642-3484
Fax: (305)642-9122
Co. E-mail: gmd@cnc.org
URL: http://www.cnc.org
Contact: Guarione M. Diaz, President
Description: Aims to identify the socioeconomic needs of the Cuban population in the U.S. and to promote needed human services. Services the needy through research and human services while advocating on behalf of Hispanics and other minority groups. **Founded:** 1972. **Publications:** *The Council Letter* (Quarterly); *Ethnic Segregation in Greater Miami: 1980-1990*; *Freedom of Speech in Miami*. **Educational Activities:** Cuban American National Council Conference (Biennial).

40680 ■ Disabled Businesspersons Association (DBA)
San Diego State University - Interwork Institute
3590 Camino del Rio N
San Diego, CA 92108
Ph: (619)594-8805
Fax: (619)594-4208
Co. E-mail: info@disabledbusiness.com
URL: http://disabledbusiness.org
Contact: Mr. Urban Miyares, President
Description: Assists active and enterprising individuals with disabilities maximize their rehabilitation and potential in the workplace and business, and work with vocational rehabilitation, government, education and business. Encourages the participation and enhances the performance of the disabled in the work force. Membership is not a prerequisite for services or assistance. **Founded:** 1985. **Publications:** *Challenged America Newsletter* (Quarterly); *DBA Advisor* (Quarterly).

40681 ■ Diversity Information Resources (DIR)
2105 Central Ave. NE
Minneapolis, MN 55418
Ph: (612)781-6819
Fax: (612)781-0109
Co. E-mail: info@diversityinforesources.com
URL: http://www.diversityinforesources.com
Contact: Leslie Bonds, Executive Director
E-mail: lbonds@diversityinforesources.com
Description: Promotes businesses with minority, women, veteran, service-disabled veteran and HUBZone ownership. Compiles and publishes minority and women-owned business directories to acquaint major corporations and government purchasing agents with the products and services of minority and women-owned firms. Sponsors national supplier diversity seminars. **Founded:** 1968. **Publications:** *Purchasing People in Major Corporations* (Annual); *Supplier Diversity Information Resource Guide* (Annual); *Supplier Diversity Information Resource Guide: Complete Guide to Public and Private Sector M/WBE Business Resources* (Annual); *TRY US National Women-Owned Business Directory*; *Guide to Obtaining Minority Business Directories*; *National Minority and Women-Owned Business Directory* (Annual).

40682 ■ Latin Business Association (LBA)
120 S San Pedro St., Ste. 530
Los Angeles, CA 90012
Ph: (213)628-8510
Fax: (213)628-8519
Co. E-mail: membership@lbausa.com
URL: http://www.lbausa.com
Contact: Ruben Guerra, Chief Executive Officer
Description: Latino business owners and corporations. Assists Latino business owners to develop their businesses. **Scope:** business, management, leadership. **Founded:** 1976. **Subscriptions:** 250 books. **Publications:** *Latin Business Association Business*

Journal (Monthly); *Latin Business Association Business Newsletter* (Monthly). **Awards:** Scholarship of Latino Business Owners; SOL Business Awards (Annual).

40683 ■ Milton S. Eisenhower Foundation
1875 Connecticut Ave. NW, Ste. 410
Washington, DC 20009
Ph: (202)234-8104
Fax: (202)234-8484
Co. E-mail: info@eisenhowerfoundation.org
URL: http://www.eisenhowerfoundation.org
Contact: Charles P. Austin, Sr., Chairman
Description: Dedicated to youth investment and economic development in the inner city by reducing the school dropout rate, crime, welfare dependency, drug abuse, unemployment, and family instability. Works as a "mediating institution" to finance, technically assist, and evaluate minority nonprofit organizations. Assists more than 30 local programs based on the themes of: organizing neighborhoods; early intervention for at-risk youth; creating extended families; facilitating employment and remedial education. Also integrates community-oriented policing to assist minority nonprofit-led ventures. Operates international exchanges with Eastern Europe, France, Great Britain, Japan, and other countries. Founded as the private sector continuation of the National Violence Commission and the Kenner Riot Commission, established by former President Johnson. **Founded:** 1981. **Publications:** *Patriotism, Democracy, and Common Sense: Restoring America's Promise at Home and Abroad.*

40684 ■ National Association of Hispanic Publications (NAHP)
529 14th St. NW, Ste. 1126
Washington, DC 20045
Ph: (202)662-7250
Co. E-mail: mgomez@nahp.org
URL: http://www.nahp.org
Contact: Amy Hinojosa, Executive Director
Description: Newspapers, magazines, and other periodicals published in Spanish (or bilingually in English and Spanish) in the United States. Promotes adherence to high standards of ethical and professional standards by members; advocates continuing professional development of Hispanic journalists and publishers. Provides technical assistance to members in areas including writing and editing skills, circulation and distribution methods, attracting advertisers, obtaining financing, design and layout, and graphic arts. Conducts public service programs including voter registration drives. **Scope:** Hispanic scholarship. **Founded:** 1982. **Subscriptions:** books. **Publications:** *The Hispanic Press* (Quarterly). **Educational Activities:** National Association of Hispanic Publications Convention (Annual). **Awards:** Amigo Awards (Annual); Corporate Recognition Awards (Annual); Hispanic Print Awards (Annual).

40685 ■ National Association of Investment Companies (NAIC)
1300 Pennsylvania Ave. NW, Ste. 700
Washington, DC 20004
Ph: (202)289-4336
Fax: (202)289-4329
Co. E-mail: info@naicpe.com
URL: http://www.naicvc.com
Contact: Ed Dandridge, President
Description: Aims to: represent the minority small business investment company industry in the public sector; provide industry education and develop research material on the activities of the industry. Collects and disseminates relevant business and trade information to members; facilitates the exchange of new ideas and financing strategies; assists organizing groups attempting to form or acquire minority enterprise small business investment companies; provide management and technical assistance to members. **Founded:** 1971. **Publications:** *NAIC Membership Directory* (Annual); *National Association of Investment Companies--Membership Directory* (Annual). **Telecommunication Services:** admin@naicvc.com.

40686 ■ National Association of Minority Automobile Dealers (NAMAD)
9475 Lottsford Rd., Ste. 150
Largo, MD 20774
Ph: (301)306-1614
Fax: (301)306-1493
Co. E-mail: damon.lester@namad.org
URL: http://www.namad.org
Contact: Damon Lester, President
Description: Automobile dealers. Acts as liaison between membership, the federal government, the community, and industry representatives; seeks to better the business conditions of its members on an ongoing basis. Serves as a confidential spokesperson for dealers. Offers business analysis, financial counseling, and short- and long-term management planning. Conducts research programs; compiles statistics. **Founded:** 1980. **Publications:** *NAMAD Newsletter.*

40687 ■ National Black MBA Association (NBMBAA)
180 N Michigan Ave., Ste. 1400
Chicago, IL 60601
Ph: (312)236-2622
Fax: (312)236-0390
Co. E-mail: mail@nbmbaa.org
URL: http://www.nbmbaa.org
Contact: William Wells, Jr., Chairman of the Board
Description: Creates educational opportunities to form professional and economic growth of African-Americans. Develops partnerships to its members and provides educational programs to increase the awareness on business field. **Founded:** 1970. **Publications:** *Black MBA* (Quarterly); *National Black MBA Association--Newsletter* (Monthly); *NBMBAA Program Book* (Annual). **Educational Activities:** National Black Masters of Business Administration Annual Conference and Exposition (Annual). **Awards:** NBMBAA Graduate Scholarships Program; NBMBAA PhD Fellowship Program.

40688 ■ National Hispanic Corporate Council (NHCC)
1050 Connecticut Ave. NW, Fl. 10
Washington, DC 20036-5334
Ph: (202)772-1100
Fax: (202)772-3101
Co. E-mail: pmartinez@nhcchq.org
URL: http://www.nhcchq.org
Contact: Pat Martinez, President
Description: Corporate think tank serving Fortune 1000 companies and their representatives as a principal resource for information, expertise and counsel about Hispanic issues affecting corporate objectives, and to advocate for increased employment, leadership and business opportunities for Hispanics in corporate America. **Scope:** Hispanic market, language, household trends, corporate America, consumer trends. **Founded:** 1985. **Publications:** *NHCC News* (Quarterly). **Educational Activities:** National Hispanic Corporate Council Conference.

40689 ■ National Minority Business Council (NMBC)
120 Broadway, 19th Fl.
New York, NY 10271
Ph: (212)693-5050
Fax: (212)693-5048
Co. E-mail: info@nmbc.org
URL: http://www.nmbc.org
Contact: John F. Robinson, President
Description: Represents minority businesses in all areas of industry and commerce. Seeks to increase profitability by developing marketing, sales, and management skills in minority businesses. Acts as an informational source for the national minority business community. Includes programs such as: legal services plan that provides free legal services to members in such areas as sales contracts, copyrights, estate planning, and investment agreement; business referral service that develops potential customer leads; international trade assistance program that provides technical assistance in developing foreign markets; executive banking program that teaches members how to package a business loan for bank approval; procurement outreach program for minority and women business owners. Conducts continuing management education and provides assistance in teaching youth the free enterprise system. **Founded:** 1972. **Publications:** *Corporate Minority Vendor Directory* (Annual); *Corporate Purchasing Directory* (Annual); *NMBC Business Report* (Biennial). **Awards:** Luncheon Award (Annual).

40690 ■ National Minority Supplier Development Council (NMSDC)
1359 Broadway, 10th Fl.
New York, NY 10018
Ph: (212)944-2430
Fax: (212)719-9611
Co. E-mail: info@nmsdc.org
URL: http://www.nmsdc.org
Contact: Joset B. Wright, President
URL(s): www.nmsdc.org/nmsdc/. **Description:** Provides a direct link between its 3,500 corporate members and minority-owned businesses (Black, Hispanic, Asian and Native American) and increases procurement and business opportunities for minority businesses of all sizes. **Scope:** business. **Founded:** 1972. **Holdings:** MBISYS is held in computer-readable form and contains data on approximately 15,000 minority suppliers. The MBIC contains periodicals, newspapers, government documents, and general reference sources. **Publications:** *Minority Supplier News* (Quarterly); *National Minority Supplier Development Council--Annual Report* (Annual); *Minority Business Information Center.* **Educational Activities:** Conference and Business Opportunity Fair (Annual); Business Opportunity Fair (Annual). **Awards:** Corporation of the Year (Annual). **Telecommunication Services:** nmsdc1@aol.com.

40691 ■ National Society of Hispanic MBAs (NSHMBA)
450 E John Carpenter Freeway, Ste. 200
Irving, TX 75062
Ph: (214)596-9338
Free: 877-467-4622
Fax: (214)596-9325
URL: http://www.nshmba.org
Contact: Manny Gonzalez, Chief Executive Officer
Description: Hispanic MBA professional business network dedicated to economic and philanthropic advancement. **Founded:** 1988. **Educational Activities:** National Society of Hispanic MBAs Conference (Annual). **Awards:** NSHMBA Scholarships; Brillante Award (Annual).

40692 ■ United States Hispanic Chamber of Commerce (USHCC)
1424 K St. NW, Ste. 401
Washington, DC 20005
Ph: (202)842-1212
Free: 800-USH-CC86
Fax: (202)842-3221
Co. E-mail: palomarez@ushcc.com
URL: http://www.ushcc.com
Contact: Javier Palomarez, President
Description: Hispanic and other business firms interested in the development of Hispanic business and promotion of business leadership and economic interests in the Hispanic community. Promotes a positive image of Hispanics and encourages corporate involvement with Hispanic firms. Conducts business-related workshops, conferences, and management training; reports on business achievements and vendor programs of major corporations; compiles statistics. **Founded:** 1979. **Educational Activities:** U.S. Hispanic Chamber of Commerce Annual National Convention (Annual). **Awards:** Corporate Advisor of the Year (Annual); Large and Small Chamber of the Year (Annual). **Telecommunication Services:** membership@ushcc.com.

REFERENCE WORKS

40693 ■ "$3.5 Million Lawsuit Points Finger at Black Firm" in Black Enterprise (Vol. 38, March 2008, No. 8)
Pub: Earl G. Graves Publishing Co. Inc.
Ed: Cliff Hocker. **Description:** World Wide Technology, the world's largest black-owned company is being sued by a former employee for racial discrimination and retaliation. Details of the lawsuit are outlined.

40694 ■ *"The 100 Fastest-Growing Companies" in Hispanic Business (Vol. 30, July-August 2008, No. 7-8, pp. 22)*
Pub: Hispanic Business, Inc.
Ed: Michael Bowker. **Description:** CEO's of the five fastest growing Hispanic-owned companies discuss the success of their companies; most of them attribute their success to proper investment and diversification, effective innovations and seeing growth opportunities where others see roadblocks.

40695 ■ *"2008 Woman of the Year Gala" in Hispanic Business (Vol. 30, July-August 2008, No. 7-8, pp. 58)*
Pub: Hispanic Business, Inc.
Ed: Brynne Chappell. **Description:** Brief report on the sixth annual Women of the Year Awards gala which was held at JW Marriott Desert Ridge Resort and Spa is given; 20 women were honored with these awards for their professional contribution, commitment to the advancement of the Hispanic community and involvement with charitable organizations.

40696 ■ *"2009 Corporate Elite: Our Top 25 Executives" in Hispanic Business (January-February 2009, pp. 16, 18, 20, 22)*
Pub: Hispanic Business
Description: Profiles of Hispanic Business Media's 2009 Corporate Elite are presented.

40697 ■ *"Accelerator Welcomes First Hispanic Firms" in Business Courier (Vol. 27, August 13, 2010, No. 15, pp. 1)*
Pub: Business Courier
Ed: Lucy May. **Description:** The Minority Business Accelerator (MBA) initiative of the Cincinnati USA Regional Chamber in Ohio has included Hispanic-owned firms Best Upon Request and Vivian Llambi and Associates Inc. to its portfolio. Vivian Llambi and Associates is a design, landscape architecture and civil engineering specialist. Prior to these firms' membership, MBA was limited to black-owned companies.

40698 ■ *"Adapt or Die" in Black Enterprise (Vol. 38, July 2008, No. 12, pp. 27)*
Pub: Earl G. Graves Publishing Co. Inc.
Ed: Oguntoyinbo Lekan. **Description:** Turbulence in the domestic auto industry is hitting auto suppliers hard and black suppliers, the majority of whom contract with the Big Three, are just beginning to establish relationships with import car manufacturers. The more savvy CEOs are adopting new technologies in order to weather the downturn in the economy and in the industry as a whole.

40699 ■ *"AG Warns Slots MBE Plan Risky" in Boston Business Journal (Vol. 29, May 27, 2011, No. 3, pp. 1)*
Pub: American City Business Journals Inc.
Ed: Scott Dance. **Description:** Attorney General Doug Gansler states that the law extending the minority business program on slots parlors contracting through 2018 could be open to lawsuits. He recommended that the state should conduct a study proving that minority- and women-owned businesses do not get a fair share in the gaming industry before it signs the bill to avoid lawsuits from majority-owned firms.

40700 ■ *"The AHA Moment" in Hispanic Business (December 2010)*
Pub: Hispanic Business
Ed: Rebecca Vallaneda. **Description:** An interview with Gisela Girard on how competitive market conditions push buttons. Girard stepped down from her 18-month position as chairwoman the Association of Hispanic Advertising Agencies. She has more than 20 years of experience in advertising and research marketing.

40701 ■ *"Amid Recession, Companies Still Value Supplier Diversity Programs" in Hispanic Business (July-August 2009, pp. 34)*
Pub: Hispanic Business
Ed: Joshua Molina. **Description:** The decline of traditionally strong industries, from automotive manufacturing to construction, has shaken today's economy and has forced small businesses, especially suppliers and minority-owned firms, turn to diversity programs in order to make changes.

40702 ■ *"As Technology Changes, So Must African American Business" in Black Enterprise (Vol. 41, August 2010, No. 1, pp. 61)*
Pub: Earl G. Graves Publishing Co. Inc.
Ed: Sonya A. Donaldson. **Description:** Social media is essential to compete in today's business environment, especially for African American firms.

40703 ■ *"AT&T To Acquire Black Telecom Firm" in Black Enterprise (Vol. 38, January 2008, No. 6, pp. 24)*
Pub: Earl G. Graves Publishing Co. Inc.
Ed: Alan Hughes. **Description:** Details of AT&T's acquisition of ChaseCom LP, a telecommunications company based in Houston, Texas, are covered.

40704 ■ *"Back Talk with Chris Gardner" in Black Enterprise (Vol. 37, January 2007, No. 6, pp. 112)*
Pub: Earl G. Graves Publishing Co. Inc.
Ed: Kenneth Meeks. **Description:** Profile of with Chris Gardner and his Chicago company, Gardner Rich L.L.C., a multimillion-dollar investment firm. During an interview, Gardner discusses his rise from homelessness. His story became a book, The Pursuit of Happyness and was recently released as a film starring Will Smith.

40705 ■ *"Best Companies for Diversity" in Black Enterprise (Vol. 38, July 2008, No. 12, pp. 12)*
Pub: Earl G. Graves Publishing Co. Inc.
Description: Maintaining excellence in a company's diversity efforts requires critical challenges such as recruiting, retaining and developing talent in the executive pipeline. Top young and diverse emerging executives in corporate America are featured.

40706 ■ *"Black On Black Business: Moorehead Buys Hank Aaron's Toyota Dealership" in Black Enterprise (Vol. 38, February 2008, No. 7, pp. 28)*
Pub: Earl G. Graves Publishing Co. Inc.
Ed: Brenda Porter. **Description:** In a move to expand his automotive business, Thomas A. Moorehead, CEO of BMW/MINI of Sterling, Georgia bought Hank Aaron's Toyota automobile dealership in McDonough, Georgia. Moorehead stated that he will call the new store Toyota of McDonough.

40707 ■ *"Bob Johnson Opens Car Dealership: Plans To Provide a Bridge To Create More Minority Owners" in Black Enterprise (December 2007)*
Pub: Earl G. Graves Publishing Co. Inc.
Ed: Wendy Isom, Jeff Fortson. **Description:** Robert L. Johnson, founder of RLJ Companies and majority owner of RLJ-McLarty Automotive Landers Automotive Partnership which carries Chrysler, Dodge, Ford, Jeep, Scion, and Toyota vehicles has a plan to create opportunity for minority car dealers.

40708 ■ *"Brewing a Love-Haiti Relationship" in The Business Journal - Serving Phoenix and the Valley of the Sun (Vol. 28, July 4, 2008, No. 44)*
Pub: American City Business Journals, Inc.
Ed: Yvonne Zusel. **Description:** Jean and Alicia Marseille have ventured into a coffee distribution company called Ka Bel LLC which markets Marabou brand of coffee imported from Haiti. Part of the proceeds of the business is donated to entrepreneurs from Jean's country, Haiti. Details of the Marseille's startup business and personal mission to help are discussed.

40709 ■ *"Businesses Owned by Minorities Proliferate" in MMR (Vol. 27, November 29, 2010, No. 18, pp. 33)*
Pub: Mass Market Retailers
Description: Ethnic minorities are launching new businesses faster than the general population of the U.S. Statistical data included.

40710 ■ *"Calendar" in Crain's Detroit Business (Vol. 24, March 31, 2008, No. 13, pp. 1)*
Pub: Crain Communications, Inc.
Description: Listing of events in the Detroit area include conferences addressing entrepreneurialism, economic development, and minority business ownership.

40711 ■ *"Calendar" in Crain's Detroit Business (Vol. 24, April 7, 2008, No. 14, pp. 27)*
Pub: Crain Communications, Inc.
Description: Listing of events in the Detroit area include conferences addressing entrepreneurialism, economic development, and minority business ownership.

40712 ■ *"Celebrate Success. Embrace Innovation" in Black Enterprise (Vol. 37, February 2007, No. 7, pp. 145)*
Pub: Earl G. Graves Publishing Co. Inc.
Description: 2007 Women of Power Summit provides networking opportunities, empowerment sessions, and nightly entertainment. More than 500 executive women of color are expected to attend this inspiring summit in Phoenix, February 7-10.

40713 ■ *"CEO Forecast" in Hispanic Business (January-February 2009, pp. 34, 36)*
Pub: Hispanic Business
Ed: Jessica Haro, Richard Kaplan. **Description:** As economic uncertainty fogs the future, executives turn to government contracts in order to boost business. Revenue sources, health care challenges, environmental consulting and remediation services, as well as technological strides are discussed.

40714 ■ *"Changing Society One Organization at a Time" in Hispanic Business (January-February 2008, pp. 55-56)*
Pub: Hispanic Business
Ed: Hildy Median. **Description:** Profile of Jerry Porras, Stanford professor, whose mission is to create a healthier society. Porras discusses what makes any business successful.

40715 ■ *Chinese Ethnic Business*
Pub: Routledge Inc.
Ed: Eric Fong; Chiu Ming Luk. **Released:** October 2006. **Description:** Impact of globalization on Chinese ethnic small businesses is covered, focusing on U.S., Australia, and Canada.

40716 ■ *"City Council Committee Votes Against Establishing Small and Minority Business Fund" in Commercial Appeal (November 10, 2010)*
Pub: Commercial Appeal
Ed: Amos Maki. **Description:** Memphis, Tennessee City Council decided against the establishment of a $1 million small and minority business fund until criteria can be set in place for disbursing the money.

40717 ■ *"City Seeks More Minorities" in Austin Business Journallnc. (Vol. 28, November 7, 2008, No. 34, pp. A1)*
Pub: American City Business Journals
Ed: Jean Kwon. **Description:** Austin, Texas is planning to increase the participation of minority- and women-owned businesses in government contracts. Contractors are required to show 'good faith' to comply with the specified goals. The city is planning to effect the changes in the construction and professional services sector.

40718 ■ *"Coca-Cola Bottler Up for Sale: CEO J. Bruce Llewellyn Seeks Retirement" in Black Enterprise (Vol. 37, December 2006, No. 5, pp. 31)*
Pub: Earl G. Graves Publishing Co. Inc.
Ed: Marcia A. Wade. **Description:** J. Bruce Llewellyn of Brucephil Inc., the parent company of the Philadelphia Coca-Cola Bottling Co. has agreed to sell its remaining shares to Coca-Cola Co., which previously owned 31 percent of Philly Coke. Analysts believe that Coca-Cola will eventually sell its shares to another bottler.

40719 ■ *"Complete Discovery Source, Inc. (CDS) Receives Minority Owned Business Certification" in Internet Wire (December 14, 2010)*
Pub: Comtex
Description: Complete Discovery Source Inc. (CDS) was granted Minority-Owned Business Enterprise status by the New York State Department of Economic Development. The certification provides CDS, an end-to-end eDiscovery services provider, with access to contracting opportunities with 130 government agencies throughout New York state.

40720 ■ *"Compounding Opportunity" in Hispanic Business (October 2007, pp. 72, 74-75)*
Pub: Hispanic Business
Ed: Hildy Medina. **Description:** New banks are targeting Hispanic entrepreneurs.

40721 ■ *"Construction Firms Support NAACP Plan" in Business Courier (Vol. 27, September 24, 2010, No. 21, pp. 1)*
Pub: Business Courier
Ed: Lucy May. **Description:** Executives of Turner Construction Company and Messer Construction Company expressed their support for the Cincinnati National Association for the Advancement of Colored People Construction Partnership Agreement. The agreement involves the setting of rules for the involvement of firms owned by African Americans in major projects in Cincinnati.

40722 ■ *"Contractors: Slots MBE Goal a Test" in Baltimore Business Journal (Vol. 27, November 20, 2009, No. 28, pp. 1)*
Pub: American City Business Journals
Ed: Scott Dance. **Description:** Slot machine manufacturers in Maryland have been searching minority business enterprises (MBEs) that will provide maintenance and delivery services to the machines. MBEs will also build the stands where the machines will be mounted.

40723 ■ *"Convention Calendar" in Black Enterprise (Vol. 37, February 2007, No. 7, pp. 68)*
Pub: Earl G. Graves Publishing Co. Inc.
Description: Listing of conventions and trade show of interest to minority and women business leaders.

40724 ■ *"Corner Office" in Hispanic Business (December 2010)*
Pub: Hispanic Business
Ed: Jesus Chavarria. **Description:** The gap opens up between government contracts and small businesses. The state of minority enterprise development in federal markets as well as other levels of government throughout the U.S. is examined.

40725 ■ *"Corporate Elite Face Steep Challenges" in Hispanic Business (January-February 2008, pp. 20, 22, 24, 26, 28, 30, 32)*
Pub: Hispanic Business
Ed: Jonathan Higuera. **Description:** Hispanic men and women are moving up corporate ranks at leading companies in the U.S., including Ralph de la Vega, president and CEO of AT&T Mobility. Profiles of Vega and other Hispanic business leaders are included.

40726 ■ *"County Limited in Awarding Contracts" in Crain's Cleveland Business (Vol. 30, June 15, 2009, No. 23, pp. 8)*
Pub: Crain Communications, Inc.
Description: Cuyahoga County government has been accused of not offering fair levels of county-issued contracts to minority-owned companies.

40727 ■ *"Crafting Kinship at Home and Work: Women Miners in Wyoming" in WorkingUSA (Vol. 11, December 2008, No. 4, pp. 439)*
Pub: Blackwell Publishers Ltd.
Ed: Jessica M. Smith. **Description:** Institutional policies and social dynamics shaping women working in the northeastern Wyoming mining industry are examined. Ethnographic research suggests that the women's successful integration into this nontraditional workplace is predicated on their ability to craft and maintain kin-like social relationships in two spheres. First, women miners have addressed the challenges of managing their home and work responsibilities by cultivating networks of friends and family to care for their children while they are at work. Second, women miners craft close relationships with coworkers in what are called 'crew families'. These relationships make their work more enjoyable and the ways in which they create camaraderie prompt a reconsideration of conventional accounts of sexual harassment in the mining industry.

40728 ■ *"Detroit Hosts Conferences on Green Building, IT, Finance" in Crain's Detroit Business (Vol. 25, June 1, 2009, No. 22, pp. 9)*
Pub: Crain Communications Inc. - Detroit
Ed: Tom Henderson. **Description:** Detroit will host three conferences in June 2009, one features green technology, one information technology and the third will gather black bankers and financial experts from across the nation.

40729 ■ *"DiversityStockIndexes" in Hispanic Business (October 2007, pp. 68)*
Pub: Hispanic Business
Description: Two proprietary stock indexes of interest to Hispanic businesses are presented.

40730 ■ *"Edible Endeavors" in Black Enterprise (March 2008)*
Pub: Earl G. Graves Publishing Co. Inc.
Ed: Carolyn M. Brown. **Description:** Profile of Jacqueline Frazer, woman entrepreneur who turned her love for cooking into a catering business. She is chef and owner of Command Performance in New York City. The firm works with more than 50 clients annually and generates annual revenues of about $350,000.

40731 ■ *"El Paso Firm Rides Boom to the Top" in Hispanic Business (Vol. 30, July-August 2008, No. 7-8, pp. 28)*
Pub: Hispanic Business, Inc.
Ed: Jeremy Nisen. **Description:** VEMAC, a commercial construction management and general contracting firm that is experiencing success despite the plummeting construction market is discussed. VEMAC's success is attributed to the Pentagons' $5 billion investment in construction for the benefit of new personnel and their families to be transferred to Fort Bliss, a U.S. army base adjacent to El Paso.

40732 ■ *"The Endless Flow of Russell Simmons" in Entrepreneur (Vol. 37, September 2009, No. 9, pp. 24)*
Pub: Entrepreneur Media, Inc.
Ed: Josh Dean. **Description:** Entrepreneur Russell Simmons has successfully grown his businesses by focusing on underserved markets. Simons has never given up on any business strategy. He has also entered the music, clothing and television industries.

40733 ■ *"Ethnic Businesses Ending Vacancies" in Business First-Columbus (Vol. 26, August 20, 2010, No. 51, pp. 1)*
Pub: Business First
Ed: Carrie Ghose. **Description:** The Morse Road commercial corridor in Columbus, Ohio has several immigrant-owned businesses that were recognized as instrumental in preventing widespread vacancies when the Northland Mall closed in 2002. The ethnic stores have created a diverse destination that attracted traffic and more businesses.

40734 ■ *"Ethnic Chambers Seek Combined Facility" in Business Journal (Vol. 28, October 8, 2010, No. 18, pp. 1)*
Pub: Minneapolis Business Journal
Ed: Jim Hammerand. **Description:** Six ethnic business and commerce groups in St. Paul and Minneapolis, Minnesota, all members of the Minnesota Multi-Ethnic Chambers of Commerce Joint Council, are planning to move in together in order to save on costs and to strengthen their organizations. The Council expects to transfer by September 2011. The project will cost about $290,000.

40735 ■ *Ethnic Solidarity for Economic Survival: Korean Greengrocers in New York City*
Pub: Russell Sage Foundation Publications
Ed: Pyong Gap Min. **Released:** August 2008. **Price:** $32.50. **Description:** Investigations into the entrepreneurial traditions of Korean immigrant families in New York City running ethnic businesses, particularly small grocery stores and produce markets. Social, cultural and economic issues facing these retailers are discussed.

40736 ■ *"FCC Adopts New Media Ownership Rules" in Black Enterprise (Vol. 38, March 2008, No. 8, pp. 26)*
Pub: Earl G. Graves Publishing Co. Inc.
Ed: Joyce Jones. **Description:** Federal Communications Commission approved a ruling that lifts a ban on newspaper and/or broadcast cross ownership. Because of declining sales in newspaper advertising and readership the ban will allow companies to share local news gathering costs across multiple media platforms.

40737 ■ *"Filling the Business Gap" in Hispanic Business (December 2010)*
Pub: Hispanic Business
Ed: Richard Larsen. **Description:** New York group seeks to increase state diversity supplier spending to help create jobs and boost the economy. According to a recent study, six out of 10 small business owners will increase capital spending but delay hiring in 2011. However, potential job creation is good among businesses owned by women and minorities.

40738 ■ *"The Final Say" in Hispanic Business (Vol. 30, March 2008, No. 3, pp. 52)*
Pub: Hispanic Business
Ed: Hildy Medina. **Description:** Vice-Chairwoman of the pensions and investments committee and Illinois State Senator Iris Martinez is the first Hispanic woman to be elected Senator and is advocating for pension funds to include Hispanic money managers and minority- and female-owned businesses in the investment plans.

40739 ■ *"Former Football Pro Closes Doors of Car Dealership" in Black Enterprise (Vol. 38, March 2008, No. 8, pp. 28)*
Pub: Earl G. Graves Publishing Co. Inc.
Ed: Brenda Porter. **Description:** Aenease Williams automobile dealerships closed their doors in Louisiana due to low sales. Williams, a former NFL safety retired in 2005. According to an expert, the image of the Lincoln as a luxury brand has been diminished.

40740 ■ *"Game On! African Americans Get a Shot at $17.9 Billion Video Game Industry" in Black Enterprise (Vol. 38, July 2008, No. 12, pp. 56)*
Pub: Earl G. Graves Publishing Co. Inc.
Ed: Carolyn M. Brown. **Description:** Despite the economic crisis, consumers are still purchasing the hottest video games and hardware. Tips for African American developers who want to become a part of this industry that lacks content targeting this demographic are offered.

40741 ■ *"Go Green Or Go Home" in Black Enterprise (Vol. 41, August 2010, No. 1, pp. 53)*
Pub: Earl G. Graves Publishing Co. Inc.
Ed: Tennille M. Robinson. **Description:** The green economy has become an essential part of every business, however, small business owners need to learn how to participate, including minority owned entrepreneurs.

40742 ■ *"Happy Trails: RV Franchiser Gives Road Traveling Enthusiasts a Lift" in Black Enterprise (Vol. 38, July 2008, No. 12, pp. 47)*
Pub: Earl G. Graves Publishing Co. Inc.
Ed: Tamara E. Holmes. **Description:** Overview of Bates International Motor Home Rental Systems Inc., a growing franchise that gives RV owners the chance to rent out their big-ticket purchases to others when they are not using them; Sandra Williams Bate launched the company as a franchise in July 1997 and now has a fleet of 30 franchises across the

country. She expects the company to reach 2.2 million for 2008 due to a marketing initiative that will expand the company's presence.

40743 ■ *"HB Diversity Stock Index" in Hispanic Business (March 2008, pp. 10)*
Pub: Hispanic Business
Description: Presentation of the Hispanic Business Diversity Stock Index as of February 1, 2008, which includes 54 publicly traded companies. Statistical data included.

40744 ■ *"HBDiversity Stock Index" in Hispanic Business (July-August 2007, pp. 58)*
Pub: Hispanic Business
Description: Listing of 43 Hispanic companies, their stock symbol, value and change over a six month period, January 3, 2007 through July 6, 2007.

40745 ■ *"HBDiversityStockIndex" in Hispanic Business (January-February 2008, pp. 10)*
Pub: Hispanic Business
Description: Presentation of the Hispanic Business Diversity Stock Index for 2007, which includes 54 publicly traded companies.

40746 ■ *"HBDiversityStockIndex" in Hispanic Business (October 2009, pp. 1)*
Pub: Hispanic Business
Description: Data covering the Hispanic Business Diversity Stock Index is highlighted. The HBDSI was up 0.12 percent through September 3, 2009. Statistical data included.

40747 ■ *"Health Care Leads Sectors Attracting Capital" in Hispanic Business (March 2008, pp. 14-16, 18)*
Pub: Hispanic Business
Ed: Scott Williams. **Description:** U. S. Hispanic healthcare, media, and food were the key industries in the U.S. gaining investors in 2007.

40748 ■ *"Health Care Leads Sectors Attracting Capital" in Hispanic Business (Vol. 30, March 2008, No. 3, pp. 14)*
Pub: Hispanic Business
Ed: Scott Williams. **Description:** Discusses the capital gains of Hispanic-owned companies and other Hispanic leaders in the investment and retail fields in the year 2007. Sectors like health care, media, food and technology saw a healthy flow of capital due to successful mergers, acquisitions and increased private equity investments.

40749 ■ *"Helping Women Grow Their Businesses One Entrepreneur at a Time" in Hispanic Business (July-August 2007, pp. 56-57)*
Pub: Hispanic Business
Ed: Hildy Medina. **Description:** American Express OPEN is a program focusing on women business owners whose companies report revenues of $200,000 or more. The program offers the chance to win a free year of mentoring, marketing and technology assistance along with a $50,000 line of credit.

40750 ■ *"Hispanic Business 100 Fastest-Growing Companies" in Hispanic Business (July-August 2007, pp. 28, 30, 32, 36)*
Pub: Hispanic Business
Description: Top 100 Hispanic businesses are ranked by sales growth 2002-2006, gross sales, profit ranges, number of employees, and year the firm was founded.

40751 ■ *"Hispanic Business 100 Fastest-Growing Companies" in Hispanic Business (July-August 2009, pp. 16-18)*
Pub: Hispanic Business
Ed: Joshua Molina. **Description:** Despite the recession, the 100 fastest growing companies profiled are able to maintain their competitive edge; federal contracts are key to their success. Service companies are at the top of the list and Texas and Florida are the states in which the top are located.

40752 ■ *"Hispanic Business 100 Fastest-Growing Companies" in Hispanic Business (July-August 2009, pp. 24-26, 28)*
Pub: Hispanic Business
Description: Comprehensive list of the top 100 Hispanic businesses for 2009; data includes company location and description, sales growth, revenues, profits and number of employees from 2004-2208.

40753 ■ *"Hispanic Business 100 Influentials" in Hispanic Business (October 2009, pp. 22)*
Pub: Hispanic Business
Description: Profiles of the top one hundred influential Hispanics in business and government are presented.

40754 ■ *"Hispanic Business 100 Influentials: Profiles of the Top 100 Influentials" in Hispanic Business (October 2009, pp. 22)*
Pub: Hispanic Business
Description: Profiles of the top one hundred influential Hispanics in business and government are presented.

40755 ■ *"The Hispanic Business 100 Most Influential Hispanics" in Hispanic Business (October 2007, pp. 30)*
Pub: Hispanic Business
Description: Profiles of the one hundred Hispanic business leaders are presented.

40756 ■ *"Hispanic Business Group Leader Continues Push for Better Inclusion" in Crain's Cleveland Business (Vol. 30, June 22, 2009, No. 24)*
Pub: Crain Communications, Inc.
Ed: Jay Miller. **Description:** Hispanic Business Association is working to create more opportunities for Hispanic business owners. The article discusses the Minority Business Accelerator 2.5 program of the Greater Cleveland Partnership that helps minority-owned small businesses.

40757 ■ *"Hispanic Businesses Try to Drum Up Cash to Battle Crime Spree" in Baltimore Business Journal (Vol. 28, September 3, 2010, No. 17)*
Pub: Baltimore Business Journal
Ed: Scott Dance. **Description:** Hispanic businesses in Baltimore, Maryland have been raising funds to pay off-duty police officers to patrol a few blocks of Broadway in Fells Point to help curb crime. Efforts to make the area a Latin Town have failed owing to muggings, prostitution and drug dealing. Comments from small business owners are also given.

40758 ■ *"Hispanic Executives Continue Their Rise to Prominence Amid a Shaky Economy" in Hispanic Business (January-February 2009, pp. 12-14)*
Pub: Hispanic Business
Ed: Michael Bowker. **Description:** Hispanic Business Media's 2009 Corporate Elite winners defied expectations and a tough economy and rose to the top of their industries; innovation being cited as key to growth of Hispanic-owned companies.

40759 ■ *"Hispanic Representation in Boardrooms Remains Static" in Hispanic Business (January-February 2008, pp. 36, 38, 40)*
Pub: Hispanic Business
Description: Estimated 3 percent of Hispanic representation in corporate boardroom in America has remained the same, despite the growth in the Hispanic population. Statistical data and board member names are included.

40760 ■ *"Hispanics Take Seats in America's Boardrooms" in Hispanic Business (January-February 2009, pp. 24, 28)*
Pub: Hispanic Business
Ed: Joshua Molina. **Description:** Three percent of those serving as directors of Fortune 500 companies in America are Hispanic. A listing of forty of these directors is included.

40761 ■ *"Hispantelligence Report" in Hispanic Business (January-February 2008, pp. 8)*
Pub: Hispanic Business
Description: Presentation of the Hispanic Business Stock Index shows the current value of fifteen Hispanic companies through December 2007. Forecasts showing increased growth for Hispanic-owned companies are also included.

40762 ■ *"Hispantelligence Report" in Hispanic Business (March 2008, pp. 8)*
Pub: Hispanic Business
Description: Listing of the Hispanic Business Stock Index covering Hispanic owned businesses; stock symbol, previous 30-day, year-to-date and one year performance is presented.

40763 ■ *"Hispantelligence Report" in Hispanic Business (July-August 2009, pp. 8)*
Pub: Hispanic Business
Description: After forty years, Hispanic-owned businesses have grown to more than three million, according to a U.S. Census report. The Hispanic business stock index is also presented. Statistical data included.

40764 ■ *"Hispantelligence Report" in Hispanic Business (January-February 2009, pp. 10)*
Pub: Hispanic Business
Description: U.S. Hispanic purchasing power is expected to reach $958 billion in 2009 and projected to reach $1.25 trillion by 2015, a rate of more than two times the overall national rate. Statistical data included.

40765 ■ *How to Be an Entrepreneur and Keep Your Sanity: The African-American Guide to Owning, Building and Maintaining Successfully Your Own Small Business*
Pub: Amber Books
Ed: Paula McCoy Pinderhughes. **Released:** June 2003. **Price:** $14.95. **Description:** Ten easy steps to becoming a successful African-American entrepreneur.

40766 ■ *"How Two Flourishing Exporters Did It" in Hispanic Business (Vol. 30, July-August 2008, No. 7-8, pp. 46)*
Pub: Hispanic Business, Inc.
Ed: Richard Kaplan. **Description:** Vigorous growth in export revenues posted by two Hispanic-owned export companies Compasa LLC and Ametza LLC is discussed; both firms have benefited from their closer locations to major Mexican markets, superior quality of their products, market knowledge and the relationships of trust developed with key business partners.

40767 ■ *Immigrant, Inc.: Why Immigrant Entrepreneurs Are Driving the New Economy*
Pub: John Wiley & Sons, Inc.
Ed: Richard T. Herman, Robert L. Smith. **Released:** November 9, 2009. **Price:** $19.77. **Description:** Immigrant entrepreneurs are driving the new economy and will play a role in saving American jobs.

40768 ■ *"The Impact of Immigrant Entrepreneurs" in Business Week (February 7, 2007)*
Pub: McGraw-Hill Companies
Ed: Kerry Miller. **Description:** Overview of immigrant entrepreneur's impact on economic development and their status as a driving force for the U.S. economy.

40769 ■ *"Impressive Numbers: Companies Experience Substantial Increases in Dollars, Employment" in Hispanic Business (July-August 2007)*
Pub: Hispanic Business
Ed: Derek Reveron. **Description:** Profiles of five fastest growing Hispanic companies reporting increases in revenue and employment include Brightstar, distributor of wireless products; Greenway Ford Inc., a car dealership; Fred Loya Insurance, auto insurance carrier; and Group O, packaging company; and Diverse Staffing, Inc., an employment and staffing firm.

40770 ■ *"In Sickness and In Wealth Management" in Hispanic Business (Vol. 30, March 2008, No. 3, pp. 28)*
Pub: Hispanic Business
Ed: Rick Munarriz. **Description:** Discusses the investment and wealth management firms owned and operated by Hispanics. There are only a handful of these firms owned by Hispanics, as most of them prefer capital preservation by investing in hard assets like cash and real estate than in capital appreciation.

40771 ■ *"In Sickness and in Wealth Management" in Hispanic Business (March 2008, pp. 28, 30)*
Pub: Hispanic Business
Ed: Rick Munarriz. **Description:** Financial advice is offered by experts, Myrna Rivera and Samuel Ramirez Jr., with an overview of Hispanic-owned investment firms.

40772 ■ *"Investment Firms Unite: Coalition Fights New Tax Law" in Black Enterprise (Vol. 38, December 2007, No. 5, pp. 52)*
Pub: Earl G. Graves Publishing Co. Inc.
Ed: Joyce Jones. **Description:** Minorities working in private equity, real estate and investment management firms have united to form the Access to Capital Coalition to oppose legislation that they feel would adversely affect their ability to attract investments and executives. Details of the group are included.

40773 ■ *"J.C. Watts First Black John Deere Dealer" in Black Enterprise (Vol. 37, November 2006, No. 4, pp. 36)*
Pub: Earl G. Graves Publishing Co. Inc.
Ed: Kiara Ashanti. **Description:** Profile of former Congressman J.C. Watts Jr., a man who grew up in rural America and is the first African American to own a John Deere Dealership.

40774 ■ *"Just Following Directions" in Entrepreneur (Vol. 36, February 2008, No. 2, pp. 56)*
Pub: Entrepreneur Media Inc.
Ed: Amanda C. Kooser. **Description:** Buyer's guide for purchasing Global Positioning System units is presented.

40775 ■ *"Kid-Friendly Business Sources" in Black Enterprise (Vol. 37, January 2007, No. 6, pp. 40)*
Pub: Earl G. Graves Publishing Co. Inc.
Ed: Carolyn M. Brown. **Description:** Financial or business camps are a great way to encourage a child who interested in starting his or her own business. A number of these camps are available each year including Kidpreneurs Conference and Bull and Bear Investment Camp. Other resources are available online. Resources included.

40776 ■ *"A Knack for Entrepreneurship" in Hispanic Business (January-February 2008, pp. 42, 44-45)*
Pub: Hispanic Business
Ed: Hildy Medina. **Description:** Profile of Carlos Antonio Garcia, CEO of Kira, is investing in young companies.

40777 ■ *"Leaps and Bounds: Liberty Power, Force 3 Ride Rapid Expansion to the Top" in Hispanic Business (July-August 2007, pp. 20-22, 24)*
Pub: Hispanic Business
Ed: Derek Reveron. **Description:** Profiles of Liberty Power Corporation, a Florida supplier of retail electricity and Force 3 Inc. of Maryland, network infrastructure developer are two of the 100 fastest growing Hispanic businesses recognized in 2007.

40778 ■ *"The Major Leagues: Have Front-Office Positions Opened Up for Blacks?" in Black Enterprise (Vol. 37, February 2007, No. 7, pp.)*
Pub: Earl G. Graves Publishing Co. Inc.
Ed: Alexis McCombs. **Description:** Major leave sports teams are hiring more African Americans to manage and coach teams. Statistical data included.

40779 ■ *"The Marathon Club: Building a Bridge to Wealth" in Hispanic Business (March 2008, pp. 24)*
Pub: Hispanic Business
Ed: Hildy Median. **Description:** Minority businesses find it more difficult to secure venture capital for entrepreneurial pursuits. Joe Watson, CEO of Without Excuses and Strategic Hire, suggests Hispanics and African Americans collaborate on issues of importance to minority entrepreneurs.

40780 ■ *"Maryland Ready to Defend Slots Minority Policy" in Boston Business Journal (Vol. 29, July 8, 2011, No. 9, pp. 3)*
Pub: American City Business Journals Inc.
Ed: Scott Dance. **Description:** The legality of Maryland's minority inclusion policy may be put under scrutiny once the lawsuit filed by rejected slots developer Baltimore City Entertainment Group on July 5, 2011 is heard in court. The lawsuit aims to stop the bidding process on a proposed casino in Baltimore because the minority policy amounts to reverse discrimination.

40781 ■ *"Merger Brings New Force to Hispanic Marketing Industry" in Hispanic Business (July-August 2007, pp. 60)*
Pub: Hispanic Business
Description: Merger between Latin Force LLC, a marketing strategy firm and Geoscape International Inc., a consumer intelligence and data analytics company is discussed.

40782 ■ *"Miami's 'Big Wheels' Keep Latin America Rolling" in Hispanic Business (July-August 2007, pp. 46-47)*
Pub: Hispanic Business
Ed: Frank Nelson. **Description:** Four top Hispanic owned exporters of tires are discussed. All four companies are based in Miami, Florida.

40783 ■ *"MicroTech: No. 1 Fastest-Growing Company" in Hispanic Business (July-August 2009, pp. 20, 22)*
Pub: Hispanic Business
Ed: Suzanne Heibel. **Description:** Profile of Tony Jimenez, former lieutenant colonel in the Army and CEO and founder of Virginia-based information technology firm, Micro Tech LLC. Jimenez was named Latinos in Information Science and Technology Association's CEO of the Year for 2008.

40784 ■ *"Minority Auto Suppliers Get Help Diversifying" in Crain's Detroit Business (Vol. 26, January 11, 2010, No. 2, pp. 3)*
Pub: Crain Communications, Inc.
Ed: Sherri Welch. **Description:** Displaced minority auto suppliers are being given assistance by the Kauffman's Foundation Urban Entrepreneur Partnership Detroit program, a three-year effort to assist 150 of the region's suppliers into more diversified businesses.

40785 ■ *"Minority Entrepreneurs, Business Advocate of the Year Named" in Daily News (November 1, 2010)*
Pub: Daily News
Ed: Aniesa Holmes. **Description:** Jacksonville-Onslow Chamber of Commerce Minority Enterprise Development Day honored outstanding entrepreneurs from the region. Candidates were chosen based on criteria such as business accomplishments, chamber involvement and dedication as well as their commitment to serving people in the community.

40786 ■ *"Mom of Eight Named Regional Minority Small Business Person of the Year" in Daily News (November 8, 2010)*
Pub: Daily News
Ed: Suzanne Ulbrich. **Description:** Profile of Melissa Leifheit, mother of eight and named Regional Minority Small Business Person of the Year by the North Carolina Small Business Administration.

40787 ■ *"Moving Into the Digital Space: How New Media Create Opportunities for Minorities" in Black Enterprise (February 2008)*
Pub: Earl G. Graves Publishing Co. Inc.
Ed: Sonia Alleyne. **Description:** The Internet is becoming an alternative to traditional sources of entertainment; nearly 16 percent of American households who use the Internet watch television online. One such Internet show features a variety of African American lifestyles.

40788 ■ *"Nation of Islam Businessman Who Became Manager for Muhamnmad Ali Dies" in Chicago Tribune (August 28, 2008)*
Pub: McClatchy-Tribune Information Services
Ed: Trevor Jensen. **Description:** Profile of Jabir Herbert Muhammad who died on August 25, after heart surgery; Muhammad lived nearly all his life on Chicago's South Side and ran a number of small businesses including a bakery and a dry cleaners before becoming the manager to famed boxer Mohammad Ali.

40789 ■ *National Minority and Women-Owned Business Directory*
Pub: Diversity Information Resources
Contact: Leslie Bonds, Executive Director
E-mail: lbonds@diversityinforesources.com
URL(s): www.diversityinforesources.com. **Ed:** Leslie Bonds. **Released:** Annual; Latest edition 2012. **Price:** $145, Individuals print. **Covers:** Information regarding minority and women-owned business directories to acquaint major corporations and government purchasing agents with the products and services of minority and women-owned firms. Covers approximately 7000 minority-owned firms. **Entries include:** Company name, address, phone, fax, e-mail, Web site, number of employees, year established, products or services, certification status, minority identification, annual sales, NAICS code. **Arrangement:** Classified by product or service, then geographical and alphabetical. **Indexes:** Commodity, keyword.

40790 ■ *"A New Breed of Entrepreneurs" in Black Enterprise (Vol. 37, November 2006, No. 4, pp. 16)*
Pub: Earl G. Graves Publishing Co. Inc.
Description: Black entrepreneurs are an important part of the chain for providing economic opportunities within the community. Many black business owners are more likely to hire black employees and apply innovative strategies in building their businesses rather than taking the traditional route.

40791 ■ *"New King Top the Charts" in The Business Journal-Portland (Vol. 25, August 8, 2008, No. 22, pp. 1)*
Pub: American City Business Journals, Inc.
Ed: Andy Giegerich. **Description:** Spanish-language KRYP-FM station's spring 2008 ratings soared to 6.4 from 2.8 for the previous year. The station timing is flawless given the fact that one of every three new Portland-area residents between 2002 and 2007 were Latino.

40792 ■ *"The Next Chapter" in Business Courier (Vol. 26, November 20, 2009, No. 30, pp. 1)*
Pub: American City Business Journals, Inc.
Ed: Lucy May. **Description:** Eric Browne and Mel Gravely purchased controlling interest in TriVersity Construction Group from CM-GC CEO Schulyler Murdoch and MBJ Consultants President Monroe Barnes. One third of the company was still owned by Cincinnati-based Messer and TriVersity and will continue to be a certified minority business enterprise.

40793 ■ *"NJ Tries to Push Stimulus Funds to Minorities" in Philadelphia Business Journal (Vol. 28, September 25, 2009, No. 32, pp. 1)*
Pub: American City Business Journals
Ed: Athena D. Merritt. **Description:** New Jersey Governor Jon S. Corzine signed an executive order that seeks to ease the way for minority and women-owned business to take on federal stimulus-funded work. New Jersey has also forged new relations with different organizations to reduce the time and cost of certifications for businesses.

40794 ■ *"Nonprofits May Lose MBE Status in MD" in Boston Business Journal (Vol. 29, September 2, 2011, No. 17, pp. 1)*
Pub: American City Business Journals Inc.
Ed: Scott Dance. **Description:** A business group has been pushing to bar nonprofits from Maryland's Minority Business program. Nonprofits have been

found to take a large portion of state contracts intended for women- and minority-owned businesses. The group is also crafting proposed legislation to remove nonprofits from the program.

40795 ■ *"On the Green: Sheila Johnson Adds $35 Million Golf Resort To Her Expanding Portfolio" in Black Enterprise (January 2008)*
Pub: Earl G. Graves Publishing Co. Inc.

Ed: Donna M. Owens. **Description:** Profile of Sheila Johnson, CEO of Salamander Hospitality LLC, made history when she purchased the Innisbrook Resort and Golf Club, making her the first African American woman to own this type of property. The resort includes four championship golf courses, six swimming pools, four restaurants, eleven tennis courts, three conference halls, and a nature preserve.

40796 ■ *Overcoming Barriers to Entrepreneurship in the United States*
Pub: Lexington Books

Ed: Diana Furchtgott-Roth. **Released:** March 28, 2008. **Price:** $24.95. **Description:** Real and perceived barriers to the founding and running of small businesses in America are discussed. Each chapter outlines how policy and economic environments can hinder business owners and offers tips to overcome these obstacles. Starting with venture capital access in Silicon Valley during the Internet bubble, the book goes on to question the link between personal wealth and entrepreneurship, examines how federal tax rates affect small business creation and destruction, explains the low rate of self-employment among Mexican immigrants, and suggests ways pension coverage can be increased in small businesses.

40797 ■ *The Peebles Principles: Insights from an Entrepreneur's Life of Business Success, Making Deals, and Creating a Fortune from Scratch*
Pub: John Wiley and Sons Inc.

Ed: R. Donahue Peebles. **Released:** April 2007. **Price:** $29.99. **Description:** Successful entrepreneur shares his business experience. Peebles went from CEO of the nation's largest Black-owned real estate development firm to founding his own firm.

40798 ■ *"Power In the Boardroom" in Black Enterprise (Vol. 38, February 2008, No. 7, pp. 112)*
Pub: Earl G. Graves Publishing Co. Inc.

Ed: Derek T. Dingle. **Description:** Comprehensive list of Black corporate directors for 250 of the largest companies in the U.S.; these leaders play a critical role in business development.

40799 ■ *"Power Partnerships" in Business Courier (Vol. 27, October 22, 2010, No. 25, pp. 1)*
Pub: Business Courier

Ed: Lucy May. **Description:** The $400 million Harrah's casino and the $47 million redevelopment and expansion of Washington Park are project aimed at boosting the economy in downtown Cincinnati, Ohio. These projects will be done in cooperation with the National Association for the Advancement of Colored People. Insights into the role of minority-owned businesses in regional economic development are explored.

40800 ■ *Prepare to Be a Teen Millionaire*
Pub: Health Communications, Inc.
Contact: Peter Vegso, President

Ed: Robyn Collins; Kimberly Spinks Burleson. **Released:** April 1, 2008. **Price:** $16.95. **Description:** Business reference for any teenager wishing to become a successful entrepreneur; advice is given from successful teenage millionaires. Topics covered include: choosing a business name, type, and location; use of the Internet; legal issues; branding, sales, and marketing; funding and financial management; return on investment; retirement; development of a sound business plan; and certification for minority or women-owned companies.

40801 ■ *"President Obama Appoints Record Number of Hispanics to High Office" in Hispanic Business (October 2009, pp. 12-13)*
Pub: Hispanic Business

Ed: Rob Kuznia. **Description:** Fourteen percent, or 43 of the Senate-approved appointees by President Obama are Hispanic; President George W. Bush appointed 34 Hispanics, Bill Clinton, 30 Hispanics.

40802 ■ *"Procurement Benefits" in Black Enterprise (Vol. 38, February 2008, No. 7, pp. 72)*
Pub: Earl G. Graves Publishing Co. Inc.

Ed: Aisha Sylvester. **Description:** Nearly 18 percent of all U.S. firms are minority-owned according to the recent report called Minorities in Business: A Demographic Review of Minority Business Ownership produced by the Small Business Administration. Issues for working with diversity suppliers are addressed.

40803 ■ *"Prominent Hispanic Businessman Signs with Choice Hotels" in Hispanic Business (March 2008, pp. 36)*
Pub: Hispanic Business

Ed: Melinda Burns. **Description:** Profile of John C. Lopez, who has signed an agreement with Choice Hotels International to build five new Cambria Suites in the U.S.; cost of the project will total $14 million.

40804 ■ *"Prominent Hispanic Businessman Signs With Choice Hotels" in Hispanic Business (Vol. 30, March 2008, No. 3, pp. 36)*
Pub: Hispanic Business

Ed: Melinda Burns. **Description:** Chairman of the board of Lopez Food Inc., John C. Lopez signs the agreement with Choice Hotels International to build five new Cambria suites in the USA. This is his first hotel venture and also the first Hispanic franchisee to enter into business with Choice Hotels.

40805 ■ *"Prudential Courts Hispanics" in Hispanic Business (March 2008, pp. 38, 40)*
Pub: Hispanic Business

Ed: Melinda Burns. **Description:** Prudential Financial Inc. is reaching out to Hispanic Chambers of Commerce in an effort to hire and do business with the Hispanic community in the U.S.

40806 ■ *"PRWT Service Acquires Pharmaceutical Plant: Firm Wins Multimillion-Dollar Contract with Merck" in Black Enterprise (March 2008)*
Pub: Earl G. Graves Publishing Co. Inc.

Ed: Tamara E. Holmes. **Description:** PRWT Services Inc. expanded through its acquisition of a chemical manufacturing plant in New Jersey. The Whitehouse Station, part of Merck & Co. Inc. produces active pharmaceutical ingredients for antibiotics, making PRWT the first minority-owned company in the U.S. to manufacture active pharmaceutical ingredients.

40807 ■ *Race and Entrepreneurial Success: Black-, Asian-, and White-Owned Businesses in the United States*
Pub: The MIT Press
Contact: Ellen W. Faran, Director
E-mail: ewfaran@mit.edu

Ed: Robert W. Fairlie. **Released:** September 30, 2008. **Price:** $35.00. **Description:** Trends in minority small business ownership are explored, focusing on the importance of human capital, financial capital, and family business background in successful business ownership.

40808 ■ *"The Racial Divide and the Class Struggle in the United States" in WorkingUSA (Vol. 11, September 2008, No. 3, pp. 311)*
Pub: Blackwell Publishers Ltd.

Ed: Michael Goldfield. **Description:** An examination of questions of race that continue to play such a prominent role in contemporary society is presented, focusing on the undermining of potential solidarity and strength of the working class movement, what sustains racists attitudes, practices and institutions, especially in the face of trends in world economic development.

40809 ■ *"Ready To Take Your Business Global?" in Black Enterprise (Vol. 41, August 2010, No. 1, pp. 89)*
Pub: Earl G. Graves Publishing Co. Inc.

Ed: Alan Hughes. **Description:** The 2010 Black Enterprise Entrepreneurs Conference held in May stressed the need for all small firms to promote a global agenda in order to stay competitive.

40810 ■ *The Rhythm of Success: How an Immigrant Produced His Own American Dream*
Pub: Penguin Group USA Inc.

Ed: Emilio Estefan. **Released:** January 10, 2010. **Price:** $24.95. **Description:** Emilio Estafan, husband to singer Gloria Estefan and founder of the Latin pop legend Miami Sound Machine, is the classic example of the American dream. He shares his guiding principles that entrepreneurs need to start and grow a business.

40811 ■ *"SBA Makes Reforms To Federal Government Contracting" in Black Enterprise (Vol. 38, January 2008, No. 6, pp. 26)*
Pub: Earl G. Graves Publishing Co. Inc.

Ed: Alexis McCombs. **Description:** U.S. Small Business Administration's new requirement that small businesses recertify size status in order to remain eligible for federal contracts lasting more than five years. Prior regulations allowed companies declared small in earlier contracts may have grown through acquisitions, making them ineligible. This move may impact black businesses.

40812 ■ *Small Business Loan Program Kit*
Pub: International Wealth Success, Inc.

Ed: Tyler G. Hicks. **Released:** 2006. **Price:** $100.00. **Description:** Guide to the Small Business Loan Program that offers loans to small and minority-owned companies doing work for government agencies, large corporations, hospitals, universities, and similar organizations.

40813 ■ *"Social Networkers for Hire" in Black Enterprise (Vol. 40, December 2009, No. 5, pp. 56)*
Pub: Earl G. Graves Publishing Co., Inc.

Ed: Brittany Hutson. **Description:** Companies are utilizing social networking sites in order to market their brand and personally connect with consumers and are increasingly looking to social media specialists to help with this task. Aliya S. King is one such web strategist, working for ICED Media by managing their Twitter, Facebook, YouTube and Flickr accounts for one of their publicly traded restaurant clients.

40814 ■ *"Sound Fundamentals" in Hispanic Business (September 2007, pp. 12, 14, 16)*
Pub: Hispanic Business

Ed: Michael T. Mena. **Description:** Profile of Ozomatli, a Los Angeles-based multicultural, multi-ethnic musical group that has topped Billboard's Latin Pop chart without relying on record sales. Members explain how they run the group like a small business.

40815 ■ *"South African Connections: Small Business Owners Work Toward Forming Strategic Alliances" in Black Enterprise (March 2008)*
Pub: Earl G. Graves Publishing Co. Inc.

Ed: Aisha Sylvester. **Description:** National Minority Supplier Development Council Inc. is working to create business partnerships between African American businesses and black-owned South African companies within the country's pharmaceutical supply industry.

40816 ■ *"The Stars Align: Trail Blazers, Headline Makers on 2007 List Set Example for Others" in Hispanic Business (October 2007, pp. 22)*
Pub: Hispanic Business

Description: Top one hundred most influential Hispanic business leaders comprise of 66 percent men and 34 percent women, distributed by 27 percent in government, 42 percent corporate, 11 percent education, five percent art and entertainment, and 15 percent in other sectors. Statistical data included.

40817 ■ *"Steering Toward Profitability" in Black Enterprise (Vol. 41, December 2010, No. 5, pp. 72)*
Pub: Earl G. Graves Publishing Co. Inc.
Ed: Alan Hughes. **Description:** Systems Electro Coating LLC had to make quick adjustments when auto manufacturers were in a slump. The minority father-daughter team discuss their strategies during the auto industry collapse.

40818 ■ *"Still Stretching" in Business Courier (Vol. 24, December 28, 2008, No. 37, pp. 1)*
Pub: American City Business Journals, Inc.
Ed: Lucy May. **Description:** Minority-owned businesses have experienced growth in 2007 as Cincinnati and Hamilton County used a workforce development and economic inclusion policy. Kroger Co., for example, has been inducted to the Billion Dollar Roundtable in 2007 for attaining $1 billion in annual spending with suppliers that are minority- owned. The need for more progress within the minority-owned enterprises is discussed.

40819 ■ *"Still Unprepared For Natural Disasters" in Black Enterprise (Vol. 38, January 2008, No. 6, pp. 28)*
Pub: Earl G. Graves Publishing Co. Inc.
Ed: Alexis McCombs. **Description:** According to a study conducted by the American Red Cross, 19 percent of African Americans are not prepared for a natural disaster, compared to 10 percent of white Americans.

40820 ■ *"Teaneck Resident Chairs National Minority Business Group" in Record (January 5, 2011)*
Pub: Record
Ed: Andrew Tangel. **Description:** National Minority Business Council Inc. is a trade group for minority women- and veteran-owned small businesses. Ben Jones began his term as chairman of the group in January 2011.

40821 ■ *"They Have Issues: New Black-Owned Investment Bank Nets $90 Million In Managed Issues" in Black Enterprise (Vol. 38, March 2008)*
Pub: Earl G. Graves Publishing Co. Inc.
Ed: Marcia A. Wade. **Description:** Castle Oak Securities LP has co-managed multiple deals for more than 35 blue-chip clients. Their first deal earned $300 million for General Electric Capital Corporation and Castle Oak has since co-managed nine more deals with GE Capital, seven for Citigroup, six for American Express, and three for Goldman Sachs.

40822 ■ *"Too Much Information?" in Black Enterprise (Vol. 37, December 2006, No. 5, pp. 59)*
Pub: Earl G. Graves Publishing Co. Inc.
Ed: James C. Johnson. **Description:** African American business owners often face the dilemma of whether or not to divulge their minority status when soliciting new customers and financial institutions. The quality of the products or services is always the key factor and race should never define one's business; however, it is appropriate to market oneself as a minority or women-owned business, especially if the company is in an industry where those clients are offered top-tier contracts.

40823 ■ *"Top 100 Consolidate Gains" in Hispanic Business (Vol. 30, July-August 2008, No. 7-8, pp. 30)*
Pub: Hispanic Business, Inc.
Ed: Richard Kaplan. **Description:** Data developed by HispanTelligence on the increase in revenue posted by the top 100 fastest-growing U.S. Hispanic firms over the last five years is reported. Despite the economic downturn, the service sector, IT and health suppliers showed an increase in revenue whereas construction companies showed a marginal slump in revenue growth.

40824 ■ *"Transform Your Life" in Black Enterprise (Vol. 37, January 2007, No. 6, pp. 14)*
Pub: Earl G. Graves Publishing Co. Inc.
Description: Through the magazine, television and radio programs, events, and the website, the various platforms of Black Enterprise will provide the tools necessary to achieve success in business ventures, career aspirations, and personal goals.

40825 ■ *"Two Local Firms Make Inc. List: Minority Business" in Indianapolis Business Journal (Vol. 31, August 30, 2010, No. 26, pp. 13A)*
Pub: Indianapolis Business Journal Corporation
Description: Smart IT staffing agency and Entap Inc., an IT outsourcing firm were among the top ten fastest growing black-owned businesses in the U.S. by Inc. magazine.

40826 ■ *"Vernon Revamp" in Business Courier (Vol. 26, October 9, 2009, No. 24, pp. 1)*
Pub: American City Business Journals, Inc.
Ed: Dan Monk. **Description:** Al Neyer Inc. will redevelop the Vernon Manor Hotel as an office building for the Cincinnati Children's Hospital Medical Center. The project will cost $35 million and would generate a new investment vehicle for black investors who plan to raise $2.7 million in private offerings to claim majority ownership of the property after its renovations.

40827 ■ *"A View to a Killer Business Model" in Black Enterprise (Vol. 40, December 2009, No. 5, pp. 50)*
Pub: Earl G. Graves Publishing Co., Inc.
Ed: Sonya A. Donaldson. **Description:** Profile of Gen2Media Corp., a production, technology and Internet marketing firm based in Florida with offices in New York; Gen2Media is utilizing the advances in technology to now include video in its online marketing offerings.

40828 ■ *"Wal-Mart Sharpens Focus on Roxbury" in Boston Business Journal (Vol. 31, July 8, 2011, No. 24, pp. 1)*
Pub: Boston Business Journal
Ed: Mary Moore. **Description:** Wal-Mart Stores is boosting its search for a possible location in the Roxbury section of Boston, Massachusetts. The search is focused on underserved communities in terms of jobs and access to reasonably-priced merchandise. The extent Boston's African American community has clashed with Mayor Thomas M. Memino over the accommodations of the retailer in Roxbury is discussed.

40829 ■ *"We Do: Copreneurs Simultaneously Build Happy Marriages and Thriving Enterprises" in Black Enterprise (Vol. 38, February 2008)*
Pub: Earl G. Graves Publishing Co. Inc.
Ed: Krissah Williams. **Description:** Of the 2.7 million businesses in the U.S. that are equally owned by male-female partnerships, about 79,000 are black-owned. One couple shares their experiences of working and growing their business together.

40830 ■ *Women Entrepreneurs*
Pub: Edward Elgar Publishing, Incorporated
Ed: Andrea Smith-Hunter. **Released:** October 2006. **Price:** $120.00. **Description:** Focus is on women entrepreneurs; information includes human capital, network structures and financial capital, with comparative analysis across racial lines.

40831 ■ *"Women of Power Summit" in Black Enterprise (Vol. 38, February 2008, No. 7, pp. 163)*
Pub: Earl G. Graves Publishing Co. Inc.
Description: Third annual Women of Power Summit, hosted by State Farm, will host over 700 executive women of color offering empowerment sessions, tips for networking, along with entertainment.

TRADE PERIODICALS

40832 ■ *Black Enterprise*
Pub: Earl Graves Publishing Co.
URL(s): www.blackenterprise.com/magazine. **Ed:** Earl G. Graves, Sr. **Released:** Monthly **Price:** $14. 95, Individuals; $29.95, Other countries; $27.95, Two years.

40833 ■ *The Columbus Times*
Pub: Columbus Times
Contact: Ophelia Mitchell, Chief Executive Officer
URL(s): www.columbustimes.com/. **Released:** Weekly (Wed.) **Price:** $65.48, Individuals; $0.50, Single issue.

40834 ■ *Hispanic Business*
Pub: Hispanic Business Inc.
URL(s): www.hispanicbusiness.com. **Released:** 10/ yr. **Price:** $9.99, Individuals.

40835 ■ *Minority Business Entrepreneur*
Pub: Minority Business Entrepreneur
Contact: Anthony Robinson, President
URL(s): www.mbemag.com/. **Released:** Bimonthly **Price:** $18, Individuals print only; $30, Two years print only.

40836 ■ *Multicultural Marketing News*
Pub: Multicultural Marketing Resources Inc.
Contact: Lisa Skriloff, Editor-in-Chief
Released: Bimonthly. **Price:** $1050 for Multicultural Marketing News only; $250 for MMN Online only. **Description:** Covers minority- and women-owned businesses and corporations that sell to them. Provides story ideas, diverse resources for journalists, and contacts for marketing executives. Recurring features include a calendar of events, business profiles, and a feature on a trend in multicultural marketing.

40837 ■ *NMBC Business Report*
Pub: National Minority Business Council Inc.
Contact: John Robinson, Publisher
Ed: Julian Reynolds, Editor. **Released:** Semiannual. **Price:** Free. **Description:** Focuses on business issues relevant to the minority business community.

VIDEOCASSETTES/ AUDIOCASSETTES

40838 ■ *Ebony/Jet Guide to Black Excellence: The Entrepreneurs*
Home Vision Cinema
c/o Image Entertainment
20525 Nordhoff St., Ste. 200
Chatsworth, CA 91311
Co. E-mail: inquiries@image-entertainment.com
URL: http://www.homevision.com
Released: 1992. **Price:** $24.95. **Description:** A look at three African-Americans who have built their own businesses: John H. Johnson of Johnson Publishing Company, Joshua I. Smith of the Maxima Corporation, and Oprah Winfrey, talk show host and CEO of Harpo Productions. **Availability:** VHS.

CONSULTANTS

40839 ■ Joel Greenstein & Associates (JGA)
6212 Nethercombe Ct.
McLean, VA 22101
Ph: (703)893-1888
Co. E-mail: jgreenstein@contractmasters.com
Contact: Joel Greenstein, Principal
E-mail: jgreenstein@contractmasters.com
Scope: Provides services to minority and women-owned businesses and government agencies. Specializes in interpreting federal, agency-specific acquisition regulations and contract terms and conditions. Offers assistance with preparing technical, cost proposals and sealed bids.

COMPUTERIZED DATABASES

40840 ■ *HispanTelligence®*
425 Pine Ave.
Santa Barbara, CA 93117-3709
Ph: (805)964-4554
Fax: (805)964-5539
URL: http://www.hispanicbusiness.com
Availability: Online: Hispanic Business Inc. **Type:** Directory.

40841 ■ *National Directory of Minority-Owned Business Firms*
7720 Wisconsin Ave., Ste. 213
Bethesda, MD 20814
Ph: (301)229-5561
Free: 800-845-8420
Fax: (301)229-6133
Co. E-mail: brspubs@sba8a.com
URL: http://www.sba8a.com

Availability: CD-ROM: Business Research Services Inc. **Type:** Directory.

TRADE PERIODICALS

40842 ▪ *Urgent Communications: Technical Information for Paging, Trunking and Private Wireless Networks*
Pub: Penton
Contact: Raymond E. Maloney, President
URL(s): urgentcomm.com/. **Ed:** Donny Jackson. **Released:** Monthly

FRANCHISES AND BUSINESS OPPORTUNITIES

40843 ▪ Altracolor Systems
Aftermarket Appearance Industries Inc.
111 Phlox Ave. 0162
Metairie, LA 70001-4537
Ph: (504)456-1714
Free: 800-727-6567
Fax: (504)456-1714
Co. E-mail: altra@altracolor.com
URL: http://www.altracolor.com
Description: Mobile auto painting and plastic repair. **No. of Franchise Units:** 60. **Founded:** 1989.. **Franchised:** 1991. **Equity Capital Needed:** $37,500-$53,950 total investment. **Franchise Fee:** $8,000-$19,950. **Royalty Fee:** $95/week. **Financial Assistance:** Limited in-house financing available. **Training:** Yes.

40844 ▪ Fast-teks On-site Computer Services
15310 Amberly Dr., Ste. 185
Tampa, FL 33647
Ph: (800)262-1671
Fax: (813)932-2485
URL: http://www.fastteks.com
Description: Onsite computer repair services. **No. of Franchise Units:** 249. **Founded:** 2003.. **Franchised:** 2004. **Equity Capital Needed:** $36,460-$62,260. **Franchise Fee:** $19,750-$42,250. **Royalty Fee:** 8%. **Financial Assistance:** Third party financing available. **Training:** Offers 2 days training at headquarters and 2 days onsite with ongoing support provided.

40845 ▪ Kidokinetics
304 Indian Trace, Ste. 121
Weston, FL 33326
Ph: (954)385-8511
Fax: (954)217-5928
Description: Children's mobile sports/fitness. **No. of Franchise Units:** 3. **No. of Company-Owned Units:** 1. **Founded:** 2000.. **Franchised:** 2007. **Equity Capital Needed:** $42,900-$57,000. **Franchise Fee:** $30,000. **Training:** Yes.

40846 ▪ Mobile Attic Franchising Company
Mobile Attic, Inc.
246 Larkin Rd.
Elba, AL 36323
Ph: (334)897-1346
Free: 866-874-8474
Fax: (334)897-1349
Description: Portable self-storage. **No. of Franchise Units:** 40. **No. of Company-Owned Units:** 4. **Founded:** 2000.. **Franchised:** 2004. **Equity Capital Needed:** $250,000+. **Financial Assistance:** Yes. **Training:** Yes.

40847 ▪ Paramount Home Beauty
100 N Main St.
Chagrin Falls, OH 44022
Ph: (440)893-0920
Fax: (440)461-4046
Description: Mobile salon & spa services for medically restricted individuals. **Founded:** 2004.. **Franchised:** 2006. **Equity Capital Needed:** $44,100. **Franchise Fee:** $14,800. **Royalty Fee:** 5%. **Training:** Includes 5 days training at headquarters, 5 days optional training onsite, and ongoing support. pport.

40848 ▪ Pop-A-Lock
SystemForward America, Inc.
1018 Harding St., Ste. 101
Lafayette, LA 70503
Ph: (337)233-6211
Co. E-mail: michaelkleimeyer@systemforward.com
URL: http://www.popalock.com
Description: Mobile locksmith/car unlocking service. There is no build-out required with quick to market/revenue generation. Your employees provide our mobile tech services to commercial & residential customers, and national accounts. **No. of Franchise Units:** 220. **Founded:** 1991.. **Franchised:** 1994. **Equity Capital Needed:** $50,000 and up, based on territory population. **Franchise Fee:** $29,000. **Training:** Offers new franchisee business training, employee advanced technical training including state-of-the-art dispatch service. Provides ongoing technical updates, public relations and marketing, business analysis, and National Accounts Support-mentor program.

Multicultural Workforce

ASSOCIATIONS AND OTHER ORGANIZATIONS

40849 ■ American Library Association - Ethnic and Peoplecultural Information Exchange Roundtable (EMIERT)
50 E Huron
Office for Literary and Outreach Studies
Chicago, IL 60611
Ph: (312)280-4295
Free: 800-545-2433
Fax: (312)280-3256
Co. E-mail: sorange@ala.org
URL: http://www.ala.org/ala/emiert/aboutemiert/aboutemiert.htm

Description: A round table of the ALA. Exchanges information about minority materials and library services for minority groups in the U.S. Conducts educational programs with a focus on multicultural librarianship. **Founded:** 1972. **Publications:** *Directory of Ethnic & Multicultural Publishers, Distributors and Resource Organizations, 5th Edition* (Periodic); *EMIE Bulletin* (Quarterly). **Educational Activities:** American Library Association I Ethnic and Peoplecultural Information Exchange Roundtable Meeting (Annual); American Library Association I Ethnic and Peoplecultural Information Exchange Roundtable Conference (Annual). **Awards:** Coretta Scott King Book Award (Annual); David Cohen/EMIERT Award (Annual); GALE/EMIERT Multicultural Award (Annual).

40850 ■ Common Destiny Alliance (CODA)
University of Maryland
2110 Benjamin Bldg.
College Park, MD 20742
Ph: (301)405-0639
Fax: (301)405-3573
Co. E-mail: mh267@umail.umd.edu
URL: http://www.education.umd.edu/CODA/index.html

Description: Organizations and scholars interested in working to end prejudice. Fosters the viewpoint that cultural diversity is "a resource that can help the nation attain goals such as improving economic productivity and the academic achievement of all children." Seeks to end racial isolation in schools, neighborhoods, and the work force. Promotes social policies, especially those related to education, that encourage racial and ethnic understanding and cooperation. Conducts research to identify the causes of racism and means to overcome racism. **Scope:** multicultural education, race relations, postsecondary education, professional development. **Founded:** 1991. **Publications:** *Tracking, Diversity, and Educational Equity: What's New in the Research*; *Toward a Common Destiny: Improving Race and Ethnic Relations in America*.

40851 ■ Institute of HeartMath (IHM)
14700 W Park Ave.
Boulder Creek, CA 95006
Ph: (831)338-8500
Free: 800-711-6221
Fax: (831)338-8504
Co. E-mail: info@heartmath.org
URL: http://www.heartmath.org
Contact: Sara Childre, President

URL(s): www.heartmath.com. **Description:** Works to create a cultural shift in how organizations view people, and how people view each other and themselves. Seeks to scientifically validate the intelligence of the heart. Conducts biomedical research programs on the sources of stress, including work with post-cardiac patients, people interested in emotional management, educators serving child populations of at risk, learning disabled, at risk for violence, and in all sectors of society. **Scope:** stress, intuition, education. **Founded:** 1991. **Subscriptions:** articles books monographs papers. **Publications:** *HeartMath Report*; *IHM Newsletters*; *Science of the Heart*; *Heartmath Solution*. **Telecommunication Services:** inquiry@heartmath.com; service@heartmath.org.

40852 ■ National MultiCultural Institute (NMCI)
1666 K St. NW, Ste. 440
Washington, DC 20006-1242
Ph: (202)483-0700
Fax: (202)483-5233
Co. E-mail: nmci@nmci.org
URL: http://www.nmci.org
Contact: Elizabeth Pathy Salett, President
E-mail: Salett@nmci.org

Description: Seeks to work with individuals, organizations, and communities in creating a society that is strengthened and empowered by its diversity. Leads efforts to increase communication, understanding, and respect among diverse groups and addresses important issues of multiculturalism facing society today. Provides organizational training and consulting on diversity issues and develops leading edge projects in the field. Cross-cultural conflict resolution, and initiating cross-cultural dialogues. Programs serve professionals in such fields as management, human resource development, education, health and mental health, social services, refugee resettlement, mediation, and law enforcement. **Scope:** A non-profit organization specializing in the areas of workforce diversity, human resource management, multicultural education and cross-cultural conflict resolution. Offers consulting programs in policy review and benchmarking; strengthening recruitment and retention programs; promoting cross-cultural communication; leading crisis interventions; and networking with affinity groups. Provides training programs for employees in building cultural competence; cultural competency in dialogue facilitation; leadership development; managing a diverse workforce; mediating multicultural conflict; organizational culture change; preventing sexual harassment; recruiting, interviewing, hiring and retaining a culturally diverse staff; strategic planning; and training of diversity trainers. **Founded:** 1983. **Publications:** "Race, Ethnicity and Self: Identity in Multicultural Perspective," 2003; "Race, Gender & Rhetoric: The True State of Race and Gender Relations in Corporate America," 1998; "Crossing Cultures in Mental Health".

EDUCATIONAL PROGRAMS

40853 ■ Developing Diversity Communication and Messaging (Onsite)
Seminar Information Service, Inc.
20 Executive Park, Ste. 120
Irvine, CA 92614
Ph: (949)261-9104
Free: 877-SEM-INFO
Fax: (949)261-1963
Co. E-mail: info@seminarinformation.com
URL: http://www.seminarinformation.com

Price: $795.00. **Description:** Covers basic concepts of developing a diversity communication strategy and key techniques for communicating a diversity crisis.

40854 ■ Diversity Awareness (Onsite)
Seminar Information Service, Inc.
20 Executive Park, Ste. 120
Irvine, CA 92614
Ph: (949)261-9104
Free: 877-SEM-INFO
Fax: (949)261-1963
Co. E-mail: info@seminarinformation.com
URL: http://www.seminarinformation.com

Price: $795.00. **Description:** Increase understanding of all aspects of diversity and begin the process of dialogue and working together productively.

40855 ■ Diversity Train-the-Trainer (Onsite)
Seminar Information Service, Inc.
20 Executive Park, Ste. 120
Irvine, CA 92614
Ph: (949)261-9104
Free: 877-SEM-INFO
Fax: (949)261-1963
Co. E-mail: info@seminarinformation.com
URL: http://www.seminarinformation.com

Price: $1,820.00. **Description:** Designed to build the confidence, knowledge, and skills of individuals charged with conducting high impact, relevant, and involved diversity education and training in their organization. **Dates and Locations:** New York, NY.

40856 ■ Training Difficult Issues in Diversity (Onsite)
Seminar Information Service, Inc.
20 Executive Park, Ste. 120
Irvine, CA 92614
Ph: (949)261-9104
Free: 877-SEM-INFO
Fax: (949)261-1963
Co. E-mail: info@seminarinformation.com
URL: http://www.seminarinformation.com

Price: $1,395.00. **Description:** Provides trainers with a step-by-step curriculum for delivering training and education on the tougher issues, including racism, privilege, religion, sexual orientation, gender identity, and oppression. Explore training techniques and models that get diversity messages across. **Dates and Locations:** New York, NY.

REFERENCE WORKS

40857 ■ *"2007 Best Schools for Hispanics: Head of the Class" in Hispanic Business (September 2007, pp. 34, 36, 38)*
Pub: Hispanic Business
Ed: Hildy Medina. **Description:** Stanford's business school recruits Hispanic students through the Charles P. Bonini Partnership for Diversity Fellowship program. A listing of the top schools for business, engineering, law, and medicine for Hispanics are included.

40858 ■ *"An Analysis of Three Labor Unions' Outreach to Brazilian Immigrant Workers in Boston" in WorkingUSA (Vol. 11, June 2008, No. 2)*
Pub: Blackwell Publishers Ltd.
Ed: Joshua Kirshner. **Description:** Author seeks to shed light on the conditions under which labor unions can include immigrants in their ranks as a means to regain their strength. It does so by focusing on the example of Brazilian immigrants in Boston and compares the approaches of three union locals in Boston toward organizing Brazilian workers, the Painters, the Teamsters, and the United Food and Commercial Workers Union. While previous studies argue that ethnicity and social networks can account for immigrants' receptivity to unions, this article highlights strategic choice on the part of union officials as an important factor in facilitating unionization of Brazilian workers.

40859 ■ *"Another Determinant of Entrepreneurship" in International Journal of Entrepreneurship and Small Business (Vol. 10, July 6, 2010)*
Pub: Publishers Communication Group
Ed: Felix Pauligard Ntep, Wilton Wilton. **Description:** Interviews were carried out with entrepreneurs of Douala, Cameroon. These entrepreneurs believe that witchcraft existed and could bring harm to them or their enterprises.

40860 ■ *"Ask Inc." in Inc. (December 2007, pp. 83-84)*
Pub: Gruner & Jahr USA Publishing
Ed: Ari Weinzweig. **Description:** Questions regarding knowledge management in the case of a retiring CFO, issues involved in opening a satellite office for a New York realtor, and information for hiring a multicultural workforce are all discussed.

40861 ■ *"Be a Better Manager: Live Abroad" in Harvard Business Review (Vol. 88, September 2010, No. 9, pp. 24)*
Pub: Harvard Business School Publishing
Ed: William W. Maddux, Adam D. Galinsky, Carmit T. Tadmor. **Description:** Interrelationship between international experience and entrepreneurship is discussed. Individuals with international experience are likelier to be promoted and to develop new products and businesses.

40862 ■ *The Big Payback: The History of the Business of Hip-Hop*
Pub: New American Library/Penguin Group
Ed: Dan Charnas. **Price:** $24.95. **Description:** The complete history of hip-hop music is presented, by following the money and the relationship between artist and merchant. In its promise of economic security and creative control for black artist-entrepreneurs, it is the culmination of dreams of black nationalists and civil rights leaders.

40863 ■ *"Bond Hill Cinema Site To See New Life" in Business Courier (Vol. 27, October 29, 2010, No. 26, pp. 1)*
Pub: Business Courier
Ed: Dan Monk. **Description:** Avondale, Ohio's Corinthian Baptist Church will redevelop the 30-acre former Showcase Cinema property to a mixed-use site that could feature a college, senior home, and retail. Corinthian Baptist, which is one of the largest African-American churches in the region, is also planning to relocate the church.

40864 ■ *"Border Boletin: UA to Take Lie-Detector Kiosk to Poland" in Arizona Daily Star (September 14, 2010)*
Pub: Arizona Daily Star
Ed: Brady McCombs. **Description:** University of Arizona's National Center for Border Security and Immigration Research will send a team to Warsaw, Poland to show border guards from 27 European Union countries the center's Avatar Kiosk. The Avatar technology is designed for use at border ports and airports to assist Customs officers detect individuals who are lying.

40865 ■ *"Buying Power of Hispanics Growing" in Austin Business JournalInc. (Vol. 29, November 27, 2009, No. 38, pp. 1)*
Pub: American City Business Journals
Ed: Sandra Zaragoza. **Description:** Hispanic Marketing Symposium presented a report stating that the buying power of Hispanics of Austin, Texas has grown by 54 percent in last five years to $9.4 billion in 2009. Details on the projected growth of the Hispanic market in the are is covered.

40866 ■ *"Casino Minority Spend: $80 Million" in Business Courier (Vol. 27, August 20, 2010, No. 16, pp. 1)*
Pub: Business Courier
Ed: Lucy May. **Description:** Real estate developers are planning to invest $80 million to build the Harrah's casino project in Cincinnati, Ohio. Rock Ventures LLC is seeking a 20 percent inclusion rate in the project.

40867 ■ *"A Cautionary Tale for Emerging Market Giants" in Harvard Business Review (Vol. 88, September 2010, No. 9, pp. 99)*
Pub: Harvard Business School Publishing
Ed: J. Stewart Black, Allen J. Morrison. **Description:** Key factors that negatively affected Japan corporate growth and organizational effectiveness include: devotion to established path, isolated domestic markets, homogenous executive teams, and a non-contentious labor force. Solutions include leadership development programs, multicultural input, and cross-cultural training.

40868 ■ *"CEOs Split on Migrant Workers" in Canadian Business (Vol. 83, September 14, 2010, No. 15, pp. 23)*
Pub: Rogers Media Ltd.
Ed: Jacqueline Nelson. **Description:** A survey of Canadian CEOs shows that 49 percent of the respondents believe it was wrong to suspend the immigration programs and companies should be allowed to hire the most skilled workers regardless of citizenship. However, 42 percent believe the suspension was right because employment of Canadians must take precedence.

40869 ■ *Chinese Ethnic Business*
Pub: Routledge Inc.
Ed: Eric Fong; Chiu Ming Luk. **Released:** October 2006. **Description:** Impact of globalization on Chinese ethnic small businesses is covered, focusing on U.S., Australia, and Canada.

40870 ■ *Chinese Ethnic Business: Global and Local Perspectives*
Pub: Routledge
Ed: Eric Fong; Chiu Luk. **Released:** May 2009. **Price:** $39.95 paperback. **Description:** Globalization impacts on the development of Chinese businesses are analyzed, focusing on economic globalization of the United States, Australia, and Canada. Information is focused on economic globalization and Chinese community development, transnational linkages, local urban structures, homogenization and place attachment, as well as methodology such as ethnographic studies, historical analysis, geographic studies and statistical analysis.

40871 ■ *"The Color of Success: ELC Focuses On Making Diversity Work" in Black Enterprise (Vol. 41, December 2010, No. 5, pp. 59)*
Pub: Earl G. Graves Publishing Co. Inc.
Ed: Sonia Alleyne. **Description:** CEOs and top ELC members at the annual recognition conference held in New York in October 2010 shared their perspective on corporate inclusion and advice for C-suite aspirants.

40872 ■ *"Construction Firms Support NAACP Plan" in Business Courier (Vol. 27, September 24, 2010, No. 21, pp. 1)*
Pub: Business Courier
Ed: Lucy May. **Description:** Executives of Turner Construction Company and Messer Construction Company expressed their support for the Cincinnati National Association for the Advancement of Colored People Construction Partnership Agreement. The agreement involves the setting of rules for the involvement of firms owned by African Americans in major projects in Cincinnati.

40873 ■ *"CSX Transportation: Supplier Diversity on the Right Track" in Hispanic Business (July-August 2009, pp. 34)*
Pub: Hispanic Business
Description: CSX Transportation is a leader in delivering essential products, operating as many as 1,200 trains and a fleet of more than 100,000 freight cars. CSX attributes its success by valuing diversity in both hiring and supplier contracts.

40874 ■ *The Diversity Code: Unlocking the Secrets to Making Differences Work in the Real World*
Pub: AMACOM
Ed: Michelle T. Johnson. **Released:** September 8, 2010. **Price:** $19.95. **Description:** The most diligent compliance with laws and regulations can't foster true work place diversity. The best organizations have become genuine cross-cultural communities that believe equality in reconciling difference and valuing them. The book promotes understanding by answering many of the toughest questions that professionals and their employers are afraid to ask.

40875 ■ *"Diversity Elite Scorecard" in Hispanic Business (September 2007, pp. 72-74, 76, 78, 80, 82, 84)*
Pub: Hispanic Business
Description: Special report on companies committed to diversity in 2007 is presented along with a brief profile of each company. Southern California Edison and AT&T Inc. topped the list.

40876 ■ *"Diversity Knocks" in Canadian Business (Vol. 83, October 12, 2010, No. 17, pp. 62)*
Pub: Rogers Media Ltd.
Ed: Angelina Chapin. **Description:** Canadian companies have a global edge because of their multicultural workforce. However, most of these organizations do not take advantage and avoid doing business abroad. Canadian firms could leverage their multicultural staff with language skills and knowledge of local customs.

40877 ■ *Doing Business Anywhere: The Essential Guide to Going Global*
Pub: John Wiley and Sons, Inc.
Ed: Tom Travis. **Released:** 2007. **Price:** $24.95. **Description:** Plans are given for new or existing businesses to organize, plan, operate and execute a business on a global basis. Trade agreements, brand protection and patents, ethics, security as well as cultural issues are among the issues addressed.

40878 ■ *"Ethnic Businesses Ending Vacancies" in Business First-Columbus (Vol. 26, August 20, 2010, No. 51, pp. 1)*
Pub: Business First
Ed: Carrie Ghose. **Description:** The Morse Road commercial corridor in Columbus, Ohio has several immigrant-owned businesses that were recognized as instrumental in preventing widespread vacancies when the Northland Mall closed in 2002. The ethnic stores have created a diverse destination that attracted traffic and more businesses.

40879 ■ *Ethnic Solidarity for Economic Survival: Korean Greengrocers in New York City*
Pub: Russell Sage Foundation Publications
Ed: Pyong Gap Min. **Released:** August 2008. **Price:** $32.50. **Description:** Investigations into the entrepreneurial traditions of Korean immigrant families in New

York City running ethnic businesses, particularly small grocery stores and produce markets. Social, cultural and economic issues facing these retailers are discussed.

40880 ■ *"Filling the Business Gap" in Hispanic Business (December 2010)*
Pub: Hispanic Business
Ed: Richard Larsen. **Description:** New York group seeks to increase state diversity supplier spending to help create jobs and boost the economy. According to a recent study, six out of 10 small business owners will increase capital spending but delay hiring in 2011. However, potential job creation is good among businesses owned by women and minorities.

40881 ■ *"Finding Your Place in the World: Global Diversity Has Become a Corporate Catchphrase" in Black Enterprise (November 2007)*
Pub: Earl G. Graves Publishing Co. Inc.
Ed: Wendy Harris. **Description:** Does the inclusion of workers from other countries mean exclusion of African American workers in the U.S.?.

40882 ■ *"Future of Diversity: Cultural Inclusion Is a Business Imperative" in Black Enterprise (Vol. 41, August 2010, No. 1, pp. 75)*
Pub: Earl G. Graves Publishing Co. Inc.
Ed: Annya M. Lott. **Description:** As globalization continues to make the world a smaller place, workforce diversity will be imperative to any small company in order to be sustainable.

40883 ■ *Gendered Processes: Korean Immigrant Small Business Ownership*
Pub: LFB Scholarly Publishing LLC
Ed: Eunju Lee. **Released:** November 2005. **Price:** $60.00. **Description:** Examination of the gender processes among Korean immigrants becoming small business owners in the New York City metropolitan area.

40884 ■ *"Get Hired Now! A 28-Day Program for Landing the Job You Want" in Black Enterprise (Vol. 37, October 2006, No. 3, pp. 119)*
Pub: Earl G. Graves Publishing Co. Inc.
Ed: C.J. Hayden; Frank Traditi. **Description:** Finding a job can be a challenge. Surveys estimate that 74 to 85 percent of those available are never advertised. Tips for searching out employment opportunities and landing the job you desire are explored.

40885 ■ *"Give Us Your Skilled" in Canadian Business (Vol. 80, October 8, 2007, No. 20, pp. 78)*
Pub: Rogers Media
Ed: Zena Olijnyk. **Description:** Demand for skilled workers in Canada is discussed. Despite a strong demand, as evidenced by shortages in both skilled and unskilled labor, the country's immigration policy is affecting the recruitment process. Peter Veress, founder and president of Vermax Group, believes the country is wasting opportunities to take advantage of its attractiveness as a destination for foreign workers.

40886 ■ *"HireDiversity: Some Companies Developing Affinity for Employee Groups" in Hispanic Business (October 2007, pp. 86-87)*
Pub: Hispanic Business
Ed: Hildy Medina. **Description:** Affinity groups, also known as employee resource networks, help companies identify and recruit candidates.

40887 ■ *"Investment Firms Unite: Coalition Fights New Tax Law" in Black Enterprise (Vol. 38, December 2007, No. 5, pp. 52)*
Pub: Earl G. Graves Publishing Co. Inc.
Ed: Joyce Jones. **Description:** Minorities working in private equity, real estate and investment management firms have united to form the Access to Capital Coalition to oppose legislation that they feel would adversely affect their ability to attract investments and executives. Details of the group are included.

40888 ■ *"It's Not Rocket Science" in Hispanic Business (September 2007, pp. 30, 32)*
Pub: Hispanic Business
Ed: Hildy Medina. **Description:** Profile of France Cordova, president of Purdue University. Cordova has established many diversity programs at the school.

40889 ■ *The Jewish Century*
Pub: Princeton University Press
Ed: Yuri Slezkins. **Released:** August 2006. **Price:** $18.95. **Description:** Success and vulnerability of individuals of Jewish descent is discussed, uncovering the 'Jewish Revolution' within the Russian Revolution.

40890 ■ *"Labor Force Data" in Montly Labor Review (Vol. 133, September 2010, No. 9, pp. 89)*
Pub: Bureau of Labor Statistics
Description: Employment status of the population of the U.S. by sex, age, race and origin is presented.

40891 ■ *"LatinWorks Cozies Up to Chevy in Detroit" in Austin Business Journal (Vol. 31, August 12, 2011, No. 23, pp. A1)*
Pub: American City Business Journals Inc.
Ed: Sandra Zaragoza. **Description:** Hispanic marketing agency LatinWorks opened an office in Detroit to better serve its client Chevrolet and to potentially secure more contracts from its parent company General Motors, whose offices are located nearby.

40892 ■ *"Leadership Counts" in Hispanic Business (January-February 2008, pp. 60, 62)*
Pub: Hispanic Business
Ed: Frank Nelson. **Description:** Small business leaders discuss the importance of including diversity initiatives into any plan.

40893 ■ *"Leaks in the Pipeline" in Hispanic Business (September 2007, pp. 18, 20, 22, 24)*
Pub: Hispanic Business
Ed: Holly Ocasio Rizzo. **Description:** Graduate schools need to focus on domestic diversity in order to attract Hispanic students in a growing global economy.

40894 ■ *"Leaps and Bounds: Liberty Power, Force 3 Ride Rapid Expansion to the Top" in Hispanic Business (July-August 2007, pp. 20-22, 24)*
Pub: Hispanic Business
Ed: Derek Reveron. **Description:** Profiles of Liberty Power Corporation, a Florida supplier of retail electricity and Force 3 Inc. of Maryland, network infrastructure developer are two of the 100 fastest growing Hispanic businesses recognized in 2007.

40895 ■ *"Legalities of Diversity" in Hispanic Business (September 2007, pp. 26)*
Pub: Hispanic Business
Ed: Francisco Ramos Jr., Bill Krutzen. **Description:** Most companies in America have diversity programs, however, critics believe diversity can be used as reverse discrimination because minorities are getting preferential treatment in hiring, promotion, and admissions.

40896 ■ *The Logic of Life: The Rational Economics of an Irrational World*
Pub: Random House
Ed: Tim Harford. **Released:** February 2009. **Price:** $15.00 paperback. **Description:** Harford excels at making economists' studies palatable for discerning but non-expert readers. The uses hard data to show why promiscuous teens are actually health-conscious, divorce hasn't gotten a fair shake, corporate bosses will always be overpaid and job prospects for minorities continue to be grim.

40897 ■ *Managing the Older Worker: How to Prepare for the New Organizational Order*
Pub: Harvard Business Press
Ed: Peter Cappelli, Bill Novelli. **Price:** $29.95. **Description:** Your organization needs older workers more than ever: They transfer knowledge between generations, transmit your company's values to new hires, make excellent mentors for younger employees, and provide a 'just in time' workforce for special projects.

40898 ■ *"Native Wisdom" in Canadian Business (Vol. 80, October 8, 2007, No. 20, pp. 121)*
Pub: Rogers Media
Ed: Bernd Christmas. **Description:** Roles of Canadian indigenous peoples in the country's economic development are discussed. It is believed that empowering Canadian natives to contribute to the country's economy will positively affect the country's future. The need for education in preparing natives for the global economy is also tackled.

40899 ■ *"A New Breed of Entrepreneurs" in Black Enterprise (Vol. 37, November 2006, No. 4, pp. 16)*
Pub: Earl G. Graves Publishing Co. Inc.
Description: Black entrepreneurs are an important part of the chain for providing economic opportunities within the community. Many black business owners are more likely to hire black employees and apply innovative strategies in building their businesses rather than taking the traditional route.

40900 ■ *"The New Face of Social Media" in Hispanic Business (December 2010)*
Pub: Hispanic Business
Ed: Gary D. Fackler. **Description:** Latina bloggers carve out a new niche in social media that helps preserve their unique cultural identities.

40901 ■ *Non-Standard Employment under Globalization*
Pub: Palgrave Macmillan
Ed: Koichi Usami. **Released:** January 19, 2010. **Price:** $100.00. **Description:** Expansion of non-standard employment under globalization is being recognized in all of the newly industrialized countries. The book examines deregulation of labor markets, social protection for nonstandard workers, and social security reforms in accordance with the transformation of employment.

40902 ■ *"The One Thing That's Holding Back Your Wellness Program" in Employee Benefit News (Vol. 25, December 1, 2011, No. 15, pp. 8)*
Pub: SourceMedia Inc.
Ed: Kelley M. Butler. **Description:** A 13-year study shows that women who sat for more than six hours a day were 94 percent more likely to die during the study period. Most women sit at their desks an average of 7.7 hours while at work.

40903 ■ *"One Workforce - Many Languages" in HRMagazine (Vol. 54, January 2009, No. 1, pp. 32)*
Pub: Society for Human Resource Management
Contact: Henry G. Jackson, President
E-mail: hjackson@shrm.org
Ed: Rita Zeidner. **Description:** Many U.S. employers are investing in English classes to upgrade their immigrant workers' skills on the job.

40904 ■ *"Overseas Overtures" in Business Journal-Portland (Vol. 24, October 26, 2007, No. 35, pp. 1)*
Pub: American City Business Journals, Inc.
Ed: Robin J. Moody. **Description:** Oregon has a workforce shortage, specifically for the health care industry. Recruiting agencies, such as the International Recruiting Network Inc., answers the high demand for workforce by recruiting foreign employees. The difficulties recruiting companies experience with regards to foreign labor laws are investigated.

40905 ■ *"Perspective: Borderline Issues" in Entrepreneur (Vol. 35, October 2007, No. 10, pp. 48)*
Pub: Entrepreneur Media Inc.
Ed: Joshua Kurlantzick. **Description:** Failure of the immigration reform bill is expected to result in increased difficulty in finding workers that would take on the dirty and perilous jobs, which are usually taken by immigrants. Regularizing immigration on the other hand will cost business owners money by making

them spend for the legality of their employees' stay in the U.S. Other effects of immigration laws on entrepreneurs are discussed.

40906 ■ *"The Power of Diversity: Southern California Utility Company Tops Elite List" in Hispanic Business (September 2007, pp. 66, 68, 70)*
Pub: Hispanic Business
Ed: Frank Nelson. **Description:** Southern California Edison is committed to recognizing diversity in its consumer base, employees and potential labor market.

40907 ■ *Profiting from Diversity: The Business Advantages and the Obstacles to Achieving Diversity*
Pub: Palgrave Macmillan
Ed: Gloria Moss. **Released:** January 5, 2010. **Price:** $95.00. **Description:** Although the benefits of diversity in small business are often discussed, specific ways in which organizations can profit from diversity and some of the obstacles faced are defined.

40908 ■ *"Race and Gender Diversity" in Business Horizons (November-December 2007, pp. 445)*
Pub: Elsevier Technology Publications
Ed: James C. Wimbush. **Description:** Research conducted on diversity building, employee recruitment, gender issues in management, and pay inequality from 2006 through present are discussed. Diversity conditions and attitudes toward it are slowly improving based on these findings.

40909 ■ *"The Racial Divide and the Class Struggle in the United States" in WorkingUSA (Vol. 11, September 2008, No. 3, pp. 311)*
Pub: Blackwell Publishers Ltd.
Ed: Michael Goldfield. **Description:** An examination of questions of race that continue to play such a prominent role in contemporary society is presented, focusing on the undermining of potential solidarity and strength of the working class movement, what sustains racists attitudes, practices and institutions, especially in the face of trends in world economic development.

40910 ■ *"Retirement Barriers: Lowering Retirement System Barriers for Women" in Employee Benefit News (Vol. 25, December 1, 2011, No. 15)*
Pub: SourceMedia Inc.
Ed: Mary Nell Billings. **Description:** Challenges faced by small business for lowering retirement benefits barriers for women and minorities, which is difficult to put into practice, is discussed.

40911 ■ *"Say What?" in Entrepreneur (Vol. 35, November 2007, No. 11, pp. 106)*
Pub: Entrepreneur Media Inc.
Ed: Gail Dutton. **Description:** Business enterprises with units and employees in different parts of the world may encounter problems with culture clashes. The employees' different cultural backgrounds can cause misunderstanding that can affect a company's operations. So before doing business in a particular region, it is important to study the history and culture of the area.

40912 ■ *"Scholarships for Minority Students" in Occupational Outlook Quarterly (Vol. 54, Fall 2010, No. 3, pp. 25)*
Pub: U.S. Bureau of Labor Statistics
Description: Gates Millennium Scholars scholarship is awarded to minority students with leadership skills, a good GPA, and college aspirations.

40913 ■ *"Senate's Effort to Reform Immigration Policies Fizzles Out" in Hispanic Business (July-August 2007, pp. 62)*
Pub: Hispanic Business
Description: Legislators predict no further work towards comprehensive immigration reform is likely to occur until a new administration is in place in Washington, DC.

40914 ■ *"Speaking In Tongues: Rosetta Stone's TOTALE Adds 'Social' To Language Learning" in Black Enterprise (Vol. 41, September 2010, No. 2)*
Pub: Earl G. Graves Publishing Co. Inc.
Ed: Sonya A. Donaldson. **Description:** As small businesses become more globalized, it is necessary to learn new languages in order to compete. Rosetta Stone's TOTALe is profiled.

40915 ■ *"Taking the 'Comprehensive' Out of Immigration Reform" in Hispanic Business (September 2007, pp. 8)*
Pub: Hispanic Business
Ed: Patricia Guadalupe. **Description:** Information about the AgJOBS bill, legislation that would grant legal residency to migrant agricultural workers is discussed.

40916 ■ *"Talent Shows" in Canadian Business (Vol. 81, December 24, 2007, No. 1, pp. 14)*
Pub: Rogers Media
Ed: Megan Harman. **Description:** Canadian companies are increasingly turning to marketing to promote themselves as employers, as concerns on employee recruitment increase with the nearing retirement age of the baby boomers. Details on skills shortage, the potential advantage for the immigrant workforce, and employee retention are discussed.

40917 ■ *"Tao of Downfall" in International Journal of Entrepreneurship and Small Business (Vol. 11, August 31, 2010, No. 2, pp. 121)*
Pub: Publishers Communication Group
Ed: Wenxian Zhang, Ilan Alon. **Description:** Through historical reviews and case studies, this research seeks to understand why some initially successful entrepreneurs failed in the economic boom of past decades. Among various factors contributing to their downfall are a unique political and business environment, fragile financial systems, traditional cultural influences and personal characteristics.

40918 ■ *"Uncovering Offshoring's Invisible Costs" in HRMagazine (Vol. 54, January 2009, No. 1, pp. 1)*
Pub: Society for Human Resource Management
Contact: Henry G. Jackson, President
E-mail: hjackson@shrm.org
Ed: Rita Zeidner. **Description:** Nearly half of all offshore service work fails, often due to the invisible costs of communication and cultural friction according to researchers. The challenges of offshore services are discussed.

40919 ■ *"Wanted: African American Professional for Hire" in Black Enterprise (Vol. 37, November 2006, No. 4, pp. 93)*
Pub: Earl G. Graves Publishing Co. Inc.
Ed: Joe Watson. **Description:** Excerpt from the book, Without Excuses: Unleash the Power of Diversity to Build Your Business, speaks to the lack of diversity in the corporate arena and why executives, recruiters, and HR professionals claim they are unable to find qualified individuals of different races when hiring.

40920 ■ *"Web Site Design, Content Can Boost Diversity" in HRMagazine (Vol. 53, August 2008, No. 8, pp. 20)*
Pub: Society for Human Resource Management
Contact: Henry G. Jackson, President
E-mail: hjackson@shrm.org
Description: Design and content of an employer's Website influences prospective young job candidates, especially young black job seekers, a new academic study has found. The findings appear in Black and White and Read All Over: Race Differences in Reactions To Recruitment Web Sites, published in the summer 2008 issue of the Human Resource Management Journal.

40921 ■ *"What Employees Worldwide Have in Common" in Gallup Management Journal (September 22, 2011)*
Pub: Gallup
Ed: Steve Crabtree. **Description:** According to a Gallup study, workplace conditions are strongly tied to personal wellbeing, regardless of geographic region. The employee study covered 116 countries.

40922 ■ *"What It Takes to Be an Effective Leader" in Black Enterprise (Vol. 41, December 2010, No. 5, pp. 62)*
Pub: Earl G. Graves Publishing Co. Inc.
Ed: Sonia Alleyne. **Description:** Redia Anderson and Lenora Billings-Harris have partnered to write the book, 'Trailblazers: How Top Business Leaders Are Accelerating Results Through Inclusion and Diversity'. The book offers insight into best practices demonstrated by some of the most influential chief diversity officers in business.

40923 ■ *"Work Force: In the Mix" in Entrepreneur (Vol. 35, October 2007, No. 10, pp. 109)*
Pub: Entrepreneur Media Inc.
Ed: Mark Henricks. **Description:** A study of 708 companies' diversity programs shows that diversity training alone is not the most effective way of increasing diversity in management. It was found that one effective way of putting minorities and women in management teams is to give a team or a person the task of improving diversity in the company. The reason why accountability succeeds in diversifying the workforce is discussed.

TRADE PERIODICALS

40924 ■ *The Columbus Times*
Pub: Columbus Times
Contact: Ophelia Mitchell, Chief Executive Officer
URL(s): www.columbustimes.com/. **Released:** Weekly (Wed.) **Price:** $65.48, Individuals; $0.50, Single issue.

40925 ■ *Insight into Diversity: The EEO Recruitment Publication*
Pub: INSIGHT Into Diversity
URL(s): www.insightintodiversity.com. **Ed:** Michael Rainey. **Released:** Monthly

VIDEOCASSETTES/ AUDIOCASSETTES

40926 ■ *Bridges: Skills to Manage a Diverse Workforce*
Learning Communications L.L.C.
5520 Trabuco Rd.
Irvine, CA 92620-5705
Free: 800-622-3610
Fax: (949)727-4323
Co. E-mail: sales@learncom.com
URL: http://www.learncom.com
Contact: Lloyd W. Singer, President
Released: 1990. **Price:** $175.00. **Description:** An eight-part series designed to train supervisors and managers to deal with a culturally diverse workforce. The tapes are available individually or as a set. Trainer's manuals and participants manuals are included. **Availability:** VHS; 3/4 U.

40927 ■ *Choices*
Learning Communications L.L.C.
5520 Trabuco Rd.
Irvine, CA 92620-5705
Free: 800-622-3610
Fax: (949)727-4323
Co. E-mail: sales@learncom.com
URL: http://www.learncom.com
Contact: Lloyd W. Singer, President
Released: 1990. **Price:** $175.00. **Description:** A 12-part training course, designed to help train managers in EEO and affirmative action. Tapes are available as a set or individually. Trainer and participant manuals are included. **Availability:** VHS; 3/4 U.

40928 ■ *Combating Racism*
Chinese for Affirmative Action (CAA)
17 Walter U. Lum Pl.
San Francisco, CA 94108
Ph: (415)274-6750

Fax: (415)397-8770
Co. E-mail: info@caasf.org
URL: http://www.caasf.org
Contact: Andy Wong, Director
Released: 1973. **Description:** In this program various community representatives from San Francisco are interviewed as to what can be done to combat racism. Among those interviewed were Leonard Carter, George Tamsak, Mack Hall, Shone Martinez, John Chinn, and Margaret Cruz. **Availability:** EJ.

40929 ■ *Making Diversity Work*
American Management Association (AMA)
1601 Broadway
New York, NY 10019-7420
Ph: (212)586-8100
Free: 877-566-9441
Fax: (212)903-8168
Co. E-mail: customerservice@amanet.org
URL: http://www.amanet.org
Contact: Charles R. Craig, Chairman
Released: 1993. **Price:** $215.00. **Description:** Contains information on today's growing diversity in the work force and offers three basic guidelines that can help make diversity work. **Availability:** VHS.

40930 ■ *Managing Cultural Differences*
Gulf Publishing Co.
2 Greenway Plz., Ste. 1020
Houston, TX 77046-0208
Ph: (713)529-4301
Free: 800-231-6275
Fax: (713)520-4433
Co. E-mail: advertising@gulfpub.com
URL: http://www.gulfpub.com
Contact: John Royall, President
Released: 1984. **Price:** $95.00. **Description:** This program gives an in-depth look at how cultural differences can affect business and management practices. **Availability:** VHS; 3/4 U.

40931 ■ *Managing Diversity*
Excellence in Training Corp.
c/o ICON Training
804 Roosevelt St.
Polk City, IA 50226
Free: 800-609-0479
Co. E-mail: info@icontraining.com
URL: http://www.icontraining.com
Released: 1991. **Price:** $725.00. **Description:** A look at how to go beyond dealing with diversity to gaining from it. **Availability:** VHS; 3/4 U; Special order formats.

40932 ■ *Meeting the Diversity Challenge*
American Management Association (AMA)
1601 Broadway
New York, NY 10019-7420
Ph: (212)586-8100
Free: 877-566-9441
Fax: (212)903-8168
Co. E-mail: customerservice@amanet.org
URL: http://www.amanet.org
Contact: Charles R. Craig, Chairman
Released: 19??. **Price:** $395.00. **Description:** Points out six major challenges that are faced by management and offers specific guidelines to promote a diverse work force. **Availability:** VHS.

40933 ■ *Prejudice: A Lesson to Forget*
Capital Communications
2357-3 S. Tamiami Tr.
Venice, FL 34293
Ph: (941)492-4688
Free: 800-822-5678
Fax: (941)492-4923
Co. E-mail: cap5678@isp.com
URL: http://labtrainingvideos.com
Released: 1973. **Description:** An interview with people who exhibit unconscious prejudices against minorities. **Availability:** VHS; 3/4 U.

40934 ■ *Understanding EEOC, Part 1-3*
RMI Media
1365 N. Winchester St.
Olathe, KS 66061-5880
Ph: (913)768-1696
Free: 800-745-5480
Fax: (800)755-6910
Co. E-mail: actmedia@act.org
URL: http://www.actmedia.com
Released: 1987. **Price:** $80.00. **Description:** In this three-part series, equal employment opportunity laws are explained and followed by suggestions for companies seeking to develop practices, policies, and procedures in this area. **Availability:** VHS; 3/4 U.

40935 ■ *Vegetable Soup 1*
GPN Educational Media
1550 Executive Drive
Elgin, IL 60123
Ph: (402)472-2007
Free: 800-228-4630
Fax: (800)306-2330
Co. E-mail: askgpn@smarterville.com
URL: http://www.shopgpn.com
Released: 1975. **Description:** By dramatizing the positive value of human diversity, this series counters the negative, destructive effects of racial prejudice and isolation. Also available in 78 15-minute programs. All programs are available individually. **Availability:** VHS; 3/4 U; CC.

40936 ■ *Vegetable Soup 2*
GPN Educational Media
1550 Executive Drive
Elgin, IL 60123
Ph: (402)472-2007
Free: 800-228-4630
Fax: (800)306-2330
Co. E-mail: askgpn@smarterville.com
URL: http://www.shopgpn.com
Released: 1978. **Description:** The second season of a series that promotes racial and ethnic harmony. Also available in 60 15-minute programs. All programs are available individually. **Availability:** VHS; 3/4 U; CC.

40937 ■ *Why Value Diversity?*
American Management Association (AMA)
1601 Broadway
New York, NY 10019-7420
Ph: (212)586-8100
Free: 877-566-9441
Fax: (212)903-8168
Co. E-mail: customerservice@amanet.org
URL: http://www.amanet.org
Contact: Charles R. Craig, Chairman
Price: $395.00. **Description:** Provides insights for managers to deal with the growing diversity of today's work force. **Availability:** VHS.

40938 ■ *Working Together: Managing Cultural Diversity*
Excellence in Training Corp.
c/o ICON Training
804 Roosevelt St.
Polk City, IA 50226
Free: 800-609-0479
Co. E-mail: info@icontraining.com
URL: http://www.icontraining.com
Released: 1991. **Description:** A video training program designed to teach viewers how to develop sensitivity to other cultures and be more effective in a multi-cultural environment. A leader's guide and workbooks are included. **Availability:** VHS; 3/4 U; Special order formats.

TRADE SHOWS AND CONVENTIONS

40939 ■ National Black Masters of Business Administration Annual Conference and Exposition
National Black MBA Association (NBMBAA)
180 N Michigan Ave., Ste. 1400
Chicago, IL 60601
Ph: (312)236-2622
Fax: (312)236-0390
Co. E-mail: mail@nbmbaa.org
URL: http://www.nbmbaa.org
Contact: William Wells, Jr., Chairman of the Board
URL(s): www.nbmbaa.org. **Frequency:** Annual. **Audience:** Minority professionals and minority graduate students. **Principal Exhibits:** Fortune 500 corporations information and job recruitment services, and entrepreneurs for the Merchants Career Fair. **Telecommunication Services:** mail@nbmbaa.org.

CONSULTANTS

40940 ■ D.C.W. Research Associates International
2606 Parkdale Dr.
Kingwood, TX 77339-2476
Ph: (281)359-4234
Co. E-mail: dcwigg@earthlink.net
Contact: David C. Wigglesworth, President
E-mail: dcwigg@earthlink.net
Scope: Provider of consulting and training services in human resources professional management and organizational development with particular emphasis on: organizational analysis; human resource strategic planning; executive education; training program design and delivery; multicultural interventions such as the economic benefits of management of diversity in the workforce and the cultural determinants of international/global management; and program monitoring, evaluation, and analysis. Industries served: private industries, start-ups, energy, education and computer organizations, nonprofits, as well as government agencies (both U.S. and foreign). **Founded:** 2001. **Publications:** "Diversity and Team Building" Cross-Cultural Team Building, McGraw-Hill Ltd, London, England, 1995; "Meeting the Needs of the Multicultural Workforce"; "International/Intercultural O.D.," Organization Development Competencies, Pfeiffer Associates Publishers, 1993; "New Directions in Career Planning and the Workplace," Consulting Psychologists Press Inc., 1992.

40941 ■ Ethnicity & Mental Health Associates
25 Parkview Ave.
Bronxville, NY 10708
Ph: (914)961-1940
Fax: (914)961-1940
Contact: Joseph Giordano, Director
Scope: Managing cultural diversity in the workplace and in the delivery of services to multi ethnic/racial groups (consumers). Also offers on-site workshops, consultations and training. Industries served: Corporations; nonprofit organizations including schools, colleges, health, mental health and human service organizations; and government agencies. **Founded:** 1990. **Publications:** "Growing Up In America: Many Families, Many Cultures". **Seminars:** Managing Cultural Diversity in the Workplace; Roots and Wings: Raising Children in a Multi-ethnic Society; Prejudice Reduction.

40942 ■ Lee Grossman Associates
9030 Forestview Rd.
Evanston, IL 60203
Ph: (847)679-6796
Contact: Lee Grossman, Owner
Scope: Offers counsel in managing change, personnel issues and organization development. **Founded:** 1974. **Publications:** "The Change Agent," American Management Association; "Fat Paper, Diets for Trimming Paperwork," McGraw Hill. **Seminars:** Making Affirmative Action Work.

40943 ■ H & A International—Huiras & Associates International Training
13815 Ella Lee Ln., Ste. 100
Houston, TX 77077
Ph: (281)496-9044
Fax: (281)496-3671
Co. E-mail: dhuiras@huirasassoc.com
URL: http://www.huirasassoc.com
Contact: Dick Huiras, President
E-mail: dhuiras@huirasassoc.com
Scope: Offers executive, business, and team coaching services. Accredited in Insights Learning and Development, an International psychometric assessment tool for personal, business, sales management,

team effectiveness and learning styles. **Founded:** 1980. **Publications:** "Bond Of Mutual Trust". **Seminars:** Management Leadership/Development Certification workshop; City Slickers for Corporate America Leadership workshop; Additional workshops in communication and team building; Handling Conflict, Criticism and Anger; Managing and Coping With Stress; Team Building For The Future; Interpersonal Communication Styles.

40944 ■ Human Resource Solutions Inc.
244 5th Ave., Ste. 2645
New York, NY 10001-7604
Ph: (212)316-2800
Fax: (212)316-6994
Contact: Dr. Gerald Olivero, President
E-mail: golivero@nyc.rr.com
Scope: Organizational performance improvement firm provides consulting services in executive coaching, process consulting, team building, organization development, management training, strategic planning retreats, quality and productivity enhancement, and conflict resolution. Industries served: manufacturing, retail, communications, computers and government. **Founded:** 1985. **Publications:** "Executive coaching as a transfer of training tool: Effects on productivity in a public agency," Public Personnel Management, 1997.

40945 ■ ITEC Inc.—International Trainers Educators & Consultants Inc.
2 Marella Dr.
San Antonio, TX 78248-2804
Ph: (210)479-4121
Free: 800-681-4832
Fax: (210)479-0024
Co. E-mail: itecinc@satx.rr.com
URL: http://www.judygates.com
Contact: Judith Rae Gates, President
Scope: Designs materials and conducts workshops for companies and agencies with culturally diverse workforces. Sees diversity as a positive factor in creativity and high productivity; specializes in supervisory/managerial development, as well as maintenance, mechanic, and support staff empowerment. Assists organizations to develop "in-house capacity" by training and developing their own employees to perform task analysis, curriculum development, job aid design, and "train the trainer" sessions. Develops surveys and assessments for all stages of strategic planning; facilitates all phases of processes, including the team building and implementation/coaching phase, for profit, non-profit, and government offices. Industries served: private and government offices. **Founded:** 1976. **Seminars:** The Challenge of Leadership; Managing Diversity via Empowerment; Basic Leadership Skills for Women; The Challenge of Team Building; Conflict Management; Controlling and Eliminating Employee Absenteeism; Managing Stress and Preventing Burnout; Managing Performance; Making Meetings Work; Taming and Training the Pen; No-Limit Secretary; Managing Organizational Change; Effective Problem Solving and Decision Making.

40946 ■ Kochman Mavrelis Associates Inc. (KMA)
PO Box 3549
Oak Park, IL 60302
Ph: (708)383-9235
Free: 888-562-4070
Fax: (708)383-9084
Co. E-mail: tomkma@aol.com
URL: http://www.kmadiversity.com
Contact: Jean Mavrelis, Chief Executive Officer
E-mail: jean.mavrelis@kmadiversity.com
Scope: Offers guidance through the various stages of growth and understanding that lead to effective management of cultural differences. Specifically, managers can learn to identify patterns of cultural difference, social experiences, issues and concerns of a socially and culturally diverse workforce; develop effective interventionist strategies; and adopt a group or organizational philosophy that recognizes the value of cultural diversity. Serves private industries as well as government agencies. **Founded:** 1986. **Publications:** "Opening Pathways to Tolerance: School Leadership in an Age of Diversity," Dec, 1997; "Corporate Tribalism: White Men/White Women and Cultural Diversity at Work"; "Black and White Styles in Conflict"; "We Hold These Truths to Be Self-Evident...An Interdisciplinary Analysis of the Roots of Racism and Slavery in America". **Telecommunication Services:** jean.mavrelis@kmadiversity.com.

40947 ■ McClure Associates Inc.
PO Box 40637
Mesa, AZ 85274-0637
Ph: (480)829-6801
Fax: (480)968-5897
Co. E-mail: lmcclure@mcclureassociates.com
URL: http://www.mcclureassociates.com
Contact: Lynne McClure, President
E-mail: lmcclure@mcclureassociates.com
Scope: Nationally recognized expert in preventing employee violence. Also training managing anger, conflict, stress and change. Provide expert witness analysis and testimony. **Founded:** 1980. **Publications:** "Angry Women: Stop Letting Anger Control Your Life," Impact Publications, 2003; "Managing High-Risk Behaviors," Impact Publications, 2003; "Angry Men: Managing Anger in Unforgiving World," 2004; "Anger & Conflict in the Workplace: Spot the Signs, Avoid the Trauma," Impact Publications, 2000; "Risky Business: Managing Employee Violence in the Workplace," "Keys to Preventing a Hostile Work Environment". **Seminars:** The Risky Business: Managing Violence in the Workplace@su1TM@su2program; How to identify high risk employee behaviors; How to intervene early, and manage high-risk behaviors; How to manage anger and conflict; How to manage change; Train-the-Trainer Services.

40948 ■ Navarro, Kim & Associates
529 N Charles St., Ste. 202
Baltimore, MD 21201-5043
Ph: (410)837-6317
Fax: (410)837-6294
Co. E-mail: bnavarro@sprynet.com
Contact: Beltran Navarro, Director
E-mail: bnavarro@sprynet.com
Scope: Specializes in bridging the gap between firms and non-traditional ethnic communities, especially in community development and institutional building. **Founded:** 1984.

40949 ■ New Dynamics Associates
72 Shore Dr.
Laconia, NH 03246-3042
Ph: (603)524-1115
Free: 800-580-4651
Fax: (603)528-7912
Contact: David Wagner, Manager
Scope: Provider of organization development consulting to a variety of organizations, specializing in the management of diversity and working in flat inclusive structures. **Founded:** 1972. **Publications:** "A Male/Female Continuum: Paths to Colleagueship"; "Sexual Orientation and Identity"; "The Power Equity Group"; "Definitions for Multicultural Dialogue". **Seminars:** Sexual Orientation and Identity; Journeys of Race and Culture; Gender Men, Women, and Colleagueship; Valuing Multicultural Diversity.

40950 ■ Pope & Associates Inc.
11800 Conrey Rd., Ste. 240
Cincinnati, OH 45249-1067
Ph: (513)671-1277
Fax: (513)671-1815
Co. E-mail: info@popeandassociates.com
URL: http://www.popeandassociates.com
Contact: Patricia C. Pope, Chief Executive Officer
E-mail: pat.pope@popeandassociates.com
Scope: Personnel Diversity consultants and trainers who have developed an approach to Workforce Diversity designed to improve working relationships and reduce inter personal barriers by focusing on the needs of all employees. Consulting services include organizational diagnosis, program design and evaluation, conflict management, personnel counseling, and organizational change interventions. Industries served agri business, banking insurance finance, chemicals pharmaceuticals, communications publishing, education, energy, entertainment, food and beverages, government, health services, manufacturing, research and development, transportation, and wholesale retail. **Founded:** 1976. **Publications:** "Relationship Mapping". **Seminars:** Managing Personnel Diversity; Diversity SOS: Skills for Ongoing Success; Diversity Learning Lab; Understanding Gender Dynamics; ConsultingPairs®.

40951 ■ ProActive English
4355 SE 29th Ave.
Portland, OR 97202
Ph: (503)231-2906
Co. E-mail: infopae@proactive-english.com
URL: http://www.proactive-english.com
Contact: Margaret Lyman, Manager
E-mail: mlyman@proactive-english.com
Scope: Offers on-site individual and small group language and communication training. Sets up learning plans tailored to the needs and schedules of managers and executives who are non-native English speakers. Serves all industries. **Founded:** 1997. **Seminars:** Communicating in Business Situations; Presentations and Pronunciation; Tailored Curriculum; One-on-One Programs.

40952 ■ Professional Psychological Services (PPS)
4130 Linden Ave., Ste. 309
Dayton, OH 45432-3034
Ph: (937)254-7301
Fax: (937)254-2117
Co. E-mail: ppsdocs@aol.com
Contact: Dr. Michael A. Williams, Partner
Scope: Offers clinical services, human relations training, multicultural and pluralistic training, and staff development and training. **Founded:** 1994.

40953 ■ Horace Williams
175 S Madison Ave., Ste. 9
Pasadena, CA 91101
Ph: (626)793-3524
Co. E-mail: hwms626@aol.com
Contact: Horace Williams, President
Scope: Management consultant specializing in multi culturalism and program evaluation.

RESEARCH CENTERS

40954 ■ Intercultural Communication Institute (ICI)
8835 SW Canyon Ln., Ste. 238
Portland, OR 97225
Ph: (503)297-4622
Fax: (503)297-4695
Co. E-mail: ici@intercultural.org
URL: http://www.intercultural.org
Contact: Milton Bennett, Director
Founded: 1986.

40955 ■ Medical College of Wisconsin - Center for the Study of Bioethics
8701 Watertown Plank Rd.
Milwaukee, WI 53226
Ph: (414)456-8498
Fax: (414)456-6511
Co. E-mail: aderse@mcw.edu
URL: http://www.mcw.edu/bioethics.htm
Contact: Dr. Arthur Derse, Director
Founded: 1982. **Publications:** *Medical Ethics Committee Network Newsletter* (Monthly). **Educational Activities:** Certificate Program in Clinical Bioethics (Daily), aims to gain an essential introduction to the philosophical, legal, and clinical foundations of bioethics through four web-based courses; Certificate Program in Research Ethics (Daily), aims to build an understanding of human subjects research regulations and their historical foundations, and explore current topics in research ethics through four web-based courses; Ethics Grand Rounds (Monthly), lecture series on current issues in bioethics. **Telecommunication Services:** bioethics@mcw.edu.

40956 ■ National MultiCultural Institute (NMCI)
1666 K St. NW, Ste. 440
Washington, DC 20006-1242
Ph: (202)483-0700

Fax: (202)483-5233
Co. E-mail: nmci@nmci.org
URL: http://www.nmci.org
Contact: John R. Kirksey, President
Founded: 1983. **Publications:** *NMCI Abstracts* (Annual). **Educational Activities:** Training in cultural awareness, cultural competency, and prejudice and bias prevention; NMCI Conferences (Semiannual).

40957 ■ University of Houston - African American Studies Program (AAS)
629 Agnes Arnold Hall
Houston, TX 77024-3303
Ph: (713)743-2811
Fax: (713)743-2818
Co. E-mail: jconyers@uh.edu
URL: http://www.uh.edu/class/aas
Contact: Dr. James L. Conyers, Jr., Director
Services: Food and clothing drives. **Founded:** 1969. **Publications:** *Ujima* (Biennial). **Educational Activities:** Cultural programs, for the community; Conferences, forums, and workshops; Graduate Fellowship Initiative; Instruction emphasizing cultural and historical heritage of Africans and black Americans, analyzing and critically examining sociological, psychological, economic, and political aspects of the black community, as it exists in the U.S. and Africa. **Awards:** Visiting Scholar Fellowship.

40958 ■ University of Texas at Arlington - Women and Minorities Research and Resource Center
Box 19599
Arlington, TX 76019
Ph: (817)272-3131
Fax: (817)272-3117
Co. E-mail: womensstudies@uta.edu
URL: http://www.uta.edu/womens_studies/
Contact: Beth Anne Shelton, Director
Founded: 1991. **Educational Activities:** Women's History Month (Annual), with speakers, mini-conferences, and other events focusing on women in private and public sectors.

ASSOCIATIONS AND OTHER ORGANIZATIONS

40959 ■ Multi-Level Marketing International Association (MLMIA)
119 Stanford Ct.
Irvine, CA 92612
Ph: (949)854-0484
Fax: (949)854-7687
Co. E-mail: info@mlmia.com
URL: http://www.mlmia.com
Contact: Doris Wood, Chairperson Founder
Description: Companies, support groups, and distributors. Seeks to strengthen and improve the Multi-Level Marketing (also known as Network Marketing) industry in the U.S. and abroad. (Multi-Level Marketing is a method of selling products directly, independently, and usually out of the home, without the medium of a retail outlet.) Provides educational services to consumers and law enforcement agencies. Serves as an information source for the industry. Offers recommendations for start-up companies; maintains speakers' bureau; conducts training programs. **Scope:** MLM industry, self-improvement, legal. **Founded:** 1985. **Subscriptions:** 100. **Publications:** *Connections and Dittos from Doris* (Monthly). **Educational Activities:** Multi-Level Marketing International Association Convention (Quarterly). **Awards:** Distributor of the Year (Annual); Hall of Fame (Periodic); International Company (Periodic); Supplier of the Year (Annual); Distributor of the Year Award; MLM Company of the Year; MLM Company of the Year (Annual); Support Company of the Year (Annual).

REFERENCE WORKS

40960 ■ *"Ask Inc." in Inc. (October 2007, pp. 73-74)*
Pub: Gruner & Jahr USA Publishing
Description: An online marketing research firm investigates the use of online communities such as MySpace and Second life in order to recruit individuals to answer surveys.

40961 ■ *"Merger Brings New Force to Hispanic Marketing Industry" in Hispanic Business (July-August 2007, pp. 60)*
Pub: Hispanic Business
Description: Merger between Latin Force LLC, a marketing strategy firm and Geoscape International Inc., a consumer intelligence and data analytics company is discussed.

40962 ■ *"Multichannel Marketing: Mindset and Program Development" in Business Horizons (September-October 2007)*
Pub: Elsevier Technology Publications
Ed: Bruce D. Weinberg, Salvatore Parise, Patricia J. Guinan. **Description:** Organizations should develop a multichannel mindset and design multichannel marketing programs in order to increase profitability and enhance customer satisfaction. Creating a holistic strategy, crating metrics that measure the impacts and overall performance, and designing organizational structure and incentives are key factors in implementing the marketing program.

40963 ■ *Steal These Ideas!: Marketing Secrets That Will Make You a Star*
Pub: Bloomberg Press
Ed: Steve Cone. **Released:** September 13, 2005. **Price:** $18.95. **Description:** The book shares information to successfully market any product or service.

40964 ■ *"Web.Preneuring: How Local TV Ads and Online Marketing Can Help You Win Big" in Small Business Opportunities (January 2008)*
Pub: Harris Publications Inc.
Ed: David Waxman. **Description:** Spot Runner, an Internet-based advertising agency offers low-cost local business television ads. The company secures the ad buy, places and tracks the ads, and analyzes viewership and demographics for clients.

40965 ■ *"Yes, No, and Somewhat Likely: Survey the World with Web Polls" in Inc. (October 2007, pp. 58-59)*
Pub: Gruner & Jahr USA Publishing
Ed: Don Steinberg. **Description:** Online tools for surveying customers, employees and the general public include Zoomergan zPro and Zoomerang Sample, software designed to send surveys and allows viewing results; SurveyMonkey software creates, administers and allows viewing online surveys and results; Vizu software places a one-question poll on a particular Website; and Vovici EFM Feedback, a subscription service providing ongoing surveys to customers or employees.

VIDEOCASSETTES/ AUDIOCASSETTES

40966 ■ *Beware the Naked Man Who Offers You His Shirt*
PBS Home Video
Catalog Fulfillment Center
Charlotte, NC 28275-1089
Ph: (800)531-4727
Free: 800-645-4PBS
Co. E-mail: info@pbs.org
URL: http://www.pbs.org
Released: 1990. **Price:** $395.00. **Description:** The author of "Swim With the Sharks Without Being Eaten Alive" offers insights and advice on increasing sales productivity. **Availability:** VHS; 3/4 U.

40967 ■ *Creating a Winner: The Real Secrets of Successful Marketing*
Warner Home Video, Inc.
5775 Linder Canyon Rd.
Westlake Village, CA 91362
URL: http://www.warnerbros.com
Released: 1989. **Price:** $59.95. **Description:** A video sponsored by Inc. Magazine and AT&T, outlining the best procedures for marketing a product. **Availability:** VHS.

40968 ■ *How to Win Marketing Wars in the 1990s*
Excellence in Training Corp.
c/o ICON Training
804 Roosevelt St.
Polk City, IA 50226
Free: 800-609-0479
Co. E-mail: info@icontraining.com
URL: http://www.icontraining.com
Released: 1991. **Price:** $395.00. **Description:** A three-part discussion of principles of global marketing strategies. **Availability:** VHS; 3/4 U; Special order formats.

40969 ■ *Marketing*
Coast Telecourses
11460 Warner Ave.
Fountain Valley, CA 92708-2597
Ph: (714)241-6109
Free: 800-547-4748
Fax: (714)241-6286
Co. E-mail: coastlearning@coastline.edu
URL: http://www.coastlearning.org
Released: 1992. **Description:** A video course in marketing. **Availability:** VHS; 3/4 U; Q.

40970 ■ *Marketing Research*
GPN Educational Media
1550 Executive Drive
Elgin, IL 60123
Ph: (402)472-2007
Free: 800-228-4630
Fax: (800)306-2330
Co. E-mail: askgpn@smarterville.com
URL: http://www.shopgpn.com
Released: 1988. **Price:** $69.95. **Description:** Looks at the format, systematic approach and the informal, casual methods of marketing research, and how companies make their marketing decisions. **Availability:** VHS.

40971 ■ *Marketing Strategy*
Advantage Media
c/o Kantola Productions
55 Sunnyside Ave.
Mill Valley, CA 94941
Ph: (415)381-9363
Free: 800-280-1180
Fax: (415)381-9801
Co. E-mail: kantola@kantola.com
URL: http://www.kantola.com/d/advantage.htm
Contact: Daniel Amos, Chief Executive Officer
Released: 1988. **Price:** $189.00. **Description:** Part one of two part program introduces the fundamentals of a solid marketing plan. In part two, Professors Thomas S. Robertson and David J. Reibstein present a marketing strategy audit that identifies the key points of a good plan. Originally presented at the Aresty Institute for Executive Education at the Wharton School. Comes with audiocassette and study guide. **Availability:** VHS.

40972 ■ *Philip Kotler on Competitive Marketing*
Video Arts, Inc.
c/o Aim Learning Group
8238-40 Lehigh
Morton Grove, IL 60053-2615
Free: 877-444-2230
Fax: (416)252-2155
Co. E-mail: service@aimlearninggroup.com
URL: http://www.aimlearninggroup.com

Released: 19??. **Price:** $995.00. **Description:** Kotler, a professor at the Kellogg Business School at Northwestern University, provides the fundamentals of successful marketing in the contemporary business environment through panel discussions with business leaders and other experts. **Availability:** VHS.

CONSULTANTS

40973 ■ Eastern Point Consulting Group Inc.
36 Glen Ave.
Newton, MA 02464
Ph: (617)965-4141
Fax: (617)965-4172
Co. E-mail: info@eastpt.com
URL: http://www.eastpt.com
Contact: Katherine A. Herzog, President
E-mail: kherzog@eastpt.com

Scope: Specializes in bringing practical solutions to complex challenges. Provides consulting and training in managing diversity; comprehensive sexual-harassment policies and programs; organizational development; benchmarks 360 skills assessment; executive coaching; strategic human resource planning; team building; leadership development for women; mentoring programs; and gender issues in the workplace. **Founded:** 1995. **Seminars:** Leadership Development for Women.

LIBRARIES

40974 ■ Alticor Inc. Corporate Library
7575 E. Fulton St.
Ada, MI 49355
Ph: (616)787-1000
Free: 800-253-6500
URL: http://www.alticor.com

Scope: Chemistry, direct selling, business, e-commerce. **Services:** Interlibrary loan; copying; SDI; library not open to the public. **Founded:** 1970. **Holdings:** Figures not available.

START-UP INFORMATION

40975 ■ *Getting Rich In Your Underwear: How To Start and Run a Profitable Home-Based Business*
Pub: HCM Publishing
Ed: Peter I. Hupalo. **Released:** April 1, 2005. **Price:** $17.95. **Description:** Book offers insight into starting a home-based business. Entrepreneurs will learn about business models and the home business; distribution and fulfillment of product or service; marketing and sales; how to overcome the fear of starting a business; personal success characteristics; naming a business; zoning and insurance; intellectual capital; copyrights, trademarks, and patents; limited liability companies and S-corporations; business expenses and accounting; taxes; fifteen basic steps for starting a home-based business, state resources for starting a home company; and seven home-based business ideas.

40976 ■ *Your Million-Dollar Idea: From Concept to Marketplace*
Pub: Adams Media Corporation
Ed: Sandy Abrams. **Released:** March 1, 2010. **Price:** $14.95. **Description:** Self-taught entrepreneur provides a 12-step plan to make a new product or service a profitable reality.

EDUCATIONAL PROGRAMS

40977 ■ New Product Research: Laying the Foundation for New Product Success (Onsite)
Seminar Information Service, Inc.
20 Executive Park, Ste. 120
Irvine, CA 92614
Ph: (949)261-9104
Free: 877-SEM-INFO
Fax: (949)261-1963
Co. E-mail: info@seminarinformation.com
URL: http://www.seminarinformation.com
Price: $1,995.00. **Description:** Learn how to design and implement marketing research studies to guide the total product development and evaluation process. **Dates and Locations:** Los Angeles, CA.

REFERENCE WORKS

40978 ■ *"3Par: Storing Up Value" in Barron's (Vol. 90, August 30, 2010, No. 35, pp. 30)*
Pub: Barron's Editorial & Corporate Headquarters
Ed: Mark Veverka. **Description:** Dell and Hewlett Packard are both bidding for data storage company 3Par. The acquisition would help Dell and Hewlett Packard provide customers with a one-stop shop as customers move to a private cloud in the Internet.

40979 ■ *"7-Eleven Considers Private Label Ice Cream" in Ice Cream Reporter (Vol. 22, December 20, 2008, No. 1, pp. 1)*
Pub: Ice Cream Reporter
Description: 7-Eleven is considering the introduction of a private label of snack foods, including ice cream desserts.

40980 ■ *"21st Century Filling Station" in Austin Business JournalInc. (Vol. 29, December 11, 2009, No. 40, pp. 1)*
Pub: American City Business Journals
Ed: Jacob Dirr. **Description:** Clean Energy Fuels Corporation announced plans for the construction of a $1 million, 17,000 square foot compressed natural gas fueling station at or near the Austin-Bergstrom International Airport (ABIA). Clean Energy Fuels hopes to encourage cab and shuttle companies in the ABIA to switch from gasoline to natural gas.

40981 ■ *"2011 FinOvation Awards" in Farm Industry News (January 19, 2011)*
Pub: Penton Business Media Inc.
Ed: Jodie Wehrspann. **Description:** The 2011 FinOvation Award winners are announced, covering new products that growers need for corn and soybean crops. Winners range from small turbines and a fuel-efficient pickup to a Class 10 combine and drought-tolerant hybrids.

40982 ■ *"ACC Game Development Program Opens" in Austin Business JournalInc. (Vol. 28, October 31, 2008, No. 33, pp. 1)*
Pub: American City Business Journals
Ed: Sandra Zaragoza. **Description:** Austin, Texas-based Austin Community College has launched its Game Development Institute. The institute was created to meet the gaming industry's demand for skilled workers. One hundred students have enrolled with the institute.

40983 ■ *Achieving Planned Innovation: A Proven System for Creating Successful New Products and Services*
Pub: Simon and Schuster
Ed: Frank R. Bacon. **Released:** August 2007. **Price:** $16.95. **Description:** Planned innovation is a disciplined and practical step-by-step sequence of procedures for reaching the intended destination point: successful products. This easy-to-read book explains the system along with an action-oriented program for continuous success in new-product innovations. Five steps outlined include: a disciplined reasoning process; lasting market orientation; proper selection criteria that reflect both strategic and tactical business objectives and goals along with dynamic matching of resources to present and future opportunities, and positive and negative requirements before making major expenditures; and proper organizational staffing. The author explains what to do and evaluating the potential of any new product or service, ranging from ventures in retail distribution to the manufacture of goods as diverse as bicycles, motorcycles, aerospace communication and navigation equipment, small business computers, food packaging, and medical products.

40984 ■ *"Acsys Interactive Announces Crowdsourcing Comes to the Hospital Industry" in Internet Wire (August 23, 2010)*
Pub: Comtex
Description: Hospital marketers are obtaining data through crowdsourcing as strategy to gain ideas and feedback. The Hospital Industry Crowdsourced Survey of Digital, Integrated and Emerging Marketing is the first initiative among hospitals.

40985 ■ *"Advancing the Ball" in Inside Healthcare (Vol. 6, December 2010, No. 7, pp. 31)*
Pub: RedCoat Publishing Inc.
Ed: Michelle McNickle. **Description:** Profile of Medicalodges an elder-care specialty company that provides both patient care and technology development. President and CEO of the firm believes that hiring good employees is key to growth for any small business.

40986 ■ *"ALA: Hot Topics for Librarianship" in Information Today (Vol. 28, September 2011, No. 8, pp. 17)*
Pub: Information Today, Inc.
Ed: Barbara Brynko. **Description:** Highlights from the American Library Association Annual Conference and Exhibition are listed. Thousands of attendees sought out services, displays, demos, new product rollouts, and freebies. Emerging technology for librarians, staff development, gray literature, interlibrary loans, and next-generation interfaces were among the topics discussed.

40987 ■ *"AMT's Partner Program Enables New Security Business Models" in Internet Wire (August 12, 2010)*
Pub: Comtex
Description: AMT, technical provider of physical access control Software as a Service (Saas) solutions, has developed a new Partner Program that allows partners to outsource any technical abilities lacking to AMT with no upfront fees.

40988 ■ *"Aptitudes for Apps" in Boston Business Journal (Vol. 31, July 1, 2011, No. 23, pp. 3)*
Pub: Boston Business Journal
Ed: Kyle Alspach. **Description:** Startups Apperian Inc. and Kinvey Inc. are aiming to accelerate the development and deployment of mobile applications and have received fund pledges from Boston-area venture capital firms.

40989 ■ *"Are You Ready for a Transformation?" in Women Entrepreneur (November 28, 2008)*
Pub: Entrepreneur Media Inc.
Ed: Aliza Sherman. **Description:** Marlene J. Waldock, an expert in women's empowerment and reinvention, discusses brand modification and what a business owner should consider before attempting to change or modify their brand.

40990 ■ *"The Art of Rapid, Hands-On Execution Innovation" in Strategy and Leadership (Vol. 39, March-April 2011, No. 2, pp. 28)*
Pub: Emerald Group Publishing Inc.
Ed: Anssi Tuulenmaki, Liisa Valikangas. **Description:** A model of 'rapid execution innovation' that can be used to increase the chances of achieving innovations that develop into successful new business

models is introduced. The model involves company experiments that inspire the radical rethinking business opportunities, and by continuing these experiments until the idea evolves into a product.

40991 ■ *"At Wine Kiosk, Show ID, Face Camera, Swipe Card and Blow" in Pittsburgh Post-Gazette (November 28, 2010)*
Pub: Pittsburgh-Post Gazette
Ed: Dennis B. Roddy. **Description:** New technology installed on wine kiosks enables sellers to abide by the law. This technology tests blood alcohol levels and warns people if they have recently used a mouthwash before testing.

40992 ■ *"Auxilium Drug's New Use: Putting Squeeze On Cellulite" in Philadelphia Business Journal (Vol. 30, September 16, 2011, No. 31, pp. 1)*
Pub: American City Business Journals Inc.
Ed: John George. **Description:** Auxilium Pharmaceuticals and BioSpecifics Technologies are getting on with their plans of finding new uses for their drug Xiaflex, a possible treatment for cellulite. The two firms have dismissed their pending litigations and mapped out an amended licensing agreement for their search for the potential uses of the drug.

40993 ■ *"Avoiding Invention Scams" in Black Enterprise (Vol. 37, January 2007, No. 6, pp. 46)*
Pub: Earl G. Graves Publishing Co. Inc.
Ed: James C. Johnson. **Description:** Invention promotion firms provide inventors assistance in developing a prototype for product development. It is important to research these companies before making a commitment to work with them because there are a number of these firms that are not legitimate and have caused independent inventors to lose thousands of dollars by making false claims as to the market potential of the inventions.

40994 ■ *"Bag It" in Entrepreneur (Vol. 36, May 2008, No. 5, pp. 48)*
Pub: Entrepreneur Media, Inc.
Ed: Amanda C. Kooser. **Description:** Buyer's guide featuring bags and carrying cases for laptops is presented. Prices and attributes of the bags are provided.

40995 ■ *"Baskin-Robbins" in Ice Cream Reporter (Vol. 23, November 20, 2010, No. 12, pp. 7)*
Pub: Ice Cream Reporter
Description: Baskin-Robbins is reintroducing its popular Turkey Ice Cream Cake for the holiday.

40996 ■ *"Baskin-Robbins" in Ice Cream Reporter (Vol. 23, September 20, 2010, No. 10, pp. 6)*
Pub: Ice Cream Reporter
Description: Baskin-Robbins will feature an old favorite called Quarterback Crunch as its September Flavor of the Month. The item was created in 1978 and features vanilla ice cream with chocolate covered rice crunchies and a carmel ribbon.

40997 ■ *"Be a Better Manager: Live Abroad" in Harvard Business Review (Vol. 88, September 2010, No. 9, pp. 24)*
Pub: Harvard Business School Publishing
Ed: William W. Maddux, Adam D. Galinsky, Carmit T. Tadmor. **Description:** Interrelationship between international experience and entrepreneurship is discussed. Individuals with international experience are likelier to be promoted and to develop new products and businesses.

40998 ■ *"Better Made's Better Idea: Diversify Despite Rising Costs" in Crain's Detroit Business (Vol. 24, September 22, 2008, No. 38, pp. 18)*
Pub: Crain Communications Inc.
Ed: Nathan Skid. **Description:** Better Made Snack Foods Inc. is planning to expand its product lines and market reach as well as boost manufacturing capability during a time in which the company is being buffeted by rising commodity and fuel costs. The company feels that diversification is the key to maintain sales and growth.

40999 ■ *"Beverage Brand Vies To Be the Latest Purple Prince" in Brandweek (Vol. 49, April 21, 2008, No. 16, pp. 20)*
Pub: VNU Business Media, Inc.
Ed: Becky Ebenkamp. **Description:** Profile on the new beverage product Purple and its founder, Ted Farnsworth; Purple is a drink that blends seven antioxidant-rich juices to create what Mr. Farnsworth calls a 'Cascade Effect' that boosts antioxidants' effectiveness. Mr. Farnsworth is marketing the brand's Oxygen Radical Absorbance Capability (ORAC) which is a value of 7,600 compared with orange juice's 1,200.

41000 ■ *"Beyond the RAZR's Edge" in Canadian Business (Vol. 79, November 6, 2006, No. 22, pp. 15)*
Pub: Rogers Media
Ed: Andrew Wahl. **Description:** Features of Motorola RAZR, such as low weight and camera accessibility, are presented.

41001 ■ *"A Big Dream That 'Was Going Nowhere" in Globe & Mail (February 4, 2006, pp. B4)*
Pub: CTVglobemedia Publishing Inc.
Ed: Konrad Yakabuski. **Description:** The reasons behind the decision of Bombardier Inc. to terminate its plans to develop jet airplanes are presented.

41002 ■ *"Biodiesel Poised to Regain Growth" in Farm Industry News (January 21, 2011)*
Pub: Penton Business Media Inc.
Description: According to Gary Haer, vice president of sales and marketing for Renewable Energy Group, the biodiesel industry is positioned to regain growth in 2011 with the reinstatement of the biodiesel blendersa tax credt of $1 per gallon.

41003 ■ *"BK Menu Gives Casual Dining Reason to Worry" in Advertising Age (Vol. 79, November 17, 2008, No. 43, pp. 12)*
Pub: Crain Communications, Inc.
Ed: Emily Bryson York. **Description:** Burger King is beginning to compete with such casual dining restaurants as Applebees and the Cheesecake Factory with new premium menu items, including thicker burgers and ribs; statistical data regarding the casual dining segment which continues to fall and Burger King, whose sales continue to rise is included.

41004 ■ *"Blue Cross to Put Kiosk in Mall" in News & Observer (November 9, 2010)*
Pub: News & Observer
Ed: Alan M. Wolf. **Description:** Blue Cross and Blue Shield of North Carolina has placed a kiosk in Durham's Streets of Southpoint in order to market its health insurance.

41005 ■ *"BMW Makes Bet on Carbon Maker" in Wall Street Journal Eastern Edition (November 19 , 2011, pp. B3)*
Pub: Dow Jones & Company Inc.
Ed: Christoph Rauwald. **Description:** Eight months ago, Volkswagen AG acquired a 10 percent holding in carbon-fiber maker SGL Carbon SE. Its rival BMW AG is catching up by acquiring 15.2 percent stake in SGL as it seeks alliances like the rest of the industry in order to share industrial costs of new product development.

41006 ■ *"Boise-based Highway 12 Invests in Crowdsourcing Platform" in Idaho Business Review (September 24, 2010)*
Pub: Dolan Media Newswires
Ed: Simon Shifrin. **Description:** The only venture capital fund in Idaho, Highway 12 Ventures, is funding Kapost a new company that helps news Websites, blogs and other online venues to pull content from a larger network of writers.

41007 ■ *"Bon Voyager" in Entrepreneur (Vol. 36, April 2008, No. 4, pp. 58)*
Pub: Entrepreneur Media, Inc.
Ed: Heather Clancy. **Description:** LG Voyager, especially made for Verizon Wireless, is a smart phone that is being compared to Apple iPhone. The Voyager has a 2.8-inch external touchscreen and has a clamshell design, which features an internal keyboard. It does not have Wi-Fi support like iPhone, but it has 3G support. Other differences between the two phones are discussed.

41008 ■ *Borrowing Brilliance: The Six Steps to Business Innovation by Building on the Ideas of Others*
Pub: Gotham
Ed: David Kord Murray. **Price:** $26.00. **Description:** The author builds the case that cherry-picking the ideas of others is a vital part of the research and development process for any small firm.??.

41009 ■ *"Bovie Medical Makes Electrosurgical Strike" in The Business Journal-Serving Greater Tampa Bay (Vol. 28, August 22, 2008, No. 35)*
Pub: American City Business Journals, Inc.
Ed: Margie Manning. **Description:** Bovie Medical Group, which manufactures electrosurgical products, is planning to sell its manufacturing plant in the Tyrone Industrial Park and to purchase the former Harland Clarke facility. The moves are expected to boost the efficiency and the development of new products. Other information on Bovie Medical Group is presented.

41010 ■ *"Brands' Mass Appeal" in ADWEEK (Vol. 51, June 14, 2010, No. 24)*
Pub: Nielsen Business Media Inc.
Ed: Lisa Thorell, James Sherret. **Description:** Engineering/science crowdsourced projects tend to result from posting and/or publishing interim results as well as from other talents building upon those results to produce even better results. However, the author does not see the same results in the creative world.

41011 ■ *"Bristol-Myers Close to Settling Lawsuit" in Globe & Mail (January 23, 2006, pp. B6)*
Pub: CTVglobemedia Publishing Inc.
Ed: Barbara Martinez. **Description:** The details of shareholder case against Bristol-Myers Squibb Co. are presented. The dispute is over the company's claim on the efficiency of Vanlev drug.

41012 ■ *"Burner Handles Everything From #2 to B100" in Indoor Comfort Marketing (Vol. 70, May 2011, No. 5, pp. 24)*
Pub: Industry Publications Inc.
Description: A new oil burner being offered by AMERIgreen Energy is profiled.

41013 ■ *"Business Diary" in Crain's Detroit Business (Vol. 24, October 6, 2008, No. 40, pp. 23)*
Pub: Crain Communications, Inc.
Description: Detailed listing of acquisitions, expansions, new products, new services, business contracts and startups from the Detroit area is provided.

41014 ■ *"Business Diary" in Crain's Detroit Business (Vol. 26, January 11, 2010, No. 2, pp. 16)*
Pub: Crain Communications Inc.
Description: Listing of local businesses involved in acquisitions, contracts, expansions, new products and services as well as startups in the region.

41015 ■ *"Can America Invent Its Way Back?" in Business Week (September 22, 2008, No. 4100, pp. 52)*
Pub: McGraw-Hill Companies, Inc.
Description: Business leaders as well as economists agree that innovative new products, services and ways of doing business may be the only way in which America can survive the downward spiral of the economy; innovation economics may be the answer and may even provide enough growth to enable Americans to prosper in the years to come.

41016 ■ *"Can a Brazilian SUV Take On the Jeep Wrangler?" in Business Week (September 22, 2008, No. 4100, pp. 50)*
Pub: McGraw-Hill Companies, Inc.
Ed: Helen Walters. **Description:** Profile of the Brazilian company TAC as well as the flourishing Brazilian

car market; TAC has launched a new urban vehicle, the Stark, which has won prizes for innovation; the company uses local technology and manufacturing expertise.

41017 ■ *"Cancer Care's Quantum Leap" in Hawaii Business (Vol. 53, October 2007, No. 4, pp. 17)*
Pub: Hawaii Business Publishing
Ed: Cathy S. Cruz-George. **Description:** TomoTherapy is an innovative device for cancer treatment that gives high-intensity radiation to more accurate parts of the body compared to conventional treatments. Hawaii has one of the 70 TomoTherapy machines in the nation, and it is expected to help advance cancer care in the area. Details on how the machine works are provided.

41018 ■ *"Cell Phone the Ticket on American Airlines" in Chicago Tribune (November 14, 2008)*
Pub: McClatchy-Tribune Information Services
Ed: Julie Johnsson. **Description:** American Airlines is testing a new mobile boarding pass at O'Hare International Airport. Travelers on American can board flights and get through security checkpoints by flashing a bar code on their phones. Passengers must have an Internet-enabled mobile device and an active e-mail address in order to utilize this service.

41019 ■ *"Changing Fuel Compositions: What It Means To You and Your Business" in Indoor Comfort Marketing (Vol. 70, June 2011, No. 6, pp. 30)*
Pub: Industry Publications Inc.
Ed: Paul Nazzaro. **Description:** Biofuels are outlined and the way it is changing the HVAC/R industry are discussed.

41020 ■ *"Cheese Spread Whips Up a Brand New Bowl" in Brandweek (Vol. 49, April 21, 2008, No. 16, pp. 17)*
Pub: VNU Business Media, Inc.
Ed: Mike Beirne. **Description:** Mrs. Kinser's Pimento Cheese Spread is launching a new container for its product in order to attempt stronger brand marketing with a better bowl in order to win over the heads of households as young as in their 30s. The company also intends to begin distribution in Texas and the West Coast. Mrs. Kinser's is hoping that the new packaging will provide a more distinct branding and will help consumers distinguish what flavor they are buying.

41021 ■ *"Chinese Fund Loans $33.5 Million to Prestolite" in Crain's Detroit Business (Vol. 26, January 18, 2010, No. 3, pp. 1)*
Pub: Crain Communications Inc.
Ed: Ryan Beene. **Description:** Prestolite Electric Inc., a distributor of alternators and starter motors for commercial and heavy-duty vehicles, looked to China for fresh capital in order to fund new product launches.

41022 ■ *"Chopping Option Added to Calmer Corn Head Kits" in Farm Industry News (January 16, 2011)*
Pub: Penton Business Media Inc.
Description: New equipment for combines, called the BT Chopper option for Calmer Corn Heads, will chop and crust BT corn stalks into confetti-sized pieces for easier decomposition in the field.

41023 ■ *"Chuck's Big Chance" in Barron's (Vol. 89, July 13, 2009, No. 28, pp. L3)*
Pub: Dow Jones & Co., Inc.
Ed: Leslie P. Norton. **Description:** Charles Schwab is cutting prices and rolling out new products to lure customers and the company is well positioned to benefit from Wall Street's misery. Their shares are trading at just 17 times earnings, which should be at least at a multiple of 20.

41024 ■ *"ClickFuel Launches New Products to Help Small and Mid-Sized Businesses Bolster Their Brand Online" in Internet Wire (Dec. 3,2009)*
Pub: Comtex News Network, Inc.
Description: Boostability, a provider of Enterprise Search Engine Optimization (SEO) software technology, has partnered with ClickFuel, a firm that designs, tracks and manages Internet marketing campaigns in order to leverage Boostability's technology in order to deliver comprehensive SEO solutions to small and mid-size businesses; three new products will also become available for these business clients to help them manage all facets of their online presence.

41025 ■ *"ClickFuel Launches New Products to Help Small and Mid-Sized Businesses Bolster Their Brand Online" in Internet Wire (Dec. 3, 2009)*
Pub: Comtex News Network, Inc.
Description: Boostability, a provider of Enterprise Search Engine Optimization (SEO) software technology, has partnered with ClickFuel, a firm that designs, tracks and manages Internet marketing campaigns in order to leverage Boostability's technology in order to deliver comprehensive SEO solutions to small and mid-size businesses; three new products will also become available for these business clients to help them manage all facets of their online presence.

41026 ■ *"The Code-Cracker" in Business Courier (Vol. 24, January 11, 2008, No. 40, pp. 1)*
Pub: American City Business Journals, Inc.
Ed: James Ritchie. **Description:** Michael Kennedy, a professor in the chemistry and biochemistry department at the Miami University, is a part of the Protein Structure Initiative, a project that is aimed at forming a catalog of three-dimensional protein structures. The initiative is a project of the Northeast Structural Genomics consortium, of which the Miami University is a member. The impacts of the research on drug development are discussed.

41027 ■ *"Cold Stone Creamery Offers New Eight-Layer Ice Cream Cakes" in Ice Cream Reporter (Vol. 23, October 20, 2010, No. 11, pp. 2)*
Pub: Ice Cream Reporter
Description: Cold Stone Creamery is introducing a new line of eight-layer ice cream cakes, which are crafted with three layers of ice cream, three layers of cake and two mid-layers of mix-ins and finished with frosting and a creative design.

41028 ■ *"Cold Stone in Licensing Agreement with Turin Chocolates" in Ice Cream Reporter (Vol. 22, December 20, 2008, No. 1, pp. 2)*
Pub: Ice Cream Reporter
Description: Cold Stone Creamery and Turin Chocolatier are teaming up to offer a new line of chocolate truffles under the Cold Stone label. The treats will feature four the most popular Cold Stone flavors: Coffee Lovers Only, Chocolate Devotion, Our Strawberry Blonde, and Peanut Butter Cup Perfection.

41029 ■ *"Colores Origenes: Martha Kruse" in Advertising Age (Vol. 77, November 13, 2006, No. 46, pp. S12)*
Pub: Crain Communications, Inc.
Ed: Laurel Wentz. **Description:** Home Depot has created a range of Latin paint colors called Colores Origenes; the new line was originally intended to launch only at locations with heavily Hispanic patrons but the company decided to make the line available at all of their stores.

41030 ■ *"Coming Soon: Electric Tractors" in Farm Industry News (November 21, 2011)*
Pub: Penton Business Media Inc.
Ed: Jodie Wehrspann. **Description:** The agricultural industry is taking another look at electric farm vehicles. John Deere Product Engineering Center said that farmers can expect to see more diesel-electric systems in farm tractors, sprayers, and implements.

41031 ■ *"Company Severs Ties with Chiquita, Starts Own Brand" in Business Journal-Serving Phoenix and the Valley of the Sun (October 5, 2007)*
Pub: American City Business Journals, Inc.
Ed: Mike Sunnucks. **Description:** Melones International is ending a deal with Chiquita Brands International Inc. Melones will now distribute its produce in the U.S. under its own brand, called Plain Jane. Alejandro N. Canelos Jr., head of the firm, stated their relationship with Chiquita was good, but wants to promote the Plain Jane brand name.

41032 ■ *"Connectors for Space, Mil/Aero and Medical Applications" in Canadian Electronics (Vol. 23, June-July 2008, No. 4, pp. 13)*
Pub: Action Communication Inc.
Ed: Gilles Parguey. **Description:** Product information on electrical connectors for use in space, military, aeronautics, and medical applications is provided. These connectors are built to withstand the extreme conditions offered by the harsh working environments in those applications.

41033 ■ *"Contest Produce Ad Designs on a Dime" in San Diego Business Journal (Vol. 31, August 23, 2010, No. 31, pp. 1)*
Pub: San Diego Business Journal
Ed: Mike Allen. **Description:** San Diego-based Prova.fm runs design contests for clients such as the U.S. Postal Service. The client then chooses the best entry from the contest. Prova.fm relies on the Internet to deliver a range of possible graphic solutions and allowing the customer to make the right selection for its business through a process called crowdsourcing.

41034 ■ *Craft, Inc.*
Pub: Chronicle Books LLC
Ed: Meg Mateo Ilasco. **Released:** August 2007. **Price:** $16.95. **Description:** Business primer for entrepreneurial crafters wishing to turn their hobbies into a small business, including tips for developing products, naming the company, writing a business plan, applying for licenses, and paying taxes.

41035 ■ *"Credit Crunch Takes Bite Out Of McDonald's" in Advertising Age (Vol. 79, September 29, 2008, No. 36, pp. 1)*
Pub: Crain Communications, Inc.
Ed: Emily Bryson York. **Description:** McDonald's will delay its launch of coffee bars inside its restaurants due to the banking crisis which has prompted Bank of America to halt loans to the franchise chains.

41036 ■ *"Criticare Sees Rapid Expansion" in Business Journal-Milwaukee (Vol. 28, December 31, 2010, No. 14, pp. A1)*
Pub: Milwaukee Business Journal
Ed: Rich Rovito. **Description:** Criticare Systems Inc. expanded its distribution network, added customers, launched two new products and transferred into a new building in Pewaukee, Wisconsin at the start of their fiscal year. Criticare expanded its workforce and now has nearly 140 full time employees.

41037 ■ *"A Crowd for the Cloud" in CIO (Vol. 24, October 2, 2010, No. 1, pp. 16)*
Pub: CIO
Ed: Stephanie Overby. **Description:** Information about a project which aimed to implement a cloud-based crowdsourcing platform and innovation-management process is provided. Chubb Group of Insurance Companies wanted to mine revenue-generating ideas from its 10,400 employees and hundreds of thousands of external agents. The company hosted its first innovation event using its new system in October 2008.

41038 ■ *"Crowdsourcing the Law" in LJN's Legal Tech Newsletter (October 1, 2010)*
Pub: Incisive Media
Contact: Lee Feldman, Manager
E-mail: lee.feldman@incisivemedia.com
Ed: Robert J. Ambrogi. **Description:** Spindle Law strives to make legal research faster and smarter using crowdsourcing as one means to reach users.

41039 ■ *"Crowdsourcing Solutions to Prepare Our Communities" in The America's*

Intelligence Wire (November 2, 2010)
Pub: HighBeam Research
Description: The 2010 TEDMED conference in San Diego, California, held in October 2010, challenged leaders from government and the public sector to offer ideas to help communities prepare for disasters.

41040 ■ *"Crowdsourcing their Way into One Big Mess" in Brandweek (Vol. 51, October 25, 2010, No. 38, pp. 26)*
Pub: Nielsen Business Media, Inc.
Ed: Gregg S. Lipman. **Description:** The Gap, was counting on crowdsourcing to provide feedback for its new logo, but it did not prove positive for the retailer. However, a massive outcry of negative opinion, via crowdsourcing, may not always equal valid, constructive criticism.

41041 ■ *"Cyberwise" in Black Enterprise (Vol. 41, December 2010, No. 5, pp. 50)*
Pub: Earl G. Graves Publishing Co. Inc.
Ed: Marica Wade Talbert. **Description:** Information is given regarding single platforms that can be used to develop applications for iPhone, Android, Blackberry, and Nokia.

41042 ■ *"Deal With Tribes Revives Revenue Stream" in Crain's Detroit Business (Vol. 24, March 24, 2008, No. 12, pp. 6)*
Pub: Crain Communications, Inc.
Ed: Amy Lane. **Description:** Michigan Bureau of State Lottery's 2003 launch of its Club Keno game caused the Little River Band of Ottawa Indians and the Little Traverse Bay Bands of Odawa Indians to halt payments of shared casino revenue with the state. The federal lawsuit that resulted has now been settled and tribal revenue-sharing will resume as well as $26 million in previous payments to the state of Michigan that the tribes had put into escrow.

41043 ■ *"Death of the PC" in Canadian Business (Vol. 83, October 12, 2010, No. 17, pp. 44)*
Pub: Rogers Media Ltd.
Ed: Joe Castaldo. **Description:** The future of the personal computer (PC) is looking bleak as consumers are relying more on new mobile devices instead of their PC. A 'Wall Street Journal' article published in September 2010 reported that the iPad had cannibalized sales of laptops by as much as 50 percent. The emergence of tablet computers running alternative operating systems is also explained.

41044 ■ *"Defense Contractor May Expand Locally; BAE Systems Ramps Up Vehicle Prototypes" in Crain's Detroit Business (March 24, 2008)*
Pub: Crain Communications, Inc.
Ed: Chad Halcom. **Description:** Profile of BAE Systems, a defense contractor, that has built a prototype in the highly competitive Joint Light Tactical Vehicle project; the company has also completed its prototype RG33L Mine Resistant Recovery Maintenance Vehicle and has plans for expansion.

41045 ■ *"Descartes Launches Ocean Shipment Management Suite" in Canadian Corporate News (May 16, 2007)*
Pub: Comtex News Network Inc.
Description: Descartes Systems Group, a global on-demand software-as-a-service (SaaS) logistics solutions provider, launched the latest release of its Descartes Ocean Shipment Management Suite. The release integrates customs compliance services with Descartes' Rate Builder solution, a central database for global shipment and rate information, and Descartes Global Logistics Network (GLN) messaging capabilities.

41046 ■ *"The Design of Things to Come" in Business Horizons (Vol. 51, January-February 2008, No. 1, pp. 74)*
Pub: Elsevier Advanced Technology Publications
Ed: Mimi Dollinger. **Description:** Review of the book that helps entrepreneurs develop and market new products, 'The Design of Things to Come: How Ordinary People Create Extraordinary Products'.

41047 ■ *"Digital Power Management and the PMBus" in Canadian Electronics (Vol. 23, June-July 2008, No. 4, pp. 8)*
Pub: Action Communication Inc.
Ed: Torbjorn Hohnberg. **Description:** PMBus is an interface that can be applied to a variety of devices including power management devices. Information on digital power management products using this interface are also provided.

41048 ■ *"Disney Has High Hopes for Duffy" in Canadian Business (Vol. 83, October 12, 2010, No. 17, pp. 14)*
Pub: Rogers Media Ltd.
Ed: James Cowan. **Description:** The reintroduction of Duffy is expected to create a new, exclusive product line that distinguishes Disney's parks and stores from competitors. Duffy, a teddy bear, was first introduced at a Disney World store in Florida in 2002. The character was incorporated into the Disney mythology when its popularity grew in Japan.

41049 ■ *"The Doctor Is In" in Canadian Business (Vol. 80, February 12, 2007, No. 4, pp. 38)*
Pub: Rogers Media
Ed: Erin Pooley. **Description:** The research at McMaster University to make a pill having imaging devices to takes pictures of any possible cancerous cells in the human body is discussed.

41050 ■ *"A Doll That Looks Like You: Will Custom Toys Take Off?" in Inc. (Volume 32, December 2010, No. 10, pp. 144)*
Pub: Inc. Magazine
Ed: Shivani Vora. **Description:** Profiles of various companies that provide custom items that look like people.

41051 ■ *"Dots Sings To New Tune With Its Radio Station" in Crain's Cleveland Business (Vol. 30, June 15, 2009, No. 23, pp. 7)*
Pub: Crain Communications, Inc.
Description: Dots LLC, a women's clothing retailer, has launched an online radio station on its Website. The station plays the in-store music to customers while they are shopping online.

41052 ■ *"Dry Idea" in Entrepreneur (Vol. 36, April 2008, No. 4, pp. 20)*
Pub: Entrepreneur Media, Inc.
Ed: Tiffany Meyers. **Description:** Lucky Earth LLC is an Inglewood, California-based company that markets 'Waterless' Carwash, an organic product that is sprayed on to the car and wiped down without using water. Businesses related to water conservation are being created, as water shortage is anticipated in 36 states in the U.S. by 2013.

41053 ■ *"DuPontas Pioneer Hi-Bred, Evogene to Develop Rust-Resistant Soybean Varieties" in Farm Industry News (November 22, 2011)*
Pub: Penton Business Media Inc.
Ed: Karen McMahon. **Description:** DuPont and Evogene have signed a new contract to work together to develop resistance in soybeans to rust. Financial terms of the agreement were not disclosed.

41054 ■ *"The Easy Route" in Entrepreneur (Vol. 36, April 2008, No. 4, pp. 60)*
Pub: Entrepreneur Media, Inc.
Ed: Amanda C. Kooser. **Description:** Buyer's guide of wireless office routers is presented. All products included in the list use the latest draft-n technology. Price and availability of the products are provided.

41055 ■ *Electronic Commerce*
Pub: Course Technology
Ed: Gary Schneider, Bryant Chrzan, Charles McCormick. **Released:** May 1, 2010. **Price:** $117.95. **Description:** E-commerce can open the door to more opportunities than ever before for small business. Packed with real-world examples and cases, the book delivers comprehensive coverage of emerging online technologies and trends and their influence on the electronic marketplace. It details how the landscape of online commerce is evolving, reflecting changes in the economy and how business and society are responding to those changes. Balancing technological issues with the strategic business aspects of successful e-commerce, the new edition includes expanded coverage of international issues, social networking, mobile commerce, Web 2.0 technologies, and updates on spam, phishing, and identity theft.

41056 ■ *"Electronic Design and a Greener Environment" in Canadian Electronics (Vol. 23, June-July 2008, No. 4, pp. 6)*
Pub: Action Communication Inc.
Ed: Nicholas Deeble. **Description:** Companies seeking to minimize their environmental impact are using Design methodologies of Cadence Design Systems Ltd. The company's Low Power Format and Low Power Design Flow help reduce carbon dioxide emissions.

41057 ■ *"Electronics Assembly" in Canadian Electronics (Vol. 23, February 2008, No. 1, pp. 12)*
Pub: CLB Media Inc.
Description: I&J Fisnar Inc. has launched a new system of bench top dispensing robots while Vitronics Soltec and KIC have introduced a new reflow soldering machine. Teknek, on the other hand, has announced a new product, called the CM10, which an be used in cleaning large format substrates. Other new products and their description are presented.

41058 ■ *"Elemental Nabs $5.5 Million" in The Business Journal-Portland (Vol. 25, July 18, 2008, No. 19, pp. 1)*
Pub: American City Business Journals, Inc.
Ed: Aliza Earnshaw. **Description:** Elemental Technologies Inc., a Portland, Oregon-based software company got $5.5 million in new funding, bringing its total invested capital to $7.1 million in nine months since October 2008. The company plans to launch Badaboom, software for converting video into various formats, later in 2008.

41059 ■ *"Ending the Ebola Death Sentence" in Canadian Business (Vol. 83, August 17, 2010, No. 13-14, pp. 22)*
Pub: Rogers Media Ltd.
Ed: Michael McCullough. **Description:** US Army Medical Research Institute of Infectious Diseases made a $140 million agreement with Tekmira Pharmaceuticals Corporation to develop both a drug delivery system and delivery technology for curing the Ebola virus. Tekmira's delivery technology, which has been shown to halt Ebola in laboratory animals, might be the key to finding a cure.

41060 ■ *"Engineering Services Supplier Launches 'Robotic Renaissance" in Modern Machine Shop (Vol. 84, September 2011, No. 4, pp. 46)*
Pub: Gardner Business Media, Inc.
Contact: Richard G. Kline, President
E-mail: rkline@gardnerweb.com
Description: Profile of Applied Manufacturing Technologies (AMT) new hiring initiative that supports continuing growth in the robotics industry. AMT is located in Orion, Michigan and supplies factory automation design, engineering and process consulting services.

41061 ■ *The Entrepreneur and Small Business Problem Solver*
Pub: John Wiley & Sons, Incorporated
Ed: William A. Cohen. **Released:** December 2005. **Price:** $24.95 (US), $31.99 (Canadian). **Description:** Revised edition of the resource for entrepreneurs and small business owners that covers everything from start-up financing and loans to new product promotion and more.

41062 ■ *"Executive Decision: To Make Inroads Against RIM, Palm Steals Its Strategy" in Globe & Mail (March 25, 2006, pp. B3)*
Pub: CTVglobemedia Publishing Inc.
Ed: Simon Avery. **Description:** The Palm Inc., global leader in portable device manufacturing, is looking forward to improve its sales of Palm Treos, a wireless portable device that connects to internet and email. Palm is also planning to build partnerships, under the efficient management of Michael Moskow-

itz, general manager and vice-president of Palm Inc., with the other companies to increase the sales of its wireless devices.

41063 ■ *The Facebook Era: Tapping Online Social Networks to Build Better Products, Reach New Audiences, and Sell More Stuff*
Pub: Prentice Hall
Ed: Clara Shih. **Price:** $24.99. **Description:** The '90s were about the World Wide Web of information and the power of linking Web pages. Today it's about the World Wide Web of people and the power of the social graph. Online social networks are fundamentally changing the way we live, work, and interact. They offer businesses immense opportunities to transform customer relationships for profit: opportunities that touch virtually every business function, from sales and marketing to recruiting, collaboration to executive decision-making, product development to innovation.

41064 ■ *"Facilitating and Rewarding Creativity During New Product Development" in Journal of Marketing (Vol. 75, July 2011, No. 4, pp. 53)*
Pub: American Marketing Association
Ed: James E. Burroughs, Darren W. Dahl, C. Page Moreau, Amitava Chattopadhay, Gerald J. Gorn. **Description:** A study to determine the effects of rewards to creativity in the process of new product development is presented. The findings show that the effect of rewards can be made positive if combined with appropriate creativity training.

41065 ■ *"FinOvation 2009" in Farm Industry News (Vol. 42, January 1, 2009, No. 1)*
Pub: Penton Media Inc.
Contact: John French, President
Ed: Karen McMahon; David Hest; Mark Moore. **Description:** New and innovative products and technologies are presented.

41066 ■ *"Five Things..For Photo Fun" in Hawaii Business (Vol. 53, October 2007, No. 4, pp. 20)*
Pub: Hawaii Business Publishing
Ed: Cathy S. Cruz-George. **Description:** Featured is a buyers guide of products used for capturing or displaying digital photos; products featured include the Digital Photo Wallet and Light Affection.

41067 ■ *"Flu is a Booster for Firms Here" in Philadelphia Business Journal (Vol. 28, September 25, 2009, No. 32, pp. 1)*
Pub: American City Business Journals
Ed: John George. **Description:** GlaxoSmithKline, AstraZeneca, CSL Biotherapies, and Sanofi Aventis were awarded contract by the US Government to supply swine flu vaccines. It is estimated that global sales of the vaccine could reach billions of dollars.

41068 ■ *"The Folly of Google's Latest Gambit" in Barron's (Vol. 89, July 13, 2009, No. 28, pp. 23)*
Pub: Dow Jones & Co., Inc.
Ed: Eric J. Savitz. **Description:** Google will enter the operating systems business with the introduction of the Google Chrome OS but its success is dubious because the project is still a year or so away while Microsoft will release an updated version of Windows by then; another problem is that Google already has another OS called Android which will overlap with the Chrome OS's market.

41069 ■ *"Foods for Thought" in Pet Product News (Vol. 64, December 2010, No. 12, pp. 16)*
Pub: BowTie Inc.
Ed: Maddy Heleine. **Description:** Manufacturers have been focused at developing species-specific fish foods due to consumer tendency to assess the benefits of the food they feed their fish. As retailers stock species-specific fish foods, manufacturers have provided in-store items and strategies to assist in efficiently selling these food products. Trends in fish food packaging and ingredients are also discussed.

41070 ■ *"For Apple, It's Showtime Again" in Barron's (Vol. 90, August 30, 2010, No. 35, pp. 29)*
Pub: Barron's Editorial & Corporate Headquarters
Ed: Eric J. Savitz. **Description:** Speculations on what Apple Inc. will unveil at its product launch event are presented. These products include a possible new iPhone Nano, a new update to its Apple TV, and possibly a deal with the Beatles to distribute their songs over iTunes.

41071 ■ *"Frito Lay Plans to Spice Up Life With New Chips" in Globe & Mail (February 21, 2006, pp. B3)*
Pub: CTVglobemedia Publishing Inc.
Ed: Andy Hoffman. **Description:** The reasons behind the launch of potato chips by Frito Lay Canada Inc., subsidiary of PepsiCo. Inc., are presented.

41072 ■ *From Concept To Consumer: How to Turn Ideas Into Money*
Pub: Pearson Education Inc.
Ed: Phil Baker. **Released:** 2009. **Price:** $24.99. **Description:** Renowned product developer Phil Baker explains how a great idea accounts for only 5 percent of all the factors of success and why the majority of success is dependent upon a myriad of other factors, including the time it takes to get to market, price, marketing and distribution. By being their own best competition, a small company can stay one step ahead of competitors.

41073 ■ *"From OTC Sellers to Surgeons, Healthcare Marketers Target Women to Achieve Growth" in Marketing to Women (February 2008)*
Pub: EPM Communications Inc.
Contact: Ira Mayer, President
E-mail: imayer@epmcom.com
Description: Healthcare companies are targeting women with ad campaigns, new product development and new technology in order to reach and develop brand loyalty.

41074 ■ *"Frosted Flakes Goes For Gold" in Marketing to Women (Vol. 21, April 2008, No. 4, pp. 3)*
Pub: EPM Communications Inc.
Contact: Ira Mayer, President
E-mail: imayer@epmcom.com
Description: Kellogg is appealing to health-conscious moms with its new product Frosted Flakes Gold.

41075 ■ *"Gadget Makers Aim for New Chapter in Reading" in Crain's Cleveland Business (Vol. 28, October 22, 2007, No. 42, pp. 20)*
Pub: Crain Communications, Inc.
Ed: Jennifer McKevitt. **Description:** Although e-books and e-audiobooks are becoming more popular, e-readers, devices that display digital books, still haven't caught on with the public. Experts feel that consumers, many of whom have to look at a computer screen all day for work, still like the feel of a real book in their hands.

41076 ■ *"Game Changer" in Canadian Business (Vol. 83, June 15, 2010, No. 10, pp. 52)*
Pub: Rogers Media Ltd.
Ed: Jordan Timm. **Description:** Ubisoft chose Ontario to be the site for its new development studio and it has appointed Jade Raymond as its managing director. Raymond was born in Montreal in 1975 and studied computer science at McGill. Raymond is said to possess the understanding of the game industry's technical, art, and business components.

41077 ■ *"Game On" in Canadian Business (Vol. 80, February 12, 2007, No. 4, pp. 15)*
Pub: Rogers Media
Ed: Calvin Leung. **Description:** The plan of president of TransGaming Vikas Gupta to create innovative software programs for games that can be played in different operating systems is discussed.

41078 ■ *"GeckoSystems Reduces Sensor Fusion Costs Due to Elder Care Robot Trials" in Internet Wire (December 14, 2010)*
Pub: Comtex
Description: GeckoSystems International Corporation has been able to reduce the cost of its sensor fusion system while maintaining reliability and performance. The firm's ongoing first in-home elder care robot trials have sparked interest regarding its business model, technologies available for licensing, and joint domestic and international ventures.

41079 ■ *"Getting Inventive With..Ed Spellman" in Crain's Cleveland Business (Vol. 28, October 22, 2007, No. 42, pp. 18)*
Pub: Crain Communications, Inc.
Ed: Kimberly Bonvissuto. **Description:** Profile featuring Ed Spellman, a mechanical engineer who decided to quit his job at Invacare Corp., a medical equipment manufacturer and distributor, in order to devote his full attention to promoting his numerous inventions, including the DV-Grip, a vehicle mount for portable DVD players.

41080 ■ *"Getting Inventive With..John Nottingham and John Spirk" in Crain's Cleveland Business (Vol. 28, October 22, 2007, No. 42, pp. 19)*
Pub: Crain Communications, Inc.
Ed: Kimberly Bonvissuto. **Description:** Profile featuring John Spirk and John Nottingham of the Cleveland-based firm, Nottingham-Spirk Design Associates; the company holds 486 issued and commercialized patents and has reported over $30 billion in new product sales.

41081 ■ *"Getting Inventive With..Richard Brindisi and Gregory Vittardi" in Crain's Cleveland Business (Vol. 28, October 22, 2007, No. 42)*
Pub: Crain Communications, Inc.
Ed: Kimberly Bonvissuto. **Description:** Profile of the SmartShopper, a handheld, voice-recognition device for dictating shopping and errand lists, and its creators, Richard G. Brindisi and Gregory Vittardi.

41082 ■ *"Getting the Word Out" in Modern Machine Shop (Vol. 84, September 2011, No. 4, pp. 16)*
Pub: Gardner Business Media, Inc.
Contact: Richard G. Kline, President
E-mail: rkline@gardnerweb.com
Ed: Derek Korn. **Description:** Many times machine shops create devices to streamline their own machining processes and find these devices can be used by other shops, thus developing a marketable product. Tips for this process are outlined.

41083 ■ *"Give 'Em a Boost" in Entrepreneur (Vol. 36, April 2008, No. 4, pp. 120)*
Pub: Entrepreneur Media, Inc.
Ed: Kristen Henning. **Description:** Amir Levin of Kaboost Corp. markets a plastic booster system that attaches to the bottom of a regular chair and raises it. He thought of the idea of creating the product after seeing his young cousins refusing to sit in their booster seats. Levin started his company in 2006.

41084 ■ *"GM Canada Revved Up Over Camaro" in Globe & Mail (February 17, 2006, pp. B4)*
Pub: CTVglobemedia Publishing Inc.
Ed: Greg Keenan. **Description:** General Manager of General Motors Canada is planning to start the production of company's muscle car Camaro in Canadian facility. The car was exhibited at Canadian International Auto Show held in Toronto.

41085 ■ *"Hello, Old Friends" in Business Courier (Vol. 24, October 12, 2008, No. 26, pp. 1)*
Pub: American City Business Journals, Inc.
Ed: Jon Newberry. **Description:** Pittsburgh-based Iron City Brewing Co., a company born out of Pittsburgh Brewing Co.'s reorganization, is resuming the production of Wiedemann Bohemian Style Special Beer. Cincinnati-based Christian Moerlein Brewing Co. is also bringing back its famous Burger beer, which hasn't been available locally for a couple of years. The two companies' plans regarding the re-introduction of their beer products are discussed.

41086 ■ *"Herrell's Launches New Corporate Identity at Fancy Food Show" in Ice Cream*

***Reporter* (Vol. 23, July 20, 2010, No. 8, pp. 3)**
Pub: Ice Cream Reporter
Description: Herrell's ice cream introduced a new corporate branding at the Summer 2010 Fancy Food Show last summer. Slightly Mad Communications advertising agency developed the new brand to reflect the era of the early 1970s.

41087 ■ *"Hey, You Can't Do That" in Green Industry Pro (Vol. 23, September 2011)*
Pub: Cygnus Business Media
Ed: Rod Dickens. **Description:** Manufacturers of landscape equipment are making better use of energy resources, such as the use of fuel-injection systems instead of carburetors, lightweight materials, better lubricants, advanced battery technology, and innovative engine designs.

41088 ■ *"The Hired Guns" in Business Courier (Vol. 26, November 13, 2009, No. 29, pp. 1)*
Pub: American City Business Journals, Inc.
Ed: Lisa Biank Fasig. **Description:** YourForce has nearly 6,000 retired scientists and researchers who work together in helping Procter & Gamble (P&G) and other companies in addressing various project needs. Operating as an online innovation community, YourEncore is a result of P&G's Connect Develop program.

41089 ■ *"Hold the IPhone" in Canadian Business (Vol. 80, January 15, 2007, No. 2, pp. 22)*
Pub: Rogers Media
Ed: Andrew Wahl. **Description:** The rise in the price of shares of Apple Inc. after the introduction of its new product, the iPhone, is discussed.

41090 ■ *"Hot Kicks, Cool Price" in Black Enterprise (Vol. 37, December 2006, No. 5, pp. 34)*
Pub: Earl G. Graves Publishing Co. Inc.
Ed: Topher Sanders. **Description:** Stephon Marbury of the New York Nicks introduced a new basketball shoe, the Starbury One, costing $14.98. The shoes are an addition to the Starbury clothing line and although the privately owned company would not disclose figures; stores sold out of a month's worth of inventory in merely three days.

41091 ■ *How Customers Think*
Pub: Harvard Business School Press
Ed: Gerald Zaltman. **Released:** February 21, 2003. **Price:** $32.95. **Description:** Despite marketing efforts and customer surveys, nearly eighty percent of all new products fail of fall short of prediction within the first six months after introduction. Consumer reactions to products and marketing programs are investigated.

41092 ■ *"How Dell Will Dial for Dollars" in Austin Business Journallnc. (Vol. 29, December 4, 2009, No. 39, pp. 1)*
Pub: American City Business Journals
Ed: Christopher Calnan. **Description:** Dell Inc. revealed plans to launch a Mini3i smartphone in China which could enable revenue sharing by bundling with wireless service subscription. Dell's smartphone plan is similar to the netbook business, which Dell sold with service provided by AT&T Inc.

41093 ■ *"How Hard Could It Be? Adventures In Software Demol'ling" in Inc. (December 2007, pp. 99-100)*
Pub: Gruner & Jahr USA Publishing
Ed: Joel Spolsky. **Description:** Founder and CEO of Fog Creek Software, a New York City software developer shares insight into his software demo tour used to promote his firm's products.

41094 ■ *"How to Manage Successful Crowdsourcing Projects" in eWeek (September 29, 2010)*
Pub: Ziff Davis Enterprise
Description: The advantages, challenges and pitfalls faced when using crowdsourcing to improve a business are outlined. Crowdsourcing helps to eliminate the need to rely on an internal workforce and the need to forecast task volume.

41095 ■ *"How to Play the Tech Mergers" in Barron's (Vol. 90, August 30, 2010, No. 35, pp. 18)*
Pub: Barron's Editorial & Corporate Headquarters
Ed: Tiernan Ray. **Description:** The intense bidding by Hewlett-Packard and Dell for 3Par was foreseen in a previous Barron's cover story and 3Par's stock has nearly tripled since reported. Other possible acquisition targets in the tech industry include Brocade Communication Systems, NetApp, Xyratex, and Isilon Systems.

41096 ■ *"How to Save Good Ideas" in Harvard Business Review (Vol. 88, October 2010, No. 10, pp. 129)*
Pub: Harvard Business School Publishing
Ed: Jeff Kehoe. **Description:** Harvard Business School Professor John P. Kotter identifies situations that may hinder the development and implementation of ideas, and discusses effective ways to counter them.

41097 ■ *"Hybrid Popularity Pushes Automakers to Add to Offerings" in Crain's Cleveland Business (Vol. 28, November 12, 2007, No. 45, pp. 30)*
Pub: Crain Communications, Inc.
Ed: David Sedgwick. **Description:** Due in part to Toyota's innovative marketing, automotive hybrids have caught on with consumers thus forcing other automakers to add hybrids to their product plans.

41098 ■ *"Idea-Generation Program Creates Winning Programs" in Business Journal-Serving Metropolitan Kansas City (October 19, 2007)*
Pub: American City Business Journals, Inc.
Ed: James Dombrook. **Description:** Eureka Ranch has developed 'Eureka! Winning Ways', a program that helps companies create new ideas for their business. Brunson Instruments is the first Missouri manufacturer to engage in the program. The procedures in the new product idea generation program are supplied.

41099 ■ *"IMRA's Ultrafast Lasers Bring Precision, profits; Ann Arbor Company Eyes Expansion" in Crain's Detroit Business (March 10, 2008)*
Pub: Crain Communications, Inc.
Ed: Tom Henderson. **Description:** IMRA America Inc. plans to expand its headquarters and has applied for permits to build a fourth building that will house research and development facilities and allow the company more room for manufacturing; the company plans to add about 20 more employees that would include research scientists, manufacturing and assembly workers, engineers and salespeople. The growth is due mainly to a new technology of ultrafast fiber lasers that reduce side effects for those getting eye surgeries and help manufacturers of computer chips to reduce their size and cost.

41100 ■ *"In Search of the Next Big Thing: It's Out There - Just Waiting For You To Find It" in Inc. (Volume 32, December 2010, No. 10, pp. 34)*
Pub: Inc. Magazine
Ed: April Joyner. **Description:** Innovation is the future for small business. A new book, Inside Real Innovation: How the Right Approach Can Move Ideas from R&D to Market - And Get the Economy Moving helps to break down the process by which innovation occurs.

41101 ■ *"InnoCentive Announces Next Generation Crowdsourcing Platform" in Internet Wire (June 15, 2010)*
Pub: Comtex
Description: InnoCentive, Inc., a world leader in open innovation, is launching InnoCentive@Work3, a third generation of its @Work enterprise platform for collaborative-driven innovation for companies. The product will help clients solve critical business and technical issues by tapping information both inside and outside of a company.

41102 ■ *"Innovating Low-Cost Business Models" in Strategy and Leadership (Vol. 39, March-April 2011, No. 2, pp. 43)*
Pub: Emerald Group Publishing Inc.
Ed: Nicholas Kachaner, Zhenya Lindgardt, David Michael. **Description:** A process that can be used to implement low-cost innovation is presented. The process can be used to address the competitive challenges presented by multinationals' practice of presenting applications and price points that are intended for developing markets into developed markets. The process involves targeting large, and low-income segments of the market.

41103 ■ *"Innovation in 3D: NextFab" in Philadelphia Business Journal (Vol. 28, January 22, 2010, No. 49, pp. 1)*
Pub: American City Business Journals
Ed: Peter Key. **Description:** NextFab Studio LLC is set to offer product development services using 3D technology. The company has developed a three-dimensional printer which fabricates objects usually made of plastic.

41104 ■ *"Invacare Plans '08 Release for Portable Oxygen Product" in Crain's Cleveland Business (Vol. 28, October 22, 2007, No. 42, pp. 5)*
Pub: Crain Communications, Inc.
Ed: Chuck Soder. **Description:** Invacare Corp., an Elyria-based maker of home health care equipment, plans the release of a new 'extremely portable' oxygen concentration machine in 2008. The XP02 is expected to increase sales due to the popularity of portable oxygen concentrators.

41105 ■ *"Inventive Doctor New Venture Partner" in Houston Business Journal (Vol. 40, January 29, 2010, No. 38, pp. A2)*
Pub: American City Business Journals
Ed: Ford Gunter. **Description:** Dr. Billy Cohn, a surgeon from Houston, Texas has been named as venture partner for venture firm Sante Ventures LLC of Austin, Texas. Cohn will be responsible for seeing marketable developing technologies in the medical industry. The motivation for Cohn's naming as venture partner is his development of a minimally invasive therapy for end-stage renal disease.

41106 ■ *"iPhone Apps Big Business" in Austin Business Journallnc. (Vol. 28, November 14, 2008, No. 35, pp. 1)*
Pub: American City Business Journals
Ed: Christopher Calnan. **Description:** Members of the computer software industry in Austin, Texas have benefited from developing applications for Apple Inc.'s iPhone. Pangea Software Inc.'s revenues have grown by developing iPhone applications. Lexcycle LLC, on the other hand, has created an application that enables users to read books on the iPhone.

41107 ■ *"IPod Killers?" in Canadian Business (Vol. 79, November 20, 2006, No. 23, pp. 68)*
Pub: Rogers Media
Ed: Gerry Blackwell. **Description:** The features of Apple iPod that distinguishes it from other MP3 players available in the market are discussed.

41108 ■ *"Irene Rosenfeld; Chairman and CEO, Kraft Foods Inc." in Crain's Chicago Business (Vol. 31, May 5, 2008, No. 18, pp. 31)*
Pub: Crain Communications, Inc.
Ed: David Sterrett. **Description:** Profile of Irene Rosenfeld who is the chairman and CEO of Kraft Foods Inc. and is entering the second year of a three-year plan to boost sales of well-known brands such as Oreo, Velveeta and Oscar Mayer while facing soaring commodity costs and a declining market-share. Ms. Rosenfeld's turnaround strategy also entails spending more on advertising and giving managers more control over their budgets and product development.

41109 ■ *"Iron Man Forges New Path" in Canadian Business (Vol. 80, February 12, 2007, No. 4, pp. 41)*
Pub: Rogers Media
Ed: Rachel Pulfer. **Description:** The research of Donald Sadoway of Massachusetts Institute of Technology in making iron in an environmentally friendly method using electrolysis is discussed.

41110 ■ *"It's New or Improved, But Does It Work?" in Contractor (Vol. 57, January 2010, No. 1, pp. 22)*
Pub: Penton Media, Inc.
Ed: Al Schwartz. **Description:** There is a place for skepticism in the HVAC and plumbing industry as not all new products that are specified may not always perform. The tradesman has the responsibility of integrating new technology into the field.

41111 ■ *"Ivorydale Looks to Clean Up" in Business Courier (Vol. 26, January 15, 2010, No. 39, pp. 1)*
Pub: American City Business Journals, Inc.
Ed: Jon Newberry. **Description:** Cincinnati-based St. Bernard Soap Company plans to focus on new services such as product development and logistics and to continue growth and put excess capacity to work. The unit of Ontario, Canada-based Trillium Health Care Products Inc. is the largest contract manufacturer of bar soap in North America.

41112 ■ *"Janitorial Equipment and Supplies US Market" in PR Newswire (October 24, 2011)*
Pub: PR Newswire
Description: United States demand for janitorial equipment and supplies (excluding chemical products) is predicted to rise 2.4 percent per year to $7.6 billion in 2013. New product development will lead to increased sales of higher-value goods in the industry.

41113 ■ *"Just Add Water and Lily Pads" in Crain's Chicago Business (Vol. 31, April 28, 2008, No. 17, pp. 50)*
Pub: Crain Communications, Inc.
Ed: Phuong Ly. **Description:** Aquascape Inc., a major manufacturer of pond-building supplies, is using the recent drought in the South which hurt its business significantly to create a new product: an upscale, decorative version of the rain barrel which will collect rainwater to circulate through a pond or a fountain.

41114 ■ *"Kaiser Permanente's Innovation on the Front Lines" in Harvard Business Review (Vol. 88, September 2010, No. 9, pp. 92)*
Pub: Harvard Business School Publishing
Ed: Lew McCreary. **Description:** Kaiser Permanente's human-centered model for organizational effectiveness emphasizes the roles of patients and providers as collaborators driving quality improvement and innovation.

41115 ■ *"Kawasaki's New Top Gun" in Brandweek (Vol. 49, April 21, 2008, No. 16, pp. 18)*
Pub: VNU Business Media, Inc.
Description: Discusses Kawasaki's marketing plan which included designing an online brochure in which visitors could create a video by building their own test track on a grid and then selecting visual special effects and musical overlay. This engaging and innovative marketing technique generated more than 166,000 unique users within the first three months of being launched.

41116 ■ *King of Capital*
Pub: John Wiley and Sons, Inc.
Ed: Amey Stone; Mike Brewster. **Released:** 2004. **Price:** $16.95. **Description:** Biography of Sandy Weill describes how he became a billionaire business giant by creating successful companies from smaller, sometimes failing firms; creating successful new products where none previously existed; and making deals no one thought possible. He is also responsible for changing the landscape of the banking industry and insurance business when he created Citigroup in 1998, the world's largest financial services firm.

41117 ■ *"Kosher Ice Cream Features Traditional Jewish Ingredients" in Ice Cream Reporter (Vol. 23, August 20, 2010, No. 9, pp. 5)*
Pub: Ice Cream Reporter
Description: Chozen Ice Cream is offering traditional Jewish dessert and snack foods using tradition Jewish ingredients to name items: regelach, coconut-almond macaroon, and chocolate matzo.

41118 ■ *"LED Screen Technology Takes Centre Stage" in Canadian Electronics (Vol. 23, June-July 2008, No. 4, pp. 17)*
Pub: Action Communication Inc.
Ed: Ed Whitaker. **Description:** Display technologies based on light emitting diodes are becoming more popular due to their flexibility, versatility and reproducibility of displays. These are being increasingly used in different applications, such as advertising and concerts.

41119 ■ *"Lee's Launches With Focus on Liqueur-based Ice Creams" in Ice Cream Reporter (Vol. 23, August 20, 2010, No. 9, pp. 6)*
Pub: Ice Cream Reporter
Description: Lee's Cream Liqueur Ice Cream Parlors launched their grand opening in Old Town Scottsdale in July, featuring premium liqueurs to create adult-only ice creams that can be served on their own or blended into exotic drinks.

41120 ■ *"Leica Beefs Up Steering Options, Steering Display Features" in Farm Industry News (January 10, 2011)*
Pub: Penton Business Media Inc.
Description: Leica Geosystems is offering a new hydraulic steering kit for older tractors, along with new steering patterns and other features on its Leica mojo3C and mojoMINI displays.

41121 ■ *"Leinie's Charts National Craft Beer Rollout" in The Business Journal-Milwaukee (Vol. 25, August 29, 2008, No. 49, pp. A1)*
Pub: American City Business Journals, Inc.
Ed: Rich Rovito. **Description:** Jacob Leinenkugel Brewing Co. is expected to complete the national rollout of its craft beer brands, while the launch of a new beer is prepared for this fall. The rollout is will likely benefit MillerCoors LLC, and will leave Alaska as the only state without Leinenkugel beer. Other views and information on Leinenkugel's national rollout are presented.

41122 ■ *"Life's Work" in Harvard Business Review (Vol. 88, July-August 2010, No. 7-8, pp. 172)*
Pub: Harvard Business School Publishing
Ed: Alison Beard. **Description:** The founder of appliance company Dyson Ltd. discusses the role of making mistakes in learning and innovation, and emphasizes the importance of hands-on involvement to make a company successful.

41123 ■ *"Liora Manne to Debut Fabric Line" in Home Textiles Today (Vol. 31, May 24, 2011, No. 13, pp. 4)*
Pub: Reed Business Information
Contact: Jeff Greisch, President
Description: Textile and product designer Liora Manne will debut her new decorative fabric collection at the Showtime in High Point, North Carolina in June 2011. More than 22 fabric patterns and solid colors using Manne's patented Lamontage textile design process will be featured and can be used for indoor/outdoor decorative fabrics, furniture, decorative pillows, upholstery and more.

41124 ■ *"Local Company Seeks Patent For Armored Trucks" in Crain's Detroit Business (Vol. 24, February 4, 2008, No. 5, pp. 10)*
Pub: Crain Communications Inc. - Detroit
Description: Profile of James LeBlanc Sr., mechanical engineer and defense contractor, discusses his eleven utility patents pending for a set of vehicles and subsystems that would work as countermeasures to explosively formed projectiles.

41125 ■ *"Local Startup Hits Big Leagues" in Austin Business JournalInc. (Vol. 28, December 19, 2008, No. 40, pp. 1)*
Pub: American City Business Journals
Ed: Christopher Calnan. **Description:** Qcue LLC, an Austin, Texas-based company founded in 2007 is developing a software system that can be used by Major League Baseball teams to change the prices of their single-game tickets based on variables affecting demand. The company recently completed a trial with the San Francisco Giants in 2008.

41126 ■ *"MaggieMoo's Ice Cream and Treatery" in Ice Cream Reporter (Vol. 23, September 20, 2010, No. 10, pp. 7)*
Pub: Ice Cream Reporter
Description: MaggieMoo's Ice Cream and Treatery has launched a new Website where visitors can learn about the brands newest ice cream innovations.

41127 ■ *"Magna Stalwart to Push for Product Coups" in Globe & Mail (April 9, 2007, pp. B1)*
Pub: CTVglobemedia Publishing Inc.
Ed: Greg Keenan. **Description:** The resignation of Fred Gingl from the vice-chairmanship of the board of directors of Magna International Inc. is described. Mr. Gingl's plans to create wealth for Magna International Inc. through the development of new products are discussed.

41128 ■ *"Making Headlines" in Entrepreneur (Vol. 36, April 2008, No. 4, pp. 126)*
Pub: Entrepreneur Media, Inc.
Ed: John Janstch. **Description:** Tips on how to get journalists to notice your business and your new product offerings are presented. These include making a list of journalists that might be interested in the industry you are in and writing comments on their blogs.

41129 ■ *"Making Waves" in Business Journal Portland (Vol. 27, November 26, 2010, No. 39, pp. 1)*
Pub: Portland Business Journal
Ed: Erik Siemers. **Description:** Corvallis, Oregon-based Columbia Power Technologies LLC is about to close a $2 million Series A round of investment initiated by $750,000 from Oregon Angel Fund. The wave energy startup company was formed to commercialize the wave buoy technology developed by Oregon State University researchers.

41130 ■ *"Manufacturing in the Middle Kingdom" in Inc. (December 2007, pp. 54-57)*
Pub: Gruner & Jahr USA Publishing
Ed: Alex Salkever. **Description:** Tips for manufacturing any new product in China as well as marketing said product is examined; five key steps for successfully managing Chinese contractors are listed.

41131 ■ *Market Rebels: How Activists Make or Break Radical Innovations*
Pub: Princeton University Press
Ed: Hayagreeva Rao. **Released:** 2009. **Price:** $24. 95. **Description:** Informal groups of enthusiasts could be the key to making a new product the next big thing to hit the marketplace.

41132 ■ *"Marketer Bets Big on U.S.'s Growing Canine Obsession" in Advertising Age (Vol. 79, April 14, 2008, No. 15, pp. 14)*
Pub: Crain Communications, Inc.
Ed: Emily Bryson York. **Description:** Overview of FreshPet, a New Jersey company that began marketing two brands of refrigerated dog food-Deli Fresh and FreshPet Select-which are made from fresh ingredients such as beef, rice and carrots. The company projects continued success due to the amount of money consumers spend on their pets as well as fears derived from the 2007 recalls that inspired consumers to look for smaller, independent manufacturers that are less likely to source ingredients from China.

41133 ■ *"Martha Stewart Launches Macys Line" in Marketing to Women (Vol. 21, March 2008, No. 3, pp. 5)*
Pub: EPM Communications Inc.
Contact: Ira Mayer, President
E-mail: imayer@epmcom.com
Description: Martha Stewart launches an exclusive line of home decor called Wedgwood as part of her relationship with Macy's stores.

41134 ■ *"Maximizing the Success of New Products" in Black Enterprise (Vol. 38, October 2007, No. 3, pp. 70)*
Pub: Earl G. Graves Publishing Co. Inc.
Description: New product development drives business growth and profitability. University of Chicago offers a weeklong New Product Development in Innovation class for executive training.

41135 ■ *"McD's Tries to Slake Consumer Thirst for Wider Choice of Drinks" in Advertising Age (Vol. 79, June 9, 2008, No. 23, pp. 1)*
Pub: Crain Communications, Inc.
Ed: Natalie Zmuda; Emily Bryson York. **Description:** McDonald's is testing the sale of canned and bottled drinks in about 150 locations in an attempt to offer more options to consumers who are going elsewhere for their beverage choices.

41136 ■ *"Media Giant Remakes Itself: Job Cuts Signal Journal Sentinel's Focus on New Products" in Business Journal-Milwaukee (Oct. 12, 2007)*
Pub: American City Business Journals, Inc.
Ed: Rich Kirchen. **Description:** Milwaukee Journal Sentinel is reducing its workforce by offering separation pay, and is willing to consider layoffs if the separation program fails. The downsizing is a result of lowered revenue, which was caused by the decline in printed news demand and increase in online competition. Strategies that the Journal Sentinel are employing, such as developing new products, to increase revenue are presented.

41137 ■ *"Microsoft Clicks Into High Speed" in Hispanic Business (Vol. 30, July-August 2008, No. 7-8, pp. 54)*
Pub: Hispanic Business, Inc.
Ed: Derek Reveron. **Description:** Microsoft's diversity hiring and vendor diversity program to capture more Hispanic consumer and business-to-business market is described. One of the main goals of these programs is to hire more Hispanic executives and managers who will help the company develop and market products and services that will appeal and benefit Hispanic consumers.

41138 ■ *"Midwest Test" in Crain's Cleveland Business (Vol. 28, November 26, 2007, No. 47, pp. 1)*
Pub: Crain Communications, Inc.
Ed: John Booth. **Description:** Provides an overview of the experimental Wal-Mart Supercenter in Elyria which researches consumer preferences with department layouts, new merchandise and even exterior architecture. Store manager Bob Butler said, 'We're trying to get out of that box-store look.'.

41139 ■ *"Milwaukee Rolls Out Major Line Expansion" in Contractor (Vol. 56, July 2009, No. 7, pp. 3)*
Pub: Penton Media, Inc.
Ed: Robert P. Mader. **Description:** Milwaukee Electric Tool Corp. introduced a new line of products that include corded tools and cordless tools, measurement instruments, and tool accessories. The products include four new Deep Cut Band Saws and the M12 Cordless 3/8-inch Impact Wrench.

41140 ■ *"MIR Growing With Help From Former Pfizer Workers" in Crain's Detroit Business (Vol. 24, January 28, 2008, No. 4, pp. 33)*
Pub: Crain Communications Inc. - Detroit
Ed: Tom Henderson. **Description:** Molecular Imaging Research Inc. helps fund research at its parent firm, Molecular Therapeutics Inc. The company provides imaging services and other in vivo and in vitro services to help pharmaceutical companies test new compounds.

41141 ■ *"Mobile Security for Business V5" in SC Magazine (Vol. 20, August 2009, No. 8, pp. 55)*
Pub: Haymarket Media, Inc.
Description: Review of F-Secure's Mobile Security for Business v5 which offers protection for business smartphones that can be centralized for protection monitoring by IT administrators.

41142 ■ *"A Model Machine for Titanium" in Modern Machine Shop (Vol. 84, October 2011, No. 5, pp. 84)*
Pub: Gardner Business Media, Inc.
Contact: Richard G. Kline, President
E-mail: rkline@gardnerweb.com
Ed: Peter Zelinski. **Description:** Researchers have developed a machine tool that controls vibration in order to mill titanium more productively. In-depth information on the machine tool as well as understanding the processes involved in milling titanium is covered.

41143 ■ *"Monsanto's Next Single-Bag Refuge Product Approved" in Farm Industry News (December 5, 2011)*
Pub: Penton Business Media Inc.
Description: Monsanto's refuge-in-a-bag (RIB) product was approved for commercialization in 2012. The Genuity VT Double Pro RIB Complete is a blend of 95 percent Genuity VT Double Pro and 5 percent refuge (non-Bt) seed and provides above-ground pest control and not corn rootworm protection.

41144 ■ *"More Than 1,000 Attend Second WaterSmart" in Contractor (Vol. 56, November 2009, No. 11, pp. 3)*
Pub: Penton Media, Inc.
Description: Over 1,000 plumbing and water conservation professionals attended the second WaterSmart Innovations Conference and Exposition in Las Vegas. Plumbing industry personalities made presentations during the conference and several innovative products were displayed at the trade show.

41145 ■ *"A Motorola Spinoff Is No Panacea" in Barron's (Vol. 88, March 31, 2008, No. 13, pp. 19)*
Pub: Dow Jones & Company, Inc.
Ed: Mark Veverka. **Description:** Motorola's plan to try and spinoff their handset division is bereft of details as to how or specifically when in 2009 the spinoff would occur. There's no reason to buy the shares since there's a lot of execution risk to the plan. Motorola needs to hire a proven cellphone executive and develop a compelling new cellphone platform.

41146 ■ *"Motorola's New Cell Phone Lineup Includes Green Effort" in Chicago Tribune (January 14, 2009)*
Pub: McClatchy-Tribune Information Services
Ed: Eric Benderoff. **Description:** Motorola Inc. introduced a new line of mobile phones at the Consumer Electronics Show in Las Vegas; the phones are made using recycled water bottles for the plastic housing.

41147 ■ *"Motors and Motion Control" in Canadian Electronics (Vol. 23, February 2008, No. 1, pp. 23)*
Pub: CLB Media Inc.
Description: A new version of MicroMo Electronics Inc.'s Smoovy Series 0303..B has been added to MicroMo's DC motor product line. United Electronic Industries, on the other hand, has introduced the new UEIPAC series of programmable automation controllers that can offer solutions to various applications such as unmanned vehicle controllers. Features and functions of other new motors and motion control devices are given.

41148 ■ *The Mousedriver Chronicles*
Pub: Perseus Books Group
Ed: John Lusk; Kyle Harrison. **Released:** 2003. **Price:** $16.95. **Description:** Entrepreneurial voyage through the startup business of two ivy-league business school graduates and the lessons they learned while developing their idea of a computer mouse that looks like a golf driver into the marketplace. The book is an inspiration for those looking to turn an idea into a company.

41149 ■ *"Nanoready?" in Entrepreneur (Vol. 36, May 2008, No. 5, pp. 20)*
Pub: Entrepreneur Media, Inc.
Ed: Andrea Cooper. **Description:** Experts predict that the medicine and energy sectors are among those that will see nanotechnology innovations in the coming years, and that nanotechnology will produce significant commercial value in new products. Some entrepreneurs are investing in nanotech and are partnering with universities. Details on nanotech funding concerns are discussed.

41150 ■ *"Nanotech Impact is Smaller Than Hoped For" in Boston Business Journal (Vol. 27, October 26, 2007, No. 39, pp. 1)*
Pub: American City Business Journals Inc.
Ed: Jackie Noblett. **Description:** Survey by the Massachusetts Technology Collaborative showed that nanotechnology firms are within the early stages of operations and need funding to make them profitable. Details on some nanotech companies and their operations and difficulties in developing or mass producing their products are discussed.

41151 ■ *"Nat'l Instruments Connects with Lego" in Austin Business JournalInc. (Vol. 28, August 22, 2008, No. 23, pp. 1)*
Pub: American City Business Journals
Ed: Laura Hipp. **Description:** Austin-based National Instruments Corporation has teamed with Lego Group from Denmark to create a robot that can be built by children and can be used to perform tasks. Lego WeDo, their latest product, uses computer connection to power its movements. The educational benefits of the new product are discussed.

41152 ■ *"Need Grub? Start Texting at Kroger" in Business Courier (Vol. 24, December 21, 2008, No. 36, pp. 1)*
Pub: American City Business Journals, Inc.
Ed: Laura Baverman. **Description:** Discusses the University of Cincinnati which is teaming up to release a technology platform called Macopay that would link a cell phone to a bank account and allow a person to make payments at participating retailers by sending a text message. Details with regard to the new service and its growth potential are discussed.

41153 ■ *"Network TV" in Canadian Business (Vol. 79, September 11, 2006, No. 18, pp. 136)*
Pub: Rogers Media
Ed: Gerry Blackwell. **Description:** The functions and features of the new Mediasmart LCD TV offered by Hewlett-Packard are discussed.

41154 ■ *"The New Alchemists" in Canadian Business (Vol. 81, October 27, 2008, No. 18, pp. 22)*
Pub: Rogers Media Ltd.
Ed: Joe Castaldo. **Description:** Ethanol industry expects second-generation ethanol or cellulosic biofuels to provide ecologically friendly technologies than the ethanol made from food crops. Government and industries are investing on producing cellulosic biofuels.

41155 ■ *"New Crop Protection Products from Monsanto, Valent, DuPont, FMC, BASF" in Farm Industry News (December 17, 2010)*
Pub: Penton Business Media Inc.
Ed: Mark Moore. **Description:** Glyphosate-dominated herbicides are declining because a more diversified market for corn and soybeans is available. New crop care includes old chemistries, new formulations and unique combinations of both giving farmers more choices to protect the yield potential of their corn and soybean crops. Profiles of new products are included.

41156 ■ *"New Ethanol Plant Planned In Iowa to Use Corn Stover" in Farm Industry News (June 27, 2011)*
Pub: Penton Business Media Inc.
Ed: Lynn Grooms. **Description:** DuPont Danisco Cellulosic Ethanol (DDCE) will buy land next to the Lincolnway Energy corn-based ethanol plant in Nevada, Iowa in order to produce ethanol from corn stover at the location.

41157 ■ *"The New Guard" in Entrepreneur (Vol. 36, February 2008, No. 2, pp. 46)*
Pub: Entrepreneur Media Inc.
Ed: Amanda C. Kooser. **Description:** A natural language search engine is being developed by Powerset for better online searching. Zannel Inc. offers Instant Media Messaging platform, which allows for social networking using phones. Ning is an online platform that allows users to customize and control their social networks.

41158 ■ *The New Innovators: How Canadians are Shaping the Knowledge-Based Economy*
Pub: James Lorimer & Company Ltd.
Ed: Roger Voyer; Patti Ryan. **Released:** January 1, 1994. **Price:** $29.95. **Description:** Details are examined showing how the innovation process works and how ideas are successfully translated into marketable products.

41159 ■ *"New Life for Old Chemistries" in Farm Industry News (Vol. 42, January 1, 2009, No. 1)*
Pub: Penton Media Inc.
Contact: John French, President
Ed: Mark Moore. **Description:** To expand the uses of familiar crop protection products, chemical companies are utilizing biotechnology research and development tools; many off-patent products are being rejuvenated with small changes to make the product even better than it was when originally conceived.

41160 ■ *"New Recipes Added to IAMS Naturals Pet Food Line" in MMR (Vol. 28, August 1, 2011, No. 11, pp. 17)*
Pub: Racher Press Inc.
Description: Procter & Gamble Company's IAMS brand has created a new pet food line called IAMS Naturals for pet owners wishing to feed their pets natural, wholesome food. IAMS Sensitive Naturals has ocean fish and its first ingredient for dogs with sensitivities. IAMS Simple & Natural features chicken with no fillers.

41161 ■ *"New Sony HD Ads Tout Digital" in Brandweek (Vol. 49, April 21, 2008, No. 16, pp. 5)*
Pub: VNU Business Media, Inc.
Description: Looking to promote Sony Electronics' digital imaging products, the company has launched another campaign effort known as HDNA, a play on the words high-definition and DNA; originally Sony focused the HDNA campaign on their televisions, the new ads will include still and video cameras as well and marketing efforts will consist of advertising in print, Online, television spots and publicity at various venues across the country.

41162 ■ *"New Sprint Phone Whets Appetite for Applications" in The Business Journal-Serving Metropolitan Kansas City (Vol. 26, July 25, 2008)*
Pub: American City Business Journals, Inc.
Ed: Suzanna Stagemeyer. **Description:** Firms supporting the applications of the new Samsung Instinct, which was introduced by Sprint Nextel Corp. in June 2008, have reported usage rates increase for their products. Handmark, whose mobile services Pocket Express comes loaded with Instinct, has redirected employees to meet the rising demand for the services. Other views and information on Instinct, are presented.

41163 ■ *"A New Way to Swing" in Canadian Business (Vol. 81, December 8, 2008, No. 21, pp. S8)*
Pub: Rogers Media Ltd.
Ed: Robert Thompson. **Description:** Golf developer Mike Keiser believes that remote is the new luxury, and finances golf projects in out-of-the-way locales in various countries. Keiser is currently developing Cabot Links in Canada, which is expected to open by 2011.

41164 ■ *"New Yetter Stubble Solution Prevents Tire, Track Damage" in Farm Industry News (November 21, 2011)*
Pub: Penton Business Media Inc.
Description: The new Yetter 5000 Stalk Devastator helps prevent premature tire and track wear and damage caused by crop stubble.

41165 ■ *"The Next Big Thing" in Farm Industry News (Vol. 42, January 1, 2009, No. 1)*
Pub: Penton Media Inc.
Contact: John French, President
Ed: David Hest. **Description:** Communication technology that allows farmers to detect equipment location, travel speed and real-time fuel and sprayer/combine tank levels will pay off with better machine use efficiency, improved maintenance and reduced downtime. These telemetry systems will be widely available in the next few years.

41166 ■ *"Next Generation Audi TT Hits Canadian Streets" in Canadian Corporate News (May 16, 2007)*
Pub: Comtex News Network Inc.
Description: Audi Canada prepares for the launch of the highly anticipated 2008 Audi TT, recipient of the 2007 World Car Design of the Year due to its contemporary look, powerful engine, and innovative technology, with a multiple touch-point marketing campaign.

41167 ■ *"No Lines, No Waiting" in The Business Journal-Serving Greater Tampa Bay (Vol. 28, August 15, 2008, No. 34, pp. 1)*
Pub: American City Business Journals, Inc.
Ed: Jane Meinhardt. **Description:** Voda LLC, which was founded to commercialize developments by David Fries, develops outdoor sensor networks used for environmental monitoring by markets like research, the security industry, and the government. Fries already licensed 12 technologies for clients for about $130,000 per technology. Other information on Voda LLC is presented.

41168 ■ *"No-Shed Dogs Lead the Way to Big Growth" in Business Courier (Vol. 26, January 8, 2010, No. 38, pp. 1)*
Pub: American City Business Journals, Inc.
Ed: Lucy May. **Description:** Ed Lukacevic of Grant County, Kentucky is developing Dinovite, a dietary supplement that minimizes shedding and scratching in dogs. Statistical data included.

41169 ■ *"Nonstop Round Baler Earns Top International Award for Krone" in Farm Industry News (November 18, 2011)*
Pub: Penton Business Media Inc.
Ed: Karen McMahon. **Description:** The new Ultima baler from Krone can make and net a bale in 40 seconds without stopping, thus producing 90 bales an hour. The new baler, still in test stage, won top honors at the Agritechnica farm equipment show in Hannover, Germany.

41170 ■ *"Now See This" in Entrepreneur (Vol. 36, April 2008, No. 4, pp. 53)*
Pub: Entrepreneur Media, Inc.
Ed: Mike Hogan. **Description:** New high definition (HD) products are to be introduced in 2008 at the Consumer Electronics Show and the Macworld Conference & Expo. HD lineup from companies such as Dell Inc. and Hewlett-Packard Co. are discussed.

41171 ■ *"OccuLogix Shares Plummet 65 Percent" in Globe & Mail (February 4, 2006, pp. B5)*
Pub: CTVglobemedia Publishing Inc.
Ed: Leonard Zehr. **Description:** The shares of OccuLogix drop by 65% in Canada. The decline in share price is attributed to failure of blood filtering system.

41172 ■ *"Ocean of Opportunity" in Hawaii Business (Vol. 53, October 2007, No. 4, pp. 61)*
Pub: Hawaii Business Publishing
Ed: Mike Markrich. **Description:** Brew Moon owner Marcus Bender and former Coca-Cola Enterprises Inc. executive Jim Stevens have introduced Kai Vodka in June 2007. The new drink is being marketed to professional women, the number of which is increasing based on a research by the Queens College Department of Sociology. The development process of the new product is also discussed.

41173 ■ *"Office Tech: A Pretty Little Vista" in Canadian Business (Vol. 80, January 29, 2007, No. 3, pp. 61)*
Pub: Rogers Media
Ed: Andrew Wahl. **Description:** The features of the new version of Microsoft Windows Vista OS and Microsoft Office 2007 are described.

41174 ■ *"One-Pass Tillage" in Farm Industry News (Vol. 42, January 1, 2009, No. 1)*
Pub: Penton Media Inc.
Contact: John French, President
Description: Bigham Brothers Inc.'s One Pass Terr-Till, a tool that breaks up compacted soil while cutting heavy residue, is reviewed.

41175 ■ *"Our Gadget of the Week" in Barron's (Vol. 88, March 24, 2008, No. 12, pp. 47)*
Pub: Dow Jones & Company, Inc.
Ed: Tiernan Ray. **Description:** Review of the $299 Apple Time Capsule, which is a 500-megabyte hard disk drive and a Wi-Fi router, rolled into one device. The device allows users to create backup files without the need for sophisticated file management software.

41176 ■ *"Our Gadget of the Week" in Barron's (Vol. 88, March 10, 2008, No. 10, pp. 36)*
Pub: Dow Jones & Company, Inc.
Ed: Jay Palmer. **Description:** Review of the $1,599 Fujitsu Lifebook T2010 tablet notebook which is a lightweight notebook offering a comfortable keyboard and a 12-inch screen illuminated by light emitting diodes. The notebook, however, also offers limited capability with its low-end processor and the lack of a built-in optical drive and a touchpad.

41177 ■ *"Our Gadget of the Week" in Barron's (Vol. 89, July 27, 2009, No. 30, pp. 26)*
Pub: Dow Jones & Co., Inc.
Ed: Jay Palmer. **Description:** Zeo Sleep Coach has a lightweight headband with built-in sensors which measures the user's brain waves and records their sleep patterns. The device details the time the users spends in deep sleep, light sleep and the restorative REM (rapid eye movement) sleep mode. Users can get lifestyle change recommendations from a website to improve their sleep.

41178 ■ *"Our Gadget of the Week: Balancing Act" in Barron's (Vol. 88, March 31, 2008, No. 13, pp. 40)*
Pub: Dow Jones & Company, Inc.
Ed: Naureen S. Malik. **Description:** Wii Fit gives users the experience of a virtual personal trainer and workouts that become progressively harder. The device turns the typical fitness regimes into fun exercises and users can choose workouts in four categories including yoga, balance, strength-training and, low impact aerobics.

41179 ■ *"Our Gadget of the Week: Business Buddy" in Barron's (Vol. 88, July 7, 2008, No. 27, pp. 26)*
Pub: Dow Jones & Co., Inc.
Ed: Jay Palmer. **Description:** Review and evaluation of the Lenovo X300 laptop computer which offers executives a variety of features despite its smaller size and weight. The laptop is about 0.73 inch thick, comes with a 64-gigabyte solid-state drive from Samsung, and weighs less than three pounds.

41180 ■ *"Our Gadget of the Week: Mostly, I Liked It" in Barron's (Vol. 88, July 14, 2008, No. 28, pp. 31)*
Pub: Dow Jones & Co., Inc.
Ed: Jay Palmer. **Description:** Review of the Apple iPhone 3G, which costs $199, has better audio and is slightly thicker than its predecessor; using the 3G wireless connection makes going online faster but drains the battery faster too.

41181 ■ *"P&G's Iams Finds Itself in a Pet-Food Dogfight" in Advertising Age (Vol. 78, March 5, 2007, No. 10, pp. 6)*
Pub: Crain Communications, Inc.
Ed: Jack Neff. **Description:** Proctor & Gamble Co.'s Iams has been slow to embrace the trend toward foods for pets that appear fit for human consumption. Competitors such as Nestle Purina have made big gains with its colorful premium Beneful brand and dry nuggets that look like chunks of vegetables and meat. Statistical data included.

41182 ■ *"Patent Pain" in Canadian Business (Vol. 80, November 19, 2007, No. 23, pp. 43)*
Pub: Rogers Media
Ed: Andrew Wahl. **Description:** James McBride of World Standard Fitness has prepared a patent for his invention, a rubberized lifting strap. The patent helped raid interest for the product, however other similar products have already been available in the market. Benefits of having an invention patented are examined.

41183 ■ *"Patently (Un)Clear" in Business Strategy Review (Vol. 21, Spring 2010, No. 1, pp. 28)*
Pub: Wiley-Blackwell
Ed: Markus Reitzig, Stefan Wagner. **Description:** After developing a great product or process, it's important to protect it. The benefits of using internal patent lawyers versus outsourcing the task are examined.

41184 ■ *"PDAs Are Great - As Long As You Can Find Them" in Crain's Chicago Business (Vol. 31, May 5, 2008, No. 18, pp. 41)*
Pub: Crain Communications, Inc.
Ed: Jennifer Olvera. **Description:** Discusses a new service from Global Lost & Found Inc. in which after paying a one-time fee, customers receive a label with an identification number and a toll free phone number so if they lose a gadget such as a cell phone, PDA or laptop the finder can return the device and are rewarded with a gift card.

41185 ■ *"The Perfect Formula to Build Your Brand" in Entrepreneur (Vol. 37, July 2009, No. 7, pp. 70)*
Pub: Entrepreneur Media, Inc.
Ed: Susan J. Linder. **Description:** Combining a product with expertise and a promise is the formula in building a brand for startups. The product will not sell itself, so one must consider what makes the product truly unique. Meanwhile, establishing trust and a foundation for a brand can be achieved by making a promise to the consumer and fulfilling it.

41186 ■ *The Perfect Scent: A Year Inside the Perfume Industry in Paris and New York*
Pub: Henry Holt and Co.
Contact: Michael Naumann, President
Ed: Chandler Burr. **Released:** 2009. **Price:** $25.00. **Description:** An insiders glimpse at the development of two new fragrances from Hermes and Coty.

41187 ■ *"Perry's Goes Organic" in Ice Cream Reporter (Vol. 22, December 20, 2008, No. 1, pp. 1)*
Pub: Ice Cream Reporter
Description: Family-owned Perry's Ice Cream is starting a new line of organic ice cream in both vanilla and chocolate flavors. All Perry's products are made with milk and cream from local dairy farmers.

41188 ■ *"Pink Label: Victoria's Sales Secret" in Advertising Age (Vol. 79, July 7, 2008, No. 26, pp. 4)*
Pub: Crain Communications, Inc.
Ed: Natalie Zmuda. **Description:** Victoria Secret's Pink label accounted for roughly 17 percent of the retailer's total sales last year. The company is launching a Collegiate Collection which will be promoted by a campus tour program.

41189 ■ *"Pinkberry" in Ice Cream Reporter (Vol. 23, October 20, 2010, No. 11, pp. 6)*
Pub: Ice Cream Reporter
Description: Pinkberry introduced its new Fresh Fruit Bowl, a made-to-order dessert with fresh cut fruit and topped with signature P:inkberry Swirly Whip whipped cream.

41190 ■ *"Pioneer Unveils Drought-Tolerant Hybrids" in Farm Industry News (January 6, 2011)*
Pub: Penton Business Media Inc.
Description: Eight new drought-tolerant hybrids are now available across five genetic platforms from Pioneer. The new hybrids, marketed under the Optimum AQUAmax brand name (previously announced as Drought Tolerant 1 Hybrids), contain a collection of native corn traits that improve water access and utilization.

41191 ■ *"Pioneering Strategies for Entrepreneurial Success" in Business Horizons (Vol. 51, January-February 2008, No. 1, pp. 21)*
Pub: Elsevier Advanced Technology Publications
Ed: Candida G. Brush. **Description:** Entrepreneurs are known for new products, services, processes, markets and industries. In order to achieve success, they have to develop a clear vision, creatively manage finances, and use social skills to persuade others to commit to the venture. Pioneering strategies and their implementation are examined.

41192 ■ *"Pioneers Get All The Perks" in Canadian Business (Vol. 81, March 3, 2008, No. 3, pp. 18)*
Pub: Rogers Media
Description: Suncor Energy Inc. will face royalty payments from 25% to 30% of net profits as it signs a new deal with Alberta. Biovail Corp., meanwhile, is under a U.S. grand jury investigation for supposed improprieties in Cardizem LA heart drug launch. The Conference Board of Canada's proposal to impose taxes on greenhouse gas emissions and other developments in the business community are discussed.

41193 ■ *"Play It Safe or Take a Stand?" in Harvard Business Review (Vol. 88, November 2010, No. 11, pp. 139)*
Pub: Harvard Business School Publishing
Ed: Trish Gorman Clifford, Jay Barney. **Description:** A fictitious leadership scenario is presented, with contributors providing comments and recommendations. A female executive ponders whether to assert a point of view on a new venture. Both experts agree that after providing careful analysis of pros and cons, the executive should come to a well-informed conclusion.

41194 ■ *"Plumbing, Heating Products Shine at Greenbuild Expo" in Contractor (Vol. 56, December 2009, No. 12, pp. 1)*
Pub: Penton Media, Inc.
Ed: Robert P. Mader. **Description:** Greenbuild Show held in Phoenix, Arizona has showcased the latest in plumbing and heating products. Zurn displayed its EcoVantage line of fixtures and valves during the event. Meanwhile, Sloan Valve offered its washdown 1-pint/flush Alphine urinal.

41195 ■ *"Pop N Go Launching Into Dollar Store Market" in Internet Wire (July 14, 2009)*
Pub: Comtex News Network, Inc.
Description: Pop N Go, Inc. announced that it will test the company's flagship popcorn vending machine in the rapidly growing dollar store distribution channel.

41196 ■ *"Portland Home Is First in U.S. to Use Variable Speed 'Inverter' Technology" in Contractor (Vol. 56, December 2009, No. 12, pp. 5)*
Pub: Penton Media, Inc.
Description: Daikin Altherma heat pump with inverter drive has been installed in a Portland, Oregon home. The heat pump provides a high coefficient of performance while delivering hydronic and domestic hot water functionality. Other product features and dimensions are also supplied.

41197 ■ *"Precision Fertilizer Spreading Shown at Agritechnica" in Farm Industry News (November 23, 2011)*
Pub: Penton Business Media Inc.
Ed: Karen McMahon. **Description:** Rauch, the German firm, introduced a new system that precisely spreads fertilizer on crops. The new product was shown at Agritechnica.

41198 ■ *"Presidential Address: Innovation in Retrospect and Prospect" in Canadian Journal of Electronics (Vol. 43, November 2010, No. 4)*
Pub: Journal of the Canadian Economics Association
Ed: James A. Brander. **Description:** Has innovation slowed in recent decades? While there has been progress in information and communications technology, the recent record of innovation in agriculture, energy, transportation and healthcare sectors is cause for concern.

41199 ■ *"Press Release: New Corn Hybrid from Seed Consultants" in Farm Industry News (January 6, 2011)*
Pub: Penton Business Media Inc.
Description: Seed Consultants Inc. is releasing its first proprietary corn line called SC 1101. The product was developed, bred, and tested for the eastern Corn Belt diseases, soils, and growing conditions.

41200 ■ *"Press Release: New Trough Drinker From Pride of the Farm" in Farm Industry News (January 5, 2011)*
Pub: Penton Business Media Inc.
Description: Model WPO70 is a 90-inch long trough drinker designed for high-capacity feedyard applications and features foam-filly poly construction and a rib-reinforced trough. A description of this new offering from Pride of the Farm is included.

41201 ■ *"Press Release: Revolver Grain Auger End from Mauer Manufacturing" in Farm Industry News (December 17, 2010)*
Pub: Penton Business Media Inc.
Description: Profile of the Revolver Grain Auger End from Mauer Manufacturing is presented. The new design eliminates grain loss/dribble, reduces grain in the next year's crop, and has a greater clearance for combine unloading auger.

41202 ■ *"Press Release: Trimble Introduces CFX-750 Display" in Farm Industry News (January 4, 2011)*
Pub: Penton Business Media Inc.
Description: Trimble is offering a touch screen display called the CFX-750. The new 8-inch full-color display allows farmers to choose the specific guidance, steering and precision agriculture capabilities that best fit their farm's particular needs. The display can be upgraded as business needs change, including the addition of GLONASS capabilities, or the addition of section and rate control for crop inputs such as seed, chemicals and fertilizer.

41203 ■ *"Probability Processing Chip: Lyric Semiconductor" in Inc. (Volume 32, December 2010, No. 10, pp. 52)*
Pub: Inc. Magazine
Ed: Christine Lagorio. **Description:** Lyric Semiconductor, a start up located in Cambridge, Massachusetts, has developed a computer chip that also uses values that fall between zero and one, resulting in a chip that can process information using probabilities, considering many possible answers that find the best fit.

41204 ■ *"Procter & Gamble Boosts Bet on Exclusive Brands" in Business Courier (Vol. 27, July 9, 2010, No. 10, pp. 1)*
Pub: Business Courier
Ed: Jon Newberry. **Description:** Procter & Gamble is creating more special versions of its brands such as Pringles and Pampers exclusively for retail partners such as Tesco in the U.K. The greater push towards this direction is seen as a way to regain market share.

41205 ■ *"Procter Gambles on Wallpaper; Putting Paint On a Roll" in Advertising Age (Vol. 77, September 18, 2006, No. 38, pp. 4)*
Pub: Crain Communications, Inc.
Ed: Jack Neff. **Description:** Procter & Gamble Co. has launched a new line of textured paints that are already applied to a wallpaper-like roll that can be hung without paste or wallpaper tools.

41206 ■ *"Protection One Introduces Home and Business Security iPhone App" in*

Wireless News (November 13, 2009)
Pub: Close-Up Media
Description: Protection One, Inc., a provider of security systems to business and residential customers, has developed an application that allows users to access their security panels and receive real-time updates from their iPhone or iPod touch devices.

41207 ■ *"Providing Expertise Required to Develop Microsystems" in Canadian Electronics (Vol. 23, February 2008, No. 1, pp. 6)*
Pub: CLB Media Inc.
Ed: Ian McWalter. **Description:** CMC Microsystems, formerly Canadian Microelectronics Corporation, is focused on empowering microelectronics and Microsystems research in Canada. Microsystems offers the basis for innovations in the fields of science, environment, technology, automotives, energy, aerospace and communications technology. CMC's strategy in developing Microsystems in Canada is described.

41208 ■ *"Put It In Drive" in Entrepreneur (Vol. 36, April 2008, No. 4, pp. 31)*
Pub: Entrepreneur Media, Inc.
Ed: Jill Amadio. **Description:** Commercial vehicle models for 2008 are presented. These new models are more user- and environment-friendly. Features and prices of car models and tips to consider before purchasing are presented.

41209 ■ *"Putting 'Extra' in Extra-Silky Shampoo" in Crain's Chicago Business (Vol. 31, April 28, 2008, No. 17, pp. 37)*
Pub: Crain Communications, Inc.
Ed: Phuong Ly. **Description:** Profile of HallStar Co., a Chicago-based company which develops and manufactures specialty chemicals to upgrade existing products such as hair dye, lotion and deodorant. HallStar has seen its annual earnings rise more than 30 percent since 2002.

41210 ■ *"Qualcomm Could Win Big as the IPhone 3G Calls" in Barron's (Vol. 88, July 4, 2008, No. 28, pp. 30)*
Pub: Dow Jones & Co., Inc.
Ed: Eric J. Savitz. **Description:** Apple iPhone 3G's introduction could widen the smartphone market thereby benefiting handset chipmaker Qualcomm in the process. Qualcomm Senior V.P., Bill Davidson sees huge potential for his company's future beyond phones with their Snapdragon processor. The prospects of Sun Microsystems' shares are also discussed.

41211 ■ *"The Quality Revolution" in Canadian Business (Vol. 81, November 10, 2008, No. 19, pp. 128)*
Pub: Rogers Media Ltd.
Ed: Andrew Nikiforuk. **Description:** John Volpe believes that the pursuit of quantity of food choices leads to tasteless meals, expanding waistlines, and food poisoning and stresses emphasis on food quality and food security.

41212 ■ *"The Quest for the Smart Prosthetic" in Canadian Business (Vol. 83, October 12, 2010, No. 17, pp. 26)*
Pub: Rogers Media Ltd.
Ed: Jacqueline Nelson. **Description:** Information about a two-year research project led by Southern Methodist University (SMU) and funded by the Defense Advance Research Projects Agency (DARPA) is provided. The agency aims to create a 'smart prosthetic' which will improve the lives of military amputees. The planned prosthetic will use a sensor that can carry nerve signals through synthetic channels.

41213 ■ *"Red Velvet Cupcake Bites" in CandyIndustry (Vol. 176, September 2011, No. 9, pp. RC4)*
Pub: BNP Media
Contact: Al Reser, President
Description: Taste of Nature's Cookie Dough Bites has launched a new candy called, Red Velvet Cupcake Bites. The new product will feature a cupcake center covered in red frosting; ingredients are listed.

41214 ■ *"Retailers Tap into War-Room Creativity of Employees" in Globe & Mail (March 12, 2007, pp. B1)*
Pub: CTVglobemedia Publishing Inc.
Ed: Marina Strauss. **Description:** The methods adopted by Canadian Tire Corporation Ltd. to utilize the creative abilities of its employees for innovation during new product development are discussed.

41215 ■ *"RIM Gets Smart" in Canadian Business (Vol. 79, October 23, 2006, No. 21, pp. 157)*
Pub: Rogers Media
Ed: Gerry Blackwell. **Description:** Details of the features of Blackberry Pearl, the new personal digital assistant from Research in Motion Inc., are presented.

41216 ■ *Risk-Free Entrepreneur*
Pub: Adams Media Corporation
Ed: Don Debelak. **Released:** June 2006. **Price:** $14. 95. **Description:** Information is offered to help entrepreneurs to develop an idea for a product or service and have other companies provide the marketing, manufacturing and staff.

41217 ■ *"Rule of the Masses: Reinventing Fashion Via Crowdsourcing" in WWD (Vol. 200, July 26, 2010, No. 17, pp. 1)*
Pub: Conde Nast Publications
Contact: David Carey, President
Ed: Cate T. Corcoran. **Description:** Large apparel brands and retailers are crowdsourcing as a way to increase customer loyalty and to build their businesses.

41218 ■ *"Rumor Has It" in Entrepreneur (Vol. 35, October 2007, No. 10, pp. 30)*
Pub: Entrepreneur Media Inc.
Ed: Chris Penttila. **Description:** Some entrepreneurs like Ren Moulton and Dan Scudder regard rumor sites and product blogs as great sources of market research. However, there are legal issues that must be studied before using these Internet sites in marketing and product development. The use and limitations of rumor sites and product blogs are provided.

41219 ■ *"Safer Ammonium-Nitrate-Based Fertilizer" in Farm Industry News (Vol. 42, January 1, 2009, No. 1)*
Pub: Penton Media Inc.
Contact: John French, President
Description: Honeywell has patented a new technology which it will use to develop a highly effective, safer ammonium-nitrate-based fertilizer that has a significantly lower potential for explosion.

41220 ■ *"Scanning the Field" in Business Courier (Vol. 26, January 8, 2010, No. 38, pp. 1)*
Pub: American City Business Journals, Inc.
Ed: Jon Newberry. **Description:** Anti-terror detection systems developer Valley Force Composite Technologies Inc. of Kentucky plans to enter the market with its high-resolution ODIN and Thor-LVX screening systems. These systems are expected to meet the increasing demand for airport security equipment.

41221 ■ *"Should You Invest in the Long Tail?" in Harvard Business Review (Vol. 86, July-August 2008, No. 8, pp. 88)*
Pub: Harvard Business School Press
Ed: Anita Elberse. **Description:** Relevance of the long tail, or the sustainability of sales after a given product's launch is examined. It is posited that niche sales are not as sustainable as those for products with broader appeal.

41222 ■ *"A Side Project Threatens To Get Totally Out of Control and I Think, 'How Fun'" in Inc. (October 2007, pp. 81-82)*
Pub: Gruner & Jahr USA Publishing
Ed: Joel Spolsky. **Description:** Profile of Fog Creek Software, makers of project-management software for other software developers. Fog Creek's owner discusses his idea to create a new product for his firm.

41223 ■ *"Similac Introduces New Packaging" in Marketing to Women (Vol. 21, February 2008, No. 2, pp. 3)*
Pub: EPM Communications Inc.
Contact: Ira Mayer, President
E-mail: imayer@epmcom.com
Description: Baby formula brand Similac introduces a new ready to feed packaging which requires no mixing, measuring or preparation.

41224 ■ *"Sinai Doctor Seeks FDA OK for Drug" in Baltimore Business Journal (Vol. 28, July 16, 2010, No. 10, pp. 1)*
Pub: Baltimore Business Journal
Ed: Emily Mullin. **Description:** Paul Gurbel, Sinai Hospital Center for Thrombosis Research director, is seeking an FDA approval of Brilinta, a drug which he helped create and test. Gurbel says that the approval could bring the drug to market as early as December 2010. The drug is expected to rival Bristol-Myers' Plavix, which generated almost $6.2 billion in 2009.

41225 ■ *Six SIGMA for Small Business*
Pub: Entrepreneur Press
Ed: Greg Brue. **Released:** October 2005. **Price:** $19.95 (US), $26.95 (Canadian). **Description:** Jack Welch's Six SIGMA approach to business covers accounting, finance, sales and marketing, buying a business, human resource development, and new product development.

41226 ■ *"The Sky's the Limit" in Retail Merchandiser (Vol. 51, July-August 2011, No. 4, pp. 64)*
Pub: Phoenix Media Corporation
Ed: John Capizzi. **Description:** Mars Retail Group (MRG) is the licensing division handling M&M's Brand Candies. Since taking over the brand they have expanded from 12 licensees to 50 licensees with new offerings.

41227 ■ *"Space Shut Hot" in Canadian Business (Vol. 80, October 22, 2007, No. 21, pp. 28)*
Pub: Rogers Media
Ed: John Gray. **Description:** Scandium, a metal first developed by the Soviet military in missile and fighter jets, sells for $700 a kilogram. The pricey metal is beginning to generate some hype, although current demand is still low. Details for marketing growth opportunities are discussed.

41228 ■ *"STAR TEC Incubator's Latest Resident Shows Promise" in The Business Journal-Serving Greater Tampa Bay (August 8, 2008)*
Pub: American City Business Journals, Inc.
Ed: Jane Meinhardt. **Description:** Field Forensics Inc., a resident of the STAR Technology Enterprise Center, has grown after being admitted into the business accelerator. The producer of defense and security devices and equipment has doubled 2007 sales as of 2008.

41229 ■ *"The Start of a Beautiful Friendship: Partnering with Your Customers on R&D" in Inc. (March 2008, pp. 37-38)*
Pub: Gruner & Jahr USA Publishing
Ed: Leigh Buchanan. **Description:** Joint research and development projects between customers and suppliers are a growing trend in the small business community; these ventures can help keep new product development costs lower. Four tips to maintain a good working relationship in these ventures are outlined.

41230 ■ *"Startup on Cusp of Trend" in Austin Business JournalInc. (Vol. 29, January 8, 2010, No. 44, pp. 1)*
Pub: American City Business Journals
Ed: Christopher Calnan. **Description:** Austin-based Socialware Inc. introduced a new business called social middleware, which is a software that is layered between the company network and social networking Website used by workers. The software was designed to give employers a measure of control over content while allowing workers to continue using online social networks.

41231 ■ *"Startup to Serve Bar Scene" in Austin Business JournalInc. (Vol. 29, December 18, 2009, No. 41, pp. 1)*
Pub: American City Business Journals
Ed: Christopher Calnan. **Description:** Startup ATX Innovation Inc. of Austin, Texas has developed a test version of TabbedOut, a Web-based tool that would facilitate mobile phone-based restaurant and bar bill payment. TabbedOut has been tested by six businesses in Austin and will be available to restaurant and bar owners for free. Income would be generated by ATX through a 99-cent convenience charge per transaction.

41232 ■ *"Stepping Up" in Baltimore Business Journal (Vol. 28, October 22, 2010, No. 24, pp. 1)*
Pub: Baltimore Business Journal
Ed: Erik Siemers. **Description:** Uner Armour Inc. will release its Micro G line of four basketball sneakers on October 23, 2010. The company's executives mentioned that Under Armour's goal is to appeal to customers, and not to chip away at Nike Inc.'s supremacy in basketball shoes. The new sneakers will range from $80 to $110.

41233 ■ *"Steve Meginniss Helped Reinvent the Toothbrush. Can He Do the Same Thing for Wheels?" in Inc. (February 2008, pp. 32)*
Pub: Gruner & Jahr USA Publishing
Ed: Dalia Fahmy. **Description:** Profile of Steve Meginniss, co-inventor of Sonicare Toothbrush and inventor of a two-gear wheel for wheelchairs. Mgeinniss discusses his need to raid $1 million to promote and cut manufacturing costs for this new product that helps reduce pain for users.

41234 ■ *"Stop the Innovation Wars" in Harvard Business Review (Vol. 88, July-August 2010, No. 7-8, pp. 76)*
Pub: Harvard Business School Publishing
Ed: Vijay Govindarajan, Chris Trimble. **Description:** Methods for managing conflicts between partners during the innovation initiative process are highlighted. These include dividing the labor, assembling a dedicated team, and mitigating likelihood for any potential conflict.

41235 ■ *"Strategy: Hurry Up and Wait" in Business Courier (Vol. 24, February 1, 2008, No. 43, pp. 50)*
Pub: American City Business Journals, Inc.
Ed: Dan Monk. **Description:** It has taken years for Enerfab Inc. chairman Dave Herche to develop new product lines, form an expert management group and come up with a strategic-planning approach. However, his patience has paid off since Enerfab's revenue has grown by 93 percent since 2005. Herche's strategy for Enerfab and its impacts on the company are analyzed further.

41236 ■ *"Stronger Corn? Take It Off Steroids, Make It All Female" in Farm Industry News (December 5, 2011)*
Pub: Penton Business Media Inc.
Ed: Brian Wallheimer. **Description:** Purdue University researcher found that higher improvements in corn crops, and possibly other crops, were yielded when steroids were discontinued.

41237 ■ *"Study: New Moms Build A Lot of Brand Buzz" in Brandweek (Vol. 49, April 21, 2008, No. 16, pp. 7)*
Pub: VNU Business Media, Inc.
Description: According to a new survey which sampled 1,721 pregnant women and new moms, this demographic is having 109 word-of-mouth conversations per week concerning products, services and brands. Two-thirds of these conversations directly involve brand recommendations. The Internet is driving these word-of-mouth, or W-O-M, conversations among this segment, beating out magazines, television and other forms of media.

41238 ■ *"Study Puts Hub On Top of the Tech Heap" in Boston Business Journal (Vol. 30, November 26, 2010, No. 44, pp. 1)*
Pub: Boston Business Journal
Ed: Galen Moore. **Description:** The Ewing Marion Kauffman Foundation ranked Massachusetts at the top in its evaluations of states' innovative industries, government leadership, and education. Meanwhile, research blog formDs.com also ranked Massachusetts number one in terms of venture-capital financings per capita.

41239 ■ *"Styles" in Ice Cream Reporter (Vol. 21, July 20, 2008, No. 8, pp. 6)*
Pub: Ice Cream Reporter
Description: British ice cream maker Styles is using sheep's milk in its new frozen dessert, Slim Ewe Iced Dessert. The products has all the natural taste, texture and health advantages of sheep's milk with less than 2.5 grams of fat and under 75 calories per serving.

41240 ■ *"Success Products" in Black Enterprise (Vol. 37, February 2007, No. 7, pp. 135)*
Pub: Earl G. Graves Publishing Co. Inc.
Ed: Tanisha A. Sykes. **Description:** Using innovative resources that are already at your fingertips instead of trying to reach out to companies first is a great way to discover whether you have a viable idea or product. Be motivated to start an e-newsletter letting people know about your products and attend conferences like The Motivation Show, the world's largest exhibition of motivational products and services related to performance in business.

41241 ■ *"Sustaining Supply" in Crain's Cleveland Business (Vol. 28, November 19, 2007, No. 46, pp. 3)*
Pub: Crain Communications, Inc.
Ed: David Bennett. **Description:** Local firms are playing key roles in preparing Wal-Mart suppliers to develop sustainable, or ecologically conscious, packaging. New products such as the innovative 'eco-bottle' - a collapsed container made of recyclable plastic that will expand to its traditional size and shape once water is added and would transform to such items as window cleaner when the water mixes with the container's dry contents - are being designed by firms such as Nottingham Spirk.

41242 ■ *"Sweet Tea; Neil Golden" in Advertising Age (Vol. 79, November 17, 2008, No. 43, pp. 4)*
Pub: Crain Communications, Inc.
Ed: Emily Bryson York. **Description:** McDonald's launch of iced coffee and sweat tea, which were promoted via price cuts over the summer, helped to boost sales at the fast-food chain.

41243 ■ *"Tabular Dreams" in Canadian Business (Vol. 80, February 12, 2007, No. 4, pp. 36)*
Pub: Rogers Media
Ed: Christina Campbell. **Description:** The research of Raymor Industries in developing carbon nanotubes by bonding carbon atoms using high technology is discussed.

41244 ■ *"Taco Bell; David Ovens" in Advertising Age (Vol. 79, November 17, 2008, No. 43, pp. S2)*
Pub: Crain Communications, Inc.
Ed: Emily Bryson York. **Description:** Due to the addition of new products such as a low-calorie, low-fat Fresco menu; a fruity iced beverage; and a value initiative, Taco Bell now accounts for half of Yum Brands' profits. The chain has also benefited from a new chief marketing officer, David Ovens, who oversees ad support.

41245 ■ *"Tale of a Gun" in Canadian Business (Vol. 80, February 26, 2007, No. 5, pp. 37)*
Pub: Rogers Media
Ed: Matthew McClearn. **Description:** The technology behind automated ballistic identification systems, which can be used to analyze fired ammunition components and link them to crime guns and suspects, developed by Canadian companies is presented.

41246 ■ *"Technology Drivers to Boost Your Bottom Line" in Franchising World (Vol. 42, August 2010, No. 8, pp. 15)*
Pub: International Franchise Association
Ed: Dan Dugal. **Description:** Technological capabilities are expanding quickly and smart franchises should stay updated on all the new developments, including smart phones, global positioning systems, and social media networks.

41247 ■ *"Thumbing Around" in Canadian Business (Vol. 79, October 9, 2006, No. 20, pp. 143)*
Pub: Rogers Media
Ed: Gerry Blackwell. **Description:** The features, functions of Cruzer Titanium, a serial bus standard to interface device developed by SanDisk Corporation are discussed.

41248 ■ *"Tim Hortons Aims for Breakfast Breakout" in Globe & Mail (February 13, 2006, pp. B3)*
Pub: CTVglobemedia Publishing Inc.
Ed: Andy Hoffman. **Description:** Fast food chain Tim Hortons will be launching its new breakfast menu with more combinations that include bacons, eggs and coffee. Tim Horton is subsidiary of Wendy's International Inc and has 290 outlets in America.

41249 ■ *"A Timely Boon for Small Investors" in Barron's (Vol. 88, March 24, 2008, No. 12, pp. 48)*
Pub: Dow Jones & Company, Inc.
Ed: Theresa W. Carey. **Description:** Nasdaq Data Store's new program called Market Replay allows investors to accurately track stock price movements. The replay can be as long as a day of market time and allows investors to determine whether they executed stock trades at the best possible price.

41250 ■ *The Tipping Point*
Pub: Back Bay/Little, Brown
Ed: Malcom Gladwell. **Price:** $14.95. **Description:** How and why certain products and ideas become fads.

41251 ■ *"Title Creep: The Chief Revenue Officer" in Inc. (March 2008, pp. 28)*
Pub: Gruner & Jahr USA Publishing
Ed: The title, Chief Revenue Officer, is growing. The marketing function of the CRO is to oversee sales, new product development, and pricing.

41252 ■ *"To Win, Create What's Scarce" in Harvard Business Review (Vol. 88, November 2010, No. 11, pp. 46)*
Pub: Harvard Business School Publishing
Ed: Seth Godin. **Description:** It is recommended to identify what is scarce yet valuable and applying this principle to business in order to be successful.

41253 ■ *"TomTom GO910: On the Road Again" in Black Enterprise (Vol. 37, January 2007, No. 6, pp. 52)*
Pub: Earl G. Graves Publishing Co. Inc.
Ed: Stephanie Young. **Description:** TomTom GO 910 is a GPS navigator that offers detailed maps of the U.S., Canada, and Europe. Consumers view their routes by a customizable LCD screen showing everything from the quickest to the shortest routes available or how to avoid toll roads. Business travelers may find this product invaluable as it also functions as a cell phone and connects to a variety of other multi-media devices.

41254 ■ *"Tool Time" in Entrepreneur (Vol. 36, March 2008, No. 3, pp. 90)*
Pub: Entrepreneur Media Inc.
Ed: Nichole A. Torres. **Description:** DaVinci Institute holds an annual event in Colorado to display new products and inventions. Innovative Design Engineering Animation is a consulting company that helps inventors develop product through various stages. NineSigma Inc. has an online marketplace where inventors can post ideas for clients needing new products.

41255 ■ *"A Torch in the Darkness" in Canadian Business (Vol. 83, August 17, 2010, No. 13-14, pp. 66)*
Pub: Rogers Media Ltd.
Ed: Joe Castaldo. **Description:** Research In Motion (RIM) unveiled the BlackBerry Touch, featuring a touch screen as well as a physical keyboard, in an

attempt to repel competitors and expand share in the consumer smart phone market. RIM shares have fallen 43 percent from its peak in 2009.

41256 ■ *"Touching the Future" in Canadian Business (Vol. 81, July 21, 2008, No. 11, pp. 41)*
Pub: Rogers Media Ltd.
Ed: Matt McClearn. **Description:** Microsoft Corp. has launched a multi-touch product which is both a software and hardware technology called Microsoft Surface. The innovative product allows people to use it at the same time, however touch-based computers are reported to be around $100,000. Other features and benefits of the product are presented.

41257 ■ *"Toy Scares Drive Business" in Boston Business Journal (Vol. 27, November 23, 2007, No. 43, pp. 1)*
Pub: American City Business Journals, Inc.
Ed: Joan Goodchild. **Description:** Several Boston businesses have tapped into the lead content scare in toys and other products manufactured in China. ConRoy Corporation LLC launched Toy Recall Alert!, an online tool to alert consumers about new recalls while Hybrivet Systems introduced screening test kit, LeadCheck. Other new products pertaining to toy safety are discussed.

41258 ■ *Trade-Off: The Ever-Present Tension Between Quality and Conscience*
Pub: Crown Business Books
Ed: Kevin Maney. **Released:** August 17, 2010. **Price:** $15.00. **Description:** The tension between fidelity (the quality of a consumer's experience) and convenience (the ease of getting and paying for a product) are shown to be the forces that determine the success or failure of new products and services in the marketplace.

41259 ■ *"Turning Green Ink to Black" in The Business Journal-Serving Metropolitan Kansas City (Vol. 26, August 8, 2008, No. 48, pp. 1)*
Pub: American City Business Journals, Inc.
Ed: James Dornbrook. **Description:** InkCycle has introduced grenk, a line of environmentally-friendly printer toner and ink cartridges. The cartridges are collected and recycled after use by the company, which separates them into their metal, cardboard, and plastic components.

41260 ■ *"Twice the Innovation, Half the Tears" in Business Courier (Vol. 24, March 7, 2008, No. 48, pp. 1)*
Pub: American City Business Journals, Inc.
Ed: Lisa Biank Fasig. **Description:** Procter & Gamble was able to develop a pant-style diaper called Pampers First Pants by creating a virtual, three-dimensional baby. The company was able to reduce the number of real mock-ups that it had to make by putting the diapers on the virtual baby first. Specifics about product designs were not revealed by the company.

41261 ■ *"UM-Dearborn to Launch Program for Entrepreneurs" in Crain's Detroit Business (Vol. 24, April 14, 2008, No. 15, pp. 7)*
Pub: Crain Communications Inc.
Ed: Chad Halcom. **Description:** Starting this fall the University of Michigan-Dearborn will begin its Product Realization and Technology Commercialization Program for entrepreneurs and innovators with lab-tested, high-technology products. Ultimately, 20 businesses will each work with the university in creating a customer base, commercializing a new high-tech product or process and connecting with venture capitalists who may invest in the new companies.

41262 ■ *"Unbreakable" in Canadian Business (Vol. 79, October 9, 2006, No. 20, pp. 111)*
Pub: Rogers Media
Ed: Robert Hercz. **Description:** The features and functions of Neutrino, an embedded operating system developed by QNX Software Systems are discussed.

41263 ■ *"Under Armour Wants to Equip Athletes, Too" in Boston Business Journal (Vol. 29, July 8, 2011, No. 9, pp. 1)*
Pub: American City Business Journals Inc.
Ed: Ryan Sharrow. **Description:** Baltimore sportswear maker Under Armour advances plans to enter into the equipment field, aiming to strengthen its hold on football, basketball and lacrosse markets where it already has a strong market share. The company is now cooking up licensing deals to bolster the firm's presence among athletes.

41264 ■ *"Unleashing the Power of Marketing" in Harvard Business Review (Vol. 88, October 2010, No. 10, pp. 90)*
Pub: Harvard Business School Publishing
Ed: Beth Comstock, Ranjay Gulati, Stephen Liguori. **Description:** Chronicle of the development of General Electric's marketing framework that focused on three key factors: Principles, people and process. GE determined that successful marketing fulfills four functions: instigating, innovating, implementing, and integrating.

41265 ■ *"US Hygiene Adds Bed Bug Fix to Its Line of Highly Effective Cleaning and Pest Control Products" in Benzinga.com (October 29, 2011)*
Pub: Benzinga.com
Ed: Benzinga Staff. **Description:** US Hygiene LLC introduced its newest product called Bed Bug Fix, which is a naturally-derived, nontoxic insecticide that kills a multitude of bugs including bed bugs and dust mites. The product is safe to use around children, plants and pets.

41266 ■ *"uTest Discusses the Evolution of Crowdsourcing Models at CrowdConf 2010" in Internet Wire (October 1, 2010)*
Pub: Comtex
Description: World's largest software testing marketplace, uTest, announces its first conference dedicated to the emerging field of crowdsourcing along with the future of distributed work. A panel of experts will discuss common misconceptions about crowdsourcing using real-world examples.

41267 ■ *"VC-Heavy, Revenue-Light Sensicore Sold to GE Division" in Crain's Detroit Business (Vol. 24, April 14, 2008, No. 15, pp. 28)*
Pub: Crain Communications Inc.
Ed: Tom Henderson. **Description:** General Electric has acquired Sensicore Inc., which although one of Michigan's most successful companies in raising venture capital was unable to generate significant revenue from its handheld water-testing devices. GE is capable of penetrating a larger market than a private company and will be able to take the devices to the municipal marketplace.

41268 ■ *"Virgin America Flies with V&S on Web" in ADWEEK (Vol. 51, July 12 2010, No. 27, pp. 31)*
Pub: Nielsen Business Media Inc.
Description: Victors & Spoils, a crowdsourcing agency is examined.

41269 ■ *"Vitabath: Sweet Smell of Success" in Retail Merchandiser (Vol. 51, September-October 2011, No. 5, pp. 82)*
Pub: Phoenix Media Corporation
Description: After taking over at Vitabath, Rich Brands developed new scents and products and while discovering new channels to distribute these items.

41270 ■ *"Vitamins to Spice Up Food" in Philadelphia Business Journal (Vol. 28, October 2, 2009, No. 33, pp. 1)*
Pub: American City Business Journals
Ed: John George. **Description:** VitaminSpice, a startup company established by Ed Bukstel, makes a line of spice and vitamin blends that come in seasoning form. The form of the blends could facilitate easier ingestion of vitamins into people's diets. A reverse merger that will allow a publicly-traded company status for VitaminSpice will be accomplished by early October 2009.

41271 ■ *"Vonage V-Phone: Use Your Laptop to Make Calls Via the Internet" in Black Enterprise (Vol. 37, January 2007, No. 6, pp. 52)*
Pub: Earl G. Graves Publishing Co. Inc.
Ed: James C. Johnson. **Description:** Overview of the Vonage V-Phone, which is small flash drive device that lets you make phone calls through a high-speed Internet connection and plugs into any computer's USB port. Business travels may find this product to be a wonderful solution as it includes 250MB of memory and can store files, digital photos, MP3s, and more.

41272 ■ *"Wall Street Is No Friend to Radical Innovation" in Harvard Business Review (Vol. 88, July-August 2010, No. 7-8, pp. 28)*
Pub: Harvard Business School Publishing
Ed: Julia Kirby. **Description:** Research indicates that investors are skittish about backing a business that proposes significant changes to its product or service status quo.

41273 ■ *"Want to Unleash the Next Best Seller? Think Like a Dog" in Advertising Age (Vol. 79, March 10, 2008, No. 10, pp. 14)*
Pub: Crain Communications, Inc.
Ed: Lenore Skenazy. **Description:** Cott Corp. has launched a new product, fortified water for pets, in flavors ranging from peanut butter to parsley to spearmint.

41274 ■ *"Wealth and Jobs: the Broken Link" in Harvard Business Review (Vol. 88, November 2010, No. 11, pp. 44)*
Pub: Harvard Business School Publishing
Ed: Nitin Nohria. **Description:** Rebuilding the link between business and job creation to shore up the middle class is advocated. A blend of government policies and business strategies that foster entrepreneurship and innovation are essential.

41275 ■ *"Well-Heeled Startup" in Business Journal Portland (Vol. 27, November 12, 2010, No. 37, pp. 1)*
Pub: Portland Business Journal
Ed: Erik Siemers. **Description:** Oh! Shoes LLC expects to receive about $1.5 million in funding from angel investors, while marketing a new line of high heel shoes that are comfortable, healthy, and attractive. The new line of shoes will use the technology of athletic footwear while having the look of an Italian designer. Oh! Shoes hopes to generate $35 million in sales by 2014.

41276 ■ *"What's New" in Crain's Cleveland Business (Vol. 30, June 29, 2009, No. 25, pp. 19)*
Pub: Crain Communications, Inc.
Description: More Than Gourmet, located in Akron, Ohio has introduced a new line of ready-to-use sauces, packed in 11-ounce containers that hold three-five servings.

41277 ■ *"What's New" in Crain's Cleveland Business (Vol. 30, June 8, 2009, No. 22, pp. 23)*
Pub: Crain Communications, Inc.
Description: Air Technical Industries in Ohio has launched a new product called the Scorpion Aircraft Tug that includes a built-in crane lift and auxiliary power unit that enables a fixed-base operator aircraft mechanic to move and precisely position aircraft weight up to 15,000 pounds.

41278 ■ *"What's New" in Crain's Cleveland Business (Vol. 30, June 1, 2009, No. 21, pp. 19)*
Pub: Crain Communications, Inc.
Description: Profile of Precision Polymer Casting, a manufacturer located in Northeast Ohio. Precision has launched its new product, Castinite HCR polymer composite pump base castings that are base plates that are used to mount a pump and electric motor for various chemical pumping operations. Details of the pump are included.

41279 ■ *"Where Good Ideas Come From: The Natural History of Innovation" in Business Owner (Vol. 35, July-August 2011, No. 4, pp. 6)*
Pub: DL Perkins Company
Description: A history of ideas, concepts, innovations and technologies that have created a successful small business environment are explored.

41280 ■ *"A Whiteboard that Peels and Sticks" in Inc. (Volume 32, December 2010, No. 10, pp. 58)*
Pub: Inc. Magazine
Ed: Issie Lapwosky. **Description:** Profile of an affordable adhesive whiteboard that can be restuck multiple times; the whiteboard was created by three college friends. The students share insight in the contacts they used in order to promote the sale of their invention.

41281 ■ *"Why Entrepreneurs Matter More Than Innovators" in Gallup Management Journal (November 22, 2011)*
Pub: Gallup
Ed: Jim Clifton. **Description:** In the race to create good jobs, leaders are not paying enough attention to cultivating talented entrepreneurs, rather they invest too much attention on innovation.

41282 ■ *"With Whom Do You Trade? Defensive Innovation and the Skill-Bias" in Canadian Journal of Electronics (Vol. 43, November 2010)*
Pub: Journal of the Canadian Economics Association
Ed: Pushan Dutt, Daniel Traca. **Description:** Examination into whether increased trade with ineffective protection of intellectual property has contributed to the skill-deepening of the 1980s. An index of effective protection of intellectual property at the country level, combining data on protection of patents and rule of law are presented. An industry-specific version of this index is given using as weights each country's trade share in the total trade of the industry. A decline is seen in this trade-weighted index, owing to a rise in trade with countries with low effective protection of intellectual property, which explains 29 percent of the rise within-industry skill-intensity.

41283 ■ *"Zit Zapper Lands New Funding" in Houston Business Journal (Vol. 40, November 27, 2009, No. 29, pp. 1)*
Pub: American City Business Journals
Ed: Mary Ann Azevedo. **Description:** Tyrell Inc. of Houston, Texas generated $20 million in funds for making a cheaper version of its acne-removing Zeno device. The upcoming product, Zeno Mini, will be targeted to a mass market with a price tag of about $89. In 2005, the original Zeno acne treatment device could only be bought through medical offices and spas at about $225.

TRADE PERIODICALS

41284 ■ *Product Safety & Liability Reporter*
Pub: Bureau of National Affairs Inc.
Ed: Gary A. Weinstein, Editor, gweinstein@bna.com. **Released:** Weekly. **Description:** Provides coverage of current administrative, legislative, judicial, and industry developments relating to product safety and product liability. Covers significant advances under the Consumer Product Safety Act, the National Highway Traffic Administration, and other consumer safety protection statutes and agencies.

CONSULTANTS

41285 ■ 2010 Fund 5
24351 Spartan St.
Mission Viejo, CA 92691-3920
Ph: (949)583-1992
Fax: (949)583-0474
Contact: Wally Eater, Principal
Scope: Funds in formation that will invest in technologies licensed from 30 universities. **Founded:** 1982.

41286 ■ Aurora Management Partners Inc.
4485 Tench Rd., Ste. 340
Suwanee, GA 30024
Ph: (770)904-5209
Fax: (770)904-5226
Co. E-mail: rturcotte@auroramp.com
URL: http://www.auroramp.com
Contact: William A. Barbee, Director
E-mail: abarbee@auroramp.com
Scope: Specializes in turnaround management and reorganization consulting. Firm develop strategic initiatives, organize and analyze solutions, deal with creditor issues, review organizational structure and develop time frames for decision making. Turnaround services offered include Recovery plans and their implementation, Viability analysis, Crisis management, Financial restructuring, Corporate and organizational restructuring, Facilities rationalization, Liquidation management, Loan workout, Litigation support and Expert testimony, Contract renegotiation, Sourcing loan refinancing and Sourcing equity investment. **Founded:** 2005. **Publications:** "TMA Turnaround of the Year Award, Small Company, Honorable Mention," Nov, 2005; "Back From The Brink - Bland Farms," Progressive Farmer, Oct, 2004; "New Breed of Turnaround Managers," Catalyst Magazine, Aug, 2004; "Key Performance Drivers - Bland Farms," The Produce News, Apr, 2004; "Corporate Governance: Averting Crisis's Before They Happen," ABJ journal, Feb, 2004.

41287 ■ C. Clint Bolte & Associates
809 Philadelphia Ave.
Chambersburg, PA 17201
Ph: (717)263-5768
Fax: (717)263-8954
Co. E-mail: clint@clintbolte.com
URL: http://www.clintbolte.com
Contact: C. Clint Bolte, Principal
E-mail: cbolte3@comcast.net
Scope: Provider of management consulting services to firms involved with the printing industry. Services include outsourcing studies, graphics supply chain management studies, company and equipment valuations, plant layout services, litigation support, fulfillment warehouse consulting and product development services. **Founded:** 1989. **Seminars:** How to compete with the majors.

41288 ■ ByrneMRG Corp.
22 Isle of Pines Dr.
Hilton Head Island, SC 29928
Ph: (215)630-7411
Free: 888-816-8080
Co. E-mail: info@byrnemrg.com
URL: http://www.byrnemrg.com
Contact: Patrick J. Boyle, President
E-mail: pjboyle@byrnemrg.com
Scope: Specializes in management consulting, including department management, equipment evaluation and selection, project management, research and development planning; and database design and management. **Founded:** 1972. **Publications:** "Implementing Solutions to Everyday Issues". **Telecommunication Services:** pjboyle@byrnemrg.com.

41289 ■ Casino, Hotel & Resort Consultants L.L.C.
4825 Quality Ct., Ste. B
Las Vegas, NV 89103
Ph: (702)528-9537
Co. E-mail: info@hraba.com
URL: http://www.hraba.com
Contact: John S. Hraba, President
E-mail: jshraba@aol.com
Scope: Casino and hospitality industry consultants. Firm specializes in developing and implementing customized forecast and labor management control systems that deliver immediate, positive impact to the company's bottom line. Involved in production planning, employ surveys and communication, inventory management, business process reviews, audits, development and implementation of key management reports. **Founded:** 1989. **Seminars:** Payroll Cost Control; Effective Staff Scheduling. **Telecommunication Services:** john.hraba@hraba.com.

41290 ■ Comer & Associates L.L.C.—Energy Alliance Group
5255 Holmes Pl.
Boulder, CO 80303
Ph: (303)786-7986
Free: 888-950-3190
Fax: (303)895-2347
Co. E-mail: jerry@comerassociates.com
URL: http://www.comerassociates.com
Contact: Jerry C. Comer, President
E-mail: jerry@comerassociates.com
URL(s): www.energyalliance.biz. **Scope:** Specialize in developing markets and businesses. Marketing support includes: Developing and writing strategic and tactical business plans; developing and writing focused, effective market plans; researching market potential and competition; implementing targeted marketing tactics to achieve company objectives; conducting customer surveys to determine satisfaction and attitudes toward client. Organization development support includes: Executive management training programs; executive coaching; team building; developing effective organization structures; and management of change in dynamic and competitive environments; individual coaching for management and leadership effectiveness. **Founded:** 1993. **Seminars:** Developing a Strategic Market Plan; Market Research: Defining Your Opportunity; Management and Leadership Effectiveness; Team Building; Developing a Business Plan; How to Close; Using Questions to Sell; Sales System Elements and Checklist; Working With Independent Reps; Features vs. Benefits; Overcoming Objections; Sales Force Automation.

41291 ■ Flor & Associates
179 Schan Dr.
Churchville, PA 18966-1619
Ph: (215)355-7466
Fax: (215)355-7464
Co. E-mail: fredflor@msn.com
Contact: Frederick Flor, President
Scope: Offers business development consulting helping companies increase the value of their businesses. Services include: market development for technologies sand products; product positioning strategies; technology assessment; competitive intelligence and analysis; team augmentation and facilitation; business growth strategies including acquisitions, licensing, and partnerships.

41292 ■ Global Technology Transfer L.L.C.
1500 Dixie Hwy.
Park Hills, KY 41011-2819
Ph: (859)431-1262
Fax: (859)431-5148
Contact: Anthony Zembrodt, President
Scope: Firm specializes in product development; quality assurance; new product development; and total quality management focusing on household chemical specialties, especially air fresheners. Utilizes latest technology from global resources. Specializes in enhancement products for home and automobile. **Founded:** 1992.

41293 ■ Gordian Concepts & Solutions
16 Blueberry Ln.
Lincoln, MA 01773
Ph: (617)259-8341
Contact: Stephen R. Low, President
Scope: Engineering and management consultancy offering general, financial, and valuation services, civil and tax litigation support. Assists clients in entering new businesses, planning new products and services, and evaluating feasibility. Targets industrial concerns engaged in manufacturing, assembly, warehousing, energy production, process systems and biotechnology, steel, paper, and electronics. Serves businesses such as retailing, financial services, health care, satellite broadcasting and cable television, outdoor advertising and professional practices. **Founded:** 1990. **Publications:** "Establishing Rural Cellular Company Values," Cellular Business.

41294 ■ Health Strategy Group Inc.
46 River Rd.
Chatham, NY 12037

Ph: (518)392-6770
Contact: Cameron Battley, President
Scope: Provides consulting services in the areas of strategic planning, feasibility studies, start-up businesses, organizational development, market research, customer service audits, new product development, marketing, public relations. **Founded:** 1981. **Publications:** "Online Consumer Surveys as a Methodology for Assessing the Quality of the United States Health Care System," 2004.

41295 ■ Hewitt Development Enterprises (HDE)
1717 N Bayshore Dr., Ste. 2154
Miami, FL 33132
Ph: (305)372-0941
Fax: (305)372-0941
Co. E-mail: info@hewittdevelopment.com
URL: http://www.hewittdevelopment.com
Contact: Robert G. Hewitt, Principal
E-mail: bob@hewittdevelopment.com
Scope: Specializes in strategic planning; profit enhancement; start-up businesses; interim management; crisis management; turnarounds; production planning; just-in-time inventory management; and project management. Serves senior management (CEOs, CFOs, division presidents, etc.) and acquirers of distressed businesses. **Founded:** 1985.

41296 ■ Hills Consulting Group Inc.
6 Partridge Ct.
Novato, CA 94945-1315
Ph: (415)898-3944
Contact: Michael R. Hills, President
Scope: Specializes in strategic planning; marketing surveys; market research; customer service audits; new product development; competitive analysis; and sales forecasting. **Founded:** 1985.

41297 ■ Hornberger & Associates (H&A)
1966 Lombard St.
San Francisco, CA 94123
Ph: (415)346-2106
Fax: (415)346-9993
Co. E-mail: info@hornbergerassociates.com
URL: http://www.hornbergerassociates.com
Contact: Deborah Hornberger, President
E-mail: deborah@hornbergerassociates.com
Scope: Specialized services include wealth management, retirement programs, small business banking, personal trust, investment management, brokerage services, mutual funds, relationship management, private banking and employee banking. Help clients by offering strategic marketing plans, market segmentation/niche marketing, website strategies and development; product development and introduction; client communications; product, sales and referral training; client retention programs and project management. **Founded:** 1992. **Publications:** "Establishing a Mini-trust Product," Bank Marketing, Oct, 1997. **Seminars:** Building a Marketing Plan Directed at Emerging Wealth Baby Boomers, Strategy Institute conference, Jun, 1999.

41298 ■ Interminds & Federer Resources Inc.
106 E 6th St., Ste. 310
Austin, TX 78701-3659
Ph: (512)476-8800
Fax: (512)476-8811
Co. E-mail: yesyoucan@interminds.com
URL: http://www.interminds.com
Contact: Frank Federer, President
E-mail: ffederer@integra100.com
Scope: Specializes in feasibility studies; startup businesses; small business management; mergers and acquisitions; joint ventures; divestitures; interim management; crisis management; turnarounds; production planning; team building; appraisals and valuations. **Founded:** 1985. **Publications:** "Yes You Can: How To Be A Success No Matter Who You Are Or Where You're From".

41299 ■ Intuition Design Inc.
508 2nd St.
Chesapeake City, MD 21915
Ph: (410)885-2513
Fax: (410)885-3094
URL: http://www.intuitiondesign.com
Contact: Robert E. Bernstein, President
E-mail: rob@intuitiondesign.com
Scope: Provider of cost-effective product development services. The firm excels in identifying problems, evaluating concepts, and providing practical product solutions. **Founded:** 1995.

41300 ■ Kubba Consultants Inc.
1255 Montgomery Dr.
Deerfield, IL 60015
Ph: (847)867-0874
URL: http://www.kubbainc.com
Contact: Ed Kubba, President
E-mail: edkubba@aol.com
Scope: Industrial and business-to-business marketing research and consulting. Services include new product research, new market evaluation, competitor analysis and customer value analysis. **Founded:** 1987.

41301 ■ Marketing Leverage Inc.
2022 Laurel Oak Ln.
Palm City, FL 34990
Ph: (772)878-6495
Free: 800-633-1422
Fax: (772)659-8664
Co. E-mail: lkelly@marketingleverage.com
Contact: Lynn C. Kelly, President
E-mail: lkelly@marketingleverage.com
Scope: Consulting and research firm focusing on the targeting, retention and satisfaction of customers. Consulting is offered for due diligence; marketing and customer retention strategy; program design and implementation. Research services offered help clients determine service improvements that increase customer loyalty; boosting sales through better understanding buyer motivations; increasing the odds of product acceptance through new product concept testing; and improving the effectiveness of advertising, collateral, publications through audience evaluation. Clients include top financial services, insurance, health care, technology and management services organizations. **Founded:** 1987. **Publications:** "Creating Strategic Leverage"; "Exploring Corporate Strategy"; "Competitive Advantage"; "Breakpoint and Beyond "; "Competitive Strategy ". **Seminars:** Best Practices in Brainstorming; Getting Results in the Real World; Finding the Leverage in Your Customer Strategy; The Role of Communications in Building Customer Loyalty; Building a Customer Centered Relationship and Making it Pay. **Special Services:** The Marketing Leverage Win/Loss Tracking System™.

41302 ■ Medical Imaging Consultants Inc. (MIC)
1037 US Highway 46, Ste. G-2
Clifton, NJ 07013-2445
Ph: (973)574-8000
Free: 800-589-5685
Fax: (973)574-8001
Co. E-mail: info@micinfo.com
URL: http://www.micinfo.com
Contact: Dr. Philip A. Femano, President
E-mail: phil@micinfo.com
Scope: Provider of professional support services for radiology management and comprehensive continuing education programs for radiologic technologists. Management services include resource-critical database logistics; customer registration in educational programs; educational program development and Category A accreditation; national agency notification (e.g., ASRT, SNM-TS) of CE credits earned; meeting planning; manpower assessment; market research; expert witness; think-tank probes and executive summaries of industry issues. **Founded:** 1991. **Seminars:** Sectional Anatomy and Imaging Strategies; CT Cross-Trainer; CT Registry Review Program; MR Cross Trainer; MRI Registry Review Program; Digital Mammography Essentials for Technologists; Radiology Trends for Technologists.

41303 ■ Mefford, Knutson & Associates Inc. (MK)
6437 Lyndale Ave. S, Ste. 103
Richfield, MN 55423-1465
Ph: (612)869-8011
Free: 800-831-0228
Fax: (612)869-8004
Co. E-mail: info@mkaonline.net
URL: http://www.mkaonline.net
Contact: Jeanette Mefford, Director
E-mail: jmefford@mkaonline.com
Scope: A consulting and licensed business brokerage firm specializing in start-up businesses; strategic planning; mergers and acquisitions; joint ventures; divestitures; business process re-engineering; personnel policies and procedures; market research; new product development and cost controls. **Founded:** 1990.

41304 ■ The New Marketing Network Inc.
300 Park Ave., 17th Fl.
New York, NY 10022
Ph: (212)572-6392
Co. E-mail: info@newmarketingnetwork.com
URL: http://www.newmarketingnetwork.com
Contact: Pamela S. Boynton, Director
Scope: Full service firm assisting companies in marketing, creative, research, branding and communications specialties. The firm assists companies achieve their growth initiatives, increase profits and establish a sustainable competitive advantage through successful new products, accurate trend identification; application; business and brand franchise expansion. Additional services include strategic planning and positioning; qualitative and quantitative research. **Founded:** 1989.

41305 ■ Partners for Market Leadership L.L.C.
400 Galleria Pky., Ste. 1500
Atlanta, GA 30339
Ph: (770)850-1409
Free: 800-984-1110
Co. E-mail: dcarpenter@market-leadership.com
URL: http://www.market-leadership.com
Contact: Nancy Surdyka, Manager
E-mail: nsurdyka@market-leadership.com
Scope: Boutique consulting firm focused on assisting clients to develop sustainable market leadership in geographic, practice area and/or industry markets. Provides consulting on market leadership, revenue enhancement, strategic development and change facilitation. Additional services are offered to legal, accounting, valuation and financial firms. **Founded:** 1995.

41306 ■ Stratamar Inc.
5661 Seapine Rd.
Hilliard, OH 43026
Ph: (614)946-4614
Fax: (614)529-2945
Co. E-mail: info@stratamar.com
URL: http://www.stratamar.com
Contact: Nancy Brown, Owner
Scope: A full-spectrum strategic marketing consulting company. Areas of concentration include product development, product management, strategic planning, development and implementation of tactical marketing plans, and Internet marketing. The primary focus is upon maximizing the benefit, cost ratio of promotions through the use of direct marketing, low cost media, and the like. **Founded:** 1998. **Publications:** "Business Plans," Feb, 2006.

41307 ■ Via Nova Consulting
1228 Winburn Dr.
Atlanta, GA 30344
Ph: (404)761-7484
Fax: (404)762-7123
Scope: Consulting services in the areas of strategic planning; privatization; executive searches; market research; customer service audits; new product development; competitive intelligence; and Total Quality Management (TQM). **Founded:** 1994.

RESEARCH CENTERS

41308 ■ Ball State University - Center for Organizational Resources (COR)
Carmichael Hall, Rm. 201
Muncie, IN 47306
Ph: (765)285-2770

Free: 800-541-9313
Fax: (765)285-1284
Co. E-mail: dboyd@bsu.edu
URL: http://www.bsu.edu/cor
Contact: Delaina Boyd, Director
Services: Contract Consulting. **Founded:** 1984. **Educational Activities:** Customized training and open-enrollment seminars (Monthly).

41309 ■ Canadian Innovation Centre (CIC)
Accelerator Ctr., Ste. 15
Waterloo Research & Technology Park
295 Hagey Blvd.
Waterloo, ON, Canada N2L 6R5
Ph: (519)885-5870
Fax: (519)513-2421
Co. E-mail: info@innovationcentre.ca
URL: http://innovationcentre.ca
Contact: Ted Cross, Chief Executive Officer
Services: Invention Assistance Program: which assesses all aspects of an invention and aids in its development; Marketing Services: which provides market research assistance to small, medium, and large companies. **Founded:** 1976.

41310 ■ IIT Research Institute (IITRI)
10 W 35th St.
Chicago, IL 60616
Ph: (312)567-4000
Fax: (312)567-4021
Co. E-mail: dmccormick@iitri.org
URL: http://www.iitri.org
Contact: David L. McCormick, Director
Founded: 1936. **Telecommunication Services:** lsginfo@iitri.org.

41311 ■ Institute for the Future (IFTF)
124 University Ave.
Palo Alto, CA 94301
Ph: (650)854-6322
Fax: (650)854-7850
Co. E-mail: info@iftf.org
URL: http://www.iftf.org
Contact: Sean Ness, Director, Business Development
Founded: 1968. **Publications:** *Ten-Year Forecast*. **Educational Activities:** IFTF Annual Conference; Summer Institute. **Telecommunication Services:** sness@iftf.org.

41312 ■ Iowa State University of Science and Technology - Center for Industrial Research and Service (CIRAS)
2272 Howe Hall, Ste. 2620
Ames, IA 50011-2272
Ph: (515)294-3420
Fax: (515)294-4925
Co. E-mail: rcox@iastate.edu
URL: http://www.ciras.iastate.edu
Contact: Ronald A. Cox, Director
Services: Consults with industry on special problems; Information retrieval: available to industry and professional groups within the state; Statewide University Center Program for Iowa Businesses. **Founded:** 1963. **Publications:** *CIRASNews* (Quarterly). **Educational Activities:** Workshops, briefings, and specialized extension courses for various phases of industry in the state. **Telecommunication Services:** ciras.info@iastate.edu.

41313 ■ Pennsylvania State University - Institute for the Study of Business Markets (ISBM)
484 Business Bldg.
Smeal College of Business
University Park, PA 16802
Ph: (814)863-2782
Fax: (814)863-0413
Co. E-mail: isbm@psu.edu
URL: http://isbm.smeal.psu.edu
Contact: Dr. Ralph A. Oliva, Executive Director
E-mail: roliva@psu.edu
Services: Business marketing research support; Doctoral dissertation support. **Founded:** 1983. **Publications:** *ISBM Insights*; *Marketplace: The ISBM Review Newsletter* (Semiannual); *ISBM Working papers*. **Educational Activities:** Joint educational programs, with Pennsylvania State Executive Programs; PhD Camp (Biennial), small group meeting to help doctoral students develop a business-to-business research proposal; faculty for the camp are leaders in the field; Seminars and special courses, for industry and academicians; Short courses and conferences; Special-interest consortia; ISBM Academic Conference (Biennial), held in the same city location as AMA, this academic meeting brings the top business-to-business researchers together to present their most recent research; Members meetings. **Awards:** ISBM Business Marketing Doctoral Award Support Competition (Annual), that provides research funding to doctoral students in business-to-business marketing. **Telecommunication Services:** glilien@psu.edu.

41314 ■ University of Missouri—St. Louis - Center for Business and Industrial Studies
220 CCB
1 University Dr.
Saint Louis, MO 63121-4499
Ph: (314)516-6108
Fax: (314)516-6827
Co. E-mail: ldsmith@umsl.edu
URL: http://www.umsl.edu/divisions/business/ncbis/index.html
Contact: Dr. L. Douglas Smith, Director
Founded: 1983.

41315 ■ University of North Dakota (CI)
Ina Mae Rude Entrepreneur Center
Grand Forks, ND 58203
Ph: (701)777-3132
Fax: (701)777-2339
Co. E-mail: info@innovators.net
URL: http://www.innovators.net
Contact: Jordan T. Schuetzle, Director
E-mail: jordan@innovators.net
Description: Provides technical and business support services to entrepreneurs, inventors, and small manufacturers. Assists specifically with the product evaluation process, the patenting process, and technology transfer. **Scope:** Offers market and demographical research, business plan development, financial forecasts and manufacturing services to entrepreneurs, particularly manufacturing technology start up enterprises. Provides assistance to innovators, entrepreneurs, and researchers to launch new ventures, commercialize new technologies, and secure access to capital from private and public sources. **Services:** Commercial Evaluations for Emerging Technologies (11/year). **Founded:** 1984. **Publications:** "The Business Plan: A State-Of-The-Art Guide"; "The Marketing Plan: Step-By-Step"; "The Ultimate Business Planner"; "Campus Entrepreneurship: A Changing Curriculum for Changing Times"; "Financing Startup Ventures"; "The Business Plan: A State-of-the-Art Guide"; "The Marketing Plan: Step-by-Step". **Educational Activities:** Center for Innovation Conferences and workshops (Monthly), Seed and Angel Capital, Entrepreneur Startups, Business Planning, Market Feasibility. **Telecommunication Services:** celia@innovators.net; bruce@innovators.net; askme@innovators.net.

41316 ■ University of Pennsylvania - SEI Center for Advanced Studies in Management
700 Jon M. Huntsman Hall
Wharton School
3730 Walnut St.
Philadelphia, PA 19104-6340
Ph: (215)898-8267
Fax: (215)898-1703
Co. E-mail: windj@wharton.upenn.edu
URL: http://seicenter.wharton.upenn.edu
Contact: Prof. Jerry Wind, Director
Founded: 1990. **Publications:** *Insights and Impact* (Occasionally). **Telecommunication Services:** seicenter@wharton.upenn.edu.

41317 ■ Virginia Polytechnic Institute and State University - Center for High Performance Manufacturing (CHPM)
102 Durham Hall
Blacksburg, VA 24061
Ph: (540)231-6201
Fax: (540)231-3322
Co. E-mail: rotaylo2@vt.edu
URL: http://www.ise.vt.edu/ResearchFacilities/Centers/CenterPages/CHPM_center.html
Contact: Robert E. Taylor, Director
Founded: 2001. **Educational Activities:** CHPM Short courses; Biannual Meeting. **Awards:** Research associateships and assistantships. **Telecommunication Services:** chpm@vt.edu.

REFERENCE WORKS

41318 ■ *"ACE Aims High With Spinoff of Repair Unit" in Globe & Mail (January 31, 2007, pp. B15)*
Pub: CTVglobemedia Publishing Inc.
Ed: Brent Jang. **Description:** The decision of ACE Aviation Holdings Inc. to sell its aircraft maintenance division and add workforce at its El Salvador plant is discussed.

41319 ■ *Adoption Resource Book*
Pub: HarperCollins
URL(s): www.harpercollins.com/Book/Browse.aspx. **Released:** Irregular; Latest edition 4th. **Price:** $16. 95, Individuals paperback. **Publication includes:** List of public and private adoption agencies, support groups, and services. **Entries include:** Agency name, address, phone, special requirements. Principal content of the publication is a discussion of adoption procedures and requirements, including adoption of foreign children and open adoption. **Arrangement:** Geographical.

41320 ■ *"Alberta Star Begins Phase 2 Drilling On Its Eldorado & Contact Lake IOCG & Uranium Projects" in Canadian Corporate News (May 16, 2007)*
Pub: Comtex News Network Inc.
Description: Profile of Alberta Star Development Corp., a Canadian mineral exploration company that identifies, acquires, and finances advanced stage exploration projects in Canada, and its current undertaking of its 2007 drill program in which the company intends to begin accelerating its uranium and poly-metallic exploration and drilling activities on all of its drill targets for 2007 now that it has been granted its permits.

41321 ■ *"CN Aims for Regional Pacts to Halt Labor Row" in Globe & Mail (April 17, 2007, pp. B2)*
Pub: CTVglobemedia Publishing Inc.
Ed: Brent Jang. **Description:** The decision of Canadian National Railway Co. to settle labor dispute with regional unions is discussed.

41322 ■ *"CN 'Extremely Optimistic' After Record Profit" in Globe & Mail (January 24, 2007, pp. B3)*
Pub: CTVglobemedia Publishing Inc.
Ed: Brent Jang. **Description:** The increase in Canadian National Railway Co.'s profits to $2.1 billion despite a harsh winter is discussed.

41323 ■ *"Decision CEO Cool to Acquisitions" in Globe & Mail (April 19, 2007, pp. B6)*
Pub: CTVglobemedia Publishing Inc.
Ed: Andy Hoffman. **Description:** The increase in the shares of Denison Mines Corp. due to hike in Uranium prices is discussed.

41324 ■ *"Diamond in the Rough" in Canadian Business (Vol. 79, October 23, 2006, No. 21, pp. 71)*
Pub: Rogers Media
Ed: Mark Brown. **Description:** The opening of a new mine 420 kilometers northeast of Yellowknife in Northwest Territories by Tahera Diamond Corp. is discussed.

41325 ■ *"Diaz Announces Financial and Operating Results for the First Three Months of 2007" in Canadian Corporate News (May 16, 2007)*
Pub: Comtex News Network Inc.
Description: Diaz Resources Ltd., an oil and gas exploration and production company, announced its financial results during the first quarter of 2007 which were hampered by lower gas prices and declining production volumes but anticipates the financial results should steadily improve in the second quarter of 2007.

41326 ■ *"Diving for the Next Big Gold Rush" in Canadian Business (Vol. 80, February 12, 2007, No. 4, pp. 28)*
Pub: Rogers Media
Ed: Thomas Watson. **Description:** The interest of Canadian mining companies led by Nautilus Minerals to invest in mining for deep sea-floor massive sulphide deposits, which have several minerals, is discussed.

41327 ■ *"eResearch Issues Initiating Report on Aldershot Resources Ltd." in Canadian Corporate News (May 14, 2007)*
Pub: Comtex News Network Inc.
Description: Overview of Bob Weir and Michael Wood's Initiating Report on Aldershot Resources Ltd., a junior Canadian-based uranium exploration company with prospective projects in Canada, Zambia, Australia, and a base metals project in Chile.

41328 ■ *"Fuel for Thought; Canadian Business Leaders on Energy Policy" in Canadian Business (Vol. 81, September 15, 2008, No. 14-15, pp. 12)*
Pub: Rogers Media Ltd.
Ed: Joe Castaldo. **Description:** Most Canadian business leaders worry about the unreliability of the oil supply but feel that Canada is in a better position to benefit from the energy supply crisis than other countries. Many respondents also highlighted the need to invest in renewable energy sources.

41329 ■ *"A Gambling Man: Career Transitions that Put a Vegas Hotshot on Top" in Black Enterprise (Vol. 37, October 2006, No. 3, pp. 89)*
Pub: Earl G. Graves Publishing Co. Inc.
Ed: Laura Egodigwe. **Description:** Interview with Lorenzo Creighton, president and chief operating officer of MGM Mirage's New York-New York Hotel and Casino. Creighton talks about his history and the challenges he faced since he didn't come from the casino industry.

41330 ■ *"Goldeye Completes Private Placement" in Canadian Corporate News (May 16, 2007)*
Pub: Comtex News Network Inc.
Description: Goldeye, a Canadian mineral exploration company acquiring, exploring, and advancing properties in Chile and Canada, announced that it has completed a partially brokered private placement for gross proceeds of $1,232,660 which will be used to finance exploration on Goldeye's mineral properties in Chile and for administrative expenses, and working capital.

41331 ■ *"Goldfingers" in Canadian Business (Vol. 81, Summer 2008, No. 9, pp. 31)*
Pub: Rogers Media Ltd.
Ed: Sharda Prashad. **Description:** Large players in the mining industry are looking for junior mining companies in Canada to be acquired. The U.S. recession and subprime mortgage crisis have made it easier for giant miners to acquire small mining companies than to conduct the operations themselves. Junior miners are those that lack cash flow and expertise to build and operate mine.

41332 ■ *"Horizon Acquires Significant Working Interest in High Impact Prospect in Southeast Texas" in Canadian Corporate News (May 14, 2007)*
Pub: Comtex News Network Inc.
Description: Horizon Industries Ltd., an emerging gas and oil exploration and production company, announced that it has entered into a Joint Venture agreement with Pan American Development Company, Inc. in which they will begin a drilling program in San Jacinto County, Texas.

41333 ■ *"Insider" in Canadian Business (Vol. 81, March 3, 2008, No. 3, pp. 96)*
Pub: Rogers Media
Description: History of gold usage and gold trading is presented in a timeline. Gold was a symbol of power and wealth in 2500 B.C., and in 1500 B.C., it became the first currency to be recognized internationally. Other remarkable events in the gold industry and laws that covered gold are discussed.

41334 ■ *"Insider" in Canadian Business (Vol. 81, Summer 2008, No. 9, pp. 170)*
Pub: Rogers Media Ltd.
Ed: Thomas Watson; Jeff Sanford. **Description:** Oil peak theory posits that the world has consumed half of the non-renewable resources is indicated by the surging oil prices. However, critics argued that the high oil prices are effects of market speculation and not the depletion of the supply. Ten reasons on why to buy and not buy peak oil are presented.

41335 ■ *"Life After Cod" in Globe & Mail (March 18, 2006, pp. B1)*
Pub: CTVglobemedia Publishing Inc.
Ed: Gordon Pitts. **Description:** Canadian fishing industry is under threat because of Chinese processing competition, high energy costs, rise of powerful retailers and the rise of Canadian dollar value. Fishing industry of Canada is analyzed.

41336 ■ *"Lufthansa-Cathay Deal Reinforces Outsourcing" in Globe & Mail (March 30, 2007, pp. B9)*
Pub: CTVglobemedia Publishing Inc.
Ed: Daniel Michaels. **Description:** Cathay Pacific Airways Ltd. signed a $300 million contract with Lufthansa Technik AG to outsource engine maintenance operations. The outsourcing of non-core operation is increasing in airline industry.

41337 ■ *"Lundin Deal Leaves Nickel Market Thin" in Globe & Mail (April 5, 2007, pp. B4)*
Pub: CTVglobemedia Publishing Inc.
Ed: Andy Hoffman. **Description:** The likely acquisition of Rio Narcea Gold Mines Ltd. by Lundin Mining Corp. and the decreasing number of nickel mining companies on the list of Toronto Stock Exchange are discussed.

41338 ■ *"Micro-Cap Companies" in Canadian Business (Vol. 81, Summer 2008, No. 9, pp. 157)*
Pub: Rogers Media Ltd.
Description: Micro-cap companies have lower than $221 million in terms of market capitalization. Burnaby, British Columbia-based Fancamp Exploration Ltd. topped the roster with 1,116.7 percent in return. A table showing the 2008 rankings of the companies is presented.

41339 ■ *National Agricultural Aviation Association--Membership Directory*
Pub: National Agricultural Aviation Association
Contact: Rick Richter, President
URL(s): www.agaviation.org. **Ed:** Andrew D. Moore. **Released:** Annual **Covers:** Nearly 1300 executives, pilots, and supplier companies engaged primarily in aerial application. **Entries include:** For chapter and supplier company members--Name, spouse's name, company name, address, phone. **Arrangement:** Classified by type of membership; chapter members are then geographical; supplier company members are then by product.

41340 ■ *National Association for Drama Therapy--Membership List*
Pub: National Association for Drama Therapy
Contact: Nisha Sajnani, President
URL(s): www.nadt.org. **Released:** Annual; August. **Covers:** About 400 registered drama therapists and NADT members. **Entries include:** Name, address, membership category. **Arrangement:** Separate alphabetical sections for registered drama therapists and regular members. **Indexes:** Geographical.

41341 ■ *National Council of Acoustical Consultants--Directory*
Pub: National Council of Acoustical Consultants
Contact: Jackie Williams, Executive Director
URL(s): www.ncac.com. **Covers:** 125 acoustical consulting firms, primarily in the United States. **Entries include:** Company name, address, phone, name of principal executive, list of services. **Arrangement:** Alphabetical.

41342 ■ *"Not in Your Backyard?" in Canadian Business (Vol. 80, March 12, 2007, No. 6, pp. 44)*
Pub: Rogers Media
Ed: John Gray. **Description:** The threat of losing residential property rights of persons whose land has rightful stakes from miners due to availability of minerals at the place is discussed.

41343 ■ *"Over a Barrel" in Canadian Business (Vol. 80, February 12, 2007, No. 4, pp. 52)*
Pub: Rogers Media
Ed: Andrew Nikoforuk. **Description:** The potential of tar sands of Alberta in becoming the largest source of oil in the world and huge investments of Canadian companies to mine for the oil there are discussed.

41344 ■ *"Playfair Receives Drill Permit for Risby, Yukon Tungsten Deposit" in Canadian Corporate News (May 16, 2007)*
Pub: Comtex News Network Inc.
Description: Playfair Mining announced that it has received a 5 year Class III land use permit from the Mineral Resources Branch, Yukon which will allow the company to carry out a drill program during the upcoming drill season on the company-owned Risby, Yukon tungsten deposit. Statistical data included.

41345 ■ *"Q&A" in Canadian Business (Vol. 81, July 22, 2008, No. 12-13, pp. 8)*
Pub: Rogers Media Ltd.
Ed: Michelle Magnan. **Description:** Interview with Scott Saxberg who discusses Crescent Point Energy Trust's discovery of resources in Saskatchewan and believes that this is a once-in-a-lifetime type of event. Crescent Point holds 75 percent of its resources in Saskatchewan; this new finding being considered the second-largest pool discovered since the 1950s. Saxberg's other views as well as information on Crescent Point's services are presented.

41346 ■ *"Reports of Banks' Revival were Greatly Exaggerated" in Barron's (Vol. 88, July 7, 2008, No. 27, pp. L14)*
Pub: Dow Jones & Co., Inc.
Ed: Jack Willoughby. **Description:** Performance of mutual funds improved for the second quarter of 2008 compared to the previous quarter, registering an average gain of 0.13 percent; funds focusing on natural resources rose the highest, their value rising by an average of 24.50 percent.

41347 ■ *"Rimfire Minerals Corporation: Jake Gold Project-Drilling Planned for 2007" in Canadian Corporate News (May 16, 2007)*
Pub: Comtex News Network Inc.
Description: Rimfire Minerals Corporation and Island Arc Exploration Corporation formed a partnership to explore the Jake Property, a high-grade gold prospect with previously unrecognized potential to host economic gold mineralization, located 13 kilometers west of Clearwater, British Columbia.

41348 ■ *"Rock Festival: High Spirited Conventioneers Celebrate Their Good Fortune" in Canadian Business (Vol. 81, March 31, 2008, No. 5)*
Pub: Rogers Media
Ed: Jeff Sanford. **Description:** Soaring prices of commodities in the mining industry have been very good for the attendees of the 76th annual conference of the Prospectors & Developers Association of Canada. A speaker at the conference expects commodity prices to come off a bit but not fall dramatically as it did in the 1980's.

41349 ■ *"The Search for Big Oil" in Canadian Business (Vol. 80, April 9, 2007, No. 8, pp. 10)*
Pub: Rogers Media
Ed: Joe Castaldo. **Description:** The continuing effort of Canmex Minerals Corp. to explore for oil in Somalia despite the failure of several other companies is discussed.

41350 ■ *"Shell Venture Aims at 'Oil Rocks'" in Globe & Mail (March 22, 2006, pp. B1)*
Pub: CTVglobemedia Publishing Inc.
Ed: Patrick Brethour. **Description:** Royal Dutch Shell PLC is all set to launch its Alberta's operations in bitumen deposits trapped in limestone. Details of the new venture are analyzed.

41351 ■ *"Ship Shape" in Hawaii Business (Vol. 53, January 2008, No. 7, pp. 46)*
Pub: Hawaii Business Publishing
Ed: David K. Choo. **Description:** Ship Maintenance LLC is in charge of repairing and maintaning the U.S. Navy ships at Pearl Harbor's Middle Noch, having renewed a five-year contract with the navy. Cleaning a ship is a difficult process, which involves degreasing and removal of sensitive items such as guns and missiles. The awards given to Ship Maintenance are also discussed.

41352 ■ *"Slick Science" in Canadian Business (Vol. 81, September 15, 2008, No. 14-15, pp. 55)*
Pub: Rogers Media Ltd.
Ed: Andrew Nikiforuk. **Description:** N-Solv Corp's John Nenniger has discovered a better alternative to steam-assisted gravity drainage methods for extracting bitumen. Nenniger's technique also relies on gravity but replaces steam with propane, which leaves behind impurities like asphaltenes and heavy metals that are too dirty to burn.

41353 ■ *"Southwestern Resources Project Update" in Canadian Corporate News (May 14, 2007)*
Pub: Comtex News Network Inc.
Description: Southwestern Resoures Corp. provides a quarterly update on its various exploration projects in both Peru and China.

41354 ■ *"Strathmore Receives Permit to Drill oca Honda Project in New Mexico" in Canadian Corporate News (May 14, 2007)*
Pub: Comtex News Network Inc.
Description: New Mexico's Mining and Minerals Division approved a permit to allow Strathmore Minerals Corp. to conduct drilling at its Roca Honda Project located in McKinley County, New Mexico.

41355 ■ *"Superior Completes Second Vertical Hole Through Morin Kimberlite and Intersects 141 Metres of Crater Facies Material at the Ville Marie Project" in*
Pub: Comtex News Network Inc.
Description: Superior Diamonds Inc., a junior Canadian exploration company that primarily searches for diamonds in the highly prospective and under-explored regions of the Canadian Shield, announced completion of a second vertical hole through the western side of Superior's Morin kimberlite pipe to try to determine the type and thickness of the kimberlite material.

41356 ■ *The Theatre Listing: A Directory of Professional Theatre in Canada*
Pub: Professional Association of Canadian Theatres
PACT Communications Centre
Contact: Nancy Webster, President
E-mail: nwebster@lktyp.ca
URL(s): www.pact.ca. **Ed:** Janet Mackenzie. **Released:** latest edition 2011. **Covers:** Over 300 English-language professional theatres in Canada. **Entries include:** Theatre name, address, phone, fax, e-mail, internet sites, contacts, key personnel, budget, mandates, facilities, submissions, repertoire, play development and other programs, affiliations. **Arrangement:** Regional. **Indexes:** Companies and Rental Spaces; Governments and Organizations; Advertisers; Last names; Festivals.

41357 ■ *"Underworld Acquires Yukon Gold Property" in Canadian Corporate News (May 16, 2007)*
Pub: Comtex News Network Inc.
Description: Underworld Resources Inc., a well-structured junior exploration company, announced that it has secured an option to earn a 100 percent right, title, and interest in the 11,850 acre White and Black Fox gold Properties in Yukon Territory, Canada. The company will be exploring both vein hosted and sedimentary hosted gold targets.

41358 ■ *"Uranerz Acquires Additional Uranium Property Adjoining Nichols Ranch" in Canadian Corporate News (May 14, 2007)*
Pub: Comtex News Network Inc.
Description: Uranerz Energy Corporation announced the successful leasing of the fee mineral lands that appear to host the 'nose' of the oxidation-rduction geochemical front and has the potential for increasing the known uranium mineralization at the Nichols Ranch project which lies west of and adjacent to Uranerz's Nichols Ranch ISR uranium project.

41359 ■ *"Uranium Energy Corp Provides an Update on Its Goliad Operations" in Canadian Corporate News (May 16, 2007)*
Pub: Comtex News Network Inc.
Description: Complaints against Uranium Energy Corp. and its Goliad Project in South Texas have been dismissed. The Railroad Commission of Texas (RRC), the regulatory authority which oversees mineral exploration in Texas, concluded that Uranium Energy Corp.'s drilling activities on the Goliad Project have not contaminated certain water wells or the related aquifier.

START-UP INFORMATION

41360 ■ *Angel Financing: How to Find and Invest in Private Equity*
Pub: John Wiley and Sons, Inc.
Ed: Gerald A. Benjamin; Joel B. Margulis. **Price:** $65. 00. **Description:** The book provides a proven strategy to help entrepreneurs find angel investors. Interviews with angel investors as well as information about investors' hedging strategies, risk assessments, syndication orientation, financial return expectations, deal structuring preferences, monitoring investments, harvesting returns, and realist exit strategies are covered.

41361 ■ *"Firefighter Wins ABC's American Inventor" in Hispanic Business (September 2007, pp. 94)*
Pub: Hispanic Business
Description: Greg Chavez, firefighter, won ABC televisions American Inventor award of $1 million for his Guardian Angel invention. The device makes Christmas trees safer.

41362 ■ *Raising Capital*
Pub: Kiplinger Books and Tapes
Ed: Andrew J. Sherman. **Price:** $34.95. **Description:** Corporate attorney provides a comprehensive guide using in-depth, practical advice on raising money to start and grow a business. A 115-page appendix contains samples of financing agreements, forms and questionnaires.

REFERENCE WORKS

41363 ■ *"Affordable Financing for Acquisitions" in Franchising World (Vol. 42, September 2010, No. 9, pp. 47)*
Pub: International Franchise Association
Ed: Gene Cerrotti. **Description:** Acquisition pricing is reasonable and interest rates are low and quality franchised resale opportunities are priced 4.5 times EBITDA. Information about Small Business Administration loans is also included.

41364 ■ *"Angel Investing 2009" in Inc. (Vol. 31, January-February 2009, No. 1, pp. 83)*
Pub: Mansueto Ventures LLC
Ed: Kasey Wehrum. **Description:** Tips for finding funding in tough economic times are presented, including secrets for closing second-round deals.

41365 ■ *"Angel Investors Across State Collaborate" in Austin Business Journal (Vol. 31, May 20, 2011, No. 11, pp. 1)*
Pub: American City Business Journals Inc.
Ed: Christopher Calnan. **Description:** Texas' twelve angel investing groups are going to launch the umbrella organization Alliance of Texas Angel Networks (ATAN) to support more syndicated deals and boost investments in Texas. In 2010, these investing groups infused more than $24 million to startups in 61 deals.

41366 ■ *The Art of the Start*
Pub: Portfolio Publishing
Ed: Guy Kawasaki. **Price:** $26.95. **Description:** Apple's Guy Kawasaki offers information to help would-be entrepreneurs create new enterprises. As founder and CEO of Garage Technology Ventures, he has field-tested his ideas with newly hatched companies and he takes readers through every phase of creating a business, from the very basics of raising money and designing a business model through the many stages that eventually lead to success and thus giving back to society.

41367 ■ *"Can You Say $1 Million? A Language-Learning Start-Up Is Hoping That Investors Can" in Inc. (Vol. 33, November 2011, No. 9, pp. 116)*
Pub: Inc. Magazine
Ed: April Joyner. **Description:** Startup, Verbling is a video platform that links language learners and native speakers around the world. The firm is working to raise money to hire engineers in order to build the product and redesign their Website.

41368 ■ *"Chasing Credit" in Canadian Business (Vol. 81, November 10, 2008, No. 19, pp. 59)*
Pub: Rogers Media Ltd.
Ed: Joe Castaldo. **Description:** Small and medium sized companies are dealing with tightening credit because they appear riskier than usual. Some of these businesses are turning to private investors, but this is not easy since many have invested everything in the stock market. The sector is expected to weaken with the broader Canadian market in the next six months from October 2008.

41369 ■ *"How Sweet It Is: a Health Hardship Leads to Cupcake Commerce" in Black Enterprise (Vol. 41, August 2010, No. 1, pp. 56)*
Pub: Earl G. Graves Publishing Co. Inc.
Ed: Tamara E. Holmes. **Description:** Profile of Andra Hall, entrepreneur who started her cupcake business when her one-year-old daughter suffered from sleep apnea and wanted the flexibility to be with her baby. Hall and her husband refinanced their home in order to start the bakery.

41370 ■ *"How To Get a Loan the Web 2.0 Way" in Black Enterprise (Vol. 41, December 2010, No. 5, pp. 23)*
Pub: Earl G. Graves Publishing Co. Inc.
Ed: John Simons. **Description:** People are turning to online peer-to-peer network for personal loans as banks are lending less money.

41371 ■ *"The King of Kincardine" in Canadian Business (Vol. 79, October 9, 2006, No. 20, pp. 101)*
Pub: Rogers Media
Ed: Paul Webster. **Description:** Motives of Duncan Hawthorne, president and chief executive officer of Bruce Power Ltd., behind investing in nuclear power plant in Ontario, Canada through private financing are discussed.

41372 ■ *"Meet UT's New Business Mind" in Austin Business Journal (Vol. 31, May 13, 2011, No. 10, pp. A1)*
Pub: American City Business Journals Inc.
Ed: Sandra Zaragoza. **Description:** University of Texas (UT) chief commercialization officer, Dr. Richard Miller, has opened a satellite office in Silicon Valley, California in the hopes of luring Californian investors to the science and technology at UT. The satellite office is just one of Miller's efforts to reshape and widen the commercialization of UT-Austin. Insights into Miller's long-term view approach to commercialization are also covered.

41373 ■ *"Microlending Seen as Having a Major Impact" in Business Journal Serving Greater Tampa Bay (Vol. 30, November 26, 2010, No. 49, pp. 1)*
Pub: Tampa Bay Business Journal
Ed: Margie Manning. **Description:** There are several organizations that are planning to offer microlending services in Tampa Bay, Florida. These include the Children's Board of Hillsborough County, and OUR Microlending Florida LLC. Organizations that are already offering these services in the area include the Small Business Administration and the Tampa Bay Black Business Investment Corp.

41374 ■ *"New Economy Initiative Gains Partners" in Crain's Detroit Business (Vol. 25, June 1, 2009, No. 22, pp. M014)*
Pub: Crain Communications Inc. - Detroit
Ed: Sherri Begin Welch. **Description:** New Economy Initiative is a $100 million philanthropic initiative that focuses on regional economic development. Recent grants awarded to Michigan companies are outlined.

41375 ■ *Raising Capital*
Pub: Raising Capital
Ed: Andrew J. Sherman. **Price:** $34.95.

41376 ■ *Raising Capital*
Pub: Greenwood Publishing Group, Inc.
Ed: David Nour. **Released:** March 1, 2009. **Price:** $39.95. **Description:** An overview to help entrepreneurs find capital for starting and maintaining a small business is presented. The author shows how to develop long-term relationships with financial partners and ways to attract financing to fund the startup and growth phases of any business. Entrepreneurs tell how they raised money from friends, family, angel investors, banks and venture capitalists and private equity firms.

41377 ■ *"Raising Money: the Bond that Lasts" in Entrepreneur (Vol. 35, October 2007, No. 10, pp. 73)*
Pub: Entrepreneur Media Inc.
Ed: Crystal Detamore-Rodman. **Description:** Tax-exempt bonds can be the solution to long-term financing needs of entrepreneurs. However, high initial costs may discourage some entrepreneurs to apply for these bonds, with transactions usually costing $3 mor more. How tax-exempt bonds work, and how rules vary with different states are discussed.

41378 ■ *"Recession-Proof Your Startup" in Crain's Chicago Business (Vol. 31, November 10, 2008, No. 45, pp. 24)*
Pub: Crain Communications, Inc.
Description: Detailed information concerning ways in which to start a business during an economic crisis is provided. Ways in which to find financing, the importance of a solid business plan, customer service, problem-solving and finding the right niche for the region are also discussed.

41379 ■ *Risk-Free Entrepreneur*
Pub: Adams Media Corporation
Ed: Don Debelak. **Released:** June 2006. **Price:** $14. 95. **Description:** Information is offered to help entrepreneurs to develop an idea for a product or service and have other companies provide the marketing, manufacturing and staff.

41380 ■ *"Savvy Solutions" in Black Enterprise (Vol. 41, December 2010, No. 5, pp. 42)*
Pub: Earl G. Graves Publishing Co. Inc.
Ed: Tennille M. Robinson. **Description:** Individual asks for advice in launching a graphic design business, particularly grants available in a slow economy.

41381 ■ *"Savvy Solutions" in Black Enterprise (Vol. 41, October 2010, No. 3, pp. 52)*
Pub: Earl G. Graves Publishing Co. Inc.
Ed: Tennille M. Robinson. **Description:** Husband and wife team seek advice for expanding their catering business. They are also seeking funding resources.

41382 ■ *The Wall Street Journal. Complete Small Business Guidebook*
Pub: Three Rivers Press
Ed: Colleen DeBaise. **Released:** December 29, 2009. **Price:** $15.00. **Description:** The mechanics of building, running and growing a profitable business are outlined, teaching how to write a business plan, ways to finding money during lean years, how to keep stress in check, time management, investment in technology, hiring, marketing, management basics, angel investing and venture capital, as well as an exit strategy.

41383 ■ *"Wanted: Angels in the Country" in Austin Business JournalInc. (Vol. 28, July 18, 2008, No. 18, pp. 1)*
Pub: American City Business Journals
Ed: Laura Hipp. **Description:** A proposal is being pushed forward by managers of Texas' Emerging Technology Fund to create an angel investors' network. The proposal is asking that tax credits for those who invest in research and development projects be granted in order to boost the number of technology companies in the state.

41384 ■ *"Where New Economy Initiative Grants Have Gone" in Crain's Detroit Business (Vol. 25, June 1, 2009, No. 22, pp. M014)*
Pub: Crain Communications Inc. - Detroit
Description: Listing of grants totaling $20.5 million focusing on talent development, attraction and retention; innovation and entrepreneurship; and shifting to a culture that values learning, work and innovation, is presented.

41385 ■ *The Worst-Case Scenario Business Survival Guide*
Pub: John Wiley & Sons, Inc.
Released: September 28, 2009. **Price:** $17.95. **Description:** Since 1999, the Worst-Case Scenario survival handbooks have provided readers with real answers for the most extreme situations. Now, in a time of economic crisis, the series returns with a new, real-world guide to avoiding the worst business cataclysms.

VIDEOCASSETTES/ AUDIOCASSETTES

41386 ■ *ESOPS: The Ultimate Way to Finance a Company*
Chesney Communications
2302 Martin St., Ste. 125
Irvine, CA 92612
Ph: (949)263-5500
Free: 800-223-8878
Fax: (949)263-5506
Co. E-mail: videocc@aol.com
URL: http://www.videocc.com
Released: 1989. **Price:** $49.95. **Description:** A way of selling stock tax free and still controlling the company is demonstrated. **Availability:** VHS; 3/4 U.

41387 ■ *Flexing Your Creative Muscle in the Financial Marketplace*
1st Financial Training Services
1515 E. Woodfield Rd., Ste. 345
Schaumburg, IL 60173
Ph: (847)969-0900
Free: 800-442-8662
Fax: (847)969-0521
URL: http://www.1stfinancialtraining.com
Released: 1987. **Price:** $299.00. **Description:** Dr. Berry shows the diverse array of areas that a financial institution can get involved in. **Availability:** VHS; 3/4 U.

41388 ■ *Raising Capital in Turbulent Times*
Chesney Communications
2302 Martin St., Ste. 125
Irvine, CA 92612
Ph: (949)263-5500
Free: 800-223-8878
Fax: (949)263-5506
Co. E-mail: videocc@aol.com
URL: http://www.videocc.com
Released: 1989. **Price:** $49.95. **Description:** Shows that, even when the economy is looking bad, there are still places for people to get capital. **Availability:** VHS; 3/4 U.

START-UP INFORMATION

41389 ▪ *Running Your Small Business on a MAC*
Pub: Peachpit Press
Ed: Doug Hanley. **Released:** November 2007. **Price:** $29.99. **Description:** Information to effectively start and run a small business using a MAC, including setting up a network and accounting.

41390 ▪ *Working for Yourself: An Entrepreneur's Guide to the Basics*
Pub: Kogan Page, Limited
Contact: Ben Glover, Director of Marketing
Ed: Jonathan Reuvid. **Released:** September 2006. **Description:** Guide for starting a new business venture, focusing on raising financing, legal and tax issues, marketing, information technology, and site location.

REFERENCE WORKS

41391 ▪ *"Agfa: M-Press Leopard Debuts" in American Printer (Vol. 128, June 1, 2011, No. 6)*
Pub: Penton Media Inc.
Description: M-Press Leopard is a new version of the machine that offers advanced ink jet technology at a lower price point. Agfa Graphics introduced the new version that allows for new applications that require more manual handling.

41392 ▪ *The Big Switch*
Pub: W. W. Norton & Company, Inc.
Ed: Nicholas Carr. **Released:** January 19, 2009. **Price:** $16.95 paperback. **Description:** Today companies are dismantling private computer systems and tapping into services provided via the Internet. This shift is remaking the computer industry, bringing competitors such as Google to the forefront ant threatening traditional companies like Microsoft and Dell. The book weaves together history, economics, and technology to explain why computing is changing and what it means for the future.

41393 ▪ *"Buyer's Guide: Room for Improvement" in Entrepreneur (Vol. 35, October 2007, No. 10, pp. 62)*
Pub: Entrepreneur Media Inc.
Ed: Amanda C. Kooser. **Description:** Buyers guide for wireless routers is presented. Price, features and availability of the Belkin N1 Vision, Buffalo Wireless-N Nfinit Router, D-Link Xtreme Gigabit Router DIR 655, Linksys Wireless-N Gigabit Security Router, Netgear RangeMax Next Wireless-N Router and Zyxel NBG-460N are provided.

41394 ▪ *Cisco Network Design Solutions for Small-Medium Businesses*
Pub: Cisco Press
Ed: Peter Rybaczyk. **Released:** August 2004. **Price:** $55.00. **Description:** Solutions for computer networking professionals using computer networks within a small to medium-sized business. Topics cover not only core networking issues and solutions, but security, IP telephony, unified communications, customer relations management, wireless LANs, and more.

41395 ▪ *"Crouser Offers UV Coating Price Report" in American Printer (Vol. 128, June 1, 2011, No. 6)*
Pub: Penton Media Inc.
Description: Crouser and Associates will offer the 'Pricing Off-Line UV Coating' report that provides background information on all three types of protective printing coatings and price guidance. The report will also offer comparisons of four popular types of offline equipment.

41396 ▪ *"Cyberwise" in Black Enterprise (Vol. 41, December 2010, No. 5, pp. 50)*
Pub: Earl G. Graves Publishing Co. Inc.
Ed: Marica Wade Talbert. **Description:** Information is given regarding single platforms that can be used to develop applications for iPhone, Android, Blackberry, and Nokia.

41397 ▪ *"Death of the PC" in Canadian Business (Vol. 83, October 12, 2010, No. 17, pp. 44)*
Pub: Rogers Media Ltd.
Ed: Joe Castaldo. **Description:** The future of the personal computer (PC) is looking bleak as consumers are relying more on new mobile devices instead of their PC. A 'Wall Street Journal' article published in September 2010 reported that the iPad had cannibalized sales of laptops by as much as 50 percent. The emergence of tablet computers running alternative operating systems is also explained.

41398 ▪ *"The Digital Revolution is Over. Long Live the Digital Revolution!" in Business Strategy Review (Vol. 21, Spring 2010, No. 1, pp. 74)*
Pub: Wiley-Blackwell
Ed: Gianvito Lanzolla, Jamie Anderson. **Description:** Many businesses are now involved in the digital marketplace. The authors argue that the new reality of numerous companies offering overlapping products means that it is critical for managers to understand digital convergence and to observe the imperatives for remaining competitive.

41399 ▪ *"Double Duty" in Black Enterprise (Vol. 38, February 2008, No. 7, pp. 56)*
Pub: Earl G. Graves Publishing Co. Inc.
Description: Pantech Wireless is offering its new Duo cellular phone that combines multiple features of a phone with the high speed data functions of a Blackberry-style smartphone.

41400 ▪ *"Featherweight Contenders: Thin and Light, But Heavy On Features" in Inc. (Vol. 33, October 2011, No. 8, pp. 44)*
Pub: Inc. Magazine
Ed: John Brandon. **Description:** Profiles of ultraportable notebooks include Sony Z Series VPCZ212GX/B, Samsung Series 9 NP900X1B, ASUS U36SJC, and Macbook Air.

41401 ▪ *"Firm Stays In the 'Family'; After Owner's Death, Employees Buy Company" in Crain's Detroit Business (Vol. 24, January 28, 2008)*
Pub: Crain Communications Inc. - Detroit
Ed: Chad Halcom. **Description:** Sterling Office Systems Inc., distributor of photocopiers and other office machines was purchased from the owner's family after his demise. The new owners would like to hit $1.75 million in sales their first year.

41402 ▪ *"For Apple, It's Showtime Again" in Barron's (Vol. 90, August 30, 2010, No. 35, pp. 29)*
Pub: Barron's Editorial & Corporate Headquarters
Ed: Eric J. Savitz. **Description:** Speculations on what Apple Inc. will unveil at its product launch event are presented. These products include a possible new iPhone Nano, a new update to its Apple TV, and possibly a deal with the Beatles to distribute their songs over iTunes.

41403 ▪ *"Funny Business" in Canadian Business (Vol. 82, April 27, 2009, No. 7, pp. 27)*
Pub: Rogers Media
Ed: Rachel Pulfer. **Description:** Companies are advised to use humor in marketing to drive more revenue. IBM Canada, for example, commissioned Second City Communications for a marketing campaign that involved humor. While IBM Canada declined to give sales or traffic figures, firm executives rank the marketing campaign as an overall success.

41404 ▪ *"gdgt: The New Online Home for Gadget Fans" in Hispanic Business (July-August 2009, pp. 15)*
Pub: Hispanic Business
Ed: Jeremy Nisen. **Description:** Profile of the new online Website for gadget lovers. The site combines a leek interface, gadget database, and social networking-type features which highlights devices for the consumer.

41405 ▪ *Greening Your Small Business: How to Improve Your Bottom Line, Grow Your Brand, Satisfy Your Customers and Save the Planet*
Pub: Prentice Hall Press
Contact: Dame Marjorie M. Scardino, Chief Executive Officer
Ed: Jennifer Kaplan. **Released:** November 3, 2009. **Price:** $19.95. **Description:** A definitive resource for anyone who wants their small business to be cutting-edge, competitive, profitable, and eco-conscious. Stories from small business owners address every aspect of going green, from basics such as recycling waste, energy efficiency, and reducing information technology footprint, to more in-depth concerns such as green marketing and communications, green business travel, and green employee benefits.

41406 ▪ *"Guide to Carbon Footprinting" in American Printer (Vol. 128, June 1, 2011, No. 6)*
Pub: Penton Media Inc.
Description: PrintCity Alliance published its new report, 'Carbon Footprint & Energy Reduction for

Graphic Industry Value Chain.' The report aims to help improve the environmental performance of printers, converters, publishers, brand owners and their suppliers.

41407 ■ *"Handle with Care" in Entrepreneur (Vol. 35, November 2007, No. 11, pp. 24)*
Pub: Entrepreneur Media Inc.
Ed: Jacquelyn Lynn. **Description:** Preventing equipment breakdown can be done by having a regular maintenance schedule. It is also recommended that companies use quality surge protectors or uninterruptible power supplies (UPSs) for electronic equipment that can be affected by power fluctuations and lightning. Other suggestions for preventive maintenance practices are outlined.

41408 ■ *"Hewlett-Packard Mini: Ultra-Portable, and Affordable" in Hispanic Business (July-August 2009, pp. 36)*
Pub: Hispanic Business
Ed: Jeremy Nisen. **Description:** Hewlett-Packard's 1151 NR computers works a lot like a smartphone online, it can dial up fast speeds on Verizon's 3G network almost anywhere.

41409 ■ *"Hoover's Mobile, MobileSP Now Available" in Information Today (Vol. 26, February 2009, No. 2, pp. 29)*
Pub: Information Today, Inc.
Description: Hoover's Inc. introduced its Hoover's Mobile for iPhone, BlackBerry and Windows Mobile smartphones along with Hoover's MobileSP for Black-Berry and Windows Mobile. Both products allow users to access customer, prospect, and partner information; analyze competitors; prepare for meetings; and find new opportunities. In addition, MobileSP adds one-click calling to executives, GPS-enabled location searches, advanced search and list building, and a custom call queue and a 'save to contacts' capabilities.

41410 ■ *IBM on Demand Technology for the Growing Business: How to Optimize Your Computing Environment for Today and Tomorrow*
Pub: Maximum Press
Ed: Jim Hoskins. **Released:** June 2005. **Price:** $29. 95. **Description:** IBM is offering computer solutions to small companies entering the On Demand trend in business.

41411 ■ *"Insert Grade Coating Improves Tool Live" in Modern Machine Shop (Vol. 84, October 2011, No. 5, pp. 124)*
Pub: Gardner Business Media, Inc.
Contact: Richard G. Kline, President
E-mail: rkline@gardnerweb.com
Ed: Emily K. Tudor. **Description:** Profile of Sumitomo Electric Carbide's AC420K insert that is a CVD-coated carbide grade that features layers of TiCN and Al.sub.2 O.sub.3 for wear, chipping and heat resistance.

41412 ■ *"The IT Department: Understanding Geeks: A Field Guide To Your Tech Staff" in Inc. (December 2007, pp. 62-63)*
Pub: Gruner & Jahr USA Publishing
Ed: Adam Bluestein. **Description:** Guide to demystify managing the information technology staff of any small business is presented, including a list of do's and don'ts and a glossary of technical terms.

41413 ■ *"Keeping Up With the Joneses: Outfitting Your Company With Up-To-Date Technology is Vital" in Black Enterprise (November 2007)*
Pub: Earl G. Graves Publishing Co. Inc.
Ed: Sonya A. Donaldson. **Description:** Small businesses, whether home-based or not, need to keep up with new technological developments including hardware, software, and the Internet.

41414 ■ *"A Labelmaker with Style" in Inc. (Vol. 33, October 2011, No. 8, pp. 48)*
Pub: Inc. Magazine
Ed: John Brandon. **Description:** Epson's first label-maker, the LabelWorks LW-400 offers many design options and has a full QWERTY keyboard that allows users to create and print labels in various sizes.

41415 ■ *"Lights, Camera, Action: Tools for Creating Video Blogs" in Inc. (Volume 32, December 2010, No. 10, pp. 57)*
Pub: Inc. Magazine
Ed: John Brandon. **Description:** A video blog is a good way to spread company news, talk about products, and stand out among traditional company blogs. New editing software can create two- to four-minute blogs using a webcam and either Windows Live Essentials, Apple iLife 2011, Powerdirector 9 Ultra, or Adobe Visual Communicator 3.

41416 ■ *"Like Being There" in Canadian Business (Vol. 79, August 14, 2006, No. 16-17, pp. 77)*
Pub: Rogers Media
Ed: Gerry Blackwell. **Description:** Latest video conferencing facilities at the Halo Collaboration Studio, are discussed.

41417 ■ *"Look, No Hands!" in Inc. (Vol. 33, September 2011, No. 7, pp. 52)*
Pub: Inc. Magazine
Ed: John Brandon. **Description:** The Jabra Freeway, a small Bluetooth speakerphone clips to a car visor and allows the user to place, answer and ignore calls by speaking commands.

41418 ■ *Microsoft Windows Small Business Server 2003 R2 Administrator's Companion*
Pub: Microsoft Press
Ed: Charlie Russel; Sharon Crawford. **Released:** July 2006. **Price:** $80.99. **Description:** Profile of Microsoft's Small Business Server R2.

41419 ■ *Mobile Office: The Essential Small Business Guide to Office Technology*
Pub: Double Storey Books
Ed: Arthur Goldstruck, Steven Ambrose. **Released:** September 1, 2009. **Price:** $6.95. **Description:** Essential pocket guide for startup businesses and entrepreneurs which provides information to create a mobile office in order to maximize business potential while using current technologies.

41420 ■ *"The New Breed of Wi-Fi Only Tablets: No Data Plan Required" in Inc. (Vol. 33, September 2011, No. 7, pp. 52)*
Pub: Inc. Magazine
Ed: John Brandon. **Description:** New Wi-Fi only tablets are available from Samsung, Hewlett Packard, Asus and Acer. A description of offerings from these companies is included.

41421 ■ *"New Ways To Think About Data Loss: Data Loss Is Costly and Painful" in Franchising World (Vol. 42, August 2010, No. 8, pp. 21)*
Pub: International Franchise Association
Ed: Ken Colburn. **Description:** Information for maintaining data securely for franchised organizations, including smart phones, tablets, copiers, computers and more is given.

41422 ■ *"Not Your Father's Whiteboard" in Inc. (Vol. 33, November 2011, No. 9, pp. 50)*
Pub: Inc. Magazine
Ed: Adam Baer. **Description:** Sharp's new interactive whiteboard is really a 70-inch touch screen monitor with software for importing presentations from any Windows 7 computer.

41423 ■ *"Note-Taking App, Supercharged" in Inc. (Vol. 33, October 2011, No. 8, pp. 48)*
Pub: Inc. Magazine
Ed: Adam Baer. **Description:** Note Taker HD is an iPad app that lets the user text by typing with finger or stylus with various colors, fonts and sizes; Extensive Notes creates notes, records audio memos, and takes photos and videos; Evernote allows users to create notes, take snapshots, and record voice memos.

41424 ■ *"One Charger, Many Devices: the Skinny on Wireless Power Pads" in Inc. (Volume 32, December 2010, No. 10, pp. 58)*
Pub: Inc. Magazine
Ed: John Brandon. **Description:** Wireless charging pads eliminate the need for multiple cords and wall outlets. Powermat 2X, Energizer Q1, Pure Energy Solutions Wildcharge Pad, and Curacell mygrid are profiled.

41425 ■ *"Panda Security for Business 4.05" in SC Magazine (Vol. 21, July 2010, No. 7, pp. 50)*
Pub: Haymarket Media Inc.
Description: Profile of Panda Security for Business, software offering endpoint security protection for computer desktops and servers is presented.

41426 ■ *"Play By Play: These Video Products Can Add New Life to a Stagnant Website" in Black Enterprise (Vol. 41, December 2010, No. 5)*
Pub: Earl G. Graves Publishing Co. Inc.
Ed: Marcia Wade Talbert. **Description:** Web Visible, provider of online marketing products and services, cites video capability as the fastest-growing Website feature for small business advertisers. Profiles of various devices for adding video to a Website are included.

41427 ■ *"Port of Call" in Entrepreneur (Vol. 35, November 2007, No. 11, pp. 66)*
Pub: Entrepreneur Media Inc.
Ed: Amanda C. Kooser. **Description:** List of the latest USB (universal serial bus) devices for upgrading technology for a small business is presented.

41428 ■ *"Power Ranger" in Inc. (November 2007, pp. 131)*
Pub: Gruner & Jahr USA Publishing
Ed: Nitasha Tiku. **Description:** Surveyor software is designed to power down computers when not in use, in order to save energy.

41429 ■ *Power Up Your Small-Medium Business: A Guide to Enabling Network Technologies*
Pub: Cisco Press
Ed: Robyn Aber. **Released:** March 2004. **Price:** $39.95 (US), $57.95 (Canadian). **Description:** Network technologies geared to small and medium-size business, focusing on access, IP telephony, wireless technologies, security, and computer network management.

41430 ■ *Practical Tech for Your Business*
Pub: Kiplinger Books and Tapes
Ed: Michael J. Martinez. **Released:** 2002. **Description:** Advice is offered to help small business owners choose the right technology for their company. The guide tells how to get started, network via the Internet, create an office network, use database software, and conduct business using mobile technology.

41431 ■ *"Presidential Address: Innovation in Retrospect and Prospect" in Canadian Journal of Electronics (Vol. 43, November 2010, No. 4)*
Pub: Journal of the Canadian Economics Association
Ed: James A. Brander. **Description:** Has innovation slowed in recent decades? While there has been progress in information and communications technology, the recent record of innovation in agriculture, energy, transportation and healthcare sectors is cause for concern.

41432 ■ *Pro Windows Small Business Server 2003*
Pub: Apress L.P.
Ed: Tony Campbell. **Released:** July 2006. **Price:** $39.99. **Description:** Profile of Microsoft's Windows Small Business Server, designed for companies with 50 or fewer employees.

41433 ■ *"Put a Projector in Your Pocket" in Inc. (Vol. 31, January-February 2009, No. 1, pp. 42)*
Pub: Mansueto Ventures LLC
Description: PowerPoint presentations can be given using the Optoma Pico Pocket Projector. The device can be connected to laptops, cell phones, digital cameras, and iPods.

41434 ■ *"Putting the App in Apple" in Inc. (Vol. 30, November 2008, No. 11, pp.)*
Pub: Mansueto Ventures LLC
Ed: Nitasha Tiku. **Description:** Aftermarket companies are scrambling to develop games and widgets for Apple's iPhone. Apple launched a kit for develop-

ers interested in creating iPhone-specific software along with the App Store, and an iTunes spinoff. Profiles of various software programs that may be used on the iPhone are given.

41435 ■ ***"Quickoffice's MobileFiles Pro App Enables Excel Editing On-the-Go" in Information Today (Vol. 26, February 2009, No. 2, pp. 31)***
Pub: Information Today, Inc.
Description: Quickoffice Inc. introduced MobileFiles Pro, which features editable Microsoft Office functionality for the iPone and iPod touch. The application allows users to edit and save Microsoft Excel files in .xls format, transfer files to and from PC and Mac desktops via Wi-Fi, and access and synchronize with Apple MobileMe accounts.

41436 ■ ***Reading Financial Reports for Dummies***
Pub: John Wiley and Sons, Inc.
Ed: Lita Epstein. **Released:** January 2009. **Price:** $21.99. **Description:** This second edition contains more new and updated information, including new information on the separate accounting and financial reporting standards for private/small businesses versus public/large businesses; updated information reflecting 2007 laws on international financial reporting standards; new content to match SEC and other governmental regulatory changes over the last three years; new information about how the analyst-corporate connection has changed the playing field; the impact of corporate communications and new technologies; new examples that reflect the current trends; and updated Websites and resources.

41437 ■ ***"Remote Control: Working From Wherever" in Inc. (February 2008, pp. 46-47)***
Pub: Gruner & Jahr USA Publishing
Ed: Ryan Underwood. **Description:** New technology allows workers to perform tasks from anywhere via the Internet. Profiles of products to help connect to your office from afar include, LogMein Pro, a Web-based service that allowsaccess to a computer from anywhere; Xdrive, an online service that allows users to store and swap files; Basecamp, a Web-based tools that works like a secure version of MySpace; MojoPac Freedom, is software that allows users to copy their computer's desktop to a removable hard drive and plug into any PC; WatchGuard Firebox X Core e-Series UTM Bundle, hardware that blocks hackers and viruses while allowing employees to work remotely; TightVNC, a free open-source software that lets you control another computer via the Internet.

41438 ■ ***"RIM Opts to Be Little Less Open" in Canadian Business (Vol. 83, October 12, 2010, No. 17, pp. 13)***
Pub: Rogers Media Ltd.
Ed: Joe Castaldo. **Description:** RIM is planning to stop releasing quarterly subscriber updates. However, some analysts are skeptical about the change due to the previous drop in company subscribers. The company also decided to stop reporting the average selling price of the BlackBerry, which analysts have also scrutinized.

41439 ■ ***"Rough and Ready: Putting Rugged Phones to the Test" in Inc. (Vol. 33, November 2011, No. 9, pp. 45)***
Pub: Inc. Magazine
Ed: John Brandon. **Description:** Smartphones were roughed up in order to discover their durability. Tests involved the Casio G'Zone Commando, the Sonim XP3300 Force, Motorola Titaniu, and the Samsung Convoy 2.

41440 ■ ***Running Your Small Business on a Mac***
Pub: Pearson Technology Group Canada
Ed: Doug Hanley. **Released:** November 2006. **Price:** $39.99. **Description:** Tips for using a Mac computer for small business is presented. The book offers shortcuts to iWork and email.

41441 ■ ***"Samsung's Metamorphosis" in Austin Business Journal (Vol. 31, May 20, 2011, No. 11, pp. 1)***
Pub: American City Business Journals Inc.
Ed: Christopher Calnan. **Description:** Samsung Austin Semiconductor LP, a developer of semiconductors for smartphones and tablet computers, plans to diversify its offerings to include niche products: flash memory devices and microprocessing devices. In light of this strategy, Samsung Austin will be hiring 300 engineers as part of a $3.6 billion expansion of its plant.

41442 ■ ***The Small Business Owner's Manual: Everything You Need to Know to Start Up and Run Your Business***
Pub: Career Press, Incorporated
Ed: Joe Kennedy. **Released:** June 2005. **Price:** $19.99 (US), $26.95 (Canadian). **Description:** Comprehensive guide for starting a small business, focusing on twelve ways to obtain financing, business plans, selling and advertising products and services, hiring and firing employees, setting up a Web site, business law, accounting issues, insurance, equipment, computers, banks, financing, customer credit and collection, leasing, and more.

41443 ■ ***"Social Networks in the Workplace" in Strategy & Leadership (Vol. 38, July-August 2010, No. 4, pp. 50-53)***
Pub: Emerald Inc.
Ed: Daniel Burrus. **Description:** The opinions of futurist Daniel Burrus on a novel trend called 'Business 2.0', which involves the use of social networking applications as business tools, are presented. His suggestion that personal social networking technology can be used by businesses to improve collaboration, problem solving, and leadership communications to achieve continuous value innovation is discussed.

41444 ■ ***"A Souped-Up Digital Pen" in Inc. (Vol. 33, November 2011, No. 9, pp. 50)***
Pub: Inc. Magazine
Ed: Adam Baer. **Description:** Wacom's Inkling is a digital pen designed to record drawings and can save layers of sketches and add or remove them at a later date. Animation of these drawings can also be played. Files can be saved on the receiver which has a 2GB memory and they can then be transferred to a computer.

41445 ■ ***"Stay in Touch, Wherever You Roam: Smartphones for Overseas Travel" in Inc. (Volume 32, December 2010, No. 10, pp. 60)***
Pub: Inc. Magazine
Description: International cell phones services are profiled, including HTC Aria, Nokia E73 Mode, Samsung Captivate, and Blackberry Bold 9650.

41446 ■ ***"Strictly Business" in Black Enterprise (Vol. 38, October 2007, No. 3, pp. 62)***
Pub: Earl G. Graves Publishing Co. Inc.
Description: Profile of the HP iPAQ hw6925 smartphone suited to small business use. The phone offers mobile word processing and messaging features great for the tech-savvy business traveler.

41447 ■ ***"Suited for Success" in Retail Merchandiser (Vol. 51, July-August 2011, No. 4, pp. 6)***
Pub: Phoenix Media Corporation
Description: MyBestFit is a size-matching body scanner that helps consumers find the perfect size clothing for themselves, giving brick and mortar retailers an edge on ecommerce competitors.

41448 ■ ***Tactical Entrepreneur: The Entrepreneur's Game Plan***
Pub: Sortis Publishing
Ed: Brian J. Hazelgren. **Released:** September 2005. **Price:** $14.95. **Description:** A smart, realistic business plan is essential for any successful entrepreneur. Besides offering products or services, small business owners must possess skills in accounting, planning, human resources management, marketing, and information technology.

41449 ■ ***"Tap the iPad and Mobile Internet Device Market" in Franchising World (Vol. 42, September 2010, No. 9, pp. 43)***
Pub: International Franchise Association
Ed: John Thomson. **Description:** The iPad and other mobile Internet devices will help franchise owners interact with customers. It will be a good marketing tool for these businesses.

41450 ■ ***"Technology Drivers to Boost Your Bottom Line" in Franchising World (Vol. 42, August 2010, No. 8, pp. 15)***
Pub: International Franchise Association
Ed: Dan Dugal. **Description:** Technological capabilities are expanding quickly and smart franchises should stay updated on all the new developments, including smart phones, global positioning systems, and social media networks.

41451 ■ ***"Thinking Strategically About Technology" in Franchising World (Vol. 42, August 2010, No. 8, pp. 9)***
Pub: International Franchise Association
Ed: Bruce Franson. **Description:** Nearly 25 percent of companies waste money from their technology budget. Most of the budget is spent on non-strategic software. Ways to spend money on technology for any franchise are examined.

41452 ■ ***"Tired of PowerPoint? Try This Instead" in Harvard Business Review (Vol. 88, September 2010, No. 9, pp. 30)***
Pub: Harvard Business School Publishing
Ed: Daniel McGinn, Stephanie Crowley. **Description:** Usefulness of graphic recording, also known as storyboarding or visual facilitation, during client meetings is illustrated.

41453 ■ ***"The Total Cost of Ignorance: Avoiding Top Tech Mistakes" in Black Enterprise (Vol. 38, October 2007, No. 3, pp. 64)***
Pub: Earl G. Graves Publishing Co. Inc.
Ed: Alwin A.D. Jones. **Description:** Cost of data loss for any small business can be devastating; lack of security is another mistake companies make when it comes to technology.

41454 ■ ***"Touch and Go" in Black Enterprise (Vol. 38, January 2008, No. 6, pp. 46)***
Pub: Earl G. Graves Publishing Co. Inc.
Ed: Anthony Calypso. **Description:** Profile of HTC Touch Smartphone, which operates on the Windows Mobile 6 Pro platform. The phone is about the size of a credit card and weighs less than four ounces and can connect to Bluetooth, GSM/GPRS/EDGE/Wi-Fi.

41455 ■ ***The Wall Street Journal. Complete Small Business Guidebook***
Pub: Three Rivers Press
Ed: Colleen DeBaise. **Released:** December 29, 2009. **Price:** $15.00. **Description:** The mechanics of building, running and growing a profitable business are outlined, teaching how to write a business plan, ways to finding money during lean years, how to keep stress in check, time management, investment in technology, hiring, marketing, management basics, angel investing and venture capital, as well as an exit strategy.

41456 ■ ***"Weathering the BlackBerry Storm" in Hispanic Business (January-February 2009, pp. 52)***
Pub: Hispanic Business
Ed: Jeremy Nisen. **Description:** Profile of BlackBerry Storm, the smartphone from Research in Motion.

41457 ■ ***"What Makes for an Effective, Production-Oriented VMC?" in Modern Machine Shop (Vol. 84, November 2011, No. 6, pp. 24)***
Pub: Gardner Business Media, Inc.
Contact: Richard G. Kline, President
E-mail: rkline@gardnerweb.com
Ed: Derek Korn. **Description:** When a machine shop's existing VMC only offers a modest spindle performance and slow, non-cutting functions, the latest VMC technology for high-volume production that minimizes cycle times and maximizes competitive-

ness could be helpful. Makino's new Production Standard (PS) series of VMCs provides not only a number of standard features to shrink cycle times, but also design elements that can effectively support a shops production elements are defined.

41458 ■ *"Wireless: Full Service" in Entrepreneur (Vol. 35, October 2007, No. 10, pp. 60)*
Pub: Entrepreneur Media Inc.
Ed: Amanda C. Kooser. **Description:** Palm Foleo, the $599 smart phone enables users to access and compose email, browse the Internet, view documents and play Powerpoint files. It weighs 2.5 pounds and has a 10-inch screen. Other features, such as built-in WiFi are described.

TRADE PERIODICALS

41459 ■ *PC WORLD: The Magazine of Business Computing*
Pub: 101 Communications
Contact: Neil Vitale, President
URL(s): www.pcworld.com. **Ed:** Edward Albro. **Released:** Quarterly **Price:** $19.97, Individuals; $29.97, Two years.

41460 ■ *Software: Practice and Experience*
Pub: John Wiley & Sons Inc.
Contact: Stephen M. Smith, President
URL(s): onlinelibrary.wiley.com/journal/10.1002/(-ISSN)1097-024X. **Ed:** Prof. Andy J. Wellings, Prof. R.N. Horspool. **Released:** 12/yr. **Price:** $4988, Institutions print; $4988, Institutions, other countries print; €3219, Institutions, other countries print; £2546, Institutions print; $4988, Institutions, Canada and Mexico print.

VIDEOCASSETTES/ AUDIOCASSETTES

41461 ■ *Business World's Guide to Computers*
MPI Home Video
16101 S. 108th Ave.
Orland Park, IL 60467
Ph: (708)460-0555
Free: 800-323-0442
Fax: (708)873-3177
URL: http://www.mpihomevideo.com
Released: 1990. **Price:** $19.98. **Description:** Constant change in the computer industry makes choosing the right computer for your long-term business needs difficult. Top business leaders provide reliable information on what may be the most important purchasing decision a company can make. **Availability:** VHS.

CONSULTANTS

41462 ■ AA Antivirus
1608 W Campbell Ave., Ste. 370
Campbell, CA 95008
Ph: (408)374-8000
Free: 800-478-1828
Fax: (408)374-2045
Co. E-mail: sales@aaantivirus.com
URL: http://www.aaantivirus.com
Contact: Roy Miehe, Chief Executive Officer
E-mail: roy@aaantivirus.com
Scope: Offers a range of local area networking and wide area networking solutions to small and medium-sized businesses. Assists business owners and administrators in planning, purchasing and installing networks. **Founded:** 1994. **Telecommunication Services:** info@aaantivirus.com; tech@aaantivirus.com. **Special Services:** Panda Security SaaS; Web Root Security SaaS; Kaspersky Anti virus; Trend Micro Anti virus; Mal Ware Bytes; Norman Anti virus; Red Condor Anti Spam SaaS; Borderware; Ironport; CyberRoam; Bloxx.

41463 ■ Warren Acuff
4133 Ponca Rd.
Omaha, NE 68112-1123
Ph: (402)451-2805
Fax: (402)451-8303
Scope: Specialists in all phases of computers: micros, minis, and mainframes.

41464 ■ Advanced Network Consulting (ANC)
12627 Gabbett Dr.
La Mirada, CA 90638
Ph: (562)903-3992
Free: 877-262-0999
Fax: (562)204-0655
Co. E-mail: info@ancsite.com
URL: http://www.ancsite.com
Contact: Cindy Staples, Controller
E-mail: cindy@ancsite.com
Scope: Provider of LAN consulting as well as hardware and software services. Offers server-based solutions that include: Backup, antivirus LAN/WAN design, implementation and support, system administration and hardware warrantee contracts, and office automation for small businesses. **Founded:** 2002.

41465 ■ Agility Computer Network Services L.L.C.
1332 N Halsted St., Ste. 405
Chicago, IL 60642
Ph: (312)587-9894
Free: 877-244-5489
Fax: (312)587-9948
Co. E-mail: support@agilitynetworks.com
URL: http://www.agilitynetworks.com
Contact: Chandler Denny, President
E-mail: cdenny@agilitynetworks.com
Scope: Provider of networking and other related computer consulting services. **Founded:** 1994. **Telecommunication Services:** info@agilitynetworks.com.

41466 ■ Alexander Associates
230 Cotuit Rd.
Marstons Mills, MA 02648
Ph: (508)428-3000
Fax: (508)428-0935
Contact: John Redfern, Manager
E-mail: jrredfern@alexsoft.com
Scope: Provider of computer technology expertise for industrial operations worldwide. Offers outsourced development and application support for a broad spectrum of commercial and not-for-profit entities in Insurance, Health-care, Bio-tech, Communications, Government. **Founded:** 1983.

41467 ■ American Topical Association, Americana Unit (AU)
17 Peckham Rd.
Poughkeepsie, NY 12603
Ph: (845)452-2126
Fax: (781)459-0392
Co. E-mail: info@americanaunit.org
URL: http://www.americanaunit.org
Contact: Dennis M. Dengel, Treasurer
Description: A study unit of the American Topical Association and the American Philatelic Society. Works to collect stamps commemorating or picturing Americans or Americana; to research and publish philatelic information concerning the Americana topic; to encourage and support topical stamp exhibitions pertaining to Americana; to share this knowledge and experience with fellow collectors. **Scope:** Philatelic club devoted to the collecting of stamps, covers and other philatelic material related to the topic of Americana. **Founded:** 1951. **Publications:** *Americana Philatelic News* (Quarterly); *Index to Americana Philatelic News, 1970-85.* **Educational Activities:** National Topical Stamp Show (Annual). **Awards:** Merit Award (Annual).

41468 ■ Analytical Solutions
20426 Blythe St.
Winnetka, CA 91306-2238
Ph: (818)998-4774
Free: 800-859-4774
Fax: (818)230-9023
Co. E-mail: sales.as@earthlink.net
Contact: Lydia I. Kasparian, Manager
Scope: Enterprise document management and retention system consulting. Data processing system consultant offering local area network expertise and providing feasibility studies, user surveys and system evaluations, systems analyses and design, system development and implementation, project management, disaster planning, corporate strategic planning and sales and marketing group optimization. Serves private industries as well as government agencies. **Founded:** 1984.

41469 ■ Bell Techlogics
8888 Keystone Crossing, Ste. 1700
Indianapolis, IN 46240
Ph: (317)704-6000
Free: 800-999-9813
Fax: (317)575-9401
Co. E-mail: bellservice@belltechlogix.com
URL: http://www.belltechlogix.com
Contact: Clinton Coleman, Chief Executive Officer
Scope: Provider of integrated technology and service solutions for organizations throughout the United States. Provides designing, implementing, and managing technology solutions that result in decreased costs, increased customer retention, improved service levels and operational efficiencies for small, mid-sized and Fortune 500 companies. Installs, configures, maintains and supports the local and wide area network technologies. Offers connectivity services that include secure Internet and Intranet communication solutions, virus scanning, and firewall protections. **Founded:** 1978. **Seminars:** Virtualization and Disaster Recovery, 2008.

41470 ■ Marion R. Boslaugh
44148 Bristow Cir.
Ashburn, VA 20147
Ph: (703)729-2526
Contact: Bruce R. Boslaugh, Owner
Scope: Consultant provides advice on computer systems engineering and integration and software engineering.

41471 ■ Branchline Income Tax Services—Branchline Services
5901 Westminster Blvd.
Westminster, CA 92683-3545
Ph: (714)892-4807
Fax: (714)892-8153
Contact: Gary S. Branch, President
Scope: Offers business financial system design and programming. Specializes in complete system design from concept to final delivery. Provides knowledge of IBM mainframes and PC. Strategic planning utilizes CASE methodology and system development LIFR cycle. Additional specialization in networking and telecommunications and in database system design for business application with very strong user interface. Industries served: aerospace, finance, retail, nonprofit, and automotive. **Founded:** 1976.

41472 ■ W.A. Buie Consulting Services
2355 Sumter Dr.
Garner, NC 27529-0857
Ph: (919)550-3747
Co. E-mail: adrian@hakpenguin.com
Contact: William Adrian Buie, Jr., Owner
E-mail: abuie@pobox.com
Scope: An Internet service provider for individuals, organizations, or companies. Services include Web site rental, Web page creation, URL submission to search engines and domain name set up.

41473 ■ Business Logic Inc.
220 E 23rd St.
New York, NY 10010-4646
Ph: (212)505-9323
Fax: (212)725-4808
Co. E-mail: blogic@blogicnyc.com
URL: http://www.blogicnyc.com
Contact: Howard P. Zien, President
Scope: Specializes in information systems and technology. Provides a high level of information technology support and development services to companies and governmental organizations of all sizes. Specializes in understanding the business and information needs of organizations and in finding, designing, developing and implementing solutions to these needs. A large percentage of current projects involve the integration of oracle and sql server databases with web sites, intranet sites, and client server applications. Business Logic is also involved

in data warehousing and data mining applications. **Founded:** 1980. **Telecommunication Services:** info@blogicnyc.com.

41474 ■ Champion Networks L.L.C.—Downtime Inc.
1081 Mere Point Rd.
Brunswick, ME 04011
Ph: (207)725-8903
Contact: Edward Hunter, Manager
E-mail: ehunter@downtime.com
Scope: Firm specializes in network integration, total wide area network solutions, and network services. **Founded:** 1990.

41475 ■ Cohn Consulting Corp. (CCC)
3605 Sandy Plains Rd., Ste. 240-416
Marietta, GA 30066
Ph: (770)321-5532
Fax: (770)321-4497
Co. E-mail: info@cohnconsultingcorp.com
URL: http://www.cohnconsultingcorp.com
Contact: Daniel S. Cohn, President
E-mail: dan@cohnconsultingcorp.com
Scope: Provider of a wide range of PC and LAN services. Specialized services includes Network administration, Backup and Disaster Recovery, Thin client computing, Internet services, Centralized fax solutions, Mainframe and midrange connectivity and Workgroup collaboration. **Founded:** 1993. **Publications:** "Total Network Solution Gets Title Insurance Agency Off To A Fast Start"; "Thin Client Solution Modernizes Psychological Practice". **Special Services:** Cohn Care™.

41476 ■ Colonial Heritage Consultants Ltd.
11202 Trailside Ct.
San Diego, CA 92127-2005
Ph: (858)254-2425
Fax: (858)451-0338
Contact: William N. Birkhoff, President
E-mail: bill@colonialheritage.com
Scope: Active in all phases of data processing consulting including scoping company requirements, organizing internal data processing organizations, education, equipment selection, and software consulting/creation. Primary industries of applications in real estate, financial planning, medical, accounting, and legal fields. Serves private industries as well as government agencies. All Pac/SBT Dealer. **Founded:** 1978. **Seminars:** Telemagic Users Group; SBT Users Group; Novell Users Group.

41477 ■ Computer Connections Inc.
1241-2 E Dixon Blvd., Ste. 2
Shelby, NC 28150
Ph: (704)482-0057
Fax: (704)482-0950
Co. E-mail: ccsales@painlesspc.net
URL: http://www.painlesspc.net
Contact: Lynne Rockwell, Sales Manager
E-mail: lynner@carolina.rr.com
Scope: Specializes in client or server networking environments. Offers service, upgrades, and repairs most IBM compatible computers. Networking services include: network design, implementation, and administration of novell and windows NT networks. **Founded:** 1996.

41478 ■ Crawley & Associates Inc.
121 Lincoln Ave.
Fair Lawn, NJ 07410
Ph: (973)636-7350
Fax: (973)636-7360
Co. E-mail: sales@crawleyinc.com
URL: http://www.crawleyinc.com
Contact: Chris Apsey, Engineer
Scope: Provider of education technology management services for both public and private schools located in New Jersey; provides experienced guidance and direction. Services include: Design, budget development, hardware and software selection, implementation, project management and system monitoring. **Founded:** 1995. **Publications:** "Give Your Servers All the Attention," Oct, 2007; "The Importance of aTechnology Audit," Jun, 2007; "Eliminate Extended Warranties on YourWorkstation Purchases," May, 2007; "Beware of Hidden Cost When PurchasingWorkstations," Apr, 2007; "Top Five Overlooked Budget Items," Feb, 2007; "Technology Budgets: When to Say No," Jan, 2007. **Seminars:** Reducing Technology Costs. **Telecommunication Services:** info@crawleyinc.com.

41479 ■ Creative Associates International Inc.
5301 Wisconsin Ave. NW, Ste. 700
Washington, DC 20015-2043
Ph: (202)966-5804
Fax: (202)363-4771
Co. E-mail: creative@creativeworldwide.com
URL: http://www.caii-dc.com
Contact: M. Charito Kruvant, President
E-mail: charitok@caii.com
Scope: Supports public, private and non-governmental institutions that are makers and managers of change and transition. It builds the individual and organizational means to join forces for progress through education, information and communication. **Founded:** 1977. **Publications:** "Tool 4 - Textbook Analysis of Equity". **Seminars:** The Principles of the Abrahamic Faiths: Traditions that Advance Education; Creative Edge Literacy Network: A Guide to integrated Post-Literacy Methodology.

41480 ■ Data Concepts
984 S Reading Rd.
Bloomfield Hills, MI 48304-2044
Ph: (248)258-5964
Fax: (248)258-5866
Co. E-mail: sales@rdataconcepts.com
URL: http://www.rdataconcepts.com
Contact: Robert Graff, Owner
Scope: Data processing consultant offering expertise in the following areas: office automation, feasibility and needs assessment, system design, hardware and software selection, custom program development, database design, networks, spreadsheet templates, computer modeling, sales, training, computer service and upgrades, accounting software and installation of hardware and software. Focus is to offer many professional computer services to small and medium-sized businesses of all types, and government agencies for short and long-term projects. Maintains a network of specialists to assist in multidimensional projects. **Founded:** 1983.

41481 ■ Del Technology Inc.
7407 E Via Estrella Ave., Ste. 10
Scottsdale, AZ 85258-1006
Ph: (480)483-7588
Fax: (480)483-7533
Co. E-mail: ddonahoe@qwest.net
Contact: Georgine Donahoe, President
Scope: Provides services including management consulting, information technology and micro business. Focuses on organizational assessment, business process reengineering, quality assurance program development, hardware software evaluation and acquisition, applications software development and systems integration. **Founded:** 1990. **Publications:** "Standards for Information Systems Development and Project Administration". **Seminars:** Organization for Future Technology; Business Reengineering; Managing Successful Projects; Planning and Implementing the Information Systems Architecture; Successfully Managing the Information Resource.

41482 ■ Dimension Data
2350 Corporate Park Dr., Ste. 425
Herndon, VA 20171
Ph: (571)203-4000
Fax: (571)203-4001
URL: http://www.dimensiondata.com
Contact: Brett Dawson, Chief Executive Officer
Scope: A global technology company. Provides solutions and services that optimize and manage the performance of IT infrastructure to enable businesses to build competitive advantage. **Founded:** 1983.

41483 ■ DLM Consultants Inc.
566 Croyden Ct., Ste. 200
Sunnyvale, CA 94087-3322
Ph: (408)736-5650
Fax: (408)736-5650
Contact: Richard S. Kent, President
E-mail: dlm@consultant.com
Scope: A full service computer consulting firm, offers Project Management, Software Development, Database design and Training on many software packages. **Founded:** 1976. **Seminars:** How to Be a Computer Consultant; Introduction to Small Business Systems; Use of Spreadsheets in a Small Business Environment; Database Applications in a Small Business Environment.

41484 ■ Thomas R. Egan Consulting Inc.
1012 Ronda Ln.
Birmingham, AL 35214
Ph: (205)796-9541
Fax: (205)744-9404
Contact: Thomas R. Egan, President
E-mail: tegan@treci.com
Scope: Provides consultation and design services, installation, and service/maintenance for several network platforms. **Founded:** 1994.

41485 ■ Electronic Solutions Co.
1414 Broadwood Ave.
Cinnaminson, NJ 08077
Ph: (856)786-3700
Fax: (856)735-0416
Co. E-mail: info.homeowner@electronicsolutionsco.com
URL: http://www.electronicsolutionsco.com
Contact: Steven M. Rosenberry, Senior Partner
E-mail: smrosenberry@electronicsolutionsco.com
Scope: Provider of services in home automation, home management systems, process control and data communications. **Founded:** 1994. **Seminars:** Lighting Control System Design; Advanced Custom System Controllers; Technical Aspects of Whole House Systems; Communication Protocols: The Good, The Bad and The Ugly. **Special Services:** ESC Home Management System.

41486 ■ EM Microelectronic-US Inc.
5475 Mark Dabling Blvd., Ste. 200
Colorado Springs, CO 80918-3848
Ph: (719)593-2883
Fax: (719)598-8106
Contact: James Lauffenburger, President
Scope: Specializes in the design of low-power, low-voltage, mixed-signal ASICs and ASSPs with non-volatile memory, as well as optoelectronics where PDICs and XOEICs are used in CD and DVD drive applications. **Founded:** 1990.

41487 ■ ePartners Inc.
12110 Sunset Hills Rd., Ste. 150
Reston, VA 20190
Ph: (703)817-1400
Free: 888-883-9797
Fax: (703)488-6799
Co. E-mail: info@epartnersolutions.com
URL: http://www.epartnersolutions.com
Contact: Michael McCarthy, Chief Executive Officer
E-mail: mmccarthy@epartnersolutions.com
Scope: A total solutions provider that designs, develops, implements, integrates, hosts, manages and supports comprehensive e-Business solutions. **Founded:** 1992.

41488 ■ William J. Fejes
7 Renda St.
New Fairfield, CT 06812
Ph: (203)746-6161
Fax: (212)467-0457
Scope: Company specializes in information and records management, retention scheduling, information systems, integrating imaging technology with optical disk, space planning, off-site record storage, and disaster planning systems.

41489 ■ Frankel and Topche P.C.
1700 Galloping Hill Rd.
Kenilworth, NJ 07033
Ph: (908)298-7700

Fax: (908)298-7701
Co. E-mail: info@frankelandtopche.com
URL: http://www.frankelandtopche.com
Contact: Mark J. Tikkanen, Director
E-mail: mtikkanen@frankelandtopche.com
Scope: Offers financial consulting for closely held businesses. Assists in mergers and acquisitions, tax planning, strategic business planning, family succession planning, accounting, auditing, and obtaining financing. The firm serves small businesses in the service, retail, wholesale, and manufacturing industries. Specializes in real estate, lumber and building materials, and service businesses. **Founded:** 1990. **Seminars:** Annual Tax Seminar.

41490 ■ Frazier Consulting Service Inc.
207 N Main St.
Leland, MS 38756
Ph: (662)686-7324
Fax: (662)686-4446
Co. E-mail: alf@tecinfo.com
Contact: A. Lee Frazier, President
E-mail: alf@tecinfo.com
Scope: Agricultural consultants interested in investigation of special agricultural problems-crop damage, chemical drift, products liability, disease, insects, weeds and other problems. Industries served: insurance companies, farmers, attorneys, and chemical companies. **Founded:** 1978.

41491 ■ Gimbel Associates
71 Longview Dr.
Churchville, PA 18966-1636
Ph: (215)357-8830
Fax: (781)723-8941
Co. E-mail: joe@gimbelassociates.com
URL: http://www.gimbelassociates.com
Contact: Roger Gimbel, President
Scope: Help organizations create, utilize, analyze and manage information. Specializes in helping small businesses select and install microcomputers and integrate microcomputer based applications into their organizations. **Founded:** 1984. **Seminars:** How to Become a Successful Consultant in Your Own Field; How to Computerize Your Small Business. **Special Services:** Fringe98; Fringe for DOS; EPAY2000.

41492 ■ Glades Crop Care Inc.
949 Turner Quay
Jupiter, FL 33458
Ph: (561)746-3740
Free: 800-330-1103
Fax: (561)746-3775
Co. E-mail: cmellinger@gladescropcare.com
URL: http://www.gladescropcare.com
Contact: Madeline Mellinger, President
Scope: Offers customized crop health management programs, development and implementation of vegetable IPM programs, professional custom field research of age chemicals and biotechnology products for residue, efficacy performance studies and breeding. Crops: vegetables, citrus, sugarcane, turf, rice and ornaments. Food safety consultation and certified 3rd party audits. **Founded:** 1972. **Publications:** "IPM Adoption Evaluated: A Strong Foundation for a Safe, Profitable Crop"; "Ring spot Damage to Florida Citrus Fruit Caused by Thrips Feeling Injury"; "Aspects of Biologically Based Pest Management in Commercial Pepper Production"; "Potential Use of Beauveria bassiana for Biological Control of Thrips in Peppers"; "Measuring Integrated Pest Management Adoption in South Florida Vegetable Crops," 1998. **Seminars:** Getting the Most for Your Money: An Effective Weed Control Program.

41493 ■ GlobalNET Corp.
2616 South Loop W
Houston, TX 77054-2662
Ph: (832)778-9591
Fax: (210)579-1192
Co. E-mail: sales@gbne.net
Contact: David F. Levy, President
Scope: Specializes in the installation, configuration, and technical support of local (LAN) and wide (WAN) Area Networks. Installs Multi-User and Multi-Platform systems (i.e. DOS, OS2, Windows NT, UNIX, NextStep, and Macintosh) which perform Accounting, client/server Database, Word Processing, Spreadsheet, and Computer Aide Design (CAD) tasks in a variety of industries. **Founded:** 1987. **Telecommunication Services:** customercare@gbne.net.

41494 ■ GSC Associates Inc.—GSC Assoc
2727 Xanthia Ct.
Denver, CO 80238-2611
Ph: (303)388-6355
Co. E-mail: info@gscassociates.com
URL: http://www.gscassociates.com
Contact: Rikk Carey, President
Scope: Computer design consultants and systems integrators. Specializes in innovation in systems engineering and in research and development. **Founded:** 1981. **Publications:** "Collaboration in Regional Civilian and Military Transportation Planning," Jun, 2007; "A Measurement and Monitoring System for Tracking and Visualizing Collaboration Metrics in Real-time and for Later Analysis," Jun, 2005; "UML and Human Performance Modeling," Mar, 2005; "Graphics Networking and Distributed Computing"; "X3H3 standards report"; "Introduction to the computer graphics reference model". **Seminars:** VRML Conformance Testing Workshop, Aug, 1996. **Special Services:** GraphPorter; MetaPICT; T-CALS; FAX2PICT; PICT2FAX.

41495 ■ High-Tech Enterprise Solutions Inc.
13 E A St.
Brunswick, MD 21716-1406
Ph: (301)834-5778
Fax: (301)834-5587
Co. E-mail: info@high-techus.com
URL: http://www.high-techus.com
Contact: Les Deneen, Owner
E-mail: ldeneen@high-techus.com
Scope: A data processing consultancy specializing in total computer systems integration and support. Provides the technical support that you expect to handle repairs, installations and other issues after the sale. **Founded:** 1985. **Seminars:** MS Navision Training; Quick Books Training; Peachtree Training; Business Works Training; Microsoft Office Training. **Special Services:** QuickBooks.

41496 ■ IMC
399 Sackett Point Rd.
North Haven, CT 06473
Ph: (203)248-5324
Free: 800-840-9989
Fax: (203)248-5384
Co. E-mail: info@imcinternet.net
URL: http://www.imcinternet.net
Contact: Robert J. Caldarella, President
E-mail: bob@imcinternet.net
Scope: Specializes in the development of total office solutions for business which includes office networking, client/server technologies, Internet access and computer sales. **Founded:** 1994.

41497 ■ Integrated Security Technologies (IST)
520 Herndon Pky., Ste. C
Herndon, VA 20170
Ph: (703)464-4766
Free: 888-291-0120
Fax: (703)464-5836
Co. E-mail: info@ntllc.com
URL: http://www.ntllc.com
Contact: Jon A. Langhorst, President
Scope: Focuses on the application of information technologies to enhance the effectiveness of the business environment including collecting, organizing and storing information; designing, building and maintaining the appropriate architecture to make information available. to assess, design and implement solutions for security and Information Technology challenges. **Publications:** "American University Wins High Marks for New Security System"; "All American Upgrade"; "IST named 77th on SDM's Top 100 System Integrators".

41498 ■ Interface Computer Associates (ICA)
7230 Native Dancer Dr.
Reno, NV 89502-9772
Ph: (775)857-8777
Fax: (775)857-2567
Co. E-mail: icanv@icanv.com
URL: http://www.icanv.com
Contact: Prince Hawkins, President
Scope: Data processing consultants offering complete system design, implementation and training for end-users, particularly in small businesses. Operates on the concept of providing systems to meet individual needs and then actually interfacing new computer users and their systems together with the goal of the computer doing business the way the client does business, not the other way around. **Founded:** 1980. **Seminars:** Individualized Workshops.

41499 ■ KCS Computer Technology Inc.
9524 Franklin Ave.
Franklin Park, IL 60131
Ph: (847)288-9820
Fax: (847)288-9822
Co. E-mail: sales@kcstech.com
URL: http://www.kcstech.com
Contact: Kenneth Kollar, President
Scope: Offers a full line of business-class computers, servers, workstations, laptops, printers, and peripherals. Offers hardware, software, installation, configuration, maintenance and management. Specializes in software and computer reselling, Windows NT, Lantastic and Novell network installation and maintenance, custom programming, network communications fax/modem server installation and maintenance, Internet setup and training, custom html programming services, network and phone cabling, computer leasing, data conversion and data recovery and maintenance contracts. **Founded:** 1993.

41500 ■ KeyLAN Consulting Inc.
2399 Lenida Dr.
North Gower, ON, Canada K0A 2T0
Ph: (613)489-2336
Fax: (613)489-4190
Co. E-mail: keylan@keylan.ca
URL: http://www.keylan.ca
Contact: James MacNabb, Principal
Scope: Specializes in all facets of local area networking, purchasing, installation, administration, training, automation, disaster planning, high security databases and security consulting. **Founded:** 1991.

41501 ■ LAN Solutions •
449 Hillway Dr.
Emerald Hills, CA 94062-3313
Ph: (650)261-1300
Fax: (650)361-8012
Co. E-mail: info@lansol.com
URL: http://www.lansol.com
Contact: Robert L. Byrd, Manager
E-mail: woodbyrd@lansol.com
Scope: Offers Microsoft MCSE certified installation, service and consulting. Services include: network design and needs analysis, CD-Rom and FAX design and installation, network and Internet email design and installation, network troubleshooting and diagnostics, network performance optimization, system manager and user training and network cabling installation. **Founded:** 1989.

41502 ■ LBC Networks
675 King St. W, Ste. 210
Toronto, ON, Canada M5V 1M9
Ph: (416)727-9200
Free: 888-437-7741
Fax: (416)929-1173
Contact: Sean Ford, Principal
E-mail: seanf@lbcnetworks.com
Scope: Network consulting group that specializes in TCP/IP, Linux and other network technologies. Services include: Novell to NT migration, firewall and internet security, support, Linux, email solutions, virtual private networks, data wiring, network management, and web design. **Founded:** 1998.

41503 ■ Jerome W. McGee & Associates—Bruce W. McGee & Associates
7826 Eastern Ave. NW, Ste. 300
Washington, DC 20012
Ph: (202)726-7272

Fax: (202)726-2946
Contact: Bruce W. McGee, President
Scope: Business consultants experienced in office automation, small business management, invention and patent counseling, technology commercialization, loan packaging and business plan development. **Founded:** 1985. **Seminars:** Marketing Research for the High-Technology Business; Introduction to Microcomputers; Marketing Technological Products to Industry; How to Evaluate Your Technical Idea; Patenting Your Own Invention.

41504 ■ MindLabs.net
317 N Broad St., Ste. 402
Philadelphia, PA 19107
Ph: (215)888-6220
Co. E-mail: email@mindlabs.net
URL: http://www.mindlabs.net
Contact: Mike Creech, Partner
Scope: Solutions include website design and development, website make over's, ongoing maintenance and support, website hosting and Internet marketing. **Founded:** 1996.

41505 ■ Morgan Parker & Johnson Inc.
50 Broadway, 26th Fl.
New York, NY 10004
Ph: (212)968-1100
Fax: (212)968-8702
Contact: M. K. Morgan, President
Scope: A New York-based corporation which serves the needs of banks, brokerage firms and other financial concerns by providing consultants and consultant teams to solve challenges in computer and people systems technology. Assists in the design and use of technology which serves users. Specializes in the areas of enterprise computing (both data driven and process control driver), methodologies/tools and object and neural technology. Also specializes in object-oriented program development and client server systems. **Founded:** 1991. **Seminars:** Objects Made Easy; Client/Server Object Oriented Development.

41506 ■ Mountain Realty Inc.
590 Main St.
Young Harris, GA 30582
Ph: (706)379-3115
Free: 800-201-5526
Fax: (706)379-2575
Co. E-mail: chuck@ssg-i.com
URL: http://www.ssg-i.com
Contact: Richard C. Albury, Jr., President
Scope: Specializes in custom applications and systems development for micro and mid range business systems. Industries served: manufacturing, retail, construction, and general office automation. **Founded:** 1971.

41507 ■ P. Murphy & Associates Inc. (PMA)
2301 W Olive Ave.
Burbank, CA 91506
Ph: (818)841-2002
Fax: (818)841-0082
Co. E-mail: jody@pmurphy.com
URL: http://www.pmurphy.com
Contact: Phyliss Murphy, President
E-mail: pmurphy@pmurphy.com
Scope: Computer consultant firm. Provides staff to businesses and government agencies on a contract, contract to hire or direct placement basis. **Founded:** 1981.

41508 ■ Richard D. Murphy
5212 Spring Ave.
Kansas City, MO 64133-2669
Ph: (816)356-5827
Fax: (816)358-3076
Contact: Richard Murphy, Owner
Scope: Offers scientific and engineering services and computer consulting. Services include: general technical advice (engineering and scientific industries), accident reconstruction (legal profession), scientific computations (advice, algorithms, program development), and small business computer assistance (software development and hardware advice). Serves private industries as well as government agencies. **Founded:** 1974.

41509 ■ NetKnowledge Technologies L.L.C. (NKT)—NKSoft Corp.
6565 N MacArthur Blvd., Ste. 800
Irving, TX 75039
Ph: (214)624-5122
Fax: (972)910-0069
Co. E-mail: aubrey.roberts@nksoft.com
Scope: Works with executives worldwide to solve pressing business problems through the integration of business strategy and operations; information technology; and change management. **Founded:** 1997.

41510 ■ Networked Solutions Inc.
4280 Caparosa Cir.
Melbourne, FL 32940
Ph: (321)259-3242
Fax: (321)259-3846
Co. E-mail: info@ensusa.com
URL: http://www.ensusa.com
Contact: John Redrup, President
E-mail: jr@ensusa.com
Scope: Specializes in simultaneous Internet web and email access via LAN. Capabilities include: requirements analysis, computer system setup, network design and installation, software development, training and support. **Founded:** 1996. **Seminars:** Network Design & Implementation; Managed Services & Support; Collection of your Personal Information; Use of your Personal Information. **Telecommunication Services:** support@ensusa.com; sales@ensusa.com. **Special Services:** SAAZ.

41511 ■ Paladin Consultants L.L.C.
11 Beech Ct.
Chatham, NJ 07928
Ph: (973)635-0080
Fax: (973)701-8151
Co. E-mail: info@paladn.com
URL: http://www.paladn.com
Contact: Chris Kemp, President
E-mail: chrisk@paladn.com
Scope: Versatile designer of business systems and custom software for small and medium sized businesses. Industries served all. **Founded:** 1988. **Publications:** "Database Design"; "Technical Complexities of Database Design"; "VB Custom Programming"; ".NET (DOTNET) Programming And Development"; "Client Server Northern New Jersey Morristown SQL Server New York Client Server Consulting Services"; "User-Defined Functions"; "Rozenshte in Method"; "Case expressions".

41512 ■ Perceptive Technology Corp. (PTC)
11309 Park Central Pl.
Dallas, TX 75230
Ph: (214)368-0900
Co. E-mail: vic@perceptive.net
Contact: Vic Summerour, President
E-mail: vic@perceptive.net
Scope: Services include: Business web site design and hosting, Internet connectivity, web server co location, Intranet design, LAN or WAN design and consulting.

41513 ■ R & S Design Computer Services Inc.
10 W Front St.
Media, PA 19063
Ph: (610)565-5523
Fax: (610)480-8398
Co. E-mail: info@rsdesign.com
URL: http://www.rsdesign.com
Contact: Bob Strain, Manager
Scope: Provider of technology solutions. Offers the sale, installation and configuration of PC software for business and home use. Offers training for a wide variety of software applications, maintenance and repair of hardware and network systems. **Founded:** 1987. **Seminars:** Quick Postings and Processes, Jan, 2012; Analysis Reports, Jan, 2012; Intro to Church Office, Feb, 2012; Stewardship Library of Reports, Feb, 2012; Intermediate Reporting in Church Office, Mar, 2012; Tuition, Mar, 2102; Communicating in Church Office, Apr, 2012; Financial Reports, Apr, 2012. **Special Services:** Parish Data Software.

41514 ■ Research Applications Inc. (RAI)
414 Hungerford Dr., Ste. 220
Rockville, MD 20850-4125
Ph: (301)251-6717
Free: 888-311-6221
Fax: (301)251-6719
Contact: David H. Friedman, President
E-mail: dfriedman@resapplinc.com
Scope: A consulting firm provides specialized design, evaluation, testing and analytic services in the fields of social, computer and mathematical sciences. It brings to its customers a senior staff with strong theoretical and scientific backgrounds in areas of expertise, coupled with extensive practical knowledge and experience in contract research. The firm focuses on providing a group of interrelated services which include human resources support and improvement, computer programming support, direct mail services, and MOBIS. **Founded:** 1975. **Seminars:** Gender Awareness in the Workplace; Humor in the Workplace; Understanding and Using Assessments (Validity/Reliability); Diversity in the Workplace; Structured Interviews; Leadership; Leadership and Humor.

41515 ■ S & S Office Solutions Inc.
3480 Johnson Ferry Rd.
Roswell, GA 30075
Ph: (770)518-0868
Fax: (770)518-4483
Co. E-mail: info@ssos.com
URL: http://www.ssos.com
Contact: Annette Stone, President
Scope: Specialists in designing, installing, and consulting for LANs (Local Area Networks) and wiring systems for professional offices (MCSE). Offers total turn-key solution to networking challenge. **Founded:** 1993.

41516 ■ SBA Computers Inc.
620 E State St.
O'Fallon, IL 62269-1540
Ph: (618)628-9590
Fax: (618)622-3717
Co. E-mail: info@sbacomputers.com
Contact: Richard Scaiefe, President
E-mail: rick@sbacomputers.com
Scope: Provider of web site and domain hosting. Offers domain registration services. **Founded:** 1997.

41517 ■ Schneider Associates
1485 Chain Bridge Rd., Ste. 201
McLean, VA 22101
Ph: (703)442-8927
Fax: (703)442-8929
Contact: Jim Schneider, President
Scope: Information consultants specializing in the design and implementation of data and information processing systems for litigation support. Specialize in the development of software packages for the storage and retrieval of information describing documents, exhibits, transcripts, and events of legal cases. **Founded:** 1977. **Special Services:** Developed FIND-IT and FINDLAW litigation support software.

41518 ■ Simplified Technology Co.
35532 Cabrillo Dr.
Fremont, CA 94536
Ph: (510)794-5520
Free: 800-782-4435
Co. E-mail: sales201008@simplifiedtechnology.com
URL: http://www.simplifiedtechnology.com
Contact: Gregory Carvalho, President
E-mail: gregoryc@simplifiedtechnology.com
Scope: Specializes in providing system security, networking, custom software development and data availability. **Founded:** 1991. **Special Services:** MRO's Maximo and Datastream's Maintenance Package 2 (MP2).

41519 ■ SON Systems International Inc.
5 Great Valley Pky., Ste. 210
Malvern, PA 19355
Ph: (949)260-2073
Free: 800-525-8211

Fax: (484)631-0513
Co. E-mail: info@sonsystems.com
URL: http://www.sonsystems.com
Contact: Joey Beitdashtoo, President
E-mail: joey.beitdashtoo@sonsystems.com
Scope: Provider of corporate performance management and business intelligence services and solutions. **Founded:** 1984.

41520 ■ Systems Alternatives International L.L.C. (SAI)
1705 Indian Wood Cir.
Maumee, OH 43537
Ph: (419)891-1100
Fax: (419)891-1045
Co. E-mail: sales@sysalt.com
URL: http://www.sysalt.com
Contact: John Underwood, President
Scope: Provider of a total solution with consulting and design, industry proven software and hardware, and training and support. Develops and delivers the highest standard in computerized systems and engineered solutions. Specializes in selling hardware and software. Provides innovative software and quality information technology services to the unique needs of the recycling and metals industries. **Founded:** 1981. **Special Services:** XSight; Version 4; CRES; CRIS; Integrated Mill Procurements and Costing System (IMPACT).

41521 ■ Verbit & Co.
19 Bala Ave.
Bala Cynwyd, PA 19004-3202
Ph: (610)668-9840
Co. E-mail: verbitcompany@earthlink.net
Contact: Alan C. Verbit, President
Scope: Management consulting firm to assist executives and managers fulfill their mission and to assure that adequate planning of day-to-day operations occurs; that controls sufficient to safeguard valuable resources; and that results of decisions reviewed in sufficient time to effect continuing action. Financial planning and control-to develop accounting, budgeting, forecasting and other information systems for the management of resources and evaluation of strategies. Services also include: Evaluation of desk-top computer systems for small firms; CAD/CAM implementation plan and orderly introduction of CAD/CAM. Industries served: manufacturing, distribution, metals casting, equipment and components, professional services, health care, retail, nonprofit and government. **Founded:** 1981. **Seminars:** Integrating Manufacturing Management Systems with Business Systems; Negotiating Information Systems Agreements with Suppliers.

41522 ■ Vocus Inc.—Gnossos Software Inc.
12051 Indian Creek Ct.
Beltsville, MD 20705-1246
Ph: (301)459-2590
Free: 800-345-5572
Fax: (301)459-2827
Co. E-mail: info@vocus.com
URL: http://www.vocus.com
Contact: Rick Rudman, President
Founded: 1991. **Publications:** *PACpro*; *GRpro*; *PRpro*; *CLIPpro*; *PRoffice*.

41523 ■ WNF Consulting Inc.
602 E Briles Rd.
Phoenix, AZ 85027-7886
Ph: (480)940-4808
Fax: (602)222-8616
Contact: Robert Murphy, President
Scope: Firm specializes in network analysis and design. Consulting engineers assist in understanding the characteristics of each network resource and segment, optimization of network hierarchy based on usage requirements, system performance and effective resource utilization, optimization of pooled server and application configurations, storage management methodology for day-to-day storage management and storage management methodology for automated storage management. **Founded:** 1995. **Special Services:** PXEGuard™; Identity Management Service.

41524 ■ Zentek Computer Consulting
5222 Woodlawn Pl.
Bellaire, TX 77401-3305
Ph: (713)667-8228
Co. E-mail: zentek@acm.org
URL: http://www.zentek.us
Contact: Bruce k. Leutwyler, President
Scope: Provider of computer management and support for small businesses. Specializes in supporting and training physicians, attorneys, and executives. Also offers software and networking support and Antivirus and data backup support. **Founded:** 1990.

COMPUTERIZED DATABASES

41525 ■ *TecTrends™*
PO Box 8120
Berkeley, CA 94707
Ph: (510)525-6220
Co. E-mail: tectrendsinfo@tectrends.com
URL: http://www.tectrends.com
Availability: Online: ProQuest LLC-Dialog; ProQuest LLC - Dialog; Information Sources Inc. - TecTrends. **Type:** Bibliographic; Directory.

LIBRARIES

41526 ■ Bluegrass Community & Technical College - Learning Resource Center
221 Oswald Bldg.
470 Cooper Dr.
Lexington, KY 40506-0235
Ph: (859)246-6380
Fax: (859)246-4675
Co. E-mail: charles.james@kctcs.edu
URL: http://www.bluegrass.kctcs.edu/Library.aspx
Contact: Charles James, Director
Scope: Associated health technologies, computer information systems, business technology, undergraduate general education, and technical degree/certificate programs. **Services:** Interlibrary loan; copying; Library open to the public. **Founded:** 1965. **Holdings:** 45,000 volumes. **Subscriptions:** 218 journals and other serials.

41527 ■ Chicago Public Library Central Library - Business/Science/Technology Division
Harold Washington Library Center
400 S. State St., 4th Fl.
Chicago, IL 60605
Ph: (312)747-4450
Fax: (312)747-4975
URL: http://www.chipublib.org/branch/details/library/harold-washington/p/Bst
Scope: Small business, marketing, technology, corporate reports, investments, management, personnel, patents, physical and biological sciences, medicine, health, computer science, careers, environmental information, gardening, cookbooks. **Services:** Interlibrary loan; copying; division open to the public. **Founded:** 1977. **Holdings:** 415,000 books; 52,100 bound periodical volumes; 33,000 reels of microfilm; Securities and Exchange Commission (SEC) reports; federal specifications and standards; American National Standards Institute standards; corporate Annual reports. **Subscriptions:** 4000 journals and other serials; 8 newspapers.

41528 ■ IBM Canada, Ltd. - Research Information Centre
3600 Steeles Ave., E.
F2/270
Markham, ON, Canada L3R 9Z7
Ph: (905)316-5000
Fax: (905)316-2535
URL: http://www.ibm.com/ca/en/
Scope: Market intelligence, information technology. **Services:** Center not open to the public. **Founded:** 1991. **Holdings:** Books; magazines. **Subscriptions:** 80 journals and other serials; 5 newspapers.

41529 ■ York Technical College - Anne Springs Close Library
452 S. Anderson Rd.
Rock Hill, SC 29730
Ph: (803)327-8025
Fax: (803)327-4535
Co. E-mail: deborah.jones@yorktech.com
URL: http://www.yorktech.com/library
Contact: Kristine Jones, Librarian
Scope: Industrial engineering technology, health and human services, business and office systems technology, liberal arts, computer science. **Services:** Interlibrary loan; Library open to the public. **Founded:** 1964. **Holdings:** 27,000 books; 50,574 microforms; 1813 videocassettes. **Subscriptions:** 475 journals and other serials; 13 newspapers; 40 databases. **Telecommunication Services:** spigford@yorktech.com.

RESEARCH CENTERS

41530 ■ Organizational Systems Research Association (OSRA)
UPO 2478
Department of Information Systems
Morehead State University
Morehead, KY 40351-1689
Ph: (606)783-2718
Fax: (606)783-5025
Co. E-mail: d.everett@morehead-st.edu
URL: http://www.osra.org
Contact: Dr. Donna R. Everett, Executive Director
Founded: 1982. **Publications:** *OSRA Newsletter* (Quarterly); *Information Technology, Learning, and Performance Journal* (Semiannual). **Educational Activities:** Research conference (Annual).

ASSOCIATIONS AND OTHER ORGANIZATIONS

41531 ■ Independent Office Products and Furniture Dealers Association (IOPFDA)
301 N Fairfax St., Ste. 200
Alexandria, VA 22314
Ph: (703)549-9040
Free: 800-542-6672
Fax: (703)683-7552
Co. E-mail: cbates@nopanet.org
URL: http://www.iopfda.org
Contact: Bob Chilton, President
E-mail: bchilton@iopfda.org

Description: Represents and serves privately owned commercial dealers and their business partners in two divisions: National Office Products Alliance (NOPA); and Office Furniture Dealers Alliance (OFDA). Offers strategic information, government advocacy, business performance benchmarking, standards development, and management education services to members located throughout the United States and in key Canadian markets. **Founded:** 1979. **Publications:** *BPIA Directory and Buyer's Guide* (Annual); *Office World News* (Bimonthly); *Business Products Industry Report* (Semimonthly). **Telecommunication Services:** info@iopfda.org.

41532 ■ International Association of Lighting Designers (IALD)
440 N Wells St., Ste. 210
Chicago, IL 60654
Ph: (312)527-3677
Fax: (312)527-3680
Co. E-mail: iald@iald.org
URL: http://www.iald.org
Contact: Kevin Theobald, President

Description: Represents professionals, educators, students, and others working in the field of lighting design worldwide. Promotes the benefits of quality lighting design and emphasizes the potential impact of lighting on architectural design and environmental quality. Furthers professional standards of lighting designers and seeks to increase their function in the interior design industry. Sponsors national awards program, summer intern program for qualified college students interested in lighting design as a profession, and career development lectures and seminars. **Scope:** lighting. **Founded:** 1969. **Subscriptions:** periodicals. **Publications:** *e-Reflections* (Monthly); *International Association of Lighting Designers--Membership Directory* (Annual); *Why Hire an IALD Lighting Designer*. **Educational Activities:** Lightfair International (Annual). **Awards:** IALD Award (Annual); IALD Scholarship (Annual); Lighting Design Awards; IALD Education Trust Scholarship Program.

41533 ■ Planning and Visual Education Partnership (PAVE)
4651 Sheridan St., Ste. 470
Hollywood, FL 33021
Ph: (954)241-4834
Fax: (954)893-8375
Co. E-mail: pave@paveinfo.org
URL: http://www.paveinfo.org
Contact: Dennis Gerdeman, President

Description: Retail executives, visual merchandisers, store planners, architects, specifiers, students. Seeks to educate and motivate members and encourage interaction among their related fields. Holds annual design competition; offers an internship program; donates proceeds of shows toward financial aid for students. **Founded:** 1992. **Educational Activities:** Planning and Visual Education Partnership Competition (Annual). **Awards:** Student Design Competition (Annual).

REFERENCE WORKS

41534 ■ *"Bag It" in Entrepreneur (Vol. 36, May 2008, No. 5, pp. 48)*
Pub: Entrepreneur Media, Inc.
Ed: Amanda C. Kooser. **Description:** Buyer's guide featuring bags and carrying cases for laptops is presented. Prices and attributes of the bags are provided.

41535 ■ *"CSE: Contractors Are Always Responsible" in Contractor (Vol. 56, November 2009, No. 11, pp. 34)*
Pub: Penton Media, Inc.
Ed: Dave Yates. **Description:** Plumbing contractors should purchase a long snorkel hose, a tripod with manual-crank hoist, and a sump pump in order to prevent accidents associated with Confined Space Entry. Liability issues surrounding confined space entry prevention and accidents are discussed.

41536 ■ *"The Dynamic DUO" in Canadian Electronics (Vol. 23, February 2008, No. 1, pp. 24)*
Pub: CLB Media Inc.
Description: Citronics Corporation not only aims to proved a good working environment for its employees, it also values the opinions of its personnel. Citronics had its employees test different workbenches before finally purchasing thirty-five of Lista's Align adjustable height workstation, which combines flexibility with aesthetics. The design of the Alin workbench is described.

41537 ■ *"The Easy Route" in Entrepreneur (Vol. 36, April 2008, No. 4, pp. 60)*
Pub: Entrepreneur Media, Inc.
Ed: Amanda C. Kooser. **Description:** Buyer's guide of wireless office routers is presented. All products included in the list use the latest draft-n technology. Price and availability of the products are provided.

41538 ■ *"Fabulous New Office Furniture: Ways to Revamp Your Workspace" in Inc. (Vol. 33, September 2011, No. 7, pp. 51)*
Pub: Inc. Magazine
Ed: Nadine Heintz. **Description:** Various new looks to revamp any office space are highlighted including a table lamp by designer Peter Stathis for Joby.

41539 ■ *"Firm Stays In the 'Family'; After Owner's Death, Employees Buy Company" in Crain's Detroit Business (Vol. 24, January 28, 2008)*
Pub: Crain Communications Inc. - Detroit
Ed: Chad Halcom. **Description:** Sterling Office Systems Inc., distributor of photocopiers and other office machines was purchased from the owner's family after his demise. The new owners would like to hit $1.75 million in sales their first year.

41540 ■ *"For Apple, It's Showtime Again" in Barron's (Vol. 90, August 30, 2010, No. 35, pp. 29)*
Pub: Barron's Editorial & Corporate Headquarters
Ed: Eric J. Savitz. **Description:** Speculations on what Apple Inc. will unveil at its product launch event are presented. These products include a possible new iPhone Nano, a new update to its Apple TV, and possibly a deal with the Beatles to distribute their songs over iTunes.

41541 ■ *"Formaspace Finds a Bigger Home" in Austin Business JournalInc. (Vol. 29, December 4, 2009, No. 39, pp. 1)*
Pub: American City Business Journals
Ed: Kate Harrington. **Description:** Formaspace Technical Furniture has signed a lease for 56,700 square feet in Harris Ridge Business Center at Northeast Austin, Texas, which represents one of the area's largest leases for 2009. The new lease enables Formaspace to hire new employees, invest in new equipment, and take advantage of a taxing designation created for manufacturers.

41542 ■ *"Handle with Care" in Entrepreneur (Vol. 35, November 2007, No. 11, pp. 24)*
Pub: Entrepreneur Media Inc.
Ed: Jacquelyn Lynn. **Description:** Preventing equipment breakdown can be done by having a regular maintenance schedule. It is also recommended that companies use quality surge protectors or uninterruptible power supplies (UPSs) for electronic equipment that can be affected by power fluctuations and lightning. Other suggestions for preventive maintenance practices are outlined.

41543 ■ *How to Make Big Money*
Pub: Hyperion Books
Ed: Jeffrey J. Fox. **Released:** May 19, 2004. **Price:** $16.95. **Description:** Entrepreneur and consultant offers advice to help others create successful startups and prosper. Fox directs new business owners with a counterintuitive style and describes essential methods that beat the competition. Tips include: setting priorities, getting a personal driver, creating a contingency plan for employees, pricing to value, saving money, and getting an office outside of the home.

41544 ■ *"How to Set Up an Effective Home Office" in Women Entrepreneur (August 22, 2008)*
Pub: Entrepreneur Media Inc.
Ed: Laura Stack. **Description:** Checklist provides ways in which one can arrange their home office to provide the greatest efficiency which will allow maximum productivity and as a result the greater the chance of success.

41545 ■ *"Intel Joins Movement to Turn Cube Farms Into Wide-Open Spaces" in Sacramento Business Journal (Vol. 28, May 27, 2011, No. 13, pp. 1)*
Pub: Sacramento Business Journal
Ed: Melanie Turner. **Description:** Intel Corporation has remodeled its facility in Folsom, California. The renovation has required some workers to give up their cubicles. Comments from executives are included.

41546 ■ *"Island Co.: Isle Style" in Entrepreneur (Vol. 35, October 2007, No. 10, pp. 172)*
Pub: Entrepreneur Media Inc.
Ed: Sara Wilson. **Description:** Island Co., producer of travel clothing and swimsuits was formed by Spencer Antle in 2002. Its office projects the Caribbean atmosphere, a strategy Antle used to promote the company's theme to its clients. Future plans for the company are also indicated.

41547 ■ *"Mexican Companies to Rent Space in TechTown, Chinese Negotiating" in Crain's Detroit Business (Vol. 24, September 29, 2008, No. 39)*
Pub: Crain Communications Inc.
Ed: Tom Henderson. **Description:** Wayne State University's TechTown, the business incubator and research park, has signed an agreement with the Mexican government that will provide temporary office space to 25 Mexican companies looking to find customers or establish partnerships in Michigan. TechTown's executive director is negotiating with economic development officials from China. To accommodate foreign visitors the incubator is equipping offices with additional equipment and resources.

41548 ■ *"Office Tech: A Pretty Little Vista" in Canadian Business (Vol. 80, January 29, 2007, No. 3, pp. 61)*
Pub: Rogers Media
Ed: Andrew Wahl. **Description:** The features of the new version of Microsoft Windows Vista OS and Microsoft Office 2007 are described.

41549 ■ *"Our Gadget of the Week" in Barron's (Vol. 88, March 24, 2008, No. 12, pp. 47)*
Pub: Dow Jones & Company, Inc.
Ed: Tiernan Ray. **Description:** Review of the $299 Apple Time Capsule, which is a 500-megabyte hard disk drive and a Wi-Fi router, rolled into one device. The device allows users to create backup files without the need for sophisticated file management software.

41550 ■ *"Our Gadget of the Week" in Barron's (Vol. 88, March 10, 2008, No. 10, pp. 36)*
Pub: Dow Jones & Company, Inc.
Ed: Jay Palmer. **Description:** Review of the $1,599 Fujitsu Lifebook T2010 tablet notebook which is a lightweight notebook offering a comfortable keyboard and a 12-inch screen illuminated by light emitting diodes. The notebook, however, also offers limited capability with its low-end processor and the lack of a built-in optical drive and a touchpad.

41551 ■ *"Our Gadget of the Week: Business Buddy" in Barron's (Vol. 88, July 7, 2008, No. 27, pp. 26)*
Pub: Dow Jones & Co., Inc.
Ed: Jay Palmer. **Description:** Review and evaluation of the Lenovo X300 laptop computer which offers executives a variety of features despite its smaller size and weight. The laptop is about 0.73 inch thick, comes with a 64-gigabyte solid-state drive from Samsung, and weighs less than three pounds.

41552 ■ *"Pick and Save" in Entrepreneur (Vol. 36, April 2008, No. 4, pp. 66)*
Pub: Entrepreneur Media, Inc.
Ed: C.J. Prince. **Description:** Business owners can purchase the needed big equipment to offset this year's expected profit. They can also switch to annualized computing of quarterly income and estimated tax payments to pay less estimated taxes for the first half of the year. Other tips on tax planning are provided.

41553 ■ *"Relationship "Farming" Tools" in Agency Sales Magazine (Vol. 39, August 2009, No. 8, pp. 46)*
Pub: MANA
Ed: Terry L. Brock. **Description:** Manufacturer's representatives should spend time, money and effort in establishing and maintaining relationships; one tool to help is the new Fujitsu S1500 scanner. The scanner can accomplish critical tasks, quickly, easily and at low cost. Other suggestions to help build better business relationships are given.

41554 ■ *"Shore Total Office Liquidates Massive Supply of Bank Furniture and Used Furniture" in Internet Wire (June 21, 2010)*
Pub: Comtex
Description: Shore Total Office, located in San Diego, California, is liquidating quality bank furniture and used furniture to customers hoping to outfit their facilities with stylish new furnishings. Shore Total Office is a leading supplier of high quality office furniture and designs.

41555 ■ *"Simply Therapeutic" in Women In Business (Vol. 61, December 2009, No. 6, pp. 34)*
Pub: American Business Women's Association
Ed: Maureen Sullivan. **Description:** Steps on minimizing office clutter are presented in an effort to also eliminate clutter from the office worker's mind. Allotting time for clutter reduction, setting realistic goals, file organization, labeling, and sticking to a clutter reduction system are suggested. Clutter reduction is expected to contribute to increased productivity in the workplace.

41556 ■ *The Small Business Owner's Manual: Everything You Need to Know to Start Up and Run Your Business*
Pub: Career Press, Incorporated
Ed: Joe Kennedy. **Released:** June 2005. **Price:** $19.99 (US), $26.95 (Canadian). **Description:** Comprehensive guide for starting a small business, focusing on twelve ways to obtain financing, business plans, selling and advertising products and services, hiring and firing employees, setting up a Web site, business law, accounting issues, insurance, equipment, computers, banks, financing, customer credit and collection, leasing, and more.

41557 ■ *"Succeed With the Right Equipment" in Pet Product News (Vol. 64, November 2010, No. 11, pp. 42)*
Pub: BowTie Inc.
Ed: Sandi Cain. **Description:** Grooming shop owners have been focusing on obtaining ergonomic, durable, and efficient products such as restraints, tables, and tubs. These products enhance the way grooming tasks are conducted. Ways pet supply manufacturers have responded to this trend are examined.

41558 ■ *Thank God It's Monday! How to Create a Workplace You and Your Customers Love*
Pub: FT Press
Ed: Roxanne Emmerich. **Released:** April 18, 2009. **Price:** $19.99. **Description:** Tips on creating a positive environment for both employees and customers.

41559 ■ *"Touching the Future" in Canadian Business (Vol. 81, July 21, 2008, No. 11, pp. 41)*
Pub: Rogers Media Ltd.
Ed: Matt McClearn. **Description:** Microsoft Corp. has launched a multi-touch product which is both a software and hardware technology called Microsoft Surface. The innovative product allows people to use it at the same time, however touch-based computers are reported to be around $100,000. Other features and benefits of the product are presented.

41560 ■ *"Welcome to a New Kind of Cubicle Culture" in Boston Business Journal (Vol. 29, August 19, 2011, No. 15, pp. 1)*
Pub: American City Business Journals Inc.
Ed: Alexander Jackson. **Description:** Beehive Baltimore offers a co-working space where independent freelancers and entrepreneurs can work. There are two other companies that provide the same service and the value of these services to these professional is that it provides them with an office that is both convenient and affordable aside from letting them network with peers.

41561 ■ *"What Is In Your Company Library?" in Modern Machine Shop (Vol. 84, October 2011, No. 5, pp. 60)*
Pub: Gardner Business Media, Inc.
Contact: Richard G. Kline, President
E-mail: rkline@gardnerweb.com
Ed: Mike Lynch. **Description:** A good company library in any machine shop can help keep employees productive. Safety as well as information are critical to complete any task in a shop.

41562 ■ *"A Whiteboard that Peels and Sticks" in Inc. (Volume 32, December 2010, No. 10, pp. 58)*
Pub: Inc. Magazine
Ed: Issie Lapwosky. **Description:** Profile of an affordable adhesive whiteboard that can be restuck multiple times; the whiteboard was created by three college friends. The students share insight in the contacts they used in order to promote the sale of their invention.

41563 ■ *"Working on the Dock of the Bay" in Canadian Business (Vol. 83, July 20, 2010, No. 11-12, pp. 76)*
Pub: Rogers Media Ltd.
Ed: Jacqueline Nelson. **Description:** A buyers guide of tools for employees working outdoors is presented. Information on price and availability are also presented.

VIDEOCASSETTES/ AUDIOCASSETTES

41564 ■ *Automating the Office*
Time-Life Video and Television
1450 Palmyra Ave.
Richmond, VA 23227-4420
Ph: (804)266-6330
Free: 800-950-7887
Fax: (757)427-7905
URL: http://www.timelife.com
Released: 1985. **Description:** A series of programs that clarify modern methods of automating workplaces for maximum efficency and productivity. **Availability:** VHS; 3/4 U; Special order formats.

CONSULTANTS

41565 ■ AA Antivirus
1608 W Campbell Ave., Ste. 370
Campbell, CA 95008
Ph: (408)374-8000
Free: 800-478-1828
Fax: (408)374-2045
Co. E-mail: sales@aaantivirus.com
URL: http://www.aaantivirus.com
Contact: Roy Miehe, Chief Executive Officer
E-mail: roy@aaantivirus.com
Scope: Offers a range of local area networking and wide area networking solutions to small and medium-sized businesses. Assists business owners and administrators in planning, purchasing and installing networks. **Founded:** 1994. **Telecommunication Services:** info@aaantivirus.com; tech@aaantivirus.com. **Special Services:** Panda Security SaaS; Web Root Security SaaS; Kaspersky Anti virus; Trend Micro Anti virus; Mal Ware Bytes; Norman Anti virus; Red Condor Anti Spam SaaS; Borderware; Ironport; CyberRoam; Bloxx.

41566 ■ ABI Designs Inc.
8555 SW Apple Way, Ste. 120
Portland, OR 97225-1775
Ph: (503)292-0151
Fax: (503)292-0685
Co. E-mail: walkinthelight@hotmail.com
Contact: Adele E. Beck, President
Scope: Provides interior design services to architectural firms and individuals. **Founded:** 1978.

41567 ■ Advanced Network Consulting (ANC)
12627 Gabbett Dr.
La Mirada, CA 90638
Ph: (562)903-3992
Free: 877-262-0999
Fax: (562)204-0655
Co. E-mail: info@ancsite.com
URL: http://www.ancsite.com
Contact: Cindy Staples, Controller
E-mail: cindy@ancsite.com
Scope: Provider of LAN consulting as well as hardware and software services. Offers server-based solutions that include: Backup, antivirus LAN/WAN design, implementation and support, system administration and hardware warrantee contracts, and office automation for small businesses. **Founded:** 2002.

41568 ■ Agility Computer Network Services L.L.C.
1332 N Halsted St., Ste. 405
Chicago, IL 60642
Ph: (312)587-9894
Free: 877-244-5489
Fax: (312)587-9948
Co. E-mail: support@agilitynetworks.com
URL: http://www.agilitynetworks.com
Contact: Chandler Denny, President
E-mail: cdenny@agilitynetworks.com
Scope: Provider of networking and other related computer consulting services. **Founded:** 1994. **Telecommunication Services:** info@agilitynetworks.com.

41569 ■ Lino J. Agosti & Associates
1901 W Tudor Rd.
Anchorage, AK 99517-3114
Ph: (907)243-3556
Co. E-mail: tim.agosti@alaska.com
Contact: Tim F. Agosti, Owner
E-mail: tim.agosti@alaska.com
Scope: Offers food facility design, interior design and feasibility planning. Service offered: Concept development, design, feasibility. **Founded:** 1965.

41570 ■ AIM Associates
100 Fair St.
Petaluma, CA 94952-2515
Ph: (707)763-3300
Fax: (707)763-6489
Co. E-mail: info@aimgreen.com
URL: http://www.aimgreen.com
Contact: George A. Beeler, Principal
E-mail: george@aimgreen.com
Scope: The firm has been providing green and high performance building consulting, integrated design team management, and full architectural and engineering services. Provides consulting to cities, school districts, AE firms, R&D facilities, other businesses, and individuals. The firm is also an architectural and project management firm that provides peer review, integrated design team management, and performance based design. **Founded:** 1982.

41571 ■ Anshen + Allen
901 Market St., Ste. 600
San Francisco, CA 94103
Ph: (415)882-9500
Fax: (415)882-9523
Co. E-mail: inquire@anshen.com
URL: http://www.anshen.com
Contact: Felicia Cleper Borkovi, President
E-mail: felicia.borkovi@anshen.com
Scope: Offers architectural consulting services from feasibility studies through construction administration. Also provides space planning and interior design services and facilities management utilizing CAD and database management. **Founded:** 1940. **Publications:** "Urban Land Green - Greening Health Care Facilties"; "Health Care Design Cost of Innovation"; "The Architecture of Medical Imaging"; "Health Facilities Management - Surolgy is Coming". **Telecommunication Services:** info@anshen.com.

41572 ■ A.P. Designs
33 Merrall Dr., Ste. 1
Lawrence, NY 11559
Ph: (516)239-2931
Fax: (516)239-2932
Contact: Ann Pollack, President
Scope: Provider of interior design business services. Industries served: All industries and individuals requiring interior design services. **Founded:** 1975.

41573 ■ Architectural Alliance
400 Clifton Ave. S
Minneapolis, MN 55403-3212
Ph: (612)871-5703
Fax: (612)871-7212
Co. E-mail: pvesterholt@archalliance.com
URL: http://www.archalliance.com
Contact: Tom Hysell, Manager
E-mail: thysell@archalliance.com
Scope: Offers architectural design, interior design, facility studies, programming, space planning, facilities master planning and renovation design services. Project types have included corporate offices, computer/data centers, retail facilities, college and university buildings, other educational facilities, airport facilities and public facilities (parks, city halls, police facilities, etc.). Industries served: public and private corporations/companies, school districts, public colleges and universities, public (state and federal) agencies, commercial developers, municipalities and other institutions. **Founded:** 1970.

41574 ■ Array Healthcare Facilities Solutions—Array HFS
2520 Renaissance Blvd., Ste. 110
King of Prussia, PA 19406
Ph: (610)270-0599
Free: 800-828-8199
Fax: (610)270-0995
Co. E-mail: info@arrayhfs.com
URL: http://www.arrayhfs.com
Contact: Carl J. Davis, President
E-mail: cdavis@blm-architects.com
Scope: Provider of comprehensive architectural, facility master planning, interior design, project management, design/building and computer-aided facilities management services. Clients include nonprofit health care corporations, academic health centers, investor-owned enterprises, start-up entrepreneurs, management companies for long-term care units, physician groups and developers serving medical niche markets. Also serves government agencies. **Founded:** 1983. **Publications:** "Drawing a Meaning from a Mission," Oct, 2009; "Constructive Thinking," Sep, 2009; "A Patient Centered ED," Aug, 2009; "Multimedia Prototypes," May, 2009; "Keys to Success to a Hybrid Cath Lab," Mar, 2009; "Acuity Adaptable Rooms: Design Considerations Can Improve Patient Care," Feb, 2009; "Healthcare Spaces," Visual Reference Publications, 2008; "Healthcare Design," Sep, 2008; "Doctors Order: Translating University Hospitals' Healing Mission Into the Built Environment," Jul, 2008.

41575 ■ BBLM Architects
924 Cherry St., Ste. 1
Philadelphia, PA 19107-2411
Ph: (215)625-2500
Fax: (215)625-0275
Contact: Paul G. Shaffer, Principal
Scope: Offers architecture, planning, and interior design consulting services, including color, furnishings, and lighting. Recent experience in health care design. Serves private institutions as well as government agencies. **Founded:** 1986.

41576 ■ Beck Powell & Parsons Inc.
29 W Susquehanna Ave., Ste. 300
Towson, MD 21204
Ph: (410)828-9220
Fax: (410)828-9661
Co. E-mail: main@beckpowell.com
URL: http://www.beckpowell.com
Contact: Mark H. Beck, Principal
E-mail: mb4833@aol.com
Scope: Architecture and interior design firm. Provides design services to governmental, corporate and institutional clients. **Founded:** 1962. **Publications:** "Active Solar Energy System Design Practice"; "Better Homes and Gardens"; "Solar Energy Analysis Guide"; "Solar Performance/Practice Guide"; "New Energy Conserving passive solar single family homes".

41577 ■ Bell Techlogics
8888 Keystone Crossing, Ste. 1700
Indianapolis, IN 46240
Ph: (317)704-6000
Free: 800-999-9813
Fax: (317)575-9401
Co. E-mail: bellservice@belltechlogix.com
URL: http://www.belltechlogix.com
Contact: Clinton Coleman, Chief Executive Officer
Scope: Provider of integrated technology and service solutions for organizations throughout the United States. Provides designing, implementing, and managing technology solutions that result in decreased costs, increased customer retention, improved service levels and operational efficiencies for small, mid-sized and Fortune 500 companies. Installs, configures, maintains and supports the local and wide area network technologies. Offers connectivity services that include secure Internet and Intranet communication solutions, virus scanning, and firewall protections. **Founded:** 1978. **Seminars:** Virtualization and Disaster Recovery, 2008.

41578 ■ Burt Hill Inc.
400 Morgan Ctr., 101 E Diamond St.
Butler, PA 16001-5923
Ph: (724)285-4761
Fax: (724)285-6815
Co. E-mail: dianne.sinz@burthill.com
URL: http://www.burthill.com
Contact: Peter H. Moriaty, President
E-mail: pete.moriaty@burthill.com
Scope: Offers architecture and engineering consulting services including space planning, facility evaluation, assessment of interior design, building infrastructure, landscape architecture and energy management. Industries served: healthcare, medical research, hospitality, high tech, education, corporate, housing, and manufacturing worldwide, with emphasis on the Eastern United States. **Founded:** 1936. **Publications:** "Metal Building Developer"; "Laboratory Design Construction and Renovation: Participants, Process, and Product," Board on Chemical Sciences and Technology, National Research Council, 1999; "Guidelines for planning and designing Biomedical Research Facilities," 1999; "Advances Technology Facilities Design," 1996; "Improving Collaboration: Architects and Engineers, Design and Construction," American Institute of Architects, 1996; "Fundamentals of Building Energy Dynamics; Energy Conservation and Management Strategies," MIT Press, 1996; "Teaching Space Utilization, Managing one of Higher Education's Most Significant Assets," 1996. **Seminars:** Advanced Technology Facilities Design and the Technology Intensive Workplace; Energy Conservation in Commercial Buildings Current Practice; Health care in the Baltics- Meeting the 21st Century; Architectural and Engineering Practice in the 21st Century; Class rooms of the Future; Class rooms of the Future; Campus-Wide Information Networks; Risk Allocation and Dispute Avoidance in Construction; Achieving Architectural and Engineering Collaboration in Building Design; Designing for Improved Occupant Comfort and Productivity; Construction Procurement; International Health Care; Campus-Wide Information Network.

41579 ■ Cambridge Seven Associates Inc. (C7A)
1050 Massachusetts Ave.
Cambridge, MA 02138
Ph: (617)492-7000
Fax: (617)492-7007
Co. E-mail: marketing@c7a.com
URL: http://www.c7a.com
Contact: Peter G. Kuttner, President
E-mail: pkuttner@c7a.com
Scope: Offers consulting in architecture, planning graphic, exhibit, habitat and interior design. Industries served: Colleges and universities, retail, corporations, museums, aquariums and government agencies, Full Service Firm, Architectural Design, Feasibility Analysis, Marketing Communications Design. **Founded:** 1962. **Publications:** "On Strip, Hard Rock has a touch of interactivity," Oct, 2009; "Architectural follies surprise contest jurors," Sep, 2009; "Buck Center for Health and Fitness opens doors," Sep, 2009; "Diehard fans hail The Hall at Patriot Place," Aug, 2009;

"Mentors - Where are They When You Need Them," Aug, 2009; "Boston may soon have a history museum," Aug, 2009; "A New Lobby for the Charles Hotel," Aug, 2009; "New Balance Foundation Marine Mammal Center opening," Jul, 2009; "How Green is Your City," Metropolis, Sep, 2006; "Designing and Building for the Class of 2020," Sep, 2006; "Dumping Steel," The Boston Globe, Jun, 2006; "Healing Architecture," Architectural Record, Jun, 2005. **Seminars:** Where We Learn seminar.

41580 ■ Carmichael Associates
4255 Auburn St.
Wichita, KS 67220
Ph: (316)681-1535
Fax: (316)681-1548
Co. E-mail: joewmc@aol.com
Contact: Joe William Carmichael, President
E-mail: joewmc@aol.com
Scope: Architectural consultant active in legal assistance, library design, church design, health care projects, nursing homes, clinics, apartments, governmental buildings, renovations and remodeling work, residential and commercial, heavy truck maintenance and operations design, and small college buildings and planning. **Founded:** 1958.

41581 ■ Cassway/Albert Ltd.
1528 Walnut St., Ste. 1100
Philadelphia, PA 19102
Ph: (215)545-4900
Fax: (215)545-8222
Co. E-mail: cal@icdc.com
Contact: Robert L. Cassway, President
Scope: Consultants in architecture, landscape architecture, urban planning, interior design, and space planning. **Founded:** 1963.

41582 ■ Champion Networks L.L.C.—Downtime Inc.
1081 Mere Point Rd.
Brunswick, ME 04011
Ph: (207)725-8903
Contact: Edward Hunter, Manager
E-mail: ehunter@downtime.com
Scope: Firm specializes in network integration, total wide area network solutions, and network services. **Founded:** 1990.

41583 ■ Chicago-Edison Electrical & Lighting
189 Poplar Pl., Ste. 3
North Aurora, IL 60542
Ph: (630)264-6940
Fax: (630)264-6942
Contact: Larry C. Jeppesen, President
Scope: Lighting systems consultants. **Founded:** 1986. **Publications:** "An Efficient Solution: The right energy investments could pay big dividends," Barron's Magazine, Feb, 2002; "The Benefits of High Efficiency Lighting".

41584 ■ Cohn Consulting Corp. (CCC)
3605 Sandy Plains Rd., Ste. 240-416
Marietta, GA 30066
Ph: (770)321-5532
Fax: (770)321-4497
Co. E-mail: info@cohnconsultingcorp.com
URL: http://www.cohnconsultingcorp.com
Contact: Daniel S. Cohn, President
E-mail: dan@cohnconsultingcorp.com
Scope: Provider of a wide range of PC and LAN services. Specialized services includes Network administration, Backup and Disaster Recovery, Thin client computing, Internet services, Centralized fax solutions, Mainframe and midrange connectivity and Workgroup collaboration. **Founded:** 1993. **Publications:** "Total Network Solution Gets Title Insurance Agency Off To A Fast Start"; "Thin Client Solution Modernizes Psychological Practice". **Special Services:** Cohn Care™.

41585 ■ Cole & Goyette Architects & Planners Inc.
540 Franklin St.
Cambridge, MA 02139
Ph: (617)491-5662
Fax: (617)492-0856
Co. E-mail: colegoyette@earthlink.net
URL: http://www.colegoyette.com
Contact: Doris Cole, President
Scope: Offers services in architecture and planning, interior design and design review for educational, commercial, residential and governmental clients. **Founded:** 1981.

41586 ■ Computer Connections Inc.
1241-2 E Dixon Blvd., Ste. 2
Shelby, NC 28150
Ph: (704)482-0057
Fax: (704)482-0950
Co. E-mail: ccsales@painlesspc.net
URL: http://www.painlesspc.net
Contact: Lynne Rockwell, Sales Manager
E-mail: lynner@carolina.rr.com
Scope: Specializes in client or server networking environments. Offers service, upgrades, and repairs most IBM compatible computers. Networking services include: network design, implementation, and administration of novell and windows NT networks. **Founded:** 1996.

41587 ■ Crawley & Associates Inc.
121 Lincoln Ave.
Fair Lawn, NJ 07410
Ph: (973)636-7350
Fax: (973)636-7360
Co. E-mail: sales@crawleyinc.com
URL: http://www.crawleyinc.com
Contact: Chris Apsey, Engineer
Scope: Provider of education technology management services for both public and private schools located in New Jersey; provides experienced guidance and direction. Services include: Design, budget development, hardware and software selection, implementation, project management and system monitoring. **Founded:** 1995. **Publications:** "Give Your Servers All the Attention," Oct, 2007; "The Importance of aTechnology Audit," Jun, 2007; "Eliminate Extended Warranties on YourWorkstation Purchases," May, 2007; "Beware of Hidden Cost When PurchasingWorkstations," Apr, 2007; "Top Five Overlooked Budget Items," Feb, 2007; "Technology Budgets: When to Say No," Jan, 2007. **Seminars:** Reducing Technology Costs. **Telecommunication Services:** info@crawleyinc.com.

41588 ■ Cutten Associates Lighting Design
PO Box 6926
Tahoe City, CA 96145-6926
Contact: Merritt E. Cutten, President
E-mail: medcut@yahoo.com
Scope: Design consultant, offer expertise in lighting design and electrical engineering. Industries served construction residential, commercial, and industrial; also government agencies. **Founded:** 1987. **Seminars:** Lighting fundamentals course. **Special Services:** Auto CAD LT capability.

41589 ■ dEpagnier Furniture
14201 Notley Rd.
Silver Spring, MD 20904
Ph: (301)384-1663
Fax: (301)384-3201
Contact: John A. D'Epagnier, President
Scope: Specializes in custom design and fabrication of furniture for corporate, residential or professional spaces. Performs architectural exterior and interior design consulting work with extensive knowledge in traditional cabinet making skills, solid woods and joinery. Design expertise in Greene and Greene genre of the American Arts and Crafts Movement. Offers advice on use, location and types of domestic woods in place of foreign exotic woods. Offers artistic high end functional quality built furniture. **Founded:** 1978. **Seminars:** Marquetry.

41590 ■ Design Collective Inc. (Columbus, Ohio)—Design Collective Architecture Inc.
151 E Nationwide Blvd.
Columbus, OH 43215-2546
Ph: (614)464-2880
Fax: (614)464-1180
Co. E-mail: dcooke@dcollective.com
URL: http://www.dcollective.com
Contact: Robert B. Valentine, President
E-mail: rvalentine@dcollective.com
Scope: Firm offers expertise in interior design to clients in the commercial trade industry. **Founded:** 1989.

41591 ■ Dimension Data
2350 Corporate Park Dr., Ste. 425
Herndon, VA 20171
Ph: (571)203-4000
Fax: (571)203-4001
URL: http://www.dimensiondata.com
Contact: Brett Dawson, Chief Executive Officer
Scope: A global technology company. Provides solutions and services that optimize and manage the performance of IT infrastructure to enable businesses to build competitive advantage. **Founded:** 1983.

41592 ■ Eaton Design Group Inc.
8115 Old Dominion Dr., Ste. 100
McLean, VA 22102-2312
Ph: (703)790-8444
Free: 800-291-8444
Fax: (703)893-3256
Co. E-mail: eatondesgn@aol.com
Contact: Carl Blake, Director
Scope: Nationally recognized McLean-based space planning and interior design firm. **Founded:** 1983.

41593 ■ Thomas R. Egan Consulting Inc.
1012 Ronda Ln.
Birmingham, AL 35214
Ph: (205)796-9541
Fax: (205)744-9404
Contact: Thomas R. Egan, President
E-mail: tegan@treci.com
Scope: Provides consultation and design services, installation, and service/maintenance for several network platforms. **Founded:** 1994.

41594 ■ Engineered Lighting Products (ELP)
10768 Lower Azusa Rd.
El Monte, CA 91731
Ph: (626)579-0943
Fax: (626)579-6803
Co. E-mail: contact@elplighting.com
URL: http://www.elplighting.com
Contact: Toni Swarens, President
E-mail: tswarens@videssence.tv
Scope: Offers lighting consulting for commercial, residential, and industrial projects. Provides design, specifications, and illumination calculations. Maintains a studio for mock-up design. **Founded:** 1985. **Telecommunication Services:** elp2@aol.com.

41595 ■ ePartners Inc.
12110 Sunset Hills Rd., Ste. 150
Reston, VA 20190
Ph: (703)817-1400
Free: 888-883-9797
Fax: (703)488-6799
Co. E-mail: info@epartnersolutions.com
URL: http://www.epartnersolutions.com
Contact: Michael McCarthy, Chief Executive Officer
E-mail: mmccarthy@epartnersolutions.com
Scope: A total solutions provider that designs, develops, implements, integrates, hosts, manages and supports comprehensive e-Business solutions. **Founded:** 1992.

41596 ■ Ergometrics Inc.—ErgoMetrics Consulting Services Inc.
192 Monroe Ct.
Southampton, PA 18966-2722
Ph: (215)968-6943
Fax: (215)968-4250
Co. E-mail: ergodave@aol.com
Contact: David A. Rose, Director
E-mail: ergodave@aol.com
Scope: Provides occupational and forensic ergonomic services addressing work-site evaluations accident investigations, office ergonomics, tool, product and equipment evaluations, product liability, workplace accidents and occupational injuries. Specializes in heavy industrial, light industrial, service and office environments. **Founded:** 1993.

41597 ■ Error Analysis Inc. (EAI)
5173 Waring Rd., Ste. 157
San Diego, CA 92120-2705
Ph: (619)464-4427
Fax: (619)464-4992
Co. E-mail: info@erroranalysis.com
URL: http://www.erroranalysis.com
Contact: Kristy Norris, Manager
Scope: Research and consulting in the fields of human factors, safety and accident reconstruction. Provides consulting and expert witness services to attorneys, the insurance industry and businesses throughout the world. **Founded:** 1988. **Publications:** "Participation on voluntary committees for standards and codes by forensic practitioners: A win-win combination,"2011; "Ergonomics in Design,"2011; "Stairway falls: An ergonomics analysis of 80 cases," Professional Safety, 2009; "The practice of forensic human factors/ergonomics and related safety professions," Lawyers & Judges Publishing Company, 2009. **Seminars:** The role of a just culture, American Society of Safety Engineers, Costa Mesa, TCA, Jan, 2009; Common trends in slip and falls, Las Vegas, NV, Sep, 2008; Safety; Risk Management; Premises and Product Liability.

41598 ■ Fowlie & Associates
630 Skyline Dr.
Ventura, CA 93003-1143
Ph: (805)644-0201
Fax: (805)644-9885
Contact: Elmore I. Fowlie, Owner
E-mail: efowliearchitect@sbcglobal.net
Scope: Offers environmentally conscious architectural services, including interior design, urban planning, building program development, and site analysis. Industries served: Educational, industrial, residential, commercial, and municipal facilities. **Founded:** 1979.

41599 ■ FRCH Design Worldwide
311 Elm St., Ste. 600
Cincinnati, OH 45202-2774
Ph: (513)241-3000
Fax: (513)241-5015
Co. E-mail: info@frch.com
URL: http://www.frch.com
Contact: James R. Tippmann, Chief Executive Officer
Scope: Offers interior design, architectural, graphic communications, graphic design, brand consulting and new media development services. **Founded:** 1980. **Seminars:** Futureshop: Inspiring Your Next Design.

41600 ■ Glaser Associates Inc.—Glaserworks
304 E 8th St.
Cincinnati, OH 45202-2231
Ph: (513)665-9555
Co. E-mail: shaber@glaserworks.com
URL: http://www.glaserworks.com
Contact: Randal J. Reifsnider, Director
E-mail: rreifsnider@glaserworks.com
Scope: Architectural consulting firm offers master planning, site and feasibility analysis, architectural and interior design, space planning, renovation and adaptive reuse. Industries served: museums, higher education and mixed-use developments. **Founded:** 1958. **Publications:** "Greyfields to Goldfields"; "A Collection Of Work From Glaser and Myers, Glaser Associates, And Glaserworks"; "Sixteen Acres : Architecture and the Outrageous Struggle for the Future of Ground Zero"; "Bauhaus Adaptations"; "Stirring an Architectural Debate".

41601 ■ GlobalNET Corp.
2616 South Loop W
Houston, TX 77054-2662
Ph: (832)778-9591
Fax: (210)579-1192
Co. E-mail: sales@gbne.net
Contact: David F. Levy, President
Scope: Specializes in the installation, configuration, and technical support of local (LAN) and wide (WAN) Area Networks. Installs Multi-User and Multi-Platform systems (i.e. DOS, OS2, Windows NT, UNIX, NextStep, and Macintosh) which perform Accounting, client/server Database, Word Processing, Spreadsheet, and Computer Aide Design (CAD) tasks in a variety of industries. **Founded:** 1987. **Telecommunication Services:** customercare@gbne.net.

41602 ■ RMJM Hillier
500 Alexander Pk.
Princeton, NJ 08543-6395
Ph: (609)452-8888
Free: 888-445-5437
Fax: (609)452-8332
Co. E-mail: princeton@rmjm.com
URL: http://www.rmjm.com
Contact: Martin M. Bloomenthal, Director
E-mail: martin.bloomenthal@hillier.com
Scope: Provider of services in architecture, planning, interior design, engineering, construction management, strategic facilities planning, real estate evaluation and graphic design. Industries served: public and private sector. **Founded:** 1966.

41603 ■ Humanics ErgoSystems Inc.—Humanics Ergonomics
22287 Mulholland Hwy., Ste. 273
Calabasas, CA 91302-5190
Ph: (818)345-3746
Fax: (818)705-3903
Co. E-mail: ergonomics@humanics-es.com
URL: http://www.humanics-es.com
Contact: Rani Lueder, Principal
E-mail: rani@humanics-es.com
Scope: Specializes in occupational ergonomics; ergonomic workplace evaluations; ergonomics research; ergonomic seminars and training; psychological and biomechanics testing (EMG, dynamic lumbar motion, strength assessment, nerve conduction); product evaluations; compliance with ergonomic standards; and expert witnessing. **Founded:** 1982. **Publications:** "The Future of Ergonomics in Children's Education," IEA 2009; "Ergonomics for Children; designing products and places for toddlers to teens," 2007; "Are Children just Little Adults? Child growth, development and age-related risk," Dec, 2003; "Rethinking Sitting," Oct, 2003; "Revisiting Ergonomics," May, 2003. **Seminars:** Teaching elder design, Las Vegas, Jul, 2008; Ergonomic considerations in seated work activities, University of California, Los Angeles, Jun, 2008; Rethinking back support: Sacral, lumbar or live backs, Dec, 2007; Adjunct Faculty, Human Factors and Design, 2006; Zen sitting and Western seating, 2005; Behavioral ergonomics, Oct, 2005; Sitting & seating in Zenmonasteries, Sep, 2005; Walking in their shoe. **Telecommunication Services:** ergoquestions@gmail.com.

41604 ■ Illuminated Concepts Inc.
22981 Triton Way, Ste. D
Laguna Hills, CA 92653
Ph: (949)455-9914
Fax: (949)951-3603
Co. E-mail: info@oclights.com
URL: http://www.oclights.com
Contact: Chuck Evans, Owner
Scope: Provider of extensive design and installation services for both interior and exterior lighting. Specialist in low voltage lighting and fiber optic systems. **Founded:** 1988.

41605 ■ IMC
399 Sackett Point Rd.
North Haven, CT 06473
Ph: (203)248-5324
Free: 800-840-9989
Fax: (203)248-5384
Co. E-mail: info@imcinternet.net
URL: http://www.imcinternet.net
Contact: Robert J. Caldarella, President
E-mail: bob@imcinternet.net
Scope: Specializes in the development of total office solutions for business which includes office networking, client/server technologies, Internet access and computer sales. **Founded:** 1994.

41606 ■ Integrated Security Technologies (IST)
520 Herndon Pky., Ste. C
Herndon, VA 20170
Ph: (703)464-4766
Free: 888-291-0120
Fax: (703)464-5836
Co. E-mail: info@ntllc.com
URL: http://www.ntllc.com
Contact: Jon A. Langhorst, President
Scope: Focuses on the application of information technologies to enhance the effectiveness of the business environment including collecting, organizing and storing information; designing, building and maintaining the appropriate architecture to make information available. to assess, design and implement solutions for security and Information Technology challenges. **Publications:** "American University Wins High Marks for New Security System"; "All American Upgrade"; "IST named 77th on SDM's Top 100 System Integrators".

41607 ■ IRI Design Associates Inc.
122 E 42nd St.
New York, NY 10168-0002
Ph: (212)922-0632
Contact: Lisa Nikol, Chief Executive Officer
Scope: Full service interior architectural and design firm. Industries served: All. **Founded:** 1984.

41608 ■ Jacobs-Schneider Interior Design Inc.
1012 E 75th St.
Indianapolis, IN 46240-2843
Ph: (317)251-0312
Fax: (317)251-0339
Co. E-mail: jjacobs@jacobs-schneider.com
URL: http://www.jacobs-schneider.com
Contact: Janie Jacobs, Principal
E-mail: jjacobs@jacobs-schneider.com
Scope: Interior design consulting firm provide a truly custom design, executed with skill and to fulfill the client's expectations creating timeless interiors. **Founded:** 1987.

41609 ■ Kajioka Design Associates
2614 Ross Rd.
Chevy Chase, MD 20815-3835
Ph: (301)565-3535
Fax: (301)565-3535
Contact: June J. Kajioka, Owner
Scope: Interior design consultant (licensed and certified in Maryland and Virginia) provides expertise in space planning, complete furnishings and installation of window treatments, floor and wall coverings, and in other areas. **Founded:** 1972.

41610 ■ KCS Computer Technology Inc.
9524 Franklin Ave.
Franklin Park, IL 60131
Ph: (847)288-9820
Fax: (847)288-9822
Co. E-mail: sales@kcstech.com
URL: http://www.kcstech.com
Contact: Kenneth Kollar, President
Scope: Offers a full line of business-class computers, servers, workstations, laptops, printers, and peripherals. Offers hardware, software, installation, configuration, maintenance and management. Specializes in software and computer reselling, Windows NT, Lantastic and Novell network installation and maintenance, custom programming, network communications fax/modem server installation and maintenance, Internet setup and training, custom html programming services, network and phone cabling, computer leasing, data conversion and data recovery and maintenance contracts. **Founded:** 1993.

41611 ■ KeyLAN Consulting Inc.
2399 Lenida Dr.
North Gower, ON, Canada K0A 2T0
Ph: (613)489-2336
Fax: (613)489-4190
Co. E-mail: keylan@keylan.ca
URL: http://www.keylan.ca
Contact: James MacNabb, Principal
Scope: Specializes in all facets of local area networking, purchasing, installation, administration, training, automation, disaster planning, high security databases and security consulting. **Founded:** 1991.

41612 ■ T. Kondos Associates
333 W 39th St., Ste. 202
New York, NY 10018-1429
Ph: (212)736-5510

Fax: (212)594-6332
Co. E-mail: info@tkondos.com
URL: http://www.tkondos.com
Contact: Caleb A. McKenzie, Manager
E-mail: cmckenzie@tkondos.com
Scope: Full service architectural lighting design firm. Expertise with product development, budgeting, production, and equipment specification. **Founded:** 1977.

41613 ■ Lam Partners Inc.
84 Sherman St.
Cambridge, MA 02140
Ph: (617)354-4502
Fax: (617)497-5038
Co. E-mail: info@lampartners.com
URL: http://www.lampartners.com
Contact: Robert J. Osten, Jr., Principal
Scope: Architectural lighting consultants experienced in all phases of lighting design including artificial lighting, day lighting, lighting for urban design, and custom fixture design. **Founded:** 1969.

41614 ■ LAN Solutions
449 Hillway Dr.
Emerald Hills, CA 94062-3313
Ph: (650)261-1300
Fax: (650)361-8012
Co. E-mail: info@lansol.com
URL: http://www.lansol.com
Contact: Robert L. Byrd, Manager
E-mail: woodbyrd@lansol.com
Scope: Offers Microsoft MCSE certified installation, service and consulting. Services include: network design and needs analysis, CD-Rom and FAX design and installation, network and Internet email design and installation, network troubleshooting and diagnostics, network performance optimization, system manager and user training and network cabling installation. **Founded:** 1989.

41615 ■ Robert J. Laughlin & Associates
255 Osceola Ct.
Winter Park, FL 32789
Ph: (407)740-0160
Fax: (407)629-0411
Co. E-mail: info@robertjlaughlin.com
URL: http://www.robertjlaughlin.com
Contact: Robert J. Laughlin, Owner
Scope: Provider of lighting design and consulting services. Its projects include offices, resorts, restaurants, bridges, museums, and churches. **Founded:** 1987. **Publications:** "Architectural Records," May, 2005; "Florida Design," 2002; "House and Garden," Sep, 2000; "Sign Business," Nov, 1997.

41616 ■ LBC Networks
675 King St. W, Ste. 210
Toronto, ON, Canada M5V 1M9
Ph: (416)727-9200
Free: 888-437-7741
Fax: (416)929-1173
Contact: Sean Ford, Principal
E-mail: seanf@lbcnetworks.com
Scope: Network consulting group that specializes in TCP/IP, Linux and other network technologies. Services include: Novell to NT migration, firewall and internet security, support, Linux, email solutions, virtual private networks, data wiring, network management, and web design. **Founded:** 1998.

41617 ■ Lighting Design Collaborative (LDC)
1216 Arch St., Ste. 3A, 3rd Fl.
Philadelphia, PA 19107-2835
Ph: (215)569-2115
Fax: (215)569-2580
Co. E-mail: info@ldc-pa.com
URL: http://www.lightingdesigncollaborative.com
Contact: Michelle Emmerick, Principal
E-mail: memmerick@ldcpa.com
Scope: Architectural lighting design firm offering expertise in commercial, interior and exterior, hotel/hospitality, retail, mixed-use, museum, healthcare, transportation, and educational projects. Serves private industries as well as government agencies. **Founded:** 1973.

41618 ■ The Luminations Group L.L.C.
9 Kilmer Dr.
Hillsborough, NJ 08844
Ph: (908)281-9027
Fax: (908)349-3270
Co. E-mail: info@luminationsgroup.com
URL: http://www.luminationsgroup.com
Contact: Lisa Kent, President
E-mail: lisa@luminationsgroup.com
Scope: Lighting consultants experienced with commercial, retail, institutional and residential projects. **Founded:** 2003. **Special Services:** FleXforce®; Namestrom®; FleXforce®.

41619 ■ M. Richler & Associates Ltd.
85 Skymark Dr., Ste. 2603
North York, ON, Canada M2H 3P2
Ph: (416)491-5264
Contact: Mitchell M. Richler, President
E-mail: mitchrichler@aol.com
Scope: A general management consulting firm specializing in acquisitions and mergers, costing and pricing, office layout design and management, production management and taxation, particularly for small businesses. Industries served: manufacturing, retail, wholesale, import/export, design services, and government agencies. **Founded:** 1951. **Seminars:** Keeping the Cottage in the Family; Maximizing Capital Gains Exemption; Minimizing Probate Fees; Plant Reorganization; Departmental Scheduling.

41620 ■ Major Electric Supply Inc.
123 High St.
Pawtucket, RI 02860
Ph: (401)724-7100
Free: 800-444-1660
Fax: (401)727-7563
Co. E-mail: showroom@majorelectricsupply.com
URL: http://www.majorelectricsupply.com
Contact: Devid Leven, President
Scope: Provider of extensive lighting design services for commercial, residential, theatrical and landscape projects.

41621 ■ E.F. Marburger Fine Flooring—E.F. Marburger and Son Inc.
9999 Allisonville Rd.
Fishers, IN 46038-2006
Ph: (317)841-7250
Fax: (317)841-7269
Co. E-mail: kshone@efmarburger.com
URL: http://www.efmarburger.com
Contact: Ron Marburger, President
E-mail: marburger@efmarburger.com
Scope: Offers counsel to architects, designers, interior decorators and institutions, on the proper type of carpeting to be used in commercial applications. Furnishes sound absorbing and sound loss transmission data on carpet wall coverings. Also offers counsel on acoustical absorption and sound transmission factors on other types of acoustical products. **Founded:** 1913. **Seminars:** Use of Glass in Your Kitchen and Bath Designs.

41622 ■ Marconi Designs
985 University Ave., Ste. 22
Los Gatos, CA 95032-0115
Ph: (408)807-8330
Fax: (408)841-7234
Co. E-mail: patricia@marconidesigns.com
URL: http://www.wahlichusa.com/design
Contact: Patricia A. Wahli, Owner
E-mail: patricia@marconidesigns.com
Scope: Provider of interior design, space planning and facility design for commercial office buildings of any size. Renovation, remodel and reconfiguration of personnel workspaces and existing buildings the firms specialties. Tenant improvements for new and existing office space also handled. Industries served electronics, medical, banking industries and government agencies in California, state-wide, with emphasis on San Francisco Bay Area. **Founded:** 1981. **Telecommunication Services:** patty.wahli@gmail.com.

41623 ■ C.E. Marquardt Lighting Design
13498 SE Wiese Rd.
Boring, OR 97009-8342
Ph: (503)658-5505
Contact: Craig E. Marquardt, Owner
Scope: Architectural lighting design firm offering services in both interior and exterior lighting. Services include custom control design, ceiling and skylight design, computer mock ups, scale models, and lighting art. **Founded:** 1990.

41624 ■ Marshall Craft Associates Inc. (MCA)
6112 York Rd.
Baltimore, MD 21212-2611
Ph: (410)532-3131
Fax: (410)532-9206
Co. E-mail: info@marshallcraft.com
URL: http://www.marshallcraft.com
Contact: Linton S. Marshall, III, President
E-mail: lsm@marshallcraft.com
Scope: Specializes in architecture, interior design, and planning. Offers professional services to healthcare, academic, corporate and government clients. **Founded:** 1986.

41625 ■ Maxdeco Interior Design Inc.
160 Fresh Ponds Rd.
East Brunswick, NJ 08816-2408
Ph: (732)821-7850
Co. E-mail: maxdeco@worldnet.att.net
Contact: Sarina Feldman, Owner
Scope: Interior design and decoration consultation and planning for commercial, institutional and residential clients. Serves private industries as well as government agencies in New Jersey, New York City and Philadelphia. **Founded:** 1986.

41626 ■ Michaels Associates Design Consultants Inc.
14809 N 73rd St.
Scottsdale, AZ 85260-3113
Ph: (480)998-7476
Fax: (480)998-9390
Co. E-mail: madinc@vsnl.com
Contact: Andrea Arthur Michaels, President
E-mail: andrea@madcap.nu
Scope: Twenty year specialization in all areas of library (public, academic, corporate and national) programming and planning, including needs assessments and interior and graphic design. Michaels Associates expertise also includes ADA audits, furniture and product design for offices, lighting and graphic design. **Founded:** 1975. **Publications:** "Forum III: Physical Spaces for the E-ssential Library," 2003; "Library facility Planning"; "Library Administration & Management"; "Enhance Security With Effective Interior Planning and Design"; "Designing for Technology in Todays Libraries". **Seminars:** Library Environments: Changing to Fit New Technologies and Services, Dowling College, Long Island, NY, Nov, 2004; Reconfiguration Strategies Library Space for the E-Library, Information Futures Institute, San Francisco, CA, Sep, 2004; Creative Learning Seminars; Library Interior Planning & Design; Accessible, Healthy, Imaginative Spaces: Old & New; Fresh Looks for Library Interiors; The Future is Now: Library Planning &Design for the 21st Century; ADA Furnishings Response for Today's Libraries; Lighting & Libraries; Library Planning Based on New Functional Space Guidelines; Crime Prevention through Environmental Design.

41627 ■ MindLabs.net
317 N Broad St., Ste. 402
Philadelphia, PA 19107
Ph: (215)888-6220
Co. E-mail: email@mindlabs.net
URL: http://www.mindlabs.net
Contact: Mike Creech, Partner
Scope: Solutions include website design and development, website make over's, ongoing maintenance and support, website hosting and Internet marketing. **Founded:** 1996.

41628 ■ Mitchell B. Architectural Lighting Consultants—Mitchell B. Kohn Lighting Design
2256 Linden Ave.
Highland Park, IL 60035-2006
Ph: (847)433-0840

Fax: (847)433-0839
Co. E-mail: mitchell@mbklightingdesign.com
URL: http://www.mbklightingdesign.com
Contact: Mitchell B. Kohn, President
E-mail: mitchell@mbklightingdesign.com
Scope: Full service architectural lighting design firm provides interior lighting design for commercial projects. **Publications:** "Lighting Today's Office Environment," Professional Lighting Design Magazine, 2002; "Lighting Focus," 1998; "Lighting Considered," Apr, 1997; "Task Lighting for Offices," Apr, 1994; "Effective Lighting for Open Plan Offices," Facilities Magazine, Feb, 1992; "Task Lighting is a Key to Productivity," Consulting-Specifying Magazine, Nov, 1990; "Lighting Design and Vdts," Electrical Business Magazine, Mar, 1990; "Office Lighting for the 1990S," Commerce Magazine, Nov, 1989; "Lighting Offices Containing Vdts," Lighting Design and Application Magazine, Dec, 1988. **Seminars:** NEOCON, Chicago, 1999; Light Fair International, San Francisco, 1996; IIDACEU accredited seminars, 2004; IBD Chicago, Office Lighting Seminar, 1993.

41629 ■ MJS Lighting Consultants—Archtectural Lighting Consultation and Design
3118 Richmond Ave., Ste. 100
Houston, TX 77098
Ph: (713)850-1488
Fax: (713)521-4505
Co. E-mail: mjsmith@mjslight.com
URL: http://www.mjslight.com
Contact: Malcolm Perry, Office Manager
E-mail: malcolm@mjslight.com
Scope: Full service architectural lighting design firm that provides expertise with interior, exterior, landscape, facade, roadway, and industrial illumination. **Founded:** 1982.

41630 ■ Networked Solutions Inc.
4280 Caparosa Cir.
Melbourne, FL 32940
Ph: (321)259-3242
Fax: (321)259-3846
Co. E-mail: info@ensusa.com
URL: http://www.ensusa.com
Contact: John Redrup, President
E-mail: jr@ensusa.com
Scope: Specializes in simultaneous Internet web and email access via LAN. Capabilities include: requirements analysis, computer system setup, network design and installation, software development, training and support. **Founded:** 1996. **Seminars:** Network Design & Implementation; Managed Services & Support; Collection of your Personal Information; Use of your Personal Information. **Telecommunication Services:** support@ensusa.com; sales@ensusa.com. **Special Services:** SAAZ.

41631 ■ Robert Newell Lighting Design
654 N Ave. W
Westfield, NJ 07090-1432
Ph: (908)654-9304
Fax: (908)654-9302
Co. E-mail: robert.newell@robertnewelllightingdesign.com
URL: http://www.robertnewelllightingdesign.com
Contact: Robert Newell, Principal
E-mail: robert.newell@robertnewelllightingdesign.com
Scope: Full service architectural lighting design firm offers experience with commercial, corporate, educational, religious and residential environments. **Founded:** 1984.

41632 ■ Notari Associates
175 W Ostend St., Ste. 100
Baltimore, MD 21230
Ph: (410)752-0330
Fax: (410)685-6364
Contact: Peter Notari, President
E-mail: pnotari@notariassociates.com
Scope: Architectural firm offering project management and interior design services. **Founded:** 1986.

41633 ■ Peckham Guyton Albers and Viets Inc. (PGAV)—PGAV
200 N Broadway, Ste. 1000
Saint Louis, MO 63102-2754
Ph: (314)231-7318
Fax: (314)231-7433
Co. E-mail: mike.konzen@pgav.com
URL: http://www.pgav.com
Contact: Robert McKim, Manager
E-mail: mckim@pgavkc.com
Scope: Provides programming, planning and urban design, architecture, engineering, interior design, space planning, graphics, landscape architecture, energy engineering, construction documents, feasibility studies, zoning and codes analysis, development analysis, computer aided design, computer based specifications, cost estimating, construction management and value engineering. Projects include the design of civic, criminal justice, educational, library, recreational, governmental/public, healthcare facilities and multi-family housing. Also experienced in historic preservation and restoration. Industries served: Governmental organizations, criminal justice, public administration, corporate administration, education and recreation. **Founded:** 1965. **Seminars:** Consensus Building in the Planning of Public Facilities; Juvenile Detention and Adult Detention Facilities.

41634 ■ Perceptive Technology Corp. (PTC)
11309 Park Central Pl.
Dallas, TX 75230
Ph: (214)368-0900
Co. E-mail: vic@perceptive.net
Contact: Vic Summerour, President
E-mail: vic@perceptive.net
Scope: Services include: Business web site design and hosting, Internet connectivity, web server co location, Intranet design, LAN or WAN design and consulting.

41635 ■ Plantkeeper Inc.—Hawiian Tropical Plant Sales
2211 N Beckley Ave.
Dallas, TX 75222
Ph: (214)752-5750
Free: 800-340-4488
Fax: (214)651-0540
Co. E-mail: sales@plantkeeperinc.com
URL: http://www.plantkeeperinc.com
Contact: Lee Hitt, President
E-mail: leehitt@plantkeperinc.com
Scope: Interior design consultants specializing in plants and containers. Serving architects, developing companies and other commercial accounts. Provides interior design and maintenance for bank, office buildings, hotels, malls and restaurants. **Founded:** 1977. **Telecommunication Services:** plants@plantkeeperinc.com.

41636 ■ Patrick B. Quigley & Associates Inc. (PBQA)
2340 Plz., Del Amo, Ste. 125
Torrance, CA 90501
Ph: (310)533-6064
Fax: (310)320-3482
Co. E-mail: lighting@pbqa.com
URL: http://www.pbqa.com
Contact: Erin Erdman, Manager
Scope: Offers full service architectural and landscape lighting design. Experienced with cruise vessels, hotels, theme parks, civic centers, libraries, office interiors, and residences. **Founded:** 1985.

41637 ■ R & S Design Computer Services Inc.
10 W Front St.
Media, PA 19063
Ph: (610)565-5523
Fax: (610)480-8398
Co. E-mail: info@rsdesign.com
URL: http://www.rsdesign.com
Contact: Bob Strain, Manager
Scope: Provider of technology solutions. Offers the sale, installation and configuration of PC software for business and home use. Offers training for a wide variety of software applications, maintenance and repair of hardware and network systems. **Founded:** 1987. **Seminars:** Quick Postings and Processes, Jan, 2012; Analysis Reports, Jan, 2012; Intro to Church Office, Feb, 2012; Stewardship Library of Reports, Feb, 2012; Intermediate Reporting in Church Office, Mar, 2012; Tuition, Mar, 2102; Communicating in Church Office, Apr, 2012; Financial Reports, Apr, 2012. **Special Services:** Parish Data Software.

41638 ■ Roeder Design
3878 Oak Lawn Ave., Ste. 220
Dallas, TX 75219
Ph: (214)528-2300
Fax: (214)521-2300
Co. E-mail: robert@roederdesign.com
Contact: Craig A. Roeder, Director
Scope: Lighting design consulting firm experienced with cruise ships, residences, hotels, casinos, office buildings, retail showrooms, and health-care facilities.

41639 ■ Rowland Design Inc.
701 E New York St.
Indianapolis, IN 46202
Ph: (317)636-3980
Fax: (317)263-2065
Co. E-mail: info@rowlanddesign.com
URL: http://www.rowlanddesign.com
Contact: Sarah Marr-Schwartzkopf, President
Scope: Architecture, interior design, environmental graphic design, club consulting, alternative workplace strategies, space planning, thematic entertainment, hospitality design, and museum/exhibit design. **Founded:** 1968.

41640 ■ RTKL Associates Inc.—RTKL Associates
901 S Bond St.
Baltimore, MD 21231-3339
Ph: (410)537-6000
Fax: (410)276-2136
URL: http://www.rtkl.com
Contact: Lance K. Josal, President
E-mail: ljosal@zrtkl.com
Scope: Provides architecture, engineering, planning and urban design, interior architecture and design, landscape architecture, and environmental graphic design services for clients in public and private sector. Engaged in office, retail, hospitality, mixed-use, health sciences, entertainment, transportation, residential, and planning projects worldwide. **Founded:** 1946. **Publications:** "Placemaking: The Critical Ingredients"; "Discovering the new urbanism"; "Showcasing success in Today's workplaces"; "Mixed-Use: The new Urban Warrior"; "What is a Brand-Rich Environment?"; "Waiting for Wi-Fi"; "The Unit Plan of the Future"; "The Keys to the District".

41641 ■ S & S Office Solutions Inc.
3480 Johnson Ferry Rd.
Roswell, GA 30075
Ph: (770)518-0868
Fax: (770)518-4483
Co. E-mail: info@ssos.com
URL: http://www.ssos.com
Contact: Annette Stone, President
Scope: Specialists in designing, installing, and consulting for LANs (Local Area Networks) and wiring systems for professional offices (MCSE). Offers total turn-key solution to networking challenge. **Founded:** 1993.

41642 ■ SBA Computers Inc.
620 E State St.
O'Fallon, IL 62269-1540
Ph: (618)628-9590
Fax: (618)622-3717
Co. E-mail: info@sbacomputers.com
Contact: Richard Scaiefe, President
E-mail: rick@sbacomputers.com
Scope: Provider of web site and domain hosting. Offers domain registration services. **Founded:** 1997.

41643 ■ Schrager Lighting Design L.L.C.
412 Main St., Ste. H
Ridgefield, CT 06877
Ph: (203)438-1188
Fax: (203)438-2299
Co. E-mail: sspublic@schragerlightingdesign.com
Contact: Sara Schrager, Principal
Scope: Provides consulting services in architectural lighting design, with experience in lighting museums, academic and religious institutions, historic preserva-

tion, public atriums, corporate interiors, exterior lighting for landscapes and hard capes, art collections, restaurants and fine homes and estates. **Founded:** 2008.

41644 ■ Chris Shaff Consulting
8641 Dasher Ave. NW
North Canton, OH 44720-4611
Ph: (330)494-1921
Contact: Grover Chris Shaff, II, President
Scope: Specializes in business forms manufacturing and administration.

41645 ■ Simplified Technology Co.
35532 Cabrillo Dr.
Fremont, CA 94536
Ph: (510)794-5520
Free: 800-782-4435
Co. E-mail: sales201008@simplifiedtechnology.com
URL: http://www.simplifiedtechnology.com
Contact: Gregory Carvalho, President
E-mail: gregoryc@simplifiedtechnology.com
Scope: Specializes in providing system security, networking, custom software development and data availability. **Founded:** 1991. **Special Services:** MRO's Maximo and Datastream's Maintenance Package 2 (MP2).

41646 ■ Spacial Design
524 San Anselmo Ave., Ste. 146
San Anselmo, CA 94960
Ph: (415)457-3195
Fax: (415)457-1876
Co. E-mail: contactus@spacialdesign.com
URL: http://www.spacialdesign.com
Contact: Susan Lund, President
E-mail: susan@spacialdesign.com
Scope: Specializes in space planning for kitchens, closets and office. Works with individual homeowners and small businesses. Also advises clients on setting up systems and then designing spaces to accommodate those systems. **Founded:** 1979. **Seminars:** Kitchen Planning Seminar, Sonoma Valley Adult School, Oct, 2006; So. . .you'dlove a new kitchen?; Where do you begin?; What should you expect from the design and your budget?. **Telecommunication Services:** clientservices@spacialdesign.com.

41647 ■ Gary Steffy Lighting Design Inc. (GSLD)
2900 S State St., Ste. 12
Ann Arbor, MI 48104
Ph: (734)747-6630
Free: 800-537-1230
Fax: (734)747-6629
Co. E-mail: grs@gsld.net
URL: http://www.gsld.net
Contact: Gary R. Steffy, President
E-mail: grs@gsld.net
URL(s): www.garysteffy.com. **Scope:** Lighting design consultants for interior and exterior lighting needs. Additional area of expertise is landscape lighting. Serves private industries as well as government agencies. **Founded:** 1982. **Publications:** "Architectural Lighting Design". **Seminars:** Office Lighting; Lighting for Electronic Offices; Lighting Design; Historic Lighting.

41648 ■ Symmes Maini & McKee Associates (SMMA)
1000 Massachusetts Ave.
Cambridge, MA 02138
Ph: (617)547-5400
Free: 800-487-4894
Fax: (800)648-4920
URL: http://www.smma.com
Contact: Ara Krafian, President
E-mail: a_krafian@smma.com
Scope: A full service architecture, master planning, urban design, and interior design firm serving healthcare, educational, financial, and commercial institutions with particular emphasis on hospitals, research laboratories, office buildings, and educational structures including athletic facilities. **Founded:** 1955.

41649 ■ Systems Alternatives International L.L.C. (SAI)
1705 Indian Wood Cir.
Maumee, OH 43537
Ph: (419)891-1100
Fax: (419)891-1045
Co. E-mail: sales@sysalt.com
URL: http://www.sysalt.com
Contact: John Underwood, President
Scope: Provider of a total solution with consulting and design, industry proven software and hardware, and training and support. Develops and delivers the highest standard in computerized systems and engineered solutions. Specializes in selling hardware and software. Provides innovative software and quality information technology services to the unique needs of the recycling and metals industries. **Founded:** 1981. **Special Services:** XSight; Version 4; CRES; CRIS; Integrated Mill Procurements and Costing System (IMPACT).

41650 ■ TLA-Lighting Consultants Inc.
7 Pond St.
Salem, MA 01970-4819
Ph: (978)745-6870
Fax: (978)741-4420
Co. E-mail: tmlattla@aol.com
Contact: Thomas M. Lemons, President
E-mail: tmlattla@aol.com
Scope: Offers counsel on lighting installation design, lighting product design, lighting energy conservation studies and day lighting, optical systems design, system evaluation and testing, and product and market planning. Serves private industries as well as government agencies. **Founded:** 1970. **Seminars:** Reflector Design - Theory and Practice.

41651 ■ Scott M. Watson Inc.—Scott M. Watson Lighting Consultant Inc.
15200 Shady Grove Rd., Ste. 202
Rockville, MD 20850
Ph: (301)869-8800
Fax: (301)869-8802
Co. E-mail: smwiald@aol.com
Contact: Scott M. Watson, Manager
E-mail: smwiald@starpower.net
Scope: Lighting design consultant for new and renovated commercial, institutional, and high-end residential projects. Particular expertise provided in lighting layouts, fixture specifications, control groupings, dimmer specifications, shop drawing review, punch-out and focus of installations. Custom fixtures and applications designed as needed. Serves architects, interior designers, and owners, as well as government agencies. **Founded:** 1987.

41652 ■ WNF Consulting Inc.
602 E Briles Rd.
Phoenix, AZ 85027-7886
Ph: (480)940-4808
Fax: (602)222-8616
Contact: Robert Murphy, President
Scope: Firm specializes in network analysis and design. Consulting engineers assist in understanding the characteristics of each network resource and segment, optimization of network hierarchy based on usage requirements, system performance and effective resource utilization, optimization of pooled server and application configurations, storage management methodology for day-to-day storage management and storage management methodology for automated storage management. **Founded:** 1995. **Special Services:** PXEGuard™; Identity Management Service.

FRANCHISES AND BUSINESS OPPORTUNITIES

41653 ■ California Closet Company
1000 4th St., Ste. 800
San Rafael, CA 94901
Ph: (415)256-8500
Free: 800-241-3222
Fax: (415)256-8501
Co. E-mail: franchising@calclosets.com
URL: http://www.californiaclosets.com
Description: Custom closet design, manufacture, and installation. **No. of Franchise Units:** 88. **Founded:** 1978.. **Franchised:** 1982. **Equity Capital Needed:** $127,500-$377,000 total investment. **Franchise Fee:** $40,000. **Royalty Fee:** 6%. **Financial Assistance:** Third party financing available. **Training:** Includes training at headquarters, franchisee's location and ongoing support.

LIBRARIES

41654 ■ Tech-U-Fit Corporation Library
400 Madison St., No. 210
Alexandria, VA 22314
Ph: (703)549-0512
Fax: (703)548-0780
Contact: John Molino
Scope: Engineering, psychology, human factors engineering, ergonomics. **Holdings:** 200 volumes.

RESEARCH CENTERS

41655 ■ New Jersey Institute of Technology - Center for Architecture and Building Science Research (CABSR)
335 Campbell Hall
323 Martin Luther King Blvd.
Newark, NJ 07102-1982
Ph: (973)596-3097
Fax: (973)596-8443
Co. E-mail: deane.evans@njit.edu
URL: http://www.cabsr.org
Contact: Deane M. Evans, Executive Director
Founded: 1985. **Telecommunication Services:** faulks@njit.edu.

41656 ■ Rensselaer Polytechnic Institute - Lighting Research Center (LRC)
School of Architecture
21 Union St.
Troy, NY 12180
Ph: (518)687-7100
Fax: (518)687-7120
Co. E-mail: ream@rpi.edu
URL: http://www.lrc.rpi.edu
Contact: Prof. Mark S. Rea, Director
Founded: 1988. **Publications:** *Delta Portfolios* (Periodic); *Design books, evaluations*; *NLPIP Lighting Answers* (Periodic); *NLPIP Specifier Reports* (Periodic). **Educational Activities:** Colloquia (Biweekly); Industrial partners program; Roundtables, workshops, teleconferences, symposia, tours, demonstrations, and presentations; Utility Personnel Training Seminars. **Awards:** Grants, scholarships. **Telecommunication Services:** lrc@rpi.edu.

41657 ■ University of Quebec at Montreal - Centre for Study of Biological Interactions Between Environment and Health—University of Quebec at Montreal - Centre de Recherche Interdisciplinaire sur la Biologie, la Santé, la Société et l'Environnement (CINBIOSE)
Succursale Centre-ville
Case postale 8888
Montreal, QC, Canada H3C 3P8
Ph: (514)987-3915
Fax: (514)987-6183
Co. E-mail: saint-charles.johanne@uqam.ca
URL: http://www.cinbiose.uqam.ca
Contact: Dr. Johanne Saint-Charles, Director
Founded: 1990. **Telecommunication Services:** cinbiose@uqam.ca.

EDUCATIONAL PROGRAMS

41658 ■ Auditing Outsourced Operations (Onsite)
Seminar Information Service, Inc.
20 Executive Park, Ste. 120
Irvine, CA 92614
Ph: (949)261-9104
Free: 877-SEM-INFO
Fax: (949)261-1963
Co. E-mail: info@seminarinformation.com
URL: http://www.seminarinformation.com
Price: $2,050.00. **Description:** Explore the prime risk factors present in outsourcing arrangements. You will identify the key areas you must cover to ensure your audits protect your organization's interest, including audit procedures, maintaining and enforcing your right to audit with guaranteed access, and creating contracts that focus on delivery, ROI, and performance metrics. **Dates and Locations:** Boston, MA.

REFERENCE WORKS

41659 ■ *"35-Year-Old Downtown Fabric Store Closes Doors" in The Times and Democrat (September 29, 2009)*
Pub: The Times and Democrat
Description: Warren's Fashion Fabrics Inc., a 35-year-old retail fabric, decor and sewing store, officially closed its doors due, in part, to the changing tide of the industry in which fewer women sew and products from countries such as China are so cheap.

41660 ■ *"Albany Molecular on Hiring Spree as Big Pharma Slashes Work Force" in Business Review, Albany New York (December 28, 2007)*
Pub: American City Business Journals, Inc.
Ed: Barbara Pinckney. **Description:** Albany Molecular Research Inc. (AMRI) is an outsourcing company that provides work forces for pharmaceutical companies due to large numbers of downsizings in the year 2007. In 2008, AMRI plans to hire several workers.

41661 ■ *"Auxis Introduces Services for Government Contracting" in Entertainment Close-Up (December 22, 2010)*
Pub: Close-Up Media
Description: Profile of Auxis Inc., a management consulting and outsourcing company has launched a new service for companies involved in or bidding for government contracts. Details of the program are provided.

41662 ■ *"Beaumont Outsources Purchasing as Route to Supply Cost Savings" in Crain's Detroit Business (Vol. 25, June 1, 2009, No. 22)*
Pub: Crain Communications Inc. - Detroit
Ed: Jay Greene. **Description:** William Beaumont Hospitals in Royal Oak have begun outsourcing the purchasing of supplies in order to cut costs. So far, Beaumont is the only hospital in southeast Michigan to outsource its purchasing department. Other hospitals employ their own purchasing supply workers.

41663 ■ *"A Change Would Do You Good" in Canadian Business (Vol. 80, November 19, 2007, No. 23, pp. 15)*
Pub: Rogers Media
Ed: Geoff Kirbyson. **Description:** Western Glove Works will be manufacturing clothing offshore, including Sheryl Crow's jeans collection, in countries such as China and the Philippines. The company decided to operate offshore after 86 years of existence due to the high price of manufacturing jeans in Canada. Western Glove's focus on producing celebrity-endorsed goods is discussed.

41664 ■ *"ChemSW Software Development Services Available for Outsourcing" in Information Today (Vol. 26, February 2009, No. 2, pp. 30)*
Pub: Information Today, Inc.
Description: ChemSW software development services include requirements analysis, specification development, design, development, testing, and system documentation as an IT outsourcing solution. The company can also develop software tracking systems for satellite stockrooms, provide asset management integration solutions and more.

41665 ■ *"The China Syndrome" in Canadian Business (Vol. 79, July 17, 2006, No. 14-15, pp. 25)*
Pub: Rogers Media
Ed: Peter Diekmeyer. **Description:** Contrasting pace of growth in China and India are presented. Reasons for the slow pace of growth of Canadian companies like CAE Inc. and Magna in India are also discussed.

41666 ■ *"Closed Minds and Open Skies" in Barron's (Vol. 88, March 10, 2008, No. 10, pp. 50)*
Pub: Dow Jones & Company, Inc.
Ed: Thomas Donlan. **Description:** American politicians have closed minds when it comes to fair trade. The American government must not interfere with the country's manufacturing industries or worry about outsourcing defense contracts to European aerospace company Airbus.

41667 ■ *"Contract Design as a Firm Capability" in Academy of Management Review (October 2007, pp. 1060)*
Pub: ScholarOne, Inc.
Ed: Nicholas Argyres, Kyle J. Mayer. **Description:** A firm's capabilities for designing detailed contracts and the role of managers, engineers, and lawyers in the design of such contracts is highlighted.

41668 ■ *"Debt-Collection Agency to Lay Off 368 in Hampton Center" in Virginian-Pilot (December 4, 2010)*
Pub: Virginian-Pilot
Ed: Tom Shean. **Description:** NCO Financial Systems Inc., provider of debt-collection and outsourcing services will permanently lay off 368 workers at its Hampton call center in 2011.

41669 ■ *"Designing Events Updates Online Suite" in Wireless News (October 25, 2009)*
Pub: Close-Up Media
Description: Designing Events, an outsourcing and consulting firm for conferences and meetings, announced the release of an update to its Designing Events Online suite of web-based management and marketing tools; features include enhanced versions of online registration and collaboration, content management, session development, social media and conference websites.

41670 ■ *"Don't Try This Offshore" in Harvard Business Review (Vol. 86, September 2008, No. 9, pp. 39)*
Pub: Harvard Business School Press
Description: Fictitious outsourcing scenario is presented, with contributors offering advice. The suggestions address the ease or complexity of offshoring business creativity, along with challenges and benefits.

41671 ■ *"Fifth Third Grapples With Account Snafu" in Business Courier (Vol. 24, December 7, 2008, No. 34, pp. 1)*
Pub: American City Business Journals, Inc.
Ed: Jon Newberry. **Description:** Fifth Third Bank's vendor committed an error which led to a badly damaged credit score for Brett and Karen Reloka. The couple reported the incident to the bank and are still waiting for action to be taken. A major outourced services vendor caused paid-off mortgages to be reported delinquent.

41672 ■ *"Five Steps for Handling Independent Contractors" in Hawaii Business (Vol. 53, January 2008, No. 7, pp. 49)*
Pub: Hawaii Business Publishing
Ed: Jason Ubay. **Description:** Small companies should be cautious in dealing with independent contractors. They must understand that they cannot dictate specific operational procedures, job duties, standards of conduct and performance standards to the contractors, and they cannot interfere with the evaluation and training of the contractors' employees. Tips on negotiating with independent contractors are given.

41673 ■ *"The Future of Work" in Black Enterprise (Vol. 41, August 2010, No. 1, pp. 65)*
Pub: Earl G. Graves Publishing Co. Inc.
Ed: Annya M. Lott. **Description:** Technology, globalization, and outsourcing will continue to shape the future of work. Social media is a means for small companies to market goods and services.

41674 ■ *"Hire Power" in Entrepreneur (Vol. 35, November 2007, No. 11, pp. 105)*
Pub: Entrepreneur Media Inc.
Ed: Mark Henricks. **Description:** Companies with big resources may hire human resource (HR) consultants to help with writing manuals, drafting policies and designing benefits for employees. HR consultants may also be hired to assist with specific functions or other strategic aspects.

41675 ■ *How to Start a Bankruptcy Forms Processing Service*
Pub: Graphico Publishing Company
Ed: Victoria Ring. **Released:** September 2004. **Price:** $39.00. **Description:** Due to the increase in bankruptcy filings, attorneys are outsourcing related jobs in order to reduce overhead.

41676 ■ *"Importers Share Safety Liability" in Feedstuffs (Vol. 80, January 21, 2008, No. 3, pp. 19)*
Pub: Miller Publishing Company, Inc.
Description: Pet food and toys containing lead paint are among products from China being recalled due to safety concerns. American Society for Quality's list of measures that outsourcing companies can take to help ensure safer products being imported to the U.S.

41677 ■ *"Intel Forges New Strategy With Chinese Fabrication Plant" in Globe & Mail (March 26, 2007, pp. B6)*
Pub: CTVglobemedia Publishing Inc.
Ed: Don Clark. **Description:** World's largest semiconductor manufacturing giant Intel Corp. is planning to construct a new chip fabrication plant in China. It will be investing an estimated $2.5 billion for this purpose.

41678 ■ *"It's Time To Swim" in Canadian Business (Vol. 81, March 3, 2008, No. 3, pp. 37)*
Pub: Rogers Media
Ed: Megan Harman. **Description:** Canadian manufacturers should consider Asian markets such as India and the United Arab Emirates as the U.S. economic downturn continues. Canada's shortage in skilled labor is also expected to negatively affect manufacturing industries. Ontario's plans to assist manufacturers are also presented.

41679 ■ *"Knox County Schools Debate Outsourcing Janitorial Services" in (March 29, 2011)*
Pub: Knoxville News Sentinel
Ed: Lola Alapo. **Description:** Custodial services of Knox County Schools in Tennessee may be outsourced in move to save money for the school district. Details of the proposed program are included.

41680 ■ *"Local Manufacturers See Tax Proposal Hurting Global Operations" in Crain's Cleveland Business (Vol. 30, May 18, 2009, No. 20)*
Pub: Crain Communications, Inc.
Ed: Dan Shingler. **Description:** New tax laws proposed by the Obama Administration could hinder the efforts of some Northeast Ohio industrial companies from expanding their overseas markets. The law is designed to prevent companies from moving jobs overseas.

41681 ■ *"Lufthansa-Cathay Deal Reinforces Outsourcing" in Globe & Mail (March 30, 2007, pp. B9)*
Pub: CTVglobemedia Publishing Inc.
Ed: Daniel Michaels. **Description:** Cathay Pacific Airways Ltd. signed a $300 million contract with Lufthansa Technik AG to outsource engine maintenance operations. The outsourcing of non-core operation is increasing in airline industry.

41682 ■ *"May I Handle That For You?" in Inc. (March 2008, pp. 40, 42)*
Pub: Gruner & Jahr USA Publishing
Ed: Taylor Mallory. **Description:** According to a recent survey, 53 percent of all companies outsource a portion of their human resources responsibilities. Ceridian, Administaff, Taleo, KnowledgeBank, and CheckPoint HR are among the companies profiled.

41683 ■ *"Meet Rebecca. She's Here to Fire You" in Inc. (November 2007, pp. 25-26)*
Pub: Gruner & Jahr USA Publishing
Ed: Max Chafkin. **Description:** Amid liability concerns as well as CEO guilt, more and more firms are using consulting companies to fire workers. These outsourced firms help small companies structure severance and document information in order to limit legal liability when firing an employee.

41684 ■ *"New Work Order" in Black Enterprise (Vol. 38, March 2008, No. 8, pp. 60)*
Pub: Earl G. Graves Publishing Co. Inc.
Description: Today's management challenges includes issues of more competition, globalization, outsourcing and technological advances. Suggestions to help create progressive leadership in small business that sustains a competitive edge are listed.

41685 ■ *"Nobel Winners Provide Insight on Outsourcing, Contract Work" in Workforce Management (Vol. 88, November 16, 2009, No. 12, pp. 11)*
Pub: Crain Communications Inc.
Ed: Jeremy Smerd. **Description:** Insights into such workforce management issues as bonuses, employee contracts and outsourcing has been recognized by the Nobel Prize winners in economics whose research sheds a light on the way economic decisions are made outside markets.

41686 ■ *Outsourcing: Information Technology, Original Equipment Manufacturer, Leo, Oursourcing, Offshoring Research Network, Crowdsourcing*
Pub: General Books LLC
Released: May 1, 2010. **Price:** $14.14. **Description:** Chapters include information for outsourcing firms and how to maintain an outsourcing business.

41687 ■ *"Overseas Overtures" in Business Journal-Portland (Vol. 24, October 26, 2007, No. 35, pp. 1)*
Pub: American City Business Journals, Inc.
Ed: Robin J. Moody. **Description:** Oregon has a workforce shortage, specifically for the health care industry. Recruiting agencies, such as the International Recruiting Network Inc., answers the high demand for workforce by recruiting foreign employees. The difficulties recruiting companies experience with regards to foreign labor laws are investigated.

41688 ■ *"Patently (Un)Clear" in Business Strategy Review (Vol. 21, Spring 2010, No. 1, pp. 28)*
Pub: Wiley-Blackwell
Ed: Markus Reitzig, Stefan Wagner. **Description:** After developing a great product or process, it's important to protect it. The benefits of using internal patent lawyers versus outsourcing the task are examined.

41689 ■ *"Prevent Disasters In Design Outsourcing" in Harvard Business Review (Vol. 86, September 2008, No. 9, pp. 30)*
Pub: Harvard Business School Press
Ed: Jason Amaral; Geoffrey Parker. **Description:** Factors that could compromise the quality and success of product platform outsourcing are examined including misaligned objectives and inadequate version control.

41690 ■ *"Rep Vs. Direct: Always an Interesting Story" in Agency Sales Magazine (Vol. 39, July 2009, No. 7, pp. 3)*
Pub: MANA
Ed: Bryan C. Shirley. **Description:** Manufacturers benefit from outsourcing their field sales to professional sales representatives in the areas of multi-line selling and customer knowledge and relationship. Some misperceptions about sales reps include the belief that they are an additional 'channel' in sales.

41691 ■ *"Research: Mind the Gap" in Business Strategy Review (Vol. 21, Summer 2010, No. 2, pp. 84)*
Pub: Wiley-Blackwell
Description: Isabel Fernandez-Mateo's cumulative gender disadvantage in contract employment is presented.

41692 ■ *"Stung by Recession, Hemmer Regroups with New Strategy" in Business Courier (Vol. 27, June 4, 2010, No. 5, pp. 1)*
Pub: Business Courier
Ed: Lucy May. **Description:** Paul Hemmer Companies reduced its work force and outsourced operations such as marketing and architecture, in order for the commercial and construction firm to survive the recession. Hammer's total core revenue in 2009 dropped to less than $30 million forcing the closure of its Chicago office.

41693 ■ *"Tata's Novi Unit Looks to Hire 200 Engineers" in Crain's Detroit Business (Vol. 26, January 18, 2010, No. 3, pp. 4)*
Pub: Crain Communications Inc.
Ed: Lindsay Chappell. **Description:** Indian conglomerate Tata Sons Ltd.'s Novi-based engineering subsidiary is expected to hire around 200 engineers in the next three months or so, in part due to a more sophisticated attitude about outsourcing vehicle engineering to other companies.

41694 ■ *"To Offshore Or Not To Offshore?" in Converting (Vol. 25, October 1, 2007, No. 10, pp. 10)*
Pub: Reed Business Information Inc.
Ed: Mark Spaulding. **Description:** Offshore manufacturing and the issue of buying raw materials from foreign suppliers by American companies is discussed. Results of a study conducted by Cap Gemini and Pro Logis regarding offshore manufacturing, especially to China, are presented.

41695 ■ *"Two Local Firms Make Inc. List: Minority Business" in Indianapolis Business Journal (Vol. 31, August 30, 2010, No. 26, pp. 13A)*
Pub: Indianapolis Business Journal Corporation
Description: Smart IT staffing agency and Entap Inc., an IT outsourcing firm were among the top ten fastest growing black-owned businesses in the U.S. by Inc. magazine.

41696 ■ *"Uncovering Offshoring's Invisible Costs" in HRMagazine (Vol. 54, January 2009, No. 1, pp. 1)*
Pub: Society for Human Resource Management
Contact: Henry G. Jackson, President
E-mail: hjackson@shrm.org
Ed: Rita Zeidner. **Description:** Nearly half of all offshore service work fails, often due to the invisible costs of communication and cultural friction according to researchers. The challenges of offshore services are discussed.

CONSULTANTS

41697 ■ C. Clint Bolte & Associates
809 Philadelphia Ave.
Chambersburg, PA 17201
Ph: (717)263-5768
Fax: (717)263-8954
Co. E-mail: clint@clintbolte.com
URL: http://www.clintbolte.com
Contact: C. Clint Bolte, Principal
E-mail: cbolte3@comcast.net
Scope: Provider of management consulting services to firms involved with the printing industry. Services include outsourcing studies, graphics supply chain management studies, company and equipment valuations, plant layout services, litigation support, fulfillment warehouse consulting and product development services. **Founded:** 1989. **Seminars:** How to compete with the majors.

FRANCHISES AND BUSINESS OPPORTUNITIES

41698 ■ Oxford Business Consulting Group, LLC
19 Beech Pl.
Huntington, NY 11743
Ph: (631)423-8570
Fax: (631)423-8580
Description: Outsourced franchise sales & development. **Founded:** 2000..

START-UP INFORMATION

41699 ■ *101 Businesses You Can Start with Less Than One Thousand Dollars: for Retirees*
Pub: Atlantic Publishing Company
Ed: Heather Lee Shepherd. **Released:** October 2007. **Price:** $21.95. **Description:** According to a study by the U.S. Department of Health and Human Resources, people starting their work careers will face the following situation when they retire at the age of 65: they will have annual incomes between $4,000 and $26,000. According to the Social Security Administration, today's retirees can count on corporate pensions and Social Security for 61 percent of their retirement income. The remainder must come from other sources. Therefore, if this holds true for the future, today's workers need to accumulate enough in personal savings to make up the 39 percent shortfall in retirement income. The solution for many will be to start a small part-time business.

ASSOCIATIONS AND OTHER ORGANIZATIONS

41700 ■ National Association of Part-Time and Temporary Employees (NAPTE)
5800 Barton, Ste. 201
Shawnee, KS 66203
Ph: (913)962-7740
Co. E-mail: napte-champion@worldnet.att.net
URL: http://www.members.tripod.com/~napte
Contact: Preston L. Conner, President

Description: Promotes the economic and social interests of persons working on a part-time, contingent, or temporary basis through research, advocacy, and member services. Offers short-term portable health insurance. **Scope:** economic and labor trends, career development, public policy. **Founded:** 1994. **Subscriptions:** books clippings periodicals.

RESEARCH CENTERS

41701 ■ New Ways to Work
103 Morris St., Ste. A
Sebastopol, CA 95472
Ph: (707)824-4000
Fax: (707)824-4410
Co. E-mail: sgtrippe@newwaystowork.org
URL: http://www.nww.org
Contact: Steve Trippe, President

Founded: 1972. **Publications:** *Work Times* (Quarterly). **Educational Activities:** Programs, to educate employers and employees in work time options and policy issues; New Ways to Work Workshops, to educate employers and employees in work time options and policy issues; International Society for Work Options Meeting. **Telecommunication Services:** newways@newwaystowork.org.

Partnerships/Mergers

START-UP INFORMATION

41702 ■ *The Mousedriver Chronicles*
Pub: Perseus Books Group
Ed: John Lusk; Kyle Harrison. **Released:** 2003. **Price:** $16.95. **Description:** Entrepreneurial voyage through the startup business of two ivy-league business school graduates and the lessons they learned while developing their idea of a computer mouse that looks like a golf driver into the marketplace. The book is an inspiration for those looking to turn an idea into a company.

41703 ■ *Partnership: Small Business Start-Up Kit*
Pub: Nova Publishing Company
Ed: Daniel Sitarz. **Released:** November 2005. **Price:** $29.95. **Description:** Guidebook detailing partnership law by state covering the formation and use of partnerships as a business form. Information on filing requirements, property laws, legal liability, standards, and the new Revised Uniform Partnership Act is covered.

41704 ■ *Structuring Your Business*
Pub: Adams Media Corporation
Contact: Gary Krebs, Director
E-mail: swatrous@adamsmedia.com
Ed: Michele Cagan. **Released:** 2004. **Price:** $19.95. **Description:** Accountant and author shares insight into starting a new company. The guide assists entrepreneurs through the process, whether it is a corporation, an LLC, a sole proprietorship, or a partnership. Tax codes, accounting practices and legislation affecting every business as well as tips on managing finances are among the topics covered.

41705 ■ *The Toilet Paper Entrepreneur: The Tell-It-Like-It-Is Guide to Cleaning Up In Business, Even If You Are At the End of Your Roll*
Pub: Obsidian Launch LLC
Ed: Mike Michalowicz. **Price:** $24.95. **Description:** The founder of three multimillion-dollar companies, including Obsidian Launch, a company that partners with first-time entrepreneurs to grow their concepts into industry leaders.

EDUCATIONAL PROGRAMS

41706 ■ AMA's Course on Mergers and Acquisitions (Onsite)
American Management Association
600 AMA Way
Saranac Lake, NY 12983-5534
Ph: (212)586-8100
Free: 877-566-9441
Fax: (518)891-0368
Co. E-mail: customerservice@amanet.org
URL: http://www.amaseminars.org
Price: $4,395.00 for non-members; $3,995.00 for AMA members; and $3,421.00 for General Services Administration (GSA) members. **Description:** Three-day seminar for executive managers; covers organizational, financial, planning, tax, and risk aspects of mergers and acquisitions. **Dates and Locations:** Las Vegas, NV; and La Jolla, CA.

REFERENCE WORKS

41707 ■ *"3Par: Storing Up Value" in Barron's (Vol. 90, August 30, 2010, No. 35, pp. 30)*
Pub: Barron's Editorial & Corporate Headquarters
Ed: Mark Veverka. **Description:** Dell and Hewlett Packard are both bidding for data storage company 3Par. The acquisition would help Dell and Hewlett Packard provide customers with a one-stop shop as customers move to a private cloud in the Internet.

41708 ■ *"13D Filings" in Barron's (Vol. 88, March 10, 2008, No. 10, pp. M11)*
Pub: Dow Jones & Company, Inc.
Description: Barington Capital and Clinton Group sent a letter to Dillard's demanding a list of the company's stockholders. Elliott Associates announced that it is prepared to take over Packeteer for $5.50 a share. Strongbow capital suggested a change in leadership in Duckwall-ALCO Stores.

41709 ■ *"13D Filings: Investors Report to the SEC" in Barron's (Vol. 88, March 31, 2008, No. 13, pp. M10)*
Pub: Dow Jones & Company, Inc.
Description: Obrem Capital Management wants Micrel to rescind Micrel's shareholder-rights plan and to boost its board to six members from five. Patricia L. Childress plans to nominate herself to the board of Sierra Bancorp, and Luther King Capital Management may consider a competing acquisition proposal for Industrial Distribution Group.

41710 ■ *"13D Filings: Investors Report to the SEC" in Barron's (Vol. 89, July 13, 2009, No. 28, pp. M9)*
Pub: Dow Jones & Co., Inc.
Description: Bulldog Investors wants Hicks Acquisition Co. to liquidate and return money to shareholders and they believe that the acquisition of Graham Packaging by Hicks will not be completed in a timely manner. Discovery Group raised their holdings to 5.2 percent of Nobel Learning Communities.

41711 ■ *"13D Filings: Investors Report to the SEC" in Barron's (Vol. 89, July 27, 2009, No. 30, pp. M14)*
Pub: Dow Jones & Co., Inc.
Description: Duquesne Capital Management is opposed to Alpha Natural Resources' proposed merger with Foundation Coal Holdings since it is against the long-term interest of shareholders. Lime Rock Partners increased their holdings of Tesco to 5,234,516 shares while Nova A/S increased their holdings of BioMimetic Therapeutics to 3,729,065 shares.

41712 ■ *"$40M Fund Created for Big Energy Project" in Austin Business JournalInc. (Vol. 29, November 27, 2009, No. 38, pp. 1)*
Pub: American City Business Journals
Ed: Christopher Calnan. **Description:** A group of Texas businessmen, called Republic Power Partners LP, is planning to raise $40 million in order to launch an alternative energy project. The 6,000-megawatt initiative would generate solar, biomass and wind power in West Texas and could cost as much as $10 billion.

41713 ■ *"2008: Year of the Rat Race" in Mergers & Acquisitions: The Dealmaker's Journal (March 1, 2008)*
Pub: SourceMedia, Inc.
Ed: Danelle Fugazy. **Description:** Although China still presents opportunities to Western investors, many are discovering that much more research needs to be done concerning doing business in that country before investing there becomes truly mainstream. According to one source, there are at least 300,000 small state-owned enterprises in China and millions of middle-market privately owned companies; the Chinese stock market can only handle about 50 to 70 IPOs a year and lists about 1,500 companies at a time.

41714 ■ *"A&E Networks" in Brandweek (Vol. 49, April 21, 2008, No. 16, pp. SR9)*
Pub: VNU Business Media, Inc.
Ed: Anthony Crupi. **Description:** Provides contact information for sales and marketing personnel for the A&E Networks as well as a listing of the station's top programming and an analysis of the current season and the target audience for those programs running in the current season. A&E has reinvented itself as a premium entertainment brand over the last five years and with its $2.5 million per episode acquisition of The Sopranos, the station signaled that it was serious about getting back into the scripted programming business. The acquisition also helped the network compete against other cable networks and led to a 20 percent increase in prime-time viewers.

41715 ■ *"Abacast, Citadel Strike Radio Ad Deal" in Business Journal Portland (Vol. 27, December 31, 2010, No. 44, pp. 3)*
Pub: Portland Business Journal
Ed: Erik Siemers. **Description:** Software firm Abacast Inc. has partnered with Citadel Media to aid the latter's advertising sales. Citadel provides radio networks and syndicated programs to 4,200 affiliate stations.

41716 ■ *"Abaddon Acquires Pukaskwa Uranium Properties in NW Ontario" in Canadian Corporate News (May 16, 2007)*
Pub: Comtex News Network Inc.
Description: Rubicon Minerals Corp. has entered into an Option Agreement with Consolidated Abaddon Resources Inc. for the acquisition of Pukaskwa uranium properties and plans to conduct an extensive exploration program to prove out the resource and geological potential of the area. Statistical data included.

41717 ■ *"Achieve Tampa Bay Thrown a Lifeline in Proposed Merger" in Tampa Bay Business Journal (Vol. 30, January 22, 2010, No. 5, pp. 1)*
Pub: American City Business Journals
Ed: Margie Manning. **Description:** Mental Health Care Inc. proposed a merger with Achieve Tampa

Bay Inc. The former proposes to administer the latter's operations and take over its assets while paying its debts.

41718 ■ *"Acquisition of a Uranium Exploration Project, Laguiche Basin, Opinaca Area, Quebec" in Canadian Corporate News (May 16, 2007)*
Pub: Comtex News Network Inc.
Description: Dios Exploration Inc. negotiated an option agreement with Sirios Resources Inc. to explore the Opinaca Nord Property with a project that comprises one main anomaly cluster for gold in association with arsenic and two detailed uranium anomaly clusters.

41719 ■ *"AdvacePierre Heats Up" in Business Courier (Vol. 27, October 29, 2010, No. 26, pp. 1)*
Pub: Business Courier
Ed: John Newberry. **Description:** Bill Toler, chief executive officer of AdvancePierre Foods, is aiming for more growth and more jobs. The company was formed after the merger of Pierre Foods with two Oklahoma-based food processing companies. Toler wants to expand production and is set to start adding employees in the next 6-12 months.

41720 ■ *"Advertising May Take a Big Hit in Southwest/AirTran Merger" in Baltimore Business Journal (Vol. 28, October 1, 2010, No. 21, pp. 1)*
Pub: Baltimore Business Journal
Ed: Gary Haber. **Description:** Advertising on television stations and the publishing industry in Baltimore could drop as a result of the merger between rival discount airlines Southwest Airlines and AirTran Airways. Southwest is among the top advertisers in the U.S., spending $126 million in 2009. No local jobs are expected to be affected because neither airline uses a local advertising firm.

41721 ■ *"Affordable Financing for Acquisitions" in Franchising World (Vol. 42, September 2010, No. 9, pp. 47)*
Pub: International Franchise Association
Ed: Gene Cerrotti. **Description:** Acquisition pricing is reasonable and interest rates are low and quality franchised resale opportunities are priced 4.5 times EBITDA. Information about Small Business Administration loans is also included.

41722 ■ *"Age-Old System of Bartering Is Being Revolutionized by Phoenix Company, Premier Barter" in Internet Wire (July 12, 2010)*
Pub: Comtex
Description: Premier Barter is helping entrepreneurs rediscover the system of bartering as a method of exchanging goods and services without cash or credit.

41723 ■ *"Aggenix Completes Merger with German Giant" in Houston Business Journal (Vol. 40, December 25, 2009, No. 33, pp. 2)*
Pub: American City Business Journals
Ed: Mary Ann Azevedo. **Description:** Agennix Inc. has completed its transformation into a German company after Germany-based GPC Biotech merged into the former publicly traded Agennix AG. One quarter of Agennix's 60 employees will remain in Houston. Details on Agennix's drug trials are examined.

41724 ■ *"AIC To Buy $350M of Real Estate" in Austin Business JournalInc. (Vol. 28, November 14, 2008, No. 35, pp. 1)*
Pub: American City Business Journals
Ed: Kate Harrington. **Description:** Austin-based AIC Ventures LP is planning to buy $350 million worth of commercial real estate. The company's move will double its acquisitions. It is also planning to acquire 30 assets for its eight fun in 2009 from middle-market companies.

41725 ■ *"Airline Mergers: United Next?" in Crain's Chicago Business (Vol. 31, April 21, 2008, No. 16, pp. 12)*
Pub: Crain Communications, Inc.
Description: Discusses a potential merger between United and Continental airlines; unions representing 48,900 pilots, mechanics, flight attendants, ticket agents and ramp workers at United have put the management on notice that they expect to be a factor in any merger discussions if the company wants their cooperation.

41726 ■ *"Airlines Mount PR Push to Win Public Support Against Big Oil" in Advertising Age (Vol. 79, July 14, 2008, No. 7, pp. 1)*
Pub: Crain Communications, Inc.
Ed: Michael Bush. **Description:** Top airline executives from competing companies have banded together in a public relations plan in which they are sending e-mails to their frequent fliers asking for aid in lobbying legislators to put a restriction on oil speculation.

41727 ■ *"Akerman Senterfitt Merger Deal Close" in The Business Journal-Serving Greater Tampa Bay (Vol. 28, July 18, 2008, No. 30, pp. 1)*
Pub: American City Business Journals, Inc.
Ed: Jeff Blumenthal. **Description:** Sources familiar to the negotiations of Akerman Senterfitt's planned merger with Wolf Block has disclosed that executive committees of both firms have approved the deal. They expect to create an 800-lawyer firm with a significant presence in the U.S. East Coast. Other views and information on the deal and its expected impact on law practice in Florida are presented.

41728 ■ *"All About The Benjamins" in Canadian Business (Vol. 81, September 29, 2008, No. 16, pp. 92)*
Pub: Rogers Media Ltd.
Ed: David Baines. **Description:** Discusses real estate developer Royal Indian Raj International Corp., a company that planned to build a $3 billion 'smart city' near the Bangalore airport; to this day nothing has ever been built. The company was incorporated in 1999 by Manoj C. Benjamin one investor, Bill Zack, has been sued by the developer for libel due to his website that calls the company a scam. Benjamin has had a previous case of fraud issued against him as well as a string of liabilities and lawsuits.

41729 ■ *"All For One, None for All?" in Canadian Business (Vol. 83, October 12, 2010, No. 17, pp. 60)*
Pub: Rogers Media Ltd.
Ed: Michael McCullogh. **Description:** The effect of the growth of Canada's overseas provincial trade offices on Canadian trade is discussed. Economic development commissions in the country have devised a single 'Consider Canada' campaign to pitch foreign investors. It is hoped that large cities will gain from banding together rather than competing against one another.

41730 ■ *"Altegrity Acquires John D. Cohen, Inc." in (November 19, 2009, pp. 14)*
Pub: Investment Weekly News
Description: John D. Cohen, Inc., a contract provider of national security policy guidance and counsel to the federal government, was acquired by Altegrity, Inc., a global screening and security solutions provider; the company will become part of US Investigations Services, LLC and operate under the auspices of Altegrity's new business, Altegrity Security Consulting.

41731 ■ *"Aluminium maker Novelis Soars on Indian Takeover Talk" in Globe & Mail (January 27, 2007, pp. B5)*
Pub: CTVglobemedia Publishing Inc.
Ed: Andy Hoffman. **Description:** The plans of India-based Kumar Mangalam Birla's Aditya Birla Group to bid for Atlanta-based rolled aluminium maker Novelis Inc. are discussed. The talks about the purchase have caused a rise in Novelis's share price.

41732 ■ *"Amcon Distributing Co." in Arkansas Business (Vol. 26, November 9, 2009, No. 45, pp. 13)*
Pub: Journal Publishing Inc.
Description: Amcon Distributing Co., a consumer products company, has bought the convenience store distribution assets of Discount Distributors from its parent, Harps Food Stores Inc., significantly increasing its wholesale distribution presence in the northwest Arkansas market. The acquisition will be funded through Amcon's existing credit facilities.

41733 ■ *"Analysts: More Mergers for the Region's Hospitals" in Boston Business Journal (Vol. 30, October 15, 2010, No. 36, pp. 1)*
Pub: Boston Business Journal
Ed: Julie M. Donnelly. **Description:** A number of hospitals in Boston, Massachusetts are engaging in mergers and acquisitions. Caritas Christi Health Care is set to be purchased by Cerberus Capital Management. The U.S. healthcare reform law is seen to drive the development.

41734 ■ *"And In This Briefcase" in Mergers & Acquisitions: The Dealmaker's Journal (March 1, 2008)*
Pub: SourceMedia, Inc.
Description: ACG San Diego decided to address the impact the changes in the economy will have on potential private equity transactions as well as what criteria private equity firms are looking for when assessing a company. At the opening of the chapter's 2008 breakfast meeting, real-world case studies were utilized with the audiences' participation in order to assess pre-deal risk scenarios.

41735 ■ *"Angel Investors Across State Collaborate" in Austin Business Journal (Vol. 31, May 20, 2011, No. 11, pp. 1)*
Pub: American City Business Journals Inc.
Ed: Christopher Calnan. **Description:** Texas' twelve angel investing groups are going to launch the umbrella organization Alliance of Texas Angel Networks (ATAN) to support more syndicated deals and boost investments in Texas. In 2010, these investing groups infused more than $24 million to startups in 61 deals.

41736 ■ *"Angiotech to Buy Top Medical Devices Company" in Globe & Mail (February 1, 2006, pp. B1)*
Pub: CTVglobemedia Publishing Inc.
Ed: Leonard Zehr. **Description:** The details on Angiotech Pharmaceuticals Inc.'s acquisition of American Medical Instruments Holdings Inc. are presented.

41737 ■ *"Arcelor Bid Wins Dofasco Board's Blessing" in Globe & Mail (January 17, 2006, pp. B1)*
Pub: CTVglobemedia Publishing Inc.
Ed: Greg Keenan. **Description:** The details surrounding Arcelor SA's proposed acquisition of Dofasco Inc., for $5.5 billion, are presented.

41738 ■ *"Area Small Businesses Enjoy Benefits of Bartering Group" in News-Herald (August 22, 2010)*
Pub: The News-Herald
Ed: Brandon C. Baker. **Description:** ITEX is a publicly traded firm that spurs cashless, business-to-business transactions within its own marketplace. Details of the bartering of goods and services within the company are outlined.

41739 ■ *"Around the World" in Entrepreneur (Vol. 36, March 2008, No. 3, pp. 82)*
Pub: Entrepreneur Media Inc.
Ed: Gail Dutton. **Description:** Joining a global consortium can improve a business greater access to services and expertise from other members around the world. The goal is to develop the company to be able to reach to a wider customer base; other details on the benefits of joining a consortium are discussed.

41740 ■ *"As Capital Gains Tax Hike Looms, Merger Activity Percolates" in Baltimore Business Journal (Vol. 28, August 27, 2010, No. 16, pp. 1)*
Pub: Baltimore Business Journal
Ed: Scott Dance. **Description:** Concerns for higher capital gains taxes in 2011 have been provoking buyers and sellers to engage in mergers and acquisitions activity, which is expected to gain momentum before the end of 2010. Companies that had saved

cash during the recession have been taking advantage of the buyer's market. Other trends in local and national mergers and acquisitions activity are presented.

41741 ■ *"'The Asian Decade" in Hawaii Business (Vol. 53, January 2008, No. 7, pp. 19)*
Pub: Hawaii Business Publishing
Ed: Cathy S. Cruz-George. **Description:** Chaney Brooks, a Hawaiian real estate company, has affiliated with commercial real estate network NAI Global. The NAI partnership will improve Hawaii's international business, particularly its Asian investments. Hawaii's diverse workforce is evaluated, with regards to being an asset for international businesses.

41742 ■ *"Astral Fine-Tunes Details of Standard Purchase" in Globe & Mail (February 26, 2007, pp. B1)*
Pub: CTVglobemedia Publishing Inc.
Ed: Grant Robertson. **Description:** The proposed acquisition of Standard Radio Inc. by Astral Media Inc. for $1.2 billion is discussed.

41743 ■ *"Astral Media Set to Broadcast Coast to Coast" in Globe & Mail (February 24, 2007, pp. B5)*
Pub: CTVglobemedia Publishing Inc.
Ed: Grant Robertson. **Description:** The decision of Astral Media Inc. to acquire Standard Broadcasting Corp. Ltd. for $1.2 billion, with a view to increase its broadcast coverage, is discussed.

41744 ■ *"ASU Explores Russian Partnership" in The Business Journal - Serving Phoenix and the Valley of the Sun (Vol. 28, September 5, 2008)*
Pub: American City Business Journals, Inc.
Ed: Mike Sunnucks. **Description:** Arizona State University is planning to partner with Russia-based St. Petersburg State University (SPSU) regarding research, faculty and student exchange, and other joint efforts. SPSU is one of Russia's leading scientific and research institutions. Arizona State's partnerships with other foreign colleges are also mentioned.

41745 ■ *"At 5-Year Mark, News 9 Makes Presence Felt in Competition for Ad Dollars" in Business Review, Albany New York (October 5, 2007)*
Pub: American City Business Journals, Inc.
Ed: Barbara Pinckney. **Description:** The 24-hour news channel Capital News 9 can be watched live by viewers on their cell phones beginning late 2007 or early 2008 as part of a deal between Time Warner Cable and Sprint Nextel Corporation to bring Sprint's Pivot technology. News 9 marked its fifth year and plans to continue expanding coverage and provide better services to viewers.

41746 ■ *"AT&T To Acquire Black Telecom Firm" in Black Enterprise (Vol. 38, January 2008, No. 6, pp. 24)*
Pub: Earl G. Graves Publishing Co. Inc.
Ed: Alan Hughes. **Description:** Details of AT&T's acquisition of ChaseCom LP, a telecommunications company based in Houston, Texas, are covered.

41747 ■ *"Atlific Adds Management of 4 Hotels to Its Portfolio in Fort McMurray" in Canadian Corporate News (May 16, 2007)*
Pub: Comtex News Network Inc.
Description: Atlific Hotels & Resorts took over management for Merit Inn & Suites, The Merit Hotel, The Nomad Hotel and The Nomad Suites in Fort McMurray. The company feels that they will be able to increase the hotels' abilities to promote their services through their vast network of sales personnel and marketing and e-commerce team.

41748 ■ *"Attorney Guides Biotech Company in $6 Million Initial Public Offering" in Miami Daily Business Review (March 26, 2008)*
Pub: ALM Media Inc.
Description: In order to raise capital to engage in a full-scale trial of MyoCell to receive clinical approval, Bioheart Inc., launched an initial public offering. Bioheart researches and develops cell therapies to treat heart damage.

41749 ■ *"Aussie Rules" in Canadian Business (Vol. 79, Winter 2006, No. 24, pp. 45)*
Pub: Rogers Media
Ed: Jeff Sanford. **Description:** The efforts of the Toronto-based private equity firm Onex, to acquire the Australian national airline, Qantas Airways Ltd., are described.

41750 ■ *"Australian Firm Buys Off Sands Engineering Company for $1 Billion" in Globe & Mail (February 8, 2007, pp. B3)*
Pub: CTVglobemedia Publishing Inc.
Ed: David Ebner. **Description:** Australia's WorleyParson Ltd. acquires Colt Engineering Corp., a private petroleum company, for $1 billion. The acquision will provide WorleyParson an opportunity to expand its operations in Australia.

41751 ■ *"Auto Show Taps Moms" in Marketing to Women (Vol. 21, April 2008, No. 4, pp. 3)*
Pub: EPM Communications Inc.
Contact: Ira Mayer, President
E-mail: imayer@epmcom.com
Description: Teamed with Mother Proof, an online site which features automotive content aimed at moms, the Chicago Auto Show will present a full day of programming with the emphasis on mom.

41752 ■ *"AV Concept Expands Into Green Energy Storage" in Wireless News (January 25, 2010)*
Pub: Close-Up Media
Description: Electronics distributor and manufacturer AV Concept Holdings Limited announced a marketing partnership with Boston-Power, a provider of lithium-ion batteries, with a focus in the Chinese and Korean markets.

41753 ■ *"Avnet Inc.'s Expansion Fueled By Mergers and Acquisitions" in The Business Journal - Serving Phoenix and the Valley of the Sun (Vol. 28, September 12, 2008, No. 53, pp. 1)*
Pub: American City Business Journals, Inc.
Ed: Patrick O'Grady. **Description:** Avnet Inc. has grown and has nearly tripled its revenue in the past ten years through the company's acquisitions and consolidation. The company's revenue in 2008 is $17.9 billion. Other details about the company's growth are discussed.

41754 ■ *"Baking Up Bigger Lance" in Charlotte Business Journal (Vol. 25, December 3, 2010, No. 37, pp. 1)*
Pub: Charlotte Business Journal
Ed: Ken Elkins. **Description:** Events that led to the merger between Charlotte, North Carolina-based snack food manufacturer Lance Inc. and Pennsylvania-based pretzel maker Snyder's of Hanover Inc. are discussed. The merger is expected to help Lance in posting a 70 percent increase in revenue, which reached $900 million in 2009. How the merger would affect Snyder's of Hanover is also described.

41755 ■ *"Baldwin Connelly Partnership Splits" in Business Journal Serving Greater Tampa Bay (Vol. 30, November 19, 2010, No. 48, pp. 1)*
Pub: Tampa Bay Business Journal
Ed: Alexis Muellner. **Description:** The fast-growing insurance brokerage Baldwin Connelly is now breaking up after five years. Two different entrepreneurial visions have developed within the organization and founders Lowry Baldwin and John Connell will not take separate tracks. Staffing levels in the firm are expected to remain the same.

41756 ■ *"The Bankrate Double Pay" in Barron's (Vol. 88, March 24, 2008, No. 12, pp. 27)*
Pub: Dow Jones & Company, Inc.
Ed: Neil A. Martin. **Description:** Shares of Bankrate may rise as much as 25 percent from their level of $45.08 a share due to a strong cash flow and balance sheet. The company's Internet business remains strong despite weakness in the online advertising industry and is a potential takeover target.

41757 ■ *"Banks Could Greet Tenants in One Year" in Business Courier (Vol. 26, October 16, 2009, No. 25, pp. 1)*
Pub: American City Business Journals, Inc.
Ed: Lucy May. **Description:** The Banks project's initial phase is expected to start in 60 days, which may mean that the project's first tenant could move in by the end of 2010 or beginning of 2011. Carter, an Atlanta-based firm has partnered with Dawson Company in this riverfront development. The first phase will include 80,000 square feet of retail and 300 apartments.

41758 ■ *"Barbarians Set Bar Low With Lowly Canadian Telco" in Globe & Mail (March 31, 2007, pp. B1)*
Pub: CTVglobemedia Publishing Inc.
Ed: Derek DeCloet. **Description:** The efforts of the private equity fund Kohlberg, Kravis, Roberts and Co. to acquire the Canadian telecommunications firm BCE are described.

41759 ■ *"Bartering, Browsing, Borrowing to Save" in Reading Eagle (July 20, 2010)*
Pub: Reading Eagle/Reading Times
Ed: Jessica Bakeman. **Description:** Various forms of bartering are outlined to help small companies as well as individuals.

41760 ■ *"Bartering Makes a Return in Hard Times" in Atlanta Journal-Constitution (October 2, 2010, pp. A15)*
Pub: Atlanta Journal-Constitution
Ed: Bill York. **Description:** The advantages of bartering are explored.

41761 ■ *"Bartering Takes Businesses Back to Basics: Broker's Exchange Helps Members to Reach New Customers" in Buffalo News (July 9, 2010)*
Pub: The Buffalo News
Ed: Dino Grandoni. **Description:** Bartering clubs can help small businesses reach new customers and to expand their business.

41762 ■ *"Bartering Trades on Talents" in Reading Eagle (June 20, 2010)*
Pub: Reading Eagle/Reading Times
Ed: Tony Lucia. **Description:** Bartering is not just a way of trading goods and services, it can be an essential tool for small business to survive in a bad economy.

41763 ■ *"BASF Launches $4.9 Billion Bid for Rival Engelhard" in Globe & Mail (January 4, 2006, pp. B7)*
Pub: CTVglobemedia Publishing Inc.
Ed: Mike Esterl; Steve Levine. **Description:** The plans of BASF AG, to acquire Engelhard Corp. for $4.9 billion, are presented.

41764 ■ *"Battle of the Titans" in Canadian Business (Vol. 81, March 17, 2008, No. 4, pp. 15)*
Pub: Rogers Media
Ed: Rachel Pulfer. **Description:** Regulatory authorities in Canada gave Thomson Corp and Reuters Group PLC the permission to go ahead with their merger. The merged companies could eclipse Bloomberg LP's market share of 33 percent. Authorities also required Thomson and Reuters to sell some of their databases to competitors.

41765 ■ *"BCE Mulls Radical Changes With Industry Under Pressure" in Globe & Mail (March 30, 2007, pp. B1)*
Pub: CTVglobemedia Publishing Inc.
Ed: Andrew Willis; Jacquie McNish; Catherine McLean. **Description:** An account on the expansion plans of BCE Inc., which plans to acquire TELUS Corp., is presented.

41766 ■ *"Beat the Buck: Bartering Tips from In-The-Know Authors" in (June 23, 2010)*
Pub: The Telegraph
Ed: Jill Moon. **Description:** The Art of Barter is a new book to help small businesses learn this art form in order to expand customer base and reserve cash flow.

41767 ■ *"Because 10 Million Zumba Lovers Can't Be Wrong" in Inc. (Volume 32, December 2010, No. 10, pp. 106)*
Pub: Inc. Magazine
Ed: Christine Lagorio. **Description:** Profile of partners, Alberto Perez, Alberto Perlman, and Alberto Aghion, founders of Zumba, a form of dance used for fitness.

41768 ■ *"Being Big By Design" in Canadian Business (Vol. 82, April 27, 2009, No. 7, pp. 39)*
Pub: Rogers Media
Ed: Andrew Wahl. **Description:** Gennum expects that its planned acquisition of Tundra Semiconductor will expand its market presence and leverage its research and development better than working alone. The proposed friendly acquisition could challenge Zarlink Semiconductor as the largest Canadian semiconductor firm in terms of revenue. The merger could expand Gennum's addressable market to about $2 billion.

41769 ■ *"Beltway Monitor" in Mergers & Acquisitions: The Dealmaker's Journal (March 1, 2008)*
Pub: SourceMedia, Inc.
Description: Discusses in detail The Foreign Investment and National Security Act of 2007 which was put into legislation due to the initially approved acquisition of certain U.S. ports by Dubai Ports World which set off a firestorm of controversy.

41770 ■ *"Benefits of Bartering" in Mail Tribune (November 22, 2010)*
Pub: Mail Tribune
Ed: Damian Mann. **Description:** Various people discuss the use of bartering for their small companies in order to improve business.

41771 ■ *"Best Growth Stocks" in Canadian Business (Vol. 81, Summer 2008, No. 9, pp. 61)*
Pub: Rogers Media Ltd.
Ed: Calvin Leung. **Description:** Table showing the one-year performance of growth stocks is presented. Edmonton-based Stantec Inc. expects to advance its sales and profits by 15 percent to 20 percent per year through tapping international markets and acquisitions. Analysts forecast a 17.1 percent growth rate annually over the next 3 to 5 years.

41772 ■ *"Best Growth Stocks" in Canadian Business (Vol. 82, Summer 2009, No. 8, pp. 28)*
Pub: Rogers Media
Ed: Calvin Leung. **Description:** Canadian stocks that are considered as the best growth stocks, and whose price-earnings ratio is less than their earnings growth rate, are suggested. Suggestions include pharmaceutical firm Paladin Labs, which was found to have 13 consecutive years of revenue growth. Paladin Labs acquires or licenses niche drugs and markets them in Canada.

41773 ■ *"Beware this Chinese Export" in Barron's (Vol. 90, August 30, 2010, No. 35, pp. 21)*
Pub: Barron's Editorial & Corporate Headquarters
Ed: Bill Alpert, Leslie P. Norton. **Description:** A look at 158 China reverse-merger stocks in the U.S. reveal that the median underperformed the index of U.S. listed Chinese companies by 75 percent in their first three years. These reverse merger stocks also lagged the Russell 2000 index of small cap stocks by 66 percent.

41774 ■ *"Beyond Microsoft and Yahoo!: Some M&A Prospects" in Barron's (Vol. 88, March 17, 2008, No. 11, pp. 39)*
Pub: Dow Jones & Company, Inc.
Ed: Eric J. Savitz. **Description:** Weak quarterly earnings report for Yahoo! could pressure the company's board to cut a deal with Microsoft. Electronic Arts is expected to win its hostile $26-a-share bid for Take-Two Interactive Software. Potential targets and buyers for mergers and acquisitions are mentioned.

41775 ■ *"Beyond Zipcar: Collaborate Consumption" in Harvard Business Review (Vol. 88, October 2010, No. 10, pp. 30)*
Pub: Harvard Business School Publishing
Ed: Rachel Botsman, Roo Rogers. **Description:** Description of the rise of collaborative consumption, the sharing or redistributing of products, rather than the purchasing thereof is discussed.

41776 ■ *"Big Boys Drawn Back to Play in Oil Sands" in Globe & Mail (March 7, 2006, pp. B2)*
Pub: CTVglobemedia Publishing Inc.
Ed: Deborah Yedlin. **Description:** The feasibility of companies such as Chevron Corp. in acquiring oil sands is discussed.

41777 ■ *"Big Gains Brewing at Anheuser-Busch InBev" in Barron's (Vol. 90, August 30, 2010, No. 35, pp. 34)*
Pub: Barron's Editorial & Corporate Headquarters
Ed: Christopher C. Williams. **Description:** Anheuser-Busch InBev is realizing cost synergies and it posted better than expected returns two years after the merger that formed the company. One analyst believes its American depositary receipt could be worth as much as 72 in a year.

41778 ■ *The Big Payback: The History of the Business of Hip-Hop*
Pub: New American Library/Penguin Group
Ed: Dan Charnas. **Price:** $24.95. **Description:** The complete history of hip-hop music is presented, by following the money and the relationship between artist and merchant. In its promise of economic security and creative control for black artist-entrepreneurs, it is the culmination of dreams of black nationalists and civil rights leaders.

41779 ■ *"Big Spenders" in Hawaii Business (Vol. 53, November 2007, No. 5, pp. 28)*
Pub: Hawaii Business Publishing
Ed: Cathy S. Cruz-George. **Description:** Blackstone Group announced its acquisition of Hilton Hotels Corp. valued at $26 billion in July 2007, one of the largest buyouts in the history of hotels. Blackstone now becomes the second most powerful landowners in Hawaii.

41780 ■ *"Big Trouble at Sony Ericsson" in Barron's (Vol. 88, March 24, 2008, No. 12, pp. M9)*
Pub: Dow Jones & Company, Inc.
Ed: Angelo Franchini. **Description:** Sony Ericsson is facing trouble as it warned that its sales and net income before taxes will fall by nearly half for the first quarter of 2008. The joint venture of Sony and Ericsson has a global mobile phone market share of nine percent as of 2007, fourth largest in the world.

41781 ■ *"A Bigger Deal" in Crain's Cleveland Business (Vol. 28, November 12, 2007, No. 45, pp. 1)*
Pub: Crain Communications, Inc.
Ed: Shawn A. Turner. **Description:** In an attempt to boost its revenue CBiz Inc., a provider of accounting and business services, is looking to balance its acquisitions of smaller companies with larger ones as part of its overall growth strategy.

41782 ■ *"Biotechs Are Using Back Door to Go Public" in Boston Business Journal (Vol. 31, May 27, 2011, No. 18, pp. 1)*
Pub: Boston Business Journal
Ed: Julie M. Donnelly. **Description:** Members of Massachusetts' biotechnology sector have been engaging in reverse mergers as an alternative to initial public offerings. Reverse mergers provide access to institutional investors and hedge funds.

41783 ■ *"Black Diamond Holdings Corp. Receives SEC Approval" in Canadian Corporate News (May 16, 2007)*
Pub: Comtex News Network Inc.
Description: Black Diamond Holdings, Corp., a British Columbia domiciled company and its two wholly owned subsidiaries are engaged in the bottling, importation, distribution, marketing, and brand creation of premium spirits and wines to worldwide consumers, announced that it has completed the SEC review process and has applied to list for trading in the United States on the OTC.BB.

41784 ■ *"Blackstone Set to Sell Stake" in Globe & Mail (March 17, 2007, pp. B6)*
Pub: CTVglobemedia Publishing Inc.
Ed: Tennille Tracy. **Description:** The plan of Blackstone Group to sell 10 percent of its stake to raise $4 billion and its proposal to go for initial public offering is discussed.

41785 ■ *"Blackstone's Outlook Still Tough" in Barron's (Vol. 88, March 17, 2008, No. 11, pp. 19)*
Pub: Dow Jones & Company, Inc.
Ed: Andrew Bary. **Description:** Earnings for the Blackstone Group may not recover soon since the company's specialty in big leveraged buyouts is floundering and may not recover until 2009. The company earns lucrative incentive fees on its funds but those fees went negative in the fourth quarter of 2007 and there could be more fee reversals in the future.

41786 ■ *"BMW Makes Bet on Carbon Maker" in Wall Street Journal Eastern Edition (November 19 , 2011, pp. B3)*
Pub: Dow Jones & Company Inc.
Ed: Christoph Rauwald. **Description:** Eight months ago, Volkswagen AG acquired a 10 percent holding in carbon-fiber maker SGL Carbon SE. Its rival BMW AG is catching up by acquiring 15.2 percent stake in SGL as it seeks alliances like the rest of the industry in order to share industrial costs of new product development.

41787 ■ *"BofA Will Reach the Top with Countrywide Deal" in Business North Carolina (Vol. 28, March 2008, No. 3, pp. 36)*
Pub: Business North Carolina
Description: Bank of America, headquartered in Charlotte, North Carolina, will add Countrywide to its let of credits. Countrywide is the largest U.S. mortgage lender. Statistical data included.

41788 ■ *"Bonds v. Stocks: Who's Right About Recession?" in Barron's (Vol. 90, August 23, 2010, No. 34, pp. M3)*
Pub: Barron's Editorial & Corporate Headquarters
Ed: Kopin Tan. **Description:** The future of treasury securities and stocks should the U.S. enter or avoid a recession are discussed. The back to school business climate and BHP Billiton's bid for Potash Corporation of Saskatchewan are also discussed.

41789 ■ *"Boom and Bust in the Book Biz" in Canadian Business (Vol. 83, August 17, 2010, No. 13-14, pp. 16)*
Pub: Rogers Media Ltd.
Ed: Jordan Timm. **Description:** Electronic book marketplace is booming with Amazon.com's e-book sales for the Kindle e-reader exceeding the hardcover sales. Kobo Inc. has registered early success with its Kobo e-reader and has partnered with Hong Kong telecom giant on an e-book store.

41790 ■ *"Border Boletin: UA to Take Lie-Detector Kiosk to Poland" in Arizona Daily Star (September 14, 2010)*
Pub: Arizona Daily Star
Ed: Brady McCombs. **Description:** University of Arizona's National Center for Border Security and Immigration Research will send a team to Warsaw, Poland to show border guards from 27 European Union countries the center's Avatar Kiosk. The Avatar technology is designed for use at border ports and airports to assist Customs officers detect individuals who are lying.

41791 ■ *"Boston Scientific Makes Formal Offer for Guidant, Possibly Thwarting J&J" in Globe & Mail (January 9, 2006, pp. B6)*
Pub: CTVglobemedia Publishing Inc.
Ed: Silvia Pagan Westphal; Thomas M. Burton; Dennis Berman. **Description:** The details on Boston Scientific Corp.'s $25 billion bid on Guidant Corp. are presented. The company makes the move to outbid Johnson & Johnson.

41792 ■ *"Brazil's New King of Food" in Barron's (Vol. 89, July 13, 2009, No. 28, pp. 28)*
Pub: Dow Jones & Co., Inc.
Ed: Kenneth Rapoza. **Description:** Perdigao and Sadia's merger has resulted in the creation of Brasil Foods and the shares of Brasil Foods provides a play on both Brazil's newly energized consumer economy and its role as a major commodities exporter. Brasil Foods shares could climb as much as 36 percent.

41793 ■ *"Breadwinner Tries on Designer Jeans" in Houston Business Journal (Vol. 40, December 18, 2009, No. 32, pp. 1)*
Pub: American City Business Journals
Ed: Allison Wollam. **Description:** Chuck Cain, the franchisee who introduced Panera Bread to Houston, Texas has partnered with tax accountant Jim Jacobsen to introduce custom-make Tattu Jeans. As more Tattu Jeans outlets are being planned, Cain is using entrepreneurial lessons learned from Panera Bread in the new venture. Both Panera Bread and Tattu Jeans were opened by Cain during economic downturns.

41794 ■ *"Breaking Up" in Canadian Business (Vol. 80, March 12, 2007, No. 6, pp. 34)*
Pub: Rogers Media
Ed: John Gray. **Description:** The need for business partners to draft a shareholder agreement in the beginning of their business to make it easier to break their relationship in case of disputes later is discussed.

41795 ■ *"Brewed to Succeed; Mokarbia Perks Up Sales for King Coffee" in Crain's Detroit Business (Vol. 24, March 17, 2008, No. 11, pp. 3)*
Pub: Crain Communications, Inc.
Ed: Brent Snavely. **Description:** Profile of King Coffee Tea Services, Royal Oak-based company, whose distributing deal with Mokarabia coffee has generated an increase in sales.

41796 ■ *"Bridging the Talent Gap Through Partnership and Innovation" in Canadian Business (Vol. 81, October 27, 2008, No. 18, pp. 88)*
Pub: Rogers Media Ltd.
Description: Research revealed that North America is short by more than 60,000 qualified networking professionals. Businesses, educators and communities are collaborating in order to address the shortfall.

41797 ■ *"Briefly" in Crain's Detroit Business (Vol. 25, June 15, 2009, No. 24, pp. 18)*
Pub: Crain Communications Inc. - Detroit
Ed: Tom Henderson, Jay Greene. **Description:** Details of the merger between Pl= anning Alternatives Ltd. and Oakland Wealth Management are highlighted. The two investment advisory firms will have a combined staff of 12 and will maintain two offices.

41798 ■ *"Bringing Big Guns" in Business Courier (Vol. 24, January 18, 2008, No. 41, pp. 1)*
Pub: American City Business Journals, Inc.
Ed: Lucy May. **Description:** Chief executive officer of Nidland Co. John Hayden was assigend as Cincinnati USA Partnership chairman. Hayden will bring his expertise to help the partnership drive economic development in the Greater Cincinnati area. Details of the parntership's plans are suplied.

41799 ■ *"Brookfield Eyes 'New World'" in Globe & Mail (February 6, 2007, pp. B1)*
Pub: CTVglobemedia Publishing Inc.
Ed: Sinclair Stewart; Elizabeth Church. **Description:** The efforts of Brookfield Asset Management Inc. to acquire American paper company, Longview Fibre Co., and Australian construction company Multiplex Ltd. are discussed.

41800 ■ *"Building His Dream" in Business Courier (Vol. 24, January 25, 2008, No. 42, pp. 1)*
Pub: American City Business Journals, Inc.
Ed: Laura Baverman. **Description:** Technology entrepreneur Mahendra Vora plans to build a more than $100 million local IT headquarters for VTech Holdings Ltd by 2010. Acquisition of four $5 million companies within 2008 are part of the owner's plan to expand the office equipment company. Other plans for the IT company are discussed.

41801 ■ *"Bumpy Ride Ahead for United" in Crain's Chicago Business (Vol. 31, May 5, 2008, No. 18, pp. 3)*
Pub: Crain Communications, Inc.
Ed: John Pletz. **Description:** Continental Airlines Inc. walked away from merger talks with United Airlines last week. Now the choices facing United boil down to going it alone in an increasingly stormy airline business or a less-desirable merger with US Airways Group Inc. Analysts expect United to lose $977 million this year due, mainly, to the high price of fuel.

41802 ■ *"The Business of Activism" in Entrepreneur (Vol. 37, September 2009, No. 9, pp. 43)*
Pub: Entrepreneur Media, Inc.
Ed: Mary Catherine O'Connor. **Description:** San Francisco, California-based business incubator Virgance has been promoting sustainable projects by partnering with businesses. The company has launched campaigns which include organizing homeowners in negotiating with solar installers. The company is also planning to expand its workforce.

41803 ■ *"Business Diary" in Crain's Detroit Business (Vol. 24, October 6, 2008, No. 40, pp. 23)*
Pub: Crain Communications, Inc.
Description: Detailed listing of acquisitions, expansions, new products, new services, business contracts and startups from the Detroit area is provided.

41804 ■ *"Business Diary" in Crain's Detroit Business (Vol. 26, January 11, 2010, No. 2, pp. 16)*
Pub: Crain Communications Inc.
Description: Listing of local businesses involved in acquisitions, contracts, expansions, new products and services as well as startups in the region.

41805 ■ *"Businesses Band Together in Destin Bartering to Keep Heads Above Water" in Destin Log (July 24, 2010)*
Pub: The Destin Log
Ed: Andrew Metz. **Description:** Profile of The Barter Company located in Destin, Florida, whose owner believes that bartering for goods and services can help small companies in a down economy.

41806 ■ *"Canadian Satellite Investors Scoop Up Stratos" in Globe & Mail (March 20, 2007, pp. B4)*
Pub: CTVglobemedia Publishing Inc.
Ed: Simon Avery. **Description:** The proposed acquisition of Stratos Global Corp. by CIP Canada Investment Inc. for $229 million is discussed.

41807 ■ *"The Canadians Are Coming!" in Canadian Business (Vol. 80, October 22, 2007, No. 21, pp. 15)*
Pub: Rogers Media
Ed: Rachel Pulfer. **Description:** Toronto-Dominion Bank declared its acquisition of the New Jersey-based Commerce Bancorp for C$8.5 billion. Royal Bank of Canada has scooped up Trinidad-based Financial Group for C$2.2 billion. Details of the foreign acquisitions, as well as the impact of high Canadian dollars on the mergers are discussed.

41808 ■ *"Cancer Therapy Raises Debate Over Shared Technology" in Crain's Detroit Business (Vol. 24, March 10, 2008, No. 10, pp. 1)*
Pub: Crain Communications, Inc.
Ed: Jay Greene. **Description:** Overview of a proposed collaborative approach among select hospitals that would allow the consortium to utilize proton-beam accelerators in order to treat cancer patients; this expensive new technology is possibly a better way to destroy cancers by using the proton beams to direct high dosages of radiation to destroy small tumors.

41809 ■ *"Capital Position" in Business Journal-Milwaukee (Vol. 28, December 24, 2010, No. 12, pp. A1)*
Pub: Milwaukee Business Journal
Ed: Rich Kirchen. **Description:** Canada-based BMO Financial Group has purchased Marshall and Isley Corporation (M and I), which dominated lending among Wisconsin businesses for decades. The sale of M and I will enable other banks to recruit M and I's customers but BMO Financial remains a stronger competitor since it possesses a more potent capital position.

41810 ■ *"Capture New Markets" in Pet Product News (Vol. 64, December 2010, No. 12, pp. 12)*
Pub: BowTie Inc.
Ed: Ethan Mizer. **Description:** Flea and tick treatments are among the product categories that can be offered in order to clinch new markets. With the help of manufacturers, pet store retailers are encouraged to educate themselves about these products considering that capturing markets involves variations in customer perceptions. Retailers would then be deemed as resources and sources for these products.

41811 ■ *"Carveouts Back in Vogue" in Mergers & Acquisitions: The Dealmaker's Journal (March 1, 2008)*
Pub: SourceMedia, Inc.
Ed: Ken MacFadyen. **Description:** Discusses ways in which companies look for hidden assets that they can exploit in worsening economic times; oftentimes firms try to sell off assets or in other instances they will look to unlock value through public spinoffs or through internal reorganizations.

41812 ■ *"Cash-Heavy Biovail on the Prowl for Deals" in Globe & Mail (March 24, 2006, pp. B1)*
Pub: CTVglobemedia Publishing Inc.
Ed: Leonard Zehr. **Description:** Biovail Corp. posted 48 percent rise in profits for 2005. The business growth plans of the company through acquisitions are presented.

41813 ■ *"Casinos See College as Job Jackpot" in The Business Journal-Serving Metropolitan Kansas City (Vol. 26, August 1, 2008, No. 47)*
Pub: American City Business Journals, Inc.
Ed: Suzanna Stagemeyer. **Description:** Wyandotte County casino managers revealed plans to develop partnerships with Kansas City Kansas Community College. The planned partnership is expected to include curriculum development and degree programs that would help train employees for the planned casinos. Other views and information on the project are presented.

41814 ■ *"CBC and Chrysler Strike Deal" in Black Enterprise (Vol. 37, December 2006, No. 5, pp. 36)*
Pub: Earl G. Graves Publishing Co. Inc.
Ed: Kiara Ashanti. **Description:** Congressional Black Foundation and Chrysler Financial have partnered to provide financial education to students at historically black colleges and universities. The prime objective of the program is to reduce the number of college students that graduate with poor credit scores and high debt.

41815 ■ *"CBC Eyes Partners for TV Downloads" in Globe & Mail (February 9, 2006, pp. B1)*
Pub: CTVglobemedia Publishing Inc.
Ed: Grant Robertson. **Description:** The details on Canadian Broadcasting Corp.'s distribution agreement with Google Inc. and Apple Computer Inc. are presented.

41816 ■ *"CE2 Carbon Capital and Dogwood Carbon Solutions Partner With Missouri Landowners" in Nanotechnolgy Business Journal (Jan. 25, 2010)*
Pub: Investment Weekly News
Description: Dogwood Carbon Solutions, a developer of agriculture and forestry based conservation projects, has partnered with CE2 Carbon Capital,

one of the largest investors and owners of U.S. carbon commodities and carbon emissions reduction projects, to develop high-quality carbon offsets from over 30,000 acres of privately-owned non-industrial forest in the Ozark mountain region of Arkansas and Missouri.

41817 ■ *"Centrue Sets Down New Roots in St. Louis; Bank Looks to Expand in Exurbs of Chicago" in Crain's Chicago Business (May 5, 2008)*
Pub: Crain Communications, Inc.
Ed: H. Lee Murphy. **Description:** Centrue Financial Corp. has moved its headquarters from Ottawa to suburban St. Louis in search of higher-growth markets. The banks acquisitions and expansion plans are also discussed.

41818 ■ *"Centurion Signs Egypt Deal With Shell" in Globe & Mail (March 21, 2006, pp. B5)*
Pub: CTVglobemedia Publishing Inc.
Ed: Dave Ebner. **Description:** Centurion Energy International Inc., a Calgary-based natural gas producer in Egypt, has signed contract with Royal Dutch Shell PLC to explore about 320,000 hectares of land in Egypt. Details of the agreement are presented.

41819 ■ *"Cerner Works the Business Circuit" in Business Journal-Serving Metropolitan Kansas City (Vol. 26, October 5, 2007, No. 4, pp. 1)*
Pub: American City Business Journals, Inc.
Ed: Rob Roberts. **Description:** Cerner Corporation is embracing the coming of the electronic medical record exchange by creating a regional health information organization (RHIO) called the CareEntrust. The RHIO convinced health insurers to share claims data with patients and clinicians. At the Center Health Conference, held October 7 to 10, Cerner will demonstrate the software it developed for CareEntrust to the 40,000 healthcare and information technology professionals.

41820 ■ *"Challenges Await Quad in Going Public" in Milwaukee Business Journal (Vol. 27, January 29, 2010, No. 18, pp. A1)*
Pub: American City Business Journals
Ed: Rich Rovito. **Description:** Sussex, Wisconsin-based Quad/Graphics Inc.'s impending acquisition of rival Canadian World Color Press Inc. will transform it into a publicly held entity for the first time. Quad has operated as a private company for nearly 40 years and will need to adjust to changes, such as the way management shares information with Quad/Graphics' employees. Details of the merger are included.

41821 ■ *"Champion Enterprises Buys UK Company" in Crain's Detroit Business (Vol. 24, March 17, 2008, No. 11, pp. 4)*
Pub: Crain Communications, Inc.
Ed: Daniel Duggan. **Description:** With the acquisition of ModularUK Building Systems Ltd., a steel-frame modular manufacturer, Champion Enterprises has continued its expansion outside the United States.

41822 ■ *The Changing Geography of Banking and Finance*
Pub: Springer Publishing Company
Ed: Pietro Alessandrini, Michele Fratianni, Alberto Zazzaro. **Released:** May 1, 2009. **Price:** $139.00. **Description:** The two contrasting trends that have emerged from the integration and consolidation processes of the banking industry in both Europe and the United States in the 1990s is examined.

41823 ■ *"Channeling for Growth" in The Business Journal-Serving Greater Tampa Bay (Vol. 28, July 11, 2008, No. 29, pp. 1)*
Pub: American City Business Journals, Inc.
Ed: Margie Manning. **Description:** HSN Inc., one of the largest employers in Tampa Bay, Florida, is expected to spend an additional $9.7 million annually as it plans to hire more accounting, internal audit, legal, treasury and tax personnel after its spin-off to a public company. Details on the company's sales growth are provided.

41824 ■ *"Chelsea Community Hospital to Merge with St. Joseph Mercy Health" in Crain's Detroit Business (Vol. 24, March 24, 2008, No. 12)*
Pub: Crain Communications, Inc.
Ed: Jay Greene. **Description:** Chelsea Community Hospital has signed a letter of intent to merge with St. Joseph Mercy Health System and will negotiate merger terms, including a plan to fund an unspecified amount of facility improvements and equipment purchases at Chelsea.

41825 ■ *"Chemed's Vitas Aims to Acquire" in Business Courier (Vol. 27, July 9, 2010, No. 10, pp. 1)*
Pub: Business Courier
Ed: James Ritchie. **Description:** Chemed Corporation's Vitas Healthcare Corporation is looking for smaller nonprofit hospices as it looks to become more streamlined in a tougher reimbursement environment. CFO David Williams syas they want to acquire these hospices as fast as they can integrate them.

41826 ■ *"Chew On This: Soul Fans to 'Chew' Games' First Play" in Philadelphia Business Journal (Vol. 30, September 30, 2011, No. 33, pp. 3)*
Pub: American City Business Journals Inc.
Ed: John George. **Description:** Arena football team Philadelphia Soul extended its marketing partnership with Just Born Inc. The team's fans will enter a contest where the winner will be allowed to select the team's first play during a home game.

41827 ■ *"China Vs. the World: Whose Technology Is It?" in Harvard Business Review (Vol. 88, December 2010, No. 12, pp. 94)*
Pub: Harvard Business School Publishing
Ed: Thomas M Hout, Pankaj Ghemawat. **Description:** Examination of the regulation the Chinese government is implementing that require foreign corporations wishing to do business in the country to give up their new technologies. These regulations avoid World Trade Organization technology transfer provisions and complicate the convergence of socialism and capitalism.

41828 ■ *"China's ZTE in Hunt for Partners" in Globe & Mail (February 27, 2006, pp. B1)*
Pub: CTVglobemedia Publishing Inc.
Ed: Gordon Pitts. **Description:** The business growth plans of ZTE Corp. in Canada, through partnership, are presented.

41829 ■ *"CIBC Spends $1.1 Billion on Caribbean Expansion" in Globe & Mail (March 14, 2006, pp. B1)*
Pub: CTVglobemedia Publishing Inc.
Ed: Sinclair Stewart. **Description:** Canadian Imperial Bank of Commerce (CIBC), the fifth-largest bank of Canada, is planning to spend $1.1billion to buy major share of Barbados-based First Caribbean International Bank. The details of the acquisition plan are presented.

41830 ■ *"Citigroup Moves to Buy Japan's Nikko" in Globe & Mail (March 7, 2007, pp. B12)*
Pub: CTVglobemedia Publishing Inc.
Ed: Jonathan Soble; Dan Wilchins. **Description:** Citigroup Inc. offered $10.8 billion to acquire troubled Nikko Cordial Corp., Japan's largest securities firm.

41831 ■ *"City a Pawn in Airlines' Chess Game" in Business Courier (Vol. 24, January 18, 2008, No. 41, pp. 1)*
Pub: American City Business Journals, Inc.
Ed: Lisa Biank Fasig. **Description:** Delta Air Lines is under negotitaions with Northwest Airlines and UAL Corp. for a proposed merger. The deal will have a negative impact on Cincinnati as a hub regardless whether it goes to UAL or Northwest. The impacts of the planned merger on Cincinnati's labor market and airport traffic are discussed.

41832 ■ *"Clean-Tech Focus Sparks Growth" in Philadelphia Business Journal (Vol. 28, January 15, 2010, No. 48, pp. 1)*
Pub: American City Business Journals
Ed: Peter Key. **Description:** Keystone Redevelopment Group and economic development organization Ben Franklin Technology Partners of Southeastern Pennsylvania have partnered in supporting the growth of new alternative energy and clean technology companies. Keystone has also been developing the Bridge Business Center.

41833 ■ *"Closures Pop Cork on Wine Bar Sector Consolidation" in Houston Business Journal (Vol. 40, January 22, 2010, No. 37, pp. A2)*
Pub: American City Business Journals
Ed: Allison Wollam. **Description:** Wine bar market in Houston, Texas is in the midst of a major shift and heads toward further consolidation due to the closure of pioneering wine bars that opened in the past decade. The Corkscrew owner, Andrew Adams, has blamed the creation of competitive establishments to the closure which helped wear out his concept.

41834 ■ *"CMS Products and Avecto Team for Business Security Product Solutions" in Wireless News (November 11, 2009)*
Pub: Close-Up Media
Description: CMS Products, a provider of data security, backup, content management and disaster recovery, has agreed on a strategic partnership with Avect, a provider in least privilege management. The partnership will allow the companies to bundle their products.

41835 ■ *"Cold Stone in Licensing Agreement with Turin Chocolates" in Ice Cream Reporter (Vol. 22, December 20, 2008, No. 1, pp. 2)*
Pub: Ice Cream Reporter
Description: Cold Stone Creamery and Turin Chocolatier are teaming up to offer a new line of chocolate truffles under the Cold Stone label. The treats will feature four the most popular Cold Stone flavors: Coffee Lovers Only, Chocolate Devotion, Our Strawberry Blonde, and Peanut Butter Cup Perfection.

41836 ■ *"Colliers Shifts Its Brokerage Home" in Charlotte Business Journal (Vol. 25, November 5, 2010, No. 33, pp. 1)*
Pub: Charlotte Business Journal
Ed: Will Boye. **Description:** Colliers International signed a long-term affiliate agreement with commercial real estate firm Clarus Properties, in a move that would allow Colliers to resume business in Charlotte, North Carolina. Colliers also hired well known brokers Brad Grow and Brent Royall.

41837 ■ *"Colt Capital Corp. Acquires Two Uranium Properties From DIAGNOS" in Canadian Corporate News (May 16, 2007)*
Pub: Comtex News Network Inc.
Description: DIAGNOS Inc., a leader in the use of artificial intelligence and advanced knowledge extraction techniques, announced an agreement with Colt Capital Corp., a Canadian mineral exploration company that will grant an exclusive option in two uranium properties.

41838 ■ *"Comcast Networks" in Brandweek (Vol. 49, April 21, 2008, No. 16, pp. SR9)*
Pub: VNU Business Media, Inc.
Ed: Anthony Crupi. **Description:** Provides contact information for sales and marketing personnel for the Comcast networks as well as a listing of the station's top programming and an analysis of the current season and the target audience for those programs running in the current season. Experts believe Comcast will continue to acquire more stations into their portfolio.

41839 ■ *"Company Severs Ties with Chiquita, Starts Own Brand" in Business Journal-Serving Phoenix and the Valley of the Sun (October 5, 2007)*
Pub: American City Business Journals, Inc.
Ed: Mike Sunnucks. **Description:** Melones International is ending a deal with Chiquita Brands International Inc. Melones will now distribute its produce in

the U.S. under its own brand, called Plain Jane. Alejandro N. Canelos Jr., head of the firm, stated their relationship with Chiquita was good, but wants to promote the Plain Jane brand name.

41840 ■ *"Competition At Last?" in Canadian Business (Vol. 81, July 22, 2008, No. 12-13, pp. 7)*
Pub: Rogers Media Ltd.
Description: Competition Policy Review Panel's 'Compete to Win' report revealed that Canada is being 'hollowed-out' by foreign acquisitions. The panel investigated competition and foreign investment policies in Canada. Key information on the report, as well as views on the Investment Canada Act and the Competition Act, is presented.

41841 ■ *"Competition Qualms Overblown: Inco" in Globe & Mail (February 15, 2006, pp. B1)*
Pub: CTVglobemedia Publishing Inc.
Ed: Wendy Stueck. **Description:** Inco Ltd. plans the acquisition of Falconbridge Ltd., for $12.5 billion. The advantages of the acquisition for Inco Ltd. are presented.

41842 ■ *"Construction Firms Support NAACP Plan" in Business Courier (Vol. 27, September 24, 2010, No. 21, pp. 1)*
Pub: Business Courier
Ed: Lucy May. **Description:** Executives of Turner Construction Company and Messer Construction Company expressed their support for the Cincinnati National Association for the Advancement of Colored People Construction Partnership Agreement. The agreement involves the setting of rules for the involvement of firms owned by African Americans in major projects in Cincinnati.

41843 ■ *"Consulting Firm Goes Shopping" in Crain's Chicago Business (Vol. 31, April 28, 2008, No. 17, pp. 45)*
Pub: Crain Communications, Inc.
Ed: Phuong Ly. **Description:** Clark & Wamberg LLC was created last year after the merger of Clark Inc. to a Dutch insurance conglomerate. Clark Inc. was a life insurance and benefits consultancy which had been on a downslide, returning just 5.6 percent a year to shareholders. In contrast Clark & Wamberg posted first-year revenue of $106.8 million, fueled by business from its executive compensation and health care clients.

41844 ■ *"A Conversation With Steven Hilfinger, Foley & Lardner L.L.P." in Crain's Detroit Business (Vol. 24, March 24, 2008, No. 12, pp. 1)*
Pub: Crain Communications, Inc.
Description: Interview with Steven Hilfinger who is a member of Foley & Lardner L.L.P.'s mergers and acquisitions practice and is co-chair of its automotive industry team. Hilfinger discusses such issues as the role a board of directors can play in the M&A process and the future of the auto market.

41845 ■ *"CoolBrands" in Canadian Business (Vol. 83, September 14, 2010, No. 15, pp. 25)*
Pub: Rogers Media Ltd.
Ed: Joe Castaldo. **Description:** CoolBrands International Inc.'s merger with Swisher International Inc., a US hygiene products and services company, has formally erased the last traces of the former ice cream company. CoolBrands began as a frozen yogurt stand in 1986 and flourished across the world. How the string of acquisitions and poor corporate governance led to its demise are cited.

41846 ■ *"Copyright Clearance Center (CCC) Partnered with cSubs" in Information Today (Vol. 28, November 2011, No. 10, pp. 14)*
Pub: Information Today, Inc.
Description: Copyright Clearance Center (CCC) partnered with cSubs to integrate CCC's point-of-content licensing solution RightsLink Basic directly into cSubs workflow. The partnership will allow cSubs' customers a user-friendly process for obtaining permissions. Csubs is a corporate subscription management service for books, newspapers, and econtent.

41847 ■ *"Corporate Elite Show Resilience" in The Business Journal-Serving Greater Tampa Bay (Vol. 28, August 1, 2008, No. 32, pp. 1)*
Pub: American City Business Journals, Inc.
Ed: Margie Manning; Alexis Muellner. **Description:** Stocks of the largest public companies in Tampa Bay, Florida, outperformed the S&P 500 index by 28 percent in the first half of 2008. The escalation is attributed to the growth orientation of the companies in the area and the lack of exposure to the real estate and financial services sectors.

41848 ■ *"Corporate Training" in Hawaii Business (Vol. 53, October 2007, No. 4, pp. 46)*
Pub: Hawaii Business Publishing
Ed: Cathy S. Cruz-George. **Description:** Kalani Pa, Mike Hann, and Li Si Yang are three of the fitness trainers who have worked with some of the participants at the Hawaii's Fittest CEO contest. Pa has trained Group Pacific Inc.'s Chip Doyle while Hann was Sharon Serene's trainer. Their insights on the profession of being a fitness trainer, and on working with executives are given.

41849 ■ *"Corporex in Battle With Hedge Fund" in Business Courier (Vol. 24, December 21, 2008, No. 36, pp. 1)*
Pub: American City Business Journals, Inc.
Ed: Jon Newberry. **Description:** Discusses a breach of contract complaint that was filed by Apollo Real Estate Advisors against Corporex Companies Inc. but Corporex said that the lawsuit was intended to counter an arbitration complaint filed by Corporex against Apollo, which seeks $11 million in termination fees. The issue is in relation to the acquisition of Eagle Hospitality by Apollo earlier in 2007.

41850 ■ *"Corporex Checks Into Hotel Niche" in Business Courier (Vol. 24, October 12, 2008, No. 26, pp. 1)*
Pub: American City Business Journals, Inc.
Ed: Laura Baverman. **Description:** Corporex Companies Inc. is investing $900 million on select-service hotels ranging from $12 million to $20 million each, with eight hotels under construction and nine sites under contract.

41851 ■ *"COSE Turns On To Electricity Market" in Crain's Cleveland Business (Vol. 30, June 22, 2009, No. 24, pp. 4)*
Pub: Crain Communications, Inc.
Ed: Jay Miller. **Description:** Council of Smaller Enterprises is working to offer small businesses and their employees electricity at discount prices set at auction by the Public Utilities Commission of Ohio and even lower prices from the Northern Ohio Public Energy Council. Details of the program are offered.

41852 ■ *"Crouching Tigers Spring to Life" in Globe & Mail (April 14, 2007, pp. B1)*
Pub: CTVglobemedia Publishing Inc.
Ed: Grant Robertson. **Description:** The prospects of the acquisition of BCE Inc, by Canadian pension funds are discussed. The effect of the growth of these pension funds on the Canadian economy is described.

41853 ■ *"CRTC Signals CHUM Deal Will Get Nod" in Globe & Mail (May 2, 2007, pp. B3)*
Pub: CTVglobemedia Publishing Inc.
Ed: Grant Robertson. **Description:** The likely approval of Canadian Radio-Television and Telecommunications Commission to the proposed acquisition of CHUM Ltd. by CTVglobemedia Inc. is discussed.

41854 ■ *"CTV's CHUM Proposal Gets Chilly Reception" in Globe & Mail (May 1, 2007, pp. B1)*
Pub: CTVglobemedia Publishing Inc.
Ed: Grant Robertson. **Description:** The possible violation of broadcast regulations in case of acquisition of CHUM Ltd. by CTV Inc. for $1.4 billion is discussed.

41855 ■ *"The CW" in Brandweek (Vol. 49, April 21, 2008, No. 16, pp. SR8)*
Pub: VNU Business Media, Inc.
Ed: John Consoli. **Description:** Provides contact information for sales and marketing personnel for the CW network as well as a listing of the station's top programming and an analysis of the current season and the target audience for those programs running in the current season. Purchases of advertising feel that Warner Bros. and CBS made a mistake merging The WB and UPN into the new CW rather than folding UPN into the more-established WB; compared to last season ratings are down more than 20 percent across the board.

41856 ■ *"Danaher to Acquire Tectronix" in Canadian Electronics (Vol. 22, November-December 2007, No. 7, pp. 1)*
Pub: CLB Media Inc.
Description: Leading supplier of measurement, test and monitoring equipment Tektronix will be acquired by Danaher Corporation for $2.8 billion. Tektronix products are expected to complement Danaher's test equipment sector. The impacts of the deal on Tektronix shareholders and Danaher's operations are discussed.

41857 ■ *"Dancing With Giants: Acquisition and Survival of the Family Firm" in Family Business Review (Vol. 19, December 2006, No. 4, pp. 289)*
Pub: Family Firm Institute
Contact: Judy L. Green, President
Ed: Adam Steen, Lawrence S. Welch. **Description:** Responses of family firms to mergers and acquisitions are analyzed taking the example of the takeover of an Australian wine producer and family firm.

41858 ■ *"David Maus Debuting New Dealership" in Orlando Business Journal (Vol. 26, February 5, 2010, No. 36, pp. 1)*
Pub: American City Business Journals
Ed: Anjali Fluker. **Description:** Automotive dealers David Maus Automotive Group and Van Tuyl Automotive Investment Group will launch David Maus Chevrolet in Sanford, Florida in fall 2010. The 12-acre site of the Chevy dealership will be located adjacent to the David Maus Toyota dealership. The new store is expected to generate nearly 125 new jobs.

41859 ■ *"Deal Braces Cramer for Growth Run" in The Business Journal-Serving Metropolitan Kansas City (Vol. 26, July 4, 2008, No. 43, pp. 1)*
Pub: American City Business Journals, Inc.
Ed: James Dornbook. **Description:** Gardner, Kansas-based Cramer Products Inc. bought 100 percent of the stocks of Louisville, Kentucky-based Active Ankle Inc. from 26 private investors increasing its revenue by 20 percent. The latter is the second largest vendor of Cramer. Other details of the merger are presented.

41860 ■ *"The Deal - Rhymes With Steal - Of A Lifetime" in Barron's (Vol. 88, March 24, 2008, No. 12, pp. 24)*
Pub: Dow Jones & Company, Inc.
Ed: Andrew Bary. **Description:** JPMorgan Chase's impending acquisition of Bear Stearns for $2.50 a share is a huge steal for the former. JPMorgan is set to acquire a company with a potential annual earnings of $1 billion while the Federal Reserve funds Bear's illiquid assets by providing $30 billion in nonrecourse loans.

41861 ■ *"Dealer Gets a Lift with Acquisitions at Year's End" in Crain's Detroit Business (Vol. 26, January 11, 2010, No. 2, pp. 3)*
Pub: Crain Communications, Inc.
Ed: Ryan Beene. **Description:** Alta Equipment Co., a forklift dealer, closed 2009 with a string of acquisitions expecting to double the firm's employee headcount and triple its annual revenue. Alta Lift Truck Services, Inc., as the company was known before the acquisitions, was founded in 1984 as Michigan's dealer for forklift manufacturer Yale Materials Handling Corp.

41862 ■ *"Dealers Trying Not to Fold" in Business First Columbus (Vol. 25, December 5, 2008, No. 15, pp. A1)*
Pub: American City Business Journals
Ed: Dan Eaton. **Description:** Increase in the number of automobile dealer closures in Ohio is seen to impact the state's economy. The trend of consolidation is forecasted to adversely affect employment and sales. Statistical data included.

41863 ■ *"Death Spiral" in Business Journal Serving Greater Tampa Bay (Vol. 30, October 29, 2010, No. 45, pp. 1)*
Pub: Tampa Bay Business Journal
Ed: Margie Manning. **Description:** Bay Cities Bank has started working on the loan portfolio of its acquisition, Progress Bank of Florida. Regulators closed Progress Bank in October 2010 after capital collapsed due to charge-offs and increases in the provision for future loan losses.

41864 ■ *"Denver Will Put Up Fight for MillerCoors HQ" in Business Journal-Milwaukee (Vol. 25, October 19, 2007, No. 3, pp. A1)*
Pub: American City Business Journals, Inc.
Ed: Rich Rovito. **Description:** A contention exists between Milwaukee and Denver over which city will become the new location of the Miller Brewing Company (Milwaukee) and Coors Brewing Company (Colorado) joint venture MillerCoors. Leaders of the breweries since the announcement of the merger, have contended frantically to prepare strategies to back up their own cities. The advantages and disadvantages of both cities are presented.

41865 ■ *"Desmarais Makes Move into U.S." in Globe & Mail (February 2, 2007, pp. B1)*
Pub: CTVglobemedia Publishing Inc.
Ed: Andrew Willis. **Description:** The decision of Desmarais family, which runs Great-West Lifeco Inc., to acquire Putnam Investment Trust for $4.6 billion to enter the United States market, is discussed.

41866 ■ *"Developer Banks On East Submarket, Slowdown Not a Hinderance" in The Business Journal-Serving Greater Tampa Bay (August 1, 2008)*
Pub: American City Business Journals, Inc.
Ed: Janet Leiser. **Description:** CLW Industrial Group and Cobalt Industrial REIT II have teamed up to develop a 14-acre area in northeast Hillsborough County, Florida. The $15 million industrial park project includes the 175,000-square-foot New Tampa Commerce Center, scheduled for completion in the first quarter of 2009.

41867 ■ *"A Different Breed of Deal Maker is Emerging" in Globe & Mail (January 14, 2006, pp. B2)*
Pub: CTVglobemedia Publishing Inc.
Ed: Eric Reguly. **Description:** The managerial strategies of chief executive officers in business acquisitions of companies, such as Dofasco Inc., are presented.

41868 ■ *"Digital Duplication" in Crain's Cleveland Business (Vol. 28, October 1, 2007, No. 39, pp. 3)*
Pub: Crain Communications, Inc.
Ed: David Bennett. **Description:** Profile of the business plan of eBlueprint Holdings LLC, a reprographics company that found success by converting customers' paper blueprints to an electronic format; the company plans to expand into other geographic markets by acquiring solid reprographics companies and converting their computer systems so that customers' blueprints can be managed electronically.

41869 ■ *"Doctors Buy In to Medical Timeshares" in Houston Business Journal (Vol. 40, December 11, 2009, No. 31, pp. 1)*
Pub: American City Business Journals
Ed: Mary Ann Azevedo. **Description:** Memorial Hermann Hospital System has leased to doctors three examination rooms and medical office space in the Memorial Hermann Medical Plaza in line with its new timeshare concept. The concept was designed to bring primary care physicians to its Texas Medical Center campus.

41870 ■ *"A Dog-Day Pooch" in Canadian Business (Vol. 79, September 11, 2006, No. 18, pp. 19)*
Pub: Rogers Media
Ed: Andrew Wahl. **Description:** Acquisition deal of Hummingbird Ltd by Canadian software maker Open Text Corp., is discussed.

41871 ■ *"Don't Count Your Millions Yet" in Business Courier (Vol. 24, January 11, 2008, No. 40, pp. 1)*
Pub: American City Business Journals, Inc.
Ed: Steve Watkins. **Description:** Merger and acquisition deals have been difficult to complete since 2007 largely due to a weaker economy and the credit crunch. Buyers have become more cautious because of the state of the economy and capital has become tougher to obtain because of the credit market crisis. The trends in mergers and acquisitions are analyzed further.

41872 ■ *"Dow Champions Innovative Energy Solutions for Auto Industry at NAIAS" in Business of Global Warming (January 25, 2010, pp. 7)*
Pub: Investment Weekly News
Description: This year's North American International Auto Show in Detroit will host the 'Electric Avenue' exhibit sponsored by the Dow Chemical Company. The display will showcase the latest in innovative energy solutions from Dow as well as electric vehicles and the technology supporting them. This marks the first time a non-automotive manufacturer is part of the main floor of the show.

41873 ■ *"Dow Jones Gives Apple-Loving Sales Professionals a Boost" in Information Today (Vol. 26, February 2009, No. 2, pp. 30)*
Pub: Information Today, Inc.
Description: Dow Jones Sales Triggers for iPhone and iPod program helps sales professionals stay current to prospects and customers in their fields by providing real-time news on business changes, including management moves, mergers, and new investments. The application presents events that trigger best opportunities and allows users to look up companies and executives to retrieve information.

41874 ■ *"Downtown Bank Got High Marks for Irwin Purchase, Is Looking For More" in Business Courier (Vol. 27, September 3, 2010, No. 18, pp. 1)*
Pub: Business Courier
Ed: Steve Watkins. **Description:** First Financial Bancorp is looking to acquire more troubled banks following its purchase of Irwin Union Bank. The bank has reported a $383 million bargain purchase gain during the third quarter of 2009.

41875 ■ *Driving With No Brakes: How a Bunch of Hooligans Built the Best Travel Company in the World*
Pub: Grand Circle Corporation
Ed: Alan and Harriet Lewis. **Price:** $19.95. **Description:** Inspirational book about how two courageous leaders built a remarkable company that can thrive in change and succeed in an unpredictable world. Important lessons for any business leader trying to create value in the 21st Century are included.

41876 ■ *"Drug-Maker Plans IPO" in Business Courier (Vol. 24, November 23, 2008, No. 32, pp. 1)*
Pub: American City Business Journals, Inc.
Ed: James Ritchie; Steve Watkins. **Description:** Xanodyne Pharmaceuticals Inc. filed plans with the Securities and Exchange Commission on November 9, 2007 for an initial public offering. The company, with annual sales of $75 million, had lost $222 million since it was founded in 2001.

41877 ■ *"DuPontas Pioneer Hi-Bred, Evogene to Develop Rust-Resistant Soybean Varieties" in Farm Industry News (November 22, 2011)*
Pub: Penton Business Media Inc.
Ed: Karen McMahon. **Description:** DuPont and Evogene have signed a new contract to work together to develop resistance in soybeans to rust. Financial terms of the agreement were not disclosed.

41878 ■ *"Earth Angels" in Playthings (Vol. 106, September 1, 2008, No. 8, pp. 10)*
Pub: Reed Business Information
Contact: Jeff Greisch, President
Ed: Karyn M. Peterson. **Description:** ImagiPlay toy company has partnered with Whole Foods Market to distribute the company's wooden playthings across the country. The company's Earth-friendly business model is outlined.

41879 ■ *The Economics of Integrity*
Pub: HarperStudio/HarperCollins
Ed: Anna Bernasek. **Released:** February 23, 2010. **Price:** $19.99. **Description:** Integrity is built over time and the importance of trust in starting and building business relationships is stressed.

41880 ■ *"EDCO Doling Out Capital Along Border" in Austin Business JournalInc. (Vol. 28, August 1, 2008, No. 20, pp. 1)*
Pub: American City Business Journals
Ed: Sandra Zaragoza. **Description:** Non-profit business incubator Economic Development Catalyst Organization Ventures is searching for promising startup companies. The company is targeting startups in green energy, technology and consumer markets. EDCO has partnered with consumer electronics repair company CherryFusion and technology firm MiniDonations.

41881 ■ *"Elevated Status" in Business Courier (Vol. 24, March 21, 2008, No. 50, pp. 1)*
Pub: American City Business Journals, Inc.
Ed: James Ritchie. **Description:** Overview of TriHealth Inc.'s growth is presented. Currently, the company's revenue is estimated to be around $1 billion. Since 2004, the company was able to build patient towers, an outpatient facility in Lebanon, and was able to acquire the Group Health Associates physician practice. TriHealth recently hired 500 nurses in order to meet its needs.

41882 ■ *"Embarq Sale Sets New Tone" in The Business Journal-Serving Metropolitan Kansas City (Vol. 27, October 31, 2008, No. 8, pp. 1)*
Pub: American City Business Journals, Inc.
Ed: Suzsanna Stagemeyer. **Description:** CenturyTel Inc. has agreed to acquire Embarq Corp., a large phone company based in Overland Park. The acquisition deal is valued at $11.6 billion. The potential impacts of the deal on Kansas City's economy are analyzed.

41883 ■ *"Empire of the Sun" in Canadian Business (Vol. 82, April 27, 2009, No. 7, pp. 42)*
Pub: Rogers Media
Ed: Jeff Sanford. **Description:** Suncor Energy Inc. and Petro-Canada announced on March 23, 2009 plans for a merger. The $19 billion merger will result in Suncor keeping their brand name and 60 percent of the company while Pe= tro-Canada will hold 40 percent. The new Suncor now has 7.5 billion barrels of proved and probable reserves of oil and could account for as much as 25 percent of North American production by 2025.

41884 ■ *"Empty Office Blues" in Business Journal Portland (Vol. 26, December 4, 2009, No. 39, pp. 1)*
Pub: American City Business Journals Inc.
Ed: Wendy Culverwell. **Description:** Portland's office vacancy rates could reach almost 15 percent by the end of 2010 due to job reductions and mergers.

41885 ■ *"EnCana Gets Top Dollar for Gas Depot Division" in Globe & Mail (March 7, 2006, pp. B6)*
Pub: CTVglobemedia Publishing Inc.
Ed: Dave Ebner. **Description:** The details on acquisition of natural gas storage assets of EnCana Corp. by Carlyle/Riverstone Global Energy and Power Fund II LP and Carlyle Group LP are presented.

41886 ■ *"Endeca Gears Up for Likely IPO Bid" in Boston Business Journal (Vol. 31, July 1, 2011, No. 23, pp. 1)*
Pub: Boston Business Journal
Ed: Kyle Alspach. **Description:** Endeca Inc. is readying itself for its plans to register as a public company. The search engine technology leader is enjoying continued growth with revenue up by 30 percent in 2010 while its expansion trend makes it an unlikely candidate for an acquisition.

41887 ■ *"Entrepreneur Column" in Entrepreneur (September 24, 2009)*
Pub: Entrepreneur Media, Inc.
Ed: Allen Moon. **Description:** In an attempt to compete with Google, Microsoft and Yahoo have entered a partnership to merge their search services; advice on the best ways to get noticed on this new search engine entitled Bing, is provided.

41888 ■ *"eResearch Issues Initiating Report on Aldershot Resources Ltd." in Canadian Corporate News (May 14, 2007)*
Pub: Comtex News Network Inc.
Description: Overview of Bob Weir and Michael Wood's Initiating Report on Aldershot Resources Ltd., a junior Canadian-based uranium exploration company with prospective projects in Canada, Zambia, Australia, and a base metals project in Chile.

41889 ■ *"ESolar Partners With Penglai on Landmark Solar Thermal Agreement for China" in Business of Global Warming (January 25, 2010, pp. 8)*
Pub: Investment Weekly News
Description: Penglai Electric, a privately-owned Chinese electrical power equipment manufacturer, and eSolar, a global provider of cost-effective and reliable solar power plants, announced a master licensing agreement in which eSolar will build at least 2 gigawatts of solar thermal power plants in China over the next 10 years.

41890 ■ *"Ethnic Chambers Seek Combined Facility" in Business Journal (Vol. 28, October 8, 2010, No. 18, pp. 1)*
Pub: Minneapolis Business Journal
Ed: Jim Hammerand. **Description:** Six ethnic business and commerce groups in St. Paul and Minneapolis, Minnesota, all members of the Minnesota Multi-Ethnic Chambers of Commerce Joint Council, are planning to move in together in order to save on costs and to strengthen their organizations. The Council expects to transfer by September 2011. The project will cost about $290,000.

41891 ■ *"Executive Decision: Just What the Doctor Ordered" in Globe & Mail (February 11, 2006, pp. B3)*
Pub: CTVglobemedia Publishing Inc.
Ed: Leonard Zehr. **Description:** The leadership ability of chief executive William Hunter of Angiotech Pharmaceuticals Inc., who acquired American Medical Instruments Holdings Inc. for $785 million, is discussed.

41892 ■ *"Executive Decision: To Make Inroads Against RIM, Palm Steals Its Strategy" in Globe & Mail (March 25, 2006, pp. B3)*
Pub: CTVglobemedia Publishing Inc.
Ed: Simon Avery. **Description:** The Palm Inc., global leader in portable device manufacturing, is looking forward to improve its sales of Palm Treos, a wireless portable device that connects to internet and email. Palm is also planning to build partnerships, under the efficient management of Michael Moskowitz, general manager and vice-president of Palm Inc., with the other companies to increase the sales of its wireless devices.

41893 ■ *"Expanding Middleby's Food Processing Biz" in Crain's Chicago Business (Vol. 31, April 21, 2008, No. 16, pp. 6)*
Pub: Crain Communications, Inc.
Ed: David Sterrett. **Description:** Profile of the executive vice-president of the food processing company, Middleby Corp, whose business plan is to develop new products, begin looking for acquisitions and simplify operations in order to expand the firm.

41894 ■ *"Export Initiative Launched" in Philadelphia Business Journal (Vol. 28, December 11, 2009, No. 43, pp. 1)*
Pub: American City Business Journals
Ed: Athena D. Merritt. **Description:** The first initiative that came out of the partnership between the Export-Import Bank of the US, the city of Philadelphia, and the World Trade Center of Greater Philadelphia is presented. A series of export finance workshops have featured Ex-Im Bank resources that can provide Philadelphia businesses with working capital, insurance protection and buyer financing.

41895 ■ *"Exposed?" in Mergers & Acquisitions: The Dealmaker's Journal (March 1, 2008)*
Pub: SourceMedia, Inc.
Ed: Jerry Abejo. **Description:** State-run pension plans' contributions are declining due to a loss of tax revenue from plummeting home values.

41896 ■ *The Facebook Era: Tapping Online Social Networks to Build Better Products, Reach New Audiences, and Sell More Stuff*
Pub: Prentice Hall
Ed: Clara Shih. **Price:** $24.99. **Description:** The '90s were about the World Wide Web of information and the power of linking Web pages. Today it's about the World Wide Web of people and the power of the social graph. Online social networks are fundamentally changing the way we live, work, and interact. They offer businesses immense opportunities to transform customer relationships for profit: opportunities that touch virtually every business function, from sales and marketing to recruiting, collaboration to executive decision-making, product development to innovation.

41897 ■ *"Fair Exchange" in Food and Drink (Winter 2010, pp. 84)*
Pub: Schofield Media Group
Ed: Don Mardak. **Description:** Bartering can assist firms in the food and beverage industry to attract new customers, maximize resources, and reduce cash expenses.

41898 ■ *Family Limited Partnership Deskbook*
Pub: American Bar Association
Contact: Carolyn Lamm, President
Ed: David T. Lewis; Andrea C. Chomakos. **Released:** March 25, 2008. **Price:** $169.95. **Description:** Forming and funding a family limited partnership or limited liability company is complicated. In-depth analysis of all facets of this business entity are examined using detailed guidance on the basic principles of drafting, forming, funding, and valuing an FLP or LLC and also covers tax concerns. Examples and extensive sample forms are included on a CD-ROM included with the book.

41899 ■ *Family Limited Partnerships Deskbook: Forming and Funding FLPs and Other Closely Held Business Entities*
Pub: American Bar Association
Contact: Carolyn Lamm, President
Ed: David T. Lewis. **Released:** March 2008. **Price:** $169.95. **Description:** Forming and funding a family limited partnership (FLP) or limited liability company (LLC) is common and complicated. This handbook offers in-depth analysis of issues facing these types of businesses. Guidance is given on the principles of drafting, forming, funding, and valuing an FLP or LLC as well as tax matters. Examples and sample forms are included on a CD-ROM.

41900 ■ *"FCC Adopts New Media Ownership Rules" in Black Enterprise (Vol. 38, March 2008, No. 8, pp. 26)*
Pub: Earl G. Graves Publishing Co. Inc.
Ed: Joyce Jones. **Description:** Federal Communications Commission approved a ruling that lifts a ban on newspaper and/or broadcast cross ownership. Because of declining sales in newspaper advertising and readership the ban will allow companies to share local news gathering costs across multiple media platforms.

41901 ■ *"Fertilizer for Growth" in Canadian Business (Vol. 83, September 14, 2010, No. 15, pp. 76)*
Pub: Rogers Media Ltd.
Ed: Bryan Borzykowski. **Description:** Australian-based BHP Billiton launches a C$38.5 billion hostile takeover bid for Saskatchewan-based Potash Corporation and some investors immediately bought Potash stock at C$130. However, Potash has resisted BHP's offer and announced a plan to try to stop the deal.

41902 ■ *"Fieldbrook Foods Acquired By Private Equity Firm" in Ice Cream Reporter (Vol. 23, October 20, 2010, No. 11, pp. 1)*
Pub: Ice Cream Reporter
Description: Fieldbrook Foods Corporation, manufacturer of frozen novelty and ice cream products was acquired by Chicago-based private equity firm Arbor Investments. Arbor partnered with Herman 'Bing' Graffunder, a long-term dairy industry partner, in its acquisition of Fieldbrook.

41903 ■ *"Fifth Third Spinoff" in Business Courier (Vol. 27, July 16, 2010, No. 11, pp. 1)*
Pub: Business Courier
Ed: Dan Monk, Steve Watkins. **Description:** Electronic-funds transfer company Fifth Third Solutions (FTPS), a spinoff of Fifth Third Bancorp, is seeking as much as 200,000 square feet of new office space in Ohio. The bank's sale of 51 percent ownership stake to Boston-based Advent International Corporation has paved the way for the growth of FTPS. How real estate brokers' plans have responded to FTPS' growth mode is discussed.

41904 ■ *"Film Giants Disney, Pixar Talk Marriage" in Globe & Mail (January 19, 2006, pp. B1)*
Pub: CTVglobemedia Publishing Inc.
Ed: Merissa Marr; Nick Wingfield. **Description:** The plans of Walt Disney Co. to acquire Pixar Animation Studios are presented.

41905 ■ *"Finalist: BlackEagle Partners L.L.C." in Crain's Detroit Business (Vol. 24, March 24, 2008, No. 12, pp. 12)*
Pub: Crain Communications, Inc.
Ed: Brent Snavely. **Description:** Overview of private-equity firm, BlackEagle Partners L.L.C., an upstart that acquired Rockford Products Corp. in order to improve the performance of the company who does business with several major tier-one automotive suppliers; Rockford manufactures highly engineered chassis and suspension components for automakers and the automotive aftermarket.

41906 ■ *Financing Growth: Strategies, Capital Structure, and M and A Transactions*
Pub: John Wiley and Sons, Inc.
Ed: Kenneth H. Marks, Larry E. Robbins, Gonzalo Fernandez, John P. Funkhouser, D.L. Williams. **Released:** September 1, 2009. **Price:** $95.00. **Description:** Guide for emerging growth and middle market companies includes information to help understand and apply the basics of corporate finance using empirical data and actual company cases to illustrate capital structures and financing approaches.

41907 ■ *Financing Your Small Business*
Pub: Barron's Educational Series Inc.
Contact: Alex Holtz, President
E-mail: aholtz@berronseduc.com
Ed: Robert Walter. **Released:** December 2003. **Description:** Tips for raising venture capital, dealing with bank officials, and initiating public offerings of stock shares for small business.

41908 ■ *"Finding Competitive Advantage in Adversity" in Harvard Business Review (Vol. 88, November 2010, No. 11, pp. 102)*
Pub: Harvard Business School Publishing
Ed: Bhaskar Chakravorti. **Description:** Four opportunities in adversity are identified and applied to business scenarios. These are matching unmet needs with unneeded resources, seeking collaboration from unlikely partners, developing small/appropriate solutions to large/complex issues, and focusing on the platform as well as the product.

41909 ■ *"Finding the Voice of the Marketplace" in Mergers & Acquisitions: The Dealmaker's Journal (March 1, 2008)*
Pub: SourceMedia, Inc.
Description: Companies oftentimes are unable to achieve their strategic goals through acquisition due, in part, to not understanding the target's market and its position in the marketplace.

41910 ■ ***"First the Merger: Then, The Culture Clash. How To Fix the Little Things That Can Tear a Company Apart" in Inc. (January 2008)***
Pub: Gruner & Jahr USA Publishing
Ed: Elaine Appleton Grant. **Description:** Ways three CEOs handled the culture classes that followed after company mergers; companies profiled include Fuel Outdoor, an outdoor advertising company; Nelson, an interior design and architecture firm; and Beber Silverstein, an ad agency.

41911 ■ ***"First U.S. :M-Press Tiger with Inline Screen Printing" in American Printer (Vol. 128, June 1, 2011, No. 6)***
Pub: Penton Media Inc.
Description: Graphic Tech located in California bought :M-Press Tiger, the first in North America with an inline screen printing unit.

41912 ■ ***"Florida's Housing Gloom May Add To Woes of National City" in Crain's Cleveland Business (Vol. 28, October 29, 2007, No. 43, pp. 1)***
Pub: Crain Communications, Inc.
Ed: Shawn A. Turner. **Description:** Already suffering by bad loans in the troubled mortgage market, National City Corp. is attempting to diversify its geographic presence beyond the slow-growth industrial Midwest by acquiring two Florida firms. Analysts worry that the acquisitions may end up making National City vulnerable to a takeover if the housing slump continues and credit quality becomes more of an issue for the bank.

41913 ■ ***"For Giving Us a Way To Say Yes To Solar: Lynn Jurich and Edward Fenster" in Inc. (Volume 32, December 2010, No. 10, pp. 110)***
Pub: Inc. Magazine
Description: Profile of entrepreneurs Lynn Jurich and Edward Fenster, cofounders of SunRun. The firm installs solar panels at little or no cost and homeowners sign 20-year contracts to buy power at a fixed price.

41914 ■ ***"For Hospitals, a Dating Game" in Business Courier (Vol. 26, December 4, 2009, No. 32, pp. 1)***
Pub: American City Business Journals, Inc.
Ed: James Ritchie. **Description:** Drake Center, Fort Hamilton Hospital, and West Chester Medical Center are among the members of Cincinnati's Health Alliance looking for potential buyers or partners. Meanwhile, Jewish Hospital, another member of the Alliance, will be bought by Mercy Health Partners by January 7, 2010.

41915 ■ ***"For Sale: Old Florida Panache" in The Business Journal-Serving Greater Tampa Bay (Vol. 28, July 4, 2008, No. 28, pp. 1)***
Pub: American City Business Journals, Inc.
Ed: Jane Meinhardt. **Description:** Linger Lodge, owned by real estate investor and developer Martin Kaplan and Senator Michael Bennett, is now on the market for a sealed bid process facilitated by Levin & Associates. The business partners bought the riverfront property for about $3 million in 2005. Other details on the sale of the property are presented.

41916 ■ ***"Former Gov. Fletcher Starts Blue Ash Firm" in Business Courier (Vol. 26, October 9, 2009, No. 24, pp. 1)***
Pub: American City Business Journals, Inc.
Ed: Lucy May. **Description:** Former Kentucky Governor Ernie Fletcher partnered with Belcan Corporation founder Ralph Anderson to purchase Blue Ash, Ohio-based Virtual Medical Network and form Alton Healthcare LLC. The company's goal is to increase practice revenues by adapting technology to reinvent clinical practices and deliver best possible care to more patients.

41917 ■ ***"Former Mayor Driving $500 Million Real Estate Equity Fund" in The Business Journal - Serving Phoenix and the Valley of the Sun (Vol. 28, August 15, 2008, No. 50, pp. 1)***
Pub: American City Business Journals, Inc.
Ed: Jan Buchholz. **Description:** Paul John, the former mayor of Phoenix, is establishing a $500 million real estate asset management fund. The fund is dubbed Southwest Next Capital Management and has attracted three local partners, namely Joseph Meyer, Jay Michalowski, and James Mullany, who all have background in finance and construction.

41918 ■ ***"Fortis Snaps Up Terasen's Gas Utility Business" in Globe & Mail (February 27, 2007, pp. B1)***
Pub: CTVglobemedia Publishing Inc.
Ed: Wendy Stueck. **Description:** The acquisition of Terasen Inc. from Kinder Morgan Inc. by Fortis Inc. is described.

41919 ■ ***"Fraser and Neave Acquires King's Creameries" in Ice Cream Reporter (Vol. 23, November 20, 2010, No. 12, pp. 1)***
Pub: Ice Cream Reporter
Description: Fraser and Neave Ltd., a Singapore-based consumer products marketer, has entered a conditional agreement to acquire all outstanding shares of King's Creameries, the leading manufacturer and distributor of frozen desserts.

41920 ■ ***"Freeing the Wheels of Commerce" in Hispanic Business (July-August 2007, pp. 50, 52, 54)***
Pub: Hispanic Business
Ed: Keith Rosenblum. **Description:** SecureOrigins, a border-based partnership with high-tech innovators is working to move goods faster, more efficiently, and securely.

41921 ■ ***"Fresh Direct's Crisis" in Crain's New York Business (Vol. 24, January 14, 2008, No. 2, pp. 3)***
Pub: Crain Communications, Inc.
Ed: Lisa Fickenscher. **Description:** Freshdirect, an Internet grocery delivery service, finds itself under siege from federal immigration authorities, customers and labor organizations due to its employment practice of hiring illegals. At stake is the grocer's reputation as well as its ambitious growth plans, including an initial public offering of its stock.

41922 ■ ***"Friedland's Next Frontier: Drilling for Oil in Iraq" in Globe & Mail (April 20, 2007, pp. B1)***
Pub: CTVglobemedia Publishing Inc.
Ed: Wendy Stueck. **Description:** The decision of the Canadian oil and gas company Ivanhoe Energy Inc. to partner with the Japanese oil and gas firm INPEX Corp. for the development of heavy oil fields in north central Iraq is discussed.

41923 ■ ***"Friends With Money" in Canadian Business (Vol. 81, Summer 2008, No. 9, pp. 22)***
Pub: Rogers Media Ltd.
Description: Two of the most well connected managers in Canadian capital markets Rob Farquharson and Brian Gibson will launch Panoply Capital Asset Management in June. The investment management company aims to raise a billion dollars from institutions and high-net worth individuals.

41924 ■ ***"From Bikes to Building" in Austin Business JournalInc. (Vol. 29, October 30, 2009, No. 34, pp. 1)***
Pub: American City Business Journals
Ed: Kate Harrington. **Description:** Tour de France champion Lance Armstrong, Bill Stapleton his long-time agent, and business manager Bart Knaggs have formed a privately held real estate investment company CSE Realty Parters in Austin, Texas. They see tremendous opportunity in the commercial real estate market in the area.

41925 ■ ***"From Lone Hero to a Culture of Leadership" in Harvard Business Review (Vol. 88, November 2010, No. 11, pp. 146)***
Pub: Harvard Business School Publishing
Ed: Charles J. Palus, John B. McGuire. **Description:** Review of the book, 'Working Together: Why Great Partnerships Succeed', is given.

41926 ■ ***"From Malls to Steel Plants" in Crain's Chicago Business (Vol. 31, April 28, 2008, No. 17, pp. 30)***
Pub: Crain Communications, Inc.
Ed: Samantha Stainburn. **Description:** Profile of the company Graycor Inc. which started out as a sand-blasting and concrete-breaking firm but has grown into four businesses due to innovation and acquisitions. Graycor's businesses include: Graycor Industrial Constructors Inc., which builds and renovates power plants and steel mills; Graycor Construction Co., which erects stores, medical centers and office buildings; Graycor Blasting Co., which uses explosives and blasts tunnels for industrial cleaning, and Graycor International Inc., which provides construction services in Mexico.

41927 ■ ***"Futures Shock for the CME" in Crain's Chicago Business (Vol. 31, November 10, 2008, No. 45, pp. 8)***
Pub: Crain Communications, Inc.
Ed: Ann Saphir. **Description:** Chicago-based CME Group Inc., the largest futures exchange operator in the U.S., is facing a potentially radically altered regulatory landscape as Congress weighs sweeping reform of financial oversight. The possible merger of the CFTC and the Securities and Exchange Commission are among CME's concerns. Other details of possible regulatory measures are provided.

41928 ■ ***"GeckoSystems Reduces Sensor Fusion Costs Due to Elder Care Robot Trials" in Internet Wire (December 14, 2010)***
Pub: Comtex
Description: GeckoSystems International Corporation has been able to reduce the cost of its sensor fusion system while maintaining reliability and performance. The firm's ongoing first in-home elder care robot trials have sparked interest regarding its business model, technologies available for licensing, and joint domestic and international ventures.

41929 ■ ***"Getting in the Swing" in Canadian Business (Vol. 80, February 26, 2007, No. 5, pp. 67)***
Pub: Rogers Media
Ed: Andrew Wahl. **Description:** The economic issues associated with the acquisition of Adams, Harkness and Hill Inc. by Canaccord Capital are presented. A large number of Canadian companies are entering into the United States.

41930 ■ ***"Giant Garages Could Rise Up Downtown" in Business Courier (Vol. 27, October 22, 2010, No. 25, pp. 1)***
Pub: Business Courier
Ed: Dan Monk. **Description:** More than 2,500 new parking spaces could rise up to the eastern edge of downtown Cincinnati, Ohio as public and private investors collect resources for new garage projects. These projects are expected to accommodate almost 1,500 monthly parkers who will lose access at Broadway Commons due to the construction of Harrah's casino.

41931 ■ ***"Give Me Liberty With DirecTV" in Barron's (Vol. 89, July 13, 2009, No. 28, pp. M5)***
Pub: Dow Jones & Co., Inc.
Ed: Fleming Meeks. **Description:** Shares of Liberty Entertainment look cheap at $25.14 and the same goes for DirecTV at $23.19. A merger between the two companies was announced and the deal will likely close by September 2009. Barclays Capital has a target of $30 for Liberty Media and $32 for DirecTV.

41932 ■ ***"Glamis Reserves Get Boost With Western Silver Deal" in Globe & Mail (February 25, 2006, pp. B3)***
Pub: CTVglobemedia Publishing Inc.
Ed: Wendy Stueck. **Description:** The details on Glamis Gold Ltd.'s proposed acquisition of Western Silver Corp., for $1.2 billion, are presented.

41933 ■ ***"Global Steel Makers Circle Stelco" in Globe & Mail (April 19, 2007, pp. B3)***
Pub: CTVglobemedia Publishing Inc.
Ed: Greg Keenan. **Description:** The details of the take over bids offered to Stelco Inc. are presented. Due to these bids the shares of Stelco Inc rose up to 70 percent.

41934 ■ *"GM-Chrysler Merger Could Cull Dealerships From Coast to Coast" in Globe & Mail (February 20, 2007, pp. B17)*
Pub: CTVglobemedia Publishing Inc.
Ed: Greg Keenan. **Description:** General Motors Corp. is planning to acquire Chrysler Group. The challenges before the possible merger are presented.

41935 ■ *"GM-Chrysler Merger: Just a Bigger Mess?" in Globe & Mail (February 17, 2007, pp. B3)*
Pub: CTVglobemedia Publishing Inc.
Ed: Barrie McKenna; Greg Keenan. **Description:** The General Motors Corp. is negotiating talks to acquire DaimlerChrysler AG's Chrysler Group. The five reasons for the possible merger of the companies are presented.

41936 ■ *"GM's Mortgage Unit Deal Brings in $9 Billion" in Globe & Mail (March 24, 2006, pp. B3)*
Pub: CTVglobemedia Publishing Inc.
Ed: Shawn McCarthy. **Description:** General Motors Corp. sells General Motors Acceptance Corp.'s commercial real estate division to Kohlberg Kravis Roberts & Co. Five Mile Capital Partners LLC and Goldman Sachs Capital Partners. The reasons behind the deal are presented.

41937 ■ *"Gold Handshake" in Canadian Business (Vol. 79, September 11, 2006, No. 18, pp. 25)*
Pub: Rogers Media
Ed: John Gray. **Description:** Goldcorp Inc.'s company's planned takeover of Glamis Gold Ltd. is discussed. Implications of the merger on its investors are presented.

41938 ■ *"Goldeye Completes Private Placement" in Canadian Corporate News (May 16, 2007)*
Pub: Comtex News Network Inc.
Description: Goldeye, a Canadian mineral exploration company acquiring, exploring, and advancing properties in Chile and Canada, announced that it has completed a partially brokered private placement for gross proceeds of $1,232,660 which will be used to finance exploration on Goldeye's mineral properties in Chile and for administrative expenses, and working capital.

41939 ■ *"Goldfingers" in Canadian Business (Vol. 81, Summer 2008, No. 9, pp. 31)*
Pub: Rogers Media Ltd.
Ed: Sharda Prashad. **Description:** Large players in the mining industry are looking for junior mining companies in Canada to be acquired. The U.S. recession and subprime mortgage crisis have made it easier for giant miners to acquire small mining companies than to conduct the operations themselves. Junior miners are those that lack cash flow and expertise to build and operate mine.

41940 ■ *"GoodNews.com and the Little Cupcake Shoppe Support Calgary Food Bank With Unique $1.00 Deal" in Marketwire Canada (March 9, 2011)*
Pub: Marketwire Canada
Description: Socially-conscious group-buying Website, GoodNews.com has partnered with The Little Cupcake Shoppe in Calgary, to raise funds for the Inter-Faith Food Bank. The fundraiser will feature a half dozen, pre-packaged assorted miniature cupcakes for $1.00. The entire amount is donated to the Calgary Food Bank.

41941 ■ *"Goodwill Haunts Local Companies; Bad Buyouts During Boom Times Producing Big Writedowns" in Crain's Chicago Business (Apr. 28, 2008)*
Pub: Crain Communications, Inc.
Ed: Ann Saphir. **Description:** Many companies are having to face the reality that they overpaid for acquisitions made in better economic times; investors often dismiss such one-time charges as mere accounting adjustments but writeoffs related to past acquisitions can signal future problems because they mean the expected profits that justified the purchase have not materialized. Writeoffs are particularly worrisome for firms with a lot of debt and whose banks require them to have enough assets to back up their borrowings.

41942 ■ *"Google, MySpace Deal Hits Snag" in Globe & Mail (February 7, 2007, pp. B11)*
Pub: CTVglobemedia Publishing Inc.
Ed: Julia Angwin; Kevin J. Delaney. **Description:** MySpace's intention to partner with eBay which is delaying the finalization of its $900 million online advertising deal signed with Google Inc. is discussed.

41943 ■ *"Great Stocks Cheap" in Canadian Business (Vol. 80, January 15, 2007, No. 2, pp. 31)*
Pub: Rogers Media
Ed: Calvin Leung. **Description:** The stock performance of top 10 international companies like Furgo, Moody's Investor Service, Adidas Group and Nestle is analyzed.

41944 ■ *"Green Acres" in Hawaii Business (Vol. 54, September 2008, No. 3, pp. 48)*
Pub: Hawaii Business Publishing
Ed: Jan Tenbruggencate. **Description:** Bill Cowern's Hawaiian Mahogany is a forestry business that processes low-value trees to be sold as wood chips, which can be burned to create biodiesel. Cowern is planning to obtain certification to market carbon credits and is also working with Green Energy Hawaii for the permit of a biomass-fueled power plant. Other details about Cowern's business are discussed.

41945 ■ *"Greenhouse Announces Merger With Custom Q, Inc." in Investment Weekly (January 30, 2010, pp. 338)*
Pub: Investment Weekly News
Description: In accordance with an Agreement and Plan of Share Exchange, GreenHouse Holdings, Inc., an innovative green solutions provider, has gone public via a reverse merger with Custom Q, Inc.

41946 ■ *"Grote Company Puts Final Wrap on Sandwich-Making Line" in Business First-Columbus (October 26, 2007, pp. A1)*
Pub: American City Business Journals, Inc.
Ed: Dan Eaton. **Description:** Grote Company acquired Oxfordshire, England-based Advanced Food Technology Ltd., giving the Ohio-based food cutting equipment company a manufacturing base in Europe. This is the company's second deal in four months. Details on Grote Company's plan to tap into the prepared fresh sandwich market are discussed.

41947 ■ *"Group-Buying Site Hones In on Hispanics" in Austin Business Journal (Vol. 31, July 1, 2011, No. 17, pp. 1)*
Pub: American City Business Journals Inc.
Ed: Vicky Garza. **Description:** Descuentl Libre is a new group-buying site from Austin, Texas that targets the Hispanic market, offering discounts of practical items and family-friendly activities. The Hispanic market constitutes 17 percent of the U.S. population and spends $23 billion yearly online.

41948 ■ *Group Genius: The Creative Power of Collaboration*
Pub: Basic Books/Perseus Books Group
Ed: Keith Sawyer. **Released:** March 2008. **Price:** $16.95 paperback. **Description:** Organizations can foster creativity and innovation through discussion, argumentation and group activities.

41949 ■ *Growing Local Value: How to Build Business Partnerships That Strengthen Your Community*
Pub: Berrett-Koehler Publishers, Incorporated
Ed: Laury Hammel; Gun Denhart. **Released:** December 2006. **Price:** $15.00. **Description:** Advice and examples are provided for building socially responsible entrepreneurship.

41950 ■ *"Hain Celestial Acquires Greek Gods Yogurt" in Ice Cream Reporter (Vol. 23, July 20, 2010, No. 8, pp. 1)*
Pub: Ice Cream Reporter
Description: Hain Celestial Group acquired The Greek Gods LLC. Hain Celestial is a natural and organic products company and Greek Gods makes all natural, Greek-style yogurt and ice cream.

41951 ■ *"Hand-Held Heaven: Smallcakes Cupcakery" in Tulsa World (February 15, 2011)*
Pub: McClatchy Company
Description: Franchisee Carolyn Archer displays her products at Smallcakes Cupcakery, a Jenks shop that's the first to be co-branded with FreshBerry under the Beautiful Brands International banner. The shop's launch is part of a franchise deal between BBI and Jeff and Brandy Martin, co-owners of Smallcakes; twelve concepts have been developed and marketed already by Tulsa-based BBI.

41952 ■ *Happy About Joint Venturing: The 8 Critical Factors of Success*
Pub: Happy About
Ed: Valerie Orsoni-Vauthey. **Released:** June 2006. **Price:** $23.95. **Description:** An overview of joint venturing is presented.

41953 ■ *"The Harder Side of Sears" in Crain's Chicago Business (Vol. 31, March 31, 2008, No. 13, pp. 68)*
Pub: Crain Communications, Inc.
Ed: Steven R. Strahler. **Description:** Discusses the history of Sears Roebuck & Co. and its merger with Kmart Corp.

41954 ■ *"Harleysville Eyes Growth After Nationwide Deal" in Philadelphia Business Journal (Vol. 30, October 7, 2011, No. 34, pp. 1)*
Pub: American City Business Journals Inc.
Ed: Jeff Blumenthal. **Description:** Harleysville Group announced growth plans after the company was sold to Columbus, Ohio-based Nationwide Mutual Insurance Company for about $1.63 billion. Nationwide gained an independent agency platform in 32 states with the Harleysville deal.

41955 ■ *"Has Microsoft Found a Way to Get at Yahoo?" in Advertising Age (Vol. 79, July 7, 2008, No. 26, pp. 4)*
Pub: Crain Communications, Inc.
Ed: Abbey Klaassen. **Description:** Microsoft's attempt to acquire Yahoo's search business is discussed as is Yahoo's plans for the future at a time when the company's shares have fallen dangerously low.

41956 ■ *"HBC Sells Credit Card Division" in Globe & Mail (February 8, 2006, pp. B1)*
Pub: CTVglobemedia Publishing Inc.
Ed: Sinclair Stewart; Marina Strauss. **Description:** The details on General Electric Co.'s acquisition of Hudson's Bay Co.'s credit card division, for $370 million, are presented.

41957 ■ *"HBC Sets Friday as Deadline to Trump Zucker Takeover Bid" in Globe & Mail (January 18, 2006, pp. B1)*
Pub: CTVglobemedia Publishing Inc.
Ed: Marina Strauss. **Description:** The reasons behind Hudson's Bay Co.'s decision to seek alternative bids on the company are presented. Investor Jerry Zucker earlier offered $1.1 billion for the company.

41958 ■ *"Health Care of the Future" in Business Journal Serving Greater Tampa Bay (Vol. 30, November 19, 2010, No. 48, pp. 1)*
Pub: Tampa Bay Business Journal
Ed: Margie Manning. **Description:** Information about accountable care organizations (ACO), which are integrated care systems with doctors and hospitals working closely together to handle patient care, is provided. The Patient Protection and Affordable Care Act paved the way for ACOs as Medicare demonstration projects.

41959 ■ *"Health Care Leads Sectors Attracting Capital" in Hispanic Business (Vol. 30, March 2008, No. 3, pp. 14)*
Pub: Hispanic Business
Ed: Scott Williams. **Description:** Discusses the capital gains of Hispanic-owned companies and other Hispanic leaders in the investment and retail fields in the year 2007. Sectors like health care, media, food

and technology saw a healthy flow of capital due to successful mergers, acquisitions and increased private equity investments.

41960 ■ *"HealthTronics Eager to Buy" in Austin Business JournalInc. (Vol. 28, September 12, 2008, No. 26, pp. 1)*
Pub: American City Business Journals
Ed: Laura Hipp. **Description:** HealthTronics Inc., an Austin, Texas urology equipment company has repeated its offer to buy Endocare Inc., an Irvine, California tumor technology firm for $26.9 million. The proposal has been revised to allow Endocare shareholders to choose between HealthTronics cash or shares. Endocare has not commented on the offer.

41961 ■ *"Healthy Fast Food Acquires Rights to U-Swirl Yogurt" in Ice Cream Reporter (Vol. 21, October 20, 2008, No. 11, pp. 5)*
Pub: Ice Cream Reporter
Description: Healthy Fast Food Inc. will acquire worldwide rights to U-Swirl Frozen Yogurt; the firm will use the new acquisition to create a yogurt superstore in a cafe setting concept for its operations.

41962 ■ *"The Heat Is On" in Crain's Chicago Business (Vol. 31, April 28, 2008, No. 17, pp. 4)*
Pub: Crain Communications, Inc.
Ed: Steve Daniels. **Description:** Discusses Nicor Inc., a natural-gas utility serving 2 million customers in Chicago's suburbs, and its potential acquirers; shares of the company have dropped 17 percent this year making Nicor the second-worst among 31 utilities in an index tracked by Standrd & Poor's. Statistical data included.

41963 ■ *"Heat's On, but Glacier Not Retreating" in Globe & Mail (January 26, 2006, pp. B3)*
Pub: CTVglobemedia Publishing Inc.
Ed: Grant Robertson. **Description:** The details on Glacier Ventures International Corp., which acquired Hollinger International Inc.'s assets, are presented.

41964 ■ *"His Way" in Inc. (February 2008, pp. 90-97)*
Pub: Gruner & Jahr USA Publishing
Ed: Stephanie Clifford. **Description:** Profile of Chris Reed, founder of a natural soda company, who undertook an initial public offering (IPO). Reed discusses the challenges he faced mediating with the Securities Exchange Commission regarding his firm's IPO.

41965 ■ *"Hispanic Business Group Leader Continues Push for Better Inclusion" in Crain's Cleveland Business (Vol. 30, June 22, 2009, No. 24)*
Pub: Crain Communications, Inc.
Ed: Jay Miller. **Description:** Hispanic Business Association is working to create more opportunities for Hispanic business owners. The article discusses the Minority Business Accelerator 2.5 program of the Greater Cleveland Partnership that helps minority-owned small businesses.

41966 ■ *"The Hollow Debate" in Canadian Business (Vol. 81, March 3, 2008, No. 3, pp. 26)*
Pub: Rogers Media
Ed: Thomas Watson. **Description:** According to a report conducted by the Conference Board of Canada, the Canadian business community is not being hollowed out by acquisitions made by foreign companies. Findings further showed that local businesses are protected by dual shares and that the economy can benefit more from foreign acquisitions than local mergers. The need to relax foreign ownership restrictions and other recommendations are presented.

41967 ■ *"Hong Kong's Boom in IPO" in Barron's (Vol. 89, July 13, 2009, No. 28, pp. M7)*
Pub: Dow Jones & Co., Inc.
Ed: Nick Lord. **Description:** Hong Kong's IPO (initial public offering) market is booming with 13 Chinese IPOs already on the market for the year as July 2009. One of them is Bawang International which raised $214 million after generating $9 billion in order which makes it 42 times oversubscribed.

41968 ■ *"Horizon Acquires Significant Working Interest in High Impact Prospect in Southeast Texas" in Canadian Corporate News (May 14, 2007)*
Pub: Comtex News Network Inc.
Description: Horizon Industries Ltd., an emerging gas and oil exploration and production company, announced that it has entered into a Joint Venture agreement with Pan American Development Company, Inc. in which they will begin a drilling program in San Jacinto County, Texas.

41969 ■ *"Hospital Fighting for Its Life; Board of St. Anthony Scrambles to Stem Losses" in Crain's Chicago Business (April 28, 2008)*
Pub: Crain Communications, Inc.
Ed: Mike Colias. **Description:** Chicago's Catholic health chain was looking to sell the money-losing hospital St. Anthony Hospital on the West Side but with the financial picture improving and no merger offers in the works the investment bank hired to shop the hospital is hoping to operate the 111-year-old facility as an independent entity. St. Anthony serves as a 'safety net' for the region since an increasing number of its patients are uninsured or on public aid, which pays far less than commercial insurers.

41970 ■ *"How to Beat Jet Lag for $550,000" in Globe & Mail (January 3, 2006, pp. B1)*
Pub: CTVglobemedia Publishing Inc.
Ed: Simon Avery. **Description:** The details on DreamWorks Animation SKG Inc., which developed videoconferencing software 'Halo' in association with Hewlett-Packard Co., are presented.

41971 ■ *How to Become a Great Boss: The Rules for Getting and Keeping the Best Employees*
Pub: Hyperion Special Markets
Ed: Jeffrey J. Fox. **Released:** May 15, 2002. **Price:** $16.95. **Description:** The book offers valuable advice to any manager or entrepreneur to improve leadership and management skills. Topics covered include: hiring, managing, firing, partnership and competition, self and organization, employee performance, attitude, and priorities.

41972 ■ *"How to Conquer New Markets With Old Skills" in Harvard Business Review (Vol. 88, November 2010, No. 11, pp. 118)*
Pub: Harvard Business School Publishing
Ed: Mauro F. Guillen, Esteban Garcia-Canal. **Description:** Exploration of business-networking factors that have helped lead to the success of Spain's multinational companies is provided. These include development of political skills, access to capabilities and resources, globalization partnerships, and speed of implementation.

41973 ■ *"How I Did It: Jack Ma" in Inc. (January 2008, pp. 94-102)*
Pub: Gruner & Jahr USA Publishing
Ed: Rebecca Fannin. **Description:** Profile of Jack Ma, who started as a guide and interpreter for Western tourists in Hangzhou. Ma used the Internet to build Alibaba.com, China's largest business-to-business site and one of the hottest IPOs in years.

41974 ■ *"How to Play the Tech Mergers" in Barron's (Vol. 90, August 30, 2010, No. 35, pp. 18)*
Pub: Barron's Editorial & Corporate Headquarters
Ed: Tiernan Ray. **Description:** The intense bidding by Hewlett-Packard and Dell for 3Par was foreseen in a previous Barron's cover story and 3Par's stock has nearly tripled since reported. Other possible acquisition targets in the tech industry include Brocade Communication Systems, NetApp, Xyratex, and Isilon Systems.

41975 ■ *"How Yamana CEO First Struck Gold With Desert Sun" in Globe & Mail (February 27, 2006, pp. B3)*
Pub: CTVglobemedia Publishing Inc.
Ed: Andrew Willis. **Description:** The role of chief executive officer Peter Marronne of Yamana Gold Inc. in the acquisition of Desert Sun Mining Corp. is discussed.

41976 ■ *I'm on LinkedIn - Now What? (Second Edition): A Guide to Getting the Most Out of LinkedIn*
Pub: Happy About
Ed: Diane Danielson. **Released:** January 7, 2009. **Price:** $19.95. **Description:** Designed to help get the most out of LinkedIn, the popular business networking site and follows the first edition and includes the latest and great approaches using LinkedIn. With over 32 million members there is a lot of potential to find and develop relationships to help in your business and personal life, but many professionals find themselves wondering what to do once they sign up. This book explains the different benefits of the system and recommends best practices (including LinkedIn Groups) so that you get the most out of LinkedIn.

41977 ■ *"Imax in Play as It Explores Options" in Globe & Mail (March 10, 2006, pp. B3)*
Pub: CTVglobemedia Publishing Inc.
Ed: Shirley Won. **Description:** Imax Corp. has put up itself for sale, and has also confirmed that it has received unsolicited offers for purchase.

41978 ■ *"iMozi Integrates Esprida LiveControl for Advanced DVD Kiosk Hardware" in Wireless News (December 20, 2010)*
Pub: Close-Up Media Inc.
Description: Provider of self-service entertainment technology, iMozi Canada has partnered with Esprida to make its automated DVD Kiosk solutions Esprida-enabled. Esprida develops remote device management solutions and will offer enhanced capabilities and to improve customer experience for users.

41979 ■ *"The Impact of Acquisitions On the Productivity of Inventors at Semiconductor Firms" in Academy of Management Journal (October 2007)*
Pub: Academy of Management
Contact: Ming-Jer Chen, President
Ed: Rahul Kapoor, Kwanghui Lim. **Description:** Study examined the relation between knowledge-based and incentive-based outlook in explaining the impact of acquisitions on the productivity of inventors at acquired semiconductor firms. Results showed a definite relation between the two perspectives.

41980 ■ *"In the Public Eye" in Entrepreneur (Vol. 35, November 2007, No. 11, pp. 75)*
Pub: Entrepreneur Media Inc.
Ed: David Worrell. **Description:** The market for initial public offerings (IPOs) was booming in 2007 and strong fundamentals for companies that would like to go public are needed. The basics that companies should review before planning an IPO are outlined.

41981 ■ *"Inco Takeover Faces Foreign Hurdles" in Globe & Mail (February 14, 2006, pp. B1)*
Pub: CTVglobemedia Publishing Inc.
Ed: Paul Waldie. **Description:** The issues that impact Inco Ltd.'s acquisition of Falconbridge Ltd., for $12.5 billion, are presented. Inco Ltd. is awaiting foreign regulatory approval in the United States and Europe.

41982 ■ *"Inco's Takeover Offer Extended Four Months" in Globe & Mail (February 22, 2006, pp. B1)*
Pub: CTVglobemedia Publishing Inc.
Ed: Wendy Stueck. **Description:** United States and Europe competition authorities wanted more time to investigate Inco Ltd.'s takeover of Falconbridge Ltd. and compelling Inco to extend its $12.5 billion offer for the third time.

41983 ■ *"Indian Buyer Gives Life to Algoma Expansion" in Globe & Mail (April 17, 2007, pp. B1)*
Pub: CTVglobemedia Publishing Inc.
Ed: Greg Keenan. **Description:** The proposed capacity expansion of Algoma Steel Inc. after its acquisition by Essar Global Ltd. is discussed.

41984 ■ *"Ingrian and Channel Management International Sign Distribution Agreement" in Canadian Corporate News (May 16, 2007)*
Pub: Comtex News Network Inc.
Description: Channel Management International (CMI), a Canadian channel management and distribution company, and Ingrian Networks, Inc., the leading

provider of data privacy solutions, announced a Canadian distribution agreement to resell Ingrian encryption solutions to the Canadian market.

41985 ■ *"Inland Snaps Up Rival REITs" in Crain's Chicago Business (Vol. 31, November 17, 2008, No. 46, pp. 3)*
Pub: Crain Communications, Inc.
Ed: Alby Gallun. **Description:** Discusses Inland American Real Estate Trust Inc., a real estate investment trust that is napping up depressed shares of publicly traded competitors, a possible first step toward taking over these companies; however, with hotel and retail properties accounting for approximately 70 percent of its portfolio, the company could soon face its own difficulties.

41986 ■ *"Inmet Selling Nunavut Mining Properties" in Globe & Mail (February 15, 2006, pp. B6)*
Pub: CTVglobemedia Publishing Inc.
Ed: Allan Robinson. **Description:** The details on Wolfden Resources Inc.'s acquisition of mining assets of Inmet Mining Corp. are presented.

41987 ■ *"Innovative Growth" in Small Business Opportunities (March 2008)*
Pub: Harris Publications Inc.
Ed: Peter Erickson. **Description:** Nine tips are outlined to help small companies and entrepreneurs to partner with larger companies.

41988 ■ *Instant Income*
Pub: McGraw-Hill Inc.
Ed: Janet Switzer. **Released:** February 2007. **Price:** $30.95 (CND). **Description:** Book covers small business advertising techniques, marketing, joint ventures, and sales.

41989 ■ *"An Insurance Roll-Up In Danger of Unraveling" in Barron's (Vol. 88, March 17, 2008, No. 11, pp. 51)*
Pub: Dow Jones & Company, Inc.
Ed: Bill Alpert. **Description:** Shares of National Financial Partners have fallen below their initial offering price as sputtering sales and management turnover leave many investors wondering. One of the company's star brokers is being sued for their 'life settlement' contracts while another broker is being pursued by the IRS for unpaid taxes.

41990 ■ *"International Nickel Ventures Corporation Reports Results for the First Quarter 2007" in Canadian Corporate News (May 16, 2007)*
Pub: Comtex News Network Inc.
Description: Profile of International Nickel Ventures Corporation (INV) including its financial report for the first quarter of fiscal 2007, its partnership and possible acquisition of Teck Cominco Limited, and its plans for the future. Statistical data included.

41991 ■ *"Internet Translation Service Helps Burmese" in News-Sentinel (May 10, 2011)*
Pub: New-Sentinel
Ed: Ellie Bogue. **Description:** Catherine Kasper Place, Parkview Health Community Outreach, Allen County-Fort Wayne Department of Health and Advantage Health have partnered to help the Burmese Community in the area by providing an online service that links doctors' offices with translators in order to provide better healthcare.

41992 ■ *"Intrawest Puts Itself on Market" in Globe & Mail (March 1, 2006, pp. B1)*
Pub: CTVglobemedia Publishing Inc.
Ed: Elizabeth Church. **Description:** The reasons behind the decision of Intrawest Corp. to go for sale or seek partnerships are presented. The company appointed Goldman Sachs & Co. to meet the purpose.

41993 ■ *"Inventive Doctor New Venture Partner" in Houston Business Journal (Vol. 40, January 29, 2010, No. 38, pp. A2)*
Pub: American City Business Journals
Ed: Ford Gunter. **Description:** Dr. Billy Cohn, a surgeon from Houston, Texas has been named as venture partner for venture firm Sante Ventures LLC of Austin, Texas. Cohn will be responsible for seeing marketable developing technologies in the medical industry. The motivation for Cohn's naming as venture partner is his development of a minimally invasive therapy for end-stage renal disease.

41994 ■ *"Investment Bank Predicts Shakeup in Farm Equipment Industry" in Farm Industry News (November 16, 2011)*
Pub: Penton Business Media Inc.
Ed: Jodie Wehrspann. **Description:** Farming can expect to see more mergers and acquisitions in the agricultural equipment industry, as it appears to be in the early stages of growth over the next few years.

41995 ■ *"Investment Firms Unite: Coalition Fights New Tax Law" in Black Enterprise (Vol. 38, December 2007, No. 5, pp. 52)*
Pub: Earl G. Graves Publishing Co. Inc.
Ed: Joyce Jones. **Description:** Minorities working in private equity, real estate and investment management firms have united to form the Access to Capital Coalition to oppose legislation that they feel would adversely affect their ability to attract investments and executives. Details of the group are included.

41996 ■ *"ITT Places Its Bet With Defense Buy; Selling Equipment to Army Pays Off" in Crain's New York Business (Vol. 24, January 7, 2008)*
Pub: Crain Communications, Inc.
Description: ITT Corp.'s revenue has jumped by 20 percent in each of the past three years due to demand for the company's radio sets and night-vision goggles. The firm has acquired EDO Corp., which specializes in battlefield communications systems, in an attempt to expand its defense-industry division.

41997 ■ *"Jamieson Eyes $175 Million Trust IPO" in Globe & Mail (March 7, 2006, pp. B1)*
Pub: CTVglobemedia Publishing Inc.
Ed: Sinclair Stewart; Leonard Zehr. **Description:** The reasons behind $175 million initial public offering plans of Jamieson Laboratories Ltd. are presented.

41998 ■ *"Janet Froetscher, CEO, United Way of Metropolitan Chicago" in Crain's Chicago Business (Vol. 31, May 5, 2008, No. 18, pp. 26)*
Pub: Crain Communications, Inc.
Ed: Emily Stone. **Description:** Profile of Janet Froetscher who is the CEO of United Way of Metropolitan Chicago who organized the country's largest-ever merger of non-profits with 53 smaller suburban chapters consolidating with the Chicago one. The consolidation saves $4 million a year with departments such as finance, information technology and communications which allows that money be spent funding job training, after-school programs and aid for 7,000 Hurricane Katrina evacuees living in the Chicago area.

41999 ■ *"Janson: Duke's Dynamo, Regional President Focuses on Economic Development" in Business Courier (Vol. 27, July 9, 2010, No. 10, pp. 1)*
Pub: Business Courier
Ed: Lucy May. **Description:** Duke Energy President Julie Janson is also chair of the Cincinnati USA Partnership for Economic Development and the co-chair of the Cincinnati Business Committee's Economic Development Task Force. Duke is launching a Site Readiness Pilot Program to help the region prepare for an economic recovery.

42000 ■ *"Jo-Ann Fabric and Craft Stores Joins ArtFire.com to Offer Free Online Craft Marketplace" in Internet Wire (January 26, 2010)*
Pub: Comtex News Network, Inc.
Description: Jo-Ann Fabric and Craft Stores has entered into a partnership with ArtFire.com which will provide sewers and crafters all the tools they need in order to make and sell their products from an online venue.

42001 ■ *"Joint Venture Plans Bronzeville Project" in Business Journal-Milwaukee (Vol. 25, October 5, 2007, No. 1, pp. A1)*
Pub: American City Business Journals, Inc.
Ed: Rich Kirchen. **Description:** Proposal for construction of an apartment building and possible expansion of Northtown Mall in Milwaukee, Wisconsin is being planned by developers in the city's Bronzeville area. The project for rehabilitating the existing mall and building of a 50-unit apartment would amount to about $12.5 million.

42002 ■ *"Juicy Feud; Deal Caps Years of Rancor in Wrigley Gum Dynasty" in Crain's Chicago Business (Vol. 31, May 5, 2008, No. 18, pp. 1)*
Pub: Crain Communications, Inc.
Ed: David Sterrett. **Description:** Discusses the sale of Wm. Wrigley Jr. Co. to Mars Inc. and Warren Buffett for $23 billion as well as the intra-family feuding which has existed for nearly a decade since William Wrigley Jr. took over as CEO of the company following his father's death.

42003 ■ *"KBA, Graphic Art System Partner on Cold Foil" in American Printer (Vol. 128, June 1, 2011, No. 6)*
Pub: Penton Media Inc.
Description: KBA North America has partnered with Graphic Art System to retrofit and equip presses with cold foil machines.

42004 ■ *"Keeping Railcars 'Busy At All Times' At TTX" in Crain's Chicago Business (Vol. 31, April 28, 2008, No. 17, pp. 6)*
Pub: Crain Communications, Inc.
Ed: Bob Tita. **Description:** Profile of the president of Chicago railcar pool operator TTX Co. and his business plan for the company which includes improving fleet management and car purchasing through better use of data on railroad demand.

42005 ■ *"Kerkorian Shakes Up Chrysler Race" in Globe & Mail (April 6, 2007, pp. B1)*
Pub: CTVglobemedia Publishing Inc.
Ed: Greg Keenan. **Description:** The bid of Kirk Kerkorian's Tracinda Corp. to acquire DaimlerChrysler AG for $4.5 billion is discussed.

42006 ■ *"Kirnross Holds Firm on Offer for Bema" in Globe & Mail (January 20, 2007, pp. B5)*
Pub: CTVglobemedia Publishing Inc.
Ed: Andy Hoffman. **Description:** The acquisition of Bema Gold Corp. by Kinross Gold Corp. is discussed.

42007 ■ *"Knight Sold as Industry Struggles" in Globe & Mail (March 14, 2006, pp. D1)*
Pub: CTVglobemedia Publishing Inc.
Ed: Christopher Rowland. **Description:** McClatchy Co. said that it would buy Knight Ridder Inc. for $4.5 billion, which is a newspaper giant in United States. The details of McClatchy acquisition plans for Knight Ridder news syndicate are analyzed.

42008 ■ *"Kodak Offers Cloud-Based Operating Option" in American Printer (Vol. 128, June 1, 2011, No. 6)*
Pub: Penton Media Inc.
Description: Kodak partnered with VMware to offer its first Virtual Operating Environment option for Kodak Unified Workflow Solutions. The new feature enables cost savings, increased efficiency and failover protection.

42009 ■ *"Kubicki Juggles Lineup at Vianda" in Business Courier (Vol. 26, December 11, 2009, No. 33, pp. 1)*
Pub: American City Business Journals, Inc.
Ed: Dan Monk. **Description:** Cincinnati real estate developer Chuck Kubicki replaced the management team of Vianda LLC and cancelled contracts with two vendors that caused a surge of customer complaints. Vianda is a direct-response marketing firm that sells and distributes dietary supplements for wellness and sexual performance.

42010 ■ *"Labatt to Swallow Lakeport" in Globe & Mail (February 2, 2007, pp. B1)*
Pub: CTVglobemedia Publishing Inc.
Ed: Keith McArthur. **Description:** The decision of Labatt Brewing Company Ltd. to acquire Lakeport Brewing Income Fund for $201.4 million is discussed.

42011 ■ *"Land Agent Taken Over" in Farmer's Weekly (March 28, 2008, No. 320)*
Pub: Reed Business Information
Contact: Jeff Greisch, President
Description: Property business Smiths Gore will take over Cluttons' rural division, one of the oldest names in land agency. Cluttons said it had decided to sell its rural business as part of a strategic repositioning that would refocus the business on commercial, residential and overseas opportunities.

42012 ■ *"The Last Ingredient?" in Canadian Business (Vol. 81, October 13, 2008, No. 17, pp. 88)*
Pub: Rogers Media Ltd.
Ed: Rachel Pulfer. **Description:** Views and information on Cookie Jar Group's plan to acquire rights for Strawberry Shortcake and the Care Bears are discussed. The move would make Cookie Jar a major player in the global children's entertainment market. Cookie Jar chief executive, Michael Hirsh is believed to be securing funds for the planned $195 million acquisition.

42013 ■ *"Late to Minivan Party, VW Hitches Ride With Daimler" in Globe & Mail (January 6, 2006, pp. B1)*
Pub: CTVglobemedia Publishing Inc.
Ed: Greg Keenan. **Description:** DaimlerChrysler AG and Volkswagen AG plans to manufacture minivan. The details of joint venture are presented.

42014 ■ *"Lathrop Finds Partner In LA" in The Business Journal-Serving Metropolitan Kansas City (Vol. 27, November 21, 2008, No. 11, pp. 1)*
Pub: American City Business Journals, Inc.
Ed: Steve Vockrodt. **Description:** Kansas, Missouri-based Lathrop and Gage LLP is planning to merge with Spillane Shaeffer Aronoff Bandlow LLP. The merging of the business law firms will add entertainment clients to Lathrop's fold. Comments from executives are also presented.

42015 ■ *"Laugh or Cry?" in Barron's (Vol. 88, March 24, 2008, No. 12, pp. 7)*
Pub: Dow Jones & Company, Inc.
Ed: Alan Abelson. **Description:** Discusses the American economy which is just starting to feel the effect of the credit and housing crises. JPMorgan Chase purchased Bear Stearns for $2 a share, much lower than its share price of $60, while quasi-government entities Fannie Mae and Freddie Mac are starting to run into trouble.

42016 ■ *"Leadership Training" in Black Enterprise (Vol. 37, January 2007, No. 6, pp. 56)*
Pub: Earl G. Graves Publishing Co. Inc.
Ed: Sonia Alleyne. **Description:** Profile of Theopolis Holman, Group Vice-President of Duke Energy, who discusses how he prepared for the merger between Duke Energy and Cinergy. Holman oversees a division of 9,000 service contractors and employees.

42017 ■ *"Leapin' Lizards, Does SoBe Have Some Work To Do On Life Water" in Brandweek (Vol. 49, April 21, 2008, No. 16, pp. 32)*
Pub: VNU Business Media, Inc.
Ed: Amy Shea. **Description:** Discusses the competing marketing campaigns of both Vitaminwater, now owned by Coca-Cola, and SoBe Life Water which is owned by Pepsi; also looks at the repositioning of Life Water as a thirst-quencher, rather than a green product as well as the company's newest advertising campaign.

42018 ■ *"Lenders Capitalize on a Thinning Bulge Bracket" in Mergers & Acquisitions: The Dealmaker's Journal (March 1, 2008)*
Pub: SourceMedia, Inc.
Description: Regardless of what the economic markets look like, private equity firms will continue to invest capital and mid-market finance firms are becoming very attractive acquisition opportunities since not as much capital is needed to buy them.

42019 ■ *"Let the Big Fish Eat" in Canadian Business (Vol. 80, March 12, 2007, No. 6, pp. 4)*
Pub: Rogers Media
Ed: Joe Chidley. **Description:** The need for profitable Canadian banks to go for mergers to enjoy the benefits of globalization and compete with global banks is discussed.

42020 ■ *Let's Buy a Company: How to Accelerate Growth Through Acquisitions*
Pub: Career Press, Incorporated
Ed: H. Lee Rust. **Released:** January 2006. **Price:** $18.99 (US), $25.95 (Canadian). **Description:** Advice for negotiating terms and pricing as well as other aspects of mergers and acquisitions in small companies.

42021 ■ *"A Lifetime of Making Deals" in Crain's Detroit Business (Vol. 24, March 24, 2008, No. 12, pp. 11)*
Pub: Crain Communications, Inc.
Ed: Tom Henderson. **Description:** Profile of Walter 'Bud' Aspatore who received Crain's Lifetime Achievement Award for mergers and acquisitions; Aspatore is chairman and co-founder of Amherst Partners L.L.C., an investment banking firm that does evaluations and financings, specializes in turnarounds and advises private and public companies on mergers and acquisitions.

42022 ■ *"Li'l Guy Rolls Up Into Bigger Company" in The Business Journal-Serving Metropolitan Kansas City (Vol. 26, September 12, 2008)*
Pub: American City Business Journals, Inc.
Ed: Suzanna Stagemeyer. **Description:** Li'l Guy Foods, a Mexican food company in Kansas City, Missouri, has merged with Tortilla King Inc. Li'l Guy's revenue in 2007 was $3.3 million, while a newspaper report said that Tortilla King's revenue in 2001 was $7.5 million. Growth opportunities for the combined companies and Li'l Guy's testing of the Wichita market are discussed.

42023 ■ *"A Limited Sphere of Influence" in Mergers & Acquisitions: The Dealmaker's Journal (March 1, 2008)*
Pub: SourceMedia, Inc.
Ed: Ken MacFadyen. **Description:** Changes to the interest rate has had little impact on the mergers and acquisitions market since the federal funds rate does not link directly to the liquidity available to the M&A market; lenders are looking at cash flows and are likely to remain cautious due to other factors impacting the market.

42024 ■ *"A Local Affair: Decisions for Tops Again Being Made at Amherst HQ" in Business First Buffalo (December 7, 2007, pp. 3)*
Pub: American City Business Journals, Inc.
Ed: James Fink. **Description:** Tops Market LLC merged with Morgan Stanley Private Equity and names its new CEO, Frank Curci. The company headquarters moved to its new location in Amherst, New York.

42025 ■ *"Local M&A Activity Sputters in 1Q" in Crain's Chicago Business (Vol. 31, April 21, 2008, No. 16, pp. 20)*
Pub: Crain Communications, Inc.
Ed: H. Lee Murphy. **Description:** Local mergers-and-acquisitions activity is down by 34 percent in the first quarter compared to the fourth quarter of last year due to the credit crisis making financing harder to obtain.

42026 ■ *"Local TV Hits Media Radar Screen" in Business Courier (Vol. 27, July 2, 2010, No. 9, pp. 1)*
Pub: Business Courier
Ed: Dan Monk. **Description:** Fort Wright, Kentucky-based broadcasting company Local TV LLC has acquired 18 television stations since its founding in 2007, potentially boosting its chances of becoming a media empire. In the last twelve months that ended in March 2010, Local TV LLC has posted total revenues of $415 million. How Local TV LLC has entered into cost-sharing deals with other stations is also discussed.

42027 ■ *"Looking For Financing?" in Hispanic Business (Vol. 30, July-August 2008, No. 7-8, pp. 16)*
Pub: Hispanic Business, Inc.
Ed: Frank Nelson. **Description:** Investment firms want to know about businesses that need funding for either expansion or acquisition; companies fitting this profile are interviewed and their perceptions are discussed. Investment firms need businesses to be realistic in their expectations and business plans which show spending of funds and expected benefits, long term goals, track record and strong management teams.

42028 ■ *"The Lost Opportunity for a Canadian Steel Giant" in Globe & Mail (April 23, 2007, pp. B1)*
Pub: CTVglobemedia Publishing Inc.
Ed: Greg Keenan. **Description:** The efforts of Algoma Steel Inc. to create a Canadian steel manufacturer that could survive the global trends of consolidation in the steel industry are described. The company's efforts to acquire Stelco Inc., Ivaco Inc. and Slater Steel Inc. are discussed.

42029 ■ *"Lundin Deal Leaves Nickel Market Thin" in Globe & Mail (April 5, 2007, pp. B4)*
Pub: CTVglobemedia Publishing Inc.
Ed: Andy Hoffman. **Description:** The likely acquisition of Rio Narcea Gold Mines Ltd. by Lundin Mining Corp. and the decreasing number of nickel mining companies on the list of Toronto Stock Exchange are discussed.

42030 ■ *"Magpower May Build Solar Panels Here" in Austin Business Journal (Vol. 31, May 13, 2011, No. 10, pp. A1)*
Pub: American City Business Journals Inc.
Ed: Christopher Calnan. **Description:** RRE Austin Solar LLC CEO Doven Mehta has revealed plans to partner with Portugal-based Magpower SA, only if Austin energy buys electricity from planned solar energy farm in Pflugerville. Austin Energy has received 100 bids from 35 companies to supply 200 megawatts of solar- and wind-generated electricity.

42031 ■ *"Making the Cut; Osprey Takes Undervalued Courses to the Leader Board" in Crain's Detroit Business (Vol. 24, April 7, 2008, No. 14)*
Pub: Crain Communications, Inc.
Ed: Jason Deegan. **Description:** Profile of Osprey Management Co., a diverse real estate company that continues to expand its golf portfolio through the company's recreation division; although many developers are getting out of the field due to Michigan's sluggish golf industry, Osprey has found success by purchasing properties in turmoil for more affordable prices.

42032 ■ *"M&T On the March?" in Baltimore Business Journal (Vol. 28, November 12, 2010, No. 27, pp. 1)*
Pub: Baltimore Business Journal
Ed: Gary Haber. **Description:** Information on the growth of M&T Bank, as well as its expansion plans are presented. M&T recently acquired Wilmington Trust and took over $500 million in deposits from the failed K Bank. Analysts believe that M&T would continue its expansion through Washington DC and Richmond, Virginia, especially after a bank executive acknowledged that the markets in those areas are attractive.

42033 ■ *"Manufacturers Become Part of Coalition" in Contractor (Vol. 56, July 2009, No. 7, pp. 40)*
Pub: Penton Media, Inc.
Description: Bradford White Water Heaters, Rheem Water Heating, Rinnai America Corp., and A.O. Smith Water Heaters have joined the Consortium for Energy Efficiency in the Coalition for Energy Star Water Heaters. The coalition seeks to increase the awareness of Energy Star water heaters.

42034 ■ *"Market Squeezes Some Lawyers" in Austin Business JournalInc. (Vol. 28, December 12, 2008, No. 39, pp. 1)*
Pub: American City Business Journals

Ed: Jean Kwon. **Description:** Austin, Texas-based lawyers have been adversely affected by the economic downtown. Fewer works for lawyers in mergers and acquisitions and other activities are being offered. Lawyers are refinancing debts and offering other services.

42035 ■ *"MBA Project Turns on Tastebuds" in The Business Journal - Serving Phoenix and the Valley of the Sun (Vol. 28, August 15, 2008, No. 50)*
Pub: American City Business Journals, Inc.

Ed: Angela Gonzales. **Description:** Amol Khade, Venkat Nallapati and Govind Arora, master of businesss administration graduates from Thunderbird School of Global Management, have opened an Indian restaurant, called The Daba, in Tempe, Arizona. The Indian name of the restaurant means 'a place for travelers to stop for rest and food'. Franchise plans for the restaurant are discussed.

42036 ■ *"McClatchy Believed Front-Runner in Knight Ridder Sale" in Globe & Mail (March 13, 2006, pp. B6)*
Pub: CTVglobemedia Publishing Inc.

Ed: Joseph T. Hallinan; Dennis K. Berman. **Description:** The details on proposed acquisition of Knight Ridder Inc. by McClatchy Co. are presented.

42037 ■ *"Meadowbrook CEO Sees 20 Percent Growth With New Acquisition" in Crain's Detroit Business (Vol. 24, March 10, 2008, No. 10, pp. 4)*
Pub: Crain Communications, Inc.

Ed: Jay Greene. **Description:** Discusses the major turnaround of Meadowbrook Insurance Group after Robert Cubbin became CEO and implemented a new business strategy.

42038 ■ *"Meadowbrook To Acquire ProCentury in $272.6 Million Deal" in Crain's Detroit Business (Vol. 24, February 25, 2008, No. 8, pp. 4)*
Pub: Crain Communications Inc. - Detroit

Description: Meadowbrook Insurance Group, based in Southfield, Michigan reports its proposed acquisition of ProCentury Corporation based in Columbus, Ohio. Meadowbrook provides risk-management to agencies, professional and trade associations and small-to-midsize businesses.

42039 ■ *"Measuring the Impact" in Mergers & Acquisitions: The Dealmaker's Journal (March 1, 2008)*
Pub: SourceMedia, Inc.

Ed: Ken MacFadyen. **Description:** Discusses a new study out of Europe which contends that the private equity market does not have as much impact on the overall economy as critics contend.

42040 ■ *"MEC, Churchill Downs Saddle Up in Racing Deal" in Globe & Mail (March 6, 2007, pp. B1)*
Pub: CTVglobemedia Publishing Inc.

Ed: Greg Keenan. **Description:** The formation of a company called TrackNet Media Group LLC by Magna Entertainment Corp. and Churchill Downs Inc. for the broadcast of horse races on television is discussed. The efforts of the two companies to revive public interest in horse racing are described.

42041 ■ *"Media Industry Collection Agency Completes Acquisition" in Collections & Credit Risk (Vol. 15, December 1, 2010, No. 11, pp. 22)*
Pub: SourceMedia Inc.

Description: Media Receivable Management Inc. (MRM) will take over the collection operations at Borden, Jones & Mitchell, in Miami, Florida. MRM clients are basically magazine and electronic media publishers.

42042 ■ *"Medicaid Insurers See Growth in Small Business Market" in Boston Business Journal (Vol. 31, July 15, 2011, No. 25, pp. 1)*
Pub: Boston Business Journal

Ed: Julie M. Donnelly. **Description:** BMC HealthNet Plan announced plans to launch small business products to serve small businesses that are priced out of rising premium rates at large Massachusetts insurers. BMC joined competitors CeltiCare Health Plan and Neighborhood Health Plan in augmenting its core business.

42043 ■ *"Medical Office Developers To Merge November 1" in The Business Journal - Serving Phoenix and the Valley of the Sun (Vol. 29, September 26, 2008, No. 4, pp. 1)*
Pub: American City Business Journals, Inc.

Ed: Angela Gonzales. **Description:** Ensemble Real Estate Services LLC and DevMan Co. will merge effective November 1, 2008 and will call the firm Ensemble DevMan of Arizona after the merger. The two companies will combine their resources and expertise on planned projects that include the Phoenix Children's Hospital's Specialty Clinic and Banner Ironwood Medical Office Building.

42044 ■ *"Melnyk Loses Round in Battle for Hemosol" in Globe & Mail (January 24, 2007, pp. B3)*
Pub: CTVglobemedia Publishing Inc.

Ed: Leonard Zehr. **Description:** Biovail Corp. chairman Eugene Melnyk's loosing of the case against Catalyst Capital Group Inc. over the acquisition of Hemosol Corp. is discussed.

42045 ■ *"Merger Brings New Force to Hispanic Marketing Industry" in Hispanic Business (July-August 2007, pp. 60)*
Pub: Hispanic Business

Description: Merger between Latin Force LLC, a marketing strategy firm and Geoscape International Inc., a consumer intelligence and data analytics company is discussed.

42046 ■ *"Merger Mania: Regional Snaps Up HVS" in The Business Journal-Serving Greater Tampa Bay (Vol. 28, September 26, 2008, No. 40, pp. 1)*
Pub: American City Business Journals, Inc.

Ed: Alexis Muellner. **Description:** It was reported that Harper Van Scoik & Co. LLP has finalized a merger with Carr Riggs & Ingram LLC. The agreement, effective October 1, 2008, is a merger of HVS assets into CRI. Bill Carr, a managing partner, revealed that HVS' $5 million in revenue will take CRI from $78 million to $82 million in revenue.

42047 ■ *Mergers and Acquisitions from A to Z*
Pub: Amacom

Ed: Andrew J. Sherman, Milledge A. Hart. **Released:** January 2006. **Price:** $35.00. **Description:** Guide for the entire process of mergers and acquisitions, including taxes, accounting, laws, and projected financial gain.

42048 ■ *"Mergers Mean Woe for Fliers; Airline Hookups Boost Fares, Diminish Service" in Crain's Chicago Business (April 21, 2008)*
Pub: Crain Communications, Inc.

Ed: John Pletz. **Description:** Discusses the impact airline mergers will have on customer service, pricing and business travel, particularly at Chicago's O'Hare International Airport.

42049 ■ *"Merrill Lynch in Talks to Buy BlackRock Stake" in Globe & Mail (February 13, 2006, pp. B4)*
Pub: CTVglobemedia Publishing Inc.

Ed: Dennis K. Breman; Randall Smith. **Description:** Financial services firm Merrill Lynch and Co. Inc. is planning to acquire money managing company BlackRock Inc. for 8 million dollars. Sources report that this deal would create 1-trillion dollar huge fund management venture.

42050 ■ *"Micro-Finance Agencies and SMEs" in International Journal of Entrepreneurship and Small Business (Vol. 11, August 3, 2010)*
Pub: Publishers Communication Group

Ed: Patricia A. Rowe, Michael J. Christie, Frank Hoy. **Description:** Institutional preparedness of economic development agencies for developing small and medium-sized enterprises (SMEs) is discussed. The cases presented illustrate variations in the microfinance lender agency-enterprise development of processes for sharing vision and interdependence.

42051 ■ *"Microsoft's Big Gamble" in Canadian Business (Vol. 81, March 3, 2008, No. 3, pp. 13)*
Pub: Rogers Media

Ed: Andrew Wahl. **Description:** Microsoft Corp. is taking a big risk in buying Yahoo, as it is expected to pay more than $31 a share to finalize the acquisition. The deal would be seven and a half times bigger than any other that Microsoft has entered before, an execution of such deal is also anticipated to become a challenge for Microsoft. Recommendations on how Microsoft should handle the integration of the two businesses are given.

42052 ■ *"Milk Producers Target Moms" in Marketing to Women (Vol. 21, January 2008, No. 1, pp. 3)*
Pub: EPM Communications Inc.
Contact: Ira Mayer, President
E-mail: imayer@epmcom.com

Description: In an attempt to encourage moms to serve milk with meals, the American Dairy Association partners with the New York State Dietetic Association to promote milk via a new logo, website and contest.

42053 ■ *"MindLeaders' Online Training Courses Come to ePath Learning" in Information Today (Vol. 26, February 2009, No. 2, pp. 4)*
Pub: Information Today, Inc.

Description: MindLeaders has partnered with ePath Learning to provide clients with over 2,200 new online courses. ePath's integrated Learning Management Service (iLMS) allows organizations to create online training programs for employees.

42054 ■ *"Minor-League Baseball's Sliders Plan Stock Offering" in Crain's Detroit Business (Vol. 25, June 15, 2009, No. 24, pp. 3)*
Pub: Crain Communications Inc. - Detroit

Ed: Bill Shea. **Description:** New minor-league baseball team is raising funds to build a new stadium in Waterford Township, Michigan because banks are unwilling to provide loans for the project. Owners of the Midwest Sliders in Ypsilanti, Michigan are waiting for the federal Securities and Exchange Commission to approve a Regulation A public offering.

42055 ■ *"Molson Coors Ends Ill-Fated Foray Into Brazil" in Globe & Mail (January 17, 2006, pp. B1)*
Pub: CTVglobemedia Publishing Inc.

Ed: Andy Hoffman. **Description:** The details of loss incurred by Molson Coors Brewing Co., from the sale of Cervejarias Kaiser SA to Fomento Economico Mexicano S.A. de C.V., are presented.

42056 ■ *"Molycorp Funds Wind Energy Technology Company" in Manufacturing Close-Up (September 19, 2011)*
Pub: Close-Up Media

Description: Molycorp Inc., producer of rare earth oxides (REO) and a REO producer outside of China, announced it will invest in Boulder Wind Power, which has designed a rare earth magnet powered wind turbine generator. This new generator can produce electricity as low as $0.04 per Kilowatt Hour. Boulder Wind Power's patented wind turbine technology allows for use of rare earth permanent magnets that do not require dysprosium, which is relatively scarce.

42057 ■ *"MoneyGram In Pact With Payday Lender" in American Banker (Vol. 173, March*

7, 2008, No. 46, pp. 6)
Pub: SourceMedia Inc.

Ed: William Launder. **Description:** Details of pact between MoneyGram International Inc. and Advance America Cash Advance Centers are examined.

42058 ■ *"Montreal Exchange Buoyed by U.S. Takeover Moves" in Globe & Mail (March 16, 2007, pp. B1)*
Pub: CTVglobemedia Publishing Inc.

Ed: Sinclair Stewart. **Description:** The rise in the share prices of Montreal Exchange due to the derivatives exchange's bid to acquire the Chicago Board of Trade is discussed. The trends pertaining to the consolidation of global stock markets are described.

42059 ■ *"Montreal Port Head Lands CP Ships Deal" in Globe & Mail (January 5, 2006, pp. B4)*
Pub: CTVglobemedia Publishing Inc.

Description: The opinions of president Dominic Taddeo, on the positive impact of TUI AG's acquisition of CP Ships Ltd. on operations at Port of Montreal, are presented.

42060 ■ *"More Jobs Moving Out of City" in Business Courier (Vol. 24, March 14, 2008, No. 49, pp. 1)*
Pub: American City Business Journals, Inc.

Ed: Steve Watkins; Laura Baverman. **Description:** UBS Financial Services Inc. is moving Gradison to Kenwood Town Place in Sycamore Township a year after UBS acquired Gradison. The township does not have a tax on earnings so the move will save Gradison's employees the 2.1 percent Cincinnati tax.

42061 ■ *"More Questions Face Huntington" in Business First-Columbus (December 7, 2007, pp. A3)*
Pub: American City Business Journals, Inc.

Ed: Adrian Burns. **Description:** Marty Adams' abrupt resignation has lead to speculation that he was dismissed by the bank in relation to the unexpected run-in with the subprime mortgage fiasco. Analysis predict Columbus-based Huntington Bancshares Inc. might be targeted for acquisition. Details on the company's revenues and shares of stock prices are presented.

42062 ■ *"Move Marks KKR's Latest Push into Retail" in Globe & Mail (March 13, 2007, pp. B17)*
Pub: CTVglobemedia Publishing Inc.

Ed: Heather Burke. **Description:** Investment giant Kohlberg Kravis Roberts and Co. has finalized a deal to acquire retail store chain Dollar General Corp. for an estimated 6.9 billion dollars. The company will be entering lucrative retail market by this acquisition.

42063 ■ *"Muddy Portfolio Raises a Question: Just What Is National City Worth?" in Crain's Detroit Business (Vol. 24, April 7, 2008, No. 14)*
Pub: Crain Communications, Inc.

Ed: Jay Miller. **Description:** National City Bank is looking at strategies to help it deal with its credit and loan problems which are reflected in its falling stock price. One possible solution is a merger with another bank, however most national banks are facing their own home-loan portfolio issues and may be unable to tackle another company's unresolved problems. Statistical data included.

42064 ■ *"Nancy Hughes Anthony" in Canadian Business (Vol. 81, October 13, 2008, No. 17, pp. 104)*
Pub: Rogers Media Ltd.

Ed: Andy Holloway. **Description:** Profile of Nancy Hughes Anthony, who believes her experience operating large enterprises as a public servant helped her earn positions that ultimately brought her to her current position as chief executive and president of the Canadian Bankers Association. She also thinks there should be more public-private sector coordination within industries.

42065 ■ *"A Nasty Russian Tale" in Canadian Business (Vol. 81, March 3, 2008, No. 3, pp. 85)*
Pub: Rogers Media

Ed: Andrew Nikiforuk. **Description:** Billionaires Alex Shnaider and Michael Shtaif entered a partnership for an oil venture which ended in a slew of litigations. Cases of breach of contract, injurious falsehood and other related lawsuits were filed against Shnaider. Details of the lawsuits and the other parties involved in the disputes are presented.

42066 ■ *"Nat'l Instruments Connects with Lego" in Austin Business JournalInc. (Vol. 28, August 22, 2008, No. 23, pp. 1)*
Pub: American City Business Journals

Ed: Laura Hipp. **Description:** Austin-based National Instruments Corporation has teamed with Lego Group from Denmark to create a robot that can be built by children and can be used to perform tasks. Lego WeDo, their latest product, uses computer connection to power its movements. The educational benefits of the new product are discussed.

42067 ■ *"Navistar, Cat Talk Truck Deal" in Crain's Chicago Business (Vol. 31, March 24, 2008, No. 12, pp. 1)*
Pub: Crain Communications, Inc.

Ed: Bob Tita. **Description:** Caterpillar Inc. and Navistar International Corp. are negotiating a partnership in which Navistar would build Cat-branded trucks with engines supplied by the Peoria-based equipment manufacturer, Caterpillar.

42068 ■ *"Need Grub? Start Texting at Kroger" in Business Courier (Vol. 24, December 21, 2008, No. 36, pp. 1)*
Pub: American City Business Journals, Inc.

Ed: Laura Baverman. **Description:** Discusses the University of Cincinnati which is teaming up to release a technology platform called Macopay that would link a cell phone to a bank account and allow a person to make payments at participating retailers by sending a text message. Details with regard to the new service and its growth potential are discussed.

42069 ■ *"Nestle Acquires Waggin' Train Dog Treat Company" in Pet Product News (Vol. 64, November 2010, No. 11, pp. 7)*
Pub: BowTie Inc.

Description: Vevey, Switzerland-based Nestle has acquired South Carolina-based dog treat firm Waggin' Train LLC from private equity firm VMG Partners in September 2010. Waggin' Train LLC, which will be operated as a wholly owned subsidiary, is expected to fill a gap in Nestle's dog treat product portfolio.

42070 ■ *"NetSpend, Payday Firm in Pact" in American Banker (Vol. 173, February 22, 2008, No. 7, pp. 7)*
Pub: SourceMedia Inc.

Ed: Daniel Wolfe. **Description:** NetSpend Corporation of Austin, Texas is providing its prepaid cards to Advance America Cash Advance Centers Inc., a Spartanburg, South Carolina payday lender.

42071 ■ *"Neuromed Strikes Major Merck Deal" in Globe & Mail (March 21, 2006, pp. B1)*
Pub: CTVglobemedia Publishing Inc.

Ed: Leonard Zehr. **Description:** Neuromed Pharmaceuticals Ltd., a spin off of British Columbia University, has struck a drug research deal valued at up to $500 million (U.S) with giant Merck &Co. Inc., the biggest collaboration in Canada. Details of the deal are presented.

42072 ■ *"Never Boring: Ad Agencies' Big Changes" in Business Courier (Vol. 24, February 8, 2008, No. 44, pp. 1)*
Pub: American City Business Journals, Inc.

Ed: Dan Monk. **Description:** Many changes are occurring in Cincinnati's advertising industry, including new clients, acquisitions, and market leaders, and an increase in employment. Bridge Worldwide passed Northlich LLC as the city's largest advertising agency.

42073 ■ *"A New Alliance For Global Change" in Harvard Business Review (Vol. 88, September 2010, No. 9, pp. 56)*
Pub: Harvard Business School Publishing

Ed: Bill Drayton, Valeria Budinich. **Description:** Collaboration between social organizations and for-profit firms through the development of hybrid value chains to target complex global issues is promoted. While social organizations offer links to communities and consumers, firms provide financing and scale expertise.

42074 ■ *"The New Arsenal of Risk Management" in Harvard Business Review (Vol. 86, September 2008, No. 9, pp. 92)*
Pub: Harvard Business School Press

Ed: Kevin Bueler; Andrew Freeman; Ron Hulme. **Description:** Goldman Sachs Group Inc. is used to illustrate methods for successful risk management. The investment bank's business principles, partnerships, and oversight practices are discussed.

42075 ■ *"New Economy Initiative Gains Partners" in Crain's Detroit Business (Vol. 25, June 1, 2009, No. 22, pp. M014)*
Pub: Crain Communications Inc. - Detroit

Ed: Sherri Begin Welch. **Description:** New Economy Initiative is a $100 million philanthropic initiative that focuses on regional economic development. Recent grants awarded to Michigan companies are outlined.

42076 ■ *"A New Flavor for Second Street: Lamberts Chef Backs New Restaurant" in Austin Business JournalInc. (Vol. 28, January 2, 2009)*
Pub: American City Business Journals

Ed: Sandra Zaragoza. **Description:** Chef Larry McGuire has teamed up with the Icon Group to develop the La Condesa restaurant and the Malverde lounge in the Second Street district. The La Condesa restaurant will be a Mexico City-inspired restaurant, while the Malverde lounge atop the La Condesa will host DJs and live music.

42077 ■ *"New Life for Porsche's VW Dreams" in Barron's (Vol. 89, July 6, 2009, No. 27, pp. 9)*
Pub: Dow Jones & Co., Inc.

Ed: Vito J. Racanelli. **Description:** Porsche and Volkswagen moved closer to a merger after the Qatar Investment Authority offered to take a stake in Porsche. The QIA could take up to a 30 percent stake in Porsche and purchase all Volkswagen calls for up to $6 billion.

42078 ■ *"New York Firm Secures Sheffield, Amherst Centers for $26 Million" in Crain's Cleveland Business (Vol. 28, December 3, 2007, No. 48)*
Pub: Crain Communications, Inc.

Ed: Stan Bullard. **Description:** Silverman Realty Group completed a $26 million transaction which made it the new owner of the Sheffield Crossing and Amherst Marketplace shopping centers in Lorain County.

42079 ■ *"New Zealand Natural Co-Branding with Mrs. Fields" in Ice Cream Reporter (Vol. 23, November 20, 2010, No. 12, pp. 2)*
Pub: Ice Cream Reporter

Description: Mrs. Fields has partnered with a New Zealand firm to co-brand ice cream and cookies in Australian markets.

42080 ■ *The Nokia Revolution: The Story of an Extraordinary Company That Transformed an Industry*
Pub: AMACOM

Ed: Dan Steinbock. **Released:** May 31, 2001. **Description:** Profile of Nokia, the world's largest wireless communications company. Nokia started in 1865 in rural Finland and merged its rubber company and a cabling firm to form the corporation around 1965. The firm's corporate strategy in the mobile communications industry is highlighted.

42081 ■ *"Nonprofit NAIC Acquires Software Developer as For-Profit Arm" in Crain's Detroit Business (Vol. 25, June 22, 2009, No. 25, pp. 10)*
Pub: Crain Communications Inc. - Detroit
Ed: Sherri Begin Welch. **Description:** Details of National Association of Investors Corporation's acquisition of a Massachusetts investment software developer in order to offer more products to investment clubs and individual investors nationwide.

42082 ■ *"Nortel Romances Chinese Rival Huawei" in Globe & Mail (February 2, 2006, pp. B1)*
Pub: CTVglobemedia Publishing Inc.
Ed: Simon Avery. **Description:** The reasons behind Nortel Networks Corp.'s joint venture with Huawei Technologies Company Ltd. are presented.

42083 ■ *"Note to Leonard: Swim Fast" in Canadian Business (Vol. 80, January 15, 2007, No. 2, pp. 29)*
Pub: Rogers Media
Ed: Zena Olijnyk. **Description:** The decision of CanWest Entertainment Inc and Goldman Sachs Capital Partners to collectively acquire Toronto-based Alliance Atlantis Communications Inc. is discussed.

42084 ■ *"NovAtel Inc. Licensed to Sell Galileo Receivers" in Canadian Corporate News (May 14, 2007)*
Pub: Comtex News Network Inc.
Description: NovAtel Inc., a leading provider of precision Global Navigation Satellite System (GNSS) components and subsystems that afford its customers rapid integration of precise positioning technology, has received a license valid for ten years that allows NovAtel to sell receivers that track Galileo signals.

42085 ■ *"NStar Feels the Heat" in Cape Cod Times (September 30, 2011)*
Pub: Cape Cod Media Group
Ed: Patrick Cassidy. **Description:** Massachusetts energy officials wish to delay a merger between NStar and Northeast Utilities until it is clear how the partnership would meet the state's green energy goals. Governor Deval Patrick supports the proposed Nantucket Sound wind farm.

42086 ■ *"N.Y. Group Top Bidder for Last Duke Sites" in Crain's Cleveland Business (Vol. 28, November 19, 2007, No. 46, pp. 1)*
Pub: Crain Communications, Inc.
Ed: Stan Bullard. **Description:** Overview of the possible portfolio sale of Duke Realty Corp.'s last Northeast Ohio properties, 14 office buildings in Independence, Seven Hills and North Olmsted, believed to be purchased by a real estate investor group led by Nightingale Properties LLC of New York.

42087 ■ *"Nymex Dissidents Rattle Sabers" in Crain's Chicago Business (Vol. 31, April 21, 2008, No. 16, pp. 2)*
Pub: Crain Communications, Inc.
Ed: Ann Saphir. **Description:** Two groups of New York Mercantile Exchange members say they have more than enough votes to stop CME Group Inc.'s $10 billion deal to acquire the oil and metals exchange and they are threatening a proxy fight if the Chicago exchange doesn't raise its offer.

42088 ■ *"Oakland County Hopes Auto Suppliers Can Drive Medical Industry Growth" in Crain's Detroit Business (March 10, 2008)*
Pub: Crain Communications, Inc.
Ed: Chad Halcom. **Description:** Oakland County officials are hoping to create further economic development for the region by pairing health care companies and medical device makers with automotive suppliers in an attempt to discover additional crossover technology.

42089 ■ *"Ocean Choice in Running to Acquire Assets of FPI" in Globe & Mail (March 15, 2007, pp. B9)*
Pub: CTVglobemedia Publishing Inc.
Description: Ocean Choice International is bidding vigorously for acquiring assets St. Johns based of FPI Ltd. Complete details of these bids are discussed.

42090 ■ *"Offer for Sears Canada 'Inadequate" in Globe & Mail (February 10, 2006, pp. B4)*
Pub: CTVglobemedia Publishing Inc.
Ed: Marina Strauss. **Description:** The financial feasibility of Sears Holdings Corp.'s proposed acquisition of Sears Canada Inc., for $835 million, is discussed.

42091 ■ *"Oil Patch Expects Richer Shell Offer" in Globe & Mail (January 3, 2006, pp. B1)*
Pub: CTVglobemedia Publishing Inc.
Ed: Andrew Willis; Patrick Brethour. **Description:** The concerns investors over the feasibility of Royal Dutch Shell PLC's acquisition of Shell Canada Ltd., for $7.6 billion, are presented. Shell Canada Ltd. reports rise in shares by ten percent.

42092 ■ *"Old Friends Make Old Buildings Successful Restaurants" in Crain's Detroit Business (Vol. 24, February 4, 2008, No. 5, pp. 14)*
Pub: Crain Communications Inc. - Detroit
Ed: Brent Snavely. **Description:** Profiles of Jon Carlson and Gregory Lobdell, founders of ten new restaurants in Ann Arbor, Royal Oak, and Traverse City, Michigan, and their plans to add four more in the near future.

42093 ■ *"Olympus is Urged to Revise Board" in Wall Street Journal Eastern Edition (November 28, 2011, pp. B3)*
Pub: Dow Jones & Company Inc. Enterprise Media Group
Contact: Clare Hart, President
Ed: Phred Dvorak. **Description:** Koji Miyata, once a director on the board of troubled Japanese photographic equipment company, is urging the company to reorganize its board, saying the present group should resign their board seats but keep their management positions. The company has come under scrutiny for its accounting practices and costly acquisitions.

42094 ■ *"OMERS Joins Bid for U.K. Port Giant" in Globe & Mail (March 28, 2006, pp. B1)*
Pub: CTVglobemedia Publishing Inc.
Ed: Paul Waldie. **Description:** The plans of Ontario Municipal Employees Retirement Board to partner with Goldman Sachs Group Inc., in order to acquire Associated British Ports PLC, are presented.

42095 ■ *"On a Mission: Ginch Gonch Wants You to Get Rid of Your Tighty Whities" in Canadian Business (Vol. 81, September 29, 2008, No. 16)*
Pub: Rogers Media Ltd.
Ed: Michelle Magnan. **Description:** New Equity Capital acquired underwear maker Ginch Gonch in July 2008; founder Jason Sutherland kept his position as creative director of the company and will retain his title as 'director of stitches and inches'. The company is known for its products, which are reminiscent of the days when people wore underwear covered in cowboys and stars as kids. The company also claims that Nelly, Justin Timberlake, and Hilary Duff have worn their products.

42096 ■ *"Online Reverse Auctions: Common Myths Versus Evolving Reality" in Business Horizons (September-October 2007, pp. 373)*
Pub: Elsevier Technology Publications
Ed: Tobias Schoenherr, Vincent A. Mabert. **Description:** Common misconceptions about online reverse auctions are examined based on the data obtained from 30 case study companies. Strategies for maintaining a good buyer-supplier relationship and implications for firms and supply managers are presented.

42097 ■ *"Operation Fusion" in Black Enterprise (Vol. 38, November 2007, No. 4, pp. 30)*
Pub: Earl G. Graves Publishing Co. Inc.
Ed: Tara C. Walker. **Description:** Entrepreneur Albert H. Frazier tells how he combined three separate acquisitions in order to create Goods Movement Inc.:-W&H Systems Inc., a systems integrator and material handler supplier and North American Conveyor Inc. which fabricates and installs conveyor and sort equipment systems for the U.S. Postal Service and Total Transportation Services, a third-party logistics provider.

42098 ■ *"The Oracle's Endgame; Wrigley Investment Isn't What Many Call a Classic Buffett Play" in Crain's Chicago Business (May 5, 2008)*
Pub: Crain Communications, Inc.
Ed: Ann Saphir. **Description:** Discusses Warren Buffett's deal with Mars Inc. to buy Wm. Wrigley Jr. Co., a move which would make Mr. Buffett a minority shareholder in a privately held company, a departure from his typical investment strategy. Mr. Buffett's Berkshire Hathaway Inc. agreed to provide $4.4 billion to help finance the $23 billion deal to pay another $2.1 billion for an equity stake in the company once it became a subsidiary of Mars.

42099 ■ *"Ottawa to Push for Gas Deal Between Petrocan, Gazprom" in Globe & Mail (February 13, 2006, pp. B1)*
Pub: CTVglobemedia Publishing Inc.
Ed: Greame Smith. **Description:** Jim Flaherty, finance minister of Canada is negotiating a 1.3 billion dollar deal between state owned Petro-Canada and Russia's OAO Gazprom. This once again highlighted the country's increasing dependence on Russia for its energy requirements.

42100 ■ *"Out of This World: Noah Samara and WorldSpace" in Black Enterprise (November 2007)*
Pub: Earl G. Graves Publishing Co. Inc.
Ed: Anthony Calypso. **Description:** Profile of Noah Samara, CEO of WorldSpace Inc. who raised $1 billion to help create the technological architecture for satellite radio.

42101 ■ *"Owner of IT Firm MK2 Tying Future to Software" in Crain's Cleveland Business (Vol. 30, June 15, 2009, No. 23, pp. 3)*
Pub: Crain Communications, Inc.
Ed: Chuck Soder. **Description:** Donald Kasper, owner of MK2 Technologies LLC of Cleveland, Ohio discusses his recent acquisition of a portion of ProSource Solution. The move will help expand the two companies' custom software development plans.

42102 ■ *"Parent Firm's Global Reach, Stricter Air Quality Rules Have Stock Smiling" in Crain's Cleveland Business (October 15, 2007)*
Pub: Crain Communications, Inc.
Ed: David Bennett. **Description:** Since Stock Equipment Co., a firm that makes industrial pollution control equipment, was acquired by Schenck Process Group, a diversified global manufacturer based in Germany, the company's orders from abroad have been on the rise. The purchase has opened the doors to regions such as Eastern and Central Europe, Latin America and Australia.

42103 ■ *"Partnering for Success" in Art Business News (Vol. 36, October 2009, No. 10, pp. 4)*
Pub: Summit Business Media
Ed: Jennifer Dulin Wiley. **Description:** In such a volatile economy many savvy artists and gallery owners are turning to out-of-the-box partnerships for continued success; these partnerships are also pervading the Internet, especially with such social media networks as Facebook and Twitter where artists and businesses can develop a loyal following.

42104 ■ *The Partnership: The Making of Goldman Sachs*
Pub: Penguin Group USA Inc.
Ed: Charles D. Ellis. **Released:** 2009. **Price:** $37.95. **Description:** The history of Goldman Sachs is presented, along with a chronicle of Wall Street.

42105 ■ *"Paterson Plots Comeback With Internet IPO" in Globe & Mail (February 20, 2006, pp. B1)*
Pub: CTVglobemedia Publishing Inc.
Ed: Grant Robertson. **Description:** The initial public offering plans of chief executive officer Scott Paterson of JumpTV.com are presented.

42106 ■ *"PC Connection Acquires Cloud Software Provider" in New Hampshire Business Review (Vol. 33, March 25, 2011, No. 6, pp. 8)*
Pub: Business Publications Inc.
Description: Merrimack-based PC Connection Inc. acquired ValCom Technology, a provider of cloud-based IT service management software. Details of the deal are included.

42107 ■ *"Peking Launches Trina Turk Bedding Collection" in Home Textiles Today (Vol. 31, May 24, 2011, No. 13, pp. 4)*
Pub: Reed Business Information
Contact: Jeff Greisch, President
Description: Peking Handicraft is launching designer Trina Turk's bedding collection of four beds that reflect her approach to contemporary fabric design using color and prints with strong graphic effects.

42108 ■ *"Pepsi Co. Breaches the Walls of Coke Fortress McDonald's" in Globe & Mail (March 13, 2007, pp. B1)*
Pub: CTVglobemedia Publishing Inc.
Ed: Keith McArthur. **Description:** Soft drinks giant Pepsi Co. has entered an agreement with fast food chain McDonald's for offering its products in outlets across Canada. Earlier Coca-Cola Co. used to offer its exclusive products in these outlets.

42109 ■ *"Pioneers Get All The Perks" in Canadian Business (Vol. 81, March 3, 2008, No. 3, pp. 18)*
Pub: Rogers Media
Description: Suncor Energy Inc. will face royalty payments from 25% to 30% of net profits as it signs a new deal with Alberta. Biovail Corp., meanwhile, is under a U.S. grand jury investigation for supposed improprieties in Cardizem LA heart drug launch. The Conference Board of Canada's proposal to impose taxes on greenhouse gas emissions and other developments in the business community are discussed.

42110 ■ *"Please Pass the Mayo" in Crain's Chicago Business (Vol. 31, April 28, 2008, No. 17, pp. 32)*
Pub: Crain Communications, Inc.
Ed: Samantha Stainburn. **Description:** Fort Dearborn Co. has come a long way since it started as on one-press print shop; the family-owned company was struggling to keep up with the technology of making consumer product labels for curvy bottles of products like V8 V-Fusion juice and in 2006 sold off to Genstar Capital LLC which has pushed for acquisitions; last year, Fort Derborn bought its biggest competitor, Renaissance Mark Inc., doubling its size and adding spirit and wine makers to its client roster.

42111 ■ *"Polite Conversation" in Mergers & Acquisitions: The Dealmaker's Journal (March 1, 2008)*
Pub: SourceMedia, Inc.
Description: In January, industry leaders and dealmakers met at Davos to discuss topics ranging from the possibility of a recession to what lies ahead in the deal market.

42112 ■ *"Poor Economy Inspires Rich Alternatives In a Modern, and Tax-Free, Twist on Bartering" in Houston Chronicle (June 7, 2010)*
Pub: Houston Chronicle Publishing Company
Ed: Michael Rubinkam. **Description:** Time banking helps individuals and firms receive goods or services by depositing time dollars into a bank reserved for receipt of goods and services.

42113 ■ *"Porsche Raises VW Stake, Makes Bid for Firm" in Globe & Mail (March 26, 2007, pp. B5)*
Pub: CTVglobemedia Publishing Inc.
Ed: Chad Thomas. Jeremy Van Logan. **Description:** Automobile giant Porsche AG has increased its stake in Volkswagen AG to $54 billion recently. The company is planning a merger by claiming 30% stake under German law.

42114 ■ *"Power Partnerships" in Business Courier (Vol. 27, October 22, 2010, No. 25, pp. 1)*
Pub: Business Courier
Ed: Lucy May. **Description:** The $400 million Harrah's casino and the $47 million redevelopment and expansion of Washington Park are project aimed at boosting the economy in downtown Cincinnati, Ohio. These projects will be done in cooperation with the National Association for the Advancement of Colored People. Insights into the role of minority-owned businesses in regional economic development are explored.

42115 ■ *"Powers Reels in Pinger" in Business Courier (Vol. 24, December 21, 2008, No. 36, pp. 1)*
Pub: American City Business Journals, Inc.
Ed: Lisa Biank Fasig. **Description:** Powers Agency has acquired Dan Pinger Public Relations Inc. after three years in planning. The new company is to be called 'Pinger PR at Powers'. Details of the deal and the new company are discussed.

42116 ■ *"Pre-Deal Trades More Common in Canada, Study Finds" in Globe & Mail (March 23, 2007, pp. B5)*
Pub: CTVglobemedia Publishing Inc.
Ed: John Kipphoff; Joe Schneider. **Description:** The results of the study conducted by Measuredmarkets Inc. to examine the impact of merger activity on insider trading of the companies are presented.

42117 ■ *"Precision Crop Control with Valley Irrigation/CropMetrics Partnership" in Farm Industry News (January 6, 2011)*
Pub: Penton Business Media Inc.
Description: Irrigation systems have become a precision farming tool since partnering with agronomic software systems to apply products across the field by prescription. Valley Irrigation and CropMetrics have partnered in order to variably control water, fertilizer and other crop management products through a center pivot irrigation system.

42118 ■ *"Preparing for Weed Control" in Farmer's Weekly (March 28, 2008, No. 320)*
Pub: Reed Business Information
Contact: Jeff Greisch, President
Description: Profile of Richard Beachell who farms in a joint venture with his neighbor. Beachell discusses nitrogen applications, fungicides and the reduction of pesticides.

42119 ■ *"Private Equity Firm Links First Arizona Deal" in Business Journal-Serving Phoenix and the Valley of the Sun (November 2, 2007)*
Pub: American City Business Journals, Inc.
Ed: Chris Cassacchia. **Description:** Pacific Investment Partners and Your Source Financial launched a $10 million fund and signed their first deal. The two companies acquires a minority stake in Dreambrands Inc. for $3 million. Dreambrands is using the capital to market its personal lubricant product Carrageenana.

42120 ■ *"Private Equity Firms Focus on Failing Banks" in Baltimore Business Journal (Vol. 28, July 16, 2010, No. 10, pp. 1)*
Pub: Baltimore Business Journal
Ed: Gary Haber. **Description:** Four deals in which assets of failed banks were acquired by private equity firms have been approved by the Federal Deposit Insurance Corporation in the past couple of years. Bay Bank FSK, for example, purchased Bay National Bank's assets in July 2010. Forecasts on more private equity acquisitions in the community banking industry are given.

42121 ■ *"Procter & Gamble Boosts Bet on Exclusive Brands" in Business Courier (Vol. 27, July 9, 2010, No. 10, pp. 1)*
Pub: Business Courier
Ed: Jon Newberry. **Description:** Procter & Gamble is creating more special versions of its brands such as Pringles and Pampers exclusively for retail partners such as Tesco in the U.K. The greater push towards this direction is seen as a way to regain market share.

42122 ■ *"Profico Takes Itself Off the Market" in Globe & Mail (March 14, 2006, pp. B1)*
Pub: CTVglobemedia Publishing Inc.
Ed: Deborah Yedlin; Dave Ebner. **Description:** Profico Energy Management Ltd., Canada's largest junior energy explorer, has backed off its potential acquisition plans. The decreased prices of the natural gas are the main reasons that caused Profico to back off from the acquisition plan.

42123 ■ *"Prominent Hispanic Businessman Signs With Choice Hotels" in Hispanic Business (Vol. 30, March 2008, No. 3, pp. 36)*
Pub: Hispanic Business
Ed: Melinda Burns. **Description:** Chairman of the board of Lopez Food Inc., John C. Lopez signs the agreement with Choice Hotels International to build five new Cambria suites in the USA. This is his first hotel venture and also the first Hispanic franchisee to enter into business with Choice Hotels.

42124 ■ *"Proposed Law Would Stop REIS Bid for Annexation by Livonia" in Crain's Detroit Business (Vol. 24, March 10, 2008, No. 10, pp. 2)*
Pub: Crain Communications, Inc.
Ed: Chad Halcom. **Description:** REIS Northville L.L.C., a joint venture made up of Real Estate Interests Group Inc. and Schostak Bros. & Co., has proposed an $800 million project called Highwood at the former Northville Psychiatric Hospital site but has been stalled due to a disagreement with Northville Township on several terms including: the amount of retail at the site and the paying for cleanup of environmental and medical waste.

42125 ■ *"Proposed Triangle Redo in Motion" in Crain's Cleveland Business (Vol. 28, October 15, 2007, No. 41, pp. 1)*
Pub: Crain Communications, Inc.
Ed: Stan Bullard. **Description:** Zaremba Homes and MRN Ltd. are partnering to redevelop the so-called Triangle section of University Circle. The proposed project will include a total of 434 new rental and for-sale residential suites and as much as 227,000 square feet of retail and restaurant space.

42126 ■ *"PRWT Service Acquires Pharmaceutical Plant: Firm Wins Multimillion-Dollar Contract with Merck" in Black Enterprise (March 2008)*
Pub: Earl G. Graves Publishing Co. Inc.
Ed: Tamara E. Holmes. **Description:** PRWT Services Inc. expanded through its acquisition of a chemical manufacturing plant in New Jersey. The Whitehouse Station, part of Merck & Co. Inc. produces active pharmaceutical ingredients for antibiotics, making PRWT the first minority-owned company in the U.S. to manufacture active pharmaceutical ingredients.

42127 ■ *"Public Media Works to Launch DVD Kiosk Operations in Toronto, Canada" in Internet Wire (November 15, 2010)*
Pub: Comtex
Description: Public Media Works Inc. along with its EntertainmentXpress Inc., have partnered with Spot Venture Distribution Inc. and Signifi Solutions Inc., both headquartered in Toronto, Canada, to manage and expand the Spot DVD movie and game kiosk business in greater Toronto and other Canadian locations.

42128 ■ *"Public Opinion" in Entrepreneur (Vol. 36, April 2008, No. 4, pp. 28)*
Pub: Entrepreneur Media, Inc.
Ed: Aliza Sherman. **Description:** According to a 2007 report from Group and Organization Management, women in top positions can lead publicly traded companies to stock price and earnings growth. Some women business owners say that going public has provided them with the capital to grow. Details on the potential of women-managed publicly traded companies are discussed.

42129 ■ *"Pulp Friction: Spin Off Mills to Boost Wood Products" in Globe & Mail (February 18, 2006, pp. B3)*
Pub: CTVglobemedia Publishing Inc.
Ed: Peter Kennedy. **Description:** The reasons behind the decision of chief executive officer Jim Shepherd of Canfor Corp. to sell pulp mills are presented.

42130 ■ *"Que Pasa? A Canadian-Cuban Credit Card Crisis" in Canadian Business (Vol. 81, March 31, 2008, No. 5, pp. 10)*
Pub: Rogers Media
Ed: Geoff Kirbyson. **Description:** Discusses the acquisition of CUETS Financial Ltd. by the Bank of America which means that CUETS-issued credit cards in Cuba are worthless since U.S. laws prohibit transactions from Cuba and other sanctioned countries. CUETS members are advised to take multiple payment methods to Cuba.

42131 ■ *"A Questionable Chemical Romance" in Barron's (Vol. 88, July 14, 2008, No. 28, pp. 28)*
Pub: Dow Jones & Co., Inc.
Ed: Andrew Bary. **Description:** Dow Chemical paid $78-a-share for the surprise takeover of Rohm & Haas. The acquisition is reducing Dow Chemical's financial flexibility at a time when chemical companies are being affected by high costs and a weak U.S. economy.

42132 ■ *"Ralcorp Investigated for Rejecting ConAgra Bid" in Saint Louis Business Journal (Vol. 32, September 16, 2011, No. 3, pp. 1)*
Pub: Saint Louis Business Journal
Ed: Evan Binns. **Description:** New York-based Levi & Korsinsky started investigating Ralcorp Holidngs Inc. after it rejected ConAgra Foods Inc.'s third and latest takeover bid of $5.17 billion. The investigation would determine whether Ralcorp's directors had acted on behalf of shareholders' best interest.

42133 ■ *"R&R Ice Cream" in Ice Cream Reporter (Vol. 23, November 20, 2010, No. 12, pp. 8)*
Pub: Ice Cream Reporter
Description: R&R Ice Cream, the United Kingdom's largest ice cream manufacturer, has completed a private offering of senior secured notes that has raised 298 million (pounds sterling) to fund expansion and acquisitions.

42134 ■ *"R&R Launches Upscale Spoony's and Low Fat Dragon's Den" in Ice Cream Reporter (Vol. 23, August 20, 2010, No. 9, pp. 3)*
Pub: Ice Cream Reporter
Description: European ice cream manufacturer R&R has acquired French ice cream maker Rolland and will position itself as an upscale challenger to brands like Ben & Jerry's.

42135 ■ *"RBC Holds Inside Card With HBC Credit Assets" in Globe & Mail (January 25, 2006, pp. B1)*
Pub: CTVglobemedia Publishing Inc.
Ed: Marina Strauss; Sinclair Stewart. **Description:** Hudson's Bay Co. (HBC) signed co-branding credit card agreement with Royal Bank of Canada are presented. The significance of the deal for HBC is discussed.

42136 ■ *"Rebels' Cause: Adult Stem Cell" in Austin Business Journal (Vol. 31, June 3, 2011, No. 13, pp. 1)*
Pub: American City Business Journals Inc.
Ed: Sandra Zaragoza. **Description:** MedRebels Foundation was launched in February 2011 with the goal of providing millions of dollars for research funding, education and advocacy for adult stem cell-focused medicine. The foundation, whose major contributor is SpineSmith LP, is a collaboration of other adult stem cell-related companies and nonprofit partners. It hopes to raise $200,000 by the end of 2011.

42137 ■ *"Recent Deals Signal an M&A Resurgence" in Austin Business JournalInc. (Vol. 29, January 22, 2010, No. 46, pp. 1)*
Pub: American City Business Journals
Ed: Jacob Dirr. **Description:** The acquisition of at least six Austin, Texas technology companies reflects the growing acquisition activity in the US. Corporations have bought 86 companies and spent $7.3 billion during the fourth quarter of 2009. Insights into the impact of the acquisition activity to Austin's entrepreneurial energy are also given.

42138 ■ *"Redcorp Ventures Ltd.: Tulsequah Camp Construction Begins" in Canadian Corporate News (May 16, 2007)*
Pub: Comtex News Network Inc.
Description: Redfern Reources Ltd., a subsidiary of Redcorp Ventures Ltd., announced that Modular Transportable Solutions LLC was selected to design and manufacture its prefabricated, modular construction camp, cookhouse, administration buildings, and mine dry at the Tulsequah Mine location in northwest British Columbia due to the virtually indestructible design of the units that withstand extreme weather conditions.

42139 ■ *"Regal Venture Puts Imax Back in the Spotlight" in Globe & Mail (March 13, 2007, pp. B5)*
Pub: CTVglobemedia Publishing Inc.
Ed: Shirley Won. **Description:** Imax Corp. has signed new contract with cinema hall operating giant Regal Entertainment Corp. for constructing two more giant screen theaters. Share prices of Imax Corp. have increased sharply after this announcement.

42140 ■ *"Regent's Signal, Once Powerful, Fading From Local Scene" in Business Courier (Vol. 27, June 4, 2010, No. 5, pp. 1)*
Pub: Business Courier
Ed: Dan Monk. **Description:** Los Angeles, California-based Oaktree Capital Management bought former Regent Communications Inc. from Chapter 11 bankruptcy and transformed it into Townsquare Media Inc., a privately held firm. Regent's corporate presence has faded fast in Cincinnati, Ohio as its operations wind down. Insights on Regent's failed business model are also given.

42141 ■ *"Rehab Will Turn Hospital Into Incubator" in The Business Journal-Serving Metropolitan Kansas City (Vol. 26, September 12, 2008)*
Pub: American City Business Journals, Inc.
Ed: Rob Roberts. **Description:** Independence Regional Health Center will be purchased by CEAH Realtors and be converted into the Independence Regional Entrepreneurial Center, a business incubator that will house startups and other tenants. Other details about the planned entrepreneurial center are provided.

42142 ■ *"Research Note" in International Journal of Globalisation and Small Business (Vol. 4, September 21, 2010, No. 1, pp. 92)*
Pub: Publishers Communication Group
Ed: Alexander Bode, Tobias B. Talmon l'Armee, Simon Alig. **Description:** The cluster concept has steadily increased its importance during the past years both from practitioners' and reearchers' points of view. Simultaneously, many corporate networks are established. Researchers from different areas (business management, economic social and geographical science) are trying to explain both phenomena.

42143 ■ *"Research Reports" in Barron's (Vol. 88, March 10, 2008, No. 10, pp. M13)*
Pub: Dow Jones & Company, Inc.
Description: Research reports on different company stocks by investment analysts are given. Shares of Cal Dive are rated Outperform by analysts, citing the shares' continued attractiveness and the company's acquisition of Horizon. Analysts recommend buying the shares of California Water Service Group.

42144 ■ *"Research Reports: How Analysts Size Up Companies" in Barron's (Vol. 88, March 31, 2008, No. 13, pp. M13)*
Pub: Dow Jones & Company, Inc.
Ed: Anita Peltonen. **Description:** Sirius Satellite's shares are ranked Outperform as it awaits approval from the Federal Communications Commission in its merger with XM. TiVo's shares are ranked Avoid as the company is in a sector that's being commoditized. Verizon Communications' rising dividend yield earns it a Focus List ranking. The shares of Bear Stearns, Churchill Downs, Corning, and Deerfield Triarc Capital are also reviewed. Statistical data included.

42145 ■ *"RIM Reinforces Claim as Top Dog by Expanding BlackBerry" in Globe & Mail (March 11, 2006, pp. B3)*
Pub: CTVglobemedia Publishing Inc.
Ed: Simon Avery. **Description:** The plans of Research In Motion Ltd. to enhance the features of BlackBerry, through acquisition of Ascendent Systems, are presented.

42146 ■ *"Rimfire Minerals Corporation: Jake Gold Project-Drilling Planned for 2007" in Canadian Corporate News (May 16, 2007)*
Pub: Comtex News Network Inc.
Description: Rimfire Minerals Corporation and Island Arc Exploration Corporation formed a partnership to explore the Jake Property, a high-grade gold prospect with previously unrecognized potential to host economic gold mineralization, located 13 kilometers west of Clearwater, British Columbia.

42147 ■ *"Roll Your Own" in Business North Carolina (Vol. 28, March 2008, No. 3, pp. 66)*
Pub: Business North Carolina
Ed: Amanda Parry. **Description:** Profile of U.S. Flue-Cured Tobacco Growers who process tobacco and make cigarettes. Details of the program are outlined.

42148 ■ *"Roundtable - The Auto Sector Shifts Gears" in Mergers & Acquisitions: The Dealmaker's Journal (March 1, 2008)*
Pub: SourceMedia, Inc.
Description: Industry professionals discuss the current state of the automotive sector as well as what they predict for the future of the industry; also provides information for investors about opportunities in the sector.

42149 ■ *"Royal Dutch's Grip Firm on Shell" in Globe & Mail (March 19, 2007, pp. B1)*
Pub: CTVglobemedia Publishing Inc.
Ed: David Ebner. **Description:** The proposed acquisition of Shell Canada Ltd. by Royal Dutch Shell PLC for $8.7 billion is discussed.

42150 ■ *"Rumors Kill Algoma Takeover Talks" in Globe & Mail (March 14, 2007, pp. B14)*
Pub: CTVglobemedia Publishing Inc.
Ed: Tara Perkins. **Description:** Canada-based steel manufacturing giant Salzgitter AG has dropped its acquisition negotiations with Algoma Steel Inc. The decision comes after the secret price quotation was leaked to competitors.

42151 ■ *"Russia Eyes Nuclear Power Co-Operation With Canada" in Globe & Mail (April 2, 2007, pp. B1)*
Pub: CTVglobemedia Publishing Inc.
Ed: Shawn McCarthy. **Description:** The plans of the Russian nuclear energy agency, Federal Atomic Energy Agency, to enter into a partnership with its Canadian counterpart Atomic Energy of Canada Ltd. for the generation of electric power are discussed.

42152 ■ *"S3 Entertainment Group Partners with WFW International for Film Services in Michigan" in Michigan Vue (July-August 2008)*
Pub: Entrepreneur Media Inc.
Description: William F. White (WFW), one of North America's largest production equipment providers has partnered with S3 Entertainment Group (S3EG), a Michigan-based full-service film production services company due to the new incentives package which currently offers the highest incentives in the United States, up to 42 percent. S3EG will actively store, lease, manage, distribute and sell WFW's equipment to the growing number of production teams that are filming in the state.

42153 ■ *"Sabathia Deal Makes Dollars and Sense" in The Business Journal-Milwaukee (Vol. 25, July 11, 2008, No. 42, pp. A1)*
Pub: American City Business Journals, Inc.
Ed: Mark Kass. **Description:** It was reported that the Milwaukee Brewers' acquisition of CC Sabathia will mean that the team will pick up an estimated $5 mil-

lion in salary that Sabathia is owed for the remainder of the season. Because of this, the team will not make a profit in 2008. The acquisition of Sabathia is expected to cause an increase in attendance and merchandise revenue over the remainder of the season.

42154 ■ *"SABMiller Deal Hit by Tax Ruling" in Wall Street Journal Eastern Edition (November 21 , 2011, pp. B9)*
Pub: Dow Jones & Company Inc.
Ed: David Fickling, Simon Zekaria. **Description:** SABMiller PLC, the giant brewer in the United Kingdom, is acquiring Australian beer icon Foster's Group Ltd. for US$9.9 billion, but will have to come up with another A$582 million following a tax ruling by the Australian Taxation Office in order that shareholders of Foster's don't lose.

42155 ■ *"SAGE Publications Announced a Partnership with Which Medical Device" in Information Today (Vol. 28, November 2011, No. 10, pp. 15)*
Pub: Information Today, Inc.
Description: SAGE Publications has partnered with Which Medical Device to offer insights, tutorials, and reviews of medical devices.

42156 ■ *"St. Elizabeth Fights for Share at St. Lukes" in Business Courier (Vol. 27, November 12, 2010, No. 28, pp. 1)*
Pub: Business Courier
Ed: James Ritchie. **Description:** Key information on how St. Elizabeth Healthcare helps partner St. Luke's Hospitals increase market share in the healthcare industry are presented. Some of St. Luke's hospitals, such as the St. Elizabeth Fort Thomas in Kentucky, are struggling with low occupancy rates, prompting St. Elizabeth to invest about $24 million to help St. Luke's increase its market share.

42157 ■ *"Save the Date" in Mergers & Acquisitions: The Dealmaker's Journal (March 1, 2008)*
Pub: SourceMedia, Inc.
Description: Listing of conferences and forums that deal with business and investing, particularly with mergers and acquisitions. Includes dates, locations and Internet addresses.

42158 ■ *The Savvy Gal's Guide to Online Networking*
Pub: Booklocker.com Inc.
Ed: Diane K. Daneilson, Lindsey Pollak. **Released:** August 10, 2007. **Price:** $14.95. **Description:** It is a truth universally acknowledged that a woman in search of a fabulous career must be in want of networking opportunities. Or so Jane Austen would say if she were writing, or more likely, blogging today. So begins the must-read guide to networking in the 21st Century. Authors and networking experts share the nuts, bolts and savvy secrets that business-women need in order to use technology to build professional relationships.

42159 ■ *"Scanning Dell's Shopping List" in Barron's (Vol. 89, July 13, 2009, No. 28, pp. 24)*
Pub: Dow Jones & Co., Inc.
Ed: Mark Veverka. **Description:** It is believed that Dell will be looking for companies to acquire since they poached an experienced mergers-and-acquisitions executive. In addition Dell's CEO is reportedly telling people he plans to go shopping. Dell executives have also stated an interest in data storage.

42160 ■ *"Scotiabank Tapped as Likely Buyer in Puerto Rico" in Globe & Mail (January 30, 2007, pp. B3)*
Pub: CTVglobemedia Publishing Inc.
Ed: Andrew Willis. **Description:** Speculation over Bank of Nova Scotia's proposed acquisition of First BanCorp is discussed.

42161 ■ *"Scripps' Dinner Bell" in Business Courier (Vol. 24, October 19, 2008, No. 27, pp. 1)*
Pub: American City Business Journals, Inc.
Ed: Dan Monk. **Description:** Discusses the split of E.W. Scripps Co.'s Food Network into a separate publicly traded company Scripps Networks Interactive could produce expansion into Asia and Europe.

42162 ■ *"Sears' Lampert Solid in Game of Valuation Chicken" in Globe & Mail (February 25, 2006, pp. B2)*
Pub: CTVglobemedia Publishing Inc.
Ed: Eric Reguly. **Description:** The feasibility of share value of Sears Canada Inc., following Sears Holdings Corp.'s acquisition, is discussed.

42163 ■ *"Sears' Profit Result Puts Ball in Parent's Court" in Globe & Mail (February 3, 2006, pp. B4)*
Pub: CTVglobemedia Publishing Inc.
Ed: Marina Strauss. **Description:** Sears Canada Inc. achieved $783.4 million in profits for fourth quarter 2005. The financial performance of the company paves way for the acquisition of Sears Holdings Corp.

42164 ■ *The Secret of Exiting Your Business Under Your Terms!*
Pub: Outskirts Press, Incorporated
Ed: Gene H. Irwin. **Released:** August 2005. **Price:** $29.95. **Description:** Topics include how to sell a business for the highest value, tax laws governing the sale of a business, finding the right buyer, mergers and acquisitions, negotiating the sale, and using a limited auction to increase future value of a business.

42165 ■ *"A Security Risk?" in Canadian Business (Vol. 80, October 22, 2007, No. 21, pp. 36)*
Pub: Rogers Media
Ed: Joe Castaldo. **Description:** Garda World Security Corporation declared a C$1.5 million loss in the second quarter of 2007. The company's securities have been falling since June and hit a 52-week low of $15.90 in September. Details of the physical and cash-handling firm's strategy to integrate its acquisitions are discussed.

42166 ■ *"Sedo Keeps Trucking in Good Times and Bad" in Crain's Chicago Business (Vol. 31, April 28, 2008, No. 17, pp. 35)*
Pub: Crain Communications, Inc.
Ed: Samantha Stainburn. **Description:** Discusses Seko Worldwide Inc., an Itasca-based freight forwarder, and its complicated road to growth and expansion on a global scale.

42167 ■ *"Sense of Discovery" in Business Journal Portland (Vol. 27, November 19, 2010, No. 38, pp. 1)*
Pub: Portland Business Journal
Ed: Erik Siemers. **Description:** Tigard, Oregon-based Exterro Inc. CEO Bobby Balachandran announced plans to go public without the help of an institutional investor. Balachandran believes Exterro could grow to a $100 million legal compliance software company in the span of three years. Insights on Exterro's growth as market leader in the $1 billion legal governance software market are also given.

42168 ■ *"Shipbuilding & Defence" in Canadian Sailings (July 7, 2008)*
Pub: UBM Global Trade
Contact: Leonard J. Corallo, President
Ed: Sharon Hobson. **Description:** Overview of the Joint Support Ship Project whose initial budget was set at $2.1 billion for the acquisition of the ships required for the Canadian navy; another $800 million was allotted for 20 years of in-service support. Four teams of competitors bid for the contract and the Department of National Defence decided to fund two teams for the project definition phase of the competition.

42169 ■ *"Shop Around" in Houston Chronicle (December 7, 2010, pp. 3)*
Pub: Houston Chronicle
Ed: Tara Dooley. **Description:** Profile of Diana Candida and Maria Martinez who partnered to open Beatniks, a shop carrying vintage clothing, art from various artists, dance shoes, and jewelry.

42170 ■ *"Sites Set" in Entrepreneur (Vol. 35, November 2007, No. 11, pp. 112)*
Pub: Entrepreneur Media Inc.
Ed: Nichole L. Torres. **Description:** Marketing information online can be a good bui9sness if you know who to target. Partnering with other online companies to provide information services that cater to specific groups of people is also helpful.

42171 ■ *"Six Tips To Maximize Networking Opportunities" in Women Entrepreneur (November 3, 2008)*
Pub: Entrepreneur Media Inc.
Ed: Tamara Monosoff. **Description:** Networking events fall into the realm of business development as opposed to immediate sales opportunities. It is important to remember that these events provide a chance to build relationships that may someday help one's business. Tips to help make the most out of networking events are provided.

42172 ■ *"Size Does Matter" in International Journal of Globalisation and Small Business (Vol. 4, September 21, 2010, No. 1, pp. 61)*
Pub: Publishers Communication Group
Ed: Julia Cornnell, Ranjit Voola. **Description:** Examination of how members of an Australian-based manufacturing and engineering cluster share knowledge through networking as a means to improve competitive advantage.

42173 ■ *"Small Firms Punch Ticket for Growth" in Houston Business Journal (Vol. 40, January 29, 2010, No. 38, pp. 1)*
Pub: American City Business Journals
Ed: Allison Wollam. **Description:** Independent ticket agencies anticipate growth as American and Canadian authorities approved a merger between Ticketmaster and concert promoter Live Nation. Expansion of service offerings and acquisition of venues have also been done by independent ticket agencies in light of the merger. Details of the merger are included.

42174 ■ *"SoBran Partners with U.S. Navy" in Black Enterprise (Vol. 37, October 2006, No. 3, pp. 38)*
Pub: Earl G. Graves Publishing Co. Inc.
Ed: Glenn Townes. **Description:** SoBran Inc., partnered with Lockheed Martin and signed a three-Tear production service contract with the Naval Aviation Depot in Jacksonville, Florida. The $44 million contract will allow SoBran to transport and warehouse materials for Navy facilities.

42175 ■ *"Software's Last Hurrah" in Canadian Business (Vol. 81, December 24, 2007, No. 1, pp. 27)*
Pub: Rogers Media
Ed: Andrew Wahl. **Description:** Canada's software industry could be facing a challenge with IBM's acquisition of Cognos, which was the country's last major independent business intelligence company and was also IBM's largest acquisition ever. Next in line to Cognos in terms of prominence is Open Text Corporation, which could also be a possible candidate for acquisition, as analysts predict.

42176 ■ *"Some Relief Possible Following Painful Week" in Barron's (Vol. 88, July 14, 2008, No. 28, pp. M3)*
Pub: Dow Jones & Co., Inc.
Ed: Kopin Tan. **Description:** Dow Chemical is offering a 74 percent premium to acquire Rohm & Haas' coatings and electronics materials operations. Frontline amassed a 5.6 percent stake in rival Overseas Shipholding Group and a merger between the two would create a giant global fleet with pricing power. Highlights of the U.S. stock market during the week that ended in July 11, 2008 are discussed. Statistical data included.

42177 ■ *"Sorrell Digs Deep to Snag TNS" in Advertising Age (Vol. 79, July 14, 2008, No. 7, pp. 1)*
Pub: Crain Communications, Inc.
Ed: Michael Bush. **Description:** Martin Sorrell's strategic vision for expansion in order to become the largest ad-agency holding company in the world is discussed.

42178 ■ *"South African Connections: Small Business Owners Work Toward Forming Strategic Alliances" in Black Enterprise (March 2008)*
Pub: Earl G. Graves Publishing Co. Inc.
Ed: Aisha Sylvester. **Description:** National Minority Supplier Development Council Inc. is working to create business partnerships between African American businesses and black-owned South African companies within the country's pharmaceutical supply industry.

42179 ■ *"Staples Advantage Receives NJPA National Contract for Janitorial Supplies" in Professional Services Close-Up (April 22, 2011)*
Pub: Close-Up Media
Description: Staples Advantage, the business-to-business division of Staples Inc. was awarded a contract for janitorial supplies to members of the National Joint Powers Alliance (NJPA). NJPA is a member-owned buying cooperative serving public and private schools, state and local governments, and nonprofit organizations.

42180 ■ *"The Start of a Beautiful Friendship: Partnering with Your Customers on R&D" in Inc. (March 2008, pp. 37-38)*
Pub: Gruner & Jahr USA Publishing
Ed: Leigh Buchanan. **Description:** Joint research and development projects between customers and suppliers are a growing trend in the small business community; these ventures can help keep new product development costs lower. Four tips to maintain a good working relationship in these ventures are outlined.

42181 ■ *"Startup Makes Attempt to 'Reform' Health Insurance" in Austin Business JournalInc. (Vol. 29, January 15, 2010, No. 45, pp. 1)*
Pub: American City Business Journals
Ed: Sandra Zaragoza. **Description:** Health insurance provider ETMG LLC of Austin, Texas plans to act as a managing general agent and a third-party administrator that can facilitate customized plans for small businesses and sole proprietors. According to CEO Mark Adams, profitability is expected for ETMG, which have also clinched $1.5 million worth of investments. Entities that have agreed to do business with ETMG are presented.

42182 ■ *"State Shock Prices Take Large Tumble" in The Business Journal-Milwaukee (Vol. 25, September 12, 2008, No. 51, pp. A1)*
Pub: American City Business Journals, Inc.
Ed: Rich Rovito. **Description:** Weak economic times have caused the stocks of most publicly traded companies in Wisconsin to dip in 2008. Companies that appeared on the worst performing stocks list also experienced drops in share price to as much as 70 percent. Information about the companies that experienced increases in stock prices is also presented. Statistical data included.

42183 ■ *"State of the Unions" in Canadian Business (Vol. 81, December 8, 2008, No. 21, pp. 23)*
Pub: Rogers Media Ltd.
Ed: Sharda Prashad. **Description:** Companies planning on joint ventures should look for partners they can trust and respect and are also competent. Joint venture deals aim to bring existing products to a a new market or in acquiring a foreign product for an existing market.

42184 ■ *"Stikemans' Ascent, Its Legacy, and Its Future" in Globe & Mail (January 29, 2007, pp. B2)*
Pub: CTVglobemedia Publishing Inc.
Ed: Jacquie McNish. **Description:** Pierre Raymond, chairman of legal firm Stikeman Elliott LLP, talks about his strategies to handle competition, his challenges, and about Canada's present mergers and acquisition scenario. Stikeman achieved the first place in 2006 M&A legal rankings.

42185 ■ *"STMicroelectronics" in Canadian Electronics (Vol. 23, February 2008, No. 1, pp. 1)*
Pub: CLB Media Inc.
Description: STMicroelectronics, a semiconductor maker, revealed that it plans to acquire Genesis Microchip Inc. Genesis develops image and video processing systems. It was reported that the acquisition has been approved by Genesis' Board of Directors. It is expected that Genesis will enhance STMicroelectronics' technological capabilities.

42186 ■ *"Stockgroup Completes US $4.5 Million Financing" in Canadian Corporate News (May 16, 2007)*
Pub: Comtex News Network Inc.
Description: Stockgroup, a financial media company focused on collaborative technologies and user-generated content, will use the proceeds of the private placement for acquisitions and general working capital.

42187 ■ *"The Story Of Diane Greene" in Barron's (Vol. 88, July 14, 2008, No. 28, pp. 31)*
Pub: Dow Jones & Co., Inc.
Ed: Mark Veverka. **Description:** Discusses the ousting of Diane Greene as a chief executive of VMWare, a developer of virtualization software, after the firm went public; in this case Greene, a brilliant engineer, should not be negatively impacted by the decision because it is common for companies to bring in new executive leadership that is more operations oriented after the company goes public.

42188 ■ *Strategic Partnerships: An Entrepreneur's Guide to Joint Ventures and Alliances*
Pub: Kaplan Publishing
Ed: Robert Wallace. **Released:** September 2004. **Description:** Ways to develop and execute joint venture relationships with larger business entities for small company owners.

42189 ■ *"Subprime Hits Huntington" in Business First-Columbus (November 23, 2007, pp. A1)*
Pub: American City Business Journals, Inc.
Ed: Adrian Burns. **Description:** Huntington Bancshares Inc. picked up a $1.5 billion exposure to the country's subprime mortgage mess. It caused the bank to set aside $450 million to cover increases in loan losses. When Huntington acquired Sky Financial, it absorbed a 17-year relationship Sky had with Franklin Credit Corporation, which is a subprime lender and servicer.

42190 ■ *"Sudbury Waits With Future Up in the Air" in Globe & Mail (February 22, 2006, pp. B1)*
Pub: CTVglobemedia Publishing Inc.
Ed: Wendy Stueck. **Description:** The takeover of Falconbridge Ltd., by Inco Ltd Sudbury, is in the process with uncertainty. The transaction has been a long overdue.

42191 ■ *"Sullivan Led Bucyrus through Unforgettable Year" in Business Journal-Milwaukee (Vol. 28, December 17, 2010, No. 11, pp. A1)*
Pub: Milwaukee Business Journal
Ed: Rich Rovito. **Description:** Bucyrus International's president and CEO, Tim Sullivan, was chosen as Milwaukee, Wisconsin's Executive of the Year for 2010. Sullivan led Bucyrus through a year of dramatic change which started with the acquisition of the mining business of Terex Corporation and culminating with a deal to sell Caterpillar Inc.

42192 ■ *"Summit, Lions Gate are in Talks to Merge Studios" in Wall Street Journal Eastern Edition (November 29, 2011, pp. B2)*
Pub: Dow Jones & Company Inc. Enterprise Media Group
Contact: Clare Hart, President
Ed: Erica Orden, Michelle Kung. **Description:** Movie studio Summit Entertainment LLC is in talks with television producer Lions Gate Entertainment Corporation about a possible merger. Previous talks have taken place, but no deal was ever reached. Such a deal would create a large, independent studio able to compete in the market with the big Hollywood giants.

42193 ■ *"Sun Capital Partners Affiliate Acquires Timothy's Coffees" in Miami Daily Business Review (March 26, 2008)*
Pub: ALM Media Inc.
Description: An affiliate of Sun Capital Partners acquired Timothy's Coffees of the World. Timothy's operates and franchises 166 stores offering coffees, muffins, and Michel's Baguette products.

42194 ■ *"SunBank Plans Expansion Via Wall-Mart" in Business Journal-Serving Phoenix and the Valley of the Sun (Vol. 10, November 9, 2007)*
Pub: American City Business Journals, Inc.
Ed: Chris Casacchia. **Description:** SunBank plans to install 12 to 14 branches in Wal-Mart stores in Arizona and hire 100 bankers by the end of 2008. Wal-Mart also offers financial products at other stores through partnerships with other banks.

42195 ■ *"Sundt, DPR Score $470 Million Biotech Project" in The Business Journal - Serving Phoenix and the Valley of the Sun (Vol. 29, September 19, 2008, No. 3, pp. 1)*
Pub: American City Business Journals, Inc.
Ed: Jan Buchholz. **Description:** Sundt Inc. and DPR Construction Inc. were awarded the winning joint-venture contract to develop the second phase of the Arizona Biomedical Collaborative on the Phoenix Biomedical Campus. Both firms declined to comment, but an employee of the Arizona Board of Regents confirmed that the firms won the bidding. Views and information on the development project are presented.

42196 ■ *"Suppliers May Follow Fiat" in Crain's Detroit Business (Vol. 25, June 15, 2009, No. 24, pp. 1)*
Pub: Crain Communications Inc. - Detroit
Ed: Ryan Beene. **Description:** Italian suppliers to Fiat SpA are looking toward Detroit after the formation of Chrysler Group LLC, the Chrysler-Fiat partnership created from Chrysler's bankruptcy. The Italian American Alliance for Business and Technology is aware of two Italy-based powertrain component suppliers that are considering a move to Detroit.

42197 ■ *"Swedes Swoop In To Save Time4" in Advertising Age (Vol. 78, January 29, 2007, No. 5, pp. 4)*
Pub: Crain Communications, Inc.
Ed: Nat Ives. **Description:** Overview of Stockholm's Bonnier Group, a family-owned publisher that is looking to expand its U.S. presence; Bonnier recently acquired a number of Time Inc. magazines.

42198 ■ *"Sweet Spot" in Canadian Business (Vol. 79, November 20, 2006, No. 23, pp. 25)*
Pub: Rogers Media
Ed: John Gray. **Description:** The plans of Kinross Gold Corp., to acquire the stake of Bema Gold Corp., are discussed. Under the terms of the deal Kinross is offering Bema stockholders 0.441 of a Kinross share for each of Bema shares.

42199 ■ *"Swope: Breakup Won't Delay Job" in The Business Journal-Serving Metropolitan Kansas City (Vol. 26, August 22, 2008, No. 50, pp. 1)*
Pub: American City Business Journals, Inc.
Ed: Rob Roberts. **Description:** Swope Community Builders said that the Kansas City Redevelopment Project will not be delayed by the breakup of their partnership with Sherman Associates Inc. Swopes will be the sole master developer of the project.

42200 ■ *"Symbility Solutions Joins Motion Computing Partner Program" in Canadian Corporate News (May 14, 2007)*
Pub: Comtex News Network Inc.
Description: Symbility Solutions Inc., a wholly owned subsidiary of Automated Benefits Corp., announced an agreement with Alliance Partner of Motion Computing, a leader in wireless communications and

mobile computing, in which both companies will invest in a sales and marketing strategy that focuses specifically on the insurance market.

42201 ■ *"Takeover Frenzy Stokes Steel Stocks" in Globe & Mail (February 7, 2006, pp. B1)*
Pub: CTVglobemedia Publishing Inc.
Description: The impact of merger speculations, on shares of steel companies such as Ipsco Inc., is discussed.

42202 ■ *"Taking Collections" in Investment Dealers' Digest (Vol. 75, October 9, 2009, No. 38, pp. 19)*
Pub: SourceMedia, Inc.
Ed: Aleksandrs Rozens. **Description:** Although the nation's debt-collection industry has grown with increased reliance by consumers on credit, valuations of these firms have lessened due to the economy which has hurt some of the success of these firms in obtaining the debt back from consumers who are experiencing trying economic times.

42203 ■ *"Taking on Intel" in Canadian Business (Vol. 79, October 23, 2006, No. 21, pp. 27)*
Pub: Rogers Media
Ed: Andrew Wahl. **Description:** The decision of ATI Technologies Inc., a Canadian computer peripherals company to acquire cash and stocks worth US$5.4-billion from American microprocessor maker Advanced Micro Devices Inc., is discussed.

42204 ■ *"Taking the Over-the-Counter Route to US" in Barron's (Vol. 88, July 7, 2008, No. 27, pp. 24)*
Pub: Dow Jones & Co., Inc.
Ed: Eric Uhlfelder. **Description:** Many multinational companies have left the New York Stock Exchange and allowed their shares to trade over-the-counter. The companies have taken advantage of a 2007 SEC rule allowing publicly listed foreign companies to change trading venues if less than 5 percent of global trading volume in the past 12 months occurred in the US.

42205 ■ *"Tampa Condo Conversion Sells for $14.8 Million Less" in The Business Journal-Serving Greater Tampa Bay (Vol. 28, September 5, 2008)*
Pub: American City Business Journals, Inc.
Ed: Janet Leiser. **Description:** Former apartment complex Village Oaks at Tampa, which was converted to condominiums, has been sold to Tennessee-based real estate investment trust Mid-America Apartment Communities Inc. for $21.2 million in August 2008. The amount was $14.2 million less than what developer Radco Management LLC paid for in 2005.

42206 ■ *"Tastee-Freez Celebrates 60th Anniversary" in Ice Cream Reporter (Vol. 23, July 20, 2010, No. 8, pp. 2)*
Pub: Ice Cream Reporter
Description: Tastee-Freez founders, Leo Moranz (inventor) and Harry Axene, an inventor partnered to market the soft-serve pump and freezer for serving frozen treats back in 1950.

42207 ■ *"Tasti D-Lite Has Franchise Agreement for Australia" in Ice Cream Reporter (Vol. 23, November 20, 2010, No. 12, pp. 3)*
Pub: Ice Cream Reporter
Description: Tasti D-Lite signed an international master franchise agreement with Friezer Australia Pty. Ltd. and will open 30 units throughout Australia over the next five years.

42208 ■ *"Tate & Lyle to Sell Redpath Division to American Sugar" in Globe & Mail (February 15, 2007, pp. B15)*
Pub: CTVglobemedia Publishing Inc.
Description: American Sugar Refining has agreed to acquire the Canadian sugar unit of Tate & Lyle PLC for $301.9 million. Tate & Lyle PLC has been selling off businesses and closing plants in order to focus on starches and Splenda.

42209 ■ *"Teachers, U.S. Fund Providence Made Moves On BCE Buyout" in Globe & Mail (April 10, 2007, pp. B17)*
Pub: CTVglobemedia Publishing Inc.
Ed: Boyd Erman; Sinclair Stewart; Jacquie McNish. **Description:** The Ontario Teachers Pension Plan, the largest shareholder of telecommunications firm BCE Inc., has called for a partnership with buyout firm Providence Equity Partners Inc. in order to acquire BCE Inc.

42210 ■ *"Tech Deal Couples Homegrown Firms" in The Business Journal-Serving Greater Tampa Bay (Vol. 28, July 4, 2008, No. 28, pp. 1)*
Pub: American City Business Journals, Inc.
Ed: Michael Hinman. **Description:** Tampa Bay, Florida-based Administrative Partners Inc. was acquired by Tribridge Inc. resulting in the strengthening of the delivery of Microsoft products to clients. Other details of the merger of the management consulting services companies are presented.

42211 ■ *"Tech's Payout Problem" in Barron's (Vol. 90, September 13, 2010, No. 37, pp. 19)*
Pub: Barron's Editorial & Corporate Headquarters
Ed: Andrew Bary. **Description:** Big tech companies have the potential to be good dividend payers, but instead just hoard their cash for acquisitions and share buybacks. If these companies offered more dividends, they could boost their shares and attract more income-oriented investors.

42212 ■ *"Tektronix Buys Arbor Networks for Security Business" in eWeek (August 9, 2010)*
Pub: Ziff Davis Enterprise
Description: Tektronix Communications, provider of communications test and network intelligence solutions will acquire Arbor Networks. The deal will help Tektronix build a brand in security. Details of the transaction are included.

42213 ■ *"TELUS Says No Thanks to Joining BCE Fray" in Globe & Mail (April 24, 2007, pp. B1)*
Pub: CTVglobemedia Publishing Inc.
Ed: Eric Reguly; Catherine McLean. **Description:** The causes of the refusal of TELUS Corp. to try and acquire BCE Inc. are discussed. The prospects of the acquisition of TELUS Corp. by private equity funds are discussed, besides the availability of cash with private equity funds.

42214 ■ *"Theme Park Sale has Vendor Upside" in Tampa Bay Business Journal (Vol. 29, October 23, 2009, No. 44, pp. 1)*
Pub: American City Business Journals
Ed: Margie Manning. **Description:** Private equity firm The Blackstone Group has concluded its $2.7 billion purchase of Busch Entertainment Corporation. Aside from enhanced business opportunities in Florida's Tampa Bay area, new attractions might be built in the Busch Gardens and Adventure Island properties that will be acquired by Blackstone. Blackstone's other plans are also discussed.

42215 ■ *"This Just In" in Crain's Detroit Business (Vol. 25, June 1, 2009, No. 22, pp. 1)*
Pub: Crain Communications Inc. - Detroit
Description: Three veterans of the auto industry have partnered to create, Revitalizing Michigan, a nonprofit dedicated to help manufacturers improve their processes. The firm is seeking federal, state and private grants to fund the mission.

42216 ■ *"Three Funds Look to Join CPP, Bypassing Teachers in BCE Hunt" in Globe & Mail (April 23, 2007, pp. B1)*
Pub: CTVglobemedia Publishing Inc.
Ed: Sinclair Stewart. **Description:** The plans of the Ontario Municipal Employees Retirement Board, British Columbia Investment Management Corp. and the Alberta Investment Corp. to join the bidding consortium led by Canadian Pension Plan Investment Board, for the buyout of BCE Inc. are discussed. The efforts of the Ontario Teachers Pension Plan Board to form a bidding consortium for the same purpose are discussed.

42217 ■ *"Tim Armstrong" in Canadian Business (Vol. 81, July 21, 2008, No. 11, pp. 10)*
Pub: Rogers Media Ltd.
Ed: Calvin Leung. **Description:** Interview with Tim Armstrong who is the president of advertising and commerce department of Google Inc. for North America; the information technology company executive talked about the emerging trends and changes to YouTube made by the company since its acquisition in 2006.

42218 ■ *"Timberland's CEO On Standing Up to 65,000 Angry Activists" in Harvard Business Review (Vol. 88, September 2010, No. 9, pp. 39)*
Pub: Harvard Business School Publishing
Ed: Jeff Swartz. **Description:** Timberland Company avoided a potential boycott by taking a two-way approach. It addressed a supplier issue that posed a threat to the environment, and launched an email campaign to keep Greenpeace activists informed of the development of a new supplier agreement.

42219 ■ *"Tiny Telecom Big Prize in Bell Aliant Bid Battle" in Globe & Mail (April 4, 2007, pp. B1)*
Pub: CTVglobemedia Publishing Inc.
Ed: Catherine McLean. **Description:** The competition between Bell Aliant Regional Communications Income Fund of BCE Inc. and Bragg Communications Inc. to bid for acquiring Amtelecom Income Fund is discussed.

42220 ■ *"TiVo, Domino's Team to Offer Pizza Ordering by DVR" in Advertising Age (Vol. 79, November 17, 2008, No. 43, pp. 48)*
Pub: Crain Communications, Inc.
Ed: Brian Steinberg. **Description:** Domino's Pizza and TiVo are teaming up to make it possible for customers to order from the restaurant straight from their DVR. The companies see that this kind of interactive television and consumer experience will only serve to generate more sales as the customer can be exposed to a fuller range of menu selections and will not have to interrupt their viewing, while workers can spend more time making the product.

42221 ■ *"To Help Maintain an Adequate Blood Supply During the Summer Months" in Ice Cream Reporter (Vol. 21, August 20, 2008, No. 9, pp. 8)*
Pub: Ice Cream Reporter
Description: Friendly's and the American Red Cross have partnered to offer blood donors a coupon for one free carton of Friendly's ice cream in order to maintain an adequate supply during summer months.

42222 ■ *"Toolmakers' New Tack" in Crain's Detroit Business (Vol. 25, June 8, 2009,)*
Pub: Crain Communications Inc. - Detroit
Ed: Ryan Beene, Amy Lane. **Description:** MAG Industrial Automation Systems LLC and Dowding Machining Inc. have partnered to advance wind-turbine technology. The goal is to cut costs of wind energy to the same level as carbon-based fuel.

42223 ■ *"Top 50 In Profits" in Canadian Business (Vol. 81, Summer 2008, No. 9, pp. 116)*
Pub: Rogers Media Ltd.
Description: Royal Bank of Canada topped the Investor 500 by profits list despite the slower economic growth in Canada and the U.S. The bank was in the runner-up position in the 2007. RBC's growth strategy is through hefty acquisitions in the U.S. A table ranking the top 50 companies in Canada in terms of profits is presented.

42224 ■ *"Top Law Firms Join Forces" in Business Journal Portland (Vol. 27, December 3, 2010, No. 40, pp. 1)*
Pub: Portland Business Journal
Ed: Andy Giegerich. **Description:** Law Firms Powell PC and Roberts Kaplan LLP will forge a collaboration, whereby 17 Roberts Kaplan attorneys will join the Portland, Oregon-based office of Lane Powell. The partnership is expected to strengthen the law firms' grip on Portland's banking clients.

42225 ■ *"Trading Down at the Supermarket" in Barron's (Vol. 88, July 14, 2008, No. 28, pp. 36)*
Pub: Dow Jones & Co., Inc.
Ed: Alexander Eule. **Description:** Shares of Ralcorp Holdings are cheap at around $49.95 after slipping 20 percent prior to their acquisition of Post cereals from Kraft. Some analysts believe its shares could climb over 60 percent to $80 as value-seeking consumers buy more private label products.

42226 ■ *"Transcontinental to Exchange Assets with Quad/Graphics" in American Printer (Vol. 128, August 1, 2011, No. 8)*
Pub: Penton Media Inc.
Description: Transcontinental Inc. and Quad/Graphics Inc. entered into an agreement where Transcontinental will indirectly acquire all shares of Quad Graphics Canada Inc.

42227 ■ *"Trust Buyouts Not My Fault, Flaherty Says" in Globe & Mail (April 3, 2007, pp. B1)*
Pub: CTVglobemedia Publishing Inc.
Ed: Tara Perkins; Doug Saunders; Steven Chase. **Description:** The causes of the acquisition of Canadian firms by foreign investors are discussed by the Canadian Finance Minister Jim Flaherty.

42228 ■ *"Trust Tax Under Fire as Drain on Revenue" in Globe & Mail (April 9, 2007, pp. B1)*
Pub: CTVglobemedia Publishing Inc.
Ed: Steven Chase. **Description:** The economic aspects of the implementation of the trust levy by the Canadian government are discussed. The acquisition of Canadian income trusts by Canadian and international financial institutions is described.

42229 ■ *"TSX Linkup Sets Stage for Battle" in Globe & Mail (March 6, 2007, pp. B1)*
Pub: CTVglobemedia Publishing Inc.
Ed: Boyd Erman; Sinclair Stewart. **Description:** The strategic alliance between TSX Group Inc. and International Securities Exchange Holdings Inc. for the establishment of a derivatives exchange in Canada is discussed. The prospects of competition between the new exchange and the Montreal Exchange are discussed.

42230 ■ *"Turner Broadcasting System" in Brandweek (Vol. 49, April 21, 2008, No. 16, pp. SR13)*
Pub: VNU Business Media, Inc.
Ed: Anthony Crupi. **Description:** Provides contact information for sales and marketing personnel for the Turner Broadcasting System networks as well as a listing of the station's top programming and an analysis of the current season and the target audience for those programs running in the current season. Recent acquisitions are also discussed.

42231 ■ *"TUSK Announces 2007 First Quarter Results" in Canadian Corporate News (May 14, 2007)*
Pub: Comtex News Network Inc.
Description: TUSK Energy Corp. announced its financial and operating results for the first quarter ending March 31, 2007.

42232 ■ *"Two Local Bakers Winners of TV's 'Cupcake Wars" in Toledo Blade (July 6, 2011)*
Pub: Toledo Times
Description: Winners of cable network Food Channel's Cupcake Wars, Lori Jacobs and Dana Iliev own Cake in a Cup in Toledo, Ohio. The partners shop features creative cupcakes with names such as Monkey Business, Pretty in Pink, and Tropical Getaway.

42233 ■ *"Tying the Knot" in Entrepreneur (Vol. 36, April 2008, No. 4, pp. 48)*
Pub: Entrepreneur Media, Inc.
Ed: Guy Kawasaki. **Description:** Tips to consider when forming business partnerships are presented.

42234 ■ *"U-Swirl To Open in Salt Lake City Metro Market" in Ice Cream Reporter (Vol. 23, November 20, 2010, No. 12, pp. 4)*
Pub: Ice Cream Reporter
Description: Healthy Fast Food Inc., parent company to U-SWIRL International Inc., the owner and franchisor of U-SWIRL Frozen Yogurt cafes signed a franchising area development agreement for the Salt Lake City metropolitan area with Regents Management and will open 5 cafes over a five year period.

42235 ■ *"UBS Buys Out Canadian Partner" in Globe & Mail (January 20, 2006, pp. B1)*
Pub: CTVglobemedia Publishing Inc.
Ed: Andrew Willis. **Description:** The details on UBS AG's acquisition of UBS Securities Canada Inc. are presented.

42236 ■ *"UMKC, Hospital Drill Down on Deal" in The Business Journal-Serving Metropolitan Kansas City (Vol. 26, July 18, 2008, No. 45, pp. 1)*
Pub: American City Business Journals, Inc.
Ed: Rob Roberts. **Description:** University of Missouri Kansas City and Children's Mercy Hospital are negotiating the hospital's potential acquisition of the university's School of Dentistry building. The deal would transfer the 240,000-square foot dental school building to Children's Mercy. Plans for a new dental school building for the UMKC are also presented.

42237 ■ *"Under Fire, Sabia Triggers Battle for BCE" in Globe & Mail (April 14, 2007, pp. B1)*
Pub: CTVglobemedia Publishing Inc.
Ed: Boyd Erman. **Description:** The announcement of negotiations for the sale of BCE Inc. by its chief executive officer Michael Sabia is discussed. The efforts of Ontario Teachers Pension Plan to submit its proposal for the sale are described.

42238 ■ *"Underworld Acquires Yukon Gold Property" in Canadian Corporate News (May 16, 2007)*
Pub: Comtex News Network Inc.
Description: Underworld Resources Inc., a well-structured junior exploration company, announced that it has secured an option to earn a 100 percent right, title, and interest in the 11,850 acre White and Black Fox gold Properties in Yukon Territory, Canada. The company will be exploring both vein hosted and sedimentary hosted gold targets.

42239 ■ *"Unilever Acquiring Danish Operations of Diplom-Is Ice Cream" in Ice Cream Reporter (Vol. 23, August 20, 2010, No. 9, pp. 1)*
Pub: Ice Cream Reporter
Description: Unilever will acquire Danish operations of the ice cream company Diplom-Is from Norwegian dairy group Tine.

42240 ■ *"Unilever Acquiring EVGA's Ice Cream Brands in Greece" in Ice Cream Reporter (Vol. 23, October 20, 2010, No. 11, pp. 1)*
Pub: Ice Cream Reporter
Description: Unilever will acquire the ice cream brands and distribution network of the Greek frozen dessert manufacturer EVGA.

42241 ■ *"United Insurance To Grow St. Pete's Corporate Base" in The Business Journal-Serving Greater Tampa Bay (August 29, 2008)*
Pub: American City Business Journals, Inc.
Ed: Margie Manning. **Description:** United Insurance Holdings LC is on its way to becoming a public company by agreeing in a reverse merger with FMG Acquisition Corp. The $104.3 million agreement will provide the company's St. Petersburg operations the opportunity to grow. The other impacts of the proposed reverse merger are examined.

42242 ■ *"U.S. Buyer Rescues KCP From Trust Tax Burden" in Globe & Mail (April 3, 2007, pp. B1)*
Pub: CTVglobemedia Publishing Inc.
Ed: Richard Blackwell. **Description:** The economic aspects of the buyout of KCP Income Fund by Caxton-Iseman Capital Inc. are discussed.

42243 ■ *"U.S. Firm to Acquire Manufacturer GSW" in Globe & Mail (January 21, 2006, pp. B4)*
Pub: CTVglobemedia Publishing Inc.
Ed: Gordon Pitts. **Description:** The details on A.O. Smith Corp.'s acquisition of GSW Inc. are presented.

42244 ■ *"U.S. Savvy Helps Fuel TD's Fortunes" in Globe & Mail (February 23, 2007, pp. B1)*
Pub: CTVglobemedia Publishing Inc.
Ed: Andrew Willis; Tavia Grant. **Description:** The rise in the revenues of Toronto-Dominion Bank due to its acquisition of American financial service providers and the rise in its domestic retail banking revenues are disussed.

42245 ■ *"U.S. Widens Rocket Field" in Wall Street Journal Eastern Edition (October 17 , 2011, pp. B4)*
Pub: Dow Jones & Company Inc. Enterprise Media Group
Contact: Clare Hart, President
Ed: Andy Pasztor. **Description:** An agreement has been reached between National Aeronautics and Space Administration, the Department of Defense and the Air Force that will assist small commercial space ventures in bidding for profitable contracts for government launching. The program will give those companies a chance to compete against larger corporations.

42246 ■ *"Uniting Spring in OP Could Reduce Static" in Business Journal-Serving Metropolitan Kansas City (October 19, 2007)*
Pub: American City Business Journals, Inc.
Ed: Jim Davis, Steve Vockrodt. **Description:** Sprint Nextel, the result of Sprint Corporation and Nextel Communications Inc. has been using Nextel's Reston office as corporate headquarters. The consolidation of Sprint Nextel's headquarters is expected to result in saving on cost of living and leases. The benefits of choosing Kansas City as the headquarters are evaluated.

42247 ■ *"Universal Energy Group Releases March 31, 2007 Financial Statements" in Canadian Corporate News (May 14, 2007)*
Pub: Comtex News Network Inc.
Description: Universal Energy Group Ltd., a company that sells electricity and natural gas to small to mid-size commercial and small industrial customers as well as residential customers, announced the release of its March 31, 2007 financial statements. Management's analysis and discussion of the company's financial condition and results of operations are listed. Statistical data included.

42248 ■ *"Unwanted News for Hospitals" in Business Courier (Vol. 24, October 26, 2008, No. 28, pp. 1)*
Pub: American City Business Journals, Inc.
Description: Christ and St. Luke Hospital might be sharing responsibility costs on the $207 million hospital being built by Health Alliance, the group they are parting with. Christ and St. Lu ke hospitals will be paying $60 million and $25 million for partial liability res pectively because the plans for the said project were already underway before they decided to withdraw. Christ Hospital is involved in a whistle-blower case that might cause $424 million in liability across the group.

42249 ■ *"Uranerz Acquires Additional Uranium Property Adjoining Nichols Ranch" in Canadian Corporate News (May 14, 2007)*
Pub: Comtex News Network Inc.
Description: Uranerz Energy Corporation announced the successful leasing of the fee mineral lands that appear to host the 'nose' of the oxidation-rduction geochemical front and has the potential for increasing the known uranium mineralization at the Nichols Ranch project which lies west of and adjacent to Uranerz's Nichols Ranch ISR uranium project.

42250 ■ *"US Airways Stock Up 5 Percent on Day Merger Try Ends" in Charlotte Observer (February 1, 2007)*
Pub: Knight-Ridder/Tribune Business News
Ed: Steve Harrison. **Description:** US Airways stock rose 5 percent on the day Doug Parker, CEO, cancelled his offer to purchase Delta Air Lines.

42251 ■ *"USAmeriBank Deals for Growth" in The Business Journal-Serving Greater Tampa Bay (Vol. 28, September 26, 2008, No. 40, pp. 1)*

Pub: American City Business Journals, Inc.

Ed: Margie Manning. **Description:** It is believed that the pending $14.9 million purchase of Liberty Bank by USAmeriBank could be at the forefront of a trend. Executives of both companies expect the deal to close by the end of 2008. USAmeriBank will have $430 million in assets and five offices in Pinellas, Florida once the deal is completed.

42252 ■ *"UT Deans Serious about Biz" in Austin Business Journal (Vol. 31, May 20, 2011, No. 11, pp. 1)*

Pub: American City Business Journals Inc.

Ed: Sandra Zaragoza. **Description:** Dean Thomas Gilligan of the University of Texas, McCombs School of Business and engineering school Dean Gregory Fenves have partnered to develop a joint engineering and business degree. Their partnership has resulted in an undergraduate course on initiating startups.

42253 ■ *"UV Suppliers Form Strategic Alliance" in American Printer (Vol. 128, June 1, 2011, No. 6)*

Pub: Penton Media Inc.

Description: British ultra-violent curing systems developer Integration Technology Ltd. formed a strategic alliance with UV technology provider IST Metz GmbH of Germany in order to offer a complete line of UV solutions for the printing industry.

42254 ■ *"Valener Announces that Gaz Metro has Achieved a Key Step in Acquiring CVPS" in CNW Group (September 30, 2011)*

Pub: CNW Group

Contact: Carolyn McGill-Davidson, President

Description: Valener Inc., which owns about 29 percent of Gaz Metro Ltd. Partnership, announced that Gaz Metro welcomes the sale of Central Vermont Public Service Corporation (CVPS). Valener owns an indirect interest of 24.5 percent in the wind power projects jointly developed by Beaupre Eole General Partnership and Boralex Inc. on private lands in Quebec. Details of the deal are included.

42255 ■ *"ValienteHernandez Acquired" in The Business Journal-Serving Greater Tampa Bay (Vol. 28, September 12, 2008, No. 38, pp. 1)*

Pub: American City Business Journals, Inc.

Ed: Alexis Muellner. **Description:** Minnesota accounting firm LarsonAllen LLP has acquired Florida-based ValienteHernandez PA, creating a company with 35 employees to be based in ValienteHernandez's newly built office in Tampa Bay Area. Other details about the merger are provided.

42256 ■ *"V&J Scores Partnership with Shaq" in Business Journal-Milwaukee (Vol. 25, October 12, 2007, No. 2, pp. A1)*

Pub: American City Business Journals, Inc.

Ed: Rich Kirchen. **Description:** O'Neal Franchise Group has agreed to a partnership with V&J Foods of Milwaukee to handle Auntie Anne's shops in New York, South Africa, Michigan, and the Caribbean. V&J O'Neal Enterprises will open six Auntie Anne's soft pretzel shops in Detroit towards the end of 2007. Planned international ventures of the partnership are presented.

42257 ■ *"VC-Heavy, Revenue-Light Sensicore Sold to GE Division" in Crain's Detroit Business (Vol. 24, April 14, 2008, No. 15, pp. 28)*

Pub: Crain Communications Inc.

Ed: Tom Henderson. **Description:** General Electric has acquired Sensicore Inc., which although one of Michigan's most successful companies in raising venture capital was unable to generate significant revenue from its handheld water-testing devices. GE is capable of penetrating a larger market than a private company and will be able to take the devices to the municipal marketplace.

42258 ■ *"Vicki Avril; Senior Vice-President of Tubular Division, Ipsco Inc." in Crain's Chicago Business (Vol. 31, May 5, 2008, No. 18)*

Pub: Crain Communications, Inc.

Ed: Miriam Gottfried. **Description:** Profile of Vicki Avril who is the senior vice-president of the tubular division at Ipsco Inc. where she supervises 2,800 employees and 13 mills throughout the United States and Canada.

42259 ■ *"Viewing Ironman As Gold, R.I. Firm Buys Its Parent" in The Business Journal-Serving Greater Tampa Bay (Vol. 28, September 19, 2008)*

Pub: American City Business Journals, Inc.

Ed: Pete Williams. **Description:** Providence Equity Partners purchased World Triathlon Corp., parent company of the Ironman Triathlon, for an undisclosed sum. The acquisition means that the World Triathlon Headquarters will move to Tampa, Florida, and allows Providence Equity Partners to stage or license rights to Ironman and half-Ironman distance events.

42260 ■ *"Vital Signs: The Big Picture" in Canadian Business (Vol. 81, Summer 2008, No. 9, pp. 153)*

Pub: Rogers Media Ltd.

Description: Results of the Investor 500 showing percentage of companies with positive returns, most actively traded companies over the past six months and market capitalization by industry are presented. Stock performance and revenues of publicly held corporations in Canada are also provided.

42261 ■ *"Vitamins to Spice Up Food" in Philadelphia Business Journal (Vol. 28, October 2, 2009, No. 33, pp. 1)*

Pub: American City Business Journals

Ed: John George. **Description:** VitaminSpice, a startup company established by Ed Bukstel, makes a line of spice and vitamin blends that come in seasoning form. The form of the blends could facilitate easier ingestion of vitamins into people's diets. A reverse merger that will allow a publicly-traded company status for VitaminSpice will be accomplished by early October 2009.

42262 ■ *"Vive La Resistance: Competing Logics and the Consolidation of U.S. Community Banking" in Academy of Management Journal (August 2007)*

Pub: Academy of Management

Contact: Ming-Jer Chen, President

Ed: Christopher Marquis, Michael Lounsbury. **Description:** Ways in which competing logics facilitate resistance to institutional change is presented, highlighting on banking professionals' resistance to large, national banks acquisitions of smaller, local banks.

42263 ■ *"Wachovia Gears Up for Major Arizona Expansion" in Business Journal-Serving Phoenix and the Valley of the Sun (Vol. 5, Oct. 5, 2007)*

Pub: American City Business Journals, Inc.

Ed: Chris Casacchia. **Description:** Wachovia, America's fourth-largest bank is finalizing a deal to build its Arizona headquarters in downtown Phoenix. The bank plans to add an additional 100 employees by June 2008 and double its financial network to 30 offices in four years. Wachovia will also convert fifteen World Savings Bank branches it acquired in 2006 through Golden West Financial Corporation.

42264 ■ *"Walgreen Takes Up Doctoring" in Crain's Chicago Business (Vol. 31, March 31, 2008, No. 13, pp. 18)*

Pub: Crain Communications, Inc.

Ed: Mark Bruno. **Description:** Walgreen Co. has agreed to acquire two firms that provide on-site medical and pharmaceutical services to large companies. Walgreen feels that these facilities mark the future of health care for a number of large corporations.

42265 ■ *"Want Leverage? Multi-Unit Franchisees Deliver Substantial Savings" in Franchising World (Vol. 42, October 2010, No. 10, pp. 39)*

Pub: International Franchise Association

Ed: Aziz Hashim. **Description:** Many retail franchises selling the same product are able to buy in bulk. Volume-buying can save money for any franchise.

42266 ■ *"Water Treatment Play Zenon Goes to GE" in Globe & Mail (March 15, 2006, pp. B1)*

Pub: CTVglobemedia Publishing Inc.

Ed: Leonard Zehr. **Description:** General Electric Co. acquires Ontario-based company, Zenon Environmental Inc., a technology giant in purifying water in northern Canada.

42267 ■ *"Wayne, Oakland Counties Create Own 'Medical Corridor'" in Crain's Detroit Business (Vol. 24, October 6, 2008, No. 40, pp. 8)*

Pub: Crain Communications, Inc.

Ed: Jay Greene. **Description:** Woodward Medical Corridor that runs along Woodward Avenue and currently encompasses twelve hospitals and is rapidly growing with additional physician offices, advanced oncology centers and new hospitals. Beaumont Hospital is building a $160 million proton-beam therapy cancer center on its Royal Oak campus in a joint venture with Procure Treatment Centers of Bloomington Ind. That is expected to open in 2010 and will employ approximately 145 new workers.

42268 ■ *"The Wealth Portfolio" in Canadian Business (Vol. 79, Winter 2006, No. 24, pp. 146)*

Pub: Rogers Media

Ed: Jeff Sanford. **Description:** The trends pertaining to the pricing of shares of public enterprises, at the Montreal stock exchange, are described.

42269 ■ *"Web Biz Brulant Surfing for Acquisition Candidates" in Crain's Cleveland Business (Vol. 28, December 3, 2007, No. 48, pp. 6)*

Pub: Crain Communications, Inc.

Ed: Chuck Soder. **Description:** Brulant Inc., a provider of web development and marketing services, is looking to acquire other companies after growing for five years straight. The company is one of the largest technology firms in Northeast Ohio.

42270 ■ *"A Week of the Worst Kind of Selling" in Barron's (Vol. 88, June 30, 2008, No. 26, pp. M3)*

Pub: Dow Jones & Co., Inc.

Ed: Kopin Tan. **Description:** In the week that ended in June 27, 2008 the selloff in the U.S. stock market was brought on by mounting bank losses and the spread of economic slowdown on top of high oil prices. The 31 percent decrease in the share price of Ingersoll-Rand since October 2007 may have factored in most of its risks. The company has completed its acquisition of Trane to morph into a refrigeration-equipment company.

42271 ■ *The Weekly Corporate Growth Report*

Pub: NVST Inc.

Contact: Walter Jurek, President

URL(s): www.nvst.com/pubs/cgr-pub.asp. **Released:** Weekly; Fifty times per year. **Publication includes:** Current acquisition and merger transactions. **Entries include:** Buyer and seller names and locations, annual sales and net income for each, seller's net worth and price-earnings ratio, and purchase price, including terms and various ratios. **Arrangement:** Classified by Standard Industrial Classification (SIC) code.

42272 ■ *"Wells Fargo Will Soon Lead Local Banks in Deposits" in Austin Business JournalInc. (Vol. 28, December 5, 2008, No. 38, pp. A1)*

Pub: American City Business Journals

Ed: Christopher Calnan. **Description:** Acquisition of Wachovia Corporation by Wells Fargo and Company will leave the latter as the top bank for deposits in Austin, Texas. The merged bank will have deposits of more than $ billion, more than the $3.9 billion deposits Bank of America maintains in the area.

42273 ■ *"Wendy's Speeds Up Tim's Spinout" in Globe & Mail (January 11, 2006, pp. B1)*
Pub: CTVglobemedia Publishing Inc.
Ed: Andrew Willis. **Description:** The reasons behind the decision of Wendy's International Inc. to bid Tim Hortons are presented.

42274 ■ *"What Players in the Midmarket Are Talking About" in Mergers & Acquisitions: The Dealmaker's Journal (March 1, 2008)*
Pub: SourceMedia, Inc.
Description: Sports Properties Acquisition Corp. went public at the end of January; according to the company's prospectus, it is not limiting its focus to just teams, it is also considering deals for stadium construction companies, sports leagues, facilities, sports-related advertising and licensing of products, in addition to other related segments.

42275 ■ *"What's In a Relationship? The Case of Commercial Lending" in Business Horizons (Vol. 51, March-April 2008, No. 2, pp. 93)*
Pub: Elsevier Advanced Technology Publications
Description: Academic literature on relationship lending and banking to small and medium enterprises is analyzed. This practice is best suited to some SME types but creates special challenges for bank managers. Relationship lending may also be better delivered by community banks.

42276 ■ *"When Anything (And Everything) Goes" in Globe & Mail (January 12, 2007, pp. B4)*
Pub: CTVglobemedia Publishing Inc.
Ed: Elizabeth Church. **Description:** The forecast on acquisition of different real estate firms is presented.

42277 ■ *"Where Are the Vultures?" in Mergers & Acquisitions: The Dealmaker's Journal (March 1, 2008)*
Pub: SourceMedia, Inc.
Ed: Ken MacFadyen. **Description:** Although the real estate market is distressed, not many acquisitions are being made by distress private equity investors; this is due, in part, to the difficulty in assessing real estate industry firms since it is a sector which is so localized.

42278 ■ *"Where Rubber Meets Road" in Canadian Business (Vol. 80, March 12, 2007, No. 6, pp. 15)*
Pub: Rogers Media
Ed: Michelle Magnan. **Description:** The partnership between Engineered Drilling Solutions Inc. and EnCana Corp. to build road from rubber wastes and follow environment-friendly methods in work is discussed.

42279 ■ *"Who's Next?" in Boston Business Journal (Vol. 27, November 16, 2007, No. 42, pp. 1)*
Pub: American City Business Journals Inc.
Ed: Lisa van der Pool. **Description:** Boston, Massachusetts' burgeoning technology and biotech industries along with rising billing rates make it a unique legal market. Law firms cross the threshold either by merging with or acquiring a smaller law firm. Boston as a unique legal market is discussed.

42280 ■ *"Why Intel Should Dump Its Flash-Memory Business" in Barron's (Vol. 88, March 10, 2008, No. 10, pp. 35)*
Pub: Dow Jones & Company, Inc.
Ed: Eric J. Savitz. **Description:** Intel Corp. must sell its NAND flash-memory business as soon as it possibly can to the highest bidder to focus on its PC processor business and take advantage of other business opportunities. Apple should consider a buyback of 10 percent of the company's shares to lift its stock.

42281 ■ *"Why Nestle Should Sell Alcon" in Barron's (Vol. 88, March 17, 2008, No. 11, pp. M12)*
Pub: Dow Jones & Company, Inc.
Ed: Sean Walters. **Description:** Nestle should sell Alcon because Nestle can't afford to be complacent as its peers have made changes to their portfolios to boost competitiveness. Nestle's stake in Alcon and L'Oreal have been ignored by investors and Nestle could realize better value by strengthening its nutrition division through acquisitions.

42282 ■ *Wikinomics: How Mass Collaboration Changes Everything*
Pub: Penguin Group
Ed: Don Tapscott. **Released:** November 2006. **Price:** $25.95. **Description:** Guide to collaborate plans change beliefs about business hierarchies.

42283 ■ *"Wikinomics: The Sequel" in Business Strategy Review (Vol. 21, Summer 2010, No. 2, pp. 64)*
Pub: Wiley-Blackwell
Description: Ever-optimistic Don Tapscott and Anthony Williams, coauthors of Wikinomics and individually, of a number of other books that study the Internet and its relation to society, are now working on a new book, one for which they're using the Internet to determine its title.

42284 ■ *"Will Work for Equity" in Inc. (March 2008, pp. 50, 52)*
Pub: Gruner & Jahr USA Publishing
Ed: Ryan McCarthy. **Description:** Profile of Dave Graham and his information technology company; Graham built his business by taking equity in client firms rather than charging fees. Four tips to consider before signing a work-for-equity business deal are outlined.

42285 ■ *"Winner: Caparo Group Plc" in Crain's Detroit Business (Vol. 24, March 24, 2008, No. 12, pp. 12)*
Pub: Crain Communications, Inc.
Ed: Brent Snavely. **Description:** London-based Caparo Group plc saw its acquisition of Voestalpine Polynorm as an opportunity to gain a foothold in the North American automotive industry. Caparo was impressed with the company's breadth of manufacturing capabilities and quality systems as well as with the management team.

42286 ■ *"A Wireless Makes 8 Store-In-Store Kiosk Acquisitions" in Wireless News (October 16, 2010)*
Pub: Close-Up Media Inc.
Description: A Wireless, a retailer for Verizon Wireless has acquired eight of Verizon's retail kiosks that are positioned in home appliance and electronics stores.

42287 ■ *"Wirtz Partners With California Liquor Wholesaler To Expand Reach" in Chicago Tribune (December 17, 2008)*
Pub: McClatchy-Tribune Information Services
Ed: Mike Hughlett. **Description:** Young's Market Co. and Wirtz Beverage Group have tentatively agreed to a joint venture that will give both companies a larger reach in the wine and liquor distribution business.

42288 ■ *"With Algoma Steel Gone, Is Stelco Next?" in Globe & Mail (April 16, 2007, pp. B1)*
Pub: CTVglobemedia Publishing Inc.
Ed: Greg Keenan. **Description:** Speculation in Canadian steel industry over possible sale of Stelco Inc. too after the sale of Algoma Steel Inc. to Essar Global Ltd. is discussed.

42289 ■ *Working Together: Why Great Partnerships Succeed*
Pub: HarperBusiness
Ed: Michael D. Eisner with Aaron Cohen. **Price:** $25.99. **Description:** Michael D. Eisner, former CEO of the Walt Disney Company interviews corporate partners from various industries, including Bill and Melinda Gates and Warren Buffet and Charlie Munger. Why certain business partnerships succeed in the corporate world is discussed.

42290 ■ *"Wrigley's a Rich Meal for Mars" in Crain's Chicago Business (Vol. 31, May 5, 2008, No. 18, pp. 2)*
Pub: Crain Communications, Inc.
Ed: Steven R. Strahler. **Description:** Mars Inc. will have to manage wisely in order to make their acquisition of Wm. Wrigley Jr. Co. profitable due to the high selling price of Wrigley which far exceeds the industry norm. Statistical data included.

42291 ■ *"XM and Sirius Satellite Radio Face Up to Their Losses and Decide to Get Hitched" in Globe & Mail (February 20, 2007, pp. B17)*
Pub: CTVglobemedia Publishing Inc.
Ed: Grant Robertson. **Description:** XM Satellite Radio and Sirius Satellite Radio are planning to merge operations, after years of losses. The possible merger could create a $13 billion company.

42292 ■ *"Xstrata's Takeover Bid Comes Up Short in Shareholder's Eyes" in Globe & Mail (March 27, 2007, pp. B16)*
Pub: CTVglobemedia Publishing Inc.
Ed: Andy Hoffman. **Description:** The share holders of LionOre Mining International have expressed dissatisfaction over $4.6 billion take over by Xstrata PLC. Share holders are demanding more prices for share value.

42293 ■ *"The Yahoo Family Tree" in Conde Nast Portfolio (Vol. 2, June 2008, No. 6, pp. 34)*
Pub: Conde Nast Publications
Contact: David Carey, President
Ed: Blaise Zerega. **Description:** Yahoo, founded in 1994 by Stanford students Jerry Yang and David Filo, is still an Internet powerhouse. The company's history is also outlined as well as the reasons in which Microsoft desperately wants to acquire the firm.

42294 ■ *"Yahoo! - Microsoft Pact: Alive Again?" in Barron's (Vol. 89, July 27, 2009, No. 30, pp. 8)*
Pub: Dow Jones & Co., Inc.
Ed: Mark Veverka. **Description:** Yahoo! reported higher than expected earnings in the second quarter of 2009 under CEO Carol Bartz who has yet to articulate her long-term vision and strategy for turning around the company. The media reported that Yahoo! and Microsoft are discussing an advertising-search partnership which should benefit both companies.

42295 ■ *"Zucker Closes Deal on HBC With Sweeter Takeover Offer" in Globe & Mail (January 27, 2006, pp. B1)*
Pub: CTVglobemedia Publishing Inc.
Ed: Marina Strauss; Sinclair Stewart; Jacquie McNish. **Description:** Jerry Zucker, vice-president of InterTech Group Inc., has finalized a deal to buy retail store Hudson Bay Co, for 1.1 billion dollars. The shares will be purchased at a rate of 15.25 dollars per share in an all cash transaction. Complete details of the buyout are discussed.

42296 ■ *"Zucker's HBC Shakeup Imminent" in Globe & Mail (February 20, 2006, pp. B3)*
Pub: CTVglobemedia Publishing Inc.
Ed: Marina Strauss. **Description:** The plans of investor Jerry Zucker to revamp Hudson's Bay Co., upon its acquisition, are presented.

VIDEOCASSETTES/ AUDIOCASSETTES

42297 ■ *Fergi Builds a Business*
Phoenix Learning Group
2349 Chaffee Dr.
Saint Louis, MO 63146-3306
Ph: (314)569-0211
Free: 800-221-1274
Fax: (314)569-2834
URL: http://www.phoenixlearninggroup.com
Released: 1990. **Price:** $400.00. **Description:** The process of forming and building a business is demonstrated. Included are dealing with success, failure, partnerships, corporations, capital and profits. **Availability:** VHS; EJ; 3/4 U; Special order formats.

42298 ■ *Partnership Series*
Excellence in Training Corp.
c/o ICON Training
804 Roosevelt St.
Polk City, IA 50226

Free: 800-609-0479
Co. E-mail: info@icontraining.com
URL: http://www.icontraining.com
Released: 1990. **Price:** $895.00. **Description:** A four-part program designed to build more effective management. **Availability:** VHS; 3/4 U; Special order formats.

42299 ■ *The Price: Update*
Commonwealth Films, Inc.
223 Commonwealth Ave.
Boston, MA 02116
Ph: (617)262-5634
Fax: (617)262-6948
Co. E-mail: info@commonwealthfilms.com
URL: http://www.commonwealthfilms.com
Released: 1989. **Price:** $395.00. **Description:** An updated version of the film on mergers, antitrust violations, and other big business dealings. **Availability:** VHS; 3/4 U.

CONSULTANTS

42300 ■ AB Associates
7380 Sherman Rd.
Chesterland, OH 44026-2050
Ph: (330)672-1219
Contact: Dr. Raj Aggarwal, Principal
Scope: Offers expertise in the areas of banking, capital budgeting, investing in emerging markets, international risk analysis, strategic planning and international accounting, management of foreign exchange and other accounting and financial policies. Additional services include acquisition and merger analysis, the valuation of a proposed purchase and development of appropriate post-merger managerial policies, and the implementation of computer-based receivable and inventory management policies. **Founded:** 1976.

42301 ■ Access Management Corp.
6135 Park S Dr.
Charlotte, NC 28220-2059
Ph: (704)554-9000
Fax: (704)554-0258
Contact: George A. Suter, President
E-mail: gasuter@webserve.net
Scope: Provider of international management services specializing in trade financing (Worldwide Factoring) market development, licensing/technology transfer, and marketing. Experienced in merger/acquisition brokering, trade financing, letter of credit discounting and forfeiting, factoring, equipment financing, and debt recovery. **Founded:** 1984.

42302 ■ AgriCapital Corp.—William Goodbar Agricapital
1410 Broadway, Ste. 1802
New York, NY 10018-5018
Ph: (212)944-9500
Fax: (212)944-9525
Co. E-mail: info@agricapital.com
URL: http://www.agricapital.com
Contact: David J. Repking, Vice President
E-mail: repking@agricapital.com
Scope: Provider of investment banking services for agribusiness clients in the United States and abroad, including financial consulting, debt and equity placements and joint ventures, and mergers and acquisitions. Industries served: Agribusiness and food companies. **Founded:** 1983. **Publications:** "The New Geogolitics of food," 2012; "What formers Can Teach Harvard Business School," 2012; "Seed world"; "Strategic Agribusiness Review," Dec, 2003; "Yield," Jun, 2003; "Feed Management," May, 2002. **Seminars:** Thoughts on Private Equity and Agribusiness, Sep, 2009; Capital Markets and the Crop Input Sector, Oct, 2006; Views on the Crop Protection Industry, Sep, 2005; Mergers and Acquisitions in the US Food and Agribusiness Industry, Sep, 2002.

42303 ■ Air Comm Corp. (ACC)—Air Comm Corporation
3300 Airport Rd.
Boulder, CO 80301
Ph: (303)440-4075
Free: 877-572-6800
Fax: (303)440-6355
Co. E-mail: info@aircommcorp.com
URL: http://www.aircommcorp.com
Contact: Keith Steiner, President
E-mail: ksteiner@aircommcorp.com
Scope: Aviation engineering consultants offering to clients design and FAA approval of aircraft accessories and aircraft modifications, as well as general business planning services, including acquisitions and mergers. **Founded:** 1987.

42304 ■ ALCO Capital Group Inc.
745 5th Ave., Ste. 1506
New York, NY 10151-1504
Ph: (212)751-9150
Free: 800-233-2526
Fax: (212)371-2768
Contact: Julian A. Schwartz, Principal
Scope: Consultants in financially troubled situations, specializing in Chapter 11 rehabilitations, Chapter 7 liquidation interface with the creditors committee, arrange for and provide funding for company rehabilitation; evaluation of company operations and procedures. Expertise includes investments, acquisitions, auctions, and liquidations. **Founded:** 1983.

42305 ■ American Appraisal Associates Inc.—American Appraisal Assoc
411 E Wisconsin Ave., Ste. 1900
Milwaukee, WI 53202-4466
Ph: (414)271-7240
Free: 800-558-8650
Co. E-mail: moreinfo@american-appraisal.com
URL: http://www.american-appraisal.com
Contact: Joseph P. Zvesper, President
Scope: Performs valuations of business enterprises and their securities for tax-related purposes, estate, gift and income taxes, mergers and acquisitions including fairness opinions, and ESOPs. **Founded:** 1896. **Publications:** "Estimation of Hospital Real Property Values for Ad Valorem Tax Purposes"; "Developing Discount Rates in a Global Environment"; "Discount Rates for Foreign Investments"; "Getting a Grip on Foreign Discount Rates".

42306 ■ Aquinas Group L.L.P.
1733 Green Valley Rd., Ste. 100
Havertown, PA 19083-2520
Ph: (610)449-2290
Contact: Charles P. Steckel, Director
Scope: Offers business, financial and management consulting services. Activities include corporate planning and finance, production and marketing, management systems, organization development, merger and acquisition, startup and venture capital. Serves private industries as well as government agencies. Investment banking services. **Founded:** 1960. **Seminars:** Productivity and Profit Improvement; Business Planning and Financing; Operational Auditing.

42307 ■ ARDITO Information & Research Inc.
1019 Sedwick Dr., Ste. G
Wilmington, DE 19803
Ph: (302)479-5373
Free: 800-836-9068
Fax: (302)479-5375
Co. E-mail: sardito@ardito.com
Contact: Stephanie C. Ardito, President
E-mail: sardito@ardito.com
Scope: A full-service information and research firm. Provides information in areas of financial data, published research, demographic data, industry-specific publications, competitor data, marketing and sales trends, new product developments, government relations, bibliographies. Industries served are pharmaceutical, health, publishing, and environment, and business. **Founded:** 1990. **Publications:** "The Swine flu pandemic: Authoritative information versus community gossip," Searcher, Oct, 2009; "The Medical blogosphere: How social networking platforms are changing medical searching," Searcher, May, 2009; "Social Networking and Video Web Sites: MySpace and YouTube Meet the Copyright Cops," Searcher, May, 2007; "Copyright Clearance Center raises transactional fees," Information Today, Jul, 2004.

42308 ■ The Argus Group
5950 Canoga Ave., Ste. 515
Woodland Hills, CA 91367
Ph: (818)990-7200
Free: 800-339-9910
Fax: (818)990-7909
Co. E-mail: cbercy@arguslending.com
URL: http://www.arguslending.com
Contact: Charles E. Bercy, President
E-mail: cbercy@arguslending.com
Scope: Provider of asset based real estate loans. It offers construction and rehabilitation services for multi-family residential, commercial, and industrial properties. **Founded:** 1990.

42309 ■ Associated Management Systems Inc.
1000 Elwell Ct., Ste. 234
Palo Alto, CA 94303-4306
Ph: (650)852-9041
Fax: (650)967-9992
Co. E-mail: amsn@rcn.com
Contact: M. A. Quraishi, President
Scope: The firm's entrepreneurial and professional expertise includes corporate management, investment banking, finance, strategic planning, risk evaluation, due diligence studies and management audits. Also assists with mergers and acquisitions, and provides management for turnaround situations. Undertakes project packaging, plant relocations, capital restructuring and funding. Industries served: Agriculture, real estate, insurance, computers, communications, retail/wholesale, electronics/instruments, paper/printing, food processing, furniture/home products, travel, transportation, recreation, heavy industry, pharmaceuticals, and government agencies. **Founded:** 1966.

42310 ■ Associated Marketers
10 E Hartshorn Dr.
Short Hills, NJ 07078
Ph: (973)376-3835
Contact: Lauren K. Hagaman, President
Scope: Consulting services limited to area of mergers and acquisitions through a network of associates. Active in serving manufacturing, distributing and service businesses seeking new corporate homes, acquiring additional businesses, or divesting divisions or subsidiaries. Fields served include appliances, house wares, advertising, industrial, publishing, building materials, printing and graphic arts, banking, insurance, apparel and textiles, automotive, transportation, home furnishings, food and confectionery products, leisure products, mail order, natural resources, plastics, packaging, and service businesses and retailing. **Founded:** 1959.

42311 ■ Atlantic Management Company Inc.
875 Greenland Rd., Orchard Pk., Ste. A12
Portsmouth, NH 03801-7124
Ph: (603)436-8009
Fax: (603)427-0146
Co. E-mail: amc@atlantic-mgmt.com
URL: http://www.atlantic-mgmt.com
Contact: John P. Murphy, President
E-mail: jpm@atlantic-mgmt.com
Scope: Offers business valuation services in connection with employee stock ownership plans, fairness opinions, management buyouts, mergers and acquisitions, divorce, stockholder disputes, estate planning and estate and gift tax. Additional ESOP advisory services include feasibility studies, equity allocations, and financing proposals. Serves private industries as well as government agencies. **Founded:** 1968. **Publications:** "Business Succession Strategies," 2006; "Selling a Company," 2006; "Case Study on Business Valuation and Industry Intelligence," 2006; "Lock, Stock, and Barrel: A Well Connected Hedge Firm Buys Bushmaster Firearms," Maine biz, May, 2006; "Buying A Company," 2006; "ESOP Questions & Answers," 2006; "Tips for Lawyers When Working with Appraisers," New Hampshire Bar Review, Oct, 2005; "A Win All Around," Worcester Telegram and Gazette, Mar, 2005. **Seminars:** Current Techniques For Successful Business Transition, Keeley the Katerer Banquet Center, Sep, 2009; Maximizing the Value of Your ESOP in Challenging Times, Mar, 2009; Business Succession Planning & ESOPs - Creating a Buyer for the Closely-Held Company, Sep, 2008;

Business Valuation II, Boston Tax Institute, Jun, 2008; Business Valuation I, Boston Tax Institute, Jun, 2008; Now That You've Built It, What Do You Want To Do With It?, May, 2008; Human Resource and Fiduciary Issues for New and Established ESOPs, Mar, 2008; Now That You've Built It; Feb, 2008; A Journey to Employee Ownership: The Future Is In Your Hands, Oct, 2007; Advanced Limited Liability Issues, Jun, 2007.

42312 ■ Bain and Company Inc.
131 Dartmouth St.
Boston, MA 02116-5134
Ph: (617)572-2000
Fax: (617)572-2427
Co. E-mail: cheryl.krauss@bain.com
URL: http://www.bain.com
Contact: Orit Gadiesh, Chairman of the Board
Scope: Management consulting firm which focuses on helping clients improve their financial performance. Specifically, the firm operates in these areas: corporate and business unit strategy, manufacturing, mergers and acquisitions, value managed relationships, information technology, retailing, customer base management and retention, distribution and logistics, high technology, cost reduction, consumer marketing, change management and healthcare. Client base represents virtually all economic sectors manufacturing, wholesaling, retailing, transportation and services. **Founded:** 1973. **Publications:** "Individual philanthropy lags in India and China"; "Profit from the core: A return to growth in turbulent times," 2010; "Management Tools 2009: An Executive's Guide," 2009; "The Breakthrough Imperative: How the Best Managers Get Outstanding Results," Harper Collins Publishers, 2008; "Memo to the CEO: Lessons from Private Equity Any Company Can Use," Harvard Business Press, 2008; "Unstoppable: Finding Hidden Assets to Renew the Core and Fuel Profitable Growth," Harvard Business School Press, 2007; "Management Tools 2007: An Executive's Guide," 2007; "Growth in a slower-growth China"; "Falling profits signal radical changes for retail banks"; "Private equity firms sharpen their focus"; "Private equity's new landscape"; "The green edge: Why carbon competitiveness matter"; "After easy money: Managing in a new era"; "Managing IT to win in the recovery". **Seminars:** Internship intro seminar.

42313 ■ Jacalyn E. S. Bennett & Co.
45 Water St.
Newburyport, MA 01950
Ph: (978)462-1966
Fax: (978)463-2062
Co. E-mail: sales@bennettcompany.com
URL: http://www.bennettcompany.com
Contact: Jacalyn E. S. Bennett, President
Scope: Developed a multitude of textile blends, including ecologically friendly fabrics, across all relevant fibers, in both knits and woven's, in silks, cottons and synthetics. Designed more than 60, 000 styles across all foundation, lingerie, sleepwear and related product categories. **Founded:** 1989.

42314 ■ Biomedical Management Resources (BMR)
PO Box 521125
Salt Lake City, UT 84152-1125
Ph: (801)272-4668
Fax: (801)277-3290
Co. E-mail: SeniorManagement@BiomedicalManagement.com
URL: http://www.biomedicalmanagement.com
Contact: Ping Fong, Jr., President
E-mail: pingfong@biomedicalmanagement.com
Scope: Provides business development, interim management, and executive search services. Assists companies in strategic alliances, corporate partnering, business acquisition. Demonstrated success in identifying recruiting, and placing key managers in difficult to hire positions. **Founded:** 1993.

42315 ■ Business Brokers Hawaii L.L.C. (BBH)
3230 Pikai Way
Kihei, HI 96753
Ph: (808)879-8833
Free: 866-239-1567
Fax: (808)879-5966
URL: http://www.business-brokers.com
Contact: Milton Docktor, Chief Executive Officer
E-mail: md@business-brokers.com
Scope: Offers buying or selling existing businesses, creation of new businesses, business evaluation and appraisal, assistance to clients on expansion and mergers, consultation with owners of businesses in trouble, and consultation on Unites States, Japan and Chinese commerce. **Founded:** 1983. **Seminars:** How to Start Your Own Business; How to Make a Sick Business Well Again; How to do Fiscal Forecasting and Cash Flow Projections.

42316 ■ The Business Place Ltd.
10 Kingsbridge Garden Cir., Ste. 506
Mississauga, ON, Canada L5R 3K6
Ph: (905)890-9245
Fax: (905)890-3229
Co. E-mail: gary.landa@thebusinessplace.com
URL: http://www.thebusinessplace.com
Contact: Gary R. Landa, President
E-mail: gary.landa@thebusinessplace.com
Scope: Assists in the buying and selling of businesses, arranging bank financing, venture capital loans/investments, mergers and acquisitions. **Founded:** 1986. **Publications:** "Did you find the right business for sale Part II," Feb, 2009; "Did you find the right business," Feb, 2009; "Buying a business what do you look for when looking at financial statements," Feb, 2009; "Business brokers how do you know if you found the right business broker," Feb, 2009; "Businesses how do you determine if you found the right one," Feb, 2009; "Start up businesses how do you value them when you are looking for equity," Feb, 2009; "Business locations time to move intone space, " Feb, 2009; Business brokers are they helpful," Feb, 2009.

42317 ■ Business Team
1901 S Bascom Ave., Ste. 400
Campbell, CA 95008
Ph: (408)246-1102
Fax: (408)246-2219
Co. E-mail: sanjose@business-team.com
URL: http://www.business-team.com
Contact: William L. Kramer, Vice President
Scope: Business consulting services offered to companies looking for buyers. Specializes in mergers and acquisitions, business brokerage, and valuations. **Founded:** 1980. **Seminars:** Business Valuation Enhancing the Value of Your Company.

42318 ■ The Change Agents
145 Columbia Ave.
Holland, MI 49423-2978
Ph: (616)392-5564
Contact: William G. Garlough, Managing Director
Scope: Provider of consulting services related to mergers, acquisitions and divestitures. Services offered include: Assisting acquiring companies in establishing and managing effective acquisition programs; representing sellers in the sale of their companies, and bringing buyers and sellers together. Additional consulting services include: Advising on the structure of leveraged buy-outs; mediating sales between partners or in family succession; business valuations; due diligence examination of the marketing function; post-acquisition integration advice; and corporate strategy and planning. **Founded:** 1983.

42319 ■ Diego Chevere & Co.
Metro Office Pk.
Pueblo Viejo, PR 00920
Ph: (787)774-9595
Fax: (787)774-9566
Co. E-mail: dcco@coqui.net
Contact: Jose G. de Cordova Figueroa, Principal
Scope: Business consultants offering assistance with financial projections, strategic business planning, mergers, reorganizations, EDP system design and cash management. Serves private industries as well as government agencies. **Founded:** 1983. **Seminars:** EDP System Development; Loan Package Preparation.

42320 ■ Cole, Warren and Long Inc. (CWL)
2 Penn Center Plz., Ste. 312
Philadelphia, PA 19102
Ph: (215)563-0701
Free: 800-394-8517
Fax: (215)563-2907
Co. E-mail: cwlserch@cwl-inc.com
URL: http://www.cwl-inc.com
Contact: Ronald J. Cole, President
E-mail: rcole@cwl-inc.com
Scope: Offers management guidance to commercial, industrial, and government organizations specializing in the areas of organization studies, executive searches, acquisitions and mergers, compensation programs, audits, and improvement seminars. Conducts marketing, economic, and systems studies counsels on profit improvement, manpower control, operations, and systems integration. **Founded:** 1970.

42321 ■ Consortium House Co.
15 Bostan Rd.
Malden on Hudson, NY 12453
Ph: (845)246-2336
Fax: (845)246-2338
Contact: Gene Schwartz, President
Scope: Offers its services to book, periodical, multimedia, and electronic publishers. Specializes in web strategies and in education, training, professional and general trade markets. Advises in financial and business development, marketing, new product development, fulfillment and distribution, venture investment, mergers and acquisitions, literary and publishing properties, project management and operating systems troubleshooting. **Founded:** 1978. **Publications:** "From Eyeballs to I Balls: Reaching the Reader," Foreword Magazine, Jan, 2001; "Need to Know Guide to Books on Demand," Foreword Magazine, Jun, 2000; "Setting Industry-Wide Distribution Standards," Small Press, Jan, 1997. **Seminars:** Has presented Electronic Publishing; Print on Demand; Money and Publishing; Managing Profitability and Strategic and Business Plan Development.

42322 ■ The Consulting Firm Inc.
64 Sierra Ct., Ste. 1200
Old Bridge, NJ 08857-3050
Ph: (732)679-5520
Fax: (732)679-9451
Co. E-mail: efields128@aol.com
URL: http://www.edfields.com
Contact: Edward Fields, President
E-mail: efields128@aol.com
Scope: Offers acquisition and venture investment services including search, evaluation, negotiation, and financing. Also advises on product, profit center evaluation, and personnel benefits. Firm assists companies with serious business problems and those whose performance should be much better. Serves all industries. **Founded:** 1976. **Publications:** "The Essentials of Finance and Accounting for Non-Financial Managers," 2002.

42323 ■ CorDev Financial Inc.
Stanford Financial Sq., 2600 El Camino Real
2600 El Camino Real, Ste. 400
Palo Alto, CA 94306-1705
Ph: (650)493-9111
Fax: (650)493-9115
Co. E-mail: robert@cordevfinancial.com
URL: http://www.cordevfinancial.com
Contact: Robert Patton Oliver, Chief Executive Officer
E-mail: robert@cordevfinancial.com
Scope: Specializes in corporate mergers and acquisitions for small to mid sized companies and CEO consulting. **Founded:** 1970.

42324 ■ Corporate Growth Assistance Ltd.
1 Benvenuto Pl., Ste. 420
Toronto, ON, Canada M4V 2L1
Ph: (416)222-7772
Fax: (416)222-6091
Co. E-mail: millard@corporategrowth.ca
URL: http://www.corporategrowthassistance.com
Contact: Millard S. Roth, Manager
E-mail: millard@corporategrowth.ca
Scope: Represents extensive experience in facilitating profitable growth and liquidity and will deliver: A broad network of contacts providing access to investment options, funding, and business development opportunities, the talent necessary to provide solid strategic and operating guidance, the experience to

generate high rates of return while effectively managing challenging situations, hands on professionalism. A commitment to execution so as to maximize profit, market share and team building. Client involvement has included: computerized car valuation database management for the insurance industry; dimensional art reproduction; dining and bedroom furniture manufacturing; employee and family assistance programs. **Founded:** 1967. **Seminars:** Expansion Equity And Management Engineering.

42325 ■ James W. Davidson Company Inc.
23 Forest View Rd.
Wallingford, PA 19086
Ph: (610)566-1462
Co. E-mail: jwdmsd@comcast.net
Contact: James W. Davidson, President
E-mail: jwdmsd@comcast.net
Scope: Offers counsel to clients to improve business strategy, organization, controls, management effectiveness and profits. Provides planning, problem-analysis and implementation assistance. Also performs thorough, in-depth executive recruiting and acquisition and divestment search and analysis. Experienced with large and small manufacturing and service companies, including new ventures. **Founded:** 1973.

42326 ■ DeVries & Company Inc.
800 W 47th St.
Kansas City, MO 64112
Ph: (816)756-0055
Fax: (816)756-0061
Contact: Robert J. de Vries, President
Scope: Investment banking/financial consulting firm which helps companies solve financial problems and achieve growth and diversification goals. Helps established companies raise capital and assists new and developing companies secure venture capital and create public markets for their stocks. Provides confidential services to companies who want to sell or merge, aids companies in acquiring other companies, helps individuals and companies structure and negotiate leveraged buyouts, provides financial guidance, shapes business strategy and develops operating and financial strategies. Also performs business valuations for estate and gift tax and ESOPS. Renders fairness opinions and expert witness services. **Founded:** 1984.

42327 ■ Dorn & Associates Inc.
8506 Bass Lake Rd.
Minneapolis, MN 55428-5304
Ph: (763)533-7689
Fax: (763)533-1143
Contact: John L. Dorn, President
Scope: Services include accounting, marketing, employment partnership, new doctor agreements, personnel issues and human resources assessment, practice management, practice merger acquisition sale and liquidation, practice surveys and valuation, staff development and training. **Founded:** 2000.

42328 ■ Executive Consultants Inc.
78 Carlton Dr. NE
Atlanta, GA 30342-3202
Ph: (404)255-4801
Fax: (404)255-4801
Contact: Stuart Schwarzschild, President
Scope: Offers mergers and acquisition consulting, estate planning, pension planning, profit sharing advice, and insurance planning services. **Founded:** 2000.

42329 ■ Fowler, Anthony & Co.
20 Walnut St.
Wellesley, MA 02481
Ph: (781)237-4201
Fax: (781)237-7718
Contact: John A. Quagliaroli, President
E-mail: jquagliaroli@mediaone.net
Scope: Offers consulting services and direct investment into small businesses in mergers and acquisitions, capital financing and venture capital. Active with the following industries: Communications, computer related, consumer, distribution, electronic components and instrumentation, multimedia, on-line database/publishing, industrial products and equipment, food processing, multimedia, health care services, medical/health related and publishing. **Founded:** 1976.

42330 ■ Frankel and Topche P.C.
1700 Galloping Hill Rd.
Kenilworth, NJ 07033
Ph: (908)298-7700
Fax: (908)298-7701
Co. E-mail: info@frankelandtopche.com
URL: http://www.frankelandtopche.com
Contact: Mark J. Tikkanen, Director
E-mail: mtikkanen@frankelandtopche.com
Scope: Offers financial consulting for closely held businesses. Assists in mergers and acquisitions, tax planning, strategic business planning, family succession planning, accounting, auditing, and obtaining financing. The firm serves small businesses in the service, retail, wholesale, and manufacturing industries. Specializes in real estate, lumber and building materials, and service businesses. **Founded:** 1990. **Seminars:** Annual Tax Seminar.

42331 ■ Haas Wheat & Partners L.P.
300 Crescent Ct., Ste. 1700
Dallas, TX 75201-1876
Ph: (214)871-8300
Fax: (214)871-8357
Co. E-mail: info@haaswheat.com
Contact: Robert B. Haas, Chairman of the Board
Scope: Business consulting firm offering expertise with mergers and acquisitions and financial investment in the United States. **Founded:** 1992.

42332 ■ Jefferies Broadview
520 Madison Ave., 10th Fl.
New York, NY 10022
Ph: (212)284-2300
Fax: (212)284-8101
Co. E-mail: info@jefferiesbroadview.com
URL: http://www.jefferies.com
Contact: Alec L. Ellison, President
E-mail: aellison@jefferies.com
Scope: A technology investment banking group, is an advisor in mergers and acquisitions to technology companies, private equity investors, media, health care technology and communications industries. **Founded:** 1973.

42333 ■ Johnson, Butler & Co. (JBC)
2600 Mission St., Ste. 206
San Marino, CA 91108
Ph: (626)799-5200
Fax: (626)799-5274
Contact: Bruce C. Juell, Chief Executive Officer
E-mail: bcj@johnsonbutler.com
Scope: Serves as a consultant and intermediary in merger-acquisition work, representing either buyer or seller. Performs acquisition searches for corporate buyers. Arranges corporate divestitures, management buyouts, joint ventures and financing. Other services include business valuations and strategic planning. Experienced in numerous industries including industrial product manufacturing, consumer goods manufacturing, distribution in all fields, hospitality industry services and life sciences. **Founded:** 1978.

42334 ■ KFA Services
4704 Pointes Dr., Ste. 103
Mukilteo, WA 98275-6074
Ph: (425)493-8020
Fax: (425)745-6860
Contact: Michael S. Katz, Owner
Scope: Offers consulting services in financial, accounting, and economic analysis including business valuations, financial projections and feasibility analysis, cost accounting, economic loss determination, mergers and acquisitions, and business policy and planning assistance. Also provides litigation support and construction claims analysis. Serves private industries as well as government agencies. **Founded:** 1983. **Seminars:** Economic Feasibility Analysis; The Use of Current Value Accounting for Measuring Port Profitability; Damages for Construction Delays: Analyzing Contractor Claims for Home Office Overhead Costs.

42335 ■ Kibel Green Inc. (KGI)
2001 Wilshire Blvd., Ste. 420
Santa Monica, CA 90403
Ph: (310)829-0255
Free: 866-875-0255
Fax: (310)453-6324
Co. E-mail: info@kginc.com
URL: http://www.kibelgreen.com
Contact: Steven J. Green, President
E-mail: sgreen@kginc.com
Scope: Provider of services in turnaround and crisis management, value creation and investment banking. Serves manufacturing, service, technology, retail, distribution and real estate industries. **Founded:** 1984. **Publications:** "Avoiding the Lose-Lose Paradigm," Apr, 2012; "Kibel Green Hits a Home Run for Defense Manufacturer," Feb, 2012; "Kibel Green Advises on $320M Restructuring," Dec, 2011; "Kibel Green helps Arlie & Co. Beat-the-Clock," Aug, 2011; "Where's My Bail Out? - Restructuring Debts and Eliminating Personal Guarantees," Jul, 2011; "Kibel Green Completes $191M Real Estate Restructuring ," Jun, 2011; " Working Wonders for a Small Equipment Distributor," Apr, 2011; "The 2010 Letter - Reflections from the President," Feb, 2011; "Winning the Loan Restructuring Battle," Aug, 2010; "Show Me the Money," May, 2010; "Shopping Center Owners Act Now or Lose Your Shirt," Apr, 2009; "Kibel Green Helps Save Media Company," Mar, 2009; "The Role of the Chief Restructuring Officer," Jan, 2009; "The Growth Paradox Effectively Resizing to Drive Profits," Dec, 2008. **Special Services:** The Kibel Green System™.

42336 ■ L.G. Kranick & Associates
1517 W Pierce St.
Milwaukee, WI 53204-1236
Ph: (414)671-3636
Fax: (414)671-4264
Contact: Thomas L. Kranick, President
Scope: Consulting services includes economic analysis of industry trends and long-range planning; market and product surveys and analysis; mergers and acquisitions; manufacturing methods and systems; organization structure and development; and interim management. **Founded:** 1957.

42337 ■ Lyons Solutions L.L.C.
4 St. Mary's Ln.
Norwalk, CT 06851
Ph: (203)642-4141
Co. E-mail: jlyons@lyonssolutions.com
URL: http://www.lyonssolutions.com
Contact: Jack Lyons, President
E-mail: jlyons@lyonssolutions.com
Scope: Strategic financial advisers to owners of health care, management consulting, marketing communications, technology and professional services firms. **Founded:** 1984. **Publications:** "Constant Progress: Keep Your Eye on the Ball," 2012; "Economic Outlook:An Interview with Alan Beaulieu," 2012; "Smart Planning vs. Gambling Your Net Worth," 2011; "It's Business Planning Time," 2011; "Business Exit: Options and Timing," 2011; "It's Never Too Early to Fix Your Company," 2011; "Perspectives From a Business Seller:An Interview with Mike Salvagno," 2011; "Using Acquisitions to Eliminate a Business Owner's Value Gap," 2011. **Seminars:** How to Become More Attractive to a Buyer, 2007; The Nuts and Bolts of M&A Hardware for Buyers and Sellers, 2007; Mind Your M&A's: Track the Trends, Find the Funding and Seal the Deal, 2006; Run It Like You Are Going to Sell It!, 2006; M&A 2006: Who's Buying, What's Selling and Why, 2006; Mergers and Acquisitions, 2006.

42338 ■ M. Richler & Associates Ltd.
85 Skymark Dr., Ste. 2603
North York, ON, Canada M2H 3P2
Ph: (416)491-5264
Contact: Mitchell M. Richler, President
E-mail: mitchrichler@aol.com
Scope: A general management consulting firm specializing in acquisitions and mergers, costing and pricing, office layout design and management, production management and taxation, particularly for small businesses. Industries served: manufacturing, retail, wholesale, import/export, design services, and government agencies. **Founded:** 1951. **Seminars:**

Keeping the Cottage in the Family; Maximizing Capital Gains Exemption; Minimizing Probate Fees; Plant Reorganization; Departmental Scheduling.

42339 ■ James V. McTevia & Associates
2401 PGA Blvd., Ste. 196
Palm Beach Gardens, FL 33410
Ph: (561)691-6270
Co. E-mail: jmctevia@mcteviallc.com
URL: http://www.mcteviallc.com
Contact: Dennis Hoyt, President
Scope: Specializes in reorganization programs for businesses with serious financial problems. Services include debt restructuring, bankruptcy trustees, liquidations, management reorganization and acquisitions and mergers. Serves private industries as well as government agencies. **Founded:** 1960. **Publications:** "Survival in The Face of Change," Jun, 2006; "Tips for Picking An Outside Adviser," Sep, 2005; "Out-of Court Problem Solving and Restructuring: Guide to a Successful Outcome," May, 2005; "Small Business: The Basics of Business Problem Solving," Mar, 2005; "Annual Business Check," Jan, 2005; "When Bad Things Happen To Good Family Businesses," Business Direct Weekly, Dec, 2001. **Seminars:** Alternative Methods of Financing for Underperforming Companies, Jun, 2009; Preventing or Structuring a Reorganization without Court Supervision, May, 2008; Business and Professions in Transition - Unlocking Your Business Potential, Jun, 2007; Professions in Transition, Oct, 2007; Preventing or Structuring a Reorganization without Court Supervision, Novi, Jun, 2006; Guiding the Customer in Preventing or Structuring a Reorganization Without Court Supervision, Atlanta, Jun, 2005.

42340 ■ Mertz Associates Inc.
N1629 County Road P
Rubicon, WI 53078
Ph: (262)523-4200
Fax: (262)523-4202
Co. E-mail: mertz@mertz.com
URL: http://www.mertz.com
Contact: Linda Mertz, Chief Executive Officer
E-mail: l.mertz@mertz.com
Scope: A merger and acquisition consulting firm representing either dedicated buyers or sellers of companies across the U.S. Clients range from small privately held companies to large public companies in all industries. **Publications:** "Why Successful Companies are Launching Acquisition Searches Now"; "On the Block"; "Selling Troubled Divisions and Companies"; "Don't Fear the D Word"; "M and A Multiples: A Key to Value Or a Distraction"; "Savvy CPA Levels the Playing Field"; "M and A Trends Strategic Focus Drives Success".

42341 ■ MRCworldwide
3020 Old Ranch Pky., 3rd Fl.
Seal Beach, CA 90740
Ph: (562)799-5510
Fax: (562)799-5594
Co. E-mail: jgollihugh@mrcworldwide.com
URL: http://www.mrcworldwide.com
Contact: Ted Johnston, Director
E-mail: tjohnston@mrcworldwide.com
Scope: Specializes in mergers and acquisitions, divestitures, strategic planning, executive leadership, product strategy, valuation, ESOPs, venture capital, and management development. Serves industries in graphic arts, printing, manufacturing, distribution, electronics, service, and high-technology and investment banking advisory services. **Founded:** 1976. **Seminars:** Executive Leadership; Integration; Strategic Planning; Valuation; Mergers and Acquisitions.

42342 ■ New Century Consultants
1600 2nd St.
Gulfport, MS 39501-2135
Ph: (228)864-3999
Fax: (228)868-4960
Contact: Stephen J. Bosarge, Principal
E-mail: new-century@cwix.com
Scope: Provider of management consulting and strategies in public relations, communications, marketing, and advertising. Specializes in consulting services to the music, entertainment and casino industries. Recent experience with new business start-ups and new business acquisitions. Serves private industries as well as government agencies. Training, Executive Search. **Founded:** 1987. **Seminars:** Communicating With Power; Writing With Power; Communicating With Employees; Communicating With the Customer; Customer Service Communications; Creativity and Communications.

42343 ■ Nimark Group Inc.
238 Osborne Rd.
Harrison, NY 10528
Ph: (914)967-7600
Contact: Leonard Lipsky, President
Scope: Specializes in mergers, acquisitions, divestiture analysis and negotiation for middle market companies. Services include business valuations. Also provides expertise in crisis management. **Founded:** 1979. **Seminars:** How to Sell Your Business for the Most Profit.

42344 ■ The Rehmann Group
5800 Gratiot Rd., Ste. 201
Saginaw, MI 48638
Ph: (989)799-9580
Free: 866-799-9580
Fax: (989)799-0227
Co. E-mail: info@rehmann.com
URL: http://www.rehmann.com
Contact: Steven D. Kelly, Chief Executive Officer
E-mail: skelly@rehmann.com
Scope: Offers general business services that include profit enhancement consulting, investigative services (Kerby Bailey), assistance in preparation of a business plan, aid in obtaining financing, employee benefit plan analysis, systems counseling, incentive plans, cash management, marketing plans and research, as well as business valuations (litigation support) and mergers and acquisitions. Specializing in services for health care, manufacturing and governmental units. **Founded:** 1941. **Publications:** "Manufacturing Monitor "; "Bwg Magazine"; "Bwd Magazine".

42345 ■ Robbinex Inc.
41 Stuart St.
Hamilton, ON, Canada L8L 1B5
Ph: (905)523-7510
Free: 888-762-2463
Fax: (905)523-4998
Co. E-mail: robbinex@robbinex.com
URL: http://www.robbinex.com
Contact: Leo Santi, Director
E-mail: leo@robbinex.com
Scope: Business consultants specializing in the merger and acquisition area and financial planning for small to medium size companies. Other services include business financing, crisis management, acquisition search, business valuations, joint ventures and venture capital, resolution of partnership problems, implementation of franchise programs, and general assistance in site selection. **Founded:** 1974. **Seminars:** Creating Transitional Strategies; How to Start a Small Business; Growing Through Acquisition: How to Buy a Business; How to Successfully Manage Medium to Small Businesses; Expansion Through Acquisition; Growth Through Franchising; How to Borrow Money from a Bank; Syndicating Equity; Global Expansion: Are You Missing the Boat; Business succession planning: What's the hurry. **Special Services:** Robbinex®.

42346 ■ Sam Rosenbaum & Co.
419 Northfield Ave.
West Orange, NJ 07052-3091
Ph: (973)736-2323
Contact: Samuel Rosenbaum, President
Scope: Specializes in mergers, acquisitions, and divestitures and also in marketing. **Founded:** 1980.

42347 ■ Siebrand-Wilton Associates Inc.
PO Box 369
Marlboro, NJ 07746-0369
Ph: (732)917-0239
Fax: (732)972-0214
Co. E-mail: clientsvcs@s-wa.com
URL: http://www.s-wa.com
Contact: John S. Sturges, President
E-mail: bencomp@s-wa.com
Scope: Assesses, plans and implements human resources aspects of mergers and acquisitions. Offers human resources consulting in compensation and benefit plan design, mergers and acquisitions (HR aspects), business ethics assessment and development, editing, writing and association management services, and contract professionals and interim executives. **Founded:** 1986. **Publications:** "Should Government or Business Try to Save Medicare," HR News; "Executive Temping," HR Horizons; "When is an Employee Truly an Employee," HR Magazine; "Examining Your Insurance Carrier," HR Magazine.

42348 ■ Stalley Associates Inc.—Rodney E. Stalley & Associates Inc.
10635 James Cir.
Minneapolis, MN 55431-4157
Ph: (952)888-0617
Contact: Rodney E. Stalley, President
E-mail: rstalley@stalley.com
Scope: Advises management of companies in the areas of finance, administrative and general management, corporate objectives, policies and procedures, and management and organization audits. Firm has developed a particular expertise in advising management of young and growing companies. Advises in strategic planning, capital planning and financing strategies, securing private and public investment capital, establishing strategic alliances, management and staff organizational restructuring, working with board of directors, shareholders and serving as chief financial officer and chief operations officer on a contract basis. **Founded:** 1978. **Publications:** "Knowledge: The Key to Business Success"; "The Board of Directors: A Ceo's Source for Advice, Insight and Support"; "Controlling the Audit Expense".

42349 ■ Stockton Bates L.L.P.
1617 JFK Blvd., Ste. 1005
Philadelphia, PA 19103-1825
Ph: (215)241-7500
Fax: (215)567-3813
Co. E-mail: info@stocktonbates.com
URL: http://www.stocktonbates.com/
Contact: Nick Andreola, Manager
E-mail: nandreola@stocktonbates.com
URL(s): www.cliftoncpa.com. **Scope:** Business consultants whose wide-ranging services include operational audits, mergers and acquisitions expertise, litigation support, and computer hardware and software consulting. Industries served: manufacturing, construction, services, banking, retail and wholesale, and government agencies. **Founded:** 1897. **Telecommunication Services:** contact@cliftoncpa.com.

42350 ■ Throne & Co.
49 N Main St.
Stewartstown, PA 17363-4030
Ph: (717)993-3201
Contact: James P. Throne, Partner
E-mail: jthrone@throneco.com
Scope: Business consultants, specializing in mergers and acquisitions with service specialization in leveraged buyouts, foreign investors, joint ventures, divestitures, marketing and licensing. Consulting also in negotiations, evaluations and structuring. **Founded:** 1980. **Seminars:** How to maximize the value of your business and exit on your own terms.

42351 ■ Value Creation Group Inc.
7820 Scotia Dr., Ste. 2000
Dallas, TX 75248-3115
Ph: (972)980-7407
Fax: (972)980-4619
Co. E-mail: john.antos@valuecreationgroup.com
URL: http://www.valuecreationgroup.com
Contact: John Antos, Chief Executive Officer
E-mail: john.antos@valuecreationgroup.com
Scope: General business experts offering predictive strategic planning, Activity Based Costing ABC, Activity Based Management ABM, mergers and acquisitions, outsourcing, re engineering, process management, web enabling technology, bench marking, installation of financial systems, executive search, training, teams, activity based budgeting, operational auditing, feature costing. Industries served financial services, food, health care, insurance, manufacturing, electronics, real estate, consumer products, nonprofit, telecommunication, oil, service, data processing, hotel and resort and government agen-

cies. **Founded:** 1984. **Publications:** "Handbook of Process Management Based Predictive Accounting," Alcpa 2002; "Cost Management for Today's Manufacturing Environment and Activity Based Management for Service Environments, Government Entities and Nonprofit Organizations"; "Risks and Opportunities in International Finance and Treasury"; "Driving Value Using Activity Based Budgeting"; "Process Based Accounting Leveraging Processes to Predict Results"; "Handbook of Supply Chain Management"; "Economic Value Management Applications and Techniques"; "The Change Handbook": "Group Methods for Creating the Future"; "Why Value Management and Performance Measurement Through U.S. Binoculars," Journal of Strategic Performance Measurement; "Real Options, Intangibles Measurement and the Benefits of Human Capital Investment to Power the Organization," Journal of Strategic Performance Measurement. **Seminars:** Activity Based Management; Predictive Accounting; Performance measures; ABM for Manufacturing; ABM for Service Organizations; Finance and Accounting for Non-Financial Executives; Return on Investment/Capital Expenditure Evaluation; Planning and Cost Control; The Next Step Intermediate Finance and Accounting for Non-financial Managers; Activity-Based Budgeting; Friendly Finance for Fund Raisers; Strategic Outsourcing. **Telecommunication Services:** assistu@valuecreationgroup.com; consultu@valuecreationgroup.com.

42352 ■ Mark Vanderstelt
9831 Gulfstream Ct.
Fishers, IN 46037
Ph: (317)576-9328
Fax: (317)576-9328
Contact: Mark Vanderstelt, Owner
Scope: Consulting services include financial planning and analysis, inventory control, cash management, return on investment, budgeting, pricing, system design and analysis, mergers and acquisitions, feasibility studies, data processing, cost systems and controls, and performance measurement. Also performs operational and financial reviews. **Founded:** 1985.

42353 ■ Vencon Management Inc. (VMI)
65 W 55th St.
New York, NY 10019
Ph: (212)581-8787
Fax: (208)955-5165
Co. E-mail: vencon@att.net
URL: http://www.venconinc.com
Contact: Irvin Barash, President
Scope: Venture capital firm and management consultants to corporations and entrepreneurs. Specializes in the areas of mergers and acquisitions evaluation and negotiation, and the preparation of marketing and business plans. Assists small or new businesses in expansion plans and financing. Also involved in new enterprise planning with industry and communities for rural economic analysis. Industries served: nanotechnology, photonics, optics, environment, semiconductor, electronics, chemicals, alternative energy, and health. **Founded:** 1973. **Seminars:** Heegaard Knot Diagrams, Sep, 2009; Issues in finite Approximation, Oct, 2009.

42354 ■ Wabash Equity Group
5460 W 84th St.
Indianapolis, IN 46268-1523
Ph: (317)579-6698
Fax: (317)228-1142
Contact: John J. Jaqua, Jr., Partner
Scope: Business and financial consultants specializing in mergers and acquisitions for small companies and investments in small companies in central Indiana. Industries served: low tech manufacturing firms. **Founded:** 1990.

42355 ■ Wellbrock Inc.
27 Tall Timbers Rd.
Watchung, NJ 07069
Ph: (908)753-0590
Fax: (908)753-7197
Contact: Dr. Richard D. Wellbrock, President
E-mail: rwelbro@webspan.net
Scope: Business consultant for small businesses regarding mergers, acquisitions, real estate and venture capital. **Founded:** 1971.

42356 ■ White, Nelson & Company L.L.P.
2875 Michelle Dr., Ste. 300
Irvine, CA 92606
Ph: (714)978-1300
Fax: (714)978-7893
Co. E-mail: info@whitenelson.com
URL: http://www.whitenelson.com
Contact: David P. Doran, Partner
E-mail: ddoran@whitenelson.com
Scope: Computer technologies and international tax consultants. Mergers and acquisitions consultants for manufacturing and distribution organizations. **Founded:** 1948. **Publications:** "Federal and California Payroll Tax Issues," 2012; "Web Tax Guide," 2011; "Fiduciary Checklist"; "Warning: Electronic Federal Tax Payment System (EFTPS) Phishing Scam"; "Deficit Reduction," 2011; "California Independent Contractors (SB459)," 2011; "Small Business Jobs Act (SBJA) Extends 179 Expensing and Reinstates," 2010; "Bonus Depreciation," 2010; "The Small Business Jobs Act," 2010; "Levels of Attestation"; "Record Retention Guide"; "Effective Business Planning"; "Types of Financial Statements"; "Financial Planning Guide"; "Small Business Guide"; "Tax Forms Library"; "IRSTax Publications Library". **Telecommunication Services:** recruiter@whitenelson.com; request@whitenelson.com.

42357 ■ Robert E. Wright Tax and Accounting
3533 Moncure Ave.
Falls Church, VA 22041-2017
Ph: (703)379-0592
Co. E-mail: rwrighttax@aol.com
Contact: Robert E. Wright, Owner
Scope: Business consultants specializing in tax and accounting services, including preparation of business and personal tax returns, quarterly reports, amended returns and special forms(1040s, 1120s, 990s, 941s, 1040Xs, 1099s, etc.). Additional services include the setup and maintenance of bookkeeping systems and the preparation of financial statements, articles of incorporation, corporate minutes and resolutions, articles of partnership, employment agreements, contracts, leases, deeds, promissory notes, etc., assistance with documentation and accounting services required for business licenses and permits, certificates of authority and tax-exempt status. **Founded:** 1987.

RESEARCH CENTERS

42358 ■ Babson College - Arthur M. Blank Center for Entrepreneurship
231 Forest St.
Babson Park, MA 02457-0310
Ph: (781)233-5023
Fax: (781)239-4178
Co. E-mail: jstrimaitis@babson.edu
URL: http://www3.babson.edu/eship
Contact: Janet Strimaitis, Director
Founded: 1978. **Publications:** *Babson Entrepreneurial Review*; *Frontiers of Entrepreneurship Research* (Annual). **Educational Activities:** Babson Entrepreneurship Research Conference (Annual). **Awards:** Sponsors Global Academy of Distinguished Entrepreneurs, for outstanding entrepreneurship; Price-Babson College Fellows Program (Annual).

Public Administration

ASSOCIATIONS AND OTHER ORGANIZATIONS

42359 ■ American Society for Public Administration (ASPA)
1301 Pennsylvania Ave. NW, Ste. 700
Washington, DC 20004-1716
Ph: (202)393-7878
Fax: (202)638-4952
Co. E-mail: info@aspanet.org
URL: http://www.aspanet.org
Contact: Kuotsai Tom Liou, President

Description: Promotes excellence in public service, including government, non-profit and private sectors, and academic community. **Founded:** 1939. **Publications:** *Public Administration Review*; *PA Times* (Monthly); *Public Administration Review* (Bimonthly). **Awards:** Louis Brownlow Award; Laverne Burchfield Award; Donald C. Stone Award; Dwight Waldo Award; James E. Webb Award; Marshall E. Dimock Award; William E. Mosher and Frederick C. Mosher Award; NASPAA/ASPA Distinguished Research Award; Equal Opportunity/Affirmative Action Exemplary Practice Award. **Telecommunication Services:** mhamilton@aspanet.org.

42360 ■ National Academy of Public Administration (NAPA)
900 7th St. NW, Ste. 600
Washington, DC 20001
Ph: (202)347-3190
Fax: (202)393-0993
URL: http://www.napawash.org
Contact: Dan G. Blair, President

Description: Works to respond to specific requests from public agencies and non-governmental organizations. Promotes discourse on emerging trends in governance through standing panels and external funding. Assists federal agencies, congressional committees, state and local governments, civic organizations, and institutions overseas through problem solving, objective research, rigorous analysis, information sharing, development strategies for change, and connecting people and ideas. Promotes forward-looking ideas and of analyzing successes and failures of government reform. **Founded:** 1967. **Awards:** National Public Service Awards; Herbert Roback Scholarship; Herbert Roback Scholarship (Annual); Louis Brownlow Book Award (Annual); National Public Service Award (Annual); Louis Brownlow Book Award.

42361 ■ National Forum for Black Public Administrators (NFBPA)
777 N Capitol St. NE, Ste. 807
Washington, DC 20002
Ph: (202)408-9300
Fax: (202)408-8558
Co. E-mail: jsaunders@nfbpa.org
URL: http://www.nfbpa.org
Contact: John E. Saunders, III, Executive Director

Description: Black city and county managers and assistant managers; chief administrative officers; agency directors; bureau and division heads; corporate executives; students. Works to promote, strengthen, and expand the role of blacks in public administration. Seeks to focus the influence of black administrators toward building and maintaining viable communities. Develops specialized training programs for managers and executives. Provides national public administrative leadership resource and skills bank. Works to further communication among black public, private, and academic institutions. Addresses issues that affect the administrative capacity of black managers. **Founded:** 1983. **Publications:** *The Forum Magazine* (Quarterly). **Educational Activities:** National Forum for Black Public Administrators Conference (Annual). **Awards:** The Future Colleagues Scholarships; Land-Use Planning Scholarships; NFBPA/CDM Scholarships; Hall of Fame Award (Annual); Marks of Excellence Award (Annual); Willie T. Loud - CH2M Hill Scholarships; RA Consulting Service/Maria Riley Scholarships; Steven D. Ford Memorial Award (Annual); CIGNA Healthcare Graduate Scholarships; CIGNA Healthcare Undergraduate Scholarships; Johnnie L. Cochran, Jr./MWH Scholarships; Marks of Excellence Award; Hall of Fame Award; Steven D. Ford Memorial Award. **Telecommunication Services:** webmaster@nfbpa.org.

42362 ■ Section for Women in Public Administration (SWPA)
2828 Mt. Isle Harbor Dr.
Charlotte, NC 28214
Ph: (202)393-7878
Co. E-mail: swpasection@gmail.com
URL: http://www.swpanet.org
Contact: Barbara Lewkowitz, Chairman

Description: Established by the American Society for Public Administration to initiate action programs appropriate to the needs and concerns of women in public administration. Promotes equal educational and employment opportunities for women in public service, and full participation and recognition of women in all areas of government. Develops strategies for implementation of ASPA policies of interest to women in public administration; recommends qualified women to elective and appointive ASPA governmental leadership positions; acts as forum for communication among professional and laypeople interested in the professional development of women in public administration. **Founded:** 1971. **Awards:** Joan Fiss Bishop Award; Rita Mae Kelly Awards; Julia Henderson Service to the Section Award.

42363 ■ Southern Public Administration Education Foundation (SPAEF)
122 W High St.
Elizabethtown, PA 17022
Ph: (717)540-6126
Co. E-mail: paq@spaef.com
URL: http://www.spaef.com

Description: Represents researchers and scholars. Produces publications to educate scholars and practitioners. Publishes electronic journals. **Founded:** 1977. **Publications:** *German Policy Studies* (Triennial); *Public Administration Quarterly* (Quarterly); *Journal of Power and Ethics: An Interdisciplinary Review* (Quarterly); *Global Virtue Ethics Review* (Quarterly); *Public Administration & Management: An Interactive Journal*; *International Journal of Economic Development*; *Journal of Health and Human Services Administration* (Quarterly).

REFERENCE WORKS

42364 ■ "1914 Proved to Be Key Year for Chevy" in Automotive News (Vol. 86, October 31, 2011, No. 6488, pp. S18)
Pub: Crain Communications Inc.

Ed: Jamie Lareau. **Description:** Chevy Bow Tie emblem was born in 1914, creating the brand's image that has carried through to current days.

42365 ■ "Adidas' Brand Ambitions" in Business Journal Portland (Vol. 27, December 10, 2010, No. 41, pp. 1)
Pub: Portland Business Journal

Ed: Erik Siemers. **Description:** Adidas AG, the second-largest sporting goods brand in the world, hopes to increase global revenue by 50 percent by 2015. The German company, which reported $14.5 billion sales, plans to improve its U.S. market. The U.S. is Adidas' largest, but also the most underperforming market for the firm.

42366 ■ "Bill Kaneko" in Hawaii Business (Vol. 53, December 2007, No. 6, pp. 32)
Pub: Hawaii Business Publishing

Ed: David K. Choo. **Description:** Hawaii Institute for Public Affairs chief executive officer and president Bill Kaneko believes that the Hawaiian economy is booming, however, he also asserts that the economy is too focused on tourism and real estate. Kaneko has also realized the that the will of the people is strong while he was helping with the Hawaiian 2050 Sustainability Plan. The difficulties of making a sustainable Hawaii are discussed.

42367 ■ "Business Plan Refines Focus" in Business Journal Portland (Vol. 27, December 10, 2010, No. 41, pp. 1)
Pub: Portland Business Journal

Ed: Wendy Culverwell. **Description:** Organizers of the Oregon Business Plan's Leadership Summit 2010 seek the opinions of nearly 1,000 business, education, political, and civic leaders in an effort to address how to rehabilitate Oregon's economy. The opinion-seeking actions recognize the organizers' belief that the economic fate of the state depends on rural Oregon.

42368 ■ "Candidates Differ On State's Green Streak" in Business Journal Portland (Vol. 27, October 22, 2010, No. 34, pp. 1)
Pub: Portland Business Journal

Ed: Andy Giegerich. **Description:** The views of Oregon gubernatorial candidates Chris Dudley and John Kitzhaber on the state's economy and on environmental policies are presented. Both Dudley, who is a Republican, and his Democratic challenger believe that biomass could help drive the state's economy. Both candidates also pledged changes in Oregon's business energy tax credit (BETC) program.

42369 ■ *"CBC Chief: Future is Now" in Business Courier (Vol. 27, August 13, 2010, No. 15, pp. 1)*
Pub: Business Courier
Ed: Lucy May. **Description:** Tom Williams, chairman of the Cincinnati Business Committee (CBC), maintains that politicians and business leaders must cooperate to ensure the competitiveness of the city for the 21st Century. Under Williams' leadership, the CBC has put emphasis on initiatives related to government efficiency, economic development, and public education. Williams' views on a proposed inland port are given.

42370 ■ *"City Consults Executives on Police Hire" in Business Courier (Vol. 27, August 27, 2010, No. 17, pp. 1)*
Pub: Business Courier
Ed: Lucy May, Dan Monk. **Description:** The City of Cincinnati, Ohio has begun a selection process for the new police chief by consulting the city's business executives. The city charter amendment known as Issue 5 has removed civil service protection from the chief's post and enables City Manager Milton Dohoney to hire a chief from outside the department.

42371 ■ *"City's Streetcar Utility Estimate Way Off Mark" in Business Courier (Vol27, November 19, 2010, No. 29. , pp. 1)*
Pub: Business Courier
Ed: Dan Monk, Lucy May. **Description:** Duke Energy Corporation has released new estimates that show moving electric and gas lines alone for Cincinnati, Ohio's proposed streetcar project could cost more than $20 million. However, the city has only estimated the relocation to cost $5 million in federal grant applications.

42372 ■ *"Councilman May Revive Labor Bill" in Baltimore Business Journal (Vol. 28, August 13, 2010, No. 14, pp. 1)*
Pub: Baltimore Business Journal
Ed: Daniel J. Sernovitz. **Description:** Baltimore, Maryland Councilman Bill Henry has started reviving controversial legislation that would force developers and contractors to give preference to union labor. The legislation requires contractors to give preference to city workers in order to lower Baltimore's unemployment rate.

42373 ■ *"County Tract Pitched for Data Center" in Baltimore Business Journal (Vol. 28, July 23, 2010, No. 11, pp. 1)*
Pub: Baltimore Business Journal
Ed: Scott Dance. **Description:** One hundred acres of land in Woodlawn, Maryland is set to be sold for use in the construction of a data center for the U.S. Social Security Administration. Baltimore County has submitted a bid for the $750M construction project.

42374 ■ *"Dark Horse Murphy Means Business In Gubernatorial Race" in Baltimore Business Journal (Vol. 28, June 25, 2010, No. 7, pp. 1)*
Pub: Baltimore Business Journal
Ed: Scott Dance. **Description:** Maryland gubernatorial candidate Brian Murphy has claimed better knowledge in helping small business owners than the other candidates, Governor Martin O'Malley and former Governor Robert Ehrlich. Murphy, who faces off against Ehrlich in the Republican primary, is banking on the benefit of his business background.

42375 ■ *"Developers Give Big to Mayor's Bid" in Boston Business Journal (Vol. 29, August 26, 2011, No. 16, pp. 1)*
Pub: American City Business Journals Inc.
Ed: Scott Dance. **Description:** Mayor Stephanie Rawlings-Blake received thousands of dollars in her political campaign from companies of real estate developers who are vying to build key development projects in Baltimore, Maryland. Rawlings-Blake created a major fundraising advantage over other mayoral candidates with the help of those contributions.

42376 ■ *"Fed May Ban Amphibian Trade" in Pet Product News (Vol. 64, November 2010, No. 11, pp. 13)*
Pub: BowTie Inc.
Description: U.S. Fish and Wildlife Service is seeking public input on a petition submitted by the conservation activist group Defenders of Wildlife. The petition involves possible classification of chytrid fungus-infected amphibians and amphibian eggs as 'injurious wildlife' under the Lacey Act. Interstate trading or importation of injurious wildlife into the U.S. is not allowed.

42377 ■ *"Gov. Kasich to Put DOD On Short Leash" in Business Courier (Vol. 27, November 26, 2010, No. 30, pp. 1)*
Pub: Business Courier
Ed: Dan Monk. **Description:** Ohio Governor-elect John Kasich proposed the privatization of the Ohio Department of Development in favor of a nonprofit corporation called JobsOhio. Kasich believes that the department has lost its focus by adding to its mission issues such as energy efficiency and tourism.

42378 ■ *"Green Energy Exec Hits State Policy" in Boston Business Journal (Vol. 30, December 3, 2010, No. 45, pp. 1)*
Pub: Boston Business Journal
Ed: Kyle Alspach. **Description:** American Superconductor Corporation President Dan McGahn believes that the state government of Massachusetts is not proactive enough to develop the state into a manufacturing hub for wind power technology. McGahn believes that while Governor Deval Patrick campaigned for wind turbines in the state, his administration does not have the focus required to build the turbines in the state.

42379 ■ *"Groundbreaking 2.0" in Philadelphia Business Journal (Vol. 30, September 23, 2011, No. 32, pp. 1)*
Pub: American City Business Journals Inc.
Ed: Natalie Kostelni. **Description:** University Place Associates, the developer of 2.0 University Place in West Philadelphia, Pennsylvania, will break ground on a five-story, 97,000-square-foot office building in December 2011. The decision follows the Citizenship and Immigration Services signing of a 15-year lease as anchor tenant.

42380 ■ *"Hotel Woes Reflect Area Struggle" in Business Journal Serving Greater Tampa Bay (Vol. 30, December 3, 2010, No. 50, pp. 1)*
Pub: Tampa Bay Business Journal
Ed: Mark Holan. **Description:** Quality Inn and Suites in East Tampa, Florida has struggled against the sluggish economy but remained open to guests despite facing a foreclosure. The hotel project is the center of East Tampa's redevelopment plans and public officials defend the $650,000 investment in public amenities near the building.

42381 ■ *"Janson: Duke's Dynamo, Regional President Focuses on Economic Development" in Business Courier (Vol. 27, July 9, 2010, No. 10, pp. 1)*
Pub: Business Courier
Ed: Lucy May. **Description:** Duke Energy President Julie Janson is also chair of the Cincinnati USA Partnership for Economic Development and the co-chair of the Cincinnati Business Committee's Economic Development Task Force. Duke is launching a Site Readiness Pilot Program to help the region prepare for an economic recovery.

42382 ■ *"Lawyers Lock Up Cops as Clients" in Sacramento Business Journal (Vol. 28, April 8, 2011, No. 6, pp. 1)*
Pub: Sacramento Business Journal
Ed: Kathy Robertson. **Description:** Sacramento-based law firm Mastagni, Holstedt and Chiurazzi has grown its client base by specializing in law enforcement labor issues. The firm represents 80,000 public sector correctional officers in the US. The firm has been experiencing an increase in new business as public sector employers face huge budget deficits.

42383 ■ *"Lotteries Scratch Their Way to Billions" in Saint Louis Business Journal (Vol. 31, August 19, 2011, No. 52, pp. 1)*
Pub: Saint Louis Business Journal
Ed: Kelsey Volkmann. **Description:** Missouri Lottery reported $1 billion in sales in 2011. A six-fold increase in the lottery's advertising budget is seen to drive the revenue increase; a 4.5 percent rise in its scratch-off tickets and new sponsorships has also contributed to the development.

42384 ■ *"Md. Tries to Recoup $73M from Actuary" in Baltimore Business Journal (Vol. 28, June 11, 2010, No. 5, pp. 1)*
Pub: Baltimore Business Journal
Ed: Gary Haber. **Description:** Maryland State Retirement and Pension System has won nearly $73 million in administrative ruling against Milliman Inc. over pension loss miscalculations. However, Milliman filed two court cases seeking to reverse the decision and to recoup to the state any money a court orders.

42385 ■ *"New Chief Walking the Talk" in Business Courier (Vol. 27, August 27, 2010, No. 17, pp. 1)*
Pub: Business Courier
Ed: Lucy May. **Description:** National Brand & Tag Company president, Eric Haas, has vowed to put his various work experiences when he assumes the presidency of North Kentucky Chamber of Commerce. Haas wants to help the Chamber influence government policies that could help various businesses through the economic depression.

42386 ■ *"Retailers, City Clash Over Wages" in Baltimore Business Journal (Vol. 28, July 9, 2010, No. 9, pp. 1)*
Pub: Baltimore Business Journal
Ed: Daniel J. Sernovitz. **Description:** A bill pending before the City Council of Baltimore, Maryland would mandate the city's major retailers to pay their employees at least $10.57 per hour, $3 higher than was state law requires. Major retailers, as defined in the said bill by Councilwoman Mary Pat Clarke, have gross sales of at least $10 million. Reactions of the retailers affected are presented.

42387 ■ *"Smart Businesses See Value, and Profit, in Promoting Women" in Crain's Chicago Business (Vol. 30, February 2007, No. 6, pp. 30)*
Pub: Crain Communications, Inc.
Ed: Marc J. Lane. **Description:** Despite U.S. corporations making little progress in advancing women to leadership positions over the past ten years, enlightened corporate decision makers understand that gender diversity is good business as the highest percentages of women officers yielded, on average, a 34 percent higher total return to shareholders and a 35.1 percent higher return on equity than those firms with the lowest percentages of women officers, according to a 2004 Catalyst study of Fortune 500 companies.

42388 ■ *"Staples Advantage Receives NJPA National Contract for Janitorial Supplies" in Professional Services Close-Up (April 22, 2011)*
Pub: Close-Up Media
Description: Staples Advantage, the business-to-business division of Staples Inc. was awarded a contract for janitorial supplies to members of the National Joint Powers Alliance (NJPA). NJPA is a member-owned buying cooperative serving public and private schools, state and local governments, and nonprofit organizations.

42389 ■ *"State Center Lease Deal High for Md." in Baltimore Business Journal (Vol. 28, August 6, 2010, No. 13, pp. 1)*
Pub: Baltimore Business Journal
Ed: Daniel J. Sernovitz. **Description:** The proposed $1.5 billion State Center development project in Midtown Baltimore might cause the State of Maryland to pay the most expensive rental rates in the city. The state will have to pay an effective rental rate of $34 per square foot, including expenses, on the leasing. Other details of the redevelopment project are discussed.

42390 ■ *"Study Puts Hub On Top of the Tech Heap" in Boston Business Journal (Vol. 30, November 26, 2010, No. 44, pp. 1)*
Pub: Boston Business Journal
Ed: Galen Moore. **Description:** The Ewing Marion Kauffman Foundation ranked Massachusetts at the top in its evaluations of states' innovative industries,

government leadership, and education. Meanwhile, research blog formDs.com also ranked Massachusetts number one in terms of venture-capital financings per capita.

42391 ■ *"Swirling Debate" in Business Courier (Vol. 27, August 20, 2010, No. 16, pp. 1)*
Pub: Business Courier
Ed: Lucy May. **Description:** The debate on whether to convert Greater Cincinnati Water Works into a public regional district is seen to impact the city's economic recovery. The utility's service area and customer base has significantly grown.

42392 ■ *"Tourism Push Rising in Fall" in Philadelphia Business Journal (Vol. 30, August 26, 2011, No. 28, pp. 1)*
Pub: American City Business Journals Inc.
Ed: Peter Van Allen. **Description:** Philadelphia is offering events for tourists this fall despite massive cuts for tourism promotion. Governor Tim Corbet slashed $5.5 million in funding for the state's tourism-promotion agencies which received $32 million in 2009. The agencies were forced to cooperate and fend for themselves using the hotel taxes that sustain them.

42393 ■ *"VA Seeking Bidders for Ft. Howard" in Baltimore Business Journal (Vol. 28, June 25, 2010, No. 7, pp. 1)*
Pub: Baltimore Business Journal
Ed: Daniel J. Sernovitz. **Description:** The Veterans Affairs Maryland Health Care Systems has requested proposals from developers to build a retirement community at Fort Howard in Baltimore County. The historic site, which has about 36 mostly vacant buildings, could become the home to hundreds of war veterans. Details of the proposed development are discussed.

42394 ■ *"Vision for Camden in Better Focus" in Philadelphia Business Journal (Vol. 30, September 30, 2011, No. 33, pp. 1)*
Pub: American City Business Journals Inc.
Ed: Natalie Kostelni. **Description:** More than $500 million worth of projects aimed at redeveloping the downtown and waterfront areas of Camden, New Jersey are being planned. These include the construction of residential, commercial, and education buildings.

42395 ■ *"Walker Seeks More Business Participation" in Business Journal-Milwaukee (Vol. 28, December 10, 2010, No. 10, pp. A1)*
Pub: Milwaukee Business Journal
Ed: Rich Kirchen. **Description:** Wisconsin governor Scott Walker is seeking the aid of Milwaukee business leaders to participate in resolving the challenges posed by the economic crisis. Walker is aiming to create 250,000 jobs. He is also planning to call a special session of the legislature to enact strategies to jumpstart the economy.

TRADE PERIODICALS

42396 ■ *American City and County*
Pub: Penton
Contact: Raymond E. Maloney, President
URL(s): americancityandcounty.com. **Released:** Monthly

42397 ■ *The American Review of Public Administration*
Pub: SAGE Publications USA
Contact: Blaise R. Simqu, President
URL(s): www.sagepub.com/journals/Journal200753. **Ed:** John Clayton Thomas, Andrew Glassberg, Guy Adams. **Released:** Quarterly **Price:** $165, Institutions single print; $23, Single issue print; $917, Institutions print & e-access; $825, Institutions e-access; $899, Institutions print; $108, Individuals print.

42398 ■ *Canadian Public Administration*
Pub: Institute of Public Administration of Canada
Contact: Robert P. Taylor, Chief Executive Officer
URL(s): www.ipac.ca/CPAJ. **Ed:** Prof. Barbara Wake Carroll. **Released:** Quarterly **Price:** $404, Institutions print plus online; €193, Institutions print only; $351, Institutions print only; €223, Institutions print plus online.

42399 ■ *Demokratizatsiya: The Journal of Post-Soviet Democratization*
Pub: Taylor & Francis Group Journals
Contact: Kevin J. Bradley, President
URL(s): www.demokratizatsiya.org. **Released:** Quarterly **Price:** $148, Institutions print or online; $57, Individuals online only; $60, Individuals print and online; $177, Institutions print and online.

42400 ■ *Governing Magazine: The Magazine of States and Localities*
Contact: Peter Harkness, Columnist
E-mail: pharkness@governing.com
URL(s): www.governing.com. **Released:** Monthly **Price:** $19.95, Individuals; $34.95, Two years.

42401 ■ *Illinois Issues*
Pub: University of Illinois
URL(s): illinoisissues.uis.edu. **Ed:** Dana Heupel. **Released:** Monthly **Price:** $39.95, Individuals.

42402 ■ *Journal of Policy Analysis and Management*
Pub: John Wiley & Sons Inc.
Contact: Stephen M. Smith, President
URL(s): onlinelibrary.wiley.com/journal/10.1002/(ISSN)1520-6688. **Ed:** Maureen Pirog. **Released:** Quarterly **Price:** $397, U.S., Canada, and Mexico print only; $397, U.S., Canada, and Mexico print only; $1278, Institutions print only; $1318, Institutions, Canada and Mexico print only; $1352, Institutions, other countries print only; $1470, Institutions print with online; $1510, Institutions, Canada and Mexico print with online; $1544, Institutions, other countries print with online.

42403 ■ *Missouri Municipal Review*
Pub: Missouri Municipal League
Contact: Patrick Bonnot, Director
E-mail: pbonnot@mocities.com
URL(s): www.mocities.com/?page=ReviewMagazine. **Ed:** Laura Holloway. **Released:** Bimonthly **Price:** $30, Individuals.

42404 ■ *Municipal World*
Pub: Municipal World Inc.
Contact: Nicholas R. Smither, President
E-mail: nick@municipalworld.com
URL(s): www.municipalworld.com/index.php. **Released:** Monthly **Price:** C$55, Individuals plus GST; C$99, Two years; C$140.75, Individuals 3 years; $7.95, Single issue back issue; $80, Other countries.

42405 ■ *PA Times*
Pub: American Society for Public Administration
Contact: Patricia Yearwood, Director
E-mail: pyearwood@aspanet.org
URL(s): www.aspanet.org/public/. **Ed:** Christine Jewett McCrehin. **Released:** Monthly **Price:** $50, Individuals first class mail; $75, Out of country.

42406 ■ *Public Administration Abstracts*
Pub: EBSCO Publishing
Contact: Tim Collins, President
E-mail: tcollins@ebscohost.com
URL(s): www.ebscohost.com/academic/public-administration-abstracts. **Released:** Quarterly **Price:** $1038, Institutions print only; $261, Individuals print only; $285, Institutions single print; $85, Individuals single print.

42407 ■ *Public Administration Review*
Pub: American Society for Public Administration
Contact: Patricia Yearwood, Director
E-mail: pyearwood@aspanet.org
URL(s): www.aspanet.org/public/www.blackwellpublishing.com/journal.asp?ref=0033-3352. **Released:** Bimonthly **Price:** $477, Institutions U.S., print + online; £600, Institutions European, print + online; £929, Institutions, other countries print + online; $415, Institutions U.S., print or online; £522, Institutions European, print or online; £807, Institutions, other countries print or online.

42408 ■ *Public Affairs Report*
Pub: Institute of Governmental Studies
Contact: Rarick Ethan, Director
E-mail: erarick@berkeley.edu
Ed: Gerald C. Lubenow, Editor. **Released:** Bimonthly, 6/year. **Price:** Free. **Description:** Publishes essays on emerging governmental and public policy issues of significance to public officials and citizens in both California and the nation. Covers such subjects as pollution, politics, finance, transportation, health and housing policy, and California-Mexico trade relations. Recurring features include bibliographies.

42409 ■ *Public Management*
Pub: International City/County Management Association
Contact: Elizabeth Kellar, President
E-mail: ekellar@icma.org
URL(s): www.icma.org/pm. **Ed:** Beth Payne. **Released:** 11/yr. **Price:** $46, Nonmembers; $62, Other countries.

42410 ■ *Tennessee Town & City*
Pub: Tennessee Municipal League
URL(s): www.tml1.org. **Ed:** Carole Graves. **Released:** Semimonthly **Price:** $6, Members; $15, Nonmembers; $1, Single issue.

TRADE SHOWS AND CONVENTIONS

42411 ■ Maryland Municipal League Convention
Maryland Municipal League (MML)
1212 W St.
Annapolis, MD 21401
Ph: (410)268-5514
Free: 800-492-7121
Fax: (410)268-7004
Co. E-mail: mml@mdmunicipal.org
URL: http://www.mdmunicipal.org
Contact: Michael E. Bennett, President
URL(s): www.mdmunicipal.org. **Frequency:** Annual. **Audience:** Municipal officials and other county and state officials. **Principal Exhibits:** Office equipment, public works equipment, insurance companies, consulting firms, recreation equipment, computers, engineering firms, police equipment, and code publishers. **Dates and Locations:** , Princess Royale Hotel. **Telecommunication Services:** mml@mdmunicipal.org.

42412 ■ New Jersey League of Municipalities Annual Conference
New Jersey League of Municipalities
222 W. State St.
Trenton, NJ 08608
Ph: (609)695-3481
Fax: (609)695-0151
Co. E-mail: league@njslom.com
URL: http://www.njslom.com
Contact: William G. Dressel, Executive Director
E-mail: bdressel@njslom.com
URL(s): www.njslom.org. **Price:** $50, Pre-registered; $100, Pre-registered non-municipal. **Frequency:** Annual. **Audience:** Municipal officials. **Principal Exhibits:** Municipal products and services.

CONSULTANTS

42413 ■ Institute of Public Administration (IPA)
295 Lafayette St., Fl. 2
New York, NY 10003
Ph: (212)992-9898
Free: 800-258-1102
Fax: (212)995-4876
Co. E-mail: p553@nyu.edu
URL: http://www.theipa.org
Contact: David Mammen, President
Scope: Provider of consulting and research services. It serves local, state and federal governments, international aid agencies, and foreign governments. **Founded:** 1906. **Publications:** "Local Governance Approach to Social Reintegration and Economic Recovery in Post Conflict Countries: The Political Context for Programs of UNDP/UNCDF Assistance";

"Local Governance Approach to Social Reintegration and Economic Recovery in Post Conflict Countries: Programming Options for UNDP/UNCDF Assistance"; "Local Governance Approach to Social Reintegration and Economic Recovery in Post Conflict Countries: The View from Mozambique"; "Local Governance Approach to Social Reintegration and Economic Recovery in Post Conflict Countries: Towards a Definition and a Rationale"; "Local Governance Approach to Post Conflict Recovery: Perspective from Cambodia"; "The Sustainable Human Development Strategy: A Proposal for Post Conflict Recovery Societies"; "Local Governance Approach to Post Conflict Recovery: Proceedings Report on the Workshop Organized by the Institute of Public Administration". **Seminars:** A Local Governance Approach to Post Conflict Recovery.

42414 ■ National Center for Public Policy Research (NCPPR)
501 Capitol Ct. NE
Washington, DC 20002
Ph: (202)543-4110
Fax: (202)543-5975
Co. E-mail: info@nationalcenter.org
URL: http://www.nationalcenter.org
Contact: Amy Moritz Ridenour, President
E-mail: aridenour@nationalcenter.org
Description: Educates the public about public policy issues. Conducts research; distributes national policy analysis papers, memorandums, brochures, newsletters, article reprints, and other materials to the public, libraries, and the media. **Scope:** A communications and research nonprofit organization offering advice and information on international affairs and United States domestic affairs. Sponsors Project 21. Gives special emphasis an environmental and regulatory issues and civil rights issues. **Founded:** 1982. **Publications:** "National Policy Analysis"; "Legal Briefs"; "White Paper: National Policy Analysis 523"; "Shattered Dreams: One Hundred Stories of Government Abuse"; "Shattered Lives: 100 Victims of Government Health Care".

42415 ■ North Carolina Fair Share (NCFS)
3824 Barrett Dr., Ste. 312
Raleigh, NC 27609
Ph: (919)786-7474
Fax: (919)786-7475
Co. E-mail: ncfslrw@aol.com
URL: http://www.ncfairshare.org
Scope: Social services firm consults on community organizing and lobbying for health issues. **Founded:** 1987.

42416 ■ Practice Development Counsel
60 Sutton Pl. S
New York, NY 10022
Ph: (212)593-1549
Fax: (212)980-7940
Co. E-mail: pwhaserot@pdcounsel.com
URL: http://www.pdcounsel.com
Contact: Phyllis Weiss Haserot, President
E-mail: pwhaserot@pdcounsel.com
Scope: Specializes in business and organizaationdal development, and conflict resolution for professional firms. It serves the law, accounting, real estate, and management consulting organizations. **Founded:** 1982. **Publications:** "The Rainmaking Machine: Marketing Planning, Strategy and Management For Law Firms"; "The Marketer's Handbook of Tips & Checklists"; "Venturesome Questions: The Law Firms Guide to Developing a New Business Venture"; "Navigating the Whitewater of Internal Politics"; "Changing Attitudes on Firm Flexibility"; "Transition Planning: A Looming Challenge"; "Don't You Think the Solution Is to Bring In a Good Rainmaker?"; "Aligning Firm Culture with the Needs of the Times"; "What New Partners Need to Know"; "Dangers of Lack of Diversity"; "Learn to Respect Emotion in Business"; "What New Partners Need to Know"; "Taking Responsibility: Implementing Personal Marketing Plans"; "How to Change Unwritten Rules"; "Mentoring and Networking Converge"; "Integrating a New Practice into the Firm"; "Using Conflict Resolution Skills for Marketing Success"; "Sports Team Models for Law Firm Management". **Seminars:** Managing Work Expectations; Effective Coaching Skills; Service Quality; End-Running the Resistance Professionals Have to Getting Client Input; Ancillary Business Activities; Marketing for Professional Firms; Marketing Ethics; Business Development Training; Trends in Professional Services Marketing; Client Relationship Management; Collaborative Culture; Reaching Consensus; Conflict Resolution; Work life Balance; Generaltional Issues; Preparing New Partners; Becoming the Employer of Choice; A Marketing Approach to Recruiting; Implementing Workplace Flexibility; The Business Case for Flexible Work Arrangements.

42417 ■ Praxis Media Inc.
9 Twilight Pl.
Norwalk, CT 06854
Ph: (203)866-6666
Co. E-mail: aldo@praxismediainc.com
Contact: Christopher Campbell, President
Scope: Media needs analysis and project planning specialists provide services in product introductions, communications planning, technology application, promotion and marketing communications. Also assists with focus groups, research, concept development, creative development, scripting and executive speech coaching/training. Industries served: Financial services, high-tech, travel and leisure, health and pharmaceutical and telecommunications. **Founded:** 1979.

42418 ■ Public Policy Communications
4163 Dingman Dr.
Sanibel, FL 33957
Ph: (941)395-6773
Fax: (941)395-6779
Contact: Robert Schaeffer, President
E-mail: bobschaeffer@earthlink.net
Scope: Provides strategic communications for progressive causes, candidates and socially-responsible businesses. These include public relations strategies, political campaign planning, organizational development and training. Substantial work in report writing, editing and design as well as production of a full range of media materials. Industries served: nonprofit, social change organizations, foundations, political campaigns, environmentally and consumer-oriented businesses, government agencies. **Founded:** 1985. **Publications:** "Winning Local and State Elections," Free Press MacMillan; "Giving the Media Your Message, and The News Media and the Big Lie". **Seminars:** Giving the Media Your Message; Effective Public Relations Practices; Winning Your Election; Understanding the Government Budget Process; How to Be an Effective Advocate; Strategic Planning for Non-Profits; How to Run a News Conference: Ten Key Steps, 1998.

42419 ■ Public Sector Consultants Inc. (PSC)
600 W St. Joseph St., Ste. 10
Lansing, MI 48933-2267
Ph: (517)484-4954
Fax: (517)484-6549
Co. E-mail: psc@pscinc.com
URL: http://www.pscinc.com
Contact: William R. Rustem, President
E-mail: wrustem@pscinc.com
Scope: Offers policy research expertise, specializing in opinion polling, public relations, conference planning, and legislative and economic analysis. Industries served: Associations, education, environment, health-care, and public finance. **Founded:** 1980. **Publications:** "The New Landscape of Civic Business: How Business Leadership Is Influencing Civic Progress in Our Metropolitan Regions Today," Feb, 2012; "Saginaw Bay Watershed and Area of Concern," Mar, 2012; "Michigan Public School Employees Retirement System: Major Changes in Recent Years and More Changes to Come," May, 2012; "Saginaw River/Bay Area of Concern: Restoration Plan for the Habitat and Populations BUIs," Sep, 2012; "Proposal 3: Key Questions and Answers," Sep, 2012; "Final Report of the Michigan State Park and Recreation Blue Ribbon Panel," Oct, 2012; "The Impact of Reducing PIP Coverage in Michigan," Sep, 2011; "Michigan Sales Tax Collection and the Internet: A Need for Fairness," Sep, 2011; "Ingham Community Voices Final Evaluation Report," Nov, 2008; "First Class Schools Analysis," Aug, 2008; "Opportunities for Achieving Efficiency in the Aging, Community Mental Health, Local Public Health, and Substance Abuse Coordinating Agency Networks," Aug, 2008; "Saginaw River Bay Area of Concern," Jun, 2008; "Portage Lake Water shed Forever Plan," May, 2008; "Smoke Free Workplaces," Apr, 2008; "Protecting and Restoring the Upper Looking Glass River," Feb, 2008; "Market Structures and the 21st Century Energy Plan," Sep, 2007; "The Growing Crisis of Aging Dams," Apr, 2007; "Financing Community Health Workers Why and How," Jan, 2007; "Hastings Area: Inter local Approaches to Growth Management," Jan, 2007; "Michigan's Part 201 Environmental Remediation Program Review," Jan, 2007.

RESEARCH CENTERS

42420 ■ Boston College - Center on Wealth and Philanthropy (CWP)
McGuinn Hall 515
140 Commonwealth Ave.
Chestnut Hill, MA 02467
Ph: (617)552-4070
Fax: (617)552-3903
Co. E-mail: paul.schervish@bc.edu
URL: http://www.bc.edu/research/cwp
Contact: Prof. Paul G. Schervish, Director
Services: Consulting. **Founded:** 1970. **Publications:** *CWP Newsletter* (Quarterly); *CWP Research reports.* **Educational Activities:** Presentations; CWP Research seminars. **Telecommunication Services:** cwp508@bc.edu.

42421 ■ California State University, Long Beach - Graduate Center for Public Policy and Administration (GCPPA)
College of Health & Human Services, SSPA-228
1250 Bellflower Blvd.
Long Beach, CA 90840-5608
Ph: (562)985-4178
Fax: (562)985-4672
Co. E-mail: wbaber@csulb.edu
URL: http://www.csulb.edu/colleges/chhs/departments/public-policy-and-administration
Contact: Walter F. Baber, Director
Founded: 1973. **Educational Activities:** Graduate education program, in public policy and administration; Graduate certificate programs, in public management analysis, public sector financial management, employer-employee relations and personnel management, transportation policy and planning, and urban executive management.

42422 ■ Carleton University - Carleton Research Unit on Innovation, Science, and Environment (CRUISE)
Dunton Twr., Rm. 1001
School of Public Policy & Administration
1125 Colonel By Dr.
Ottawa, ON, Canada K1S 5B6
Ph: (613)520-2547
Fax: (613)520-2551
Co. E-mail: glen_toner@carleton.ca
URL: http://www2.carleton.ca/sppa/research/research-centres/carleton-research-unit-oninnovation-science-environment-cruise
Contact: Prof. Glen Toner, Director
Services: Consulting. **Founded:** 1997. **Publications:** *CRUISE Journal* (Annual). **Educational Activities:** CRUISE Conference (Annual).

42423 ■ Carleton University - Centre for Policy and Program Assessment (CPPA)
Dunton Twr., 10th Fl.
School of Public Policy & Administration
1125 Colonel By Dr.
Ottawa, ON, Canada K1S 5B6
Ph: (613)520-2547
Fax: (613)520-2551
Co. E-mail: susan_phillips@carleton.ca
URL: http://www2.carleton.ca/sppa/research/research-centres/centre-for-policy-and-progr am-assessment-cppa
Contact: Dr. Susan Phillips, Director
Founded: 1988. **Publications:** *How Ottawa Spends.* **Educational Activities:** Conferences, short courses. **Telecommunication Services:** sppa@carleton.ca.

42424 ■ Citizens Budget Commission (CBC)
2 Penn Plz., 5th Fl.
New York, NY 10121

Ph: (212)279-2605
Fax: (212)868-4745
Co. E-mail: info@cbcny.org
URL: http://www.cbcny.org
Contact: Carol Kellerman, President
E-mail: ckellermann@cbcny.org
Founded: 1932. **Publications:** *CBC Research Reports*. **Awards:** Prize for Public Service Innovation (Annual); Award for High Civic Service to New York (Annual).

42425 ■ Cornell University - Program in International Studies in Planning
106 W Sibley Hall
Ithaca, NY 14853-3901
Ph: (607)255-4331
Fax: (607)255-1971
Co. E-mail: wwg2@cornell.edu
URL: http://www.aap.cornell.edu/crp/programs/grad/mrp.cfm
Contact: Prof. William Goldsmith, Chairperson
Founded: 1972. **Educational Activities:** Courses abroad; Program in International Studies in Planning Seminars; Program in International Studies in Planning Seminars, held Fridays with visiting lecturers in the spring; Annual one-semester lecture series; Program in International Studies in Planning Student travel grants.

42426 ■ Council on Foreign Relations (CFR)
The Harold Pratt House
58 E 68th St.
New York, NY 10065
Ph: (212)434-9400
Fax: (212)434-9800
Co. E-mail: communications@cfr.org
URL: http://www.cfr.org
Contact: Richard N. Haass, President
Founded: 1921. **Publications:** *CFR Annual Report*; *Foreign Affairs* (Bimonthly). **Educational Activities:** CFR Seminars; Frequent meetings, on international affairs (primarily for members only); CFR Meetings (Occasionally), for corporate executives of 200 subscribing companies.

42427 ■ Florida State University - Florida Center for Public Management (FCPM)
227 N Bronough St., Ste. 4600
Tallahassee, FL 32301
Ph: (850)644-6460
Fax: (850)644-0152
Co. E-mail: cpm@admin.fsu.edu
URL: http://www.fcpm.fsu.edu
Contact: Ben Green, Director
Services: Conference planning. **Educational Activities:** Florida Certified Public Manager Program; Florida Government Technology Conference; Management consulting and training. **Telecommunication Services:** bgreen@admin.fsu.edu.

42428 ■ George Washington University - Center for International Science and Technology Policy (CISTP)
Elliott School of International Affairs
1957 E St. NW, Ste. 403
Washington, DC 20052
Ph: (202)994-7292
Fax: (202)994-1639
Co. E-mail: vonortas@gwu.edu
URL: http://www.gwu.edu/~cistp
Contact: Prof. Nicholas S. Vonortas, Director
Founded: 1968. **Educational Activities:** CISTP Seminar series, in science and technology policy; CISTP Symposia. **Awards:** CISTP Fellowships, for graduate study in science and technology policy and space policy. **Telecommunication Services:** cistp@gwu.edu.

42429 ■ Harvard University - A. Alfred Taubman Center for State and Local Government
John F. Kennedy School of Government
79 John F. Kennedy St.
Cambridge, MA 02138
Ph: (617)495-2199
Fax: (617)496-1722
Co. E-mail: edward_glaeser@hks.harvard.edu
URL: http://www.hks.harvard.edu/centers/taubman
Contact: Prof. Edward L. Glaeser, Director
Founded: 1988. **Publications:** *A. Alfred Taubman Center for State and Local Government Annual Report*. **Educational Activities:** Forums and conferences (Periodic). **Telecommunication Services:** taubman@harvard.edu.

42430 ■ Murray State University - Bureau of Business and Economic Research (BBER)
307 Business Bldg.
College of Business & Public Affairs
Murray, KY 42071
Ph: (270)809-4433
Fax: (270)809-3788
Co. E-mail: cbpa.bber@murraystate.edu
URL: http://www.murraystate.edu/qacd/cbpa/bber
Contact: Dr. Jim McCoy, Executive Director
Founded: 1991. **Publications:** *Business and Public Affairs Journal* (Periodic); *BBER Research reports*; *State of the Economy in Western Kentucky* (Semiannual); *Western Kentucky Quarterly Economic Report* (Quarterly). **Educational Activities:** BBER Seminars (Semiannual), for local civic and educational organizations. **Telecommunication Services:** jim.mccoy@murraystate.edu.

42431 ■ Ohio University - Institute for Local Government Administration and Rural Development (ILGARD)
The Ridges, Bldg. 22
Voinovich School of Leadership & Public Affairs
1 Ohio University
Athens, OH 45701
Ph: (740)593-4388
Fax: (740)593-4398
Co. E-mail: gvsinfo@ohio.edu
URL: http://www.voinovichschool.ohio.edu
Contact: Mark L. Weinberg, Director
Services: Training programs and technical assistance: for local government and non-profits. **Founded:** 1981. **Publications:** *Educational Access*; *Employment and Business Opportunities for Low Income Populations in SE Ohio*; *Environmental Risk*. **Educational Activities:** Business Assistance and Capital Access (Daily); Environmental remediation, including watershed planning, assessment, restoration and evaluation; Facilitation and evaluation; Public administration and policy innovation and research; Survey analysis; Value-added research. **Awards:** Undergraduate research scholar positions (Annual), for undergraduate students engaged in research.

42432 ■ Oklahoma State University - Center for Local Government Technology (CLGT)
5202 N Richmond Hills Rd.
Stillwater, OK 74078-8088
Ph: (405)744-6049
Fax: (405)744-7268
Co. E-mail: clgt@okstate.edu
URL: http://clgt.okstate.edu
Contact: Dr. Michael Hughes, Director
Founded: 1974. **Publications:** *Workbooks*; *CLGT Manuals*; *CLGT Newsletters* (Quarterly); *Project Journals*; *Technical Fact Sheets*. **Educational Activities:** Certification program, for county assessors and deputies; CLGT Seminars; CLGT Workshops; Equipment Maintenance Management Conference (Annual), in October; Road and Street Conference (Annual), in April.

42433 ■ Public/Private Ventures (P/PV)
2000 Market St., Ste. 550
Philadelphia, PA 19103
Ph: (215)557-4400
Fax: (215)557-4469
Co. E-mail: publications@ppv.org
URL: http://www.ppv.org
Contact: Chelsea Farley, Vice President, Communications
Founded: 1978. **Publications:** *P/PV Annual reports*; *Case Studies*; *Executive Summaries*; *Policy briefs*; *Practitioner Guides*; *P/PV Research Reports*. **Educational Activities:** P/PV Conferences (Periodic), research- and policy-focused convenings on issues such as employment, crime reduction and prisoner re-entry, mentoring, in-school and out-ofschool-time initiatives and community health; P/PV Meetings (Periodic). **Awards:** P/PV Summer internships. **Telecommunication Services:** cfarley@ppv.org.

42434 ■ Queen's University at Kingston - Institute of Intergovernmental Relations (IIGR)
Robert Sutherland Hall, Rm. 301
School of Policy Studies
138 Union St.
Kingston, ON, Canada K7L 3N6
Ph: (613)533-2080
Fax: (613)533-6868
Co. E-mail: ajuneau@queensu.ca
URL: http://www.queensu.ca/iigr/index.html
Contact: André Juneau, Director
Founded: 1965. **Publications:** *IIGR Annual Reports*; *Bibliographies on Federalism*; *Canada: The State of the Federation* (Annual); *IIGR Monographs*; *Reflections Series*; *Research Paper Series*. **Educational Activities:** Institute's Advisory Council; Kenneth R. MacGregor Lectureship in Intergovernmental Relations; IIGR Seminars, on regionalism, economic policy, fiscal relations, interest groups, and other topics pertinent to Canadian federalism; IIGR Conferences (Semiannual), for government officials, university faculty, journalists, representatives of interest organizations, and the private sector. **Telecommunication Services:** iigr@queensu.ca.

42435 ■ Rutgers University - National Center for Public Productivity (NCPP)
School of Public Affairs & Administration
111 Washington St.
Newark, NJ 07102
Ph: (973)353-5093
Fax: (973)353-5907
Co. E-mail: mholzer@pipeline.com
URL: http://ncpp.us
Contact: Dr. Marc Holzer, Executive Director
Services: Technical training and assistance. **Founded:** 1975. **Publications:** *NCPP Newsletter* (Quarterly); *Public Productivity and Management Review* (Quarterly). **Educational Activities:** NCPP Conferences; NCPP Forums. **Telecommunication Services:** ncpp@andromeda.rutgers.edu.

42436 ■ Tennessee State University - Institute of Government
330-10th Ave. N, Ste. F-400
Nashville, TN 37203-3401
Ph: (615)963-7241
Fax: (615)963-7245
Co. E-mail: arizzo@tnstate.edu
URL: http://www.tnstate.edu/interior.asp?mid=299
Contact: Ann Marie Rizzo, Director
Services: Training and consultation programs for government and nonprofit organizations. **Founded:** 1988. **Publications:** *The Public Servant* (3/year).

42437 ■ University of California, Berkeley - Institute of Governmental Studies (IGS)
109 Moses Hall, No. 2370
Berkeley, CA 94720-2370
Ph: (510)642-1473
Fax: (510)642-3020
Co. E-mail: gojack@berkeley.edu
URL: http://igs.berkeley.edu
Contact: Jack Citrin, Director
Founded: 1919. **Publications:** *IGS Monographs*; *Public Affairs Report* (Quarterly); *IGS Research Reports*. **Educational Activities:** IGS Conferences; IGS Lectures; IGS Seminars, on government policies and social issues; IGS Workshops. **Awards:** John Gardner Fellowships, to undergraduate students; John Gardner Public Service Fellowships.

42438 ■ University of Delaware - Institute for Public Administration (IPA)
180 Graham Hall
College of Education & Public Policy
Newark, DE 19716-7380
Ph: (302)831-8971

Fax: (302)831-3488
Co. E-mail: jlewis@udel.edu
URL: http://www.ipa.udel.edu
Contact: Jerome R. Lewis, Director
Founded: 1973. **Publications:** *IPA Reports.* **Educational Activities:** Policy forums; Training workshops, certificate programs. **Awards:** IPA Internship program; Legislative Fellows program.

42439 ■ University of Georgia - Carl Vinson Institute of Government
201 N Milledge Ave.
Athens, GA 30602-5482
Ph: (706)542-2736
Fax: (706)542-9301
Co. E-mail: lmeadows@uga.edu
URL: http://www.cviog.uga.edu
Contact: Laura Meadows, Director (Acting)
Services: Technical and consultative advice and assistance: to state and local government officials. **Founded:** 1928. **Publications:** *Project Reports*; *Books and reports* (7/year); *State and Local Government Review* (3/year). **Educational Activities:** Carl Vinson Institute of Government Workshops; Carl Vinson Institute of Government Short courses, for state and local government officials.

42440 ■ University of Maryland at College Park - Institute for Governmental Service and Research (IGSR)
4321 Hartwick Rd., Ste. 208
College Park, MD 20742-3225
Ph: (301)405-4905
Fax: (301)314-9258
Co. E-mail: igsr@umd.edu
URL: http://www.igsr.umd.edu
Contact: Dr. Robin Parker Cox, Director
Founded: 1959. **Publications:** *Compensation Survey of Maryland Local Governments* (Occasionally); *Did You Know* (Occasionally); *Handbook for Maryland Municipal Officials* (Annual); *Home Rule Options in Maryland* (5/year); *Maryland Government Report* (Annual); *Outreach Newsletter* (5/year). **Telecommunication Services:** rcox2@umd.edu.

42441 ■ University of Minnesota, Duluth - Center for Community and Regional Research (CCRR)
329A Cina Hall
Department of Geography
1123 University Dr.
Duluth, MN 55812
Ph: (218)726-7331
Fax: (218)726-6540
Co. E-mail: okuhlke@d.umn.edu
URL: http://www.d.umn.edu/cla/CCRR/main/index.php
Contact: Olaf Kuhlke, Director (Acting)
Founded: 1985.

42442 ■ University of North Florida - Center for Community Initiatives (CCI)
Bldg. 1/Ste. 1901
Department of Sociology & Anthropology
1 UNF Dr.
Jacksonville, FL 32224
Ph: (904)620-2463
Fax: (904)620-4415
Co. E-mail: jwill@unf.edu
URL: http://www.unf.edu/coas/cci
Contact: Jeffry A. Will, Director
Founded: 1995.

42443 ■ University of South Dakota - Government Research Bureau (GRB)
USD Farber House
414 E Clark St.
Vermillion, SD 57069
Ph: (605)677-5708
Fax: (605)677-6968
Co. E-mail: grb@usd.edu
URL: http://www.usd.edu/arts-and-sciences/political-science/government-research-bureau
Contact: Bryan Dettrey, Director
Services: Clearinghouse: for information on governmental administration; Consultation services: for governmental officials. **Founded:** 1939. **Publications:** *Public Affairs* (Quarterly).

42444 ■ University of Utah - Center for Public Policy and Administration (CPPA)
260 S Central Campus Dr., Rm. 214
Salt Lake City, UT 84112-9154
Ph: (801)581-6781
Fax: (801)587-7861
Co. E-mail: robinson@cppa.utah.edu
URL: http://www.cppa.utah.edu
Contact: Jennifer Robinson, Director (Acting)
Services: Consultation: to local, county, and state governments; Technical assistance; Training. **Founded:** 1979. **Publications:** *Policy briefing papers* (Occasionally); *Policy Perspectives* (Monthly). **Educational Activities:** Policy Conference; Master Public Administration Alumni Conference; Public administration educational programs; Utah Leadership Education and Development Program; Women's Conference. **Awards:** Dalmas Nelson Lectureship; Dalmas Nelson Student Award; Morita Endowed Scholarship. **Telecommunication Services:** megan.crowley@cppa.utah.edu.

42445 ■ Virginia Commonwealth University - Center for Public Policy
L. Douglas Wilder School of Government & Public Affairs
Richmond, VA 23284-3061
Ph: (804)828-6837
Fax: (804)828-6838
Co. E-mail: clfunk@vcu.edu
URL: http://www.vcu.edu/cppweb/ppa
Contact: Carolyn L. Funk, Director
Founded: 1994. **Telecommunication Services:** ppa@vcu.edu.

Public Relations

ASSOCIATIONS AND OTHER ORGANIZATIONS

42446 ■ Public Relations Society of America (PRSA)
33 Maiden Ln., 11th Fl.
New York, NY 10038-5150
Ph: (212)460-1400
Fax: (212)995-0757
Co. E-mail: william.murray@prsa.org
URL: http://www.prsa.org
Contact: William Murray, President
Description: Professional society of public relations practitioners in business and industry, counseling firms, government, associations, hospitals, schools, and nonprofit organizations. Conducts professional development programs. Maintains a Professional Resource Center. Offers accreditation program. **Scope:** Public relations firm specializes in counseling firms and training programs. **Founded:** 1947. **Subscriptions:** 1000 archival material. **Publications:** "Tactics"; "Professional Development". **Educational Activities:** Public Relations Society of America Conference & Expo (Annual). **Awards:** PR Professional of the Year; Gold Anvil Award; Outstanding Educator Award; Bronze Anvil Awards; Silver Anvil Awards; Bronze Anvil Awards (Annual); Gold Anvil Award (Annual); Outstanding Educator Award (Annual); Paul M. Lund Public Service Award (Annual); Silver Anvil Awards (Annual); Paul M. Lund Public Service Award; MacEachern Chief Executive Officer Award. **Seminars:** PR Boot Camp: Key Concepts and Techniques of Effective Public Relations, New York, Dec, 2009. **Telecommunication Services:** ppc@prsa.org; hq@prsa.org; info@prsany.org.

REFERENCE WORKS

42447 ■ *"Airlines Mount PR Push to Win Public Support Against Big Oil" in Advertising Age (Vol. 79, July 14, 2008, No. 7, pp. 1)*
Pub: Crain Communications, Inc.
Ed: Michael Bush. **Description:** Top airline executives from competing companies have banded together in a public relations plan in which they are sending e-mails to their frequent fliers asking for aid in lobbying legislators to put a restriction on oil speculation.

42448 ■ *"AllHipHop.com's Founders Thought a Weeklong Event Would Raise the Company" in Inc. (February 2008, pp. 48-51)*
Pub: Gruner & Jahr USA Publishing
Ed: Kermit Pattison. **Description:** Co-founders Greg Watkins and Chuck Creekmur, planned a weeklong festival to promote their company, AllHipHop.com; the event nearly ruined the firm. The online firm provides news about hip hop artists and the industry and is updated daily.

42449 ■ *"Back Talk With Terrie M. Williams" in Black Enterprise (Vol. 38, December 2007, No. 5, pp. 204)*
Pub: Earl G. Graves Publishing Co. Inc.
Ed: Tennille M. Robinson. **Description:** Profile of Terrie M. Williams, president of a public relations agency as well as founder of a youth empowerment organization called Stay Strong Foundation. Williams reflects on her bouts with depression and how the disease impacts sufferers and talks about her book that will inspire others dealing with depression.

42450 ■ *"Banks Deposit Reassurance, Calm Customers" in The Business Journal-Serving Greater Tampa Bay (Vol. 28, August 22, 2008)*
Pub: American City Business Journals, Inc.
Ed: Margie Manning. **Description:** Community banks in the Tampa Bay Area are training tellers and other customer care workers to help reassure customers that their deposits are safe. Other measures to reassure depositors include joining a network that allows banks to share deposits. Additional information on moves community banks are making to reassure consumers is presented.

42451 ■ *"Banks Fret About Gist Of Bailout" in The Business Journal-Serving Metropolitan Kansas City (Vol. 27, September 26, 2008, No. 2)*
Pub: American City Business Journals, Inc.
Ed: James Dornbrook. **Description:** Banks from the Kansas City area hope that the proposed $700 billion bailout will not send the wrong message. UMB Financial Corp. chairman says that he hopes that the bailout would benefit companies that were more risk restrained and punish those that took outsized risk. Other bank executives' perceptions on the planned bailout are given.

42452 ■ *"BBB Hires Marketing Firm to Attract More Businesses" in Baltimore Business Journal (Vol. 27, January 1, 2010, No. 35, pp. 1)*
Pub: American City Business Journals
Ed: Julekha Dash. **Description:** Better Business Bureau (BBB) of Greater Maryland hired Bystry Carson & Associates Ltd. to assist in its rebranding efforts in order to entice more businesses. Bystry Carson will promote BBB's new mission at lectures, seminars, and networking events, as well as educate businesses about the agency through blogs and Twitter. BBB's services are also outlined.

42453 ■ *"BBB Reworks Logo, Grading System" in Crain's Cleveland Business (Vol. 28, October 8, 2007, No. 40, pp. 5)*
Pub: Crain Communications, Inc.
Ed: John Booth. **Description:** During the next year, the Better Business Bureau will adopt a grading system that will establish performance minimums that will make it tougher for some types of businesses to become accredited; this nationwide rebranding effort is part of a campaign to sharpen the Better Business Bureau's image.

42454 ■ *"Better ROI Or Your Money Back, Says Buzz Agency" in Advertising Age (Vol. 79, July 14, 2008, No. 7, pp. 1)*
Pub: Crain Communications, Inc.
Ed: Michael Bush. **Description:** Word-of-mouth marketing is discussed as well as the impact on the advertising industry. Although many firms specializing in this form of marketing have opened over the past few years, many marketers are reluctant to try this route.

42455 ■ *"Brand Imaging" in Small Business Opportunities (November 2010)*
Pub: Harris Publications Inc.
Ed: Karen Harnesk. **Description:** Design and branding pro shares strategies and tips to help guide any small business' image development.

42456 ■ *"Branding Your Way" in Canadian Business (Vol. 80, February 12, 2007, No. 4, pp. 31)*
Pub: Rogers Media
Ed: Erin Pooley. **Description:** The trend in involving consumers in brand marketing by seeking their views through contests or inviting them to produce and submit commercials through Internet is discussed.

42457 ■ *"Building Confidence" in Black Enterprise (Vol. 38, January 2008, No. 6, pp. 50)*
Pub: Earl G. Graves Publishing Co. Inc.
Ed: Marcia A. Reed-Woodard. **Description:** Patriot Management in Chicago offers courses at its Investment Management Training Academy for the institutional asset management and investment sector. Classes are designed to help build investor confidence amid the scandals that hit the financial, investment and asset management industry.

42458 ■ *"The Business Value of Social Networks" in Agency Sales Magazine (Vol. 39, July 2009, No. 7, pp. 44)*
Pub: MANA
Ed: Daniel Burrus. **Description:** Personal and business uses of several Web 2.0 tools for salespeople are discussed. Leading questions which will guide salespeople in finding out if one particular tool will benefit them are presented.

42459 ■ *"Calming Customers" in The Business Journal-Portland (Vol. 25, August 29, 2008, No. 25, pp. 1)*
Pub: American City Business Journals, Inc.
Ed: Kirsten Grind; Rob Smith. **Description:** Credit unions and banks in the Portland area are reaching out to clients in an effort to reassure them on the security of their money and the firms' financial stability. Roy Whitehead of Washington Federal Savings, for instance, wrote 41,000 customers of the bank to reassure them. The strategies of different banks and credit unions to answer their client's worries are discussed.

42460 ■ *"Canon Focuses on New Moms" in Marketing to Women (Vol. 21, January 2008,*

No. 1, pp. 3)
Pub: EPM Communications Inc.
Contact: Ira Mayer, President
E-mail: imayer@epmcom.com
Description: Canon launches a photo contest aimed at spotlighting baby's first pictures in an attempt to connect with new mothers.

42461 ■ *"Change Agent; What Peter Francese Says You Need to Know" in Advertising Age (Vol. 79, July 7, 2008, No. 26, pp. 13)*
Pub: Crain Communications, Inc.
Ed: Peter Francese. **Description:** Advice for marketers on how to deal effectively with a changing consumer base is given.

42462 ■ *"The Changing Face of the U.S. Consumer" in Advertising Age (Vol. 79, July 7, 2008, No. 26, pp. 1)*
Pub: Crain Communications, Inc.
Ed: Peter Francese. **Description:** It is essential for marketers to examine demographic shifts when looking at ways in which to market brands. The average head-of-households is aging and marketers must not continue to ignore them. Statistical data included.

42463 ■ *"Creative Marketing: How to Cultivate a Network of Endless Referrals" in Agency Sales Magazine (Vol. 39, July 2009, No. 7, pp. 38)*
Pub: MANA
Ed: Bob Burg. **Description:** Tips on how a salesperson can build a network of people that will bring them referrals are presented. Asking a person about their business and re-introducing one's self to an earlier acquaintance while remembering their names are some elements in the process of building this network.

42464 ■ *"The Customer Is Right Even If He's Wrong" in Contractor (Vol. 57, February 2010, No. 2, pp. 12)*
Pub: Penton Media, Inc.
Ed: Al Schwarz. **Description:** Mechanical contractors should note that customers will make a judgment based upon the impression that they form on their first meeting. Contractors can maintain a professional image by washing their trucks and having the personnel dress uniformly. Contractors have every right to demand that employees clean up and make a better impression on customers.

42465 ■ *"Do the Math on Discounts" in Entrepreneur (Vol. 37, October 2009, No. 10, pp. 82)*
Pub: Entrepreneur Media, Inc.
Ed: Jennifer Lawler. **Description:** Small business owners should consider all effects of discounts before implementing them. Some entrepreneurs do not discount prices for fear of damaging brands or their company's reputation.

42466 ■ *"Down on the Boardwalk" in Retail Merchandiser (Vol. 51, September-October 2011, No. 5, pp. 56)*
Pub: Phoenix Media Corporation
Ed: Eric Slack. **Description:** Classic board game, Monopoly, continues to be the most recognized game brand while staying fresh by entering new markets and gaming platforms for all walks of life. Monopoly is available in over 100 countries, translated into 43 languages and played by more than 1 billion people since its introduction, and the game is tailored to each geographic market it enters.

42467 ■ *"Effective Use of Field Time" in Agency Sales Magazine (Vol. 39, July 2009, No. 7, pp. 40)*
Pub: MANA
Description: Sales representatives need to consider the value of field visits to themselves and their customers ahead of time. Several anecdotes about field visits from the perspective of manufacturers and sale representatives are presented.

42468 ■ *"Emotional Brand Attachment and Brand Personality" in Journal of Marketing (Vol. 75, July 2011, No. 4, pp. 35)*
Pub: American Marketing Association
Ed: Lucia Malar, Harley Krohmer, Wayne D. Hoyer, Bettin Nyffeneger. **Description:** A study on whether the brand's personality should match the consumer's actual self or ideal self is presented. Actual self-congruence is found to have the most impact on emotional brand attachment.

42469 ■ *"Empowered" in Harvard Business Review (Vol. 88, July-August 2010, No. 7-8, pp. 94)*
Pub: Harvard Business School Publishing
Ed: Josh Bernoff, Ted Schadler. **Description:** HERO concept (highly empowered and resourceful operative) which builds a connection between employees, managers, and IT is outlined. The resultant additional experience and knowledge gained by employees improves customer relationship management.

42470 ■ *Facebook Marketing: Designing Your Next Marketing Campaign*
Pub: Que
Ed: Justin R. Levy. **Released:** May 1, 2010. **Price:** $24.99. **Description:** Detailed steps are given in order to develop, use, and create awareness for any business. The book provides detailed instructions, along with case studies from known brands, for launching marketing campaigns on Facebook.

42471 ■ *"For Baxter, A Lingering PR Problem; Ongoing Focus On Heparin Deaths Ups Heat On CEO" in Crain's Chicago Business (April 21, 2008)*
Pub: Crain Communications, Inc.
Ed: Mike Colias. **Description:** Baxter International Inc.'s recall of the blood-thinning medication heparin has exposed the company to costly litigation and put the perils of overseas drug manufacturing in the spotlight. Wall Street investors predict that an indefinite halt in production of the drug should not hurt the company's bottom line since heparin represents a tiny sliver of the business. Since Baxter began recalling the drug in January its shares have continued to outpace most other medical stocks.

42472 ■ *"FTC Takes Aim At Foreclosure 'Rescue' Firm" in The Business Journal-Serving Greater Tampa Bay (Vol. 28, September 19, 2008, No. 39)*
Pub: American City Business Journals, Inc.
Ed: Michael Hinman. **Description:** United Home Savers LLP has been ordered to halt its mortgage foreclosure rescue services after the Federal Trade Commission accused it of deceptive advertising. The company is alleged to have charged customers $1,200 in exchange for unfulfilled promises to keep them in their homes.

42473 ■ *"Good Questions and the Basics of Selling" in Agency Sales Magazine (Vol. 39, September-October 2009, No. 9, pp. 14)*
Pub: MANA
Ed: Dave Kahle. **Description:** Six basic elements to enhance the job of a sales person in regards to his relationship to a customer are presented.

42474 ■ *Groundswell: Winning in a World Transformed by Social Technologies*
Pub: Harvard Business School Press
Ed: Charlene Li; Josh Bernoff. **Released:** April 21, 2008. **Price:** $29.95. **Description:** Individuals are using online social technologies such as blogs, social networking sites, YouTube, and podcasts to discuss products and companies, write their own news, and find their own deals. When consumers you've never met are rating your company's products in public forums with which you have no experience or influence, your company is vulnerable. This book teaches the tools and data necessary to turn this treat into an opportunity.

42475 ■ *Groundswell: Winning in a World Transformed by Social Technologies*
Pub: Harvard Business School Press
Ed: Charlene Li, Josh Bernoff. **Released:** 2008. **Price:** $29.95. **Description:** Corporate executives are struggling with a new trend: people using online social technologies (blogs, social networking sites, YouTube, podcasts) to discuss products and companies, write their own news, and find their own deals.

42476 ■ *"Help Employees Give Away Some Of That Bonus" in Harvard Business Review (Vol. 86, July-August 2008, No. 8, pp. 1)*
Pub: Harvard Business School Press
Ed: Michael I. Norton; Elizabeth W. Dunn. **Description:** Research indicates that how employees spend their bonuses is key to their resultant happiness, rather than simply receiving the bonus itself. Firms that offer donation options can thereby increase employee satisfaction.

42477 ■ *"'Help Wanted' Meets 'Buy It Now': Why More Companies Are Integrating Marketing and Recruiting" in Inc. (November 2007, pp. 50-52)*
Pub: Gruner & Jahr USA Publishing
Ed: Ryan McCarthy. **Description:** Five tips to merge marketing and recruiting together include: thinking every help wanted ad as a marketing opportunity, treating every job candidate as a potential customer, involving the youngest employees in the interview process, look for way to promote recruiting events, and to sponsor community-oriented events.

42478 ■ *"Hopkins' Security, Reputation Face Challenges in Wake of Slaying" in Baltimore Business Journal (Vol. 28, August 6, 2010, No. 13)*
Pub: Baltimore Business Journal
Ed: Gary Haber. **Description:** The slaying of Johns Hopkins University researcher Stephen Pitcairn has not tarnished the reputation of the elite school in Baltimore, Maryland among students. Maintaining Hopkins' reputation is important since it is Baltimore's largest employer with nearly 32,000 workers. Insights on the impact of the slaying among the Hopkins' community are also given.

42479 ■ *"How to Boost Your Super Bowl ROI" in Advertising Age (Vol. 80, December 7, 2009, No. 41, pp. 3)*
Pub: Crain's Communications
Ed: Abbey Klaassen. **Description:** Internet marketing is essential, even for the corporations that can afford to spend $3 million on a 30-second Super Bowl spot; last year, Super Bowl advertising reached an online viewership of 99.5 million while 98.7 million people watched the game on television validating the idea that public relations must go farther than a mere television ad campaign. Social media provides businesses with a longer shelf life for their ad campaigns. Advice is also given regarding ways in which to strategize a smart and well-thought plan for utilizing the online marketing options currently available.

42480 ■ *"How Hard Could It Be? The Four Pillars of Organic Growth" in Inc. (January 2008, pp. 69-70)*
Pub: Gruner & Jahr USA Publishing
Ed: Joel Spolsky. **Description:** Revenue, head count, public relations, and quality are the four most important aspects of any growing business.

42481 ■ *"How to Ramp Up Marketing in a Downturn" in Entrepreneur (Vol. 37, July 2009, No. 7, pp. 55)*
Pub: Entrepreneur Media, Inc.
Ed: Jeff Wuorio. **Description:** How businesses can save money while boosting their marketing efforts during a down economy is discussed. Using price-driven marketing, online social networks, and cause-driven marketing are among the suggested ways companies can attract more customers. Guarantees and warrantees, as well as contests, can also be used as marketing tools.

42482 ■ *"How To Live To Be 100; John E. Green Co. Grows Through Diversification" in Crain's Detroit Business (February 18, 2008)*
Pub: Crain Communications Inc. - Detroit
Ed: Chad Halcom. **Description:** Continuity, name recognition, and inventiveness are keys to continuing growth for Highland Park, Michigan's John E. Green Company, designer of pipe systems and mechanical contractor.

42483 ■ *"How Two Flourishing Exporters Did It" in Hispanic Business (Vol. 30, July-August*

2008, No. 7-8, pp. 46)
Pub: Hispanic Business, Inc.

Ed: Richard Kaplan. **Description:** Vigorous growth in export revenues posted by two Hispanic-owned export companies Compasa LLC and Ametza LLC is discussed; both firms have benefited from their closer locations to major Mexican markets, superior quality of their products, market knowledge and the relationships of trust developed with key business partners.

42484 ■ *If You Have to Cry, Go Outside: And Other Things Your Mother Never Told You*
Pub: HarperOne

Ed: Kelly Cutrone. **Released:** February 2, 2010. **Price:** $22.99. **Description:** Women's mentor advices on how to make it in one of the most competitive industries in the world, fashion. She has kicked people out of fashion shows, forced some of reality television's shiny start to fire their friends, and built her own company which is one of the most powerful public relations firms in the fashion business.

42485 ■ *"In the Wake of Pet-Food Crisis, Iams Sales Plummet Nearly 17 Percent" in Advertising Age (Vol. 78, May 14, 2007, No. 18, pp. 3)*
Pub: Crain Communications, Inc.

Ed: Jack Neff. **Description:** Although the massive U.S. pet-food recall impacted more than 100 brands, Procter & Gamble Co.'s Iams lost more sales and market share than any other industry player. According to Information Resources Inc. data, the brand's sales dropped 16.5 percent in the eight-week period ended April 22. Many analysts feel that the company could have handled the crisis in a better manner.

42486 ■ *"Insurance: Marathon Effort" in Canadian Business (Vol. 80, January 29, 2007, No. 3, pp. 11)*
Pub: Rogers Media

Ed: Jeff Sanford. **Description:** The efforts of the insurance firm ING Canada Inc. to manage its relations with its customers are described. The enhancement of the insurance services provided by the company is discussed.

42487 ■ *It's Not Who You Know - It's Who Knows You!: The Small Business Guide to Raising Your Profits by Raising Your Profile*
Pub: John Wiley & Sons, Inc.

Ed: David Avrin. **Released:** November 9, 2010. **Price:** $24.95. **Description:** When it comes to promoting a small business or a brand, it is essential to know how valuable high-profile attention can be. But for most small companies, the cost of hiring an outside firm to increase attention can be too expensive.

42488 ■ *"It's Time to Take Full Responsibility" in Harvard Business Review (Vol. 88, October 2010, No. 10, pp. 42)*
Pub: Harvard Business School Publishing

Ed: Rosabeth Moss Kanter. **Description:** A case for corporate responsibility is cited, focusing on long-term impact and the effects of public accountability.

42489 ■ *"Kraft Not Alone" in Crain's Chicago Business (Vol. 30, February 2007, No. 6, pp. 8)*
Pub: Crain Communications, Inc.

Description: Consumer watchdog group, The Center for Science in the Public Interest, has been putting pressure on food companies to be more truthful on their product labels. Listing of companies who have had misleading claims on their products is included.

42490 ■ *"Kuno Creative to Present B2B Social Media Campaign Webinar" in Entertainment Close-Up (August 25, 2011)*
Pub: Close-Up Media

Description: Kuno Creative, an inbound marketing agency, will host Three Steps of a Successful B2B Social Media Campaign. The firm is a provider of Website development, branding, marketing strategy, public relations, Internet marketing, and inbound marketing.

42491 ■ *"Leadership in Flight" in Women In Business (Vol. 63, Fall 2011, No. 3, pp. 24)*
Pub: American Business Women's Association

Ed: Leigh Elmore. **Description:** Flight attendants in major airlines are trained to keep passengers comfortable and to calmly deal with emergencies. They also have a significant role in brand image and customer loyalty as they interact with the customers directly. Examples of teamwork leadership for flight attendants are given.

42492 ■ *"Making Sense of Ambiguous Evidence" in Harvard Business Review (Vol. 86, September 2008, No. 9, pp. 53)*
Pub: Harvard Business School Press

Ed: Lisa Burrell. **Description:** Documentary filmmaker Errol Morris emphasizes the role of perception in portraying objective reality, and how investigation and analysis enhance the accuracy of that portrayal.

42493 ■ *Marketing in a Web 2.0 World - Using Social Media, Webinars, Blogs, and More to Boost Your Small Business on a Budget*
Pub: Atlantic Publishing Company

Ed: Peter VanRysdam. **Released:** June 1, 2010. **Price:** $24.95. **Description:** Web 2.0 technologies have leveled the playing field for small companies trying to boost their presence by giving them an equal voice against larger competitors. Advice is given to help target your audience using social networking hubs.

42494 ■ *"Massage the Message" in Canadian Business (Vol. 79, Winter 2006, No. 24, pp. 137)*
Pub: Rogers Media

Ed: Erin Pooley. **Description:** The methods adopted by Canadian billionaires to manage their public images are described.

42495 ■ *"McD's Warms Up For Olympics Performance" in Advertising Age (Vol. 79, July 7, 2008, No. 26, pp. 8)*
Pub: Crain Communications, Inc.

Description: Overview of McDonald's marketing plans for the company's sponsorship of the Olympics which includes a website, an alternate-reality game, names featured on U.S. athletes and on-the-ground activities.

42496 ■ *Media, Organizations and Identity*
Pub: Palgrave Macmillan

Ed: Lilie Chouliaraki, Mette Morsing. **Released:** January 19, 2010. **Price:** $90.00. **Description:** The mass media, press and television are a essential in the formation of corporate identity and the promotion of business image and reputation. This book offers a new perspective into the interrelationships between media and organizations over three dimensions: media as business, media in business and business in the media.

42497 ■ *"Menu Foods Seeks Answers in Death of Ten Pets" in Globe & Mail (March 19, 2007, pp. B2)*
Pub: CTVglobemedia Publishing Inc.

Ed: Thomas M. Burton. **Description:** The failure of Menu Foods Inc. to ascertain the cause of ten deaths of house pets, which were fed its food products, prompting the government to recall the products from the market, is discussed.

42498 ■ *"Microsoft Clicks Into High Speed" in Hispanic Business (Vol. 30, July-August 2008, No. 7-8, pp. 54)*
Pub: Hispanic Business, Inc.

Ed: Derek Reveron. **Description:** Microsoft's diversity hiring and vendor diversity program to capture more Hispanic consumer and business-to-business market is described. One of the main goals of these programs is to hire more Hispanic executives and managers who will help the company develop and market products and services that will appeal and benefit Hispanic consumers.

42499 ■ *"Network Like A Boy Scout" in Women Entrepreneur (January 15, 2009)*
Pub: Entrepreneur Media Inc.

Ed: Merrily Orsini. **Description:** Marketing for businesses that provide products or services that people only seek during emergencies or natural disasters such as hurricanes can be a challenge; tips for branding such businesses, networking and establishing a strong customer base that will refer your business to others are given.

42500 ■ *O'Dwyer's Directory of Public Relations Firms*
Pub: J.R. O'Dwyer Company Inc.

URL(s): www.odwyerpr.com. **Ed:** Kevin McCauley. **Released:** Annual; Latest edition 2012. **Price:** $95, Individuals. **Covers:** Over 1,600 public relations firms; international coverage. **Entries include:** Firm name, address, phone, principal executives, branch and overseas offices, billings, date founded, and 7,750 clients are cross-indexed. **Database includes:** List of top 50 public relations firms. **Arrangement:** Geographical by country. **Indexes:** Specialty (beauty and fashions, finance/investor, etc.), geographical, client.

42501 ■ *"Personal File: Laura Laing" in Canadian Business (Vol. 80, April 23, 2007, No. 9, pp. 58)*
Pub: Rogers Media

Description: A brief profile of Laura Laing, director of public relations at AdFarm, including her services, is presented.

42502 ■ *"Pet-Food Crisis a Boon to Organic Players" in Advertising Age (Vol. 78, April 9, 2007, No. 15, pp. 3)*
Pub: Crain Communications, Inc.

Ed: Jack Neff. **Description:** In the wake of the pet-food recall crisis, the natural-and-organic segment of the market is gaining recognition and sales; one such manufacturer, Blue Buffalo, has not only seen huge sale increases but also has witnessed a 50-60 percent increase in traffic to the brand's website which has led to the decision to move up the timetable for the brand's first national ad campaign.

42503 ■ *"Pet-Food Industry Too Slow" in Advertising Age (Vol. 78, March 26, 2007, No. 13, pp. 29)*
Pub: Crain Communications, Inc.

Description: Many crisis-communications experts believe that the pet-food industry mishandled the problem by waiting almost a month to recall the 60 million 'wet-food' products after numerous consumer complaints. Experts site that the first 24 to 49 hours are the most important in dealing with a crisis of this nature.

42504 ■ *"Powers Reels in Pinger" in Business Courier (Vol. 24, December 21, 2008, No. 36, pp. 1)*
Pub: American City Business Journals, Inc.

Ed: Lisa Biank Fasig. **Description:** Powers Agency has acquired Dan Pinger Public Relations Inc. after three years in planning. The new company is to be called 'Pinger PR at Powers'. Details of the deal and the new company are discussed.

42505 ■ *"Promote Your Business Through New Media" in Business Week (November 5, 2009)*
Pub: McGraw-Hill Companies

Ed: Karen E. Klein. **Description:** Traditional public relations strategies are becoming more and more outdated due to the rapid shift in Internet marketing opportunities. Ideas for marketing your company online are presented.

42506 ■ *Public Relations Tactics--Member Services Directory--The Blue Book: The PRSA Membership Networking Issue*
Pub: Public Relations Society of America
Contact: William Murray, President

URL(s): www.prsa.orgauth.iweb.prsa.org/xmembernet/main/directory.cfm. **Released:** Annual; latest edition 2007. **Covers:** PRSA members--headquaters, staff contacts, and chapter, section, and district information. **Entries include:** Name, professional affiliation and title, address, phone, membership rank. **Arrangement:** Alphabetical. **Indexes:** Geographical, organizational.

42507 ■ *"The Question: Who Do You Think Is the Most Genuine?" in Advertising Age (Vol. 79, July 7, 2008, No. 26, pp. 4)*
Pub: Crain Communications, Inc.
Ed: Ken Wheaton. **Description:** According to a survey conducted by Harris Interactive Reputation Quotient, Johnson & Johnson was deemed the most genuine brand. Google came in second followed by UPS.

42508 ■ *"Recalls Cause Consumers to Put More Stock in Online Reviews" in Crain's Cleveland Business (Vol. 28, November 12, 2007, No. 45)*
Pub: Crain Communications, Inc.
Ed: Jack Neff. **Description:** Due to the string of product recalls over the last year, consumers are looking at online product reviews to help them make purchasing decisions which could reshape marketing for a wide range of products.

42509 ■ *"Relationship "Farming" Tools" in Agency Sales Magazine (Vol. 39, August 2009, No. 8, pp. 46)*
Pub: MANA
Ed: Terry L. Brock. **Description:** Manufacturer's representatives should spend time, money and effort in establishing and maintaining relationships; one tool to help is the new Fujitsu S1500 scanner. The scanner can accomplish critical tasks, quickly, easily and at low cost. Other suggestions to help build better business relationships are given.

42510 ■ *"Report: McD's Pepsi Score Best With Young Hispanics" in Brandweek (Vol. 49, April 21, 2008, No. 16, pp. 8)*
Pub: VNU Business Media, Inc.
Ed: Della de Lafuente. **Description:** According to a new report, in order to reach Hispanic Gen Yers, marketing strategists need to understand this demographic's 'bi-dentity,' something which has proved an elusive task to many marketers. Another trend is the emergence of Latinas who have careers, as opposed to just jobs. There is an opportunity to tap this new, young and empowered female market with innovative messaging. Statistical data included.

42511 ■ *"Reputation Warfare" in Harvard Business Review (Vol. 88, December 2010, No. 12, pp. 70)*
Pub: Harvard Business School Publishing
Ed: Leslie Gaines-Ross. **Description:** Steps are presented for addressing attacks on corporate public image. These include responding promptly, avoiding disproportionate displays of force, empowering employees to present the firm's position, and stockpiling credentials to bolster credence.

42512 ■ *"Restaurants Dish Up Meal Deals To Attract Customers" in Crain's Detroit Business (Vol. 24, October 6, 2008, No. 40, pp. 1)*
Pub: Crain Communications, Inc.
Ed: Nathan Skid. **Description:** Restaurateurs are devising many creative and rewarding incentives to get customers to frequent their establishments during this economic crisis. Innovative ways in which even higher-end establishments are drawing in business are discussed.

42513 ■ *"Rich Returns: Media Master" in Entrepreneur (Vol. 35, October 2007, No. 10, pp. 42)*
Pub: Entrepreneur Media Inc.
Ed: Robert Kiyosaki. **Description:** Advertising is a powerful way of reaching clients, however, public relations is a less expensive method which is just as effective as advertising. Entrepreneurs must also be ready to try something new to be noticed by the public. Insights on how to master the use of media are given.

42514 ■ *Sarbanes-Oxley for Dummies, 2nd Ed.*
Pub: John Wiley and Sons, Inc.
Ed: Jill Gilbert Welytok. **Released:** February 2008. **Price:** $21.99. **Description:** Provides the latest Sarbanes-Oxley (SOX) legislation with procedures to safely and effectively reduce compliance costs. Topics include way to: establish SOX standards for IT professionals, minimize compliances costs for every aspect of a business, survive a Section 404 audit, avoid litigation under SOX, anticipate future rules and trends, create a post-SOX paper trail, increase a company's standing and reputation, work with SOX in a small business, meet new SOX standards, build a board that can't be bought, and to comply with all SOX management mandates.

42515 ■ *"The Seat-Of-The-Pants School of Marketing" in Brandweek (Vol. 49, April 21, 2008, No. 16, pp. 24)*
Pub: VNU Business Media, Inc.
Ed: David Vinjamuri. **Description:** Excerpt from the book 'Accidental Branding: How Ordinary People Build Extraordinary Brands,' by David Vinjamuri, discusses six shared principles for creating a brand that is unique and will be successful over the long-term.

42516 ■ *"Shoestring-Budget Marketing" in Women Entrepreneur (January 5, 2009)*
Pub: Entrepreneur Media Inc.
Ed: Maria Falconer. **Description:** Pay-per-click search engine advertising is the traditional type of e-marketing that may not only be too expensive for certain kinds of businesses but also may not attract the quality customer base a business looking to grow needs to find. Social networking websites have become a mandatory marketing tool for business owners who want to see growth in their sales; tips are provided for utilizing these networking websites in order to gain more visibility on the Internet which can, in turn, lead to the more sales.

42517 ■ *"Sick of Trends? You Should Be" in Brandweek (Vol. 49, April 21, 2008, No. 16, pp. 22)*
Pub: VNU Business Media, Inc.
Ed: Eric Zeitoun. **Description:** Eric Zeitoun, the president of Dragon Rouge, a global brand consultancy, discusses the importance of macrotrends as opposed to microtrends which he feels are often irrelevant, create confusion and cause marketers to lose site of the larger picture of their industry. Macrotrends, on the other hand, create a fundamental, societal shift that influences consumer attitudes over a long period of time.

42518 ■ *"Smart Businesses See Value, and Profit, in Promoting Women" in Crain's Chicago Business (Vol. 30, February 2007, No. 6, pp. 30)*
Pub: Crain Communications, Inc.
Ed: Marc J. Lane. **Description:** Despite U.S. corporations making little progress in advancing women to leadership positions over the past ten years, enlightened corporate decision makers understand that gender diversity is good business as the highest percentages of women officers yielded, on average, a 34 percent higher total return to shareholders and a 35.1 percent higher return on equity than those firms with the lowest percentages of women officers, according to a 2004 Catalyst study of Fortune 500 companies.

42519 ■ *"Sound Check" in Agency Sales Magazine (Vol. 39, August 2009, No. 8, pp. 14)*
Pub: MANA
Ed: Dave Kahle. **Description:** Most customers believe salespersons are unable to do well in terms of listening, which is one of the four fundamental competencies of a sales person. Listening is the primary tool to uncover deeper and more powerful needs and motivations of the customer. A guide on how to listen better and improve listening effectiveness is presented.

42520 ■ *Start Your Own Blogging Business, Second Edition*
Pub: Entrepreneur Press
Contact: Perlman Neil, President
Released: July 1, 2010. **Price:** $17.95. **Description:** Interviews with professional bloggers from some of the most popular blogs on the Internet will help anyone interested in starting their own blogging business.

42521 ■ *"Stock Delisting Could Hamper First Mariner" in Boston Business Journal (Vol. 29, July 29, 2011, No. 12, pp. 1)*
Pub: American City Business Journals Inc.
Ed: Gary Haber. **Description:** Possible delisting of First Mariner Bancorp from the Nasdaq stock exchange could adversely impact the bank's ability to attract institutional investors. Some institutions limit their investments to companies trading on the Nasdaq.

42522 ■ *"The Sure Thing That Flopped" in Harvard Business Review (Vol. 86, July-August 2008, No. 8, pp. 29)*
Pub: Harvard Business School Press
Ed: Gerald Zaltman; Lindsay Zaltman. **Description:** Fictitious brand extension scenario is presented, with contributors providing suggestions and advice. The company's struggles with expanding the brand may be alleviated by improving consumer research, focusing on emotional responses to products and services.

42523 ■ *"Suspense Hangs Over Fledging Film Industry" in Crain's Detroit Business (Vol. 26, January 18, 2010, No. 3, pp. 3)*
Pub: Crain Communications Inc.
Ed: Bill Shea. **Description:** Overview of the film incentive package which has fostered a growth in the industry with 52 productions completed in 2009, bringing in $223.6 million in gross in-state production expenditures of which the state will refund $87.2 million. Opposition to the incentives has been growing among legislatures who believe that the initiatives cost more than they ultimately bring into the state. Experts believe that the initiatives will remain since they have already fostered economic growth and are good for the state's image.

42524 ■ *"A Team Sport" in Business Courier (Vol. 26, October 2, 2009, No. 23, pp. 1)*
Pub: American City Business Journals, Inc.
Ed: Lisa Biank Fasig. **Description:** Procter & Gamble (P&G) revised the way it works with marketing, design and public relations firms. Creative discussions will be managed by only two representatives, the franchise leader and the brand agency leader in order for P&G to simplify operations as it grows larger and more global.

42525 ■ *"The Tech 100" in Canadian Business (Vol. 81, July 21, 2008, No. 11, pp. 48)*
Pub: Rogers Media Ltd.
Ed: Calvin Leung. **Description:** Absolute Software Corp. Day4 Energy Inc., Sandvine Corp., Norsat International Inc. and Call Genie Inc. are the five technology firms included in the annual ranking of top companies in Canada by market capitalization. The services and the one-year total return potential of the companies are presented.

42526 ■ *"Timberland's CEO On Standing Up to 65,000 Angry Activists" in Harvard Business Review (Vol. 88, September 2010, No. 9, pp. 39)*
Pub: Harvard Business School Publishing
Ed: Jeff Swartz. **Description:** Timberland Company avoided a potential boycott by taking a two-way approach. It addressed a supplier issue that posed a threat to the environment, and launched an email campaign to keep Greenpeace activists informed of the development of a new supplier agreement.

42527 ■ *"Toss the Gum Before You Speak" in Agency Sales Magazine (Vol. 39, July 2009, No. 7, pp. 34)*
Pub: MANA
Ed: Stephen D. Boyd. **Description:** When preparing to present to a prospective principal, a salesperson should anticipate the speaking situation and find out in advance the program events that occur around their speech. They should also practice their material in front of a friend or colleague.

42528 ■ *"Traits that Makes Blogs Attractive to Book Publishers" in Marketing to Women*

(Vol. 22, July 2009, No. 7, pp. 1)
Pub: EPM Communications Inc.
Contact: Ira Mayer, President
E-mail: imayer@epmcom.com
Description: Book publishers are finding a beneficial relationship between themselves and women bloggers on the Internet. A high visitor count, frequent updates and active readership are criteria for identifying the blogs with the most clout and therefore providing the greatest benefit to publishers.

42529 ■ *"Tweaking On-Board Activities, Equipment Saves Fuel, Reduces CO2" in Canadian Sailings (June 30, 2008)*
Pub: UBM Global Trade
Contact: Leonard J. Corallo, President
Description: Optimizing ship activities and equipment uses less fuel and therefore reduces greenhouse gas emissions. Ways in which companies are implementing research and development techniques in order to monitor ship performance and analyze data in an attempt to become more efficient are examined.

42530 ■ *"Utah Technology Council: Social Media Is Here to Stay; Embrace It" in Wireless News (December 14, 2009)*
Pub: Close-Up Media
Description: Social media outlets such as Facebook and Twitter are blurring the lines between advertising, public relations, branding and marketing; businesses must stop thinking in terms of traditional marketing versus Internet marketing if they want to succeed in today's marketing climate.

42531 ■ *"The Valuation of Players" in Canadian Business (Vol. 80, October 22, 2007, No. 21, pp. 39)*
Pub: Rogers Media
Ed: Jeff Sanford. **Description:** Business professionals are supplementing their Masters in Business Administration degrees with CBV or chartered business valuator. CBVs are trained, not only in business tangibles, but also in business intangibles such as market position, reputation, intellectual property, and patent. Details of employment opportunities for chartered business valuators are discussed.

42532 ■ *"Vanity Plates" in Canadian Business (Vol. 82, April 27, 2009, No. 7, pp. 26)*
Pub: Rogers Media
Ed: Andy Holloway. **Description:** Politicians in the U.S. called for the review of firms that availed of the bailout money but are under deals for naming rights of sports stadiums. Angus Reid's Corporate Reputation and Sponsorship Index found for example, that there is little correlation between sponsoring arenas on having a better brand image. It is suggested that firms who enter these deals build closer to people's homes.

42533 ■ *"Voice: Rebuilding Trust" in Business Strategy Review (Vol. 21, Summer 2010, No. 2, pp. 79)*
Pub: Wiley-Blackwell
Ed: David De Cremer. **Description:** The financial world's attempts to rebuild trust are charted. Three steps to jump-start that process are outlined.

42534 ■ *"Wait for the Call" in Canadian Business (Vol. 80, April 9, 2007, No. 8, pp. 74)*
Pub: Rogers Media
Ed: Andrew Wahl. **Description:** The effort of chief executive of BCE Inc. Michael Sabia to deal with rumors about the company's private equity deal with Kohlberg Kravis Roberts & Co. is discussed.

42535 ■ *"'We Had to Won the Mistakes" in Harvard Business Review (Vol. 88, July-August 2010, No. 7-8, pp. 108)*
Pub: Harvard Business School Publishing
Ed: Adi Ignatius. **Description:** Interview with Howard Schultz, CEO of Starbucks, covers topics that include investment in retraining, the impact of competition, premium quality, authenticity, customer services, strategy development, work-and-life issues, and international presence.

42536 ■ *"What School Did You Attend?" in Hawaii Business (Vol. 53, December 2007, No. 6, pp. 14)*
Pub: Hawaii Business Publishing
Ed: Kelli Abe Trifonovitch. **Description:** Discusses the question 'what school did you attend?' which is observed to be the most important inquiry in Hawaiian business discourse. The principle behind the question is based on establishing connections. The relation between the aforementioned inquiry and Hawaiian culture is explained.

42537 ■ *When the Headline Is You: An Insider's Guide to Handling the Media*
Pub: Jossey-Bass
Ed: Jeff Ansell, Jeff Lesson. **Price:** $29.95. **Description:** How-to guide for executives and other professionals whose high-visibility requires frequent interviews with the media. Tested techniques, tools, and insights for how to respond to all types of media in tough situation are provided. The books also reveals the lessons learned and the pitfalls to avoid by referencing actual news stores from around the world and provides exercises for readers who wish to sharpen their media-handling skills.

42538 ■ *"Wise Guy: Get In Good" in Entrepreneur (Vol. 35, October 2007, No. 10, pp. 46)*
Pub: Entrepreneur Media Inc.
Ed: Guy Kawasaki. **Description:** Good public relations are a requirement for business entrepreneurs, and it can be achieved through proper communication. Giving of and asking for favors are some of the ways to build relationships in the business world. Other tips on how to build good business relationships are provided.

42539 ■ *"Women-Centric Events Can Captivate Consumers" in Crain's Cleveland Business (Vol. 28, November 12, 2007, No. 45, pp. 24)*
Pub: Crain Communications, Inc.
Ed: Kimberly Bonvissuto. **Description:** Discusses innovative ways that companies are targeting the female consumer market including arranging networking and social events.

42540 ■ *"You Have to Lead From Everywhere" in Harvard Business Review (Vol. 88, November 2010, No. 11, pp. 76)*
Pub: Harvard Business School Publishing
Ed: Scott Berinato. **Description:** U.S. Coast Guard Admiral Thad W. Allen discusses effective leadership in successful crises management. Topics include influence of media and public perspective, the applicability of military training to the business arena, and the responsibility of a leader to set morale.

42541 ■ *"Your Big Give" in Small Business Opportunities (September 2008)*
Pub: Entrepreneur Press
Contact: Perlman Neil, President
Ed: Michael Guld. **Description:** Cause related marketing is beneficial to businesses as well as the communities they inhabit; three small businesses that are elevating their standing in the community while at the same time increasing their customer base are profiled.

TRADE PERIODICALS

42542 ■ *The Levison Letter*
Pub: Ivan Levison & Associates
Ed: Ivan Levison, Editor, ivan@levison.com. **Released:** Monthly. **Price:** Free. **Description:** Offers tips for improving marketing.

VIDEOCASSETTES/ AUDIOCASSETTES

42543 ■ *The Crisis Interview: A Media Relations Guide for Field Personnel*
Gulf Publishing Co.
2 Greenway Plz., Ste. 1020
Houston, TX 77046-0208
Ph: (713)529-4301
Free: 800-231-6275
Fax: (713)520-4433
Co. E-mail: advertising@gulfpub.com
URL: http://www.gulfpub.com
Contact: John Royall, President
Released: 19??. **Price:** $495.00. **Description:** Offers media relations training for managers, supervisors, and field personnel. Dramatization shows a chemical company supervisor who is in the unaccustomed role of spokesperson as he arrives to oversee a cleanup of a chemical spill. Illustrates issues such as the community's right to know, how to take control of a situation, what is expected from a spokesperson, and how to end an interview on your own terms. Includes reference guide. **Availability:** VHS.

CONSULTANTS

42544 ■ Sol Abrams Public Relations Counsel & Marketing Consultants
331 Webster Dr.
New Milford, NJ 07646
Ph: (201)262-4111
Fax: (201)262-7669
Contact: Sol Abrams, Owner
E-mail: solbabrams@aol.com
Scope: Independent consulting provides publicity, public relations and marketing counsel and services to management of private and public enterprises. Also serves as public relations consultants to other public relations consulting firms, advertising agencies and marketing companies. Provides expert witness services involving public relations. Also lectures, trains, teaches, and conducts seminars in public relations and marketing. Industries served: Corporate management, businesses large and small including real estate, construction, entertainment, food, fashion, fundraising, automotive, aviation, franchising, government agencies, and nonprofit organizations. **Founded:** 1962. **Seminars:** How to Select a Public Relations Firm; Publicity and Promotion for Small Business Owner; Expose Yourself - Don't Be a Secret Agent -Increase Your Sales, Incomes, Images, Publicity, Profits and Prestige via Professional Public Relations.

42545 ■ Bitner Goodman
701 W Cypress Creek Rd., Ste. 204
Fort Lauderdale, FL 33309-2045
Ph: (954)730-7730
Fax: (954)730-7130
Co. E-mail: gary@bitnergoodman.com
URL: http://www.bitnergoodman.com
Contact: Gary Bitner, President
Scope: A public relations, advertising and marketing consultancy. Serves industries including: travel, technology, telecommunications, financial services, consumer products, health-care, government, automotive, real estate and retail. **Founded:** 1980. **Telecommunication Services:** info@bitnergoodman.com.

42546 ■ Burns Public Relations Services Inc.—Dargan Burns Public Relations Services
1660 W 2nd St., Ste. 410
Cleveland, OH 44113-1454
Ph: (216)621-5950
Fax: (216)241-7300
Contact: D.J. Burns, President
Scope: Full service public communicators and consultants. Specializations: marketing strategies, urban affairs, minority business enterprise; and Affirmative Action programming. **Founded:** 1959.

42547 ■ Kelley Chunn & Associates (KCA)
184 Dudley St., Ste. 106
Boston, MA 02119
Ph: (617)427-0997
Fax: (617)427-3997
Co. E-mail: kc4info@aol.com
URL: http://www.kelleychunn.com
Contact: Kelley C. Chunn, President
E-mail: kcprmail@aol.com
Scope: Consulting firm that specializes in multicultural and cause-related public relations and marketing. Services include: Cause-related marketing, strategic planning, community relations, corporate

communications, guerrilla marketing, event planning and management, public affairs, media relations and training. **Founded:** 1991. **Publications:** "The Tipping point of social marketing Color Magazine"; "Community Voices, Bay State Banner"; "Education: Inner City Slickers," 2006. **Seminars:** Crisis communications; Guerrilla marketing; Ethnic marketing.

42548 ■ Coyne Associates
4010 E Lake St.
Minneapolis, MN 55406-2201
Ph: (612)724-1188
Fax: (612)722-1379
Contact: John T. Coyne, Chief Executive Officer
Scope: A marketing and public relations consulting firm that specializes in assisting architectural, engineering, and contractor/developer firms. Services include: marketing plains and audits, strategic planning, corporate identity, turnarounds, and sales training. **Founded:** 2008.

42549 ■ Wayne Dean Public Relations—W. Dean Productions
1064 Palmetto St.
Mobile, AL 36604-3041
Ph: (334)335-3601
Co. E-mail: revchief@fcbl.net
Contact: Bennett Wayne Dean, Sr., President
Scope: Provider of public relations consulting services to all industries, including government agencies, religious organizations, and small businesses and organizations. Services include programming and budgeting, publicity (news releases, electronic spots, features), advertising, promotions, writing and editing, staff training, speeches and internal communication. Also does publicist work for entertainment industry. Operates internet vending of collectible and other items-goods and services. **Founded:** 1985. **Publications:** "The Swarming Bee Hive," 1984.

42550 ■ Devillier Communications Inc.
3315 Fessenden St., NW
Washington, DC 20008-2034
Ph: (202)362-4429
Fax: (202)966-5754
Co. E-mail: info@devillier.com
URL: http://www.devillier.com
Contact: Linda Devillier, President
Scope: Firm marketing consultancy. Firm develops innovative solutions for a wide range of extra ordinary clients. **Founded:** 1984.

42551 ■ Donna Cornell Enterprises Inc.—Cornell Career Center
68 N Plank Rd., Ste. 204
Newburgh, NY 12550-2122
Ph: (845)565-0088
Free: 888-769-3792
Fax: (845)565-0084
Co. E-mail: rc@cornellcareercenter.com
Contact: Donna Cornell, President
E-mail: rc@cornellcareercenter.com
Scope: Offers services in career consultant, professional search, job placement and national professional search. **Founded:** 1996. **Publications:** "The Power of the Woman Within"; "Juggling it All!"; "Journey: A Woman's Guide to Success"; "Shatter the Traditions".

42552 ■ Russ Fons Public Relations
7509 Turtle Dove Ct.
Las Vegas, NV 89129-6032
Ph: (702)658-7654
Free: 888-658-7654
Fax: (702)658-1349
Co. E-mail: russfons@cox.net
Contact: Russ Fons, Owner
E-mail: russfons@cox.net
Scope: Offers corporate counseling and image development; media relations; marketing communications and product publicity; event management and special promotions; and graphic design and production. Industries served: All worldwide. Licensing and merchandising, literary services, Hispanic communications. Revenue Sharing/PI Advertising. **Founded:** 1980. **Publications:** "The Executive Crisis Manager, a planning guide to surviving corporate crisis".

42553 ■ Health Strategy Group Inc.
46 River Rd.
Chatham, NY 12037
Ph: (518)392-6770
Contact: Cameron Battley, President
Scope: Provides consulting services in the areas of strategic planning, feasibility studies, start-up businesses, organizational development, market research, customer service audits, new product development, marketing, public relations. **Founded:** 1981. **Publications:** "Online Consumer Surveys as a Methodology for Assessing the Quality of the United States Health Care System," 2004.

42554 ■ hightechbiz.com—Leahy & Associates Inc.
4209 Santa Monica Blvd., Ste. 201
Los Angeles, CA 90029-3027
Ph: (323)913-3355
Free: 877-648-4753
Fax: (323)913-3355
URL: http://www.hightechbiz.com
Contact: Steven L. Hayes, Principal
Scope: A full service marketing agency specializing in integrated marketing solutions. Services include: marketing surveys; positioning surveys; strategic and tactical plans; implementation plans; management consulting; product brochures; product catalogs; product packaging; product data sheets; direct mail programs; media research; competitive research; complete creative; production and film; media placement; corporate identity; in-house creative; public relations. **Founded:** 1980.

42555 ■ C. W. Hines and Associates Inc.—C&W Associates Inc.
344 Churchill Cir., Sanctuary Bay
White Stone, VA 22578
Ph: (804)435-8844
Fax: (804)435-8855
Co. E-mail: turtlecwh@aol.com
URL: http://www.cwhinesassociates.org
Contact: Dr. Carolyn C.W. Hines, President
Scope: Management consultants with expertise in the following categories: advertising and public relations; health and human resources; management sciences; organizational development; computer sciences; financial management; behavioral sciences; environmental design; technology transfer; project management; facility management; program evaluation; and business therapy. Also included are complementary areas such as sampling procedures; job training; managerial effectiveness; corporate seminars; gender harassment; training for trainers and leadership and management skills development. **Founded:** 1979. **Publications:** "Money Muscle, 120 Exercises To Build Spiritual And Financial Strength," 2004; "Inside Track: Executives Coaching Executives"; "Money Muscle: 122 Exercises to Build Financial Strength"; "Nuts and Bolts of Work Force Diversity"; "Legal Issues, published in the Controllers Business Advisor"; "Identifying Racism: Specific Examples"; "BOSS Spelled Backwards is double SSOB! Or is it?"; "A No-Nonsense Guide to Being Stressed". **Seminars:** Career Development; Coaching and Counseling for Work Success; Communicating More Effectively in a Diverse Work Environment; Communications 600: Advanced Skills for Relationship Building; Customer Service: Building a Caring Culture.

42556 ■ Jeffrey Lant Associates Inc.
50 Follen St., Ste. 507
Cambridge, MA 02138
Ph: (617)547-6372
Fax: (617)547-0061
URL: http://www.jeffreylant.com
Contact: Dr. Jeffrey L. Lant, President
E-mail: drjlant@worldprofit.com
Description: Description: Publishes technical assistance books for nonprofit organizations, consultants, independent professionals and small and home-based businesses. Offers audio cassettes, workshops and consultation services. Also publishes twice monthly Worlgram newsletter. Reaches market through commission representatives, direct mail, telephone sales and the Internet. Accepts unsolicited manuscripts. **Scope:** Sets up businesses online, design websites and assists with marketing. **Founded:** 1979. **Publications:** "E-mail El Dorado," JLA Publications, 1998; "Web Wealth: How to Turn the World Wide Web Into a Cash Hose for Your Business. Whatever You're Selling," 1997; "Multi-Level Money," JLA Publications, 1994; "No More Cold Calls," JLA Publications, 1997; "Cash Copy"; "How to make at least $100000 a year"; "E-Money". **Seminars:** Business and personal development, including Establishing and Operating Your Successful Consulting Business; Successfully Promoting Your Small Business and Professional Practice; Succeeding in Your Mail Order Business; Successfully Raising Money for Your Nonprofit Organization from Foundations, Corporations and Individuals; Money Making Marketing: Finding the People Who Need What You're Selling and Making Sure They Buy It; Getting Corporations, Foundations, and Individuals to Give You the Money Your Nonprofit Organization Needs.

42557 ■ Gary Ruben Inc., Marketing Communications Consultants
931 E 86th St., Ste. 206
Indianapolis, IN 46240-1860
Ph: (317)251-5330
Contact: Gary A. Ruben, President
Scope: A communications and marketing consulting firm whose services include: advertising agency selection, advertising agency performance review, advertising program structuring, creative assistance, advertising program measurement, public relations program structuring, advertising department personnel development, in house agency structuring, and executive counseling. Industries served include supermarket chains, franchise systems, and retail products and services. **Founded:** 1976.

42558 ■ S & S Public Relations Inc.
2700 Patriot Blvd., Ste. 430
Glenview, IL 60026
Ph: (847)955-0700
Free: 800-287-2279
Fax: (847)955-7720
Co. E-mail: ssimon@sspr.com
URL: http://www.sspr.com
Contact: Steve Simon, President
E-mail: ssimon@sspr.com
Scope: Offers a wide range of public relations consulting services particularly for franchisers, authors, consultants, and various products. **Founded:** 1978.

42559 ■ Shannon Staffing Inc.
636 Chestnut St.
Coshocton, OH 43812
Ph: (740)622-2600
Fax: (740)622-9638
Co. E-mail: coshocton@shannonstaffing.com
Contact: Edward A. Seitz, President
E-mail: eseitz@shannonstaffing.com
Scope: Serving broad range of industries and public sector organizations and foundations. Specializing in human resources recruiting and outplacement counseling on international scale for businesses of all sizes. Offers expertise in human resources policies and procedures, supervisor development, manager leadership style development, interview training, etc. Provides consulting to small business in human resources, advertising, marketing, sales, public relations and community relations. **Founded:** 1985. **Publications:** "Powells Rules for Picking People". **Seminars:** Time Management workshop.

42560 ■ Tom Shillock Consulting
5545 SW Windsor Ct.
Portland, OR 97221-2150
Ph: (503)291-7928
Fax: (503)221-2052
Co. E-mail: tomsh@qwest.net
Contact: Tom Shillock, Principal
E-mail: tomsh@qwest.net
Scope: Offers consulting services in marketing and communications including public relations and advertising. Industries served: high technology. **Founded:** 1988.

42561 ■ Sparkworks Media
325 W Republican St.
Seattle, WA 98119-4008
Ph: (206)284-5500

Fax: (206)284-6611
Co. E-mail: info@sparkworksmedia.com
URL: http://www.sparkworksmedia.com
Contact: Heath Ward, Director

Scope: Offers counsel on media and video production for medium and small businesses, governmental and educational institutions. Editing and other post production work as required. Distribution and marketing for products produced. Full service production firm for video and new media. **Founded:** 1979.

42562 ■ Alan J. Zell

PO Box 69
Portland, OR 97207-0069
Ph: (503)241-1988
Fax: (503)241-1989
Co. E-mail: azell@aol.com
URL: http://www.sellingselling.com
Contact: Alan J. Zell, Owner
E-mail: azell@aol.com

Scope: An advisory service for those who sell their services, products or their organization's ideas, information, and skills through face-to-face and telephone conversations, printed materials, the media, electronic communications, schools, guilds, trade shows, and display presentations. Industries served: minority and woman-owned businesses; government and education; medicine, law, accounting, technology, manufacturers, distributors, and retailers; professional and trade associations; and nonprofit organizations. **Founded:** 1983. **Publications:** "Elements of Selling"; "An Unconventional Look at the Complex Subject of Selling"; "The Art Of Selling Art"; "Selling Situations"; "What Customers need to know"; "Turnover & Return on Investment"; "The Ultimate Business Oxymoron"; "Walkin The Aisles, Looking at the Booths, etc"; "Four Uses Of Internet". **Seminars:** Ambassador Of Selling; An Unconventional Look at the Complex Subject of Selling; Selling Change . . . Pain or Progress, Revolution or Evolution?; Giving GOOD SERVICE When Giving Good Service Is Not Good Enough; Two Sides Of A Trade Show; Selling For People Who Do Not Like To Sell; The Art Of Selling Art; Yes, Technically Trained People Can Learn To Sell; Beginning Business, How To Achieve Your Goals. **Telecommunication Services:** alan@sellingselling.com.

START-UP INFORMATION

42563 ■ *"Revel in Riches!" in Small Business Opportunities (May 2008)*
Pub: Harris Publications Inc.
Description: Profile of Proforma, a business-to-business franchise firm providing print and promotional products.

ASSOCIATIONS AND OTHER ORGANIZATIONS

42564 ■ Advertising Club of New York (ACNY)
989 Ave. of the Americas, 7th Fl.
New York, NY 10018
Ph: (212)533-8080
Fax: (212)533-1929
Co. E-mail: gina@theadvertisingclub.org
URL: http://www.theadvertisingclub.org
Contact: Beth-Ann Eason, Chairwoman
Description: Professionals in advertising, publishing, marketing and business. Sponsors educational and public service activities, promotional and public relations projects and talks by celebrities and advertising persons. Conducts annual advertising and marketing course, which offers classes in copywriting, special graphics, verbal communication, advertising production, sale promotion, marketing and management. Sponsors competitions and charitable programs. **Founded:** 1906. **Publications:** *ACNY Membership Roster* (Annual); *Auction Catalogue and Program* (Annual); *ANDY Souvenir Journal* (Annual). **Awards:** ANDY Awards; ANDY Award (Annual); The Silver Medal Award (Annual).

42565 ■ Advertising Council (AC)
815 2nd Ave., 9th Fl.
New York, NY 10017
Ph: (212)922-1500
Fax: (212)922-1676
Co. E-mail: info@adcouncil.org
URL: http://www.adcouncil.org
Contact: Andrew Robertson, Chairman
Description: Founded and supported by American business, media, and advertising sectors to conduct public service advertising campaigns. Encourages advertising media to contribute time and space and advertising agencies to supply creative talent and facilities to further timely national causes. Specific campaigns include: Drug Abuse Prevention; AIDS Prevention; Teen-Alcoholism; Child Abuse; Crime Prevention; Forest Fire Prevention. **Founded:** 1941. **Publications:** *PSA Bulletin* (Bimonthly). **Awards:** Public Service Award (Annual); Silver Bell Award (Annual); Public Service Award.

42566 ■ Advertising and Marketing International Network (AMIN)
3587 Northshore Dr.
Wayzata, MN 55391
Ph: (952)457-1116
Fax: (952)471-7752
Co. E-mail: jsundby@aminworldwide.com
URL: http://www.aminworldwide.com
Contact: Janna Sperry Sundby, Manager, Member Services
Description: Comprised of cooperative worldwide network of non-competing independent advertising agencies organized to provide facilities and branch office services for affiliated agencies. **Founded:** 1932. **Educational Activities:** Advertising and Marketing International Network Seminar (Annual).

42567 ■ Advertising Research Foundation (ARF)
432 Park Ave. S, 6th Fl.
New York, NY 10016-8013
Ph: (212)751-5656
Fax: (212)319-5265
Co. E-mail: info@thearf.org
URL: http://www.thearf.org
Contact: Robert Barocci, President
E-mail: bb@thearf.org
URL(s): www.arfsite.org. **Description:** Advertisers, advertising agencies, research organizations, associations, and the media are regular members of the foundation; colleges and universities are associate members. Objectives are to: further scientific practices and promote greater effectiveness of advertising and marketing by means of objective and impartial research; develop new research methods and techniques; analyze and evaluate existing methods and techniques, and define proper applications; establish research standards, criteria, and reporting methods. Compiles statistics and conducts research programs. **Scope:** advertising, marketing. **Founded:** 1936. **Subscriptions:** 2500 clippings periodicals reports. **Publications:** *Journal of Advertising Research* (Quarterly; Bimonthly). **Educational Activities:** Re:think (Annual); ARF Annual Convention (Annual). **Awards:** David Ogilvy Awards (Annual); Rising Star Award; Innovation Award; Member Recognition Award; Michael J. Naples Award (Annual). **Telecommunication Services:** journal@thearf.org.

42568 ■ Advertising Women of New York (AWNY)
25 W 45th St., Ste. 403
New York, NY 10036
Ph: (212)221-7969
Fax: (212)221-8296
Co. E-mail: awny@awny.org
URL: http://www.awny.org
Contact: Arlene Manos, President
E-mail: amanos@awny.org
Description: Women in advertising and related industries that provides a forum for professional growth, serves as catalyst for enhancement and advancement of women; promotes philanthropic endeavors. Conducts events of interest and benefit to members and non-members involved in the industry. Membership concentrated in the metropolitan New York area. **Founded:** 1912. **Awards:** Silver Medal Award; Advertising Woman of the Year (Annual); President's Award; Crystal Prism Award.

42569 ■ American Academy of Advertising (AAA)
Florida International University
831 Langdon
831 Fearrington Post
Pittsboro, NC 27312
Ph: (786)393-3333
Free: 866-607-8512
Co. E-mail: director@aaasite.org
URL: http://www.aaasite.org
Contact: Patricia B. Rose, Executive Director
Description: Serves as a professional organization for college and university teachers of advertising and for industry professionals who wish to contribute to the development of advertising education. **Founded:** 1958. **Publications:** *Journal of Advertising* (Quarterly); *Journal of Interactive Advertising* (Semiannual); *Proceedings of the Conference of the American Academy of Advertising* (Annual); *Roster of Members* (Annual). **Awards:** Distinguished Service Award; Doctoral Dissertation Grant Competition; Distinguished Service Award (Periodic); Fellow of the American Academy of Advertising Award (Periodic); Journal of Advertising Best Article Award (Annual); Outstanding Contribution to Research Award (Periodic).

42570 ■ American Advertising Federation (AAF)—AAF
1101 Vermont Ave. NW, Ste. 500
Washington, DC 20005-6306
Ph: (202)898-0089
Free: 800-999-2231
Fax: (202)898-0159
Co. E-mail: aaf@aaf.org
URL: http://www.aaf.org
Contact: James Edmund Datri, President
Description: Works to advance the business of advertising as a vital and essential part of the American economy and culture through government and public relations; professional development and recognition; community service, social responsibility and high standards; and benefits and services to members. Operates Advertising Hall of Fame, Hall of Achievement, and National Student Advertising Competition. Maintains speakers' bureau. **Founded:** 1967. **Publications:** *AAF Government Report*; *American Advertising Federation--Speakers Directory* (Annual); *Communicator* (Monthly); *Newsline* (Monthly); *American Advertising*; *American Advertising: The American Advertising Federation Magazine* (Quarterly). **Educational Activities:** National Advertising (Annual); American Advertising Federation Annual Conference (Annual). **Awards:** ADDY Awards (Annual); Barton A. Cummings Gold Medal Award (Annual); Betty Riehl Excellence in Service Award (Annual); Distinguished Advertising Educator Award (Annual); Silver Medal Award; Advertising Hall of Fame; Club Achievement Awards; Distinguished Advertising Educator Award; National Student Advertising Competition; Silver Medal; Advertising Hall of Achievement (Annual); James S. Fish Aid to Advertising Education Award. **Telecommunication Services:** acroot@aaf.org.

42571 ■ American Association of Advertising Agencies (AAAA)
1065 Ave. of the Americas, 16th Fl.
New York, NY 10018
Ph: (212)682-2500
Fax: (212)682-8391
Co. E-mail: nhill@aaaa.org
URL: http://www.aaaa.org
Contact: Nancy Hill, President
Description: Fosters development of the advertising industry; assists member agencies to operate more efficiently and profitably. Sponsors member information and international services. Maintains 47 committees. Conducts government relations. **Scope:** advertising, marketing. **Services:** Interlibrary loan; primarily serves association members. **Founded:** 1917. **Holdings:** 2000 books; 300 VF drawers of clippings, reports, and pamphlets. **Subscriptions:** 250 journals and other serials. **Publications:** *AAAA Publications Catalog* (Periodic); *The Reporter* (Bimonthly); *Roster of Members* (Annual); *Cable Broadcast Traffic Guide*; *American Association of Advertising Agencies--Roster and Organization* (Annual); *Advertising Agency Accounting/Finance/Collaboration Software Directory*. **Educational Activities:** American Association of Advertising Agencies Conference (Annual). **Awards:** O'Toole Agency Awards; O'Toole Award (Annual); Bill Bernbach Diversity Scholarships; Multicultural Advertising Intern Program; O'Toole Multicultural Advertising Award; O'Toole Public Service Award; AAAA Operation Jumpstart III Scholarships. **Telecommunication Services:** research@aaaa.org; webmaster@aaaa.org.

42572 ■ American Lutheran Publicity Bureau (ALPB)
4 Court St.
Delhi, NY 13753-0327
Ph: (607)746-7511
Fax: (607)746-7511
Co. E-mail: dkralpb@aol.com
URL: http://www.alpb.org
Contact: Rev. John R. Hannah, President
Description: Organized by laymen and pastors of the Lutheran church to publicize its teachings, work, and activities in a movement towards Lutheran unity. Helps Lutherans to explain their faith to non-Lutherans and the unchurched and to discuss important issues in church and society. **Founded:** 1914. **Publications:** *Forum Letter* (Monthly); *Lutheran Forum* (Quarterly); *For All the Saints: A Prayer Book For and By the Church*; *Heaven on Earth: A Lutheran-Orthodox Odyssey*; *O Lord, Teach Me to Pray: A Catechetical Prayer Book for Personal Use*; *We Believe: A Prayer Book Based on the Augsburg Confession*. **Educational Activities:** Inter-Lutheran Forum (Biennial).

42573 ■ Association of Free Community Papers (AFCP)
7445 Morgan Rd., Ste. 103
Liverpool, NY 13090
Free: 877-203-2327
Fax: (781)459-7770
Co. E-mail: afcp@afcp.org
URL: http://www.afcp.org
Contact: Scott Patterson, President
Description: Represents publishers of nearly 3,000 free circulation papers and shopping/advertising guides. Offers national classified advertising placement service and national marketing for industry recognition. Conducts charitable programs. Sponsors competitions and compiles industry statistics. **Founded:** 1950. **Publications:** *Free Paper INK* (Monthly).

42574 ■ Association of Independent Commercial Producers (AICP)
3 W 18th St., 5th Fl.
New York, NY 10011
Ph: (212)929-3000
Fax: (212)929-3359
Co. E-mail: info@aicp.com
URL: http://www.aicp.com
Contact: Matt Miller, President
Description: Represents the interests of companies that specialize in producing television commercials for advertisers and agencies, and the businesses that furnish supplies and services to this industry. Serves as a collective voice for the industry before government and business councils, and in union negotiations; disseminates information; works to develop industry standards and tools; provides professional development; and markets American production. **Founded:** 1972. **Publications:** *AICP National Newsletter*. **Awards:** The Jay B. Eisenstat Award (Periodic); The AICP Show: The Art and Technique of the American Television Commercial (Annual).

42575 ■ Association of National Advertisers (ANA)
708 3rd Ave., 33rd Fl.
New York, NY 10017-4270
Ph: (212)697-5950
Fax: (212)687-7310
Co. E-mail: info@ana.net
URL: http://www.ana.net
Contact: Robert D. Liodice, President
Description: Serves the needs of members by providing marketing and advertising industry leadership in traditional and e-marketing, legislative leadership, information resources, professional development and industry-wide networking. Maintains offices in New York City and Washington, DC. **Founded:** 1910. **Publications:** *The Advertiser* (Bimonthly). **Educational Activities:** Agency Relationship Forum (Annual). **Awards:** Multicultural Excellence Awards; Robert V. Goldstein Award (Annual).

42576 ■ Eight Sheet Outdoor Advertising Association (ESOAA)
PO Box 2680
Bremerton, WA 98310-0344
Ph: (360)377-9867
Free: 800-874-3387
Fax: (360)377-9870
Co. E-mail: ddjesoaa@comcast.net
URL: http://www.esoaa.com
Contact: Carla Osmus, President
Description: Promotes the use of 8-sheet poster panels in outdoor advertising. (8-sheet signs are smaller than the usual 24-sheet ones, and are most commonly composed of 1 or 3 sheets covering an area of 6 x 12 feet.). **Founded:** 1953. **Publications:** *Rates and Allotments: 8 Sheet Poster Panels in the Top Population Ranked Markets* (Annual); *Eight Sheet Outdoor Advertising Association-Sources: A Guide to Suppliers of Outdoor Materials and Services* (Annual); *Eight Sheet Outdoor Advertising Association-Sources: A Guide to Suppliers of Outdoor Materials and Services* (Annual); *Rates and Allotments: 8 Sheet Poster Panels in the Top Population Ranked Markets* (Annual). **Educational Activities:** Eight Sheet Outdoor Advertising Association Annual Conference (Annual). **Telecommunication Services:** dave@jacobsbillboards.com.

42577 ■ Intermarket Agency Network (IAN)
c/o Cameron Green, Pres.
1938 Fairview Ave. E, Ste. 200
Seattle, WA 98102-3650
Ph: (206)447-4747
Fax: (206)447-9494
Co. E-mail: camg@greenrubino.com
URL: http://www.intermarketnetwork.com
Contact: Cam Green, President
Description: An active network of high-powered marketing/communications agencies in the United States, Canada, Central and South America, and Europe. **Founded:** 1967.

42578 ■ International Advertising Association (IAA)
275 Madison Ave., Ste. 2102
New York, NY 10016
Ph: (212)557-1133
Fax: (212)983-0455
Co. E-mail: membership@iaaglobal.org
URL: http://www.iaaglobal.org
Contact: Luis Mendiola Codina, President
Description: Global network of advertisers, advertising agencies, the media and related services, spanning 99 countries. Demonstrates to governments and consumers the benefits of advertising as the foundation of diverse, independent media. Protects and advances freedom of commercial speech and consumer choice, encourages greater practice and acceptance of advertising self-regulation, provides a forum to debate emerging professional marketing communications issues and their consequences in the fast-changing world environment, and takes the lead in state-of-the-art professional development through education and training for the marketing communications industry of tomorrow. Conducts research on such topics as restrictions and taxes on advertising, advertising trade practices and related information, and advertising expenditures around the world. Sponsors IAA Education Program. Has compiled recommendations for international advertising standards and practices. **Scope:** advertising/marketing communications, regulatory issues affecting the industry. **Founded:** 1938. **Subscriptions:** audiovisuals books clippings monographs periodicals. **Publications:** *IAA Membership Directory* (Annual); *International Advertising Association--Membership Directory* (Continuous); *IAA National & World News*; *The Case for Advertising Self-Regulation*; *IAA Annual Report* (Annual); *IAA Membership Directory* (Annual); *International Advertising Association Membership Directory*; *IAA National & World News*. **Educational Activities:** World Advertising (Biennial); International Advertising Association - World Advertising Congress (Biennial). **Awards:** Samir Fares Award (Biennial). **Telecommunication Services:** iaa@iaaglobal.org.

42579 ■ International Communications Agency Network (ICOM)
PO Box 490
Rollinsville, CO 80474-0490
Ph: (303)258-9511
Fax: (303)484-4087
Co. E-mail: info@icomagencies.com
URL: http://www.icomagencies.com
Contact: Mr. Gary Burandt, Executive Director
Description: Network of non-competing advertising agencies. Provides an interchange of management information, international facilities, and branch office service for partner agencies. Provides discounts on syndicated services and access to 1,000 computer databases. **Founded:** 1950. **Publications:** *Agency Client Lists* (Monthly); *Agency Client Lists* (Monthly); *The Globe* (Monthly); *Membership Roster* (Annual). **Educational Activities:** International Management Conference (Annual). **Awards:** Creative Award (Annual).

42580 ■ Mailing and Fulfillment Service Association (MFSA)
1421 Prince St., Ste. 410
Alexandria, VA 22314-2806
Ph: (703)836-9200
Free: 800-333-6272
Fax: (703)548-8204
Co. E-mail: mfsa-mail@mfsanet.org
URL: http://www.mfsanet.org
Contact: Michael Kellogg, Chairman of the Board
Description: Commercial direct mail producers, letter shops, mailing list houses, fulfillment operations, and advertising agencies. Conducts special interest group meetings. Offers specialized education; conducts research programs. **Founded:** 1920. **Publications:** *Postscripts* (Monthly); *MFSA Wage Salary, and Fringe Benefit Survey* (Semiannual); *Performance Profiles: The Financial Ratios for the Mailing Service Industry* (Annual); *Who's Who: MASA's Buyers' Guide to Blue Ribbon Mailing Services* (Annual). **Educational Activities:** Mid-Winter Executive Conference (Annual). **Awards:** Leo G. Bill Bernheimer Award (Annual); Miles Kimball Medallion (Annual); Henry Hoke, Sr. Award; Miles Kimball Medallion; Mailing Industry Ingenuity Award; President's Plaque; John Howie Wright Cup; L.V. Luke Kaiser Educational Award (Annual); Robert M. Huse Chapter Achievement Award (Annual); Leo G. Bill Bernheimer, Jr. Award; L. U. "Luke" Kaiser Educational Award.

42581 ■ Marketing and Advertising Global Network (MAGNET)
1017 Perry Hwy., Ste. 5
Pittsburgh, PA 15237
Ph: (412)366-6850
Fax: (412)366-6840
Co. E-mail: mxdirector@verizon.net
URL: http://www.magnetglobal.org
Contact: Cheri D. Gmiter, Executive Director
Description: Cooperative network of non-competing advertising, marketing, merchandising, and public

relations agencies. Aims to bring about, through mutual cooperation, greater accomplishment and efficiency in the management of member advertising agencies. Other goals are: to raise standards of the advertising agency business through the exchange of information relative to agency management and all phases of advertising; to exchange information on all common problems, such as management, sales development, market studies, agency functions, and operations. Aims to inform the general public of current global marketing trends. **Founded:** 1946. **Publications:** *MAGNET Matters* (3/year); *This Week at MAGNET* (Weekly). **Educational Activities:** Marketing and Advertising Global Network Annual Meeting (Annual). **Awards:** Indie Awards Competition (Annual). **Telecommunication Services:** cheri@magnetglobal.org.

42582 ■ National Advertising Review Board (NARB)
70 W 36th St., 13th Fl.
New York, NY 10018
Ph: (212)705-0114
Co. E-mail: bhopewell@asrcreviews.org
URL: http://www.asrcreviews.org/category/narb
Contact: Bruce Hopewell, Director
Description: Individuals from industry and the public. Sponsored by the National Advertising Review Council for the purpose of sustaining high standards of truth and accuracy in national advertising. Aims to maintain a self-regulatory mechanism that responds constructively to public complaints about national advertising and which significantly improves advertising performance and credibility. **Scope:** advertising disputes. **Founded:** 1971. **Subscriptions:** 84 reports. **Publications:** *NARB Panel Reports.*

42583 ■ National Association of Publishers' Representatives (NAPR)
1901 N Roselle Rd., Ste. 920
Schaumburg, IL 60195
Ph: (847)885-2410
Fax: (847)885-8393
Co. E-mail: info@napronline.org
URL: http://www.napronline.org
Contact: Ian McDonald, President
Description: Independent publishers' representatives selling advertising space for more than one publisher of consumer, industrial, direct response, and trade publications. **Founded:** 1950. **Publications:** *NAPR Newsletter* (Monthly).

42584 ■ Outdoor Advertising Association of America (OAAA)
1850 M St. NW, Ste. 1040
Washington, DC 20036
Ph: (202)833-5566
Fax: (202)833-1522
Co. E-mail: nfletcher@oaaa.org
URL: http://www.oaaa.org
Contact: Nancy Fletcher, President
Description: Firms owning, erecting, and maintaining standardized poster panels and painted display advertising facilities. Aims to provide leadership, services, and standards to promote, protect and advance the outdoor advertising industry. **Founded:** 1891. **Awards:** OBIE Awards; Awards for Excellence in Operations Management (Biennial); Industry Awards (Annual); OBIE Awards (Annual); Out of Home Media Plan Awards (Annual); Myles Standish Award of Excellence; L. Ray Vahue Award of Merit.

42585 ■ Point-of-Purchase Advertising International (POPAI)
440 N Wells St., Ste. 740
Chicago, IL 60654
Ph: (312)863-2900
Fax: (312)229-1152
Co. E-mail: rwinter@popai.com
URL: http://www.popai.com
Contact: Richard Winter, President
Description: Producers and suppliers of point-of-purchase advertising signs and displays and national and regional advertisers and retailers interested in use and effectiveness of signs, displays and other point-of-purchase media. Conducts student education programs; maintains speakers' bureau. **Scope:** marketing. **Founded:** 1936. **Subscriptions:** articles books. **Publications:** *Marketing at Retail Global Journal of Research* (Quarterly). **Educational Activities:** Point-of-Purchase Advertising Institute Marketplace (Annual). **Awards:** Chief Award (Annual); Digital Signage Award Contest (Annual); Industry Achievement Award (Annual); Outstanding Marketing at-Retail Achievement Award (Annual); Outstanding Merchandising Achievement Awards Competition.

42586 ■ Promotional Products Association International (PPAI)
3125 Skyway Cir. N
Irving, TX 75038-3526
Ph: (972)252-0404
Free: 888-426-7724
Fax: (972)258-3004
Co. E-mail: membership@ppai.org
URL: http://www.ppai.org
Contact: Steven Meyer, Chairman of the Board
Description: Suppliers and distributors of promotional products including incentives, imprinted ad specialties, premiums, and executive gifts. Promotes industry contacts in 60 countries. Holds executive development and sales training seminars. Conducts research and compiles statistics. Administers industry advertising and public relations program. Maintains speakers' bureau. Conducts trade shows, regional training, publishes educational resources. **Scope:** management, professional development, technology, sales management. **Founded:** 1903. **Subscriptions:** 200. **Publications:** *PPB Newslink*; *Promotional Products Business* (Monthly); *Promotional Products Association International--Membership Directory and Reference Guide* (Annual). **Awards:** Distributor Web Award (Annual); Golden Pyramid Competition (Annual); Industry Hall of Fame (Annual); Supplier Web Award (Annual); Suppliers Golden Achievement (Annual); Suppliers Golden Achievement Award; Golden Pyramid Competition; Industry Hall of Fame; Distributor Web Awards; Supplier Web Awards.

42587 ■ Radio Advertising Bureau (RAB)
1320 Greenway Dr., Ste. 500
Irving, TX 75038-2587
Ph: (212)681-7214
Free: 800-232-3131
Co. E-mail: efarber@rab.com
URL: http://www.rab.com
Contact: Erica Farber, President
Description: Includes radio stations, radio networks, station sales representatives, and allied industry services, such as producers, research firms, schools, and consultants. Calls on advertisers and agencies to promote the sale of radio time as an advertising medium. Sponsors program to increase professionalism of radio salespeople, awarding Certified Radio Marketing Consultant designation to those who pass examination. Sponsors regional marketing conferences. Conducts extensive research program into all phases of radio sales. Issues reports on use of radio by national, regional, and local advertisers. Speaks before conventions and groups to explain benefits of radio advertising. Sponsors Radio Creative Fund. Compiles statistics. **Scope:** advertising, retailing, demographics, marketing. **Founded:** 1951. **Subscriptions:** 500 archival material books clippings periodicals. **Publications:** *Radio Co-op Sources* (Annual); *Guide to Competitive Media* (Biennial); *RAB Media Fact Book* (Annual). **Educational Activities:** Managing Sales Conference (Annual). **Awards:** Radio Mercury Awards; Radio-Mercury Award (Annual).

42588 ■ Scenic America (SA)
1634 I St., NW, Ste. 510
Washington, DC 20006
Ph: (202)638-0550
Fax: (202)638-3171
Co. E-mail: tracy@scenic.org
URL: http://www.scenic.org
Contact: Kevin Fry, President
E-mail: fry@scenic.org
Description: Safeguards natural beauty and community character through billboard and sign control, appropriate siting of cellular towers and other utilities, promotion of scenic byways, context-sensitive highway design, and protection of scenic landscapes and cityscapes. Advocates for the preservation of scenic beauty, open space, and quality of life. Fights billboard proliferation and other forms of visual pollution; works for the conservation of scenic byways and for context-sensitive highway design. **Founded:** 1982. **Publications:** *Taming Wireless Telecommunications Towers*; *Viewpoints* (Quarterly); *Fighting Billboard Blight: An Action for Citizens and Public Officials*; *Getting It Right In the Right-of-Way: Citizen Participation in Context-Sensitive Solutions*; *Power to the People: Strategies for Reducing the Visual Impact of Overhead Utilities*; *Tree Conservation Ordinances: Land Use Regulations Go Green*; *Aesthetics, Community Character, and the Law*; *Gift of the Journey: America's Scenic Roadways*; *Looking at Change Before it Occurs*; *Trees Are Treasure: Sustaining the Community Forest.* **Awards:** Stafford Award (Biennial).

42589 ■ Television Bureau of Advertising (TVB)
3 E 54th St., 10th Fl.
New York, NY 10022-3108
Ph: (212)486-1111
Fax: (212)935-5631
Co. E-mail: info@tvb.org
URL: http://www.tvb.org
Contact: Steve Lanzano, President
Description: Television stations, station sales representatives, and program producers/syndicates. Strives to increase advertiser dollars to U.S. spot television. Represents television stations to the advertising community. **Scope:** broadcasting. **Founded:** 1954. **Subscriptions:** 200. **Educational Activities:** Television Bureau of Advertising Annual Conference (Annual). **Awards:** TVB Automotive Commercial Competition (Annual).

42590 ■ thinkLA
4223 Glencoe Ave., Ste. C100
Marina del Rey, CA 90292
Ph: (310)823-7320
Fax: (310)823-7325
Co. E-mail: info@thinkla.org
URL: http://www.thinkla.org
Contact: Eric Johnson, Co-President
Description: Assists heads of advertising agencies in the Western U.S. to operate their agencies more effectively and profitably. Offers assistance to agency management and staff. Provides a forum for discussion and exchange of information. Promotes members' interests. **Founded:** 1946. **Awards:** Lifetime Achievement Award/Leader of the Year (Annual).

42591 ■ Traffic Audit Bureau for Media Measurement (TAB)
271 Madison Ave., Ste. 1504
New York, NY 10016
Ph: (212)972-8075
Fax: (212)972-8928
Co. E-mail: larryhennessy@tabonline.com
URL: http://www.tabonline.com
Contact: Joseph C. Philport, President
Description: Advertisers, advertising agencies, operators of outdoor advertising plants, bus shelter advertising companies, and backlighted display and painted bulletin companies. Sets standard practices for the evaluation of circulation and visibility of outdoor advertising; issues statements on the circulation values of outdoor advertising plants. Encourages standardization of terminology and practices in the industry. Seeks to educate those involved in out-of-home media on ways of developing circulation data for advertising sites. Compiles statistics. **Founded:** 1933. **Publications:** *TABBriefs*; *Building Accountability for Out of Home Media*; *TAB Eyes On Out of Home*; *What You Should Know About the New TAB Audit.* **Educational Activities:** Conference and Marketing Expo (Annual); Traffic Audit Bureau for Media Measurement Out of Home Media Conference & Marketing Expo (Annual). **Telecommunication Services:** inquiry@tabonline.com.

42592 ■ Transworld Advertising Agency Network (TAAN)
814 Watertown St.
Newton, MA 02465
Ph: (617)795-1706

Fax: (419)730-1706
Co. E-mail: peterg@taan.org
URL: http://www.taan.org
Contact: Mark Gale, Chairman of the Board
Description: Independently owned advertising agencies that cooperate for exchange of management education and information, reciprocal service, and personal local contact. Allows members to seek aid of other members in campaign planning, creative services, merchandising, public relations, publicity, media, research, and test facilities. Conducts annual expertise audit. **Founded:** 1936.

EDUCATIONAL PROGRAMS

42593 ■ Design and Page Layout Skills (Onsite)
Padgett-Thompson Seminars
Rockhurst University CEC
14502 W. 105th St.
Lenexa, KS 66215
Free: 800-349-1935
URL: http://www.findaseminar.com/tpd/Padgett-Thompson-Seminars.asp
Price: $249.00. **Description:** Workshop teaches participants to create publications, newsletters, brochures, fliers, and reports. **Dates and Locations:** Cities throughout the United States.

DIRECTORIES OF EDUCATIONAL PROGRAMS

42594 ■ *CounselorConnect*
Pub: Public Relations Society of America
Contact: William Murray, President
URL(s): www.prsa.orgwww.prsa.org/publications/. **Released:** Latest edition 2007. **Covers:** Public relations firms and academy members. **Entries include:** Name and contact information. **Database includes:** Editorials on selecting a PR firm, geographic cross reference, industry cross reference. **Indexes:** Practice area.

REFERENCE WORKS

42595 ■ *6 Steps to Free Publicity*
Pub: ReadHowYouWant.com, Ltd.
Ed: Marcia Yudkin. **Released:** July 9, 2010. **Price:** $15.99. **Description:** Six steps to help promote a small business are given. The history of the Internet and its use to help provide free publicity to small firms is outlined.

42596 ■ *49 Marketing Secrets (That Work) to Grow Sales*
Pub: Morgan James Publishing, LLC
Ed: Ronald Finklestein. **Released:** October 2007. **Price:** $19.95/. **Description:** This book was written to fill the void on marketing books and is tailored to the small business owner. The author helps the small business owner to understand marketing and who they can trust while doing business. The book includes information to help entrepreneurs discover winning marketing strategies, branding and corporate image, media strategies, networking tips, technology-based marketing ideas, event strategies, and sales strategies.

42597 ■ *"1914 Proved to Be Key Year for Chevy" in Automotive News (Vol. 86, October 31, 2011, No. 6488, pp. S18)*
Pub: Crain Communications Inc.
Ed: Jamie Lareau. **Description:** Chevy Bow Tie emblem was born in 1914, creating the brand's image that has carried through to current days.

42598 ■ *"Airlines Mount PR Push to Win Public Support Against Big Oil" in Advertising Age (Vol. 79, July 14, 2008, No. 7, pp. 1)*
Pub: Crain Communications, Inc.
Ed: Michael Bush. **Description:** Top airline executives from competing companies have banded together in a public relations plan in which they are sending e-mails to their frequent fliers asking for aid in lobbying legislators to put a restriction on oil speculation.

42599 ■ *"AllHipHop.com's Founders Thought a Weeklong Event Would Raise the Company" in Inc. (February 2008, pp. 48-51)*
Pub: Gruner & Jahr USA Publishing
Ed: Kermit Pattison. **Description:** Co-founders Greg Watkins and Chuck Creekmur, planned a weeklong festival to promote their company, AllHipHop.com; the event nearly ruined the firm. The online firm provides news about hip hop artists and the industry and is updated daily.

42600 ■ *"Alto Ventures Retains Investor Relations Professional" in Canadian Corporate News (May 16, 2007)*
Pub: Comtex News Network Inc.
Description: Alto Ventures Ltd., a gold exploration and development company with a portfolio of eleven properties in the Canadian Shield, announced that it has engaged the consulting services of Mark Prosser in order to focus on increasing investor awareness and exposure to the investment community through the dissemination of corporate information to a network of North American and European institutions, retail brokerage firms, and private investors.

42601 ■ *"Ampm Focus Has BP Working Overtime; New Convenience-Store Brand Comes to Chicago" in Crain's Chicago Business (April 28, 2008)*
Pub: Crain Communications, Inc.
Ed: John T. Slania. **Description:** Britian's oil giant BP PLC is opening its ampm convenience stores in the Chicago market and has already begun converting most of its 78 Chicago-area gas stations to ampms. The company has also started to franchise the stores to independent operators. BP is promoting the brand with both traditional and unconventional marketing techniques such s real or simulated 3D snacks embedded in bus shelter ads and an in-store Guitar Hero contest featuring finalists from a recent contest at the House of Blues.

42602 ■ *"AVT Featured on TD Waterhouse Market News Website and in Vending Times Magazine" in Benzinga.com (August 17, 2011)*
Pub: Benzinga.com
Ed: Benzinga Staff. **Description:** AVT Inc. was featured online and in an article reporting the firm's plan to install automated vending machines in high-profile areas including malls, office buildings, stadiums and arenas.

42603 ■ *"Banks Deposit Reassurance, Calm Customers" in The Business Journal-Serving Greater Tampa Bay (Vol. 28, August 22, 2008)*
Pub: American City Business Journals, Inc.
Ed: Margie Manning. **Description:** Community banks in the Tampa Bay Area are training tellers and other customer care workers to help reassure customers that their deposits are safe. Other measures to reassure depositors include joining a network that allows banks to share deposits. Additional information on moves community banks are making to reassure consumers is presented.

42604 ■ *"BBB Reworks Logo, Grading System" in Crain's Cleveland Business (Vol. 28, October 8, 2007, No. 40, pp. 5)*
Pub: Crain Communications, Inc.
Ed: John Booth. **Description:** During the next year, the Better Business Bureau will adopt a grading system that will establish performance minimums that will make it tougher for some types of businesses to become accredited; this nationwide rebranding effort is part of a campaign to sharpen the Better Business Bureau's image.

42605 ■ *"Best Buy's CEO On Learning to Love Social Media" in Harvard Business Review (Vol. 88, December 2010, No. 12, pp. 43)*
Pub: Harvard Business School Publishing
Ed: Brian J. Dunn. **Description:** Effective utilization of online social networks to enhance brand identity, connect with consumers, and address bad publicity scenarios is examined.

42606 ■ *"Better ROI Or Your Money Back, Says Buzz Agency" in Advertising Age (Vol. 79, July 14, 2008, No. 7, pp. 1)*
Pub: Crain Communications, Inc.
Ed: Michael Bush. **Description:** Word-of-mouth marketing is discussed as well as the impact on the advertising industry. Although many firms specializing in this form of marketing have opened over the past few years, many marketers are reluctant to try this route.

42607 ■ *Beyond Buzz: The Next Generation of Word-of-Mouth Marketing*
Pub: AMACOM
Ed: Lois Kelly. **Released:** March 2007. **Price:** $24. 95. **Description:** New marketing ideas to bring attention to any small business are showcased.

42608 ■ *"Brand Imaging" in Small Business Opportunities (November 2010)*
Pub: Harris Publications Inc.
Ed: Karen Harnesk. **Description:** Design and branding pro shares strategies and tips to help guide any small business' image development.

42609 ■ *Briefs for Building Better Brands: Tips, Parables and Insight into Market Leaders*
Pub: AGCD Brandspa Books
Ed: Allan Gorman. **Released:** September 2004. **Description:** In today's marketplace, a company needs to gain consumer trust in order to build a brand. By gaining trust, the brand gets sold by word-of-mouth publicity. The author calls this type of marketing: guerrilla marketing, and he believes it to be more effective than traditional advertising.

42610 ■ *"The Buck Stops Here" in Canadian Business (Vol. 81, November 10, 2008, No. 19, pp. 25)*
Pub: Rogers Media Ltd.
Ed: Sarka Halas. **Description:** Reputation strategist Leslie Gaines-Ross says that minimizing the damage followed by the identification of what went wrong are the first steps that companies need to take when trying to salvage their reputation. Gaines-Ross states that it is up to the CEO to ensure the company's speedy recovery and they need to be at the forefront of the process.

42611 ■ *"Building Confidence" in Black Enterprise (Vol. 38, January 2008, No. 6, pp. 50)*
Pub: Earl G. Graves Publishing Co. Inc.
Ed: Marcia A. Reed-Woodard. **Description:** Patriot Management in Chicago offers courses at its Investment Management Training Academy for the institutional asset management and investment sector. Classes are designed to help build investor confidence amid the scandals that hit the financial, investment and asset management industry.

42612 ■ *"Canon Focuses on New Moms" in Marketing to Women (Vol. 21, January 2008, No. 1, pp. 3)*
Pub: EPM Communications Inc.
Contact: Ira Mayer, President
E-mail: imayer@epmcom.com
Description: Canon launches a photo contest aimed at spotlighting baby's first pictures in an attempt to connect with new mothers.

42613 ■ *"Change Agent; What Peter Francese Says You Need to Know" in Advertising Age (Vol. 79, July 7, 2008, No. 26, pp. 13)*
Pub: Crain Communications, Inc.
Ed: Peter Francese. **Description:** Advice for marketers on how to deal effectively with a changing consumer base is given.

42614 ■ *"City Slickers" in Canadian Business (Vol. 81, March 31, 2008, No. 5, pp. 36)*
Pub: Rogers Media
Ed: Joe Castaldo. **Description:** Richard Florida believes that the creative class drives the economy and the prosperity of countries depends on attracting and retaining these people. Florida has brought attention to developing livable and economically vibrant

cities thanks in part to his promotional skills. However, he has also drawn critics who see his data on his theories as flimsy and inadequate.

42615 ■ *"Conversations Need to Yield Actions Measured in Dollars" in Advertising Age (Vol. 79, July 7, 2008, No. 26, pp. 18)*
Pub: Crain Communications, Inc.
Ed: Jonathan Salem Baskin. **Description:** New ways in which to market to consumers are discussed.

42616 ■ *"Dramatic Results: Making Opera (Yes, Opera) Seem Young and Hip" in Inc. (October 2007, pp. 61-62)*
Pub: Gruner & Jahr USA Publishing
Description: Profile of Peter Gelb, who turned New York's Metropolitan Opera into one of the most media-savvy organizations in the country, using a multifaceted marketing strategy through the media. Gelb used streaming audio and simulcasts on satellite radio and movie theaters to promote a message that opera is hip.

42617 ■ *"Easy Answers? Hall No" in Charlotte Business Journal (Vol. 25, December 17, 2010, No. 39, pp. 1)*
Pub: Charlotte Business Journal
Ed: Erik Spanberg. **Description:** Charlotte, North Carolina-based NASCAR Hall of Fame has been trying to recover from its shaky start, but still bullish on the future as officials intensify promotions. Sports museums and halls of fame are mainly dependent on families and always search for new exhibits and great appearances to boost attendance.

42618 ■ *"Economy Should Play Big Role When Presidential Spotlight Returns" in Business First-Columbus (November 9, 2007, pp. A1)*
Pub: American City Business Journals, Inc.
Ed: Jeff Bell. **Description:** Ohio leaders, including the president of Columbus Chamber, Ty Marsh, suggests that Ohio has benefited from past campaigns as candidates spend money on advertising along with the media exposure the state received. The significance of Ohio in determining the winner in the 2008 presidential elections is discussed.

42619 ■ *"Emotional Brand Attachment and Brand Personality" in Journal of Marketing (Vol. 75, July 2011, No. 4, pp. 35)*
Pub: American Marketing Association
Ed: Lucia Malar, Harley Krohmer, Wayne D. Hoyer, Bettin Nyffeneger. **Description:** A study on whether the brand's personality should match the consumer's actual self or ideal self is presented. Actual self-congruence is found to have the most impact on emotional brand attachment.

42620 ■ *"Empowered" in Harvard Business Review (Vol. 88, July-August 2010, No. 7-8, pp. 94)*
Pub: Harvard Business School Publishing
Ed: Josh Bernoff, Ted Schadler. **Description:** HERO concept (highly empowered and resourceful operative) which builds a connection between employees, managers, and IT is outlined. The resultant additional experience and knowledge gained by employees improves customer relationship management.

42621 ■ *"FTC Takes Aim At Foreclosure 'Rescue' Firm" in The Business Journal-Serving Greater Tampa Bay (Vol. 28, September 19, 2008, No. 39)*
Pub: American City Business Journals, Inc.
Ed: Michael Hinman. **Description:** United Home Savers LLP has been ordered to halt its mortgage foreclosure rescue services after the Federal Trade Commission accused it of deceptive advertising. The company is alleged to have charged customers $1,200 in exchange for unfulfilled promises to keep them in their homes.

42622 ■ *"Fueling Business" in The Business Journal-Milwaukee (Vol. 25, July 25, 2008, No. 44, pp. A1)*
Pub: American City Business Journals, Inc.
Ed: David Doege. **Description:** Several businesses in Wisconsin's Milwaukee area are offering gas cards in order to attract customers. Examples of this include apartment manager Nancy Randle offering a $400 gas card to new tenants with a 1 year lease and dentist Perry Sukowatey giving a $25 gas card after examining patients. Other details on gas card promotions are discussed.

42623 ■ *"Get Personal" in Entrepreneur (Vol. 36, April 2008, No. 4)*
Pub: Entrepreneur Media, Inc.
Ed: Romanus Wolter. **Description:** Customers appreciate personal contact, and communicating with them can help business owners' customer relations. Some ways on how to keep a personal touch with customers and improve business dealings include blending technology with personal interaction and knowing what the customers want. Other tips are provided.

42624 ■ *"Get Real" in Entrepreneur (Vol. 36, April 2008, No. 4, pp. 86)*
Pub: Entrepreneur Media, Inc.
Ed: Kim T. Gordon. **Description:** Selling points of a product or service must show real benefits to women. Provide detailed information as women look at details more deeply before purchasing. Other tips on how to market products designed for women consumers are provided.

42625 ■ *Groundswell: Winning in a World Transformed by Social Technologies*
Pub: Harvard Business School Press
Ed: Charlene Li; Josh Bernoff. **Released:** April 21, 2008. **Price:** $29.95. **Description:** Individuals are using online social technologies such as blogs, social networking sites, YouTube, and podcasts to discuss products and companies, write their own news, and find their own deals. When consumers you've never met are rating your company's products in public forums with which you have no experience or influence, your company is vulnerable. This book teaches the tools and data necessary to turn this treat into an opportunity.

42626 ■ *Groundswell: Winning in a World Transformed by Social Technologies*
Pub: Harvard Business School Press
Ed: Charlene Li, Josh Bernoff. **Released:** 2008. **Price:** $29.95. **Description:** Corporate executives are struggling with a new trend: people using online social technologies (blogs, social networking sites, YouTube, podcasts) to discuss products and companies, write their own news, and find their own deals.

42627 ■ *"Half of Canadian Firms to Boost Marketing Budgets" in Globe & Mail (January 22, 2007, pp. B1)*
Pub: CTVglobemedia Publishing Inc.
Ed: Keith McArthur. **Description:** The advertising and marketing spending plans of different companies are presented.

42628 ■ *"'Help Wanted' Meets 'Buy It Now': Why More Companies Are Integrating Marketing and Recruiting" in Inc. (November 2007, pp. 50-52)*
Pub: Gruner & Jahr USA Publishing
Ed: Ryan McCarthy. **Description:** Five tips to merge marketing and recruiting together include: thinking every help wanted ad as a marketing opportunity, treating every job candidate as a potential customer, involving the youngest employees in the interview process, look for way to promote recruiting events, and to sponsor community-oriented events.

42629 ■ *"Hopkins' Security, Reputation Face Challenges in Wake of Slaying" in Baltimore Business Journal (Vol. 28, August 6, 2010, No. 13)*
Pub: Baltimore Business Journal
Ed: Gary Haber. **Description:** The slaying of Johns Hopkins University researcher Stephen Pitcairn has not tarnished the reputation of the elite school in Baltimore, Maryland among students. Maintaining Hopkins' reputation is important since it is Baltimore's largest employer with nearly 32,000 workers. Insights on the impact of the slaying among the Hopkins' community are also given.

42630 ■ *"How To Live To Be 100; John E. Green Co. Grows Through Diversification" in Crain's Detroit Business (February 18, 2008)*
Pub: Crain Communications Inc. - Detroit
Ed: Chad Halcom. **Description:** Continuity, name recognition, and inventiveness are keys to continuing growth for Highland Park, Michigan's John E. Green Company, designer of pipe systems and mechanical contractor.

42631 ■ *I Love You More Than My Dog*
Pub: Portfolio
Ed: Jeanne Bliss. **Price:** $22.95. **Description:** Ways to win passionate, loyal and vocal customers in order to build a small business is outlined.

42632 ■ *If You Have to Cry, Go Outside: And Other Things Your Mother Never Told You*
Pub: HarperOne
Ed: Kelly Cutrone. **Released:** February 2, 2010. **Price:** $22.99. **Description:** Women's mentor advices on how to make it in one of the most competitive industries in the world, fashion. She has kicked people out of fashion shows, forced some of reality television's shiny start to fire their friends, and built her own company which is one of the most powerful public relations firms in the fashion business.

42633 ■ *"The Impact of Incomplete Typeface Logos on Perceptions of the Firms" in Journal of Marketing (Vol. 75, July 2011, No. 4, pp. 86)*
Pub: American Marketing Association
Ed: Henrik Hagtvedt. **Description:** A study of the influence of incomplete typeface logos on consumer perceptions of the company is presented. The findings suggest that companies should avoid incomplete typeface logos if perceptions of trustworthiness are critical or if consumers are likely to have a prevention focus.

42634 ■ *"Increasing Building Work at Ryan Cos." in Crain's Chicago Business (Vol. 34, May 23, 2011, No. 21, pp. 6)*
Pub: Crain Communications Inc.
Ed: Eddie Baeb. **Description:** Profile of Tim Hennelly, who is working to make Ryan Company known as a pure builder rather than a developer-builder.

42635 ■ *"Industry Vet To Spread Glory's Word" in Business First-Columbus (November 9, 2007, pp. A1)*
Pub: American City Business Journals, Inc.
Ed: Dan Eaton. **Description:** Glory Foods, Inc. chose Jacqueline Neal as its new president in October 2007. Neal has eleven years experience in brand management and has worked with food industry leaders such as Mars Inc., Kraft Foods Inc., and Nabisco Holdings Corporation. Neil's plans for the company are presented.

42636 ■ *It's Not Who You Know - It's Who Knows You!: The Small Business Guide to Raising Your Profits by Raising Your Profile*
Pub: John Wiley & Sons, Inc.
Ed: David Avrin. **Released:** November 9, 2010. **Price:** $24.95. **Description:** When it comes to promoting a small business or a brand, it is essential to know how valuable high-profile attention can be. But for most small companies, the cost of hiring an outside firm to increase attention can be too expensive.

42637 ■ *"Kraft Not Alone" in Crain's Chicago Business (Vol. 30, February 2007, No. 6, pp. 8)*
Pub: Crain Communications, Inc.
Description: Consumer watchdog group, The Center for Science in the Public Interest, has been putting pressure on food companies to be more truthful on their product labels. Listing of companies who have had misleading claims on their products is included.

42638 ■ *"Kuno Creative to Present B2B Social Media Campaign Webinar" in Entertainment Close-Up (August 25, 2011)*
Pub: Close-Up Media
Description: Kuno Creative, an inbound marketing agency, will host Three Steps of a Successful B2B

Social Media Campaign. The firm is a provider of Website development, branding, marketing strategy, public relations, Internet marketing, and inbound marketing.

42639 ■ *"Leadership in Flight" in Women In Business (Vol. 63, Fall 2011, No. 3, pp. 24)*
Pub: American Business Women's Association
Ed: Leigh Elmore. **Description:** Flight attendants in major airlines are trained to keep passengers comfortable and to calmly deal with emergencies. They also have a significant role in brand image and customer loyalty as they interact with the customers directly. Examples of teamwork leadership for flight attendants are given.

42640 ■ *"Making Headlines" in Entrepreneur (Vol. 36, April 2008, No. 4, pp. 126)*
Pub: Entrepreneur Media, Inc.
Ed: John Janstch. **Description:** Tips on how to get journalists to notice your business and your new product offerings are presented. These include making a list of journalists that might be interested in the industry you are in and writing comments on their blogs.

42641 ■ *"Making Sense of Ambiguous Evidence" in Harvard Business Review (Vol. 86, September 2008, No. 9, pp. 53)*
Pub: Harvard Business School Press
Ed: Lisa Burrell. **Description:** Documentary filmmaker Errol Morris emphasizes the role of perception in portraying objective reality, and how investigation and analysis enhance the accuracy of that portrayal.

42642 ■ *Marketing in a Web 2.0 World - Using Social Media, Webinars, Blogs, and More to Boost Your Small Business on a Budget*
Pub: Atlantic Publishing Company
Ed: Peter VanRysdam. **Released:** June 1, 2010. **Price:** $24.95. **Description:** Web 2.0 technologies have leveled the playing field for small companies trying to boost their presence by giving them an equal voice against larger competitors. Advice is given to help target your audience using social networking hubs.

42643 ■ *"McD's Warms Up For Olympics Performance" in Advertising Age (Vol. 79, July 7, 2008, No. 26, pp. 8)*
Pub: Crain Communications, Inc.
Description: Overview of McDonald's marketing plans for the company's sponsorship of the Olympics which includes a website, an alternate-reality game, names featured on U.S. athletes and on-the-ground activities.

42644 ■ *"MEC, Churchill Downs Saddle Up in Racing Deal" in Globe & Mail (March 6, 2007, pp. B1)*
Pub: CTVglobemedia Publishing Inc.
Ed: Greg Keenan. **Description:** The formation of a company called TrackNet Media Group LLC by Magna Entertainment Corp. and Churchill Downs Inc. for the broadcast of horse races on television is discussed. The efforts of the two companies to revive public interest in horse racing are described.

42645 ■ *Media, Organizations and Identity*
Pub: Palgrave Macmillan
Ed: Lilie Chouliaraki, Mette Morsing. **Released:** January 19, 2010. **Price:** $90.00. **Description:** The mass media, press and television are a essential in the formation of corporate identity and the promotion of business image and reputation. This book offers a new perspective into the interrelationships between media and organizations over three dimensions: media as business, media in business and business in the media.

42646 ■ *"New Sony HD Ads Tout Digital" in Brandweek (Vol. 49, April 21, 2008, No. 16, pp. 5)*
Pub: VNU Business Media, Inc.
Description: Looking to promote Sony Electronics' digital imaging products, the company has launched another campaign effort known as HDNA, a play on the words high-definition and DNA; originally Sony focused the HDNA campaign on their televisions, the new ads will include still and video cameras as well and marketing efforts will consist of advertising in print, Online, television spots and publicity at various venues across the country.

42647 ■ *"Next Generation Audi TT Hits Canadian Streets" in Canadian Corporate News (May 16, 2007)*
Pub: Comtex News Network Inc.
Description: Audi Canada prepares for the launch of the highly anticipated 2008 Audi TT, recipient of the 2007 World Car Design of the Year due to its contemporary look, powerful engine, and innovative technology, with a multiple touch-point marketing campaign.

42648 ■ *"Org to Moms: Eat Your Veggies" in Marketing to Women (Vol. 21, April 2008, No. 4, pp. 3)*
Pub: EPM Communications Inc.
Contact: Ira Mayer, President
E-mail: imayer@epmcom.com
Description: In order to increase the purchase and consumption of fruit and vegetables to moms, the non profit Produce for Better Health Foundation is launching a series of initiatives.

42649 ■ *The Power of Social Networking: Using the Whuffie Factor to Build Your Business*
Pub: Crown Business Books
Ed: Tara Hunt. **Released:** May 4, 2010. **Price:** $15.00. **Description:** This book shows how any small business can harness its power by increasing whuffie, the store of social capital that is the currency of the digital world. Blogs and social networks such as Facebook and Twitter are used to help grow any small firm.

42650 ■ *"Psst..Spread the Word" in Boston Business Journal (Vol. 27, November 23, 2007, No. 43, pp. 1)*
Pub: American City Business Journals Inc.
Ed: Lisa van der Pool. **Description:** More and more Boston companies are using word-of-mouth marketing to boost sales, and spending on it rose to $981 million in 2006. It is projected that spending on word-of-mouth marketing will reach $1.4 billion in 2007, and marketing companies using this type of method are getting higher funding. Trends in word-of-mouth marketing are discussed.

42651 ■ *"Report: McD's Pepsi Score Best With Young Hispanics" in Brandweek (Vol. 49, April 21, 2008, No. 16, pp. 8)*
Pub: VNU Business Media, Inc.
Ed: Della de Lafuente. **Description:** According to a new report, in order to reach Hispanic Gen Yers, marketing strategists need to understand this demographic's 'bi-dentity,' something which has proved an elusive task to many marketers. Another trend is the emergence of Latinas who have careers, as opposed to just jobs. There is an opportunity to tap this new, young and empowered female market with innovative messaging. Statistical data included.

42652 ■ *"Restaurants Dish Up Meal Deals To Attract Customers" in Crain's Detroit Business (Vol. 24, October 6, 2008, No. 40, pp. 1)*
Pub: Crain Communications, Inc.
Ed: Nathan Skid. **Description:** Restaurateurs are devising many creative and rewarding incentives to get customers to frequent their establishments during this economic crisis. Innovative ways in which even higher-end establishments are drawing in business are discussed.

42653 ■ *"Rich Returns: Media Master" in Entrepreneur (Vol. 35, October 2007, No. 10, pp. 42)*
Pub: Entrepreneur Media Inc.
Ed: Robert Kiyosaki. **Description:** Advertising is a powerful way of reaching clients, however, public relations is a less expensive method which is just as effective as advertising. Entrepreneurs must also be ready to try something new to be noticed by the public. Insights on how to master the use of media are given.

42654 ■ *"Roadside Attraction" in Hawaii Business (Vol. 53, January 2008, No. 7, pp. 39)*
Pub: Hawaii Business Publishing
Ed: Jason Ubay. **Description:** Businesses beside the Kamehameha Highway find ways to survive in a rural community. Sunshine Arts Hawaii, for instance, uses a bright-colored and huge mural to attract tourists who drive along the highway. Other techniques employed by businesses in the aforementioned are des cribed.

42655 ■ *"The Seat-Of-The-Pants School of Marketing" in Brandweek (Vol. 49, April 21, 2008, No. 16, pp. 24)*
Pub: VNU Business Media, Inc.
Ed: David Vinjamuri. **Description:** Excerpt from the book 'Accidental Branding: How Ordinary People Build Extraordinary Brands,' by David Vinjamuri, discusses six shared principles for creating a brand that is unique and will be successful over the long-term.

42656 ■ *"Shoestring-Budget Marketing" in Women Entrepreneur (January 5, 2009)*
Pub: Entrepreneur Media Inc.
Ed: Maria Falconer. **Description:** Pay-per-click search engine advertising is the traditional type of e-marketing that may not only be too expensive for certain kinds of businesses but also may not attract the quality customer base a business looking to grow needs to find. Social networking websites have become a mandatory marketing tool for business owners who want to see growth in their sales; tips are provided for utilizing these networking websites in order to gain more visibility on the Internet which can, in turn, lead to the more sales.

42657 ■ *"Show and Tell" in Entrepreneur (Vol. 36, May 2008, No. 5, pp. 54)*
Pub: Entrepreneur Media, Inc.
Ed: Heather Clancy. **Description:** FreshStart Telephone uses recorded video testimonials of customers, by using Pure Digital Flip Video that downloads content directly to the computer, and uploads it in the company's website to promote their wireless phone service.

42658 ■ *The Small Business Bible: Everything You Need to Know to Succeed in Your Small Business*
Pub: John Wiley and Sons, Inc.
Ed: Steven D. Strauss. **Released:** September 2008. **Price:** $19.95 (US), $28.99 (Canadian). **Description:** Comprehensive guide to starting and running a successful small business. Topics include bookkeeping and financial management, marketing, publicity, and advertising.

42659 ■ *"Sponsorship, Booths Available for Spring Business Showcase" in Bellingham Business Journal (Vol. February 2010, pp. 3)*
Pub: Sound Publishing Inc.
Description: Third Annual Spring Business Showcase still have space available for vendors and sponsors. The event gives local businesses the opportunity to increase their visibility and provides a means to increase sales and build relationships.

42660 ■ *Start Your Own Blogging Business, Second Edition*
Pub: Entrepreneur Press
Contact: Perlman Neil, President
Released: July 1, 2010. **Price:** $17.95. **Description:** Interviews with professional bloggers from some of the most popular blogs on the Internet will help anyone interested in starting their own blogging business.

42661 ■ *Start Your Own Fashion Accessories Business*
Pub: Entrepreneur Press
Contact: Perlman Neil, President
Released: March 1, 2009. **Price:** $17.95. **Description:** Entrepreneurs wishing to start a fashion accessories business will find important information for setting up a home workshop and office, exploring the market, managing finances, publicizing and advertising the business and more.

42662 ■ *"Staying Power" in Canadian Business (Vol. 79, November 6, 2006, No. 22, pp. 73)*
Pub: Rogers Media

Ed: John Gray. **Description:** The effects on brand image on customer choices are analyzed. The need of maintaining brand image is also emphasized.

42663 ■ *"Stock Delisting Could Hamper First Mariner" in Boston Business Journal (Vol. 29, July 29, 2011, No. 12, pp. 1)*
Pub: American City Business Journals Inc.

Ed: Gary Haber. **Description:** Possible delisting of First Mariner Bancorp from the Nasdaq stock exchange could adversely impact the bank's ability to attract institutional investors. Some institutions limit their investments to companies trading on the Nasdaq.

42664 ■ *"Technology Protects Lottery" in Arkansas Business (Vol. 26, September 28, 2009, No. 39, pp. 1)*
Pub: Journal Publishing Inc.

Ed: George Waldon. **Description:** Arkansas Lottery Commission was initially criticized for what was seen as a major breach in security protocol by revealing the exact location of 26 million lottery tickets during a publicity stunt in which the media was invited to the main distribution center; however, due to the high-tech security that has been implemented the tickets are worthless until their status is changed after passing through multiple security scans.

42665 ■ *"Timberland's CEO On Standing Up to 65,000 Angry Activists" in Harvard Business Review (Vol. 88, September 2010, No. 9, pp. 39)*
Pub: Harvard Business School Publishing

Ed: Jeff Swartz. **Description:** Timberland Company avoided a potential boycott by taking a two-way approach. It addressed a supplier issue that posed a threat to the environment, and launched an email campaign to keep Greenpeace activists informed of the development of a new supplier agreement.

42666 ■ *"To Be Seen Is to Be Successful" in Pet Product News (Vol. 64, December 2010, No. 12, pp. 12)*
Pub: BowTie Inc.

Ed: David Arvin. **Description:** Guidelines on how pet business retailers can boost customer visibility are described considering that complacency could hamper retailers' efforts to effectively market their businesses. To enhance customer base and stand out from competing businesses, being different, strategic, creative, and differentiated is emphasized.

42667 ■ *"Too Much Information?" in Black Enterprise (Vol. 37, December 2006, No. 5, pp. 59)*
Pub: Earl G. Graves Publishing Co. Inc.

Ed: James C. Johnson. **Description:** African American business owners often face the dilemma of whether or not to divulge their minority status when soliciting new customers and financial institutions. The quality of the products or services is always the key factor and race should never define one's business; however, it is appropriate to market oneself as a minority or women-owned business, especially if the company is in an industry where those clients are offered top-tier contracts.

42668 ■ *Twitterville: How Businesses Can Thrive in the New Global Neighborhoods*
Pub: Portfolio Hardcover

Ed: Shel Israel. **Price:** $23.95. **Description:** Twitter is the most rapidly adopted communication tool in history, going from zero to ten million users in just over two years. On Twitter, word can spread faster than wildfire. Companies no longer have the option of ignoring the conversation. Unlike other hot social media spaces, Twitterville is dominated by professionals, not students. And despite its size, it still feels like a small town. Twitter allows people to interact much the way they do face-to-face, honestly and authentically.

42669 ■ *"UAlbany on the Hunt for New Brand" in Business Review, Albany New York (Vol. 34, October 5, 2007, No. 27, pp. 1)*
Pub: American City Business Journals, Inc.
Ed: Richard A. D'Errico. **Description:** State University of New York at Albany is working on a new marketing and branding initiative to help communicate its message better. The initiative is for the school to better understand its target audiences and their perception of the university.

42670 ■ *"Vanity Plates" in Canadian Business (Vol. 82, April 27, 2009, No. 7, pp. 26)*
Pub: Rogers Media
Ed: Andy Holloway. **Description:** Politicians in the U.S. called for the review of firms that availed of the bailout money but are under deals for naming rights of sports stadiums. Angus Reid's Corporate Reputation and Sponsorship Index found for example, that there is little correlation between sponsoring arenas on having a better brand image. It is suggested that firms who enter these deals build closer to people's homes.

42671 ■ *"'We Had to Won the Mistakes" in Harvard Business Review (Vol. 88, July-August 2010, No. 7-8, pp. 108)*
Pub: Harvard Business School Publishing
Ed: Adi Ignatius. **Description:** Interview with Howard Schultz, CEO of Starbucks, covers topics that include investment in retraining, the impact of competition, premium quality, authenticity, customer services, strategy development, work-and-life issues, and international presence.

42672 ■ *"What You Look Like Online" in Black Enterprise (Vol. 37, January 2007, No. 6, pp. 56)*
Pub: Earl G. Graves Publishing Co. Inc.
Ed: Marcia A. Reed-Woodard. **Description:** Of 100 executive recruiters 77 percent stated that they use search engines to check the backgrounds of potential job candidates, according to a survey conducted by ExecuNet. Of those surveyed 35 percent stated that they eliminate potential candidates based on information they find online so it is important to create a positive Web presence which highlights professional image qualities.

42673 ■ *"What's In Your Toolbox" in Women In Business (Vol. 61, August-September 2009, No. 4, pp. 7)*
Pub: American Business Women's Association
Ed: Mimi Kopulos. **Description:** Business owners are increasingly turning to using social networking websites, such as Facebook, LinkedIn and Twitter, to promote their companies. The number of adult social media users has increased from 8 percent in 2005 to 35 percent in 2009.

42674 ■ *When the Headline Is You: An Insider's Guide to Handling the Media*
Pub: Jossey-Bass
Ed: Jeff Ansell, Jeff Lesson. **Price:** $29.95. **Description:** How-to guide for executives and other professionals whose high-visibility requires frequent interviews with the media. Tested techniques, tools, and insights for how to respond to all types of media in tough situation are provided. The books also reveals the lessons learned and the pitfalls to avoid by referencing actual news stores from around the world and provides exercises for readers who wish to sharpen their media-handling skills.

42675 ■ *"Women-Centric Events Can Captivate Consumers" in Crain's Cleveland Business (Vol. 28, November 12, 2007, No. 45, pp. 24)*
Pub: Crain Communications, Inc.
Ed: Kimberly Bonvissuto. **Description:** Discusses innovative ways that companies are targeting the female consumer market including arranging networking and social events.

42676 ■ *"You Have to Lead From Everywhere" in Harvard Business Review (Vol. 88, November 2010, No. 11, pp. 76)*
Pub: Harvard Business School Publishing
Ed: Scott Berinato. **Description:** U.S. Coast Guard Admiral Thad W. Allen discusses effective leadership in successful crises management. Topics include influence of media and public perspective, the applicability of military training to the business arena, and the responsibility of a leader to set morale.

42677 ■ *"Your Big Give" in Small Business Opportunities (September 2008)*
Pub: Entrepreneur Press
Contact: Perlman Neil, President
Ed: Michael Guld. **Description:** Cause related marketing is beneficial to businesses as well as the communities they inhabit; three small businesses that are elevating their standing in the community while at the same time increasing their customer base are profiled.

TRADE PERIODICALS

42678 ■ *Accutips*
Pub: Accudata America
Released: Monthly. **Price:** Free. **Description:** Discusses promotion and marketing issues relevant to businesses.

42679 ■ *The Gauge*
Pub: Delahaye Medialink
Contact: Katharine Delahaye Paine, Publisher
E-mail: kpaine@delahaye.com
Ed: William Teunis Paarlberg, Editor, wpaarlberg@aol.com. **Released:** Bimonthly. **Price:** $75. **Description:** Provides information on and evaluates marketing communications activities of companies. Recurring features include interviews, news of research, and a calendar of events.

42680 ■ *The Publicity Hound*
Pub: Joan Stewart
Contact: Joan Stewart, Publisher
E-mail: jstewart@publicityhound.com
Released: Weekly. **Price:** Free internet service. **Description:** Provides techniques and strategies on self-promotion and inexpensive publicity. Recurring features include letters to the editor, interviews, news of research, book reviews, news of educational opportunities, notices of publications available, and columns titled Advice From Media People, Seasonal Story Ideas, Resource Page, Success Stories, and Media Insider Secrets. Does not report public relations agency staff changes.

VIDEOCASSETTES/ AUDIOCASSETTES

42681 ■ *Ad Campaigns That Work*
Instructional Video
2219 C St.
Lincoln, NE 68502
Ph: (402)475-6570
Free: 800-228-0164
Fax: (402)475-6500
Co. E-mail: feedback@insvideo.com
URL: http://www.insvideo.com
Released: 19??. **Price:** $89.95. **Description:** Three successful ad agency executives furnish information on successful ad campaigns and why they were successful. Covers principles of successful advertising.
Availability: VHS.

42682 ■ *Advertising the Small Business*
NETCHE
1800 N. 33rd St.
Lincoln, NE 68583
Ph: (402)472-3611
Free: 800-698-3426
Fax: (402)472-1785
Co. E-mail: netche@unl.edu
URL: http://www.netche.org
Released: 1981. **Price:** $100.00. **Description:** These two tapes, provide a step-by-step instructional course on how to best publicize a small business, from research/planning to managing/implementation.
Availability: VHS; 3/4 U.

42683 ■ *Advertising: The Hidden Language*
First Light Video Publishing
2321 Abbot Kinney Blvd.
Venice, CA 90291
Ph: (310)577-8581
Free: 800-262-8862

Fax: (310)574-0886
Co. E-mail: sale@firslightvideo.com
URL: http://www.firstlightvideo.com
Released: 19??. **Description:** Features Dr. Phillip Bell as he demostrates how successful ads grab the consumer and make them want to purchase the product. **Availability:** VHS.

42684 ■ *Advertising Tricks Without the Gimmicks*
Instructional Video
2219 C St.
Lincoln, NE 68502
Ph: (402)475-6570
Free: 800-228-0164
Fax: (402)475-6500
Co. E-mail: feedback@insvideo.com
URL: http://www.insvideo.com
Released: 19??. **Price:** $79.00. **Description:** Offers an overview and practical hints on the basics of advertising. **Availability:** VHS.

42685 ■ *Promotion: Polishing the Apple*
RMI Media
1365 N. Winchester St.
Olathe, KS 66061-5880
Ph: (913)768-1696
Free: 800-745-5480
Fax: (800)755-6910
Co. E-mail: actmedia@act.org
URL: http://www.actmedia.com
Released: 1991. **Price:** $89.95. **Description:** Presents promotional mixes developed by Apple Computers for the Apple IIc, the Macintosh, and the Macintosh Office to demonstrate successful uses of print and television advertising. **Availability:** VHS.

CONSULTANTS

42686 ■ Sol Abrams Public Relations Counsel & Marketing Consultants
331 Webster Dr.
New Milford, NJ 07646
Ph: (201)262-4111
Fax: (201)262-7669
Contact: Sol Abrams, Owner
E-mail: solbabrams@aol.com
Scope: Independent consulting provides publicity, public relations and marketing counsel and services to management of private and public enterprises. Also serves as public relations consultants to other public relations consulting firms, advertising agencies and marketing companies. Provides expert witness services involving public relations. Also lectures, trains, teaches, and conducts seminars in public relations and marketing. Industries served: Corporate management, businesses large and small including real estate, construction, entertainment, food, fashion, fundraising, automotive, aviation, franchising, government agencies, and nonprofit organizations. **Founded:** 1962. **Seminars:** How to Select a Public Relations Firm; Publicity and Promotion for Small Business Owner; Expose Yourself - Don't Be a Secret Agent -Increase Your Sales, Incomes, Images, Publicity, Profits and Prestige via Professional Public Relations.

42687 ■ COMsciences Inc.
4712 Admiralty Way, Ste. 870
Marina del Rey, CA 90292
Ph: (310)823-5257
Fax: (323)937-0160
Co. E-mail: info@comsciences.com
URL: http://www.comsciences.com
Contact: Dr. Jack Torobin, Chief Executive Officer
E-mail: jtorobin@comsciences.com
Scope: Offers research services to support public relations, corporate advertising, impact of new communications media, communication entertainment, and internet/web development. Also provides strategic management consulting on communications, marketing, opinion surveys, and organizational development and assessment. The company specializes in media campaigns and evaluation tools. Also conducts government sponsored and media sponsored surveys. Serves all industry sectors, especially. com, wireless telecommunications, interactive media, and consumer electronics. **Founded:** 1989. **Publications:** "Wanted: Radical Thinking," Pmg World Magazine, Mar, 2003. **Telecommunication Services:** info@imovio.com. **Special Services:** iKIT®; imovio®.

42688 ■ Russ Fons Public Relations
7509 Turtle Dove Ct.
Las Vegas, NV 89129-6032
Ph: (702)658-7654
Free: 888-658-7654
Fax: (702)658-1349
Co. E-mail: russfons@cox.net
Contact: Russ Fons, Owner
E-mail: russfons@cox.net
Scope: Offers corporate counseling and image development; media relations; marketing communications and product publicity; event management and special promotions; and graphic design and production. Industries served: All worldwide. Licensing and merchandising, literary services, Hispanic communications. Revenue Sharing/PI Advertising. **Founded:** 1980. **Publications:** "The Executive Crisis Manager, a planning guide to surviving corporate crisis".

42689 ■ Holcomb Gallagher Adams Advertising Inc.—Holcomb Design
300 Marconi Blvd., Ste. 305
Columbus, OH 43215
Ph: (614)221-3343
Fax: (614)221-3367
Co. E-mail: radams@hgainc.com
URL: http://www.hgainc.com
Contact: Rick Adams, Partner
E-mail: radams@hgainc.com
Scope: Consults in strategic marketing planning, and new business, brand equity, creative strategy, and media strategy development. Industries served: Consumer goods and services, manufacturing, retail, business-to-business products and services, education, travel, and tourism. **Founded:** 1993.

42690 ■ Westlife Consultants & Counsellors
95 October Ln.
Aurora, ON, Canada L4G 7A1
Ph: (905)867-0686
Fax: (416)799-5242
Co. E-mail: westlifeconsultant@hotmail.com
URL: http://www.westlifeconsultants.com
Contact: Dr. Syed N. Hussain, President
E-mail: westlifeconsultant@hotmail.com
Scope: Provider of entrepreneurs and businesses with a highly commercial and global perspectives on the international business development ideas under consideration. **Founded:** 1990. **Publications:** "Innovative Management"; "Team Building and Leadership"; "Financial Planning"; "Estate Planning"; "Risk Management"; "Export/Import Trade Finance Mechanics"; "Marketing and Sales Management"; "What Your Banker Needs to Know"; "Building A Successful Financial Plan".

42691 ■ Alan J. Zell
PO Box 69
Portland, OR 97207-0069
Ph: (503)241-1988
Fax: (503)241-1989
Co. E-mail: azell@aol.com
URL: http://www.sellingselling.com
Contact: Alan J. Zell, Owner
E-mail: azell@aol.com
Scope: An advisory service for those who sell their services, products or their organization's ideas, information, and skills through face-to-face and telephone conversations, printed materials, the media, electronic communications, schools, guilds, trade shows, and display presentations. Industries served: minority and woman-owned businesses; government and education; medicine, law, accounting, technology, manufacturers, distributors, and retailers; professional and trade associations; and nonprofit organizations. **Founded:** 1983. **Publications:** "Elements of Selling"; "An Unconventional Look at the Complex Subject of Selling"; "The Art Of Selling Art"; "Selling Situations"; "What Customers need to know"; "Turnover & Return on Investment"; "The Ultimate Business Oxymoron"; "Walkin The Aisles, Looking at the Booths, etc"; "Four Uses Of Internet". **Seminars:** Ambassador Of Selling; An Unconventional Look at the Complex Subject of Selling; Selling Change . . . Pain or Progress, Revolution or Evolution?; Giving GOOD SERVICE When Giving Good Service Is Not Good Enough; Two Sides Of A Trade Show; Selling For People Who Do Not Like To Sell; The Art Of Selling Art; Yes, Technically Trained People Can Learn To Sell; Beginning Business, How To Achieve Your Goals. **Telecommunication Services:** alan@sellingselling.com.

COMPUTERIZED DATABASES

42692 ■ *ABI/INFORM®*
789 E Eisenhower Pkwy.
Ann Arbor, MI 48106-1346
Ph: (734)761-4700
Free: 800-521-0600
Co. E-mail: info@il.proquest.com
URL: http://www.il.proquest.com
Contact: Matt Dunie, President
Availability: Online: ProQuest Co.; ProQuest LLC-Dialog; ProQuest LLC - Dialog; LexisNexis Group; STN International; Wolters Kluwer Health - Ovid. **Type:** Full-text; Bibliographic; Image.

42693 ■ *Advertiser & Agency Red Books Plus*
9443 Springboro Pke.
Dayton, OH 45342
Ph: (937)865-6800
Free: 800-227-4908
Co. E-mail: customerservice.customer.support@lexisnexis.com
URL: http://www.bender.com/
Contact: Michael Walsh, President
URL(s): www.redbooks.com. **Released:** Quarterly; Latest edition January, 2007. **Price:** $2195, Individuals. **Description:** CD-ROM. Covers 15,750 of the world's top advertisers, their products and what media they use, as well as 13,900 U.S. and international ad agencies and nearly 100,000 key executives worldwide in management, creative, and media positions. **Entries include:** For advertisers--Company name, job function/title, product/brand name, advertising expenditures by media. For personnel--Name and title.

42694 ■ *PR Newswire (PRN)*
350 Hudson St., Ste. 300
New York, NY 10014
Ph: (212)596-1500
Free: 800-776-8090
Fax: (212)793-9313
Co. E-mail: information@prnewswire.com
URL: http://www.prnewswire.com
Availability: Online: ProQuest LLC - Dialog; Dow Jones & Company Inc.; Mzinga Inc.; LexisNexis Group; LexisNexis Group; Bloomberg L.P.; Track Data Corp. **Type:** Directory; Full-text.

LIBRARIES

42695 ■ Burson-Marsteller Knowledge Center
230 Park Ave. S.
New York, NY 10003
Ph: (212)614-4000
Fax: (212)598-5581
Co. E-mail: tony.telloni@bm.com
URL: http://www.burson-marsteller.com/default.aspx
Contact: Tony Telloni, Manager
Scope: Advertising, public relations, marketing research. **Services:** Interlibrary loan; library open to clients and librarians; copying. **Founded:** 1955. **Holdings:** 1000 books. **Subscriptions:** 100 journals and other serials. **Telecommunication Services:** contactbm@bm.com.

42696 ■ Campbell Mithun Library & Information Services
222 S. 9th St.
Minneapolis, MN 55402
Ph: (612)347-1759
Co. E-mail: psjolander@cmithun.com
URL: http://www.campbell-mithun.com
Contact: Peggy Sjolander, Associate Director
Scope: Advertising, marketing. **Services:** Interlibrary loan; copying; library open with permission. **Founded:**

1953. **Holdings:** 1000 books; 500 data files (reports, studies, and clippings by subject). **Subscriptions:** 350 journals and other serials.

42697 ■ D'Arcy Masius Benton & Bowles Information Center
1 Memorial Dr.
St. Louis, MO 63102
Ph: (314)342-3925
Fax: (314)342-3584
URL: http://library.duke.edu/digitalcollections/rbmscl/dmbb/inv/
Scope: Advertising agency records from 1929-1995. **Services:** Library open to the researchers by appointment with restrictions. **Founded:** 1985. **Holdings:** 750 volumes; 375 VF drawers of pamphlets and clippings. **Subscriptions:** 750 journals and other serials.

42698 ■ Grey Worldwide Information Center
200 5th Ave.
New York, NY 10010
Ph: (212)546-2000
Fax: (212)546-2001
Co. E-mail: espross@grey.com
URL: http://www.grey.com/
Contact: Jim Heekin, Chief Executive Officer
Scope: Advertising, marketing, business, new business development. **Services:** Interlibrary loan. **Founded:** 1948. **Holdings:** 500 books; 200 directories. **Subscriptions:** 200 journals and other serials; 5 newspapers. **Telecommunication Services:** odougherty@grey.com; jim.heekin@grey.com.

42699 ■ Ketchum Advertising - Library Services
1285 Avenue of the Americas, 4th Fl.
New York, NY 10019
Ph: (646)935-3900
Co. E-mail: kelley.skoloda@ketchum.com
URL: http://www.ketchum.com
Contact: Ray Kotcher, Chairman
Scope: Advertising, marketing, general reference. **Services:** Interlibrary loan. **Founded:** 1949. **Holdings:** 1100 books; 40 VF drawers of marketing material; reference collection; Annual reports. **Subscriptions:** 450 journals and other serials. **Telecommunication Services:** ray.kotcher@ketchum.com.

42700 ■ Martin/Williams Advertising Library
60 S. 6th St., Ste. 2800
Minneapolis, MN 55402
Ph: (612)340-0800
Fax: (612)342-9700
URL: http://www.martinwilliams.com
Scope: Advertising, marketing, business. **Services:** Library open to agency employees and clients; open to the public with special permission. **Founded:** 1977. **Holdings:** Figures not available.

42701 ■ McCann-Erickson Advertising of Canada Ltd. Information Centre
10 Bay St., Ste. 1012
Toronto, ON, Canada M5J 2S3
Ph: (416)594-6400
Fax: (416)594-6272
Co. E-mail: contact@mccann.com
URL: http://www.mccann.com/
Contact: Valerie Walton, Manager
Scope: Advertising, marketing, business, industry. **Services:** Center not open to the public. **Founded:** 1960. **Holdings:** 1000 books. **Subscriptions:** 90 journals and other serials.

42702 ■ Reader's Digest - Marketing Information Center
260 Madison Ave.
New York, NY 10016
Ph: (212)850-7100
Free: 800-310-2181
Fax: (212)696-0587
Co. E-mail: letters@rd.com
URL: http://www.rd.com
Scope: Advertising, marketing, and media research. **Services:** Interlibrary loan. **Holdings:** 800 volumes; 23 lateral file drawers of commodity and industry data. **Subscriptions:** 74 journals and other serials.

RESEARCH CENTERS

42703 ■ Boston College - Center for Corporate Citizenship
Carroll School of Management
55 Lee Rd.
Chestnut Hill, MA 02467-3942
Ph: (617)552-4545
Fax: (617)552-8499
Co. E-mail: bradley.googins.1@bc.edu
URL: http://www.bcccc.net
Contact: Bradley K. Googins, Executive Director
Services: Contract research and consulting. **Founded:** 1985. **Publications:** *Corporate Citizen magazine* (Annual); *Center for Corporate Citizenship Research reports* (Periodic); *Voice of Corporate Citizenship newsletter* (Monthly). **Educational Activities:** Center for Corporate Citizenship Conferences; Executive education, professional development courses in managing community involvement and corporate citizenship; Seminars and institutes. **Awards:** Paid internship. **Telecommunication Services:** ccc@bc.edu.

42704 ■ Massachusetts College of Art - Design Research Unit (DRU)
621 Huntington Ave.
Boston, MA 02115
Ph: (617)879-7793
Fax: (617)566-4034
Co. E-mail: rstreit@massart.edu
URL: http://babel.massart.edu/dru
Contact: Dan Wallis, President
Services: Provides design services to educational, research, charitable, and non-profit organizations. **Founded:** 1972. **Educational Activities:** Educational training in design, printing, and business.

Purchasing

ASSOCIATIONS AND OTHER ORGANIZATIONS

42705 ■ American Purchasing Society (APS)
PO Box 256
Aurora, IL 60506
Ph: (630)859-0250
Fax: (630)859-0270
Co. E-mail: propurch@propurch.com
URL: http://www.american-purchasing.com
Contact: Mr. Richard H. Hough, Executive Vice President
Description: Seeks to certify qualified purchasing personnel. Maintains speakers' bureau and placement service. Conducts research programs; compiles statistics including salary surveys. Provides consulting service for purchasing, materials management, and marketing. Conducts seminars and online courses. **Scope:** purchasing, materials management, supply chain, inventory. **Founded:** 1969. **Subscriptions:** 1500 articles audio recordings books periodicals. **Publications:** *Professional Purchasing*; *Benchmarking Purchasing* (Annual); *Professional Purchasing*; *Benchmarking Purchasing* (Annual); *Handbook of Buying and Purchasing Management*; *Annual Report of Purchasing Salaries and Employment Trends* (Annual); *How To Get the Best Results from your Purchasing Department* (Biennial). **Awards:** Certified Purchasing Professional (Periodic); Excellent Supplier Award (Annual). **Telecommunication Services:** propurch@mgci.com.

42706 ■ National Purchasing Institute (NPI)
PO Box 370192
Las Vegas, NV 89137-0192
Ph: (702)989-8095
Free: 866-877-7641
Fax: (702)967-0744
Co. E-mail: info@npiconnection.org
URL: http://www.npiconnection.org/home/index.asp
Contact: Harold Good, President
Description: Purchasing agents, directors of purchasing and procurement, buyers, and others employed by governmental, educational, or other tax-supported agencies. Seeks to improve the field through development of simplified standards of specifications, improved communication, and promotion of uniform purchasing laws. Compiles statistics. **Scope:** purchasing specifications. **Founded:** 1968. **Publications:** *Annual Conference Program* (Annual); *Membership Roster* (Annual); *Public Purchasing Review* (Bimonthly). **Educational Activities:** National Purchasing Institute Conference (Annual). **Awards:** Achievement of Excellence in Procurement (Annual); Carlton N. Parker Award for Outstanding Service (Annual).

EDUCATIONAL PROGRAMS

42707 ■ Fundamentals of Purchasing (Canada)
Canadian Management Centre (CMC)
150 York St., 5th Fl.
Toronto, ON, Canada M5H 3S5
Ph: (416)214-5678
Free: 877-262-2519
Fax: (416)313-4985
Co. E-mail: cmcinfo@cmctraining.org
URL: http://www.cmctraining.org
Contact: John Wright, President
Price: $2,395.00 Canadian for non-members; $2,195.00 Canadian for CMC members. **Description:** Covers the steps involved in purchasing, negotiating, working with vendors and suppliers, cost and price analysis, and types of purchase contracts. **Dates and Locations:** Toronto, ON; and Mississauga, ON.

42708 ■ Fundamentals of Purchasing for the New Buyer (Onsite)
American Management Association
600 AMA Way
Saranac Lake, NY 12983-5534
Ph: (212)586-8100
Free: 877-566-9441
Fax: (518)891-0368
Co. E-mail: customerservice@amanet.org
URL: http://www.amaseminars.org
Price: $2,345.00 for non-members; $2,095.00 for AMA members; and $1,794.00 for General Services Administration (GSA) members. **Description:** Covers the steps involved in purchasing, negotiating, working with vendors and suppliers, using e-procurement, and the materials management process. **Dates and Locations:** Atlanta, GA; Chicago, IL; New Yory, NY; Washington, DC; and Arlington, VA.

42709 ■ How to Bargain & Negotiate with Vendors and Suppliers (Onsite)
Fred Pryor Seminars & CareerTrack
5700 Broadmoor St., Ste. 300
Mission, KS 66202
Free: 800-780-8476
Fax: (913)967-8849
Co. E-mail: customerservice@pryor.com
URL: http://www.pryor.com
Price: $179.00; $169.00 for groups of 5 or more. **Description:** Learn how to get lower prices, quicker delivery, higher quality and better service through negotiation. **Dates and Locations:** Cities throughout the United States.

REFERENCE WORKS

42710 ■ *Common Sense Purchasing: Hard Knock Lessons Learned from a Purchasing Pro*
Pub: Booksurge, LLC
Ed: Tom DePaoli. **Released:** February 2004. **Price:** $9.99. **Description:** Guide to purchasing and negotiating deals.

42711 ■ *"Many Procter Products To Get Price Increase" in Business Courier (Vol. 24, November 16, 2008, No. 31, pp. 1)*
Pub: American City Business Journals, Inc.
Ed: Lisa Biank Fasig. **Description:** Procter & Gamble Co. is increasing the prices of its products as a means to offset the rising costs of gas, plastics and raw materials. The price increase will be somewhere between 3 to 12 percent, depending on the product.

42712 ■ *"New Beginnings for VIBE" in Black Enterprise (Vol. 37, November 2006, No. 4, pp. 34)*
Pub: Earl G. Graves Publishing Co. Inc.
Ed: Mashaun D. Simon. **Description:** Danyel Smith replaced Mimi Valdes as editor-in-chief of VIBE magazine after the Wicks Group, private equity firm focused on selected segments of the media, communications, and information industries, purchased the magazine.

42713 ■ *"Suiting Up; Yes, You're Smart, But Can You Look the Part" in Crain's Chicago Business (Vol. 30, February 2007, No. 6, pp. 39)*
Pub: Crain Communications, Inc.
Ed: Kate Ryan. **Description:** For investment bankers, fashion is a must. Advice for men and women included.

TRADE PERIODICALS

42714 ■ *Business Consumer's Advisor*
Pub: Buyers Laboratory Inc.
Contact: Michael Danziger, Chief Executive Officer
Ed: Daria Hoffman, Editor. **Released:** Monthly. **Price:** $20. **Description:** Focuses on office equipment and supplies, offering purchasing advice and exploring methods of increasing office productivity through appropriate management of the equipment and its operators. Offers readers a chance to share their experiences, evaluate products and equipment, and gives results of Buyers Laboratory's testing.

42715 ■ *Caveat Emptor*
Pub: Ontario Public Buyers Association
Ed: C.B. Bott, Editor. **Released:** 4/year. **Price:** $99, individuals $99/year. **Description:** Contains information of interest to anyone who spends public funds. Recurring features include updates on OPBA's Internet Bid Document Advertising System and internal databank and articles dealing with new technology, management issues, and methodology related to the expenditure of public funds.

42716 ■ *Inside Supply Management: Resources to Create Your Future*
Pub: Institute for Supply Management
URL(s): www.ism.ws/Pubs/ISMMag/index.cfm. **Released:** Monthly

42717 ■ *The Journal of Supply Chain Management: A Global Review of Purchasing and Supply*
Pub: Institute for Supply Management
URL(s): www.ism.ws/pubs/journalscm/index.cfm-?navItemNumber=5474. **Released:** Quarterly **Price:** $109, Individuals Americas print + online; €103, Individuals print + online; £68, Individuals rest of world print + online; $279, Institutions print + online; €255, Institutions print + online; £201, Institutions, other countries print + online.

42718 ■ *NAEP Bulletin*
Pub: National Association of Educational Procurement
Contact: Doreen Murner, Chief Executive Officer
Ed: Doreen Murner, Editor, dmurner@naeb.org. **Released:** Monthly, except May and April. **Price:** Included in membership. **Description:** Features information on institutional purchasing and news of the Association. Recurring features include a calendar of events, reports of meetings, news of educational opportunities, job listings, book reviews, notices of publications available, and columns titled Professional Perspective, Market Index, and Roamin' With Yeoman.

42719 ■ *NASPO Newsletter*
Pub: National Association of State Procurement Officials
Contact: Carol Wilson, President
E-mail: carol.wilson@ct.gov
Ed: Leslie Scott, Editor, lflynn@iglov.rom. **Released:** Quarterly, 2/year. **Price:** Included in membership. **Description:** Covers Association activities and purchasing innovations in state governments. Reports on developments in energy efficiency and recycling. Recurring features include news from the states, resources available, a calendar of events, and reports of state and federal legislation.

42720 ■ *Professional Purchasing*
Pub: American Purchasing Society
Contact: Mr. Richard H. Hough, Executive Vice President
Ed: Harry E. Hough, Ph.D., Editor, hehough@mgci.com. **Released:** Monthly. **Description:** Provides information on policies, procedures, methods, and prices of purchasing. Features price indexes. Recurring features include letters to the editor, news of research, reports of meetings, news of educational opportunities, job listings, book reviews, and notices of publications available.

42721 ■ *Progressive Purchasing*
Pub: Purchasing Management Association of Canada
Ed: A. Marshall, Editor, amarshall@pmac.ca. **Released:** Bimonthly. **Price:** Included in membership. **Description:** Presents news on the association's C.P.P. Accreditation program, new developments in purchasing, industry trends, and profiles of membership. Recurring features include a calendar of events, summary of national activities, and a column titled the National President's Message. Remarks: Also available in French.

42722 ■ *Purchasing b2b*
Pub: Business Information Group
Contact: Bruce Creighton, President
URL(s): www.canadianmanufacturing.com/purchasing-and-procurement. **Ed:** Michael Power. **Released:** 10/yr.

TRADE SHOWS AND CONVENTIONS

42723 ■ ISM Annual International Supply Management Conference
Institute for Supply Management
2055 E. Centennial Cir.
Tempe, AZ 85285-2160
Ph: (480)752-6276
Free: 800-888-6276
Fax: (480)752-7890
URL: http://www.ism.ws
Contact: Sidney Johnson, Chairman of the Board
URL(s): www.ism.ws. **Price:** $1229, Pre-registered, members early bird; $1579, Pre-registered, non-members early bird. **Frequency:** Annual. **Audience:** Purchasing professionals and general public. **Principal Exhibits:** Auctions, business service, capital equipment, computer hardware/software, consulting services, e-business services/software, logistics and transportation, MRO, office supply, procurement card services.

CONSULTANTS

42724 ■ Mark Vanderstelt
9831 Gulfstream Ct.
Fishers, IN 46037
Ph: (317)576-9328
Fax: (317)576-9328
Contact: Mark Vanderstelt, Owner
Scope: Consulting services include financial planning and analysis, inventory control, cash management, return on investment, budgeting, pricing, system design and analysis, mergers and acquisitions, feasibility studies, data processing, cost systems and controls, and performance measurement. Also performs operational and financial reviews. **Founded:** 1985.

RESEARCH CENTERS

42725 ■ Arizona State University - CAPS Research
2055 E Centennial Cir.
Tempe, AZ 85285-2160
Ph: (480)752-2277
Fax: (480)491-7885
Co. E-mail: research@capsresearch.org
URL: http://www.capsresearch.org
Contact: Phillip Carter, Executive Director
Founded: 1986. **Publications:** *Critical Issue reports* (Quarterly); *Practix* (Quarterly); *CAPS Research Research reports* (Quarterly). **Educational Activities:** Focus study research, benchmarking, critical issues reports, focused on executive participation in supply management research; Executive Roundtable, Best Practices Forums/Workshops (10/year), for senior purchasing and supply management practitioners. **Telecommunication Services:** pcarter@capsresearch.org.

TRADE SHOWS AND CONVENTIONS

42726 ■ Society for Human Resource Management Exposition (SHRM)
Society for Human Resource Management (SHRM)
1800 Duke St.
Alexandria, VA 22314
Ph: (703)548-3440
Free: 800-283-7476
Fax: (703)535-6490
Co. E-mail: shrm@shrm.org
URL: http://www.shrm.org
Contact: Henry G. Jackson, President
E-mail: hjackson@shrm.org
URL(s): www.shrm.org. **Frequency:** Annual. **Audience:** Human resource management and related professionals. **Principal Exhibits:** Human resource management products and services; including relocation human resource information systems, recruitment, executive search, temporary/contact personnel employee compensation and benefits, incentive program information, childcare/eldercare, and drug testing information.

CONSULTANTS

42727 ■ Ambler Growth Strategy Consultants Inc.
3432 Reading Ave.
Hammonton, NJ 08037-8008
Ph: (609)567-9669
Free: 888-253-6662
Fax: (609)567-3810
Co. E-mail: thegrowthstrategist@ambler.com
URL: http://www.ambler.com
Contact: Aldonna R. Ambler, Chief Executive Officer
E-mail: aldonna@ambler.com
Scope: Growth strategies, strategic assessments, CEO coaching. **Founded:** 1979. **Publications:** "A joint venture can deliver more than growth"; "Achieving competitive advantage"; "Achieving resilience for your business during difficult times"; "Achieving resilient growth during challenging times"; "Acquisitions: A growth strategy to consider"; "Attracting and retaining longterm corporate sponsors"; "Celebrate Selling: The Consultative Relationship Way"; "A Joint Venture Can Deliver More Than Growth"; "Achieving Competitive Advantage"; "Achieving Resilience for Your Business During Difficult Times"; "Balancing Revenue Growth with Growth of a Business"; "Capture Your Competitive Advantage"; "Ease Succession Planning"; "Games Employees Play"; "How to Spark Innovation in an Existing Company"; "Managers demands must change with growth"; "Motivating Generation employees"; "Knowing when to hire ratios provide answers"; "Better customer service can bring black ink". **Seminars:** Strategic Leadership; Managing Innovation; Breaking Through Classic Barriers to Growth; Energize Your Enterprise; Capture Your Competitive Advantage; Four Entrepreneurial Styles; Perservance and Resilience; Real-Time Strategic Planning/RO1. **Special Services:** The Growth Strategist™.

42728 ■ Effectiveness Resource Group Inc.
2529 170th Pl. SE
Bellevue, WA 98008-5520
Ph: (206)949-4171
Fax: (425)957-9186
Co. E-mail: don@consultdon.com
Contact: Donald H. Swartz, President
E-mail: dhsergsri@aol.com
Scope: Provider of problem solving help to client organizations in public and private sectors so they can release and mobilize the full potential of their personnel to achieve productive and satisfying results. Emphasis is on technical or human productivity improvement projects and systems, total human resource systems design and implementation, and a whole systems approach to organizational change design and implementation. Serves private industries as well as government agencies. Consults with both internal and external consultants via e-mail and phone. Also offers executive coaching. **Founded:** 1973. **Seminars:** Life/Work Goals Exploration; Influencing Change Thru Consultation; Designing and Leading Participative Meetings; Designing, Leading and Managing Change; Project Management and Leadership; Performance Management; Productive Management of Differences; Performance Correction.

42729 ■ Goldore Consulting Inc.
120-5 St. NW, Ste. 1
Linden, AB, Canada T0M 1J0
Ph: (403)546-4208
Fax: (403)546-4208
Co. E-mail: goldore@leadershipessentials.com
Contact: Robert A. Orr, President
E-mail: orr@leadershipessentials.com
Description: Description: Publishes materials on leadership and management skills for churches and charitable organizations that provide services to developing countries. Also publishes in Spanish and Portuguese. Does not accept unsolicited manuscripts. Reaches market through direct mail and wholesalers and distributors, including Leadership Training Ministry Foundation, Inc. **Scope:** Provides consulting service in leadership and management skills. Industries served: primarily charities, non-profits; some businesses. **Founded:** 1990. **Seminars:** The Challenge Of Leadership.

42730 ■ Organizational Improvement Associates L.L.C. (OIA)—OIAUS L.L.C.
40 Gilbert St.
Ridgefield, CT 06877
Ph: (203)417-4957
Fax: (203)244-5737
Co. E-mail: daveknibbe@oiaus.com
URL: http://www.oiaus.com
Contact: Dr. David S. Knibbe, President
E-mail: daveknibbe@oiaus.com
Scope: Specializes in high-performance team development, executive coaching, employee development programs, performance management and reward systems and dispute mediation. Industries served: Consumer products, telecommunications, finance, health-care, amusement/leisure, hospitality/lodging, retail and pharmaceuticals. **Founded:** 1991.

42731 ■ Performance Dynamics Group L.L.C.
1 Ridge Rd.
Green Brook, NJ 08812
Free: 888-720-7337
Co. E-mail: info@performance-dynamics.net
URL: http://www.performance-dynamics.net
Contact: Mark E. Green, President
E-mail: mark.green@performance-dynamics.net
Scope: An organizational consulting group whose approach to learning and employee empowerment is designed to be both effective and efficient in achieving the specific knowledge and skill goals of a given program, in developing changes in thinking and behavior and also to foster and develop initiative, self confidence, creative problem-solving ability and interpersonal effectiveness of all participants. Brings improvement in areas of revenue growth, profitability, sales, marketing effectiveness, and employee and customer loyalty. **Founded:** 2003. **Seminars:** Accelerated Approach to Change; Commitment to Quality; Managing Cultural Diversity; The Corporate Energizer; The Power Pole Experience; Team Assessment; Self-Directed Work Teams.

42732 ■ Sanford Consulting
52 Perry Corners Rd., RR 1
Amenia, NY 12501
Ph: (845)373-8960
Fax: (845)373-8961
Co. E-mail: sanford@mohawk.com
Contact: Anne Sanford, President
E-mail: sanford@mohawk.com
Scope: Helps businesses find, sell, to, and keep customers. Provides management and marketing services, including problem analysis and solution design for new business development, market analysis and segmentation, departmental organization and administrative policies and procedures. Industries served: small business, telecommunications, professional services, health care and nonprofits in the continental United States. **Founded:** 1986. **Seminars:** Trade show success; Finding customers; Business attitudes at not for profit and others.

42733 ■ The Walk The Talk Co.—Performance Systems Corp.
1100 Parker Sq., Ste. 250
Flower Mound, TX 75028-7458
Ph: (972)899-8300
Free: 800-888-2811
Fax: (972)899-9291
Co. E-mail: info@walkthetalk.com
URL: http://www.walkthetalk.com
Contact: Eric L. Harvey, President
E-mail: ericharvey@walkthetalk.com
Scope: Assists a wide variety of organizations in implementing proprietary performance management system developed by the firm which concentrates on individual responsibility and decision making instead of disciplinary penalties. Helps organizations develop and implement peer review, a proven system that helps solve employee problems in a remarkable way-

through employees and an evaluation process software is used whereby feedback is compiled from a full-range of sources, including a self-evaluation, leadership development workshops and keynote presentations and publications. **Founded:** 1977. **Publications:** "Positive Discipline"; "Leadership Secrets of Santa Claus"; "Start Right-Stay Right"; "Walk Awhile in My Shoes"; "Listen Up, Leader!"; "Five Star Teamwork"; "Ethics4Everyone"; "Leadership Courage"; "The Manager's Communication Handbook"; "180 Ways to Walk the Recognition Talk"; "The Manager's Coaching Handbook"; "The Best Leadership Advice I Ever Got"; "Power Exchange". **Seminars:** Walk the Talk; Coaching for Continuous Improvement; Managing Employee Performance; Customized Management Development Forums; Keynote presentations; Leadership Development Workshops; Consulting Services and Publications; Customer service training; Ethics and Values training.

RESEARCH CENTERS

42734 ■ Institute for the Development of Emotional and Life Skills (IDEALS)
4400 E W Hwy.
Bethesda, MD 20814
Ph: (301)986-1479
Fax: (301)680-3756
Co. E-mail: bguerney@nire.org
Contact: Dr. Bernard Guerney, Jr., President

Founded: 1972. **Educational Activities:** Training programs for professionals and the public.

42735 ■ Manchester College - Peace Studies Institute - Program in Conflict Resolution
604 E College Ave.
North Manchester, IN 46962-1276
Ph: (260)982-5343
Free: 800-852-3648
Fax: (260)982-5043
Co. E-mail: klgraybrown@manchester.edu
URL: http://www.manchester.edu/academics/departments/peace_studies/index.shtml
Contact: Katy Gray Brown, Director

Founded: 1948. **Publications:** *Bulletin of the Peace Studies Institute* (Annual); *Connections Newsletter* (Quarterly). **Educational Activities:** Church as Peacemaker and the Ropchan Lecture series (5/year). **Awards:** Graduate peace studies internship (Annual); Program in Conflict Resolution Scholarships, for undergraduate peace studies majors; Program in Conflict Resolution Summer internships (Annual).

42736 ■ National Institute of Relationship Enhancement (NIRE)
4400 East-West Hwy., Ste. 28
Bethesda, MD 20814-4501
Ph: (301)680-8977
Fax: (301)680-3756
Co. E-mail: niremd@nire.org
URL: http://www.nire.org
Contact: Dr. Bernard Guerney, Jr., Director

Founded: 1992. **Educational Activities:** Practicum training; Workshops for training professionals, organizational personnel, and families.

Research and Development

START-UP INFORMATION

42737 ▪ *Entrepreneurship: Frameworks and Empirical Investigations from Forthcoming Leaders of European Research*
Pub: Elsevier Science and Technology Books
Ed: Johan Wiklund; Dimo Dimov; Jerome A. Katz; Dean Shepherd. **Released:** July 2006. **Price:** $99. 95. **Description:** Entrepreneurial research and theory cover the early growth of research-based startups and the role of learning in international entrepreneurship, focusing on Europe.

42738 ▪ *"Incubator Cooking Up Expansion Plans" in Business First Columbus (Vol. 25, December 5, 2008, No. 15, pp.)*
Pub: American City Business Journals
Ed: Kevin Kemper. **Description:** United States-based Science and Technology Campus Corporation is planning to build additional office space in Columbus, Ohio. The site is designed to accommodate three large tenants. Comment from company executives are presented.

42739 ▪ *"Online Fortunes" in Small Business Opportunities (Fall 2008)*
Pub: Entrepreneur Media Inc.
Description: Fifty hot, e-commerce enterprises for the aspiring entrepreneur to consider are featured; virtual assistants, marketing services, party planning, travel services, researching, web design and development, importing as well as creating an online store are among the businesses featured.

42740 ▪ *Small Business Tool Kit*
Pub: Lessons Professional Publishing
Ed: Linda M. Magoon. **Released:** April 10, 2010. **Price:** $40.00. **Description:** When starting a business, new managers and entrepreneurs require many resources to get the company up and running successfully. This book covers a wide range of topics that are critical for any new business owner.

42741 ▪ *"Troy Patent Law Firm Launches Rent-Free Tech Incubator" in Crain's Detroit Business (Vol. 25, June 8, 2009, No. 23, pp. 4)*
Pub: Crain Communications Inc. - Detroit
Ed: Tom Henderson. **Description:** Young Basile Hanlon MacFarlane & Helmholdt PC, a patent law firm located in Troy, Michigan has created a small, rent-free technology incubator on site. The incubator will be called North Woodward Tech Incubator and has room for four or five startups. The incubator is for the earliest or pre-seed stage for entrepreneurs who have not yet gotten significant investment capital.

42742 ▪ *"Wanted: Angels in the Country" in Austin Business JournalInc. (Vol. 28, July 18, 2008, No. 18, pp. 1)*
Pub: American City Business Journals
Ed: Laura Hipp. **Description:** A proposal is being pushed forward by managers of Texas' Emerging Technology Fund to create an angel investors' network. The proposal is asking that tax credits for those who invest in research and development projects be granted in order to boost the number of technology companies in the state.

REFERENCE WORKS

42743 ▪ *"The 100 Fastest-Growing Companies" in Hispanic Business (Vol. 30, July-August 2008, No. 7-8, pp. 22)*
Pub: Hispanic Business, Inc.
Ed: Michael Bowker. **Description:** CEO's of the five fastest growing Hispanic-owned companies discuss the success of their companies; most of them attribute their success to proper investment and diversification, effective innovations and seeing growth opportunities where others see roadblocks.

42744 ▪ *"2011 U.S. Smart Grid - Saving Energy/Saving Money" in Ecology,Environment & Conservation Business (October 8, 2011, pp. 3)*
Pub: HighBeam Research
Description: Highlights of the '2011 U.S. Smart Grid —Saving Energy/Saving Money Customers' Prospective Demand-Response assesses residential energy consumers' willingness to decrease their power consumption in order to mitigate power issues. Statistical details included.

42745 ▪ *"Abraxis Bets On Biotech Hub" in Business Journal-Serving Phoenix and the Valley of the Sun (Vol. 10, November 9, 2007, No. 28)*
Pub: American City Business Journals, Inc.
Ed: Angela Gonzales. **Description:** Abraxis BioScience Inc. purchased a 200,000 square foot manufacturing facility in Phoenix, Arizona from Watson Pharmaceuticals Inc. The company has the technology to allow chemotherapy drugs to be injected directly into tumor cell membranes. A human protein, albumin is used to deliver the chemotherapy.

42746 ▪ *"Adapt or Die" in Black Enterprise (Vol. 38, July 2008, No. 12, pp. 27)*
Pub: Earl G. Graves Publishing Co. Inc.
Ed: Oguntoyinbo Lekan. **Description:** Turbulence in the domestic auto industry is hitting auto suppliers hard and black suppliers, the majority of whom contract with the Big Three, are just beginning to establish relationships with import car manufacturers. The more savvy CEOs are adopting new technologies in order to weather the downturn in the economy and in the industry as a whole.

42747 ▪ *"Aggenix Completes Merger with German Giant" in Houston Business Journal (Vol. 40, December 25, 2009, No. 33, pp. 2)*
Pub: American City Business Journals
Ed: Mary Ann Azevedo. **Description:** Agennix Inc. has completed its transformation into a German company after Germany-based GPC Biotech merged into the former publicly traded Agennix AG. One quarter of Agennix's 60 employees will remain in Houston. Details on Agennix's drug trials are examined.

42748 ▪ *"Alberta Star Begins Phase 2 Drilling On Its Eldorado & Contact Lake IOCG & Uranium Projects" in Canadian Corporate News (May 16, 2007)*
Pub: Comtex News Network Inc.
Description: Profile of Alberta Star Development Corp., a Canadian mineral exploration company that identifies, acquires, and finances advanced stage exploration projects in Canada, and its current undertaking of its 2007 drill program in which the company intends to begin accelerating its uranium and poly-metallic exploration and drilling activities on all of its drill targets for 2007 now that it has been granted its permits.

42749 ▪ *"Angel Investments Tripled in 2009" in Austin Business JournalInc. (Vol. 29, January 8, 2010, No. 44, pp. 1)*
Pub: American City Business Journals
Ed: Christopher Calnan. **Description:** Central Texas Angel Network (CTAN) has invested $3.5 million in 12 ventures, which include 10 in Austin, Texas in 2009 to triple the amount it invested during 2008. The largest recipient of CTAN's investments is life sciences, which attracted 20 percent of the capital, while software investments fell to 18 percent. The new screening process that helps startups secure CTAN capital is explored.

42750 ▪ *"Another Baby Step" in Canadian Business (Vol. 81, March 31, 2008, No. 5, pp. 32)*
Pub: Rogers Media
Ed: Andrew Wahl. **Description:** Discusses the Canadian government's federal budget which makes it easier to tap into tax credits for corporate research and development. However, these steps do not really go far enough to boost industrial research levels in Canada. Making these incentives at least partially refundable could help during tough economic times.

42751 ▪ *"Apples, Decoded: WSU Scientist Unraveling the Fruit's Genetics" in Puget Sound Business Journal (Vol. 29, September 5, 2008, No. 20)*
Pub: American City Business Journals
Ed: Clay Holtzman. **Description:** Washington State University researcher is working to map the apple's genome in order to gain information about how the fruit grows, looks and tastes. His work, funded by a research grant from the US Department of Agriculture and the Washington Apple Commission is crucial to improving the state's position as an apple-producing region.

42752 ▪ *"Ask Inc." in Inc. (October 2007, pp. 73-74)*
Pub: Gruner & Jahr USA Publishing
Description: An online marketing research firm investigates the use of online communities such as MySpace and Second life in order to recruit individuals to answer surveys.

42753 ▪ *"Asterand Eyes Jump to Ann Arbor; TechTown Tenant" in Crain's Detroit Business*

(Vol. 25, June 22, 2009)
Pub: Crain Communications Inc. - Detroit
Ed: Tom Henderson. **Description:** Asterand PLC is considering a move to Ann Arbor from its current location as anchor tenant at TechTown, an incubator and technology park associated with Wayne State University. The university believes the Ann Arbor location's rent is too expensive for the tissue bank company.

42754 ■ *"ATI Now Ready to Pounce on Biotech" in Austin Business JournalInc. (Vol. 28, August 22, 2008, No. 23, pp. 1)*
Pub: American City Business Journals
Ed: Laura Hipp. **Description:** Austin Technology Incubator has entered the biotechnology sector through a program of the University of Texas incubator. The company's bioscience program was set off by a grant from the City of Austin worth $125,000. The growth of Austin's biotechnology sector is examined.

42755 ■ *"Attorney Guides Biotech Company in $6 Million Initial Public Offering" in Miami Daily Business Review (March 26, 2008)*
Pub: ALM Media Inc.
Description: In order to raise capital to engage in a full-scale trial of MyoCell to receive clinical approval, Bioheart Inc., launched an initial public offering. Bioheart researches and develops cell therapies to treat heart damage.

42756 ■ *"Auctions and Bidding: a Guide for Computer Scientists" in ACM Computing Surveys (Vol. 43, Summer 2011, No. 2, pp. 10)*
Pub: Association for Computing Machinery
Ed: Simon Parsons, Juan A. Rodriguez-Aguilar, Mark Klein. **Description:** There are various actions: single dimensional, multi-dimensional, single-sided, double-sided, first-price, second-price, English, Dutch, Japanese, sealed-bid, and these have been extensively discussed and analyzed in economics literature. This literature is surveyed from a computer science perspective, primarily from the viewpoint of computer scientists who are interested in learning about auction theory, and to provide pointers into the economics literature for those who want a deeper technical understanding. In addition, since auctions are an increasingly important topic in computer science, the article also looks at work on auctions from the computer science literature. The aim is to identify what both bodies of work tell us about creating electronic auctions.

42757 ■ *"Auxilium Drug's New Use: Putting Squeeze On Cellulite" in Philadelphia Business Journal (Vol. 30, September 16, 2011, No. 31, pp. 1)*
Pub: American City Business Journals Inc.
Ed: John George. **Description:** Auxilium Pharmaceuticals and BioSpecifics Technologies are getting on with their plans of finding new uses for their drug Xiaflex, a possible treatment for cellulite. The two firms have dismissed their pending litigations and mapped out an amended licensing agreement for their search for the potential uses of the drug.

42758 ■ *"Avoiding Invention Scams" in Black Enterprise (Vol. 37, January 2007, No. 6, pp. 46)*
Pub: Earl G. Graves Publishing Co. Inc.
Ed: James C. Johnson. **Description:** Invention promotion firms provide inventors assistance in developing a prototype for product development. It is important to research these companies before making a commitment to work with them because there are a number of these firms that are not legitimate and have caused independent inventors to lose thousands of dollars by making false claims as to the market potential of the inventions.

42759 ■ *"Banking on Cord Blood" in Business Journal-Serving Phoenix & the Valley of the Sun (Vol. 31, September 10, 2010, No. 1, pp. 1)*
Pub: Phoenix Business Journal
Ed: Angela Gonzales. **Description:** Celebration Stem Cell Centre obtained contracts from Mercy Gilbert Medical Center and its two sister hospitals, St. Joseph Hospital and Medical Center in Phoenix, Arizona and Chandler Regional Medical Center. The contract will facilitate the donation of unused umbilical cord blood for research.

42760 ■ *"Bar Hopping: Your Numbers At a Glance" in Inc. (January 2008, pp. 44-45)*
Pub: Gruner & Jahr USA Publishing
Ed: Michael Fitzgerald. **Description:** Software that helps any company analyze data include Crystal Xcelsius, a program that takes data from Excel documents and turns them into animated gauges, charts and graphs; CashView, a Web-based application that tracks receivables and payables; iDashboards, a Web-based programs that produces animated gauges, maps, pie charts and graphs; Corda Human Capital Management, that transforms stats like head count, productivity, and attrition into graphs and dials; NetSuite, a Web-based application that tracks key indicators; and Cognos Now, that gauges, dials, and graphs data.

42761 ■ *"Being Big By Design" in Canadian Business (Vol. 82, April 27, 2009, No. 7, pp. 39)*
Pub: Rogers Media
Ed: Andrew Wahl. **Description:** Gennum expects that its planned acquisition of Tundra Semiconductor will expand its market presence and leverage its research and development better than working alone. The proposed friendly acquisition could challenge Zarlink Semiconductor as the largest Canadian semiconductor firm in terms of revenue. The merger could expand Gennum's addressable market to about $2 billion.

42762 ■ *"Biotechnology Wants a Lead Role" in Business North Carolina (Vol. 28, March 2008, No. 3, pp. 14)*
Pub: Business North Carolina
Description: According to experts, North Carolina is poised as a leader in the biotechnology sector. Highlights of a recent roundtable discussion sponsored by the North Carolina Biotechnology Center in Research Triangle Park are presented.

42763 ■ *"Bloomberg Law Upgraded Its Online Legal Research Platform" in Information Today (Vol. 28, September 2011, No. 8, pp. 28)*
Pub: Information Today, Inc.
Description: Bloomberg Law upgraded its online legal research platform for law practices. The new services includes a redesigned interface, improved search capabilities, and expanded collaboration and workflow features, while maintaining it comprehensive law resources such as mergers and acquisitions, antitrust, and securities.

42764 ■ *"Border Boletin: UA to Take Lie-Detector Kiosk to Poland" in Arizona Daily Star (September 14, 2010)*
Pub: Arizona Daily Star
Ed: Brady McCombs. **Description:** University of Arizona's National Center for Border Security and Immigration Research will send a team to Warsaw, Poland to show border guards from 27 European Union countries the center's Avatar Kiosk. The Avatar technology is designed for use at border ports and airports to assist Customs officers detect individuals who are lying.

42765 ■ *"Born of Culture of Innovation" in Canadian Business (Vol. 81, October 27, 2008, No. 18, pp. 98)*
Pub: Rogers Media Ltd.
Description: MaRS, an independent nonprofit organization, aims to better capture the relevant commercial potential of Ontario's research and to connect the worlds of science, business, and capital as well as to stimulate a culture of innovation. Profile of MaRS and its 'MaRS Innovation' program is included.

42766 ■ *Borrowing Brilliance: The Six Steps to Business Innovation by Building on the Ideas of Others*
Pub: Gotham
Ed: David Kord Murray. **Price:** $26.00. **Description:** The author builds the case that cherry-picking the ideas of others is a vital part of the research and development process for any small firm.??.

42767 ■ *"Bridging the Worlds" in Academy of Management Journal (Vol. 50, No. 5, October 2007, pp. 1043)*
Pub: Academy of Management
Contact: Ming-Jer Chen, President
Ed: Lise Saari. **Description:** Need to transfer human resource research information published in journals to practitioners and organizations is investigated, along with suggestions on ways of achieving this goal.

42768 ■ *"Business as Usual at RIM, Balsillie Says" in Globe & Mail (March 6, 2007, pp. B1)*
Pub: CTVglobemedia Publishing Inc.
Ed: Simon Avery. **Description:** The continuation of normal business at Research In Motion Ltd., after the resignation of Jim Balsillie from the chairman's post, is described. The investigation of securities fraud at Research In Motion Ltd., and the continuation of Jim Balsillie as the co-chief executive officer of the company is discussed.

42769 ■ *"California Company Suing City's Lupin Over its Generic Diabetes Drug" in Baltimore Business Journal (Vol. 27, January 1, 2010)*
Pub: American City Business Journals
Ed: Gary Haber. **Description:** California-based Depomed Inc. is suing Baltimore, Maryland-based Lupin Pharmaceuticals Inc. and its parent company in India over the patents to a diabetes drug. Lupin allegedly infringed on Depomed's four patents for Glumetza when it filed for permission to sell its own version of the drug with the US Food and Drug Administration. Details on generic pharmaceutical manufacturer tactics are discussed.

42770 ■ *"Can America Invent Its Way Back?" in Business Week (September 22, 2008, No. 4100, pp. 52)*
Pub: McGraw-Hill Companies, Inc.
Description: Business leaders as well as economists agree that innovative new products, services and ways of doing business may be the only way in which America can survive the downward spiral of the economy; innovation economics may be the answer and may even provide enough growth to enable Americans to prosper in the years to come.

42771 ■ *"Canadian Research Generates Innovation and Prosperity" in Canadian Business (Vol. 81, October 27, 2008, No. 18, pp. 87)*
Pub: Rogers Media Ltd.
Description: Universities play a key role in helping Canadians achieve prosperity, competitiveness, and quality of life by conducting more than a third of Canada's research. Research in universities help train graduates to apply sophisticated knowledge to real problems.

42772 ■ *"Cancer-Fighting Entrepreneurs" in Austin Business Journal (Vol. 31, August 5, 2011, No. 22, pp. 1)*
Pub: American City Business Journals Inc.
Ed: Sandra Zaragoza. **Description:** Cancer Prevention and Research Institute of Texas has invested $10 million in recruiting known faculty to the University of Texas. The move is seen to bolster Austin's position as a major cancer research market. The institute has awarded grants to researchers Jonghwan Kim, Guangbin Dong and Kyle Miller.

42773 ■ *"Cannabis Science Signs Exclusive and Non-Exclusive Agreement with Prescription Vending Machines" in Benzinga.com (October 29, 2011)*
Pub: Benzinga.com
Ed: Benzinga Staff. **Description:** Cannabis Science Inc., a biotech company developing pharmaceutical cannabis products has partnered with Prescription Vending Machines Inc. and its principal Vincent Meddizadeh to provide industry specific consulting and advisory services to Cannabis Science.

42774 ■ *"Caterpillar to Expand Research, Production in China" in Chicago Tribune*

(August 27, 2008)
Pub: McClatchy-Tribune Information Services
Ed: James P. Miller. **Description:** Caterpillar Inc., the Peoria-based heavy-equipment manufacturer, plans to establish a new research-and-development center at the site of its rapidly growing campus in Wuxi.

42775 ■ *"Clean Wind Energy Tower Transitions from R&D Stage Company" in Professional Services Close-Up (September 30, 2011)*
Pub: Close-Up Media
Description: Clean Wind Energy designed and is developing large downdraft towers that use benevolent, non-toxic natural elements to generate electricity and clean water. The firm is closing its internally staffed engineering office in Warrenton, Virginia and transitioning a development team to oversee and coordinate industry consultants and advisors to construct their first dual renewable energy tower.

42776 ■ *"The CMO of Consequence" in Business Strategy Review (Vol. 21, Autumn 2010, No. 3, pp. 42)*
Pub: Wiley-Blackwell
Ed: D. Eric Boyd, Rajesh K. Chandy, Marcus Cunha. **Description:** Do chief marketing officers matter? Some say that CMOs have limited effect on corporate performance and don't add significant value to the firm. The authors agree that the job in many firms is in great peril, but their research has uncovered why the contributions of some CMOs are invaluable.

42777 ■ *"Commercial Water Efficiency Initiatives Announced" in Contractor (Vol. 56, November 2009, No. 11, pp. 5)*
Pub: Penton Media, Inc.
Ed: Robert P. Mader. **Description:** Plumbing engineers John Koeller and Bill Gauley are developing a testing protocol for commercial toilets. The team said commercial toilets should have a higher level of flush performance than residential toilets for certification. The Environmental Protection Agency's WaterSense program wants to expand the program into the commercial/institutional sector.

42778 ■ *"Congestion Relief" in Canadian Business (Vol. 80, February 12, 2007, No. 4, pp. 31)*
Pub: Rogers Media
Ed: Andrea Jezovit. **Description:** The development of a satellite-based system for traffic management including paying for parking fees by Skymeter Corp. is discussed.

42779 ■ *"Craig Muhlhauser" in Canadian Business (Vol. 81, September 15, 2008, No. 14-15, pp. 6)*
Pub: Rogers Media Ltd.
Ed: Andrew Wahl. **Description:** Interview with Craig Muhlhauser who is the CEO of Celestica, a manufacturing company that provides services for the electronics sector; Muhlhauser discusses the company's restructuring program, which he feels was the secret to their surprising first-quarter results. Muhlhauser states that the company is operating with more forward visibility and that understanding the opportunities during the current economic situation presents the biggest challenge.

42780 ■ *"A Curious Appeal (Market for Scientific Toys)" in Playthings (Vol. 106, October 1, 2008, No. 9, pp. 26)*
Pub: Reed Business Information
Contact: Jeff Greisch, President
Ed: Pamela Brill. **Description:** Science and nature toys are still popular with children. Kits allow kids to make candy, soap, grow miniature gardens, catch bugs and more. These hands-on kits have manufacturers watching trends to create more toys in this category.

42781 ■ *"Dean Foods" in Ice Cream Reporter (Vol. 23, September 20, 2010, No. 10, pp. 8)*
Pub: Ice Cream Reporter
Description: Dean Foods promoted Joseph Scalzo to President and Chief Operating Officer to oversee the firm's operational turnaround and near-term strategic initiatives as well as business units. Key functions will include worldwide supply chain and research and development.

42782 ■ *"Defense Contractor May Expand Locally; BAE Systems Ramps Up Vehicle Prototypes" in Crain's Detroit Business (March 24, 2008)*
Pub: Crain Communications, Inc.
Ed: Chad Halcom. **Description:** Profile of BAE Systems, a defense contractor, that has built a prototype in the highly competitive Joint Light Tactical Vehicle project; the company has also completed its prototype RG33L Mine Resistant Recovery Maintenance Vehicle and has plans for expansion.

42783 ■ *"Describing the Entrepreneurial Profile" in International Journal of Entrepreneurship and Small Business (Vol. 11, November 1, 2010)*
Pub: Publishers Communication Group
Ed: Serena Cubico, Elisa Bortolani, Giuseppe Favretto, Riccardo Sartori. **Description:** An illustration of metric characteristics and selected research applications of an instrument that can be used to define aptitude for an entrepreneurial profile (created in the 1990s) is examined. The entrepreneurial aptitude test (TAI) describes entrepreneurial potential with regard to eight factors.

42784 ■ *"Dow AgroSciences Buys Wheat Breeding Firm in Pacific Northwest" in Farm Industry News (July 29, 2011)*
Pub: Penton Business Media Inc.
Description: Dow AgroSciences purchased Northwest Plant Breeding Company, a cereals breeding station in Washington in 2011. The acquisition will help Dow expand its Hyland Seeds certified wheat seed program foundation in the Pacific Northwest. Financial terms of the deal were not disclosed.

42785 ■ *"DuPontas Pioneer Hi-Bred, Evogene to Develop Rust-Resistant Soybean Varieties" in Farm Industry News (November 22, 2011)*
Pub: Penton Business Media Inc.
Ed: Karen McMahon. **Description:** DuPont and Evogene have signed a new contract to work together to develop resistance in soybeans to rust. Financial terms of the agreement were not disclosed.

42786 ■ *"East Coast Solar" in Contractor (Vol. 57, February 2010, No. 2, pp. 17)*
Pub: Penton Media, Inc.
Ed: Dave Yates. **Description:** U.S. Department of Energy's Solar Decathlon lets 20 college student-led teams from around the world compete to design and build a solar-powered home. A mechanical contractor discusses his work as an advisor during the competition.

42787 ■ *"Ed Otto, Director of Biotechnology at RCCC" in Charlotte Observer (February 8, 2007)*
Pub: Knight-Ridder/Tribune Business News
Ed: Gail Smith-Arrants. **Description:** Profile of Ed Otto, director of biotechnology at Rowan-Cabarrus Community College. Before taking the position at RCCC, Otto directed the Food and Drug Administration office responsible for regulating cellular, tissue and gene therapies products.

42788 ■ *"EMU, Spark Plan Business Incubator for Ypsilanti" in Crain's Detroit Business (Vol. 23, October 15, 2007, No. 42, pp. 3)*
Pub: Crain Communications Inc. - Detroit
Ed: Chad Halcom. **Description:** Eastern Michigan University is seeking federal grants and other funding for a new business incubator program that would be in cooperation with Ann Arbor Spark. The site would become a part of a network of three Spark incubator programs with a focus on innovation in biotechnology and pharmaceuticals.

42789 ■ *"Ending the Ebola Death Sentence" in Canadian Business (Vol. 83, August 17, 2010, No. 13-14, pp. 22)*
Pub: Rogers Media Ltd.
Ed: Michael McCullough. **Description:** US Army Medical Research Institute of Infectious Diseases made a $140 million agreement with Tekmira Pharmaceuticals Corporation to develop both a drug delivery system and delivery technology for curing the Ebola virus. Tekmira's delivery technology, which has been shown to halt Ebola in laboratory animals, might be the key to finding a cure.

42790 ■ *"Entrepreneurial Orientation and Firm Performance" in Journal of Small Business and Entrepreneurship (Vol. 23, Winter 2010, No. 1)*
Pub: Canadian Council for Small Business and Entrepreneurship
Description: The article develops a theoretical model of the relationship between firm-level entrepreneurship and firm performance. This model is intended to further clarify the consequences of an 'entrepreneurial orientation', paying particular attention to the differential relationship that exists between the three sub-dimensions of entrepreneurial orientation and firm performance. Included in the theoretical model are other important variables (such as organizational structure and environmental characteristics) that may impact the EO-performance relationship. Propositions are developed regarding the various configurations of the sub-dimensions of EO and organizational structure that would be most appropriate in a given environmental context. Future research may also benefit from considering the important role that organizational strategy and life cycle stage play in this model. The implications of this model for both researchers and managers are discussed.

42791 ■ *"The Executive Brain" in Canadian Business (Vol. 80, October 22, 2007, No. 21, pp. 41)*
Pub: Rogers Media
Ed: Rachel Pulfer. **Description:** Studies by Jordan Petersen, Frank Schmidt, and John Hunter show that leaders have highly evolved capacities to think using the prefrontal cortex of the brain. Inspirational leadership ability is located in the parietal lobe. Other details of the research are discussed.

42792 ■ *"Family Business Research" in International Journal of Entrepreneurship and Small Business (Vol. 12, December 3, 2010, No. 1)*
Pub: Publishers Communication Group
Ed: A. Bakr Ibrahim, Jean B. McGuire. **Description:** Assessment of the growing field of family business and suggestions for an integrated framework. The paper addresses a number of key issues facing family business research.

42793 ■ *"Feedback From Payers Will Be Vital For Future Developments" in Farmer's Weekly (March 28, 2008, No. 320)*
Pub: Reed Business Information
Contact: Jeff Greisch, President
Description: Potato Council staff will carry on working with levy payers to retain the same high caliber of marketing, research and other activities.

42794 ■ *"Five New Scientists Bring Danforth Center $16 Million" in Saint Louis Business Journal (Vol. 32, October 7, 2011, No. 6, pp. 1)*
Pub: Saint Louis Business Journal
Ed: E.B. Solomont. **Description:** Donald Danforth Plant Science Center's appointment of five new lead scientists has increased its federal funding by $16 million. Cornell University scientist Tom Brutnell is one of the five new appointees.

42795 ■ *"Flu is a Booster for Firms Here" in Philadelphia Business Journal (Vol. 28, September 25, 2009, No. 32, pp. 1)*
Pub: American City Business Journals
Ed: John George. **Description:** GlaxoSmithKline, AstraZeneca, CSL Biotherapies, and Sanofi Aventis were awarded contract by the US Government to supply swine flu vaccines. It is estimated that global sales of the vaccine could reach billions of dollars.

42796 ■ *"Flue Vaccines are Going Green" in Canadian Business (Vol. 83, September 14, 2010, No. 15, pp. 24)*
Pub: Rogers Media Ltd.
Ed: Angelia Chapman. **Description:** Quebec-based Medicago has found a solution to the bottleneck in the production of influenza vaccines by using plant-

based processes instead of egg-based systems. Medicago's US Department of Defense funded research has produced the technology that speeds up the production time for vaccines by almost two-thirds. Insights into Medicago's patented process are also given.

42797 ■ *"Funding Drought Stalls Biotech Incubators" in Saint Louis Business Journal (Vol. 31, July 29, 2011, No. 49, pp. 1)*
Pub: Saint Louis Business Journal
Ed: Angela Mueller. **Description:** Economic slowdown took its toll on cash-strapped startups that fill incubators such as the Bio-Research and Development Growth (BRDG) Park in Creve Coeur, Missouri and the Center for Emerging Technologies in Midtown St. Louis. BRDG put a hold on construction of of its two buildings.

42798 ■ *"The Future of Work" in Business Strategy Review (Vol. 21, Autumn 2010, No. 3, pp. 16)*
Pub: Blackwell Publishers Ltd.
Ed: Lynda Gratton. **Description:** Work is universal. But how, why, where and when we work has never been so open to individual interpretation. The certainties of the past have been replaced by ambiguity, questions and the steady hum of technology. Now, in a groundbreaking research project covering 21 global companies and more than 200 executives, the author is making sense of the future of work.

42799 ■ *"Galvanizing the Scientific Community" in Information Today (Vol. 26, February 2009, No. 2, pp. 20)*
Pub: Information Today, Inc.
Ed: Barbara Brynko. **Description:** Profile of John Haynes, newly appointed vice president of publishing for the American Institute of Physics; the Institute consists of ten organizations specializing in STM publishing as well as providing publishing services for over 170 science and engineering journals.

42800 ■ *"Giving Biotech Startups a Hand" in Philadelphia Business Journal (Vol. 28, January 8, 2010, No. 47, pp. 1)*
Pub: American City Business Journals
Ed: John George. **Description:** Elkins Park, Pennsylvania-based BioStrategy Partners is a virtual life sciences incubator that is seeking to improve the dull ranking of Philadelphia in the small business vitality index of life sciences. BioStrategy provides technology and business development services to startup life sciences companies and university-based research projects.

42801 ■ *Global Electronic Business Research: Opportunities and Directions*
Pub: Idea Group Publishing
Ed: Nabeel A.Y. Al-Qirim. **Released:** December 2005. **Price:** $ 74.95. **Description:** Importance electronic commerce research plays in small to medium-sized enterprises in various countries.

42802 ■ *Handbook of Quality Research in Entrepreneurship*
Pub: Edward Elgar Publishing, Incorporated
Ed: Neergaard. **Released:** March 2007. **Price:** $215.00. **Description:** Advice for researchers to make informed choices and to design more stringent and sophisticated studies in the field of entrepreneurship.

42803 ■ *"The Hidden Advantages of Quiet Bosses" in Harvard Business Review (Vol. 88, December 2010, No. 12, pp. 28)*
Pub: Harvard Business School Publishing
Ed: Adam M. Grant, Francesca Gino, David A. Hofmann. **Description:** Research on organizations behavior indicates that, while extroverts most often become managers, introvert managers paired with proactive employees make a highly efficient and effective combination.

42804 ■ *"Hopkins' Security, Reputation Face Challenges in Wake of Slaying" in Baltimore Business Journal (Vol. 28, August 6, 2010, No. 13)*
Pub: Baltimore Business Journal
Ed: Gary Haber. **Description:** The slaying of Johns Hopkins University researcher Stephen Pitcairn has not tarnished the reputation of the elite school in Baltimore, Maryland among students. Maintaining Hopkins' reputation is important since it is Baltimore's largest employer with nearly 32,000 workers. Insights on the impact of the slaying among the Hopkins' community are also given.

42805 ■ *"Hopkins, UMd Worry Reduced NIH Budget Will Impact Research" in Boston Business Journal (Vol. 29, August 19, 2011, No. 15, pp. 1)*
Pub: American City Business Journals Inc.
Ed: Scott Dance. **Description:** The budget for the National Institutes of Health (NIH) is slated to be cut by at least 7.9 percent to $2.5 billion in 2013. This will have a big negative effect on medical and biotech research in Maryland, especially Johns Hopkins University and University of Maryland, Baltimore which could face stiffer completion for grants from the NIH.

42806 ■ *"How Green Is The Valley?" in Barron's (Vol. 88, July 4, 2008, No. 28, pp. 13)*
Pub: Dow Jones & Co., Inc.
Description: San Jose, California has made a good start towards becoming a leader in alternative energy technology through the establishment of United Laboratories' own lab in the city. The certification process for photovoltaic cells will be dramatically shortened with this endeavor.

42807 ■ *How to Write a Business Plan*
Pub: Kogan Page, Limited
Contact: Ben Glover, Director of Marketing
Ed: Brian Finch. **Released:** February 10, 2010. **Price:** $17.95. **Description:** Starting with the premise that there's only one chance to make a good impression, this book covers all the issues involved in producing a successful business plan, from profiling competitors to forecasting marketing development.

42808 ■ *"Human Activity Analysis: a Review" in ACM Computing Surveys (Vol. 43, Fall 2011, No. 3, pp. 16)*
Pub: Association for Computing Machinery
Ed: J.K. Aggarwal, M.S. Ryoo. **Description:** Human activity recognition is an important area of computer vision research and is studied in this report.

42809 ■ *"Human Bone Breakthrough" in Houston Business Journal (Vol. 40, January 8, 2010, No. 35, pp. 1)*
Pub: American City Business Journals
Ed: Casey Wooten. **Description:** Biotech startup company Osteosphere in Houston, Texas aims to market a technology in which laboratory-grown bone tissues can be processed to appear like a real human bone tissue. The technology was developed by a co-founder of the startup and it can be applied to bone disease and injury treatment. Osteophere's future plans, such as the search for possible investors, is also outlined.

42810 ■ *"In Search of the Next Big Thing: It's Out There - Just Waiting For You To Find It" in Inc. (Volume 32, December 2010, No. 10, pp. 34)*
Pub: Inc. Magazine
Ed: April Joyner. **Description:** Innovation is the future for small business. A new book, Inside Real Innovation: How the Right Approach Can Move Ideas from R&D to Market - And Get the Economy Moving helps to break down the process by which innovation occurs.

42811 ■ *Innovation Methodologies in Enterprise Research*
Pub: Edward Elgar Publishing, Incorporated
Ed: Hine. **Released:** December 2006. **Price:** $75.00. **Description:** The importance of qualitative, interpretist research in the field of enterprise research is discussed. The book stresses how enterprise research is a new method and permits a wide scope for new and innovative research studies.

42812 ■ *"Innovation Station" in Canadian Business (Vol. 80, October 8, 2007, No. 20, pp. 42)*
Pub: Rogers Media
Ed: Andrew Wahl. **Description:** Study and teaching of entrepreneurship at the University of Waterloo is discussed. Research projects in the university are expected to be influential in Canada's economic development. In spite of the success of these studies, financing is still a problem for the university, especially in technological innovations.

42813 ■ *"The Innovator: Rob McEwen's Unique Vision of Philanthropy and Business" in Canadian Business (Vol. 81, November 10, 2008, No. 19)*
Pub: Rogers Media Ltd.
Ed: Alex Mlynek. **Description:** Rob McEwen says that his donation to the Schulich School of Business is his first large donation. He went to the University Health Network and was told about their pan for regenerative medicine, helping him make the decision. McEwan wants to be involved in philanthropy in the areas of leadership and education.

42814 ■ *International Entrepreneurship*
Pub: Edward Elgar Publishing, Incorporated
Ed: Oviatt. **Released:** March 2007. **Price:** $295.00. **Description:** Universities are focusing research efforts on international entrepreneurship. The book features critical articles on the topic.

42815 ■ *"The Interplay Between Theory and Method" in Academy of Management Review (October 2007, pp. 1145)*
Pub: ScholarOne, Inc.
Ed: John Van Maanen, Jesper B. Sorensen, Terence R. Mitchell. **Description:** Discussion about the role of theory and method in particular organization and management studies, stressing the importance of balancing primacy of theory and evidence for better research results.

42816 ■ *"Inventive Doctor New Venture Partner" in Houston Business Journal (Vol. 40, January 29, 2010, No. 38, pp. A2)*
Pub: American City Business Journals
Ed: Ford Gunter. **Description:** Dr. Billy Cohn, a surgeon from Houston, Texas has been named as venture partner for venture firm Sante Ventures LLC of Austin, Texas. Cohn will be responsible for seeing marketable developing technologies in the medical industry. The motivation for Cohn's naming as venture partner is his development of a minimally invasive therapy for end-stage renal disease.

42817 ■ *"Key FDA Approval Yanked for Avastin" in Wall Street Journal Eastern Edition (November 19 , 2011, pp. B1)*
Pub: Dow Jones & Company Inc.
Ed: Thomas M. Burton, Jennifer Corbett Dooren. **Description:** Avastin, a drug manufactured by Genetech Inc. and used in the treatment of metastatic breast cancer in women, has had its approval by the US Food and Drug Administration withdrawn by the agency, which says there is no evidence the widely-used drug is successful in increasing the longevity of breast cancer patients.

42818 ■ *"The Life Changers" in Canadian Business (Vol. 81, October 27, 2008, No. 18, pp. 86)*
Pub: Rogers Media Ltd.
Description: The first season of 'The Life Changers' was produced in September 2007 to feature stories about research and development (R&D) efforts by universities in Atlantic Canada. The program addresses the need to inform the public about university R&D and its outcomes.

42819 ■ *"Life Sciences Become State's Growth Powerhouse" in Crain's Detroit Business (Vol. 25, June 1, 2009, No. 22, pp. M008)*
Pub: Crain Communications Inc. - Detroit
Ed: Amy Lane. **Description:** According to a study conducted by Anderson Economic Group, Michigan's University Research Corridor has helped grow the life sciences industry. Statistical details included.

42820 ■ *"Li'l Guy Rolls Up Into Bigger Company" in The Business Journal-Serving Metropolitan Kansas City (Vol. 26, September 12, 2008)*
Pub: American City Business Journals, Inc.
Ed: Suzanna Stagemeyer. **Description:** Li'l Guy Foods, a Mexican food company in Kansas City, Missouri, has merged with Tortilla King Inc. Li'l Guy's

revenue in 2007 was $3.3 million, while a newspaper report said that Tortilla King's revenue in 2001 was $7.5 million. Growth opportunities for the combined companies and Li'l Guy's testing of the Wichita market are discussed.

42821 ■ *"Local Green Technology on Display" in Crain's Detroit Business (Vol. 26, January 18, 2010, No. 3, pp. 1)*
Pub: Crain Communications Inc.
Ed: Ryan Beene. **Description:** Detroit's 2010 North American International Auto Show put the newest, most innovative green technologies on display showing that the Southeast Michigan automobile industry is gaining traction with its burgeoning e-vehicle infrastructure. Think, a Norwegian electric city-car manufacturer is eyeing sites in Southeast Michigan in which to locate its corporate headquarters and technical center for its North American branch.

42822 ■ *"Local Researchers Get Cash Infusion" in Business Courier (Vol. 26, October 9, 2009, No. 24, pp. 1)*
Pub: American City Business Journals, Inc.
Ed: James Ritchie. **Description:** Cincinnati's Children's Hospital Medical Center and the University of Cincinnati researchers are set to receive at least $56 million from the stimulus bill. The cash infusion has reenergized research scientists and enhances Cincinnati's national clout as a major research center.

42823 ■ *"Luster Lost" in Saint Louis Business Journal (Vol. 32, September 16, 2011, No. 3, pp. 1)*
Pub: Saint Louis Business Journal
Ed: E.B. Solomont. **Description:** Express Cripts shares have plunged 22.71 percent since late July amid regulatory concerns, as the luster of the second-largest deal announced for 2011 wore off. Express Scripts has become the largest pharmacy benefit manager in the country after the $29 billion deal to take rival Medco Health Solutions.

42824 ■ *"Making Waves" in Business Journal Portland (Vol. 27, November 26, 2010, No. 39, pp. 1)*
Pub: Portland Business Journal
Ed: Erik Siemers. **Description:** Corvallis, Oregon-based Columbia Power Technologies LLC is about to close a $2 million Series A round of investment initiated by $750,000 from Oregon Angel Fund. The wave energy startup company was formed to commercialize the wave buoy technology developed by Oregon State University researchers.

42825 ■ *Marketing for Entrepreneurs*
Pub: FT Press
Ed: Jurgen Wolff. **Released:** December 9, 2010. **Price:** $24.99. **Description:** This text identifies marketing as the entire process of researching, creating, distributing and selling a product or service. It isn't about theory and metrics, rather it is a practical guide that starts with the basics of all marketing aspects.

42826 ■ *"McD's Tries to Slake Consumer Thirst for Wider Choice of Drinks" in Advertising Age (Vol. 79, June 9, 2008, No. 23, pp. 1)*
Pub: Crain Communications, Inc.
Ed: Natalie Zmuda; Emily Bryson York. **Description:** McDonald's is testing the sale of canned and bottled drinks in about 150 locations in an attempt to offer more options to consumers who are going elsewhere for their beverage choices.

42827 ■ *"Meet UT's New Business Mind" in Austin Business Journal (Vol. 31, May 13, 2011, No. 10, pp. A1)*
Pub: American City Business Journals Inc.
Ed: Sandra Zaragoza. **Description:** University of Texas (UT) chief commercialization officer, Dr. Richard Miller, has opened a satellite office in Silicon Valley, California in the hopes of luring Californian investors to the science and technology at UT. The satellite office is just one of Miller's efforts to reshape and widen the commercialization of UT-Austin. Insights into Miller's long-term view approach to commercialization are also covered.

42828 ■ *Memos to the Prime Minister: What Canada Could Be in the 21st Century*
Pub: John Wiley & Sons, Incorporated
Ed: Harvey Schacter. **Released:** April 11, 2003. **Price:** $16.95. **Description:** A look into the business future of Canada. Topics include business, healthcare, think tanks, policy groups, education, the arts, economy, and social issues.

42829 ■ *"Methodological Fit in Management Field Research" in Academy of Management Review (October 2007, pp. 1155)*
Pub: ScholarOne, Inc.
Ed: Amy C. Edmondson, Stacy E. McManus. **Description:** The importance of methodological fit in management field research is investigated in order to produce high quality results.

42830 ■ *"MIR Growing With Help From Former Pfizer Workers" in Crain's Detroit Business (Vol. 24, January 28, 2008, No. 4, pp. 33)*
Pub: Crain Communications Inc. - Detroit
Ed: Tom Henderson. **Description:** Molecular Imaging Research Inc. helps fund research at its parent firm, Molecular Therapeutics Inc. The company provides imaging services and other in vivo and in vitro services to help pharmaceutical companies test new compounds.

42831 ■ *"Monsanto Acquires Targeted-Pest Control Technology Start-Up; Terms Not Disclosed" in Benzinga.com (, 2011)*
Pub: Benzinga.com
Ed: Benzinga Staff. **Description:** Monsanto Company acquired Beelogics, a firm that researches and develops biological tools that control pests and diseases. Research includes a product that will help protect bee health.

42832 ■ *"More Pain" in Canadian Business (Vol. 81, December 24, 2007, No. 1, pp. 12)*
Pub: Rogers Media
Ed: Lauren McKeon. **Description:** Manufacturing sector in Canada is sinking with a forecast by as much as 23 percent for 2008, which can be offset as manufacturers say they plan to increase productivity by 25 percent. Details on the sector's competitiveness, workforce, importing of machinery from the U.S. and financial needs for research and development are examined.

42833 ■ *"MPI Expansion Goes Back to Family Roots" in Crain's Detroit Business (Vol. 25, June 1, 2009, No. 22, pp. M007)*
Pub: Crain Communications Inc. - Detroit
Ed: Sherri Begin Welch. **Description:** William Parfet, grandson of Upjohn Company founder, is expanding MPI Research's clinical and early clinical research operations into two buildings in Kalamazoo, land which was once part of his grandfather's farm.

42834 ■ *"NASA Taps Younger Talent Pool to Supplement Aging Work Force" in Crain's Cleveland Business (Vol. 30, June 22, 2009, No. 24, pp. 1)*
Pub: Crain Communications, Inc.
Ed: Chuck Soder. **Description:** NASA's Glenn Research Center has reversed the trend towards hiring older workers with more experience by recruiting for entry-level positions as part of a pilot program to attract younger talent.

42835 ■ *"New Institutional Accounting and IFRS" in Accounting and Business Research (Vol. 41, Summer 2011, No. 3, pp. 309)*
Pub: American Institute of Certified Public Accountants
Contact: Barry C. Melancon, President
E-mail: bmelancon@aicpa.org
Ed: Peter Wysocki. **Description:** A new framework for institutional accounting research is presented. It has five fundamental components — efficient versus inefficient results, interdependencies, causation, level of analysis, and institutional structure. The use of the framework for evaluation accounting institutions such as the international financial reporting standards is discussed.

42836 ■ *"Nine Sectors to Watch: Biotech" in Canadian Business (Vol. 81, December 24, 2007, No. 1, pp. 48)*
Pub: Rogers Media
Ed: Calvin Leung. **Description:** Forecasts on the Canadian biotechnology sector for 2008 are presented. Details on the increase in the number of biotechnology companies and prediction on the government's plan for business incentives are discussed.

42837 ■ *"The One Thing That's Holding Back Your Wellness Program" in Employee Benefit News (Vol. 25, December 1, 2011, No. 15, pp. 8)*
Pub: SourceMedia Inc.
Ed: Kelley M. Butler. **Description:** A 13-year study shows that women who sat for more than six hours a day were 94 percent more likely to die during the study period. Most women sit at their desks an average of 7.7 hours while at work.

42838 ■ *Our Daily Meds: How the Pharmaceutical Companies Transformed Themselves into Slick Marketing Machines*
Pub: Farrar, Straus and Giroux
Ed: Melody Petersen. **Released:** 2009. **Price:** $26.00. **Description:** Petersen, using industry memos, transcripts of meetings, and other sources shows how some drug companies are more concerned with the bottom line than with helping patients. Some of these firms are actually inventing 'diseases' in order to sell marginal medicines.

42839 ■ *"PA Tax Reforms See Some Progress" in Philadelphia Business Journal (Vol. 28, October 16, 2009, No. 35, pp. 1)*
Pub: American City Business Journals
Ed: Athena D. Merritt. **Description:** It was reported that Pennsylvania's $27.8 billion budget arrived 101 days late, but business groups are encouraged that progress continues to be made on long-called-for tax reforms. The Research and Development Tax Credit, currently at $40 million, will drop to $20 million in 2009-2010.

42840 ■ *"P&G vs. IRS: Split Decision" in Business Courier (Vol. 27, July 16, 2010, No. 11, pp. 1)*
Pub: Business Courier
Ed: Jon Newberry. **Description:** Implications of a court ruling in a $435 million legal dispute between Procter & Gamble Company (P&G) and the Internal Revenue Service (IRS) are discussed. A $21 million win has been realized for P&G for its interpretation of research and development tax credits. However, the said case might involve more than $700 million in P&G tax deductions from 2001 through 2004 that the IRS had disallowed.

42841 ■ *"Paralysis Foundation has Big Plans" in Austin Business JournalInc. (Vol. 29, December 11, 2009, No. 40, pp. 1)*
Pub: American City Business Journals
Ed: Sandra Zaragoza. **Description:** Lone Star Paralysis Foundation revealed plans to launch a fund-raising effort for the advancement of cures for spinal cord injuries via adult stem cells and also fund a new spinal injury rehabilitation center. Efforts to raise about $3 million will begin as soon as the adult stem cell research study by Dr. Wise Young receives Food and Drug Administration approval.

42842 ■ *"Patently Absurd" in Globe & Mail (January 28, 2006, pp. B4)*
Pub: CTVglobemedia Publishing Inc.
Ed: Barrie McKenna; Paul Waldie; Simon Avery. **Description:** An overview of facts about patent dispute between Research In Motion Ltd. and NTP Inc. is presented.

42843 ■ *"Physics for Females" in Occupational Outlook Quarterly (Vol. 55, Summer 2011, No. 2, pp. 22)*
Pub: U.S. Bureau of Labor Statistics
Description: Free resources to help females investigate careers in medical physics and health physics are available from the American Physical Society. The booklet is designed for girls in middle and high

school and describes the work of 15 women who use physics to solve medical mysteries, discover planets, research new materials, and more.

42844 ■ *"Positive Social Interactions and the Human Body at Work" in Academy of Management Review (January 2008, pp. 137)*
Pub: ScholarOne, Inc.
Ed: Emily D. Heaphy, Jane E. Dutton. **Description:** Research is recommended for the manner in which positive social interactions in organizational contexts can influence employees' health and physiological resourcefulness.

42845 ■ *"The Power of Innovation" in Canadian Business (Vol. 81, March 17, 2008, No. 4, pp. 57)*
Pub: Rogers Media
Ed: Andrew Wahl. **Description:** Canada ranks badly in terms innovation yardsticks that directly translate to economic growth such as business R&D as a percentage of GDP and R&D per capita. Canada's reliance on natural resources does not provide incentives to innovate unlike smaller countries with little natural resources. Canada could spur innovation through regulations that encourage industrial research.

42846 ■ *"Providing Expertise Required to Develop Microsystems" in Canadian Electronics (Vol. 23, February 2008, No. 1, pp. 6)*
Pub: CLB Media Inc.
Ed: Ian McWalter. **Description:** CMC Microsystems, formerly Canadian Microelectronics Corporation, is focused on empowering microelectronics and Microsystems research in Canada. Microsystems offers the basis for innovations in the fields of science, environment, technology, automotives, energy, aerospace and communications technology. CMC's strategy in developing Microsystems in Canada is described.

42847 ■ *"Putting 'Extra' in Extra-Silky Shampoo" in Crain's Chicago Business (Vol. 31, April 28, 2008, No. 17, pp. 37)*
Pub: Crain Communications, Inc.
Ed: Phuong Ly. **Description:** Profile of HallStar Co., a Chicago-based company which develops and manufactures specialty chemicals to upgrade existing products such as hair dye, lotion and deodorant. HallStar has seen its annual earnings rise more than 30 percent since 2002.

42848 ■ *"The Quest for the Smart Prosthetic" in Canadian Business (Vol. 83, October 12, 2010, No. 17, pp. 26)*
Pub: Rogers Media Ltd.
Ed: Jacqueline Nelson. **Description:** Information about a two-year research project led by Southern Methodist University (SMU) and funded by the Defense Advance Research Projects Agency (DARPA) is provided. The agency aims to create a 'smart prosthetic' which will improve the lives of military amputees. The planned prosthetic will use a sensor that can carry nerve signals through synthetic channels.

42849 ■ *"Race and Gender Diversity" in Business Horizons (November-December 2007, pp. 445)*
Pub: Elsevier Technology Publications
Ed: James C. Wimbush. **Description:** Research conducted on diversity building, employee recruitment, gender issues in management, and pay inequality from 2006 through present are discussed. Diversity conditions and attitudes toward it are slowly improving based on these findings.

42850 ■ *"R&D Will Remain a Key Priority" in Farmer's Weekly (March 28, 2008, No. 320)*
Pub: Reed Business Information
Contact: Jeff Greisch, President
Description: Executives as well as the board of the new Horticultural Development Company (HDC) remain committed to the efficient delivery of research and development, a promotional drive and communications over the coming year.

42851 ■ *"Reading the Public Mind" in Harvard Business Review (Vol. 88, October 2010, No. 10, pp. 27)*
Pub: Harvard Business School Publishing
Ed: Andrew O'Connell. **Description:** Examination of the various methods for obtaining public opinion and consumer preferences is provided; an outline of the disadvantages and benefits of both are also given.

42852 ■ *"Real Estate Ambitions" in Black Enterprise (Vol. 37, January 2007, No. 6, pp. 101)*
Pub: Earl G. Graves Publishing Co. Inc.
Description: National Real Estate Investors Association is a nonprofit trade association for both advanced as well as novice real estate investors that offers information on builders to contractors to banks. When looking to become a real estate investor utilize this organization, talk to various investors like the president of your local chapter, let people know your aspirations, and see if you can find a partner who has experience in the field. Resources included.

42853 ■ *"Rebels' Cause: Adult Stem Cell" in Austin Business Journal (Vol. 31, June 3, 2011, No. 13, pp. 1)*
Pub: American City Business Journals Inc.
Ed: Sandra Zaragoza. **Description:** MedRebels Foundation was launched in February 2011 with the goal of providing millions of dollars for research funding, education and advocacy for adult stem cell-focused medicine. The foundation, whose major contributor is SpineSmith LP, is a collaboration of other adult stem cell-related companies and nonprofit partners. It hopes to raise $200,000 by the end of 2011.

42854 ■ *"Red One and The Rain Chronicles" in Michigan Vue (Vol. 13, July-August 2008, No. 4, pp. 30)*
Pub: Entrepreneur Media Inc.
Ed: Evan Cornish. **Description:** Troy-based film school the Motion Picture Institute (MPI) implemented the latest technology by shooting the second of their trilogy, 'The Rain Chronicles', on the Red One camera. This is the first feature film in Michigan to utilize this exciting new camera, which includes proprietary software for rendering and color correction. Brian K. Johnson heads up the visual effects team as visual effects supervisor and lead CG artist. His company, Dream Conduit Studios, had to tackle the task of employing the new work flow through a post-production pipeline that would allow him to attack complex visual effects shots, many of which were shot with a moving camera, a technique rarely seen in films at this budgetary level where the camera is traditionally locked off.

42855 ■ *"Region to Be Named Innovation Hub" in Business Courier (Vol. 27, July 2, 2010, No. 9, pp. 1)*
Pub: Business Courier
Ed: Dan Monk. **Description:** The selection of Cincinnati's consumer-marketing cluster as a 'Hub of Innovation' by the Ohio Department of Development could boost Cincinnati's chances of receiving $100 million in grants from Ohio's Third Frontier program and other funding sources. Implications of the University of Cincinnati's designation as a Center of Excellence in Advanced Transportation and Aerospace are also discussed.

42856 ■ *"Region Ready to Dig Deeper into Tech Fund" in Business Courier (Vol. 26, October 30, 2009, No. 27, pp. 1)*
Pub: American City Business Journals, Inc.
Ed: James Ritchie. **Description:** Southwest Ohio region aims for a bigger share in the planned renewal of Ohio's Third Frontier technology funding program. Meanwhile, University of Cincinnati vice president Sarah Degen will be appointed to the program's advisory board if the renewal proceeds.

42857 ■ *"Renewable Energy Market Opportunities: Wind Testing" in PR Newswire (September 22, 2011)*
Pub: United Business Media
Description: Global wind energy test systems markets are discussed. Research conducted covers both non-destructive test equipment and condition monitoring equipment product segments.

42858 ■ *"A Research Firm With More Than One Foe" in Globe & Mail (February 24, 2006, pp. B1)*
Pub: CTVglobemedia Publishing Inc.
Ed: Shawn McCarthy. **Description:** The details of Biovail Corp.'s securities fraud case against Gradient Analytics Inc. are presented.

42859 ■ *"Research Note" in International Journal of Globalisation and Small Business (Vol. 4, September 21, 2010, No. 1, pp. 92)*
Pub: Publishers Communication Group
Ed: Alexander Bode, Tobias B. Talmon l'Armee, Simon Alig. **Description:** The cluster concept has steadily increased its importance during the past years both from practitioners' and reearchers' points of view. Simultaneously, many corporate networks are established. Researchers from different areas (business management, economic social and geographical science) are trying to explain both phenomena.

42860 ■ *"Research in Personnel and Human Resources Management, Vol. 28" in Human Resource Management (Vol. 49, July-August 2010, No. 4)*
Pub: John Wiley
Ed: Mukta Kulkarni. **Description:** An overview of the book, 'Research in Personnel and Human Resources Management', Vol. 28 is presented.

42861 ■ *"Research Reports: How Analysts Size Up Companies" in Barron's (Vol. 90, September 13, 2010, No. 37, pp. M12)*
Pub: Barron's Editorial & Corporate Headquarters
Description: Shares of Adtran and Redwood City-based Informatica both get an 'Outperform' rating while the shares of Phillips-Van Heusen are given a 'Neutral' rating. The shares of Melco Crown Entertainment, Sonic Solutions, Jamba, Warnaco Group are also rated.

42862 ■ *"Research Reports: How Analysts Size Up Companies" in Barron's (Vol. 90, August 23, 2010, No. 34, pp. M13)*
Pub: Barron's Editorial & Corporate Headquarters
Description: Shares of Sirius XM Radio, Target and Deere and Company received an eBuyE rating, while shares of Research in Motion got an eNeutralE rating.

42863 ■ *Research Services Directory*
Pub: Gale Group Inc.
URL(s): www.greyhouse.com/research.htm. **Released:** Annual; latest edition 9th, 2003/04. **Price:** $450, Individuals softcover. **Covers:** More than 8,000 commercial laboratories, consultants, firms, data collection and analysis centers, individuals, and facilities in the private sector that conduct contractual or proprietary research in all areas of business, government, humanities, social science, and science and technology. **Entries include:** Firm name, address, phone, fax, toll-free number, e-mail name of chief executive, name and title of contact, date founded, staff size and composition, rates charged, annual revenues, professional memberships, parent and/or affiliate organizations, description of research services and principal clients, affiliates, patents, licenses, special equipment. **Arrangement:** Alphabetical. **Indexes:** Research firm name, geographical, personal name, subject. **Type:** Directory.

42864 ■ *"The Right Remedy: Entrepreneur's Success Is a Matter of Life and Death" in Black Enterprise (Vol. 38, February 2008, No. 7, pp. 46)*
Pub: Earl G. Graves Publishing Co. Inc.
Ed: Tamara E. Holmes. **Description:** Profile of Leah Brown, whose company conducts clinical trials to determine if specific drugs will relieve particular symptoms. Her company will also visit physician's offices to make certain doctors are following proper protocol for a clinical trial or will collect data from patients.

42865 ■ *"RIM Allegedly Caused 'Substantial Harm" in Globe & Mail (January 18, 2006, pp. B6)*
Pub: CTVglobemedia Publishing Inc.
Ed: Simon Avery. **Description:** The details of dispute between Research In Motion Ltd. and NTP Inc. are presented.

42866 ■ *"RIM Reinforces Claim as Top Dog by Expanding BlackBerry" in Globe & Mail (March 11, 2006, pp. B3)*
Pub: CTVglobemedia Publishing Inc.
Ed: Simon Avery. **Description:** The plans of Research In Motion Ltd. to enhance the features of BlackBerry, through acquisition of Ascendent Systems, are presented.

42867 ■ *"The Role for Canada's Research Universities" in Canadian Business (Vol. 81, October 27, 2008, No. 18, pp. 84)*
Pub: Rogers Media Ltd.
Description: Great students tend to be the foundation of a great research-intensive university, enabling it to attract great teachers and researchers. Success is likely to attract the brightest graduate students to do research, leading to further success.

42868 ■ *"Roswell Park Researcher Gets $1.5M From M&T" in Business First Buffalo (October 19, 2007, pp. 1)*
Pub: American City Business Journals, Inc.
Ed: Annmarie Franczyk. **Description:** Roswell Park Cancer Institute researcher Dr. Thomas Tomasi has received the M&T Bank Endowed Chair in Cancer Research, wherein $1.5 million in research funds is included. The funding is an addition to Roswell Park's Leaders for Life endowment campaign which aims to raise $20 for research. Tomasi's plans and background are also given.

42869 ■ *"RS Information Systems Signs Buyout Deal" in Black Enterprise (February 2008)*
Pub: Earl G. Graves Publishing Co. Inc.
Ed: Alan Hughes. **Description:** Details of the RS Information Systems buyout by Wyle, a privately held provider of high-tech aerospace engineering, testing, and research services.

42870 ■ *"Rumor Has It" in Entrepreneur (Vol. 35, October 2007, No. 10, pp. 30)*
Pub: Entrepreneur Media Inc.
Ed: Chris Penttila. **Description:** Some entrepreneurs like Ren Moulton and Dan Scudder regard rumor sites and product blogs as great sources of market research. However, there are legal issues that must be studied before using these Internet sites in marketing and product development. The use and limitations of rumor sites and product blogs are provided.

42871 ■ *"Scanning the Field" in Business Courier (Vol. 26, January 8, 2010, No. 38, pp. 1)*
Pub: American City Business Journals, Inc.
Ed: Jon Newberry. **Description:** Anti-terror detection systems developer Valley Force Composite Technologies Inc. of Kentucky plans to enter the market with its high-resolution ODIN and Thor-LVX screening systems. These systems are expected to meet the increasing demand for airport security equipment.

42872 ■ *Science Lessons: What the Business of Biotech Taught Me About Management*
Pub: Harvard Business School Press
Ed: Gordon Binder, Philip Bashe. **Released:** 2009. **Price:** $29.95. **Description:** Former CFO of biotechnology startup Amgen and veteran of Ford Motor Company provides a universal guide to management based on some of the same scientific principles used to create new drugs.

42873 ■ *"Scientific American Builds Novel Blog Network" in Information Today (Vol. 28, September 2011, No. 8, pp. 12)*
Pub: Information Today, Inc.
Ed: Kurt Schiller. **Description:** Scientific American launched a new blog network that joins a diverse lineup of bloggers cover various scientific topics under one banner. The blog network includes 60 bloggers providing insights into the ever-changing world of science and technology.

42874 ■ *"The Service Imperative" in Business Horizons (Vol. 51, January-February 2008, No. 1, pp. 39)*
Pub: Elsevier Advanced Technology Publications
Ed: Mary Jo Bitner, Stephen W. Brown. **Description:** The importance of services is growing in developing countries like India and China, but little attention is given to service research, education and innovation. The 'service imperative' seeks to promote the advancement of services. The scope, objectives and philosophy of the service imperative platform are outlined.

42875 ■ *"A Set-Theoretic Approach to Organizational Configurations" in Academy of Management Review (October 2007, pp. 1180)*
Pub: ScholarOne, Inc.
Ed: Peer C. Fiss. **Description:** The author argues about the mismatch between theory and methods that have led to decline in research on organizational configurations. He suggests adoption of set-theoretic methods to overcome this mismatch.

42876 ■ *"Shire Seeking New Digs for Headquarters" in Philadelphia Business Journal (Vol. 30, September 2, 2011, No. 29, pp. 1)*
Pub: American City Business Journals Inc.
Ed: Natalie Kostelni. **Description:** Dublin, Ireland-based Shire PLC announced plans to relocate its North American headquarters from Chesterbrook Corporate Center in Wayne, Pennsylvania and currently evaluating their options. The specialty biopharmaceutical firm is also considering a move to New Jersey or Delaware.

42877 ■ *"Slow but Steady into the Future" in Barron's (Vol. 88, July 7, 2008, No. 27, pp. M)*
Pub: Dow Jones & Co., Inc.
Ed: Mark Veverka. **Description:** Investors are advised to maintain their watch on the shares of business software company NetSuite. The company's chief executive officer, Zach Nelson, claims that the company has a 10-year lead on its competitors with the development of software-as-a service.

42878 ■ *"Some Women Warming Up to Economy's Prospects" in Crain's Cleveland Business (Vol. 30, June 1, 2009, No. 21, pp. 9)*
Pub: Crain Communications, Inc.
Ed: Mark Dodosh. **Description:** According to a recent survey conducted by the Center for Women's Business Research and KeyBank focusing on the experience and opinions of women business owners, 48 percent of respondents believe the economy will improve over the next six months. Statistical data included.

42879 ■ *"The Start of a Beautiful Friendship: Partnering with Your Customers on R&D" in Inc. (March 2008, pp. 37-38)*
Pub: Gruner & Jahr USA Publishing
Ed: Leigh Buchanan. **Description:** Joint research and development projects between customers and suppliers are a growing trend in the small business community; these ventures can help keep new product development costs lower. Four tips to maintain a good working relationship in these ventures are outlined.

42880 ■ *Start and Run a Delicatessen: Small Business Starters Series*
Pub: How To Books
Ed: Deborah Penrith. **Released:** November 9, 2010. **Price:** $30.00. **Description:** Information for starting and running a successful delicatessen is provided. Insight is offered into selecting a location, researching the market, writing a business plan and more.

42881 ■ *Start-ups That Work: Surprise Research on What Makes or Breaks a New Company*
Pub: Penguin Group
Ed: Joel Kurtzman; Glenn Rifkin. **Released:** October 2005. **Price:** $25.95.

42882 ■ *"Stronger Corn? Take It Off Steroids, Make It All Female" in Farm Industry News (December 5, 2011)*
Pub: Penton Business Media Inc.
Ed: Brian Wallheimer. **Description:** Purdue University researcher found that higher improvements in corn crops, and possibly other crops, were yielded when steroids were discontinued.

42883 ■ *"Study Puts Hub On Top of the Tech Heap" in Boston Business Journal (Vol. 30, November 26, 2010, No. 44, pp. 1)*
Pub: Boston Business Journal
Ed: Galen Moore. **Description:** The Ewing Marion Kauffman Foundation ranked Massachusetts at the top in its evaluations of states' innovative industries, government leadership, and education. Meanwhile, research blog formDs.com also ranked Massachusetts number one in terms of venture-capital financings per capita.

42884 ■ *"Surfing's Next Safari" in Entrepreneur (Vol. 37, July 2009, No. 7, pp. 24)*
Pub: Entrepreneur Media, Inc.
Ed: Dennis Romero. **Description:** Profile of Firewire Surfboards, a San Diego-based maker of lightweight surfboards, aims to capture surfing enthusiasts' attention with its use of unusual and high-tech materials. Firewire's biggest challenge is the preference for old-school surfboards, but the company is determined to revolutionize how surfboards should be made. The company's various innovations and experiences are also discussed.

42885 ■ *Technological Entrepreneurship*
Pub: Edward Elgar Publishing, Incorporated
Ed: Donald Siegel. **Released:** October 2006. **Price:** $230.00. **Description:** Technological entrepreneurship at universities is discussed. The book covers four related topics: university licensing and patenting; science parks and incubators; university-based startups; and the role of academic science in entrepreneurship.

42886 ■ *"Testing Firm to Add Jobs" in Business Courier (Vol. 26, December 11, 2009, No. 33, pp. 1)*
Pub: American City Business Journals, Inc.
Ed: Dan Monk. **Description:** Cincinnati-based Q Laboratories announced plans to add dozens of jobs with the $1.6 million stimulus assisted expansion. The company hired Michael Lichtenberg & Sons Construction Co. to build a new 9,000 square foot laboratory building.

42887 ■ *"Thinking Aloud" in Business Strategy Review (Vol. 21, Summer 2010, No. 2, pp. 47)*
Pub: Wiley-Blackwell
Ed: Yiorgos Mylonadis. **Description:** In each issue we ask an academic to explain the big question on which their research hopes to shed light. Yiorgos Mylonadis looks at how people define and solve problems.

42888 ■ *"Thinking Aloud: Julian Franks" in Business Strategy Review (Vol. 21, Autumn 2010, No. 3, pp. 35)*
Pub: Blackwell Publishers Ltd.
Ed: Stuart Crainer. **Description:** Julian Franks is Academic Director of the Centre for Corporate Governance at London Business School and lead investigator for a 1.4 million (sterling pounds) grand for research into corporate governance.

42889 ■ *"Thinking Aloud: Julian Franks" in Business Strategy Review (Vol. 21, Autumn 2010, No. 3, pp. 35)*
Pub: Wiley-Blackwell
Ed: Stuart Crainer. **Description:** Julian Franks is academic director of the Centre for Corporate Governance at London Business School and lead investigator for a (pounds sterling) 1.4 million grant for research into corporate governance.

42890 ■ *"Top Worst Weeds in Corn" in Farm Industry News (November 29, 2011)*
Pub: Penton Business Media Inc.
Ed: John Pocock. **Description:** Effective weed control for profitable crops is discussed with information from leading weed scientists from the University of Illinois Extension. It is important for farmers to know what their worst weed is in order to choose the best product, or mix of products, to control them.

42891 ■ *"Twice the Innovation, Half the Tears" in Business Courier (Vol. 24, March 7, 2008, No. 48, pp. 1)*
Pub: American City Business Journals, Inc.
Ed: Lisa Biank Fasig. **Description:** Procter & Gamble was able to develop a pant-style diaper called Pampers First Pants by creating a virtual, three-dimensional baby. The company was able to reduce the number of real mock-ups that it had to make by putting the diapers on the virtual baby first. Specifics about product designs were not revealed by the company.

42892 ■ *"UA, BP Test Unmanned Aircraft" in Alaska Business Monthly (Vol. 27, October 2011, No. 10, pp. 8)*
Pub: Alaska Business Publishing Company
Ed: Nancy Pounds. **Description:** University of Alaska Fairbanks Geophysical Institute and BP Exploration Alaska tested the oil-spill capabilities of an unmanned aircraft. The aircraft will be used to gather 3-D ariel data to aid in oil-spill cleanup.

42893 ■ *"UC Lobbies for Big Chunk of New Funds" in Business Courier (Vol. 24, February 22, 2008, No. 46, pp. 1)*
Pub: American City Business Journals, Inc.
Ed: Laura Baverman. **Description:** Discusses the University of Cincinnati (UC) which has requested $192 million funding from the Ohio Innovation Partnership. The program was launched by governor Stickland in an attempt to drive research and innovation in the studies of biotechnology, aeronautics, and other fields that reflects Ohio's strengths. Details of UC's grant proposals are supplied.

42894 ■ *Unique 3-in-1 Research & Development Directory*
Pub: Government Data Publications Inc.
Contact: Siegfried Lobel, President
URL(s): www.govdata.com. **Released:** Annual **Price:** $49.50, Individuals. **Covers:** Firms that received research and development contracts from the federal government during preceding fiscal year. **Entries include:** Awardees name, address, agency, description of work, dollar amount of contract, and other pertinent data. Additional contracts are listed in 'R&D Contracts Monthly,' published in the same arrangement; $96 per year. **Arrangement:** First section alphabetical by name of firm; second section geographical by awarding agency; third section classified by nature of work. Similar information in each section.

42895 ■ *U.S. Source Book of R & D Spenders*
Pub: Schonfeld and Associates Inc.
Contact: Carol Greenhut, President
E-mail: cgreenhut@saibooks.com
URL(s): www.saibooks.com/rnd.html. **Released:** Annual **Price:** $395, Individuals book; $495, Individuals book and disk. **Covers:** 5,700 public companies in the U.S. That spend money on research and development. **Entries include:** Company name, address, phone, names and titles of key personnel, financial data, research and development budgets, fiscal year close, Standard Industrial Classification (SIC) code. **Arrangement:** Geographical by state, then classified by ZIP code. **Indexes:** Company name.

42896 ■ *"USM Focuses on Turning Science Into New Companies, Cash" in Boston Business Journal (Vol. 29, July 1, 2011, No. 8, pp. 1)*
Pub: American City Business Journals Inc.
Ed: Alexander Jackson. **Description:** University System of Maryland gears up to push for its plan for commercializing its scientific discoveries which by 2020 could create 325 companies and double the $1.4 billion the system's eleven schools garner in yearly research grants. It is talking with University of Utah and University Maryland, Baltimore to explore ways to make this plan a reality.

42897 ■ *Values and Opportunities in Social Entrepreneurship*
Pub: Palgrave Macmillan
Ed: Kai Hockerts. **Released:** November 1, 2009. **Price:** $90.00. **Description:** Social entrepreneurship has grown as a research field. This book discusses social entrepreneurship as well as the identification and exploitation of social venturing opportunities.

42898 ■ *"Voices: Breaking the Corruption Habit" in Business Strategy Review (Vol. 21, Autumn 2010, No. 3, pp. 67)*
Pub: Wiley-Blackwell
Ed: David De Cremer. **Description:** In times of crisis, it seems natural that people will work together for the common good. David De Cremer cautions that, on the contrary, both economic and social research prove otherwise. He proposes steps for organizations to take to prevent corrupt behaviors.

42899 ■ *"Where the Future is Made" in Indoor Comfort Marketing (Vol. 70, May 2011, No. 5, pp. 48)*
Pub: Industry Publications Inc.
Description: Research being performed at Brookhaven National Laboratory, located in Upton, New York, is discussed, focusing on new energy sources for our nation.

42900 ■ *"Yes, No, and Somewhat Likely: Survey the World with Web Polls" in Inc. (October 2007, pp. 58-59)*
Pub: Gruner & Jahr USA Publishing
Ed: Don Steinberg. **Description:** Online tools for surveying customers, employees and the general public include Zoomergan zPro and Zoomerang Sample, software designed to send surveys and allows viewing results; SurveyMonkey software creates, administers and allows viewing online surveys and results; Vizu software places a one-question poll on a particular Website; and Vovici EFM Feedback, a subscription service providing ongoing surveys to customers or employees.

TRADE PERIODICALS

42901 ■ *Dentaletter*
Pub: MPL Communications Inc.
Contact: Barrie Martland, President
E-mail: bmartland@mplcomm.com
Ed: Dr. Brian Waters, Editor. **Released:** 11/year. **Price:** $119. **Description:** Publishes news of dental research. Also covers related web sites.

CONSULTANTS

42902 ■ Health Strategy Group Inc.
46 River Rd.
Chatham, NY 12037
Ph: (518)392-6770
Contact: Cameron Battley, President
Scope: Provides consulting services in the areas of strategic planning, feasibility studies, start-up businesses, organizational development, market research, customer service audits, new product development, marketing, public relations. **Founded:** 1981. **Publications:** "Online Consumer Surveys as a Methodology for Assessing the Quality of the United States Health Care System," 2004.

42903 ■ Hills Consulting Group Inc.
6 Partridge Ct.
Novato, CA 94945-1315
Ph: (415)898-3944
Contact: Michael R. Hills, President
Scope: Specializes in strategic planning; marketing surveys; market research; customer service audits; new product development; competitive analysis; and sales forecasting. **Founded:** 1985.

42904 ■ Kubba Consultants Inc.
1255 Montgomery Dr.
Deerfield, IL 60015
Ph: (847)867-0874
URL: http://www.kubbainc.com
Contact: Ed Kubba, President
E-mail: edkubba@aol.com
Scope: Industrial and business-to-business marketing research and consulting. Services include new product research, new market evaluation, competitor analysis and customer value analysis. **Founded:** 1987.

42905 ■ Margiloff & Associates
621 Royalview St.
Duarte, CA 91010-1346
Ph: (626)303-1266
Fax: (626)303-0127
Contact: Dorine Margiloff, Manager
Scope: Energy and water conservation studies, analysis of research and development, licensing, economics and project management. Projects involve development, training, utility review, cost analysis, manufacturing system improvement, process modeling and expert witness services. Clients include in the field of food, chemical, fermentation, energy, financial and legal services, government and general manufacturing fields. **Founded:** 1983.

42906 ■ Medical Imaging Consultants Inc. (MIC)
1037 US Highway 46, Ste. G-2
Clifton, NJ 07013-2445
Ph: (973)574-8000
Free: 800-589-5685
Fax: (973)574-8001
Co. E-mail: info@micinfo.com
URL: http://www.micinfo.com
Contact: Dr. Philip A. Femano, President
E-mail: phil@micinfo.com
Scope: Provider of professional support services for radiology management and comprehensive continuing education programs for radiologic technologists. Management services include resource-critical database logistics; customer registration in educational programs; educational program development and Category A accreditation; national agency notification (e.g., ASRT, SNM-TS) of CE credits earned; meeting planning; manpower assessment; market research; expert witness; think-tank probes and executive summaries of industry issues. **Founded:** 1991. **Seminars:** Sectional Anatomy and Imaging Strategies; CT Cross-Trainer; CT Registry Review Program; MR Cross Trainer; MRI Registry Review Program; Digital Mammography Essentials for Technologists; Radiology Trends for Technologists.

42907 ■ Miller, Hellwig Associates
150 W End Ave.
New York, NY 10023-5713
Ph: (212)799-0471
Fax: (212)877-0186
Co. E-mail: millerhelwig@earthlink.net
Contact: Ernest C. Miller, President
Scope: Consulting services in the areas of start-up businesses; small business management; employee surveys and communication; performance appraisals; executive searches; team building; personnel policies and procedures; market research. Also involved in improving cross-cultural and multi-cultural relationships, particularly with Japanese clients. **Founded:** 1984. **Seminars:** Objectives and standards/recruiting for boards of directors.

42908 ■ New Commons
545 Pawtucket Ave., Studio 106A
Pawtucket, RI 02860
Ph: (401)351-7110
Fax: (401)351-7158
Co. E-mail: info@newcommons.com
URL: http://www.newcommons.com
Contact: Robert Leaver, Chief Executive Officer
E-mail: rleaver@newcommons.com
Scope: Builder of agile human networks to champion innovation and mobilize change; to pursue business opportunities; to custom design agile organizations and communities, to foster civic engagement. Clients include organizations on-profits, corporations, government agencies, educational institutions; networks-Trade/professional groups, IT services collaborations, service-sharing collectives; and communities- municipalities, states and statewide agencies, regional collaborations. **Founded:** 1982. **Publications:** "Plexus Imperative," Sep, 2005; "Creating 21st Century Capable Innovation Systems," Aug, 2004; "Call to Action: Building Providences Creative and Innovative Economy"; "Getting Results from Meetings"; "The Entrepreneur as Artist," Commonwealth Publications; "Leader and Agent of Change," Commonwealth Publications; "Achieving our Providence: Lessons of City-Building," Commonwealth Publications. **Seminars:** Introduction to Social Computing (Web 2.0), Jan, 2009; Every Company Counts, Jun, 2009;

Facilitating for Results; Story-Making and Story-Telling. **Telecommunication Services:** inquiries@newcommons.com.

42909 ■ Plans and Solutions Inc.
7823 Mistic View Ct.
Derwood, MD 20855
Ph: (301)947-8150
Fax: (240)525-5601
Co. E-mail: info@plansandsolutions.com
URL: http://www.plansandsolutions.com
Contact: Kenneth D. Weiss, President
E-mail: kw@plansandsolutions.com
Scope: Market research and competitive analysis; marketing and promotion planning, and executing promotion plans. Specializes in registration and problem solving services that include food canning establishment and process registration, registration under the terrorism act, assistance in case of detention of shipments, and on-site inspection of processing plants and records. Most clients are minority-owned businesses in the USA and companies overseas that want to begin or increase exports to the United States and Canada. **Founded:** 1996. **Publications:** "Building an Import/Export Business," John Wiley & Sons, 2002; "How to Conquer the U.S. Market"; "Going Global (Getting Started in International Trade)". **Seminars:** U.S. Import Regulations on Food Products.

42910 ■ Via Nova Consulting
1228 Winburn Dr.
Atlanta, GA 30344
Ph: (404)761-7484
Fax: (404)762-7123
Scope: Consulting services in the areas of strategic planning; privatization; executive searches; market research; customer service audits; new product development; competitive intelligence; and Total Quality Management (TQM). **Founded:** 1994.

FRANCHISES AND BUSINESS OPPORTUNITIES

42911 ■ Supperworks
481 North Service Rd. W, Unit A24
Oakville, ON, Canada L6M 2V6
Ph: (905)599-4392
Fax: (905)481-0785
URL: http://www.supperworks.com
Description: Meal preparation. **No. of Franchise Units:** 14. **No. of Company-Owned Units:** 1. **Founded:** 2005.. **Franchised:** 2006. **Equity Capital Needed:** $200,000 start-up capital required; $300,000 investment required. **Franchise Fee:** $40,000. **Training:** Includes 3 weeks training.

LIBRARIES

42912 ■ Allen County Public Library - Business and Technology Department
900 Library Plaza
Fort Wayne, IN 46802-3600
Ph: (260)421-1200
Fax: (260)421-1386
Co. E-mail: ask@acpl.info
URL: http://www.acpl.lib.in.us
Contact: Cheryl Mathews
Scope: Business, economics, investments, sciences, medicine, agriculture, automobiles, home economics, management, manufacturing, engineering, law. **Services:** Interlibrary loan; copying; Wi-Fi. **Founded:** 1900. **Holdings:** 80,000 books; 22,000 bound periodical volumes. **Subscriptions:** 1500 journals and other serials; 45 newspapers. **Telecommunication Services:** genealogy@acpl.info; webcat@acpl.lib.in.us.

42913 ■ Honeywell - Federal Manufacturing and Technologies - Technical Information Center
2000 E. 95th St.
Kansas City, MO 64141-6159
Ph: (816)997-2000
Free: 800-225-8829
Fax: (816)997-3686
Co. E-mail: customer_inquiry@kcp.com
URL: http://honeywell.com/sites/aero-kcp/About-Us/Pages/contact-us.aspx
Contact: Luis Perez
Scope: Materials, processing, computers, manufacturing. **Services:** Interlibrary loan; center not open to the public. **Founded:** 1970. **Holdings:** 6000 books; military and federal specifications and standards; technical reports; vendor catalogs. **Subscriptions:** 300 journals and other serials. **Telecommunication Services:** customer_feedback@kcp.com.

RESEARCH CENTERS

42914 ■ Midwest Research Institute (MRI)
425 Volker Blvd.
Kansas City, MO 64110-2241
Ph: (816)753-7600
Fax: (816)753-8420
Co. E-mail: info@mriresearch.org
URL: http://www.mriglobal.org/Pages/Default.aspx
Contact: Michael F. Helmstetter, President
Services: Science Pioneers program: that provides science related activities, written materials, and services to students and teachers in the 36 school districts of Greater Kansas City. **Founded:** 1944. **Publications:** *Innovations*; *Midwest Research Institute Annual Report*. **Educational Activities:** Science Pioneers; MRI Workshops, seminars. **Awards:** MRI Internship programs, with colleges and universities.

42915 ■ National Conference on the Advancement of Research (NCAR)
Georgia Tech Savannah
210 Technology Cir.
Savannah, GA 31407
Ph: (912)966-6765
Co. E-mail: kristy.reeves@gtsav.gatech.edu
URL: http://www.ncar.org
Founded: 1947. **Educational Activities:** NCAR Annual conference, to discuss policy issues relating to research; NCAR Forums, for members on problems in the field; International conferences and seminars, for academic, industry, government and research associated organizations.

START-UP INFORMATION

42916 ■ *55 Surefire Food-Related Businesses: You Can Start for Under $5000*
Pub: Entrepreneur Press
Contact: Perlman Neil, President
Ed: Cheryl Kimball. **Released:** March 1, 2009. **Price:** $17.95. **Description:** Advice is given to start 55 various food-related companies and goes beyond restaurant or catering services. Home-based, retail and mail order ventures are covered, as well as food safety and standards.

42917 ■ *Cute Little Store: Between the Entrepreneurial Dream and Business Reality*
Pub: Outskirts Press, Incorporated
Ed: Adeena Mignogna. **Released:** May 2006. **Price:** $11.95. **Description:** Challenges of starting and growing a retail business are profiled.

42918 ■ *Design and Launch Your Online Boutique in a Week*
Pub: Entrepreneur Press
Ed: Melissa Campanelli. **Released:** June 26, 2008. **Price:** $17.95. **Description:** Tips for starting an online boutique in a short amount of time are given. The books shows how to build the online boutique with designer goods or your own product, ways to create eye-catching content, online tools to handle payments and accept orders, marketing and advertising techniques, and customer service.

42919 ■ *EBay Income: How ANYONE of Any Age, Location, and/or Background Can Build a Highly Profitable Online Business with eBay*
Pub: Atlantic Publishing Company
Released: December 1, 2010. **Price:** $24.95. **Description:** A complete overview of eBay is given and guides any small company through the entire process of creating the auction and auction strategies, photography, writing copy, text and formatting, multiple sales, programming tricks, PayPal, accounting, creating marketing, merchandising, managing email lists, advertising plans, taxes and sales tax, best time to list items and for how long, sniping programs, international customers, opening a storefront, electronic commerce, buy-it now pricing, keywords, Google marketing and eBay secrets.

42920 ■ *How to Open and Operate a Financially Successful Bookstore on Amazon and Other Web Sites: With Companion CD-ROM*
Pub: Atlantic Publishing Company
Released: December 1, 2010. **Price:** $39.95. **Description:** This book was written for every used book aficionado and bookstore owner who currently wants to take advantage of the massive collection of online resources available to start and run your own online bookstore business.

42921 ■ *How to Start a Home-Based Online Retail Business*
Pub: Globe Pequot Press
Ed: Jeremy Shepherd. **Released:** February 2007. **Price:** $18.95. **Description:** Information for starting an online retail, home-based business is shared.

42922 ■ *How to Use the Internet to Advertise, Promote, and Market Your Business or Web Site: With Little or No Money*
Pub: Atlantic Publishing Company
Released: December 1, 2010. **Price:** $24.95. **Description:** Information is given to help build, promote, and make money from your Website or brick and mortar store using the Internet, with minimal costs.

42923 ■ *In Fashion: From Runway to Retail, Everything You Need to Know to Break Into the Fashion Industry*
Pub: Crown Business Books
Ed: Annemarie Iverson. **Released:** August 10, 2010. **Price:** $16.99. **Description:** Whether your dream is to photograph models, outfit celebrities, design fashions, this book provides details into every aspect for working in the fashion industry.

42924 ■ *Mommy Millionaire: How I Turned My Kitchen Table Idea Into a Million Dollars and How You Can, Too!*
Pub: St. Martin's Press LLC
Ed: Kim Lavine. **Released:** February 19, 2008. **Price:** $14.95. **Description:** Advice, secrets and lessons for making a million dollars from a mom who turned her kitchen into a successful business; tools cover developing and patenting an idea, cold calling, trade shows, QVC, big retailers, manufacturing, and raising venture capital.

42925 ■ *Scrapbooking for Profit: Cashing in on Retail, Home-Based and Internet Opportunities*
Pub: Allworth Press
Ed: Rebecca Pittman. **Released:** June 2005. **Price:** $19.95 (US), $22.95 (Canadian). **Description:** Eleven strategies for starting a scrapbooking business, including brick-and-mortar stores, home-based businesses, and online retail and wholesale outlets.

42926 ■ *Small Business Desk Reference*
Pub: Penguin Books USA Inc.
Ed: Gene Marks. **Released:** December 2004. **Description:** Comprehensive guide for starting or running a successful small business, focusing on buying a business or franchise, writing a business plan, financial management, accounting, legal issues, human resources management, operations, marketing, sales, customer service, taxes, insurance, and ethics. Information for launching a restaurant, property management firm, retail outlet, consulting firm, and service business is included.

42927 ■ *The Specialty Shop: How to Create Your Own Unique and Profitable Retail Business*
Pub: AMACOM
Ed: Dorothy Finell. **Released:** February 27, 2007. **Price:** $21.95. **Description:** Advise to start retail businesses, including bakeries, gift shops, toy stores, book shops, tea houses, clothing boutiques, and other unique stores.

42928 ■ *Starting a Yahoo! Business for Dummies*
Pub: John Wiley & Sons, Incorporated
Ed: Rob Snell. **Released:** June 2006. **Price:** $24.99. **Description:** Rob Snell offers advice for turning online browsers into buyers, increase online traffic, and build an online store from scratch.

ASSOCIATIONS AND OTHER ORGANIZATIONS

42929 ■ Electronic Retailing Association (ERA)
607 14th St. NW, Ste. 530
Washington, DC 20005
Ph: (703)841-1751
Free: 800-987-6462
Fax: (425)977-1036
Co. E-mail: webadmin@retailing.org
URL: http://www.retailing.org
Contact: Steven Feinberg, Chairman
Description: Serves companies that use the power of electronic media to sell goods and services to the public. Its global membership includes television, radio and Internet retailers, along with expert back-end suppliers. **Founded:** 1991. **Publications:** *E-News Weekly* (Weekly); *Marketing, Meetings and Membership* (Monthly); *Retailing.org* (Bimonthly); *Retailing.org Daily* (Daily). **Educational Activities:** Asia Meeting (Annual); European Conference (Annual). **Awards:** ERA Awards (Annual).

42930 ■ National Association for Retail Marketing Services (NARMS)
2095 W 6th Ave., Ste. 213
Broomfield, CO 80020
Ph: (720)442-9011
Co. E-mail: admin@narms.com
URL: http://www.narms.com
Contact: Steve Donzelli, Chairman
Description: Individuals and businesses providing retail merchandising services. Seeks to advance the retail merchandising industries. Represents members' collective interests; facilitates communication and cooperation among members. **Founded:** 1995.

42931 ■ National Retail Federation (NRF)
325 7th St. NW, Ste. 1100
Washington, DC 20004
Ph: (202)783-7971
Free: 800-673-4692
Fax: (202)737-2849
Co. E-mail: bookinquiries@nrf.com
URL: http://www.nrf.com
Contact: Terry J. Lundgren, President
E-mail: shaym@nrf.com
Description: Represents state retail associations, several dozen national retail associations, as well as large and small corporate members representing the breadth and diversity of the retail industry's establishment and employees. Conducts informational and educational conferences related to all phases of retailing including financial planning and cash management, taxation, economic forecasting, expense

planning, shortage control, credit, electronic data processing, telecommunications, merchandise management, buying, traffic, security, supply, materials handling, store planning and construction, personnel administration, recruitment and training, and advertising and display. **Scope:** retail management, fashion merchandising. **Founded:** 1911. **Subscriptions:** 1000. **Publications:** *NRF Foundation Focus* (Quarterly); *NRF Update*; *STORES Magazine* (Monthly); *Washington Retail Report* (Weekly); *STORES--Top 100 Retailers Issue* (Annual). **Educational Activities:** Human Resources Summit (Annual); Retail's Big Show (Annual); Loss Prevention Conference & Exhibition (Annual); National Retail Federation Annual Convention & Expo (Annual). **Awards:** American Spirit Award (Annual); Gold Medal in Retailing (Annual); Leadership/Public Service Award (Annual); Gold Medal Award; International Retailer of the Year; Silver Plaque Award; Distinguished Service Award; Leadership in Public Service Award; American Spirit Award; J. Thomas Weyant Lifetime Achievement Award. **Telecommunication Services:** shaym@nrf.com.

42932 ■ Planning and Visual Education Partnership (PAVE)
4651 Sheridan St., Ste. 470
Hollywood, FL 33021
Ph: (954)241-4834
Fax: (954)893-8375
Co. E-mail: pave@paveinfo.org
URL: http://www.paveinfo.org
Contact: Dennis Gerdeman, President

Description: Retail executives, visual merchandisers, store planners, architects, specifiers, students. Seeks to educate and motivate members and encourage interaction among their related fields. Holds annual design competition; offers an internship program; donates proceeds of shows toward financial aid for students. **Founded:** 1992. **Educational Activities:** Planning and Visual Education Partnership Competition (Annual). **Awards:** Student Design Competition (Annual).

DIRECTORIES OF EDUCATIONAL PROGRAMS

42933 ■ *Directory of Private Accredited Career Schools and Colleges of Technology*
Pub: Accrediting Commission of Career Schools and Colleges of Technology
Contact: Michale S. McComis, Executive Director

Released: On web page. **Price:** Free. **Description:** Covers 3900 accredited post-secondary programs that provide training programs in business, trade, and technical fields, including various small business endeavors. Entries offer school name, address, phone, description of courses, job placement assistance, and requirements for admission. Arrangement is alphabetical.

REFERENCE WORKS

42934 ■ *"13D Filings" in Barron's (Vol. 88, March 10, 2008, No. 10, pp. M11)*
Pub: Dow Jones & Company, Inc.

Description: Barington Capital and Clinton Group sent a letter to Dillard's demanding a list of the company's stockholders. Elliott Associates announced that it is prepared to take over Packeteer for $5.50 a share. Strongbow capital suggested a change in leadership in Duckwall-ALCO Stores.

42935 ■ *"$50 Million Project for West Chester" in Business Courier (Vol. 24, December 14, 2008, No. 35, pp. 1)*
Pub: American City Business Journals, Inc.

Ed: Laura Baverman. **Description:** Commercial developer Scott Street Partners is planning to invest $50 million for the development of a site south of the Streets of West Chester retail center. The 31-acre project will generate 1,200 jobs, and will bring in offices, restaurants and a hotel. The development plans and the features of the site are discussed as well.

42936 ■ *"The ABCs of a Good Show" in Playthings (Vol. 106, October 1, 2008, No. 9, pp. 18)*
Pub: Reed Business Information
Contact: Jeff Greisch, President

Ed: Karyn M. Peterson. **Description:** ABC Kids Expo 2008 made a strong showing with products for babies, kids and new/expecting parents. The new Naturally Kids section promoting eco-friendly products was the highlight of the show.

42937 ■ *"Add Aquatics to Boost Business" in Pet Product News (Vol. 64, December 2010, No. 12, pp. 20)*
Pub: BowTie Inc.

Ed: David Lass. **Description:** Pet stores are encouraged to add aquatics departments to increase profitability through repeat sales. This goal can be realized by sourcing, displaying, and maintaining high quality live fish. Other tips regarding the challenges associated with setting up an aquatics department are presented.

42938 ■ *"Amid Recession, Companies Still Value Supplier Diversity Programs" in Hispanic Business (July-August 2009, pp. 34)*
Pub: Hispanic Business

Ed: Joshua Molina. **Description:** The decline of traditionally strong industries, from automotive manufacturing to construction, has shaken today's economy and has forced small businesses, especially suppliers and minority-owned firms, turn to diversity programs in order to make changes.

42939 ■ *"Apparel Apparatchic at Kmart" in Barron's (Vol. 88, March 17, 2008, No. 11, pp. 16)*
Pub: Dow Jones & Company, Inc.

Description: Kmart began a nationwide search for women to represent the company in a national advertising campaign. Contestants need to upload their photos to Kmart's website and winners will be chosen by a panel of celebrity judges. The contest aims to reverse preconceived negative notions about the store's quality and service.

42940 ■ *"Aquatic Medications Engender Good Health" in Pet Product News (Vol. 64, November 2010, No. 11, pp. 47)*
Pub: BowTie Inc.

Ed: Madelaine Heleine. **Description:** Pet supply manufacturers and retailers have been exerting consumer education and preparedness efforts to help aquarium hobbyists in tackling ornamental fish disease problems. Aquarium hobbyists have been also assisted in choosing products that facilitate aquarium maintenance before disease attacks their pet fish.

42941 ■ *"Are You Looking for an Environmentally Friendly Dry Cleaner?" in Inc. (Vol. 30, December 2008, No. 12, pp. 34)*
Pub: Mansueto Ventures LLC

Ed: Shivani Vora. **Description:** Greenopia rates the greenness of 52 various kinds of businesses, including restaurants, nail salons, dry cleaners, and clothing stores. The guidebooks are sold through various retailers including Barnes & Noble and Amazon.com.

42942 ■ *"Attention, Shoppers Take a Deep Breath: Why It Pays to Help Customers Relax" in Inc. (Vol. 33, November 2011, No. 9, pp. 26)*
Pub: Inc. Magazine

Ed: J.J. McCorvey. **Description:** According to a current study, along with festive music and decorations for holiday shoppers, some merchants are considering back messages and pedicures to keep customers happy.

42943 ■ *"Austin to Make it Easier for Stores to Just Pop In" in Austin Business Journal (Vol. 31, August 19, 2011, No. 24, pp. A1)*
Pub: American City Business Journals Inc.

Ed: Vicky Garza. **Description:** Temporary retail stores may soon become common in Austin as City Council has urged the city manager to look into the possibility of amending the city codes to permit businesses to temporarily fill the vacant spaces downtown.

42944 ■ *"Bangles, BMWs Elbow Out Delis and Discount Shops" in Crain's New York Business (Vol. 24, January 14, 2008, No. 2, pp. 35)*
Pub: Crain Communications, Inc.

Ed: Wendy Davis. **Description:** Lured by a growing number of affluent residents and high-earning professionals, a number of upscale retailers have opened locations downtown which is driving up rents and forcing out longtime independent merchants.

42945 ■ *"Banks Could Greet Tenants in One Year" in Business Courier (Vol. 26, October 16, 2009, No. 25, pp. 1)*
Pub: American City Business Journals, Inc.

Ed: Lucy May. **Description:** The Banks project's initial phase is expected to start in 60 days, which may mean that the project's first tenant could move in by the end of 2010 or beginning of 2011. Carter, an Atlanta-based firm has partnered with Dawson Company in this riverfront development. The first phase will include 80,000 square feet of retail and 300 apartments.

42946 ■ *"Banks, Retailers Squabble Over Fees" in Baltimore Business Journal (Vol. 28, June 18, 2010, No. 6, pp. 1)*
Pub: Baltimore Business Journal

Ed: Gary Haber. **Description:** How an amendment to the financial regulatory reform bill would affect the bankers' and retailers' conflict over interchange fees is discussed. Interchange fees are paid for by retailers every time consumers make purchases through debit cards. Industry estimates indicate that approximately $50 million in such fees are paid by retailers.

42947 ■ *"Bedding a Leader in Kohl's Q1 Gains" in Home Textiles Today (Vol. 31, May 24, 2011, No. 13, pp. 1)*
Pub: Reed Business Information
Contact: Jeff Greisch, President

Description: Kohl's credited home furnishings, particularly bedding, as the leading source of its first-quarter sales and profit gains in 2011. Statistical data included.

42948 ■ *"Beer Sales 'Foament' a Dispute" in Philadelphia Business Journal (Vol. 28, October 9, 2009, No. 34, pp. 1)*
Pub: American City Business Journals

Ed: Peter van Allen. **Description:** Malt Beverages Distributors Association of Pennsylvania filed a case against the Liquor Control Board (LCB) at the Pennsylvania Supreme Court in order to further restrict store sales. The dispute stems from the supermarket chains circumventing the liquor law with the blessings of LCB.

42949 ■ *"Best Buy's CEO On Learning to Love Social Media" in Harvard Business Review (Vol. 88, December 2010, No. 12, pp. 43)*
Pub: Harvard Business School Publishing

Ed: Brian J. Dunn. **Description:** Effective utilization of online social networks to enhance brand identity, connect with consumers, and address bad publicity scenarios is examined.

42950 ■ *"Better Than New" in Bellingham Business Journal (Vol. February 2010, pp. 16)*
Pub: Sound Publishing Inc.

Ed: Ashley Mitchell. **Description:** Profile of family owned Better Than New clothing store that sells overstock items from department stores and clothing manufacturers. The stores location makes it easy to miss and its only advertising is a large sign posted outside. This is the sixth store owned by the couple, Keijeo and Sirba Halmekanqas.

42951 ■ *"Betting on the Glitz" in Canadian Business (Vol. 79, October 9, 2006, No. 20, pp. 104)*
Pub: Rogers Media

Ed: Zena Olijnyk. **Description:** Holt, Renfrew & Comany's expansion plans to cash on the booming demand for high end retail luxury markets are discussed.

42952 ■ *Big-Box Swindle: The True Cost of Mega-Retailers and the Fight for America's Independent Businesses*
Pub: Beacon Press
Ed: Stacy Mitchell. **Released:** October 2007. **Price:** $15.00. **Description:** Examination of the economic, environmental, and social damage done by big-box retailers like Wal-Mart, Costco, and Home Depot. Labor policies of these retailers, particularly those enforced by Wal-Mart, are discussed at length.

42953 ■ *The Big Payback: The History of the Business of Hip-Hop*
Pub: New American Library/Penguin Group
Ed: Dan Charnas. **Price:** $24.95. **Description:** The complete history of hip-hop music is presented, by following the money and the relationship between artist and merchant. In its promise of economic security and creative control for black artist-entrepreneurs, it is the culmination of dreams of black nationalists and civil rights leaders.

42954 ■ *"Birdcage Optimization" in Pet Product News (Vol. 64, November 2010, No. 11, pp. 54)*
Pub: BowTie Inc.
Description: Manufacturers have been emphasizing size, security, quality construction, stylish design, and quick cleaning when guiding consumers on making birdcage options. Selecting a birdcage is gaining importance considering that cage purchases have become the highest expense associated with owning a bird. Other avian habitat trends are also examined.

42955 ■ *"Blues at the Toy Fair: Industry Reeling From Recalls, Lower Sales Volumes" in Crain's New York Business (February 18, 2008)*
Pub: Crain Communications Inc.
Ed: Elisabeth Cordova. **Description:** Over 1,500 toy developers and vendors will attend the American International Toy Fair, expected to be low-key due to recent recalls of toys not meeting American safety standards. Toy retailers and manufacturers, as well as the Chinese government, are promoting product testing to prevent toxic metals in toys.

42956 ■ *"Bond Hill Cinema Site To See New Life" in Business Courier (Vol. 27, October 29, 2010, No. 26, pp. 1)*
Pub: Business Courier
Ed: Dan Monk. **Description:** Avondale, Ohio's Corinthian Baptist Church will redevelop the 30-acre former Showcase Cinema property to a mixed-use site that could feature a college, senior home, and retail. Corinthian Baptist, which is one of the largest African-American churches in the region, is also planning to relocate the church.

42957 ■ *"Boom and Bust in the Book Biz" in Canadian Business (Vol. 83, August 17, 2010, No. 13-14, pp. 16)*
Pub: Rogers Media Ltd.
Ed: Jordan Timm. **Description:** Electronic book marketplace is booming with Amazon.com's e-book sales for the Kindle e-reader exceeding the hardcover sales. Kobo Inc. has registered early success with its Kobo e-reader and has partnered with Hong Kong telecom giant on an e-book store.

42958 ■ *"Boots Treat Street Rolls Out Trolley Dash App on Androis and iPhone OS" in Entertainment Close-Up (October 24, 2011)*
Pub: Close-Up Media
Description: Shoppers using Boots Treat Street can now download the Trolley Dash app game, available from the Apple Store and the Android Market, and enjoy the pastel colored street featuring favorite retailers such as eBay, New Look and Play.com collecting prizes while avoiding hazards.

42959 ■ *"The Bottom Line" in Retail Merchandiser (Vol. 51, July-August 2011, No. 4, pp. 60)*
Pub: Phoenix Media Corporation
Description: Hanky Panky believes that comfort and style don't have to be mutually exclusive when designing their line of intimate apparel for women. The lingerie retailer was launched in 1977.

42960 ■ *Building Buzz to Beat the Big Boys*
Pub: Greenwood Publishing Group, Inc.
Ed: Steve O'Leary; Kim Sheehan. **Released:** March 30, 2008. **Price:** $39.95. **Description:** Seventy to eighty percent of small retail stores fail within the first five years of opening due to competition from big-box retailers and online stores. Service providers and small retailers should capitalize on the fact that they are local and can connect on a personal level with customers in a way the big stores cannot. Word of mouth marketing methods are very critical to any small retail or service company. This book is designed to help any small business compete against large competitors.

42961 ■ *Building Buzz to Beat the Big Boys*
Pub: Greenwood Publishing Group Inc.
Contact: Janann Sherman, Manager
Ed: Steve O'Leary. **Released:** March 2008. **Price:** $39.95. **Description:** Marketing methods to help small retailers compete against big box stores are examined. It is important for local stores to create a strong customer base.

42962 ■ *"Building Your Business: A Strong Web Presence Is a Must" in Black Enterprise (Vol. 38, December 2007, No. 5, pp. 74)*
Pub: Earl G. Graves Publishing Co. Inc.
Ed: Tennille M. Robinson. **Description:** Building a strong presence on the Internet is crucial to any growing business. Websites can provide information or sell merchandise, but the site must also make sure the customer knows how to use and navigate around within the site. Common mistakes to avoid when designing a small business Website are outlined.

42963 ■ *"Burritos New Bag for Shopping Developer" in Houston Business Journal (Vol. 40, December 4, 2009, No. 30, pp. 4A)*
Pub: American City Business Journals
Ed: Allison Wollam. **Description:** Houston, Texas-based Rob Johnson is the newest franchisee for Bullritos and plans to open eight area locations to market the quick-casual burrito concept. The former shopping center developer was looking for a new business sector after selling off his shopping center holdings.

42964 ■ *"The Business Case for Mobile Content Acceleration" in Streaming Media (November 2011, pp. 78)*
Pub: Information Today Inc.
Ed: Dan Rayburn. **Description:** Last holiday season, eBay became a mobile commerce (m-commerce) giant when sales rose by 134 percent, as most online retailers offered customers the ability to purchase items using their mobile devices.

42965 ■ *"Buy Local to Land Great Deals" in Inside Business (Vol. 13, September-October 2011, No. 5, pp. SS8)*
Pub: Great Lakes Publishing Co.
Description: Buy Lakewood! Loyalty Program offers residents great bargains for shopping at local retailers. Residents sign up online and the city mails them a letter of appreciations along with a key card. Showing the key card at any participating businesses listed on the Website will provide discounts.

42966 ■ *"Buying Chanel (All Of It)" in Conde Nast Portfolio (Vol. 2, June 2008, No. 6, pp. 34)*
Pub: Conde Nast Publications
Contact: David Carey, President
Ed: Willow Duttge. **Description:** Overview of the luxury company Chanel and an estimated guess as to what the company is worth.

42967 ■ *"Buying In" in Harvard Business Review (Vol. 86, September 2008, No. 9, pp. 36)*
Pub: Harvard Business School Press
Ed: Andrew O'Connell. **Description:** Review of the book entitled, 'Buying In: The Secret Dialogue between What We Buy and Who We Are' which offers tips that those in the field of marketing will find useful.

42968 ■ *"Buying Power of Hispanics Growing" in Austin Business JournalInc. (Vol. 29, November 27, 2009, No. 38, pp. 1)*
Pub: American City Business Journals
Ed: Sandra Zaragoza. **Description:** Hispanic Marketing Symposium presented a report stating that the buying power of Hispanics of Austin, Texas has grown by 54 percent in last five years to $9.4 billion in 2009. Details on the projected growth of the Hispanic market in the are is covered.

42969 ■ *"Can Avenue be Fashionable Again? Livernois Merchants, City Want Revival" in Crain's Detroit Business (March 10, 2008)*
Pub: Crain Communications, Inc.
Ed: Nancy Kaffer. **Description:** Once a busy retail district, the Avenue of Fashion, a Livernois Avenue strip between Six Mile and Eight Mile roads, is facing a community business effort being backed by city support whose aim is to restore the area to its former glory.

42970 ■ *"Capture New Markets" in Pet Product News (Vol. 64, December 2010, No. 12, pp. 12)*
Pub: BowTie Inc.
Ed: Ethan Mizer. **Description:** Flea and tick treatments are among the product categories that can be offered in order to clinch new markets. With the help of manufacturers, pet store retailers are encouraged to educate themselves about these products considering that capturing markets involves variations in customer perceptions. Retailers would then be deemed as resources and sources for these products.

42971 ■ *"Casey's Buys Second Marion Convenience Store" in Gazette (December 14, 2010)*
Pub: Gazette
Ed: Dave DeWitte. **Description:** Casey's General Stores Inc. has acquired a Short Stop convenience store on Marion's west side in Iowa. The new store includes a car and truck wash.

42972 ■ *Cheap: The High Cost of Discount Culture*
Pub: Penguin Group USA Inc.
Ed: Ellen Ruppel Shell. **Released:** July 2, 2009. **Price:** $25.95. **Description:** The American drive toward bargain-hunting and low-price goods has hidden costs in lower wages for workers and reduced quality of goods for consumers.

42973 ■ *"Christ Hospital to Expand" in Business Courier (Vol. 27, June 25, 2010, No. 8, pp. 3)*
Pub: Business Courier
Ed: Dan Monk, James Ritchie. **Description:** Christ Hospital intends to invest more than $300 million and generate 200 jobs in an expansion of its Mount Auburn campus in Cincinnati, Ohio. About $22 million in retail activity can be created by the hospital expansion, which will also include a replacement garage and new surgery facilities.

42974 ■ *"Clothier Delays Opening" in The Business Journal-Serving Metropolitan Kansas City (Vol. 27, November 14, 2008, No. 10, pp. 1)*
Pub: American City Business Journals, Inc.
Ed: Suzanna Stagemeyer. **Description:** Jos A. Bank Clothiers Inc. has delayed the opening of its store at the Kansas City Power and Light District in Missouri for the first quarter of 2009. The company is still waiting for other tenants to open shop in the district. Comments from officials concerning the retail sector are also presented.

42975 ■ *"Come Together" in Pet Product News (Vol. 64, December 2010, No. 12, pp. 28)*
Pub: BowTie Inc.
Ed: Lizett Bond. **Description:** Pet supply retailers have posted improved sales and improved customer service by bundling their offerings. Bundling pertains to grouping related items such as collars and leashes into a single unit for marketing purposes. Aside from providing convenience and enhanced product information to customers, bundling has facilitated more efficient purchases.

42976 ■ *"Commercial Builders Take It on the Chin" in Crain's Chicago Business (Vol. 31, April 28, 2008, No. 17, pp. 16)*
Pub: Crain Communications, Inc.
Ed: Alby Gallun. **Description:** Although the health care development sector has seen growth, the rest of Chicago's local commercial building industry has seen steep declines in the first quarter of this year. According to McGraw-Hill Construction, Chicago-area non-residential construction starts totaled $731 million in the quarter, a 60 percent drop from the year-earlier period. Volume in the retail, office and hotel markets fell by nearly 70 percent.

42977 ■ *Consumer Behavior*
Pub: Prentice Hall Business Publishing
Contact: Jerome Grant, President
Ed: Leon Schiffman, Leslile Kanuk. **Released:** August 7, 2009. **Price:** $180.00. **Description:** Consumer behavior is central to the planning, development and implementation of marketing strategies.

42978 ■ *"Convenience Store Expanding" in Clovis News Journal (November 9, 2010)*
Pub: Freedom Communications Inc.
Description: Allsup's convenience store on North Prince Street in Clovis, New Mexico will expand its facilities. The current building is being demolished to make way for the new construction.

42979 ■ *"Convenience Store Owners Will Request New Zoning Once More" in Daily Republic (November 1, 2010)*
Pub: McClatchy Tribune Information Services
Ed: Tom Lawrence. **Description:** Zoning change has been requested for a proposed convenience store in Mitchell, South Dakota. Details are included.

42980 ■ *"A Counter Offer" in Inc. (February 2008, pp.)*
Pub: Gruner & Jahr USA Publishing
Ed: Elaine Appleton Grant. **Description:** Online retailer offering a line of kitchen and home products has upgraded its Website in order to make the business more attractive to possible buyers of the company. The firm is asking $9.9 million and reported gross revenue of $12.7 in 2007. The owner suggests that a buyer add product lines geared towards more rooms of the home than currently offer on the retail site.

42981 ■ *"Crowdsourcing their Way into One Big Mess" in Brandweek (Vol. 51, October 25, 2010, No. 38, pp. 26)*
Pub: Nielsen Business Media, Inc.
Ed: Gregg S. Lipman. **Description:** The Gap, was counting on crowdsourcing to provide feedback for its new logo, but it did not prove positive for the retailer. However, a massive outcry of negative opinion, via crowdsourcing, may not always equal valid, constructive criticism.

42982 ■ *"A Curious Appeal (Market for Scientific Toys)" in Playthings (Vol. 106, October 1, 2008, No. 9, pp. 26)*
Pub: Reed Business Information
Contact: Jeff Greisch, President
Ed: Pamela Brill. **Description:** Science and nature toys are still popular with children. Kits allow kids to make candy, soap, grow miniature gardens, catch bugs and more. These hands-on kits have manufacturers watching trends to create more toys in this category.

42983 ■ *"Cyber Thanksgiving Online Shopping a Growing Tradition" in Marketing Weekly News (December 12, 2009, pp. 137)*
Pub: Investment Weekly News
Description: According to e-commerce analysts, Thanksgiving day is becoming increasingly important to retailers in terms of online sales. Internet marketers are realizing that consumers are already searching for Black Friday sales and if they find deals on the products they are looking for, they are highly likely to make their purchase on Thanksgiving day instead of waiting.

42984 ■ *"Deltona to Get First Movie Theater, Shopping Center" in Orlando Business Journal (Vol. 26, December 4, 2009, No. 26, pp. 1)*
Pub: American City Business Journals
Ed: Anjali Fluker. **Description:** Epic Theaters Inc. revealed plans to build a new 900,000 square foot retail center anchored by a 12-screen movie theater in the city of Deltona in Volusia County, Florida by 2010. The project, dubbed Deltona Village, would provide the city with its first movie theater and shopping center.

42985 ■ *"Despite Hot Toys, Holiday Sales Predicted To Be Ho-Ho-Hum" in Drug Store News (Vol. 29, November 12, 2007, No. 14, pp. 78)*
Pub: Drug Store News
Ed: Doug Desjardins. **Description:** Summer toy recalls have retailers worried about holiday sales in 2007. Mattel was heavily impacted from the recall of millions of toys manufactured in China.

42986 ■ *"Developer Backs Out of Major Bastrop Project" in Austin Business JournalInc. (Vol. 28, December 19, 2008, No. 40, pp. 1)*
Pub: American City Business Journals
Ed: Kate Harrington. **Description:** Weingarten Realty Investors, a Houston, Texas-based real estate company, has backed out of its contract on more than 1 million square feet of retail space at the County Road 304 and State Highway 71 corner in Bastrop, Texas, according to landowner Tom Brundage. Analysts say that the Bastrop area is not ready for big retail projects.

42987 ■ *Directory of Department Stores*
Pub: Chain Store Guide
Contact: Lisa Patterson, President
URL(s): www.chainstoreguide.com. **Released:** Annual; Latest edition 2011. **Price:** $395, Individuals directory; $445, Individuals online lite; $1075, Individuals online pro; $1375, Individuals online pro plus. **Covers:** 6,000 department store companies, 1,600 shoe store companies, jewelry store companies, 95 optical store companies, and 70 leather and luggage store companies in the United States and Canada, with annual sales of $160 billion. **Entries include:** Company name; physical and mailing addresses; phone and fax numbers, company e-mail and web addresses; listing type; total sales; industry sales; total selling square footage; store prototype sizes; total units; units by trade name; trading areas; projected openings and remodeling; self-distributing indicator; distribution center locations; resident buyers' name and location; leased departments area, name, and location; mail order catalog indicator; Internet order processing indicator; private label softlines, hardlines, and credit card indicators; furniture styles and price lines; average number of checkouts; year founded; public company indicator; parent company name and location; subsidiaries' names and locations; regional and divisional office locations; key personnel with titles; store locations, with address, phone number, and manager name (department stores only); 3,000 personnel email addresses. **Arrangement:** Geographical. **Indexes:** Alphabetical, product lines, exclusions.

42988 ■ *"Discount Shopping: Holiday Shopping Meets Social Media" in Employee Benefit News (Vol. 25, December 1, 2011, No. 15)*
Pub: SourceMedia Inc.
Ed: Rob J. Thurston. **Description:** Offering employees access to discount shopping using social media sites for Christmas bonuses, could be the gift that keeps on giving.

42989 ■ *"Dollar General Selects GSI Commerce to Launch Its eCommerce Business" in Benzinga.com (October 29, 2011)*
Pub: Benzinga.com
Ed: Benzinga Staff. **Description:** Dollar General Corporation chose GSI Commerce, a leading provider of ecommerce and interactive marketing solutions, to launch its online initiative. GSI Commerce is an eBay Inc. company.

42990 ■ *"Dollar Tree Store To Open Mid-July in Shelby Mall" in La Crosse Tribune (June 20, 2010)*
Pub: La Crosse Tribune
Ed: Steve Cahalan. **Description:** Dollar Tree Inc. plans to open a new store in the location formerly occupied by Family Dollar.

42991 ■ *"Dots Sings To New Tune With Its Radio Station" in Crain's Cleveland Business (Vol. 30, June 15, 2009, No. 23, pp. 7)*
Pub: Crain Communications, Inc.
Description: Dots LLC, a women's clothing retailer, has launched an online radio station on its Website. The station plays the in-store music to customers while they are shopping online.

42992 ■ *"Down by the Bay" in Canadian Business (Vol. 81, December 8, 2008, No. 21, pp. 15)*
Pub: Rogers Media Ltd.
Ed: Calvin Leung. **Description:** Hudsons Bay Company chief executive Jeffrey Sherman believes that his vast experience in retail will help him find the company's customer base. Sales are estimated to increase 3.6 percent in 2009 after posting average annual retail sales increases of 5 percent between 2006 and 2008.

42993 ■ *"Downtown Detroit Needs More Retail" in Crain's Detroit Business (Vol. 24, March 10, 2008, No. 10, pp. 9)*
Pub: Crain Communications, Inc.
Ed: Robin Boyle; James Bieri. **Description:** Although Detroit is doing well with event-driven traffic, the city remains far off the site selection rosters of major national retailers as well as smaller retail outlets.

42994 ■ *"Downtown Retail Site Sold to ATCO" in Austin Business JournalInc. (Vol. 29, November 20, 2009, No. 37, pp. 1)*
Pub: American City Business Journals
Ed: Kate Harrington. **Description:** New York-based real estate company ATCO Advisory Services purchased a 13,700 square foot retail space in Austin, Texas from 360 Condominiums. The selection of the retail space, named the Shops at 360 has been attributed to the local tenant mix and its location in downtown Austin. Meanwhile, ATCO may continue investing in the area in the near future.

42995 ■ *"Eastland Future Unclear: Local Merchants Say They're OK Amid Closings of 4 More Stores" in Charlotte Observer (February 8, 2007)*
Pub: Knight-Ridder/Tribune Business News
Ed: Nichole Monroe Bell. **Description:** Retailers in the Eastland Mall that market goods to shoppers looking for the urban, hip-hop look are most successful.

42996 ■ *"eBay Introduces Open Commerce Ecosystem" in Entertainment Close-Up (October 24, 2011)*
Pub: Close-Up Media
Description: eBay's new X.commerce is an open commerce ecosystem that will arm developers and merchants with the technology tools required to keep pace with the ever-changing industry. X.commerce brings together the technology assets and developer communities of eBay, PayPal, Magento and partners to expand on eBays vision for enabling commerce.

42997 ■ *"eBay and Jonathan Adler Team to Launch 'The eBay Inspiration Shop" in Entertainment Close-Up (October 25, 2011)*
Pub: Close-Up Media
Description: Designer Jonathan Adler partnered with eBay to create a collection of new must-have merchandise for the fall season. Top trendsetters, including actors, designers, bloggers, stylists, editors, photographers, models and musicians helped curate the items being featured in the windows by sharing their shopping wish lists with users.

42998 ■ *"Eckerd Sales Spell Relief for Coutu" in Globe & Mail (January 18, 2006, pp. B4)*
Pub: CTVglobemedia Publishing Inc.
Ed: Bertrand Marotte. **Description:** The details on Eckerd Corp., which posted rise in sales by 2.7 percent in December 2005, are presented. Eckerd Corp. is a unit of Jean Coutu Group (PJC) Inc.

42999 ■ *The Essential Online Solution: The 5-Step Formula for Small Business Success*
Pub: John Wiley & Sons, Incorporated
Ed: Rick Segel; Barbara Callan-Bogia. **Released:** October 2006. **Price:** $22.95. **Description:** Strategies to help any small business increase its online presence and compete with big retail chains. Tips for success Web design are included.

43000 ■ *"Ethnic Businesses Ending Vacancies" in Business First-Columbus (Vol. 26, August 20, 2010, No. 51, pp. 1)*
Pub: Business First
Ed: Carrie Ghose. **Description:** The Morse Road commercial corridor in Columbus, Ohio has several immigrant-owned businesses that were recognized as instrumental in preventing widespread vacancies when the Northland Mall closed in 2002. The ethnic stores have created a diverse destination that attracted traffic and more businesses.

43001 ■ *Ethnic Solidarity for Economic Survival: Korean Greengrocers in New York City*
Pub: Russell Sage Foundation Publications
Ed: Pyong Gap Min. **Released:** August 2008. **Price:** $32.50. **Description:** Investigations into the entrepreneurial traditions of Korean immigrant families in New York City running ethnic businesses, particularly small grocery stores and produce markets. Social, cultural and economic issues facing these retailers are discussed.

43002 ■ *"Executives Exit at Wal-Mart in China" in Wall Street Journal Eastern Edition (October 17 , 2011, pp. B3)*
Pub: Dow Jones & Company Inc.
Ed: Laurie Burkitt. **Description:** Woes for Wal-Mart Inc.'s subsidiary in China are adding up as Wal-Mart China president and chief executive Ed Chan stepped down, as well as the company's senior vice president for human resources, Clara Wong. The company has been charged by regulators with mislabeling pork products, the result which has forced stores to close. Sales in China have been slow at the retail stores.

43003 ■ *"Experts Strive to Educate on Proper Pet Diets" in Pet Product News (Vol. 64, November 2010, No. 11, pp. 40)*
Pub: BowTie Inc.
Ed: John Hustace Walker. **Description:** Pet supply manufacturers have been bundling small mammal food and treats with educational sources to help retailers avoid customer misinformation. This action has been motivated by the customer's quest to seek proper nutritional advice for their small mammal pets.

43004 ■ *"Familiar Fun" in Crain's Cleveland Business (Vol. 28, October 22, 2007, No. 42, pp. 3)*
Pub: Crain Communications Inc.
Ed: John Booth. **Description:** Marketing for the 2007 holiday season has toy retailers focusing on American-made products because of recent recalls of toys produced in China that do not meet U.S. safety standards.

43005 ■ *"Feldman Pushing Past 'Pain' of Cost Overruns, Delays at Colonie Center" in Business Review, Albany New York (November 9, 2007)*
Pub: American City Business Journals, Inc.
Ed: Michael DeMasi. **Description:** Details of major improvements at Colonie Center are presented. The total cost for these projects increased by $15 million, and the construction of the nearly ten-story theater in the mall is experiencing delays. According to Larry Feldman, chairman of Feldman Mall Properties, which owns a minority stake in the mall, the cost overruns have pushed the company's renovation costs to around $85 million.

43006 ■ *"Fifty Percent of Global Online Retail Visits Were to Amazon, eBay and Alibaba in June 2011" in Benzinga.com (October 29, 2011)*
Pub: Benzinga.com
Ed: Benzinga Staff. **Description:** Current statistics and future forecasts through the year 2015 for Amazon, eBay and Alibaba are explored.

43007 ■ *"Filling the Gap" in Canadian Business (Vol. 80, March 12, 2007, No. 6, pp. 62)*
Pub: Rogers Media
Ed: Andrew Wahl. **Description:** The chief executive officer of GAP, Bruce Poon Tip, shares his experience and efforts in the growth of the company to a leading position in Canada.

43008 ■ *"The Final Piece; Lowe's to Fill Last Big Parcel Near Great Lakes Crossing" in Crain's Detroit Business (March 10, 2008)*
Pub: Crain Communications, Inc.
Ed: Daniel Duggan. **Description:** Silverman Development Co. is developing a Lowe's home-improvement store on the last major retail parcel near the intersection of I-75 and Joslyn Road, an area which was once desolate but is now home to several restaurants and other retail facilities.

43009 ■ *"Financo Panel Lauds Product, Online Marketing" in Home Textiles Today (Vol. 31, January 25, 2010, No. 3, pp. 1)*
Pub: Reed Business Information, Inc.
Ed: James Mammarella. **Description:** Overview of the Financo Annual Merchandising Industry Chief Executives Event during which there was much discussion on the merits of e-commerce, online marketing as well as the traditional methods of brand recognition and retailing.

43010 ■ *"Finishing Touches: the Fashion Statement is in the Detail" in Black Enterprise (Vol. 37, January 2007, No. 6, pp. 106)*
Pub: Earl G. Graves Publishing Co. Inc.
Ed: Sonia Alleyne. **Description:** Men are discovering the importance of dressing for success. Paying attention to the details such as shoes, socks, cuffs, and collars are just as important as finding the right suit.

43011 ■ *"Fire Destroys Surplus Store, Sets Off Live Rounds Near Jacksonville NAS" in Florida Times-Union (December 5, 2010)*
Pub: Florida Times-Union
Ed: John Leacock. **Description:** Fire which caused numerous explosions at a military surplus store near Jacksonville Naval Air Station is under investigation. Heat and flames ignited lighter fluid and set off live rounds of ammunition sold in the store.

43012 ■ *"Five Reasons Why the Gap Fell Out of Fashion" in Globe & Mail (January 27, 2007, pp. B4)*
Pub: CTVglobemedia Publishing Inc.
Ed: Keith McArthur. **Description:** The five major market trends that have caused the decline of fashion clothing retailer Gap Inc.'s sales are discussed. The shift in brand, workplace fashion culture, competition, demographics, and consumer preferences have lead to the Gap's brand identity.

43013 ■ *"Fledgling Brands May Take the Fall With Steve & Barry's" in Advertising Age (Vol. 79, July 7, 2008, No. 26, pp. 6)*
Pub: Crain Communications, Inc.
Ed: Natalie Zmuda. **Description:** Steve & Barry's, a retailer that holds licensing deals with a number of designers and celebrities, may have to declare bankruptcy; this leaves the fate of the retailer's hundreds of licensing deals and exclusive celebrity lines in question.

43014 ■ *"Food Fight" in Canadian Business (Vol. 79, November 6, 2006, No. 22, pp. 18)*
Pub: Rogers Media
Ed: Zena Olijnyk. **Description:** The war between Canadian grocers and Wal-Mart due to its plans for opening new stores is analyzed.

43015 ■ *"Food as Nature Intended" in Pet Product News (Vol. 64, November 2010, No. 11, pp. 30)*
Pub: BowTie Inc.
Ed: Nikki Moustaki. **Description:** Dog owners have been extending their health-consciousness to their pets by seeking natural products that will address their pets' raw food diet. Retailers response to this trend are outlined.

43016 ■ *"For $150 Million Mall, Failure to Launch" in Business Courier (Vol. 24, January 25, 2008, No. 42, pp. 1)*
Pub: American City Business Journals, Inc.
Ed: Lisa Biank Fasig. **Description:** Blue Ash-based Bear Creek Capital and Chattanooga, Tennessee-based CBL & Associates Properties had abandoned their plan to build a mixed-use project in South Lebanon. The construction of the proposed $475 million open-air mall was cancelled when real estate developer CBL failed to secure retailers.

43017 ■ *"Forget Your Pants, Calvin Klein Wants Into Your Bedroom" in Globe & Mail (March 31, 2007, pp. B4)*
Pub: CTVglobemedia Publishing Inc.
Ed: Barrie McKenna. **Description:** The plans of Phillips-Van Heusen Corp. to open more Calvin Klein stores for selling the new ranges of clothing, personal care products, luggage and mattresses are discussed.

43018 ■ *"Free Your Mind" in Entrepreneur (Vol. 37, October 2009, No. 10, pp. 24)*
Pub: Entrepreneur Media Inc.
Ed: Joe Robinson. **Description:** Writer Chris Anderson believes that firms in the digital age should allow products and services to initially be sold for free. These companies could then charge for premium versions of these products and services after the free versions have gained attention.

43019 ■ *"From Craft Biz To Wholesale Giant" in Women Entrepreneur (January 19, 2009)*
Pub: Entrepreneur Media Inc.
Ed: Maria Falconer. **Description:** Advice is given on how to turn a small craft business into a full-time venture; tips to help one transition from a part-time designer to a full-time wholesaler and brand are also included.

43020 ■ *"Furniture Chain Moving to Harford" in Baltimore Business Journal (Vol. 27, January 22, 2010, No. 38, pp. 1)*
Pub: American City Business Journals
Ed: David J. Sernovitz. **Description:** Manchester, Connecticut-based Bob's Discount Furniture signed a lease for 672,000 square feet of space in Harford County, Maryland. The site will become the discount furniture retailer's distribution center in mid-Atlantic US. As many as 200 jobs could be generated when the center opens.

43021 ■ *"Gables Unveils Plan for Downtown Tower" in Austin Business JournalInc. (Vol. 28, August 8, 2008, No. 21, pp. A1)*
Pub: American City Business Journals
Ed: Jean Kwon. **Description:** Gables Residential plans to develop a residential tower with 220 units and 15,000 square feet of retail and commercial spaces in the Warehouse District in Ohio. The development is expected to start in late 2009 and be completed in 18 to 24 months.

43022 ■ *"Gateway Delays Start" in The Business Journal-Serving Metropolitan Kansas City (Vol. 27, October 31, 2008, No. 8, pp. 1)*
Pub: American City Business Journals, Inc.
Ed: Rob Roberts. **Description:** Economic problems caused, in part, by the Wall Street crisis has resulted in the setback of a proposed mixed-use redevelopment project, The Gateway. The $307 million project, which includes the Kansas Aquarium, will be delayed due to financing problems. Details of the project are given.

43023 ■ *"Get Real" in Entrepreneur (Vol. 36, April 2008, No. 4, pp. 86)*
Pub: Entrepreneur Media, Inc.
Ed: Kim T. Gordon. **Description:** Selling points of a product or service must show real benefits to women. Provide detailed information as women look at details more deeply before purchasing. Other tips on how to market products designed for women consumers are provided.

43024 ■ *"Give It Your All, and Don't Worry About the Rest" in Inc. (Vol. 33, November 2011, No. 9, pp. 37)*
Pub: Inc. Magazine
Ed: Norm Brodsky. **Description:** In the early stage of a service company, the owners sell themselves to the customers.

43025 ■ *"GM's Decision to Boot Dealer Prompts Sale" in Baltimore Business Journal (Vol. 27, November 6, 2009, No. 26, pp. 1)*
Pub: American City Business Journals
Ed: Daniel J. Sernovitz. **Description:** General Motors Corporation's (GM) decision to strip Baltimore's Anderson Automotive Group Inc. of its GM franchise has prompted the owner, Bruce Mortimer, to close the automotive dealership and sell the land to a developer. The new project could make way for new homes, a shopping center and supermarket.

43026 ■ *"Going Green, Going Slowly" in Playthings (Vol. 106, September 1, 2008, No. 8, pp. 17)*
Pub: Reed Business Information
Contact: Jeff Greisch, President
Ed: Nancy Zwiers. **Description:** Sustainability and greener materials for both product and packaging in the toy industry has become important for protecting our environment. However, in a recent survey nearly 60 percent of responders stated environmental issues did not play a part in purchasing a toy or game for their children.

43027 ■ *"Good Price, Best Brands" in Retail Merchandiser (Vol. 51, July-August 2011, No. 4, pp. 58)*
Pub: Phoenix Media Corporation
Description: Flemington Department Store has been a family-owned and operated retailer for over 50 years. Customer service is key to the store's success.

43028 ■ *"Good Things Happen When We Buy Local" in Crain's Detroit Business (Vol. 24, October 6, 2008, No. 40, pp. 7)*
Pub: Crain Communications, Inc.
Description: Michigan is facing incredibly difficult economic times. One way in which each one of us can help the state and the businesses located here is by purchasing our goods and services from local vendors. The state Agriculture Department projected that if Michigan households earmarked $10 per week in their grocery purchases to made-in-Michigan products, this would generate $30 million a week in economic impact.

43029 ■ *"Grand Letdown" in The Business Journal-Milwaukee (Vol. 25, September 12, 2008, No. 51, pp. A1)*
Pub: American City Business Journals, Inc.
Ed: Rich Kirchen. **Description:** Overview of retail trade in Milwaukee, Wisconsin is presented. It has been observed that vacancies in storefronts both east and west of the Milwaukee River have increased, and the Shops of Grand Avenue has yet to attract new retailers or shoppers. The completion of the Marquette Interchange is also discussed.

43030 ■ *"Green and Clean" in Retail Merchandiser (Vol. 51, July-August 2011, No. 4, pp. 56)*
Pub: Phoenix Media Corporation
Description: Green Valley Grocery partnered with Paragon Solutions consulting firm to make their stores environmentally green.

43031 ■ *"Green Counting" in Canadian Business (Vol. 81, October 13, 2008, No. 17, pp. 27)*
Pub: Rogers Media Ltd.
Ed: Joe Castaldo. **Description:** Procter and Gamble research revealed that only 10 percent of North American consumers are willing to accept trade-offs for a greener product. Three out of four North American consumers will not accept a higher price or a decrease in a product's performance for an environmental benefit. Details on green marketing are also discussed.

43032 ■ *"Group-Buying Site Hones In on Hispanics" in Austin Business Journal (Vol. 31, July 1, 2011, No. 17, pp. 1)*
Pub: American City Business Journals Inc.
Ed: Vicky Garza. **Description:** Descuentl Libre is a new group-buying site from Austin, Texas that targets the Hispanic market, offering discounts of practical items and family-friendly activities. The Hispanic market constitutes 17 percent of the U.S. population and spends $23 billion yearly online.

43033 ■ *"H&M Offers a Dress for Less" in Canadian Business (Vol. 83, September 14, 2010, No. 15, pp. 20)*
Pub: Rogers Media Ltd.
Ed: Laura Cameron. **Description:** Swedish clothing company H&M has implemented loss leader strategy by pricing some dresses at extremely low prices. The economy has forced retailers to keep prices down despite the increasing cost of manufacturing, partly due to Chinese labor becoming more expensive. How the trend will affect apparel companies is discussed.

43034 ■ *"The Harder Side of Sears" in Crain's Chicago Business (Vol. 31, March 31, 2008, No. 13, pp. 68)*
Pub: Crain Communications, Inc.
Ed: Steven R. Strahler. **Description:** Discusses the history of Sears Roebuck & Co. and its merger with Kmart Corp.

43035 ■ *"Hartco Income Fund Announces the Completion of the CompuSmart Strategic Review" in Canadian Corporate News (May 14, 2007)*
Pub: Comtex News Network Inc.
Description: Hartco Income Fund announced that it has completed the process of exploring strategic options for CompuSmart and found that it should implement a plan to sell select stores and assets while consolidating remaining CompuSmart locations over the next sixty days.

43036 ■ *"HBC Enlists IBM to Help Dress Up Its On-Line Shopping" in Globe & Mail (February 7, 2006, pp. B3)*
Pub: CTVglobemedia Publishing Inc.
Ed: Simon Avery. **Description:** The details of management contract between Hudson's Bay Co. and International Business Machines Corp. are presented.

43037 ■ *"HBC Sets Friday as Deadline to Trump Zucker Takeover Bid" in Globe & Mail (January 18, 2006, pp. B1)*
Pub: CTVglobemedia Publishing Inc.
Ed: Marina Strauss. **Description:** The reasons behind Hudson's Bay Co.'s decision to seek alternative bids on the company are presented. Investor Jerry Zucker earlier offered $1.1 billion for the company.

43038 ■ *"Health Care Leads Sectors Attracting Capital" in Hispanic Business (Vol. 30, March 2008, No. 3, pp. 14)*
Pub: Hispanic Business
Ed: Scott Williams. **Description:** Discusses the capital gains of Hispanic-owned companies and other Hispanic leaders in the investment and retail fields in the year 2007. Sectors like health care, media, food and technology saw a healthy flow of capital due to successful mergers, acquisitions and increased private equity investments.

43039 ■ *"High Anxiety" in Canadian Business (Vol. 80, November 19, 2007, No. 23, pp. 11)*
Pub: Rogers Media
Ed: Zena Olijnyk. **Description:** Value of Canadian dollar continues to rise, and consumers are asking for lower prices of goods. Retailers, on the other hand, are facing concerns over losing sales. The impacts of the rising Canadian dollar on the business sector and consumer behavior are examined.

43040 ■ *"High Growth Reported for the Natural Supermarket Pet Department Close-Up" in Canadian Corporate News (October 20, 2008)*
Pub: Comtex News Network Inc.
Description: Leading natural supermarket chains have been outperforming mainstream grocers by carrying natural and organic pet products. Statistical data included.

43041 ■ *"Hispantelligence Report" in Hispanic Business (January-February 2009, pp. 10)*
Pub: Hispanic Business
Description: U.S. Hispanic purchasing power is expected to reach $958 billion in 2009 and projected to reach $1.25 trillion by 2015, a rate of more than two times the overall national rate. Statistical data included.

43042 ■ *"Ho, Ho, Ho!" in Retail Merchandiser (Vol. 51, September-October 2011, No. 5, pp. 10)*
Pub: Phoenix Media Corporation
Ed: Ted Vaughan. **Description:** Despite consumer caution and economic woes, retail leaders are expecting a high volume holiday selling season for 2011 Christmas. Statistical data covering holiday sales expectations is included.

43043 ■ *"Holiday Sales Look Uncertain for Microsoft and PC Sellers" in Puget Sound Business Journal (Vol. 29, November 28, 2008, No. 32)*
Pub: American City Business Journals
Ed: Todd Bishop. **Description:** Personal computer makers face uncertain holiday sales for 2008 as a result of the weak U.S. economy and a shift toward low-cost computers. Personal computer shipments for the fourth quarter 2008 are forecast to drop 1 percent compared to the same quarter 2007.

43044 ■ *"Home Depot Eyes Wholesale Spinoff" in Globe & Mail (February 13, 2007, pp. B13)*
Pub: CTVglobemedia Publishing Inc.
Description: Home Depot Inc. is planning to sell or spinoff its professional supply business to focus on retail stores. The weakening sales and profits are the main driving force behind the company's decision.

43045 ■ *"Home Helps Push Macy's to First-Quarter Profit" in Home Textiles Today (Vol. 31, May 24, 2011, No. 13, pp. 2)*
Pub: Reed Business Information
Contact: Jeff Greisch, President
Description: Macy's Inc. reported home goods as one of the three strong performing categories for first quarter 2011. Home goods sales, both big and small ticket items, have improved significantly for the retailer.

43046 ■ *"Home Improvement Marketers Target Women With New Products, New Campaigns and Plenty of Pink" in Marketing to Women (March 2008)*
Pub: EPM Communications Inc.
Contact: Ira Mayer, President
E-mail: imayer@epmcom.com
Description: From creating tools that fit a woman's ergonomics to designs that fit a woman's fashion sense, home improvement is finding new ways in which to market to women.

43047 ■ *"Home Shows Signs of Life at Target" in Home Textiles Today (Vol. 31, May 24, 2011, No. 13, pp. 1)*
Pub: Reed Business Information
Contact: Jeff Greisch, President
Description: Retailer, Target, is experience a boost in sales for apparel and products for the home.

43048 ■ *"Home Sits Out Q1 Surge at JCP" in Home Textiles Today (Vol. 31, May 24, 2011, No. 13, pp. 1)*
Pub: Reed Business Information
Contact: Jeff Greisch, President
Ed: James Mammarella. **Description:** JCPenney chairman and CEO, Mike Ullman, reported sales gains for first quarter 2011 in all products except home goods.

43049 ■ *"Hometown Value" in Retail Merchandiser (Vol. 51, July-August 2011, No. 4, pp. 50)*
Pub: Phoenix Media Corporation
Ed: Todd Vowell. **Description:** Profile of family-owned Vowell's Marketplace located in Noxapater, Mississippi. The 10-store chain caters to its Southern roots and is run by the third generation of the Vowell family.

43050 ■ *"Hot Kicks, Cool Price" in Black Enterprise (Vol. 37, December 2006, No. 5, pp. 34)*
Pub: Earl G. Graves Publishing Co. Inc.
Ed: Topher Sanders. **Description:** Stephon Marbury of the New York Nicks introduced a new basketball shoe, the Starbury One, costing $14.98. The shoes are an addition to the Starbury clothing line and although the privately owned company would not disclose figures; stores sold out of a month's worth of inventory in merely three days.

43051 ■ *"How Growers Buy" in Farm Industry News (Vol. 42, January 1, 2009, No. 1)*
Pub: Penton Media Inc.
Contact: John French, President
Ed: Karen McMahon. **Description:** According to a survey regarding the buying habits among large commercial growers, most prefer to purchase from local retailers, customer service is important concerning their decision on who to buy products from, and price and convenience seem to be more important then brand.

43052 ■ *How to Market and Sell Your Art, Music, Photographs, and Handmade Crafts Online*
Pub: Atlantic Publishing Group, Inc.
Ed: Lee Rowley. **Released:** May 2008. **Price:** $24. 95. **Description:** The book provides all the basics for starting and running an online store selling arts, crafts, photography or music. There are more than 300 Websites listed to help anyone market and promote their arts and/or crafts online.

43053 ■ *How Walmart is Destroying America (And the World): And What You Can Do About It*
Pub: Celestial Arts Publishing Co.
Contact: Patricia Kelly, Manager
Ed: Bill Quinn. **Released:** April 2005. **Price:** $10.95. **Description:** Wal-Mart employs 1.5 million employees and operates more than 3,500 stores, making it the largest private employer globally. Wal-Mart's impact on mom-and-pop business is discussed.

43054 ■ *"Hy-Vee Plans Expansion, Convenience Store in Cedar Rapids" in Gazette (November 26, 2010)*
Pub: Gazette
Ed: George Ford. **Description:** Hy-Vee Inc. is awaiting approval to expand its supermarket in Cedar Rapids, Iowa. Hy-Vee is a food and drug store chain will construct a convenience store and gas station on the site.

43055 ■ *"Hyde Park Hungry for Expansion at Cap" in Business First-Columbus (October 12, 2007, pp. A1)*
Pub: American City Business Journals, Inc.
Ed: Dan Eaton. **Description:** The Cap, an area developed for the retail and restaurant industry, is experiencing major changes such as Hyde Park Restaurant System's planned expansion, and the expected departure of other tenants. The expansion of Hyde Park will lead to the relocation of Schakolad Chocolate Factory.

43056 ■ *"An Ill Wind: Icelandic Bank Failures Chill Atlantic Canada" in Canadian Business (Vol. 81, November 10, 2008, No. 19, pp. 10)*
Pub: Rogers Media Ltd.
Ed: Charles Mandel. **Description:** Bank failures in Iceland have put a stop to flights ferrying Icelanders to Newfoundland to purchase Christmas gifts, thereby threatening Newfoundland's tourism industry. The credit of Newfoundland's fisheries is also being squeezed since most of Atlantic Canadian seafood processors hold lines of credit from Icelandic banks.

43057 ■ *"Inland Snaps Up Rival REITs" in Crain's Chicago Business (Vol. 31, November 17, 2008, No. 46, pp. 3)*
Pub: Crain Communications, Inc.
Ed: Alby Gallun. **Description:** Discusses Inland American Real Estate Trust Inc., a real estate investment trust that is napping up depressed shares of publicly traded competitors, a possible first step toward taking over these companies; however, with hotel and retail properties accounting for approximately 70 percent of its portfolio, the company could soon face its own difficulties.

43058 ■ *"Inside Out" in Playthings (Vol. 107, January 1, 2009, No. 1, pp. 3)*
Pub: Reed Business Information
Contact: Jeff Greisch, President
Description: Mattel signed on as the global master toy licensee for Cartoon Network's The Secret Saturdays while Toy Island signed a deal for wooden toys based on several leading Nick Jr. properties.

43059 ■ *"It's All in the Details" in Canadian Business (Vol. 80, December 25, 2006, No. 1, pp. 11)*
Pub: Rogers Media
Description: The failure of several Canadian clothing retailers to disclose their labor practices is discussed.

43060 ■ *"Izod, Loft Outlets Coming To Tanger" in New Hampshire Business Review (Vol. 33, March 25, 2011, No. 6, pp. 30)*
Pub: Business Publications Inc.
Description: Izod and Lots stores will open at the Tanger Outlet Center in Tilton, New Hampshire. Both stores will feature fashions and accessories.

43061 ■ *"Keeping Customers Satisfied" in Pet Product News (Vol. 64, December 2010, No. 12, pp. 10)*
Pub: BowTie Inc.
Ed: Devon McPhee. **Description:** Windsor, California-based Debbie's Pet Boutique, recipient of Pet Product News International's Outstanding Customer Service Award, has been dedicated to combining topnotch grooming services with a robust retail selection. These features might gain return customers for Debbie's Pet Boutique.

43062 ■ *"Kent Officials Seek Further KSU, City Unity" in Crain's Cleveland Business (Vol. 28, December 3, 2007, No. 48, pp. 3)*
Pub: Crain Communications, Inc.
Ed: Jay Miller. **Description:** Kent State University and Portage County are searching for a developer who will use a three-acre parcel to bring new life to the city's sagging downtown and create an area that will better link the town and the Kent State campus. The project will include a hotel and conference center as well as retail and restaurant space.

43063 ■ *"Killings Remind Convenience Store Workers of Job's Potential Risks" in Waterloo Courier (November 19, 2010)*
Pub: Gazette
Ed: Tina Hinz. **Description:** Potential risks for convenience store workers is stressed citing shootings in area shops; safety plans are important for these stores.

43064 ■ *The Leadership Challenge*
Pub: Jossey-Bass Publishers
Ed: James M. Kouzes, Barry Z. Posner. **Released:** June 30, 1995. **Price:** $22.00. **Description:** According to research by the authors, people can make extraordinary things happen by liberating the leader within everyone around them. This handbook gives practical tips to aspire leaders in retail, manufacturing, government, community, church and school settings.

43065 ■ *"Leaning Tower" in Business Courier (Vol. 27, June 4, 2010, No. 5, pp. 1)*
Pub: Business Courier
Ed: Jon Newberry. **Description:** New York-based developer Armand Lasky, owner of Tower Place Mall in downtown Cincinnati, Ohio has sued Birmingham, Alabama-based Regions Bank to prevent the bank's foreclosure on the property. Regions Bank claims Lasky was in default on an $18 million loan agreement. Details on the mall's leasing plan is also discussed.

43066 ■ *"Leasing Midway; Look for Higher Parking Fees, More Retail Under Private Airport Operator" in Crain's Chicago Business (May 5, 2008)*
Pub: Crain Communications, Inc.
Ed: Paul Merrion. **Description:** According to experts, bids for the first privatization of a major U.S. airport could run as high as $3.5 billion. Information-gathering and negotiations will soon get under way with some or all of the six major international investor groups that recently expressed interest in running Midway.

43067 ■ *"Let Emerging Market Customers Be Your Teachers" in Harvard Business Review (Vol. 88, December 2010, No. 12, pp. 115)*
Pub: Harvard Business School Publishing
Ed: Guillermo D'Andrea, David Marcotte, Gwen Dixon Morrison. **Description:** Examination of effective strategies for emerging markets is presented. These include helping educate customers as well as selling to them, adapting to customers' habits, and focusing brands appropriately. Magazine Luiza, a chain store in Brazil, is used to illustrate these points.

43068 ■ *"Let's Go Team: When a Retail Professional Leads by Example, Everyone Benefits" in Black Enterprise (Vol. 41, November 2010, No. 4)*
Pub: Earl G. Graves Publishing Co. Inc.
Ed: Aisha I. Jefferson. **Description:** Profile of Derek Jenkins, senior vice president of Target Stores Northeast Region is presented. Jenkins oversees the management of 450 retail stores with nearly 75,000 workers. He shares insight into managing by making sure every interaction with his team counts.

43069 ■ *"Life After Cod" in Globe & Mail (March 18, 2006, pp. B1)*
Pub: CTVglobemedia Publishing Inc.
Ed: Gordon Pitts. **Description:** Canadian fishing industry is under threat because of Chinese processing competition, high energy costs, rise of powerful retailers and the rise of Canadian dollar value. Fishing industry of Canada is analyzed.

43070 ■ *"Loblaw's Apparel Guru No Average Joe" in Globe & Mail (March 13, 2006, pp. B1)*
Pub: CTVglobemedia Publishing Inc.
Ed: Marina Strauss. **Description:** The details on Loblaw Companies Ltd., which unveiled Joe Fresh Style line of clothing, are presented.

43071 ■ *"Local Firms Will Feel Impact Of Wall St. Woes" in The Business Journal-Milwaukee (Vol. 25, September 19, 2008, No. 52, pp. A1)*
Pub: American City Business Journals, Inc.
Ed: Rich Kirchen. **Description:** Wall Street's crisis is expected to affect businesses in Wisconsin, in terms of decreased demand for services and products and increased financing costs. Businesses in Milwaukee area may face higher interest rates and tougher loan standards. The potential impacts of the Wall Street crisis on local businesses are examined further.

43072 ■ *"A Look Ahead Into 2007" in Canadian Business (Vol. 80, December 25, 2006, No. 1, pp. 40)*
Pub: Rogers Media
Description: The 2007 forecasts for various industrial sectors like telecom, information technology, manufacturing, retail, financial and energy among others is discussed.

43073 ■ *"Look Who's Eating Loblaw's Lunch" in Canadian Business (Vol. 80, February 26, 2007, No. 5, pp. 44)*
Pub: Rogers Media
Ed: Zena Olijnyk. **Description:** Loblaw Cos. Ltd. and Shoppers Drug Mart Corp. of Canada are finding increased competition from the global retail giant Wal-Mart Inc. The financial performance of the companies is analyzed.

43074 ■ *"Looking For Good Buys" in Black Enterprise (Vol. 38, November 2007, No. 4, pp. 39)*
Pub: Earl G. Graves Publishing Co. Inc.
Ed: Steve Garmhausen. **Description:** Lower interest rates mean consumers generally have more money to spend, which could spur economic growth in the retail sector of the U.S.

43075 ■ *"Looking for a Sales Tax Extension" in Milwaukee Business Journal (Vol. 27, January 29, 2010, No. 18, pp. A1)*
Pub: American City Business Journals
Ed: Mark Kass. **Description:** Milwaukee, Wisconsin-area business executives believe the extension of the Miller Park 0.1 percent sales tax could help fund a new basketball arena to replace the 21-year-old Bradley Center in downtown Milwaukee. However, any sales tax expansion that includes the new basketball arena would need approval by Wisconsin's legislature.

43076 ■ *"Loyalty Cards Score Points" in Crain's Cleveland Business (Vol. 30, June 8, 2009, No. 22, pp. 1)*
Pub: Crain Communications, Inc.
Ed: Chuck Soder. **Description:** Northeast Ohio retailers are promoting loyalty and rewards programs in order to attract and maintain loyal customers.

43077 ■ *"Luxe Men Are In Style" in Brandweek (Vol. 49, April 21, 2008, No. 16, pp. 12)*
Pub: VNU Business Media, Inc.
Description: According to a recent survey by Unity Marketing, among 1,300 luxury shoppers found that men spent an average of $2,401 on fashion items over a three-month period which is nearly $1,000 more than women. Men also spring for more luxury items such as vehicles and memberships to exclusive clubs.

43078 ■ *"Luxury Still Sells Well" in Puget Sound Business Journal (Vol. 29, September 5, 2008, No. 20, pp. 1)*
Pub: American City Business Journals
Ed: Jeanne Lang Jones. **Description:** High fashion retailers are planning to open stores in the Puget Sound area despite the economic slowdown, citing high incomes in the area despite the weak U.S. dollar.

43079 ■ *"Macy's Seeks Balance in All Things Ad-Related" in Crain's Chicago Business (Vol. 31, March 31, 2008, No. 13, pp. 19)*
Pub: Crain Communications, Inc.
Ed: Natalie Zmuda. **Description:** Macy's Inc. is seeking to balance its national television campaign with locally tailored promotions and products.

43080 ■ *"Major Golf Retail Show in the Rough for 2010" in Orlando Business Journal (Vol. 26, January 15, 2010, No. 33, pp. 1)*
Pub: American City Business Journals
Ed: Anjali Fluker. **Description:** The 57th Annual PGA Merchandise Show in Orlando, Florida is projected to attract 39,000 attendees in 2010, compared with 41,000 in 2009. According to the Orange County Convention Center, economic benefits that could be obtained from the 2010 edition of the golf retail show might reach only $77 million, compared with $78 million generated last year.

43081 ■ *"Major Renovation Planned for Southridge" in Business Journal-Milwaukee (Vol. 28, November 12, 2010, No. 6, pp. A1)*
Pub: Milwaukee Business Journal
Ed: Stacy Vogel Davis. **Description:** Simon Property Group plans to invest more than $20 million in upgrading and renovating Southridge Mall in Milwaukee County, Wisconsin. The project, which is partially financed by a $10 million grant from the Village of Greendale, could boost the property's value by $52.5 million.

43082 ■ *"Many Retailers Soften Return Policies" in Austin Business JournalInc. (Vol. 28, December 26, 2008, No. 41, pp. 1)*
Pub: American City Business Journals
Ed: Jean Kwon. **Description:** National Retail Federation reported the percentage of retailers saying their holiday return policy in 2008 will slacken compared to last season has increased from 3.4 percent to 11 percent. An increasing percentage of retailers are also getting stingier, as 17.1 percent revealed that their return policies will be stricter.

43083 ■ *"Marathon Money" in Hawaii Business (Vol. 53, December 2007, No. 6, pp. 127)*
Pub: Hawaii Business Publishing
Ed: Jolyn Okimoto Rosa. **Description:** Discusses the effects of the Honolulu Marathon on small businesses' sales. The Running Room, for instance, experience growth in sales starting from the training season up to the end of the race, as a surge of Hawaiian residents and tourists come into the store for items such as running shoes and blister kits. The marathon's impact on Hawaii's tourism is examined as well.

43084 ■ *"Market for Retail Space Flat, but Recovery Still Uncertain" in Sacramento Business Journal (Vol. 28, August 26, 2011, No. 26, pp. 1)*
Pub: Sacramento Business Journal
Ed: Kelly Johnson. **Description:** The retail market in the Sacramento, California region remains challenged with the stock market volatility being the latest of its hurdles. The overall vacancy was 13.1 percent as of mid-2011, but retail real estate professionals express hopes that the worst is behind. A list and description of the region's winners and losers in retail vacancies is provided.

43085 ■ *"Market Share" in Business Journal-Milwaukee (Vol. 28, December 3, 2010, No. 9, pp. A1)*
Pub: Milwaukee Business Journal
Ed: Stacy Vogel Davis. **Description:** Roundy's Supermarkets' market share has decreased with the expansion of low-price grocery chains in Milwaukee, Wisconsin. Wal-Mart stores Inc., Aldi Inc., and Target Corporation have all opened new stores in the area.

43086 ■ *"Marketers Push for Mobile Tuesday as the New Black Friday" in Advertising Age (Vol. 79, December 1, 2008, No. 44, pp. 21)*
Pub: Crain Communications, Inc.
Ed: Natalie Zmuda. **Description:** Marketers are using an innovative approach in an attempt to stimulate business on the Tuesday following Thanksgiving by utilizing consumer's cell phones to alert them of sales or present them with coupons for this typically slow retail business day; with this campaign both advertisers and retailers are hoping to start Mobile Tuesday, another profitable shopping day in line with Black Friday and Cyber Monday.

43087 ■ *"Marketing: 'Twill Be the Season" in Entrepreneur (Vol. 35, October 2007, No. 10, pp. 108)*
Pub: Entrepreneur Media Inc.
Ed: Kim T. Gordon. **Description:** Entrepreneurs should plan ahead in order to promote products for the holiday season, since it is peak sales time. They can unify their business theme, use customer incentives, advertise early using TV or radio, and reorganize the company Website. Other ways to market for the holiday season are provided.

43088 ■ *"Mars Advertising's Orbit Grows as Other Ad Segments Fall" in Crain's Detroit Business (Vol. 25, June 1, 2009, No. 22, pp. 10)*
Pub: Crain Communications Inc. - Detroit
Ed: Bill Shea. **Description:** An electrical fire burned at Mars Advertising's headquarters in Southfield, Michigan. The company talks about its plans for regrouping and rebuilding. The family firm specializes in in-store marketing that targets consumers already in the buying mode.

43089 ■ *"Martha Stewart Launches Macys Line" in Marketing to Women (Vol. 21, March 2008, No. 3, pp. 5)*
Pub: EPM Communications Inc.
Contact: Ira Mayer, President
E-mail: imayer@epmcom.com
Description: Martha Stewart launches an exclusive line of home decor called Wedgwood as part of her relationship with Macy's stores.

43090 ■ *"Maternity Wear Goes Green" in Marketing to Women (Vol. 21, March 2008, No. 3, pp. 3)*
Pub: EPM Communications Inc.
Contact: Ira Mayer, President
E-mail: imayer@epmcom.com
Description: Mother's Work Inc. has launched a series of environmentally-friendly products made from such sustainable fibers as organic cotton and bamboo.

43091 ■ *"Mattel's Got a Monster Holiday Hit, But Will Franchise Have Staying Power?" in Advertising Age (Vol. 81, December 6, 2010, No. 43)*
Pub: Crain Communications, Inc.
Ed: Beth Snyder Bulik. **Description:** Monster High transmedia play expands beyond dolls to merchandise, apparel and entertainment.

43092 ■ *"Men May Wear the Pants in the Family, But Women Retain the Power of the Purse" in Marketing to Women (Vol. 22, August 2009, No. 8)*
Pub: EPM Communications Inc.
Contact: Ira Mayer, President
E-mail: imayer@epmcom.com
Description: Nearly 8 in 10 women say that their opinion holds the most sway in the families' financial decisions. Significant factors that influence women's $100 or more purchases include Online reviews, the opinion of spouse or significant other and expert recommendations. Statistical data included.

43093 ■ *"Midtown Tampa Bay Taking Shape" in The Business Journal-Serving Greater Tampa Bay (Vol. 28, September 12, 2008, No. 38, pp. 1)*
Pub: American City Business Journals, Inc.
Ed: Janet Leiser. **Description:** Midtown Tampa Bay's 610,000 square foot shopping and entertainment center is being planned in Florida and is to replace the Tampa Bay One project proposed years earlier. The retail center is to be developed by Bromley Cos. and Opus South Corp. and is expected to have five buildings. Other details about the plan are discussed.

43094 ■ *"Midwest Test" in Crain's Cleveland Business (Vol. 28, November 26, 2007, No. 47, pp. 1)*
Pub: Crain Communications, Inc.
Ed: John Booth. **Description:** Provides an overview of the experimental Wal-Mart Supercenter in Elyria which researches consumer preferences with department layouts, new merchandise and even exterior architecture. Store manager Bob Butler said, 'We're trying to get out of that box-store look.'.

43095 ■ *"Millennials: The Great White Hope for Wine Industry" in Advertising Age (Vol. 81, December 6, 2010, No. 43, pp. 2)*
Pub: Crain Communications, Inc.
Ed: E.J. Shultz. **Description:** Generation offers category of most growth potential in 30 years and 7-Eleven and vintner are taking notice.

43096 ■ *Million Dollar Website: Simple Steps to Help You Compete with the Big Boys-Even on a Small Business Budget*
Pub: Prentice Hall Press
Ed: Lori Culwell. **Released:** May 9, 2010. **Price:** $19.95. **Description:** Resource for any small business owner wishing to build a successful Website in order to compete with big box stores.

43097 ■ *"Minimizing Import Risks" in Canadian Sailings (July 7, 2008)*
Pub: UBM Global Trade
Contact: Leonard J. Corallo, President
Ed: Jack Kohane. **Description:** New food and product safety laws may be enacted by Canada's Parliament; importers, retailers and manufacturers could face huge fines if the new laws are passed.

43098 ■ *"Modern Bride Unveiled Exclusively at JCPenney" in Benzinga.com (February 3, 2011)*
Pub: Benzinga.com
Ed: Benzinga Staff. **Description:** JCPenney created its new Modern Bride concept in its bridal find jewelry

departments. The new shopping experience is a collaboration between the retailer and Conde Nast catering to the bridal customer.

43099 ■ *The Mom and Pop Store: How the Unsung Heroes of the American Economy Are Surviving and Thriving*
Pub: Walker & Company
Ed: Robert Spector. **Released:** September 1, 2009. **Price:** $26.00. **Description:** The history of small independent retail enterprises and how mom and pop stores in the U.S. continue to thrive through customer service and renewed community support for local businesses.

43100 ■ *"Moms Are Still Shopping" in Marketing to Women (Vol. 21, February 2008, No. 2, pp. 1)*
Pub: EPM Communications Inc.
Contact: Ira Mayer, President
E-mail: imayer@epmcom.com
Description: According to a monthly poll by Parenting Magazine, although the economic signs worsen many moms are still shopping. Statistical data included.

43101 ■ *"More Details Emerge on Maersk Plan" in Charlotte Business Journal (Vol. 25, August 13, 2010, No. 21, pp. 1)*
Pub: Charlotte Business Journal
Ed: Will Boye. **Description:** Children Klen Properties has announced the details of its redevelopment plan for a property in Charlotte, North Carolina. The plan includes office and retail space and residential units. The construction of a hotel has also been proposed.

43102 ■ *"More Leading Retailers Using Omniture Conversion Solutions to Boost Sales and Ecommerce Performance" in Internet Wire (Sept. 22,2009)*
Pub: Comtex News Network, Inc.
Description: Many retailers are utilizing Omniture conversion solutions to improve the performance of their ecommerce businesses; recent enhancements to Omniture Merchandising and Omniture Recommendations help clients drive increased conversion to their Internet ventures.

43103 ■ *"More Leading Retailers Using Omniture Conversion Solutions to Boost Sales and Ecommerce Performance" in Internet Wire (Sept. 22,2009)*
Pub: Comtex News Network, Inc.
Description: Many retailers are utilizing Omniture conversion solutions to improve the performance of their ecommerce businesses; recent enhancements to Omniture Merchandising and Omniture Recommendations help clients drive increased conversion to their Internet ventures.

43104 ■ *"More SouthPark Shopping" in Charlotte Business Journal (Vol. 25, July 16, 2010, No. 17, pp. 1)*
Pub: Charlotte Business Journal
Ed: Will Boye. **Description:** Charlotte, North Carolina-based Bissel Companies has announced plans to expand its retail presence at the Siskey and Sharon properties in SouthPark. Bissel Companies has requested a rezoning to a mixed-use development classification so that it can utilize the entire ground floor of the Siskey building for restaurant and retail uses.

43105 ■ *"Move Marks KKR's Latest Push into Retail" in Globe & Mail (March 13, 2007, pp. B17)*
Pub: CTVglobemedia Publishing Inc.
Ed: Heather Burke. **Description:** Investment giant Kohlberg Kravis Roberts and Co. has finalized a deal to acquire retail store chain Dollar General Corp. for an estimated 6.9 billion dollars. The company will be entering lucrative retail market by this acquisition.

43106 ■ *"A Muddle at Marks & Spencer" in Barron's (Vol. 88, July 7, 2008, No. 27, pp. M7)*
Pub: Dow Jones & Co., Inc.
Ed: Molly Neal. **Description:** British retail outfit Marks & Spencer is encountering turbulent financial conditions but remains confident in spending 900 million pounds sterling. The company has not made a profit forecast for the first half of 2008 and is suffering from a shrinking cash flow.

43107 ■ *"Murdock Carrousel Sold" in Charlotte Observer (January 31, 2007)*
Pub: Knight-Ridder/Tribune Business News
Ed: Bob Fliss. **Description:** Details on the sale of the Murdock Carrousel shopping center are highlighted. The deal was reported at $281 million.

43108 ■ *"Must Work for Food" in Pet Product News (Vol. 64, November 2010, No. 11, pp. 24)*
Pub: BowTie Inc.
Ed: Wendy Bedwell-Wilson. **Description:** Pet supply retailers can benefit from stocking foods and treats that address obesity, which according to the American Veterinary Medical Association, has become the most prevalent nutritional disorder in dogs. With the rise in dog obesity, products like work-for-their food toys have been sought by dog owners.

43109 ■ *"National Cattlemen's Beef Association" in Retail Merchandiser (Vol. 51, September-October 2011, No. 5, pp. 77)*
Pub: Phoenix Media Corporation
Description: National Cattlemen's Beef Association offers a wide range of tools and information to keep its members informed regarding the state of the beef industry. Their Website provides tools to help cattle producers improve operations.

43110 ■ *"Neighbors Rally for Dollar Store" in Chattanooga Times/Free Press (August 4, 2010)*
Pub: Chattanooga Times/Free Press
Description: Neighbors are rallying to keep the Family Dollar Store in their city open. The proposed new store would expand the grocery portion of its retail discount shop.

43111 ■ *"New Dollar Store Opens in Shoppes at Richland" in Aiken Standard (October 15, 2010)*
Pub: Aiken Standard
Ed: Haley Hughes. **Description:** Information regarding the opening of Froogle's Dollar Store is given. The store opened in Richland area of South Carolina.

43112 ■ *"New Family Dollar Store Now Open in Hermon" in Bangor Daily News (August 12, 2010)*
Pub: Bangor Daily News
Ed: Dawn Gagnon. **Description:** A new Family Dollar Store opened its doors at the newly expanded Hermon Shopping Center in Bangor, Maine.

43113 ■ *"A New Mix of Tenants Settles In" in Crain's New York Business (Vol. 24, January 14, 2008, No. 2, pp. 26)*
Pub: Crain Communications, Inc.
Ed: Andrew Marks. **Description:** More and more nonfinancial firms are relocating downtown due to the new retailers and restaurants that are reshaping the look and feel of lower Manhattan.

43114 ■ *"New York Firm Secures Sheffield, Amherst Centers for $26 Million" in Crain's Cleveland Business (Vol. 28, December 3, 2007, No. 48)*
Pub: Crain Communications, Inc.
Ed: Stan Bullard. **Description:** Silverman Realty Group completed a $26 million transaction which made it the new owner of the Sheffield Crossing and Amherst Marketplace shopping centers in Lorain County.

43115 ■ *"Nine Sectors to Watch: Retail" in Canadian Business (Vol. 81, December 24, 2007, No. 1, pp. 56)*
Pub: Rogers Media
Ed: Zena Olijnyk. **Description:** Canadian consumers are expected to spend more in 2008 as the Canadian dollar hit par with the U.S. greenback after the slowdown in the U.S. economy. Forecasts on retail sales growth are presented.

43116 ■ *"No Frills - And No Dodge" in Crain's Detroit Business (Vol. 24, September 22, 2008, No. 38, pp. 3)*
Pub: Crain Communications Inc.
Ed: Bradford Wernie. **Description:** Chrysler LLC is in the middle of a business plan known as Project Genesis, a five-year strategy in which the company will reduce the dealer count by combining its Jeep, Chrysler and Dodge brands under one rooftop wherever possible. Not every dealer will be able to arrange this deal because of the investment required to expand stores in which have low-overhead; many of these stores feel that low-overhead structures are more likely to survive difficult times than the larger stores in which the Genesis consolidation plan intends to implement.

43117 ■ *"Nordstrom Points for Richmond Heights" in Saint Louis Business Journal (Vol. 31, August 5, 2011, No. 50, pp. 1)*
Pub: Saint Louis Business Journal
Ed: E.B. Solomont. **Description:** Nordstrom is set to upgrade its offerings for its second full-line store in St. Louis, Missouri. The new store is expected to benefit nearby shops.

43118 ■ *"Offer for Sears Canada 'Inadequate'" in Globe & Mail (February 10, 2006, pp. B4)*
Pub: CTVglobemedia Publishing Inc.
Ed: Marina Strauss. **Description:** The financial feasibility of Sears Holdings Corp.'s proposed acquisition of Sears Canada Inc., for $835 million, is discussed.

43119 ■ *On the Make: Clerks and the Quest for Capital in Nineteenth-Century America*
Pub: New York University Press
Contact: Steve Maikowski, Director
E-mail: steve.maikowski@nyu.edu
Ed: Brian Luskey. **Released:** January 1, 2010. **Price:** $48.00. **Description:** Through exploration into the diaries, newspapers, credit reports, census data, advice literature and fiction, the book presents the origins of the white collar culture, the antebellum clerk.

43120 ■ *"Online All the Time" in Retail Merchandiser (Vol. 51, July-August 2011, No. 4, pp. 18)*
Pub: Phoenix Media Corporation
Description: Ecommerce sales are rising at a steady pace and for cross-channel retailers it is boosting sales in the weak economy. Online sales are expected to reach $188 billion in 2011, boasting a 13.7 rate of growth.

43121 ■ *"Online Security Crackdown: Scanning Service Oversees Site Security at David's Bridal" in (Vol. 84, July 2008, No. 7, pp. 46)*
Pub: Chain Store Age
Ed: Samantha Murphy. **Description:** Online retailers are beefing up security on their Websites. Cyber thieves use retail systems in order to gain entry to consumer data. David's Bridal operates over 275 bridal showrooms in the U.S. and has a one-stop wedding resource for new brides planning weddings.

43122 ■ *"Options Abound in Winter Wares" in Pet Product News (Vol. 64, November 2010, No. 11, pp. 1)*
Pub: BowTie Inc.
Ed: Maggie M. Shein. **Description:** Pet supply manufacturers emphasize creating top-notch construction and functional design in creating winter clothing for pets. Meanwhile, retailers and pet owners seek human-inspired style, quality, and versatility for pets' winter clothing. How retailers generate successful sales of pets' winter clothing outside of traditional brand marketing is also examined.

43123 ■ *Over the Counter*
Pub: The Mercier Press, Ltd.
Ed: Keogh. **Released:** January 1, 2009. **Price:** $54.95. **Description:** An overview of the changing landscape of Cork, Ireland's retail stores is presented.

43124 ■ *"Peacocks Launches Its First Wedding Dress" in Benzinga.com (July 1, 2011)*
Pub: Benzinga.com
Ed: Benzinga Staff. **Description:** Peacocks, a leading fashion retailer in the United Kingdom launched its first wedding dress available for sale in August 2011.

43125 ■ *"Penney's Buys Wal-Mart Site" in Crain's Chicago Business (Vol. 31, March 31, 2008, No. 13, pp. 13)*
Pub: Crain Communications, Inc.
Ed: Eddie Baeb. **Description:** J.C. Penny Co. bought the closed Wal-Mart location in Crystal Lake and plans to open a store next year in its push to become more prominent in non-mall locations; Penney plans to expand and renovate the store.

43126 ■ *"Penny Chief Shops For Shares" in Barron's (Vol. 88, July 7, 2008, No. 27, pp. 29)*
Pub: Dow Jones & Co., Inc.
Ed: Teresa Rivas. **Description:** Myron Ullman III, chairman and chief executive officer of J.C. Penney, purchased $1 million worth of shares of the company. He now owns 393,140 shares of the company and an additional 1,282 on his 401(k) plan.

43127 ■ *"People; E-Commerce, Online Games, Mobile Apps" in Advertising Age (Vol. 80, October 19, 2009, No. 35, pp. 14)*
Pub: Crain's Communications
Ed: Nat Ives. **Description:** Profile of People Magazine and the ways in which the publisher is moving its magazine forward by exploring new concepts in a time of declining newsstand sales and advertising pages; among the strategies are e-commerce such as the brand People Style Watch in which consumers are able highlight clothing and jewelry and then connect to retailers' sites and a channel on Taxi TV, the network of video-touch screens in New Your City taxis.

43128 ■ *"People; E-Commerce, Online Games, Mobile Apps: This Isn't Your Mom's People" in Advertising Age (Vol. 80, October 19, 2009, No. 35)*
Pub: Crain's Communications
Ed: Nat Ives. **Description:** Profile of People Magazine and the ways in which the publisher is moving its magazine forward by exploring new concepts in a time of declining newsstand sales and advertising pages; among the strategies are e-commerce such as the brand People Style Watch in which consumers are able highlight clothing and jewelry and then connect to retailers' sites and a channel on Taxi TV, the network of video-touch screens in New Your City taxis.

43129 ■ *"Perfecting Customer Services" in Pet Product News (Vol. 64, November 2010, No. 11, pp. 18)*
Pub: BowTie Inc.
Description: Pet supply retailers are encouraged to emphasize customer experience and sales representatives' knowledge of the store's product offerings to foster repeat business. Employee protocols could be implemented to improve customer interaction. Other guidelines on developing a pet supply retail environment that advances repeat business are presented.

43130 ■ *"PGA Tour: Course Management" in Retail Merchandiser (Vol. 51, September-October 2011, No. 5, pp. 38)*
Pub: Phoenix Media Corporation
Ed: Eric Slack. **Description:** PGA Tour must reach new customers and solidify relationships with its traditional base in order to continue its success. The PGA brand equity has translated into one of the largest retail licensing operations worldwide.

43131 ■ *"Phillips Edison Launches $1.8B Retail REIT" in Business Courier (Vol. 27, October 15, 2010, No. 24, pp. 1)*
Pub: Business Courier
Ed: Dan Monk. **Description:** Retail center operator Phillips Edison & Company is organizing a real estate investment trust (REIT) to raise $1.8 billion to finance the planned purchase of 150 grocery-centered shopping centers around the U.S. The offering would be Phillips largest. Phillips Edison employesss 174 workers and operates 250 shopping centers nationwide.

43132 ■ *"Pink Label: Victoria's Sales Secret" in Advertising Age (Vol. 79, July 7, 2008, No. 26, pp. 4)*
Pub: Crain Communications, Inc.
Ed: Natalie Zmuda. **Description:** Victoria Secret's Pink label accounted for roughly 17 percent of the retailer's total sales last year. The company is launching a Collegiate Collection which will be promoted by a campus tour program.

43133 ■ *"Plans for $160M Condo Resort in Wisconsin Dells Moves Forward" in Commercial Property News (March 18, 2008)*
Pub: Nielsen Company
Description: Plans for the Grand Cambrian Resort in the Wisconsin Dells is discussed. The luxury condominium resort will include condos, townhomes, and condo-hotel style residences, two water parts, meeting space and indoor entertainment space, as well as a spa, four restaurants and retail offerings.

43134 ■ *"Point, Click, Buy" in Barron's (Vol. 90, September 6, 2010, No. 36, pp. 11)*
Pub: Barron's Editorial & Corporate Headquarters
Ed: Vito J. Racanelli. **Description:** Non-travel online retail sales from January to July 2010 increased nine percent which indicates that online shopping for the coming holidays will be good. Online sales are outpacing traditional shopping, but pricing is still critical.

43135 ■ *"Pop N Go Launching Into Dollar Store Market" in Internet Wire (July 14, 2009)*
Pub: Comtex News Network, Inc.
Description: Pop N Go, Inc. announced that it will test the company's flagship popcorn vending machine in the rapidly growing dollar store distribution channel.

43136 ■ *"Population Growing Faster Than Retail, Service Sector" in Crain's New York Business (Vol. 24, January 14, 2008, No. 2, pp. 30)*
Pub: Crain Communications, Inc.
Ed: Andrew Marks. **Description:** Downtown Manhattan is seeing more residential development; however, as more families call the area home the need for more retail and services is becoming evident.

43137 ■ *"'Pre-Sale' for Planned Could Mich Tower" in Crain's Chicago Business (Vol. 31, March 24, 2008, No. 12, pp. 14)*
Pub: Crain Communications, Inc.
Ed: Eddie Baeb. **Description:** Condominium developer William Warman is planning to build a mixed-use tower at 300 North Michigan Avenue which would include a hotel, retail space, apartments and a parking garage. Mr. Warman is looking for investors to buy part or all of the space in order to make it easier to land financing.

43138 ■ *"Prepaid Cards and State Unclaimed Property Laws" in Franchise Law Journal (Vol. 27, Summer 2007, No. 1, pp. 23)*
Pub: American Bar Association
Contact: Carolyn Lamm, President
Ed: Phillip W. Bohl, Kathryn J. Bergstrom, Kevin J. Moran. **Description:** Unredeemed value of electronic prepaid stored-value credit cards for retail purchases is known as breakage. Laws governing unclaimed property as it relates to these gift cards is covered.

43139 ■ *"Procter & Gamble Boosts Bet on Exclusive Brands" in Business Courier (Vol. 27, July 9, 2010, No. 10, pp. 1)*
Pub: Business Courier
Ed: Jon Newberry. **Description:** Procter & Gamble is creating more special versions of its brands such as Pringles and Pampers exclusively for retail partners such as Tesco in the U.K. The greater push towards this direction is seen as a way to regain market share.

43140 ■ *"Profit Strong Rona to Maintain Acquisition Strategy" in Globe & Mail (February 22, 2007, pp. B14)*
Pub: CTVglobemedia Publishing Inc.
Description: Canada-based Rona Inc., home improvement retailer that reported record annual profit in 2006, will continue its strategy of acquisitions. The company has reported profits of $190.6 million in 2006.

43141 ■ *"Promotions Create a Path to Better Profit" in Pet Product News (Vol. 64, December 2010, No. 12, pp. 1)*
Pub: BowTie Inc.
Ed: Joan Hustace Walker. **Description:** Pet store retailers can boost small mammal sales by launching creative marketing and promotions such as social networking and adoption days.

43142 ■ *"Proposed Triangle Redo in Motion" in Crain's Cleveland Business (Vol. 28, October 15, 2007, No. 41, pp. 1)*
Pub: Crain Communications, Inc.
Ed: Stan Bullard. **Description:** Zaremba Homes and MRN Ltd. are partnering to redevelop the so-called Triangle section of University Circle. The proposed project will include a total of 434 new rental and for-sale residential suites and as much as 227,000 square feet of retail and restaurant space.

43143 ■ *"Pssst! Buzz About Target" in Barron's (Vol. 89, July 27, 2009, No. 30, pp. 15)*
Pub: Dow Jones & Co., Inc.
Ed: Katherine Cheng. **Description:** Target rebutted the rumor that they will disassociate themselves from a line of clothing inspired by the television show 'Gossip Girl'. Target's spokesman says that the retailer intends to remain closely identified with the show. Target's sales should benefit from the hotly anticipated clothing line.

43144 ■ *"Q&A: David Labistour" in Canadian Business (Vol. 81, March 17, 2008, No. 4, pp. 10)*
Pub: Rogers Media
Ed: Lauren McKeon. **Description:** David Labistour says that the difference between being a co-op retailer and a corporate-owned retailer in the case of Mountain Equipment Co-op (MEC) is that the company is owned by their customers and not by shareholders. Labistour also says that MEC works with their factories to ensure that these maintain ethical standards in the manufacturing process.

43145 ■ *QuickBooks X for Dummies*
Pub: John Wiley & Sons, Incorporated
Ed: Stephen L. Nelson. **Released:** November 2006. **Price:** $21.99. **Description:** Key features of QuickBooks software for small business are introduced. Invoicing and credit memos, recoding sales receipts, accounting, budgeting, taxes, payroll, financial reports, job estimating, billing, tracking, data backup, are among the features.

43146 ■ *"Recovery on Tap for 2010?" in Orlando Business Journal (Vol. 26, January 1, 2010, No. 31, pp. 1)*
Pub: American City Business Journals
Ed: Melanie Stawicki Azam, Richard Bilbao, Christopher Boyd, Anjali Fluker. **Description:** Economic forecasts for Central Florida's leading business sectors in 2010 are presented. These sectors include housing, film and TV, sports business, law, restaurants, aviation, tourism and hospitality, banking and finance, commercial real estate, retail, health care, insurance, higher education, and manufacturing. According to some local executives, Central Florida's economy will slowly recover in 2010.

43147 ■ *"Rent Check" in Boston Business Journal (Vol. 31, July 29, 2011, No. 27, pp. 1)*
Pub: Boston Business Journal
Ed: Lisa van der Pool. **Description:** Merchants at Newbury Street in Boston, Massachusetts are concerned with the annual increase of already inflated rents that prevent many small businesses from expanding.

43148 ■ *"Report: McD's Pepsi Score Best With Young Hispanics" in Brandweek (Vol. 49, April 21, 2008, No. 16, pp. 8)*
Pub: VNU Business Media, Inc.
Ed: Della de Lafuente. **Description:** According to a new report, in order to reach Hispanic Gen Yers, marketing strategists need to understand this demographic's 'bi-dentity,' something which has proved an elusive task to many marketers. Another trend is the emergence of Latinas who have careers, as opposed to just jobs. There is an opportunity to tap this new, young and empowered female market with innovative messaging. Statistical data included.

43149 ■ *"Research Reports: How Analysts Size Up Companies" in Barron's (Vol. 90, August 23, 2010, No. 34, pp. M13)*
Pub: Barron's Editorial & Corporate Headquarters
Description: Shares of Sirius XM Radio, Target and Deere and Company received an eBuyE rating, while shares of Research in Motion got an eNeutralE rating.

43150 ■ *"Rest Easy, Retailers" in Pet Product News (Vol. 64, December 2010, No. 12, pp. S1)*
Pub: BowTie Inc.
Ed: Wendy Bedwell-Wilson. **Description:** Pointers on how retailers can market all-natural beds and bedding products for pets are provided. The demand for these pet beds and bedding products has been increasing as customers become aware of the benefits of natural rest and relaxation products.

43151 ■ *"Retail in Austin Strong, Will Continue to Be" in Austin Business JournalInc. (Vol. 29, January 22, 2010, No. 46, pp. 1)*
Pub: American City Business Journals
Ed: Jacob Dirr. **Description:** Retail sector in Austin, Texas has outpaced the national average in value, mid-tier, high-end and drugs retail sectors, according to a report by Pitney Bowes. The national consulting firm's report has projected growth in every sector until the end of fiscal 2012. Data regarding other sectors is also included.

43152 ■ *"Retail Briefs - Dollar Store Opens in Long Leaf Mall" in Star-News (November 5, 2010)*
Pub: Star-News Media
Ed: Judy Royal. **Description:** Dollar Delight$ opened a new shop in Long Leaf Mall in Wilmington, North Carolina. The store will carry gift bags, balloons, party supplies, greeting cards, school supplies, health and beauty products, hardware, baby items, toys, Christmas goods, crafts, housewares and jewelry in its inventory.

43153 ■ *"Retail Center Pitched" in Business Courier (Vol. 27, June 18, 2010, No. 7, pp. 1)*
Pub: Business Courier
Ed: Dan Monk. **Description:** Jeffrey R. Anderson Real Estate Inc.'s plan for a retail center in Butler County, Ohio could have three department stores in the 1.1 million-square-foot property. An outdoor sports retailer is also part of the plans.

43154 ■ *"Retail Center Planned for Canton Site" in Boston Business Journal (Vol. 29, May 20, 2011, No. 2, pp. 1)*
Pub: American City Business Journals Inc.
Ed: Daniel J. Sernovitz. **Description:** A real estate development team is planning to build a shopping center at Canton Crossing in Baltimore, Maryland and is near closing the deal with ExxonMobil Corporation who owns the waterfront site.

43155 ■ *"Retail Franchises to Start Now" in Entrepreneur (Vol. 37, August 2009, No. 8, pp. 88)*
Pub: Entrepreneur Media, Inc.
Ed: Tracy Stapp. **Description:** Listing of retail franchises is presented and is categorized based on their products sold. The total cost of the franchise and the website are also included as well as additional statistical data.

43156 ■ *"Retail: Loblaw Goes for Broke" in Canadian Business (Vol. 80, January 29, 2007, No. 3, pp. 7)*
Pub: Rogers Media
Ed: Zena Oiljnyk. **Description:** The efforts of Loblaw Companies Limited to reduce its operational expenses are described. The company's decision to reduce the number of employees at its national and regional offices, besides closing some of its facilities, is discussed.

43157 ■ *The Retail Revolution: How Wal-Mart Created a Brave New World of Business*
Pub: Metropolitan Books
Ed: Nelson Lichtenstein. **Released:** July 21, 2009. **Price:** $25.00. **Description:** Comprehensive discussion on how Wal-Mart changed retailing, and its place in the changing global economy.

43158 ■ *"Retail Slump Deflates Local Development" in Business Courier (Vol. 24, February 29, 2008, No. 47, pp. 1)*
Pub: American City Business Journals, Inc.
Ed: Lisa Biank Fasig. **Description:** 2007 sales of the retail industry are the slowest since the year 2003, driving retail stores to reconsider their expansion plans for 2008. A number of retail projects have been delayed, cancelled or altered, including Newport Pavilion, Rivers Crossing, Wal-Mart Supercenters, Legacy Place and Millworks. The impacts of retail slowdown on development projects are analyzed further.

43159 ■ *"Retail Woes: The Shoe Doesn't Fit for Gerald Loftin's Stock Picks" in Black Enterprise (Vol. 38, July 2008, No. 12, pp. 40)*
Pub: Earl G. Graves Publishing Co. Inc.
Ed: Steve Garmhausen. **Description:** Each of the three stocks that Gerald Loftin picked in May 2007 have lost money; DSW, the designer shoe retailer, fell by 63.7 percent; paint and coatings retailer Sherwin-Williams Co. fell by 7.2 percent; and Verizon Communications Inc. fell by 1.4 percent. Statistical data included.

43160 ■ *"Retailers, City Clash Over Wages" in Baltimore Business Journal (Vol. 28, July 9, 2010, No. 9, pp. 1)*
Pub: Baltimore Business Journal
Ed: Daniel J. Sernovitz. **Description:** A bill pending before the City Council of Baltimore, Maryland would mandate the city's major retailers to pay their employees at least $10.57 per hour, $3 higher than was state law requires. Major retailers, as defined in the said bill by Councilwoman Mary Pat Clarke, have gross sales of at least $10 million. Reactions of the retailers affected are presented.

43161 ■ *"Retailers Dig In For Holiday Shopping Push" in Business Review, Albany New York (Vol. 34, November 30, 2007, No. 35, pp. 1)*
Pub: American City Business Journals, Inc.
Ed: Michael DeMasi. **Description:** Tough economic conditions have led to lower consumer spending and retailers in Albany, New York and nationwide experienced mix results during the Black Friday weekend. Local retailers enjoyed higher sales in 2007 compared to 2006 and the National Retail Federation projects that retail sales will climb by four percent. Holiday retail trade forecasts are discussed.

43162 ■ *"Retailers Pull Out All Stops to Combat Poor Projections" in Austin Business JournalInc. (Vol. 28, November 21, 2008, No. 36, pp. 1)*
Pub: American City Business Journals
Ed: Jean Kwon. **Description:** Report from Wachovia Economics Group reports that holiday sales for 2008 are expected to decline by 2 percent and local retailers are planning to boost holiday sales through marketing efforts, which include giving freebies to early shoppers. Details on marketing strategies of several retailers are provided.

43163 ■ *"Retailers Report 'Shrinkage' of Inventory on the Rise" in Arkansas Business (Vol. 26, September 28, 2009, No. 39, pp. 17)*
Pub: Journal Publishing Inc.
Ed: Mark Friedman. **Description:** According to a National Retail Security Survey report released last June, retailers across the country have lost about $36.5 billion in shrinkage, most of it at the hands of employees and shoplifters alike. Statistical data included.

43164 ■ *"Retailers Tap into War-Room Creativity of Employees" in Globe & Mail (March 12, 2007, pp. B1)*
Pub: CTVglobemedia Publishing Inc.
Ed: Marina Strauss. **Description:** The methods adopted by Canadian Tire Corporation Ltd. to utilize the creative abilities of its employees for innovation during new product development are discussed.

43165 ■ *"Retailers, Your Will, and More" in Agency Sales Magazine (Vol. 39, July 2009, No. 7, pp. 46)*
Pub: MANA
Ed: Melvin H. Daskal. **Description:** IRS audit guide for small retail businesses is presented. Tips on how to make a will with multiple beneficiaries are discussed together with medical expenses that can not be deducted.

43166 ■ *"The Return of the Infomercial" in Canadian Business (Vol. 83, September 14, 2010, No. 15, pp. 19)*
Pub: Rogers Media Ltd.
Ed: James Cowan. **Description:** Infomercials or direct response ads have helped some products succeed in the marketplace. The success of infomercials is due to the cheap advertising rates, expansion into retail stores and the products' oddball appeal. Insights into the popularity of infomercial products on the Internet and on television are given.

43167 ■ *"Riding High" in Small Business Opportunities (November 2008)*
Pub: Entrepreneur Press
Contact: Perlman Neil, President
Ed: Stan Roberts. **Description:** Profile of David Sanborn who found a way to turn his passion for biking into a moneymaking opportunity by opening his own bicycle shops; Sanborn's goal is to become the largest independent bike retailer in the United States.

43168 ■ *"The Rise of Pompei" in Retail Merchandiser (Vol. 51, September-October 2011, No. 5, pp. 13)*
Pub: Phoenix Media Corporation
Description: Soho creative consulting group follows its C3 philosophy to create an invigorated brand experience that transforms customers from consumers to empowered buyers. Pompei AD is a leading creative consultancy that specializes in design and branding for retail, museum, hospitality, and other sectors.

43169 ■ *"The Role of Human and Financial Capital in the Profitability and Growth of Women-Owned Small Firms" in Journal of Small Business Management*
Pub: Blackwell Publishing Inc.
Contact: Gordon Tibbitts, President
Ed: Susan Coleman. **Description:** Examines the relationship between the human and financial capital in both men and women-owned businesses and firm performance in the service and retail sectors.

43170 ■ *"Ross Stores Reports Spectacular First Quarter" in Home Textiles Today (Vol. 31, May 24, 2011, No. 13, pp. 2)*
Pub: Reed Business Information
Contact: Jeff Greisch, President
Ed: James Mammarella. **Description:** Retailer Ross Stores reported strong sales and profit gains for first quarter 2011, with their home department helping to lead the way.

43171 ■ *"Rough Q1 Begs Question: Is the Crocs Craze Over?" in Brandweek (Vol. 49, April 21, 2008, No. 16, pp. 16)*
Pub: VNU Business Media, Inc.
Ed: Eric Newman. **Description:** Crocs, a rubber shoemaker, announced last week that it missed its expected first quarter revenues by 15 percent. The

popular rubber sandals are suffering in sales due to a number of factors including a tougher economic environment, less expensive, knock-off brands, the cold weather delay of the spring season and fading consumer interest in plastic shoes.

43172 ■ *"Roundtable: Functional Foods and Treats" in Pet Product News (Vol. 64, December 2010, No. 12, pp. S1)*
Pub: BowTie Inc.
Description: Executives and business owners from the pet supplies industries deliberate on the role of functional foods in the retail sector. Functional foods pertain to foods with specified health benefits. Insight into marketing functional foods and convincing pet owners to make the transition to these products is examined.

43173 ■ *"Rule of the Masses: Reinventing Fashion Via Crowdsourcing" in WWD (Vol. 200, July 26, 2010, No. 17, pp. 1)*
Pub: Conde Nast Publications
Contact: David Carey, President
Ed: Cate T. Corcoran. **Description:** Large apparel brands and retailers are crowdsourcing as a way to increase customer loyalty and to build their businesses.

43174 ■ *"Sears' Profit Result Puts Ball in Parent's Court" in Globe & Mail (February 3, 2006, pp. B4)*
Pub: CTVglobemedia Publishing Inc.
Ed: Marina Strauss. **Description:** Sears Canada Inc. achieved $783.4 million in profits for fourth quarter 2005. The financial performance of the company paves way for the acquisition of Sears Holdings Corp.

43175 ■ *"Secrets To Trade Show Success" in Women Entrepreneur (September 12, 2008)*
Pub: Entrepreneur Media Inc.
Ed: Lesley Spencer Pyle. **Description:** Trade shows require an enormous amount of work, but they are an investment that can pay off handsomely because they allow a business to get their product or service in front of their target market. Advice regarding trade shows is given including selecting the correct venue, researching the affair and following up on leads obtained at the event.

43176 ■ *Selling Online: Canada's Bestselling Guide to Becoming a Successful E-Commerce Merchant*
Pub: John Wiley and Sons Canada Ltd.
Ed: Jim Carroll; Rick Broadhead. **Released:** September 6, 2002. **Description:** Helps individuals build online retail enterprises; this updated version includes current tools, information and success strategies, how to launch an online storefront, security, marketing strategies, and mistakes to avoid.

43177 ■ *"Sheets Makers Optimistic Amid Price, Delivery Issues" in Home Textiles Today (Vol. 31, May 24, 2011, No. 13, pp. 8)*
Pub: Reed Business Information
Contact: Jeff Greisch, President
Ed: Jill Rowen. **Description:** Retail sales of sheets and pillowcases dropped 4.7 percent in volume in 2009. Retailers pulled back inventory significantly in 2010. Statistical data included.

43178 ■ *"Shopped Out; Retailing Gloom" in The Economist (Vol. 390, January 3, 2009, No. 8612, pp. 26)*
Pub: The Economist Newspaper Inc.
Description: Economic volatility in the retail sector is having an impact on a number of countries around the globe. Europe is experiencing hard economic times as well and unless businesses have a strong business plan banks feel unable to lend the money necessary to tide the retailers over. The falling pound has increased the cost of imported goods and small to midsize retail chains may not be able to weather such an unforgiving economic climate.

43179 ■ *"Shoppers Targets an Upscale Move" in Globe & Mail (January 19, 2007, pp. B4)*
Pub: CTVglobemedia Publishing Inc.
Ed: Marina Strauss. **Description:** Shoppers Drug Mart Corp.'s plan to boost sales of cosmetics and take up global sourcing to offer new products is discussed.

43180 ■ *"Shoppes of Kenwood Files Chap. 11" in Business Courier (Vol. 26, December 18, 2009, No. 34, pp. 1)*
Pub: American City Business Journals, Inc.
Ed: Jon Newberry. **Description:** Shoppes of Kenwood filed for Chapter 11 reorganization in US Bankruptcy Court just as the property was scheduled to be offered at a sheriff's auction. Details of the filing are included.

43181 ■ *"Shopping Around for New Ideas" in Canadian Business (Vol. 79, July 17, 2006, No. 14-15, pp. 76)*
Pub: Rogers Media
Description: Pensions should be a win-win situation for both the employer and the employee. The perspective of both parties concerning pension plans is explored as well as the need to amend laws in order to make sure that one class of merchant does not suffer at the cost of another.

43182 ■ *"Silver Springs Creamery Opens Retail" in Bellingham Business Journal (Vol. March 2010, pp. 3)*
Pub: Sound Publishing Inc.
Description: Eric Sundstrom, owner of Silver Springs Creamery, announced the opening of its on-site retail store that will sell the farm's goat and cow cheese, yogurt, ice cream and flesh milk.

43183 ■ *"Six Sears Board Members to Resign in April" in Globe & Mail (March 1, 2006, pp. B1)*
Pub: CTVglobemedia Publishing Inc.
Ed: Marina Strauss. **Description:** The reasons behind the departure of six board members of Sears Canada Inc. are presented.

43184 ■ *"The Sky's the Limit" in Retail Merchandiser (Vol. 51, July-August 2011, No. 4, pp. 64)*
Pub: Phoenix Media Corporation
Ed: John Capizzi. **Description:** Mars Retail Group (MRG) is the licensing division handling M&M's Brand Candies. Since taking over the brand they have expanded from 12 licensees to 50 licensees with new offerings.

43185 ■ *"Small Business Sales" in Small Business Economic Trends (April 2008, pp. 7)*
Pub: National Federation of Independent Business
Ed: William C. Dunkelberg, Holly Wade. **Description:** Two tables and a graph resenting sales figures of small businesses in the U.S. is presented. Statistics for sales changes and sales expectations are provided. The figures in the graph include data from 1986 to 2008.

43186 ■ *"Small Business Sales" in Small Business Economic Trends (March 2008, pp. 7)*
Pub: National Federation of Independent Business
Ed: William C. Dunkelberg, Holly Wade. **Description:** Two tables and a graph that present sales figures for small businesses in the U.S. are given. Statistics for sales changes and sales expectations are provided. The figures in the graph include data from 1986 to 2008.

43187 ■ *"Small Business Sales" in Small Business Economic Trends (February, pp. 7)*
Pub: National Federation of Independent Business
Ed: William C. Dunkelberg, Holly Wade. **Description:** Two tables and a graph that present sales figures for small businesses in the U.S. are given. Statistics for sales changes and sales expectations are provided. The figures in the graph include data from 1974 to 2008.

43188 ■ *"Small Business Sales" in Small Business Economic Trends (January, pp. 7)*
Pub: National Federation of Independent Business
Description: Graph from a survey of small businesses in the U.S. is given, representing sales from January 1986 to December 2007. Actual sales (prior three months) and expected sales (next three months) were compared in the graph. Tables of actual sales changes and sales expectations from January 2002 to December 2007 are also given.

43189 ■ *"Small Fish, Big Box Stores" in Hawaii Business (Vol. 53, November 2007, No. 5, pp. 55)*
Pub: Hawaii Business Publishing
Ed: Jolyn Okimoto Rosa. **Description:** Ohana Seafoods can be found at big-box stores such as Costco, Marukai and Don Quijote. Owner Jeffrey Yee spends his weekend at a farmers market to have direct contact with his customers and get feedback right away. Ohana offers ready-to cook fish products, sauces and fish.

43190 ■ *"Smarts Drive Sales" in Pet Product News (Vol. 64, December 2010, No. 12, pp. 1)*
Pub: BowTie Inc.
Ed: Karen Shugart. **Description:** Retailers could make smart decisions by deciding how to best attract customers into their stores or resolving whether to nurture in-store or buy herps (reptiles) from suppliers. Paying attention to these smart decisions could help boost customer interest in herps and address customer demands.

43191 ■ *"Smoke Signals: Johnny Drake On What To Expect In a Fine Cigar" in Black Enterprise (Vol. 38, December 2007, No. 5, pp. 195)*
Pub: Earl G. Graves Publishing Co. Inc.
Ed: Alan Hughes. **Description:** Profile of Johnny Drake, co-owner of the retail tobacco company Renaissance Cigar Emporium. According to the Retail Tobacco Dealers of America, 320 million handmade cigars are sold in the U.S. annually.

43192 ■ *"Some Atlantic Beach Leaders Leery About Convenience Store Safety Measure" in Florida Times-Union (November 3, 2010)*
Pub: Florida Times-Union
Ed: Drew Dixon. **Description:** Jacksonville, Florida authorities are proposing a new ordinance that would require convenience stores to upgrade safety measures to protect store workers and customers from robbery and other crimes.

43193 ■ *"Staples Advantage Receives NJPA National Contract for Janitorial Supplies" in Professional Services Close-Up (April 22, 2011)*
Pub: Close-Up Media
Description: Staples Advantage, the business-to-business division of Staples Inc. was awarded a contract for janitorial supplies to members of the National Joint Powers Alliance (NJPA). NJPA is a member-owned buying cooperative serving public and private schools, state and local governments, and nonprofit organizations.

43194 ■ *"The State of the Stores" in Playthings (Vol. 106, November 1, 2008, No. 10, pp. 8)*
Pub: Reed Business Information
Contact: Jeff Greisch, President
Ed: Dana French. **Description:** Investigation into the top twenty-five toy and game retailers shows that video games and related handheld and console systems as well as computer games were number one with America's children in 2007.

43195 ■ *"Staying Power" in Canadian Business (Vol. 79, November 6, 2006, No. 22, pp. 73)*
Pub: Rogers Media
Ed: John Gray. **Description:** The effects on brand image on customer choices are analyzed. The need of maintaining brand image is also emphasized.

43196 ■ *"Steady Spending in Retail" in Business Week (September 22, 2008, No. 4100, pp. 13)*
Pub: McGraw-Hill Companies, Inc.
Ed: Tara Kalwarski. **Description:** Retail jobs have begun to decline on the national level despite the two percent growth in the industry over the last year; much of the growth has been attributed to the sales of higher-priced oil products.

43197 ■ *"Storm Takes Toll On Area Businesses" in The Business Journal - Serving Phoenix and the Valley of the Sun*

(Vol. 28, September 5, 2008, No. 52, pp. 1)
Pub: American City Business Journals, Inc.

Ed: Chris Casacchia. **Description:** Many small businesses in Phoenix, Arizona have lost sales and goods from storms and power outages. Retailers were forced to dispose of spoiled products. Details of damages inflicted by the storm are also presented.

43198 ■ *"Studies Mixed on State's 2008 Retail Outlook" in Crain's Detroit Business (Vol. 24, March 24, 2008, No. 12, pp. 28)*
Pub: Crain Communications, Inc.

Ed: Nancy Kaffer. **Description:** Marcus and Millichap Real Estate Investment Services and the Michigan Retailers Association have released two separate studies concerning Michigan retailers in 2008. According to its report, MRA is forecasting modest retail growth later this year; however, the study conducted by national commercial real estate brokers Marcus and Millichap predicts increasing vacancy rates, flat employment and decreasing sales for Detroit-area retailers.

43199 ■ *"Study: New Moms Build A Lot of Brand Buzz" in Brandweek (Vol. 49, April 21, 2008, No. 16, pp. 7)*
Pub: VNU Business Media, Inc.

Description: According to a new survey which sampled 1,721 pregnant women and new moms, this demographic is having 109 word-of-mouth conversations per week concerning products, services and brands. Two-thirds of these conversations directly involve brand recommendations. The Internet is driving these word-of-mouth, or W-O-M, conversations among this segment, beating out magazines, television and other forms of media.

43200 ■ *"Suited for Success" in Retail Merchandiser (Vol. 51, July-August 2011, No. 4, pp. 6)*
Pub: Phoenix Media Corporation

Description: MyBestFit is a size-matching body scanner that helps consumers find the perfect size clothing for themselves, giving brick and mortar retailers an edge on ecommerce competitors.

43201 ■ *"SunBank Plans Expansion Via Wall-Mart" in Business Journal-Serving Phoenix and the Valley of the Sun (Vol. 10, November 9, 2007)*
Pub: American City Business School Journals, Inc.

Ed: Chris Casacchia. **Description:** SunBank plans to install 12 to 14 branches in Wal-Mart stores in Arizona and hire 100 bankers by the end of 2008. Wal-Mart also offers financial products at other stores through partnerships with other banks.

43202 ■ *"Sunbrella Engages Consumers Via Social Media" in Home Textiles Today (Vol. 31, May 24, 2011, No. 13, pp. 4)*
Pub: Reed Business Information
Contact: Jeff Greisch, President

Description: Performance fabric brand Sunbrella is marketing to social media, such as Facebook and Twitter, in order to boost consumer interest and retailer support.

43203 ■ *"The Sure Thing That Flopped" in Harvard Business Review (Vol. 86, July-August 2008, No. 8, pp. 29)*
Pub: Harvard Business School Press

Ed: Gerald Zaltman; Lindsay Zaltman. **Description:** Fictitious brand extension scenario is presented, with contributors providing suggestions and advice. The company's struggles with expanding the brand may be alleviated by improving consumer research, focusing on emotional responses to products and services.

43204 ■ *"Surplus Store Rebuilding Again" in Spokesman-Review (November 17, 2010)*
Pub: Spokesman Review

Ed: Chelsea Bannach. **Description:** Retail business owner, David Arnold Sr., is rebuilding his Army Surplus store in Spokane, Washington after a truck crashed into the building.

43205 ■ *"Survey Says Commercial Real Estate Headed for Turbulence" in Commercial Property News (March 17, 2008)*
Pub: Nielsen Company

Description: Commercial real estate sector is declining due to the sluggish U.S. economy. According to a recent survey, national office, retail and hospitality markets are also on the decline.

43206 ■ *"Survival Guide: There Can Be an Upside to Managing a Downturn" in Canadian Business (Vol. 81, November 10, 2008, No. 19, pp. 54)*
Pub: Rogers Media Ltd.

Ed: Sharda Prashad. **Description:** Canada-based Foxy is already limiting its exposure to retailers who could be a credit problem in case of recession. Retirement Life Communities is entering into fixed-rate and fixed-term loans for them to have sufficient financing to grow. Business owners need to realize that customers want more for less.

43207 ■ *"Sustaining Health" in Pet Product News (Vol. 64, November 2010, No. 11, pp. 28)*
Pub: BowTie Inc.

Ed: Angela Pham. **Description:** How pet supply retailers have responded to dog owners' interest in health supplements and their ingredients is discussed. Dog owners are showing interest in the ingredients inside the supplements and are reading labels. Retailers must now prove the beneficial effects of these ingredients in order to make the sale.

43208 ■ *"Sustaining Supply" in Crain's Cleveland Business (Vol. 28, November 19, 2007, No. 46, pp. 3)*
Pub: Crain Communications, Inc.

Ed: David Bennett. **Description:** Local firms are playing key roles in preparing Wal-Mart suppliers to develop sustainable, or ecologically conscious, packaging. New products such as the innovative 'eco-bottle' - a collapsed container made of recyclable plastic that will expand to its traditional size and shape once water is added and would transform to such items as window cleaner when the water mixes with the container's dry contents - are being designed by firms such as Nottingham Spirk.

43209 ■ *"Take 'Em Out of the Ball Game" in Canadian Business (Vol. 79, November 20, 2006, No. 23, pp. 19)*
Pub: Rogers Media

Ed: Andy Holloway. **Description:** Strategies adopted by retailers to retain profitable customers are discussed.

43210 ■ *"Tapping the 'Well' in Wellness" in Pet Product News (Vol. 64, November 2010, No. 11, pp. 1)*
Pub: BowTie Inc.

Ed: Wendy-Bedwell Wilson. **Description:** Healthy food and treats are among the leading wellness products being sought by customers from specialty retailers to keep their pets healthy. With this demand for pet wellness products, retailers suggest making sure that staff know key ingredients to emphasize to customers. Other insights into this trend and ways to engage customers are discussed.

43211 ■ *"Target Gets Exclusive with Ben & Jerry's" in Ice Cream Reporter (Vol. 23, July 20, 2010, No. 8, pp. 1)*
Pub: Ice Cream Reporter

Description: Target Corporation will launch two new Ben & Jerry's ice cream flavors at its retail stores in 49 states. The new ice cream flavors will be available in mini cups and pints and are called Berry Voluntary and Brownie Chew Gooder.

43212 ■ *"Tax-Free Zones Need Shows; Out-of-State Shoppers Are Key To Success" in Crain's Detroit Business (Vol. 24, January 28, 2008, No. 4)*
Pub: Crain Communications Inc. - Detroit

Ed: Daniel Duggan. **Description:** Sales tax-free zones are being considered by Michigan's legislators in order to promote the state as a conference destination.

43213 ■ *"Teachable Moments: Worth Every Penny" in Pet Product News (Vol. 64, December 2010, No. 12, pp. 34)*
Pub: BowTie Inc.

Ed: Cheryl Reeves. **Description:** Pet bird retailers can attain both outreach to customers and enhanced profitability by staging educational events such as the annual Parrot Palooza event of Burlington, New Jersey-based Bird Paradise. Aside from attracting a global audience, Parrot Palooza features seminars, workshops, classes, and bird-related contests.

43214 ■ *"Things Really Clicking for Macy's Online" in Business Courier (Vol. 24, November 30, 2008, No. 33, pp. 1)*
Pub: American City Business Journals, Inc.

Ed: Lisa Biank Fasig. **Description:** Retailer Macy's online division Macys.com are projecting sales at $1billion in 2007, compared to $620 million in 2006. Macy's new online features and products and the growth of online retail sector are also discussed.

43215 ■ *"Three Trails Blazes Tax Credit Deal" in The Business Journal-Serving Metropolitan Kansas City (Vol. 27, November 7, 2008, No. 9)*
Pub: American City Business Journals, Inc.

Ed: Rob Roberts. **Description:** Three Trails Redevelopment LLC plans to redevelop the Bannister Mall area. The Missouri Development Finance Board is expected to approve $30 million in tax credits for the project. A verbal agreement on the terms and conditions has already been reached according to the agency's executive director.

43216 ■ *"To Be Seen Is to Be Successful" in Pet Product News (Vol. 64, December 2010, No. 12, pp. 12)*
Pub: BowTie Inc.

Ed: David Arvin. **Description:** Guidelines on how pet business retailers can boost customer visibility are described considering that complacency could hamper retailers' efforts to effectively market their businesses. To enhance customer base and stand out from competing businesses, being different, strategic, creative, and differentiated is emphasized.

43217 ■ *"Too Much too Soon" in Barron's (Vol. 89, July 27, 2009, No. 30, pp. 33)*
Pub: Dow Jones & Co., Inc.

Ed: Leslie P. Norton. **Description:** Shares of hhgregg have risen 85 percent in the year leading up to July 2009 and analysts believe the stock could hit 25. However, their 113 outlets are concentrated in states where unemployment is above 10 percent and expanding into areas already overstored. Competition is also rife and credit availability is still tight.

43218 ■ *"Tough Climate for Nurseries" in Crain's Cleveland Business (Vol. 30, June 29, 2009, No. 25, pp. 1)*
Pub: Crain Communications, Inc.

Ed: Stan Bullard. **Description:** After 81 years in the business, Sunnybrook Farms & Nursery is closing its doors. The owner sites the bad economy along with cold weather the reason for lack of sales. Other nursery owners discuss the bad economy and weather conditions and how they are affecting their business.

43219 ■ *"Tough-Love Boss at BMO Demands Retail Turnaround" in Globe & Mail (March 2, 2007, pp. B13)*
Pub: CTVglobemedia Publishing Inc.

Ed: Andrew Willis. **Description:** William Downe, the newly appointed chief executive of Bank of Montreal (BMO), discusses strategies to improve the number of retail customers. The BMO reported $292 million profits in the first quarter of 2007.

43220 ■ *"Tower City Hopes Restrictions on Minors Boost Retail Center" in Crain's Cleveland Business (Vol. 28, November 5, 2007, No. 44)*
Pub: Crain Communications, Inc.

Ed: John Booth. **Description:** Tower City Center, a shopping mall in downtown Cleveland, hopes to generate more business with their new rules restricting the access of unaccompanied minors after 2:30 p.m.

43221 ■ *"Toy Story: U.S.-Made a Hot Seller" in Crain's Detroit Business (Vol. 23, December 17, 2007, No. 51, pp. 3)*
Pub: Crain Communications Inc. - Detroit
Ed: Chad Halcom. **Description:** American Plastic Toys, located in Walled Lake, Michigan reports all its toys are made in the U.S. and have passed all U.S. safety standards. Revenue for American Plastic Toys reached nearly $33 million in 2005, and the company expects to exceed that because of recent toy safety recalls of products produced in China.

43222 ■ *"Tradeshow Attendance Incentives Add Up" in Pet Product News (Vol. 64, December 2010, No. 12, pp. 14)*
Pub: BowTie Inc.
Ed: Mark E. Battersby. **Description:** Pointers on how pet specialty retailers can claim business travel tax and income tax deductions for expenses paid or incurred in participation at tradeshows, conventions, and meetings are presented. Incentives in form of these deductions could allow pet specialty retailers to gain business benefits, aside from the education and enjoyment involved with the travel.

43223 ■ *Treasure Hunt*
Pub: Penguin Group Incorporated
Ed: Michael J. Silverstein; John Butman. **Released:** May 4, 2006. **Description:** Explanation of people's spending habits and how to capitalize on retail sales.

43224 ■ *"The Trouble With $150,000 Wine" in Barron's (Vol. 88, July 7, 2008, No. 27, pp. 33)*
Pub: Dow Jones & Co., Inc.
Ed: Orley Ashenfelter. **Description:** Review of the book, 'The Billionaire's Vinegar: The Mystery of the World's Most Expensive Bottle of Wine,' which discusses vintners along with the marketing and distribution of wine as well as the winemaking industry as a whole.

43225 ■ *"Turmoil Means Changes For Retailers" in The Business Journal-Serving Metropolitan Kansas City (Vol. 27, October 10, 2008, No. 4)*
Pub: American City Business Journals, Inc.
Ed: Suzanna Stagemeyer. **Description:** Impacts of the financial crisis on Kansas Metropolitan Area retailers are varied. Rob Dalzell, for instance, found it difficult to secure a loan for his new self-serve yogurt store Yummo. The trends in retailing in the area are examined further as well as ways in which local businesses are changing in an attempt to stay solvent during the economic downturn.

43226 ■ *"Turning Trust Into Success" in Retail Merchandiser (Vol. 51, July-August 2011, No. 4, pp. 52)*
Pub: Phoenix Media Corporation
Ed: Karen Kondilis. **Description:** Shopko Stores employs tenured and trustworthy pharmacists and believes it is the core to their success.

43227 ■ *"The Twittering Class" in Entrepreneur (Vol. 37, September 2009, No. 9, pp. 40)*
Pub: Entrepreneur Media, Inc.
Ed: Mikal E. Belicove. **Description:** Advice on how entrepreneurs can use online social networks to promote their businesses is presented. Facebook offers applications and advertising solutions to promote Websites, products and services. Twitter, on the other hand, provides instant messaging, which can be done through computer or cell phone.

43228 ■ *"U.S. Retailer Eyes 'Tween' Market" in Globe & Mail (January 30, 2007, pp. B1)*
Pub: CTVglobemedia Publishing Inc.
Ed: Marina Strauss. **Description:** The decision of Tween Brands Inc. (Too Incorporated) to open 100 new stores in Canada as part of its expansion is discussed. The company's focus on targeting girls for its products is detailed.

43229 ■ *"U.S. Savvy Helps Fuel TD's Fortunes" in Globe & Mail (February 23, 2007, pp. B1)*
Pub: CTVglobemedia Publishing Inc.
Ed: Andrew Willis; Tavia Grant. **Description:** The rise in the revenues of Toronto-Dominion Bank due to its acquisition of American financial service providers and the rise in its domestic retail banking revenues are disussed.

43230 ■ *Up the Loyalty Ladder*
Pub: HarperCollins Publishers Inc.
Ed: Murray Rephel; Neil Raphel. **Released:** September 1996. **Description:** Marketing consultants share insight into growing any retail business and gain customer loyalty.

43231 ■ *"Uptick in Clicks: Nordstrom's Online Sales Surging" in Puget Sound Business Journal (Vol. 29, August 22, 2008, No. 18, pp. 1)*
Pub: American City Business Journals
Ed: Gregg Lamm. **Description:** Nordstrom Inc.'s online division grew its sales by 15 percent in the second quarter of 2008, compared to 2007's 4.3 percent in overall decline. The company expects their online net sales to reach $700 million in 2008 capturing eight percent of overall sales.

43232 ■ *"US Cavalry Store" in Retail Merchandiser (Vol. 51, September-October 2011, No. 5, pp. 70)*
Pub: Phoenix Media Corporation
Description: US Cavalry Store serves enlisted military members. The store has launched a newly upgraded Website and has expanded its distribution center.

43233 ■ *"VeriFone Announces Global Security Solutions Business" in Marketing Weekly News (October 3, 2009)*
Pub: Investment Weekly News
Description: Focused on delivering innovative security solutions, VeriFone Holdings, Inc. announced the formation of its Global Security Solutions Business Unit, including VeriShield Protect, an end-to-end encryption to protect cardholder data throughout the merchant and processor systems. The business will focus on consulting, sales and implementation of these new products in order to help retailers and processors protect customer data.

43234 ■ *"Wal-Mart Doesn't Sell Council" in The Business Journal-Serving Metropolitan Kansas City (Vol. 26, July 4, 2008, No. 43, pp. 1)*
Pub: American City Business Journals, Inc.
Ed: Steve Vockrodt. **Description:** Wal-Mart Stores Inc. announced that it will move the location of its annual convention from Kansas City, Missouri to Orlando, Florida. The change of venue came after Rick Hughes, Kansas City Convention and Visitors Association president rejected Wal-Mart's proposal to subsidize a new hotel in the downtown area that is needed for the event.

43235 ■ *"'Wal-Mart Effect' Feeds Grocer Price Wars" in Globe & Mail (March 15, 2007, pp. B14)*
Pub: CTVglobemedia Publishing Inc.
Ed: Marina Strauss. **Description:** The decrease in profit reports by Canadian grocery giants amidst high expansion plans by Wal-Mart Stores Inc. are discussed. This industry is witnessing the most severe pricing competitions in recent times.

43236 ■ *"Wal-Mart Expansion Plans Hit Roadblock" in Crain's Chicago Business (Vol. 31, March 24, 2008, No. 12, pp. 2)*
Pub: Crain Communications, Inc.
Ed: Monee Fields-White. **Description:** Wal-Mart Stores Inc.'s expansion plans in Chicago have suffered a series of setbacks due to a shifting political landscape in which may require the company to pay higher wages. Wal-Mart claims that its hourly pay and benefits are fair; however, the labor force does not agree.

43237 ■ *"Wal-Mart Proposed for Timmerman Plaza" in Business Journal-Milwaukee (Vol. 28, December 31, 2010, No. 14, pp. A1)*
Pub: Milwaukee Business Journal
Ed: Sean Ryan. **Description:** Dickson, Tennessee-based Gatlin Development Company Inc. owner Franklin C. Gatlin III revealed plans for a new Wal-Mart store in Timmerman Plaza in Milwaukee, Wisconsin. Wal-Mart plans to open up approximately 18 new stores in southeast Wisconsin in 2012 and the Timmerman project is the first of four that Gatlin will submit for city approval.

43238 ■ *"Wal-Mart Relaunches Private Brand, Reimagines Stores Layout" in Marketing to Women (Vol. 22, July 2009, No. 7, pp. 5)*
Pub: EPM Communications Inc.
Contact: Ira Mayer, President
E-mail: imayer@epmcom.com
Description: Wal-Mart is focusing its strategies by centering on new store layouts that they believe will match their new branding of 'fast, friendly, and clean' and enable mothers to 'just get on with what they need to do.'.

43239 ■ *"Wal-Mart Sharpens Focus on Roxbury" in Boston Business Journal (Vol. 31, July 8, 2011, No. 24, pp. 1)*
Pub: Boston Business Journal
Ed: Mary Moore. **Description:** Wal-Mart Stores is boosting its search for a possible location in the Roxbury section of Boston, Massachusetts. The search is focused on underserved communities in terms of jobs and access to reasonably-priced merchandise. The extent Boston's African American community has clashed with Mayor Thomas M. Memino over the accommodations of the retailer in Roxbury is discussed.

43240 ■ *"Wal-Mart Takes Expansion Up a Notch" in Globe & Mail (March 21, 2007, pp. B8)*
Pub: CTVglobemedia Publishing Inc.
Ed: Shirley Won. **Description:** Retail giant Wal-Mart Canada Corp. is planning to invest $500 million for expanding its business in Ontario region. It will open 21 new outlets by the end of 2007.

43241 ■ *"Walmart, Target Moving to Convenience Store Near You" in Hardware Retailing (Vol. 199, November 2010, No. 5, pp. 60)*
Pub: North American Retail Hardware Association
Contact: Mike O'Hara, President
Description: Walmart has plans to move into small convenience stores in Chicago, Detroit, San Francisco, and Los Angeles.

43242 ■ *"Want Leverage? Multi-Unit Franchisees Deliver Substantial Savings" in Franchising World (Vol. 42, October 2010, No. 10, pp. 39)*
Pub: International Franchise Association
Ed: Aziz Hashim. **Description:** Many retail franchises selling the same product are able to buy in bulk. Volume-buying can save money for any franchise.

43243 ■ *"Wary Investors Turn to a Different Market for Strong Returns" in Boston Business Journal (Vol. 29, September 2, 2011, No. 17, pp. 1)*
Pub: American City Business Journals Inc.
Ed: Daniel J. Sernovitz. **Description:** Maryland-based investors have been choosing to put their money in the supermarket business. Retail property sales have increased during the second quarter of 2011.

43244 ■ *"Wattles Plugs Back Into State" in Business Journal Portland (Vol. 27, November 19, 2010, No. 38, pp. 1)*
Pub: Portland Business Journal
Ed: Wendy Culverwell. **Description:** Denver, Colorado-based Ultimate Electronics Inc.'s first store in Oregon was opened in Portland and the 46th store in the chain of electronic superstores is expected to employ 70-80 workers. The venture is the latest for Mark Wattles, one of Oregon's most successful entrepreneurs, who acquired Ultimate from bankruptcy.

43245 ■ *"Waugh Chapel to Expand" in Baltimore Business Journal (Vol. 28, August 27, 2010, No. 16, pp. 1)*
Pub: Baltimore Business Journal
Ed: Daniel J. Sernovitz. **Description:** Developer Greenberg Gibbons Corporation has broken ground on a $275 million, 1.2 million-square-foot addition to

its Village at the Waugh Chapel mixed-use complex. Aside from creating 2,600 permanent jobs, the addition, named Village South, is expected to lure Target and Wegmans Food Markets to Crofton, Maryland. Funding for this project is discussed.

43246 ■ *"Weaving a Stronger Fabric: Organizing a Global Sweat-Free Apparel Production Agreement" in WorkingUSA (Vol. 11, June 2008, No. 2)*
Pub: Blackwell Publishers Ltd.
Ed: Eric Dirnbach. **Description:** Tens of millions of workers working under terrible sweatshop conditions in the global apparel industry. Workers are employed at apparel contractors and have been largely unsuccessful in organizing and improving their working conditions. The major apparel manufacturers and retailers have the most power in this industry, and they have adopted corporate social responsibility programs as a false solution to the sweatshop problem. The major North American apparel unions dealt with similar sweatshop conditions a century ago by organizing the contractors and brands into joint association contracts that significantly raised standards. Taking inspiration from their example, workers and their anti-sweatshop allies need to work together to coordinate a global organizing effort that builds worker power and establishes a global production agreement that negotiates with both contractors and the brands for improved wages, benefits, and working conditions.

43247 ■ *"Web Sight: Do You See What I See?" in Entrepreneur (Vol. 35, October 2007, No. 10, pp. 58)*
Pub: Entrepreneur Media Inc.
Ed: Heather Clancy. **Description:** Owners of Trunkt, a boutique in New York that showcases independent designs, have created a new style of Website called Trunkt.org. The Website allows buyers to select the products they want to see and designers can choose anytime which of their items will be displayed on the site. An explanation of the strategy that helped bring Trunkt closer to its clients is presented.

43248 ■ *"Website for Women 50 Launches" in Marketing to Women (Vol. 21, April 2008, No. 4, pp. 5)*
Pub: EPM Communications Inc.
Contact: Ira Mayer, President
E-mail: imayer@epmcom.com
Description: Vibrantnation.com is an online community targeting women over age 50; members can share recommendations on a variety of topics such as vacation spots, retailers and financial issues.

43249 ■ *"Wedding Present Shopping - What to Get the Couple Who Have Everything" in Benzinga.com (April 19, 2011)*
Pub: Benzinga.com
Ed: Benzinga Staff. **Description:** Tips for purchasing the perfect wedding gift are outlined.

43250 ■ *"Well-Heeled Startup" in Business Journal Portland (Vol. 27, November 12, 2010, No. 37, pp. 1)*
Pub: Portland Business Journal
Ed: Erik Siemers. **Description:** Oh! Shoes LLC expects to receive about $1.5 million in funding from angel investors, while marketing a new line of high heel shoes that are comfortable, healthy, and attractive. The new line of shoes will use the technology of athletic footwear while having the look of an Italian designer. Oh! Shoes hopes to generate $35 million in sales by 2014.

43251 ■ *"Welsh Meat Sales on the Rise" in Farmer's Weekly (March 28, 2008, No. 320)*
Pub: Reed Business Information
Contact: Jeff Greisch, President
Description: Due, in part, to marketing efforts, retail sales of Welsh lamb and beef rose significantly in the first two months of 2008.

43252 ■ *"What Dead Zone?" in Entrepreneur (Vol. 37, October 2009, No. 10, pp. 128)*
Pub: Entrepreneur Media, Inc.
Ed: Jason Daley. **Description:** Joe Purifico, Halloween Adventure franchises co-owner and chief executive officer, discusses the Halloween superstore phenomenon. Malls allow seasonal leasing for Halloween stores due to the high number of customers these stores attract.

43253 ■ *"What the Future Holds for Consumers" in Black Enterprise (Vol. 41, August 2010, No. 1, pp. 47)*
Pub: Earl G. Graves Publishing Co. Inc.
Ed: Sheiresa Ngo. **Description:** The way people purchase goods and service has changed with technology. With an increased focus on security (as well as privacy and fairness) the U.S. Congress began regulating the credit card industry with the Fair Credit Reporting Act of 1970 and the Credit Card Accountability, Responsibility, and Disclosure (CARD) Act of 2009.

43254 ■ *"What Slump? Davis Likely to Fill Borders Gap Quickly" in Sacramento Business Journal (Vol. 28, July 29, 2011, No. 22, pp. 1)*
Pub: Sacramento Business Journal
Ed: Kelly Johnson. **Description:** The nationwide shutdown of Borders bookstores worry most cities, but not Davis, California, which is experiencing a relatively low retail vacancy rate of 6.3 percent.

43255 ■ *"When Virtue Is A Vice" in Harvard Business Review (Vol. 86, July-August 2008, No. 8, pp. 22)*
Pub: Harvard Business School Press
Ed: Anat Keinan; Ran Kivetz. **Description:** Negative consequences of habitually denying self-indulgence, from work and life balance to consumer shopping behaviors are discussed.

43256 ■ *"White Cat Media Tells You Where to Get a Bargain. Now It's Shopping for $1.5 Million" in Inc. (March 2008, pp. 48)*
Pub: Gruner & Jahr USA Publishing
Ed: Athena Schindelheim. **Description:** Profile of White Cat Media which runs two shopping Websites: SheFinds.com for fashion and beauty items, and MomFinds.com for mothers. The New York City firm reported revenues for 2007 at $400,000 and is looking for funding capital in the amount of $1.7 million.

43257 ■ *"Will mCommerce Make Black Friday Green?" in Retail Merchandiser (Vol. 51, September-October 2011, No. 5, pp. 8)*
Pub: Phoenix Media Corporation
Ed: Scott Miller. **Description:** Retailers speculate the possibilities of mobile commerce and are implementing strategies at their stores. Consumers using mobile devices accounted for only 0.1 percent of visits to retail Websites on Black Friday 2009 and rose to 5.6 percent in 2010; numbers are expected to rise for 2011.

43258 ■ *"Williams-Sonoma Beats Expectations in Q1" in Home Textiles Today (Vol. 31, May 24, 2011, No. 13, pp. 2)*
Pub: Reed Business Information
Contact: Jeff Greisch, President
Description: Both retail nameplates, Williams-Sonoma and Pottery Barn reported gains in 2011's first quarter, accredited to the way shoppers responded to new opening price point programs for several of its brands.

43259 ■ *"The Wine Spectator" in Business Courier (Vol. 27, November 26, 2010, No. 30, pp. 1)*
Pub: Business Courier
Ed: Dan Monk. **Description:** Vintner Select, a wine distributor, will introduce an internationally known portfolio of more than 50 German and Austrian wines. The company now distributes about 900 different wine labels from 220 producers in 10 countries to smaller, independent retailers in Indiana, Kentucky and Ohio.

43260 ■ *"A Wireless Makes 8 Store-In-Store Kiosk Acquisitions" in Wireless News (October 16, 2010)*
Pub: Close-Up Media Inc.
Description: A Wireless, a retailer for Verizon Wireless has acquired eight of Verizon's retail kiosks that are positioned in home appliance and electronics stores.

43261 ■ *"WNY Casing In On Loonie's Climb" in Business First Buffalo (November 23, 2007, pp. 1)*
Pub: American City Business Journals, Inc.
Ed: Scott Thomas. **Description:** Economy of Western New York has rebounded since the 9/11 recession and the rise of the Canadian dollar, which has contributed to the areas economic growth. Canadian shoppers are frequenting markets in the area due to the parity of the U.S. and Canadian dollar. Details of the cross-border shopping and its impact in WNY are discussed.

43262 ■ *"Woes Portend Consumer Shift" in The Business Journal-Serving Metropolitan Kansas City (Vol. 27, September 26, 2008, No. 2, pp. 1)*
Pub: American City Business Journals, Inc.
Ed: Suzanna Stagemeyer. **Description:** Black Bamboo owner Tim Butt believes that prolonged tightening of the credit market will result in consumer spending becoming more cash-driven that credit card driven. The financial crisis has already constricted spending among consumers. Forecasts for the US economy are provided.

43263 ■ *"Women: Send Me An Angel" in Entrepreneur (Vol. 35, October 2007, No. 10, pp. 38)*
Pub: Entrepreneur Media Inc.
Ed: Aliza Sherman. **Description:** Golden Seeds has invested in Enter Artemis Woman LLC when the latter decided to put its products into Wal-Mart. Golden Seeds was formed by angel investors who aim to help women build their own businesses. Tips on how to approach angel investors and getting angel funding are given.

43264 ■ *"Worldwide Food Services (EREI) Tests Mini Dollar Store Program" in Internet Wire (August 6, 2009)*
Pub: Comtex News Network, Inc.
Description: Mini Dollar Stores and Eagle View LLC, wholly-owned subsidiaries of Worldwide Food Services, Inc., recently met with government officials and purchasing agents to lay out a test program which would distribute Mini Dollar Store items into VA hospital gift shops.

43265 ■ *"Young Adult, Childless May Help Fuel Post-Recession Rebound" in Pet Product News (Vol. 64, November 2010, No. 11, pp. 4)*
Pub: BowTie Inc.
Description: Pet industry retailers and marketers are encouraged to tap into the young adult and childless couple sectors to boost consumer traffic and sales to pre-recession levels. Among young adult owners, pet ownership increased from 40 percent in 2003 to 49 percent in 2009. Meanwhile, the childless couple sector represented 63 percent of all dog/cat owners in 2009.

43266 ■ *"Zebra's Changing Stripes" in Crain's Chicago Business (Vol. 31, November 17, 2008, No. 46, pp. 4)*
Pub: Crain Communications, Inc.
Ed: John Pletz. **Description:** Zebra Technologies Corp., the world's largest manufacturer of bar-code printers is profiled; the company's stock has plunged with shares declining 40 percent in the past three months grinding the firm's growth to a halt. Zebra's plans to regain revenue growth are also discussed.

43267 ■ *"Zeon Solutions Teams with Endeca for SaaS Version of Endeca InFront" in Entertainment Close-Up (October 25, 2011)*
Pub: Close-Up Media
Description: Zeon Solutions, an enterprise e-commerce and Website development firm announced a special licensing partnership with Endecca Technologies. Endeca is an information management software company that provides small and mid-size retailers with high-performance Customer Experience Management technology.

43268 ■ *"Zucker Closes Deal on HBC With Sweeter Takeover Offer" in Globe & Mail*

(January 27, 2006, pp. B1)
Pub: CTVglobemedia Publishing Inc.

Ed: Marina Strauss; Sinclair Stewart; Jacquie McNish. **Description:** Jerry Zucker, vice-president of InterTech Group Inc., has finalized a deal to buy retail store Hudson Bay Co, for 1.1 billion dollars. The shares will be purchased at a rate of 15.25 dollars per share in an all cash transaction. Complete details of the buyout are discussed.

STATISTICAL SOURCES

43269 ■ *RMA Annual Statement Studies*
Pub: Risk Management Association
Contact: Kevin M. Blakey, President

Released: Annual. **Price:** $175.00 2006-07 edition, $105.00. **Description:** Contains composite balance sheets and income statements for more than 360 industries, including the accounting, auditing, and bookkeeping industries. Also contains five years of comparative historical data for discerning trends. Includes 16 commonly used ratios, computed for most of the size groupings for nearly every industry.

43270 ■ *Value Retailing in the 1990s: Off-Pricers, Factory Outlets, and Closeout*
Pub: John Wiley & Sons, Inc.

Released: 1994. **Price:** $425.00 (Print on Demand). **Description:** Published by Packaged StoresCloseout Stores Facts. Examines off-price stores and manufacturers' outlets, covering market size and growth, competition, industry trends, and consumers. Also includes profiles of value retailers and regional outlet mall developers.

TRADE PERIODICALS

43271 ■ *Barnard's Retail Trend Report*
Pub: Barnard Enterprises Inc.
Contact: Kurt Barnard, Editor
E-mail: kbarnard@retailtrends.com

Released: Bimonthly. **Price:** $179; $199, other countries; $45, single issue. **Description:** Forecasts predictions, analyzes, explains, and identifies trends and events affecting retail operations. Recurring features include market statistics and news of research.

43272 ■ *Loeb Retail Letter*
Pub: Loeb Associates Inc.

Ed: Walter F. Loeb, Editor, loeb@idt.net. **Released:** 11/year. **Price:** $300, U.S.; $325, Canada; $350, elsewhere. **Description:** Publishes articles on the retail industry. Recurring features include news of research.

43273 ■ *NSSRA Newsletter*
Pub: National Ski and Snowboard Retailers Association
Contact: Thomas B. Doyle, President
E-mail: tdoyle@nssra.com

Released: Quarterly. **Price:** Included in membership. **Description:** Informs ski and snowboard retail stores on critical industry issues such as guidelines and litigation exposure and marketing.

43274 ■ *Retail Info Systems News: Fusing Technology Solutions to Corporate Vision*
Pub: Edgell Communications Inc.
Contact: Gerald C. Ryerson, President
E-mail: gryerson@edgellmail.com

URL(s): risnews.edgl.com/homewww.edgellcommunications.com/print.html. **Ed:** Adam Blair. **Released:** Monthly **Price:** Free to qualified professionals.

43275 ■ *Retailing Today*
Pub: Lebhar-Friedman Inc.

Ed: Tim Craig, Editor. **Released:** Biweekly. **Price:** $229, U.S.; $350, elsewhere. **Description:** Provides up-to-date information on what is happening in the retail industry and how current economic conditions affect retailing. Summarizes actions, acquisitions, and policies of major retail chains across the U.S. Discusses problems facing retail operations, i.e., shoplifting and retaining customer loyalty.

43276 ■ *Western-English Industry Report*
Pub: Western English Retailers Association
Contact: Susan Leach, Executive Editor

Released: Bimonthly. **Price:** $29. **Description:** Disseminates information on trends, markets, business techniques, and issues on the nation's retailers of Western and English apparel, tack, and equipment.

VIDEOCASSETTES/ AUDIOCASSETTES

43277 ■ *Beware the Naked Man Who Offers You His Shirt*
PBS Home Video
Catalog Fulfillment Center
Charlotte, NC 28275-1089
Ph: (800)531-4727
Free: 800-645-4PBS
Co. E-mail: info@pbs.org
URL: http://www.pbs.org

Released: 1990. **Price:** $395.00. **Description:** The author of "Swim With the Sharks Without Being Eaten Alive" offers insights and advice on increasing sales productivity. **Availability:** VHS; 3/4 U.

43278 ■ *Shoplifting Prevented*
American Media, Inc.
4621 121st St.
Urbandale, IA 50323-2311
Ph: (515)224-0919
Free: 888-776-8268
Fax: (515)327-2555
Co. E-mail: custsvc@ammedia.com
URL: http://www.ammedia.com

Released: 1988. **Price:** $450.00. **Description:** Employees are shown some simple things they can do to keep their store from getting ripped off. **Availability:** VHS; 3/4 U.

TRADE SHOWS AND CONVENTIONS

43279 ■ EuroShop - Global Retail Trade Fair
Messe Dusseldorf North America—MDNA
150 N. Michigan Ave., Ste. 2920
Chicago, IL 60601
Ph: (312)781-5180
Fax: (312)781-5188
Co. E-mail: info@mdna.com
URL: http://www.mdna.com

URL(s): www.euroshop.de. **Frequency:** Triennial. **Principal Exhibits:** International trade fair for retail information, communications and security technology. **Telecommunication Services:** euroshop@messe-duesseldorf.de.

CONSULTANTS

43280 ■ G.G.W. and Associates
1213 Hampton Dr.
Jackson, MI 49203-5004
Ph: (517)782-2255
Fax: (517)784-1256
Contact: Gerard G. Wood, President

Scope: Consultants to retail businesses with services that include profit and loss strategy, business planning short or long term, marketing strategies, market survey analysis, advertising budget, merchandise control systems and effective internal security and employee communications programs. Serves private industries as well as government agencies. **Founded:** 1985. **Seminars:** Retraining for the 90's; How to Start and Manage a Small Business.

43281 ■ Gordian Concepts & Solutions
16 Blueberry Ln.
Lincoln, MA 01773
Ph: (617)259-8341
Contact: Stephen R. Low, President

Scope: Engineering and management consultancy offering general, financial, and valuation services, civil and tax litigation support. Assists clients in entering new businesses, planning new products and services, and evaluating feasibility. Targets industrial concerns engaged in manufacturing, assembly, warehousing, energy production, process systems and biotechnology, steel, paper, and electronics. Serves businesses such as retailing, financial services, health care, satellite broadcasting and cable television, outdoor advertising and professional practices. **Founded:** 1990. **Publications:** "Establishing Rural Cellular Company Values," Cellular Business.

43282 ■ Stan Knipe & Associates
3176 Silver Sands Cir.
Virginia Beach, VA 23451-1185
Ph: (757)496-5475
Fax: (757)560-7631
Co. E-mail: sknipe3566@aol.com
Contact: Stan W. Knipe, President

Scope: Specializes in retail management, strategic and organizational planning and operations, and consumer repair service. **Founded:** 1992. **Seminars:** Leadership and management development.

43283 ■ Kurt Salmon Associates Inc.—Kurt Salmon AssociatesSalmon (Kurt) Assoc;
1355 Peachtree St. NE, Ste. 900
Atlanta, GA 30309-3257
Ph: (404)892-0321
Fax: (404)872-7271
Co. E-mail: infoksaweb@kurtsalmon.com
URL: http://www.kurtsalmon.com
Contact: William B. Pace, President

URL(s): www.mcgplc.com. **Scope:** Offers retail consulting services for retailers and consumer products makers in strategic planning, product development and sourcing, merchandising and planning, supply chain services, store operations services, customer experience, information technology and private equity. Health care consulting services include strategy setting; facility development; operational planning and information technology. **Founded:** 1935. **Publications:** "Europe's 2009 Global Sourcing Reference"; "The Three Stages of Retail PLM Adoption"; "Optimizing Your Outsourced Sourcing Strategy"; "Using Strategic Sourcing to Cut Costs"; "Supply Chain Effectiveness"; "Managing the Assortment Lifecycle"; "Managing a Supply Chain of Proprietary Products"; "Creating a Successful Product Development Operation". **Seminars:** Leading the Surf Industry; Time to Talk Turnaround. **Telecommunication Services:** ehford@kurtsalmon.com.

43284 ■ Lougheed Resource Group Inc. (LRG)
17608 Deer Isle Cir.
Winter Garden, FL 34787
Ph: (407)654-1212
Fax: (407)654-5419
Co. E-mail: info@lrgconstruction.com
URL: http://www.lrgconstruction.com
Contact: Karen Lougheed, Owner
E-mail: karen@lrgmanagement.com

Scope: Construction consultants specializing in project strategies, scope preparation, contract negotiation, project management, document and code evaluation, peer reviews, scheduling/estimates, dispute resolution, and forensic analysis expert testimony. **Founded:** 1987.

FRANCHISES AND BUSINESS OPPORTUNITIES

43285 ■ Aarons Sales & Lease Ownership
Aaron's Inc.
309 E Paces Ferry Rd. NE
Atlanta, GA 30305
Ph: (404)231-0011
Free: 877-607-9999
Fax: (404)240-6583
Co. E-mail: IR@aaronrents.com
URL: http://www.aaronrents.com

Description: Furniture, electronics, computer, and appliance leasing and sales. **No. of Franchise Units:** 668. **No. of Company-Owned Units:** 1,272. **Founded:** 1955.. **Franchised:** 1992. **Equity Capital Needed:** $263,870-$692,580. **Franchise Fee:** $15,000-$50,000. **Royalty Fee:** 6%. **Financial Assistance:** Limited third party financing available.

Training: Provides 3 days at headquarters, less than 30 days at franchisee's location and 1 week at regional locations with ongoing support.

43286 ■ Adam & Eve Stores
AEFC, Inc.
302 Meadowland Dr.
Hillsborough, NC 27278
Ph: (800)217-7423
Fax: (919)644-1704
Co. E-mail: franchising@adameve.com
URL: http://www.adameve.com/stores
Description: The adult industry is now offering retail store franchise opportunities. With over 30 years experience and over 4 million customers nationwide, you benefit from the Adam & Eve brand name recognized around the country. **No. of Franchise Units:** 33. **Founded:** 1970. **Franchised:** 2004. **Equity Capital Needed:** $192,000-$345,000; cash $50,000. **Franchise Fee:** $30,000. **Training:** Training and support program will show you everything from planning 'open buys' to buying, working with vendors, merchandise inventory control, and the merchandising and display products in your store. Onsite training prior to opening.

43287 ■ Beehive Co-op LLC
66 Farrington Rd.
Croton-on-Hudson, NY 10520
Ph: (678)429-1418
Fax: (404)929-6695
Description: Retail cooperative for local designers. **No. of Franchise Units:** 1. **No. of Company-Owned Units:** 1. **Founded:** 2004. **Franchised:** 2007. **Equity Capital Needed:** $71,800-$130,750. **Franchise Fee:** $25,000. **Royalty Fee:** 4%. **Training:** 2 days at headquarters, 3 days at franchisee's location and ongoing support.

43288 ■ Brilliant Sky Toys & Books
TT & B, Inc.
5100 Marsh Rd., Ste. D-2
Okemos, MI 48823
Ph: (517)381-1655
Fax: (517)381-1622
Description: Retail, toys, games, and books. **No. of Franchise Units:** 15. **Founded:** 2002.. **Franchised:** 2007. **Equity Capital Needed:** $100,000 liquid, investment. **Franchise Fee:** $35,000. **Training:** Yes.

43289 ■ Buck or Two Plus!
11B Director Court
Vaughan, ON, Canada L4L 4S5
Ph: (905)265-3168
Free: 800-890-8633
Fax: (905)265-3162
Co. E-mail: fburt@extremeretail.ca
URL: http://www.buckortwo.com
Description: Buck or Two is a Canada-wide chain of specialty retail stores offering everyday quality basics with an ever changing mix of seasonable and extreme value products, as well as special deals. **No. of Franchise Units:** 60. **No. of Company-Owned Units:** 1. **Founded:** 1990.. **Franchised:** 1990. **Equity Capital Needed:** $300,000-$600,000 total investment; $75,000-$100,000 start-up capital needed. **Franchise Fee:** $25,000. **Training:** Includes 10 days training.

43290 ■ DirectBuy
8450 Broadway
Merrillville, IN 46410
Ph: (219)641-6480
Free: 800-827-6400
Fax: (219)756-2859
Co. E-mail: franchising@directbuy.com
URL: http://franchise.directbuy.com
Description: DirectBuy is an international leader in providing the best alternative to conventional retail buying. Members of DirectBuy are able to avoid traditional markups and purchase from an unprecedented selection of quality merchandise, direct from manufacturers, at unparalleled prices. **No. of Franchise Units:** 14. **No. of Company-Owned Units:** 1. **Founded:** 1971.. **Franchised:** 1972. **Equity Capital Needed:** $200,000 start-up capital required; $354,000-$800,000 investment required. **Franchise Fee:** $75,000. **Training:** Provides 9 weeks training and support.

43291 ■ Discount Sport Nutrition
Discount Sport Nutrition Franchising, L.P.
7324 Gaston Ave., Ste. 124-422
Dallas, TX 75214
Ph: (972)489-7925
Fax: (214)292-8619
Co. E-mail: franchising@sportsupplements.com
URL: http://www.sportsupplements.com
Description: Nutritional sport supplements retail store. **No. of Franchise Units:** 6. **Founded:** 1996.. **Franchised:** 2000. **Equity Capital Needed:** $92,774-$185,344. **Franchise Fee:** $25,000. **Financial Assistance:** Yes. **Training:** 3 phase initial hands on training program located at current stores, as well as your location. Provides assistance with site location, leases, layout design, suppliers, advertising, marketing, and ongoing assistance.

43292 ■ Dollar Chest Franchising Corporation Inc.
3535 St. Charles Boul., St. 305
Kirkland, QC, Canada H9H 5B9
Ph: (514)693-9776
Fax: (514)693-9775
Co. E-mail: info@dollarchest.com
URL: http://www.dollarchest.com
Description: Value dollar stores, offering consumers cleaning supplies, disposables, health and beauty, plastic wares, household, home decors, kitchen, and accessories, picture frames, hardware, electronics, lighting, stationary, candies, snacks, beverages, party supplies, novelties, gifts, pet supplies, outdoor products, foods and all basic home and household accessories, all at a unique price of one dollar. **No. of Franchise Units:** 5. **No. of Company-Owned Units:** 1. **Founded:** 2006.. **Franchised:** 2006. **Equity Capital Needed:** $170,000-$203,000. **Franchise Fee:** $25,000. **Training:** Provides complete training and full range of online support.

43293 ■ EmbroidMe
1959 Upper Water St., Ste. 1713
Halifax, NS, Canada B3J 3N2
Ph: (416)238-6934
Free: 866-933-6337
Fax: (866)497-3533
Co. E-mail: franchise@embroidme.ca
URL: http://www.embroidme.com
Description: Full service promotional products, screen printing and corporate apparel franchise. Showrooms feature a large selection of casual apparel of various sizes, colours and styles. **No. of Franchise Units:** 18. **Founded:** 2003 Canada; 2000 U.S.. **Franchised:** 2000. **Equity Capital Needed:** $195,000-$245,000. **Franchise Fee:** $49,500. **Training:** Includes 2 weeks training at headquarters and 2 weeks onsite.

43294 ■ Eola Wine Company Franchising
Eola Wine Company
500 E Central Ave.
Orlando, FL 32801
Ph: (813)935-5087
Fax: (813)425-5799
Description: Wine company. **No. of Company-Owned Units:** 1. **Founded:** 2004.. **Franchised:** 2007. **Equity Capital Needed:** $338,000-$460,000. **Franchise Fee:** $50,000. **Training:** Yes.

43295 ■ Furla
Furla Licensing USA Inc.
389 Fifth Ave., Ste. 700
New York, NY 10016
Ph: (212)213-1177
Fax: (212)685-5910
Co. E-mail: bruce@furlausa.com
URL: http://www.furlausa.com
Description: Furla sells women's handbags, shoes, belts, small leather goods, watches, jewelry and accessories. All products are exclusively designed by our own cadre of designers and primarily manufactured in Italy. Furla products are updated classic in styling and targeted towards the upscale modern woman with prices ranging between $180-$350 for handbags and shoes. Our brand is known worldwide through over 200 exclusive shops. **No. of Franchise Units:** 18. **No. of Company-Owned Units:** 15. **Founded:** 1927. **Franchised:** 1998. **Equity Capital Needed:** $284,000-$480,000. **Franchise Fee:** $25,000. **Training:** 1 week training program at New York City office and in our corporate stores. Provides initial store set-up and opening training and ongoing training as requested.

43296 ■ Giant Tiger/Tigre Geant
Giant Tiger Stores Limited
2480 Walkley Rd.
Ottawa, ON, Canada K1G 6A9
Ph: (613)521-8222
Fax: (613)260-6398
Co. E-mail: careers@giantiger.com
URL: http://www.gianttiger.com
Description: Franchise involves retailing services. **No. of Franchise Units:** 208. **No. of Company-Owned Units:** 1. **Founded:** 1961.. **Franchised:** 1964. **Training:** Training, site selection, lease negotiations and advisory council are provided.

43297 ■ Great Canadian Dollar Store 1993 Ltd.
2957 Jutland Rd., Ste. 101
Victoria, BC, Canada V8T 5J9
Ph: (250)388-0123
Free: 877-388-0123
Fax: (250)388-9763
Co. E-mail: franchise@dollarstores.com
URL: http://www.dollarstores.com
Description: Offers an excellent opportunity to market a wide range of exciting merchandise. **No. of Franchise Units:** 120. **Founded:** 1993.. **Franchised:** 1993. **Equity Capital Needed:** $150,000-$400,000; $100,000 start-up capital required. **Franchise Fee:** $19,880. **Training:** Offers training (3P's) and ongoing support.

43298 ■ Hempire Sales Ltd.
1462 10th Ave.
Fernie, BC, Canada V0B 1M0
Ph: (250)423-3970
Free: 866-877-4367
Co. E-mail: marsha@hempirecanada.com
URL: http://www.hempirecanada.com
Description: Unique retail store specializing in the sale of hemp and hemp related products. Offers a wide variety of environmentally friendly products, as well as smoking supplies. **No. of Franchise Units:** 4. **No. of Company-Owned Units:** 1. **Founded:** 1998.. **Franchised:** 2006. **Equity Capital Needed:** $80,000-$100,000; $40,000-$50,000 start-up capital required. **Franchise Fee:** $20,000. **Royalty Fee:** 5%. **Training:** Provides 1-2 weeks training; initial onsite and ongoing support.

43299 ■ Marcello's Market & Deli Inc.
2450 Lancaster Rd., Unit 41
Ottawa, ON, Canada K1B 5N3
Ph: (613)260-3773
Fax: (613)738-2699
URL: http://www.marcellos.ca
Description: European style market and deli takeout restaurant. **No. of Franchise Units:** 15. **No. of Company-Owned Units:** 6. **Founded:** 1998.. **Franchised:** 1998. **Equity Capital Needed:** $350,000-$1,000,000 investment required; $150,000-$400,000 start-up capital required. **Franchise Fee:** $25,000. **Training:** Provides 4-6 weeks training.

43300 ■ Max Muscle Sports Nutrition
210 W Taft Ave.
Orange, CA 92865
Ph: (714)456-0700
Fax: (714)456-0725
Description: The franchise deals mainly with retailing. **No. of Franchise Units:** 151. **No. of Company-Owned Units:** 1. **Founded:** 1991.. **Franchised:** 2001. **Equity Capital Needed:** $50,000-$75,000. **Franchise Fee:** $35,000. **Financial Assistance:** Yes. **Training:** Yes.

43301 ■ Nicholby's Franchise Systems Inc.
170 Main St.
Unionville, ON, Canada L3R 2G9
Ph: (905)940-1515

Fax: (905)940-1516
Co. E-mail: info@nicholbys.com
URL: http://www.nicholbys.com
Description: Retail stores operating in hospitals, hotels, highways and office buildings. **No. of Franchise Units:** 25. **No. of Company-Owned Units:** 2. **Founded:** 1980.. **Equity Capital Needed:** $27,000-$66,000. **Franchise Fee:** $9,900. **Training:** Offers 3-4 weeks training and ongoing support.

43302 ■ Nutrition House Canada Inc.
80 West Beaver Creek Rd., Unit 12
Richmond Hill, ON, Canada L4B 1H3
Ph: (905)707-7633
Free: 888-466-3085
Fax: (905)707-5102
URL: http://www.nutritionhouse.com
Description: Retail 'Lifesyle' stores featuring proprietary and national brands of vitamins, supplements, body care, weight loss, sports nutrition and health related products. Stores feature a 'Sante Fe' design and are located in major malls and Big Box 'Lifestyle' centres across Canada. **No. of Franchise Units:** 54. **No. of Company-Owned Units:** 10. **Founded:** 1979.. **Franchised:** 1993. **Equity Capital Needed:** $50-$75,000. **Franchise Fee:** $25,000. **Training:** Includes 3 weeks training.

43303 ■ Panda Franchises Ltd.
259 Labelle Blvd. Suite 201
Rosemere, QC, Canada J7A 2H3
Ph: (450)818-9741
Fax: (450)622-2939
URL: http://www.pandashoes.com
Description: Children's shoes. **No. of Franchise Units:** 28. **No. of Company-Owned Units:** 3. **Founded:** 1972. **Franchised:** 1974. **Equity Capital Needed:** $125,000 start-up capital; $250,000-$350,000 investment required. **Franchise Fee:** $25,000. **Training:** Complete training to franchisees and staff, buying, selling, administration, merchandising, advertising, etc.

43304 ■ Party Central
True Value Specialty Company, LLC
203 Jandus Rd.
Cary, IL 60013-2861
Free: 800-833-3004
Description: Rental store. **No. of Franchise Units:** 475. **Founded:** 1910.. **Franchised:** 1985. **Equity Capital Needed:** $250,000-$325,000. **Franchise Fee:** $1,500. **Training:** Yes.

43305 ■ Personal Edge
Centre Du Rasoir
10200 Cote de Liesse
Lachine, QC, Canada H8T 1A3
Ph: (514)636-4512
Fax: (514)636-8356
Co. E-mail: jean-claude@cdrem.com
URL: http://www.personaledge.com
Description: Our stores, located in major shopping malls, feature one of Canada's largest selection of electric shavers and other personal grooming products, as well as small household appliances and specialty gifts from leading manufacturers. We have a unique mix of quality brand name products and onsite repair services. **No. of Franchise Units:** 64. **Founded:** 1959. **Franchised:** 1980. **Equity Capital Needed:** $50,000-$80,000. **Franchise Fee:** No franchise fee for new store. **Training:** Includes 6 weeks training.

43306 ■ Planet Clean
1609 Derwent Way
Delta, BC, Canada V3M 6K8
Ph: (604)540-5300
Free: 877-877-5877
Fax: (604)540-5302
Co. E-mail: info@janitors-warehouse.ca
URL: http://www.planetclean.com
Description: Retail of commercial cleaning supplies, equipment and training needs. Planet Clean brings you the highest quality, most innovative and environmentally considerate products. **No. of Franchise Units:** 4. **No. of Company-Owned Units:** 12. **Founded:** 1982.. **Franchised:** 2006. **Equity Capital Needed:** $15,000/$50,000. **Franchise Fee:** $25,000. **Training:** Yes.

43307 ■ Port City Java
PCJ Franchising Co., LLC
2101 Market St.
Wilmington, NC 28403
Ph: (910)796-6646
Fax: (910)796-6611
Description: Gourmet coffee cafe with wireless web. **No. of Franchise Units:** 28. **No. of Company-Owned Units:** 12. **Founded:** 1995. **Franchised:** 2003. **Equity Capital Needed:** $210,300-$413,900 total investment; $300,000 liquid capital; $500,000 net worth. **Franchise Fee:** $20,000. **Royalty Fee:** 5%. **Financial Assistance:** Limited third party financing available. **Training:** Offers 18 days at headquarters and 14 days at franchisee's location with ongoing support.

43308 ■ Printwear Xpress
Printwear Xpress Franchise Corp.
1819 Wazee St.
Denver, CO 80202
Ph: (303)771-7100
Free: 888-241-0337
Fax: (303)771-7133
Co. E-mail: info@printwearxpress.com
URL: http://www.printwearxpress.com
Description: Printwear Xpress (PWX) combines shopping experience, technology & customer service to deliver a highly competitive business model. PWX stores are modern, attractive & well merchandised to help customers select the right product for their needs. Production is showcased to illustrate the capabilities of the business & customer service is second to none. PWX stores are located in neighborhood strip centers & don't require an anchor tenant. **No. of Company-Owned Units:** 1. **Founded:** 2007.. **Franchised:** 2007. **Equity Capital Needed:** $148,200-$169,600. **Franchise Fee:** $29,900. **Royalty Fee:** 5%. **Financial Assistance:** Limited third party financing available. **Training:** Offers 1 week classroom in Denver and 1 week onsite during opening, as well as vendor training.

43309 ■ Saxbys Coffee Worldwide, LLC
Proven Record, Inc.
401 Parkway Dr.
Broomall, PA 19008
Ph: (484)472-6100
Co. E-mail: info@saxbyscoffee.com
URL: http://www.saxbyscoffee.com
Description: Coffee retail store, specializing in gourmet espresso drinks, smoothies, and tea. An affordable initial investment, a rewarding career, a simple business to own and operate, and an easy restaurant to staff. **No. of Franchise Units:** 30. **Founded:** 2002.. **Franchised:** 2003. **Equity Capital Needed:** $50,000 cash, $200,000 equity. **Franchise Fee:** $30,000. **Training:** 5 day owner training before opening the store and a 5 day owner and employee training upon opening the store.

43310 ■ Sports Experts 2000 Inc.
The Forzani Group, Ltd.
4855 Louis-B Mayer St.
Laval, QC, Canada H7P 6C8
Ph: (450)687-5200
Fax: (450)687-0502
URL: http://www.sportsexperts.ca
Description: Retailer and wholesaler of sporting goods clothing, footwear and equipment. **No. of Franchise Units:** 228. **No. of Company-Owned Units:** 260. **Founded:** 1967.. **Franchised:** 1967. **Equity Capital Needed:** Varies. **Franchise Fee:** Banner specific. **Training:** Yes.

43311 ■ Tastings - A Wine Experience
201 N Illinois St., Ste. 1632
Indianapolis, IN 46204
Free: 877-425-0071
Co. E-mail: info@awineexperience.com
Description: Wine tasting store. **No. of Franchise Units:** 12. **Founded:** 2005.. **Franchised:** 2006. **Franchise Fee:** $50,000. **Training:** Yes. Yes.

43312 ■ Theater Xtreme
140 Bradford Dr.
West Berlin, NJ 08091
Ph: (302)455-1334
Fax: (302)455-1612
Description: Home theaters and furnishings. **No. of Franchise Units:** 6. **No. of Company-Owned Units:** 5. **Founded:** 2003.. **Franchised:** 2004. **Equity Capital Needed:** $400,000-$700,000. **Franchise Fee:** $40,000. **Royalty Fee:** 4%. **Training:** Offers 2 weeks at headquarters, onsite and ongoing electronic training. ing.

43313 ■ Vintage Stock
202 E 32nd St.
Joplin, MO 64804
Ph: (417)623-1550
Fax: (417)782-0024
Description: DVDs, videogames, music and sports cards. **No. of Company-Owned Units:** 13. **Founded:** 1980.. **Franchised:** 2005. **Equity Capital Needed:** $337,700-$585,400. **Franchise Fee:** $30,000. **Royalty Fee:** 5%. **Training:** Offers 1 week of training at headquarters, 2-3 weeks onsite and ongoing support.

43314 ■ Watch It! Inc.
10544B-82 Ave.
Edmonton, AB, Canada T6E 2A4
Ph: (780)435-2824
Free: 877-404-2824
Fax: (780)434-5039
Co. E-mail: partner@watchit.ca
URL: http://www.watchit.ca
Description: Watch It! Is a cool and funky retail boutique that offers a wide selection of premium brand name watches, sunglasses and accessories. With its trademarked names, a consistent look and feel across stores, low start-up costs and operating procedures that are polished and efficient, purchasing a Watch It franchise is a sensible investment. **No. of Franchise Units:** 17. **No. of Company-Owned Units:** 7. **Founded:** 1999.. **Franchised:** 2004. **Equity Capital Needed:** $200,000-$400,000. **Franchise Fee:** $25,000. **Training:** Yes.

COMPUTER SYSTEMS/ SOFTWARE

43315 ■ *Business Controller*
17075 Newhope St., Ste. A
Fountain Valley, CA 92708
Ph: (800)726-3282
Fax: (201)785-1568
Co. E-mail: info@microbiz.com
URL: http://www.microbiz.com
Price: Contact MicroBiz for pricing. **Description:** This new version of the Business Controller Plus for Windows is a true 32 bit program that runs in Windows or NT. The software does inventory, invoicing, customer tracking, accounts receivable, reordering, purchasing and much more. It also includes a Query module that allows you to design your own reports and it's Internet Ready!.

CPSIA information can be obtained
at www.ICGtesting.com
Printed in the USA
FFOW051001250313
1030FF

9 781414 479613